Table of Contents

iv - v .... How to Use the Atlas

The Real World
vi - vii .... Introduction
viii - ix .... Climate
x - xi .... Population
xii - xv .... Peoples and Countries
xvi .... World Time Zones

Maps and Index of the United States
S·1 .... Introduction
S·2 - S·3 .... United States
S·4 .... Alabama
S·5 .... Alaska
S·6 .... Arizona
S·7 .... Arkansas
S·8 .... California
S·9 .... Colorado
S·10 .... Connecticut
S·11 .... Delaware
S·12 .... Florida
S·13 .... Georgia
S·14 .... Hawaii
S·15 .... Idaho
S·16 .... Illinois
S·17 .... Indiana
S·18 .... Iowa
S·19 .... Kansas
S·20 .... Kentucky
S·21 .... Louisiana
S·22 .... Maine
S·23 .... Maryland
S·24 .... Massachusetts
S·25 .... Michigan
S·26 .... Minnesota

S·27 .... Mississippi
S·28 .... Missouri
S·29 .... Montana
S·30 .... Nebraska
S·31 .... Nevada
S·32 .... New Hampshire
S·33 .... New Jersey
S·34 .... New Mexico
S·35 .... New York
S·36 .... North Carolina
S·37 .... North Dakota
S·38 .... Ohio
S·39 .... Oklahoma
S·40 .... Oregon
S·41 .... Pennsylvania
S·42 .... Rhode Island
S·43 .... South Carolina
S·44 .... South Dakota
S·45 .... Tennessee
S·46 .... Texas
S·47 .... Utah
S·48 .... Vermont
S·49 .... Virginia
S·50 .... Washington
S·51 .... West Virginia
S·52 .... Wisconsin
S·53 .... Wyoming
S·54 - S·64 .... Index

Maps and Index of the World
1 .... Introduction
2-3 .... World, Political
4-5 .... World, Physical

Chairman, President, & CEO,
Rand McNally & Company
Henry J. Feinberg

Senior Vice President, Marketing
Margaret A. Stender

Director, Reference Publishing
Kendra L. Ensor

Editors
Kathryn Martin O'Neil
Brett R. Gover
Ann T. Natunewicz

Art Direction and Design
John C. Nelson
Peggy R. Hogan

Marketing
Amy C. Krouse
JoEllen A. Klein

Photo Research
Feldman and Associates, Inc.

Manufacturing
Terry D. Rieger

Cartography Directors
V. Patrick Healy
Jon M. Leverenz

Cartography (U.S.)
Robert K. Argersinger
Barbara Benstead-Strassheim
David M. Bukala
Kerry B. Chambers
Marzee L. Eckhoff
Julie A. Geyer
Winifred V. Farbman
Susan K. Hudson
Elizabeth A. Hunt
Gwynn A. Hurshman
William R. Karbler
Brian M. Lash
Nina Lusterman
Erik A. Pedersen
Thomas F. Vitacco
David R. Walters
Richard A. Wanzo
James Wooden
David C. Zapenski

Cartography (U.K.)
Craig Asquith

Cartography (Italy)
Giovanni Baselli
Ubaldo Uberti

Credits

Jacket
© Earth Image/Tony Stone Images (globe), © PhotoDisc (coastline)

The Real World
Developed by Rand McNally with Dr. Marvin W. Mikesell, University of Chicago.

Satellite image on pages vi-vii: Mendoza, Argentina. Processed by Earth Information Systems Corporation, Austin, TX.; Laser film by Cirrus Technologies, Inc., Nashau, NH.

Rand McNally Atlas of the World

This edition published by Barnes & Noble, Inc., by arrangement with Rand McNally & Company

Copyright © 1999 by Rand McNally & Company
1999 Barnes & Noble Books

www.randmcnally.com

This product is protected under copyright law. It is illegal to reproduce or transmit it in whole or in part, in any form or by any means (including mechanical, photographic, or electronic methods), without the written permission of Rand McNally.

M 10 9 8 7 6 5 4 3 2 1

ISBN 0-7607-1889-X

Published and printed in the United States of America.

Rand McNally & Company.
　　Atlas of the world.
　　　　p.　cm.
　　Includes index.
　　　ISBN (TC)
　　1. Atlases.　　I. Title.
　G1021 .R43 1999 <G&M>
　912—DC21
　　　　　　　　　　　　　98-8663
　　　　　　　　　　　　　　CIP
　　　　　　　　　　　　　　MAPS

Europe
6-7 .... Europe, Political
8-9 .... Northern Europe and Scandinavia
10-11 .... Baltic Regions and Moscow
12-13 .... British Isles
14-15 .... Northern France, Belgium, and
                   the Netherlands
16-17 .... Germany, Czech Republic, Slovakia,
                   and Poland
18-19 .... Southern France and Switzerland
20-21 .... Spain and Portugal
22-23 .... Northern Italy, Austria, and the Balkans
24-25 .... Southern Italy
26-27 .... Hungary, Yugoslavia, Romania, and
                   Bulgaria
28-29 .... Greece and Western Turkey

Asia
30-31 .... Asia, Political
32-33 .... Northwestern Asia
34-35 .... Northeastern Asia
36-37 .... China, Korea, and Japan
38-39 .... Japan, Korea, and Northeastern China
40-41 .... Central and Southern Japan
42-43 .... Eastern China
44-45 .... Southeast Asia
46-47 .... Southern Asia
48-49 .... Myanmar, Thailand, and Singapore
50-51 .... Borneo, Java, and Sumatra
52 .... Philippines
53 .... Southern India
54-55 .... Northern India
56-57 .... Southwestern Asia
58-59 .... Israel, Lebanon, and Jordan

Africa
60-61 .... Africa, Political
62-63 .... Northeastern Africa
64-65 .... Northwestern Africa
66-67 .... Central Africa
68-69 .... Southern Africa
70-71 .... South Africa

Australia and Oceania
72-73 .... Australia and Oceania, Political
74-75 .... Australia
76-77 .... Southeastern Australia
78-79 .... Islands of the Pacific
80 .... New Zealand
81 .... Antarctica

South America
82-83 .... South America, Political
84-85 .... Northern South America
86-87 .... Venezuela and Colombia
88-89 .... Eastern Brazil
90-91 .... Southern South America
92-93 .... Central Argentina and Chile

North America
94-95 .... North America, Political
96-97 .... Mexico, Central America, and
                  the Caribbean
98-99 .... Northwestern Mexico and Southwestern
                  United States
100-101 .... Central Mexico
102-103 .... Central America
104-105 .... Islands of the Caribbean
106-107 .... Canada
108-109 .... United States
110-111 .... Northeastern United States and
                 Southeastern
112-113 .... Great Lakes
114-115 .... Central Atlantic States
116-117 .... Southeastern United States
118-119 .... Northern Midwest
120-121 .... Midwest
122-123 .... Mississippi Delta
124-125 .... Northern Great Plains
126-127 .... Central Great Plains
128-129 .... Southern Great Plains
130-131 .... Southern Texas
132-133 .... Arizona and Utah
134-135 .... California, Nevada, and Hawaii
136-137 .... Northwestern United States
138-139 .... Southwestern Canada
140 .... Alaska and the Aleutians
141 .... Greenland

142-143 .... Pacific and Indian Oceans
144 .... Atlantic Ocean

I·1 to I·64 ...... Index

How to use the Atlas

What is an Atlas?

A set of maps bound together is called an atlas. Abraham Ortelius' *Theatrum orbis terrarum*, published in 1570, is considered to be the first modern "atlas," although it was not referred to as such for almost 20 years. In 1589, Gerardus Mercator *(figure 1)* coined the term when he named his collection of maps after Atlas, the mythological Titan who carried Earth on his shoulders as punishment for warring against Zeus. Since then, the definition of "atlas" has been expanded, and atlases often include additional geographic information in diagrams, tables, and text.

figure 1

Latitude and Longitude

The terms "latitude" and "longitude" refer to the grid of horizontal and vertical lines found on most maps and globes. Any point on Earth can be located by its precise latitude and longitude coordinates.

The imaginary horizontal line that circles Earth halfway between the North and South poles is called the equator; it represents 0° latitude and lies 90° from either pole. The other lines of latitude, or parallels, measure distances north or south from the equator *(figure 2)*. The imaginary vertical line that measures 0° longitude runs through the Greenwich Observatory in the United Kingdom, and is called the Prime Meridian. The other lines of longitude, or meridians, measure distances east or west from the prime meridian *(figure 3)*, up to a maximum of 180°. Lines of latitude and longitude cross each other, forming a grid *(figure 4)*.

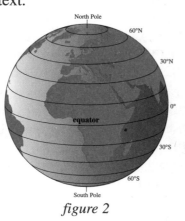

figure 2

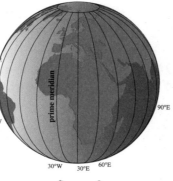

figure 3

Map Projections

Every cartographer is faced with the problem of transforming the curved surface of Earth onto a flat plane with a minimum of distortion. The systematic transformation of locations on Earth (a spherical surface) to locations on a map (a flat surface) is called projection.

figure 4

It is not possible to represent on a flat map the spatial relationships of angle, distance, direction, and area that only a globe can show faithfully. As a result, projections inevitably involve some distortion. On large-scale maps representing a few square miles, the distortion is generally negligible. But on maps depicting large countries, continents, or the entire world, the amount of distortion can be significant. On maps which use the Mercator Projection *(figure 5)*, for example, distortion increases with distance from the equator. Thus the island of Greenland appears larger than the entire continent of South America,

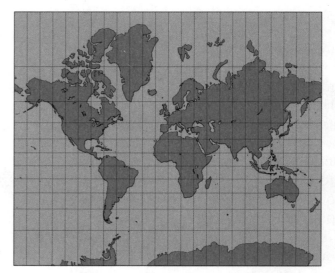

figure 5

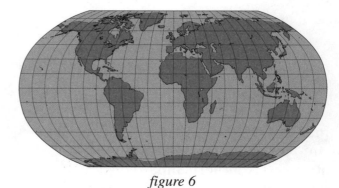

figure 6

although South America is in fact nine time larger. In contrast, the Robinson Projection *(figure 6)* renders the world's major land areas in generally correct proportion to one another, although distortion is still apparent in areas such as Antarctica, which is actually smaller than all of the continents except Europe and Australia.

There are an infinite number of possible map projections, all of which distort one or more of the characteristics of the globe in varying degrees. The projection that a cartographer chooses depends on the size and location of the area being projected and the purpose of the map. In this atlas, most of the maps are drawn on projections that give a consistent or only slightly distorted area scale, good land and ocean shape, parallels that are parallel, and as consistent a linear scale as possible throughout the projection.

Map Scale

The scale of a map is the relationship between distances or areas shown on the map and the corresponding distances or areas on Earth's surface. Large-scale maps show relatively small areas in greater detail than do small-scale maps, such as those of individual continents or of the world.

There are three different ways to express scale. Most often scale is given as a fraction, such as 1:10,000,000, which means that the ratio of distances on the map to actual distances on Earth is 1 to 10,000,000. Scale can also be expressed as a phrase, such as "One inch represents approximately ten million miles." Finally, scale can be illustrated via a bar scale on which various distances are labeled *(figure 7)*. Any of these three scale expressions can be used to calculate distances on a map.

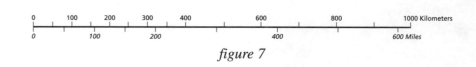

figure 7

Measuring Distances

Using a bar scale, it is possible to calculate the distance between any two points on a map. To find the approximate distance between São Paulo and Rio de Janeiro, Brazil, for example, follow these steps:

1) Lay a piece of paper on the right-hand page of the "Eastern Brazil" map found on pages 88-89, lining up its edge with the city dots for São Paulo and Rio de Janeiro. Make a mark on the paper next to each dot (figure 8).

2) Place the paper along the scale bar found below the map, and position the first mark at 0. The second mark falls about a quarter of the way between the 200-mile tick and the 300-mile tick, indicating that the distance separating the two cities is approximately 225 miles (figure 9).

figure 8

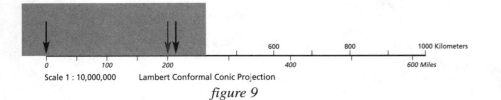

figure 9

3) To confirm this measurement, make a third pencil mark (shown in red in figure 9) at the 200-mile tick. Slide the paper to the left so that this mark lines up with 0. The Rio de Janeiro mark now falls very close to the 25-mile tick, which is unlabelled. Thus, São Paulo and Rio de Janeiro are indeed approximately 225 (200 + 25) miles apart.

Using the Index to Find Places

One of the most important purposes of an atlas is to help the reader locate cities, towns, and geographic features such as rivers, lakes, and mountains. This atlas uses a "bingo key" indexing system. In the index, found on pages I•1 through I•64, every entry is assigned an alpha-numeric code that consists of a letter and a number. This code relates to the red letters and numbers that run along the perimeter of each map. To locate places or features, follow the steps outlined in this example for the city of Bratsk, Russia.

1) Look up Bratsk in the index. The entry (figure 10) contains the following information: the place name (Bratsk), the name of the country (Russia) in which Bratsk is located, the map reference key (C18) that corresponds to Bratsk's location on the map, and the page number (32) of the map on which Bratsk can be found.

Brassey, Banjaran, mts.,		
Malay	A10	50
Brass Islands, is., V.I.U.S.	o7	104 b
Brasstown Bald, mtn., Ga.,		
U.S.	B2	116
Bratca, Rom.	C9	26
Bratislava, Slov.	H13	16
Bratislava, state, Slov.	H13	16
Bratsk, Russia	C18	32
Bratskoe vodohranilisce,		
res., Russia	C18	32

figure 10

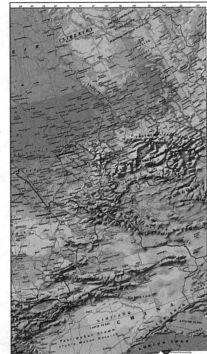

figure 11

2) Turn to the Northwestern Asia map on pages 32-33. Look along either the left or right-hand margin for the red letter "C"—the letter code given for Bratsk. The "C" denotes a band that arcs horizontally across the map, between the grid lines representing 55° and 60° North latitude. Then, look along either the top or bottom margin for the red number "18"—the numerical part of the code given for Bratsk. The "18" denotes a widening vertical band, between the grid lines representing 100° and 105° East longitude, which angles from the top center of the map to right-hand edge.

3) Using your finger, follow the horizontal "C" band and the vertical "18" band to the area where they overlap (figure 11). Bratsk lies within this overlap area.

Physical Maps and Political Maps

Most of the maps in the Atlas of the World are physical maps, like the one shown in figure 12, emphasizing terrain, landforms, and elevation. Political maps, as in figure 13, emphasize countries and other political units over topography. The atlas includes political maps of the world and each of the continents except Antarctica.

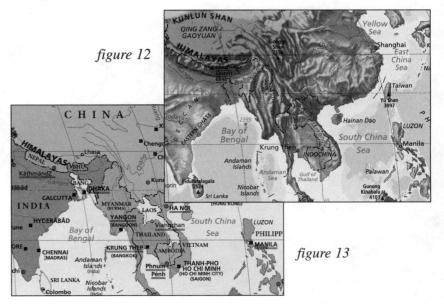

figure 12

figure 13

How Maps Show Topography

The physical maps in this atlas use two techniques to depict Earth's topography. Variations in elevation are shown through a series of colors called hypsometric tints. Areas below sea level appear as a dark green; as the elevation rises, the tints move successively through lighter green, yellow, and orange. Similarly, variations in ocean depth are represented by bathymetric tints. The shallowest areas appear as light blue; darker tints of blue indicate greater depths. The hypsometric/bathymetric scale that accompanies each map identifies, in feet and meters, all of the elevation and depth categories that appear on the map.

Principal landforms, such as mountain ranges and valleys, are rendered in shades of gray, a technique known as shaded relief. The combination of hypsometric tints and shaded relief provides the map reader with a three-dimensional picture of Earth's surface (figure 14).

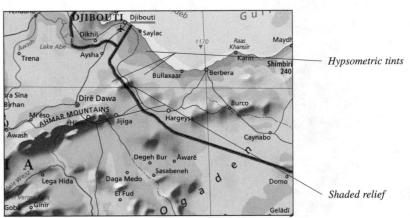

figure 14

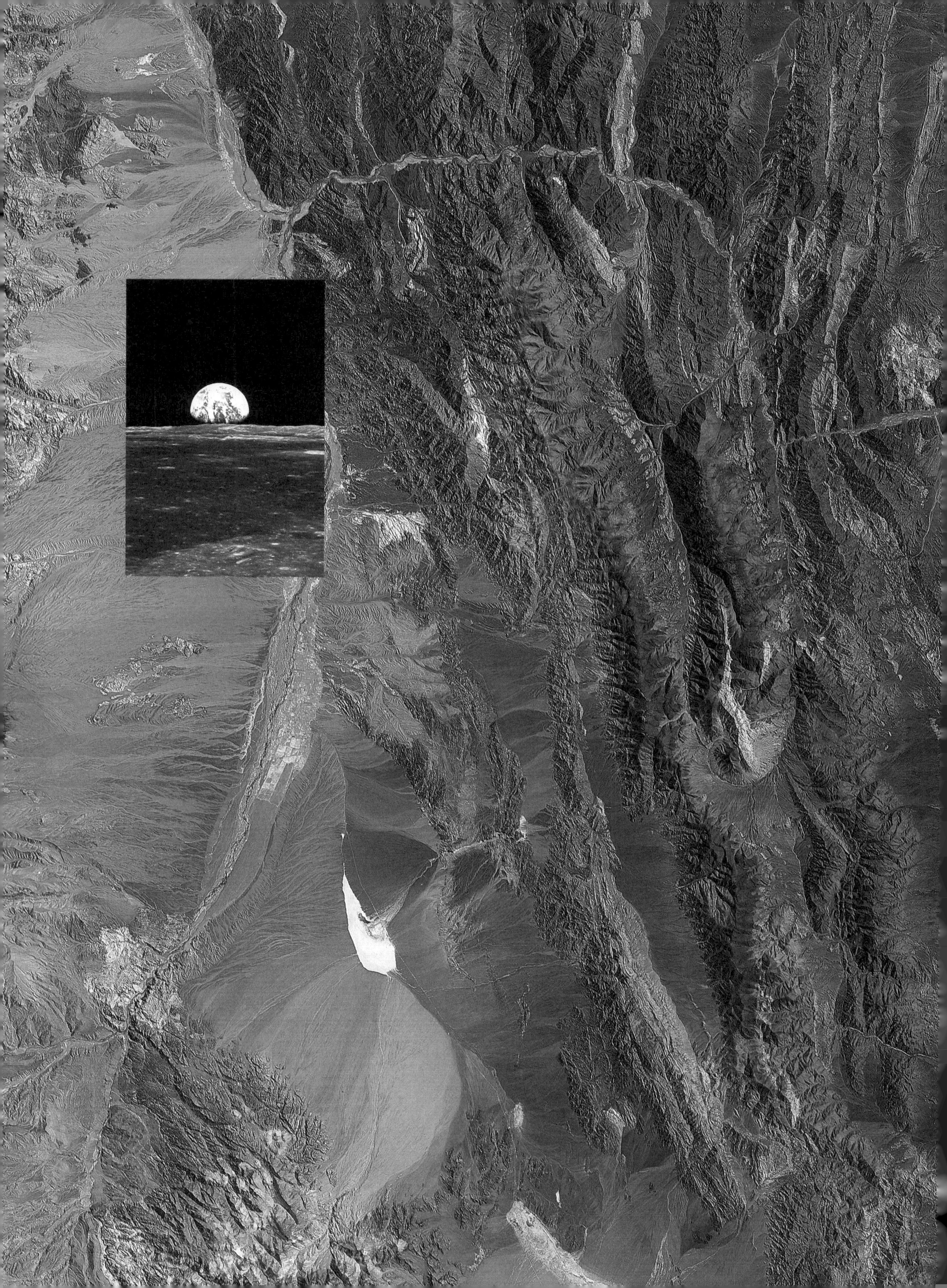

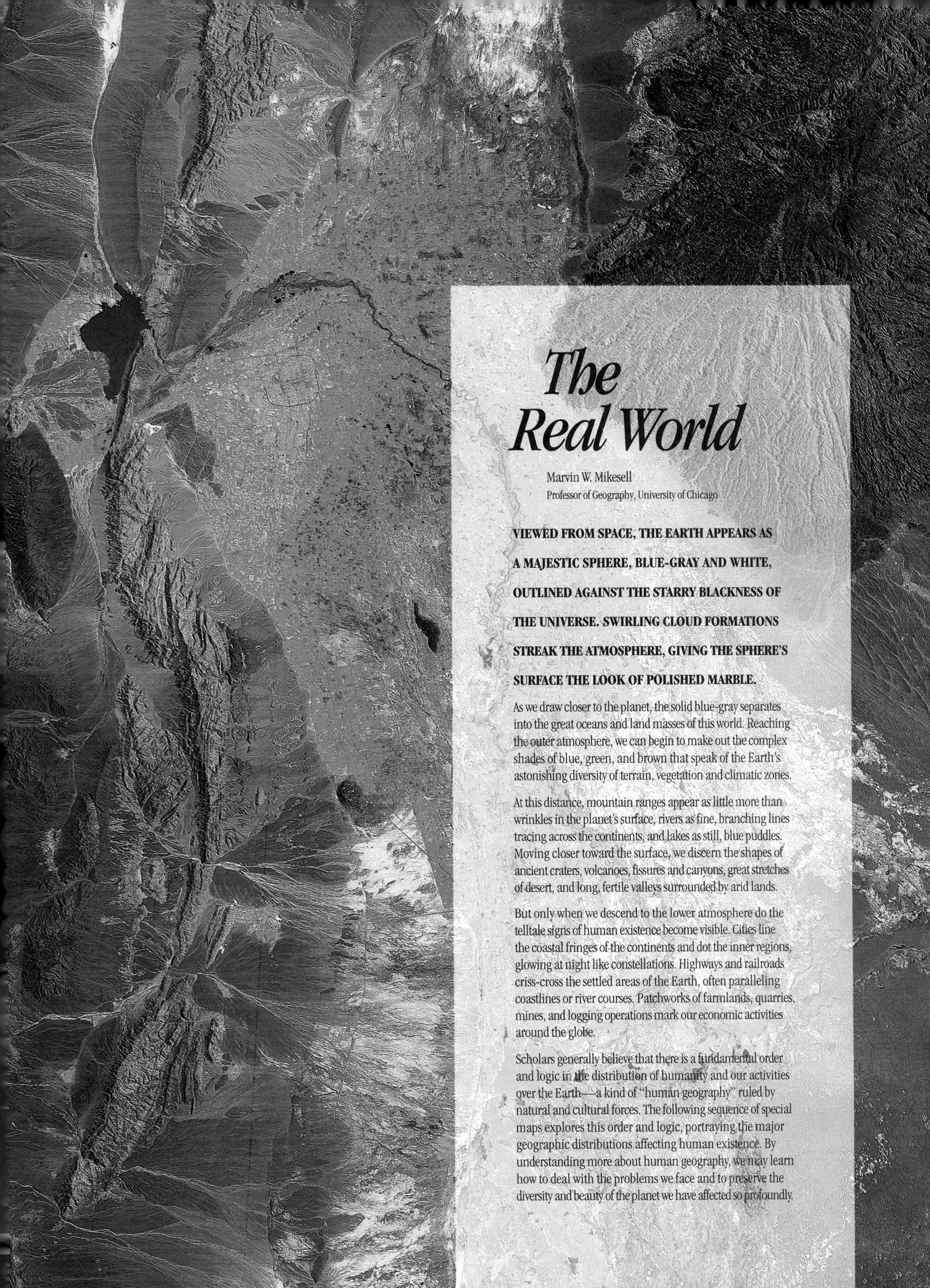

The Real World

Marvin W. Mikesell
Professor of Geography, University of Chicago

VIEWED FROM SPACE, THE EARTH APPEARS AS A MAJESTIC SPHERE, BLUE-GRAY AND WHITE, OUTLINED AGAINST THE STARRY BLACKNESS OF THE UNIVERSE. SWIRLING CLOUD FORMATIONS STREAK THE ATMOSPHERE, GIVING THE SPHERE'S SURFACE THE LOOK OF POLISHED MARBLE.

As we draw closer to the planet, the solid blue-gray separates into the great oceans and land masses of this world. Reaching the outer atmosphere, we can begin to make out the complex shades of blue, green, and brown that speak of the Earth's astonishing diversity of terrain, vegetation and climatic zones.

At this distance, mountain ranges appear as little more than wrinkles in the planet's surface, rivers as fine, branching lines tracing across the continents, and lakes as still, blue puddles. Moving closer toward the surface, we discern the shapes of ancient craters, volcanoes, fissures and canyons, great stretches of desert, and long, fertile valleys surrounded by arid lands.

But only when we descend to the lower atmosphere do the telltale signs of human existence become visible. Cities line the coastal fringes of the continents and dot the inner regions, glowing at night like constellations. Highways and railroads criss-cross the settled areas of the Earth, often paralleling coastlines or river courses. Patchworks of farmlands, quarries, mines, and logging operations mark our economic activities around the globe.

Scholars generally believe that there is a fundamental order and logic in the distribution of humanity and our activities over the Earth—a kind of "human geography" ruled by natural and cultural forces. The following sequence of special maps explores this order and logic, portraying the major geographic distributions affecting human existence. By understanding more about human geography, we may learn how to deal with the problems we face and to preserve the diversity and beauty of the planet we have affected so profoundly.

CLIMATE

WHILE CALM, CLEAR SKIES PREVAIL OVER NORTH AMERICA'S GREAT PLAINS, A VIOLENT HURRICANE BATTERS A CHAIN OF CARIBBEAN ISLANDS. IN EASTERN AFRICA, RAINSTORMS break a two-year drought, but northern European farmers watch their crops dry up in a heat wave. Mild spring winds arrive over Argentina, and in southeast Asia monsoon winds bring lightning and torrential rains.

The infinite variety of our planet's weather is created by the complex relationship of air, water, and land. Air masses ebb and flow around the globe, as moist tropical air moves toward the poles and drier polar air descends toward the equator. The spinning of the Earth helps to direct the air masses. Ocean currents circulate "rivers" of warmer and cooler waters around the globe. Great mountain ranges trap air masses and disrupt the world-wide flow. The 23½° inclination of our planet as it revolves around the sun creates the yearly cycle of seasons.

Over time, this constant interaction of natural forces establishes consistent weather patterns which, in turn, define the major climatic regions of the world, which are depicted on the adjacent map. Within each region, characteristic soils and related plant and animal life evolve.

Generally predictable patterns of weather within these regions have permitted humanity to develop an array of economic and cultural systems, each closely related to the area's normal climatic conditions.

It is the abnormal climatic occurrence—sometimes called a "climatic anomaly"—that causes the most human turmoil, as well as shock to the natural order. For example, a combination of cold Pacific currents and dry air masses makes the northern coast of Chile one of the driest places on Earth. The lifestyle of the region is based upon this prevailing climate. When the phenomenon known as *El Niño* occurs, the usual northerly flow of cold air and water reverses itself, and warm equatorial air and water flow south onto the coast of Chile. These unexpected conditions dramatically increase rainfall, leading to disastrous flooding, and completely disrupting the cultural and natural order.

Today there is growing awareness and concern about humanity's increasing impact on climate. In many large urban areas, the heat-absorbing artificial terrain, combined with air pollution from automobiles and industry, has created "micro-climates" characterized by higher temperatures and excessive smog. A far greater potential problem is global warming resulting from the so-called "greenhouse effect." The burning of fossil fuels adds carbon dioxide to the atmosphere, which causes the atmosphere to trap heat that would normally radiate out into space. If global temperatures rise even a few degrees, the consequences could be disastrous.

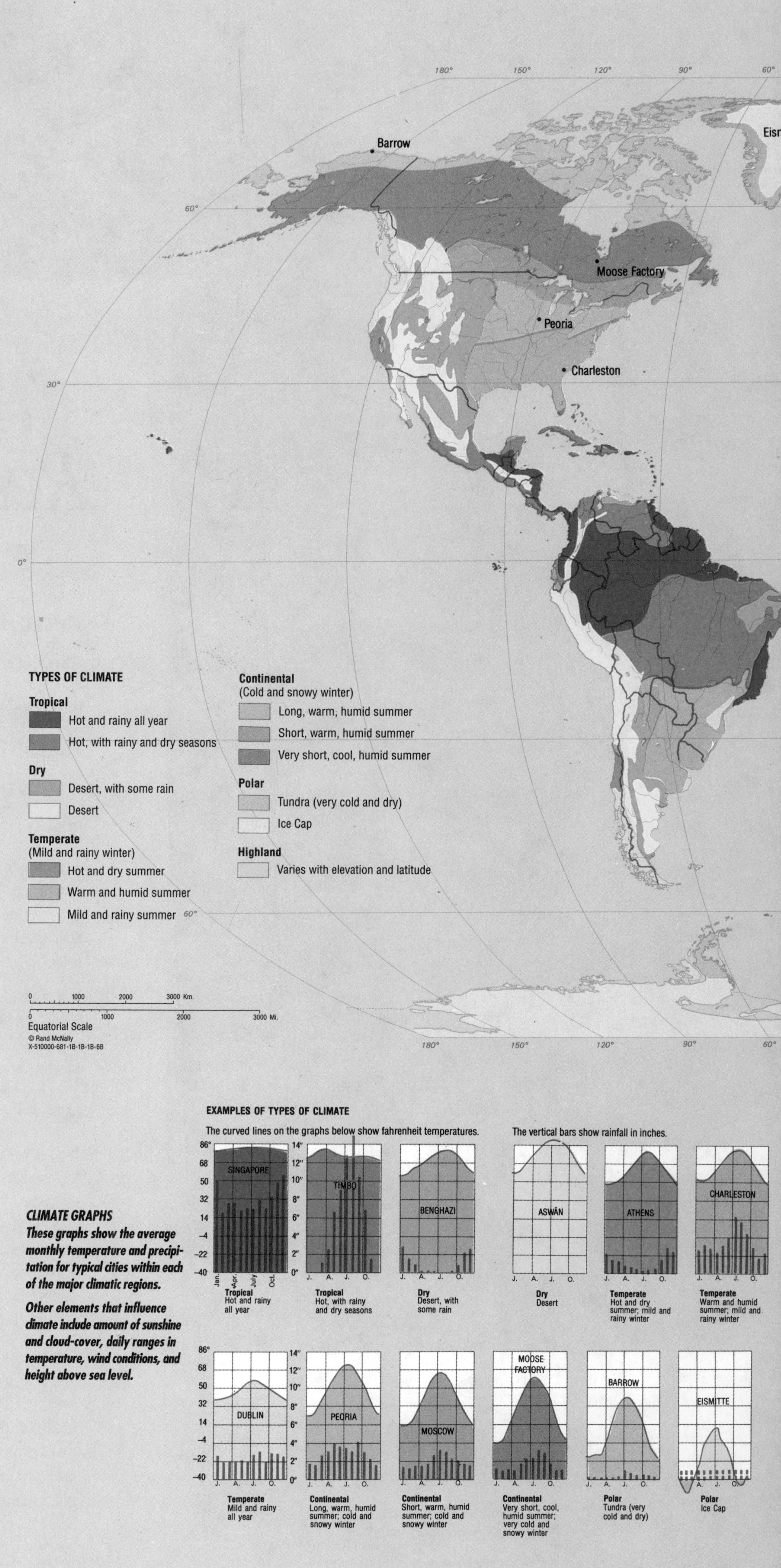

TYPES OF CLIMATE

Tropical
- Hot and rainy all year
- Hot, with rainy and dry seasons

Dry
- Desert, with some rain
- Desert

Temperate
(Mild and rainy winter)
- Hot and dry summer
- Warm and humid summer
- Mild and rainy summer

Continental
(Cold and snowy winter)
- Long, warm, humid summer
- Short, warm, humid summer
- Very short, cool, humid summer

Polar
- Tundra (very cold and dry)
- Ice Cap

Highland
- Varies with elevation and latitude

Equatorial Scale
© Rand McNally
X-510000-681-1B-1B-1B-6B

EXAMPLES OF TYPES OF CLIMATE

The curved lines on the graphs below show fahrenheit temperatures.   The vertical bars show rainfall in inches.

CLIMATE GRAPHS
These graphs show the average monthly temperature and precipitation for typical cities within each of the major climatic regions.

Other elements that influence climate include amount of sunshine and cloud-cover, daily ranges in temperature, wind conditions, and height above sea level.

SINGAPORE — Tropical / Hot and rainy all year
TIMBO — Tropical / Hot, with rainy and dry seasons
BENGHAZI — Dry / Desert, with some rain
ASWAN — Dry / Desert
ATHENS — Temperate / Hot and dry summer; mild and rainy winter
CHARLESTON — Temperate / Warm and humid summer; mild and rainy winter
DUBLIN — Temperate / Mild and rainy all year
PEORIA — Continental / Long, warm, humid summer; cold and snowy winter
MOSCOW — Continental / Short, warm, humid summer; cold and snowy winter
MOOSE FACTORY — Continental / Very short, cool, humid summer; very cold and snowy winter
BARROW — Polar / Tundra (very cold and dry)
EISMITTE — Polar / Ice Cap

WORLD CLIMATE REGIONS

The climates shown on the map tend to align with major zones that parallel the equator. Tropical climates hug the equator, where the air is hot and moist most of the year. Dry, desertic conditions often form north and south of the equator, where descending air causes moisture to remain in vapor form rather than falling as rain. In the mid-latitudes a variety of climates exist, called "temperate" because extreme air masses meet and are modified in this zone. Continental climates prevail in a broad band that covers much of North America, eastern Europe, and northern Asia. Extremely cold climates characterize the polar regions.

30°   0°   30°   60°   90°   120°   150°   180°

60°

Moscow •

Dublin •

30°

Athens •

Benghazi

Aswān •

EQUATOR

Timbo •

PRIME MERIDIAN

Singapore •   0°

30°

60°

30°   0°   30°   60°   90°   120°   150°   180°

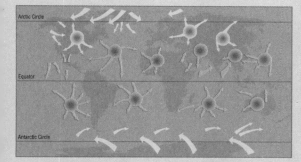

Arctic Circle

Equator

Antarctic Circle

Cold Air   Warm Air

AIR AND WATER

These two maps show the direction and movement of the Earth's major air masses and ocean currents. The world's weather and its climatic regions result from the movement of these huge masses of air and water. The boundaries and direction of these masses are altered by factors such as vertical motion, surface friction, continental and seabed topography, and the Earth's rotation.

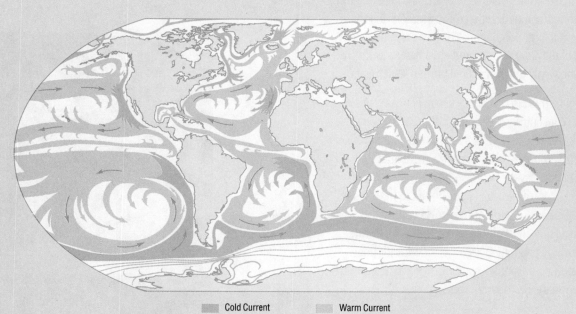

Cold Current   Warm Current

NEARLY 1.6 MILLION YEARS AGO, OUR

HUMAN ANCESTORS STRUGGLED TO SURVIVE

IN THE FORESTS AND FERTILE PLAINS

OF EASTERN AFRICA. TODAY, HUMANITY

inhabits every continent on earth. World population is approaching 6 billion, with 80 million new lives added every year. More people are alive now than have existed since the dawn of human history.

This explosive growth is fueled not only by a rising birth rate but by longer average life spans and by a sharp reduction in the number of children who die young. With births far outstripping deaths, predictions are that world population will not stablize until the year 2010, when over 10 billion people will share the planet.

The most densely settled parts of the Earth appear in the industrial areas of Europe, North America, and Japan, and the predominantly rural areas of India, China, and Southeast Asia. In developed areas, modern technology has encouraged the growth of large urban districts. The heavily populated rural areas of Asian countries reflect nearly 4,000 years of agricultural civilization.

Even with the surge in population, however, substantial areas of the Earth remain underpopulated or virtually empty. Some regions offer striking contrasts between crowded and open spaces. In Russia, a narrow band of population stretches along the Trans-Siberian Railway. The eastern shore of the Mediterranean Sea, with its crowded coastal fringe of Israel, Lebanon, and Syria, stands out sharply against the barren, uninhabited land beyond.

Several natural and cultural factors help explain the uneven distribution of humanity. Nature imposes limits on agricultural development: many areas are too dry or mountainous or have growing seasons too short to support a large population. The harsher climate and terrain of the polar regions and great deserts of the world show only widely scattered human settlements.

Cultural factors also influence where populations are likely to concentrate. Nearly 2.5 billion people now live in urban centers, half of them in cities that number 500,000 or more. By the year 2000, the urban population in less-developed countries will double, as the rural poor seek greater opportunities in the already-crowded cities. Religion and cultural values also influence a nation's ability to control its birth rate. Until curbing population becomes a worldwide goal, our growing numbers will continue to exert increasing pressure on the Earth's resources.

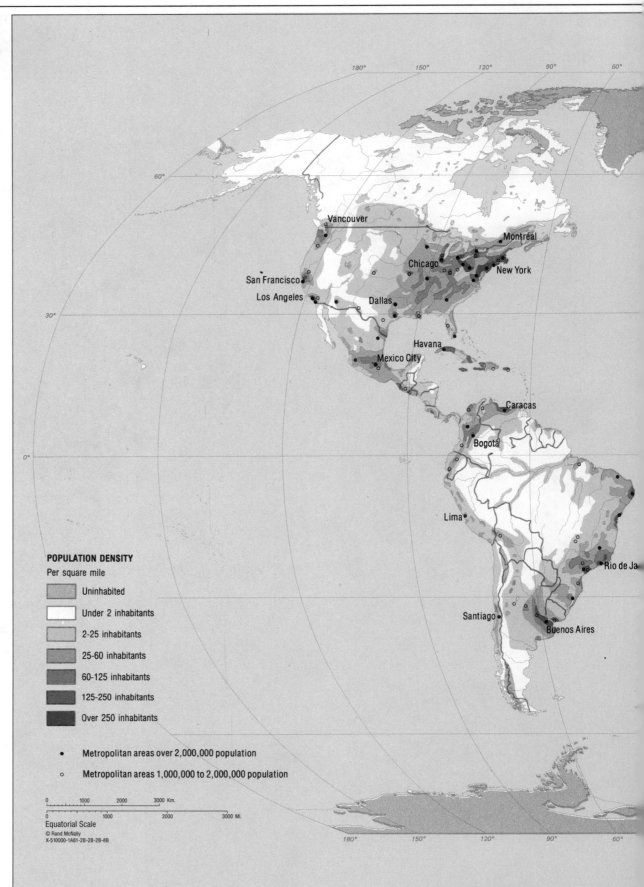

POPULATION DENSITY
Per square mile

- Uninhabited
- Under 2 inhabitants
- 2-25 inhabitants
- 25-60 inhabitants
- 60-125 inhabitants
- 125-250 inhabitants
- Over 250 inhabitants

• Metropolitan areas over 2,000,000 population

○ Metropolitan areas 1,000,000 to 2,000,000 population

Equatorial Scale
© Rand McNally
X-510000-1A81-2B-2B-2B-8B

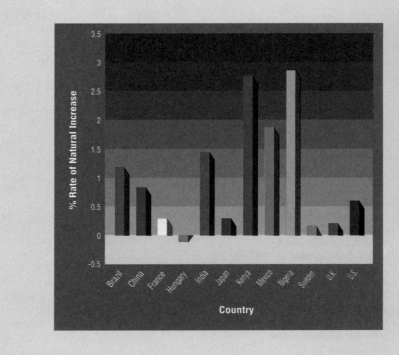

POPULATION GROWTH
In densely populated countries, extremely high growth rates can cripple efforts to develop viable economies. Through state-encouraged family planning, China has managed to decrease its growth rate and thus improve the economic well-being of its people. Low rates of growth in industrialized countries have resulted in economies which are able to support relatively high standards of living.

(Rate of natural growth per year = birth rate minus death rate. Immigration and emigration are not included in this formulation.)

PATTERNS OF POPULATION DENSITY

This map strikingly portrays the great expanses of population density in south-east Asia, Europe, and the northeastern United States. Dramatic, too, are smaller areas where sharp differences occur between crowded and open places, as between Egypt's fertile Nile River delta and the surrounding desert. Russia's narrow east-west band of population is partly explained by the presence of the Trans-Siberian Railway. Coastal densities exist on all of the continents. It is always a complex combination of physical and human geographic factors that explains these and the other density patterns of the world.

Stockholm
Moscow
Novosibirsk
London
Volgograd
Madrid
Rome
Tashkent
Beijing
Casablanca
Damascus
Tōkyō
Cairo
Tehrān
Khartoum
Mumbai (Bombay)
Xianggang (Hong Kong)
Lagos
Bangkok
Nairobi
Kinshasa
Jakarta
Johannesburg
Cape Town
Sydney

PRIME MERIDIAN

AGE AND SEX COMPOSITION

The varying shapes of these graphs illustrate the vast differences between youth and age throughout the world. Brazil, with a high birth rate and declining death rate, exemplifies many developing countries. Sudan's jagged structure results largely from recurring periods of famine. Typical of many developed countries, Japan's graph shows a declining birth rate. Warfare and family planning are other factors affecting the age composition of countries.

Age and Sex Composition ■ Male □ Female

Age: 85+, 80-84, 75-79, 70-74, 65-69, 60-64, 55-59, 50-54, 45-49, 40-44, 35-39, 30-34, 25-29, 20-24, 15-19, 10-14, 5-9, 0-4

Brazil | China | Japan | Sudan | United Kingdom | United States

Percent

FOOD AND POPULATION

In this cartogram, the size of each country is proportional to the size of its population. Per capita calorie supply is indicated through five gradations of coloration, as shown in the legend. The worst malnutrition problems are found in underdeveloped areas of the world such as India, Bangladesh, and much of Africa. The developed countries of Europe and North America all enjoy calorie supplies well above requirements.

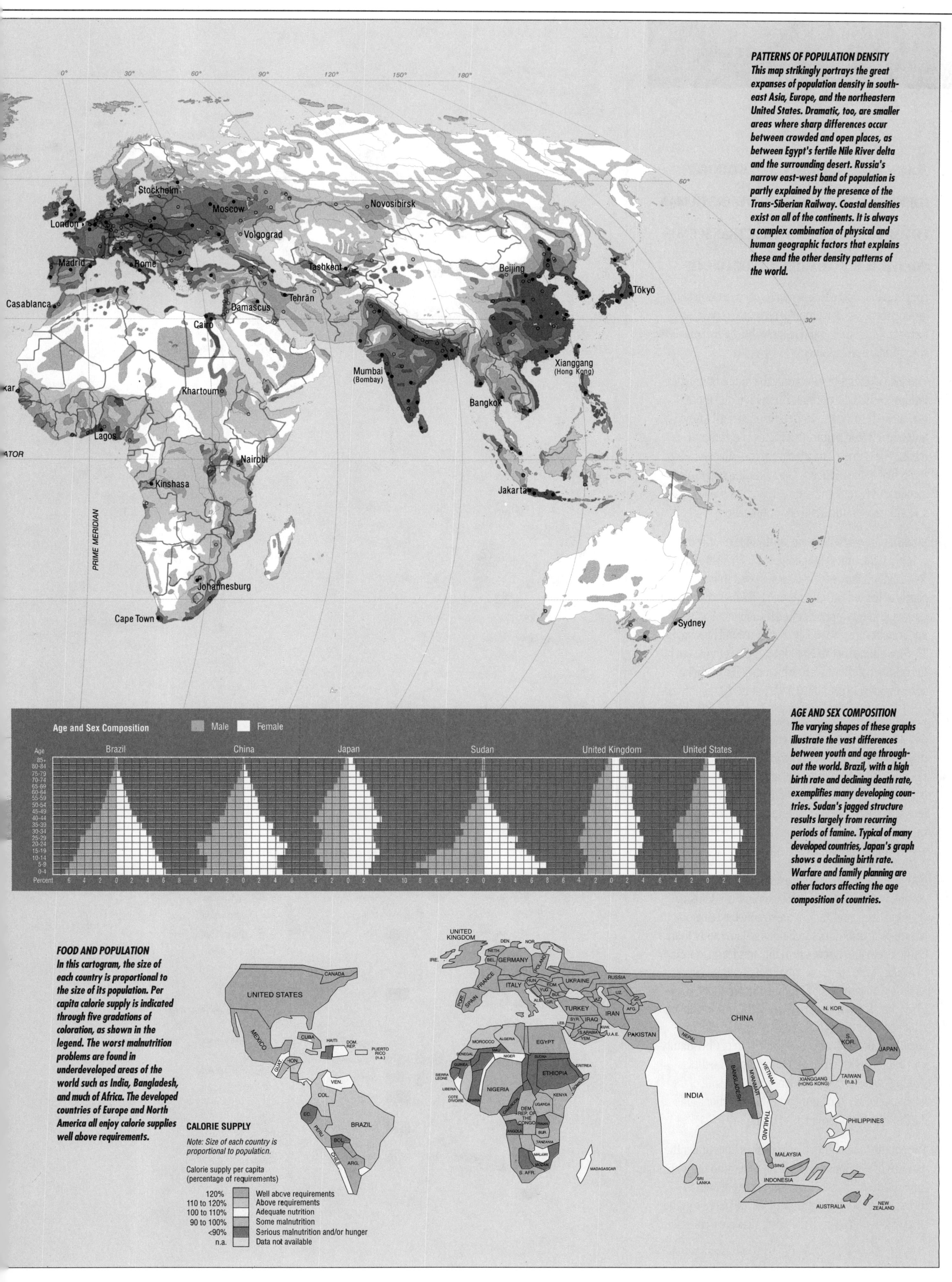

CALORIE SUPPLY

Note: Size of each country is proportional to population.

Calorie supply per capita (percentage of requirements)

120%	Well above requirements
110 to 120%	Above requirements
100 to 110%	Adequate nutrition
90 to 100%	Some malnutrition
<90%	Serious malnutrition and/or hunger
n.a.	Data not available

UNITED KINGDOM
CANADA
IRE.
DEN. NOR.
NETH.
BEL. GERMANY POLAND
PORT. FRANCE ITALY UKRAINE RUSSIA
SPAIN TURKEY
MEXICO CUBA HAITI DOM. REP.
PUERTO RICO (n.a.)
IRAN AFG.
MOROCCO ALGERIA EGYPT
PAKISTAN NEPAL CHINA N. KOR.
S. KOR.
JAPAN
NIGERIA ETHIOPIA
INDIA BANGLADESH
VIETNAM
XIANGGANG (HONG KONG)
TAIWAN (n.a.)
VEN. COL. THAILAND PHILIPPINES
BRAZIL MALAYSIA SING.
PERU BOL. INDONESIA
CHILE ARG.
MADAGASCAR
S. AFR.
SRI LANKA
AUSTRALIA NEW ZEALAND

LANGUAGE, RELIGION, AND ETHNIC IDENTITY—THESE HELP TO DEFINE HUMAN COMMUNITIES IN A WAY THAT TRANSCENDS POLITICAL BOUNDARIES. LANGUAGE, OF course, is the most effective means of communication among members of a group. It serves as a cohesive force for the members and helps to distinguish one community from another.

The map to the right shows only the major language groups, such as the Germanic branch of the Indo-European family. A map that displayed all known languages would require thousands of colors and labels. The Chinese branch of the Sino-Tibetan family ranks first in the number of speakers. English ranks second, but is the world's most important medium for scientific and commercial communication.

English enjoys absolute predominance in only four countries: the United Kingdom, the U.S., Australia, and New Zealand. However, it is spoken by a majority of people in Ireland and Canada and is the preferred second language in many other countries. French, Spanish, and Russian are also widely used as second languages. The importance of two other languages is suggested by the number of countries in which they have official status: Arabic (18 countries) and Spanish (20 countries).

Religion, like language, is a means of communication and a mechanism that promotes social cohesion. The map here shows the most important universalizing religions (Christianity, Islam, and Buddhism) that are held to be appropriate for all of humankind and so are propagated by missionary activities. Religions associated with particular peoples, such as Judaism and Hinduism, seldom entail missionary activity.

Countries cannot always be neatly divided into religious groups, however. In China, for example, Buddhism, Confucianism, and Taoism are so entwined that one has to speak of a Chinese religious system rather than a Chinese religion. Elsewhere in thé world, and especially in Africa, a wide array of tribal religions can be identified, and many of these have incorporated some of the practices and beliefs of one of the universalizing religions. Over time, most religions tend to split into factions or denominations. The division of Christianity into Catholic, Orthodox, and Protestant branches is striking evidence of this tendency, as is the split of the Islamic religion into Sunni and Shi'ite factions after the death of Muhammad in A.D. 632.

The country boundaries that appear as lines under the patterns of religions and languages remind us of an important fact about our world: very few of the 184 member states of the United Nations are nations in the strict or singular sense of the word. Most are a collection

Continued on page xiv

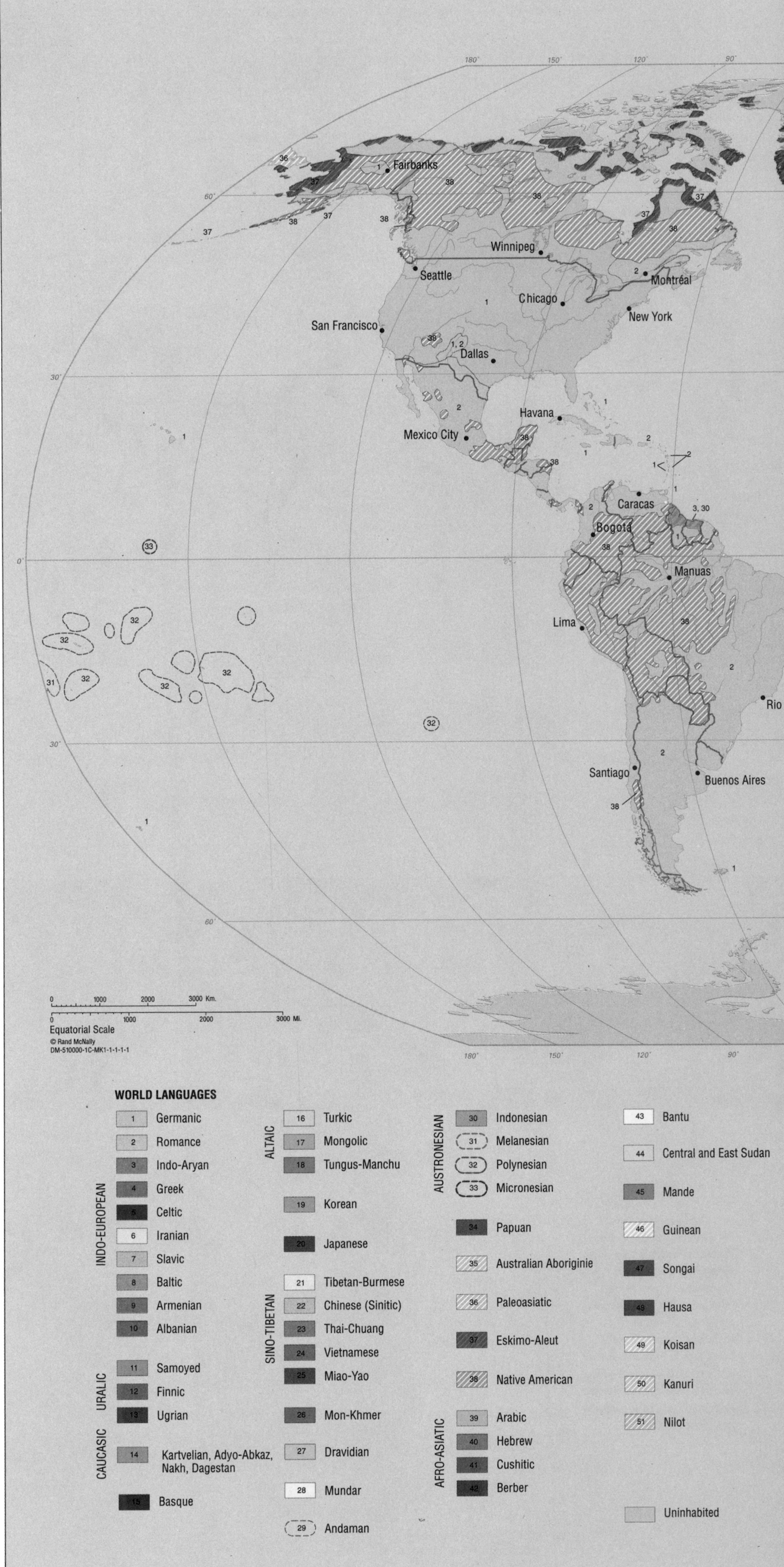

WORLD LANGUAGES

INDO-EUROPEAN		
1	Germanic
2	Romance
3	Indo-Aryan
4	Greek
5	Celtic
6	Iranian
7	Slavic
8	Baltic
9	Armenian
10	Albanian

URALIC
11	Samoyed
12	Finnic
13	Ugrian

CAUCASIC
| 14 | Kartvelian, Adyo-Abkaz, Nakh, Dagestan |
| 15 | Basque |

ALTAIC
16	Turkic
17	Mongolic
18	Tungus-Manchu
19	Korean
20	Japanese

SINO-TIBETAN
21	Tibetan-Burmese
22	Chinese (Sinitic)
23	Thai-Chuang
24	Vietnamese
25	Miao-Yao
26	Mon-Khmer
27	Dravidian
28	Mundar
29	Andaman

AUSTRONESIAN
30	Indonesian
31	Melanesian
32	Polynesian
33	Micronesian
34	Papuan
35	Australian Aboriginie
36	Paleoasiatic
37	Eskimo-Aleut
38	Native American

AFRO-ASIATIC
39	Arabic
40	Hebrew
41	Cushitic
42	Berber

43	Bantu
44	Central and East Sudan
45	Mande
46	Guinean
47	Songai
48	Hausa
49	Koisan
50	Kanuri
51	Nilot

Uninhabited

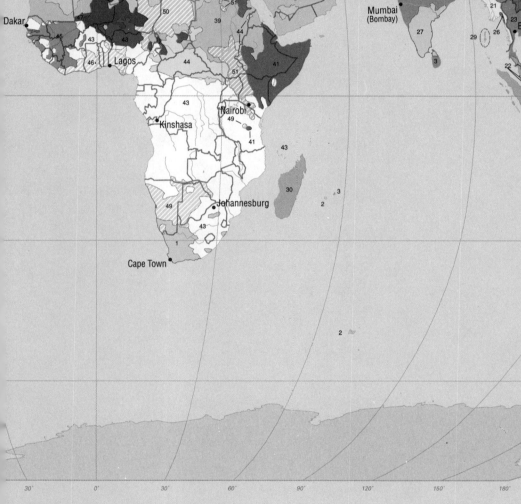

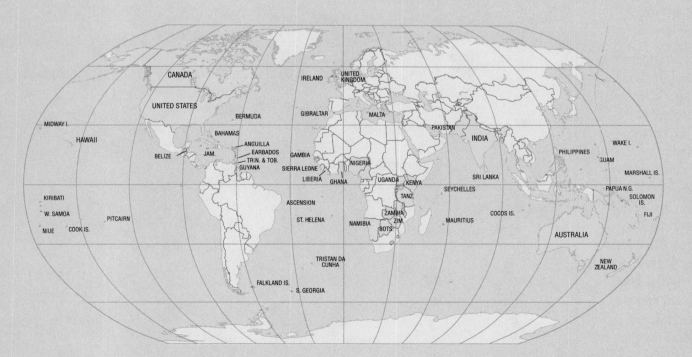

MAJOR LANGUAGE GROUPS

How languages are mapped depends upon how they are classified. The map offered here shows major language groups, not specific languages (of which there are more than 2,000).

English is one of several Germanic languages which have a common grammatical structure. French is one of several Romance languages, so-named because they evolved from Latin, the language of the Roman Empire. Some languages, such as Basque and Japanese, stand alone without well established connections with other languages.

Several of the groups identified on this map, such as Papuan and Bantu, include hundreds of specific languages. Linguists are able to place some language groups under even larger headings, which they call language families. Indo-European was the first such family identified by scholars. The Sino-Tibetan family includes language groups and specific languages spoken by more than a billion people.

THE REALM OF ENGLISH

English has become the world's most useful language. This map shows where it has official status. A map showing where English is used without such status would extend its realm to most of the world.

Continued from page xii

of different groups speaking a variety of languages and maintaining diverse religious and cultural beliefs. In Western Europe, only Denmark and Portugal are homogeneous countries where everyone speaks the same language and belongs to the same church. In Africa, only Tunisia shares this distinction.

It is hard to find a comparable example in the Middle East, even among countries predominantly Islamic in faith and Arabic in speech. Saudi Arabia, if its large foreign labor population is ignored, is the only example of a true nation state in this region. Elsewhere in Asia, Japan and the two Korean states are rare exceptions to the more common pattern of cultural complexity. In Latin America, Spanish or Portuguese speech and Roman Catholicism are cultural common denominators, but Native American languages are still spoken in most countries. In contrast, Argentina and Brazil are cultural melting pots like the United States. Costa Rica and Uruguay may be the only New World states without significant minorities.

The fact that cultural uniformity is so rare, and only one perfect example can be cited (Iceland), means that the familiar political map not only differs from the less familiar maps of language and religion, but may actually conflict with them. Some countries have laws and institutions that permit citizens of different faiths and languages to live in peace and prosperity. For example, the Swiss live in harmony in spite of speaking four languages (German, French, Italian, and Romansch) and having Catholic and Protestant affiliations. Unfortunately, such happy examples of cultural accommodation are offset by numerous instances of tension and conflict. The ethnic warfare within recent decades in Sri Lanka, Bosnia, Sudan, Lebanon, and Rwanda are conspicuous examples of the potential for violence that often exists in states that are not true nation states or have borders that do not coincide with ethnic realities. The collapse of the Soviet Union exposed many problems of this nature.

Since the world is never likely to have only one language or one religion, comparison of maps showing cultural patterns with those indicating political jurisdiction reveals an important truth about our troubled world. In order to understand why ethnic conflict occurs so frequently we need an appropriate vocabulary. We need to be able to distinguish among the following cultural-political categories: *nation states* (homogeneous countries, such as Iceland and Denmark); *multinational states* (countries made up of diverse ethnic and linguistic groups, such as India); *multi-state nations* (multiple countries that share language and religion, such as the Arabic-Islamic realm); *non-nation states* (Vatican City is the only example); and, finally, *non-state nations* (regions where people share language and religion but have no political state, such as Kurdistan and Palestine).

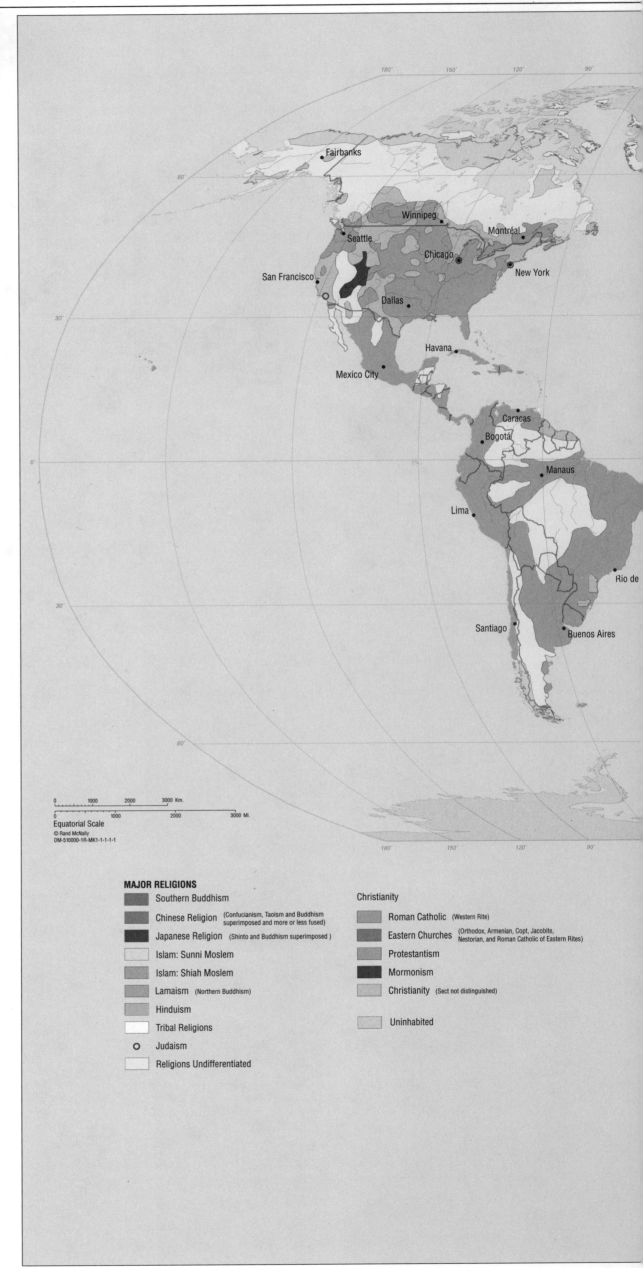

Equatorial Scale
© Rand McNally
DM-510000-1R-MK1-1-1-1-1

MAJOR RELIGIONS

- Southern Buddhism
- Chinese Religion (Confucianism, Taoism and Buddhism superimposed and more or less fused)
- Japanese Religion (Shinto and Buddhism superimposed)
- Islam: Sunni Moslem
- Islam: Shiah Moslem
- Lamaism (Northern Buddhism)
- Hinduism
- Tribal Religions
- ○ Judaism
- Religions Undifferentiated

Christianity
- Roman Catholic (Western Rite)
- Eastern Churches (Orthodox, Armenian, Copt, Jacobite, Nestorian, and Roman Catholic of Eastern Rites)
- Protestantism
- Mormonism
- Christianity (Sect not distinguished)

- Uninhabited

MAJOR WORLD RELIGIONS

Religion, like language, is one of the basic divisions of humankind. The 14 categories shown on this map indicate the range and diversity of religious beliefs.

Christianity, Buddhism, and Islam are universalizing religions proclaimed by adherents to be appropriate for all peoples. Other religions, such as Judaism and Hinduism, are associated with particular peoples and so are exclusive rather than inclusive. As the map indicates, China and Japan are characterized by composite or superimposed religions. "Tribal religions" is a vague but useful designation for the many religious beliefs, practices, and systems of authority found in parts of Africa, Siberia, and Southeastern Asia.

Religious distribution, even more than linguistic distribution, is in perpetual flux. The frontier of Islam has been advancing rapidly in Africa, and Christian missionary activity has been a persistent global force for several centuries.

MAJOR ETHNIC GROUPS

Majority Presence (50% or more)

Czechs
Slovaks
Hungarians
Romanians
Bulgarians
Slovenes
Croats
Serbs
Muslims
Montenegrins
Albanians
Macedonians
Turks

No Majority Present

CULTURAL COMPLEXITY IN EASTERN EUROPE

The boundaries of the states of Eastern Europe have seldom coincided with cultural realities. At present, Hungarians are found not only in Hungary but also in Slovakia, Romania, and Serbia. The former state of Yugoslavia had within its borders Roman Catholic and Eastern Orthodox Christians, Muslims, and speakers of Serbo-Croatian, Slovenian, and Macedonian languages. In Bosnia, ancient disputes among religious and linguistic groups still encourage tension and conflict.

Copyright by Rand McNally & Co
DM-559800-1D-MK1-1-1-1-1

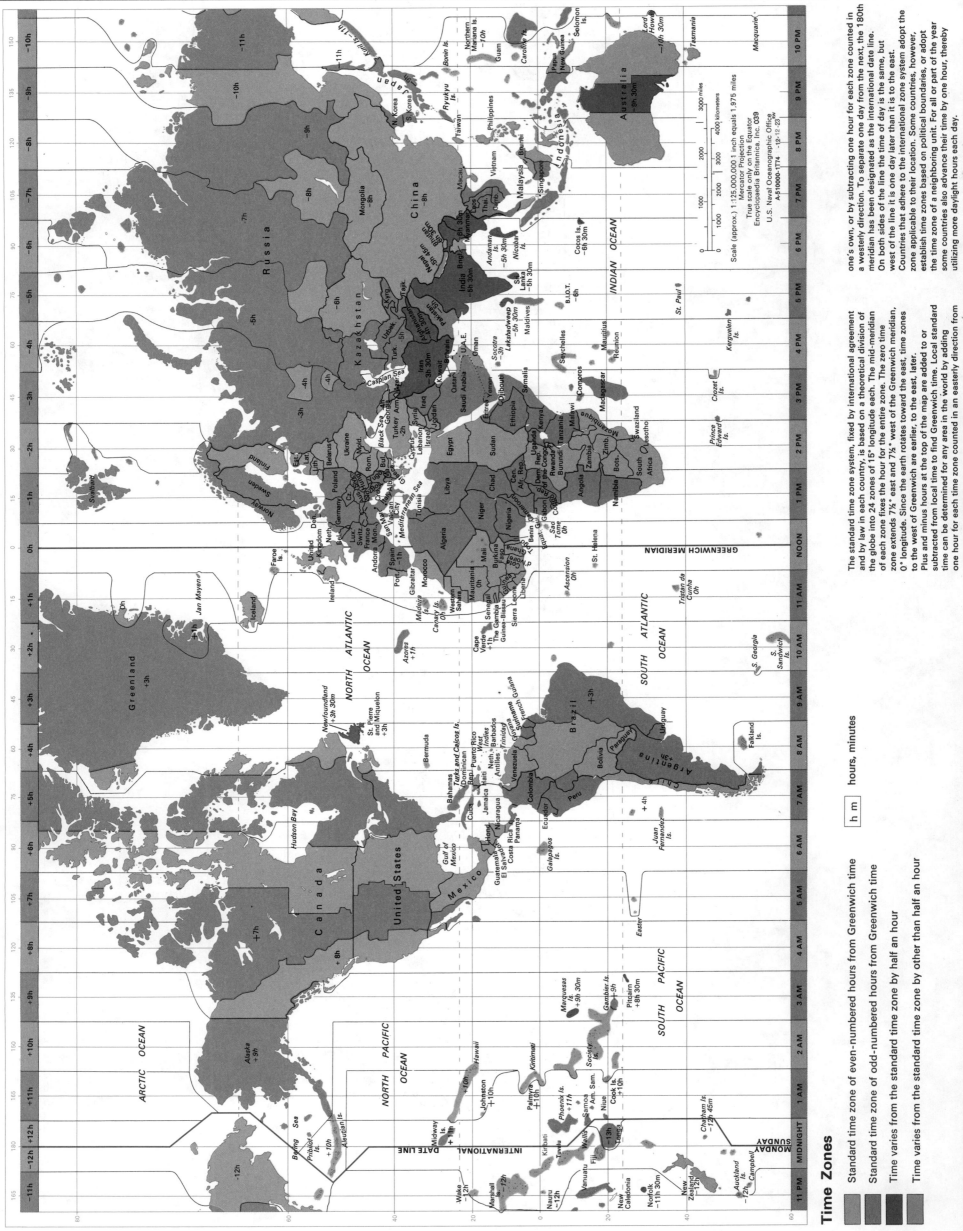

Time Zones

The standard time zone system, fixed by international agreement and by law in each country, is based on a theoretical division of the globe into 24 zones of 15° longitude each. The mid-meridian of each zone fixes the hour for the entire zone. The zero time zone extends 7½° east and 7½° west of the Greenwich meridian, 0° longitude. Since the earth rotates toward the east, time zones to the west of Greenwich are earlier, to the east, later. Plus and minus hours at the top of the map are added to or subtracted from local time to find Greenwich time. Local standard time can be determined for any area in the world by adding one hour for each time zone counted in an easterly direction from one's own, or by subtracting one hour for each zone counted in a westerly direction. To separate one day from the next, the 180th meridian has been designated as the international date line. On both sides of the line the time of day is the same, but west of the line it is one day later than it is to the east. Countries that adhere to the international zone system adopt the zone applicable to their location. Some countries, however, establish time zones based on political boundaries, or adopt the time zone of a neighboring unit. For all or part of the year some countries also advance their time by one hour, thereby utilizing more daylight hours each day.

☐ h m   hours, minutes

Standard time zone of even-numbered hours from Greenwich time

Standard time zone of odd-numbered hours from Greenwich time

Time varies from the standard time zone by half an hour

Time varies from the standard time zone by other than half an hour

Scale (approx.) 1:125,000,000 1 inch equals 1,975 miles
True scale only on the Equator
Mercator Projection
Encyclopaedia Britannica, Inc. 039
U.S. Naval Oceanographic Office
A-510000-1T14   12-12-23

Maps and Index of the United States

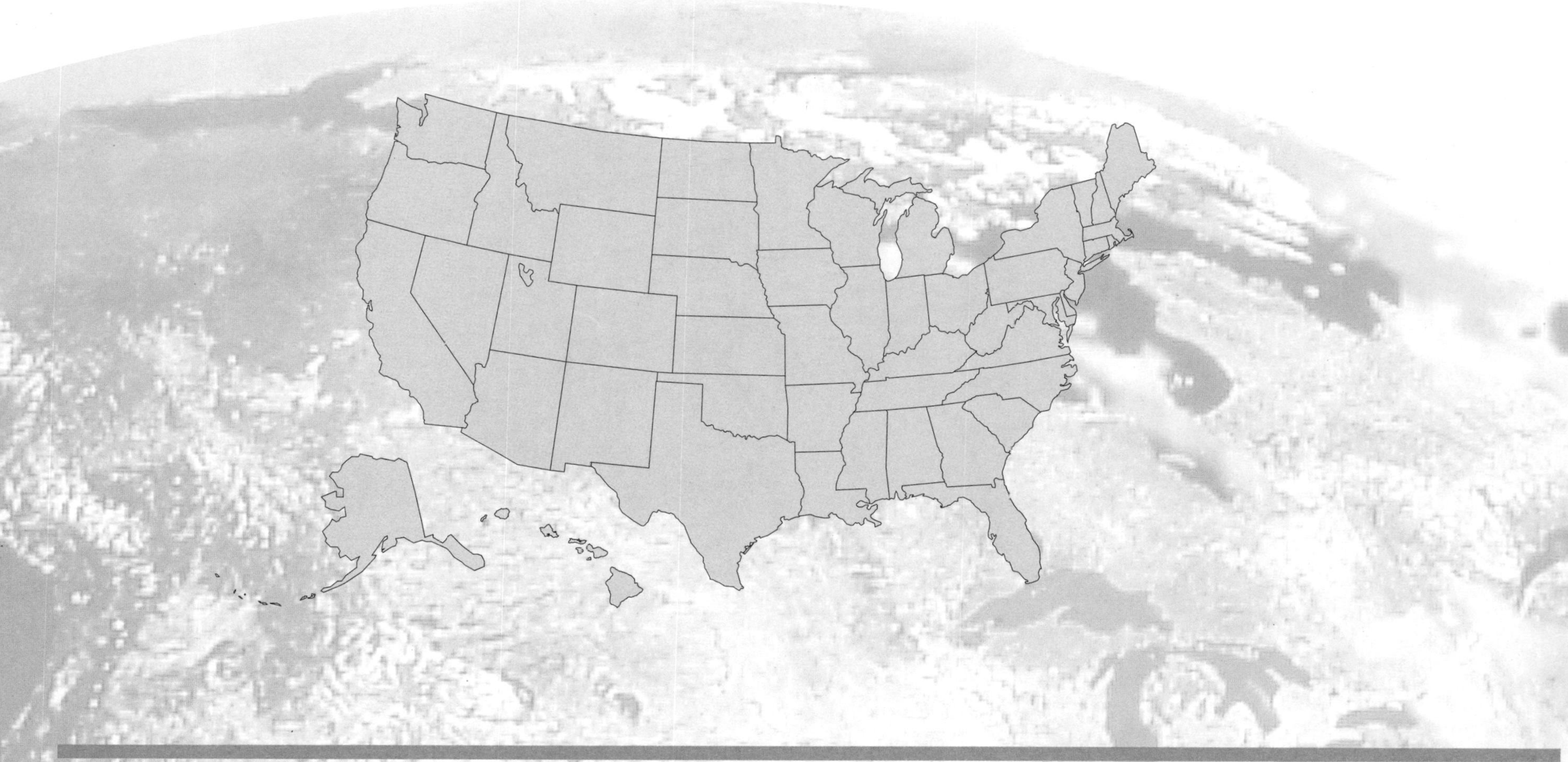

Legend

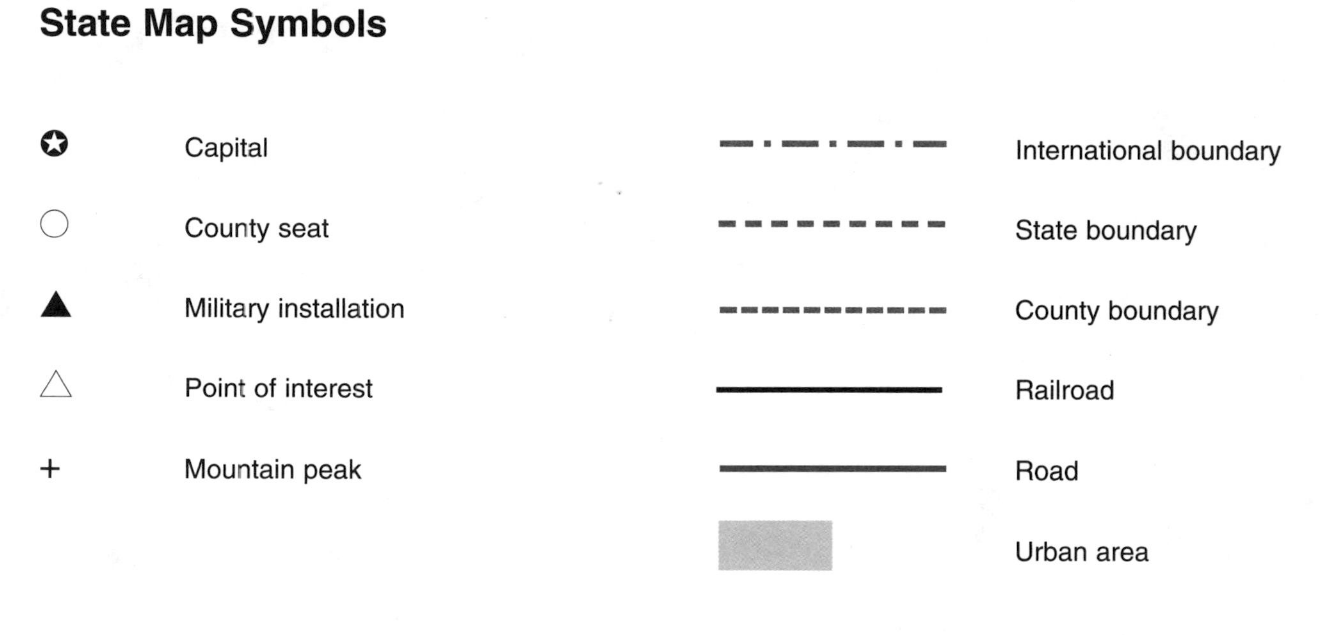

State Map Symbols

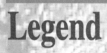

Capital		⎯·⎯·⎯·⎯	International boundary
○ County seat		⎯ ⎯ ⎯ ⎯	State boundary
▲ Military installation		- - - - - -	County boundary
△ Point of interest		⎯⎯⎯⎯	Railroad
+ Mountain peak		⎯⎯⎯⎯	Road
		▨	Urban area

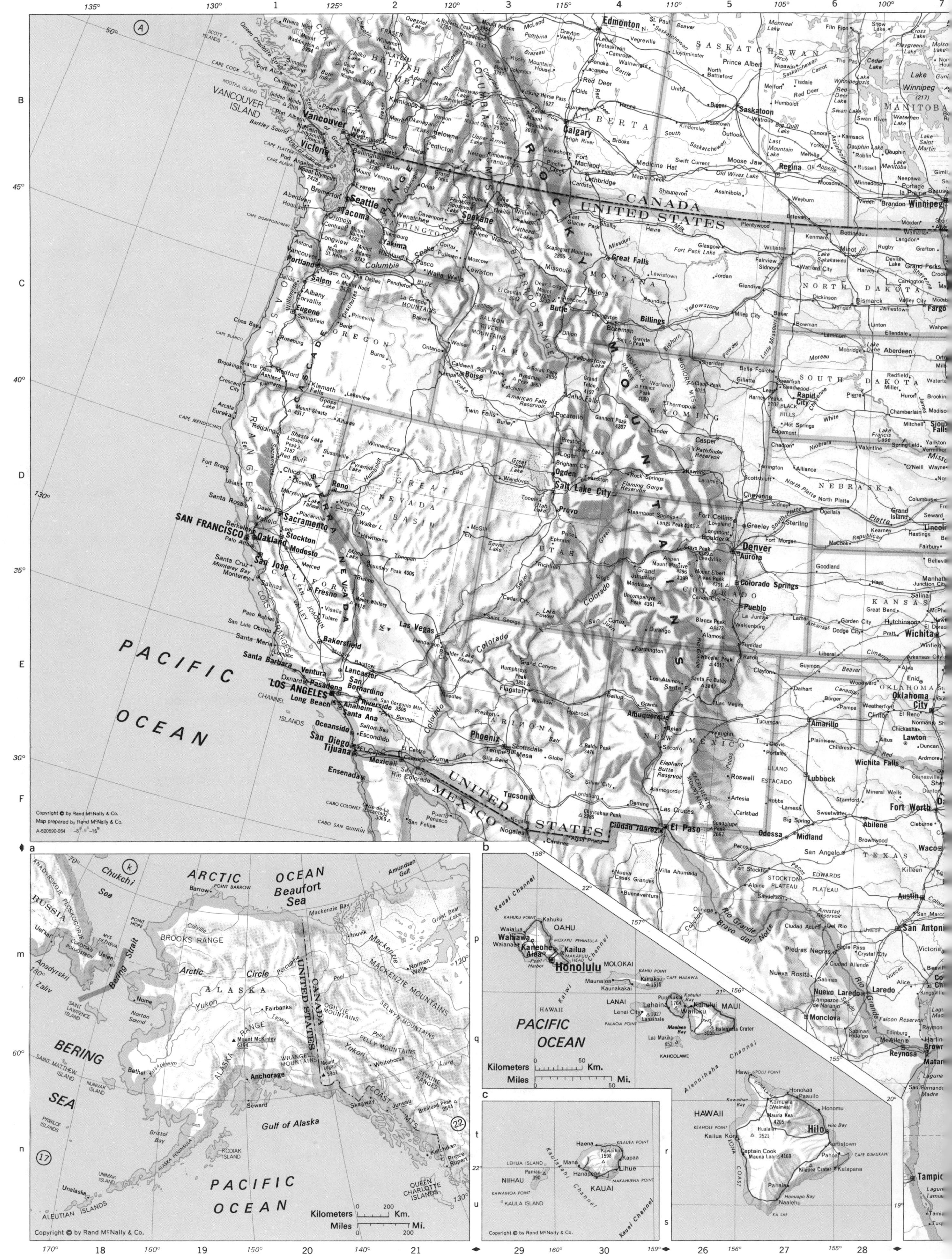

PACIFIC OCEAN

PACIFIC OCEAN

CANADA
UNITED STATES

UNITED STATES
MEXICO

VANCOUVER ISLAND

BRITISH COLUMBIA

ALBERTA

SASKATCHEWAN

MANITOBA

WASHINGTON

OREGON

IDAHO

MONTANA

NORTH DAKOTA

SOUTH DAKOTA

WYOMING

NEBRASKA

NEVADA

UTAH

COLORADO

KANSAS

CALIFORNIA

ARIZONA

NEW MEXICO

OKLAHOMA

TEXAS

GREAT BASIN

ROCKY MOUNTAINS

SIERRA NEVADA

COAST RANGE

SAN FRANCISCO
Oakland
San Jose
Sacramento
Stockton
Modesto
Fresno
Bakersfield
Santa Barbara
LOS ANGELES
Long Beach
Anaheim
San Diego
Tijuana

Seattle
Tacoma
Olympia
Portland
Salem
Eugene

Spokane
Yakima

Vancouver
Victoria

Boise

Salt Lake City
Provo
Ogden

Las Vegas

Phoenix
Tucson
Mesa

Denver
Aurora
Colorado Springs
Pueblo

Albuquerque

El Paso
Ciudad Juárez

Edmonton
Calgary
Saskatoon
Regina

Winnipeg
Brandon

Great Falls
Billings

Rapid City

Cheyenne

Oklahoma City
Lawton

Wichita

Amarillo
Lubbock

Wichita Falls
Fort Worth
Abilene
Midland
Odessa
San Angelo
Austin
San Antonio

Copyright © by Rand McNally & Co.
Map prepared by Rand McNally & Co.
A-520590-264

ARCTIC OCEAN
Beaufort Sea
Chukchi Sea

RUSSIA

BROOKS RANGE

ALASKA

Arctic Circle

Bering Strait

Nome

Fairbanks

Anchorage

Mount McKinley 6194

BERING SEA

ALEUTIAN ISLANDS

Gulf of Alaska

PACIFIC OCEAN

CANADA
UNITED STATES

MACKENZIE MOUNTAINS

Yukon

Whitehorse

Juneau

Kilometers 200 Km.
Miles 200 Mi.

Copyright © by Rand McNally & Co.

OAHU
Waialua
Wahiawa
Waianae
Kaneohe
Aiea
Honolulu

MOLOKAI

LANAI
Lanai City

MAUI
Lahaina
Wailuku
Kahului
Haleakala Crater

KAHOOLAWE

PACIFIC OCEAN

Kilometers 50 Km.
Miles 50 Mi.

NIIHAU

KAUAI
Lihue
Kapaa
Hanapepe

HAWAII
Kailua Kona
Captain Cook
Mauna Loa 4169
Mauna Kea 4205
Hilo

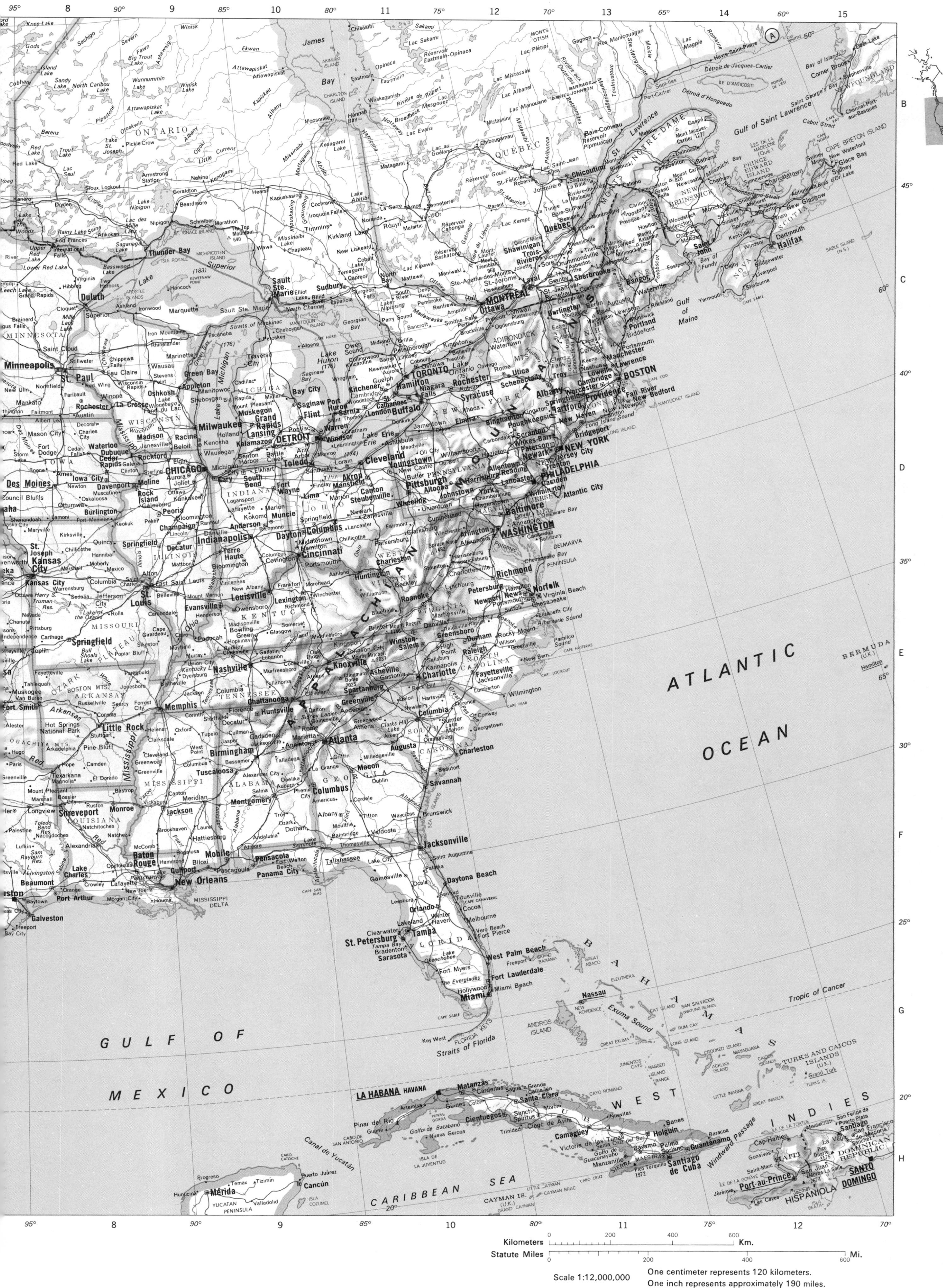

Kilometers
Statute Miles
Scale 1:12,000,000   One centimeter represents 120 kilometers.
One inch represents approximately 190 miles.
Albers Conical Equal-Area Projection

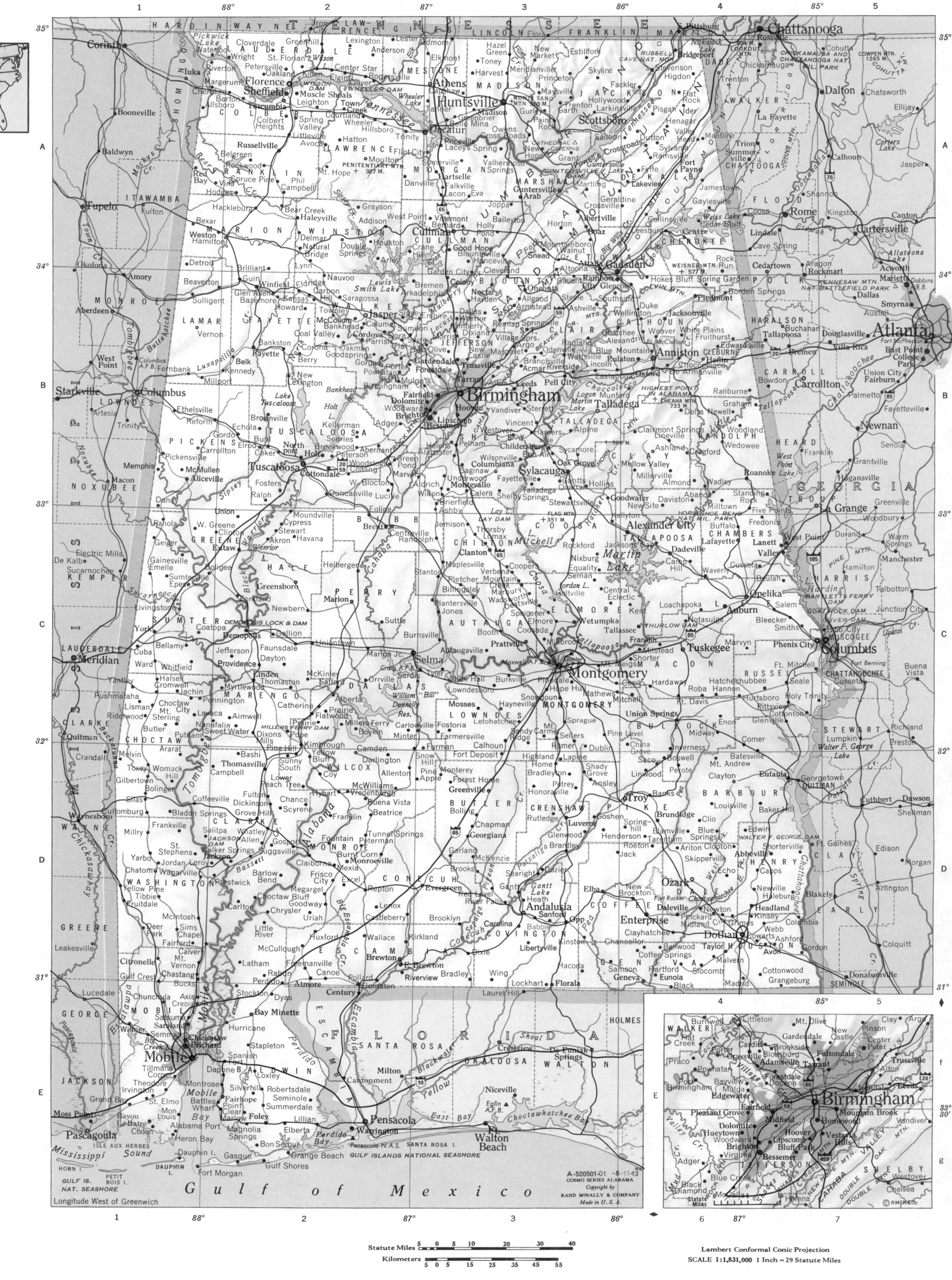

Statute Miles

Kilometers

Lambert Conformal Conic Projection
SCALE 1:1,831,000 1 Inch = 29 Statute Miles

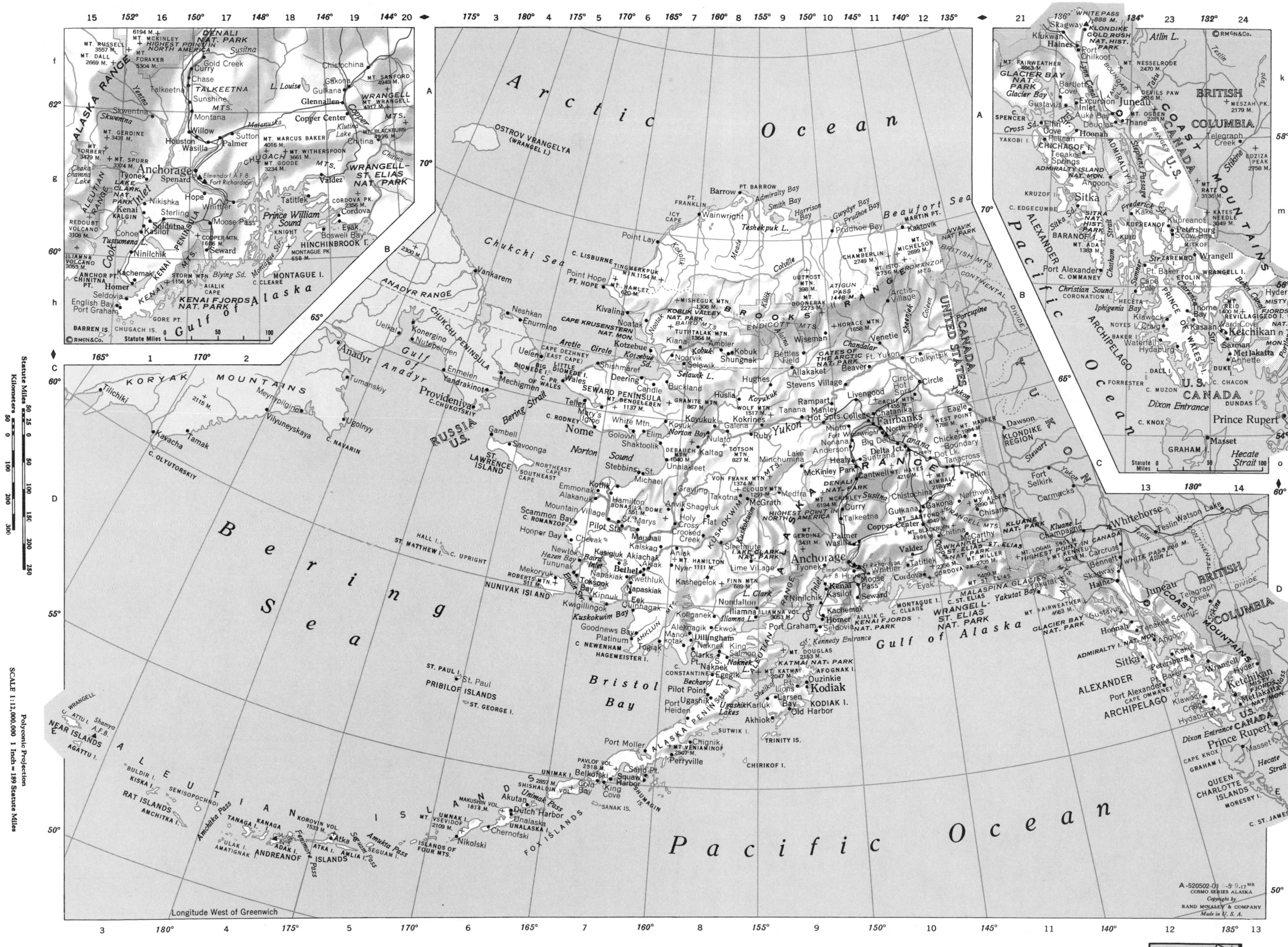
Arctic Ocean
Beaufort Sea
Chukchi Sea
Bering Sea
Bristol Bay
Gulf of Alaska
Pacific Ocean
Gulf of Anadyr
CANADA
UNITED STATES
RUSSIA
U.S.
BROOKS RANGE
ALASKA RANGE
ALEUTIAN ISLANDS
ALEXANDER ARCHIPELAGO
COAST MOUNTAINS
Anchorage
Fairbanks
Juneau
Nome
Kodiak
Prince Rupert
Whitehorse
Dawson
Statute Miles 50 25 0 50 100 150 200 250
Kilometers 50 0 100 200 300
Polyconic Projection
SCALE 1:12,000,000 1 Inch = 189 Statute Miles
Longitude West of Greenwich
COSMO SERIES ALASKA
Copyright by RAND McNALLY & COMPANY
Made in U. S. A.

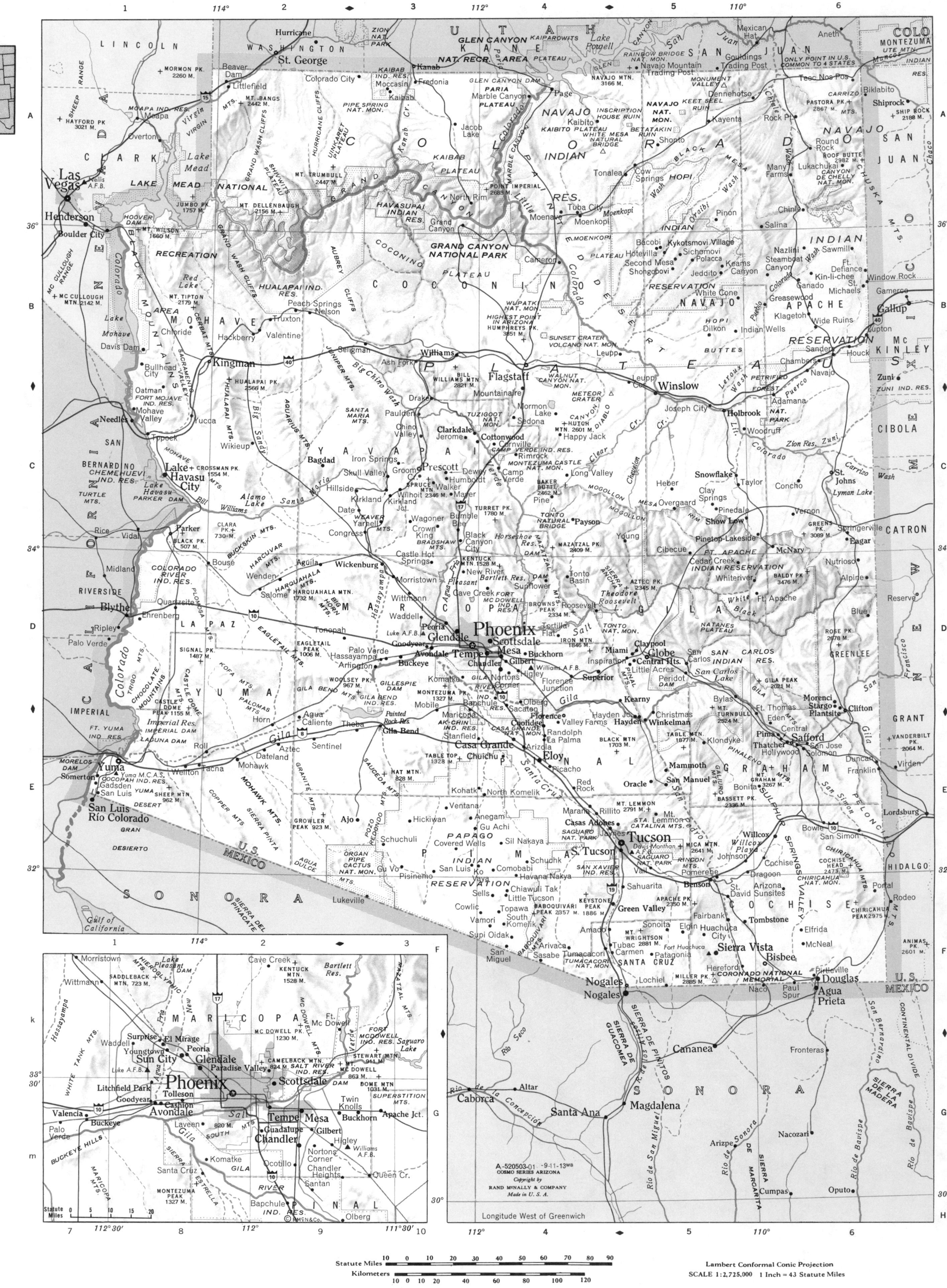

Lambert Conformal Conic Projection
SCALE 1:2,725,000   1 Inch = 43 Statute Miles

Statute Miles

Kilometers

Longitude West of Greenwich

A-520503-01 · 9-11-13MB
COSMO SERIES ARIZONA
Copyright by
RAND McNALLY & COMPANY
Made in U.S.A.

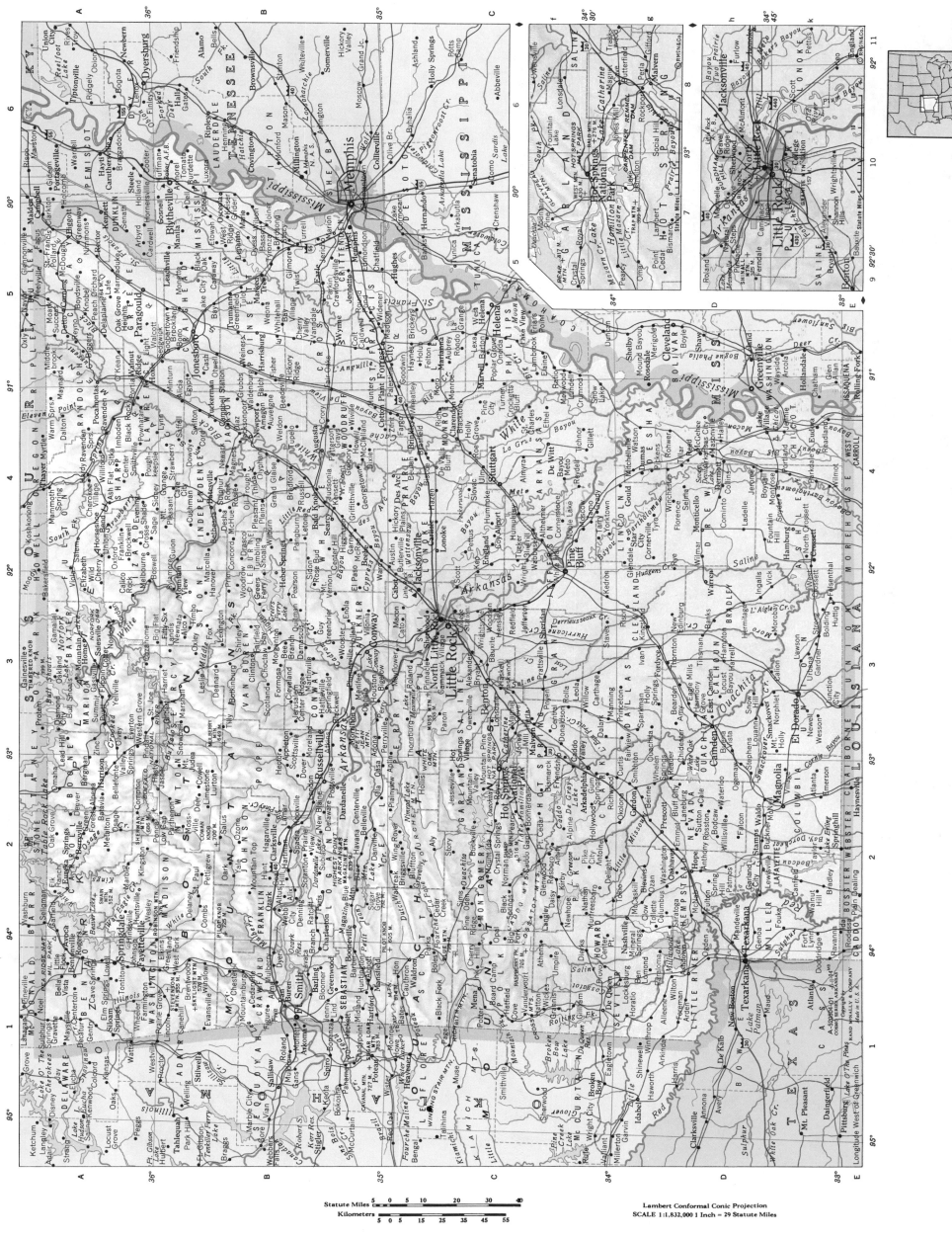

Statute Miles 5 0 5 10 20 30 40
Kilometers 5 0 5 15 25 35 45 55

Lambert Conformal Conic Projection
SCALE 1:1,832,000 1 Inch = 29 Statute Miles

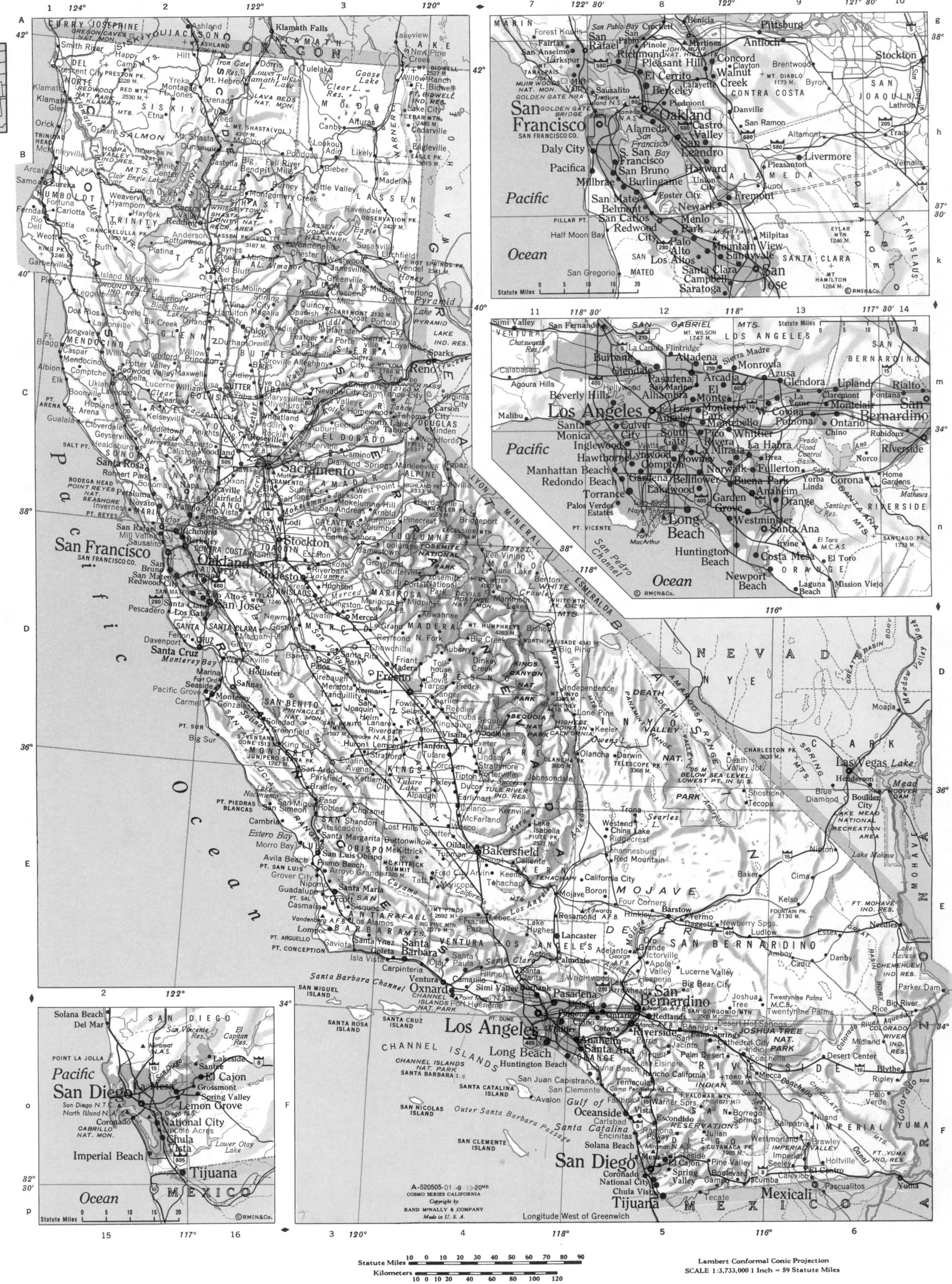

Statute Miles 10 0 10 20 30 40 50 60 70 80 90

Kilometers 10 0 10 20 40 60 80 100 120

Lambert Conformal Conic Projection
SCALE 1:3,733,000 1 Inch = 59 Statute Miles

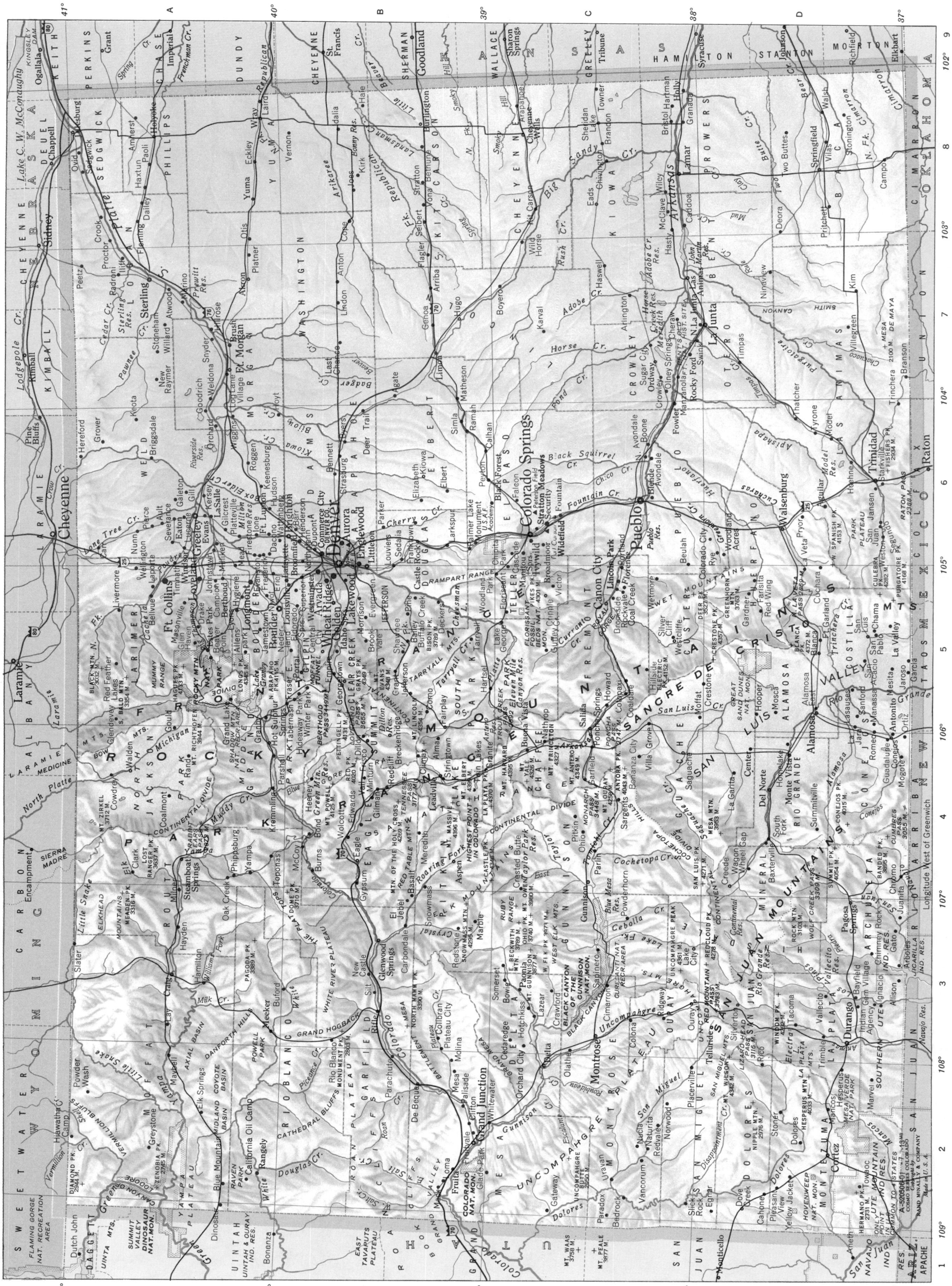

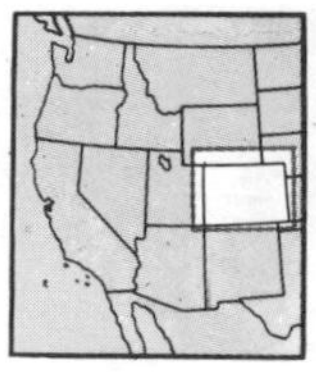

Colorado

COLORADO

ROCKY MOUNTAINS

SANGRE DE CRISTO MTS

SAN JUAN MOUNTAINS

CONTINENTAL DIVIDE

NORTH PARK MIDDLE PARK SOUTH PARK

Denver Colorado Springs Pueblo Boulder Ft. Collins Greeley Sterling Grand Junction Durango Trinidad Alamosa Montrose Cheyenne Sidney Laramie

NEBRASKA KANSAS OKLAHOMA NEW MEXICO WYOMING UTAH ARIZONA

Statute Miles 5 0 5 10 20 30 40 50
Kilometers 5 0 5 15 25 35 45 55 65 75

Lambert Conformal Conic Projection
SCALE 1:2,186,000   1 Inch = 34.5 Statute Miles

RAND MCNALLY & COMPANY

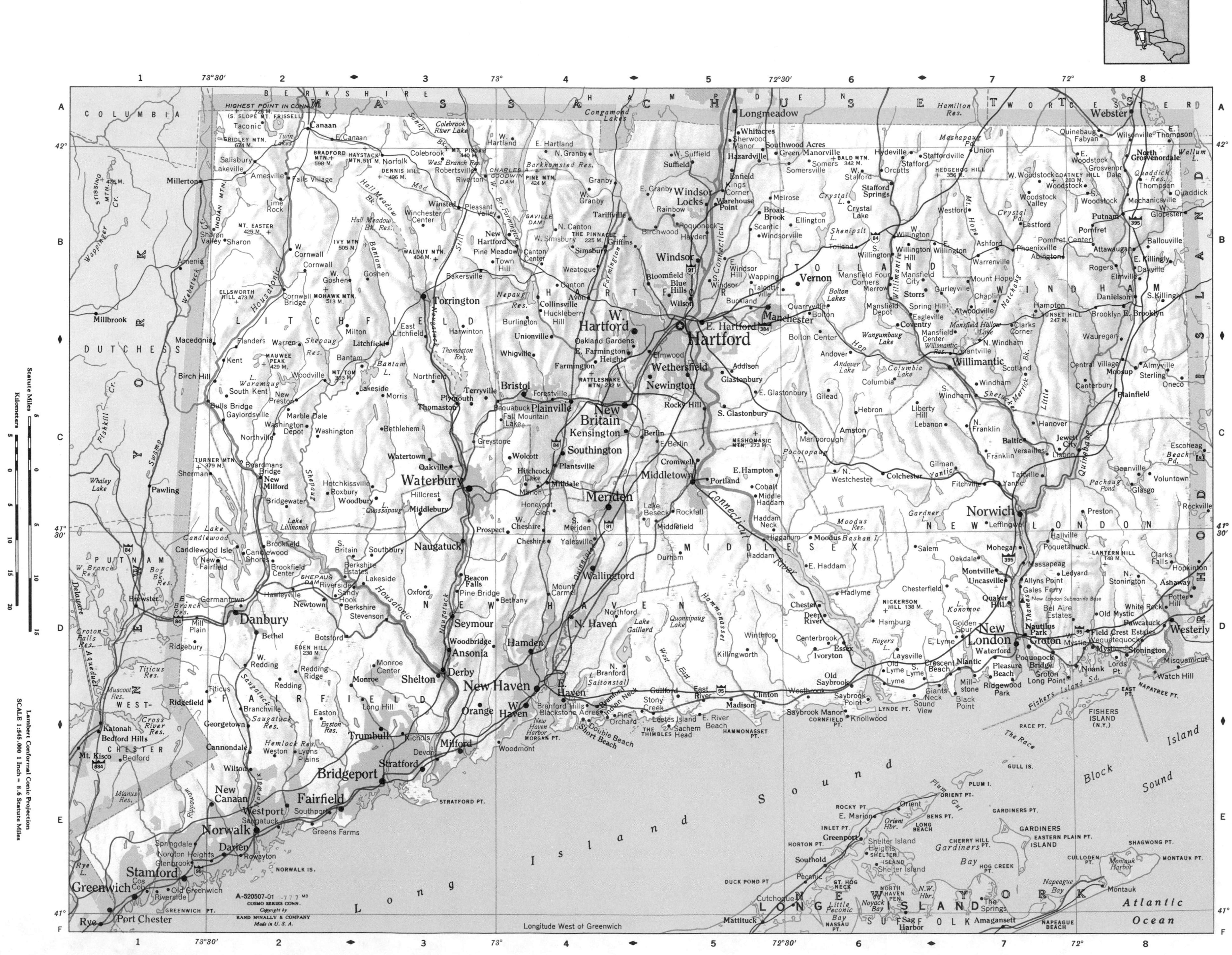

Statute Miles

Kilometers

Lambert Conformal Conic Projection
SCALE 1:545,000 1 Inch = 8.6 Statute Miles

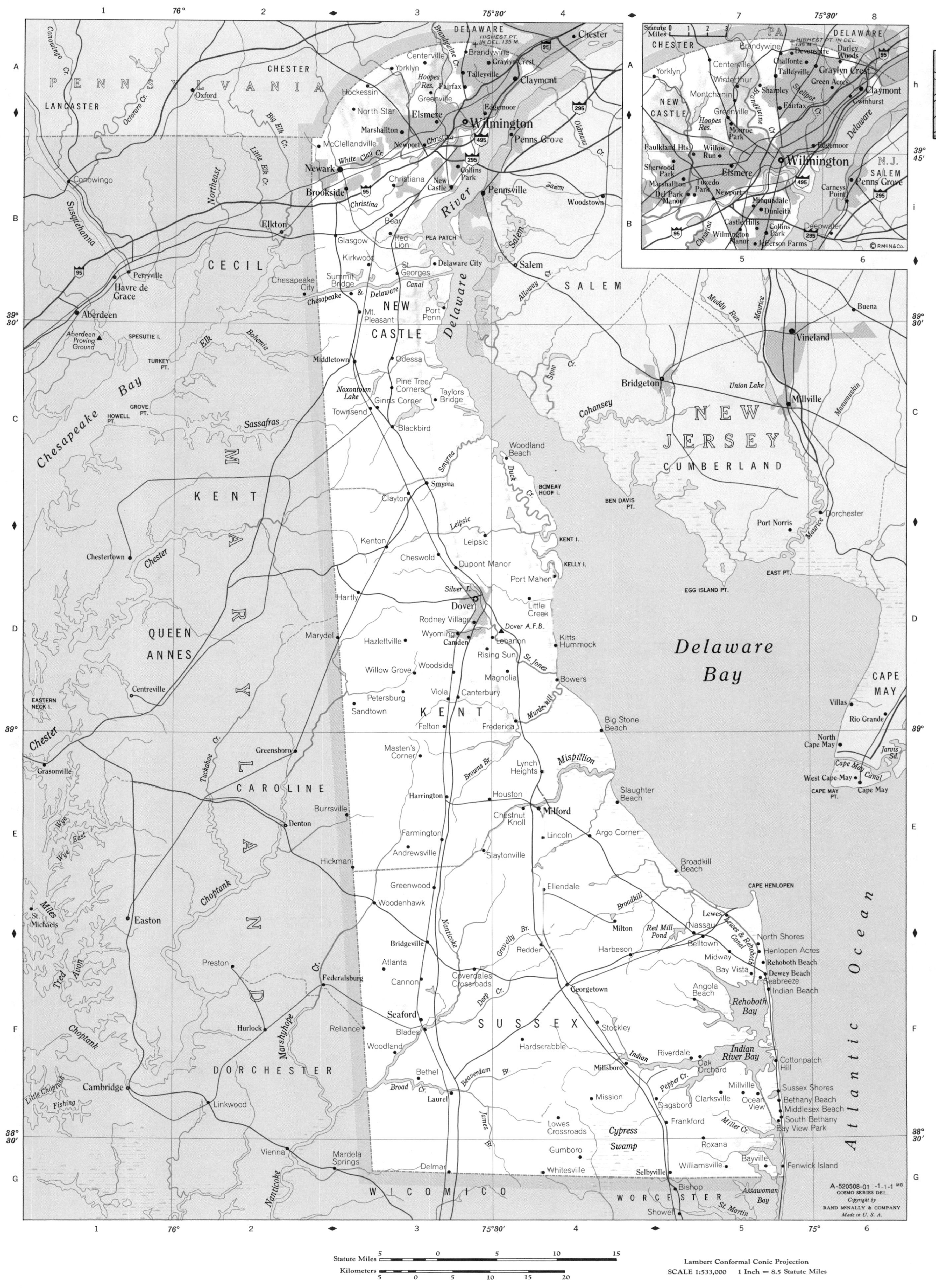

Lambert Conformal Conic Projection
SCALE 1:533,000   1 Inch = 8.5 Statute Miles

Statute Miles
Kilometers

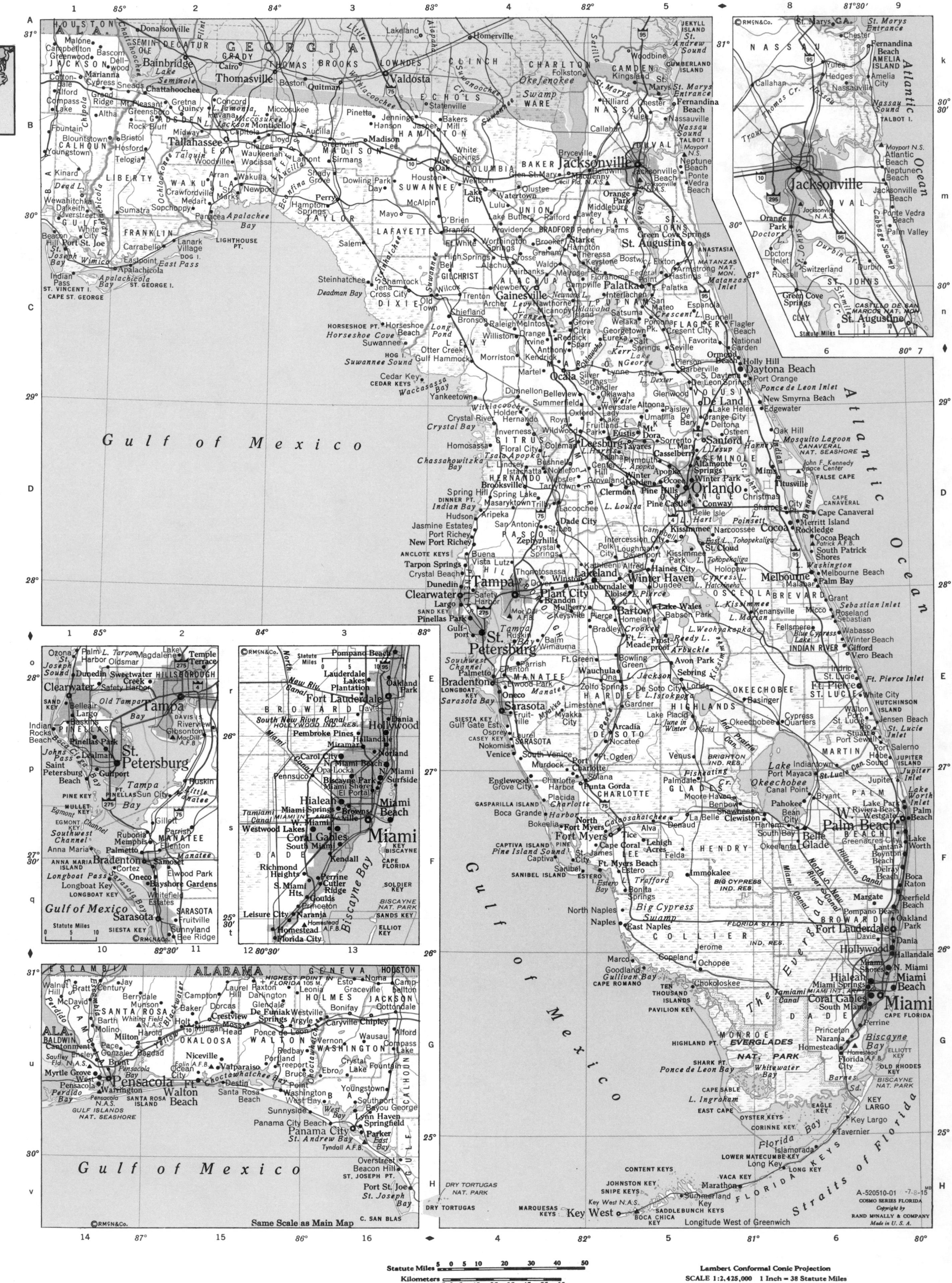

Statute Miles 5 0 5 10 20 30 40 50
Kilometers 5 0 5 15 25 35 45 55 65

Lambert Conformal Conic Projection
SCALE 1:2,425,000 1 Inch = 38 Statute Miles

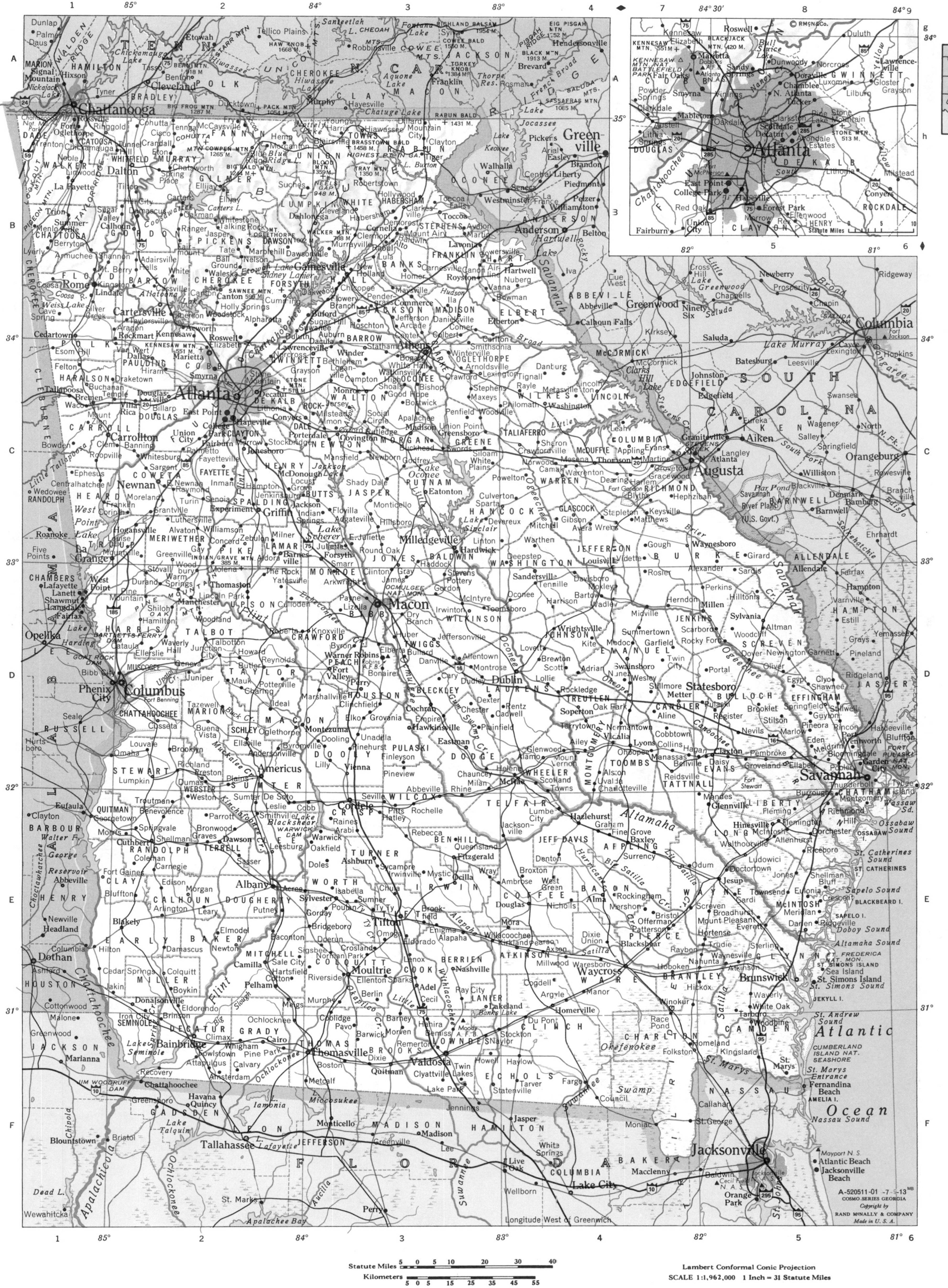

Statute Miles   5 0 5 10   20   30   40

Kilometers   5 0 5   15   25   35   45   55

Lambert Conformal Conic Projection
SCALE 1:1,962,000   1 Inch = 31 Statute Miles

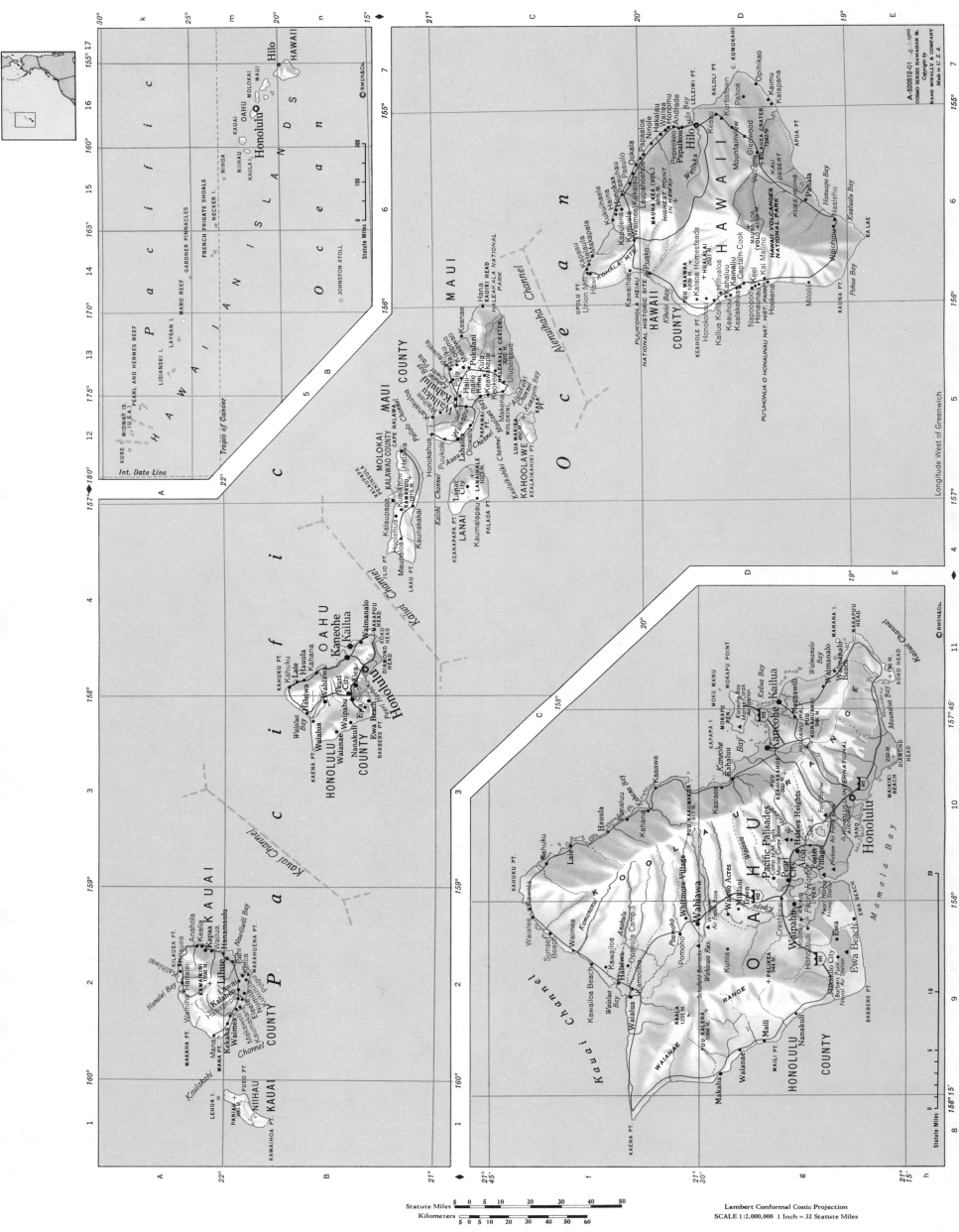

Statute Miles 5 0 5 10   20   30   40   50
Kilometers 5 0 5 10 20 30 40 50 60

Lambert Conformal Conic Projection
SCALE 1:2,000,000   1 Inch = 32 Statute Miles

Statute Miles 5 0 5 10 20 30 40 50 60

Kilometers 5 0 5 15 25 35 45 55 65 75

Lambert Conformal Conic Projection

SCALE 1:2,633,000 1 Inch = 41.5 Statute Miles

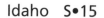

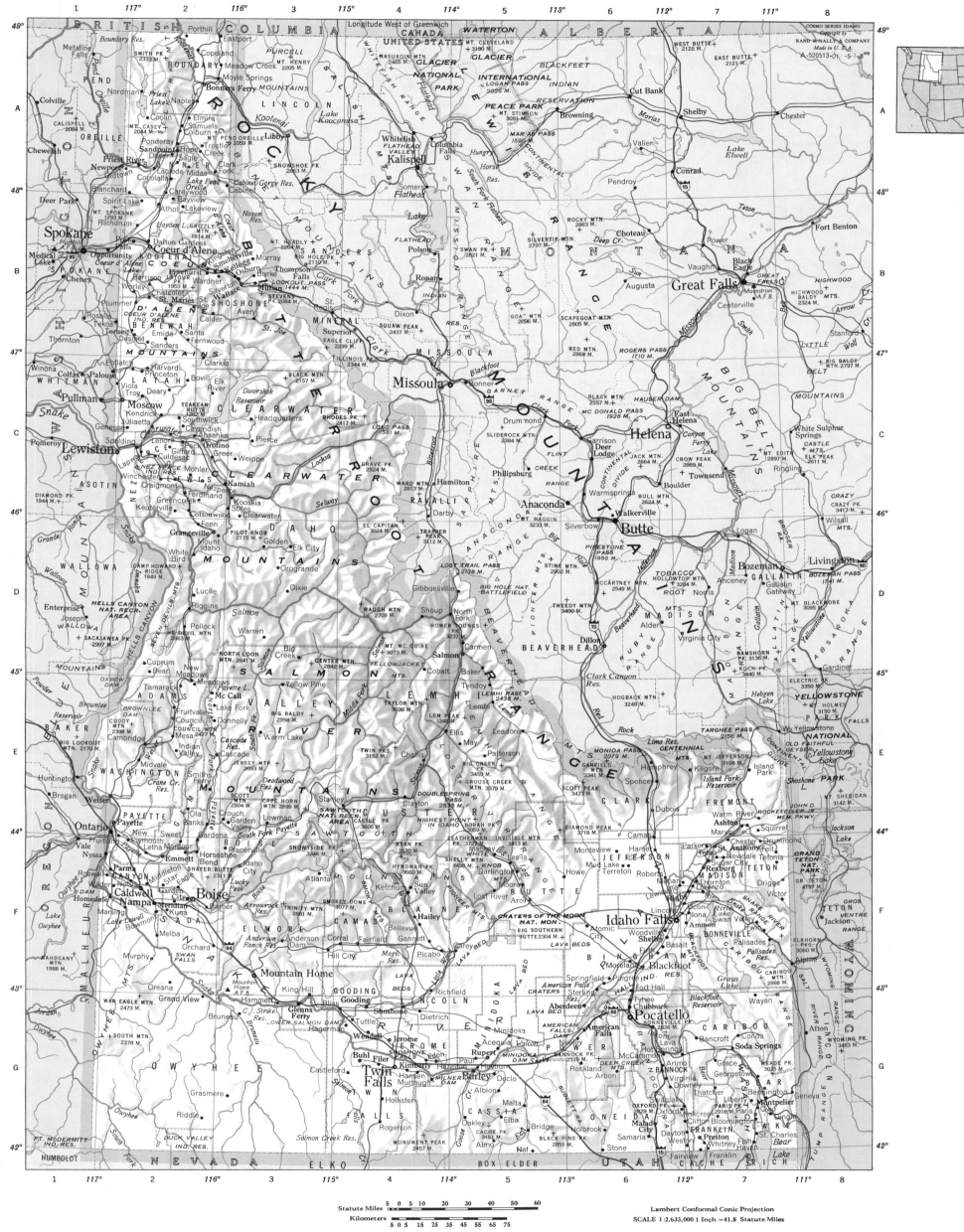

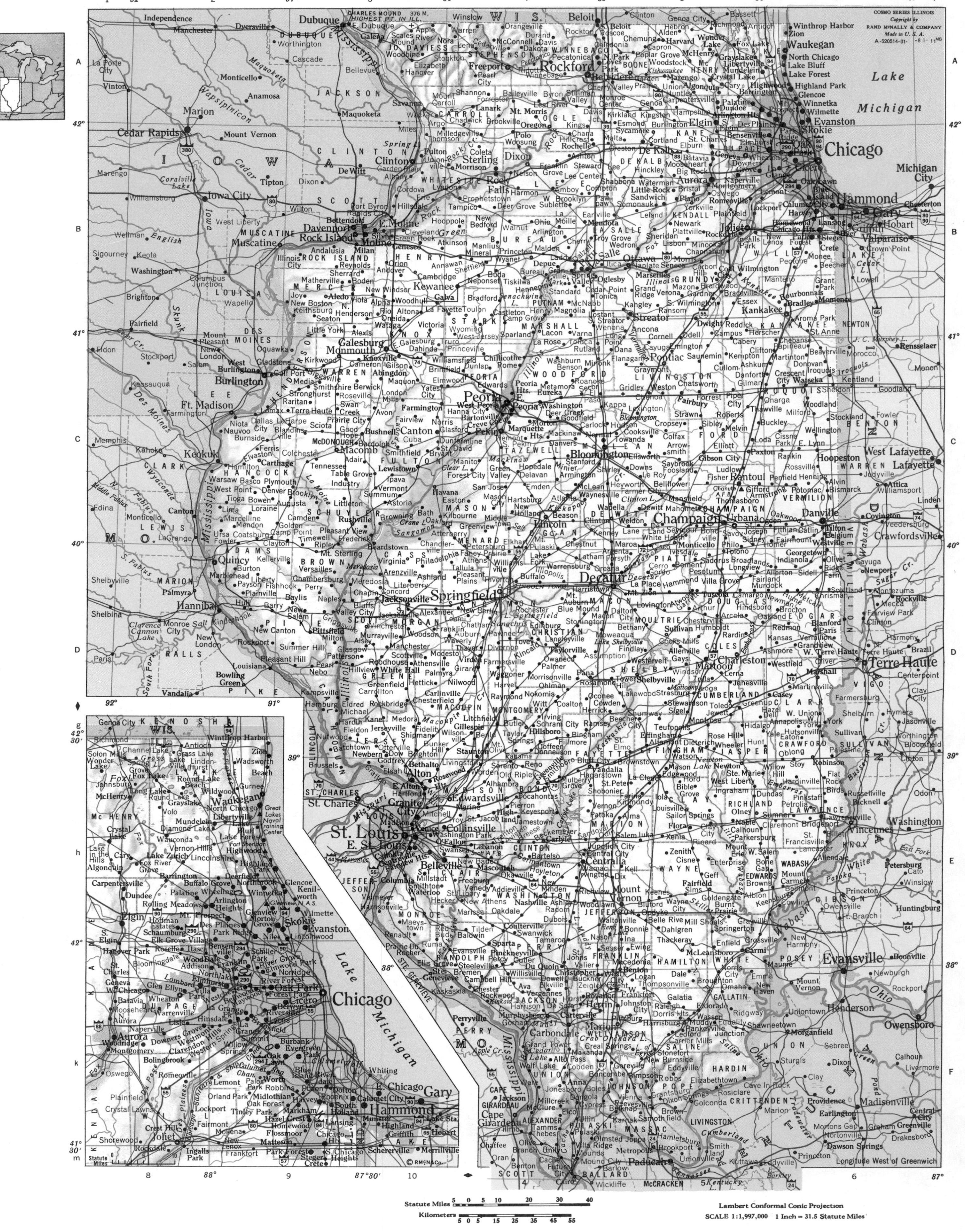

Statute Miles 5 0 5 10 20 30 40

Kilometers 5 0 5 15 25 35 45 55

Lambert Conformal Conic Projection
SCALE 1:1,997,000 1 Inch = 31.5 Statute Miles

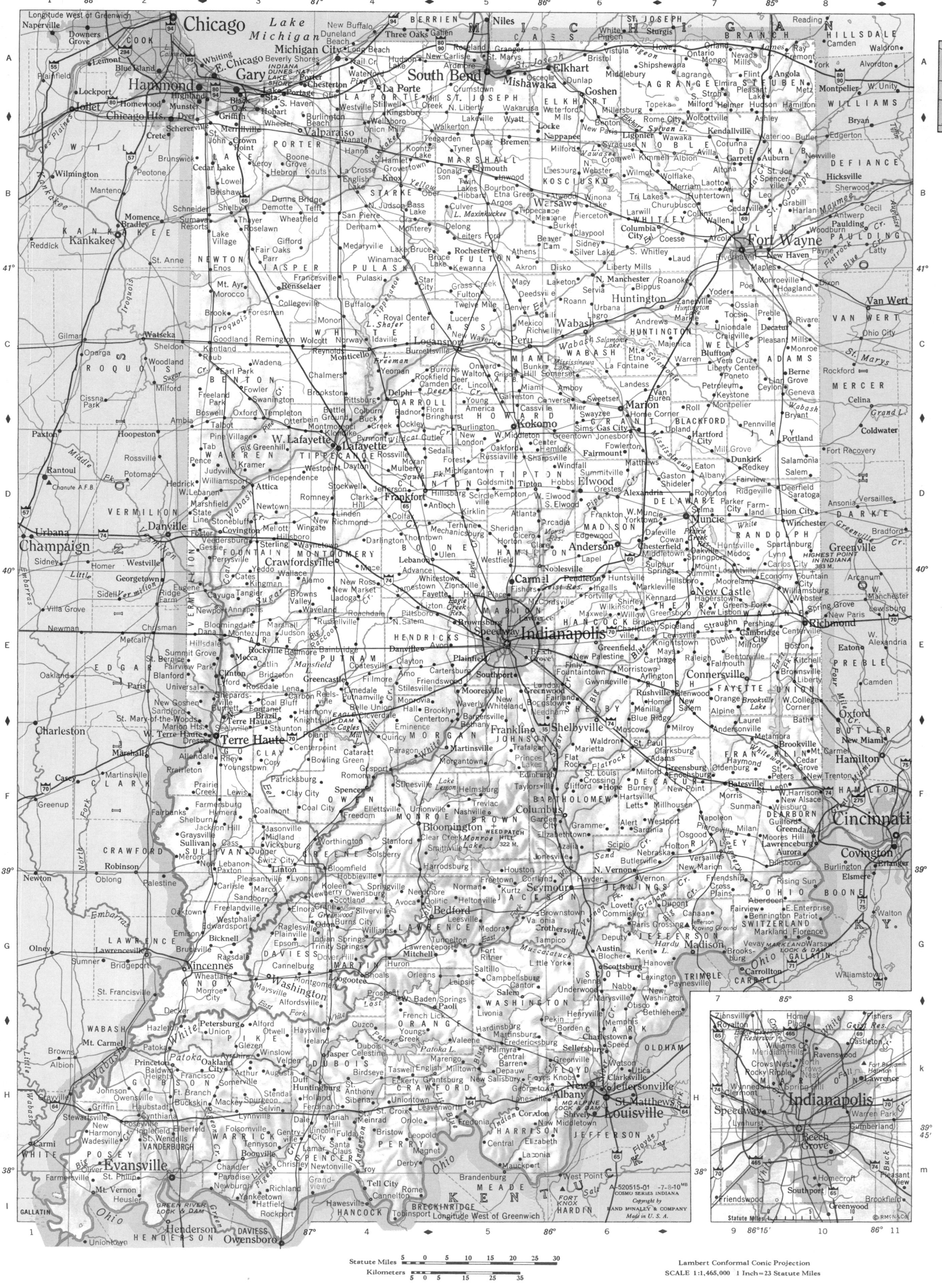

Lambert Conformal Conic Projection
SCALE 1:1,465,000   1 Inch=23 Statute Miles

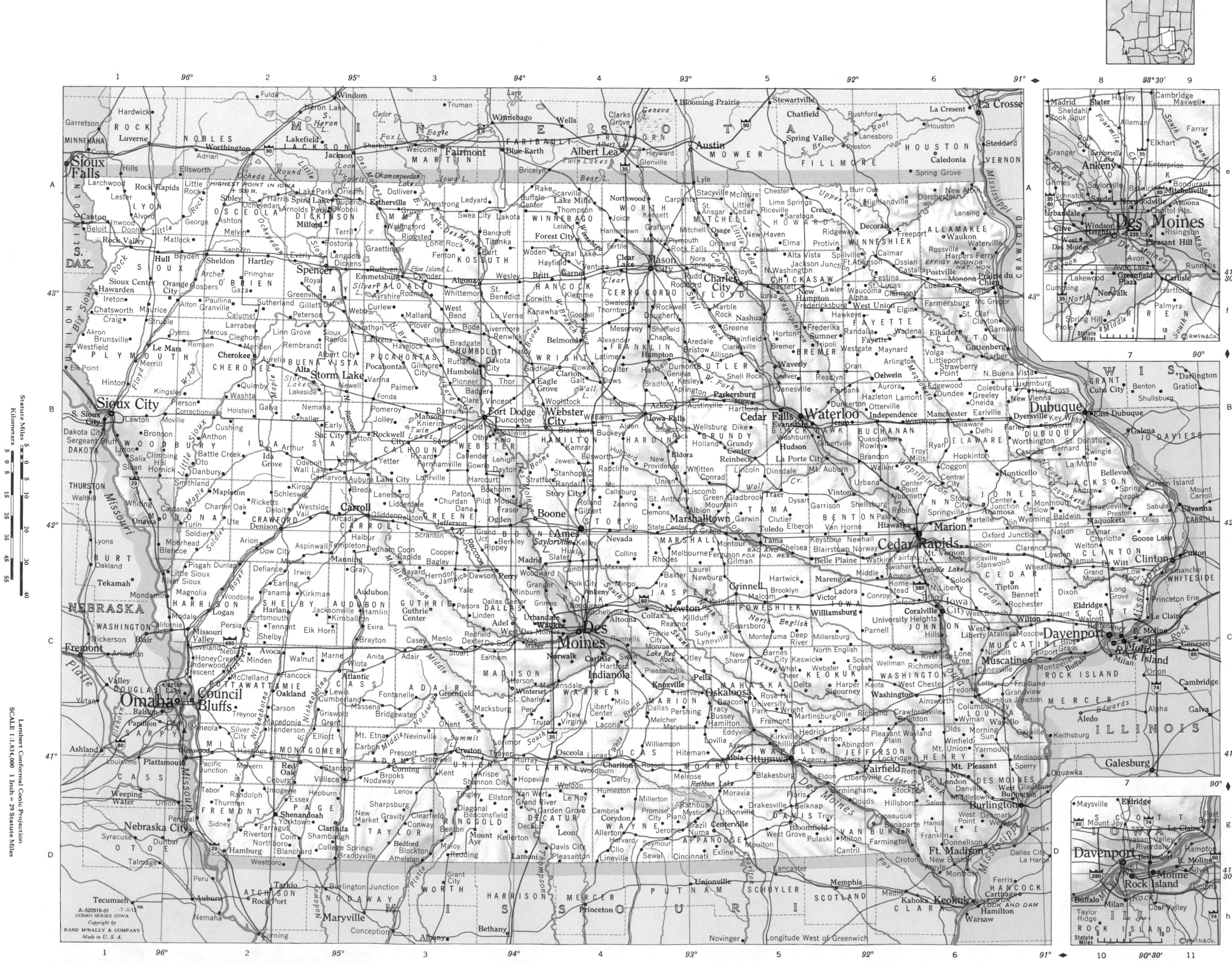

Statute Miles 5 0 5 10   20   30   40

Kilometers 5 0 5 15   25   35   45   55

Lambert Conformal Conic Projection
SCALE 1:1,834,000   1 Inch = 29 Statute Miles

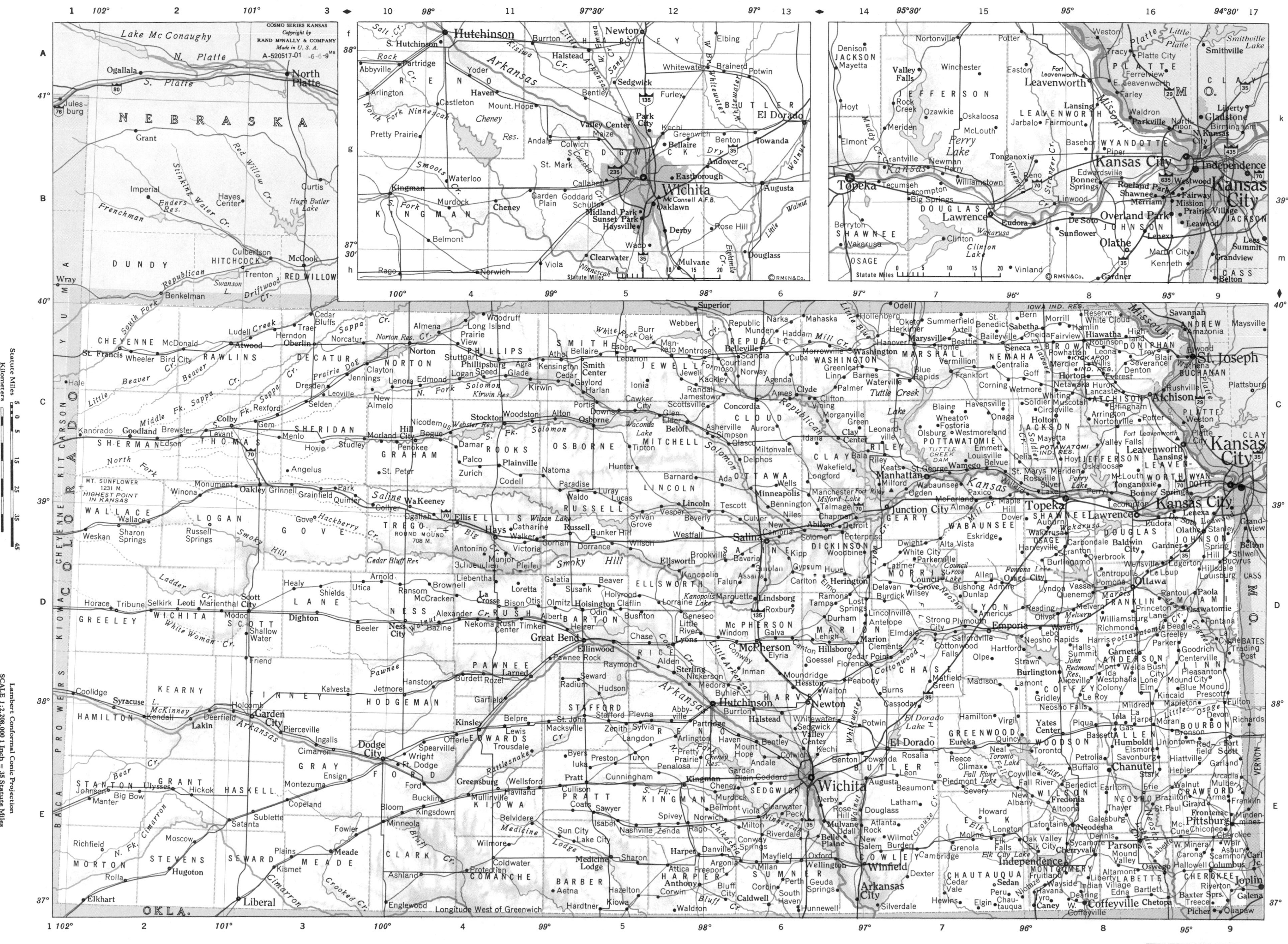
KANSAS
NEBRASKA
OKLA.
MO.
COLORADO
Topeka
Wichita
Kansas City
Lawrence
Manhattan
Salina
Hutchinson
Dodge City
Garden City
Great Bend
Emporia
Leavenworth
Olathe
Independence
Coffeyville
Pittsburg
Liberal
Goodland
Colby
Hays
Junction City
Newton
El Dorado
Arkansas City
Winfield
Chanute
Parsons
St. Joseph
Joplin
North Platte
McCook
Lambert Conformal Conic Projection
SCALE 1:2,208,000 1 Inch = 35 Statute Miles
Statute Miles
Kilometers
Longitude West of Greenwich
MT. SUNFLOWER 1231 M. HIGHEST POINT IN KANSAS
COSMO SERIES KANSAS
Copyright by RAND McNALLY & COMPANY
Made in U. S. A.
A-520517-01

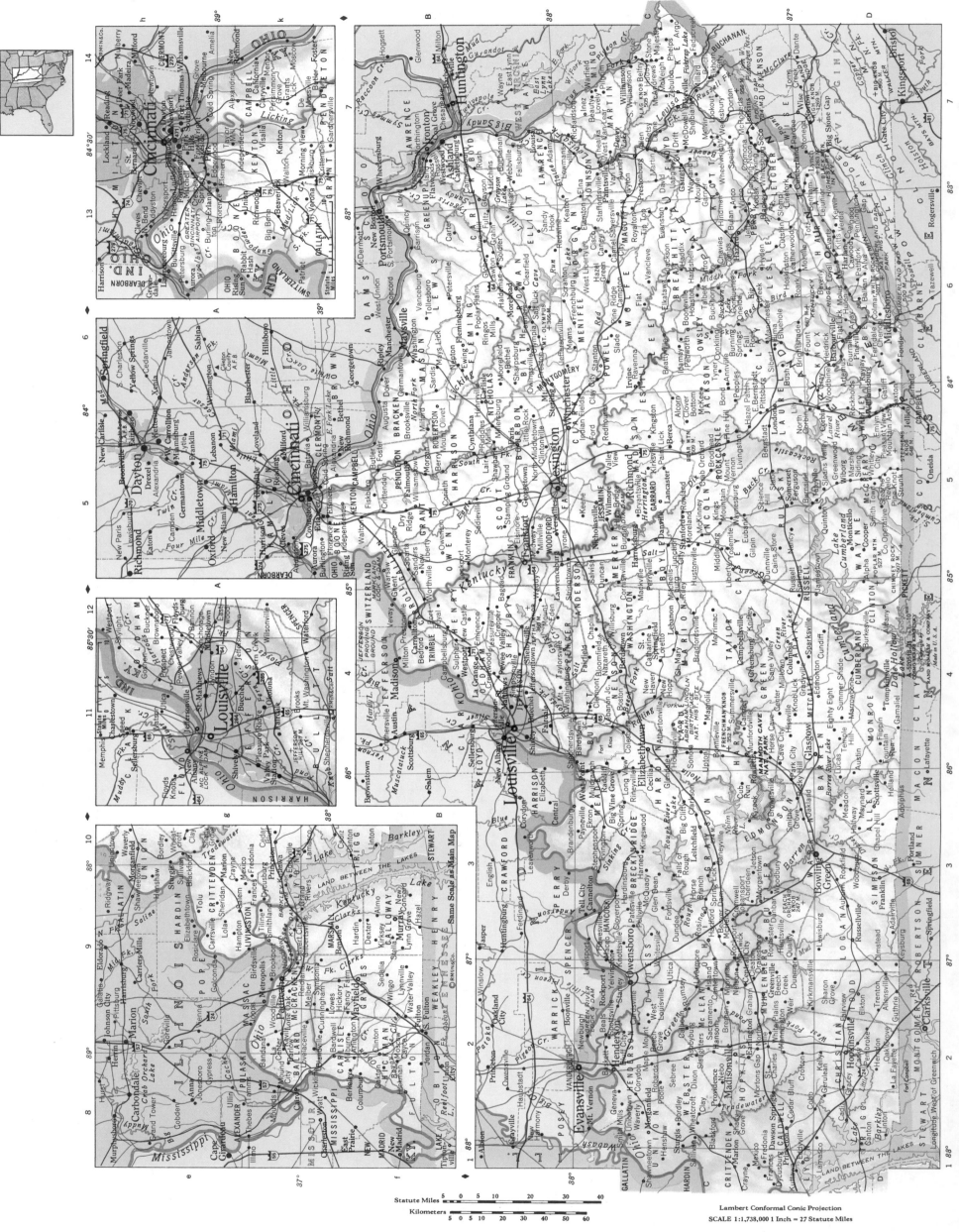

Statute Miles

Kilometers

Lambert Conformal Conic Projection
SCALE 1:1,738,000 1 Inch = 27 Statute Miles

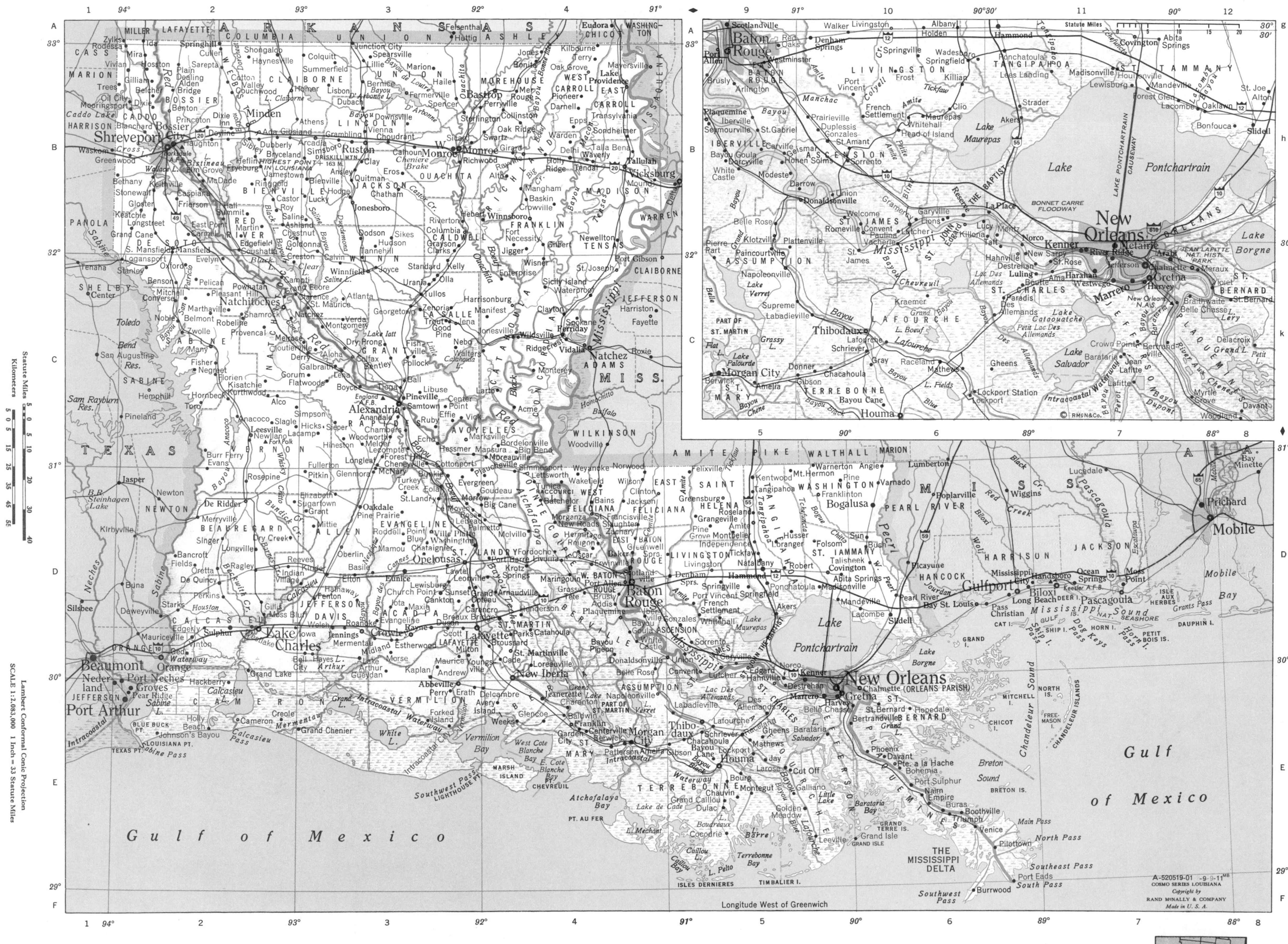

Statute Miles

Kilometers

Lambert Conformal Conic Projection

SCALE 1:2,083,000   1 Inch = 33 Statute Miles

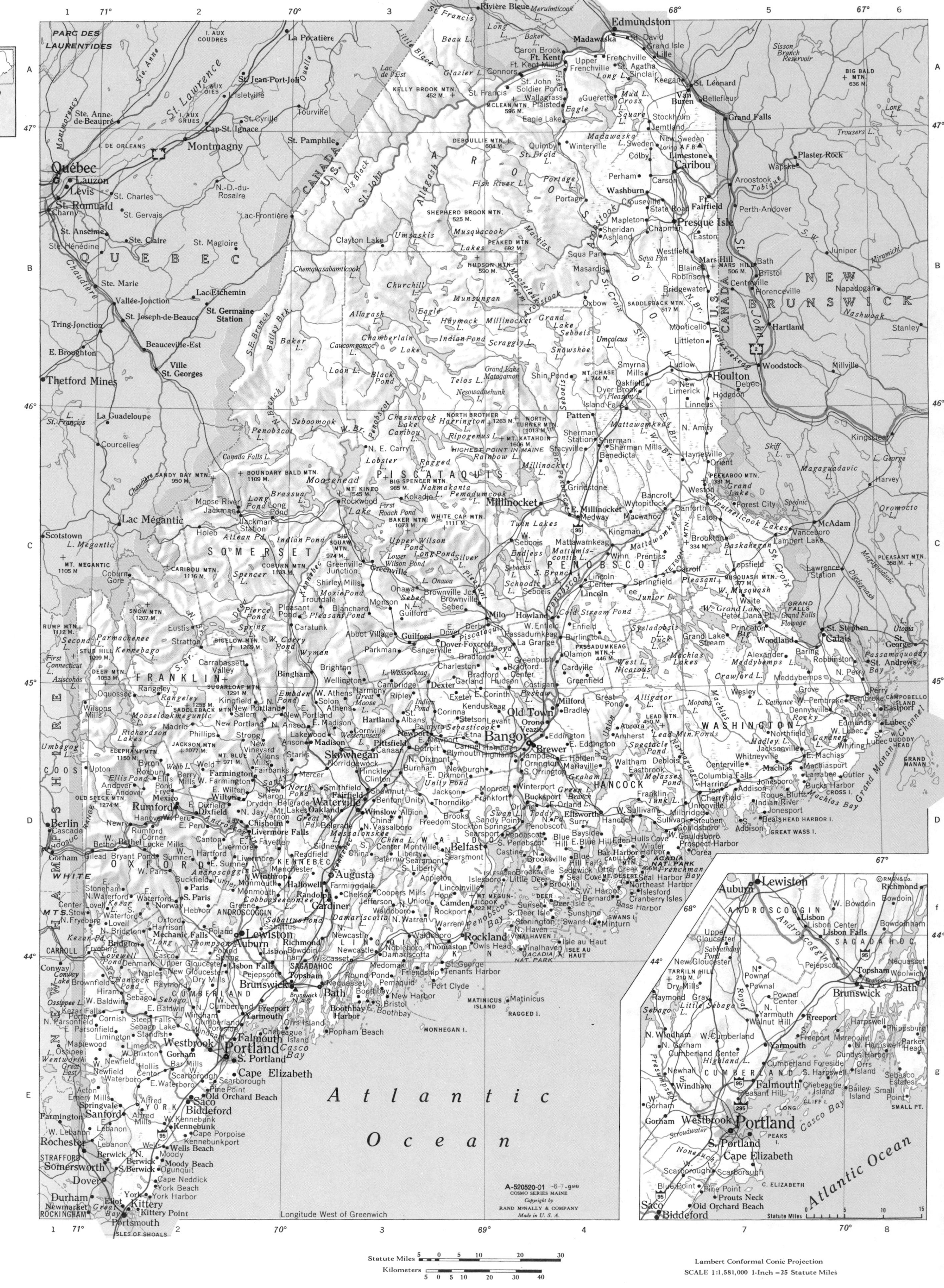

Atlantic Ocean

A-520520-01 -6-7-gmB
COSMO SERIES MAINE
Copyright by
RAND MCNALLY & COMPANY
Made in U.S.A.

Longitude West of Greenwich

Statute Miles 5 0 5 10   20   30
Kilometers   5 0 5 10 20   30 40

Lambert Conformal Conic Projection
SCALE 1:1,581,000 1-Inch = 25 Statute Miles

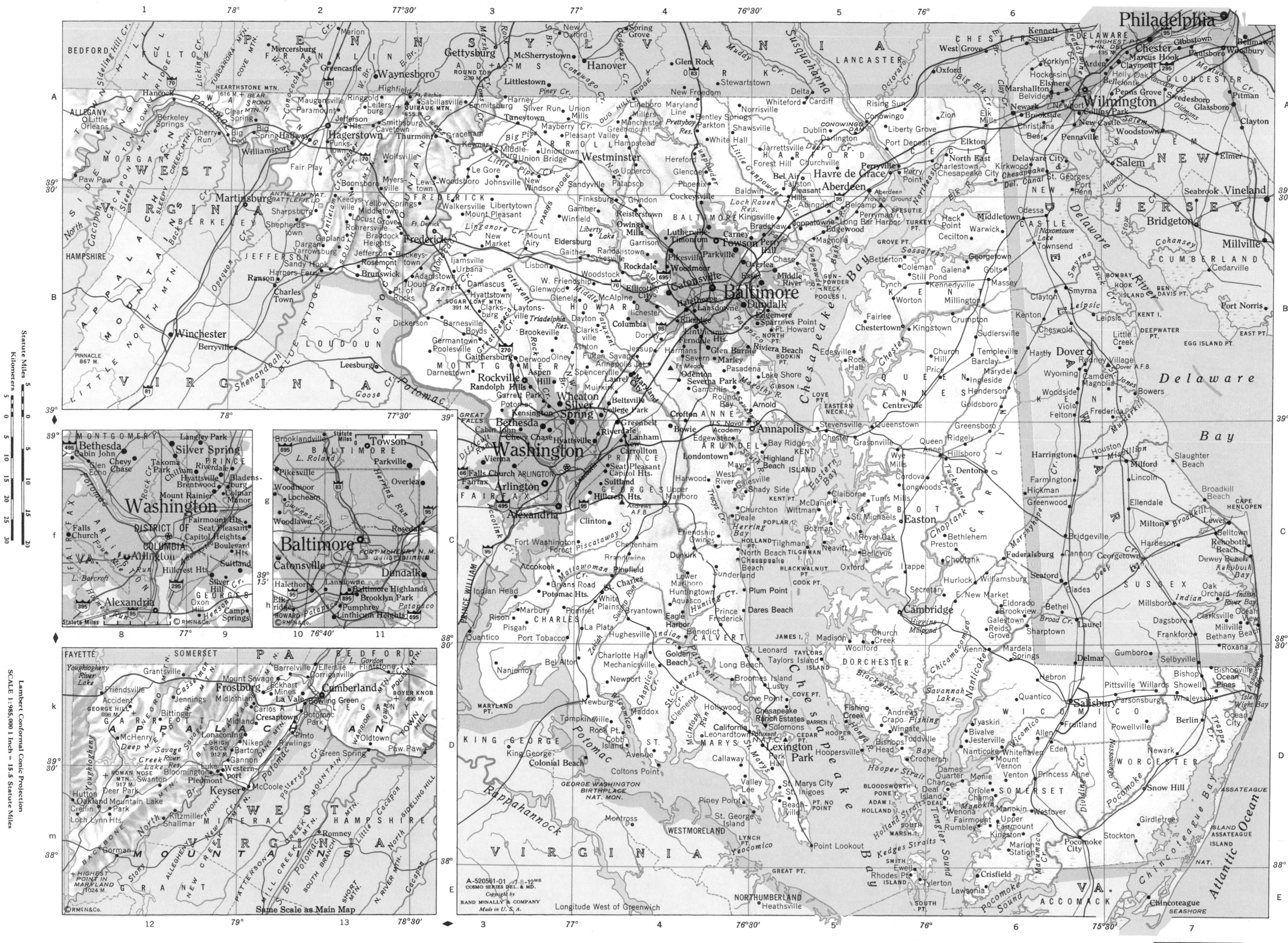

Statute Miles 5 0 5 10 15 20
Kilometers 5 0 5 10 15 20 25 30

Lambert Conformal Conic Projection
SCALE 1:985,000 1 Inch = 15.5 Statute Miles

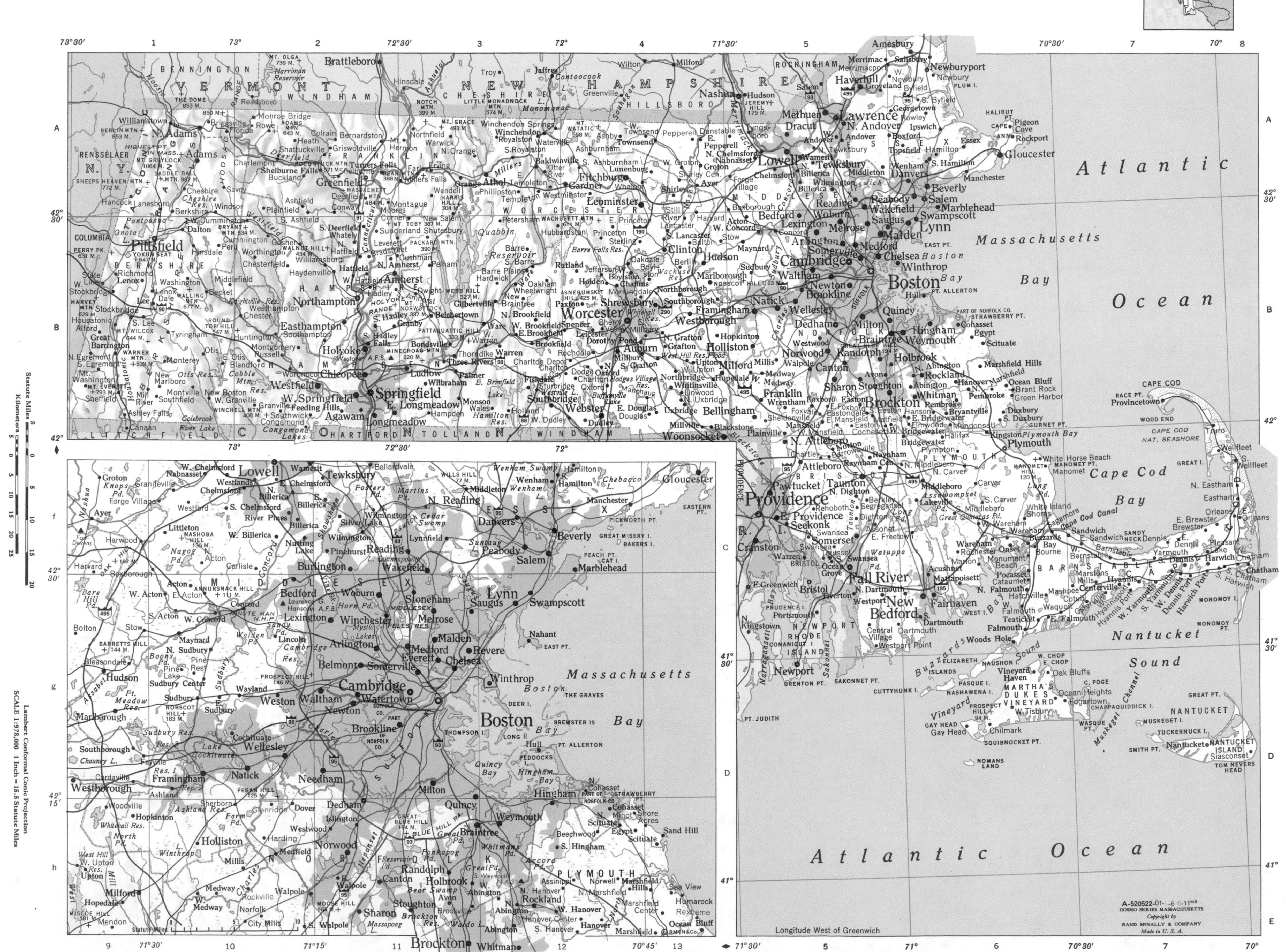

Statute Miles
Kilometers

Lambert Conformal Conic Projection
SCALE 1:978,000   1 Inch = 15.5 Statute Miles

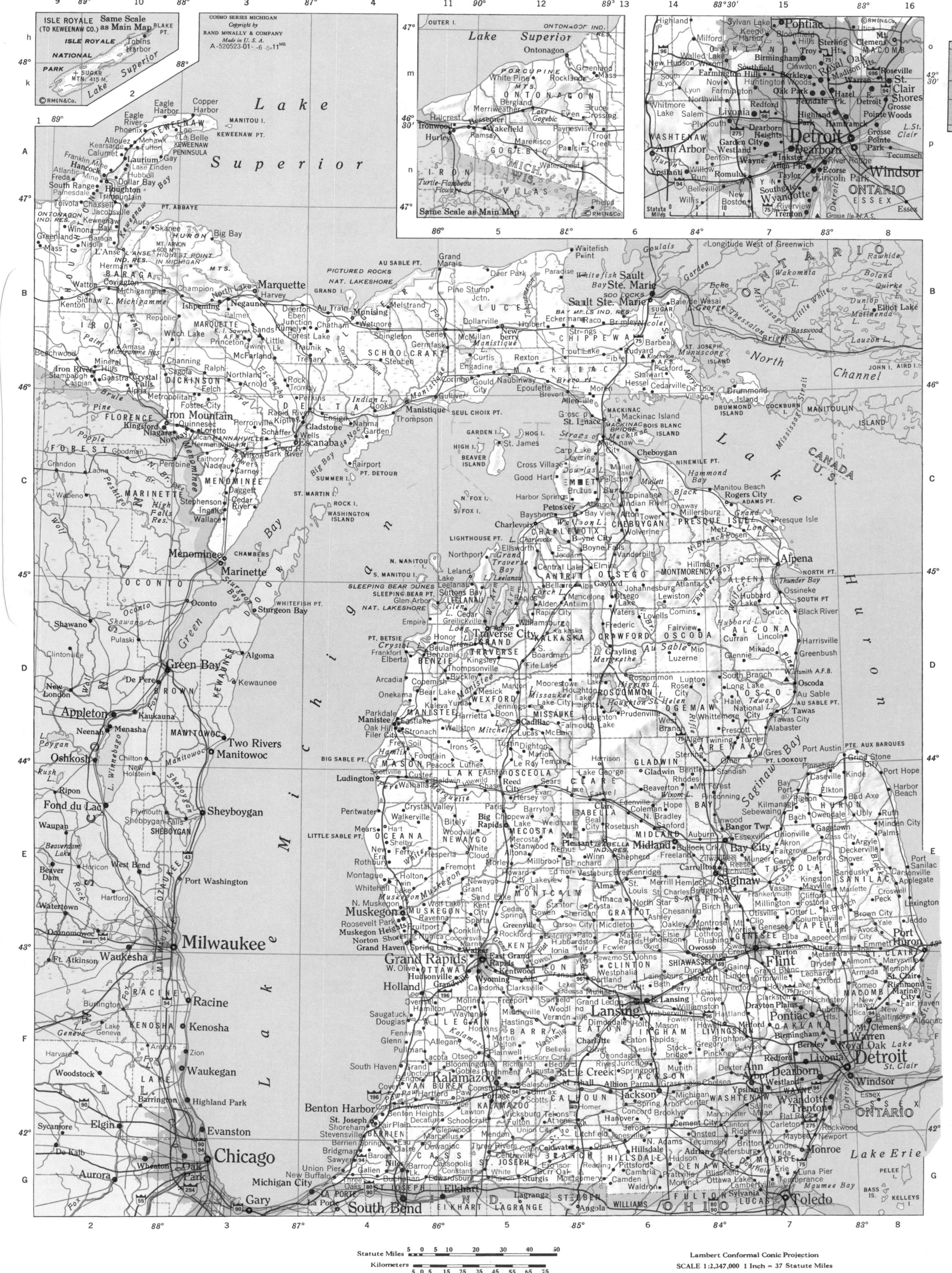

Statute Miles 5 0 5 10 20 30 40 50

Kilometers 5 0 5 15 25 35 45 55 65 75

Lambert Conformal Conic Projection

SCALE 1:2,347,000 1 Inch = 37 Statute Miles

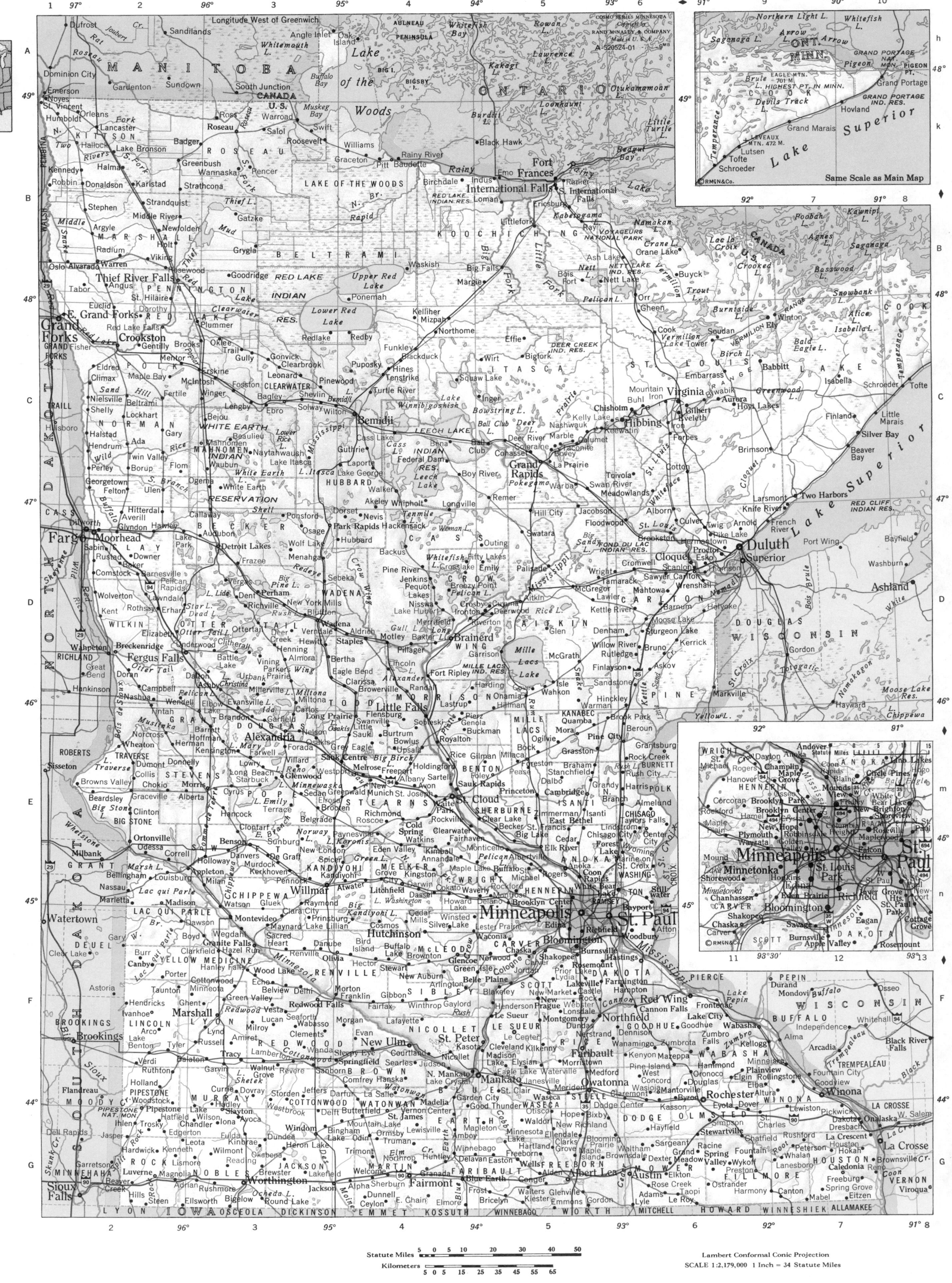
Longitude West of Greenwich
MANITOBA
ONTARIO
CANADA
U.S.
Lake of the Woods
Rainy River
International Falls
Fort Frances
Upper Red Lake
Lower Red Lake
RED LAKE INDIAN RES.
KOOCHICHING
BELTRAMI
ROSEAU
KITTSON
MARSHALL
PENNINGTON
POLK
NORMAN
CLEARWATER
ITASCA
ST. LOUIS
LAKE
COOK
Lake Superior
Same Scale as Main Map
Thief River Falls
Crookston
Grand Forks
E. Grand Forks
Bemidji
Grand Rapids
Hibbing
Virginia
Duluth
Superior
Two Harbors
Moorhead
Fargo
Detroit Lakes
Fergus Falls
Brainerd
Mille Lacs Lake
Little Falls
Alexandria
St. Cloud
Willmar
Minneapolis
St. Paul
Hutchinson
Red Wing
Mankato
New Ulm
Marshall
Rochester
Winona
Owatonna
Albert Lea
Austin
Worthington
Fairmont
Sioux Falls
La Crosse
NORTH DAKOTA
SOUTH DAKOTA
IOWA
WISCONSIN
Lake Pepin
Mississippi
Minnesota
Minnetonka
Bloomington
St. Louis Park
Richfield
Eagan
Statute Miles 5 0 5 10 20 30 40 50
Kilometers 5 0 5 15 25 35 45 55 65
Lambert Conformal Conic Projection
SCALE 1:2,179,000 1 Inch = 34 Statute Miles

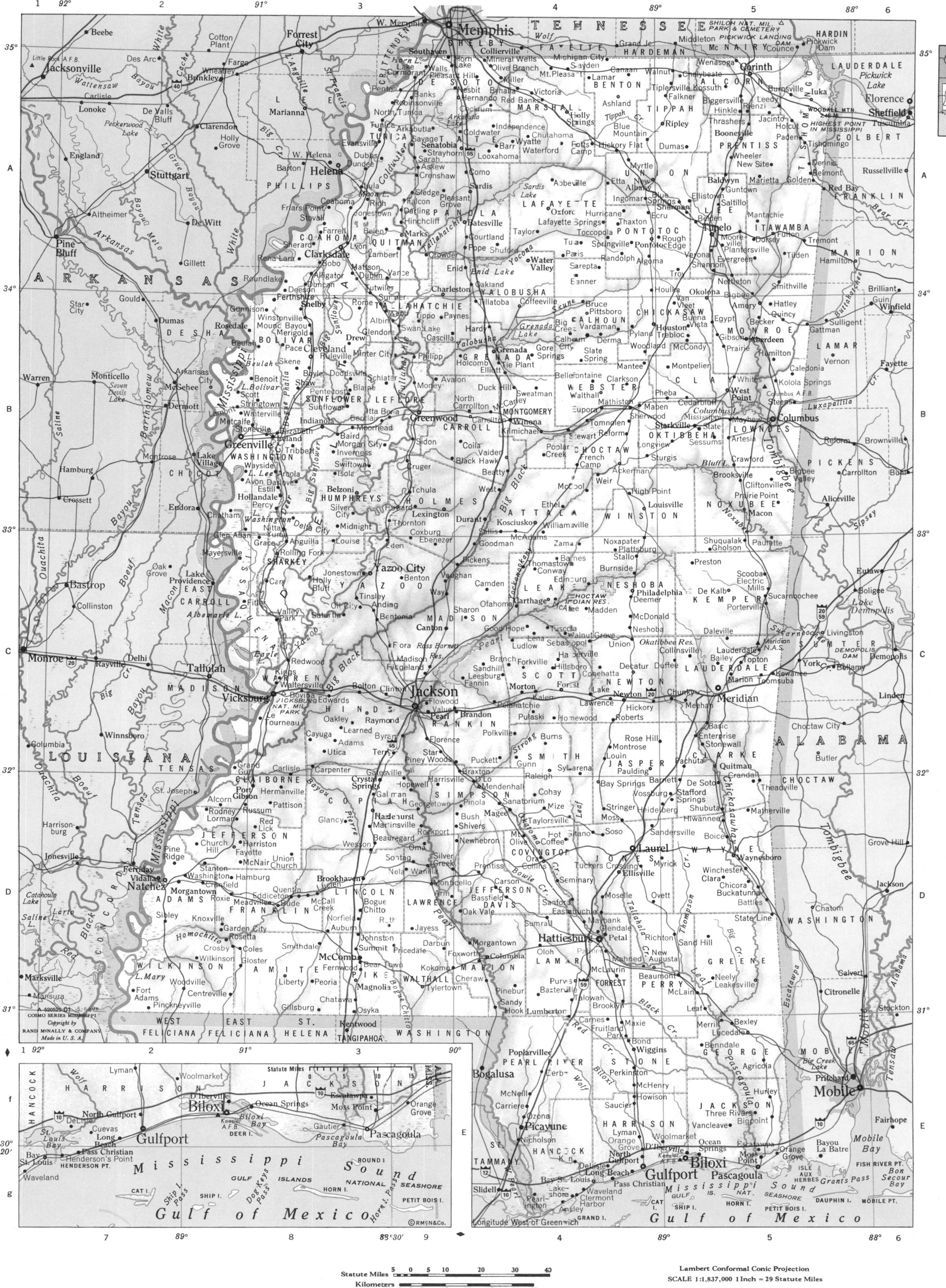

Statute Miles 5 0 5 10 20 30 40

Kilometers 5 0 5 15 25 35 45 55

Lambert Conformal Conic Projection
SCALE 1:1,837,000 1 Inch = 29 Statute Miles

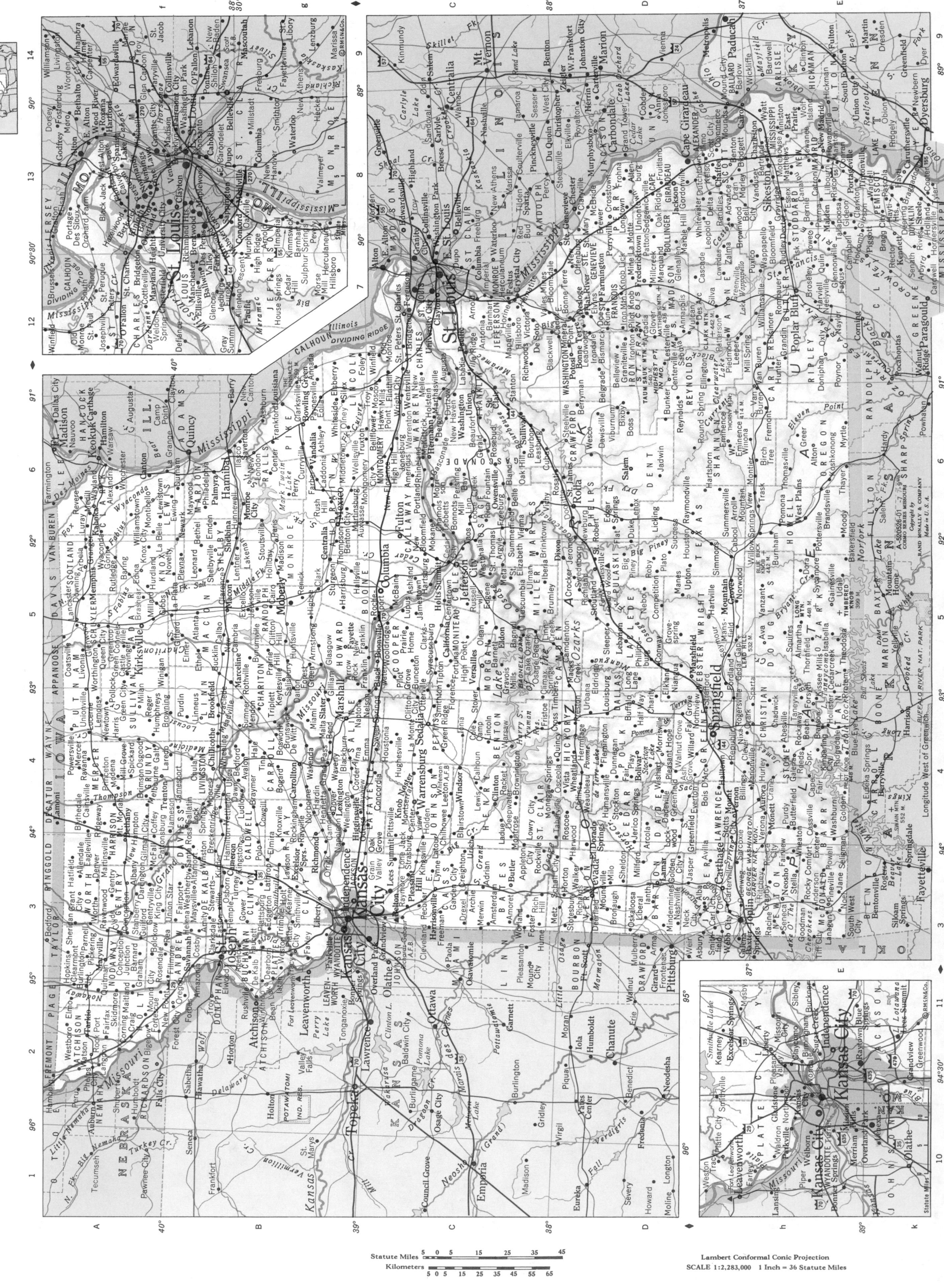

Statute Miles 5 0 5 15 25 35 45
Kilometers 5 0 5 15 25 35 45 55 65

Lambert Conformal Conic Projection
SCALE 1:2,283,000 1 Inch = 36 Statute Miles

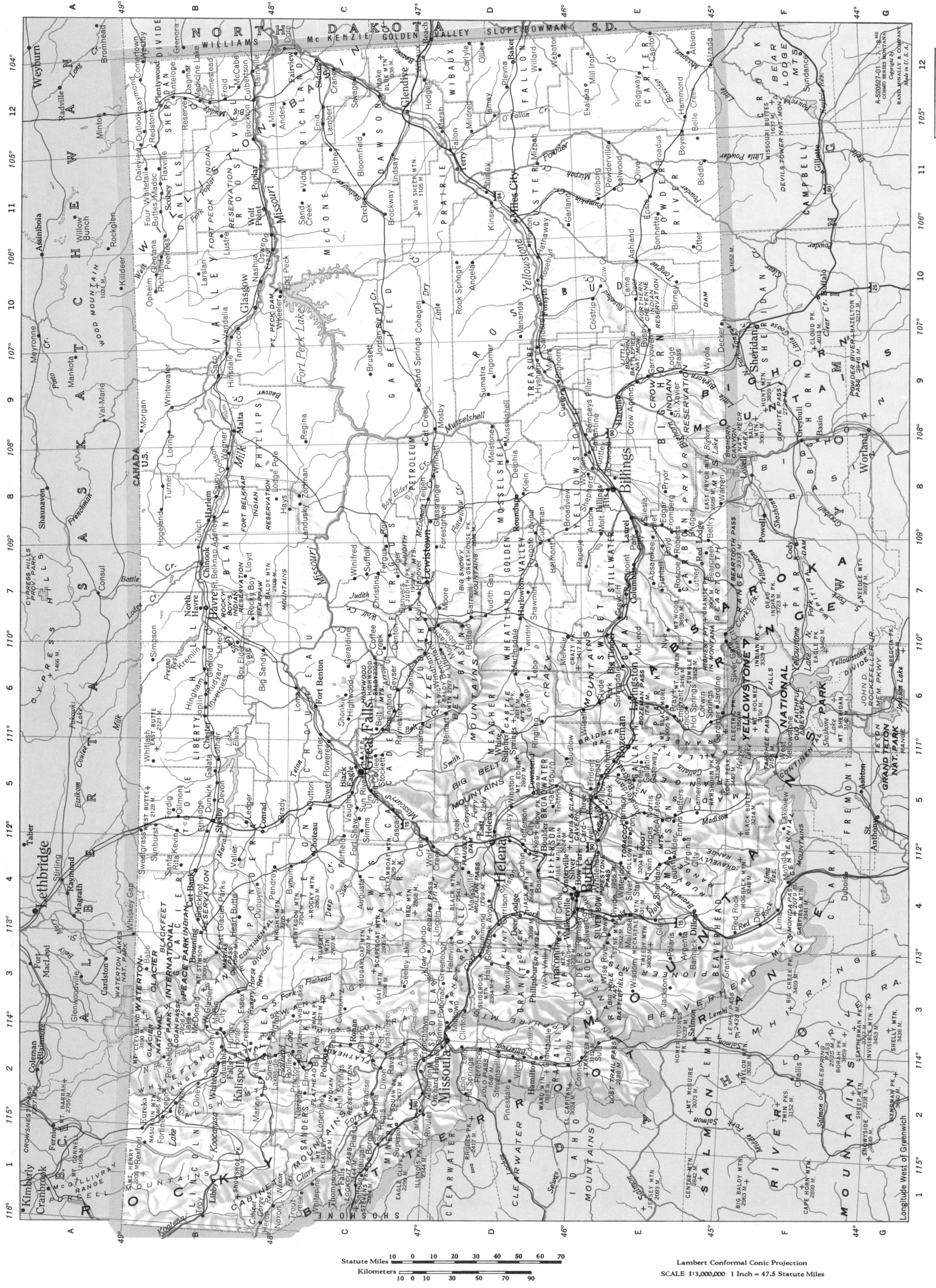

Statute Miles 10 0 10 20 30 40 50 60 70
Kilometers 10 0 10 30 50 70 90

Lambert Conformal Conic Projection
SCALE 1:3,000,000 1 Inch = 47.5 Statute Miles

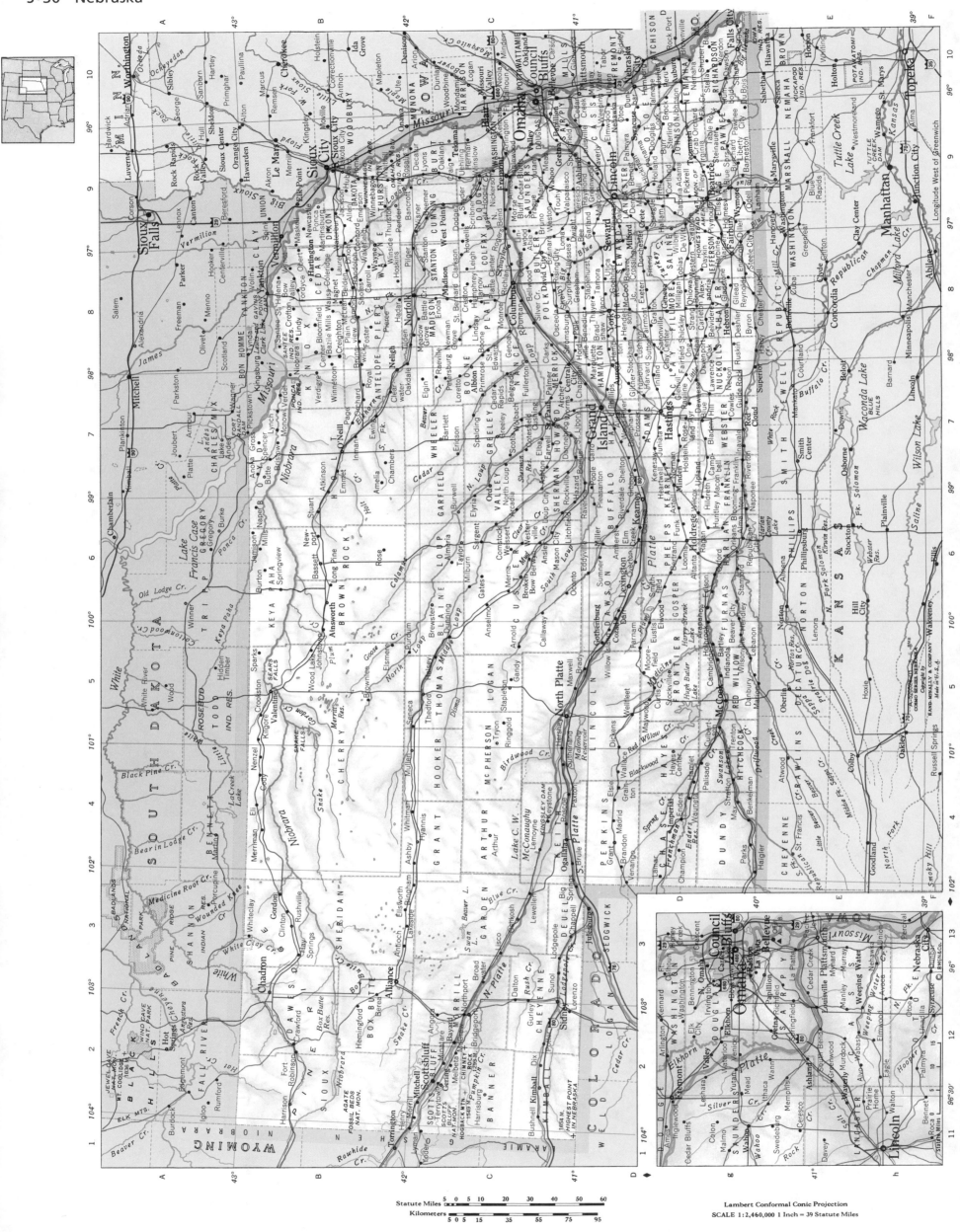

Statute Miles 5 0 5 10 20 30 40 50 60
Kilometers 5 0 5 15 35 55 75 95

Lambert Conformal Conic Projection
SCALE 1:2,460,000 1 Inch = 39 Statute Miles

OREGON
IDAHO
UTAH
ARIZONA
CALIFORNIA
HARNEY
MALHEUR
OWYHEE
TWIN FALLS
CASSIA
LAKE
MODOC
WASHOE
HUMBOLDT
PERSHING
ELKO
LANDER
EUREKA
CHURCHILL
WHITE PINE
STOREY
LYON
DOUGLAS
MINERAL
ESMERALDA
NYE
LINCOLN
CLARK
MONO
INYO
SAN BERNARDINO
BOX ELDER
TOOELE
JUAB
MILLARD
BEAVER
IRON
WASHINGTON
MOHAVE
Reno
Sparks
Carson City
Winnemucca
Elko
Ely
Las Vegas
N. Las Vegas
Henderson
Boulder City
Tonopah
Fallon
Lovelock
Battle Mountain
Wells
Caliente
Fresno
Bakersfield
Visalia
Lake Tahoe
Pyramid L.
Walker Lake
Lake Mead
Lake Mohave
Death Valley
Yosemite National Park
Kings Canyon Nat. Park
Sequoia Nat. Park
Great Basin Nat. Park
Death Valley National Monument
Lake Mead National Rec. Area
China Lake Naval Weapons Center
Humboldt
Colorado
Mt. Whitney 4418 M. Highest Point in California
Boundary Pk. 4006 M. Highest Point in Nevada
86 M. below sea level lowest point in U.S.
A-520529-01 -5-9-10
COSMO SERIES NEVADA
Copyright by
RAND McNALLY & COMPANY
Made in U.S.A.
Longitude West of Greenwich
Statute Miles 5 0 5 10 20 30 40 50 60 70 80
Kilometers 5 0 10 20 40 60 80 100 120
Lambert Conformal Conic Projection
SCALE 1:2,630,000 1 Inch = 41.5 Statute Miles

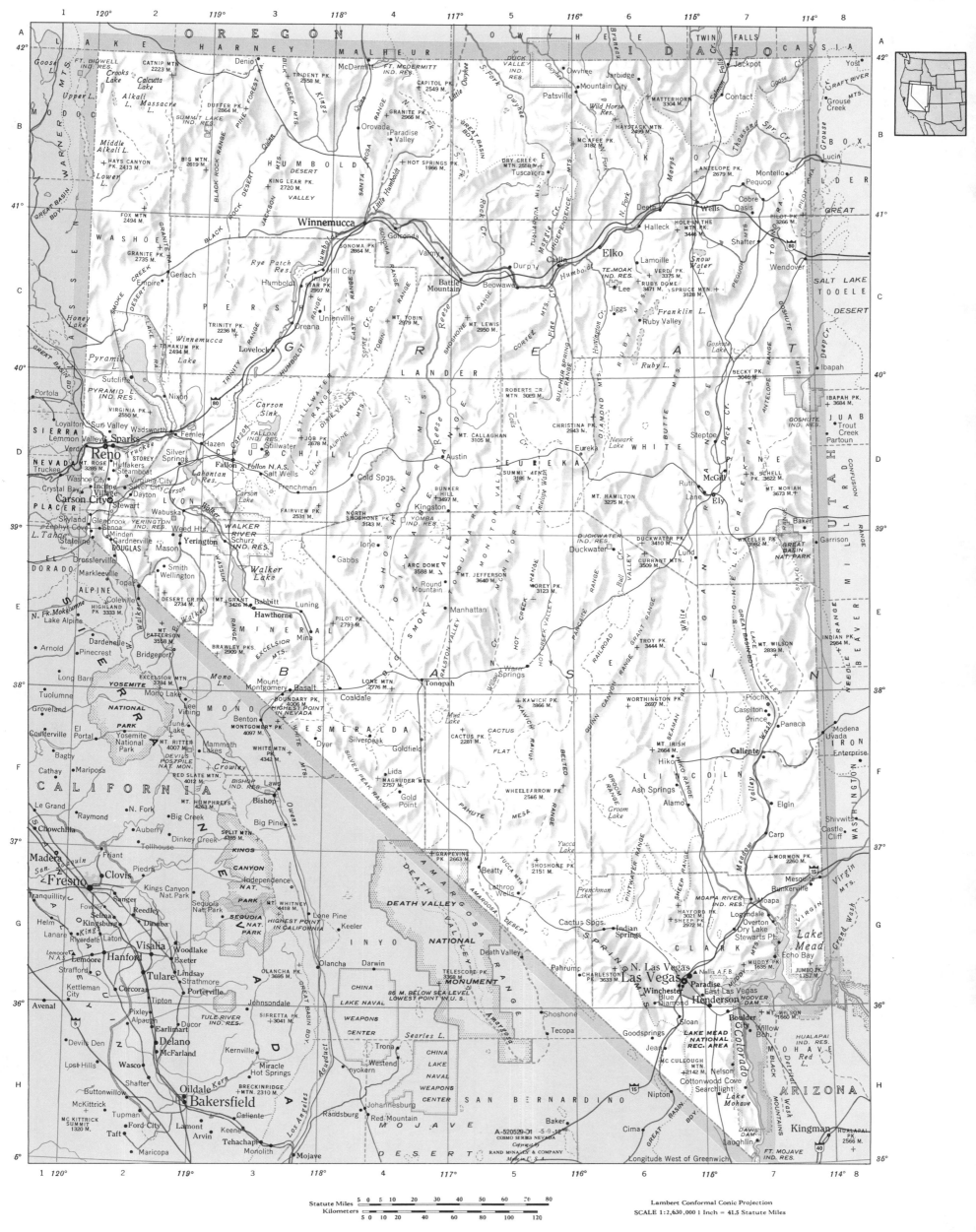

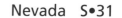

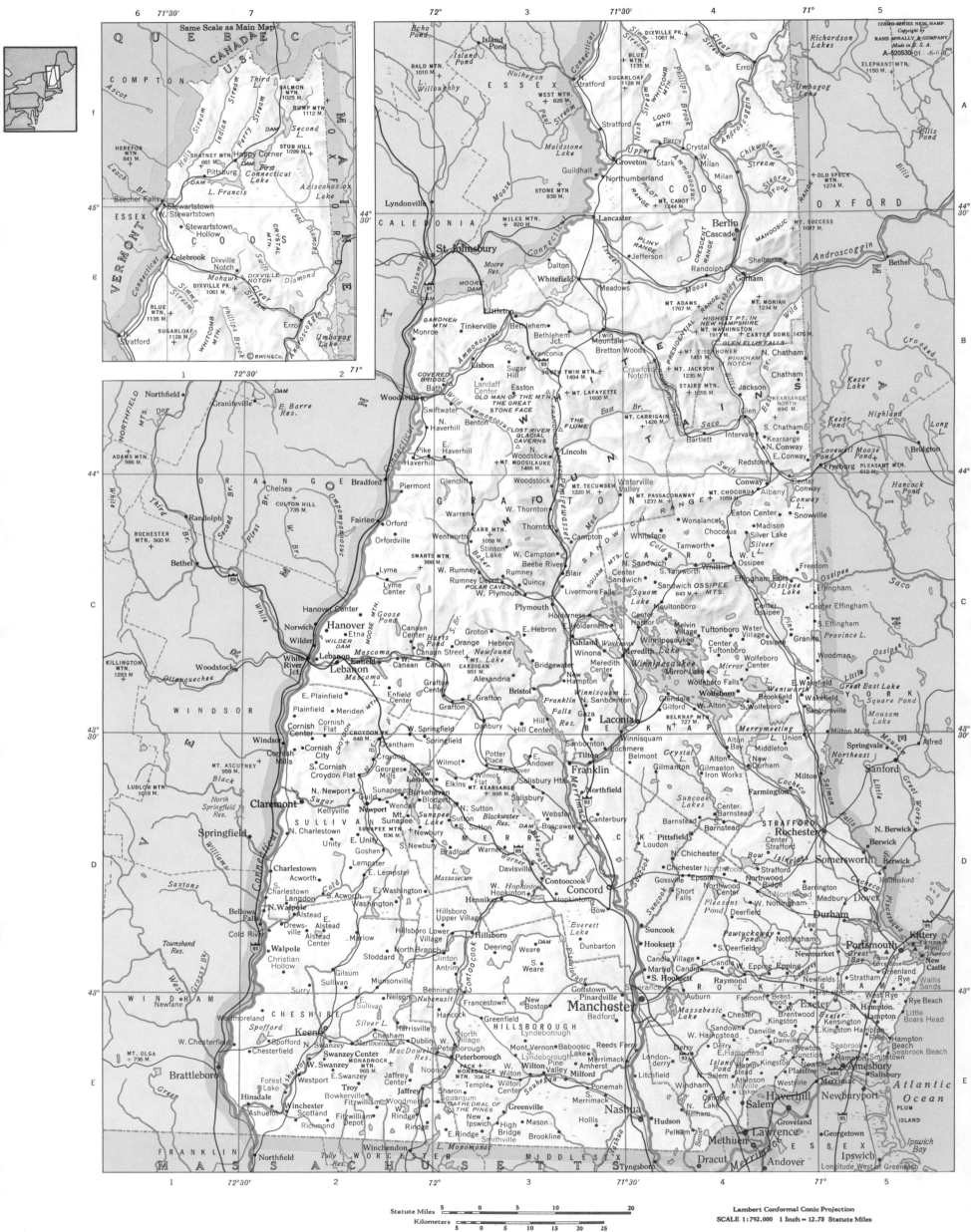

Statute Miles   5   0   5   10   20

Kilometers   5   0   5   10   15   20   25

Lambert Conformal Conic Projection
SCALE 1:792,000   1 Inch = 12.75 Statute Miles

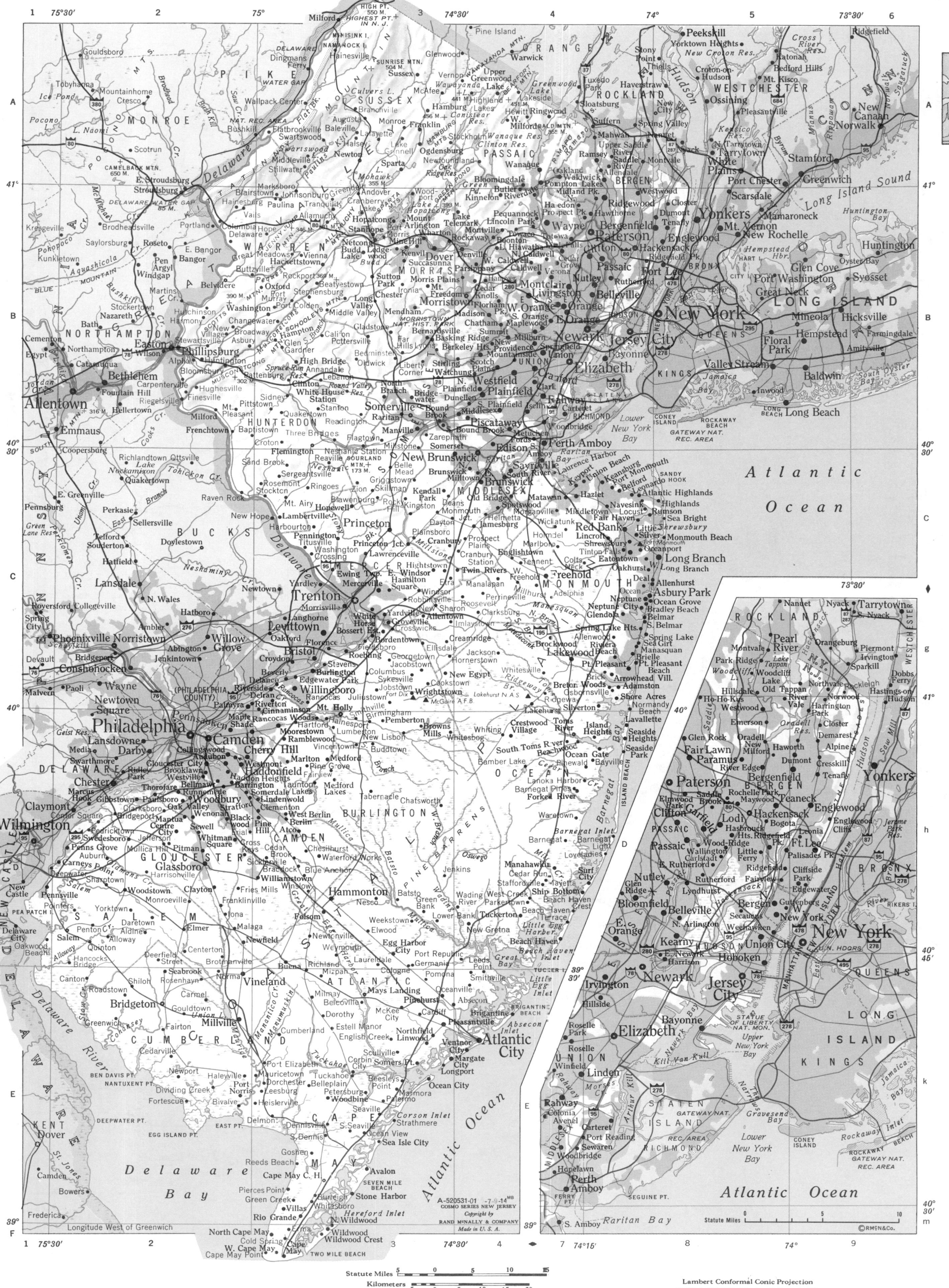

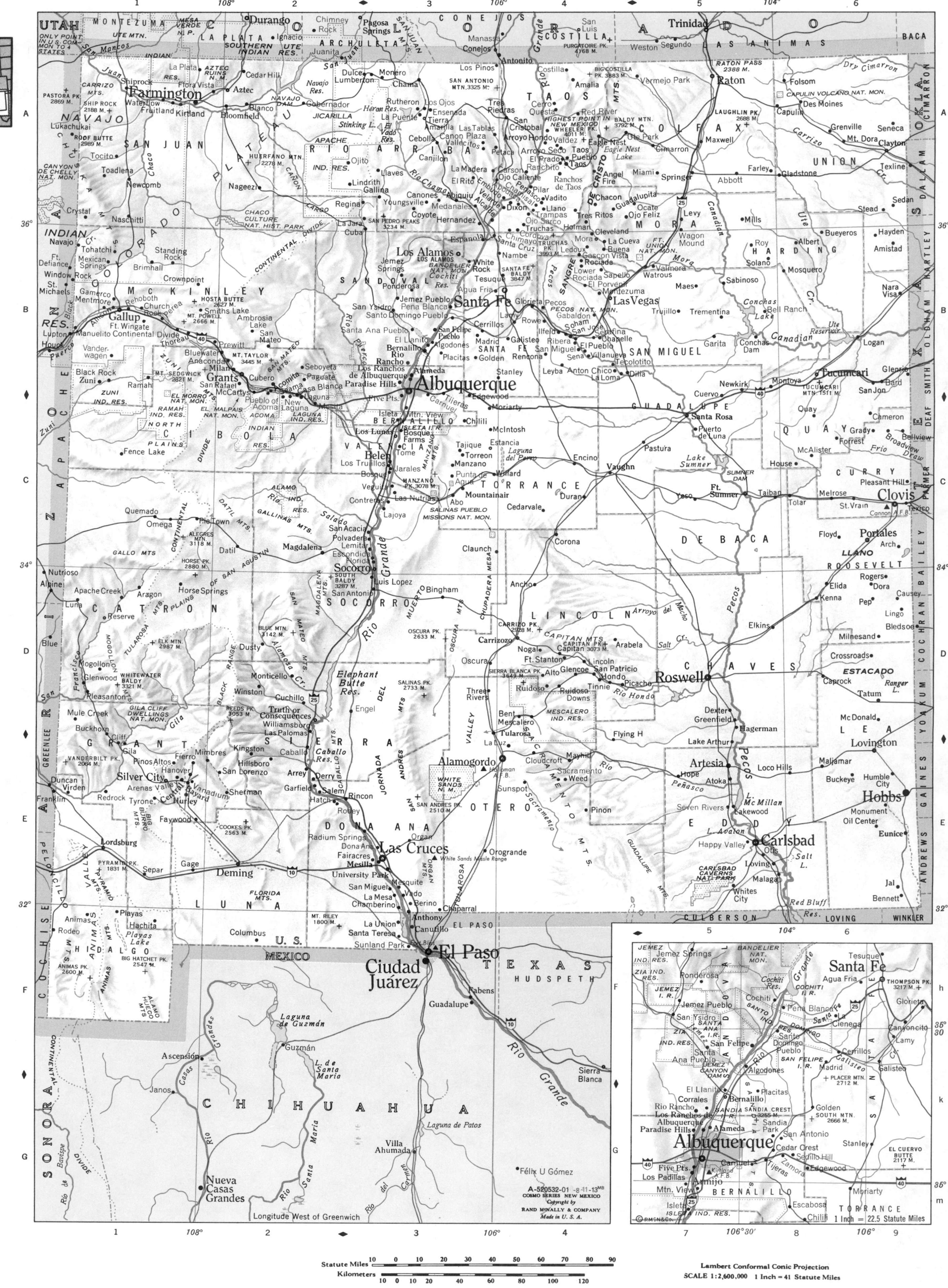
UTAH
C O L O R A D O
O K L A.
T E X A S
MEXICO
C H I H U A H U A
SONORA
Durango
Trinidad
Farmington
Gallup
Grants
Santa Fe
Los Alamos
Albuquerque
Las Vegas
Raton
Tucumcari
Clovis
Portales
Roswell
Artesia
Carlsbad
Hobbs
Lovington
Alamogordo
Las Cruces
Deming
Lordsburg
Silver City
Socorro
Belen
Santa Rosa
El Paso
Ciudad Juárez
Nueva Casas Grandes
Rio Grande
Pecos
Canadian
SAN JUAN
RIO ARRIBA
TAOS
COLFAX
UNION
MORA
HARDING
SAN MIGUEL
SANDOVAL
McKINLEY
CIBOLA
VALENCIA
BERNALILLO
SANTA FE
TORRANCE
GUADALUPE
QUAY
CURRY
DE BACA
ROOSEVELT
LINCOLN
CHAVES
LEA
EDDY
OTERO
DONA ANA
SIERRA
SOCORRO
CATRON
GRANT
LUNA
HIDALGO
A-520532-01 -8-11-13
COSMO SERIES NEW MEXICO
Copyright by RAND McNALLY & COMPANY
Made in U. S. A.
Longitude West of Greenwich
Statute Miles
Kilometers
Lambert Conformal Conic Projection
SCALE 1:2,600,000 1 Inch = 41 Statute Miles
1 Inch = 22.5 Statute Miles

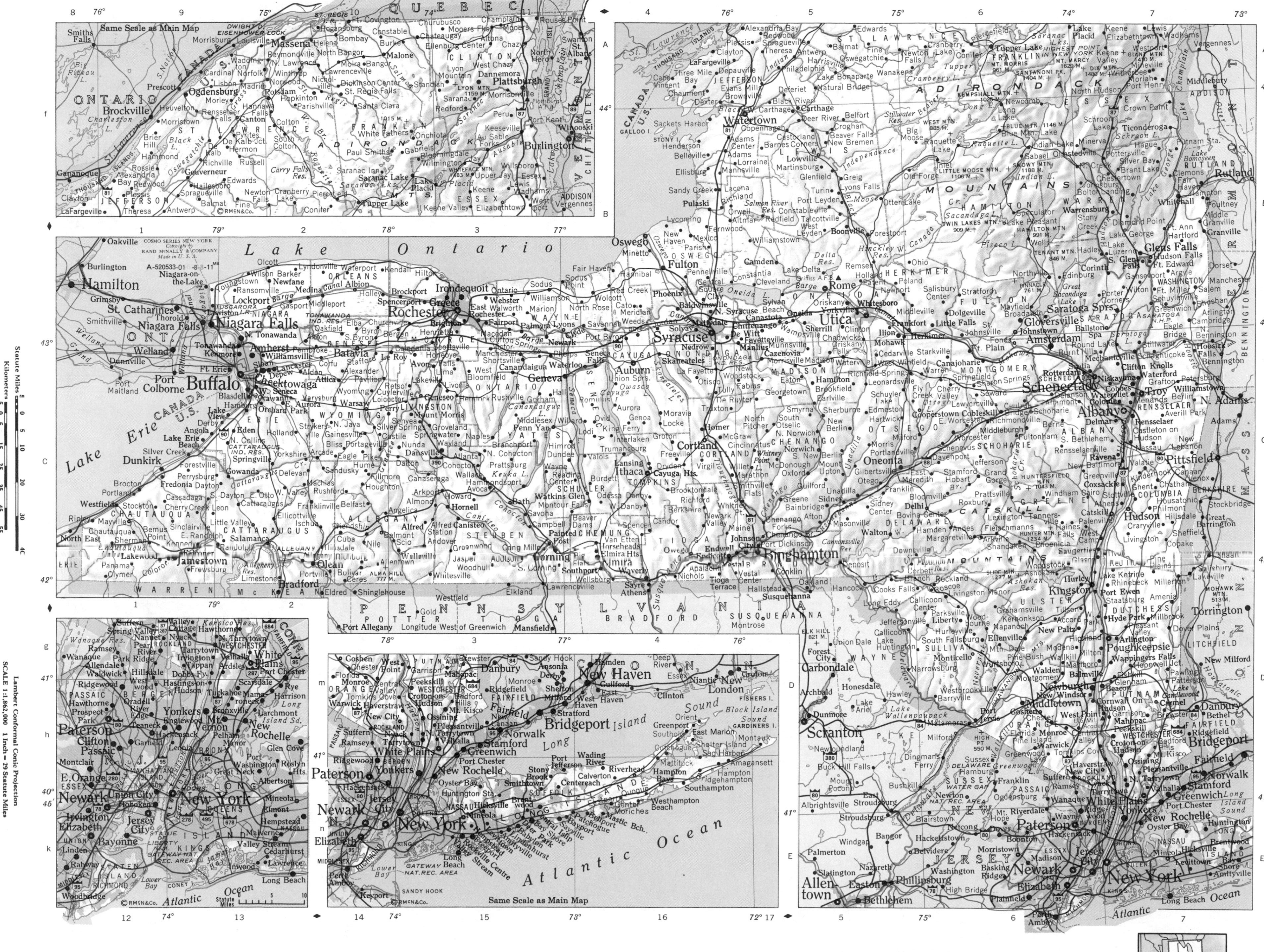

Statute Miles

Kilometers

Lambert Conformal Conic Projection
SCALE 1:1,862,000   1 Inch = 29 Statute Miles

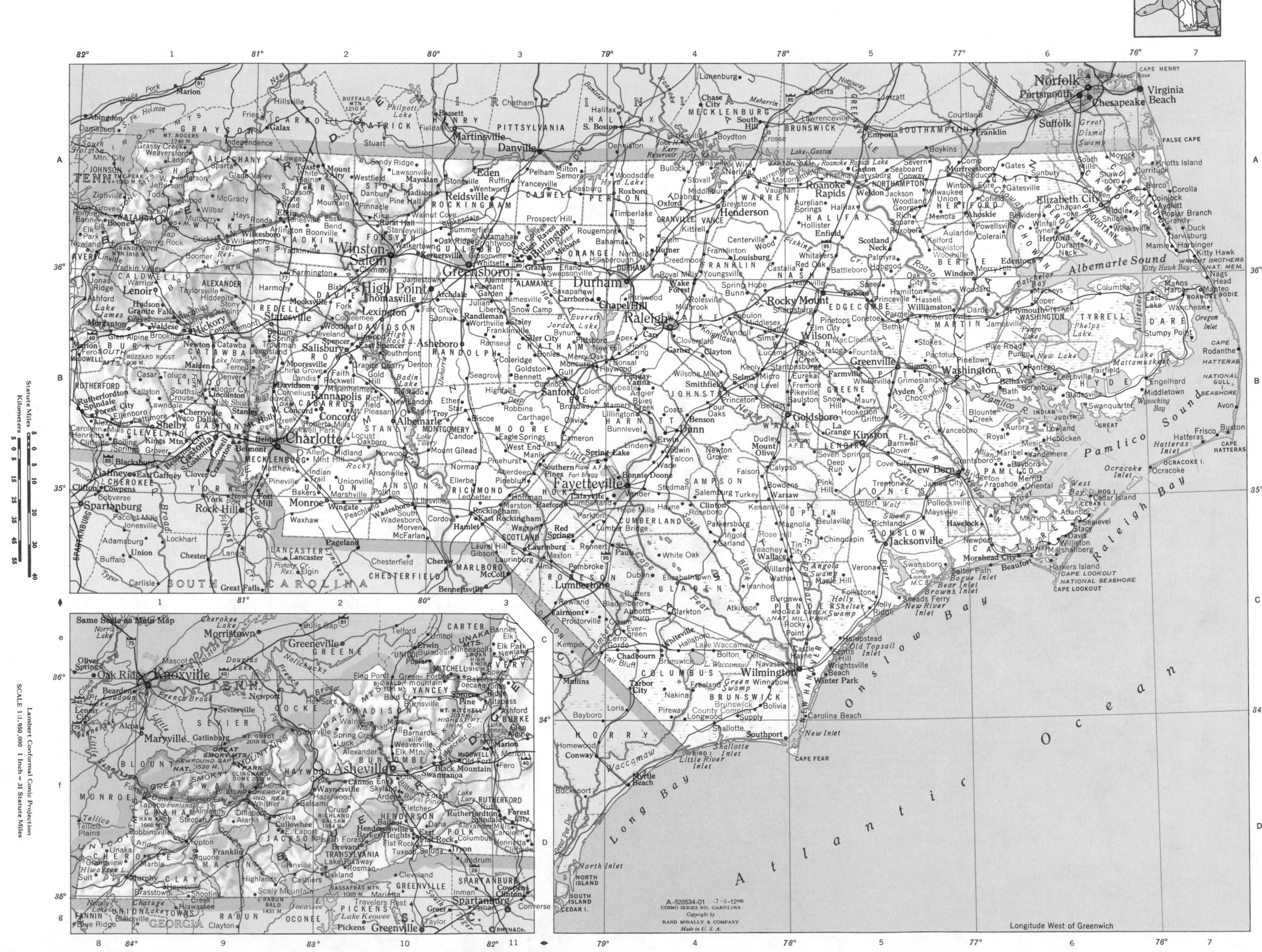

Statute Miles 5 0 5 10 20 30 40
Kilometers 5 0 5 15 25 35 45 55

Lambert Conformal Conic Projection
SCALE 1:1,950,000 1 Inch = 31 Statute Miles

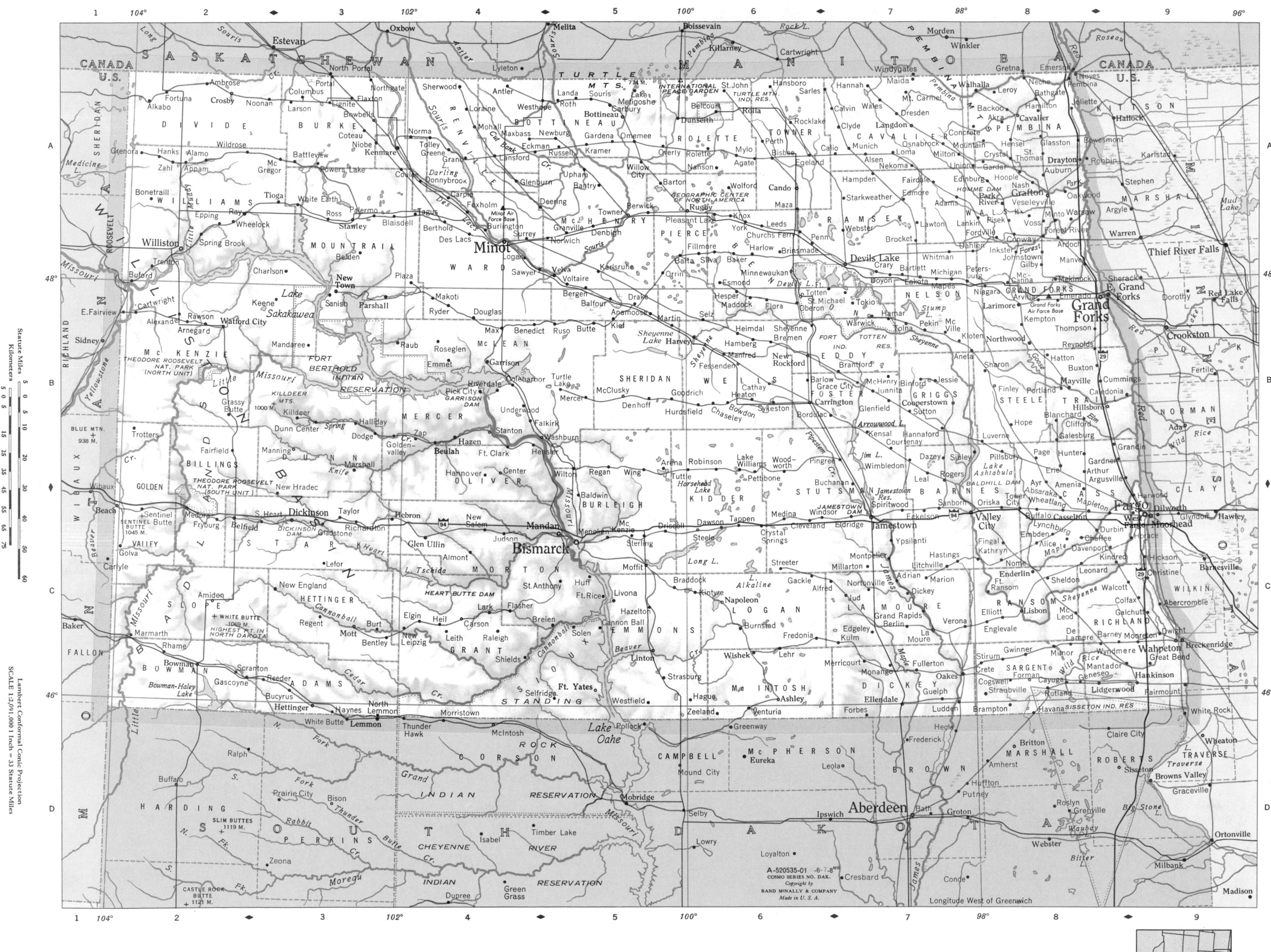

Statute Miles 5 0 5 10   20   30   40   50   60

Kilometers 5 0 5   15 25 35 45 55 65 75

Lambert Conformal Conic Projection
SCALE 1:2,091,000 1 Inch = 33 Statute Miles

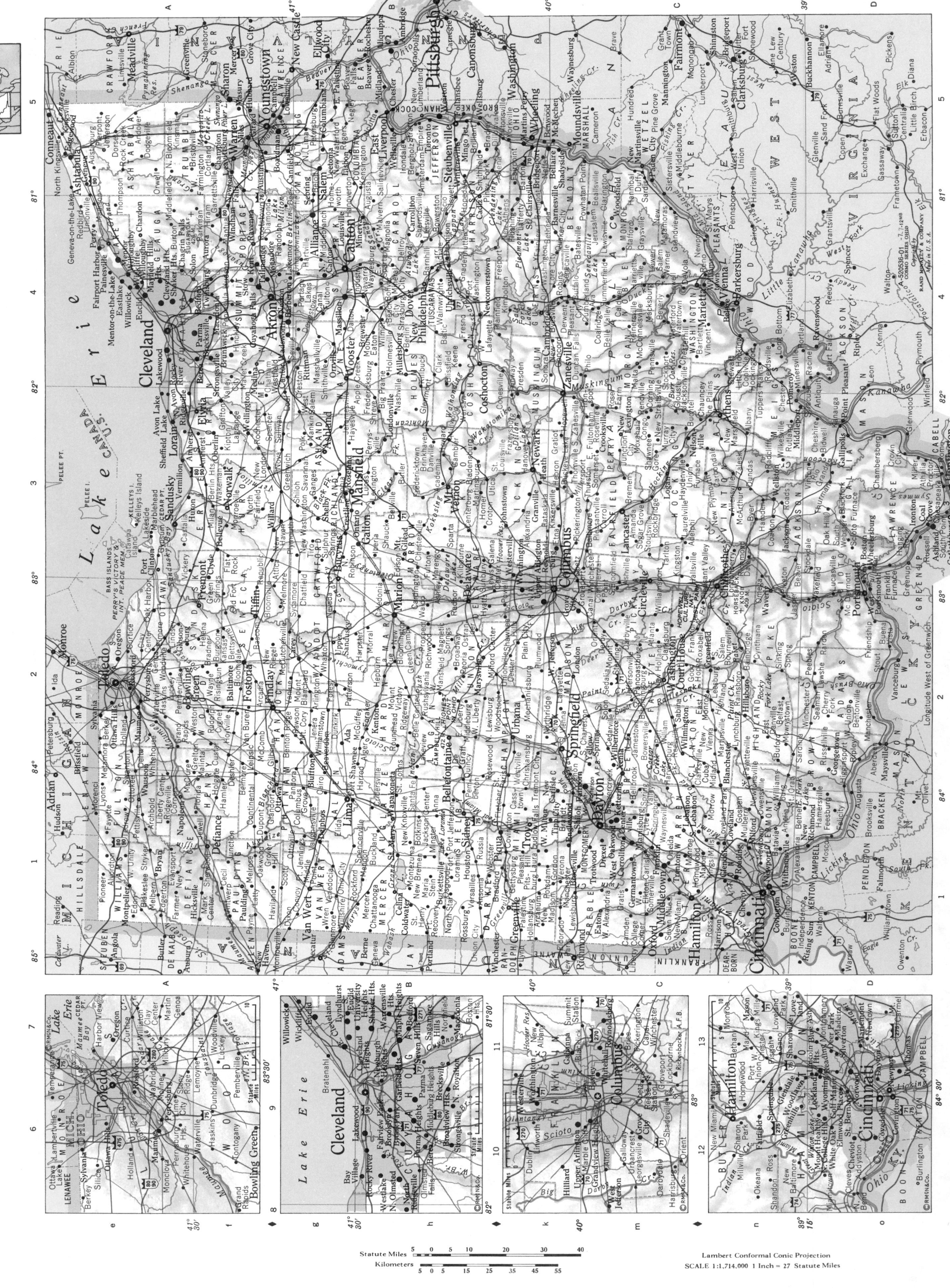

Statute Miles 5 0 5 10 20 30 40
Kilometers 5 0 5 15 25 35 45 55

Lambert Conformal Conic Projection
SCALE 1:1,714,000 1 Inch = 27 Statute Miles

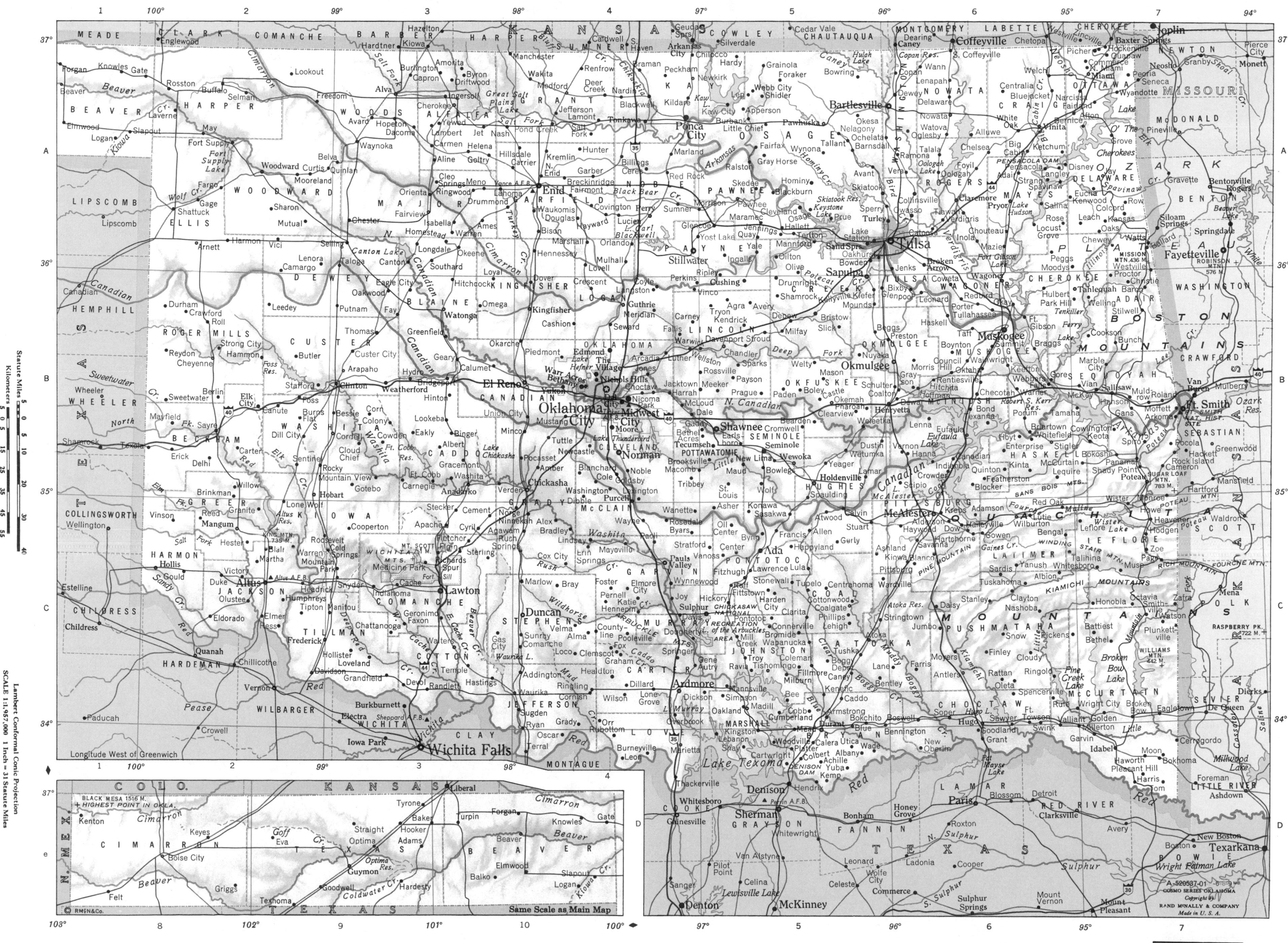

Statute Miles

Kilometers

Lambert Conformal Conic Projection
SCALE 1:1,957,000 1 Inch = 31 Statute Miles

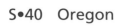

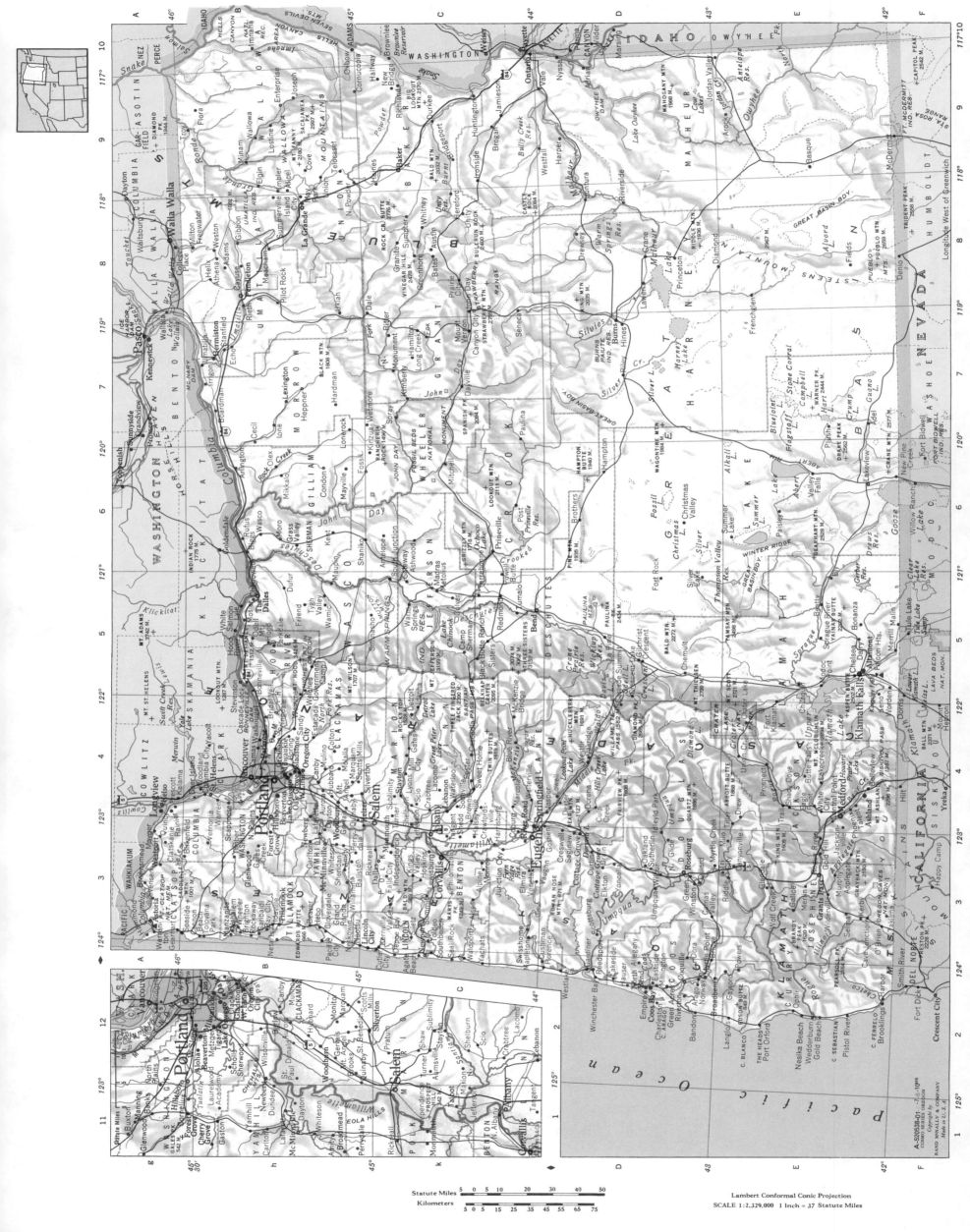

Lambert Conformal Conic Projection
SCALE 1:2,329,000 1 Inch = 37 Statute Miles

Statute Miles
Kilometers

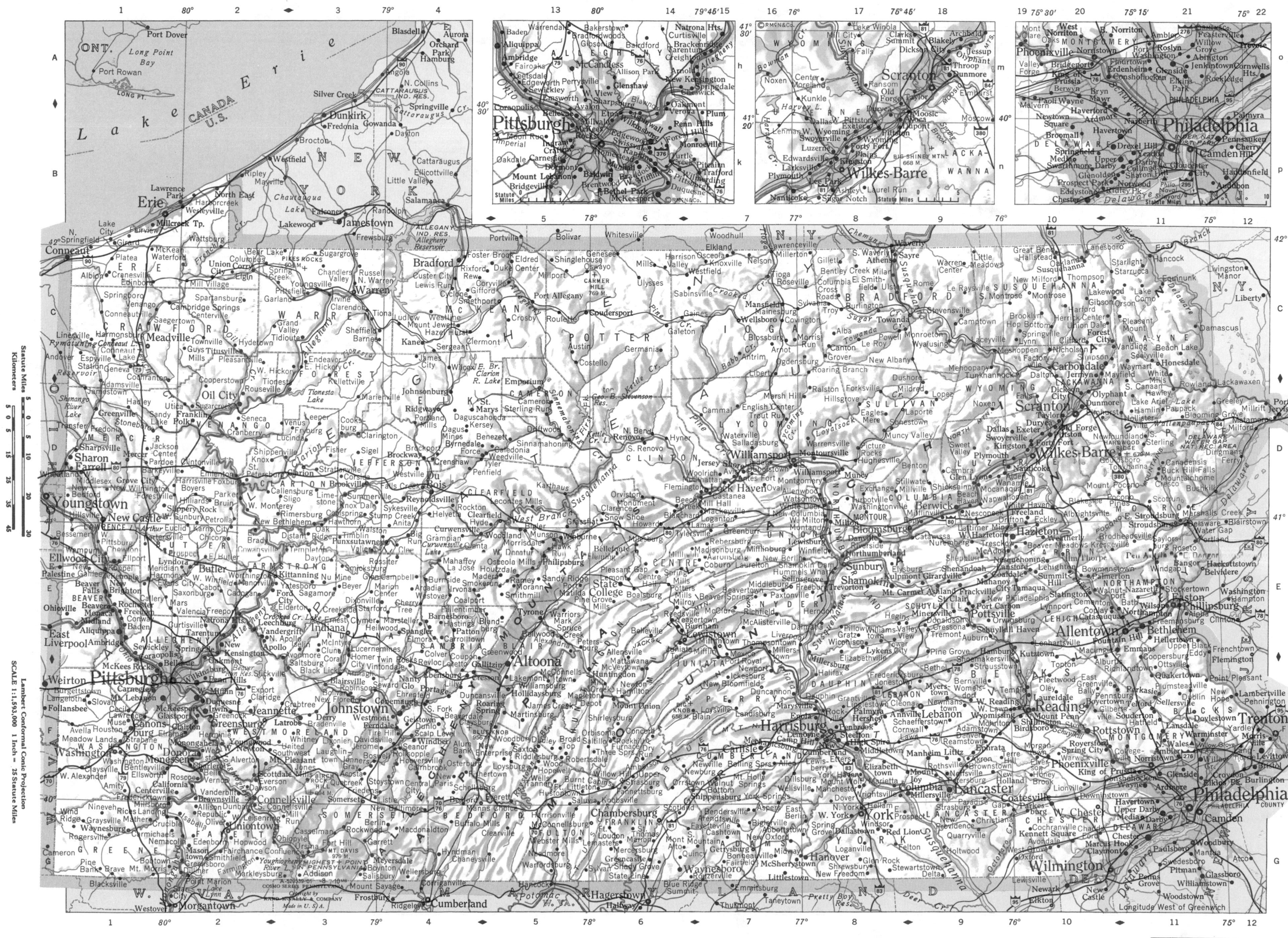

Statute Miles
Kilometers

Lambert Conformal Conic Projection
SCALE 1:1,593,000   1 Inch = 25 Statute Miles

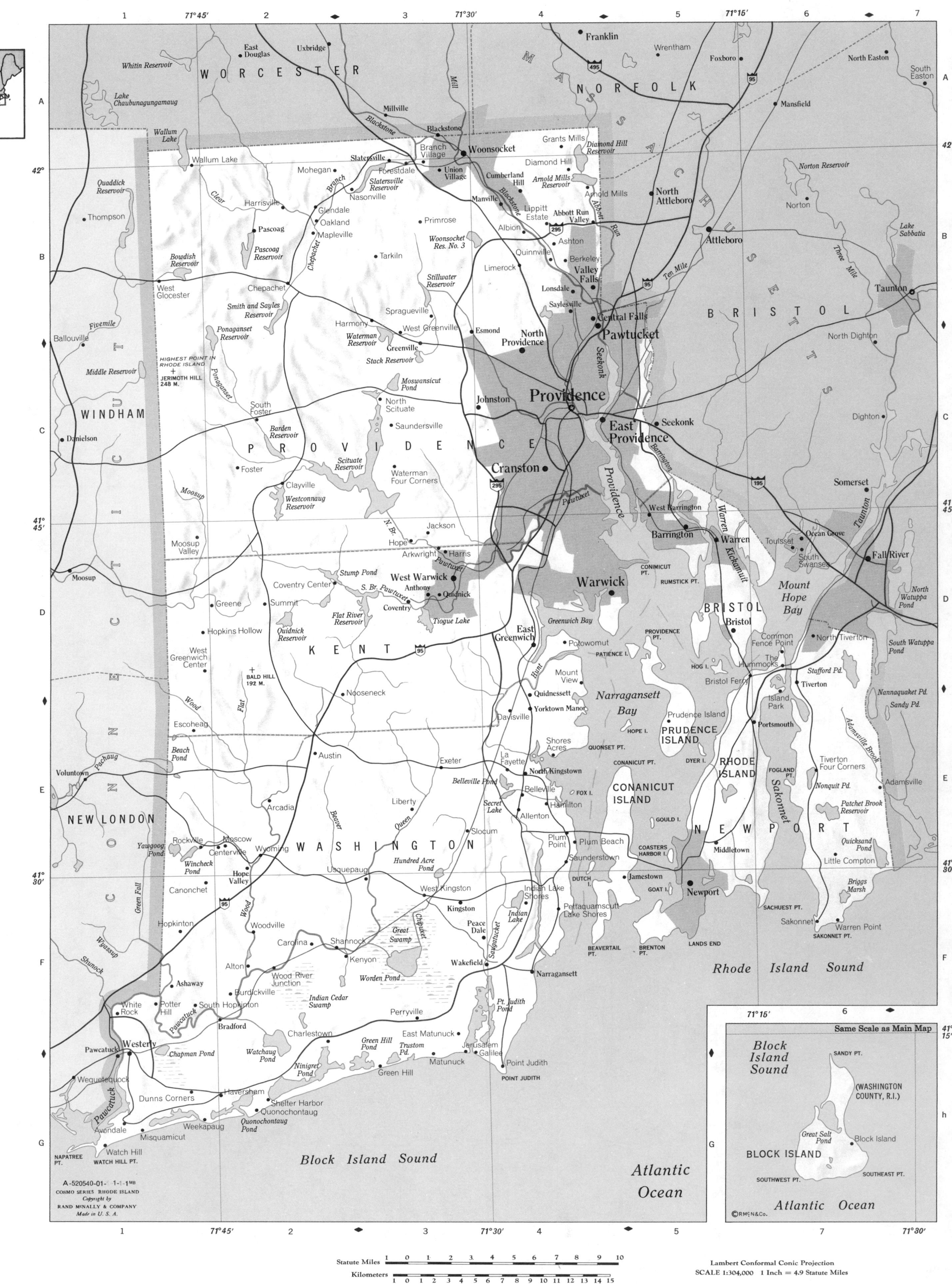

Statute Miles
Kilometers

Lambert Conformal Conic Projection
SCALE 1:304,000 1 Inch = 4.9 Statute Miles

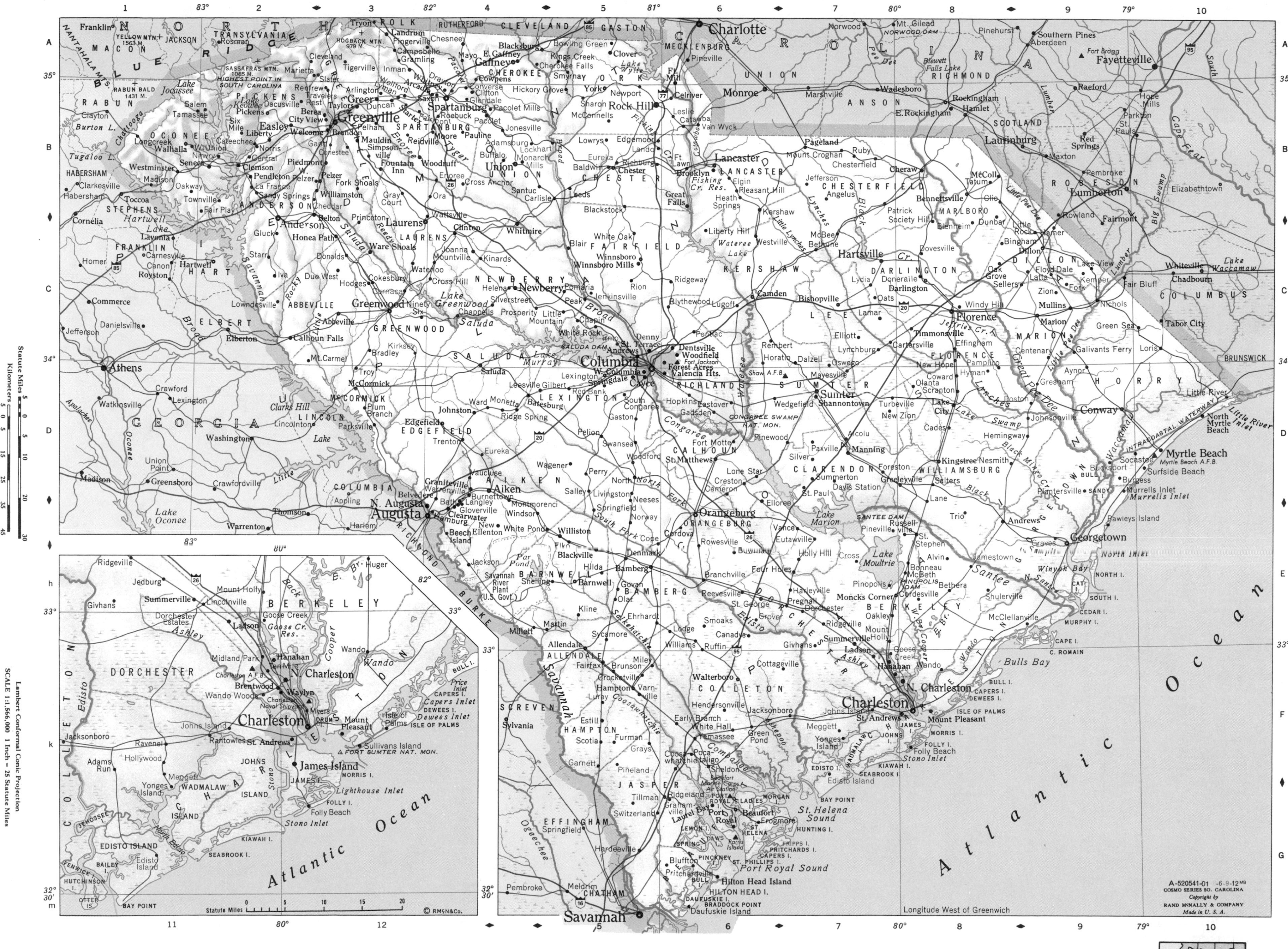
Atlantic Ocean
GEORGIA
Charlotte
Columbia
Charleston
Savannah
Augusta
Greenville
Spartanburg
Florence
Myrtle Beach
Sumter
Orangeburg
Anderson
Rock Hill
Athens
Fayetteville
Longitude West of Greenwich
A-520541-01 -6-9-12MB
COSMO SERIES SO. CAROLINA
Copyright by
RAND McNALLY & COMPANY
Made in U. S. A.
Lambert Conformal Conic Projection
SCALE 1:1,566,000 1 Inch = 25 Statute Miles
Statute Miles 5 0 5 10 20 30
Kilometers 5 0 5 15 25 35 45
© RMcN&Co.

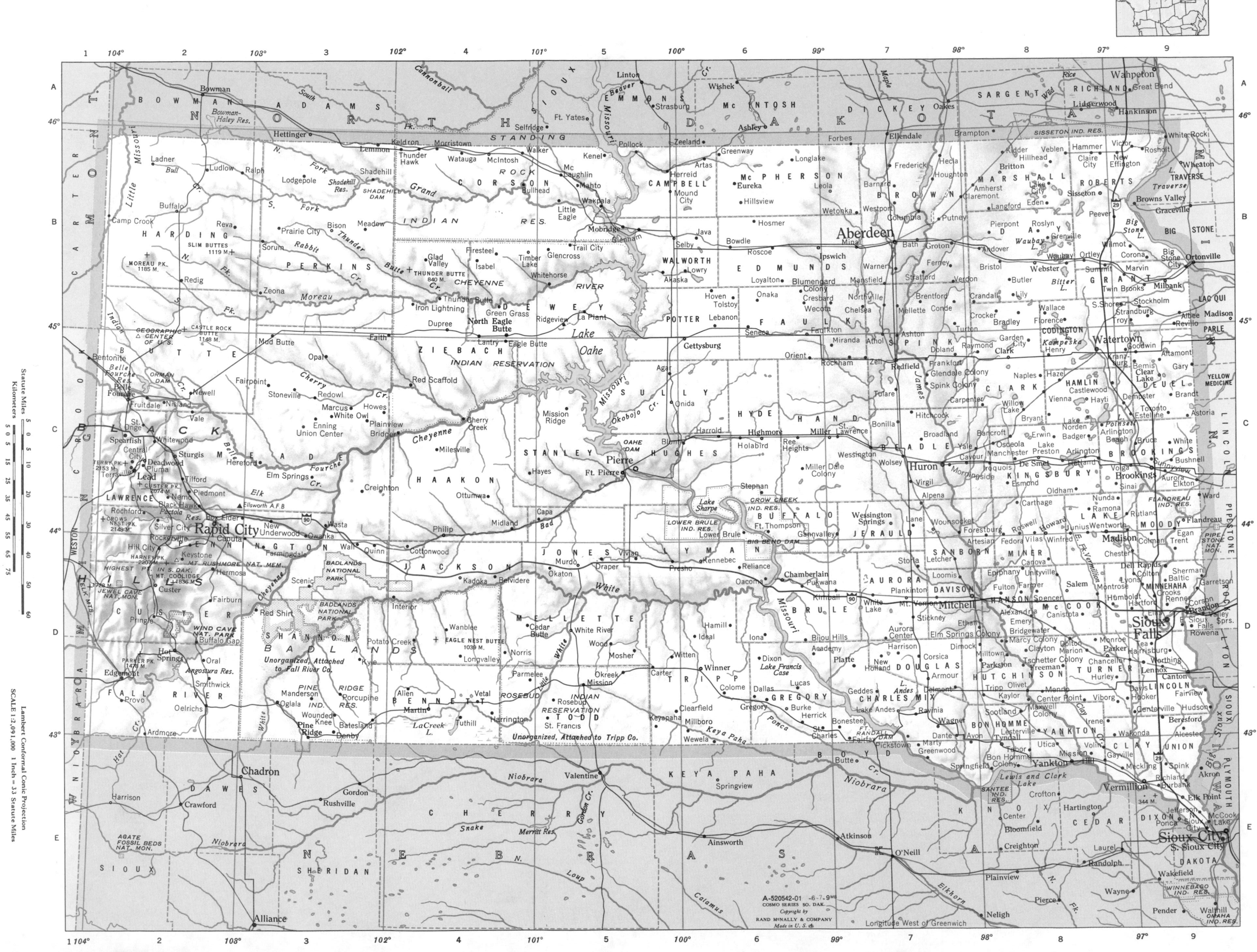

Statute Miles
Kilometers

Lambert Conformal Conic Projection
SCALE 1:2,091,000   1 Inch = 33 Statute Miles

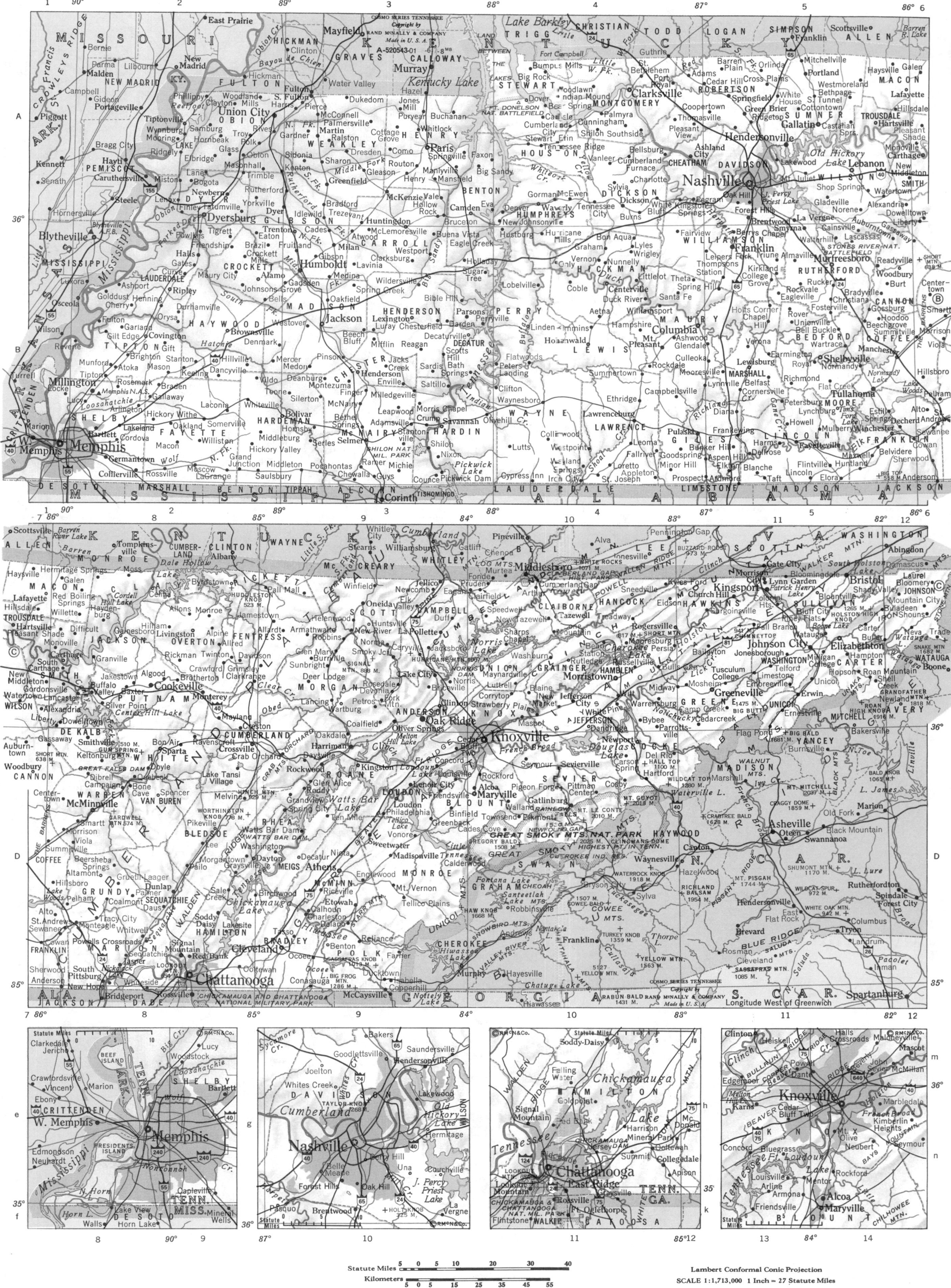

Statute Miles   5 0 5 10   20   30   40
Kilometers   5 0 5 15 25 35 45 55

Lambert Conformal Conic Projection
SCALE 1:1,713,000   1 Inch = 27 Statute Miles

Same Scale as Main Map

Longitude West of Greenwich

A-520544-01 7-10-12MB
COSMO SERIES TEXAS
Copyright by
RAND McNALLY & COMPANY
Made in U. S. A.

Statute Miles 10 0 10 20 30 40 50 60 70 80 90 100

Kilometers 10 0 10 20 40 60 80 100 120 140

Lambert Conformal Conic Projection
SCALE 1:4,118,000 1 Inch = 65 Statute Miles

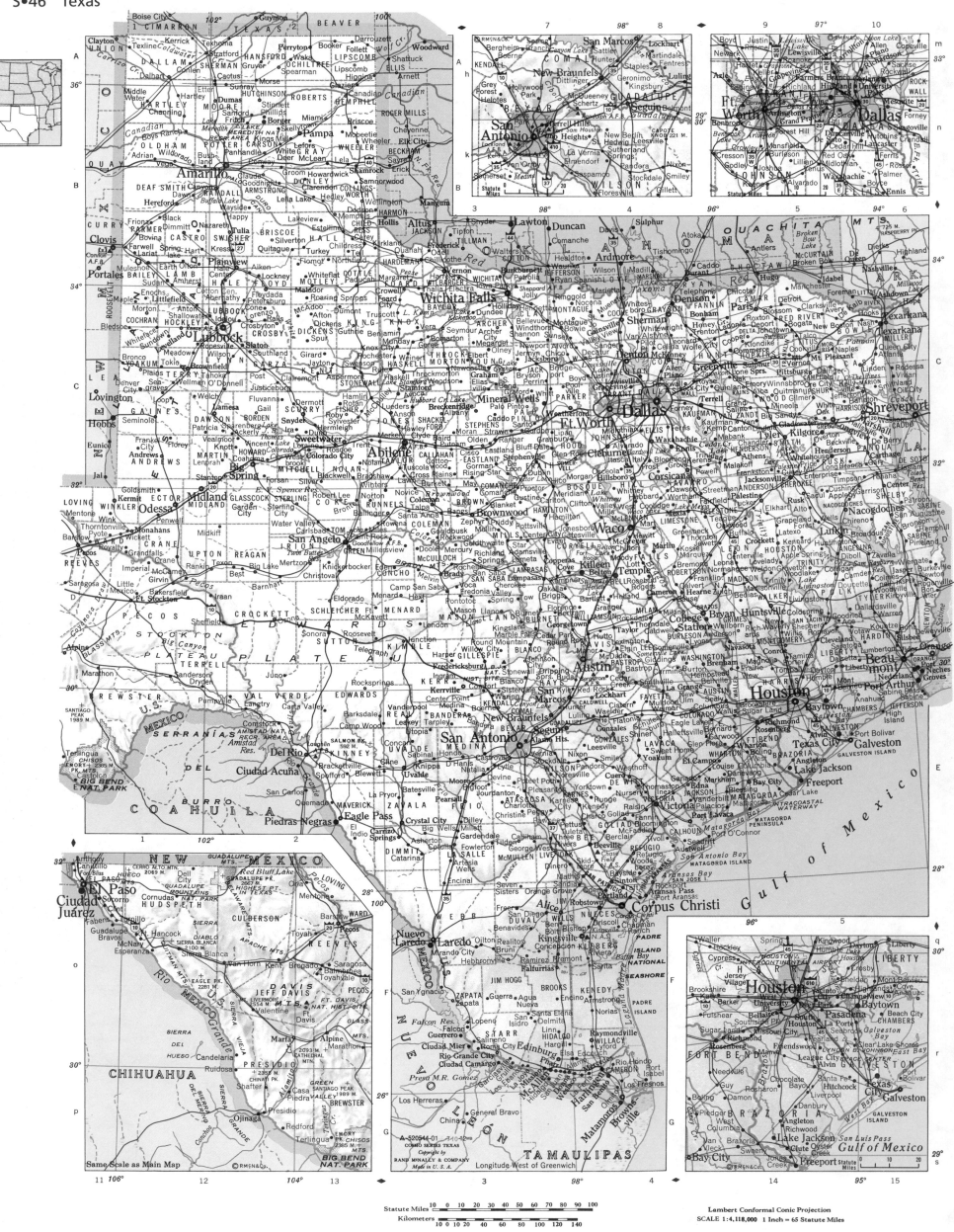

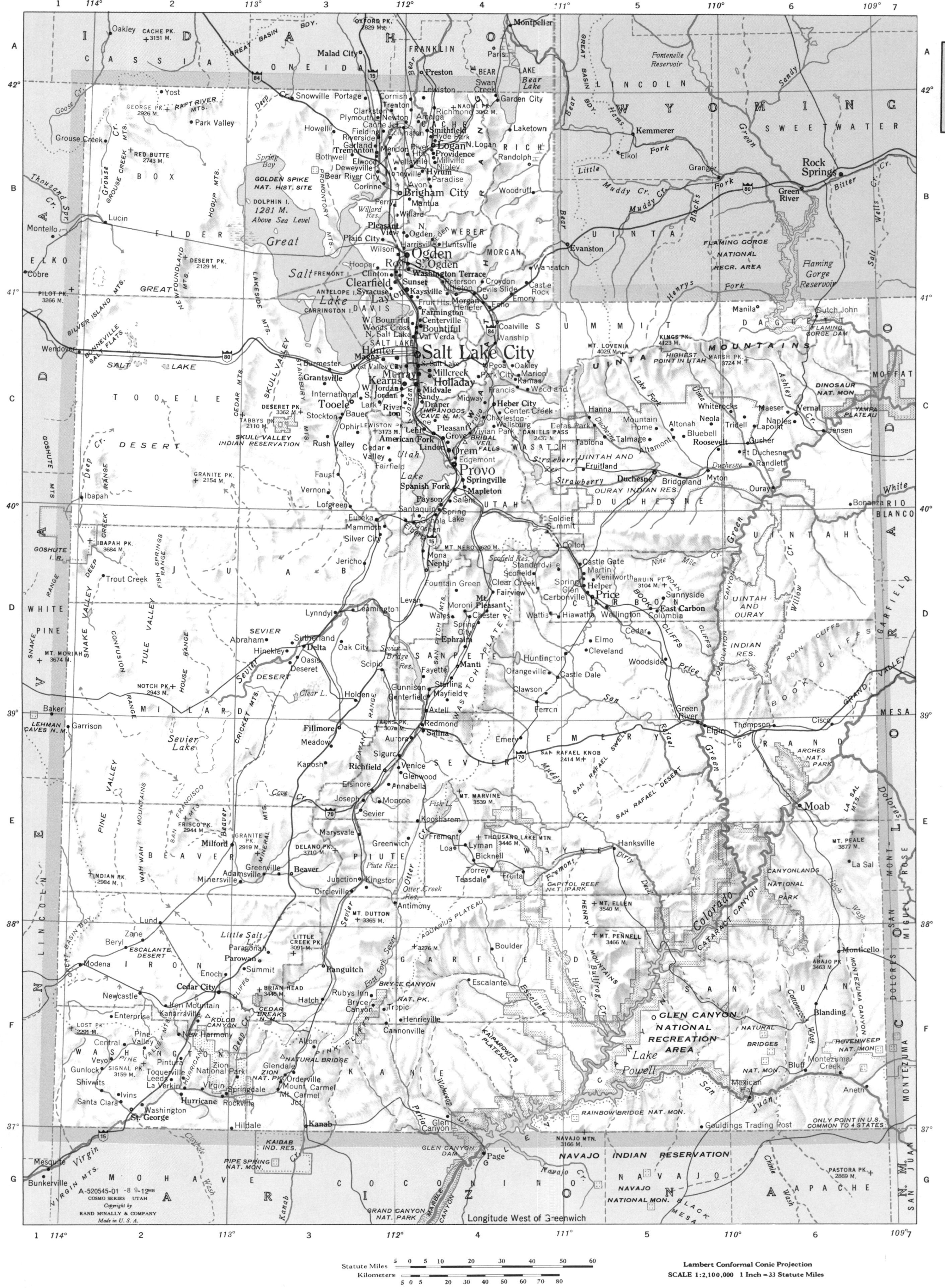

Statute Miles

Kilometers

Lambert Conformal Conic Projection
SCALE 1:2,100,000   1 Inch = 33 Statute Miles

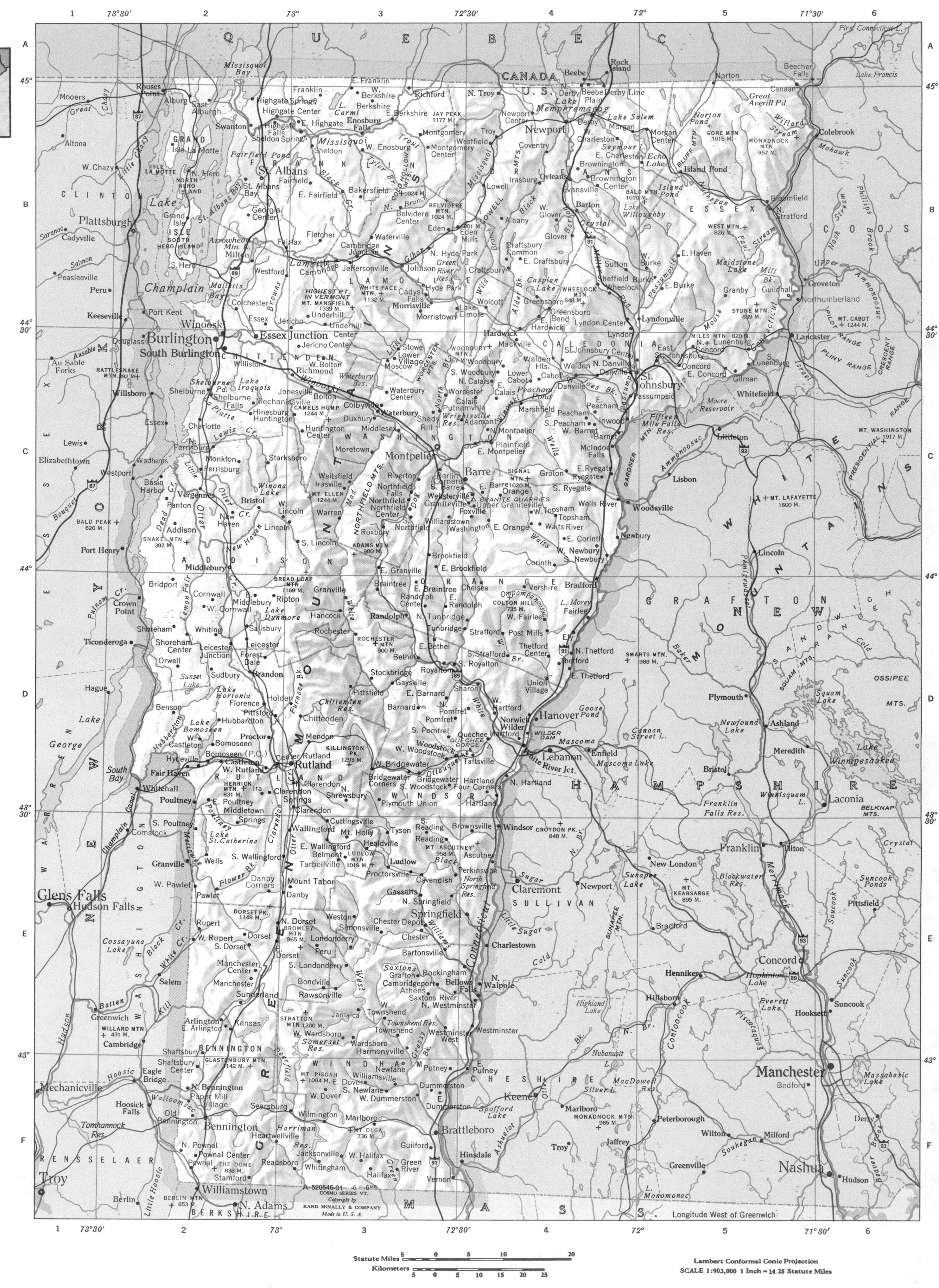

Statute Miles 5 0 5 10 20

Kilometers 5 0 5 10 15 20 25

Lambert Conformal Conic Projection

SCALE 1:903,000 1 Inch = 14.25 Statute Miles

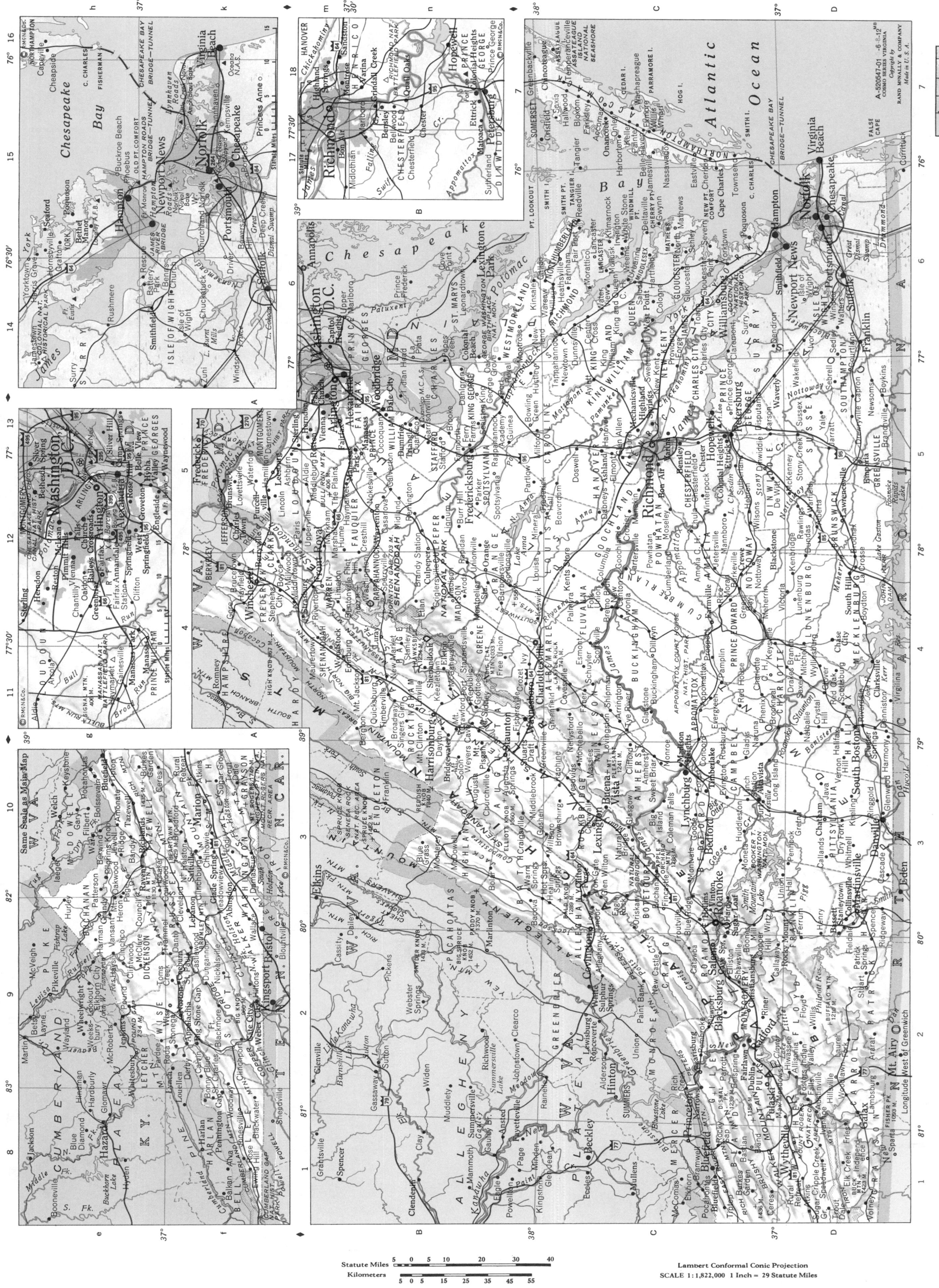

Lambert Conformal Conic Projection
SCALE 1:1,822,000   1 Inch = 29 Statute Miles

Statute Miles 5 0 5   10   20   30   40
Kilometers   5 0 5 15   25   35   45   55

Statute Miles 5 0 5 10 20 30 40 50

Kilometers 5 0 5 15 25 35 45 55 65

Lambert Conformal Conic Projection
SCALE 1:2,068,000 Inch = 33 Statute Miles

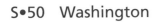

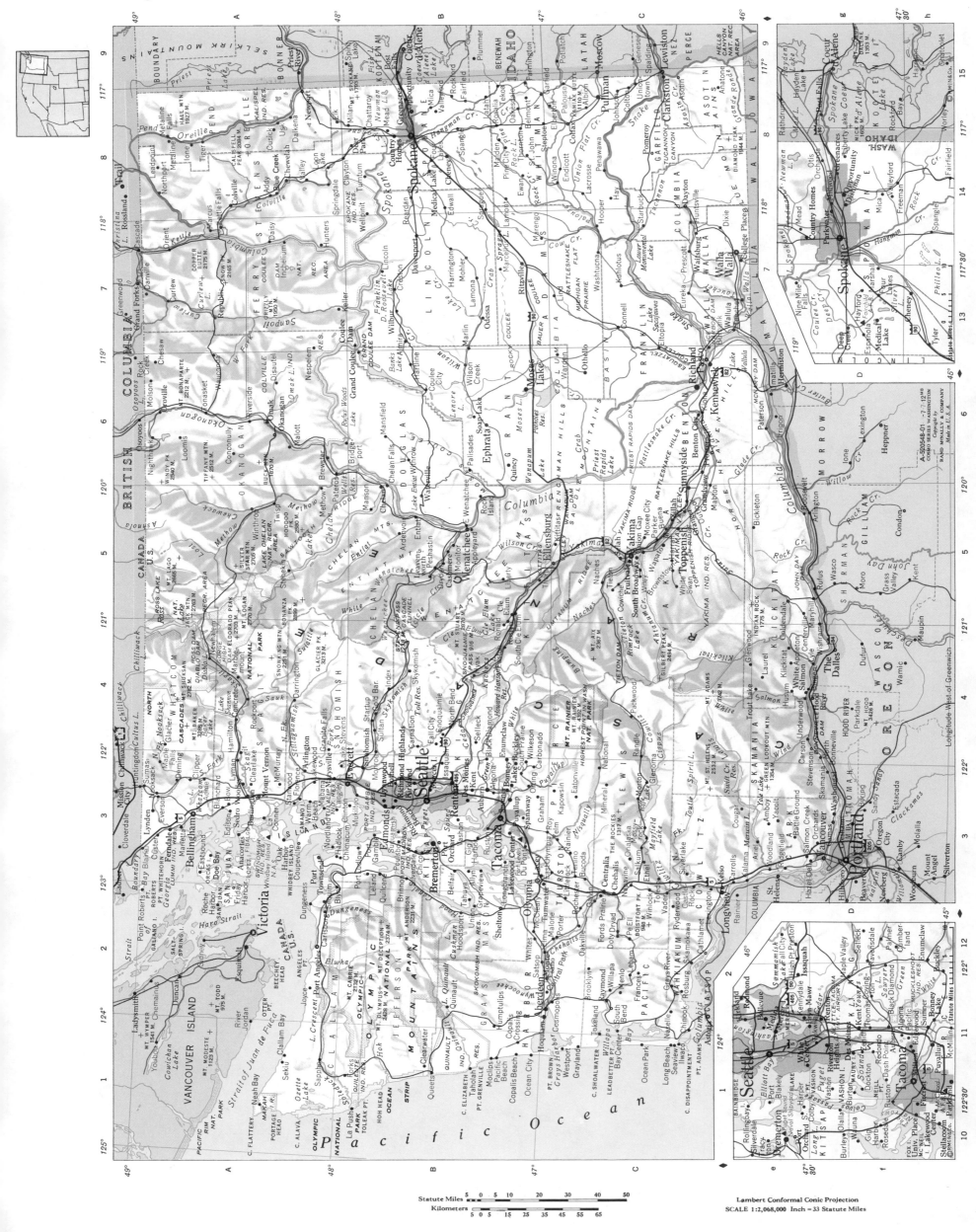

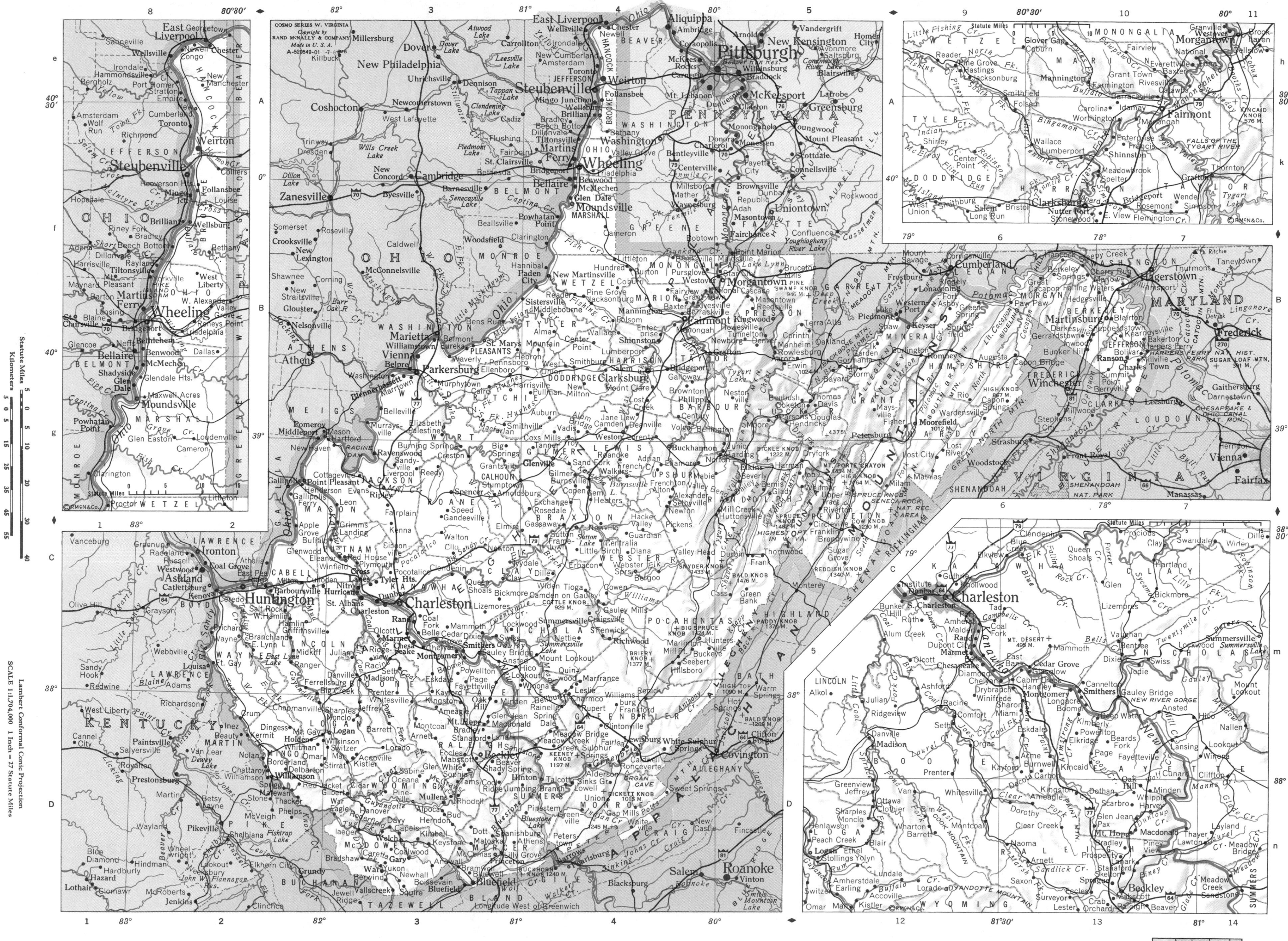

Lambert Conformal Conic Projection
SCALE 1:1,704,000   1 Inch = 27 Statute Miles

Statute Miles 5 0 5 10 20 30 40
Kilometers 5 0 5 15 25 35 45 55

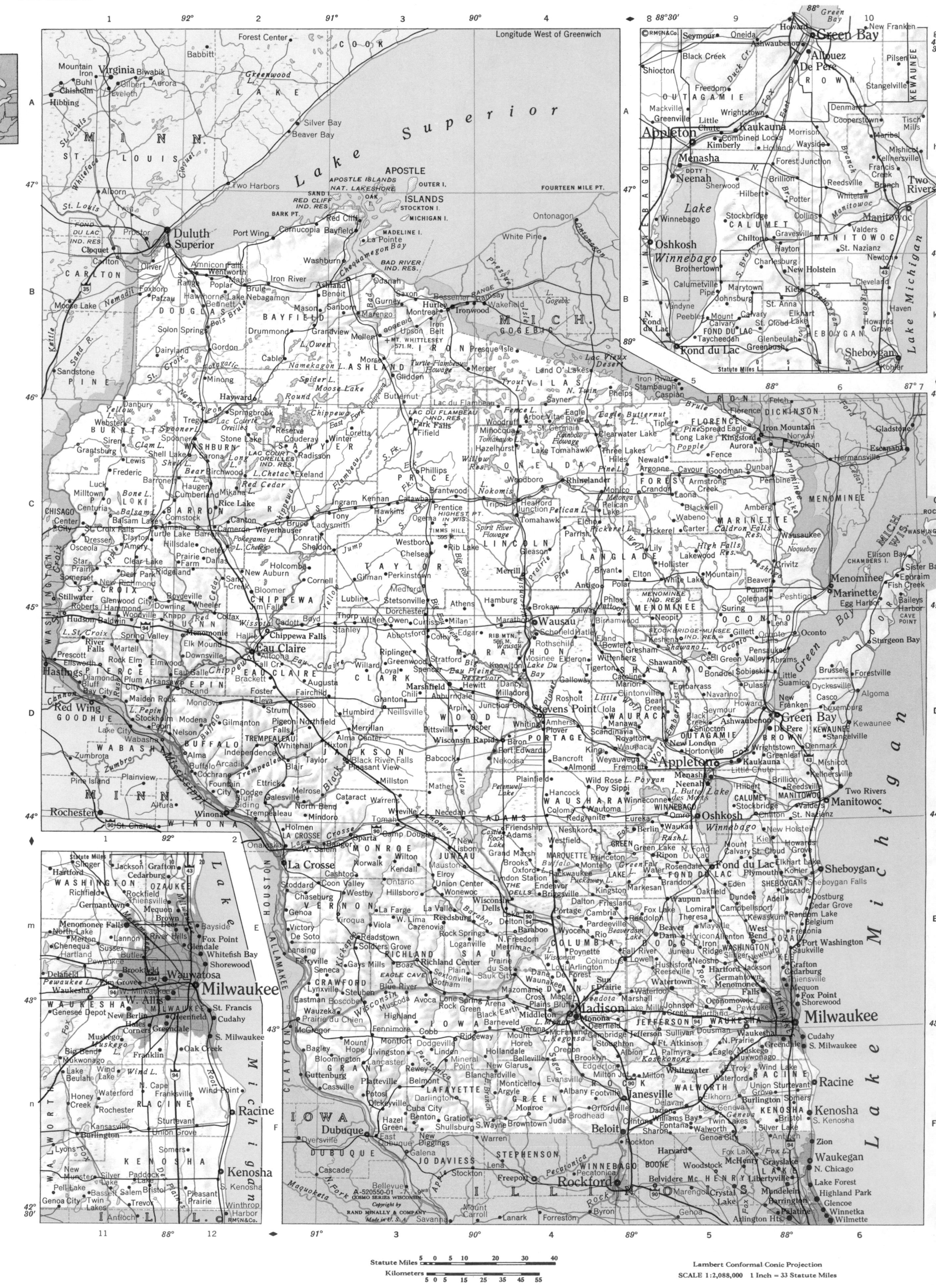

Statute Miles 5 0 5 10 20 30 40
Kilometers 5 0 5 15 25 35 45 55

Lambert Conformal Conic Projection
SCALE 1:2,088,000   1 Inch = 33 Statute Miles

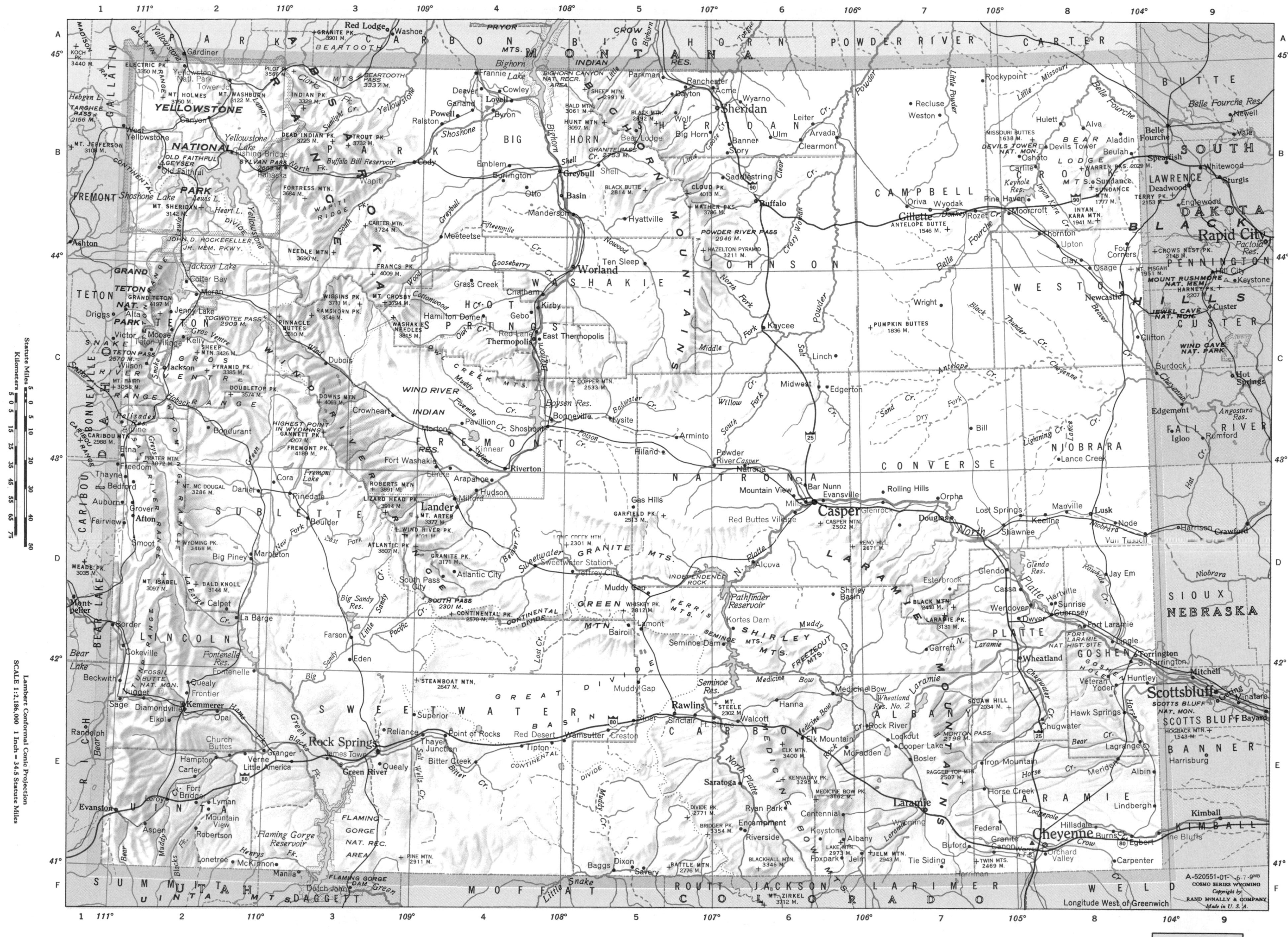

Statute Miles 5 0 5 10   20   30   40   50
Kilometers 5 0 5 15 25 35 45 55 65 75

Lambert Conformal Conic Projection
SCALE 1:2,186,000   1 Inch = 34.5 Statute Miles

Index to State Maps

In a single alphabetical list, this index includes the names of features that appear on the individual state maps. The names of cities and towns appear in regular type. The names of all other features appear in *italics.*

The names of physical features may be inverted, since they are always alphabetized under the proper, not the generic, part of the name. For example, Lake Erie is listed as *Erie, Lake.* Otherwise every entry, whether consisting of one word or more, is alphabetized as a single continuous entity. In the case of identical names, towns are listed first, then political divisions, then physical features. Entries that are completely identical are listed alphabetically by state name.

The map reference keys and page references are found in the last two columns of each entry. Each map reference key consists of a letter and a number. The letters correspond to letters along the sides of the maps. The numbers correspond to numbers that appear across the tops and bottoms of the maps.

List of Abbreviations

AK	Alaska	**LA**	Louisiana	**OH**	Ohio
AL	Alabama	**MA**	Massachusetts	**OK**	Oklahoma
AR	Arkansas	**MD**	Maryland	**OR**	Oregon
AZ	Arizona	**ME**	Maine	**PA**	Pennsylvania
CA	California	**MI**	Michigan	***r.***	river
CO	Colorado	**MN**	Minnesota	**RI**	Rhode Island
CT	Connecticut	**MO**	Missouri	**SC**	South Carolina
DC	District of Columbia	**MS**	Mississippi	**SD**	South Dakota
DE	Delaware	**MT**	Montana	**TN**	Tennessee
FL	Florida	**NA**	North America	**TX**	Texas
GA	Georgia	**NC**	North Carolina	**US**	United States
HI	Hawaii	**ND**	North Dakota	**UT**	Utah
IA	Iowa	**NE**	Nebraska	**VA**	Virginia
ID	Idaho	**NH**	New Hampshire	**VT**	Vermont
IL	Illinois	**NJ**	New Jersey	**WA**	Washington
IN	Indiana	**NM**	New Mexico	**WI**	Wisconsin
KS	Kansas	**NV**	Nevada	**WV**	West Virginia
KY	Kentucky	**NY**	New York	**WY**	Wyoming

A

Name	Map Ref.	Page
Abajo Peak, UT	F6	47
Abbaye, Point, MI	B2	25
Abbeville, AL	D4	4
Abbeville, LA	E3	21
Abbeville, SC	C3	43
Aberdeen, ID	G6	15
Aberdeen, MD	A5	23
Aberdeen, MS	B5	27
Aberdeen, SD	B7	44
Aberdeen, WA	C2	50
Abert, Lake, OR	E6	40
Abilene, KS	D6	19
Abilene, TX	C3	46
Abingdon, IL	C3	16
Abingdon, VA	f10	49
Abington, MA	B6	24
Abington [Township], PA	o21	41
Abraham Lincoln Birthplace National Historic Site, KY	C4	20
Absaroka Range, US	F7	53
Absarokee, MT	E7	29
Acadia National Park, ME	D4	22
Accokeek, MD	C3	23
Ackerman, MS	B4	27
Ackley, IA	B4	18
Acomita, NM	B2	34
Acworth, GA	B2	13
Ada, MN	C2	26
Ada, OK	C5	39
Adairsville, GA	B2	13
Adak Island, AK	E4	5
Adams, Mount, NH	B4	32
Adams, Mount, WA	C4	50
Adamsville, AL	f7	4
Addison, CT	C5	10
Addison, IL	k8	16
Adel, GA	E3	13
Adel, IA	C3	18
Adirondack Mountains, NY	A6	35
Admiralty Bay, AK	A9	5
Admiralty Island, AK	m22	5
Adrian, MI	G6	25
Afognak Island, AK	D9	5
Afton, MN	F6	26
Afton, WY	D2	53
Agawam, MA	B2	24
Agua Fria, NM	B3	34
Agua Fria, r., AZ	D3	6
Ahoskie, NC	A6	36
Aiea, HI	B4	14
Aiken, SC	D4	43
Ainsworth, NE	B6	30
Aitkin, MN	D5	26
Ajo, AZ	E3	6
Akiachak, AK	C7	5
Akron, CO	A7	9
Akron, IA	B1	18
Akron, OH	A4	38
Alabama, state, US	C3	4
Alabama, r., AL	D2	4
Alabaster, AL	B3	4
Alameda, CA	h8	8
Alameda, NM	B3	34
Alamo, TN	B2	45
Alamo, TX	F3	46
Alamogordo, NM	E4	34
Alamosa, CO	D5	9
Alamosa, r., CO	D5	9
Alamosa East, CO	D5	9
Alapaha, r., US	E3	13
Alaska, state, US	C9	5
Alaska, Gulf of, AK	D10	5
Alaska Peninsula, AK	D8	5
Alaska Range, AK	C9	5
Alava, Cape, WA	A1	50
Albany, GA	E2	13
Albany, IN	D7	17
Albany, KY	D4	20
Albany, MO	A3	28
Albany, NY	C7	35
Albany, OR	C3	40
Albemarle, NC	B2	36
Albemarle Sound, NC	A6	36
Albert Lea, MN	G5	26
Albertville, AL	A3	4
Albia, IA	C5	18
Albion, IN	B7	17
Albion, MI	F6	25
Albion, NE	C7	30
Albuquerque, NM	B3	34
Alcalde, NM	A3	34
Alcester, SD	D9	44
Alcoa, TN	D10	45
Alderson, WV	D4	51
Aldrich, AL	B3	4
Aledo, IL	B3	16
Alegres Mountain, NM	C2	34
Alenuihaha Channel, HI	C5	14
Aleutian Islands, AK	E3	5
Aleutian Range, AK	D9	5
Alexander City, AL	C4	4
Alexandria, IN	D6	17
Alexandria, KY	B5	20
Alexandria, LA	C3	21
Alexandria, MN	E3	26
Alexandria, VA	B5	49
Alfred, ME	E2	22
Algoma, WI	D6	52
Algona, IA	A3	18
Algonquin, IL	A5	16
Algood, TN	C8	45
Alhambra, CA	m12	8
Alice, TX	F3	46
Aliceville, AL	B1	4
Aliquippa, PA	E1	41
Allagash, r., ME	B3	22
Allatoona Lake, GA	B2	13
Allegheny, r., US	E2	41
Allegheny Mountain, US	B3	49
Allegheny Plateau, US	E1	41
Allegheny Reservoir, US	B4	41
Allemands, Lac Des, LA	E5	21
Allen, TX	C4	46
Allendale, SC	E5	43
Allen Park, MI	p15	25
Allentown, PA	E11	41
Alliance, NE	B3	30
Alliance, OH	B4	38
Alligator, r., NC	B6	36
Allison Park, PA	h14	41
Allouez, WI	h9	52
Alma, AR	B1	7
Alma, GA	E4	13
Alma, MI	E6	25
Alma, NE	D6	30
Aloha, OR	h12	40
Alpena, MI	C7	25
Alpharetta, GA	B2	13
Alstead, NH	D2	32
Alta, IA	B2	18
Altamaha, r., GA	E4	13
Altamont, OR	E5	40
Altamonte Springs, FL	D5	12
Altavista, VA	C3	49
Altheimer, AR	C4	7
Alton, IL	E3	16
Alton, MO	E6	28
Alton, NH	D4	32
Alton Bay, NH	D4	32
Altoona, IA	C4	18
Altoona, PA	E5	41
Altoona, WI	D2	52
Altus, OK	C2	39
Altus Reservoir, OK	C2	39
Alva, OK	A3	39
Alvin, TX	E5	46
Amargosa, r., US	D5	8
Amargosa Desert, US	G5	31
Amargosa Range, US	G5	31
Amarillo, TX	B2	46
Ambler, PA	F11	41
Ambridge, PA	E1	41
American Falls, ID	G6	15
American Falls Reservoir, ID	F5	15
American Fork, UT	C4	47
Americus, GA	D2	13
Amery, WI	C1	52
Ames, IA	B4	18
Amesbury, MA	A6	24
Amherst, MA	B2	24
Amherst, NH	E3	32
Amherst, NY	C2	35
Amherst, OH	A3	38
Amherstdale, WV	n12	51
Amite, LA	D5	21
Amite, r., LA	D5	21
Amityville, NY	E7	35
Ammon, ID	F7	15
Ammonoosuc, r., NH	B3	32
Amory, MS	B5	27
Amsterdam, NY	C6	35
Anaconda, MT	D4	29
Anaconda Range, MT	E3	29
Anacortes, WA	A3	50
Anacostia, r., US	C4	23
Anadarko, OK	B3	39
Anaheim, CA	F5	8
Anamosa, IA	B6	18
Anchorage, AK	C10	5
Anchorage, KY	g11	20
Anchor Point, AK	D9	5
Andalusia, AL	D3	4
Anderson, AK	C10	5
Anderson, IN	D6	17
Anderson, MO	E3	28
Anderson, SC	B2	43
Anderson Ranch Reservoir, ID	F3	15
Andover, KS	g12	19
Andover, MA	A5	24
Andover, MN	m12	26
Andreanof Islands, AK	E4	5
Andrews, NC	f9	36
Andrews, SC	E8	43
Andrews, TX	C1	46
Andrews Air Force Base, MD	C4	23
Androscoggin, r., ME	D2	22
Angle Inlet, MN	A3	26
Angleton, TX	E5	46
Angola, IN	A8	17
Animas, r., US	D3	9
Ankeny, IA	C4	18
Ann, Cape, MA	A6	24
Anna, IL	F4	16
Anna, Lake, VA	B5	49
Annandale, VA	g12	49
Annapolis, MD	C5	23
Ann Arbor, MI	F7	25
Anniston, AL	B4	4
Annville, PA	F8	41
Anoka, MN	E5	26
Anson, ME	D3	22
Ansonia, CT	D3	10
Ansted, WV	C3	51
Antelope Island, UT	B3	47
Antelope Peak, NV	B7	31
Anthony, KS	E5	19
Anthony, NM	F3	34
Anthony, RI	D3	42
Antietam National Battlefield, MD	B2	23
Antigo, WI	C4	52
Antioch, CA	h9	8
Antioch, IL	A5	16
Antlers, OK	C6	39
Antrim, NH	D3	32
Apache Junction, AZ	m9	6
Apalachee Bay, FL	B2	12
Apalachicola, r., FL	B1	12
Apalachicola Bay, FL	C2	12
Apex, NC	B4	36
Apopka, FL	D5	12
Apopka, Lake, FL	D5	12
Apostle Islands, WI	A3	52
Apostle Islands National Lakeshore, WI	A3	52
Appalachian Mountains, NA	C11	2
Apple, r., WI	C1	52
Apple Orchard Mountain, VA	C3	49
Appleton, MN	E2	26
Appleton, WI	D5	52
Apple Valley, CA	E5	8
Apple Valley, MN	n12	26
Appomattox, r., VA	C4	49
Appomattox Court House National Historical Park, VA	C4	49
Arab, AL	A3	4
Arabi, LA	k11	21
Aransas Bay, TX	E4	46
Arapahoe, NE	D6	30
Arbuckle Mountains, OK	C4	39
Arcadia, CA	m12	8
Arcadia, IN	D5	17
Arc Dome, NV	E4	31
Archbald, PA	m18	41
Archdale, NC	B3	36
Arches National Park, UT	E6	47
Arco, ID	F5	15
Ardmore, IN	A5	17
Ardmore, OK	C4	39
Ardmore, PA	F11	41
Arena, Point, CA	C2	8
Argos, IN	B5	17
Arizona, state, US	C4	6
Arkadelphia, AR	C2	7
Arkansas, state, US	C3	7
Arkansas, r., US	C9	2
Arkansas City, AR	D4	7
Arkansas City, KS	E6	19
Arkoma, OK	B7	39
Arlington, MA	B5	24
Arlington, NE	C9	30
Arlington, NY	D7	35
Arlington, SD	C8	44
Arlington, TX	n9	46
Arlington, VT	E2	48
Arlington, VA	B5	49
Arlington, WA	A3	50
Arlington Heights, IL	A5	16
Arma, KS	E9	19
Armijo, NM	k7	34
Armour, SD	D7	44
Arnold, MD	B5	23
Arnold, MO	C7	28
Arnold, NE	C5	30
Arnold, PA	h14	41
Artesia, NM	E5	34
Arthur, Lake, PA	E1	41
Arvada, CO	B5	9
Arvon, Mount, MI	B2	25
Asbury Park, NJ	C4	33
Ashburn, GA	E3	13
Ashdown, AR	D1	7
Asheboro, NC	B3	36
Asheville, NC	f10	36
Ashford, AL	D4	4
Ashland, AL	B4	4
Ashland, KY	B7	20
Ashland, MA	g10	24
Ashland, NE	C9	30
Ashland, NH	C3	32
Ashland, OH	B3	38
Ashland, OR	E4	40
Ashland, VA	C5	49
Ashland, WI	B3	52
Ashland City, TN	A4	45
Ashley, ND	C6	37
Ashokan Reservoir, NY	D6	35
Ashtabula, OH	A5	38
Ashton, ID	E7	15
Ashuelot, r., NH	E2	32
Ashwaubenon, WI	D5	52
Aspen, CO	B4	9
Aspen Butte, OR	E4	40
Aspen Hill, MD	B3	23
Assateague Island, US	D7	23
Assateague Island National Seashore, US	D7	23
Astoria, OR	A3	40
Atchafalaya, r., LA	D4	21
Atchafalaya Bay, LA	E4	21
Atchison, KS	C8	19
Athens, AL	A3	4
Athens, GA	C3	13
Athens, OH	C3	38
Athens, TN	D9	45
Athens, TX	C5	46
Athol, MA	A3	24
Atkins, AR	B3	7
Atkinson, NE	B7	30
Atkinson, NH	E4	32
Atlanta, GA	C2	13
Atlantic, IA	C2	18
Atlantic Beach, FL	m9	12
Atlantic City, NJ	E4	33
Atlantic Peak, WY	D3	53
Atmore, AL	D2	4
Atoka, OK	C5	39
Attalla, AL	A3	4
Attica, IN	D3	17
Attleboro, MA	C5	24
Attu Island, AK	E2	5
Atwood, KS	C2	19
Auau Channel, HI	C5	14
Auburn, AL	C4	4
Auburn, GA	B3	13
Auburn, IL	D4	16
Auburn, IN	B7	17
Auburn, ME	D2	22
Auburn, MA	B4	24
Auburn, NE	D10	30
Auburn, NY	C4	35
Auburn, WA	B3	50
Auburn Heights, MI	F7	25
Audubon, IA	C3	18
Auglaize, r., OH	A1	38
Augusta, AR	B4	7
Augusta, GA	C5	13
Augusta, KS	E7	19
Augusta, ME	D3	22
Augusta, MT	C4	29
Ault, CO	A6	9
Aurora, CO	B6	9
Aurora, IL	B5	16
Aurora, IN	F8	17
Aurora, MN	C6	26
Aurora, MO	E4	28
Aurora, NE	D7	30
Aurora, OH	A4	38
Au Sable, r., MI	D6	25
Ausable, r., NY	f11	35
Au Sable Point, MI	D7	25
Austell, GA	h7	13
Austin, IN	G6	17
Austin, MN	G6	26
Austin, NV	D4	31
Austin, TX	D4	46
Austintown, OH	A5	38
Ava, MO	E5	28
Avalon, PA	h13	41
Avenel, NJ	k7	33
Avilla, IN	B7	17
Avoca, IA	C2	18
Avon, CT	B4	10
Avon, OH	A3	38
Avon, SD	E7	44
Avondale, AZ	D3	6
Avondale Estates, GA	h8	13
Avon Lake, OH	A3	38
Ayden, NC	B5	36
Azle, TX	n9	46
Aztec, NM	A2	34

B

Name	Map Ref.	Page
Babbitt, NV	E3	31
Baboquivari Mountains, AZ	F4	6
Baboquivari Peak, AZ	F4	6
Babylon, NY	n15	35
Backbone Mountain, US	m12	23
Bad, r., SD	C5	44
Bad Axe, MI	E8	25
Baden, PA	E1	41
Badlands, SD	D3	44
Badlands National Park, SD	D3	44
Bagley, MN	C3	26
Baileys Crossroads, VA	g12	49
Bainbridge, GA	F2	13
Bainbridge Island, WA	e10	50
Baker, LA	D4	21
Baker, MT	D12	29
Baker, OR	C9	40
Baker, Mount, WA	A4	50
Baker Mountain, ME	C3	22
Bakersfield, CA	E4	8
Bald Knob, AR	B4	7
Bald Knob, VA	c3	49
Bald Knob, WV	C5	51
Baldwin, PA	k14	41
Baldwin City, KS	D8	19
Baldwinsville, NY	B4	35
Baldwyn, MS	A5	27
Baldy Peak, AZ	D6	6
Ball, LA	C3	21
Ballwin, MO	f12	28
Baltimore, MD	B4	23
Baltimore Highlands, MD	h11	23
Bamberg, SC	E5	43
Banana River, FL	D6	12
Bangor, ME	D4	22
Bangor, PA	E11	41
Bangor Township, MI	E7	25
Bankhead Lake, AL	B2	4
Banks Lake, WA	B6	50
Bannock Peak, ID	F6	15
Baraboo, WI	E4	52
Baranof Island, AK	m22	5
Barataria Bay, LA	E6	21
Barbers Point, HI	B3	14
Barberton, OH	A4	38
Barboursville, WV	C2	51
Barbourville, KY	D6	20
Bardstown, KY	C4	20
Bargersville, IN	E5	17
Bar Harbor, ME	D4	22
Barkley, Lake, US	f10	20
Barling, AR	B1	7
Barnegat Bay, NJ	D4	33
Barnesville, GA	C2	13
Barnesville, MN	D2	26
Barnstable, MA	C7	24
Bar Nunn, WY	D6	53
Barnwell, SC	E5	43
Barques, Pointe aux, MI	D8	25
Barrackville, WV	B4	51
Barre, VT	C4	48
Barren, r., KY	C3	20
Barren River Lake, KY	D3	20
Barrington, IL	A5	16
Barrington, RI	D5	42
Barron, WI	C2	52
Barrow, AK	A8	5
Barrow, Point, AK	A8	5
Barstow, CA	E5	8
Bartlesville, OK	A6	39
Bartlett, NH	B4	32
Bartlett, TN	B2	45
Barton, VT	B4	48
Bartonville, IL	C4	16
Bartow, FL	E5	12
Basalt, CO	B3	9
Basehor, KS	k16	19
Basin, WY	B4	53
Bass Harbor, ME	D4	22
Bass Islands, OH	A3	38
Bass Lake, IN	B4	17
Basswood Lake, MN	B7	26
Bastrop, LA	B4	21
Batavia, IL	B5	16
Batavia, NY	C2	35
Batesburg, SC	D4	43
Batesville, AR	B4	7
Batesville, IN	F7	17
Batesville, MS	A4	27
Bath, ME	E3	22
Baton Rouge, LA	D4	21
Battle Creek, MI	F5	25
Battle Creek, NE	C8	30
Battle Ground, WA	D3	50
Battle Lake, MN	D3	26
Battle Mountain, NV	C5	31
Baxley, GA	E4	13
Baxter, MN	D4	26
Baxter Springs, KS	E9	19
Bay, AR	B5	7
Bayard, NE	C2	30
Bayard, NM	E1	34
Bay City, MI	E7	25
Bay City, TX	E5	46
Bayfield, CO	D3	9
Bay Minette, AL	E2	4
Bayonne, NJ	B4	33
Bayou Cane, LA	E5	21
Bayou D'Arbonne Lake, LA	B3	21
Bayou La Batre, AL	E1	4
Bayport, MN	E6	26
Bay Saint Louis, MS	E4	27
Bay Shore, NY	E7	35
Bayshore Gardens, FL	q10	12
Bayside, WI	m12	52
Bays Mountain, TN	C10	45
Bay Springs, MS	D4	27
Baytown, TX	E5	46
Bay Village, OH	h9	38
Beach, IL	h9	16
Beach, ND	C1	37
Beacon, NY	D7	35
Beals, ME	D5	22
Bearden, AR	D3	7
Beardstown, IL	C3	16
Bear Lake, US	A4	47
Bear Mountain, AR	f7	7
Beartooth Pass, WY	B3	53
Beartooth Range, US	E7	29
Beatrice, NE	D9	30
Beatty, NV	G5	31
Beaufort, NC	C6	36
Beaufort, SC	G6	43
Beaumont, TX	D5	46
Beaver, OK	A1	39
Beaver, PA	E1	41
Beaver, WV	D3	51
Beaver, r., US	A2	39
Beavercreek, OH	C1	38
Beaver Dam, KY	C3	20
Beaver Dam, WI	E5	52
Beaverdam Lake, WI	E5	52
Beaver Falls, PA	E1	41
Beaverhead, r., MT	E4	29
Beaverhead Mountains, US	D5	15
Beaver Island, MI	C5	25
Beaver Lake, AR	A2	7
Beavertail Point, RI	F4	42
Beaverton, OR	B4	40
Beckley, WV	D3	51
Bedford, IN	G5	17
Bedford, IA	D3	18
Bedford, MA	B5	24
Bedford, NH	E3	32
Bedford, OH	A4	38
Bedford, VA	C3	49
Beebe, AR	B4	7
Beech Grove, IN	E5	17
Beeville, TX	E4	46
Bel Air, MD	A5	23
Belen, NM	C3	34
Belfast, ME	D3	22
Belfield, ND	C2	37
Belgrade, MT	E5	29
Belington, WV	B5	51
Belknap Crater, OR	C5	40
Bellaire, KS	g12	19
Bellaire, OH	C5	38
Bellaire, TX	r14	46
Bella Vista, AR	A1	7
Bellbrook, OH	C1	38
Belle, WV	C3	51
Belle Chasse, LA	E5	21
Bellefontaine, OH	B2	38
Bellefonte, PA	E6	41
Belle Fourche, SD	C2	44
Belle Fourche, r., US	C3	44
Belle Glade, FL	F6	12
Belle Meade, TN	g10	45
Belle Plaine, IA	C5	18
Belle Plaine, KS	E6	19
Belle Plaine, MN	F5	26
Belle View, VA	g12	49
Belleville, IL	E4	16
Belleville, KS	C6	19
Belleville, NJ	B4	33
Bellevue, ID	F4	15
Bellevue, IA	B7	18
Bellevue, KY	h13	20
Bellevue, NE	C10	30
Bellevue, OH	A3	38
Bellevue, PA	F1	41
Bellevue, WA	e11	50
Bellflower, CA	n12	8
Bellingham, WA	A3	50
Bellmawr, NJ	D2	33
Bellows Falls, VT	E4	48
Bellwood, IL	k9	16
Bellwood, VA	n18	49
Belmond, IA	B4	18
Belmont, CA	h8	8
Belmont, MA	g11	24
Belmont, MS	A5	27
Belmont, NH	D4	32
Belmont, NC	B1	36
Beloit, KS	C5	19
Beloit, WI	F4	52
Belpre, OH	C4	38
Belton, MO	C3	28
Belton, SC	B3	43
Belton, TX	D4	46
Belton Lake, TX	D4	46
Beltsville, MD	B4	23
Belvedere, SC	D4	43
Belvidere, IL	A5	16
Belzoni, MS	B3	27
Bemidji, MN	C4	26
Benbrook, TX	n9	46
Bend, OR	C5	40
Benicia, CA	C2	8
Benkelman, NE	D4	30
Bennett, CO	B6	9
Bennettsville, SC	B8	43
Bennington, NH	D3	32
Bennington, VT	F2	48
Bensenville, IL	B6	16
Bensley, VA	C5	49
Benson, AZ	F5	6
Benson, MN	E3	26
Benton, AR	C3	7
Benton, IL	E5	16
Benton, KY	f9	20
Benton, TN	B7	45
Benton Harbor, MI	F4	25
Bentonville, AR	A1	7
Benwood, WV	f8	51
Berea, KY	C5	20
Berea, OH	A4	38
Berea, SC	B3	43
Beresford, SD	D9	44
Bergenfield, NJ	B4	33
Berkeley, CA	D2	8
Berkeley, MO	f13	28
Berkeley Heights, NJ	B4	33
Berkley, MI	F7	25

Name — Map Ref. — Page

Berkshire Hills, MA B1 24
Berlin, NH B4 32
Berlin, PA G4 41
Berlin, WI E5 52
Berlin Lake, OH A4 38
Bernalillo, NM B3 34
Berne, IN C8 17
Bernie, MO E8 28
Berryessa, Lake, CA C2 8
Berrys Chapel, TN B5 45
Berryville, AR A2 7
Berryville, VA A5 49
Berthoud, CO A5 9
Berthoud Pass, CO B5 9
Berwick, LA E4 21
Berwick, ME E2 22
Berwick, PA D9 41
Berwyn, IL k9 16
Berwyn, PA o20 41
Bessemer, AL B3 4
Bessemer, MI n11 25
Bessemer City, NC B1 36
Bethalto, IL E3 16
Bethany, MO A3 28
Bethany, OK B4 39
Bethany, WV A4 51
Bethel, AK C7 5
Bethel, CT D2 10
Bethel, VT D3 48
Bethel Acres, OK B5 39
Bethel Park, PA k14 41
Bethesda, MD C3 23
Bethlehem, NH B3 32
Bethlehem, PA E11 41
Bettendorf, IA C7 18
Beulah, ND B4 37
B. Everett Jordan Lake, NC B3 36
Beverly, MA A6 24
Beverly Hills, CA m12 8
Bexley, OH m11 38
Bickle Knob, WV C5 51
Bicknell, IN G3 17
Biddeford, ME E2 22
Big Bay De Noc, MI C4 25
Big Belt Mountains, MT D5 29
Big Bend National Park, TX E1 46
Big Black, r., ME B3 22
Big Black, r., MS C3 27
Big Butt, TN C11 45
Big Costilla Peak, NM A4 34
Big Cypress Swamp, FL F5 12
Big Eau Pleine, r., WI D3 52
Bigelow, Mount, ME C2 22
Bigfork, MT B2 29
Big Fork, r., MN B5 26
Bighorn, r., US B6 2
Bighorn Lake, US E8 29
Bighorn Mountains, US B5 53
Big Lake, MN E5 26
Big Lake, ME C5 22
Big Lost, r., ID F5 15
Big Muddy, r., IL F4 16
Big Nemaha, r., NE D10 30
Big Piney, WY D2 53
Big Rapids, MI E5 25
Big Sable Point, MI D4 25
Big Sandy, MT B6 29
Big Sandy, r., US C2 51
Big Sandy, r., AZ C2 6
Big Sandy, r., TN B3 45
Big Sandy, r., WY D3 53
Big Sandy Creek, r., CO C8 9
Big Sioux, r., US E9 44
Big Spring, TX C2 46
Big Spruce Knob, WV C4 51
Big Stone Gap, VA f9 49
Big Stone Lake, US E2 26
Big Sunflower, r., MS B3 27
Big Sur, CA D3 8
Big Thompson, r., CO A5 9
Big Timber, MT E7 29
Big Wood, r., ID F4 15
Bijou Creek, r., CO B6 9
Billerica, MA A5 24
Billings, MT E8 29
Biloxi, MS E5 27
Binghamton, NY C5 35
Birdsboro, PA F10 41
Birmingham, AL B3 4
Birmingham, MI F7 25
Bisbee, AZ F6 6
Biscayne, Key, FL s13 12
Biscayne Bay, FL G6 12
Biscayne National Monument, FL G6 12
Bishopville, SC C7 43
Bismarck, ND C5 37
Bistineau, Lake, LA B2 21
Bitter Creek, r., WY E4 53
Bitterroot, r., MT D2 29
Bitterroot Range, US B3 15
Bixby, OK B6 39
Black, r., AZ D5 6
Black, r., AR B4 7
Black, r., LA C4 21
Black, r., MI E8 25
Black, r., SC D8 43
Black, Bayou, r., LA E5 21
Blackburn, Mount, AK C11 5
Black Butte, MT F5 29
Black Canyon, CO C3 9
Black Canyon City, AZ C3 6
Black Canyon of the Gunnison National Monument, CO C3 9
Black Creek, r., SC B7 43
Blackduck, MN C4 26
Blackfoot, ID F6 15
Black Forest, CO C6 9
Black Hawk, SD C2 44
Black Hills, US C2 44
Black Lake, NY f9 35
Black Mesa, OK e8 39
Black Mountain, NC f10 36
Black Mountain, US D7 20
Black Mountain, MT D4 29
Black Mountains, AZ B1 6
Black River Falls, WI D3 52
Blacksburg, VA C2 49
Blacks Fork, r., US E3 53
Blackshear, GA E4 13
Blackstone, VA C5 49
Blackstone, r., RI B4 42
Black Warrior, r., AL C2 4
Blackwater, r., VA D6 49
Blackwell, OK A4 39
Bladensburg, MD f9 23
Blaine, MN m12 26
Blaine, WA A3 50
Blair, NE C9 30
Blakely, GA E2 13
Blakely, PA m18 41
Blake Point, MI h10 25
Blanca, Sierra, TX o12 46
Blanca Peak, CO D5 9
Blanco, Cape, OR E2 40
Blanding, UT F6 47
Blende, CO C6 9
Blennerhassett, WV B3 51
Block Island, RI h7 42
Block Island Sound, US G2 42
Bloodsworth Island, MD D5 23
Bloomer, WI C2 52
Bloomfield, CT B5 10
Bloomfield, IN F4 17
Bloomfield, IA D5 18
Bloomfield, NE B8 30
Bloomfield, NJ h8 33
Bloomfield, NM A2 34
Bloomfield Hills, MI o15 25
Bloomingdale, GA D5 13
Bloomingdale, IL k8 16
Bloomingdale, TN C11 45
Blooming Prairie, MN G5 26
Bloomington, IL C4 16
Bloomington, IN F4 17
Bloomington, MN F5 26
Bloomsburg, PA E9 41
Blountsville, AL A3 4
Blountville, TN C11 45
Blue Ash, OH o13 38
Blue Earth, MN G4 26
Blue Earth, r., MN G4 26
Bluefield, VA C1 49
Bluefield, WV D3 51
Blue Hills, CT B5 10
Blue Island, IL B6 16
Blue Mountain, NY B6 35
Blue Mountain, PA F6 41
Blue Mountains, US A4 2
Blue Ridge, US C11 2
Blue Springs, MO h11 28
Bluestone Lake, US D4 51
Bluewell, WV D3 51
Bluff Park, AL g7 4
Bluffton, IN C7 17
Blytheville, AR B6 7
Boardman, OH A5 38
Boaz, AL A3 4
Boca Chica Key, FL H5 12
Boca Raton, FL F6 12
Boeuf, r., LA C4 21
Boeuf, Bayou, r., LA D3 21
Bogalusa, LA D6 21
Bogue Chitto, r., US D5 21
Bois Blanc Island, MI C6 25
Boise, ID F2 15
Boise City, OK e8 39
Bolingbrook, IL k8 16
Bolivar, MO D4 28
Bolivar, TN B3 45
Bolivar, WV B7 51
Bomoseen, Lake, VT D2 48
Bon Air, VA C5 49
Bonanza Peak, WA A5 50
Bondurant, IA C4 18
Bonita Springs, FL F5 12
Bonners Ferry, ID A2 15
Bonner Springs, KS C9 19
Bonnet Carre Floodway, LA h11 21
Bonne Terre, MO D7 28
Bonneville Peak, ID F6 15
Bonneville Salt Flats, UT C2 47
Bonney Lake, WA B3 50
Bono, AR B5 7
Bon Secour, AL E2 4
Boomer, WV C3 51
Boone, IA B4 18
Boone, NC A1 36
Boone, r., IA B4 18
Booneville, AR B2 7
Booneville, MS A5 27
Boonville, IN H3 17
Boonville, MO C5 28
Boothbay, ME E3 22
Boothbay Harbor, ME E3 22
Borah Peak, ID E5 15
Borger, TX B2 46
Borgne, Lake, LA D6 21
Boscobel, WI E3 52
Bosque Farms, NM C3 34
Bossier City, LA B2 21
Boston, MA B5 24
Boston Bay, MA B6 24
Boston Mountains, AR B2 7
Bothell, WA B3 50
Bottineau, ND A5 37
Boulder, CO A5 9
Boulder City, NV H7 31
Boundary Bald Mountain, ME C2 22
Boundary Bay, WA A3 50
Boundary Peak, NV F3 31
Bountiful, UT C4 47
Bourbon, IN B5 17
Bourbonnais, IL B6 16
Bow, NH D3 32
Bowdon, GA C1 13
Bowie, MD C4 23
Bowling Green, KY D3 20
Bowling Green, MO B6 28
Bowling Green, OH A2 38
Bowman, ND C2 37
Bowman-Haley Lake, ND C2 37
Box Elder, SD C2 44
Box Elder Creek, r., CO A6 9
Boyer, r., IA C2 18
Boynton Beach, FL F6 12
Boysen Reservoir, WY C4 53
Boys Town, NE g12 30
Bozeman, MT E5 29
Brackenridge, PA h15 41
Braddock, PA k14 41
Braddock Heights, MD B2 23
Bradenton, FL E4 12
Bradford, PA C4 41
Bradford, VT D4 48
Bradley, IL B6 16
Bradley, WV D3 51
Braidwood, IL B5 16
Brainerd, MN D4 26
Braintree, MA B5 24
Brandenburg, KY C3 20
Brandon, FL E4 12
Brandon, MS C4 27
Brandon, SD D9 44
Brandon, VT D2 48
Branford, CT D4 10
Branford Hills, CT D4 10
Branson, MO E4 28
Brasstown Bald, GA B3 13
Brattleboro, VT F3 48
Brawley Peaks, NV E3 31
Brazil, IN E3 17
Brazos, r., TX D4 46
Brea, CA n13 8
Bread Loaf Mountain, VT D3 48
Breaux Bridge, LA D4 21
Breckenridge, CO B4 9
Breckenridge, MN D2 26
Brecksville, OH A4 38
Breese, IL E4 16
Bremen, GA C1 13
Bremen, IN B5 17
Bremerton, WA B3 50
Brenham, TX D4 46
Brent, FL u14 12
Brenton Point, RI F5 42
Brentwood, MO f13 28
Brentwood, NY E7 35
Brentwood, PA k14 41
Brentwood, TN A5 45
Breton Islands, LA E6 21
Breton Sound, LA E6 21
Brevard, NC f10 36
Brewer, ME D4 22
Brewster Islands, MA g12 24
Brewton, AL D2 4
Brick [Township], NJ C4 33
Bridgeport, AL A4 4
Bridgeport, CT E3 10
Bridgeport, MI E7 25
Bridgeport, NE C2 30
Bridgeport, PA o20 41
Bridgeport, WV B4 51
Bridgeton, MO C7 28
Bridgeton, NJ E2 33
Bridgeville, PA k13 41
Bridgewater, VA B4 49
Bridgton, ME D2 22
Briery Knob, WV C4 51
Brigantine, NJ E4 33
Brigham City, UT B3 47
Brighton, AL B3 4
Brighton, CO B6 9
Brighton, MI F7 25
Brighton, NY B3 35
Brillion, WI D5 52
Brinkley, AR C4 7
Bristol, CT C4 10
Bristol, NH C3 32
Bristol, RI D5 42
Bristol, TN C11 45
Bristol, VT C2 48
Bristol, VA f9 49
Bristol Bay, AK D7 5
Bristol [Township], PA F12 41
Bristow, OK B5 39
Britt, IA A4 18
Britton, SD B8 44
Broad, r., SC C5 43
Broadview Heights, OH h9 38
Brockport, NY B3 35
Brockton, MA B5 24
Brodhead, WI F4 52
Broken Arrow, OK A6 39
Broken Bow, NE C6 30
Broken Bow, OK C7 39
Broken Bow Lake, OK C7 39
Brookfield, IL k9 16
Brookfield, MA B3 24
Brookfield, MO B4 28
Brookfield, WI m11 52
Brookhaven, MS D3 27
Brookhaven, WV h11 51
Brookings, OR E2 40
Brookings, SD C9 44
Brookline, MA B5 24
Brooklyn, IA C5 18
Brooklyn, OH h9 38
Brooklyn Center, MN E5 26
Brooklyn Park, MD h11 23
Brooklyn Park, MN m12 26
Brook Park, OH h9 38
Brooks, KY g11 20
Brookside, AL f7 4
Brookside, DE B3 11
Brooks Range, AK B9 5
Brookston, IN C4 17
Brookville, IN F8 17
Brookville Lake, IN E7 17
Broomall, PA p20 41
Broomfield, CO B5 9
Browerville, MN D4 26
Brown Deer, WI m12 52
Brownfield, TX C1 46
Browning, MT B3 29
Brownlee Reservoir, US C10 40
Brownsburg, IN E5 17
Browns Mills, NJ D3 33
Brownstown, IN G5 17
Brownsville, FL s13 12
Brownsville, TN B2 45
Brownsville, TX G4 46
Brownville Junction, ME C3 22
Brownwood, TX D3 46
Bruce, MS B4 27
Brundidge, AL D4 4
Bruneau, r., US G3 15
Brunswick, GA E5 13
Brunswick, ME E3 22
Brunswick, MD B2 23
Brunswick, OH A4 38
Brush, CO A7 9
Bryan, OH A1 38
Bryan, TX D4 46
Bryant, AR C3 7
Bryant Pond, ME D2 22
Bryce Canyon National Park, UT F3 47
Buchanan, MI G4 25
Buckatunna, MS D5 27
Buckeye, AZ D3 6
Buckfield, ME D2 22
Buckhannon, WV C4 51
Buckley, WA B3 50
Buck Mountain, VA D1 49
Buckner, MO h11 28
Bucksport, ME D4 22
Bucyrus, OH B3 38
Buena Park, CA n12 8
Buena Vista, CO C4 9
Buena Vista, VA C3 49
Buffalo, MN E5 26
Buffalo, MO D4 28
Buffalo, NY C2 35
Buffalo, SD B2 44
Buffalo, WV C3 51
Buffalo, WY B6 53
Buffalo, r., AR B3 7
Buffalo, r., TN B4 45
Buffalo, r., WI D2 52
Buffalo Bill Reservoir, WY B3 53
Buffalo Grove, IL h9 16
Buford, GA B2 13
Buhl, ID G4 15
Buhler, KS D6 19
Bullhead City, AZ B1 6
Bull Run, r., VA g11 49
Bulls Bay, SC F8 43
Bull Shoals, AR A3 7
Bull Shoals Lake, US A3 7
Bunker Hill, NV D4 31
Bunkie, LA D3 21
Burbank, CA E4 8
Burbank, IL k9 16
Burkburnett, TX B3 46
Burke, SD D6 44
Burkesville, KY D4 20
Burleson, TX n9 46
Burley, ID G5 15
Burlington, CO B8 9
Burlington, IA D6 18
Burlington, KS D8 19
Burlington, KY A5 20
Burlington, MA f11 24
Burlington, NJ C3 33
Burlington, NC A3 36
Burlington, ND A4 37
Burlington, VT C2 48
Burlington, WA A3 50
Burlington, WI F5 52
Burns, OR D7 40
Burnsville, MN F5 26
Burnt Mills, Lake, VA k14 49
Burt Lake, MI C6 25
Burton, MI F7 25
Burwell, NE C6 30
Bushnell, IL C3 16
Butler, AL C1 4
Butler, IN B8 17
Butler, MO C3 28
Butler, PA E2 41
Butner, NC A4 36
Butte, MT E4 29
Butte des Morts, Lake, WI D5 52
Buzzards Bay, MA C6 24
Buzzards Bay, MA C6 24
Byron, GA D3 13
Byron, MN F6 26
Byron, WY B4 53

C

Cabin Creek, WV m13 51
Cabinet Gorge Reservoir, US B1 29
Cabinet Mountains, MT B1 29
Cabool, MO D5 28
Cabot, AR C3 7
Cacapon, r., WV B6 51
Cache, OK C3 39
Cache, r., AR C4 7
Cache la Poudre, r., CO A5 9
Cache Peak, ID G5 15
Caddo, r., AR C2 7
Caddo Mountains, AR C2 7
Caddo Valley, AR C2 7
Cadillac, MI D5 25
Cadiz, KY D2 20
Caesar Creek Lake, OH C2 38
Cahaba, r., AL C2 4
Cahokia, IL E3 16
Cairo, GA F2 13
Cairo, IL F4 16
Calais, ME C5 22
Calcasieu, r., LA D2 21
Calcasieu Lake, LA E2 21
Calcasieu Pass, LA E2 21
Caldwell, ID F2 15
Caldwell, KS E6 19
Caledonia, MN G7 26
Calera, AL B3 4
Calera, OK D5 39
Calhoun, GA B2 13
Calhoun City, MS B4 27
Calhoun Falls, SC C2 43
Caliente, NV F7 31
California, MD D4 23
California, MO C5 28
California, PA F2 41
California, state, US D4 8
California Aqueduct, CA E4 8
Caloosahatchee, r., FL F5 12
Calumet, Lake, IL k9 16
Calumet City, IL B6 16
Calvert City, KY e9 20
Camanche, IA C7 18
Camano Island, WA A3 50
Camarillo, CA E4 8
Camas, WA D3 50
Cambridge, MD C5 23
Cambridge, MA B5 24
Cambridge, MN E5 26
Cambridge, NE D5 30
Cambridge, OH B4 38
Cambridge City, IN E7 17
Camden, AL D2 4
Camden, AR D3 7
Camden, DE D3 11
Camden, ME D3 22
Camden, NJ D2 33
Camden, SC C6 43
Camden, TN A3 45
Camdenton, MO D5 28
Camelback Mountain, AZ k9 6
Camels Hump, VT C3 48
Cameron, LA E2 21
Cameron, MO B3 28
Cameron, WV B4 51
Camilla, GA E2 13
Campbell, MO E7 28
Campbell, OH A5 38
Campbell Hill, OH B2 38
Campbellsville, KY C4 20
Camp Hill, AL C4 4
Camp Hill, PA F8 41
Camp Lejeune Marine Corps Base, NC C5 36
Camp Springs, MD f9 23
Campton, NH C3 32
Camp Verde, AZ C4 6
Canaan, NH C2 32
Canadian, r., US C7 2
Canandaigua, NY C3 35
Canandaigua Lake, NY C3 35
Canaveral, Cape, FL D6 12
Canaveral National Seashore, FL D6 12
Canby, MN F2 26
Canby, OR B4 40
Candlewood, Lake, CT D1 10
Cando, ND A6 37
Cane, r., LA C2 21
Caney, KS E8 19
Caney Fork, r., TN C8 45
Canisteo, r., NY C3 35
Cannelton, IN I4 17
Cannon, r., MN F5 26
Cannonball, r., ND C5 37
Cannon Falls, MN F6 26
Cannonsville Reservoir, NY C5 35
Canon City, CO C5 9
Canonsburg, PA F1 41
Canton, GA B2 13
Canton, IL C3 16
Canton, ME D2 22
Canton, MA B5 24
Canton, MS C3 27
Canton, MO A6 28
Canton, NC f10 36
Canton, OH B4 38
Canton, SD D9 44
Canyon, TX B2 46
Canyon de Chelly National Monument, AZ A6 6
Canyon Ferry Lake, MT D5 29
Canyon Lake, TX E3 46
Canyonlands National Park, UT E6 47
Cape Cod Bay, MA C7 24
Cape Cod Canal, MA C6 24
Cape Cod National Seashore, MA C7 24
Cape Coral, FL F5 12
Cape Elizabeth, ME E2 22
Cape Fear, r., NC C4 36
Cape Girardeau, MO D8 28
Cape Hatteras National Seashore, NC B7 36
Cape Lookout National Seashore, NC C6 36
Cape Porpoise, ME E2 22
Capitan, NM D4 34
Capitan Peak, NM D4 34
Capitol Reef National Park, UT E4 47
Caraway, AR B5 7
Carbondale, CO B3 9
Carbondale, IL F4 16
Carbondale, KS D8 19
Carbondale, PA C10 41
Carencro, LA D3 21
Caribou, ME B5 22
Caribou Mountain, ME C2 22
Carlin, NV C5 31
Carlinville, IL D4 16
Carlisle, AR C4 7
Carlisle, IA C4 18
Carlisle, KY B5 20
Carlisle, PA F7 41
Carl Junction, MO D3 28
Carlsbad, CA F5 8
Carlsbad, NM E5 34
Carlsbad Caverns National Park, NM E5 34
Carlyle, IL E4 16
Carlyle Lake, IL E4 16
Carmel, IN E5 17
Carmi, IL E5 16
Carnegie, PA F1 41
Carney, MD B4 23
Carol City, FL s13 12
Carolina Beach, NC C5 36
Carpentersville, IL A5 16
Carrboro, NC B3 36
Carrington, ND B6 37
Carrington Island, UT C3 47
Carrizozo, NM D4 34
Carroll, IA B3 18
Carrollton, AL B1 4
Carrollton, GA C1 13
Carrollton, KY B4 20
Carrollton, MO B4 28
Carrollton, TX n10 46
Carry Falls Reservoir, NY f10 35
Carson, r., NV D2 31
Carson City, NV D2 31
Carson Sink, NV D3 31
Carter Dome, NH B4 32
Carteret, NJ B4 33
Carter Lake, IA C2 18
Cartersville, GA B2 13
Carterville, IL F4 16
Carterville, MO D3 28
Carthage, MS C4 27
Carthage, MO D3 28
Carthage, TN C8 45
Caruthersville, MO E8 28
Cary, IL A5 16
Cary, NC B4 36
Casa Grande, AZ E4 6
Casas Adobes, AZ E5 6
Cascade, IA B6 18
Cascade Range, NA B3 2
Cascade Reservoir, ID E3 15
Casco, ME D2 22
Casco Bay, ME E3 22
Casey, Mount, ID A2 15
Cashion, AZ m8 6
Cashmere, WA B5 50
Casper, WY D6 53
Casselberry, FL D5 12
Casselton, ND C8 37
Cass Lake, MN C4 26
Cassopolis, MI G4 25
Cassville, MO E4 28
Castle Dome Peak, AZ D1 6
Castle Hills, DE i7 11
Castle Point, MO f13 28
Castle Rock, CO B6 9
Castle Rock Lake, WI E4 52
Castleton, VT D2 48
Castro Valley, CA h8 8
Catahoula Lake, LA C3 21
Catasauqua, PA E11 41
Catawba, r., SC B6 43
Cathedral City, CA F5 8
Catlettsburg, KY B7 20
Catoctin Mountain, US B2 23
Catonsville, MD B4 23
Catoosa, OK A6 39
Catskill, NY C7 35
Catskill Mountains, NY C6 35
Cavalier, ND A8 37
Cave City, AR B4 7
Cave City, KY C4 20
Cave Run Lake, KY B6 20
Cave Spring, VA C2 49
Cayce, SC D5 43
Cayuga Lake, NY C4 35
Cedar, r., US C6 18
Cedar Bluff, AL A4 4
Cedar Breaks National Monument, UT F3 47
Cedarburg, WI E6 52
Cedar City, UT F2 47
Cedar Creek, r., ND C3 37
Cedar Creek Lake, TX C4 46
Cedar Crest, NM k8 34
Cedaredge, CO C3 9
Cedar Falls, IA B5 18
Cedar Grove, NJ B4 33
Cedar Grove, WV C3 51
Cedar Hill, TX n10 46
Cedar Lake, IN B3 17
Cedar Point, OH A3 38
Cedar Rapids, IA C6 18
Cedar Springs, MI E5 25
Cedartown, GA B1 13
Celina, OH B1 38
Center, CO D4 9
Center, ND B4 37
Centereach, NY n15 35
Center Harbor, NH C4 32
Center Hill Lake, TN C8 45
Center Ossipee, NH C4 32
Center Point, AL f7 4
Center Point, IA B6 18
Center Rutland, VT D2 48
Centerville, IN E8 17
Centerville, IA D5 18
Centerville, MA C7 24
Centerville, OH C1 38
Centerville, SD D9 44
Centerville, TN B4 45
Centerville, UT C4 47
Central, NM E1 34
Central City, KY C2 20
Central City, NE C7 30
Central Falls, RI B4 42
Centralia, IL E4 16
Centralia, MO B5 28
Centralia, WA C3 50
Central Islip, NY n15 35
Central Park, WA C2 50
Central Point, OR E4 40
Centre, AL A4 4
Centreville, IL E3 16
Centreville, MS D2 27
Ceredo, WV C2 51
Ceresco, NE C9 30
Chacon, Cape, AK n24 5
Chadron, NE B3 30
Chaffee, MO D8 28
Chagrin Falls, OH A4 38
Chalfonte, DE h7 11
Chalmette, LA E6 21
Chama, NM A3 34
Chama, Rio, r., NM A3 34
Chamberlain, SD D6 44
Chamberlin, Mount, AK B10 5
Chambersburg, PA G6 41
Chambers Island, WI C6 52
Chamblee, GA h8 13
Champaign, IL C5 16
Champlin, MN m12 26
Chandalar, r., AK B10 5
Chandeleur Islands, LA E7 21
Chandeleur Sound, LA E6 21
Chandler, AZ D4 6
Chandler, IN H3 17
Chandler, OK B5 39
Chanhassen, MN n11 26
Channahon, IL B5 16
Channel Islands, CA F4 8
Channelview, TX r14 46
Chantilly, VA g12 49
Chanute, KS E8 19
Chaparral, NM E3 34
Chapel Hill, NC B3 36
Chapman, KS D6 19
Chapmanville, WV D2 51
Chappaquiddick Island, MA D7 24
Chappell, NE C3 30
Chariton, IA C4 18
Chariton, r., US A5 28
Charleroi, PA F2 41
Charles, r., MA B5 24
Charles, Cape, VA C6 49
Charles City, IA A5 18
Charles Mound, IL A3 16
Charleston, AR B1 7
Charleston, IL D5 16
Charleston, MS A3 27
Charleston, MO E8 28
Charleston, SC F8 43
Charleston, WV C3 51
Charleston Peak, NV G6 31
Charlestown, IN H6 17
Charlestown, NH D2 32
Charles Town, WV B7 51
Charlevoix, MI C5 25
Charlotte, MI F6 25
Charlotte, NC B2 36
Charlottesville, VA B4 49
Chase, Mount, ME B4 22
Chaska, MN F5 26
Chatfield, MN G6 26
Chatham, IL D4 16
Chatham Strait, AK m22 5
Chatsworth, GA B2 13
Chattahoochee, r., US E1 13
Chattanooga, TN D8 45
Chattaroy, WV D2 51
Chattooga, r., US B1 43
Chautauqua, NY C1 35
Chautauqua Lake, NY C1 35
Chauvin, LA E5 21
Cheaha Mountain, AL B4 4
Chebeague Island, ME E2 22
Cheboygan, MI C6 25
Checotah, OK B6 39
Cheektowaga, NY C2 35
Chehalis, WA C3 50
Chehalis, r., WA C2 50
Chelan, WA B5 50
Chelan Mountains, WA A5 50
Chelmsford, MA A5 24
Chelsea, AL g7 4
Chelsea, MA B5 24
Chelsea, MI F6 25
Chelsea, VT D4 48
Cheney, KS E6 19
Cheney, WA B8 50
Chenoweth, OR B5 40
Chequamegon Bay, WI B3 52
Cheraw, SC B8 43
Cherokee, AL A2 4
Cherokee, IA B2 18
Cherokee, OK A3 39
Cherokee Lake, TN C10 45
Cherokees, Lake O' The, OK A7 39
Cherokee Village, AR A4 7
Cherry Creek, r., SD C3 44
Cherry Hill, NJ D2 33
Cherryvale, KS E8 19
Cherryville, NC B1 36
Chesapeake, VA D6 49
Chesapeake, WV C3 51
Chesapeake Bay, US C12 2
Chesapeake Bay Bridge-Tunnel, VA D7 49
Cheshire, CT D4 10
Chester, IL F4 16
Chester, MT B6 29
Chester, NH E4 32
Chester, PA G11 41
Chester, SC B5 43
Chester, VT E3 48
Chester, VA C5 49
Chester, WV A4 51
Chester, r., MD B5 23
Chester Depot, VT E3 48
Chesterfield, IN D6 17
Chesterton, IN A3 17
Chetopa, KS E8 19
Cheviot, OH C1 38
Chevy Chase, MD C3 23
Cheyenne, WY E8 53
Cheyenne, r., US C4 44
Cheyenne Wells, CO C8 9
Chicago, IL B6 16
Chicago Heights, IL B6 16
Chicago Sanitary and Ship Canal, IL k8 16
Chickahominy, r., VA C5 49
Chickamauga, GA B1 13
Chickamauga Lake, TN D8 45
Chickasaw, AL E1 4
Chickasawhay, r., MS D5 27
Chickasha, OK B4 39
Chico, CA C3 8
Chicopee, MA B2 24
Childersburg, AL B3 4
Chillicothe, IL C4 16
Chillicothe, MO B4 28
Chillicothe, OH C3 38
Chillum, MD f9 23
Chilton, WI D5 52
Chimayo, NM A4 34
Chimney Rock, NE C2 30
China, ME D3 22
Chinati Peak, TX p12 46
Chincoteague, VA C7 49
Chincoteague Bay, US D7 23
Chinle, AZ A6 6
Chino, CA F5 8
Chinook, MT B7 29
Chinook, Lake, OR C5 40
Chino Valley, AZ C3 6
Chippewa, r., WI D2 52
Chippewa, Lake, WI C2 52
Chippewa Falls, WI D2 52
Chiricahua Peak, AZ F6 6
Chisago City, MN E6 26
Chisholm, MN C6 26
Chisos Mountains, TX E1 46
Chocolate Mountains, US F6 8
Choctaw, OK B4 39
Choctawhatchee Bay, FL u15 12
Choptank, r., MD C6 23
Choteau, MT C4 29
Chowan, r., NC A6 36
Christiansburg, VA C2 49
Christina, r., DE B3 11
Christina Peak, NV D6 31
Chubbuck, ID G6 15
Chula Vista, CA F5 8
Church Hill, TN C11 45
Church Point, LA D3 21
Churubusco, IN B7 17
Cicero, IL B6 16
Cicero, IN D5 17
Cimarron, KS E3 19
Cimarron, r., US C8 2
Cincinnati, OH C1 38
Cinnaminson, NJ D3 33
Circle, MT C11 29

Name	Map Ref.	Page
Circle Pines, MN	m12	26
Circleville, OH	C3	38
Citronelle, AL	D1	4
City of Refuge National Historical Park, HI	D5	14
C.J. Strike Reservoir, ID	G3	15
Clair Engle Lake, CA	B2	8
Clairton, PA	F2	41
Clanton, AL	C3	4
Clare, MI	E6	25
Claremont, NH	D2	32
Claremore, OK	A6	39
Clarence Strait, AK	n23	5
Clarendon, AR	C4	7
Clarendon Hills, IL	k9	16
Clarinda, IA	D2	18
Clarion, IA	B4	18
Clarion, PA	D3	41
Clarion, r., PA	D3	41
Clark, NJ	B4	33
Clark, SD	C8	44
Clark, Lake, AK	C9	5
Clarkdale, AZ	C3	6
Clark Fork, r., US	C1	29
Clarksburg, WV	B4	51
Clarksdale, MS	A3	27
Clarks Summit, PA	m18	41
Clarkston, GA	h8	13
Clarkston, WA	C8	50
Clarksville, AR	B2	7
Clarksville, IN	H6	17
Clarksville, IA	B5	18
Clarksville, TN	A4	45
Clawson, MI	o15	25
Claxton, GA	D5	13
Clay Center, KS	C6	19
Clay Center, NE	D7	30
Claymont, DE	A4	11
Claypool, AZ	D5	6
Clayton, MO	f13	28
Clayton, NM	A6	34
Clayton, NC	B4	36
Clear Boggy Creek, r., OK	C5	39
Cleare, Cape, AK	D10	5
Clearfield, PA	D5	41
Clearfield, UT	B3	47
Clear Lake, IA	A4	18
Clear Lake, SD	C9	44
Clearwater, FL	E4	12
Clearwater, KS	E6	19
Clearwater, SC	E4	43
Clearwater, r., ID	C2	15
Clearwater Mountains, ID	C2	15
Cleburne, TX	C4	46
Clemmons, NC	A2	36
Clemson, SC	B2	43
Clendenin, WV	C3	51
Cleveland, MS	B3	27
Cleveland, OH	A4	38
Cleveland, OK	A5	39
Cleveland, TN	D9	45
Cleveland, Mount, MT	B3	29
Cleveland Heights, OH	A4	38
Cliffside Park, NJ	h9	33
Clifton, AZ	D6	6
Clifton, CO	B2	9
Clifton, NJ	B4	33
Clifton Forge, VA	C3	49
Clinch, r., US	D9	45
Clinch Mountain, US	C10	45
Clingmans Dome, US	D10	45
Clinton, AR	B3	7
Clinton, CT	D5	10
Clinton, IL	C5	16
Clinton, IN	E3	17
Clinton, IA	C7	18
Clinton, KY	f9	20
Clinton, MD	C4	23
Clinton, MS	C3	27
Clinton, MO	C4	28
Clinton, NC	C4	36
Clinton, OK	B3	39
Clinton, SC	C4	43
Clinton, TN	C9	45
Clinton, UT	B3	47
Clinton, Lake, IL	C5	16
Clintonville, WI	D5	52
Clintwood, VA	e9	49
Clio, MI	E7	25
Clive, IA	e8	18
Cloquet, MN	D6	26
Cloud Peak, WY	B5	53
Clover, SC	A5	43
Cloverdale, IN	E4	17
Clovis, CA	D4	8
Clovis, NM	C6	34
Clute, TX	r14	46
Clyde, OH	A3	38
Coal City, IL	B5	16
Coal Fork, WV	C3	51
Coalgate, OK	C5	39
Coaling, AL	B2	4
Coast Ranges, US	B3	2
Coatesville, PA	G10	41
Cobble Mountain Reservoir, MA	B2	24
Cochran, GA	D3	13
Cockeysville, MD	B4	23
Cocoa, FL	D6	12
Cocoa Beach, FL	D6	12
Cod, Cape, MA	C7	24
Coden, AL	E1	4
Cody, WY	B3	53
Coeur d'Alene, ID	B2	15
Coeur d'Alene, r., ID	B2	15
Coeur d'Alene Lake, ID	B2	15
Coeur d'Alene Mountains, ID	B2	15
Coffeyville, KS	E8	19
Cohoes, NY	C7	35
Cokeville, WY	D2	53
Colbert Heights, AL	A2	4
Colby, KS	C2	19
Colchester, CT	C6	10
Cold Spring, KY	A5	20
Cold Spring, MN	E4	26
Coldwater, MI	G5	25
Coldwater, MS	A4	27
Colebrook, NH	g7	32
Colfax, IA	C4	18
Colfax, WA	C8	50
College, AK	B10	5
Collegedale, TN	h11	45
College Park, GA	C2	13
College Park, MD	C4	23
College Place, WA	C7	50
College Station, AR	C3	7
College Station, TX	D4	46
Collegeville, PA	F11	41
Collierville, TN	B2	45
Collingdale, PA	p20	41
Collingswood, NJ	D2	33
Collins, MS	D4	27
Collins Park, DE	B3	11
Collinsville, CT	B4	10
Collinsville, IL	E4	16
Collinsville, OK	A6	39
Colonial Beach, VA	B6	49
Colonial Heights, TN	C11	45
Colonial Heights, VA	C5	49
Colonial National Historical Park, VA	C6	49
Colonie, NY	C7	35
Colorado, state, US	B5	9
Colorado, r., NA	D5	2
Colorado, r., TX	D3	46
Colorado City, AZ	A3	6
Colorado City, CO	D6	9
Colorado Plateau, US	B4	6
Colorado River Aqueduct, CA	F6	8
Colorado Springs, CO	C6	9
Colquitt, GA	E2	13
Colstrip, MT	E10	29
Columbia, IL	E3	16
Columbia, KY	C4	20
Columbia, MD	B4	23
Columbia, MS	D4	27
Columbia, MO	C5	28
Columbia, PA	F9	41
Columbia, SC	C5	43
Columbia, TN	B4	45
Columbia, r., NA	A3	2
Columbia City, IN	B7	17
Columbia Falls, MT	B2	29
Columbia Heights, MN	m12	26
Columbiana, AL	B3	4
Columbus, GA	D2	13
Columbus, IN	F6	17
Columbus, KS	E9	19
Columbus, MS	B5	27
Columbus, MT	E7	29
Columbus, NE	C8	30
Columbus, OH	C2	38
Columbus, WI	E4	52
Columbus Junction, IA	C6	18
Colville, WA	A8	50
Colville, r., AK	B9	5
Colville, r., WA	A8	50
Colvos Passage, WA	f10	50
Combahee, r., SC	F6	43
Commerce, GA	B3	13
Commerce, OK	A7	39
Commerce City, CO	B6	9
Como, MS	A4	27
Compton, CA	n12	8
Conanicut Island, RI	E5	42
Conception, Point, CA	E3	8
Conchas Lake, NM	B5	34
Concord, CA	h8	8
Concord, MA	B5	24
Concord, NH	D3	32
Concord, NC	B2	36
Concord, TN	D9	45
Concordia, KS	C6	19
Concordia, MO	C4	28
Conecuh, r., US	D3	4
Congamond Lakes, US	A4	10
Congaree, r., SC	D6	43
Conneaut, OH	A5	38
Connecticut, state, US	C5	10
Connellsville, PA	F2	41
Connersville, IN	E7	17
Conover, NC	B1	36
Conrad, MT	B5	29
Conroe, TX	D5	46
Conshohocken, PA	F11	41
Contoocook, NH	D3	32
Contoocook, r., NH	D3	32
Conway, AR	B3	7
Conway, FL	D5	12
Conway, NH	C4	32
Conway, SC	D9	43
Conway Springs, KS	E6	19
Conyers, GA	C2	13
Cookes Peak, NM	E2	34
Cookeville, TN	C8	45
Cook Inlet, AK	D9	5
Cook Point, MD	C5	23
Coolidge, AZ	E4	6
Coon Rapids, MN	E5	26
Cooper Mountain, AK	g17	5
Cooperstown, NY	C6	35
Cooperstown, ND	B7	37
Coosa, r., US	C3	4
Coosawhatchie, r., SC	F5	43
Coos Bay, OR	D2	40
Copperas Cove, TX	D4	46
Copper Harbor, MI	A3	25
Coquille, OR	D2	40
Coral Gables, FL	G6	12
Coralville, IA	C6	18
Coralville Lake, IA	C5	18
Coraopolis, PA	E1	41
Corbin, KY	D5	20
Corcoran, MN	m11	26
Cordele, GA	E3	13
Cordell, OK	B3	39
Cordell Hull Lake, TN	C8	45
Cordova, AL	B2	4
Cordova, AK	C10	5
Corea, ME	D5	22
Corinth, MS	A5	27
Cornelia, GA	B3	13
Cornelius, OR	g11	40
Corning, AR	A5	7
Corning, IA	D3	18
Corning, NY	C3	35
Cornish, ME	E2	22
Corona, CA	F5	8
Coronado, CA	F5	8
Corpus Christi, TX	F4	46
Corrales, NM	k7	34
Corry, PA	C2	41
Corsicana, TX	C4	46
Cortez, CO	D2	9
Cortland, NY	C4	35
Cortland, OH	A5	38
Corvallis, OR	C3	40
Corydon, IN	H5	17
Corydon, IA	D4	18
Coshocton, OH	B4	38
Costa Mesa, CA	n13	8
Cottage Grove, MN	n13	26
Cottage Grove, OR	D3	40
Cottleville, MO	f12	28
Cottondale, AL	B2	4
Cotton Plant, AR	B4	7
Cottonwood, AZ	C3	6
Cottonwood, r., KS	D7	19
Coudersport, PA	C5	41
Coulee Dam National Recreation Area, WA	A7	50
Council Bluffs, IA	C2	18
Council Grove, KS	D7	19
Country Homes, WA	B8	50
Courtland, AL	A2	4
Covedale, OH	o12	38
Coventry, CT	B6	10
Coventry, RI	D3	42
Cove Point, MD	D5	23
Covina, CA	m13	8
Covington, GA	C3	13
Covington, IN	D3	17
Covington, KY	A5	20
Covington, LA	D5	21
Covington, TN	B2	45
Covington, VA	C3	49
Cowen, Mount, MT	E6	29
Coweta, OK	B6	39
Cowley, WY	B4	53
Cowlitz, r., WA	C3	50
Cowpasture, r., VA	B3	49
Cozad, NE	D6	30
Crab Orchard, WV	n13	51
Crab Orchard Lake, IL	F4	16
Crafton, PA	k13	41
Craig, CO	A3	9
Craigsville, WV	C4	51
Cranberry Lake, NY	A6	35
Crandon, WI	C5	52
Cranford, NJ	B4	33
Cranston, RI	C4	42
Crater Lake, OR	E4	40
Crater Lake National Park, OR	E4	40
Craters of the Moon National Monument, ID	F5	15
Crawford, NE	B2	30
Crawford Notch State Park, NH	B4	32
Crawfordsville, IN	D4	17
Creighton, NE	B8	30
Creola, AL	E1	4
Cresaptown, MD	k13	23
Crescent Springs, KY	h13	20
Cresco, IA	A5	18
Cresskill, NJ	h9	33
Crest Hill, IL	k8	16
Creston, IA	C3	18
Crestone Peak, CO	D5	9
Crestview, FL	u15	12
Crete, IL	B6	16
Crete, NE	D9	30
Creve Coeur, IL	C4	16
Crisfield, MD	E6	23
Crofton, MD	B4	23
Crofton, NE	B8	30
Croix, Lac la, MN	B6	26
Crooked, r., OR	C6	40
Crooked Lake, MN	B7	26
Crookston, MN	C2	26
Crosby, MN	D5	26
Crosby, ND	A2	37
Crossett, AR	D4	7
Cross Lanes, WV	C3	51
Crossville, AL	A4	4
Crossville, TN	D8	45
Croswell, MI	E8	25
Crothersville, IN	G6	17
Croton-on-Hudson, NY	D7	35
Crow Agency, MT	E9	29
Crowley, LA	D3	21
Crown Point, IN	B3	17
Crownpoint, NM	B1	34
Crows Nest Peak, SD	C2	44
Crow Wing, r., MN	D4	26
Croydon, PA	F12	41
Crystal, MN	m12	26
Crystal Bay, NV	D1	31
Crystal City, MO	C7	28
Crystal City, TX	E3	46
Crystal Falls, MI	B2	25
Crystal Lake, IL	A5	16
Crystal Lake, MI	D4	25
Crystal Springs, MS	D3	27
Cuba, MO	C6	28
Cudahy, WI	F6	52
Culebra Peak, CO	D5	9
Cullman, AL	A3	4
Culloden, WV	C2	51
Culpeper, VA	B4	49
Culver, IN	B5	17
Culver City, CA	m12	8
Cumberland, KY	D7	20
Cumberland, MD	k13	23
Cumberland, r., US	C11	2
Cumberland, Lake, KY	D5	20
Cumberland Foreside, ME	E2	22
Cumberland Gap, US	D6	20
Cumberland Gap National Historical Park, US	D6	20
Cumberland Hill, RI	B4	42
Cumberland Island National Seashore, GA	F5	13
Cumberland Mountain, TN	C9	45
Cumberland Plateau, US	D8	45
Cumbres Pass, CO	D4	9
Cumming, GA	B2	13
Currant Mountain, NV	E6	31
Current, r., US	A5	7
Cushing, OK	B5	39
Custer, SD	D2	44
Custer Battlefield National Monument, MT	E9	29
Custer Peak, SD	C2	44
Cut Bank, MT	B4	29
Cuthbert, GA	E2	13
Cutler Ridge, FL	s13	12
Cut Off, LA	E5	21
Cuyahoga, r., OH	A4	38
Cuyahoga Falls, OH	A4	38
C.W. McConaughy, Lake, NE	C4	30
Cynthiana, KY	B5	20

D

Name	Map Ref.	Page
Dacono, CO	A6	9
Dacula, GA	C3	13
Dadeville, AL	C4	4
Dahlonega, GA	B3	13
Dakota City, NE	B9	30
Dale, IN	H4	17
Dale City, VA	B5	49
Dale Hollow Lake, US	C8	45
Daleville, AL	D4	4
Daleville, IN	D6	17
Dalhart, TX	A1	46
Dall, Mount, AK	f15	5
Dallas, GA	C2	13
Dallas, NC	B1	36
Dallas, OR	C3	40
Dallas, TX	C4	46
Dallas Center, IA	C4	18
Dalton, GA	B2	13
Dalton Gardens, ID	B2	15
Daly City, CA	h8	8
Damariscotta, ME	D3	22
Damascus, MD	B3	23
Dan, r., US	D3	49
Danbury, CT	D2	10
Danforth, ME	C5	22
Dania, FL	F6	12
Danielson, CT	B8	10
Daniels Pass, UT	C4	47
Danvers, MA	A6	24
Danville, AR	B2	7
Danville, IL	C6	16
Danville, IN	E4	17
Danville, KY	C5	20
Danville, NH	E4	32
Danville, PA	E8	41
Danville, VA	D3	49
Daphne, AL	E2	4
D'Arbonne, Bayou, r., LA	B3	21
Darby, PA	G11	41
Dardanelle, AR	B2	7
Darien, CT	E2	10
Darling, Lake, ND	A4	37
Darlington, SC	C8	43
Dauphin Island, AL	E1	4
Davenport, IA	C7	18
David City, NE	C8	30
Davidson, NC	B2	36
Davie, FL	F6	12
Davis, CA	C3	8
Davis, OK	C4	39
Davis, Mount, PA	G3	41
Davis Mountains, TX	o12	46
Dawson, GA	E2	13
Dawson Springs, KY	C2	20
Dayton, KY	h14	20
Dayton, OH	C1	38
Dayton, TN	D8	45
Dayton, WA	C8	50
Dayton, WY	B5	53
Daytona Beach, FL	C5	12
Deadwood, SD	C2	44
Dearborn, MI	F7	25
Dearborn Heights, MI	p15	25
Death Valley, CA	D5	8
Death Valley National Park, US	D5	8
Decatur, AL	A3	4
Decatur, GA	C2	13
Decatur, IL	D5	16
Decatur, IN	C8	17
Decatur, Lake, IL	D5	16
Decherd, TN	B5	45
Decorah, IA	A6	18
Dedham, MA	B5	24
Deep Creek Lake, MD	K12	23
Deep Fork, r., OK	B5	39
Deep River, CT	D6	10
Deerfield, IL	h9	16
Deerfield, r., US	A2	24
Deerfield Beach, FL	F6	12
Deer Isle, ME	D4	22
Deer Lodge, MT	D4	29
Deer Park, NY	n15	35
Deer Park, OH	o13	38
Deer Park, TX	r14	46
Deer River, MN	C5	26
Defiance, OH	A1	38
De Forest, WI	E4	52
De Kalb, IL	B5	16
Delafield, WI	m11	52
De Land, FL	C5	12
Delano, MN	E5	26
Delano Peak, UT	E3	47
Delavan, WI	F5	52
Delaware, OH	B2	38
Delaware, state, US	D3	11
Delaware, r., US	E2	33
Delaware, r., KS	C8	19
Delaware Bay, US	C12	2
Delaware City, DE	B3	11
Delaware Water Gap National Recreation Area, US	B2	33
Del City, OK	B4	39
Dellenbaugh, Mount, AZ	A2	6
Dell Rapids, SD	D9	44
Delmar, DE	G3	11
Delmar, NY	C7	35
Del Norte, CO	D4	9
Del Park Manor, DE	i7	11
Delphi, IN	C4	17
Delphos, OH	B1	38
Delran, NJ	C3	33
Delray Beach, FL	F6	12
Del Rio, TX	E2	46
Delta, CO	C2	9
Delta, UT	D3	47
Delta, MS	B3	27
Deltona, FL	D5	12
Deming, NM	E2	34
Demopolis, AL	C2	4
Demotte, IN	B3	17
Denali National Park, AK	C9	5
Denham Springs, LA	D5	21
Denison, IA	B2	18
Denison, TX	C4	46
Denmark, SC	E5	43
Dennis, MA	C7	24
Dennis Port, MA	C7	24
Denton, MD	C6	23
Denton, TX	C4	46
Dentsville, SC	C6	43
Denver, CO	B6	9
Denver, IA	B5	18
Denville, NJ	B4	33
De Pere, WI	D5	52
Depew, NY	C2	35
De Queen, AR	C1	7
De Quincy, LA	D2	21
Derby, CT	D3	10
Derby, KS	E6	19
Derby, VT	B4	48
Derby Line, VT	A4	48
De Ridder, LA	D2	21
Dermott, AR	D4	7
Dernieres, Isles, LA	E5	21
Derry, NH	E4	32
Des Arc, AR	C4	7
Deschutes, r., OR	B6	40
Deseret Peak, UT	C3	47
Desert Creek Peak, NV	E2	31
Desert Hot Springs, CA	F5	8
Des Lacs, r., ND	A4	37
Desloge, MO	D7	28
De Smet, SD	C8	44
Des Moines, IA	C4	18
Des Moines, WA	B3	50
Des Moines, r., US	D5	18
De Soto, KS	D9	19
De Soto, MO	C7	28
De Soto, TX	n10	46
Despard, WV	k10	51
Des Peres, MO	f13	28
Des Plaines, IL	A6	16
Des Plaines, r., US	k8	16
Destrehan, LA	E5	21
Detroit, MI	F7	25
Detroit Lakes, MN	D3	26
DeView, Bayou, r., AR	B4	7
Devils Lake, ND	A7	37
Devils Tower National Monument, WY	B8	53
Devonshire, DE	h7	11
Dewey, OK	A6	39
De Witt, AR	C4	7
De Witt, IA	C7	18
De Witt, NY	B4	35
Dexter, ME	C3	22
Dexter, MO	E8	28
Dexter, NM	D5	34
Diablo, Canyon, AZ	C4	6
Diablo, Mount, CA	h9	8
Diamond Head, HI	B4	14
Diamondville, WY	E2	53
Diaz, AR	B4	7
D'Iberville, MS	E5	27
Dickinson, ND	C3	37
Dickson, TN	A4	45
Dickson City, PA	D10	41
Dierks, AR	C1	7
Dighton, KS	D3	19
Dillingham, AK	D8	5
Dillon, MT	E4	29
Dillon, SC	C9	43
Dillon Lake, OH	B3	38
Dilworth, MN	D2	26
Dinosaur National Monument, US	C6	47
Dirty Devil, r., UT	E5	47
Disappointment, Cape, WA	C1	50
Dishman, WA	g14	50
District of Columbia, US	f8	23
Dixfield, ME	D2	22
Dix Mountain, NY	A7	35
Dixon, IL	B4	16
Dixon, NM	A4	34
Dobbs Ferry, NY	g13	35
Docena, AL	f7	4
Dodge Center, MN	F6	26
Dodge City, KS	E3	19
Dodgeville, WI	F3	52
Dolomite, AL	B3	4
Dolton, IL	k9	16
Dona Ana, NM	E3	34
Donaldsonville, LA	D4	21
Donalsonville, GA	E2	13
Doniphan, MO	E7	28
Donna, TX	F3	46
Donner Pass, CA	C3	8
Donora, PA	F2	41
Dora, AL	B2	4
Doraville, GA	h8	13
Dormont, PA	k13	41
Dorset, VT	E2	48
Dorset Peak, VT	E2	48
Dothan, AL	D4	4
Double Springs, AL	A2	4
Douglas, AZ	F6	6
Douglas, GA	E4	13
Douglas, WY	D7	53
Douglas, Mount, AK	D9	5
Douglas Lake, TN	D10	45
Douglass, KS	E7	19
Douglasville, GA	C2	13
Dover, AR	B2	7
Dover, DE	D3	11
Dover, NH	D5	32
Dover, NJ	B3	33
Dover, OH	B4	38
Dover Air Force Base, DE	D4	11
Dover-Foxcroft, ME	C3	22
Dowagiac, MI	G4	25
Downers Grove, IL	B5	16
Downey, CA	n12	8
Downingtown, PA	F10	41
Doylestown, PA	F11	41
Dracut, MA	A5	24
Drake Peak, OR	E6	40
Draper, UT	C4	47
Drayton, ND	A8	37
Drayton Plains, MI	F7	25
Dresden, TN	A3	45
Drew, MS	B3	27
Driskill Mountain, LA	B3	21
Drummond Island, MI	C7	25
Drumright, OK	B5	39
Dryden, ME	D2	22
Dry Ridge, KY	B5	20
Dry Tortugas, FL	H5	12
Dublin, GA	D4	13
Dublin, NH	E2	32
Dublin, OH	k10	38
Du Bois, PA	D4	41
Dubois, WY	C3	53
Dubuque, IA	B7	18
Duck, r., TN	B4	45
Dudley, MA	B4	24
Dulce, NM	A2	34
Duluth, GA	B2	13
Duluth, MN	D6	26
Dumas, AR	D4	7
Dumas, TX	B2	46
Dumfries, VA	B5	49
Dumont, NJ	B5	33
Dunbar, WV	C3	51
Duncan, OK	C4	39
Duncanville, TX	n10	46
Dundalk, MD	B4	23
Dundee, IL	A5	16
Dundee, MI	G7	25
Dunedin, FL	D4	12
Dunkirk, IN	D7	17
Dunkirk, NY	C1	35
Dunlap, IN	A6	17
Dunlap, TN	D8	45
Dunleith, DE	i7	11
Dunmore, PA	D10	41
Dunn, NC	B4	36
Dunseith, ND	A5	37
Dunwoody, GA	h8	13
Du Page, r., IL	k8	16
Dupont, CO	B6	9
Dupont, PA	n18	41
Duquesne, PA	F2	41
Du Quoin, IL	E4	16
Durand, MI	F6	25
Durango, CO	D3	9
Durant, IA	C7	18
Durant, MS	B4	27
Durant, OK	D5	39
Durham, CT	D5	10
Durham, NH	D5	32
Durham, NC	B4	36
Duryea, PA	D10	41
Dwight, IL	B5	16
Dwight D. Eisenhower Lock, NY	f9	35
Dworshak Reservoir, ID	C3	15
Dyer, IN	A2	17
Dyer, TN	A3	45
Dyersburg, TN	A2	45
Dyersville, IA	B6	18

E

Name	Map Ref.	Page
Eagan, MN	n12	26
Eagar, AZ	C6	6
Eagle, CO	B4	9
Eagle, ID	F2	15
Eagle, NE	h12	30
Eagle Creek Reservoir, IN	E5	17
Eagle Grove, IA	B4	18
Eagle Lake, ME	A4	22
Eagle Mountain, MN	k9	26
Eagle Pass, TX	E2	46
Eagle Peak, TX	o12	46
Eagle Point, OR	E4	40
Earle, AR	B5	7
Earlington, KY	C2	20
Easley, SC	B2	43
East Alton, IL	E3	16
East Arlington, VT	E2	48
East Aurora, NY	C2	35
East Barre, VT	C4	48
East Bethel, MN	E5	26
East Brewton, AL	D2	4
East Bridgewater, MA	B6	24
East Brimfield Lake, MA	B3	24
East Brunswick, NJ	C4	33
East Chicago, IN	A3	17
East Cleveland, OH	g9	38
East Cote Blanche Bay, LA	E4	21
East Derry, NH	E4	32
East Detroit, MI	p16	25
Eastern Bay, MD	C5	23
Eastern Neck Island, MD	B5	23
East Flat Rock, NC	f10	36
East Grand Forks, MN	C2	26
East Grand Rapids, MI	F5	25
East Greenwich, RI	D4	42
East Hampstead, NH	E4	32
East Hampton, CT	C5	10
Easthampton, MA	B2	24
East Hartford, CT	B5	10
East Haven, CT	D4	10
East Helena, MT	D5	29
Eastlake, OH	A4	38
East Lansing, MI	F6	25
East Las Vegas, NV	G6	31
East Liverpool, OH	B5	38
East Longmeadow, MA	B2	24
East Los Angeles, CA	m12	8
East Lynn Lake, WV	C2	51
East Machias, ME	D5	22
Eastman, GA	D3	13
East Middlebury, VT	D2	48
East Moline, IL	B3	16
East Montpelier, VT	C4	48
East Naples, FL	F5	12
East Nishnabotna, r., IA	C2	18
East Norriton, PA	o20	41
Easton, MD	C5	23
Easton, PA	E11	41
East Orange, NJ	B4	33
East Pea Ridge, WV	C2	51
East Peoria, IL	C4	16
East Point, GA	C2	13
East Point, MA	B6	24
Eastport, ME	D6	22
East Poultney, VT	D2	48
East Prairie, MO	E8	28
East Providence, RI	C4	42
East Ridge, TN	h11	45
East River, CT	D5	10
East Rochester, NY	B3	35
East Rockingham, NC	C3	36
East Saint Louis, IL	E3	16
East Sebago, ME	E2	22
East Stroudsburg, PA	D11	41
East Troy, WI	F5	52
East View, WV	k10	51
East Wenatchee, WA	B5	50
East Windsor, NJ	C3	33
Eaton, CO	A6	9
Eaton, IN	D7	17
Eaton, OH	C1	38
Eaton Rapids, MI	F6	25
Eatonton, GA	C3	13
Eatontown, NJ	C4	33
Eau Claire, WI	D2	52
Eccles, WV	n13	51
Eclectic, AL	C3	4
Ecorse, MI	p15	25
Eddyville, KY	e9	20
Eden, NC	A3	36
Eden Prairie, MN	n12	26
Edenton, NC	A6	36
Edgeley, ND	C7	37
Edgemere, MD	B5	23
Edgemont, SD	D2	44
Edgemoor, DE	A3	11
Edgerton, KS	D8	19
Edgerton, WI	F4	52
Edgewater, AL	f7	4
Edgewater, FL	D6	12
Edgewood, IN	D6	17
Edgewood, KY	h13	20
Edgewood, MD	B5	23
Edgewood, WA	f11	50
Edina, MN	F5	26
Edina, MO	A5	28
Edinboro, PA	C1	41
Edinburg, TX	F3	46
Edinburgh, IN	F6	17
Edison, NJ	B4	33
Edisto, r., SC	E6	43
Edisto Island, SC	F7	43
Edmond, OK	B4	39
Edmonds, WA	B3	50
Edwardsville, IL	E4	16
Edwardsville, KS	k16	19
Edwardsville, PA	n17	41
Eel, r., IN	C6	17
Eel, r., IN	F3	17
Effingham, IL	D5	16
Egan Range, NV	E7	31
Egg Island Point, NJ	E2	33
Eglin Air Force Base, FL	u15	12
Egypt, Lake of, IL	F5	16
Elba, AL	D3	4
Elbert, Mount, CO	B4	9
Elberton, GA	B4	13
El Cajon, CA	F5	8
El Campo, TX	E4	46
El Cerrito, CA	h8	8
Eldersburg, MD	B4	23
Eldon, MO	C5	28
Eldora, IA	B4	18
El Dorado, AR	D3	7
Eldorado, IL	F5	16
El Dorado, KS	E7	19
Eldorado Peak, WA	A4	50
El Dorado Springs, MO	D3	28
Eldridge, IA	C7	18
Eleanor, WV	C3	51
Elephant Butte Reservoir, NM	D2	34
Elephant Mountain, ME	D2	22
Eleven Point, r., US	A4	7
Elgin, IL	A5	16
Elgin, ND	C4	37
Elizabeth, NJ	B4	33
Elizabeth City, NC	A6	36
Elizabeth Islands, MA	D6	24
Elizabethton, TN	C11	45
Elizabethtown, KY	C4	20
Elizabethtown, NC	C4	36
Elizabethtown, PA	F8	41
Elk, r., WV	C3	51
Elkader, IA	B6	18
Elk City, OK	B2	39
Elk Grove Village, IL	h9	16
Elkhart, IN	A6	17
Elkhart, KS	E2	19
Elkhorn, NE	g12	30
Elkhorn, WI	F5	52
Elkhorn, r., NE	B7	30
Elkin, NC	A2	36
Elkins, WV	C5	51
Elk Mountain, NM	D1	34
Elko, NV	C6	31
Elk Point, SD	E9	44
Elkridge, MD	B4	23
Elk River, MN	E5	26
Elkton, KY	D2	20
Elkton, MD	A6	23
Elkview, WV	m13	51
Ellen, Mount, UT	E5	47
Ellen, Mount, VT	C3	48
Ellendale, ND	C7	37
Ellensburg, WA	C5	50
Ellettsville, IN	F4	17
Ellicott City, MD	B4	23
Ellinwood, KS	D5	19
Ellis, KS	D4	19
Ellisville, MS	D4	27
Ellisville, MO	f12	28
Ellsworth, KS	D5	19
Ellsworth, ME	D4	22
Ellsworth, WI	D1	52
Ellwood City, PA	E1	41
Elma, WA	C2	50
Elm Creek, NE	D6	30
Elm Grove, WI	m11	52
Elmhurst, IL	B6	16
Elmira, NY	C4	35
El Mirage, AZ	k8	6
Elmont, NY	k13	35
El Monte, CA	m12	8
Elmwood Park, IL	k9	16
Elmwood Park, NJ	h8	33
Elon College, NC	A3	36
Eloy, AZ	E4	6
El Paso, TX	o11	46
El Reno, OK	B4	39
Elsberry, MO	B7	28
Elsmere, DE	B3	11
Elsmere, KY	B5	20
El Toro, CA	n13	8
Elwell, Lake, MT	B5	29

Name	Map Ref.	Page
Elwood, IN	D6	17
Ely, MN	C7	26
Ely, NV	D7	31
Elyria, OH	A3	38
Embarras, r., IL	E6	16
Eminence, KY	B4	20
Emmaus, PA	E11	41
Emmetsburg, IA	A3	18
Emmett, ID	F2	15
Emory Peak, TX	E1	46
Empire, NV	C2	31
Emporia, KS	D7	19
Emporia, VA	D5	49
Encampment, WY	E6	53
Encinitas, CA	F5	8
Enderlin, ND	C8	37
Endicott, NY	C4	35
Endicott Mountains, AK	B9	5
Endwell, NY	C4	35
Enfield (Thompsonville), CT	B5	10
Enfield, NH	C2	32
Enfield, NC	A5	36
England, AR	C4	7
Engleside, VA	g12	49
Englewood, CO	B6	9
Englewood, FL	F4	12
Englewood, NJ	B5	33
Englewood, OH	C1	38
Enid, OK	A4	39
Enid Lake, MS	A4	27
Enka, NC	f10	36
Ennis, TX	C4	46
Enola, PA	F8	41
Enoree, r., SC	B3	43
Enosburg Falls, VT	B3	48
Ensley, FL	u14	12
Enterprise, AL	D4	4
Enterprise, WV	B4	51
Entiat, r., WA	B5	50
Entiat, Lake, WA	B5	50
Enumclaw, WA	B4	50
Ephrata, PA	F9	41
Ephrata, WA	B6	50
Epping, NH	D4	32
Erie, CO	A5	9
Erie, KS	E8	19
Erie, PA	B1	41
Erie, Lake, NA	B11	2
Erie Canal, NY	B5	35
Erlanger, KY	A5	20
Erwin, TN	C11	45
Escalante, UT	F4	47
Escambia, r., FL	u14	12
Escanaba, MI	C3	25
Escanaba, r., MI	B3	25
Escatawpa, MS	E5	27
Escondido, CA	F5	8
Esmond, RI	B4	42
Espanola, NM	B3	34
Essex, CT	D6	10
Essex, MD	B5	23
Essex, VT	B2	48
Essex Junction, VT	C2	48
Estes Park, CO	A5	9
Estherville, IA	A3	18
Etolin Island, AK	m23	5
Etowah, TN	D9	45
Etowah, r., GA	B2	13
Ettrick, VA	C5	49
Euclid, OH	A4	38
Eudora, AR	D4	7
Eudora, KS	D8	19
Eufaula, AL	D4	4
Eufaula, OK	B6	39
Eufaula Lake, OK	B6	39
Eugene, OR	C3	40
Eunice, LA	D3	21
Eunice, NM	E6	34
Eupora, MS	B4	27
Eureka, CA	B1	8
Eureka, IL	C4	16
Eureka, KS	E7	19
Eureka, MO	f12	28
Eureka, MT	B1	29
Eureka, NV	D6	31
Eureka, SD	B6	44
Eureka Springs, AR	A2	7
Eustis, FL	D5	12
Evans, CO	A6	9
Evans, GA	C4	13
Evans, Mount, CO	B5	9
Evansdale, IA	B5	18
Evanston, IL	A6	16
Evanston, WY	E2	53
Evansville, IN	I2	17
Evansville, WI	F4	52
Evansville, WY	D6	53
Eveleth, MN	C6	26
Everett, MA	g11	24
Everett, WA	B3	50
Everett, Mount, MA	B1	24
Everglades National Park, FL	G5	12
Evergreen, AL	D3	4
Evergreen, CO	B5	9
Evergreen Park, IL	k9	16
E.V. Spence Reservoir, TX	D2	46
Ewa, HI	B3	14
Ewa Beach, HI	B3	14
Ewing Township, NJ	C3	33
Excelsior Springs, MO	B3	28
Exeter, NH	E5	32
Exeter, PA	D10	41
Experiment, GA	C2	13

F

Name	Map Ref.	Page
Fairbanks, AK	C10	5
Fairborn, OH	C1	38
Fairburn, GA	C2	13
Fairbury, IL	C5	16
Fairbury, NE	D8	30
Fairdale, KY	B4	20
Fairfax, DE	A3	11
Fairfax, VA	B5	49
Fairfield, AL	B3	4
Fairfield, CA	C2	8
Fairfield, CT	E2	10
Fairfield, IL	E5	16
Fairfield, IA	C6	18
Fairfield, ME	D3	22
Fairfield, OH	n12	38
Fairfield Bay, AR	B3	7
Fairhaven, MA	C6	24
Fair Haven, VT	D2	48
Fairhope, AL	E2	4
Fair Lawn, NJ	h8	33
Fairlea, WV	D4	51
Fairmont, MN	G4	26
Fairmont, WV	B4	51
Fairmount, IN	D6	17
Fair Oaks, GA	h7	13
Fair Plain, MI	F4	25
Fairview, NJ	h8	33
Fairview, OK	A3	39
Fairview, TN	B4	45
Fairview Heights, IL	E3	16
Fairview Park, IN	E3	17
Fairview Park, OH	g9	38
Fairway, KS	k16	19
Falcon Heights, MN	n12	26
Fallon, NV	D3	31
Fall River, MA	C5	24
Falls Church, VA	g12	49
Falls City, NE	D10	30
Fallston, MD	A5	23
Falmouth, KY	B5	20
Falmouth, ME	E2	22
Falmouth, MA	C6	24
Falmouth, VA	B5	49
Fargo, ND	C9	37
Faribault, MN	F5	26
Farley, IA	B6	18
Farmers Branch, TX	n10	46
Farmerville, LA	B3	21
Farmington, AR	A1	7
Farmington, CT	C4	10
Farmington, ME	D2	22
Farmington, MI	p15	25
Farmington, MN	F5	26
Farmington, MO	D7	28
Farmington, NH	D4	32
Farmington, NM	A1	34
Farmington, UT	C4	47
Farmington, r., CT	B4	10
Farmington Hills, MI	o15	25
Farmland, IN	D7	17
Farmville, NC	B5	36
Farmville, VA	C4	49
Farrell, PA	D1	41
Faulkland Heights, DE	i7	11
Faulkton, SD	B6	44
Fayette, AL	B2	4
Fayette, IA	B6	18
Fayette, MS	D2	27
Fayette, MO	B5	28
Fayetteville, AR	A1	7
Fayetteville, GA	C2	13
Fayetteville, NC	B4	36
Fayetteville, TN	B5	45
Fayetteville, WV	C3	51
Fear, Cape, NC	D5	36
Feather, r., CA	C3	8
Fennimore, WI	F3	52
Fenton, MI	F7	25
Fer, Point au, LA	E4	21
Ferdinand, IN	H4	17
Fergus Falls, MN	D2	26
Ferguson, MO	C7	28
Fern Creek, KY	g11	20
Ferndale, MD	B4	23
Ferndale, MI	P15	25
Ferndale, WA	A3	50
Fernley, NV	D2	31
Ferriday, LA	C4	21
Fessenden, ND	B6	37
Festus, MO	C7	28
Fidalgo Island, WA	A3	50
Filer, ID	G4	15
Findlay, OH	A2	38
Fircrest, WA	f10	50
Firestone, CO	A6	9
First Connecticut Lake, NH	f7	32
Fishers, IN	E5	17
Fishers Island, NY	m16	35
Fishing Bay, MD	D5	23
Fitchburg, MA	A4	24
Fitzgerald, GA	E3	13
Fitzwilliam, NH	E2	32
Five Points, NM	B3	34
Flagstaff, AZ	B4	6
Flaming Gorge Reservoir, US	E3	53
Flandreau, SD	C9	44
Flathead Lake, MT	C2	29
Flat River, MO	D7	28
Flat Rock, MI	F7	25
Flattery, Cape, WA	A1	50
Flatwoods, KY	B7	20
Flemingsburg, KY	B6	20
Flint, MI	E7	25
Flint, r., GA	E2	13
Flint City, AL	A3	4
Flippin, AR	A3	7
Flomaton, AL	D2	4
Flora, IL	E5	16
Flora, IN	C4	17
Flora, MS	C3	27
Florala, AL	D3	4
Florence, AL	A2	4
Florence, AZ	D4	6
Florence, CO	C5	9
Florence, KY	A5	20
Florence, MS	C3	27
Florence, OR	D2	40
Florence, SC	C8	43
Florida, state, US	E5	12
Florida, Cape, FL	G6	12
Florida Bay, FL	H6	12
Florida Keys, FL	H6	12
Florissant, MO	f13	28
Flossmoor, IL	k9	16
Flourtown, PA	o21	41
Flowood, MS	C3	27
Flushing, MI	E7	25
Foley, AL	E2	4
Folkston, GA	F4	13
Follansbee, WV	A4	51
Fond du Lac, WI	E5	52
Fond du Lac Indian Reservation, MN	D6	26
Fontana, CA	m14	8
Fontenelle Reservoir, WY	D2	53
Foraker, Mount, AK	f16	5
Fords, NJ	B4	33
Fords Prairie, WA	C2	50
Fordyce, AR	D3	7
Foreman, AR	D1	7
Forest, MS	C4	27
Forest Acres, SC	C6	43
Forest City, IA	A4	18
Forest City, NC	B1	36
Forestdale, AL	B3	4
Forest Grove, OR	B3	40
Forest Hill, TX	n9	46
Forest Hills, PA	k14	41
Forest Hills, TN	A5	45
Forest Lake, MN	E6	26
Forest Park, GA	h8	13
Forest Park, IL	k9	16
Forked Deer, r., TN	B2	45
Forks, WA	B1	50
Forman, ND	C8	37
Forrest City, AR	B5	7
Forsyth, GA	C3	13
Forsyth, MT	D10	29
Fort Ashby, WV	B6	51
Fort Atkinson, WI	F5	52
Fort Belvoir, VA	g12	49
Fort Benning, GA	D2	13
Fort Benton, MT	C6	29
Fort Bragg, NC	B3	36
Fort Branch, IN	H2	17
Fort Carson, CO	C6	9
Fort Cobb Reservoir, OK	B3	39
Fort Collins, CO	A5	9
Fort Davis, TX	o13	46
Fort Davis National Historic Site, TX	o13	46
Fort Defiance, AZ	B6	6
Fort Dix, NJ	C3	33
Fort Dodge, IA	B3	18
Fort Gibson, OK	B6	39
Fort Gibson Lake, OK	A6	39
Fort Gordon, GA	C4	13
Fort Greely, AK	C10	5
Fort Hall, ID	F6	15
Fort Jefferson National Monument, FL	H4	12
Fort Kent, ME	A4	22
Fort Knox, KY	B4	20
Fort Lauderdale, FL	F6	12
Fort Leavenworth, KS	C9	19
Fort Lee, NJ	B5	33
Fort Loudoun Lake, TN	D9	45
Fort Lupton, CO	A6	9
Fort Madison, IA	D6	18
Fort McHenry National Monument And Historic Shrine, MD	g11	23
Fort Meade, MD	B4	23
Fort Mill, SC	A6	43
Fort Mitchell, KY	h13	20
Fort Morgan, CO	A7	9
Fort Myers, FL	F5	12
Fort Myers Beach, FL	F5	12
Fort Oglethorpe, GA	B1	13
Fort Payne, AL	A4	4
Fort Peck Lake, MT	C9	29
Fort Pierce, FL	E6	12
Fort Pierre, SD	C5	44
Fort Richardson, AK	C10	5
Fort Scott, KS	E9	19
Fort Sill, OK	C3	39
Fort Smith, AR	B1	7
Fort Stewart, GA	D5	13
Fort Stockton, TX	D1	46
Fort Sumner, NM	C5	34
Fort Sumter National Monument, SC	k12	43
Fort Thomas, KY	h14	20
Fort Totten, ND	B7	37
Fort Valley, GA	D3	13
Fortville, IN	E6	17
Fort Wainwright, AK	C10	5
Fort Walton Beach, FL	u15	12
Fort Wayne, IN	B7	17
Fort Wingate, NM	B1	34
Fort Worth, TX	C4	46
Fort Wright, KY	h13	20
Forty Fort, PA	D10	41
Fort Yukon, AK	B10	5
Foss Reservoir, OK	B2	39
Foster Village, HI	g10	14
Fostoria, OH	A2	38
Fountain, CO	C6	9
Fountain Hill, PA	E11	41
Fountain Inn, SC	B3	43
Fourche Mountain, AR	C2	7
Four Mountains, Islands of, AK	E6	5
Fowler, CO	C6	9
Fowler, IN	C3	17
Fowlerville, MI	F6	25
Fox, r., US	B5	16
Fox, r., WI	D5	52
Foxboro, MA	B5	24
Fox Islands, AK	E6	5
Fox Lake, IL	A5	16
Fox Point, WI	E6	52
Fox River Grove, IL	h8	16
Frackville, PA	E9	41
Framingham, MA	B5	24
Francis Case, Lake, SD	D6	44
Franconia, NH	B3	32
Franconia Notch, NH	B3	32
Francs Peak, WY	C3	53
Frankenmuth, MI	E7	25
Frankfort, IL	m9	16
Frankfort, IN	D4	17
Frankfort, KY	B5	20
Frankfort, MI	D4	25
Franklin, IN	F5	17
Franklin, KY	D3	20
Franklin, LA	E4	21
Franklin, MA	B5	24
Franklin, NE	D7	30
Franklin, NH	D3	32
Franklin, NJ	A3	33
Franklin, NC	f9	36
Franklin, OH	C1	38
Franklin, PA	D2	41
Franklin, TN	B5	45
Franklin, VA	D6	49
Franklin, WI	n11	52
Franklin D. Roosevelt Lake, WA	B7	50
Franklin Falls Reservoir, NH	C3	32
Franklin Park, IL	k9	16
Franklinton, LA	D5	21
Frankton, IN	D6	17
Frederica, DE	D4	11
Frederick, MD	B3	23
Frederick, OK	C2	39
Fredericksburg, VA	B5	49
Fredericktown, MO	D7	28
Fredonia, AZ	A3	6
Fredonia, KS	E8	19
Fredonia, NY	C1	35
Freeburg, IL	E4	16
Freedom, WY	D2	53
Freehold, NJ	C4	33
Freeman, SD	D8	44
Freeport, IL	A4	16
Freeport, NY	n15	35
Freeport, TX	E5	46
Fremont, CA	D2	8
Fremont, IN	A8	17
Fremont, NE	C9	30
Fremont, OH	A2	38
Fremont Peak, WY	C3	53
French Broad, r., US	D10	45
French Lick, IN	G4	17
Frenchman Bay, ME	D4	22
Frenchville, ME	A4	22
Fresno, CA	D4	8
Fridley, MN	m12	26
Friend, NE	D8	30
Friendswood, TX	r14	46
Frio, r., TX	E3	46
Frisco, CO	B4	9
Frissell, Mount, US	A2	10
Frontenac, KS	E9	19
Front Range, CO	A5	9
Front Royal, VA	B4	49
Frostburg, MD	k13	23
Fruita, CO	B2	9
Fruit Heights, UT	B4	47
Fruitland, ID	F2	15
Fruitvale, WA	C5	50
Fruitville, FL	E4	12
Fullerton, CA	n13	8
Fullerton, NE	C8	30
Fulton, IL	B3	16
Fulton, KY	f9	20
Fulton, MS	A5	27
Fulton, MO	C6	28
Fulton, NY	B4	35
Fultondale, AL	f7	4
Fuquay-Varina, NC	B4	36

G

Name	Map Ref.	Page
Gadsden, AL	A3	4
Gaffney, SC	A4	43
Gahanna, OH	k11	38
Gainesville, FL	C4	12
Gainesville, GA	B3	13
Gainesville, MO	E5	28
Gainesville, TX	C4	46
Gaithersburg, MD	B3	23
Galax, VA	D2	49
Galena, IL	A3	16
Galena, KS	E9	19
Galesburg, IL	C3	16
Galion, OH	B3	38
Gallatin, TN	A5	45
Galliano, LA	E5	21
Gallup, NM	B1	34
Galveston, IN	C5	17
Galveston, TX	E5	46
Galveston Bay, TX	E5	46
Galveston Island, TX	E5	46
Ganado, AZ	B6	6
Gannett Peak, WY	C3	53
Gantt, SC	B3	43
Gardena, CA	n12	8
Garden City, GA	D5	13
Garden City, ID	F2	15
Garden City, KS	E3	19
Garden City, MI	p15	25
Gardendale, AL	B3	4
Garden Grove, CA	n13	8
Gardiner, ME	D3	22
Gardiners Island, NY	m16	35
Gardner, KS	D9	19
Gardner, MA	A4	24
Gardnerville, NV	E2	31
Garfield, NJ	h8	33
Garfield Heights, OH	h9	38
Garfield Mountain, MT	F4	29
Garland, TX	n10	46
Garner, IA	A4	18
Garner, NC	B4	36
Garnett, KS	D8	19
Garretson, SD	D9	44
Garrett, IN	B7	17
Garrison, MD	B4	23
Garrison, ND	B4	37
Gary, IN	A3	17
Gary, WV	D3	51
Gas City, IN	D6	17
Gasconade, r., MO	C6	28
Gassville, AR	A3	7
Gaston, Lake, US	A5	36
Gastonia, NC	B1	36
Gates of the Arctic National Park, AK	B9	5
Gatesville, TX	D4	46
Gatlinburg, TN	D10	45
Gauley, r., WV	C3	51
Gautier, MS	f8	27
Gay Head, MA	D6	24
Gaylord, MI	C6	25
Genesee, r., NY	C2	35
Geneseo, IL	B3	16
Geneseo, NY	C3	35
Geneva, AL	D4	4
Geneva, IL	B5	16
Geneva, NE	D8	30
Geneva, NY	C4	35
Geneva, OH	A5	38
Genoa, IL	A5	16
Genoa, NE	C8	30
Gentry, AR	A1	7
George, Lake, FL	C5	12
George, Lake, NY	B7	35
Georgetown, DE	F4	11
Georgetown, IL	D6	16
Georgetown, IN	H6	17
Georgetown, KY	B5	20
Georgetown, OH	D2	38
Georgetown, SC	E9	43
Georgetown, TX	D4	46
George Washington Birthplace National Monument, VA	B6	49
Georgia, state, US	D3	13
Georgiana, AL	D3	4
Gering, NE	C2	30
Germantown, MD	B3	23
Germantown, TN	B2	45
Germantown, WI	E5	52
Gettysburg, PA	G7	41
Gettysburg, SD	C6	44
Gibbon, NE	D7	30
Gibson City, IL	C5	16
Gibsonton, FL	p11	12
Gibsonville, NC	A3	36
Gig Harbor, WA	B3	50
Gila, r., US	D5	2
Gila Bend, AZ	E3	6
Gila Bend Mountains, AZ	D2	6
Gilbert, AZ	D4	6
Gilbert, MN	C6	26
Gilbert Peak, WA	C4	50
Gilcrest, CO	A6	9
Gillespie, IL	D4	16
Gillette, WY	B7	53
Gilman, VT	C5	48
Gilmanton, NH	D4	32
Gilsum, NH	D2	32
Girard, KS	E9	19
Girard, OH	A5	38
Glacier Bay, AK	k21	5
Glacier Bay National Park, AK	D12	5
Glacier National Park, MT	B2	29
Glacier Peak, WA	A4	50
Gladstone, MO	h10	28
Gladstone, OR	B4	40
Glasgow, KY	C4	20
Glasgow, MO	B5	28
Glasgow, MT	B10	29
Glassboro, NJ	D2	33
Glassport, PA	F2	41
Glastenbury Mountain, VT	F2	48
Glastonbury, CT	C5	10
Glen Allen, VA	C5	49
Glen Burnie, MD	B4	23
Glen Canyon, US	G4	47
Glencoe, AL	B4	4
Glencoe, IL	A6	16
Glencoe, MN	F4	26
Glen Cove, NY	h13	35
Glendale, AZ	D3	6
Glendale, CA	m12	8
Glen Dale, WV	B4	51
Glendale, WI	m12	52
Glendive, MT	C12	29
Glendora, CA	m13	8
Glendo Reservoir, WY	D8	53
Glen Ellyn, IL	k8	16
Glenns Ferry, ID	G3	15
Glennville, GA	E5	13
Glenolden, PA	p20	41
Glenpool, OK	B5	39
Glen Rock, NJ	h8	33
Glenrock, WY	D7	53
Glens Falls, NY	B7	35
Glenside, PA	F11	41
Glen Ullin, ND	C4	37
Glenview, IL	h9	16
Glenville, WV	C4	51
Glenwood, AR	C2	7
Glenwood, IA	C2	18
Glenwood, MN	E3	26
Glenwood Springs, CO	B3	9
Globe, AZ	D5	6
Gloucester, MA	A6	24
Gloucester City, NJ	D2	33
Gloucester Point, VA	C6	49
Gloversville, NY	B6	35
Goat Mountain, MT	C3	29
Goddard, KS	E6	19
Godfrey, IL	E3	16
Goffstown, NH	D3	32
Golden, CO	B5	9
Goldendale, WA	D5	50
Golden Gate Bridge, CA	h7	8
Golden Spike National Historic Site, UT	B3	47
Golden Valley, MN	n12	26
Goldsboro, NC	B5	36
Gonzales, LA	D5	21
Good Hope, AL	A3	4
Gooding, ID	G4	15
Goodland, KS	C2	19
Goodlettsville, TN	g10	45
Goodview, MN	F7	26
Goodwater, AL	B3	4
Goodyear, AZ	D3	6
Goose Creek, SC	F7	43
Gordon, GA	D3	13
Gordon, NE	B3	30
Gorham, ME	E2	22
Gorham, NH	B4	32
Goshen, IN	A6	17
Gosnell, AR	B6	7
Gothenburg, NE	D5	30
Gould, AR	D4	7
Grafton, ND	A8	37
Grafton, WV	B4	51
Grafton, WI	E6	52
Graham, NC	A3	36
Graham, TX	C3	46
Graham, Mount, AZ	E6	6
Graham Lake, ME	D4	22
Grain Valley, MO	B3	28
Grambling, LA	B3	21
Granby, CT	B4	10
Granby, MO	E3	28
Granby, Lake, CO	A5	9
Grand, r., MI	E5	25
Grand, r., MO	A3	28
Grand, r., OH	A4	38
Grand, r., SD	B4	44
Grand Bay, AL	E1	4
Grand Blanc, MI	F7	25
Grand Canyon, AZ	A3	6
Grand Canyon, AZ	A3	6
Grand Canyon National Park, AZ	B3	6
Grand Coulee Dam, WA	B6	50
Grande, Rio, r., NA	E7	2
Grande Ronde, r., US	C8	50
Grand Falls, ME	C5	22
Grandfather Mountain, NC	A1	36
Grand Forks, ND	B8	37
Grand Haven, MI	E4	25
Grand Island, NE	D7	30
Grand Island, MI	B4	25
Grand Isle, LA	E6	21
Grand Junction, CO	B2	9
Grand Lake, LA	E6	21
Grand Lake, LA	E3	21
Grand Lake, OH	B1	38
Grand Ledge, MI	F6	25
Grand Portage Indian Reservation, MN	k10	26
Grand Portage National Monument, MN	h10	26
Grand Prairie, TX	n10	46
Grand Rapids, MI	F5	25
Grand Rapids, MN	C5	26
Grand Teton, WY	C2	53
Grand Teton National Park, WY	C2	53
Grand Traverse Bay, MI	C5	25
Grandview, MO	C3	28
Grandview, WA	C6	50
Grandview Heights, OH	m10	38
Grandville, MI	F5	25
Grand Wash Cliffs, AZ	B2	6
Granger, IN	A5	17
Grangeville, ID	D2	15
Granite, OK	C2	39
Granite City, IL	E3	16
Granite Falls, MN	F3	26
Granite Falls, NC	B1	36
Granite Falls, WA	A4	50
Granite Pass, WY	B5	53
Granite Peak, MT	E7	29
Granite Peak, NV	B4	31
Graniteville, VT	C4	48
Grant, NE	D4	30
Grant, Mount, NV	E3	31
Grants, NM	B2	34
Grants Pass, OR	E3	40
Grantsville, UT	C3	47
Grapevine, TX	C4	46
Gravel Ridge, AR	h10	7
Gravette, AR	A1	7
Gray, GA	C3	13
Grayling, MI	D6	25
Graylyn Crest, DE	A3	11
Grays Harbor, WA	C1	50
Grayslake, IL	A5	16
Grayson, KY	B7	20
Grays Peak, CO	B5	9
Graysville, AL	f7	4
Great Barrington, MA	B1	24
Great Basin, US	C4	2
Great Basin National Park, NV	E7	31
Great Bay, NJ	D4	33
Great Bend, KS	D5	19
Great Dismal Swamp, US	D6	49
Great Divide Basin, WY	E4	53
Great Egg Harbor, r., NJ	D3	33
Great Falls, MT	C5	29
Great Falls, MD	B3	23
Great Lakes Naval Training Center, IL	h9	16
Great Miami, r., US	C1	38
Great Pee Dee, r., US	D9	43
Great Sacandaga Lake, NY	C6	35
Great Salt Lake, UT	B3	47
Great Salt Lake Desert, UT	C2	47
Great Salt Plains Lake, OK	A3	39
Great Sand Dunes National Monument, CO	D5	9
Great Smoky Mountains, US	D10	45
Great Smoky Mountains National Park, US	D10	45
Great Valley, US	C2	49
Greece, NY	B3	35
Greeley, CO	A6	9
Green, OR	D3	40
Green, r., US	C6	2
Green, r., US	F3	48
Green, r., IL	B4	16
Green, r., KY	C2	20
Greenacres, WA	B8	50
Greenacres City, FL	F6	12
Green Bay, WI	D6	52
Green Bay, US	D3	25
Greenbelt, MD	C4	23
Greenbrier, VA	g12	49
Greenbrier, AR	B3	7
Green Brier, TN	A5	45
Greenbrier, r., WV	D4	51
Greenbush, MN	B2	26
Greencastle, IN	E4	17
Greendale, IN	F8	17
Greendale, WI	F6	52
Greene, ME	D2	22
Greeneville, TN	C11	45
Greenfield, IN	E6	17
Greenfield, IA	C3	18
Greenfield, MA	A2	24
Greenfield, MO	D4	28
Greenfield, NH	E3	32
Greenfield, TN	A3	45
Greenfield, WI	n12	52
Greenfield Plaza, IA	e8	18
Green Forest, AR	A2	7
Greenland, NH	D5	32
Green Mountains, VT	F2	48
Green Peter Lake, OR	C4	40
Green River, UT	E5	47
Green River, WY	E3	53
Green River Lake, KY	C4	20
Green River Reservoir, VT	B3	48
Greensboro, AL	C2	4
Greensboro, GA	C3	13
Greensboro, NC	A3	36
Greensburg, IN	F7	17
Greensburg, KS	E4	19
Greensburg, KY	C4	20
Greensburg, PA	F2	41
Greentown, IN	D6	17
Green Valley, AZ	F5	6
Greenville, AL	D3	4
Greenville, IL	E4	16
Greenville, KY	C2	20
Greenville, ME	C3	22
Greenville, MI	E5	25
Greenville, MS	B2	27
Greenville, NH	E3	32
Greenville, NC	B5	36
Greenville, OH	B1	38
Greenville, PA	D1	41
Greenville, RI	C3	42
Greenville, SC	B3	43
Greenville, TX	C4	46
Greenwich, CT	E1	10
Greenwood, AR	B1	7
Greenwood, IN	E5	17
Greenwood, MS	B3	27
Greenwood, MO	k11	28
Greenwood, SC	C3	43
Greenwood, Lake, SC	C4	43
Greer, SC	B3	43
Greers Ferry Lake, AR	B3	7
Gregory, SD	D6	44
Grenada, MS	B4	27
Grenada Lake, MS	B4	27
Gresham, OR	B4	40
Gretna, LA	E5	21
Gretna, NE	C9	30
Greybull, WY	B4	53
Greybull, r., WY	B4	53
Greylock, Mount, MA	A1	24
Griffin, GA	C2	13
Griffith, IN	A3	17
Grimes, IA	C4	18
Grinnell, IA	C5	18
Grosse Pointe Park, MI	p16	25
Grosse Pointe Woods, MI	p16	25
Gros Ventre Range, WY	C2	53
Groton, CT	D7	10
Groton, SD	B7	44
Grove, OK	A7	39
Grove City, OH	C2	38
Grove City, PA	D1	41
Grove Point, MD	B5	23
Groves, TX	E6	46
Groveton, NH	A3	32
Groveton, VA	g12	49
Grovetown, GA	C4	13
Grundy Center, IA	B5	18
Guadalupe, AZ	m9	6
Guadalupe Mountains, US	E5	34
Guadalupe Mountains National Park, TX	o12	46
Guadalupe Peak, TX	o12	46
Guernsey, WY	D8	53
Guilford, CT	D5	10
Guilford, ME	C3	22
Gulf Gate Estates, FL	E4	12
Gulf Islands National Seashore, US	E5	27
Gulfport, FL	E4	12
Gulfport, MS	E4	27
Gulf Shores, AL	E2	4
Gunnison, CO	C4	9
Gunnison, r., CO	C2	9
Gunpowder Neck, MD	B5	23
Gunpowder River, MD	B5	23
Guntersville, AL	A3	4
Guntersville Lake, AL	A3	4
Gurdon, AR	D2	7
Gurnee, IL	h9	16
Guthrie, OK	B4	39
Guthrie Center, IA	C3	18
Guttenberg, IA	B6	18
Guyandotte, r., WV	C2	51
Guymon, OK	e9	39
Guyot, Mount, US	D10	45
Gwinhurst, DE	h8	11
Gypsum, CO	B4	9

H

Name	Map Ref.	Page
Hackensack, NJ	B4	33
Haddonfield, NJ	D2	33
Hagerman, NM	D5	34
Hagerstown, IN	E7	17
Hagerstown, MD	A2	23
Haggin, Mount, MT	D3	29
Hailey, ID	F4	15
Haines City, FL	D5	12
Halawa, Cape, HI	B5	14
Halawa Heights, HI	g10	14
Haleakala Crater, HI	C5	14
Haleakala National Park, HI	C6	14
Hales Corners, WI	n11	52
Halethorpe, MD	B4	23
Haleyville, AL	A2	4
Half Moon Bay, CA	k8	8
Halfway, MD	A2	23
Hallandale, FL	G6	12
Hallock, MN	B2	26
Hallowell, ME	D3	22
Halls, TN	B2	45
Halls Crossroads, TN	m14	45
Halstead, KS	E6	19
Hamburg, AR	D4	7
Hamburg, NY	C2	35
Hamden, CT	D4	10
Hamilton, AL	A2	4
Hamilton, IL	C2	16
Hamilton, MT	D2	29
Hamilton, OH	C1	38
Hamilton, Mount, NV	D6	31
Hamilton Square, NJ	C3	33
Hamlet, NC	C3	36
Hamlin, WV	C2	51
Hammond, IN	A2	17
Hammond, LA	D5	21
Hammonton, NJ	D3	33
Hampden, ME	D4	22
Hampstead, NH	E4	32
Hampton, AR	D3	7
Hampton, GA	C2	13
Hampton, IA	B4	18
Hampton, NH	E5	32
Hampton, SC	F5	43
Hampton, TN	C11	45
Hampton, VA	C6	49
Hampton Bays, NY	n16	35
Hampton Beach, NH	E5	32
Hampton Falls, NH	E5	32
Hams Fork, r., WY	E2	53
Hamtramck, MI	p15	25

Name	Map Ref.	Page
Hanahan, SC	F7	43
Hanamaulu, HI	B2	14
Hanceville, AL	A3	4
Hancock, ME	D4	22
Hancock, MI	A2	25
Hankinson, ND	C9	37
Hanna, WY	E6	53
Hannibal, MO	B6	28
Hanover, IN	G7	17
Hanover, NH	C2	32
Hanover, PA	G8	41
Hanover Park, IL	k8	16
Hapeville, GA	C2	13
Harahan, LA	k11	21
Harcuvar Mountains, AZ	D2	6
Hardeeville, SC	G5	43
Hardin, MT	E9	29
Hardinsburg, KY	C3	20
Hardwick, GA	C3	13
Hardwick, VT	B4	48
Harlan, IA	C2	18
Harlan, KY	D6	20
Harlan County Lake, NE	E6	30
Harlem, GA	C4	13
Harlem, MT	B8	29
Harlingen, TX	F4	46
Harlowton, MT	D7	29
Harney Lake, OR	D7	40
Harney Peak, SD	D2	44
Harper, KS	E5	19
Harpers Ferry National Historical Park, WV	B7	51
Harpersville, AL	B3	4
Harpeth, r., TN	A5	45
Harquahala Mountain, AZ	D2	6
Harrah, OK	B4	39
Harriman, TN	D9	45
Harriman Reservoir, VT	F3	48
Harrington, DE	E3	11
Harrington, ME	D5	22
Harrisburg, AR	B5	7
Harrisburg, IL	F5	16
Harrisburg, PA	F8	41
Harrisburg, SD	D9	44
Harrison, AR	A2	7
Harrison, ME	D2	22
Harrison, MI	D6	25
Harrison, NJ	k8	33
Harrison, NY	h13	35
Harrison, OH	C1	38
Harrison, TN	h11	45
Harrisonburg, VA	B4	49
Harrisonville, MO	C3	28
Harrisville, RI	B2	42
Harrisville, WV	B3	51
Harrodsburg, KY	C5	20
Harry S. Truman Reservoir, MO	C4	28
Hartford, AL	D4	4
Hartford, CT	B5	10
Hartford, KY	C3	20
Hartford, MI	F4	25
Hartford, SD	D9	44
Hartford, VT	D4	48
Hartford, WI	E5	52
Hartford City, IN	D7	17
Hartington, NE	B8	30
Hartland, VT	D4	48
Hartland, WI	E5	52
Hartley, IA	A2	18
Hartselle, AL	A3	4
Hartshorne, OK	C6	39
Hartsville, SC	C7	43
Hartsville, TN	A5	45
Hartwell, GA	B4	13
Hartwell Lake, US	B1	43
Harvard, IL	A5	16
Harvard, NE	D7	30
Harvard, Mount, CO	C4	9
Harvey, IL	B6	16
Harvey, LA	E5	21
Harvey, ND	B6	37
Harwinton, CT	B3	10
Harwood, ND	C9	37
Hasbrouck Heights, NJ	h8	33
Haskell, AR	C3	7
Haskell, OK	B6	39
Hastings, MI	F5	25
Hastings, MN	F6	26
Hastings, NE	D7	30
Hatch, NM	E2	34
Hatchie, r., TN	B2	45
Hatteras, Cape, NC	B7	36
Hattiesburg, MS	D4	27
Hatton, ND	B8	37
Haubstadt, IN	H2	17
Haut, Isle au, ME	D4	22
Hauula, HI	B4	14
Havana, IL	C3	16
Havasu, Lake, US	C1	6
Havelock, NC	C6	36
Haven, KS	E6	19
Haverford [Township], PA	o20	41
Haverhill, MA	A5	24
Haverstraw, NY	D7	35
Havre, MT	B7	29
Havre de Grace, MD	A5	23
Hawaii, state, US	C5	14
Hawaii, HI	D6	14
Hawaiian Islands, HI	m14	14
Hawaii Volcanoes National Park, HI	D6	14
Hawarden, IA	A1	18
Hawkinsville, GA	D3	13
Hawthorne, CA	n12	8
Hawthorne, NV	E3	31
Hawthorne, NJ	B4	33
Hayden, CO	A3	9
Hayden Lake, ID	B2	15
Hayes, Mount, AK	C10	5
Hayford Peak, NV	G6	31
Hays, KS	D4	19
Hays, MT	C8	29
Haysville, KS	g12	19
Hayti, MO	E8	28
Hayward, CA	h8	8
Hazard, KY	C6	20
Hazardville, CT	B5	10
Hazel Crest, IL	k9	16
Hazel Dell, WA	D3	50
Hazel Green, AL	A3	4
Hazel Park, MI	p15	25
Hazen, AR	C4	7
Hazen, ND	B4	37
Hazlehurst, GA	E4	13
Hazlehurst, MS	D3	27
Hazlet, NJ	C4	33
Hazleton, PA	E10	41
Headland, AL	D4	4
Healdton, OK	C4	39
Heart, r., ND	C3	37
Heath, OH	B3	38
Heavener, OK	C7	39
Heber City, UT	C4	47
Heber Springs, AR	B3	7
Hebron, IN	B3	17
Hebron, NE	D8	30
Hebron, ND	C3	37
He Devil, ID	D2	15
Heflin, AL	B4	4
Helena, AL	B3	4
Helena, AR	C5	7
Helena, MT	D4	29
Hellertown, PA	E11	41
Hells Canyon, US	B10	40
Hemet, CA	F5	8
Hemingford, NE	B2	30
Hempstead, NY	n15	35
Henagar, AL	A4	4
Henderson, KY	C2	20
Henderson, NE	D8	30
Henderson, NV	G7	31
Henderson, NC	A4	36
Henderson, TN	B3	45
Henderson, TX	C5	46
Hendersonville, NC	f10	36
Hendersonville, TN	A5	45
Henlawson, WV	n12	51
Henlopen, Cape, DE	E5	11
Hennessey, OK	A4	39
Henniker, NH	D3	32
Henning, MN	D3	26
Henryetta, OK	B6	39
Henry Mountains, UT	E5	47
Henrys Fork, r., US	E2	53
Hephzibah, GA	C4	13
Hereford, TX	B1	46
Herington, KS	D7	19
Herkimer, NY	B6	35
Hermann, MO	C6	28
Hermano Peak, CO	D2	9
Hermantown, MN	D6	26
Hermiston, OR	B7	40
Hernando, MS	A4	27
Herndon, VA	B5	49
Herrin, IL	F4	16
Hershey, PA	F8	41
Hesperia, CA	E5	8
Hesston, KS	D6	19
Hettinger, ND	D3	37
Hewitt, TX	D4	46
Heyburn, ID	G5	15
Hialeah, FL	G6	12
Hiawatha, IA	B6	18
Hiawatha, KS	C8	19
Hibbing, MN	C6	26
Hickam Air Force Base, HI	g10	14
Hickman, KY	f8	20
Hickman, NE	D9	30
Hickory, NC	B1	36
Hicksville, NY	E7	35
Hico, WV	C3	51
Higgins Lake, MI	D6	25
Higginsville, MO	B4	28
High Knob, US	A4	49
Highland, IL	E4	16
Highland, IN	A3	17
Highland Park, IL	A6	16
Highland Park, MI	p15	25
Highland Park, TX	n10	46
Highland Springs, VA	C5	49
Highmore, SD	C6	44
High Point, NC	B2	36
High Rock Lake, NC	B2	36
Highwood, IL	A6	16
Hill City, KS	C4	19
Hillcrest Heights, MD	C4	23
Hilliard, OH	k10	38
Hillsboro, IL	D4	16
Hillsboro, KS	D6	19
Hillsboro, NH	D3	32
Hillsboro, ND	B8	37
Hillsboro, OH	C2	38
Hillsboro, OR	B4	40
Hillsboro Canal, FL	F6	12
Hillsborough, NC	A3	36
Hillsdale, MI	G6	25
Hillside, NJ	k8	33
Hilo, HI	D6	14
Hilton Head Island, SC	G6	43
Hilton Head Island, SC	G6	43
Hinesville, GA	E5	13
Hingham, MA	B6	24
Hingham Bay, MA	g12	24
Hinsdale, IL	k9	16
Hinsdale, NH	E2	32
Hinton, WV	D4	51
Hiwassee, r., TN	D9	45
Hiwassee Lake, NC	f8	36
Hobart, IN	A3	17
Hobart, OK	B2	39
Hobbs, NM	E6	34
Hobe Sound, FL	E6	12
Hoboken, NJ	k8	33
Hockessin, DE	A3	11
Hocking, r., OH	C3	38
Hodgenville, KY	C4	20
Hoffman Estates, IL	h8	16
Hogansville, GA	C2	13
Hogback Mountain, MT	F4	29
Hohenwald, TN	B4	45
Hoisington, KS	D5	19
Hokes Bluff, AL	B4	4
Holbrook, AZ	C5	6
Holbrook, MA	B5	24
Holcomb, KS	E3	19
Holden, MO	C4	28
Holden, WV	D2	51
Holdenville, OK	B5	39
Holdrege, NE	D6	30
Hole in the Mountain Peak, NV	C6	31
Holladay, UT	C4	47
Holland, MI	F4	25
Hollandale, MS	B3	27
Hollidaysburg, PA	F5	41
Hollins, VA	C3	49
Hollis, OK	C2	39
Hollister, MO	E4	28
Holliston, MA	B5	24
Hollowtop Mountain, MT	E4	29
Holly Hill, FL	C5	12
Holly Springs, GA	B2	13
Holly Springs, MS	A4	27
Hollywood, AL	A4	4
Hollywood (part of Los Angeles), CA	m12	8
Hollywood, FL	F6	12
Holmen, WI	E2	52
Holstein, IA	B2	18
Holston, r., TN	C11	45
Holt, AL	B2	4
Holt, MI	F6	25
Holton, KS	C8	19
Holualoa, HI	D6	14
Holy Cross, Mountain of the, CO	B4	9
Holyoke, CO	A8	9
Holyoke, MA	B2	24
Holyoke Range, MA	B2	24
Homedale, ID	F2	15
Homer, AK	D9	5
Homer, LA	B2	21
Homerville, GA	E4	13
Homestead, FL	G6	12
Homestead National Monument of America, NE	D9	30
Homewood, AL	g7	4
Homewood, IL	B6	16
Hominy, OK	A5	39
Hondo, Rio, r., NM	D4	34
Honea Path, SC	C3	43
Honesdale, PA	C11	41
Honolulu, HI	B4	14
Hood, Mount, OR	B5	40
Hood Canal, WA	B2	50
Hoodoo Peak, WA	A5	50
Hood River, OR	B5	40
Hooker, OK	e9	39
Hooksett, NH	D4	32
Hooper, NE	C9	30
Hoopeston, IL	C6	16
Hoosac Range, US	A1	24
Hoover, AL	B3	4
Hoover Dam, US	G7	31
Hoover Reservoir, OH	B3	38
Hooverson Heights, WV	f8	51
Hopatcong, NJ	B3	33
Hopatcong, Lake, NJ	A3	33
Hope, AR	D2	7
Hope, IN	F6	17
Hope Mills, NC	C4	36
Hopewell, VA	C5	49
Hopi Indian Reservation, AZ	A5	6
Hopkins, MN	n12	26
Hopkinsville, KY	D2	20
Hoquiam, WA	C2	50
Horace, ND	C9	37
Horicon, WI	E5	52
Hornell, NY	C3	35
Horn Lake, MS	A3	27
Horse Cave, KY	C4	20
Horseheads, NY	C4	35
Horseshoe Bend, AR	A4	7
Horton, KS	C8	19
Hot Springs, SD	D2	44
Hot Springs National Park, AR	C2	7
Hot Springs National Park, AR	C2	7
Hot Springs Village, AR	C2	7
Houghton, MI	A2	25
Houghton Lake, MI	D6	25
Houghton Lake, MI	D6	25
Houlton, ME	B5	22
Houma, LA	E5	21
Housatonic, r., US	D3	10
Houston, MS	B4	27
Houston, MO	D6	28
Houston, TX	E5	46
Howard, SD	C8	44
Howard, WI	D5	52
Howards Grove-Millersville, WI	E6	52
Howell, MI	F7	25
Howland, ME	C4	22
Hoxie, AR	A5	7
Hoxie, KS	C3	19
Hoyt Lakes, MN	C6	26
Huachuca City, AZ	F5	6
Hualapai Mountains, AZ	C2	6
Hualapai Peak, AZ	B2	6
Hubbard, OH	A5	38
Hubbard Creek Lake, TX	C3	46
Hudson, IA	B5	18
Hudson, MA	B4	24
Hudson, NH	E4	32
Hudson, NY	C7	35
Hudson, WI	D1	52
Hudson, r., US	E7	35
Hudson, Lake, OK	A6	39
Hudson Falls, NY	B7	35
Hudson Lake, IN	A4	17
Hudsonville, MI	F5	25
Hueytown, AL	g6	4
Hugh Butler Lake, NE	D5	30
Hughes, AR	C5	7
Hugo, MN	m13	26
Hugo, OK	C6	39
Hugoton, KS	E2	19
Hull, IA	A1	18
Hull, MA	B6	24
Humble, TX	E5	46
Humboldt, IA	B3	18
Humboldt, KS	E8	19
Humboldt, NE	D10	30
Humboldt, TN	B3	45
Humboldt, r., NV	C3	31
Humphreys Peak, AZ	B4	6
Hungry Horse Reservoir, MT	B3	29
Hunter Mountain, NY	C6	35
Huntertown, IN	B7	17
Huntingburg, IN	H4	17
Huntingdon, PA	F6	41
Huntingdon, TN	A3	45
Huntington, IN	C7	17
Huntington, NY	E7	35
Huntington, WV	C2	51
Huntington Beach, CA	F4	8
Huntington Lake, IN	C7	17
Huntsville, AL	A3	4
Huntsville, AR	A2	7
Huntsville, MO	B5	28
Huntsville, TX	D5	46
Hurley, NM	E1	34
Huron, OH	A3	38
Huron, SD	C7	44
Huron, r., MI	p14	25
Huron, Lake, NA	B11	2
Huron Mountains, MI	B3	25
Hurricane, UT	F2	47
Hurricane, WV	C2	51
Hutchinson, KS	D6	19
Hutchinson, MN	F4	26
Huxley, IA	C4	18
Hyannis, MA	C7	24
Hyattsville, MD	C4	23
Hybla Valley, VA	g12	49
Hyco Lake, NC	A3	36
Hyde Park, VT	B3	48
Hydeville, VT	D2	48
Hyndman Peak, ID	F4	15
Hyrum, UT	B4	47
I		
Ibapah Peak, UT	D2	47
Icy Cape, AK	A7	5
Idabel, OK	D7	39
Ida Grove, IA	B2	18
Idaho, state, US	E3	15
Idaho Falls, ID	F6	15
Idaho Springs, CO	B5	9
Iliamna Lake, AK	D8	5
Iliamna Volcano, AK	C9	5
Ilion, NY	B5	35
Illinois, state, US	C4	16
Illinois, r., US	A7	39
Illinois, r., IL	B5	16
Immokalee, FL	F5	12
Imnaha, r., OR	B10	40
Imperial, NE	D4	30
Imperial Beach, CA	o15	8
Imperial Reservoir, US	E1	6
Imperial Valley, CA	F6	8
Incline Village, NV	D2	31
Independence, IA	B6	18
Independence, KS	E8	19
Independence, KY	B5	20
Independence, MO	B3	28
Independence, OR	C3	40
Independence National Historical Park, PA	p21	41
Independence Rock, WY	D5	53
Indiana, PA	E3	41
Indiana, state, US	E5	17
Indiana Dunes National Lakeshore, IN	A3	17
Indianapolis, IN	E5	17
Indian Neck, CT	D4	10
Indianola, IA	C4	18
Indianola, MS	B3	27
Indian River, FL	D6	12
Indian River Bay, DE	F5	11
Indio, CA	F5	8
Inglewood, CA	n12	8
Inkster, MI	p15	25
Institute, WV	m12	51
International Falls, MN	B5	26
Intracoastal Waterway, US	E4	21
Inver Grove Heights, MN	n12	26
Inwood, NY	k13	35
Inwood, WV	B6	51
Iola, KS	E8	19
Ionia, MI	F5	25
Iowa, state, US	C4	18
Iowa, r., IA	C6	18
Iowa City, IA	C6	18
Iowa Falls, IA	B4	18
Ipswich, SD	B6	44
Irmo, SC	C5	43
Irondale, AL	f7	4
Irondequoit, NY	B3	35
Iron Mountain, MI	C2	25
Iron Mountains, US	D1	49
Iron River, MI	B2	25
Ironton, OH	D3	38
Ironwood, MI	n11	25
Iroquois, r., US	C6	16
Irvine, CA	n13	8
Irvine, KY	C6	20
Irving, TX	n10	46
Irvington, NJ	k8	33
Irwin, PA	F2	41
Iselin, NJ	B4	33
Ishpeming, MI	B3	25
Island Pond, VT	B5	48
Isle of Palms, SC	k12	43
Isle of Wight Bay, MD	D7	23
Isle Royale National Park, MI	h9	25
Islesboro Island, ME	D4	22
Isleta, NM	C3	34
Issaquah, WA	B3	50
Isto, Mount, AK	B11	5
Istokpoga, Lake, FL	E5	12
Itasca, IL	k8	16
Ithaca, NY	C4	35
Itta Bena, MS	B3	27
Iuka, MS	A5	27
Ivanhoe, MN	F2	26
Ivoryton, CT	D6	10
J		
Jacinto City, TX	r14	46
Jackman, ME	C2	22
Jack Mountain, MT	D4	29
Jack Mountain, WA	A5	50
Jacks Mountain, PA	E6	41
Jackson, AL	D2	4
Jackson, GA	C3	13
Jackson, KY	C6	20
Jackson, LA	D4	21
Jackson, MI	F6	25
Jackson, MN	G4	26
Jackson, MS	C3	27
Jackson, MO	D8	28
Jackson, OH	C3	38
Jackson, TN	B3	45
Jackson, WI	E5	52
Jackson, WY	C2	53
Jackson Lake, WY	C2	53
Jackson Mountain, ME	D2	22
Jacksonville, AL	B4	4
Jacksonville, AR	C3	7
Jacksonville, FL	B5	12
Jacksonville, IL	D3	16
Jacksonville, NC	C5	36
Jacksonville, TX	D5	46
Jacksonville Beach, FL	B5	12
Jaffrey, NH	E2	32
Jal, NM	E6	34
Jamaica Bay, NY	k13	35
James, r., US	A8	2
James, r., MO	E4	28
James, r., VA	C5	49
James City, NC	B5	36
James Island, SC	k12	43
Jamestown, KY	D4	20
Jamestown, NY	C1	35
Jamestown, ND	C7	37
Jamestown, RI	F5	42
Janesville, WI	F4	52
Jasmine Estates, FL	D4	12
Jasonville, IN	F3	17
Jasper, AL	B2	4
Jasper, IN	H4	17
Jasper, TN	D8	45
Jay, OK	A7	39
Jay Peak, VT	B3	48
Jeanerette, LA	E4	21
Jeannette, PA	F2	41
Jefferson, GA	B3	13
Jefferson, IA	B3	18
Jefferson, LA	k11	21
Jefferson, WI	E5	52
Jefferson, r., MT	E5	29
Jefferson, Mount, ID	E7	15
Jefferson, Mount, NV	E5	31
Jefferson, Mount, OR	C5	40
Jefferson City, MO	C5	28
Jefferson City, TN	C10	45
Jefferson Farms, DE	i7	11
Jeffersontown, KY	B4	20
Jeffersonville, IN	H6	17
Jeffersonville, KY	C6	20
Jeffersonville, VT	B3	48
Jeffrey City, WY	D5	53
Jekyll Island, GA	E5	13
Jellico, TN	C9	45
Jemez Pueblo, NM	B3	34
Jenkins, KY	C7	20
Jenkintown, PA	o21	41
Jenks, OK	A6	39
Jennings, LA	D3	21
Jennings, MO	f13	28
Jensen Beach, FL	E6	12
Jericho, VT	C3	48
Jerimoth Hill, RI	C1	42
Jerome, ID	G4	15
Jersey City, NJ	B4	33
Jersey Shore, PA	D7	41
Jerseyville, IL	D3	16
Jessup, MD	B4	23
Jessup, PA	m18	41
Jesup, GA	E5	13
Jesup, IA	B5	18
Jesup, Lake, FL	D5	12
Jewett City, CT	C8	10
Jim Thorpe, PA	E10	41
Job Peak, NV	D3	31
Jocassee, Lake, US	B1	43
John Day, r., OR	B6	40
John F. Kennedy Space Center, FL	D6	12
John H. Kerr Reservoir, US	D4	49
John Martin Reservoir, CO	C7	9
John Redmond Reservoir, KS	D8	19
Johnson, KS	E2	19
Johnson, VT	B3	48
Johnson City, NY	C5	35
Johnson City, TN	C11	45
Johnston, IA	e8	18
Johnston, RI	C4	42
Johnston City, IL	F5	16
Johnstown, CO	A6	9
Johnstown, NY	B6	35
Johnstown, PA	F4	41
John W. Flannagan Reservoir, VA	e9	49
Joliet, IL	B5	16
Jones, OK	B4	39
Jonesboro, AR	B5	7
Jonesboro, GA	C2	13
Jonesboro, IN	D6	17
Jonesboro, LA	B3	21
Jonesborough, TN	C11	45
Jones Mill, AR	C3	7
Jonestown, MS	A3	27
Joplin, MO	D3	28
Joppatowne, MD	B5	23
Jordan, MT	C10	29
Jordan, r., UT	C4	47
Jornado del Muerto, NM	D3	34
J. Percy Priest Lake, TN	A5	45
Juan de Fuca, Strait of, NA	A1	50
Judsonia, AR	B4	7
Julesburg, CO	A8	9
Junction City, KS	C7	19
Junction City, KY	C5	20
Junction City, OR	C3	40
Juneau, AK	D13	5
June in Winter, Lake, FL	E5	12
Juniata, r., PA	F7	41
Jupiter, FL	F6	12
Jupiter Inlet, FL	F6	12
K		
Kaala, HI	f9	14
Kabetogama Lake, MN	B5	26
Kadoka, SD	D4	44
Kaena Point, HI	B3	14
Kahoka, MO	A6	28
Kahoolawe, HI	C5	14
Kahuku Point, HI	B4	14
Kahului, HI	C5	14
Kaibab Plateau, AZ	A3	6
Kailua, HI	B4	14
Kailua Kona, HI	D6	14
Kaiwi Channel, HI	B4	14
Ka Lae, HI	E6	14
Kalaheo, HI	B2	14
Kalamazoo, MI	F5	25
Kalamazoo, r., MI	F5	25
Kalispell, MT	B2	29
Kalona, IA	C6	18
Kamuela (Waimea), HI	C6	14
Kanab, UT	F3	47
Kanawha, r., WV	C3	51
Kane, PA	C4	41
Kaneohe, HI	B4	14
Kaneohe Bay, HI	g10	14
Kankakee, IL	B6	16
Kankakee, r., US	B5	16
Kannapolis, NC	B2	36
Kansas, state, US	D5	19
Kansas, r., KS	C7	19
Kansas City, KS	C9	19
Kansas City, MO	B3	28
Kapaa, HI	A2	14
Kaplan, LA	D3	21
Karns, TN	n13	45
Kaskaskia, r., IL	D5	16
Kasson, MN	F6	26
Katahdin, Mount, ME	C4	22
Kates Needle, AK	m24	5
Katmai, Mount, AK	D9	5
Katmai National Park, AK	D9	5
Katy, TX	r14	46
Kauai, HI	A2	14
Kauai Channel, HI	B3	14
Kauiki Head, HI	C6	14
Kaukauna, WI	D5	52
Kaulakahi Channel, HI	A2	14
Kawaikini, HI	A2	14
Kaw Lake, OK	A5	39
Kayenta, AZ	A5	6
Kaysville, UT	B4	47
Keahole Point, HI	D5	14
Keansburg, NJ	C4	33
Kearney, MO	B3	28
Kearney, NE	D6	30
Kearns, UT	C4	47
Kearny, AZ	D5	6
Kearny, NJ	h8	33
Keene, NH	E2	32
Keizer, OR	C3	40
Kekaha, HI	B2	14
Keller, TX	n9	46
Kellogg, ID	B2	15
Kelso, WA	C3	50
Kemmerer, WY	E2	53
Kenai, AK	C9	5
Kenai Fjords National Park, AK	D10	5
Kenai Mountains, AK	h16	5
Kenai Peninsula, AK	h16	5
Kendall, FL	s13	12
Kendallville, IN	B7	17
Kenduskeag, ME	C4	22
Kenesaw, NE	D7	30
Kenmare, ND	A3	37
Kenmore, NY	C2	35
Kennebec, r., ME	D3	22
Kennebunk, ME	E2	22
Kennebunkport, ME	E2	22
Kenner, LA	E5	21
Kennesaw, GA	B2	13
Kennett, MO	E7	28
Kennett Square, PA	G10	41
Kennewick, WA	C6	50
Kenosha, WI	F6	52
Kenova, WV	C2	51
Kensett, AR	B4	7
Kensington, CT	C4	10
Kent, OH	A4	38
Kent, WA	B3	50
Kent Island, MD	C5	23
Kentland, IN	C3	17
Kenton, OH	B2	38
Kent Point, MD	C5	23
Kentucky, state, US	C4	20
Kentucky, r., KY	B5	20
Kentucky Lake, US	C10	2
Kentwood, MI	F5	25
Keokuk, IA	D6	18
Keowee, Lake, SC	B2	43
Kern, r., CA	E4	8
Kernersville, NC	A2	36
Kerrville, TX	D3	46
Ketchikan, AK	D13	5
Ketchum, ID	F4	15
Kettering, OH	C1	38
Kettle Falls, WA	A7	50
Keuka Lake, NY	C3	35
Kewanee, IL	B4	16
Kewaskum, WI	E5	52
Kewaunee, WI	D6	52
Keweenaw Bay, MI	B2	25
Keweenaw Peninsula, MI	A3	25
Keweenaw Point, MI	A3	25
Keya Paha, r., US	A5	30
Keyhole Reservoir, WY	B8	53
Key Largo, FL	G6	12
Keyser, WV	B6	51
Keystone Lake, OK	A5	39
Key West, FL	H5	12
Kiamichi, r., OK	C6	39
Kiel, WI	E5	52
Kihei, HI	C5	14
Kilauea Crater, HI	D6	14
Kilgore, TX	C5	46
Killdeer, ND	B3	37
Killeen, TX	D4	46
Killen, AL	A2	4
Killington Peak, VT	D3	48
Kimball, NE	C2	30
Kimball, SD	D7	44
Kimberly, AL	B3	4
Kimberly, ID	G4	15
Kimberly, WI	h9	52
Kinchafoonee Creek, r., GA	E2	13
King, NC	A2	36
Kingfield, ME	D2	22
Kingfisher, OK	B4	39
Kingman, AZ	B1	6
Kingman, KS	E5	19
King of Prussia, PA	F11	41
Kings, r., CA	D4	8
King Salmon, AK	D8	5
Kings Canyon National Park, CA	D4	8
Kingsford, MI	C2	25
Kingsland, GA	F5	13
Kings Mountain, NC	B1	36
Kings Peak, UT	C5	47
Kingsport, TN	C11	45
Kingston, NH	E4	32
Kingston, NY	D6	35
Kingston, PA	D10	41
Kingston, RI	F3	42
Kingston, TN	D9	45
Kingstree, SC	D8	43
Kingsville, TX	F4	46
Kingwood, TX	q14	46
Kingwood, WV	B5	51
Kinsley, KS	E4	19
Kinston, NC	B5	36
Kiowa, KS	E5	19
Kiowa Creek, r., CO	B6	9
Kirkland, WA	B3	50
Kirksville, MO	A5	28
Kirkwood, MO	f13	28
Kirtland, NM	A1	34
Kissimmee, FL	D5	12
Kissimmee, r., FL	E5	12
Kissimmee, Lake, FL	E5	12
Kittanning, PA	E2	41
Kittatinny Mountain, US	B2	33
Kittery, ME	E2	22
Kitty Hawk, NC	A7	36
Klamath, r., US	B2	8
Klamath Falls, OR	E5	40
Klamath Mountains, US	E2	40
Klickitat, r., WA	C4	50
Klondike Gold Rush National Historical Park, AK	k22	5
Knife, r., ND	B3	37
Knightstown, IN	E6	17
Knob Noster, MO	C4	28
Knollwood, WV	m12	51
Knox, IN	B4	17
Knoxville, IL	C3	16
Knoxville, IA	C4	18
Knoxville, TN	D10	45
Koch Peak, MT	E5	29
Kodiak, AK	D9	5
Kodiak Island, AK	D9	5
Koko Head, HI	B4	14
Kokomo, IN	D5	17
Koolau Range, HI	f10	14
Koontz Lake, IN	B5	17
Korovin Volcano, AK	E5	5
Kosciusko, MS	B4	27
Koshkonong, Lake, WI	F5	52
Kotzebue, AK	B7	5
Kouts, IN	B3	17
Koyukuk, r., AK	B8	5
Kremmling, CO	A4	9
Kumukahi, Cape, HI	D7	14
Kuna, ID	F2	15
Kure Island, HI	k12	14
Kuskokwim, r., AK	C8	5
Kuskokwim Mountains, AK	C8	5
Kutztown, PA	E10	41
L		
Laau Point, HI	B4	14
La Barge, WY	D2	53
Lacey, WA	B3	50
Lackawanna, NY	C2	35
Lacombe, LA	D6	21
Laconia, NH	C4	32
La Crescent, MN	G7	26
La Crosse, KS	D4	19
La Crosse, WI	E2	52
Ladson, SC	F7	43
Ladysmith, WI	C2	52
Lafayette, AL	C4	4
Lafayette, CO	B5	9
Lafayette, GA	B1	13
Lafayette, IN	D4	17
Lafayette, LA	D3	21
Lafayette, NC	B3	36
Lafayette, TN	A5	45
Lafayette, Mount, NH	B3	32
La Follette, TN	C9	45
Lafourche, Bayou, r., LA	E5	21
La Grande, OR	B8	40
La Grange, GA	C1	13
La Grange, IL	B6	16
Lagrange, IN	A7	17
La Grange, KY	B4	20
La Grange, MO	A6	28
La Grange Park, IL	k9	16
Laguna Beach, CA	F5	8
La Habra, CA	n13	8
Lahaina, HI	C5	14
Lahontan Reservoir, NV	D2	31
Laie, HI	B4	14
La Junta, CO	D7	9
Lake Andes, SD	D7	44
Lake Bluff, IL	A6	16
Lake Charles, LA	D2	21
Lake Chelan National Recreation Area, WA	A5	50
Lake City, AR	B5	7
Lake City, FL	B4	12
Lake City, IA	B3	18
Lake City, MN	F6	26
Lake City, SC	D8	43
Lake City, TN	C9	45
Lake Elsinore, CA	F5	8
Lake Forest, IL	A6	16
Lake Geneva, WI	F5	52
Lake Hamilton, AR	g7	7
Lake Havasu City, AZ	C1	6
Lake in the Hills, IL	h8	16
Lake Jackson, TX	r14	46
Lakeland, FL	D5	12
Lakeland, GA	E3	13
Lake Magdalene, FL	o11	12
Lake Mead National Recreation Area, US	H7	31
Lake Mills, IA	A4	18
Lake Mills, WI	E5	52
Lake Orion, MI	F7	25
Lake Oswego, OR	B4	40
Lake Placid, NY	A7	35
Lake Pontchartrain Causeway, LA	h11	21

Name | Map Ref. | Page

Lake Providence, LA B4 21
Lake Shore, MD B5 23
Lakeside Park, KY h13 20
Lake Station, IN A3 17
Lake Stevens, WA A3 50
Lake View, IA B2 18
Lake Village, AR D4 7
Lakeville, MN F5 26
Lake Wales, FL E5 12
Lakewood, CA n12 8
Lakewood, CO B5 9
Lakewood, IA f8 18
Lakewood, NJ C4 33
Lakewood, OH A4 38
Lakewood, WA B3 50
Lake Worth, FL F6 12
Lake Zurich, IL h8 16
Lakin, KS E2 19
Lakota, ND A7 37
La Luz, NM E4 34
Lamar, CO C8 9
Lamar, MO D3 28
Lambertville, MI G7 25
Lame Deer, MT E10 29
La Mesa, CA F5 8
La Mesa, NM E3 34
Lamesa, TX C2 46
Lamoille, r., VT B3 48
La Moine, r., IL C3 16
Lamoni, IA D4 18
La Motte, Isle, VT B2 48
La Moure, ND C7 37
Lanai, HI C4 14
Lancaster, CA E4 8
Lancaster, KY C5 20
Lancaster, NH B3 32
Lancaster, NY C2 35
Lancaster, OH C3 38
Lancaster, PA F9 41
Lancaster, SC B6 43
Lancaster, TX n10 46
Lancaster, WI F3 52
Land Between the Lakes, US f9 20
Lander, WY D4 53
Landess, IN C6 17
Landrum, SC A3 43
Lanett, AL C4 4
Langdon, ND A7 37
Langley Park, MD f9 23
Lanham, MD C4 23
Lansdale, PA F11 41
Lansdowne, MD B4 23
L'Anse, MI B2 25
Lansford, PA E10 41
Lansing, IL B6 16
Lansing, KS C9 19
Lansing, MI F6 25
Lapeer, MI E7 25
Lapel, IN D6 17
La Place, LA h11 21
La Plata, MD C4 23
La Plata, MO A5 28
La Plata Peak, CO B4 9
Laporte, CO A5 9
La Porte, IN A4 17
La Porte, TX r14 46
La Porte City, IA B5 18
Laramie, WY E7 53
Laramie, r., US E7 53
Laramie Mountains, WY D7 53
Laredo, TX F3 46
Largo, FL E4 12
Largo, Key, FL G6 12
Larimore, ND B8 37
Larksville, PA n17 41
Larned, KS D4 19
Larose, LA E5 21
La Salle, CO A6 9
La Salle, IL B4 16
La Sal Mountains, UT E6 47
Las Animas, CO C7 9
Las Cruces, NM E3 34
Lassen Peak, CA B3 8
Lassen Volcanic National Park, CA B3 8
Las Vegas, NV G6 31
Las Vegas, NM B4 34
Lathrop, MO B3 28
Latrobe, PA F3 41
Lauderdale Lakes, FL r13 12
Laurel, DE F3 11
Laurel, MD B4 23
Laurel, MS D4 27
Laurel, MT E8 29
Laurel, NE B8 30
Laurel, VA C5 49
Laurel Bay, SC G6 43
Laurel River Lake, KY D5 20
Laurens, IA B3 18
Laurens, SC C3 43
Laurinburg, NC C3 36
Lavaca, AR B1 7
La Vale, MD k13 23
La Vergne, TN A5 45
La Vista, NE g12 30
Lawrence, IN E5 17
Lawrence, KS D8 19
Lawrence, MA A5 24
Lawrenceburg, IN F8 17
Lawrenceburg, KY B5 20
Lawrenceburg, TN B4 45
Lawrence Park, PA B1 41
Lawrenceville, GA C3 13
Lawrenceville, IL E6 16
Lawson, MO B3 28
Lawton, OK C3 39
Layton, UT B4 47
Leachville, AR B5 7
Lead, SD C2 44
Leadville, CO B4 9
Leaf, r., MS D5 27
League City, TX r14 46
Leakesville, MS D5 27
Lealman, FL p10 12
Leatherman Peak, ID E5 15
Leavenworth, KS C9 19
Leawood, KS D9 19
Lebanon, IL E4 16
Lebanon, IN D5 17
Lebanon, KY C4 20
Lebanon, MO D5 28
Lebanon, NH C2 32
Lebanon, OH C1 38
Lebanon, OR C4 40
Lebanon, PA F9 41
Lebanon, TN A5 45
Lebanon, VA f9 49
Lebanon Junction, KY C4 20
Le Claire, IA C7 18
Leconte, Mount, TN D10 45
Leech Lake, MN C4 26
Leech Lake Indian Reservation, MN C4 26
Leeds, AL B3 4
Leesburg, FL D5 12
Leesburg, VA A5 49
Lees Summit, MO C3 28
Leesville, LA C2 21
Lehi, UT C4 47
Lehigh, r., PA E10 41
Lehigh Acres, FL F5 12
Lehighton, PA E10 41
Leighton, AL A2 4
Leipsic, r., DE C3 11
Leisure City, FL s13 12
Leitchfield, KY C3 20
Leland, MS B3 27
Le Mars, IA B1 18
Lemhi, r., ID E5 15
Lemhi Range, ID E5 15
Lemmon, SD B3 44
Lemmon, Mount, AZ E5 6
Lemmon Valley, NV D2 31
Lemon Grove, CA o15 8
Lemont, IL B5 16
Lenexa, KS D9 19
Lennox, SD D9 44
Lenoir, NC B1 36
Lenoir City, TN D9 45
Lenox, IA D3 18
Leominster, MA A4 24
Leon, IA D4 18
Leonia, NJ h9 33
Leoti, KS D2 19
Lepanto, AR B5 7
Le Sueur, MN F5 26
Levelland, TX C1 46
Levisa Fork, r., US C7 20
Levittown, NY E7 35
Levittown, PA F12 41
Lewes, DE E5 11
Lewis, r., WA C4 50
Lewis, Mount, NV C5 31
Lewis and Clark Lake, US E8 44
Lewisburg, PA E8 41
Lewisburg, TN B5 45
Lewisburg, WV D4 51
Lewisport, KY C3 20
Lewis Smith Lake, AL B2 4
Lewiston, ID C1 15
Lewiston, ME D2 22
Lewistown, MT C7 29
Lewistown, PA E6 41
Lewisville, AR D2 7
Lewisville, TX C4 46
Lewisville Lake, TX C4 46
Lexington, KY B5 20
Lexington, MA B5 24
Lexington, MS B3 27
Lexington, MO B4 28
Lexington, NE D6 30
Lexington, NC B2 36
Lexington, TN B3 45
Lexington, VA C3 49
Lexington Park, MD D5 23
Libby, MT B1 29
Liberal, KS E3 19
Liberty, IN E8 17
Liberty, KY C5 20
Liberty, MO B3 28
Liberty, TX D5 46
Libertyville, IL A6 16
Licking, r., KY B6 20
Lidgerwood, ND C8 37
Lighthouse Point, MI C5 25
Ligonier, IN B6 17
Lihue, HI B2 14
Lilburn, GA h8 13
Lillinonah, Lake, CT C2 10
Lilly Grove, WV D3 51
Lima, OH B1 38
Limon, CO B7 9
Lincoln, AL B3 4
Lincoln, AR B1 7
Lincoln, IL C4 16
Lincoln, KS C5 19
Lincoln, ME C4 22
Lincoln, NE D9 30
Lincoln, NH B3 32
Lincoln City, OR C3 40
Lincoln Park, CO C5 9
Lincoln Park, MI p15 25
Lincolnshire, IL h9 16
Lincoln Tomb State Memorial, IL D4 16
Lincolnton, NC B1 36
Lincolnwood, IL h9 16
Lindale, GA B1 13
Linden, NJ k8 33
Lindenhurst, IL h8 16
Lindenhurst, NY n15 35
Lindenwold, NJ D3 33
Lindon, UT C4 47
Lindsay, OK C4 39
Lindsborg, KS D6 19
Lindstrom, MN E6 26
Lingle, WY D8 53
Lino Lakes, MN m12 26
Linton, IN F3 17
Linton, ND C5 37
Lipscomb, AL B3 4
Lisbon, IA C6 18
Lisbon, NH B3 32
Lisbon, ND C8 37
Lisbon Falls, ME E2 22
Lisburne, Cape, AK B6 5
Lisle, IL k8 16
Litchfield, IL D4 16
Litchfield, MN E4 26
Litchfield Park, AZ m8 6
Lithia Springs, GA h7 13
Lithonia, GA C2 13
Lititz, PA F9 41
Little, r., LA C3 21
Little Arkansas, r., KS D6 19
Little Belt Mountains, MT D6 29
Little Blue, r., US C6 19
Little Boars Head, NH E5 32
Little Chute, WI D5 52
Little Colorado, r., AZ B4 6
Little Diomede Island, AK B6 5
Little Egg Harbor, NJ D4 33
Little Falls, MN E4 26
Little Falls, NJ B4 33
Little Fork, r., MN B5 26
Little Gunpowder Falls, r., MD A4 23
Little Humboldt, r., NV B4 31
Little Kanawha, r., WV C4 51
Little Lake, LA E5 21
Little Missouri, r., US A7 2
Little Missouri, r., AR D2 7
Little Pee Dee, r., SC C9 43
Little Red, r., AR B4 7
Little Rock, AR C3 7
Little Sandy, r., KY B6 20
Little Sioux, r., US B2 18
Little Tennessee, r., US D9 45
Littleton, CO B6 9
Littleton, NH B3 32
Little Wabash, r., IL E5 16
Livermore, CA h9 8
Livermore, KY C2 20
Livermore, Mount, TX o12 46
Livermore Falls, ME D2 22
Livingston, AL C1 4
Livingston, MT E6 29
Livingston, NJ B4 33
Livingston, TN C8 45
Livonia, MI F7 25
Lizard Head Pass, CO D3 9
Lizard Head Peak, WY D3 53
Llano, r., TX D3 46
Lochearn, MD g10 23
Loch Raven Reservoir, MD B4 23
Lockhart, TX E4 46
Lock Haven, PA D7 41
Lockport, IL B5 16
Lockport, NY B2 35
Lockwood, MT E8 29
Lodi, CA C3 8
Lodi, NJ h8 33
Logan, IA C2 18
Logan, NM B6 34
Logan, OH C3 38
Logan, UT B4 47
Logan, WV D3 51
Logan Pass, MT B2 29
Logansport, IN C5 17
Loganville, GA C3 13
Lolo, MT D2 29
Lolo Pass, US C4 15
Lombard, IL k8 16
London, KY C5 20
London, OH C2 38
Londonderry, NH E4 32
Londontown, MD C4 23
Lone Grove, OK C4 39
Long Beach, CA F4 8
Long Beach, IN A4 17
Long Beach, MS g7 27
Long Beach, NY E7 35
Long Branch, NJ C5 33
Long Island, NY E7 35
Long Island Sound, US E7 35
Long Lake, ND C6 37
Longmeadow, MA B2 24
Longmont, CO A5 9
Long Prairie, MN E4 26
Longs Peak, CO A5 9
Long View, NC B1 36
Longview, TX C5 46
Longview, WA C3 50
Lonoke, AR C4 7
Lonsdale, RI B4 42
Loogootee, IN G4 17
Lookout, Cape, NC C6 36
Lookout Mountain, US E6 41
Lookout Pass, US B3 15
Loosahatchie, r., TN B2 45
Lopez Island, WA A3 50
Lorain, OH A3 38
Lordsburg, NM E1 34
Loris, SC C10 43
Los Alamos, NM B3 34
Los Altos, CA k8 8
Los Angeles, CA E4 8
Los Angeles Aqueduct, CA E4 8
Los Gatos, CA D2 8
Los Lunas, NM C3 34
Los Padillas, NM m7 34
Los Ranchos de Albuquerque, NM B3 34
Lost River Range, ID E5 15
Lost Trail Pass, US D5 15
Loudon, TN D9 45
Louisa, KY B7 20
Louisburg, KS D9 19
Louisburg, NC A4 36
Louisiana, MO B6 28
Louisiana, state, US C3 21
Louisiana Point, LA E2 21
Louisville, CO B5 9
Louisville, GA C4 13
Louisville, KY B4 20
Louisville, MS B4 27
Louisville, NE D9 30
Louisville, OH B4 38
Loup, r., NE C8 30
Loup City, NE C7 30
Loveland, CO A5 9
Loveland, OH n13 38
Loveland Pass, CO B5 9
Lovell, WY B4 53
Lovelock, NV C3 31
Lovenia, Mount, UT C5 47
Love Point, MD B5 23
Loves Park, IL A4 16
Loving, NM E5 34
Lovington, NM E6 34
Lowell, AR A1 7
Lowell, IN B3 17
Lowell, MA A5 24
Lower Klamath Lake, CA B3 8
Lower New York Bay, NJ B4 33
Lower Red Lake, MN C3 26
Loxley, AL E2 4
Lubbock, TX C2 46
Lubec, ME D6 22
Lucedale, MS E5 27
Lucky Peak Lake, ID F3 15
Ludington, MI E4 25
Ludlow, KY h13 20
Ludlow, MA B3 24
Ludlow, VT E3 48
Lufkin, TX D5 46
Lumberport, WV B4 51
Lumberton, MS D4 27
Lumberton, NC C3 36
Lund, NV E6 31
Luray, VA B4 49
Lusk, WY D8 53
Lutcher, LA D5 21
Lutherville-Timonium, MD B4 23
Lutz, FL D4 12
Luverne, AL D3 4
Luverne, MN G2 26
Luxora, AR B6 7
Lyman, WY E2 53
Lynchburg, TN B5 45
Lynchburg, VA C3 49
Lynches, r., SC D8 43
Lynden, WA A3 50
Lyndhurst, NJ h8 33
Lyndhurst, OH g9 38
Lyndon, KY g11 20
Lyndon, VT B4 48
Lyndon B. Johnson National Historical Site, TX D3 46
Lyndon B. Johnson Space Center, TX r14 46
Lyndonville, VT B4 48
Lynn, MA B6 24
Lynn, Lake, WV B5 51
Lynnfield, MA f11 24
Lynn Garden, TN C11 45
Lynn Haven, FL u16 12
Lynnwood, WA B3 50
Lynwood, CA n12 8
Lyons, CO A5 9
Lyons, GA D4 13
Lyons, IL k9 16
Lyons, KS D5 19
Lyons, NE C9 30

M

Mableton, GA h7 13
Mabscott, WV D3 51
Machias, ME D5 22
Machias Bay, ME D5 22
Mackinac, Straits of, MI C6 25
Mackinac Bridge, MI C6 25
Mackinac Island, MI C6 25
Mackinaw City, MI C6 25
Macomb, IL C3 16
Macon, GA D3 13
Macon, MS B5 27
Macon, MO B5 28
Madawaska, ME A4 22
Madeira, OH o13 38
Madelia, MN F4 26
Madeline Island, WI B3 52
Madill, OK C5 39
Madison, AL A3 4
Madison, AR B5 7
Madison, GA C3 13
Madison, IL E3 16
Madison, IN G7 17
Madison, ME D3 22
Madison, MN E2 26
Madison, MS C3 27
Madison, NE C8 30
Madison, NJ B4 33
Madison, SD D8 44
Madison, WV C3 51
Madison, WI E4 52
Madison, r., MT E5 29
Madison Heights, MI o15 25
Madison Heights, VA C3 49
Madisonville, KY C2 20
Madisonville, TN D9 45
Madras, OR C5 40
Madre, Laguna, TX F4 46
Madrid, IA C4 18
Magazine, AR B2 7
Magazine Mountain, AR B2 7
Magdalena, NM C2 34
Magee, MS D4 27
Magna, UT C3 47
Magnolia, AR D2 7
Magnolia, MS D3 27
Mahanoy City, PA E9 41
Mahomet, IL C5 16
Mahopac, NY D7 35
Maili, HI g9 14
Maine, state, US C3 22
Maize, KS g12 19
Makaha, HI g9 14
Makakilo City, HI g9 14
Makapuu Head, HI B4 14
Makawao, HI C5 14
Makushin Volcano, AK E6 5
Malad City, ID G6 15
Malden, MA B5 24
Malden, MO E8 28
Malheur, r., OR D9 40
Malheur Lake, OR D8 40
Malibu, CA m11 8
Malone, NY f10 35
Malta, MT B9 29
Malvern, AR C3 7
Malvern, PA o19 41
Malverne, NY k13 35
Mamaroneck, NY h13 35
Mammoth Cave National Park, KY C4 20
Mammoth Spring, AR A4 7
Mamou, LA D3 21
Manassas, VA B5 49
Manassas National Battlefield Park, VA g11 49
Manassas Park, VA B5 49
Manatee, r., FL E4 12
Manchester, CT B5 10
Manchester, GA D2 13
Manchester, IA B6 18
Manchester, KY C6 20
Manchester, MO f12 28
Manchester, NH E4 32
Manchester, TN B5 45
Manchester, VT E2 48
Manchester Center, VT E2 48
Mandan, ND C5 37
Mandeville, LA D5 21
Mangum, OK C2 39
Manhattan, KS C7 19
Manhattan Beach, CA n12 8
Manhattan Island, NY h13 35
Manheim, PA F9 41
Manila, AR B5 7
Manistee, MI D4 25
Manistee, r., MI D5 25
Manistique, MI C4 25
Manistique, r., MI B4 25
Manistique Lake, MI B5 25
Manitou Springs, CO C6 9
Manitowoc, WI D6 52
Mankato, MN F5 26
Manly, IA A4 18
Mannford, OK A5 39
Manning, IA C2 18
Manning, SC D7 43
Mannington, WV B4 51
Mansfield, AR B1 7
Mansfield, LA B2 21
Mansfield, OH B3 38
Mansfield, PA C7 41
Mansfield, TX n9 46
Mansfield, Mount, VT B3 48
Mansfield Hollow Lake, CT B7 10
Manson, IA B3 18
Manteno, IL B6 16
Manti, UT D4 47
Manville, NJ B3 33
Manville, RI B4 42
Many, LA C2 21
Maple, r., IA B2 18
Maple, r., ND C8 37
Maple Grove, MN m12 26
Maple Heights, OH h9 38
Maple Shade, NJ D2 33
Mapleton, ND C8 37
Maplewood, MN n12 26
Maplewood, MO f13 28
Maplewood, NJ B4 33
Maquoketa, IA B7 18
Maquoketa, r., IA B6 18
Marana, AZ E4 6
Marble Canyon, AZ A4 6
Marblehead, MA B6 24
Marbleton, WY D2 53
Marceline, MO B5 28
Marco, FL G5 12
Marcus Baker, Mount, AK g18 5
Marcy, Mount, NY A7 35
Marengo, IL A5 16
Marengo, IA C5 18
Margaret, AL B3 4
Margate, FL F6 12
Marianna, AR C5 7
Marianna, FL B1 12
Marias Pass, MT B3 29
Maricopa, AZ E3 6
Maricopa Mountains, AZ m7 6
Marietta, GA C2 13
Marietta, OH C4 38
Marietta, OK D4 39
Marine City, MI F8 25
Marinette, WI C6 52
Marion, AL C2 4
Marion, AR B5 7
Marion, IL F5 16
Marion, IN C6 17
Marion, IA B6 18
Marion, KS D6 19
Marion, KY e9 20
Marion, MS C5 27
Marion, NC B1 36
Marion, OH B2 38
Marion, SC C9 43
Marion, SD D8 44
Marion, VA f10 49
Marion, Lake, SC E7 43
Marionville, MO D4 28
Marked Tree, AR B5 7
Markham, IL k9 16
Marks, MS A3 27
Marksville, LA C3 21
Mark Twain Lake, MO B6 28
Marlborough, CT C6 10
Marlborough, MA B4 24
Marlborough, NH E2 32
Marley, MD B4 23
Marlinton, WV C4 51
Marlow, OK C4 39
Marlton, NJ D3 33
Marmaduke, AR A5 7
Marmet, WV C3 51
Marquesas Keys, FL H4 12
Marquette, MI B3 25
Marquette Heights, IL C4 16
Marrero, LA E5 21
Marseilles, IL B5 16
Marshall, AR B3 7
Marshall, IL D6 16
Marshall, MI F6 25
Marshall, MN F3 26
Marshall, MO B4 28
Marshall, TX C5 46
Marshall, WI E4 52
Marshallton, DE B3 11
Marshalltown, IA B5 18
Marshfield, MA B6 24
Marshfield, MO D5 28
Marshfield, WI D3 52
Mars Hill, ME B5 22
Marsh Island, LA E4 21
Marsh Peak, UT C6 47
Martha's Vineyard, MA D6 24
Martin, SD D4 44
Martin, TN A3 45
Martin City, MT B3 29
Martinez, GA C4 13
Martin Lake, AL C4 4
Martinsburg, WV B7 51
Martins Ferry, OH B5 38
Martinsville, IN F5 17
Martinsville, VA D3 49
Marvell, AR C5 7
Marvine, Mount, UT E4 47
Maryland, state, US B4 23
Maryland City, MD B4 23
Maryland Heights, MO f13 28
Maryland Point, MD D3 23
Marys, r., NV B6 31
Marysville, KS C7 19
Marysville, MI F8 25
Marysville, OH B2 38
Marysville, WA A3 50
Maryville, MO A3 28
Maryville, TN D10 45
Mascoma, r., NH C2 32
Mascot, TN C10 45
Mascoutah, IL E4 16
Mason, OH C1 38
Mason, WV B2 51
Mason City, IA A4 18
Massachusetts, state, US B4 24
Massachusetts Bay, MA B6 24
Massena, NY f10 35
Massillon, OH B4 38
Massive, Mount, CO B4 9
Mastic Beach, NY n16 35
Matagorda Bay, TX E4 46
Matagorda Island, TX E4 46
Matagorda Peninsula, TX E5 46
Matanuska, r., AK g18 5
Mattapoisett, MA C6 24
Mattaponi, r., VA C5 49
Mattawamkeag, ME C4 22
Mattawamkeag, r., ME C4 22
Matterhorn, NV B6 31
Matteson, IL k9 16
Matthews, NC B2 36
Mattoon, IL D5 16
Maui, HI C6 14
Mauldin, SC B3 43
Maumee, OH A2 38
Maumee, r., US A2 38
Maumelle, AR h10 7
Maumelle, Lake, AR C3 7
Mauna Kea, HI D6 14
Mauna Loa, HI D6 14
Maunawili, HI g10 14
Maurepas, Lake, LA D5 21
Maurice, r., NJ E2 33
Mauston, WI E3 52
Maxwell Acres, WV g8 51
Mayfield, KY f9 20
Mayfield Heights, OH A4 38
Mayflower, AR C3 7
Maynard, MA B5 24
Maysville, KY B6 20
Mayville, ND B8 37
Mayville, WI E5 52
Maywood, IL k9 16
McAfee Peak, NV B6 31
McAlester, OK C6 39
McAllen, TX F3 46
McAlmont, AR h10 7
McCall, ID E2 15
McCandless, PA h13 41
McComb, MS D3 27
McCook, NE D5 30
McCormick, SC D3 43
McCrory, AR B4 7
McDonough, GA C2 13
McDowell Peak, AZ k9 6
McFarland, WI E4 52
McGehee, AR D4 7
McGill, NV D7 31
McGrath, AK C8 5
McGuire Air Force Base, NJ C3 33
McHenry, IL A5 16
McIntosh, MN C3 26
McKeesport, PA F2 41
McKees Rocks, PA F1 41
McKenzie, TN A3 45
McKenzie, r., OR C4 40
McKinley, Mount, AK C9 5
McKinney, TX C4 46
McLaughlin, SD B5 44
McLean, VA g12 49
McLoud, OK B4 39
McLoughlin, Mount, OR D4 40
McMechen, WV B4 51
McMillan, Lake, NM E5 34
McMinnville, OR B3 40
McMinnville, TN D8 45
McPherson, KS D6 19
McRae, GA D4 13
Mead, Lake, US A1 6
Meade, KS E3 19
Meade Peak, ID G7 15
Meadville, PA C1 41
Mebane, NC A3 36
Mechanic Falls, ME D2 22
Mechanicsburg, PA F7 41
Mechanicsville, VA C5 49
Medford, MA B5 24
Medford, OR E4 40
Medford, WI C3 52
Media, PA G11 41
Mediapolis, IA C6 18
Medical Lake, WA B8 50
Medicine Bow, r., WY E6 53
Medicine Bow Mountains, US E6 53
Medicine Bow Peak, WY E6 53
Medicine Lodge, KS E5 19
Medicine Lodge, r., US E4 19
Medina, NY B2 35
Medina, OH A4 38
Medina, WA e11 50
Medway, MA B5 24
Meeker, CO A3 9
Mehlville, MO f13 28
Melbourne, AR A4 7
Melbourne, FL D6 12
Melrose, MA B5 24
Melrose, MN E4 26
Melton Hill Lake, TN D9 45
Memphis, MO A5 28
Memphis, TN B1 45
Mena, AR C1 7
Menasha, WI D5 52
Mendenhall, MS D4 27
Mendota, IL B4 16
Mendota, Lake, WI E4 52
Menlo Park, CA k8 8
Menno, SD D8 44
Menominee, MI C3 25
Menominee, r., US C6 52
Menomonee Falls, WI E5 52
Menomonie, WI D2 52
Mentone, AL A4 4
Mentor, OH A4 38
Mentor-on-the-Lake, OH A4 38
Mequon, WI E6 52
Meramec, r., MO C7 28
Meraux, LA k12 21
Merced, CA D3 8
Merced, r., CA D3 8
Mercedes, TX F4 46
Mercer Island, WA B3 50
Mercerville, NJ C3 33
Meredith, NH C3 32
Meredith, Lake, TX B2 46
Meriden, CT C4 10
Meridian, ID F2 15
Meridian, MS C5 27
Meridian Hills, IN k10 17
Meridianville, AL A3 4
Merriam, KS k16 19
Merrill, WI C4 52
Merrillville, IN B3 17
Merrimac, MA A5 24
Merrimack, NH E4 32
Merrimack, r., US A5 24
Merritt Island, FL D6 12
Mesa, AZ D4 6
Mesabi Range, MN C6 26
Mesa Verde National Park, CO D2 9
Mescalero, NM D4 34
Mesilla, NM E3 34
Mesquite, NV G7 31
Mesquite, TX n10 46
Metairie, LA k11 21
Meteor Crater, AZ C4 6
Methow, r., WA A5 50
Methuen, MA A5 24
Meto, Bayou, r., AR C4 7
Metropolis, IL F5 16
Metter, GA D4 13
Metuchen, NJ B4 33
Metzger, OR h12 40
Mexico, ME D2 22
Mexico, MO B6 28
Miami, AZ D5 6
Miami, FL G6 12
Miami, OK A7 39
Miami Beach, FL G6 12
Miami Canal, FL F6 12
Miamisburg, OH C1 38
Miami Shores, FL G6 12
Miami Springs, FL G6 12
Michelson, Mount, AK B11 5
Michigamme Reservoir, MI B2 25
Michigan, state, US E6 25
Michigan, Lake, US B10 2
Michigan Center, MI F6 25
Michigan City, IN A4 17
Middleboro (Middleborough Center), MA C6 24
Middleburg Heights, OH h9 38
Middlebury, CT C3 10
Middlebury, IN A6 17
Middlebury, VT C2 48
Middle River, MD B5 23
Middlesboro, KY D6 20
Middlesex, NJ B4 33
Middleton, ID F2 15
Middleton, WI E4 52
Middletown, CT C5 10
Middletown, DE C3 11
Middletown, IN D6 17
Middletown, KY g11 20
Middletown, NJ C4 33
Middletown, NY D6 35
Middletown, OH C1 38
Middletown, PA F8 41
Middletown, RI E5 42
Midfield, AL g7 4
Midland, MI E6 25
Midland, TX D1 46
Midland City, AL D4 4
Midland Park, KS g12 19
Midlothian, IL k9 16
Midvale, UT C4 47
Midwest, WY C6 53
Midwest City, OK B4 39
Milan, IL B3 16
Milan, IN F7 17
Milan, MI F7 25
Milan, MO A4 28
Milan, NM B2 34
Milan, TN B3 45
Milbank, SD B9 44
Miles City, MT D11 29
Milford, CT E3 10
Milford, DE E4 11
Milford, IN B6 17
Milford, IA A2 18
Milford, ME D4 22
Milford, MA B4 24
Milford, MI F7 25
Milford, NE D8 30
Milford, NH E3 32
Milford, UT E2 47
Milford Lake, KS C6 19
Mililani Town, HI g9 14
Millbrook, AL C3 4
Millburn, NJ B4 33
Millcreek, UT C4 47
Millcreek Township, PA B1 41
Milledgeville, GA C3 13
Mille Lacs Lake, MN D5 26
Millen, GA D5 13
Miller, SD C7 44
Millersville, PA F9 41
Milliken, CO A6 9
Millington, TN B2 45
Millinocket, ME C4 22
Millinocket Lake, ME B4 22
Millport, AL B1 4
Mills, WY D6 53
Millsboro, DE F4 11
Millstone, r., NJ C4 33
Millvale, PA k14 41
Millville, NJ E2 33
Millville Lake, NH E4 32
Millwood Lake, AR D1 7
Milnor, ND C8 37
Milo, ME C4 22
Milpitas, CA k9 8
Milton, MA B5 24
Milton, NH D5 32

S•60 Milt-Ozar

Name	Map Ref.	Page
Milton, PA	D8	41
Milton, VT	B2	48
Milton, WA	f11	50
Milton, WV	C2	51
Milton, WI	F5	52
Milton-Freewater, OR	B8	40
Milwaukee, WI	E6	52
Milwaukie, OR	B4	40
Mims, FL	D6	12
Minatare, NE	C2	30
Minden, LA	B2	21
Minden, NE	D7	30
Minden, WV	D3	51
Mineola, NY	E7	35
Mineral Point, WI	F3	52
Mineral Springs, AR	D2	7
Mineral Wells, TX	C3	46
Minersville, PA	E9	41
Minneapolis, KS	C6	19
Minneapolis, MN	F5	26
Minnesota, state, US	E4	26
Minnesota, r., MN	F2	26
Minnetonka, MN	n12	26
Minnetonka, Lake, MN	n11	26
Minot, ND	A4	37
Mint Hill, NC	B2	36
Minute Man National Historical Park, MA	g10	24
Miramar, FL	s13	12
Mishawaka, IN	A5	17
Mispillion, r., DE	E4	11
Mission, KS	m16	19
Mission, SD	D5	44
Mission, TX	F3	46
Mission Viejo, CA	n13	8
Missisquoi, r., VT	B3	48
Missisquoi Bay, VT	A2	48
Mississinewa, r., US	D7	17
Mississinewa Lake, IN	C6	17
Mississippi, state, US	C4	27
Mississippi, r., US	D9	2
Mississippi Delta, LA	E6	21
Mississippi Sound, US	E5	27
Mississippi State, MS	B5	27
Missoula, MT	D2	29
Missouri, state, US	C5	28
Missouri, r., US	B8	2
Missouri Buttes, WY	B8	53
Missouri City, TX	r14	46
Missouri Valley, IA	C2	18
Mitchell, IN	G5	17
Mitchell, NE	C2	30
Mitchell, SD	D7	44
Mitchell, Mount, NC	f10	36
Mitchellville, IA	C4	18
Moab, UT	E6	47
Moberly, MO	B5	28
Mobile, AL	E1	4
Mobile, r., AL	E1	4
Mobile Bay, AL	E1	9
Mobridge, SD	B5	44
Mocksville, NC	B2	36
Modesto, CA	D3	8
Moffat Tunnel, CO	B5	9
Mogollon Mesa, AZ	C4	6
Mogollon Rim, AZ	C5	6
Mohall, ND	A4	37
Mohave, Lake, US	H7	31
Mohawk, r., NY	C6	35
Mojave, r., CA	E5	8
Mojave Desert, CA	E5	8
Mokapu Peninsula, HI	g10	14
Mokelumne, r., CA	C3	8
Mokena, IL	k9	16
Molalla, OR	B4	40
Moline, IL	B3	16
Molokai, HI	B5	14
Momence, IL	B6	16
Monaca, PA	E1	41
Monadnock, Mount, NH	E2	32
Monahans, TX	D1	46
Monarch Pass, CO	C4	9
Moncks Corner, SC	E7	43
Mondovi, WI	D2	52
Monessen, PA	F2	41
Monett, MO	E4	28
Monette, AR	B5	7
Monida Pass, US	E6	15
Monmouth, IL	C3	16
Monmouth, ME	D2	22
Monmouth, OR	C3	40
Monocacy, r., MD	B3	23
Mono Lake, CA	D4	8
Monomoy Point, MA	C7	24
Monon, IN	C4	17
Monona, IA	A6	18
Monona, WI	E4	52
Monongah, WV	B4	51
Monongahela, PA	F2	41
Monongahela, r., US	G2	41
Monroe, GA	C3	13
Monroe, IA	C4	18
Monroe, LA	B3	21
Monroe, MI	G7	25
Monroe, NY	D6	35
Monroe, NC	C2	36
Monroe, WA	B4	50
Monroe, WI	F4	52
Monroe Center, CT	D3	10
Monroe City, MO	B6	28
Monroe Lake, IN	F5	17
Monroeville, AL	D2	4
Monroeville, PA	k14	41
Monrovia, CA	m13	8
Montague Island, AK	D10	5
Montana, state, US	D7	29
Montclair, NJ	B4	33
Montebello, CA	m12	8
Monterey, CA	D3	8
Monterey, TN	C8	45
Monterey Bay, CA	D2	8
Monterey Park, CA	m12	8
Montesano, WA	C2	50
Montevallo, AL	B3	4
Montevideo, MN	F3	26
Monte Vista, CO	D4	9
Montezuma, GA	D2	13
Montezuma, IA	C5	18
Montgomery, AL	C3	4
Montgomery, IL	B5	16
Montgomery, OH	o13	38
Montgomery, WV	C3	51
Montgomery City, MO	C6	28
Monticello, AR	D4	7
Monticello, GA	C3	13
Monticello, IL	C5	16
Monticello, IN	C4	17
Monticello, IA	B6	18
Monticello, KY	D5	20
Monticello, ME	B5	22
Monticello, MN	E5	26
Monticello, MS	D3	27
Monticello, NY	D6	35
Montoursville, PA	D8	41
Montpelier, ID	G7	15
Montpelier, IN	C7	17
Montpelier, VT	C3	48
Montrose, AL	E2	4
Montrose, CO	C3	9
Montrose, VA	m18	49
Montville, CT	D7	10
Monument Peak, ID	G4	15
Monument Valley, AZ	A5	6
Moorcroft, WY	B8	53
Moore, OK	B4	39
Moorefield, WV	B6	51
Moore Reservoir, US	B3	32
Moorestown, NJ	D3	33
Mooresville, IN	E5	17
Mooresville, NC	B2	36
Moorhead, MN	D2	26
Moorhead, MS	B3	27
Moosehead Lake, ME	C3	22
Mooselookmeguntic Lake, ME	D2	22
Moosic, PA	m18	41
Moosilauke, Mount, NH	B3	32
Moosup, CT	C8	10
Mora, MN	E5	26
Mora, NM	B4	34
Moreau, r., SD	B3	44
Morehead, KY	B6	20
Morehead City, NC	C6	36
Morenci, AZ	D6	6
Morgan City, LA	E4	21
Morganfield, KY	C2	20
Morganton, NC	B1	36
Morgantown, KY	C3	20
Morgantown, MS	D2	27
Morgantown, WV	B5	51
Moriah, Mount, NV	D7	31
Moriarty, NM	C3	34
Morrill, NE	C2	30
Morrilton, AR	B3	7
Morris, IL	B5	16
Morris, MN	E3	26
Morrison, IL	B4	16
Morristown, NJ	B4	33
Morristown, TN	C10	45
Morrisville, PA	F12	41
Morrisville, VT	B3	48
Morro Bay, CA	E3	8
Morrow, GA	C2	13
Morton, IL	C4	16
Morton, MS	C4	27
Morton Grove, IL	h9	16
Moscow, ID	C2	15
Moses Lake, WA	B6	50
Mosinee, WI	D4	52
Mosquito Creek Lake, OH	A5	38
Mosquito Lagoon, FL	D6	12
Moss Bluff, LA	D2	21
Moss Point, MS	E5	27
Mott, ND	C3	37
Moulton, AL	A2	4
Moultrie, GA	E3	13
Moultrie, Lake, SC	E7	43
Mound, MN	n11	26
Mound Bayou, MS	B3	27
Mound City, MO	A2	28
Moundridge, KS	D6	19
Mounds View, MN	m12	26
Moundsville, WV	B4	51
Mountainair, NM	C3	34
Mountain Brook, AL	g7	4
Mountain City, TN	C12	45
Mountain Grove, MO	D5	28
Mountain Home, AR	A3	7
Mountain Home, ID	F3	15
Mountain Iron, MN	C6	26
Mountain Lake, MN	G4	26
Mountain View, AR	B3	7
Mountain View, CA	k8	8
Mountain View, MO	D6	28
Mountain View, NM	C3	34
Mountain View, WY	E2	53
Mountain View, WY	D6	53
Mount Airy, NC	A2	36
Mount Angel, OR	B4	40
Mount Ayr, IA	D3	18
Mount Carmel, IL	E6	16
Mount Carmel, PA	E9	41
Mount Clemens, MI	F8	25
Mount Desert Island, ME	D4	22
Mount Gay, WV	D2	51
Mount Healthy, OH	o12	38
Mount Holly, NJ	D3	33
Mount Holly, NC	B1	36
Mount Hope, WV	D3	51
Mount Horeb, WI	E4	52
Mount Ida, AR	C2	7
Mount Joy, PA	F9	41
Mount Juliet, TN	A5	45
Mount Kisco, NY	D7	35
Mount Lebanon, PA	F1	41
Mount Olive, AL	B3	4
Mount Olive, NC	B4	36
Mount Olive, TN	n14	45
Mount Pleasant, IA	D6	18
Mount Pleasant, MI	E6	25
Mount Pleasant, PA	F2	41
Mount Pleasant, SC	F8	43
Mount Pleasant, TN	B4	45
Mount Pleasant, TX	C5	46
Mount Prospect, IL	A6	16
Mount Rainier, MD	f9	23
Mount Rainier National Park, WA	C4	50
Mount Rushmore National Memorial, SD	D2	44
Mount Sterling, KY	B6	20
Mount Vernon, AL	D1	4
Mount Vernon, IL	E5	16
Mount Vernon, IN	I2	17
Mount Vernon, IA	C6	18
Mount Vernon, KY	C5	20
Mount Vernon, MO	D4	28
Mount Vernon, NY	h13	35
Mount Vernon, OH	B3	38
Mount Vernon, WA	A3	50
Mount Washington, KY	B4	20
Mount Zion, IL	D5	16
Moville, IA	B1	18
Muddy Boggy Creek, r., OK	C6	39
Mukilteo, WA	B3	50
Mukwonago, WI	F5	52
Mulberry, AR	B1	7
Muldrow, OK	B7	39
Mullen, NE	B4	30
Mullens, WV	D3	51
Mullett Lake, MI	C6	25
Mullica, r., NJ	D3	33
Mullins, SC	C9	43
Mulvane, KS	E6	19
Muncie, IN	D7	17
Mundelein, IL	A5	16
Munford, AL	B4	4
Munford, TN	B2	45
Munfordville, KY	C4	20
Munhall, PA	k14	41
Munising, MI	B4	25
Munster, IN	A2	17
Murderkill, r., DE	D4	11
Murfreesboro, AR	C2	7
Murfreesboro, TN	B5	45
Murphy, MO	g13	28
Murphy, NC	f8	36
Murphysboro, IL	F4	16
Murray, KY	f9	20
Murray, UT	C4	47
Murray, Lake, SC	C5	43
Murrells Inlet, SC	D9	43
Muscatatuck, r., IN	G5	17
Muscatine, IA	C6	18
Muscle Shoals, AL	A2	4
Musconetcong, r., NJ	B4	33
Muskego, WI	F5	52
Muskegon, MI	E4	25
Muskegon, r., MI	E4	25
Muskegon Heights, MI	E4	25
Muskingum, r., OH	C4	38
Muskogee, OK	B6	39
Musselshell, r., MT	D9	29
Mustang, OK	B4	39
Myrtle Beach, SC	D10	43
Myrtle Grove, FL	u14	12
Myrtle Point, OR	D2	40
Mystic, CT	D8	10

N

Name	Map Ref.	Page
Naches, r., WA	C5	50
Nacogdoches, TX	D5	46
Nags Head, NC	B7	36
Nambe, NM	B4	34
Namekagon, r., WI	B2	52
Nampa, ID	F2	15
Nanakuli, HI	B3	14
Nanticoke, PA	D10	41
Nanticoke, r., US	D6	23
Nantucket, MA	D7	24
Nantucket Island, MA	D7	24
Nantucket Sound, MA	C7	24
Nanuet, NY	g12	35
Napa, CA	C2	8
Napatree Point, RI	G1	42
Naperville, IL	B5	16
Naples, FL	F5	12
Naples, ME	E2	22
Napoleon, ND	C6	37
Napoleon, OH	A1	38
Nappanee, IN	B5	17
Narberth, PA	p20	41
Narragansett, RI	F4	42
Narragansett Bay, RI	E5	42
Nashua, IA	B5	18
Nashua, NH	E4	32
Nashville, AR	D2	7
Nashville, GA	E3	13
Nashville, IL	E4	16
Nashville, NC	B5	36
Nashville, TN	A5	45
Nashwauk, MN	C5	26
Natchez, MS	D2	27
Natchitoches, LA	C2	21
Natick, MA	B5	24
National City, CA	F5	8
Natrona Heights, PA	E2	41
Natural Bridges National Monument, UT	F6	47
Naugatuck, CT	D3	10
Naugatuck, r., CT	D3	10
Naushon Island, MA	D6	24
Nautilus Park, CT	D7	10
Navajo, NM	B1	34
Navajo Indian Reservation, US	A4	6
Navajo Mountain, UT	F5	47
Navajo Reservoir, US	A2	34
Nazareth, PA	E11	41
Neah Bay, WA	A1	50
Nebo, Mount, UT	D4	47
Nebraska, state, US	C6	30
Nebraska City, NE	D10	30
Nederland, CO	B5	9
Nederland, TX	E6	46
Needham, MA	g11	24
Neenah, WI	D5	52
Neillsville, WI	D3	52
Nekoosa, WI	D4	52
Neligh, NE	B7	30
Nemadji, r., US	B1	52
Neodesha, KS	E8	19
Neosho, MO	E3	28
Nephi, UT	D4	47
Neponset, r., MA	h11	24
Neptune, NJ	C4	33
Ness City, KS	D4	19
Nett Lake Indian Reservation, MN	B6	26
Nettleton, MS	A5	27
Neuse, r., NC	B6	36
Nevada, IA	B4	18
Nevada, MO	D3	28
Nevada, state, US	D5	31
Nevada, Sierra, CA	D4	8
New, r., US	C3	51
New Albany, IN	H6	17
New Albany, MS	A4	27
Newark, AR	B4	7
Newark, CA	h8	8
Newark, DE	B3	11
Newark, NJ	B4	33
Newark, NY	B3	35
Newark, OH	B3	38
New Bedford, MA	C6	24
Newberg, OR	B4	40
New Berlin, WI	n11	52
New Bern, NC	B5	36
Newbern, TN	A2	45
Newberry, MI	B5	25
Newberry, SC	C4	43
New Braunfels, TX	E3	46
New Brighton, MN	m12	26
New Brighton, PA	E1	41
New Britain, CT	C4	10
New Brunswick, NJ	C4	33
Newburgh, IN	I3	17
Newburgh, NY	D6	35
Newburyport, MA	A6	24
New Canaan, CT	E2	10
New Carlisle, IN	A4	17
New Carrollton, MD	C4	23
New Castle, AL	B3	4
New Castle, DE	B3	11
New Castle, IN	E7	17
Newcastle, OK	B4	39
New Castle, PA	D1	41
Newcastle, WY	C8	53
New City, NY	D6	35
New Cumberland, PA	F8	41
New Cumberland, WV	A4	51
Newell, WV	A4	51
New England, ND	C3	37
Newenham, Cape, AK	D7	5
New Fairfield, CT	D2	10
Newfields, NH	D5	32
Newfound Gap, US	f9	36
Newfound Lake, NH	C3	32
New Gloucester, ME	E2	22
New Hampshire, state, US	C3	32
New Hampton, IA	A5	18
New Harbor, ME	E3	22
New Haven, CT	D4	10
New Haven, IN	B7	17
New Haven, WV	C3	51
New Holland, PA	F9	41
New Holstein, WI	E5	52
New Hope, AL	A3	4
New Hope, MN	m12	26
New Iberia, LA	D4	21
Newington, CT	C5	10
New Ipswich, NH	E3	32
New Jersey, state, US	C4	33
New Kensington, PA	E2	41
Newkirk, OK	A4	39
New Lenox, IL	B6	16
New London, CT	D7	10
New London, IA	D6	18
New London, NH	D3	32
New London, WI	D5	52
New Madrid, MO	E8	28
Newmarket, NH	D5	32
New Martinsville, WV	B4	51
New Mexico, state, US	C3	34
New Milford, CT	C2	10
New Milford, NJ	h8	33
Newnan, GA	C2	13
New Orleans, LA	E5	21
New Philadelphia, OH	B4	38
New Plymouth, ID	F2	15
New Point Comfort, VA	C6	49
Newport, AR	B4	7
Newport, KY	A5	20
Newport, ME	D3	22
Newport, MN	n13	26
Newport, NH	D2	32
Newport, OR	C2	40
Newport, RI	F5	42
Newport, TN	D10	45
Newport, VT	B4	48
Newport Beach, CA	n13	8
Newport News, VA	D6	49
New Port Richey, FL	D4	12
New Prague, MN	F5	26
New Providence, NJ	B4	33
New Richmond, OH	D1	38
New Richmond, WI	C1	52
New Roads, LA	D4	21
New Rochelle, NY	E7	35
New Rockford, ND	B6	37
New Salem, ND	C4	37
New Site, AL	B4	4
New Smyrna Beach, FL	C6	12
Newton, AL	D4	4
Newton, IL	E5	16
Newton, IA	C4	18
Newton, KS	D6	19
Newton, MA	B5	24
Newton, MS	C4	27
Newton, NJ	A3	33
Newton, NC	B1	36
New Town, ND	B3	37
Newtown Square, PA	p20	41
New Ulm, MN	F4	26
New Whiteland, IN	E5	17
New Windsor, NY	D6	35
New York, NY	E7	35
New York, state, US	C6	35
Niagara Falls, NY	B1	35
Niantic, CT	D7	10
Niceville, FL	u15	12
Nicholasville, KY	C5	20
Nichols Hills, OK	B4	39
Nickajack Lake, TN	D8	45
Nicoma Park, OK	B4	39
Niihau, HI	B1	14
Niles, IL	h9	16
Niles, MI	G4	25
Niles, OH	A5	38
Nimrod Lake, AR	C2	7
Ninnescah, r., KS	E6	19
Niobrara, r., US	B7	30
Nisqually, r., WA	C3	50
Nitro, WV	C3	51
Niwot, CO	A5	9
Nixa, MO	D4	28
Noble, OK	B4	39
Noblesville, IN	D6	17
Nogales, AZ	F5	6
Nolichucky, r., TN	C10	45
Nomans Land, MA	D6	24
Nome, AK	C6	5
Noorvik, AK	B7	5
No Point, Point, MD	D5	23
Nora Springs, IA	A5	18
Norco, LA	E5	21
Norcross, GA	C2	13
Norfolk, NE	B8	30
Norfolk, VA	D6	49
Norfork, AR	A3	7
Norfork Lake, US	A3	7
Norland, FL	s13	12
Normal, IL	C5	16
Norman, OK	B4	39
Norman, Lake, NC	B2	36
Normandy, MO	f13	28
Norridge, IL	k9	16
Norris Lake, TN	C10	45
Norristown, PA	F11	41
North Adams, MA	A1	24
North Albany, OR	k11	40
Northampton, MA	B2	24
Northampton, PA	E11	41
North Andover, MA	A5	24
North Arlington, NJ	h8	33
North Atlanta, GA	h8	13
North Attleboro, MA	C5	24
North Augusta, SC	D4	43
North Aurora, IL	k8	16
North Belmont, NC	B1	36
North Bend, NE	C9	30
North Bend, OR	D2	40
North Bend, WA	B4	50
North Bennington, VT	F2	48
North Bergen, NJ	h8	33
North Branch, NH	D3	32
North Branford, CT	D4	10
Northbridge, MA	B4	24
Northbrook, IL	h9	16
North Brother, ME	C4	22
North Brunswick, NJ	C4	33
North Canadian, r., OK	A5	39
North Canton, OH	B4	38
North Carolina, state, US	B3	36
North Cascades National Park, WA	A4	50
North Charleston, SC	F8	43
North Chicago, IL	A6	16
North Clarendon, VT	D3	48
North College Hill, OH	o12	38
North Conway, NH	B4	32
North Corbin, KY	D5	20
North Crossett, AR	D4	7
North Dakota, state, US	B5	37
North Eagle Butte, SD	B4	44
North East, PA	B2	41
Northeast Harbor, ME	D4	22
Northfield, MN	F5	26
Northfield, NH	D3	32
Northfield, VT	C3	48
Northfield Falls, VT	C3	48
North Fond du Lac, WI	E5	52
Northford, CT	D4	10
North Fort Myers, FL	F5	12
Northglenn, CO	B6	9
North Gulfport, MS	E4	27
North Hampton, NH	E5	32
North Haven, CT	D4	10
North Haven, ME	D4	22
North Hero Island, VT	B2	48
North Judson, IN	B4	17
North Kansas City, MO	h10	28
North Kingstown, RI	E4	42
Northlake, IL	k9	16
North Las Vegas, NV	G6	31
North Liberty, IN	A5	17
North Liberty, IA	C6	18
North Little Rock, AR	C3	7
North Manchester, IN	C6	17
North Manitou Island, MI	C4	25
North Mankato, MN	F4	26
North Miami, FL	G6	12
North Miami Beach, FL	s13	12
North Myrtle Beach, SC	D10	43
North Naples, FL	F5	12
North New River Canal, FL	F6	12
North Ogden, UT	B4	47
North Olmsted, OH	h9	38
North Park, IL	A4	16
North Pembroke, MA	B6	24
North Plainfield, NJ	B4	33
North Platte, NE	C5	30
North Platte, r., US	B7	2
North Point, MI	C7	25
North Pole, AK	C10	5
Northport, AL	B2	4
North Providence, RI	C4	42
North Raccoon, r., IA	C3	18
North Reading, MA	f11	24
North Richland Hills, TX	n9	46
Northridge, OH	C2	38
North Ridgeville, OH	A3	38
North Royalton, OH	h9	38
North Salem, NH	E4	32
North Salt Lake, UT	C4	47
North Sioux City, SD	E9	44
North Skunk, r., IA	C5	18
North Springfield, VT	E3	48
North St. Paul, MN	m13	26
North Stratford, NH	A3	32
North Sudbury, MA	g10	24
North Swanzey, NH	E2	32
North Syracuse, NY	B4	35
North Tarrytown, NY	D7	35
North Terre Haute, IN	E3	17
North Tonawanda, NY	B2	35
North Troy, VT	B4	48
North Turner Mountain, ME	C4	22
North Vernon, IN	F6	17
North Walpole, NH	D2	32
North Wilkesboro, NC	A1	36
North Windham, ME	E2	22
Northwood, IA	A4	18
Northwood, ND	B8	37
North Woodstock, NH	B3	32
Norton, KS	C4	19
Norton, OH	A4	38
Norton, VA	f9	49
Norton Shores, MI	E4	25
Norton Sound, AK	C6	5
Norwalk, CA	n12	8
Norwalk, CT	E2	10
Norwalk, IA	C4	18
Norwalk, OH	A3	38
Norwalk, r., CT	E2	10
Norway, ME	D2	22
Norwich, CT	C7	10
Norwich, NY	C5	35
Norwich, VT	D4	48
Norwood, MA	B5	24
Norwood, OH	o13	38
Norwood, PA	p20	41
Nottoway, r., VA	D5	49
Novato, CA	C2	8
Novi, MI	p15	25
Nowata, OK	A6	39
Nowood, r., WY	B5	53
Noxon Reservoir, MT	C1	29
Noxubee, r., US	B5	27
Nueces, r., TX	E3	46
Nulhegan, r., VT	B5	48
Nunivak Island, AK	D6	5
Nutley, NJ	B4	33
Nutter Fort, WV	k10	51

O

Name	Map Ref.	Page
Oahe, Lake, US	A7	2
Oahu, HI	B4	14
Oak Creek, WI	n12	52
Oakdale, LA	D3	21
Oakes, ND	C7	37
Oak Forest, IL	k9	16
Oak Grove, KY	D2	20
Oak Grove, OR	B4	40
Oak Harbor, WA	A3	50
Oak Hill, TN	A5	45
Oak Hill, WV	D3	51
Oakhurst, OK	A5	39
Oakland, CA	D2	8
Oakland, IA	C2	18
Oakland, ME	D3	22
Oakland, NE	C9	30
Oakland, NJ	A4	33
Oakland City, IN	H3	17
Oakland Park, FL	r13	12
Oak Lawn, IL	B6	16
Oaklawn, KS	g12	19
Oakley, KS	C3	19
Oakmont, PA	E2	41
Oak Park, IL	B6	16
Oak Park, MI	p15	25
Oakridge, OR	D4	40
Oak Ridge, TN	C9	45
Oakton, VA	g12	49
Oakville, CT	C3	10
Oakville, MO	g13	28
Oberlin, KS	C3	19
Oberlin, OH	A3	38
Obion, r., TN	A2	45
Ocala, FL	C4	12
Oceana, WV	D3	51
Ocean Bluff, MA	B6	24
Ocean City, MD	D7	23
Ocean City, NJ	E3	33
Oceanside, CA	F5	8
Ocean Springs, MS	E5	27
Ocean [Township], NJ	C4	33
Ochlockonee, r., FL	B2	12
Ocilla, GA	E3	13
Ocmulgee, r., GA	D3	13
Ocoee, FL	D5	12
Oconee, r., GA	C3	13
Oconee, Lake, GA	C3	13
Oconomowoc, WI	E5	52
Oconto, WI	D6	52
Oconto, r., WI	D5	52
Oconto Falls, WI	D5	52
Ocracoke Island, NC	B7	36
Odenton, MD	B4	23
Odessa, MO	C4	28
Odessa, TX	D1	46
Odon, IN	G4	17
Oelwein, IA	B6	18
O'Fallon, IL	E4	16
O'Fallon, MO	f12	28
Ogallala, NE	C4	30
Ogden, IA	B3	18
Ogden, KS	C7	19
Ogden, UT	B4	47
Ogdensburg, NY	f9	35
Ogeechee, r., GA	D5	13
Oglesby, IL	B4	16
Ohatchee, AL	B3	4
Ohio, state, US	B3	38
Ohio, r., US	C11	2
Oil City, PA	D2	41
Okeechobee, Lake, FL	F6	12
Okefenokee Swamp, US	F4	13
Okemah, OK	B5	39
Oklahoma, state, US	B4	39
Oklahoma City, OK	B4	39
Oklawaha, r., FL	C5	12
Oklawaha, Lake, FL	C5	12
Okmulgee, OK	B6	39
Okolona, KY	g11	20
Okolona, MS	B5	27
Ola, AR	B2	7
Olathe, CO	C3	9
Olathe, KS	D9	19
Old Bridge, NJ	C4	33
Old Faithful Geyser, WY	B2	53
Old Forge, PA	D10	41
Old Hickory Lake, TN	A5	45
Old Man of the Mountain, NH	B3	32
Old Orchard Beach, ME	E2	22
Old Point Comfort, VA	h15	49
Old Speck Mountain, ME	D2	22
Old Town, ME	D4	22
Olean, NY	C2	35
Olive Branch, MS	A4	27
Olive Hill, KY	B6	20
Oliver Springs, TN	C9	45
Olivia, MN	F4	26
Olmsted Falls, OH	h9	38
Olney, IL	E5	16
Olney, MD	B3	23
Olympia, WA	B3	50
Olympic Mountains, WA	B2	50
Olympic National Park, WA	B2	50
Olympus, Mount, WA	B2	50
Olyphant, PA	D10	41
Omaha, NE	C10	30
Omak, WA	A6	50
Omro, WI	D5	52
Onalaska, WI	E2	52
Onawa, IA	B1	18
Oneida, NY	B5	35
Oneida, TN	C9	45
Oneida Lake, NY	B5	35
O'Neill, NE	B7	30
Oneonta, AL	B3	4
Oneonta, NY	C5	35
Onida, SD	C5	44
Onslow Bay, NC	C5	36
Ontario, CA	E5	8
Ontario, OR	C10	40
Ontario, Lake, NA	B12	2
Ontonagon, MI	m12	25
Oolitic, IN	G4	17
Oologah Lake, OK	A6	39
Opa-Locka, FL	s13	12
Opelika, AL	C4	4
Opelousas, LA	D3	21
Opp, AL	D3	4
Opportunity, WA	B8	50
Optima Reservoir, OK	e9	39
Oracle, AZ	E5	6
Orange, CA	n13	8
Orange, CT	D3	10
Orange, NJ	B4	33
Orange, TX	D6	46
Orange Beach, AL	E2	4
Orangeburg, SC	E6	43
Orange City, IA	B1	18
Orange Grove, MS	E5	27
Orange Park, FL	B5	12
Orcas Island, WA	A3	50
Orchard City, CO	C3	9
Orchard Homes, MT	D2	29
Orchards, WA	D3	50
Orchard Valley, WY	E8	53
Ord, NE	C7	30
Oregon, IL	A4	16
Oregon, MO	B2	28
Oregon, OH	A2	38
Oregon, WI	F4	52
Oregon, state, US	C6	40
Oregon City, OR	B4	40
Orem, UT	C4	47
Orlando, FL	D5	12
Orland Park, IL	k9	16
Orleans, IN	G5	17
Orleans, VT	B4	48
Ormond Beach, FL	C5	12
Orofino, ID	C2	15
Orono, ME	D4	22
Oroville, Lake, CA	C3	8
Orrington, ME	D4	22
Orrville, OH	B4	38
Ortonville, MN	E2	26
Osage, IA	A5	18
Osage, r., MO	C3	28
Osage Beach, MO	C5	28
Osage City, KS	D8	19
Osawatomie, KS	D9	19
Osborne, KS	C5	19
Osburn, ID	B3	15
Osceola, AR	B6	7
Osceola, IN	A5	17
Osceola, IA	C4	18
Osceola, NE	C8	30
Osgood, IN	F7	17
Oshkosh, NE	C3	30
Oshkosh, WI	D5	52
Oskaloosa, IA	C5	18
Ossabaw Island, GA	E5	13
Ossian, IN	C7	17
Ossining, NY	D7	35
Ossipee, r., US	C5	32
Oswegatchie, r., NY	f9	35
Oswego, IL	B5	16
Oswego, KS	E8	19
Oswego, NY	B4	35
Othello, WA	C6	50
Otis Orchards, WA	g14	50
Ottawa, IL	B5	16
Ottawa, KS	D8	19
Ottawa Hills, OH	e6	38
Otter Creek, r., VT	C2	48
Otter Tail, r., MN	D2	26
Otter Tail Lake, MN	D3	26
Ottumwa, IA	C5	18
Ouachita, Lake, AR	C2	7
Ouachita Mountains, US	D9	2
Outer Island, WI	A3	52
Overland, MO	f13	28
Overland Park, KS	m16	19
Overlea, MD	B4	23
Owasco Lake, NY	C4	35
Owasso, OK	A6	39
Owatonna, MN	F5	26
Owens, r., CA	D4	8
Owensboro, KY	C2	20
Owens Lake, CA	D5	8
Owensville, MO	C6	28
Owings Mills, MD	B4	23
Owls Head, ME	D3	22
Owosso, MI	E6	25
Owyhee, NV	B5	31
Owyhee, r., US	E9	40
Owyhee, Lake, OR	D9	40
Owyhee Mountains, US	G2	15
Oxford, AL	B4	4
Oxford, KS	E6	19
Oxford, MA	B4	24
Oxford, MS	A4	27
Oxford, NE	D6	30
Oxford, NC	A4	36
Oxford, OH	C1	38
Oxnard, CA	E4	8
Oxon Hill, MD	f9	23
Oyster Bay, NY	E7	35
Ozark, AL	D4	4
Ozark, AR	B2	7
Ozark, MO	D4	28
Ozark Escarpment, US	B4	7
Ozark Plateau, US	C9	2
Ozark Reservoir, AR	B1	7
Ozarks, Lake of the, MO	C5	28

Name | Map Ref. | Page

P

Pacific, MO C7 28
Pacific, WA f11 50
Pacifica, CA h8 8
Pacific Grove, CA D3 8
Pacific Palisades, HI g10 14
Packwood, WA C4 50
Paddock Lake, WI n11 52
Paden City, WV B4 51
Padre Island, TX F4 46
Padre Island National Seashore, TX F4 46
Paducah, KY e9 20
Page, AZ A4 6
Pageland, SC B7 43
Pagoda Peak, CO A3 9
Pagosa Springs, CO D3 9
Pahrump, NV G6 31
Painesville, OH A4 38
Painted Desert, AZ B4 6
Painted Rock Reservoir, AZ D3 6
Paintsville, KY C7 20
Palatine, IL A5 16
Palatka, FL C5 12
Palestine, TX D5 46
Palisade, CO B2 9
Palisades Park, NJ h8 33
Palisades Reservoir, US F7 15
Palm Bay, FL D6 12
Palm Beach, FL F6 12
Palmdale, CA E4 8
Palm Desert, CA F5 8
Palmer, AK C10 5
Palmer, MS D4 27
Palmer Lake, CO B6 9
Palmerton, PA E10 41
Palmetto, GA C2 13
Palm Harbor, FL o10 12
Palm Springs, CA F5 8
Palm Valley, FL m9 12
Palmyra, MO B6 28
Palmyra, NJ C2 33
Palmyra, PA F8 41
Palo Alto, CA D2 8
Palos Park, IL k9 16
Palos Verdes Estates, CA n12 8
Palouse, r., WA C7 50
Pamlico, r., NC B6 36
Pamlico Sound, NC B6 36
Pampa, TX B2 46
Pamunkey, r., VA C5 49
Pana, IL D4 16
Panama City, FL u16 12
Paola, KS D9 19
Paoli, IN G5 17
Paoli, PA o20 41
Paonia, CO C3 9
Papillion, NE C9 30
Paradise, NV G6 31
Paradise Hills, NM B3 34
Paradise Valley, AZ k9 6
Paragould, AR A5 7
Paramus, NJ h8 33
Paris, AR B2 7
Paris, IL D6 16
Paris, KY B5 20
Paris, MO B5 28
Paris, TN A3 45
Paris, TX C5 46
Park City, KS g12 19
Park City, UT C4 47
Parker, AZ C1 6
Parker, CO B6 9
Parker, SD D8 44
Parker City, IN D7 17
Parkersburg, IA B5 18
Parkersburg, WV B3 51
Park Falls, WI C3 52
Park Forest, IL B6 16
Park Hills, KY h13 20
Parkin, AR B5 7
Parkland, WA f11 50
Park Range, CO A4 9
Park Rapids, MN D3 26
Park Ridge, IL B6 16
Park River, ND A8 37
Parkrose, OR B4 40
Parkston, SD D8 44
Parkville, MD B4 23
Parkville, MO B3 28
Parkwater, WA g14 50
Parkwood, NC B4 36
Parma, ID F2 15
Parma, OH A4 38
Parma Heights, OH h9 38
Parrish, AL B2 4
Parshall, ND B3 37
Parsons, KS E8 19
Parsons, WV B5 51
Pasadena, CA E4 8
Pasadena, MD B4 23
Pasadena, TX r14 46
Pascagoula, MS E5 27
Pascagoula, r., MS E5 27
Pasco, WA C6 50
Pascoag, RI B2 42
Passaic, NJ B4 33
Passaic, r., NJ h8 33
Passamaquoddy Bay, ME C6 22
Pass Christian, MS E4 27
Passumpsic, r., VT C4 48
Patapsco, r., MD B4 23
Patchogue, NY n15 35
Paterson, NJ B4 33
Pathfinder Reservoir, WY D6 53
Patoka, r., IN H2 17
Patoka Lake, IN H4 17
Patrick Air Force Base, FL D6 12
Patten, ME C4 22
Patterson, LA E4 21
Patuxent, r., MD D4 23
Paulina Peak, OR E5 40
Paulins Kill, r., NJ A3 33
Pauls Valley, OK C4 39
Pavlof Volcano, AK D7 5
Pawcatuck, CT D8 10
Pawcatuck, r., RI G1 42
Pawhuska, OK A5 39
Pawnee, OK A5 39
Pawnee City, NE D9 30
Paw Paw, MI F5 25
Pawtucket, RI C4 42
Pawtuxet, r., RI C4 42
Paxton, IL C5 16
Payette, ID E2 15
Paynesville, MN E4 26
Payson, AZ C4 6
Payson, UT C4 47
Pea, r., AL D3 4
Peabody, KS D6 19
Peabody, MA A6 24
Peace, r., FL E5 12
Peace Dale, RI F3 42
Peale, Mount, UT E6 47
Pea Ridge, AR A1 7
Pearl, MS C3 27
Pearl, r., US D3 27
Pearland, TX r14 46
Pearl City, HI B4 14
Pearl Harbor, HI B3 14
Pearl River, NY g12 35
Pecatonica, r., US A4 16
Pecos, NM B4 34
Pecos, TX D1 46
Pecos, r., US D7 2
Peekskill, NY D7 35
Pekin, IL C4 16
Pelahatchie, MS C4 27
Pelham, AL B3 4
Pelham, GA E2 13
Pelham, NH E4 32
Pelican Rapids, MN D2 26
Pella, IA C5 18
Pell City, AL B3 4
Peloncillo Mountains, US E1 34
Pemadumcook Lake, ME C3 22
Pembina, ND A8 37
Pembroke Pines, FL r13 12
Pemigewasset, r., NH C3 32
Pender, NE B9 30
Pendleton, IN E6 17
Pendleton, OR B8 40
Pendleton, SC B2 43
Pend Oreille, Lake, ID A2 15
Pennell, Mount, UT F5 47
Penn Hills, PA k14 41
Pennington Gap, VA f8 49
Pennsauken, NJ D2 33
Pennsboro, WV B4 51
Pennsville, NJ D1 33
Pennsylvania, state, US E7 41
Penobscot, r., ME C4 22
Penobscot Bay, ME D3 22
Pensacola, FL u14 12
Pentagon Mountain, MT C3 29
Peoria, AZ D3 6
Peoria, IL C4 16
Peoria Heights, IL C4 16
Peotone, IL B6 16
Pepin, Lake, US D1 52
Pepperell, MA A4 24
Pequannock, NJ B4 33
Pequot Lakes, MN D4 26
Perdido Bay, AL E2 4
Perham, MN D3 26
Perkasie, PA F11 41
Perrine, FL G6 12
Perry, FL B3 12
Perry, GA D3 13
Perry, IA C3 18
Perry, OK A4 39
Perry Hall, MD B5 23
Perry Lake, KS C8 19
Perrysburg, OH A2 38
Perryton, TX A2 46
Perryville, AR B3 7
Perryville, MO D8 28
Perth Amboy, NJ B4 33
Peru, IL B4 16
Peru, IN C5 17
Peru, NE D10 30
Peshtigo, WI C6 52
Peshtigo, r., WI C5 52
Petal, MS D4 27
Petenwell Lake, WI D4 52
Peterborough, NH E3 32
Petersburg, AK D13 5
Petersburg, IN H3 17
Petersburg, VA C5 49
Petersburg, WV B5 51
Petersville, AL A2 4
Petit Bois Island, MS E5 27
Petit Jean, r., AR B2 7
Petoskey, MI C6 25
Petrified Forest National Park, AZ B6 6
Pevely, MO g13 28
Pewaukee, WI E5 52
Pharr, TX F3 46
Phelps Lake, NC B6 36
Phenix City, AL C4 4
Philadelphia, MS C4 27
Philadelphia, PA G11 41
Phil Campbell, AL A2 4
Philip, SD C4 44
Philippi, WV B4 51
Philipsburg, MT D3 29
Phillips, ME D2 22
Phillipsburg, KS C4 19
Phillipsburg, NJ B2 33
Philomath, OR C3 40
Philpott Reservoir, VA D2 49
Phoenix, AZ D3 6
Phoenix, OR E4 40
Phoenixville, PA F10 41
Picayune, MS E4 27
Pickerington, OH C3 38
Pickwick Lake, US A6 27
Pico Rivera, CA n12 8
Pictured Rocks National Lakeshore, MI B4 25
Piedmont, AL B4 4
Piedmont, MO D7 28
Piedmont, OK B4 39
Piedmont, SC B3 43
Piedmont, WV B5 51
Pierce, NE B8 30
Pierce, Lake, FL E5 12
Pierce City, MO E3 28
Pierre, SD C5 44
Pierre Part, LA k9 21
Pigeon, MI E7 25
Pigeon Forge, TN D10 45
Pigeon Point, MN h10 26
Pigg, r., VA D3 49
Piggott, AR A5 7
Pikes Peak, CO C5 9
Pikesville, MD B4 23
Pikeville, KY C7 20
Pilot Peak, NV B7 31
Pima, AZ E6 6
Pimmit Hills, VA g12 49
Pinardville, NH E3 32
Pinckney, MI F7 25
Pinckneyville, IL E4 16
Pinconning, MI E7 25
Pine Barrens, NJ D3 33
Pine Bluff, AR C3 7
Pine Bluffs, WY E8 53
Pine City, MN E6 26
Pine Creek Lake, OK C6 39
Pinedale, WY D3 53
Pinefield, MD C4 23
Pine Hills, FL D5 12
Pinehurst, NC B3 36
Pine Island, MN F6 26
Pine Knot, KY D5 20
Pine Lawn, MO f13 28
Pinellas Park, FL E4 12
Pine Mountain, US D6 20
Pine Ridge, SD D3 44
Pines, Lake O' the, TX C5 46
Pineville, KY D6 20
Pineville, LA C3 21
Pineville, NC B2 36
Piney View, WV n13 51
Pinson, AL f7 4
Pioche, NV F7 31
Pipestone, MN G2 26
Pipestone National Monument, MN G2 26
Piqua, OH B1 38
Piscataway, NJ B4 33
Pisgah, AL A4 4
Pisgah, OH n13 38
Pismo Beach, CA E3 8
Pittsburg, KS E9 19
Pittsburgh, PA F1 41
Pittsfield, IL D3 16
Pittsfield, ME D3 22
Pittsfield, MA B1 24
Pittsfield, NH D4 32
Pittsford, VT D2 48
Pittston, PA D10 41
Placitas, NM B3 34
Plainfield, CT C8 10
Plainfield, IL B5 16
Plainfield, IN E5 17
Plainfield, NJ B4 33
Plainfield, VT C4 48
Plains, MT C2 29
Plains, PA n17 41
Plainview, MN F6 26
Plainview, NE B8 30
Plainview, TX B2 46
Plainville, CT C4 10
Plainville, KS C4 19
Plainwell, MI F5 25
Plaistow, NH E4 32
Plano, IL B5 16
Plano, TX C4 46
Plantation, FL r13 12
Plant City, FL D4 12
Plantsville, CT C4 10
Plaquemine, LA D4 21
Platte, SD D7 44
Platte, r., US B3 28
Platte, r., NE D6 30
Platte City, MO B3 28
Platteville, CO A6 9
Platteville, WI F3 52
Plattsburg, MO B3 28
Plattsburgh, NY f11 35
Plattsmouth, NE D10 30
Pleasant Grove, AL g7 4
Pleasant Grove, UT C4 47
Pleasant Hill, IA e8 18
Pleasant Hill, MO C3 28
Pleasanton, CA h9 8
Pleasanton, KS D9 19
Pleasant Prairie, WI n12 52
Pleasantville, IA C4 18
Pleasantville, NJ E3 33
Pleasantville, NY D7 35
Pleasure Ridge Park, KY g11 20
Plentywood, MT B12 29
Plover, WI D4 52
Plum, PA k14 41
Plum Bayou, r., AR k10 7
Plymouth, IN B5 17
Plymouth, MA C6 24
Plymouth, MI p15 25
Plymouth, MN m12 26
Plymouth, NH C3 32
Plymouth, NC B6 36
Plymouth, PA D10 41
Plymouth, WI E6 52
Plymouth Bay, MA C6 24
Pocahontas, AR A5 7
Pocahontas, IA B3 18
Pocatalico, WV C3 51
Pocatello, ID G6 15
Pocola, OK B7 39
Pocomoke, r., MD D7 23
Pocomoke Sound, MD E6 23
Pocono Mountains, PA E11 41
Point Clear, AL E2 4
Point Hope, AK B6 5
Point Pleasant, NJ C4 33
Point Pleasant, WV C2 51
Polk City, IA C4 18
Polson, MT C2 29
Pomme de Terre Lake, MO D4 28
Pomona, CA E5 8
Pompano Beach, FL F6 12
Pompton Lakes, NJ A4 33
Ponca, NE B9 30
Ponca City, OK A4 39
Ponchatoula, LA D5 21
Pontchartrain, Lake, LA D5 21
Pontiac, IL C5 16
Pontiac, MI F7 25
Pontotoc, MS A4 27
Pooler, GA D5 13
Poplar, MT B11 29
Poplar Bluff, MO E7 28
Poplarville, MS E4 27
Poquonock Bridge, CT D7 10
Poquoson, VA C6 49
Porcupine Mountains, MI m12 25
Portage, IN A3 17
Portage, ME B4 22
Portage, MI F5 25
Portage, WI E4 52
Portage Lakes, OH B4 38
Portageville, MO E8 28
Portales, NM C6 34
Port Allen, LA D4 21
Port Angeles, WA A2 50
Port Arthur, TX E6 46
Port Charlotte, FL F4 12
Port Chester, NY E7 35
Port Clinton, OH A3 38
Port Clyde, ME E3 22
Porte Crayon, Mount, WV C5 51
Porter, IN A3 17
Port Gibson, MS D3 27
Port Huron, MI F8 25
Port Jervis, NY D6 35
Portland, CT C5 10
Portland, IN D8 17
Portland, ME E2 22
Portland, MI F6 25
Portland, ND B8 37
Portland, OR B4 40
Portland, TN A5 45
Portland, TX F4 46
Port Lavaca, TX E4 46
Port Neches, TX E6 46
Port Orange, FL C6 12
Port Orchard, WA B3 50
Port Royal, SC G6 43
Port Royal Sound, SC G6 43
Port Saint Lucie, FL E6 12
Portsmouth, NH D5 32
Portsmouth, OH D3 38
Portsmouth, RI E6 42
Portsmouth, VA D6 49
Port Sulphur, LA E6 21
Port Townsend, WA A3 50
Port Washington, NY h13 35
Port Washington, WI E6 52
Port Wentworth, GA D5 13
Posen, IL k9 16
Post Falls, ID B2 15
Postville, IA A6 18
Poteau, OK B7 39
Potholes Reservoir, WA B6 50
Potomac, MD B3 23
Potomac, r., US D4 23
Potosi, MO D7 28
Potsdam, NY f10 35
Pottstown, PA F10 41
Pottsville, AR B2 7
Pottsville, PA E9 41
Poughkeepsie, NY D7 35
Poulsbo, WA B3 50
Poultney, VT D2 48
Pound Gap, US C7 20
Poway, CA F5 8
Powder, r., US A6 2
Powder Springs, GA h8 13
Powell, TN m13 45
Powell, WY B4 53
Powell, Lake, US F5 47
Powell Mountain, US C10 45
Powell's Crossroads, AL A4 4
Powellton, WV C3 51
Poygan, Lake, WI D5 52
Prairie City, IA C4 18
Prairie du Chien, WI E2 52
Prairie du Sac, WI E4 52
Prairie Grove, AR B1 7
Prairie Village, KS m16 19
Pratt, KS E5 19
Prattville, AL C3 4
Prentiss, MS D4 27
Prescott, AZ C3 6
Prescott, AR D2 7
Prescott, WI D1 52
Presidential Range, NH B4 32
Presidio, TX p12 46
Presque Isle, ME B5 22
Preston, ID G7 15
Prestonsburg, KY C7 20
Prettyboy Reservoir, MD A4 23
Pribilof Islands, AK D5 5
Price, UT D5 47
Priceville, AL A3 4
Prichard, AL E1 4
Priest Lake, ID A2 15
Priest Rapids Lake, WA C6 50
Priest River, ID A2 15
Prince of Wales, Cape, AK B6 5
Prince of Wales Island, AK n23 5
Princeton, IL B4 16
Princeton, IN H2 17
Princeton, KY C2 20
Princeton, MN E5 26
Princeton, MO A4 28
Princeton, NJ C3 33
Princeton, WV D3 51
Princeton, Mount, CO C4 9
Prince William Sound, AK g18 5
Prineville, OR C6 40
Prior Lake, MN F5 26
Proctor, MN D6 26
Proctor, VT D2 48
Proctorsville, VT E3 48
Prospect, CT C4 10
Prospect, KY g11 20
Prospect Harbor, ME D4 22
Prospect Park, PA p20 41
Prosperity, WV n13 51
Prosser, WA C6 50
Providence, KY C2 20
Providence, RI C4 42
Providence, r., RI C5 42
Provincetown, MA B7 24
Provo, UT C4 47
Provo, r., UT C4 47
Prudence Island, RI E5 42
Pryor, OK A6 39
Pueblo, CO C6 9
Pueblo Mountain, OR E8 40
Pueblo of Acoma, NM C2 34
Puerco, r., US C6 6
Puget Sound, WA B3 50
Pukalani, HI C5 14
Pulaski, TN B4 45
Pulaski, VA C2 49
Pullman, WA C8 50
Pumphrey, MD h11 23
Punta Gorda, FL F4 12
Punxsutawney, PA E4 41
Purcell, OK B4 39
Purgatoire Peak, CO D5 9
Purvis, MS D4 27
Putnam, CT B8 10
Putney, VT F3 48
Puyallup, WA B3 50
Pymatuning Reservoir, US C1 41
Pyramid Lake, NV C2 31

Q

Quabbin Reservoir, MA B3 24
Quakertown, PA F11 41
Quartzsite, AZ D1 6
Quechee, VT D4 48
Questa, NM A4 34
Quidnessett, RI E4 42
Quidnick, RI D3 42
Quinault, r., WA B1 50
Quincy, IL D2 16
Quincy, MA B5 24
Quincy, WA B6 50
Quinebaug, r., CT C8 10
Quinhagak, AK D7 5
Quinn, r., NV B3 31
Quinnipiac, r., CT D4 10
Quitman, GA F3 13
Quitman, MS C5 27

R

Raceland, KY B7 20
Raceland, LA E5 21
Race Point, MA B7 24
Racine, WI F6 52
Radcliff, KY C4 20
Radford, VA C2 49
Raeford, NC C3 36
Raft, r., ID G5 15
Raft River Mountains, UT B2 47
Rahway, NJ B4 33
Rainbow Bridge National Monument, UT F5 47
Rainelle, WV D4 51
Rainier, Mount, WA C4 50
Rainsville, AL A4 4
Rainy Lake, MN B5 26
Raleigh, NC B4 36
Raleigh Bay, NC C6 36
Ralston, NE g12 30
Ramapo, r., NJ A4 33
Ramsey, NJ A4 33
Ramshorn Peak, MT E5 29
Ranchester, WY B5 53
Ranchos de Taos, NM A4 34
Rand, WV C3 51
Randallstown, MD B4 23
Randolph, MA B5 24
Randolph, NE B8 30
Randolph, VT D3 48
Randolph Hills, MD B3 23
Rangeley, ME D2 22
Rangely, CO A2 9
Ranson, WV B7 51
Rantoul, IL C5 16
Rapid City, SD C2 44
Raquette, r., NY f10 35
Raritan, r., NJ C4 33
Raritan Bay, NJ C4 33
Rathbun Lake, IA D5 18
Rathdrum, ID B2 15
Raton, NM A5 34
Raton Pass, NM A5 34
Ravenna, NE C7 30
Ravenna, OH A4 38
Ravenswood, WV C3 51
Rawlins, WY E5 53
Ray, ND A2 37
Raymond, ME E2 22
Raymond, NH D4 32
Raymond, WA C2 50
Raymondville, TX F4 46
Raymore, MO C3 28
Rayne, LA D3 21
Raynham, MA C5 24
Raytown, MO h11 28
Rayville, LA B4 21
Readfield, ME D3 22
Reading, MA A5 24
Reading, OH C1 38
Reading, PA F10 41
Rector, AR A5 7
Red, r., NA A8 2
Red, r., US D9 2
Red, r., KY C6 20
Red, r., TN A4 45
Red Bank, NJ C4 33
Red Bank, SC D5 43
Red Bank, TN D8 45
Red Bay, AL A1 4
Red Bluff Lake, US o12 46
Red Cedar, r., WI C2 52
Red Cloud, NE D7 30
Redcloud Peak, CO D3 9
Redding, CA B2 8
Redfield, AR C3 7
Redfield, SD C7 44
Redford, MI F7 25
Redkey, IN D7 17
Red Lake, AZ B1 6
Red Lake, r., MN C2 26
Red Lake Indian Reservation, MN B3 26
Redlands, CA E5 8
Red Lion, PA G8 41
Red Lodge, MT E7 29
Redmond, OR C5 40
Redmond, WA e11 50
Red Mountain, MT C4 29
Red Oak, GA h7 13
Red Oak, IA D2 18
Redondo Beach, CA n12 8
Redoubt Volcano, AK g15 5
Red Rock, Lake, IA C4 18
Red Springs, NC C3 36
Red Wing, MN F6 26
Redwood City, CA D2 8
Redwood Falls, MN F3 26
Redwood National Park, CA B2 8
Reed City, MI E5 25
Reedsburg, WI E3 52
Reedsport, OR D2 40
Reelfoot Lake, TN A2 45
Reese, r., NV C4 31
Rehoboth Bay, DE F5 11
Rehoboth Beach, DE F5 11
Reidland, KY e9 20
Reidsville, GA D4 13
Reidsville, NC A3 36
Reinbeck, IA B5 18
Reisterstown, MD B4 23
Reliance, WY E3 53
Remsen, IA B2 18
Rend Lake, IL E5 16
Reno, NV D2 31
Rensselaer, IN C3 17
Rensselaer, NY C7 35
Renton, WA B3 50
Republic, MO D4 28
Republican, r., US C6 19
Reserve, LA h10 21
Reston, VA B5 49
Revere, MA g11 24
Rexburg, ID F7 15
Reyes, Point, CA C2 8
Reynoldsburg, OH C3 38
Rhinelander, WI C4 52
Rhode Island, state, US D3 42
Rhode Island, RI E5 42
Rhode Island Sound, US F5 42
Rialto, CA m14 8
Rib Mountain, WI D4 52
Rice Lake, WI C2 52
Richardson, TX n10 46
Richardson Lakes, ME D2 22
Richardton, ND C3 37
Richfield, MN F5 26
Richfield, UT E3 47
Richford, VT B3 48
Richland, MO D5 28
Richland, WA C6 50
Richland Balsam, NC f10 36
Richland Center, WI E3 52
Richlands, VA e10 49
Richmond, CA D2 8
Richmond, IN E8 17
Richmond, KY C5 20
Richmond, ME D3 22
Richmond, MO B4 28
Richmond, TX E5 46
Richmond, VT C3 48
Richmond, VA C5 49
Richmond Heights, MO f13 28
Richmond Hill, GA E5 13
Richwood, WV C4 51
Ridgefield, CT D2 10
Ridgefield Park, NJ B4 33
Ridgeland, MS C3 27
Ridgewood, NJ B4 33
Ridgway, PA D4 41
Ridley Park, PA p20 41
Riffe Lake, WA C3 50
Rifle, CO B3 9
Rigby, ID F7 15
Rincon, GA D5 13
Ringwood, NJ A4 33
Rio Grande 20 Grande, Rio, r., NA E7 2
Rio Grande City, TX F3 46
Rio Rancho, NM B3 34
Ripley, MS A5 27
Ripley, TN B2 45
Ripley, WV C3 51
Ripon, WI E5 52
Rising Sun, IN G8 17
Rison, AR D3 7
Ritter, Mount, CA D4 8
Rittman, OH B4 38
Rivanna, r., VA C4 49
Riverdale, IL k9 16
Riverdale, MD C4 23
River Edge, NJ h8 33
River Falls, WI D1 52
River Forest, IL k9 16
River Grove, IL k9 16
Riverhead, NY n16 35
River Pines, MA f10 24
River Ridge, LA k11 21
River Road, OR C3 40
River Rouge, MI p15 25
Riverside, AL B3 4
Riverside, CA F5 8
Riverside, IL k9 16
Riverton, UT C4 47
Riverton, WY C4 53
Riverton Heights, WA f11 50
Riverview, MI p15 25
Rivesville, WV B4 51
Riviera Beach, FL F6 12
Riviera Beach, MD B4 23
Roanoke, AL B4 4
Roanoke, VA C3 49
Roanoke, r., US A5 36
Roanoke Rapids, NC A5 36
Roaring Fork, r., CO C4 9
Robbins, IL k9 16
Robbinsdale, MN m12 26
Roberts, MT E7 29
Robertsdale, AL E2 4
Robert S. Kerr Reservoir, OK B6 39
Roberts Mountain, WY D3 53
Robinson, IL D6 16
Robstown, TX F4 46
Rochelle, IL B4 16
Rochester, IN B5 17
Rochester, MN F6 26
Rochester, NH D5 32
Rochester, NY B3 35
Rochester, VT D3 48
Rock, r., US B3 16
Rock, r., US A1 18
Rock Creek Butte, OR C8 40
Rockdale, MD B4 23
Rock Falls, IL B4 16
Rockford, IL A4 16
Rock Hill, SC B5 43
Rockingham, NC C3 36
Rock Island, IL B3 16
Rockland, ME D3 22
Rockland, MA B6 24
Rockledge, FL D6 12
Rockmart, GA B1 13
Rockport, IN I3 17
Rockport, MA A6 24
Rock Port, MO A2 28
Rock Rapids, IA A1 18
Rock Springs, WY E3 53
Rockton, IL A4 16
Rock Valley, IA A1 18
Rockville, IN E3 17
Rockville, MD B3 23
Rockville Centre, NY n15 35
Rockwall, TX C4 46
Rockwell City, IA B3 18
Rockwood, TN D9 45
Rocky Ford, CO C7 9
Rocky Hill, CT C5 10
Rocky Mount, NC B5 36
Rocky Mount, VA D3 49
Rocky Mountain, MT C4 29
Rocky Mountain National Park, CO A5 9
Rocky River, OH A4 38
Roderfield, WV D3 51
Rodney Village, DE D3 11
Roeland Park, KS k16 19
Rogers, AR A1 7
Rogers, Mount, VA f10 49
Rogersville, AL A2 4
Rogersville, TN C10 45
Rogue, r., OR E2 40
Rohnert Park, CA C2 8
Roland, OK B7 39
Rolette, ND A6 37
Rolla, MO D6 28
Rolla, ND A6 37
Rolling Fork, MS C3 27
Rolling Fork, r., KY C4 20
Rolling Meadows, IL h8 16
Rollinsford, NH D5 32
Roma, TX F3 46
Roman Nose Mountain, MD m12 23
Romanzof, Cape, AK C6 5
Rome, GA B1 13
Rome, NY B5 35
Romeo, MI F7 25
Romeoville, IL k8 16
Romney, WV B6 51
Romulus, MI p15 25
Ronan, MT C2 29
Ronceverte, WV D4 51
Roosevelt, UT C5 47
Rose, Mount, NV D2 31
Roseau, MN B3 26
Rosebud, SD D5 44
Roseburg, OR D3 40
Rosedale, MD g11 23
Rosedale, MS B2 27
Rose Hill, KS E6 19
Roselle, IL k8 16
Roselle, NJ k7 33
Roselle Park, NJ k7 33
Rosemount, MN F5 26
Rosenberg, TX E5 46
Roseville, MI o16 25
Roseville, MN m12 26
Rosewood Heights, IL E3 16
Ross Barnett Reservoir, MS C3 27
Rossford, OH A2 38
Ross Lake National Recreation Area, WA A5 50
Rossville, GA B1 13
Roswell, GA B2 13
Roswell, NM D5 34
Rothschild, WI D4 52
Rotterdam, NY C6 35
Rough River Lake, KY C3 20
Round Lake, IL h8 16
Round Lake Beach, IL h8 16
Round Rock, TX D4 46
Roundup, MT D8 29
Roxboro, NC A4 36
Roy, UT B3 47
Royale, Isle, MI h9 25
Royal Gorge, CO C5 9
Royal Oak, MI F7 25
Royersford, PA F10 41
Royston, GA B3 13
Rubidoux, CA n14 8
Ruby Dome, NV C6 31
Rufus Woods Lake, WA A6 50
Rugby, ND A6 37
Ruidoso, NM D4 34
Ruidoso Downs, NM D4 34
Ruleville, MS B3 27
Rumford, ME D2 22
Rupert, ID G5 15
Rupert, WV D4 51
Rushville, IL C3 16
Rushville, IN E7 17
Rushville, NE B3 30
Russell, KS D5 19
Russell, KY B7 20
Russell Springs, KY C4 20
Russellville, AL A2 4
Russellville, AR B2 7
Russellville, KY D3 20
Russian, r., CA C2 8
Ruston, LA B3 21
Rutherford, NJ B4 33
Rutherfordton, NC B1 36
Rutland, VT D3 48
Rye, NH D5 32
Rye, NY h13 35
Rye Beach, NH E5 32

S

Sabattus, ME D2 22
Sabetha, KS C8 19
Sabine, r., US D6 46
Sabine Lake, US E2 21
Sable, Cape, FL G5 12
Sacajawea, Lake, WA C7 50
Sacajawea Peak, OR B9 40
Sac City, IA B2 18
Saco, ME E2 22

Name	Map Ref.	Page
Saco, r., US	E2	22
Sacramento, CA	C3	8
Sacramento, r., CA	C3	8
Sacramento Mountains, NM	E4	34
Sacramento Valley, AZ	B1	6
Sacramento Valley, CA	C2	8
Saddle Ball Mountain, MA	A1	24
Saddle Brook, NJ	h8	33
Safety Harbor, FL	E4	12
Safford, AZ	E6	6
Saginaw, MI	E7	25
Saginaw, TX	n9	46
Saginaw Bay, MI	E7	25
Saint Agatha, ME	A4	22
Saint Albans, VT	B2	48
Saint Albans, WV	C3	51
Saint Andrews, SC	F7	43
Saint Anthony, ID	F7	15
Saint Augustine, FL	C5	12
Saint Bernard, AL	A3	4
Saint Catherines Island, GA	E5	13
Saint Charles, IL	B5	16
Saint Charles, MD	C4	23
Saint Charles, MN	G6	26
Saint Charles, MO	C7	28
Saint Clair, MI	F8	25
Saint Clair, MO	C6	28
Saint Clair Shores, MI	p16	25
Saint Cloud, FL	D5	12
Saint Cloud, MN	E4	26
Saint Croix, r., US	C1	52
Saint Edward, NE	C8	30
Saint Elias, Cape, AK	D11	5
Saint Francis, KS	C2	19
Saint Francis, SD	D5	44
Saint Francis, WI	n12	52
Saint Francis, r., US	A5	7
Saint Francois Mountains, MO	D7	28
Sainte Genevieve, MO	D7	28
Saint George, UT	F2	47
Saint George, Cape, FL	C1	12
Saint George Island, AK	D6	5
Saint Helena Island, SC	G6	43
Saint Helens, OR	B4	40
Saint Helens, Mount, WA	C3	50
Saint Ignace, MI	C6	25
Saint Ignatius, MT	C2	29
Saint James, MN	G4	26
Saint James, MO	D6	28
Saint Joe, r., ID	B3	15
Saint John, IN	B3	17
Saint John, KS	E5	19
Saint Johns, AZ	C6	6
Saint Johns, MI	F6	25
Saint Johns, r., FL	B5	12
Saint Johnsbury, VT	C4	48
Saint Johnsbury Center, VT	C4	48
Saint Jones, r., DE	D4	11
Saint Joseph, MI	F4	25
Saint Joseph, MN	E4	26
Saint Joseph, MO	B3	28
Saint Joseph, r., US	F5	25
Saint Joseph Bay, FL	C1	12
Saint Joseph Point, FL	v16	12
Saint Lawrence Island, AK	C5	5
Saint Louis, MI	E6	25
Saint Louis, MO	C7	28
Saint Louis, r., US	D6	26
Saint Louis Bay, MS	f7	27
Saint Louis Park, MN	n12	26
Saint Lucie Canal, FL	F6	12
Saint Maries, ID	B2	15
Saint Martinville, LA	D4	21
Saint Marys, GA	F5	13
Saint Marys, IN	A5	17
Saint Marys, KS	C7	19
Saint Marys, OH	B1	38
Saint Marys, PA	D4	41
Saint Marys, WV	B3	51
Saint Marys, r., US	F5	13
Saint Marys, r., US	C8	17
Saint Matthew Island, AK	C5	5
Saint Matthews, KY	B4	20
Saint Paul, MN	F5	26
Saint Paul, NE	C7	30
Saint Paul Island, AK	D5	5
Saint Paul Park, MN	n12	26
Saint Peter, MN	F5	26
Saint Peters, MO	C7	28
Saint Petersburg, FL	E4	12
Saint Simons Island, GA	E5	13
Saint Simons Island, GA	E5	13
Sakakawea, Lake, ND	B3	37
Sakonnet, r., RI	E6	42
Sakonnet Point, RI	F6	42
Salamonie, r., IN	C6	17
Salamonie Lake, IN	C6	17
Salem, AR	A4	7
Salem, IL	E5	16
Salem, IN	G5	17
Salem, MA	A6	24
Salem, MO	D6	28
Salem, NH	E4	32
Salem, OH	B5	38
Salem, OR	C4	40
Salem, SD	D8	44
Salem, VA	C2	49
Salem, WV	B4	51
Salida, CO	C5	9
Salina, KS	D6	19
Salina, UT	E4	47
Salinas, CA	D3	8
Saline, MI	F7	25
Saline, r., AR	D4	7
Saline, r., KS	C5	19
Salisbury, MD	D6	23
Salisbury, MA	A6	24
Salisbury, MO	B5	28
Salisbury, NC	B2	36
Salkehatchie, r., SC	E5	43
Sallisaw, OK	B7	39
Salmon, ID	D5	15
Salmon, r., ID	D3	15
Salmon Creek, WA	D3	50
Salmon Falls, r., US	D5	32
Salmon River Mountains, ID	E3	15
Salt, r., AZ	D4	6
Salt, r., KY	C4	20
Salt, r., MO	B6	28
Salt Fork Lake, OH	B4	38
Saltillo, MS	A5	27
Salt Lake, HI	g10	14
Salt Lake City, UT	C4	47
Salton Sea, CA	F5	8
Saluda, r., SC	C4	43
Salvador, Lake, LA	E5	21
Salyersville, KY	C6	20
Sam Rayburn Reservoir, TX	D5	46
Samson, AL	D3	4
Samtown, LA	C3	21
San Agustin, Plains of, NM	C2	34
San Angelo, TX	D2	46
San Antonio, TX	E3	46
San Antonio Bay, TX	E4	46
San Antonio Mountain, NM	A3	34
San Benito, TX	F4	46
San Bernardino, CA	E5	8
San Blas, Cape, FL	v16	12
Sanborn, IA	A2	18
Sanbornville, NH	C4	32
San Bruno, CA	D2	8
San Carlos, AZ	D5	6
San Clemente, CA	F5	8
San Clemente Island, CA	F4	8
Sandersville, GA	D4	13
Sandia Mountains, NM	k8	34
San Diego, CA	F5	8
Sand Island, HI	g10	14
Sand Mountain, US	A3	4
Sandpoint, ID	A2	15
Sand Springs, OK	A5	39
Sandston, VA	m18	49
Sandstone, MN	D6	26
Sandusky, OH	A3	38
Sandusky, r., OH	B2	38
Sandusky Bay, OH	A3	38
Sandwich, IL	B5	16
Sandwich, MA	C7	24
Sandy, OR	B4	40
Sandy, UT	C4	47
Sandy Hook, NJ	C5	33
Sandy Springs, GA	h8	13
San Felipe Pueblo, NM	B3	34
San Fernando, CA	m12	8
Sanford, FL	D5	12
Sanford, ME	E2	22
Sanford, NC	B3	36
Sanford, Mount, AK	C11	5
San Francisco, CA	D2	8
San Francisco Bay, CA	h8	8
San Gabriel Mountains, CA	m12	8
Sangamon, r., IL	C3	16
Sanibel Island, FL	F4	12
San Jacinto, CA	F5	8
San Joaquin, r., CA	D3	8
San Joaquin Valley, CA	D3	8
San Jose, CA	D3	8
San Jose Island, TX	E4	46
San Juan, TX	F3	46
San Juan, r., US	C6	2
San Juan Capistrano, CA	F5	8
San Juan Island, WA	A2	50
San Juan Mountains, CO	D3	9
San Leandro, CA	h8	8
San Luis, AZ	E1	6
San Luis Obispo, CA	E3	8
San Luis Valley, CO	D4	9
San Manuel, AZ	E5	6
San Marcos, TX	E4	46
San Mateo, CA	D2	8
San Pablo, CA	h8	8
San Pedro, r., AZ	E5	6
San Pedro Peaks, NM	A3	34
Sanpoil, r., WA	A7	50
San Rafael, CA	D2	8
San Rafael, r., UT	D5	47
San Simon, r., AZ	E6	6
Santa Ana, CA	F5	8
Santa Barbara, CA	E4	8
Santa Catalina Island, CA	F4	8
Santa Clara, CA	D2	8
Santa Cruz, CA	D2	8
Santa Cruz, NM	B3	34
Santa Cruz, r., AZ	E4	6
Santa Cruz Island, CA	F4	8
Santa Fe, NM	B4	34
Santa Fe, TX	r14	46
Santa Maria, CA	E3	8
Santa Maria, r., AZ	C2	6
Santa Monica, CA	m12	8
Santa Paula, CA	E4	8
Santa Rosa, CA	C2	8
Santa Rosa, NM	C5	34
Santa Rosa Island, CA	F3	8
Santa Teresa, NM	F3	34
Santee, CA	o16	8
Santee, r., SC	E8	43
Santiam Pass, OR	C4	40
Santo Domingo Pueblo, NM	B3	34
Sapelo Island, GA	E5	13
Sapulpa, OK	B5	39
Saraland, AL	E1	4
Saranac, r., NY	F11	35
Saranac Lake, NY	f10	35
Sarasota, FL	E4	12
Sarasota Bay, FL	E4	12
Saratoga, CA	k8	8
Saratoga, WY	E6	53
Saratoga National Historical Park, NY	B7	35
Saratoga Springs, NY	B7	35
Sarcoxie, MO	D3	28
Sardis, MS	A4	27
Sardis Lake, MS	A4	27
Sargent, NE	C6	30
Sartell, MN	E4	26
Sassafras Mountain, US	A2	43
Satilla, r., GA	E5	13
Satsuma, AL	E1	4
Saugus, MA	B5	24
Sauk, r., WA	A4	50
Sauk Centre, MN	E4	26
Sauk City, WI	E4	52
Sauk Rapids, MN	E4	26
Saukville, WI	E6	52
Sault Sainte Marie, MI	B6	25
Sausalito, CA	D2	8
Savage, r., MD	k12	23
Savanna, IL	A3	16
Savannah, GA	D5	13
Savannah, MO	B3	28
Savannah, TN	B3	45
Savannah, r., US	F5	13
Sawtooth Mountains, ID	F4	15
Saxtons River, VT	E3	48
Saydel, IA	e8	18
Saylesville, RI	B4	42
Saylorville Lake, IA	C4	18
Sayre, OK	B2	39
Sayre, PA	C8	41
Sayreville, NJ	C4	33
Sayville, NY	n15	35
Scapegoat Mountain, MT	C3	29
Scappoose, OR	B4	40
Scarborough, ME	E2	22
Scarsdale, NY	h13	35
Schaumburg, IL	h8	16
Schell Creek Range, NV	D7	31
Schenectady, NY	C7	35
Schererville, IN	B3	17
Schertz, TX	h7	46
Schiller Park, IL	k9	16
Schofield, WI	D4	52
Schofield Barracks, HI	g9	14
Schuyler, NE	C8	30
Schuylkill, r., PA	F10	41
Schuylkill Haven, PA	E9	41
Scioto, r., OH	B2	38
Scituate, MA	B6	24
Scituate Reservoir, RI	C3	42
Scobey, MT	B11	29
Scotch Plains, NJ	B4	33
Scotia, NY	C7	35
Scotland, SD	D8	44
Scotlandville, LA	D4	21
Scott, LA	D3	21
Scott, Mount, OR	E4	40
Scott City, KS	D3	19
Scott City, MO	D8	28
Scottdale, GA	h8	13
Scottdale, PA	F2	41
Scottsbluff, NE	C2	30
Scotts Bluff National Monument, NE	C2	30
Scottsboro, AL	A3	4
Scottsburg, IN	G6	17
Scottsdale, AZ	D4	6
Scottsville, KY	D3	20
Scranton, PA	D10	41
Scribner, NE	C9	30
Seabrook, NH	E5	32
Seaford, DE	F3	11
Seaford, VA	h15	49
Seagoville, TX	n10	46
Searcy, AR	B4	7
Seaside, OR	B3	40
Seat Pleasant, MD	C4	23
Seattle, WA	B3	50
Sebastian, FL	E6	12
Sebec Lake, ME	C3	22
Sebree, KY	C2	20
Secaucus, NJ	h8	33
Section, AL	A4	4
Security, CO	C6	9
Sedalia, MO	C4	28
Sedan, KS	E7	19
Sedgwick, KS	E6	19
Sedona, AZ	C4	6
Sedro Woolley, WA	A3	50
Seekonk, MA	C5	24
Seeley Lake, MT	C3	29
Seguin, TX	E4	46
Selah, WA	C5	50
Selby, SD	B5	44
Selbyville, DE	G5	11
Selinsgrove, PA	E8	41
Sellersburg, IN	H6	17
Sellersville, PA	F11	41
Sells, AZ	F4	6
Selma, AL	C2	4
Selma, NC	B4	36
Selmer, TN	B3	45
Selway, r., ID	C3	15
Seminoe Reservoir, WY	D6	53
Seminole, OK	B5	39
Seminole, Lake, US	F2	13
Semmes, AL	E1	4
Senath, MO	E7	28
Senatobia, MS	A4	27
Seneca, KS	C7	19
Seneca, MO	E3	28
Seneca, SC	B2	43
Seneca Falls, NY	C4	35
Seneca Lake, NY	C4	35
Sequatchie, r., TN	D8	45
Sequim, WA	A2	50
Sequoia National Park, CA	D4	8
Sergeant Bluff, IA	B1	18
Seven Devils Mountains, ID	D2	15
Seven Hills, OH	h9	38
Severn, MD	B4	23
Severna Park, MD	B4	23
Sevier, r., UT	D3	47
Sevier Bridge Reservoir, UT	D4	47
Sevier Lake, UT	E2	47
Sevierville, TN	D10	45
Sewanee, TN	D8	45
Seward, AK	C10	5
Seward, NE	D8	30
Seward Peninsula, AK	B7	5
Seymour, CT	D3	10
Seymour, IN	G6	17
Seymour, MO	D5	28
Seymour, TN	D10	45
Seymour, WI	D5	52
Seymourville, LA	h9	21
Shady Spring, WV	D3	51
Shaker Heights, OH	A4	38
Shakopee, MN	F5	26
Shamokin, PA	E8	41
Shannon, MS	A5	27
Shannon Hills, AR	k10	7
Shannontown, SC	D7	43
Sharon, PA	D1	41
Sharon Hill, PA	p20	41
Sharonville, OH	n13	38
Sharpe, Lake, SD	C6	44
Sharpsville, PA	D1	41
Shasta, Mount, CA	B2	8
Shasta Lake, CA	B2	8
Shattuck, OK	A2	39
Shaw, MS	B3	27
Shawangunk Mountains, NY	D6	35
Shawano, WI	D5	52
Shawnee, KS	k16	19
Shawnee, OK	B5	39
Sheboygan, WI	E6	52
Sheboygan Falls, WI	E6	52
Sheenjek, r., AK	B11	5
Sheffield, AL	A2	4
Sheffield Lake, OH	A3	38
Shelbina, MO	B5	28
Shelby, MI	E4	25
Shelby, MS	B3	27
Shelby, MT	B5	29
Shelby, NC	B1	36
Shelby, OH	B3	38
Shelbyville, IL	D5	16
Shelbyville, IN	F6	17
Shelbyville, KY	B4	20
Shelbyville, TN	B5	45
Shelbyville, Lake, IL	D5	16
Sheldon, IA	A2	18
Shelley, ID	F6	15
Shell Rock, IA	B5	18
Shelton, CT	D3	10
Shelton, NE	D7	30
Shelton, WA	B2	50
Shenandoah, IA	D2	18
Shenandoah, PA	E9	41
Shenandoah, r., US	A5	49
Shenandoah National Park, VA	B4	49
Shepherdstown, WV	B7	51
Shepherdsville, KY	C4	20
Sheridan, AR	C3	7
Sheridan, IN	D5	17
Sheridan, OR	B3	40
Sheridan, WY	B6	53
Sherman, TX	C4	46
Sherman Reservoir, NE	C7	30
Sherwood, AR	C3	7
Sherwood, OR	h12	40
Sherwood Manor, CT	B5	10
Sherwood Park, DE	i7	11
Shetucket, r., CT	C7	10
Sheyenne, r., ND	C8	37
Shillington, PA	F10	41
Shiloh, OH	C1	38
Shiloh National Military Park, TN	B3	45
Shinnston, WV	B4	51
Shippensburg, PA	F6	41
Shiprock, NM	A1	34
Ship Rock, NM	A1	34
Shishaldin Volcano, AK	E7	5
Shively, KY	B4	20
Shoreview, MN	m12	26
Shorewood, IL	k8	16
Shorewood, WI	E6	52
Short Beach, CT	D4	10
Shoshone, ID	G4	15
Shoshone, r., WY	B4	53
Shoshone Falls, ID	G4	15
Shoshone Mountains, NV	E4	31
Shoshoni, WY	C4	53
Show Low, AZ	C5	6
Shreveport, LA	B2	21
Shrewsbury, MA	B4	24
Shuksan, Mount, WA	A4	50
Sibley, IA	A2	18
Sidney, MT	C12	29
Sidney, NE	C3	30
Sidney, OH	B1	38
Sidney Lanier, Lake, GA	B2	13
Sierra Blanca Peak, NM	D4	34
Sierra Madre, CA	m12	8
Sierra Vista, AZ	F5	6
Signal Mountain, TN	D8	45
Sigourney, IA	C5	18
Sikeston, MO	E8	28
Siler City, NC	B3	36
Siloam Springs, AR	A1	7
Silt, CO	B3	9
Silver Bay, MN	C7	26
Silver City, NM	E1	34
Silverdale, WA	B3	50
Silver Lake, KS	C8	19
Silver Spring, MD	C3	23
Silver Springs, NV	D2	31
Silver Star Mountain, WA	A5	50
Silvertip Mountain, MT	C3	29
Silverton, OH	o13	38
Silverton, OR	C4	40
Silview, DE	B3	11
Silvis, IL	B3	16
Simi Valley, CA	E4	8
Simpsonville, SC	B3	43
Simsbury, CT	B4	10
Sinclair, WY	E5	53
Sinclair, Lake, GA	C3	13
Sioux Center, IA	A1	18
Sioux City, IA	B1	18
Sioux Falls, SD	D9	44
Siskiyou Mountains, US	F3	40
Siskiyou Pass, OR	E4	40
Sisseton, SD	B8	44
Sistersville, WV	B4	51
Sitka, AK	D12	5
Sitka National Historical Park, AK	m22	5
Sitka Sound, AK	m22	5
Skagway, AK	D12	5
Skaneateles Lake, NY	C4	35
Skiatook, OK	A5	39
Skokie, IL	A6	16
Skowhegan, ME	D3	22
Skunk, r., IA	D6	18
Skykomish, r., WA	B4	50
Slater, MO	B4	28
Slatersville, RI	A3	42
Slatington, PA	E10	41
Slayton, MN	G3	26
Sleeping Bear Dunes National Lakeshore, MI	D4	25
Sleepy Eye, MN	F4	26
Slidell, LA	D6	21
Slide Mountain, NY	D6	35
Slinger, WI	E5	52
Smackover, AR	D3	7
Smith Center, KS	C5	19
Smithers, WV	C3	51
Smithfield, NC	B4	36
Smithfield, UT	B4	47
Smithfield, VA	D6	49
Smith Mountain Lake, VA	C3	49
Smith Point, VA	C6	49
Smithtown, NY	n15	35
Smithville, MO	B3	28
Smithville, TN	D8	45
Smoky Hill, r., US	D5	19
Smyrna, DE	C3	11
Smyrna, GA	C2	13
Smyrna, TN	B5	45
Snake, r., US	A4	2
Snohomish, WA	B3	50
Snoqualmie, r., WA	B4	50
Snoqualmie Pass, WA	B4	50
Snowflake, AZ	C5	6
Snowmass Mountain, CO	B3	9
Snow Mountain, ME	C2	22
Snowshoe Peak, MT	B1	29
Snowy Mountain, NY	B6	35
Snyder, TX	C2	46
Socastee, SC	D9	43
Social Circle, GA	C3	13
Socorro, NM	C3	34
Socorro, TX	o11	46
Soda Springs, ID	G7	15
Soddy-Daisy, TN	D8	45
Soldotna, AK	g16	5
Solomon, r., KS	C6	19
Solon, OH	A4	38
Solvay, NY	B4	35
Somers, CT	B6	10
Somerset, KY	C5	20
Somerset, MA	C5	24
Somerset, NJ	B3	33
Somerset, PA	F3	41
Somerset Reservoir, VT	E3	48
Somers Point, NJ	E3	33
Somersworth, NH	D5	32
Somerton, AZ	E1	6
Somerville, MA	B5	24
Somerville, NJ	B3	33
Sonoma Peak, NV	C4	31
Sonora, TX	D2	46
Soperton, GA	D4	13
Sophia, WV	D3	51
Souderton, PA	F11	41
Souris, r., ND	A7	2
Southaven, MS	A3	27
South Baldy, NM	D2	34
South Barre, VT	C3	48
South Beloit, IL	A4	16
South Bend, IN	A5	17
South Berwick, ME	E2	22
South Boston, VA	D4	49
Southbridge, MA	B3	24
South Bristol, ME	E3	22
South Broadway, WA	C5	50
South Burlington, VT	C2	48
Southbury, CT	D3	10
South Carolina, state, US	D6	43
South Charleston, WV	C3	51
South Chicago Heights, IL	m9	16
South Dakota, state, US	C5	44
South Dartmouth, MA	C6	24
South Daytona, FL	C5	12
South Elgin, IL	B5	16
Southern Pines, NC	B3	36
South Euclid, OH	g9	38
Southfield, MI	o15	25
South Fulton, TN	A3	45
South Gastonia, NC	B1	36
South Gate, CA	n12	8
Southgate, KY	h14	20
Southgate, MI	p15	25
South Haven, IN	A3	17
South Hero Island, VT	B2	48
South Hill, VA	D4	49
South Holland, IL	k9	16
South Hooksett, NH	D4	32
South Houston, TX	r14	46
South Hutchinson, KS	f11	19
Southington, CT	C4	10
South International Falls, MN	B5	26
South Jacksonville, IL	D3	16
South Jordan, UT	C3	47
South Lake Tahoe, CA	C4	8
South Manitou Island, MI	C4	25
South Marsh Island, MD	D5	23
South Miami, FL	G6	12
South Miami Heights, FL	s13	12
South Milwaukee, WI	F6	52
South Ogden, UT	B4	47
South Orange, NJ	B4	33
South Paris, ME	D2	22
South Pass, WY	D4	53
South Pass, LA	F6	21
South Patrick Shores, FL	D6	12
South Pittsburg, TN	D8	45
South Plainfield, NJ	B4	33
South Platte, r., US	B7	2
Southport, IN	E5	17
Southport, NY	C4	35
South Portland, ME	E2	22
South River, NJ	C4	33
South Royalton, VT	D3	48
South Ryegate, VT	C4	48
South Saint Paul, MN	n12	26
South San Francisco, CA	h8	8
Southside, AL	B3	4
South Sioux City, NE	B9	30
South Skunk, r., IA	C4	18
South Tucson, AZ	E5	6
South Venice, FL	E4	12
South Wellfleet, MA	C8	24
Southwest Harbor, ME	D4	22
Southwest Pass, LA	F6	21
Southwest Pass, LA	E3	21
South Whitley, IN	B6	17
South Williamsport, PA	D7	41
South Windsor, CT	B5	10
Southwood Acres, CT	A5	10
South Yarmouth, MA	C7	24
Spanaway, WA	B3	50
Spanish Fork, UT	C4	47
Spanish Fort, AL	E2	4
Spanish Lake, MO	f13	28
Sparks, NV	D2	31
Sparta, IL	E4	16
Sparta (Lake Mohawk), NJ	A3	33
Sparta, TN	D8	45
Sparta, WI	E3	52
Spartanburg, SC	B4	43
Spearfish, SD	C2	44
Speedway, IN	E5	17
Spencer, IN	F4	17
Spencer, IA	A2	18
Spencer, MA	B4	24
Spencer, NC	B2	36
Spencer, WV	C3	51
Spesutie Island, MD	B5	23
Spindale, NC	B1	36
Spirit Lake, IA	A2	18
Spiro, OK	B7	39
Spokane, WA	B8	50
Spokane, r., US	B8	50
Spoon, r., IL	C3	16
Spooner, WI	C2	52
Sprague, WV	n13	51
Spring, TX	q14	46
Spring, r., AR	A4	7
Springboro, OH	C1	38
Spring City, TN	D9	45
Springdale, AR	A1	7
Springdale, OH	n13	38
Springer, NM	A5	34
Springfield, CO	D8	9
Springfield, IL	D4	16
Springfield, KY	C4	20
Springfield, MA	B2	24
Springfield, MO	D4	28
Springfield, NE	C9	30
Springfield, NJ	B4	33
Springfield, OH	C2	38
Springfield, OR	C4	40
Springfield, PA	p20	41
Springfield, SD	E8	44
Springfield, TN	A5	45
Springfield, VT	E4	48
Springfield, VA	g12	49
Springfield, Lake, IL	D4	16
Spring Hill, FL	D4	12
Spring Hill, KS	D9	19
Springhill, LA	A2	21
Spring Lake, MI	E4	25
Spring Lake, NC	B4	36
Spring Lake, ME	C2	22
Spring Mountains, NV	G6	31
Springvale, ME	E2	22
Spring Valley, CA	o16	8
Spring Valley, IL	B4	16
Spring Valley, MN	G6	26
Spring Valley, NY	g12	35
Springville, UT	C4	47
Spruce Knob, WV	C6	51
Spruce Knob-Seneca Rocks National Recreation Area, WV	C5	51
Spruce Mountain, NV	C7	31
Spurr, Mount, AK	g15	5
Squam Lake, NH	C4	32
Square Lake, ME	A4	22
Squibnocket Point, MA	D6	24
Stafford, KS	E5	19
Stafford Springs, CT	B6	10
Stamford, CT	E1	10
Stamps, AR	D2	7
Stanaford, WV	D3	51
Stanberry, MO	A3	28
Standish, MI	E7	25
Stanford, KY	C5	20
Stanley, ND	A3	37
Stanleyville, NC	A2	36
Stanton, KY	C6	20
Stanton, MI	E5	25
Stanton, NE	C8	30
Staples, MN	D4	26
Stapleton, AL	E2	4
Star City, AR	D4	7
Star City, WV	B5	51
Starkville, MS	B5	27
Star Peak, NV	C3	31
State College, PA	E6	41
Stateline, NV	E2	31
Staten Island, NY	k12	35
Statesboro, GA	D5	13
Statesville, NC	B2	36
Statue of Liberty National Monument, NJ	k8	33
Staunton, IL	D4	16
Staunton, VA	B3	49
Stayton, OR	C4	40
Steamboat Springs, CO	A4	9
Stearns, KY	D5	20
Stebbins, AK	C7	5
Steele, AL	B3	4
Steele, MO	E8	28
Steele, ND	C6	37
Steelton, PA	F8	41
Steelville, MO	D6	28
Steens Mountain, OR	E8	40
Steep Falls, ME	E2	22
Steger, IL	B6	16
Steilacoom, WA	f10	50
Stephens, AR	D2	7
Stephenville, TX	C3	46
Sterling, AK	g16	5
Sterling, CO	A7	9
Sterling, IL	B4	16
Sterling, KS	D5	19
Sterling, VA	A5	49
Sterling Heights, MI	o15	25
Steubenville, OH	B5	38
Stevens Pass, WA	B4	50
Stevens Point, WI	D4	52
Stewartville, MN	G6	26
Stigler, OK	B6	39
Stikine, r., AK	D13	5
Stillhouse Hollow Lake, TX	D4	46
Stillwater, MN	E6	26
Stillwater, OK	A4	39
Stilwell, OK	B7	39
Stimson, Mount, MT	B3	29
Stockbridge, GA	C2	13
Stockton, CA	D3	8
Stockton, KS	C4	19
Stockton Lake, MO	D4	28
Stockton Springs, ME	D4	22
Stollings, WV	n12	51
Stoneham, MA	g11	24
Stone Mountain, GA	C2	13
Stone Mountains, US	A1	36
Stonewood, WV	k10	51
Stony Brook, NY	n15	35
Storm Lake, IA	B2	18
Storrs, CT	B7	10
Story, WY	B6	53
Story City, IA	B4	18
Stoughton, MA	B5	24
Stoughton, WI	F4	52
Stow, OH	A4	38
Stowe, VT	C3	48
Strasburg, PA	G9	41
Strasburg, VA	B4	49
Stratford, CT	E3	10
Stratford Point, CT	E3	10
Stratham, NH	D5	32
Stratton Mountain, VT	E3	48
Strawberry, r., UT	C5	47
Strawberry Mountain, OR	C8	40
Strawberry Point, IA	B6	18
Streator, IL	B5	16
Stromsburg, NE	C8	30
Strongsville, OH	A4	38
Stroud, OK	B5	39
Stroudsburg, PA	E11	41
Struthers, OH	A5	38
Stuart, FL	E6	12
Stuart, IA	C3	18
Stuart, Mount, WA	B5	50
Stuarts Draft, VA	B3	49
Sturgeon Bay, WI	D6	52
Sturgis, KY	e10	20
Sturgis, MI	G5	25
Sturgis, SD	C2	44
Sturtevant, WI	F6	52
Stuttgart, AR	C4	7
Sublette, KS	E3	19
Suffern, NY	D6	35
Suffolk, VA	D6	49
Sugar, r., NH	D2	32
Sugar City, ID	F7	15
Sugar Creek, MO	h11	28
Sugarcreek, PA	D2	41
Sugar Hill, GA	B2	13
Sugar Island, MI	B6	25
Sugar Land, TX	E5	46
Sugarloaf Mountain, ME	C2	22
Suiattle, r., WA	A4	50
Suitland, MD	C4	23
Sullivan, IL	D5	16
Sullivan, IN	F3	17
Sullivan, MO	C6	28
Sulphur, LA	D2	21
Sulphur, OK	C5	39
Sulphur Springs, TX	C5	46
Sulphur Springs Valley, AZ	E6	6
Sumiton, AL	B2	4
Summer Lake, OR	E6	40
Summersville, WV	C4	51
Summersville Lake, WV	C4	51
Summerville, GA	B1	13
Summerville, SC	E7	43
Summit, IL	k9	16
Summit, MS	D3	27
Summit, NJ	B4	33
Summit, TN	h11	45
Summit Mountain, NV	D5	31
Sumner, IA	B5	18
Sumner, WA	B3	50
Sumter, SC	D7	43
Sunapee, NH	D2	32
Sunapee Lake, NH	D2	32
Sunbury, PA	E8	41
Sun City, AZ	k8	6
Suncook, NH	D4	32
Sundance, WY	B8	53
Sunflower, Mount, KS	C2	19
Sunland Park, NM	F3	34
Sunnyside, WA	C5	50
Sunnyvale, CA	k8	8
Sun Prairie, WI	E4	52
Sunset, UT	B4	47
Sun Valley, NV	D2	31
Superior, AZ	D4	6
Superior, MT	C2	29
Superior, NE	D7	30
Superior, WI	B1	52
Superior, Lake, NA	A10	2
Superstition Mountains, AZ	m10	6
Suquamish, WA	B3	50
Surfside Beach, SC	D10	43
Surprise, AZ	k8	6
Surrey, ND	A4	37
Susquehanna, r., US	A5	23
Sussex, WI	m11	52
Sutherland, NE	C4	30
Sutherlin, OR	D3	40
Sutton, NE	D8	30
Sutton Lake, WV	C4	51
Suwanee, GA	B2	13
Suwannee, r., US	C4	12
Swainsboro, GA	D4	13
Swampscott, MA	B6	24
Swannanoa, NC	f10	36
Swan Peak, MT	C3	29
Swansea, IL	E4	16
Swanson Lake, NE	D4	30
Swanton, OH	A2	38
Swanton, VT	B2	48
Swanzey Center, NH	E2	32
Swarthmore, PA	p20	41
Sweet Home, OR	C4	40
Sweetwater, TN	D9	45
Sweetwater, TX	C2	46
Sweetwater, r., WY	D4	53
Sweetwater Creek, FL	p10	12
Swissvale, PA	k14	41
Switzer, WV	D3	51
Swoyerville, PA	D10	41
Sycamore, IL	B5	16
Sylacauga, AL	B3	4
Sylvania, AL	A4	4
Sylvania, GA	D5	13
Sylvania, OH	A2	38
Sylvester, GA	E3	13
Syracuse, IN	B6	17
Syracuse, KS	E2	19
Syracuse, NE	D9	30
Syracuse, NY	B4	35
Syracuse, UT	B3	47

T

Name	Map Ref.	Page
Table Rock Lake, US	E4	28
Tacoma, WA	B3	50
Taconic Range, US	A1	24
Tahlequah, OK	B7	39
Tahoe, Lake, US	E1	31
Tahquamenon, r., MI	B5	25
Takoma Park, MD	f8	23
Talent, OR	E4	40
Talladega, AL	B3	4
Tallahassee, FL	B2	12
Tallahatchie, r., MS	B3	27
Tallapoosa, GA	C1	13

Name | Map Ref. | Page

Tallapoosa, r., AL C3 4
Tallassee, AL C4 4
Talleyville, DE A3 11
Tallmadge, OH A4 38
Tallulah, LA B4 21
Tama, IA C5 18
Tamalpais, Mount, CA h7 8
Tamaqua, PA E10 41
Tamiami Canal, FL G6 12
Tampa, FL E4 12
Tampa Bay, FL E4 12
Tamworth, NH C4 32
Tanana, r., AK C10 5
Taneytown, MD A3 23
Tangier Sound, MD D6 23
Tangipahoa, r., LA D5 21
Taos, NM A4 34
Taos Pueblo, NM A4 34
Tar, r., NC B5 36
Tarboro, NC B5 36
Tarentum, PA E2 41
Targhee Pass, US E7 15
Tarkio, MO A2 28
Tarpon Springs, FL D4 12
Tarrant, AL B3 4
Tarrytown, NY D7 35
Taum Sauk Mountain, MO D6 28
Taunton, MA C5 24
Tawakoni, Lake, TX C4 46
Tawas City, MI D7 25
Taylor, AZ C5 6
Taylor, MI p15 25
Taylor, PA D10 41
Taylor, TX D4 46
Taylor, Mount, NM B2 34
Taylor Mill, KY k14 20
Taylor Mountain, ID E4 15
Taylors, SC B3 43
Taylors Island, MD D5 23
Taylorsville, MS D4 27
Taylorville, IL D4 16
Tazewell, TN C10 45
Tazewell, VA e10 49
Tchula, MS B3 27
Tea, SD D9 44
Teaneck, NJ h8 33
Teaticket, MA C6 24
Teche, Bayou, r., LA D4 21
Tecumseh, MI G7 25
Tecumseh, NE D9 30
Tecumseh, OK B5 39
Tekamah, NE C9 30
Telescope Peak, CA D5 8
Telford, PA F11 41
Tell City, IN I4 17
Telluride, CO D3 9
Temecula, CA F5 8
Tempe, AZ D4 6
Temperance, MI G7 25
Temple, TX D4 46
Temple Terrace, FL o11 12
Tenafly, NJ B5 33
Tenants Harbor, ME E3 22
Tenkiller Ferry Lake, OK B6 39
Tennessee, state, US B5 45
Tennessee, r., US D10 2
Tennessee Pass, CO B4 9
Tensas, r., LA B4 21
Tensaw, r., AL E2 4
Ten Thousand Islands, FL G5 12
Terra Alta, WV B5 51
Terrebonne Bay, LA E5 21
Terre Haute, IN F3 17
Terrell, TX C4 46
Terrell Hills, TX k7 46
Terry, MT D11 29
Terry Peak, SD C2 44
Terryville, CT C3 10
Tesuque, NM B4 34
Teton Range, WY C2 53
Tewksbury, MA A5 24
Texarkana, AR D1 7
Texarkana, TX C5 46
Texas, state, US D3 46
Texas City, TX E5 46
Texico, NM C6 34
Texoma, Lake, US D5 39
Thames, r., CT D7 10
Thatcher, AZ E6 6
Thayer, MO E6 28
The Dalles, OR B5 40
The Dells, WI E4 52
The Everglades, FL G6 12
The Flume, NH B3 32
The Narrows, WA f10 50
Theodore, AL E1 4
Theodore Roosevelt Lake, AZ D4 6
Theodore Roosevelt National Park (South Unit), ND C2 37
Theodore Roosevelt National Park (North Unit), ND B2 37
Thermopolis, WY C4 53
The Village, OK B4 39
Thibodaux, LA E5 21
Thief River Falls, MN B2 26
Thielsen, Mount, OR D4 40
Thiensville, WI E6 52
Thomaston, CT C3 10
Thomaston, GA D2 13
Thomaston, ME D3 22
Thomasville, AL D2 4
Thomasville, GA F3 13
Thomasville, NC B2 36
Thompson, ND B8 37
Thompson Falls, MT C1 29
Thomson, GA C4 13
Thoreau, NM B1 34
Thorntown, IN D4 17
Thorsby, AL C3 4
Thousand Islands, NY A4 35
Thousand Lake Mountain, UT E4 47
Three Forks, MT E5 29
Three Rivers, MI G5 25
Three Sisters, OR C5 40
Thunder Bay, MI D7 25
Thunder Bay, r., MI D6 25
Thunderbolt, GA D5 13
Tickfaw, r., LA C5 21
Ticonderoga, NY B7 35
Tierra Amarilla, NM A3 34
Tiffin, OH A2 38
Tifton, GA E3 13
Tigard, OR h12 40
Tilden, NE B8 30
Tillamook, OR B3 40
Tillery, Lake, NC B2 36
Tillmans Corner, AL E1 4
Tilton, NH D3 32
Timberlake, VA C3 49
Timms Hill, WI C3 52
Tims Ford Lake, TN B5 45
Tinley Park, IL k9 16
Tinton Falls, NJ C4 33
Tioga, ND A3 37
Tioughnioga, r., NY C4 35
Tippecanoe, r., IN C4 17
Tipton, IN D5 17
Tipton, IA C6 18
Tipton, Mount, AZ B1 6
Tiptonville, TN A2 45
Tishomingo, OK C5 39
Titusville, FL D6 12
Titusville, PA C2 41
Tiverton, RI D6 42
Tobin, Mount, NV C4 31
Toccoa, GA B3 13
Toccoa, r., GA B2 13
Togwotee Pass, WY C2 53
Toiyabe Range, NV D4 31
Tok, AK C11 5
Toledo, IA B5 18
Toledo, OH A2 38
Toledo, OR C3 40
Toledo Bend Reservoir, US C2 21
Tolleson, AZ m8 6
Tomah, WI E3 52
Tomahawk, WI C4 52
Tombigbee, r., US D1 4
Tombstone, AZ F5 6
Tom Nevers Head, MA D8 24
Tompkinsville, KY D4 20
Toms River, NJ D4 33
Tonawanda, NY B2 35
Tonganoxie, KS C8 19
Tongue, r., MT E10 29
Tonkawa, OK A4 39
Tonopah, NV E4 31
Taum Sauk

Tooele, UT C3 47
Topeka, KS C8 19
Toppenish, WA C5 50
Topsham, ME E3 22
Toronto, OH B5 38
Torrance, CA n12 8
Torrington, CT B3 10
Torrington, WY D8 53
Towanda, KS E7 19
Towner, ND A5 37
Townley, AL B2 4
Townsend, MT D5 29
Towson, MD B4 23
Tracy, MN F3 26
Tracyton, WA e10 50
Tradewater, r., KY C2 20
Traer, IA B5 18
Trail Creek, IN A4 17
Traverse, Lake, US B9 44
Traverse City, MI D5 25
Tremonton, UT B3 47
Trenton, GA B1 13
Trenton, MI F7 25
Trenton, MO A4 28
Trenton, NJ C3 33
Trenton, OH C1 38
Trenton, TN B3 45
Triangle, VA B5 49
Tri City, OR E3 40
Tri Lakes, IN B7 17
Trinidad, CO D6 9
Trinity, r., CA B2 8
Trinity, r., TX D5 46
Trotwood, OH C1 38
Troy, AL D4 4
Troy, IL E4 16
Troy, MI o15 25
Troy, MT B1 29
Troy, NH E2 32
Troy, NY C7 35
Troy, NC B3 36
Troy, OH B1 38
Troy Peak, NV E6 31
Truchas Peak, NM B4 34
Truckee, r., US D2 31
Trumann, AR B5 7
Trumbull, CT E3 10
Trumbull, Mount, AZ A2 6
Trussville, AL B3 4
Truth or Consequences (Hot Springs), NM D2 34
Tsala Apopka Lake, FL D4 12
Tuba City, AZ A4 6
Tucker, GA h8 13
Tuckerman, AR B4 7
Tucson, AZ E5 6
Tucumcari, NM B6 34
Tugaloo Lake, US B1 43
Tug Fork, r., US C2 51
Tukwila, WA f11 50
Tulare, CA D4 8
Tularosa, NM D3 34
Tularosa Valley, NM E3 34
Tullahoma, TN B5 45
Tulsa, OK A6 39
Tumwater, WA B3 50
Tupelo, MS A5 27
Turkey, r., IA B6 18
Turlock, CA D3 8
Turnbull, Mount, AZ D5 6
Turrell, AR B5 7
Turtle Creek, PA k14 41
Turtle Lake, ND B5 37
Tuscaloosa, AL B2 4
Tuscola, IL D5 16
Tuscumbia, AL A2 4
Tuskegee, AL C4 4
Tuttle, OK B4 39
Tuttle Creek Lake, KS C7 19
Tutwiler, MS A3 27
Tuxedo Park, DE i7 11
Tweedy Mountain, MT E4 29
Twentynine Palms, CA E5 8
Twin Falls, ID G4 15
Twin Knolls, AZ m9 6
Twin Lakes, WI F5 52
Twinsburg, OH A4 38
Twin Valley, MN C2 26
Two Harbors, MN C7 26
Two Rivers, WI D6 52
Tybee Island, GA D6 13
Tygart Lake, WV B5 51
Tygart Valley, r., WV B4 51
Tyler, MN F2 26
Tyler, TX C5 46
Tyler Heights, WV C3 51
Tylertown, MS D3 27
Tyndall, SD E8 44
Tyrone, NM E1 34
Tyrone, PA E5 41

U

Ugashik Lakes, AK D8 5
Uhrichsville, OH B4 38
Uinta Mountains, UT C5 47
Ulysses, KS E2 19
Umatilla, OR B7 40
Umnak Island, AK E6 5
Umpqua, r., OR D3 40
Unaka Mountains, US C11 45
Unalaska, AK E6 5
Unalaska Island, AK E6 5
Uncompahgre Peak, CO C3 9
Underwood, ND B4 37
Unicoi Mountains, US D9 45
Unimak Island, AK D7 5
Union, KY k13 20
Union, ME D3 22
Union, MS C4 27
Union, MO C6 28
Union, SC B4 43
Union City, CA h8 8
Union City, GA C2 13
Union City, IN D8 17
Union City, NJ h8 33
Union City, TN A2 45
Union Gap, WA C5 50
Union Grove, WI F5 52
Union Springs, AL C4 4
Uniontown, PA G2 41
Union Village, RI B3 42
Unionville, CT B4 10
Unionville, MO A4 28
United States, NA C8 2
United States Air Force Academy, CO B6 9
United States Military Academy, NY C6 35
United States Naval Academy, MD C4 23
University City, MO C7 28
University Heights, OH h9 38
University Park, NM E3 34
University Park, TX n10 46
University Place, WA f10 50
Upland, CA E5 8
Upland, IN D7 17
Upolu Point, HI C6 14
Upper Arlington, OH B2 38
Upper Darby, PA G11 41
Upper Iowa, r., IA A5 18
Upper Klamath Lake, OR E4 40
Upper Red Lake, MN B4 26
Upper Sandusky, OH B2 38
Upton, WY B8 53
Urbana, IL C5 16
Urbana, OH B2 38
Urbandale, IA C4 18
Utah, state, US D4 47
Utah Lake, UT C4 47
Ute Reservoir, NM B6 34
Utica, NY B5 35
Uvalde, TX E3 46

V

Vacaville, CA C3 8
Vail, CO B4 9
Valdese, NC B1 36
Valdez, AK C10 5
Valdosta, GA F3 13
Valencia Heights, SC D6 43
Valentine, NE B5 30
Vallejo, CA C2 8
Valley, NE C9 30
Valley Center, KS E6 19
Valley City, ND C8 37
Valley Cottage, NY g13 35
Valley Falls, KS C8 19
Valley Falls, RI B4 42
Valley Park, MO f12 28
Valley Springs, SD D9 44
Valley Station, KY g11 20
Valley Stream, NY n15 35
Valliant, OK D6 39
Valparaiso, IN B3 17
Van Buren, AR B1 7
Van Buren, ME A5 22
Vanceboro, ME C5 22
Vanceburg, KY B6 20
Vancleave, MS E5 27
Vancouver, WA D3 50
Vandalia, IL E4 16
Vandalia, MO B6 28
Vandergrift, PA E2 41
Van Horn, TX o12 46
Van Kull, Kill, r., NJ k8 33
Van Wert, OH B1 38
Vashon Island, WA f11 50
Vaughn, MT C5 29
Veedersburg, IN D3 17
Velva, ND A5 37
Veniaminof, Mount, AK D8 5
Venice, FL E4 12
Venice, IL E3 16
Ventnor City, NJ E4 33
Ventura (San Buenaventura), CA E4 8
Verde, r., AZ C4 6
Verdi, NV D2 31
Verdigre, NE B7 30
Verdigris, r., US A6 39
Vergennes, VT C2 48
Vermilion, OH A3 38
Vermilion, r., IL C5 16
Vermilion, r., LA E3 21
Vermilion Bay, LA E3 21
Vermilion Lake, MN C6 26
Vermilion Range, MN C7 26
Vermillion, SD E9 44
Vermont, state, US D3 48
Vernal, UT C6 47
Vernon, AL B1 4
Vernon, TX B3 46
Vernon Hills, IL h9 16
Vero Beach, FL E6 12
Verona, MS A5 27
Verona, WI E4 52
Verret, Lake, LA E4 21
Versailles, IN F7 17
Versailles, KY B5 20
Versailles, MO C5 28
Vestavia Hills, AL g7 4
Vevay, IN G7 17
Viborg, SD D8 44
Vicksburg, MS C3 27
Victoria, KS D4 19
Victoria, TX E4 46
Victorville, CA E5 8
Vidalia, GA D4 13
Vidalia, LA C4 21
Vidor, TX D5 46
Vienna, GA D3 13
Vienna, VA B5 49
Vienna, WV B3 51
Villa Park, IL k8 16
Villa Rica, GA C2 13
Ville Platte, LA D3 21
Villisca, IA D3 18
Vilonia, AR B3 7
Vinalhaven, ME D4 22
Vinalhaven Island, ME D4 22
Vincennes, IN G3 17
Vinegar Hill, OR C8 40
Vine Grove, KY C4 20
Vineland, NJ E2 33
Vinita, OK A6 39
Vinton, IA B5 18
Vinton, VA C3 49
Violet, LA k12 21
Virden, IL D4 16
Virgin, r., US G8 31
Virginia, MN C6 26
Virginia, state, US C4 49
Virginia Beach, VA D7 49
Virginia Peak, NV D2 31
Virgin Mountains, US A1 6
Viroqua, WI E3 52
Visalia, CA D4 8
Vista, CA F5 8
Vivian, LA B2 21
Volga, SD C9 44
Voyageurs National Park, MN B5 26
Vsevidof, Mount, AK E6 5

W

Wabash, IN C6 17
Wabash, r., US H2 17
Wabasha, MN F6 26
Waccamaw, Lake, NC C4 36
Wachusett Reservoir, MA B4 24
Waco, TX D4 46
Waconda Lake, KS C5 19
Waconia, MN F5 26
Wadena, MN D3 26
Wadesboro, NC C2 36
Wadley, GA D4 13
Wadsworth, OH A4 38
Wagner, SD D7 44
Wagoner, OK B6 39
Wahiawa, HI B3 14
Wahoo, NE C9 30
Wahpeton, ND C9 37
Waialua, HI B3 14
Waianae, HI B3 14
Waikiki Beach, HI g10 14
Wailuku, HI C5 14
Waimanalo, HI B4 14
Waimea, HI B2 14
Wainwright, AK A8 5
Waipahu, HI B3 14
Waipio Acres, HI g9 14
Waite Park, MN E4 26
Wakarusa, IN A5 17
WaKeeney, KS C4 19
Wakefield, MA B5 24
Wakefield, MI n12 25
Wakefield, NE B9 30
Wakefield, RI F3 42
Wake Forest, NC B4 36
Walbridge, OH e6 38
Walcott, IA C7 18
Walcott, Lake, ID G5 15
Walden Pond, MA g10 24
Walden Ridge, TN D8 45
Waldo, AR D2 7
Waldron, AR C1 7
Walhalla, ND A8 37
Walhalla, SC B1 43
Walker, LA g10 21
Walker, MI E5 25
Walker, MN C4 26
Walker Lake, NV E3 31
Walkerton, IN B5 17
Wall, SD D3 44
Wallace, NC B4 36
Walla Walla, WA C7 50
Wallenpaupack, Lake, PA D11 41
Wallingford, CT D4 10
Wallingford, VT E3 48
Wallington, NJ h8 33
Wallowa Mountains, OR B9 40
Wallula, Lake, US C7 50
Walnut, r., KS E6 19
Walnut Creek, CA h8 8
Walnut Ridge, AR A5 7
Walpole, MA B5 24
Walpole, NH D2 32
Walsenburg, CO D6 9
Walterboro, SC F6 43
Walter F. George Lake, US D4 4
Walters, OK C3 39
Waltham, MA B5 24
Walthourville, GA E5 13
Walton, KY B5 20
Wamego, KS C7 19
Wanapum Lake, WA B6 50
Wanaque Reservoir, NJ A4 33
Wando Woods, SC k11 43
Wapakoneta, OH B1 38
Wapato, WA C5 50
Wapello, IA C6 18
Wapsipinicon, r., IA B6 18
War, WV D3 51
Ward, AR B4 7
Ward Mountain, MT D2 29
Ware, r., MA B3 24
Wareham, MA C6 24
Warminster, PA F11 41
Warm Springs Reservoir, OR D8 40
Warner, NH D3 32
Warner Peak, OR E7 40
Warner Robins, GA D3 13
Warr Acres, OK B4 39
Warren, AR D3 7
Warren, MI F7 25
Warren, OH A5 38
Warren, PA C3 41
Warren, RI D5 42
Warren Park, IN k10 17
Warrensburg, MO C4 28
Warrensville Heights, OH h9 38
Warrenton, GA C4 13
Warrenton, MO C6 28
Warrenton, VA B5 49
Warrenville, IL k8 16
Warrington, FL u14 12
Warrior, AL B3 4
Warsaw, IN B6 17
Warwick, RI D4 42
Waseca, MN F5 26
Washburn, IA B5 18
Washburn, ME B4 22
Washburn, ND B5 37
Washington, DC C3 23
Washington, GA C4 13
Washington, IL C4 16
Washington, IN G3 17
Washington, IA C6 18
Washington, KS C6 19
Washington, MO C6 28
Washington, NC B5 36
Washington, PA F1 41
Washington, UT F2 47
Washington, state, US B5 50
Washington, Lake, WA e11 50
Washington, Mount, NH B4 32
Washington Court House, OH C2 38
Washington Island, WI C7 52
Washington Park, IL E3 16
Washington Terrace, UT B4 47
Washita, r., OK C4 39
Washougal, WA D3 50
Wasilla, AK C10 5
Wasatch, Mount, MA A4 24
Watauga Lake, TN C12 45
Watch Hill, RI G1 42
Waterboro, ME E2 22
Waterbury, CT C3 10
Waterbury, VT C3 48
Waterbury Center, VT C3 48
Wateree, r., SC D6 43
Wateree Lake, SC C6 43
Waterford, CT D7 10
Waterford, WI F5 52
Waterloo, IL E3 16
Waterloo, IN B7 17
Waterloo, IA B5 18
Waterloo, WI E5 52
Watertown, CT C3 10
Watertown, MA g11 24
Watertown, NY B5 35
Watertown, SD C8 44
Watertown, WI E5 52
Water Valley, MS A4 27
Waterville, ME D3 22
Watervliet, NY C7 35
Watford City, ND B2 37
Wathena, KS C9 19
Watkins Glen, NY C4 35
Watonga, OK B3 39
Watseka, IL C6 16
Watts Bar Lake, TN D9 45
Wauconda, IL h8 16
Waukee, IA C4 18
Waukegan, IL A6 16
Waukesha, WI F5 52
Waukon, IA A6 18
Waunakee, WI E4 52
Waupaca, WI D4 52
Waupun, WI E5 52
Waurika, OK C4 39
Wausau, WI D4 52
Wauseon, OH A1 38
Wauwatosa, WI m12 52
Waveland, MS E4 27
Waverly, IA B5 18
Waverly, NE D9 30
Waverly, TN A4 45
Waxahachie, TX C4 46
Waycross, GA E4 13
Wayne, MI p15 25
Wayne, NE B8 30
Wayne, NJ B4 33
Wayne, WV C2 51
Waynesboro, GA C4 13
Waynesboro, MS D5 27
Waynesboro, PA G6 41
Waynesboro, VA B4 49
Waynesburg, PA G1 41
Waynesville, MO D5 28
Waynesville, NC f10 36
Waynewood, VA g12 49
Weatherford, OK B3 39
Weatherford, TX C4 46
Weatogue, CT B4 10
Weaver, AL B4 4
Webb City, MO D3 28
Webster, MA B4 24
Webster, SD B8 44
Webster City, IA B4 18
Webster Groves, MO f13 28
Websterville, VT C4 48
Wedgewood, MO f13 28
Wedowee, AL B4 4
Weehawken, NJ h8 33
Weeping Water, NE D9 30
Weirton, WV A4 51
Weiser, ID E2 15
Weiss Lake, US A4 4
Welch, WV D3 51
Welcome, SC B3 43
Wellesley, MA B5 24
Wellington, CO A5 9
Wellington, KS E6 19
Wells, ME E2 22
Wells, MN G5 26
Wells, NV B7 31
Wellsburg, WV A4 51
Wellston, OH C3 38
Wellsville, KS D8 19
Wenatchee, WA B5 50
Wenatchee, r., WA B5 50
Wenatchee Mountains, WA B5 50
Wendell, ID G4 15
Wendover, UT C1 47
Wentzville, MO C7 28
Weslaco, TX F4 46
Wessington Springs, SD C7 44
Wesson, MS D3 27
West Allis, WI m11 52
West Bend, WI E5 52
West Blocton, AL B2 4
Westborough, MA B4 24
West Bountiful, UT C4 47
West Branch, IA C6 18
Westbrook, ME E2 22
West Burlington, IA D6 18
West Buxton, ME E2 22
West Carrollton, OH C1 38
Westchester, IL k9 16
West Chester, PA G10 41
West Chicago, IL k8 16
West Columbia, SC D5 43
West Concord, NC B2 36
West Cote Blanche Bay, LA E4 21
West Covina, CA m13 8
West Crossett, AR D4 7
West Des Moines, IA C4 18
West Enfield, ME C4 22
Westerly, RI F1 42
Western Springs, IL k9 16
Westerville, OH B3 38
West Fargo, ND C9 37
Westfield, IN D5 17
Westfield, MA B2 24
Westfield, NJ B4 33
West Fork, AR B1 7
West Frankfort, IL F5 16
West Freehold, NJ C4 33
West Glacier, MT B3 29
West Grand Lake, ME C5 22
West Hartford, CT B4 10
West Haven, CT D4 10
West Helena, AR C5 7
West Jordan, UT C3 47
West Lafayette, IN D4 17
Westlake, LA D2 21
Westlake, OH h9 38
Westland, MI F7 25
West Laramie, WY E7 53
West Liberty, IA C6 18
West Liberty, KY C6 20
West Liberty, WV f8 51
West Linn, OR B4 40
West Memphis, AR B5 7
West Mifflin, PA F2 41
West Milford, NJ A4 33
West Milwaukee, WI m12 52
Westminster, CA n12 8
Westminster, CO B5 9
Westminster, MD A4 23
West Monroe, LA B3 21
Westmont, IL k9 16
Westmont, PA F4 41
West Mystic, CT D8 10
West New York, NJ h8 33
West Nishnabotna, r., IA C2 18
West Norriton, PA o20 41
Weston, MA g10 24
Weston, WV B4 51
West Orange, NJ B4 33
Westover, WV B5 51
West Palm Beach, FL F6 12
West Pensacola, FL u14 12
West Peoria, IL C4 16
West Pittston, PA m17 41
West Plains, MO E6 28
West Point, GA D1 13
West Point, MS B5 27
West Point, NE C9 30
West Point, NY D7 35
West Point Lake, US C1 13
Westport, CT E2 10
Westport, IN F6 17
Westport, WA C1 50
West Quoddy Head, ME D6 22
West Rutland, VT D2 48
West Saint Paul, MN n12 26
West Salem, WI E2 52
West Seneca, NY C2 35
West Slope, OR g12 40
West Springfield, MA B2 24
West Springfield, VA g12 49
West Swanzey, NH E2 32
West Terre Haute, IN F3 17
West Union, IA B6 18
West University Place, TX r14 46
West Valley City, UT C4 47
West View, PA h13 41
Westville, IL C6 16
Westville, IN A4 17
Westville, NH E4 32
West Virginia, state, US C4 51
West Warwick, RI D3 42
Westwego, LA k11 21
Westwood, KS k16 19
Westwood, KY B7 20
Westwood Lakes, FL s13 12
West Yellowstone, MT F5 29
West York, PA G8 41
Wethersfield, CT C5 10
Wet Mountains, CO C5 9
Wetumpka, AL C3 4
Wewoka, OK B5 39
Weymouth, MA B6 24
Wharton, TX E4 46
Whatcom, Lake, WA A3 50
Wheatland, WY D8 53
Wheaton, IL B5 16
Wheaton, MD B3 23
Wheat Ridge, CO B5 9
Wheeler Air Force Base, HI g9 14
Wheeler Lake, AL A2 4
Wheeler Peak, NV E7 31
Wheeler Peak, NM A4 34
Wheelersburg, OH D3 38
Wheeling, IL h9 16
Wheeling, WV A4 51
Whidbey Island, WA A3 50
Whitacres, CT A5 10
White, r., US D5 44
White, r., US C7 47
White, r., IN H2 17
White, r., NV E6 31
White, r., TX C2 46
White, r., VT D4 48
White Bear Lake, MN E5 26
White Butte, ND C2 37
White Cap Mountain, ME C3 22
White Center, WA e11 50
White City, OR E4 40
White Earth Indian Reservation, MN C3 26
Whiteface Mountain, NY f11 35
White Face Mountain, VT B3 48
Whitefield, NH B3 32
Whitefish, MT B2 29
Whitefish Bay, WI m12 52
Whitefish Bay, MI B6 25
White Hall, AR C3 7
Whitehall, OH m11 38
White House, TN A5 45
White Lake, LA E3 21
White Mountain Peak, CA D4 8
White Mountains, US D4 8
White Mountains, NH B3 32
White Oak, OH o12 38
White Plains, NY D7 35
Whiteriver, AZ D6 6
White River Junction, VT D4 48
White Rock, NM B3 34
White Salmon, WA D4 50
White Sands Missile Range, NM E3 34
White Sands National Monument, NM E3 34
Whitesburg, KY C7 20
White Sulphur Springs, MT D6 29
White Sulphur Springs, WV D4 51
White Tank Mountains, AZ k7 6
Whiteville, NC C4 36
Whitewater, WI F5 52
Whitewater, r., US F7 17
Whitewood, SD C2 44
Whiting, IN A3 17
Whitman, MA B6 24
Whitman, WV D2 51
Whitmore Village, HI f9 14
Whitney, SC B4 43
Whitney, Mount, CA D4 8
Whittier, CA F4 8
Wichita, KS E6 19
Wichita Falls, TX C3 46
Wichita Mountains, OK C3 39
Wickenburg, AZ D3 6
Wickiup Reservoir, OR E5 40
Wickliffe, OH A4 38
Wicomico, r., MD D6 23
Widefield, CO C6 9
Wiggins, MS E4 27
Wilber, NE D9 30
Wilbraham, MA B3 24
Wilburton, OK C6 39
Wilder, VT D4 48
Wilkes-Barre, PA D10 41
Wilkinsburg, PA F2 41
Willamette, r., OR C3 40
Willamette Pass, OR D4 40
Willapa Bay, WA C1 50
Willard, MO D4 28
Willard, OH A3 38
Willcox, AZ E6 6
Willcox Playa, AZ E5 6
William Bill Dannelly Reservoir, AL C2 4
Williams, AZ B3 6
Williams, r., WV C4 51
Williamsburg, IA C5 18
Williamsburg, KY D5 20
Williamsburg, VA C6 49
Williamson, WV D2 51
Williamsport, IN D3 17
Williamsport, PA D7 41
Williamston, MI F6 25
Williamston, NC B5 36
Williamston, SC B3 43
Williamstown, KY B5 20
Williamstown, NJ D3 33
Williamstown, VT C3 48
Williamstown, WV B3 51
Willimantic, CT C7 10
Willimantic, r., CT B6 10
Willingboro, NJ C3 33
Williston, ND A2 37
Willmar, MN E3 26
Willoughby, OH A4 38
Willoughby Hills, OH A4 38
Willow Grove, PA F11 41
Willowick, OH A4 38
Willow Run, DE i7 11
Willow Run, MI p14 25
Willow Springs, IL k9 16
Willow Springs, MO E6 28
Wilmette, IL A6 16
Wilmington, DE B3 11
Wilmington, IL B5 16
Wilmington, MA A5 24
Wilmington, NC C5 36
Wilmington, OH C2 38
Wilmington, VT F3 48
Wilmington Manor, DE i7 11
Wilmore, KY C5 20
Wilmot, AR D4 7
Wilson, AR B5 7
Wilson, NC B5 36

Name	Map Ref.	Page
Wilson, PA	E11	41
Wilson, WY	C2	53
Wilson, Mount, CA	m12	8
Wilson Lake, AL	A2	4
Wilsonville, OR	h12	40
Wilton, CT	E2	10
Wilton, IA	C6	18
Wilton, ME	D2	22
Wilton, NH	E3	32
Wilton, ND	B5	37
Winamac, IN	B4	17
Winchester, IN	D8	17
Winchester, KY	C5	20
Winchester, MA	g11	24
Winchester, NV	G6	31
Winchester, NH	E2	32
Winchester, TN	B5	45
Winchester, VA	A4	49
Wind, r., WY	C4	53
Windber, PA	F4	41
Winder, GA	C3	13
Wind Lake, WI	F5	52
Windmill Point, VA	C6	49
Windom, MN	G3	26
Window Rock, AZ	B6	6
Wind River Peak, WY	D3	53
Wind River Range, WY	C3	53
Windsor, CO	A6	9
Windsor, CT	B5	10
Windsor, MO	C4	28
Windsor, VT	E4	48
Windsor Heights, IA	e8	18
Windsor Locks, CT	B5	10
Winfield, AL	B2	4
Winfield, KS	E7	19
Winfield, WV	C3	51
Winnebago, r., IA	A4	18
Winnebago, Lake, WI	E5	52
Winnemucca, NV	C4	31
Winner, SD	D6	44
Winnetka, IL	A6	16
Winnfield, LA	C3	21
Winnibigoshish, Lake, MN	C4	26
Winnipesaukee, Lake, NH	C4	32
Winnisquam, NH	C3	32
Winnisquam Lake, NH	C3	32
Winnsboro, LA	B4	21
Winnsboro, SC	C5	43
Winona, MN	F7	26
Winona, MS	B4	27
Winona Lake, IN	B6	17
Winooski, VT	C2	48
Winooski, r., VT	C3	48
Winslow, AZ	C5	6
Winslow, ME	D3	22
Winsted, CT	B3	10
Winston, OR	D3	40
Winston-Salem, NC	A2	36
Winter Garden, FL	D5	12
Winter Harbor, ME	D4	22
Winter Haven, FL	D5	12
Winter Park, FL	D5	12
Winter Park, NC	C5	36
Winterset, IA	C4	18
Winthrop, ME	D3	22
Winthrop, MA	B6	24
Winthrop Harbor, IL	A6	16
Wiscasset, ME	D3	22
Wisconsin, state, US	D4	52
Wisconsin, r., WI	E3	52
Wisconsin, Lake, WI	E4	52
Wisconsin Dells, WI	E4	52
Wisconsin Rapids, WI	D4	52
Wise, VA	f9	49
Wishek, ND	C6	37
Wisner, NE	C9	30
Wister Lake, OK	C7	39
Withlacoochee, r., US	B3	12
Withlacoochee, r., FL	C4	12
Wixom, MI	o14	25
Woburn, MA	B5	24
Wolcott, CT	C4	10
Wolf, r., WI	C5	52
Wolfeboro, NH	C4	32
Wolfeboro Falls, NH	C4	32
Wolf Lake, IL	k9	16
Wolf Point, MT	B11	29
Wonder Lake, IL	A5	16
Wood, r., RI	F2	42
Wood, Mount, MT	E7	29
Woodall Mountain, MS	A5	27
Woodbine, IA	C2	18
Woodbridge, CT	D3	10
Woodbridge, VA	B5	49
Woodbridge [Township], NJ	B4	33
Woodburn, IN	B8	17
Woodburn, OR	B4	40
Woodbury, MN	F6	26
Woodbury, NJ	D2	33
Woodbury, TN	B5	45
Wood Dale, IL	k9	16
Woodfield, SC	C6	43
Woodland, ME	C5	22
Woodland, WA	D3	50
Woodland Park, CO	C5	9
Woodlawn, KY	e9	20
Woodlawn, MD	g10	23
Woodmoor, MD	B4	23
Woodridge, IL	k8	16
Wood River, IL	E3	16
Wood River, NE	D7	30
Woodruff, SC	B3	43
Woods Cross, UT	C4	47
Woods Hole, MA	C6	24
Woodstock, GA	B2	13
Woodstock, IL	A5	16
Woodstock, VT	D3	48
Woodstock, VA	B4	49
Woodsville, NH	B2	32
Woodville, MS	D2	27
Woodward, OK	A2	39
Woonsocket, RI	A3	42
Woonsocket, SD	C7	44
Wooster, OH	B4	38
Worcester, MA	B4	24
Worden Pond, RI	F3	42
Worland, WY	B5	53
Worth, IL	k9	16
Worthington, IN	F4	17
Worthington, KY	B7	20
Worthington, MN	G3	26
Worthington, OH	B2	38
Wrangell, AK	D13	5
Wrangell, Cape, AK	E2	5
Wrangell, Mount, AK	f19	5
Wrangell Island, AK	m24	5
Wrangell Mountains, AK	C11	5
Wrangell-Saint Elias National Park, AK	C11	5
Wray, CO	A8	9
Wrens, GA	C4	13
Wright, WY	B7	53
Wright, Mount, MT	C4	29
Wright Brothers National Memorial, NC	A7	36
Wright-Patterson Air Force Base, OH	C1	38
Wrightsville, AR	C3	7
Wrightsville, GA	D4	13
Wrightsville Beach, NC	C5	36
Wyandotte, MI	F7	25
Wylie, Lake, US	A5	43
Wymore, NE	D9	30
Wynne, AR	B5	7
Wyoming, MI	F5	25
Wyoming, MN	E6	26
Wyoming, OH	o13	38
Wyoming, state, US	C5	53
Wyomissing, PA	F10	41
Wytheville, VA	D1	49

X

Name	Map Ref.	Page
Xenia, OH	C2	38

Y

Name	Map Ref.	Page
Yadkin, r., NC	B2	36
Yakima, WA	C5	50
Yakima, r., WA	C6	50
Yakutat Bay, AK	D11	5
Yale, Mount, CO	C5	9
Yampa, r., CO	A2	9
Yamsay Mountain, OR	E5	40
Yankton, SD	E8	44
Yarmouth, ME	E2	22
Yates Center, KS	E8	19
Yazoo, r., MS	C3	27
Yazoo City, MS	C3	27
Yeadon, PA	p21	41
Yellow, r., US	u15	12
Yellow, r., GA	h8	13
Yellow, r., WI	D3	52
Yellow, r., WI	C3	52
Yellowstone, r., US	D10	29
Yellowstone Lake, WY	B2	53
Yellowstone National Park, US	B2	53
Yellville, AR	A3	7
Yerington, NV	E2	31
Yonkers, NY	E7	35
Yorba Linda, CA	n13	8
York, AL	C1	4
York, ME	E2	22
York, NE	D8	30
York, PA	G8	41
York, SC	B5	43
York, r., VA	C6	49
York Harbor, ME	E2	22
Yorktown, IN	D7	17
Yorktown Manor, RI	E4	42
Yorkville, IL	B5	16
Yosemite National Park, CA	D4	8
Youghiogheny, r., US	F2	41
Youghiogheny River Lake, US	G3	41
Youngstown, OH	A5	38
Youngtown, AZ	k8	6
Ypsilanti, MI	F7	25
Yuba, r., CA	C3	8
Yuba City, CA	C3	8
Yukon, OK	B4	39
Yuma, AZ	E1	6
Yuma, CO	A8	9

Z

Name	Map Ref.	Page
Zachary, LA	D4	21
Zanesville, OH	C4	38
Zeeland, MI	F5	25
Zephyr Cove, NV	E2	31
Zion, IL	A6	16
Zion National Park, UT	F3	47
Zionsville, IN	E5	17
Zumbrota, MN	F6	26
Zuni (Zuni Pueblo), NM	B1	34
Zuni, r., US	C6	6

Maps and Index of the World

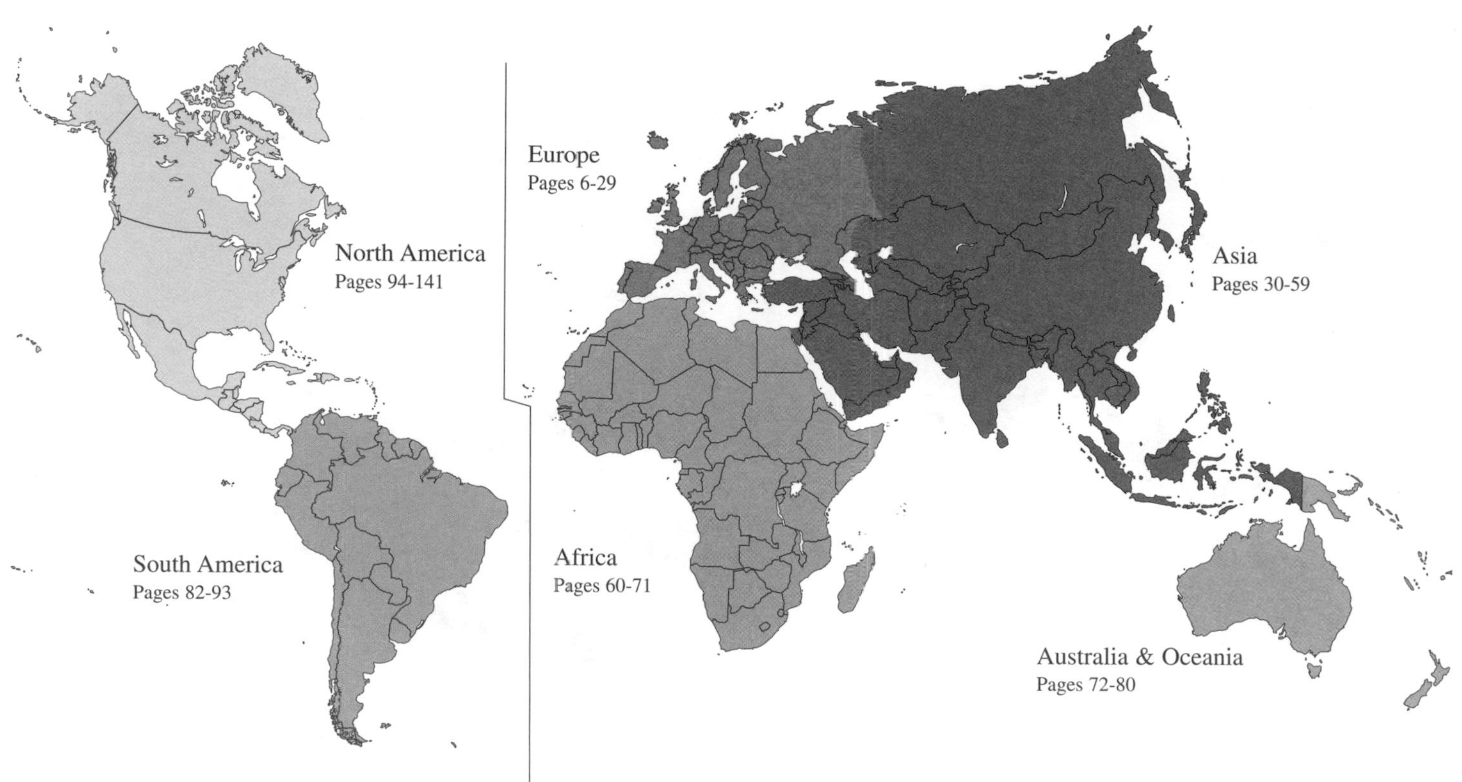

North America
Pages 94-141

Europe
Pages 6-29

Asia
Pages 30-59

South America
Pages 82-93

Africa
Pages 60-71

Australia & Oceania
Pages 72-80

Legend

Hydrographic Features

	Perennial river
	Seasonal river
Aswan High Dam	Dam
Salto Ángel	Falls
Los Angeles Aqueduct	Aqueduct
	Lake, reservoir
	Seasonal lake
	Salt lake
	Seasonal salt lake
	Dry lake
395	Lake surface elevation
	Swamp, marsh
	Reef
	Glacier/ice sheet

Topographic Features
All elevations and depths are given in meters.

764	Depth of water
2278	Elevation above sea level
1700	Elevation below sea level
⌣	Mountain pass
Huo Shan 1774	Mountain peak/elevation

The highest elevation on each continent is underlined.

The highest elevation in each country is shown in boldface.

Transportation Features

	Motorway/Special Highway
	Major road
	Other road
	Trail
	Major railway
	Other railway
	Navigable canal
	Tunnel
	Ferry
✈	International airport
✈	Other airport

Political Features
International boundaries

	Demarcated
	Disputed (de facto)
	Disputed (de jure)
	Indefinite/undefined
	Demarcation line

Internal boundaries

	State/province
	Third-order (counties, oblasts, etc.)
NORMANDIE	Cultural/historic region
(Denmark)	Administering country

Cities and Towns
The size of symbol and type indicates the relative importance of the locality.

■	**LONDON**
▣	**CHICAGO**
◉	**Milwaukee**
◎	Tacna
⊙	Iquitos
○	Old Crow
○	Mettawa
●	Urban area

Capitals

MEXICO CITY / Bonn	Country, dependency
RIO DE JANEIRO / Perth	State, province
MANCHESTER / Chester	County

Cultural Features

⬚ or ▪	National park, reservation
•	Point of interest
⌁⌁⌁⌁⌁	Wall
∴	Ruins
⬚	Military installation
•	Polar research station

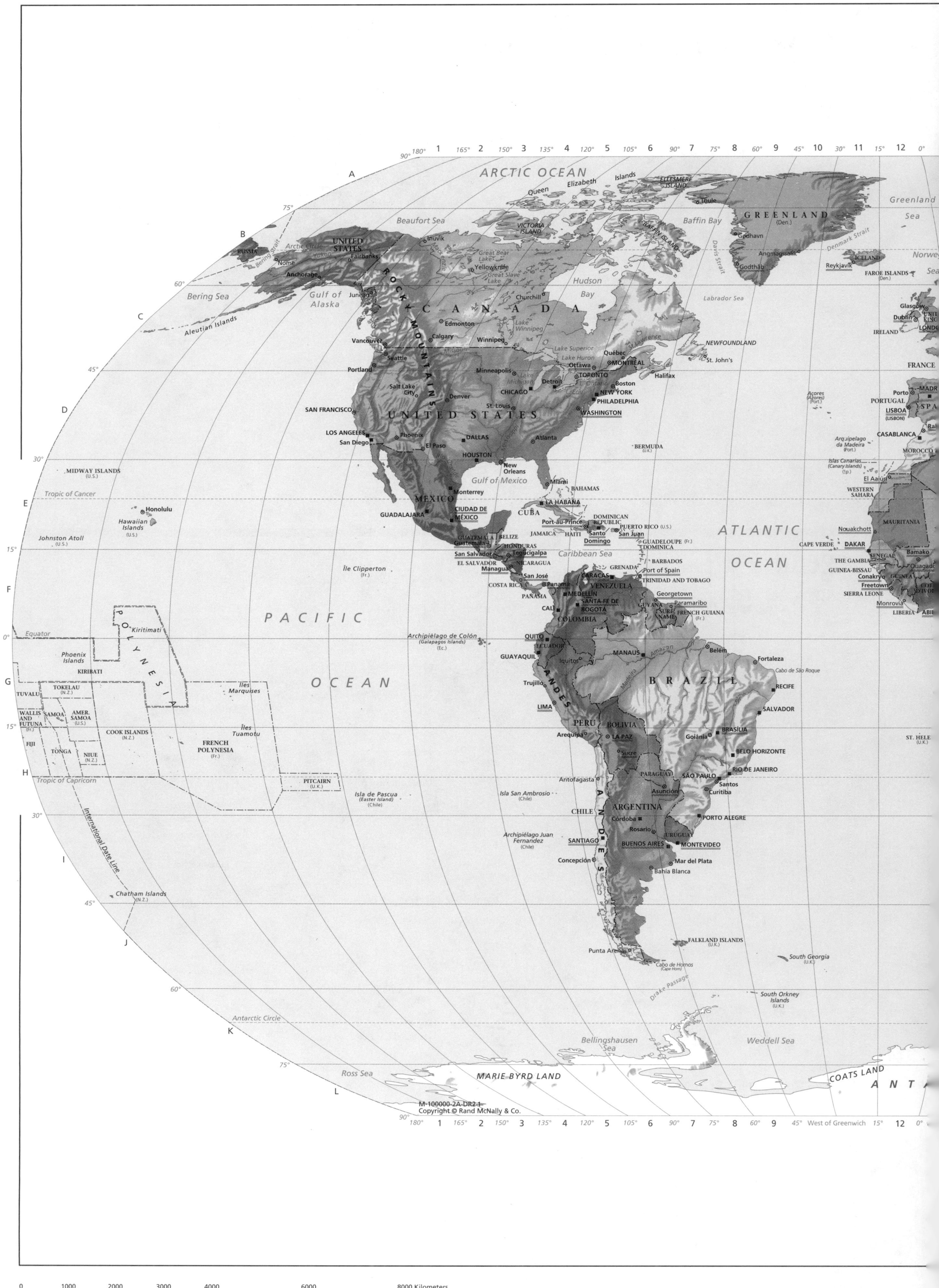

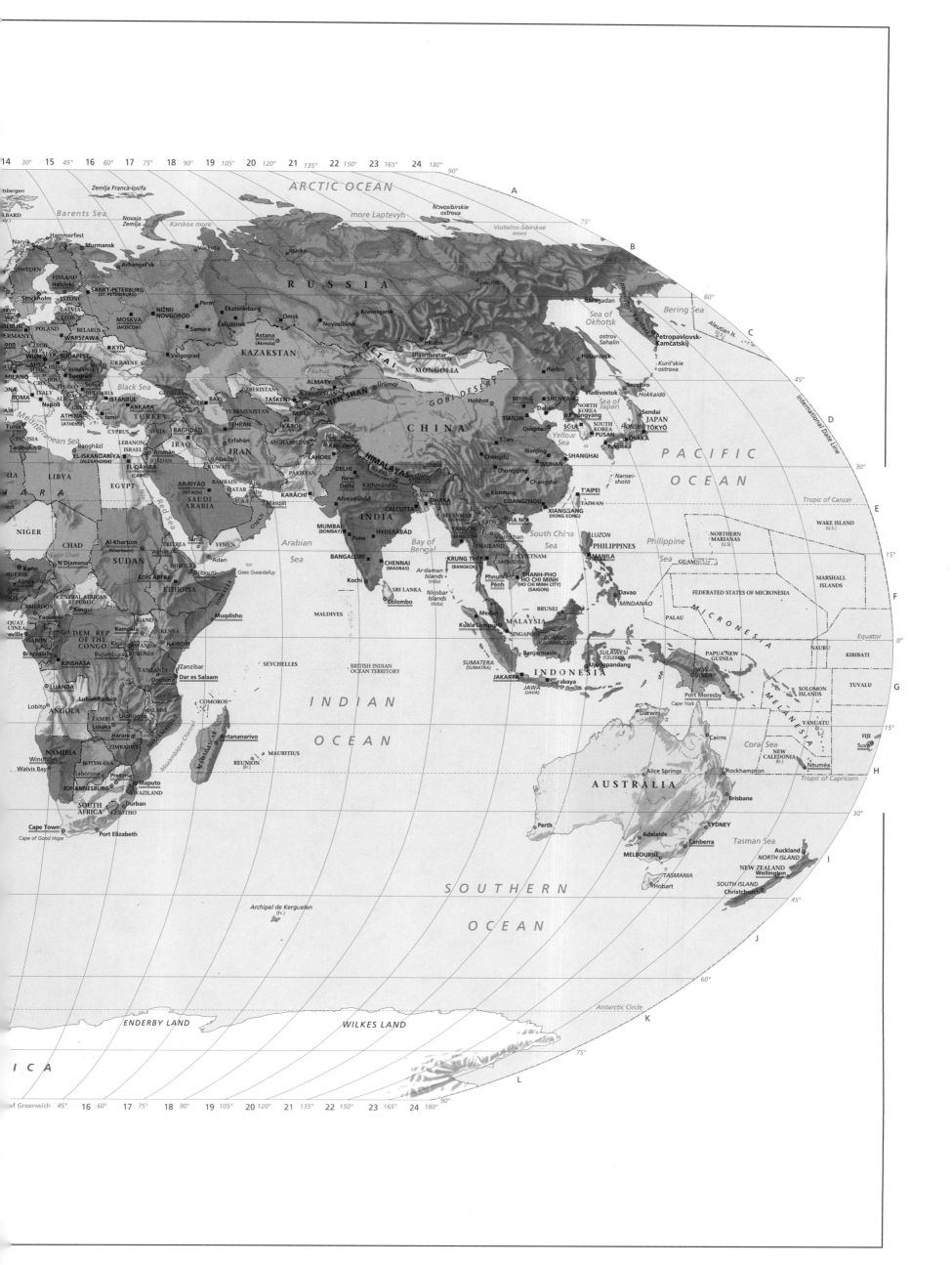

ARCTIC OCEAN

Zemlja Franca-Iosifa

tsbergen

LBARD

Barents Sea

Novaja
Zemlja

Karskoe more

Novosibirskie
ostrova

Tiksi

more Laptevyh

Vostočno-Sibirskoe
more

75°

90°

A

Naryik   Hammerfest

Murmansk

SWEDEN FINLAND

Stockholm Helsinki

ravn

EST'ONI

LATVIA

BERLIN

ERMANY

onn

LITH.

POLAND BELARUS

WARSZAWA

Arhangel'sk

Niznij
NovGOROD

SANKT-PETERBURG
(ST. PETERBURG)

MOSKVA
(MOSCOW)

Perm'

Ekaterinburg

Vorkuta

Igarka

RUSSIA

Krasnojarsk

Jakutsk

Magadan

Bering Sea

Arctic Circle

60°

Sea of
Okhotsk

ostrov
Sahalin

Petropavlovsk-
Kamčatskij

Aleutian Is.
(U.S.)

C

CZECH
REP.

MILANO

ROMA

ITALY

WIEN SLOV.

ROSS.

BUDAPEST

UKRAINE

KYIV

Volgograd

Samara

Celjabinsk

Astana
(Akmola)

Omsk

Novosibirsk

ALTAI

Irkutsk

Ulaanbaatar

Čita

Habarovsk

Harbin

Vladivostok

Sapporo

Hokkaido

45°

D

ROMANIA

SLOV.

BULGARIA

Beograd

Black Sea

KAZAKSTAN

ALMATY

Urümqi

Hohhot

MONGOLIA

GOBI DESERT

BEIJING

SHENYANG

NORTH
KOREA
Pyongyang

Dalian

SEOUL

SOUTH
KOREA
PUSAN

Sea
of
Japan

Sendai

HONSHU

TOKYO

OSAKA

JAPAN

Fukuoka

ATHINA
(ATHENS)

GREECE

ISTANBUL

ANKARA

TURKEY

GEORGIA

AZER.

BAKI

UZBEKISTAN

TASKENT

KYRGYZSTAN

TIEN SHAN

Kasgar

CHINA

Xi'an

Chengdu

Chongqing

WUHAN

SHANGHAI

Nanjing

Qingdao

TIANJIN

Yellow
Sea

Nansei-
shoto

PACIFIC

OCEAN

30°

Tunis

TUNISIA

Tarabulus

Banghazi

EL-ISKANDARIYA
(ALEXANDRIA)

EL-QAHIRA
(CAIRO)

CYPRUS

LEBANON

ISRAEL

SYRIA

BAGHDAD

JORDAN

AR-RIYAD
(RIYADH)

IRAQ

KUWAIT

BAHRAIN

QATAR

Abu
Zaby

U.A.E.

Abadan

TEHRAN

IRAN

Esfahan

KABOL

AFGHANISTAN

Rawalpindi

Islamabad

LAHORE

PAKISTAN

DELHI

New
Delhi

Kathmandu

NEPAL

HIMALAYAS

Lhasa

Kunming

Changsha

GUANGZHOU

XIANGGANG
(HONG KONG)

HA NOI

T'AIPEI

TAIWAN

Tropic of Cancer

WAKE ISLAND
(U.S.)

E

IA

LIBYA

EGYPT

SAUDI
ARABIA

Masqat

OMAN

KARACHI

Ahmadabad

MUMBAI
(BOMBAY)

Pune

HYDERABAD

INDIA

CALCUTTA

DHAKA

MYANMAR
(BURMA)

YANGON
(RANGOON)

LAOS

Viangchan

THAILAND

South China

Sea

Philippine

NORTHERN
MARIANAS
(U.S.)

15°

ARA

NIGER

CHAD

N'Djamena

Al-Khartum
(Khartoum)

ERITREA

Asmera

YEMEN

Adan

Gees Gwardafuy

Arabian

Sea

BANGALORE

CHENNAI
(MADRAS)

Kochi

SRI LANKA

Colombo

Andaman
Islands
(India)

Nicobar
Islands
(India)

KRUNG THEP
(BANGKOK)

Phnum
Penh

CAMBODIA

VIETNAM

THANH-PHO
HO CHI MINH
(HO CHI MINH CITY)
(SAIGON)

MANILA

PHILIPPINES

Davao

MINDANAO

Sea

GUAM (U.S.)

MARSHALL
ISLANDS

FEDERATED STATES OF MICRONESIA

F

NIGERIA

Kano

Abuja

AGOS

CAMEROON

Yaoundé

QUAT.
GUINEA

aville

GABON

Brazzaville

CENTRAL AFRICAN
REPUBLIC

Bangui

SUDAN

ADIS ABEBA

ETHIOPIA

Djibouti

DJIBOUTI

SOMALIA

Muqdisho

MALDIVES

BRUNEI

MALAYSIA

Medan

Kuala Lumpur

SINGAPORE

SUMATERA
(SUMATRA)

BORNEO
(KALIMANTAN)

Banjarmasin

PALAU

SULAWESI
(CELEBES)

Ujungpandang

MICRONESIA

NAURU

Equator

KIRIBATI

0°

CONGO

DEM. REP.
OF THE
CONGO

KINSHASA

LUANDA

UGANDA

Kampala

RWANDA

BURUNDI

Bujumbura

KENYA

TANZANIA

Dodoma

Zanzibar

Dar es Salaam

SEYCHELLES

BRITISH INDIAN
OCEAN TERRITORY

JAKARTA

JAWA
(JAVA)

Surabaya

INDONESIA

PAPUA NEW
GUINEA

NEW
GUINEA

Port Moresby

Cape York

SOLOMON
ISLANDS

MELANESIA

TUVALU

G

ANGOLA

Lobito

Luhumbashi

ZAMBIA

Lusaka

MALAWI

Lilongwe

Harare

ZIMBABWE

COMOROS

MADAGASCAR

Antananarivo

INDIAN

OCEAN

Darwin

Cairns

Coral Sea

VANUATU

NEW
CALEDONIA
(Fr.)

Nouméa

FIJI

Suva

15°

NAMIBIA

Windhoek

Walvis Bay

BOTSWANA

Gaborone

Pretoria

JOHANNESBURG

Maputo

SWAZILAND

REUNION
(Fr.)

MAURITIUS

OCEAN

Mozambique Channel

Alice Springs

Rockhampton

AUSTRALIA

Brisbane

Tropic of Capricorn

H

Cape Town

Cape of Good Hope

SOUTH
AFRICA

LESOTHO

Durban

Port Elizabeth

Perth

Adelaide

SYDNEY

Canberra

MELBOURNE

Darling

Tasman Sea

Auckland

NORTH ISLAND

NEW ZEALAND

Wellington

30°

I

SOUTHERN

Archipel de Kerguelen
(Fr.)

TASMANIA

Hobart

SOUTH ISLAND

Christchurch

45°

OCEAN

J

60°

Antarctic Circle

ENDERBY LAND

WILKES LAND

K

ICA

75°

L

90°

4

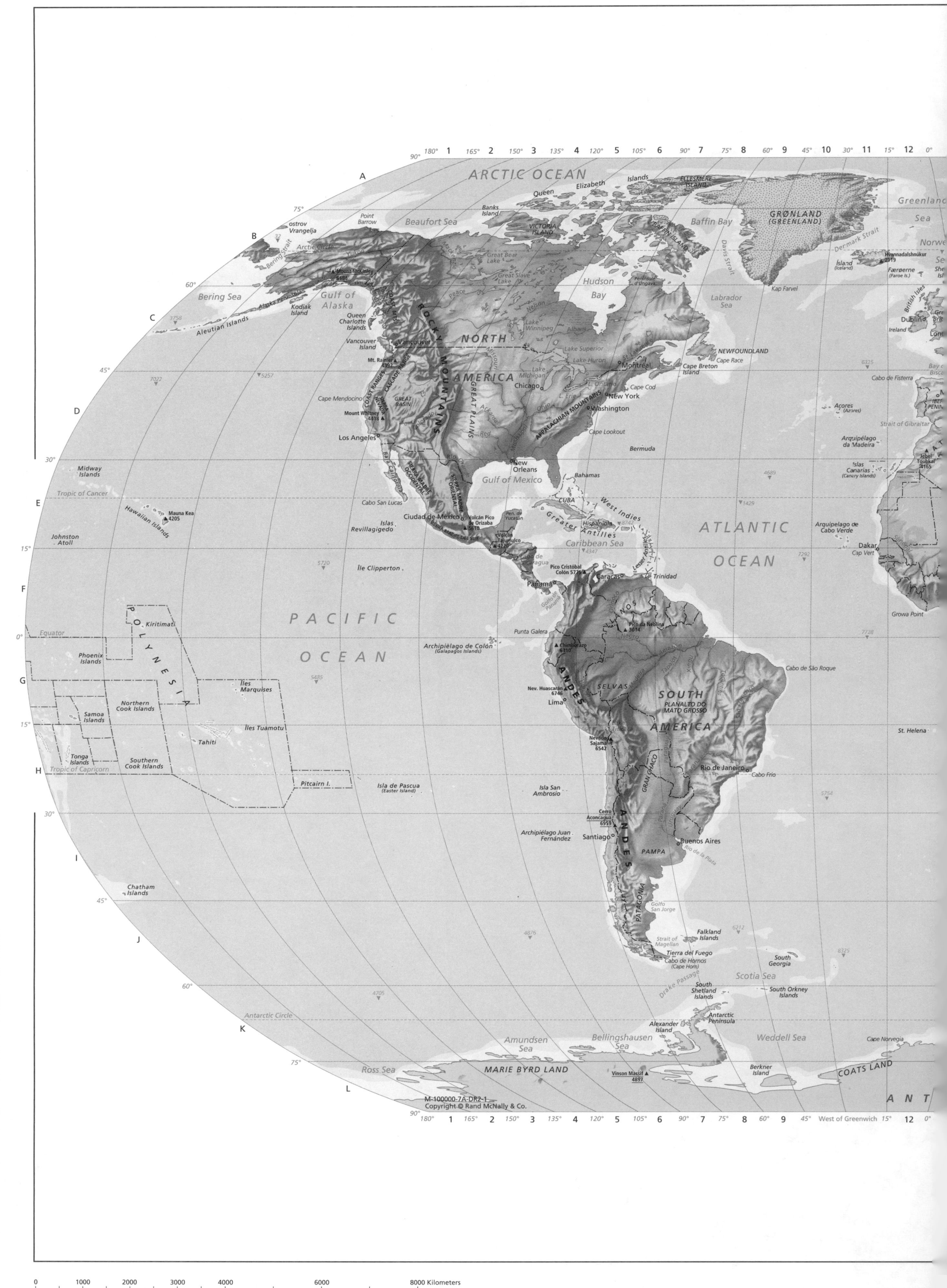

Meters
Feet

6000
19680

4000
13120

3000
9840

2000
6560

1000
3280

500
1640

200
656

Sea Level

200
656

2000
6560

| 0 | 1000 | 2000 | 3000 | 4000 | | 6000 | | 8000 Kilometers |

| 0 | 500 | 1000 | 1500 | 2000 | | 3000 | | 4000 | | 5000 Miles |

Scale 1 : 80,000,000   Robinson Projection

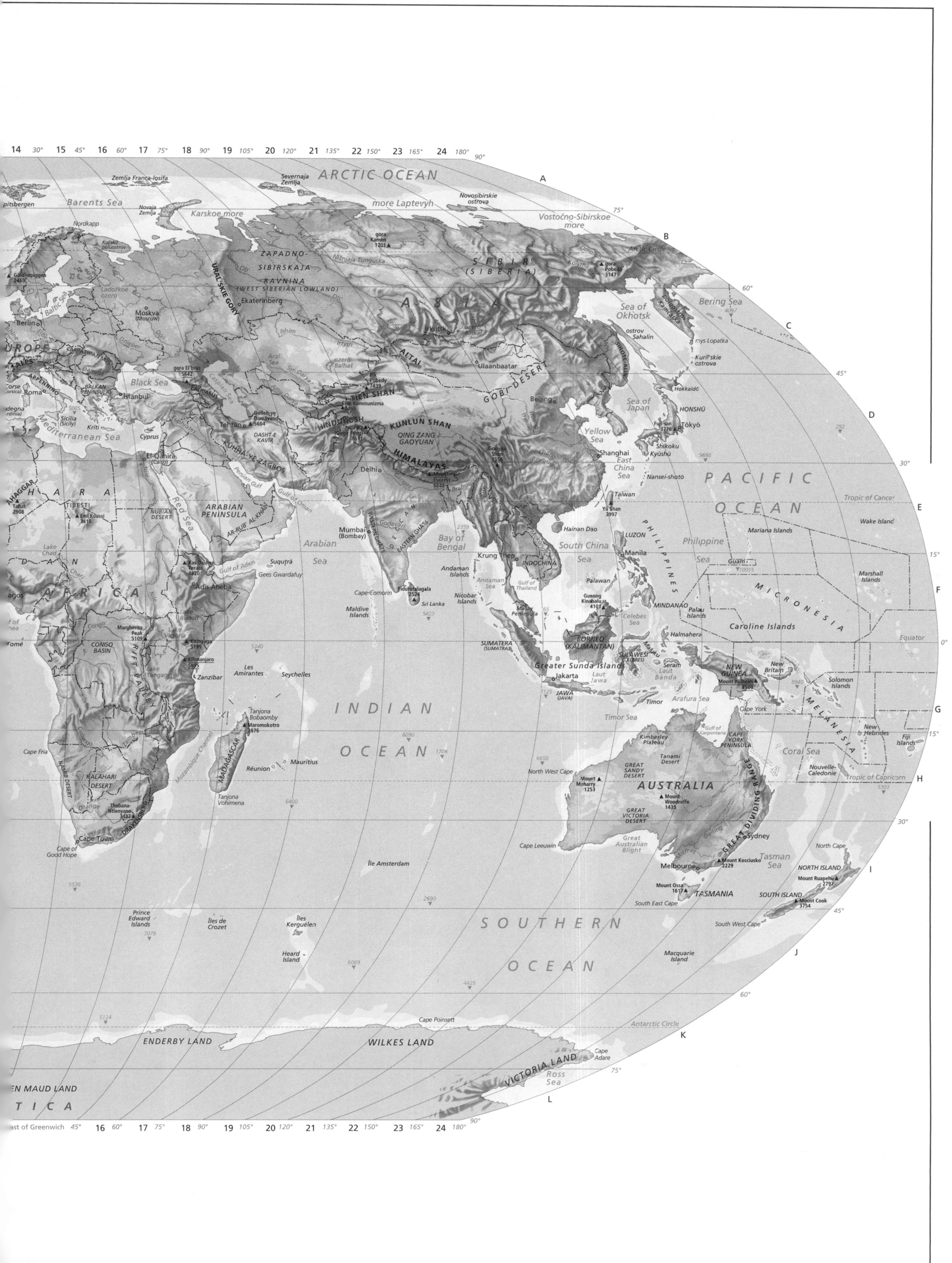
ARCTIC OCEAN
Barents Sea
more Laptevyh
Karskoe more
Vostočno-Sibirskoe more
ASIA
SIBIR' (SIBERIA)
ZAPADNO-SIBIRSKAJA RAVNINA (WEST SIBERIAN LOWLAND)
URAL'SKIE GORY
ALTAI
TIEN SHAN
GOBI DESERT
KUNLUN SHAN
QING ZANG GAOYUAN
HIMALAYAS
HINDU KUSH
EUROPE
ALPS
Black Sea
Mediterranean Sea
Caspian Sea
Aral Sea
ARABIAN PENINSULA
AR-RUB' AL-KHALI
Red Sea
Persian Gulf
Gulf of Oman
Gulf of Aden
Arabian Sea
Bay of Bengal
AFRICA
CONGO BASIN
KALAHARI DESERT
NAMIB DESERT
DRAKENSBERG
MADAGASCAR
INDIAN OCEAN
PACIFIC OCEAN
Philippine Sea
South China Sea
East China Sea
Yellow Sea
Sea of Japan
Sea of Okhotsk
Bering Sea
MICRONESIA
MELANESIA
Caroline Islands
Mariana Islands
Marshall Islands
Wake Island
Solomon Islands
New Hebrides
Fiji Islands
Coral Sea
Tasman Sea
Arafura Sea
Timor Sea
AUSTRALIA
GREAT DIVIDING RANGE
GREAT SANDY DESERT
GREAT VICTORIA DESERT
Great Australian Bight
TASMANIA
NORTH ISLAND
SOUTH ISLAND
NEW GUINEA
BORNEO (KALIMANTAN)
SUMATERA (SUMATRA)
JAWA (JAVA)
SULAWESI (CELEBES)
Greater Sunda Islands
INDOCHINA
PHILIPPINES
LUZON
MINDANAO
HONSHŪ
Hokkaidō
Shikoku
Kyūshū
Taiwan
Hainan Dao
SOUTHERN OCEAN
ENDERBY LAND
WILKES LAND
VICTORIA LAND
Ross Sea
Moskva (Moscow)
Berlin
Roma
İstanbul
Tehrān
El Qâhira (Cairo)
Mumbai (Bombay)
Delhi
Beijing
Shanghai
Tōkyō
Ulaanbaatar
Ekaterinburg
Krung Thep
Jakarta
Sydney
Melbourne
Cape Town
Adis Abeba
Zanzibar
Cape of Good Hope
Cape Comorin
Cape York
Cape Leeuwin
North West Cape
South East Cape
South West Cape
North Cape
Cape Adare
Cape Poinsett
Antarctic Circle
Arctic Circle
Tropic of Cancer
Tropic of Capricorn
Equator
gora El'brus 5642
Kilimanjaro 5895
Kirinyaga 5199
Mount Everest 8848
K2 8611
Mount Kosciusko 2229
Mount Cook 3754
Mount Ruapehu 2797
Mount Wilhelm 4509
Mount Woodroffe 1435
Gunong Kinabalu 4101
Fuji-san 3776
Yü Shan 3997
Maldive Islands
Sri Lanka
Seychelles
Mauritius
Réunion
Îles Kerguélen
Îles de Crozet
Heard Island
Prince Edward Islands
Macquarie Island
Île Amsterdam
Andaman Islands
Nicobar Islands
Nouvelle-Calédonie
New Britain
Halmahera
Timor
Seram
Palau Islands
Guam
Kuril'skie ostrova
ostrov Sahalin
Novosibirskie ostrova
Severnaja Zemlja
Zemlja Franca-Iosifa
Novaja Zemlja
14 30° 15 45° 16 60° 17 75° 18 90° 19 105° 20 120° 21 135° 22 150° 23 165° 24 180°
A B C D E F G H I J K L

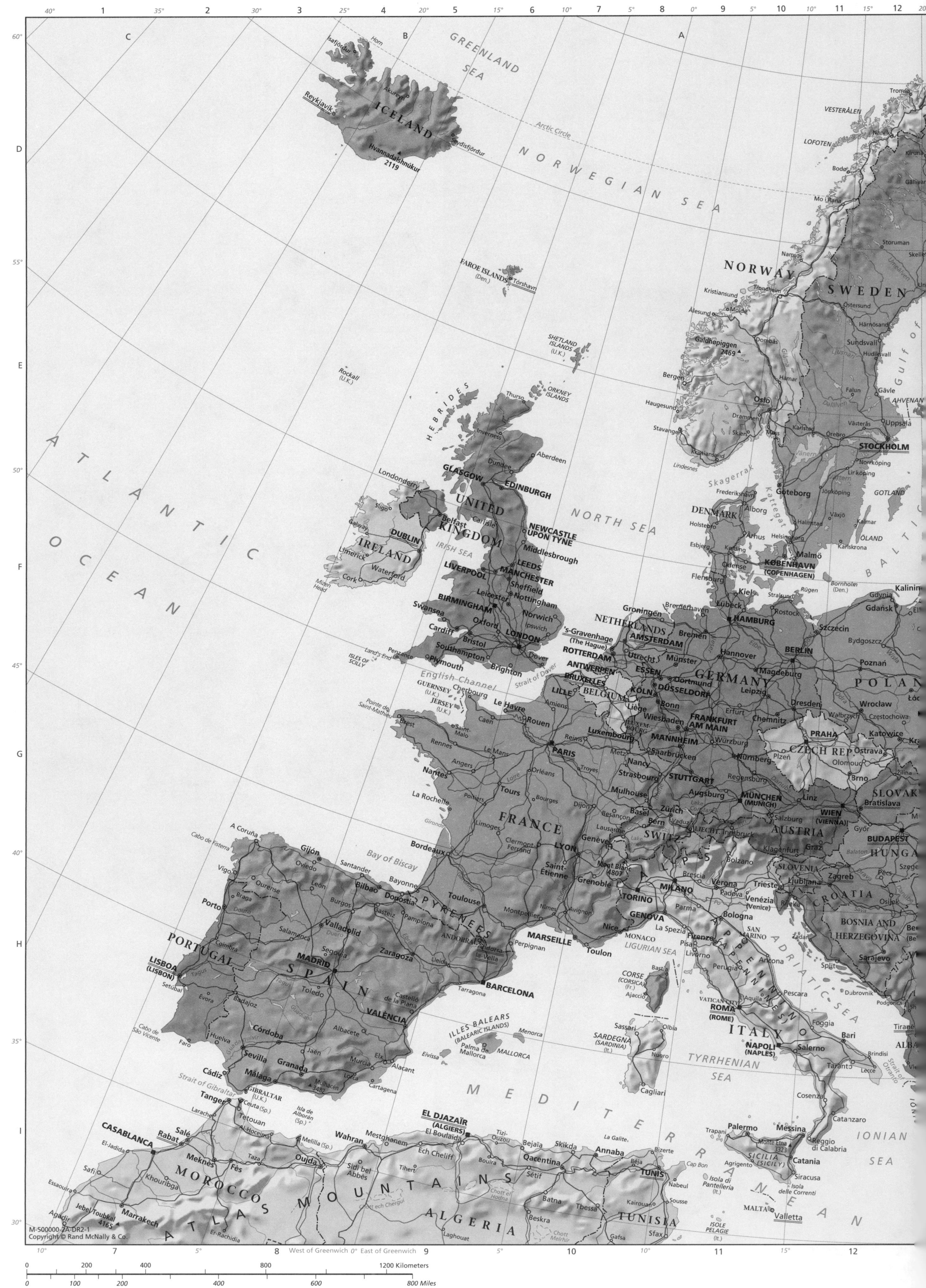

West of Greenwich 0° East of Greenwich

Scale 1 : 12,500,000   Conic Equidistant Projection

0   100   200   400   600   800 Miles

0   200   400   800   1200 Kilometers

M-500000-2A-DR2-1
Copyright © Rand McNally & Co.

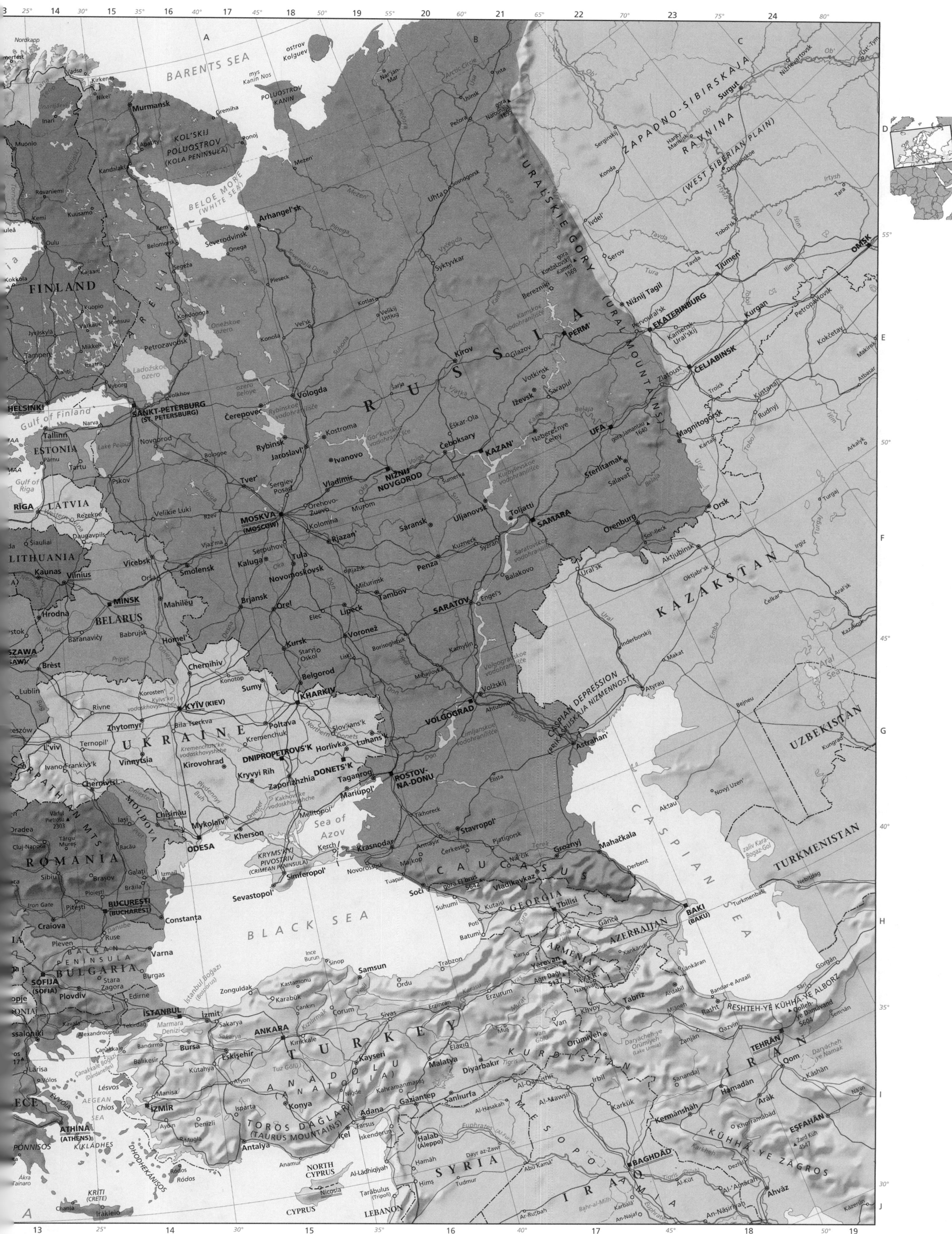
BARENTS SEA
ostrov Kolguev
POLUOSTROV KANIN
KOL'SKIJ POLUOSTROV (KOLA PENINSULA)
BELOE MORE (WHITE SEA)
Murmansk
Arkhangel'sk
FINLAND
HELSINKI
Gulf of Finland
Tallinn
ESTONIA
Gulf of Riga
RIGA
LATVIA
LITHUANIA
Vilnius
MINSK
BELARUS
SANKT-PETERBURG (ST. PETERSBURG)
Ladožskoe ozero
Onežskoe ozero
Petrozavodsk
Vologda
Novgorod
Tver'
MOSKVA (MOSCOW)
Jaroslavl'
Rybinsk
Kostroma
Ivanovo
Vladimir
NIŽNIJ NOVGOROD
Rjazan'
Tula
Kaluga
Smolensk
Brjansk
Orel
Kursk
Voronež
Lipeck
Tambov
Penza
Saransk
Uljanovsk
KAZAN'
Čeboksary
Kirov
Syktyvkar
Uhta
Kotlas
Iževsk
PERM'
UFA
Toljatti
SAMARA
SARATOV
Orenburg
Orsk
EKATERINBURG
ČELJABINSK
Magnitogorsk
Tjumen'
Kurgan
OMSK
R U S S I A
URAL'SKIE GORY (URAL MOUNTAINS)
ZAPADNO-SIBIRSKAJA RAVNINA (WEST SIBERIAN PLAIN)
Surgut
Nižnij Tagil
Arctic Circle
KAZAKSTAN
Aktjubinsk
Ural'sk
Atyrau
Aral Sea
UZBEKISTAN
TURKMENISTAN
CASPIAN DEPRESSION
PRIKASPIJSKAJA NIZMENNOST'
Astrahan'
VOLGOGRAD
ROSTOV-NA-DONU
Stavropol'
Krasnodar
Mahačkala
Groznyj
CAUCASUS
GEORGIA
Tbilisi
ARMENIA
Yerevan
AZERBAIJAN
BAKI (BAKU)
CASPIAN SEA
UKRAINE
KYÏV (KIEV)
KHARKIV
DNIPROPETROVS'K
DONETS'K
Zaporizhzhia
Kryvyi Rih
Odesa
Mykolaïv
Kherson
Sevastopol'
Simferopol'
KRYMS'KYI PIVOSTRIV (CRIMEAN PENINSULA)
Sea of Azov
MOLDOVA
Chişinău
ROMANIA
BUCUREŞTI (BUCHAREST)
Constanţa
BULGARIA
SOFIJA (SOFIA)
Plovdiv
Varna
BLACK SEA
ISTANBUL
ANKARA
TURKEY
İZMIR
Bursa
Konya
Adana
Antalya
TOROS DAĞLARI (TAURUS MOUNTAINS)
ATHÍNA (ATHENS)
KRÍTI (CRETE)
NORTH CYPRUS
CYPRUS
Nicosia
SYRIA
Halab (Aleppo)
LEBANON
IRAQ
BAGHDĀD
IRAN
TEHRĀN
EŞFAHĀN
Tabrīz
KŪHHĀ-YE ZĀGROS
RESHTEH-YE KŪHHĀ-YE ALBORZ
KURDISTAN
MESOPOTAMIA

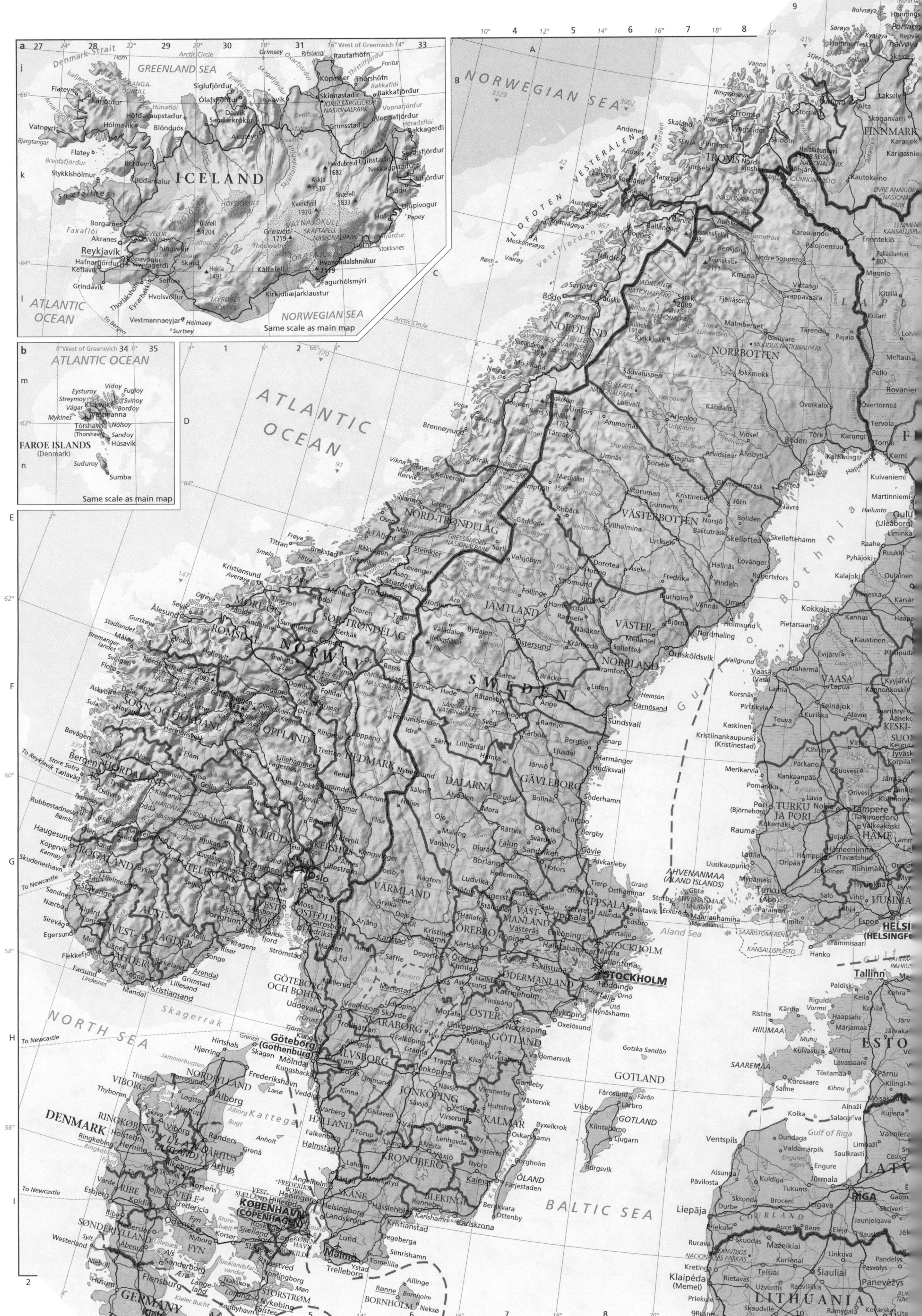

GREENLAND SEA
Denmark Strait
ICELAND
Reykjavík
Akureyri
Faxaflói
ATLANTIC OCEAN
NORWEGIAN SEA
Same scale as main map
ATLANTIC OCEAN
FAROE ISLANDS
(Denmark)
Tórshavn
Same scale as main map
NORWEGIAN SEA
ATLANTIC OCEAN
LOFOTEN
VESTERÅLEN
Arctic Circle
NORWAY
SWEDEN
FINNMARK
TROMS
NORDLAND
NORRBOTTEN
VÄSTERBOTTEN
NORD-TRØNDELAG
SØR-TRØNDELAG
MØRE OG ROMSDAL
SOGN OG FJORDANE
OPPLAND
HEDMARK
HORDALAND
BUSKERUD
ROGALAND
TELEMARK
AUST-AGDER
VEST-AGDER
AKERSHUS
ØSTFOLD
VESTFOLD
JÄMTLAND
VÄSTERNORRLAND
GÄVLEBORG
DALARNA
VÄRMLAND
UPPSALA
VÄSTMANLAND
ÖREBRO
SÖDERMANLAND
STOCKHOLM
ÖSTERGÖTLAND
SKARABORG
ÄLVSBORG
GÖTEBORG OCH BOHUS
JÖNKÖPING
KALMAR
HALLAND
KRONOBERG
BLEKINGE
SKÅNE
GOTLAND
ÖLAND
Gulf of Bothnia
Aland Sea
AHVENANMAA (ÅLAND ISLANDS)
BALTIC SEA
NORTH SEA
Skagerrak
Kattegat
DENMARK
KØBENHAVN (COPENHAGEN)
JYLLAND (JUTLAND)
NORDJYLLAND
VIBORG
RINGKØBING
ÅRHUS
VEJLE
RIBE
SØNDERJYLLAND
FYN
STORSTRØM
BORNHOLM
GERMANY
Oslo
STOCKHOLM
Göteborg (Gothenburg)
Bergen
Trondheim
Malmö
Tallinn
Riga
LATVIA
LITHUANIA
ESTONIA
Gulf of Riga
SAAREMAA
HIIUMAA
COURLAND
LAPLAND
VAASA
TURKU JA PORI
HÄME
UUSIMAA
Helsinki (Helsingfors)
To Newcastle
To Reykjavík
To Bergen

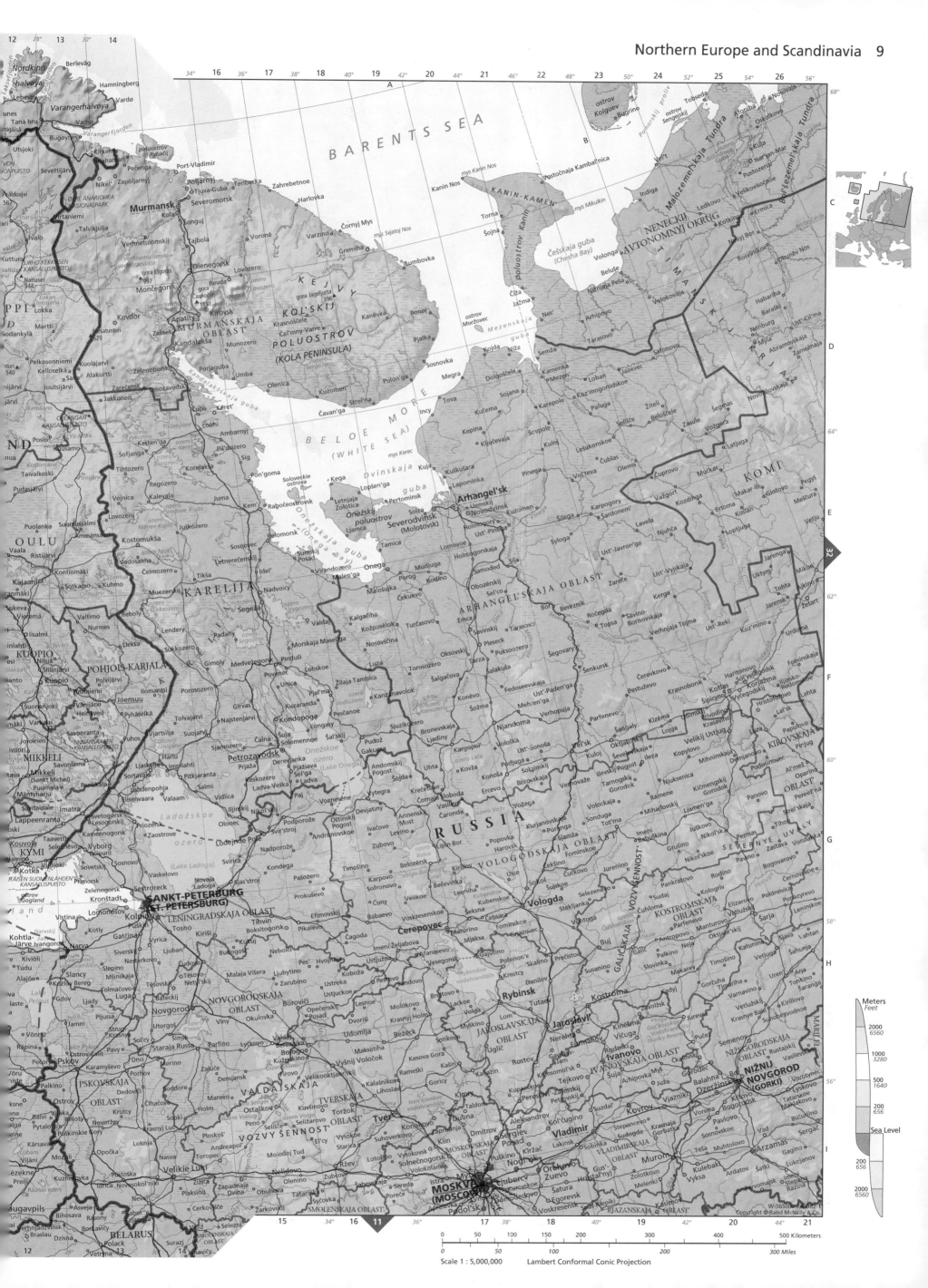

Scale 1 : 5,000,000   Lambert Conformal Conic Projection

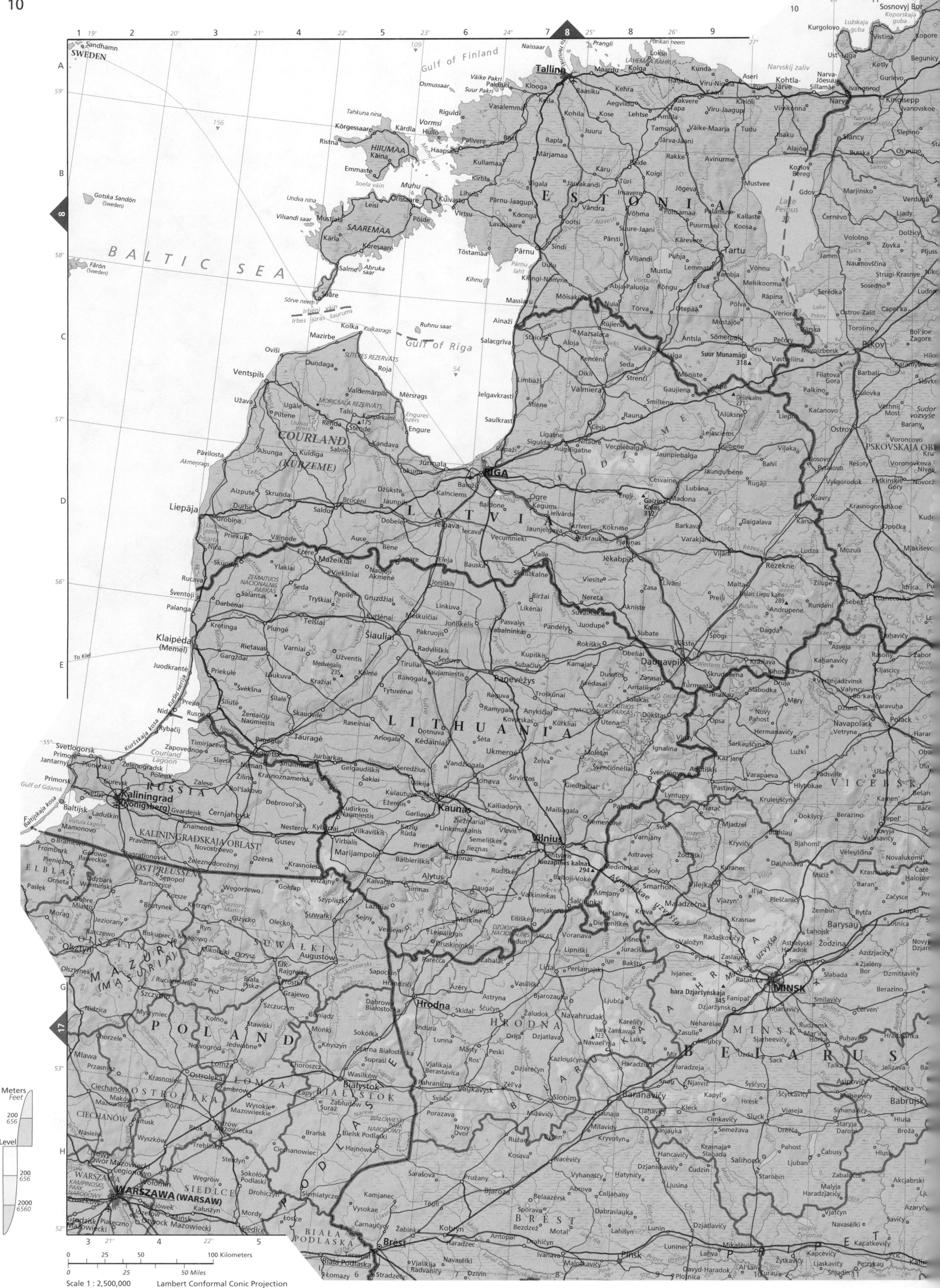

Meters
Feet

200
656

Sea Level

200
656

2000
6560

0   25   50   100 Kilometers

0   25   50 Miles

Scale 1 : 2 500 000   Lambert Conformal Conic Projection

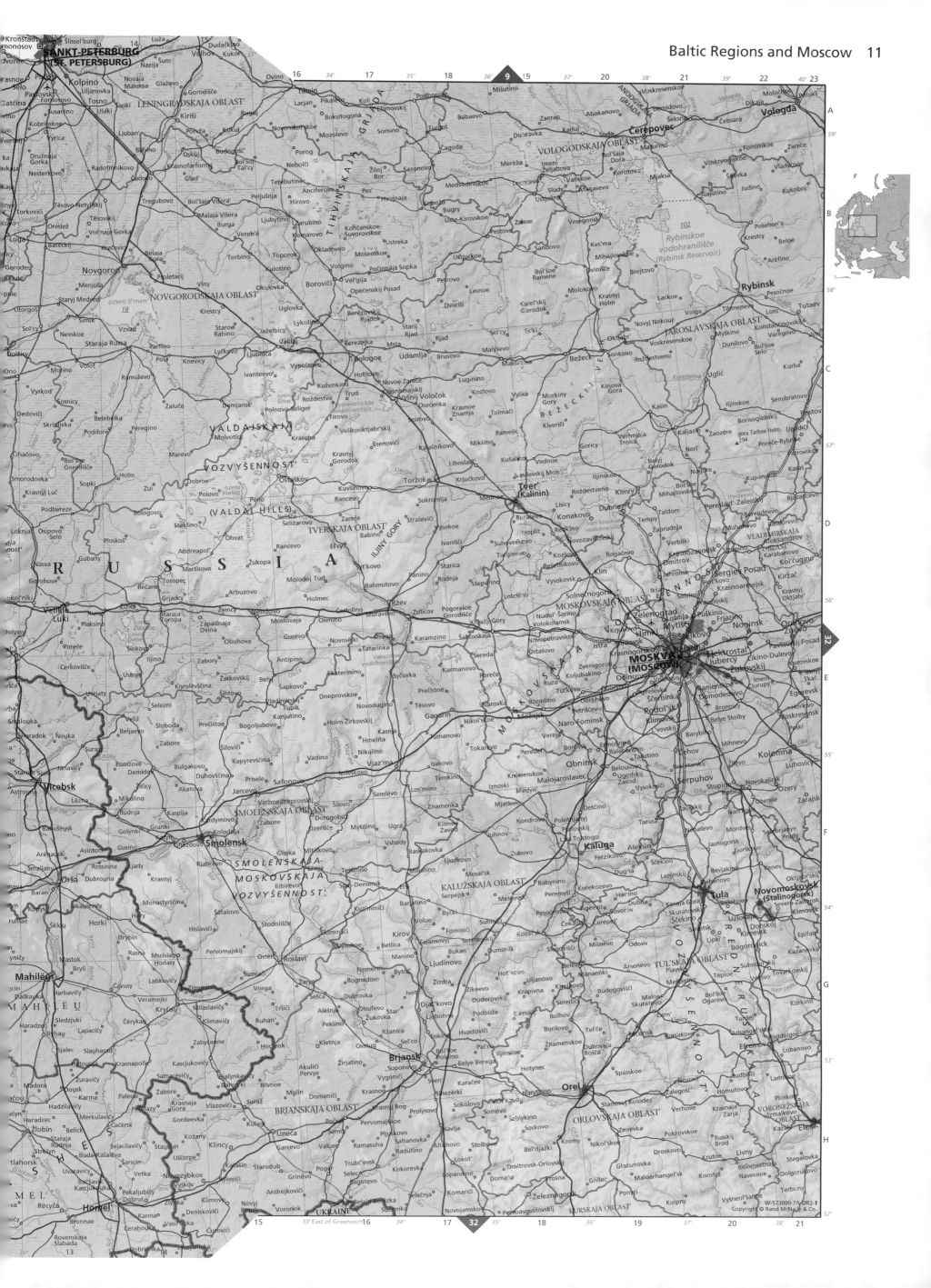

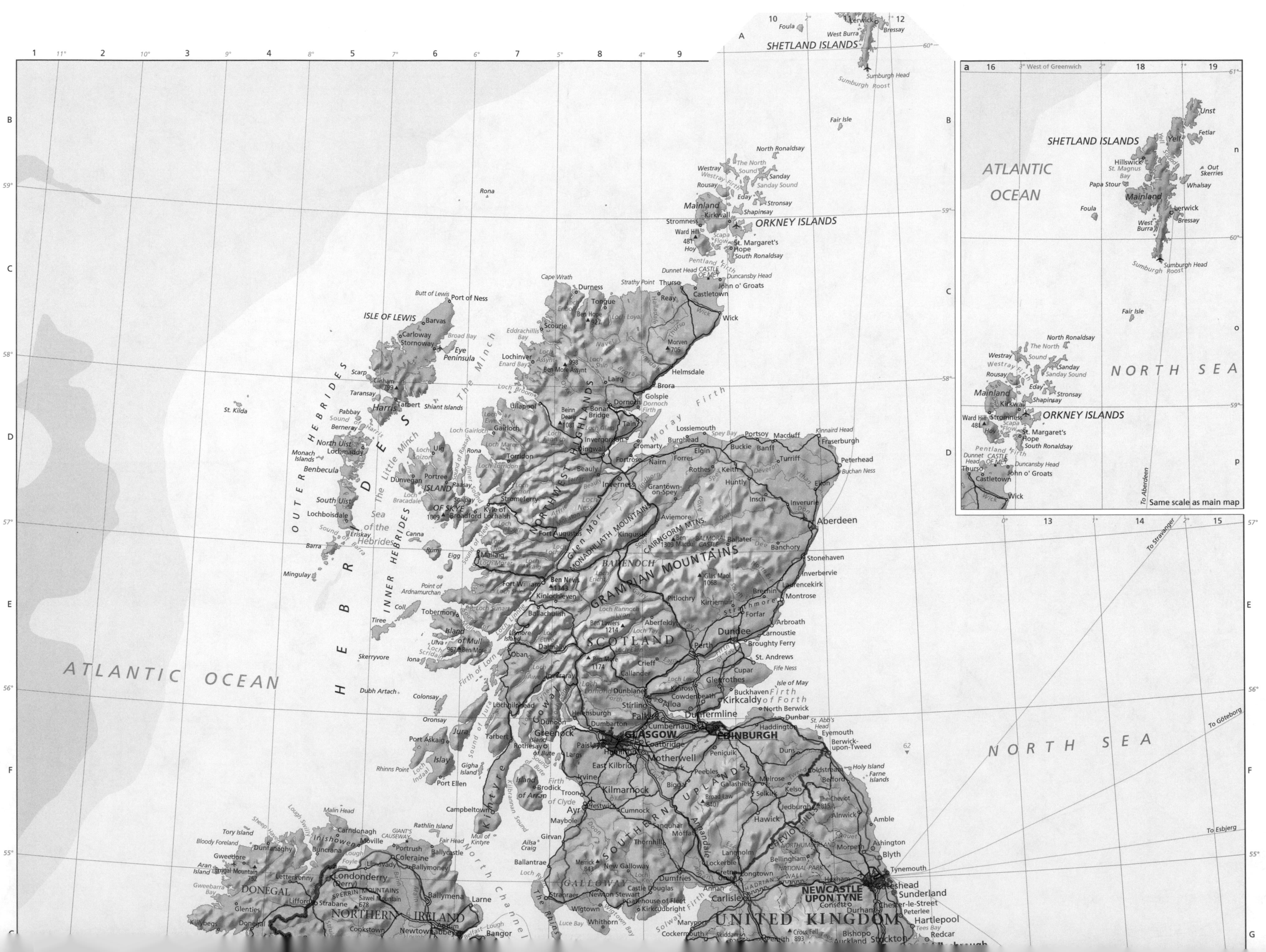
ATLANTIC OCEAN
NORTH SEA
HEBRIDES
OUTER HEBRIDES
INNER HEBRIDES
SHETLAND ISLANDS
ORKNEY ISLANDS
ISLE OF LEWIS
ISLAND OF SKYE
NORTHWEST HIGHLANDS
GRAMPIAN MOUNTAINS
CAIRNGORM MTNS.
MONADHLIATH MOUNTAINS
BADENOCH
SOUTHERN UPLANDS
SCOTLAND
UNITED KINGDOM
NORTHERN IRELAND
DONEGAL
GALLOWAY
The Minch
The Little Minch
Sea of the Hebrides
Moray Firth
Firth of Forth
Firth of Clyde
Firth of Lorn
Solway Firth
North Channel
Kilbrannan Sound
Sound of Jura
Pentland Firth
Scapa Flow
Kintyre
Fair Isle
Foula
Rona
St. Kilda
Butt of Lewis
Port of Ness
Barvas
Carloway
Stornoway
Eye Peninsula
Broad Bay
Scarp
Taransay
Harris
Tarbert
Shiant Islands
Pabbay
Berneray
North Uist
Lochmaddy
Monach Islands
Benbecula
South Uist
Lochboisdale
Eriskay
Barra
Mingulay
Canna
Rum
Eigg
Coll
Tiree
Tobermory
Island of Mull
Ulva
Iona
Skerryvore
Dubh Artach
Colonsay
Oronsay
Jura
Port Askaig
Islay
Port Ellen
Rhinns Point
Gigha Island
Campbeltown
Portree
Dunvegan
Uig
Raasay
Scalpay
Broadford
Kyle of Lochalsh
Mallaig
Point of Ardnamurchan
Cape Wrath
Durness
Tongue
Ben Hope
Strathy Point
Thurso
Reay
Dunnet Head
Castletown
Duncansby Head
John o' Groats
Wick
Morven
Helmsdale
Brora
Golspie
Dornoch
Tain
Bonar Bridge
Lairg
Scourie
Eddrachillis Bay
Lochinver
Enard Bay
Ben More Assynt
Ullapool
Gairloch
Loch Gairloch
Torridon
Beinn Dearg
Invergordon
Dingwall
Cromarty
Fortrose
Inverness
Beauly
Nairn
Forres
Elgin
Lossiemouth
Burghead
Spey Bay
Buckie
Portsoy
Macduff
Banff
Turriff
Fraserburgh
Kinnaird Head
Peterhead
Buchan Ness
Ellon
Inverurie
Aberdeen
Stonehaven
Inverbervie
Laurencekirk
Montrose
Brechin
Forfar
Arbroath
Carnoustie
Dundee
Broughty Ferry
St. Andrews
Fife Ness
Cupar
Glenrothes
Kirkcaldy
Buckhaven
Isle of May
North Berwick
Dunbar
Haddington
St. Abb's Head
Eyemouth
Berwick-upon-Tweed
Holy Island
Farne Islands
Amble
Ashington
Blyth
Tynemouth
NEWCASTLE UPON TYNE
Gateshead
Sunderland
Chester-le-Street
Peterlee
Hartlepool
Redcar
Stockton
Durham
Consett
Bishop Auckland
Cross Fell
Morpeth
Alnwick
Hexham
Bellingham
The Cheviot
Kelso
Coldstream
Jedburgh
Hawick
Selkirk
Melrose
Galashiels
Peebles
Penicuik
EDINBURGH
Dunfermline
Alloa
Stirling
Falkirk
Cumbernauld
GLASGOW
Paisley
Coatbridge
Motherwell
Hamilton
East Kilbride
Lanark
Biggar
Kilmarnock
Irvine
Troon
Ayr
Prestwick
Cumnock
Sanquhar
Maybole
Girvan
Ailsa Craig
Ballantrae
Stranraer
Newton Stewart
Wigtown
Whithorn
Luce Bay
Kirkcudbright
Gatehouse of Fleet
Castle Douglas
Dumfries
Moffat
Lockerbie
Langholm
Annan
Gretna
Longtown
Carlisle
Maryport
Cockermouth
Greenock
Dunoon
Rothesay
Largs
Brodick
Isle of Arran
Lochgilphead
Tarbert
Oban
Dalmally
Ballachulish
Kinlochleven
Fort William
Ben Nevis
Fort Augustus
Glen Mor
Kingussie
Aviemore
Grantown-on-Spey
Rothes
Keith
Huntly
Insch
Ballater
Balmoral Castle
Ben Macdui
Glas Maol
Banchory
Pitlochry
Kirriemuir
Aberfeldy
Ben Lawers
Loch Rannoch
Loch Tay
Crieff
Callander
Ben More
Perth
Dunblane
Kinross
Cowdenbeath
Dumbarton
Helensburgh
Loch Lomond
Malin Head
Carndonagh
Moville
Buncrana
Inishowen
Lough Swilly
Sheep Haven
Tory Island
Bloody Foreland
Gweedore
Aran Island
Errigal Mountain
Dunfanaghy
Letterkenny
Gweebarra Bay
Glenties
Killybegs
Donegal
Lifford
Strabane
Londonderry (Derry)
Sperrin Mountains
Sawel Mountain
Cookstown
Limavady
Coleraine
Portrush
Giant's Causeway
Ballycastle
Rathlin Island
Fair Head
Mull of Kintyre
Ballymoney
Ballymena
Larne
Antrim
Newtownabbey
Belfast
Bangor
Belfast Lough
Stromness
Ward Hill
Hoy
Mainland
Kirkwall
Rousay
Westray
Westray Firth
The North Sound
North Ronaldsay
Sanday
Sanday Sound
Stronsay
Eday
Shapinsay
St. Margaret's Hope
South Ronaldsay
Lerwick
Bressay
West Burra
Sumburgh Head
Sumburgh Roost
Unst
Yell
Yell Sound
Fetlar
Out Skerries
Whalsay
Hillswick
St. Magnus Bay
Papa Stour
3° West of Greenwich
Same scale as main map
To Aberdeen
To Stravanger
To Göteborg
To Esbjerg

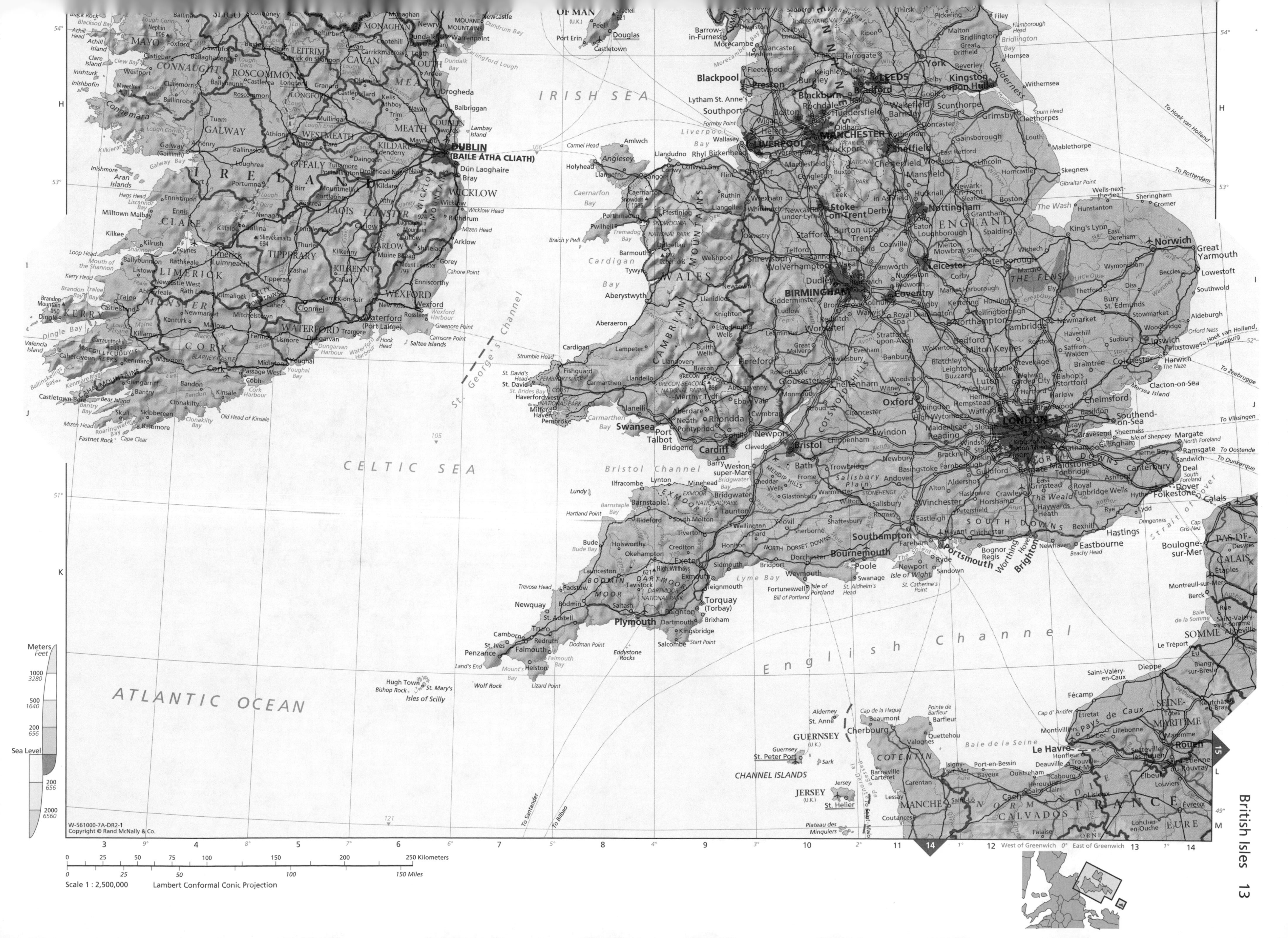

Scale 1 : 2,500,000

Lambert Conformal Conic Projection

W-561000-7A-D&2-1
Copyright © Rand McNally & Co.

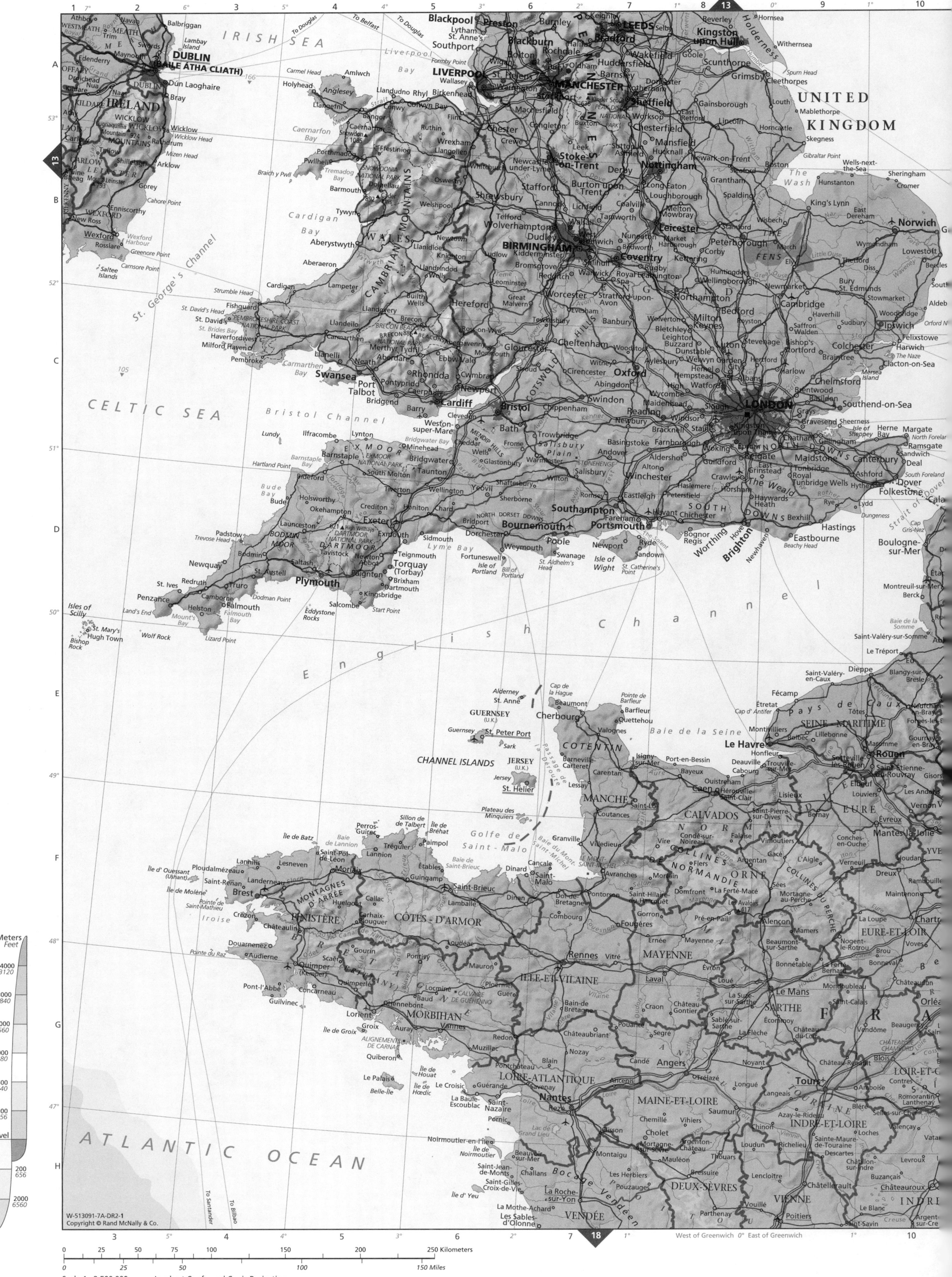

Meters
Feet

4000
13120

3000
9840

2000
6560

1000
3280

500
1640

200
656

Sea Level

200
656

2000
6560

W-513091-7A-DR2-1
Copyright © Rand McNally & Co.

0   25   50   75   100   150   200   250 Kilometers
0   25   50   100   150 Miles

Scale 1 : 2,500,000   Lambert Conformal Conic Projection

West of Greenwich 0° East of Greenwich

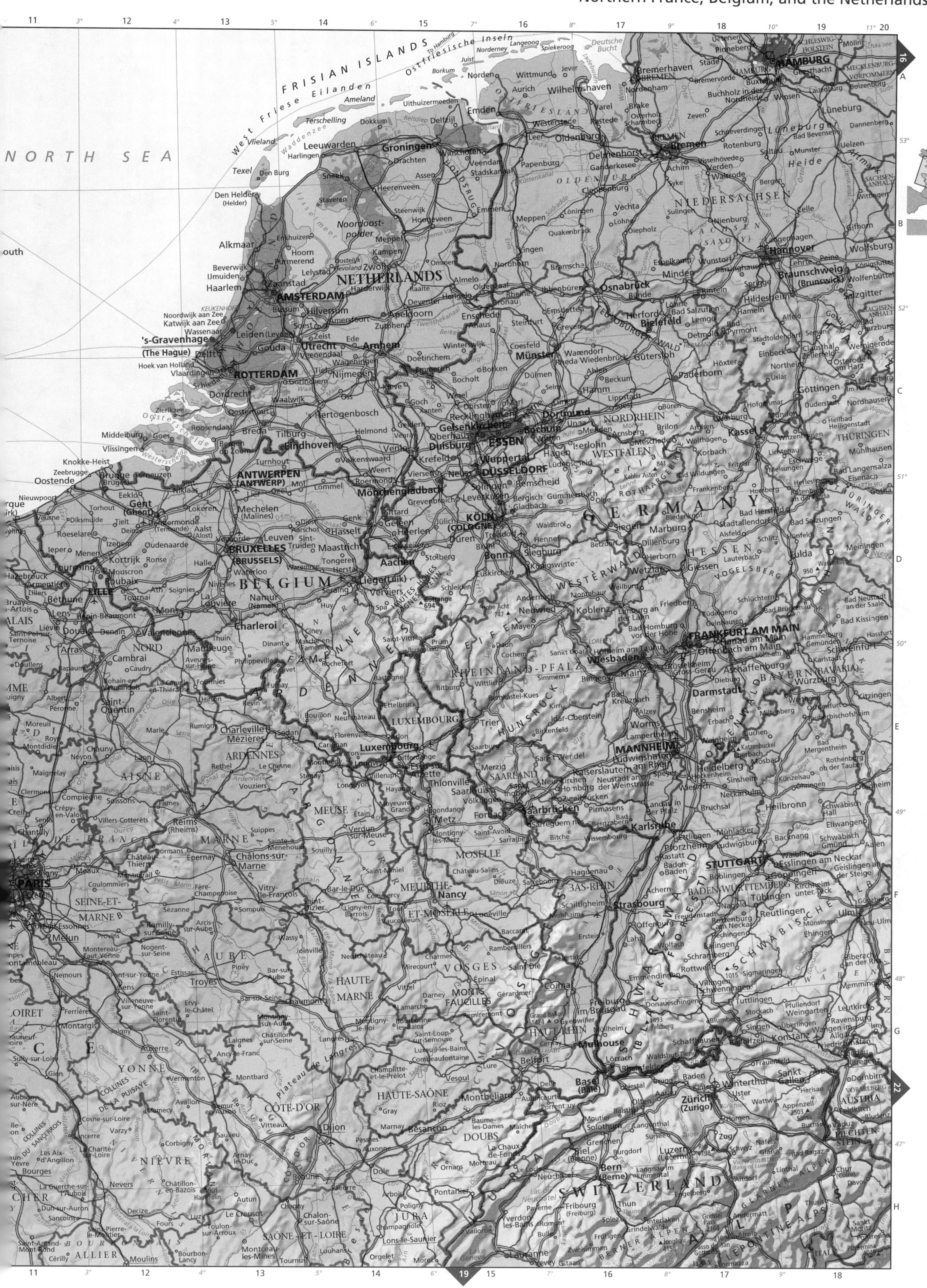
NORTH SEA
FRISIAN ISLANDS
West Friese Eilanden
Ostfriesische Inseln
NETHERLANDS
BELGIUM
LUXEMBOURG
GERMANY
SWITZERLAND
AMSTERDAM
ROTTERDAM
's-Gravenhage
(The Hague)
Utrecht
Groningen
Leeuwarden
Arnhem
Nijmegen
Eindhoven
ANTWERPEN
(ANTWERP)
BRUXELLES
(BRUSSELS)
Gent
(Ghent)
Liège (Luik)
Namur
Charleroi
Luxembourg
Oostende
LILLE
PARIS
Reims
(Rheims)
Metz
Nancy
Strasbourg
Mulhouse
Dijon
Besançon
Basel
(Bâle)
Zürich
(Zurigo)
Bern
(Berne)
Luzern
(Lucerne)
HAMBURG
Bremen
Bremerhaven
Hannover
Braunschweig
(Brunswick)
Osnabrück
Bielefeld
Münster
Dortmund
ESSEN
Duisburg
Gelsenkirchen
Bochum
DÜSSELDORF
Wuppertal
KÖLN
(COLOGNE)
Bonn
Aachen
Koblenz
Wiesbaden
Mainz
FRANKFURT AM MAIN
Darmstadt
MANNHEIM
Heidelberg
Karlsruhe
STUTTGART
Saarbrücken
Kassel
Göttingen
NIEDERSACHSEN
NORDRHEIN
WESTFALEN
RHEINLAND-PFALZ
HESSEN
SAARLAND
BADEN-WÜRTTEMBERG
BAYERN (BAVARIA)
THÜRINGEN
ARDENNES
EIFEL
HUNSRÜCK
VOSGES
JURA
ALPS
AUSTRIA
LIECHTENSTEIN

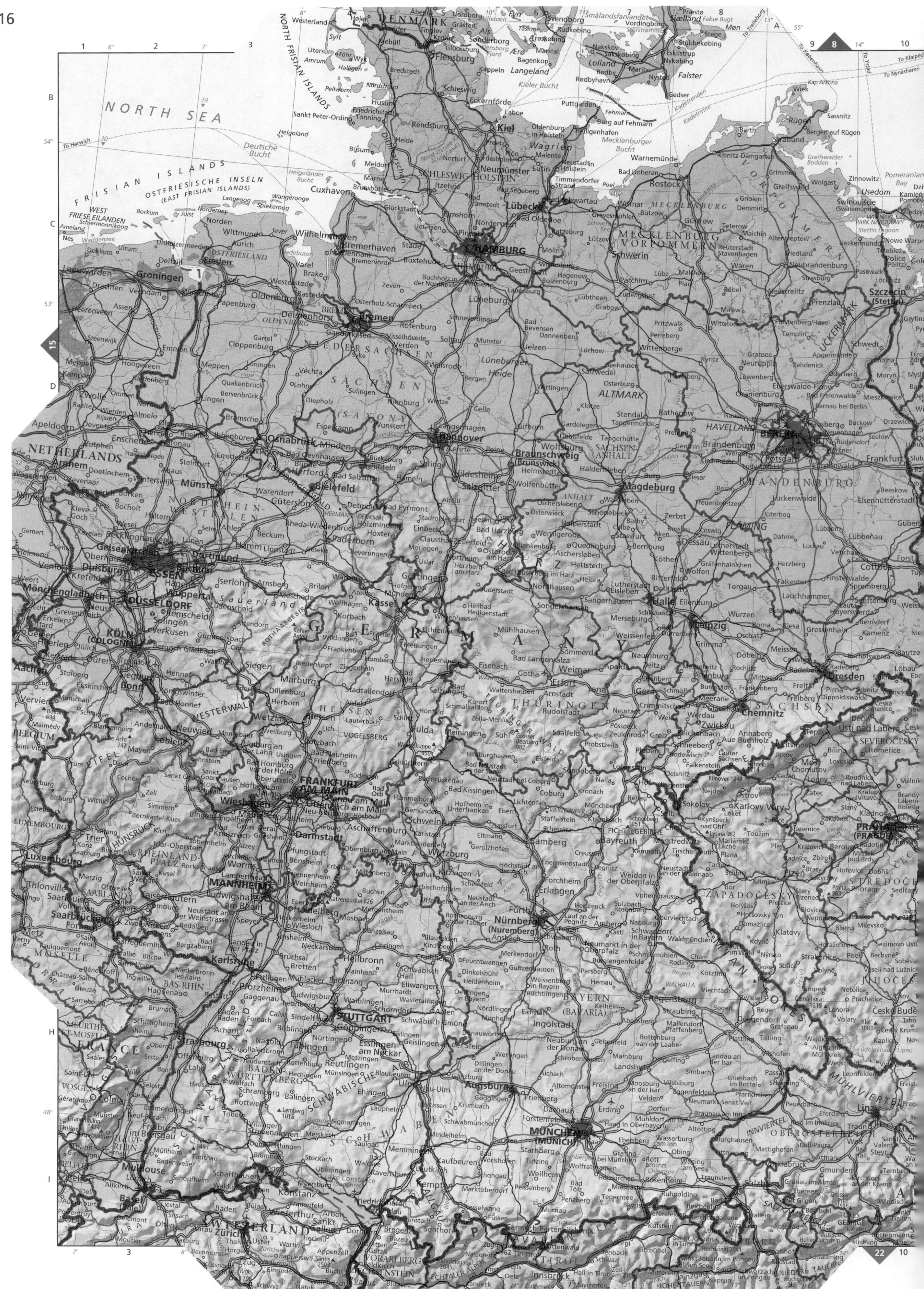
NORTH SEA
FRISIAN ISLANDS
OSTFRIESISCHE INSELN
(EAST FRISIAN ISLANDS)
WEST FRIESE EILANDEN
NORTH FRISIAN ISLANDS
Deutsche Bucht
Helgoländer Bucht
Kieler Bucht
Mecklenburger Bucht
DENMARK
Fyn
Sjælland
Lolland
Falster
Møn
Flensburg
Kiel
Lübeck
HAMBURG
Bremen
Bremerhaven
Cuxhaven
Wilhelmshaven
Emden
Oldenburg
Groningen
NETHERLANDS
Arnhem
Apeldoorn
Zwolle
Osnabrück
Münster
Bielefeld
Hannover
Braunschweig
(Brunswick)
Magdeburg
BERLIN
Potsdam
Frankfurt
Rostock
Schwerin
Stralsund
Rügen
Szczecin
(Stettin)
MECKLENBURG
VORPOMMERN
NIEDERSACHSEN
(SAXONY)
SACHSEN-ANHALT
BRANDENBURG
ALTMARK
UCKERMARK
Lüneburger Heide
Dortmund
ESSEN
Duisburg
DÜSSELDORF
Wuppertal
Mönchengladbach
KÖLN
(COLOGNE)
Bonn
Aachen
Kassel
Göttingen
HARZ
Halle
Leipzig
Dresden
Chemnitz
Erfurt
Weimar
Jena
Gera
Eisenach
THÜRINGEN
SACHSEN
HESSEN
GERMANY
NORDRHEIN-WESTFALEN
Sauerland
Westerwald
Vogelsberg
Fulda
Koblenz
Wiesbaden
FRANKFURT AM MAIN
Darmstadt
Mainz
Würzburg
Bamberg
Bayreuth
Nürnberg
(Nuremberg)
Erlangen
Regensburg
Ingolstadt
Augsburg
MÜNCHEN
(MUNICH)
BAYERN
(BAVARIA)
SCHWABEN
MANNHEIM
Heidelberg
Karlsruhe
STUTTGART
Ulm
Freiburg
Trier
Saarbrücken
Luxembourg
LUXEMBOURG
BELGIUM
FRANCE
Metz
Strasbourg
Mulhouse
Basel
(Bâle)
Zürich
SWITZERLAND
Konstanz
Innsbruck
TIROL
Salzburg
Linz
PRAHA
(PRAGUE)
Plzeň
Karlovy Vary
Ústí nad Labem
ZÁPADOČESKÝ
SEVEROČESKÝ
ČESKÁ
Rheinland-Pfalz
Hunsrück
Eifel
Schwäbische Alb
Bodensee

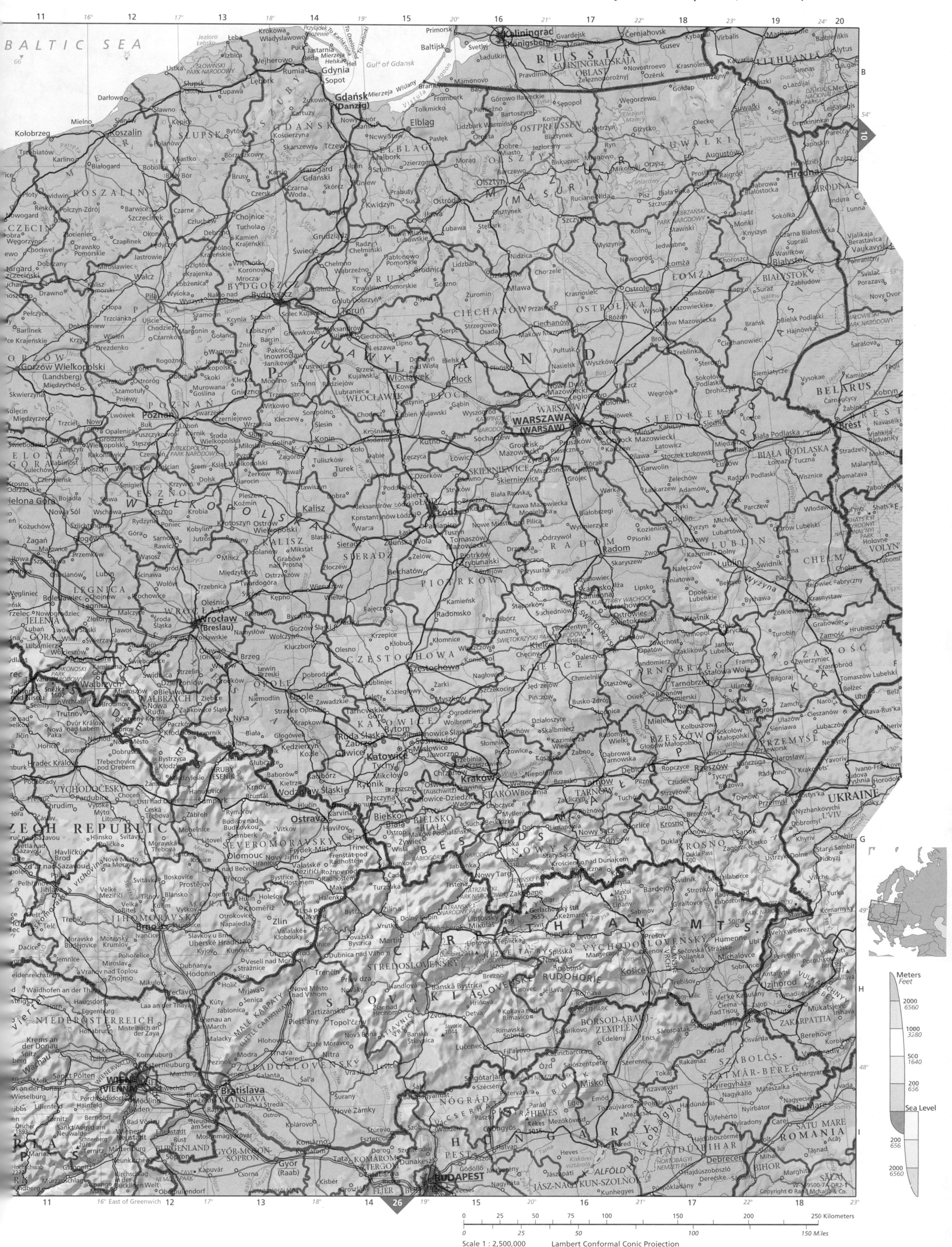
BALTIC SEA
RUSSIA
LITHUANIA
BELARUS
UKRAINE
POLAND
CZECH REPUBLIC
SLOVAKIA
HUNGARY
ROMANIA
CARPATHIAN MTS.
WARSZAWA (WARSAW)
Kaliningrad (Königsberg)
Gdańsk (Danzig)
Wrocław (Breslau)
WIEN (VIENNA)
Bratislava
BUDAPEST
Meters
Feet
2000
6560
1000
3280
500
1640
200
656
Sea Level
200
656
2000
6560
Scale 1 : 2,500,000
Lambert Conformal Conic Projection
0
25
50
75
100
150
200
250 Kilometers
0
25
50
100
150 Miles
16° East of Greenwich
Copyright © Rand McNally & Co.

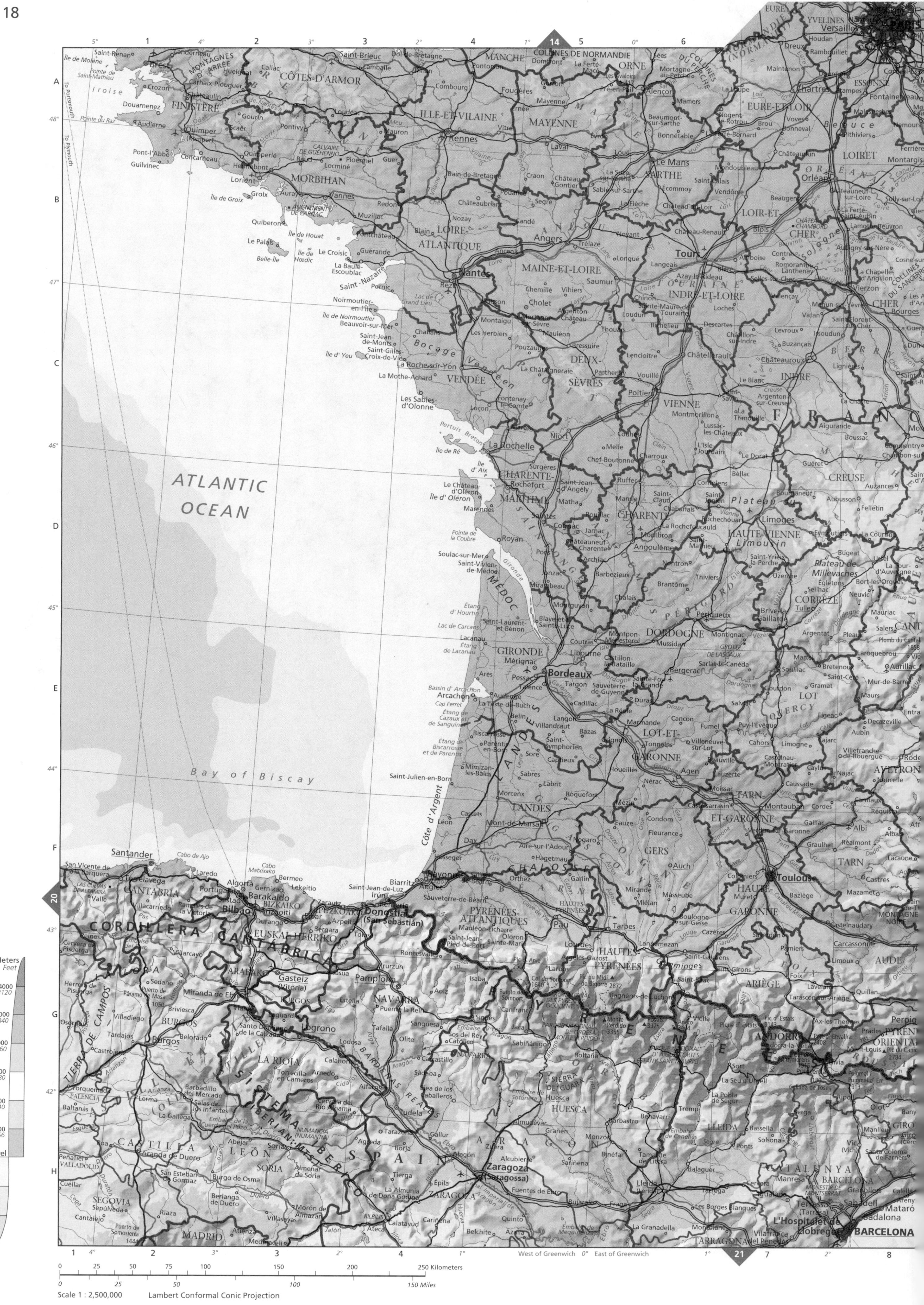

ATLANTIC
OCEAN

Bay of Biscay

Meters
Feet

4000
13120

3000
9840

2000
6560

1000
3280

500
1640

200
656

Sea Level

200
656

2000
6560

0   25   50   75   100   150   200   250 Kilometers
0   25   50   100   150 Miles

Scale 1 : 2,500,000   Lambert Conformal Conic Projection

West of Greenwich 0° East of Greenwich

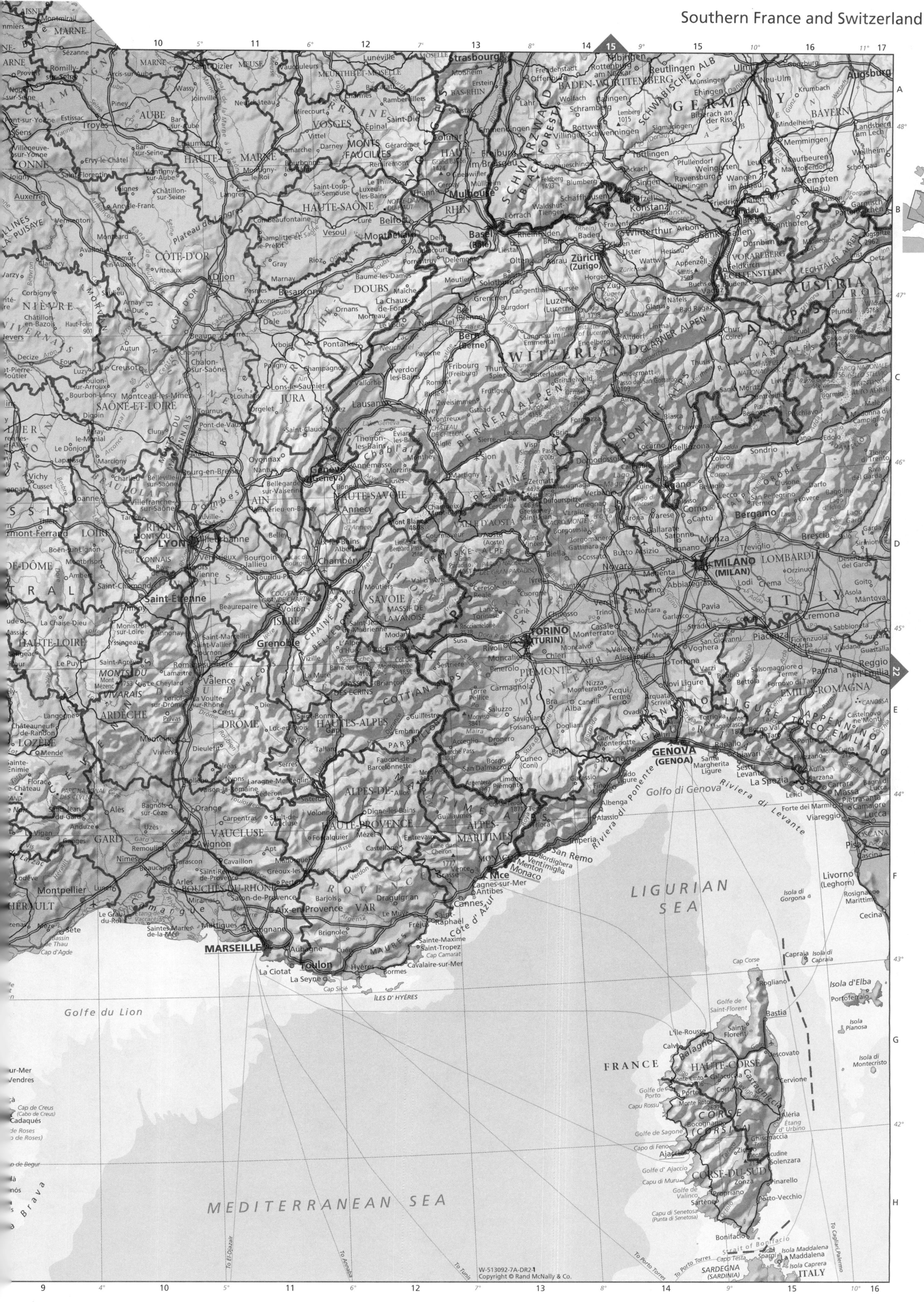
SWITZERLAND
GERMANY
AUSTRIA
ITALY
FRANCE
LIGURIAN SEA
MEDITERRANEAN SEA
Golfe du Lion
Golfo di Genova
Riviera di Levante
Riviera di ponente
Côte d'Azur
Strasbourg
Mulhouse
Basel (Bâle)
Zürich (Zurigo)
Bern (Berne)
Luzern (Lucerne)
Lausanne
Genève (Geneva)
Lyon
Saint-Étienne
Grenoble
Valence
Avignon
Montpellier
MARSEILLE
Toulon
Nice
Monaco
Cannes
TORINO (TURIN)
MILANO (MILAN)
GENOVA (GENOA)
Bergamo
Brescia
Livorno (Leghorn)
Ajaccio
Bastia
Bonifacio
Dijon
Besançon
Augsburg
Konstanz
BERNER ALPEN
PENNINE ALPS
ALPES MARITIMES
COTTIAN ALPS
JURA
VOSGES
SCHWARZWALD (BLACK FOREST)
CORSE (CORSICA)
HAUTE-CORSE
CORSE-DU-SUD
SARDEGNA (SARDINIA)
Isola d'Elba
Cap Corse
Strait of Bonifacio
To El-Djazaïr
To Annaba
To Tunis
To Porto Torres
To Cagliari, Palermo

Bay of Biscay

ATLANTIC OCEAN

ALBORAN SEA

Golfo de Cádiz

PORTUGAL

SPAIN

MOROCCO

Meters	Feet
3000	9840
2000	6560
1000	3280
500	1640
200	656
Sea Level	
200	656
2000	6560

W-556200-7A-DR2-1

0 25 50 75 100 150 200 Kilometers

0 25 50 100 Miles

Scale 1 : 2,500,000

Lambert Conformal Conic Projection

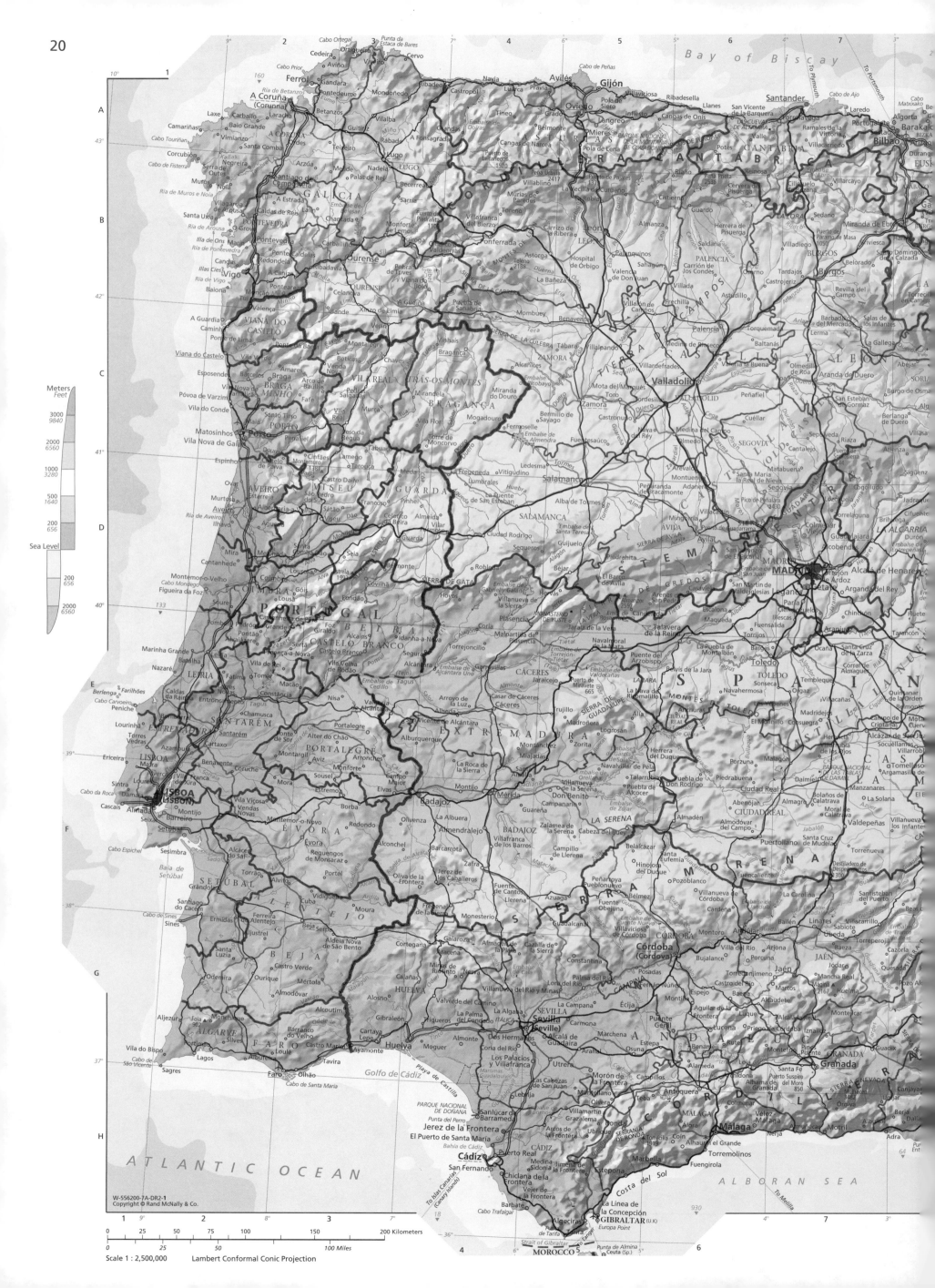

9 10 11 18 12 13 14 15

Golfe du Lion

Pyrénées-Atlantiques
Hautes-Pyrénées
Haute-Garonne
Ariège
Aude
Hérault
Pyrénées-Orientales
Gers
Béarn
Landes
Tarn

F R A N C E

P Y R É N É E S

Bayonne
Biarritz
Saint-Jean-de-Luz
Irún
Donostia (San Sebastián)
Pamplona
Navarra
Estella
Logroño
Tudela
Tarazona
Zaragoza (Saragossa)
Aragón
Huesca
Jaca
Lourdes
Pau
Tarbes
Toulouse
Carcassonne
Narbonne
Béziers
Sète
Perpignan
Port-Vendres
Andorra
Andorra la Vella
La Seu d'Urgell
Figueres
Girona
Olot
Vic
Manresa
Terrassa
Mataró
Badalona
BARCELONA
L'Hospitalet de Llobregat
Vilanova i la Geltrú
Tarragona
Reus
Lleida
Catalunya
Costa Brava
Cap de Creus
Cadaqués
Golf de Sant Jordi
Tortosa
Amposta
Delta de l'Ebre
Vinaròs
Benicarló
Peñíscola
Castelló de la Plana
Illes Columbrets
Teruel
Cuenca
Sagunt
Golf de València
VALÈNCIA
València
Gandia
Dénia
Xàbia
Cap de la Nau
Benidorm
Alcoi
Elx
Alacant (Alicante)
Albacete
Murcia
Cartagena
Torrevella
Lorca
Águilas
Mojácar
Cabo de Gata

ILLES BALEARS (BALEARIC ISLANDS)
Menorca (Minorca)
Ciutadella de Menorca
Maó
Mallorca (Majorca)
Palma de Mallorca
Badia de Palma
Alcúdia
Manacor
Cabrera
Eivissa (Ibiza)
Formentera
Sant Antoni de Portmany

MEDITERRANEAN SEA

EL DJAZAÏR (ALGIERS)
Tizi-Ouzou
Dellys
Cherchell
Ténès
Ech Cheliff
Blida
Médéa
Kabylie
ALGERIA
ATLAS MOUNTAINS

2° 9 1° 10 West of Greenwich 0° East of Greenwich 11 1° 12 2° 64 13 3° 14 4° 15

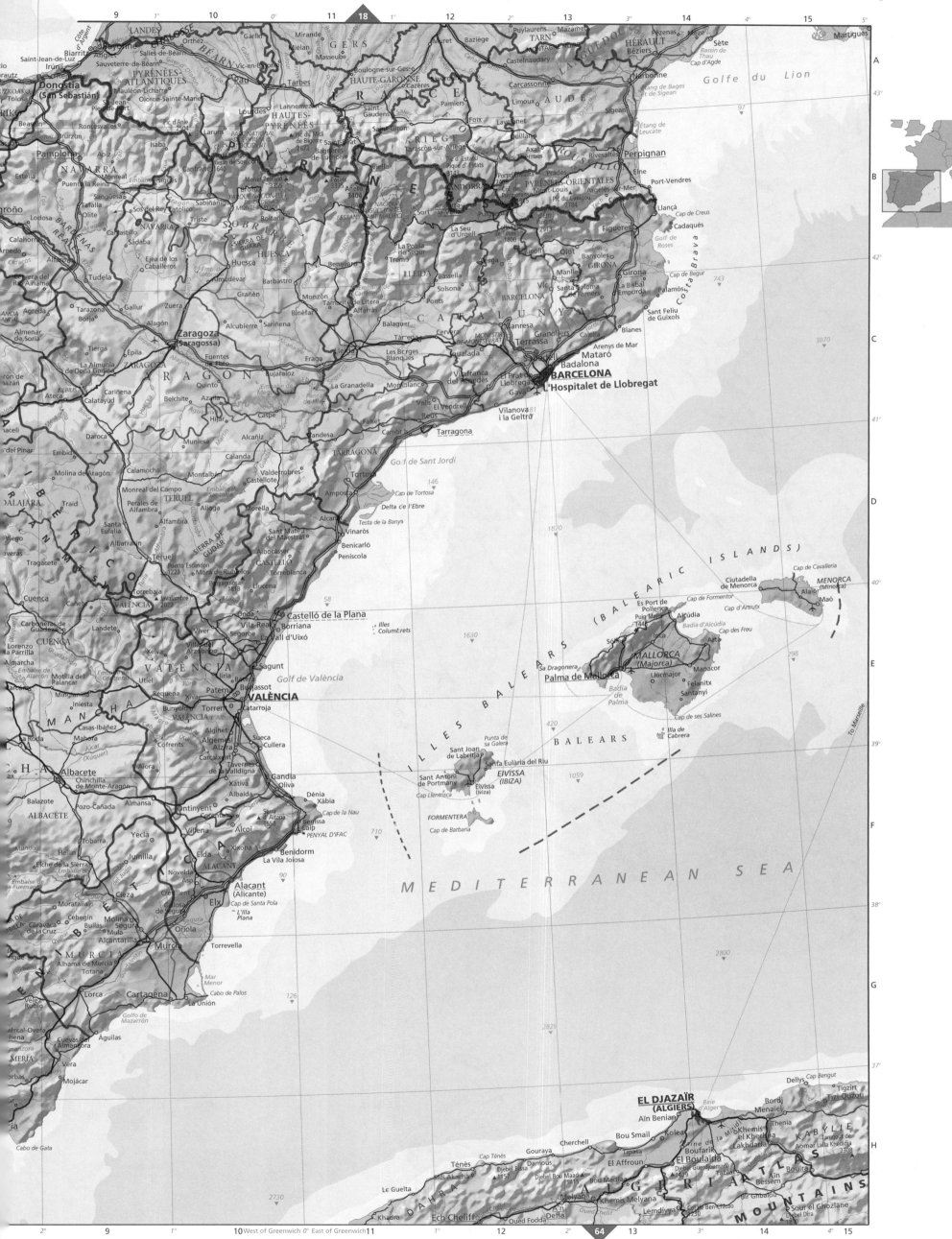

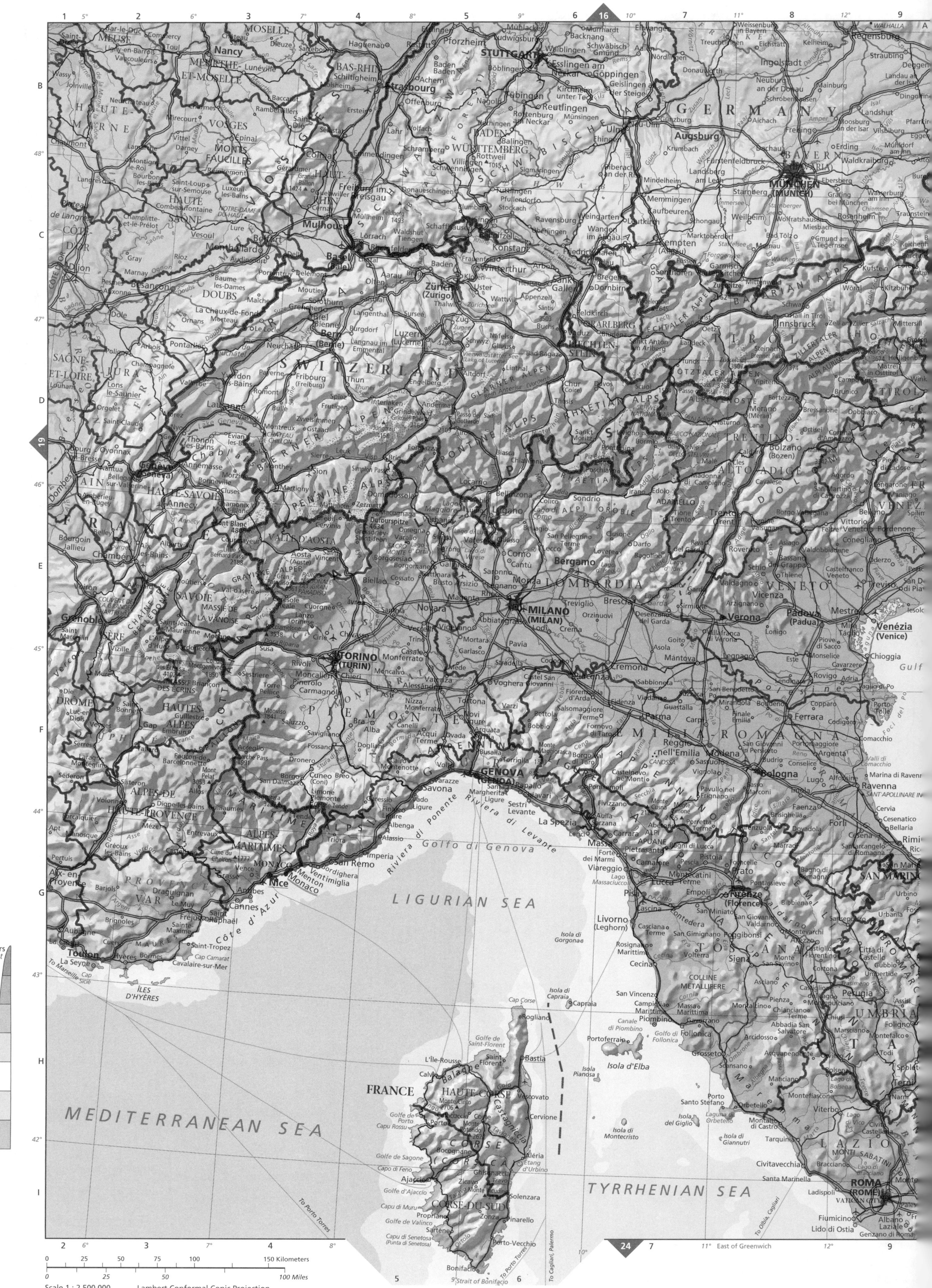
GERMANY
SWITZERLAND
FRANCE
LIGURIAN SEA
MEDITERRANEAN SEA
TYRRHENIAN SEA
Golfo di Genova
STUTTGART
MÜNCHEN (MUNICH)
Augsburg
Strasbourg
Nancy
Mulhouse
Basel (Bâle)
Zürich (Zurigo)
Bern (Berne)
Luzern (Luzerne)
Genève (Geneva)
Lausanne
Grenoble
Annecy
Chambéry
Besançon
Dijon
MILANO (MILAN)
TORINO (TURIN)
GENOVA (GENOA)
Bergamo
Brescia
Verona
Padova (Padua)
Venézia (Venice)
Bologna
Ferrara
Ravenna
Parma
Modena
Firenze (Florence)
Livorno (Leghorn)
Pisa
Siena
Perugia
ROMA (ROME)
Innsbruck
Bolzano (Bozen)
Trento
Nice
Monaco
Cannes
Toulon
Bastia
Ajaccio
Isola d'Elba
LOMBARDIA
PIEMONTE
EMILIA-ROMAGNA
VENETO
TOSCANA
UMBRIA
LAZIO
TIROL
BAYERN
CORSE
PENNINE ALPS
BERNER ALPEN
MARITIME ALPS
Meters
Feet
4000
13120
3000
9840
2000
6560
1000
3280
500
1640
200
656
Sea Level
200
656
2000
6560
0
25
50
75
100
150 Kilometers
0
25
50
100 Miles
Scale 1 : 2,500,000
Lambert Conformal Conic Projection
East of Greenwich

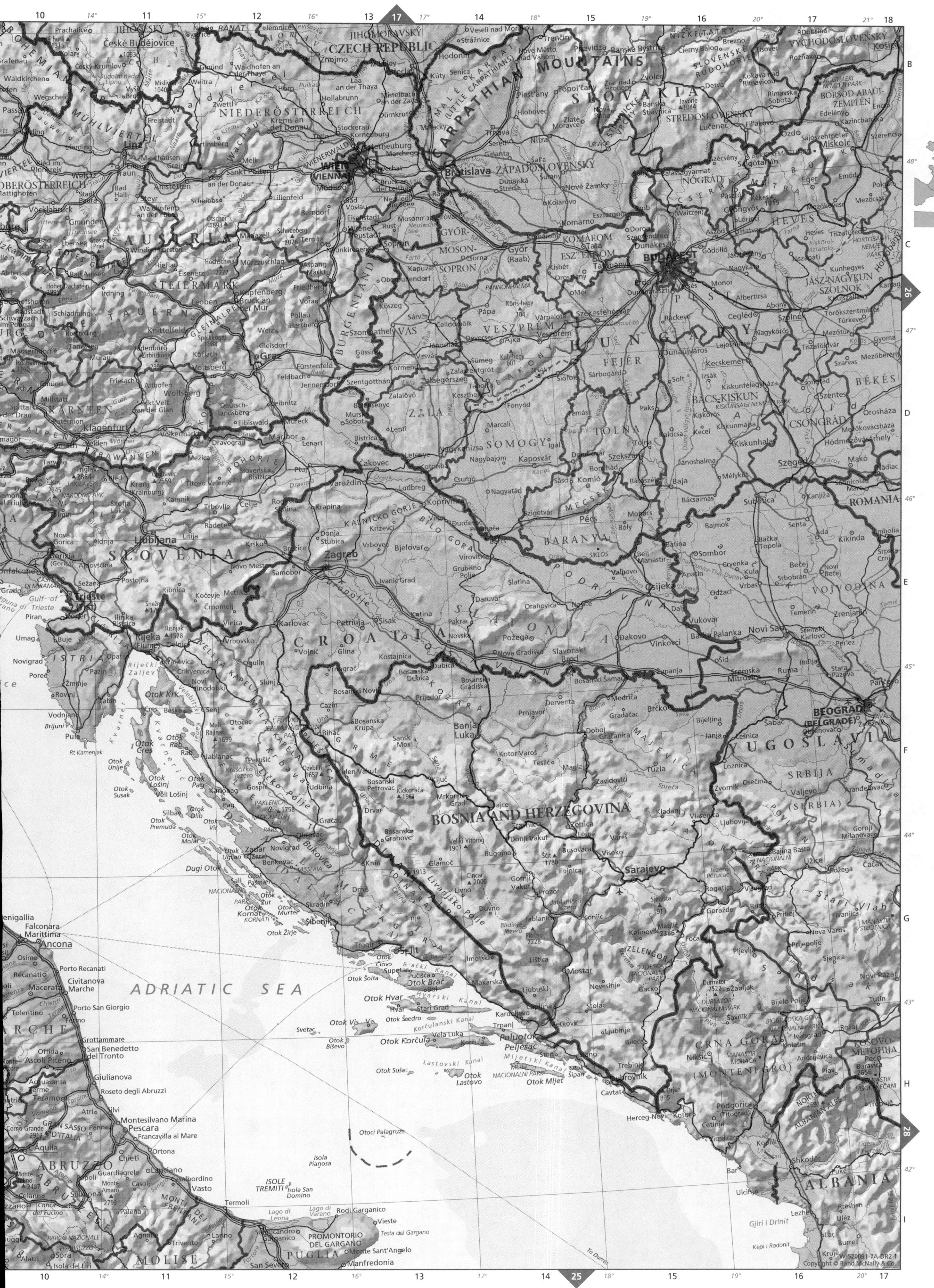
CZECH REPUBLIC
CARPATHIAN MOUNTAINS
SLOVAKIA
NIEDERÖSTERREICH
OBERÖSTERREICH
AUSTRIA
STEIERMARK
KÄRNTEN
BURGENLAND
WIEN (VIENNA)
Bratislava
ZÁPADOSLOVENSKÝ
STREDOSLOVENSKÝ
VÝCHODOSLOVENSKÝ
BORSOD-ABAÚJ-ZEMPLÉN
Miskolc
BUDAPEST
PEST
HUNGARY
VESZPRÉM
FEJÉR
TOLNA
SOMOGY
ZALA
BARANYA
BÁCS-KISKUN
CSONGRÁD
BÉKÉS
JÁSZ-NAGYKUN SZOLNOK
HEVES
NÓGRÁD
GYŐR-MOSON-SOPRON
KOMÁROM ESZTERGOM
VAS
Győr (Raab)
Linz
Graz
Klagenfurt
Ljubljana
SLOVENIA
Trieste
Gulf of Trieste
Zagreb
CROATIA
ISTRIA
Rijeka (Fiume)
Osijek
Novi Sad
VOJVODINA
ROMANIA
BEOGRAD (BELGRADE)
YUGOSLAVIA
SRBIJA (SERBIA)
Sarajevo
BOSNIA AND HERZEGOVINA
Banja Luka
Tuzla
Split
Dubrovnik
CRNA GORA (MONTENEGRO)
Podgorica (Titograd)
KOSOVO METOHIJA
ALBANIA
NORTH ALBANIAN ALPS
ADRIATIC SEA
Ancona
Pescara
ABRUZZO
MARCHE
MOLISE
PUGLIA
PROMONTORIO DEL GARGANO
ISOLE TREMITI
Manfredonia
Otok Hvar
Otok Brač
Otok Korčula
Otok Mljet
Otok Krk
Dugi Otok
Otok Vis
Otok Lastovo
Copyright © Rand McNally & Co.

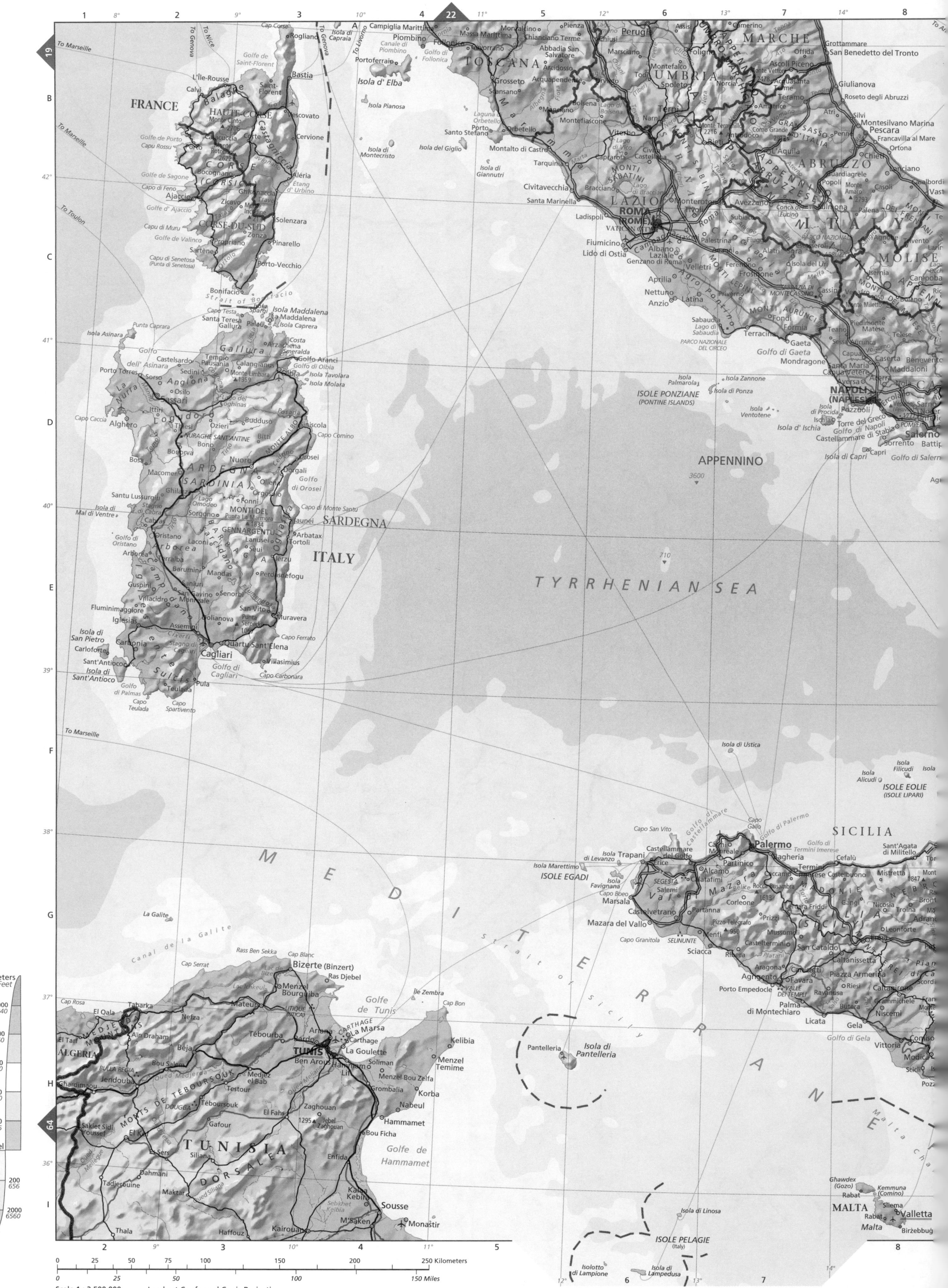
FRANCE
ITALY
SARDEGNA
TYRRHENIAN SEA
MEDITERRANEAN
SICILIA
TUNISIA
ALGERIA
MALTA
TOSCANA
UMBRIA
MARCHE
LAZIO
ABRUZZO
MOLISE
CORSE
Roma (Rome)
Napoli (Naples)
Palermo
Cagliari
Tunis
Bastia
Ajaccio
Isola d' Elba
Strait of Bonifacio
Strait of Sicily
Golfe de Tunis
Golfe de Hammamet
ISOLE EGADI
ISOLE EOLIE (ISOLE LIPARI)
ISOLE PONZIANE (PONTINE ISLANDS)
ISOLE PELAGIE
Isola di Pantelleria
APPENNINO
Meters
Feet
3000
9840
2000
6560
1000
3280
500
1640
200
656
Sea Level
200
656
2000
6560
Scale 1 : 2,500,000
Lambert Conformal Conic Projection
0
25
50
75
100
150
200
250 Kilometers
0
25
50
100
150 Miles

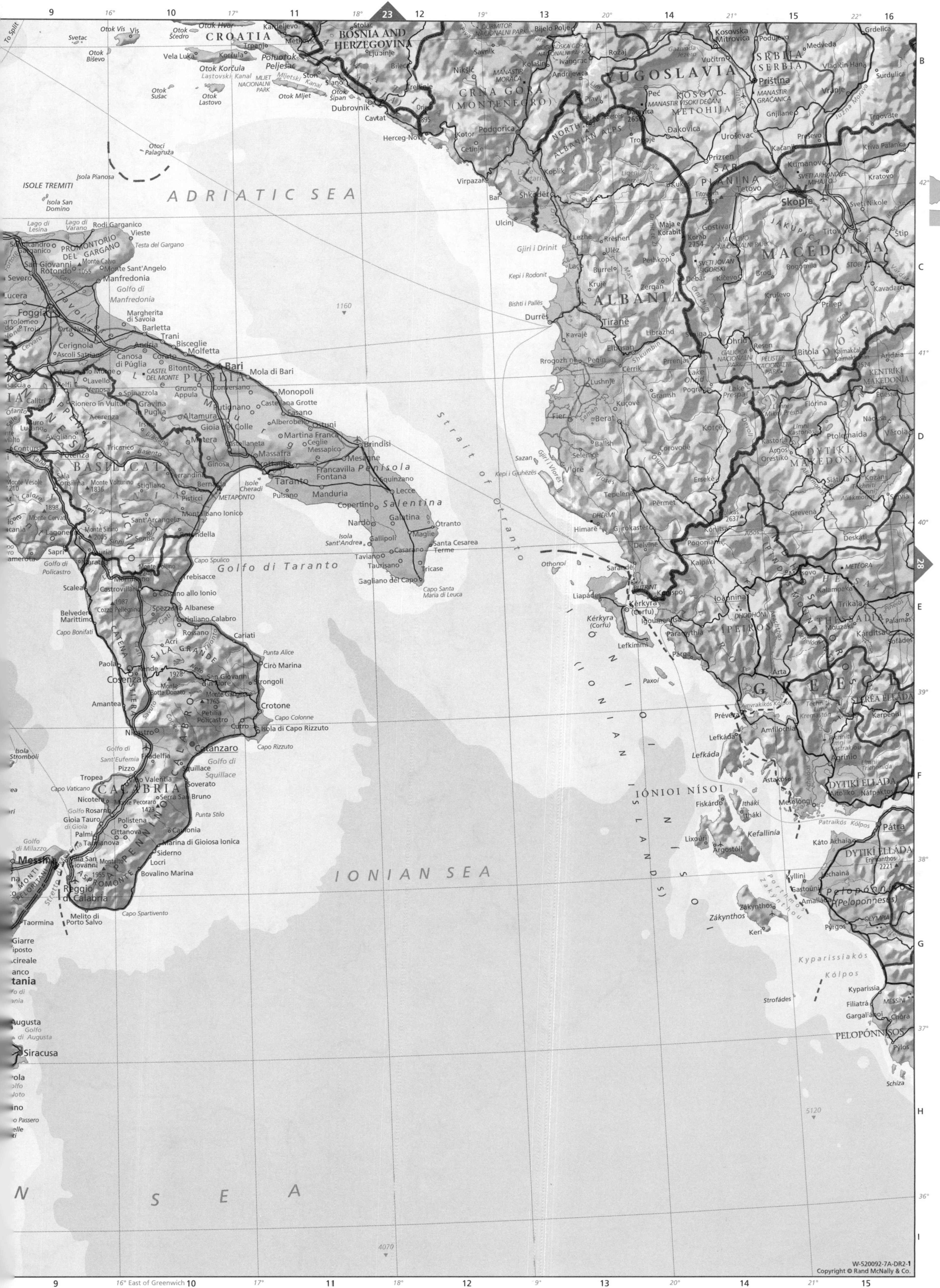

CROATIA
BOSNIA AND HERZEGOVINA
CRNA GORA (MONTENEGRO)
YUGOSLAVIA
SRBIJA (SERBIA)
KOSOVO-METOHIJA
ALBANIA
MACEDONIA
GREECE
ADRIATIC SEA
IONIAN SEA
Strait of Otranto
Golfo di Taranto
Golfo di Manfredonia
ISOLE TREMITI
PROMONTORIO DEL GARGANO
PUGLIA
BASILICATA
CALABRIA
SILA GRANDE
Penisola Salentina
IÓNIOI NÍSOI
IONIAN ISLANDS
Kérkyra (Corfu)
Kefallinía
Zákynthos
Lefkáda
Ithákí
Dubrovnik
Podgorica
Shkodër
Durrës
Tiranë
Elbasan
Berat
Vlorë
Skopje
Prištinа
Bari
Foggia
Barletta
Trani
Molfetta
Monopoli
Brindisi
Lecce
Taranto
Gallipoli
Otranto
Matera
Potenza
Cosenza
Catanzaro
Crotone
Reggio di Calabria
Messina
Taormina
Catania
Siracusa
Augusta
Ioánnina
Árta
Préveza
Pátra
Kalamáta
Pýrgos
Kyparissía
Pelopónnisos (Peloponnesus)

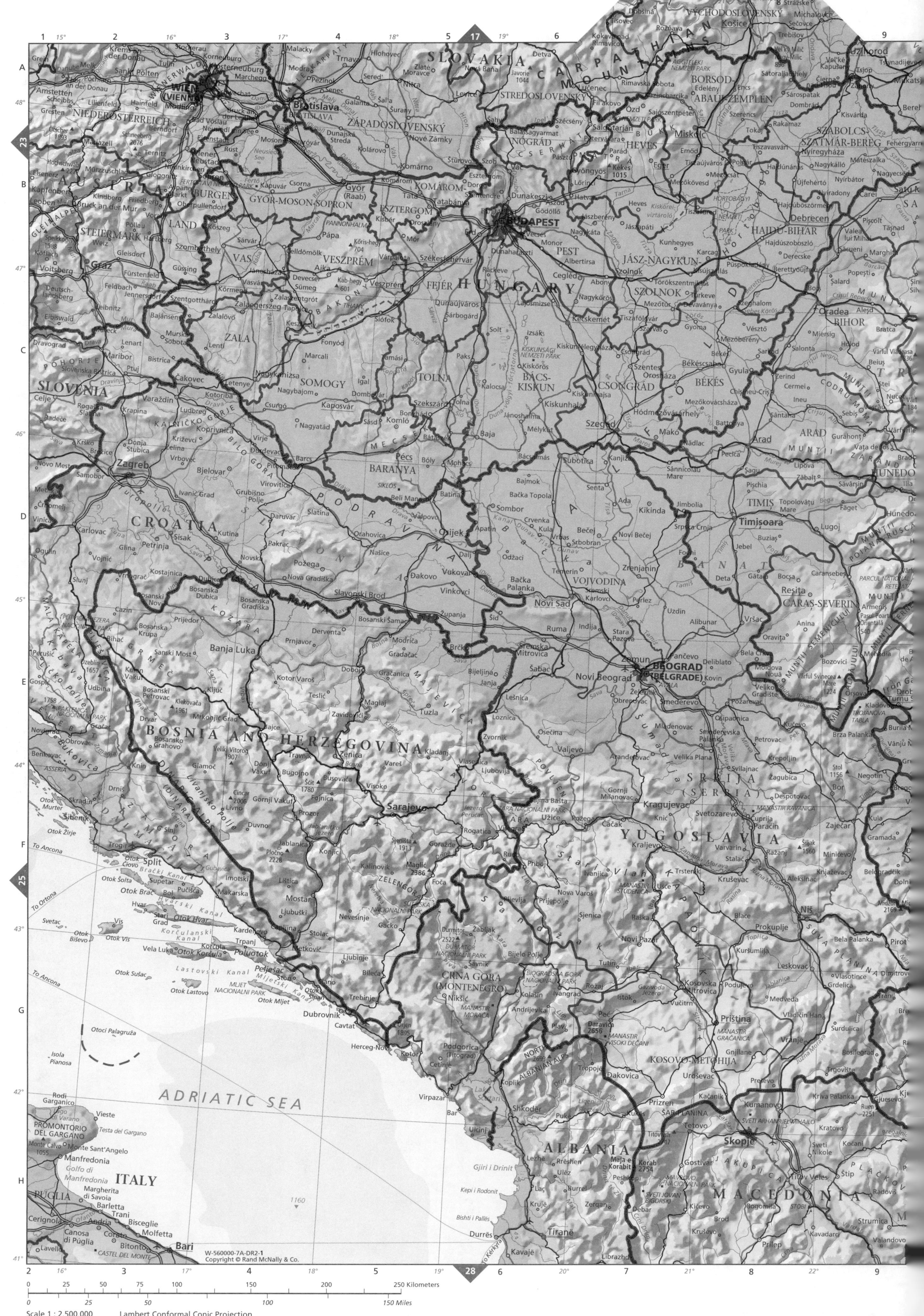

SLOVAKIA
CARPATHIAN MOUNTAINS
HUNGARY
SLOVENIA
CROATIA
BOSNIA AND HERZEGOVINA
YUGOSLAVIA
SRBIJA (SERBIA)
CRNA GORA (MONTENEGRO)
ALBANIA
MACEDONIA
ITALY
ADRIATIC SEA
WIEN (VIENNA)
Bratislava
BUDAPEST
Zagreb
Sarajevo
BEOGRAD (BELGRADE)
Novi Sad
Skopje
Podgorica (Titograd)
Tiranë
Bari
Split
Dubrovnik
Debrecen
Szeged
Timişoara
Pécs
Győr (Raab)
Miskolc
Košice
Graz
Niš
Priština
VOJVODINA
KOSOVO-METOHIJA
SLAVONIJA
PODRAVINA
BANAT
DINARA
Meters
Feet
2000
6560
1000
3280
500
1640
200
656
Sea Level
200
656
2000
6560
W-560000-7A-DR2-1
Copyright © Rand McNally & Co.
0
25
50
75
100
150
200
250 Kilometers
0
25
50
100
150 Miles
Scale 1 : 2,500,000
Lambert Conformal Conic Projection

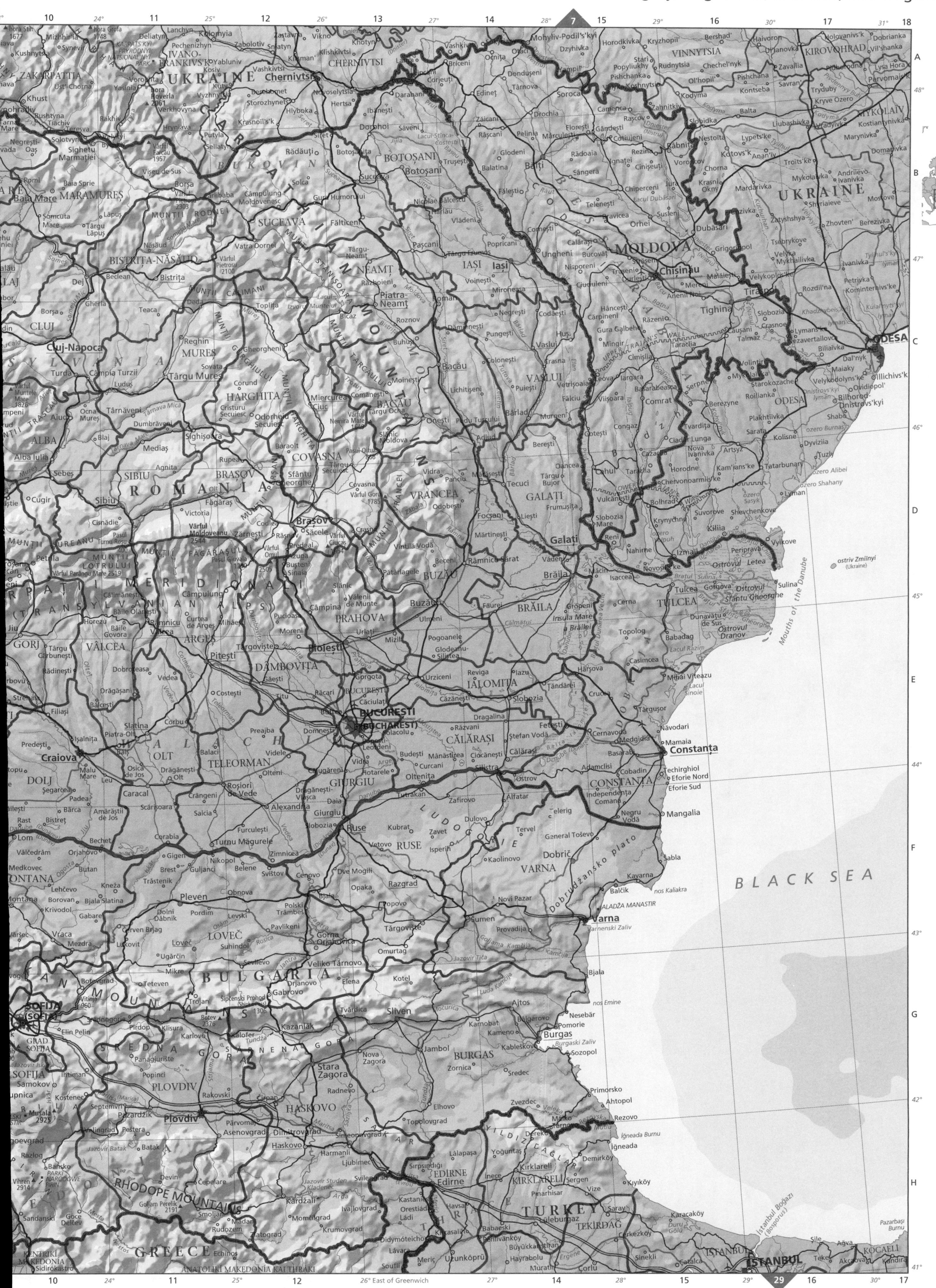
UKRAINE
MOLDOVA
ROMANIA
BULGARIA
TURKEY
GREECE
BLACK SEA
Chernivtsi
Chişinău
Iaşi
Bacău
Galaţi
Brăila
Braşov
Ploieşti
BUCUREŞTI (BUCHAREST)
Constanţa
Craiova
Pleven
Ruse
Varna
Burgas
Plovdiv
SOFIJA (SOFIA)
Edirne
İSTANBUL
ODESA
Cluj-Napoca
26° East of Greenwich

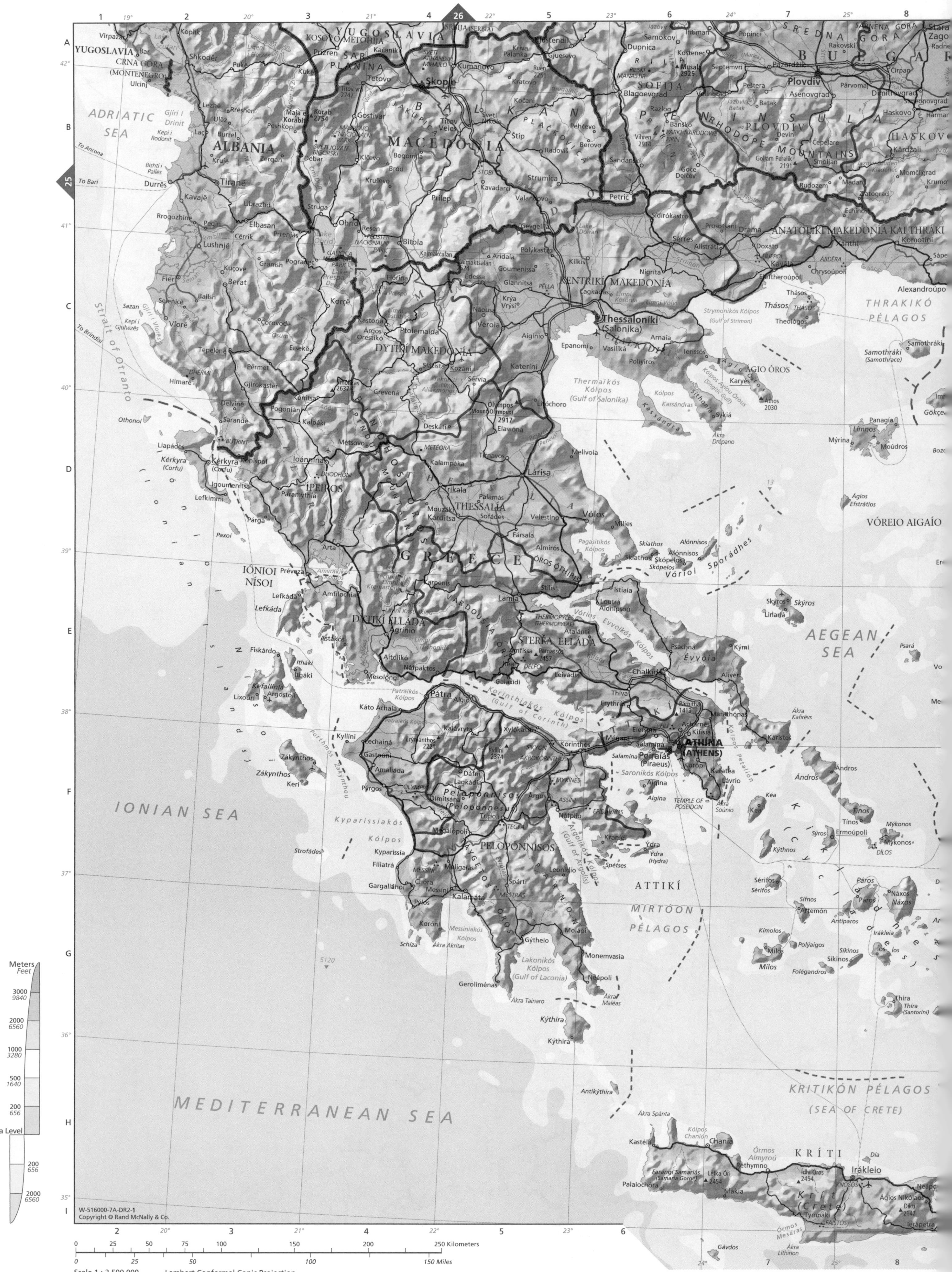

YUGOSLAVIA

CRNA GORA
(MONTENEGRO)

ALBANIA

Tiranë

Durrës

ADRIATIC
SEA

To Ancona

To Bari

To Brindisi

Strait of Otranto

YUGOSLAVIA

SRBIJA (SERBIA)

KOSOVO
METOHIJA

ŠAR
PLANINA

Skopje

MACEDONIA

BALKAN

Bitola

PINDHOS

DYTIKÍ MAKEDONIA

ÍPEIROS

IÓNIOI
NÍSOI

GREECE

Kérkyra
(Corfu)

Ioánnina

THESSALIA

Lárisa

Vólos

DYTIKÍ ELLÁDA

STEREÁ ELLÁDA

Lamía

Pátra

Pelopónnisos
(Peloponnesus)

PELOPÓNNISOS

ATTIKÍ

ATHÍNA
(ATHENS)

Peiraiás
(Piraeus)

IONIAN SEA

MEDITERRANEAN SEA

BULGARIA

Plovdiv

RHODOPE
MOUNTAINS

SOFIJA

ANATOLIKÍ MAKEDONÍA KAI THRÁKI

KENTRIKÍ MAKEDONÍA

Thessaloníki
(Salonika)

THRAKIKÓ
PÉLAGOS

Thermaïkós
Kólpos
(Gulf of Salonika)

ÁGIO ÓROS

VÓREIO AIGAÍO

Sporádhes

AEGEAN
SEA

Évvoia

Korinthiakós Kólpos
(Gulf of Corinth)

MIRTÓON
PÉLAGOS

KRITIKÓN PÉLAGOS
(SEA OF CRETE)

KRÍTI
(CRETE)

Irákleio

Meters
Feet

3000
9840

2000
6560

1000
3280

500
1640

200
656

Sea Level

200
656

2000
6560

W-516000-7A-DR2-1
Copyright © Rand McNally & Co.

0   25   50   75   100   150   200   250 Kilometers

0   25   50   100   150 Miles

Scale 1 : 2,500,000   Lambert Conformal Conic Projection

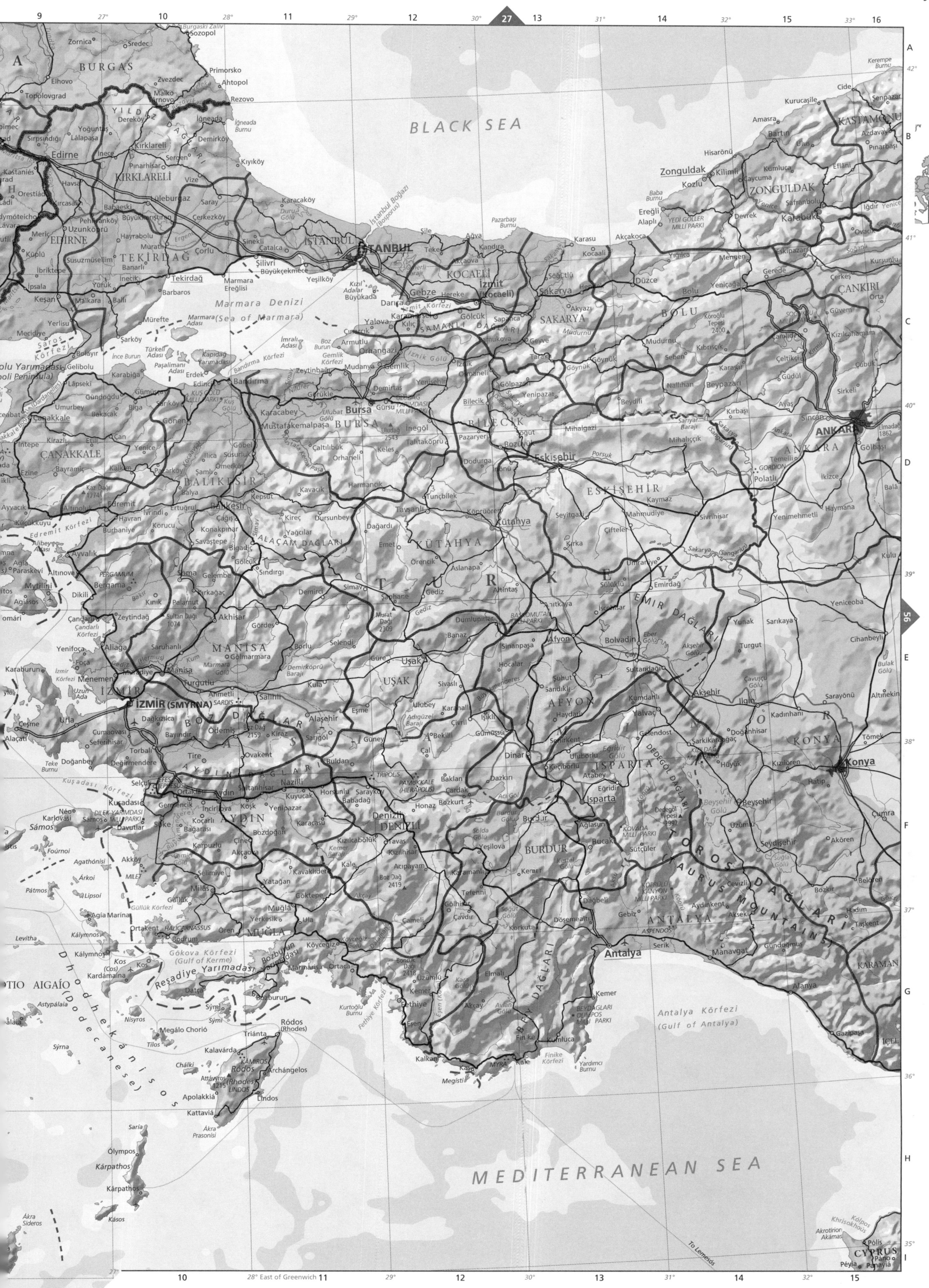
BLACK SEA
MEDITERRANEAN SEA
Marmara Denizi
(Sea of Marmara)
Antalya Körfezi
(Gulf of Antalya)
BURGAS
Sozopol
Primorsko
Ahtopol
Rezovo
Edirne
EDİRNE
KIRKLARELİ
Kırklareli
TEKİRDAĞ
Tekirdağ
İSTANBUL
İstanbul Boğazı
(Bosporus)
Şile
KOCAELİ
İzmit
(Kocaeli)
Gebze
SAKARYA
Sakarya
Düzce
BOLU
Bolu
Zonguldak
ZONGULDAK
Karabük
Amasra
KASTAMONU
ÇANKIRI
ANKARA
Ankara
Gölbaşı
Polatlı
GORDION
Eskişehir
ESKİŞEHİR
BİLECİK
Bilecik
Bursa
BURSA
Yalova
Gemlik
Mudanya
Bandırma
Gelibolu
Çanakkale
ÇANAKKALE
BALIKESİR
Balıkesir
Edremit
Ayvalık
Bergama
PERGAMUM
Mytilíni
Manisa
MANİSA
Akhisar
İZMİR
İZMİR (SMYRNA)
SARDIS
Çeşme
Urla
Kuşadası
EFES
EPHESUS
Söke
Aydın
AYDIN
Nazilli
Denizli
DENİZLİ
PAMUKKALE
(HIERAPOLIS)
UŞAK
Uşak
KÜTAHYA
Kütahya
AFYON
Afyon
Emirdağ
Bolvadin
Akşehir
KONYA
Konya
ISPARTA
Isparta
Eğirdir
BURDUR
Burdur
Beyşehir
ANTALYA
Antalya
ASPENDOS
Manavgat
Alanya
Kemer
Finike
Kaş
Kalkan
Fethiye
MUĞLA
Muğla
Milâs
Bodrum
HALICARNASSUS
Marmaris
Datça
Kos
Sámos
Rhódos
(Rhodes)
Ródos
LINDOS
Kárpathos
Kásos
Dhodhekánisos
(Dodecanese)
TOROS DAĞLARI
TAURUS MOUNTAINS
EMİR DAĞLARI
BOZ DAĞLAR
AYDIN DAĞLARI
ALAÇAM DAĞLARI
SULTAN DAĞLARI
T U R K E Y
CYPRUS
Pólis
Kelbey
To Lemesós
28° East of Greenwich
9
10
11
12
13
14
15
16
A
B
C
D
E
F
G
H
I
27
56

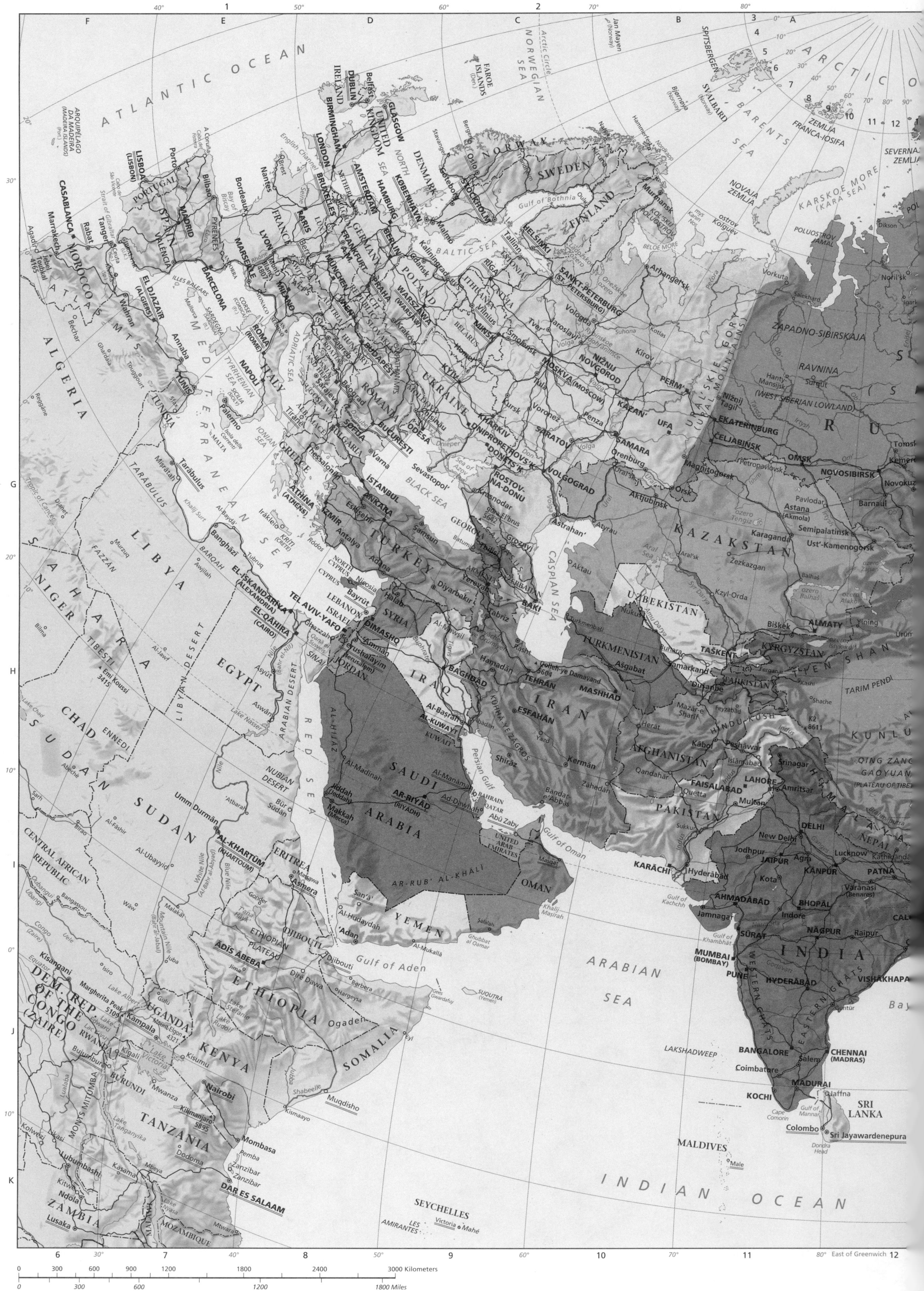

Scale 1 : 30,000,000   Lambert Azimuthal Equal Area Projection

A   B   C   D   E   F   G   H   I   J   K

PACIFIC OCEAN

BERING SEA

Bering Strait

St.Lawrence Island (U.S.)

ostrov Vrangelja

proliv Longa

MORE LAPTEVYH (LAPTEV SEA)

NOVOSIBIRSKIE OSTROVA

VOSTOČNO-SIBIRSKOE MORE

ALEUTIAN ISLANDS (U.S.)

Attu   Kiska

KOMANDORSKIE OSTROVA

HAWAIIAN ISLANDS (U.S.)

MIDWAY ISLANDS (U.S.)

HREBET ČERSKOGO

VERHOJANSKIJ HREBET

SEA OF OKHOTSK

POLUOSTROV KAMCATKA

Petropavlovsk-Kamčatskij

Tropic of Cancer

STANOVOJ HREBET

KURIL'SKIE OSTROVA (KURIL ISLANDS)

OSTROV SAHALIN

WAKE (U.S.)

SIHOTE-ALIN'

Komsomol'sk-na-Amure

Tatarskij proliv

HOKKAIDO

Sapporo   Hakodate

Vladivostok

Aomori

Sendai

SEA OF JAPAN

HONSHŪ

Niigata

TŌKYŌ

Minami-Tori-Shima (Japan)

Irkutsk

Ulan-Ude

Čita

Blagoveščensk

Harbin

HARBIN

Qiqihar

CHANGCHUN

Jilin

FUSHUN

SHENYANG

Ch'ŏngjin

NORTH KOREA

P'yongyang

SOUL (SEOUL)

Kanazawa

KYŌTO

NAGOYA

YOKOHAMA

JAPAN

Kazan-Retto (Japan)

Ogasawara-Gunto (Japan)

MONGOLIA

HANGAYN NURUU

Har-Us nuur

Ulaanbaatar

Hohhot

BEIJING

Zhangjiakou

DALIAN

Bo Hai

TAEGU

SOUTH KOREA

PUSAN

HIROSHIMA

OSAKA

FUKUOKA

SHIKOKU

KYŪSHŪ

Mokp'o

Korea Strait

Cheju-do

Kagoshima

Amami-Ō-shima

NORTHERN MARIANAS (U.S.)

Farallon de Pajaros

Agrihan

Alamagan   Pagan

GOBI DESERT

Baotou

TAIYUAN   TIANJIN

Yinchuan

Shijiazhuang

JINAN

Qingdao

YELLOW SEA

Okinawa-jima

Naha

NANSEI-SHOTO (RYUKYU ISLANDS)

Anatahan

Guguan

Saipan

Tinian

Rota

GUAM (U.S.)

Agana

MARIANA ISLANDS

Gaferut

Ulul

MICRONESIA

HALL ISLANDS

MORTLOCK ISLANDS

CHUUK

SENYAVIN ISLANDS

Oroluk

Pohnpei

Kolonia

Xining

Lanzhou

Baoji

XI'AN

Zhengzhou

Kaifeng

Xuzhou

Huainan

Nanjing

SHANGHAI

Ningbo

EAST CHINA SEA

CHINA

Qinghai Hu

Lhasa

CHENGDU

CHONGQING

WUHAN

Nanchang

CHANGSHA

Hangzhou

Wenzhou

T'AIPEI

TAIWAN

Tainan

KAOHSIUNG

Taiwan Strait

PHILIPPINE SEA

YAP

Sorol

Woleai

Eauripik

Ngulu

Faraulep

Lamotrek

Pulap

Ulul

FEDERATED STATES OF MICRONESIA

CAROLINE ISLANDS

Kapingamarangi

Zigong

Guiyang

Liuzhou

Kunming

GUANGZHOU

Nanning

MACAU

XIANGGANG (HONG KONG)

Zhanjiang

Luzon Strait

LUZON

Quezon City

MANILA

PHILIPPINES

Equator

Ngulu

BANGLADESH

DHAKA (DACCA)

CHITTAGONG

MYANMAR (BURMA)

Mandalay

LAOS

HA NOI (HANOI)

Hai Phong

Gulf of Tonkin

Haikou

HAINAN DAO

VIETNAM

XISHA QUNDAO (PARACEL ISLANDS)

SOUTH CHINA SEA

Mindoro

Panay

Iloilo

Cebu

Samar

Leyte

Bohol

MINDANAO

Davao

PALAU ISLANDS

SONSOROL ISLANDS

PALAU

Koror

ADMIRALTY ISLANDS

Manus Island

NEW HANOVER

NEW IRELAND

Rabaul

BISMARCK SEA

Sittwe

YANGON (RANGOON)

Gulf of Martaban

THAILAND

KRUNG THEP (BANGKOK)

CAMBODIA

Phnum Pénh

THANH PHO HO CHI MINH (HO CHI MINH CITY) (SAIGON)

Da Nang

Palawan

Zamboanga

Moro Gulf

Mount Apo 2954

Tinaca Point

Jolo Island

KEPULAUAN TALAUD

Morotai

NEW BRITAIN

BISMARCK ARCHIPELAGO

Talasea

NEW IRELAND

SOLOMON SEA

ANDAMAN ISLANDS (India)

COCO ISLANDS

Dawei

SPRATLY ISLANDS

Balabac Island

SULU SEA

Jolo Island

Gunung Kinabalu 4101

Bandar Seri Begawan

BRUNEI

HALMAHERA

Pulau Waigeo

Pulau Yapen

Biak

Jayapura

Wewak

Madang

Mount Wilhelm 4509

Puncak Jaya 5030

Lae

NEW GUINEA

PAPUA NEW GUINEA

Port Moresby

Gulf of Papua

Mui Ca Mau

MALAY PENINSULA

Phuket

George Town (Penang)

MALAYSIA

KUALA LUMPUR

Kampong Saóm

Gulf of Thailand

ANDAMAN SEA

NICOBAR ISLANDS (India)

Banda Aceh

MEDAN

Pulau Nias

KEPULAUAN MENTAWAI

Pulau Siberut

SINGAPORE

Kuching

BORNEO (KALIMANTAN)

Pontianak

Balikpapan

Banjarmasin

P. Laut

CELEBES SEA

Manado

SULAWESI (CELEBES)

Teluk Tomini

KEPULAUAN SANGIHE

KEPULAUAN NATUNA BESAR

Selat Makasar

Ujungpandang

KEPULAUAN SULA

Buru

LAUT MALUKU

KEPULAUAN OBI

MALUKU (MOLUCCAS)

SERAM (CERAM)

KEPULAUAN KAI

Pulau Yos Sudarso

KEPULAUAN ARU

Pulau Buton

LAUT BANDA

ARAFURA SEA

Cape Arnhem

Cape Wessel

KEPULAUAN TANIMBAR

Pulau Wetar

TIMOR SEA

Melville Island

Gulf of Carpentaria

CAPE YORK PENINSULA

Great Barrier Reef

CORAL SEA

Padang

Palembang

Pulau Bangka

Pulau Belitung

SUMATERA (SUMATRA)

Selat Sunda

Tanjungkarang-Telukbetung

JAKARTA

BANDUNG

SURABAYA

JAWA (JAVA)

Madura

Bali

Lombok

Sumbawa

LAUT JAWA

LAUT FLORES

FLORES

LAUT SAWU

Kupang

TIMOR

Sumba

INDONESIA

AUSTRALIA

M-600000-2A-DR2-1
Copyright © Rand McNally & Co.

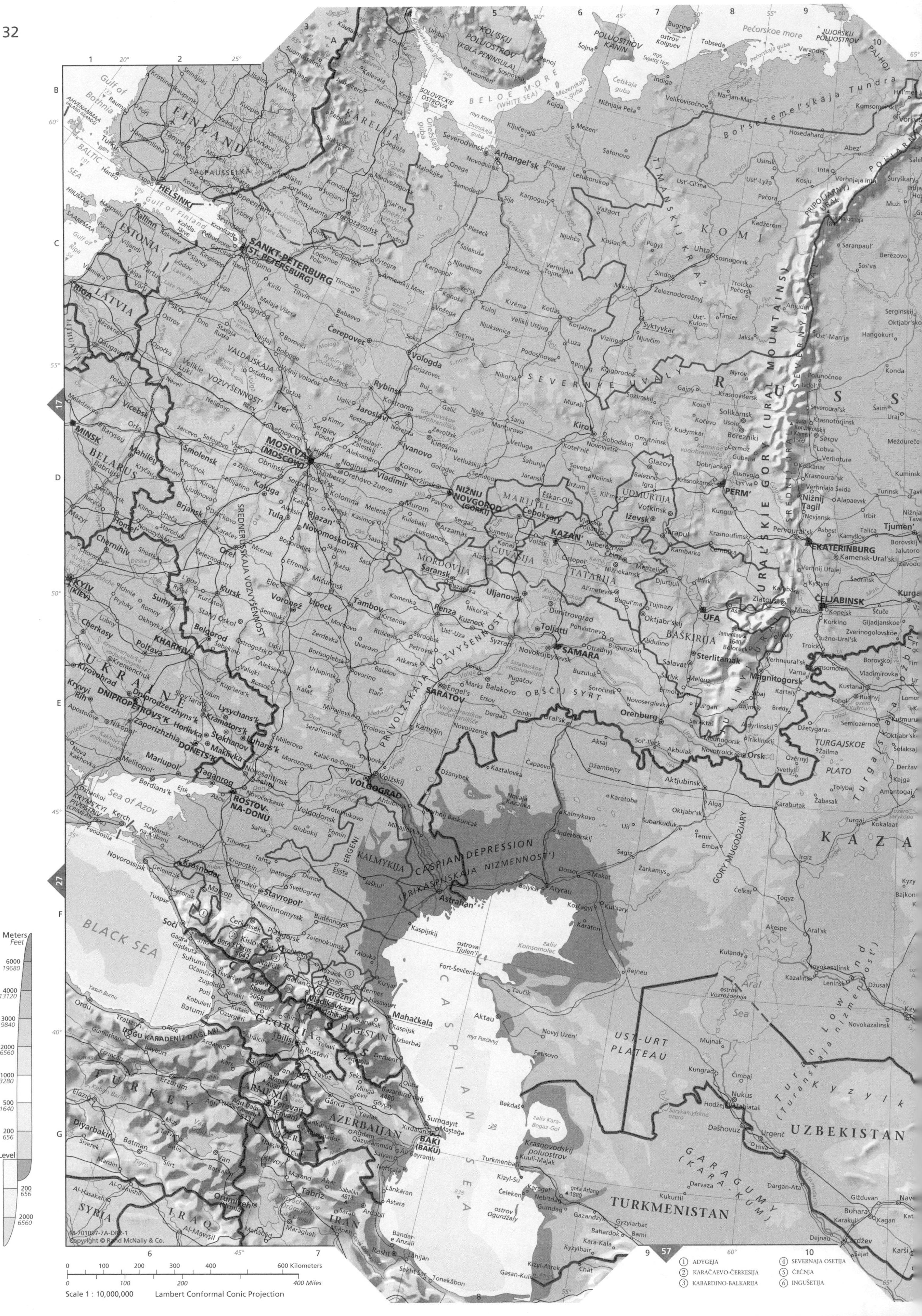

BELOE MORE
(WHITE SEA)

FINLAND

HELSINKI

ESTONIA

BALTIC
SEA

LATVIA

LITHUANIA

RIGA

SANKT-PETERBURG
(ST. PETERSBURG)

KARELIJA

KOLÏSKIJ
POLUOSTROV
(KOLA PENINSULA)

POLUOSTROV
KANIN

JUJORSKIJ
POLUOSTROV

PAJ-HOJ

Pečorskoe more

KOMI

PRIPOLIARNYJ
URAL

R   U   S   S

BELARUS

MINSK

MOSKVA
(MOSCOW)

Smolensk

SREDNE-RUSSKAJA VOZVYŠENNOST'

SEVERNYE UVALY

SREDNIJ URAL

SEVERNYJ URAL

URAL'SKIE GORY (URAL MOUNTAINS)

NIŽNIJ
NOVGOROD
(GORKI)

MARIJEL

Čeboksary

UDMURTIJA

PERM'

KAZAN'

ČUVAŠIJA

IževsK

EKATERINBURG

Kamensk-Ural'skij

Nižnij
Tagil

Tjumen'

KYJIV
(KIEV)

UKRAINE

KHARKIV

MORDOVIJA

Saransk

TATARIJA

UFA

BAŠKIRIJA

ČELJABINSK

Kurga

Magnitogorsk

PRIVOLŽSKAJA VOZVYŠENNOST'

SARATOV

SAMARA

Sterlitamak

Orenburg

Orsk

DNIPROPETROVS'K

Zaporizhzhia

DONETS'K

Mariupol'

Taganrog

VOLGOGRAD

OBŠČIJ SYRT

PLATO

TURGAJSKOE

K   A   Z   A

ROSTOV-
NA-DONU

Sea of Azov

Kerch

ARKYMS'KYJ
PIVOSTRIV
(CRIMEA)

ERGENI

KALMYKIJA

CASPIAN DEPRESSION
(PRIKASPIJSKAJA NIZMENNOST')

Astrahan'

GORY MUGODŽARY

Turanskaja nizmennost' (Turan Lowland)

BLACK SEA

Novorossijsk

Krasnodar

Stavropol'

Elista

Atyrau

Aral'sk

UZBEKISTAN

Soči

Maxop

Čerkessk

Grozny

Vladikavkaz

Mahačkala

CASPIAN SEA

UST-URT
PLATEAU

Aral
Sea

GEORGIA

Tbilisi

DAGESTAN

C   A   S   P   I   A   N

Kara
Bogaz-Gol

GARAGUMY
(KARA-KUMY)

TURKEY

ARMENIA

Yerevan

AZERBAIJAN

BAKI
(BAKU)

S   E   A

TURKMENISTAN

SYRIA

IRAQ

IRAN

Meters
Feet

6000
19680

4000
13120

3000
9840

2000
6560

1000
3280

500
1640

200
656

Sea Level

200
656

2000
6560

1 ADYGEJA
2 KARAČAEVO-ČERKESIJA
3 KABARDINO-BALKARIJA
4 SEVERNAJA OSETIJA
5 ČEČNJA
6 INGUŠETIJA

0   100   200   300   400   600 Kilometers

0   100   200   400 Miles

Scale 1 : 10,000,000   Lambert Conformal Conic Projection

Copyright © Rand McNally & Co.

70° 12 75° 13 80° 14 85° 15 90° 16 95° 17 100° 18 105° 19 110° 20 115°

ZAPADNO-SIBIRSKAJA RAVNINA (WEST SIBERIAN PLAIN)

SIBIR' (SIBERIA)

SREDNESIBIRSKOE PLOSKOGOR'E (CENTRAL SIBERIAN PLATEAU)

CENTRALNO-TUNGUSSKOE PLATO

ENISEJSKIJ KRJAŽ

VOSTOČNYJ SAJAN

ZAPADNYJ SAJAN

SAYAN MOUNTAINS

TANNU-OLA HREBET

TUVA

HAKASIJA

BURJATIJA

ALTAJ

MONGOLIA

HANGAYN NURUU

MONGOL ALTAYN NURUU

KAZAHSKIJ MELKOSOPOČNIK (KAZAKH HILLS)

Kulundinskaja ravnina

Barabinskaja step'

Išimskaja ravnina

Betpak-Dala

PESKI MOJYNKUM

DZHUNGARIAN ALATAU

HREBET TARBAGATAJ

JUNGGAR PENDI

BOROHORO SHAN

BOGDA SHAN

Turpan Pendi (Turfan Depression)

KURUKTAG

TIEN SHAN

XINJIANG

CHINA

TARIM PENDI

Taklimakan Shamo (Takla Makan Desert)

ALTUN SHAN

KUNLUN SHAN

QAIDAM PENDI

QINGHAI

GANSU

KYRGYZSTAN

TAJIKISTAN

PAMIR

AFG.

KAZAKHSTAN

NOVOSIBIRSK

OMSK

Tomsk

Kemerovo

Novokuzneck

Barnaul

Krasnojarsk

Irkutsk

Bratsk

Astana (Akmola)

Karaganda

Pavlodar

Semipalatinsk

Ust'-Kamenogorsk

ALMATY

Biškek

TAŠKENT

Ürümqi

Surgut

Nižnevartovsk

Petropavlovsk

34

36 90° East of Greenwich 16

B C D E F G

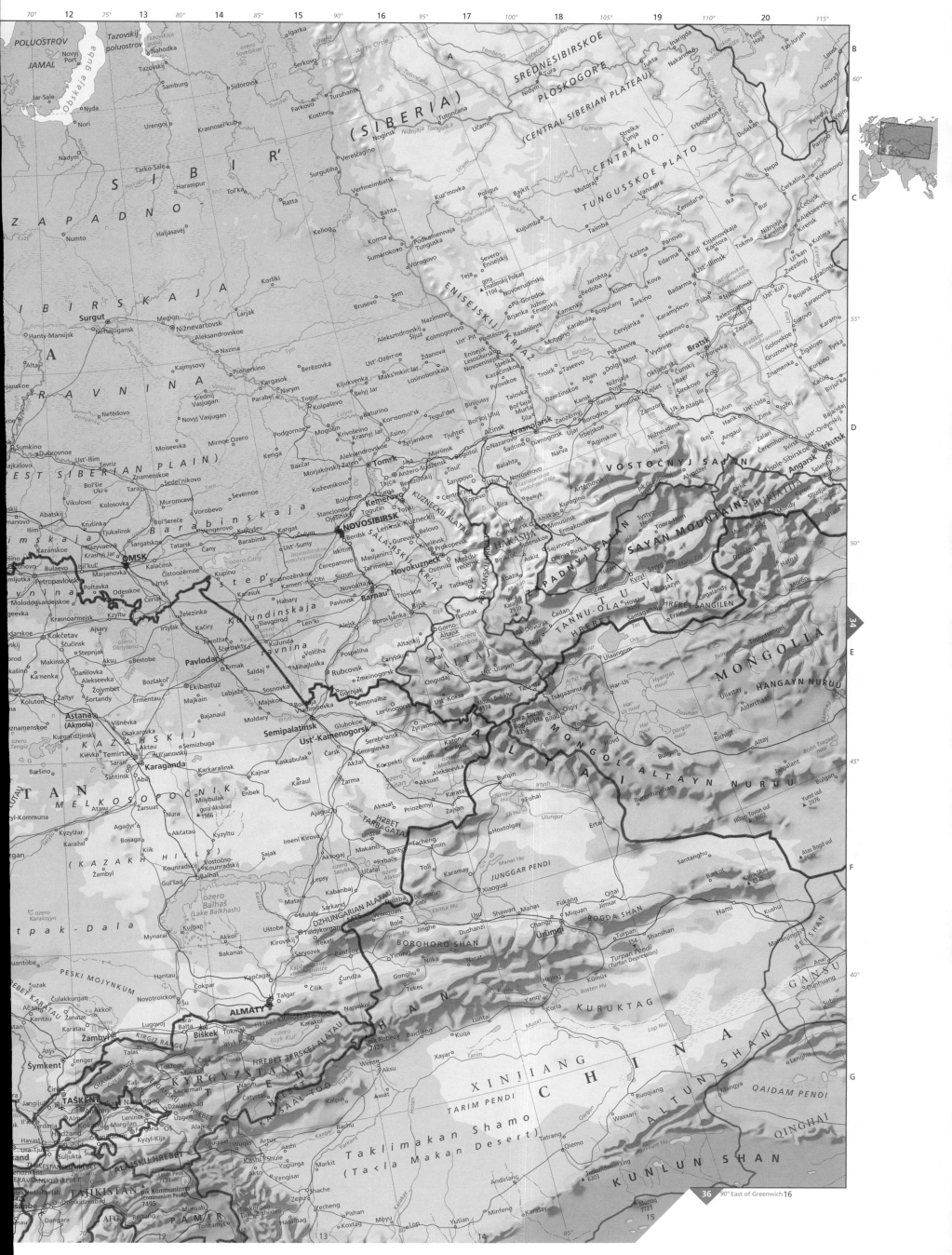

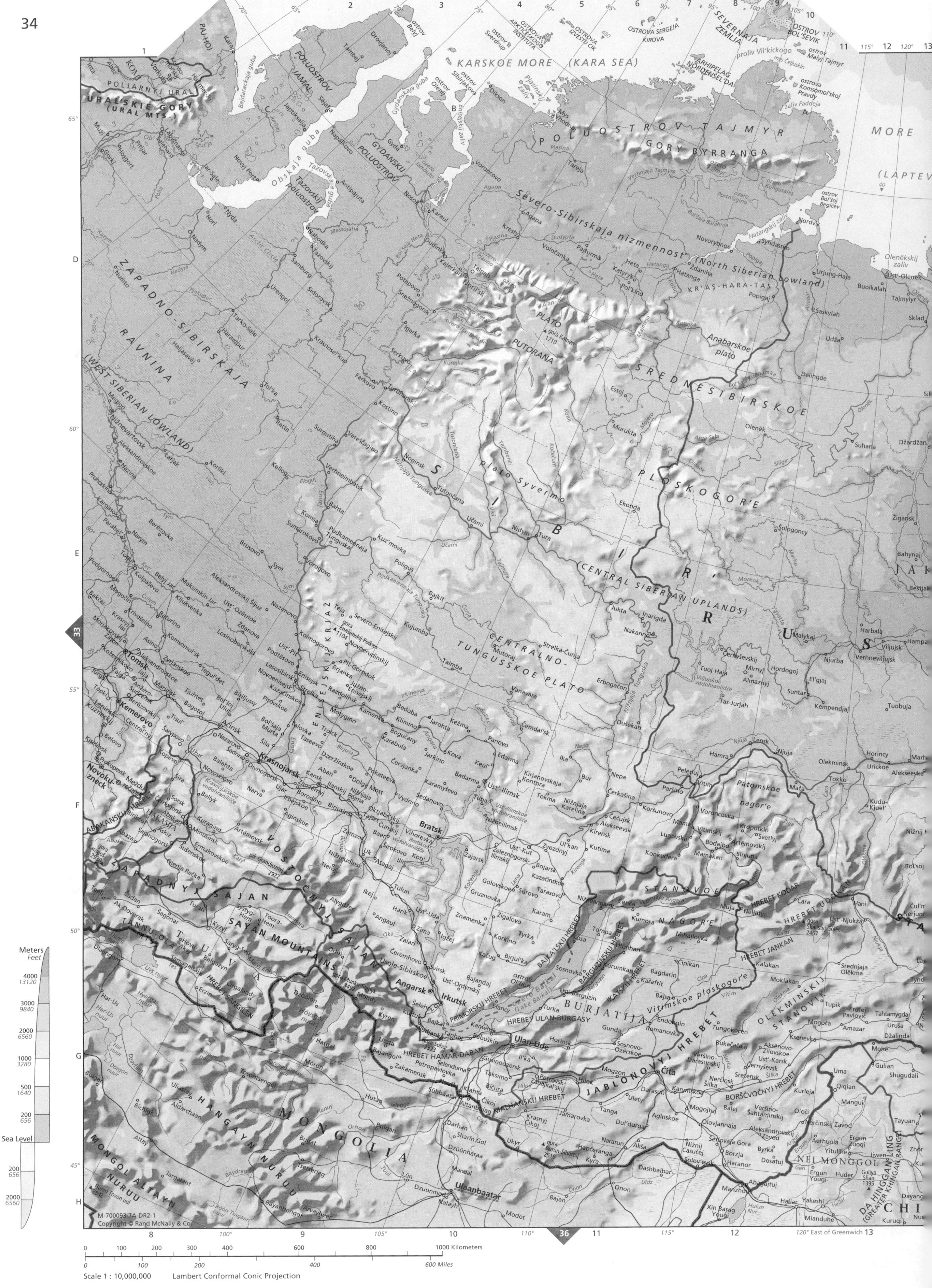

Meters
Feet

4000
13120

3000
9840

2000
6560

1000
3280

500
1640

200
656

Sea Level

200
656

2000
6560

M-700093-7A-DR2-1
Copyright © Rand McNally & Co.

0 100 200 300 400   600   800   1000 Kilometers

0   100   200   400   600 Miles

Scale 1 : 10,000,000   Lambert Conformal Conic Projection

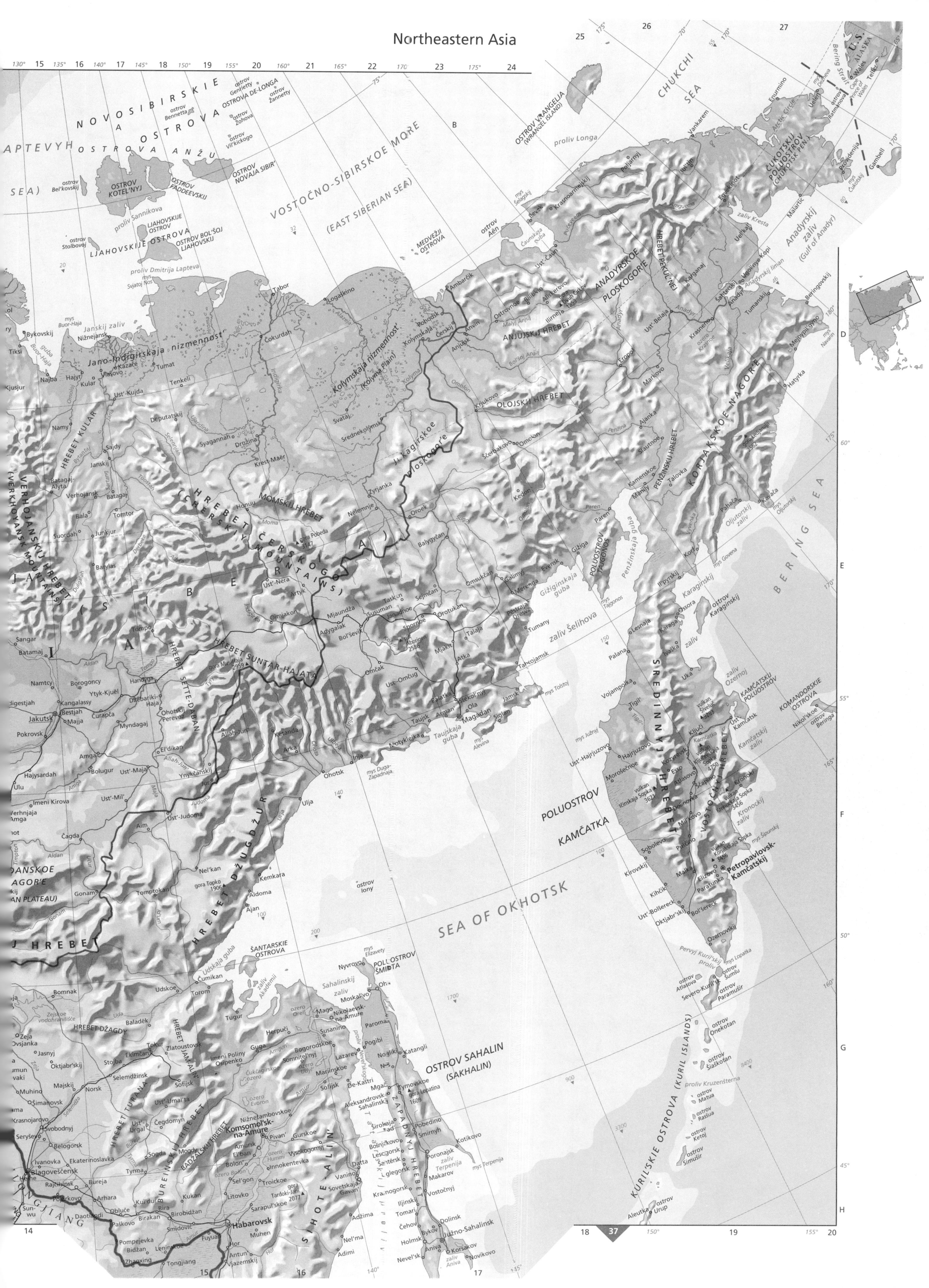

NOVOSIBIRSKIE OSTROVA

APTEVYH (SEA) OSTROVA ANŽU

OSTROVA DE-LONGA

ostrov Genrietty
ostrov Bennetta
ostrov Žannetty

ostrov Vil'kickogo

ostrov Žoxova

OSTROV KOTEL'NYJ

OSTROV FADDEEVSKIJ

LJAHOVSKIJE OSTROV

OSTROV NOVAJA SIBIR'

OSTROV BOL'ŠOJ LJAHOVSKIJ

ostrov Bel'kovskij

proliv Sannikova

LJAHOVSKIJE OSTROVA

proliv Dmitrija Lapteva

ostrov Stolbovoj

VOSTOČNO-SIBIRSKOE MORE

(EAST SIBERIAN SEA)

OSTROV VRANGELJA (WRANGEL ISLAND)

proliv Longa

CHUKCHI SEA

Bering Strait

U.S. ALASKA

Arctic Circle

ČUKOTSKIJ POLUOSTROV (CHUKOTSK PEN.)

MEDVEŽJI OSTROVA

Svjatoj Nos

Bykovskij

Tiksi

Janskij zaliv

Nižnejansk

Jano-Indigirskaja nizmennost'

Kolymskaja nizmennost'

Kolyma Plain

ANADYRSKOE PLOSKOGORE

HREBET PEKUL'NEJ

ANJUJSKIJ HREBET

Anadyrskij zaliv (Gulf of Anadyr)

Anadyr

KORJAKSKOE NAGORE

OLOJSKIJ HREBET

Čerskij

VERHOJANSKIJ HREBET (VERKHOYANSK MOUNTAINS)

HREBET KULAR

HREBET ČERSKOGO (ČERSKIJ) (CHERSKY MOUNTAINS)

MOMSKIJ HREBET

gora Pobeda 3147

Oroek

ILIRNEJSKOE PLOSKOGORE

Jakutsk

HREBET SETTE-DABAN

HREBET SUNTAR-HAJATA

PENŽINSKIJ HREBET

BERING SEA

Magadan

POLUOSTROV TAJGONOS

Gižiginskaja guba

Penžinskaja guba

zaliv Šelihova

ostrov Karaginskij

Ohotsk

HREBET DŽUGDŽUR

Ajan

POLUOSTROV KAMČATKA

SREDINNYJ HREBET

VOSTOČNYJ HREBET

KOMANDORSKIE OSTROVA

ostrov Beringa

Petropavlovsk-Kamčatskij

SEA OF OKHOTSK

ŠANTARSKIE OSTROVA

POL.OSTROV ŠMIDTA

Sahalinskij zaliv

OSTROV SAHALIN (SAKHALIN)

Komsomol'sk-na-Amure

HREBET TURANA

HREBET BADŽAL'SKIJ

BUREINSKIJ HREBET

ZAPADNYJ HREBET

KURIL'SKIE OSTROVA (KURIL ISLANDS)

proliv Kruzenšterna

SIHOTE-ALIN'

Habarovsk

Južno-Sahalinsk

zaliv Aniva

HREBET DŽAGDY

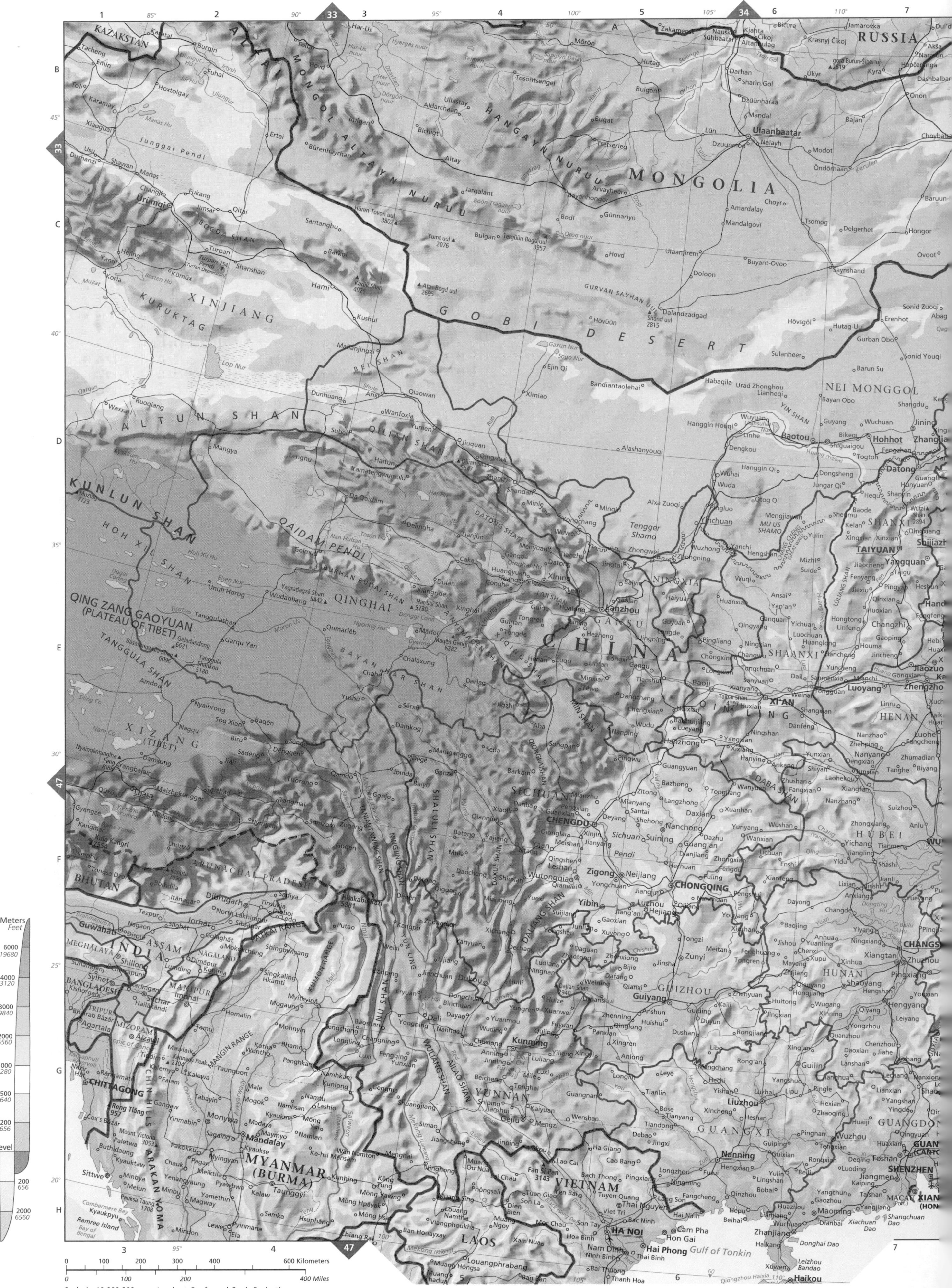
RUSSIA
KAZAKSTAN
MONGOLIA
CHINA
GOBI DESERT
XINJIANG
QINGHAI
XIZANG (TIBET)
QING ZANG GAOYUAN (PLATEAU OF TIBET)
NEI MONGGOL
NINGXIA
GANSU
SHAANXI
SHANXI
HENAN
HUBEI
HUNAN
SICHUAN
CHONGQING
GUIZHOU
YUNNAN
GUANGXI
GUANGDONG
INDIA
ASSAM
ARUNACHAL PRADESH
BHUTAN
BANGLADESH
MYANMAR (BURMA)
LAOS
VIETNAM
HANGAYN NURUU
MONGOL ALTAYN NURUU
GURVAN SAYHAN UUL
Junggar Pendi
BOGDA SHAN
KURUKTAG
ALTUN SHAN
KUNLUN SHAN
HOH XIL SHAN
TANGGULA SHAN
QILIAN SHAN
QAIDAM PENDI
BAYAN HAR SHAN
BEI SHAN
YIN SHAN
QIN LING
DABA SHAN
LÜLIANG SHAN
DAXUE SHAN
SHALUILI SHAN
NU SHAN
WULIANG SHAN
AILAO SHAN
CHIN HILLS
ARAKAN YOMA
Tengger Shamo
MU US SHAMO
Sichuan Pendi
Ulaanbaatar
Ürümqi
Lanzhou
Xining
CHENGDU
Kunming
Guiyang
Nanning
Baotou
Hohhot
Datong
TAIYUAN
XI'AN
Zhengzhou
Luoyang
Yinchuan
Lhasa
Mandalay
HA NOI
Hai Phong
Gulf of Tonkin
Haikou
SHENZHEN
Zhanjiang
Kula Kangri 7554
Scale 1 : 10,000,000
Lambert Conformal Conic Projection
0 100 200 300 400 600 Kilometers
0 100 200 400 Miles
Meters Feet
6000 19680
4000 13120
3000 9840
2000 6560
1000 3280
500 1640
200 656
Sea Level
200 656
2000 6560

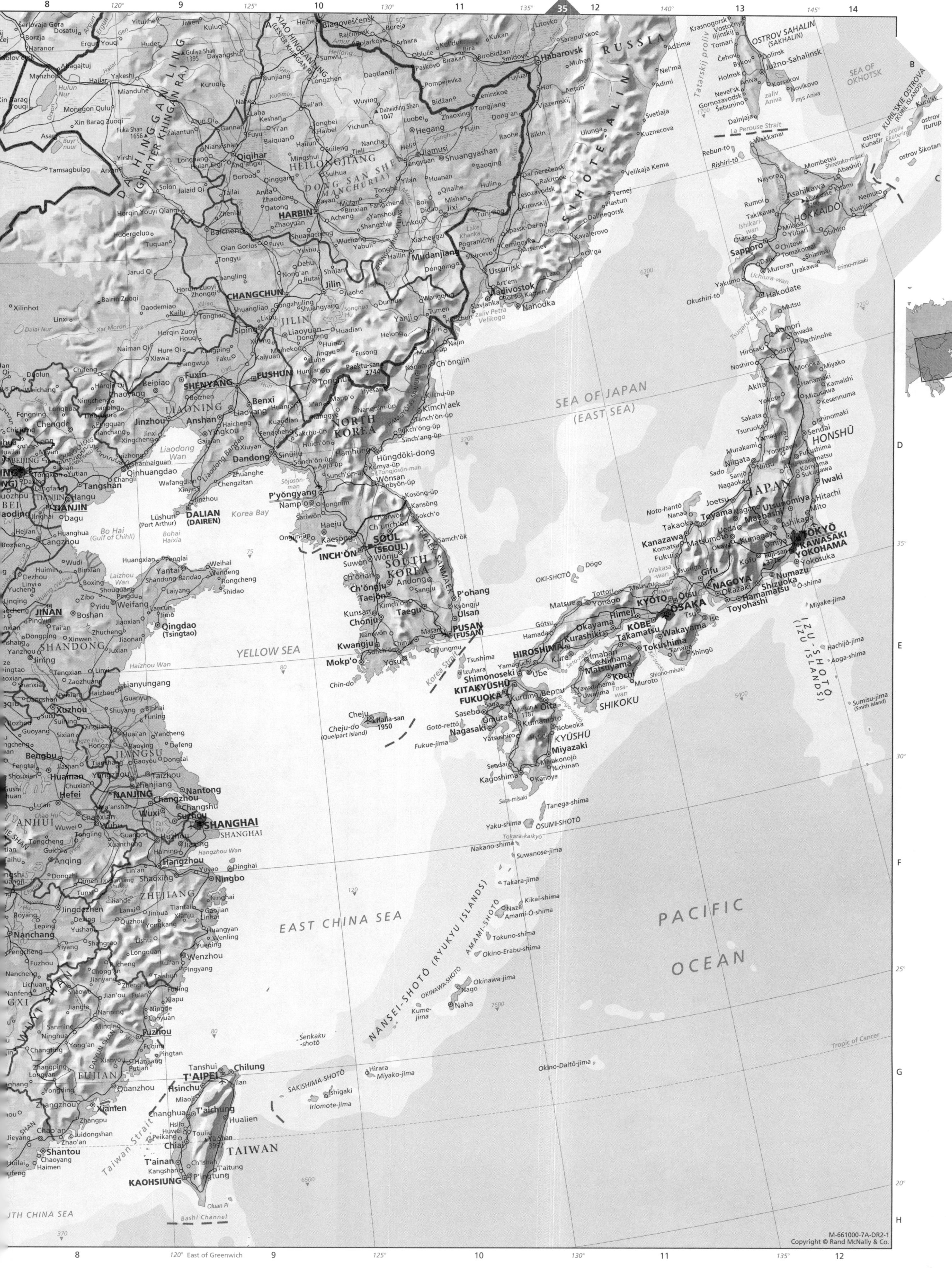
RUSSIA
SIKHOTE-ALIN
DA HINGGAN LING (GREATER KHINGAN RA.)
XIAO HINGGAN LING (LESSER KHINGAN RA.)
HEILONGJIANG
DONG SAN SHENG (MANCHURIA)
JILIN
LIAONING
HEBEI
SHANDONG
JIANGSU
ANHUI
ZHEJIANG
FUJIAN
TAIWAN
NORTH KOREA
SOUTH KOREA
JAPAN
HOKKAIDŌ
HONSHŪ
SHIKOKU
KYŪSHŪ
OSTROV SAHALIN (SAKHALIN)
KURIL'SKIE OSTROVA (KURIL ISLANDS)
SEA OF OKHOTSK
SEA OF JAPAN (EAST SEA)
YELLOW SEA
EAST CHINA SEA
PACIFIC OCEAN
Korea Bay
Bo Hai (Gulf of Chihli)
Liaodong Wan
Korea Strait
Taiwan Strait
Bashi Channel
La Perouse Strait
Tatarskij proliv
Tsugaru-kaikyō
NANSEI-SHOTŌ (RYUKYU ISLANDS)
IZU-SHOTŌ (IZU ISLANDS)
AMAMI-SHOTŌ
OKINAWA-SHOTŌ
SAKISHIMA-SHOTŌ
ŌSUMI-SHOTŌ
OKI-SHOTŌ
Tropic of Cancer
Blagoveščensk
Habarovsk
Vladivostok
Nahodka
Ussurijsk
Južno-Sahalinsk
HARBIN
Qiqihar
CHANGCHUN
Jilin
SHENYANG
FUSHUN
Anshan
DALIAN (DAIREN)
BEIJING
TIANJIN
Tangshan
JINAN
Qingdao (Tsingtao)
Xuzhou
NANJING
SHANGHAI
Hangzhou
Ningbo
Wenzhou
Fuzhou
Xiamen
Shantou
P'yŏngyang
SŎUL (SEOUL)
INCH'ŎN
Taegu
PUSAN (FUSAN)
Kwangju
Taejŏn
Sapporo
Hakodate
Aomori
Sendai
TŌKYŌ
KAWASAKI
YOKOHAMA
NAGOYA
KYŌTO
ŌSAKA
KŌBE
HIROSHIMA
KITAKYŪSHŪ
FUKUOKA
Nagasaki
Kagoshima
Naha
T'AIPEI
Chilung
KAOHSIUNG
Paektu-san 2744
Halla-san 1950
Fuji-san 3776
Cheju-do (Quelpart Island)
Okinawa-jima
120° East of Greenwich
M-661000-7A-DR2-1
Copyright © Rand McNally & Co.

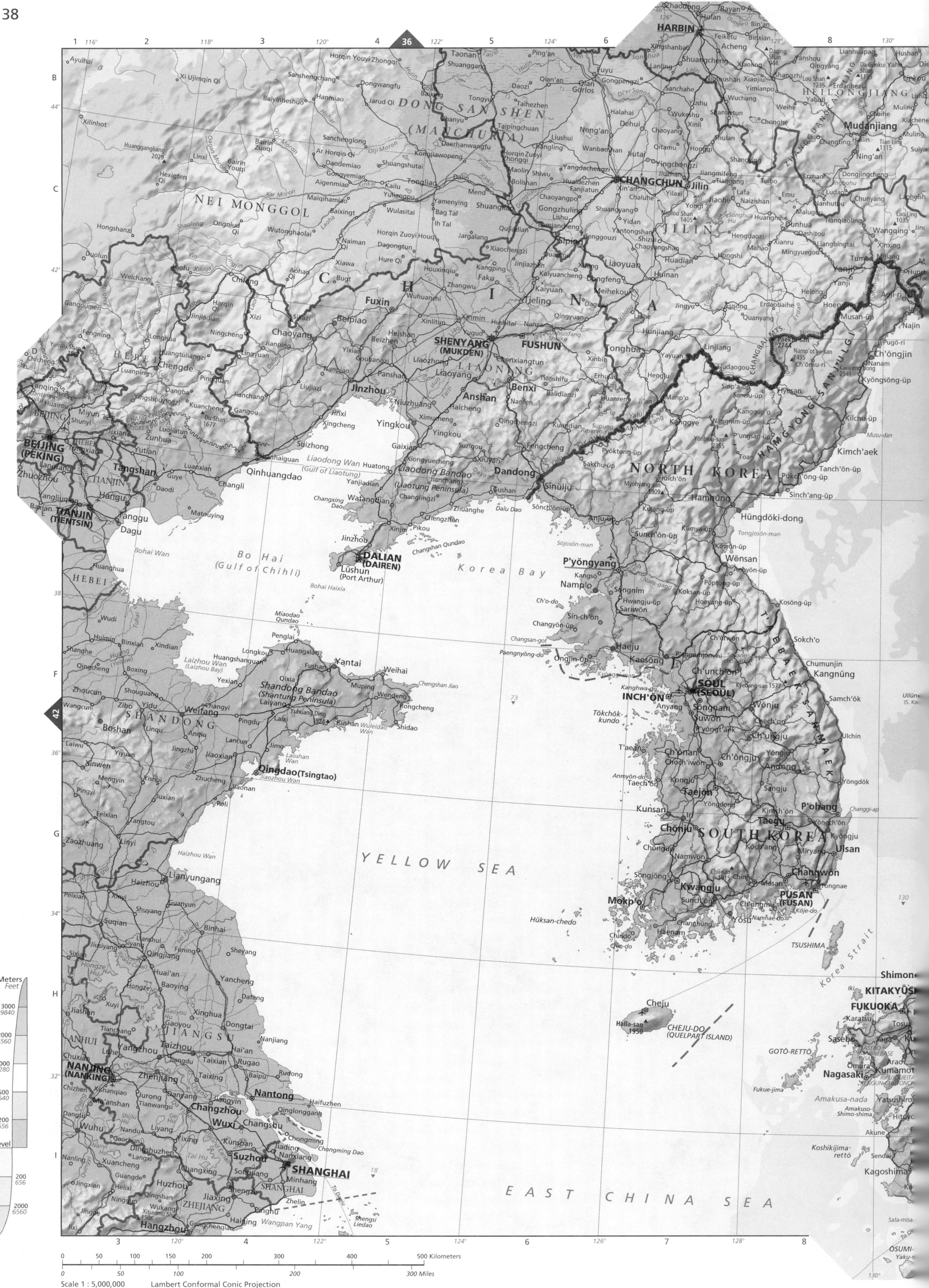

NEI MONGGOL
DONG SAN SHEN (MANCHURIA)
HEILONGJIANG
JILIN
LIAONING
HEBEI
SHANDONG
JIANGSU
ANHUI
ZHEJIANG
SHANGHAI
CHINA
NORTH KOREA
SOUTH KOREA
HARBIN
CHANGCHUN
Jilin
SHENYANG (MUKDEN)
FUSHUN
Anshan
Benxi
Dandong
Jinzhou
Yingkou
BEIJING (PEKING)
TIANJIN (TIENTSIN)
Tangshan
Qinhuangdao
DALIAN (DAIREN)
Lüshun (Port Arthur)
Yantai
Qingdao (Tsingtao)
Weifang
Lianyungang
NANJING (NANKING)
Changzhou
Wuxi
Suzhou
Nantong
Hangzhou
P'yŏngyang
Namp'o
Wŏnsan
Hamhŭng
Ch'ŏngjin
SŎUL (SEOUL)
INCH'ŎN
Taejŏn
Taegu
Kwangju
PUSAN (FUSAN)
Ulsan
P'ohang
Cheju
CHEJU-DO (QUELPART ISLAND)
Halla-san 1950
TSUSHIMA
FUKUOKA
KITAKYŪSHŪ
Nagasaki
Kagoshima
Bo Hai (Gulf of Chihli)
Liaodong Wan (Gulf of Liaotung)
Liaodong Bandao (Liaotung Peninsula)
Shandong Bandao (Shantung Peninsula)
Korea Bay
YELLOW SEA
EAST CHINA SEA
Korea Strait
CHANGBAI MTS.
HAMGYŎNG SANMAEK
T'AEBAEK SANMAEK
Meters / Feet
3000 / 9840
2000 / 6560
1000 / 3280
500 / 1640
200 / 656
Sea Level
200 / 656
2000 / 6560
0 50 100 150 200 300 400 500 Kilometers
0 50 100 200 300 Miles
Scale 1 : 5,000,000
Lambert Conformal Conic Projection

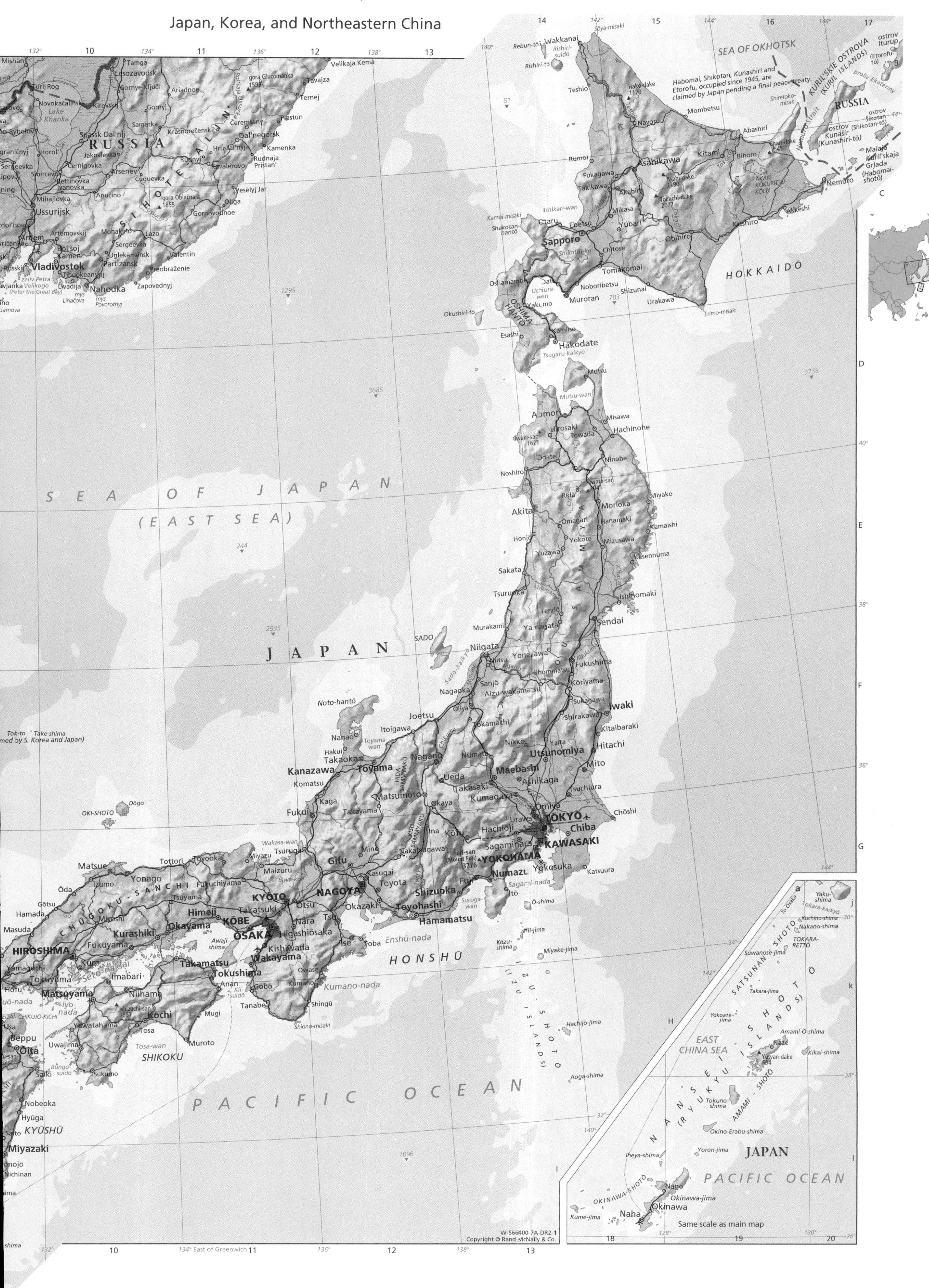

SEA OF OKHOTSK
Habomai, Shikotan, Kunashiri and Etorofu, occupied since 1945, are claimed by Japan pending a final peace treaty.
KURIL'SKIE OSTROVA (KURIL ISLANDS)
RUSSIA
HOKKAIDŌ
Wakkanai
Sōya-misaki
Rebun-tō
Rishiri-tō
Teshio
Mombetsu
Abashiri
Nayoro
Asahikawa
Kitami
Rumoi
Fukagawa
Takikawa
Bihoro
Nemuro
Kushiro
Akkeshi
Obihiro
Ishikari-wan
Otaru
Ebetsu
Sapporo
Chitose
Tomakomai
Noboribetsu
Muroran
Shizunai
Urakawa
Erimo-misaki
Oshamambe
Okushiri-tō
Esashi
Hakodate
Tsugaru-kaikyō
Mutsu
Mutsu-wan
Aomori
Misawa
Hachinohe
Hirosaki
Towada
Ninohe
Noshiro
Miyako
Morioka
Hanamaki
Kamaishi
Akita
Omagari
Honjō
Yokote
Mizusawa
Yuzawa
Kesennuma
Sakata
Tsuruoka
Ishinomaki
Tendō
Yamagata
Sendai
Murakami
SADO
Niigata
Yonezawa
Fukushima
Sado-kaikyō
Sanjō
Koriyama
Nagaoka
Aizu-wakamatsu
Iwaki
Noto-hantō
Joetsu
Itoigawa
Kitaibaraki
Hitachi
Nanao
Toyama-wan
Nikkō
Utsunomiya
Hakui
Takaoka
Toyama
Nagano
Numata
Mito
Kanazawa
Komatsu
Ueda
Maebashi
Ashikaga
Takasaki
Kumagaya
Tsuchiura
Kaga
Matsumoto
Okaya
Fukui
Takayama
Ōmiya
TŌKYŌ
Chōshi
Urawa
Chiba
Kōfu
Hachiōji
KAWASAKI
Sagamihara
YOKOHAMA
Fuji-san (Mount Fuji) 3776
Yokosuka
Katsuura
Gifu
Numazu
Kasugai
Fuji
NAGOYA
Toyota
Shizuoka
Okazaki
Toyohashi
Hamamatsu
Ō-shima
Tsu
Enshū-nada
Toba
Ise
HONSHŪ
Miyake-jima
Kumano-nada
Shingū
Hachijō-jima
Aoga-shima
IZU-SHOTŌ (IZU ISLANDS)
Wakasa-wan
Tsuruga
Maizuru
Biwa-ko
KYŌTO
Ōtsu
Nara
Higashiōsaka
ŌSAKA
KŌBE
Himeji
Okayama
Kurashiki
Fukuyama
HIROSHIMA
Kure
Wakayama
Kishiwada
Tokushima
Takamatsu
Imabari
Niihama
Matsuyama
Kōchi
Tosa
Tosa-wan
Muroto
SHIKOKU
Uwajima
Sukumo
Anan
Tanabe
Shiono-misaki
Tottori
Matsue
Izumo
Yonago
CHŪGOKU-SANCHI
Fukuchiyama
Tsuyama
Hamada
Masuda
Ōda
Gōtsu
Yamaguchi
Tokuyama
Hōfu
Beppu
Ōita
Saiki
Nobeoka
Hyūga
KYŪSHŪ
Miyazaki
Nichinan
OKI-SHOTŌ
Dōgo
Tok-to Take-shima
(claimed by S. Korea and Japan)
SEA OF JAPAN
(EAST SEA)
JAPAN
PACIFIC OCEAN
RUSSIA
Vladivostok
Ussurijsk
Nahodka
Artem
Partizansk
Lesozavodsk
Spassk-Dal'nij
Lake Khanka
Dal'negorsk
Kavalerovo
Rudnaja Pristan'
Ternej
Plastun
Velikaja Kema
Olga
Preobraženie
Zaliv Petra Velikogo (Peter the Great Bay)
SIKHOTE-ALIN'
Same scale as main map
EAST CHINA SEA
NANSEI-SHOTŌ (RYUKYU ISLANDS)
SATSUNAN-SHOTŌ
TOKARA-RETTŌ
AMAMI-SHOTŌ
OKINAWA-SHOTŌ
Yaku-shima
Tanega-shima
Tokara-kaikyō
Kuchino-shima
Nakano-shima
Suwanose-jima
Takara-jima
Yokoate-jima
Amami-Ō-shima
Naze
Kikai-shima
Tokuno-shima
Okino-Erabu-shima
Yoron-jima
Iheya-shima
Nago
Okinawa-jima
Okinawa
Naha
Kume-jima

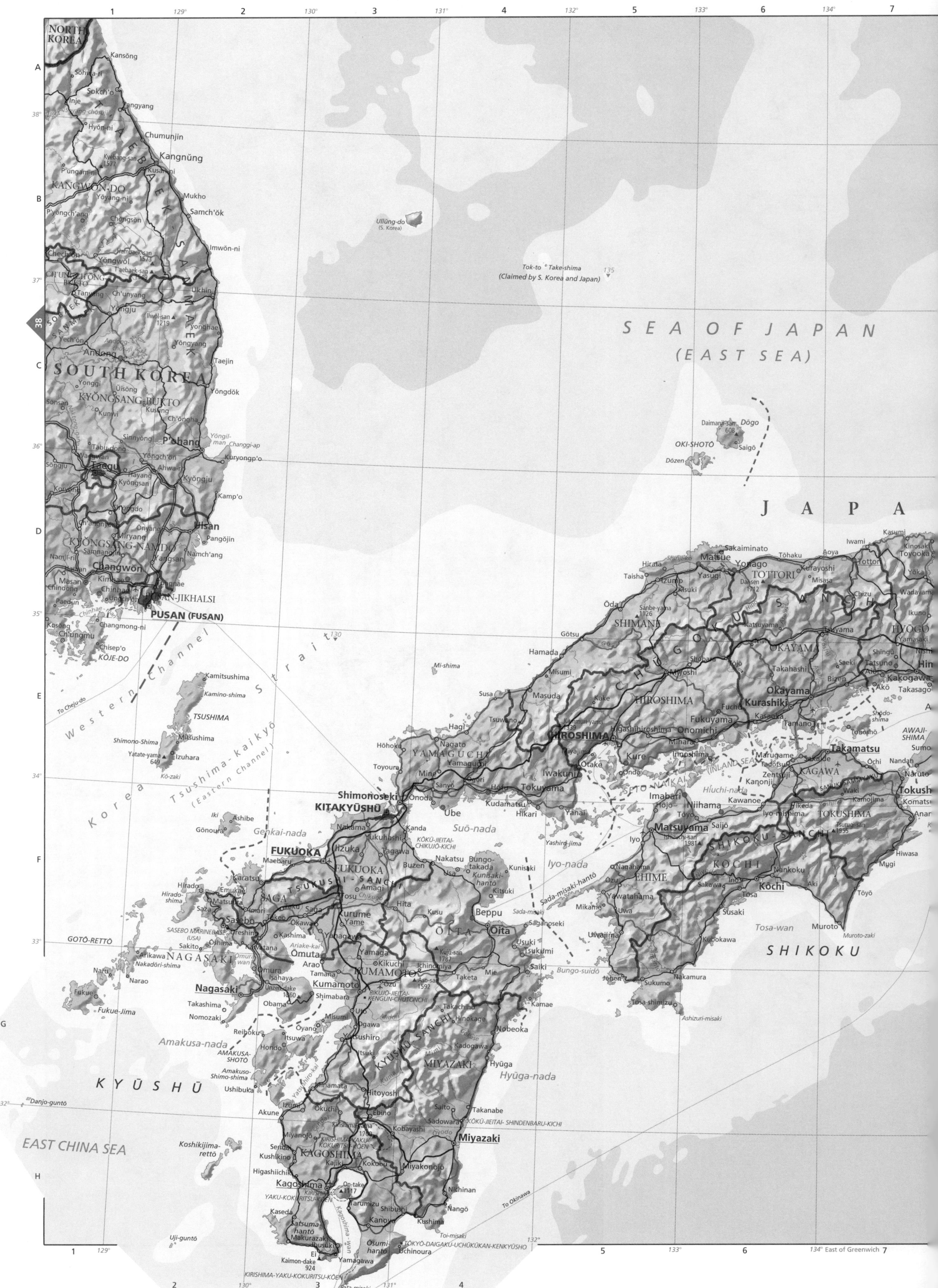

NORTH KOREA

Kansŏng
Sohwa-ri
Sokch'o
Inje
Kumgang-chŏsuji
Zangyang
Hyŏn-ni
Chumunjin
Kangnŭng
KANGWON-DO
Kyebang-san
1577
Yŏyang-ni
Mukho
Samch'ŏk
P'yongch'ang
Chŏngson
Chech'on
Yongwŏl
Hambaek-san
1573
T'aebaek-san
Uljin
CH'UNG CH'ŎNG
BUK-TO
Tanyang
Iwŏl-san
1219
Ch'unyang
P'yonghae
Yŏngyang
SOUTH KOREA
Andong
Taejin
Yonggi
Uisŏng
Yŏngdŏk
KYŎNGSANG-BUKTO
Kunwi
Ch'ŏnga
Songsan
Sinnyŏng
Yŏngch'ŏn
P'ohang
Taegu
Hayang
Kyŏngsan
Yŏngil-man
Changgi-ap
Kuryongp'o
Ahwa-ri
Kyŏngju
Kamp'o
Onyang
Ulsan
Miryang
Pangojin
KYŎNGSANG-NAMDO
Namji-ri
Sammangdin
Yangsan
Namch'ang
Changwŏn
Kimhae
Masan
Ch'inhae
Chinhae
Ungch'ŏn
PUSAN (FUSAN)
Paedun
Kosŏng
Ch'ungmu
Changmong-ni
Chisep'o
KÔJE-DO
To Cheju-do

SEA OF JAPAN
(EAST SEA)

North Korea / South Korea / Japan

Ullŭng-do
(S. Korea)

Tok-to °Take-shima
(Claimed by S. Korea and Japan)
135

Daimani-san Dōgo
608
OKI-SHOTŌ Saigō
Dōzen

JAPA

Sakaiminato Tōhaku Aoya Iwami Kasumi Kinosaki
Hirata Shinji Matsue Yonago TOTTORI Kurayoshi Toyooka
Taisha Izumo Yasugi Daisen Misasa Yōka
Izumo 1712 Chizu Wadayama
Ōda Sanbe-yama Kōjō Tsuyama Ikuno
1126 Shōbara Miyoshi OKAYAMA Bizen Tatsuno Shingu Hin
Gōtsu SHIMANE GŌ Tottori Yamasaki Nishi
Hamada GŌ HIROSHIMA Kurashiki Akō Kagogawa
Misumi Kake Fuchū Okayama Takasago
Tsuwano Higashihiroshima Kasaoka Tamano Shōdo- AWAJI-
Hagi HIROSHIMA Onomichi Minara shima SHIMA
Susa Masuda YAMAGUCHI Mihara Innoshima Marugame Sumo
Hōhoku Yamaguchi HIROSHIMA Kure Takamatsu
Nagato Kudamatsu Otake Ondo KAGAWA Naruto
Toyoura Sanyō Tokuyama Iwakuni Niihama Kamojima Tokush
Mine Hofu Hikari Imabari Saijō Ikeda
Ube Kanda Suō-nada Yashiro-jima Hōjō SHIKOKU-SANCHI TOKUSHIMA
Onoda Kawanoe Anar
Shimonoseki Hikari Kunisaki Iyo-nada Matsuyama EHIME KŌCHI Mugi
KITAKYŪSHŪ KŌKŪ-JIEITAI- Bungo- hantō Iyo Hiwasa
CHIKUJŌ-KICHI takada Kunisaki Ōzu Kōchi
FUKUOKA Nakatsu Kitsuki Yawatahama Nankoku
Izuka Tagawa Buzen Kitsuki Mikame Tōyō
Maebaru Yukuhashi Hita Kusu Beppu Uwa Susaki
Karatsu FUKUOKA Amagi Ōita Usuki Uwajima Kubokawa
Hirado- TSUKUSHI-SANCHI Chikugo Ōita Tsukumi Ashizuri-misaki
shima Saga Yame Saiki
Matsura SAGA Kurume Taketa Nakamura
Emukae Okawa Yamaga Kikuchi Mie Kamae
Sasebo Ariake-kai Kuju-san Nobeoka
Greshima Ōmura Tamana 1787 Takachiho
NAGASAKI wan Arao Kumamoto Shintomiya
Ōmuta KUMAMOTO Kadogawa
Nagasaki Isahaya Kikuchi Hinokage
Takashima Unzen-dake Shimabara KYŪSHŪ-SANCHI MIYAZAKI
Obama 1360 Misumi Hyūga
Nomozaki Ogawa Takachiho Hyūga-nada
Reihoku Oyano Usuki Hinokage Nobeoka
KYŪSHŪ Hondo Itsuwa Sushiro Mimi
Amakusa-nada AMAKUSA- Kadogawa
SHOTŌ MIYAZAKI
Amakuso- Hitoyoshi
Shimo-shima Ushibuka
Danjo-guntō Akune Okuchi Ebino Saito Takanabe
EAST CHINA SEA Kobayashi RIKUJŌ-JIEITAI- SHINDENBARU-KICHI
Koshikijima- Sendai Kirishima-yama Oyodo Miyazaki
rettō 1700 KIRISHIMA YAKU
Kushikino KOKURITSU-KŌEN
KAGOSHIMA Kajiki
Higashiichiki Kokubu Miyakonojō
Kagoshima On-take Nichinan
1117 Nangō
Kaseda Shibushi Kushima
Satsuma- Kanoya
hantō Ōsumi- Toi-misaki
Makurazaki hantō TŌKYŌ-DAIGAKU-UCHŪKŪKAN-KENKYŪSHO
Kaimon-dake Uchinoura
924 KIRISHIMA-YAKU-KOKURITSU-KŌEN

GOTŌ-RETTŌ
Arikawa
Nakadōri-shima
Naru
Fukue
Narao
Fukue-Jima

Genkai-nada
Iki
Ashibe
Gōnoura

TSUSHIMA
Kamitsushima
Kamino-shima
Shimono-Shima
Mitsushima
Izuhara
Yatate-yama
649
Kō-zaki

Korea Strait
Tsushima-kaikyō
(Eastern Channel)

Western Channel

SHIKOKU

Mi-shima

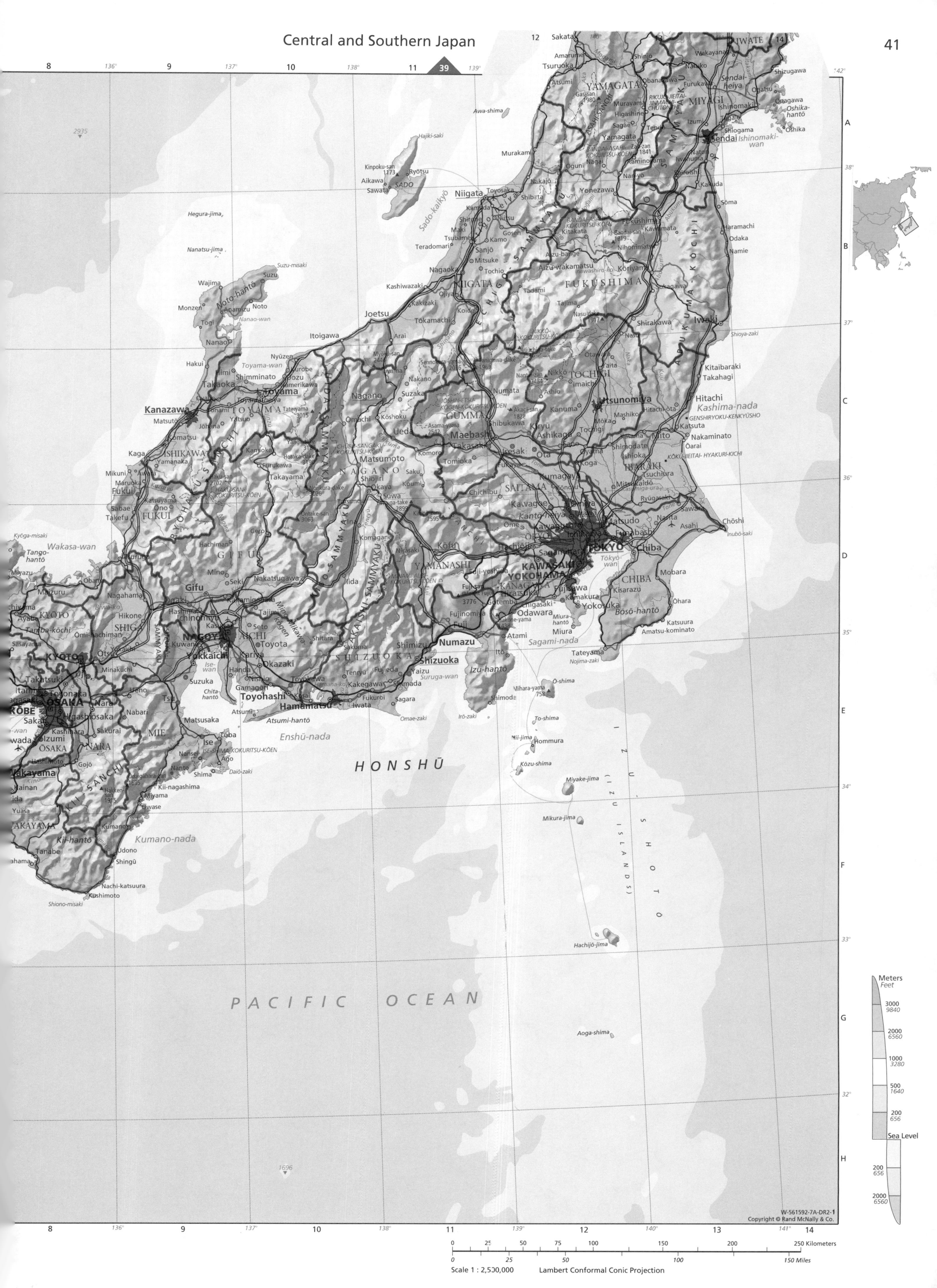

PACIFIC OCEAN

HONSHŪ

Meters
Feet

3000
9840

2000
6560

1000
3280

500
1640

200
656

Sea Level

200
656

2000
6560

W-561592-7A-DR2-1
Copyright © Rand McNally & Co.

0 25 50 75 100 150 200 250 Kilometers

0 25 50 100 150 Miles

Scale 1 : 2,500,000   Lambert Conformal Conic Projection

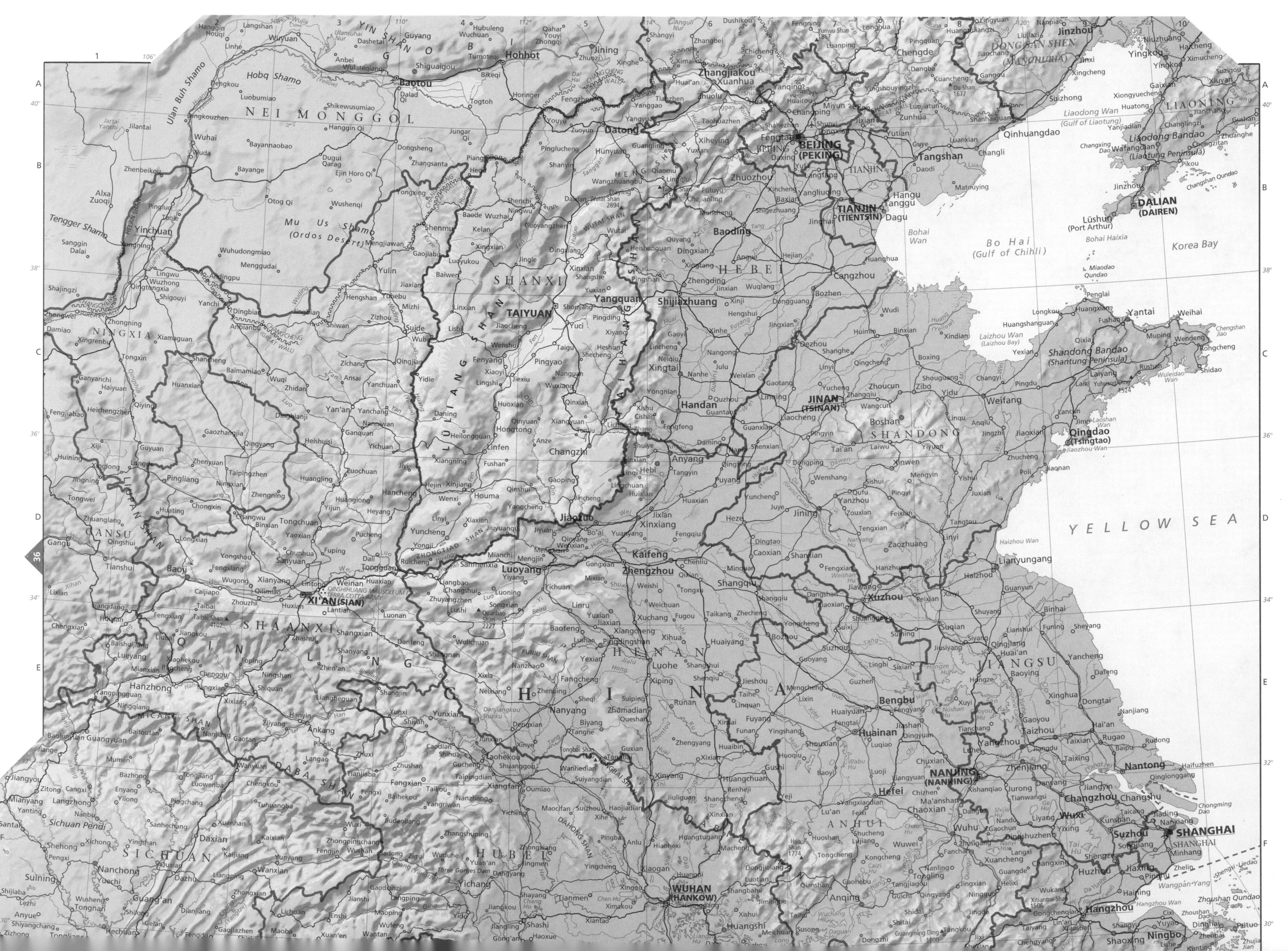
YELLOW SEA
Korea Bay
Bo Hai (Gulf of Chihli)
Bohai Wan
Laizhou Wan (Laizhou Bay)
Liaodong Wan (Gulf of Liaotung)
LIAONING
Liaodong Bandao (Liaotung Peninsula)
DALIAN (DAIREN)
Lüshun (Port Arthur)
Shandong Bandao (Shantung Peninsula)
Qingdao (Tsingtao)
Yantai
Weihai
BEIJING (PEKING)
TIANJIN (TIENTSIN)
Tanggu
Dagu
Tangshan
Qinhuangdao
Jinzhou
Yingkou
Chengde
Zhangjiakou
Datong
Hohhot
Baotou
Yinchuan
Shijiazhuang
Baoding
Handan
Xingtai
Cangzhou
JINAN (TSINAN)
Weifang
Lianyungang
Xuzhou
Bengbu
Huainan
Hefei
Wuhu
NANJING (NANKING)
Zhenjiang
Changzhou
Wuxi
Suzhou
Nantong
SHANGHAI
Hangzhou
Ningbo
Anqing
Huangshi
WUHAN (HANKOW)
Kaifeng
Zhengzhou
Luoyang
Nanyang
Jiaozuo
Anyang
Changzhi
Yangquan
TAIYUAN
Linfen
Houma
Yuncheng
XI'AN (SIAN)
Baoji
Tianshui
Hanzhong
Ankang
Yichang
Nanchong
Guang'an
HEBEI
SHANDONG
SHANXI
SHAANXI
HENAN
HUBEI
ANHUI
JIANGSU
NEI MONGGOL
NINGXIA
GANSU
SICHUAN
CHINA
LÜLIANG SHAN
TAIHANG SHAN
QINLING
DABA SHAN
DABIE SHAN
LIUPAN SHAN
YIN SHAN
Mu Us Shamo (Ordos Desert)
Hobq Shamo
Ulan Buh Shamo
Tengger Shamo
36

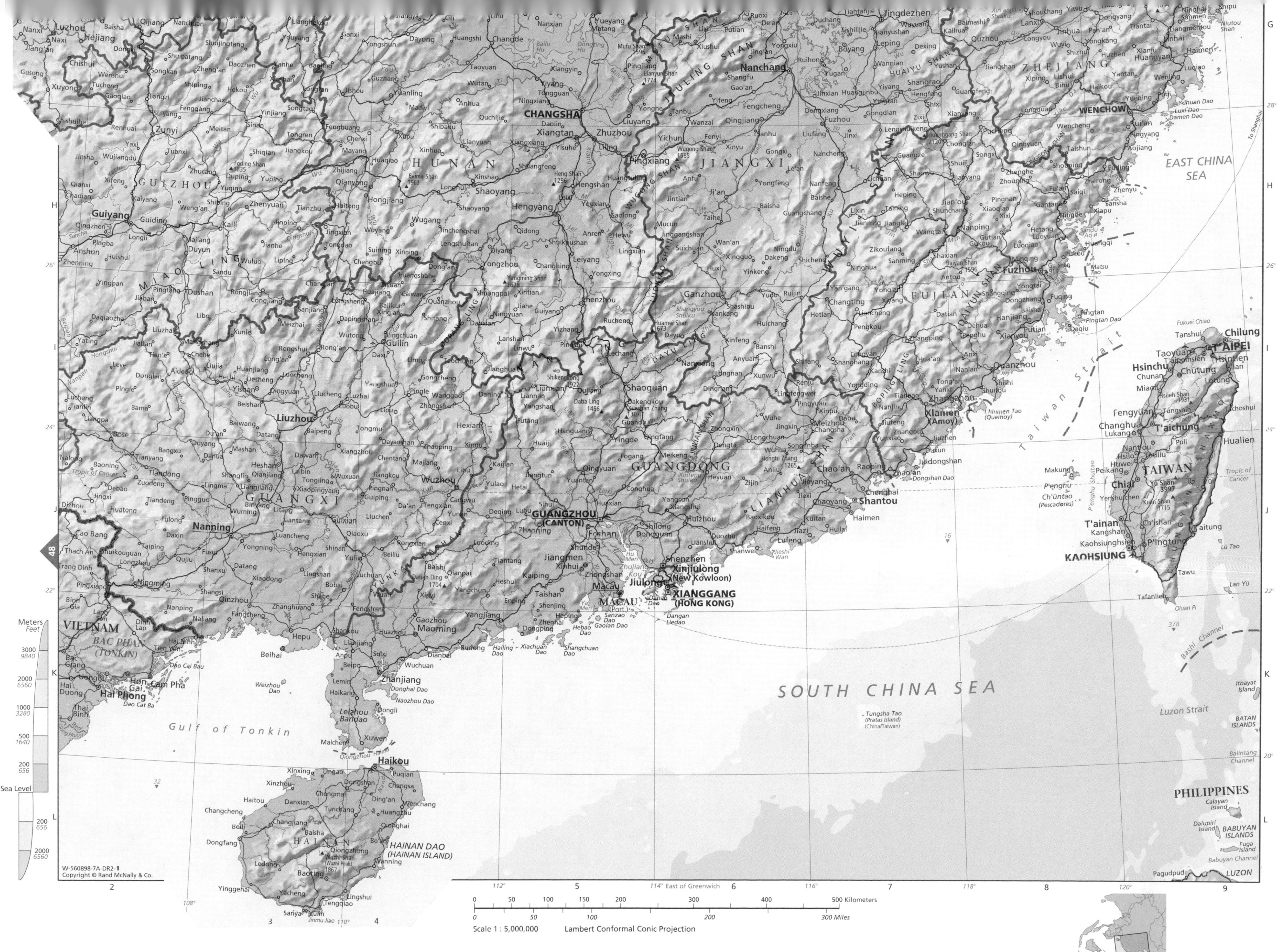
EAST CHINA SEA
SOUTH CHINA SEA
Taiwan Strait
Luzon Strait
Gulf of Tonkin
PHILIPPINES
TAIWAN
VIETNAM
LUZON
HAINAN DAO
(HAINAN ISLAND)
ZHEJIANG
FUJIAN
JIANGXI
HUNAN
GUANGDONG
GUANGXI
GUIZHOU
HAINAN
CHANGSHA
Nanchang
GUANGZHOU
(CANTON)
XIANGGANG
(HONG KONG)
MACAU
Shantou
WENCHOW
Fuzhou
Xiamen
(Amoy)
Guiyang
Nanning
Haikou
Zhanjiang
Guilin
Liuzhou
Hengyang
Xiangtan
Zhuzhou
Ganzhou
Shaoguan
Jingdezhen
T'AIPEI
Chilung
Hsinchu
T'aichung
T'ainan
KAOHSIUNG
Hualien
Beihai
Hai Phong
Scale 1 : 5,000,000
0 50 100 150 200 300 400 500 Kilometers
0 50 100 200 300 Miles
Lambert Conformal Conic Projection
114° East of Greenwich
W-560898-7A-DR2-1
Copyright © Rand McNally & Co.
Meters Feet
3000 9840
2000 6560
1000 3280
500 1640
200 656
Sea Level
200 656
2000 6560

MYANMAR (BURMA)
THAILAND
LAOS
VIETNAM
CAMBODIA
MALAYSIA
CHINA
BRUNEI
INDOCHINA
SOUTH CHINA SEA
Gulf of Tonkin
Gulf of Thailand
Andaman Sea
Gulf of Martaban
Mouths of the Ayeyarwady
Isthmus of Kra
Strait of Malacca
MALAY PENINSULA
SEMENANJUNG MALAYSIA
INDIAN OCEAN
LAUT JAWA (JAVA SEA)
GREATER SUNDA I
IND
Selat Karimata (Karimata Strait)
Selat Sunda
Selat Mentawai
Selat Bangka
Selat Gelasa
Selat Berhala
Selat Madura
Selat Lombok
Selat Serasan
Laut Bali (Bali Sea)

HA NOI
Hai Phong
Thai Binh
Nam Dinh
Ninh Binh
Thanh Hoa
Sam Son
Vinh
Ha Tinh
Ky Anh
Bo Trach
Dong Hoi
Lao Bao
Tam Lo
Hue
Da Nang
Hoi An
Tam Ky
Binh Son
Quang Ngai
Dac Glei
Dac To
Kon Tum
Sa Huynh
Tam Quan
Play Ku
An Nhon
Quy Nhon
Song Cau
Tuy Hoa
Buon Ma Thuot
Nha Trang
Cam Ranh
Phan Rang
Da Lat
Di Linh
Bao Lac
Loc Ninh
Tay Ninh
Bien Hoa
Phan Thiet
THANH PHO HO CHI MINH (HO CHI MINH CITY) (SAIGON)
Tan An
My Tho
Vinh Long
Tra Vinh
Long Xuyen
Rach Gia
Can Tho
Soc Trang
Bac Lieu
Ca Mau
Mui Ca Mau
Hon Khoai
Con Son
Dao Phu Quoc
Quan Dao Nam Du
Iles Catwick
Moc Chau
Xam Nua
Bai Thuong
Ky Son
Khe Bo
Phou Bia 2819
Muang Pakxan
Ban Nahin
Khamkeut
Ban Signo
Nakhon Phanom
Muang Khammouan
Savannakhet
Muang Phalang
Muang Xepon
Kalasin
Saravan
Muang Khôngxédôn
Pakxe
Champasak
Attapu
Ban Pakha
Muang Khong
Virôchey
Bà Kêv
Lumphăt
Phumĭ Sre Khtum
Krâchéh
Phumĭ Dăk Dăm
Stœng Trêng
Phumĭ Kâmpóng Srâlau
Choâm Khsant
Phumĭ Kântuŏt Sâmraông
Phumĭ Moŭng
Sisŏphŏn
Bătdâmbâng
ANGKOR WAT
Kâmpóng Thum
Poŭthĭsăt
Krakŏr
Kâmpóng Chhnăng
Phnum Aôral 1813
Ŏdŏngk
Kâmpóng Cham
Phnum Pénh (Phnom Penh)
Phumĭ Châmbák
Phumĭ Chhuk
Svay Riĕng
Takêv
Kâmpôt
Kaôh Rŭng
Kâmpóng Saôm
Krŏng Kaôh Kŏng
Phumĭ Kaôh Kŏng
Ko Chang
Ko Kut
Trat
Chanthaburi
Rayong
Chon Buri
Si Racha
Samut Prakan
KRUNG THEP (BANGKOK)
Aranyaprathet
PHANOM DONGRAK RANGE
Nakhon Ratchasima
Buri Ram
Surin
Si Sa Ket
Ubon Ratchathani
Tha Tum
Warin Chamrap
Roi Et
Maha Sarakham
Khon Kaen
Udon Thani
Sakon Nakhon
Nong Khai
Loei
Lom Sak
Phetchabun
Phitsanulok
Sukhothai
Sawankhalok
Uttaradit
Phichit
Nakhon Sawan
Chaiyaphum
Chaturat
Bang Mun Nak
Chum Saeng
Uthai Thani
Chai Nat
Takhli
Chai Badan
Bua Yai
Lop Buri
Saraburi
Phra Nakhon Si Ayutthaya
Suphan Buri
Nam Tok
Nakhon Pathom
Ban Pong
Samut Songkhram
Phetchaburi
Cha-am
Hua Hin
Prachuap Khiri Khan
Chumphon
Ranong
Ko Tao
Ko Phangan
Ko Samui
Ao Ban Don
Surat Thani
Nakhon Si Thammarat
Pak Phanang
Thung Song
Phangnga
Phuket
Ko Phuket
Trang
Kantang
Phatthalung
Thale Luang
Songkhla
Hat Yai
Pattani
Yala
Narathiwat
Satun
Kangar
Pulau Langkawi
Kota Bharu
Pasir Mas
Sungai Kolok
Betong
Alor Setar
Sungai Petani
George Town (Penang)
Butterworth
Kuala Krai
Kuala Terengganu
Taiping
Kuala Kangsar
Ipoh
Gunung Tahan 2187
Kuala Lipis
Kampar
Teluk Intan
Raub
Bentung
Gunung Benum 2107
Cukai
Kuantan
Pahang
KUALA LUMPUR
Shah Alam
Kajang
Klang
Seremban
Kuala Pilah
Melaka
Segamat
Labis
Mersing
Keluang
Pulau Tioman
Muar
Batu Pahat
Johor Bahru
SINGAPORE
Tak
Mae Sot
Kamphaeng Phet
Taphan Hin
Mawlamyine
Thaton
Pha-an
Thongwa
YANGON (RANGOON)
Syriam
Wakema
Pathein
Myaungmya
Bogale
Pyapon
Kyaunggon
Henzada
Gwa
Kyeintali
Sandoway
Prome
Paungde
Oktwin
Pyu
Kyaukkyi
Toungoo
Thayetmyo
Allanmyo
PEGU YOMA
Pyinmana
Loi-kaw
Ela
Mattaunt 2620
Nyaunglebin
Thanatpin
Tharrawaddy
Thonze
Bago
Kyaikto
Papun
Myanaung
Mae Sariang
Mae Hong Son
Doi Inthanon 2600
Chiang Mai
Lamphun
Lampang
Phrae
Nan
Phayao
Chiang Rai
Chiang Kham
Hsum Hsai
Mong Hsat
Ban Houayxay
Louangphrabang
Muang Xaignabouri
Muang Thadua
Muang Phiang
Ban Thieng
Ban Nalé
Muang Vangviang
Muang Pak-Lay
Viangchan (Vientiane)
Chiang Khan
Nam Pat
Thoen
Viangphoukha
Muang Ngoy
DAWNA RA.
TAUNGNYO RANGE
BILAUKTAUNG RANGE
TANEN TAUNGGYI
Myitta
Dawei
Myinmoletkat Taung 2075
Palaw
Mergui
Tenasserim
Kadan Kyun
MERGUI ARCHIPELAGO
Daung Kyun
Bentinck Island
Letsok-aw Kyun
Kanmaw Kyun
Lenya
Lanbi Kyun
Ye
Paya Chedi Sam Ong 282
ANNAMITIQUE (CHAINE ANNAMITIQUE)
Xuwen
Leizhou Bandao
Qiongzhou Haixia
Haikou
Lingao
Chengmai
Danxian
Wenchang
Qionghai
Changjiang
Dongfang
Wuzhi Shan 1867
Baoting
Wanning
Lingshui
Sanya
HAINAN DAO (HAINAN ISLAND)
XISHA QUNDAO (PARACEL ISLANDS) (Claimed by China, Taiwan and Vietnam)
SPRATLY ISLANDS (Claimed by Brunei, China, Malaysia, Philippines, Taiwan and Vietnam)
Nanshan Island
Mount Mantalingajan 2085
Balabac Island
Balabac Strait
Pulau Balambangan
Kudat
Kota Belud
Gunung Kinabalu 4101
Kota Kinabalu
SABAH
Pulau Labuan
Labuan
Bandar Seri Begawan
Seria
Miri
Gunung Mulu 2377
Niah
Bintulu
SARAWAK
Mukah
Sibu
Sarikei
Kapit
Kuching
Betong
Serian
Gunung Murud 2422
Nameh
Kong Kemul 2053
Tarakan
Bengara
Datum
Tanjungredeb
Lasan
Gunung Menyapa 2000
IRAN MTS.
UPPER KAPUAS MTS.
PEG. MULLER
Putussibau
Semitau
Sanggau
Sintang
Pontianak
Mempawah
Singkawang
Sambas
Cape Datu
Bontang
Longiram
Samarinda
Balikpapan
BORNEO (KALIMANTAN)
Gunung Saran 1758
Bukit Raya 2278
Telukbatang
Sukadana
Pulau Karimata
Ketapang
Nangatayap
Sukaraja
Kendawangan
Palangkaraya
Sampit
Buntok
Amuntai
Kandangan
Kumai
Teluk Kumai
Teluk Sampit
Kualakapuas
Banjarmasin
Martapura
Tanjung Puting
Tanjung Selatan
Pulau Laut
Pulau Sebuku
Selat Laut
Tanjung Aru
KEPULAUAN NATUNA BESAR
Pulau Laut
Natuna Besar
KEPULAUAN ANAMBAS
Pulau Jemaja
Pulau Midai
KEPULAUAN NATUNA SELATAN
Pulau Subi
Pulau Serasan
KEPULAUAN TAMBELAN
Pulau Pejantan
Pulau We
Banda Aceh
Lhokseumawe
Langsa
Gunung Abongabong 2985
Meulaboh
Gunung Leuser 3381
Binjai
MEDAN
Tebingtinggi
Blangpidie
Tapaktuan
Gunung Sinabung 2451
Kisaran
Pematangsiantar
Danau Toba
Tanjungbalai
Pulau Simeulue
Sinabang
Pulau Babi
Tarutung
Pulau Tuangku
Sibolga
Bagansiapiapi
Rantauprapat
Pulau Rupat
Dumai
Pulau Bengkalis
Pulau Mursala
Gunungsitoli
Padangsidempuan
Pulau Nias
Pulau Padang
Pulau Tebingtinggi
Pulau Batam
Pulau Kundur
Pulau Bintan
Tanjungpinang
KEPULAUAN RIAU
SUMATERA (SUMATRA)
Pekanbaru
Bangkinang
Pulau Pini
Talu
Kampar Kanan
Pulau Sebangka
Pulau Lingga
KEPULAUAN LINGGA
Pulau Singkep
Pulau Basu
Equator
Pulau Tanahmasa
KEPULAUAN BATU
Pulau Tanahbala
Bukittinggi
Payakumbuh
Padangpanjang
Pariaman
Padang
Tembilahan
Rengat
Taluk
Pulau Siberut
Sungaidareh
Painan
Muarabungo
Gunung Kerinci 3800
Jambi
Hari
KEPULAUAN MENTAWAI
Pulau Sipura
Pulau Pagai Utara
Pulau Pagai Selatan
Mukomuko
Bangko
Surulangun
PEGUNUNGAN BARISAN
Muntok
Pangkalpinang
Pulau Bangka
Tanjungpandan
Manggar
Belitung
Pulau Lepar
Palembang
Musi
Kayuagung
Prabumulih
Lubuklinggau
Muaraenim
Lais
Bengkulu
Lahat
Gunung Dempo 3159
Baturaja
Martapura
Tulangbawang
Menggala
Tanjung Lumut
Manna
Bintuhan
Kotabumi
Krui
Kotaagung
Tanjungkarang-Telukbetung
Panjang
Pulau Enggano
Tanjung Cina
Serang
JAKARTA
Karawang
Indramayu
Purwakarta
Bogor
Cianjur
Cirebon
Sumedang
Pekalongan
Kudus
Rembang
Tuban
Madura
Sukabumi
BANDUNG
Tegal
Garut
Gunung Slamet 3428
Purwokerto
SEMARANG
Gresik
SURABAYA
Bangkalan
Sumenep
Pamekasan
Surakarta
Gunung Lawu 3265
Kediri
Pasuruan
Probolinggo
Cilacap
Yogyakarta
Tulungagung
Blitar
Malang
Jember
Banyuwangi
JAWA (JAVA)
Ujunggenteng
Sindangbarang
Tanjung Cangkuang
Kepulauan Karimunjawa
Pulau Bawean
Pulau Masalembu Besar
Pulau Kangean
Pulau Sepanjang
Bali
Gunung Agung 3142m
Denpasar
Nusa Penida
Lombok
Praya
Mataram
Taliwang
Gunung Rinjani 3726

Meters / Feet
4000 13120
3000 9840
2000 6560
1000 3280
500 1640
200 656
Sea Level
200 656
2000 6560

0 100 200 300 400 600 800 1000 Kilometers
0 100 200 400 600 Miles
Scale 1 : 10,000,000 Sinusoidal Projection

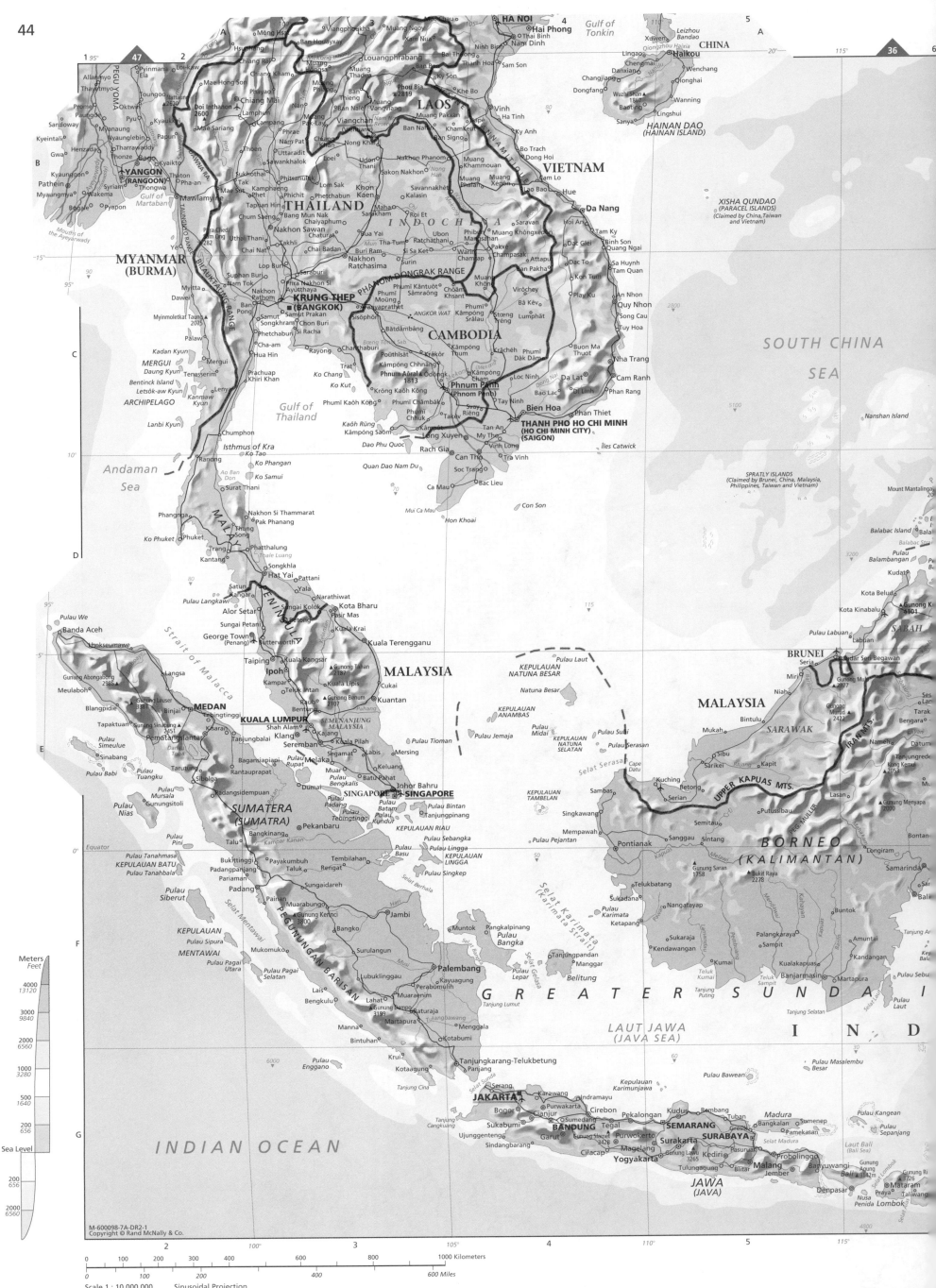

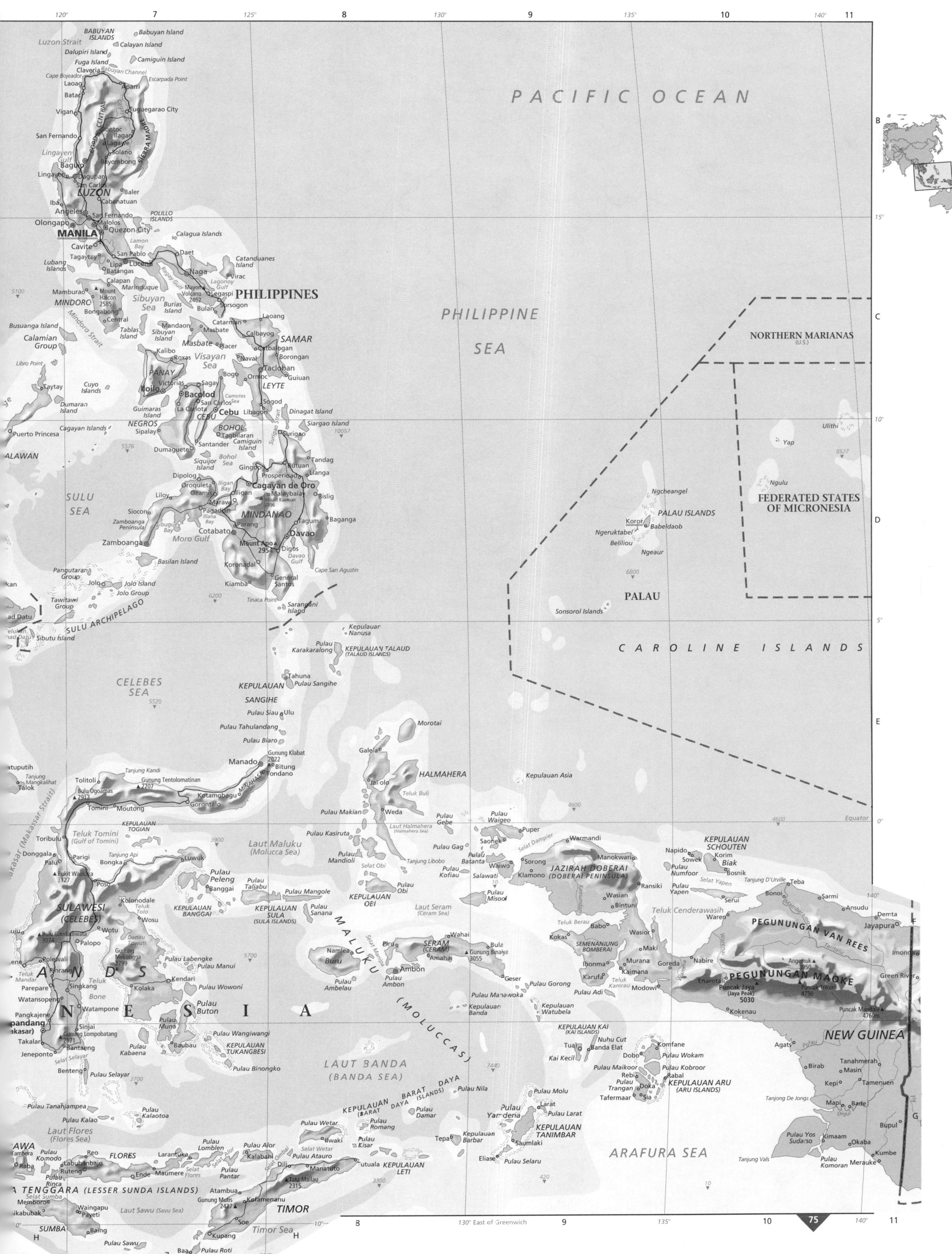

PACIFIC OCEAN

PHILIPPINE

SEA

PHILIPPINES

NORTHERN MARIANAS
(U.S.)

FEDERATED STATES
OF MICRONESIA

PALAU ISLANDS

Koror
Babeldaob
Ngeruktabel
Beliliou
Ngeaur

PALAU

Sonsorol Islands

CAROLINE ISLANDS

Yap

Ulithi

Ngulu

LUZON

MANILA

MINDORO

Sibuyan
Sea

SAMAR

PANAY

Visayan
Sea

Iloilo
Bacolod
CEBU
Cebu

LEYTE

NEGROS
BOHOL
Bohol
Sea

Cagayan de Oro

MINDANAO

Davao

Mount Apo
2954

Zamboanga

Cotabato
Moro Gulf

General
Santos

SULU
SEA

SULU ARCHIPELAGO

CELEBES
SEA

KEPULAUAN
SANGIHE

KEPULAUAN TALAUD
(TALAUD ISLANDS)

Kepulauan
Nanusa

Pulau
Karakaralong

Tahuna
Pulau Sangihe

Pulau Siau
Ulu
Pulau Tahulandang
Pulau Biaro

Manado
Gunung Klabat
2022
Bitung
Tondano

Morotai

Galela

HALMAHERA

Kepulauan Asia

Equator

Tolitoli
Bulu Ogoamas
2313

Tomini
Moutong

Gunung Tentolomatinan
2207

Kotamobagu
Gorontalo

Jailolo

Weda

Teluk Buli

Pulau Makian

Pulau
Gebe

Pulau
Waigeo

Selat Dampier

Warmandi

SULAWESI
(CELEBES)

Palu

Poso

KEPULAUAN
TOGIAN

Teluk Tomini
(Gulf of Tomini)

Luwuk

Pulau
Peleng

Banggai

KEPULAUAN
BANGGAI

Pulau
Taliabu

Pulau Mangole

KEPULAUAN
SULA
(SULA ISLANDS)

Laut Maluku
(Molucca Sea)

Pulau
Mandioli

Selat Obi

Pulau
Obi

KEPULAUAN
OBI

Laut Halmahera
(Halmahera Sea)

Pulau Kasiruta

Pulau Gag

Pulau
Batanta
Waigeo
Salawati

Sorong
Klamono

JAZIRAH DOBERAI
(DOBERAI PENINSULA)

Manokwari

KEPULAUAN
SCHOUTEN

Biak

Napido
Sowek
Korim
Bosnik

Pulau
Numfoor

Ransiki

Pulau
Yapen

Selat Yapen

Tanjung D'Urville

Teba

Bonoi

Sarmi

Ansudu

PEGUNUNGAN VAN REES

Demta
Jayapura

NEW GUINEA

Kolonodale
Teluk
Tolo

Wosu

Wotu
Palopo

SULAWESI

Danau
Poso

Pulau Labengke

Pulau Manui

KEPULAUAN
OEI

Pulau
Sanana

Piru
Wahai

SERAM
(CERAM)
Amahai

Laut Seram
(Ceram Sea)

Gunung Binaiya
3055

Bula

Geser

Wasian

Bintuni

SEMENANJUNG
BOMBERAI

Babo

Kokas

Wasior

Teluk Berau

Maki

Kaimana

Teluk Cenderawasih

Waren

Serui

Nabire

Angemuk
3950

PEGUNUNGAN MAOKE

Puncak Trikora
4750

Green River

Imonda

Kendari

Kolaka

Pulau Wowoni

Pulau
Muna

SULAWESI

Watampone

Sinjai

Kolaka

Pulau
Buton

Pulau Wangiwangi

KEPULAUAN
TUKANGBESI

Baubau

Pulau
Kabaena

Namlea
Buru

Pulau
Ambelau

Ambon
Pulau
Ambon

Pulau Manawoka

Pulau Gorong

Pulau Adi

Teluk
Kamrau

Modowi

Murana

Ibonma

Karufu

Goreda

Kaimana

Enarotali

Puncak Jaya
(Jaya Peak)
5030

Puncak Mandala
4760m

Kokenau

Agats

MALUKU
(MOLUCCAS)

Kepulauan
Banda

Kepulauan
Watubela

KEPULAUAN KAI
(KAI ISLANDS)

Nuhu Cut
Banda Elat

Tual

Kai Kecil

Dobo
Pulau Wokam

Komfane

Pulau Kobroor

KEPULAUAN ARU
(ARU ISLANDS)

Birab

Masin

Kepi

Tamenuen

Mapi
Bade

Bupul

Pulau
Yos
Sudarso

Kimaam

Okaba

Kumbe

Merauke

Pangkajene
Pandang
(Makasar)

Takalar

Jeneponto

Benteng

Gunung Lompobatang
2871

Pulau Selayar

LAUT BANDA
(BANDA SEA)

Pulau Binongko

Pulau Nila

Pulau
Damar

KEPULAUAN
BARAT
DAYA
(ISLANDS)

BARAT
DAYA

Pulau
Yamdena

Larat
Pulau Larat

KEPULAUAN
TANIMBAR

Saumlaki

ARAFURA SEA

Tanjong De Jongs

Tanjung Vals

Pulau
Tanahjampea

Pulau Kalao

Pulau Kalaotoa

Laut Flores
(Flores Sea)

FLORES

Reo
Ruteng

Ende
Maumere

Larantuka

Pulau Lomblen

Pulau Pantar

Pulau Alor

Kalabahi

Selat Ombai

Dili

Manatuto

TIMOR

Gunung Mutis
2427

Soe

Kupang

Timor Sea

NUSA TENGGARA (LESSER SUNDA ISLANDS)

Selat Flores

Pulau
Wetar

Ilwaki

Pulau Romang

Pulau Kisar

Tepa

Kepulauan
Barbar

Eliasa

KEPULAUAN
LETI

Selat Wetar

Tata Mailau
2315

Atambua

Kefamenanu

SUMBA

Waingapu

Waikabubak

Pulau Sawu

Laut Sawu
(Savu Sea)

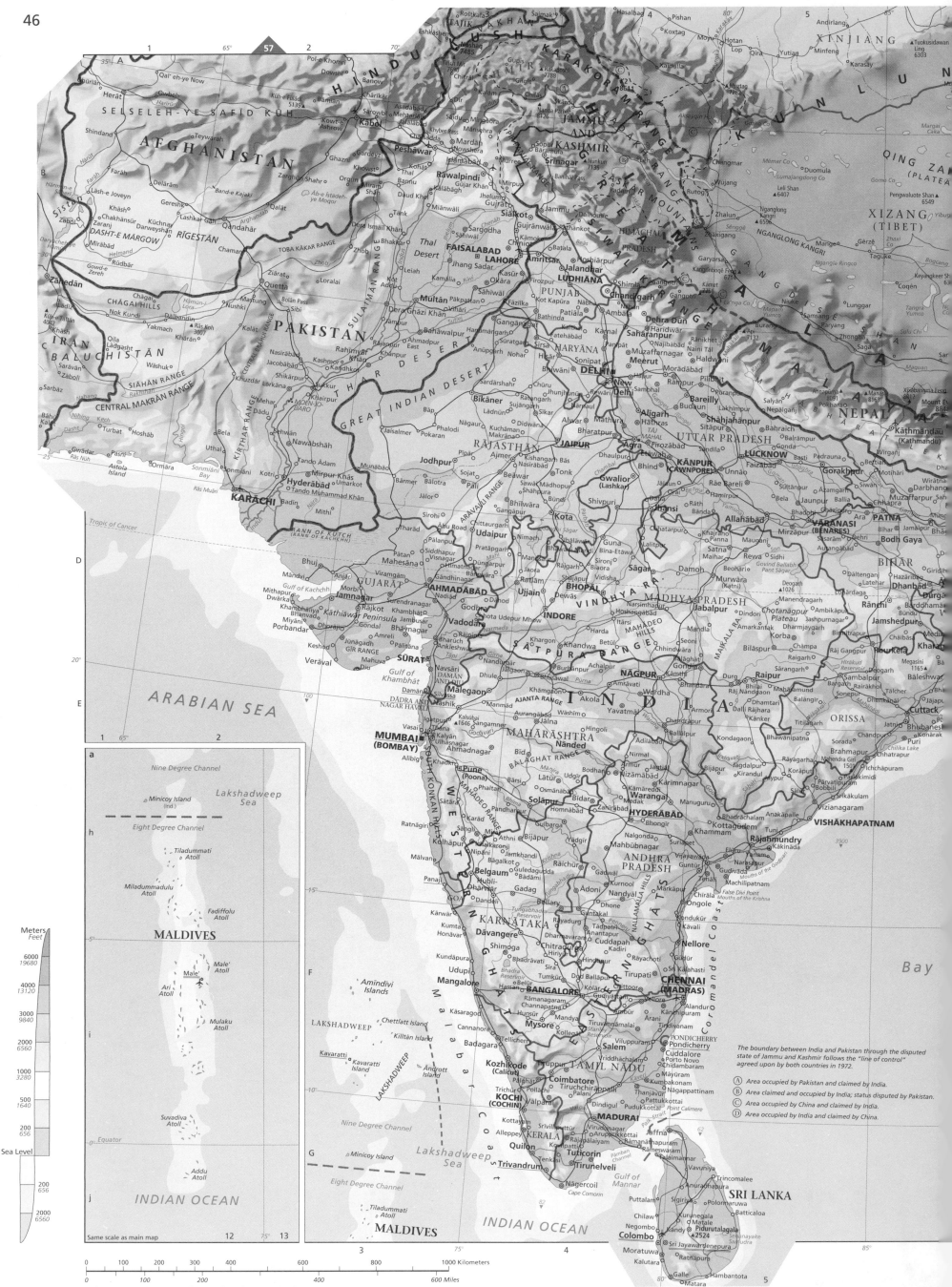

The boundary between India and Pakistan through the disputed state of Jammu and Kashmir follows the "line of control" agreed upon by both countries in 1972.

(A) Area occupied by Pakistan and claimed by India.
(B) Area claimed and occupied by India; status disputed by Pakistan.
(C) Area occupied by China and claimed by India.
(D) Area occupied by India and claimed by China.

Scale 1 : 10,000,000   Lambert Conformal Conic Projection

CHINA
YUNNAN
GUANGXI
HAINAN
HAINAN DAO (HAINAN ISLAND)
Gulf of Tonkin
SOUTH CHINA SEA
VIETNAM
LAOS
CAMBODIA
THAILAND
INDOCHINA
MYANMAR (BURMA)
SHAN
KAYAH
KAYIN
MON
MANDALAY
SAGAING
MAGWAY
BAGO
YANGON
AYEYARWADY
RAKHINE
CHIN
TANINTHARYI
HA NOI
Hai Phong
Da Nang
Hue
Vinh
Viangchan (Vientiane)
Louangphrabang
KRUNG THEP (BANGKOK)
Chiang Mai
Nakhon Ratchasima
Mandalay
YANGON (RANGOON)
Mawlamyine
Taunggyi
Bay of Bengal
Gulf of Martaban
Nanning
Quy Nhon
Nha Trang

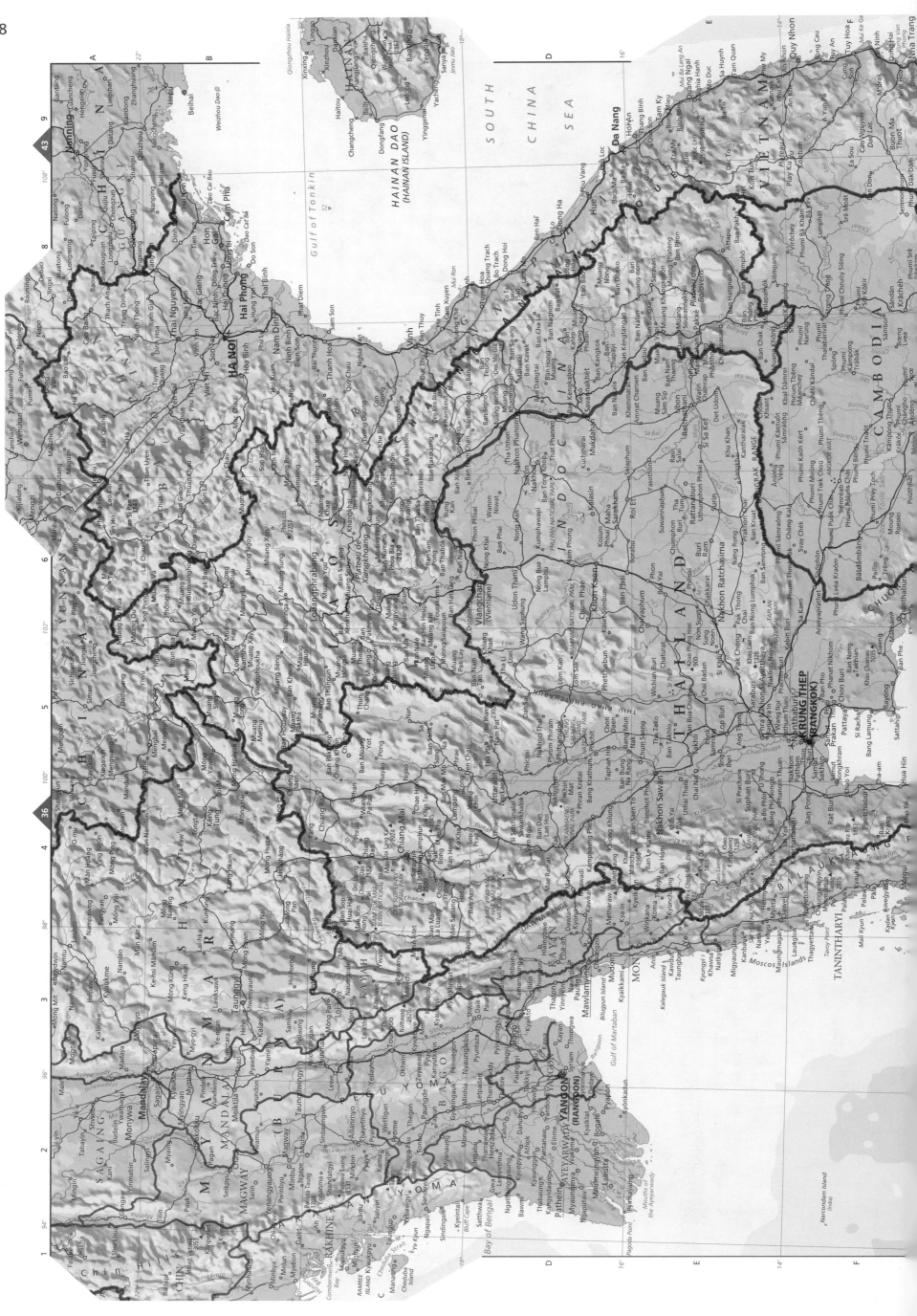

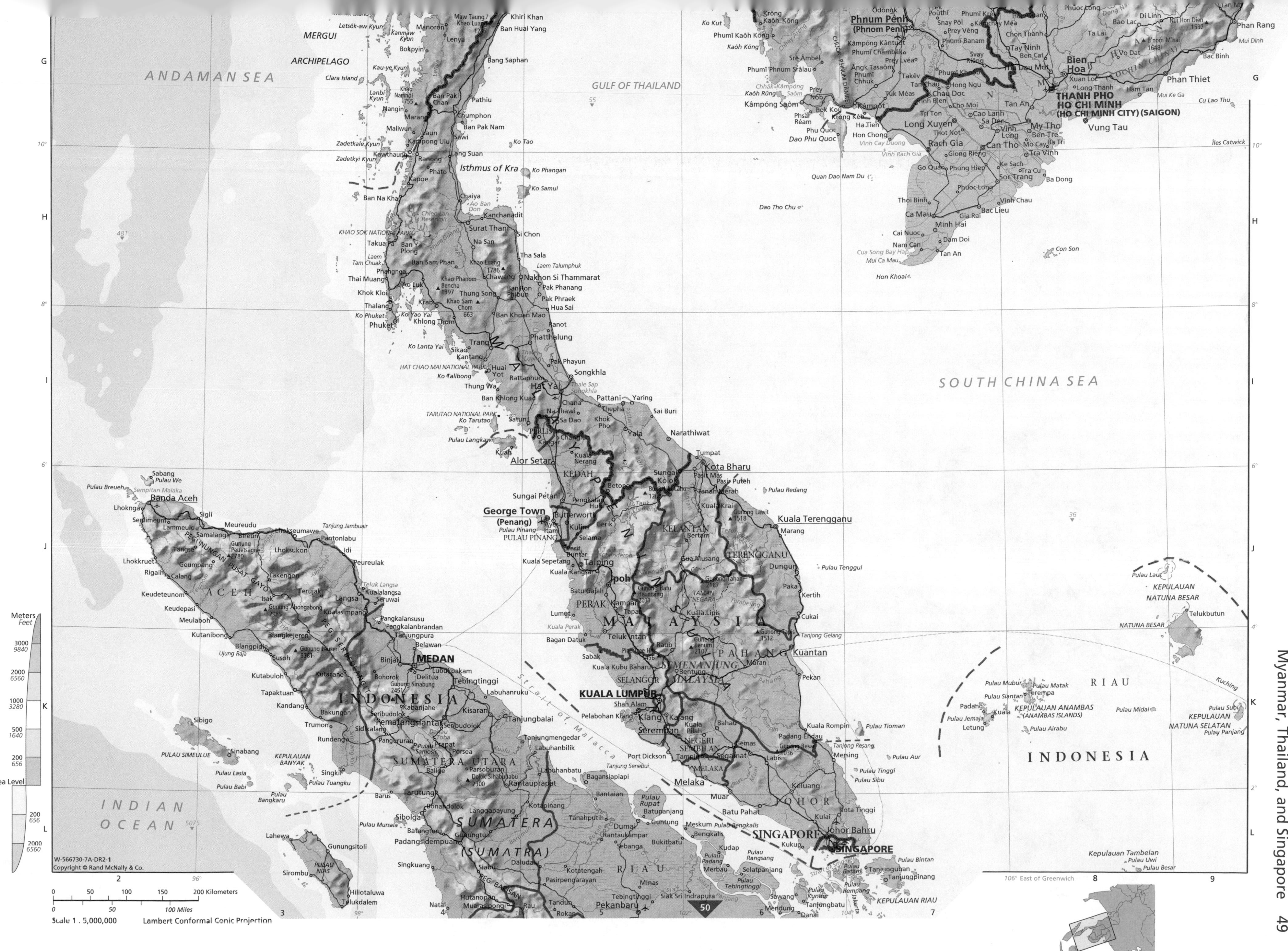

ANDAMAN SEA
MERGUI
ARCHIPELAGO
GULF OF THAILAND
SOUTH CHINA SEA
INDIAN OCEAN
Strait of Malacca
Isthmus of Kra
Phnom Penh
(Phnom Penh)
THANH PHO
HO CHI MINH
(HO CHI MINH CITY) (SAIGON)
Vung Tau
Phan Thiet
Phuket
Songkhla
Hat Yai
Alor Setar
George Town
(Penang)
Kota Bharu
Kuala Terengganu
Kuantan
Ipoh
MALAYSIA
KUALA LUMPUR
Melaka
SINGAPORE
Johor Bahru
Banda Aceh
MEDAN
INDONESIA
SUMATERA
(SUMATRA)
RIAU
KEPULAUAN
NATUNA BESAR
Pekanbaru
50
W-566730-7A-DR2-1
Copyright © Rand McNally & Co.
Scale 1:5,000,000
Lambert Conformal Conic Projection
200 Kilometers
100 Miles
106° East of Greenwich
Meters
Feet
Sea Level

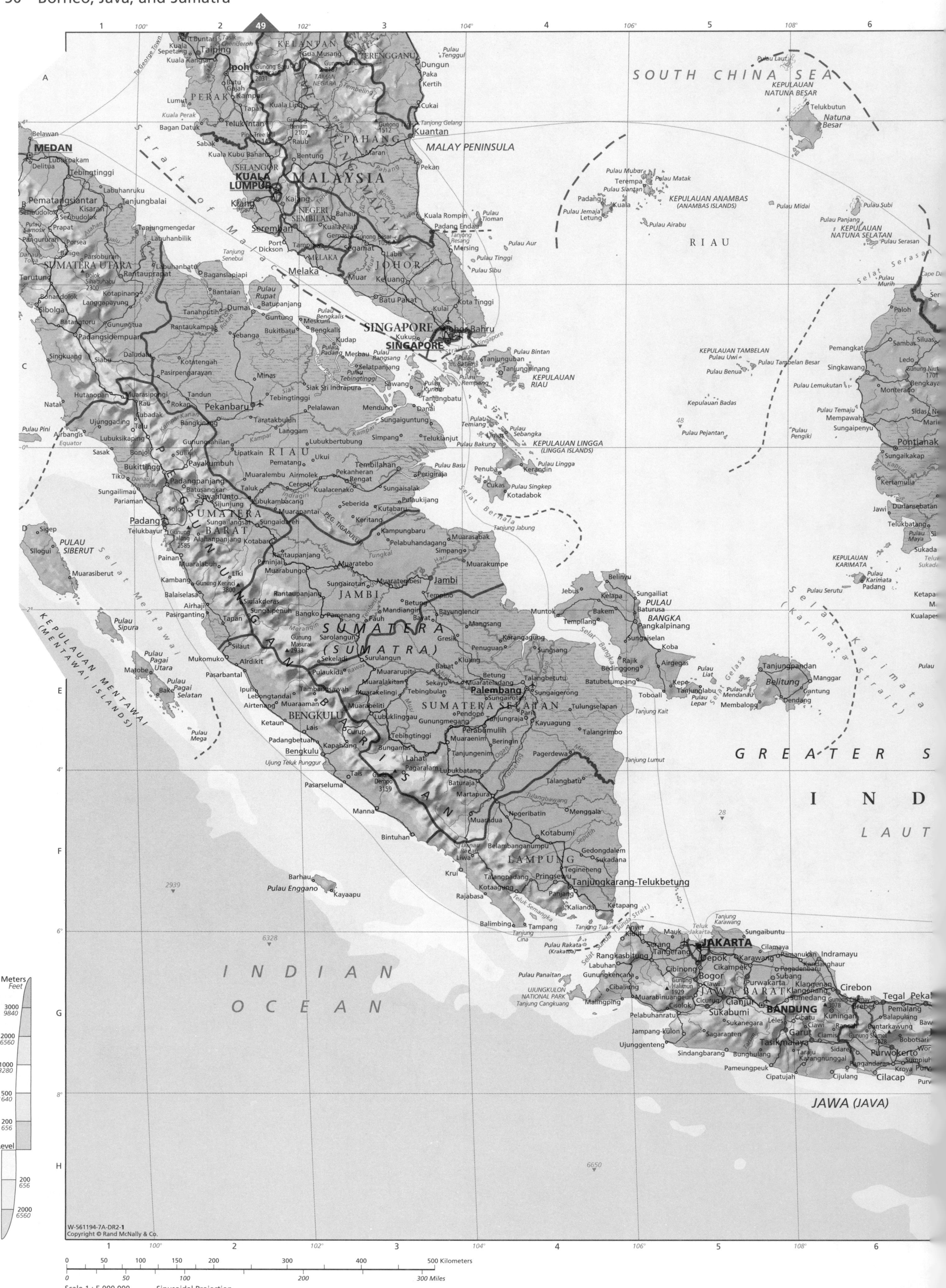

Meters
Feet

3000
9840

2000
6560

1000
3280

500
1640

200
656

Sea Level

200
656

2000
6560

W-561194-7A-DR2-1
Copyright © Rand McNally & Co.

0   50   100   150   200   300   400   500 Kilometers

0   50   100   200   300 Miles

Scale 1 : 5,000,000   Sinusoidal Projection

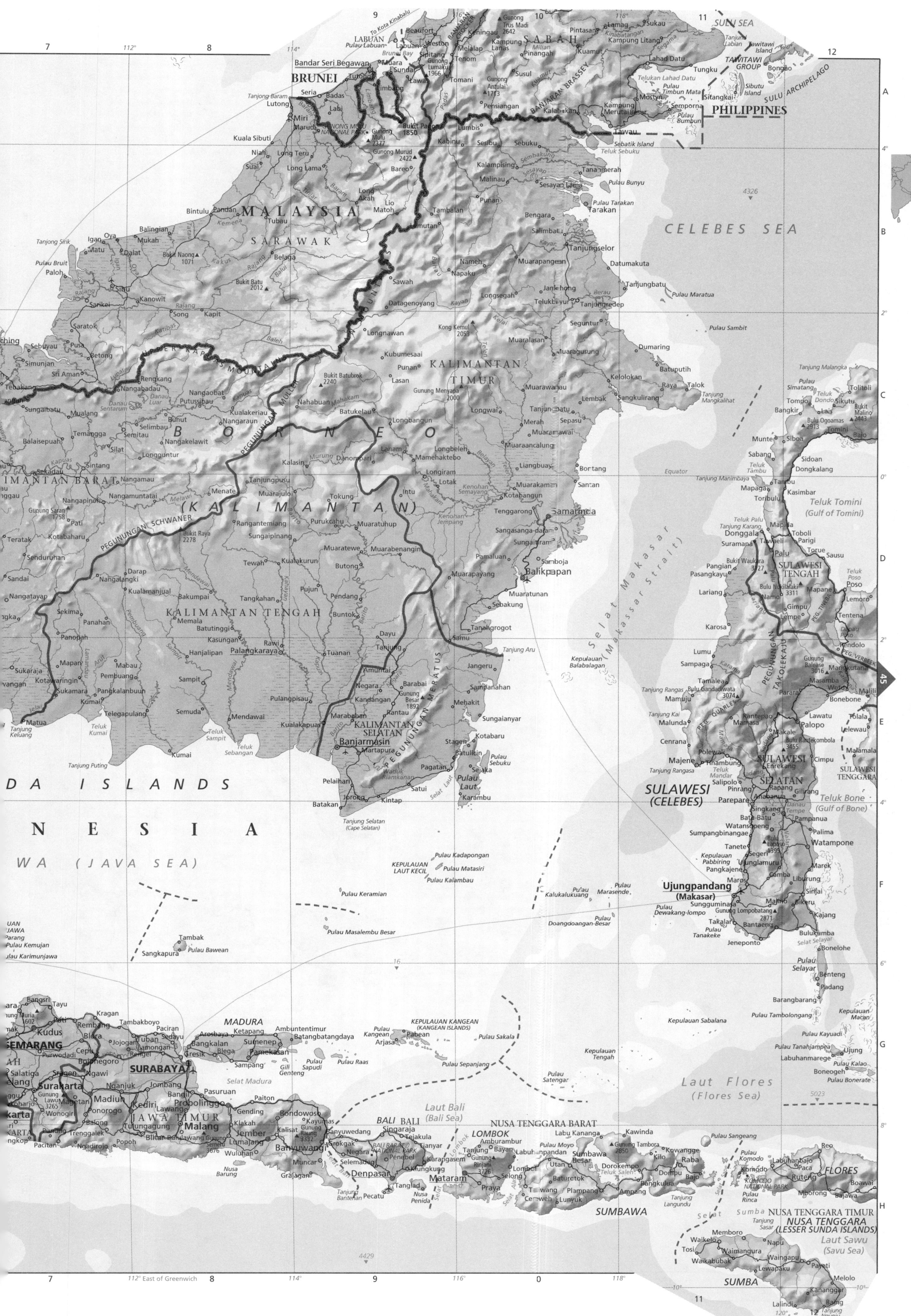

BRUNEI
Bandar Seri Begawan
MALAYSIA
SARAWAK
SABAH
PHILIPPINES
SULU SEA
CELEBES SEA
BORNEO
(KALIMANTAN)
KALIMANTAN TIMUR
KALIMANTAN TENGAH
KALIMANTAN SELATAN
Banjarmasin
Samarinda
Balikpapan
Selat Makasar
(Makassar Strait)
SULAWESI
(CELEBES)
SULAWESI TENGAH
SULAWESI SELATAN
Ujungpandang
(Makasar)
Teluk Tomini
(Gulf of Tomini)
Teluk Bone
(Gulf of Bone)
Laut Flores
(Flores Sea)
Laut Bali
(Bali Sea)
DA ISLANDS
NESIA
WA (JAVA SEA)
MADURA
SURABAYA
SEMARANG
Surakarta
JAWA TIMUR
Malang
BALI
Denpasar
NUSA TENGGARA BARAT
LOMBOK
Mataram
SUMBAWA
FLORES
NUSA TENGGARA TIMUR
NUSA TENGGARA
(LESSER SUNDA ISLANDS)
Laut Sawu
(Savu Sea)
SUMBA
45
112° East of Greenwich

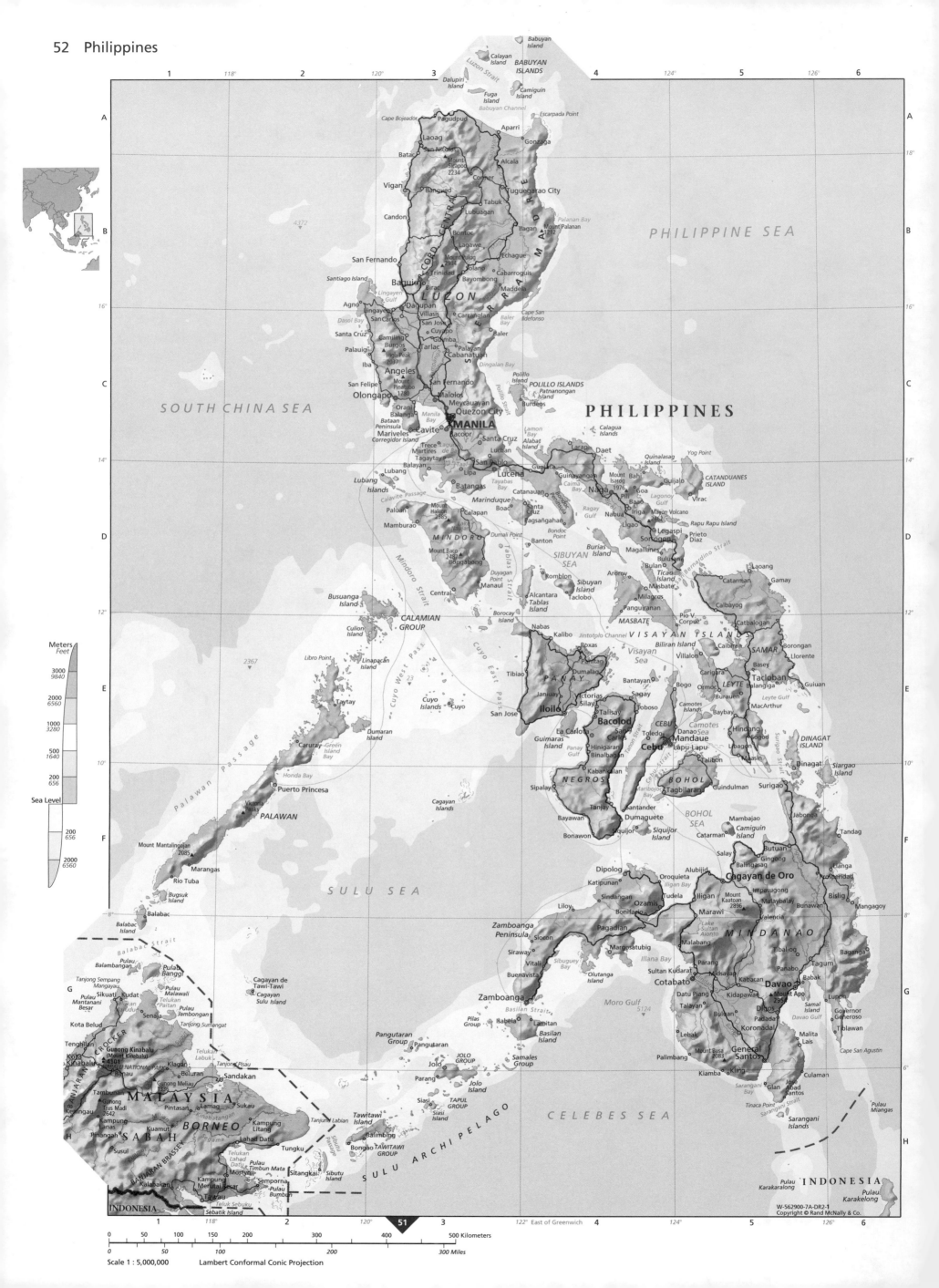

Meters / Feet

2000 / 6560

1000 / 3280

500 / 1640

200 / 656

Sea Level

200 / 656

2000 / 6560

0 50 100 150 200 300 400 500 Kilometers

0 50 100 200 300 Miles

Scale 1 : 5,000,000

Lambert Conformal Conic Projection

76° East of Greenwich

W-561092-7A-DR2-1

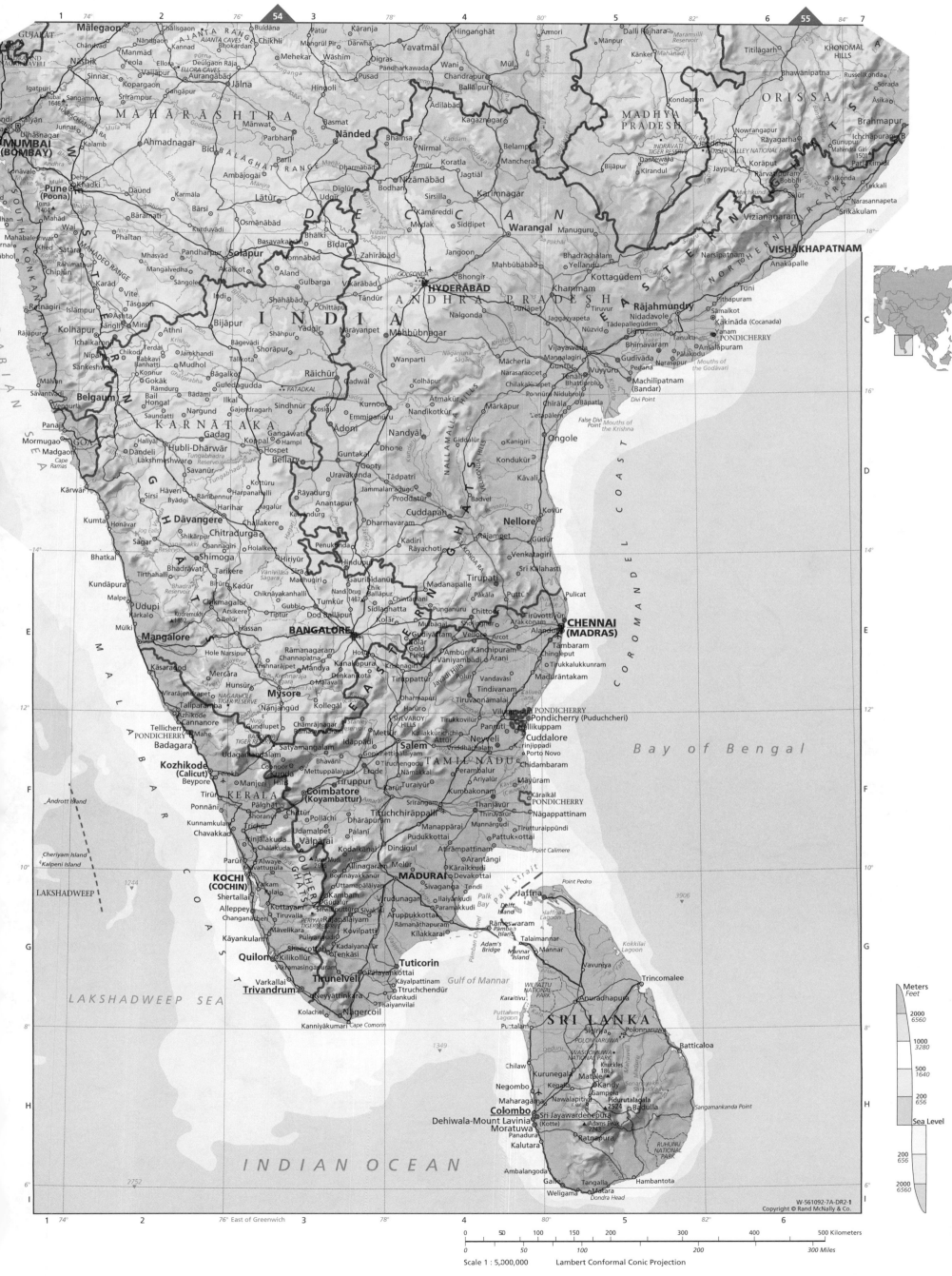

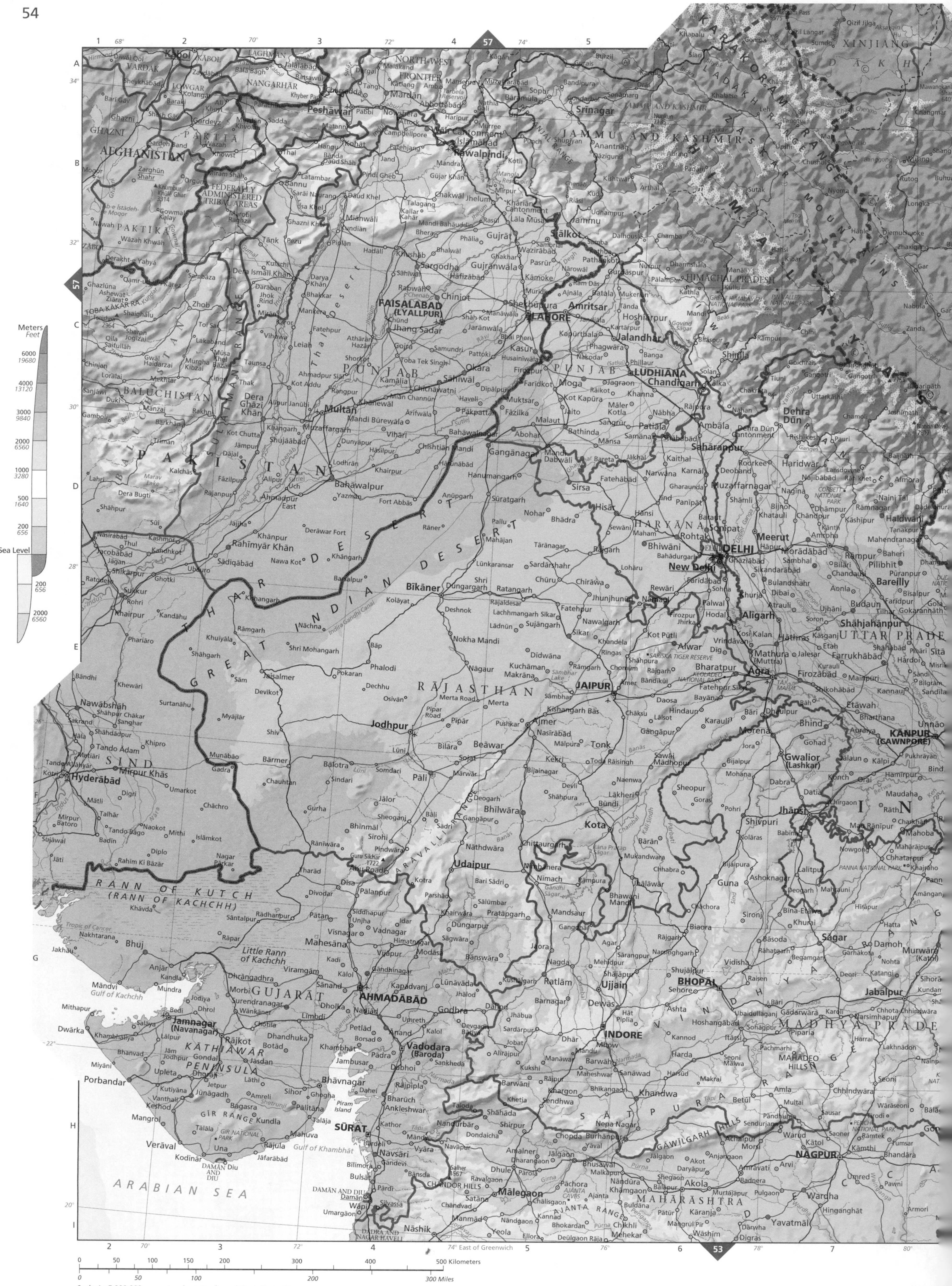
AFGHANISTAN
PAKISTAN
BALUCHISTAN
FEDERALLY ADMINISTERED TRIBAL AREAS
NORTH-WEST FRONTIER
PUNJAB
SIND
JAMMU AND KASHMIR
HIMACHAL PRADESH
HARYANA
RĀJASTHAN
GUJARĀT
UTTAR PRADE
MADHYA PRADE
MAHĀRĀSHTRA
XINJIANG
KĀTHIĀWĀR PENINSULA
THAR DESERT
GREAT INDIAN DESERT
RANN OF KUTCH
(RANN OF KACHCHH)
Little Rann of Kachchh
Gulf of Kachchh
Gulf of Khambhāt
ARABIAN SEA
KARAKORAM RANGE
LADAKH RANGE
ZASKAR MOUNTAINS
SULAIMAN RANGE
ARAVALLI RANGE
VINDHYA RANGE
SĀTPURA RANGE
GĪR RANGE
Kābul
Peshāwar
Islāmābād
Rāwalpindi
Srīnagar
Lahore
Faisalabad (Lyallpur)
Multān
Amritsar
Ludhiāna
Chandīgarh
DELHI
New Delhi
Jaipur
Jodhpur
Bīkāner
Hyderābād
Ahmadābād
Vadodara (Baroda)
Sūrat
Indore
Bhopāl
Kanpur (Cawnpore)
Āgra
Gwalior (Lashkar)
Nāgpur
Meerut
Udaipur
Kota
Ajmer
Jabalpur
Ujjain
Rājkot
Jamnagar (Navanagar)
Bhāvnagar
Mālegaon
Akola
Bareilly
Dehra Dūn
Meters
Feet
6000
19680
4000
13120
3000
9840
2000
6560
1000
3280
500
1640
200
656
Sea Level
200
656
2000
6560
0
50
100
150
200
300
400
500 Kilometers
0
50
100
200
300 Miles
Scale 1 : 5,000,000
Lambert Conformal Conic Projection
74° East of Greenwich

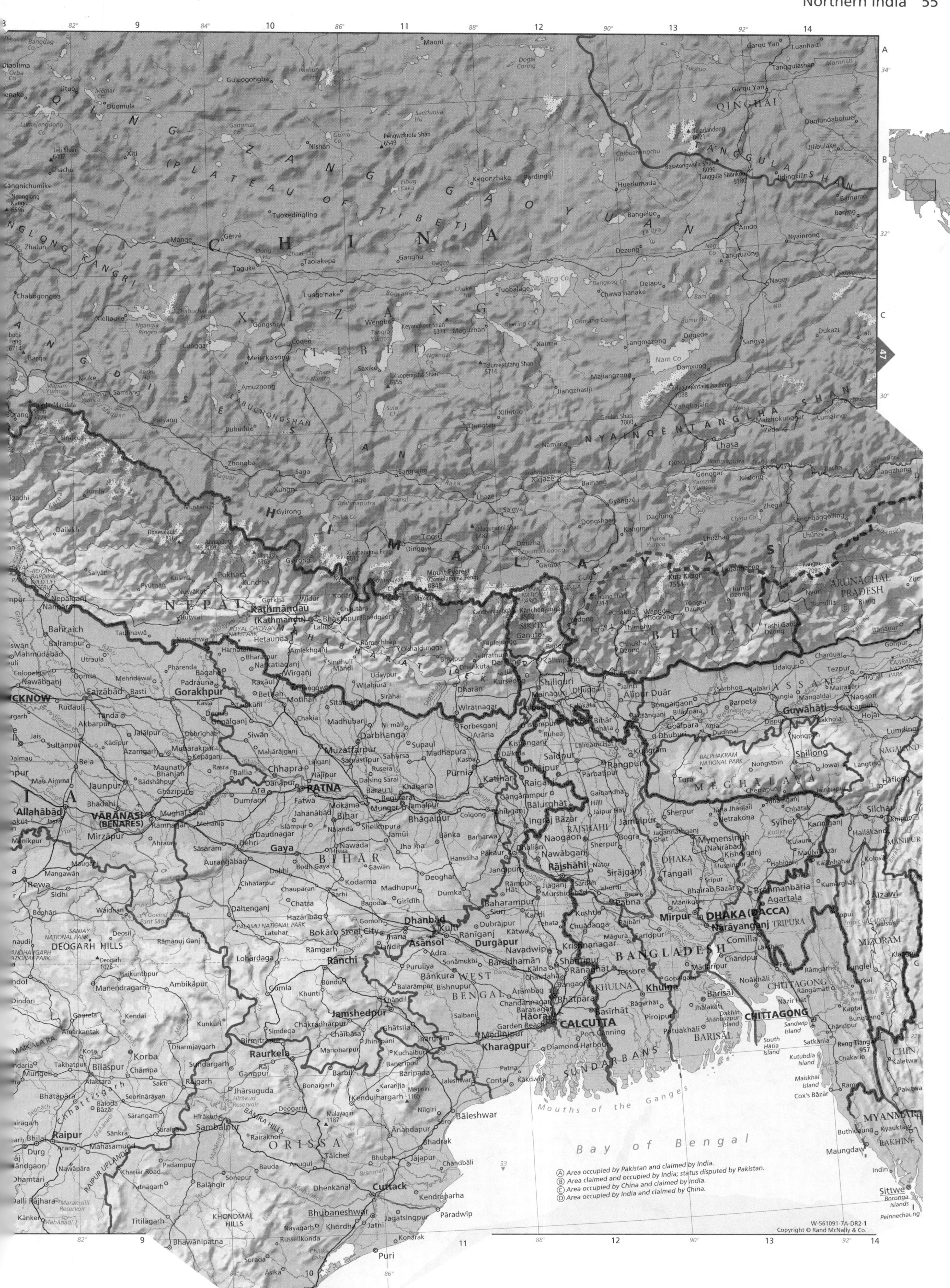

A Area occupied by Pakistan and claimed by India.
B Area claimed and occupied by India; status disputed by Pakistan.
C Area occupied by China and claimed by India.
D Area occupied by India and claimed by China.

W-561091-7A-DR2-1
Copyright © Rand McNally & Co.

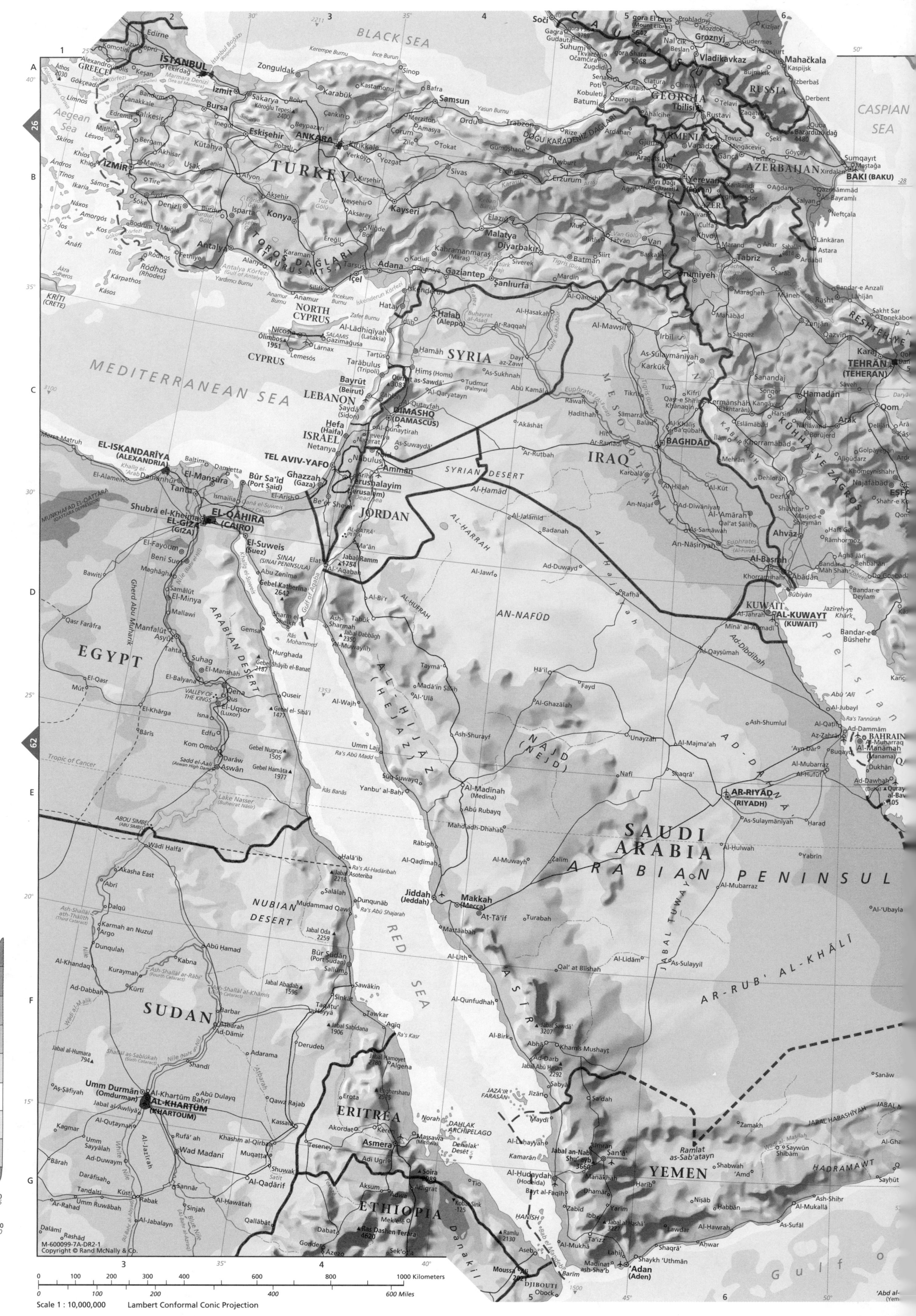

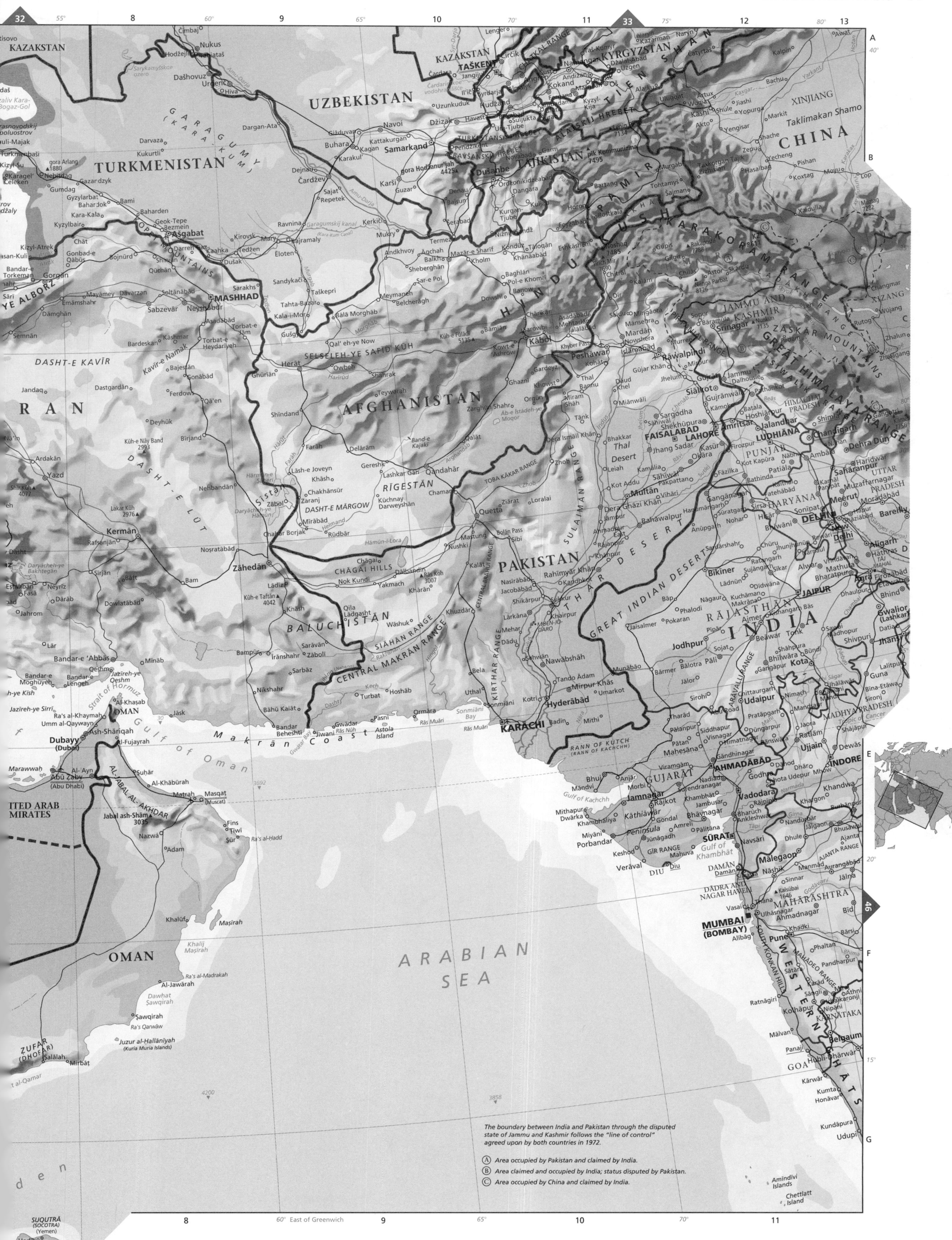

The boundary between India and Pakistan through the disputed
state of Jammu and Kashmir follows the "line of control"
agreed upon by both countries in 1972.

Ⓐ Area occupied by Pakistan and claimed by India.

Ⓑ Area claimed and occupied by India; status disputed by Pakistan.

Ⓒ Area occupied by China and claimed by India.

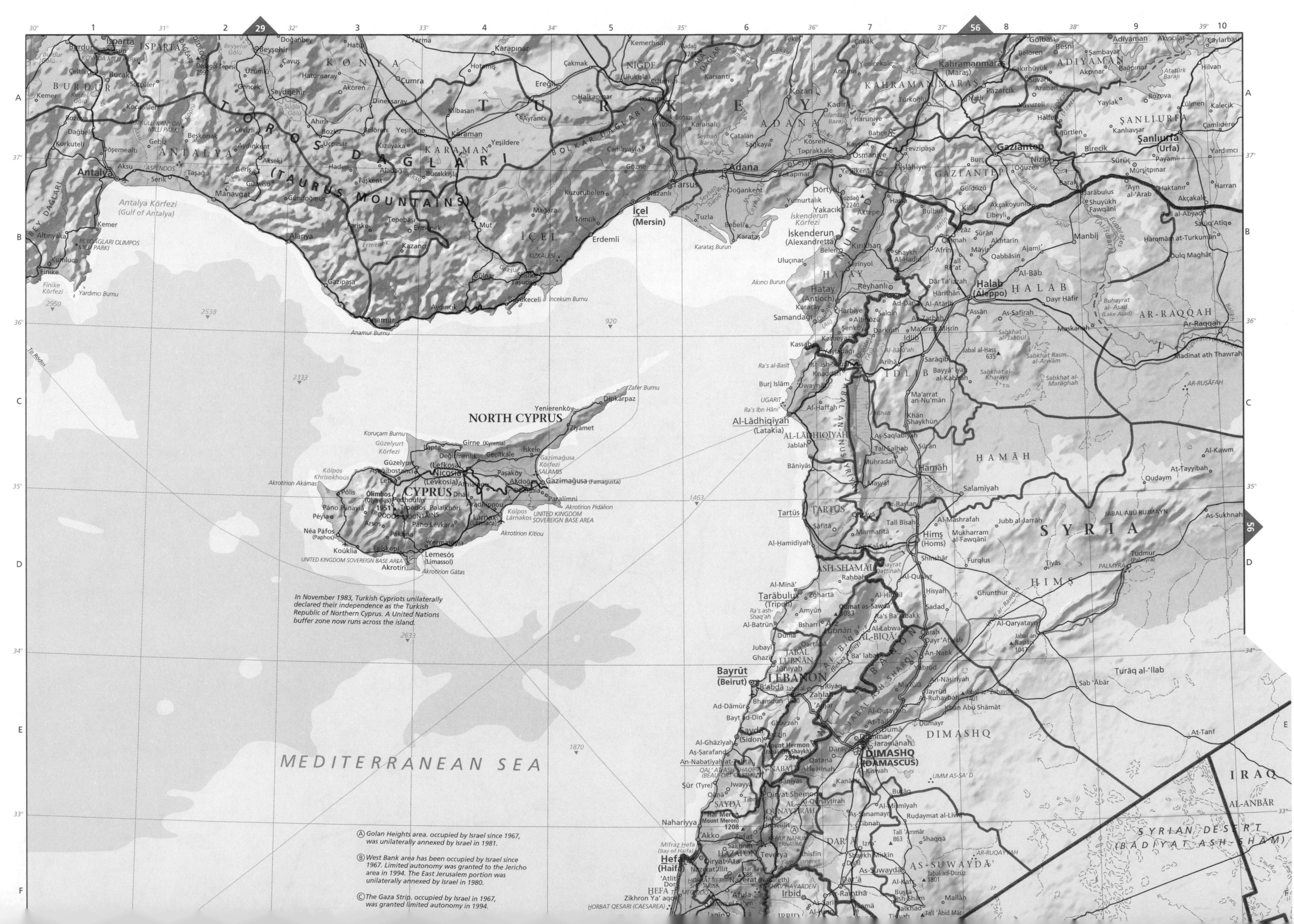
TURKEY
SYRIA
LEBANON
CYPRUS
NORTH CYPRUS
IRAQ
MEDITERRANEAN SEA
TOROS DAĞLARI (TAURUS MOUNTAINS)
SYRIAN DESERT (BĀDIYAT ASH-SHĀM)
Antalya Körfezi (Gulf of Antalya)
İskenderun Körfezi
Antalya
Adana
İçel (Mersin)
Tarsus
İskenderun (Alexandretta)
Hatay (Antioch)
Gaziantep
Şanlıurfa (Urfa)
Kahramanmaraş (Maraş)
Halab (Aleppo)
Al-Lādhiqīyah (Latakia)
Ḥamāh
Ḥimṣ (Homs)
Ṭarṭūs
Ṭarābulus (Tripoli)
Bayrūt (Beirut)
Dimashq (Damascus)
Ṣaydā (Sidon)
Ṣūr (Tyre)
Ḥefa (Haifa)
Nicosia (Lefkoşa) (Levkosía)
Gazimağusa (Famagusta)
Lemesós (Limassol)
Lárnax (Larnaca)
Néa Páfos (Paphos)
Ar-Raqqah
Tudmur (Palmyra)
In November 1983, Turkish Cypriots unilaterally declared their independence as the Turkish Republic of Northern Cyprus. A United Nations buffer zone now runs across the island.
Ⓐ Golan Heights area, occupied by Israel since 1967, was unilaterally annexed by Israel in 1981.
Ⓑ West Bank area has been occupied by Israel since 1967. Limited autonomy was granted to the Jericho area in 1994. The East Jerusalem portion was unilaterally annexed by Israel in 1980.
Ⓒ The Gaza Strip, occupied by Israel in 1967, was granted limited autonomy in 1994.

Scale 1 : 2,500,000   Lambert Conformal Conic Projection

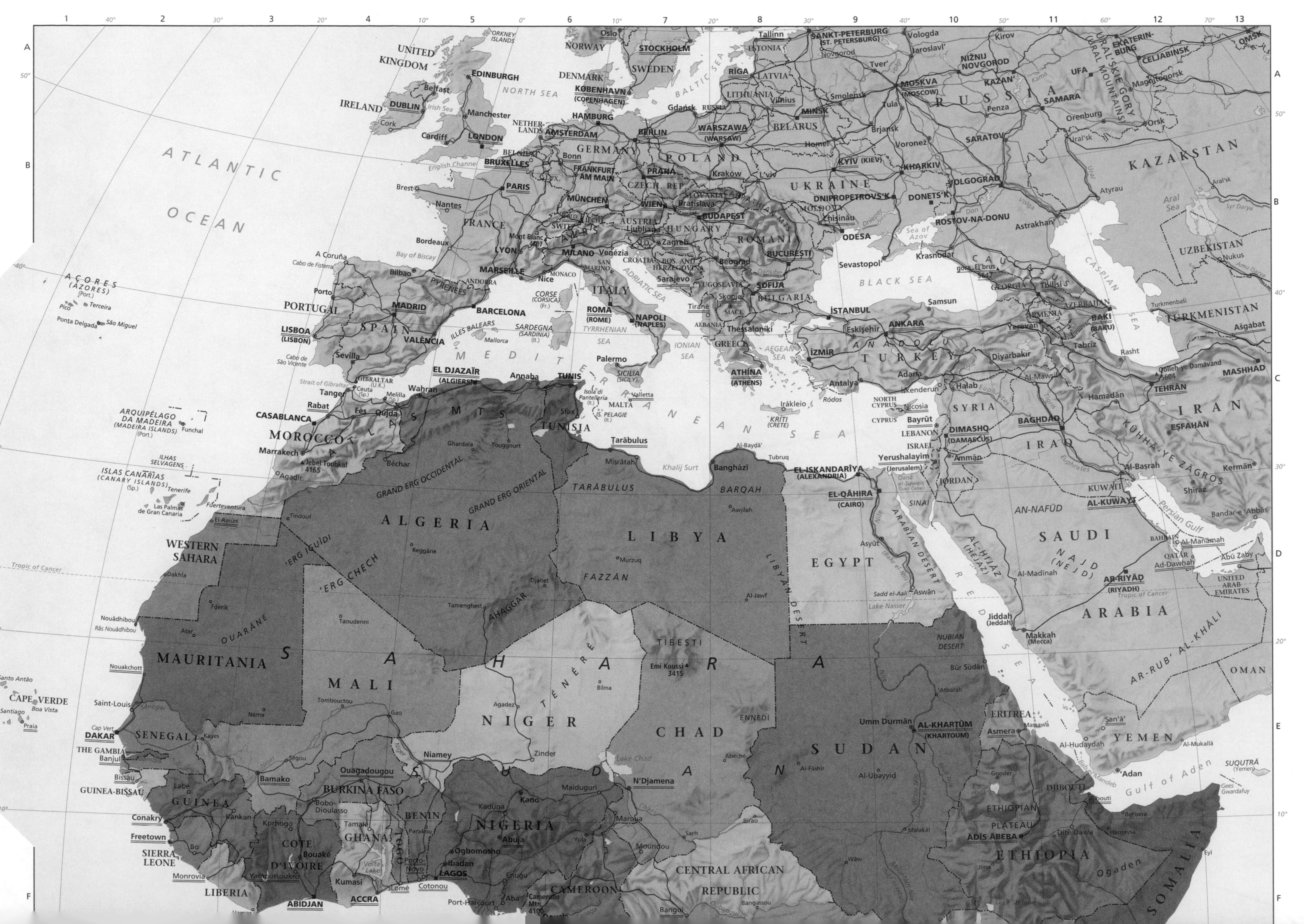
ATLANTIC
OCEAN
NORTH SEA
BALTIC SEA
BLACK SEA
CASPIAN SEA
MEDITERRANEAN SEA
ADRIATIC SEA
TYRRHENIAN SEA
IONIAN SEA
AEGEAN SEA
RED SEA
Persian Gulf
Gulf of Aden
UNITED KINGDOM
IRELAND
NORWAY
SWEDEN
DENMARK
FRANCE
SPAIN
PORTUGAL
ITALY
GERMANY
POLAND
BELARUS
UKRAINE
RUSSIA
KAZAKSTAN
UZBEKISTAN
TURKMENISTAN
TURKEY
SYRIA
IRAQ
IRAN
SAUDI ARABIA
YEMEN
OMAN
EGYPT
LIBYA
TUNISIA
ALGERIA
MOROCCO
WESTERN SAHARA
MAURITANIA
MALI
NIGER
CHAD
SUDAN
ERITREA
DJIBOUTI
ETHIOPIA
SOMALIA
SENEGAL
THE GAMBIA
GUINEA-BISSAU
GUINEA
SIERRA LEONE
LIBERIA
CÔTE D'IVOIRE
GHANA
BURKINA FASO
BENIN
NIGERIA
CAMEROON
CENTRAL AFRICAN REPUBLIC
CAPE VERDE
SAHARA
LONDON
PARIS
MADRID
LISBOA (LISBON)
ROMA (ROME)
BERLIN
WARSZAWA (WARSAW)
MOSKVA (MOSCOW)
KYIV (KIEV)
ISTANBUL
ANKARA
EL-QÂHIRA (CAIRO)
AL-KHARṬŪM (KHARTOUM)
AR-RIYĀḌ (RIYADH)
BAGHDAD
TEHRĀN
ADIS ABEBA
DAKAR
ABIDJAN
ACCRA
LAGOS
Ṭarābulus
TUNIS
EL DJAZAÏR (ALGIERS)
CASABLANCA
Tropic of Cancer

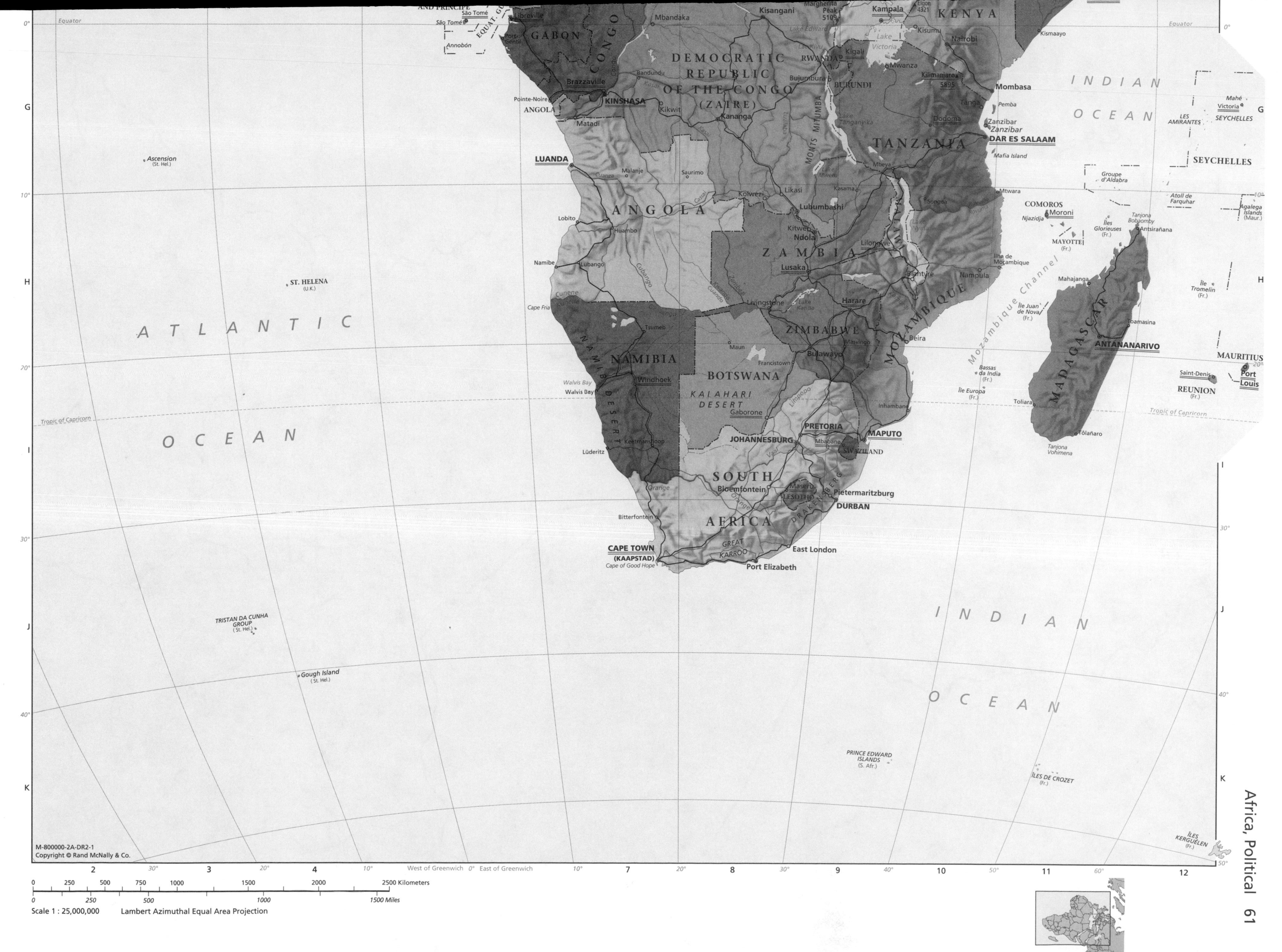

INDIAN OCEAN

SEYCHELLES
Victoria
Mahé

LES AMIRANTES

Atoll de Farquhar

Groupe d'Aldabra

Îles Glorieuses (Fr.)

MAYOTTE (Fr.)
COMOROS
Moroni
Njazidja

Aldabra Islands (Maur.)

MAURITIUS
Port Louis

Saint-Denis
RÉUNION (Fr.)

Île Tromelin (Fr.)

Tropic of Capricorn

Antsiranana

Toamasina

ANTANANARIVO

MADAGASCAR

Mahajanga

Toliara

Tôlanaro

Tarjona Vohimena

Mozambique Channel

Île Juan de Nova (Fr.)

Île Europa (Fr.)

Bassas da India (Fr.)

Îlha de Moçambique

KENYA
Nairobi
Kisumu
Eldoret
Kilimanjaro 5895

TANZANIA
Dodoma
Mwanza
Tabora

Lake Victoria

Kampala
Kigali
RWANDA
BURUNDI
Bujumbura

DEMOCRATIC REPUBLIC OF THE CONGO (ZAIRE)

Kisangani
Mbandaka
Bandundu
KINSHASA
Matadi

CONGO
Brazzaville
Pointe-Noire

GABON
Libreville

SÃO TOMÉ & PRÍNCIPE
São Tomé
Annobón

EQUAT. G.

Mombasa
Pemba
Zanzibar
Tanga
DAR ES SALAAM
Mafia Island

MALAWI
Lilongwe
Blantyre

Lake Malawi

MONTS MITUMBA

Lubumbashi
Likasi
Kolwezi
Kananga
Mbuji-Mayi

ZAMBIA
Lusaka
Livingstone
Kitwe
Ndola

ANGOLA
LUANDA
Lobito
Benguela
Huambo
Namibe
Cape Frio

Zambezi

MOZAMBIQUE
Beira
Quelimane
Nampula
Pemba

ZIMBABWE
Harare
Bulawayo

BOTSWANA
Gaborone
Francistown
Maun

KALAHARI DESERT

NAMIBIA
Windhoek
Tsumeb
Keetmanshoop
Lüderitz
Walvis Bay

NAMIB DESERT

SWAZILAND
Mbabane

MAPUTO

Pietermaritzburg
DURBAN

PRETORIA
JOHANNESBURG
Bloemfontein

LESOTHO

SOUTH AFRICA

East London
Port Elizabeth

GREAT KARROO

CAPE TOWN (KAAPSTAD)
Cape of Good Hope

Bitterfontein

Orange

INDIAN OCEAN

ATLANTIC OCEAN

ST. HELENA (U.K.)

Ascension (St. Hel.)

TRISTAN DA CUNHA GROUP (St. Hel.)

Gough Island (St. Hel.)

PRINCE EDWARD ISLANDS (S. Afr.)

ÎLES DE CROZET (Fr.)

ÎLES KERGUÉLEN (Fr.)

West of Greenwich 0° East of Greenwich

Scale 1 : 25,000,000

Lambert Azimuthal Equal Area Projection

M-800000-2A-DR2-1
Copyright © Rand McNally & Co.

0 250 500 750 1000 1500 2000 2500 Kilometers
0 250 500 1000 1500 Miles

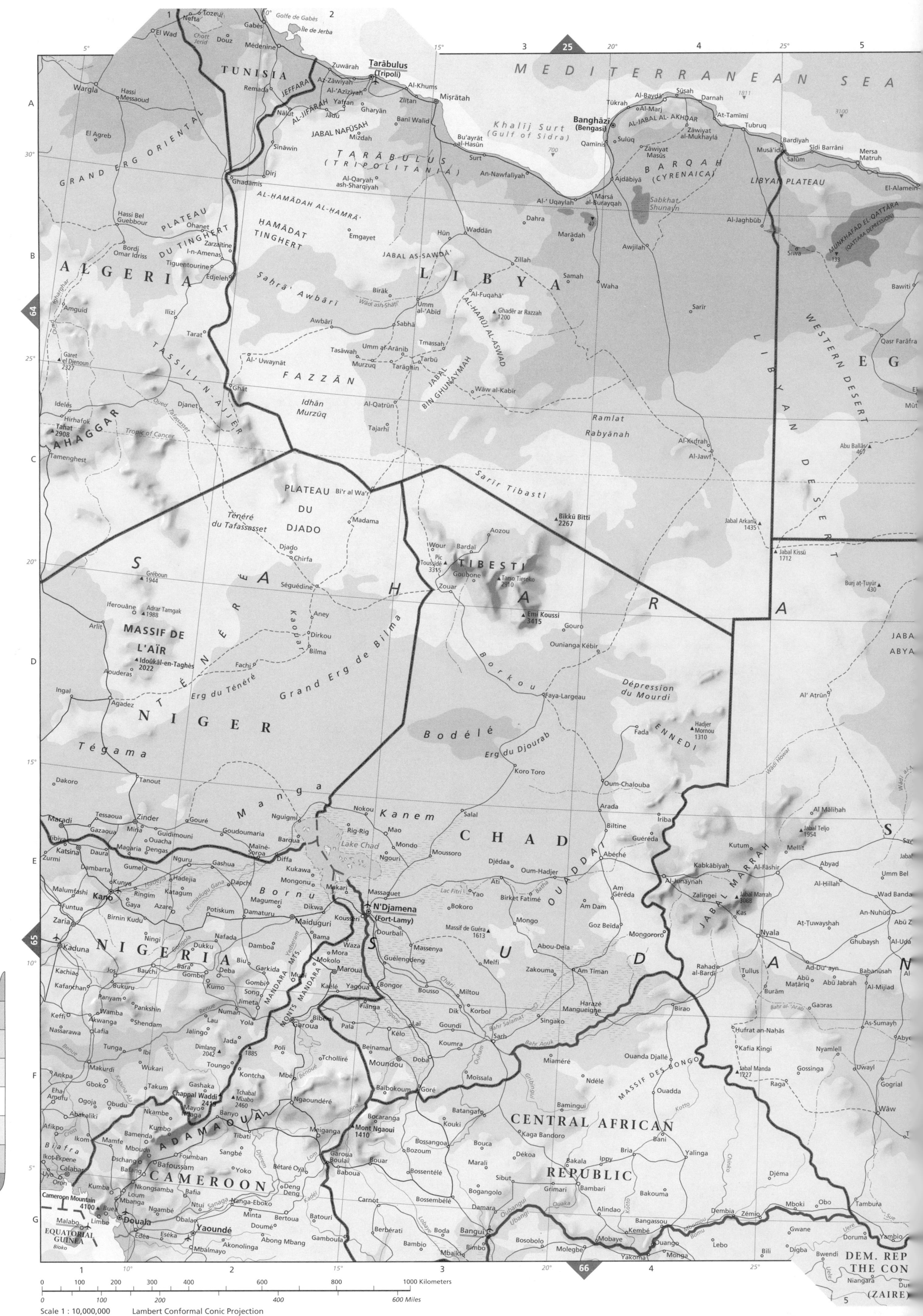

MEDITERRANEAN SEA

TUNISIA

ALGERIA

LIBYA

EGYPT

NIGER

CHAD

SUDAN

NIGERIA

CAMEROON

CENTRAL AFRICAN REPUBLIC

EQUATORIAL GUINEA

DEM. REP THE CON (ZAIRE)

SAHARA

Scale 1 : 10,000,000   Lambert Conformal Conic Projection

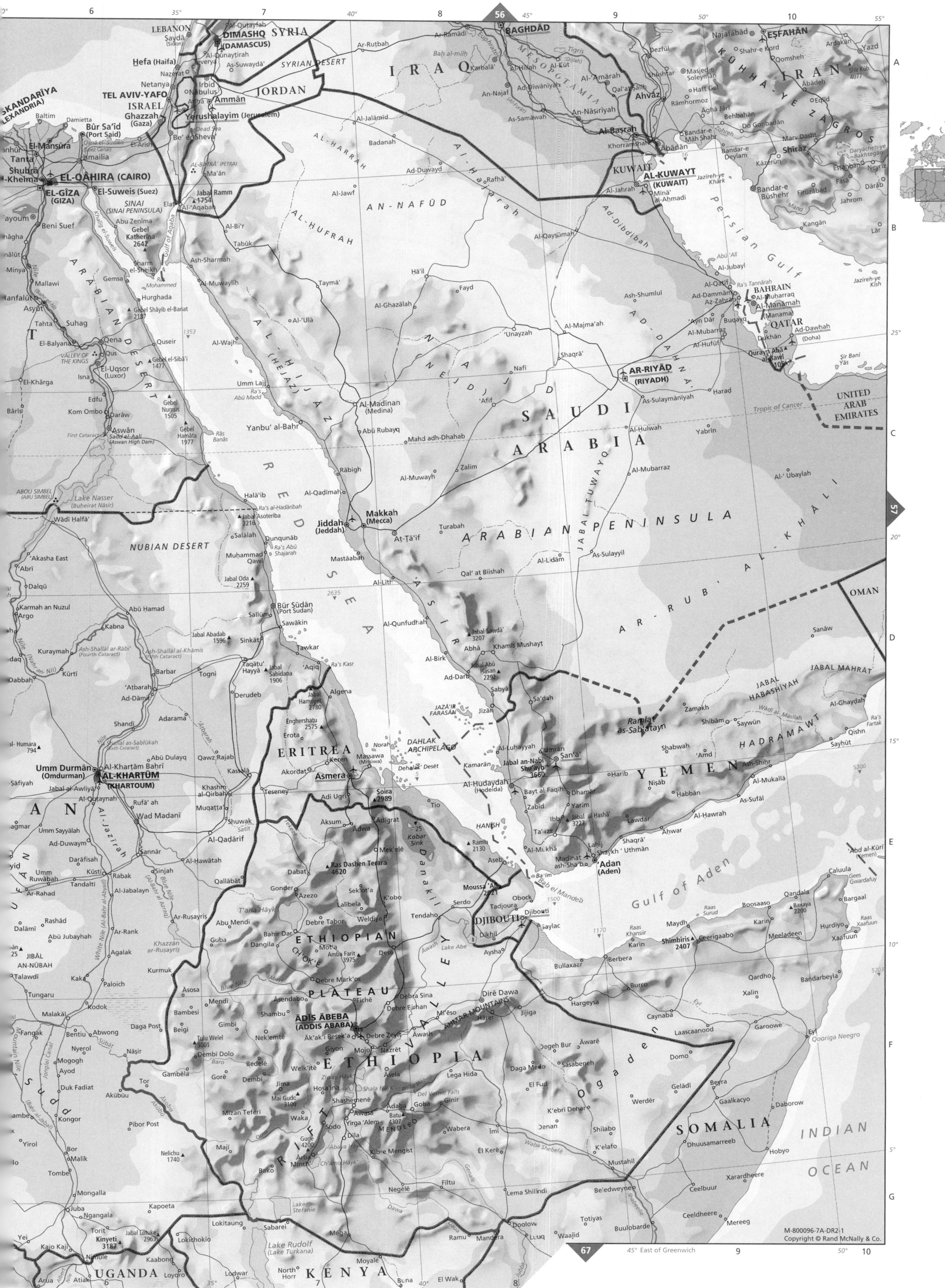
LEBANON
DIMASHQ (DAMASCUS)
SYRIA
SYRIAN DESERT
IRAQ
BAGHDĀD
MESOPOTAMIA
JORDAN
'Ammān
ISRAEL
TEL AVIV-YAFO
Yerushalayim (Jerusalem)
EL-QÂHIRA (CAIRO)
EL-GÎZA (GIZA)
Bûr Sa'îd (Port Said)
El-Suweis (Suez)
SINAI (SINAI PENINSULA)
ARABIAN DESERT
AN-NAFŪD
AL-ḤIJĀZ (HEJAZ)
NAJD
SAUDI ARABIA
AR-RIYĀḌ (RIYADH)
Al-Madīnah (Medina)
Makkah (Mecca)
Jiddah (Jeddah)
ARABIAN PENINSULA
AR-RUB' AL-KHĀLĪ
KUWAIT
AL-KUWAYT (KUWAIT)
Persian Gulf
BAHRAIN
Al-Manāmah (Manama)
QATAR
Ad-Dawḥah (Doha)
UNITED ARAB EMIRATES
Tropic of Cancer
IRAN
KŪHHĀ-YE ZĀGROS
EṢFAHĀN
Shīrāz
OMAN
YEMEN
Ṣan'ā'
'Adan (Aden)
HAḌRAMAWT
RED SEA
NUBIAN DESERT
Bûr Sûdân (Port Sudan)
Lake Nasser
Aswân
El-Uqṣor (Luxor)
Umm Durmān (Omdurman)
AL-KHARṬŪM (KHARTOUM)
ERITREA
Asmera
DAHLAK ARCHIPELAGO
DJIBOUTI
Djibouti
Gulf of Aden
ETHIOPIAN PLATEAU
ĀDĪS ĀBEBA (ADDIS ABABA)
ETHIOPIA
RIFT VALLEY
Danakil
Ogaden
SOMALIA
INDIAN OCEAN
Lake Rudolf (Lake Turkana)
KENYA
UGANDA
45° East of Greenwich
M-800096-7A-DR2-1
Copyright © Rand McNally & Co.

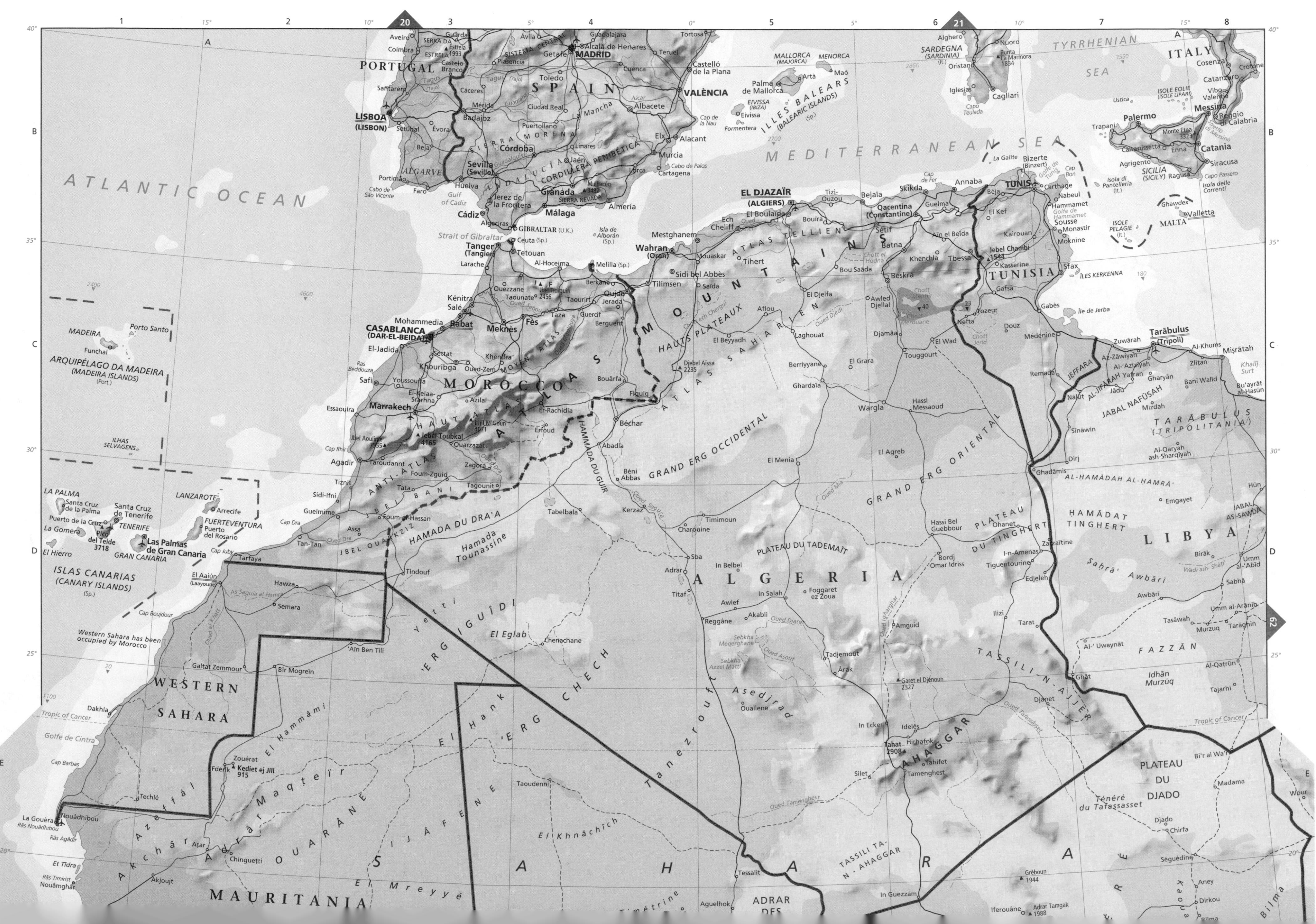
ATLANTIC OCEAN
MEDITERRANEAN SEA
TYRRHENIAN SEA
PORTUGAL
SPAIN
ITALY
MOROCCO
ALGERIA
TUNISIA
LIBYA
WESTERN SAHARA
MAURITANIA
LISBOA (LISBON)
MADRID
VALÈNCIA
EL DJAZAÏR (ALGIERS)
TUNIS
RABAT
CASABLANCA (DAR-EL-BEIDA)
Marrakech
Fès
Meknès
Tanger (Tangier)
Wahran (Oran)
Qacentina (Constantine)
Annaba
Ṭarābulus (Tripoli)
Valletta
MALTA
Palermo
Catania
Messina
Cagliari
SARDEGNA (SARDINIA) (It.)
SICILIA (SICILY)
ILLES BALEARS (BALEARIC ISLANDS) (Sp.)
Palma de Mallorca
Sevilla (Seville)
Córdoba
Granada
Málaga
Cádiz
GIBRALTAR (U.K.)
Strait of Gibraltar
Ceuta (Sp.)
Melilla (Sp.)
ISLAS CANARIAS (CANARY ISLANDS) (Sp.)
Las Palmas de Gran Canaria
Santa Cruz de Tenerife
ARQUIPÉLAGO DA MADEIRA (MADEIRA ISLANDS) (Port.)
Funchal
El Aaiún (Layoune)
Western Sahara has been occupied by Morocco
Tropic of Cancer
ATLAS MOUNTAINS
HAUT ATLAS
ANTI-ATLAS
GRAND ERG OCCIDENTAL
GRAND ERG ORIENTAL
HAMADA DU DRA'A
HAMMADA DU GUIR
PLATEAU DU TADEMAÏT
TASSILI-N-AJJER
AHAGGAR
PLATEAU DU DJADO
FAZZĀN
JABAL NAFŪSAH
ERG CHECH
HAUTS PLATEAUX

66

a Same scale as main map

Scale 1 : 10,000,000

0 100 200 300 400 600 800 1000 Kilometers

0 100 200 400 600 Miles

Lambert Conformal Conic Projection

Meters	Feet
4000	13120
3000	9840
2000	6560
1000	3280
500	1640
200	656
Sea Level	
200	656
2000	6560

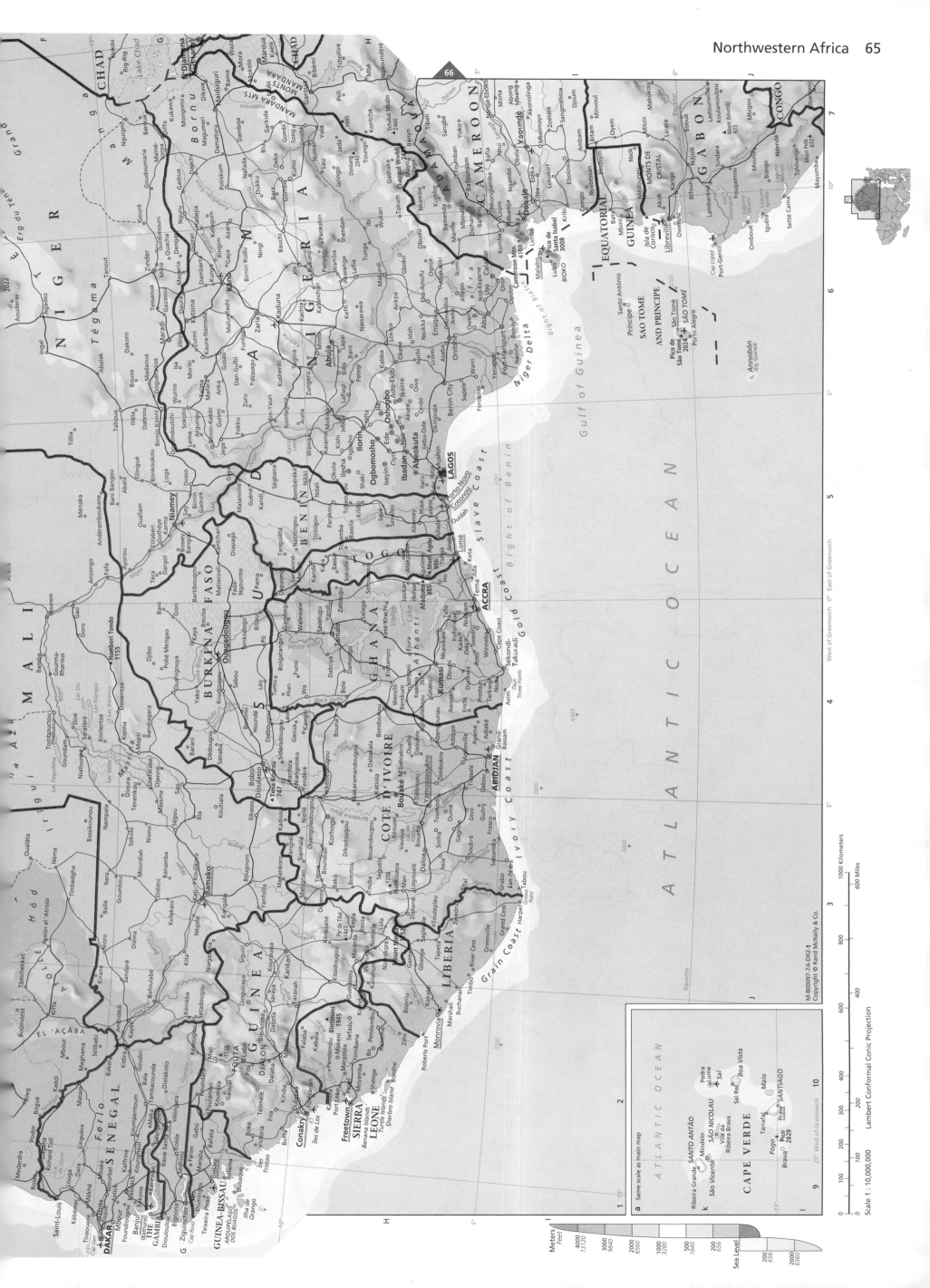

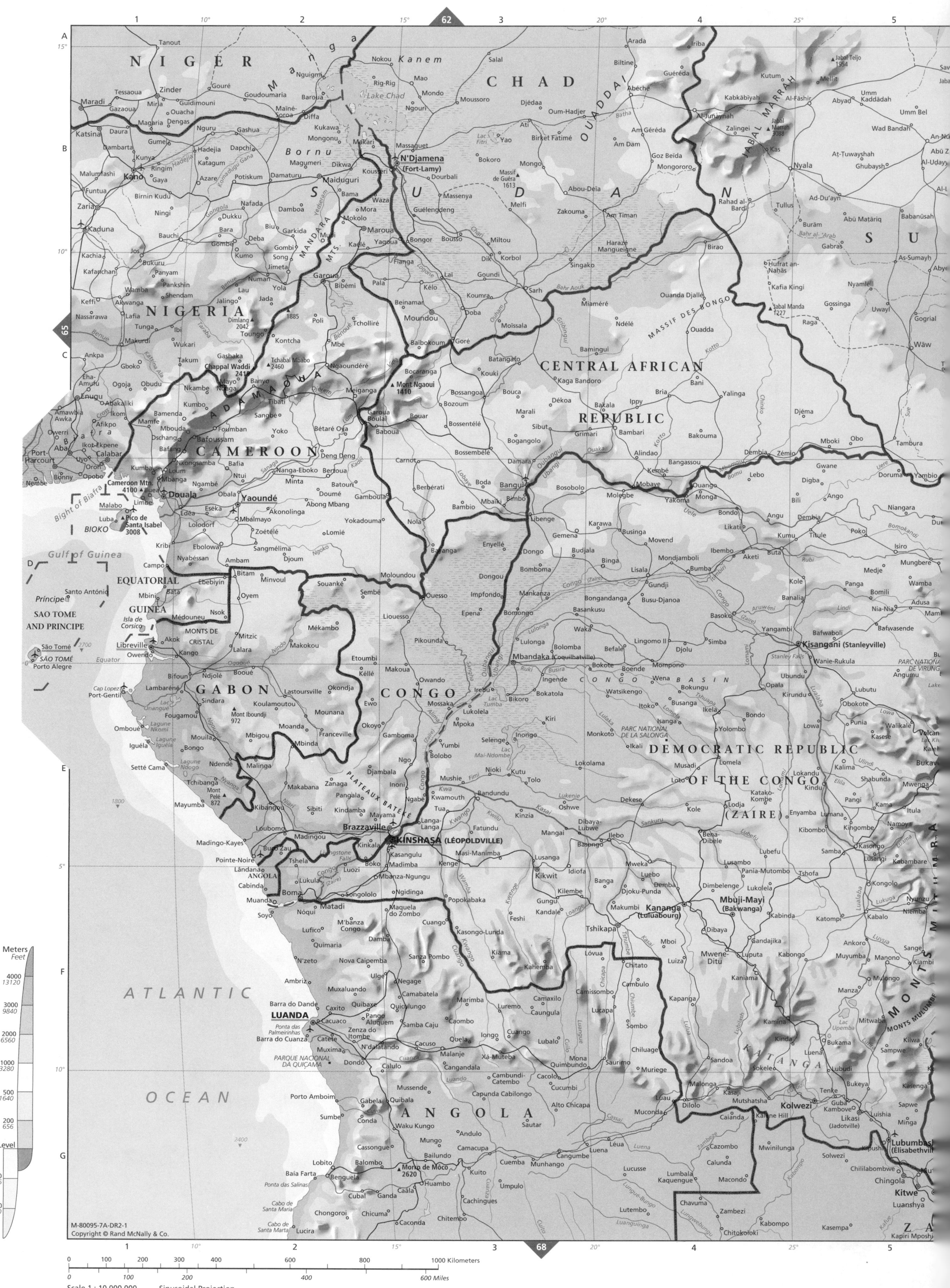

Meters
Feet

4000
13120

3000
9840

2000
6560

1000
3280

500
1640

200
656

Sea Level

200
656

2000
6560

M-80095-7A-DR2-1
Copyright © Rand McNally & Co.

0   100   200   300   600   1000 Kilometers
0   100   200   400   600 Miles

Scale 1 : 10,000,000   Sinusoidal Projection

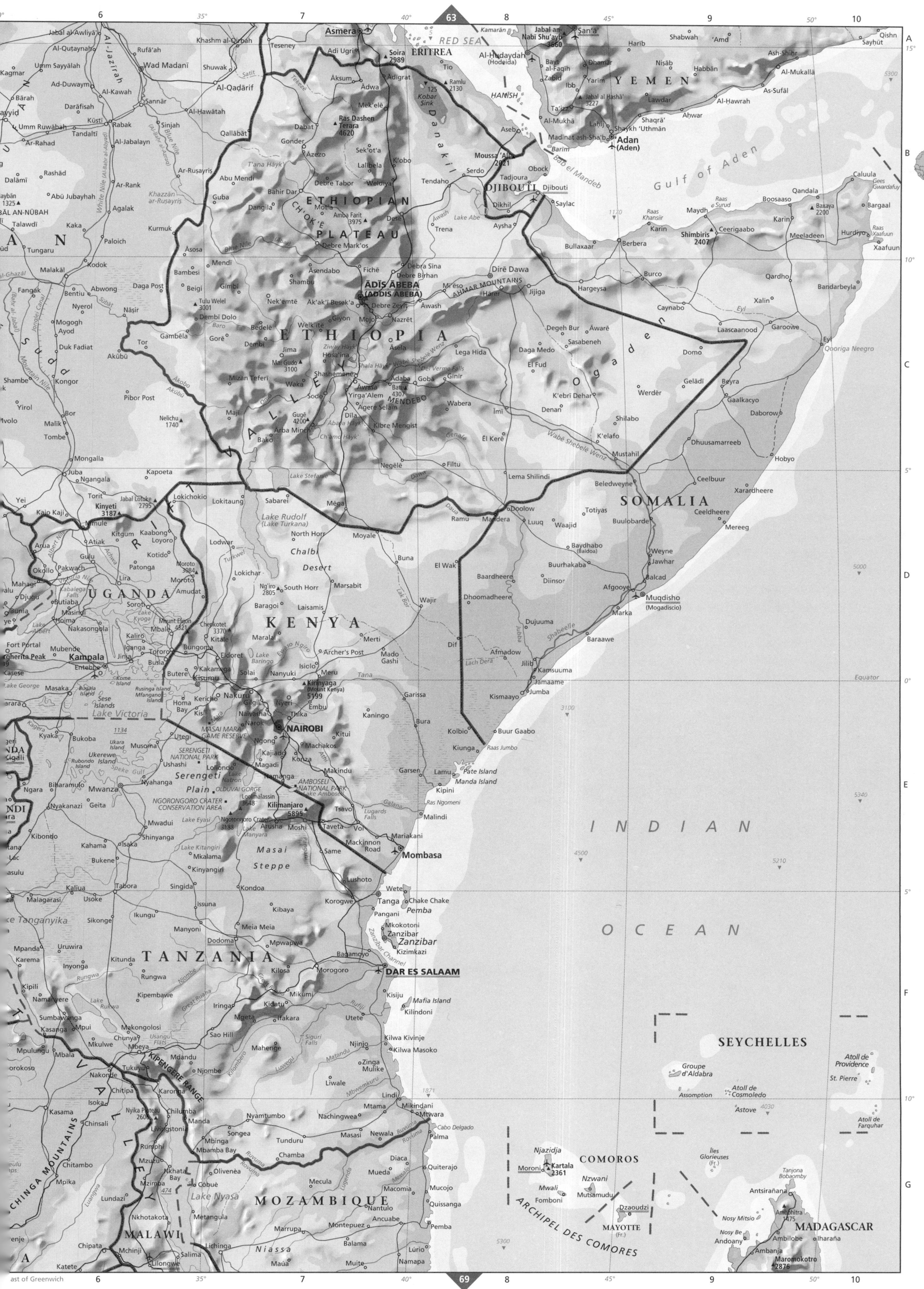
RED SEA
Asmera
ERITREA
Soira 2989
Adi Ugri
Aksum
Adwa
Adigrat
Mek'elē
Kobar Sink
Ramlu 2130
Tio
Danakil
Ras Dashen Terara 4620
Dabat
Gonder
Azezo
Sek'ot'a
K'obo
Lalibela
Weldiya
T'ana Hayk'
Bahir Dar
Debre Tabor
ETHIOPIAN
CH'OK'Ē
PLATEAU
Mota
Amba Farit 3975
Dangila
Dese
Debre Mark'os
Debre Sīna
Debre Birhan
Āsendabo
Fichē
Shambu
ĀDĪS ĀBEBA (ADDIS ABEBA)
Āk'ak'ī Besek'a
Debre Zeyit
Nazrēt
Giyon
Mojo
Awash
Nek'emtē
Bambesi
Beigi
Gimbi
Mendī
Tulu Welel 3001
Dembī Dolo
Gambēla
Gorē
Bedelē
Dembī
ETHIOPIA
Jīma
Mat Gudo 3100
Hosa'ina
Ziway Hayk'
Āsela
Shashemenē
Ādaba
Goba
Ginir
Awasa
Yirga'Alem
Batu 4307
MENDEBO
Agere Selam
Dīla
Abaya Hayk'
Ch'amo Hayk'
Kibre Mengist
Gugē 4200
Arba Minch'
Bako
Mīzan Teferī
Waka
Sodo
Maji
Negēlē
Filtu
Lake Stefanie
Mēga
Moyale
Lake Rudolf (Lake Turkana)
North Horr
Chalbi Desert
Marsabit
Wajir
Buna
El Wak
Mandera
Ramu
Doolow
Luuq
Waajid
Lokitaung
Sabarei
Lokichokio
Kinyeti 3187
Jabal Lotuke 2795
Torit
Kapoeta
Juba
Ngangala
Mongalla
Tombe
Malik
Yirol
Pibor Post
Nelichu 1740
Akobo
Tor
Akūbū
Gambēla
Nāṣir
Abwong
Daga Post
Kodok
Malakāl
Fangak
Bentiu
Nyerol
Mogogh
Ayod
Duk Fadiat
Kongor
Bor
Shambe
Khashm al-Qirbah
Tesenev
Wad Madanī
Shuwak
Al-Qaḍārif
Rufā'ah
Al-Jazīrah
Jabal al-Awliyā'
Al-Quṭaynah
Umm Sayyālah
Ad-Duwaym
Al-Kawah
Kagmar
Bārah
Darāfisah
Sannār
Sinjah
Al-Hawātah
Kūstī
Rabak
Umm Ruwābah
Tandaltī
Ar-Rahad
Al-Jabalayn
Qallābāt
Ar-Ruṣayris
Rashād
Dalāmī
Abū Jubayhah
Ar-Rank
Agalak
Abu Mendi
Guba
Kaka
Kurmuk
Paloich
Tungaru
Talawdī
Āsosa
Kamarān
Jabal an-Nabi Shu'ayb 3660
Ṣan'ā'
Al-Hudaydah (Hodeida)
Bayt al-Faqīh
Zabīd
Dhamār
Yarīm
Ibb
YEMEN
Ta'izz
Jabal al Hasha' 3227
Al-Mukhā
Lahij
Shaykh 'Uthmān
Adan (Aden)
Madīnat ash-Sha'b
Barīm
Bab el Mandeb
HANISH
Harib
Shabwah
'Amd
Niṣāb
Habbān
Lawdar
Aḥwar
Shaqrā'
Al-Hawrah
As-Sufāl
Al-Mukallā
Ash-Shihr
Qishn
Sayhūt
Asab
Moussa 'Ali 2021
Serdo
Obock
Tadjoura
DJIBOUTI
Djibouti
Dikhil
Saylac
Lake Abe
Tendaho
Trena
Aysha
Gulf of Aden
Raas Surud
Maydh
Raas Khansiir
Karin
Berbera
Bullaxaar
Shimbiris 2407
Ceerigaabo
Boosaaso
Qandala
Baxaya 2200
Bargaal
Caluula
Raas Gees Gwardafuy
Hurdiyo
Raas Xaafuun
Xaafuun
Meeleeden
Qardho
Bandarbeyla
Xalin
Burco
Hargeysa
Dirē Dawa
AHMAR MOUNTAINS
Hārer
Jījiga
Caynabo
Eyl
Laascaanood
Garoowe
Degeh Bur
Āwarē
Sasabeneh
Daga Medo
El Fud
Ogaden
Domo
Werdēr
K'ebrī Dehar
Gelādī
Beyra
Gaalkacyo
Dabarow
Denan
Īmī
Shilabo
K'elafo
Mustahīl
Ēl Kerē
Dhuusamarreeb
Hobyo
Wabē Shebelē Wenz
Genalē
Lema Shilindi
Beledweyne
Ceelbuur
Xarardheere
SOMALIA
Totiyas
Ceeldheere
Buulobarde
Mereeg
Baydhabo (Baidoa)
Buurhakaba
Weyne
Jawhar
Balcad
Baardheere
Diinsor
Afgooye
Muqdisho (Mogadishu)
Marka
Dhoomadheere
Dujuuma
Baraawe
Shabeelle
Afmadow
Jilib
Kamsuuma
Jamaame
Jumba
Kismaayo
Buur Gaabo
Kolbio
Kiunga
Raas Jumbo
Pate Island
Manda Island
Lamu
Kipini
Ras Ngomeni
Malindi
Garsen
Bura
Garissa
Kaningo
Dif
Lach Dera
Tana
Mado Gashi
Merti
Archer's Post
Isiolo
Meru
Kirinyaga (Mount Kenya) 5199
Nyeri
Embu
Thika
NAIROBI
Kitui
Machakos
Makindu
Kajiado
Magadi
Namanga
Konza
Tsavo
Taveta
Voi
Mackinnon Road
Mariakani
Mombasa
Lugards Falls
KENYA
Laisamis
Baragoi
South Horr
Ng'iro 2805
Lodwar
Lokichar
Turkwel
Kakuma
Moroto 3084
Moroto
Amudat
Kotido
Kaabong
Loyoro
Kitgum
Patonga
Lira
Gulu
Atiak
Arua
Okollo
Pakwach
Nimule
Kajo Kaji
Yei
UGANDA
Soroti
Mbale
Mount Elgon 4321
Cherangani 3370
Kitale
Bungoma
Eldoret
Maralal
Lake Baringo
Kisumu
Kakamega
Busia
Tororo
Iganga
Jinja
Kampala
Entebbe
Mubende
Fort Portal
Hoima
Masindi
Nakasongola
Kabalega Falls
Butiaba
Bunia
Kome Island
Bugala Island
Sese Islands
Masaka
Lake George
Rusinga Island
Mfangano Island
Homa Bay
Kisii
Kericho
Nakuru
Gilgil
Naivasha
Narok
Nanyuki
Solai
Lake Victoria
Kagera
Kyaka
Bukoba
Ukara Island
Ukerewe Island
Musoma
Rubondo Island
Speke Gulf
Utegi
MASAI MARA GAME RESERVE
SERENGETI NATIONAL PARK
Ushashi
Serengeti Plain
Loliondo
OLDUVAI GORGE
Lake Natron
NGORONGORO CRATER CONSERVATION AREA
Loolmalassin 3648
Ngorongoro Crater 3133
Lake Manyara
Kilimanjaro 5895
AMBOSELI NATIONAL PARK
Lake Amboseli
Arusha
Moshi
Nyahanga
Bihara mulo
Mwanza
Ngara
Nyakanazi
Geita
Mwadui
Lake Eyasi
Shinyanga
Kibondo
Kahama
Isaka
Lake Kitangiri
Mkalama
Bukene
Kinyangiri
Masai Steppe
Pangani
Same
Lushoto
Kondoa
Singida
Tabora
Kaliua
Malagarasi
Usoke
Ikungu
Issuna
Kibaya
Korogwe
Tanga
Wete
Chake Chake
Pemba
Mkokotoni
Zanzibar
Kizimkazi
Zanzibar Channel
Bagamoyo
DAR ES SALAAM
Lake Tanganyika
Sikonge
Manyoni
Meia Meia
Dodoma
Mpwapwa
Uruwira
Mpanda
Karema
Inyonga
Kitunda
TANZANIA
Rungwa
Kilosa
Morogoro
Kipili
Namanyere
Kipembawe
Lake Rukwa
Mikumi
Great Ruaha
Iringa
Kidatu
Ifakara
Kisiju
Mafia Island
Kilindoni
Rufiji
Utete
Sumbawanga
Kasanga
Mpui
Makongolosi
Mgeta
Sao Hill
Mpulungu
Mbala
Mkulwe
Chunya
Usangu Flats
Mbeya
Mahenge
Matandu
Kilwa Kivinje
Kilwa Masoko
Njinjo
Sigiri Falls
Luwegu
Kilombero
Tukuyu
KIPENGERE RANGE
Mdandu
Njombe
Zinga Mulike
Liwale
Lindi
Mbemkuru
Nakonde
Chitipa
Karonga
Isoka
Nyika Plateau 2606
Chilumba
Livingstonia
Manda
Kasama
Chinsali
Nyamtumbo
Nachingwea
Mtama
Mikindani
Mtwara
Cabo Delgado
Palma
Masasi
Newala
Rovuma
Songea
Tunduru
Mbinga
Mbamba Bay
Rumphi
Mzuzu
Chamba
Diaca
Mueda
Quiterajo
Mucojo
Macomia
Quissanga
Chitambo
Mpika
Luangwa
Lundazi
MUCHINGA MOUNTAINS
Nkhata Bay
Mzimba
Olivenca
Cóbuè
Lake Nyasa
474
Mecula
Lugenda
Montepuez
MOZAMBIQUE
Nantulo
Ancuabe
Pemba
Metangula
Nkhotakota
Marrupa
Balama
Lúrio
Namapa
Niassa
Chipata
MALAWI
Mchinji
Lichinga
Salima
Lilongwe
Katete
Maúa
Muite
Mossuril
INDIAN OCEAN
SEYCHELLES
Groupe d'Aldabra
Assumption
Atoll de Cosmoledo
Astove
Atoll de Providence
St. Pierre
Atoll de Farquhar
Îles Glorieuses (Fr.)
COMOROS
Njazidja
Moroni
Kartala 2361
Nzwani
Mwali
Fomboni
Mutsamudu
Dzaoudzi
MAYOTTE (Fr.)
ARCHIPEL DES COMORES
Tanjona Bobaomby
Antsiraṅana
Ambilobe
Nosy Mitsio
Nosy Be
Andoany
Ambanja
Iharaña
Maromokotro 2876
MADAGASCAR
Equator
5300
1120
5000
3100
5340
4500
5210
4030
1871
63
69
6
7
8
9
10
35°
40°
45°
50°
15°
10°
5°
0°
A
B
C
D
E
F
G
ast of Greenwich

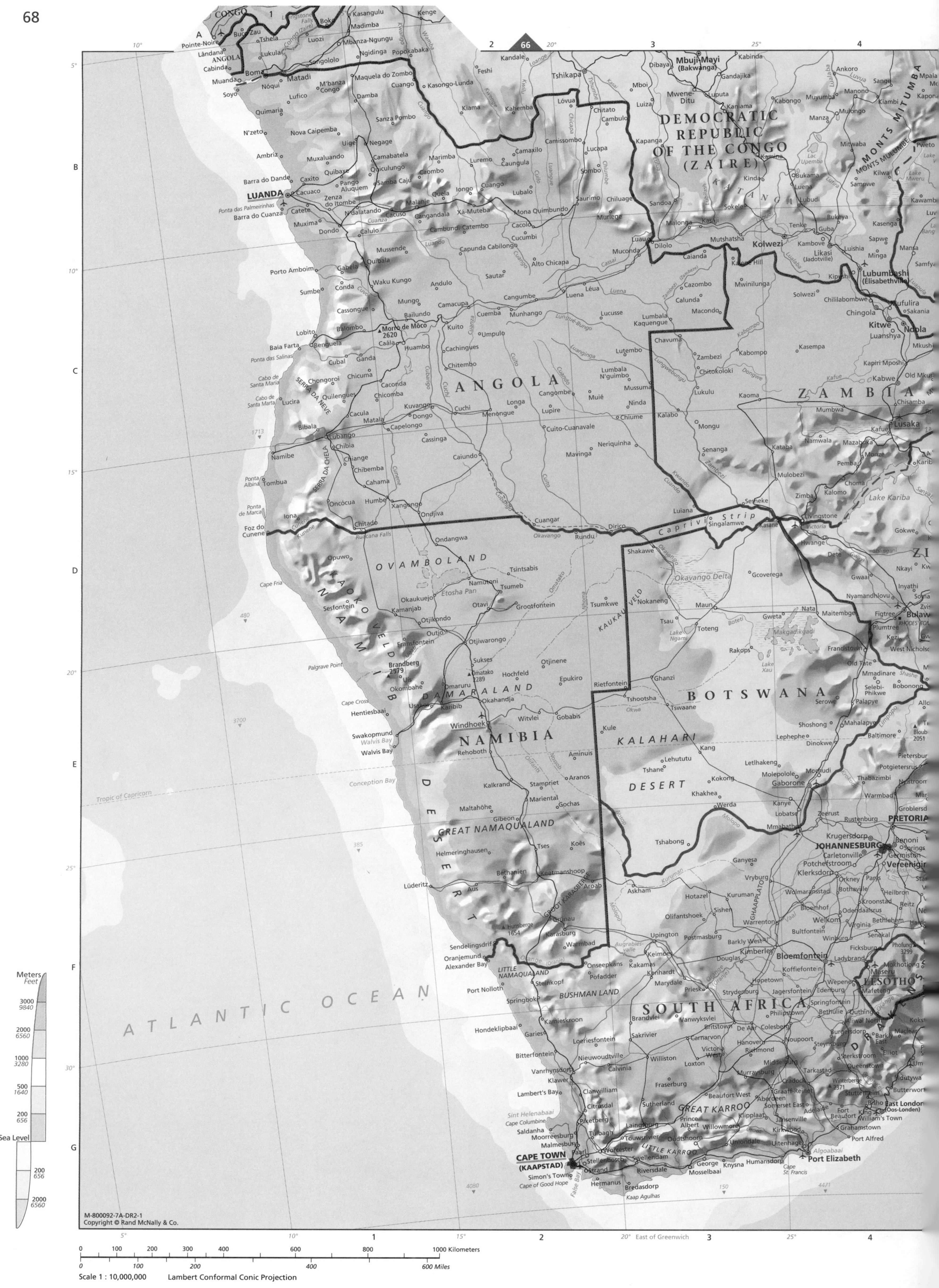

ATLANTIC OCEAN

Meters
Feet
3000
9840
2000
6560
1000
3280
500
1640
200
656
Sea Level
200
656
2000
6560

M-800092-7A-DR2-1
Copyright © Rand McNally & Co.

0   100   200   300   400   600   800   1000 Kilometers
0   100   200   400   600 Miles
Scale 1 : 10,000,000   Lambert Conformal Conic Projection

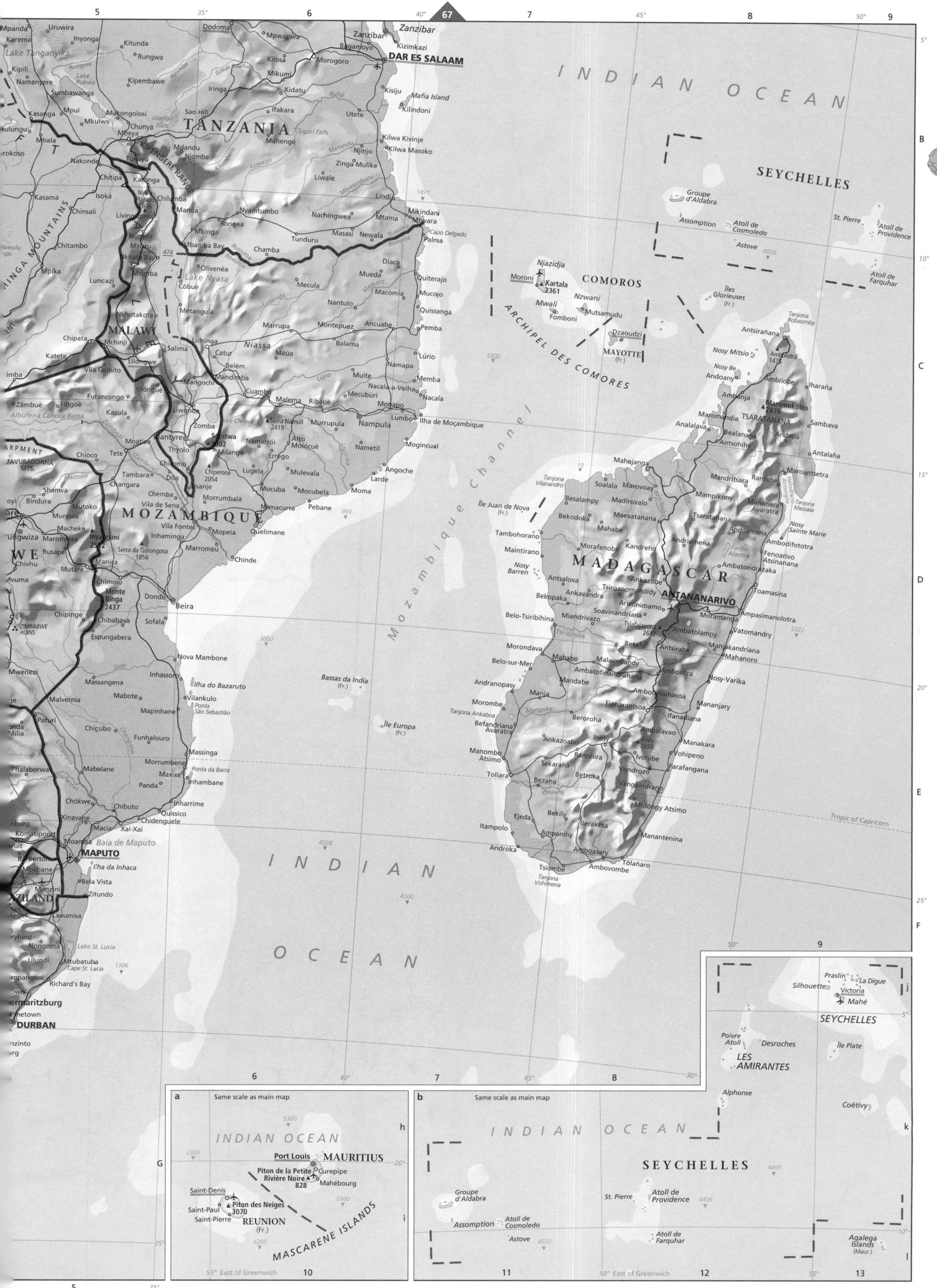

INDIAN OCEAN

SEYCHELLES

Groupe d'Aldabra
Assomption
Atoll de Cosmoledo
Astove
St. Pierre
Atoll de Providence
Atoll de Farquhar

TANZANIA

DAR ES SALAAM
Zanzibar
Mafia Island
Kilwa Kivinje
Kilwa Masoko

MALAWI
Lake Nyasa

COMOROS
Njazidja
Moroni
Kartala 2361
Mwali
Fomboni
Nzwani
Mutsamudu
MAYOTTE (Fr.)
Dzaoudzi

ARCHIPEL DES COMORES

Iles Glorieuses (Fr.)

Antsiranana
Nosy Mitsio
Nosy Be
Ambilobe
Maromokotro 2876
TSARATANANA
Sambava
Andapa
Antalaha

MOZAMBIQUE
Nampula
Ilha de Moçambique

Mozambique Channel

Ile Juan de Nova (Fr.)

MADAGASCAR
Mahajanga
ANTANANARIVO
Toamasina
Antsirabe

Beira

Bassas da India (Fr.)

Ile Europa (Fr.)

MAPUTO

Bassas da India

INDIAN OCEAN

Tropic of Capricorn

DURBAN

INDIAN OCEAN

SEYCHELLES
Praslin
Silhouette
La Digue
Victoria
Mahé
Poivre Atoll
Desroches
Ile Plate
LES AMIRANTES
Alphonse
Coëtivy

a Same scale as main map

INDIAN OCEAN

Port Louis MAURITIUS
Piton de la Petite
Rivière Noire 828
Curepipe
Mahébourg
Saint-Denis
Saint-Paul
Piton des Neiges 3070
Saint-Pierre REUNION (Fr.)

MASCARENE ISLANDS

b Same scale as main map

INDIAN OCEAN

SEYCHELLES
Groupe d'Aldabra
Assomption
Atoll de Cosmoledo
Astove
St. Pierre
Atoll de Providence
Atoll de Farquhar
Agalega Islands (Maur.)

55° East of Greenwich
50° East of Greenwich

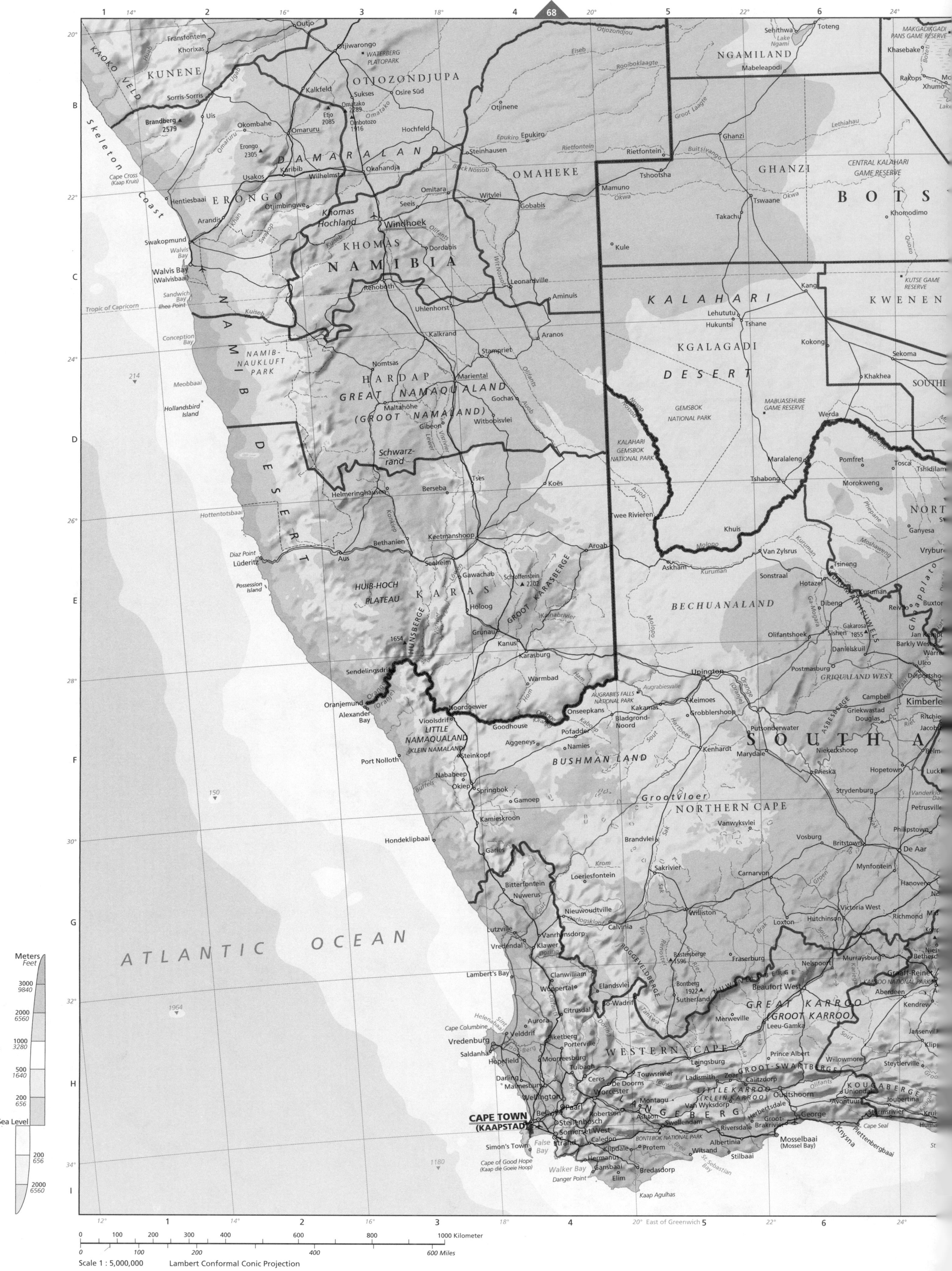
ATLANTIC OCEAN
NAMIBIA
BOTS
SOUTH A
KALAHARI
KGALAGADI DESERT
NAMIB DESERT
Windhoek
CAPE TOWN (KAAPSTAD)
Lüderitz
Walvis Bay (Walvisbaai)
Swakopmund
Upington
NORTHERN CAPE
WESTERN CAPE
GREAT KARROO (GROOT KAROO)
BUSHMAN LAND
BECHUANALAND
KUNENE
ERONGO
KHOMAS
HARDAP
KARAS
OMAHEKE
OTJOZONDJUPA
NGAMILAND
GHANZI
KWENEN
Scale 1 : 5,000,000
Lambert Conformal Conic Projection
1000 Kilometer
600 Miles
Meters
Feet
Sea Level

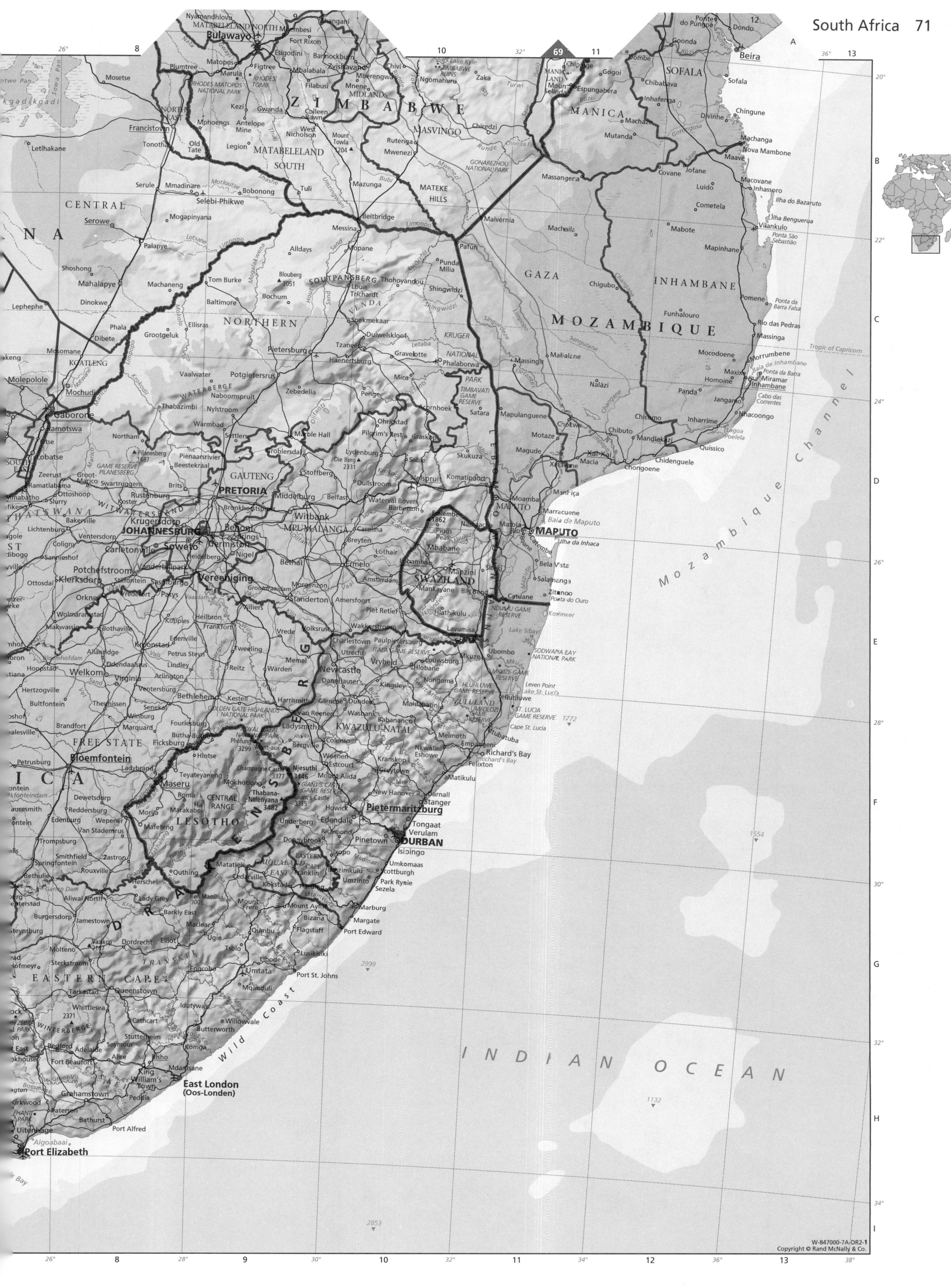

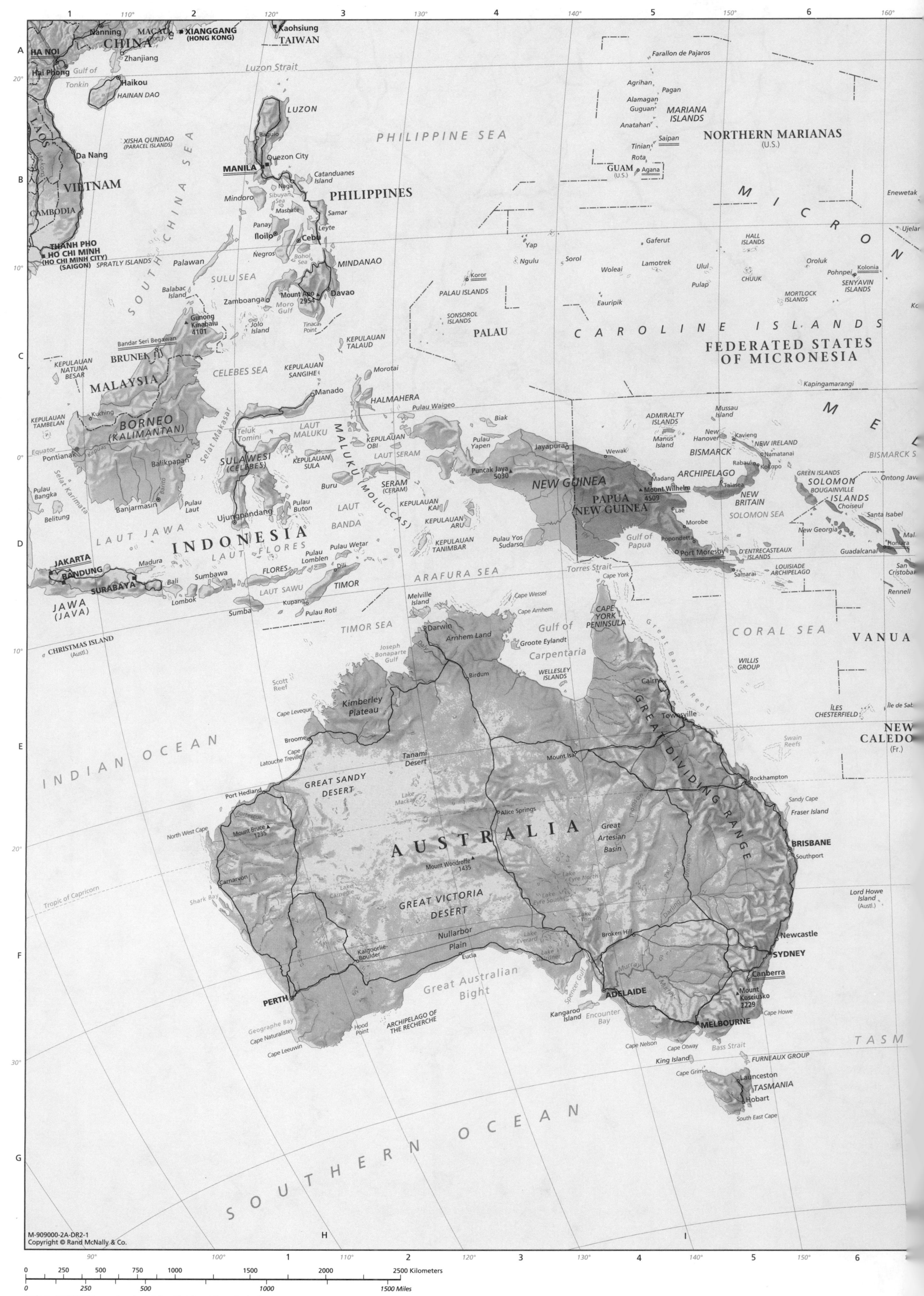

Scale 1 : 25,000,000   Lambert Azimuthal Equal Area Projection

M-909000-2A-DR2-1
Copyright © Rand McNally & Co.

0   250   500   750   1000   1500   2000   2500 Kilometers

0   250   500   1000   1500 Miles

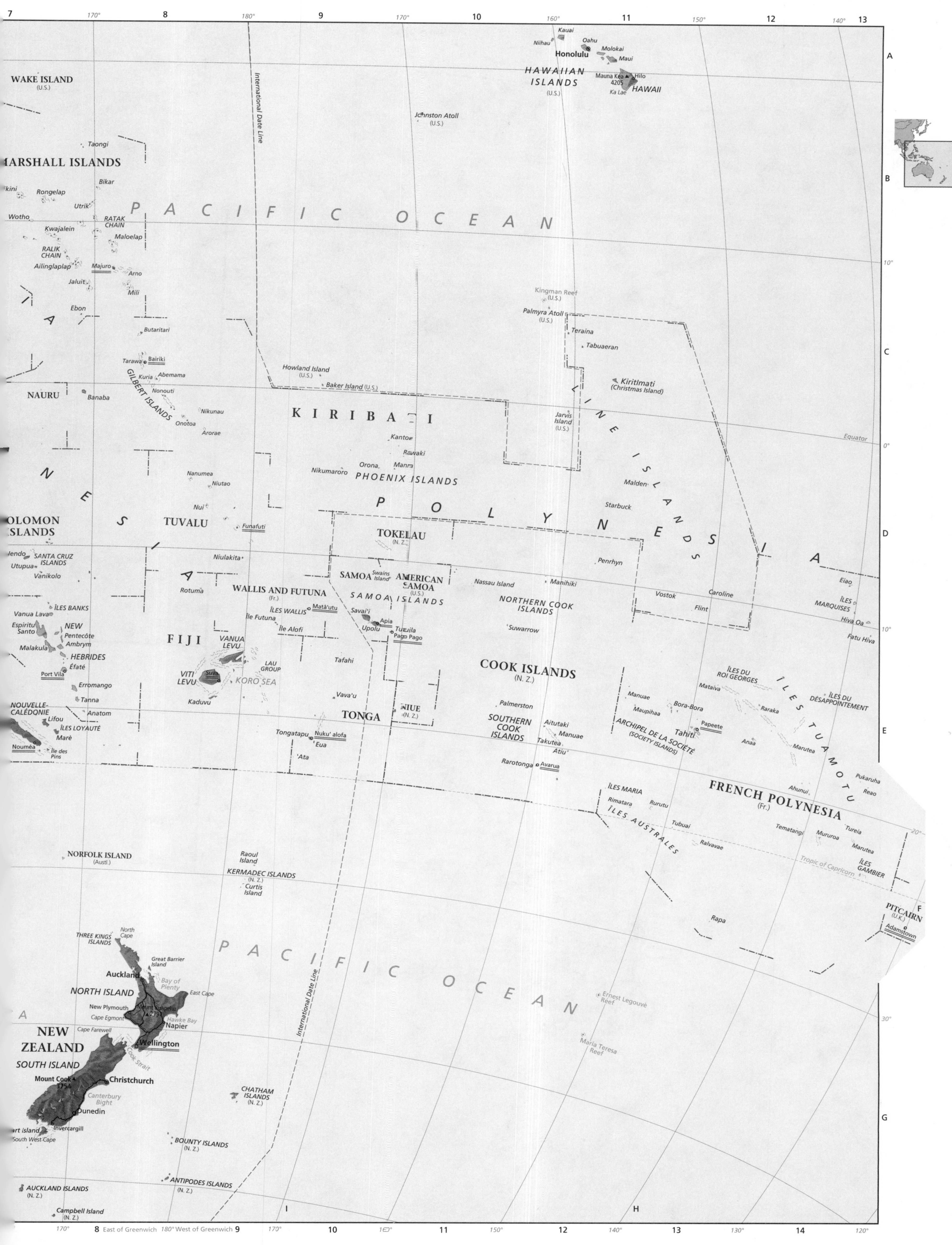

WAKE ISLAND
(U.S.)

HAWAIIAN
ISLANDS
(U.S.)

Niihau   Kauai   Oahu   Molokai
Honolulu   Maui
Mauna Kea ▲ Hilo
4205   HAWAII
Ka Lae

Johnston Atoll
(U.S.)

Taongi

MARSHALL ISLANDS

kini   Rongelap   Bikar
Utrik
Wotho   Kwajalein   RATAK
CHAIN
Maloelap
RALIK
CHAIN
Ailinglaplap   Majuro   Arno
Jaluit   Mili
Ebon

Butaritari

Tarawa Bairiki
Kuria Abemama
Kuria
Nonouti
NAURU   Banaba
Nikunau
Onotoa
Arorae

PACIFIC   OCEAN

Kingman Reef
(U.S.)
Palmyra Atoll
(U.S.)
Teraina

Tabuaeran

Kiritimati
(Christmas Island)

Howland Island
(U.S.)
Baker Island (U.S.)

KIRIBATI
Kanton
Rawaki
Orona   Manra
Nikumaroro
PHOENIX ISLANDS

Jarvis
Island
(U.S.)

Malden

Starbuck

GILBERT ISLANDS

Nanumea
Niutao
Nui
TUVALU
Funafuti
Niulakita

POLYNESIA

LINE ISLANDS

Vostok
Flint
Caroline

Equator

TOKELAU
(N.Z.)

Penrhyn

Manihiki

SOLOMON
ISLANDS
endo   SANTA CRUZ
ISLANDS
Utupua
Vanikolo

Rotuma

SAMOA   Swains
Island
AMERICAN
SAMOA
(U.S.)

Nassau Island

NORTHERN COOK
ISLANDS

Eiao

ÎLES
MARQUISES

Hiva Oa

ÎLES BANKS
Vanua Lava
Espiritu   NEW
Santo   Pentecôte
Ambrym
Malakula   HEBRIDES
Efate
Port Vila

WALLIS AND FUTUNA
(Fr.)
ÎLES WALLIS   Matà'utu
Ile Futuna
Ile Alofi
SAMOA   ISLANDS
Savai'i
Apia
Upolu   Tutuila
Pago Pago

Suwarrow

Fatu Hiva

FIJI
VANUA
LEVU
Tafahi
Tafahi

Manuae

ÎLES DU
ROI GEORGES
Mataiva   ÎLES DU
DÉSAPPOINTEMENT

NOUVELLE-
CALÉDONIE
Lifou
ÎLES LOYAUTÉ
Maré
Nouméa   Ile des
Pins

Erromango
Tanna   Anatom

VITI
LEVU   Suva
KORO SEA
Kaduvu

LAU
GROUP
Vava'u

COOK ISLANDS
(N.Z.)

Palmerston

Manuae
Maupihaa
Bora-Bora
Raraka

Anaa

Marutea

Pukaruha
Reao

TONGA
NIUE
(N.Z.)

SOUTHERN
COOK
ISLANDS

Aitutaki
Manuae
Takutea
Atiu

Tahiti
Papeete
ARCHIPEL DE LA SOCIÉTÉ
(SOCIETY ISLANDS)

ÎLES TUAMOTU

Tongatapu   Nuku'alofa
'Ata   'Eua

Rarotonga   Avarua

ÎLES MARIA
Rimatara   Rururu
Tubuai
Ralvavae
Rapa

FRENCH POLYNESIA
(Fr.)

Ahunui
Tematangi   Mururoa   Marutea
ÎLES AUSTRALES

Turela
Reao

ÎLES
GAMBIER

Tropic of Capricorn

NORFOLK ISLAND
(Austl.)

Raoul
Island
KERMADEC ISLANDS
(N.Z.)
Curtis
Island

PACIFIC   OCEAN

PITCAIRN
(U.K.)
Adamstown

THREE KINGS
ISLANDS
North
Cape
Great Barrier
Island
Auckland
Bay of
Plenty
East Cape
NORTH ISLAND
New Plymouth
Mount Egmont
Cape Egmont
Napier
Hawke Bay
NEW
ZEALAND
Wellington
SOUTH ISLAND
Cook Strait
Mount Cook ▲
3754
Christchurch
Canterbury
Bight
Dunedin
art island   Invercargill
South West Cape

CHATHAM
ISLANDS
(N.Z.)

Ernest Legouvé
Reef

Maria Teresa
Reef

AUCKLAND ISLANDS
(N.Z.)
Campbell Island
(N.Z.)

ANTIPODES ISLANDS
(N.Z.)

BOUNTY ISLANDS
(N.Z.)

PACIFIC   OCEAN

International Date Line

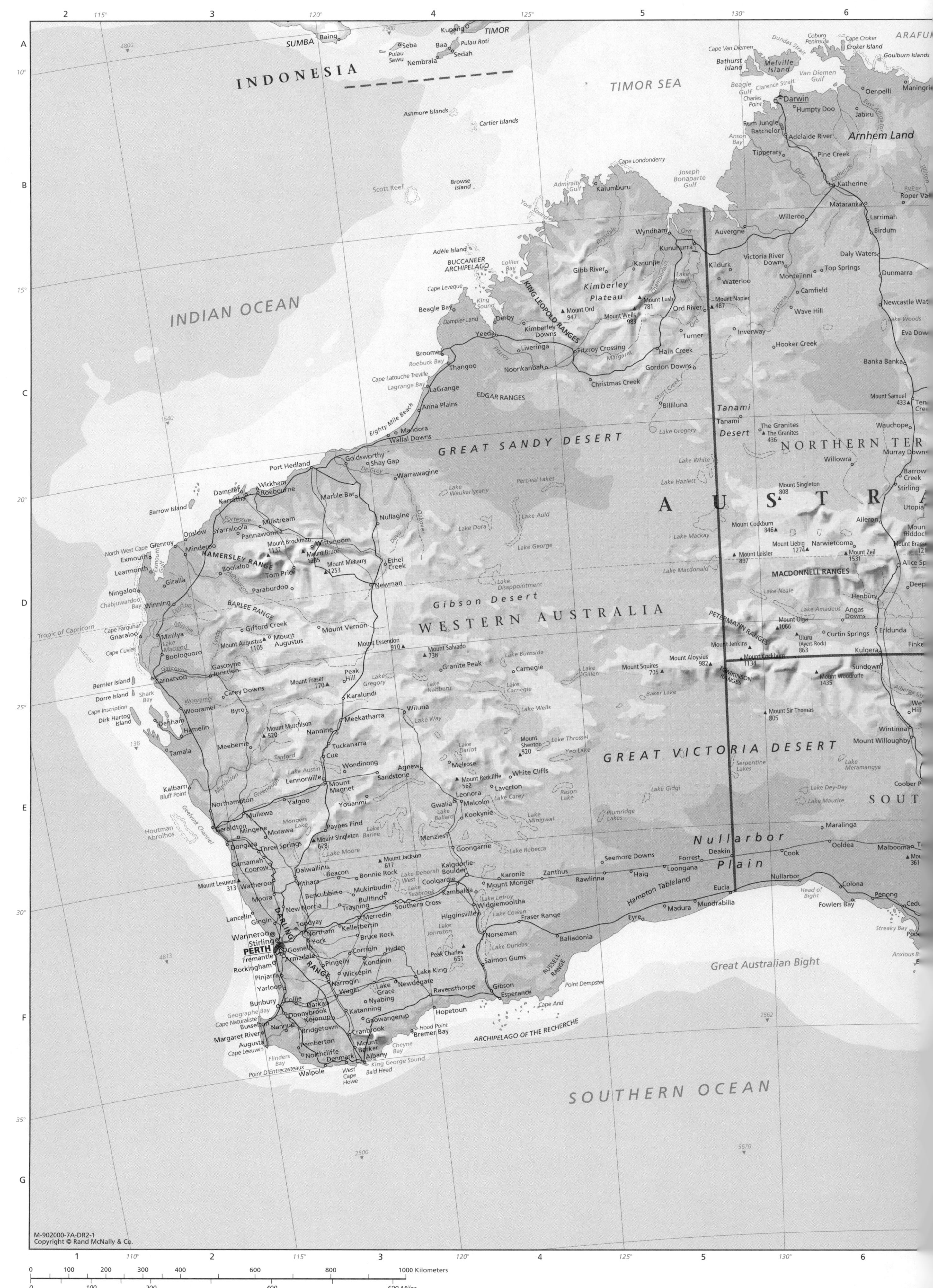

Meters
Feet

2000
6560

1000
3280

500
1640

200
656

Sea Level

200
656

2000
6560

M-902000-7A-DR2-1
Copyright © Rand McNally & Co.

| 0 | 100 | 200 | 300 | 400 | 600 | 800 | 1000 Kilometers |

0   200   400   600 Miles

Scale 1 : 10,000,000   Lambert Conformal Conic Projection

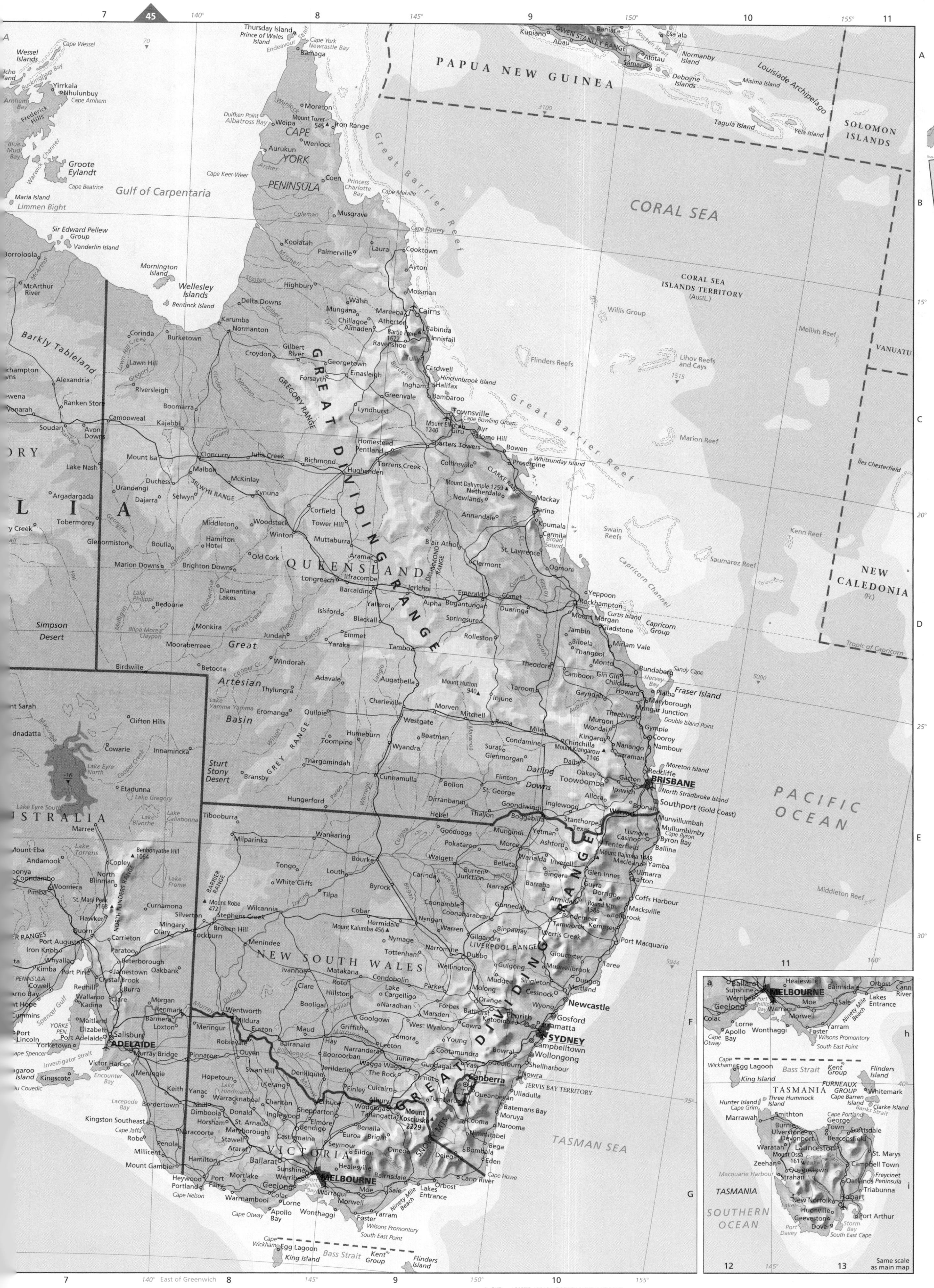
PAPUA NEW GUINEA
CORAL SEA
CORAL SEA ISLANDS TERRITORY (Austl.)
SOLOMON ISLANDS
VANUATU
NEW CALEDONIA (Fr.)
PACIFIC OCEAN
TASMAN SEA
Gulf of Carpentaria
CAPE YORK PENINSULA
Great Barrier Reef
GREAT DIVIDING RANGE
QUEENSLAND
NEW SOUTH WALES
VICTORIA
Great Artesian Basin
BRISBANE
SYDNEY
Canberra
MELBOURNE
ADELAIDE
Newcastle
Wollongong
Townsville
Cairns
Rockhampton
Bass Strait
TASMANIA
SOUTHERN OCEAN
Hobart
Launceston
Same scale as main map
A.C.T. = AUSTRALIAN CAPITAL TERRITORY

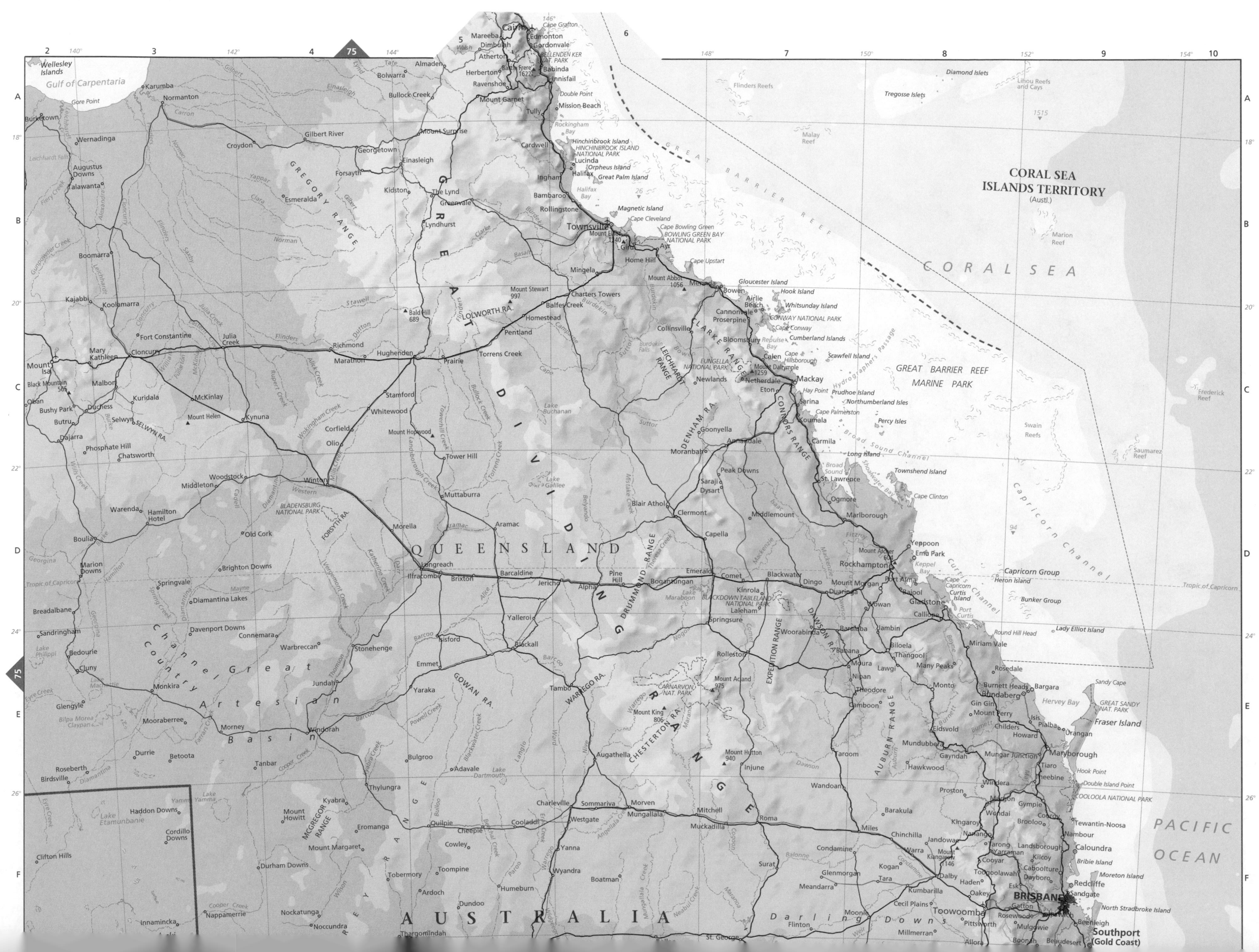

CORAL SEA
ISLANDS TERRITORY
(Aust.)

CORAL SEA

PACIFIC OCEAN

GREAT BARRIER REEF MARINE PARK

QUEENSLAND

AUSTRALIA

GREAT DIVIDING RANGE

Gulf of Carpentaria

Brisbane

Southport
(Gold Coast)

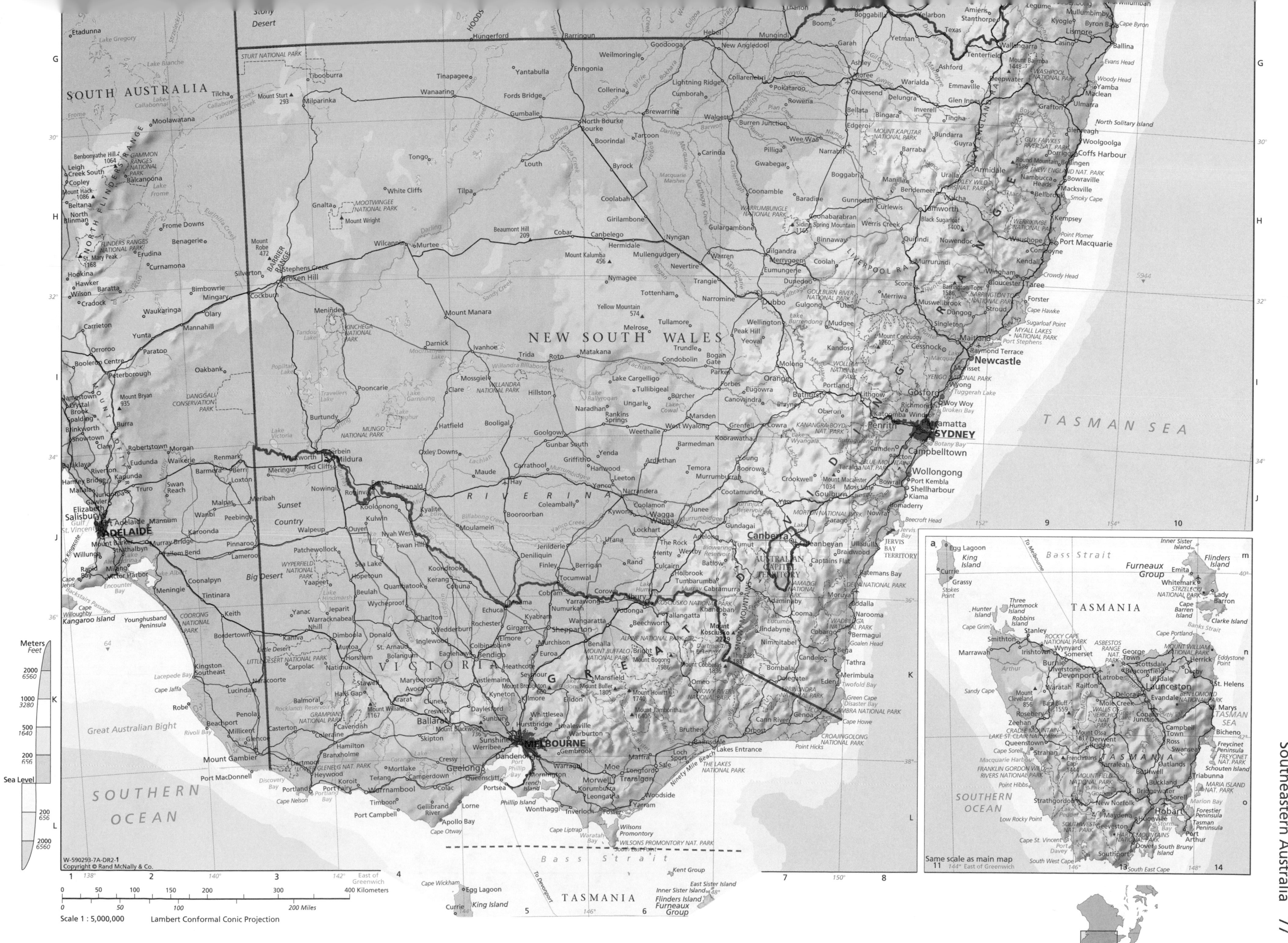

Meters / Feet
2000 / 6560
1000 / 3280
500 / 1640
200 / 656
Sea Level
200 / 656
2000 / 6560

Scale 1 : 5,000,000

Lambert Conformal Conic Projection

W-590293-7A-DR2-1
Copyright © Rand McNally & Co.

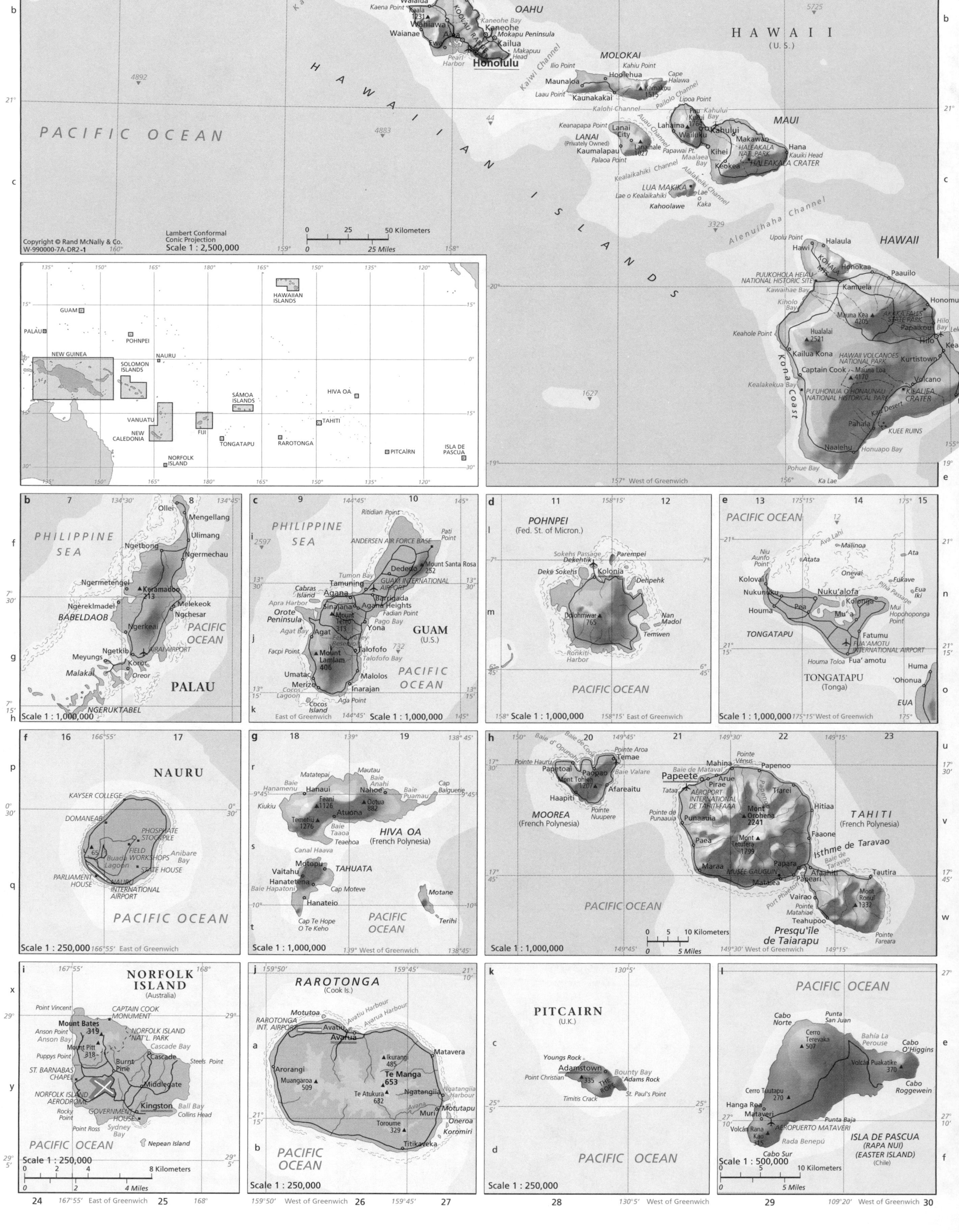
HAWAII (U.S.)
PACIFIC OCEAN
HAWAIIAN ISLANDS
KAUAI
OAHU
MOLOKAI
LANAI
MAUI
HAWAII
Honolulu
Kauai Channel
Copyright © Rand McNally & Co.
Lambert Conformal Conic Projection
Scale 1 : 2,500,000
PALAU
GUAM (U.S.)
POHNPEI (Fed. St. of Micron.)
TONGATAPU (Tonga)
NAURU
HIVA OA (French Polynesia)
TAHITI (French Polynesia)
MOOREA (French Polynesia)
NORFOLK ISLAND (Australia)
RAROTONGA (Cook Is.)
PITCAIRN (U.K.)
ISLA DE PASCUA (RAPA NUI) (EASTER ISLAND) (Chile)
PHILIPPINE SEA
Scale 1 : 1,000,000
Scale 1 : 250,000
Scale 1 : 500,000

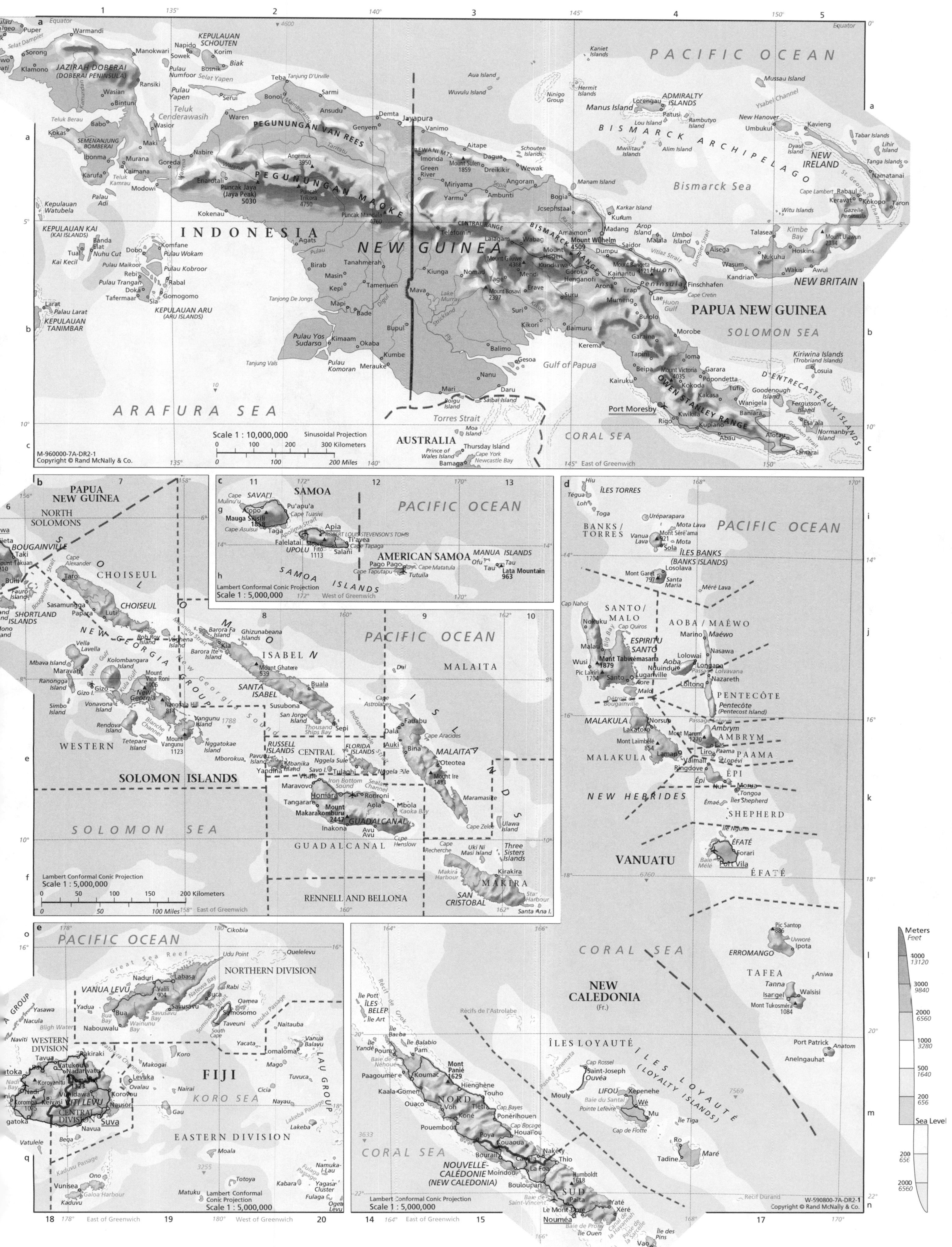

Scale 1 : 10,000,000
Sinusoidal Projection
0   100   200   300 Kilometers
0   100   200 Miles

M-960000-7A-DR2-1
Copyright © Rand McNally & Co.

Lambert Conformal Conic Projection
Scale 1 : 5,000,000

Lambert Conformal Conic Projection
Scale 1 : 5,000,000
0   50   100   200 Kilometers
0   50   100 Miles

Lambert Conformal Conic Projection
Scale 1 : 5,000,000

Lambert Conformal Conic Projection
Scale 1 : 5,000,000

W-590800-7A-DR2-1
Copyright © Rand McNally & Co.

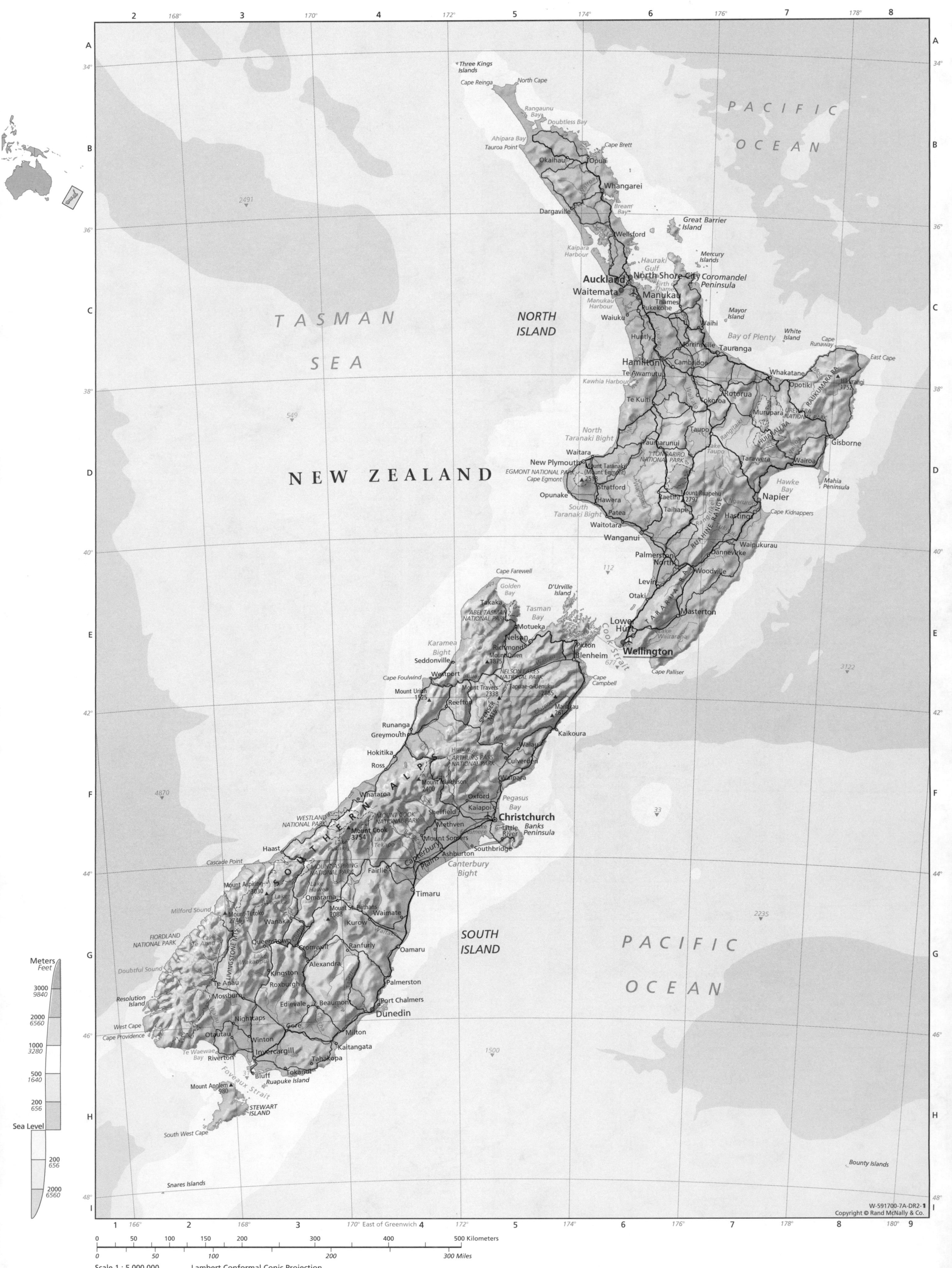

NEW ZEALAND

TASMAN SEA

PACIFIC OCEAN

NORTH ISLAND

SOUTH ISLAND

PACIFIC OCEAN

Three Kings Islands
Cape Reinga
North Cape
Rangaunu Bay
Doubtless Bay
Ahipara Bay
Tauroa Point
Cape Brett
Okaihau
Opua
Whangarei
Dargaville
Bream Bay
Wellsford
Great Barrier Island
Kaipara Harbour
Hauraki Gulf
Mercury Islands
Auckland
Waitemata
North Shore City
Coromandel Peninsula
Manukau
Firth of Thames
Thames
Manukau Harbour
Waiuku
Pukekohe
Waihi
Mayor Island
Huntly
Morrinsville
Tauranga
White Island
Bay of Plenty
Cape Runaway
Hamilton
Cambridge
Whakatane
East Cape
Te Awamutu
Opotiki
Kawhia Harbour
Rotorua
Hikurangi 1753
Te Kuiti
Tokoroa
Murupara
UREWERA NATIONAL PARK
North Taranaki Bight
Taupo
Tongariro
Rangitaiki
Gisborne
Taumarunui
Lake Taupo
TONGARIRO NATIONAL PARK
Tarawera
Waikaremoana
Wairoa
Waitara
New Plymouth
Mount Taranaki (Mount Egmont) 2518
EGMONT NATIONAL PARK
Cape Egmont
Stratford
Mount Ruapehu 2797
Hawke Bay
Napier
Mahia Peninsula
Opunake
Raetihi
Hawera
Taihape
Hastings
Cape Kidnappers
South Taranaki Bight
Patea
Waitotara
Waipukurau
Wanganui
RUAHINE RANGE
Dannevirke
Woodville
Palmerston North
Levin
Otaki
Masterton
Cape Farewell
D'Urville Island
Golden Bay
Takaka
ABEL TASMAN NATIONAL PARK
Tasman Bay
Lower Hutt
Motueka
Nelson
Richmond
Picton
Wellington
Karamea Bight
Mount Owen 1875
Blenheim
Cook Strait
Seddonville
NELSON LAKES NATIONAL PARK
Cape Campbell
Cape Palliser
Cape Foulwind
Westport
Mount Travers 2338
Tapuae-o-uenuku 2885
Mount Uriah 1925
Reefton
Manakau
Kaikoura
Runanga
Greymouth
Waiau
Hokitika
ARTHUR'S PASS NATIONAL PARK
Culverden
Ross
Waipara
Mount Murchison 2400
Oxford
Pegasus Bay
Whataroa
Kaiapoi
WESTLAND NATIONAL PARK
Sheffield
Christchurch
MOUNT COOK NATIONAL PARK
Methven
Little River
Banks Peninsula
Mount Cook 3754
Mount Somers
Haast
Ashburton
Southbridge
MOUNT ASPIRING NATIONAL PARK
Lake Tekapo
Canterbury Bight
Cascade Point
Fairlie
Mount Aspiring 3030
SOUTHERN ALPS
Mount Tutoko
Mount St. Bathans 2088
Waimate
Milford Sound
Wanaka
Kurow
Timaru
LIVINGSTONE MTS
Queenstown
Cromwell
Ranfurly
Oamaru
FIORDLAND NATIONAL PARK
Doubtful Sound
Te Anau
Alexandra
Palmerston
Resolution Island
Kingston
Roxburgh
West Cape
Mossburn
Edievale
Beaumont
Port Chalmers
Nightcaps
Dunedin
Cape Providence
Otautau
Gore
Milton
Te Waewae Bay
Winton
Tahakopa
Riverton
Invercargill
Kaitangata
Bluff
Tokanui
Ruapuke Island
Mount Anglem 980
STEWART ISLAND
Foveaux Strait
Snares Islands
South West Cape
Bounty Islands

2491
549
112
4870
33
2235
1500
3122

Meters / Feet
3000 / 9840
2000 / 6560
1000 / 3280
500 / 1640
200 / 656
Sea Level
200 / 656
2000 / 6560

0 50 100 150 200 300 400 500 Kilometers
0 50 100 200 300 Miles
Scale 1 : 5,000,000   Lambert Conformal Conic Projection

W-591700-7A-DR2-1
Copyright © Rand McNally & Co.

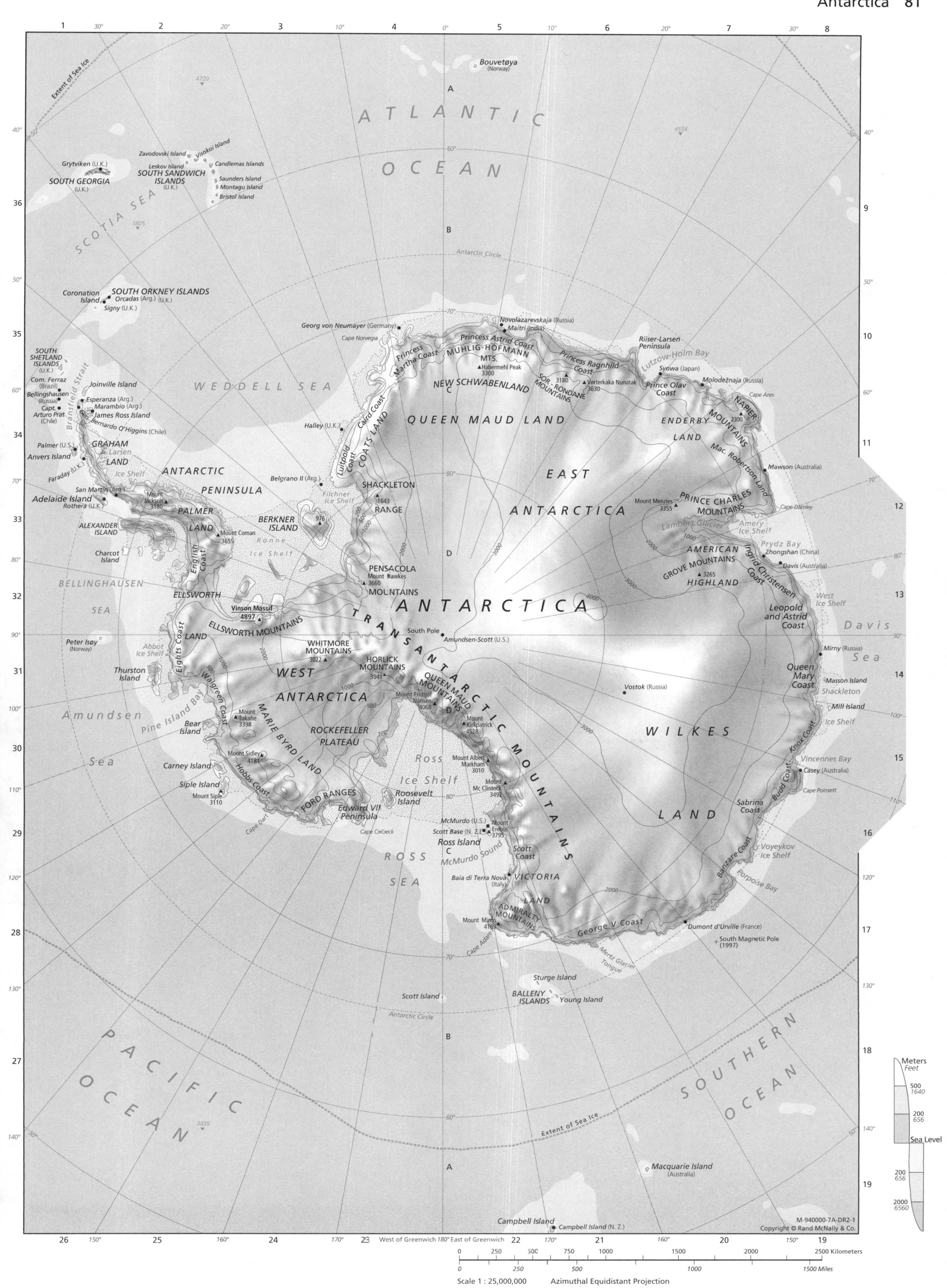

| 1 | 30° | 2 | 20° | 3 | 10° | 4 | 0° | 5 | 10° | 6 | 20° | 7 | 30° | 8 |

ATLANTIC

Bouvetøya
(Norway)

4720

4554

OCEAN

A

40°   40°

60°

Grytviken (U.K.)   Zavodovski Island
SOUTH GEORGIA   Leskov Island   Visokoi Island
(U.K.)   SOUTH SANDWICH   Candlemas Islands
              ISLANDS
              (U.K.)   Saunders Island
36°   Montagu Island   9
                        Bristol Island

SCOTIA SEA   3805

B

Antarctic Circle

50°   50°

Coronation   SOUTH ORKNEY ISLANDS
Island   Orcadas (Arg.) (U.K.)
       Signy (U.K.)

Georg von Neumayer (Germany)   Novolazarevskaja (Russia)
                            Maitri (India)
60°   Cape Norvegia   Princess   Princess Astrid Coast   Riiser-Larsen   Lützow-Holm Bay   60°
SOUTH   Martha   MÜHLIG-HOFMANN   Princess Ragnhild   Peninsula
SHETLAND   Coast   MTS.   Coast   Syowa (Japan)
ISLANDS   WEDDELL SEA   Habermehl Peak   SØR-   3180   Prince Olav   Molodežnaja (Russia)
(U.K.)   NEW SCHWABENLAND 3300 RONDANE Vorterkaka Nunatak Coast   Cape Ann
Com. Ferraz   MOUNTAINS 3630
(Brazil)   Joinville Island   3355   NAPIER
Bellingshausen Esperanza (Arg.)   QUEEN MAUD LAND   ENDERBY   2300
(Russia)   Marambio (Arg.)   LAND   MOUNTAINS
Capt.   James Ross Island   Mac. Robertson Land
Arturo Prat Bernardo O'Higgins (Chile)   Halley (U.K.)   EAST   Mawson (Australia)
(Chile)   GRAHAM   ANTARCTICA
Palmer (U.S.) LAND   Larsen   Cape Darnley
Anvers Island   Ice Shelf   Belgrano II (Arg.)   SHACKLETON   Mount Menzies   PRINCE CHARLES
Faraday (U.K.)   ANTARCTIC   RANGE   1643   3355   MOUNTAINS   Prydz Bay
       Mount   PENINSULA   Filchner   Lambert Glacier   Amery   Zhongshan (China)
San Martin (Arg.) Jackson   Ice Shelf   Ice Shelf   Ingrid Christensen
Adelaide Island 3180   PALMER   AMERICAN   Davis (Australia)   Coast
Rothera (U.K.)   LAND   BERKNER   976   GROVE MOUNTAINS
ALEXANDER   Mount Coman ISLAND   3265 HIGHLAND   West
ISLAND   3655   Ronne   Leopold   Ice Shelf
Charcot   Vinson Massif Ice Shelf   and Astrid
Island   English   ELLSWORTH   4897   PENSACOLA   Coast   Davis
BELLINGHAUSEN Coast   ELLSWORTH MOUNTAINS Mount Hawkes MOUNTAINS   Sea
SEA   3660   Mirny (Russia)
                  WHITMORE   ANTARCTICA   South Pole   Queen
Peter Isøy   Abbot   MOUNTAINS TRANSANTARCTIC   Amundsen-Scott (U.S.)   Mary   Masson Island
(Norway)   Ice Shelf 3022   HORLICK   Coast   Shackleton
Thurston   Eights Coast   MOUNTAINS   MOUNTAINS   Vostok (Russia)   Ice Shelf
Island   WEST   3941   QUEEN MAUD   WILKES   Mill Island
Amundsen   ANTARCTICA   MOUNTAINS Mount Friedjof   Vincennes Bay
       Pine Island Bay   Mount   Nansen   LAND   Casey (Australia)
Sea   Bear   ROCKEFELLER   Takahe 4068   Mount   Cape Poinsett
      Island   PLATEAU   3398   Kirkpatrick   Sabrina
Mount Sidley   4528   Budd   Coast
Carney Island 4181   MARIE BYRD LAND   Mount Albert   Banzare Coast
Siple Island   Hobbs Coast   Ross   Markham   Voyeykov
Mount Siple   FORD RANGES   Ice Shelf 3010   Mount   Ice Shelf
3110   Edward VII   Mc Clintock   Porpoise Bay
          Peninsula   Roosevelt 3492
       Cape Dart   Island   Mount Minto
             Cape Colbeck   McMurdo (U.S.)   Erebus   VICTORIA
ROSS   Scott Base (N.Z.) 3795   Scott   LAND
                  Ross Island   Coast
SEA   McMurdo Sound   ADMIRALTY   George V Coast   Dumont d'Urville (France)
                  Baia di Terra Nova (Italy)   MOUNTAINS   South Magnetic Pole
                                 Mount Minto   (1997)
                         Cape Adare 4163   Mertz Glacier
                                    Tongue
Antarctic Circle

PACIFIC   Sturge Island
                  Scott Island   BALLENY   Young Island
                         ISLANDS

3335   **SOUTHERN**

OCEAN   **OCEAN**

Campbell Island
       Campbell Island (N.Z.)   Macquarie Island
                                 (Australia)

| 26 | 150° | 25 | 160° | 24 | 170° | 23 | West of Greenwich 180° East of Greenwich | 22 | 170° | 21 | 160° | 20 | 150° | 19 |

M-940000-7A-DR2-1
Copyright © Rand McNally & Co.

Meters
Feet

500
1640

200
656

Sea Level

200
656

2000
6560

0   250   500   750   1000   1500   2000   2500 Kilometers
0   250   500   1000   1500 Miles

Scale 1 : 25,000,000   Azimuthal Equidistant Projection

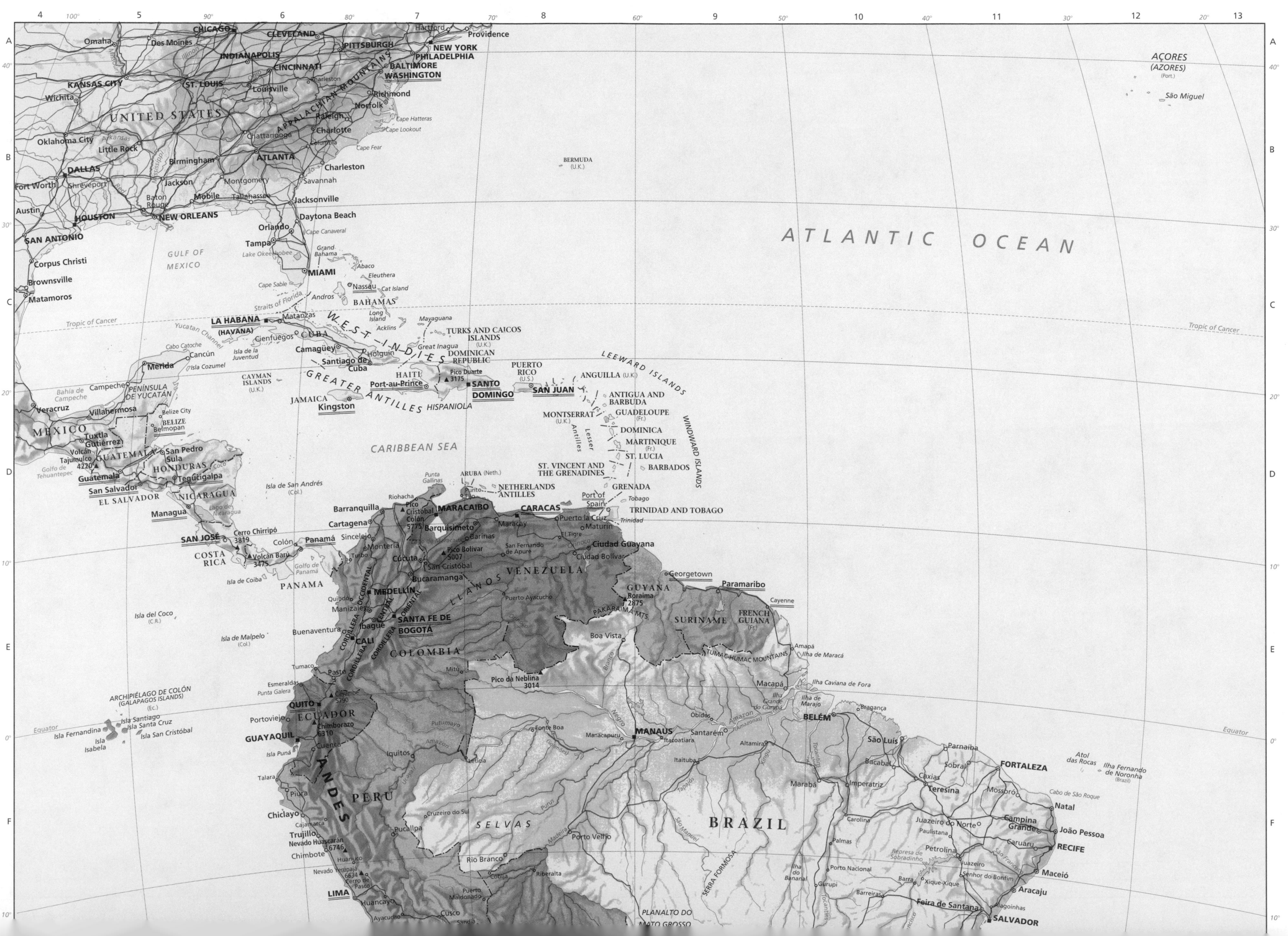
ATLANTIC OCEAN
AÇORES (AZORES) (Port.)
São Miguel
Tropic of Cancer
Equator
BERMUDA (U.K.)
UNITED STATES
APPALACHIAN MOUNTAINS
CHICAGO
Des Moines
Omaha
KANSAS CITY
Wichita
Oklahoma City
DALLAS
Fort Worth
Austin
SAN ANTONIO
HOUSTON
Corpus Christi
Brownsville
Matamoros
Shreveport
Little Rock
ST. LOUIS
INDIANAPOLIS
CLEVELAND
CINCINNATI
Louisville
PITTSBURGH
NEW YORK
PHILADELPHIA
BALTIMORE
WASHINGTON
Providence
Hartford
Richmond
Norfolk
Cape Hatteras
Cape Lookout
Cape Fear
Raleigh
Charlotte
Charleston
Savannah
Jacksonville
Daytona Beach
Cape Canaveral
Orlando
Tampa
MIAMI
Lake Okeechobee
ATLANTA
Chattanooga
Montgomery
Tallahassee
Birmingham
Jackson
Mobile
Baton Rouge
NEW ORLEANS
GULF OF MEXICO
MEXICO
Veracruz
Bahía de Campeche
Campeche
Villahermosa
Mérida
Cancún
Cabo Catoche
Isla Cozumel
Yucatan Channel
PENÍNSULA DE YUCATÁN
Tuxtla Gutiérrez
Golfo de Tehuantepec
BELIZE
Belize City
Belmopan
GUATEMALA
Guatemala
EL SALVADOR
San Salvador
HONDURAS
San Pedro Sula
Tegucigalpa
NICARAGUA
Managua
COSTA RICA
SAN JOSÉ
Cerro Chirripó 3819
Volcán Barú 3475
PANAMA
Panamá
Colón
Golfo de Panamá
Isla de Coiba
Isla de San Andrés (Col.)
Isla de Malpelo (Col.)
Isla del Coco (C.R.)
ARCHIPIÉLAGO DE COLÓN (GALAPAGOS ISLANDS) (Ec.)
Isla Santiago
Isla Santa Cruz
Isla San Cristóbal
Isla Fernandina
Isla Isabela
Straits of Florida
BAHAMAS
Grand Bahama
Abaco
Andros
Nassau
Eleuthera
Cat Island
Long Island
Acklins
Mayaguana
Great Inagua
LA HABANA (HAVANA)
Matanzas
Cienfuegos
Isla de la Juventud
CUBA
Camagüey
Holguín
Santiago de Cuba
CAYMAN ISLANDS (U.K.)
WEST INDIES
GREATER ANTILLES
JAMAICA
Kingston
HAITI
Port-au-Prince
HISPANIOLA
DOMINICAN REPUBLIC
Pico Duarte 3175
SANTO DOMINGO
TURKS AND CAICOS ISLANDS (U.K.)
PUERTO RICO (U.S.)
SAN JUAN
LEEWARD ISLANDS
ANGUILLA (U.K.)
ANTIGUA AND BARBUDA
MONTSERRAT (U.K.)
GUADELOUPE (Fr.)
DOMINICA
MARTINIQUE (Fr.)
ST. LUCIA
BARBADOS
WINDWARD ISLANDS
ST. VINCENT AND THE GRENADINES
GRENADA
TRINIDAD AND TOBAGO
Tobago
Trinidad
Port of Spain
Lesser Antilles
CARIBBEAN SEA
ARUBA (Neth.)
NETHERLANDS ANTILLES
Punta Gallinas
Riohacha
Pico Cristóbal Colón 5775
MARACAIBO
Barranquilla
Cartagena
Sincelejo
Montería
Barquisimeto
CARACAS
Maracay
Barinas
Pico Bolívar 5007
San Cristóbal
Cúcuta
Bucaramanga
MEDELLÍN
SANTA FE DE BOGOTÁ
Ibagué
Manizales
CALI
Buenaventura
Pasto
Tumaco
CORDILLERA OCCIDENTAL
CORDILLERA CENTRAL
CORDILLERA ORIENTAL
COLOMBIA
LLANOS
VENEZUELA
Puerto Ayacucho
San Fernando de Apure
Ciudad Bolívar
Ciudad Guayana
Puerto la Cruz
Maturín
GUYANA
Georgetown
PAKARAIMA MTS.
Roraima 2875
SURINAME
Paramaribo
FRENCH GUIANA (Fr.)
Cayenne
TUMUC-HUMAC MOUNTAINS
Boa Vista
Pico da Neblina 3014
ECUADOR
QUITO
Esmeraldas
Punta Galera
Portoviejo
GUAYAQUIL
Isla Puná
Chimborazo 6310
Cuenca
Talara
Piura
Chiclayo
Trujillo
Nevado Huascarán 6746
Chimbote
LIMA
Huancayo
Ayacucho
Cusco
PERU
ANDES
Iquitos
Pucallpa
Cruzeiro do Sul
Rio Branco
Porto Velho
SELVAS
Amazon
Negro
MANAUS
Itacoatiara
Santarém
Óbidos
Itaituba
Macapá
Amapá
Ilha de Maracá
Ilha Caviana de Fora
Ilha de Marajó
BELÉM
Bragança
São Luís
Bacabal
Imperatriz
Marabá
Altamira
Carolina
Palmas
Porto Nacional
Gurupi
Barreiras
Ilha do Bananal
BRAZIL
SERRA FORMOSA
PLANALTO DO MATO GROSSO
Teresina
Caxias
Parnaíba
Sobral
FORTALEZA
Mossoró
Natal
Campina Grande
João Pessoa
RECIFE
Caruaru
Maceió
Aracaju
SALVADOR
Feira de Santana
Juazeiro do Norte
Juazeiro
Petrolina
Senhor do Bonfim
Xique-Xique
Barra
Represa de Sobradinho
Paulistana
Cabo de São Roque
Atol das Rocas
Ilha Fernando de Noronha (Brazil)

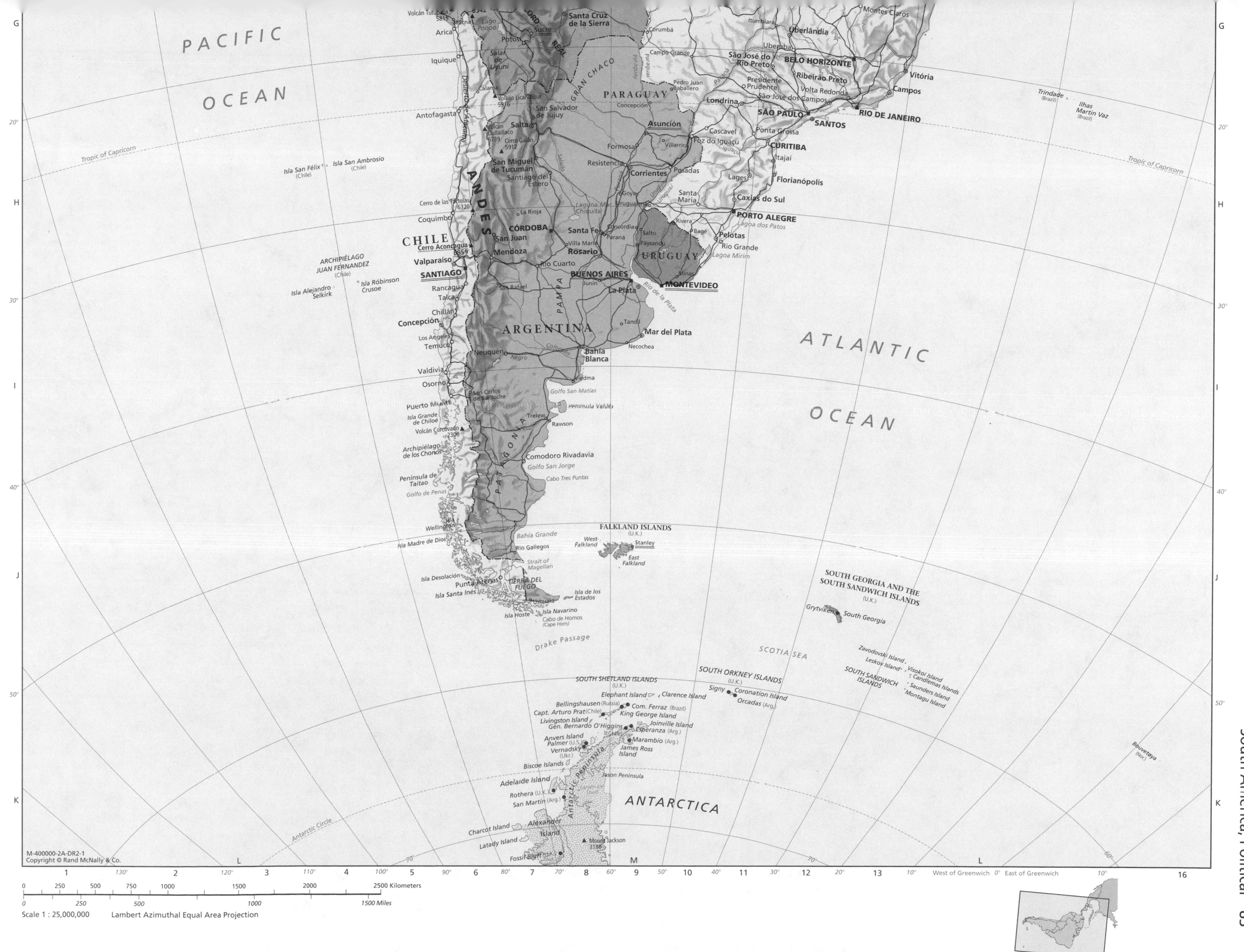
PACIFIC
OCEAN
ATLANTIC
OCEAN
SCOTIA SEA
Drake Passage
ANTARCTICA
ANDES
GRAN CHACO
PAMPA
PATAGONIA
CHILE
ARGENTINA
PARAGUAY
URUGUAY
FALKLAND ISLANDS (U.K.)
West Falkland
East Falkland
Stanley
SOUTH GEORGIA AND THE SOUTH SANDWICH ISLANDS (U.K.)
South Georgia
Grytviken
SOUTH SANDWICH ISLANDS
Zavodovski Island
Leskov Island
Visokoi Island
Candlemas Island
Saunders Island
Montagu Island
SOUTH ORKNEY ISLANDS (U.K.)
Coronation Island
Signy
Orcadas (Arg.)
SOUTH SHETLAND ISLANDS (U.K.)
Elephant Island
Clarence Island
Bellingshausen (Russia)
Com. Ferraz (Brazil)
Capt. Arturo Prat (Chile)
King George Island
Livingston Island
Gen. Bernardo O'Higgins
Joinville Island
Esperanza (Arg.)
Marambio (Arg.)
James Ross Island
Anvers Island
Palmer (U.S.)
Vernadsky (Ukr.)
Biscoe Islands
Adelaide Island
Rothera (U.K.)
San Martín (Arg.)
Alexander Island
Charcot Island
Latady Island
Fossil Bluff (U.K.)
Mount Jackson 3184
Antarctic Peninsula
Jason Peninsula
Bouvetøya (Nor.)
Trindade (Brazil)
Ilhas Martin Vaz (Brazil)
Isla San Félix (Chile)
Isla San Ambrosio (Chile)
ARCHIPIÉLAGO JUAN FERNÁNDEZ (Chile)
Isla Róbinson Crusoe
Isla Alejandro Selkirk
TIERRA DEL FUEGO
Isla de los Estados
Isla Navarino
Cabo de Hornos (Cape Horn)
Isla Hoste
Strait of Magellan
Isla Santa Inés
Isla Desolación
Isla Wellington
Isla Madre de Dios
Golfo de Penas
Península de Taitao
Archipiélago de los Chonos
Isla Grande de Chiloé
Golfo San Jorge
Golfo San Matías
Península Valdés
Bahía Grande
Cabo Tres Puntas
Río de la Plata
Lagoa dos Patos
Lagoa Mirim
Desierto de Atacama
Salar de Uyuni
Lago Poopó
Tropic of Capricorn
Antarctic Circle
RIO DE JANEIRO
SÃO PAULO
SANTOS
BELO HORIZONTE
CURITIBA
PORTO ALEGRE
Florianópolis
Vitória
Campos
Montes Claros
Uberlândia
Uberaba
Ribeirão Preto
Volta Redonda
São José dos Campos
São José do Rio Preto
Presidente Prudente
Londrina
Ponta Grossa
Itajaí
Caxias do Sul
Lages
Cascavel
Foz do Iguaçu
Santa Maria
Pelotas
Rio Grande
Bagé
Rivera
Corumbá
Campo Grande
Pedro Juan Caballero
Asunción
Concepción
Villarrica
Posadas
Corrientes
Resistencia
Formosa
Goya
MONTEVIDEO
Salto
Paysandú
Minas
BUENOS AIRES
La Plata
Junín
Mar del Plata
Tandil
Necochea
Bahía Blanca
Rosario
Santa Fe
Paraná
Concordia
CÓRDOBA
Río Cuarto
Villa María
San Miguel de Tucumán
Santiago del Estero
Salta
San Salvador de Jujuy
La Rioja
San Juan
Mendoza
San Rafael
Neuquén
San Carlos de Bariloche
Viedma
Rawson
Trelew
Comodoro Rivadavia
Río Gallegos
Ushuaia
Punta Arenas
SANTIAGO
Valparaíso
Cerro Aconcagua 6959
Cerro de las Tórtolas 6320
Rancagua
Talca
Chillán
Concepción
Los Angeles
Temuco
Valdivia
Osorno
Puerto Montt
Volcán Corcovado 2300
Coquimbo
Antofagasta
Iquique
Arica
Calama
Potosí
Sucre
Santa Cruz de la Sierra
Volcán Llullaillaco 6739
Cerro Galán 5912
Volcán Licancabur 5916
Volcán Tutupaca 5815
M-400000-2A-DR2-1
Copyright © Rand McNally & Co.
Scale 1 : 25,000,000
Lambert Azimuthal Equal Area Projection
2500 Kilometers
1500 Miles
West of Greenwich 0° East of Greenwich

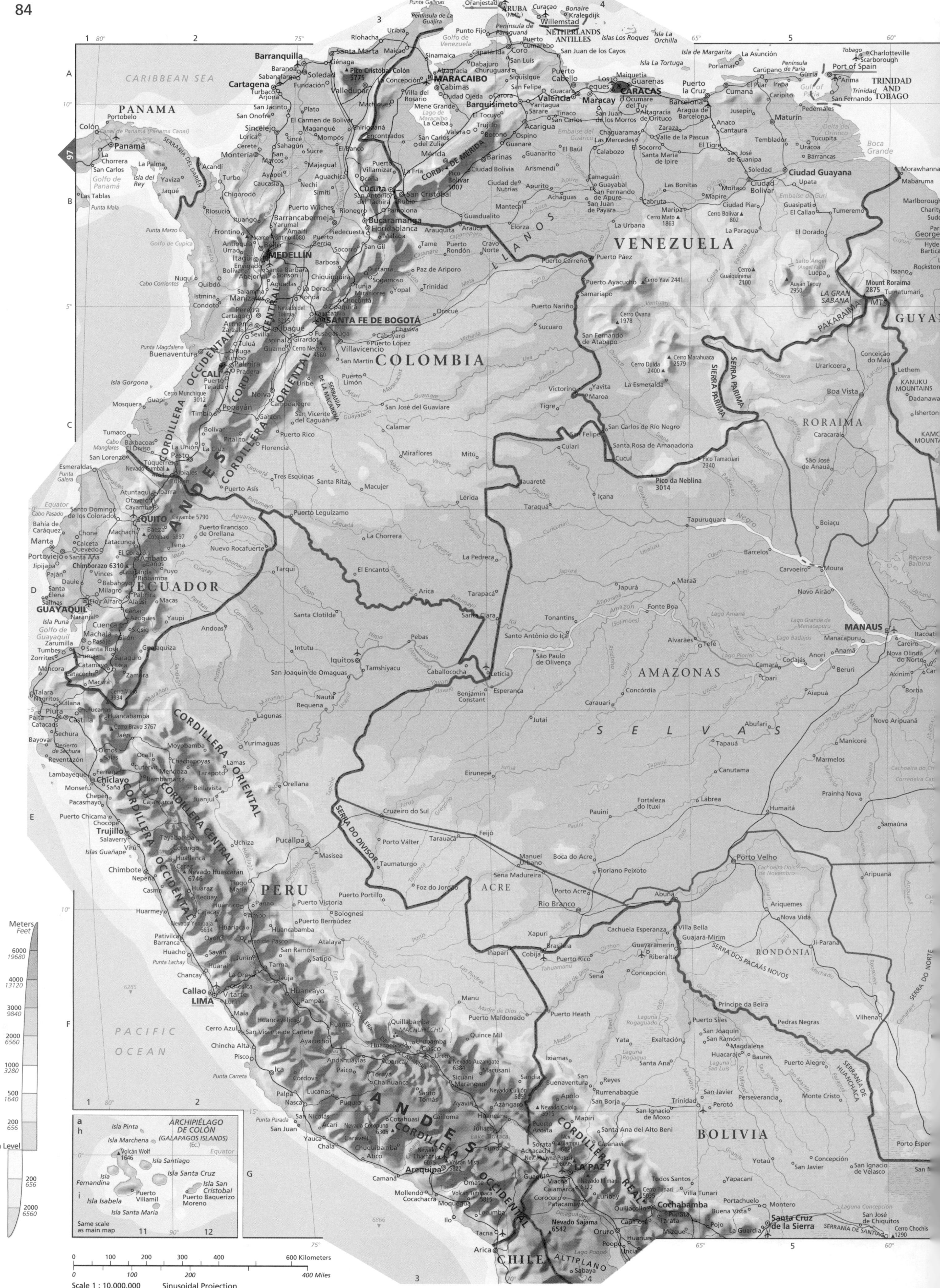
CARIBBEAN SEA
PANAMA
COLOMBIA
VENEZUELA
ECUADOR
PERU
BOLIVIA
CHILE
AMAZONAS
S E L V A S
ACRE
RONDÔNIA
RORAIMA
TRINIDAD AND TOBAGO
ARUBA (Neth.)
NETHERLANDS ANTILLES
PACIFIC OCEAN
LLANOS
ANDES
CORDILLERA OCCIDENTAL
CORDILLERA CENTRAL
CORDILLERA ORIENTAL
CORDILLERA REAL
ALTIPLANO
SIERRA PARIMA
SERRA DO DIVISOR
PAKARAIMA MTS.
LA GRAN SABANA
SANTA FE DE BOGOTÁ
CARACAS
QUITO
LIMA
LA PAZ
MEDELLÍN
CALI
MARACAIBO
GUAYAQUIL
MANAUS
Barranquilla
Cartagena
Panamá
Valencia
Barquisimeto
Maracay
Ciudad Guayana
Port of Spain
Willemstad
Cúcuta
Bucaramanga
Trujillo
Chiclayo
Callao
Arequipa
Cochabamba
Santa Cruz de la Sierra
Iquitos
Leticia
Porto Velho
Rio Branco
Boa Vista
Pico Cristóbal Colón 5775
Nevado Huascarán 6746
Chimborazo 6310
Mount Roraima 2875
Pico da Neblina 3014
Meters
Feet
6000
19680
4000
13120
3000
9840
2000
6560
1000
3280
500
1640
200
656
Sea Level
200
656
2000
6560
ARCHIPIÉLAGO DE COLÓN (GALAPAGOS ISLANDS) (Ec.)
Isla Pinta
Isla Marchena
Volcán Wolf 1646
Isla Santiago
Isla Santa Cruz
Isla Fernandina
Isla Isabela
Puerto Villamil
Isla San Cristobal
Puerto Baquerizo Moreno
Isla Santa Maria
Same scale as main map
0 100 200 300 400 600 Kilometers
0 100 200 400 Miles
Scale 1 : 10,000,000
Sinusoidal Projection
97

ATLANTIC OCEAN

SURINAME

FRENCH GUIANA

BRAZIL

AMAPÁ

PARÁ

MARANHÃO

PIAUÍ

CEARÁ

RIO GRANDE DO NORTE

PARAÍBA

PERNAMBUCO

ALAGOAS

SERGIPE

BAHIA

TOCANTINS

GOIÁS

DISTRITO FEDERAL

MINAS GERAIS

MATO GROSSO

MATO GROSSO DO SUL

PLANALTO DO MATO GROSSO

TUMUC-HUMAC MOUNTAINS

SERRA DO CACHIMBO

SERRA FORMOSA

SERRA DO RONCADOR

SERRA DOS CARAJÁS

SERRA DO ESTRONDO

CHAPADA DAS MANGABEIRAS

SERRA DO PENITENTE

SERRA GERAL DE GOIÁS

SERRA GRANDE

CHAPADA DO ARARIPE

SERRA DO ESPINHAÇO

SERRA DO CAIAPÓ

SERRA DE SÃO JERÔNIMO

ILHA DE MARAJÓ

Equator

Paramaribo

Cayenne

Macapá

BELÉM

São Luís

Teresina

FORTALEZA

Natal

João Pessoa

RECIFE

Maceió

Aracaju

SALVADOR

Palmas

BRASÍLIA

GOIÂNIA

Cuiabá

Santarém

Marabá

Imperatriz

Petrolina

Juazeiro

Feira de Santana

Vitória da Conquista

Ilhéus

Montes Claros

Campina Grande

Mossoró

Parnaíba

Anápolis

M-400091-7A-DR2-1

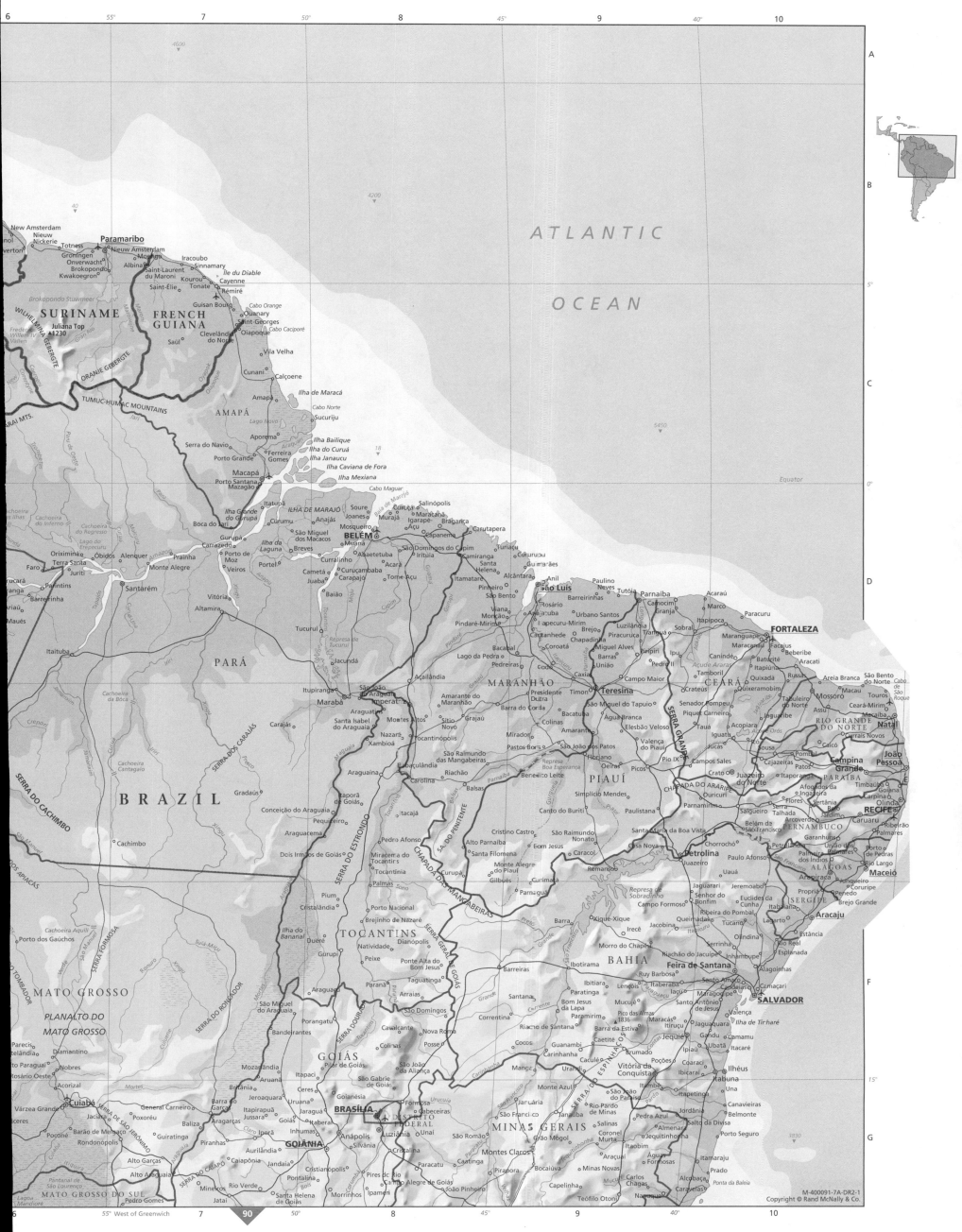

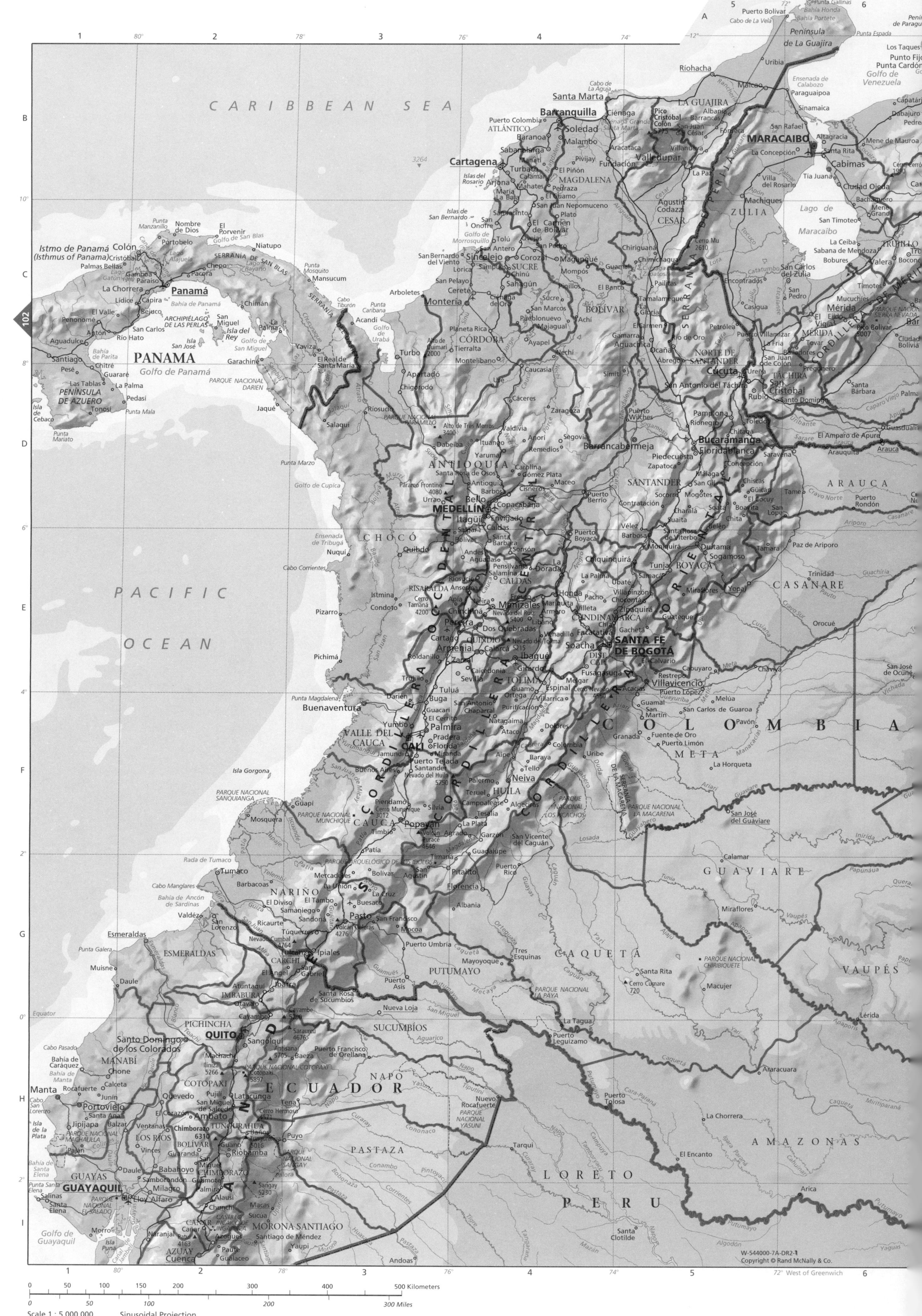

Meters / Feet

4000 / 13120
3000 / 9840
2000 / 6560
1000 / 3280
500 / 1640
200 / 656
Sea Level
200 / 656
2000 / 6560

0 50 100 150 200 300 400 500 Kilometers

0 50 100 200 300 Miles

Scale 1 : 5,000,000 Sinusoidal Projection

ARUBA (Neth.)
Curaçao
Willemstad
Bonaire
NETHERLANDS ANTILLES
LESSER ANTILLES
Isla de Margarita
TRINIDAD AND TOBAGO
Port of Spain
Tobago
Trinidad
FALCÓN
CARACAS
Maracay
Valencia
Puerto Cabello
Barquisimeto
Cumaná
Barcelona
Maturín
SUCRE
MONAGAS
ANZOÁTEGUI
GUÁRICO
Delta del Orinoco
Tucupita
DELTA AMACURO
Ciudad Guayana
Ciudad Bolívar
VENEZUELA
APURE
San Fernando de Apure
ATLANTIC OCEAN
Gulf of Paria
BOLÍVAR
GUIANA HIGHLANDS (MACIZO DE GUAYANA)
PARQUE NACIONAL CANAIMA
LA GRAN SABANA
PAKARAIMA MOUNTAINS
GUYANA
BARIMA-WAINI
CUYUNI-MAZARUNI
POTARO-SIPARUNI
UPPER TAKUTU-UPPER ESSEQUIBO
Puerto Ayacucho
AMAZONAS
SIERRA PARIMA
GUAINÍA
VICHADA
Boa Vista
RORAIMA
Pico da Neblina 3014
BRAZIL
AMAZONAS
Equator
MANAUS
Manacapuru
Barcelos
Novo Airão
Fonte Boa

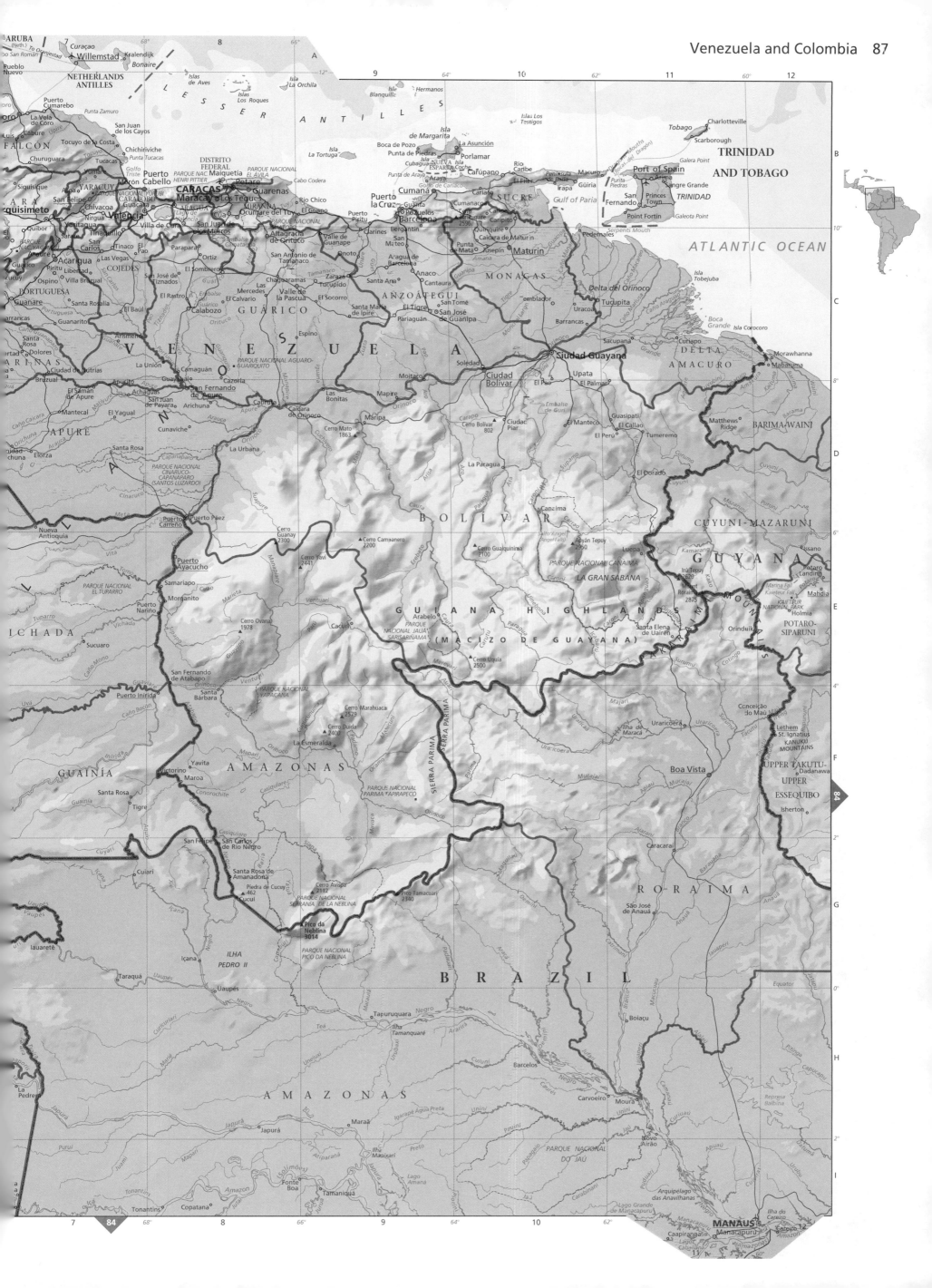

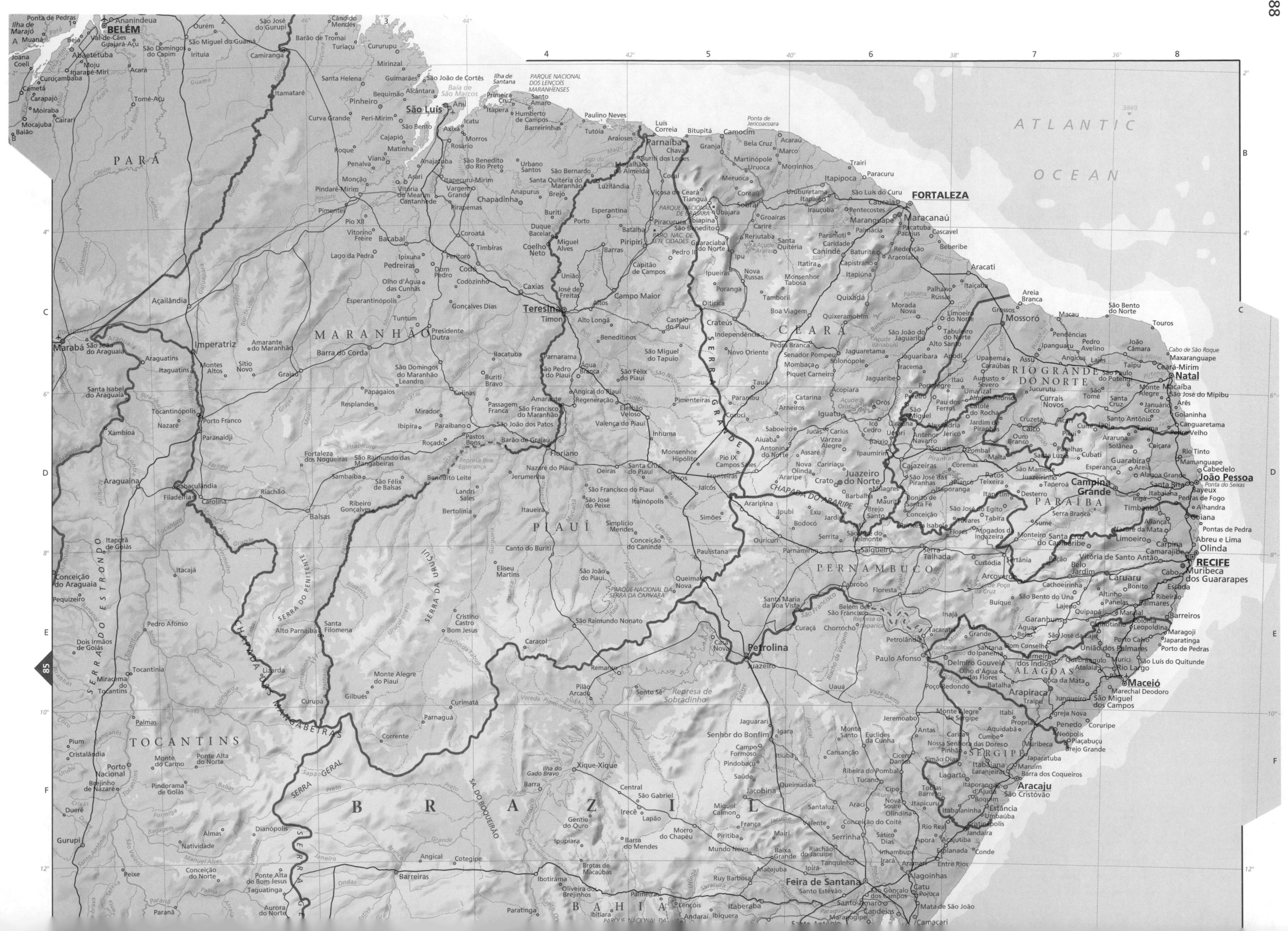
ATLANTIC
OCEAN
FORTALEZA
RECIFE
João Pessoa
Natal
Maceió
Aracaju
Teresina
São Luís
BELÉM
Campina Grande
Juazeiro do Norte
Petrolina
Feira de Santana
Imperatriz
Parnaíba
Mossoró
CEARÁ
RIO GRANDE DO NORTE
PARAÍBA
PERNAMBUCO
ALAGOAS
SERGIPE
PIAUÍ
MARANHÃO
PARÁ
TOCANTINS
BAHIA
BRAZIL
SERRA GRANDE
CHAPADA DO ARARIPE
SERRA DA URUÇUÍ
SERRA DO PENITENTE
CHAPADA DAS MANGABEIRAS
SERRA GERAL
SA. DO BOQUEIRÃO
SERRA DO ESTRONDO
Represa de Sobradinho
85

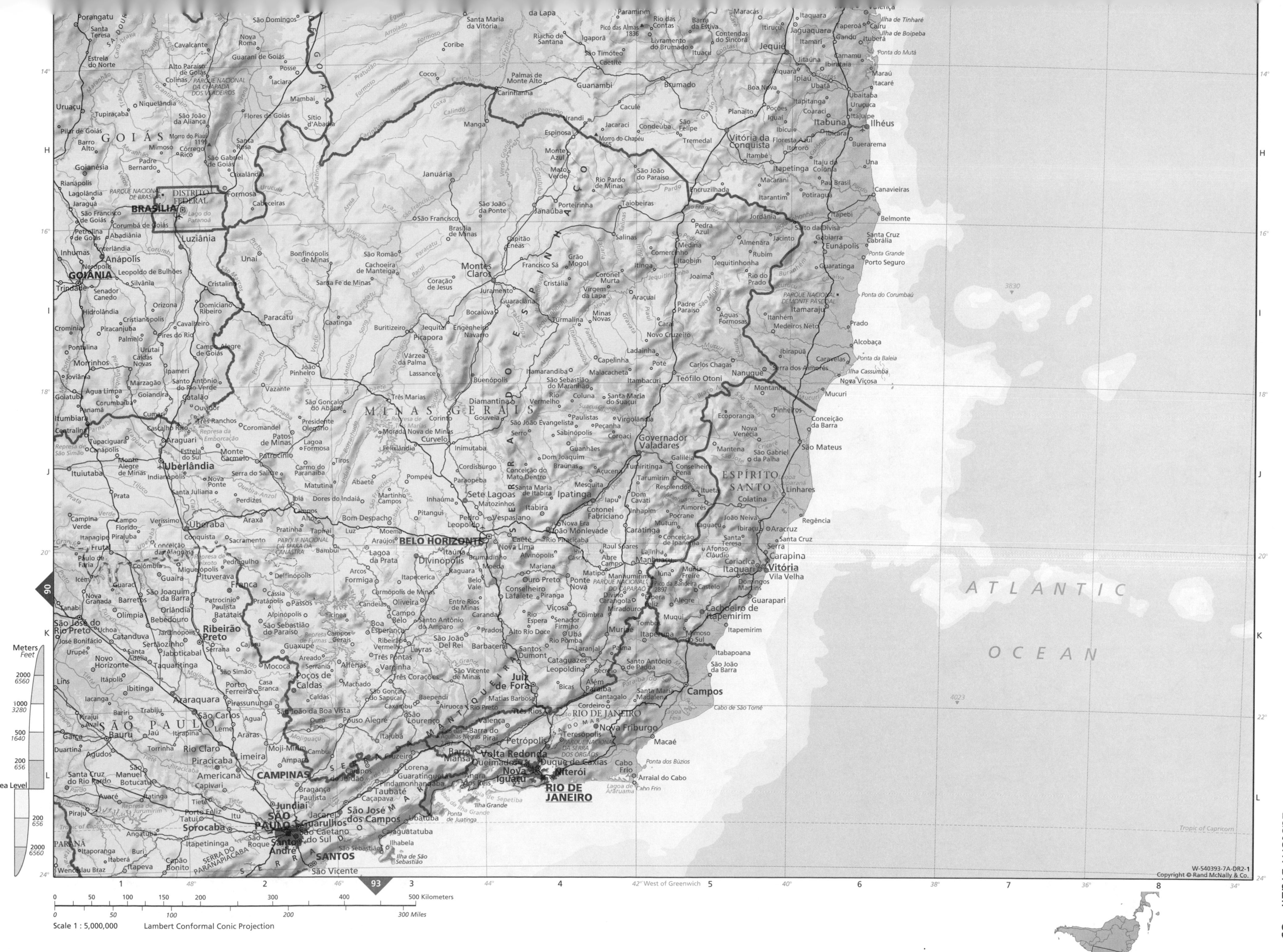

Scale 1 : 5,000,000

Lambert Conformal Conic Projection

500 Kilometers

300 Miles

Meters
Feet
2000 · 6560
1000 · 3280
500 · 1640
200 · 656
Sea Level
200 · 656
2000 · 6560

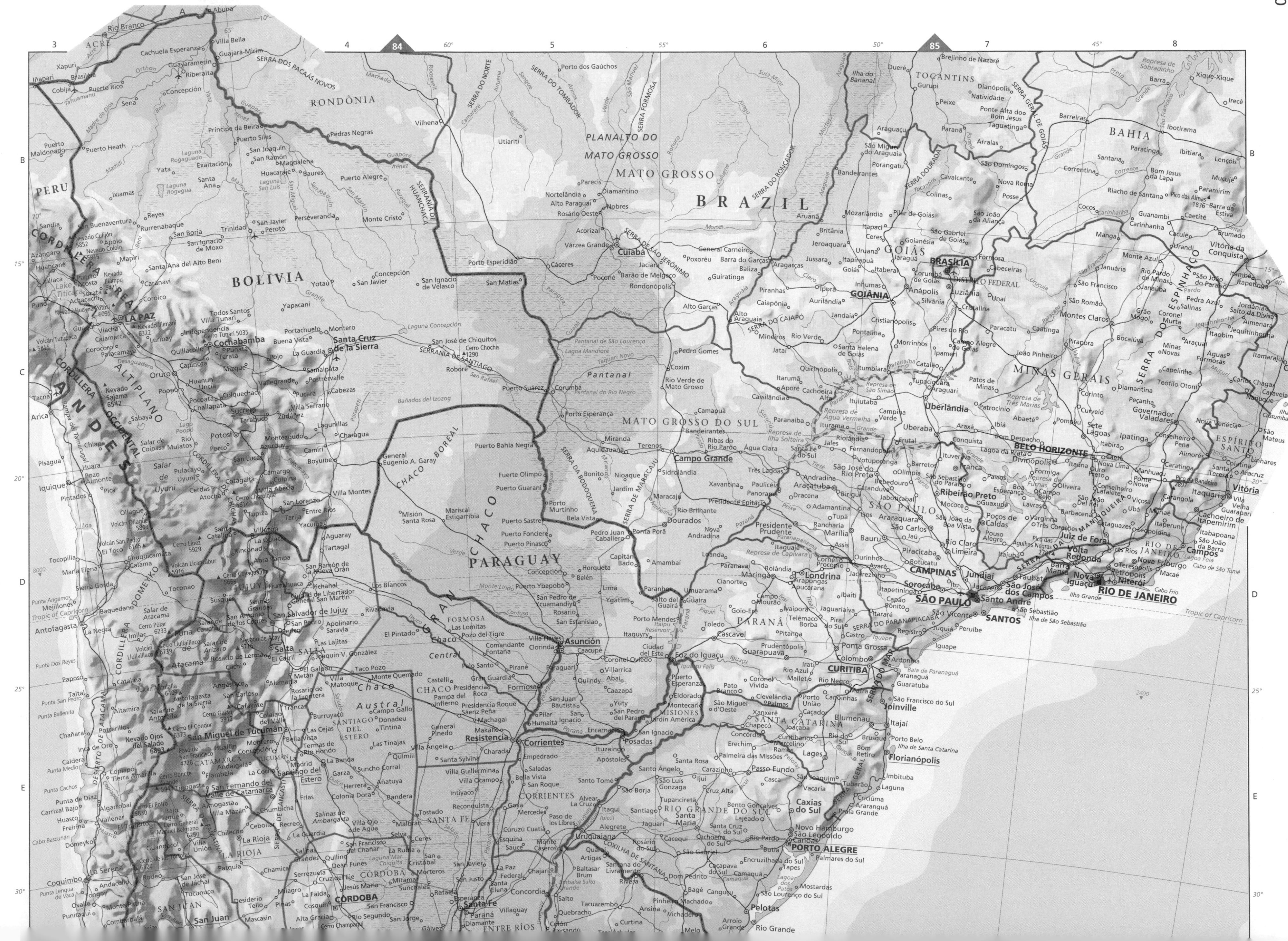
BRAZIL
BOLIVIA
PARAGUAY
PERU
ANDES
BAHIA
MINAS GERAIS
GOIÁS
TOCANTINS
MATO GROSSO
MATO GROSSO DO SUL
SÃO PAULO
RIO DE JANEIRO
ESPÍRITO SANTO
PARANÁ
SANTA CATARINA
RIO GRANDE DO SUL
RONDÔNIA
ACRE
FORMOSA
CORRIENTES
MISIONES
SANTA FE
CÓRDOBA
SAN JUAN
LA RIOJA
CATAMARCA
SALTA
JUJUY
ENTRE RÍOS
PLANALTO DO MATO GROSSO
SERRA DO RONCADOR
SERRA DOS PACAÁS NOVOS
SERRA DO NORTE
SERRA DO TOMBADOR
SERRA FORMOSA
SERRA DO ESPINHAÇO
SERRA DA MANTIQUEIRA
SERRA DO MAR
SERRA GERAL DE GOIÁS
SERRA DOURADA
SERRA DO CAIAPÓ
SERRA DE MARACAJU
SERRA DA BODOQUENA
SERRANIA DE HUANCHACA
ALTIPLANO
CORDILLERA OCCIDENTAL
CORDILLERA REAL
CHACO BOREAL
Pantanal
Tropic of Capricorn
BRASÍLIA
DISTRITO FEDERAL
GOIÂNIA
BELO HORIZONTE
RIO DE JANEIRO
SÃO PAULO
SANTOS
CAMPINAS
CURITIBA
Florianópolis
PORTO ALEGRE
Vitória
Campo Grande
Cuiabá
Asunción
LA PAZ
Cochabamba
Santa Cruz de la Sierra
Sucre
Potosí
Oruro
Salta
Resistencia
Corrientes
CÓRDOBA
San Miguel de Tucumán
Santa Fe
Antofagasta
Iquique
Arica
Coquimbo
Rio Branco
Londrina
Uberlândia
Juiz de Fora
Campos
Joinville
Pelotas
Caxias do Sul
Ribeirão Preto
Foz do Iguaçu
Posadas
Corumbá

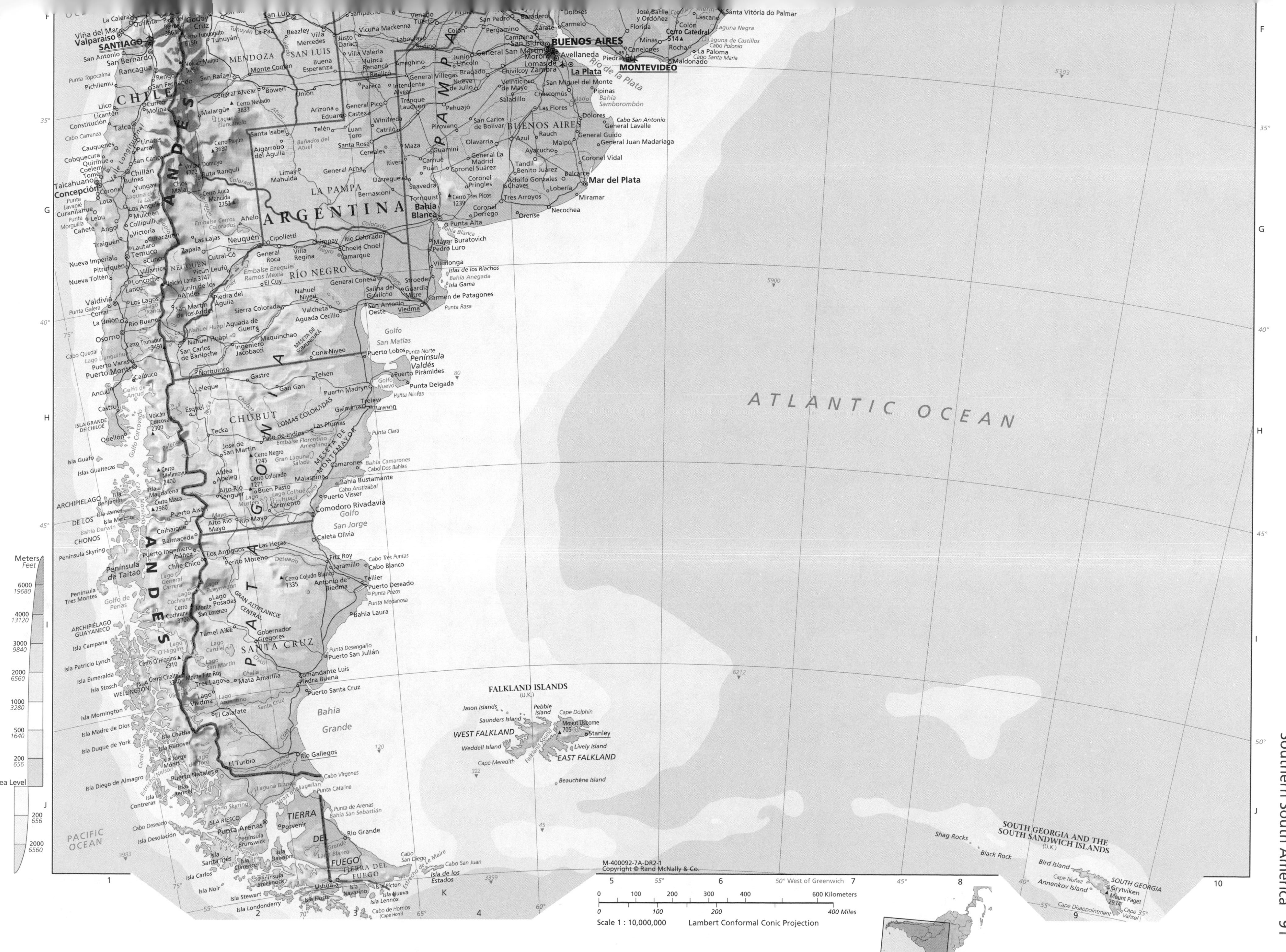

ATLANTIC OCEAN

PACIFIC OCEAN

SOUTH GEORGIA AND THE
SOUTH SANDWICH ISLANDS
(U.K.)

SOUTH GEORGIA

FALKLAND ISLANDS
(U.K.)

WEST FALKLAND

EAST FALKLAND

ARGENTINA

CHILE

ANDES

PAMPA

PATAGONIA

TIERRA DEL FUEGO

BUENOS AIRES

MONTEVIDEO

SANTIAGO

Mar del Plata

Bahía
Blanca

50° West of Greenwich

Scale 1 : 10,000,000

Lambert Conformal Conic Projection

M-400092-7A-DR2:1
Copyright © Rand McNally & Co.

Meters/	Feet
6000	19680
4000	13120
3000	9840
2000	6560
1000	3280
500	1640
200	656
Sea Level	
200	656
2000	6560

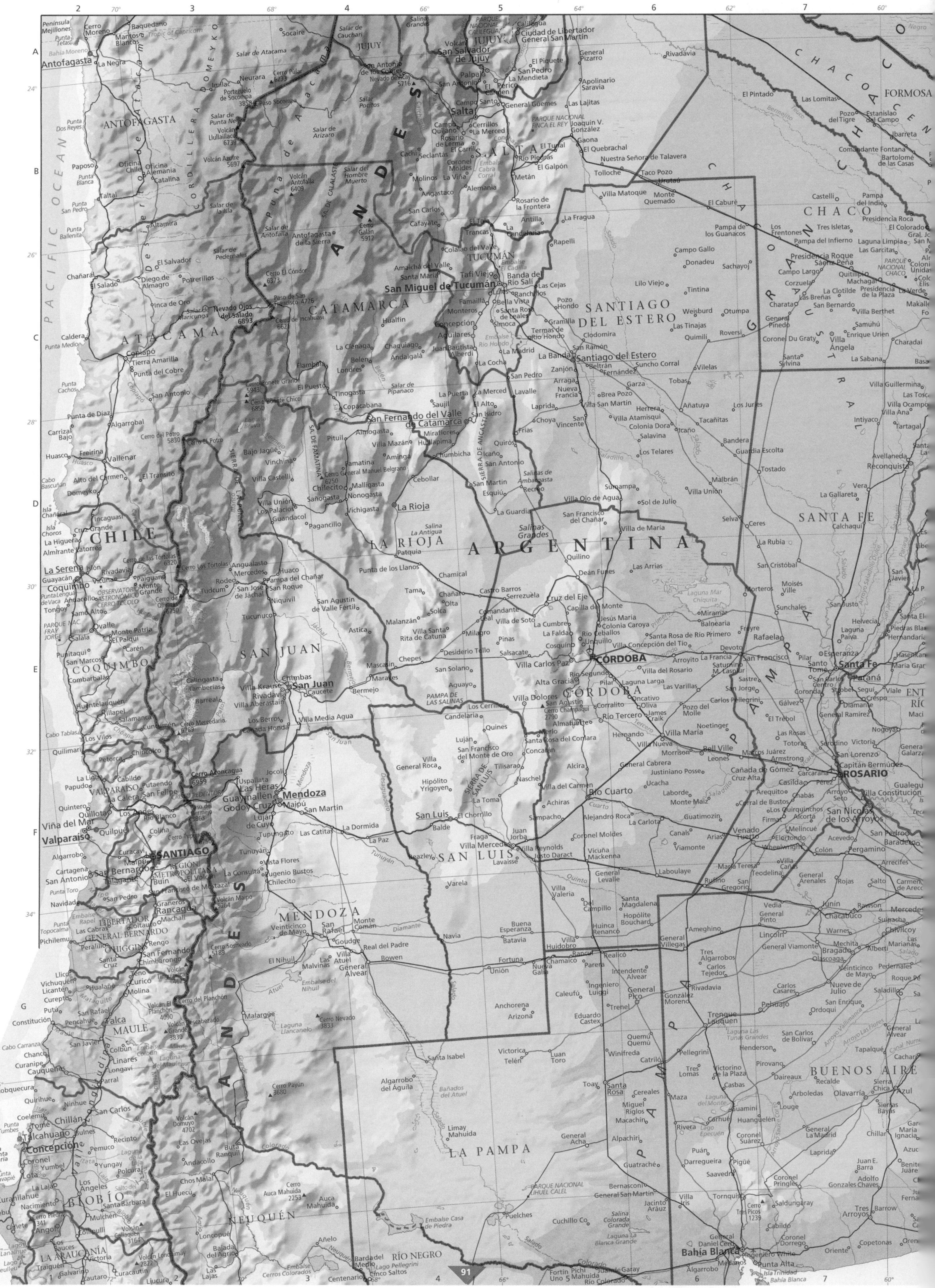

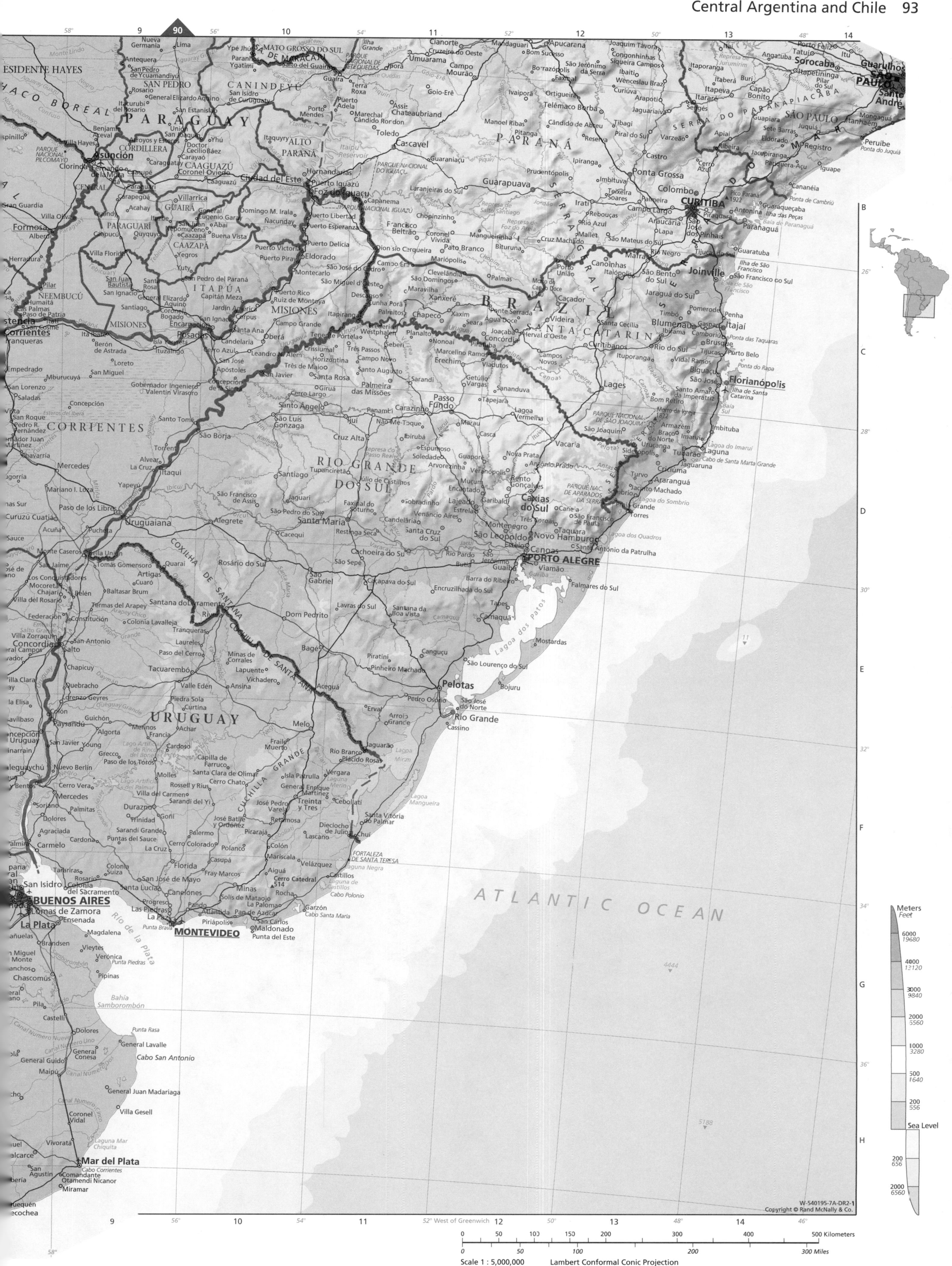

0   50   100   150   200   300   400   500 Kilometers

0   50   100   200   300 Miles

Scale 1 : 5,000,000   Lambert Conformal Conic Projection

Meters	
6000	19680
4000	13120
3000	9840
2000	6560
1000	3280
500	1640
200	656
Sea Level	
200	656
2000	6560

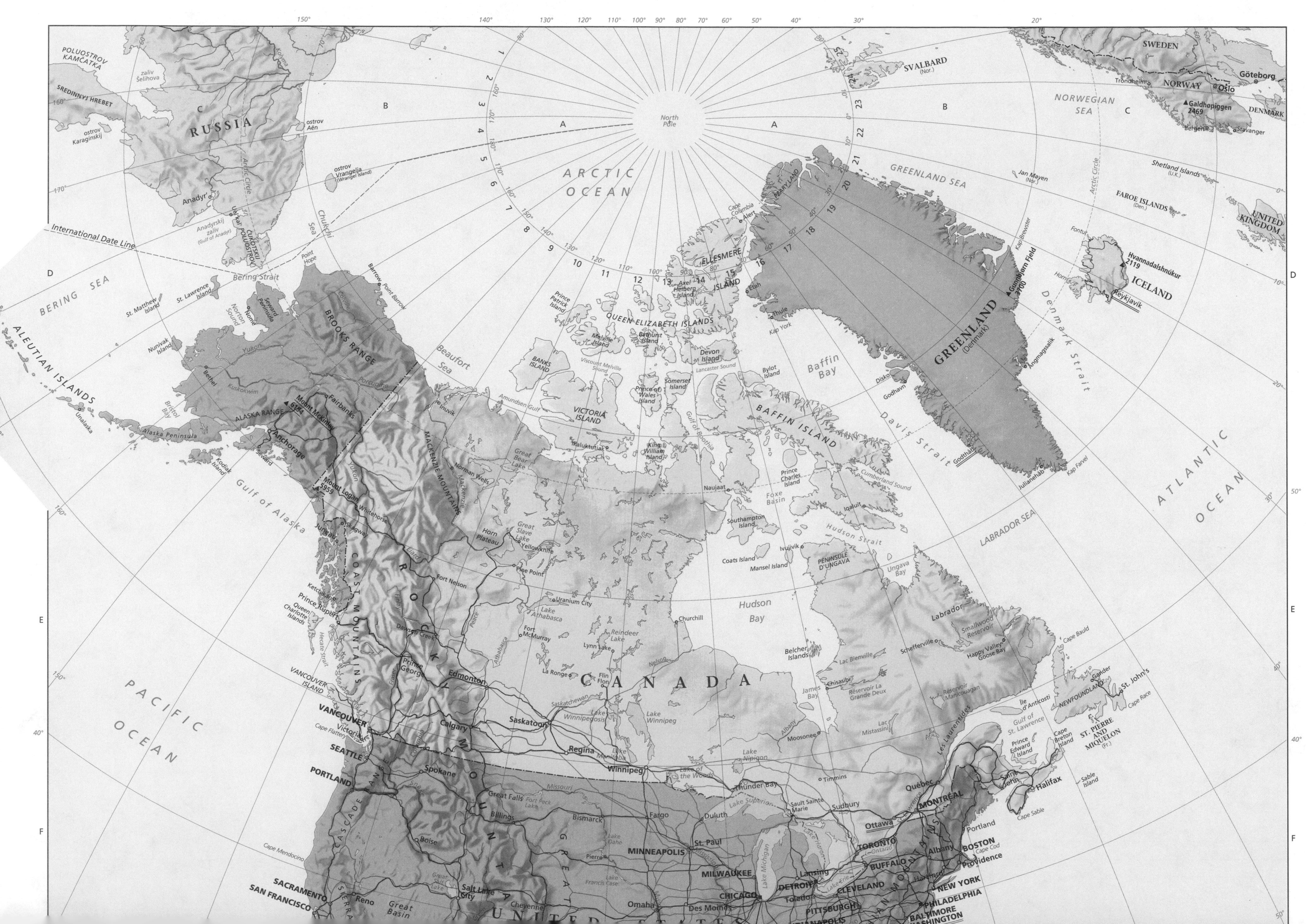

SWEDEN
Göteborg
Oslo
Galdhøpiggen 2469
NORWAY
Trondheim
Stavanger
DENMARK
UNITED KINGDOM
Shetland Islands (U.K.)
FAROE ISLANDS (Den.)
Hvannadalshnúkur 2119
ICELAND
Reykjavik
Surtsey

ATLANTIC OCEAN

NORWEGIAN SEA
Arctic Circle
Jan Mayen (Nor.)

SVALBARD (Nor.)

Denmark Strait

Kujalleq
Scoresbysund
Kulusuk

GREENLAND (Denmark)
Gunnbjørn Fjeld 3700

Denmark Strait

LABRADOR SEA

ST. PIERRE AND MIQUELON
St. John's
NEWFOUNDLAND
Cape Race
Sable Island

ARCTIC OCEAN

North Pole

GREENLAND SEA

Davis Strait

Baffin Bay

BAFFIN ISLAND

Godthåb
Godhavn

Ellesmere Island
Bylot Island
Devon Island

Cumberland Sound

Hudson Strait

PENINSULE D'UNGAVA

Labrador

Cape Chidley

Ungava Bay

Lac Bienville

Portland
Quebec
MONTREAL
Halifax
Cape Breton Island
Prince Edward Island
Gulf of St. Lawrence
Anticosti Island
Les Laurentides
Ottawa

QUEEN-ELIZABETH ISLANDS
Prince Charles Island
Foxe Basin
Southampton Island
Coats Island
Mansel Island

Hudson Bay

Belcher Islands

James Bay

Lake Mistassini

Réservoir La Grande Deux

Schefferville

Moosonee

Sudbury
Sault Ste. Marie
Thunder Bay
Lake Superior
Lake Huron
TORONTO
BUFFALO
Lake Ontario
Lake Michigan
Lake Erie
DETROIT
CLEVELAND
PITTSBURGH
BOSTON
Cape Cod
Providence
NEW YORK
PHILADELPHIA
BALTIMORE
WASHINGTON

VICTORIA ISLAND
BANKS ISLAND
Melville Island
Prince Patrick Island
Somerset Island
Prince of Wales Island
King William Island
Boothia Peninsula
Gulf of Boothia

Amundsen Gulf

Great Bear Lake

Great Slave Lake
Yellowknife

Lake Athabasca
Fort McMurray

Churchill

Reindeer Lake
Lake Winnipeg
Flin Flon
La Ronge
Lynn Lake

CANADA

Winnipeg
Regina
Saskatoon

Fort Nelson

Horn Plateau
Norman Wells
Fort Good Hope
Mackenzie

MACKENZIE MOUNTAINS

Beaufort Sea

Point Barrow
Barrow

BROOKS RANGE

Fairbanks
ALASKA RANGE
Mount McKinley 6194
Anchorage

Yukon

COAST MOUNTAINS

Prince George
Finlay
Prince Rupert
Queen Charlotte Islands
Hecate Strait

VANCOUVER ISLAND
VANCOUVER
Victoria
Cape Flattery
SEATTLE
Spokane
PORTLAND

ROCKY MOUNTAINS

Calgary
Edmonton

Great Falls
Billings
Bismarck
Fargo

GREAT PLAINS

UNITED STATES

Duluth
St. Paul
MINNEAPOLIS
Des Moines
MILWAUKEE
CHICAGO
INDIANAPOLIS
Omaha

Missouri

Pierre

CASCADE RANGE
SIERRA NEVADA
Boise
Salt Lake City
Great Basin
Reno
SACRAMENTO
SAN FRANCISCO
Cape Mendocino

PACIFIC OCEAN

Gulf of Alaska
Kodiak Island
Kenai Peninsula

ALEUTIAN ISLANDS
Unalaska

Bristol Bay
Bethel
Nushagak
Nunivak Island
St. Matthew Island
St. Lawrence Island
Norton Sound
Nome
Seward Peninsula
Port Hope

Chukchi Sea

International Date Line

BERING SEA

Bering Strait
ČUKOTSKI POLUOSTROV
Uelen
Anadyr
Anadyrskij zaliv

Arctic Circle

RUSSIA

ostrov Vrangelja Island
ostrov Ajon
Kolyma

zaliv Sel'nova

POLUOSTROV KAMCATKA
SREDINNYJ CHREBET
ostrov Karaginski

25 24 23 22 21 20 19 18 17 16 15 14 13 12 11 10 9 8 7 6 5 4 3 2 1

Scale 1 : 25,000,000

Lambert Azimuthal Equal Area Projection

0 250 500 750 1000 1500 2000 2500 Kilometers

0 250 500 1000 1500 Miles

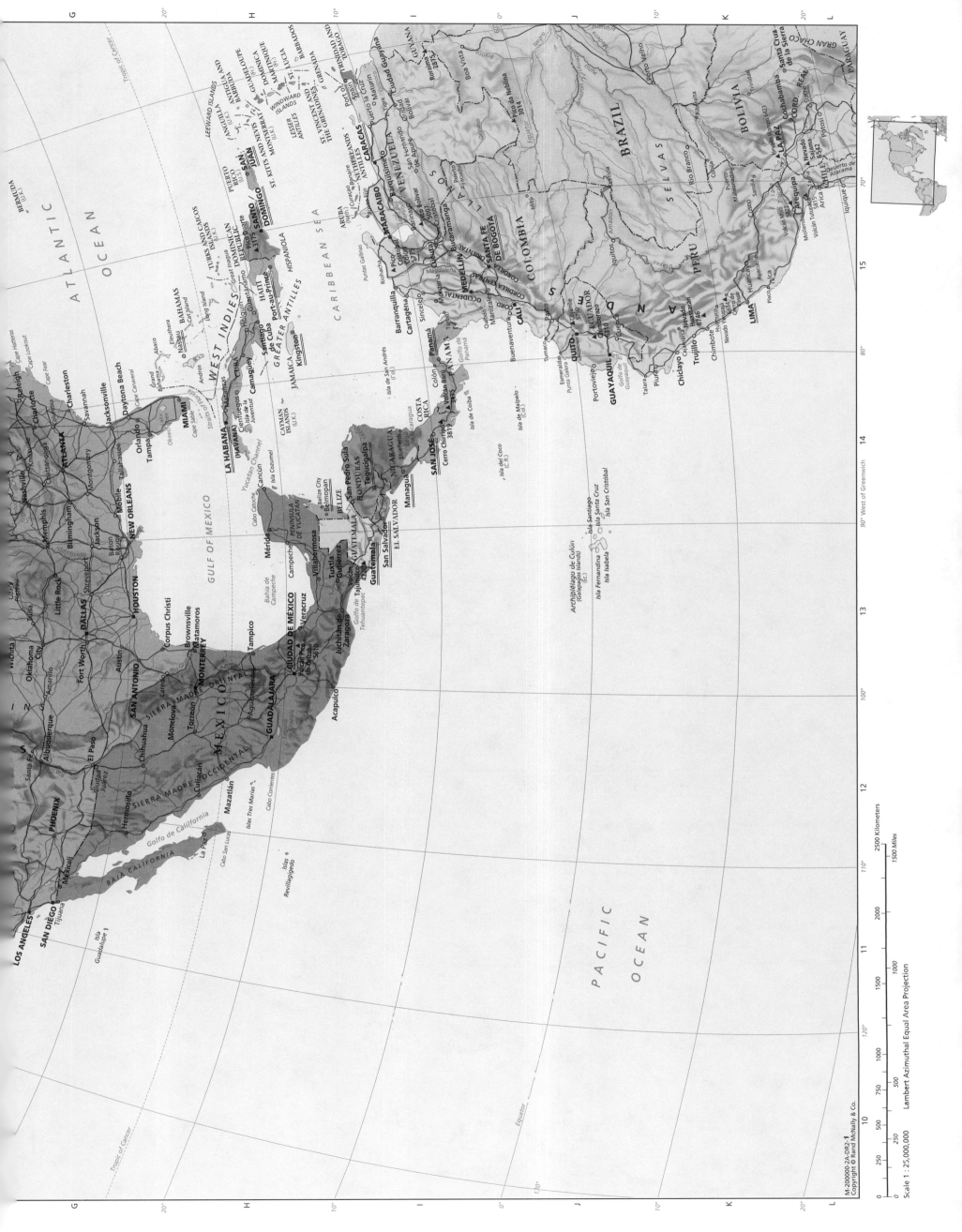

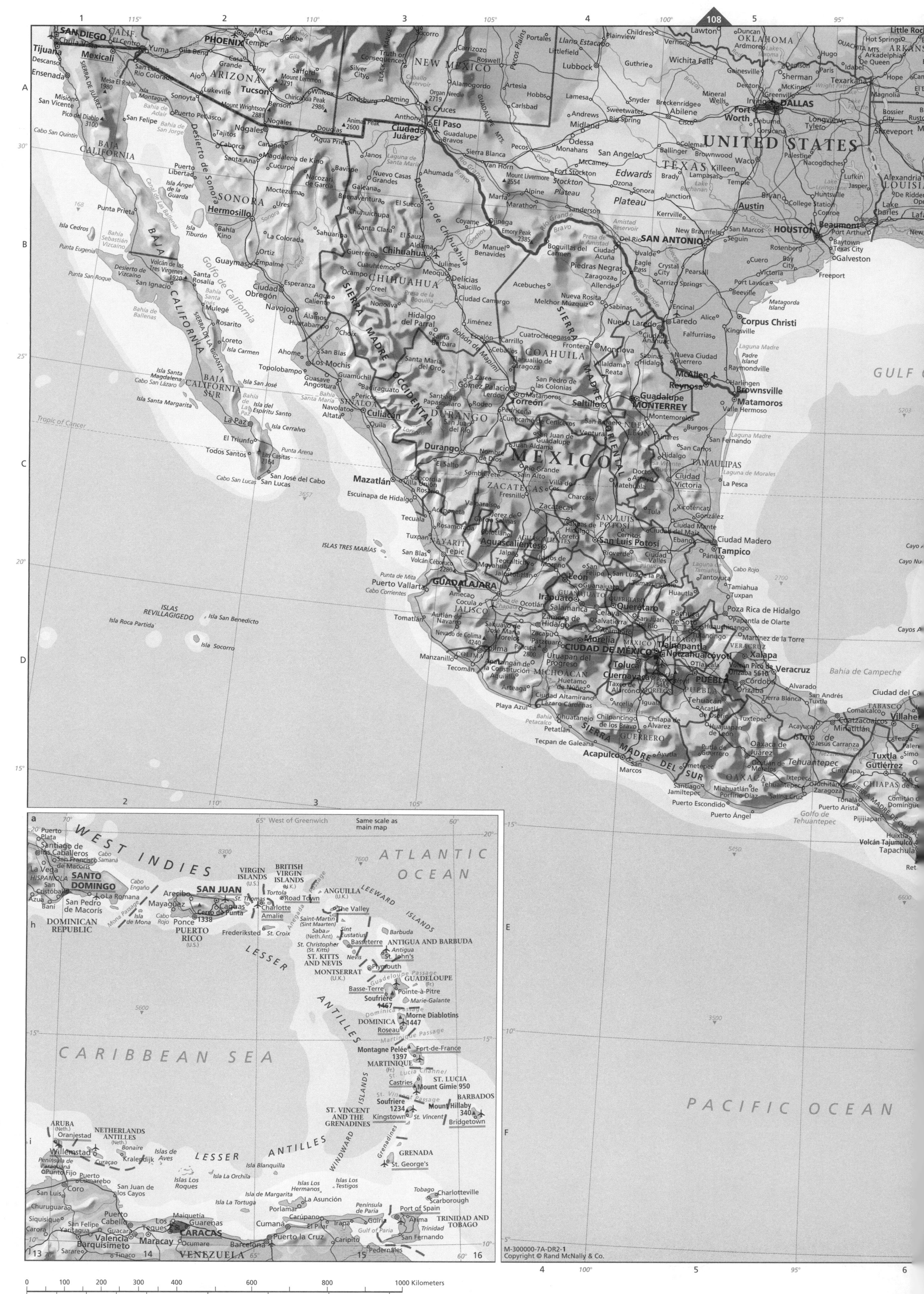

Meters / Feet
4000 / 13120
3000 / 9840
2000 / 6560
1000 / 3280
500 / 1640
200 / 656
Sea Level
200 / 656
2000 / 6560

0 100 200 300 400 600 800 1000 Kilometers
0 100 200 400 600 Miles
Scale 1 : 10,000,000 Lambert Conformal Conic Projection

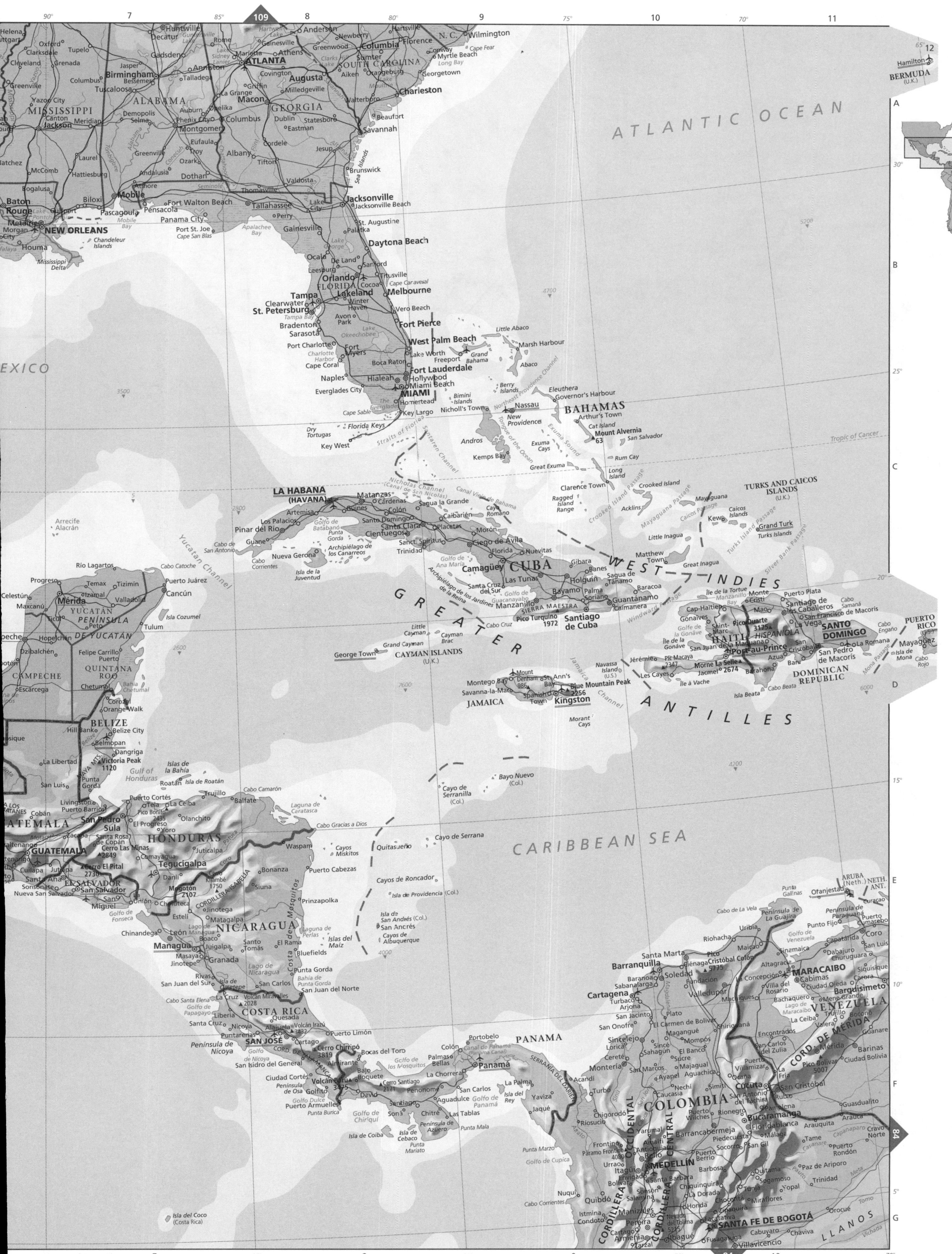

ATLANTIC OCEAN

Hamilton

109

7   85°   8   80°   9   75°   10   70°   11

Helena
Stuttgart

Cleveland
Clarksdale
Oxford
Tupelo

Greenville
Columbus

Grenada

Yazoo City
Canton

Jackson

Natchez
McComb

Bogalusa
Baton
Rouge

Metairie
New Orleans

Houma

Mississippi
Delta

MISSISSIPPI

Laurel
Hattiesburg

Biloxi
Pascagoula

Mobile

Huntsville
Decatur

Gadsden

Talladega

Tuscaloosa
Bessemer
Birmingham

Anniston

La Grange

Columbus
Phenix City

Eufaula

Montgomery

Greenville
Auburn
Opelika

Andalusia
Dothan

ALABAMA

Rome
Marietta
ATLANTA

Covington
Athens

Augusta

Macon
Milledgeville

Dublin
Statesboro

Eastman

GEORGIA

Cordele
Tifton

Albany

Thomasville

Valdosta

Anderson
Newberry
Greenwood
Columbia
Florence
N. C.
Wilmington

Hartwell
Lake

Sidney Lanier

Clarks Hill
Lake

SOUTH CAROLINA

Aiken
Sumter

Charleston

Beaufort

Savannah

Brunswick

Jesup

Conway
Myrtle Beach

Georgetown

Long Bay

Cape Fear

MEXICO

Celestún
Maxcanú

Mérida

Progreso
Temax
Tizimín

Río Lagartos

Valladolid

Campeche

Hopelchén

Dzibalchén

CAMPECHE

YUCATÁN
PENINSULA

DE YUCATÁN

Felipe Carrillo
Puerto

Tulum

QUINTANA
ROO

Isla Cozumel

Cabo Catoche
Puerto Juárez
Cancún

Chetumal

GUATEMALA

Coban

Cuilapa
GUATEMALA

Chiquimula

Santa Ana
Sonsonate
Nueva San Salvador

EL SALVADOR
San Salvador

San Miguel

BELIZE

Orange Walk

Corozal

Belize City

Belmopan

Dangriga

Victoria Peak
1120

Punta
Gorda

San Luis

Livingston
Puerto Barrios

Pico Bonito

San Pedro
Sula

El Progreso

Olanchito

Santa Rosa
de Copán

Cerro Las Minas
2849

Tegucigalpa
Comayagua

Juticalpa

HONDURAS

Islas de
la Bahía

Roatán
Isla de Roatán

Trujillo

Balfate

Cabo Camarón

Gulf of
Honduras

Arrecife
Alacrán

3500

3500

2800

2600

GREATER

WEST - INDIES

Little Abaco

Marsh Harbour

Abaco

Grand
Bahama

Freeport

Bimini
Islands

The
Everglades

Nicholl's Town

New
Providence

Nassau

Berry
Islands

Andros

Kemps Bay

BAHAMAS

Eleuthera
Governor's Harbour

Cat Island
Mount Alvernia
63

Arthur's Town

San Salvador

Rum Cay

Long
Island

Clarence Town

Exuma
Cays

Great Exuma

Crooked Island

Acklins

Ragged
Island
Range

Mayaguana

Caicos
Islands

TURKS AND CAICOS
ISLANDS
(U.K.)

Grand Turk
Turks Islands

Little Inagua

Great Inagua

Matthew
Town

Silver Bank Passage

Puerto Plata

Monte
Cristi

Cabo
Samaná

Santiago de
los Caballeros

San Francisco de Macorís
La Vega

SANTO
DOMINGO

Cabo
Engaño

La Romana
San Pedro
de Macorís

DOMINICAN
REPUBLIC

Isla de
Mona

PUERTO
RICO

Mayagüez

Cabo
Rojo

HISPANIOLA

HAITI

Cap-Haïtien

Gonaïves

Pic Duarte
3175

Île de la Tortue

Môle
Saint-Nicolas

Jérémie

Les Cayes

Pic Macaya
2347

Île de la
Gonâve

Port-au-Prince

Morne la Selle
2674

Jacmel

Île à Vache

San Juan de la
Maguana

Azua

Barahona

Isla Beata

Cabo Beata

6000

4200

Tropic of Cancer

20°

D

Key Largo

Cape Sable

Key West

Dry
Tortugas

Florida Keys

Straits of Florida

Nicholas Channel (Canal de San Nicolás)

LA HABANA
(HAVANA)

Artemisa

Los Palacios

Pinar del Río

Guane

Cabo de
San Antonio

Yucatán Channel

Nueva Gerona

Isla de la
Juventud

Matanzas
Cárdenas

Colón

Santo Domingo

Cienfuegos

Archipiélago de
los Canarreos

Sagua la Grande

Santa Clara

Placetas

Cabo
Corrientes

Golfo de
Batabanó

Punta
Gorda

Caibarién

Cayo
Romano

Morón

Sancti Spíritus

Trinidad

Ciego de Ávila

Florida

Golfo de
Ana María

Camagüey

CUBA

Nuevitas

Las Tunas

Gibara

Banes

Holguín

Bayamo

Palma
Soriano

Baracoa

Guantánamo

Caimanera

Sagua de
Tánamo

Sierra Maestra

Manzanillo

Archipiélago de los Jardines
de la Reina

Golfo de
Guacanayabo

Pico Turquino
1972

Santiago
de Cuba

Cabo Cruz

Golfo de
Batabanó

Little
Cayman

Grand Cayman

George Town

CAYMAN ISLANDS
(U.K.)

Cayman
Brac

Windward Passage

Navassa
Island
(U.S.)

Mona
Passage

Canal Viejo de Bahama

Santa Cruz
del Sur

Crooked Island Passage

Mayaguana Passage

Caicos Passage

Turks Island Passage

Kew

7600

4700

5200

C

B

Tampa

St. Petersburg
Clearwater

Bradenton

Sarasota

Port Charlotte

Cape Coral

Naples

Everglades City

FLORIDA

Orlando

Lakeland

Winter
Haven

Avon
Park

Lake
Okeechobee

West Palm Beach

Boca Raton

Fort Lauderdale

Hollywood
Miami Beach

MIAMI

Hialeah

Homestead

Fort
Myers

Charlotte
Harbor

Melbourne

Vero Beach

Fort Pierce

Titusville
Cocoa
Cape Canaveral

Ocala
De Land

Sanford

Leesburg

Gainesville

Palatka
St. Augustine

Daytona Beach

Jacksonville
Jacksonville Beach

Lake
City

Perry

Tallahassee

Panama City

Apalachee
Bay

Port St. Joe
Cape San Blas

Chandeleur
Islands

Fort Walton Beach
Pensacola

Jasper
Marianna

Seminole

3500

Little Abaco

Northwest Providence Channel

Nicholl's Town

Northeast Providence Channel

Tongue of the Ocean

Exuma Sound

GREATER

CARIBBEAN SEA

Cayo de
Serranilla
(Col.)

Bayo Nuevo
(Col.)

Cayo de Serrana

Quita Sueño

Cayos
de Miskitos

Cayos de Roncador

Isla de Providencia (Col.)

Isla de
San Andrés (Col.)
San Andrés

Cayos de
Albuquerque

ARUBA
(Neth.)

Oranjestad

NETH.
ANT.

Punta
Gallinas

Cabo de La Vela

Península de
La Guajira

Riohacha

Uribia

Maicao

Península de
Paraguaná

Punto Fijo

Coro

San Luis

Dabajuro

Golfo de
Venezuela

La Concepción

MARACAIBO

Cabimas

Ciudad Ojeda

Lago de
Maracaibo

VENEZUELA

Trujillo

Mérida

CORD. DE MÉRIDA

Pico Bolívar
5007

Barinas

Ciudad Bolivia

Guasdualito

Arauca

Tame

Cravo
Norte

Capanaparo

LLANOS

Vichada

Meta

El
Nula

San Cristóbal

Cúcuta

San Antonio
del Táchira

Bucaramanga

Arauquita

84

70°

84

E

F

G

San José

Cartagena

Barranquilla

Santa Marta

Ciénaga

Pico Cristóbal Colón
5775

Soledad

Sabanalarga

Fundación

Valledupar

Turbaco

Arjona

San Jacinto

El Carmen de Bolívar

Magangué

Mompós

San Marcos

Sincelejo

Corozal

Lorica

Cereté

Montería

El Banco

Aguachica

Ocaña

Ayapel

Caucasia

Nechí

Segovia

Tarazá

Turbo

Acandí

Riosucio

Frontino

Urrao

Quibdó

Istmina

Condoto

Nuquí

Cabo Corrientes

MEDELLÍN

Itagüí

Sonsón

La Ceja

La Dorada

Puerto
Berrío

Barbosa

Chiquinquirá

Zipaquirá

SANTA FE DE BOGOTÁ

Girardot

Honda

Manizales

Pereira

Armenia

Ibagué

Neiva

COLOMBIA

CORDILLERA OCCIDENTAL

CORDILLERA CENTRAL

Nevado del Tolima
5215

Facatativá

Villavicencio

Orocué

Yopal

Sogamoso

Duitama

Tunja

Chiquinquirá

Puerto
López

Acacías

Puerto
Rico

ANTILLES

Montego Bay

Savanna-la-Mar

JAMAICA

Spanish
Town

Kingston

Blue Mountain Peak
2256

Mount
Denham
886

Mandeville
St. Ann's
Bay

Morant
Cays

NICARAGUA

Managua

Masaya

Granada

Jinotepe

Rivas

San Juan del Sur

León

Chinandega

Corinto

Estelí

Matagalpa

Jinotega

Ocotal

Somoto

Madriz

Mogotón
2107

Lago de
Nicaragua

Lago de
Managua

Juigalpa

Santo
Tomás

Boaco

Camoapa

El Rama

Bluefields

Punta Gorda

Bahía de
Punta Gorda

San Juan del Norte

Waspán

Siuna

Bonanza

Prinzapolka

Puerto Cabezas

Isla del
Maíz

Islas del
Maíz

CORDILLERA ISABELIA

MOSQUITOS

Bocay

Río Coco

4000

COSTA RICA

San José

Puntarenas

Liberia

Santa Cruz

Península de
Nicoya

Golfo de
Nicoya

Nicoya

Cabo Santa Elena

Golfo de
Papagayo

Volcán Miravalles
2028

Volcán Irazú
3432

Cerro Chirripó
3819

Quesada

Puerto Limón

San Isidro del General

Ciudad Cortés

Península
de Osa

Puerto Armuelles

Punta Burica

Golfo
de Osa

Golfo Dulce

Volcán Barú
3475

David

Bajo
Boquete

PANAMA

Santiago

Aguadulce

Penonomé

Chitré

Las Tablas

Península
de Azuero

Punta Mala

Sons

Isla del Coco
(Costa Rica)

Cabo Gracias a Dios

Laguna de
Caratasca

Danlí

Comayagua

CORDILLERA

Colón

Portobelo

Bocas del Toro

Palmas
Bellas

La Chorrera

Panamá

Golfo de
Panamá

Isla de
San José

Isla del
Rey

La Palma

Yaviza

Jaqué

SERRANÍA DEL DARIÉN

Punta Marzo

Golfo de Cupica

Canal de Panamá (Panama Canal)

San Carlos

Cañazas

Golfo de
los Mosquitos

Golfo
Dulce

Golfo de
Chiriquí

Isla de Coiba

Isla de
Cébaco

Punta
Mariato

2600

7600

4200

4700

30°

25°

Tropic of Cancer

20°

15°

10°

5°

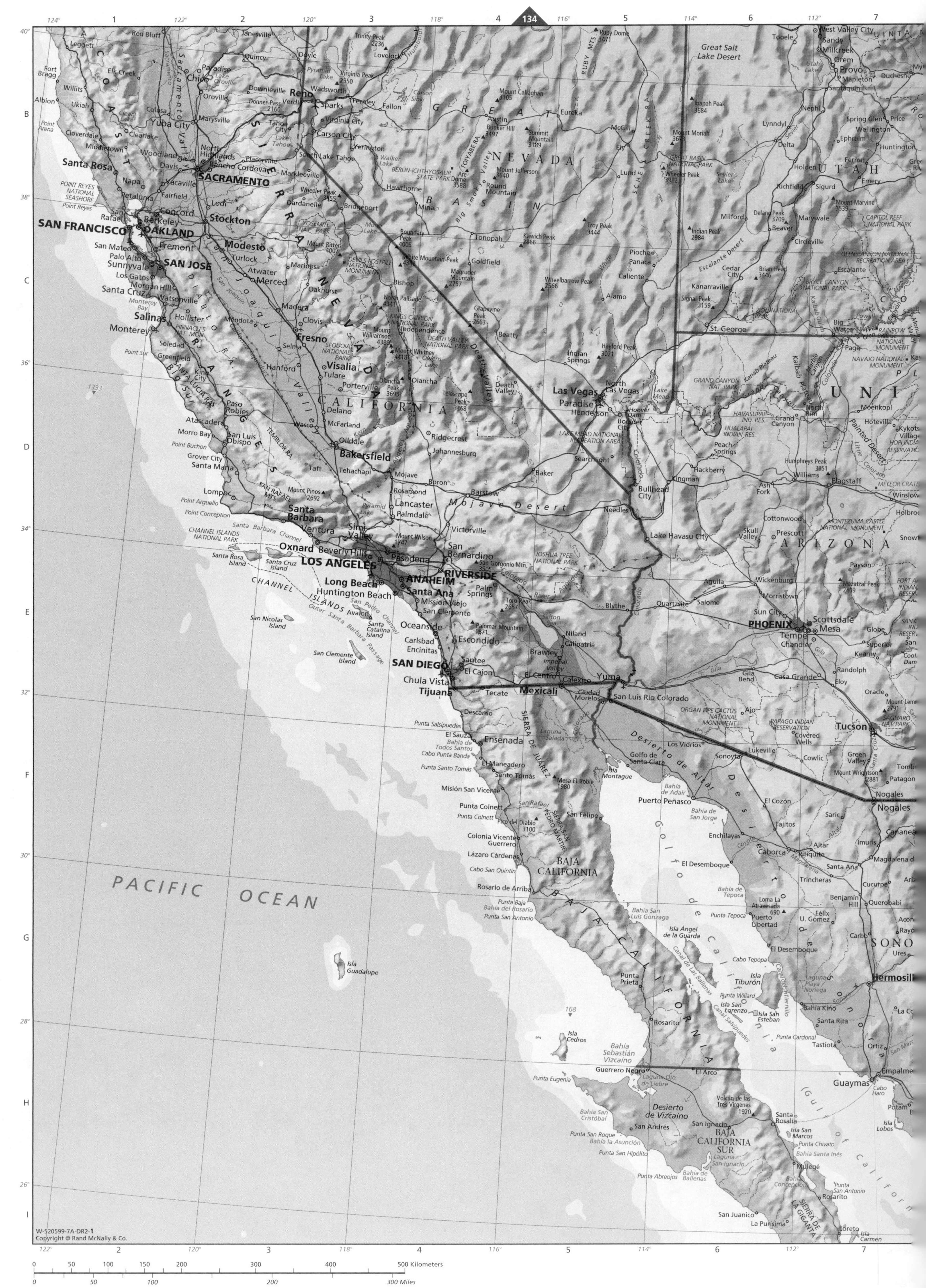

134

Meters
Feet

4000
13120

3000
9840

2000
6560

1000
3280

500
1640

200
656

Sea Level

200
656

2000
6560

W-520599-7A-DR2-1
Copyright © Rand McNally & Co.

0   50   100   150   200   300   400   500 Kilometers

0   50   100   200   300 Miles

Scale 1 : 5,000,000   Lambert Conformal Conic Projection

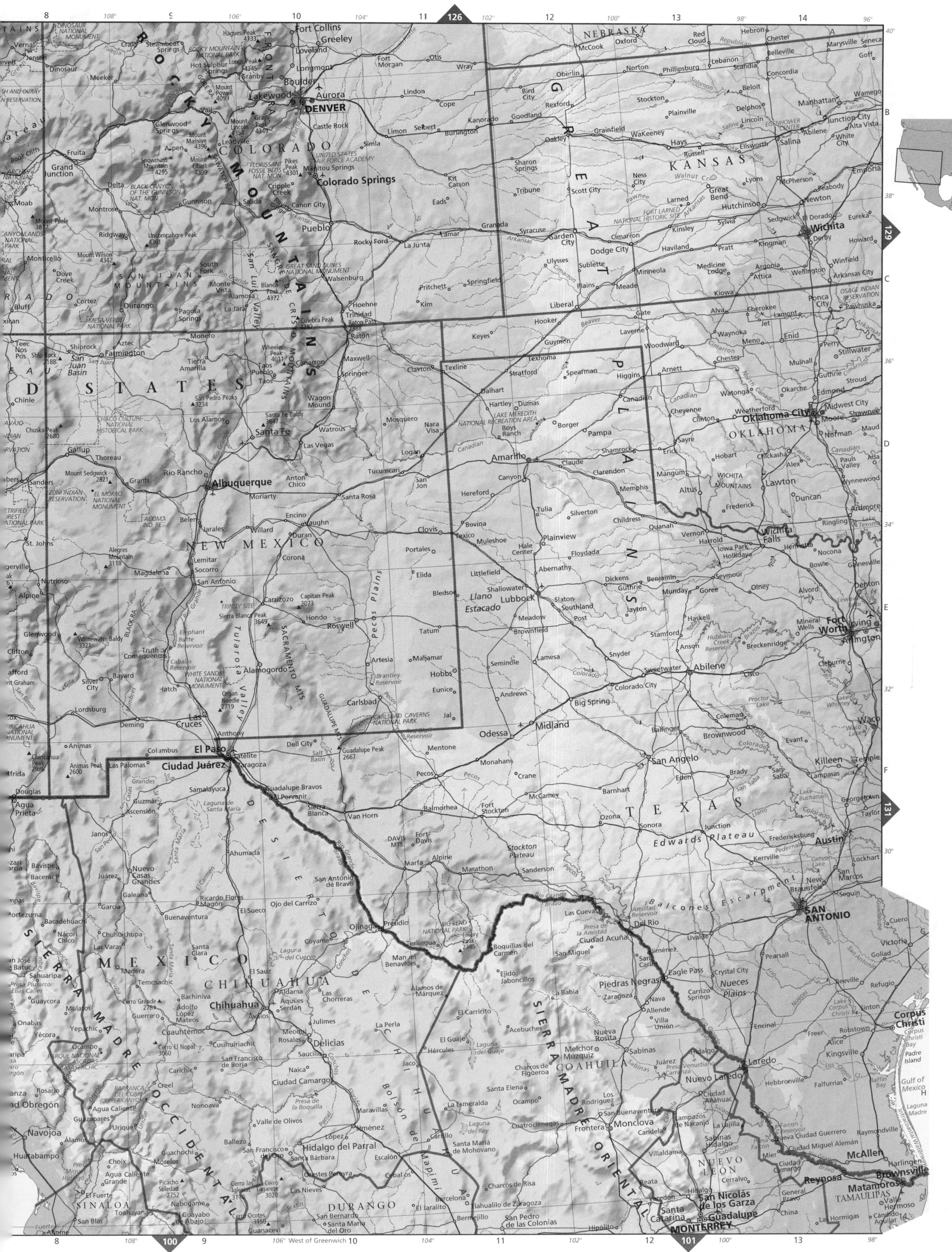
ROCKY MOUNTAINS
COLORADO
KANSAS
NEBRASKA
GREAT PLAINS
OKLAHOMA
NEW MEXICO
TEXAS
MEXICO
CHIHUAHUA
COAHUILA
NUEVO LEÓN
DURANGO
SINALOA
TAMAULIPAS
DESIERTO DE CHIHUAHUA
SIERRA MADRE OCCIDENTAL
SIERRA MADRE ORIENTAL
SAN JUAN MOUNTAINS
SANGRE DE CRISTO MOUNTAINS
SACRAMENTO MTS
GUADALUPE MTS
WICHITA MOUNTAINS
Llano Estacado
Pecos Plains
Edwards Plateau
Balcones Escarpment
Bolsón de Mapimí
Fort Collins
Greeley
Boulder
Aurora
DENVER
Lakewood
Colorado Springs
Pueblo
Grand Junction
Durango
Farmington
Santa Fe
Albuquerque
Las Cruces
El Paso
Ciudad Juárez
Chihuahua
Amarillo
Lubbock
Midland
Odessa
Abilene
San Angelo
Oklahoma City
Wichita
Wichita Falls
Fort Worth
Arlington
Waco
Austin
SAN ANTONIO
Laredo
Nuevo Laredo
Corpus Christi
McAllen
Reynosa
Brownsville
Matamoros
Monclova
MONTERREY
San Nicolás de los Garza
Guadalupe
Delicias
Hidalgo del Parral
Ciudad Obregón
Navojoa
Gulf of Mexico
West of Greenwich

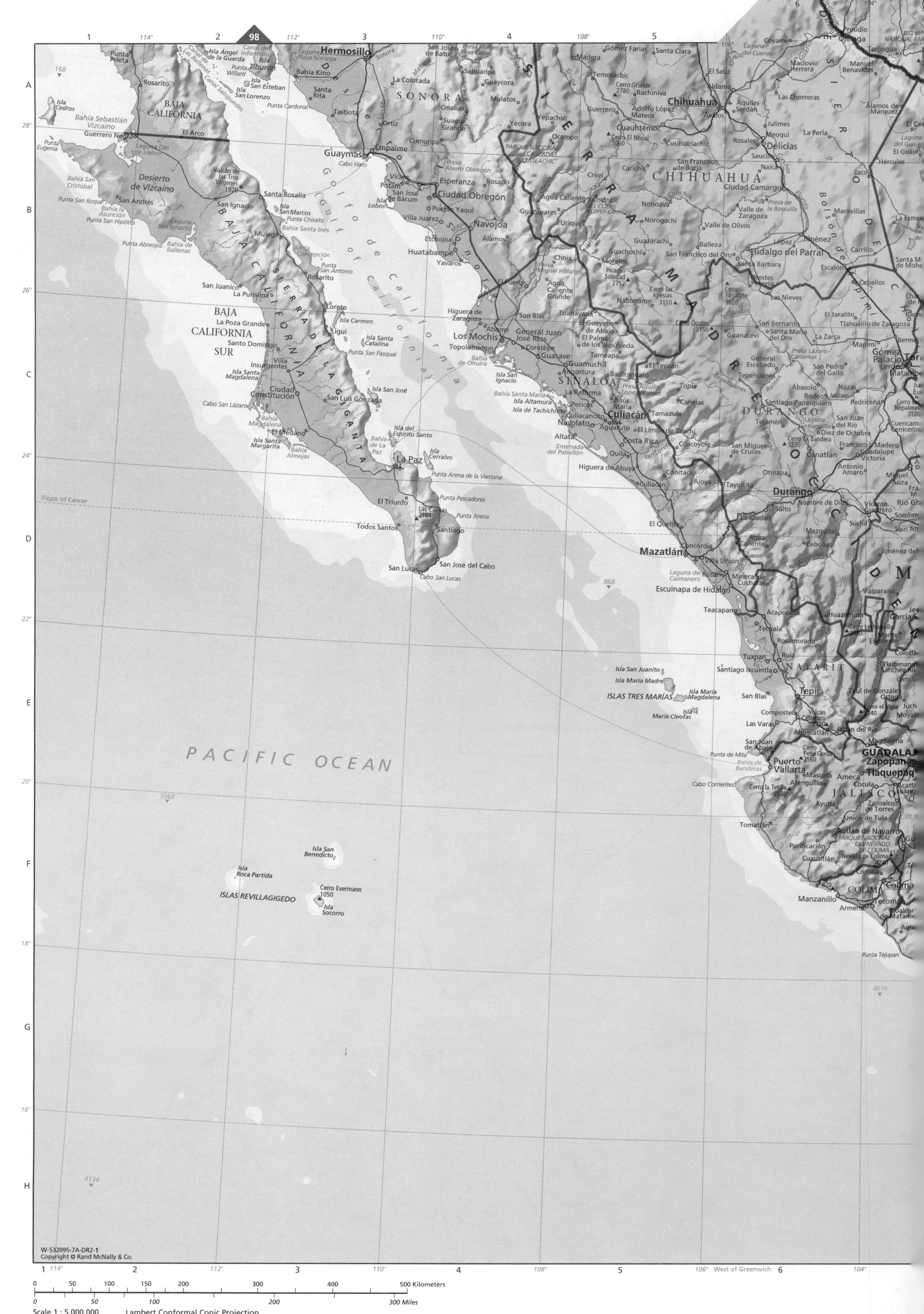

PACIFIC OCEAN

W-532095-7A-DR2-1
Copyright © Rand McNally & Co.

Scale 1 : 5,000,000   Lambert Conformal Conic Projection

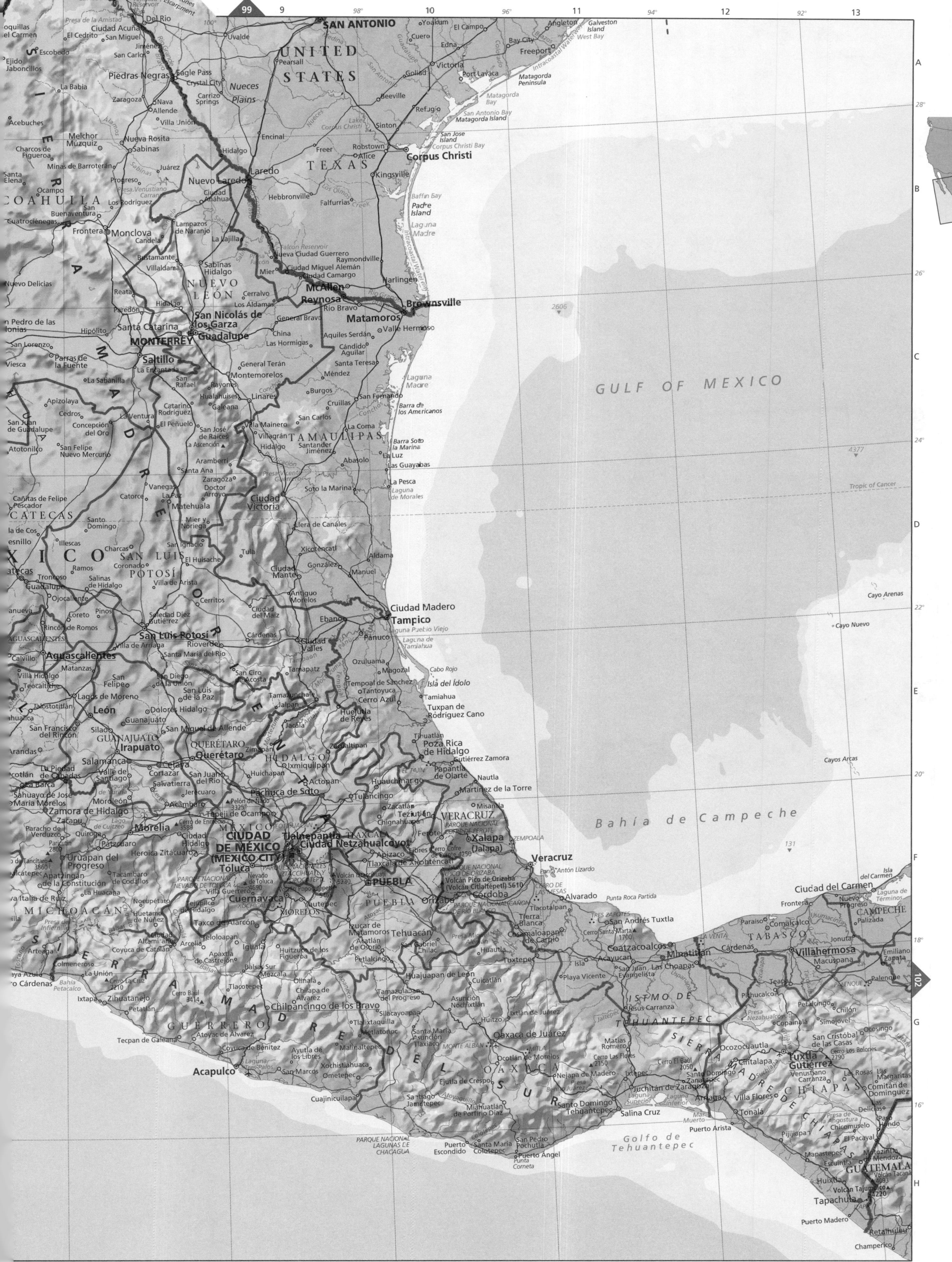
UNITED STATES
TEXAS
SAN ANTONIO
Corpus Christi
Laredo
Brownsville
McAllen
Matamoros
Reynosa
MONTERREY
Saltillo
Monclova
COAHUILA
NUEVO LEÓN
TAMAULIPAS
SAN LUIS POTOSÍ
San Luis Potosí
Aguascalientes
León
Irapuato
Querétaro
Morelia
CIUDAD DE MÉXICO (MEXICO CITY)
Toluca
Cuernavaca
PUEBLA
Tlalnepantla
Ciudad Netzahualcoyotl
Ciudad Victoria
Ciudad Madero
Tampico
Poza Rica de Hidalgo
Xalapa (Jalapa)
Veracruz
Acapulco
Oaxaca de Juarez
Chilpancingo de los Bravo
Coatzacoalcos
Minatitlán
Villahermosa
Ciudad del Carmen
Tuxtla Gutiérrez
Tapachula
GUATEMALA
GULF OF MEXICO
Bahía de Campeche
Golfo de Tehuantepec
SIERRA MADRE ORIENTAL
SIERRA MADRE DEL SUR
SIERRA MADRE DE CHIAPAS
VERACRUZ
HIDALGO
PUEBLA
GUERRERO
OAXACA
MICHOACÁN
TABASCO
CHIAPAS
CAMPECHE
ISTMO DE TEHUANTEPEC
Tropic of Cancer
99
102

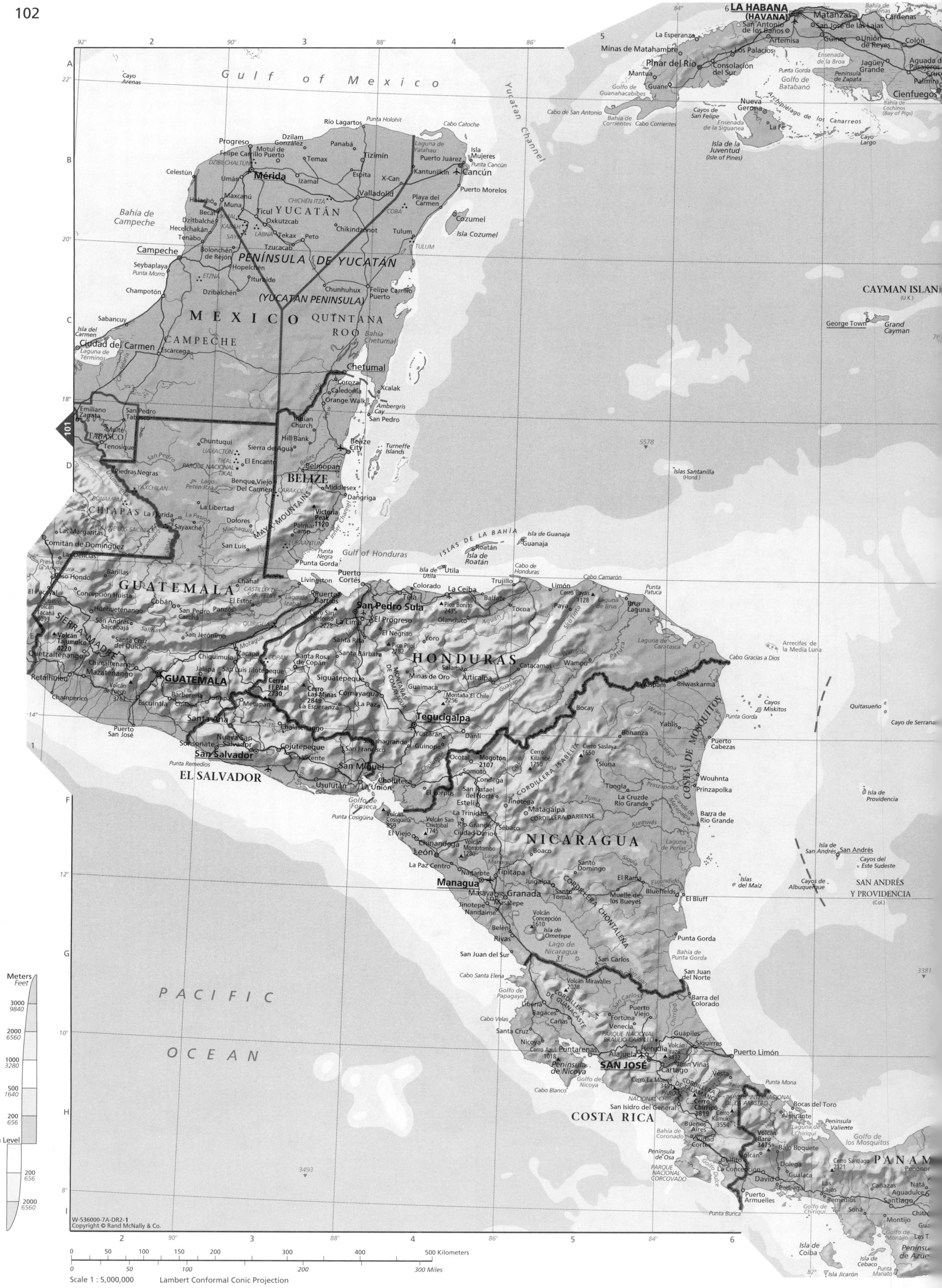

Gulf of Mexico

PACIFIC OCEAN

PENÍNSULA DE YUCATÁN
(YUCATAN PENINSULA)

MEXICO

QUINTANA ROO

CAMPECHE

YUCATÁN

CHIAPAS

TABASCO

BELIZE

GUATEMALA

HONDURAS

EL SALVADOR

NICARAGUA

COSTA RICA

PANAMÁ

LA HABANA (HAVANA)

CAYMAN ISLANDS (U.K.)

SAN ANDRÉS Y PROVIDENCIA (Col.)

Gulf of Honduras

Yucatan Channel

Mérida

Cancún

Campeche

Chetumal

Belize City

Belmopan

San Pedro Sula

Tegucigalpa

San Salvador

Managua

San José

Scale 1:5,000,000   Lambert Conformal Conic Projection

Meters / Feet
3000 / 9840
2000 / 6560
1000 / 3280
500 / 1640
200 / 656
Sea Level
200 / 656
2000 / 6560

W-536000-7A-DR2-1
Copyright © Rand McNally & Co.

0 50 100 150 200 300 400 500 Kilometers
0 50 100 200 300 Miles

CUBA
8   78°   9   76°   Deadman's   Clarence   74°   Samana
Canal de San Nicolás   Cay   Long   Town   Cay
Canal Viejo de Bahama   Island   11

Sagua
la Grande
Caibarién   Cayo Coco   Cay Lobos
Yaguajay   Bahía de Perros   Cayo Romano
Placetas   Moron
Sancti   Ciego   Cayo Guajaba
Spiritus   de Avila   Cayo Sabinal
Trinidad   Camagüey   Puerto   Nuevitas
Golfo de   Minas   Padre
Ana María   Vertientes   Puerto   Antilla
Holguín
Las Tunas
Manzanillo   Bayamo   Palma   Sagua
Campechuela   Jiguaní   Soriano   de Tánamo   Baracoa
Niquero   SIERRA   San   Guantánamo
Cabo Cruz   Marea de   MAESTRA   Luis   Caimanera
Portillo   Pico Turquino   Santiago   GUANTANAMO BAY
1972   de Cuba   NAVAL STATION (U.S.)

BAHAMAS

WEST

INDIES

Long
Island
Cape Verde   Crooked
Island

Ragged   Bight of
Island   Acklins   Acklins
Salina Point

Matthew
Town   Great
Inagua

Mayaguana

TURKS AND
CAICOS ISLANDS
(U.K.)
Kew
Providenciales   North
Caicos   Middle
Caicos
West   CAICOS   East
Caicos   ISLANDS   Caicos
Little   Grand Turk
Inagua   TURKS
Palacca Point   ISLANDS
Lake   Seal Cays
Rosa

ATLANTIC

OCEAN

22°

A

72°   12   70°   13

Mayaguana Passage

Caicos Passage

Silver Bank Passage

Mouchoir Passage

Windward Passage

HISPANIOLA
Monte
Cristi   Cabo Isabela
Cap-à-Foux   Cap-Haïtien   Manzanillo   Puerto Plata   Cabo Macorís
Port-de-Paix   Limbé   Bay   Pico Diego   Cabo Francés Viejo
Île de la Tortue   SANS   Fort-Liberté   de Ocampo   Moca   Nagua   Bahía
SOUCI   Dajabón   Mao   4749   Escocesa
Cap à Foux   CITADELLE   Santiago de los   San Francisco   Samaná
Golfe de   Gonaïves   Desdunes   Caballeros   de Macorís   Sabana   Bahía de Samaná
la Gonâve   Pico Duarte   La Vega   de la Mar   Miches
Île de la   Morne Bonhomme   3175   Bonao   Hato Mayor del Rey   El Seibo
Gonâve   1786   Comendador   Alto Bandera   Cabo Engaño
Saint-Marc   Canal de Saint-Marc   2630   SANTO   Higüey
HAITI   San Juan   DOMINGO   Bahía
Jérémie   Canal du Sud   de la Maguana   San   de Yuma
Grande   Port-au-Prince   Neiba   Cristóbal   Isla
Cayemite   Petit-Goâve   Pétion-Ville   Azua   San Pedro   Saona
Anse-d'Hainault   Pic Macaya   Léogâne   Lago   de Macorís
Pointe   2347   Morne   Enriquillo   Barahona   La Romana
Fantasio   Aquin   La Selle   Bahía
Coteaux   Jacmel   2674   Bahía   Palenque   Mona Passage
Les Cayes   Pedernales   de Ocoa   Punta
Île à Vache   Cabo Falso   Enriquillo   DOMINICAN
Pointe   Cabo Rojo   Isla Beata   REPUBLIC
Abacou   Cabo Beata
Navassa Island
(U.S.)

GREATER

ANTILLES

22°

B

C

18°

JAMAICA
Falmouth   Ocho   Port
Montego Bay   Saint Ann's   Rios   Maria   Port
Bay   Antonio
South Negril Point   Denham   986
Savanna-la-Mar   Mount   Kingston   Blue Mountain Peak
Mandeville   Spanish   2256
Town   Morant   Morant Point
Portland   Bay
Point   Portland
Bight
Portland Point   2184   Morant
Cays

Pedro
Cays

JAMAICA

Jamaica Channel

D

CARIBBEAN   SEA

16°

E

Cayo de Serranilla
(Col.)   Bajo Nuevo
(Col.)

os de Roncador

LESSER   ANTILLES

F

14°

5102

ARUBA
(Neth.)
Oranjestad   NETHERLANDS
ANTILLES
(Neth.) Bonaire
Curaçao   Willemstad

12°

Punta Gallinas
Bahía Honda   Bahía
Puerto Bolívar   Portete   Punta Espada
Cabo de La Vela   Península   Cabo San Román   Punto   Pueblo
de La Guajira   Fijo   Nuevo   Puerto
Uribia   Golfo de   Punta   Península   Cumarebo   Punta
Ensenada   Venezuela   Cardón   de Paraguaná   Zamuro
Riohacha   de Calabozo   Golfete   Puerto
Maicao   Paraguaipoa   San Rafael   de Coro   La Vela
Santa Marta   LA GUAJIRA   Sinamaica   Coro   de Coro
Barranquilla   Pico   Barrancas   Albania   Capatárida   San Luis   Cabure
Ciénaga   Cristóbal   Fonseca   Dabajuro   Churuguara
ATLÁNTICO   Colón   Mene de Mauroa   FALCON
Soledad   5775   Villanueva   MARACAIBO   Altagracia
Baranoa   Malambo   Santa   La
Cartagena   Sabanalarga   Valledupar   Rita   Siquisique   PARQUE   YARACUY
Islas del   Manatí   del   La   Cabimas   NACIONAL
Rosario   Turbaco   Fundación   Cesar   Paz   Santa   Cerro Cocuy   ARUBI   San Felipe
Arjona   El Piñón   Villa del   Tía Juana   1990   VENEZUELA
Islas de   María La Baja   Calamar   Rosario   Ciudad Ojeda   Carora   LARA   Barquisimeto
San Bernardo   San   Pedraza   Agustín   Machiques   Lago de   Quíbor
San Onofre   Jacinto   Codazzi   Maracaibo   La Ceiba   10°
Sincelejo   El Carmen   Chinú   El Banco   ZULIA   Sabana de Mendoza   PORTUGUESA
SUCRE   de Bolívar   CESAR   Bobures   Trujillo   Acarigua
Istmo de Panamá   Golfo de   MAGDALENA   San   Valera   TRUJILLO   Piritu
(Isthmus of Panama)   Morrosquillo   Tolú   Cerro Mu   Carlos   Guanare
Punta   Toluviejo   2610   del Zulia   Boconó   Bocono   PARQUE NAC
Manzanillo   Nombre   Coveñas   La Gloria   Encontrados   San Pedro   Mérida
bobelo   de Dios   SERRANÍA DE SAN BLAS   Sincé   Ciénaga   Timotes
Golfo de San Blas   Magangué   de Oro   Petróleo   Mucuchíes   88
rrera   Punta Mosquito   Sampués   Aguachica   Ocaña   Tovar   Barinitas
Panamá   Mansucum   Cereté   San   Gamarra   CÓRDOBA   Pico Bolívar   Santa
Chepo   Sinú   Marcos   El Carmen   NORTE DE   5002   Rosa
Bahía de Panamá   SERRAN   Cabo   Planeta   Majagual   SANTANDER   La Grita   Dolores   MÉRIDA
San Carlos   Tiburón   Punta   Rica   Achí   Ocaña   Libertad   BARINAS
San Miguel   Caribana   ANTIOQUIA   Tierralta   Ayapel   Nechí   COLOMBIA   Táchira   Ciudad
ARCHIPIÉLAGO   Acandí   Tierralta   2000   San Juan   de Nutrias
DE LAS PERLAS   Isla del   Gari   Caucasia   Cúcuta   Santa
Rey   Golfo de   Montelíbano   ANTIOQUIA   San Antonio del Táchira   Bárbara
Isla   San Miguel   Yaviza   Simití   Rubio   Palmarito
San José   El Real de   Turbo   San Cristóbal   LLANOS
Golfo de Panamá   Santa María   Apartadó   PARQUE NACIONAL DARIEN   APURE

G

87

H

8°

I

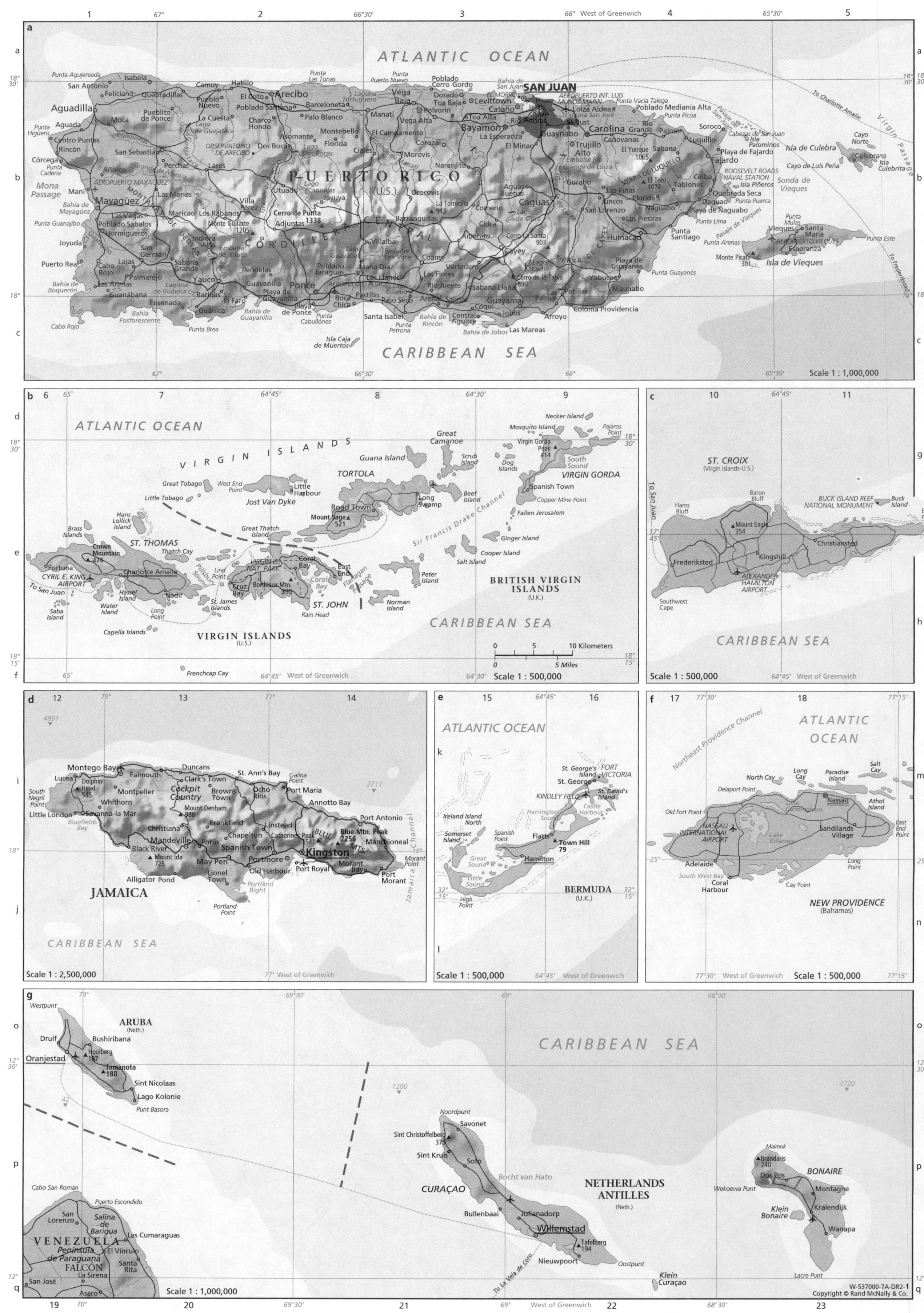
ATLANTIC OCEAN
CARIBBEAN SEA
PUERTO RICO
(U.S.)
CORDILLERA CENTRAL
SAN JUAN
Aguadilla
Arecibo
Mayagüez
Ponce
Bayamón
Caguas
Carolina
Guaynabo
Humacao
Fajardo
Cayey
Guayama
Yauco
Utuado
Isla de Culebra
Isla de Vieques
Mona Passage
Virgin Passage
Scale 1 : 1,000,000
VIRGIN ISLANDS
TORTOLA
Road Town
Jost Van Dyke
VIRGIN GORDA
Spanish Town
Anegada
ST. THOMAS
Charlotte Amalie
ST. JOHN
Cruz Bay
Coral Bay
Sir Francis Drake Channel
BRITISH VIRGIN ISLANDS
(U.K.)
VIRGIN ISLANDS
(U.S.)
Scale 1 : 500,000
0 5 10 Kilometers
0 5 Miles
ST. CROIX
(Virgin Islands-U.S.)
Christiansted
Frederiksted
Kingshill
BUCK ISLAND REEF NATIONAL MONUMENT
ALEXANDER HAMILTON AIRPORT
CARIBBEAN SEA
Scale 1 : 500,000
JAMAICA
Montego Bay
Kingston
Spanish Town
Mandeville
May Pen
Ocho Rios
St. Ann's Bay
Port Antonio
Port Maria
Lucea
Savanna-la-Mar
Black River
Port Royal
Morant Bay
Blue Mtn. Peak 2256
BLUE MTS.
Cockpit Country
Jamaica Channel
CARIBBEAN SEA
Scale 1 : 2,500,000
ATLANTIC OCEAN
BERMUDA
(U.K.)
Hamilton
St. George's
St. David's Island
Somerset Island
Ireland Island North
Town Hill 79
KINDLEY FIELD
FORT VICTORIA
Scale 1 : 500,000
ATLANTIC OCEAN
Northeast Providence Channel
NEW PROVIDENCE
(Bahamas)
Nassau
NASSAU INTERNATIONAL AIRPORT
Adelaide
Coral Harbour
Sandilands Village
Lake Killarney
Scale 1 : 500,000
CARIBBEAN SEA
ARUBA
(Neth.)
Oranjestad
Sint Nicolaas
Jamanota 188
Hooiberg 167
CURAÇAO
Willemstad
Sint Christoffelberg 372
Tafelberg 194
Klein Curaçao
NETHERLANDS ANTILLES
(Neth.)
BONAIRE
Kralendijk
Klein Bonaire
Brandaris 240
VENEZUELA
Península de Paraguaná
FALCÓN
Scale 1 : 1,000,000
W-537000-7A-DR2-1
Copyright © Rand McNally & Co.

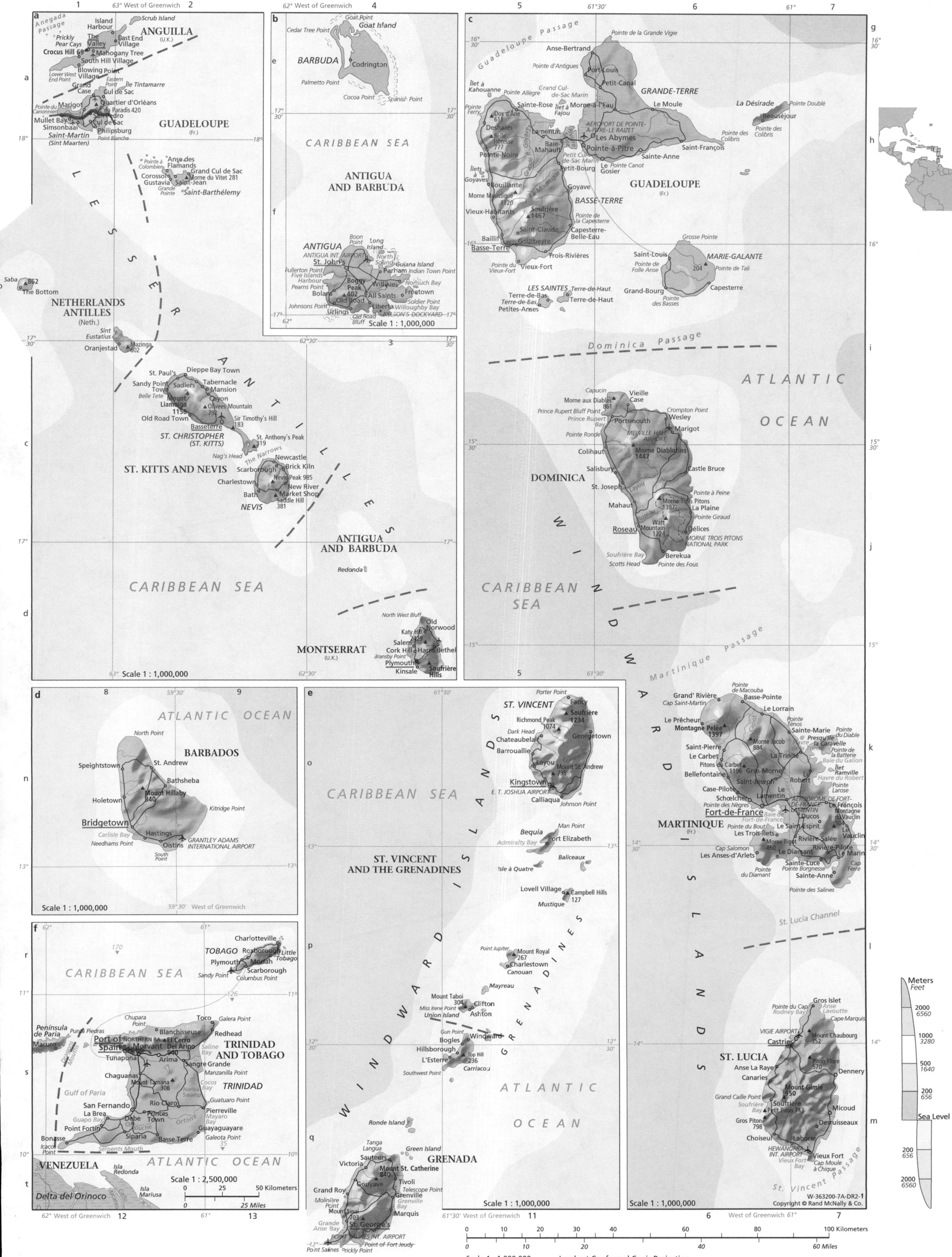

a

63° West of Greenwich   2

Anegada Passage
Scrub Island
Island Harbour
Prickly Pear Cays
ANGUILLA
(U.K.)
Crocus Hill 69
The Valley
East End Village
South Hill Village
Mahogany Tree
Blowing Point
Lower West End Point
Eastern Point
Grand Case
Île Tintamarre
Quartier d'Orléans
Pointe du Canonnier
Marigot
Pic du Paradis 420
Pedro
GUADELOUPE
(Fr.)
Mullet Bay
Cul de Sac
Simsonbaai
Philipsburg
Saint-Martin
(Sint Maarten)
Point Blanche

18°

Pointe à Colombier
Anse des Flamands
Grand Cul de Sac
Corossol
Morne du Vitet 281
Gustavia
Saint-Jean
Grande Pointe
°**Saint-Barthélemy**

b
Saba 862
The Bottom

NETHERLANDS ANTILLES
(Neth.)

17°30'

Sint Eustatius
Oranjestad
Mazinga 602

c

St. Paul's
Dieppe Bay Town
Sandy Point Town
Sadlers
Tabernacle
Mansion
Belle Tete
Mount Liamuiga 1156
Ottleys
Olivees Mountain 791
Old Road Town
Basseterre
Sir Timothy's Hill 183
ST. CHRISTOPHER (ST. KITTS)
Nag's Head
St. Anthony's Peak 319
The Narrows
Newcastle
Brick Kiln
ST. KITTS AND NEVIS
Scarborough
Nevis Peak 985
Charlestown
New River
Bath
Market Shop
NEVIS
Saddle Hill 381

17°

CARIBBEAN SEA

d

Redonda

ANTIGUA AND BARBUDA

North West Bluff
Old Norwood
Katy Hill
Salem
Cork Hill
Harris
Bethel
Bransby Point
Plymouth
MONTSERRAT
(U.K.)
Soufrière Hills
Kinsale

Scale 1 : 1,000,000

---

b   62° West of Greenwich   4

Cedar Tree Point
Goat Point
Goat Island
BARBUDA
Codrington

e
Palmetto Point
Cocoa Point
Spanish Point

17°30'

CARIBBEAN SEA

ANTIGUA AND BARBUDA

f

Boon Point
Long Island
ANTIGUA
ANTIGUA INT. AIRPORT
North Sound
St. John's
Guiana Island
Fullerton Point
Five Islands Harbour
Parham
Indian Town Point
Pearns Point
Nonsuch Bay
Boggy Peak 402
Freetown
Bolans
All Saints
Liberta
Soldier Point
Willoughby Bay
Johnsons Point
Urlings
Old Road
NELSON'S DOCKYARD
Old Road Bluff

Scale 1 : 1,000,000

---

c   5   61°30'   6   61°   7

g
Guadeloupe Passage
Pointe de la Grande Vigie
Anse-Bertrand
Pointe d'Antigues
Port-Louis
Îlet à Kahouanne
Pointe Allègre
Sainte-Rose
Petit-Canal
Grand Cul-de-Sac Marin
Îlet à Morne-à-l'Eau
Fajou
GRANDE-TERRE
Le Moule
La Désirade
Pointe Doublé
Pointe Ferry
Dos d'Âne
Beauséjour
Deshaies
AÉROPORT DE POINTE-À-PITRE-LE RAIZET
Les Abymes
Pointe des Colibris
Belle Hôtesse
Baie-Mahault
Pointe-à-Pitre
Sainte-Anne
Saint-François
Pointe-Noire
Petit-Bourg
Le Pointe Canot
Gosier
GUADELOUPE
(Fr.)
Îlets à Goyaves
Goyave
Morne Mistique 720
La Soufrière
BASSE-TERRE
Vieux-Habitants
Soufrière 1467
Saint-Claude
Capesterre-Belle-Eau
Baillif
Goubeyre
Grosse Pointe
Basse-Terre
Pointe de la Capesterre
Saint-Louis
MARIE-GALANTE
Pointe du Vieux-Fort
Vieux-Fort
Trois-Rivières
Pointe de Folle Anse
204
Pointe de Tali
LES SAINTES
Grand-Bourg
Capesterre
Terre-de-Bas
Terre-de-Haut
Pointe des Basses
Terre-de-Bas
Petites-Anses
Terre-de-Haut

16°30'

16°

h

i
Dominica Passage

ATLANTIC OCEAN

Capucin
Vieille Case
Morne aux Diables 861
Prince Rupert Bluff Point
Portsmouth
Crompton Point
Wesley
Prince Rupert Bay
Marigot
Pointe Ronde
MELVILLE HALL AIRPORT
Colihaut
Morne Diablotins 1447
Castle Bruce
Salisbury
St. Joseph
DOMINICA
Mahaut
Layou
Morne Trois Pitons 1387
La Plaine
Pointe à Peine
Roseau
Watt Mountain 1224
Pointe Giraud
Délices
MORNE TROIS PITONS NATIONAL PARK
Soufrière Bay
Berekua
Scotts Head
Pointe des Fous

15°30'

15°

j

CARIBBEAN SEA

Martinique Passage

---

d   8   59°30'   9

ATLANTIC OCEAN

BARBADOS

North Point
n
Speightstown
St. Andrew
Bathsheba
Holetown
Mount Hillaby 340
Bridgetown
Carlisle Bay
Hastings
Needhams Point
Oistins
GRANTLEY ADAMS INTERNATIONAL AIRPORT
Kitridge Point
South Point

13°

Scale 1 : 1,000,000   59°30'   West of Greenwich

---

f   62°   61°

Charlotteville
r   170
TOBAGO
Roxborough
Plymouth
Moriah
Little Tobago
Scarborough
CARIBBEAN SEA
Sandy Point
Columbus Point

11°

Chupara Point
Toco
Galera Point
Peninsula de Paria
Punta Piedras
Blanchisseuse
Redhead
Macuro
El Cerro Del Aripo 940
Port of Spain
NORTHERN RA
Morvant
TRINIDAD AND TOBAGO
Tunapuna
Arima
Chaguanas
Sangre Grande
Manzanilla Point
TRINIDAD
Mount Tamana 308
s
Gulf of Paria
San Fernando
Rio Claro
Guataro Point
La Brea
Debe
Pierreville
Mayaro
Point Fortin
Princes Town
Guayaguayare
Galeota Point
Bonasse
Siparia
Basse Terre
Icacos Point
Guapo Bay
Serpents Mouth
VENEZUELA
Isla Redonda

10°

Isla Mariusa
t
Delta del Orinoco

Scale 1 : 2,500,000
0   25   50 Kilometers
0   25 Miles

---

e   61°30'

Porter Point
ST. VINCENT
Fancy
Soufrière 1234
Richmond Peak 1074
Georgetown
Dark Head
o
Chateaubelair
Barrouallie
Layou
Mount St. Andrew 735
Kingstown
E. T. JOSHUA AIRPORT
Calliaqua
Johnson Point

CARIBBEAN SEA

Man Point
Bequia
Port Elizabeth
Admiralty Bay
ST. VINCENT AND THE GRENADINES
Isle à Quatre
Baleaux

13°

Lovell Village
Campbell Hills 127
Mustique

p

Point Jupiter
Mount Royal 267
Charlestown
Canouan
Mayreau
Mount Taboi 304
Clifton
Miss Irene Point
Union Island
Ashton
Gun Point
Bogles
Windward
GRENADINES
Hillsborough
Top Hill 236
L'Esterre
Carriacou

12°

Southwest Point

ATLANTIC OCEAN

Ronde Island

q
Tanga Langua
Green Island
Sauteurs
Victoria
Mount St. Catherine 840
Tivoli
GRENADA
Grand Roy
Gouyave
Telescope Point
Molinière Point
Grenville Bay
Mount Sinai 703
Grenville
Marquis
St. George's
POINT SALINES INT. AIRPORT
Point Salines
Prickly Point
Point of Fort Jeudy

61°30'   West of Greenwich   11   6
Scale 1 : 1,000,000

---

c   61°30'

Grand' Rivière
Pointe de Macouba
Cap Saint-Martin
Basse-Pointe
Le Prêcheur
Le Lorrain
Montagne Pelée 1397
Sainte-Marie
Pointe du Diable
Saint-Pierre
Morne Jacob 884
Presqu'île de la Caravelle
Le Carbet
La Trinité
Pointe de la Batterie
Pitons du Carbet 1196
Gros-Morne
Baie du Galion
k
Bellefontaine
Îlet Ramville
Saint-Joseph
Robert
Havre du Robert
Case-Pilote
Schoelcher
Lamentin
Pointe Larose
Fort-de-France
AÉRODROME DE FORT-DE-FRANCE LAMENTIN
Le François
Pointe du Bout
Ducos
Montagne du Vauclin
Les Trois-Îlets
Le Saint-Esprit
MARTINIQUE
(Fr.)
Rivière-Salée
Vauclin
Morne Bigot 460
Le Diament
Rivière-Pilote
Le Marin
Cap Salomon
Les Anses-d'Arlets
Sainte-Anne
Pointe Borgnesse
Sainte-Luce
Cap Ferré
Pointe du Diamant
Pointe des Salines

14°30'

14°

l
St. Lucia Channel

Gros Islet
Pointe du Cap
Anse Lavoutte
Rodney Bay
VIGIE AIRPORT
Cape Marquis
Castries
Mount Chaubourg 352
ST. LUCIA
Anse La Raye
Canaries
Dennery
Grand Caille Point
Mount Gimie 950
m
Soufrière
Soufrière
Gros Piton 798
Petit Piton 743
Micoud
Choiseul
Laborie
HEWANORRA INT. AIRPORT
Vieux Fort
Cap Moule à Chique

14°

St. Vincent Passage

Scale 1 : 1,000,000

Meters / Feet
2000 / 6560
1000 / 3280
500 / 1640
200 / 656
Sea Level
200 / 656
2000 / 6560

W-363200-7A-DR2-1
Copyright © Rand McNally & Co.

0   10   20   30   40   50   60   100 Kilometers
0   10   20   30   40   50   60 Miles
Scale 1 : 1,000,000   Lambert Conformal Conic Projection

Meters
Feet

4000
13120

3000
9840

2000
6560

1000
3280

500
1640

200
656

Sea Level

200
656

2000
6560

0 100 200 300 400 600 800 1000 Kilometers

0 100 200 400 600 Miles

Scale 1 : 10,000,000 Lambert Conformal Conic Projection

140

108

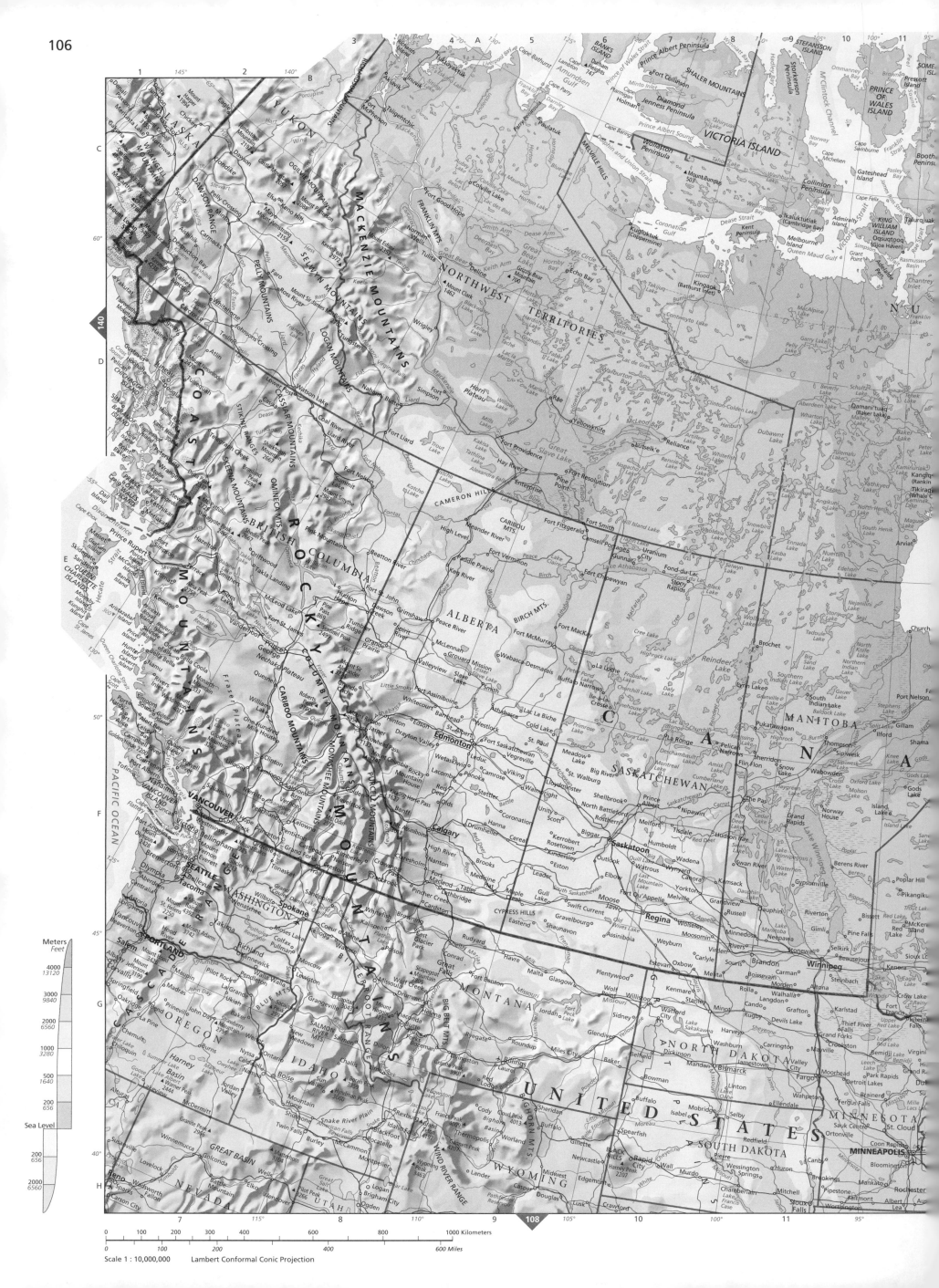

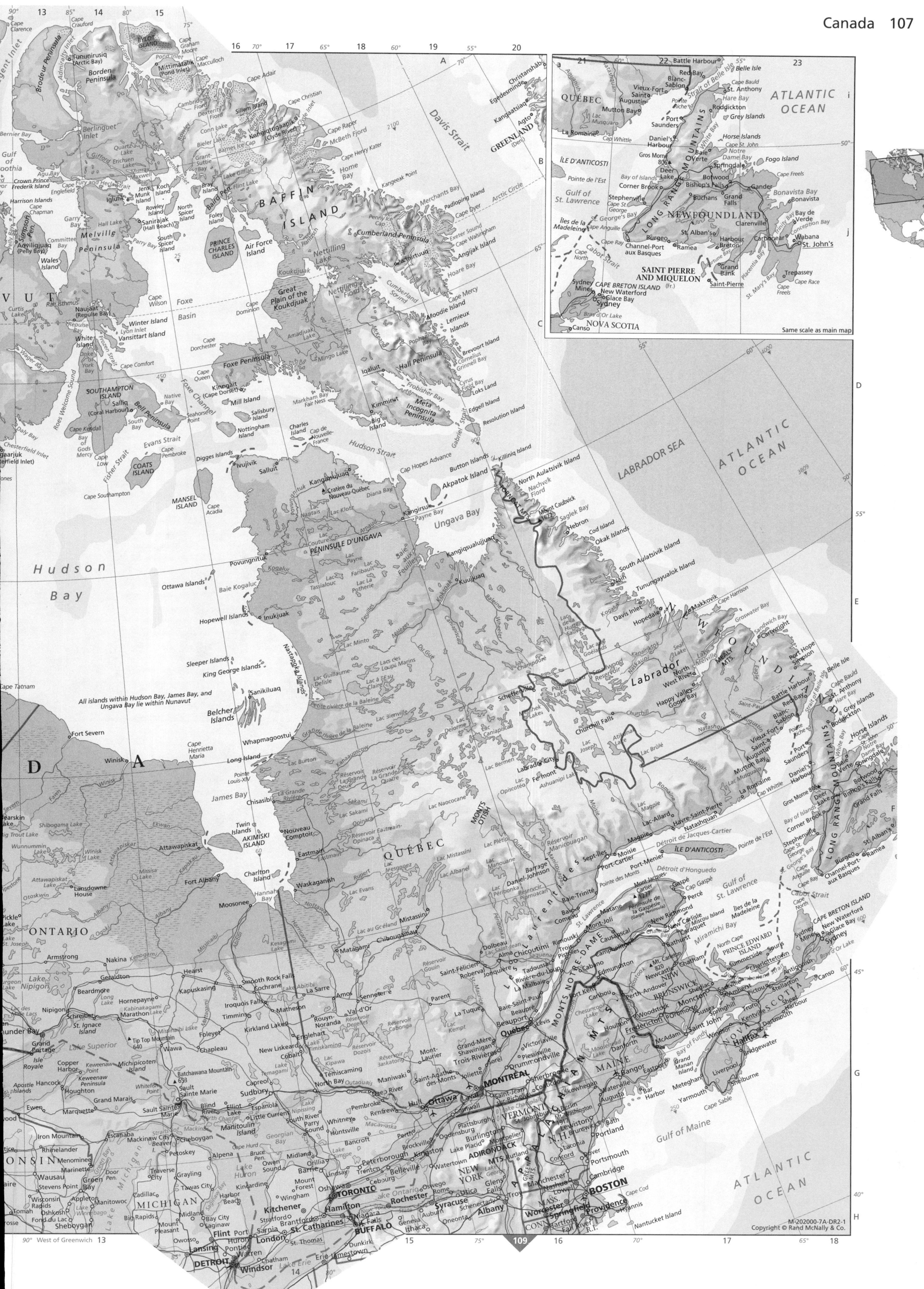
Same scale as main map
All islands within Hudson Bay, James Bay, and Ungava Bay lie within Nunavut
M-202000-7A-DR2-1
Copyright © Rand McNally & Co.
90° West of Greenwich

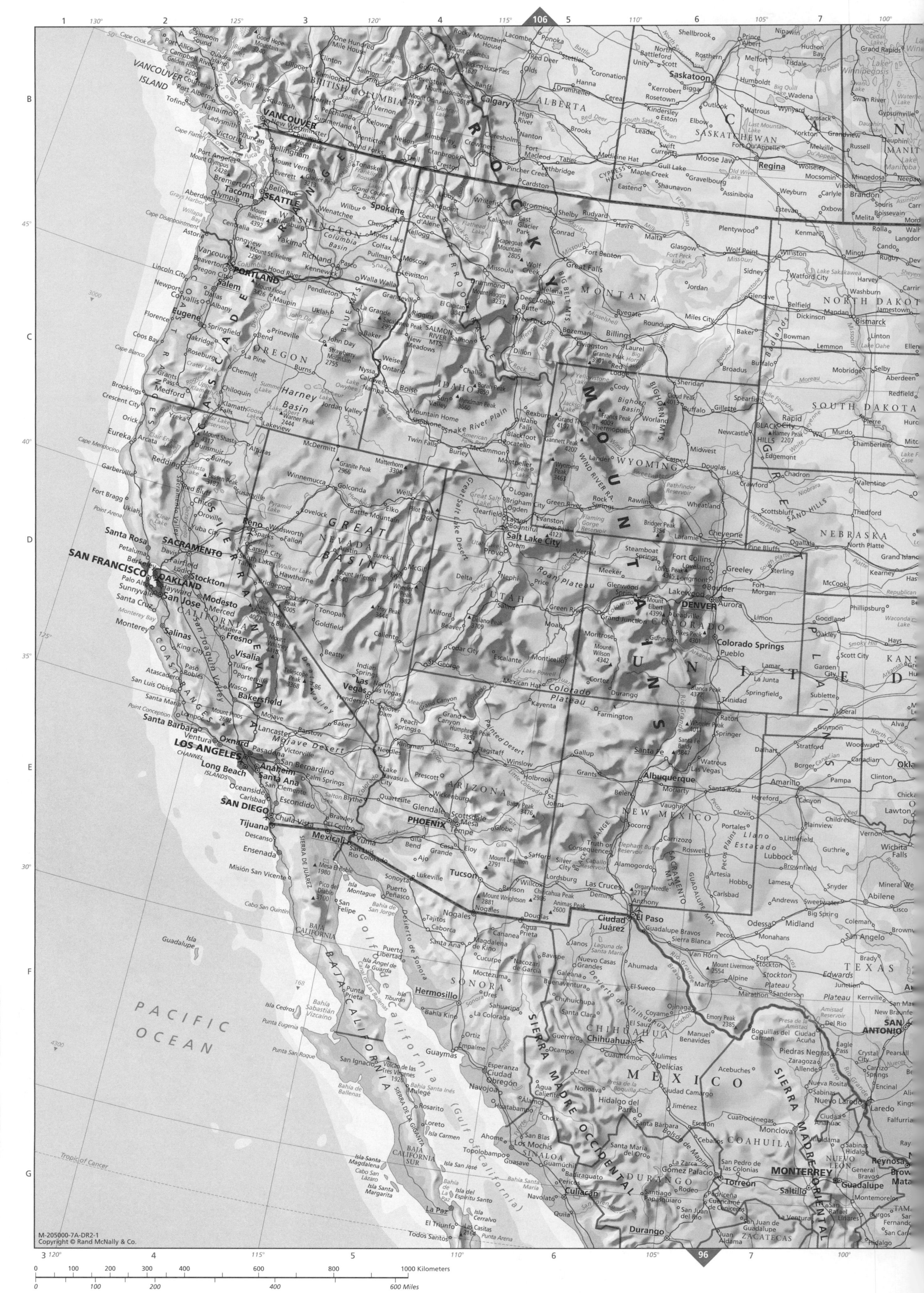

PACIFIC
OCEAN

Meters
Feet
3000
9840

2000
6560

1000
3280

500
1640

200
656

Sea Level

200
656

2000
6560

M-205000-7A-DR2-1
Copyright © Rand McNally & Co.

0   100   200   300   400   600 Miles
0   100   200   300   400   600   800   1000 Kilometers

Scale 1 : 10,000,000   Lambert Conformal Conic Projection

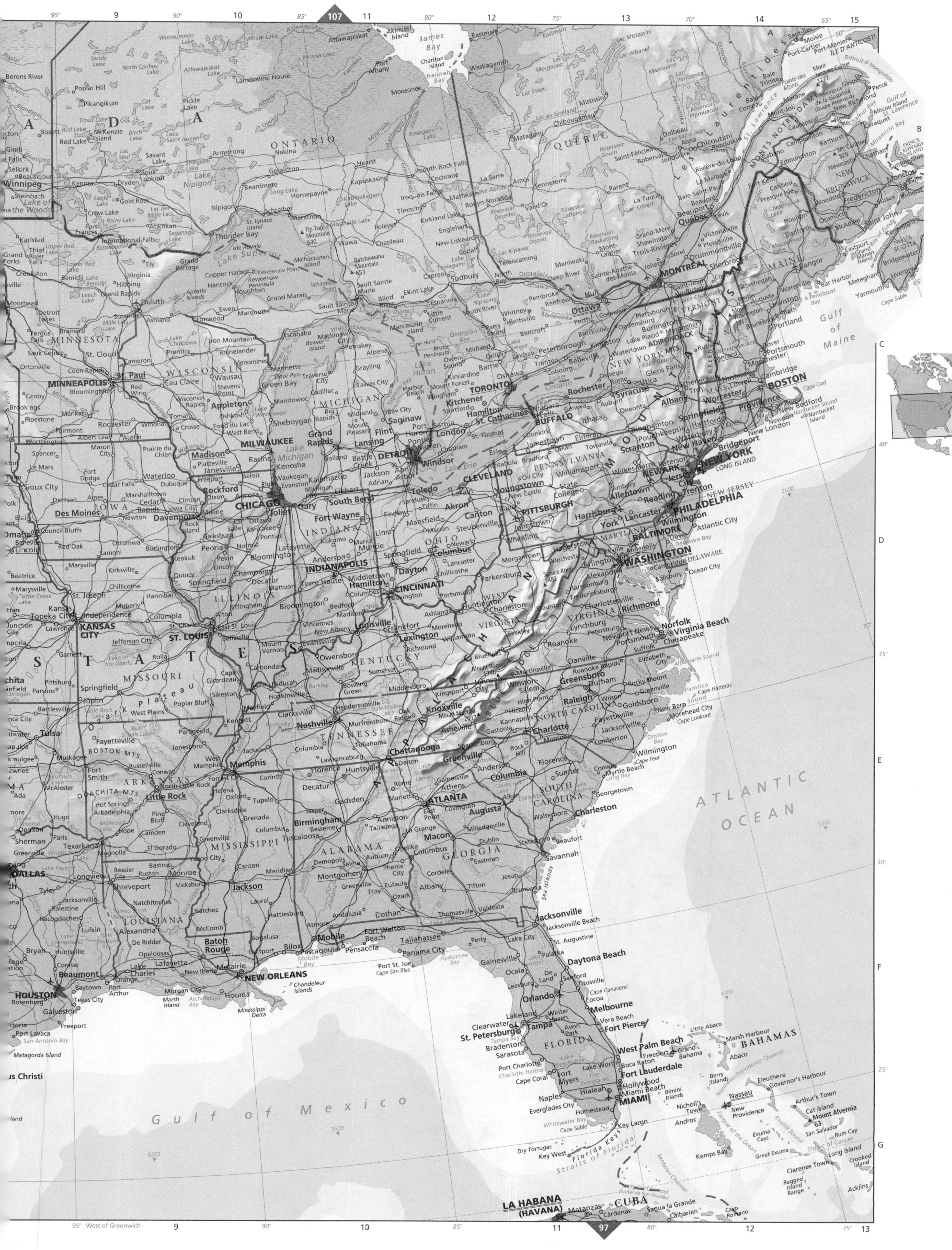

107
97
ONTARIO
QUÉBEC
MINNESOTA
WISCONSIN
MICHIGAN
IOWA
ILLINOIS
INDIANA
OHIO
PENNSYLVANIA
NEW YORK
NEW JERSEY
MARYLAND
DELAWARE
WEST VIRGINIA
VIRGINIA
KENTUCKY
MISSOURI
TENNESSEE
NORTH CAROLINA
SOUTH CAROLINA
GEORGIA
ALABAMA
MISSISSIPPI
LOUISIANA
FLORIDA
MAINE
VERMONT
NEW BRUNSWICK
NOVA SCOTIA
BAHAMAS
CUBA
James Bay
Lake Superior
Lake Michigan
Lake Huron
Lake Erie
Lake Ontario
Gulf of Maine
ATLANTIC OCEAN
Gulf of Mexico
Straits of Florida
Winnipeg
Thunder Bay
Duluth
MINNEAPOLIS
St. Paul
Green Bay
MILWAUKEE
CHICAGO
Des Moines
Madison
Grand Rapids
DETROIT
Windsor
TORONTO
Hamilton
MONTREAL
Ottawa
Québec
BUFFALO
Rochester
Syracuse
Albany
BOSTON
Providence
Hartford
New Haven
NEW YORK
NEWARK
PHILADELPHIA
BALTIMORE
WASHINGTON
PITTSBURGH
CLEVELAND
Toledo
Columbus
CINCINNATI
INDIANAPOLIS
Louisville
ST. LOUIS
KANSAS CITY
Nashville
Knoxville
Memphis
Little Rock
Chattanooga
ATLANTA
Birmingham
Charlotte
Raleigh
Norfolk
Virginia Beach
Richmond
Charleston
Savannah
Jacksonville
Jackson
Mobile
NEW ORLEANS
Baton Rouge
HOUSTON
DALLAS
Tampa
St. Petersburg
Orlando
Miami
West Palm Beach
Fort Lauderdale
Key West
Nassau
LA HABANA (HAVANA)
West of Greenwich

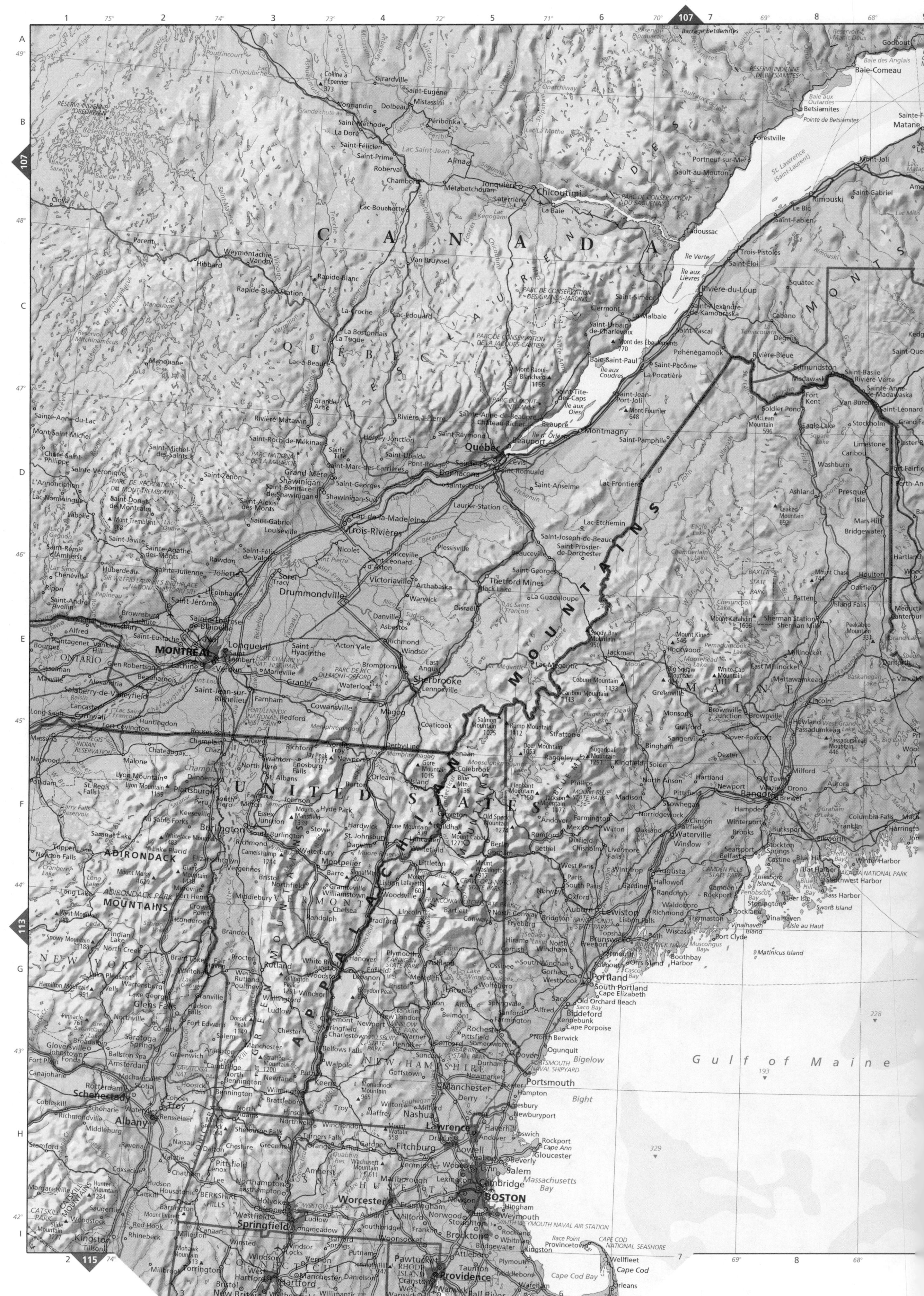

C A N A D A
Q U É B E C
L A U R E N T I D E S
M O N T S
N O T R E - D A M E
O N T A R I O
U N I T E D S T A T E S
M A I N E
V E R M O N T
N E W H A M P S H I R E
N E W Y O R K
APPALACHIAN
MOUNTAINS
ADIRONDACK
MOUNTAINS
WHITE MOUNTAINS
GREEN MOUNTAINS
CATSKILL MOUNTAINS
G u l f o f M a i n e
Bigelow
Bight
Cape Cod Bay
Massachusetts Bay
St. Lawrence (Saint-Laurent)
MONTRÉAL
Québec
Lac Saint-Jean
Chicoutimi
Jonquière
La Baie
Alma
Roberval
Saint-Félicien
Dolbeau
Mistassini
Girardville
Chibougamau
Baie-Comeau
Godbout
Forestville
Betsiamites
Matane
Mont-Joli
Rimouski
Saint-Gabriel
Le Bic
Saint-Fabien
Trois-Pistoles
Tadoussac
Rivière-du-Loup
La Malbaie
Saint-Siméon
Clermont
Baie-Saint-Paul
Montmagny
Lévis
Beauport
Sainte-Anne-de-Beaupré
La Pocatière
Saint-Pascal
Pohénégamook
Dégelis
Cabano
Edmundston
Madawaska
Fort Kent
Trois-Rivières
Shawinigan
Grand-Mère
La Tuque
Louiseville
Victoriaville
Drummondville
Thetford Mines
Plessisville
Sherbrooke
Granby
Magog
Coaticook
Lac-Mégantic
Saint-Georges
Saint-Jérôme
Longueuil
Lachine
Verdun
Saint-Jean-sur-Richelieu
Salaberry-de-Valleyfield
Cornwall
Hawkesbury
Rawdon
Joliette
Sorel
Mont Tremblant
Parent
Clova
Réservoir Gouin
Burlington
Montpelier
Barre
Rutland
St. Albans
St. Johnsbury
Newport
Middlebury
Brattleboro
Bennington
Plattsburgh
Malone
Massena
Lake Placid
Saranac Lake
Glens Falls
Saratoga Springs
Amsterdam
Schenectady
Albany
Troy
Kingston
Gloversville
Hudson
Pittsfield
North Adams
Springfield
Worcester
Fitchburg
Lowell
Lawrence
Haverhill
Salem
Cambridge
BOSTON
Brockton
Plymouth
Providence
Pawtucket
Hartford
New Britain
Keene
Concord
Manchester
Nashua
Portsmouth
Dover
Laconia
Lebanon
Hanover
Berlin
Portland
South Portland
Biddeford
Lewiston
Auburn
Augusta
Waterville
Skowhegan
Bangor
Brewer
Orono
Old Town
Millinocket
Houlton
Presque Isle
Caribou
Ellsworth
Bar Harbor
Rockland
Camden
Belfast
Bath
Brunswick
Farmington
Rumford
Gloucester
Provincetown
Cape Cod
Mount Katahdin 1606
Mount Washington 1917

Scale 1 : 2,500,000   Lambert Conformal Conic Projection

W-520298-7A-DR2-1
Copyright © Rand McNally & Co.

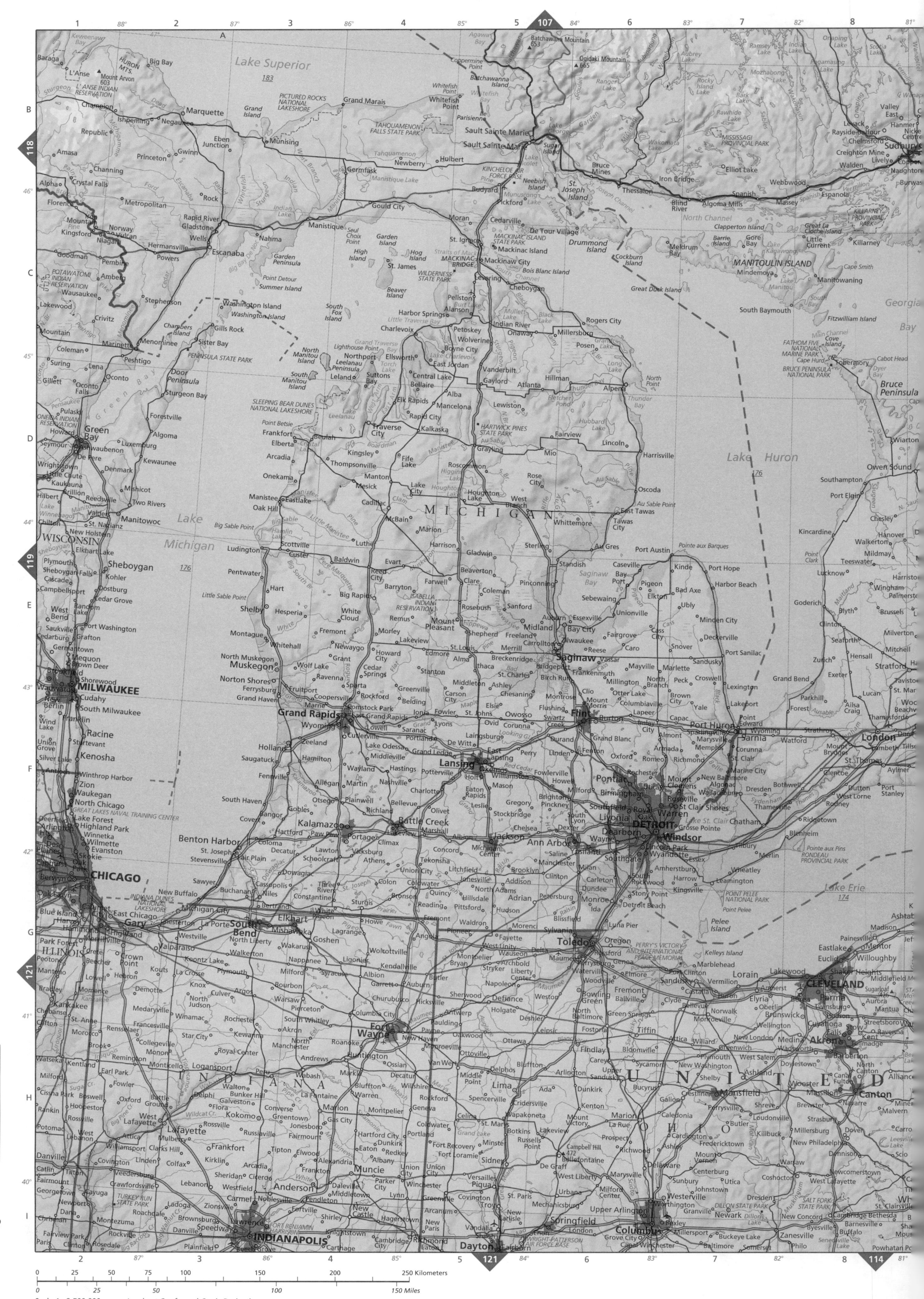

Meters
Feet

1000
3280

500
1640

200
656

Sea Level

200
656

2000
6560

0   25   50   75   100   150   200   250 Kilometers
0   25   50   100   150 Miles
Scale 1 : 2,500,000   Lambert Conformal Conic Projection

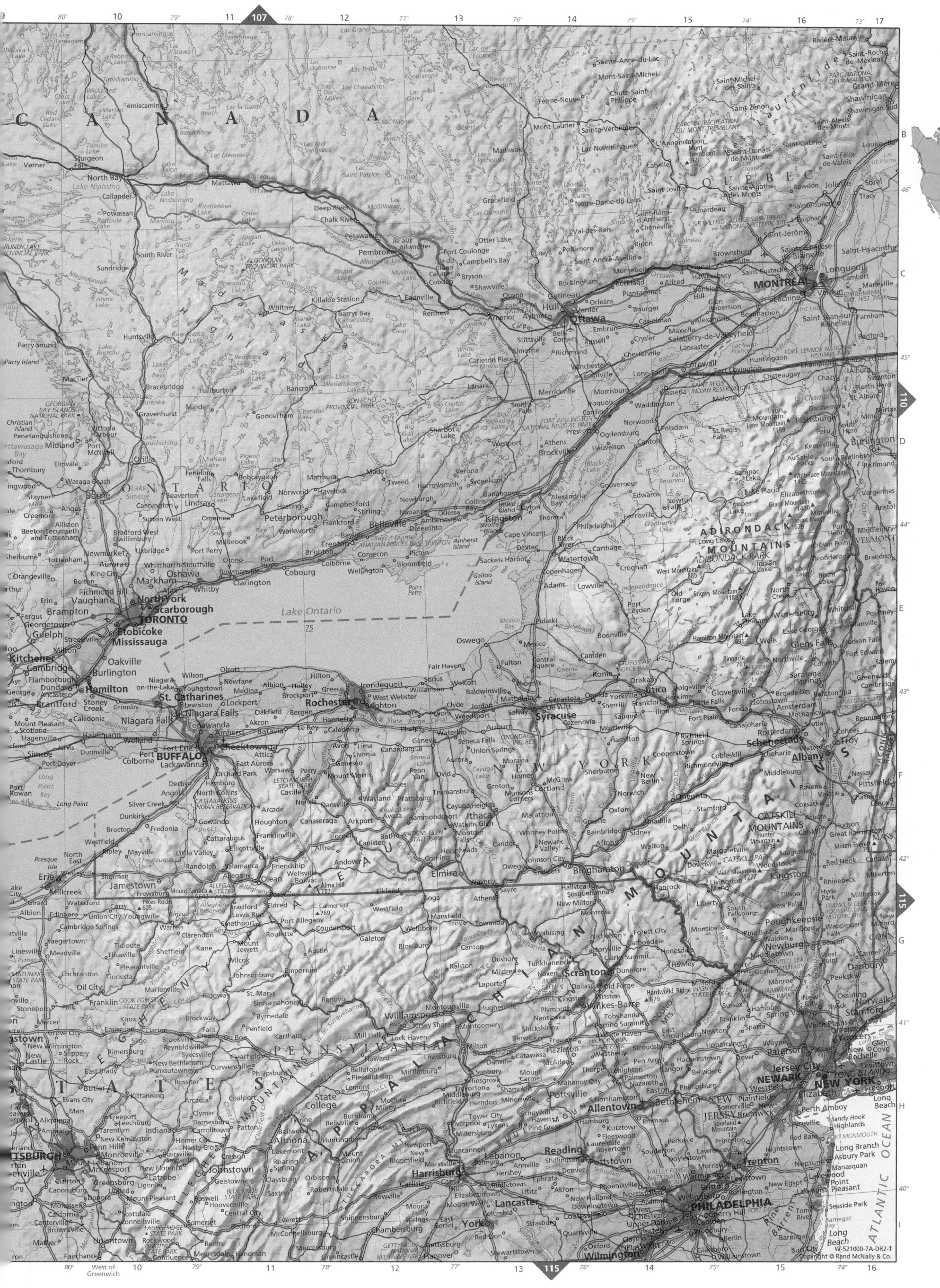
C A N A D A
ONTARIO
QUÉBEC
NEW YORK
PENNSYLVANIA
NEW JERSEY
VERMONT
MASS
CONN
U N I T E D S T A T E S
Lake Ontario
ATLANTIC OCEAN
ADIRONDACK MOUNTAINS
ADIRONDACK PARK
CATSKILL MOUNTAINS
APPALACHIAN MOUNTAINS
ALLEGHENY PLATEAU
ALLEGHENY MOUNTAINS
Laurentides
Madawaska Highlands
ALGONQUIN PROVINCIAL PARK
TORONTO
North York
Scarborough
Etobicoke
Mississauga
Hamilton
St. Catharines
Niagara Falls
BUFFALO
Cheektowaga
Rochester
Syracuse
Utica
Schenectady
Albany
Troy
Binghamton
Kingston
Ottawa
Hull
Gatineau
MONTRÉAL
Longueuil
Verdun
Laval
Oshawa
Peterborough
Belleville
Barrie
Orillia
Kitchener
Cambridge
Guelph
Brampton
Oakville
Burlington
North Bay
Pembroke
Cornwall
Watertown
Oswego
Ithaca
Elmira
Jamestown
Erie
Scranton
Wilkes-Barre
Williamsport
State College
Altoona
Johnstown
PITTSBURGH
Harrisburg
Lancaster
York
Reading
Allentown
Bethlehem
Trenton
PHILADELPHIA
Wilmington
NEWARK
Jersey City
Paterson
NEW YORK
LONG ISLAND
Yonkers
Stamford
Danbury
Poughkeepsie
Newburgh
Kingston
Pittsfield
Glens Falls
Saratoga Springs
Plattsburgh
Burlington
Lake Placid
Chalk River
Deep River
Mattawa
Sorel
Saint-Jérôme
Saint-Hyacinthe
Trois-Rivières
Shawinigan
Grand-Mère
Mont-Laurier
West of Greenwich
W-521000-7A-DR2-1 Copyright © Rand McNally & Co.

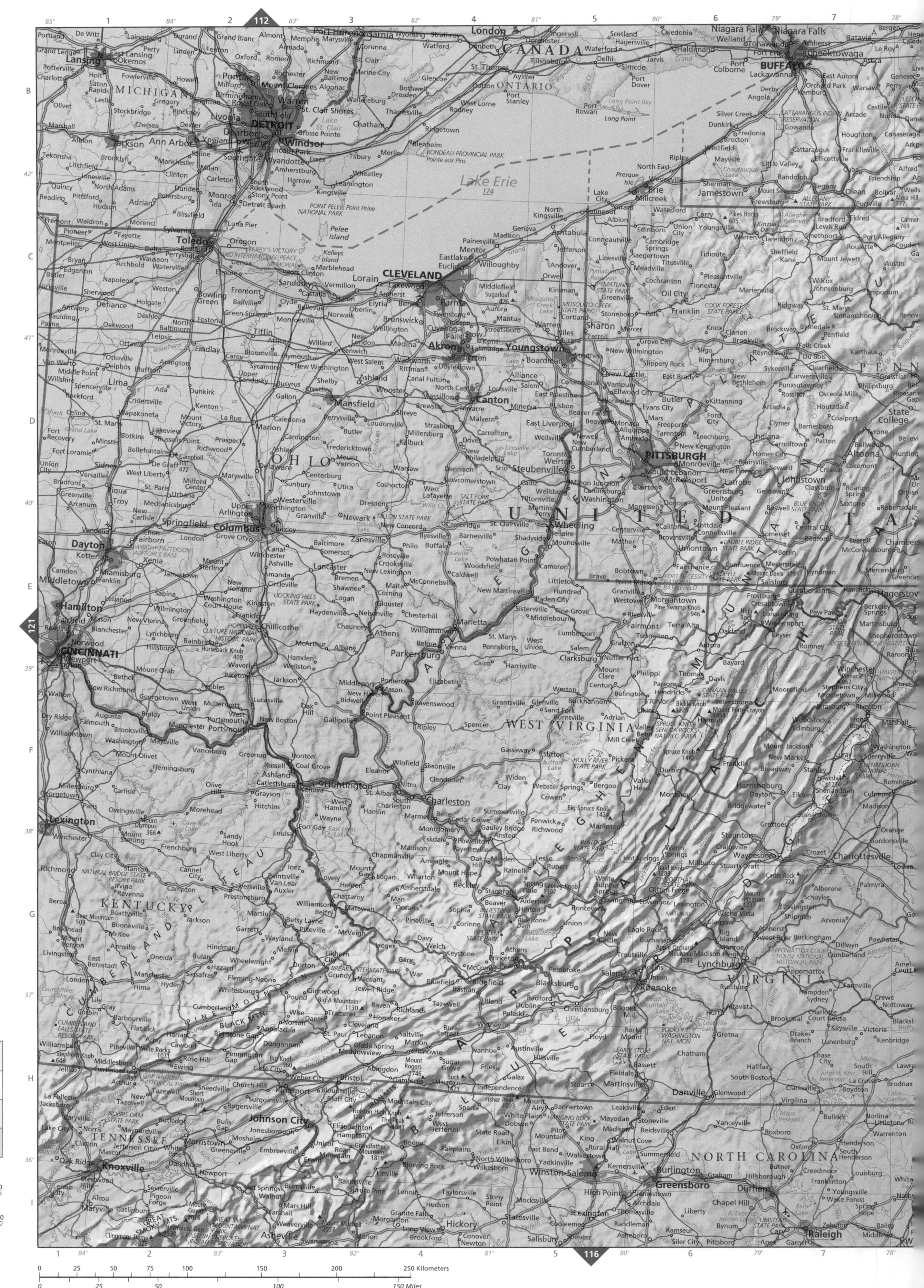
112
121
116
CANADA
ONTARIO
MICHIGAN
OHIO
PENNSYLVANIA
UNITED STATES
WEST VIRGINIA
KENTUCKY
TENNESSEE
VIRGINIA
NORTH CAROLINA
Lake Erie
174
Lake St. Clair
ALLEGHENY PLATEAU
ALLEGHENY MOUNTAINS
APPALACHIAN MOUNTAINS
CUMBERLAND PLATEAU
PINE MOUNTAIN
BLACK MTN.
BLUE RIDGE
GREAT SMOKY MTS.
DETROIT
Windsor
Lansing
Ann Arbor
Toledo
CLEVELAND
Akron
Canton
Youngstown
Mansfield
Columbus
Dayton
Hamilton
CINCINNATI
Lexington
Erie
BUFFALO
Niagara Falls
PITTSBURGH
Wheeling
Parkersburg
Huntington
Charleston
Morgantown
Roanoke
Lynchburg
Charlottesville
Johnson City
Knoxville
Asheville
Winston-Salem
Greensboro
Durham
Raleigh
Meters
Feet
1000
3280
500
1640
200
656
Sea Level
200
656
2000
6560
0 25 50 75 100 150 200 250 Kilometers
0 25 50 100 150 Miles
Scale 1 : 2,500,000
Lambert Conformal Conic Projection

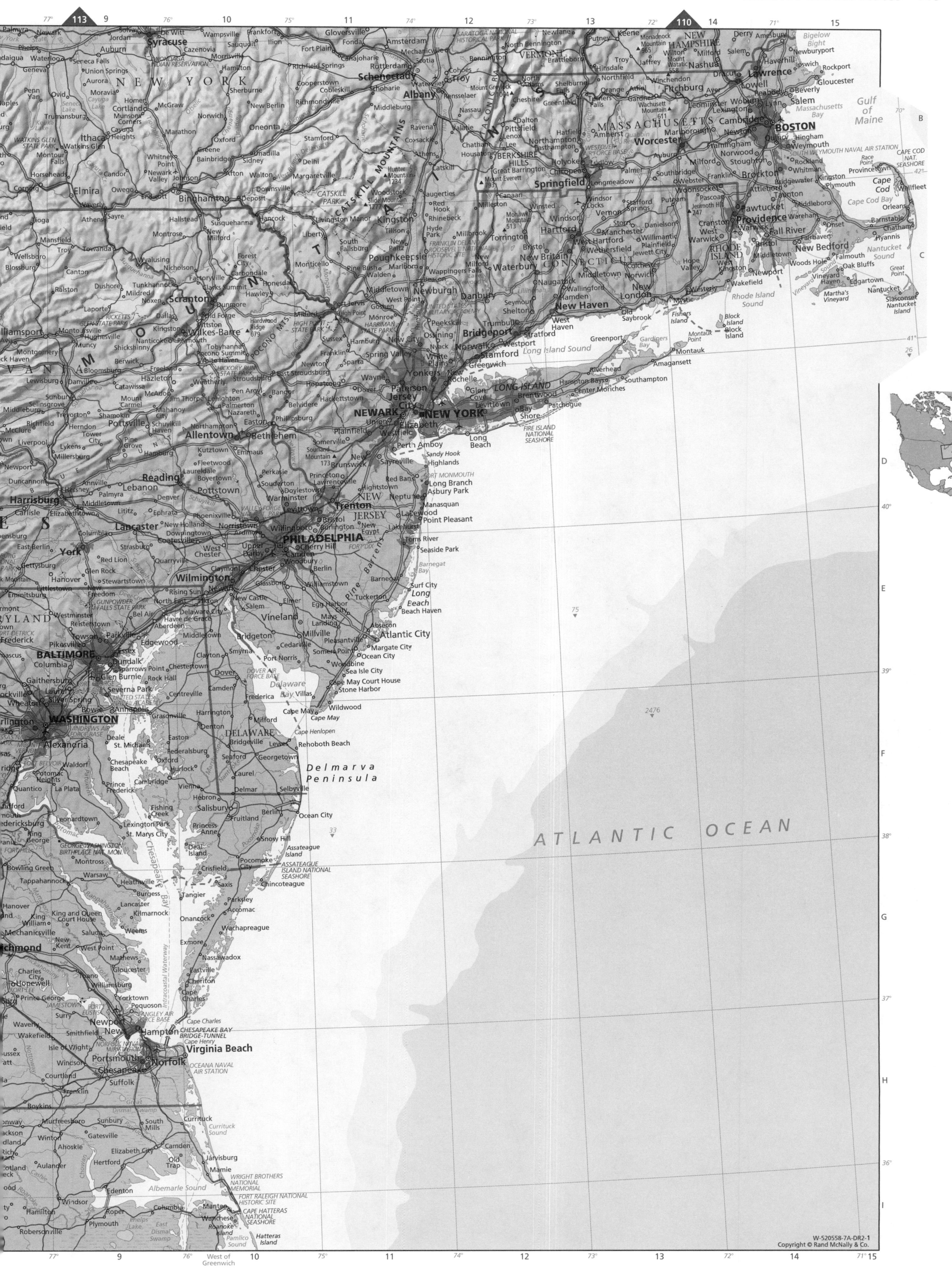

NEW YORK
MASSACHUSETTS
CONNECTICUT
RHODE ISLAND
NEW JERSEY
DELAWARE
VERMONT
NEW HAMPSHIRE
CATSKILL MOUNTAINS
Syracuse
Albany
Schenectady
Binghamton
Scranton
Wilkes-Barre
Allentown
Bethlehem
Reading
Lancaster
Harrisburg
York
Springfield
Hartford
Worcester
BOSTON
Providence
New Haven
Bridgeport
Stamford
Trenton
NEWARK
NEW YORK
PHILADELPHIA
Wilmington
BALTIMORE
WASHINGTON
Alexandria
Atlantic City
Cape May
Virginia Beach
Norfolk
Portsmouth
Chesapeake
LONG ISLAND
Long Island Sound
Gulf of Maine
Massachusetts Bay
Cape Cod Bay
Nantucket Sound
Rhode Island Sound
Delaware Bay
Chesapeake Bay
Albemarle Sound
Delmarva Peninsula
ATLANTIC OCEAN
W-520558-7A-DR2-1
Copyright © Rand McNally & Co.

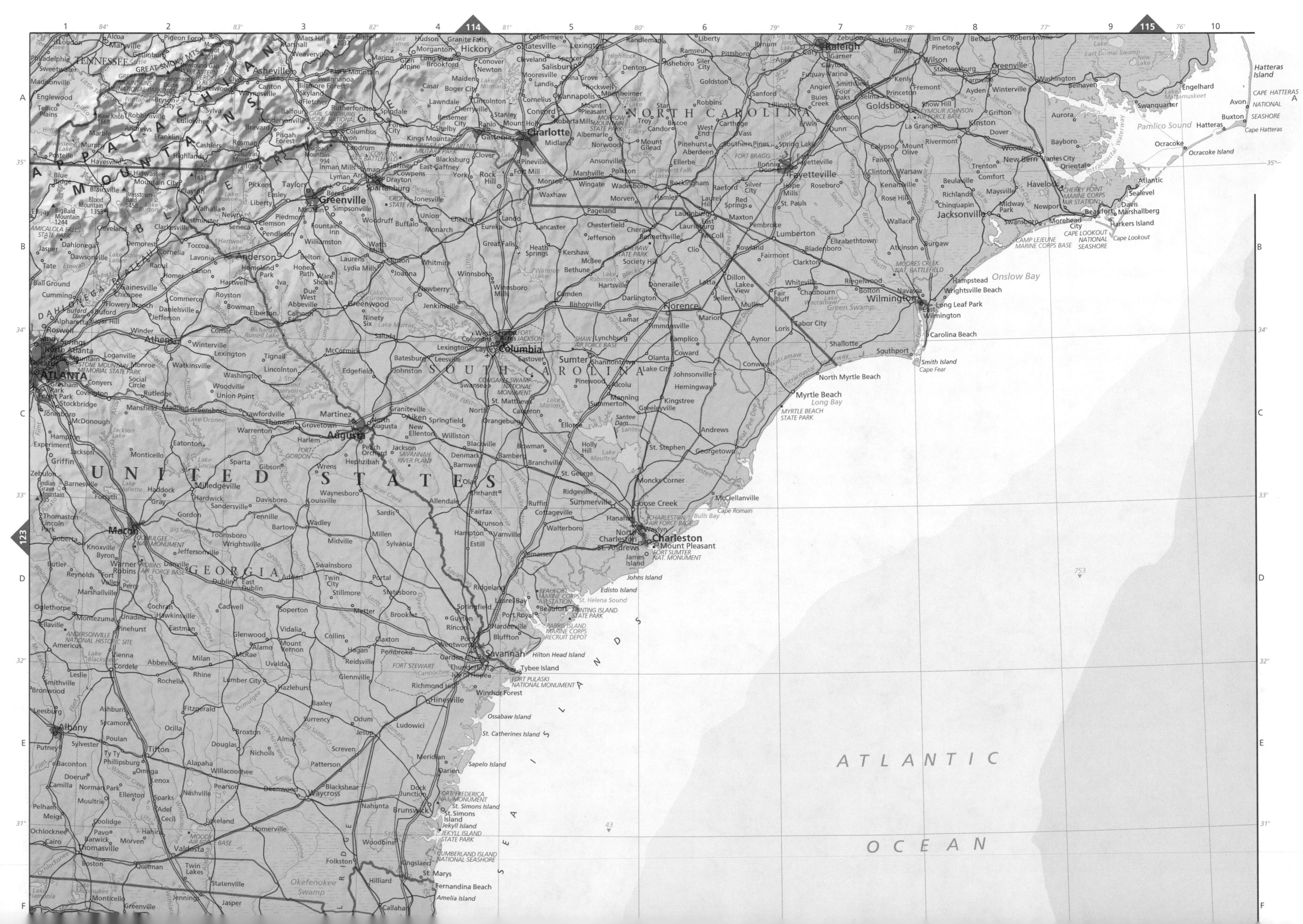
ATLANTIC
OCEAN
NORTH CAROLINA
SOUTH CAROLINA
GEORGIA
UNITED STATES
TENNESSEE
APPALACHIAN MOUNTAINS
BLUE RIDGE
SEA ISLANDS
Onslow Bay
Long Bay
Pamlico Sound
Hatteras Island
Cape Hatteras
Cape Lookout
Cape Fear
Cape Romain
Raleigh
Charlotte
Columbia
Charleston
Savannah
Wilmington
Fayetteville
Greenville
Augusta
Macon
ATLANTA
Albany
Asheville
Florence
Sumter
Myrtle Beach
Jacksonville
Goldsboro
Valdosta
Okefenokee Swamp
114
115
123

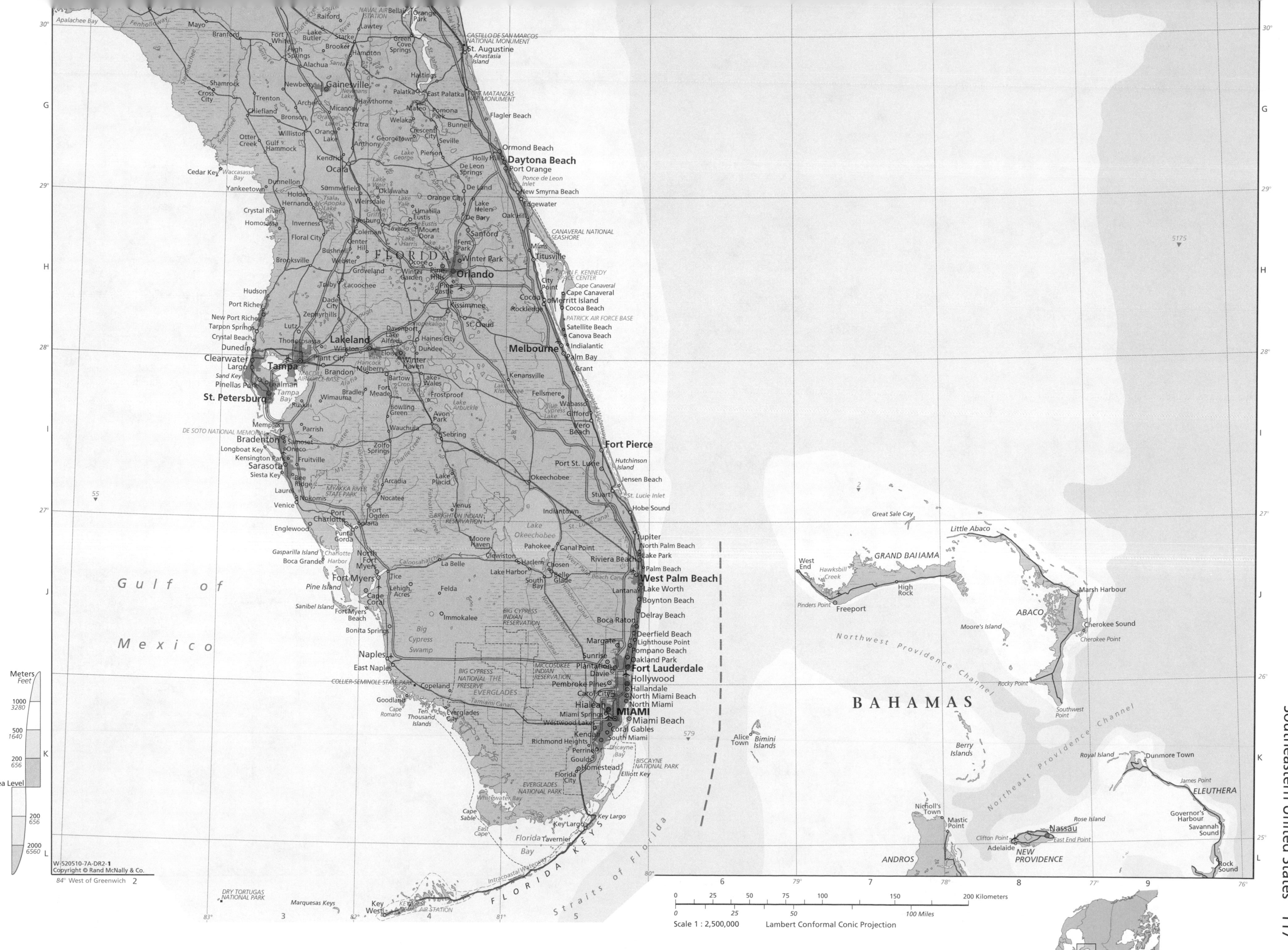

BAHAMAS

Gulf of Mexico

Straits of Florida

FLORIDA

200 Kilometers
100 Miles
Scale 1 : 2,500,000
Lambert Conformal Conic Projection

Meters / Feet
1000 / 3280
500 / 1640
200 / 656
Sea Level
200 / 656
2000 / 6560

W520510-7A-DR2-1
Copyright © Rand McNally & Co.

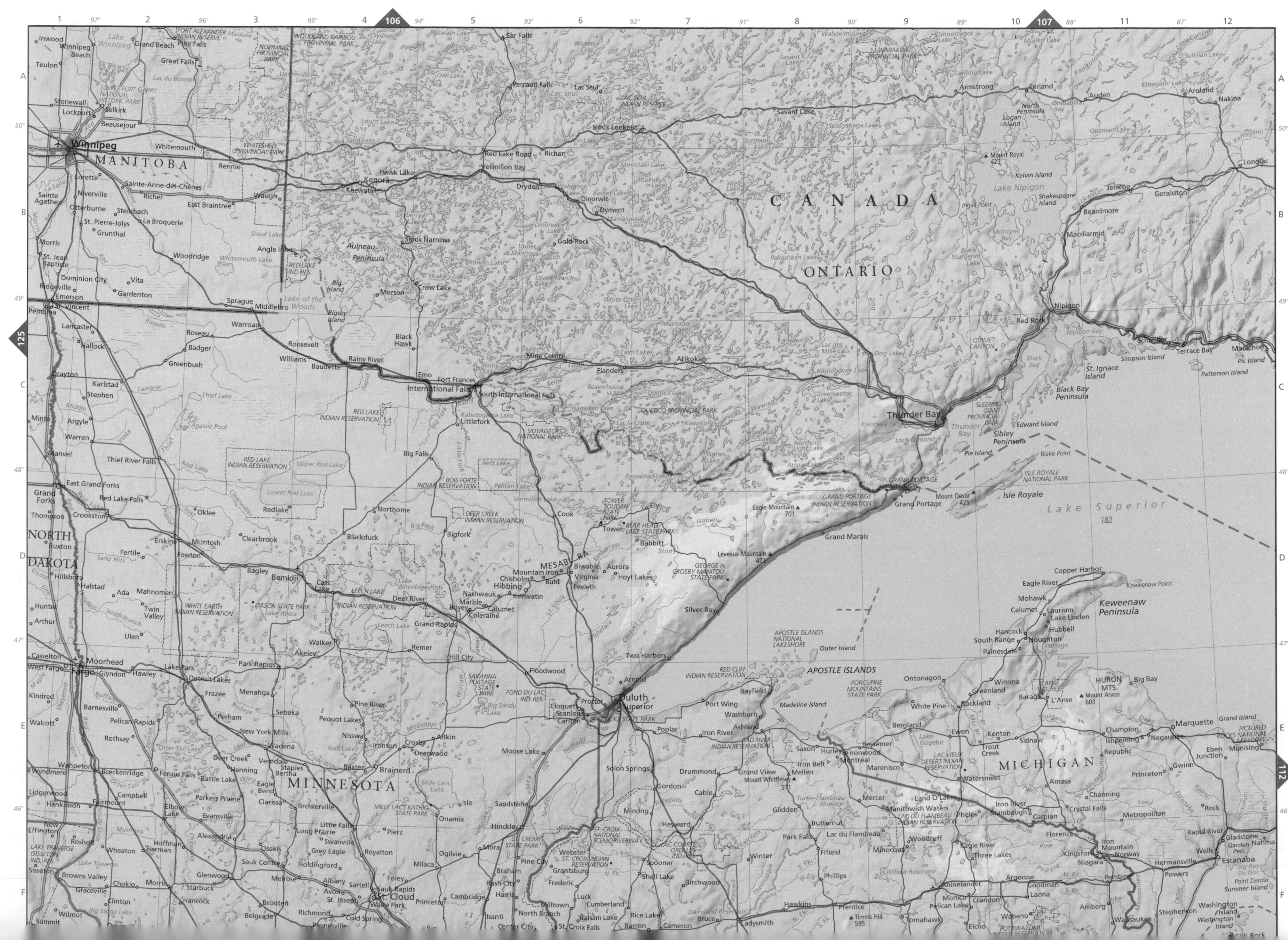

CANADA
ONTARIO
MANITOBA
MINNESOTA
MICHIGAN
NORTH DAKOTA
Lake Superior
Isle Royale
Keweenaw Peninsula
APOSTLE ISLANDS
Lake Nipigon
Thunder Bay
Duluth
Superior
Winnipeg
Marquette
International Falls
Grand Forks
Fargo
Moorhead
St. Cloud
Escanaba
107
106
112
125

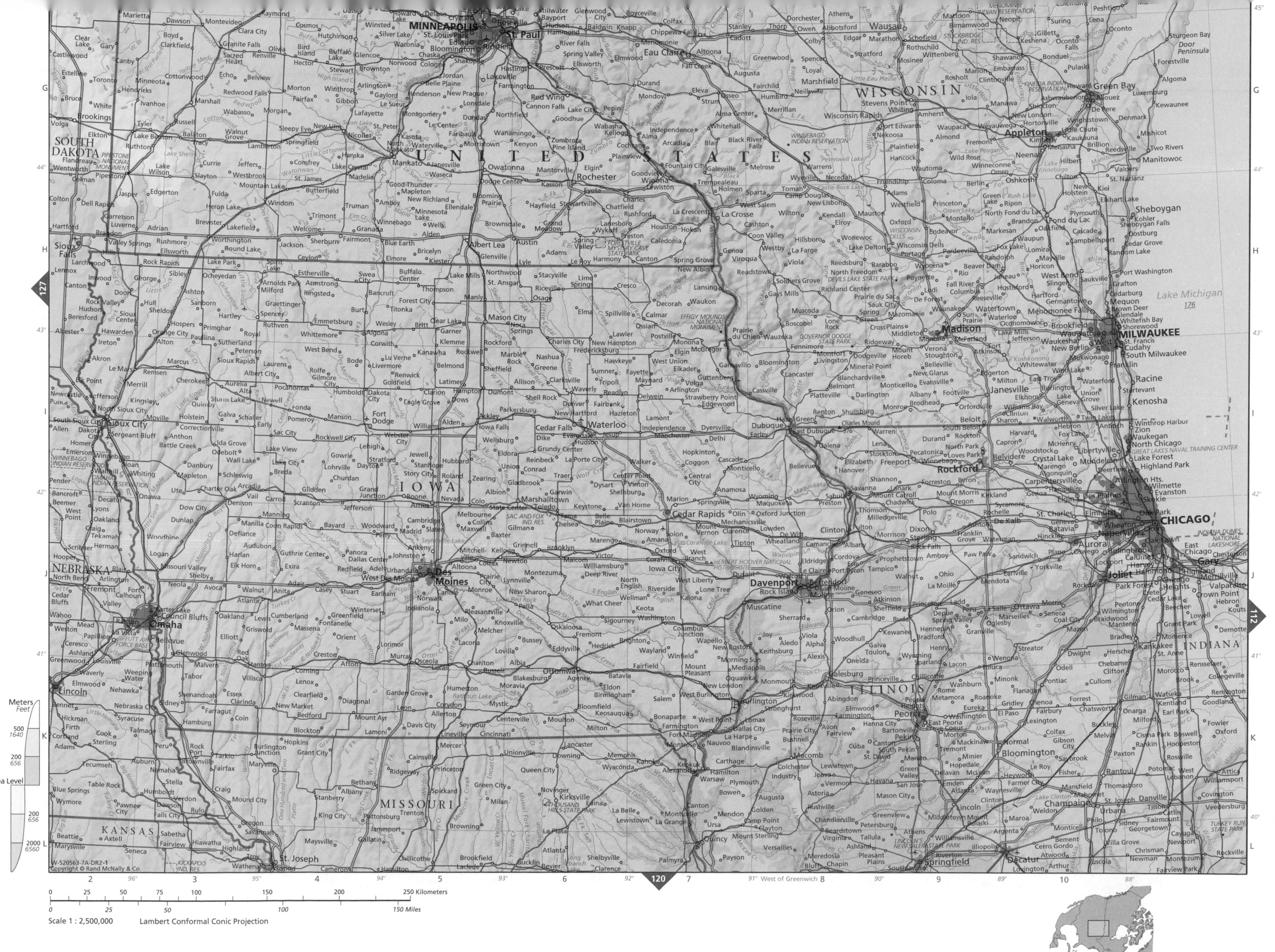
WISCONSIN
IOWA
ILLINOIS
INDIANA
MISSOURI
KANSAS
NEBRASKA
SOUTH DAKOTA
UNITED STATES
MINNEAPOLIS
St. Paul
MILWAUKEE
CHICAGO
Madison
Des Moines
Cedar Rapids
Davenport
Rockford
Springfield
Peoria
Omaha
Lincoln
Sioux City
Sioux Falls
Green Bay
Appleton
Dubuque
Waterloo
Rochester
Lake Michigan
112
120
127
Meters
Feet
Sea Level
Scale 1 : 2,500,000
Lambert Conformal Conic Projection
250 Kilometers
150 Miles
91° West of Greenwich
W-520563-7A-DR2-1
Copyright © Rand McNally & Co.

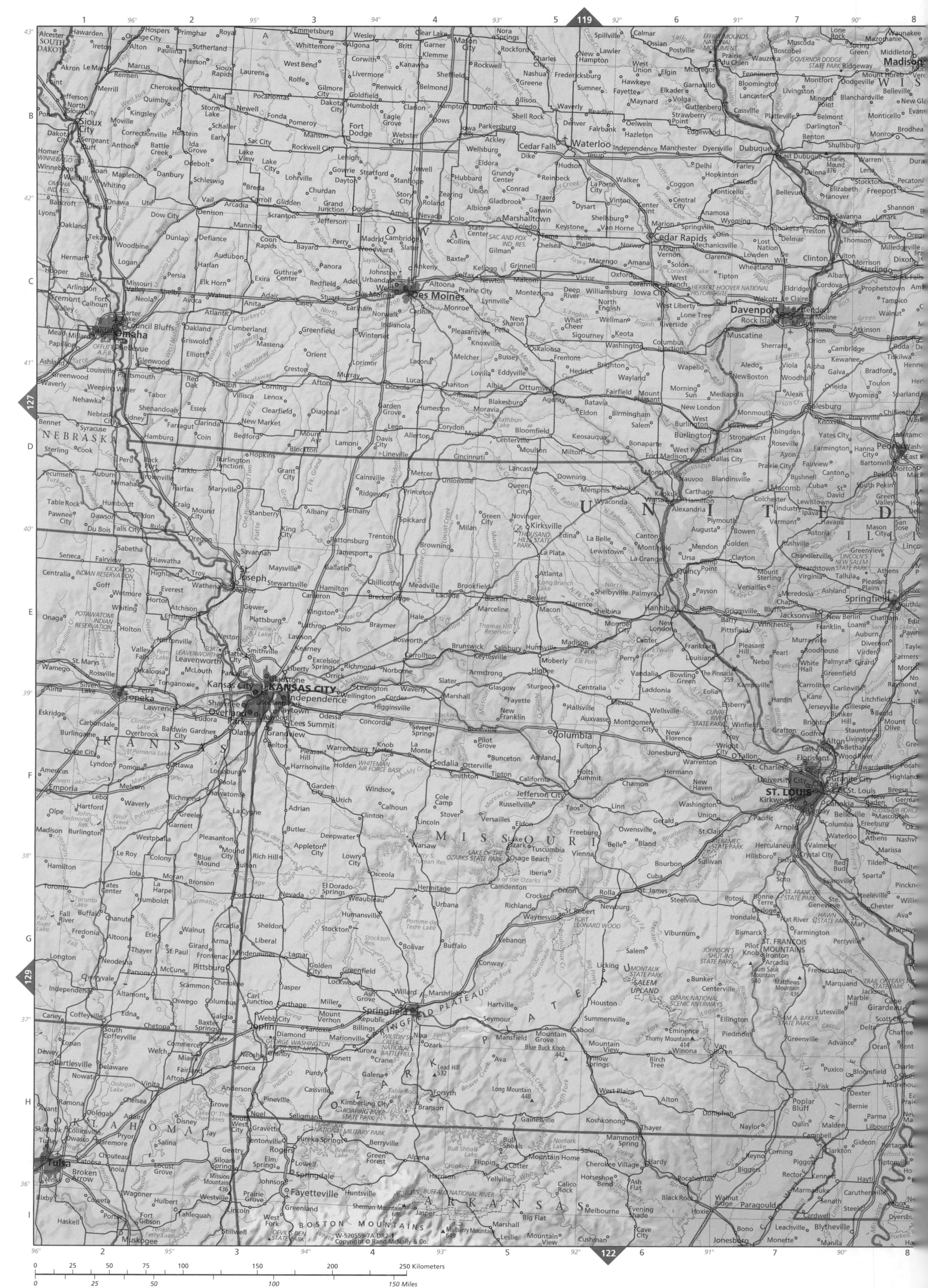

Meters
Feet

1000
3280

500
1640

200
656

Sea Level

200
656

2000
6560

0   25   50   75   100   150   200   250 Kilometers

0   25   50   100   150 Miles

Scale 1 : 2,500,000   Lambert Conformal Conic Projection

W-5205599-7A-DR21
Copyright © Rand McNally & Co.

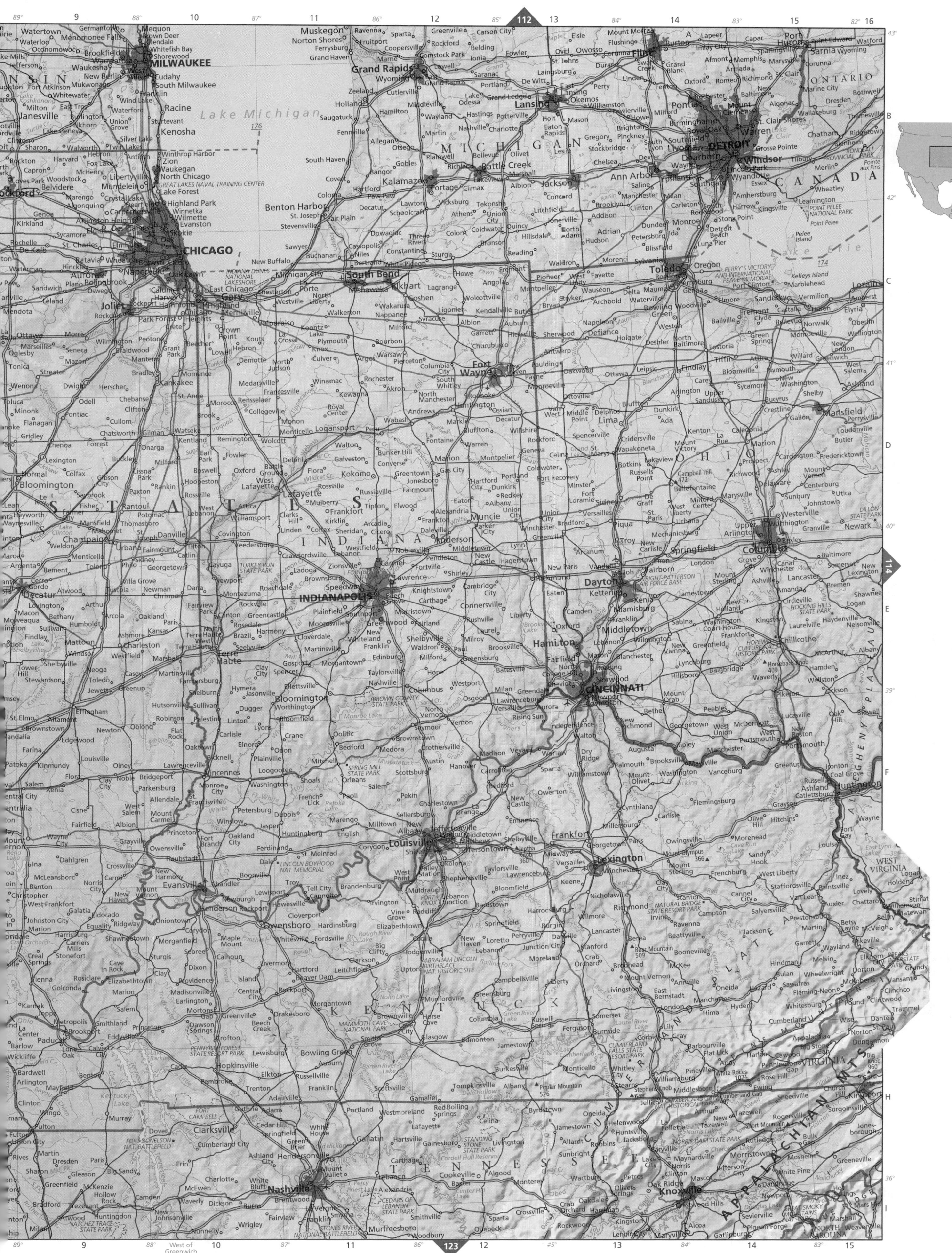
MICHIGAN
INDIANA
OHIO
KENTUCKY
TENNESSEE
ONTARIO
CANADA
WEST VIRGINIA
VIRGINIA
NORTH CAROLINA
Lake Michigan
Lake Erie
MILWAUKEE
CHICAGO
DETROIT
Windsor
Grand Rapids
Lansing
Flint
Toledo
South Bend
Fort Wayne
INDIANAPOLIS
Dayton
CINCINNATI
Columbus
Louisville
Lexington
Nashville
Knoxville
Kalamazoo
Gary
Joliet
Champaign
Decatur
Terre Haute
Evansville
Bloomington
Lafayette
Muncie
Springfield
Frankfort
Owensboro
Bowling Green
Clarksville
Huntington
Mansfield
Sarnia
APPALACHIAN MTS
GREAT LAKES NAVAL TRAINING CENTER
INDIANA DUNES NATIONAL LAKESHORE
PERRY'S VICTORY AND INTERNATIONAL PEACE MEMORIAL
POINT PELEE NATIONAL PARK
WRIGHT-PATTERSON AIR FORCE BASE
MAMMOTH CAVE NATIONAL PARK
ABRAHAM LINCOLN BIRTHPLACE NAT. HISTORIC SITE
LINCOLN BOYHOOD NAT. MEMORIAL
FORT DONELSON NAT. BATTLEFIELD
STONES RIVER NATIONAL BATTLEFIELD
NATCHEZ TRACE STATE PARK
West of Greenwich
112
114
123

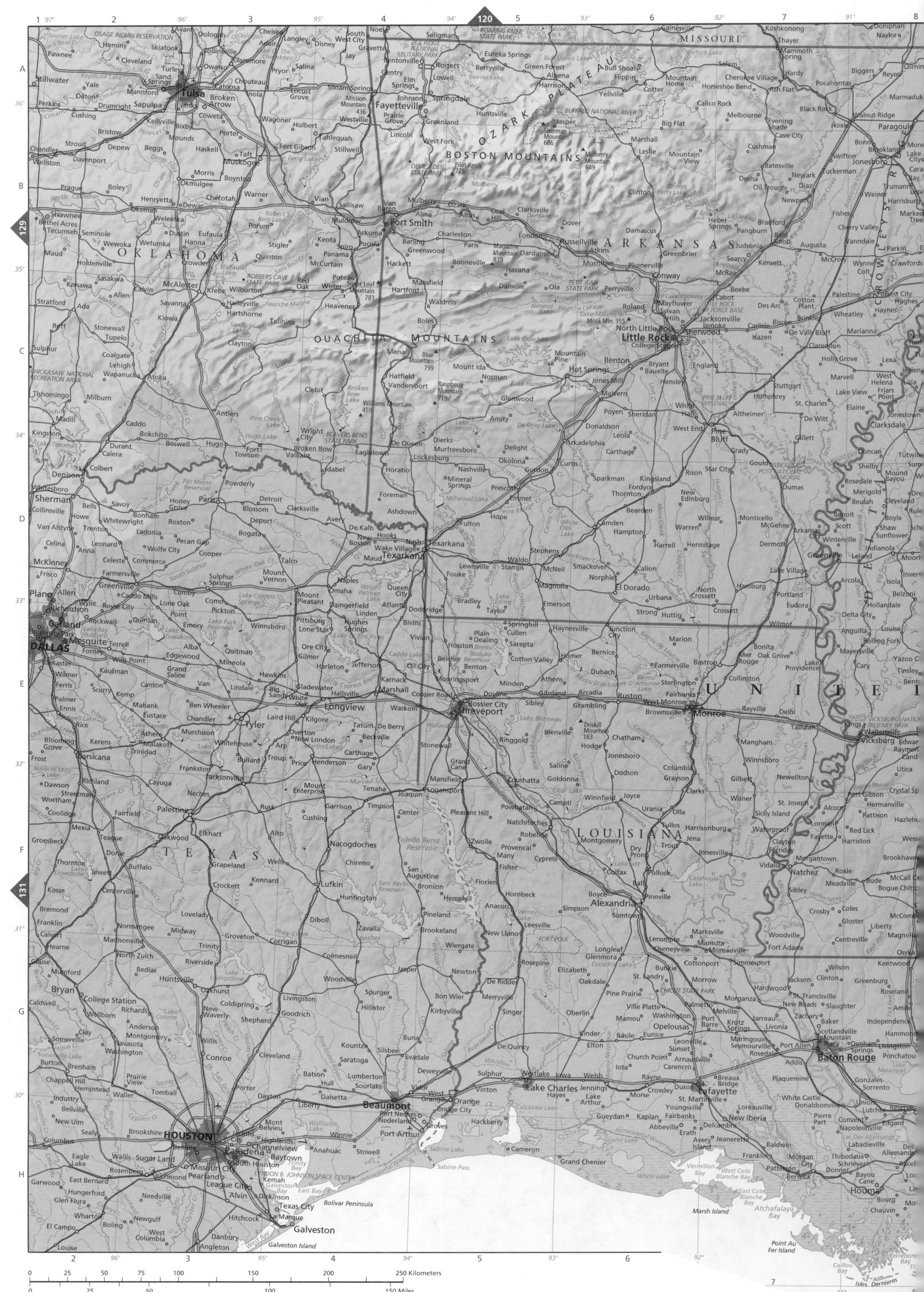

120
129
131
MISSOURI
OKLAHOMA
ARKANSAS
TEXAS
LOUISIANA
OZARK PLATEAU
BOSTON MOUNTAINS
OUACHITA MOUNTAINS
CROWLEY'S RIDGE
Tulsa
Fayetteville
Fort Smith
Little Rock
North Little Rock
Texarkana
Shreveport
Bossier City
Monroe
Dallas
Plano
Garland
Mesquite
Tyler
Longview
Nacogdoches
Lufkin
Bryan
College Station
Houston
Pasadena
Baytown
Galveston
Texas City
Beaumont
Port Arthur
Orange
Lake Charles
Lafayette
Baton Rouge
Alexandria
Natchez
Vicksburg
Pine Bluff
Hot Springs
El Dorado
Camden
Muskogee
McAlester
Sherman
Denison
Corsicana
Palestine
Galveston Island
Bolivar Peninsula
Sabine Lake
Sabine Pass
Marsh Island
Atchafalaya Bay
Vermilion Bay
Meters
Feet
2000
6560
1000
3280
500
1640
200
656
Sea Level
200
656
2000
6560
0 25 50 75 100 150 200 250 Kilometers
0 25 50 100 150 Miles
Scale 1 : 2,500,000
Lambert Conformal Conic Projection

KENTUCKY

TENNESSEE

MISSISSIPPI

ALABAMA

GEORGIA

FLORIDA

NORTH CAROLINA

STATES

APPALACHIAN MOUNTAINS

CUMBERLAND PLATEAU

Gulf of Mexico

W-520565-2A-DR2-1

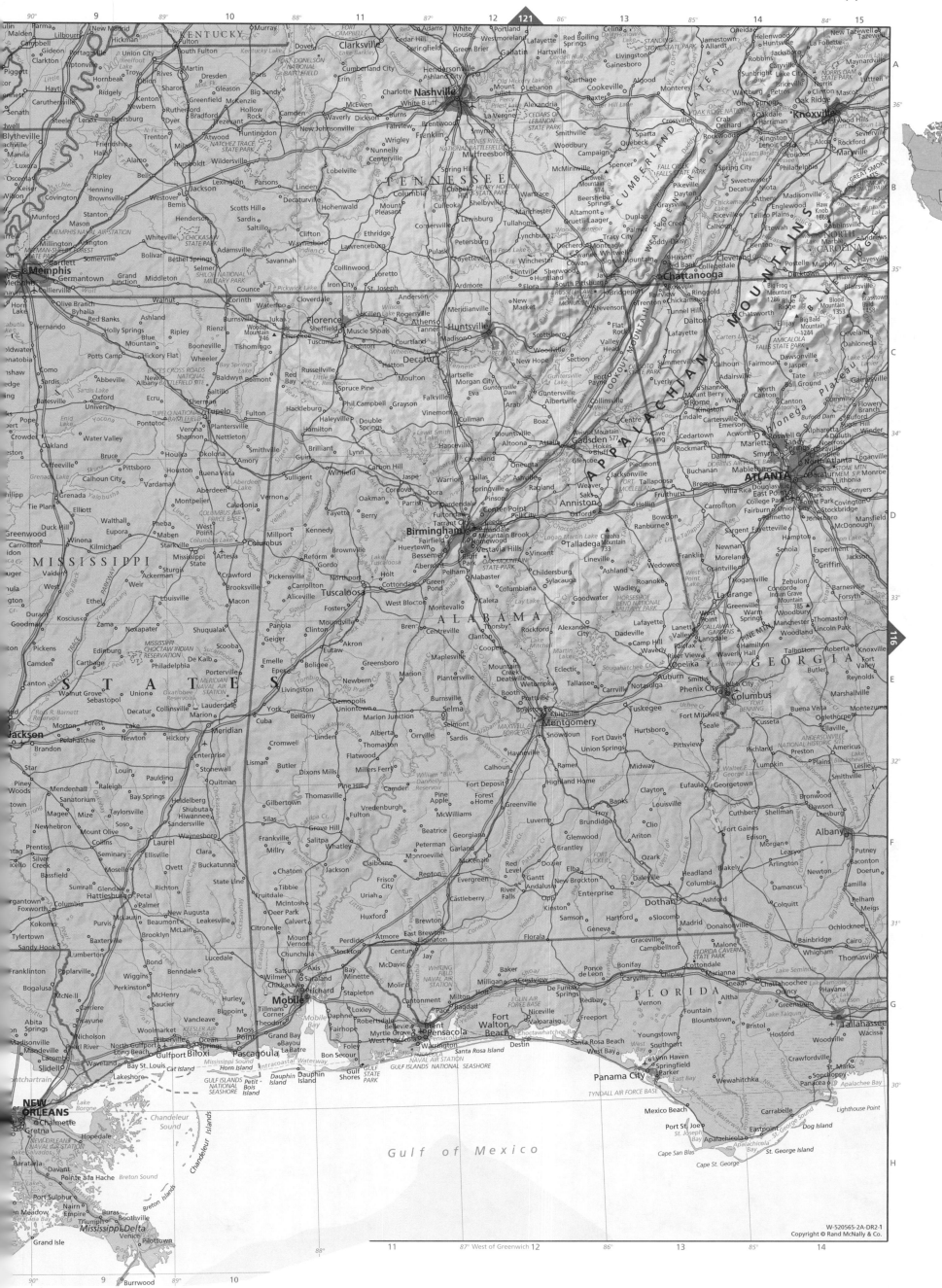

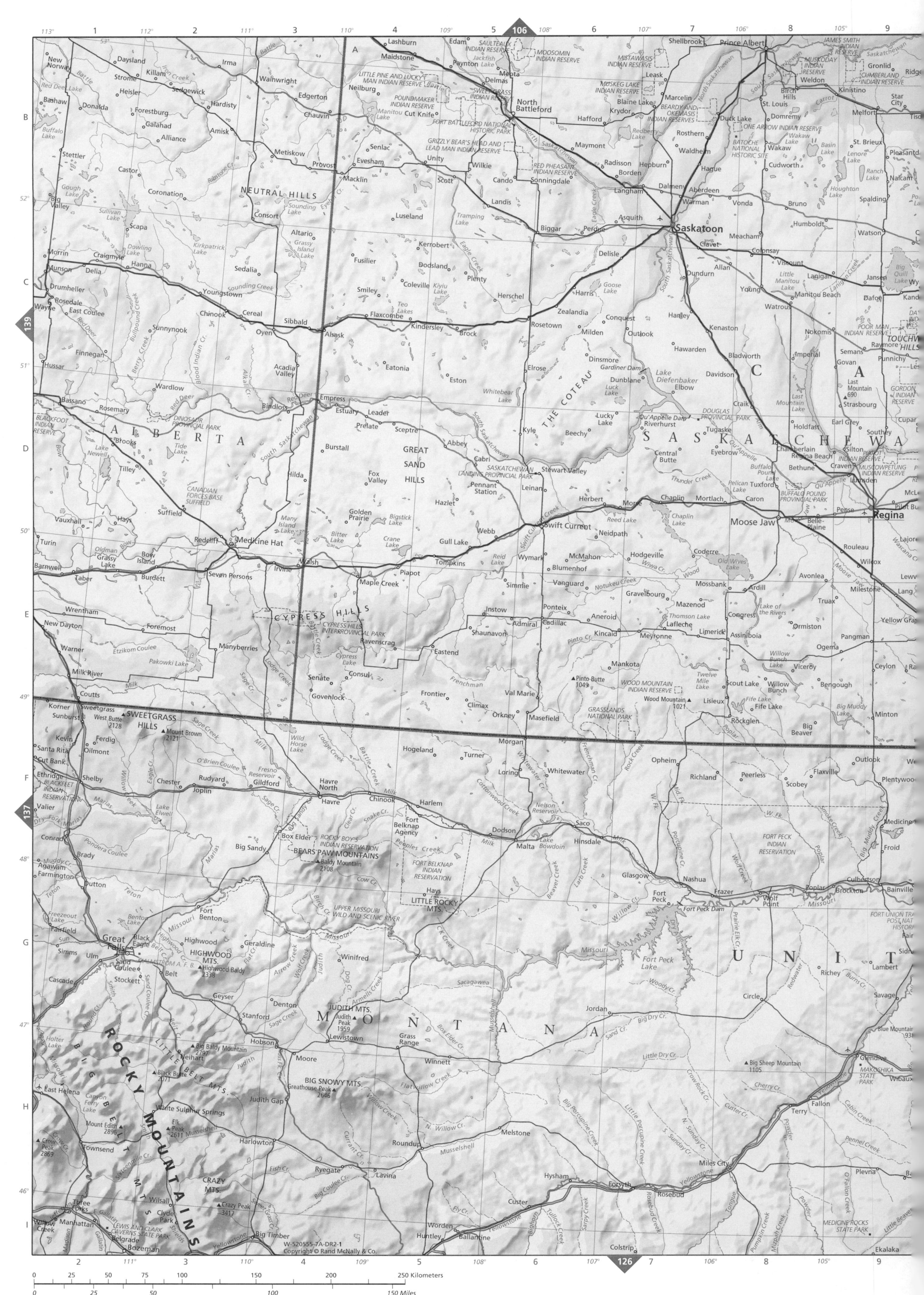
106
139
137
126
ALBERTA
SASKATCHEWAN
MONTANA
UNIT
ROCKY MOUNTAINS
BIG BELT MTS.
LITTLE BELT MTS.
NEUTRAL HILLS
GREAT SAND HILLS
THE COTEAU
CYPRESS HILLS
SWEETGRASS HILLS
BEARS PAW MOUNTAINS
LITTLE ROCKY MTS.
HIGHWOOD MTS.
JUDITH MTS.
BIG SNOWY MTS.
CRAZY MTS.
Saskatoon
Regina
Moose Jaw
Swift Current
Medicine Hat
Prince Albert
North Battleford
Lashburn
Maidstone
Edam
Shellbrook
Irma
Wainwright
Edgerton
Chauvin
Hardisty
Sedgewick
Killam
Daysland
Strome
Heisler
Forestburg
Galahad
Alliance
Amisk
Donalda
Bashaw
Stettler
Castor
Coronation
Consort
Provost
Metiskow
Macklin
Evesham
Senlac
Unity
Scott
Wilkie
Cut Knife
Neilburg
Paynton
Delmas
Meota
Blaine Lake
Leask
Marcelin
Krydor
Hafford
Duck Lake
Rosthern
Waldheim
Hague
Langham
Dalmeny
Aberdeen
Warman
Vonda
Radisson
Borden
Hepburn
Maymont
Cando
Sonningdale
Landis
Biggar
Perdue
Asquith
Luseland
Kerrobert
Dodsland
Plenty
Coleville
Smiley
Fusilier
Herschel
Harris
Zealandia
Rosetown
Delisle
Dundurn
Allan
Clavet
Meacham
Colonsay
Viscount
Young
Watrous
Manitou Beach
Lanigan
Humboldt
Bruno
Watson
Spalding
St. Brieux
Melfort
Kinistino
Birch Hills
St. Louis
Domremy
Wakaw
Cudworth
Star City
Weldon
Gronlid
Conquest
Outlook
Milden
Hanley
Kenaston
Hawarden
Bladworth
Davidson
Dinsmore
Dunblane
Elbow
Elrose
Eston
Eatonia
Kindersley
Flaxcombe
Brock
Alsask
Oyen
Sibbald
Cereal
Chinook
Youngstown
Sedalia
Hanna
Craigmyle
Delia
Morrin
Munson
Drumheller
Rosedale
East Coulee
Wayne
Sunnynook
Finnegan
Hussar
Acadia Valley
Altario
Wardlow
Bassano
Rosemary
Bindloss
Empress
Estuary
Leader
Prelate
Sceptre
Abbey
Cabri
Burstall
Brooks
Tilley
Hilda
Fox Valley
Pennant Station
Stewart Valley
Leinan
Kyle
Beechy
Lucky Lake
Riverhurst
Tugaske
Central Butte
Eyebrow
Craik
Holdfast
Strasbourg
Chamberlain
Bethune
Craven
Lumsden
Pense
Belle Plaine
Mortlach
Caron
Chaplin
Morse
Herbert
Hazlet
Golden Prairie
Suffield
Vauxhall
Hays
Turin
Redcliff
Barnwell
Taber
Grassy Lake
Bow Island
Burdett
Seven Persons
Irvine
Walsh
Piapot
Maple Creek
Tompkins
Gull Lake
Webb
Wymark
Neidpath
McMahon
Blumenhof
Hodgeville
Coderre
Vanguard
Simmie
Gravelbourg
Mazenod
Mossbank
Ardill
Avonlea
Rouleau
Wilcox
Milestone
Truax
Congress
Lafleche
Limerick
Assiniboia
Ormiston
Pangman
Ogema
Viceroy
Ceylon
Bengough
Willow Bunch
Scout Lake
Fife Lake
Minton
Big Beaver
Rockglen
Lisieux
Wood Mountain
Mankota
Kincaid
Meyronne
Aneroid
Ponteix
Cadillac
Admiral
Instow
Shaunavon
Eastend
Ravenscrag
Consul
Senate
Govenlock
Frontier
Climax
Val Marie
Orkney
Masefield
Manyberries
Foremost
Wrentham
New Dayton
Warner
Milk River
Coutts
Sweetgrass
Sunburst
Kevin
Ferdig
Oilmont
Santa Rita
Cut Bank
Ethridge
Shelby
Valier
Conrad
Brady
Dutton
Agawam
Farmington
Fairfield
Chester
Rudyard
Joplin
Gildford
Havre
Havre North
Chinook
Harlem
Box Elder
Big Sandy
Fort Belknap Agency
Hays
Dodson
Malta
Saco
Hinsdale
Glasgow
Nashua
Fort Peck
Frazer
Wolf Point
Poplar
Brockton
Culbertson
Bainville
Hogeland
Turner
Loring
Whitewater
Opheim
Richland
Peerless
Scobey
Flaxville
Outlook
Plentywood
Morgan
Fort Benton
Great Falls
Black Eagle
Highwood
Geraldine
Ulm
Simms
Sun River
Cascade
Stockett
Belt
Geyser
Denton
Stanford
Winifred
Hobson
Moore
Lewistown
Grass Range
Winnett
Jordan
Circle
Richey
Lambert
Savage
Glendive
Fallon
Terry
Miles City
Plevna
Ekalaka
Melstone
Roundup
Harlowton
Judith Gap
White Sulphur Springs
Neihart
Townsend
East Helena
Wilsall
Clyde Park
Livingston
Big Timber
Bozeman
Belgrade
Manhattan
Three Forks
Ryegate
Lavina
Custer
Hysham
Forsyth
Rosebud
Worden
Huntley
Ballantine
Colstrip
Saskatchewan
South Saskatchewan
North Saskatchewan
Red Deer
Battle
Milk
Missouri
Yellowstone
Musselshell
Fort Peck Lake
Lake Diefenbaker
Old Wives Lake
Mount Brown 2121
West Butte 2128
Baldy Mountain 2108
Highwood Baldy 2338
Judith Peak 1959
Big Baldy Mountain 2797
Black Butte 2071
Greathouse Peak 2646
Elk Peak 2611
Mount Edith 2896
Crow Peak 2869
Crazy Peak 3417
Big Sheep Mountain 1105
Pinto Butte 1049
Wood Mountain 1021
Last Mountain 690
W-520555-7A-DR2-1
Copyright © Rand McNally & Co.
Meters
Feet
4000 13120
3000 9840
2000 6560
1000 3280
500 1640
200 656
Sea Level
200 656
2000 6560
0 25 50 75 100 150 200 250 Kilometers
0 25 50 100 150 Miles
Scale 1 : 2,500,000
Lambert Conformal Conic Projection

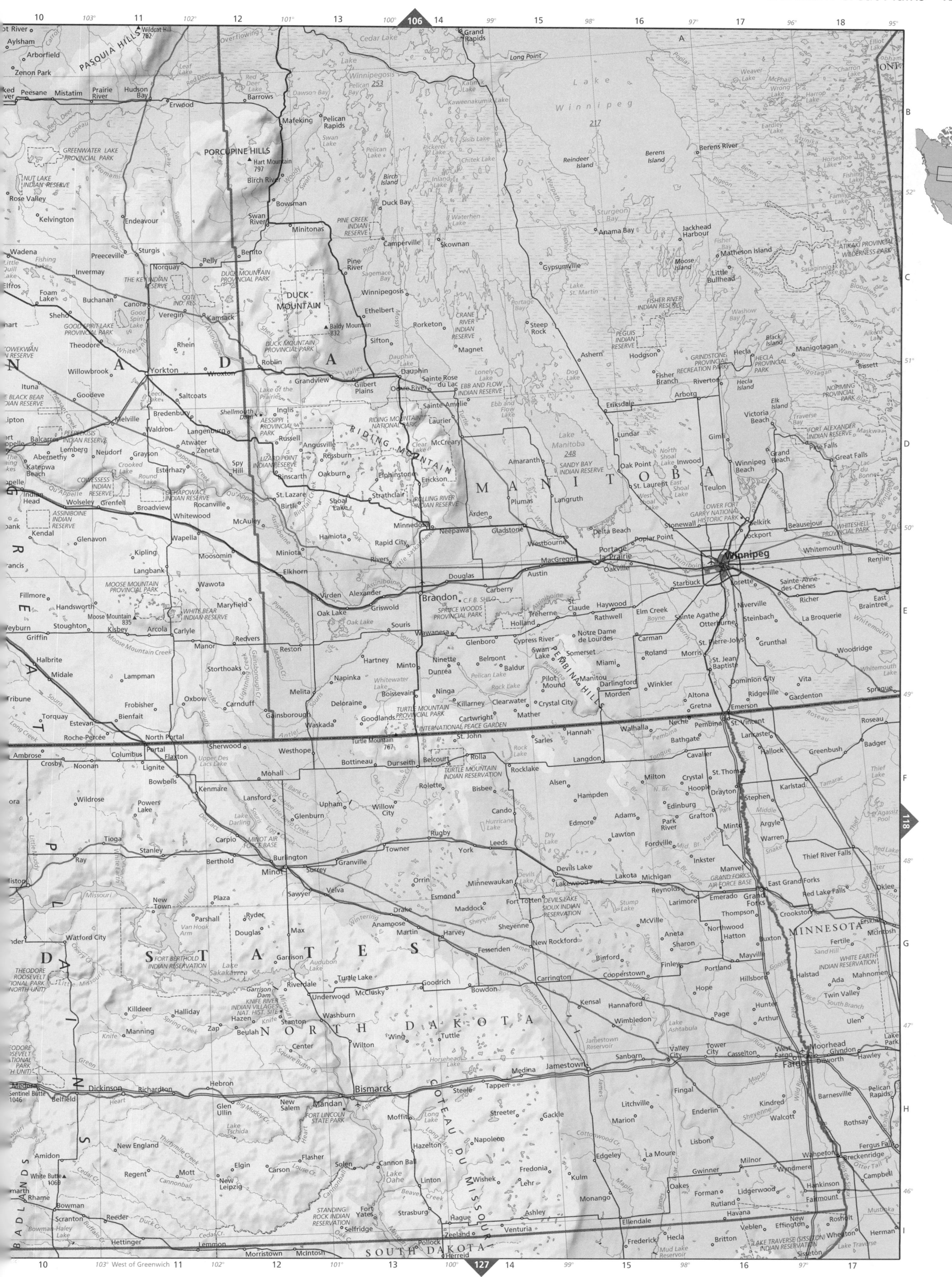

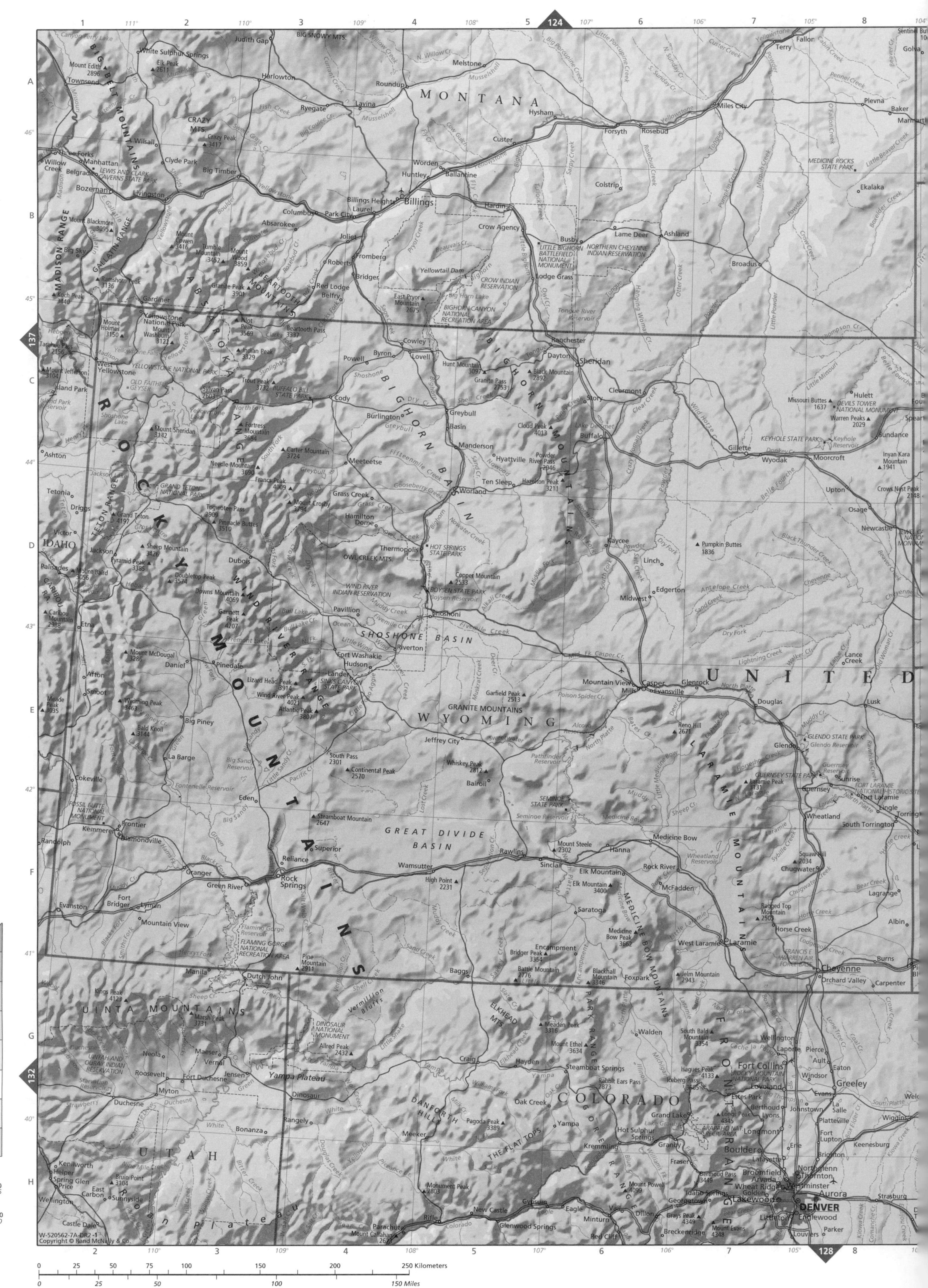

Meters
Feet

6000
19680

4000
13120

3000
9840

1000
3280

500
1640

200
656

Sea Level

200
656

2000
6560

W-520562-7A-DR2-1
Copyright © Rand McNally & Co.

0   25   50   75   100   150   200   250 Kilometers

0   25   50   100   150 Miles

Scale 1 : 2,500,000   Lambert Conformal Conic Projection

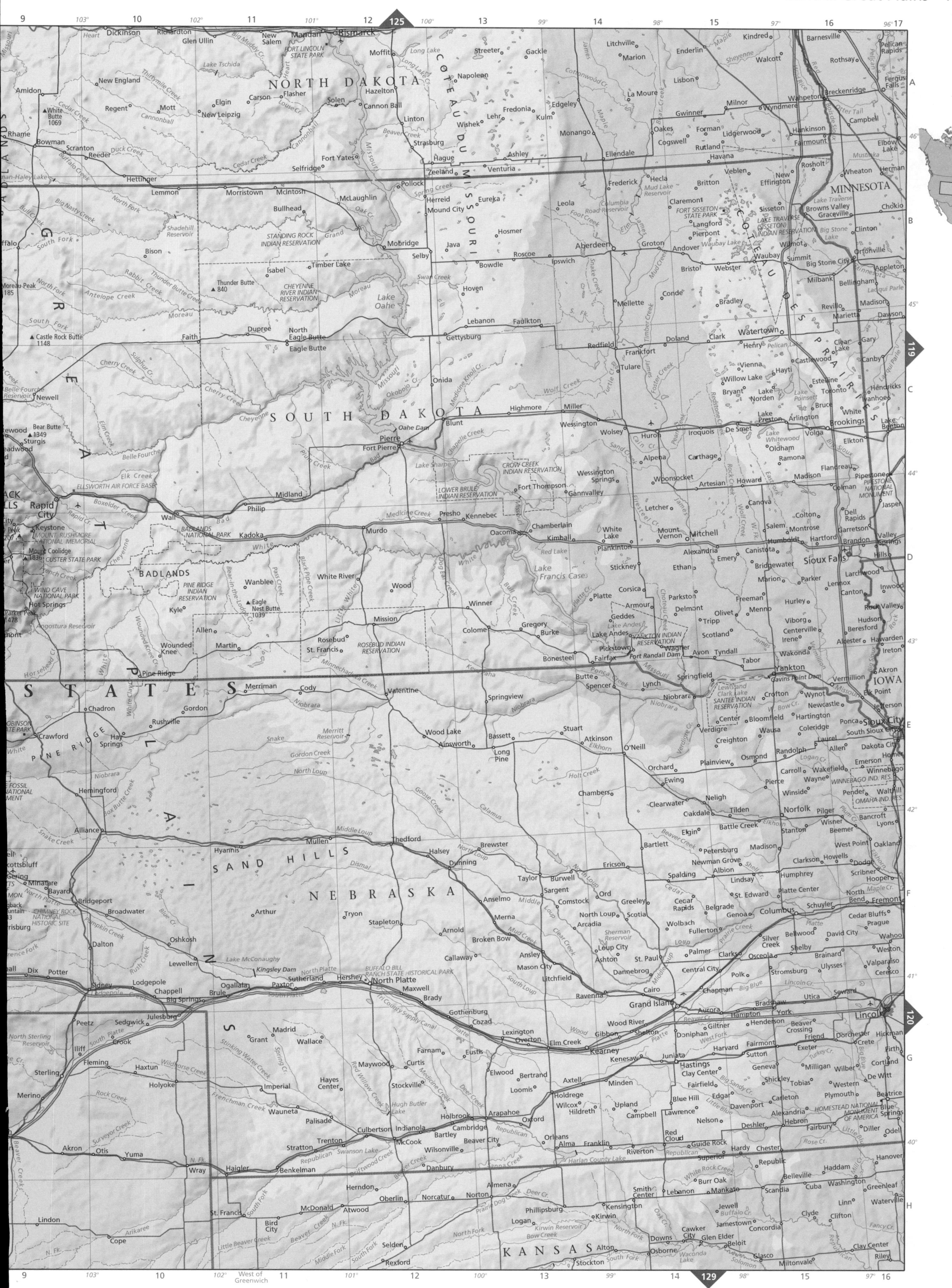
NORTH DAKOTA
SOUTH DAKOTA
NEBRASKA
KANSAS
MINNESOTA
IOWA
COTEAU DU MISSOURI
COTEAU DES PRAIRIES
SAND HILLS
PINE RIDGE
BADLANDS
BLACK HILLS
GREAT PLAINS
STATES
Bismarck
Pierre
Lincoln
Sioux Falls
Rapid City
Aberdeen
Watertown
Grand Island
North Platte
Kearney
Sioux City
West of Greenwich

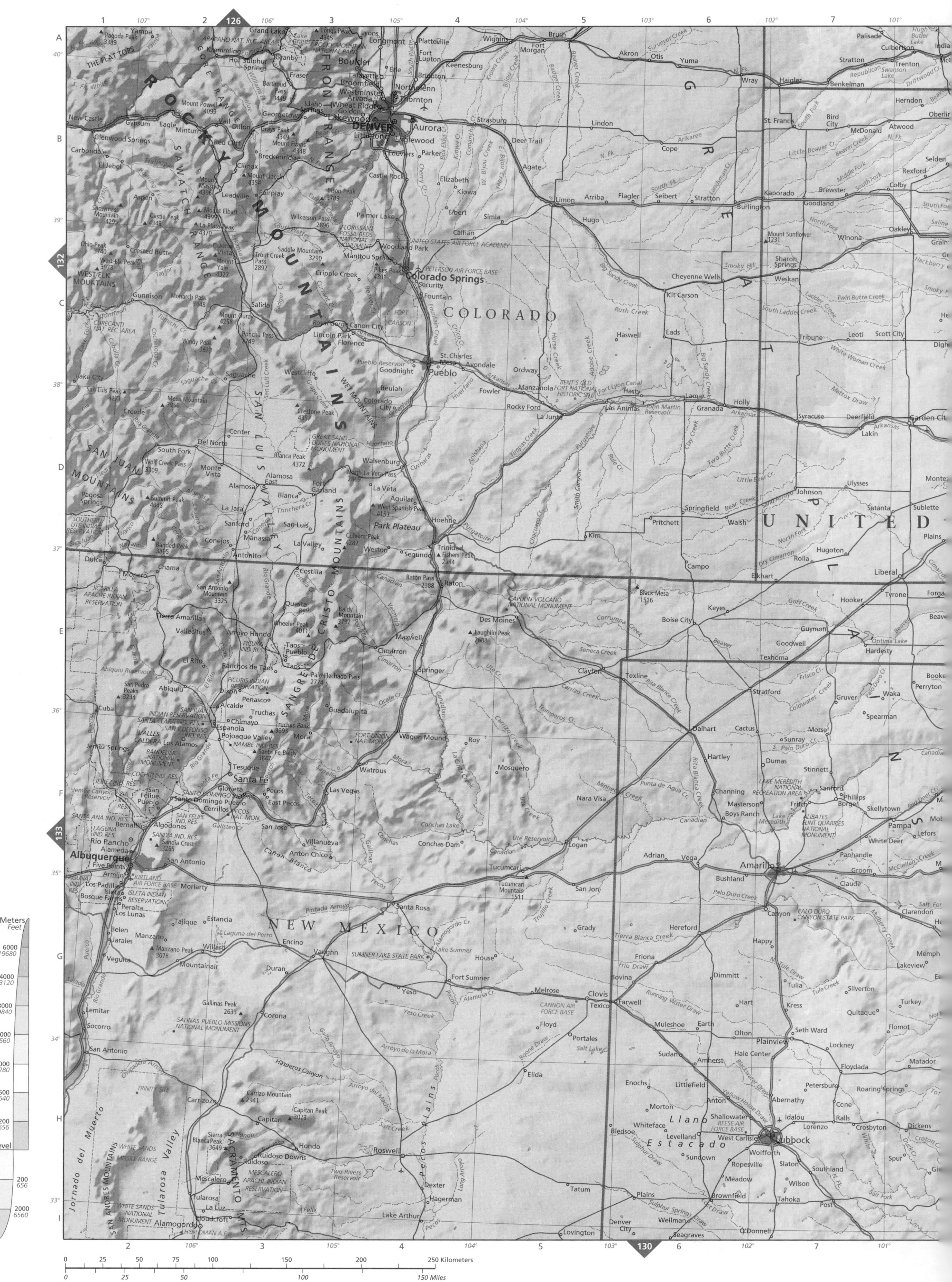

Scale 1 : 2 500 000   Lambert Conformal Conic Projection

NEBRASKA

KANSAS

MISSOURI

OKLAHOMA

TEXAS

ARKANSAS

LOUISIANA

FLINT HILLS

BOSTON MOUNTAINS

OUACHITA MOUNTAINS

OZARK PLATEAU

100° West of Greenwich

127 120 131 122

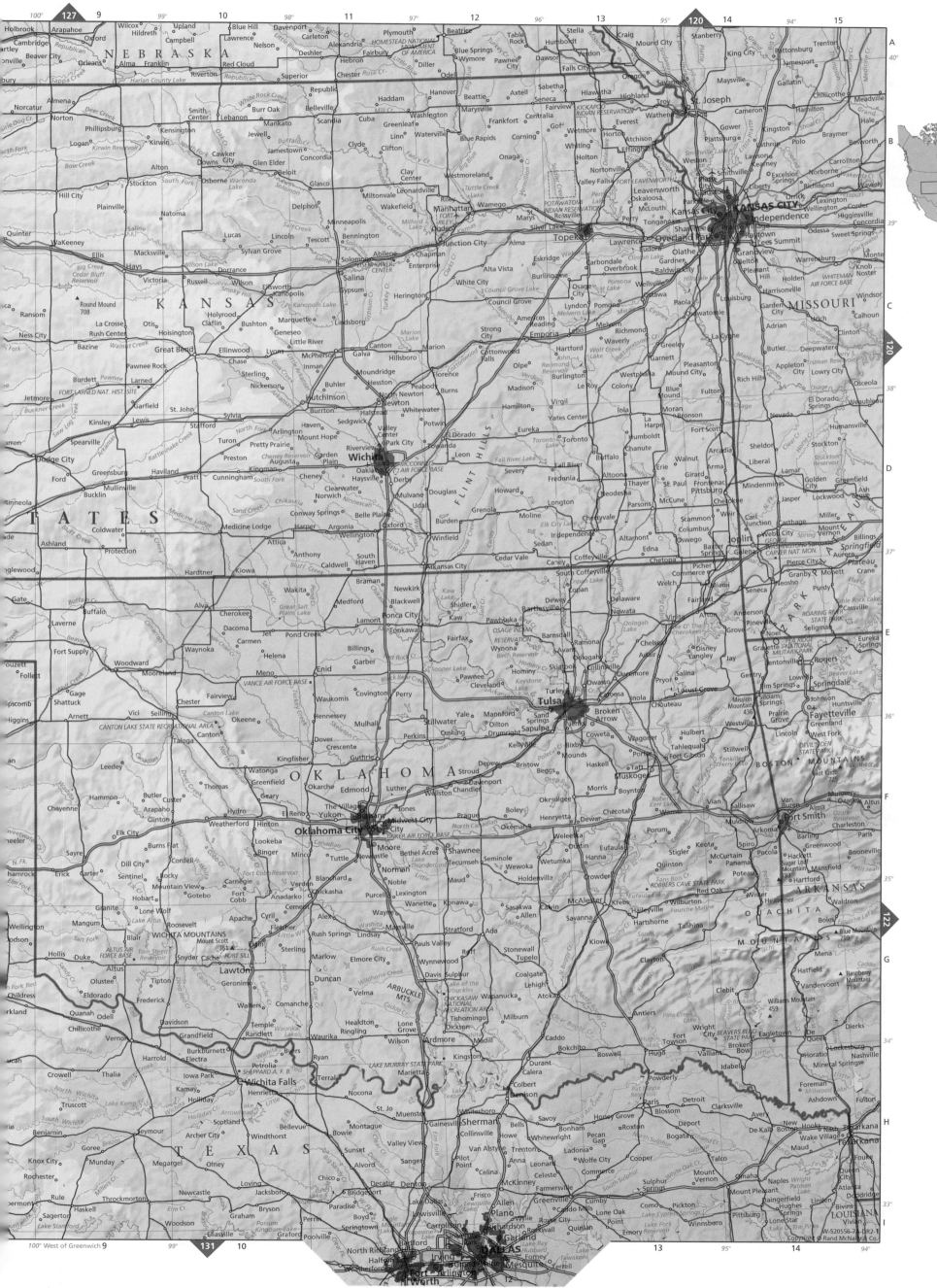

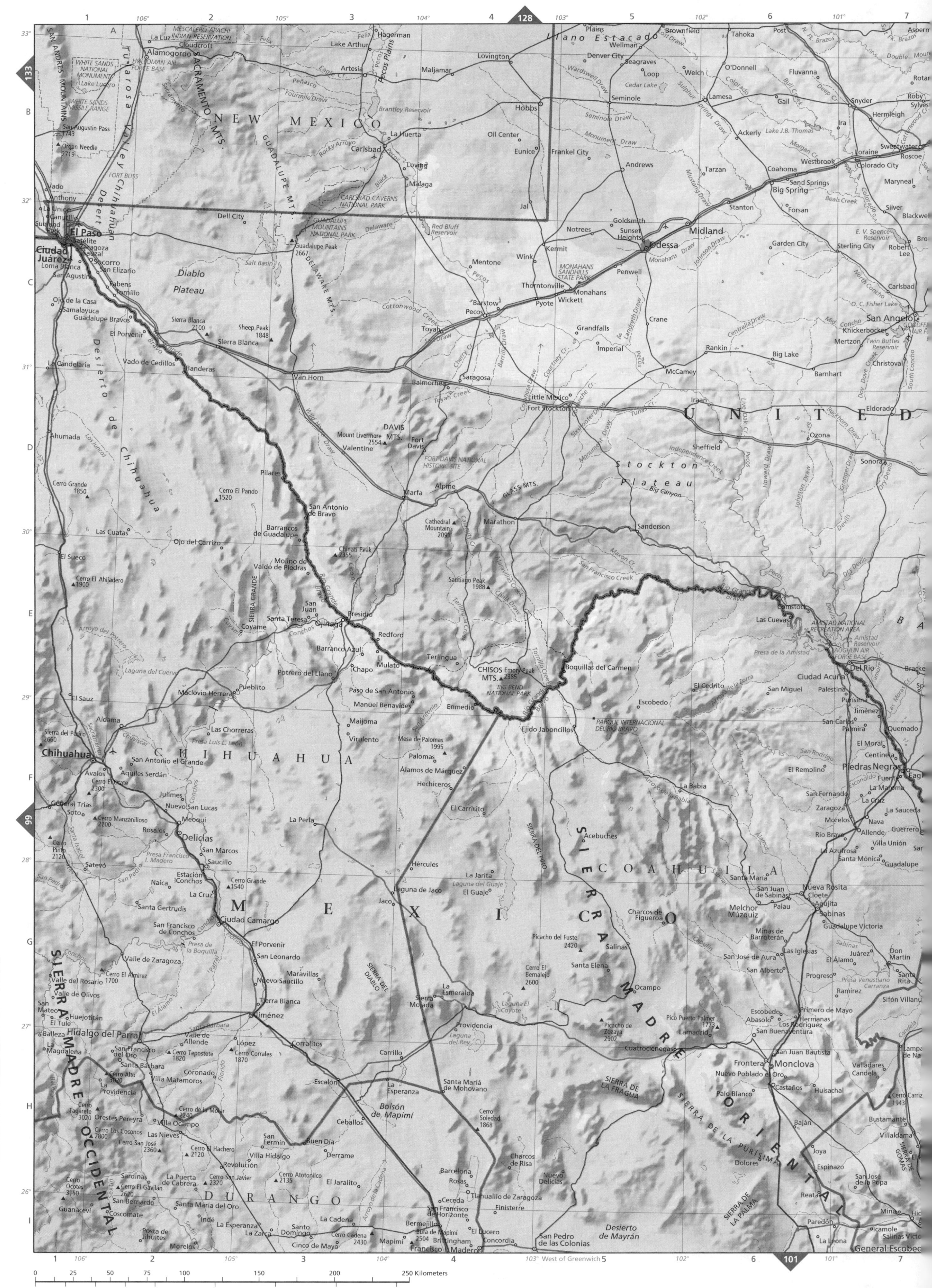
NEW MEXICO
UNITED
CHIHUAHUA
COAHUILA
DURANGO
MEXICO
SIERRA MADRE OCCIDENTAL
SIERRA MADRE ORIENTAL
Llano Estacado
Stockton Plateau
Diablo Plateau
Desierto de Chihuahua
Chihuahuan Desert
Bolsón de Mapimí
Desierto de Mayrán
SACRAMENTO MTS.
GUADALUPE MTS.
DELAWARE MTS.
GLASS MTS.
CHISOS MTS.
DAVIS MTS.
El Paso
Ciudad Juárez
Chihuahua
Midland
Odessa
San Angelo
Del Rio
Ciudad Acuña
Piedras Negras
Monclova
Hidalgo del Parral
Delicias
Ciudad Camargo
Ojinaga
Presidio
Big Spring
Alamogordo
Carlsbad
Hobbs
Fort Stockton
Pecos
Van Horn
Marfa
Alpine
BIG BEND NATIONAL PARK
CARLSBAD CAVERNS NATIONAL PARK
GUADALUPE MOUNTAINS NATIONAL PARK
WHITE SANDS NATIONAL MONUMENT
AMISTAD NATIONAL RECREATION AREA
PARQUE INTERNACIONAL DEL RIO BRAVO
Meters / Feet
4000 13120
3000 9840
2000 6560
1000 3280
500 1640
200 656
Sea Level
200 656
2000 6560
West of Greenwich
0 25 50 75 100 150 200 250 Kilometers
0 25 50 100 150 Miles
Scale 1 : 2,500,000
Lambert Conformal Conic Projection

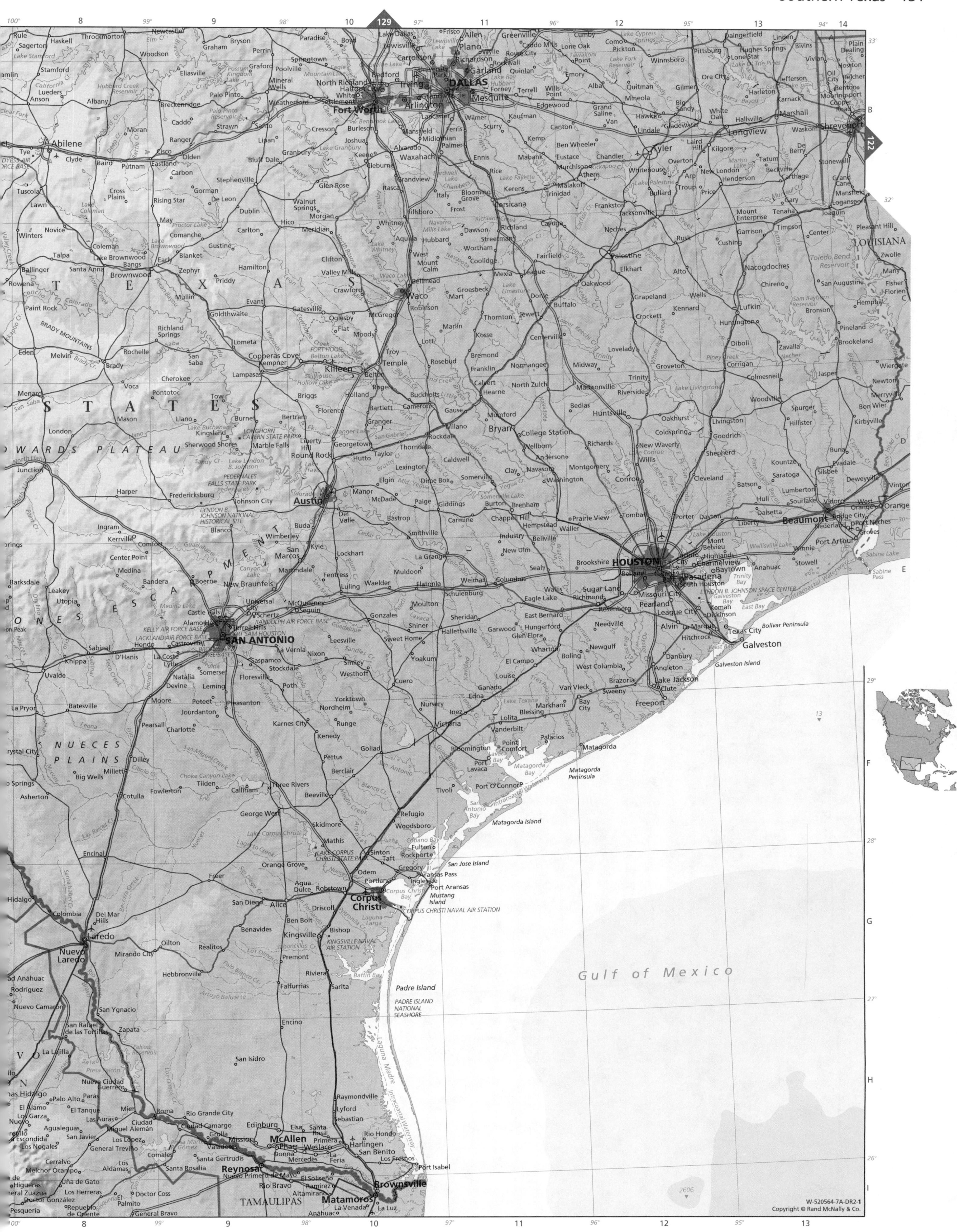
T E X A S
S T A T E S
EDWARDS PLATEAU
BALCONES ESCARPMENT
NUECES PLAINS
BRADY MOUNTAINS
LOUISIANA
TAMAULIPAS
Gulf of Mexico
DALLAS
Fort Worth
Arlington
Garland
Mesquite
Irving
Plano
Abilene
Waco
Killeen
Temple
Austin
SAN ANTONIO
HOUSTON
Pasadena
Baytown
Galveston
Texas City
Beaumont
Port Arthur
Orange
Shreveport
Tyler
Longview
Bryan
College Station
Victoria
Corpus Christi
Laredo
Nuevo Laredo
McAllen
Brownsville
Matamoros
Reynosa
Harlingen
San Marcos
New Braunfels
Huntsville
Lufkin
Nacogdoches
Palestine
Corsicana
Galveston Island
Bolivar Peninsula
Matagorda Peninsula
Matagorda Island
San Jose Island
Mustang Island
Padre Island
PADRE ISLAND NATIONAL SEASHORE
Laguna Madre
Matagorda Bay
Corpus Christi Bay
Toledo Bend Reservoir
Sam Rayburn Reservoir
Lake Livingston
LYNDON B. JOHNSON SPACE CENTER
CORPUS CHRISTI NAVAL AIR STATION
KINGSVILLE NAVAL AIR STATION
KELLY AIR FORCE BASE
LACKLAND AIR FORCE BASE
RANDOLPH AIR FORCE BASE
FORT HOOD
LAKE CORPUS CHRISTI STATE PARK
PEDERNALES FALLS STATE PARK
LONGHORN CAVERN STATE PARK
LYNDON B. JOHNSON NATIONAL HISTORICAL SITE
Intracoastal Waterway
129
122
W-520564-7A-DR2-1

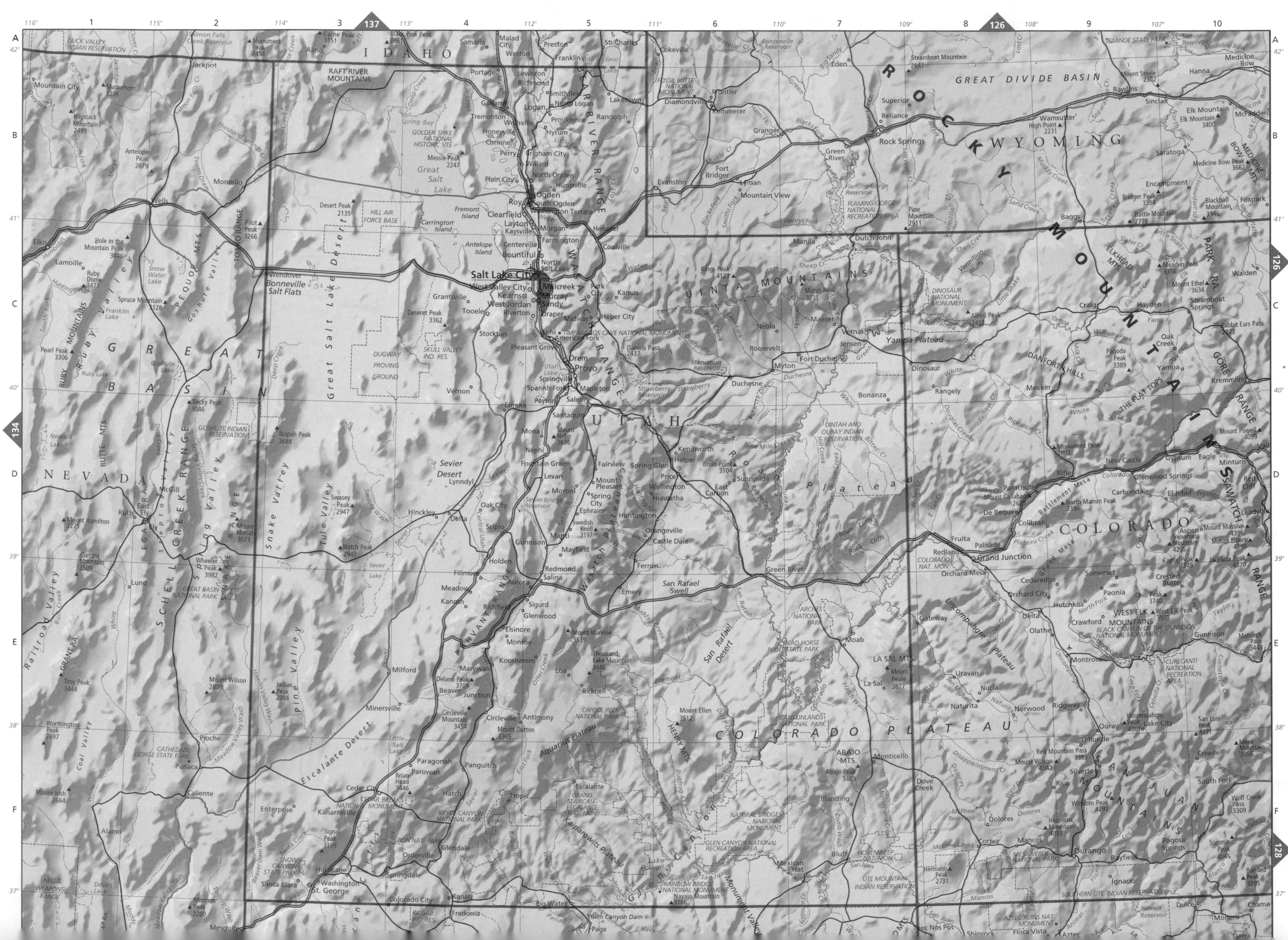

ROCKY MOUNTAINS

WYOMING

COLORADO

UTAH

IDAHO

NEVADA

GREAT BASIN

MEDICINE BOW MTS.

PARK RA.

GORE RANGE

SAWATCH RANGE

SAN JUAN MOUNTAINS

GREAT DIVIDE BASIN

ELKHEAD MTS.

DANFORTH HILLS

Yampa Plateau

UINTA MOUNTAINS

COLORADO PLATEAU

LA SAL MTS.

HENRY MTS.

WASATCH RANGE

Salt Lake City

Great Salt Lake

Great Salt Lake Desert

Sevier Desert

Escalante Desert

PEQUOP MTS.

TOANO RANGE

RAFT RIVER MOUNTAINS

BEAR RIVER RANGE

RUBY MOUNTAINS

SCHELL CREEK RANGE

EGAN RANGE

Pine Valley

Snake Valley

Tule Valley

Steamboat Mountain 2467

Medicine Bow Peak 3662

Ogden

Provo

Grand Junction

Durango

Moab

Monticello

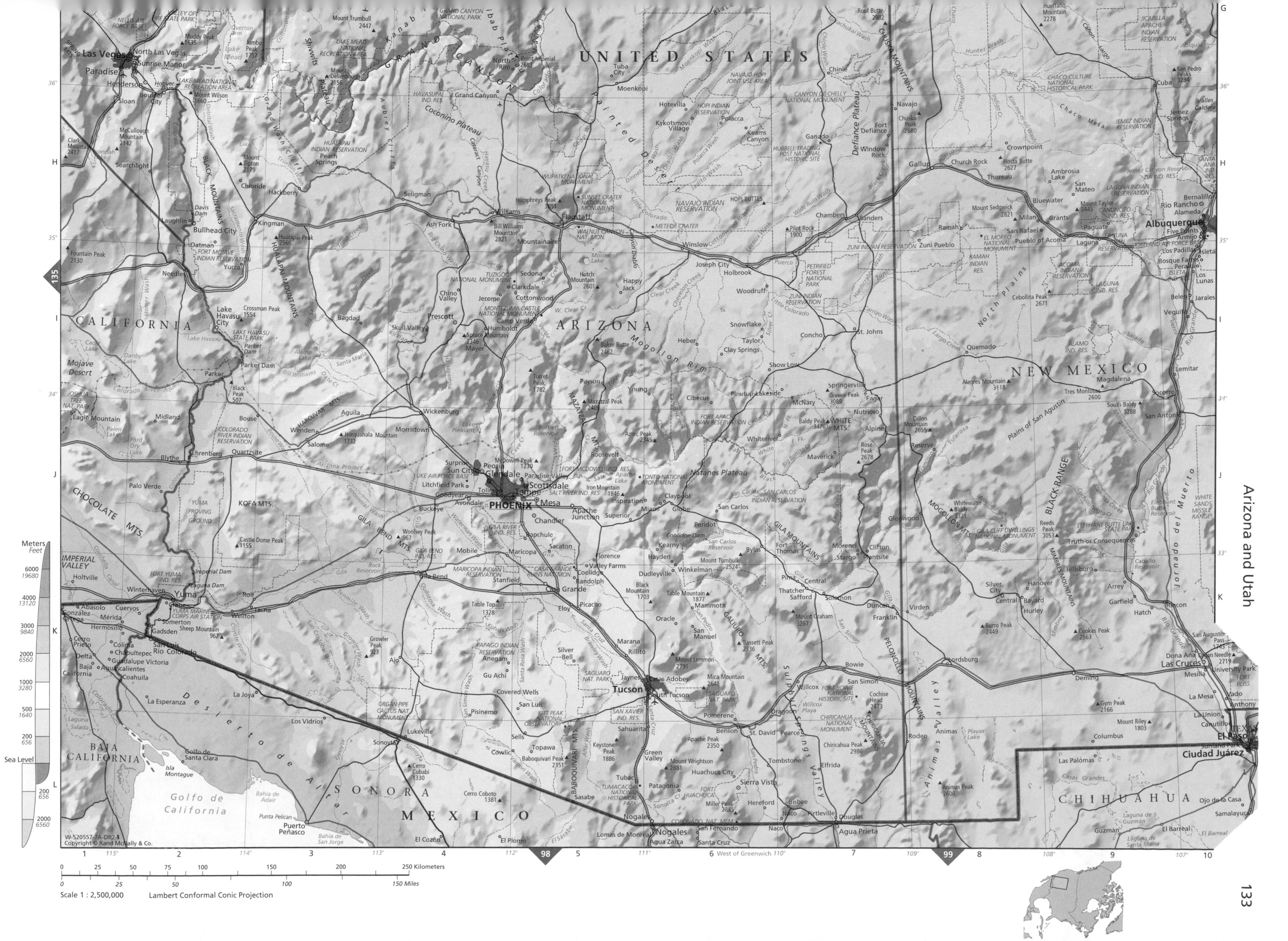
UNITED STATES
MEXICO
ARIZONA
NEW MEXICO
CALIFORNIA
SONORA
CHIHUAHUA
BAJA CALIFORNIA
Golfo de California
Desierto de Altar
PHOENIX
Tucson
Albuquerque
Las Vegas
Flagstaff
Yuma
Ciudad Juárez
El Paso
Las Cruces
Nogales
Scale 1 : 2,500,000
Lambert Conformal Conic Projection
250 Kilometers
150 Miles
Meters Feet
6000 19680
4000 13120
3000 9840
2000 6560
1000 3280
500 1640
200 656
Sea Level
200 656
2000 6560
W-520557-7A-DR2-1
Copyright © Rand McNally & Co.

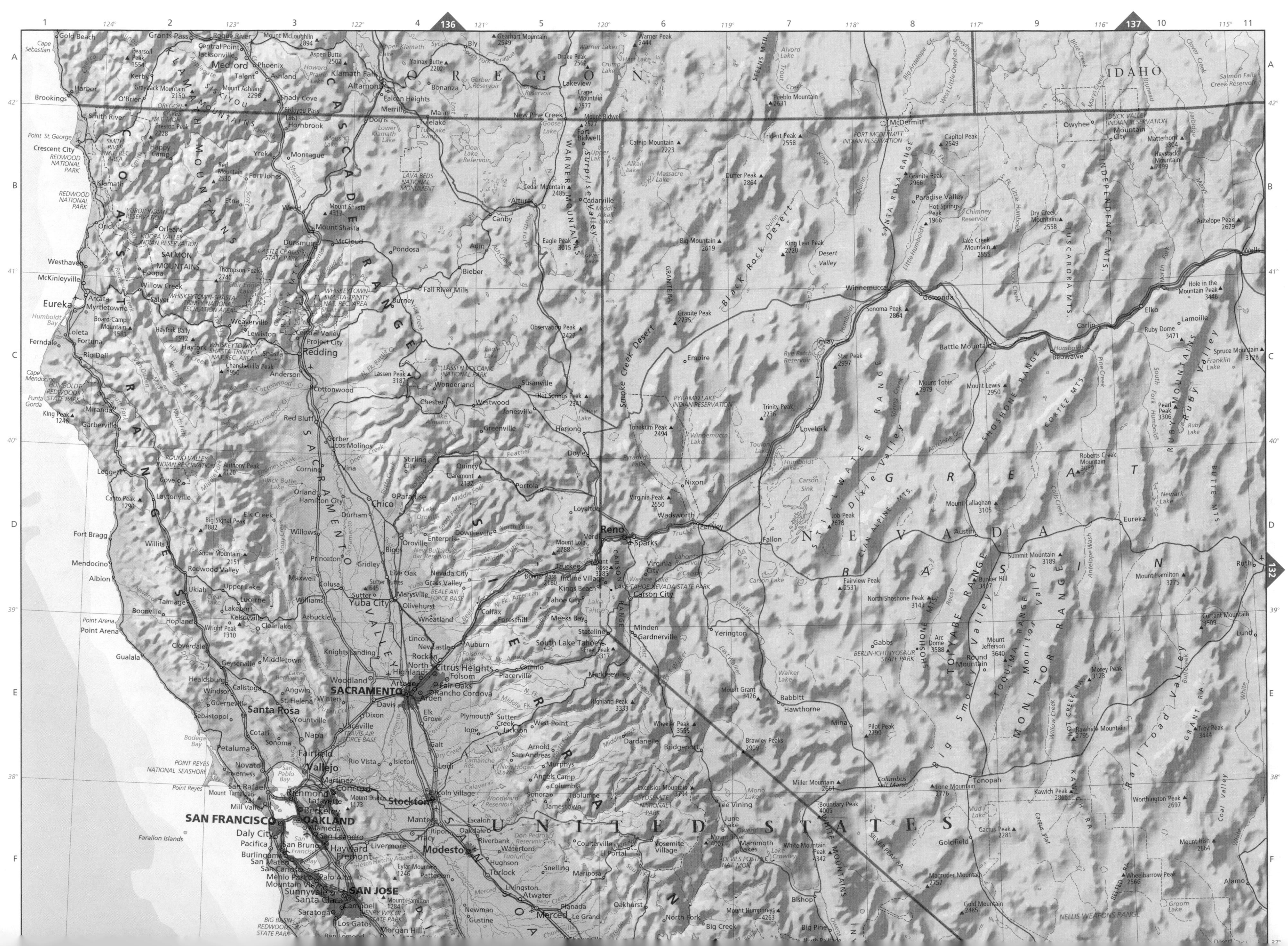
IDAHO
OREGON
NEVADA
GREAT BASIN
UNITED STATES
CASCADE RANGE
COAST RANGES
SIERRA NEVADA
SACRAMENTO VALLEY
SAN JOAQUIN VALLEY
KLAMATH MOUNTAINS
SALMON MOUNTAINS
INDEPENDENCE MTS.
TUSCARORA MTS.
SANTA ROSA RANGE
SHOSHONE RANGE
TOIYABE RANGE
TOQUIMA RANGE
MONITOR RANGE
WHITE MOUNTAINS
WARNER MOUNTAINS
CARSON RANGE
RUBY MOUNTAINS
Black Rock Desert
Smoke Creek Desert
Surprise Valley
Smoky Valley
Monitor Valley
Railroad Valley
Ruby Valley
Dixie Valley
SAN FRANCISCO
OAKLAND
SAN JOSE
SACRAMENTO
Stockton
Modesto
Reno
Sparks
Carson City
Eureka
Redding
Medford
Klamath Falls
Elko
Winnemucca
Tonopah
Fallon
Lovelock
Santa Rosa
Vallejo
Chico
Yuba City
Ukiah
Crescent City
Lakeview
Susanville
Hawthorne
Bishop
Lake Tahoe
Farallon Islands
NELLIS WEAPONS RANGE
136
137
132

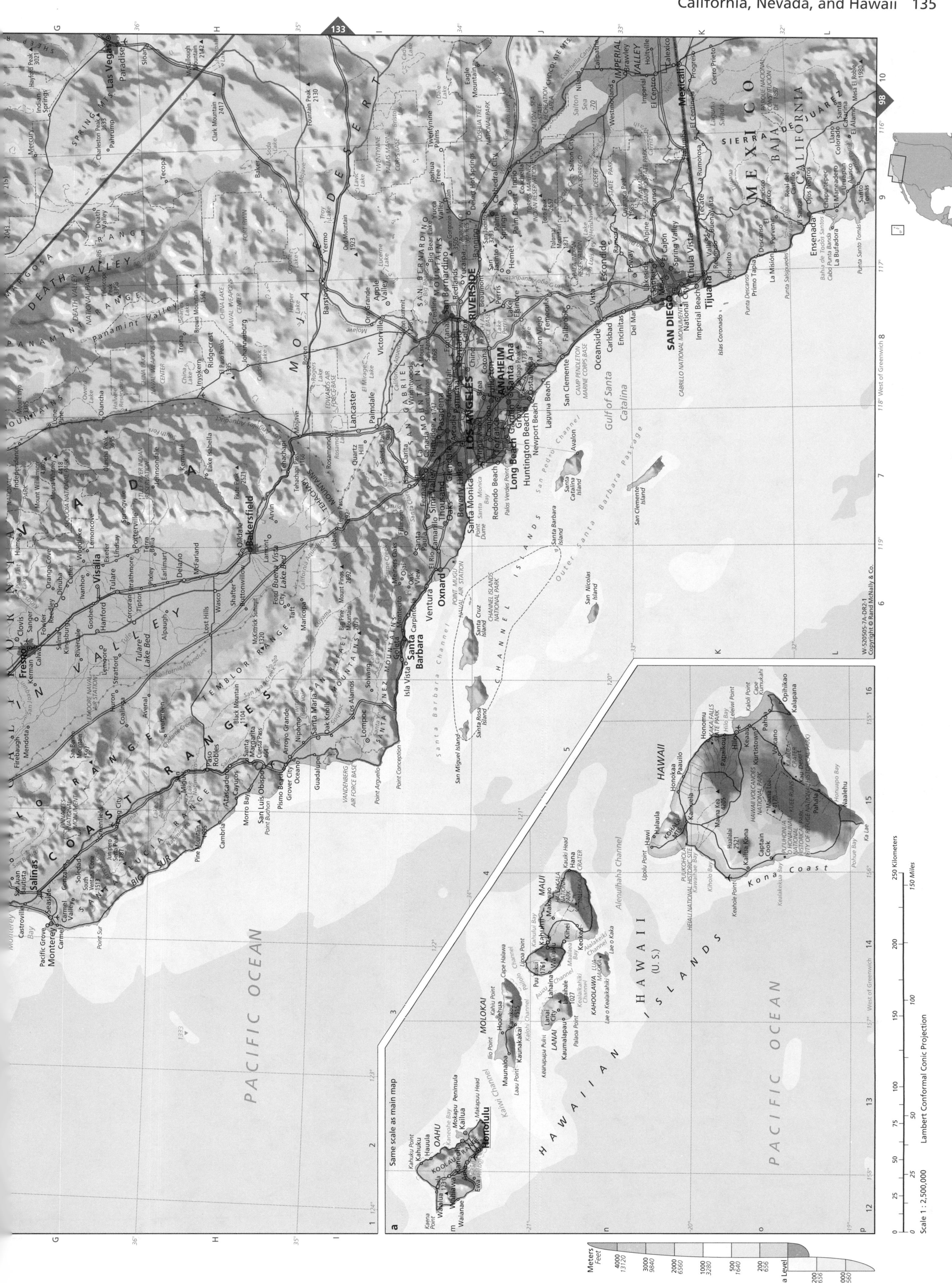
PACIFIC OCEAN
Same scale as main map
HAWAIIAN ISLANDS
HAWAII (U.S.)
Scale 1 : 2,500,000
Lambert Conformal Conic Projection
Meters
Feet
Sea Level
W-520505-7A-DR2-1
Copyright © Rand McNally & Co.

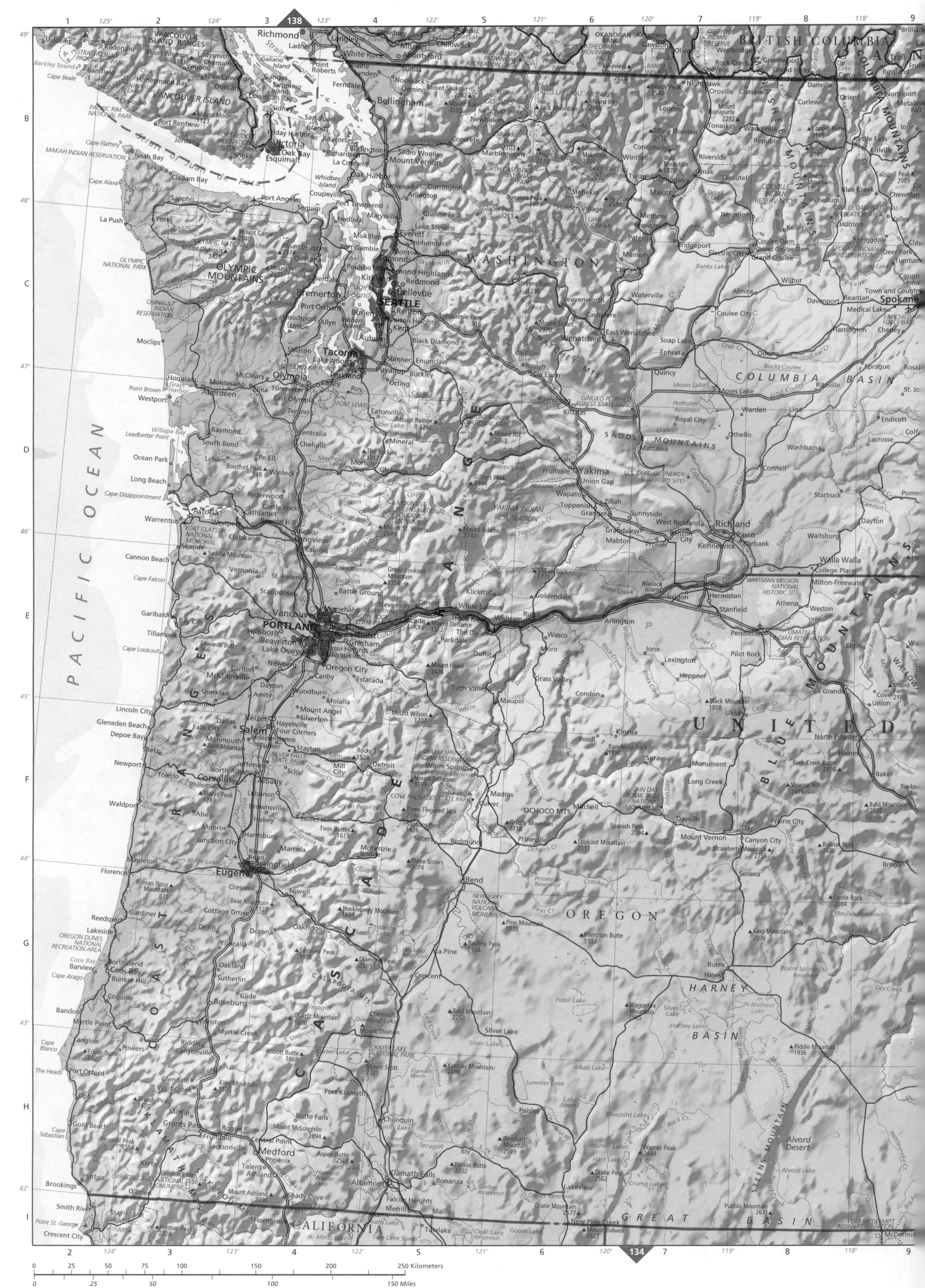

Scale 1 : 2,500,000   Lambert Conformal Conic Projection

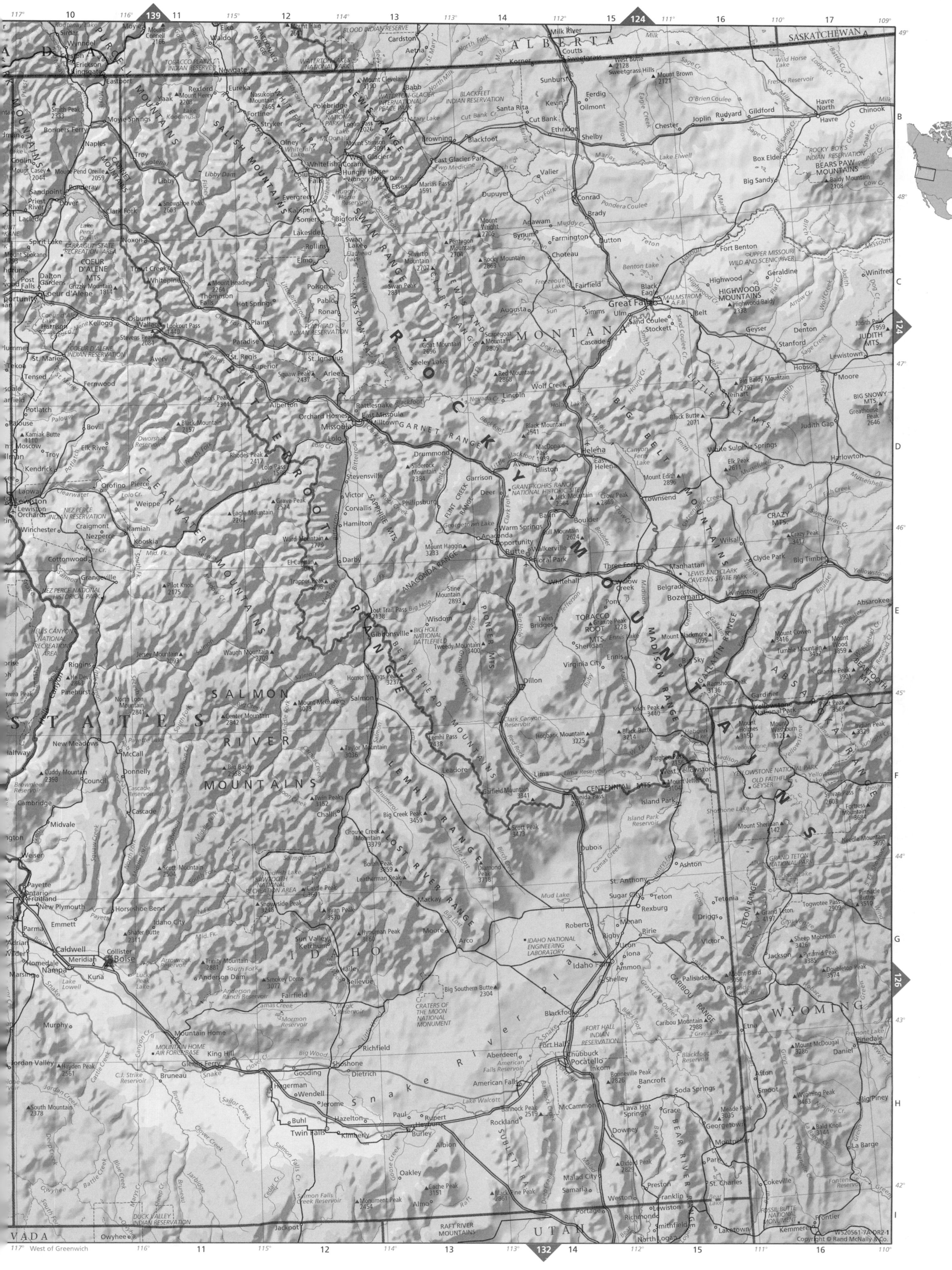
ALBERTA
SASKATCHEWAN
MONTANA
IDAHO
WYOMING
UTAH
ROCKY MOUNTAINS
SALMON RIVER MOUNTAINS
Great Falls
Helena
Missoula
Butte
Bozeman
Boise
Pocatello
Idaho Falls
Twin Falls
Lewiston
Coeur d'Alene
Kalispell
Yellowstone National Park
Copyright © Rand McNally & Co.

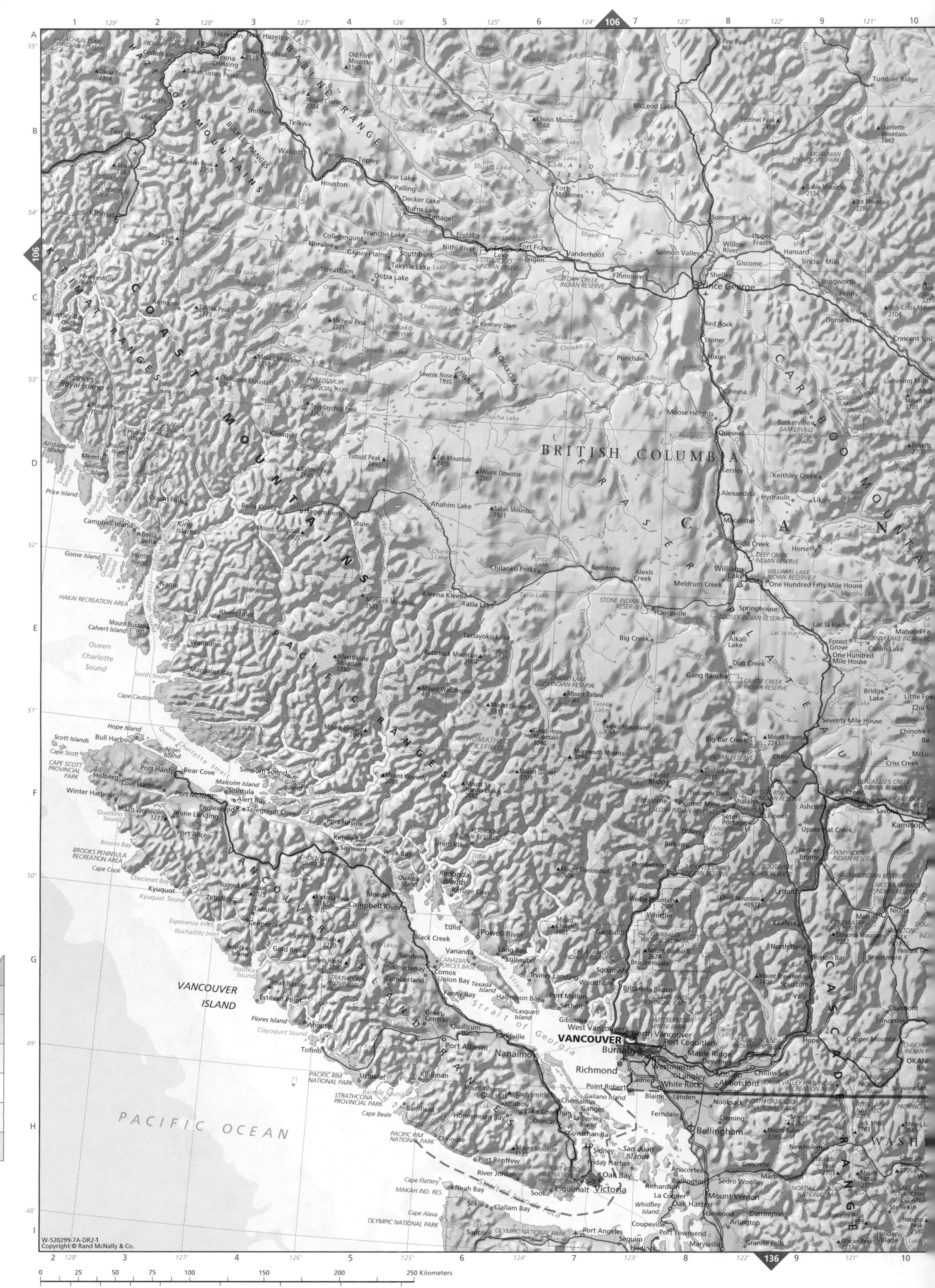

Meters
Feet

4000
13120

3000
9840

2000
6560

1000
3280

500
1640

200
656

Sea Level

200
656

2000
6560

0   25   50   75   100   150   200   250 Kilometers

0   25   50   100   150 Miles

Scale 1 : 2,500,000   Lambert Conformal Conic Projection

PACIFIC OCEAN

VANCOUVER ISLAND

BRITISH COLUMBIA

WASH.

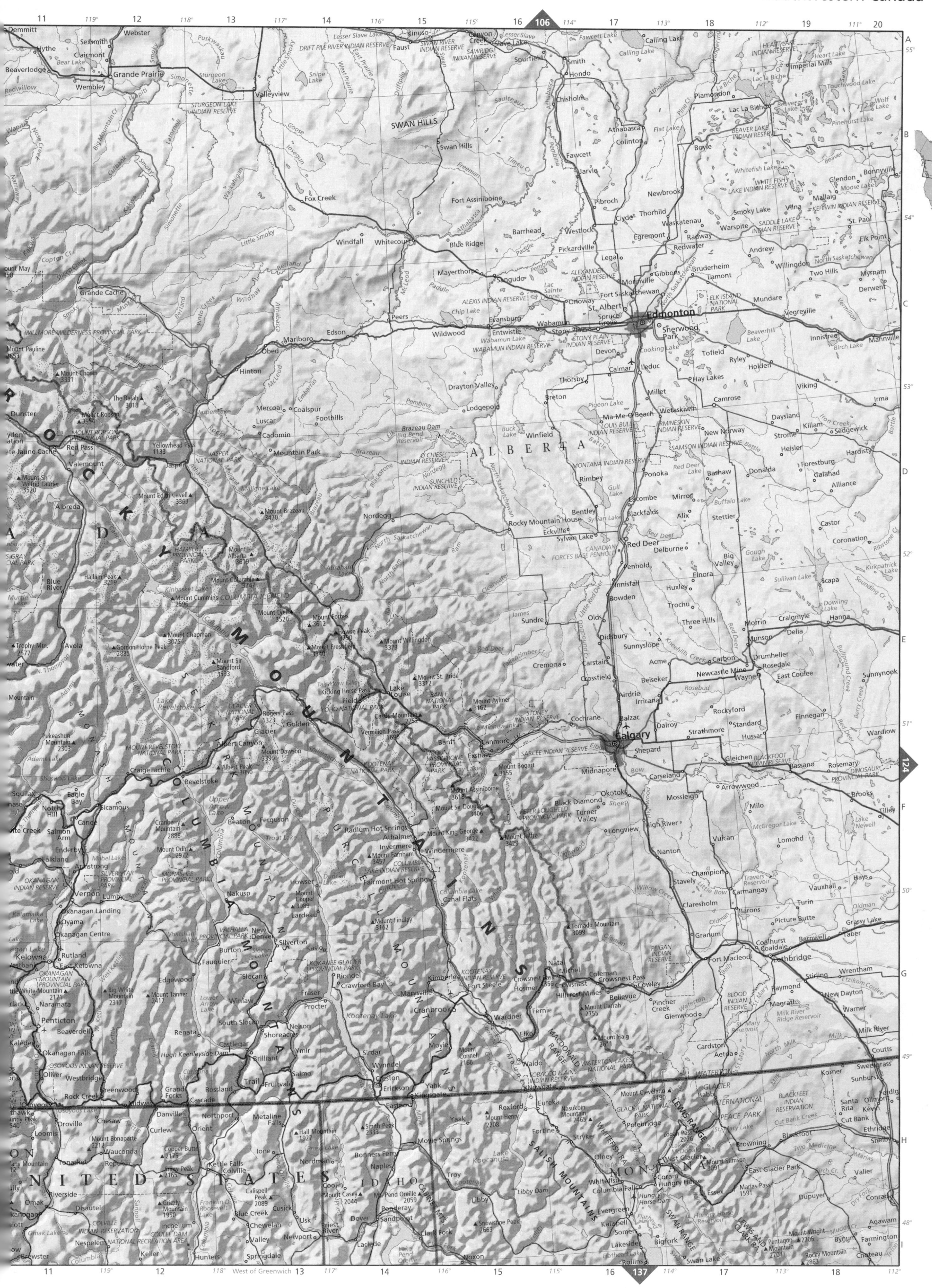
ALBERTA
ROCKY MOUNTAINS
COLUMBIA MOUNTAINS
PURCELL MOUNTAINS
SELKIRK MOUNTAINS
MONASHEE MOUNTAINS
UNITED STATES
IDAHO
MONTANA
SALISH MOUNTAINS
WHITEFISH RANGE
LEWIS RANGE
SWAN RANGE
CLARK FORK
SWAN HILLS
Edmonton
Calgary
Red Deer
Lethbridge
Grande Prairie
Grande Cache
Jasper
Banff
Canmore
Hinton
Edson
Whitecourt
Athabasca
Camrose
Wetaskiwin
Lacombe
Olds
Airdrie
Cochrane
Okotoks
High River
Claresholm
Fort Macleod
Cardston
Drumheller
Hanna
Brooks
Vegreville
Mannville
St. Albert
Sherwood Park
Leduc
Stony Plain
Sylvan Lake
Rocky Mountain House
Sundre
Pincher Creek
Crowsnest Pass
Milk River
Coutts
Revelstoke
Golden
Kelowna
Vernon
Penticton
Salmon Arm
Nelson
Trail
Castlegar
Cranbrook
Kimberley
Fernie
Invermere
Radium Hot Springs
Creston
Valemount
Blue River
Mount Robson
Lake Louise
Field
Glacier
Yellowhead Pass
Rogers Pass
Kicking Horse Pass
Crowsnest Pass
JASPER NATIONAL PARK
BANFF NATIONAL PARK
YOHO NATIONAL PARK
KOOTENAY NATIONAL PARK
GLACIER NATIONAL PARK
MOUNT REVELSTOKE NATIONAL PARK
WATERTON LAKES NATIONAL PARK
WATERTON GLACIER INTERNATIONAL PEACE PARK
ELK ISLAND NATIONAL PARK
WILLMORE WILDERNESS PROVINCIAL PARK
DINOSAUR PROVINCIAL PARK
BLACKFEET INDIAN RESERVATION
COLVILLE INDIAN RESERVATION
Kootenay Lake
Upper Arrow Lake
Lower Arrow Lake
Okanagan Lake
Lesser Slave Lake
Lac La Biche
Pigeon Lake
Gull Lake
Buffalo Lake
Kalispell
Whitefish
Columbia Falls
Polebridge
Browning
East Glacier Park
Shelby
Libby
Troy
Eureka
Bonners Ferry
Sandpoint
Newport
Colville
Kettle Falls
Oroville
Omak
Cut Bank
West of Greenwich

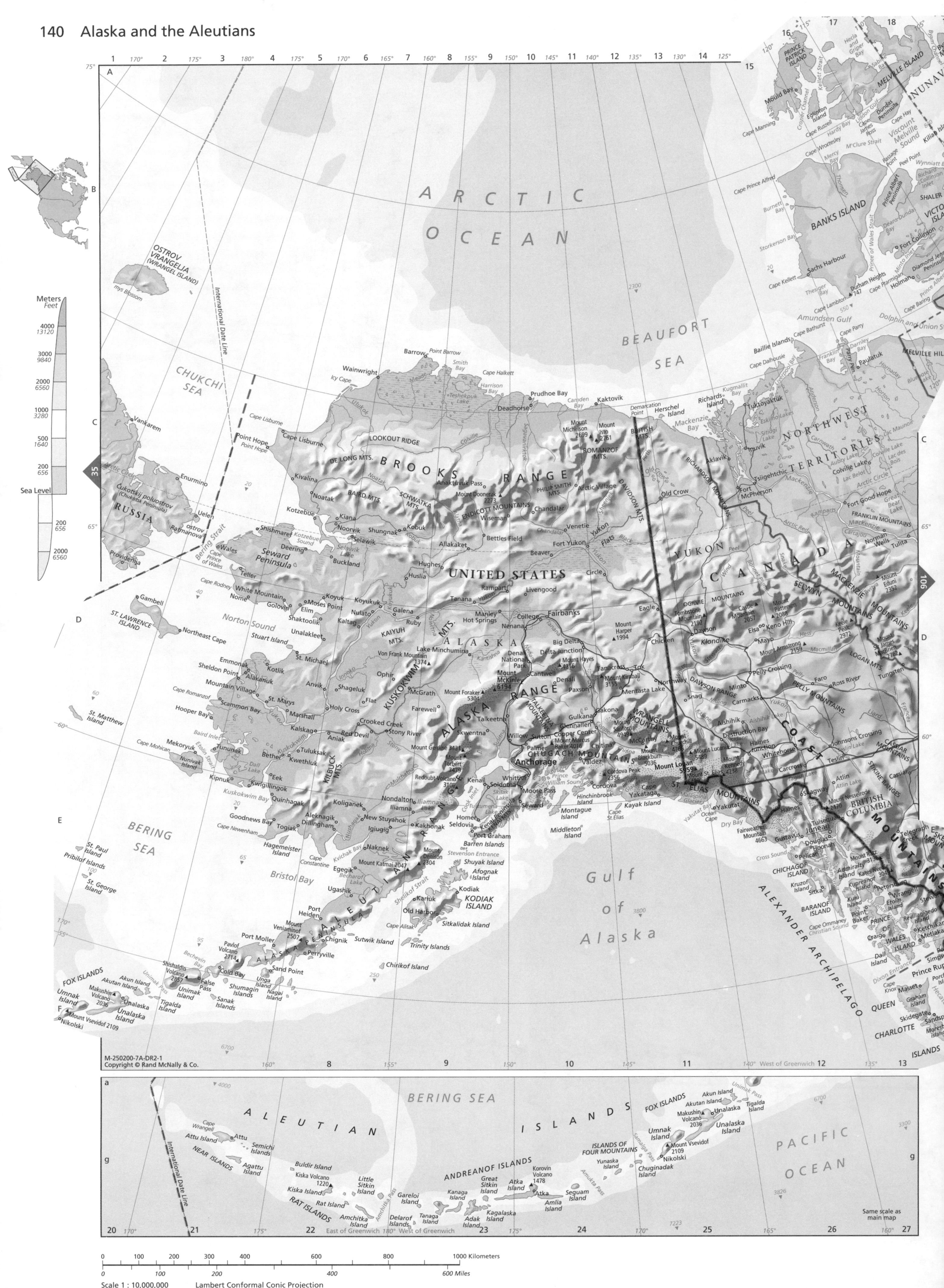

Meters
Feet

4000
13120

3000
9840

2000
6560

1000
3280

500
1640

200
656

Sea Level

200
656

2000
6560

ARCTIC OCEAN

BEAUFORT SEA

CHUKCHI SEA

RUSSIA

BROOKS RANGE

UNITED STATES

CANADA

YUKON

NORTHWEST TERRITORIES

BRITISH COLUMBIA

BERING SEA

Bristol Bay

Gulf of Alaska

PACIFIC OCEAN

ALEUTIAN ISLANDS

NEAR ISLANDS

RAT ISLANDS

ANDREANOF ISLANDS

FOX ISLANDS

ISLANDS OF FOUR MOUNTAINS

0   100   200   300   400   600   800   1000 Kilometers

0   100   200   400   600 Miles

Scale 1 : 10,000,000   Lambert Conformal Conic Projection

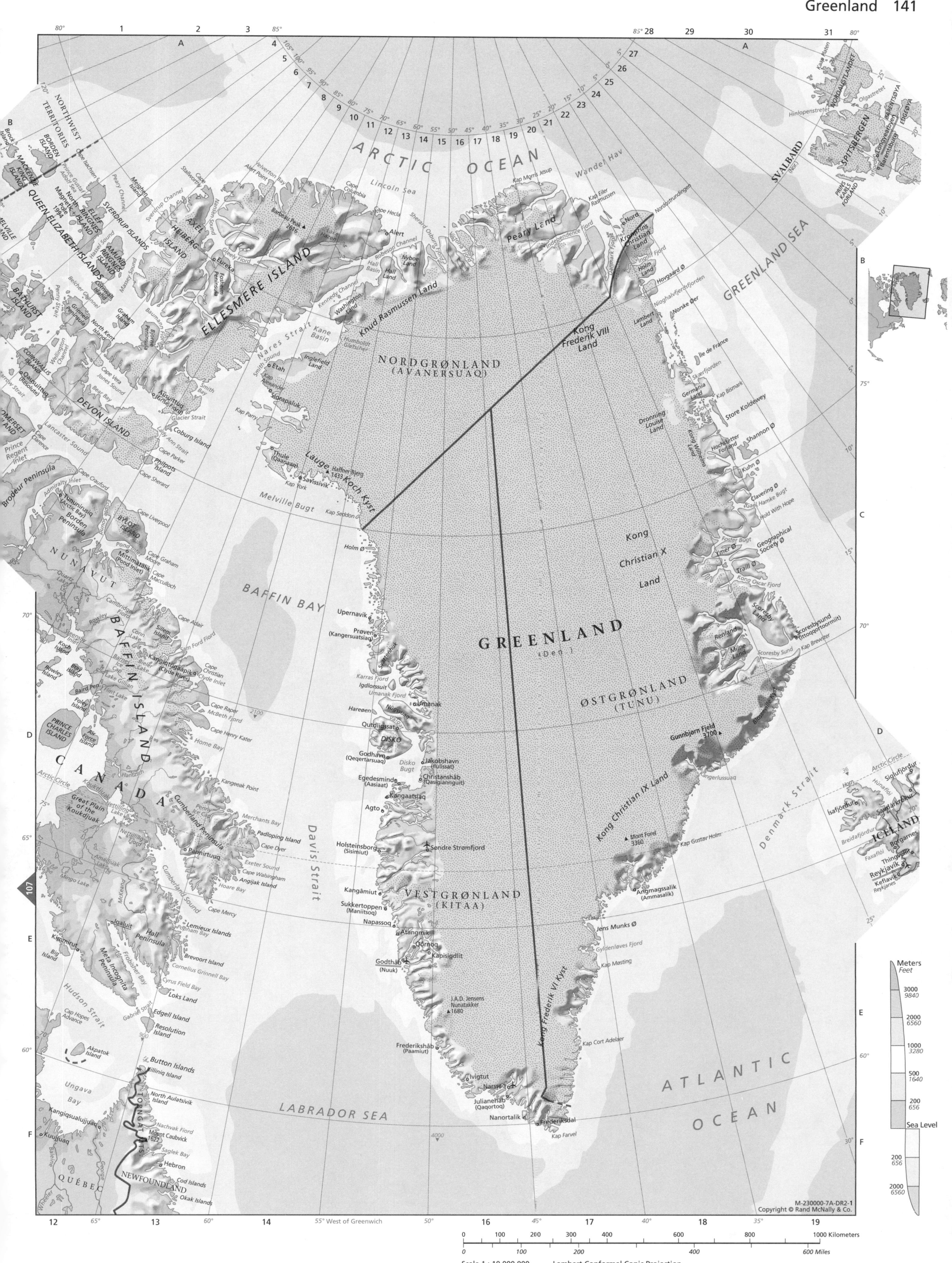

Scale 1 : 10,000,000   Lambert Conformal Conic Projection

M-230000-7A-DR2-1
Copyright © Rand McNally & Co.

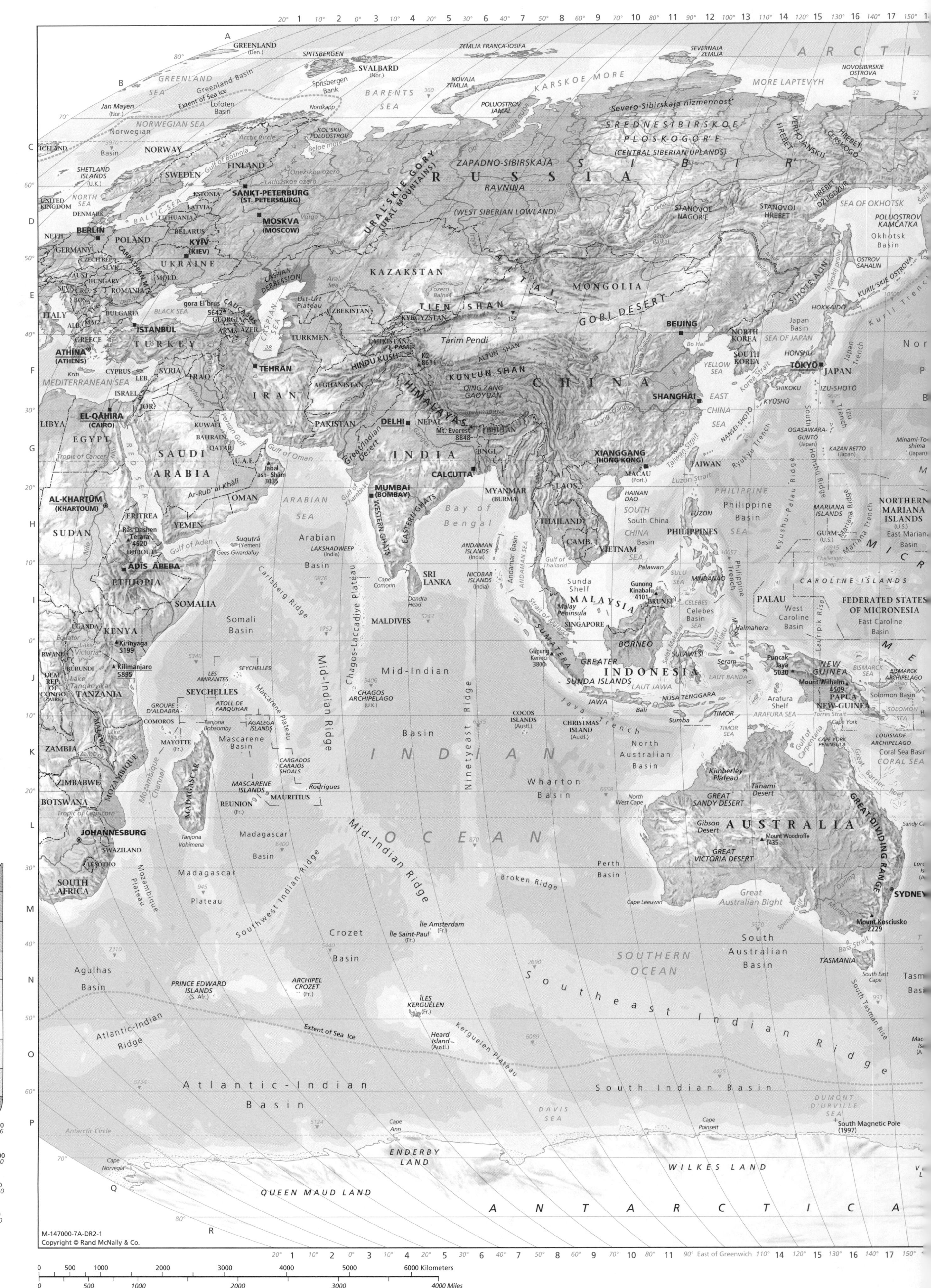

Meters
Feet

6000
19680

4000
13120

3000
9840

2000
6560

1000
3280

500
1640

200
656

Sea Level

200
656

2000
6560

4000
13120

6000
19680

M-147000-7A-DR2-1
Copyright © Rand McNally & Co.

0   500   1000   2000   3000   4000   5000   6000 Kilometers

0   500   1000   2000   3000   4000 Miles

Scale 1 : 60,000,000   Robinson Projection

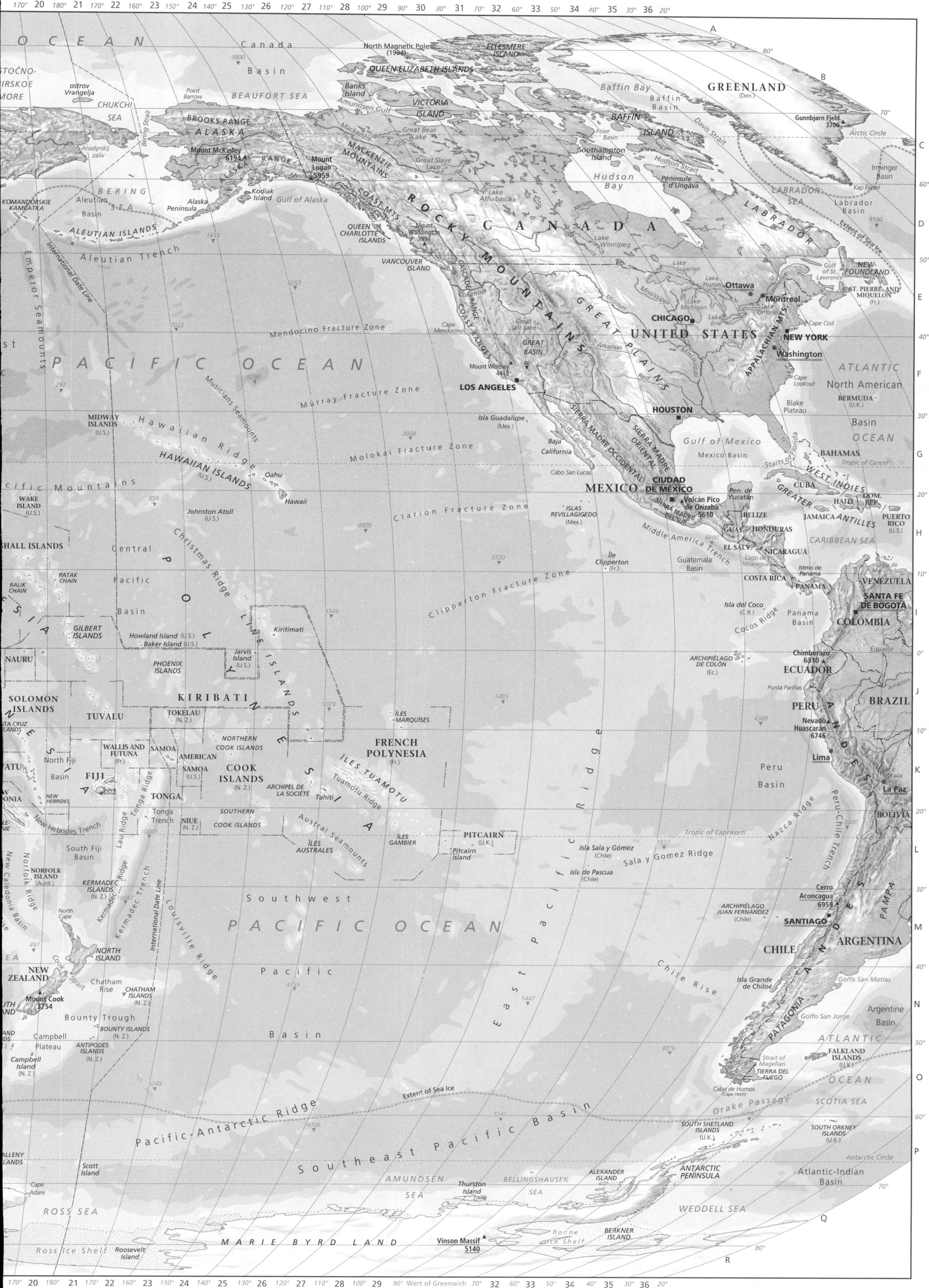
PACIFIC OCEAN
Southwest
PACIFIC OCEAN
CANADA
UNITED STATES
MEXICO
GREENLAND
ALASKA
ROCKY MOUNTAINS
GREAT PLAINS
Hudson Bay
Gulf of Mexico
CARIBBEAN SEA
HAWAIIAN ISLANDS
KIRIBATI
FRENCH POLYNESIA
COOK ISLANDS
FIJI
TONGA
TUVALU
NAURU
SOLOMON ISLANDS
NEW ZEALAND
COLOMBIA
ECUADOR
PERU
BRAZIL
BOLIVIA
CHILE
ARGENTINA
VENEZUELA
LOS ANGELES
CHICAGO
NEW YORK
HOUSTON
Washington
Ottawa
Montreal
CIUDAD DE MÉXICO
SANTA FE DE BOGOTÁ
Lima
La Paz
SANTIAGO
East Pacific Ridge
Pacific-Antarctic Ridge
Southeast Pacific Basin
AMUNDSEN SEA
BELLINGSHAUSEN SEA
WEDDELL SEA
ROSS SEA
MARIE BYRD LAND
Vinson Massif 5140
Drake Passage
SCOTIA SEA
ATLANTIC OCEAN
West of Greenwich

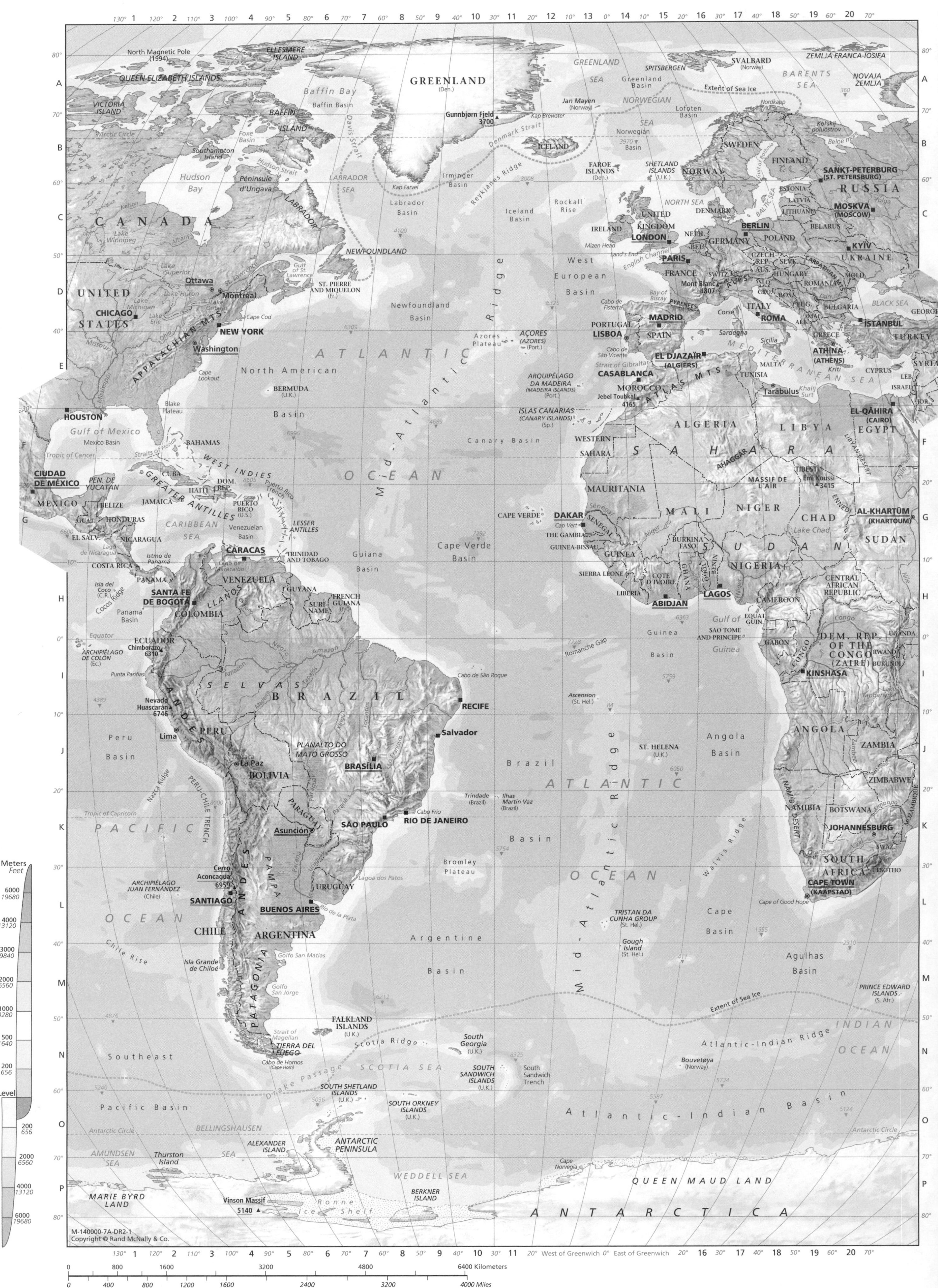

Scale 1 : 60,000,000   Robinson Projection

Index to World Reference Maps

Introduction to the Index

This index includes in a single alphabetical list approximately 54,000 names of places and geographical features that appear on the reference maps. Each name is followed by the name of the country or continent in which it is located, an alpha-numeric map reference key, and a page reference.

Names The names of cities and towns appear in the index in regular type. The names of all other features appear in *italics*, followed by descriptive terms (hill, mtn., state) to indicate their nature.

Abbreviations of names on the maps have been standardized as much as possible. Names that are abbreviated on the maps are generally spelled out in full in the index.

Country names and names of features that extend beyond the boundaries of one country are followed by the name of the continent in which each is located. Country designations follow the names of all other places in the index. The locations of places in the United States, Canada, and the United Kingdom are further defined by abbreviations that indicate the state, province, or other political division in which each is located.

All abbreviations used in the index are defined in the List of Abbreviations to the right.

Alphabetization Names are alphabetized in the order of the letters of the English alphabet. Spanish *ll* and *ch*, for example, are not treated as distinct letters. Furthermore, diacritical marks are disregarded in alphabetization—German or Scandinavian *ä* or *ö* are treated as *a* or *o*.

The names of physical features may appear inverted, since they are always alphabetized under the proper, not the generic, part of the name, thus: "Gibraltar, Strait of". Otherwise every entry, whether consisting of one word or more, is alphabetized as a single continuous entity. "Lakeland", for example, appears after "La Crosse" and before "La Salle". Names beginning with articles (Le Havre, Den Helder, Al-Manāmah) are not inverted. Names beginning "St.", "Ste." and "Sainte" are alphabetized as though spelled "Saint".

In the case of identical names, towns are listed first, then political divisions, then physical features. Entries that are completely identical are listed alphabetically by country name.

Map Reference Keys and Page References The map reference keys and page references are found in the last two columns of each entry.

Each map reference key consists of a letter and number. The letters correspond to letters along the sides of the maps. Lowercase letters refer to inset maps. The numbers correspond to numbers that appear across the tops and bottoms of the maps.

Map reference keys for point features, such as cities and mountain peaks, indicate the locations of the symbols for these features. For other features, such as countries, mountain ranges, or rivers, the map reference keys indicate the locations of the names.

The page number generally refers to the main map for the country in which the feature is located. Page references for two-page maps always refer to the left-hand page.

List of Abbreviations

Ab., Can.	Alberta, Can.
Afg.	Afghanistan
Afr.	Africa
Ak., U.S.	Alaska, U.S.
Al., U.S.	Alabama, U.S.
Alb.	Albania
Alg.	Algeria
Am. Sam.	American Samoa
anch.	anchorage
And.	Andorra
Ang.	Angola
Ant.	Antarctica
Antig.	Antigua and Barbuda
aq.	aqueduct
Ar., U.S.	Arkansas, U.S.
Arg.	Argentina
Arm.	Armenia
at.	atoll
Aus.	Austria
Austl.	Australia
Az., U.S.	Arizona, U.S.
Azer.	Azerbaijan
b.	bay, gulf, inlet, lagoon
B.C., Can.	British Columbia, Can.
Bah.	Bahamas
Bahr.	Bahrain
Barb.	Barbados
bas.	basin
Bdi.	Burundi
Bel.	Belgium
Bela.	Belarus
Ber.	Bermuda
Bhu.	Bhutan
B.I.O.T.	British Indian Ocean Territory
Blg.	Bulgaria
Bngl.	Bangladesh
Bol.	Bolivia
Bos.	Bosnia and Hercegovina
Bots.	Botswana
Braz.	Brazil
Bru.	Brunei
Br. Vir. Is.	British Virgin Islands
Burkina	Burkina Faso
c.	cape, point
Ca., U.S.	California, U.S.
Cam.	Cameroon
Camb.	Cambodia
Can.	Canada
can.	canal
C.A.R.	Central African Republic
Cay. Is.	Cayman Islands
Christ. I.	Christmas Island
C. Iv.	Cote d'Ivoire
clf.	cliff, escarpment
Co., U.S.	Colorado, U.S.
co.	county, district, etc.
Cocos Is.	Cocos (Keeling) Islands
Col.	Colombia
Com.	Comoros
cont.	continent
Cook Is.	Cook Islands
C.R.	Costa Rica
crat.	crater
Cro.	Croatia
cst.	coast, beach
Ct., U.S.	Connecticut, U.S.
ctry.	independent country
C.V.	Cape Verde
cv.	cave
Cyp.	Cyprus
Czech Rep.	Czech Republic
D.C., U.S.	District of Columbia, U.S.
De., U.S.	Delaware, U.S.
Den.	Denmark
dep.	dependency, colony
depr.	depression
des.	desert
Dji.	Djibouti
Dom.	Dominica
Dom. Rep.	Dominican Republic
D.R.C.	Democratic Republic of the Congo
Ec.	Ecuador
El Sal.	El Salvador
Eng., U.K.	England, U.K.
Eq. Gui.	Equatorial Guinea
Erit.	Eritrea
Est.	Estonia
est.	estuary
Eth.	Ethiopia
Eur.	Europe
Falk. Is.	Falkland Islands
Far. Is.	Faroe Islands
Fin.	Finland
Fl., U.S.	Florida, U.S.
for.	forest, moor
Fr.	France
Fr. Gu.	French Guiana
Fr. Poly.	French Polynesia
Ga., U.S.	Georgia, U.S.
Gam.	The Gambia
Gaza	Gaza Strip
Geor.	Georgia
Ger.	Germany
Gib.	Gibraltar
Golan	Golan Heights
Grc.	Greece
Gren.	Grenada
Grnld.	Greenland

Guad.	Guadeloupe
Guat.	Guatemala
Guern.	Guernsey
Gui.	Guinea
Gui.-B.	Guinea-Bissau
Guy.	Guyana
gysr.	geyser
Hi., U.S.	Hawaii, U.S.
hist.	historic site, ruins
hist. reg.	historic region
Hond.	Honduras
Hung.	Hungary
i.	island
Ia., U.S.	Iowa, U.S.
Ice.	Iceland
ice	ice feature, glacier
Id., U.S.	Idaho, U.S.
Il., U.S.	Illinois, U.S.
In., U.S.	Indiana, U.S.
Indon.	Indonesia
I. of Man	Isle of Man
Ire.	Ireland
is.	islands
Isr.	Israel
isth.	isthmus
Jam.	Jamaica
Jer.	Jericho Area
Jord.	Jordan
Kaz.	Kazakhstan
Kir.	Kiribati
Kor., N.	Korea, North
Kor., S.	Korea, South
Ks., U.S.	Kansas, U.S.
Kuw.	Kuwait
Ky., U.S.	Kentucky, U.S.
Kyrg.	Kyrgyzstan
l.	lake, pond
La., U.S.	Louisiana, U.S.
Lat.	Latvia
lav.	lava flow
Leb.	Lebanon
Leso.	Lesotho
Lib.	Liberia
Liech.	Liechtenstein
Lith.	Lithuania
Lux.	Luxembourg
Ma., U.S.	Massachusetts, U.S.
Mac.	Macedonia
Madag.	Madagascar
Malay.	Malaysia
Mald.	Maldives
Marsh. Is.	Marshall Islands
Mart.	Martinique
Maur.	Mauritania
May.	Mayotte
Mb., Can.	Manitoba, Can.
Md., U.S.	Maryland, U.S.
Me., U.S.	Maine, U.S.
Mex.	Mexico
Mi., U.S.	Michigan, U.S.
Micron.	Micronesia, Federated States of
Mid. Is.	Midway Islands
misc. cult.	miscellaneous cultural
Mn., U.S.	Minnesota, U.S.
Mo., U.S.	Missouri, U.S.
Mol.	Moldova
Mon.	Monaco
Mong.	Mongolia
Monts.	Montserrat
Mor.	Morocco
Moz.	Mozambique
Mrts.	Mauritius
Ms., U.S.	Mississippi, U.S.
Mt., U.S.	Montana, U.S.
mth.	river mouth or channel
mtn.	mountain
mts.	mountains
Mwi.	Malawi
Mya.	Myanmar
N.A.	North America
N.B., Can.	New Brunswick, Can.
N.C., U.S.	North Carolina, U.S.
N. Cal.	New Caledonia
N. Cyp.	North Cyprus
N.D., U.S.	North Dakota, U.S.
Ne., U.S.	Nebraska, U.S.
Neth.	Netherlands
Neth. Ant.	Netherlands Antilles
Nf., Can.	Newfoundland, Can.
ngh.	neighborhood
N.H., U.S.	New Hampshire, U.S.
Nic.	Nicaragua
Nig.	Nigeria
N. Ire., U.K.	Northern Ireland, U.K.
N.J., U.S.	New Jersey, U.S.
N.M., U.S.	New Mexico, U.S.
N. Mar. Is.	Northern Mariana Islands
Nmb.	Namibia
Nor.	Norway
Norf. I.	Norfolk Island
N.S., Can.	Nova Scotia, Can.
N.T., Can.	Northwest Territories, Can.
Nu., Can.	Nunavut, Can.
Nv., U.S.	Nevada, U.S.
N.Y., U.S.	New York, U.S.
N.Z.	New Zealand
Oc.	Oceania
Oh., U.S.	Ohio, U.S.

Ok., U.S.	Oklahoma, U.S.
On., Can.	Ontario, Can.
Or., U.S.	Oregon, U.S.
p.	pass
Pa., U.S.	Pennsylvania, U.S.
Pak.	Pakistan
Pan.	Panama
Pap. N. Gui.	Papua New Guinea
Para.	Paraguay
P.E., Can.	Prince Edward Island, Can.
pen.	peninsula
Phil.	Philippines
Pit.	Pitcairn
pl.	plain, flat
plat.	plateau, highland
p.o.i.	point of interest
Pol.	Poland
Port.	Portugal
P.R.	Puerto Rico
Qc., Can.	Quebec, Can.
r.	rock, rocks
reg.	physical region
res.	reservoir
Reu.	Reunion
rf.	reef, shoal
R.I., U.S.	Rhode Island, U.S.
Rom.	Romania
Rw.	Rwanda
S.A.	South America
S. Afr.	South Africa
Samoa	Samoa
sand	sand area
Sau. Ar.	Saudi Arabia
S.C., U.S.	South Carolina, U.S.
sci.	scientific station
Scot., U.K.	Scotland, U.K.
S.D., U.S.	South Dakota, U.S.
Sen.	Senegal
Sey.	Seychelles
S. Geor.	South Georgia
Sing.	Singapore
Sk., Can.	Saskatchewan, Can.
S.L.	Sierra Leone
Slov.	Slovakia
Slvn.	Slovenia
S. Mar.	San Marino
Sol. Is.	Solomon Islands
Som.	Somalia
Sp. N. Afr.	Spanish North Africa
Sri L.	Sri Lanka
state	state, province, etc.
St. Hel.	St. Helena
St. K./N.	St. Kitts and Nevis
St. Luc.	St. Lucia
stm.	stream (river, creek)
S. Tom./P.	Sao Tome and Principe
St. P./M.	St. Pierre and Miquelon
strt.	strait, channel, etc.
St. Vin.	St. Vincent and the Grenadines
Sur.	Suriname
sw.	swamp, marsh
Swaz.	Swaziland
Swe.	Sweden
Switz.	Switzerland
Tai.	Taiwan
Taj.	Tajikistan
Tan.	Tanzania
T./C. Is.	Turks and Caicos Islands
Thai.	Thailand
Tn., U.S.	Tennessee, U.S.
Tok.	Tokelau
Trin.	Trinidad and Tobago
Tun.	Tunisia
Tur.	Turkey
Turkmen.	Turkmenistan
Tx., U.S.	Texas, U.S.
U.A.E.	United Arab Emirates
Ug.	Uganda
U.K.	United Kingdom
Ukr.	Ukraine
unds.	undersea feature
Ur.	Uruguay
U.S.	United States
Ut., U.S.	Utah, U.S.
Uzb.	Uzbekistan
Va., U.S.	Virginia, U.S.
val.	valley, watercourse
Vat.	Vatican City
Ven.	Venezuela
Viet.	Vietnam
V.I.U.S.	Virgin Islands (U.S.)
vol.	volcano
Vt., U.S.	Vermont, U.S.
Wa., U.S.	Washington, U.S.
Wake I.	Wake Island
Wal./F.	Wallis and Futuna
W.B.	West Bank
well	well, spring, oasis
Wi., U.S.	Wisconsin, U.S.
W. Sah.	Western Sahara
wtfl.	waterfall, rapids
W.V., U.S.	West Virginia, U.S.
Wy., U.S.	Wyoming, U.S.
Yk., Can.	Yukon Territory, Can.
Yugo.	Yugoslavia
Zam.	Zambia
Zimb.	Zimbabwe

Index

A

Name | Map Ref. | Page

Å, Nor. C5 8
Aachen, Ger. F1 16
Aalen, Ger. H6 16
Aali, Sadd el- (Aswan High Dam), dam, Egypt C6 62
Aalst (Alost), Bel. D13 14
Äänekoski, Fin. E11 8
Aarau, Switz. C4 22
Aare, stm., Switz. C5 22
Aarlen see Arlon, Bel. E14 14
Aarschot, Bel. D14 14
Aasiaat see Egedesminde, Grnld. D15 141
Aat see Ath, Bel. D12 14
Aba, China E5 36
Aba, D.R.C. D6 66
Aba, Nig. H6 64
Abā al-Bawl, Qurayn, hill, Qatar E7 56
Abacaxis, stm., Braz. E6 84
Abaco, i., Bah. B9 96
Abacou, Pointe, c., Haiti D10 102
Abadab, Jabal, mtn., Sudan D7 62
Ābādān, Iran C6 56
Ābādeh, Iran C7 56
Abadla, Alg. C4 64
Abaeté, Braz. J3 88
Abaeté, stm., Braz. J3 88
Abaetetuba, Braz. A1 88
Abag Qi, China C7 36
Abaí, Para. C10 92
Abaj, Kaz. E12 32
Abakaliki, Nig. H6 64
Abakan, Russia D16 32
Abakan, stm., Russia D15 32
Abakanovo, Russia A20 10
Abakanskij hrebet, mts., Russia D15 32
Abala, Niger G5 64
Abalak, Niger F6 64
Aban, Russia C17 32
Abancay, Peru F3 84
Abashiri, Japan B16 38
Abasolo, Mex. C6 100
Abasolo, Mex. I7 130
Abasolo, Mex. G6 130
Abau, Pap. N. Gui. c4 79a
Abay see Abaj, Kaz. E12 32
Ābay see Blue Nile, stm., Afr. E6 62
Abaya, Lake see Ābaya Hāyk', l., Eth. F7 62
Ābaya Hāyk', l., Eth. F7 62
Abaza, Russia D15 32
Abbadia San Salvatore, Italy H8 22
Abbé, Lac see Abe, Lake, l., Afr. E8 62
Abbeville, Fr. D10 14
Abbeville, Ga., U.S. D2 116
Abbeville, La., U.S. H6 122
Abbeville, S.C., U.S. B3 116
Abbey, Sk., Can. D5 124
Abbeyfeale, Ire. I3 12
Abbiategrasso, Italy E5 22
Abbot, Mount, mtn., Austl. B6 76
Abbot Ice Shelf, ice, Ant. C31 81
Abbotsford, B.C., Can. G8 138
Abbottābād, Pak. A4 54
'Abd al-Kūrī, i., Yemen G7 56
Ábdēra, hist., Grc. B7 28
Abdulino, Russia D8 32
Abe, Lake, l., Afr. E8 62
Abéché, Chad E4 62
Abel Tasman National Park, p.o.i., N.Z. E5 80
Abemama, at., Kir. C8 72
Abengourou, C. Iv. H4 64
Abenójar, Spain F6 20
Åbenrå, Den. I3 8
Abensberg, Ger. H7 16
Abeokuta, Nig. H5 64
Aberdare, Wales, U.K. J9 12
Aberdeen, S. Afr. H6 70
Aberdeen, Scot., U.K. D10 12
Aberdeen, Id., U.S. H14 136
Aberdeen, Md., U.S. E9 114
Aberdeen, Ms., U.S. D10 122
Aberdeen, N.C., U.S. A6 116
Aberdeen, S.D., U.S. B14 126
Aberdeen, Wa., U.S. D3 136
Aberdeen Lake, l., Nu., Can. C10 106
Aberdeen Lake, res., Ms., U.S. D10 122
Aberfeldy, Scot., U.K. E9 12
Abergavenny, Wales, U.K. J9 12
Abernant, Al., U.S. D11 122
Abernathy, Tx., U.S. H7 128
Abernethy, Sk., Can. D10 124
Abert, Lake, l., Or., U.S. H6 136
Aberystwyth, Wales, U.K. I8 12
Abez', Russia A10 32
Abhā, Sau. Ar. F5 56
Abidjan, C. Iv. H4 64
Abilene, Tx., U.S. B8 130
Abingdon, Eng., U.K. J11 12
Abingdon, Il., U.S. D7 120
Abingdon, Va., U.S. H4 114
Abiquiu, N.M., U.S. E2 128
Abiquiu Reservoir, res., N.M., U.S. E2 128
Abisko, Swe. B8 8
Abitibi, stm., On., Can. E14 106
Abitibi, Lake, l., Can. F15 106
Abja-Paluoja, Est. B8 10
Abnûb, Egypt K2 58
Åbo see Turku, Fin. F9 8
Abohar, India C5 54
Abomey, Benin H5 64
Abongabong, Gunung, mtn., Indon. J3 48
Abong Mbang, Cam. D2 66
Abony, Hung. B6 26
Aborigen, pik, mtn., Russia D18 34
Abou-Deïa, Chad E3 62
Abou Simbel (Abu Simbel), hist., Egypt C6 62
Abraham Lake, res., Ab., Can. D14 138
Abra Pampa, Arg. D3 90
Abre Campo, Braz. K4 88
Abreu e Lima, Braz. D8 88
Abring, India B6 54
Abrud, Rom. C10 26
Abruzzo, state, Italy H10 22
Abruzzo, Parco Nazionale d', p.o.i., Italy C7 24
Absaroka Range, mts., U.S. C3 126
Absarokee, Mt., U.S. E17 136
Absecon, N.J., U.S. E11 114
Abū 'Alī, i., Sau. Ar. D6 56
Abu Ballâs, mtn., Egypt C5 62
Abu Dhabi see Abū Ẓaby, U.A.E. E7 56
Abū Dulayq, Sudan D6 62
Abū el-Ḥul (Sphinx), hist., Egypt I1 58
Abufari, Braz. E5 84
Abū Ḥamad, Sudan D6 62
Abu Ḥammâd, Egypt H2 58
Abuja, Nig. H6 64
Abū Jabrah, Sudan E5 62
Abū Jubayhah, Sudan E6 62
Abū Kamāl, Syria C5 56
Abukuma, stm., Japan B13 40
Abukuma-kōchi, plat., Japan B13 40
Abū Madd, Ra's, c., Sau. Ar. E4 56
Abu Mendi, Eth. E7 62
Abunã, Braz. E4 84
Abu Qîr, Khalîg, b., Egypt G1 58
Abu Qurqâs, Egypt K1 58
Ābu Road, India F4 54
Abū Rubayq, Sau. Ar. E4 56
Abū Shajarah Ra's, c., Sudan C7 62
Abu Shâma, Gebel, mtn., Egypt I2 58
Abu Simbel see Abou Simbel, hist., Egypt C6 62
Abu Tîg, Egypt K2 58
Abū Zabad, Sudan E5 62
Abū Ẓaby (Abu Dhabi), U.A.E. E7 56
Abwong, Sudan F6 62
Abyei, Sudan F5 62
Abyssinia see Ethiopia, ctry., Afr. F7 62
Acacías, Col. E5 86
Acadia National Park, p.o.i., Me., U.S. F8 110
Acadia Valley, Ab., Can. C3 124
Açailândia, Braz. C2 88
Acajutiba, Braz. F7 88
Acámbaro, Mex. E8 100
Acandí, Col. C3 86
Acaponeta, Mex. D6 100
Acaponeta, stm., Mex. D6 100
Acapulco de Juárez, Mex. G8 100
Acará, Braz. A1 88
Acará, stm., Braz. A1 88
Acarai Mountains, mts., S.A. C6 84
Acará-Mirim, stm., Braz. B1 88
Acaraú, Braz. B5 88
Acaraú, stm., Braz. B5 88
Acaray, stm., Para. B10 92
Acarí, Peru G3 84
Acari, stm., Braz. H3 88
Acarigua, Ven. C7 86
Acatlán de Osorio, Mex. F9 100
Acay, Nevado de, mtn., Arg. B4 92
Acayucan, Mex. F11 100
Acceglio, Italy F3 22
Accomac, Va., U.S. G10 114
Accra, Ghana H5 64
Acebuches, Mex. A7 100
Aceguá, Braz. E10 92
Aceh, state, Indon. J3 48
Acerra, Italy D8 24
Achacachi, Bol. C3 90
Achaguas, Ven. D7 86
Achalpur, India H6 54
Achar, Ur. F9 92
Acharnés, Grc. E6 28
Achelóos, stm., Grc. E4 28
Acheng, China B7 38
Achern, Ger. H4 16
Achill Head, c., Ire. G2 12
Achill Island, i., Ire. H2 12
Achiras, Arg. F5 92
Achit nuur, l., Mong. E16 32
Achwa, stm., Afr. D6 66
Acı Göl, l., Tur. F12 28
Ačinsk, Russia C16 32
Acıpayam, Tur. F12 28
Acireale, Italy G9 24
Ačisaj, Kaz. F11 32
Ackerly, Tx., U.S. B6 130
Ackley, Ia., U.S. B4 120
Acklins, i., Bah. C10 96
Acklins, Bight of, b., Bah. A10 102
Acme, Ab., Can. E17 138
Aconcagua, Cerro, mtn., Arg. F3 92
Aconchi, Mex. G7 98
Acopiara, Braz. D6 88
Açores (Azores), is., Port. C3 60
Acorizal, Braz. G6 84
A Coruña (Corunna), Spain A2 20
A Coruña, co., Spain A2 20
Acquasanta Terme, Italy H10 22
Acqui Terme, Italy F5 22
Acre see 'Akko, Isr. F6 58
Acre, state, Braz. E4 84
Acre, stm., S.A. F4 84
Acri, Italy E10 24
Acton Vale, Qc., Can. E4 110
Actopan, Mex. E9 100
Açucena, Braz. J4 88
Acuña, Arg. D8 92
Ada, Mn., U.S. D2 118
Ada, Oh., U.S. D2 114
Ada, Ok., U.S. C2 122
Ādaba, Eth. F7 62
Adair, Ia., U.S. C3 120
Adair, Bahía de, b., Mex. F6 98
Adair, Cape, c., Nu., Can. A16 106
Adairsville, Ga., U.S. C14 122
Adairville, Ky., U.S. H11 120
Adaja, stm., Spain C6 20
Adak Island, i., Ak., U.S. g23 140a
Adam, Oman E8 56
Adamantina, Braz. D6 90
Adamaoua, mts., Afr. C2 66
Adamclisi, Rom. E14 26
Adamello, mts., Italy D7 22
Adaminaby, Austl. K7 76
Adams, Mn., U.S. H6 118
Adams, Ne., U.S. K2 118
Adams, N.Y., U.S. E13 112
Adams, N.D., U.S. F15 124
Adams, stm., B.C., Can. E11 138
Adams, Mount, vol., Wa., U.S. D5 136
Adam's Bridge, rf., Asia G4 53
Adams Lake, l., B.C., Can. E11 138
Adams Peak, mtn., Sri L. H5 53
Adams Rock, r., Pit. c28 78k
Adamstown, Pit. c28 78k
Adamsville, Tn., U.S. B10 122
'Adan (Aden), Yemen G6 56
Adana, Tur. A6 58
Adana, state, Tur. A6 58
Adanero, Spain D6 20
Adarama, Sudan D6 62
Adare, Cape, c., Ant. C22 81
Adavale, Austl. E5 76
Adda, stm., Italy E6 22
Ad-Dabbah, Sudan D6 62
Ad-Dahnā', des., Sau. Ar. D6 56
Ad-Dāmir, Sudan D6 62
Ad-Dammām, Sau. Ar. D7 56
Ad-Dānā, Syria B7 58
Ad-Dawḥah (Doha), Qatar D7 56
Ad-Dibdibah, reg., Sau. Ar. D6 56
Addis, La., U.S. G7 122
Addis Ababa see Ādīs Ābeba, Eth. F7 62
Addis Abeba see Ādīs Ābeba, Eth. F7 62
Addison, Mi., U.S. F5 112
Ad-Dīwānīyah, Iraq C6 56
Addo Elephant National Park, p.o.i., S. Afr. H7 70
Addu Atoll, at., Mald. j12 46a
Ad-Du'ayn, Sudan E5 62
Ad-Duwayd, Sau. Ar. C5 56
Ad-Duwaym, Sudan E6 62
Adel, Ga., U.S. E2 116
Adelaide, Austl. J2 76
Adelaide, Bah. n18 104f
Adelaide Island, i., Ant. B33 81
Adelaide Peninsula, pen., Nu., Can. B11 106
Adelaide River, Austl. B6 74
Adèle Island, i., Austl. C4 74
Adélie, Terre, cst., Ant. B18 81
Adelie Coast see Adélie, Terre, cst., Ant. B18 81
Adelong, Austl. J6 76
Aden see 'Adan, Yemen G6 56
Aden, Gulf of, b. E9 62
Adendorp, S. Afr. H7 70
Adi, Pulau, i., Indon. F9 44
Adiaké, C. Iv. H4 64
Adige (Etsch), stm., Italy E8 22
Ādīgrat, Eth. E7 62
Adıgüzel Barajı, res., Tur. E12 28
Ādilābād, India B4 53
Adimi, Russia G16 34
Adin, Ca., U.S. B5 134
Adirondack Mountains, mts., N.Y., U.S. E15 112
Ādīs Ābeba (Addis Abeba), Eth. F7 62
Adi Ugri, Erit. E7 62
Adıyaman, Tur. A9 58
Adıyaman, state, Tur. A9 58
Adjuntas, Presa de las see Vicente Guerrero, Presa, res., Mex. D9 100
Admiral, Sk., Can. E5 124
Admiralty Gulf, b., Austl. B5 74
Admiralty Inlet, b., Nu., Can. A13 106
Admiralty Island, i., Nu., Can. B10 106
Admiralty Island, i., Ak., U.S. E13 140
Admiralty Islands, is., Pap. N. Gui. a4 79a
Admiralty Mountains, mts., Ant. C21 81
Ado, Nig. H5 64
Ado-Ekiti, Nig. H6 64
Adolfo Gonzales Chaves, Arg. H7 92
Adolfo López Mateos, Mex. A5 100
Adolfo López Mateos, Presa, res., Mex. C5 100
Adolfo Rodriguez Sáa see Santa Rosa del Conlara, Arg. F5 92
Ādoni, India D3 53
Adour, stm., Fr. F4 18
Ādra, India G11 54
Adra, Spain H7 20
Adrano, Italy G8 24
Adrar, Alg. D4 64
Adrâr, reg., Maur. E2 64
Adria, Italy E9 22
Adrian, Mi., U.S. C1 114
Adrian, Mo., U.S. F3 120
Adrian, Or., U.S. G9 136
Adrian, Tx., U.S. F6 128
Adrian, W.V., U.S. F5 114
Adriatic Sea, Eur. G11 22
A Dun, stm., Viet. F9 48
Adutiškis, Lith. E9 10
Advance, Mo., U.S. G7 120
Advocate Harbour, N.S., Can. E11 110
Ādwa, Eth. E7 62
Adyča, stm., Russia C16 34
Adygea see Adygeja, state, Russia F6 32
Adygeja, state, Russia F6 32
Adygheya see Adygeja, state, Russia F6 32
Adzopé, C. Iv. H4 64
Aegean Sea E7 28
Aegina see Aígina, i., Grc. F6 28
Aegviidu, Est. A8 10
Aën, ostrov, i., Russia B22 34
Aerku Hu, l., China C9 54
Ærø, i., Den. I4 8
Ærøskøbing, Den. B6 16
A Estrada, Spain B2 20
Aetna, Ab., Can. G17 138
Afaahiti, Fr. Poly. v22 78h
Afadjoto, mtn., Ghana H5 64
Afareaitu, Fr. Poly. v20 78h
Afars and Issas see Djibouti, ctry., Afr. E8 62
Affton, Mo., U.S. F7 120
Afghanistan, ctry., Asia C9 56
Afgooye, Som. D8 66
Afikpo, Nig. H6 64
Aflou, Alg. C5 64
Afmadow, Som. D8 66
Afogados da Ingazeira, Braz. D7 88
Afognak Island, i., Ak., U.S. E9 140
Afoniha, Russia B25 8
A Fonsagrada, Spain A3 20
Africa, cont. F14 4
'Afrīn, Syria B7 58
Afton, N.Y., U.S. B10 114
Afton, Ok., U.S. H2 120
Afton, Wy., U.S. H16 136
'Afula, Isr. F6 58
Afyon, Tur. E13 28
Afyon, state, Tur. E13 28
Agadez, Niger F6 64
Agadir, Mor. C2 64
Agâdîr, Râs, c., Maur. E1 64
Agadyr', Kaz. E12 32
Agalak, Sudan E6 62
Agalega Islands, is., Mrts. K8 142
Agan, stm., Russia B13 32
Agana, Guam j10 78c
Agana Heights, Guam j10 78c
Agano, stm., Japan B12 40
Agapa, Russia B6 34
Aga Point, c., Guam k10 78c
Agar, India G5 54
Agartala, India G13 54
Agassiz, B.C., Can. G9 138
Agassiz Pool, res., Mn., U.S. C3 118
Agate, Co., U.S. B5 128
Agate Fossil Beds National Monument, p.o.i., Ne., U.S. E9 126
Agattu Island, i., Ak., U.S. g21 140a
Agawa Bay, b., On., Can. A5 112
Agawam, Mt., U.S. B14 136
Agboville, C. Iv. H4 64
Ağdam, Azer. B6 56
Ageevo, Russia F19 10
Agen, Fr. E6 18
Agency, Ia., U.S. D5 120
Agency Lake, l., Or., U.S. H5 136
Aggeneys, S. Afr. F4 70
Aggteleki Nemzeti Park, p.o.i., Hung. A7 26
Āghā Jārī, Iran C6 56
Agía Marína, Grc. F9 28
Agiásos, Grc. D9 28
Aginskoe, Russia F11 34
Ágio Óros, state, Grc. C7 28
Ágio Óros, pen., Grc. C7 28
Ágios Nikólaos, Grc. H8 28
Ağlasun, Tur. F13 28
Agnes Lake, l., On., Can. C7 118
Agnew, Austl. E4 74
Agnibilékrou, C. Iv. H4 64
Agno, Phil. B2 52
Agno, stm., Phil. C3 52
Ago, Japan E9 40
Agogna, stm., Italy E5 22
Agou, Mont, mtn., Togo H5 64
Agout, stm., Fr. F8 18
Āgra, India E6 54
Agraciada, Ur. F8 92
Agreda, Spain C8 20
Ağrı, Tur. B5 56
Agri, stm., Italy D9 24
Ağrı Dağı (Ararat, Mount), mtn., Tur. B5 56
Agrigento, Italy G7 24
Agrihan, i., N. Mar. Is. B5 72
Agrínio, Grc. E4 28
Agrio, stm., Arg. H2 92
Agrópoli, Italy D9 24
Agro Pontino, reg., Italy C6 24
Agto, Grnld. D15 141
Água Branca, Braz. C4 88
Agua Caliente, Mex. B4 100
Agua Caliente Grande, Mex. B4 100
Aguachica, Col. C5 86
Água Clara, Braz. D6 90
Aguada Cecilio, Arg. H3 90
Aguada de Guerra, Arg. H3 90
Aguada de Pasajeros, Cuba A7 102
Aguadas, Col. E4 86
Aguadilla, P.R. B1 104a
Água Doce, Braz. C12 92
Aguadulce, Pan. H7 102
Agua Dulce, Tx., U.S. G9 130
Agua Fria, stm., Az., U.S. I4 132
Aguaí, Braz. L2 88
Agualeguas, Mex. H8 130
Aguán, stm., Hond. E4 102
Aguanaval, stm., Mex. C7 100
Aguapey, stm., Arg. D9 92
Água Preta, Igarapé, stm., Braz. H9 86
Agua Prieta, Mex. F8 98
Aguaray Guazú, stm., Para. A9 92
A Guardia, Spain C1 20
Aguarico, stm., S.A. H3 86
Aguaro-Guariquito, Parque Nacional, p.o.i., Ven. C8 86
Aguaruto, Mex. C5 100
Aguasabon, stm., On., Can. C11 118
Águas Belas, Braz. E7 88
Aguas Buenas, P.R. B3 104a
Aguascalientes, Mex. E7 100
Aguascalientes, state, Mex. D7 100
Águas Formosas, Braz. I5 88
Água Vermelha, Represa de, res., Braz. C6 90
Aguayo, Arg. E4 92
Agu Bay, b., Nu., Can. A13 106
Agudos, Braz. L1 88
Águeda, stm., Eur. D4 20
Aguelhok, Mali F5 64
Aguilar, Co., U.S. D4 128
Aguilar de la Frontera, Spain G6 20
Aguilares, Arg. C5 92
Águilas, Spain G9 20
Aguililla, Mex. F7 100
Agujereada, Punta, c., P.R. A1 104a
Agujita, Mex. G6 130
Agulhas, Kaap, c., S. Afr. I5 70
Agulhas Basin, unds. M15 144
Agulhas Negras, Pico das, mtn., Braz. L3 88
Agung, Gunung, vol., Indon. G6 44
Agusan, stm., Phil. F5 52
Agustín Codazzi, Col. C5 86
Ağva, Tur. B12 28
Ahaggar, mts., Alg. E6 64
Ahaggar, Tassili ta-n-, plat., Alg. E5 64
Ahalcihe, Geor. F6 32
Ahar, Iran B6 56
Ahaus, Ger. D3 16
Ahipara Bay, b., N.Z. B5 80
Ahlen, Ger. E3 16
Ahmadābād, India G4 54
Ahmadnagar, India B2 53
Ahmadpur East, Pak. D3 54
Ahmadpur Siāl, Pak. C3 54
Ahmar Mountains, mts., Eth. F8 62
Ahmetli, Tur. E10 28
Ahmic Lake, l., On., Can. C10 112
Ahoskie, N.C., U.S. H9 114
Ahousat, B.C., Can. G4 138
Ahraura, India F9 54
Ahtuba, stm., Russia E7 32
Ahtubinsk, Russia E7 32
Ahuacatlán, Mex. E6 100
Ahumada, Mex. D1 130
Ahunui, at., Fr. Poly. E12 72
Ahvāz, Iran C6 56
Ahvenanmaa (Åland), state, Fin. F9 8
Ahvenanmaa (Aland Islands), is., Fin. F8 8
Aḥwar, Yemen G6 56
Ahwa-ri, Kor., S. D2 40
Å i Åfjord, Nor. D4 8
Aibonito, P.R. B3 104a
Aichi, state, Japan D10 40
Aidong, China I2 42
Aiea, Hi., U.S. B3 78a
Aígina, Grc. F6 28
Aígina, i., Grc. F6 28
Aígio, Grc. E5 28
Aigle, Switz. D3 22
Aigle, stm., Qc., Can. A1 110
Aiguá, Ur. G10 92
Aigüestortes i Estany Sant Maurici, Parque Nacional d', p.o.i., Spain B11 20
Aigüestortes i Llac de Sant Maurici, Parc Nacional d' see Aigüestortes i Esta, p.o.i., Spain B11 20
Aikawa, Japan A11 40
Aiken, S.C., U.S. C4 116
Aikens Lake, l., Mb., Can. C18 124
Ailao Shan, mts., China G5 36
Aileron, Austl. D6 74
Ailinglaplap, at., Marsh. Is. C7 72
Ailsa Craig, On., Can. E8 112
Ailsa Craig, i., Scot., U.K. F7 12
Aim, Russia E15 34
Aimorés, Braz. J5 88
Ain, state, Fr. D11 18
Ain, stm., Fr. D11 18
Aïn Benian, Alg. H13 20
Aïn Bessem, Alg. H14 20
Aïn Defla, Alg. H12 20
Aïn Draham, Tun. H2 24
Aïn el Beïda, Alg. B6 64
Ainslie Lake, l., N.S., Can. D15 110
Aioi, Japan E7 40
Aiora, Spain E9 20
Aipe, Col. F4 86
Aïr, Massif de l', mts., Niger F6 64
Airai Airport, Palau g8 78b
Airbangis, Indon. C1 50
Airdrie, Ab., Can. E16 138
Aire, stm., Fr. F14 14
Aire, stm., Eng., U.K. H11 12
Aire-sur-l'Adour, Fr. F5 18
Air Force Island, i., Nu., Can. B16 106
Airhaji, Indon. D2 50
Airlie Beach, Austl. C7 76
Airolo, Switz. D5 22
Airuoca, Braz. L3 88
Aishihik, Yk., Can. C3 106
Aishihik Lake, l., Yk., Can. C3 106
Aisne, state, Fr. E12 14
Aisne, stm., Fr. E12 14
Aïssa, Djebel, mtn., Alg. C4 64
Aitape, Pap. N. Gui. a3 79a
Aitkin, Mn., U.S. E5 118
Aitolikó, Grc. E4 28
Aitutaki, at., Cook Is. E11 72
Aiuaba, Braz. D5 88
Aiud, Rom. C10 26
Aix, Île d', i., Fr. C4 18
Aix, Mount, mtn., Wa., U.S. D5 136
Aix-en-Provence, Fr. F11 18
Aix-la-Chapelle see Aachen, Ger. F1 16
Aix-les-Bains, Fr. D11 18
Āīzawl, India G14 54
Aizkraukle, Lat. D8 10
Aizu-bange, Japan B12 40
Aizu-wakamatsu, Japan B12 40
Ajaccio, Fr. H14 18
Ajaccio, Golfe d', b., Fr. H14 18
Ajaguz, Kaz. E13 32
Ajaguz, stm., Kaz. E13 32
Ajajú, stm., Col. G5 86
Ajan, Russia E16 34
Ajan, stm., Russia C7 34
Ajanta, India H5 54
Ajanta Caves, hist., India H5 54
Ajanta Range, mts., India H5 54
Ajarani, stm., Braz. F11 86
Ajax, On., Can. E10 112
Ajdābiyā, Libya A4 62
Ajdyrlinskij, Russia D9 32
Ajjer, Tassili-n-, plat., Alg. D6 64
Ajka, Hung. B4 26
'Ajlūn, Jord. F6 58
Ajmer, India E5 54
Ajnāla, India C5 54
Ajo, Az., U.S. K4 132
Ajtos, Blg. G14 26
Ajusco, Mex. L9 134
Akabira, Japan C15 38
Akabli, Alg. D5 64
Akademii, zaliv, b., Russia F16 34
Akagi-san, vol., Japan C12 40
Akaishi-sammyaku, mts., Japan D11 40
Āk'ak'ī Besek'a, Eth. F7 62
Akalkot, India C2 53
Akámas, Akrotírion, c., Cyp. C3 58
Akan-kokuritsu-kōen, p.o.i., Japan C16 38
'Akasha East, Sudan C6 62
'Akāshāt, Iraq C5 56
Akashi, Japan E7 40
Akbarpur, India E9 54
Akbulak, Russia D9 32
Akçakale, Tur. B9 58
Akçakoca, Tur. B14 28
Akçakoyunlu, Tur. B8 58
Akçaova, Tur. F11 28
Akçay, Tur. G12 28
Akçay, stm., Tur. F11 28
Akchâr, reg., Maur. E2 64
Akdoğan, N. Cyp. C4 58
Ak-Dovurak, Russia D15 32
Akeley, Mn., U.S. D4 118
Aken, Ger. E8 16
Akershus, state, Nor. F4 8
Aketi, D.R.C. D4 66
Akhaltsikhe see Ahalcihe, Geor. F6 32
Akhḍar, Al-Jabal al-, mts., Libya A4 62
Akhḍar, Al-Jabal al-, mts., Oman E8 56
Akhḍar, Wādī al-, stm., Sau. Ar. J7 58
Akhisar, Tur. E10 28
Akhtarīn, Syria B8 58
Akhtubinsk see Ahtubinsk, Russia E7 32
Aki, Japan F6 40
Akimiski Island, i., Nu., Can. E14 106
Akıncı Burun, c., Tur. B6 58
Akita, Japan E13 38
Akjoujt, Maur. F2 64
Akkeshi, Japan C16 38
'Akko, Isr. F6 58
Akkol', Kaz. E13 32
Akkol', Kaz. F12 32
Akköy, Tur. F10 28
Aklavik, N.T., Can. B4 106
'Aklé 'Aouâna, reg., Afr. F3 64
Akmeņrags, c., Lat. D3 10
Akmola see Astana, Kaz. D12 32
Akō, Japan E7 40
Ākobo (Akūbū), stm., Afr. F6 62
Akola, India H6 54
Akonolinga, Cam. D2 66
Akordat, Erit. D7 62
Akören, Tur. F15 28
Akot, India H6 54
Akpatok Island, i., Nu., Can. C17 106
Akpınar, Tur. A9 58
Akrítas, Ákra, c., Grc. G4 28
Akrokórinthos, hist., Grc. F5 28
Akron, Co., U.S. A5 128
Akron, In., U.S. G4 112
Akron, N.Y., U.S. E11 112
Akron, Oh., U.S. C4 114
Akron, Pa., U.S. H13 112
Akrotíri, Cyp. D3 58
Akša, Russia F11 34
Aksaj, Kaz. D8 32
Aksaray, Tur. B3 56
Aksayqin Hu, l., China A7 54
Akşehir, Tur. E14 28
Akşehir Gölü, l., Tur. E14 28
Akseki, Tur. F14 28
Aksu, China F14 32
Aksu, Kaz. D12 32
Aksu, stm., Kaz. E13 32
Aksu, stm., Tur. F13 28
Aksu, stm., Tur. A8 58
Aksuat, Kaz. E14 32
Aksuat, Kaz. E14 32
Āksum, Eth. E7 62
Aktau, Kaz. F8 32
Aktau, Kaz. D12 32
Aktjubinsk, Kaz. D9 32
Akto, China B12 56
Akūbū, Sudan F6 62
Akūbū (Ākobo), stm., Afr. F6 62
Akuliči Pervye, Russia G16 10
Akune, Japan G3 40
Akure, Nig. H5 64
Akureyri, Ice. k30 8a
Akutan Island, i., Ak., U.S. F6 140
Akwanga, Nig. H6 64
Akyazı, Tur. C13 28
Ål, Nor. F3 8
Alabama, state, U.S. E12 122
Alabama, stm., Al., U.S. F11 122
Alabaster, Al., U.S. D12 122
Alacant (Alicante), Spain F10 20
Alacant, co., Spain F10 20
Alaçatı, Tur. E9 28
Alachua, Fl., U.S. G3 116
Alacrán, Arrecife, rf., Mex. C7 96
Alacranes, Presa, res., Cuba A7 102
Aladağ, mtn., Tur. A6 58
Alagoa Grande, Braz. D8 88
Alagoas, state, Braz. E7 88
Alagoinhas, Braz. G6 88
Alagón, Spain C9 20
Alagón, stm., Spain E4 20
Alahanpanjang, Indon. D2 50
Alaior, Spain E15 20
Alajku, Kyrg. F12 32
Alajskij hrebet, mts., Asia B11 56
Alajuela, C.R. H5 102
Alajuela, Lago, res., Pan. H8 102
Alakanuk, Ak., U.S. D7 140
Alakol', ozero, l., Kaz. E14 32
Alaköl Köli see Alakol', ozero, l., Kaz. E14 32
Al-'Akrīshah, Egypt G1 58
Alaktara, India H9 54
Alakurtti, Russia C13 8
Alalakeiki Channel, strt., Hi., U.S. C5 78a
Alalaú, stm., Braz. H11 86
Alamagan, i., N. Mar. Is. B5 72
Al-'Amārah, Iraq C6 56
Alameda, Ca., U.S. F3 134
Alameda, N.M., U.S. H10 132
Alamo, Ga., U.S. D3 116
Alamo, Tn., U.S. B9 122
Alamo, stm., Ca., U.S. K1 132
Alamogordo, N.M., U.S. B2 130
Alamo Heights, Tx., U.S. E9 130
Alamo Lake, res., Az., U.S. I3 132
Álamos, Mex. B4 100
Álamos, stm., Mex. A8 100
Alamosa, Co., U.S. D3 128
Alamosa East, Co., U.S. D3 128
Álamos de Márquez, Mex. A7 100
Åland, India C3 53
Åland see Ahvenanmaa, state, Fin. F9 8
Åland see Ahvenanmaa, is., Fin. F8 8
Aland Islands see Ahvenanmaa, is., Fin. F8 8
Aland Sea, Eur. G8 8
Alandur, India E5 53
Alanya, Tur. G15 28
Alaotra, Farihy, l., Madag. D8 68
Alapaevsk, Russia C10 32
Alapaha, Ga., U.S. E2 116
Alapaha, stm., U.S. F2 116
Alaplı, Tur. B14 28
Alappuzha see Alleppey, India G3 53
Al-'Aqabah, Jord. I6 58
Alarcón, Spain E8 20
Alarcón, Embalse de, res., Spain E9 20
Alas, stm., Indon. K3 48
Alas, Selat, strt., Indon. H10 50
Alaşehir, Tur. E11 28
Alashanyouqi, China C5 36
Alaska, state, U.S. D9 140
Alaska, Gulf of, b., Ak., U.S. E10 140
Alaska Peninsula, pen., Ak., U.S. E7 140
Alaska Range, mts., Ak., U.S. D9 140
Alassio, Italy F5 22
Alatan'aola see Xin Barag Youqi, China B8 36
Alatri, Italy I10 22
Alatyr', Russia D7 32
Alausí, Ec. I2 86
Alava see Arabako, co., Spain B8 20
Alava, Cape, c., Wa., U.S. B2 136
Al-'Ayn, U.A.E. E8 56
Alayor see Alaior, Spain E15 20
Alazeja, stm., Russia B19 34
Al-'Azīzīyah, Libya A2 62
Alba, Italy F5 22
Alba, Mi., U.S. D5 112
Alba, Tx., U.S. E3 122
Alba, state, Rom. C10 26
Al-Bāb, Syria B8 58
Albacete, Spain E9 20
Albacete, co., Spain F9 20
Al-Bad', Sau. Ar. J6 58
Alba de Tormes, Spain D5 20
Albaida, Spain F10 20
Alba Iulia, Rom. C10 26
Al-Balqā', state, Jord. F6 58
Al-Bālū'ah, l., Syria C7 58
Albanel, Lac, l., Qc., Can. E16 106
Albania, Col. B5 86
Albania, ctry., Eur. C14 24
Albano Laziale, Italy I9 22
Albany, Ga., U.S. E1 116
Albany, In., U.S. H4 112
Albany, Ky., U.S. H12 120
Albany, Mn., U.S. F4 118
Albany, Mo., U.S. D3 120
Albany, N.Y., U.S. B12 114
Albany, Oh., U.S. E3 114
Albany, Or., U.S. F3 136
Albany, Tx., U.S. B8 130
Albany, stm., On., Can. E14 106
Albarracín, Spain D9 20
Al-Baṣrah, Iraq C6 56
Al-Batrā' (Petra), hist., Jord. H6 58
Albatross Bay, b., Austl. B8 74
Al-Bayḍā', Libya A4 62
Albemarle, N.C., U.S. A5 116
Albemarle Island see Isabela, Isla, i., Ec. i11 84a
Albemarle Sound, strt., N.C., U.S. H9 114
Albenga, Italy F5 22
Alberche, stm., Spain D6 20
Alberdi, Para. C8 92
Alberga Creek, stm., Austl. E6 74
Alberni Inlet, b., B.C., Can. G6 138
Alberobello, Italy D11 24
Albert, Fr. E11 14
Albert, Lake, l., Afr. D6 66
Albert, Lake, l., Austl. J2 76
Alberta, Al., U.S. E11 122
Alberta, state, Can. E8 106
Alberta, Mount, mtn., Ab., Can. D13 138
Albert Canyon, B.C., Can. E13 138
Albert City, Ia., U.S. I3 118
Albert Edward Bay, b., Nu., Can. B10 106
Alberti, Arg. G7 92
Albertirsa, Hung. B6 26
Albertkanaal, can., Bel. D14 14
Albert Lea, Mn., U.S. H5 118
Albert Markham, Mount, mtn., Ant. D21 81
Albert Nile, stm., Afr. D6 66
Alberton, P.E., Can. D12 110
Albertville, Fr. D12 18
Albertville, Al., U.S. C12 122
Albi, Fr. F8 18
Albia, Ia., U.S. C5 120
Albin, Wy., U.S. F8 126
Albina, Sur. B7 84
Albina, Ponta, c., Ang. D1 68
Albion, Ca., U.S. D2 134
Albion, Id., U.S. H13 136
Albion, Il., U.S. F9 120
Albion, In., U.S. G4 112
Albion, Mi., U.S. B1 114
Albion, N.Y., U.S. E11 112
Albion, Pa., U.S. C5 114
Albion, Wa., U.S. D9 136
Al-Biqā', state, Leb. D7 58
Al-Biqā' (Bekaa Valley), val., Leb. D7 58
Al-Bi'r, Sau. Ar. J7 58
Albocàsser, Spain D10 20
Alboran Sea B4 64
Ålborg, Den. H4 8
Ålborg Bugt, b., Den. H4 8
Alborz, Reshteh-ye Kūhhā-ye, mts., Iran B7 56
Albuñol, Spain H7 20
Albuquerque, N.M., U.S. H10 132
Albuquerque, Cayos de, is., Col. F6 102
Alburg, Vt., U.S. E3 110
Alburquerque, Spain E3 20
Albury, Austl. J6 76
Alcains, Port. E3 20
Alcalá de Guadaira, Spain G5 20
Alcalá de Henares, Spain D7 20
Alcalá la Real, Spain G7 20
Alcalde, N.M., U.S. E2 128
Alcamo, Italy G6 24
Alcanar, Spain D11 20
Alcañices, Spain C4 20
Alcañiz, Spain C10 20
Alcântara, Braz. B3 88
Alcántara, Spain E3 20
Alcantarilla, Spain G9 20
Alcaraz, Spain F8 20
Alcaudete, Spain G6 20
Alcázar de San Juan, Spain E7 20
Alcester, S.D., U.S. A1 120
Alcira, Arg. F5 92
Alcira see Alzira, Spain E10 20
Alcobaça, Braz. I6 88
Alcobendas, Spain D7 20
Alcoi, Spain F10 20
Alcolea del Pinar, Spain C8 20
Alcolu, S.C., U.S. C5 116

Name | Map Ref. | Page

Alcorn, Ms., U.S. F7 122
Alcorta, Arg. F7 92
Alcoutim, Port. G3 20
Alcoy see Alcoi, Spain F10 20
Alcúdia, Spain E14 20
Alcúdia, Badia d', b., Spain E14 20
Aldabra, Groupe d', is., Sey. k11 69b
Aldama, Mex. D9 100
Aldama, Mex. A5 100
Aldan, Russia E14 34
Aldan, stm., Russia D15 34
Aldan Plateau see Aldanskoe nagor'e, plat., Russia E14 34
Aldanskoe nagor'e (Aldan Plateau), plat., Russia E14 34
Aldarchaan, Mong. B4 36
Aldeia Nova de São Bento, Port. G3 20
Alden, Mn., U.S. H5 118
Alderney, i., Guern. E6 14
Aldershot, Eng., U.K. J12 12
Alderson, W.V., U.S. G5 114
Aledo, Il., U.S. C7 120
Aleg, Maur. F2 64
Alegre, Braz. K5 88
Alegrete, Braz. D10 92
Alej, stm., Russia D14 32
Alejandro Roca, Arg. F5 92
Alejandro Selkirk, Isla, i., Chile I6 82
Alejsk, Russia D14 32
Aleksandrov, Russia D21 10
Aleksandrovskij Zavod, Russia F12 34
Aleksandrovskoe, Russia B13 32
Aleksandrovsk-Sahalinskij, Russia F17 34
Aleksandrów Kujawski, Pol. D14 16
Alekseevka, Kaz. D12 32
Alekseevka, Kaz. E14 32
Alekseevka, Russia D5 32
Alekseevsk, Russia C19 32
Aleksejevka see Alekseevka, Kaz. D12 32
Alekseyevka see Alekseevka, Kaz. D12 32
Aleksin, Russia F19 10
Aleksinac, Yugo. F8 26
Alemania, Arg. B5 92
Além Paraíba, Braz. K4 88
Alençon, Fr. F9 14
Alenquer, Braz. D7 84
Alentejo, hist. reg., Port. F3 20
Alenuihaha Channel, strt., Hi., U.S. C5 78a
Aleppo see Ḥalab, Syria B8 58
Aléria, Fr. G15 18
Alert, Nu., Can. A13 141
Alert Bay, B.C., Can. F4 138
Alert Point, c., Nu., Can. A8 141
Alès, Fr. E10 18
Alëšnja, Russia G16 10
Alessándria, Italy F5 22
Ålesund, Nor. E1 8
Aleutian Basin, unds. D20 142
Aleutian Islands, is., Ak., U.S. g22 140a
Aleutian Range, mts., Ak., U.S. E8 140
Aleutian Trench, unds. E21 142
Aleutka, Russia G19 34
Alevina, mys, c., Russia E19 34
Alex, Ok., U.S. G11 128
Alexander, Mb., Can. E13 124
Alexander, N.D., U.S. G10 124
Alexander, Kap, c., Grnld. B11 141
Alexander Archipelago, is., Ak., U.S. E12 140
Alexander Bay, S. Afr. F3 70
Alexander City, Al., U.S. E12 122
Alexander Island, i., Ant. B33 81
Alexandra, N.Z. G3 80
Alexandra, stm., Austl. B3 76
Alexandra Falls, wtfl, N.T., Can. C7 106
Alexandretta see İskenderun, Tur. B6 58
Alexandretta, Gulf of see İskenderun Körfezi, b., Tur. B6 58
Alexandria, Braz. D6 88
Alexandria, B.C., Can. D8 138
Alexandria, On., Can. E2 110
Alexandria see El-Iskandarīya, Egypt A6 62
Alexandria, Rom. F12 26
Alexandria, La., U.S. F6 122
Alexandria, Mn., U.S. F3 118
Alexandria, Mo., U.S. D6 120
Alexandria, S.D., U.S. D15 126
Alexandria, Tn., U.S. H11 120
Alexandria, Va., U.S. F8 114
Alexandria Bay, N.Y., U.S. D14 112
Alexandrina, Lake, l., Austl. J2 76
Alexandroúpoli, Grc. C8 28
Alexis, Il., U.S. C7 120
Alfambra, Spain D9 20
Alfaro, Spain B9 20
Alfarràs, Spain C11 20
Alfarrás see Alfarràs, Spain C11 20
Al-Fāshir, Sudan E5 62
Alfeiós, stm., Grc. F4 28
Alfeld, Ger. D5 16
Alfenas, Braz. K3 88
Alföld, pl., Hung. C7 26
Alfonsine, Italy F9 22
Alfred, On., Can. E2 110
Alfred, Me., U.S. G6 110
Alfred, N.Y., U.S. B8 114
Al-Fujayrah, U.A.E. D8 56
Al-Fuqahā', Libya B3 62
Al-Furāt see Euphrates, stm., Asia C6 56
Alga, Kaz. E9 32
Ålgård, Nor. G1 8
Algarrobal, Chile D2 92
Algarrobo, Chile F2 92
Algarrobo del Águila, Arg. H4 92
Algarve, hist. reg., Port. G2 20
Algeciras, Col. F4 86
Algeciras, Spain H5 20
Algemesí, Spain E10 20
Algeria, ctry., Afr. D5 64
Algérie see Algeria, ctry., Afr. D5 64
Al-Ghāb, sw., Syria C7 58
Al-Ghayḍah, Yemen F7 56
Al-Ghāzīyah, Leb. E6 58
Alghero, Italy D2 24
Algiers see El Djazaïr, Alg. B5 64
Alginet, Spain E10 20
Algoabaai, b., S. Afr. H7 70
Algoa Bay see Algoabaai, b., S. Afr. H7 70
Algodón, stm., Peru I5 86
Algodones, N.M., U.S. F2 128
Algoma Mills, On., Can. B7 112
Algona, Ia., U.S. A3 120
Algonac, Mi., U.S. B3 114
Algonquin, Il., U.S. B9 120
Algorta, Spain A7 20
Algorta, Ur. F9 92
Al-Ḥaffah, Syria C7 58
Al-Ḥajarah, reg., Asia C5 56
Al-Ḥamād, pl., Sau. Ar. C4 56
Alhama de Murcia, Spain G9 20
Alhandra, Braz. D8 88
Al-Ḥarrah, lav., Sau. Ar. C4 56
Al-Harūj al-Aswad, hills, Libya B3 62
Al-Ḥasakah, Syria B5 56
Alhaurín el Grande, Spain H6 20
Al-Ḥawātah, Sudan E7 62
Al-Ḥawrah, Yemen G6 56
Al-Ḥijāz (Hejaz), reg., Sau. Ar. D4 56
Al-Ḥillah, Iraq C5 56
Al-Hirmil, Leb. D7 58
Al-Hoceima, Mor. B4 64
Al-Ḥudaydah (Hodeida), Yemen G5 56
Al-Ḥufrah, reg., Sau. Ar. J9 58
Al-Hufūf, Sau. Ar. D6 56
Al Hūj, hills, Sau. Ar. J9 58
Al-Ḥulwah, Sau. Ar. E6 56
Alía, Spain E5 20
Aliağa, Tur. E9 28
Aliákmonas, stm., Grc. C4 28
Aliança, Braz. D8 88
Alībāg, India B1 53
Alibates Flint Quarries National Monument, p.o.i., Tx., U.S. F7 128
Äli Bayramlı, Azer. B6 56
Alibei, ozero, l., Ukr. D17 26
Alibey Adası, i., Tur. D9 28
Alibunar, Yugo. D7 26
Alicante see Alacant, Spain F10 20
Alicante see Alacant, co., Spain F10 20
Alice, S. Afr. H8 70
Alice, Tx., U.S. G9 130
Alice, stm., Austl. D5 76
Alice, Punta, c., Italy E11 24
Alice Springs, Austl. D6 74
Alice Town, Bah. K6 116
Aliceville, Al., U.S. D10 122
Alick Creek, stm., Austl. C4 76
Alīgarh, India E6 54
Alignements de Carnac, hist., Fr. G5 14
Alīgūdarz, Iran C6 56
'Alī Kheyl, Afg. B2 54
Al-Ikhṣāṣ al-Qiblīyah, Egypt I2 58
Alima, stm., Congo E3 66
Alim Island, i., Pap. N. Gui. a4 79a
Alindao, C.A.R. C4 66
Alingsås, Swe. G5 8
Alīpur, Pak. D3 54
Ālīpur Duār, India E12 54
Aliquippa, Pa., U.S. D5 114
Alīrājpur, India G5 54
Aliseda, Spain E4 20
Alitak, Cape, c., Ak., U.S. E9 140
Alivéri, Grc. E7 28
Aliwal North, S. Afr. G8 70
Alix, Ab., Can. D17 138
Al-Jabalayn, Sudan E6 62
Al-Jafr, Jord. H7 58
Al-Jaghbūb, Libya B4 62
Al-Jahrah, Kuw. D6 56
Al-Jawārah, Oman F8 56
Al-Jawf, Libya C4 62
Al-Jawf, Sau. Ar. D4 56
Al-Jazaïr see El Djazaïr, Alg. B5 64
Al-Jazīrah, reg., Sudan E6 62
Al-Jifārah (Jeffara), pl., Afr. C7 64
Al-Jubayl, Sau. Ar. D6 56
Al-Junaynah, Sudan E4 62
Aljustrel, Port. G2 20
Al-Kafr, Syria F7 58
Al-Karak, Jord. G6 58
Al-Karak, state, Jord. G6 58
Al-Khalīl (Hebron), W.B. G5 58
Al-Khāliṣ, Iraq C5 56
Al-Khandaq, Sudan D6 62
Al-Kharṭām Baḥrī, Sudan D6 62
Al-Kharṭūm (Khartoum), Sudan D6 62
Al-Khaṣab, Oman D8 56
Al-Khums, Libya A2 62
Alkmaar, Neth. B13 14
Al-Kufrah, Libya C4 62
Al-Kūt, Iraq C6 56
Al-Kuwayt (Kuwait), Kuw. D6 56
Al-Labwah, Leb. D7 58
Al-Lādhiqīyah (Latakia), Syria C6 58
Al-Lādhiqīyah, state, Syria C6 58
Allagash, stm., Me., U.S. D7 110
Allahābād, India F8 54
Allah-Jun', Russia D16 34
Allakaket, Ak., U.S. C9 140
Allan, Sk., Can. C7 124
Allanmyo, Mya. C2 48
Allanridge, S. Afr. E8 70
Allatoona Lake, res., Ga., U.S. C14 122
Alldays, S. Afr. C9 70
Allegan, Mi., U.S. F4 112
Allegany, N.Y., U.S. B7 114
Allegheny, stm., U.S. D6 114
Allegheny Mountains, mts., U.S. E6 114
Allegheny Plateau, plat., U.S. D5 114
Allegheny Reservoir, res., U.S. C7 114
Allemands, Lac des, l., La., U.S. H8 122
Allen, Ne., U.S. I2 118
Allen, Ok., U.S. C2 122
Allen, Tx., U.S. D2 122
Allen, Lough, l., Ire. G4 12
Allendale, Il., U.S. F10 120
Allendale, S.C., U.S. C4 116
Allende, Mex. A8 100
Allenstein see Olsztyn, Pol. C16 16
Allentown, Pa., U.S. D10 114
Alleppey, India G3 53
Aller, stm., Ger. D5 16
Allevard, Fr. D12 18
Allgäu see Kempten, Ger. I6 16
Allgäu, reg., Ger. I6 16
Alliance, Ab., Can. D19 138
Alliance, Ne., U.S. E10 126
Alliance, Oh., U.S. D4 114
Al-Lidām, Sau. Ar. E5 56
Allier, state, Fr. C9 18
Allier, stm., Fr. C9 18
Alligator Pond, Jam. j13 104d
Allinagaram, India F3 53
Allison, Ia., U.S. B5 120
Al-Līth, Sau. Ar. E5 56
Alloa, Scot., U.K. E9 12
Allos, Fr. E12 18
Allouez, Wi., U.S. G11 118
Allred Peak, mtn., Co., U.S. C8 132
All Saints, Antig. f4 105b
Al-Luḥayyah, Yemen F5 56
Allumette Lake, l., Can. C12 112
Allumettes, Île aux, i., Qc., Can. C12 112
Alma, N.B., Can. E12 110
Alma, Qc., Can. B5 110
Alma, Ar., U.S. B4 122
Alma, Ga., U.S. E3 116
Alma, Ks., U.S. E1 120
Alma, Mi., U.S. E5 112
Alma, Wi., U.S. G7 118
Almada, Port. F1 20
Almaden, Austl. A5 76
Almadén, Spain F6 20
Al-Madīnah (Medina), Sau. Ar. E4 56
Al-Mafraq, Jord. F7 58
Al-Mafraq, state, Jord. F8 58
Almafuerte, Arg. F5 92
Almagro, Spain F7 20
Alma Hill, hill, N.Y., U.S. B8 114
Al Māliḥah, Sudan D5 62
Almalyk, Uzb. F11 32
Al-Manāmah (Manama), Bahr. D7 56
Almanor, Lake, res., Ca., U.S. C4 134
Almansa, Spain F9 20
Almanza, Spain B5 20
Almanzor, mtn., Spain D5 20
Al-Marj, Libya A4 62
Almas, Braz. F2 88
Almas, Pico das, mtn., Braz. G4 88
Al-Mashrafah, Syria D7 58
Almaty, Kaz. F13 32
Al-Mawṣil, Iraq B5 56
Almeida, Port. D3 20
Almejas, Bahía, b., Mex. C3 100
Almelo, Neth. B15 14
Almena, Ks., U.S. B9 128
Almenara, Braz. I5 88
Almendra, Embalse de, res., Spain C4 20
Almendralejo, Spain F4 20
Almería, Spain H8 20
Almería, co., Spain G8 20
Almería, Golfo de, b., Spain H8 20
Al'metevsk, Russia D8 32
Al-Mijlad, Sudan E5 62
Al-Mīnā', Leb. D6 58
Almira, Wa., U.S. C7 136
Almirante, Pan. H6 102
Almirante Latorre, Chile D2 92
Almirós, Grc. D5 28
Almo, Id., U.S. A3 132
Almodóvar del Campo, Spain F6 20
Almont, Mi., U.S. B2 114
Almonte, On., Can. C13 112
Almonte, Spain G4 20
Almonte, stm., Spain E4 20
Almora, India D7 54
Al-Mubarraz, Sau. Ar. E6 56
Al-Mubarraz, Sau. Ar. D6 56
Al-Mudawwarah, Jord. I6 58
Almudévar, Spain B10 20
Al-Muḥarraq, Bahr. D7 56
Al-Mukallā, Yemen G6 56
Al-Mukhā, Yemen G5 56
Almuñécar, Spain H7 20
Al-Muwayliḥ, Sau. Ar. K6 58
Almyroú, Órmos, b., Grc. H7 28
Alnwick, Eng., U.K. F11 12
Alofi, Île, i., Wal./F. E9 72
Alónnisos, Grc. D6 28
Alónnisos, i., Grc. D6 28
Alor, Pulau, i., Indon. G7 44
Alor, Selat, strt., Indon. G7 44
Alor Setar, Malay. I5 48
Alosno, Spain G3 20
Alost see Aalst, Bel. D13 14
Alotau, Pap. N. Gui. c5 79a
Aloysius, Mount, mtn., Austl. E5 74
Alpachiri, Arg. H5 92
Alpaugh, Ca., U.S. H6 134
Alpena, Mi., U.S. C6 112
Alpena, S.D., U.S. C14 126
Alpercatas, stm., Braz. D3 88
Alpes-de-Haute-Provence, state, Fr. E12 18
Alpes-Maritimes, state, Fr. F13 18
Alpha, Austl. D6 76
Alpha, Il., U.S. C7 120
Alpha, Mi., U.S. B1 112
Alpharetta, Ga., U.S B1 116
Alphonse, i., Sey. k12 69b
Alpine, Ca., U.S. K9 134
Alpine, Tx., U.S. D4 130
Alpine National Park, p.o.i., Austl. K6 76
Alpinópolis, Braz. K2 88
Alps, mts., Eur. D6 22
Al-Qaḍārif, Sudan E7 62
Al-Qaḍīmah, Sau. Ar. E4 56
Al-Qāmishlī, Syria B5 56
Al-Qaryah ash-Sharqīyah, Libya A2 62
Al-Qaryatayn, Syria D8 58
Al-Qaṭīf, Sau. Ar. D6 56
Al-Qaṭrānah, Jord. G7 58
Al-Qaṭrūn, Libya C2 62
Al-Qayṣūmah, Sau. Ar. D6 56
Al-Qunayṭirah, Syria E6 58
Al-Qunayṭirah, state Syria E6 58
Al-Qunfudhah, Sau. Ar. F5 56
Al-Quṭayfah, Syria E7 58
Al-Quṭaynah, Sudan E6 62
Als, i., Den. I3 8
Alsace, hist. reg., Fr. F16 14
Al'šany, Bela. H10 10
Alsask, Sk., Can. C4 124
Alsasua, Spain B8 20
Alsea, Or., U.S. F3 136
Alsek, stm., N.A. D3 106
Alsen, N.D., U.S. F15 124
Alsfeld, Ger. F5 16
Alta, Nor. B10 8
Altaelva, stm., Nor. B10 8
Alta Gracia, Arg. E5 92
Altagracia, Ven. B6 86
Altagracia de Orituco, Ven. C8 86
Altai, mts., Asia E15 32
Altaj, state, Russia D15 32
Altajskij, Russia D14 32
Altamaha, stm., Ga., U.S. E4 116
Altamira, Braz. D7 84
Altamira, Chile B3 92
Altamirano, Mex. I10 130
Altamont, Ks., U.S. G2 120
Altamont, Or., U.S. A4 134
Altamont, Tn., U.S. B13 122
Altamura, Italy D10 24
Altamura, Isla, i., Mex. C4 100
Altanbulag, Mong. A6 36
Altar, Mex. F7 98
Altar, stm., Mex. F7 98
Altar, Desierto de, des., Mex. F6 98
Altar de Los Sacrificios, hist., Guat. D2 102
Altario, Ab., Can. C3 124
Altata, Mex. C4 100
Alta Vista, Ks., U.S. C12 128
Altay, China E15 32
Altay, Mong. B4 36
Altay see Altaj, state, Russia D15 32
Altay Mountains see Altai, mts., Asia E15 32
Altdorf, Switz. D5 22
Altenburg, Ger. E8 16
Altentreptow, Ger. C9 16
Alter do Chão, Port. E3 20
Altevatnet, l., Nor. B8 8
Altha, Fl., U.S. G13 122
Altheimer, Ar., U.S C7 122
Altınekin, Tur. E15 28
Altinho, Braz. E7 88
Altınova, Tur. D9 28
Altıntaş, Tur. D13 28
Altiplano, plat., S.A. G4 84
Altmark, reg., Ger. D7 16
Altmühl, stm., Ger. G6 16
Alto, Tx., U.S. F3 122
Alto Araguaia, Braz. G7 84
Alto Chicapa, Ang. C2 68
Alto Garças, Braz. G7 84
Alto Longá, Braz. C4 88
Altomünster, Ger. H7 16
Alton, Eng., U.K. J11 12
Alton, Il., U.S. F7 120
Alton, Ia., U.S. B1 120
Alton, Ks., U.S. B9 128
Alton, N.H., U.S. G5 110
Altona, Mb., Can. E16 124
Altoona, Al., U.S. C12 122
Altoona, Ia., U.S. C4 120
Altoona, Pa., U.S. D7 114
Altoona, Wi., U.S. G7 118
Alto Paraguai, Braz. F6 84
Alto Paraíso de Goiás, Braz. G2 88
Alto Paraná, state, Para. B10 92
Alto Parnaíba, Braz. E2 88
Alto Río Mayo, Arg. I2 90
Alto Río Senguer, Arg. I2 90
Altos, Braz. C4 88
Alto Santo, Braz. C6 88
Altötting, Ger. H8 16
Altun Shan, mts., China D2 36
Alturas, Ca., U.S. B5 134
Altus, Ar., U.S. B5 122
Altus, Ok., U.S. G9 128
Alu see Shortland Island, i., Sol. Is. d6 79b
Al-'Ubaylah, Sau. Ar. E7 56
Al-Ubayyiḍ, Sudan E6 62
Alubijid, Phil. F5 52
Al-Uḍayyah, Sudan E5 62
Alūksne, Lat. C9 10
Al-'Ulā, Sau. Ar. D4 56
Al-'Uqaylah, Libya A3 62
Al-'Uwaynāt, Libya B2 62
Alva, Ok., U.S. E10 128
Alvaiázere, Port. E2 20
Alvarado, Mex. F11 100
Alvarado, Tx., U.S. B10 130
Álvaro Obregón, Presa, res., Mex. B4 100
Alvear, Arg. D9 92
Alverca, Port. F1 20
Alvernia, Mount, hill, Bah. C10 96
Alvesta, Swe. H6 8
Alvin, Tx., U.S. H3 122
Alvinópolis, Braz. K4 88
Älvkarleby, Swe. F7 8
Alvord, Tx., U.S. H11 128
Alvord Desert, des., Or., U.S. H8 136
Al-Wajh, Sau. Ar. D4 56
Alwar, India E6 54
Alwaye, India F3 53
Alxa Zuoqi, China B1 42
Alytus, Lith. F6 10
Alzey, Ger. G4 16
Alzira, Spain E10 20
Amacuro (Amakura), stm., S.A. C11 86
Amadeus, Lake, l., Austl. D6 74
Amadjuak Lake, l., Nu., Can. B16 106
Amagasaki, Japan E8 40
Amagi, Japan F3 40
Amahai, Indon. F8 44
Amaichá del Valle, Arg. C4 92
Amaimon, Pap. N. Gui. b4 79a
Amajac, stm., Mex. E9 100
Amakura (Amacuro), stm., S.A. D11 86
Amakusa-nada, Japan G2 40
Amakusa-shotō, is., Japan G2 40
Åmål, Swe. G5 8
Amalāpuram, India C6 53
Amalfi, Col. B2 84
Amaliáda, Grc. F4 28
Amalner, India H5 54
Amambaí, Braz. D5 90
Amami Islands see Amami-Ō-shima, i., Japan k19 39a
Amami-Ō-shima, i., Japan k19 39a
Amami-shotō, is., Japan l19 39a
Amana, Ia., U.S. C6 120
Amana, stm., Ven. C10 86
Amanã, Lago, l., Braz. I9 86
Amanda, Oh., U.S. E3 114
Amantea, Italy E9 24
Amapá, Braz. C7 84
Amapá, state, Braz. C7 84
Amarante, Braz. D4 88
Amaranth, Mb., Can. D15 124
Amarapura, Mya. B3 48
Amărăştii de Jos, Rom. F11 26
Amarāvati, stm., India F3 53
Amares, Port. C2 20
Amargosa, Braz. G6 88
Amargosa, stm., U.S. H9 134
Amarillo, Tx., U.S. F7 128
Amarkantak, India G8 54
Amaro, Monte, mtn., Italy H11 22
Amasra, Tur. B15 28
Amasya, Tur. A4 56
aMatikulu, S. Afr. F10 70
Amatsu-kominato, Japan D13 40
Amawbia Awka, Nig. H6 64
Amazar, Russia F13 34
Amazon (Amazonas) (Solimões), stm., S.A. D7 84
Amazonas, state, Braz. D4 84
Amazonas, state, Col. H6 86
Amazonas, state, Ven. F8 86
Ambājogāi, India B3 53
Ambāla, India C6 54
Ambalangoda, Sri L. H4 53
Ambalavao, Madag. E8 68
Ambam, Cam. D2 66
Ambanja, Madag. C8 68
Ambarčik, Russia C21 34
Ambargasta, Salinas de, pl., Arg. D5 92
Ambato, Ec. H2 86
Ambatolampy, Madag. D8 68
Ambatondrazaka, Madag. D8 68
Ambelau, Pulau, i., Indon. F8 44
Amberg, Ger. G7 16
Amberg, Wi., U.S. C2 112
Ambergris Cay, i., Belize C4 102
Ambérieu-en-Bugey, Fr. D11 18
Ambert, Fr. D9 18
Ambidédi, Mali G2 64
Ambikāpur, India G9 54
Ambilobe, Madag. C8 68
Ambla, Est. A8 10
Amble, Eng., U.K. F11 12
Ambo, Peru F2 84
Ambodifototra, Madag. D8 68
Ambohimahasoa, Madag. E8 68
Amboise, Fr. G10 14
Ambon, Indon. F8 44
Ambon, Pulau, i., Indon. F8 44
Amboseli, Lake, l., Afr. E7 66
Amboseli National Park, p.o.i., Kenya E7 66
Ambositra, Madag. E8 68
Ambovombe, Madag. F8 68
Amboy, Il., U.S. C8 120
Amboy, Mn., U.S. H4 118
Ambridge, Pa., U.S. D5 114
Ambriz, Ang. B1 68
Ambrosia Lake, N.M., U.S. H9 132
Ambrym, state, Vanuatu k17 79d
Ambrym, i., Vanuatu k17 79d
Ambuntentimur, Indon. G8 50
Ambunti, Pap. N. Gui. a3 79a
Āmbūr, India E4 53
Amchitka Island, i., Ak., U.S. g22 140a
Amchitka Pass, strt., Ak., U.S. g22 140a
Am Dam, Chad E4 62
Amdo, China B13 54
Ameagle, W.V., U.S. G4 114
Ameca, Mex. E6 100
Ameca, stm., Mex. E6 100
Ameghino, Arg. G6 92
Ameland, i., Neth. A14 14
Amelia Court House, Va., U.S. G8 114
Amelia Island, i., Fl., U.S. F4 116
Āmer, India E5 54
American, North Fork, stm., Ca., U.S. D5 134
American, South Fork, stm., Ca., U.S. E5 134
Americana, Braz. L2 88
American Falls Reservoir, res., Id., U.S. H13 136
American Fork, Ut., U.S. C5 132
American Highland, plat., Ant. C12 81
Americanos, Barra de los, i., Mex. C10 100
American Samoa, dep., Oc. h12 79c
Americus, Ga., U.S. D1 116
Americus, Ks., U.S. F1 120
Amersfoort, Neth. B14 14
Amery, Wi., U.S. F6 118
Amery Ice Shelf, ice, Ant. B12 81
Ames, Ia., U.S. B4 120
Amesbury, Ma., U.S. B14 114
Amfilochía, Grc. E4 28
Ámfissa, Grc. E5 28
Amga, Russia D15 34
Amga, stm., Russia D15 34
Amguema, stm., Russia C24 34
Amguid, Alg. D6 64
Amgun', stm., Russia F16 34
Amherst, N.S., Can. E12 110
Amherst, Ma., U.S. B13 114
Amherst, N.Y., U.S. A7 114
Amherst, Oh., U.S. C3 114
Amherst, Tx., U.S. G6 128
Amherst, Wi., U.S. G9 118
Amherstburg, On., Can. F6 112
Amherstdale, W.V., U.S. G4 114
Amherst Island, i., On., Can. D13 112
Amherstview, On., Can. D13 112
Amiens, Austl. G8 76
Amiens, Fr. E11 14
Amīndīvi Islands, is., India F3 46
Amino, Japan D8 40
Aminuis, Nmb. C4 70
Amirantes, Les, is., Sey. k12 69b
Amisk, Ab., Can. B2 124
Amisk Lake, l., Sk., Can. E10 106
Amistad, Parque Internacional de la, p.o.i., C.R. H6 102
Amistad, Presa de la (Amistad Reservoir), res., N.A. E6 130
Amistad National Recreation Area, p.o.i., Tx., U.S. E6 130
Amistad Reservoir (Amistad, Presa de la), res., N.A. E6 130
Amite, La., U.S. G8 122
Amite, stm., La., U.S. G8 122
Amity, Ar., U.S. C5 122
Āmla, India H7 54
Åmli, Nor. G3 8
'Ammān, Jord. G6 58
'Ammān, state, Jord. G7 58
Ämmänsaari, Fin. D13 8
'Ammār, Tall, hill, Syria F7 58
Ammasalik see Angmagssalik, Grnld. D18 141
Ammon, Id., U.S. G15 136
Amnat Charoen, Thai. E7 48
Amnok-kang (Yalu), stm., Asia D7 38
Amo (Torsa), stm., Asia E12 54
Amo, stm., China A5 48
Āmol, Iran B7 56
Amorgós, i., Grc. G8 28
Amory, Ms., U.S. D10 122
Amos, Qc., Can. F15 106
Åmot, Nor. G2 8
Amoy see Xiamen, China I7 42
Ampanihy, Madag. E7 68
Amparo, Braz. L2 88
Ampasimanolotra, Madag. D8 68
Amposta, Spain D11 20
Amqui, Qc., Can. B9 110
Amrāvati, India H6 54
Amreli, India H3 54
Amritsar, India C5 54
Amroha, India D7 54
Amrum, i., Ger. B4 16
Amsterdam, Neth. B13 14
Amsterdam, S. Afr. E10 70
Amsterdam, N.Y., U.S. B11 114
Amsterdam, Île, i., Afr. M10 142
Amstetten, Aus. B11 22
Am Timan, Chad E4 62
Amu Darya, stm., Asia F10 32
Amugulang see Xin Barag Zuoqi, China B8 36
Amund Ringnes Island, i., Nu., Can. B6 141
Amundsen Gulf, b., Can. B14 140
Amundsen-Scott, sci., Ant. D19 81
Amundsen Sea, Ant. P27 142
Amuntai, Indon. E9 50
Amur (Heilong), stm., Asia F16 34
Amursk, Russia F16 34
Amuzhong, China C10 54
Amvrakikós Kólpos, b., Grc. E3 28
An, Mya. C2 48
Ana, Parque Nacional dedo see Doñana, Parque Nacional de, p.o.i., Spain H4 20
Anaa, at., Fr. Poly. E12 72
Anabar, stm., Russia B11 34
Anaco, Ven. C9 86
Anaconda, Mt., U.S. D14 136
Anaconda Range, mts., Mt., U.S. E13 136
Anacortes, Wa., U.S. B4 136
Anadarko, Ok., U.S. F10 128
Anadolu (Anatolia), hist. reg., Tur. H15 6
Anadyr', Russia D24 34
Anadyr, stm., Russia C23 34
Anadyr, Gulf of see Anadyrskij zaliv, b., Russia C21 142
Anadyr Mountains see Anadyrskoe ploskogor'e, plat., Russia C23 34
Anadyrskij liman, b., Russia D24 34
Anadyrskij zaliv, b., Russia C21 142
Anadyrskoe ploskogor'e, plat., Russia C23 34
Anáfi, i., Grc. G8 28
Anagni, Italy C7 24
Anaheim, Ca., U.S. J8 134
Anahim Lake, B.C., Can. D5 138
Anáhuac, Mex. I10 130
Ānai Mudi, mtn., India F3 53
Anajás, Braz. D8 84
Anakāpalle, India C6 53
Anaktuvuk Pass, Ak., U.S. C9 140
Analalava, Madag. C8 68
Anamã, Braz. D5 84
Anama Bay, Mb., Can. C15 124
Ana María, Golfo de, b., Cuba B8 102
Anambas, Kepulauan (Anambas Islands), is., Indon. B5 50
Anambas Islands see Anambas, Kepulauan, is., Indon. B5 50
Anamizu, Japan B9 40
Anamoose, N.D., U.S. G13 124
Anamur, Tur. B3 58
Anamur Burnu, c., Tur. B3 58
Anan, Japan F7 40
Ānand, India G4 54
Ānandapur, India H11 54
Ananindeua, Braz. A1 88
Anan'iv, Ukr. B16 26
Anantapur, India D3 53
Anantnāg, India B5 54
Anápolis, Braz. I1 88
Anapurus, Braz. B4 88
Añasco, P.R. B1 104a
Anastasia Island, i., Fl., U.S. G4 116
Anatahan, i., N. Mar. Is. B5 72
Anatolia see Anadolu, hist. reg., Tur. H15 6
Anatolikí Makedonía kai Thráki, state, Grc. B8 28
Anatom, i., Vanuatu m17 79d
Añatuya, Arg. D6 92
Anauá, stm., Braz. G11 86
Anavilhanas, Arquipélago das, is., Braz. I11 86
Anbei, China F17 32
Anbianbu, China C2 42
Anbyŏn-ŭp, Kor., N. E7 38
Ancaster, On., Can. E9 112
Ancasti, Sierra de, mts., Arg. D5 92
Anchiang see Qianyang, China H3 42
Anch'ing see Anqing, China F7 42
Anchorage, Ak., U.S. D10 140
Anchuras, Spain E6 20
Ancona, Italy G10 22
Ancón de Sardinas, Bahía de, b., S.A. G2 86
Ancuabe, Moz. C6 68
Ancud, Chile H2 90
Ancy-le-Franc, Fr. G13 14
Anda, China B10 36
Andacollo, Arg. H2 92
Andahuaylas, Peru F3 84
Andalgalá, Arg. C4 92
Andalucía, state, Spain G6 20
Andalusia see Jan Kempdorp, S. Afr. E7 70
Andalusia, Al., U.S. F12 122
Andalusia see Andalucía, state, Spain G6 20
Andaman and Nicobar Islands, state, India F7 46
Andaman Basin, unds. H12 142
Andaman Islands, is., India F7 46
Andaman Sea, Asia G8 46
Andamook, Austl. F7 74
Andapa, Madag. C8 68
Andenes, Nor. B6 8
Andéramboukane, Mali F5 64
Andernach, Ger. F3 16
Anderson, Ca., U.S. C3 134
Anderson, In., U.S. H4 112
Anderson, Mo., U.S. H3 120
Anderson, S.C., U.S. B3 116
Anderson, Tx., U.S. G3 122
Anderson, stm., N.T., Can. B5 106
Anderson, Mount, mtn., Wa., U.S. C3 136
Anderson Dam, Id., U.S. G11 136
Andes, Col. E4 86
Andes, mts., S.A. F7 82
Andfjorden, strt., Nor. B7 8
Andhra Lake, res., India B1 53
Andhra Pradesh, state, India C4 53
Andilamena, Madag. D8 68
Andingpu, China B2 42
Andirlang, China A5 46
Andižan, Uzb. F12 32
Andkhvoy, Afg. B10 56
Andoany, Madag. C8 68
Andoga, stm., Russia A19 10
Andong, Kor., S. C1 40
Andong-chŏsuji, res., Kor., S. C1 40
Andorra, ctry., Eur. B12 20
Andorra, ctry., Eur. B12 20
Andorra-la-Vella, And. B12 20
Andover, Eng., U.K. J11 12
Andover, Me., U.S. F6 110
Andover, Ma., U.S. H5 110
Andover, Oh., U.S. C5 114
Andover, S.D., U.S. B15 126
Andøya, i., Nor. B6 8
Andradina, Braz. D6 90
Andranopasy, Madag. E7 68
Andreanof Islands, is., Ak., U.S. g23 140a
Andreapol', Russia D15 10
Andrews, In., U.S. H4 112
Andrews, N.C., U.S. A2 116
Andrews, S.C., U.S. C6 116
Andrews, Tx., U.S. B5 130
Andria, Italy C10 24
Andriamena, Madag. D8 68
Andriievo-Ivanivka, Ukr. B17 26
Androka, Madag. F7 68
Andronovskoe, Russia F16 8
Andros, i., Bah. C9 96
Ándros, i., Grc. F7 28
Androscoggin, stm., Me., U.S. F6 110
Āndrott Island, i., India F1 53
Andrupene, Lat. D10 10
Andudu, D.R.C. D5 66
Andújar, Spain F6 20
Andulo, Ang. C2 68
Anduze, Fr. E9 18
Anegada, Bahía, b., Arg. H4 90
Anegada Passage, strt., N.A. h15 96a
Aného, Togo H5 64
Añelo, Arg. I3 92
Anemata, Passe d', strt., N. Cal. m16 79d
Anenii Noi, Mol. C16 26
Aneroid, Sk., Can. E6 124
Aneta, N.D., U.S. G16 124
Anétis, Mali F5 64
Aneto, mtn., Spain B11 20
Anfu, China H6 42
Angamos, Punta, c., Chile D2 90
Ang'angxi, China B9 36
Angara, stm., Russia E8 34
Angarsk, Russia D18 32
Angas Downs, Austl. D6 74
Angastaco, Arg. B4 92
Angaul, Russia D18 32
Ånge, Swe. E6 8
Ángel, Salto (Angel Falls), wtfl, Ven. E10 86
Ángel de la Guarda, Isla, i., Mex. G6 98
Angeles, Phil. C3 52
Angel Falls see Ángel, Salto, wtfl, Ven. E10 86
Ängelholm, Swe. H5 8
Angelina, stm., Tx., U.S. F4 122
Angellala Creek, stm., Austl. F6 76
Angels Camp, Ca., U.S. E5 134
Angemuk, mtn., Indon. F10 44
Ångermanälven, stm., Swe. E7 8
Angermünde, Ger. C9 16
Angers, Fr. G8 14
Angical, Braz. F3 88
Angical do Piauí, Braz. D4 88
Angicos, Braz. C7 88
Angijak Island, i., Nu., Can. D13 141
Angikuni Lake, l., Nu., Can. C11 106
Angkor Wat, hist., Camb. F6 48
Ângk Tasaôm, Camb. G7 48
Angle Inlet, Mn., U.S. B3 118
Anglem, Mount, mtn., N.Z. H2 80
Anglesey, i., Wales, U.K. H8 12
Anglet, Fr. F4 18
Angleton, Tx., U.S. H3 122
Anglona, reg., Italy D2 24
Angmagssalik (Ammasalik), Grnld. D18 141
Angoche, Moz. D6 68
Angol, Chile H1 92
Angola, In., U.S. G5 112
Angola, N.Y., U.S. B6 114
Angola, ctry., Afr. C2 68
Angola Basin, unds. J14 144
Angora see Ankara, Tur. D15 28
Angoram, Pap. N. Gui. a3 79a
Angostura, Presa de la, res., Mex. H12 100
Angoulême, Fr. D6 18

Name	Map Ref.	Page
Angoumois, hist. reg., Fr.	D5	18
Angra dos Reis, Braz.	L3	88
Angren, Uzb.	F12	32
Angu, D.R.C.	D4	66
Angualasto, Arg.	D3	92
Anguilla, Ms., U.S.	E8	122
Anguilla, dep., N.A.	h15	96a
Anguille, Cape, c., Nf., Can.	C17	110
Anguli Nur, l., China	A6	42
Anguo, China	B6	42
Angus, On., Can.	D10	112
Angusville, Mb., Can.	D13	124
Anhalt, hist. reg., Ger.	D7	16
Anholt, i., Den.	H4	8
Anhua, China	G4	42
Anhui, state, China	F7	42
Anhwei see Anhui, state, China	F7	42
Aniak, Ak., U.S.	D8	140
Anibare Bay, b., Nauru	q17	78f
Anie, Pic d', mtn., Fr.	F5	18
Anil, Braz.	B3	88
Animas, N.M., U.S.	L8	132
Animas, stm., U.S.	G9	132
Animas Valley, val., N.A.	L8	132
Anina, Rom.	D8	26
Anita, Ia., U.S.	C3	120
Anıtkaya, Tur.	E13	28
Aniva, mys, c., Russia	B13	36
Aniva, zaliv, b., Russia	G17	34
Aniwa, i., Vanuatu	I17	79d
Anjangaon, India	H6	54
Anjār, India	G2	54
'Anjar, Leb.	E6	58
Anjou, hist. reg., Fr.	G8	14
Anjouan see Nzwani, i., Com.	C7	68
Anjudin, Russia	B9	32
Anjujsk, Russia	C21	34
Anjujskij hrebet, mts., Russia	C21	34
Anju-ŭp, Kor., N.	E6	38
Anka, Nig.	G6	64
Ankaboa, Tanjona, c., Madag.	E7	68
Ankang, China	E3	42
Ankara, Tur.	D15	28
Ankara, state, Tur.	D15	28
Ankavandra, Madag.	D8	68
Ankazoabo, Madag.	E7	68
Ankazobe, Madag.	D8	68
Ankeny, Ia., U.S.	C4	120
Anking see Anqing, China	F7	42
Ankleshwar, India	H4	54
Ankoro, D.R.C.	F5	66
Anlong, China	F6	36
Ânlóng Vêng, Camb.	E6	48
Anlu, China	F5	42
An Muileann gCearr see Mullingar, Ire.	H5	12
Ånn, l., Swe.	E5	8
Ann, Cape, c., Ant.	B10	81
Ann, Cape, pen., Ma., U.S.	H6	110
Anna, Il., U.S.	G8	120
Anna, Lake, res., Va., U.S.	F8	114
Annaba, Alg.	B6	64
An-Nabaṭīyah, state, Leb.	E6	58
An-Nabaṭīyah at-Taḥtā, Leb.	E6	58
Annaberg-Buchholz, Ger.	F9	16
An-Nabk, Syria	D7	58
An-Nafūd, des., Sau. Ar.	D5	56
An-Najaf, Iraq	C5	56
Annam see Trung Phan, hist. reg., Viet.	D8	48
Annamitique, Chaîne, mts., Asia	D8	48
Annan, Scot., U.K.	G9	12
Annandale, Austl.	C7	76
Annandale, Mn., U.S.	F4	118
Annandale, val., Scot., U.K.	F9	12
Anna Plains, Austl.	C4	74
Annapolis, Md., U.S.	F9	114
Annapolis Royal, N.S., Can.	F11	110
Annapūrṇa, mtn., Nepal	D9	54
Ann Arbor, Mi., U.S.	B2	114
An Nás see Naas, Ire.	H6	12
An-Nāṣirīyah, Iraq	C6	56
An-Nāṣirīyah, Syria	E7	58
An-Nawfalīyah, Libya	A3	62
Annecy, Fr.	D12	18
Annecy, Lac d', l., Fr.	D12	18
Annemasse, Fr.	C12	18
Annenkov Island, i., S. Geor.	J9	90
An Nhon, Viet.	F9	48
Anning, China	G5	36
Anniston, Al., U.S.	D13	122
Annobón, i., Eq. Gui.	J6	64
Annonay, Fr.	D10	18
An-Nuhūd, Sudan	E5	62
Annville, Ky., U.S.	G2	114
Annville, Pa., U.S.	D9	114
Anoka, Mn., U.S.	F5	118
Anori, Braz.	D5	84
Anpu, China	K3	42
Anqing, China	F7	42
Anqiu, China	C8	42
Anren, China	H5	42
Ansai, China	C3	42
Ansbach, Ger.	G6	16
Anse-d'Hainault, Haiti	C10	102
Anse La Raye, St. Luc.	m6	105c
Anselmo, Ne., U.S.	F13	126
Anserma, Col.	E4	86
Anshan, China	D5	38
Anshun, China	H1	42
Ansina, Ur.	E10	92
Ansley, Ne., U.S.	F13	126
Anson Bay, b., Austl.	B5	74
Anson Bay, b., Norf. I.	y24	78i
Ansongo, Mali	F5	64
Ansonville, N.C., U.S.	A5	116
Ansted, W.V., U.S.	F4	114
Antakya see Hatay, Tur.	B7	58
Antalaha, Madag.	C9	68
Antalieptė, Lith.	E8	10
Antalya, Tur.	G13	28
Antalya, state, Tur.	F14	28
Antalya, Gulf of see Antalya Körfezi, b., Tur.	G14	28
Antalya Körfezi (Antalya, Gulf of), b., Tur.	G14	28
Antananarivo, Madag.	D8	68
An tAonach see Nenagh, Ire.	I4	12
Antarctica, cont.	D11	81
Antarctic Peninsula, pen., Ant.	C35	81
Antas, Braz.	F6	88
Antas, stm., Braz.	D12	92
Antelope Island, i., Ut., U.S.	C4	132
Antelope Mine, Zimb.	B9	70
Antelope Peak, mtn., Nv., U.S.	B1	132
Antenor Navarro, Braz.	D6	88
Antequera, Para.	A9	92
Antequera, Spain	H6	20
Anthon, Ia., U.S.	B2	120
Anthony, Ks., U.S.	D10	128
Anthony, N.M., U.S.	K10	132
Anthony, Tx., U.S.	E9	98
Anti-Atlas, mts., Mor.	D3	64
Antibes, Fr.	F13	18
Anticosti, Île d', i., Qc., Can.	F18	106
Antifer, Cap d', c., Fr.	E8	14
Antigonish, N.S., Can.	E14	110
Antigua, i., Antig.	f4	105b
Antigua and Barbuda, ctry., N.A.	h15	96a
Antigua International Airport, Antig.	f4	105b
Antiguo Morelos, Mex.	D9	100
Antikýthira, i., Grc.	H6	28
Anti-Lebanon (Sharqī, Al-Jabal ash-), mts., Asia	E7	58
Antilla, Cuba	B10	102
Antillen, Nederlandse see Netherlands Antilles, dep., N.A.	i14	96a
Antimony, Ut., U.S.	E5	132
Antioch see Hatay, Tur.	B7	58
Antioch, Il., U.S.	F1	112
Antioquia, Col.	D4	86
Antioquia, state, Col.	D4	86
Antipajuta, Russia	C4	34
Antipodes Islands, is., N.Z.	H9	72
Antisana, vol., Ec.	H2	86
Antler, stm., N.A.	E12	124
Antofagasta, Chile	A2	92
Antofagasta, state, Chile	B3	92
Antofagasta de la Sierra, Arg.	C4	92
Antofalla, Salar de, pl., Arg.	C3	92
Antofalla, Volcán, vol., Arg.	B4	92
Antón, Pan.	H7	102
Anton, Tx., U.S.	H6	128
Anton Chico, N.M., U.S.	F3	128
Antongila, Helodrano, b., Madag.	D8	68
Antonina, Braz.	B13	92
Antonina do Norte, Braz.	D5	88
Antônio Prado, Braz.	D12	92
Antonito, Co., U.S.	D2	128
Antón Lizardo, Punta, c., Mex.	F10	100
Antopal', Bela.	H7	10
Antrim, N. Ire., U.K.	G6	12
Antropovo, Russia	G20	8
Antsalova, Madag.	D7	68
Antsirabe, Madag.	D8	68
Antsiranana, Madag.	C8	68
Antsohihy, Madag.	C8	68
Antulai, Gunong, mtn., Malay.	A10	50
Antun', Russia	G16	34
Antung see Dandong, China	D5	38
Antwerp see Antwerpen, Bel.	C13	14
Antwerp, Oh., U.S.	C1	114
Antwerpen (Antwerp), Bel.	C13	14
An Uaimh see Navan, Ire.	H6	12
Anugul, India	H10	54
Anūpgarh, India	D4	54
Anuradhapura, Sri L.	G5	53
Anvers see Antwerpen, Bel.	C13	14
Anvers Island, i., Ant.	B34	81
Anvik, Ak., U.S.	D7	140
Anxi, China	C4	36
Anxi, China	I8	42
Anxiang, China	G5	42
Anxious Bay, b., Austl.	F6	74
Anyang, China	C6	42
Anyang, Kor., S.	F7	38
A'nyêmaqên Shan, mts., China	D4	36
Anyer Kidul, Indon.	G4	50
Anykščiai, Lith.	E7	10
Anyuan, China	I6	42
Anyuanyi see Tianzhu, China	D5	36
Anyue, China	F1	42
Anze, China	C5	42
Anžero-Sudžensk, Russia	C15	32
Anzio, Italy	C6	24
Anzoátegui, state, Ven.	C9	86
Anžu, ostrova, is., Russia	A17	34
Aoba, i., Vanuatu	j16	79d
Aoba / Maéwo, state, Vanuatu	j17	79d
Aoga-shima, i., Japan	G12	40
Aohan Qi, China	C3	38
Aojiang, China	H9	42
Aoji-ri, Kor., N.	C9	38
Ao Luk, Thai.	H4	48
Aomar, Alg.	H14	20
Aomen see Macau, Macau	J5	42
Aomen see Macau, dep., Asia	J5	42
Aomori, Japan	D14	38
Aonla, India	D7	54
Aóös (Vjosës), stm., Eur.	D13	24
A'opo, Samoa	g11	79c
Aôral, Phnum, mtn., Camb.	F7	48
Aore, i., Vanuatu	j16	79d
Aosta (Aoste), Italy	E4	22
Aoste see Aosta, Italy	E4	22
Aouderas, Niger	F6	64
Aouk, Bahr, stm., Afr.	F3	62
Aoukâr, reg., Maur.	F3	64
Aoya, Japan	D7	40
Aozou, Chad	C3	62
Apache Junction, Az., U.S.	J5	132
Apache Peak, mtn., Az., U.S.	L6	132
Apalachee, stm., Ga., U.S.	C2	116
Apalachicola, Fl., U.S.	H13	122
Apalachicola, stm., Fl., U.S.	H14	122
Apalachicola Bay, b., Fl., U.S.	H13	122
Apaporis, stm., S.A.	H7	86
Aparados da Serra, Parque Nacional de, p.o.i., Braz.	D12	92
Aparri, Phil.	A3	52
Apartadó, Col.	D3	86
Apatin, Yugo.	D5	26
Apatity, Russia	C15	8
Apatzingán de la Constitución, Mex.	F7	100
Apaxtla de Castrejón, Mex.	F8	100
Apeldoorn, Neth.	B15	14
Apennines see Appennino, mts., Italy	G11	6
Apex, N.C., U.S.	I7	114
Api, mtn., Nepal	D8	54
Apía, Col.	E4	86
Apia, Samoa	g12	79c
Apiacás, Serra dos, plat., Braz.	E6	84
Apiaí, Braz.	B13	92
Apiaú, stm., Braz.	F11	86
Apishapa, stm., Co., U.S.	D4	128
Apizaco, Mex.	F9	100
Apo, Mount, mtn., Phil.	G5	52
Apodi, Braz.	C7	88
Apodi, stm., Braz.	C7	88
Apolakkiá, Grc.	G10	28
Apolda, Ger.	E7	16
Apolinario Saravia, Arg.	B6	92
Apolo, Bol.	B3	90
Apón, stm., Ven.	B5	86
Aponguao, stm., Ven.	E11	86
Apopka, Lake, l., Fl., U.S.	H4	116
Aporá, Braz.	F6	88
Aporé, Braz.	C6	90
Apostle Islands, is., Wi., U.S.	E8	118
Apostle Islands National Lakeshore, p.o.i., Wi., U.S.	D8	118
Apóstoles, Arg.	C10	92
Apostolove, Ukr.	E4	32
Appalaches, Les see Appalachian Mountains, mts., N.A.	D12	108
Appalachia, Va., U.S.	H3	114
Appalachian Mountains, mts., N.A.	D12	108
Appennino see Apennines, mts., Italy	G11	6
Appennino, Calabro, mts., Italy	E10	24
Appennino Abruzzese, mts., Italy	B7	24
Appennino Ligure, mts., Italy	F6	22
Appennino Lucano, mts., Italy	D9	24
Appennino Tosco-Emiliano, mts., Italy	F8	22
Appennino Umbro-Marchigiano, mts., Italy	G9	22
Appenzell, Switz.	C6	22
Apple Orchard Mountain, mtn., Va., U.S.	G6	114
Appleton, Mn., U.S.	F3	118
Appleton, Wi., U.S.	G10	118
Appleton City, Mo., U.S.	F3	120
Apple Valley, Ca., U.S.	I8	134
Appomattox, Va., U.S.	G7	114
Appomattox, stm., Va., U.S.	G7	114
Aprelevka, Russia	E20	10
Aprilia, Italy	C6	24
Apšeronsk, Russia	F5	32
Apt, Fr.	F11	18
Apucarana, Braz.	A12	92
Apulia see Puglia, state, Italy	C10	24
Apure, state, Ven.	D7	86
Apure, stm., Ven.	D8	86
Apurímac, stm., Peru	F3	84
Apurito, Ven.	D7	86
Aqaba, Gulf of, b.	J5	58
Āqchah, Afg.	B10	56
'Aqīq, Sudan	D7	62
Aqtaū see Aktau, Kaz.	F8	32
Aqtöbe see Aktjubinsk, Kaz.	D9	32
Aquidabã, Braz.	F7	88
Aquidauana, Braz.	D5	90
Aquila, Mex.	F7	100
Aquiles Serdán, Mex.	A6	100
Aquiles Serdán, Mex.	C9	100
Aquin, Haiti	C11	102
Aquio, stm., Col.	F8	86
Ara, India	F10	54
Ara, stm., Japan	D12	40
Arab, Al., U.S.	C12	122
'Arab, Bahr al-, stm., Sudan	E5	62
'Araba, Wadi ('Arabah, Wādī), stm., Egypt	I3	58
'Arabah, Wādī al- (Ha'Arava), val., Asia	H6	58
Arabako, co., Spain	B8	20
Araban, Tur.	A8	58
Arabian Basin, unds.	H9	142
Arabian Desert (Eastern Desert), des., Egypt	B6	62
Arabian Gulf see Persian Gulf, b., Asia	D7	56
Arabian Peninsula, pen., Asia	E6	56
Arabian Sea	F9	56
Araçá, stm., Braz.	G10	86
Aracaju, Braz.	F7	88
Aracataca, Col.	B4	86
Aracati, Braz.	C7	88
Araçatuba, Braz.	D6	90
Aracena, Spain	G4	20
Araci, Braz.	F6	88
Aracides, Cape, c., Sol. Is.	e9	79b
Aracoiaba, Braz.	C6	88
Aracruz, Braz.	J5	88
Araçuaí, Braz.	I4	88
Araçuaí, stm., Braz.	I4	88
'Arad, Isr.	G6	58
Arad, Rom.	C8	26
Arad, state, Rom.	C8	26
Aradhíppou, Cyp.	D4	58
Arafura Sea	J16	142
Arafura Shelf, unds.	K16	142
Aragarças, Braz.	G7	84
Aragats Lerr, mtn., Arm.	A5	56
Aragón, state, Spain	C10	20
Aragón, stm., Spain	B9	20
Aragona, Italy	G7	24
Aragua, state, Ven.	B8	86
Araguacema, Braz.	E8	84
Araguaçu, Braz.	F8	84
Aragua de Barcelona, Ven.	C9	86
Araguaia, stm., Braz.	E8	84
Araguaína, Braz.	D1	88
Araguao, Caño, stm., Ven.	C11	86
Araguari, Braz.	J1	88
Araguari, stm., Braz.	C7	84
Araguari, stm., Braz.	J1	88
Araguatins, Braz.	C1	88
Arahal, Spain	G5	20
Arai, Japan	B11	40
Araioses, Braz.	B4	88
Ârak, Alg.	D5	64
Arāk, Iran	C6	56
Arakan see Rakhine, state, Mya.	C1	48
Arakan Yoma, mts., Mya.	C2	48
Arakkonam, India	E4	53
Araks see Aras, stm., Asia	B6	56
Araks see Araz, stm., Asia	B6	56
Aral Sea, l., Asia	E9	32
Aral'sk, Kaz.	E10	32
Aralsk see Aral'sk, Kaz.	E10	32
Aramac, Austl.	D5	76
Aramac, stm., Austl.	D5	76
Ārāmbāg, India	G11	54
Aramberri, Mex.	C8	100
Ārān, Iran	C7	56
Aranda de Duero, Spain	C7	20
Arandas, Mex.	E7	100
Arandis, Nmb.	C2	70
Arang, India	H8	54
Ārani, India	E4	53
Aran Island, i., Ire.	G4	12
Aran Islands, is., Ire.	H3	12
Aranjuez, Spain	D7	20
Aranos, Nmb.	D4	70
Aransas, stm., Tx., U.S.	F10	130
Arantāngi, India	F4	53
Aranyaprathet, Thai.	F6	48
Arao, Japan	G3	40
Araouane, Mali	F4	64
Arapaho, Ok., U.S.	F9	128
Arapahoe, Ne., U.S.	A9	128
Arapey Grande, stm., Ur.	E9	92
Arapiraca, Braz.	E7	88
Arapongas, Braz.	D6	90
Arapoti, Braz.	B12	92
Araranguá, Braz.	D13	92
Araraquara, Braz.	K1	88
Araras, Braz.	L2	88
Araras, Açude, res., Braz.	C5	88
Ararat, Austl.	K4	76
Ararat, Mount see Ağrı Dağı, mtn., Tur.	B5	56
Arari, Braz.	B3	88
Arāria, India	E11	54
Araripe, Braz.	D5	88
Araripe, Chapada do, plat., Braz.	D6	88
Araripina, Braz.	D5	88
Ararirá, stm., Braz.	H10	86
Araruama, Lagoa de, b., Braz.	L4	88
Araruna, Braz.	D8	88
Aras (Araz), stm., Asia	B6	56
Aratuípe, Braz.	G6	88
Arauca, Col.	D6	86
Arauca, state, Col.	D6	86
Arauca, stm., S.A.	D8	86
Araucária, Braz.	B13	92
Arauquita, Col.	D6	86
Araure, Ven.	C7	86
Arāvalli Range, mts., India	F4	54
Arawa, Pap. N. Gui.	d6	79b
Araxá, Braz.	J2	88
Araya, Ven.	B9	86
Araya, Punta de, c., Ven.	B9	86
Araz (Aras), stm., Asia	B6	56
Ārba Minch', Eth.	F7	62
Arbatax, Italy	E3	24
Arboga, Swe.	G6	8
Arboledas, Arg.	H7	92
Arbon, Switz.	C6	22
Arborea, Italy	E2	24
Arborea, reg., Italy	E2	24
Arborfield, Sk., Can.	A10	124
Arbroath, Scot., U.K.	E10	12
Arbuckle, Ca., U.S.	D3	134
Arc, stm., Fr.	D12	18
Arcachon, Fr.	E4	18
Arcachon, Bassin d', b., Fr.	E4	18
Arcade, Ca., U.S.	E4	134
Arcade, N.Y., U.S.	B7	114
Arcadia, Ca., U.S.	I7	134
Arcadia, Fl., U.S.	I4	116
Arcadia, Ia., U.S.	B2	120
Arcadia, Ks., U.S.	G3	120
Arcadia, La., U.S.	E6	122
Arcadia, Mi., U.S.	D3	112
Arcadia, Mo., U.S.	G7	120
Arcadia, S.C., U.S.	B3	116
Arcadia, Wi., U.S.	G7	118
Arcanum, Oh., U.S.	D1	114
Arcas, Cayos, is., Mex.	E12	100
Arcata, Ca., U.S.	C1	134
Arc Dome, mtn., Nv., U.S.	E8	134
Arcelia, Mex.	F8	100
Arcevia, Italy	G9	22
Archangel see Arhangel'sk, Russia	D19	8
Archbold, Oh., U.S.	C1	114
Archer, Fl., U.S.	G3	116
Archer, stm., Austl.	B8	74
Archer, Mount, mtn., Austl.	D8	76
Archer City, Tx., U.S.	H10	128
Archer's Post, Kenya	D7	66
Arches National Park, p.o.i., Ut., U.S.	E7	132
Archiac, Fr.	D5	18
Archidona, Spain	G6	20
Arcis-sur-Aube, Fr.	F13	14
Arco, Id., U.S.	G13	136
Arcola, Il., U.S.	E9	120
Arcola, Ms., U.S.	D8	122
Arcos, Braz.	K3	88
Arcos de la Frontera, Spain	H5	20
Arcot, India	E4	53
Arcoverde, Braz.	E7	88
Arctic Bay, Nu., Can.	A14	106
Arctic Ocean	A21	4
Arctic Red, stm., N.T., Can.	B4	106
Arctic Village, Ak., U.S.	C10	140
Arda, stm., Eur.	H12	26
Ardabīl, Iran	B6	56
Ardahan, Tur.	A5	56
Ardakān, Iran	C7	56
Ardatov, Russia	I20	8
Ardèche, state, Fr.	E10	18
Arden, Ca., U.S.	E4	134
Ardennes, state, Fr.	E13	14
Ardennes, reg., Eur.	D14	14
Ardennes, Canal des, can., Fr.	E13	14
Ardestān, Iran	C7	56
Ardila, stm., Eur.	F3	20
Ardill, Sk., Can.	E8	124
Ardlethan, Austl.	J6	76
Ardmore, Al., U.S.	B12	122
Ardmore, Ok., U.S.	G11	128
Ardmore, Pa., U.S.	D10	114
Åre, Swe.	E5	8
Areado, Braz.	K2	88
Arecibo, P.R.	B2	104a
Arecibo, Observatorio de, sci., P.R.	B2	104a
Arecibo Observatory see Arecibo, Observatorio de, sci., P.R.	B2	104a
Arèḫausk, Bela.	F13	10
Areia, Braz.	D8	88
Areia, stm., Braz.	H3	88
Areia Branca, Braz.	C7	88
Arena, Point, c., Ca., U.S.	E2	134
Arena, Punta, c., Mex.	D4	100
Arena de la Ventana, Punta, c., Mex.	C4	100
Arenal, P.R.	C3	104a
Arenas, Cayo, i., Mex.	D13	100
Arenas, Punta de, c., Arg.	J3	90
Arenas de San Pedro, Spain	D5	20
Arendal, Nor.	G3	8
Arenys de Mar, Spain	C13	20
Arequipa, Peru	G3	84
Arequito, Arg.	F7	92
Arévalo, Spain	C6	20
Arezzo, Italy	G8	22
Arga, stm., Spain	B9	20
Argadargada, Austl.	D7	74
Argamasilla de Alba, Spain	E7	20
Arganda del Rey, Spain	D7	20
Arga-Sala, stm., Russia	C10	34
Argelès-Gazost, Fr.	F5	18
Argens, stm., Fr.	F12	18
Argent, Côte d', cst., Fr.	F4	18
Argenta, Italy	F8	22
Argentan, Fr.	F8	14
Argentat, Fr.	D7	18
Argenteuil, Fr.	F11	14
Argentina, ctry., S.A.	G3	90
Argentine Basin, unds.	L10	144
Argentino, Lago, l., Arg.	J2	90
Argenton-sur-Creuse, Fr.	H10	14
Argeș, state, Rom.	E11	26
Argeș, stm., Rom.	E13	26
Arghandāb, stm., Afg.	C10	56
Argolikós Kólpos (Argolis, Gulf of), b., Grc.	F6	28
Argolis, Gulf of see Argolikós Kólpos, b., Grc.	F6	28
Argonia, Ks., U.S.	D11	128
Argonne, Wi., U.S.	F10	118
Argonne, reg., Fr.	E14	14
Árgos, Grc.	F5	28
Argos, In., U.S.	G3	112
Argostóli, Grc.	E3	28
Arguello, Point, c., Ca., U.S.	I5	134
Argun' (Ergun), stm., Asia	F12	34
Argungu, Nig.	G5	64
Argyle, Lake, l., Austl.	C5	74
Arhangel'sk, Russia	D19	8
Arhangel'skaja oblast', co., Russia	E20	8
Arhangel'skoe, Russia	G20	10
Arhara, Russia	G15	34
Arhipovo, Russia	C21	8
Århus, Den.	H4	8
Århus, state, Den.	H4	8
Ariake-kai, b., Japan	F3	40
Ariana, Tun.	H4	24
Ariano Irpino, Italy	C9	24
Ariari, stm., Col.	F5	86
Arias, Arg.	F6	92
Ari Atoll, at., Mald.	i12	46a
Arica, Chile	C2	90
Arica, Col.	I6	86
Arichat, N.S., Can.	E16	110
Arichuna, Ven.	D8	86
Arid, Cape, c., Austl.	F4	74
Arida, Japan	E8	40
Aridaía, Grc.	C5	28
Ariège, state, Fr.	G7	18
Ārifwāla, Pak.	C4	54
Ariguaní, stm., Col.	C5	86
Arīḥā (Jericho), Gaza	G6	58
Arīḥā, Syria	C7	58
Arikaree, stm., U.S.	B6	128
Arima, Trin.	s12	105f
Arinos, stm., Braz.	F6	84
Ariogala, Lith.	E6	10
Ariporo, stm., Col.	D6	86
Aripuanã, Braz.	E5	84
Aripuanã, stm., Braz.	E5	84
Ariquemes, Braz.	E5	84
Arisa, stm., Ven.	D9	86
Arish, Wadi el- ('Arīsh, Wādī al-), stm., Egypt	H4	58
Aristazabal Island, i., B.C., Can.	E5	106
Ariton, Al., U.S.	F13	122
Arivonimamo, Madag.	D8	68
Ariyalūr, India	F4	53
Arizaro, Salar de, pl., Arg.	B4	92
Arizgoiti, Spain	A8	20
Arizona, Arg.	G5	92
Arizona, state, U.S.	I5	132
Arizpe, Mex.	F7	98
Arja, Russia	H22	8
Arjasa, Indon.	G9	50
Arjona, Col.	B4	86
Arjona, Spain	G6	20
Arka, Russia	D17	34
Arkadelphia, Ar., U.S.	C5	122
Arkalyk, Kaz.	D11	32
Arkansas, state, U.S.	B6	122
Arkansas, stm., U.S.	E9	108
Arkansas, Salt Fork, stm., U.S.	D7	122
Arkansas City, Ar., U.S.	D7	122
Arkansas City, Ks., U.S.	D11	128
Arkanū, Jabal, mtn., Libya	C4	62
Arkhara see Arhara, Russia	G15	34
Arklow, Ire.	I6	12
Arkoma, Ok., U.S.	B4	122
Arkona, Kap, c., Ger.	B9	16
Arkport, N.Y., U.S.	B8	114
Arktičeskogo Instituta, ostrova, is., Russia	A5	34
Arlanza, stm., Spain	B7	20
Arlanzón, stm., Spain	B7	20
Arles, Fr.	F10	18
Arlington, S. Afr.	E8	70
Arlington, Ga., U.S.	F14	122
Arlington, Ks., U.S.	D10	128
Arlington, Ky., U.S.	H9	120
Arlington, Ne., U.S.	C1	120
Arlington, Oh., U.S.	D2	114
Arlington, Or., U.S.	E6	136
Arlington, Tn., U.S.	B9	122
Arlington, Tx., U.S.	B10	130
Arlington, Vt., U.S.	G3	110
Arlington, Va., U.S.	F8	114
Arlington, Wa., U.S.	B4	136
Arlington Heights, Il., U.S.	F2	112
Arlit, Niger	F6	64
Arlon, Bel.	E14	14
Arm, stm., Sk., Can.	D8	124
Arma, Ks., U.S.	G3	120
Armada, Mi., U.S.	B3	114
Armadale, Austl.	F3	74
Armageddon see Tel Megiddo, hist., Isr.	F6	58
Armagh, N. Ire., U.K.	G6	12
Armançon, stm., Fr.	G13	14
Armavir, Russia	E6	32
Armenia, Col.	E4	86
Armenia, ctry., Asia	A5	56
Armenija see Armenia, ctry., Asia	A5	56
Armenistís, Grc.	F9	28
Armentières, Fr.	D11	14
Armería, Mex.	F6	100
Armero, Col.	E4	86
Armidale, Austl.	H8	76
Armijo, N.M., U.S.	H10	132
Armour, S.D., U.S.	D14	126
Armstrong, Arg.	F7	92
Armstrong, B.C., Can.	F11	138
Armstrong, On., Can.	A9	118
Armstrong, Mo., U.S.	E5	120
Armstrong, Mount, mtn., Yk., Can.	C4	106
Ārmūr, India	B4	53
Armutlu, Tur.	C11	28
Arnarfjörður, b., Ice.	k27	8a
Arnaud, stm., Qc., Can.	D16	106
Arnaudville, La., U.S.	G6	122
Arnay-le-Duc, Fr.	G13	14
Arnedo, Spain	B8	20
Arneiros, Braz.	D5	88
Arnhem, Neth.	B14	14
Arnhem, Cape, c., Austl.	B7	74
Arnhem Bay, b., Austl.	B7	74
Arnhem Land, reg., Austl.	B6	74
Arno, at., Marsh. Is.	C8	72
Arno, stm., Italy	G7	22
Arnold, Ca., U.S.	E5	134
Arnold, Mn., U.S.	E6	118
Arnold, Mo., U.S.	F7	120
Arnold, Ne., U.S.	F12	126
Arnolds Park, Ia., U.S.	H3	118
Arnon, stm., Fr.	C8	18
Arnprior, On., Can.	C13	112
Arnsberg, Ger.	E4	16
Arnstadt, Ger.	F6	16
Aro, stm., Ven.	D9	86
Aroa, Ven.	B7	86
Aroa, Pointe, c., Fr. Poly.	u20	78h
Aroab, Nmb.	E4	70
Aroland, On., Can.	A12	118
Arolsen, Ger.	E5	16
Arona, Italy	E5	22
Arona, Pap. N. Gui.	b4	79a
Aroostook, stm., N.A.	D8	110
Arop Island (Long Island), i., Pap. N. Gui.	b4	79a
Arorae, i., Kir.	D8	72
Aroroy, Phil.	D4	52
Arosa, Ría de see Arousa, Ría de, est., Spain	B1	20
Arousa, Ría de, est., Spain	B1	20
Arp, Tx., U.S.	E3	122
Arqalyq see Arkalyk, Kaz.	D11	32
Arquata Scrivia, Italy	F5	22
Arraga, Arg.	D5	92
Ar-Rahad, Sudan	E6	62
Arraial do Cabo, Braz.	L5	88
Arraias, Braz.	G2	88
Ar-Ramādī, Iraq	C5	56
Ar-Ramthā, Jord.	F7	58
Arran, Island of, i., Scot., U.K.	F7	12
Ar-Rank, Sudan	E6	62
Ar-Raqqah, Syria	B9	58
Ar-Raqqah, state, Syria	B9	58
Arras, Fr.	D11	14
Ar-Rastan, Syria	D7	58
Arrecifes, Arg.	G7	92
Arrey, N.M., U.S.	K9	132
Arriaga, Mex.	G11	100
Ar-Riyāḍ (Riyadh), Sau. Ar.	E6	56
Arroio Grande, Braz.	F11	92
Arrojado, stm., Braz.	G3	88
Arronches, Port.	E3	20
Arros, stm., Fr.	F6	18
Arroux, stm., Fr.	B10	18
Arrowhead, Lake, res., Tx., U.S.	H10	128
Arrowwood, Ab., Can.	F17	138
Arroyito, Arg.	E6	92
Arroyo, P.R.	C3	104a
Arroyo de la Luz, Spain	E4	20
Arroyo Grande, Ca., U.S.	H5	134
Arroyo Hondo, N.M., U.S.	E3	128
Arroyo Seco, Arg.	F7	92
Arroyos y Esteros, Para.	B9	92
Ar-Rub' al-Khālī, des., Asia	E6	56
Ar-Ruqayyah, hist., Syria	F8	58
Ar-Ruṣāfah, hist., Syria	C9	58
Ar-Ruṣayfah, Jord.	F7	58
Ar-Ruṣayriṣ, Sudan	E6	62
Ar-Ruṭbah, Iraq	C5	56
Arsenev, Russia	B10	38
Arsenevka, stm., Russia	B10	38
Arsikere, India	E3	53
Ársoș, Cyp.	D3	58
Art, Île, i., N. Cal.	I14	79d
Árta, Grc.	D3	28
Artà, Spain	E14	20
Artá see Artà, Spain	E14	20
Arteaga, Mex.	F7	100
Art'em, Russia	C9	38
Artemisa, Cuba	A6	102
Artëmovsk, Russia	D16	32
Artëmovskij, Russia	E12	34
Artëmovskij, Russia	C10	38
Artesia, Ms., U.S.	D10	122
Artesia, N.M., U.S.	B3	130
Arthabaska, ngh., Qc., Can.	D5	110
Arthal, India	B6	54
Arthur, On., Can.	E9	112
Arthur, Il., U.S.	E9	120
Arthur, N.D., U.S.	D1	118
Arthur, Tn., U.S.	H2	114
Arthur, stm., Austl.	n12	77a
Arthur's Pass National Park, p.o.i., N.Z.	F5	80
Arthur's Town, Bah.	C9	96
Artibonite, stm., Haiti	C11	102
Artigas, Ur.	E9	92
Artillery Lake, l., N.T., Can.	C9	106
Artois, hist. reg., Fr.	D11	14
Artsyz, Ukr.	D16	26
Artyk, Russia	D18	34
Aru, Kepulauan (Aru Islands), is., Indon.	G10	44
Aru, Tanjung, c., Indon.	E10	50
Arua, Ug.	D6	66
Aruanã, Braz.	F7	84
Aruba, dep., N.A.	F12	102
Aru Islands see Aru, Kepulauan, is., Indon.	G10	44
Arunāchal Pradesh, state, India	C7	46
Arun Qi, China	B9	36
Aruppukkottai, India	G4	53
Arurandeua, stm., Braz.	C1	88
Arusha, Tan.	E7	66
Arut, stm., Indon.	E7	50
Aruvi, stm., Sri L.	G5	53
Aruwimi, stm., D.R.C.	D4	66
Arvada, Co., U.S.	B3	128
Arvayheer, Mong.	B5	36
Arvi, India	H7	54
Arviat, Nu., Can.	C12	106
Arvidsjaur, Swe.	D8	8
Arvika, Swe.	G5	8
Arvin, Ca., U.S.	H7	134
Arvon, Mount, mtn., Mi., U.S.	B1	112
Arvorezinha, Braz.	D11	92
Arxan, China	B8	36
Arys', Kaz.	F11	32
Arys, ozero, l., Kaz.	E11	32
Arzachena, Italy	C3	24
Arzamas, Russia	I20	8
Arzignano, Italy	E8	22
Arz Lubnān, for., Leb.	D7	58
Aš, Czech Rep.	F8	16
Aša, Russia	D9	32
Asa, stm., Ven.	D10	86
Asaba, Nig.	H6	64
Asad, Buḥayrat al- (Assad, Lake), res., Syria	B9	58
Asadābād, Afg.	C11	56
Asadābād, Iran	B8	56
Aşağibostancı, N. Cyp.	C3	58
Asahan, stm., Indon.	B1	50
Asahi, Japan	D13	40
Asahi, stm., Japan	E6	40
Asahi-dake, vol., Japan	C15	38
Asahigawa see Asahikawa, Japan	C15	38
Asahikawa, Japan	C15	38
Asama-yama, vol., Japan	C11	40
Asan-man, b., Kor., S.	F7	38
Āsānsol, India	G11	54
Åsarna, Swe.	E6	8
Asaro, Ven.	q20	104g
Asbest, Russia	C10	32
Asbestos, Qc., Can.	E4	110
Asbestos Range National Park, p.o.i., Austl.	n13	77a
Asbury Park, N.J., U.S.	D12	114
Ascensión, Mex.	F9	98
Ascension, i., St. Hel.	G4	60
Aschaffenburg, Ger.	G5	16
Aschersleben, Ger.	E7	16
Ascoli Piceno, Italy	H10	22
Ascoli Satriano, Italy	C9	24
Ascör (Ostër), stm., Eur.	G14	10
Āseb, Erit.	E8	62
Åseda, Swe.	H6	8
Āsela, Eth.	F7	62
Åsele, Swe.	D7	8
Āsendabo, Eth.	F7	62
Asenovgrad, Blg.	G11	26
Aseri, Est.	A9	10
Ašgabat, Turkmen.	B8	56
Ashāqif, Jabal al-, hills, Jord.	F8	58
Ashburton, N.Z.	F4	80
Ashburton, stm., Austl.	D3	74
Ashcroft, B.C., Can.	F9	138
Ashdod, Isr.	G5	58
Ashdod, Tel, hist., Isr.	G5	58
Ashdown, Ar., U.S.	D4	122
Asheboro, N.C., U.S.	I6	114
Ashern, Mb., Can.	C15	124
Asheville, N.C., U.S.	I3	114
Ash Flat, Ar., U.S.	H6	120
Ashford, Eng., U.K.	J13	12
Ashford, Al., U.S.	F13	122
Ash Fork, Az., U.S.	H4	132
Ashgabat see Ašgabat, Turkmen.	B8	56
Ash Grove, Mo., U.S.	G4	120
Ashibe, Japan	F2	40
Ashikaga, Japan	C12	40
Ashington, Eng., U.K.	F11	12
Ashio, Japan	C12	40
Ashizuri-misaki, c., Japan	G6	40
Ashland, Al., U.S.	D13	122
Ashland, Il., U.S.	E7	120
Ashland, Ks., U.S.	D9	128
Ashland, Ky., U.S.	F3	114
Ashland, Mo., U.S.	F5	120
Ashland, Mt., U.S.	B6	126
Ashland, Ne., U.S.	C1	120
Ashland, N.H., U.S.	G5	110
Ashland, Oh., U.S.	D3	114
Ashland, Or., U.S.	A3	134
Ashland, Va., U.S.	G8	114
Ashland, Wi., U.S.	E7	118
Ashland, Mount, mtn., Or., U.S.	A3	134
Ashley, Austl.	G7	76
Ashley, Il., U.S.	F8	120
Ashley, Mi., U.S.	E5	112
Ashley, Oh., U.S.	D3	114
Ashmore, Il., U.S.	E9	120
Ashmore Islands, is., Austl.	B4	74
Ashoknagar, India	F6	54
Ashqelon, Isr.	G5	58
Ash-Shamāl, state, Leb.	D7	58
Ash-Shaqrā' see Shaqrā', Sau. Ar.	D6	56
Ash-Shāriqah, U.A.E.	D8	56
Ash-Shawbak, Jord.	H6	58
Ash-Shiḥr, Yemen	G6	56
Ash-Shurayf, Sau. Ar.	D4	56
Ashta, India	C2	53
Ashta, India	G6	54
Ashtabula, Oh., U.S.	C5	114
Ashtabula, Lake, res., N.D., U.S.	G16	124
Ashton, St. Vin.	p11	105e
Ashton, S. Afr.	H5	70
Ashton, Id., U.S.	F15	136
Ashton, Il., U.S.	C8	120
Ashton, Ne., U.S.	F14	126
Ashuanipi Lake, l., Nf., Can.	E17	106
Ashuapmushuan, stm., Qc., Can.	B3	110
Ashûm, Egypt	H1	58
Ashville, Al., U.S.	D12	122
Ashwaubenon, Wi., U.S.	D1	112

Name	Map Ref.	Page
Asi see Orontes, stm., Asia	B7	58
Asia, cont.	C19	4
Asia, Kepulauan, is., Indon.	E9	44
Asia Minor, hist. reg., Tur.	E13	28
Āsika, India	I10	54
Asinara, Golfo dell', b., Italy	D2	24
Asinara, Isola, i., Italy	C2	24
Asino, Russia	C15	32
Asintorf, Bela.	F13	10
Asipovičy, Bela.	G11	10
'Asīr, reg., Sau. Ar.	F5	56
Askham, S. Afr.	E5	70
Askiz, Russia	D16	32
Askja, vol., Ice.	k31	8a
Aslanapa, Tur.	D12	28
Aslantaş Barajı, res., Tur.	A7	58
Asmara see Asmera, Erit.	D7	62
Asmera, Erit.	D7	62
Ašmjany, Bela.	F8	10
Asola, Italy	E7	22
Asomante, P.R.	B2	104a
Āsosa, Eth.	E6	62
Asoteriba, Jabal, mtn., Sudan	C7	62
Asotin, Wa., U.S.	D9	136
Asouf, Oued, stm., Alg.	D5	64
Asp, Spain	F10	20
Aspe see Asp, Spain	F10	20
Aspen, Co., U.S.	D10	132
Aspendos, hist., Tur.	G14	28
Aspermont, Tx., U.S.	A7	130
Aspiring, Mount, mtn., N.Z.	G3	80
Assad, Lake see Asad, Buḥayrat al-, res., Syria	B9	58
As-Safīrah, Syria	B8	58
Aş-Şāfiyah, Sudan	D6	62
As-Salṭ, Jord.	F6	58
Assam, state, India	C7	46
As-Samāwah, Iraq	C6	56
Aş-Şanamayn, Syria	E7	58
Aş-Şarafand, Leb.	E6	58
Assaré, Braz.	D6	88
Assateague Island, i., U.S.	F10	114
Assateague Island National Seashore, p.o.i., U.S.	G10	114
Assemini, Italy	E2	24
Assen, Neth.	A15	14
Asseria, hist., Cro.	F12	22
Assíni, hist., Grc.	F5	28
Assiniboia, Sk., Can.	E8	124
Assiniboine, stm., Can.	E16	124
Assiniboine, Mount, mtn., Can.	F15	138
Assis, Braz.	D6	90
Assis Chateaubriand, Braz.	B11	92
Assisi, Italy	G9	22
Assomption, i., Sey.	k11	69b
Assu, Braz.	C7	88
As-Sudd, reg., Sudan	F6	62
As-Sufāl, Yemen	G6	56
As-Sulaymānīyah, Iraq	B6	56
As-Sulaymānīyah, Sau. Ar.	E6	56
As-Sulayyil, Sau. Ar.	E6	56
Assumption, Il., U.S.	E8	120
As-Suwaydā', Syria	F7	58
As-Suwaydā', state, Syria	F7	58
Astakós, Grc.	E3	28
Astana (Akmola), Kaz.	D12	32
Astara, Azer.	B6	56
Asti, Italy	F5	22
Astica, Arg.	E4	92
Astola Island, i., Pak.	D9	56
Astorga, Spain	B4	20
Astoria, Il., U.S.	D7	120
Astoria, Or., U.S.	D3	136
Astove, i., Sey.	I11	69b
Astrahan', Russia	E7	32
Astrakhan see Astrahan', Russia	E7	32
Astrašycki Haradok, Bela.	F10	10
Astrolabe, Cape, c., Sol. Is.	e9	79b
Astrolabe, Récifs de l', rf., N. Cal.	I15	79d
Astrolabe Reefs see Astrolabe, Récifs de l', rf., N. Cal.	I15	79d
Astrouna, Bela.	E12	10
Astudillo, Spain	B6	20
Asturias, state, Spain	A5	20
Astypálaia, i., Grc.	G9	28
Asunción, Para.	B9	92
Asunción, Bahía la, b., Mex.	B1	100
Asunción Nochixtlán, Mex.	G10	100
Åsunden, l., Swe.	H5	8
Asveja, Bela.	E11	10
Asvejskae, vozero, l., Bela.	D10	10
Aswân, Egypt	C6	62
Aswan High Dam see Aali, Sadd el-, dam, Egypt	C6	62
Asyût, Egypt	K2	58
Asyûti, Wadi el- (Asyūṭī, Wādī al-), stm., Egypt	K2	58
'Ata, i., Tonga	F9	72
Atabapo, stm., S.A.	F8	86
Atacama, state, Chile	C3	92
Atacama, Desierto de, des., Chile	E2	90
Atacama, Puna de, plat., S.A.	B4	92
Atacama, Salar de, pl., Chile	D3	90
Atacama Desert see Atacama, Desierto de, des., Chile	B3	92
Ataco, Col.	F4	86
Atagaj, Russia	C17	32
Atakpamé, Togo	H5	64
Atalaia, Braz.	E7	88
Atambua, Indon.	G7	44
Atami, Japan	D12	40
Atangmik, Grnld.	E15	141
Aṭar, Maur.	E2	64
Atascadero, Ca., U.S.	H5	134
Atascosa, stm., Tx., U.S.	F9	130
Atasu, Kaz.	E12	32
Atata, i., Tonga	n14	78e
Atatürk Barajı, res., Tur.	A9	58
Atauro, Pulau, i., Indon.	G8	44
'Aṭbarah, Sudan	D6	62
'Aṭbarah, stm., Afr.	D7	62
Atbasar, Kaz.	D11	32
Atchafalaya, stm., La., U.S.	G7	122
Atchafalaya Bay, b., La., U.S.	H7	122
Atchison, Ks., U.S.	E2	120
Ateca, Spain	C9	20
Aterno, stm., Italy	H10	22
Atfîh, Egypt	I2	58
Ath, Bel.	D12	14
Athabasca, Ab., Can.	B17	138
Athabasca, stm., Ab., Can.	D8	106
Athabasca, Lake, l., Can.	D9	106
Athalmer, B.C., Can.	F14	138
Athboy, Ire.	H6	12
Athena, Or., U.S.	E8	136
Athens, On., Can.	D14	112
Athens see Athína, Grc.	E6	28
Athens, Al., U.S.	C11	122
Athens, Ga., U.S.	C2	116
Athens, Il., U.S.	E8	120
Athens, La., U.S.	E5	122
Athens, Mi., U.S.	F4	112
Athens, Oh., U.S.	E3	114
Athens, Pa., U.S.	C9	114
Athens, Tn., U.S.	B14	122
Athens, Tx., U.S.	E3	122
Athens, W.V., U.S.	G5	114
Atherton, Austl.	A5	76
Athi, stm., Kenya	E7	66
Athiaínou, Cyp.	C4	58
Athína (Athens), Grc.	E6	28
Athlone, Ire.	H4	12
Athni, India	C2	53
Athok, Mya.	D2	48
Athol, Ma., U.S.	B13	114
Áthos, mtn., Grc.	C7	28
Athos, Mount see Áthos, mtn., Grc.	C7	28
Ati, Chad	E3	62
Atiak, Ug.	D6	66
Atico, Peru	G3	84
Atienza, Spain	C8	20
Atikokan, On., Can.	C7	118
Atirāmpattinam, India	F4	53
Atiu, i., Cook Is.	F11	72
Atka, Russia	D19	34
Atka Island, i., Ak., U.S.	g24	140a
Atkarsk, Russia	D6	32
Atkins, Ar., U.S.	B6	122
Atkinson, Il., U.S.	C8	120
Atkinson, N.C., U.S.	B7	116
Atlanta, Ga., U.S.	C1	116
Atlanta, Il., U.S.	D8	120
Atlanta, Mi., U.S.	C5	112
Atlanta, Mo., U.S.	E5	120
Atlantic, Ia., U.S.	C2	120
Atlantic, N.C., U.S.	B9	116
Atlantic Beach, Fl., U.S.	F4	116
Atlantic City, N.J., U.S.	E11	114
Atlantic-Indian Basin, unds.	O5	142
Atlantic-Indian Ridge, unds.	N15	144
Atlántico, state, Col.	B4	86
Atlantic Ocean	E9	144
Atlantic Peak, mtn., Wy., U.S.	E3	126
Atlas Mountains, mts., Afr.	C4	64
Atlasova, ostrov, i., Russia	F20	34
Atlas Saharien, mts., Alg.	C4	64
Atlin, B.C., Can.	D4	106
Atlin Lake, l., Can.	D4	106
'Atlit, Isr.	F5	58
Ātmakūr, India	D4	53
Atmore, Al., U.S.	F11	122
Atnarko, stm., B.C., Can.	D5	138
Atocha, Bol.	D3	90
Atoka, Ok., U.S.	C2	122
Atotonilco, Cerro, mtn., Mex.	H3	130
Atoyac, stm., Mex.	F9	100
Atoyac de Álvarez, Mex.	G8	100
Atrak (Atrek), stm., Asia	B7	56
Ätran, stm., Swe.	H5	8
Atrato, stm., Col.	D3	86
Atrauli, India	D7	54
Atrek (Atrak), stm., Asia	B7	56
Atri, Italy	H10	22
Atsumi, Japan	E10	40
Atsumi-hantō, pen., Japan	E10	40
Aṭ-Ṭafīlah, Jord.	H6	58
Aṭ-Ṭafīlah, state, Jord.	H6	58
Aṭ-Ṭā'if, Sau. Ar.	E5	56
At-Tall, Syria	E7	58
Attalla, Al., U.S.	C12	122
Attapu, Laos	E8	48
Attawapiskat, On., Can.	E14	106
Attawapiskat, stm., On., Can.	E13	106
Attawapiskat Lake, l., On., Can.	E13	106
Aṭ-Ṭawīl, mts., Sau. Ar.	D4	56
Aṭ-Ṭayyibah, Syria	C9	58
Attendorn, Ger.	E3	16
Attersee, l., Aus.	C10	22
Attica, In., U.S.	H2	112
Attica, Ks., U.S.	D10	128
Attica, N.Y., U.S.	B7	114
Attica see Attikí, hist. reg., Grc.	E6	28
Attikí, state, Grc.	F6	28
Attikí, hist. reg., Grc.	E6	28
Attleboro, Ma., U.S.	C14	114
Attock, Pak.	B4	54
Attu, Ak., U.S.	g21	140a
Attu Island, i., Ak., U.S.	g21	140a
Āttūr, India	F4	53
Aṭ-Ṭuwayshah, Sudan	E5	62
Atuel, stm., Arg.	G3	92
Atuel, Bañados del, sw., Arg.	H4	92
Atuntaqui, Ec.	G2	86
Atuona, Fr. Poly.	s18	78g
Atwater, Ca., U.S.	F5	134
Atwater, Mn., U.S.	F4	118
Atwood, Il., U.S.	E9	120
Atwood, Ks., U.S.	B7	128
Atwood, Tn., U.S.	I9	120
Atyrau, Kaz.	E8	32
Aua Island, i., Pap. N. Gui.	a3	79a
Auari, stm., Braz.	F9	86
Auau Channel, strt., Hi., U.S.	C5	78a
Aubagne, Fr.	F11	18
Aube, state, Fr.	F13	14
Aube, stm., Fr.	F13	14
Aubigny-sur-Nère, Fr.	G11	14
Aubinadong, stm., On., Can.	A6	112
Aubrey Cliffs, clf, Az., U.S.	H3	132
Aubrey Lake, res., On., Can.	A6	112
Aubry Lake, l., N.T., Can.	B5	106
Auburn, Al., U.S.	E13	122
Auburn, Ca., U.S.	E4	134
Auburn, Il., U.S.	E8	120
Auburn, In., U.S.	G4	112
Auburn, Ky., U.S.	H11	120
Auburn, Me., U.S.	F6	110
Auburn, Ma., U.S.	B14	114
Auburn, Mi., U.S.	E5	112
Auburn, N.Y., U.S.	B9	114
Auburn, Wa., U.S.	C4	136
Auburn, stm., Austl.	E8	76
Aubusson, Fr.	D8	18
Auca Mahuida, Cerro, mtn., Arg.	H3	92
Auce, Lat.	D5	10
Auch, Fr.	F6	18
Auchi, Nig.	H6	64
Aucilla, stm., U.S.	F2	116
Auckland, N.Z.	C6	80
Auckland Islands, is., N.Z.	I7	72
Aude, state, Fr.	F8	18
Aude, stm., Fr.	F9	18
Auden, On., Can.	A11	118
Audenarde see Oudenaarde, Bel.	D12	14
Audierne, Fr.	F4	14
Audincourt, Fr.	G15	14
Audubon Lake, res., N.D., U.S.	G12	124
Aue, Ger.	F8	16
Augathella, Austl.	E6	76
Augrabies Falls National Park, p.o.i., S. Afr.	F4	70
Augrabiesvalle, wtfl, S. Afr.	F5	70
Augsburg, Ger.	H6	16
Augusta, Austl.	F2	74
Augusta, Italy	G9	24
Augusta, Ar., U.S.	B7	122
Augusta, Ga., U.S.	C3	116
Augusta, Il., U.S.	D6	120
Augusta, Ky., U.S.	F1	114
Augusta, Me., U.S.	F7	110
Augusta, Mt., U.S.	C14	136
Augusta, Wi., U.S.	G7	118
Augusto Severo, Braz.	C7	88
Augustów, Pol.	C18	16
Augustowski, Kanał, can., Eur.	C19	16
Augustus, Mount, mtn., Austl.	D3	74
Auki, Sol. Is.	e9	79b
Aukštaitijos nacionalnis parkas, p.o.i., Lith.	E8	10
Aulander, N.C., U.S.	H8	114
Auld, Lake, l., Austl.	D4	74
Aulla, Italy	F6	22
Aulne, stm., Fr.	F5	14
Aulneau Peninsula, pen., On., Can.	B4	118
Aumale, Fr.	E10	14
Auna, Nig.	G5	64
Auob, stm., Afr.	E5	70
Auraiya, India	E7	54
Aurangābād, India	B2	53
Aurangābād, India	F10	54
Aure, Nor.	E3	8
Aurelia, Ia., U.S.	B2	120
Aurich, Ger.	C3	16
Aurilândia, Braz.	G7	84
Aurillac, Fr.	E8	18
Aurine, Alpi (Zillertaler Alpen), mts., Eur.	C8	22
Aurora, On., Can.	D10	112
Aurora, Co., U.S.	B4	128
Aurora, Il., U.S.	C9	120
Aurora, In., U.S.	E13	120
Aurora, Me., U.S.	F8	110
Aurora, Mn., U.S.	D6	118
Aurora, N.Y., U.S.	B9	114
Aurora, N.C., U.S.	A9	116
Aurora, Oh., U.S.	C4	114
Aurora, Ut., U.S.	E4	132
Aurora, W.V., U.S.	E6	114
Aurora do Norte, Braz.	G2	88
Aursunden, l., Nor.	E4	8
Aurukun, Austl.	B8	74
Aus, Nmb.	E3	70
Ausable, stm., On., Can.	E8	112
Au Sable, stm., Mi., U.S.	D6	112
Au Sable Forks, N.Y., U.S.	F3	110
Au Sable Point, c., Mi., U.S.	D6	112
Auschwitz see Oświęcim, Pol.	F15	16
Aust-Agder, state, Nor.	G3	8
Austin, In., U.S.	F12	120
Austin, Mn., U.S.	H6	118
Austin, Nv., U.S.	D8	134
Austin, Pa., U.S.	C7	114
Austin, Tx., U.S.	D10	130
Austin, Lake, l., Austl.	E3	74
Australes, Îles, is., Fr. Poly.	F11	72
Australia, ctry., Oc.	D5	74
Australian Capital Territory, state, Austl.	J7	76
Austral Islands see Australes, Îles, is., Fr. Poly.	F11	72
Austral Seamounts, unds.	L24	142
Austria, ctry., Eur.	C11	22
Austvågøya, i., Nor.	B6	8
Autlán de Navarro, Mex.	F6	100
Autun, Fr.	H13	14
Auvergne, hist. reg., Fr.	D8	18
Auxerre, Fr.	G12	14
Auxier, Ky., U.S.	G3	114
Auxi-le-Château, Fr.	D11	14
Auxvasse, Mo., U.S.	E6	120
Auyán Tepuy, mtn., Ven.	E10	86
Auzances, Fr.	C8	18
Auzangate, Nevado, mtn., Peru	F3	84
Ava, Mo., U.S.	H5	120
Avaí, Braz.	L1	88
Avala, hist., Yugo.	E7	26
Avallon, Fr.	G12	14
Avalon, Ca., U.S.	J7	134
Ávalos, Mex.	A5	100
Avanersuaq see Nordgrønland, state, Grnld.	B14	141
Avant, Ok., U.S.	H1	120
Avaré, Braz.	L1	88
Avarua, Cook Is.	a26	78j
Avarua Harbour, b., Cook Is.	a26	78j
Avatiu Harbour, b., Cook Is.	a26	78j
'Avedat, Horvot, hist., Isr.	H5	58
Aveiro, Port.	D2	20
Aveiro, state, Port.	D2	20
Aveiro, Ria de, mth., Port.	D1	20
Avellaneda, Arg.	D8	92
Avellaneda, Arg.	G8	92
Avellino, Italy	D8	24
Averøya, i., Nor.	E2	8
Aversa, Italy	D8	24
Avery, Id., U.S.	C11	136
Avery, Tx., U.S.	D4	122
Avery Island, La., U.S.	H6	122
Aves, Islas de, is., Ven.	B8	86
Avesnes-sur-Helpe, Fr.	D12	14
Avesta, Swe.	F6	8
Aveyron, state, Fr.	E8	18
Aveyron, stm., Fr.	E7	18
Avezzano, Italy	H10	22
Avigliano, Italy	D9	24
Avignon, Fr.	F10	18
Ávila, Spain	D6	20
Ávila, co., Spain	D6	20
Ávila, Sierra de, mts., Spain	D5	20
Avilés, Spain	A4	20
Aviño, Spain	A2	20
Avinurme, Est.	B9	10
Avispa, Cerro, mtn., Ven.	G9	86
Avoca, Austl.	K4	76
Avoca, Ia., U.S.	C2	120
Avoca, N.Y., U.S.	B8	114
Avoca, stm., Austl.	K4	76
Avola, B.C., Can.	E11	138
Avola, Italy	H9	24
Avon, Il., U.S.	D7	120
Avon, Mn., U.S.	F4	118
Avon, N.Y., U.S.	B8	114
Avon, N.C., U.S.	A10	116
Avon, stm., Eng., U.K.	K11	12
Avon, stm., Eng., U.K.	I11	12
Avon, stm., Eng., U.K.	J10	12
Avondale, Az., U.S.	J4	132
Avondale, Co., U.S.	C4	128
Avon Downs, Austl.	D7	74
Avon Park, Fl., U.S.	I4	116
Avontuur, S. Afr.	H6	70
Avranches, Fr.	F7	14
Awaaso, Ghana	H4	64
Awaji, Japan	E8	40
Awaji-shima, i., Japan	E7	40
Awara, Japan	C9	40
Āwarē, Eth.	F8	62
Āwasa, Eth.	F7	62
Āwash, Eth.	F8	62
Āwash, stm., Eth.	E8	62
Awa-shima, i., Japan	A12	40
Awbārī, Libya	B2	62
Awbārī, Şaḥrā', reg., Libya	B2	62
Awe, Loch, l., Scot., U.K.	E7	12
Awegyun, Mya.	F4	48
Awjilah, Libya	B4	62
Awled Djellal, Alg.	C6	64
Awlef, Alg.	D5	64
Awul, Pap. N. Gui.	b5	79a
Axel Heiberg Island, i., Nu., Can.	A7	141
Axim, Ghana	I4	64
Axiós (Vardar), stm., Eur.	C5	28
Axis, Al., U.S.	G10	122
Axixá, Braz.	B3	88
Axtell, Ks., U.S.	L2	118
Axtell, Ne., U.S.	G13	126
Ayabe, Japan	D8	40
Ayacucho, Arg.	H8	92
Ayacucho, Peru	F3	84
Ayakkum Hu, l., China	D2	36
Ayakoz see Ajaguz, Kaz.	E13	32
Ayam, C. Iv.	H4	64
Ayamonte, Spain	G3	20
Ayapel, Col.	C4	86
Ayaş, Tur.	C15	28
Ayaviri, Peru	F3	84
Aydın, Tur.	F10	28
Aydın, state, Tur.	F11	28
Aydınkent, Tur.	F14	28
Ayer, Ma., U.S.	B14	114
Ayers Rock see Uluru, mtn., Austl.	E6	74
Ayeyarwady, state, Mya.	D2	48
Ayeyarwady (Irrawaddy), stm., Mya.	E8	46
Ayeyarwady, Mouths of the, mth., Mya.	E7	46
Ayíou Órous, Kólpos (Singitic Gulf), b., Grc.	C6	28
Aylesbury, Eng., U.K.	J12	12
Aylmer, On., Can.	F8	112
Aylmer, Qc., Can.	C14	112
Aylmer Lake, l., N.T., Can.	C9	106
Aylsham, Sk., Can.	A10	124
'Ayn Dār, Sau. Ar.	D6	56
Aynor, S.C., U.S.	B6	116
'Aynūnah, Sau. Ar.	J6	58
Ayon Island see Aën, ostrov, i., Russia	B22	34
Ayora see Aiora, Spain	E9	20
Ayorou, Niger	G5	64
'Ayoûn el 'Atroûs, Maur.	F3	64
Ayr, Austl.	B6	76
Ayr, Scot., U.K.	F8	12
Ayrancı, Tur.	A4	58
Ayre, Point of, c., I. of Man	G8	12
Āysha, Eth.	E8	62
Aytos see Ajtos, Blg.	G14	26
Ayutla, Mex.	E6	100
Ayutla de los Libres, Mex.	G9	100
Ayvacık, Tur.	D9	28
Ayvalık, Tur.	D9	28
Azaila, Spain	C10	20
Āzamgarh, India	E9	54
Azángaro, Peru	F3	84
Azaouâd, reg., Mali	F4	64
Azare, Nig.	G6	64
Azaryčy, Bela.	H12	10
A'zāz, Syria	B8	58
Azdavay, Tur.	B16	28
Azeffâl, sand, Afr.	E2	64
Azerbaijan, ctry., Asia	A6	56
Azëry, Bela.	G7	10
Āzezo, Eth.	E7	62
Azhikode, India	F2	53
Azilal, Mor.	C3	64
Azogues, Ec.	I2	86
Azores see Açores, is., Port.	C3	60
Azores Plateau, unds.	E10	144
Azov, Russia	E5	32
Azov, Sea of, Eur.	E5	32
Azovskoje more see Azov, Sea of, Eur.	E5	32
Azraq, Al-Baḥr al- see Blue Nile, stm., Afr.	E6	62
Aztec, N.M., U.S.	G9	132
Aztec Peak, mtn., Az., U.S.	J5	132
Aztec Ruins National Monument, p.o.i., N.M., U.S.	G8	132
Azua, Dom. Rep.	C12	102
Azuaga, Spain	F5	20
Azuay, state, Ec.	I2	86
Azuer, stm., Spain	F7	20
Azuero, Península de, pen., Pan.	D1	86
Azufre, Volcán, vol., S.A.	B3	92
Azuga, Rom.	D12	26
Azul, Arg.	H8	92
Azur, Côte d', cst., Fr.	F13	18
Azurduy, Bol.	C4	90
Azure Lake, l., B.C., Can.	D10	138
Az-Zahrān, Sau. Ar.	D6	56
Az-Zarqā', Jord.	F7	58
Az-Zarqā', state, Jord.	G8	58
Az-Zāwiyah, Libya	A2	62
Azzel Matti, Sebkha, pl., Alg.	D5	64

B

Name	Map Ref.	Page
Ba, Fiji	p18	79e
Ba, stm., China	F6	42
Ba, stm., China	F2	42
Ba, stm., Viet.	F9	48
Baa, Indon.	H7	44
Baaba, Île, i., N. Cal.	I14	79d
Baao, Phil.	D4	52
Baardheere, Som.	D8	66
Baba Burnu, c., Tur.	D9	28
Babadağ, Tur.	F11	28
Babaeski, Tur.	B10	28
Babaevo, Russia	A18	10
Babahoyo, Ec.	H2	86
Babak, Phil.	G5	52
Babanango, S. Afr.	F10	70
Babanūsah, Sudan	E5	62
Babar, Kepulauan, is., Indon.	G8	44
Babbitt, Mn., U.S.	D7	118
Babbitt, Nv., U.S.	E7	134
B'abdā, Leb.	E6	58
Babeldaob, i., Palau	g7	78b
Bab el Mandeb see Mandeb, Bab el, strt.	E8	62
Babia, Arroyo de la, stm., Mex.	F5	130
Babian, stm., China	A5	48
Babičy, Bela.	H12	10
Babīna, India	F7	54
Babinda, Austl.	A5	76
Babine, stm., B.C., Can.	D5	106
Babine Lake, l., B.C., Can.	B5	138
Babine Range, mts., B.C., Can.	B4	138
Babino, Russia	A14	10
Babiogórski Park Narodowy, p.o.i., Pol.	G15	16
Babo, Indon.	F9	44
Bābol, Iran	B7	56
Baboquivari Peak, mtn., Az., U.S.	L5	132
Baborów, Pol.	F13	16
Babrujsk, Bela.	G12	10
Babuškin, Russia	F10	34
Babuyan Channel, strt., Phil.	A3	52
Babuyan Island, i., Phil.	A4	52
Babuyan Islands, is., Phil.	A3	52
Bacabal, Braz.	C3	88
Bacadéhuachi, Mex.	G8	98
Bacatuba, Braz.	C4	88
Bacău, Rom.	C13	26
Bacău, state, Rom.	C13	26
Bac Binh, Viet.	G9	48
Baccarat, Fr.	F15	14
Bačèjkava, Bela.	F12	10
Bac Giang, Viet.	B8	48
Bachaquero, Ven.	B6	86
Bachiniva, Mex.	A5	100
Bach Ma, Viet.	D8	48
Bach Thong, Viet.	A7	48
Bachu, China	B12	56
Back, stm., Nu., Can.	B11	106
Bačka, reg., Eur.	E16	22
Bačka Palanka, Yugo.	D6	26
Bačka Topola, Yugo.	D6	26
Back Creek, stm., Va., U.S.	F6	114
Backnang, Ger.	H5	16
Backstairs Passage, strt., Austl.	J1	76
Bac Lieu, Viet.	H7	48
Bac Ninh, Viet.	B8	48
Baco, Mount, mtn., Phil.	D3	52
Bacoachi, Mex.	F8	98
Bacolod, Phil.	E4	52
Baconton, Ga., U.S.	E1	116
Bacoor, Phil.	C3	52
Bac Phan, hist. reg., Viet.	A7	48
Bács-Kiskun, state, Hung.	C6	26
Bâcu, stm., Mol.	C15	26
Bacuri, Lago do, l., Braz.	B4	88
Bād, Iran	C7	56
Bad, stm., Mi., U.S.	E5	112
Bad, stm., S.D., U.S.	C12	126
Badagara, India	F2	53
Badajós, Lago, l., Braz.	D5	84
Badajoz, Spain	F4	20
Badajoz, co., Spain	F4	20
Badalona, Spain	C13	20
Bādāmi, India	D2	53
Badanah, Sau. Ar.	C5	56
Badarīnāth, India	C7	54
Badas, Bru.	A9	50
Badas, Kepulauan, is., Indon.	C5	50
Bad Axe, Mi., U.S.	E7	112
Bad Bergzabern, Ger.	G3	16
Bad Bevensen, Ger.	C6	16
Bad Bramstedt, Ger.	C5	16
Baddeck, N.S., Can.	D16	110
Bad Doberan, Ger.	B7	16
Bad Dürrenberg, Ger.	E8	16
Bad Ems, Ger.	F3	16
Baden, Switz.	C5	22
Baden-Baden, Ger.	H4	16
Badenoch, hist. reg., Scot., U.K.	E8	12
Badenweiler, Ger.	I3	16
Baden-Württemberg, state, Ger.	H4	16
Bad Freienwalde, Ger.	D9	16
Badgastein, Aus.	C10	22
Badger, Mn., U.S.	C3	118
Bad Hall, Aus.	B11	22
Bad Harzburg, Ger.	E6	16
Bad Hersfeld, Ger.	F5	16
Bad Homburg vor der Höhe, Ger.	F4	16
Bad Honnef, Ger.	F3	16
Badin Lake, res., N.C., U.S.	A5	116
Bad Ischl, Aus.	C10	22
Bad Kissingen, Ger.	F6	16
Bad Kreuznach, Ger.	G3	16
Badlands, hills, U.S.	A9	126
Badlands, hills, S.D., U.S.	D10	126
Badlands National Park, p.o.i., S.D., U.S.	D10	126
Bad Langensalza, Ger.	E6	16
Bad Lauterberg im Harz, Ger.	E6	16
Bad Mergentheim, Ger.	G5	16
Bad Muskau, Ger.	E10	16
Bad Nauheim, Ger.	F4	16
Badnera, India	H6	54
Bad Neustadt an der Saale, Ger.	F6	16
Bad Oeynhausen, Ger.	D4	16
Bad Oldesloe, Ger.	C6	16
Badong, China	F4	42
Bad Orb, Ger.	F5	16
Bad Pyrmont, Ger.	E5	16
Bad Reichenhall, Ger.	I8	16
Bad Salzuflen, Ger.	D4	16
Bad Salzungen, Ger.	F6	16
Bad Schwalbach, Ger.	F3	16
Bad Schwartau, Ger.	C6	16
Bad Segeberg, Ger.	C6	16
Bādshāhpur, India	F9	54
Bad Tölz, Ger.	I7	16
Badulla, Sri L.	H5	53
Badvel, India	D4	53
Bad Vöslau, Aus.	C13	22
Bad Waldsee, Ger.	I5	16
Bad Wildungen, Ger.	E4	16
Bad Wörishofen, Ger.	I6	16
Badžalskij hrebet, mts., Russia	F15	34
Baena, Spain	G6	20
Baependi, Braz.	K3	88
Baer, Russia	C17	32
Baeza, Spain	G7	20
Baezaeko, stm., B.C., Can.	D7	138
Bafang, Cam.	C1	66
Bafatá, Gui.-B.	G2	64
Baffin Basin, unds.	A7	144
Baffin Bay, b., N.A.	C12	141
Baffin Bay, b., Tx., U.S.	G10	130
Baffin Island, i., Nu., Can.	B16	106
Bafia, Cam.	D2	66
Bafing, stm., Afr.	G2	64
Bafoulabé, Mali	G2	64
Bafoussam, Cam.	C2	66
Bafra, Tur.	A4	56
Bāft, Iran	D8	56
Bafwaboli, D.R.C.	D5	66
Bafwasende, D.R.C.	D5	66
Bagaces, C.R.	G5	102
Bagagem, stm., Braz.	H1	88
Bagaha, India	E9	54
Bāgalkot, India	C2	53
Bagamoyo, Tan.	F7	66
Bagan Datuk, Malay.	K5	48
Baganga, Phil.	G6	52
Bagansiapiapi, Indon.	B2	50
Bagasra, India	H3	54
Bagdad, Az., U.S.	I3	132
Bagdad, Fl., U.S.	G11	122
Bagdarin, Russia	F11	34
Bagé, Braz.	E10	92
Bagenkop, Den.	B6	16
Bāgerhāt, Bngl.	G12	54
Bāgevādi, India	C2	53
Baghdād, Iraq	C5	56
Bagheria, Italy	F7	24
Baghlān, Afg.	B10	56
Bagley, Mn., U.S.	D3	118
Bagnères-de-Luchon, Fr.	G6	18
Bagni di Lucca, Italy	F7	22
Bagnols-sur-Cèze, Fr.	E10	18
Bago (Pegu), Mya.	D3	48
Bago, state, Mya.	C2	48
Bagodar, India	F10	54
Bagoé, stm., Afr.	G3	64
Bağpınar, Tur.	A9	58
Baguio, Phil.	B3	52
Bāh, India	E7	54
Bahādurgarh, India	D6	54
Bahama, Canal Viejo de, strt., N.A.	A8	102
Bahamas, ctry., N.A.	C9	96
Baharampur, India	F11	54
Bahau, Malay.	K6	48
Bahau, stm., Indon.	B9	50
Bahāwalnagar, Pak.	C4	54
Bahāwalpur, Pak.	D3	54
Bahçe, Tur.	A7	58
Baheri, India	D7	54
Bahi, Phil.	D4	52
Bahia see Salvador, Braz.	G6	88
Bahia, state, Braz.	G4	88
Bahía, Islas de la, is., Hond.	D4	102
Bahía Blanca, Arg.	I6	92
Bahía Bustamante, Arg.	I3	90
Bahía de Caráquez, Ec.	H1	86
Bahía Kino, Mex.	A3	100
Bahir Dar, Eth.	E7	62
Bahraich, India	E8	54
Bahrain, ctry., Asia	D7	56
Bahta, Russia	B15	32
Bahtîm, Egypt	H2	58
Bahty, Kaz.	E14	32
Bahušèusk, Bela.	F13	10
Bai, stm., China	A7	42
Bai, stm., China	E5	42
Baia de Aramă, Rom.	E9	26
Baia di Terra Nova, sci., Ant.	C21	81
Baía Farta, Ang.	C1	68
Baia Mare, Rom.	B10	26
Baião, Braz.	B1	88
Baicheng, China	F14	32
Baicheng, China	B9	36
Baidoa see Baydhabo, Som.	D8	66
Baie-Comeau, Qc., Can.	A8	110
Baiersbronn, Ger.	H4	16
Baie-Saint-Paul, Qc., Can.	C6	110
Baie-Trinité, Qc., Can.	A9	110
Baie Verte, Nf., Can.	j22	107a
Baihe, China	B11	46
Baijnāth, India	D7	54
Baikal, Lake see Bajkal, ozero, l., Russia	F10	34
Baikal Mountains see Bajkal'skij hrebet, mts., Russia	F10	34
Baikonur see Bajkonur, Kaz.	E11	32
Bailadores, Ven.	C6	86
Baile Átha Cliath see Dublin, Ire.	H6	12
Baile Átha Luain see Athlone, Ire.	H4	12
Băile Govora, Rom.	D11	26
Bailén, Spain	F7	20
Băileşti, Rom.	F10	26
Bailey, N.C., U.S.	I7	114
Bail Hongal, India	D2	53
Bailicun, China	I4	42
Bailique, Ilha, i., Braz.	C8	84
Baillie Islands, is., N.T., Can.	B14	140
Baillif, Guad.	h5	105c
Bailong, stm., China	E1	42
Bailu Hu, l., China	G5	42
Bailundo, Ang.	C2	68
Baimamiao, China	C2	42
Baima Shan, mtn., China	H4	42
Baimuru, Pap. N. Gui.	b3	79a
Bainbridge, Ga., U.S.	G14	122
Bainbridge, N.Y., U.S.	B10	114
Bain-de-Bretagne, Fr.	G7	14
Baing, Indon.	I12	50
Bainville, Mt., U.S.	F9	124
Baio Grande, Spain	A2	20
Baiona, Spain	B2	20
Baipeng, China	I3	42
Baipu, China	E9	42
Baiquan, China	B10	36
Baird, Tx., U.S.	B8	130
Baird Mountains, mts., Ak., U.S.	C7	140
Baird Peninsula, pen., Nu., Can.	B15	106
Bairiki, Kir.	C8	72
Bairin Zuoqi, China	C8	36
Bairnsdale, Austl.	K6	76
Baïse, stm., Fr.	F6	18
Baisha, China	G2	42
Baisha, China	L3	42
Baisha, China	I8	42
Baishe, China	H7	42
Baishuijiang, China	E2	42
Baisogala, Lith.	E6	10
Baiwang, China	I3	42
Baixingt, China	C4	38
Baixio, Braz.	D6	88
Baiyan Shan, mtn., China	H8	42
Baiyin, China	D5	36
Baiyü, China	E4	36
Baja, Hung.	C5	26
Baja, Punta, c., Chile	e29	78l
Baja California, state, Mex.	F5	98
Baja California, pen., Mex.	B2	96
Baja California Sur, state, Mex.	C2	100
Bajada del Agrio, Arg.	I2	92
Baján, Mex.	H6	130
Bajan, Mong.	B7	36
Bajanaul, Kaz.	D13	32
Bajangol, Russia	F9	34
Bajánsenye, Hung.	C3	26
Bajawa, Indon.	H12	50
Bajdarackaja guba, b., Russia	C2	34
Bajestān, Iran	C8	56
Bajkal, Russia	F9	34
Bajkal, ozero (Baikal, Lake), l., Russia	F10	34
Bajkal'skij hrebet, mts., Russia	F10	34
Bajkit, Russia	B17	32
Bajkonur, Kaz.	E11	32
Bajmak, Russia	D9	32
Bajmok, Yugo.	D6	26
Bajo, Indon.	H11	50
Bajo Boquete, Pan.	H6	102
Bajool, Austl.	D8	76
Bajramaly, Turkmen.	B9	56
Bajsun, Uzb.	G11	32
Bakacak, Tur.	C10	28
Bakala, C.A.R.	C4	66
Bakanas, Kaz.	F13	32
Bake, Indon.	E2	50
Bakel, Sen.	G2	64
Baker, Ca., U.S.	H9	134
Baker, Fl., U.S.	G12	122
Baker, La., U.S.	G7	122
Baker, Mt., U.S.	A8	126
Baker, Or., U.S.	F9	136
Baker, Mount, vol., Wa., U.S.	B5	136
Baker Butte, mtn., Az., U.S.	I5	132
Baker Island, i., Oc.	C9	72
Baker Lake, Nu., Can.	C11	106
Baker Lake, l., Austl.	E5	74
Baker Lake, l., Nu., Can.	C11	106
Bakersfield, Ca., U.S.	H7	134
Bâ Kêv, Camb.	F8	48
Bakharden, Turkmen.	B8	56
Bakhardok, Turkmen.	B8	56
Bakhtegān, Daryācheh-ye, l., Iran	D7	56
Bakı (Baku), Azer.	A6	56
Bakkafjörður, Ice.	j32	8a
Bakkaflói, b., Ice.	j32	8a
Baklan, Tur.	F12	28
Bako, C. Iv.	H3	64
Bako, Eth.	F7	62
Bakony, mts., Hung.	C4	26
Bakouma, C.A.R.	C4	66
Baku see Bakı, Azer.	A6	56
Bakumpai, Indon.	D8	50
Bakung, Pulau, i., Indon.	C4	50
Bakungan, Indon.	K3	48
Bakwanga see Mbuji-Mayi, D.R.C.	F4	66
Balâ, Tur.	D16	28
Balabac, Phil.	F1	52
Balabac Island, i., Phil.	G1	52
Balabac Strait, strt., Asia	G1	52
Ba'labakk, Leb.	D7	58
Balabalagan, Kepulauan, is., Indon.	E10	50
Balabanovo, Russia	E19	10
Balabio, Île, i., N. Cal.	m15	79d
Balad, Iraq	C5	56
Baladëk, Russia	F15	34
Bālāghāt, India	H8	54
Bālāghāt Range, mts., India	B3	53
Balagne, reg., Fr.	G14	18
Balaguer, Spain	C11	20
Balahna, Russia	H20	8
Balaikarangan, Indon.	C7	50
Balaisepuah, Indon.	C7	50
Balakirevo, Russia	D21	10
Balaklava, Austl.	J2	76
Balakovo, Russia	D7	32
Balama, Moz.	C6	68
Balambangan, Pulau, i., Malay.	G1	52
Bālā Morghāb, Afg.	B9	56
Balanga, Phil.	C3	52
Balāngīr, India	H9	54
Balapulang, Indon.	G6	50
Balarāmpur, India	G11	54
Balašiha, Russia	E20	10
Balašov, Russia	D6	32
Balassagyarmat, Hung.	A6	26
Balatina, Mol.	B14	26
Balaton, Mn., U.S.	G3	118

I•6 Bala-Bayr

Name — Map Ref. — Page

Balaton, l., Hung. C4 26
Balayan, Phil. D3 52
Balbieriškis, Lith. F6 10
Balbina, Represa, res., Braz. H12 86
Balcanoona, Austl. H2 76
Balcarce, Arg. H8 92
Balcarres, Sk., Can. D10 124
Bălcești, Rom. E10 26
Balcones Escarpment, clf, Tx., U.S. D9 130
Balde, Arg. F4 92
Bald Knob, Ar., U.S. B7 122
Bald Knob, mtn., Va., U.S. G6 114
Bald Mountain, mtn., Or., U.S. G5 136
Bald Mountain, mtn., Or., U.S. F3 136
Baldock Lake, l., Mb., Can. D11 106
Baldone, Lat. D7 10
Baldwin, La., U.S. H7 122
Baldwin, Mi., U.S. E4 112
Baldwin, Wi., U.S. G6 118
Baldwinsville, N.Y., U.S. E13 112
Baldwyn, Ms., U.S. C10 122
Baldy Mountain, mtn., Mb., Can. C13 124
Baldy Mountain, mtn., N.M., U.S. E3 128
Baldy Peak, mtn., Az., U.S. J7 132
Bâle see Basel, Switz. C4 22
Baleares see Balears, state, Spain E13 20
Baleares, Islas see Balears, Illes, is., Spain E12 20
Balearic Islands see Balears, state, Spain E13 20
Balearic Islands see Balears, Illes, is., Spain E12 20
Balears, state, Spain E13 20
Balears, Illes (Balearic Islands), is., Spain E12 20
Balease, Gunung, mtn., Indon. E12 50
Baleh, stm., Malay. C8 50
Baleia, Ponta da, c., Braz. I6 88
Baleine, stm., Qc., Can. D17 106
Baleine, Grande rivière de la, stm., Qc., Can. D15 106
Baleine, Petite rivière de la, stm., Qc., Can. D15 106
Balej, Russia F12 34
Baler, Phil. C3 52
Baler Bay, b., Phil. C3 52
Bāleshwar, India H11 54
Balezino, Russia C8 32
Balfate, Hond. E4 102
Balfour, N.C., U.S. A3 116
Balgazyn, Russia D17 32
Balhaš, ozero (Balkhash, Lake), l., Kaz. E13 32
Bāli, India F4 54
Bali, state, Indon. G9 50
Bali, i., Indon. G9 50
Bali, Laut (Bali Sea), Indon. G9 50
Bali, Selat, strt., Indon. H9 50
Bali Barat National Park, p.o.i., Indon. H9 50
Baliceaux, i., St. Vin. p11 105e
Balige, Indon. B1 50
Balıkesir, Tur. D10 28
Balıkesir, state, Tur. D10 28
Balīkh, stm., Syria B10 58
Balikpapan, Indon. D10 50
Balimbing, Indon. F4 50
Balimbing, Phil. H2 52
Balimo, Pap. N. Gui. b3 79a
Balingen, Ger. H4 16
Balingian, Malay. B8 50
Balintang Channel, strt., Phil. K9 42
Bali Sea see Bali, Laut, Indon. G9 50
Bali Strait see Bali, Selat, strt., Indon. H9 50
Baliza, Braz. G7 84
Balkan Mountains, mts., Eur. G11 26
Balkan Peninsula, pen., Eur. B6 28
Balkaria see Kabardino-Balkarija, state, Russia F6 32
Balkh, Afg. B10 56
Balkhash, Lake see Balhaš, ozero, l., Kaz. E13 32
Ballachulish, Scot., U.K. E7 12
Balladonia, Austl. F4 74
Ballālpur, India B4 53
Ballangen, Nor. B7 8
Ballantine, Mt., U.S. B4 126
Ballarat, Austl. K4 76
Ballard, Lake, l., Austl. E4 74
Ballater, Scot., U.K. D9 12
Ball Bay, b., Norf. I. y25 78i
Ballenas, Bahía de, b., Mex. B2 100
Ballenita, Punta, c., Chile B2 92
Balleny Islands, is., Ant. B21 81
Balleza, Mex. B5 100
Balleza, stm., Mex. B5 100
Ball Ground, Ga., U.S. B1 116
Ballia, India F10 54
Ballina, Austl. G9 76
Ballina, Ire. G3 12
Ballina, Ire. I4 12
Ballinrobe, Ire. H3 12
Ballston Spa, N.Y., U.S. G2 110
Ballville, Oh., U.S. C2 114
Ballybunnion, Ire. I3 12
Ballyhaunis, Ire. H4 12
Ballymena, N. Ire., U.K. G6 12
Ballymoney, N. Ire., U.K. F6 12
Ballyrogan, Lake, l., Austl. I6 76
Balmaceda, Chile I2 90
Balmoral, Austl. K3 76
Balmorhea, Tx., U.S. C4 130
Balnearia, Arg. E6 92
Baloda Bāzār, India H9 54
Balombo, Ang. C1 68
Balong, Indon. G7 50
Balonne, stm., Austl. G7 76
Bālotra, India F4 54
Balphakram National Park, p.o.i., India F13 54
Balqash Köli see Balhaš, ozero, l., Kaz. E13 32
Balrāmpur, India E8 54
Balranald, Austl. J4 76
Balș, Rom. E11 26
Balsam Lake, Wi., U.S. F6 118
Balsam Lake, l., On., Can. D11 112
Balsas, Braz. D2 88
Balsas, stm., Braz. F2 88
Balsas, stm., Braz. D3 88
Balsas, stm., Mex. F8 100
Balsas, stm., Pan. C3 86
Balsthal, Switz. C4 22
Balta, Ukr. B16 26
Baltasar Brum, Ur. E9 92
Bălți, Mol. B14 26
Baltic Sea, Eur. D12 6
Baltijsk, Russia F2 10
Baltijskaja kosa, spit, Eur. F2 10
Baltijskoje more see Baltic Sea, Eur. D12 6
Baltim, Egypt G2 58
Baltimore, Ire. J3 12
Baltimore, Md., U.S. E9 114
Baltimore, Oh., U.S. E3 114
Ba Lu, stm., Viet. E9 48
Baluchistān, state, Pak. C2 54
Baluchistan, hist. reg., Asia D9 56
Balui, stm., Malay. B8 50
Bālurghāt, India F12 54
Balvi, Lat. C10 10
Balygyčan, Russia D19 34
Balykši, Kaz. E8 32
Balzac, Ab., Can. E16 138
Balzar, Ec. H2 86
Bam, Iran D8 56
Bama, China I2 42
Bama, Nig. G7 64
Bamaga, Austl. B8 74
Bamako, Mali G3 64
Bamba, Mali F4 64
Bambamarca, Peru E2 84
Bambana, stm., Nic. F6 102
Bambari, C.A.R. C4 66
Bambaroo, Austl. B6 76
Bamberg, Ger. G6 16
Bamberg, S.C., U.S. C4 116
Bambio, C.A.R. D3 66
Bambuí, Braz. K2 88
Bam Co, l., China C13 54
Bamenda, Cam. C1 66
Bami, Turkmen. B8 56
Bāmīān, Afg. C10 56
Bamingui, C.A.R. C4 66
Bampūr, Iran D9 56
Bāmra Hills, hills, India H10 54
Bamumo, China B14 54
Banaba, i., Kir. D7 72
Banabuiú, stm., Braz. C6 88
Banabuiú, Açude, l., Braz. C6 88
Banalia, D.R.C. D5 66
Banamba, Mali G3 64
Banana Islands, is., S.L. H2 64
Bananal, stm., Braz. E1 88
Bananal, Ilha do, i., Braz. F7 84
Banarlı, Tur. B10 28
Banās, stm., India E6 54
Banâs, Râs, c., Egypt C7 62
Banat, hist. reg., Eur. D7 26
Banaz, Tur. E12 28
Ban Ban, Laos C6 48
Ban Bouang-nom, Laos E8 48
Banbridge, N. Ire., U.K. G6 12
Ban Bung Na Rang, Thai. D5 48
Banbury, Eng., U.K. I11 12
Ban Cha La, Laos D7 48
Bancroft, On., Can. C12 112
Bancroft, Id., U.S. H15 136
Bancroft, Ia., U.S. H4 118
Bancroft, Ne., U.S. C1 120
Bānda, India F8 54
Banda, Kepulauan, is., Indon. F9 44
Banda, Laut (Banda Sea), Indon. G8 44
Banda Aceh, Indon. J2 48
Bānda Dāūd Shāh, Pak. B3 54
Banda del Río Salí, Arg. C5 92
Bandai-Asahi-kokuritsu-kōen, p.o.i., Japan B12 40
Bandai-san, vol., Japan B13 40
Bandama, stm., C. Iv. H3 64
Bandama Blanc, stm., C. Iv. H3 64
Ban Dan, Thai. E7 48
Ban Dangtai, Laos D7 48
Bandar Beheshtī, Iran D9 56
Bandarbeyla, Som. C10 66
Bandar-e ʿAbbās, Iran D8 56
Bandar-e Anzalī, Iran B6 56
Bandar-e Būshehr, Iran D7 56
Bandar-e Deylam, Iran D7 56
Bandar-e Lengeh, Iran D7 56
Bandar-e Māh Shahr, Iran C6 56
Bandar-e Moghūyeh, Iran D7 56
Bandar-e Torkeman, Iran B7 56
Bandar Seri Begawan, Bru. A9 50
Banda Sea see Banda, Laut, Indon. G8 44
Bandeira, Pico da, mtn., Braz. K5 88
Bandeirantes, Braz. F7 84
Bandelier National Monument, p.o.i., N.M., U.S. F2 128
Bandera, Arg. D6 92
Bandera, Alto, mtn., Dom. Rep. C12 102
Banderas, Mex. C2 130
Banderas, Bahía de, b., Mex. E6 100
Bandhavgarh National Park, p.o.i., India G8 54
Bāndhi, Pak. E2 54
Bandiagara, Mali G4 64
Bandiantaolehai, China C5 36
Bāndīkūi, India E6 54
Bandipura, India A5 54
Bandipur Tiger Reserve, India F3 53
Bandırma, Tur. C11 28
Bandon, Or., U.S. G2 136
Ban Don, Ao, b., Thai. H4 48
Ban Donhiang, Laos C5 48
Bandundu, D.R.C. E3 66
Bandung, Indon. G5 50
Banes, Cuba B10 102
Banff, Ab., Can. E15 138
Banff, Scot., U.K. D10 12
Banff National Park, p.o.i., Ab., Can. E15 138
Banfora, Burkina G4 64
Banga, D.R.C. F4 66
Banga, India C6 54
Banga, stm., Phil. G5 52
Bangalore, India E3 53
Bangaon, India G12 54
Bangassou, C.A.R. D4 66
Bangdag Co, l., China A8 54
Banggai, Indon. F7 44
Banggai, Kepulauan, is., Indon. F7 44
Banggi, Pulau, i., Malay. G1 52
Banggong Co, l., China B7 54
Banghāzī (Bengasi), Libya A3 62
Banghiang, stm., Laos D7 48
Bangil, Indon. G8 50
Bangka, Pulau, i., Indon. E5 50
Bangka, Selat, strt., Indon. E4 50
Bangkalan, Indon. G8 50
Bangkaru, Pulau, i., Indon. L3 48
Bangkinang, Indon. C2 50
Bangkir, Indon. C12 50
Bangko, Indon. E3 50
Bangkog Co, l., China C12 54
Bangkok see Krung Thep, Thai. F5 48
Bangladesh, ctry., Asia G13 54
Bang Lamung, Thai. F5 48
Bang Mun Nak, Thai. D5 48
Bangor, N. Ire., U.K. G7 12
Bangor, Wales, U.K. H8 12
Bangor, Me., U.S. F8 110
Bangor, Pa., U.S. D10 114
Bangriposi, India G11 54
Bangs, Tx., U.S. C8 130
Bangs, Mount, mtn., Az., U.S. G3 132
Bang Saphan, Thai. G4 48
Bangued, Phil. B3 52
Bangui, C.A.R. D3 66
Bangweulu, Lake, l., Zam. C4 68
Bangweulu Swamps, sw., Zam. C5 68
Bangxu, China J2 42
Ban Hatgnao, Laos E8 48
Ban Hèt, Laos E8 48
Ban Hom, Thai. E4 48
Ban Hong Muang, Laos D7 48
Ban Houayxay, Laos B5 48
Bani, C.A.R. C4 66
Baní, Dom. Rep. C12 102
Bani, Jbel, mts., Mor. D3 64
Baniara, Pap. N. Gui. b4 79a
Bani Bangou, Niger F5 64
Banihāl Pass, p., India B4 46
Banī Walīd, Libya A2 62
Bāniyās, Golan E6 58
Bāniyās, Syria C6 58
Banja Luka, Bos. E4 26
Banjarmasin, Indon. E9 50
Banjul (Bathurst), Gam. G1 64
Bānka, India F11 54
Banka Banka, Austl. C6 74
Ban Katèp, Laos D7 48
Ban Kèngkabao, Laos D7 48
Ban Kèngtangan, Laos D7 48
Ban Kheun, Laos B5 48
Ban Khuan Mao, Thai. I4 48
Ban Kruat, Thai. E6 48
Banks, Al., U.S. F13 122
Banks, Îles (Banks Islands), is., Vanuatu i16 79d
Banks Island, i., B.C., Can. E4 106
Banks Island, i., N.T., Can. B15 140
Banks Islands see Banks, Îles, is., Vanuatu i16 79d
Banks Lake, res., Wa., U.S. C7 136
Banks Peninsula, pen., N.Z. F5 80
Banks Strait, strt., Austl. n13 77a
Banks / Torres, state, Vanuatu i16 79d
Bānkura, India G11 54
Ban Mae La Luang, Thai. C3 48
Ban Mit, Laos C5 48
Ban Muangngat, Laos C6 48
Bann, stm., N. Ire., U.K. F6 12
Ban Nadou, Laos E7 48
Ban Nahin, Laos C7 48
Ban Nalan, Laos E7 48
Ban Nam Chan, Thai. C6 48
Ban Namnga, Laos B6 48
Ban Nam Thaeng, Thai. E7 48
Ban Naxouang, Laos C7 48
Bannertown, N.C., U.S. H5 114
Banning, Ca., U.S. J9 134
Ban Nong Lumphuk, Thai. E6 48
Bannu, Pak. B3 54
Bañolas see Banyoles, Spain B13 20
Baños, Ec. H2 86
Banow, Afg. B10 56
Ban Pak Bong, Thai. C4 48
Ban Pakkhop, Laos C5 48
Ban Pak Nam, Thai. G4 48
Ban Phai, Thai. D6 48
Ban Phai, Thai. D6 48
Ban Pho, Thai. F5 48
Ban Phông Pho, Laos E7 48
Ban Pong, Thai. F4 48
Ban Sa-ang, Laos D7 48
Ban Salik, Thai. C5 48
Ban Sam Pong, Laos C6 48
Ban Samrong, Thai. E6 48
Bānsda, India H4 54
Banshadhāra, stm., India B6 53
Banská Bystrica, Slov. H15 16
Banská Štiavnica, Slov. H14 16
Bansko, Blg. H10 26
Ban Songkhon, Laos C7 48
Bānswāra, India G5 54
Bantaeng, Indon. F11 50
Ban Takhlo, Thai. E5 48
Bantarkawung, Indon. G6 50
Bantayan, Phil. E4 52
Ban Thabôk, Laos C6 48
Ban Thapayi, Laos D7 48
Ban Tian Sa, Laos C6 48
Bantry, Ire. J3 12
Bantry Bay, b., Ire. J3 12
Ban Van Hom, Laos C7 48
Ban Xènkhalôk, Laos C5 48
Banya, Testa de la, c., Spain D11 20
Banyak, Kepulauan, is., Indon. K3 48
Ban Ya Plong, Thai. H4 48
Banyo, Cam. C2 66
Banyoles, Spain B13 20
Banyuwangi, Indon. H9 50
Banzare Coast, cst., Ant. B17 81
Baode, China B4 42
Baoding, China B6 42
Baofeng, China E5 42
Bao Ha, Viet. A7 48
Baoji, China D2 42
Baojing, China G3 42
Bao Lac, Viet. G8 48
Bao Lac, Viet. A7 48
Baolunyuan, China E1 42
Baoqing, China B11 36
Baoshan, China F4 36
Baoting, China L3 42
Baotou, China A4 42
Baoulé, stm., Mali G3 64
Baowei, China A8 48
Baoyi, China E7 42
Baoying, China E8 42
Bāpatla, India D5 53
Bapaume, Fr. D11 14
Baptiste Lake, res., On., Can. C12 112
Bāqa el Gharbiyya, Isr. F6 58
Baqing, China B14 54
Baʿqūbah, Iraq C5 56
Baquedano, Chile A3 92
Bar, Yugo. G6 26
Bara, Nig. G7 64
Baraawe, Som. D8 66
Barabinsk, Russia C13 32
Barabinskaja step', pl., Russia C13 32
Baraboo, Wi., U.S. H9 118
Baraboo, stm., Wi., U.S. H8 118
Baracaldo see Barakaldo, Spain A8 20
Baracoa, Cuba B10 102
Baradero, Arg. F8 92
Baradine, Austl. H7 76
Baraga, Mi., U.S. B1 112
Bārah, Sudan E6 62
Barahona, Dom. Rep. C12 102
Barak, Tur. B8 58
Barāk, stm., India F14 54
Barakaldo, Spain A8 20
Baraki, Afg. B2 54
Barakula, Austl. F8 76
Baralaba, Austl. E7 76
Baram, stm., Malay. A9 50
Barama, stm., Guy. D12 86
Bārāmati, India B2 53
Bārāmūla, India A5 54
Baran', Bela. F13 10
Bārān, India F6 54
Baranagar, India G12 54
Baranavičy, Bela. G9 10
Barangbarang, Indon. G12 50
Baranoa, Col. B4 86
Baranof Island, i., Ak., U.S. E12 140
Barany, Russia C12 10
Baranya, state, Hung. D5 26
Barão de Grajaú, Braz. D4 88
Barão de Melgaço, Braz. G6 84
Barão de Tromaí, Braz. A3 88
Baraški, Russia D24 8
Barataria, La., U.S. H8 122
Barataria Bay, b., La., U.S. H8 122
Barat Daya, Kepulauan (Barat Daya Islands), is., Indon. G8 44
Barat Daya Islands see Barat Daya, Kepulauan, is., Indon. G8 44
Barauana, stm., Braz. G11 86
Barauni, India F10 54
Baraut, India D6 54
Baraya, Col. F4 86
Barbacena, Braz. K4 88
Barbacoas, Col. G2 86
Barbadillo del Mercado, Spain B7 20
Barbados, ctry., N.A. h16 96a
Barbalha, Braz. D6 88
Barbar, Sudan D6 62
Barbaria, Cap de, c., Spain F12 20
Barbas, Cap, c., W. Sah. E1 64
Barbaši, Russia C11 10
Barbastro, Spain B10 20
Barbate, Spain H4 20
Barbeau Peak, mtn., Nu., Can. A10 141
Barberena, Guat. E2 102
Barberton, S. Afr. D10 70
Barberton, Oh., U.S. C4 114
Barbil, India G10 54
Barbosa, Col. E5 86
Barbuda, i., Antig. e4 105b
Barby, Ger. E7 16
Bârca, Rom. F10 26
Barcaldine, Austl. D5 76
Barcău (Berettyó), stm., Eur. B8 26
Barcellona Pozzo di Gotto, Italy F9 24
Barcelona, Mex. B7 100
Barcelona, Spain C13 20
Barcelona, Ven. B9 86
Barcelona, co., Spain C13 20
Barceloneta, P.R. B2 104a
Barcelos, Braz. H10 86
Barcelos, Port. C2 20
Barcin, Pol. D13 16
Barcoo, stm., Austl. E4 76
Barczewo, Pol. C16 16
Barda del Medio, Arg. I3 92
Bardaï, Chad C3 62
Bardawîl, Sabkhet el-, b., Egypt G4 58
Barddhamān, India G11 54
Bardejov, Slov. G17 16
Bardeskan, Iran B8 56
Bardīyah, Libya A5 62
Bardo, Tun. H4 24
Bārdoli, India H4 54
Bardstown, Ky., U.S. G12 120
Bardwell Lake, res., Tx., U.S. E2 122
Bareilly, India D7 54
Barentsburg, Nor. B29 141
Barentsøya, i., Nor. B30 141
Barents Sea, Eur. B7 30
Bareta, India D5 54
Barfleur, Fr. E7 14
Bargaal, Som. B10 66
Bargara, Austl. E9 76
Bargarh, India D5 46
Barguzin, stm., Russia F11 34
Barguzinskij hrebet, mts., Russia F11 34
Bar Harbor, Me., U.S. F8 110
Barharwa, India F11 54
Barhi, India F10 54
Bāri, India E6 54
Bari, Italy C10 24
Baria, stm., Ven. G8 86
Barī Gāv, Afg. B1 54
Barigua, Salina de, pl., Ven. p20 104g
Barillas, Guat. E2 102
Barīm, i., Yemen G5 56
Barima, stm., S.A. C12 86
Barima-Waini, state, Guy. D12 86
Barinas, P.R. B2 104a
Barinas, Ven. C6 86
Barinas, state, Ven. C7 86
Baring, Cape, c., N.T., Can. A7 106
Baringo, Lake, l., Kenya D7 66
Bāripada, India H11 54
Bariri, Braz. L1 88
Bârîs, Egypt C6 62
Bari Sādri, India F5 54
Barisāl, Bngl. G13 54
Barisāl, state, Bngl. G13 54
Barisan, Pegunungan, mts., Indon. E2 50
Barito, stm., Indon. E9 50
Barjols, Fr. F11 18
Barkam, China E5 36
Barkava, Lat. D9 10
Barkerville, B.C., Can. C9 138
Bark Lake, l., On., Can. C12 112
Barkley, Lake, res., U.S. H10 120
Barkley Sound, strt., B.C., Can. H5 138
Barkly East, S. Afr. G8 70
Barkly Tableland, plat., Austl. C7 74
Barkly West, S. Afr. F7 70
Barkol, China C3 36
Bârlad, Rom. C14 26
Bârlad, stm., Rom. D14 26
Bar-le-Duc, Fr. F14 14
Barlee, Lake, l., Austl. E3 74
Barletta, Italy C10 24
Barlinek, Pol. D11 16
Barling, Ar., U.S. B4 122
Barlow, Ky., U.S. G8 120
Barmedman, Austl. J6 76
Bārmer, India F3 54
Barmera, Austl. J3 76
Barnagar, India G5 54
Barnard Castle, Eng., U.K. G11 12
Barnaul, Russia D14 32
Barn Bluff, mtn., Austl. n12 77a
Barnegat, N.J., U.S. E11 114
Barnegat Bay, b., N.J., U.S. E11 114
Barnes Ice Cap, ice, Nu., Can. A16 106
Barnesville, Ga., U.S. C1 116
Barnesville, Mn., U.S. E2 118
Barnesville, Oh., U.S. E4 114
Barneville-Carteret, Fr. E7 14
Barnsdall, Ok., U.S. E12 128
Barnsley, Eng., U.K. H11 12
Barnstable, Ma., U.S. C15 114
Barnstaple, Eng., U.K. J8 12
Barnstaple Bay, b., Eng., U.K. J8 12
Barnwell, Ab., Can. G18 138
Barnwell, S.C., U.S. C4 116
Baro, stm., Afr. F7 62
Baron Bluff, clf, V.I.U.S. g10 104c
Baron'ki, Bela. G15 10
Barora Fa Island, i., Sol. Is. d8 79b
Barora Ite Island, i., Sol. Is. d8 79b
Baroua, Niger G7 64
Barpeta, India E13 54
Barqah (Cyrenaica), hist. reg., Libya A4 62
Barques, Pointe aux, c., Mi., U.S. D7 112
Barquisimeto, Ven. B7 86
Barra, Braz. F4 88
Barra, i., Scot., U.K. D5 12
Barra, Ponta da, c., Moz. C12 70
Barraba, Austl. H8 76
Barra da Estiva, Braz. G5 88
Barra del Colorado, C.R. G6 102
Barra de Rio Grande, Nic. F6 102
Barra do Corda, Braz. C3 88
Barra do Cuanza, Ang. B1 68
Barra do Garças, Braz. G7 84
Barra do Mendes, Braz. F4 88
Barra do Piraí, Braz. L3 88
Barra do Ribeiro, Braz. E12 92
Barra Falsa, Ponta da, c., Moz. C12 70
Barra Mansa, Braz. L3 88
Barranca, Peru F2 84
Barrancabermeja, Col. D4 86
Barrancas, Ven. C10 86
Barrancas, Ven. C7 86
Barrancas, stm., Arg. H2 92
Barranco Azul, Mex. E3 130
Barranco do Velho, Port. G3 20
Barranqueras, Arg. C8 92
Barranquilla, Col. B4 86
Barranquitas, P.R. B3 104a
Barras, Braz. C4 88
Barre, Vt., U.S. F4 110
Barreal, Arg. E3 92
Barreiras, Braz. G3 88
Barreirinha, Braz. D6 84
Barreiro, Port. F1 20
Barreiros, Braz. E8 88
Barren, stm., Ky., U.S. H11 120
Barren, Nosy, is., Madag. D7 68
Barren Islands, is., Ak., U.S. E9 140
Barren River Lake, res., Ky., U.S. H11 120
Barretos, Braz. K1 88
Barrhead, Ab., Can. B16 138
Barrie, On., Can. D10 112
Barrie Island, i., On., Can. C7 112
Barrière, B.C., Can. E10 138
Barrier Range, mts., Austl. H3 76
Barrigada, Guam j10 78c
Barrington, N.S., Can. G11 110
Barrington Tops National Park, p.o.i., Austl. I8 76
Barringun, Austl. G5 76
Barrouallie, St. Vin. o11 105e
Barrow, Arg. I7 92
Barrow, Ak., U.S. B8 140
Barrow, stm., Ire. I5 12
Barrow, Point, c., Ak., U.S. B8 140
Barrow Creek, Austl. D6 74
Barrow-in-Furness, Eng., U.K. G9 12
Barrow Island, i., Austl. D2 74
Barrows, Mb., Can. B12 124
Barrow Strait, strt., Nu., Can. C6 141
Barry, Wales, U.K. J9 12
Barry, Il., U.S. E6 120
Barryton, Mi., U.S. E4 112
Barsalpur, India D4 54
Bārsi, India B2 53
Barsinghausen, Ger. D5 16
Barstow, Ca., U.S. I8 134
Barstow, Tx., U.S. C4 130
Bar-sur-Seine, Fr. F13 14
Bartang, Taj. B11 56
Barth, Ger. B8 16
Barthélemy, Deo, p., Viet. C6 48
Bartholomew, Bayou, stm., U.S. E7 122
Bartibougou, Burkina G5 64
Bartica, Guy. B6 84
Bartın, Tur. B15 28
Bartle Frere, mtn., Austl. A5 76
Bartlesville, Ok., U.S. H2 120
Bartlett, N.H., U.S. F5 110
Bartlett, Tn., U.S. B9 122
Bartlett, Tx., U.S. D10 130
Bartley, Ne., U.S. A8 128
Barton, Vt., U.S. F4 110
Bartoszyce, Pol. B16 16
Bartow, Fl., U.S. I4 116
Bartow, Ga., U.S. D3 116
Barú, Volcán, vol., Pan. H6 102
Bārūk, Jabal al-, mtn., Leb. E6 58
Barumini, Italy E2 24
Barumun, stm., Indon. C2 50
Barung, Nusa, i., Indon. H8 50
Barus, Indon. L4 48
Baruun-Urt, Mong. B7 36
Barvas, Scot., U.K. C6 12
Barview, Or., U.S. G2 136
Barwāh, India G5 54
Barwāni, India H5 54
Barwick, Ga., U.S. F2 116
Barwon, stm., Austl. H6 76
Barybino, Russia E20 10
Barycz, stm., Pol. E13 16
Barysau, Bela. F11 10
Basail, Arg. C8 92
Basalt, stm., Austl. B5 76
Basankusu, D.R.C. D3 66
Basarabeasca, Mol. C15 26
Basatongwula Shan, mtn., China B13 54
Basavakalyān, India C3 53
Basavilbaso, Arg. F8 92
Bascuñán, Cabo, c., Chile D2 92
Basel (Bâle), Switz. C4 22
Basella see Bassella, Spain B12 20
Basey, Phil. E5 52
Bashi Channel, strt., Asia K9 42
Bashkortostan see Baškirija, state, Russia D9 32
Basilan Island, i., Phil. G4 52
Basilan Strait, strt., Phil. G4 52
Basildon, Eng., U.K. J13 12
Basile, La., U.S. G6 122
Basilicata, state, Italy D10 24
Basin, Mt., U.S. D14 136
Basin, Wy., U.S. C4 126
Basingstoke, Eng., U.K. J11 12
Basin Lake, l., Sk., Can. B8 124
Basīrhāt, India G12 54
Baskahegan Lake, l., Me., U.S. E8 110
Baskakovka, Russia F17 10
Başkale, Tur. B5 56
Baskatong, Réservoir, res., Qc., Can. B13 112
Basket Lake, l., On., Can. B6 118
Baškirija, state, Russia D9 32
Baskomutan Milli Parkı, p.o.i., Tur. E13 28
Basmat, India B3 53
Bāsoda, India G6 54
Basoko, D.R.C. D4 66
Basora, Punt, c., Aruba p20 104g
Basque Provinces see Euskal Herriko, state, Spain A8 20
Basra see Al-Başrah, Iraq C6 56
Bas-Rhin, state, Fr. F16 14
Bassano, Ab., Can. F18 138
Bassano del Grappa, Italy E8 22
Bassari, Togo H5 64
Bassas da India, rf., Reu. E6 68
Bassein, stm., Mya. D2 48
Bassella, Spain B12 20
Basse Santa Su, Gam. G2 64
Basse-Terre, Guad. i5 105c
Basseterre, St. K./N. C2 105a
Basse Terre, Trin. s12 105f
Basse-Terre, i., Guad. h5 105c
Bassett, Ne., U.S. E13 126
Bassett, Va., U.S. H6 114
Bassfield, Ms., U.S. F9 122
Bassikounou, Maur. F3 64
Bassila, Benin H5 64
Bass River, N.S., Can. E13 110
Bass Strait, strt., Austl. L6 76
Basswood Lake, l., N.A. C6 118
Båstad, Swe. H5 8
Bastenaken see Bastogne, Bel. D14 14
Bastersberge, hill, S. Afr. G5 70
Basti, India E9 54
Bastia, Fr. G15 18
Bastogne, Bel. D14 14
Bastrop, La., U.S. E6 122
Bastrop, Tx., U.S. D10 130
Basu, Pulau, i., Indon. D3 50
Basutoland see Lesotho, ctry., Afr. F9 70
Bata, Eq. Gui. I6 64
Bataan Peninsula, pen., Phil. C3 52
Batabanó, Golfo de, b., Cuba A6 102
Batac, Phil. A3 52
Batagaj, Russia C15 34
Batagaj-Alyta, Russia C15 34
Batak, Blg. H11 26
Batala, India C5 54
Batalha, Braz. E7 88
Batalha, Port. E2 20
Batam, Pulau, i., Indon. C3 50
Batamaj, Russia D14 34
Batang, China E5 36
Batangafo, C.A.R. C3 66
Batangas, Phil. D3 52
Batangtoru, Indon. C1 50
Batan Islands, is., Phil. K9 42
Batanta, Pulau, i., Indon. F9 44
Batatais, Braz. K2 88
Batavia, Arg. G5 92
Batavia see Jakarta, Indon. G5 50
Batavia, Il., U.S. C9 120
Batavia, Ia., U.S. D5 120
Batavia, N.Y., U.S. A7 114
Batchelor, Austl. B6 74
Bătdâmbâng, Camb. F6 48
Bateckij, Russia B13 10
Batemans Bay, Austl. J8 76
Bates, Mount, mtn., Norf. I. y24 78i
Batesburg, S.C., U.S. C4 116
Batesville, Ar., U.S. B7 122
Batesville, Ms., U.S. C9 122
Batesville, Tx., U.S. F8 130
Bath, N.B., Can. D9 110
Bath, Eng., U.K. J10 12
Bath, Me., U.S. G7 110
Bath, N.Y., U.S. B8 114
Batha, stm., Chad E3 62
Bathgate, N.D., U.S. F16 124
Bathinda, India C5 54
Bathsheba, Barb. n8 105d
Bathurst, Austl. I7 76
Bathurst, N.B., Can. C11 110
Bathurst see Banjul, Gam. G1 64
Bathurst, Cape, c., N.T., Can. A5 106
Bathurst Inlet, Nu., Can. B9 106
Bathurst Island, i., Austl. B5 74
Bathurst Island, i., Nu., Can. B5 141
Batlow, Austl. J6 76
Batman, Tur. B5 56
Batna, Alg. B6 64
Ba To, Viet. E9 48
Baton Rouge, La., U.S. G7 122
Batouri, Cam. D2 66
Batsawul, Afg. A3 54
Batson, Tx., U.S. G4 122
Batterie, Pointe de la, c., Mart. k7 105c
Batticaloa, Sri L. H5 53
Battipaglia, Italy D8 24
Battle, stm., Can. D19 138
Battle Creek, Mi., U.S. F4 112
Battle Creek, Ne., U.S. F15 126
Battle Creek, stm., N.A. F4 124
Battle Ground, In., U.S. H3 112
Battle Ground, Wa., U.S. E4 136
Battle Harbour, Nf., Can. i22 107a
Battle Mountain, Nv., U.S. C8 134
Battle Mountain, mtn., Wy., U.S. B9 132
Batu, mtn., Eth. F7 62
Batu, Kepulauan, is., Indon. F2 44
Batu-Batu, Indon. F11 50
Batu Berincang, Gunong, mtn., Malay. J5 48
Batubrok, Bukit, mtn., Indon. C9 50
Batu Gajah, Malay. J5 48
Batukelau, Indon. C9 50
Batumi, Geor. F6 32
Batu Pahat, Malay. L6 48
Batupanjang, Indon. C2 50
Baturaja, Indon. F3 50
Baturino, Russia C15 32
Baturité, Braz. C6 88
Baturusa, Indon. D5 50
Batusangkar, Indon. D2 50
Batz, Île de, i., Fr. F4 14
Bau, Malay. C7 50
Baubau, Indon. G7 44
Bauchi, Nig. G6 64
Bauda, India H10 54
Baudette, Mn., U.S. C4 118
Baudó, stm., Col. E3 86
Bauld, Cape, c., Nf., Can. i22 107a
Bauman Fiord, b., Nu., Can. B8 141
Baume-les-Dames, Fr. G15 14
Baures, Bol. B4 90
Bauru, Braz. L1 88
Bauska, Lat. D7 10
Bautzen, Ger. E10 16
Bauxite, Ar., U.S. C6 122
Bavaria see Bayern, state, Ger. H7 16
Bavarian Alps, mts., Eur. I7 16
Båven, l., Swe. G7 8
Bavispe, Mex. F8 98
Bavispe, stm., Mex. F8 98
Bawang, Indon. G6 50
Bawdwin, Mya. A3 48
Bawean, Pulau, i., Indon. F8 50
Bawiti, Egypt B5 62
Bawmi, Mya. D2 48
Baxaya, mtn., Som. B9 66
Baxian, China G2 42
Baxian, China B7 42
Baxter, Ia., U.S. C4 120
Baxter, Mn., U.S. E4 118
Baxter, Tn., U.S. H12 120
Baxterville, Ms., U.S. F9 122
Bay, Ar., U.S. B8 122
Bay, Laguna de, l., Phil. C3 52
Bayamo, Cuba B9 102
Bayamón, P.R. B3 104a
Bayan, China A7 38
Bayan, Indon. H10 50
Bayāna, India E6 54
Bayan Har Shan, mts., China E4 36
Bayanhongor, Mong. B5 36
Bayannaobao, China B2 42
Bayano, Lago, res., Pan. H8 102
Bayan Obo, China C7 36
Bayard, Ia., U.S. C3 120
Bayard, N.M., U.S. K8 132
Bayard, W.V., U.S. E6 114
Bayawan, Phil. F4 52
Baybay, Phil. E5 52
Bayboro, N.C., U.S. A9 116
Bayburt, Tur. A5 56
Bay City, Mi., U.S. E6 112
Bay City, Or., U.S. E3 136
Bay City, Tx., U.S. F12 130
Baydhabo (Baidoa), Som. D8 66
Baydrag, stm., Mong. B4 36
Bayern (Bavaria), state, Ger. H7 16
Bayeux, Braz. D8 88
Bayeux, Fr. E8 14
Bayfield, Co., U.S. F9 132
Bayfield, Wi., U.S. E8 118
Bayındır, Tur. E10 28
Baykonur see Bajkonur, Kaz. E11 32
Bay Minette, Al., U.S. G11 122
Bayombong, Phil. B3 52
Bayona see Baiona, Spain B2 20
Bayonne, Fr. F4 18
Bayou Bodcau Reservoir, res., La., U.S. E5 122
Bayou Cane, La., U.S. H8 122
Bayou D'Arbonne Lake, res., La., U.S. E6 122
Bayovar, Peru E1 84
Bay Port, Mi., U.S. E6 112
Bayport, Mn., U.S. F6 118
Bayramiç, Tur. D9 28
Bayreuth, Ger. G7 16

Name	Map Ref.	Page
Bayrūt (Beirut), Leb.	E6	58
Bays, Lake of, l., On., Can.	C10	112
Bay Saint Louis, Ms., U.S.	G9	122
Bay Shore, N.Y., U.S.	D12	114
Bayside, On., Can.	D12	112
Bay Springs Lake, res., Ms., U.S.	C10	122
Bayt ad-Dīn, Leb.	E6	58
Bayt al-Faqīh, Yemen	G5	56
Bayt Laḥm (Bethlehem), W.B.	G6	58
Baytown, Tx., U.S.	H4	122
Bayyā'īyah al-Kabīrah, Syria	C8	58
Baza, Spain	G8	20
Bazardüzü dağ, mtn., Azer.	A6	56
Bazaruto, Ilha do, i., Moz.	B12	70
Bazhong, China	F2	42
Baziège, Fr.	F7	18
Bazine, Ks., U.S.	C9	128
Be, stm., Viet.	G8	48
Be, Nosy, i., Madag.	C8	68
Beach Haven, N.J., U.S.	E11	114
Beachport, Austl.	K3	76
Beachville, On., Can.	E9	112
Beachy Head, c., Eng., U.K.	K13	12
Beacon, Austl.	F3	74
Beacon, N.Y., U.S.	C12	114
Beacon Hill, Wa., U.S.	D3	136
Beaconsfield, Austl.	n13	77a
Beagle Gulf, b., Austl.	B5	74
Bealanana, Madag.	C8	68
Bealdoaivi see Peäldoajvi, mtn., Fin.	B12	8
Beale, Cape, c., B.C., Can.	H5	138
Beals Creek, stm., Tx., U.S.	B7	130
Bear, stm., U.S.	I14	136
Bear, stm., Ca., U.S.	D4	134
Bear Bay, b., Nu., Can.	B8	141
Bear Creek, stm., U.S.	C10	122
Bear Creek, stm., U.S.	D6	128
Bearden, Ar., U.S.	D6	122
Beardmore, On., Can.	B11	118
Bear Island, i., Ant.	C29	81
Bear Island, i., Ire.	J3	12
Bear Island see Bjørnøya, i., Nor.	B5	30
Bear Lake, l., Ab., Can.	A11	138
Bear Lake, l., U.S.	A5	132
Bear Mountain, mtn., Or., U.S.	G3	136
Béarn, hist. reg., Fr.	F5	18
Bear River, N.S., Can.	F11	110
Bear River Range, mts., U.S.	B5	132
Beartooth Pass, p., Wy., U.S.	C3	126
Bear Town, Ms., U.S.	F8	122
Beās, stm., India	C6	54
Beasain, Spain	A8	20
Beata, Cabo, c., Dom. Rep.	D12	102
Beata, Isla, i., Dom. Rep.	D12	102
Beaton, B.C., Can.	F13	138
Beatrice, Al., U.S.	F11	122
Beatrice, Ne., U.S.	A12	128
Beatrice, Cape, c., Austl.	B7	74
Beattie, Ks., U.S.	L2	118
Beatton, stm., B.C., Can.	D6	106
Beatty, Nv., U.S.	G9	134
Beattyville, Ky., U.S.	G2	114
Beaucaire, Fr.	F10	18
Beauce, reg., Fr.	F10	14
Beauceville, Qc., Can.	D6	110
Beauchêne, Lac, l., Qc., Can.	B11	112
Beauchêne Island, i., Falk. Is.	J5	90
Beaudesert, Austl.	F9	76
Beaufort, Malay.	A9	50
Beaufort, S.C., U.S.	D5	116
Beaufort Castle see Qal'at ash-Shaqīf, hist., Leb.	E6	58
Beaufort Sea, N.A.	B12	140
Beaufort West, S. Afr.	H6	70
Beaugency, Fr.	G10	14
Beauharnois, Qc., Can.	E2	110
Beaujolais, hist. reg., Fr.	C10	18
Beaumont, Fr.	E7	14
Beaumont, N.Z.	G3	80
Beaumont, Ca., U.S.	J8	134
Beaumont, Ms., U.S.	F9	122
Beaumont, Tx., U.S.	G4	122
Beaumont Hill, hill, Austl.	H5	76
Beaune, Fr.	G13	14
Beauport, Qc., Can.	D5	110
Beaupré, Qc., Can.	C6	110
Beaurepaire, Fr.	D11	18
Beausejour, Mb., Can.	D17	124
Beauséjour, Guad.	h6	105c
Beauvais, Fr.	E11	14
Beauvoir-sur-Mer, Fr.	H6	14
Beaver, Ak., U.S.	C10	140
Beaver, Ok., U.S.	E8	128
Beaver, Pa., U.S.	D5	114
Beaver, Ut., U.S.	E4	132
Beaver, stm., Can.	D9	106
Beaver, stm., Can.	C6	106
Beaver, stm., U.S.	E9	128
Beaver, stm., Ut., U.S.	E3	132
Beaver Creek, stm., U.S.	G9	124
Beaver Creek, stm., U.S.	D8	126
Beaver Creek, stm., U.S.	A8	128
Beaver Creek, stm., Co., U.S.	G9	126
Beaver Creek, stm., Mt., U.S.	F6	124
Beaver Creek, stm., Ne., U.S.	F14	126
Beaver Creek, stm., Ne., U.S.	G14	126
Beaver Creek, stm., Ok., U.S.	G10	128
Beaver Creek, stm., Tx., U.S.	H9	128
Beaver Crossing, Ne., U.S.	G15	126
Beaver Dam, Ky., U.S.	G11	120
Beaver Dam, Wi., U.S.	H9	118
Beaverdell, B.C., Can.	G11	138
Beaver Falls, Pa., U.S.	D5	114
Beaverhead, stm., Mt., U.S.	E14	136
Beaverhead Mountains, mts., U.S.	E13	136
Beaverhill Lake, l., Ab., Can.	C18	138
Beaverhouse Lake, l., On., Can.	C6	118
Beaver Island, i., Mi., U.S.	C4	112
Beaver Lake, l., Ab., Can.	B19	138
Beaver Lake, res., Ar., U.S.	H4	120
Beaverlodge, Ab., Can.	A11	138
Beaverton, On., Can.	D10	112
Beaverton, Mi., U.S.	E5	112
Beaverton, Or., U.S.	E4	136
Beāwar, India	E5	54
Beazley, Arg.	F4	92
Bebedouro, Braz.	K1	88
Becal, Mex.	B2	102
Bécancour, stm., Qc., Can.	D5	110
Beccles, Eng., U.K.	I14	12
Bečej, Yugo.	D6	26
Beceni, Rom.	D13	26
Bečevinka, Russia	G17	8
Béchar, Alg.	C4	64
Becharof Lake, l., Ak., U.S.	E8	140
Bechevin Bay, b., Ak., U.S.	E7	140
Bechuanaland, hist. reg., S. Afr.	E5	70
Bechuanaland see Botswana, ctry., Afr.	E3	68
Bechyně, Czech Rep.	G10	16
Beckley, W.V., U.S.	G4	114
Beckum, Ger.	E4	16
Bédarieux, Fr.	F9	18
Bedelē, Eth.	F7	62
Bedford, Qc., Can.	E4	110
Bedford, S. Afr.	H8	70
Bedford, Eng., U.K.	I12	12
Bedford, In., U.S.	F11	120
Bedford, Ia., U.S.	D3	120
Bedford, Ky., U.S.	F12	120
Bedford, Pa., U.S.	D7	114
Bedford, Tx., U.S.	B10	130
Bedi, India	G3	54
Bedoba, Russia	C17	32
Bedourie, Austl.	E2	76
Bedworth, Eng., U.K.	I11	12
Beebe, Ar., U.S.	B7	122
Beechal Creek, stm., Austl.	F5	76
Beech Creek, Ky., U.S.	G10	120
Beech Fork, stm., Ky., U.S.	G12	120
Beech Grove, In., U.S.	I3	112
Beechworth, Austl.	K6	76
Beechy, Sk., Can.	D6	124
Beecroft Head, c., Austl.	J8	76
Beemer, Ne., U.S.	J2	118
Beenleigh, Austl.	F9	76
Bee Ridge, Fl., U.S.	I3	116
Beersheba see Be'ér Sheva', Isr.	G6	58
Beersheba Springs, Tn., U.S.	B13	122
Be'ér Sheva'(Beersheba), Isr.	G6	58
Beeskow, Ger.	D10	16
Beeville, Tx., U.S.	F10	130
Befale, D.R.C.	D4	66
Befandriana Avaratra, Madag.	E7	68
Bega, Austl.	K7	76
Bega, stm., Eur.	D9	26
Begamganj, India	G7	54
Begur, Cap de, c., Spain	C14	20
Begusarai, India	F11	54
Behbahān, Iran	C7	56
Behshahr, Iran	B7	56
Bei, stm., China	J5	42
Bei'an, China	B10	36
Beibei, China	G2	42
Beicheng, China	G5	36
Beigi, Eth.	F6	62
Beihai, China	K3	42
Beijing (Peking), China	B7	42
Beijing, state, China	B6	42
Beili, China	L3	42
Beiliu, China	J4	42
Beinamar, Chad	F3	62
Beipa, Pap. N. Gui.	b4	79a
Beipan, stm., China	I1	42
Beipiao, China	D4	38
Beira, Moz.	A12	70
Beira, hist. reg., Port.	E3	20
Beiru, stm., China	D5	42
Beirut see Bayrūt, Leb.	E6	58
Beiseker, Ab., Can.	E17	138
Beishan, China	I3	42
Bei Shan, mts., China	C4	36
Beitbridge, Zimb.	C10	70
Beizhen, China	D4	38
Beja, Port.	G3	20
Béja, Tun.	H3	24
Beja, state, Port.	G3	20
Bejaïa, Alg.	B6	64
Béjar, Spain	D5	20
Bejhi, stm., Pak.	D2	54
Bejneu, Kaz.	E9	32
Bejuco, Pan.	H8	102
Bekaa Valley see Al-Biqā', val., Leb.	D7	58
Bekabad, Uzb.	F11	32
Bekdaš, Turkmen.	A7	56
Békés, Hung.	C8	26
Békés, state, Hung.	C7	26
Békéscsaba, Hung.	C7	26
Bekilli, Tur.	E12	28
Bekily, Madag.	E8	68
Bekodoka, Madag.	D7	68
Bekopaka, Madag.	D7	68
Bela, India	F9	54
Bela, Pak.	D10	56
Belaazërsk, Bela.	H8	10
Bela Crkva, Yugo.	E8	26
Belaga, Malay.	B8	50
Bel Air, Md., U.S.	E9	114
Belaja, stm., Russia	C8	32
Belaja Gora, Russia	B14	10
Belambanganumpu, Indon.	F4	50
Belampalli, India	B4	53
Bela Palanka, Yugo.	F9	26
Belarus, ctry., Eur.	E14	6
Belaruskaja hrada, mts., Bela.	F10	10
Belau see Palau, ctry., Oc.	g8	78b
Bela Vista, Braz.	D5	90
Bela Vista, Moz.	E11	70
Belawan, Indon.	B1	50
Belayan, stm., Indon.	C10	50
Bełchatów, Pol.	E15	16
Belcher, La., U.S.	E5	122
Belcherāgh, Afg.	B10	56
Belcher Channel, strt., Nu., Can.	B6	141
Belcher Islands, is., Nu., Can.	D14	106
Belding, Mi., U.S.	E4	112
Belebelka, Russia	C13	10
Beledweyne, Som.	D8	66
Belém, Braz.	A1	88
Belém, Moz.	C6	68
Belém de São Francisco, Braz.	E6	88
Belén, Arg.	C4	92
Belén, Nic.	G4	102
Belén, Para.	D5	90
Belen, Tur.	B7	58
Belen, N.M., U.S.	I10	132
Belén, Ur.	E9	92
Belén, stm., Arg.	C4	92
Belep, Îles, is., N. Cal.	I14	79d
Belesar, Embalse de, res., Spain	B3	20
Belëv, Russia	G19	10
Belfast, S. Afr.	D9	70
Belfast, N. Ire., U.K.	G6	12
Belfast, Me., U.S.	F7	110
Belfield, N.D., U.S.	H10	124
Belford, Eng., U.K.	F11	12
Belfort, Fr.	G15	14
Belfry, Mt., U.S.	B3	126
Belgaum, India	D2	53
Belgium, ctry., Eur.	D13	14
Belgorod, Russia	D5	32
Belgrade, Mt., U.S.	E15	136
Belgrade, Ne., U.S.	F14	126
Belgrade see Beograd, Yugo.	E7	26
Belgrano II, sci., Ant.	C36	81
Belhaven, N.C., U.S.	A9	116
Belick, Bela.	H13	10
Beliliou, i., Palau	D9	44
Belin, Fr.	E5	18
Belin-Béliet see Belin, Fr.	E5	18
Belington, W.V., U.S.	E5	114
Belinyu, Indon.	D4	50
Belitung, i., Indon.	E5	50
Belize, ctry., N.A.	D3	102
Belize, stm., Belize	D3	102
Belize City, Belize	D3	102
Belkovski, ostrov see Bel'kovskij, ostrov, i., Russia	A16	34
Bel'kovskij, ostrov, i., Russia	A16	34
Bella Bella, B.C., Can.	D2	138
Bellac, Fr.	C7	18
Bella Coola, B.C., Can.	D4	138
Bella Coola, stm., B.C., Can.	D4	138
Bellair, Fl., U.S.	F4	116
Bellaire, Oh., U.S.	D5	114
Bellaire, Tx., U.S.	H3	122
Bellamy, Al., U.S.	E10	122
Bellaria, Italy	F9	22
Bellary, India	D3	53
Bellata, Austl.	G7	76
Bella Unión, Ur.	E9	92
Bella Vista, Arg.	C5	92
Bella Vista, Arg.	D8	92
Bellavista, Peru	E2	84
Bellbrook, Austl.	H9	76
Belle, W.V., U.S.	F4	114
Bellefontaine, Mart.	k6	105c
Bellefontaine, Oh., U.S.	D2	114
Bellefonte, Pa., U.S.	D8	114
Belle Fourche, S.D., U.S.	C9	126
Belle Fourche, stm., U.S.	C10	126
Bellegarde-sur-Valserine, Fr.	C11	18
Belle Glade, Fl., U.S.	J5	116
Belle Hôtesse, mtn., Guad.	h5	105c
Belle-Île, i., Fr.	G5	14
Belle Isle, i., Nf., Can.	i22	107a
Belle Isle, Strait of, strt., Nf., Can.	i22	107a
Bellenden Ker National Park, p.o.i., Austl.	A5	76
Belle Plaine, Ia., U.S.	C5	120
Belle Plaine, Ks., U.S.	D11	128
Belle Plaine, Mn., U.S.	G5	118
Belleview, Fl., U.S.	G11	122
Belleville, On., Can.	D12	112
Belleville, Il., U.S.	F8	120
Belleville, Ks., U.S.	B11	128
Belleville, Pa., U.S.	D8	114
Belleville-sur-Saône, Fr.	C10	18
Bellevue, Ab., Can.	G16	138
Bellevue, Id., U.S.	G12	136
Bellevue, Ia., U.S.	B7	120
Bellevue, Mi., U.S.	F4	112
Bellevue, Ne., U.S.	C2	120
Bellevue, Oh., U.S.	C3	114
Bellevue, Wa., U.S.	C4	136
Belley, Fr.	D11	18
Bellingham, Mn., U.S.	F2	118
Bellingham, Wa., U.S.	B4	136
Bellinghausen, sci., Ant.	B35	81
Bellingshausen Sea, Ant.	P29	142
Bellinzona, Switz.	D6	22
Bell Lake, l., On., Can.	B7	118
Bellmead, Tx., U.S.	C10	130
Bello, Col.	D4	86
Bellot Strait, strt., Nu., Can.	A12	106
Bell Peninsula, pen., Nu., Can.	C14	106
Bells, Tn., U.S.	B9	122
Bells, Tx., U.S.	D2	122
Bells Corners, On., Can.	C14	112
Belluno, Italy	D9	22
Bell Ville, Arg.	F6	92
Bellville, S. Afr.	H4	70
Bellwood, Ne., U.S.	F15	126
Bellwood, Pa., U.S.	D7	114
Belly, stm., N.A.	G17	138
Bellyk, Russia	D16	32
Belmond, Ia., U.S.	B4	120
Belmont, N.S., Can.	E13	110
Belmont, S. Afr.	F7	70
Belmont, N.H., U.S.	G5	110
Belmont, Wi., U.S.	B7	120
Belmonte, Braz.	H6	88
Belmonte, Port.	D3	20
Belmonte, Spain	A4	20
Belmopan, Belize	D3	102
Beloe, Russia	B22	10
Beloe, ozero, l., Russia	F17	8
Beloe more (White Sea), Russia	D18	8
Belogorsk, Russia	F14	34
Belo Horizonte, Braz.	J3	88
Beloit, Ks., U.S.	B10	128
Beloit, Wi., U.S.	B8	120
Belo Jardim, Braz.	E7	88
Belomestnaja, Russia	H20	10
Belomorsk, Russia	D16	8
Beloreck, Russia	D9	32
Belören, Tur.	F15	28
Belorussia see Belarus, ctry., Eur.	E14	6
Beloščele, Russia	D22	8
Belo sur Mer, Madag.	E7	68
Belot, Lac, l., N.T., Can.	B5	106
Belo Tsiribihina, Madag.	D7	68
Belousovo, Russia	E19	10
Belovo, Russia	D15	32
Belozërsk, Russia	F17	8
Belpre, Oh., U.S.	E4	114
Belt, Mt., U.S.	C16	136
Beltana, Austl.	H2	76
Belt Creek, stm., Mt., U.S.	C16	136
Belton, Mo., U.S.	F3	120
Belton, Tx., U.S.	C10	130
Belton Lake, res., Tx., U.S.	C10	130
Beltrán, Arg.	C5	92
Belukha, Mount, mtn., Asia	E15	32
Belūr, India	E2	53
Beluran, Malay.	H1	52
Belvedere Marittimo, Italy	E9	24
Belvidere, Il., U.S.	B9	120
Belvidere, N.J., U.S.	D10	114
Belview, Mn., U.S.	G3	118
Belvoir see Kokhav HaYarden, hist., Isr.	F6	58
Belyando, stm., Austl.	D6	76
Belye Berega, Russia	G17	10
Belye Stolby, Russia	E20	10
Belyj Gorodok, Russia	C20	10
Belyj Jar, Russia	C15	32
Bełżec, Pol.	F19	16
Belzig, Ger.	D8	16
Belzoni, Ms., U.S.	D8	122
Bement, Il., U.S.	E9	120
Bemidji, Mn., U.S.	D3	118
Benaco see Garda, Lago di, l., Italy	E7	22
Bena-Dibele, D.R.C.	E4	66
Benagerie, Austl.	H3	76
Benalla, Austl.	K6	76
Benares see Vārānasi, India	F9	54
Ben Arous, Tun.	H4	24
Benavarri, Spain	B11	20
Benavente, Spain	B5	20
Benbecula, i., Scot., U.K.	D5	12
Ben Bolt, Tx., U.S.	G9	130
Ben Cat, Viet.	G8	48
Bencha, Khao Phanom, mtn., Thai.	H4	48
Ben-Chicao, Col de, p., Alg.	H13	20
Bencubbin, Austl.	F3	74
Bend, Or., U.S.	F5	136
Bendemeer, Austl.	H8	76
Bender Cassim see Boosaaso, Som.	B9	66
Bendigo, Austl.	K5	76
Bēne, Lat.	D6	10
Benedito Leite, Braz.	D3	88
Benepú, Rada, anch., Chile	f29	78l
Benevento, Italy	C8	24
Bèng, stm., Laos	B5	48
Bengal, Bay of, b., Asia	F6	46
Bengara, Indon.	B10	50
Bengasi see Banghāzī, Libya	A3	62
Bengbu, China	E7	42
Benghazi see Banghāzī, Libya	A3	62
Bengkalis, Indon.	C3	50
Bengkalis, Pulau, i., Indon.	C3	50
Bengkayang, Indon.	C6	50
Bengkulu, Indon.	E3	50
Bengkulu, state, Indon.	E3	50
Bengough, Sk., Can.	E8	124
Benguela, Ang.	C1	68
Benguerua, Ilha, i., Moz.	B12	70
Benha, Egypt	H2	58
Beni, D.R.C.	D5	66
Beni, stm., Bol.	B3	90
Béni Abbas, Alg.	C4	64
Beni'Adi el-Baharîya, Egypt	K1	58
Beni Ahmad, Egypt	J1	58
Benicarló, Spain	D11	20
Benidorm, Spain	F10	20
Beni Mazâr, Egypt	J1	58
Beni Muhammadîyat, Egypt	K2	58
Benin, ctry., Afr.	G5	64
Benin, Bight of, b., Afr.	I5	64
Benin City, Nig.	H6	64
Benisa see Benissa, Spain	F11	20
Benissa, Spain	F11	20
Beni Suef, Egypt	I2	58
Benito, Mb., Can.	C12	124
Benito Juárez, Arg.	H8	92
Benito Juárez, Presa, res., Mex.	G10	100
Benjamin, Tx., U.S.	H9	128
Benjamín, Isla, i., Chile	H2	90
Benjamin Constant, Braz.	D3	84
Benkelman, Ne., U.S.	A7	128
Benkovac, Cro.	F12	22
Benld, Il., U.S.	E8	120
Ben Lomond, Ca., U.S.	F3	134
Ben Lomond National Park, p.o.i., Austl.	n13	77a
Benndale, Ms., U.S.	G10	122
Bennetta, ostrov, i., Russia	A18	34
Bennett Island see Bennetta, ostrov, i., Russia	A18	34
Bennettsville, S.C., U.S.	B6	116
Bennington, Ks., U.S.	B11	128
Bennington, Vt., U.S.	B12	114
Benoit, Ms., U.S.	D7	122
Benoni, S. Afr.	E9	70
Ben Sekka, Rass, c., Tun.	G3	24
Bensheim, Ger.	G4	16
Benson, Az., U.S.	L6	132
Benson, Mn., U.S.	F3	118
Benson, N.C., U.S.	A7	116
Benteng, Indon.	G12	50
Ben Thuy, Viet.	C7	48
Bentinck Island, i., Austl.	C7	74
Bentinck Island, i., Mya.	G3	48
Bentiu, Sudan	F6	62
Bento Gonçalves, Braz.	D12	92
Benton, Ar., U.S.	C6	122
Benton, Il., U.S.	F9	120
Benton, Ky., U.S.	H9	120
Benton, La., U.S.	E5	122
Benton, Mo., U.S.	G8	120
Benton, Tn., U.S.	B14	122
Benton, Wi., U.S.	B7	120
Benton Harbor, Mi., U.S.	F3	112
Bentonia, Ms., U.S.	E8	122
Bentonville, Ar., U.S.	H3	120
Ben Tre, Viet.	G8	48
Bentung, Malay.	K5	48
Benua, Pulau, i., Indon.	C5	50
Benue, stm., Afr.	H6	64
Ben Wheeler, Tx., U.S.	E3	122
Benxi, China	D5	38
Beograd (Belgrade), Yugo.	E7	26
Beohāri, India	F8	54
Béoumi, C. Iv.	H3	64
Beowawe, Nv., U.S.	C9	134
Beppu, Japan	F4	40
Bequia, i., St. Vin.	o11	105e
Bequimão, Braz.	B3	88
Berat, Alb.	D13	24
Berati see Berat, Alb.	D13	24
Berau, stm., Indon.	B10	50
Berau, Teluk, b., Indon.	F9	44
Berazino, Bela.	F11	10
Berazino, Bela.	G11	10
Berbera, Som.	B9	66
Berbérati, C.A.R.	D3	66
Berchtesgaden, Ger.	I8	16
Berck, Fr.	D10	14
Berclair, Tx., U.S.	F10	130
Berdians'k, Ukr.	E5	32
Berdigestjah, Russia	D14	34
Berdsk, Russia	D14	32
Berea, Oh., U.S.	C4	114
Berea, S.C., U.S.	B3	116
Berehomet, Ukr.	A12	26
Berehove, Ukr.	A9	26
Berekua, Dom.	j6	105c
Berekum, Ghana	H4	64
Berens, stm., Can.	B17	124
Berens Island, i., Mb., Can.	B16	124
Berens River, Mb., Can.	B16	124
Beresford, N.B., Can.	C11	110
Beresford, S.D., U.S.	H2	118
Berești, Rom.	C14	26
Berettyó (Barcău), stm., Eur.	B8	26
Berettyóújfalu, Hung.	B8	26
Berezivka, Ukr.	B17	26
Bereznik, Russia	E20	8
Berezniki, Russia	C9	32
Berëzovo, Russia	B10	32
Berëzovskij, Russia	C15	32
Berëzovskij Rjadok, Russia	B17	10
Berga, Spain	B12	20
Bergama, Tur.	D10	28
Bergamo, Italy	E6	22
Bergantín, Ven.	C9	86
Bergby, Swe.	F7	8
Bergen see Mons, Bel.	D12	14
Bergen, Ger.	D5	16
Bergen, Nor.	F1	8
Bergen, N.Y., U.S.	A7	114
Bergen auf Rügen, Ger.	B9	16
Bergen op Zoom, Neth.	C13	14
Bergerac, Fr.	E6	18
Bergisch Gladbach, Ger.	F3	16
Bergoo, W.V., U.S.	F5	114
Bergsjö, Swe.	E7	8
Berguent, Mor.	C4	64
Bergville, S. Afr.	F9	70
Berhala, Selat, strt., Indon.	D4	50
Beringa, ostrov, i., Russia	F22	34
Bering Glacier, ice, Ak., U.S.	D11	140
Beringovskij, Russia	D24	34
Bering Sea	D21	142
Bering Strait, strt.	C6	140
Berja, Spain	H8	20
Berkåk, Nor.	E4	8
Berkakit, Russia	E14	34
Berkane, Mor.	C4	64
Berkeley, Ca., U.S.	F3	134
Berkeley Springs, W.V., U.S.	E7	114
Berkner Island, i., Ant.	C35	81
Berkshire Hills, hills, Ma., U.S.	B12	114
Berland, stm., Ab., Can.	B13	138
Berlevåg, Nor.	A13	8
Berlin, Ger.	D9	16
Berlin, N.H., U.S.	F5	110
Berlin, N.J., U.S.	E11	114
Berlin, Pa., U.S.	E7	114
Berlin, Wi., U.S.	H9	118
Berlin, state, Ger.	D9	16
Berlinguet Inlet, b., Nu., Can.	A14	106
Bermagui, Austl.	K8	76
Bermejillo, Mex.	C7	100
Bermejito, stm., Arg.	B7	92
Bermejo, stm., Arg.	E4	92
Bermejo, stm., S.A.	C8	92
Bermejo, Paso del, p., S.A.	F2	92
Bermen, Lac, l., Qc., Can.	E17	106
Bermeo, Spain	A8	20
Bermuda, dep., N.A.	k16	104e
Bern (Berne), Switz.	C4	22
Bernalda, Italy	D10	24
Bernasconi, Arg.	H5	92
Bernau bei Berlin, Ger.	D9	16
Bernay, Fr.	E9	14
Bernburg, Ger.	E7	16
Berndorf, Aus.	C12	22
Berne see Bern, Switz.	C4	22
Berner Alpen, mts., Switz.	D4	22
Berneray, i., Scot., U.K.	D5	12
Bernese Alps see Berner Alpen, mts., Switz.	D4	22
Bernice, La., U.S.	E6	122
Bernie, Mo., U.S.	H8	120
Bernier Bay, b., Nu., Can.	A12	106
Bernier Island, i., Austl.	D2	74
Bernina, Piz, mtn., Eur.	H18	14
Bernkastel-Kues, Ger.	G3	16
Bernsdorf, Ger.	E10	16
Berón de Astrada, Arg.	C9	92
Beroroha, Madag.	E8	68
Beroun, Czech Rep.	G9	16
Berounka, stm., Czech Rep.	F9	16
Berre, Étang de, l., Fr.	F11	18
Berri, Austl.	J3	76
Berriyyane, Alg.	C5	64
Berry, Al., U.S.	D11	122
Berry, hist. reg., Fr.	H11	14
Berry, Canal du, can., Fr.	G10	14
Berry Creek, stm., Ab., Can.	E19	138
Berryessa, Lake, res., Ca., U.S.	E3	134
Berry Islands, is., Bah.	B9	96
Berseba, Nmb.	D3	70
Bersenbrück, Ger.	D3	16
Bershad', Ukr.	A16	26
Bertha, Mn., U.S.	E3	118
Berthold, N.D., U.S.	F12	124
Berthoud, Co., U.S.	G7	126
Berthoud Pass, p., Co., U.S.	B3	128
Bertoua, Cam.	D2	66
Bertrand, Mi., U.S.	G3	112
Bertrand, Ne., U.S.	G13	126
Beruri, Braz.	D5	84
Berwick, La., U.S.	H7	122
Berwick, Pa., U.S.	C9	114
Berwick-upon-Tweed, Eng., U.K.	F11	12
Berwyn, Il., U.S.	G2	112
Besalampy, Madag.	D7	68
Besançon, Fr.	G14	14
Bešankovičy, Bela.	E12	10
Besar, Gunong, mtn., Malay.	K6	48
Besar, Gunung, vol., Indon.	E9	50
Besedz', stm., Eur.	H14	10
Beskid Mountains see Beskids, mts., Eur.	G15	16
Beskids, mts., Eur.	G15	16
Beskra, Alg.	C6	64
Beslan, Russia	F6	32
Besni, Tur.	A8	58
Bessarabia, hist. reg., Eur.	C15	26
Bessemer, Al., U.S.	D11	122
Bessemer, Mi., U.S.	E8	118
Bessemer City, N.C., U.S.	A4	116
Bestjah, Russia	D15	34
Bestobe, Kaz.	D12	32
Bestuževo, Russia	F20	8
Betafo, Madag.	D8	68
Betanzos, Spain	A2	20
Bétaré Oya, Cam.	C2	66
Bétera, Spain	E10	20
Bethal, S. Afr.	E9	70
Bethalto, Il., U.S.	F7	120
Bethanien, Nmb.	E3	70
Bethany, Mo., U.S.	D3	120
Bethany, Ok., U.S.	F11	128
Bethel, Monts.	D3	105a
Bethel, Ak., U.S.	D7	140
Bethel, Me., U.S.	F6	110
Bethel, N.C., U.S.	I8	114
Bethel Acres, Ok., U.S.	B2	122
Bethel Springs, Tn., U.S.	B10	122
Bethlehem, S. Afr.	F9	70
Bethlehem, Pa., U.S.	D10	114
Bethlehem, W.V., U.S.	H9	112
Bethlehem see Bayt Laḥm, W.B.	G6	58
Bethune, Sk., Can.	D8	124
Béthune, Fr.	D11	14
Bethune, S.C., U.S.	B5	116
Betong, Malay.	C7	50
Betong, Thai.	J5	48
Betoota, Austl.	E3	76
Betpak-Dala, des., Kaz.	E11	32
Betroka, Madag.	E8	68
Bet She'arim, Ḥorbat, hist., Isr.	F6	58
Betsiamites, stm., Qc., Can.	A8	110
Betsiamites, Barrage, dam, Qc., Can.	A7	110
Betsiamites, Pointe de, c., Qc., Can.	B8	110
Betsiboka, stm., Madag.	D8	68
Betsie, Point, c., Mi., U.S.	D3	112
Betsy Layne, Ky., U.S.	G3	114
Bettendorf, Ia., U.S.	C7	120
Bettiah, India	E10	54
Bettles Field, Ak., U.S.	C9	140
Bettola, Italy	F6	22
Betūl, India	H6	54
Betung, Indon.	E4	50
Betwa, stm., India	F7	54
Betzdorf, Ger.	F3	16
Beulah, Austl.	J4	76
Beulah, Co., U.S.	C4	128
Beulah, Mi., U.S.	D3	112
Beulah, Ms., U.S.	D8	122
Beulaville, N.C., U.S.	B8	116
Beuvron, stm., Fr.	G11	14
B. Everett Jordan Lake, res., N.C., U.S.	I6	114
Beverley, Eng., U.K.	H12	12
Beverly, Ma., U.S.	B15	114
Beverly Hills, Ca., U.S.	I7	134
Beverly Lake, l., Nu., Can.	C10	106
Beverungen, Ger.	E5	16
Beverwijk, Neth.	B13	14
Bewani Mountains, mts., Pap. N. Gui.	a3	79a
Bexhill, Eng., U.K.	K13	12
Bexley, Oh., U.S.	E3	114
Bey Dağları, mts., Tur.	G13	28
Beydagları Olimpos Milli Parkı, p.o.i., Tur.	G13	28
Beyla, Gui.	H3	64
Beypazarı, Tur.	C14	28
Beypore, India	F2	53
Beyra, Som.	C9	66
Beyşehir, Tur.	F14	28
Beyşehir Gölü, l., Tur.	F14	28
Bežanickaja vozvyšennost', plat., Russia	D12	10
Bežanicy, Russia	D12	10
Bežeck, Russia	C19	10
Béziers, Fr.	F9	18
Bezmein, Turkmen.	B8	56
Bhadohi, India	F9	54
Bhādra, India	D5	54
Bhadrāchalam, India	C5	53
Bhadrak, India	H11	54
Bhadra Reservoir, res., India	E2	53
Bhadrāvati, India	E2	53
Bhāgalpur, India	F11	54
Bhainsa, India	B3	53
Bhāi Pheru, Pak.	C4	54
Bhairab Bāzār, Bngl.	F13	54
Bhaironghāti, India	C7	54
Bhakkar, Pak.	C3	54
Bhaktapur (Bhādgāon), Nepal	E10	54
Bhālki, India	C3	53
Bhalwāl, Pak.	B4	54
Bhamo, Mya.	D8	46
Bhandāra, India	H7	54
Bhanvad, India	H2	54
Bharatpur, India	E6	54
Bharatpur, Nepal	E10	54
Bharthana, India	E7	54
Bharūch, India	H4	54
Bhātāpāra, India	H8	54
Bhātghar Lake, res., India	B1	53
Bhatkal, India	E2	53
Bhātpāra, India	G12	54
Bhattiprolu, India	C5	53
Bhavāni, India	F3	53
Bhāvnagar, India	H4	54
Bhawani Mandi, India	F5	54
Bhawānipatna, India	I9	54
Bhera, Pak.	B4	54
Bhīkangaon, India	H5	54
Bhilai, India	H8	54
Bhīlwāra, India	F5	54
Bhīma, stm., India	C3	53
Bhīmavaram, India	C5	53
Bhind, India	E7	54
Bhīnmāl, India	F4	54
Bhiwandi, India	B1	53
Bhiwāni, India	D6	54
Bhojpur, Nepal	E11	54
Bhokardan, India	H5	54
Bhongīr, India	C4	53
Bhopāl, India	G6	54
Bhuban, India	H10	54
Bhubaneshwar, India	H10	54
Bhuj, India	G2	54
Bhusāwal, India	H5	54
Bhutan, ctry., Asia	E13	54
Bia, Phou, mtn., Laos	C6	48
Biafra, Bight of, b., Afr.	I6	64
Biak, i., Indon.	F10	44
Biała Piska, Pol.	C18	16
Biała Podlaska, Pol.	D19	16
Biała Podlaska, state, Pol.	E19	16
Białobrzegi, Pol.	E16	16
Białogard, Pol.	B12	16
Białowieski Park Narodowy, p.o.i., Pol.	D19	16
Białystok, Pol.	C19	16
Białystok, state, Pol.	C19	16
Bianco, Monte see Blanc, Mont, mtn., Eur.	D12	18
Biankouma, C. Iv.	H3	64
Biaora, India	F6	54
Biaro, Pulau, i., Indon.	E8	44
Biarritz, Fr.	F4	18
Biasca, Switz.	D5	22
Biba, Egypt	J2	58
Bibala, Ang.	C1	68
Bibb City, Ga., U.S.	E14	122
Bibbiena, Italy	G8	22
Bibémi, Cam.	C2	66
Bicas, Braz.	K4	88
Bicaz, Rom.	C13	26
Biche, Lac la, l., Ab., Can.	B18	138
Bichigt, Mong.	B4	36
Bicknell, In., U.S.	F10	120
Bicknell, Ut., U.S.	E5	132
Bicudo, stm., Braz.	J3	88
Bičura, Russia	F10	34
Bīd, India	B2	53
Bida, Nig.	H6	64
Bīdar, India	C3	53
Biddeford, Me., U.S.	G6	110
Bideford, Eng., U.K.	J8	12
Bieber, Ca., U.S.	B4	134
Biebrza, stm., Pol.	C18	16
Biebrzański Park Narodowy, p.o.i., Pol.	C18	16
Biecz, Pol.	G17	16
Biedenkopf, Ger.	F4	16
Biel (Bienne), Switz.	C4	22
Bielawa, Pol.	F12	16
Bielefeld, Ger.	D4	16
Bieler Lake, l., Nu., Can.	A15	106
Biella, Italy	E4	22
Bielsko-Biała, Pol.	G14	16
Bielsko-Biała, state, Pol.	G15	16
Bielsk Podlaski, Pol.	D19	16
Bienfait, Sk., Can.	E11	124
Bien Hoa, Viet.	G8	48
Bienne see Biel, Switz.	C4	22
Bien Son, Viet.	B7	48
Bienville, La., U.S.	E5	122
Bienville, Lac, l., Qc., Can.	D16	106
Bierutów, Pol.	E13	16
Bieszczadzki Park Narodowy, p.o.i., Pol.	G18	16
Bifoun, Gabon	E2	66
Big, stm., Mo., U.S.	F7	120
Biga, Tur.	C10	28
Bigadiç, Tur.	D11	28
Big A Mountain, mtn., Va., U.S.	G3	114
Big Bald Mountain, mtn., Ga., U.S.	B1	116
Big Baldy Mountain, mtn., Mt., U.S.	D16	136
Big Bay, Mi., U.S.	B2	112
Big Bay, b., Vanuatu	j16	79d
Big Bay De Noc, b., Mi., U.S.	C3	112
Big Bear Lake, Ca., U.S.	I9	134
Big Beaver, Sk., Can.	E8	124
Big Belt Mountains, mts., Mt., U.S.	D15	136
Big Bend, Swaz.	E10	70
Big Bend National Park, p.o.i., Tx., U.S.	E4	130
Big Bend Reservoir, res., Ab., Can.	D15	138
Big Black, stm., Ms., U.S.	E8	122
Big Blue, stm., U.S.	G16	126
Big Blue, West Fork, stm., Ne., U.S.	G15	126
Big Bonito Creek, stm., Az., U.S.	J7	132
Big Canyon, val., Tx., U.S.	D5	130
Big Chino Wash, stm., Az., U.S.	H4	132
Big Creek, B.C., Can.	E7	138
Big Creek, Ca., U.S.	F6	134
Big Creek, stm., B.C., Can.	E8	138
Big Creek, stm., Ar., U.S.	C8	122
Big Creek, stm., Ks., U.S.	C9	128
Big Cypress National Preserve, Fl., U.S.	J4	116
Big Cypress Swamp, sw., Fl., U.S.	J4	116
Big Delta, Ak., U.S.	D10	140
Big Desert, des., Austl.	J3	76
Big Diomede Island see Ratmanova, ostrov, i., Russia	C27	34
Big Dry Creek, stm., Mt., U.S.	G7	124
Bigelow Bight, b., U.S.	G6	110
Big Flat, Ar., U.S.	I5	120
Bigfork, Mn., U.S.	D5	118
Big Fork, stm., Mn., U.S.	C5	118
Big Frog Mountain, mtn., Tn., U.S.	C14	122
Biggar, Sk., Can.	B6	124
Biggers, Ar., U.S.	H7	120
Biggs, Ca., U.S.	D4	134
Big Gull Lake, l., On., Can.	D12	112
Big Hole, stm., Mt., U.S.	E14	136
Bighorn, stm., U.S.	A5	126
Bighorn Basin, bas., U.S.	C4	126
Bighorn Canyon National Recreation Area, p.o.i., U.S.	B4	126
Bighorn Lake, res., U.S.	B4	126
Bighorn Mountains, mts., U.S.	C5	126
Bight, Head of, b., Austl.	F6	74
Big Island, Va., U.S.	G6	114
Big Island, i., Nu., Can.	C17	106
Big Lake, Mn., U.S.	F5	118
Big Lake, l., Me., U.S.	E9	110
Big Lookout Mountain, mtn., Or., U.S.	F9	136
Big Lost, stm., Id., U.S.	G13	136
Big Muddy, stm., Il., U.S.	G8	120

Name	Map Ref.	Page
Big Muddy Creek, stm., Mt., U.S.	F9	124
Big Nemaha, North Fork, stm., Ne., U.S.	K2	118
Bignona, Sen.	G1	64
Big Pine, Ca., U.S.	F7	134
Big Pine Mountain, mtn., Ca., U.S.	I6	134
Big Piney, Wy., U.S.	H16	136
Big Piney, stm., Mo., U.S.	G6	120
Bigpoint, Ms., U.S.	G10	122
Big Porcupine Creek, stm., Mt., U.S.	H6	124
Big Prairie Creek, stm., Al., U.S.	E11	122
Big Quill Lake, l., Sk., Can.	C9	124
Big Raccoon Creek, stm., In., U.S.	I2	112
Big Rapids, Mi., U.S.	E4	112
Big Rideau Lake, l., On., Can.	D13	112
Big River, Sk., Can.	E9	106
Big Sable Point, c., Mi., U.S.	D3	112
Big Sand Lake, l., Mb., Can.	D11	106
Big Sandy, Tn., U.S.	H9	120
Big Sandy, Tx., U.S.	E3	122
Big Sandy, stm., U.S.	F3	114
Big Sandy, stm., Wy., U.S.	F3	126
Big Sandy Creek, stm., Co., U.S.	C6	128
Bigsby Island, i., On., Can.	B4	118
Big Signal Peak, mtn., Ca., U.S.	D2	134
Big Sioux, stm., U.S.	E16	126
Big Sky, Mt., U.S.	E15	136
Big Smoky Valley, val., Nv., U.S.	E8	134
Big Spring, Tx., U.S.	B6	130
Big Spruce Knob, mtn., W.V., U.S.	F5	114
Big Stone City, S.D., U.S.	F2	118
Big Stone Gap, Va., U.S.	H3	114
Big Stone Lake, l., U.S.	F2	118
Big Sunflower, stm., Ms., U.S.	D8	122
Big Sur, reg., Ca., U.S.	H4	134
Big Timber, Mt., U.S.	E16	136
Big Trout Lake, l., On., Can.	E12	106
Biguaçu, Braz.	C13	92
Big Water, Ut., U.S.	F5	132
Big Wells, Tx., U.S.	F8	130
Big White Mountain, mtn., B.C., Can.	G12	138
Big Wood, stm., Id., U.S.	G12	136
Bihać, Bos.	E2	26
Bīhar, India	F10	54
Bihār, state, India	F10	54
Biharamulo, Tan.	E6	66
Bihor, state, Rom.	C9	26
Bihor, Vârful, mtn., Rom.	C9	26
Bihoro, Japan	C16	38
Bihosava, Bela.	E10	10
Bihu, China	G8	42
Bija, stm., Russia	D15	32
Bijagós, Arquipélago dos, is., Gui.-B.	G1	64
Bijainagar, India	F5	54
Bijaipur, India	E6	54
Bījāpur, India	C2	53
Bījāpur, India	B5	53
Bijeljina, Bos.	E6	26
Bijelo Polje, Yugo.	F6	26
Bijie, China	F6	36
Bijlikol', ozero, l., Kaz.	F12	32
Bijnor, India	D7	54
Bijsk, Russia	D15	32
Bīkāner, India	D4	54
Bikar, at., Marsh. Is.	B8	72
Bikeqi, China	A4	42
Bikin, Russia	B11	36
Bikini, at., Marsh. Is.	B7	72
Bīkkū Bīttī, mtn., Libya	C3	62
Bikoro, D.R.C.	E3	66
Bilāra, India	E4	54
Bilāri, India	D7	54
Bilāsipāra, India	E13	54
Bilāspur, India	C6	54
Bilāspur, India	G9	54
Bila Tserkva, Ukr.	F15	6
Bilauktaung Range, mts., Asia	F4	48
Bilbao, Spain	A7	20
Bilbeis, Egypt	H2	58
Bilbilis, hist., Spain	C9	20
Bileća, Bos.	G5	26
Bilecik, Tur.	C12	28
Bilecik, state, Tur.	C13	28
Biłgoraj, Pol.	F18	16
Bilgrām, India	E8	54
Bilhorod-Dnistrovs'kyi, Ukr.	C17	26
Bili, D.R.C.	D5	66
Biliaïvka, Ukr.	C17	26
Bīlimora, India	H4	54
Bilin, Mya.	D3	48
Bilin, stm., Mya.	D3	48
Bílina, Czech Rep.	F9	16
Biliran Island, i., Phil.	E5	52
Billabong Creek, stm., Austl.	J5	76
Billings, Mo., U.S.	G4	120
Billings, Mt., U.S.	B4	126
Billings Heights, Mt., U.S.	B4	126
Billiton see Belitung, i., Indon.	E5	50
Bill Williams, stm., Az., U.S.	I3	132
Billy Chinook, Lake, res., Or., U.S.	F5	136
Bilma, Niger	F7	64
Biloela, Austl.	E8	76
Biloxi, Ms., U.S.	G10	122
Bilpa Morea Claypan, l., Austl.	E2	76
Bilqas Qism Awwal, Egypt	G2	58
Biltine, Chad	E4	62
Biltmore Forest, N.C., U.S.	A3	116
Bilugyun Island, i., Mya.	D3	48
Bimbo, C.A.R.	D3	66
Bimbowrie, Austl.	H3	76
Bimini Islands, is., Bah.	B9	96
Bīna-Etāwa, India	F7	54
Binaiya, Gunung, mtn., Indon.	F9	44
Binalbagan, Phil.	E4	52
Bin'an, China	B7	38
Bindki, India	E8	54
Bindloss, Ab., Can.	D3	124
Bindura, Zimb.	D5	68
Binéfar, Spain	C11	20
Binford, N.D., U.S.	G15	124
Binga, D.R.C.	D4	66
Binga, Monte, mtn., Afr.	D5	68
Bingara, Austl.	G8	76
Bingen, Ger.	G3	16
Binger, Ok., U.S.	F10	128
Binghamton, N.Y., U.S.	B10	114
Bin Ghunaymah, Jabal, mts., Libya	B3	62
Binhai, China	D8	42
Binh Gia, Viet.	B8	48
Binjai, Indon.	K4	48
Binnaway, Austl.	H7	76
Binongko, Pulau, i., Indon.	G7	44
Binscarth, Mb., Can.	D12	124
Bintan, Pulau, i., Indon.	C4	50
Bintimani, mtn., S.L.	H2	64
Bintuhan, Indon.	F3	50
Bintulu, Malay.	B8	50
Bintuni, Indon.	F9	44
Binxian, China	B7	38
Binxian, China	C7	42
Binxian, China	D3	42
Binyang, China	J3	42
Bin-Yauri, Nig.	G5	64
Biobío, state, Chile	H1	92
Biobío, stm., Chile	G2	90
Biogradska Gora Nacionalni Park, p.o.i., Yugo.	G6	26
Bioko, i., Eq. Gui.	I6	64
Bira, Russia	G15	34
Birac, Phil.	B3	52
Birāk, Libya	B2	62
Birakan, Russia	G15	34
Bi'r al Wa'r, Libya	C2	62
Birao, C.A.R.	B4	66
Birch, stm., Ab., Can.	D8	106
Birch Creek, stm., Mt., U.S.	B14	136
Birch Hills, Sk., Can.	B8	124
Birch Island, B.C., Can.	E10	138
Birch Island, i., Mb., Can.	B13	124
Birch Mountains, hills, Ab., Can.	D8	106
Birch Run, Mi., U.S.	E6	112
Birch Tree, Mo., U.S.	H6	120
Birchwood, Wi., U.S.	F7	118
Bird Creek, stm., Ok., U.S.	E13	128
Bird Island, Mn., U.S.	G4	118
Bird Island, sci., S. Geor.	J9	90
Birdsville, Austl.	E2	76
Birdtail Creek, stm., Mb., Can.	D13	124
Birdum, Austl.	C6	74
Birecik, Tur.	A9	58
Bireun, Indon.	J3	48
Bir Ghbalou, Alg.	H14	20
Birigui, Braz.	D6	90
Biriljussy, Russia	C16	32
Bīrjand, Iran	C8	56
Birjul'ka, Russia	D19	32
Birjusa, stm., Russia	C17	32
Birjusinsk, Russia	C17	32
Birken, B.C., Can.	F8	138
Birkenfeld, Ger.	G3	16
Birkenhead, Eng., U.K.	H9	12
Birmingham, Eng., U.K.	I10	12
Birmingham, Al., U.S.	D11	122
Birmingham, Ia., U.S.	D6	120
Birmingham, Mi., U.S.	B2	114
Birmitrapur, India	G10	54
Bîr Mogreïn, Maur.	D2	64
Birnin Gaouré, Niger	G5	64
Birnin-Kebbi, Nig.	G5	64
Birnin Konni, Niger	G5	64
Birnin Kudu, Nig.	G6	64
Birobidžan, Russia	G15	34
Birrie, stm., Austl.	G6	76
Birsk, Russia	C9	32
Birštonas, Lith.	F7	10
Birtle, Mb., Can.	D12	124
Birūr, India	E2	53
Biržai, Lith.	D7	10
Birżebbuġa, Malta	I8	24
Bisaccia, Italy	C9	24
Bīsalpur, India	D7	54
Bisbee, Az., U.S.	L7	132
Bisbee, N.D., U.S.	F14	124
Biscarrosse et de Parentis, Étang de, l., Fr.	E4	18
Biscay, Bay of, b., Eur.	E2	18
Biscayne Bay, b., Fl., U.S.	K5	116
Biscayne National Park, p.o.i., Fl., U.S.	K5	116
Bisceglie, Italy	C10	24
Bischofshofen, Aus.	C10	22
Bischofswerda, Ger.	E10	16
Biscoe, N.C., U.S.	A6	116
Bishnupur, India	G11	54
Bisho, S. Afr.	H8	70
Bishop, Ca., U.S.	F7	134
Bishop, Tx., U.S.	G10	130
Bishop Auckland, Eng., U.K.	G11	12
Bishop Rock, r., Eng., U.K.	L6	12
Bishop's Falls, Nf., Can.	j22	107a
Bishop's Stortford, Eng., U.K.	J13	12
Bishopville, S.C., U.S.	B5	116
Biškek, Kyrg.	F12	32
Biskupiec, Pol.	C16	16
Bislig, Phil.	F6	52
Bismarck, Mo., U.S.	G7	120
Bismarck, N.D., U.S.	A12	126
Bismarck Archipelago, is., Pap. N. Gui.	a4	79a
Bismarck Range, mts., Pap. N. Gui.	b3	79a
Bismarck Sea, Pap. N. Gui.	a4	79a
Bismark, Kap, c., Grnld.	B22	141
Bissa, Djebel, mtn., Alg.	H12	20
Bissau, Gui.-B.	G1	64
Bissett, Mb., Can.	C18	124
Bissikrima, Gui.	G2	64
Bistcho Lake, l., Ab., Can.	D7	106
Bistineau, Lake, res., La., U.S.	E5	122
Bistrica, Slvn.	D13	22
Bistrița, Rom.	B11	26
Bistrița, stm., Rom.	C13	26
Bistrița-Năsăud, state, Rom.	B11	26
Biswān, India	E8	54
Bitam, Gabon	D2	66
Bitburg, Ger.	G2	16
Bitche, Fr.	E16	14
Bitlis, Tur.	B5	56
Bitola, Mac.	B4	28
Bitolj see Bitola, Mac.	B4	28
Bitonto, Italy	C10	24
Bitou, Burkina	G4	64
Bitter Creek, stm., Wy., U.S.	B8	132
Bitterfeld, Ger.	E8	16
Bitterfontein, S. Afr.	G4	70
Bitterroot, stm., Mt., U.S.	D13	136
Bitterroot, West Fork, stm., Mt., U.S.	E12	136
Bitterroot Range, mts., U.S.	C11	136
Bitung, Indon.	E8	44
Bitupitá, Braz.	B5	88
Biu, Nig.	G7	64
Bivins, Tx., U.S.	E4	122
Biwabik, Mn., U.S.	D6	118
Biwa-ko, l., Japan	D8	40
Bixby, Ok., U.S.	I2	120
Biyala, Egypt	G2	58
Biyang, China	E5	42
Bizana, S. Afr.	G9	70
Bizen, Japan	E7	40
Bizerte (Binzert), Tun.	G3	24
Bizerte, Lac de, l., Tun.	G3	24
Bizkaiko, co., Spain	A8	20
Bjahoml', Bela.	F10	10
Bjala, Blg.	G14	26
Bjala Slatina, Blg.	F10	26
Bjalyničy, Bela.	F12	10
Bjarèzina, stm., Bela.	H13	10
Bjarèzina, stm., Bela.	G9	10
Bjaroza, Bela.	H7	10
Bjarozauka, Bela.	G8	10
Bjelovar, Cro.	E13	22
Björna, Swe.	E8	8
Björneborg see Pori, Fin.	F9	8
Bjorne Peninsula, pen., Nu., Can.	B8	141
Bjørnøya, i., Nor.	B5	30
Bla, Mali	G3	64
Blace, Yugo.	F8	26
Black (Da, Song) (Lixian), stm., Asia	D9	46
Black, stm., Mb., Can.	D18	124
Black, stm., U.S.	I6	120
Black, stm., Ak., U.S.	C11	140
Black, stm., Az., U.S.	J6	132
Black, stm., La., U.S.	F7	122
Black, stm., Mi., U.S.	E7	112
Black, stm., N.Y., U.S.	E14	112
Black, stm., Wi., U.S.	G7	118
Blackall, Austl.	E5	76
Black Bay, b., On., Can.	C10	118
Black Bay Peninsula, pen., On., Can.	C10	118
Black Bear Creek, stm., Ok., U.S.	E11	128
Blackburn, Eng., U.K.	H10	12
Blackburn, Mount, mtn., Ak., U.S.	D11	140
Black Butte, mtn., Mt., U.S.	D15	136
Black Canyon of the Gunnison National Monument, p.o.i., Co., U.S.	E9	132
Black Creek, stm., Ms., U.S.	G9	122
Black Creek, stm., S.C., U.S.	B6	116
Black Diamond, Ab., Can.	F16	138
Black Diamond, Wa., U.S.	C5	136
Blackdown Tableland National Park, p.o.i., Austl.	D7	76
Blackduck, Mn., U.S.	D4	118
Black Eagle, Mt., U.S.	C15	136
Blackfoot, Id., U.S.	G14	136
Blackfoot, Mt., U.S.	B14	136
Blackfoot, stm., Id., U.S.	G15	136
Blackfoot, stm., Mt., U.S.	D13	136
Blackfoot Reservoir, res., Id., U.S.	H15	136
Black Forest see Schwarzwald, mts., Ger.	H4	16
Black Hills, mts., U.S.	C9	126
Black Island, i., Mb., Can.	C17	124
Black Lake, Qc., Can.	D5	110
Black Lake, l., Sk., Can.	D10	106
Black Lake, l., Mi., U.S.	C5	112
Black Lake, l., N.Y., U.S.	D14	112
Black Mesa, mtn., U.S.	E6	128
Blackmore, Mount, mtn., Mt., U.S.	E15	136
Black Mountain, N.C., U.S.	A3	116
Black Mountain, mtn., Az., U.S.	K5	132
Black Mountain, mtn., Ca., U.S.	H5	134
Black Mountain, mtn., Mt., U.S.	D14	136
Black Mountain, hill, Austl.	C2	76
Black Mountain, mts., U.S.	H2	114
Black Nossob, stm., Nmb.	C4	70
Black Pine Peak, mtn., Id., U.S.	A3	132
Blackpool, Eng., U.K.	H9	12
Black Range, mts., N.M., U.S.	J9	132
Black River, N.Y., U.S.	D14	112
Black River Falls, Wi., U.S.	G8	118
Black Rock, Ar., U.S.	H6	120
Black Rock, r., Ire.	G2	12
Black Rock, r., S. Geor.	J8	90
Black Rock Desert, des., Nv., U.S.	B7	134
Blacksburg, S.C., U.S.	A4	116
Blacksburg, Va., U.S.	G5	114
Black Sea	G15	6
Blacks Fork, stm., U.S.	B7	132
Blackshear, Lake, res., Ga., U.S.	D2	116
Blackstone, Va., U.S.	G8	114
Black Sturgeon Lake, l., On., Can.	B9	118
Blackville, S.C., U.S.	C4	116
Black Volta (Volta Noire) (Mouhoun), stm., Afr.	H4	64
Blackwater, Austl.	D7	76
Blackwater, stm., Ire.	I4	12
Blackwater, stm., Mo., U.S.	E4	120
Blackwater Creek, stm., Austl.	E5	76
Blackwater Draw, stm., Tx., U.S.	H7	128
Blackwater Lake, l., N.T., Can.	C6	106
Blackwell, Tx., U.S.	B7	130
Bladenboro, N.C., U.S.	B7	116
Bladensburg National Park, p.o.i., Austl.	D4	76
Bladgrond-Noord, S. Afr.	F4	70
Bladworth, Sk., Can.	C7	124
Bláfell, mtn., Ice.	k30	8a
Blagoevgrad, Blg.	G10	26
Blagoveščensk, Russia	D16	34
Blaine, Mn., U.S.	F5	118
Blaine, Wa., U.S.	B4	136
Blair, Ne., U.S.	C1	120
Blair, Ok., U.S.	G9	128
Blair, Wi., U.S.	G7	118
Blair Athol, Austl.	D6	76
Blairsville, Ga., U.S.	B2	116
Blairsville, Pa., U.S.	D6	114
Blaj, Rom.	C10	26
Blakely, Ga., U.S.	F13	122
Blake Plateau, unds.	E6	144
Blake Point, c., Mi., U.S.	C10	118
Blalock Island, i., Wa., U.S.	E7	136
Blanc, Mont, mtn., Eur.	D12	18
Blanca, Co., U.S.	D3	128
Blanca, Bahía, b., Arg.	G4	90
Blanca, Laguna, l., Chile	J2	90
Blanca, Punta, c., Chile	B2	92
Blanca, Sierra, mtn., Tx., U.S.	C2	130
Blanca Peak, mtn., Co., U.S.	D3	128
Blanchard, Ok., U.S.	F11	128
Blanchard, stm., Oh., U.S.	D2	114
Blanche, Lake, l., Austl.	G2	76
Blanche Channel, strt., Sol. Is.	e7	79b
Blanchester, Oh., U.S.	E1	114
Blanchisseuse, Trin.	s12	105f
Blanco, Tx., U.S.	D9	130
Blanco, stm., Arg.	D3	92
Blanco, stm., Ec.	G2	86
Blanco, stm., Tx., U.S.	E9	130
Blanco, Cabo, c., C.R.	H5	102
Blanco, Cañon, val., N.M., U.S.	F3	128
Blanco, Cape, c., Or., U.S.	H2	136
Blanco, Lago, l., Chile	J3	90
Blanc-Sablon, Qc., Can.	i22	107a
Bland, Va., U.S.	G4	114
Blanda, stm., Ice.	k30	8a
Blanding, Ut., U.S.	F7	132
Blandinsville, Il., U.S.	D7	120
Blanes, Spain	C13	20
Blangkejeren, Indon.	K3	48
Blangy-sur-Bresle, Fr.	E10	14
Blankenburg, Ger.	E6	16
Blanquilla, Isla, i., Ven.	B9	86
Blansko, Czech Rep.	G12	16
Blantyre, Mwi.	D6	68
Blarney Castle, hist., Ire.	J4	12
Błaszki, Pol.	E14	16
Blaubeuren, Ger.	H5	16
Blaufelden, Ger.	G5	16
Błażowa, Pol.	G18	16
Bledsoe, Tx., U.S.	H5	128
Blega, Indon.	G8	50
Bleik see Andenes, Nor.	B6	8
Blekinge, state, Swe.	H6	8
Blenheim, On., Can.	F8	112
Blenheim, N.Z.	E5	80
Blessing, Tx., U.S.	F11	130
Bletchley, Eng., U.K.	J12	12
Bligh Water, strt., Fiji	p18	79e
Blind River, On., Can.	B6	112
Blissfield, Mi., U.S.	C2	114
Blitar, Indon.	H8	50
Block Island, i., R.I., U.S.	C14	114
Blockton, Ia., U.S.	D3	120
Bloedel, B.C., Can.	F5	138
Bloemfontein, S. Afr.	F8	70
Bloemhof, S. Afr.	E7	70
Bloemhofdam, res., S. Afr.	E7	70
Blois, Fr.	G10	14
Blönduós, Ice.	k29	8a
Bloodvein, stm., Can.	E11	106
Bloody Foreland, c., Ire.	F4	12
Bloomer, Wi., U.S.	F7	118
Bloomfield, On., Can.	E12	112
Bloomfield, Ky., U.S.	G12	120
Bloomfield, Mo., U.S.	H8	120
Bloomfield, Ne., U.S.	E15	126
Bloomfield, N.M., U.S.	G9	132
Blooming Grove, Tx., U.S.	E2	122
Blooming Prairie, Mn., U.S.	H5	118
Bloomington, Il., U.S.	D9	120
Bloomington, In., U.S.	E11	120
Bloomington, Mn., U.S.	G5	118
Bloomington, Tx., U.S.	F11	130
Bloomington, Wi., U.S.	B7	120
Bloomsburg, Pa., U.S.	C9	114
Bloomsbury, Austl.	C7	76
Bloomville, Oh., U.S.	C2	114
Blora, Indon.	G7	50
Blosseville Kyst, cst., Grnld.	D20	141
Blossom, Tx., U.S.	D3	122
Blouberg, mtn., S. Afr.	C9	70
Blountstown, Fl., U.S.	G13	122
Blountsville, Al., U.S.	C12	122
Blowering Reservoir, res., Austl.	J6	76
Blowing Point Village, Anguilla	A1	105a
Blowing Rock, N.C., U.S.	H4	114
Bludenz, Aus.	C6	22
Blue, stm., Az., U.S.	J7	132
Blue, stm., Ok., U.S.	C2	122
Blue Creek, Wa., U.S.	B8	136
Blue Cypress Lake, l., Fl., U.S.	I5	116
Blue Earth, Mn., U.S.	H4	118
Blue Earth, stm., U.S.	H4	118
Bluefield, Va., U.S.	G4	114
Bluefield, W.V., U.S.	G4	114
Bluefields, Nic.	F6	102
Blue Hill, Ne., U.S.	A10	128
Blue Hill Bay, b., Me., U.S.	F8	110
Blue Island, Il., U.S.	G2	112
Blue Mound, Ks., U.S.	F3	120
Blue Mountain, Ms., U.S.	C9	122
Blue Mountain, mtn., Ar., U.S.	C4	122
Blue Mountain, mtn., Mt., U.S.	G9	124
Blue Mountain, mts., Pa., U.S.	D8	114
Blue Mountain Peak, mtn., Jam.	i14	104d
Blue Mountains, mts., Jam.	i14	104d
Blue Mountains, mts., U.S.	E8	136
Blue Mountains, mts., Me., U.S.	F6	110
Blue Mountains National Park, p.o.i., Austl.	J8	76
Blue Mud Bay, b., Austl.	B7	74
Blue Nile (Azraq, Al-Baḥr al-) (Ābay), stm., Afr.	E6	62
Bluenose Lake, l., Nu., Can.	B6	106
Blue Ridge, Ab., Can.	B15	138
Blue Ridge, Ga., U.S.	B1	116
Blue Ridge, mts., U.S.	H4	114
Blue River, B.C., Can.	D11	138
Bluestone Dam, dam, W.V., U.S.	G5	114
Bluestone Lake, res., W.V., U.S.	G5	114
Bluewater, N.M., U.S.	H9	132
Bluff, N.Z.	H3	80
Bluff, Ut., U.S.	F7	132
Bluff Cape, c., Mya.	D2	48
Bluff Creek, stm., U.S.	D11	128
Bluff Dale, Tx., U.S.	B9	130
Bluff Park, Al., U.S.	D12	122
Bluffs, Il., U.S.	E7	120
Bluffton, In., U.S.	H4	112
Bluffton, S.C., U.S.	D5	116
Blumberg, Ger.	I4	16
Blumenau, Braz.	C13	92
Blumenhof, Sk., Can.	D6	124
Bly, Or., U.S.	A4	134
Blyth, On., Can.	E8	112
Blyth, Eng., U.K.	F11	12
Blythe, Ca., U.S.	J2	132
Blytheville, Ar., U.S.	I7	120
Bø, Nor.	G3	8
Bo, S.L.	H2	64
Boac, Phil.	D3	52
Boaco, Nic.	F5	102
Boa Esperança, Braz.	K3	88
Boa Esperança, Represa, res., Braz.	D3	88
Bo'ai, China	D5	42
Boane, Moz.	E11	70
Board Camp Mountain, mtn., Ca., U.S.	C2	134
Boardman, Oh., U.S.	C5	114
Boatman, Austl.	F6	76
Boa Viagem, Braz.	C5	88
Boa Vista, Braz.	F11	86
Boa Vista, i., C.V.	k10	65a
Boawai, Indon.	H12	50
Boaz, Al., U.S.	C12	122
Bobai, China	J3	42
Bobaomby, Tanjona, c., Madag.	C8	68
Bobbili, India	B6	53
Bobcaygeon, On., Can.	D11	112
Bobigny, Fr.	F11	14
Böblingen, Ger.	H4	16
Bobo-Dioulasso, Burkina	G4	64
Bobolice, Pol.	C12	16
Bobonaza, stm., Ec.	H3	86
Bobonong, Bots.	B9	70
Bobr, Bela.	F12	10
Bobtown, Pa., U.S.	E5	114
Bobures, Ven.	C6	86
Boby, mtn., Madag.	E8	68
Bôca da Mata, Braz.	E7	88
Boca do Acre, Braz.	E4	84
Boca do Jari, Braz.	D7	84
Bocage, Cap, c., N. Cal.	m15	79d
Boca Grande, Fl., U.S.	J3	116
Bocaiúva, Braz.	I3	88
Bocaranga, C.A.R.	C3	66
Boca Raton, Fl., U.S.	J5	116
Bocas del Toro, Pan.	H6	102
Bocay, Nic.	E5	102
Bochnia, Pol.	G16	16
Bocholt, Ger.	E2	16
Bochum, Ger.	E3	16
Bocón, Caño, stm., Col.	F7	86
Boconó, Ven.	C6	86
Bocșa, Rom.	D8	26
Boda, C.A.R.	D3	66
Bodajbo, Russia	E11	34
Bodalla, Austl.	K8	76
Bodcau Creek, stm., Ar., U.S.	D5	122
Bode, Ia., U.S.	I4	118
Bodélé, reg., Chad	D3	62
Boden, Swe.	D9	8
Bodensee see Constance, Lake, l., Eur.	I5	16
Bodhan, India	B3	53
Bodh Gaya, India	F10	54
Bodināyakkanūr, India	G3	53
Bodmin, Eng., U.K.	K8	12
Bodø, Nor.	C6	8
Bodoquena, Serra da, plat., Braz.	D5	90
Bodrum, Tur.	F10	28
Bodzentyn, Pol.	F16	16
Boende, D.R.C.	E4	66
Bœng Lvea, Camb.	F7	48
Boeo, Capo, c., Italy	G6	24
Boesmans, stm., S. Afr.	H7	70
Boeuf, stm., U.S.	E7	122
Boffa, Gui.	G2	64
Bogale, Mya.	D2	48
Bogalusa, La., U.S.	G9	122
Bogan, stm., Austl.	H6	76
Bogan Gate, Austl.	I6	76
Bogangolo, C.A.R.	C3	66
Bogata, Tx., U.S.	D3	122
Bogcang, stm., China	C11	54
Bogda Shan, mts., China	C2	36
Bogen, Ger.	H8	16
Boger City, N.C., U.S.	A4	116
Boggabilla, Austl.	G8	76
Boggabri, Austl.	H7	76
Boggy Peak, mtn., Antig.	f4	105b
Bogles, Gren.	p11	105e
Bognor Regis, Eng., U.K.	K12	12
Bogo, Phil.	E5	52
Bogoljubovo, Russia	E15	10
Bogong, Mount, mtn., Austl.	K6	76
Bogor, Indon.	G5	50
Bogorodick, Russia	G21	10
Bogorodsk, Russia	H20	8
Bogorodskoe, Russia	F17	34
Bogotá see Santa Fe de Bogotá, Col	E4	86
Bogotol, Russia	C15	32
Bogra, Bngl.	F12	54
Bogučany, Russia	C17	32
Bogué, Maur.	F2	64
Bogue Chitto, stm., U.S.	G8	122
Bogue Phalia, stm., Ms., U.S.	D8	122
Böğürtlen, Tur.	A8	58
Bo Hai (Chihli, Gulf of), b., China	B8	42
Bohai Haixia, strt., China	B9	42
Bohain-en-Vermandois, Fr.	D12	14
Bohai Wan, b., China	B8	42
Bohemian Forest, mts., Eur.	G8	16
Böhmer Wald see Bohemian Forest, mts., Eur.	G8	16
Bohol, i., Phil.	F4	52
Bohol Sea, Phil.	F5	52
Boiaçu, Braz.	H11	86
Boiano, Italy	C8	24
Boiestown, N.B., Can.	D10	110
Boipeba, Ilha de, i., Braz.	G6	88
Bois, stm., Braz.	C6	90
Bois, Lac des, l., N.T., Can.	B6	106
Bois Blanc Island, i., Mi., U.S.	C5	112
Bois de Sioux, stm., U.S.	F2	118
Boise, Id., U.S.	G10	136
Boise, stm., Id., U.S.	G10	136
Boise, Middle Fork, stm., Id., U.S.	G11	136
Boise, South Fork, stm., Id., U.S.	G11	136
Boise City, Ok., U.S.	E6	128
Boissevain, Mb., Can.	E13	124
Boistfort Peak, mtn., Wa., U.S.	D3	136
Boizenburg, Ger.	C6	16
Boja, Indon.	G7	50
Bojadła, Pol.	E11	16
Bojeador, Cape, c., Phil.	A3	52
Bojnūrd, Iran	B8	56
Bojonegoro, Indon.	G7	50
Bojuru, Braz.	E12	92
Bokāro Steel City, India	G10	54
Bokchito, Ok., U.S.	C2	122
Boké, Gui.	G2	64
Bokhara, stm., Austl.	G6	76
Bok Koŭ, Camb.	G6	48
Boknafjorden, strt., Nor.	G1	8
Boko, Congo	E2	66
Bokoro, Chad	E3	62
Bokote, D.R.C.	E4	66
Boksitogorsk, Russia	A16	10
Bokungu, D.R.C.	E4	66
Bol, Cro.	G13	22
Bolama, Gui.-B.	G1	64
Bolaños, stm., Mex.	E7	100
Bolaños de Calatrava, Spain	F7	20
Bolān Pass, p., Pak.	D10	56
Bolayır, Tur.	C9	28
Bolbec, Fr.	E9	14
Bole, China	F14	32
Bole, Ghana	H4	64
Boles, Ar., U.S.	C4	122
Bolesławiec, Pol.	E11	16
Boley, Ok., U.S.	B2	122
Bolgatanga, Ghana	G4	64
Bolhov, Russia	G18	10
Bolhrad, Ukr.	D15	26
Boli, China	B11	36
Boligee, Al., U.S.	E10	122
Bolingbrook, Il., U.S.	C9	120
Bolishan, China	C5	38
Bolívar, Col.	G3	86
Bolívar, Col.	G3	86
Bolivar, Mo., U.S.	G4	120
Bolivar, N.Y., U.S.	B7	114
Bolivar, Tn., U.S.	B9	122
Bolívar, state, Col.	C4	86
Bolívar, state, Ec.	H2	86
Bolívar, state, Ven.	D10	86
Bolívar, Cerro, mtn., Ven.	D10	86
Bolívar, Pico (La Columna), mtn., Ven.	C6	86
Bolivar Peninsula, pen., Tx., U.S.	H4	122
Bolivia, ctry., S.A.	G5	84
Bollnäs, Swe.	F7	8
Bollon, Austl.	G6	76
Bolmen, l., Swe.	H5	8
Bolobo, D.R.C.	E3	66
Bologna, Italy	F8	22
Bolognesi, Peru	F3	84
Bologoe, Russia	C17	10
Bologovo, Russia	D14	10
Bolohovo, Russia	F20	10
Bol'ŏj Anjuj, stm., Russia	C21	34
Bolomba, D.R.C.	D3	66
Bolon', ozero, l., Russia	G16	34
Bolotnoe, Russia	C14	32
Bolovens, Plateau des, plat., Laos	E8	48
Bol'šaja Balahnja, stm., Russia	B9	34
Bol'šaja Heta, stm., Russia	C5	34
Bol'šaja Kuonamka, stm., Russia	C10	34
Bol'šaja Murta, Russia	C16	32
Bol'šaja Ussurka, stm., Russia	B11	38
Bol'šaja Višera, Russia	B15	10
Bol'šakovo, Russia	F4	10
Bolsena, Italy	H8	22
Bolsena, Lago di, l., Italy	H9	22
Bol'šereče, Russia	C13	32
Bol'šereck, Russia	F20	34
Bol'ševik, Russia	D18	34
Bol'ševik, ostrov, i., Russia	A10	34
Bol'šezemel'skaja Tundra, reg., Russia	A9	32
Bolshevik see Bol'ševik, ostrov, i., Russia	A10	34
Bol'šie Uki, Russia	C12	32
Bol'šoe Mihajlovskoe, Russia	D20	10
Bol'šoe Polpino, Russia	G17	10
Bol'šoe Selo, Russia	C21	10
Bol'šoj Begičev, ostrov, i., Russia	B11	34
Bol'šoj Jugan, stm., Russia	B12	32
Bol'šoj Kamen', Russia	C10	38
Bol'šoj Ljahovskij, ostrov, i., Russia	B17	34
Bol'šoj Tal'cy, Russia	A15	10
Bolton, On., Can.	E10	112
Bolton, Eng., U.K.	H10	12
Bolton, Ms., U.S.	E8	122
Bolton, N.C., U.S.	B7	116
Bolu, Tur.	C14	28
Bolu, state, Tur.	C14	28
Bolva, stm., Russia	G17	10
Bolvadin, Tur.	E13	28
Bóly, Hung.	C5	26
Bolzano (Bozen), Italy	D8	22
Boma, D.R.C.	F2	66
Bomaderry, Austl.	J8	76
Bombala, Austl.	K7	76
Bombay see Mumbai, India	B1	53
Bomberai, Semenanjung, pen., Indon.	F9	44
Bomboma, D.R.C.	D3	66
Bom Conselho, Braz.	E7	88
Bom Despacho, Braz.	J3	88
Bomdila, India	E14	54
Bom Jesus, Braz.	E3	88
Bom Jesus da Lapa, Braz.	G4	88
Bomnak, Russia	F14	34
Bomokandi, stm., D.R.C.	D5	66
Bomongo, D.R.C.	D3	66
Bom Retiro, Braz.	C13	92
Bomu, stm., Afr.	D4	66
Bon, Cap, c., Tun.	G5	24
Bon Air, Va., U.S.	G8	114
Bonaire, i., Neth. Ant.	p23	104g
Bonampak, hist., Mex.	D2	102
Bonandolok, Indon.	C1	50
Bonanza, Or., U.S.	A4	134
Bonanza, Ut., U.S.	C7	132
Bonanza Peak, mtn., Wa., U.S.	B5	136
Bonao, Dom. Rep.	C12	102
Bonaparte, Ia., U.S.	D6	120
Bonaparte, stm., B.C., Can.	F9	138
Bonaparte, Mount, mtn., Wa., U.S.	B7	136
Bonaparte Lake, l., B.C., Can.	E10	138
Bonar Bridge, Scot., U.K.	D8	12
Bonasse, Trin.	s12	105f
Bonaventure, Qc., Can.	B11	110
Bonaventure, stm., Qc., Can.	B11	110
Bonaventure, Île, i., Qc., Can.	B12	110
Bonavista, Nf., Can.	j23	107a
Bonavista Bay, b., Nf., Can.	j23	107a
Bondeno, Italy	F8	22
Bondo, D.R.C.	E4	66
Bondo, D.R.C.	D4	66
Bondoc Peninsula, pen., Phil.	D4	52
Bondoukou, C. Iv.	H4	64
Bondowoso, Indon.	G8	50
Bonduel, Wi., U.S.	G10	118
Bone, Teluk, b., Indon.	F7	44
Bonebone, Indon.	E12	50
Boneogeh, Indon.	G12	50
Bonerate, Pulau, i., Indon.	G12	50
Bonesteel, S.D., U.S.	D13	126
Bonete Chico, Cerro, mtn., Arg.	D3	92
Bonete Grande, Cerro, mtn., Arg.	C3	92
Bongabong, Phil.	D3	52
Bongaigaon, India	E13	54
Bongandanga, D.R.C.	D4	66
Bongka, Indon.	F7	44
Bongo, Gabon	E2	66
Bongo, Massif des, mts., C.A.R.	C4	66
Bongor, Chad	E3	62
Bonham, Tx., U.S.	D2	122
Bonhomme, Morne, mtn., Haiti	C11	102
Bonifacio, Fr.	H15	18
Bonifacio, Strait of, strt., Eur.	H15	18
Bonifati, Capo, c., Italy	E9	24
Bonin Islands see Ogasawara-guntō, is., Japan	G18	30
Bonita, La., U.S.	E7	122
Bonita Springs, Fl., U.S.	J4	116
Bonito, Braz.	E8	88
Bonito, Braz.	D5	90
Bonito de Santa Fé, Braz.	D6	88
Bonn, Ger.	F2	16
Bonners Ferry, Id., U.S.	B10	136
Bonnet, Lac du, res., Mb., Can.	D17	124
Bonnétable, Fr.	F9	14
Bonne Terre, Mo., U.S.	G7	120
Bonnet Plume, stm., Yk., Can.	B3	106
Bonneville, Fr.	C12	18
Bonneville Peak, mtn., Id., U.S.	H14	136
Bonneville Salt Flats, pl., Ut., U.S.	C2	132
Bonney SE, Lake, l., Austl.	K3	76
Bonnie Rock, Austl.	F3	74
Bonny, Nig.	I6	64
Bonnyville, Ab., Can.	B20	138
Bono, Ar., U.S.	I7	120
Bonoi, Indon.	F10	44
Bonshaw, P.E., Can.	D13	110
Bontang, Indon.	C10	50
Bontebok National Park, p.o.i., S. Afr.	I5	70
Bonthe, S.L.	H2	64
Bontoc, Phil.	B3	52
Bon Wier, Tx., U.S.	G5	122
Booker, Tx., U.S.	E8	128
Booker T. Washington National Monument, p.o.i., Va., U.S.	H6	114
Boola, Gui.	H3	64
Boolaloo, Austl.	D3	74
Booleroo Centre, Austl.	I2	76
Boologooro, Austl.	D2	74
Boomarra, Austl.	B3	76
Boonah, Austl.	F9	76
Boone, Ia., U.S.	I5	118
Boone, N.C., U.S.	H4	114
Boone, stm., Ia., U.S.	B4	120
Booneville, Ar., U.S.	B5	122
Booneville, Ky., U.S.	G2	114
Booneville, Ms., U.S.	C10	122
Böön Tsagaan nuur, l., Mong.	B4	36
Boonville, Ca., U.S.	D2	134
Boonville, Mo., U.S.	F5	120
Boonville, N.Y., U.S.	E14	112
Boorindal, Austl.	H6	76
Booroorban, Austl.	J5	76
Boosaaso, Som.	B9	66
Booth, Al., U.S.	E12	122
Boothbay Harbor, Me., U.S.	G7	110
Boothia, Gulf of, b., Nu., Can.	A12	106
Boothia Peninsula, pen., Nu., Can.	A12	106
Boothville, La., U.S.	H9	122
Booué, Gabon	E2	66
Bophuthatswana, hist. reg., S. Afr.	E7	70
Boping Ling, mts., China	I7	42
Bopolu, Lib.	H2	64
Boqueirão, Serra do, hills, Braz.	F4	88
Boquilla, Presa de la, res., Mex.	B6	100
Boquim, Braz.	F7	88
Bor, Russia	H20	8
Bor, Russia	E20	8
Bor, Sudan	F6	62
Bor, Tur.	B3	56
Bor, Yugo.	E9	26
Bor, Lak, stm., Kenya	D7	66
Bora-Bora, i., Fr. Poly.	E11	72
Borabu, Thai.	E6	48
Borah Peak, mtn., Id., U.S.	F13	136

Name — Map Ref. — Page

Borås, Swe. H5 8
Borba, Braz. D6 84
Bordeaux, Fr. E5 18
Bordeaux Mountain, hill, V.I.U.S. e8 104b
Borden, Sk., Can. B6 124
Borden Peninsula, pen., Nu., Can. A14 106
Bordertown, Austl. K3 76
Bordesholm, Ger. B6 16
Bordighera, Italy G4 22
Bordj Menaïel, Alg. H14 20
Bordj Omar Idriss, Alg. D6 64
Borđoy, i., Far. Is. m34 8b
Borgå see Porvoo, Fin. F11 8
Borgarnes, Ice. k28 8a
Børgefjell Nasjonalpark, p.o.i., Nor. D5 8
Borger, Tx., U.S. F7 128
Borgholm, Swe. H7 8
Borgne, Lake, b., La., U.S. G9 122
Borgnesse, Pointe, c., Mart. I7 105c
Borgomanero, Italy E5 22
Borgo San Dalmazzo, Italy F4 22
Borgosesia, Italy E5 22
Borgo Val di Taro, Italy F6 22
Borgworm see Waremme, Bel. D14 14
Borikhan, Laos C6 48
Borisoglebsk, Russia D6 32
Borisoglebskij, Russia C21 10
Borjas Blancas see Les Borges Blanques, Spain C11 20
Borkavičy, Bela. E11 10
Borken, Ger. E2 16
Borkou, reg., Chad D3 62
Borkum, i., Ger. C2 16
Borlänge, Swe. F6 8
Bormes, Fr. F12 18
Borna, Ger. E9 16
Borneo (Kalimantan), i., Asia E5 44
Bornholm, state, Den. I6 8
Bornholm, i., Den. I6 8
Borocay Island, i., Phil. E3 52
Borodino, Russia C17 32
Borogoncy, Russia D15 34
Borohoro Shan, mts., China F14 32
Boromo, Burkina G4 64
Boron, Ca., U.S. H8 134
Boronga Islands, is., Mya. I14 54
Borongan, Phil. E5 52
Borovan, Blg. F10 26
Boroviči, Russia B16 10
Borovljanka, Russia D14 32
Borovsk, Russia E19 10
Borovskij, Russia C11 32
Borovskoj, Kaz. D10 32
Borrachudo, stm., Braz. J3 88
Borrazópolis, Braz. A12 92
Borriana, Spain E10 20
Borroloola, Austl. C7 74
Borș, Rom. B8 26
Borșa, Rom. B11 26
Borsad, India G4 54
Borščovočnyj hrebet, mts., Russia F12 34
Borsod-Abaúj-Zemplén, state, Hung. A8 26
Bort-les-Orgues, Fr. D8 18
Borūjerd, Iran C6 56
Borzja, Russia F12 34
Bosa, Italy D2 24
Bosanska Dubica, Bos. D3 26
Bosanska Gradiška, Bos. D4 26
Bosanska Krupa, Bos. E3 26
Bosanski Novi, Bos. D3 26
Bosanski Šamac, Bos. D5 26
Bosavi, Mount, mtn., Pap. N. Gui. b3 79a
Boscobel, Wi., U.S. A7 120
Bose, China J2 42
Boshan, China C7 42
Boshof, S. Afr. F7 70
Bosilegrad, Yugo. G9 26
Bosna, stm., Bos. E5 26
Bosnia and Herzegovina, ctry., Eur. E3 26
Bosnik, Indon. F10 44
Bošnjakovo, Russia G17 34
Bosobolo, D.R.C. D3 66
Bōsō-hantō, pen., Japan D13 40
Bosporus see İstanbul Boğazı, strt., Tur. B12 28
Bossangoa, C.A.R. C3 66
Bossembélé, C.A.R. C3 66
Bossey Bangou, Niger G5 64
Bossier City, La., U.S. E5 122
Bosten Hu, l., China C2 36
Boston, Eng., U.K. H12 12
Boston, Ga., U.S. F2 116
Boston, Ma., U.S. B14 114
Boston Bar, B.C., Can. G9 138
Boston Mountains, mts., Ar., U.S. B5 122
Boswell, In., U.S. H2 112
Boswell, Ok., U.S. C3 122
Bosworth, Mo., U.S. E4 120
Botād, India G3 54
Botany Bay, b., Austl. J8 76
Boteti, stm., Bots. E3 68
Bothaville, S. Afr. E8 70
Bothnia, Gulf of, b., Eur. E9 8
Bothwell, On., Can. F8 112
Boticas, Port. C3 20
Botna, stm., Mol. C15 26
Botoșani, Rom. B13 26
Botoșani, state, Rom. B13 26
Bo Trach, Viet. D8 48
Botrange, mtn., Bel. D15 14
Botswana, ctry., Afr. E3 68
Botte Donato, Monte, mtn., Italy E10 24
Bottineau, N.D., U.S. F13 124
Botucatu, Braz. L1 88
Botwood, Nf., Can. j22 107a
Bouaflé, C. Iv. H3 64
Bouaké, C. Iv. H3 64
Bouar, C.A.R. C3 66
Bouârfa, Mor. C4 64
Bouca, C.A.R. C3 66
Boucher, stm., Qc., Can. A7 110
Bouches-du-Rhône, state, Fr. F11 18
Bouctouche, N.B., Can. D12 110
Boufarik, Alg. H13 20
Bou Ficha, Tun. H4 24
Bougainville, i., Pap. N. Gui. d7 79b
Bougainville, Détroit de, strt., Vanuatu j16 79d
Bougainville Strait, strt., Oc. d7 79b
Bougouni, Mali G3 64
Bouillante, Guad. h5 105c
Bouillon, Bel. E14 14
Bouïra, Alg. B5 64
Boujdour, Cap, c., W. Sah. D2 64
Boularderie Island, i., N.S., Can. D16 110
Boulder, Co., U.S. A3 128
Boulder, Mt., U.S. D14 136
Boulder, stm., Mt., U.S. D15 136
Boulder City, Nv., U.S. H2 132
Boulia, Austl. D2 76
Boulogne-sur-Mer, Fr. D10 14
Bouloupari, N. Cal. m15 79d
Boulsa, Burkina G4 64
Bou Medfaa, Alg. H13 20
Bouna, C. Iv. H4 64
Boundary Peak, mtn., Nv., U.S. F7 134
Boundiali, C. Iv. H3 64
Boun Nua, Laos B5 48
Bountiful, Ut., U.S. C4 132
Bounty Bay, b., Pit. c28 78k
Bounty Islands, is., N.Z. H8 80
Bounty Trough, unds. N20 142
Bourail, N. Cal. m15 79d
Bourbeuse, stm., Mo., U.S. F6 120
Bourbon, In., U.S. G3 112
Bourbonnais, hist. reg., Fr. C9 18
Bourbonne-les-Bains, Fr. G14 14
Bourem, Mali F4 64
Bourg, La., U.S. H8 122
Bourg-en-Bresse, Fr. C11 18
Bourges, Fr. G11 14
Bourget, On., Can. E1 110
Bourget, Lac du, l., Fr. D11 18
Bourgogne (Burgundy), hist. reg., Fr. B10 18
Bourgogne, Canal de, can., Fr. G13 14
Bourgoin-Jallieu, Fr. D11 18
Bourke, Austl. H5 76
Bournemouth, Eng., U.K. K11 12
Bou Saâda, Alg. B5 64
Bou Salem, Tun. H2 24
Bouse Wash, stm., Az., U.S. J3 132
Bou Smail, Alg. H13 20
Boussac, Fr. C8 18
Bousso, Chad E3 62
Boutilimit, Maur. F2 64
Bouvetøya, i., Ant. A5 81
Bouza, Niger G6 64
Bøvågen, Nor. F1 8
Bovec, Slvn. D10 22
Bovey, Mn., U.S. D5 118
Bovill, Id., U.S. D10 136
Bovina, Tx., U.S. G6 128
Bow, stm., Ab., Can. G19 138
Bo-Wadrif, S. Afr. H4 70
Bowbells, N.D., U.S. F11 124
Bow Creek, stm., Ks., U.S. B9 128
Bowden, Ab., Can. E16 138
Bowdle, S.D., U.S. B13 126
Bowdon, N.D., U.S. G14 124
Bowen, Arg. G4 92
Bowen, Austl. C7 76
Bowen, Il., U.S. D7 120
Bowen, stm., Austl. C6 76
Bowie, Az., U.S. K7 132
Bowie, Md., U.S. F9 114
Bowling Green, Fl., U.S. I4 116
Bowling Green, Ky., U.S. H11 120
Bowling Green, Mo., U.S. E6 120
Bowling Green, Oh., U.S. C2 114
Bowling Green, Va., U.S. F8 114
Bowling Green, Cape, c., Austl. B6 76
Bowling Green Bay National Park, p.o.i., Austl. B6 76
Bowman, N.D., U.S. A9 126
Bowman, S.C., U.S. C5 116
Bowman, Mount, mtn., B.C., Can. E9 138
Bowmanville, On., Can. E11 112
Bowral, Austl. J8 76
Bowraville, Austl. H9 76
Bowron, stm., B.C., Can. C9 138
Bowsman, Mb., Can. B12 124
Boxelder Creek, stm., U.S. B8 126
Box Elder Creek, stm., Mt., U.S. G5 124
Boxelder Creek, stm., S.D., U.S. C10 126
Boxing, China C8 42
Boyacá, state, Col. E5 86
Boyang, China G7 42
Boyce, La., U.S. F6 122
Boyceville, Wi., U.S. F6 118
Boyd, Tx., U.S. A10 130
Boyd, stm., Austl. G9 76
Boydton, Va., U.S. H7 114
Boyer, stm., Ia., U.S. C2 120
Boyertown, Pa., U.S. D10 114
Boykins, Va., U.S. H8 114
Boyle, Ms., U.S. D8 122
Boylston, Al., U.S. E12 122
Boyne, stm., Austl. E8 76
Boyne, stm., Mb., Can. E16 124
Boyne, stm., Ire. H5 12
Boyne City, Mi., U.S. C5 112
Boynton Beach, Fl., U.S. J5 116
Boysen Reservoir, res., Wy., U.S. D4 126
Boys Ranch, Tx., U.S. F6 128
Bozburun, Tur. G11 28
Bozburun Yarımadası, pen., Tur. G11 28
Boz Dağ, mtn., Tur. E11 28
Boz Dağlar, mts., Tur. E10 28
Bozdoğan, Tur. F11 28
Bozeman, Mt., U.S. E15 136
Bozen see Bolzano, Italy D8 22
Bozhen, China B7 42
Bozhou, China E6 42
Bozkurt, Tur. F12 28
Bozoum, C.A.R. C3 66
Bozova, Tur. A9 58
Bozovici, Rom. E9 26
Bozšakol', Kaz. D12 32
Bozüyük, Tur. D13 28
Bra, Italy F4 22
Brač, Otok, i., Cro. G13 22
Bracciano, Italy H9 22
Bracciano, Lago di, l., Italy H9 22
Bracebridge, On., Can. C10 112
Brackendale, B.C., Can. G7 138
Brackettville, Tx., U.S. E7 130
Bracknell, Eng., U.K. J12 12
Braço do Norte, Braz. D13 92
Brad, Rom. C9 26
Bradano, stm., Italy D10 24
Bradenton, Fl., U.S. I3 116
Bradford, Eng., U.K. H11 12
Bradford, Ar., U.S. B7 122
Bradford, Pa., U.S. C7 114
Bradford, Tn., U.S. H9 120
Bradford, Vt., U.S. G4 110
Bradford West Gwillimbury, On., Can. D10 112
Bradley, Ar., U.S. D5 122
Bradley, Fl., U.S. I3 116
Bradley, Il., U.S. G2 112
Bradley, S.D., U.S. B15 126
Brady, Mt., U.S. B15 136
Brady, Ne., U.S. F12 126
Brady, Tx., U.S. C8 130
Brady Creek, stm., Tx., U.S. C8 130
Braga, Port. C2 20
Braga, state, Port. C2 20
Bragado, Arg. G7 92
Bragança, Braz. D8 84
Bragança, Port. C4 20
Bragança, state, Port. C4 20
Bragança Paulista, Braz. L2 88
Brāhmanbāria, Bngl. F13 54
Brāhmani, stm., India H10 54
Brahmapur, India B7 53
Brahmaputra (Yarlung), stm., Asia C7 46
Braich y Pwll, c., Wales, U.K. I8 12
Braidwood, Austl. J7 76
Braidwood, Il., U.S. C9 120
Brăila, Rom. D14 26
Brăila, state, Rom. D14 26
Brainard, Ne., U.S. F15 126
Brainerd, Mn., U.S. E4 118
Braintree, Eng., U.K. J13 12
Brak, stm., S. Afr. G6 70
Brake, Ger. C4 16
Bralorne, B.C., Can. F8 138
Brampton, On., Can. E10 112
Bramsche, Ger. D3 16
Branchville, S.C., U.S. C5 116
Branco, stm., Braz. H11 86
Branco, stm., Braz. F3 88
Brandaris, hill, Neth. Ant. p23 104g
Brandberg, mtn., Nmb. B2 70
Brandbu, Nor. F4 8
Brandenburg, Ger. D8 16
Brandenburg, Ky., U.S. G11 120
Brandenburg, state, Ger. D9 16
Brandfort, S. Afr. F8 70
Brandon, Mb., Can. E14 124
Brandon, Fl., U.S. I3 116
Brandon, Ms., U.S. E9 122
Brandon, S.D., U.S. H2 118
Brandon, Vt., U.S. G3 110
Brandsen, Arg. G8 92
Brandvlei, S. Afr. G5 70
Brandy Peak, mtn., Or., U.S. H3 136
Brandýs nad Labem-Stará Boleslav, Czech Rep. F10 16
Branford, Fl., U.S. G2 116
Braniewo, Pol. B15 16
Bransby, Austl. G4 76
Bransby Point, c., Monts. D3 105a
Bransfield Strait, strt., Ant. B35 81
Branson, Mo., U.S. H4 120
Brantford, On., Can. E9 112
Brantley, Al., U.S. F12 122
Brantley Tank, res., N.M., U.S. B3 130
Brantôme, Fr. D6 18
Brantville, N.B., Can. C12 110
Bras d'Or Lake, l., N.S., Can. E16 110
Brasiléia, Braz. F4 84
Brasília, Braz. H1 88
Brasília, Parque Nacional de, p.o.i., Braz. H1 88
Brasília de Minas, Braz. I3 88
Braslau, Bela. E9 10
Brașov, Rom. D12 26
Brașov, state, Rom. D12 26
Brassey, Banjaran, mts., Malay. A10 50
Brass Islands, is., V.I.U.S. e7 104b
Brasstown Bald, mtn., Ga., U.S. B2 116
Bratca, Rom. C9 26
Bratislava, Slov. H13 16
Bratislava, state, Slov. H13 16
Bratsk, Russia C18 32
Bratskoe vodohranilišče, res., Russia C18 32
Bratsk Reservoir see Bratskoe vodohranilišče, res., Russia C18 32
Brattleboro, Vt., U.S. B13 114
Braulio Carrillo, Parque Nacional, p.o.i., C.R. G5 102
Braúnas, Braz. J4 88
Braunau am Inn, Aus. B10 22
Braunschweig (Brunswick), Ger. D6 16
Brava, i., C.V. I10 65a
Brava, Costa, cst., Spain C14 20
Brava, Laguna, l., Arg. D3 92
Brava, Punta, c., Ur. G9 92
Brave, Pa., U.S. E5 114
Bravo (Rio Grande), stm., N.A. H13 98
Bravo, Cerro, mtn., Peru E2 84
Bravo del Norte see Bravo, stm., N.A. H13 98
Brawley, Ca., U.S. K10 134
Bray, Ire. H6 12
Bray Island, i., Nu., Can. B15 106
Brazeau, stm., Ab., Can. D15 138
Brazeau, Mount, mtn., Ab., Can. D13 138
Brazeau Dam, dam, Ab., Can. C15 138
Brazil, In., U.S. E10 120
Brazil, ctry., S.A. F9 82
Brazil Basin, unds. J11 144
Brazoria, Tx., U.S. E12 130
Brazos, stm., Tx., U.S. E8 108
Brazos, Clear Fork, stm., Tx., U.S. B8 130
Brazos, Double Mountain Fork, stm., Tx., U.S. H8 128
Brazos, North Fork, stm., Tx., U.S. H3 122
Brazzaville, Congo E2 66
Brčko, Bos. E5 26
Brda, stm., Pol. C13 16
Bré see Bray, Ire. H6 12
Brea, Ca., U.S. J8 134
Bream Bay, b., N.Z. B6 80
Brea Pozo, Arg. D6 92
Breaux Bridge, La., U.S. G7 122
Brebes, Indon. G6 50
Brechin, Scot., U.K. E10 12
Breckenridge, Mi., U.S. E5 112
Breckenridge, Mn., U.S. E2 118
Breckenridge, Mo., U.S. E4 120
Brecknock, Península, pen., Chile J2 90
Břeclav, Czech Rep. H12 16
Brecon, Wales, U.K. J9 12
Brecon Beacons, hills, Wales, U.K. J9 12
Brecon Beacons National Park, p.o.i., Wales, U.K. J9 12
Breda, Neth. C13 14
Breda, Ia., U.S. B3 120
Bredasdorp, S. Afr. I5 70
Bredenbury, Sk., Can. D11 124
Bredy, Russia D9 32
Breë, stm., S. Afr. I5 70
Breese, Il., U.S. F8 120
Bregalnica, stm., Mac. A5 28
Bregenz, Aus. C6 22
Bregovo, Blg. E9 26
Bréhat, Île de, i., Fr. F6 14
Breiðafjörður, b., Ice. k28 8a
Brejinho de Nazaré, Braz. F1 88
Brejo, Braz. B4 88
Brejo Grande, Braz. F7 88
Brejo Santo, Braz. D6 88
Brekstad, Nor. E3 8
Bremen, Ger. C4 16
Bremen, Ga., U.S. D13 122
Bremen, Oh., U.S. E3 114
Bremen, state, Ger. C4 16
Bremer Bay, Austl. F3 74
Bremer Bay, b., Austl. F3 74
Bremerhaven, Ger. C4 16
Bremerton, Wa., U.S. C4 136
Bremervörde, Ger. C4 16
Bremond, Tx., U.S. F2 122
Brenham, Tx., U.S. G2 122
Brenner Pass, p., Eur. C8 22
Brent, Fl., U.S. G11 122
Brenta, stm., Italy D8 22
Brentwood, Eng., U.K. J13 12
Brentwood, N.Y., U.S. D12 114
Brentwood, Tn., U.S. H11 120
Breo, Italy F4 22
Brescia, Italy E7 22
Breslau see Wrocław, Pol. E13 16
Bressanone, Italy D8 22
Bressay, i., Scot., U.K. n18 12a
Bresse, reg., Fr. C11 18
Bressuire, Fr. H8 14
Brèst, Bela. H6 10
Brest, Fr. F4 14
Brèst, state, Bela. H8 10
Bretagne (Brittany), hist. reg., Fr. F5 14
Bretenoux, Fr. E7 18
Breton, Ab., Can. C16 138
Breton Islands, is., La., U.S. H9 122
Breton Sound, strt., La., U.S. H9 122
Brett, Cape, c., N.Z. B6 80
Bretten, Ger. G4 16
Breueh, Pulau, i., Indon. J2 48
Breuil-Cervinia, Italy E4 22
Brevard, N.C., U.S. A3 116
Breves, Braz. D7 84
Brevoort Island, i., Nu., Can. E13 141
Brewarrina, Austl. G6 76
Brewer, Me., U.S. F8 110
Brewster, Mn., U.S. H3 118
Brewster, Ne., U.S. F13 126
Brewster, Wa., U.S. B7 136
Brewster, Kap, c., Grnld. C21 141
Brewton, Al., U.S. F11 122
Breyten, S. Afr. E10 70
Březnice, Czech Rep. G9 16
Brezno, Slov. H15 16
Bria, C.A.R. C4 66
Brian Boru Peak, mtn., B.C., Can. A3 138
Briançon, Fr. E12 18
Brian Head, mtn., Ut., U.S. F4 132
Briare, Canal de, can., Fr. G11 14
Bribie Island, i., Austl. F9 76
Bricelyn, Mn., U.S. H5 118
Briceni, Mol. A14 26
Briceville, Tn., U.S. A14 122
Bri Chuallan see Bray, Ire. H6 12
Bridge, stm., B.C., Can. F7 138
Bridge City, Tx., U.S. G5 122
Bridge Lake, B.C., Can. E10 138
Bridgend, Wales, U.K. J9 12
Bridgeport, Ca., U.S. E6 134
Bridgeport, Ct., U.S. C12 114
Bridgeport, Mi., U.S. E6 112
Bridgeport, Ne., U.S. F9 126
Bridgeport, Tx., U.S. H11 128
Bridgeport, Wa., U.S. C7 136
Bridgeport, Lake, res., Tx., U.S. H10 128
Bridger, Mt., U.S. B4 126
Bridger Peak, mtn., Wy., U.S. B9 132
Bridgeton, N.J., U.S. E10 114
Bridgetown, Austl. F3 74
Bridgetown, Barb. n8 105d
Bridgetown, N.S., Can. F11 110
Bridgeville, De., U.S. F10 114
Bridgewater, N.S., Can. F12 110
Bridgewater, Ma., U.S. B15 114
Bridgewater, S.D., U.S. D15 126
Bridgewater, Va., U.S. F6 114
Bridgwater, Eng., U.K. J9 12
Bridgwater Bay, b., Eng., U.K. J9 12
Bridlington, Eng., U.K. G12 12
Bridport, Eng., U.K. K10 12
Brie, reg., Fr. F12 14
Brier Creek, stm., Ga., U.S. C4 116
Brig, Switz. D5 22
Briggs, Tx., U.S. D10 130
Brigham City, Ut., U.S. B4 132
Bright, Austl. K6 76
Brighton, On., Can. D12 112
Brighton, Eng., U.K. K12 12
Brighton, Co., U.S. A4 128
Brighton, Ia., U.S. C6 120
Brighton, Mi., U.S. B2 114
Brighton, N.Y., U.S. E12 112
Brighton Downs, Austl. D3 76
Brignoles, Fr. F11 18
Brijuni, i., Cro. F10 22
Brilliant, B.C., Can. G13 138
Brilliant, Al., U.S. C11 122
Brillion, Wi., U.S. D1 112
Brilon, Ger. E4 16
Brindisi, Italy D11 24
Brinkworth, Austl. I2 76
Brion, Île, i., Qc., Can. C15 110
Brioude, Fr. D9 18
Brisbane, Austl. F9 76
Brisighella, Italy F8 22
Bristol, Eng., U.K. J10 12
Bristol, Ct., U.S. C12 114
Bristol, Fl., U.S. G14 122
Bristol, N.H., U.S. G5 110
Bristol, Pa., U.S. D11 114
Bristol, R.I., U.S. C14 114
Bristol, Tn., U.S. H3 114
Bristol, Vt., U.S. F3 110
Bristol Bay, b., Ak., U.S. E7 140
Bristol Channel, strt., U.K. J8 12
Bristol Island, i., S. Geor. A2 81
Bristol Lake, l., Ca., U.S. I10 134
Bristow, Ok., U.S. B2 122
Britannia Beach, B.C., Can. G7 138
British Columbia, state, Can. E5 106
British Guiana see Guyana, ctry., S.A. C6 84
British Honduras see Belize, ctry., N.A. D3 102
British Indian Ocean Territory, dep., Afr. G17 2
British Isles, is., Eur. C12 4
British Mountains, mts., N.A. C11 140
British Solomon Islands see Solomon Islands, ctry., Oc. D7 72
British Virgin Islands, dep., N.A. h15 96a
Brits, S. Afr. D8 70
Britstown, S. Afr. G6 70
Britt, Ia., U.S. A4 120
Brittany see Bretagne, hist. reg., Fr. F5 14
Britton, S.D., U.S. B15 126
Brive-la-Gaillarde, Fr. D7 18
Brixen see Bressanone, Italy D8 22
Brixham, Eng., U.K. K9 12
Brixton, Austl. D5 76
Brjanka, Russia C16 32
Brjansk, Russia G17 10
Brjanskaja oblast', co., Russia H16 10
Brno, Czech Rep. G12 16
Broa, Ensenada de la, b., Cuba A6 102
Broad, stm., U.S. B4 116
Broad, stm., Ga., U.S. B2 116
Broadalbin, N.Y., U.S. G2 110
Broad Sound, b., Austl. D7 76
Broad Sound Channel, strt., Austl. C8 76
Broadus, Mt., U.S. B7 126
Broadwater, Ne., U.S. F10 126
Broadway, Va., U.S. F7 114
Brocēni, Lat. D5 10
Brochet, Mb., Can. D10 106
Brock, Sk., Can. C5 124
Brockman, Mount, mtn., Austl. D3 74
Brockton, Ma., U.S. B14 114
Brockton, Mt., U.S. F9 124
Brockville, On., Can. D14 112
Brockway, Pa., U.S. C7 114
Brocton, N.Y., U.S. B6 114
Brodeur Peninsula, pen., Nu., Can. A13 106
Brodhead, Wi., U.S. B8 120
Brodick, Scot., U.K. F7 12
Brodnax, Va., U.S. H7 114
Brodnica, Pol. C15 16
Brogan, Or., U.S. F9 136
Brok, Pol. D17 16
Broken Arrow, Ok., U.S. H2 120
Broken Bay, b., Austl. I8 76
Broken Bow, Ok., U.S. C4 122
Broken Bow Lake, res., Ok., U.S. C4 122
Broken Hill, Austl. H3 76
Broken Hill see Kabwe, Zam. C4 68
Broken Ridge, unds. M12 142
Brokopondo, Sur. B6 84
Brokopondo Stuwmeer, res., Sur. C6 84
Bromley Plateau, unds. K10 144
Bromptonville, Qc., Can. E4 110
Bromsgrove, Eng., U.K. I10 12
Bronkhorstspruit, S. Afr. D9 70
Bronlund Peak, mtn., B.C., Can. D5 106
Bronnae, Bela. H13 10
Bronnicy, Russia E21 10
Bronson, Fl., U.S. G3 116
Bronson, Ks., U.S. G2 120
Bronson, Mi., U.S. G4 112
Bronte, Italy G8 24
Bronte, Tx., U.S. C7 130
Brook, In., U.S. H2 112
Brookeland, Tx., U.S. F5 122
Brooker, Fl., U.S. G3 116
Brookfield, N.S., Can. E13 110
Brookfield, Wi., U.S. E1 112
Brookford, N.C., U.S. I4 114
Brookhaven, Ms., U.S. F8 122
Brookings, Or., U.S. A1 134
Brookings, S.D., U.S. G2 118
Brookland, Ar., U.S. B8 122
Brooklyn, N.S., Can. F12 110
Brooklyn, Ia., U.S. J6 118
Brooklyn, Mi., U.S. B1 114
Brooklyn Center, Mn., U.S. F5 118
Brookmere, B.C., Can. G10 138
Brookneal, Va., U.S. G7 114
Brookport, Il., U.S. G9 120
Brooks, Ab., Can. F19 138
Brooks Bay, b., B.C., Can. F2 138
Brookshire, Tx., U.S. H3 122
Brooks Range, mts., Ak., U.S. C8 140
Brooksville, Fl., U.S. H3 116
Brooksville, Ms., U.S. D10 122
Brookville, In., U.S. E12 120
Brookville, Pa., U.S. C6 114
Brookville Lake, res., In., U.S. E13 120
Broome, Austl. C4 74
Broomfield, Co., U.S. B3 128
Brooten, Mn., U.S. F3 118
Brora, Scot., U.K. C9 12
Brosna, stm., Ire. H5 12
Brotas de Macaúbas, Braz. G4 88
Brou, Fr. F10 14
Broughton, Mount, mtn., Austl. K5 76
Broughty Ferry, Scot., U.K. E10 12
Browerville, Mn., U.S. E4 118
Brown, Mount, mtn., Mt., U.S. B15 136
Brown, Point, c., Wa., U.S. D2 136
Brown Deer, Wi., U.S. E2 112
Browne Bay, b., Nu., Can. A11 106
Brownfield, Tx., U.S. A5 130
Browning, Mo., U.S. D4 120
Browning, Mt., U.S. B13 136
Brownlee Reservoir, res., U.S. F9 136
Brownsburg, Qc., Can. E2 110
Brownsburg, In., U.S. I3 112
Brownsdale, Mn., U.S. H5 118
Browns Town, Jam. i13 104d
Brownstown, In., U.S. F11 120
Brownsville, Ky., U.S. G11 120
Brownsville, La., U.S. E6 122
Brownsville, Or., U.S. F4 136
Brownsville, Tn., U.S. B9 122
Brownsville, Tx., U.S. I10 130
Brownton, Mn., U.S. G4 118
Brownville, Me., U.S. E7 110
Brownville, Ne., U.S. D2 120
Brownville Junction, Me., U.S. E7 110
Brownwood, Tx., U.S. C8 130
Brownwood, Lake, res., Tx., U.S. C9 130
Browse Island, i., Austl. B4 74
Broxton, Ga., U.S. E3 116
Broža, Bela. H12 10
Bruay-en-Artois, Fr. D11 14
Bruce, S.D., U.S. G2 118
Bruce, Wi., U.S. F7 118
Bruce, Mount, mtn., Austl. D3 74
Bruce Mines, On., Can. B6 112
Bruce Peninsula, pen., On., Can. C8 112
Bruce Peninsula National Park, p.o.i., On., Can. C8 112
Bruce Rock, Austl. F3 74
Bruchsal, Ger. G4 16
Bruck an der Leitha, Aus. B13 22
Bruck an der Mur, Aus. C12 22
Bruges see Brugge, Bel. C12 14
Brugg, Switz. C5 22
Brugge (Bruges), Bel. C12 14
Brühl, Ger. F2 16
Bruit, Pulau, i., Malay. B7 50
Brule, Ne., U.S. F11 126
Brumado, Braz. H5 88
Brundidge, Al., U.S. F13 122
Bruneau, Id., U.S. H11 136
Bruneau, stm., U.S. H11 136
Bruneck see Brunico, Italy D8 22
Brunei, ctry., Asia A9 50
Brunico, Italy D8 22
Brunsbüttel, Ger. C4 16
Brunson, S.C., U.S. D4 116
Brunswick see Braunschweig, Ger. D6 16
Brunswick, Ga., U.S. E4 116
Brunswick, Me., U.S. G6 110
Brunswick, Md., U.S. E8 114
Brunswick, Mo., U.S. E4 120
Brunswick, Oh., U.S. C4 114
Brunswick, Península, pen., Chile J2 90
Bruntál, Czech Rep. F13 16
Brus, Laguna de, b., Hond. E5 102
Brush, Co., U.S. A5 128
Brusovo, Russia C18 10
Brusque, Braz. C13 92
Brussel see Bruxelles, Bel. D13 14
Brussels see Bruxelles, Bel. D13 14
Brussels, On., Can. E8 112
Bruthen, Austl. K6 76
Bruxelles (Brussels), Bel. D13 14
Bruzual, Ven. D7 86
Bryan, Oh., U.S. C1 114
Bryan, Tx., U.S. G2 122
Bryan, Mount, mtn., Austl. I2 76
Bryant, Ar., U.S. C6 122
Bryce Canyon National Park, p.o.i., Ut., U.S. F4 132
Bryli, Bela. G13 10
Bryson, Qc., Can. C13 112
Bryson, Tx., U.S. A9 130
Brzeg, Pol. F13 16
Brześć Kujawski, Pol. D14 16
Brzesko, Pol. F16 16
Brzeziny, Pol. E15 16
Bsharrī, Leb. D6 58
Bua, Fiji p19 79e
Bua Bay, b., Fiji p19 79e
Buada Lagoon, b., Nauru q17 78f
Buala, Sol. Is. e8 79b
Bua Yai, Thai. E6 48
Bubanza, Bdi. E5 66
Bubaque, Gui.-B. G1 64
Bubi, stm., Zimb. B10 70
Būbiyān, i., Kuw. D6 56
Bubuduo, China C10 54
Bucak, Tur. F13 28
Bucaramanga, Col. D5 86
Buccaneer Archipelago, is., Austl. C4 74
Buchanan, Sk., Can. C11 124
Buchanan, Lib. H2 64
Buchanan, Ga., U.S. D13 122
Buchanan, Mi., U.S. G3 112
Buchanan, Lake, l., Austl. C5 76
Buchanan, Lake, l., Tx., U.S. D9 130
Buchan Ness, c., Scot., U.K. D11 12
Buchans, Nf., Can. j22 107a
Bucharest see București, Rom. E13 26
Buchen, Ger. G5 16
Buchholz in der Nordheide, Ger. C5 16
Buchloe, Ger. H6 16
Buchon, Point, c., Ca., U.S. H4 134
Buchs, Switz. C6 22
Buckatunna, Ms., U.S. F10 122
Buckatunna Creek, stm., Ms., U.S. F10 122
Bückeburg, Ger. D5 16
Buckeye, Az., U.S. J4 132
Buckeye Lake, Oh., U.S. I7 112
Buckhaven, Scot., U.K. E9 12
Buckholts, Tx., U.S. D10 130
Buckhorn Draw, stm., Tx., U.S. D7 130
Buckie, Scot., U.K. D10 12
Buckingham, Qc., Can. C14 112
Buckingham, Va., U.S. G7 114
Buckingham Bay, b., Austl. B7 74
Buck Island, i., V.I.U.S. g11 104c
Buck Island Reef National Monument, p.o.i., V.I.U.S. g11 104c
Buck Lake, l., Ab., Can. D16 138
Buckland, Ak., U.S. C7 140
Buckley, Wa., U.S. C4 136
Bucklin, Ks., U.S. D9 128
Bucklin, Mo., U.S. E5 120
Buck Mountain, mtn., Wa., U.S. B7 136
Bucovăț, Mol. B15 26
Buco Zau, Ang. A1 68
București (Bucharest), Rom. E13 26
București, state, Rom. E13 26
Bucyrus, Oh., U.S. D3 114
Buda, Il., U.S. C8 120
Buda, Tx., U.S. D10 130
Budalin, Mya. A2 48
Budapest, Hung. B6 26
Budapest, state, Hung. B6 26
Budaun, India D7 54
Budd Coast, cst., Ant. B16 81
Buddh Gaya see Bodh Gaya, India F10 54
Buddusò, Italy D3 24
Bude, Ms., U.S. F8 122
Bude Bay, b., Eng., U.K. K8 12
Budënnovsk, Russia F6 32
Budești, Rom. E13 26
Büdingen, Ger. F5 16
Budišov nad Budišovkou, Czech Rep. G13 16
Budjala, D.R.C. D3 66
Budogovišči, Russia G19 10
Budrio, Italy F8 22
Budweis see České Budějovice, Czech Rep. H10 16
Buea, Cam. D1 66
Buena Esperanza, Arg. G5 92
Buenaventura, Col. F3 86
Buenaventura, Mex. G9 98
Buena Vista, Bol. C4 90
Buena Vista, Mex. K9 134
Buenavista, Phil. G4 52
Buena Vista, Co., U.S. C2 128
Buena Vista, Ga., U.S. E14 122
Buena Vista, Va., U.S. G6 114
Buena Vista Lake Bed, reg., Ca., U.S. H6 134
Buendía, Embalse de, res., Spain D8 20
Buenópolis, Braz. I3 88
Buenos Aires, Arg. G8 92
Buenos Aires, Col. F3 86
Buenos Aires, C.R. H6 102
Buenos Aires, state, Arg. G5 90
Buenos Aires, Lago see General Carrera, Lago, l., S.A. I2 90
Buen Pasto, Arg. I3 90
Buerarema, Braz. H6 88
Buffalo, Ks., U.S. G2 120
Buffalo, Mn., U.S. F5 118
Buffalo, Mo., U.S. G4 120
Buffalo, N.Y., U.S. B7 114
Buffalo, Oh., U.S. E4 114
Buffalo, S.C., U.S. B4 116
Buffalo, S.D., U.S. B9 126
Buffalo, Tx., U.S. F2 122
Buffalo, stm., Can. C8 106
Buffalo, stm., Ar., U.S. H4 120
Buffalo, stm., Tn., U.S. B11 122
Buffalo Creek, stm., Mn., U.S. G4 118
Buffalo Lake, Mn., U.S. G4 118
Buffalo Lake, l., Ab., Can. D18 138
Buffalo Lake, l., N.T., Can. C7 106
Buffalo Narrows, Sk., Can. D8 106
Buffalo Pound Lake, l., Sk., Can. D8 124
Buffels, stm., S. Afr. F10 70
Buffels, stm., S. Afr. F3 70
Buford, Ga., U.S. B2 116
Buford Dam, dam, Ga., U.S. B1 116
Buftea, Rom. E12 26
Bug (Buh) (Zakhidnyy Buh), stm., Eur. D17 16
Buga, Col. F3 86
Bugala Island, i., Ug. E6 66
Bugeat, Fr. D7 18
Bugojno, Bos. E4 26
Bugrino, Russia B23 8
Bugsuk Island, i., Phil. F1 52
Bugt, China C4 38
Bugul'ma, Russia D8 32
Buguruslan, Russia D8 32
Buh, stm., China D4 36
Buh (Bug) (Zakhidnyy Buh), stm., Eur. D19 16
Buhara, Uzb. G10 32
Buhl, Mn., U.S. D6 118
Buhler, Ks., U.S. C11 128
Buhuși, Rom. C13 26
Buies Creek, N.C., U.S. A7 116
Builth Wells, Wales, U.K. I9 12
Buin, Chile F2 92
Buin, Pap. N. Gui. d6 79b
Buíque, Braz. E7 88
Buitsivango (Rietfontein), stm., Afr. B4 70
Buj, Russia G19 8
Bujalance, Spain G6 20
Buje, Cro. E10 22
Bujnaksk, Russia F7 32
Bujumbura, Bdi. E5 66
Bukačača, Russia F12 34
Bukama, D.R.C. F5 66
Bukan', Russia G17 10
Bukavu, D.R.C. E5 66
Bukeya, D.R.C. G5 66
Bukhara see Buhara, Uzb. G10 32
Bukittinggi, Indon. D2 50
Bükki Nemzeti Park, p.o.i., Hung. A7 26
Bukoba, Tan. E6 66
Bukovica, reg., Cro. F12 22
Bukovina, hist. reg., Eur. B12 26
Bukuru, Nig. H6 64
Bula, Indon. F9 44
Bulaevo, Kaz. C12 32
Bulajevo see Bulaevo, Kaz. C12 32
Bulan, Phil. D4 52
Bulandshahr, India D6 54
Bulawayo, Zimb. B9 70
Bulbul, Syria B7 58

Name	Map Ref.	Page
Buldan, Tur.	E11	28
Buldāna, India	H6	54
Buldir Island, i., Ak., U.S.	g22	140a
Bulgan, Mong.	B3	36
Bulgan, Mong.	B5	36
Bulgaria, ctry., Eur.	G12	26
Bulkley, stm., B.C., Can.	B3	138
Bullard, Tx., U.S.	E3	122
Bulla Regia, hist., Tun.	H2	24
Bullas, Spain	F9	20
Bullaxaar, Som.	B8	66
Bulle, Switz.	D4	22
Buller, stm., N.Z.	E5	80
Buller, Mount, mtn., Austl.	K6	76
Bullfinch, Austl.	F3	74
Bull Harbour, B.C., Can.	F2	138
Bullhead, S.D., U.S.	B11	126
Bullhead City, Az., U.S.	H2	132
Bullock, N.C., U.S.	H7	114
Bullock Creek, Austl.	A5	76
Bullock Creek, stm., Austl.	C5	76
Bulloo, stm., Austl.	G4	76
Bullpound Creek, stm., Ab., Can.	E19	138
Bulls Gap, Tn., U.S.	H2	114
Bull Shoals, Ar., U.S.	H5	120
Bull Shoals Lake, res., U.S.	H5	120
Bulnes, Chile	H1	92
Bulolo, Pap. N. Gui.	b4	79a
Bulsār, India	H4	54
Buluan, Phil.	G5	52
Bulukumba, Indon.	F12	50
Bululawang, Indon.	H8	50
Bumba, D.R.C.	D4	66
Bumpus, Mount, hill, Nu., Can.	B8	106
Bumu Hu, l., China	C13	54
Buna, Kenya	D7	66
Bunawan, Phil.	F5	52
Bunbury, Austl.	F3	74
Bunceton, Mo., U.S.	F5	120
Bundaberg, Austl.	E9	76
Bundarra, Austl.	H8	76
Bünde, Ger.	D4	16
Būndi, India	F5	54
Bundoran, Ire.	G4	12
Būndu, India	G10	54
Bungamas, Indon.	E3	50
Bungo-suidō, strt., Japan	G5	40
Bungo-takada, Japan	F4	40
Bungtlang, India	G14	54
Bunia, D.R.C.	D6	66
Bunker, Mo., U.S.	G6	120
Bunker Group, is., Austl.	D9	76
Bunker Hill, In., U.S.	H3	112
Bunker Hill, Or., U.S.	G2	136
Bunker Hill, mtn., Nv., U.S.	D8	134
Bunkie, La., U.S.	G6	122
Bunnell, Fl., U.S.	G4	116
Buñol see Bunyolo, Spain	E10	20
Buntok, Indon.	D9	50
Bunyolo, Spain	E10	20
Bunyu, Pulau, i., Indon.	B10	50
Buolkalah, Russia	B12	34
Buolkalakh see Buolkalah, Russia	B12	34
Buon Ma Thuot, Viet.	F9	48
Buor-Haja, guba, b., Russia	B15	34
Buor-Haja, mys, c., Russia	B15	34
Bupul, Indon.	G11	44
Buqayq, Sau. Ar.	D6	56
Bura, Kenya	E7	66
Burām, Sudan	E5	62
Burang, China	C8	54
Buranhém, stm., Braz.	I6	88
Burāq, Syria	E7	58
Burauen, Phil.	E5	52
Burbank, Wa., U.S.	D8	136
Burç, Tur.	A8	58
Burcher, Austl.	I6	76
Burco, Som.	C9	66
Burdekin, stm., Austl.	C6	76
Burdekin Falls, wtfl, Austl.	C6	76
Burden, Ks., U.S.	D12	128
Burdett, Ks., U.S.	C9	128
Burdur, Tur.	F13	28
Burdur, state, Tur.	F13	28
Burdur Gölü, l., Tur.	F12	28
Bureinskij hrebet, mts., Russia	G15	34
Bureja, Russia	G15	34
Bureja, stm., Russia	F15	34
Büren, Ger.	E4	16
Bürenhayrhan, Mong.	B3	36
Burford, On., Can.	E9	112
Burg, Ger.	D7	16
Burg, Den see Den Burg, Neth.	A13	14
Burgas, Blg.	G14	26
Burgas, state, Blg.	G13	26
Burgas, Gulf of see Burgaski Zaliv, b., Blg.	G14	26
Burgaski Zaliv, b., Blg.	G14	26
Burg auf Fehmarn, Ger.	B7	16
Burgaw, N.C., U.S.	B8	116
Burgdorf, Switz.	C4	22
Burgenland, state, Aus.	C13	22
Burgeo, Nf., Can.	j22	107a
Burgersdorp, S. Afr.	G8	70
Burghausen, Ger.	H8	16
Burghead, Scot., U.K.	D9	12
Burgin, Ky., U.S.	G13	120
Burgo de Osma, Spain	C7	20
Burgos, Mex.	C9	100
Burgos, Phil.	C3	52
Burgos, Spain	B7	20
Burgos, co., Spain	B7	20
Burgstädt, Ger.	F8	16
Burgundy see Bourgogne, hist. reg., Fr.	B10	18
Burhan Budai Shan, mts., China	D4	36
Burhaniye, Tur.	D9	28
Burhānpur, India	H5	54
Burias Island, i., Phil.	D4	52
Burica, Punta, c., N.A.	I6	102
Burien, Wa., U.S.	C4	136
Burila Mare, Rom.	E9	26
Buri Ram, Thai.	E6	48
Buriti, Braz.	B4	88
Buriti Bravo, Braz.	C4	88
Buriticupu, stm., Braz.	C2	88
Buriti dos Lopes, Braz.	B5	88
Buritizeiro, Braz.	I3	88
Burjasot see Burjassot, Spain	E10	20
Burjassot, Spain	E10	20
Burjatija, state, Russia	F11	34
Burkburnett, Tx., U.S.	G10	128
Burke, S.D., U.S.	D13	126
Burke, stm., Austl.	D2	76
Burketown, Austl.	A2	76
Burkina Faso, ctry., Afr.	G4	64
Burleson, Tx., U.S.	B10	130
Burley, Id., U.S.	H13	136
Burlingame, Ca., U.S.	F3	134
Burlingame, Ks., U.S.	F2	120
Burlington, On., Can.	E10	112
Burlington, Co., U.S.	B6	128
Burlington, Ia., U.S.	D6	120
Burlington, Ks., U.S.	F2	120
Burlington, N.C., U.S.	H6	114
Burlington, Vt., U.S.	F3	110
Burlington, Wa., U.S.	B4	136
Burlington, Wi., U.S.	B9	120
Burlington, Wy., U.S.	C4	126
Burlington Junction, Mo., U.S.	D2	120
Burma see Myanmar, ctry., Asia	D8	46
Burnaby, B.C., Can.	G7	138
Burnet, Tx., U.S.	D9	130
Burnett, stm., Austl.	E8	76
Burnett Bay, b., N.T., Can.	B14	140
Burney, Ca., U.S.	C4	134
Burnie, Austl.	n12	77a
Burnley, Eng., U.K.	H10	12
Burns, Ks., U.S.	C12	128
Burns, Or., U.S.	G7	136
Burns, Tn., U.S.	H10	120
Burns, Wy., U.S.	F8	126
Burnside, Ky., U.S.	G13	120
Burnside, stm., Nu., Can.	B8	106
Burnside, Lake, l., Austl.	E4	74
Burns Lake, B.C., Can.	B5	138
Burnsville, Ms., U.S.	C10	122
Burnsville, N.C., U.S.	I3	114
Burnsville, W.V., U.S.	F5	114
Burnt, stm., Or., U.S.	F9	136
Burnt Pine, Norf. I.	y25	78i
Burntwood, stm., Mb., Can.	D11	106
Burqin, China	B2	36
Burra, Austl.	I2	76
Burragorang, Lake, res., Austl.	J7	76
Burrel, Alb.	C13	24
Burreli see Burrel, Alb.	C13	24
Burrendong, Lake, res., Austl.	I7	76
Burren Junction, Austl.	H7	76
Burriana see Borriana, Spain	E10	20
Burrinjuck Reservoir, res., Austl.	J7	76
Burr Oak, Ks., U.S.	B10	128
Burrton, Ks., U.S.	C11	128
Burruyacú, Arg.	E4	90
Bursa, Tur.	C11	28
Bursa, state, Tur.	C11	28
Bûr Sa'îd (Port Said), Egypt	G3	58
Burstall, Sk., Can.	D4	124
Būr Sūdān (Port Sudan), Sudan	D7	62
Burt, Ia., U.S.	H4	118
Burt Lake, l., Mi., U.S.	C5	112
Burtnieks ezers, l., Lat.	C8	10
Burton, Mi., U.S.	E6	112
Burton, Tx., U.S.	G2	122
Burton upon Trent, Eng., U.K.	I11	12
Buru, i., Indon.	F8	44
Burullus, Buheirat el-, l., Egypt	G1	58
Burundi, ctry., Afr.	E6	66
Burun-Šibertuj, gora, mtn., Russia	G10	34
Bururi, Bdi.	E5	66
Burwash, On., Can.	B9	112
Burwell, Ne., U.S.	F13	126
Bury, Eng., U.K.	H10	12
Buryatia see Burjatija, state, Russia	F11	34
Bury Saint Edmunds, Eng., U.K.	I13	12
Burzil, Pak.	A5	54
Busa, Mount, mtn., Phil.	G5	52
Busan see Pusan-jikhalsi, state, Kor., S.	D2	40
Busanga, D.R.C.	E4	66
Busby, Mt., U.S.	B5	126
Bûsh, Egypt	I2	58
Bushire see Bandar-e Būshehr, Iran	D7	56
Bushland, Tx., U.S.	F6	128
Bushman Land, reg., S. Afr.	F4	70
Bushnell, Fl., U.S.	H3	116
Bushnell, Il., U.S.	D7	120
Bushtyna, Ukr.	A10	26
Busia, Ug.	D6	66
Businga, D.R.C.	D4	66
Busira, stm., D.R.C.	E3	66
Buskerud, state, Nor.	F3	8
Busko-Zdrój, Pol.	F16	16
Buṣrá ash-Shām, Syria	F7	58
Busselton, Austl.	F3	74
Bussey, Ia., U.S.	C5	120
Bussum, Neth.	B14	14
Bustamante, Mex.	B8	100
Busto Arsizio, Italy	E5	22
Busuanga Island, i., Phil.	D2	52
Busu-Djanoa, D.R.C.	D4	66
Büsum, Ger.	B4	16
Buta, D.R.C.	D4	66
Buta Ranquil, Arg.	H2	92
Butare, Rw.	E5	66
Butaritari, at., Kir.	C8	72
Bute, Island of, i., Scot., U.K.	F7	12
Bute Inlet, b., B.C., Can.	F5	138
Butembo, D.R.C.	D5	66
Butera, Italy	G8	24
Butere, Kenya	D6	66
Butha-Buthe, Leso.	F9	70
Buthidaung, Mya.	D7	46
Butiá, Braz.	E11	92
Butler, Ga., U.S.	D1	116
Butler, In., U.S.	C1	114
Butler, Mo., U.S.	F3	120
Butler, Oh., U.S.	D3	114
Butler, Pa., U.S.	D6	114
Butner, N.C., U.S.	H7	114
Buto, hist., Egypt	G1	58
Buton, Pulau, i., Indon.	F7	44
Butrint, hist., Alb.	E14	24
Butru, Austl.	C2	76
Butte, Mt., U.S.	D14	136
Butte, Ne., U.S.	E14	126
Butte Creek, stm., Ca., U.S.	D4	134
Butte Falls, Or., U.S.	H4	136
Butternut, Wi., U.S.	E8	118
Butterworth, Malay.	J5	48
Butterworth, S. Afr.	H9	70
Buttle Lake, l., B.C., Can.	G5	138
Button Islands, is., Nu., Can.	C17	106
Buttonwillow, Ca., U.S.	H6	134
Butuan, Phil.	F5	52
Buturlino, Russia	I21	8
Butwal, Nepal	E9	54
Butzbach, Ger.	F4	16
Bützow, Ger.	C7	16
Buulobarde, Som.	D9	66
Buur Gaabo, Som.	E8	66
Buurgplaatz, mtn., Lux.	D15	14
Buxtehude, Ger.	C5	16
Buxton, S. Afr.	E7	70
Buxton, Eng., U.K.	H11	12
Buxton, N.C., U.S.	A10	116
Buxton, Mount, mtn., B.C., Can.	E2	138
Buyr nuur, l., Asia	B8	36
Büyükada, Tur.	C12	28
Büyükçekmece, Tur.	B11	28
Büyükkarıştıran, Tur.	B10	28
Büyükkemikli Burnu, c., Tur.	C9	28
Büyükmenderes, stm., Tur.	F10	28
Buzău, Rom.	D13	26
Buzău, state, Rom.	D13	26
Buzău, stm., Rom.	D13	26
Buzen, Japan	F4	40
Búzi, stm., Moz.	A12	70
Buziaș, Rom.	D8	26
Buzuluk, Russia	D8	32
Byādgi, India	D2	53
Byam Channel, strt., Nu., Can.	A19	140
Byam Martin Island, i., Nu., Can.	B19	140
Bycen', Bela.	H8	10
Byčki, Russia	F17	10
Byczyna, Pol.	E14	16
Bydgoszcz, Pol.	C13	16
Bydgoszcz, state, Pol.	C13	16
Byelorussia see Belarus, ctry., Eur.	E14	6
Byers, Tx., U.S.	G10	128
Byesville, Oh., U.S.	E4	114
Bygdin, l., Nor.	F3	8
Byhalia, Ms., U.S.	C9	122
Byhau, Bela.	G13	10
Bykle, Nor.	G2	8
Bylnice, Czech Rep.	G14	16
Bylot Island, i., Nu., Can.	A15	106
Byng Inlet, On., Can.	C9	112
Bynum, Mt., U.S.	C14	136
Bynum, N.C., U.S.	I6	114
Byrd, Lac, l., Qc., Can.	A13	112
Byrnedale, Pa., U.S.	C7	114
Byro, Austl.	E3	74
Byron, Ga., U.S.	D2	116
Byron, Il., U.S.	B8	120
Byron, Cape, c., Austl.	G9	76
Byron Bay, Austl.	G9	76
Byrranga, gory, mts., Russia	B8	34
Bystřice pod Hostýnem, Czech Rep.	G13	16
Bytantaj, stm., Russia	C15	34
Bytča, Slov.	G14	16
Bytom, Pol.	F14	16
Bytoš', Russia	G17	10
Bytów, Pol.	B13	16

C

Name	Map Ref.	Page
Ca, stm., Asia	C7	48
Caacupé, Para.	B9	92
Caaguazú, Para.	B9	92
Caaguazú, state, Para.	B10	92
Caála, Ang.	C2	68
Caapiranga, Braz.	I11	86
Caatinga, Braz.	I3	88
Caazapá, Para.	C9	92
Caazapá, state, Para.	C9	92
Cabaiguán, Cuba	A8	102
Cabaliana, Lago, l., Braz.	I11	86
Caballococha, Peru	D3	84
Caballo Reservoir, res., N.M., U.S.	K9	132
Cabanatuan, Phil.	C3	52
Cabano, Qc., Can.	C8	110
Cabarroguis, Phil.	B3	52
Cabedelo, Braz.	D8	88
Cabeza del Buey, Spain	F5	20
Cabezas, Bol.	C4	90
Cabildo, Arg.	I7	92
Cabimas, Ven.	B6	86
Cabinda, Ang.	B1	68
Cabinda, state, Ang.	B1	68
Cabinet Mountains, mts., U.S.	B10	136
Cable, Wi., U.S.	E7	118
Cabo, Braz.	E8	88
Cabo Blanco, Arg.	I3	90
Cabo Frio, Braz.	L4	88
Cabonga, Réservoir, res., Qc., Can.	F15	106
Cabool, Mo., U.S.	G5	120
Caboolture, Austl.	F9	76
Caborca, Mex.	F6	98
Cabo Rojo, P.R.	B1	104a
Cabot, Ar., U.S.	C7	122
Cabot Head, c., On., Can.	C8	112
Cabot Strait, strt., Can.	j21	107a
Cabourg, Fr.	E8	14
Cabra Corral, Embalse, res., Arg.	B5	92
Cabramurra, Austl.	J7	76
Cabrera, stm., Col.	F4	86
Cabrera, Illa de, i., Spain	E13	20
Cabri, Sk., Can.	D5	124
Cabriel, stm., Spain	E9	20
Cabrillo National Monument, p.o.i., Ca., U.S.	K8	134
Cabrobó, Braz.	E6	88
Cabruta, Ven.	D8	86
Çabullónes, Punta, c., P.R.	C2	104a
Čabusy, Bela.	H11	10
Cabuyaro, Col.	E5	86
Çaçador, Braz.	C12	92
Čačak, Yugo.	F7	26
Caçapava, Braz.	L3	88
Caçapava do Sul, Braz.	E11	92
Cacapon, stm., W.V., U.S.	E7	114
Cacequi, Braz.	D10	92
Cáceres, Braz.	G6	84
Cáceres, Col.	D4	86
Cáceres, Spain	E4	20
Cáceres, co., Spain	E4	20
Čačèrsk, Bela.	H13	10
Cache, stm., Ar., U.S.	B7	122
Cache, stm., Il., U.S.	G8	120
Cache Creek, B.C., Can.	F9	138
Cache Creek, stm., Ca., U.S.	E3	134
Cache la Poudre, stm., Co., U.S.	G7	126
Cache Peak, mtn., Id., U.S.	A3	132
Cachi, Arg.	B4	92
Cachimbo, Braz.	E7	84
Cachimbo, Serra do, mts., Braz.	E6	84
Cachoeira Alta, Braz.	C6	90
Cachoeira de Manteiga, Braz.	I3	88
Cachoeira do Sul, Braz.	E11	92
Cachoeiro de Itapemirim, Braz.	K5	88
Cachos, Punta, c., Chile	C2	92
Cachuela Esperanza, Bol.	B3	90
Căciulați, Rom.	E13	26
Cacolo, Ang.	C2	68
Caconda, Ang.	C2	68
Cactus, Tx., U.S.	E6	128
Cactus Flat, pl., Nv., U.S.	F9	134
Cacuaco, Ang.	B1	68
Caculé, Braz.	H4	88
Çacuri, Ven.	E9	86
Čadan, Russia	D16	32
Čadca, Slov.	G14	16
Caddo, Ok., U.S.	C2	122
Caddo, stm., Ar., U.S.	C5	122
Caddo Lake, res., U.S.	E4	122
Caddo Mills, Tx., U.S.	D2	122
Cadell, stm., Austl.	D3	76
Cadena, Cerro, mtn., Mex.	I3	130
Cadena, Punta, c., P.R.	B1	104a
Cadillac, Sk., Can.	E6	124
Cadillac, Fr.	E5	18
Cadillac, Mi., U.S.	D4	112
Cádiz, Spain	H4	20
Cadiz, Ky., U.S.	H10	120
Cádiz, co., Spain	H5	20
Cádiz, Bahía de, b., Spain	H4	20
Çadiz Lake, l., Ca., U.S.	I1	132
Čadobec, stm., Russia	C17	32
Cadomin, Ab., Can.	C13	138
Cadore, reg., Italy	D9	22
Cadott, Wi., U.S.	G7	118
Çadwell, Ga., U.S.	D2	116
Čaek, Kyrg.	F12	32
Caen, Fr.	E8	14
Caengo (Kwenge), stm., Afr.	B2	68
Caernarfon, Wales, U.K.	H8	12
Caernarfon Bay, b., Wales, U.K.	H8	12
Caerphilly, Wales, U.K.	J9	12
Caesarea see Qesari, Horbat, hist., Isr.	F5	58
Caeté, Braz.	J4	88
Caetité, Braz.	H4	88
Cafayate, Arg.	C4	92
Cagayan, stm., Phil.	A3	52
Cagayan de Oro, Phil.	F5	52
Cagayan Islands, is., Phil.	F3	52
Çagayan Sulu Island, i., Phil.	G2	52
Čagda, Russia	E15	34
Çağış, Tur.	D10	28
Cagliari, Italy	E3	24
Cagliari, Golfo di, b., Italy	E3	24
Cagliari, Stagno di, l., Italy	E2	24
Çagnes-sur-Mer, Fr.	F13	18
Čagoda, stm., Russia	A17	10
Čagodošča, stm., Russia	A18	10
Caguán, stm., Col.	G4	86
Caguas, P.R.	B3	104a
Cahaba, stm., Al., U.S.	E11	122
Cahama, Ang.	D1	68
Caher, Ire.	I4	12
Cahokia, Il., U.S.	F7	120
Cahora Bassa, Albufeira, res., Moz.	D5	68
Cahors, Fr.	E7	18
Cahto Peak, mtn., Ca., U.S.	D2	134
Cahuinari, stm., Col.	H6	86
Cahul, Mol.	D15	26
Caí, stm., Braz.	D12	92
Caianda, Ang.	C3	68
Caiapó, Serra do, mts., Braz.	G7	84
Caibarién, Cuba	A8	102
Cai Bau, Dao, i., Viet.	B8	48
Caiçara, Braz.	D8	88
Caicara, Caño, stm., Ven.	D7	86
Caicara de Maturín, Ven.	C10	86
Caicara de Orinoco, Ven.	D8	86
Caicedonia, Col.	E4	86
Caicó, Braz.	D7	88
Caicos Islands, is., T./C. Is.	B11	102
Caicos Passage, strt., N.A.	B11	102
Caijiapo, China	D2	42
Caima Bay, b., Phil.	D4	52
Caimanera, Cuba	C10	102
Caimanero, Laguna del, l., Mex.	D5	100
Cain Creek, stm., S.D., U.S.	C14	126
Cai Nuoc, Viet.	H7	48
Cairari, Braz.	B1	88
Caird Coast, cst., Ant.	C3	81
Cairns, Austl.	A5	76
Cairo see El-Qâhira, Egypt	H2	58
Cairo, Ga., U.S.	F1	116
Cairo, Il., U.S.	G8	120
Cairo, Ne., U.S.	F14	126
Cairo, W.V., U.S.	E4	114
Cairo Montenotte, Italy	F5	22
Cairu, Braz.	G6	88
Caisleán an Bharraigh see Castlebar, Ire.	H3	12
Caiundo, Ang.	D2	68
Caiwan, China	I4	42
Caizi Hu, l., China	F7	42
Caja de Muertos, Isla, i., P.R.	C2	104a
Cajamarca, Peru	E2	84
Cajapió, Braz.	B3	88
Cajazeiras, Braz.	D6	88
Cajon Summit, p., Ca., U.S.	I8	134
Cajuru, Braz.	K2	88
Caka, China	D4	36
Çakmak, Tur.	A5	58
Čakovec, Cro.	D13	22
Calabar, Nig.	H6	64
Calabozo, Ven.	C8	86
Calabozo, Ensenada de, b., Ven.	B6	86
Calabria, state, Italy	F10	24
Calafat, Rom.	F9	26
Calagua Islands, is., Phil.	C4	52
Calahorra, Spain	B8	20
Calais, Fr.	C10	14
Calalaste, Sierra de, mts., Arg.	B4	92
Calama, Chile	D3	90
Calamar, Col.	B4	86
Calamar, Col.	F5	86
Calamian Group, is., Phil.	E3	52
Calamus, stm., Ne., U.S.	E13	126
Calañas, Spain	G4	20
Calang, Indon.	J2	48
Calapan, Phil.	D3	52
Călărași, Mol.	B15	26
Călărași, Rom.	E14	26
Călărași, state, Rom.	E14	26
Calarcá, Col.	E4	86
Calatafimi, Italy	G6	24
Calatayud, Spain	C9	20
Calau, Ger.	E9	16
Calavite Passage, strt., Phil.	D3	52
Calayan Island, i., Phil.	A3	52
Calbayog, Phil.	D5	52
Calbe, Ger.	E7	16
Calbuco, Chile	H2	90
Calcasieu, stm., La., U.S.	G5	122
Calcasieu Lake, l., La., U.S.	G5	122
Calceta, Ec.	H1	86
Calchaquí, Arg.	D7	92
Calchaquí, stm., Arg.	B4	92
Calçoene, Braz.	C7	84
Calcutta, India	G12	54
Caldaro, Italy	D8	22
Caldas, Col.	D4	86
Caldas, state, Col.	E4	86
Caldas da Rainha, Port.	E1	20
Caldas de Reis, Spain	B2	20
Caldas de Reyes see Caldas de Reis, Spain	B2	20
Caldas Novas, Braz.	I1	88
Caldera, Chile	C2	92
Caldwell, Id., U.S.	G10	136
Caldwell, Ks., U.S.	D11	128
Caldwell, Oh., U.S.	E4	114
Caldwell, Tx., U.S.	G2	122
Caledon, S. Afr.	I4	70
Caledon (Mohokare), stm., Afr.	F8	70
Caledonia, Belize	C3	102
Caledonia, N.S., Can.	F11	110
Caledonia, Ms., U.S.	D10	122
Caledonia, N.Y., U.S.	A8	114
Caledonia, Oh., U.S.	D3	114
Calella, Spain	C13	20
Calen, Austl.	C7	76
Calera, Al., U.S.	D12	122
Caleta Olivia, Arg.	I3	90
Caleufú, Arg.	G5	92
Calexico, Ca., U.S.	K10	134
Calgary, Ab., Can.	E16	138
Calhan, Co., U.S.	B4	128
Calhoun, Al., U.S.	E12	122
Calhoun, Ga., U.S.	C14	122
Calhoun, Mo., U.S.	F4	120
Calhoun, Tn., U.S.	B14	122
Calhoun City, Ms., U.S.	D9	122
Cali, Col.	F3	86
Calico Rock, Ar., U.S.	H5	120
Calicut see Kozhikode, India	F2	53
Caliente, Nv., U.S.	F2	132
California, Mo., U.S.	F5	120
California, state, U.S.	D3	108
California, Golfo de (California, Gulf of), b., Mex.	B2	96
California, Gulf of see California, Golfo de, b., Mex.	B2	96
California Aqueduct, aq., Ca., U.S.	I8	134
Calilegua, Parque Nacional, p.o.i., Arg.	A5	92
Calimere, Point, c., India	F4	53
Calingasta, Arg.	E3	92
Calion, Ar., U.S.	D6	122
Calipatria, Ca., U.S.	J10	134
Calispell Peak, mtn., Wa., U.S.	B9	136
Calistoga, Ca., U.S.	E3	134
Calitri, Italy	D9	24
Calitzdorp, S. Afr.	H5	70
Callabonna, Lake, l., Austl.	G2	76
Callabonna Creek, stm., Austl.	G3	76
Callahan, Mount, mtn., Co., U.S.	D8	132
Callan, Ire.	I5	12
Callander, On., Can.	B10	112
Callao, Peru	F2	84
Callaquén, Volcán, vol., Chile	H2	92
Callaway, Ne., U.S.	F12	126
Calliaqua, St. Vin.	o11	105e
Calling Lake, Ab., Can.	A17	138
Calling Lake, l., Ab., Can.	A17	138
Callosa de Segura, Spain	F9	20
Calmar, Ab., Can.	C17	138
Calmar, Ia., U.S.	A6	120
Çalm Lake, l., On., Can.	C6	118
Çal'mny-Varre, Russia	C17	8
Čalna, Russia	F15	8
Caloundra, Austl.	F9	76
Calp, Spain	F11	20
Calpe see Calp, Spain	F11	20
Caltagirone, Italy	G8	24
Caltanissetta, Italy	G8	24
Călugăreni, Rom.	E12	26
Calulo, Ang.	B2	68
Calumet, Mn., U.S.	D5	118
Calumet City, Il., U.S.	G2	112
Calunda, Ang.	C3	68
Caluula, Som.	B10	66
Calvados, state, Fr.	E8	14
Calvert, Al., U.S.	F10	122
Calvert, Tx., U.S.	G2	122
Calvert Island, i., B.C., Can.	E2	138
Calvillo, Mex.	E7	100
Calvin, Ok., U.S.	C2	122
Calvinia, S. Afr.	G4	70
Calw, Ger.	H4	16
Calwa, Ca., U.S.	G6	134
Calypso, N.C., U.S.	A7	116
Camabatela, Ang.	B2	68
Camaçari, Braz.	G6	88
Camacupa, Ang.	C2	68
Camaguán, Ven.	C8	86
Camagüey, Cuba	B9	102
Camaiore, Italy	G7	22
Camajuaní, Cuba	A8	102
Camaná, Peru	G3	84
Camaná, stm., Peru	G3	84
Camanaú, stm., Braz.	H11	86
Camanche Reservoir, res., Ca., U.S.	E4	134
Camapuã, Braz.	C6	90
Camaquã, Braz.	E12	92
Camaquã, stm., Braz.	E11	92
Camará, Braz.	D5	84
Camarajibe, Braz.	D8	88
Camararé, stm., Braz.	F6	84
Camarat, Cap, c., Fr.	F12	18
Camarès, Fr.	F8	18
Camargo, Bol.	D3	90
Camargue, reg., Fr.	F10	18
Camarillo, Ca., U.S.	I6	134
Camarón, Arroyo, stm., Mex.	G7	130
Camarón, Cabo, c., Hond.	D5	102
Camarones, Arg.	H3	90
Camarones, Bahía, b., Arg.	H3	90
Camas Creek, stm., Id., U.S.	F14	136
Camatagua, Embalse de, l., Ven.	C8	86
Ca Mau, Viet.	H7	48
Ca Mau, Mui, c., Viet.	H7	48
Camba, Indon.	F11	50
Cambodia, ctry., Asia	C3	48
Camboon, Austl.	E8	76
Camboriú, Braz.	C13	92
Camborne, Eng., U.K.	K7	12
Cambrai, Fr.	D12	14
Cambria, Ca., U.S.	H4	134
Cambrian Mountains, mts., Wales, U.K.	I9	12
Cambridge, On., Can.	E9	112
Cambridge, N.Z.	C6	80
Cambridge, Eng., U.K.	I12	12
Cambridge, Il., U.S.	C7	120
Cambridge, Ia., U.S.	C4	120
Cambridge, Md., U.S.	F9	114
Cambridge, Ma., U.S.	B14	114
Cambridge, Mn., U.S.	F5	118
Cambridge, Ne., U.S.	A8	128
Cambridge, N.Y., U.S.	G3	110
Cambridge, Oh., U.S.	D4	114
Cambridge Bay, Nu., Can.	B10	106
Cambridge Fiord, b., Nu., Can.	A15	106
Cambridge Springs, Pa., U.S.	C5	114
Cambrils, Spain	C11	20
Cambuí, Braz.	L2	88
Cambulo, Ang.	B3	68
Cambundi-Catembo, Ang.	C2	68
Camden, Austl.	J8	76
Camden, Al., U.S.	F11	122
Camden, Ar., U.S.	D6	122
Camden, Me., U.S.	F7	110
Camden, N.J., U.S.	E10	114
Camden, N.Y., U.S.	E14	112
Camden, N.C., U.S.	H9	114
Camden, Oh., U.S.	E1	114
Camden, S.C., U.S.	B5	116
Camden, Tn., U.S.	H9	120
Camden Bay, b., Ak., U.S.	B11	140
Camdenton, Mo., U.S.	G5	120
Camels Hump, mtn., Vt., U.S.	F3	110
Camenca, Mol.	A15	26
Camerino, Italy	G10	22
Cameron, Mo., U.S.	E3	120
Cameron, Tx., U.S.	D10	130
Cameron, W.V., U.S.	E5	114
Cameron, Wi., U.S.	F7	118
Cameron Hills, hills, Can.	D7	106
Cameroon, ctry., Afr.	C2	66
Cameroon Mountain, vol., Cam.	D1	66
Camerota, Italy	D9	24
Cametá, Braz.	B1	88
Çamiçi Gölü, l., Tur.	F10	28
Camiguin Island, i., Phil.	F5	52
Camiguin Island, i., Phil.	A3	52
Camiling, Phil.	C3	52
Camilla, Ga., U.S.	E1	116
Camino, Ca., U.S.	E5	134
Camiranga, Braz.	A2	88
Camiri, Bol.	D4	90
Camissombo, Ang.	B3	68
Çamlıdere, Tur.	C15	28
Çamlıdere, Tur.	A10	58
Cam Lo, Viet.	D8	48
Camocim, Braz.	B5	88
Camooweal, Austl.	C7	74
Camorta Island, i., India	G7	46
Camotes Islands, is., Phil.	E5	52
Camotes Sea, Phil.	E5	52
Campagna di Roma, reg., Italy	C6	24
Campaign, Tn., U.S.	B13	122
Campana, Arg.	G8	92
Campana, Isla, i., Chile	I1	90
Campanario, Spain	F5	20
Campania, state, Italy	D8	24
Campano, Appennino, mts., Italy	C8	24
Campaspe, stm., Austl.	C6	76
Campbell, S. Afr.	F6	70
Campbell, Ca., U.S.	F4	134
Campbell, Mo., U.S.	H7	120
Campbell, Ne., U.S.	A10	128
Campbell, Cape, c., N.Z.	E6	80
Campbellford, On., Can.	D12	112
Campbell Hill, hill, Oh., U.S.	D2	114
Campbell Hills, hill, St. Vin.	p11	105e
Campbell Island, B.C., Can.	D2	138
Campbell Island, i., N.Z.	I7	72
Campbell Lake, l., B.C., Can.	G5	138
Campbell Plateau, unds.	O20	142
Campbellpore, Pak.	B4	54
Campbell River, B.C., Can.	F5	138
Campbell's Bay, Qc., Can.	C13	112
Campbellsport, Wi., U.S.	E1	112
Campbellton, N.B., Can.	C10	110
Campbellton, P.E., Can.	D12	110
Campbellton, Fl., U.S.	G13	122
Campbelltown, Austl.	J8	76
Campbell Town, Austl.	n13	77a
Campbeltown, Scot., U.K.	F7	12
Campeche, Mex.	C2	102
Campeche, state, Mex.	C2	102
Campeche, Bahía de, b., Mex.	D6	96
Campeche, Gulf of see Campeche, Bahía de, b., Mex.	E13	100
Campechuela, Cuba	B9	102
Câmpeni, Rom.	C10	26
Camperdown, Austl.	L4	76
Camperville, Mb., Can.	C13	124
Cam Pha, Viet.	B8	48
Camp Hill, Al., U.S.	E13	122
Camp Hill, Pa., U.S.	H12	112
Câmpia Turzii, Rom.	C10	26
Campidano, val., Italy	E2	24
Campiglia Marittima, Italy	G7	22
Campillos, Spain	G6	20
Câmpina, Rom.	D12	26
Campina, reg., Spain	G5	20
Campina Grande, Braz.	D7	88
Campinas, Braz.	L2	88
Campina Verde, Braz.	J1	88
Campoalegre, Col.	F4	86
Campo Alegre de Goiás, Braz.	I2	88
Campobasso, Italy	C8	24
Campo Belo, Braz.	K3	88
Campo de Criptana, Spain	E7	20
Campo Erê, Braz.	C11	92
Campo Florido, Braz.	J1	88
Campo Formoso, Braz.	F5	88
Campo Gallo, Arg.	C6	92
Campo Grande, Braz.	D6	90
Campo Largo, Arg.	C7	92
Campo Largo, Braz.	B13	92
Campo Maior, Braz.	C4	88
Campo Maior, Port.	F3	20
Campo Mourão, Braz.	A11	92
Campo Novo, Braz.	C11	92
Campos, Braz.	K5	88
Campos Altos, Braz.	J2	88
Campo Santo, Arg.	B5	92
Campos Belos, Braz.	G2	88
Campos do Jordão, Braz.	L3	88
Campos Gerais, Braz.	K2	88
Campos Novos, Braz.	C12	92
Campos Sales, Braz.	D5	88
Camp Point, Il., U.S.	D6	120
Campti, La., U.S.	F5	122
Campton, Ky., U.S.	G2	114
Câmpulung, Rom.	D11	26
Câmpulung Moldovenesc, Rom.	B12	26
Campuya, stm., Peru	H4	86
Camp Verde, Az., U.S.	I4	132
Cam Ranh, Viet.	G9	48
Cam Ranh, Vinh, b., Viet.	G9	48
Cam Ranh Bay see Cam Ranh, Vinh, b., Viet.	G9	48
Camrose, Ab., Can.	C18	138
Camsell, stm., N.T., Can.	B7	106
Camuy, P.R.	B2	104a
Çan, Tur.	C10	28
Čanaan, Vt., U.S.	E5	110
Cana-brava, stm., Braz.	G1	88
Cana-brava, stm., Braz.	G1	88
Canada, ctry., N.A.	D9	106
Canada Basin, unds.	A25	142
Cañada de Gómez, Arg.	F7	92
Cañada Honda, Arg.	F3	92
Canadian, Tx., U.S.	F8	128
Canadian, stm., U.S.	F13	128
Canadian, Deep Fork, stm., Ok., U.S.	F13	128
Canaguá, stm., Ven.	D7	86
Canaima, Parque Nacional, p.o.i., Ven.	E10	86
Canajoharie, N.Y., U.S.	B11	114
Çanakkale, Tur.	C9	28
Çanakkale, state, Tur.	D9	28
Çanakkale Boğazı (Dardanelles), strt., Tur.	C9	28
Canala, N. Cal.	m15	79d
Canal Fulton, Oh., U.S.	D4	114
Canal Point, Fl., U.S.	J5	116
Canals, Arg.	F6	92
Canal Winchester, Oh., U.S.	E3	114
Canandaigua, N.Y., U.S.	B8	114
Cananea, Mex.	F7	98
Canápolis, Braz.	J1	88
Cañar, Ec.	I2	86
Cañar, state, Ec.	I2	86
Canarias, Islas (Canary Islands), is., Spain	D1	64
Canarreos, Archipiélago de los, is., Cuba	B6	102
Canary Basin, unds.	F11	144
Canary Islands see Canarias, Islas, is., Spain	D1	64
Cañas, C.R.	G5	102
Canaseraga, N.Y., U.S.	B8	114
Canastota, N.Y., U.S.	E14	112
Canatlán, Mex.	C6	100
Canaveral, Cape, c., Fl., U.S.	H5	116
Canaveral National Seashore, p.o.i., Fl., U.S.	H5	116
Cañaveras, Spain	D8	20
Canavese, hist. reg., Italy	E4	22
Canavieiras, Braz.	H6	88
Canbelego, Austl.	H6	76
Canberra, Austl.	J7	76
Canby, Ca., U.S.	B5	134
Canby, Mn., U.S.	G2	118
Canby, Or., U.S.	E4	136
Cancon, Fr.	E6	18
Cancún, Mex.	B4	102
Cancún, Punta, c., Mex.	B4	102
Çandarlı Körfezi, b., Tur.	E9	28
Čandé, Fr.	G7	14
Candeias, Braz.	G6	88
Candeias, Braz.	K3	88
Candela, stm., Mex.	B8	100
Candelaria, Arg.	C10	92
Candelária, Braz.	D11	92
Candelaria, stm., Mex.	C2	102
Candelo, Austl.	K7	76
Cándido Aguilar, Mex.	C9	100
Cândido Mendes, Braz.	A3	88
Candlemas Islands, is., S. Geor.	K12	82
Candlestick, Ms., U.S.	E8	122
Cando, N.D., U.S.	F14	124
Candon, Phil.	B3	52
Candor, N.Y., U.S.	B9	114
Candor, N.C., U.S.	A6	116
Canea see Chaniá, Grc.	H7	28
Canela, Braz.	D12	92
Canelas, Mex.	C5	100
Canelli, Italy	F5	22
Canelones, Ur.	G9	92
Cañete, Chile	H1	92
Caney, stm., U.S.	E13	128
Caney Creek, stm., Tx., U.S.	F12	130
Canfranc, Spain	B10	20
Cangas de Narcea, Spain	A4	20
Cangas de Onís, Spain	A5	20

Name — Map Ref. — Page

Cangkuang, Tanjung, c., Indon. G4 50
Cangombe, Ang. C2 68
Canguaretama, Braz. D8 88
Canguçu, Braz. E11 92
Cangumbe, Ang. C2 68
Cangxi, China F1 42
Cangzhou, China B7 42
Caniapiscau, stm., Qc., Can. D17 106
Caniapiscau, Lac, res., Qc., Can. E17 106
Canicattì, Italy G7 24
Canim Lake, B.C., Can. E10 138
Canim Lake, l., B.C., Can. E9 138
Canindé, Braz. C6 88
Canindé, stm., Braz. D4 88
Canindeyú, state, Para. B10 92
Canisteo, N.Y., U.S. B8 114
Canistota, S.D., U.S. D15 126
Cañitas de Felipe Pescador, Mex. D7 100
Canjáyar, Spain G8 20
Çankırı, Tur. A3 56
Çankırı, state, Tur. C15 28
Canmore, Ab., Can. E15 138
Cannanore, India F2 53
Cannelton, In., U.S. G11 120
Cannes, Fr. F13 18
Canning, N.S., Can. E12 110
Cannington, On., Can. D10 112
Cannock, Eng., U.K. I10 12
Cannon, stm., Mn., U.S. G5 118
Cannonball, stm., N.D., U.S. A11 126
Cannon Beach, Or., U.S. E2 136
Cannon Falls, Mn., U.S. G6 118
Cannonvale, Austl. C7 76
Cann River, Austl. K7 76
Canoas, Braz. D12 92
Canoas, stm., Braz. C12 92
Canoe, B.C., Can. F11 138
Canoe, stm., B.C., Can. D12 138
Canoinhas, Braz. C12 92
Canon City, Co., U.S. C3 128
Cañon de Río Blanco, Parque Nacional, p.o.i., Mex. F10 100
Canonsburg, Pa., U.S. D5 114
Canoochee, stm., Ga., U.S. E4 116
Canora, Sk., Can. C11 124
Canosa di Púglia, Italy C10 24
Canossa, hist., Italy F7 22
Canouan, i., St. Vin. p11 105e
Canova, S.D., U.S. D15 126
Canova Beach, Fl., U.S. H5 116
Cañovanas, P.R. B4 104a
Canowindra, Austl. I7 76
Canso, N.S., Can. E16 110
Cantabria, state, Spain A6 20
Cantabrian Mountains see Cantábrica, Cordillera, mts., Spain A5 20
Cantábrica, Cordillera, mts., Spain A5 20
Cantagalo, Braz. K4 88
Cantal, state, Fr. D8 18
Cantalejo, Spain C7 20
Cantanhede, Braz. B3 88
Cantaura, Ven. C9 86
Canterbury, Eng., U.K. J14 12
Canterbury Bight, b., N.Z. G4 80
Canterbury Plains, pl., N.Z. G4 80
Can Tho, Viet. G7 48
Canton see Guangzhou, China J5 42
Canton, Il., U.S. D7 120
Canton, Ks., U.S. C11 128
Canton, Mn., U.S. H7 118
Canton, Ms., U.S. E8 122
Canton, Mo., U.S. D6 120
Canton, N.Y., U.S. D14 112
Canton, Oh., U.S. D4 114
Canton, Ok., U.S. E10 128
Canton, Pa., U.S. C9 114
Canton, S.D., U.S. H2 118
Canton, Tx., U.S. E3 122
Canton see Kanton, i., Kir. D9 72
Canton Lake, res., Ok., U.S. E10 128
Cantonment, Fl., U.S. G11 122
Cantù, Italy E6 22
Cantu, stm., Braz. B11 92
Cantwell, Ak., U.S. D10 140
Cañuelas, Arg. G8 92
Canumã, Braz. D6 84
Çanutama, Braz. E5 84
Čany, Russia C13 32
Čany, ozero, l., Russia D13 32
Canyon, Tx., U.S. G7 128
Canyon City, Or., U.S. F8 136
Canyon Creek, Ab., Can. A15 138
Canyon de Chelly National Monument, p.o.i., Az., U.S. G7 132
Canyon Ferry Lake, res., Mt., U.S. D15 136
Canyon Lake, res., Tx., U.S. E9 130
Canyonlands National Park, p.o.i., Ut., U.S. E6 132
Canyonville, Or., U.S. H3 136
Cao, stm., China D5 38
Cao Bang, Viet. A7 48
Cao Lanh, Viet. G7 48
Caombo, Ang. B2 68
Caorle, Italy E9 22
Caoxian, China D6 42
Cap, Pointe du, c., St. Luc. I7 105c
Çapac, Mi., U.S. E7 112
Čapaevo, Kaz. D8 32
Capanaparo, stm., S.A. D8 86
Capanema, Braz. D8 84
Capão Bonito, Braz. L1 88
Capão Doce, Morro do, mtn., Braz. C12 92
Caparaó, Parque Nacional do, p.o.i., Braz. K4 88
Caparo Viejo, stm., Ven. D6 86
Capatárida, Ven. B6 86
Cap aux Meules, Île du, i., Qc., Can. C14 110
Cap-Chat, Qc., Can. A10 110
Cap-de-la-Madeleine, Qc., Can. D4 110
Cape, stm., Austl. C5 76
Cape Barren Island, i., Austl. n13 77a
Cape Basin, unds. L14 144
Cape Breton Highlands National Park, p.o.i., N.S., Can. D16 110
Cape Breton Island, i., N.S., Can. D16 110
Cape Charles, Va., U.S. G9 114
Cape Coast, Ghana H4 64
Cape Cod Bay, b., Ma., U.S. C15 114
Cape Cod National Seashore, p.o.i., Ma., U.S. B16 114
Cape Coral, Fl., U.S. J4 116
Cape Dorset, Nu., Can. C15 106
Cape Elizabeth, Me., U.S. G6 110
Cape Fear, stm., N.C., U.S. B8 116
Cape Girardeau, Mo., U.S. G8 120
Cape Hatteras National Seashore, p.o.i., N.C., U.S. A10 116
Capelinha, Braz. I4 88
Cape Lisburne, Ak., U.S. C6 140
Capel'ka, Russia B11 10
Capella, Austl. D7 76
Capelongo, Ang. C2 68
Cape Lookout National Seashore, p.o.i., N.C., U.S. B9 116
Cape May, N.J., U.S. F10 114
Cape May Court House, N.J., U.S. E11 114
Cape Porpoise, Me., U.S. G6 110
Capernaum see Kefar Nahum, hist., Isr. F6 58
Cape Sable Island, i., N.S., Can. G11 110
Capesterre, Guad. i6 105c
Capesterre, Pointe de la, c., Guad. h5 105c
Capesterre-Belle-Eau, Guad. h5 105c
Cape Tormentine, N.B., Can. D12 110
Cape Town (Kaapstad), S. Afr. H4 70
Cape Verde, ctry., Afr. k9 65a
Cape Verde Basin, unds. G10 144
Cape Vincent, N.Y., U.S. D13 112
Cape York Peninsula, pen., Austl. B8 74
Cap-Haïtien, Haiti C11 102
Capilla del Monte, Arg. E5 92
Capim, stm., Braz. A2 88
Capinota, Bol. C3 90
Capira, Pan. H8 102
Capitan, N.M., U.S. H3 128
Capitán Arturo Prat, sci., Ant. B34 81
Capitán Bado, Para. D5 90
Capitán Bermúdez, Arg. F7 92
Capitán Meza, Para. C10 92
Capitão Enéas, Braz. I4 88
Capitola, Ca., U.S. G4 134
Capitol Peak, mtn., Nv., U.S. B8 134
Capitol Reef National Park, p.o.i., Ut., U.S. E5 132
Capivara, Represa de, res., Braz. D6 90
Capivari, Braz. L2 88
Capivari, stm., Braz. G6 88
Cap-Pelé, N.B., Can. D12 110
Cappella Islands, is., V.I.U.S. e7 104b
Capraia, Italy G6 22
Capraia, Isola di, i., Italy G6 22
Caprara, Punta, c., Italy C2 24
Caprarola, Italy B6 24
Capreol, On., Can. B9 112
Caprera, Isola, i., Italy C3 24
Capri, Italy D8 24
Capri, Isola di, i., Italy D8 24
Capricorn Channel, strt., Austl. D9 76
Capricorn Group, is., Austl. D9 76
Caprivi Strip, hist. reg., Nmb. D3 68
Capron, Il., U.S. B9 120
Captain Cook, Hi., U.S. D6 78a
Captain Cook Monument, hist., Norf. I. x25 78i
Captains Flat, Austl. J7 76
Capua, Italy C8 24
Capucapu, stm., Braz. H12 86
Capucin, c., Dom. i5 105c
Capulin Volcano National Monument, p.o.i., N.M., U.S. E5 128
Caquetá, state, Col. G4 86
Çaquetá (Japurá), stm., S.A. H7 86
Čara, Russia E12 34
Čara, stm., Russia E12 34
Carabinani, stm., Braz. I10 86
Carabobo, state, Ven. B7 86
Caracal, Rom. E11 26
Caracaraí, Braz. G11 86
Caracas, Ven. B8 86
Caracol, Braz. E4 88
Caraguatatuba, Braz. L3 88
Caraguatay, Para. B9 92
Carajás, Braz. E7 84
Carajás, Serra dos, hills, Braz. E7 84
Carakol, hist., Belize D3 102
Caranavi, Bol. C3 90
Carandaí, Braz. K4 88
Carangola, Braz. K4 88
Caransebeș, Rom. D9 26
Carapá, stm., Para. B10 92
Carapajó, Braz. B1 88
Cara-Paraná, stm., Col. H5 86
Carapina, Braz. K5 88
Caraquet, N.B., Can. C11 110
Caraș-Severin, state, Rom. D8 26
Caratasca, Laguna de, b., Hond. E5 102
Caratinga, Braz. J4 88
Carauari, Braz. D4 84
Caraúbas, Braz. C7 88
Caravaca de la Cruz, Spain F8 20
Caravelas, Braz. I6 88
Caravelí, Peru G3 84
Caravelle, Presqu'île la, pen., Mart. k7 105c
Caraway, Ar., U.S. B8 122
Carayaó, Para. B9 92
Carazinho, Braz. D11 92
Carballiño, Spain B2 20
Carballo, Spain A2 20
Carberry, Mb., Can. E14 124
Carbon, Ab., Can. E17 138
Carbon, Tx., U.S. B9 130
Carbonara, Capo, c., Italy E3 24
Carbondale, Co., U.S. D9 132
Carbondale, Il., U.S. G8 120
Carbondale, Pa., U.S. C10 114
Carbonear, Nf., Can. j23 107a
Carboneras de Guadazaón, Spain E9 20
Carbon Hill, Al., U.S. D11 122
Carbonia, Italy E2 24
Carcagente see Carcaixent, Spain E10 20
Carcaixent, Spain E10 20
Carcajou, stm., N.T., Can. B5 106
Carcans, Lac de, b., Fr. D4 18
Carcarañá, Arg. F7 92
Carcarañá, stm., Arg. F7 92
Carcassonne, Fr. F8 18
Carchi, state, Ec. G3 86
Carcross, Yk., Can. C3 106
Çardak, Tur. F12 28
Čardara, Kaz. F11 32
Čardarinskoe vodohranilišče, res., Asia A10 56
Cárdenas, Cuba A7 102
Cárdenas, Mex. F12 100
Cárdenas, Mex. D9 100
Cárdenas, Bahía de, b., Cuba A7 102
Cardiel, Lago, l., Arg. I2 90
Cardiff, Wales, U.K. J9 12
Cardigan, P.E., Can. D14 110
Cardigan, Wales, U.K. I8 12
Cardigan Bay, b., Wales, U.K. I8 12
Cardinal, On., Can. D14 112
Cardona, Ur. F9 92
Cardonal, Punta, c., Mex. A3 100
Cardoso, Ur. F9 92
Cardston, Ab., Can. G17 138
Cardwell, Austl. B5 76
Cardwell, Mo., U.S. H7 120
Cardwell Mountain, mtn., Tn., U.S. B13 122
Čardžev, Turkmen. B9 56
Carei, Rom. B9 26
Careiro, Braz. I12 86
Çareiro, Ilha do, i., Braz. I12 86
Čarèja, Bela. F12 10
Carencro, La., U.S. G6 122
Carey, Oh., U.S. D2 114
Carey, Lake, l., Austl. E4 74
Carey Downs, Austl. E3 74
Cargados Carajos Shoals, is., Mrts. K9 142
Carhaix-Plouguer, Fr. F5 14
Carhué, Arg. H6 92
Cariacica, Braz. K5 88
Cariaco, Golfo de, b., Ven. B9 86
Caribbean Sea D7 82
Cariboo, stm., B.C., Can. D9 138
Cariboo Mountains, mts., B.C., Can. D10 138
Caribou, Me., U.S. D8 110
Caribou Lake, l., On., Can. A9 118
Caribou Mountain, mtn., Me., U.S. E6 110
Caribou Mountains, mts., Ab., Can. D7 106
Carichic, Mex. B5 100
Caridade, Braz. C6 88
Carigara, Phil. E5 52
Carignan, Fr. E14 14
Carinda, Austl. H6 76
Carinhanha, Braz. H4 88
Carinhanha, stm., Braz. H3 88
Carini, Italy F7 24
Carinthia see Kärnten, state, Aus. D10 22
Caripito, Ven. B10 86
Carira, Braz. F7 88
Cariré, Braz. C5 88
Cariús, Braz. D6 88
Carleton, Mi., U.S. B2 114
Carleton, Mount, mtn., N.B., Can. C10 110
Carleton Place, On., Can. C13 112
Carletonville, S. Afr. E8 70
Cârlibaba, Rom. B12 26
Carlin, Nv., U.S. C9 134
Carlingford Lough, b., Eur. H7 12
Carlinville, Il., U.S. E8 120
Carlisle, Eng., U.K. G9 12
Carlisle, In., U.S. F10 120
Carlisle, Ia., U.S. C4 120
Carlisle, Ky., U.S. F1 114
Carlisle, Pa., U.S. D8 114
Carl Junction, Mo., U.S. G3 120
Carlos, Isla, i., Chile J2 90
Carlos Casares, Arg. G7 92
Carlos Chagas, Braz. I5 88
Carlos Pellegrini, Arg. E6 92
Carlow, Ire. I5 12
Carlow, state, Ire. I6 12
Carloway, Scot., U.K. C6 12
Carlsbad see Karlovy Vary, Czech Rep. F8 16
Carlsbad, Ca., U.S. J8 134
Carlsbad, N.M., U.S. B3 130
Carlsbad, Tx., U.S. C7 130
Carlsbad Caverns National Park, p.o.i., N.M., U.S. B3 130
Carlsberg Ridge, unds. I9 142
Carlton, Or., U.S. E3 136
Carlton, Tx., U.S. C9 130
Carlyle, Sk., Can. E11 124
Carlyle Lake, res., Il., U.S. F8 120
Carmacks, Yk., Can. C3 106
Carmagnola, Italy F4 22
Carman, Mb., Can. E16 124
Carmangay, Ab., Can. F17 138
Carmarthen, Wales, U.K. J8 12
Carmarthen Bay, b., Wales, U.K. J8 12
Carmel, Ca., U.S. G3 134
Carmel, In., U.S. I3 112
Carmel, N.Y., U.S. G16 112
Carmel Head, c., Wales, U.K. H8 12
Carmelo, Ur. F8 92
Carmel Valley, Ca., U.S. G4 134
Carmen see Ciudad del Carmen, Mex. F12 100
Carmen, stm., Chile D2 92
Carmen, Isla, i., Mex. C3 100
Carmen, Isla del, i., Mex. F13 100
Carmen de Areco, Arg. G8 92
Carmen de Patagones, Arg. H4 90
Carmi, Il., U.S. F9 120
Carmila, Austl. C7 76
Carmine, Tx., U.S. D11 130
Carmo do Paranaíba, Braz. J2 88
Carmona, Spain G5 20
Carmópolis de Minas, Braz. K3 88
Carnarvon, Austl. D2 74
Carnarvon, S. Afr. G5 70
Carnarvon National Park, p.o.i., Austl. E6 76
Čarnaučycy, Bela. H6 10
Carnduff, Sk., Can. E12 124
Carnegie, Austl. E4 74
Carnegie, Lake, l., Austl. E4 74
Carney Island, i., Ant. C29 81
Carnia, reg., Italy D9 22
Carnic Alps, mts., Eur. D9 22
Car Nicobar Island, i., India G7 46
Carnot, C.A.R. D3 66
Carnoustie, Scot., U.K. E10 12
Carnsore Point, c., Ire. I6 12
Carnwath, stm., N.T., Can. B5 106
Caro, Mi., U.S. E6 112
Carol City, Fl., U.S. K5 116
Carolina, Braz. D2 88
Carolina, P.R. B4 104a
Carolina, S. Afr. E10 70
Carolina Beach, N.C., U.S. B8 116
Caroline, at., Kir. D12 72
Caroline Islands, is., Oc. C5 72
Caron, Sk., Can. D8 124
Caroní, stm., Ven. C10 86
Carora, Ven. B6 86
Carpathian Mountains, mts., Eur. B13 26
Carpații Meridionali (Transylvanian Alps), mts., Rom. D11 26
Carpentaria, Gulf of, b., Austl. B7 74
Carpenter, Wy., U.S. F8 126
Carpenter Lake, res., B.C., Can. F8 138
Carpentersville, Il., U.S. B9 120
Carpentras, Fr. E11 18
Carpi, Italy F7 22
Carpina, Braz. D8 88
Cărpineni, Mol. C15 26
Carpinteria, Ca., U.S. I6 134
Carpio, N.D., U.S. F12 124
Carp Lake, l., B.C., Can. B7 138
Carpolac, Austl. K3 76
Carrabelle, Fl., U.S. H14 122
Carranza, Cabo, c., Chile G1 92
Carrara, Italy F7 22
Carrathool, Austl. J5 76
Carrauntoohil, mtn., Ire. I3 12
Carreta, Punta, c., Peru F2 84
Carriacou, i., Gren. q11 105e
Carrick on Shannon, Ire. H4 12
Carrick-on-suir, Ire. I5 12
Carrie, Mount, mtn., Wa., U.S. C3 136
Carriers Mills, Il., U.S. G9 120
Carrieton, Austl. I2 76
Carrillo, Mex. B6 100
Carrington, N.D., U.S. G14 124
Carrión, stm., Spain B6 20
Carrión de los Condes, Spain B6 20
Carrizal Bajo, Chile D2 92
Carrizo Creek, stm., U.S. E5 128
Carrizo Mountain, mtn., N.M., U.S. H3 128
Carrizo Springs, Tx., U.S. F7 130
Carroll, Ia., U.S. B3 120
Carroll, Ne., U.S. E15 126
Carrollton, Al., U.S. D10 122
Carrollton, Ga., U.S. D13 122
Carrollton, Mi., U.S. E5 112
Carrollton, Ms., U.S. D8 122
Carrollton, Mo., U.S. E4 120
Carrollton, Oh., U.S. D4 114
Carrollton, Tx., U.S. A10 130
Carrolltown, Pa., U.S. D7 114
Carron, stm., Austl. A3 76
Carrot, stm., Can. E10 106
Carrot River, Sk., Can. A10 124
Carry Falls Reservoir, res., N.Y., U.S. F2 110
Çarseland, Ab., Can. F17 138
Čarsk, Kaz. E14 32
Carson, N.D., U.S. A11 126
Carson, Wa., U.S. E5 136
Carson, East Fork, stm., U.S. E6 134
Carson City, Nv., U.S. D6 134
Carson Lake, res., Nv., U.S. D7 134
Carson Range, mts., U.S. D6 134
Carson Sink, l., Nv., U.S. D7 134
Carstairs, Ab., Can. E16 138
Cartagena, Chile F2 92
Cartagena, Col. B4 86
Cartagena, Spain G9 20
Cartago, Col. E3 86
Cartago, C.R. H6 102
Cartaxo, Port. E2 20
Cartaya, Spain G3 20
Carter, Ok., U.S. F9 128
Carter Lake, Ia., U.S. C2 120
Cartersville, Ga., U.S. C14 122
Carthage, Tun. H4 24
Carthage, Ar., U.S. C6 122
Carthage, Ms., U.S. E9 122
Carthage, Mo., U.S. G3 120
Carthage, N.C., U.S. A6 116
Carthage, S.D., U.S. C15 126
Carthage, Tn., U.S. H11 120
Carthage, Tx., U.S. E4 122
Carthage, hist., Tun. H4 24
Cartier Islands, is., Austl. B4 74
Cartwright, Mb., Can. E14 124
Caruaru, Braz. E8 88
Carúpano, Ven. B10 86
Carutapera, Braz. D8 84
Caruthersville, Mo., U.S. H8 120
Carutu, stm., Ven. E10 86
Carvoeiro, Braz. H10 86
Carvoeiro, Cabo, c., Port. E1 20
Cary, Ms., U.S. E8 122
Çary, N.C., U.S. I7 114
Čaryšskoe, Russia D14 32
Caryville, Fl., U.S. G13 122
Casablanca (Dar-el-Beida), Mor. C3 64
Casa Branca, Braz. K2 88
Casa de Piedra, Embalse, res., Arg. I4 92
Casa Grande, Az., U.S. K5 132
Casa Grande Ruins National Monument, p.o.i., Az., U.S. K5 132
Casale Monferrato, Italy E5 22
Casanare, state, Col. E6 86
Casanare, stm., Col. D6 86
Casa Nova, Braz. E5 88
Casar, N.C., U.S. A4 116
Casarano, Italy D12 24
Casar de Cáceres, Spain E4 20
Casas Adobes, Az., U.S. K6 132
Casas Grandes, stm., Mex. F9 98
Casavieja, Spain D6 20
Casca, Braz. D12 92
Cascadas Basaseachic, Parque Nacional, p.o.i., Mex. A4 100
Cascade, B.C., Can. G12 138
Cascade, Norf. I. y25 78i
Cascade, Ia., U.S. B6 120
Cascade, Mt., U.S. C15 136
Cascade, Wi., U.S. E1 112
Cascade Bay, b., Norf. I. y25 78i
Cascade Mountains see Cascade Range, mts., N.A. C3 108
Cascade Range, mts., N.A. C3 108
Cascade Reservoir, res., Id., U.S. F10 136
Cascais, Port. F1 20
Cascapédia, stm., Qc., Can. B10 110
Cascavel, Braz. C6 88
Cascavel, Braz. B11 92
Cascina, Italy G7 22
Case-Pilote, Mart. k6 105c
Caserta, Italy C8 24
Caseville, Mi., U.S. E6 112
Casey, Il., U.S. E9 120
Casey, sci., Ant. B16 81
Casey, Mount, mtn., Id., U.S. B10 136
Cashel, Ire. I5 12
Cashiers, N.C., U.S. A2 116
Cashmere, Wa., U.S. C6 136
Cashton, Wi., U.S. H8 118
Casigua, Ven. C5 86
Casilda, Arg. F7 92
Casino, Austl. G9 76
Çasiquiare, stm., Ven. F8 86
Čáslav, Czech Rep. G11 16
Çasma, Peru E2 84
Čašniki, Bela. F12 10
Casoli, Italy H11 22
Caspe, Spain C10 20
Casper, Wy., U.S. E6 126
Caspian Depression (Prikaspijskaja nizmennost'), pl. E7 32
Caspian Sea F7 32
Cass, stm., Mi., U.S. E6 112
Cassano allo Ionio, Italy E10 24
Cass City, Mi., U.S. E6 112
Casselman, On., Can. E1 110
Cássia, Braz. K2 88
Cassiar, B.C., Can. D5 106
Cassiar Mountains, mts., Can. D5 106
Cassilândia, Braz. C6 90
Cassinga, Ang. D2 68
Cassino, Italy C7 24
Cass Lake, Mn., U.S. D4 118
Cass Lake, res., Mn., U.S. D4 118
Cassongue, Ang. C1 68
Cassopolis, Mi., U.S. G3 112
Cassumba, Ilha, i., Braz. I6 88
Cassville, Mo., U.S. H4 120
Cassville, Wi., U.S. B7 120
Castagniccia, reg., Fr. G15 18
Castaños, Mex. H6 130
Castelbuono, Italy G8 24
Castelfranco Veneto, Italy E8 22
Castellammare, Golfo di, b., Italy F6 24
Castellammare del Golfo, Italy F6 24
Castellammare di Stabia, Italy D8 24
Castellana Grotte, Italy D11 24
Castellane, Fr. F12 18
Castellaneta, Italy D10 24
Castelli, Arg. B7 92
Castelli, Arg. H9 92
Castelló, co., Spain D10 20
Castelló de la Plana, Spain E11 20
Castellón de la Plana see Castelló de la Plana, Spain E11 20
Castellón de la Plana see Castelló, co., Spain D10 20
Castelnaudary, Fr. F7 18
Castelnau-Montratier, Fr. E7 18
Castelo, Braz. K5 88
Castelo Branco, Port. E3 20
Castelo Branco, state, Port. E3 20
Castelo de Paiva, Port. C2 20
Castel San Giovanni, Italy E6 22
Castelsarrasin, Fr. E6 18
Casteltermini, Italy G7 24
Castelvetrano, Italy G6 24
Casterton, Austl. K3 76
Castets, Fr. F4 18
Castiglione del Lago, Italy G8 22
Castile, N.Y., U.S. B7 114
Castilla, Peru E1 84
Castilla, Playa de, cst., Spain G4 20
Castilla-La Mancha, state, Spain E9 20
Castilla la Nueva, hist. reg., Spain E7 20
Castilla la Vieja (Old Castille), hist. reg., Spain C7 20
Castilla y León, state, Spain C6 20
Castillo de San Marcos National Monument, p.o.i., Fl., U.S. F5 116
Castillo Incaico de Ingapirca, hist., Ec. I2 86
Castillon-la-Bataille, Fr. E5 18
Castillos, Ur. G11 92
Castillos, Laguna de, l., Ur. G11 92
Castine, Me., U.S. F8 110
Castlebar, Ire. H3 12
Castle Bruce, Dom. j6 105c
Castle Dome Peak, mtn., Az., U.S. J2 132
Castlegar, B.C., Can. G13 138
Castle Hills, Tx., U.S. E9 130
Castleisland, Ire. I3 12
Castlemaine, Austl. K5 76
Castle Mountain, mtn., Yk., Can. C3 106
Castle Peak, mtn., Co., U.S. D9 132
Castlerea, Ire. H4 12
Castlereagh, stm., Austl. H7 76
Castle Rock, Co., U.S. B3 128
Castle Rock, Wa., U.S. D3 136
Castle Rock, mtn., Or., U.S. F8 136
Castle Rock Butte, mtn., S.D., U.S. B9 126
Castle Rock Lake, res., Wi., U.S. H8 118
Castletown, I. of Man G8 12
Castlewood, S.D., U.S. G1 118
Castor, Ab., Can. D19 138
Castor, stm., Mo., U.S. G7 120
Castres, Fr. F8 18
Castries, St. Luc. I6 105c
Castro, Braz. B13 92
Castro, Chile H2 90
Castro Barros, Arg. E5 92
Castro Daire, Port. D3 20
Castro del Río, Spain G6 20
Castronuño, Spain C5 20
Castro Verde, Port. G2 20
Castrovillari, Italy E10 24
Castroville, Ca., U.S. G4 134
Catacamas, Hond. E5 102
Catacaos, Peru E1 84
Catacocha, Ec. D2 84
Cataguazes, Braz. K4 88
Catahoula Lake, l., La., U.S. F6 122
Çatalan, Tur. A6 58
Catalão, Braz. J2 88
Çatalca, Tur. B11 28
Catalina, Chile B3 92
Catalina see Santa Catalina Island, i., Ca., U.S. J7 134
Catalina, Punta, c., Chile J3 90
Catalonia see Catalunya, state, Spain C12 20
Cataluña see Catalunya, state, Spain C12 20
Catalunya, state, Spain C12 20
Catamarca, state, Arg. C4 92
Catamayo, Ec. D2 84
Catanauan, Phil. D4 52
Catanduanes Island, i., Phil. D5 52
Catanduva, Braz. K1 88
Catania, Italy G9 24
Catania, Golfo di, b., Italy G9 24
Cataño, P.R. B3 104a
Catanzaro, Italy F10 24
Cataract Canyon, val., Az., U.S. H4 132
Catarina, Braz. D6 88
Catarino Rodríguez, Mex. C8 100
Catarman, Phil. F5 52
Catarman, Phil. D5 52
Catarroja, Spain E10 20
Catatumbo, stm., Ven. C5 86
Catawba, stm., U.S. B5 116
Catawissa, Pa., U.S. D9 114
Cat Ba, Dao, i., Viet. B8 48
Catbalogan, Phil. E5 52
Catedral, Cerro, hill, Ur. G10 92
Catete, Ang. B1 68
Cathcart, S. Afr. H8 70
Cathedral City, Ca., U.S. J9 134
Catherine, Mount see Katherîna, Gebel, mtn., Egypt J4 58
Catherines Peak, mtn., Jam. i14 104d
Cat Island, i., Bah. C9 96
Cat Lake, l., On., Can. E12 106
Catlettsburg, Ky., U.S. F3 114
Catlin, Il., U.S. H2 112
Catoche, Cabo, c., Mex. B4 102
Catolé do Rocha, Braz. D7 88
Catoosa, Ok., U.S. H2 120
Catriló, Arg. H6 92
Catrimani, stm., Braz. G11 86
Catskill, N.Y., U.S. B12 114
Catskill Mountains, mts., N.Y., U.S. B11 114
Catt, Mount, mtn., B.C., Can. B2 138
Cattaraugus, N.Y., U.S. B7 114
Cattolica, Italy G9 22
Catu, Braz. G6 88
Catuane, Moz. E11 70
Catur, Moz. C6 68
Çatwick, Îles, is., Viet. G9 48
Čatyrtaš, Kyrg. F13 32
Cau, stm., Viet. A7 48
Cauaburi, stm., Braz. G8 86
Caubvick, Mount, mtn., Can. F13 141
Cauca, state, Col. F3 86
Cauca, stm., Col. D4 86
Caucaia, Braz. B6 88
Caucasia, Col. D4 86
Caucasus, mts. F6 32
Caucete, Arg. E3 92
Cauchari, Salar de, pl., Arg. D3 90
Caudry, Fr. D12 14
Çaungula, Ang. B2 68
Čaunskaja guba, b., Russia C22 34
Cauquenes, Chile G1 92
Caura, stm., Ven. D9 86
Caurés, stm., Braz. H10 86
Căușani, Mol. C16 26
Causapscal, Qc., Can. B9 110
Caussade, Fr. E7 18
Cauto, stm., Cuba B9 102
Caux, Pays de, reg., Fr. E9 14
Cávado, stm., Port. C3 20
Cavaillon, Fr. F11 18
Cavalcante, Braz. G2 88
Cavalese, Italy D8 22
Cavalier, N.D., U.S. F16 124
Cavalla (Cavally), stm., Afr. H3 64
Cavalleria, Cap de, c., Spain D15 20
Cavally (Cavalla), stm., Afr. H3 64
Cavan, Ire. G5 12
Cavan, state, Ire. H5 12
Cavarzere, Italy E9 22
Çavdır, Tur. F12 28
Čave City, Ky., U.S. G11 120
Cave In Rock, Il., U.S. G9 120
Caveiras, stm., Braz. C12 92
Cavendish, Austl. K4 76
Cave Run Lake, res., Ky., U.S. F2 114
Cave Spring, Ga., U.S. C13 122
Caviana de Fora, Ilha, i., Braz. C8 84
Cavite, Phil. C3 52
Cavour, Canale, can., Italy E5 22
Çavuș, Tur. A2 58
Čavusy, Bela. G14 10
Cawood, Ky., U.S. H2 114
Cawston, B.C., Can. G11 138
Caxambu, Braz. K3 88
Caxias, Braz. C4 88
Caxias do Sul, Braz. D12 92
Caxito, Ang. B1 68
Çay, Tur. E13 28
Čayambe, Ec. G2 86
Cayambe, vol., Ec. G3 86
Cayce, S.C., U.S. C4 116
Çaycuma, Tur. B15 28
Čay Duong, Vinh, b., Viet. G7 48
Cayenne, Fr. Gu. C7 84
Cayey, P.R. B3 104a
Caylus, Fr. E7 18
Cayman Brac, i., Cay. Is. C8 102
Cayman Islands, dep., N.A. C7 102
Caynaba, Som. C9 66
Cayon, St. K./N. C2 105a
Cayuga, In., U.S. I2 112
Cayuga, Tx., U.S. F3 122
Cayuga Heights, N.Y., U.S. B9 114
Cayuga Lake, res., N.Y., U.S. B9 114
Cazalla de la Sierra, Spain G5 20
Cazaux et de Sanguinet, Étang de, l., Fr. E4 18
Cazères, Fr. F6 18
Cazombo, Ang. C3 68
Cazorla, Spain G7 20
Cea, stm., Spain B5 20
Ceanannas see Kells, Ire. H6 12
Ceará, state, Braz. C6 88
Ceará-Mirim, Braz. C8 88
Ceará-Mirim, stm., Braz. C8 88
Ceatharlach see Carlow, Ire. I5 12
Cebaco, Isla de, i., Pan. I7 102
Çeballos, Mex. B6 100
Čeboksary, Russia C7 32
Cebollar, Arg. D4 92
Cebollas, Mex. D6 100
Cebollatí, Ur. F11 92
Cebollatí, stm., Ur. F10 92
Céboruco, Volcán, vol., Mex. E6 100
Cebu, Phil. E4 52
Cebu, i., Phil. E4 52
Cebu Strait, strt., Phil. F4 52
Çeceda, Mex. H4 130
Çechtice, Czech Rep. G11 16
Čechy, hist. reg., Czech Rep. G10 16
Cecilia, Ky., U.S. G12 120
Cecil Plains, Austl. F8 76
Çecina, Italy G7 22
Čečnja, state, Russia F7 32
Cedar, stm., U.S. J7 118
Cedar, stm., Ne., U.S. F14 126
Cedar Bluffs, Ne., U.S. J2 118
Cedar Breaks National Monument, p.o.i., Ut., U.S. F3 132
Cedarburg, Wi., U.S. E1 112
Cedar City, Ut., U.S. F3 132
Cedar Creek, stm., Id., U.S. B2 132
Cedar Creek, stm., Ia., U.S. C5 120
Cedar Creek, stm., N.D., U.S. A11 126
Cedar Falls, Ia., U.S. B5 120
Cedar Grove, Wi., U.S. E2 112
Cedar Hill, Tn., U.S. H10 120
Cedar Key, Fl., U.S. G2 116
Cedar Lake, In., U.S. J11 118
Cedar Lake, l., On., Can. B11 112
Cedar Lake, res., Mb., Can. E10 106
Cedar Mountain, mtn., Ca., U.S. B5 134
Cedar Rapids, Ia., U.S. C6 120
Cedars of Lebanon see Arz Lubnān, for., Leb. D7 58
Cedar Springs, Mi., U.S. E4 112
Cedartown, Ga., U.S. C13 122
Cedar Tree Point, c., Antig. e4 105b
Cedarvale, B.C., Can. A2 138
Cedar Vale, Ks., U.S. D12 128
Cedarville, Ca., U.S. B5 134
Cedarville, Mi., U.S. B5 112
Cedeira, Spain A2 20
Cedillo, Embalse de, res., Eur. E3 20
Cedro, Braz. D6 88
Cedros, Mex. C8 100
Cedros, Isla, i., Mex. A1 100
Ceduna, Austl. F6 74
Ceelbuur, Som. D9 66
Ceepeecee, B.C., Can. G4 138
Ceerigaabo, Som. B9 66
Cefalonia see Kefallinía, i., Grc. E3 28
Cefalù, Italy F8 24
Çega, stm., Spain C6 20
Čegdomyn, Russia F15 34
Cegléd, Hung. B6 26
Ceglie Messapico, Italy D11 24
Çehegín, Spain F9 20
Čehov, Russia E20 10
Čehov, Russia G17 34
Çekalin, Russia F19 10
Çekuevo, Russia E18 8
Čelákovice, Czech Rep. F10 16
Celano, Italy H10 22
Celaya, Mex. E8 100
Celebes see Sulawesi, i., Indon. F7 44
Celebes Basin, unds. I15 142
Çelebes Sea, Asia E7 44
Čeleken, Turkmen. B7 56
Celeste, Tx., U.S. D2 122
Celestún, Mex. B2 102
Celina, Tn., U.S. H12 120
Çelina, Tx., U.S. D2 122
Čeljabinsk, Russia C10 32
Celjahany, Bela. H8 10
Çelje, Slvn. D12 22
Čeljuskin, mys, c., Russia A9 34
Čelkar, Kaz. E9 32
Çelle, Ger. D6 16
Čelmozero, Russia D14 8
Celtic Sea, Eur. J6 12
Çeltikçi, Tur. A1 58
Čemal, Russia D15 32
Cement, Ok., U.S. G10 128
Cenajo, Embalse del, res., Spain F9 20
Cenderawasih, Teluk, b., Indon. F10 44
Cenovo, Blg. F12 26
Centenario, Arg. I3 92
Center, Co., U.S. D2 128
Center, Mo., U.S. E6 120
Center, N.D., U.S. G12 124
Center, Tx., U.S. F4 122
Centerburg, Oh., U.S. D3 114
Center Hill, Fl., U.S. H3 116
Center Hill Lake, res., Tn., U.S. H12 120
Center Moriches, N.Y., U.S. D13 114
Center Point, Al., U.S. D12 122
Center Point, Ia., U.S. B6 120
Centerville, Ia., U.S. D5 120
Centerville, Mo., U.S. G7 120

Name — Map Ref. — Page

Centerville, Pa., U.S. D5 114
Centerville, Tn., U.S. B11 122
Centerville, Tx., U.S. F2 122
Centerville, Ut., U.S. C4 132
Central, Braz. F4 88
Central, Phil. D3 52
Central, Az., U.S. K7 132
Central, N.M., U.S. K8 132
Central, state, Bots. C8 70
Central, state, Para. B9 92
Central, state, Sol. Is. e8 79b
Central, Cordillera, mts., Col. E4 86
Central, Cordillera, mts., Peru E2 84
Central, Cordillera, mts., Phil. B3 52
Central, Cordillera, mts., P.R. B2 104a
Central, Massif, mts., Fr. D8 18
Central, Sistema, mts., Spain D6 20
Central African Republic, ctry., Afr. C4 66
Central Aguirre, P.R. C3 104a
Central Arizona Project Aqueduct, aq., U.S. J3 132
Central Bohemia see Středočeský, state, Czech Rep. G10 16
Central Borneo see Kalimantan Tengah, state, Indon. D8 50
Central Brāhui Range, mts., Pak. D10 56
Central Celebes see Sulawesi Tengah, state, Indon. D12 50
Central City, Il., U.S. F8 120
Central City, Ia., U.S. B6 120
Central City, Ky., U.S. G10 120
Central City, Pa., U.S. D7 114
Central Division, state, Fiji q19 79e
Centralia, Il., U.S. F8 120
Centralia, Ks., U.S. E1 120
Centralia, Mo., U.S. E5 120
Centralia, Wa., U.S. D4 136
Centralina, Braz. J1 88
Central Java see Jawa Tengah, state, Indon. G7 50
Central Kalahari Game Reserve, Bots. C6 70
Central Lake, Mi., U.S. C4 112
Central Makrān Range, mts., Pak. D9 56
Central'nyj, Russia C15 32
Central Pacific Basin, unds. I21 142
Central Point, Or., U.S. A2 134
Central Range, mts., Pap. N. Gui. a3 79a
Central Russian Upland see Srednerusskaja vozvyšennost', plat., Russia H20 10
Central Siberian Plateau see Srednesibirskoe ploskogor'e, plat., Russia C13 34
Central Siberian Uplands see Srednesibirskoe ploskogor'e, plat., Russia C13 34
Central Slovakia see Stredoslovenský Kraj, state, Slov. H15 16
Central Utah Canal, can., Ut., U.S. D4 132
Central Valley, Ca., U.S. C3 134
Central Valley see Longitudinal, Valle, val., Chile H1 92
Centre, Canal du, can., Fr. C10 18
Centreville, Al., U.S. E11 122
Centreville, Md., U.S. E9 114
Centreville, Ms., U.S. F7 122
Centro Puntas, P.R. B1 104a
Century, Fl., U.S. G11 122
Ceos see Kéa, i., Grc. F7 28
Čepelare, Blg. H11 26
Cephalonia see Kefallinía, i., Grc. E3 28
Cepu, Indon. G7 50
Ceram see Seram, i., Indon. F8 44
Ceram Sea see Seram, Laut, Indon. F8 44
Čerčany, Czech Rep. G10 16
Cerdas, Bol. D3 90
Cereal, Ab., Can. C3 124
Čereha, stm., Russia C11 10
Čeremhovo, Russia D18 32
Čeremšany, Russia B11 38
Čerepanovo, Russia D14 32
Čerepet', Russia F19 10
Čerepovec, Russia A20 10
Ceres, Arg. D7 92
Ceres, Braz. G8 84
Ceres, S. Afr. H4 70
Ceresco, Ne., U.S. J2 118
Ceresio see Lugano, Lago di, l., Eur. D14 18
Cereté, Col. C4 86
Čerevkovo, Russia F21 8
Cerignola, Italy C9 24
Cérilly, Fr. H11 14
Çerkeş, Tur. C15 28
Čerkessk, Russia F6 32
Çerkezköy, Tur. B10 28
Čerlak, Russia D12 32
Cermei, Rom. C8 26
Čermoz, Russia C9 32
Cerna, Rom. D15 26
Černá hora, mtn., Czech Rep. G9 16
Cernavodă, Rom. E15 26
Cernay, Fr. G16 14
Černigovka, Russia B10 38
Černjahovsk, Russia F4 10
Černogorsk, Russia D16 32
Černuška, Russia C9 32
Černyševsk, Russia F12 34
Černyševskij, Russia D11 34
Cerralvo, Isla, i., Mex. C4 100
Cërrik, Alb. C14 24
Cërriku see Cërrik, Alb. C14 24
Cerrillos, Arg. B5 92
Cerrillos, N.M., U.S. F2 128
Cerritos, Mex. D8 100
Cerro Azul, Arg. C10 92
Cerro Azul, Mex. E9 100
Cerro Azul, Peru F2 84
Cerro Chato, Ur. F10 92
Cerro de las Mesas, hist., Mex. F10 100
Cerro de Pasco, Peru F2 84
Cerro Gordo, Il., U.S. E9 120
Cerro Largo, Braz. D10 92
Cerro Moreno, Chile A2 92
Cerrón, Cerro, mtn., Ven. B6 86
Cerrón Grande, Embalse, res., El Sal. E3 102
Cerro Prieto, Mex. K10 134
Cerros Colorados, Embalse, res., Arg. I3 92
Cerro Tololo, Observatorio Astronómico, sci., Chile E2 92
Čerskij, Russia C21 34
Čerskogo, hrebet (Cherskiy Mountains), mts., Russia C17 34
Čertolino, Russia D16 10
Červen', Bela. G11 10
Červen Brjag, Blg. F11 26
Cervera, Spain C12 20
Cervera de Pisuerga, Spain B6 20
Cervia, Italy F9 22
Cervialto, Monte, mtn., Italy D9 24
Cervino see Matterhorn, mtn., Eur. D13 18
Cervione, Fr. G15 18
Cervo, Spain A3 20
Cesar, state, Col. C5 86
Cesar, stm., Col. B5 86
Cesena, Italy F9 22
Cesenatico, Italy F9 22
Cēsis, Lat. C8 10
Česká Kamenice, Czech Rep. F10 16
Česká Lípa, Czech Rep. F10 16
Česká Třebová, Czech Rep. G12 16
České Budějovice, Czech Rep. H10 16
Český Brod, Czech Rep. F10 16
Çeşme, Tur. E9 28
Češskaja guba (Chesha Bay), b., Russia C21 8
Cessnock, Austl. I8 76
Cesvaine, Lat. D9 10
Cetina, stm., Cro. G13 22
Cetinje, Yugo. G5 26
Ceuta, Sp. N. Afr. B3 64
Cévennes, reg., Fr. E9 18
Cévennes, Parc National des, p.o.i., Fr. E9 18
Cevizli, Tur. F14 28
Ceyhan, Tur. A6 58
Ceyhan, stm., Tur. B6 58
Ceylon, Mn., U.S. H4 118
Ceylon see Sri Lanka, ctry., Asia G5 53
Cèze, stm., Fr. E10 18
Cha-am, Thai. F5 48
Chabanais, Fr. D6 18
Chabás, Arg. F7 92
Chabjuwardoo Bay, b., Austl. D2 74
Chablais, reg., Fr. C12 18
Chacabuco, Arg. G7 92
Chachani, Nevado, vol., Peru G3 84
Chachapoyas, Peru E2 84
Chāchora, India F6 54
Chāchro, Pak. F3 54
Chaco, state, Arg. C7 92
Chaco, stm., N.M., U.S. G8 132
Chaco, Parque Nacional, p.o.i., Arg. C8 92
Chaco Austral, reg., Arg. C7 92
Chaco Boreal, reg., Para. D4 90
Chaco Central, reg., Arg. D4 90
Chaco Mesa, mtn., N.M., U.S. H9 132
Chad, ctry., Afr. E3 62
Chad, Lake, l., Afr. G7 64
Chadbourn, N.C., U.S. B7 116
Chadian, China H1 42
Chadron, Ne., U.S. E10 126
Chadwick, Il., U.S. I9 118
Chaem, stm., Thai. C4 48
Chāgai, Pak. D9 56
Chāgai Hills, hills, Asia D9 56
Chagos Archipelago, is., B.I.O.T. J10 142
Chagos-Lacadive Plateau, unds. J10 142
Chaguanas, Trin. s12 105f
Chaguaramas, Ven. C8 86
Chahal, Guat. E3 102
Chahanwusu see Dulan, China D4 36
Chahār Borjak, Afg. C9 56
Chahe, China E4 36
Chāībāsa, India G10 54
Chaihe, China B8 38
Chai Nat, Thai. E4 48
Chaiya, Thai. H4 48
Chaiyaphum, Thai. E6 48
Chajarí, Arg. E8 92
Chakaria, Bngl. H14 54
Chākdaha, India G12 54
Chake Chake, Tan. F7 66
Chākia, India E10 54
Chakkarat, Thai. E6 48
Chakradharpur, India G10 54
Chāksu, India E5 54
Chakwāl, Pak. B4 54
Chala, Peru G3 84
Chalais, Fr. D6 18
Chalatenango, El Sal. F3 102
Chalaxung, China E4 36
Chalbi Desert, des., Kenya D7 66
Chalcidice see Chalkidikí, hist. reg., Grc. C6 28
Chalcis see Chalkída, Grc. E6 28
Chaleur Bay, b., Can. C11 110
Chalía, stm., Arg. I2 90
Chālisgaon, India H5 54
Chalke see Chálki, i., Grc. G10 28
Chálki, i., Grc. G10 28
Chalkída, Grc. E6 28
Chalkidikí, hist. reg., Grc. C6 28
Chalk River, On., Can. B12 112
Challakere, India D3 53
Challapata, Bol. C3 90
Challenger Deep, unds. H17 142
Chalmette, La., U.S. H9 122
Châlons-sur-Marne, Fr. F13 14
Chalon-sur-Saône, Fr. H13 14
Chalosse, reg., Fr. F5 18
Chaltel, Cerro (Fitz Roy, Monte), mtn., S.A. I2 90
Chaluhe, China C6 38
Cham, Ger. G8 16
Chama, N.M., U.S. G10 132
Chama, stm., U.S. E2 128
Chama, stm., Ven. C6 86
Chamaicó, Arg. G5 92
Chaman, Pak. C10 56
Chamba, India B6 54
Chambal, stm., India E6 54
Chamberlain, Sk., Can. D8 124
Chamberlain, S.D., U.S. D13 126
Chamberlain, stm., Austl. C5 74
Chamberlain Lake, l., Me., U.S. D7 110
Chambers, Ne., U.S. E14 126
Chambersburg, Pa., U.S. E8 114
Chambers Island, i., Wi., U.S. C2 112
Chambéry, Fr. D11 18
Chambi, Jebel, mtn., Tun. B6 64
Chamblee, Ga., U.S. D14 122
Chambord, Qc., Can. B4 110
Chamdo see Qamdo, China E4 36
Chamical, Arg. E4 92
Chamo, Lake see Ch'amo Hāyk', l., Eth. F7 62
Ch'amo Hāyk', l., Eth. F7 62
Chamois, Mo., U.S. F6 120
Chamoli, India C7 54
Chamonix-Mont-Blanc, Fr. D12 18
Chāmpa, India G9 54
Champagne, hist. reg., Fr. F13 14
Champagne Castle, mtn., S. Afr. F9 70
Champagnole, Fr. H14 14
Champaign, Il., U.S. D9 120
Champaquí, Cerro, mtn., Arg. F5 92
Champasak, Laos E7 48
Champdoré, Lac, l., Qc., Can. D17 106
Champion, Ab., Can. F17 138
Champion, Mi., U.S. B1 112
Champion, Oh., U.S. G9 112
Champlain, Lake, l., N.A. D16 112
Champlitte-et-le-Prélot, Fr. G14 14
Champotón, Mex. C2 102
Chāmrājnagar Rāmasamudram, India F3 53
Chana, Thai. I5 48
Chañar, Arg. E4 92
Chañaral, Chile C2 92
Chañaral, Isla, i., Chile D2 92
Chancay, Peru F2 84
Chanchiang see Zhanjiang, China K4 42
Chanco, Chile G1 92
Chandalar, Ak., U.S. C10 140
Chandalar, stm., Ak., U.S. C10 140
Chandannagar, India G11 54
Chandausi, India D7 54
Chāndbāli, India H11 54
Chandeleur Islands, is., La., U.S. H10 122
Chandeleur Sound, strt., La., U.S. H9 122
Chandīgarh, India C6 54
Chandler, Qc., Can. B12 110
Chandler, Az., U.S. J5 132
Chandler, In., U.S. F10 120
Chandler, Tx., U.S. E3 122
Chandlerville, Il., U.S. D7 120
Chāndpur, Bngl. G13 54
Chāndpur, Bngl. G14 54
Chāndpur, India D7 54
Chandrapur, India B4 53
Chāndvad, India H5 54
Chang (Yangtze), stm., China F8 36
Chang, stm., China G1 42
Chang, Ko, i., Thai. F6 48
Changan see Xi'an, China D3 42
Changanācheri, India G3 53
Changane, stm., Moz. D11 70
Changcheng, China L3 42
Chang Cheng (Great Wall), misc. cult., China D6 36
Chang Chenmo, stm., Asia A7 54
Changchiak'ou see Zhangjiakou, China A6 42
Ch'angchih see Changzhi, China C5 42
Changchou see Changzhou, China F8 42
Changchou see Zhangzhou, China I7 42
Changchow see Changzhou, China F8 42
Changchow see Zhangzhou, China I7 42
Changchun, China C6 38
Changde, China G4 42
Chang Hu, l., China F5 42
Changhua, Tai. I9 42
Changhŭng, Kor., S. G7 38
Changji, China C2 36
Changjiang, China L3 42
Changkiakow see Zhangjiakou, China A6 42
Changli, China B8 42
Changling, China B5 38
Changlun, Malay. I5 48
Changmar, China A7 54
Changning, China G4 36
Changning, China H5 42
Ch'angnyŏng, Kor., S. D1 40
Changping, China A7 42
Changsa, China L4 42
Changsan-got, c., Kor., N. E6 38
Changsha, China G5 42
Changshan Qundao, is., China B10 42
Changshou, China G2 42
Changshu, China F9 42
Ch'angte see Changde, China G4 42
Changteh see Anyang, China C6 42
Changtien see Zibo, China C8 42
Changting, China B8 38
Changting, China I7 42
Changwŏn, Kor., S. D1 40
Changwu, China D2 42
Changxing, China F8 42
Changxing Dao, i., China B9 42
Changyi, China C8 42
Changyŏn-ŭp, Kor., N. E6 38
Changzhi, China C5 42
Changzhou, China F8 42
Chaniá, Grc. H7 28
Chanión, Kólpos, b., Grc. H6 28
Chankiang see Zhanjiang, China K4 42
Channagiri, India D2 53
Channapatna, India E3 53
Channel Country, reg., Austl. E3 76
Channel Islands, is., Eur. L10 12
Channel Islands, is., Ca., U.S. J6 134
Channel Islands National Park, p.o.i., Ca., U.S. J6 134
Channel-Port aux Basques, Nf., Can. j22 107a
Channelview, Tx., U.S. H3 122
Channing, Mi., U.S. B1 112
Channing, Tx., U.S. F6 128
Chan-si see Shanxi, state, China B5 42
Chantada, Spain B3 20
Chanthaburi, Thai. F6 48
Chantilly, Fr. E11 14
Chan-tong see Shandong, state, China C7 42
Chantrey Inlet, b., Nu., Can. B11 106
Chanute, Ks., U.S. G2 120
Chao, stm., China A7 42
Chao'an, China J7 42
Ch'aochou see Chao'an, China J7 42
Chaochow see Chao'an, China J7 42
Chao Hu, l., China F7 42
Chao Phraya, stm., Thai. E5 48
Chaor, stm., China B9 36
Chaoxian, China F7 42
Chaoyang, China D4 38
Chaoyang, China B7 38
Chaoyang, China J7 42
Chaoyangshan, China C6 38
Chapada dos Veadeiros, Parque Nacional da, p.o.i., Braz. H2 88
Chapadinha, Braz. B4 88
Chapala, Mex. E7 100
Chapala, Laguna de, l., Mex. E7 100
Chāparmukh, India E14 54
Chaparral, Col. F4 86
Chapecó, Braz. C11 92
Chapel Hill, N.C., U.S. I6 114
Chapelton, Jam. i13 104d
Chapéu, Morro do, mtn., Braz. H4 88
Chapicuy, Ur. E9 92
Chapin, Il., U.S. E7 120
Chapleau, On., Can. F14 106
Chaplin, Sk., Can. D7 124
Chaplin Lake, l., Sk., Can. D7 124
Chapman, Ne., U.S. F14 126
Chapman, Cape, c., Nu., Can. B13 106
Chapmanville, W.V., U.S. G3 114
Chapo, Mex. E3 130
Chappal, Waddi, mtn., Afr. H7 64
Chappell Hill, Tx., U.S. G2 122
Chapultepec, Mex. L9 134
Chaquiago, Arg. C4 92
Charadai, Arg. C8 92
Charalá, Col. D5 86
Charata, Arg. C7 92
Charcas, Mex. D8 100
Charco Hondo, P.R. B2 104a
Charcos de Risa, Mex. B7 100
Charcot Island, i., Ant. B33 81
Chard, Eng., U.K. K10 12
Charente, state, Fr. D6 18
Charente, stm., Fr. C6 18
Charente-Maritime, state, Fr. C5 18
Chari, stm., Afr. E3 62
Chārīkār, Afg. B10 56
Chariton, Ia., U.S. C4 120
Chariton, stm., U.S. E5 120
Chariton, Mussel Fork, stm., Mo., U.S. E5 120
Charity, Guy. B6 84
Charkhāri, India F7 54
Charkhlik see Ruoqiang, China D2 36
Charleroi, Bel. D13 14
Charles, Cape, c., Va., U.S. G10 114
Charles, Peak, mtn., Austl. F4 74
Charles City, Ia., U.S. A5 120
Charles City, Va., U.S. G8 114
Charles Island, i., Nu., Can. C16 106
Charles Mound, hill, Il., U.S. B7 120
Charles Point, c., Austl. B6 74
Charleston, Ar., U.S. B4 122
Charleston, Il., U.S. E9 120
Charleston, Ms., U.S. C8 122
Charleston, Mo., U.S. H8 120
Charleston, S.C., U.S. D6 116
Charleston, W.V., U.S. F4 114
Charleston Peak, mtn., Nv., U.S. G10 134
Charlestown, St. K./N. C2 105a
Charlestown, St. Vin. p11 105e
Charlestown, S. Afr. E9 70
Charlestown, In., U.S. F12 120
Charleville, Austl. F5 76
Charleville-Mézières, Fr. E13 14
Charlevoix, Lake, l., Mi., U.S. C5 112
Charlieu, Fr. C10 18
Charlotte, Mi., U.S. B1 114
Charlotte, N.C., U.S. A5 116
Charlotte, Tn., U.S. H10 120
Charlotte, Tx., U.S. F9 130
Charlotte Amalie, V.I.U.S. e7 104b
Charlotte Harbor, b., Fl., U.S. J3 116
Charlotte Lake, l., B.C., Can. D5 138
Charlottesville, Va., U.S. F7 114
Charlottetown, P.E., Can. D13 110
Charlotteville, Trin. r13 105f
Charlton Island, i., Nu., Can. E14 106
Charouine, Alg. D4 64
Charron Lake, l., Mb., Can. B18 124
Charroux, Fr. C6 18
Chārsadda, Pak. A3 54
Charter Oak, Ia., U.S. I3 118
Charters Towers, Austl. C6 76
Chartres, Fr. F10 14
Chascomús, Arg. G8 92
Chase, B.C., Can. F11 138
Chase, Mount, mtn., Me., U.S. D8 110
Chase City, Va., U.S. H7 114
Chaska, Mn., U.S. G5 118
Chateaubelair, St. Vin. o11 105e
Châteaubriant, Fr. G7 14
Château-du-Loir, Fr. G9 14
Châteaudun, Fr. F10 14
Chateaugay (Châteauguay), stm., N.A. D15 112
Châteaulin, Fr. F4 14
Châteauneuf-sur-Charente, Fr. D5 18
Château-Renault, Fr. G9 14
Château-Richer, Qc., Can. C5 110
Châteauroux, Fr. H10 14
Château-Thierry, Fr. E12 14
Châtellerault, Fr. H9 14
Chatfield, Mn., U.S. H6 118
Chatham, N.B., Can. C11 110
Chatham, On., Can. F7 112
Chatham, Eng., U.K. J13 12
Chatham, Il., U.S. E8 120
Chatham, La., U.S. E6 122
Chatham, Ma., U.S. C15 114
Chatham, N.Y., U.S. B12 114
Chatham, Isla, i., Chile J2 90
Chatham Islands, is., N.Z. H9 72
Chatham Rise, unds. N20 142
Chatham Strait, strt., Ak., U.S. E13 140
Châtillon-en-Bazois, Fr. G12 14
Châtillon-sur-Seine, Fr. G13 14
Chatkal Range, mts., Asia F12 32
Chatom, Al., U.S. F10 122
Chatra, India F10 54
Chatsworth, Austl. C3 76
Chatsworth, Ga., U.S. C14 122
Chatsworth, Il., U.S. D9 120
Chattahoochee, stm., U.S. G14 122
Chattanooga, Tn., U.S. B13 122
Chattaroy, W.V., U.S. G3 114
Chaturat, Thai. E5 48
Chaubourg, Mount, hill, St. Luc. I7 105c
Chaudière, stm., Qc., Can. D5 110
Chau Doc, Viet. G7 48
Chauk, Mya. B2 48
Chaumont, Fr. F13 14
Chauncey, Oh., U.S. E3 114
Chaungwabyin, Mya. F4 48
Chauny, Fr. E12 14
Chaupāran, India F10 54
Chautauqua Lake, l., N.Y., U.S. B6 114
Chauvin, La., U.S. H8 122
Chavakkad, India F2 53
Chavarría, Arg. D8 92
Chaves, Port. C3 20
Cháviva, Col. E5 86
Chawa'nanake, China C12 54
Chay, stm., Viet. A7 48
Chayuan, China G9 42
Chazy, N.Y., U.S. F3 110
Chbar, stm., Camb. F8 48
Cheaha Mountain, mtn., Al., U.S. D13 122
Cheat, stm., U.S. E6 114
Cheat, Shavers Fork, stm., W.V., U.S. E6 114
Cheb, Czech Rep. F8 16
Chebanse, Il., U.S. G2 112
Cheboygan, Mi., U.S. C5 112
Chech, 'Erg, des., Afr. E4 64
Chechnya see Čečnja, state, Russia F7 32
Chech'on, Kor., S. B1 40
Chęciny, Pol. F16 16
Checleset Bay, b., B.C., Can. F3 138
Checotah, Ok., U.S. B3 122
Chedabucto Bay, b., N.S., Can. E15 110
Cheduba Island, i., Mya. C1 48
Cheduba Strait, strt., Mya. C1 48
Cheektowaga, N.Y., U.S. B7 114
Cheepie, Austl. F5 76
Chef-Boutonne, Fr. C5 18
Chefoo see Yantai, China C9 42
Chehalis, Wa., U.S. D4 136
Chehalis, stm., Wa., U.S. D3 136
Cheju, Kor., S. H7 38
Cheju-do (Quelpart Island), i., Kor., S. H7 38
Chekiang see Zhejiang, state, China G8 42
Chela, Serra da, mts., Ang. D1 68
Chelan, Lake, res., Wa., U.S. B6 136
Chelif, Oued, stm., Alg. B5 64
Chełm, Pol. E19 16
Chełm, state, Pol. E19 16
Chełmno, Pol. C14 16
Chelmsford, On., Can. B8 112
Chelmsford, Eng., U.K. J13 12
Chełmża, Pol. C14 16
Chelsea, Ia., U.S. C5 120
Chelsea, Mi., U.S. B1 114
Chelsea, Vt., U.S. F4 110
Cheltenham, Eng., U.K. J10 12
Chelva see Xelva, Spain E9 20
Chelyuskin, Cape see Čeljuskin, mys, c., Russia A9 34
Chemainus, B.C., Can. H7 138
Chemba, Moz. D5 68
Chemnitz, Ger. F8 16
Chemult, Or., U.S. G5 136
Chenāb, stm., Asia D3 54
Chenango, stm., N.Y., U.S. B10 114
Chenchiang see Zhenjiang, China E8 42
Chenderoh, Tasik, l., Malay. J5 48
Chénéville, Qc., Can. E1 110
Cheney, Wa., U.S. C9 136
Cheney Reservoir, res., Ks., U.S. D10 128
Cheneyville, La., U.S. F6 122
Chengbu, China H4 42
Chengchou see Zhengzhou, China D5 42
Chengchow see Zhengzhou, China D5 42
Chengde, China A7 42
Chengdu, China E5 36
Chenggu, China E2 42
Chenghai, China J7 42
Chengmai, China L3 42
Chengshan Jiao, c., China C10 42
Chengteh see Chengde, China A7 42
Chengtu see Chengdu, China E5 36
Chengxian, China E1 42
Chengyang, China G8 42
Chengzitan, China B10 42
Ch'enhsien see Chenzhou, China I5 42
Chen Hu, l., China F5 42
Chenliu, China D6 42
Chennai (Madras), India E5 53
Chenoa, Il., U.S. D9 120
Chen-si see Shaanxi, state, China E3 42
Chentang, China J4 42
Chenxi, China H3 42
Chenxiangtun, China D5 38
Chenyang see Shenyang, China D5 38
Chenzhou, China I5 42
Cheonan see Ch'ŏnan, Kor., S. F7 38
Cheongju see Ch'ŏngju, Kor., S. F7 38
Chepén, Peru E2 84
Chepes, Arg. E4 92
Chepkotet, mtn., Kenya D7 66
Chepo, Pan. H8 102
Cher, state, Fr. B8 18
Cher, stm., Fr. B7 18
Cheradi, Isole, i., Italy D11 24
Cherbourg, Fr. E7 14
Cherchell, Alg. H13 20
Chergui, Chott ech, l., Alg. C5 64
Cheriton, Va., U.S. G10 114
Cheriyam Island, i., India F1 53
Cherkassy see Cherkasy, Ukr. E4 32
Cherkasy, Ukr. E4 32
Cherkessia see Karačaevo-Čerkesija, state, Russia F6 32
Chernihiv, Ukr. D4 32
Chernivtsi, Ukr. A12 26
Chernivtsi, co., Ukr. A13 26
Chernobyl see Chornobyl', Ukr. D4 32
Cherokee, Ia., U.S. B2 120
Cherokee, Ks., U.S. G3 120
Cherokee, Ok., U.S. E10 128
Cherokee, Tx., U.S. C9 130
Cherokee Lake, res., Tn., U.S. H2 114
Cherokee Point, c., Bah. J8 116
Cherokees, Lake O' The, res., Ok., U.S. H2 120
Cherokee Sound, Bah. J8 116
Cherrapunji, India F13 54
Cherry Creek, stm., S.D., U.S. C11 126
Cherry Hill, N.J., U.S. E10 114
Cherryvale, Ks., U.S. G2 120
Cherry Valley, Ar., U.S. B8 122
Cherryville, N.C., U.S. A4 116
Cherskiy Mountains see Čerskogo, hrebet, mts., Russia C17 34
Chesapeake, Va., U.S. H9 114
Chesapeake Bay, b., U.S. F9 114
Chesapeake Bay Bridge-Tunnel, Va., U.S. G9 114
Chesapeake Beach, Md., U.S. F9 114
Chesaw, Wa., U.S. B7 136
Chesha Bay see Češskaja guba, b., Russia C21 8
Cheshire, Ma., U.S. B12 114
Cheslatta Lake, l., B.C., Can. C5 138
Chesnee, S.C., U.S. A4 116
Chest Creek, stm., Pa., U.S. D7 114
Chester, Eng., U.K. H10 12
Chester, Ca., U.S. C4 134
Chester, Il., U.S. G8 120
Chester, Mt., U.S. B15 136
Chester, Ne., U.S. A11 128
Chester, Ok., U.S. E10 128
Chester, Pa., U.S. E10 114
Chester, Va., U.S. G8 114
Chester Basin, N.S., Can. F12 110
Chesterfield, Eng., U.K. H11 12
Chesterfield, S.C., U.S. B5 116
Chesterfield, Îles, is., N. Cal. E6 72
Chesterfield Inlet, Nu., Can. C12 106
Chesterfield Inlet, b., Nu., Can. C12 106
Chesterfield Islands see Chesterfield, Îles, is., N. Cal. E6 72
Chesterhill, Oh., U.S. E4 114
Chester-le-Street, Eng., U.K. G11 12
Chestertown, Md., U.S. E9 114
Chesterville, On., Can. C14 112
Chesuncook Lake, l., Me., U.S. E7 110
Chetek, Wi., U.S. F7 118
Chéticamp, N.S., Can. D16 110
Chetumal, Mex. C3 102
Chetumal, Bahía, b., N.A. C3 102
Chevelon Creek, stm., Az., U.S. I6 132
Cheviot, Oh., U.S. E13 120
Cheviot Hills, hills, U.K. F10 12
Ch'ew Bahir see Stefanie, Lake, l., Afr. G7 62
Chewelah, Wa., U.S. B9 136
Cheyenne, Ok., U.S. F9 128
Cheyenne, Wy., U.S. F8 126
Cheyenne, stm., U.S. C11 126
Cheyenne Wells, Co., U.S. C6 128
Cheyne Bay, b., Austl. F3 74
Chhabra, India F6 54
Chhapra, India F10 54
Chhātak, Bngl. F13 54
Chhatarpur, India F7 54
Chhatrapur, India E6 46
Chhattīsgarh, pl., India H9 54
Chhay Arêng, stm., Camb. G6 48
Chhêb Kândal, Camb. F7 48
Chhindwāra, India H7 54
Chhlong, stm., Camb. F8 48
Chhota-Chhindwāra, India G7 54
Chhota Udepur Mhow, India D3 46
Chi, stm., China E7 42
Chi, stm., Thai. E7 48
Chía, Col. E4 86
Chiahsing see Jiaxing, China F9 42
Chiai, Tai. J9 42
Chiamussu see Jiamusi, China B11 36
Chian see Ji'an, China H6 42
Chiang Dao, Thai. C4 48
Chiange, Ang. D1 68
Chiang Kham, Thai. C5 48
Chiang Khan, Thai. D5 48
Chiang Mai, Thai. C4 48
Chiangmen see Jiangmen, China J5 42
Chiang Rai, Thai. C4 48
Chiang Saen, Thai. B4 48
Chiangtu see Yangzhou, China E8 42
Chiangyin see Jiangyin, China F9 42
Chiaohsien see Jiaoxian, China C8 42
Chiaotso see Jiaozuo, China D5 42
Chiapas, state, Mex. D6 96
Chiavari, Italy F6 22
Chiavenna, Italy D6 22
Chiba, Japan D13 40
Chiba, state, Japan D13 40
Chibabava, Moz. B11 70
Chibemba, Ang. D1 68
Chibougamau, Qc., Can. F15 106
Chibuto, Moz. D11 70
Chibuzhangchu Hu, l., China B13 54
Chicago, Il., U.S. G2 112
Chicago Heights, Il., U.S. C10 120
Chicapa, stm., Afr. B3 68
Chichagof Island, i., Ak., U.S. E12 140
Chīchāwatni, Pak. C4 54
Chicheng, China A6 42
Chichén Itzá, hist., Mex. B3 102
Chichester, Eng., U.K. K12 12
Chichibu, Japan C11 40
Ch'ich'ihaerh see Qiqihar, China B9 36
Chichiriviche, Ven. B7 86
Chickamauga, Ga., U.S. C13 122
Chickamauga Lake, res., Tn., U.S. B14 122
Chickasaw, Al., U.S. G10 122
Chickasawhay, stm., Ms., U.S. F10 122
Chickasaw National Recreation Area, p.o.i., Ok., U.S. G12 128
Chickasha, Ok., U.S. F11 128
Chicken, Ak., U.S. D11 140
Chiclana de la Frontera, Spain H4 20
Chiclayo, Peru E2 84
Chico, Ca., U.S. D4 134
Chico, Tx., U.S. H11 128
Chico, stm., Arg. I2 90
Chico, stm., Arg. I3 90
Chico, stm., Phil. B3 52
Chicomba, Ang. C2 68
Chicopee, Ga., U.S. B2 116
Chicopee, Ma., U.S. B13 114
Chicoutimi, Qc., Can. B5 110
Chicoutimi, stm., Qc., Can. B5 110
Chicuma, Ang. C1 68
Chidambaram, India F4 53
Chidenguele, Moz. D12 70
Chiefland, Fl., U.S. G3 116
Chiehyang see Jieyang, China J7 42
Chiemsee, l., Ger. I8 16
Chieo Lan Reservoir, res., Thai. H4 48
Chieri, Italy F4 22
Chiese, stm., Italy E7 22
Chieti, Italy H11 22
Chifeng, China C3 38
Chigasaki, Japan D12 40
Chignahuapan, Mex. F9 100
Chignecto, Cape, c., N.S., Can. E11 110
Chignecto Bay, b., Can. E12 110
Chignik, Ak., U.S. E8 140
Chigoubiche, Lac, l., Qc., Can. A3 110
Chigubo, Moz. C11 70
Chigu Co, l., China D13 54
Ch'ihfeng see Chifeng, China C3 38
Chihli, Gulf of see Bo Hai, b., China B8 42
Chihsi see Jixi, China B9 38
Chihuahua, Mex. A5 100
Chihuahua, state, Mex. B3 96
Chihuahua, Desierto de, des., N.A. F6 108
Chihuahuan Desert see Chihuahua, Desierto de, des., N.A. F6 108
Chii-san, mtn., Kor., S. G7 38
Chikaskia, stm., U.S. E11 128
Chik Ballāpur, India E3 53
Chikhli, India H6 54
Chikmagalūr, India E2 53
Chiknāyakanhalli, India E3 53
Chikodi, India C2 53
Chikrêng, stm., Camb. F7 48
Chikuma, stm., Japan C11 40
Chi-kyaw, Mya. B1 48
Chilakalūrupet, India C4 53
Chilako, stm., B.C., Can. C7 138
Chilanko Forks, B.C., Can. D6 138
Chilapa de Álvarez, Mex. G9 100
Chilās, Pak. B11 56
Chilcotin, stm., B.C., Can. E8 138
Childers, Austl. E9 76
Childersburg, Al., U.S. D12 122
Childress, Tx., U.S. G8 128
Chile, ctry., S.A. F2 90
Chile Chico, Chile I2 90
Chilecito, Arg. F3 92
Chilecito, Arg. D4 92
Chile Rise, unds. M5 144
Chilhowie, Va., U.S. H4 114
Chilia, Brațul, stm., Eur. D16 26
Chilika Lake, l., India I10 54
Chililabombwe, Zam. C4 68
Chilin see Jilin, China C7 38
Chilko, stm., B.C., Can. D7 138
Chilko Lake, l., B.C., Can. E6 138
Chillagoe, Austl. C8 74
Chillán, Chile H1 92
Chillicothe, Mo., U.S. E4 120
Chillicothe, Oh., U.S. E3 114
Chillicothe, Tx., U.S. G9 128
Chilliwack, B.C., Can. G9 138
Chiloé, Isla Grande de, i., Chile H2 90
Chilón, Mex. G12 100
Chiloquin, Or., U.S. H5 136
Chilpancingo de los Bravo, Mex. G9 100
Chiluage, Ang. B3 68
Chilumba, Mwi. C5 68
Chilung, Tai. I9 42
Chilwa, Lake, l., Afr. D6 68
Chimaltenango, Guat. E2 102
Chimán, Pan. H8 102

Name | Map Ref. | Page

Chimayo, N.M., U.S. E3 128
Chimbarongo, Chile G2 92
Chimbas, Arg. E3 92
Chimborazo, state, Ec. H2 86
Chimborazo, vol., Ec. H2 86
Chimbote, Peru E2 84
Chimoio, Moz. D5 68
Chimpay, Arg. G3 90
Chin, state, Mya. B1 48
China, Mex. C9 100
China, ctry., Asia B8 46
Chinan see Jinan, China C7 42
Chinandega, Nic. F4 102
Chinati Peak, mtn., Tx., U.S. E3 130
Chincha Alta, Peru F2 84
Chinchaga, stm., Can. D7 106
Chinchilla, Austl. F8 76
Chinchilla de Monte-Aragón, Spain F9 20
Chinchiná, Col. E4 86
Chinchou see Jinzhou, China A9 42
Chinchow see Jinzhou, China A9 42
Chincolco, Chile F2 92
Chincoteague, Va., U.S. G10 114
Chinde, Moz. D6 68
Chindo, Kor., S. G7 38
Chin-do, i., Kor., S. G7 38
Chindong, Kor., S. D1 40
Chindwinn, stm., Mya. D7 46
Ch'ingchiang see Qingjiang, China E8 42
Chingleput, India E4 53
Chingola, Zam. C4 68
Chingshih see Jinshi, China G4 42
Ch'ingtao see Qingdao, China C9 42
Chingtechen see Jingdezhen, China G7 42
Chinguetti, Maur. E2 64
Chinhae, Kor., S. D1 40
Chin Hills, hills, Mya. D7 46
Chinhoyi, Zimb. D5 68
Chinhsien see Jinzhou, China B9 42
Chinhua see Jinhua, China G8 42
Ch'inhuangtao see Qinhuangdao, China B8 42
Chining see Jining, China D7 42
Chining see Jining, China A5 42
Chiniot, Pak. C4 54
Chinit, stm., Camb. F7 48
Chinjan, Pak. C1 54
Chinju, Kor., S. G7 38
Chinkiang see Zhenjiang, China E8 42
Chinko, stm., C.A.R. C4 66
Chinle, Az., U.S. G7 132
Chinle Wash, stm., Az., U.S. G7 132
Chinmen Tao (Quemoy), i., Tai. I8 42
Chino, Ca., U.S. J8 134
Chinon, Fr. G9 14
Chinook, Ab., Can. C2 124
Chinook Cove, B.C., Can. E10 138
Chino Valley, Az., U.S. I4 132
Chinquapin, N.C., U.S. B8 116
Chinsali, Zam. C5 68
Chintāmani, India E4 53
Chinú, Col. C4 86
Chinwangtao see Qinhuangdao, China B8 42
Chioco, Moz. D5 68
Chioggia, Italy E9 22
Chíos, Grc. E9 28
Chíos, i., Grc. E8 28
Chios see Chíos, i., Grc. E8 28
Chipata, Zam. C5 68
Chip Lake, l., Ab., Can. C15 138
Chiplūn, India C1 53
Chipman, N.B., Can. D11 110
Chipola, stm., Fl., U.S. G13 122
Chippenham, Eng., U.K. J10 12
Chippewa, stm., Mn., U.S. F3 118
Chippewa, stm., Wi., U.S. G6 118
Chippewa, East Fork, stm., Wi., U.S. F8 118
Chippewa Falls, Wi., U.S. G7 118
Chiquimula, Guat. E3 102
Chiquinquirá, Col. E4 86
Chīrāla, India D5 53
Chirāwa, India D5 54
Chiredzi, Zimb. B10 70
Chireno, Tx., U.S. F4 122
Chirfa, Niger E7 64
Chīrgaon, India F7 54
Chiribiquete, Parque Nacional, p.o.i., Col. G5 86
Chiricahua Mountains, mts., Az., U.S. L7 132
Chiricahua National Monument, p.o.i., Az., U.S. L7 132
Chiricahua Peak, mtn., Az., U.S. L7 132
Chiriguaná, Col. C5 86
Chirikof Island, i., Ak., U.S. E8 140
Chiriquí, Golfo de, b., Pan. H6 102
Chiriquí, Laguna de, b., Pan. H6 102
Chiromo, Mwi. D5 68
Chirpan see Čirpan, Blg. G12 26
Chirripó, Cerro, mtn., C.R. H6 102
Chirripó, Parque Nacional, p.o.i., C.R. H6 102
Chisago City, Mn., U.S. F5 118
Chisamba, Zam. C4 68
Chisasibi, Qc., Can. E15 106
Chisep'o, Kor., S. E1 40
Ch'ishan, Tai. J9 42
Chisholm, Ab., Can. B16 138
Chisholm, Me., U.S. F6 110
Chisholm, Mn., U.S. D5 118
Chishtiān Mandi, Pak. D4 54
Chishui, China G1 42
Chishui, stm., China F6 36
Chisimayu see Kismaayo, Som. E8 66
Chişinău, Mol. B15 26
Chişineu-Criş, Rom. C8 26
Chita, Col. D5 86
Chitado, Ang. D1 68
Chitagá, Col. D5 86
Chita-hantō, pen., Japan E9 40
Chitato, Ang. B3 68
Chitek Lake, l., Mb., Can. B14 124
Chitembo, Ang. C2 68
Chitina, Ak., U.S. D11 140
Chitina, stm., Ak., U.S. D11 140
Chitipa, Mwi. B5 68
Chitokoloki, Zam. C3 68
Chitose, Japan C14 38
Chitradurga, India D3 53
Chitrakūt Dham, India F8 54
Chitrāl, Pak. B11 56
Chitrāvati, stm., India D3 53
Chitré, Pan. H7 102
Chittagong, Bngl. G13 54
Chittagong, state, Bngl. G13 54
Chittāpur, India C3 53
Chittaurgarh, India F5 54
Chittoor, India E4 53
Chittūr, India F3 53
Chitungwiza, Zimb. D5 68
Chiuchiang see Jiujiang, China G6 42
Chiumbe (Tshumbe), stm., Afr. B3 68
Chiume, Ang. D3 68
Chiusi, Italy G8 22
Chiva see Xiva, Spain E10 20
Chivacoa, Ven. B7 86
Chivasso, Italy E4 22
Chivi, Zimb. B10 70
Chivilcoy, Arg. G7 92
Chivirira Falls, wtfl, Zimb. B11 70
Chizu, Japan D7 40
Chloride, Az., U.S. H2 132
Chmielnik, Pol. F16 16
Chŏâm Khsant, Camb. E7 48
Choapa, stm., Chile E2 92
Choceň, Czech Rep. F12 16
Chochis, Cerro, mtn., Bol. C5 90
Choch'iwŏn, Kor., S. F7 38
Chociwel, Pol. C11 16
Chocó, state, Col. E3 86
Chocolate Mountains, mts., U.S. J1 132
Chocontá, Col. E5 86
Chocope, Peru E2 84
Choctawhatchee, West Fork, stm., Al., U.S. G13 122
Choctawhatchee Bay, b., Fl., U.S. G12 122
Chodzież, Pol. D12 16
Choele Choel, Arg. G3 90
Choiseul, St. Luc. m6 105c
Choiseul, state, Sol. Is. d7 79b
Choiseul, i., Sol. Is. d7 79b
Chojna, Pol. D10 16
Chojnice, Pol. C13 16
Chojnów, Pol. E11 16
Ch'ok'ē, mts., Eth. E7 62
Choke Canyon Reservoir, res., Tx., U.S. F9 130
Chokio, Mn., U.S. F2 118
Chókwe, Moz. D11 70
Cholet, Fr. G8 14
Choluteca, Hond. F4 102
Choluteca, stm., Hond. F4 102
Choma, Zam. D4 68
Chomo Lhāri, mtn., Asia E12 54
Chomūm, India E5 54
Chomutov, Czech Rep. F9 16
Ch'ŏnan, Kor., S. F7 38
Chon Buri, Thai. F5 48
Chon Daen, Thai. D5 48
Chone, Ec. H1 86
Chong'an, China H8 42
Ch'ŏngdo, Kor., S. D1 40
Ch'ŏngjin, Kor., N. D8 38
Ch'ŏngju, Kor., S. F7 38
Chŏng Kal, Camb. E6 48
Chongming, China I4 38
Chongming Dao, i., China F9 42
Chongoroi, Ang. C1 68
Chongqing (Chungking), China G2 42
Chŏngsŏn, Kor., S. B1 40
Chŏngŭp, Kor., S. G7 38
Chongxin, China D2 42
Chongzuo, China A8 48
Chŏnju, Kor., S. G7 38
Chonos, Archipiélago de los, is., Chile I1 90
Ch'ŏnsu-ri, Kor., N. D8 38
Chontaleña, Cordillera, mts., Nic. G5 102
Cho Oyu see Chopu, mtn., Asia D11 54
Cho Oyu see Qowowuyag, mtn., Asia D11 54
Chop, Ukr. A9 26
Chopda, India H5 54
Chopim, stm., Braz. C11 92
Chopinzinho, Braz. B11 92
Chopu (Qowowuyag), mtn., Asia D11 54
Chorna, Ukr. B16 26
Chornobyl', Ukr. D4 32
Choros, Isla, i., Chile D2 92
Ch'ŏrwŏn, Kor., S. E7 38
Chorzele, Pol. C16 16
Chosen, Fl., U.S. J5 116
Chōshi, Japan D13 40
Chosica, Peru F2 84
Chos Malal, Arg. H2 92
Choszczno, Pol. C11 16
Choteau, Mt., U.S. C14 136
Chotila, India G3 54
Chouchiak'ou see Shangshui, China E6 42
Chouk'ou see Shangshui, China E6 42
Choushan Islands see Zhoushan Qundao, is., China F10 42
Chowchilla, Ca., U.S. F5 134
Chown, Mount, mtn., Ab., Can. C11 138
Choya, Arg. D5 92
Choybalsan, Mong. B7 36
Choyr, Mong. B6 36
Chrisman, Il., U.S. I2 112
Christanshåb (Qasigiannguit), Grnld. D15 141
Christchurch, N.Z. F5 80
Christian, Cape, c., Nu., Can. A17 106
Christian, Point, c., Pit. c28 78k
Christiana, Jam. i13 104d
Christiana, S. Afr. E7 70
Christian Island, i., On., Can. D9 112
Christiansburg, Va., U.S. G5 114
Christian Sound, strt., Ak., U.S. E12 140
Christianstad, V.I.U.S. h11 104c
Christmas Island, dep., Oc. K13 142
Christmas Island, i., Christ. I. E1 72
Christmas Island see Kiritimati, at., Kir. C11 72
Christmas Ridge, unds. I22 142
Christoval, Tx., U.S. C7 130
Chrudim, Czech Rep. G11 16
Chrzanów, Pol. F15 16
Chu (Xam), stm., Asia B7 48
Chuādanga, Bngl. G12 54
Chuanchou see Quanzhou, China I8 42
Chubbuck, Id., U.S. H14 136
Chūbu-Sangaku-kokuritsu-kōen, p.o.i., Japan C10 40
Chubut, state, Arg. H3 90
Chubut, stm., Arg. H3 90
Ch'üchiang see Shaoguan, China I5 42
Chuchi Lake, l., B.C., Can. A6 138
Chuchou see Zhuzhou, China H5 42
Chuchow see Zhuzhou, China H5 42
Chu Chua, B.C., Can. E10 138
Chucunaque, stm., Pan. H9 102
Chugach Mountains, mts., Ak., U.S. D10 140
Chuginadak Island, i., Ak., U.S. g25 140a
Chūgoku-sanchi, mts., Japan D6 40
Chugwater Creek, stm., Wy., U.S. F8 126
Chuhuichupa, Mex. G8 98
Chuí, Braz. F11 92
Chukchi Sea C5 94
Chuke Hu, l., China C11 54
Chukotsk Peninsula see Čukotskij poluostrov, pen., Russia C26 34
Chula Vista, Ca., U.S. K8 134
Chulucanas, Peru E1 84
Chumbicha, Arg. D4 92
Chum Phae, Thai. D6 48
Chumphon, Thai. G4 48
Chumphon Buri, Thai. E6 48
Chum Saeng, Thai. E5 48
Chumunjin, Kor., S. B1 40
Chun'an, China G8 42
Chunan, Tai. I9 42
Chuncheon see Ch'unch'ŏn, Kor., S. F7 38
Chunchi, Ec. I2 86
Ch'unch'ŏn, Kor., S. F7 38
Chunchula, Al., U.S. G10 122
Ch'ungch'ŏng-bukto, state, Kor., S. B1 40
Ch'ungju, Kor., S. F7 38
Chungking see Chongqing, China G2 42
Ch'ungmu, Kor., S. E1 40
Chungshan see Zhongshan, China J5 42
Chungyang Shanmo, mts., Tai. J9 42
Chunhua, China D3 42
Chunhuhux, Mex. C3 102
Chuquibamba, Peru G3 84
Chuquicamata, Chile D3 90
Chur (Coire), Switz. D6 22
Church Hill, Tn., U.S. H3 114
Churchill, Mb., Can. D12 106
Churchill, stm., Can. D11 106
Churchill, stm., Nf., Can. E18 106
Churchill, Mount, mtn., B.C., Can. G7 138
Churchill, Mount, vol., Ak., U.S. D11 140
Churchill Falls, wtfl, Nf., Can. E17 106
Churchill Lake, l., Sk., Can. D9 106
Church Point, La., U.S. G6 122
Church Rock, N.M., U.S. H8 132
Chūru, India D5 54
Churubusco, In., U.S. G4 112
Churuguara, Ven. B7 86
Chushul, India B7 54
Chute-Saint-Philippe, Qc., Can. D1 110
Chutung, Tai. I9 42
Chuuk, is., Micron. C6 72
Chuvashia see Čuvašija, state, Russia C7 32
Chuxian, China E8 42
Chuxiong, China F5 36
Ci, stm., China B6 42
Ci, stm., China E6 42
Ciadâr Lunga, Mol. C15 26
Ciales, P.R. B3 104a
Ciamis, Indon. G6 50
Cianjur, Indon. G5 50
Cianorte, Braz. A11 92
Čiatura, Geor. F6 32
Ciawi, Indon. G5 50
Cibaliung, Indon. G4 50
Cibatu, Indon. G6 50
Cibinong, Indon. G5 50
Cibolo Creek, stm., Tx., U.S. E3 130
Cibolo Creek, stm., Tx., U.S. E10 130
Cicero, Il., U.S. G2 112
Cicero, In., U.S. H3 112
Cícero Dantas, Braz. F6 88
Cicurug, Indon. G5 50
Cidra, P.R. B3 104a
Ciechanów, Pol. D16 16
Ciechanów, state, Pol. C16 16
Ciechanowiec, Pol. D18 16
Ciego de Ávila, Cuba B8 102
Ciempozuelos, Spain D7 20
Ciénaga, Col. B4 86
Ciénega de Flores, Mex. H7 130
Cienfuegos, Cuba A7 102
Cíes, Illas, is., Spain B1 20
Cies, Islas see Cíes, Illas, is., Spain B1 20
Cieszanów, Pol. F19 16
Cieszyn, Pol. G14 16
Cieza, Spain F9 20
Çifteler, Tur. D13 28
Cifuentes, Spain D8 20
Cigüela, stm., Spain E7 20
Çihanbeyli, Tur. E15 28
Čiili, Kaz. F11 32
Cijara, Embalse de, res., Spain E6 20
Cijulang, Indon. G6 50
Cikampek, Indon. G5 50
Čikobia, i., Fiji o20 79e
Čikoj, Russia F10 34
Cilacap, Indon. G6 50
Cilamaya, Indon. G5 50
Cilento, reg., Italy D9 24
Cili, China G4 42
Cilician Gates see Gülek Boğazı, p., Tur. A5 58
Čilik, Kaz. F13 32
Cill Chainnigh see Kilkenny, Ire. I5 12
Cilleruelo de Bezana, Spain B7 20
Cil'ma, stm., Russia D24 8
Cimarron, N.M., U.S. E4 128
Cimarron, stm., U.S. F12 128
Cimarron, North Fork, stm., U.S. D7 128
Čimbaj, Uzb. F9 32
Cimişlia, Mol. C15 26
Cimljanskoe vodohranilišče, res., Russia E6 32
Cimone, Monte, mtn., Italy F7 22
Cimpu, Indon. E12 50
Cina, Tanjung, c., Indon. G4 50
Cinaruco, stm., Ven. D7 86
Cinaruco-Capanaparo Santos Luzardo, Parque Nacional, p.o.i., Ven. D8 86
Cinca, stm., Spain C11 20
Cincinnati, Ia., U.S. D4 120
Cincinnati, Oh., U.S. E1 114
Cinco, Canal Numero, can., Arg. H9 92
Cinco de Mayo, Mex. I3 130
Cinco Saltos, Arg. I3 92
Çine, Tur. F10 28
Ciney, Bel. D14 14
Cinfães, Port. C2 20
Cinişeuţi, Mol. B15 26
Cintalapa, Mex. G12 100
Cinto, Monte, mtn., Fr. G14 18
Cintra, Golfe de, b., W. Sah. E1 64
Ciociaria, reg., Italy I10 22
Cipa, stm., Russia F11 34
Cipatujah, Indon. G5 50
Cipó, Braz. F6 88
Cipó, stm., Braz. J4 88
Cipolletti, Arg. G3 90
Circeo, Parco Nazionale del, p.o.i., Italy C6 24
Čirčik, Uzb. F11 32
Circle, Ak., U.S. C11 140
Circle, Mt., U.S. G8 124
Circleville, Oh., U.S. E3 114
Circleville, Ut., U.S. E4 132
Circleville Mountain, mtn., Ut., U.S. E4 132
Cirebon, Indon. G6 50
Ciremay, Gunung, vol., Indon. G6 50
Cirencester, Eng., U.K. J11 12
Cirgalandy, Russia D17 32
Ciriè, Italy E4 22
Cirò Marina, Italy E11 24
Cirpan, Blg. G12 26
Ciskei, hist. reg., S. Afr. H8 70
Cisnădie, Rom. D11 26
Cisne, Il., U.S. F9 120
Cisne, Islas del see Santanilla, Islas, is., Hond. D6 102
Cisneros, Col. D4 86
Cisolok, Indon. G5 50
Çissna Park, Il., U.S. H2 112
Čistoozërnoe, Russia D13 32
Čistopol', Russia C8 32
Čita, Russia F11 34
Citlaltépetl, Volcán see Pico de Orizaba, Volcán, vol., Mex. F10 100
Citra, Fl., U.S. G3 116
Citrus Heights, Ca., U.S. E4 134
Città di Castello, Italy G9 22
Cittanova, Italy F10 24
City of Sunrise see Sunrise, Fl., U.S. J5 116
City Point, Fl., U.S. H5 116
Ciudad Acuña, Mex. A8 100
Ciudad Altamirano, Mex. F8 100
Ciudad Anáhuac, Mex. B8 100
Ciudad Bolívar, Ven. C10 86
Ciudad Bolivia, Ven. C6 86
Ciudad Camargo, Mex. B6 100
Ciudad Camargo, Mex. B9 100
Ciudad Constitución, Mex. C3 100
Ciudad Cortés, C.R. H6 102
Ciudad Darío, Nic. F4 102
Ciudad del Carmen, Mex. F12 100
Ciudad del Este, Para. B10 92
Ciudad de Libertador General San Martín, Arg. A5 92
Ciudad de México (Mexico City), Mex. F9 100
Ciudad de Nutrias, Ven. C7 86
Ciudadela see Ciutadella de Menorca, Spain D14 20
Ciudad Guayana, Ven. C10 86
Ciudad Hidalgo, Mex. F8 100
Ciudad Jiménez see Jiménez, Mex. B6 100
Ciudad Juárez, Mex. C1 130
Ciudad Lerdo see Lerdo, Mex. C7 100
Ciudad Madero, Mex. D10 100
Ciudad Mante, Mex. D9 100
Ciudad Miguel Alemán, Mex. B9 100
Ciudad Morelos, Mex. E5 98
Ciudad Netzahualcóyotl, Mex. F9 100
Ciudad Obregón, Mex. B4 100
Ciudad Ojeda, Ven. B6 86
Ciudad Piar, Ven. D10 86
Ciudad Real, Spain F6 20
Ciudad Real, co., Spain F6 20
Ciudad Rodrigo, Spain D4 20
Ciudad Valles, Mex. E9 100
Ciudad Victoria, Mex. D9 100
Ciutadella de Menorca, Spain D14 20
Civita Castellana, Italy H9 22
Civitanova Marche, Italy G10 22
Civitavecchia, Italy H8 22
Çivril, Tur. E12 28
Çixi, China F9 42
Čiža, Russia C21 8
Cjaluša, Bela. G12 10
Čkalovsk, Russia H20 8
Clackamas, stm., Or., U.S. E4 136
Clacton-on-Sea, Eng., U.K. J14 12
Claflin, Ks., U.S. C10 128
Claiborne, Al., U.S. F11 122
Clain, stm., Fr. C6 18
Claire, Lake, l., Ab., Can. D8 106
Clair Engle Lake, res., Ca., U.S. C3 134
Clairton, Pa., U.S. D6 114
Clallam Bay, Wa., U.S. B2 136
Clanton, Al., U.S. E12 122
Clanwilliam, S. Afr. H4 70
Clapperton Island, i., On., Can. B7 112
Clara, Ire. H5 12
Clara, Ms., U.S. F10 122
Clara, stm., Austl. B4 76
Clara, Punta, c., Arg. H4 90
Clare, Austl. I4 76
Clare, Mi., U.S. E5 112
Clare, state, Ire. I3 12
Clare Island, i., Ire. H2 12
Claremont, N.H., U.S. G4 110
Claremont, S.D., U.S. B15 126
Claremont, mtn., Ca., U.S. D4 134
Claremore, Ok., U.S. H2 120
Clarence, Mo., U.S. E5 120
Clarence, stm., Austl. G9 76
Clarence, stm., N.Z. F5 80
Clarence, Cape, c., Nu., Can. A13 106
Clarence, Isla, i., Chile J2 90
Clarence Strait, strt., Austl. B6 74
Clarence Strait, strt., Ak., U.S. E13 140
Clarence Town, Bah. C9 96
Clarendon, Ar., U.S. C7 122
Clarendon, Tx., U.S. G8 128
Clarenville, Nf., Can. j23 107a
Claresholm, Ab., Can. F17 138
Clarinda, Ia., U.S. D2 120
Clarines, Ven. C9 86
Clarington, On., Can. E11 112
Clarion, Ia., U.S. B4 120
Clarion, Pa., U.S. C6 114
Clarion, stm., Pa., U.S. C6 114
Clarion Fracture Zone, unds. H25 142
Clarissa, Mn., U.S. E3 118
Clark, Mount, mtn., N.T., Can. C6 106
Clarke, stm., Austl. B5 76
Clarke Island, i., Austl. n14 77a
Clarkesville, Ga., U.S. B2 116
Clarkfield, Mn., U.S. G3 118
Clark Fork, Id., U.S. B10 136
Clark Fork, stm., U.S. C11 136
Clarks, La., U.S. E6 122
Clarksburg, W.V., U.S. E5 114
Clarksdale, Ms., U.S. C8 122
Clark's Harbour, N.S., Can. G11 110
Clarks Hill, In., U.S. H3 112
Clarkson, Ky., U.S. G11 120
Clarks Summit, Pa., U.S. C10 114
Clarkston, Wa., U.S. D9 136
Clark's Town, Jam. i13 104d
Clarksville, Ar., U.S. B5 122
Clarksville, Ia., U.S. I6 118
Clarksville, Tn., U.S. H10 120
Clarksville, Va., U.S. H7 114
Clarkton, Mo., U.S. H7 120
Clarkton, N.C., U.S. B7 116
Claro, stm., Braz. G7 84
Claude, Tx., U.S. F7 128
Clausthal-Zellerfeld, Ger. E5 16
Claveria, Phil. B7 44
Clavering Ø, i., Grnld. C22 141
Clavet, Sk., Can. B7 124
Claxton, Ga., U.S. D4 116
Clay, Ky., U.S. G10 120
Clay, Tx., U.S. G2 122
Clay Center, Ne., U.S. G14 126
Clay City, Il., U.S. F9 120
Clay City, In., U.S. E10 120
Clay City, Ky., U.S. G1 114
Claymont, De., U.S. E10 114
Claypool, Az., U.S. J6 132
Claysburg, Pa., U.S. D7 114
Clayton, Al., U.S. F13 122
Clayton, Ga., U.S. B2 116
Clayton, Il., U.S. D7 120
Clayton, La., U.S. F7 122
Clayton, Mo., U.S. F7 120
Clayton, N.M., U.S. E5 128
Clayton, N.Y., U.S. D13 112
Clayton, Ok., U.S. C3 122
Clayton, Wa., U.S. B9 136
Clear, Cape, c., Ire. J3 12
Clear Boggy Creek, stm., Ok., U.S. C2 122
Clearbrook, Mn., U.S. D3 118
Clear Creek, stm., Wy., U.S. C6 126
Clearfield, Pa., U.S. C7 114
Clearfield, Ut., U.S. B4 132
Clearlake, Ca., U.S. E3 134
Clear Lake, Ia., U.S. A4 120
Clear Lake, S.D., U.S. G2 118
Clear Lake, Wi., U.S. F6 118
Clear Lake, l., Mb., Can. D14 124
Clear Lake, l., Ca., U.S. D3 134
Clear Lake, res., La., U.S. F5 122
Clear Lake Reservoir, res., Ca., U.S. B4 134
Clearmont, Wy., U.S. C6 126
Clearwater, B.C., Can. E10 138
Clearwater, Mb., Can. E14 124
Clearwater, Fl., U.S. I3 116
Clearwater, Ne., U.S. E14 126
Clearwater, stm., Can. D8 106
Clearwater, stm., Ab., Can. D15 138
Clearwater, stm., B.C., Can. D10 138
Clearwater, stm., Id., U.S. D10 136
Clearwater, stm., Mn., U.S. D3 118
Clearwater, stm., Mt., U.S. C13 136
Clearwater, Middle Fork, stm., Id., U.S. D11 136
Clearwater, North Fork, stm., Id., U.S. D11 136
Clearwater Lake, l., B.C., Can. D10 138
Clearwater Mountains, mts., Id., U.S. D11 136
Clebit, Ok., U.S. C4 122
Cleburne, Tx., U.S. B10 130
Cle Elum, stm., Wa., U.S. C5 136
Cle Elum Lake, res., Wa., U.S. C6 136
Cleethorpes, Eng., U.K. H12 12
Clementsport, N.S., Can. F11 110
Clemson, S.C., U.S. B3 116
Clermont, Austl. D6 76
Clermont, Qc., Can. C6 110
Clermont, Fr. E11 14
Clermont-Ferrand, Fr. D9 18
Clevedon, Eng., U.K. J10 12
Cleveland, Al., U.S. D12 122
Cleveland, Ms., U.S. D8 122
Cleveland, N.C., U.S. A5 116
Cleveland, Oh., U.S. C4 114
Cleveland, Ok., U.S. A2 122
Cleveland, Tn., U.S. B14 122
Cleveland, Tx., U.S. G3 122
Cleveland, Va., U.S. H3 114
Cleveland, Cape, c., Austl. B6 76
Cleveland, Mount, mtn., Mt., U.S. B13 136
Clevelândia, Braz. C11 92
Cleves see Kleve, Ger. E2 16
Clew Bay, b., Ire. H3 12
Clewiston, Fl., U.S. J4 116
Clifton, St. Vin. p11 105e
Clifton, Az., U.S. J7 132
Clifton, Tn., U.S. B11 122
Clifton, Tx., U.S. C10 130
Clifton Forge, Va., U.S. G6 114
Clifton Hills, Austl. F2 76
Climax, Sk., Can. E5 124
Climax, Co., U.S. B2 128
Clinch, stm., U.S. I13 120
Clinchco, Va., U.S. G15 120
Clingmans Dome, mtn., U.S. I2 114
Clinton, B.C., Can. E9 138
Clinton, On., Can. E8 112
Clinton, Al., U.S. E11 122
Clinton, Ar., U.S. B6 122
Clinton, In., U.S. I2 112
Clinton, Ia., U.S. C7 120
Clinton, Ky., U.S. H9 120
Clinton, La., U.S. G7 122
Clinton, Mi., U.S. B2 114
Clinton, Mn., U.S. F2 118
Clinton, Ms., U.S. E8 122
Clinton, N.C., U.S. A7 116
Clinton, Ok., U.S. F9 128
Clinton, S.C., U.S. B4 116
Clinton, Wi., U.S. B9 120
Clinton, Cape, c., Austl. D8 76
Clinton, Lake, res., Il., U.S. D9 120
Clinton-Colden Lake, l., N.T., Can. C9 106
Clinton Lake, res., Ks., U.S. F2 120
Clintonville, Wi., U.S. G10 118
Clintwood, Va., U.S. G3 114
Clio, Mi., U.S. E6 112
Clio, S.C., U.S. B6 116
Clipperton, Île, at., Oc. H28 142
Clipperton Fracture Zone, unds. I25 142
Clipperton Island see Clipperton, Île, at., Oc. H28 142
Clisson, Fr. G7 14
Clodomira, Arg. C5 92
Cloete, Mex. G6 130
Cloncurry, Austl. C3 76
Cloncurry, stm., Austl. B3 76
Clonmel, Ire. I5 12
Clo-oose, B.C., Can. H6 138
Cloppenburg, Ger. D3 16
Cloquet, Mn., U.S. E6 118
Clorinda, Arg. B9 92
Cloud Peak, mtn., Wy., U.S. C5 126
Clova, Qc., Can. B1 110
Clover, S.C., U.S. A4 116
Cloverdale, Ca., U.S. E2 134
Cloverdale, In., U.S. E11 120
Cloverport, Ky., U.S. G11 120
Clovis, Ca., U.S. G6 134
Clovis, N.M., U.S. G5 128
Cluain Meala see Clonmel, Ire. I5 12
Cluj, state, Rom. C10 26
Cluj-Napoca, Rom. C10 26
Clunes, Austl. K4 76
Cluny, Austl. E2 76
Cluny, Fr. C10 18
Clusone, Italy E7 22
Clute, Tx., U.S. E12 130
Clutha, stm., N.Z. H3 80
Clyde, Ks., U.S. B11 128
Clyde, N.C., U.S. A3 116
Clyde, Oh., U.S. C3 114
Clyde, Tx., U.S. B8 130
Clyde, stm., Scot., U.K. F9 12
Clyde, Firth of, b., Scot., U.K. F7 12
Clyde Inlet, b., Nu., Can. A17 106
Clyde Park, Mt., U.S. E16 136
Clyde River, Nu., Can. A16 106
Clymer, Pa., U.S. D6 114
Ćmielów, Pol. F17 16
Cna, stm., Russia C17 10
Cna, stm., Russia D6 32
Cnossus see Knosós, hist., Grc. H8 28
Côa, stm., Port. D3 20
Coachella, Ca., U.S. J9 134
Coachella Canal, can., Ca., U.S. K1 132
Coahoma, Tx., U.S. B6 130
Coahuila, state, Mex. B7 100
Coal City, Il., U.S. J10 118
Coalcomán de Matamoros, Mex. F7 100
Coal Creek, stm., Wa., U.S. C8 136
Coaldale, Ab., Can. G18 138
Coalgate, Ok., U.S. C2 122
Coal Grove, Oh., U.S. F3 114
Coal Hill, Ar., U.S. B5 122
Coalinga, Ca., U.S. G5 134
Coalmont, B.C., Can. G10 138
Coalport, Pa., U.S. D7 114
Coal River, B.C., Can. D5 106
Coal Valley, val., Nv., U.S. F1 132
Coalville, Eng., U.K. I11 12
Coalville, Ut., U.S. C5 132
Coamo, P.R. B3 104a
Coaraci, Braz. H6 88
Coari, Braz. D5 84
Coari, stm., Braz. D5 84
Coast Mountains, mts., N.A. D4 106
Coast Ranges, mts., U.S. C2 134
Coatbridge, Scot., U.K. F9 12
Coatesville, Pa., U.S. E10 114
Coaticook, Qc., Can. E5 110
Coats Island, i., Nu., Can. C14 106
Coats Land, reg., Ant. C2 81
Coatzacoalcos, Mex. F11 100
Cobá, hist., Mex. B4 102
Cobalt, On., Can. F14 106
Cobán, Guat. E2 102
Cobar, Austl. H5 76
Cobberas, Mount, mtn., Austl. K6 76
Cobden, On., Can. C13 112
Cobequid Bay, b., N.S., Can. E13 110
Cobh, Ire. J4 12
Cobham, stm., Can. B18 124
Cobija, Bol. B3 90
Coblence see Koblenz, Ger. F3 16
Coblenz see Koblenz, Ger. F3 16
Cobleskill, N.Y., U.S. B11 114
Cobourg, On., Can. E11 112
Cobquecura, Chile H1 92
Cobram, Austl. J5 76
Cobre, Barranca del (Copper Canyon), misc. cult., Mex. B5 100
Cóbuè, Moz. C5 68
Coburg, Ger. F6 16
Coburg Island, i., Nu., Can. B10 141
Coburg Peninsula, pen., Austl. B6 74
Coca, stm., Ec. H3 86
Cocal, Braz. B5 88
Cocentaina, Spain F10 20
Cöch, stm., Asia B6 36
Cochabamba, Bol. C3 90
Coche, Isla, i., Ven. B10 86
Cochem, Ger. F3 16
Cochin see Kochi, India G3 53
Cochin China see Nam Phan, hist. reg., Viet. G8 48
Cochinos, Bahía de (Pigs, Bay of), b., Cuba B7 102
Cochise Head, mtn., Az., U.S. K7 132
Cochrane, Ab., Can. E16 138
Cochrane, On., Can. F14 106
Cochrane, Wi., U.S. G7 118
Cochrane, Lago (Pueyrredón, Lago), l., S.A. I2 90
Cochranton, Pa., U.S. C5 114
Cockburn, Austl. I3 76
Cockburn, Mount, mtn., Austl. E5 74
Cockburn, Mount, mtn., Austl. D5 74
Cockburn Island, i., On., Can. C6 112
Cockermouth, Eng., U.K. G9 12
Cockpit Country, reg., Jam. i13 104d
Côco, stm., Braz. F1 88
Coco, stm., N.A. E6 102
Coco, Cayo, i., Cuba A8 102
Coco, Isla del, i., C.R. F7 96
Cocoa, Fl., U.S. H5 116
Cocoa Beach, Fl., U.S. H5 116
Coco Channel, strt., Asia F7 46
Cocodrie Lake, res., La., U.S. G6 122
Coco Islands, is., Mya. F7 46
Coconino Plateau, plat., Az., U.S. H4 132
Cocos, Braz. H3 88
Cocos Islands, dep., Oc. K12 142
Cocos Lagoon, b., Guam k9 78c
Cocos Ridge, unds. H5 144
Cocula, Mex. E7 100
Cod, Cape, pen., Ma., U.S. C15 114
Codajás, Braz. D5 84
Codera, Cabo, c., Ven. B8 86
Coderre, Sk., Can. D7 124
Codigoro, Italy F9 22
Cod Island, i., Nf., Can. F13 141
Codlea, Rom. D12 26
Codó, Braz. C3 88
Codogno, Italy E6 22
Codòzinho, Braz. C3 88
Codroy, Nf., Can. C17 110
Cody, Ne., U.S. E11 126
Cody, Wy., U.S. C3 126
Coelho Neto, Braz. C4 88
Coen, Austl. B8 74
Coëtivy, i., Sey. k13 69b
Coeur d'Alene, Id., U.S. C10 136
Coeur d'Alene, stm., Id., U.S. C10 136
Coeur d'Alene Lake, res., Id., U.S. C10 136
Coffeeville, Ms., U.S. D9 122
Coffeyville, Ks., U.S. G2 120
Coffs Harbour, Austl. H9 76
Cofre de Perote, Cerro, mtn., Mex. F10 100
Cofre de Perote, Parque Nacional, p.o.i., Mex. F10 100
Cofrentes see Cofrents, Spain E9 20
Cofrents, Spain E9 20
Cogâlnic (Kohyl'nyk), stm., Eur. C15 26
Coggon, Ia., U.S. B6 120
Cognac, Fr. D5 18
Cogolludo, Spain D7 20
Cogoon, stm., Austl. F7 76
Cogswell, N.D., U.S. A15 126
Cohocton, stm., N.Y., U.S. F12 112
Cohoes, N.Y., U.S. B12 114
Cohuna, Austl. J5 76
Coiba, Isla de, i., Pan. I6 102
Coig, stm., Arg. J3 90
Coihaique, Chile I2 90
Coimbatore (Koyambattur), India F3 53
Coimbra, Braz. K4 88
Coimbra, Port. D2 20
Coimbra, state, Port. D2 20
Coín, Spain H6 20
Coipasa, Lago, l., Bol. C3 90
Coipasa, Salar de, pl., S.A. C3 90
Coire see Chur, Switz. D6 22
Cojedes, state, Ven. C7 86
Cojudo Blanco, Cerro, mtn., Arg. I3 90
Cojutepeque, El Sal. F3 102
Cokato, Mn., U.S. F4 118
Çokeville, Wy., U.S. A6 132
Çokpar, Kaz. F12 32
Čokurdah, Russia B18 34
Colac, Austl. L4 76
Colatina, Braz. J5 88
Colbeck, Cape, c., Ant. C25 81
Colbert, Ok., U.S. D2 122
Colbinabbin, Austl. K5 76
Colbún, Chile G2 92
Colbún, Embalse, res., Chile G2 92
Colby, Ks., U.S. B7 128
Colby, Wi., U.S. G8 118
Colchester, Eng., U.K. J13 12
Colchester, Il., U.S. D7 120
Cold Bay, Ak., U.S. E7 140
Cold Lake, Ab., Can. E8 106
Cold Spring, Mn., U.S. F4 118
Coldstream, Scot., U.K. F10 12
Coldwater, Ks., U.S. D9 128

Name | Map Ref. | Page

Coldwater, Mi., U.S. G4 112
Coldwater, Oh., U.S. H5 112
Coldwater, stm., Ms., U.S. C8 122
Coldwater Creek, stm., U.S. E7 128
Coleambally, Austl. J5 76
Colebrook, N.H., U.S. F5 110
Cole Camp, Mo., U.S. F4 120
Coleman, Ab., Can. G16 138
Coleman, Fl., U.S. H3 116
Coleman, Mi., U.S. E5 112
Coleman, Wi., U.S. C1 112
Coleman, stm., Austl. B8 74
Colenso, S. Afr. F9 70
Coleraine, Austl. K3 76
Coleraine, N. Ire., U.K. F6 12
Coleridge, Ne., U.S. E15 126
Coles, Ms., U.S. F7 122
Colesberg, S. Afr. G7 70
Coleville, Sk., Can. C4 124
Colfax, In., U.S. H3 112
Colfax, Ia., U.S. C4 120
Colfax, La., U.S. F6 122
Colfax, Wa., U.S. D9 136
Colfax, Wi., U.S. F7 118
Colgong, India F11 54
Colhué Huapi, Lago, l., Arg. I3 90
Colibris, Pointe des, c., Guad. h6 105c
Colico, Italy D6 22
Coligny, S. Afr. E8 70
Colihaut, Dom. j5 105c
Colima, Mex. F7 100
Colima, state, Mex. F7 100
Colima, Nevado de, vol., Mex. F7 100
Colinas, Braz. D3 88
Colinas, Braz. H1 88
Colinton, Ab., Can. B17 138
Coll, i., Scot., U.K. E6 12
Collarenebri, Austl. G7 76
College, Ak., U.S. D10 140
Collegedale, Tn., U.S. B13 122
College Park, Ga., U.S. D14 122
College Place, Wa., U.S. D8 136
College Station, Ar., U.S. C6 122
College Station, Tx., U.S. G2 122
Collerina, Austl. G6 76
Colleymount, B.C., Can. B4 138
Collie, Austl. F3 74
Collier Bay, b., Austl. C4 74
Collierville, Tn., U.S. B9 122
Collingwood, On., Can. D9 112
Collins, Ga., U.S. D3 116
Collins, Ms., U.S. F9 122
Collins Bay, On., Can. D13 112
Collins Head, c., Norf. I. y25 78i
Collinston, La., U.S. E7 122
Collinsville, Austl. C6 76
Collinsville, Al., U.S. C13 122
Collinsville, Ok., U.S. H2 120
Collinsville, Tx., U.S. D2 122
Collinwood, Tn., U.S. B11 122
Collipulli, Chile H1 92
Colman, S.D., U.S. H2 118
Colmar, Fr. F16 14
Colmenar, Spain H6 20
Colmenar Viejo, Spain D7 20
Colmeneros, Mex. F8 100
Colmesneil, Tx., U.S. G4 122
Colnett, Punta, c., Mex. F4 98
Cologne see Köln, Ger. F2 16
Cologne, Mn., U.S. G5 118
Coloma, Mi., U.S. F3 112
Coloma, Wi., U.S. G9 118
Colomb-Béchar see Béchar, Alg. C4 64
Colombia, Col. F4 86
Colombia, ctry., S.A. C3 84
Colombie-Britannique see British Columbia, state, Can. E5 106
Colombo, Braz. B13 92
Colombo, Sri L. H4 53
Colome, S.D., U.S. D13 126
Colomiers, Fr. F7 18
Colón, Arg. F8 92
Colón, Arg. F7 92
Colón, Cuba A7 102
Colón, Pan. H7 102
Colon, Mi., U.S. G4 112
Colón, Ur. F10 92
Colón, Archipiélago de (Galapagos Islands), is., Ec. h12 84a
Colona, Austl. F6 74
Colonelganj, India E8 54
Colônia, stm., Braz. H6 88
Colonia Alvear Norte see General Alvear, Arg. G3 92
Colonia del Sacramento, Ur. G9 92
Colonia Dora, Arg. D6 92
Colonia Elisa, Arg. C8 92
Colonia Lavalleja, Ur. E9 92
Colonial Heights, Va., U.S. G8 114
Colonia Providencia, P.R. C4 104a
Colonia Suiza, Ur. G9 92
Colonias Unidas, Arg. C8 92
Colonne, Capo, c., Italy E11 24
Colonsay, Sk., Can. B8 124
Colonsay, i., Scot., U.K. E6 12
Colony, Ks., U.S. F2 120
Colorada Grande, Salina, pl., Arg. I5 92
Coloradas, Lomas, hills, Arg. H3 90
Colorado, Hond. E4 102
Colorado, state, U.S. D6 108
Colorado, stm., Arg. G4 90
Colorado, stm., N.A. E5 98
Colorado, stm., Tx., U.S. F11 130
Colorado, Cerro, mtn., Arg. H3 90
Colorado City, Co., U.S. C4 128
Colorado City, Tx., U.S. B7 130
Colorado Kolonie see Lago Kolonie, Aruba p20 104g
Colorado National Monument, p.o.i., Co., U.S. D8 132
Colorado Plateau, plat., U.S. E7 132
Colorado River Aqueduct, aq., Ca., U.S. E5 98
Colorado Springs, Co., U.S. C4 128
Colotlán, Mex. D7 100
Colquechaca, Bol. C3 90
Colstrip, Mt., U.S. B6 126
Colt, Ar., U.S. B8 122
Coltauco, Chile G2 92
Colton, Ca., U.S. I8 134
Colton, S.D., U.S. H2 118
Columbia, Ca., U.S. E5 134
Columbia, Il., U.S. F7 120
Columbia, Ky., U.S. G12 120
Columbia, La., U.S. E6 122
Columbia, Md., U.S. E9 114
Columbia, Mo., U.S. F5 120
Columbia, N.C., U.S. I9 114
Columbia, Pa., U.S. D9 114
Columbia, S.C., U.S. C4 116
Columbia, Tn., U.S. B11 122
Columbia, stm., N.A. D3 136
Columbia, Cape, c., Nu., Can. A11 141
Columbia, Mount, mtn., Ab., Can. D13 138
Columbia Basin, bas., Wa., U.S. C8 136
Columbia City, In., U.S. G4 112
Columbia Falls, Me., U.S. F9 110
Columbia Icefield, ice, Can. D13 138
Columbia Mountains, mts., N.A. G13 138
Columbiana, Al., U.S. D12 122
Columbiana, Oh., U.S. D5 114
Columbine, Cape, c., S. Afr. H3 70
Columbrets, Illes, is., Spain E11 20
Columbus, Ga., U.S. E14 122
Columbus, In., U.S. E12 120
Columbus, Ks., U.S. G3 120
Columbus, Ms., U.S. D10 122
Columbus, Ne., U.S. F15 126
Columbus, N.M., U.S. L9 132
Columbus, N.C., U.S. A3 116
Columbus, N.D., U.S. F11 124
Columbus, Oh., U.S. E2 114
Columbus, Tx., U.S. H2 122
Columbus, Wi., U.S. H9 118
Columbus Point, c., Trin. r13 105f
Columbus Salt Marsh, pl., Nv., U.S. E8 134
Colusa, Ca., U.S. D3 134
Colville, Wa., U.S. B9 136
Colville, stm., Ak., U.S. C9 140
Colville Lake, l., N.T., Can. B5 106
Colwyn Bay, Wales, U.K. H9 12
Comacchio, Italy F9 22
Comacchio, Valli di, l., Italy F9 22
Comala, Mex. F7 100
Comalcalco, Mex. F12 100
Comales, Mex. H9 130
Coman, Mount, mtn., Ant. C34 81
Comana, Rom. F15 26
Comanche, Ok., U.S. G10 128
Comandante Ferraz, sci., Ant. B35 81
Comandante Fontana, Arg. B7 92
Comandante Leal, Arg. E5 92
Comandante Luis Piedra Buena, Arg. I3 90
Comănești, Rom. C13 26
Comayagua, Hond. E4 102
Combarbalá, Chile E2 92
Combermere Bay, b., Mya. C1 48
Combourg, Fr. F7 14
Comboyne, Austl. H9 76
Comendador, Dom. Rep. C12 102
Comer, Ga., U.S. B2 116
Comercinho, Braz. I5 88
Comet, stm., Austl. E7 76
Cometela, Moz. B12 70
Comfort, N.C., U.S. B8 116
Comfort, Tx., U.S. E8 130
Comfort, Cape, c., Nu., Can. B14 106
Comfrey, Mn., U.S. G4 118
Comilla, Bngl. G13 54
Comino see Kemmuna, i., Malta H8 24
Comiso, Italy H8 24
Comitán de Domínguez, Mex. G12 100
Commerce, Ga., U.S. B2 116
Commerce, Ok., U.S. H3 120
Commercy, Fr. F14 14
Comminges, reg., Fr. F6 18
Committee Bay, b., Nu., Can. B13 106
Communism Peak see Kommunizma, pik, mtn., Taj. B11 56
Como, Italy E6 22
Como, Tx., U.S. D3 122
Como, Lago di, l., Italy D6 22
Comodoro Rivadavia, Arg. I3 90
Comores, Archipel des, is., Afr. C7 68
Comorin, Cape, c., India G3 53
Comoros, ctry., Afr. C7 68
Comox, B.C., Can. G6 138
Compiègne, Fr. E11 14
Compostela, Mex. E6 100
Compton, Ca., U.S. J7 134
Comrat, Mol. C15 26
Comstock, Ne., U.S. F13 126
Comstock, Tx., U.S. E6 130
Comstock Park, Mi., U.S. E4 112
Çon, stm., Viet. C7 48
Čona, stm., Russia B19 32
Co Nag, l., China B13 54
Conakry, Gui. H2 64
Conambo, stm., Ec. H3 86
Cona Niyeo, Arg. H3 90
Conasauga, stm., U.S. C14 122
Concarán, Arg. F5 92
Concarneau, Fr. G5 14
Conceição, Braz. D6 88
Conceição da Barra, Braz. J6 88
Conceição das Alagoas, Braz. J1 88
Conceição do Araguaia, Braz. E1 88
Conceição do Canindé, Braz. D5 88
Conceição do Coité, Braz. F6 88
Conceição do Mato Dentro, Braz. J4 88
Conceição do Norte, Braz. G2 88
Concepción, Arg. D9 92
Concepción, Arg. C5 92
Concepción, Bol. C4 90
Concepción, Chile H1 92
Concepción, Col. D5 86
Concepción, Para. D5 90
Concepción, Bahía, b., Mex. B2 100
Concepción, Canal, strt., Chile J2 90
Concepción, Laguna, l., Bol. C4 90
Concepción, Volcán, vol., Nic. G5 102
Concepción de la Sierra, Arg. D10 92
Concepción del Oro, Mex. C8 100
Concepción del Uruguay, Arg. F8 92
Conception, Point, c., Ca., U.S. I5 134
Conception Bay, b., Nf., Can. j23 107a
Conception Bay, b., Nmb. C2 70
Conchas, stm., Arg. B5 92
Conchas Dam, N.M., U.S. F4 128
Conchas Lake, res., N.M., U.S. F4 128
Concho, Az., U.S. I7 132
Concho, stm., Tx., U.S. C8 130
Conchos, stm., Mex. A6 100
Conchos, stm., Mex. C10 100
Conconully, Wa., U.S. B7 136
Concord, Ca., U.S. E4 134
Concord, Ga., U.S. D14 122
Concord, N.H., U.S. G5 110
Concord, N.C., U.S. A5 116
Concordia, Arg. E8 92
Concórdia, Braz. C11 92
Concordia, Mex. D5 100
Concordia, Mex. I4 130
Concordia, Mo., U.S. F4 120
Concrete, Wa., U.S. B5 136
Con Cuong, Viet. C7 48
Conda, Ang. C1 68
Condamine, Austl. F7 76
Condamine, stm., Austl. F8 76
Condat, Fr. D8 18
Conde, S.D., U.S. B14 126
Condeúba, Braz. H5 88
Condobolin, Austl. I6 76
Condom, Fr. F6 18
Condon, Or., U.S. E6 136
Condoto, Col. E3 86
Condroz, hist. reg., Bel. D14 14
Cone, Tx., U.S. H7 128
Conecuh, stm., U.S. F12 122
Conegliano, Italy E9 22
Conejos, Co., U.S. D2 128
Conejos, stm., Co., U.S. D3 128
Confuso, stm., Para. B8 92
Congaree Swamp National Monument, p.o.i., S.C., U.S. C5 116
Congaz, Mol. C15 26
Conghua, China J5 42
Congjiang, China I3 42
Congleton, Eng., U.K. H10 12
Congo, ctry., Afr. E3 66
Congo (Zaire), stm., Afr. F2 66
Congo, Democratic Republic of the (Zaire), ctry., Afr. E4 66
Congo, République démocratique du see Congo, Democratic Republic of the, ctry., Afr. E4 66
Congo Basin, bas., Afr. E4 66
Congonhinhas, Braz. A12 92
Congress, Sk., Can. E8 124
Conitaca, Mex. C5 100
Conn, Lough, l., Ire. G3 12
Connacht see Connaught, hist. reg., Ire. H3 12
Connaught, hist. reg., Ire. H3 12
Conneaut, Oh., U.S. C5 114
Conneautville, Pa., U.S. C5 114
Connecticut, state, U.S. C13 114
Connecticut, stm., U.S. H4 110
Connellsville, Pa., U.S. D6 114
Connemara, reg., Ire. H3 12
Connersville, In., U.S. E12 120
Conn Lake, l., Nu., Can. A15 106
Connors Range, mts., Austl. C7 76
Cononaco, stm., Ec. H3 86
Conorochite, stm., Ven. F8 86
Conover, N.C., U.S. I4 114
Conquest, Sk., Can. C6 124
Conquista, Braz. J2 88
Conrad, Ia., U.S. B5 120
Conroe, Tx., U.S. G3 122
Conroe, Lake, res., Tx., U.S. G3 122
Consecon, On., Can. D12 112
Conselheiro Lafaiete, Braz. K4 88
Conselheiro Pena, Braz. J5 88
Conselice, Italy F8 22
Consett, Eng., U.K. G10 12
Consolación del Sur, Cuba A6 102
Con Son, is., Viet. H8 48
Consort, Ab., Can. B3 124
Constance see Konstanz, Ger. I4 16
Constance, Lake (Bodensee), l., Eur. I5 16
Constância, Port. E2 20
Constanța, Rom. E15 26
Constanța, state, Rom. E15 26
Constantina, Spain G5 20
Constantine see Qacentina, Alg. B6 64
Constantine, Mi., U.S. G4 112
Constantine, Cape, c., Ak., U.S. E8 140
Constantinople see İstanbul, Tur. B12 28
Constitución, Chile G1 92
Constitución, Ur. E9 92
Constitución de 1857, Parque Nacional, p.o.i., Mex. K10 134
Consuegra, Spain E7 20
Contai, India H11 54
Contas, stm., Braz. H6 88
Contentnea Creek, stm., N.C., U.S. A8 116
Continental Peak, mtn., Wy., U.S. E4 126
Contratación, Col. D5 86
Contreras, Embalse de, res., Spain E9 20
Contreras, Isla, i., Chile J1 90
Contursi, Italy D9 24
Contwoyto Lake, l., Can. B8 106
Convent, La., U.S. G8 122
Conversano, Italy D10 24
Converse, In., U.S. H4 112
Conway, Ar., U.S. B6 122
Conway, Mo., U.S. G5 120
Conway, N.H., U.S. F5 110
Conway, N.C., U.S. H8 114
Conway, S.C., U.S. C6 116
Conway, Lake, res., Ar., U.S. C6 122
Conway National Park, p.o.i., Austl. C7 76
Conway Springs, Ks., U.S. D11 128
Conwy, Wales, U.K. H9 12
Coober Pedy, Austl. E6 74
Cook, Austl. F6 74
Cook, Mn., U.S. D6 118
Cook, Ne., U.S. D1 120
Cook, Cape, c., B.C., Can. F2 138
Cook, Mount, mtn., N.Z. F4 80
Cook, Récif de, rf., N. Cal. I14 79d
Cookeville, Tn., U.S. H12 120
Cooking Lake, l., Ab., Can. C17 138
Cook Inlet, b., Ak., U.S. D9 140
Cook Islands, dep., Oc. E10 72
Cook Strait, strt., N.Z. E6 80
Cooktown, Austl. C9 74
Coolabah, Austl. H6 76
Cooladdi, Austl. F5 76
Coolamon, Austl. J6 76
Coolangatta, Austl. G9 76
Cooleemee, N.C., U.S. I5 114
Coolgardie, Austl. F4 74
Coolidge, Ga., U.S. E2 116
Coolidge, Tx., U.S. F2 122
Coolidge, Mount, mtn., S.D., U.S. D9 126
Coolidge Dam, dam, Az., U.S. J6 132
Coolin, Id., U.S. B10 136
Cooloola National Park, p.o.i., Austl. F9 76
Cooma, Austl. K7 76
Coonabarabran, Austl. H7 76
Coonalpyn, Austl. J2 76
Coonamble, Austl. H7 76
Coonoor, India F3 53
Coon Rapids, Mn., U.S. F5 118
Coon Valley, Wi., U.S. H8 118
Cooper, Tx., U.S. D3 122
Cooper Creek, stm., Austl. G2 76
Cooper Road, La., U.S. E5 122
Coopers, Al., U.S. E12 122
Cooperstown, N.Y., U.S. B11 114
Coopersville, Mi., U.S. E4 112
Coopracambra National Park, p.o.i., Austl. K7 76
Coorong National Park, p.o.i., Austl. K2 76
Coorow, Austl. E3 74
Cooroy, Austl. F9 76
Coosa, stm., U.S. E12 122
Coos Bay, Or., U.S. G2 136
Cootamundra, Austl. J7 76
Cootehill, Ire. G5 12
Copacabana, Arg. D4 92
Copacabana, Col. D4 86
Copainalá, Mex. G12 100
Copan, Ok., U.S. H2 120
Copán, hist., Hond. E3 102
Copatana, Braz. I8 86
Copeland, Fl., U.S. K4 116
Copenhagen see København, Den. I4 8
Copenhagen, N.Y., U.S. E14 112
Copertino, Italy D11 24
Copiapó, Chile C2 92
Copiapó, stm., Chile C2 92
Copley, Austl. H2 76
Copparo, Italy F8 22
Copper, stm., Ak., U.S. D11 140
Copperas Cove, Tx., U.S. C9 130
Copper Butte, mtn., Wa., U.S. B8 136
Copper Canyon see Cobre, Barranca del, misc. cult., Mex. B5 100
Copper Center, Ak., U.S. D10 140
Copper Harbor, Mi., U.S. D10 118
Coppermine, stm., Can. B7 106
Copper Mine Point, c., Br. Vir. Is. e9 104b
Copper Mountain, B.C., Can. G10 138
Coquí, P.R. C3 104a
Coquilhatville see Mbandaka, D.R.C. D3 66
Coquimbo, Chile E2 92
Coquimbo, state, Chile E2 92
Corabia, Rom. F11 26
Coração de Jesus, Braz. I3 88
Coradi, Isole see Cheradi, Isole, i., Italy D11 24
Coral Gables, Fl., U.S. K5 116
Coral Harbour, Bah. n18 104f
Coral Harbour, Nu., Can. C14 106
Coral Sea, Oc. E6 72
Coral Sea Basin, unds. K18 142
Coral Sea Islands Territory, dep., Oc. B9 76
Coralville, Ia., U.S. C6 120
Coram, Mt., U.S. B12 136
Corangamite, Lake, l., Austl. K4 76
Corato, Italy C10 24
Corbeil-Essonnes, Fr. F11 14
Corbett National Park, p.o.i., India D7 54
Corbigny, Fr. G12 14
Corbin, Ky., U.S. H1 114
Corbones, stm., Spain G5 20
Corby, Eng., U.K. I12 12
Corcaigh see Cork, Ire. J4 12
Córcega, P.R. B1 104a
Corcoran, Ca., U.S. G6 134
Corcovado, Golfo, b., Chile H2 90
Corcovado, Parque Nacional, p.o.i., C.R. H6 102
Corcovado, Volcán, vol., Chile H2 90
Corcubión, Spain B1 20
Cordeiro, Braz. L4 88
Cordele, Ga., U.S. E2 116
Cordell Hull Reservoir, res., Tn., U.S. H12 120
Corder, Mo., U.S. E4 120
Cordillera, state, Para. B9 92
Cordillo Downs, Austl. F3 76
Córdoba, Arg. E5 92
Córdoba, Mex. F10 100
Córdoba (Cordova), Spain G6 20
Córdoba, state, Arg. E5 92
Córdoba, state, Col. C4 86
Córdoba, co., Spain F6 20
Córdova, Peru F2 84
Cordova see Córdoba, Spain G6 20
Cordova, Al., U.S. D11 122
Cordova, Ak., U.S. D10 140
Cordova, Il., U.S. C7 120
Cordova Peak, mtn., Ak., U.S. D10 140
Coreaú, Braz. B5 88
Coreaú, stm., Braz. B5 88
Corentyne, stm., S.A. C6 84
Corfield, Austl. C4 76
Corfu see Kérkyra, Grc. D2 28
Corfu see Kérkyra, i., Grc. D2 28
Coria, Spain D4 20
Coria del Río, Spain G4 20
Coribe, Braz. G3 88
Coricudgy, Mount, mtn., Austl. I8 76
Corigliano Calabro, Italy E10 24
Corinne, Ut., U.S. B4 132
Corinne, W.V., U.S. G4 114
Corinth see Kórinthos, Grc. F5 28
Corinth, Ms., U.S. C10 122
Corinth, N.Y., U.S. G3 110
Corinth, Gulf of see Korinthiakós Kólpos, b., Grc. E5 28
Corinto, Braz. J3 88
Corisco, Isla de, i., Eq. Gui. I6 64
Corjeuți, Mol. A14 26
Cork, Ire. J4 12
Cork, state, Ire. I4 12
Corleone, Italy G7 24
Çorlu, Tur. B10 28
Cornelia, Ga., U.S. B2 116
Cornélio Procópio, Braz. D6 90
Cornelius, N.C., U.S. A5 116
Cornelius Grinnell Bay, b., Nu., Can. E13 141
Cornell, Wi., U.S. F7 118
Corner Brook, Nf., Can. j22 107a
Cornești, Mol. B14 26
Corneta, Punta, c., Mex. H10 100
Corning, Ar., U.S. H7 120
Corning, Ca., U.S. D3 134
Corning, Ia., U.S. D3 120
Corning, Ks., U.S. B12 128
Corning, N.Y., U.S. B8 114
Çornish, Me., U.S. G6 110
Čornoe more see Black Sea G15 6
Corno Grande, mtn., Italy H10 22
Cornwall, On., Can. E2 110
Cornwallis Island, i., Nu., Can. B7 141
Cornwall Island, i., Nu., Can. B6 141
Coro, Ven. B7 86
Coro, Golfete de, b., Ven. B6 86
Coroaci, Braz. J4 88
Coroatá, Braz. C3 88
Corocoro, Bol. C3 90
Corocoro, Isla, i., S.A. C11 86
Coroico, Bol. C3 90
Coromandel, Braz. J2 88
Coromandel Coast, cst., India E5 53
Coromandel Peninsula, pen., N.Z. C6 80
Corona, Ca., U.S. J8 134
Corona, N.M., U.S. G3 128
Coronado, Mex. D8 100
Coronado, Bahía de, b., C.R. H6 102
Coronado, Islas, is., Mex. K8 134
Coronation, Ab., Can. D19 138
Coronation Gulf, b., Nu., Can. B8 106
Coronation Island, i., Ant. B36 81
Coronda, Arg. E7 92
Coronel, Chile H1 92
Coronel Bogado, Para. C9 92
Coronel Dorrego, Arg. I7 92
Coronel Fabriciano, Braz. J4 88
Coronel Moldes, Arg. B5 92
Coronel Moldes, Arg. F5 92
Coronel Oviedo, Para. B9 92
Coronel Pringles, Arg. H7 92
Coronel Suárez, Arg. H6 92
Coronel Vidal, Arg. H9 92
Coronel Vivida, Braz. C11 92
Corongo, Peru E2 84
Coropuna, Nevado, vol., Peru G3 84
Corossol, Guad. B2 105a
Çorovodë, Alb. D14 24
Čorowa, Austl. J6 76
Corozal, Belize C3 102
Corozal, Col. C4 86
Corozal, P.R. B3 104a
Corpus Christi, Tx., U.S. G10 130
Corpus Christi, Lake, res., Tx., U.S. F9 130
Corpus Christi Bay, b., Tx., U.S. G10 130
Corral, Chile H2 90
Corral de Almaguer, Spain E7 20
Corral de Bustos, Arg. F6 92
Corrales, Cerro, mtn., Mex. H2 130
Corralito, Arg. F5 92
Correctionville, Ia., U.S. B2 120
Corregidor Island, i., Phil. C3 52
Corrente, Braz. F3 88
Corrente, stm., Braz. G4 88
Correntes, Cabo das, c., Moz. D12 70
Correntina, Braz. G3 88
Corrèze, state, Fr. D7 18
Corrib, Lough, l., Ire. H3 12
Corrientes, Arg. C8 92
Corrientes, state, Arg. D9 92
Corrientes, stm., Arg. D8 92
Corrientes, stm., S.A. D2 84
Corrientes, Bahía de, b., Cuba B5 102
Corrientes, Cabo, c., Arg. I9 92
Corrientes, Cabo, c., Col. E3 86
Corrientes, Cabo, c., Mex. E6 100
Corrigan, Tx., U.S. F4 122
Corrigin, Austl. F3 74
Corriverton, Guy. B6 84
Corrumpa Creek, stm., U.S. E5 128
Corry, Pa., U.S. C6 114
Corse (Corsica), i., Fr. G15 18
Corse, Cap, c., Fr. F15 18
Corse-du-Sud, state, Fr. H15 18
Corsica see Corse, i., Fr. G15 18
Corsicana, Tx., U.S. E2 122
Cort Adelaer, Kap, c., Grnld. E17 141
Cortazar, Mex. E8 100
Corte, Fr. G15 18
Cortés, Mar de see California, Golfo de, b., Mex. B2 96
Cortez, Co., U.S. F8 132
Cortez, Sea of see California, Golfo de, b., Mex. B2 96
Cortina d'Ampezzo, Italy D8 22
Cortland, Ne., U.S. K2 118
Cortland, N.Y., U.S. B9 114
Cortland, Oh., U.S. C5 114
Cortona, Italy G8 22
Corubal, stm., Afr. G2 64
Coruche, Port. F2 20
Çorum, Tur. A4 56
Čorumbá, Braz. C5 90
Corumbá, stm., Braz. I1 88
Corumbaíba, Braz. J1 88
Corumbataí, stm., Braz. B11 92
Corumo, stm., Ven. D11 86
Corunna see A Coruña, Spain A2 20
Corunna, Mi., U.S. F5 112
Coruripe, Braz. F7 88
Corvallis, Mt., U.S. D12 136
Corvallis, Or., U.S. F3 136
Corwith, Ia., U.S. B3 120
Corydon, In., U.S. F11 120
Corydon, Ky., U.S. G10 120
Corzu, Rom. E10 26
Corzuela, Arg. C7 92
Cos see Kos, i., Grc. G10 28
Cosamaloapan de Carpio, Mex. F10 100
Coscomate, Mex. I2 130
Cosenza, Italy E10 24
Coshocton, Oh., U.S. D4 114
Cosigüina, Punta, c., Nic. F4 102
Cosigüina, Volcán, vol., Nic. F4 102
Cosmoledo, Atoll de, i., Sey. k11 69b
Cosmos, Mn., U.S. G4 118
Cosne-sur-Loire, Fr. G11 14
Cosquín, Arg. E5 92
Cossato, Italy E5 22
Cossatot, stm., Ar., U.S. C4 122
Costa Mesa, Ca., U.S. J8 134
Costa Rica, Mex. C5 100
Costa Rica, ctry., N.A. H5 102
Coswig, Ger. E9 16
Coswig, Ger. E8 16
Cotabato, Phil. G4 52
Cotahuasi, Peru G3 84
Cotati, Ca., U.S. E3 134
Coteaux, Haiti C10 102
Cote d'Ivoire, ctry., Afr. H3 64
Côte-d'Or, state, Fr. G13 14
Cotegipe, Braz. F3 88
Cotentin, pen., Fr. E7 14
Côtes-d'Armor, state, Fr. F6 14
Cotingo, stm., Braz. E11 86
Cotiujeni, Mol. B15 26
Cotonou, Benin H5 64
Cotopaxi, state, Ec. H2 86
Cotopaxi, vol., Ec. H2 86
Cotopaxi, Parque Nacional, p.o.i., Ec. H2 86
Cotswold Hills, hills, Eng., U.K. J10 12
Cottage Grove, Or., U.S. G3 136
Cottbus, Ger. E10 16
Cotter, Ar., U.S. H5 120
Cottian Alps, mts., Eur. E12 18
Cottondale, Fl., U.S. G13 122
Cotton Plant, Ar., U.S. C7 122
Cottonport, La., U.S. G6 122
Cotton Valley, La., U.S. E5 122
Cottonwood, Az., U.S. I5 132
Cottonwood, Ca., U.S. C3 134
Cottonwood, Mn., U.S. G3 118
Cottonwood, stm., Ks., U.S. C12 128
Cottonwood, stm., Mn., U.S. G3 118
Cottonwood Creek, stm., Mt., U.S. F5 124
Cottonwood Falls, Ks., U.S. C12 128
Coubre, Pointe de la, c., Fr. D4 18
Couchiching, Lake, l., On., Can. D10 112
Coudersport, Pa., U.S. C8 114
Coudres, Île aux, i., Qc., Can. C6 110
Coulee City, Wa., U.S. C7 136
Coulee Dam, Wa., U.S. B8 136
Coulommiers, Fr. F12 14
Coulonge, stm., Qc., Can. C13 112
Coulterville, Il., U.S. F8 120
Counce, Tn., U.S. B10 122
Council, Id., U.S. F10 136
Council Bluffs, Ia., U.S. C2 120
Council Grove, Ks., U.S. C12 128
Coupeville, Wa., U.S. B4 136
Courantyne see Corentyne, stm., S.A. C6 84
Courland (Kurzeme), hist. reg., Lat. C5 10
Courland Lagoon, b., Eur. E3 10
Courmayeur, Italy E3 22
Courtenay, B.C., Can. G5 138
Courtland, Al., U.S. C11 122
Courtland, Va., U.S. H8 114
Courtrai see Kortrijk, Bel. D12 14
Coutras, Fr. D5 18
Coutts, Ab., Can. G19 138
Couture, Lac, l., Qc., Can. C16 106
Covasna, state, Rom. C12 26
Cove, Or., U.S. E9 136
Cove Island, i., On., Can. C8 112
Covelo, Ca., U.S. D2 134
Coventry, Eng., U.K. I11 12
Covert, Mi., U.S. F3 112
Covilhã, Port. D3 20
Covington, Ga., U.S. C2 116
Covington, In., U.S. H2 112
Covington, Ky., U.S. E1 114
Covington, La., U.S. G8 122
Covington, Oh., U.S. H5 112
Covington, Ok., U.S. E11 128
Covington, Tn., U.S. B9 122
Covington, Va., U.S. G5 114
Cowal, pen., Scot., U.K. E7 12
Cowal, Lake, l., Austl. I6 76
Cowan, Tn., U.S. B13 122
Cowan, Lake, l., Austl. F4 74
Cowansville, Qc., Can. E4 110
Cowarie, Austl. E7 74
Cow Creek, stm., Ks., U.S. C10 128
Cow Creek, stm., Or., U.S. H3 136
Cowdenbeath, Scot., U.K. E9 12
Cowell, Austl. F7 74
Cowen, W.V., U.S. F5 114
Coweta, Ok., U.S. I2 120
Cowhouse Creek, stm., Tx., U.S. C10 130
Cowichan Bay, B.C., Can. H7 138
Cowichan Lake, l., B.C., Can. H6 138
Cowley, Austl. F5 76
Cowley, Wy., U.S. C4 126
Cowlic, Az., U.S. L4 132
Cowlitz, stm., Wa., U.S. D4 136
Cowpasture, stm., Va., U.S. F6 114
Cowpens, S.C., U.S. A4 116
Cowra, Austl. I7 76
Coxá, stm., Braz. H3 88
Coxim, Braz. C6 90
Cox's Bāzār, Bngl. H13 54
Coyaguaima, Cerro, mtn., Arg. D3 90
Coyame, Mex. A6 100
Coyle see Coig, stm., Arg. J3 90
Coyote, stm., Mex. F6 98
Coyote Wash, stm., N.M., U.S. G8 132
Coyuca de Benítez, Mex. G8 100
Coyuca de Catalán, Mex. F8 100
Cozad, Ne., U.S. G13 126
Cozumel, Mex. B4 102
Cozumel, Isla, i., Mex. B4 102
Crab Orchard, Tn., U.S. I13 120
Crab Orchard Lake, res., Il., U.S. G9 120
Cradle Mountain-Lake Saint Clair National Park, p.o.i., Austl. n12 77a
Cradock, S. Afr. H7 70
Craig, Co., U.S. C9 132
Craig, Mo., U.S. D2 120
Craig, Ne., U.S. J2 118
Craigellachie, B.C., Can. E12 138
Craigmont, Id., U.S. D10 136
Craigsville, Va., U.S. F6 114
Craik, Sk., Can. C8 124
Crailsheim, Ger. G6 16
Craiova, Rom. E10 26
Cranberry Lake, l., N.Y., U.S. F1 110
Cranbrook, Austl. F3 74
Cranbrook, B.C., Can. G15 138
Crandon, Wi., U.S. F9 118
Crane, Az., U.S. K2 132
Crane, In., U.S. F11 120
Crane, Tx., U.S. C5 130
Crane Lake, l., Sk., Can. D4 124
Crane Mountain, mtn., Or., U.S. A5 134
Crângeni, Rom. E11 26
Cranston, R.I., U.S. C14 114
Crasna, Rom. D13 26
Crasna, stm., Eur. I18 16
Crasnoe, Mol. C16 26
Crater Lake, l., Or., U.S. H4 136
Crater Lake National Park, p.o.i., Or., U.S. H5 136
Craters of the Moon National Monument, p.o.i., Id., U.S. G13 136
Crateús, Braz. C5 88
Crato, Braz. D6 88
Crauford, Cape, c., Nu., Can. A14 106
Cravo Norte, Col. D6 86
Cravo Norte, stm., Col. D6 86
Cravo Sur, stm., Col. E6 86
Crawford, Co., U.S. E9 132
Crawford, Ms., U.S. D10 122
Crawford, Tx., U.S. C10 130
Crawford Bay, B.C., Can. G14 138
Crawfordsville, Ar., U.S. B8 122
Crawfordsville, In., U.S. H2 112
Crawfordville, Ga., U.S. C3 116
Crawley, Eng., U.K. J12 12
Crazy Woman Creek, stm., Wy., U.S. C6 126
Creal Springs, Il., U.S. G9 120
Cree, stm., Sk., Can. D9 106
Creede, Co., U.S. F10 132
Creedmoor, N.C., U.S. H7 114
Cree Lake, l., Sk., Can. D9 106
Creemore, On., Can. D9 112
Creighton, Ne., U.S. E15 126
Creighton Mine, On., Can. B8 112
Creil, Fr. E11 14
Crema, Italy E6 22
Cremona, Italy E7 22
Crenshaw, Ms., U.S. C8 122
Crepori, stm., Braz. E6 84
Crépy-en-Valois, Fr. E11 14
Cres, Cro. E11 22
Cres, Otok, i., Cro. F11 22
Cresaptown, Md., U.S. E7 114
Crescent, Or., U.S. G5 136
Crescent City, Ca., U.S. B1 134
Crescent City, Fl., U.S. G4 116
Crescent Spur, B.C., Can. C10 138
Cresco, Ia., U.S. H6 118
Crespo, Arg. F7 92
Cresson, Tx., U.S. B10 130
Cressy, Austl. K4 76
Crested Butte, Co., U.S. E9 132
Crestline, Ca., U.S. I8 134
Creston, B.C., Can. G14 138
Creston, Ia., U.S. C3 120
Crestone Peak, mtn., Co., U.S. D3 128
Crestview, Fl., U.S. G12 122
Crestwood Hills, Tn., U.S. I1 114
Creswell, Or., U.S. G3 136
Creswell Bay, b., Nu., Can. A12 106
Crete, Il., U.S. G2 112
Crete, Ne., U.S. G16 126
Crete see Kríti, i., Grc. H7 28
Crete, Sea of see Kritikón Pélagos, Grc. H8 28
Créteil, Fr. F11 14
Cretin, Cape, c., Pap. N. Gui. b4 79a
Creus, Cap de, c., Spain B14 20
Creuse, state, Fr. C8 18
Creuse, stm., Fr. C6 18
Creussen, Ger. G7 16
Creve Coeur, Il., U.S. K9 118
Crevillent, Spain F10 20
Crevillente see Crevillent, Spain F10 20
Crewe, Eng., U.K. H10 12
Crewe, Va., U.S. G7 114
Cricaré, stm., Braz. J5 88
Criciúma, Braz. D13 92
Crikvenica, Cro. E11 22
Crimea see Kryms'kyi pivostriv, pen., Ukr. E4 32
Crimean Peninsula see Kryms'kyi pivostriv, pen., Ukr. E4 32
Crimmitschau, Ger. F8 16
Cripple Creek, Co., U.S. C3 128
Crisfield, Md., U.S. F10 114
Criss Creek, B.C., Can. E10 138
Crissiumal, Braz. C10 92
Cristal, Monts de, mts., Afr. I7 64
Cristalândia, Braz. F1 88

Name	Map Ref.	Page
Cristália, Braz.	I4	88
Cristalina, Braz.	I2	88
Cristinápolis, Braz.	F7	88
Cristino Castro, Braz.	E3	88
Cristóbal Colón, Pico, mtn., Col.	B5	86
Crișul Alb, stm., Eur.	C8	26
Crișul Negru, stm., Eur.	C8	26
Crișul Repede (Sebes Körös), stm., Eur.	B8	26
Crivitz, Wi., U.S.	C1	112
Crna, stm., Mac.	B4	28
Crna Gora (Montenegro), state, Yugo.	G6	26
Crni Drim (Drinit të Zi), stm., Eur.	C14	24
Črnomelj, Slvn.	E12	22
Croajingolong National Park, p.o.i., Austl.	K7	76
Croatia, ctry., Eur.	E13	22
Croche, stm., Qc., Can.	C4	110
Crocker, Mo., U.S.	G5	120
Crocker, Banjaran, mts., Malay.	H1	52
Crockett, Tx., U.S.	F3	122
Crocodilopilos, hist., Egypt	I1	58
Crocus Hill, hill, Anguilla	A1	105a
Crofton, Ky., U.S.	G10	120
Croghan, N.Y., U.S.	E14	112
Croix, Lac la, l., N.A.	C6	118
Croker, Cape, c., Austl.	B6	74
Croker, Cape, c., On., Can.	D9	112
Croker Island, i., Austl.	B6	74
Cromer, Eng., U.K.	I14	12
Cromínia, Braz.	I1	88
Crompton Point, c., Dom.	i6	105c
Cromwell, N.Z.	G3	80
Cromwell, Al., U.S.	E10	122
Crooked, stm., Or., U.S.	F5	136
Crooked Creek, Ak., U.S.	D8	140
Crooked Creek, stm., U.S.	D8	128
Crooked Island, i., Bah.	A10	102
Crooked Island Passage, strt., Bah.	A10	102
Crooked River, Sk., Can.	B10	124
Crookston, Mn., U.S.	D2	118
Crooksville, Oh., U.S.	E3	114
Crosby, Mn., U.S.	E5	118
Crosby, N.D., U.S.	F10	124
Crosby, Mount, mtn., Wy., U.S.	D3	126
Crosbyton, Tx., U.S.	H7	128
Cross, stm., Afr.	H6	64
Crossett, Ar., U.S.	D7	122
Cross Lake, res., Mb., Can.	E11	106
Crossman Peak, mtn., Az., U.S.	I2	132
Cross Plains, Tx., U.S.	B8	130
Cross Plains, Wi., U.S.	H9	118
Cross Sound, strt., Ak., U.S.	E12	140
Crossville, Il., U.S.	F9	120
Crossville, Tn., U.S.	I12	120
Croswell, Mi., U.S.	E7	112
Crotone, Italy	E11	24
Crow, North Fork, stm., Mn., U.S.	F5	118
Crow, South Fork, stm., Mn., U.S.	G4	118
Crow Agency, Mt., U.S.	B5	126
Crow Creek, stm., U.S.	G8	126
Crowder, Ms., U.S.	C8	122
Crowduck Lake, l., Mb., Can.	A3	118
Crowdy Head, c., Austl.	H9	76
Crowell, Tx., U.S.	H9	128
Crow Lake, On., Can.	B5	118
Crowley, La., U.S.	G6	122
Crowleys Ridge, mts., U.S.	B8	122
Crown Mountain, mtn., V.I.U.S.	e7	104b
Crown Point, In., U.S.	G2	112
Crownpoint, N.M., U.S.	H8	132
Crown Point, N.Y., U.S.	G3	110
Crown Prince Frederik Island, i., Nu., Can.	A13	106
Crowsnest Pass, Ab., Can.	G16	138
Crowsnest Pass, p., Can.	G16	138
Crows Nest Peak, mtn., S.D., U.S.	C8	126
Crow Wing, stm., Mn., U.S.	E4	118
Croydon, Austl.	B4	76
Croydon Station, B.C., Can.	C11	138
Crozet, Va., U.S.	F7	114
Crozet, Îles, is., Afr.	J16	4
Crozet Basin, unds.	M9	142
Crucea, Rom.	E15	26
Cruces, Cuba	A7	102
Cruger, Ms., U.S.	D8	122
Crump Lake, l., Or., U.S.	A6	134
Cruz, Cabo, c., Cuba	C9	102
Cruz Alta, Arg.	F6	92
Cruz Alta, Braz.	D11	92
Cruz Bay, V.I.U.S.	e7	104b
Cruz del Eje, Arg.	E5	92
Cruzeiro, Braz.	L3	88
Cruzeiro do Oeste, Braz.	A11	92
Cruzeiro do Sul, Braz.	E3	84
Cruzeta, Braz.	D7	88
Cruz Grande, Chile	D2	92
Crysler, On., Can.	C14	112
Crystal, Mn., U.S.	F5	118
Crystal, N.D., U.S.	F16	124
Crystal Brook, Austl.	I2	76
Crystal City, Mb., Can.	E15	124
Crystal City, Mo., U.S.	F7	120
Crystal City, Tx., U.S.	F8	130
Crystal Falls, Mi., U.S.	B1	112
Crystal Lake, Il., U.S.	B9	120
Crystal Lake, l., Mi., U.S.	D3	112
Crystal Springs, Ms., U.S.	E8	122
Csongrád, Hung.	C7	26
Csongrád, state, Hung.	C7	26
Csorna, Hung.	B4	26
Cu, stm., Asia	F11	32
Cúa, Ven.	B8	86
Cuajinicuilapa, Mex.	G9	100
Cuamba, Moz.	C6	68
Cuando (Kwando), stm., Afr.	D3	68
Cuangar, Ang.	D2	68
Cuango, Ang.	B2	68
Cuango see Kwango, stm., Afr.	F3	66
Cuanza, stm., Ang.	C2	68
Cuao, stm., Ven.	E8	86
Cuareim (Quaraí), stm., S.A.	E9	92
Cuaró, Ur.	E9	92
Cuarto, stm., Arg.	F5	92
Cuatrociénegas, Mex.	B7	100
Cuauhtémoc, Mex.	A5	100
Cuautitlán, Mex.	F6	100
Cuba, Port.	F3	20
Cuba, Al., U.S.	E10	122
Cuba, Il., U.S.	D7	120
Cuba, Mo., U.S.	F6	120
Cuba, N.M., U.S.	G10	132
Cuba, ctry., N.A.	C9	96
Cubagua, Isla, i., Ven.	B9	86
Cubal, Ang.	C1	68
Cubango (Okavango), stm., Afr.	D2	68
Cubati, Braz.	D7	88
Čublas, Russia	D21	8
Cubuk, Tur.	C15	28
Cuchi, stm., Ang.	C2	68
Cuchillo Co, Arg.	I5	92
Cuchivero, stm., Ven.	D9	86
Cucuí, Braz.	G8	86
Cucurpe, Mex.	F7	98
Cúcuta, Col.	D5	86
Cucuy, Piedra de, hill, Ven.	G8	86
Cudahy, Wi., U.S.	F2	112
Cuddalore, India	F4	53
Cuddapah, India	D4	53
Čudovo, Russia	A14	10
Cudworth, Sk., Can.	B8	124
Čudzin, Bela.	H9	10
Cue, Austl.	E3	74
Cuemba, Ang.	C2	68
Cuenca, Ec.	I2	86
Cuenca, Spain	D8	20
Cuenca, co., Spain	E9	20
Cuencamé de Ceniceros, Mex.	C7	100
Cuernavaca, Mex.	F9	100
Cuero, Tx., U.S.	E10	130
Cuers, Fr.	F12	18
Cuervo, Laguna del, l., Mex.	A6	100
Cuesta Pass, p., Ca., U.S.	H5	134
Cueto, Cuba	B9	102
Cugir, Rom.	D10	26
Čuguevka, Russia	B10	38
Čuhlomskoe, ozero, l., Russia	G19	8
Cuiabá, Braz.	G6	84
Cuiabá, stm., Braz.	G6	84
Cuiari, Braz.	G7	86
Cuicatlán, Mex.	G10	100
Cuilapa, Guat.	E2	102
Cuilco see Grijalva, stm., N.A.	G12	100
Cuilo (Kwilu), stm., Afr.	F3	66
Cuité, Braz.	D7	88
Cuíto, stm., Ang.	D2	68
Cuito Cuanavale, Ang.	D2	68
Cuitzeo, Lago de, l., Mex.	F8	100
Cuiuni, stm., Braz.	H10	86
Cukai, Malay.	J6	48
Cukas, Indon.	D4	50
Čukotskij, mys, c., Russia	D26	34
Čukotskij poluostrov (Chukotsk Peninsula), pen., Russia	C26	34
Čulakkurgan, Kaz.	F11	32
Culbertson, Mt., U.S.	F9	124
Cul de Sac, Guad.	A1	105a
Cul de Sac, Neth. Ant.	A1	105a
Culebra, P.R.	B5	104a
Culebra, Isla de, i., P.R.	B5	104a
Culebra Peak, mtn., Co., U.S.	D3	128
Culfa, Azer.	B6	56
Culgoa, stm., Austl.	G6	76
Culiacán, Mex.	C5	100
Culiacán, Mex.	C5	100
Culion Island, i., Phil.	E2	52
Cúllar, Spain	G8	20
Cullen, La., U.S.	E5	122
Culleoka, Tn., U.S.	B12	122
Cullera, Spain	E10	20
Cullman, Al., U.S.	C12	122
Cullom, Il., U.S.	D9	120
Čul'man, Russia	E13	34
Culpeper, Va., U.S.	F7	114
Culpina, Bol.	D4	90
Culuene, stm., Braz.	F7	84
Culver, In., U.S.	G3	112
Culver, Or., U.S.	F5	136
Culverden, N.Z.	F5	80
Čulym, Russia	C14	32
Čulym, stm., Russia	C14	32
Čum, Russia	C1	34
Cumaná, Ven.	B9	86
Cumare, Cerro, hill, Col.	G5	86
Cumari, Braz.	J1	88
Cumbal, Nevado, vol., Col.	G2	86
Cumbe, Braz.	F7	88
Cumberland, B.C., Can.	G5	138
Cumberland, Ky., U.S.	G2	114
Cumberland, Md., U.S.	E7	114
Cumberland, Va., U.S.	G7	114
Cumberland, Wi., U.S.	F6	118
Cumberland, stm., U.S.	H2	114
Cumberland, Lake, res., Ky., U.S.	H13	120
Cumberland, South Fork, stm., U.S.	H13	120
Cumberland Gap, p., U.S.	H2	114
Cumberland Island National Seashore, p.o.i., Ga., U.S.	F4	116
Cumberland Islands, is., Austl.	C7	76
Cumberland Lake, l., Sk., Can.	E10	106
Cumberland Peninsula, pen., Nu., Can.	B17	106
Cumberland Plateau, plat., U.S.	G14	120
Cumberland Sound, strt., Nu., Can.	B17	106
Cumbernauld, Scot., U.K.	F9	12
Cumbrian Mountains, mts., Eng., U.K.	G9	12
Cumby, Tx., U.S.	D3	122
Čumikan, Russia	F16	34
Cumming, Ga., U.S.	B1	116
Cummins, Austl.	F7	74
Cumnock, Scot., U.K.	F8	12
Cumpas, Mex.	F8	98
Cumra, Tur.	F15	28
Čumyš, stm., Russia	D15	32
Čuna, stm., Russia	C17	32
Cunani, Braz.	C7	84
Cunaviche, Ven.	D8	86
Cunco, Chile	G2	90
Cundinamarca, state, Col.	E4	86
Čundža, Kaz.	F13	32
Cunene (Kunene), stm., Afr.	D1	68
Cuneo (Coni), Italy	F4	22
Cunha Porã, Braz.	C11	92
Čunja, stm., Russia	B17	32
Cunnamulla, Austl.	G5	76
Cunningham, Ks., U.S.	D10	128
Čunskij, Russia	C17	32
Cunucunuma, stm., Ven.	F9	86
Čuny, Russia	G17	8
Cuorgnè, Italy	E4	22
Cupar, Sk., Can.	D9	124
Cupar, Scot., U.K.	E9	12
Cupica, Golfo de, b., Col.	D3	86
Čuprovo, Russia	D22	8
Cuquenán, stm., Ven.	E11	86
Curaçá, Braz.	E6	88
Curaçao, i., Neth. Ant.	p21	104g
Curacautín, Chile	I2	92
Curanilahue, Chile	H1	92
Curanipe, Chile	G1	92
Čurapča, Russia	D15	34
Curaray, stm., S.A.	H4	86
Curepipe, Mrts.	i10	69a
Curepto, Chile	G1	92
Curicó, Chile	G2	92
Curicuriari, stm., Braz.	H8	86
Curimatá, Braz.	E3	88
Curitiba, Braz.	B13	92
Curitibanos, Braz.	C12	92
Curiuaú, stm., Braz.	H11	86
Curiúva, Braz.	B12	92
Curlew, Wa., U.S.	B8	136
Curnamona, Austl.	H2	76
Čurovići, Russia	H15	10
Currais Novos, Braz.	D7	88
Curralinho, Braz.	D8	84
Currant Mountain, mtn., Nv., U.S.	E1	132
Current, stm., U.S.	H7	120
Currie, Austl.	m12	77a
Currituck, N.C., U.S.	H9	114
Currituck Sound, strt., N.C., U.S.	H10	114
Curtea de Argeș, Rom.	D11	26
Curtina, Ur.	F9	92
Curtis, Ar., U.S.	D5	122
Curtis, Ne., U.S.	G12	126
Curtis, Port, b., Austl.	D8	76
Curtis Channel, strt., Austl.	D8	76
Curtis Island, i., Austl.	D8	76
Curtis Island, i., N.Z.	G9	72
Curu, stm., Braz.	B6	88
Curuá, stm., Braz.	D7	84
Curuá, stm., Braz.	E7	84
Curuá, Ilha do, i., Braz.	C7	84
Curuá-Una, stm., Braz.	D7	84
Curuçá, Braz.	D8	84
Curumu, Braz.	D7	84
Curup, Indon.	E3	50
Curupá, Braz.	E2	88
Cururupu, Braz.	A3	88
Curuzú Cuatiá, Arg.	D8	92
Curvelo, Braz.	J3	88
Cusco, Peru	F3	84
Cushing, Ok., U.S.	B2	122
Cushing, Tx., U.S.	F4	122
Cushman, Ar., U.S.	I6	120
Cusiana, stm., Col.	E5	86
Cusihuiriachic, Mex.	A5	100
Čusovaja, stm., Russia	C9	32
Čusovoj, Russia	C9	32
Cusset, Fr.	C9	18
Cusseta, Ga., U.S.	E14	122
Čust, Uzb.	F12	32
Custer, Mi., U.S.	E3	112
Custer, Mt., U.S.	A5	126
Custer, S.D., U.S.	D9	126
Custódia, Braz.	E7	88
Cut, Nuhu, i., Indon.	G9	44
Cut Bank, Mt., U.S.	B14	136
Cutbank, stm., Ab., Can.	B12	138
Cut Bank Creek, stm., U.S.	F12	124
Cut Bank Creek, stm., Mt., U.S.	B14	136
Cutervo, Peru	E2	84
Cuthbert, Ga., U.S.	F14	122
Cutler, Ca., U.S.	G6	134
Cutler, Me., U.S.	F9	110
Cutlerville, Mi., U.S.	F4	112
Cutral-Có, Arg.	G3	90
Cutro, Italy	E10	24
Cuttack, India	H10	54
Cutzamalá, stm., Mex.	F8	100
Čuvašija, state, Russia	C7	32
Cuvier, Cape, c., Austl.	D2	74
Cuvo, stm., Ang.	C1	68
Cuxhaven, Ger.	C4	16
Cuyahoga Falls, Oh., U.S.	C4	114
Cuyama, stm., Ca., U.S.	I6	134
Cuyamaca Peak, mtn., Ca., U.S.	J9	134
Cuyarí, stm., S.A.	G7	86
Cuyo, Phil.	E3	52
Cuyo East Pass, strt., Phil.	E3	52
Cuyo Islands, is., Phil.	E3	52
Cuyo West Pass, strt., Phil.	E3	52
Cuyubini, stm., Ven.	D11	86
Cuyuni, stm., S.A.	B6	84
Cuyuni-Mazaruni, state, Guy.	D11	86
Cwmbran, Wales, U.K.	J10	12
Cyclades see Kikládhes, is., Grc.	F7	28
Cypress, La., U.S.	F5	122
Cypress Hills, hills, Can.	E4	124
Cypress River, Mb., Can.	E14	124
Cypress Springs, Lake, res., Tx., U.S.	D3	122
Cyprus, ctry., Asia	C4	58
Cyprus, i., Asia	D15	4
Cyprus, North, ctry., Asia	C4	58
Cyrenaica see Barqah, hist. reg., Libya	A4	62
Cyril, Ok., U.S.	G10	128
Cyril E. King Airport, V.I.U.S.	e7	104b
Cyrus Field Bay, b., Nu., Can.	E13	141
Čyrvonae, vozero, l., Bela.	H10	10
Cythera see Kýthira, i., Grc.	G5	28
Czaplinek, Pol.	C12	16
Czarna Woda, Pol.	C14	16
Czarnków, Pol.	D12	16
Czechoslovakia see Czech Republic, ctry., Eur.	G11	16
Czechowice-Dziedzice, Pol.	G15	16
Czech Republic, ctry., Eur.	G11	16
Czerniejewo, Pol.	D13	16
Czerwieńsk, Pol.	D11	16
Częstochowa, Pol.	F15	16
Częstochowa, state, Pol.	F15	16
Człuchów, Pol.	C13	16

D

Name	Map Ref.	Page
Da, stm., China	G8	42
Da, Song see Black, stm., Asia	D9	46
Da'an, China	J4	42
Dabajuro, Ven.	B6	86
Daba Ling, mtn., China	I5	42
Daba Shan, mts., China	E3	42
Dabat, Eth.	E7	62
Dabeiba, Col.	D3	86
Dabhoi, India	G4	54
Dąbie, Pol.	D14	16
Dabie Shan, mts., China	F6	42
Dabnou, Niger	G5	64
Dabola, Gui.	G2	64
Dabou, C. Iv.	H4	64
Daboya, Ghana	H4	64
Dabra, India	F7	54
Dąbrowa Białostocka, Pol.	C19	16
Dabu, China	I7	42
Dacca see Dhaka, Bngl.	G13	54
Dac Glei, Viet.	E8	48
Dachau, Ger.	H7	16
Dačice, Czech Rep.	G11	16
Dacoma, Ok., U.S.	E10	128
Dadanawa, Guy.	F12	86
Dade City, Fl., U.S.	H3	116
Dadeldhurā, Nepal	D8	54
Dadeville, Al., U.S.	E13	122
Dādra and Nagar Haveli, state, India	I4	54
Dādu, Pak.	D10	56
Daegu see Taegu, Kor., S.	D1	40
Daejeon see Taejŏn, Kor., S.	F7	38
Daerhanwangfu, China	B5	38
Daet, Phil.	C4	52
Dafang, China	F6	36
Dafeng, China	E9	42
Dáfni, Grc.	F5	28
Dafoe, Sk., Can.	C9	124
Dafu, stm., China	F5	42
Dagā, stm., Mya.	D2	48
Dagana, Sen.	F1	64
Daga Post, Sudan	F6	62
Dağardı, Tur.	D12	28
Dagda, Lat.	D10	10
Dagestan, state, Russia	F7	32
Daglung, China	D13	54
Dagu, China	B7	42
Dagua, Pap. N. Gui.	a3	79a
Daguan, China	F5	36
Daguan Hu, l., China	F7	42
Daguao, P.R.	B4	104a
Dagujia, China	C6	38
Dagupan, Phil.	B3	52
Dagzê Co, l., China	B11	54
Dahab, Egypt	J5	58
Dahei, India	H4	54
Daheiding Shan, mtn., China	B10	36
Da Hinggan Ling (Greater Khingan Range), mts., China	B9	36
Dahlak Archipelago, is., Erit.	D8	62
Dahlonega, Ga., U.S.	B1	116
Dahlonega Plateau, plat., U.S.	C14	122
Dahmani, Tun.	I2	24
Dahme, Ger.	E9	16
Dāhod, India	G5	54
Dahomey see Benin, ctry., Afr.	G5	64
Dahra, Libya	B3	62
Dahra, mts., Alg.	H11	20
Dahshur, Pyramides de (Dashur, Pyramids of), hist., Egypt	I1	58
Dai, i., Sol. Is.	d9	79b
Daia, Rom.	E12	26
Dai Hai, l., China	A5	42
Daik-u, Mya.	D3	48
Dā'il, Syria	F7	58
Daimiel, Spain	E7	20
Daingean, Ire.	H5	12
Daingerfield, Tx., U.S.	D4	122
Dainkog, China	E4	36
Daireaux, Arg.	H7	92
Dairen see Dalian, China	B9	42
Dairût, Egypt	K1	58
Dai-sen, vol., Japan	D6	40
Daisetta, Tx., U.S.	G4	122
Daixian, China	B5	42
Daiyun Shan, mts., China	I8	42
Dajarra, Austl.	C2	76
Dajian Shan, mtn., China	F5	36
Dakar, Sen.	G1	64
Dakeng, China	H6	42
Dakhin Shāhbāzpur Island, i., Bngl.	G13	54
Dakhla, W. Sah.	E1	64
Dākoānk, India	G7	46
Dakoro, Niger	G6	64
Dakota City, Ia., U.S.	B3	120
Dakota City, Ne., U.S.	B1	120
Đakovica, Yugo.	G7	26
Đakovo, Cro.	E15	22
Dala, Sol. Is.	e9	79b
Dalaba, Gui.	G2	64
Dalad Qi, China	A4	42
Dalälven, stm., Swe.	F7	8
Dalaman, stm., Tur.	G11	28
Dalāmī, Sudan	E6	62
Dalandzadgad, Mong.	C5	36
Dalarna, state, Swe.	F6	8
Da Lat, Viet.	F9	48
Dālbandin, Pak.	D9	56
Dalbosjön, b., Swe.	G5	8
Dalby, Austl.	F8	76
Dale, Nor.	F1	8
Dale, In., U.S.	F10	120
Dale Hollow Lake, res., U.S.	H12	120
Dalet, Mya.	B1	48
Daleville, In., U.S.	H4	112
Dalga, Egypt	K1	58
Dalhart, Tx., U.S.	E6	128
Dalhousie, N.B., Can.	B10	110
Dalhousie, India	B5	54
Dalhousie, Cape, c., N.T., Can.	B14	140
Dali, China	F5	36
Dali, China	D3	42
Dalian (Dairen), China	B9	42
Daliang Shan, mts., China	F5	36
Dalin, China	C5	38
Daling, stm., China	D4	38
Dalj, Cro.	E15	22
Dālkola, India	F11	54
Dallas, Ga., U.S.	D14	122
Dallas, Or., U.S.	F3	136
Dallas, Pa., U.S.	C9	114
Dallas, Tx., U.S.	B11	130
Dallas, Wi., U.S.	F7	118
Dallas Center, Ia., U.S.	J4	118
Dallas City, Il., U.S.	D6	120
Dalli Rājhara, India	H8	54
Dall Island, i., Ak., U.S.	F13	140
Dall Lake, l., Ak., U.S.	D7	140
Dalmacija see Dalmatia, hist. reg., Eur.	G12	22
Dalmatia, hist. reg., Eur.	G12	22
Dalmau, India	E8	54
Dal'negorsk, Russia	B11	38
Dal'nerečensk, Russia	B11	36
Dal'nyk, Ukr.	C17	26
Daloa, C. Iv.	H3	64
Dalqū, Sudan	C6	62
Dalroy, Ab., Can.	E17	138
Dalrymple, Mount, mtn., Austl.	C7	76
Dalsing Sarai, India	F10	54
Dāltenganj, India	F10	54
Dalton, Ga., U.S.	C13	122
Dalton, Ma., U.S.	B12	114
Dalton, Ne., U.S.	F10	126
Daludalu, Indon.	C2	50
Dalupiri Island, i., Phil.	A3	52
Dalwallinu, Austl.	F3	74
Daly, stm., Austl.	B6	74
Daly Bay, b., Nu., Can.	C13	106
Daly City, Ca., U.S.	F3	134
Daly Lake, l., Sk., Can.	D9	106
Daly Waters, Austl.	C6	74
Dam, stm., China	B14	54
Damaia, Port.	F1	20
Damān, India	H4	54
Damān and Diu, state, India	H4	54
Damanhûr, Egypt	G1	58
Damar, Pulau, i., Indon.	G8	44
Damaraland, hist. reg., Nmb.	E2	68
Damascus see Dimashq, Syria	E7	58
Damascus, Ar., U.S.	B6	122
Damascus, Ga., U.S.	F14	122
Damascus, Md., U.S.	E8	114
Damaturu, Nig.	G7	64
Damāvand, Qolleh-ye, vol., Iran	B7	56
Damba, Ang.	B2	68
Dambarta, Nig.	G6	64
Damboa, Nig.	G7	64
Dâmbovița, state, Rom.	E12	26
Dâmbovița, stm., Rom.	D12	26
Dam Doi, Viet.	H7	48
Damen Dao, i., China	H9	42
Dāmghān, Iran	B7	56
Damiao, China	C1	42
Damietta, Egypt	G2	58
Damietta Mouth see Dumyât, Masabb, mth., Egypt	G3	58
Daming, China	C6	42
Dāmodar, stm., India	G11	54
Damoh, India	G7	54
Damongo, Ghana	H4	64
Dampier, Austl.	D3	74
Dampier, Selat, strt., Indon.	F9	44
Dampier Land, pen., Austl.	C4	74
Dampier Strait, strt., Pap. N. Gui.	b4	79a
Dâmrei, Chuŏr Phnum, mts., Camb.	G7	48
Damxung, China	C13	54
Dan, stm., China	E4	42
Dan, stm., U.S.	H6	114
Dana, In., U.S.	I2	112
Danai, Indon.	C3	50
Danakil, reg., Afr.	E8	62
Danané, C. Iv.	H3	64
Da Nang, Viet.	D9	48
Danao, Phil.	E5	52
Dānāpur, India	F10	54
Danba, China	E5	36
Danbury, Ct., U.S.	C12	114
Danbury, Ia., U.S.	B2	120
Danbury, Ne., U.S.	A8	128
Danby Lake, l., Ca., U.S.	I1	132
Dandeli, India	D2	53
Dandenong, Austl.	K5	76
Dandong, China	D5	38
Dandridge, Tn., U.S.	H2	114
Danfeng, China	E4	42
Danforth, Me., U.S.	E9	110
Dang, stm., China	F16	32
Dangan Liedao, is., China	K6	42
Dangara, Taj.	B10	56
Dangchang, China	E5	36
Danger Point, c., S. Afr.	I4	70
Danggali Conservation Park, p.o.i., Austl.	I3	76
Dangila, Eth.	E7	62
Dangriga, Belize	D3	102
Dangshan, China	D7	42
Dangtu, China	F8	42
Dan-Gulbi, Nig.	G6	64
Dangyang, China	F4	42
Daniel, Wy., U.S.	H16	136
Daniel-Johnson, Barrage, dam, Qc., Can.	E17	106
Daniëlskuil, S. Afr.	F6	70
Danielson, Ct., U.S.	C13	114
Daniels Pass, p., Ut., U.S.	C5	132
Danielsville, Ga., U.S.	B2	116
Danilov, Russia	G18	8
Danilovka, Kaz.	D12	32
Daning, China	I4	42
Danjiangkou Shuiku, res., China	E4	42
Danjo-guntō, is., Japan	G1	40
Danlí, Hond.	F4	102
Danmark Fjord, b., Grnld.	A22	141
Dannebrog, Ne., U.S.	F14	126
Dannenberg, Ger.	C6	16
Dannevirke, N.Z.	E7	80
Danshui, China	J6	42
Dansville, N.Y., U.S.	B8	114
Dante, Va., U.S.	H3	114
Dantewāra, India	B5	53
Danube, stm., Eur.	F11	6
Danube, Mouths of the, mth., Eur.	E16	26
Danubyu, Mya.	D2	48
Danvers, Il., U.S.	D8	120
Danville, Qc., Can.	E4	110
Danville, Ga., U.S.	D2	116
Danville, Il., U.S.	H2	112
Danville, Ky., U.S.	G13	120
Danville, Pa., U.S.	D9	114
Danville, Vt., U.S.	F4	110
Danville, Va., U.S.	H6	114
Danville, Wa., U.S.	B8	136
Danxian, China	L3	42
Danyang, China	F8	42
Danzig see Gdańsk, Pol.	B14	16
Danzig, Gulf of see Gdansk, Gulf of, b., Eur.	B15	16
Daocheng, China	F5	36
Daodi, China	B8	42
Daohu, China	G7	42
Daosa, India	E6	54
Daotiandi, China	B10	36
Daoukro, C. Iv.	H4	64
Daoxian, China	I4	42
Daozhen, China	G2	42
Dapaong, Togo	G5	64
Dapchi, Nig.	G7	64
Daphnae, hist., Egypt	H3	58
Daphne, Al., U.S.	G11	122
Dapingshan, China	I3	42
Da Qaidam, China	D4	36
Daqiu, China	I8	42
Dara, Sen.	F1	64
Dar'ā, Syria	F7	58
Dar'ā, state, Syria	F7	58
Dārāb, Iran	D7	56
Darāban, Pak.	C3	54
Darabani, Rom.	A13	26
Darasun, Russia	F11	34
Đaravica, mtn., Yugo.	G7	26
Darâw, Egypt	C6	62
Dārayyā, Syria	E7	58
Darb al-Ḥajj, Jabal, mtn., Jord.	H6	58
Darbhanga, India	E10	54
D'Arbonne, Bayou, stm., La., U.S.	E6	122
Darby, Mt., U.S.	D12	136
Dardanelle, Ar., U.S.	B5	122
Dardanelle Lake, res., Ar., U.S.	B5	122
Dardanelles see Çanakkale Boğazı, strt., Tur.	C9	28
Dar-el-Beida see Casablanca, Mor.	C3	64
Dar es Salaam, Tan.	F7	66
Darfo, Italy	E7	22
Dargai, Pak.	A3	54
Dargan-Ata, Turkmen.	A9	56
Dargaville, N.Z.	B5	80
Dargol, Niger	G5	64
Darhan, Mong.	B6	36
Darıca, Tur.	C12	28
Darién, Col.	F3	86
Darien, Ga., U.S.	E4	116
Darien, Parque Nacional, p.o.i., Pan.	D2	86
Darién, Serranía del, mts.	C3	86
Dārjiling, India	E12	54
Dark Head, c., St. Vin.	o11	105e
Darlag, China	E4	36
Darling, S. Afr.	H4	70
Darling, Ms., U.S.	C8	122
Darling, stm., Austl.	I4	76
Darling Downs, reg., Austl.	F8	76
Darlingford, Mb., Can.	E15	124
Darling Range, mts., Austl.	F3	74
Darlington, Eng., U.K.	G11	12
Darlington, Wi., U.S.	B7	120
Darlington Dam, res., S. Afr.	H7	70
Darlot, Lake, l., Austl.	E4	74
Darłowo, Pol.	B12	16
Darmstadt, Ger.	G4	16
Darnah, Libya	A4	62
Darnall, S. Afr.	F10	70
Darney, Fr.	F15	14
Darnley, Cape, c., Ant.	B11	81
Darnley Bay, b., N.T., Can.	B6	106
Darr, stm., Austl.	D4	76
Darregueira, Arg.	H6	92
Darreh Gaz, Iran	B8	56
Darrington, Wa., U.S.	B5	136
Darrouzett, Tx., U.S.	E8	128
Dart, Cape, c., Ant.	C27	81
Dartmoor, Austl.	K3	76
Dartmoor, for., Eng., U.K.	K9	12
Dartmoor National Park, p.o.i., Eng., U.K.	K9	12
Dartmouth, N.S., Can.	F13	110
Dartmouth, Eng., U.K.	K9	12
Dartmouth, Lake, l., Austl.	E5	76
Dartmouth Reservoir, res., Austl.	K6	76
Daru, Pap. N. Gui.	b3	79a
Daruvar, Cro.	E14	22
Darvaza, Turkmen.	A8	56
Dārwha, India	H6	54
Darwin, Austl.	B6	74
Darwin, Bahía, b., Chile	I2	90
Darya Khān, Pak.	C3	54
Dashbalbar, Mong.	B7	36
Dashitou, China	C8	38
Dašhovuz, Turkmen.	A8	56
Dasht, stm., Pak.	D9	56
Dashur, Pyramids of see Dahshur, Pyramides de, hist., Egypt	I1	58
Dashutang, China	A6	48
Dasol Bay, b., Phil.	C2	52
Dastgardān, Iran	C8	56
Datang, China	I3	42
Datça, Tur.	G10	28
Date, Japan	C14	38
Datia, India	F7	54
Datian, China	I7	42
Datian Ding, mtn., China	J4	42
Datong, China	D5	36
Datong, China	B9	36
Datong, China	A5	42
Datong Shan, mts., China	D4	36
Datu, Cape, c., Asia	E4	44
Datumakuta, Indon.	B10	50
Datu Piang, Phil.	G5	52
Daua (Dawa), stm., Afr.	G8	62
Daudnagar, India	F10	54
Daugai, Lith.	F7	10
Daugavpils, Lat.	E9	10
Dauhinava, Bela.	F10	10
Daule, Ec.	H2	86
Daule, stm., Ec.	H1	86
Daund, India	B2	53
Daung Kyun, i., Mya.	F3	48
Dauphin, Mb., Can.	C13	124
Dauphin, stm., Mb., Can.	C15	124
Dauphiné, hist. reg., Fr.	E11	18
Dauphin Island, Al., U.S.	G10	122
Dauphin Island, i., Al., U.S.	G10	122
Dauphin Lake, l., Mb., Can.	C13	124
Daura, Nig.	G6	64
Dāvangere, India	D2	53
Davant, La., U.S.	H9	122
Davao, Phil.	G5	52
Davao Gulf, b., Phil.	G5	52
Dāvarzan, Iran	B8	56
Davenport, Fl., U.S.	H4	116
Davenport, Ia., U.S.	C7	120
Davenport, Ok., U.S.	B2	122
Davenport, Wa., U.S.	C8	136
Davenport Downs, Austl.	E3	76
Davey, Port, b., Austl.	o12	77a
David, Pan.	H6	102
David City, Ne., U.S.	F15	126
Davidson, Sk., Can.	C7	124
Davidson Mountains, mts., Ak., U.S.	C11	140
Davie, Fl., U.S.	J5	116
Davis, Ca., U.S.	E4	134
Davis, N.C., U.S.	B9	116
Davis, Ok., U.S.	G11	128
Davis, W.V., U.S.	E6	114
Davis, stm., Austl.	D4	74
Davis, sci., Ant.	B12	81
Davis, Mount, mtn., Pa., U.S.	E6	114
Davisboro, Ga., U.S.	C3	116
Davis Dam, dam, U.S.	H2	132
Davis Inlet, Nf., Can.	D18	106
Davis Mountains, mts., Tx., U.S.	D3	130
Davis Sea, Ant.	P11	142
Davis Strait, strt., N.A.	D14	141
Davos, Switz.	D6	22
Davy, W.V., U.S.	G4	114
Davyd-Haradok, Bela.	H9	10
Dawa (Daua), stm., Afr.	G7	62
Dawei (Tavoy), Mya.	E4	48
Dawen, stm., China	D7	42
Dawlan, Mya.	D4	48
Dawna Range, mts., Mya.	D4	48
Dawson, Yk., Can.	C3	106
Dawson, Ga., U.S.	F14	122
Dawson, Ne., U.S.	D2	120
Dawson, Tx., U.S.	F2	122
Dawson, stm., Austl.	D7	76
Dawson, Isla, i., Chile	J2	90
Dawson Bay, b., Mb., Can.	B13	124
Dawson Creek, B.C., Can.	D7	106
Dawson Inlet, b., Nu., Can.	C12	106
Dawson Range, mts., Yk., Can.	C3	106
Dawsonville, Ga., U.S.	B1	116
Dax, Fr.	F4	18
Daxian, China	F2	42
Daxing, China	B7	42
Daxu, China	I4	42
Daxue Shan, mts., China	F5	36
Dayang, stm., China	D5	38
Dayangshu, China	B9	36
Dayao, China	F5	36
Daye, China	F6	42
Daying, China	B5	42
Daylesford, Austl.	K5	76
Daymán, stm., Ur.	E9	92
Dayong, China	G4	42
Dayr az-Zawr, Syria	B4	56
Dayr Ḥāfir, Syria	B8	58
Daysland, Ab., Can.	D18	138
Dayton, Oh., U.S.	E1	114
Dayton, Or., U.S.	E3	136
Dayton, Tn., U.S.	B13	122
Dayton, Tx., U.S.	G4	122
Dayton, Wa., U.S.	D9	136
Dayton, Wy., U.S.	C5	126
Daytona Beach, Fl., U.S.	G5	116
Dayu, China	I6	42
Dayu Ling, mts., China	I6	42
Da Yunhe (Grand Canal), can., China	E8	42
Dayville, Or., U.S.	F7	136
Dazhu, China	F2	42
Dazkırı, Tur.	F12	28
De Aar, S. Afr.	G7	70
Deadhorse, Ak., U.S.	B10	140
Deadman's Cay, Bah.	A10	102
Dead Sea, l., Asia	G6	58
Deadwood, S.D., U.S.	C9	126
Deakin, Austl.	F5	74
Deal, Eng., U.K.	J14	12
Dealesville, S. Afr.	F7	70
Deal Island, Md., U.S.	F10	114
De'an, China	G6	42
Dean, stm., B.C., Can.	D4	138
Deán Funes, Arg.	E5	92
Deans Dundas Bay, b., N.T., Can.	B16	140
Dearborn, Mi., U.S.	B2	114
Dearg, Beinn, mtn., Scot., U.K.	D8	12
Dease, stm., B.C., Can.	D5	106
Dease Arm, b., N.T., Can.	B6	106
Dease Strait, strt., Nu., Can.	B9	106
Death Valley, Ca., U.S.	G9	134
Death Valley, val., Ca., U.S.	G9	134
Death Valley National Park, p.o.i., U.S.	G8	134
Deatsville, Al., U.S.	E12	122
Deauville, Fr.	E8	14
Deba, Nig.	G7	64
Debao, China	J2	42
Debar, Mac.	B3	28
De Bary, Fl., U.S.	H4	116
Debe, Trin.	s12	105f
De Berry, Tx., U.S.	E4	122
Dębica, Pol.	F17	16
Dęblin, Pol.	E17	16
Débo, Lac, l., Mali	F4	64
Deborah West, Lake, l., Austl.	F3	74
Deboyne Islands, is., Pap. N. Gui.	B10	74
Debre Birhan, Eth.	F7	62
Debrecen, Hung.	B8	26
Debre Mark'os, Eth.	E7	62
Debre Tabor, Eth.	E7	62
Debre Zeyit, Eth.	F7	62
Debrzno, Pol.	C13	16
Decatur, Al., U.S.	C11	122
Decatur, Ga., U.S.	C1	116
Decatur, Il., U.S.	E9	120
Decatur, In., U.S.	H4	112
Decatur, Mi., U.S.	F3	112
Decatur, Ne., U.S.	C1	120
Decatur, Tn., U.S.	B14	122
Decaturville, Tn., U.S.	B10	122
Decazeville, Fr.	E8	18
Deccan, plat., India	B4	53
Decelles, Réservoir, res., Qc., Can.	F15	106
Deception, stm., Bots.	B6	70

Name — Map Ref. — Page

Deception, Mount, mtn., Wa., U.S. C3 136
Decherd, Tn., U.S. B12 122
Dechhu, India E4 54
Děčín, Czech Rep. F10 16
Decize, Fr. H12 14
Decker Lake, B.C., Can. B5 138
Decorah, Ia., U.S. H7 118
Dedaye, Mya. D2 48
Dededo, Guam i10 78c
Dedegöl Tepesi, mtn., Tur. F14 28
De Doorns, S. Afr. H4 70
Dédougou, Burkina G4 64
Dedoviči, Russia C12 10
Dedovsk, Russia E20 10
Deduru, stm., Sri L. H5 53
Dee, stm., U.K. I9 12
Dee, stm., Scot., U.K. D10 12
Deenwood, Ga., U.S. E3 116
Deep, stm., N.C., U.S. A6 116
Deep Creek, stm., U.S. H14 136
Deep River, On., Can. B12 112
Deep River, Ia., U.S. C5 120
Deepwater, Mo., U.S. F4 120
Deep Well, Austl. D6 74
Deer Creek, stm., Ms., U.S. D8 122
Deerfield, Il., U.S. F2 112
Deerfield, Ks., U.S. C7 128
Deerfield Beach, Fl., U.S. J5 116
Deering, Ak., U.S. C7 140
Deer Island, i., N.B., Can. F10 110
Deer Isle, Me., U.S. F8 110
Deer Lake, Nf., Can. j22 107a
Deer Lodge, Mt., U.S. D14 136
Deer Park, Al., U.S. F10 122
Deer Park, Wa., U.S. C9 136
Deerpass Bay, b., N.T., Can. B6 106
Deer Trail, Co., U.S. B4 128
Defiance, Ia., U.S. C2 120
Defiance, Oh., U.S. C1 114
Defiance, Mount, mtn., Or., U.S. E5 136
De Forest, Wi., U.S. H9 118
De Funiak Springs, Fl., U.S. G12 122
Dêgê, China E4 36
Degeh Bur, Eth. F8 62
Dégelis, Qc., Can. C8 110
Degerfors, Swe. G6 8
Deggendorf, Ger. H8 16
Degh, stm., Asia B5 54
Değirmendere, Tur. E10 28
De Gray Lake, res., Ar., U.S. C5 122
De Grey, stm., Austl. D3 74
Dehalak' Desēt, i., Erit. D8 62
Dehiwala-Mount Lavinia, Sri L. H4 53
Dehlorān, Iran C6 56
Dehra Dūn, India C7 54
Dehra Dūn Cantonment, India C6 54
Dehri, India F10 54
Dehu, India B1 53
Dehua, China I8 42
Dehui, China B6 38
Deinze, Bel. D12 14
Deir Mawâs, Egypt K1 58
Dej, Rom. B10 26
Dejnau, Turkmen. B9 56
De Kalb, Il., U.S. C9 120
De Kalb, Ms., U.S. E10 122
De Kalb, Tx., U.S. D4 122
Dekese, D.R.C. E4 66
Deke Sokehs, i., Micron. m11 78d
Dékoa, C.A.R. C3 66
De Land, Fl., U.S. G4 116
Delanggu, Indon. G7 50
Delano, Ca., U.S. H6 134
Delano, Mn., U.S. F5 118
Delaport Point, c., Bah. m18 104f
Delapu, China C13 54
Delarof Islands, is., Ak., U.S. g23 140a
Delaware, Oh., U.S. D2 114
Delaware, Ok., U.S. H2 120
Delaware, state, U.S. F10 114
Delaware, stm., U.S. D10 114
Delaware, stm., Ks., U.S. E2 120
Delaware, East Branch, stm., N.Y., U.S. B10 114
Delaware, West Branch, stm., U.S. B11 114
Delaware Bay, b., U.S. E10 114
Delaware City, De., U.S. E10 114
Delburne, Ab., Can. D17 138
Del Campillo, Arg. G5 92
Del City, Ok., U.S. F11 128
Delegate, Austl. K7 76
Delémont, Switz. C4 22
De Leon, Tx., U.S. B9 130
Delfinópolis, Braz. K2 88
Délfoi, hist., Grc. E5 28
Delft, Neth. B13 14
Delft Island, i., Sri L. G4 53
Delfzijl, Neth. A15 14
Delgado, Cabo, c., Moz. C7 68
Delger, stm., Mong. G8 34
Delgerhet, Mong. B7 36
Delhi, On., Can. F9 112
Delhi, India D6 54
Delhi, Ia., U.S. B6 120
Delhi, La., U.S. E7 122
Delhi, N.Y., U.S. B11 114
Delhi, state, India D6 54
Delia, Ab., Can. E18 138
Deliblato, Yugo. E8 26
Delicias, Mex. A6 100
Delight, Ar., U.S. C5 122
Delījān, Iran C7 56
Deline, N.T., Can. B6 106
Delingde, Russia B11 34
Delingha, China D4 36
Dēliņkalns, hill, Lat. C9 10
Delisle, Sk., Can. C6 124
Delitzsch, Ger. E8 16
Dell City, Tx., U.S. C2 130
Delle, Fr. G16 14
Dellys, Alg. H14 20
Del Mar, Ca., U.S. K8 134
Delmar, Ia., U.S. C7 120
Delmar, Md., U.S. F10 114
Delmarva Peninsula, pen., U.S. F10 114
Delmas, Sk., Can. B5 124
Delmenhorst, Ger. C4 16
Delmiro Gouveia, Braz. E7 88
Delnice, Cro. E11 22
Del Norte, Co., U.S. D2 128
De-Longa, ostrova, is., Russia A19 34
De Long Mountains, mts., Ak., U.S. C7 140
Deloraine, Mb., Can. E13 124
Delorme, Lac, l., Qc., Can. E16 106
Delos see Dílos, hist., Grc. F8 28
Delphi, In., U.S. H3 112
Delphi see Délfoi, hist., Grc. E5 28
Delphos, Ks., U.S. B11 128
Delportshoop, S. Afr. F7 70
Delray Beach, Fl., U.S. J5 116
Del Rio, Tx., U.S. E7 130
Delta, Co., U.S. E8 132
Delta, Mo., U.S. G8 120
Delta, Ut., U.S. D4 132
Delta Amacuro, state, Ven. C11 86
Delta Beach, Mb., Can. D15 124
Delta City, Ms., U.S. D8 122
Delta Downs, Austl. C8 74
Delta Junction, Ak., U.S. D10 140
Delta Peak, mtn., B.C., Can. D4 106
Del Valle, Tx., U.S. D10 130
Del Verme Falls, wtfl, Eth. F8 62
Delvinë, Alb. E14 24
Demak, Indon. G7 50
Demarcation Point, c., Ak., U.S. C11 140
Demavend, Mount see Damāvand, Qolleh-ye, vol., Iran B7 56
Demba, D.R.C. F4 66
Dembī, Eth. F7 62
Dembia, C.A.R. C4 66
Dembī Dolo, Eth. F6 62
Demidov, Russia E14 10
Deming, N.M., U.S. K9 132
Demini, stm., Braz. H10 86
Demirci, Tur. D11 28
Demirköprü Barajı, res., Tur. E11 28
Demirköy, Tur. B10 28
Demjanka, stm., Russia C12 32
Demjanovo, Russia F22 8
Demjanskoe, Russia C11 32
Demmin, Ger. C8 16
Demmitt, Ab., Can. A11 138
Demopolis, Al., U.S. E11 122
Demorest, Ga., U.S. B2 116
Dempo, Gunung, vol., Indon. F3 50
Demta, Indon. F11 44
Denain, Fr. D12 14
Denali, Ak., U.S. D10 140
Denali National Park, Ak., U.S. D10 140
Denan, Eth. F8 62
Denau, Uzb. G11 32
Den Burg, Neth. A13 14
Dendang, Indon. E5 50
Dendermonde (Termonde), Bel. C12 14
Deng Deng, Cam. C2 66
Dengkou, China A2 42
Dêngqên, China E4 36
Dengxian, China E5 42
Denham, Austl. E2 74
Denham, Mount, mtn., Jam. i13 104d
Denham Range, mts., Austl. C6 76
Denham Springs, La., U.S. G8 122
Den Helder (Helder), Neth. B13 14
Dénia, Spain F11 20
Deniliquin, Austl. J5 76
Deniskoviči, Russia H14 10
Denison, Tx., U.S. D2 122
Denison, Mount, vol., Ak., U.S. E9 140
Denizli, Tur. F12 28
Denizli, state, Tur. F12 28
Denkanikota, India E3 53
Denmark, Austl. F3 74
Denmark, S.C., U.S. C4 116
Denmark, Wi., U.S. D2 112
Denmark, ctry., Eur. D10 6
Denmark Strait, strt. C20 94
Dennery, St. Luc. m7 105c
Denpasar, Indon. H9 50
Denton, Md., U.S. F10 114
Denton, Mt., U.S. C17 136
Denton, N.C., U.S. A5 116
Denton, Tx., U.S. H11 128
Denton Creek, stm., Tx., U.S. H11 128
D'Entrecasteaux, Point, c., Austl. F3 74
D'Entrecasteaux Islands, is., Pap. N. Gui. D6 72
Denver, Co., U.S. B3 128
Denver, Pa., U.S. D9 114
Denver City, Tx., U.S. A5 130
Deoband, India D6 54
Deogarh, India F4 54
Deogarh, India F7 54
Deogarh, mtn., India G9 54
Deogarh Hills, hills, India G9 54
Deoghar, India F11 54
Deori, India G7 54
Deoria, India E9 54
De Pere, Wi., U.S. D1 112
Depew, Ok., U.S. B2 122
Depoe Bay, Or., U.S. F2 136
Depok, Indon. G5 50
Deposit, N.Y., U.S. B10 114
Depue, Il., U.S. C8 120
Dêqên, China F4 36
Deqing, China J4 42
De Queen, Ar., U.S. C4 122
De Quincy, La., U.S. G5 122
Dera, Lach, stm., Afr. D8 66
Dera Bugti, Pak. D2 54
Dera Ghāzi Khān, Pak. C3 54
Dera Ismāīl Khān, Pak. C3 54
Derāwar Fort, Pak. D3 54
Derbent, Russia F7 32
Derby, Austl. C4 74
Derby, Austl. n13 77a
Derby, Eng., U.K. I11 12
Derby, Ks., U.S. D11 128
Derby, N.Y., U.S. B6 114
Dereköy, Tur. B10 28
Derg, Lough, l., Ire. I4 12
Dergači, Russia D7 32
De Ridder, La., U.S. G5 122
Dermott, Ar., U.S. D7 122
Dernieres, Isles, is., La., U.S. H8 122
Dêrong, China F4 36
Derrame, Mex. H3 130
Derry see Londonderry, N. Ire., U.K. F6 12
Derry, N.H., U.S. B14 114
Derudeb, Sudan D7 62
Derventa, Bos. E4 26
Derwent, Ab., Can. C19 138
Derwent, stm., Austl. o13 77a
Derwent, stm., Eng., U.K. G12 12
Derwent Water, l., Eng., U.K. G9 12
Deržavinsk, Kaz. D11 32
Desaguadero, stm., Arg. F4 92
Desaguadero, stm., S.A. G4 84
Désappointement, Îles du, is., Fr. Poly. E12 72
Des Arc, Ar., U.S. C7 122
Descabezado Grande, Volcán, vol., Chile G2 92
Descanso, Braz. C11 92
Descanso, Ca., U.S. K9 134
Descanso, Punta, c., Mex. K8 134
Descartes, Fr. G9 14
Deschambault Lake, l., Sk., Can. E10 106
Deschutes, stm., Or., U.S. E6 136
Desdunes, Haiti C11 102
Desē, Eth. E7 62
Deseado, stm., Arg. I3 90
Desengaño, Punta, c., Arg. I3 90
Desenzano del Garda, Italy E7 22
Deseret Peak, mtn., Ut., U.S. C4 132
Deseronto, On., Can. D12 112
Désert, stm., Qc., Can. B13 112
Désert, Lac, l., Qc., Can. B13 112
Desert Hot Springs, Ca., U.S. J9 134
Desert Lake, l., Nv., U.S. F1 132
Desert Peak, mtn., Ut., U.S. B3 132
Desert Valley, val., Nv., U.S. B7 134
Desha, Ar., U.S. B7 122
Deshaies, Guad. h5 105c
Deshler, Oh., U.S. C1 114
Deshnok, India E4 54
Desiderio Tello, Arg. E4 92
Deskáti, Grc. D4 28
Desloge, Mo., U.S. G7 120
Des Moines, Ia., U.S. C4 120
Des Moines, N.M., U.S. E5 128
Des Moines, stm., U.S. K7 118
Des Moines, East Fork, stm., U.S. H4 118
Desna, stm., Eur. D4 32
Desolación, Isla, i., Chile J2 90
De Soto, Il., U.S. G8 120
De Soto, Mo., U.S. F7 120
Despatch, S. Afr. H7 70
Despeñaperros, Desfiladero de, p., Spain F7 20
Des Plaines, Il., U.S. F1 112
Des Plaines, stm., U.S. C9 120
Desroches, i., Sey. k12 69b
Desruisseaux, St. Luc. m7 105c
Dessau, Ger. E8 16
Destruction Bay, Yk., Can. C3 106
Desvres, Fr. D10 14
Detčino, Russia F19 10
Dete, Zimb. D4 68
Detmold, Ger. E4 16
Detour, Point, c., Mi., U.S. C3 112
De Tour Village, Mi., U.S. C5 112
Detrital Wash, stm., Az., U.S. H2 132
Detroit, Mi., U.S. B2 114
Detroit, Or., U.S. F4 136
Detroit, Tx., U.S. D3 122
Detroit Beach, Mi., U.S. C2 114
Dettifoss, wtfl, Ice. k31 8a
Det Udom, Thai. E7 48
Detva, Slov. H15 16
Deua National Park, p.o.i., Austl. J7 76
Deūlgaon Rāja, India H5 54
Deutsche Bucht, b., Ger. C4 16
Deutschlandsberg, Aus. D12 22
Deux-Sèvres, state, Fr. C5 18
Deva, Rom. D9 26
Devakottai, India G4 53
Dévaványa, Hung. B7 26
Deventer, Neth. B15 14
Deveron, stm., Scot., U.K. D10 12
Devgadh Bāriva, India G4 54
De View, Bayou, stm., Ar., U.S. B8 122
Devīkot, India E3 54
Devils, stm., Tx., U.S. E6 130
Devils Island see Diable, Île du, i., Fr. Gu. B7 84
Devils Lake, N.D., U.S. F15 124
Devils Lake, l., N.D., U.S. F14 124
Devils Postpile National Monument, p.o.i., Ca., U.S. F6 134
Devils Tower National Monument, p.o.i., Wy., U.S. C8 126
Devine, B.C., Can. F8 138
Devine, Tx., U.S. E9 130
Devjatiny, Russia F17 8
Devli, India F5 54
Devoll, stm., Alb. D14 24
Devon, Ab., Can. C17 138
Devon Island, i., Nu., Can. B8 141
Devonport, Austl. n13 77a
Devoto, Arg. E6 92
Devrek, Tur. B14 28
Dewakang-lompo, Pulau, i., Indon. F11 50
Dewar, Ok., U.S. B3 122
Dewās, India G5 54
Dewey, Ok., U.S. H1 120
Deweyville, Tx., U.S. G5 122
De Witt, Ar., U.S. C7 122
De Witt, Ia., U.S. C7 120
De Witt, Ne., U.S. G16 126
De Witt, N.Y., U.S. A9 114
Dexing, China G7 42
Dexter, Me., U.S. E7 110
Dexter, Mi., U.S. B2 114
Dexter, N.M., U.S. H4 128
Dexter, N.Y., U.S. D13 112
Dexterity Fiord, b., Nu., Can. A16 106
Deyang, China E5 36
Dey-Dey, Lake, l., Austl. E6 74
Dezfūl, Iran C6 56
Dezhou, China C7 42
Dežneva, mys, c., Russia C27 34
Dezong, China B13 54
Dhahran see Az-Zahrān, Sau. Ar. D6 56
Dhaka (Dacca), Bngl. G13 54
Dhaka, state, Bngl. F13 54
Dhamār, Yemen G5 56
Dhāmpur, India D7 54
Dhamtari, India H8 54
Dhanbād, India G11 54
Dhandhuka, India G3 54
Dhangadhī, Nepal D8 54
D'Hanis, Tx., U.S. E8 130
Dhankuṭa, Nepal E11 54
Dhār, India G5 54
Dharān, Nepal E11 54
Dhārāpuram, India F3 53
Dharmābād, India B3 53
Dharmapuri, India E4 53
Dharmavaram, India D3 53
Dharmjaygarh, India G9 54
Dharmshāla, India B6 54
Dhaulpur, India E6 54
Dhawalāgiri, mtn., Nepal D9 54
Dhenkānāl, India H10 54
Dherínia, Cyp. C4 58
Dhodhekánisos (Dodecanese), is., Grc. G10 28
Dhodhóni, hist., Grc. D3 28
Dhofar see Ẓufar, reg., Oman F7 56
Dholka, India G4 54
Dhone, India D3 53
Dhoomadheere, Som. D8 66
Dhorāji, India H3 54
Dhrāngadhra, India G3 54
Dhrol, India G3 54
Dhuburi, India E13 54
Dhule, India H5 54
Dhuliān, India F12 54
Dhupgāri, India E12 54
Dhuusamarreeb, Som. C9 66
Diable, Île du (Devils Island), i., Fr. Gu. B7 84
Diable, Pointe du, c., Mart. k7 105c
Diables, Morne aux, vol., Dom. i5 105c
Diablo, Canyon, val., Az., U.S. H5 132
Diablo, Mount, mtn., Ca., U.S. F4 134
Diablo, Pico del, mtn., Mex. F4 98
Diablo Range, mts., Ca., U.S. G4 134
Diablotins, Morne, vol., Dom. j6 105c
Diaca, Moz. C6 68
Dialakoto, Sen. G2 64
Diamante, Arg. F7 92
Diamante, stm., Arg. G4 92
Diamantina, Braz. J4 88
Diamantina, stm., Austl. E2 76
Diamantina Lakes, Austl. D3 76
Diamantino, Braz. F6 84
Diamond, Mo., U.S. G3 120
Diamond Harbour, India G12 54
Diamond Islets, is., Austl. A8 76
Diamond Peak, mtn., Id., U.S. F13 136
Diamond Peak, mtn., Wa., U.S. D9 136
Diamondville, Wy., U.S. B6 132
Diana Bay, b., Can. C16 106
Dianbai, China K4 42
Dian Chi, l., China G5 36
Dianjiang, China F2 42
Dianópolis, Braz. F2 88
Diapaga, Burkina G5 64
Diaz, Ar., U.S. B7 122
Diaz Point, c., Nmb. E2 70
Dibai, India D7 54
Dibaya, D.R.C. F4 66
Dibeng, S. Afr. E6 70
D'Iberville, Ms., U.S. G9 122
Dibete, Bots. C8 70
Dibrugarh, India C7 46
Dickens, Tx., U.S. H8 128
Dickinson, N.D., U.S. A10 126
Dickinson, Tx., U.S. H3 122
Dickson, Tn., U.S. H10 120
Didao, China B9 38
Didsbury, Ab., Can. E16 138
Dīdwāna, India E5 54
Didymóteicho, Grc. B9 28
Dieburg, Ger. G4 16
Dieciocho de Julio, Ur. F11 92
Diefenbaker, Lake, res., Sk., Can. C7 124
Diego de Almagro, Chile C2 92
Diego de Almagro, Isla, i., Chile J1 90
Diego de Ocampo, Pico, mtn., Dom. Rep. C12 102
Diégo-Suarez see Antsirañana, Madag. C8 68
Diemuchuoke, China B7 54
Dien Bien, Viet. B6 48
Dien Bien Phu see Dien Bien, Viet. B6 48
Diepholz, Ger. D4 16
Dieppe, N.B., Can. D12 110
Dieppe, Fr. E9 14
Dieppe Bay Town, St. K./N. C2 105a
Dierks, Ar., U.S. C4 122
Di'er Songhua, stm., China B6 38
Diest, Bel. D14 14
Dieulefit, Fr. E10 18
Dieveniškės, Lith. F8 10
Diez de Octubre, Mex. C6 100
Dif, Kenya D8 66
Diffa, Niger G7 64
Differdange, Lux. E14 14
Dīg, India E6 54
Digba, D.R.C. D5 66
Digboi, India C8 46
Digby, N.S., Can. F11 110
Digby Neck, pen., N.S., Can. F10 110
Digges Islands, is., Nu., Can. C15 106
Dighton, Ks., U.S. C8 128
Dīglūr, India B3 53
Digne-les-Bains, Fr. E12 18
Digoin, Fr. C9 18
Digos, Phil. G5 52
Digras, India H6 54
Digul, stm., Indon. G10 44
Diinsor, Som. D8 66
Dijon, Fr. G14 14
Dikaja, Russia A22 10
Dike, Ia., U.S. B5 120
Dikhil, Dji. E8 62
Dikili, Tur. D9 28
Dikirnis, Egypt G2 58
Dikodougou, C. Iv. H3 64
Diksmuide, Bel. C11 14
Dikson, Russia B5 34
Dikwa, Nig. G7 64
Dīla, Eth. F7 62
Dilek Yarımdası Milli Parkı, p.o.i., Tur. F10 28
Dili, Indon. G8 44
Dillenburg, Ger. F4 16
Diller, Ne., U.S. A12 128
Dilley, Tx., U.S. F8 130
Dilling, Sudan E5 62
Dillingen an der Donau, Ger. H6 16
Dillingham, Ak., U.S. E8 140
Dillon, Mt., U.S. E14 136
Dillon, S.C., U.S. B6 116
Dillon Mountain, mtn., N.M., U.S. J8 132
Dillwyn, Va., U.S. G7 114
Dilolo, D.R.C. G4 66
Dílos, hist., Grc. F8 28
Dilworth, Mn., U.S. H17 124
Dimāpur, India C7 46
Dimashq (Damascus), Syria E7 58
Dimashq, state, Syria E7 58
Dimbelenge, D.R.C. F4 66
Dimbokro, C. Iv. H4 64
Dimbulah, Austl. A5 76
Dimitrovgrad, Blg. G12 26
Dimitrovgrad, Russia D8 32
Dimitsána, Grc. F4 28
Dimlang, mtn., Nig. H7 64
Dimmitt, Tx., U.S. G6 128
Dimona, Isr. G6 58
Dinagat, Phil. E5 52
Dinagat Island, i., Phil. E5 52
Dinājpur, Bngl. F12 54
Dinan, Fr. F6 14
Dinant, Bel. D13 14
Dinar, Tur. E13 28
Dinard, Fr. F6 14
Dinaric Alps (Dinara), mts., Eur. G13 22
Dindi, stm., India C4 53
Dindigul, India F4 53
Dindori, India G8 54
Dingalan Bay, b., Phil. C3 52
Ding'an, China L4 42
Dingbian, China C2 42
Dingbianji, China C3 42
Dinggyê, China D11 54
Dinghai, China F9 42
Dingle, Ire. I2 12
Dingle Bay, b., Ire. I2 12
Dingnan, China I6 42
Dingo, Austl. D7 76
Dingolfing, Ger. H8 16
Dingshuzhen, China F8 42
Dingtao, China D6 42
Dinguiraye, Gui. G2 64
Dingwall, N.S., Can. D16 110
Dingxian, China B6 42
Dingxiang, China B5 42
Dingyuan, China E7 42
Dinhāta, India E12 54
Dinh Hoa, Viet. B7 48
Dinh Lap, Viet. B8 48
Dinkelsbühl, Ger. G6 16
Dinnebito Wash, stm., Az., U.S. H5 132
Dinorwic, On., Can. B6 118
Dinorwic Lake, l., On., Can. B6 118
Dinosaur National Monument, p.o.i., U.S. C8 132
Dinsmore, Sk., Can. C6 124
Dinuba, Ca., U.S. G6 134
Dinwiddie, Va., U.S. G8 114
Dionísio Cerqueira, Braz. C11 92
Diouloulou, Sen. G1 64
Diourbel, Sen. G1 64
Dīpālpur, Pak. C4 54
Diplo, Pak. F2 54
Dipolog, Phil. F4 52
Dippoldiswalde, Ger. F9 16
Dīr, Pak. B11 56
Diré, Mali F4 64
Dirē Dawa, Eth. F8 62
Dirico, Ang. D3 68
Dirj, Libya A2 62
Dirk Hartog Island, i., Austl. E2 74
Dirkou, Niger F7 64
Dirranbandi, Austl. G7 76
Dīsa, India F4 54
Disappointment, Cape, c., S. Geor. J9 90
Disappointment, Cape, c., Wa., U.S. D2 136
Disappointment, Lake, l., Austl. D4 74
Disaster Bay, b., Austl. K8 76
Disautel, Wa., U.S. B7 136
Discovery Bay, b., Austl. L3 76
Dishman, Wa., U.S. C9 136
Disko, i., Grnld. D15 141
Disko Bugt, b., Grnld. D15 141
Dismal, stm., Ne., U.S. F12 126
Dispur, India E13 54
Disraëli, Qc., Can. E5 110
Distrito Capital, state, Col. E4 86
Distrito Federal, state, Braz. H2 88
Distrito Federal, state, Mex. F9 100
Distrito Federal, state, Ven. B8 86
Dis Ûq, Egypt G1 58
Dithmarschen, reg., Ger. B5 16
Diu, India H3 54
Dive, can., Fr. B5 18
Divenskaja, Russia A12 10
Divernon, Il., U.S. E8 120
Divinhe, Moz. B12 70
Divinópolis, Braz. K3 88
Divi Point, c., India D5 53
Divisor, Serra do, plat., S.A. E3 84
Divnoe, Russia E6 32
Divnogorsk, Russia C16 32
Divo, C. Iv. H3 64
Dīwāl Qol, Afg. A1 54
Dix, Ne., U.S. F9 126
Dixie Valley, val., Nv., U.S. D8 134
Dixon, Ca., U.S. E4 134
Dixon, Il., U.S. C8 120
Dixon, Ky., U.S. G10 120
Dixon, Mo., U.S. G5 120
Dixon, N.M., U.S. E3 128
Dixon Entrance, strt., N.A. E4 106
Diyarbakır, Tur. B4 56
Dizhou, China J2 42
Djado, Niger E7 64
Djado, Plateau du, plat., Niger E7 64
Djakarta see Jakarta, Indon. G5 50
Djamâa, Alg. C6 64
Djambala, Congo E2 66
Djanet, Alg. E6 64
Djaret, Oued, stm., Alg. D5 64
Djat'kovo, Russia G17 10
Djedi, Oued, stm., Alg. C5 64
Djéma, C.A.R. C5 66
Djenné, Mali G4 64
Djenoun, Garet el, mtn., Alg. D6 64
Djérem, stm., Cam. C2 66
Djibo, Burkina G4 64
Djibouti, Dji. E8 62
Djibouti, ctry., Afr. E8 62
Djoku-Punda, D.R.C. F4 66
Djolu, D.R.C. D4 66
Djougou, Benin H5 64
Djourab, Erg du, sand, Chad D3 62
Djugu, D.R.C. D6 66
Djurås, Swe. F6 8
Djurtjuli, Russia C8 32
Dmitrija Lapteva, proliv, strt., Russia B16 34
Dmitrov, Russia D20 10
Dneprovskoe, Russia E16 10
Dnieper, stm., Eur. F15 6
Dniester (Dnister), stm., Eur. G19 16
Dniprodzerzhyns'k, Ukr. E5 32
Dnipropetrovs'k, Ukr. E4 32
Dnistrovs'kyi lyman, l., Ukr. C17 26
Dnjaprouska Buhski, kanal, can., Bela. I8 10
Dno, Russia C12 10
Do, Lac, l., Mali F4 64
Dôa, Moz. D5 68
Doaktown, N.B., Can. D10 110
Doangdoangan-Besar, Pulau, i., Indon. F10 50
Doba, Chad F3 62
Dobczyce, Pol. G15 16
Dobele, Lat. D6 10
Döbeln, Ger. E8 16
Doberai, Jazirah (Doberai Peninsula), pen., Indon. F9 44
Doberai Peninsula see Doberai, Jazirah, pen., Indon. F9 44
Dobo, Indon. G9 44
Doboj, Bos. E4 26
Dobra, Pol. E14 16
Dobre Miasto, Pol. C16 16
Dobrič, Blg. F14 26
Dobříš, Czech Rep. G10 16
Dobrjanka, Russia C9 32
Dobroe, Russia C15 10
Dobroteasa, Rom. E11 26
Dobruja, hist. reg., Eur. E15 26
Dobruš, Bela. H14 10
Dobruška, Czech Rep. F12 16
Dobrzyń nad Wisłą, Pol. D15 16
Dobson, N.C., U.S. H5 114
Dobzha, China D12 54
Doce, stm., Braz. J6 88
Dock Junction, Ga., U.S. E4 116
Doctor Cecilio Báez, Para. B9 92
Doctor Coss, Mex. I8 130
Doctor González, Mex. I8 130
Dod Ballāpur, India E3 53
Doddridge, Ar., U.S. D4 122
Dodecanese see Dhodhekánisos, is., Grc. G10 28
Dodge Center, Mn., U.S. G5 118
Dodge City, Ks., U.S. D9 128
Dodgeville, Wi., U.S. B7 120
Dodoma, Tan. F7 66
Dodsland, Sk., Can. C5 124
Dodson, Mt., U.S. F5 124
Dodson, Tx., U.S. G8 128
Doerun, Ga., U.S. E1 116
Doetinchem, Neth. C15 14
Dogai Coring, l., China A12 54
Doğanbey, Tur. E9 28
Doğanhisar, Tur. E14 28
Dog Island, i., Fl., U.S. H14 122
Dog Islands, is., Br. Vir. Is. e9 104b
Dog Lake, l., Mb., Can. C15 124
Dog Lake, l., On., Can. C9 118
Dogliani, Italy F4 22
Dōgo, i., Japan C6 40
Do Gonbadān, Iran C7 56
Dogondoutchi, Niger G5 64
Doğu Karadeniz Dağları, mts., Tur. A5 56
Doha see Ad-Dawḥah, Qatar D7 56
Dohrīghāt, India E9 54
Doiran, Lake, l., Eur. B5 28
Dois Irmãos de Goiás, Braz. E1 88
Doi Suthep-Pui National Park, p.o.i., Thai. C4 48
Doka, Indon. G9 44
Dokkum, Neth. A14 14
Doksy, Czech Rep. F10 16
Doland, S.D., U.S. C14 126
Dolbeau, Qc., Can. B4 110
Dol-de-Bretagne, Fr. F7 14
Dole, Fr. G14 14
Dolega, Pan. H6 102
Dolgeville, N.Y., U.S. E15 112
Dolgij Most, Russia C17 32
Dolgoščele, Russia C20 8
Dolinsk, Russia G17 34
Dolj, state, Rom. E10 26
Dolni Dăbnik, Blg. F11 26
Dolný Kubín, Slov. G15 16
Dolomites see Dolomiti, mts., Italy D8 22
Dolomiti, mts., Italy D8 22
Dolores, Arg. H9 92
Dolores, Col. F4 86
Dolores, Guat. D3 102
Dolores, Mex. H6 130
Dolores, Ur. F8 92
Dolores, stm., U.S. E7 132
Dolores Hidalgo, Mex. E8 100
Dolphin, Cape, c., Falk. Is. J5 90
Dolphin and Union Strait, strt., Nu., Can. B7 106
Dolphin Head, mtn., Jam. i12 104d
Dolsk, Pol. D13 16
Dolžicy, Russia C12 10
Domaniči, Russia G16 10
Domažlice, Czech Rep. G8 16
Dombås, Nor. E3 8
Dombes, reg., Fr. D11 18
Dombóvár, Hung. C4 26
Dom Cavati, Braz. J4 88
Dôme, Puy de, mtn., Fr. D8 18
Dome Creek, B.C., Can. C9 138
Domeyko, Chile D2 92
Domeyko, Cordillera, mts., Chile D3 90
Domfront, Fr. F8 14
Domiciano Ribeiro, Braz. I2 88
Domingo M. Irala, Para. B10 92
Dominica, ctry., N.A. j5 105c
Dominica Channel see Martinique Passage, strt., N.A. k6 105c
Dominicana, República see Dominican Republic, ctry., N.A. D10 96
Dominican Republic, ctry., N.A. D10 96
Dominica Passage, strt., N.A. i6 105c
Dominion, Cape, c., Nu., Can. B15 106
Dominion City, Mb., Can. E16 124
Dom Joaquim, Braz. J4 88
Domo, Eth. F9 62
Domodedovo, Russia E20 10
Domodossola, Italy D5 22
Dom Pedrito, Braz. E10 92
Dom Pedro, Braz. C3 88
Dompu, Indon. H11 50
Domremy, Sk., Can. B8 124
Domuyo, Volcán, vol., Arg. H2 92
Dom Yai, stm., Thai. E7 48
Don, stm., India C2 53
Don, stm., Laos E7 48
Don, stm., Russia E6 32
Don, stm., Scot., U.K. D10 12
Donadeu, Arg. C6 92
Donaghadee, N. Ire., U.K. G7 12
Donald, Austl. K4 76
Donalda, Ab., Can. D18 138
Donaldson, Ar., U.S. C6 122
Donaldsonville, La., U.S. G7 122
Doñana, Parque Nacional de, p.o.i., Spain H4 20
Donau, stm., Eur. F11 6
Donaueschingen, Ger. I4 16
Donauwörth, Ger. H6 16
Don Benito, Spain F5 20
Doncaster, Eng., U.K. H11 12
Dondaicha, India H5 54
Dondo, Ang. B1 68
Dondo, Moz. A12 70
Dondo, Teluk, b., Indon. C12 50
Dondra Head, c., Sri L. I5 53
Dondușeni, Mol. A14 26
Donegal, Ire. G4 12
Donegal, state, Ire. G5 12
Donegal Bay, b., Ire. G4 12
Doneraile, S.C., U.S. B6 116
Donets'k, Ukr. E5 32
Dong, stm., China J6 42
Dong'an, China B11 36
Dong'an, China H4 42
Dongara, Austl. E3 74
Dongchuan, China F5 36
Dongfang, China L3 42
Dongfeng, China C6 38
Donggala, Indon. D11 50
Donggi Cona, l., China D4 36
Donggong Shan, mts., China H8 42
Dongguan, China J5 42
Dongguang, China C7 42
Dong Ha, Viet. D8 48
Donghai Dao, i., China K4 42
Dong Hoi, Viet. D8 48
Dong Hu, l., China B10 54
Dongjielang, China F6 42
Dongjingcheng, China B8 38
Donglan, China I2 42
Dongliao, stm., China C5 38
Dong Nai, stm., Viet. G8 48
Dongning, China B9 38
Dongo, D.R.C. D3 66
Dongou, Congo D3 66
Dongping, China K5 42
Dongping, China D7 42
Dong San Shen (Manchuria), hist. reg., China B5 38
Dongshan, China L4 42
Dongshan Dao, i., China J7 42
Dongsheng, China B4 42
Dongtai, China E9 42
Dongting Hu, l., China G5 42
Dong Trieu, Viet. B8 48
Dongwe, stm., Zam. C3 68
Dongxi, China G2 42
Dongxiang, China G7 42
Dongyang, China G9 42
Dongzhi, China F7 42
Donie, Tx., U.S. F2 122
Doniphan, Ne., U.S. G14 126
Donja Stubica, Cro. E12 22
Donjek, stm., Yk., Can. C3 106
Don Martín, Mex. G7 130
Donna, Tx., U.S. H9 130
Donnacona, Qc., Can. D5 110
Donnelly, Id., U.S. F10 136
Donner, La., U.S. H7 122
Donner Pass, p., Ca., U.S. D5 134
Donner und Blitzen, stm., Or., U.S. G8 136
Donnybrook, Austl. F3 74
Donora, Pa., U.S. D6 114
Donostia (San Sebastián), Spain A9 20
Donostia-San Sebastián see Donostia, Spain A9 20
Don Pedro Reservoir, res., Ca., U.S. F5 134
Don Peninsula, pen., B.C., Can. D2 138
Donskoj, Russia G21 10
Doolow, Som. D8 66
Doonerak, Mount, mtn., Ak., U.S. C9 140
Doornik see Tournai, Bel. D12 14
Door Peninsula, pen., Wi., U.S. D2 112
Dor, Isr. F5 58
Dora, Al., U.S. D11 122
Dora, Lake, l., Austl. D4 74
Dora Baltea, stm., Italy E4 22
Dorado, P.R. B3 104a
Doraville, Ga., U.S. D14 122
Dorcheat, Bayou, stm., U.S. D5 122
Dorchester, N.B., Can. E12 110
Dorchester, On., Can. F8 112
Dorchester, Eng., U.K. K10 12
Dorchester, Ne., U.S. G15 126
Dorchester, Cape, c., Nu., Can. B15 106
Dordabis, Nmb. C3 70
Dordogne, state, Fr. D6 18
Dordogne, stm., Fr. D8 18
Dordrecht, Neth. C13 14
Dordrecht, S. Afr. G8 70
Dore Lake, l., Sk., Can. E9 106
Dorena, Or., U.S. G4 136
Dores do Indaiá, Braz. J3 88
Dorfen, Ger. H8 16
Dorgali, Italy D3 24

Dorg-Elat I•17

Name	Map Ref.	Page
Dörgön nuur, l., Mong.	B3	36
Dori, Burkina	G4	64
Doring, stm., S. Afr.	G4	70
Dornbirn, Aus.	C6	22
Dornoch, Scot., U.K.	D8	12
Dorog, Hung.	B5	26
Dorogobuž, Russia	F16	10
Dorohoi, Rom.	A13	26
Dorokempo, Indon.	H11	50
Dorre Island, i., Austl.	E2	74
Dorrigo, Austl.	H9	76
Dorris, Ca., U.S.	B4	134
Dorsale, mts., Tun.	I3	24
Dort see Dordrecht, Neth.	C13	14
Dortmund, Ger.	E3	16
Dorton, Ky., U.S.	G3	114
Dörtyol, Tur.	B7	58
Doruma, D.R.C.	D5	66
Dos, Canal Numero, can., Arg.	H9	92
Dosatuj, Russia	A8	36
Dos Bahías, Cabo, c., Arg.	H3	90
Dos Bocas, P.R.	B2	104a
Döşemealtı, Tur.	F13	28
Dos Hermanas, Spain	G4	20
Do Son, Viet.	B8	48
Dos Pos, Neth. Ant.	p23	104g
Dos Quebradas, Col.	E4	86
Dosso, Niger	G5	64
Dossor, Kaz.	E8	32
Dothan, Al., U.S.	F13	122
Dotnuva, Lith.	E6	10
Dou, stm., China	B8	42
Douai, Fr.	D11	14
Douala, Cam.	D1	66
Douarnenez, Fr.	F4	14
Doublé, Pointe, c., Guad.	h7	105c
Double Island Point, c., Austl.	E9	76
Double Springs, Al., U.S.	C11	122
Doubletop Peak, mtn., Wy., U.S.	G16	136
Doubs, state, Fr.	G15	14
Doubs, stm., Eur.	H14	14
Doubtful Sound, strt., N.Z.	G2	80
Doubtless Bay, b., N.Z.	B5	80
Douentza, Mali	F4	64
Dougga, hist., Tun.	H3	24
Douglas, Mb., Can.	E14	124
Douglas, I. of Man	G8	12
Douglas, S. Afr.	F6	70
Douglas, Ak., U.S.	E13	140
Douglas, Az., U.S.	L7	132
Douglas, Ga., U.S.	E3	116
Douglas, Wy., U.S.	E7	126
Douglas Channel, strt., B.C., Can.	C1	138
Douglas Lake, B.C., Can.	F10	138
Douglas Lake, res., Tn., U.S.	H2	114
Douglasville, Ga., U.S.	D14	122
Doullens, Fr.	D11	14
Dourada, Serra, plat., Braz.	G1	88
Dourados, Braz.	D6	90
Dourbali, Chad	E3	62
Douro (Duero), stm., Eur.	C2	20
Dousk, Bela.	G13	10
Douz, Tun.	C6	64
Dove Bugt, strt., Grnld.	B21	141
Dove Creek, Co., U.S.	F7	132
Dover, Austl.	o13	77a
Dover, Eng., U.K.	J14	12
Dover, De., U.S.	E10	114
Dover, Id., U.S.	B10	136
Dover, N.H., U.S.	G6	110
Dover, N.J., U.S.	D11	114
Dover, N.C., U.S.	A8	116
Dover, Oh., U.S.	D4	114
Dover, Ok., U.S.	E11	128
Dover, Tn., U.S.	H10	120
Dover, Strait of, strt., Eur.	K14	12
Dover-Foxcroft, Me., U.S.	E7	110
Dovrefjell Nasjonalpark, p.o.i., Nor.	E3	8
Dow City, Ia., U.S.	C2	120
Dowlatābād, Iran	D8	56
Downey, Id., U.S.	H14	136
Downieville, Ca., U.S.	D5	134
Downing, Mo., U.S.	D5	120
Downingtown, Pa., U.S.	D10	114
Downpatrick, N. Ire., U.K.	G7	12
Downs, Ks., U.S.	B10	128
Downton, Mount, mtn., B.C., Can.	D6	138
Dows, Ia., U.S.	B4	120
Dowshī, Afg.	B10	56
Doyle, Ca., U.S.	C5	134
Doyles, Nf., Can.	C17	110
Doylestown, Pa., U.S.	D10	114
Doyline, La., U.S.	E5	122
Dōzen, is., Japan	C5	40
Dozier, Al., U.S.	F12	122
Dra, Cap, c., Mor.	D2	64
Dra'a, Hamada du, des., Alg.	D3	64
Drâa, Oued, stm., Afr.	D2	64
Drac, stm., Fr.	E2	22
Dracena, Braz.	D6	90
Drachten, Neth.	A15	14
Dracut, Ma., U.S.	B14	114
Dragalina, Rom.	E14	26
Drăgănești-Vlașca, Rom.	E12	26
Drăgășani, Rom.	E11	26
Dragonera, Sa, i., Spain	E13	20
Dragons Mouths, strt.	s12	105f
Dragoon, Az., U.S.	K6	132
Draguignan, Fr.	F12	18
Drahičyn, Bela.	H8	10
Drake, N.D., U.S.	G13	124
Drakensberg, mts., Afr.	F9	70
Drake Passage, strt.	K8	82
Drakesboro, Ky., U.S.	G10	120
Drakes Branch, Va., U.S.	H7	114
Dráma, Grc.	B7	28
Drammen, Nor.	G3	8
Drang, stm., Asia	F8	48
Drangajökull, ice, Ice.	j28	8a
Dranov, Ostrovul, i., Rom.	E16	26
Drau (Dráva), stm., Eur.	D11	22
Dráva (Drau), stm., Eur.	D14	22
Dravograd, Slvn.	D12	22
Drawsko Pomorskie, Pol.	C11	16
Drayton, N.D., U.S.	C1	118
Drayton, S.C., U.S.	B4	116
Drayton Valley, Ab., Can.	C15	138
Dresden, On., Can.	F7	112
Dresden, Ger.	E9	16
Dresden, Oh., U.S.	D3	114
Drètun', Bela.	E12	10
Dreux, Fr.	F10	14
Drew, Ms., U.S.	D8	122
Drienov, Slov.	H17	16
Driftwood, B.C., Can.	D5	106
Driftwood, stm., In., U.S.	E12	120
Driggs, Id., U.S.	G15	136
Drin, stm., Alb.	C13	24
Drina, stm., Eur.	F16	22
Drinit, Gjiri i, b., Alb.	C13	24
Drinit të Zi (Crni Drim), stm., Eur.	C14	24
Driskill Mountain, hill, La., U.S.	E6	122
Drissa (Drysa), stm., Eur.	E11	10
Drniš, Cro.	G13	22
Drobeta-Turnu Severin, Rom.	E9	26
Drochia, Mol.	A14	26
Drogheda, Ire.	H6	12
Droichead Átha see Drogheda, Ire.	H6	12
Droichead Nua, Ire.	H6	12
Drôme, state, Fr.	E11	18
Dronero, Italy	F4	22
Dronne, stm., Fr.	D6	18
Dronning Louise Land, reg., Grnld.	B20	141
Druc', stm., Bela.	G12	10
Druif, Aruba	o19	104g
Druja, Bela.	E10	10
Drūkšiai, l., Eur.	E9	10
Drumheller, Ab., Can.	E18	138
Drummond, Mt., U.S.	D13	136
Drummond, Wi., U.S.	E7	118
Drummond Island, i., Mi., U.S.	C6	112
Drummondville, Qc., Can.	E4	110
Druskininkai, Lith.	F7	10
Družba, Kaz.	E14	32
Druzhba see Družba, Kaz.	E14	32
Družina, Russia	C18	34
Drvar, Bos.	E3	26
Dry Arm, b., Mt., U.S.	G7	124
Dry Bay, b., Ak., U.S.	E12	140
Dryberry Lake, l., On., Can.	B4	118
Dry Cimarron, stm., U.S.	B2	122
Dry Creek Mountain, mtn., Nv., U.S.	B9	134
Dryden, On., Can.	B6	118
Dry Devils, stm., Tx., U.S.	D7	130
Dry Prong, La., U.S.	F6	122
Dry Ridge, Ky., U.S.	F1	114
Drysdale, stm., Austl.	C5	74
Dry Tortugas, is., Fl., U.S.	G11	108
Dry Tortugas National Park, p.o.i., Fl., U.S.	L3	116
Drzewica, Pol.	E16	16
Dschang, Cam.	C1	66
Du, stm., China	E4	42
Du'an, China	I3	42
Duaringa, Austl.	D7	76
Duarte, Pico, mtn., Dom. Rep.	C12	102
Duartina, Braz.	L1	88
Ḍubā, Sau. Ar.	K6	58
Dubach, La., U.S.	E6	122
Dubai see Dubayy, U.A.E.	D8	56
Dubăsari, Mol.	B16	26
Dubăsari, Lacul, res., Mol.	B15	26
Dubawnt, stm., Can.	C10	106
Dubawnt Lake, l., Can.	C10	106
Dubayy (Dubai), U.A.E.	D8	56
Dubbo, Austl.	I7	76
Dubh Artach, r., Scot., U.K.	E6	12
Dublin (Baile Átha Cliath), Ire.	H6	12
Dublin, Ga., U.S.	D3	116
Dublin, Tx., U.S.	B9	130
Dublin, Va., U.S.	G5	114
Dublin, state, Ire.	H6	12
Dubna, Russia	F19	10
Dubna, Russia	D20	10
Dubna, stm., Russia	D21	10
Dubnica nad Váhom, Slov.	H14	16
Dubois, In., U.S.	F11	120
Du Bois, Ne., U.S.	D1	120
Du Bois, Pa., U.S.	C7	114
Dubois, Wy., U.S.	D3	126
Dubossary Reservoir see Dubăsari, Lacul, res., Mol.	B15	26
Dubovka, Russia	E6	32
Dubrājpur, India	G11	54
Dubréka, Gui.	H2	64
Dubrouna, Bela.	F13	10
Dubrovka, Russia	G16	10
Dubrovnik, Cro.	H15	22
Dubrovnoe, Russia	C11	32
Dubuque, Ia., U.S.	B7	120
Dubysa, stm., Lith.	E6	10
Duchang, China	G7	42
Duchesne, Ut., U.S.	C6	132
Duchesne, stm., Ut., U.S.	C7	132
Duchess, Austl.	C2	76
Duck, stm., Tn., U.S.	B11	122
Duck Creek, stm., Nv., U.S.	D2	132
Duck Hill, Ms., U.S.	D9	122
Duck Lake, Sk., Can.	B7	124
Ducktown, Tn., U.S.	B14	122
Duda, stm., Col.	F4	86
Dudačkino, Russia	A15	10
Duderstadt, Ger.	E6	16
Dudinka, Russia	C6	34
Dudley, Eng., U.K.	I10	12
Dudleyville, Az., U.S.	K6	132
Dudna, stm., India	B2	53
Dudorovskij, Russia	G18	10
Dudwa National Park, p.o.i., India	D8	54
Dueré, stm., Braz.	F1	88
Duero (Douro), stm., Eur.	C2	20
Due West, S.C., U.S.	B3	116
Dufourspitze, mtn., Eur.	D13	18
Dufur, Or., U.S.	E5	136
Duga-Zapadnaja, mys, c., Russia	E18	34
Dugdemona, stm., La., U.S.	F6	122
Dugi Otok, i., Cro.	F11	22
Dugna, Russia	F19	10
Du Gué, stm., Qc., Can.	D16	106
Duhovščina, Russia	E15	10
Duida, Cerro, mtn., Ven.	F9	86
Duisburg, Ger.	E2	16
Duitama, Col.	E5	86
Duiwelskloof, S. Afr.	C10	70
Dujuuma, Som.	D8	66
Duke, Ok., U.S.	G9	128
Duke of York Bay, b., Nu., Can.	B13	106
Duk Fadiat, Sudan	F6	62
Dukhān, Qatar	D7	56
Duki, Pak.	C2	54
Dukla Pass, p., Eur.	G17	16
Dukou, China	F5	36
Dūkštas, Lith.	E9	10
Dulan, China	D4	36
Dulce, N.M., U.S.	G9	132
Dulce, stm., Arg.	D6	92
Dulce, Golfo, b., C.R.	H6	102
Dul'durga, Russia	F11	34
Dulgalah, stm., Russia	C15	34
Dullstroom, S. Afr.	D10	70
Dulovka, Russia	C11	10
Dulq Maghār, Syria	B9	58
Duluth, Ga., U.S.	C14	122
Duluth, Mn., U.S.	E6	118
Dūmā, Syria	E7	58
Dumaguete, Phil.	F4	52
Dumai, Indon.	C2	50
Dumalag, Phil.	E4	52
Dumali Point, c., Phil.	D3	52
Dumaran Island, i., Phil.	E2	52
Dumaresq, stm., Austl.	G8	76
Dumaring, Indon.	C11	50
Dumas, Tx., U.S.	F7	128
Dumbarton, Scot., U.K.	F8	12
Dumbrăveni, Rom.	C11	26
Dume, Point, c., Ca., U.S.	J7	134
Dumfries, Scot., U.K.	F9	12
Dumka, India	F11	54
Dumlupınar, Tur.	E12	28
Dummar, Syria	E7	58
Dumoine, Lac, l., Qc., Can.	B12	112
Dumont, Ia., U.S.	B4	120
Dumont d'Urville, sci., Ant.	B18	81
Dumpu, Pap. N. Gui.	b4	79a
Dumraon, India	F10	54
Dumyât, Masabb (Damietta Mouth), mth., Egypt	G3	58
Duna see Danube, stm., Eur.	F11	6
Dunaharaszti, Hung.	B6	26
Dunaj see Danube, stm., Eur.	F11	6
Dunajec, stm., Eur.	F16	16
Dunajská Streda, Slov.	H13	16
Dunakeszi, Hung.	B6	26
Dunărea Veche, Brațul, stm., Rom.	E15	26
Dunaújváros, Hung.	C5	26
Dunavățu de Sus, Rom.	E16	26
Duna-völgyi-főcsatorna, can., Hung.	C6	26
Dunav-Tisa-Dunav, Kanal, can., Yugo.	D6	26
Dunbar, Scot., U.K.	E10	12
Dunblane, Sk., Can.	C6	124
Duncan, B.C., Can.	H7	138
Duncan, Az., U.S.	K7	132
Duncan, Ok., U.S.	G11	128
Duncan, stm., B.C., Can.	F13	138
Duncan Lake, res., B.C., Can.	F14	138
Duncannon, Pa., U.S.	D8	114
Duncan Passage, strt., India	F7	46
Duncans, Jam.	i13	104d
Duncansby Head, c., Scot., U.K.	C9	12
Dundaga, Lat.	C5	10
Dundalk, On., Can.	D9	112
Dundalk (Dún Dealgan), Ire.	G6	12
Dundalk, Md., U.S.	E9	114
Dundalk Bay, b., Ire.	H6	12
Dundas, On., Can.	E9	112
Dundas, Lake, l., Austl.	F4	74
Dundas Peninsula, pen., Can.	B17	140
Dundas Strait, strt., Austl.	B6	74
Dún Dealgan see Dundalk, Ire.	G6	12
Dundee, S. Afr.	F10	70
Dundee, Scot., U.K.	E10	12
Dundee, Fl., U.S.	H4	116
Dundee, Mi., U.S.	C2	114
Dundurn, Sk., Can.	C7	124
Dunedin, N.Z.	G4	80
Dunedin, Fl., U.S.	H3	116
Dunedoo, Austl.	I7	76
Dunfermline, Scot., U.K.	E9	12
Dungannon, N. Ire., U.K.	G6	12
Dūngarpur, India	G4	54
Dungarvan, Ire.	I5	12
Dungeness, c., Eng., U.K.	K13	12
Dungog, Austl.	I8	76
Dungu, D.R.C.	D5	66
Dungun, Malay.	J6	48
Dunhua, China	C8	38
Dunhuang, China	C3	36
Dunilovo, Russia	C21	10
Dunkerque (Dunkirk), Fr.	C11	14
Dunkirk see Dunkerque, Fr.	C11	14
Dunkirk, In., U.S.	H4	112
Dunkirk, N.Y., U.S.	B6	114
Dunkirk, Oh., U.S.	D2	114
Dunkwa, Ghana	H4	64
Dún Laoghaire, Ire.	H6	12
Dunlap, Tn., U.S.	B13	122
Dunmore, Pa., U.S.	C10	114
Dunmore Town, Bah.	K9	116
Dunn, N.C., U.S.	A7	116
Dunnellon, Fl., U.S.	G3	116
Dunnet Head, c., Scot., U.K.	C9	12
Dunning, Ne., U.S.	F12	126
Dunnville, On., Can.	F10	112
Dunoon, Scot., U.K.	F8	12
Dunqulah, Sudan	D5	62
Dunqunāb, Sudan	C7	62
Duns, Scot., U.K.	F10	12
Dunseith, N.D., U.S.	F13	124
Dunsmuir, Ca., U.S.	B3	134
Dunstable, Eng., U.K.	J12	12
Dunster, B.C., Can.	C11	138
Dunyāpur, Pak.	D3	54
Duolun, China	C2	38
Duolundabohuer, China	B14	54
Duomula, China	A9	54
Duozhu, China	J6	42
Dupang Ling, mts., China	I4	42
Dupnica, Blg.	G10	26
Dupnitsa see Dupnica, Blg.	G10	26
Dupuyer, Mt., U.S.	B14	136
Duque Bacelar, Braz.	C4	88
Duque de Caxias, Braz.	L4	88
Duque de York, Isla, i., Chile	J1	90
Duran, N.M., U.S.	G3	128
Durance, stm., Fr.	F11	18
Durand, Il., U.S.	B8	120
Durand, Wi., U.S.	G7	118
Durand, Récif, rf., N. Cal.	n17	79d
Durand Reef see Durand, Récif, rf., N. Cal.	n17	79d
Durango, Mex.	C6	100
Durango, Spain	A8	20
Durango, Co., U.S.	F9	132
Durango, state, Mex.	C6	100
Durant, Ia., U.S.	C6	120
Durant, Ms., U.S.	D9	122
Durant, Ok., U.S.	D2	122
Duras, Fr.	E6	18
Durazno, Ur.	F9	92
Durban, S. Afr.	F10	70
Đurđevac, Cro.	D14	22
Düren, Ger.	F2	16
Durg, India	H8	54
Durgāpur, India	G11	54
Durham, On., Can.	D9	112
Durham, Eng., U.K.	G11	12
Durham, Ca., U.S.	D4	134
Durham, N.H., U.S.	G5	110
Durham, N.C., U.S.	H6	114
Durham Downs, Austl.	F3	76
Durham Heights, mtn., N.T., Can.	A6	106
Durlas éile see Thurles, Ire.	I5	12
Durlești, Mol.	B15	26
Durmitor, mtn., Yugo.	F5	26
Durmitor Nacionalni Park, p.o.i., Yugo.	F6	26
Dürnkrut, Aus.	B13	22
Durrës, Alb.	C13	24
Durrësi see Durrës, Alb.	C13	24
Durrie, Austl.	E3	76
Dursunbey, Tur.	D11	28
Duru Gölü, l., Tur.	B11	28
Durūz, Jabal ad-, mtn., Syria	F7	58
D'Urville, Tanjung, c., Indon.	F10	44
D'Urville Island, i., N.Z.	E5	80
Dušak, Turkmen.	B9	56
Dusa Marreb see Dhuusamarreeb, Som.	C9	66
Dušanbe, Taj.	B10	56
Dušekan, Russia	B19	32
Dusetos, Lith.	E8	10
Dushan, China	I2	42
Du Shan, mtn., China	A8	42
Dushanzi, China	C1	36
Duson, La., U.S.	G6	122
Düsseldorf, Ger.	E2	16
Dustin, Ok., U.S.	B2	122
Dutch John, Ut., U.S.	C7	132
Dutton, Mt., U.S.	C15	136
Dutton, stm., Austl.	C4	76
Duvno, Bos.	F4	26
Duxun, China	J7	42
Duyfken Point, c., Austl.	B8	74
Duyun, China	H2	42
Düzce, Tur.	C14	28
Dve Mogili, Blg.	F12	26
Dvine, ozero, l., Russia	D14	10
Dvinskaja guba, b., Russia	D17	8
Dvuh Cirkov, gora, mtn., Russia	C22	34
Dvůr Králové nad Labem, Czech Rep.	F11	16
Dwārka, India	G2	54
Dwight, Il., U.S.	C9	120
Dworshak Reservoir, res., Id., U.S.	D11	136
Dwyka, stm., S. Afr.	H5	70
Dyer, Tn., U.S.	H8	120
Dyer, Cape, c. Nu., Can.	D13	141
Dyer Bay, b., On., Can.	C8	112
Dyersburg, Tn., U.S.	H8	120
Dyje (Thaya), stm., Eur.	H12	16
Dyment, On., Can.	B6	118
Dynów, Pol.	G18	16
Dysart, Sk., Can.	D9	124
Dysart, Ia., U.S.	B5	120
Dysna (Dzisna), stm., Eur.	E9	10
Dytikí Elláda, state, Grc.	E4	28
Dytikí Makedonía, state, Grc.	C4	28
Džagdy, hrebet, mts., Russia	F15	34
Džalal-Abad, Kyrg.	F12	32
Džalinda, Russia	F13	34
Džambejty, Kaz.	D8	32
Džanybek, Kaz.	E7	32
Dzaoudzi, May.	C8	68
Džardžan, Russia	C13	34
Dzavhan, stm., Mong.	B3	36
Dzeržinsk, Russia	H20	8
Dzeržinskoe, Russia	C16	32
Džetygara, Kaz.	D10	32
Dzhankoi, Ukr.	E4	32
Dzhugdzhur Mountains see Džugdžur, hrebet, mts., Russia	E16	34
Dzhungarian Alatau Mountains, mts., Asia	E14	32
Działoszyce, Pol.	F16	16
Dzibilchaltún, hist., Mex.	B3	102
Dzierżoniów, Pol.	F12	16
Dzilam González, Mex.	B3	102
Dzisna, Bela.	E11	10
Dzisna (Dysna), stm., Eur.	E9	10
Dzitbalché, Mex.	B2	102
Dziwnów, Pol.	B10	16
Džizak, Uzb.	F11	32
Dzjarèčyn, Bela.	G7	10
Dzjaršynskaja hara, hill, Bela.	G9	10
Dzjaržynsk, Bela.	G9	10
Dzjatlavičy, Bela.	H9	10
Dzöölön, Mong.	F8	34
Džugdžur, hrebet, mts., Russia	E16	34
Dzūkijos nacionalinis parkas, p.o.i., Lith.	F7	10
Dzungarian Basin see Junggar Pendi, bas., China	B2	36
Dzungarian Gate, p., Asia	E14	32
Džusaly, Kaz.	E10	32
Dzüünharaa, Mong.	B6	36
Dzuunmod, Mong.	B6	36
Dzyhivka, Ukr.	A15	26

E

Name	Map Ref.	Page
Eads, Co., U.S.	C6	128
Eagle, Ak., U.S.	D11	140
Eagle, Co., U.S.	D10	132
Eagle, stm., Co., U.S.	B2	128
Eagle Bay, B.C., Can.	F11	138
Eagle Butte, S.D., U.S.	C11	126
Eagle Creek, stm., Sk., Can.	B6	124
Eagle Grove, Ia., U.S.	B4	120
Eaglehawk, Austl.	K4	76
Eagle Lake, Tx., U.S.	H2	122
Eagle Lake, l., On., Can.	B5	118
Eagle Lake, l., Ca., U.S.	C5	134
Eagle Lake, l., Me., U.S.	D7	110
Eagle Mountain, Ca., U.S.	J1	132
Eagle Mountain, mtn., Id., U.S.	D11	136
Eagle Mountain, mtn., Mn., U.S.	D8	118
Eagle Mountain Lake, res., Tx., U.S.	A10	130
Eagle Pass, Tx., U.S.	F7	130
Eagle Peak, mtn., Ca., U.S.	B5	134
Eagle River, Mi., U.S.	D10	118
Eagle River, Wi., U.S.	F9	118
Eagletown, Ok., U.S.	C4	122
Ear Falls, On., Can.	A5	118
Earle, Ar., U.S.	B8	122
Earl Grey, Sk., Can.	D9	124
Earlham, Ia., U.S.	C3	120
Earlimart, Ca., U.S.	H6	134
Earlville, Il., U.S.	C8	120
Early, Ia., U.S.	B2	120
Early, Tx., U.S.	C9	130
Eas, Vanuatu	k17	79d
Easley, S.C. U.S.	B3	116
East Alton, Il., U.S.	F7	120
East Angus, Qc., Can.	E5	110
East Antarctica, reg., Ant.	C8	81
East Aurora, N.Y., U.S.	B7	114
East Bay, b., Tx., U.S.	H4	122
East Bend, N.C., U.S.	H5	114
East Bernard, Tx., U.S.	H2	122
East Bernstadt, Ky., U.S.	G1	114
East Borneo see Kalimantan Timur, state, Indon.	C10	50
Eastbourne, Eng., U.K.	K13	12
East Brady, Pa., U.S.	D6	114
East Brewton, Al., U.S.	F11	122
East Cache Creek, stm., Ok., U.S.	G10	128
East Caicos, i., T./C. Is.	B12	102
East Cape, c., N.Z.	C8	80
East Cape, c., Fl., U.S.	K4	116
East Carbon, Ut., U.S.	D6	132
East Caroline Basin, unds.	I17	142
East Chicago, In., U.S.	G2	112
East China Sea, Asia	F9	36
East Cote Blanche Bay, b., La., U.S.	H7	122
East Coulee, Ab., Can.	E18	138
East Dereham, Eng., U.K.	I13	12
East Dismal Swamp, sw., N.C., U.S.	A9	116
East Dubuque, Il., U.S.	B7	120
East Ely, Nv., U.S.	D2	132
East End, V.I.U.S.	e8	104b
Easter Island see Pascua, Isla de, i. Chile	f30	78l
Eastern Cape, state, S. Afr.	G8	70
Eastern Channel see Tsushima-kaikyō, strt., Japan	F2	40
Eastern Creek, stm., Austl.	C3	76
Eastern Desert see Arabian Desert, des., Egypt	B6	62
Eastern Division, state, Fiji	q20	79e
Eastern Ghāts, mts., India	E4	53
Eastern Point, c., Guad.	A1	105a
Eastern Sayans see Vostočnyj Sajan, mts., Russia	D17	32
East Falkland, i., Falk. Is.	J5	90
East Fayetteville, N.C., U.S.	A7	116
East Frisian Islands see Ostfriesische Inseln, is., Ger.	C3	16
East Gaffney, S.C., U.S.	A4	116
East Germany see Germany, ctry., Eur.	E6	16
East Glacier Park, Mt., U.S.	B13	136
East Grand Forks, Mn., U.S.	D2	118
East Grand Rapids, Mi., U.S.	F4	112
East Grinstead, Eng., U.K.	J12	12
Easthampton, Ma., U.S.	B13	114
East Java see Jawa Timur, state, Indon.	G8	50
East Jordan, Mi., U.S.	C4	112
East Kelowna, B.C., Can.	G11	138
East Kilbride, Scot., U.K.	F8	12
Eastlake, Mi., U.S.	D3	112
Eastlake, Oh., U.S.	C4	114
Eastland, Tx., U.S.	B9	130
East Lansing, Mi., U.S.	B1	114
East Laurinburg, N.C., U.S.	B6	116
Eastleigh, Eng., U.K.	K11	12
East Liverpool, Oh., U.S.	D5	114
East London (Oos-Londen), S. Afr.	H9	70
Eastmain, Qc., Can.	E15	106
Eastmain, stm., Qc., Can.	E15	106
Eastmain-Opinaca, Réservoir, res., Qc., Can.	E15	106
Eastman, Ga., U.S.	D2	116
East Mariana Basin, unds.	H18	142
East Matagorda Bay, b., Tx., U.S.	F11	130
East Missoula, Mt., U.S.	D13	136
East Moline, Il., U.S.	C7	120
East Naples, Fl., U.S.	J4	116
East Nishnabotna, stm., Ia., U.S.	C2	120
East Nusa Tenggara see Nusa Tenggara Timur, state, Indon.	H12	50
East Olympia, Wa., U.S.	D3	136
Easton, Md., U.S.	F9	114
Easton, Pa., U.S.	D10	114
East Pacific Rise, unds.	N27	142
East Palatka, Fl., U.S.	G4	116
East Pecos, N.M., U.S.	F3	128
East Peoria, Il., U.S.	D8	120
Eastpoint, Fl., U.S.	H14	122
East Point, Ga., U.S.	D14	122
East Point, c., P.E., Can.	D15	110
East Point, c., V.I.U.S.	g11	104c
Eastport, Id., U.S.	B10	136
Eastport, Me., U.S.	F9	110
East Prairie, Mo., U.S.	H8	120
East Prairie, stm., Ab., Can.	A14	138
East Pryor Mountain, mtn., Mt., U.S.	B4	126
East Retford, Eng., U.K.	H12	12
East Saint Louis, Il., U.S.	F7	120
East Sea (Japan, Sea of), Asia	D11	38
East Shoal Lake, l., Mb., Can.	D16	124
East Siberian Sea see Vostočno-Sibirskoe more, Russia	B20	34
East Sister Island, i., Austl.	L6	76
East Slovakia see Východoslovenský Kraj, state, Slov.	H17	16
East Stroudsburg, Pa., U.S.	D11	114
East Troy, Wi., U.S.	B9	120
Eastville, Va., U.S.	G10	114
East Wenatchee, Wa., U.S.	C6	136
East Wilmington, N.C., U.S.	B8	116
Eaton, In., U.S.	H4	112
Eaton, Oh., U.S.	E1	114
Eaton Rapids, Mi., U.S.	B1	114
Eatonton, Ga., U.S.	C2	116
Eatonville, Wa., U.S.	D4	136
Eau Claire, Wi., U.S.	G7	118
Eau Claire, Lac à l', l., Qc., Can.	D16	106
Eauripik, at., Micron.	C5	72
Eauripik Rise, unds.	I17	142
Eauze, Fr.	F6	18
Ebano, Mex.	D9	100
Ebb and Flow Lake, l., Mb., Can.	D14	124
Ebbw Vale, Wales, U.K.	J9	12
Ebebiyín, Eq. Gui.	I7	64
Eben Junction, Mi., U.S.	B2	112
Ebensee, Aus.	C10	22
Eberbach, Ger.	G4	16
Eber Gölü, l., Tur.	E14	28
Ebern, Ger.	F6	16
Ebersbach, Ger.	E10	16
Eberswalde-Finow, Ger.	D9	16
Ebetsu, Japan	C14	38
Ebino, Japan	G3	40
Ebinur Hu, l., China	F14	32
Eboli, Italy	D9	24
Ebolowa, Cam.	D2	66
Ebon, at., Marsh. Is.	C7	72
Ebre see Ebro, stm., Spain	C11	20
Ebre, Delta de l', Spain	D11	20
Ebro (Ebre), stm., Spain	C11	20
Ebro, Delta del see Ebre, Delta de l', Spain	D11	20
Ebro, Embalse del, res., Spain	B7	20
Eceabat, Tur.	C9	28
Ech Cheliff, Alg.	B5	64
Echeng, China	E7	36
Echínos, Grc.	B7	28
Echt, Neth.	E1	16
Echuca, Austl.	K5	76
Écija, Spain	G5	20
Eckernförde, Ger.	B5	16
Eckerö, i., Fin.	F8	8
Eckville, Ab., Can.	D16	138
Eclectic, Al., U.S.	E12	122
Eclipse Sound, strt., Nu., Can.	A14	106
Ecoporanga, Braz.	J5	88
Écorce, Lac de l', res., Qc., Can.	B13	112
Écrins, Barre des, mtn., Fr.	E12	18
Écrins, Massif des, plat., Fr.	E12	18
Ecru, Ms., U.S.	C9	122
Ecuador, ctry., S.A.	D2	84
Ed, Swe.	G4	8
Edam, Sk., Can.	A5	124
Eddrachillis Bay, b., Scot., U.K.	C7	12
Eddystone Rocks, r., Eng., U.K.	K8	12
Eddyville, Ia., U.S.	C5	120
Eddyville, Ky., U.S.	G9	120
Ede, Neth.	B14	14
Ede, Nig.	H5	64
Edéa, Cam.	D2	66
Edehon Lake, l., Nu., Can.	C11	106
Edelény, Hung.	A7	26
Eden, Austl.	K7	76
Eden, Ms., U.S.	D8	122
Eden, N.C., U.S.	H6	114
Eden, Wy., U.S.	A7	132
Eden, stm., Eng., U.K.	G10	12
Edendale, S. Afr.	F10	70
Eden Valley, Mn., U.S.	F4	118
Edenville, S. Afr.	E8	70
Eder, stm., Ger.	E4	16
Édessa, Grc.	C4	28
Edfu, Egypt	C6	62
Edgar, Ne., U.S.	G14	126
Edgar, Wi., U.S.	G8	118
Edgard, La., U.S.	H8	122
Edgartown, Ma., U.S.	C15	114
Edgeley, N.D., U.S.	A14	126
Edgell Island, i., Grnld.	E13	141
Edgemont, S.D., U.S.	D9	126
Edgeøya, i., Nor.	B30	141
Edgeroi, Austl.	H7	76
Edgerton, Ab., Can.	B3	124
Edgerton, Mn., U.S.	H2	118
Edgerton, Oh., U.S.	C1	114
Edgerton, Wi., U.S.	B8	120
Edgewater, Fl., U.S.	H5	116
Edgewood, Il., U.S.	F9	120
Edgewood, Ia., U.S.	B6	120
Edgewood, Md., U.S.	E9	114
Edgewood, Tx., U.S.	E3	122
Edina, Mn., U.S.	G5	118
Edina, Mo., U.S.	D5	120
Edinburg, Il., U.S.	E8	120
Edinburg, In., U.S.	E11	120
Edinburg, Ms., U.S.	E9	122
Edinburg, Tx., U.S.	H9	130
Edinburg, Va., U.S.	F7	114
Edinburgh, Scot., U.K.	F9	12
Edincik, Tur.	C10	28
Edineț, Mol.	A14	26
Edirne, Tur.	B9	28
Edirne, state, Tur.	B9	28
Edison, Ga., U.S.	F14	122
Edisto, stm., S.C., U.S.	D5	116
Edisto, North Fork, stm., S.C., U.S.	C4	116
Edisto Island, i., S.C., U.S.	D5	116
Edith, Mount, mtn., Mt., U.S.	D15	136
Edith Cavell, Mount, mtn., Ab., Can.	D12	138
Edjeleh, Alg.	D6	64
Edmond, Ok., U.S.	F11	128
Edmonds, Wa., U.S.	C4	136
Edmonton, Austl.	A5	76
Edmonton, Ab., Can.	C17	138
Edmonton, Ky., U.S.	G12	120
Edmore, N.D., U.S.	F15	124
Edmundston, N.B., Can.	C8	110
Edna, Ks., U.S.	G2	120
Edna, Tx., U.S.	E11	130
Edremit, Tur.	D10	28
Edremit Körfezi, b., Tur.	D9	28
Edrovo, Russia	C16	10
Edson, Ab., Can.	C14	138
Eduardo Castex, Arg.	G5	92
Eduni, Mount, mtn., N.T., Can.	C5	106
Edward, stm., Austl.	J5	76
Edward, Lake, l., Afr.	E5	66
Edward Island, i., On., Can.	C10	118
Edwards, Ms., U.S.	E8	122
Edwards Air Force Base, Ca., U.S.	I8	134
Edwards Plateau, plat., Tx., U.S.	D7	130
Edwardsville, Il., U.S.	F8	120
Edward VII Peninsula, pen., Ant.	C25	81
Eek, Ak., U.S.	D7	140
Eeklo, Bel.	C12	14
Eel, stm., Ca., U.S.	D2	134
Eel, stm., In., U.S.	G4	112
Eel, stm., In., U.S.	E10	120
Eems (Ems), stm., Eur.	A16	14
Éfaté, state, Vanuatu	k17	79d
Éfaté, i., Vanuatu	k17	79d
Eferding, Aus.	B10	22
Efes (Ephesus), hist., Tur.	F10	28
Effigy Mounds National Monument, p.o.i., Ia., U.S.	A6	120
Effingham, Il., U.S.	E9	120
Effingham, Ks., U.S.	E2	120
Eflâni, Tur.	B15	28
Eforie Nord, Rom.	E15	26
Eforie Sud, Rom.	F15	26
Efremov, Russia	G20	10
Eg, stm., Mong.	F9	34
Egadi, Isole, is., Italy	G5	24
Egaña, Arg.	H8	92
Egan Range, mts., Nv., U.S.	D2	132
Egedesminde (Aasiaat), Grnld.	D15	141
Egegik, Ak., U.S.	E8	140
Eger, Hung.	B7	26
Egersund, Nor.	G1	8
Eggenfelden, Ger.	H8	16
Egg Harbor City, N.J., U.S.	E11	114
Égletons, Fr.	D7	18
Egmont, Cape, c., N.Z.	D5	80
Egmont, Mount see Taranaki, Mount, vol., N.Z.	D6	80
Egmont Bay, b., P.E., Can.	D12	110
Egmont National Park, p.o.i., N.Z.	D5	80
Egorevsk, Russia	E22	10
Egremont, Ab., Can.	B17	138
Eğridir, Tur.	F13	28
Eğridir Gölü, l., Tur.	E13	28
Éguas, stm., Braz.	G3	88
Egvekinot, Russia	C25	34
Egypt, ctry., Afr.	B5	62
Eha-Amufu, Nig.	H6	64
Ehime, state, Japan	F5	40
Ehingen, Ger.	H5	16
Ehrhardt, S.C., U.S.	C4	116
Eibar, Spain	A8	20
Eibiswald, Aus.	D12	22
Eichstätt, Ger.	H7	16
Eidsvold, Austl.	E8	76
Eifel, mts., Ger.	F2	16
Eigg, i., Scot., U.K.	E6	12
Eight Degree Channel, strt., Asia	h12	46a
Eights Coast, cst., Ant.	C31	81
Eighty Mile Beach, cst., Austl.	C4	74
Eildon, Austl.	K5	76
Eildon, Lake, res., Austl.	K5	76
Eilenburg, Ger.	E8	16
Eiler Rasmussen, Kap, c., Grnld.	A21	141
Einasleigh, Austl.	B5	76
Einasleigh, stm., Austl.	A4	76
Einbeck, Ger.	E5	16
Eindhoven, Neth.	C14	14
Einme, Mya.	D2	48
Eirunepé, Braz.	E4	84
Eiseb, stm., Afr.	B4	70
Eisenach, Ger.	E6	16
Eisenberg, Ger.	F7	16
Eisenerz, Aus.	C11	22
Eisenhüttenstadt, Ger.	D10	16
Eisenstadt, Aus.	C13	22
Eisfeld, Ger.	F6	16
Eišiškės, Lith.	F7	10
Eislingen, Ger.	H5	16
Eitorf, Ger.	F3	16
Eivissa (Iviza), Spain	F12	20
Eivissa (Ibiza), i., Spain	F12	20
Ejea de los Caballeros, Spain	B9	20
Ejeda, Madag.	E7	68
Ejido Jaboncillos, Mex.	A7	100
Ejin Horo Qi, China	B3	42
Ejin Qi, China	C5	36
Ejsk, Russia	E5	32
Ejura, Ghana	H4	64
Ejutla de Crespo, Mex.	G10	100
Ekaterinburg, Russia	C10	32
Ekaterinino, Russia	E16	10
Ekateriny, proliv, strt., Russia	B17	38
Ekenäs see Tammisaari, Fin.	G10	8
Ekibastuz, Kaz.	D13	32
Ekimčan, Russia	F15	34
Ekonda, Russia	C10	34
Ekwan, stm., On., Can.	E14	106
Ela, Mya.	C3	48
El Aaiún (Laayoune), W. Sah.	D2	64
El 'Açâba, plat., Maur.	F2	64
El Affroun, Alg.	H13	20
El Agreb, Alg.	C6	64
El Ahijadero, Cerro, mtn., Mex.	E1	130
Elaine, Ar., U.S.	C8	122
El-'Aiyât, Egypt	I2	58
El-Alamein, Egypt	A5	62
El Álamo, Mex.	G7	130
El Álamo, Mex.	H8	130
El Álamo, Mex.	L9	134
El Alto, Arg.	D5	92
Elan', Russia	D6	32
Elancy, Russia	F10	34
El Ángel, Ec.	G2	86
El-Arish, Egypt	G4	58
Elat, Isr.	I5	58

Name	Map Ref.	Page
Elat, Gulf of see Aqaba, Gulf of, b.	J5	58
El Ávila, Parque Nacional, p.o.i., Ven.	B8	86
Elazığ, Tur.	B4	56
Elba, Isola d', i., Italy	H7	22
El-Badâri, Egypt	K2	58
El-Bahnasa, Egypt	J1	58
El-Balyana, Egypt	B6	62
El'ban, Russia	F16	34
El Banco, Col.	C4	86
El Barco de Ávila, Spain	D5	20
Elbasan, Alb.	C13	24
Elbasani see Elbasan, Alb.	C13	24
El Baúl, Ven.	C7	86
El Baúl, Cerro, mtn., Mex.	G11	100
Elbe (Labe), stm., Eur.	C5	16
Elbe-Havel-Kanal, can., Ger.	D8	16
Elbert, Co., U.S.	B4	128
Elbert, Mount, mtn., Co., U.S.	D10	132
Elberta, Mi., U.S.	D3	112
Elberton, Ga., U.S.	B3	116
Elbeuf, Fr.	E10	14
Elbeyli, Tur.	B8	58
El Beyyadh, Alg.	C5	64
Elbląg, Pol.	B15	16
Elbląg, state, Pol.	B15	16
El Bluff, Nic.	G6	102
El Bonillo, Spain	F8	20
El Boulaïda, Alg.	B5	64
Elbow, stm., Ab., Can.	E16	138
Elbow Lake, Mn., U.S.	E3	118
El'brus, gora, mtn., Russia	F6	32
Elbrus, Mount see El'brus, gora, mtn., Russia	F6	32
El-Burg, Egypt	G1	58
El-Burgâya, Egypt	J1	58
Elburs see Alborz, Reshteh-ye Kūhhā-ye, mts., Iran	B7	56
Elburz Mountains see Alborz, Reshteh-ye Kūhhā-ye, mts., Iran	B7	56
El Cadilla, Embalse, res., Arg.	C5	92
El Cajon, Ca., U.S.	K9	134
El Calafate, Arg.	J2	90
El Callao, Ven.	D11	86
El Calvario, Ven.	C8	86
El Campamento, P.R.	B3	104a
El Campo, Tx., U.S.	H2	122
El Capitan, mtn., Mt., U.S.	D12	136
El Carmen, Arg.	B5	92
El Carmen, Col.	C5	86
El Carmen, stm., Mex.	F9	98
El Carmen de Bolívar, Col.	C4	86
El Carricito, Mex.	A7	100
El Carril, Arg.	B5	92
El Centinela, Mex.	K10	134
El Centro, Ca., U.S.	K10	134
El Cerrito, Col.	F3	86
El Cerro Del Aripo, mtn., Trin.	s12	105f
Elche see Elx, Spain	F10	20
El Chile, Montaña, mtn., Nic.	E4	102
Elcho, Wi., U.S.	F9	118
Elcho Island, i., Austl.	B7	74
El Cocuy, Col.	D5	86
El Colorado, Arg.	C8	92
El Cóndor, Cerro, vol., Arg.	C3	92
El Corazón, Ec.	H2	86
El Corpus, Hond.	F4	102
El Coto, P.R.	B2	104a
El'cy, Russia	D16	10
Elda, Spain	F10	20
El Desemboque, Mex.	G6	98
El Desemboque, Mex.	F6	98
El'dikan, Russia	D16	34
El-Dilingât, Egypt	H1	58
El Diviso, Col.	G2	86
El Djazaïr (Algiers), Alg.	B5	64
El Djelfa, Alg.	C5	64
Eldon, Ia., U.S.	D5	120
Eldora, Ia., U.S.	B4	120
Eldorado, Arg.	C10	92
Eldorado, Braz.	B13	92
El Dorado, Ar., U.S.	D6	122
Eldorado, Il., U.S.	G9	120
El Dorado, Ks., U.S.	D12	128
Eldorado, Ok., U.S.	G9	128
El Dorado, Ven.	D11	86
El Dorado Springs, Mo., U.S.	G3	120
Eldoret, Kenya	D7	66
Eldred, Pa., U.S.	C7	114
Eldridge, Ia., U.S.	C7	120
Eleanor, W.V., U.S.	F3	114
Elec, Russia	H21	10
Electric City, Wa., U.S.	C7	136
Elefantes (Olifants), stm., Afr.	D10	70
Elefsína, Grc.	E6	28
Eleftheroúpoli, Grc.	C7	28
Elektrostal', Russia	E21	10
Elena, Blg.	G12	26
El Encanto, Col.	H5	86
Elephant Butte Reservoir, res., N.M., U.S.	J9	132
Elephant Mountain, mtn., Me., U.S.	F6	110
Elesbão Veloso, Braz.	D4	88
El Estor, Guat.	E3	102
Eleuthera, i., Bah.	B9	96
Eleva, Wi., U.S.	G7	118
Eleven Point, stm., U.S.	H6	120
El Fahs, Tun.	H3	24
El Faro, P.R.	C2	104a
El-Fashn, Egypt	J1	58
El-Fayoum, Egypt	I1	58
El Ferrol del Caudillo see Ferrol, Spain	A2	20
El-Fiqriya, Egypt	K1	58
Elfrida, Az., U.S.	L7	132
El Fuerte, Mex.	B4	100
El Galpón, Arg.	B5	92
Elgin, Scot., U.K.	D9	12
Elgin, Il., U.S.	B9	120
Elgin, Ia., U.S.	B6	120
Elgin, Mn., U.S.	G6	118
Elgin, Ne., U.S.	F14	126
Elgin, N.D., U.S.	A11	126
Elgin, Ok., U.S.	G10	128
Elgin, Or., U.S.	E8	136
El-Gindîya, Egypt	J1	58
El-Gîza (Giza), Egypt	H1	58
Elgon, Mount, mtn., Afr.	D6	66
El Grara, Alg.	C5	64
El Grove see O Grove, Spain	B2	20
El Guaje, Mex.	A7	100
El Guamo, Col.	B4	86
El Guapo, Ven.	B9	86
El Hachero, Cerro, mtn., Mex.	H2	130
El Hammâmi, reg., Maur.	E2	64
El-Hamûl, Egypt	G2	58
El Hank, clf, Afr.	E3	64
El-Hawâmdîya, Egypt	I2	58
Elhovo, Blg.	G13	26
El Huisache, Mex.	D8	100
Eliase, Indon.	G9	44
Elida, N.M., U.S.	H5	128
Elila, stm., D.R.C.	E5	66
Elim, Ak., U.S.	D7	140
Elisenvaara, Russia	F13	8
Eliseu Martins, Braz.	E4	88
El-Iskandarîya (Alexandria), Egypt	A6	62
Elista, Russia	E6	32
Elizabeth, Austl.	J2	76
Elizabeth, Co., U.S.	B4	128
Elizabeth, Il., U.S.	B7	120
Elizabeth, N.J., U.S.	D11	114
Elizabeth, W.V., U.S.	E4	114
Elizabeth City, N.C., U.S.	H9	114
Elizabethton, Tn., U.S.	H3	114
Elizabethtown, Il., U.S.	G9	120
Elizabethtown, Ky., U.S.	G11	120
Elizabethtown, N.Y., U.S.	F3	110
Elizabethtown, Pa., U.S.	D9	114
Elizavety, mys, c., Russia	F17	34
Elizovo, Russia	F20	34
El-Jadida, Mor.	C3	64
El Jaralito, Mex.	B6	100
El Jebel, Co., U.S.	D9	132
Ełk, Pol.	C18	16
Elk, stm., B.C., Can.	F16	138
Elk, stm., U.S.	C12	122
Elk, stm., Ks., U.S.	D12	128
Elk, stm., W.V., U.S.	F4	114
Elkader, Ia., U.S.	B6	120
Elk City, Ok., U.S.	F9	128
Elk Creek, Ca., U.S.	D3	134
Elk Creek, stm., S.D., U.S.	C10	126
El Kef, Tun.	H2	24
El-Kelaa-Srarhna, Mor.	C3	64
Ēl Kerē, Eth.	F8	62
Elk Grove, Ca., U.S.	E4	134
El-Khânka, Egypt	H2	58
El-Khârga, Egypt	B6	62
Elkhart, In., U.S.	G4	112
Elkhart, Ks., U.S.	D7	128
Elkhart, Tx., U.S.	F3	122
El Khnâchîch, clf, Mali	E4	64
Elkhorn, Mb., Can.	D12	124
Elk Horn, Ia., U.S.	C2	120
Elkhorn, Wi., U.S.	B9	120
Elkhorn, stm., Ne., U.S.	F16	126
Elkhorn City, Ky., U.S.	G3	114
Elkhorn Mountain, mtn., B.C., Can.	G4	138
Elkhovo see Elhovo, Blg.	G13	26
Elkins, W.V., U.S.	F6	114
Elk Island, i., Mb., Can.	D17	124
Elk Island National Park, p.o.i., Ab., Can.	C18	138
Elkland, Pa., U.S.	C8	114
Elk Mountain, mtn., Wy., U.S.	B10	132
Elko, B.C., Can.	G15	138
Elko, Nv., U.S.	C1	132
Elk Point, Ab., Can.	C19	138
Elk Point, S.D., U.S.	B1	120
Elk Rapids, Mi., U.S.	D4	112
Elk River, Mn., U.S.	F5	118
Elkton, Md., U.S.	E10	114
Elkton, Mi., U.S.	E6	112
Elkton, S.D., U.S.	G2	118
Elkton, Va., U.S.	F7	114
Ellaville, Ga., U.S.	D1	116
Ellef Ringnes Island, i., Nu., Can.	B5	141
Ellen, Mount, mtn., Ut., U.S.	E6	132
Ellendale, Mn., U.S.	H5	118
Ellendale, N.D., U.S.	A14	126
Ellensburg, Wa., U.S.	C6	136
Ellenton, Ga., U.S.	E2	116
Ellesmere, Lake, l., N.Z.	F5	80
Ellesmere Island, i., Nu., Can.	B9	141
Ellettsville, In., U.S.	E11	120
Ellice, stm., Nu., Can.	B10	106
Ellice Islands see Tuvalu, ctry., Oc.	D8	72
Ellicottville, N.Y., U.S.	B7	114
Ellijay, Ga., U.S.	B1	116
Ellinwood, Ks., U.S.	C10	128
Elliot, S. Afr.	G8	70
Elliot, Mount, mtn., Austl.	B6	76
Elliot Lake, On., Can.	B7	112
Elliot Lake, l., Mb., Can.	B18	124
Elliott, Ia., U.S.	C2	120
Elliott, Ms., U.S.	D9	122
Ellisras, S. Afr.	C8	70
Elliston, Austl.	F6	74
Elliston, Mt., U.S.	D14	136
Ellisville, Ms., U.S.	F9	122
Ellon, Scot., U.K.	D10	12
Ellora, India	H5	54
Ellora Caves, hist., India	A2	53
Elloree, S.C., U.S.	C5	116
Ellsworth, Ks., U.S.	C10	128
Ellsworth, Me., U.S.	F8	110
Ellsworth, Mi., U.S.	C4	112
Ellsworth, Mn., U.S.	H3	118
Ellsworth, Wi., U.S.	G6	118
Ellsworth Land, reg., Ant.	C32	81
Ellsworth Mountains, mts., Ant.	C32	81
El Lucero, Mex.	I4	130
Ellwangen, Ger.	H5	16
Ellwood City, Pa., U.S.	D5	114
Elm, stm., U.S.	B14	126
Elma, Wa., U.S.	D3	136
El-Mahalla el-Kubra, Egypt	H2	58
El-Maimûn, Egypt	I2	58
Elmalı, Tur.	G12	28
El Maneadero, Mex.	L9	134
El-Mansûra, Egypt	G2	58
El Manteco, Ven.	D10	86
El-Manzala, Egypt	G2	58
El-Matariya, Egypt	G3	58
Elm Creek, Mb., Can.	E16	124
Elm Creek, Ne., U.S.	G13	126
El Médano, Mex.	C3	100
El Menia, Alg.	C5	64
Elmer, N.J., U.S.	E10	114
Elmhurst, Il., U.S.	G2	112
El-Minya (Minya), Egypt	J1	58
Elmira, On., Can.	E9	112
Elmira, P.E., Can.	D14	110
Elmira, N.Y., U.S.	B9	114
El Moral, Mex.	F7	130
Elmore, Austl.	K5	76
Elmore, Mn., U.S.	H4	118
Elmore, Oh., U.S.	C2	114
Elmore City, Ok., U.S.	G11	128
El Morro, hist., P.R.	B3	104a
El Morro National Monument, p.o.i., N.M., U.S.	H8	132
El Mreyyé, reg., Maur.	F3	64
Elmshorn, Ger.	C5	16
Elm Springs, Ar., U.S.	H3	120
El Mulato, Mex.	E3	130
El-Mutîʻa, Egypt	K2	58
Elmvale, On., Can.	D10	112
Elmwood, Il., U.S.	K8	118
Elmwood, Ne., U.S.	K2	118
El Negrito, Hond.	E4	102
Elnora, Ab., Can.	D17	138
Elnora, In., U.S.	F10	120
Eloguj, stm., Russia	B15	32
Eloise, Fl., U.S.	H4	116
Elora, On., Can.	E9	112
Elorza, Ven.	D7	86
El Otate, Cerro, mtn., Mex.	F1	130
Ėloten, Turkmen.	B9	56
Eloy, Az., U.S.	K5	132
Eloy Alfaro, Ec.	I2	86
El Palmar, Ven.	D10	86
El Palmar de los Sepúlveda, Mex.	C5	100
El Palmito, Mex.	I8	130
El Palqui, Chile	E2	92
El Pao, Ven.	C7	86
El Paso, Il., U.S.	D8	120
El Paso, Tx., U.S.	L10	132
El Paso de Robles see Paso Robles, Ca., U.S.	H5	134
El Paso Peaks, mtn., Ca., U.S.	H8	134
El Perú, Ven.	D11	86
Elphinstone, Mb., Can.	D13	124
El Piñón, Col.	B4	86
El Pintado, Arg.	B7	92
El Pital, Cerro, mtn., N.A.	E3	102
El Planchón, Volcán (Planchón, Cerro del), vol., S.A.	G2	92
El Polvorín, P.R.	B3	104a
El Portal, Ca., U.S.	F6	134
El Porvenir, Mex.	G3	130
El Porvenir, Mex.	K9	134
El Porvenir, Pan.	H8	102
El Potrero, Mex.	H7	130
El Potro, Cerro (Potro, Cerro del), mtn., S.A.	D3	92
El Prat de Llobregat, Spain	C12	20
El Progreso, Hond.	E4	102
El Puerto de Santa María, Spain	H4	20
El Puesto, Arg.	C4	92
El-Qâhira (Cairo), Egypt	H2	58
El-Qantara el-Sharqîya, Egypt	H3	58
El-Qasr, Egypt	B5	62
El Quebrachal, Arg.	B5	92
El Quelite, Mex.	D5	100
Elqui, stm., Chile	D2	92
El-Qûsîya, Egypt	K1	58
El Real de Santa María, Pan.	H9	102
El Remolino, Mex.	F6	130
El Reno, Ok., U.S.	F10	128
El Rio, Ca., U.S.	I6	134
El Roble, Mesa, mtn., Mex.	L10	134
Elroy, Wi., U.S.	H8	118
Elsa, Yk., Can.	C3	106
Elsa, Tx., U.S.	H9	130
El-Saff, Egypt	I2	58
El-Saʻîd (Upper Egypt), hist. reg., Egypt	J2	58
El Salado, Chile	C2	92
El Salado, Parque Nacional, p.o.i., Ec.	I1	86
El Salto, Mex.	D6	100
El Salvador, Chile	C3	92
El Salvador, ctry., N.A.	F3	102
El Samán de Apure, Ven.	D7	86
El Sauz, Mex.	A5	100
El Sauzal, Mex.	L9	134
Elsberry, Mo., U.S.	E7	120
El Seibo, Dom. Rep.	C13	102
Elsen Nur, l., China	D3	36
El-Simbillawein, Egypt	H2	58
Elsinore see Helsingør, Den.	H5	8
Elsinore, Ut., U.S.	E4	132
El Sombrero, Ven.	C8	86
Elsterwerda, Ger.	E9	16
El Sueco, Mex.	E1	130
El-Suweis (Suez), Egypt	I3	58
El Tajín, hist., Mex.	E10	100
El Tala, Arg.	C5	92
El Tanque, Mex.	H8	130
El Tecuán, Mex.	C5	100
El-Thamad, Egypt	I5	58
El Tigre, Ven.	C9	86
Eltmann, Ger.	G6	16
El Toco, Chile	D3	90
El Tocuyo, Ven.	C7	86
Elton, La., U.S.	G6	122
El Tránsito, Chile	D2	92
El Trébol, Arg.	F7	92
El Tule, Mex.	G1	130
El Tuparro, Parque Nacional, p.o.i., Col.	E7	86
El-Tûr, Egypt	J4	58
El Turbio, Arg.	J2	90
El-Uqsor (Luxor), Egypt	B6	62
Elūru, India	C5	53
El Valle, Pan.	H7	102
Elvas, Port.	F3	20
El Vendrell, Spain	C12	20
Elverum, Nor.	F4	8
El Viejo, Nic.	F4	102
El Vigía, Ven.	C6	86
El Vínculo, Ven.	p20	104g
Elvira, Arg.	G8	92
El Volcán, Chile	F2	92
El Wad, Alg.	C6	64
El-Wâsta, Egypt	I2	58
Elwell, Lake, res., Mt., U.S.	B15	136
Elwood, In., U.S.	H4	112
Elwood, Ne., U.S.	G13	126
Elx, Spain	F10	20
Ely, Eng., U.K.	I13	12
Ely, Mn., U.S.	D7	118
Ely, Nv., U.S.	D2	132
El Yagual, Ven.	D7	86
Elyria, Oh., U.S.	C3	114
El Yunque, mtn., P.R.	B4	104a
El-Zarqa, Egypt	G2	58
Émaé, i., Vanuatu	k17	79d
Emajõgi, stm., Est.	B9	10
Emāmshahr, Iran	B8	56
Emba, Kaz.	E9	32
Emba, stm., Kaz.	E9	32
Embarras, stm., Il., U.S.	F10	120
Embarrass, Wi., U.S.	G10	118
Emborcação, Represa da, res., Braz.	J2	88
Embreeville, Tn., U.S.	H3	114
Embrun, Fr.	E12	18
Embu, Kenya	E7	66
Emca, stm., Russia	E19	8
Emden, Ger.	C3	16
Emden, Il., U.S.	K9	118
Emelle, Al., U.S.	E10	122
Emerado, N.D., U.S.	G16	124
Emerald, Austl.	D6	76
Emerson, Mb., Can.	E16	124
Emerson, Ar., U.S.	D5	122
Emerson, Ia., U.S.	C2	120
Emery, S.D., U.S.	D15	126
Emery, Ut., U.S.	E5	132
Emet, Tur.	D12	28
Emiliano Zapata, Mex.	G13	100
Emilia-Romagna, state, Italy	F8	22
Emin, China	B1	36
Emine, nos, c., Blg.	G14	26
Eminence, Mo., U.S.	G6	120
Emirdağ, Tur.	D14	28
Emır Dağları, mts., Tur.	E14	28
Emita, Austl.	m13	77a
Emlembe, mtn., Afr.	D10	70
Emlenton, Pa., U.S.	G10	112
Emmaste, Est.	B5	10
Emmaus, Pa., U.S.	D10	114
Emmaville, Austl.	G8	76
Emmen, Neth.	B15	14
Emmendingen, Ger.	H3	16
Emmerich, Ger.	E2	16
Emmet, Ar., U.S.	D5	122
Emmetsburg, Ia., U.S.	A3	120
Emmiganūru, India	D3	53
Emmitsburg, Md., U.S.	E8	114
Emmonak, Ak., U.S.	D7	140
Emo, On., Can.	C5	118
Emory Peak, mtn., Tx., U.S.	E4	130
Empalme, Mex.	A3	100
Empangeni, S. Afr.	F10	70
Empedrado, Arg.	C8	92
Emperor Seamounts, unds.	E19	142
Empire, La., U.S.	H9	122
Empire, Nv., U.S.	C6	134
Empoli, Italy	G7	22
Emporia, Ks., U.S.	F1	120
Emporia, Va., U.S.	H8	114
Emporium, Pa., U.S.	C7	114
Empty Quarter see Ar-Rubʻ al-Khālī, des., Asia	E6	56
Ems, stm., Eur.	C3	16
Emsdetten, Ger.	D3	16
Emu, China	C8	38
Emu Park, Austl.	D8	76
Enarotali, Indon.	F10	44
Enašimskij Polkan, gora, mtn., Russia	C16	32
Encampment, Wy., U.S.	B10	132
Encantado, Braz.	D11	92
Encarnación, Para.	C9	92
Enchi, Ghana	H4	64
Enchilayas, Mex.	F6	98
Encinal, Tx., U.S.	F8	130
Encinitas, Ca., U.S.	J8	134
Encino, N.M., U.S.	G3	128
Encontrados, Ven.	C5	86
Encounter Bay, b., Austl.	J2	76
Encruzilhada, Braz.	H5	88
Encruzilhada do Sul, Braz.	E11	92
Encs, Hung.	A8	26
Endako, B.C., Can.	B5	138
Ende, Indon.	G7	44
Endeavor, Wi., U.S.	H9	118
Endeavour Strait, strt., Austl.	B8	74
Enderby, B.C., Can.	F11	138
Enderby Land, reg., Ant.	B10	81
Enderlin, N.D., U.S.	A15	126
Endicott, N.Y., U.S.	B9	114
Endicott, Wa., U.S.	D9	136
Endicott Mountains, mts., Ak., U.S.	C9	140
Ene, stm., Peru	F3	84
Enewetak, at., Marsh. Is.	B7	72
Enez, Tur.	C9	28
Enfield, N.C., U.S.	H8	114
Engaño, Cabo, c., Dom. Rep.	C13	102
Engcobo, S. Afr.	G9	70
Engelhard, N.C., U.S.	A10	116
Engel's, Russia	D7	32
Engen, B.C., Can.	B6	138
Engenheiro Navarro, Braz.	I3	88
Enggano, Pulau, i., Indon.	F2	50
England, state, U.K.	I12	12
Englefield, Cape, c., Nu., Can.	B13	106
Englehart, On., Can.	F15	106
Englewood, B.C., Can.	F3	138
Englewood, Co., U.S.	B4	128
Englewood, Fl., U.S.	J3	116
Englewood, Ks., U.S.	D8	128
Englewood, Tn., U.S.	A1	116
English, stm., On., Can.	A4	118
English Channel, strt., Eur.	D7	14
English Coast, cst., Ant.	C33	81
Engure, Lat.	C6	10
Engures ezers, l., Lat.	C6	10
Enid, Ok., U.S.	E11	128
Enid Lake, res., Ms., U.S.	C9	122
Enisej, stm., Russia	C6	34
Enisejsk, Russia	C16	32
Enisejskij krjaž, mts., Russia	C16	32
Enisejskij zaliv, b., Russia	B5	34
Eniwetok see Enewetak, at., Marsh. Is.	B7	72
Enka, N.C., U.S.	A3	116
Enkhuizen, Neth.	B14	14
Enköping, Swe.	G7	8
Enmedio, Mex.	E4	130
Enmedio, Cerro de, mtn., Mex.	F8	100
Enna, Italy	G8	24
Ennadai Lake, l., Nu., Can.	C10	106
Ennedi, plat., Chad	D4	62
Ennis, Ire.	I3	12
Ennis, Mt., U.S.	E15	136
Ennis, Tx., U.S.	E2	122
Enniscorthy, Ire.	I6	12
Enniskillen, N. Ire., U.K.	G5	12
Enns, Aus.	B11	22
Enns, stm., Aus.	B11	22
Enon, Oh., U.S.	E2	114
Enontekiö, Fin.	B10	8
Enoree, stm., S.C., U.S.	B3	116
Enosburg Falls, Vt., U.S.	F4	110
Enping, China	J5	42
Enrekang, Indon.	E11	50
Enrique Urien, Arg.	C7	92
Enriquillo, Dom. Rep.	D12	102
Enriquillo, Lago, l., Dom. Rep.	C12	102
Enschede, Neth.	B15	14
Ensenada, Arg.	G9	92
Ensenada, Mex.	L9	134
Enshi, China	F3	42
Enshū-nada, Japan	E10	40
Entebbe, Ug.	D6	66
Enterprise, N.T., Can.	C7	106
Enterprise, Al., U.S.	F13	122
Enterprise, Ca., U.S.	D4	134
Enterprise, Ms., U.S.	E10	122
Enterprise, Or., U.S.	E9	136
Enterprise, Ut., U.S.	F3	132
Entrepeñas, Embalse de, res., Spain	D8	20
Entre Ríos, Bol.	D4	90
Entre Rios, Braz.	G7	88
Entre Ríos, state, Arg.	F8	92
Entrevaux, Fr.	F12	18
Entroncamento, Port.	E2	20
Entwistle, Ab., Can.	C16	138
Enugu, Nig.	H6	64
Enurmino, Russia	C26	34
Envalira, Port d', p., And.	B12	20
Envigado, Col.	D4	86
Envira, stm., Braz.	E3	84
Enyamba, D.R.C.	E5	66
Enyellé, Congo	D3	66
Eolia, Mo., U.S.	E6	120
Eolie, Isole (Lipari, Isole), is., Italy	F8	24
Epanomí, Grc.	C5	28
Epecuén, Lago, l., Arg.	H6	92
Épernay, Fr.	E12	14
Epes, Al., U.S.	E10	122
Ephesus see Efes, hist., Tur.	F10	28
Ephraim, Ut., U.S.	D5	132
Ephrata, Pa., U.S.	D9	114
Ephrata, Wa., U.S.	C7	136
Épi, state, Vanuatu	k17	79d
Épi, i., Vanuatu	k17	79d
Epídavros, hist., Grc.	F6	28
Épila, Spain	C9	20
Épinal, Fr.	F15	14
Epirus see Ípeiros, hist. reg., Grc.	D3	28
Epsom, Eng., U.K.	J12	12
Epukiro, Nmb.	B4	70
Epukiro, stm., Nmb.	B4	70
Eqlīd, Iran	C7	56
Equatorial Guinea, ctry., Afr.	I6	64
Erap, Pap. N. Gui.	b4	79a
Erath, La., U.S.	H6	122
Erave, Pap. N. Gui.	b3	79a
Erawan National Park, p.o.i., Thai.	E4	48
Erbach, Ger.	G5	16
Erbogačon, Russia	B19	32
Ercevo, Russia	F18	8
Ercolano, Italy	D8	24
Érd, Hung.	B5	26
Erdao, stm., China	C8	38
Erdaohezi, China	B8	38
Erdek, Tur.	C10	28
Erdemli, Tur.	B5	58
Erding, Ger.	H7	16
Erebato, stm., Ven.	E9	86
Erebus, Mount, mtn., Ant.	C21	81
Erechim, Braz.	C11	92
Ereğli, Tur.	B14	28
Ereğli, Tur.	A4	58
Erenhot, China	C7	36
Erepecuru, Lago do, l., Braz.	D6	84
Erfoud, Mor.	C4	64
Erft, stm., Ger.	E2	16
Erfurt, Ger.	F7	16
Ergene, stm., Tur.	B10	28
Ergeni, hills, Russia	E6	32
Ērgļi, Lat.	D8	10
Ergun Youqi, China	A9	36
Ergun Zuoqi, China	F13	34
Er Hai, l., China	F5	36
Erice, Italy	F6	24
Ericeira, Port.	F1	20
Erichsen Lake, l., Nu., Can.	A14	106
Erick, Ok., U.S.	F9	128
Erickson, Mb., Can.	D14	124
Ericson, Ne., U.S.	F14	126
Erie, Co., U.S.	A3	128
Erie, Il., U.S.	C7	120
Erie, Pa., U.S.	B5	114
Erie, Lake, l., N.A.	B4	114
Erie Canal see New York State Barge Canal, can., N.Y., U.S.	E12	112
Eriksdale, Mb., Can.	D15	124
Erimo-misaki, c., Japan	D15	38
Erin, On., Can.	E9	112
Erin, Tn., U.S.	H10	120
Eriskay, i., Scot., U.K.	D5	12
Eritrea, ctry., Afr.	D7	62
Erivan see Yerevan, Arm.	A5	56
Erkelenz, Ger.	E2	16
Erkner, Ger.	D9	16
Erlangen, Ger.	G7	16
Ermak, Kaz.	D13	32
Ermelo, S. Afr.	E10	70
Ermenek, Tur.	B3	58
Ermenek, stm., Tur.	B3	58
Ermentau, Kaz.	D12	32
Ermica, Russia	C25	8
Ermolaevo, Russia	D9	32
Ermolino, Russia	E19	10
Ermoúpoli, Grc.	F7	28
Erne, Lower Lough, l., N. Ire., U.K.	G4	12
Erne, Upper Lough, l., Eur.	G5	12
Ernée, Fr.	F8	14
Erode, India	F3	53
Erofej Pavlovič, Russia	F13	34
Eromanga, Austl.	F4	76
Erongo, state, Nmb.	C2	70
Erongo, mtn., Nmb.	B2	70
Eropol, Russia	C22	34
Erota, Erit.	D7	62
Er-Rachidia, Mor.	C4	64
Errego, Moz.	D6	68
Errigal Mountain, mtn., Ire.	F4	12
Errinundra National Park, p.o.i., Austl.	K7	76
Erris Head, c., Ire.	G2	12
Errol Heights, Or., U.S.	E4	136
Erromango, i., Vanuatu	I17	79d
Erši, Russia	F17	10
Eršov, Russia	D7	32
Erstein, Fr.	F16	14
Ertai, China	B3	36
Ertix see Irtysh, stm., Asia	E15	32
Ertoma, Russia	E22	8
Erval, Braz.	F11	92
Ervy-le-Châtel, Fr.	F12	14
Erwin, N.C., U.S.	A7	116
Erwin, Tn., U.S.	H3	114
Erwood, Sk., Can.	B11	124
Erýmanthos, mtn., Grc.	F4	28
Eryuan, China	F4	36
Erzhan, China	B8	38
Erzin, Russia	D17	32
Erzincan, Tur.	B4	56
Erzurum, Tur.	B5	56
Esaʻala, Pap. N. Gui.	b5	79a
Esashi, Japan	D13	38
Esbjerg, Den.	I3	8
Esbo see Espoo, Fin.	F11	8
Escada, Braz.	E8	88
Escalante, stm., Ut., U.S.	F6	132
Escalante, stm., Ven.	C5	86
Escalón, Mex.	B6	100
Escalon, Ca., U.S.	F5	134
Escambia, stm., Fl., U.S.	G11	122
Escanaba, Mi., U.S.	C2	112
Escanaba, stm., Mi., U.S.	B2	112
Escandón, Puerto, p., Spain	D10	20
Escárcega, Mex.	C2	102
Escarpada Point, c., Phil.	A4	52
Escatawpa, stm., U.S.	G10	122
Esch-sur-Alzette, Lux.	E15	14
Escobedo, Mex.	G6	130
Escocesa, Bahía, b., Dom. Rep.	C13	102
Escondido, Ca., U.S.	J8	134
Escondido, stm., Mex.	F7	130
Escondido, stm., Nic.	F6	102
Escuinapa de Hidalgo, Mex.	D5	100
Escuintla, Guat.	E2	102
Escuintla, Mex.	H12	100
Eséka, Cam.	D2	66
Eşen, Tur.	G12	28
Eşfahān, Iran	C7	56
Esgueva, stm., Spain	C6	20
Eshkāshem, Afg.	B11	56
Eshowe, S. Afr.	F10	70
Esil', Kaz.	D11	32
Esil see Ishim, stm., Asia	C12	32
Esk, Austl.	F9	76
Ěškar-Ola, Russia	C7	32
Eskdale, W.V., U.S.	F4	114
Es'ki, Russia	C19	10
Eskilstrup, Den.	B7	16
Eskilstuna, Swe.	G7	8
Eskimo Lakes, l., N.T., Can.	B4	106
Eskimo Point see Arviat, Nu., Can.	C12	106
Eskişehir, Tur.	D13	28
Eskişehir, state, Tur.	D13	28
Eskridge, Ks., U.S.	F1	120
Esla, stm., Spain	C5	20
Eslāmābād, Iran	C6	56
Eşme, Tur.	E11	28
Esmeralda, Austl.	B4	76
Esmeralda, Cuba	B8	102
Esmeralda, Isla, i., Chile	I1	90
Esmeraldas, Ec.	G2	86
Esmeraldas, state, Ec.	G2	86
Esmeraldas, stm., Ec.	G2	86
Esnagami Lake, l., On., Can.	A11	118
Espada, Punta, c., Col.	A6	86
Espalion, Fr.	E8	18
Espanola, On., Can.	B8	112
Espanola, N.M., U.S.	F2	128
Espejo, Spain	G6	20
Espelkamp, Ger.	D4	16
Espera Feliz, Braz.	K5	88
Esperança, Braz.	D4	84
Esperança, Braz.	D7	88
Esperance, Austl.	F4	74
Esperantina, Braz.	B4	88
Esperanza, Arg.	E7	92
Esperanza, Mex.	B4	100
Esperanza, P.R.	B5	104a
Esperanza, sci., Ant.	B35	81
Espichel, Cabo, c., Port.	F1	20
Espinal, Col.	E4	86
Espinazo, Mex.	H6	130
Espinhaço, Serra do, mts., Braz.	I4	88
Espinho, Port.	D2	20
Espinillo, Arg.	B8	92
Espino, Ven.	C9	86
Espinosa, Braz.	H4	88
Espírito Santo, state, Braz.	J5	88
Espiritu Santo, i., Vanuatu	j16	79d
Espíritu Santo, Isla del, i., Mex.	C3	100
Espita, Mex.	B3	102
Esplanada, Braz.	F7	88
Espoo, Fin.	F11	8
Espungabera, Moz.	B11	70
Esquel, Arg.	H2	90
Esquimalt, B.C., Can.	H7	138
Esquina, Arg.	D8	92
Esquiú, Arg.	D5	92
Essaouira, Mor.	C3	64
Essej, Russia	C9	34
Essen, Ger.	E3	16
Essendon, Mount, mtn., Austl.	D3	74
Essequibo, stm., Guy.	C6	84
Es Sers, Tun.	H2	24
Essex, On., Can.	F7	112
Essex, Md., U.S.	E9	114
Essex, Mt., U.S.	B13	136
Essex Junction, Vt., U.S.	F3	110
Essexville, Mi., U.S.	E6	112
Esslingen am Neckar, Ger.	H5	16
Essonne, state, Fr.	F11	14
Est, Pointe de l', c., Qc., Can.	A15	110
Estacada, Or., U.S.	E4	136
Estaca de Bares, Punta da, c., Spain	A3	20
Estaca de Bares, Punta de la see Estaca de Bares, Punta da, c., Spain	A3	20
Estacado, Llano, pl., U.S.	H6	128
Estación Adolfo Rodriguez Sáa see Santa Rosa del Conlara, Arg.	F5	92
Estación Colonia Alvear Norte see General Alvear, Arg.	G3	92
Estación Foguista J. F. Juárez see El Galpón, Arg.	B5	92
Estación Gobernador Vera see Vera, Arg.	D7	92
Estación J. J. Castelli see Castelli, Arg.	B7	92
Estación Justino Solari see Mariano I. Loza, Arg.	D8	92
Estación Manuel F. Mantilla see Pedro R. Fernández, Arg.	D8	92
Estación Vela see María Ignacia, Arg.	H8	92
Estados, Isla de los, i., Arg.	J4	90
Eşţahbān, Iran	D7	56
Estância, Braz.	F7	88
Estancia, N.M., U.S.	G2	128
Estanislao del Campo, Arg.	B7	92
Estarreja, Port.	D2	20
Estats, Pic d' (Estats, Pique d'), mtn., Eur.	G7	18
Estats, Pico de see Estats, Pic d', mtn., Eur.	G7	18
Estats, Pique d' (Estats, Pic d'), mtn., Eur.	G7	18
Estcourt, S. Afr.	F9	70
Este, Italy	E8	22
Esteio, Braz.	D12	92
Estelí, Nic.	F4	102
Estella, Spain	B8	20
Estelline, S.D., U.S.	G2	118
Estelline, Tx., U.S.	G8	128
Estepa, Spain	G6	20
Estepona, Spain	H5	20
Estes Park, Co., U.S.	G7	126
Este Sudeste, Cayos del, is., Col.	F7	102
Estevan, Sk., Can.	E10	124
Estevan Point, B.C., Can.	G4	138
Estherville, Ia., U.S.	H4	118
Estill, S.C., U.S.	D4	116
Estiva, stm., Braz.	G3	88
Eston, Sk., Can.	C5	124
Estonia, ctry., Eur.	G11	8
Estrela, Braz.	D11	92
Estrela, mtn., Port.	D3	20
Estrela do Sul, Braz.	J2	88
Estremadura, hist. reg., Port.	E1	20
Estremoz, Port.	F3	20
Estrondo, Serra do, plat., Braz.	E1	88
Esztergom, Hung.	B5	26
Etadunna, Austl.	G2	76
Etah, Grnld.	B11	141
Etah, India	E7	54
Étain, Fr.	E14	14
Étampes, Fr.	F11	14
Etamunbanie, Lake, l., Austl.	F2	76
Étaples, Fr.	D10	14
Etāwah, India	E7	54
Etchojoa, Mex.	B4	100
Ethan, S.D., U.S.	D14	126
Ethel, Ms., U.S.	D9	122
Ethel, Mount, mtn., Co., U.S.	C10	132
Ethiopia, ctry., Afr.	F7	62
Ethiopian Plateau, plat., Eth.	E7	62
Ethridge, Mt., U.S.	B14	136
Ethridge, Tn., U.S.	B11	122
Etigo-heiya, pl., Japan	B12	40
Etive, Loch, l., Scot., U.K.	E7	12
E. T. Joshua Airport, St. Vin.	o11	105e
Etna, Ca., U.S.	B3	134
Etna, Monte, vol., Italy	G8	24
Etobicoke, ngh., On., Can.	E10	112
Etolin Island, i., Ak., U.S.	E13	140
Etolin Strait, strt., Ak., U.S.	D6	140
Etomami, stm., Sk., Can.	B11	124
Eton, Austl.	C7	76
Etorofu-tō (Iturup, ostrov), i., Russia	B17	38
Etosha Pan, pl., Nmb.	D2	68
Etoumbi, Congo	D2	66
Etowah, Tn., U.S.	B14	122
Etowah, stm., Ga., U.S.	C14	122
Étretat, Fr.	E9	14
Etsch see Adige, stm., Italy	E8	22
Et Tîdra, i., Maur.	F1	64
Ettlingen, Ger.	H4	16
Etzikom Coulee, stm., Ab., Can.	E2	124
Etzná, hist., Mex.	C2	102
Eu, Fr.	D10	14
Eua, i., Tonga	F9	72
Eua Iki, i., Tonga	n15	78e
Euboea see Évvoia, i., Grc.	E6	28
Euboea, Gulf of see Vórios Evvoikós Kólpos, b., Grc.	E5	28
Eucla, Austl.	F5	74
Euclid, Oh., U.S.	C4	114
Euclides da Cunha, Braz.	F6	88
Eucumbene, Lake, res., Austl.	K7	76
Eudora, Ar., U.S.	D7	122
Eudora, Ks., U.S.	F2	120
Eufaula, Al., U.S.	F13	122
Eufaula Lake, res., Ok., U.S.	B3	122
Eugene, Or., U.S.	F3	136
Eugenia, Punta, c., Mex.	B1	100
Eugenio Bustos, Arg.	F3	92
Eugowra, Austl.	I7	76
Eumungerie, Austl.	H7	76
Eunápolis, Braz.	I6	88
Eungella National Park, p.o.i., Austl.	C7	76
Eunice, La., U.S.	G6	122
Eunice, N.M., U.S.	B4	130
Euphrates (Al-Furāt), stm., Asia	C6	56
Eupora, Ms., U.S.	D9	122
Eure, state, Fr.	E9	14
Eure, stm., Fr.	E10	14
Eure-et-Loir, state, Fr.	F10	14
Eureka, Can.	A8	141
Eureka, Ca., U.S.	C1	134
Eureka, Il., U.S.	K9	118
Eureka, Ks., U.S.	D12	128
Eureka, Mt., U.S.	B11	136
Eureka, Nv., U.S.	D10	134

Name — Map Ref. — Page

Eureka, S.C., U.S. B4 116
Eureka Springs, Ar., U.S. H4 120
Eurinilla Creek, stm., Austl. H3 76
Euroa, Austl. K5 76
Europa, Île, i., Reu. E7 68
Europa, Picos de, mts., Spain A6 20
Europa Island see Europa, Île, i., Reu. E7 68
Europa Point, c., Gib. H5 20
Europe, cont. C13 4
Euskal Herriko, state, Spain A8 20
Euskirchen, Ger. F2 16
Eustace, Tx., U.S. E2 122
Eustis, Fl., U.S. H4 116
Eustis, Lake, l., Fl., U.S. H4 116
Euston, Austl. J4 76
Eutaw, Al., U.S. E11 122
Eutin, Ger. B6 16
Eutsuk Lake, l., B.C., Can. C4 138
Eva, Al., U.S. C12 122
Evadale, Tx., U.S. G4 122
Evandale, Austl. n13 77a
Evans, Lac, l., Qc., Can. E15 106
Evans, Mount, mtn., Co., U.S. B3 128
Evansburg, Ab., Can. C15 138
Evans City, Pa., U.S. D5 114
Evansdale, Ia., U.S. I6 118
Evans Strait, strt., Nu., Can. C14 106
Evanston, Il., U.S. F2 112
Evanston, Wy., U.S. B6 132
Evansville, In., U.S. F10 120
Evansville, Mn., U.S. E3 118
Evansville, Wi., U.S. B8 120
Evansville, Wy., U.S. E6 126
Evart, Mi., U.S. E4 112
Eveleth, Mn., U.S. D6 118
Evening Shade, Ar., U.S. H6 120
Evensk, Russia D20 34
Everard, Lake, l., Austl. F6 74
Everest, Mount (Qomolangma Feng), mtn., Asia D11 54
Everett, Pa., U.S. E7 114
Everett, Wa., U.S. C4 136
Everett, Mount, mtn., Ma., U.S. B12 114
Everglades, The, sw., Fl., U.S. K4 116
Everglades City, Fl., U.S. K4 116
Everglades National Park, p.o.i., Fl., U.S. K5 116
Evergreen, Al., U.S. F12 122
Evergreen, Mt., U.S. B12 136
Evermann, Cerro, vol., Mex. F3 100
Evesham, Sk., Can. B4 124
Evesham, Eng., U.K. I11 12
Évian-les-Bains, Fr. C12 18
Evje, Nor. G2 8
Évora, Port. F3 20
Évora, state, Port. F3 20
Evoron, ozero, l., Russia F16 34
Évreux, Fr. E10 14
Évry, Fr. F11 14
E. V. Spence Reservoir, res., Tx., U.S. C7 130
Évvoia, i., Grc. E6 28
Ewa, Hi., U.S. B3 78a
Ewing, Ne., U.S. E14 126
Ewing, Va., U.S. H2 114
Ewo, Congo E2 66
Exaltación, Bol. B3 90
Excelsior Mountain, mtn., Ca., U.S. E6 134
Excelsior Springs, Mo., U.S. E3 120
Exeter, On., Can. E8 112
Exeter, Eng., U.K. K9 12
Exeter, Ca., U.S. G6 134
Exeter, N.H., U.S. G6 110
Exeter Sound, strt., Nu., Can. D13 141
Exira, Ia., U.S. C3 120
Exmoor, plat., Eng., U.K. J9 12
Exmoor National Park, p.o.i., Eng., U.K. J9 12
Exmore, Va., U.S. G10 114
Exmouth, Austl. D2 74
Exmouth, Eng., U.K. K9 12
Exmouth Gulf, b., Austl. D2 74
Exshaw, Ab., Can. E15 138
Extremadura, state, Spain E4 20
Exuma Cays, is., Bah. C9 96
Exuma Sound, strt., Bah. C9 96
Eyasi, Lake, l., Tan. E6 66
Eyebrow, Sk., Can. D7 124
Eyemouth, Scot., U.K. F10 12
Eye Peninsula, pen., Scot., U.K. C6 12
Eyjafjördur, b., Ice. j30 8a
Eyl, Som. C9 66
Eyl, val., Som. C9 66
Eylar Mountain, mtn., Ca., U.S. F4 134
Eyota, Mn., U.S. H6 118
Eyrarbakki, Ice. I29 8a
Eyre, Austl. F5 74
Eyre Creek, stm., Austl. F2 76
Eyre North, Lake, l., Austl. E7 74
Eyre Peninsula, pen., Austl. F7 74
Eyre South, Lake, l., Austl. E7 74
Ezequiel Ramos Mexía, Embalse, res., Arg. G3 90
Ežerėlis, Lith. F6 10
Ezine, Tur. D9 28

F

Faaone, Fr. Poly. v22 78h
Faber Lake, l., N.T., Can. C7 106
Fabriano, Italy G9 22
Facatativá, Col. E4 86
Fachi, Niger F7 64
Facpi Point, c., Guam j9 78c
Factoryville, Pa., U.S. C10 114
Fada, Chad D4 62
Fada-Ngourma, Burkina G5 64
Faddeevskij, ostrov, i., Russia A18 34
Faddeja, zaliv, b., Russia A10 34
Fadiffolu Atoll, at., Mald. h12 46a
Faenza, Italy F8 22
Fafe, Port. C2 20
Făgăraș, Rom. D11 26
Fagernes, Nor. F3 8
Fagersta, Swe. F6 8
Faguibine, Lac, l., Mali F4 64
Fagurhólsmýri, Ice. I31 8a
Fairbank, Ia., U.S. B5 120
Fairbanks, Ak., U.S. D10 140
Fairbanks, La., U.S. E6 122
Fair Bluff, N.C., U.S. B6 116
Fairborn, Oh., U.S. E1 114
Fairbury, Il., U.S. K10 118
Fairbury, Ne., U.S. A11 128
Fairchance, Pa., U.S. E6 114
Fairchild, Wi., U.S. G8 118
Fairfax, Mn., U.S. G4 118
Fairfax, Mo., U.S. D2 120
Fairfax, S.C., U.S. D4 116
Fairfax, S.D., U.S. D14 126
Fairfax, Vt., U.S. F3 110
Fairfax, Va., U.S. F8 114
Fairfield, Al., U.S. D11 122
Fairfield, Ca., U.S. E3 134
Fairfield, Id., U.S. G12 136
Fairfield, Il., U.S. F9 120
Fairfield, Me., U.S. F7 110
Fairfield, Ne., U.S. G14 126
Fairfield, Oh., U.S. E1 114
Fairfield, Tx., U.S. F2 122
Fairgrove, Mi., U.S. E6 112
Fairhaven, Ma., U.S. C15 114
Fair Haven, N.Y., U.S. E13 112
Fair Head, c., N. Ire., U.K. F6 12
Fairhope, Al., U.S. G11 122
Fair Isle, i., Scot., U.K. B11 12
Fairland, In., U.S. E12 120
Fairlie, N.Z. G4 80
Fairmont, Mn., U.S. H4 118
Fairmont, Ne., U.S. G15 126
Fairmont, N.C., U.S. B6 116
Fairmont, W.V., U.S. E5 114
Fairmont Hot Springs, B.C., Can. F14 138
Fairmount, Il., U.S. H2 112
Fairmount, In., U.S. H4 112
Fairmount, N.D., U.S. E2 118
Fair Ness, c., Nu., Can. C16 106
Fair Oaks, Ca., U.S. E4 134
Fair Plain, Mi., U.S. F3 112
Fairplay, Co., U.S. B3 128
Fairview, Ga., U.S. C13 122
Fairview, Il., U.S. D7 120
Fairview, Mi., U.S. D5 112
Fairview, Mt., U.S. G9 124
Fairview, Tn., U.S. I10 120
Fairview, Ut., U.S. D5 132
Fairview Park, In., U.S. I2 112
Fairview Peak, mtn., Nv., U.S. D7 134
Fairweather Mountain, mtn., N.A. D3 106
Faisalabad (Lyallpur), Pak. C4 54
Faison, N.C., U.S. A7 116
Faistós, hist., Grc. H7 28
Faith, S.D., U.S. B10 126
Faizābād, India E9 54
Fajardo, P.R. B4 104a
Fajou, Îlet à, i., Guad. h5 105c
Fajr, Bi'r, well, Sau. Ar. J8 58
Fajr, Wādī, stm., Sau. Ar. H9 58
Fajr, Wādī, stm., Sau. Ar. J8 58
Fakse Bugt, b., Den. A8 16
Faku, China C5 38
Falaba, S.L. H2 64
Falaise, Fr. F8 14
Fālākāta, India E12 54
Falam, Mya. A1 48
Falcón, state, Ven. B7 86
Falcón, Presa (Falcon Reservoir), res., N.A. H8 130
Falconara Marittima, Italy G10 22
Falcon Reservoir (Falcón, Presa), res., N.A. H8 130
Falelatai, Samoa g11 79c
Falémé, stm., Afr. G2 64
Fălești, Mol. B14 26
Falfurrias, Tx., U.S. G9 130
Falkenberg, Ger. E9 16
Falkenberg, Swe. H5 8
Falkensee, Ger. D9 16
Falkenstein, Ger. F8 16
Falkirk, Scot., U.K. E9 12
Falkland, B.C., Can. F11 138
Falkland Islands, dep., S.A. J4 90
Falkland Sound, strt., Falk. Is. J5 90
Falköping, Swe. G5 8
Falkville, Al., U.S. C11 122
Fall, stm., Ks., U.S. D13 128
Fallbrook, Ca., U.S. J8 134
Fallon, Nv., U.S. D7 134
Fall River, Ks., U.S. G1 120
Fall River, Ma., U.S. C14 114
Fall River, Wi., U.S. H9 118
Fall River Mills, Ca., U.S. C4 134
Falls City, Ne., U.S. D2 120
Falls City, Or., U.S. F3 136
Falls Creek, Pa., U.S. C7 114
Falls Lake, res., N.C., U.S. I7 114
Falmouth, Jam. i13 104d
Falmouth, Eng., U.K. K7 12
Falmouth, Me., U.S. G6 110
Falmouth, Ma., U.S. C15 114
False Bay, b., S. Afr. I4 70
False Divi Point, c., India D5 53
False Pass, Ak., U.S. F7 140
Falset, Spain C11 20
Falso, Cabo, c., Dom. Rep. D12 102
Falster, i., Den. I4 8
Fălticeni, Rom. B13 26
Falun, Swe. F6 8
Famagusta see Gazimağusa, N. Cyp. C4 58
Famaillá, Arg. C5 92
Famatina, Sierra de, mts., Arg. D4 92
Famenne, reg., Bel. D14 14
Family Lake, l., Mb., Can. B18 124
Fanchang, China F8 42
Fanch'eng see Xiangfan, China F4 42
Fanchon, Pointe, c., Haiti C10 102
Fancy, St. Vin. o11 105e
Fang, Thai. C4 48
Fangak, Sudan F6 62
Fangcheng, China E5 42
Fangxian, China E4 42
Fangzheng, China B10 36
Fanipal', Bela. G10 10
Fanjiatun, China C6 38
Fanny Bay, B.C., Can. G6 138
Fano, Italy G10 22
Fan Si Pan, mtn., Viet. A6 48
Faraday, sci., Ant. B34 81
Faradje, D.R.C. D5 66
Farafangana, Madag. E8 68
Farāh, Afg. C9 56
Farāh, stm., Afg. C9 56
Farallon de Pajaros, i., N. Mar. Is. A5 72
Farallon Islands, is., Ca., U.S. F2 134
Faranah, Gui. G2 64
Farasān, Jazā'ir, is., Sau. Ar. F5 56
Fareham, Eng., U.K. K11 12
Farewell, Ak., U.S. D9 140
Farewell, Cape, c., N.Z. E5 80
Fargo, N.D., U.S. E2 118
Faribault, Mn., U.S. G5 118
Faribault, Lac, l., Qc., Can. D16 106
Farīdābad, India D6 54
Farīdkot, India C5 54
Farīdpur, Bngl. G12 54
Farīdpur, India D7 54
Farilhões, is., Port. E1 20
Farim, Gui.-B. G2 64
Farina, Il., U.S. F9 120
Farinha, stm., Braz. D2 88
Fâriskur, Egypt G2 58
Farit, Amba, mtn., Eth. E7 62
Färjestaden, Swe. H7 8
Farley, Ia., U.S. B7 120
Farmer City, Il., U.S. D9 120
Farmersville, Il., U.S. E8 120
Farmersville, Tx., U.S. D2 122
Farmerville, La., U.S. E6 122
Farmington, Il., U.S. D7 120
Farmington, Me., U.S. F6 110
Farmington, Mn., U.S. G5 118
Farmington, Mo., U.S. G7 120
Farmington, Mt., U.S. C14 136
Farmington, N.H., U.S. G5 110
Farmington, N.M., U.S. G8 132
Farmington, Ut., U.S. C5 132
Far Mountain, mtn., B.C., Can. D5 138
Farmville, N.C., U.S. A8 116
Farmville, Va., U.S. G7 114
Farnborough, Eng., U.K. J12 12
Farne Islands, is., Eng., U.K. F11 12
Farnham, Qc., Can. E3 110
Faro, Braz. D6 84
Faro, Yk., Can. C4 106
Faro, Port. H3 20
Faro, state, Port. G3 20
Faroe Islands, dep., Eur. n34 8b
Fårön, i., Swe. H8 8
Farquhar, Atoll de, i., Sey. I12 69b
Farquhar, Cape, c., Austl. D2 74
Farragut, Ia., U.S. D2 120
Farrars Creek, stm., Austl. E3 76
Farrell, Pa., U.S. C5 114
Farrukhābād, India E7 54
Fársala, Grc. D5 28
Fartak, Ra's, c., Yemen F7 56
Farvel, Kap, c., Grnld. F17 141
Farwell, Mi., U.S. E5 112
Fasā, Iran D7 56
Fasano, Italy D11 24
Fastnet Rock, r., Ire. J3 12
Fatehābād, India D5 54
Fatehjang, Pak. B4 54
Fatehpur, India F8 54
Fatehpur, India E5 54
Fatehpur Sīkri, India E6 54
Fathom Five National Marine Park, p.o.i., On., Can. C8 112
Fatick, Sen. G1 64
Fátima, Port. E2 20
Fatshan see Foshan, China J5 42
Fatu Hiva, i., Fr. Poly. E13 72
Fatumu, Tonga n14 78e
Fatwā, India F10 54
Fauabu, Sol. Is. e9 79b
Faucilles, Monts, mts., Fr. F15 14
Faulkton, S.D., U.S. B13 126
Fauquier, B.C., Can. G12 138
Făurei, Rom. D14 26
Fauresmith, S. Afr. F7 70
Fauro Island, i., Sol. Is. d6 79b
Fauske, Nor. C6 8
Faust, Ab., Can. A15 138
Favara, Italy G7 24
Fawcett Lake, l., Ab., Can. A17 138
Fawn, stm., On., Can. E13 106
Fawnie Nose, mtn., B.C., Can. C5 138
Faxaflói, b., Ice. k28 8a
Faxinal do Soturno, Braz. D11 92
Faya-Largeau, Chad D3 62
Fayette, Al., U.S. D11 122
Fayette, Ia., U.S. B6 120
Fayette, Ms., U.S. F7 122
Fayette, Mo., U.S. E5 120
Fayette, Lake, res., Tx., U.S. E2 122
Fayetteville, Ar., U.S. H3 120
Fayetteville, Ga., U.S. D14 122
Fayetteville, N.C., U.S. A7 116
Fayetteville, W.V., U.S. F4 114
Fâyid, Egypt H3 58
Fāzilka, India C5 54
Fāzilpur, Pak. D3 54
Fazzān, hist. reg., Libya B2 62
Fdérik, Maur. E2 64
Fear, Cape, c., N.C., U.S. C8 116
Feather, stm., Ca., U.S. D4 134
Feather, Middle Fork, stm., Ca., U.S. D5 134
Feather, North Fork, East Branch, stm., Ca., U.S. C5 134
Fécamp, Fr. E9 14
Federación, Arg. E8 92
Federal, Arg. E8 92
Federally Administered Tribal Areas, state, Pak. B2 54
Federal Republic of Germany see Germany, ctry., Eur. E6 16
Federalsburg, Md., U.S. F10 114
Federated States of Micronesia see Micronesia, Federated States of, ctry., Oc. C6 72
Fehérgyarmat, Hung. A9 26
Fehmarn, i., Ger. B7 16
Feia, Lagoa, b., Braz. L5 88
Fei Huang, stm., China D8 42
Feijó, Braz. E3 84
Feiketu, China B7 38
Feira de Santana, Braz. G6 88
Feixi, China F7 42
Feixian, China D7 42
Fejér, state, Hung. B5 26
Felanitx, Spain E14 20
Felda, Fl., U.S. J4 116
Feldbach, Aus. D12 22
Feldberg, mtn., Ger. I4 16
Feldkirch, Aus. C6 22
Feliciano, P.R. B1 104a
Feliciano, Arroyo, stm., Arg. E8 92
Felipe Carrillo Puerto, Mex. C4 102
Felix, Cape, c., Nu., Can. B11 106
Felixlândia, Braz. J3 88
Felixstowe, Eng., U.K. I14 12
Felletin, Fr. D8 18
Fellsmere, Fl., U.S. I5 116
Feltre, Italy E8 22
Femunden, l., Nor. E4 8
Femundsmarka Nasjonalpark, p.o.i., Nor. E4 8
Fen, stm., China D4 42
Fenelon Falls, On., Can. D11 112
Fengcheng, China D6 38
Fengcheng, China G6 42
Fengdu, China G2 42
Fengfeng, China C6 42
Fenggang, China G2 42
Fenghuang, China H3 42
Fengjiabao, China C1 42
Fengjie, China F3 42
Fengning, China A7 42
Fengqing, China G4 36
Fengqiu, China D6 42
Fengtai, China B7 42
Fengtai, China E7 42
Fengtien see Shenyang, China D5 38
Fengxi, China F3 42
Fengxian, China D7 42
Fengxiang, China D2 42
Fengyang, China E7 42
Fengyüan, Tai. I9 42
Fengzhen, China A5 42
Feni, Bngl. G13 54
Fennimore, Wi., U.S. B7 120
Fenoarivo Atsinanana, Madag. D8 68
Fenton, Mi., U.S. B2 114
Fentress, Tx., U.S. E10 130
Fenwick, W.V., U.S. F5 114
Fenyang, China C4 42
Fenyi, China H6 42
Feodosiia, Ukr. F5 32
Fer, Cap de, c., Alg. B6 64
Ferdinand, In., U.S. F10 120
Ferdows, Iran C8 56
Ferentino, Italy I10 22
Fergana, Uzb. F12 32
Fergana Mountains see Ferganskij hrebet, mts., Kyrg. F12 32
Ferganskij hrebet, mts., Kyrg. F12 32
Fergus, On., Can. E9 112
Fergus Falls, Mn., U.S. E2 118
Ferguson, B.C., Can. F13 138
Ferguson, Ky., U.S. G13 120
Ferguson, Mo., U.S. F7 120
Fergusson Island, i., Pap. N. Gui. b5 79a
Ferkéssédougou, C. Iv. H4 64
Ferlo, reg., Sen. F2 64
Ferme-Neuve, Qc., Can. B14 112
Fermo, Italy G10 22
Fermont, Qc., Can. E17 106
Fermoselle, Spain C4 20
Fernández, Arg. C6 92
Fernandina, Isla, i., Ec. i11 84a
Fernandina Beach, Fl., U.S. F4 116
Fernando de la Mora, Para. B9 92
Fernando de Noronha, Ilha, i., Braz. F11 82
Fernandópolis, Braz. D6 90
Fernando Póo see Bioko, i., Eq. Gui. I6 64
Fernán-Núñez, Spain G6 20
Ferndale, Ca., U.S. C1 134
Fernie, B.C., Can. G15 138
Fernley, Nv., U.S. D6 134
Fern Park, Fl., U.S. H4 116
Fern Ridge Lake, res., Or., U.S. F3 136
Fernwood, Id., U.S. C10 136
Ferokh, India F2 53
Ferrandina, Italy D10 24
Ferrara, Italy F8 22
Ferrato, Capo, c., Italy E3 24
Ferreira Gomes, Braz. C7 84
Ferreñafe, Peru E2 84
Ferret, Cap, c., Fr. E4 18
Ferrières, Fr. F11 14
Ferris, Tx., U.S. E2 122
Ferrol, Spain A2 20
Ferron, Ut., U.S. D5 132
Ferrysburg, Mi., U.S. E3 112
Ferto-tavi Nemzeti Park, p.o.i., Hung. B3 26
Fès, Mor. C3 64
Feshi, D.R.C. F3 66
Fessenden, N.D., U.S. G14 124
Festus, Mo., U.S. F7 120
Fetești, Rom. E14 26
Fethiye, Tur. G12 28
Fetisovo, Kaz. F8 32
Fetlar, i., Scot., U.K. n19 12a
Feucht, Ger. G7 16
Feuchtwangen, Ger. G6 16
Feuilles, stm., Qc., Can. D16 106
Feuilles, Baie aux, b., Qc., Can. D16 106
Feurs, Fr. D10 18
Feyzābād, Afg. B11 56
Fez see Fès, Mor. C3 64
Fezzan see Fazzān, hist. reg., Libya B2 62
Ffestiniog, Wales, U.K. I9 12
Fianarantsoa, Madag. E8 68
Fianga, Chad F3 62
Fichē, Eth. F7 62
Fichtelgebirge, mts., Eur. F7 16
Ficksburg, S. Afr. F8 70
Fidalgo, stm., Braz. E5 88
Fidenza, Italy F7 22
Field, B.C., Can. E14 138
Fier, Alb. D13 24
Fieri see Fier, Alb. D13 24
Fiery Creek, stm., Austl. B2 76
Fierzës, Liqeni i, res., Alb. B14 24
Fife Lake, Sk., Can. E8 124
Fife Lake, Mi., U.S. D4 112
Fife Lake, l., Sk., Can. E8 124
Fife Ness, c., Scot., U.K. E10 12
Fifield, Wi., U.S. F8 118
Fifth Cataract see Khāmis, Ash-Shallāl al-, wtfl, Sudan D6 62
Figeac, Fr. E7 18
Figtree, Zimb. B9 70
Figueira da Foz, Port. D1 20
Figueras see Figueres, Spain B13 20
Figueres, Spain B13 20
Figuig, Mor. C4 64
Fiji, ctry., Oc. E8 72
Filabusi, Zimb. B9 70
Filadelfia, Italy F10 24
Filchner Ice Shelf, ice, Ant. C1 81
Filey, Eng., U.K. G12 12
Filí, hist., Grc. E6 28
Filiatrá, Grc. F4 28
Filingué, Niger G5 64
Fílippoi, hist., Grc. B7 28
Fillmore, Sk., Can. E10 124
Fillmore, Ca., U.S. I7 134
Fīltu, Eth. F8 62
Fimi, stm., D.R.C. E3 66
Finale Emilia, Italy F8 22
Finale Ligure, Italy F5 22
Finca El Rey, Parque Nacional, p.o.i., Arg. B5 92
Findlay, Il., U.S. E9 120
Findlay, Oh., U.S. C2 114
Findlay, Mount, mtn., B.C., Can. F14 138
Fingal, N.D., U.S. H16 124
Fíngoè, Moz. D5 68
Finistère, state, Fr. F5 14
Finisterre, Cabo de see Fisterra, Cabo de, c., Spain B1 20
Finke, Austl. E6 74
Finland, ctry., Eur. C12 8
Finland, Gulf of, b., Eur. G11 8
Finlay, stm., B.C., Can. D5 106
Finley, Austl. J5 76
Finley, N.D., U.S. G16 124
Finmoore, B.C., Can. C7 138
Finnegan, Ab., Can. E18 138
Finnis, Cape, c., Austl. F6 74
Finnmark, state, Nor. B11 8
Finnsnes, Nor. B8 8
Finschhafen, Pap. N. Gui. b4 79a
Finse, Nor. F2 8
Finspång, Swe. G6 8
Finsterwalde, Ger. E9 16
Fiordland National Park, p.o.i., N.Z. G2 80
Fiorenzuola d'Arda, Italy F6 22
Fire Island National Seashore, p.o.i., N.Y., U.S. D12 114
Firenze (Florence), Italy G8 22
Firmat, Arg. F7 92
Firminy, Fr. D10 18
Firovo, Russia C16 10
Fīrozābād, India E7 54
Fīrozpur, India C5 54
Firozpur Jhirka, India E6 54
First Cataract, wtfl, Egypt C6 62
Firth, Ne., U.S. K2 118
Firth, stm., N.A. C11 140
Fīrūzābād, Iran D7 56
Fisher, Ar., U.S. B7 122
Fisher, Il., U.S. D9 120
Fisher Bay, b., Mb., Can. C17 124
Fisher Branch, Mb., Can. C16 124
Fisher Peak, mtn., Va., U.S. H5 114
Fishers Island, i., N.Y., U.S. C14 114
Fisher Strait, strt., Nu., Can. C14 106
Fishing Creek, Md., U.S. F9 114
Fishing Creek, stm., N.C., U.S. H8 114
Fishing Lake, l., Mb., Can. B18 124
Fisk, Mo., U.S. H7 120
Fiskárdo, Grc. E3 28
Fisterra, Cabo de, c., Spain B1 20
Fitchburg, Ma., U.S. B14 114
Fito, Mount, vol., Samoa g12 79c
Fitri, Lac, l., Chad E3 62
Fitz Roy, Arg. I3 90
Fitzroy, stm., Austl. C4 74
Fitzroy, stm., Austl. D8 76
Fitz Roy, Monte (Chaltel, Cerro), mtn., S.A. I2 90
Fitzroy Crossing, Austl. C5 74
Fitzwilliam Island, i., On., Can. C8 112
Fiuggi, Italy I10 22
Fiume see Rijeka, Cro. E11 22
Fiumicino, Italy I9 22
Five Islands, N.S., Can. E12 110
Five Islands Harbour, b., Antig. f4 105b
Fivemile Creek, stm., Wy., U.S. D4 126
Five Points, N.M., U.S. H10 132
Fivizzano, Italy F7 22
Fizi, D.R.C. E5 66
Fjällåsen, Swe. C8 8
Flagler, Co., U.S. B5 128
Flagstaff, Az., U.S. H5 132
Flagstaff Lake, res., Me., U.S. E6 110
Flamands, Anse des, Guad. B2 105a
Flambeau, stm., Wi., U.S. F8 118
Flamborough, On., Can. E9 112
Flamborough Head, c., Eng., U.K. G12 12
Fläming, reg., Ger. E8 16
Flaming Gorge National Recreation Area, p.o.i., U.S. B7 132
Flaming Gorge Reservoir, res., U.S. B7 132
Flanagan, Il., U.S. D9 120
Flanders, On., Can. C6 118
Flasher, N.D., U.S. A11 126
Flåsjön, l., Swe. D6 8
Flat, Ak., U.S. D8 140
Flat, Tx., U.S. C10 130
Flat, stm., N.T., Can. C5 106
Flat, stm., Mi., U.S. E4 112
Flatey, Ice. k28 8a
Flathead (Flathead, North Fork), stm., N.A. H16 138
Flathead, stm., Mt., U.S. C12 136
Flathead, Middle Fork, stm., Mt., U.S. B13 136
Flathead, North Fork (Flathead), stm., N.A. H16 138
Flathead, South Fork, stm., Mt., U.S. B13 136
Flathead Lake, l., Mt., U.S. C12 136
Flat Lake, l., Ab., Can. B17 138
Flatonia, Tx., U.S. E10 130
Flat River, P.E., Can. D13 110
Flat River, Mo., U.S. G7 120
Flat Rock, Al., U.S. C13 122
Flattery, Cape, c., Wa., U.S. B2 136
Flatts, Ber. k15 104e
Flatwillow Creek, stm., Mt., U.S. H5 124
Flatwood, U.S. E11 122
Flaxton, N.D., U.S. F11 124
Flaxville, Mt., U.S. F8 124
Fleetwood, Eng., U.K. H10 12
Fleetwood, Pa., U.S. D10 114
Flekkefjord, Nor. G2 8
Fleming-Neon, Ky., U.S. G3 114
Flemingsburg, Ky., U.S. F2 114
Flen, Swe. G7 8
Flensburg, Ger. B5 16
Fletcher, N.C., U.S. A3 116
Fletcher Pond, l., Mi., U.S. D5 112
Fleurance, Fr. F6 18
Flinders, stm., Austl. A3 76
Flinders Bay, b., Austl. F3 74
Flinders Island, i., Austl. m14 77a
Flinders Ranges National Park, p.o.i., Austl. H2 76
Flinders Reefs, rf., Austl. A7 76
Flin Flon, Mb., Can. E10 106
Flint, Wales, U.K. H9 12
Flint, Mi., U.S. E6 112
Flint, i., Kir. E11 72
Flint, stm., U.S. C12 122
Flint, stm., Ga., U.S. G14 122
Flint Lake, l., Nu., Can. B16 106
Flinton, Austl. F7 76
Flintville, Tn., U.S. B12 122
Flippin, Ar., U.S. H5 120
Flix, Pantà de, res., Spain C11 20
Flomaton, Al., U.S. F11 122
Floodwood, Mn., U.S. E6 118
Flora, Il., U.S. F9 120
Flora, In., U.S. H3 112
Florac, Fr. E9 18
Floral City, Fl., U.S. H3 116
Floral Park, Mt., U.S. E14 136
Flora Vista, N.M., U.S. G8 132
Flore, Piton, mtn., St. Luc. m7 105c
Florence see Firenze, Italy G8 22
Florence, Al., U.S. C11 122
Florence, Az., U.S. J5 132
Florence, Co., U.S. C3 128
Florence, Ks., U.S. C12 128
Florence, S.C., U.S. B6 116
Florence, Tx., U.S. D10 130
Florence, Wi., U.S. C1 112
Florencia, Col. G4 86
Florentino Ameghino, Embalse, res., Arg. H3 90
Flores, Braz. D7 88
Flores, i., Indon. G7 44
Flores, Laut (Flores Sea), Indon. G11 50
Flores, Selat, strt., Indon. G7 44
Flores de Goiás, Braz. H2 88
Flores Island, i., B.C., Can. G4 138
Flores Sea see Flores, Laut, Indon. G11 50
Floresta, Braz. E6 88
Florești, Mol. B15 26
Floresville, Tx., U.S. E9 130
Floriano, Braz. D4 88
Floriano Peixoto, Braz. E4 84
Florianópolis, Braz. C13 92
Florida, Col. F3 86
Florida, Cuba B8 102
Florida, P.R. B4 104a
Florida, Ur. G9 92
Florida, state, U.S. F11 108
Florida, Straits of, strt., N.A. G11 108
Florida Bay, b., Fl., U.S. K5 116
Floridablanca, Col. D5 86
Florida City, Fl., U.S. K5 116
Florida Islands, is., Sol. Is. e9 79b
Florida Keys, is., Fl., U.S. L4 116
Floridia, Italy G9 24
Florido, stm., Mex. B6 100
Florien, La., U.S. F5 122
Flórina, Grc. C4 28
Florissant, Mo., U.S. F7 120
Florissant Fossil Beds National Monument, p.o.i., Co., U.S. B3 128
Florø, Nor. F1 8
Flotte, Cap de, c., N. Cal. m16 79d
Floyd, N.M., U.S. G5 128
Floyd, Va., U.S. H5 114
Floyd, stm., Ia., U.S. I2 118
Floydada, Tx., U.S. G7 128
Flumendosa, stm., Italy E3 24
Fluminimaggiore, Italy E2 24
Flushing see Vlissingen, Neth. C12 14
Fluvanna, Tx., U.S. B6 130
Fly, stm. b3 79a
Foam Lake, Sk., Can. C10 124
Foča, Bos. F5 26
Foça, Tur. E9 28
Focșani, Rom. D14 26
Fogang, China J5 42
Foggaret ez Zoua, Alg. D5 64
Foggia, Italy C9 24
Fogo, i., C.V. k10 65a
Fogo Island, i., Nf., Can. j23 107a
Foguista J. F. Juárez see El Galpón, Arg. B5 92
Föhr, i., Ger. B4 16
Fóia, mtn., Port. G2 20
Foix, Fr. G7 18
Foix, hist. reg., Fr. F7 18
Fojnica, Bos. F4 26
Fokino, Russia G17 10
Folda, b., Nor. C6 8
Foley, Al., U.S. G11 122
Foleyet, On., Can. F14 106
Foley Island, i., Nu., Can. B15 106
Folgefonni, ice, Nor. G2 8
Foligno, Italy H9 22
Folkestone, Eng., U.K. J14 12
Folkston, Ga., U.S. F3 116
Follett, Tx., U.S. E8 128
Föllinge, Swe. E6 8
Follonica, Italy H7 22
Follonica, Golfo di, b., Italy H7 22
Folsom, Ca., U.S. E4 134
Folsom Lake, res., Ca., U.S. E4 134
Fomboni, Com. C7 68
Fominiči, Russia F17 10
Fominskoe, Russia A22 10
Fonda, N.Y., U.S. B11 114
Fond-du-Lac, Sk., Can. D9 106
Fond du Lac, Wi., U.S. H10 118
Fond du Lac, stm., Sk., Can. D9 106
Fondi, Italy C7 24
Fonni, Italy D3 24
Fonseca, Col. B5 86
Fonseca, Golfo de, b., N.A. F4 102
Fontainebleau, Fr. F11 14
Fontana, Arg. C8 92
Fontana, Ca., U.S. I8 134
Fontana Lake, res., N.C., U.S. A2 116
Fontanelle, Ia., U.S. J4 118
Fontas, stm., Can. D6 106
Fonte Boa, Braz. I8 86
Fontenay-le-Comte, Fr. C5 18
Fontenelle, Qc., Can. B12 110
Fontenelle Reservoir, res., Wy., U.S. A6 132
Fontur, c., Ice. j32 8a
Fonyód, Hung. C4 26
Foochow see Fuzhou, China H8 42
Foothills, Ab., Can. C14 138
Forari, Vanuatu k17 79d
Forbach, Fr. E15 14
Forbach, Ger. H4 16
Forbes, Austl. I7 76
Forbes, Mount, mtn., Ab., Can. E14 138
Forbesganj, India E11 54
Forchheim, Ger. G7 16
Ford, Ks., U.S. D9 128
Ford, stm., Mi., U.S. B2 112
Ford City, Ca., U.S. H6 134
Ford City, Pa., U.S. D6 114
Førde, Nor. F1 8
Ford Ranges, mts., Ant. C26 81
Fords Bridge, Austl. G5 76
Fordville, N.D., U.S. F16 124
Fordyce, Ar., U.S. D6 122
Forécariah, Gui. H2 64
Forel, Mont, mtn., Grnld. D18 141
Foreman, Ar., U.S. D4 122
Forest, On., Can. E8 112
Forest, Ms., U.S. E9 122
Forest Acres, S.C., U.S. B4 116
Forestburg, Ab., Can. D18 138
Forest City, N.C., U.S. A4 116
Forest City, Pa., U.S. C10 114
Forest Grove, B.C., Can. E9 138
Foresthill, Ca., U.S. D5 134
Forestier Peninsula, pen., Austl. o14 77a
Forest Lake, Mn., U.S. F5 118
Forest Park, Ga., U.S. C1 116
Forestville, Qc., Can. B7 110
Forgan, Ok., U.S. E8 128
Forges-les-Eaux, Fr. E10 14
Forillon, Parc national de, p.o.i., Qc., Can. B12 110
Forked Deer, stm., Tn., U.S. I8 120
Forks, Wa., U.S. C2 136
Forlì, Italy F9 22
Formby Point, c., Eng., U.K. H9 12
Formentera, i., Spain F12 20
Formentor, Cap de, c., Spain E14 20
Formia, Italy C7 24
Formiga, Braz. K3 88
Formosa, Arg. C8 92
Formosa, Braz. H2 88
Formosa, state, Arg. D4 90
Formosa see Taiwan, ctry., Asia J9 42
Formosa, Serra, plat., Braz. F6 84
Formosa Strait see Taiwan Strait, strt., Asia I8 42
Formoso, stm., Braz. G3 88
Forncelle, Italy G8 22
Forney, Tx., U.S. E2 122
Fornosovo, Russia A13 10
Forres, Scot., U.K. D9 12
Forrest, Austl. F5 74
Forrest, Il., U.S. D9 120
Forrest City, Ar., U.S. B8 122
Forreston, Il., U.S. I9 118
Forsayth, Austl. B4 76
Forst, Ger. E10 16
Forster, Austl. I9 76
Forsyth, Ga., U.S. C2 116
Forsyth, Mo., U.S. H4 120
Forsyth, Mt., U.S. A6 126
Fort Abbās, Pak. D4 54
Fort Albany, On., Can. E14 106
Fortaleza, Braz. B6 88
Fortaleza do Ituxi, Braz. E4 84
Fort Assiniboine, Ab., Can. B15 138
Fort Atkinson, Wi., U.S. B9 120
Fort Bayard see Zhanjiang, China K4 42
Fort Beaufort, S. Afr. H8 70
Fort Belknap Agency, Mt., U.S. F5 124
Fort Benton, Mt., U.S. C16 136
Fort Bragg, Ca., U.S. D2 134
Fort Branch, In., U.S. F10 120
Fort Bridger, Wy., U.S. B6 132
Fort Calhoun, Ne., U.S. C1 120
Fort Chipewyan, Ab., Can. D8 106
Fort Collins, Co., U.S. G7 126
Fort-Coulonge, Qc., Can. C13 112
Fort Covington, N.Y., U.S. E2 110
Fort Davis, Al., U.S. E13 122
Fort Davis, Tx., U.S. D4 130
Fort-de-France, Mart. k6 105c
Fort-de-France-Lamentin, Aérodrome de, Mart. k7 105c
Fort Deposit, Al., U.S. F12 122
Fort Dodge, Ia., U.S. B3 120
Fort Duchesne, Ut., U.S. C7 132
Forte dei Marmi, Italy G7 22
Fort Edward, N.Y., U.S. G3 110
Fort Erie, On., Can. F10 112
Fortescue, stm., Austl. D3 74
Fortezza, Italy D8 22
Fort Frances, On., Can. C5 118
Fort Fraser, B.C., Can. B6 138
Fort Frederica National Monument, p.o.i., Ga., U.S. E4 116
Fort Gaines, Ga., U.S. F13 122
Fort Garland, Co., U.S. D3 128
Fort Gibson, Ok., U.S. I2 120
Fort Good Hope, N.T., Can. B5 106
Forth, Firth of, b., Scot., U.K. E10 12

Name	Map Ref.	Page
Fort Hall, Id., U.S.	G14	136
Fortine, Mt., U.S.	B12	136
Fortín Uno, Arg.	I5	92
Fort Jones, Ca., U.S.	B3	134
Fort Klamath, Or., U.S.	H4	136
Fort Knox, Ky., U.S.	G12	120
Fort-Lamy see N'Djamena, Chad	E3	62
Fort Laramie, Wy., U.S.	E8	126
Fort Lauderdale, Fl., U.S.	J5	116
Fort Liard, N.T., Can.	C6	106
Fort Loramie, Oh., U.S.	D1	114
Fort Loudoun Lake, res., Tn., U.S.	B15	122
Fort Lyon Canal, can., Co., U.S.	C5	128
Fort MacKay, Ab., Can.	D8	106
Fort Macleod, Ab., Can.	G17	138
Fort Madison, Ia., U.S.	D6	120
Fort Matanzas National Monument, p.o.i., Fl., U.S.	G4	116
Fort McMurray, Ab., Can.	D8	106
Fort McPherson, N.T., Can.	B4	106
Fort Meade, Fl., U.S.	I4	116
Fort Mill, S.C., U.S.	A5	116
Fort Morgan, Co., U.S.	A5	128
Fort Myers, Fl., U.S.	J3	116
Fort Myers Beach, Fl., U.S.	J3	116
Fort Nelson, B.C., Can.	D6	106
Fort Nelson, stm., B.C., Can.	D6	106
Fort Ogden, Fl., U.S.	I4	116
Fort Payne, Al., U.S.	C13	122
Fort Peck, Mt., U.S.	F7	124
Fort Peck Dam, dam, Mt., U.S.	G7	124
Fort Peck Lake, res., Mt., U.S.	G7	124
Fort Pierce, Fl., U.S.	I5	116
Fort Plain, N.Y., U.S.	B11	114
Fort Portal, Ug.	D6	66
Fort Providence, N.T., Can.	C7	106
Fort Pulaski National Monument, p.o.i., Ga., U.S.	E5	116
Fort Qu'Appelle, Sk., Can.	D10	124
Fort Randall Dam, dam, S.D., U.S.	D14	126
Fort Recovery, Oh., U.S.	D1	114
Fort Resolution, N.T., Can.	C8	106
Fort Rixon, Zimb.	B9	70
Fort Saint James, B.C., Can.	B6	138
Fort Saint John, B.C., Can.	D6	106
Fort Saskatchewan, Ab., Can.	C17	138
Fort Scott, Ks., U.S.	G3	120
Fort-Ševčenko, Kaz.	F7	32
Fort Severn, On., Can.	D13	106
Fort Simpson, N.T., Can.	C6	106
Fort Smith, N.T., Can.	C8	106
Fort Smith, Ar., U.S.	B4	122
Fort Stockton, Tx., U.S.	D4	130
Fort Sumner, N.M., U.S.	G4	128
Fort Sumter National Monument, p.o.i., S.C., U.S.	D6	116
Fort Supply, Ok., U.S.	E9	128
Fort Thomas, Az., U.S.	J7	132
Fort Totten, N.D., U.S.	G14	124
Fort Towson, Ok., U.S.	D3	122
Fortuna, Arg.	G5	92
Fortuna, C.R.	G5	102
Fortuna, Ca., U.S.	C1	134
Fortuna, V.I.U.S.	e6	104b
Fortune Bay, b., Nf., Can.	j22	107a
Fortuneswell, Eng., U.K.	K10	12
Fort Union National Monument, p.o.i., N.M., U.S.	F3	128
Fort Valley, Ga., U.S.	D2	116
Fort Vermilion, Ab., Can.	D7	106
Fort Victoria, hist., Ber.	k16	104e
Fort Walton Beach, Fl., U.S.	G12	122
Fort Wayne, In., U.S.	G4	112
Fort White, Fl., U.S.	G3	116
Fort William, Scot., U.K.	E7	12
Fort Worth, Tx., U.S.	B10	130
Fort Yates, N.D., U.S.	A12	126
Fort Yukon, Ak., U.S.	C10	140
Foshan, China	J5	42
Fosheim Peninsula, pen., Nu., Can.	B9	141
Foso, Ghana	H4	64
Fossano, Italy	F4	22
Fossil, Or., U.S.	F6	136
Fossil Butte National Monument, p.o.i., Wy., U.S.	B6	132
Fossil Lake, l., Or., U.S.	G6	136
Fossombrone, Italy	G9	22
Fosston, Mn., U.S.	D3	118
Foster, Austl.	L6	76
Foster Bugt, strt., Grnld.	C21	141
Fosters, Al., U.S.	D11	122
Fostoria, Oh., U.S.	C2	114
Fougamou, Gabon	E2	66
Fougères, Fr.	F7	14
Fouhsin see Fuxin, China	C4	38
Fou-kien see Fujian, state, China	I7	42
Foula, i., Scot., U.K.	n17	12a
Fouling see Fuling, China	G2	42
Foulwind, Cape, c., N.Z.	E4	80
Foumban, Cam.	C2	66
Foum-el-Hassan, Mor.	D3	64
Foum-Zguid, Mor.	C3	64
Foundiougne, Sen.	G1	64
Fountain, Co., U.S.	C4	128
Fountain, Fl., U.S.	G13	122
Fountain City, Wi., U.S.	G7	118
Fountain Green, Ut., U.S.	D5	132
Fountain Peak, mtn., Ca., U.S.	I1	132
Fountain Place, La., U.S.	G7	122
Fourche LaFave, stm., Ar., U.S.	C6	122
Fourchu, N.S., Can.	E16	110
Four Corners, Or., U.S.	F4	136
Fourmies, Fr.	D13	14
Four Mountains, Islands of, is., Ak., U.S.	g24	140a
Four Oaks, N.C., U.S.	A7	116
Fourth Cataract see Rābiʿ, Ash-Shallāl ar-, wtfl, Sudan	D6	62
Fous, Pointe des, c., Dom.	j6	105c
Fouta Djalon, reg., Gui.	G2	64
Foux, Cap à, c., Haiti	C11	102
Fouyang see Fuyang, China	E6	42
Foveaux Strait, strt., N.Z.	H3	80
Fowler, Co., U.S.	C4	128
Fowler, In., U.S.	H2	112
Fowler, Mi., U.S.	E5	112
Fowlers Bay, Austl.	F6	74
Fowlerville, Mi., U.S.	B1	114
Fox, stm., U.S.	C9	120
Fox, stm., U.S.	D5	120
Fox, stm., Wi., U.S.	H10	118
Fox Creek, Ab., Can.	B14	138
Foxe Basin, b., Nu., Can.	B15	106
Foxe Channel, strt., Nu., Can.	C15	106
Foxe Peninsula, pen., Nu., Can.	C15	106
Foxford, Ire.	H3	12
Fox Islands, is., Ak., U.S.	g25	140a
Fox Lake, Il., U.S.	B9	120
Foxpark, Wy., U.S.	B10	132
Fox Valley, Sk., Can.	D4	124
Foxworth, Ms., U.S.	F9	122
Foyle, Lough, b., Eur.	F5	12
Foz do Areia, Represa de, res., Braz.	B12	92
Foz do Cunene, Ang.	D1	68
Foz do Iguaçu, Braz.	B10	92
Foz do Jordão, Braz.	E3	84
Foz Giraldo, Port.	E3	20
Fraga, Spain	C11	20
Fraile Muerto, Ur.	F10	92
Framingham, Ma., U.S.	B14	114
França, Braz.	F5	88
Franca, Braz.	K2	88
Franca-Iosifa, Zemlja, is., Russia	B9	30
Francavilla al Mare, Italy	H11	22
Francavilla Fontana, Italy	D11	24
France, ctry., Eur.	C8	18
Frances, stm., Yk., Can.	C5	106
Frances Lake, l., Yk., Can.	C4	106
Francés Viejo, Cabo, c., Dom. Rep.	C13	102
Franceville, Gabon	E2	66
Franche-Comté, hist. reg., Fr.	B12	18
Francis, Sk., Can.	D10	124
Francis Case, Lake, res., S.D., U.S.	D13	126
Francisco Beltrão, Braz.	B11	92
Francisco I. Madero, Mex.	C6	100
Francisco I. Madero, Mex.	I4	130
Francisco Murguía, Mex.	C7	100
Francisco Sá, Braz.	I4	88
Francistown, Bots.	B8	70
Francofonte, Italy	G8	24
François Lake, B.C., Can.	B5	138
Francois Lake, l., B.C., Can.	C5	138
Francs Peak, mtn., Wy., U.S.	C3	126
Frankel City, Tx., U.S.	B5	130
Franken, hist. reg., Ger.	G6	16
Frankenberg, Ger.	F9	16
Frankenberg, Ger.	E4	16
Frankenmuth, Mi., U.S.	E6	112
Frankford, On., Can.	D12	112
Frankford, Mo., U.S.	E6	120
Frankfort, S. Afr.	E9	70
Frankfort, In., U.S.	H3	112
Frankfort, Ks., U.S.	B12	128
Frankfort, Ky., U.S.	F13	120
Frankfort, N.Y., U.S.	A10	114
Frankfort, Oh., U.S.	E2	114
Frankfort, S.D., U.S.	C14	126
Frankfurt, Ger.	D10	16
Frankfurt am Main, Ger.	F4	16
Franklin, Az., U.S.	K7	132
Franklin, Ga., U.S.	D13	122
Franklin, Id., U.S.	A5	132
Franklin, Il., U.S.	E7	120
Franklin, In., U.S.	E11	120
Franklin, Ma., U.S.	B14	114
Franklin, Ne., U.S.	A9	128
Franklin, N.H., U.S.	G5	110
Franklin, N.J., U.S.	C11	114
Franklin, N.C., U.S.	A2	116
Franklin, Oh., U.S.	E1	114
Franklin, Pa., U.S.	C6	114
Franklin, Tn., U.S.	I11	120
Franklin, Tx., U.S.	F2	122
Franklin, Va., U.S.	H9	114
Franklin, Wi., U.S.	F2	112
Franklin Bay, b., N.T., Can.	B5	106
Franklin D. Roosevelt Lake, res., Wa., U.S.	B4	108
Franklin Gordon Wild Rivers National Park, p.o.i., Austl.	o12	77a
Franklin Grove, Il., U.S.	C8	120
Franklin Lake, l., Nu., Can.	B12	106
Franklin Mountains, mts., N.T., Can.	B5	106
Franklin Strait, strt., Nu., Can.	A11	106
Franklinton, La., U.S.	G8	122
Franklinville, N.Y., U.S.	B7	114
Frankston, Tx., U.S.	E3	122
Frankton, In., U.S.	H4	112
Fransfontein, Nmb.	B2	70
Franzensfeste see Fortezza, Italy	D8	22
Franz Josef Land see Franca-Iosifa, Zemlja, is., Russia	B9	30
Frascati, Italy	I9	22
Fraser, B.C., Can.	G13	138
Fraser, Co., U.S.	B3	128
Fraser, stm., B.C., Can.	G9	138
Fraser, Mount, mtn., Austl.	E3	74
Fraserburgh, Scot., U.K.	D11	12
Fraser Island, i., Austl.	E9	76
Fraser Lake, B.C., Can.	B6	138
Fraser Lake, l., B.C., Can.	B6	138
Fraser Plateau, plat., B.C., Can.	E8	138
Fraser Range, Austl.	F4	74
Frauenfeld, Switz.	C5	22
Fray Bentos, Ur.	F8	92
Fray Jorge, Parque Nacional, p.o.i., Chile	E2	92
Fray Marcos, Ur.	G10	92
Frazer, Mt., U.S.	F7	124
Frederic, Wi., U.S.	F6	118
Frederica, De., U.S.	E10	114
Fredericia, Den.	I3	8
Frederick, Md., U.S.	E8	114
Frederick, S.D., U.S.	B14	126
Frederick Hills, hills, Austl.	B7	74
Frederick Reef, rf., Austl.	C10	76
Fredericksburg, Ia., U.S.	B5	120
Fredericksburg, Tx., U.S.	D9	130
Fredericksburg, Va., U.S.	F8	114
Fredericktown, Oh., U.S.	D3	114
Frederico Westphalen, Braz.	C11	92
Fredericton, N.B., Can.	E10	110
Fredericton Junction, N.B., Can.	E10	110
Frederiksborg, state, Den.	H5	8
Frederiksdal, Grnld.	E17	141
Frederikshåb (Paamiut), Grnld.	E15	141
Frederikshavn, Den.	H4	8
Frederiksted, V.I.U.S.	h10	104c
Fredonia, Ks., U.S.	G2	120
Fredonia, N.Y., U.S.	B6	114
Fredonia, N.D., U.S.	A13	126
Fredrika, Swe.	D8	8
Fredrikstad, Nor.	G4	8
Freeburg, Il., U.S.	F8	120
Freeland, Mi., U.S.	E5	112
Freeland, Pa., U.S.	C9	114
Freel Peak, mtn., Ca., U.S.	E5	134
Freels, Cape, c., Nf., Can.	j23	107a
Freeman, S.D., U.S.	D15	126
Freeport, Bah.	B9	96
Freeport, N.S., Can.	F10	110
Freeport, Fl., U.S.	G12	122
Freeport, Il., U.S.	B8	120
Freeport, N.Y., U.S.	H16	112
Freeport, Pa., U.S.	D6	114
Freeport, Tx., U.S.	F12	130
Free State, state, S. Afr.	F8	70
Freetown, Antig.	f4	105b
Freetown, S.L.	H2	64
Fregenal de la Sierra, Spain	F4	20
Freiberg, Ger.	F9	16
Freiburg see Fribourg, Switz.	D4	22
Freiburg im Breisgau, Ger.	I3	16
Freirina, Chile	D2	92
Freising, Ger.	H7	16
Freistadt, Aus.	B11	22
Freital, Ger.	F9	16
Fréjus, Fr.	F12	18
Fremantle, Austl.	F3	74
Fremont, Ca., U.S.	F4	134
Fremont, In., U.S.	C1	114
Fremont, Ia., U.S.	C5	120
Fremont, Mi., U.S.	E4	112
Fremont, Ne., U.S.	C1	120
Fremont, Oh., U.S.	C2	114
Fremont, Wi., U.S.	G10	118
Fremont, stm., Ut., U.S.	E6	132
French, stm., On., Can.	B9	112
French Broad, stm., U.S.	I3	114
Frenchcap Cay, i., V.I.U.S.	f7	104b
French Guiana, dep., S.A.	C7	84
French Island, i., Austl.	L5	76
French Lick, In., U.S.	F11	120
Frenchman (Frenchman Creek), stm., N.A.	E5	124
Frenchman Creek (Frenchman), stm., N.A.	E5	124
Frenchman Creek, stm., U.S.	G11	126
Frenchmans Cap, mtn., Austl.	o12	77a
French Polynesia, dep., Oc.	K24	142
French Somaliland see Djibouti, ctry., Afr.	E8	62
Fresco, C. Iv.	H3	64
Fresco, stm., Braz.	E7	84
Fresnillo, Mex.	D7	100
Fresno, Ca., U.S.	G6	134
Fresno, stm., Ca., U.S.	F6	134
Fresno Reservoir, res., Mt., U.S.	B16	136
Freu, Cap des, c., Spain	E14	20
Freudenstadt, Ger.	H4	16
Frewena, Austl.	C7	74
Frewsburg, N.Y., U.S.	B6	114
Freycinet National Park, p.o.i., Austl.	o14	77a
Freycinet Peninsula, pen., Austl.	o14	77a
Freyre, Arg.	E6	92
Fria, Gui.	G2	64
Fria, Cape, c., Nmb.	D1	68
Friant, Ca., U.S.	G6	134
Friars Point, Ms., U.S.	C8	122
Frías, Arg.	D5	92
Fribourg (Freiburg), Switz.	D4	22
Fridley, Mn., U.S.	F5	118
Fridtjof Nansen, Mount, mtn., Ant.	D25	81
Friedberg, Aus.	C12	22
Friedberg, Ger.	F4	16
Friedberg, Ger.	H7	16
Friedland, Ger.	C9	16
Friedrichshafen, Ger.	I5	16
Friend, Ne., U.S.	G15	126
Friendship, N.Y., U.S.	B7	114
Friendship, Tn., U.S.	I8	120
Fries, Va., U.S.	H4	114
Friesach, Aus.	D11	22
Frio, stm., Tx., U.S.	F9	130
Frio, Cabo, c., Braz.	L5	88
Frio Draw, stm., U.S.	G6	128
Friona, Tx., U.S.	G6	128
Frisco, Tx., U.S.	D2	122
Frisian Islands, is., Eur.	A14	14
Fritch, Tx., U.S.	F7	128
Fritzlar, Ger.	E5	16
Friuli, hist. reg., Italy	E9	22
Friuli-Venezia Giulia, state, Italy	D9	22
Frjazino, Russia	E21	10
Frobisher, Sk., Can.	E11	124
Frobisher Bay, b., Nu., Can.	C17	106
Frobisher Lake, l., Sk., Can.	D9	106
Froid, Mt., U.S.	F9	124
Frolovo, Russia	E6	32
Frome, Eng., U.K.	J10	12
Frome, stm., Austl.	G2	76
Frome, Lake, l., Austl.	H2	76
Fronteiras, Braz.	D5	88
Frontenac, Ks., U.S.	G3	120
Frontera, Mex.	F12	100
Frontera, Mex.	B8	100
Frontier, Sk., Can.	E5	124
Frontier, Wy., U.S.	B6	132
Frontino, Col.	B2	84
Frontino, Páramo, mtn., Col.	D3	86
Front Range, mts., Co., U.S.	H7	126
Front Royal, Va., U.S.	F7	114
Frosinone, Italy	C7	24
Frostburg, Md., U.S.	E6	114
Frostproof, Fl., U.S.	I4	116
Frøya, i., Nor.	E3	8
Fruges, Fr.	D11	14
Fruita, Co., U.S.	D8	132
Fruitdale, Or., U.S.	H3	136
Fruithurst, Al., U.S.	D13	122
Fruitland, Id., U.S.	F10	136
Fruitport, Mi., U.S.	E3	112
Fruitvale, B.C., Can.	G13	138
Fruitvale, Wa., U.S.	D6	136
Frunzivka, Ukr.	B16	26
Frutal, Braz.	J1	88
Frutigen, Switz.	D4	22
Frýdek-Místek, Czech Rep.	G14	16
Fryeburg, Me., U.S.	G6	110
Fu, stm., China	G7	42
Fu, stm., China	F2	42
Fu, stm., China	G6	42
Fua'amotu International Airport, Tonga	n14	78e
Fu'an, China	H8	42
Fuchou see Fuzhou, China	H8	42
Fuchow see Fuzhou, China	G7	42
Fuchū, Japan	E6	40
Fuchun, stm., China	G8	42
Fuding, China	H9	42
Fuego, Volcán de, vol., Guat.	E2	102
Fuencaliente, Spain	F6	20
Fuengirola, Spain	H6	20
Fuensalida, Spain	D6	20
Fuente, Mex.	F7	130
Fuente de Cantos, Spain	F4	20
Fuente de Oro, Col.	F5	86
Fuentes de Ebro, Spain	C10	20
Fuerte, stm., Mex.	B4	100
Fuerte Olimpo, Para.	D5	90
Fuga Island, i., Phil.	A3	52
Fugou, China	D6	42
Fuhai, China	B2	36
Fuhsien see Wafangdian, China	B9	42
Fuji, Japan	D11	40
Fuji, Mount see Fuji-san, vol., Japan	D11	40
Fujian, state, China	I7	42
Fujieda, Japan	E11	40
Fujin, China	B11	36
Fujinomiya, Japan	D11	40
Fuji-san (Fuji, Mount), vol., Japan	D11	40
Fujisawa, Japan	D12	40
Fujiyama see Fuji-san, vol., Japan	D11	40
Fuji-yoshida, Japan	D11	40
Fukagawa, Japan	C14	38
Fukang, China	C2	36
Fukave, i., Tonga	n14	78e
Fukaya, Japan	C12	40
Fukien see Fujian, state, China	I7	42
Fukuchiyama, Japan	D8	40
Fukue, Japan	G1	40
Fukue-jima, i., Japan	G1	40
Fukui, Japan	C9	40
Fukui, state, Japan	D9	40
Fukuoka, Japan	F3	40
Fukuoka, state, Japan	F3	40
Fukuroi, Japan	E10	40
Fukushima, Japan	B13	40
Fukushima, state, Japan	B12	40
Fukuyama, Japan	E6	40
Fūlādī, Kūh-e, mtn., Afg.	C10	56
Fulaga Passage, strt., Fiji	q20	79e
Fulda, Ger.	F5	16
Fulda, Mn., U.S.	H3	118
Fulda, stm., Ger.	E5	16
Fuling, China	G2	42
Fullarton, stm., Austl.	C3	76
Fullerton, Ca., U.S.	J8	134
Fullerton Point, c., Antig.	f4	105b
Fulong, China	J2	42
Fulton, Al., U.S.	F11	122
Fulton, Ar., U.S.	D5	122
Fulton, Il., U.S.	C7	120
Fulton, Ks., U.S.	F3	120
Fulton, Ky., U.S.	H9	120
Fulton, Mo., U.S.	F5	120
Fulton, N.Y., U.S.	E13	112
Fulton, Tx., U.S.	F10	130
Fumay, Fr.	D13	14
Funabashi, Japan	D12	40
Funafuti, i., Tuvalu	D8	72
Funan, China	E6	42
Funchal, Port.	C1	64
Fundación, Col.	B4	86
Fundão, Port.	D3	20
Fundy, Bay of, b., Can.	F10	110
Fundy National Park, p.o.i., N.B., Can.	E11	110
Funhalouro, Moz.	C12	70
Funing, China	E8	42
Funiu Shan, mts., China	E5	42
Funsi, Ghana	G4	64
Funtua, Nig.	G6	64
Fuping, China	D3	42
Fuqing, China	I8	42
Fuquay-Varina, N.C., U.S.	A7	116
Furculești, Rom.	F12	26
Furmanov, Russia	H19	8
Furnas, Represa de, res., Braz.	K2	88
Furneaux Group, is., Austl.	m13	77a
Furnes see Veurne, Bel.	C11	14
Fürstenberg / Havel, Ger.	C9	16
Fürstenfeld, Aus.	C12	22
Fürstenfeldbruck, Ger.	H7	16
Fürstenwalde, Ger.	D9	16
Fürth, Ger.	G6	16
Furth im Wald, Ger.	G8	16
Furukawa, Japan	C10	40
Furukawa, Japan	A13	40
Fury and Hecla Strait, strt., Nu., Can.	B14	106
Fusagasugá, Col.	E4	86
Fusan see Pusan, Kor., S.	D2	40
Fushan, China	C9	42
Fushan, China	D4	42
Fushih see Yan'an, China	C3	42
Fushun, China	D5	38
Fushun, China	G1	42
Fusilier, Sk., Can.	C4	124
Fusong, China	C7	38
Füssen, Ger.	I6	16
Fuste, Picacho del, mtn., Mex.	G5	130
Fusui, China	J2	42
Futun, stm., China	H7	42
Futuna, Île, i., Wal./F.	E9	72
Futuyu, China	B6	42
Fuwa, Egypt	G1	58
Fuxian Hu, l., China	G5	36
Fuxin, China	C4	38
Fuyang, China	E6	42
Fuyang, stm., China	C6	42
Fuyu, China	B9	36
Fuyu, China	B6	38
Fuyuan see Tongjiang, China	B11	36
Fuyuan, China	F5	36
Fuyuan, China	B11	36
Fuzhou, China	G7	42
Fuzhou, China	H8	42
Fyn, state, Den.	I4	8
Fyn, i., Den.	I4	8
Fyne, Loch, b., Scot., U.K.	E7	12
Fyresvatnet, l., Nor.	G2	8

G

Name	Map Ref.	Page
Gaalkacyo, Som.	C9	66
Gabare, Blg.	F10	26
Gabarus, N.S., Can.	E16	110
Gabela, Ang.	C1	68
Gaberones see Gaborone, Bots.	D7	70
Gabès, Tun.	C7	64
Gabiarra, Braz.	I6	88
Gabon, ctry., Afr.	E2	66
Gaborone, Bots.	D7	70
Gabras, Sudan	E5	62
Gabriel Strait, strt., Nu., Can.	C17	106
Gabriel y Galán, Embalse de, res., Spain	D4	20
Gabrovo, Blg.	G12	26
Gacé, Fr.	F9	14
Gackle, N.D., U.S.	A13	126
Gadag, India	D2	53
Gādarwāra, India	G7	54
Gäddede, Swe.	D6	8
Gado Bravo, Ilha do, i., Braz.	F4	88
Gádor, Spain	H8	20
Gadsden, Al., U.S.	C12	122
Gadsden, Az., U.S.	K2	132
Gadwāl, India	C3	53
Gael Hamke Bugt, b., Grnld.	C22	141
Găești, Rom.	E12	26
Gaeta, Italy	C7	24
Gaeta, Golfo di, b., Italy	C7	24
Gaferut, i., Micron.	C5	72
Gaffney, S.C., U.S.	A4	116
Gafour, Tun.	H3	24
Gafsa, Tun.	C6	64
Gag, Pulau, i., Indon.	F8	44
Gagarin, Russia	E17	10
Gage, Ok., U.S.	E9	128
Gaggenau, Ger.	H4	16
Gagliano del Capo, Italy	E12	24
Gagnoa, C. Iv.	H3	64
Gagra, Geor.	F5	32
Gaibandha, Bngl.	F12	54
Gail, Tx., U.S.	B6	130
Gaillac, Fr.	F7	18
Gaillimh see Galway, Ire.	H3	12
Gaimán, Arg.	H3	90
Gainesboro, Tn., U.S.	H12	120
Gainesville, Fl., U.S.	G3	116
Gainesville, Ga., U.S.	B2	116
Gainesville, Mo., U.S.	H5	120
Gainesville, Tx., U.S.	H11	128
Gainsborough, Eng., U.K.	H12	12
Gainsborough Creek, stm., Can.	E12	124
Gairdner, Lake, l., Austl.	F7	74
Gaithersburg, Md., U.S.	E8	114
Gaixian, China	A10	42
Gaizina Kalns, hill, Lat.	D8	10
Gajendragarh, India	D2	53
Gajny, Russia	B8	32
Gajuapara, stm., Braz.	C2	88
Gajutino, Russia	B21	10
Gakarosa, mtn., S. Afr.	E6	70
Gakona, Ak., U.S.	D10	140
Galahad, Ab., Can.	D19	138
Galâla el Baharîya, Gebel el-, mts., Egypt	I3	58
Galâla el-Qiblîya, Gebel el-, mts., Egypt	J3	58
Galán, Cerro, mtn., Arg.	C4	92
Galana, stm., Kenya	E7	66
Galanta, Slov.	H13	16
Galapagos Islands see Colón, Archipiélago de, is., Ec.	h12	84a
Galashiels, Scot., U.K.	F9	12
Galați, Rom.	D14	26
Galați, state, Rom.	D14	26
Galatia, Il., U.S.	G9	120
Galatina, Italy	D12	24
Galaxídi, Grc.	E5	28
Galdhøpiggen, mtn., Nor.	F2	8
Galeana, Mex.	F9	98
Galeana, Mex.	C8	100
Galela, Indon.	E8	44
Galena, Ak., U.S.	D8	140
Galena, Il., U.S.	B7	120
Galena, Mo., U.S.	H4	120
Galena Park, Tx., U.S.	E12	130
Galeota Point, c., Trin.	s13	105f
Galera, Punta, c., Chile	G2	90
Galera, Punta, c., Ec.	G1	86
Galera Point, c., Trin.	s13	105f
Galeras, Volcán, vol., Col.	G3	86
Galesburg, Il., U.S.	D7	120
Galesville, Wi., U.S.	G7	118
Galeton, Pa., U.S.	C8	114
Galiano Island, i., B.C., Can.	H7	138
Galič, Russia	G20	8
Galicia, state, Spain	B3	20
Galicia, hist. reg., Eur.	G18	16
Galičica Nacionalni Park, p.o.i., Mac.	C3	28
Galičskaja vozvyšennost', hills, Russia	G20	8
Galičskoe, ozero, l., Russia	G20	8
Galilee, Lake, l., Austl.	D5	76
Galilee, Sea of see Kinneret, Yam, l., Isr.	F6	58
Galiléia, Braz.	J5	88
Galina Point, c., Jam.	i14	104d
Galion, Oh., U.S.	D3	114
Galite, Canal de la, strt., Tun.	G3	24
Gallarate, Italy	E5	22
Gallatin, Tn., U.S.	H11	120
Gallatin, stm., U.S.	E15	136
Galle, Sri L.	H5	53
Gállego, stm., Spain	B10	20
Gallegos, stm., Arg.	J3	90
Galliano, La., U.S.	H8	122
Gallinas, stm., N.M., U.S.	F4	128
Gallinas, Punta, c., Col.	A6	86
Gallipoli, Italy	D11	24
Gallipoli see Gelibolu, Tur.	C9	28
Gallipoli Peninsula see Gelibolu Yarımadası, pen., Tur.	C9	28
Gallipolis, Oh., U.S.	F3	114
Gällivare, Swe.	C9	8
Gallo, Capo, c., Italy	F7	24
Gallo Arroyo, stm., N.M., U.S.	G3	128
Galloo Island, i., N.Y., U.S.	E13	112
Galloway, hist. reg., Scot., U.K.	G8	12
Galloway, Mull of, c., Scot., U.K.	G8	12
Gallup, N.M., U.S.	H8	132
Gallura, reg., Italy	C3	24
Galoa Harbour, b., Fiji	q19	79e
Galt, Ca., U.S.	E4	134
Galtat Zemmour, W. Sah.	D2	64
Galty Mountains, mts., Ire.	I4	12
Galva, Il., U.S.	C7	120
Galva, Ks., U.S.	C11	128
Galveston, In., U.S.	H3	112
Galveston, Tx., U.S.	H4	122
Galveston Bay, b., Tx., U.S.	H4	122
Galveston Island, i., Tx., U.S.	E13	130
Gálvez, Arg.	F7	92
Galway (Gaillimh), Ire.	H3	12
Galway, state, Ire.	H4	12
Galway Bay, b., Ire.	H3	12
Gam (Jin), stm., Asia	A7	48
Gama, Isla, i., Arg.	H4	90
Gamagōri, Japan	E10	40
Gamarra, Col.	C5	86
Gamay, Phil.	D5	52
Gamba, China	D12	54
Gambaga, Ghana	G4	64
Gambēla, Eth.	F6	62
Gambell, Ak., U.S.	D5	140
Gambia (Gambie), stm., Afr.	G1	64
Gambia, The, ctry., Afr.	G1	64
Gambie (Gambia), stm., Afr.	G2	64
Gambier, Îles, is., Fr. Poly.	F13	72
Gamboa, Pan.	C2	86
Gamboma, Congo	E3	66
Gamboula, C.A.R.	D2	66
Gamka, stm., S. Afr.	H5	70
Gamlakarleby see Kokkola, Fin.	E10	8
Gamleby, Swe.	H7	8
Gammon Ranges National Park, p.o.i., Austl.	H2	76
Ga-Mogara, stm., S. Afr.	E6	70
Gan, stm., China	B10	36
Gan, stm., China	G6	42
Ganado, Az., U.S.	H7	132
Ganado, Tx., U.S.	E11	130
Gananoque, On., Can.	D13	112
Gäncä, Azer.	A6	56
Gand see Gent, Bel.	C12	14
Ganda, Ang.	C1	68
Gandadiwata, Bulu, mtn., Indon.	E11	50
Gandajika, D.R.C.	F4	66
Gandak (Nārāyani), stm., Asia	E10	54
Gándara, Spain	A2	20
Gander, Nf., Can.	j23	107a
Ganderkesee, Ger.	C4	16
Gandesa, Spain	C11	20
Gandevi, India	H4	54
Gāndhinagar, India	G4	54
Gandhi Reservoir see Gāndhi Sāgar, res., India	F5	54
Gāndhi Sāgar, res., India	F5	54
Gandia, Spain	F10	20
Gandu, Braz.	G6	88
Ganga see Ganges, stm., Asia	F11	54
Gan Gan, Arg.	H3	90
Gangānagar, India	D4	54
Gangāpur, India	B2	53
Gangāpur, India	F5	54
Gangāpur, India	E6	54
Gangārāmpur, India	F12	54
Gangaw, Mya.	A2	48
Gangāwati, India	D3	53
Gangdhār, India	G5	54
Gangdisê Shan, mts., China	C9	54
Ganges, B.C., Can.	H7	138
Ganges (Ganga) (Padma), stm., Asia	G13	54
Ganges, Mouths of the, mth., Asia	H12	54
Ganghu, China	B11	54
Gangmar Co, l., China	B10	54
Gangneung see Kangnŭng, Kor., S.	B1	40
Gangoa, China	D5	36
Gangotri, India	C7	54
Gangotri, India	C7	54
Gangoumen, China	D2	38
Gangtok, India	E12	54
Gangu, China	D1	42
Gangweon see Kangwŏn-do, state, Kor., S.	B1	40
Gannan, China	B9	36
Gannett Peak, mtn., Wy., U.S.	D3	126
Gannvalley, S.D., U.S.	C14	126
Ganquan, China	C3	42
Gansbaai, S. Afr.	I4	70
Gansu, state, China	D5	36
Gantang, China	H8	42
Gantt, Al., U.S.	F12	122
Gantung, Indon.	E6	50
Ganyanchi, China	C1	42
Ganyesa, S. Afr.	E7	70
Ganzê, China	E4	36
Ganzhou, China	I6	42
Gao, Mali	F4	64
Gao'an, China	G6	42
Gaochun, China	F8	42
Gaohebu, China	F7	42
Gaojian, China	F9	36
Gaolan, China	D5	36
Gaolong, China	H5	42
Gaona, Arg.	B5	92
Gaoping, China	D5	42
Gaotan, China	E3	42
Gaotang, China	C7	42
Gaoua, Burkina	G4	64
Gaoual, Gui.	G2	64
Gaoxian, China	F5	36
Gaoyi, China	C6	42
Gaoyou, China	E8	42
Gaoyou Hu, l., China	E8	42
Gaozhou, China	K4	42
Gap, Fr.	E12	18
Gar, China	B8	54
Gar, stm., China	C8	54
Gara, Lough, l., Ire.	H4	12
Garagumskij kanal (Kara-Kum Canal), can., Turkmen.	B9	56
Garagumy (Kara-Kum), des., Turkmen.	A8	56
Garaina, Pap. N. Gui.	b4	79a
Garanhuns, Braz.	E7	88
Garapan, N. Mar. Is.	B5	72
Garara, Pap. N. Gui.	b4	79a
Garber, Ok., U.S.	E11	128
Garberville, Ca., U.S.	C2	134
Gârbovu, Rom.	E10	26
Garça, Braz.	L1	88
García, Mex.	G8	98
García de Sola, Embalse de, res., Spain	E5	20
Gard, state, Fr.	F10	18
Garda, Italy	E7	22
Garda, Lago di, l., Italy	E7	22
Gardelegen, Ger.	D7	16
Garden City, Ks., U.S.	C8	128
Garden City, Mo., U.S.	F3	120
Garden City, Tx., U.S.	C6	130
Gardendale, Al., U.S.	D12	122
Garden Grove, Ca., U.S.	J7	134
Garden Grove, Ia., U.S.	D4	120
Garden Island, i., Mi., U.S.	C4	112
Garden Peninsula, pen., Mi., U.S.	C3	112
Garden Reach, India	G11	54
Gardenton, Mb., Can.	E17	124
Gardey, Arg.	H8	92
Gardeyz, Afg.	C10	56
Gardiner, Mt., U.S.	E16	136
Gardiner, Or., U.S.	G2	136
Gardiner Dam, dam, Sk., Can.	C6	124
Gardner, Ks., U.S.	F2	120
Gardner, Ma., U.S.	B13	114
Gardner Canal, b., B.C., Can.	C2	138
Gardnerville, Nv., U.S.	E6	134
Garessio, Italy	F5	22
Garet, Mont, vol., Vanuatu	j16	79d
Garfield, Ks., U.S.	C9	128
Garfield, N.M., U.S.	K9	132
Garfield Mountain, mtn., Mt., U.S.	F14	136
Gargano, Promontorio del, mts., Italy	I12	22
Gargano, Testa del, c., Italy	I13	22
Gargždai, Lith.	E4	10
Garhākota, India	G7	54
Garibaldi, Braz.	D12	92
Garibaldi, B.C., Can.	G7	138
Garibaldi, Or., U.S.	E2	136
Garibaldi, Mount, vol., B.C., Can.	G8	138
Gariep Dam, res., S. Afr.	G7	70
Garies, S. Afr.	G4	70
Garigliano, stm., Italy	C7	24
Gariglione, Monte, mtn., Italy	E10	24
Garissa, Kenya	E7	66
Garland, Tx., U.S.	E2	122
Garland, Ut., U.S.	B4	132
Garlasco, Italy	E5	22
Garlin, Fr.	F5	18
Garm, Taj.	B11	56
Garmisch-Partenkirchen, Ger.	I7	16
Garnavillo, Ia., U.S.	B6	120
Garner, Ia., U.S.	A4	120
Garner, N.C., U.S.	I7	114
Garnpung Lake, l., Austl.	I4	76
Garona (Garonne), stm., Eur.	E5	18
Garonne (Garona), stm., Eur.	E5	18
Garoowe, Som.	C9	66
Garoua, Cam.	C2	66
Garoua Boulaï, Cam.	C2	66
Garqu Yan, China	B14	54
Garqu Yan, China	A14	54
Garrel, Ger.	D3	16
Garretson, S.D., U.S.	H2	118
Garrett, In., U.S.	G4	112
Garrett, Ky., U.S.	G3	114
Garrison, N.D., U.S.	G12	124
Garrison, Tx., U.S.	F4	122
Garrison Dam, dam, N.D., U.S.	G12	124
Garry Bay, b., Nu., Can.	B13	106
Garry Lake, l., Nu., Can.	B10	106
Garsen, Kenya	E7	66
Garson, On., Can.	B9	112
Garut, Indon.	G5	50
Garwolin, Pol.	E17	16
Garwood, Tx., U.S.	H2	122
Gary, In., U.S.	G2	112
Gary, Tx., U.S.	E4	122
Gary, W.V., U.S.	G4	114
Garyarsa, China	C8	54
Garza, Arg.	D6	92
Garza Ayala, Mex.	H7	130
Garzón, Col.	F4	86
Garzón, Ur.	G10	92
Gasan-Kuli, Turkmen.	B7	56
Gas City, In., U.S.	H4	112
Gascogne (Gascony), hist. reg., Fr.	F6	18
Gasconade, stm., Mo., U.S.	F6	120
Gasconade, Osage Fork, stm., Mo., U.S.	G5	120
Gascony see Gascogne, hist. reg., Fr.	F6	18
Gascoyne, stm., Austl.	D2	74
Gashaka, Nig.	H7	64
Gashua, Nig.	G7	64
Gaspar, Braz.	C13	92
Gasparilla Island, i., Fl., U.S.	J3	116
Gaspé, Qc., Can.	B12	110
Gaspé, Baie de, b., Qc., Can.	B12	110
Gaspé, Cap, c., Qc., Can.	B12	110
Gaspe Peninsula see Gaspésie, Péninsule de la, pen., Qc., Can.	B11	110
Gaspésie, Péninsule de la (Gaspe Peninsula), pen., Qc., Can.	B11	110
Gassaway, W.V., U.S.	F5	114
Gasteiz (Vitoria), Spain	B8	20
Gaston, Lake, res., U.S.	H7	114
Gastonia, N.C., U.S.	A4	116
Gastre, Arg.	H3	90
Gata, Cabo de, c., Spain	H8	20

Name	Map Ref.	Page
Gata, Sierra de, mts., Spain	D4	20
Gătaia, Rom.	D8	26
Gátas, Akrotírion, c., Cyp.	D4	58
Gatčina, Russia	A12	10
Gate City, Va., U.S.	H3	114
Gateshead, Eng., U.K.	G11	12
Gateshead Island, i., Nu., Can.	A11	106
Gatesville, N.C., U.S.	H9	114
Gatesville, Tx., U.S.	C10	130
Gateway, Co., U.S.	E8	132
Gatineau, Qc., Can.	C14	112
Gatineau, stm., Qc., Can.	C14	112
Gatineau, Parc de la, p.o.i., Qc., Can.	C13	112
Gatlinburg, Tn., U.S.	I2	114
Gattinara, Italy	E5	22
Gatton, Austl.	F9	76
Gatún, Lago, res., Pan.	H7	102
Gatun Lake see Gatún, Lago, res., Pan.	H7	102
Gauer Lake, l., Mb., Can.	D11	106
Gauja (Koiva), stm., Eur.	C7	10
Gaujiena, Lat.	C9	10
Gauley, stm., W.V., U.S.	F4	114
Gauley Bridge, W.V., U.S.	F4	114
Gaurela, India	G8	54
Gauribidanūr, India	E3	53
Gause, Tx., U.S.	G2	122
Gaustatoppen, mtn., Nor.	G3	8
Gauteng, state, S. Afr.	D9	70
Gavà, Spain	C12	20
Gávdos, i., Grc.	I7	28
Gavião, stm., Braz.	H5	88
Gavins Point Dam, dam, U.S.	E15	126
Gävle, Swe.	F7	8
Gävleborg, state, Swe.	F7	8
Gavorrano, Italy	H7	22
Gavrilov-Jam, Russia	H18	8
Gawachab, Nmb.	E3	70
Gāwān, India	F10	54
Gawler, Austl.	J2	76
Gawler Ranges, mts., Austl.	F7	74
Gaya, India	F10	54
Gaya, Niger	G5	64
Gaya, Nig.	G6	64
Gaylord, Mn., U.S.	G4	118
Gayndah, Austl.	E8	76
Gays Mills, Wi., U.S.	H8	118
Gaza see Ghazzah, Gaza	G5	58
Gaza, state, Moz.	C11	70
Gazandzhyk see Gazandzyk, Turkmen.	B8	56
Gazandzyk, Turkmen.	B8	56
Gazaoua, Niger	G6	64
Gaza Strip, dep., Asia	G5	58
Gazelle Peninsula, pen., Pap. N. Gui.	a5	79a
Gaziantep, Tur.	A8	58
Gaziantep, state, Tur.	B8	58
Gazimağusa (Famagusta), N. Cyp.	C4	58
Gazimağusa Körfezi, b., N. Cyp.	C4	58
Gazipaşa, Tur.	G15	28
Gazivoda Jezero, res., Yugo.	G7	26
Gbanga, Lib.	H3	64
Gboko, Nig.	H6	64
Gdańsk (Danzig), Pol.	B14	16
Gdańsk, state, Pol.	B14	16
Gdansk, Gulf of, b., Eur.	B15	16
Gdov, Russia	B10	10
Gdynia, Pol.	B14	16
Gearhart Mountain, mtn., Or., U.S.	A5	134
Geary, N.B., Can.	E10	110
Geary, Ok., U.S.	F10	128
Gebe, Pulau, i., Indon.	E8	44
Gebze, Tur.	C12	28
Geçitkale, N. Cyp.	C4	58
Gediz, Tur.	D12	28
Gediz (Hermus), stm., Tur.	E10	28
Gedser, Den.	B7	16
Geel, Bel.	C13	14
Geelong, Austl.	L5	76
Geelvink Channel, strt., Austl.	E2	74
Geesthacht, Ger.	C6	16
Geeveston, Austl.	o13	77a
Ge Hu, l., China	F8	42
Geiger, Al., U.S.	E10	122
Geikie, stm., Sk., Can.	D9	106
Geisenfeld, Ger.	H7	16
Geislingen an der Steige, Ger.	H5	16
Geistown, Pa., U.S.	D7	114
Geita, Tan.	E6	66
Gejiu, China	G5	36
Gela, Italy	G8	24
Gela, Golfo di, b., Italy	H7	24
Geladī, Eth.	F9	62
Gelang, Tanjong, c., Malay.	K6	48
Gelasa, Selat, strt., Indon.	E5	50
Geleen, Neth.	D14	14
Gelembe, Tur.	D10	28
Gelendžik, Russia	F5	32
Gelgaudiškis, Lith.	E6	10
Gelibolu, Tur.	C9	28
Gelibolu Yarımadası (Gallipoli Peninsula), pen., Tur.	C9	28
Gellibrand River, Austl.	L4	76
Gelsenkirchen, Ger.	E2	16
Gemas, Malay.	K6	48
Gemena, D.R.C.	D3	66
Gemert, Neth.	E1	16
Gemlik, Tur.	C12	28
Gemlik Körfezi, b., Tur.	C11	28
Gemona del Friuli, Italy	D10	22
Gemsa, Egypt	K4	58
Gemsbok National Park, p.o.i., Bots.	D5	70
Gemünden, Ger.	F5	16
Gen, stm., China	A9	36
Genalē (Jubba), stm., Afr.	C8	66
Gending, Indon.	G8	50
General Acha, Arg.	H5	92
General Alvear, Arg.	G3	92
General Alvear, Arg.	H8	92
General Belgrano, Arg.	G8	92
General Bernardo O'Higgins, sci., Ant.	B35	81
General Bravo, Mex.	C9	100
General Cabrera, Arg.	F6	92
General Campos, Arg.	E8	92
General Carrera, Lago, l., S.A.	I2	90
General Conesa, Arg.	H4	90
General Conesa, Arg.	H9	92
General Daniel Cerri, Arg.	I6	92
General Elizardo Aquino, Para.	C9	92
General Enrique Martínez, Ur.	F10	92
General Escobedo, Mex.	I7	130
General Eugenio A. Garay, Para.	D4	90
General Galarza, Arg.	F8	92
General Güemes, Arg.	B5	92
General Guido, Arg.	H8	92
General José de San Martín, Arg.	C8	92
General Juan José Ríos, Mex.	C4	100
General Juan Madariaga, Arg.	H9	92
General La Madrid, Arg.	H7	92
General Lavalle, Arg.	H9	92
General Levalle, Arg.	G5	92
General Manuel Belgrano, Cerro, mtn., Arg.	D4	92
General Pico, Arg.	G6	92
General Pinedo, Arg.	C7	92
General Pizarro, Arg.	B6	92
General Ramírez, Arg.	F7	92
General Roca, Arg.	G3	90
General San Martin, Arg.	G8	92
General Santos, Phil.	G5	52
General Terán, Mex.	C9	100
General Toševo, Blg.	F14	26
General Toshevo see General Toševo, Blg.	F14	26
General Treviño, Mex.	H8	130
General Trias, Mex.	F1	130
General Viamonte, Arg.	G7	92
General Villegas, Arg.	G6	92
Genesee, Id., U.S.	D9	136
Genesee, stm., U.S.	F12	112
Geneseo, Il., U.S.	C7	120
Geneseo, Ks., U.S.	C10	128
Geneseo, N.Y., U.S.	B8	114
Geneva see Genève, Switz.	D3	22
Geneva, Il., U.S.	J10	118
Geneva, In., U.S.	H5	112
Geneva, Ne., U.S.	G15	126
Geneva, N.Y., U.S.	B8	114
Geneva, Oh., U.S.	C4	114
Geneva, Lake, l., Eur.	C12	18
Genève (Geneva), Switz.	D3	22
Genève, Lac de see Geneva, Lake, l., Eur.	C12	18
Genf see Genève, Switz.	D3	22
Gengma, China	G4	36
Genil, stm., Spain	G5	20
Genk, Bel.	C14	14
Genkai-nada, Japan	F2	40
Genoa, Austl.	K7	76
Genoa see Genova, Italy	F5	22
Genoa, Ne., U.S.	F15	126
Genoa, Oh., U.S.	C2	114
Genoa, Wi., U.S.	H7	118
Genova (Genoa), Italy	F5	22
Genova, Golfo di, b., Italy	G5	22
Genrietty, ostrov, i., Russia	A20	34
Gens de Terre, stm., Qc., Can.	B13	112
Genshiryoku-kenkyūsho, sci., Japan	C13	40
Gent (Ghent), Bel.	C12	14
Genteng, Gili, i., Indon.	G8	50
Genthin, Ger.	D8	16
Gentio do Ouro, Braz.	F4	88
Genzano di Roma, Italy	I9	22
Geographe Bay, b., Austl.	F3	74
Geographical Society Ø, i., Grnld.	C21	141
Geok-Tepe, Turkmen.	B8	56
George, S. Afr.	H6	70
George, Ia., U.S.	H2	118
George, stm., Qc., Can.	D17	106
George, Lake, l., Austl.	D4	74
George, Lake, l., Austl.	J7	76
George, Lake, l., Ug.	E6	66
George, Lake, l., Fl., U.S.	G4	116
George, Lake, res., N.Y., U.S.	G3	110
Georgetown, Austl.	B4	76
George Town, Austl.	n13	77a
Georgetown, On., Can.	E9	112
Georgetown, P.E., Can.	D14	110
George Town, Cay. Is.	C7	102
Georgetown, Gam.	G2	64
Georgetown, Guy.	B6	84
George Town (Penang), Malay.	J4	48
Georgetown, St. Vin.	o11	105e
Georgetown, Co., U.S.	B3	128
Georgetown, De., U.S.	F10	114
Georgetown, Fl., U.S.	G4	116
Georgetown, Id., U.S.	H15	136
Georgetown, Ky., U.S.	F1	114
Georgetown, Ms., U.S.	F8	122
Georgetown, Oh., U.S.	F2	114
Georgetown, S.C., U.S.	C6	116
Georgetown, Tx., U.S.	D10	130
George V Coast, cst., Ant.	B19	81
George Washington Birthplace National Monument, p.o.i., Va., U.S.	F9	114
George Washington Carver National Monument, p.o.i., Mo., U.S.	H3	120
George West, Tx., U.S.	F9	130
Georgia, ctry., Asia	F6	32
Georgia, state, U.S.	E11	108
Georgia, Strait of, strt., N.A.	G7	138
Georgian Bay, b., On., Can.	C8	112
Georgian Bay Islands National Park, p.o.i., On., Can.	D9	112
Georgievka, Kaz.	E14	32
Georgina, stm., Austl.	D2	76
Georg von Neumayer, sci., Ant.	B3	81
Gera, Ger.	F7	16
Geral, Serra, mts., Braz.	C12	92
Geral, Serra, clf, Braz.	F2	88
Gerald, Mo., U.S.	F6	120
Geral de Goiás, Serra, clf, Braz.	G2	88
Geraldine, Mt., U.S.	C16	136
Geraldton, Austl.	E2	74
Geraldton, On., Can.	B11	118
Gérardmer, Fr.	F15	14
Gerber, Ca., U.S.	C3	134
Gerdine, Mount, mtn., Ak., U.S.	D9	140
Gerede, Tur.	C15	28
Gereshk, Afg.	C9	56
Gérgal, Spain	G8	20
Gerik, Malay.	J5	48
Gerlachovský štít, mtn., Slov.	G16	16
German Democratic Republic see Germany, ctry., Eur.	E6	16
Germania Land, reg., Grnld.	B21	141
Germantown, Il., U.S.	F8	120
Germantown, Tn., U.S.	B9	122
Germantown, Wi., U.S.	E1	112
Germany, ctry., Eur.	E6	16
Germany, Federal Republic of see Germany, ctry., Eur.	E6	16
Germencik, Tur.	F10	28
Germfask, Mi., U.S.	B4	112
Germiston, S. Afr.	E9	70
Gernika, Spain	A8	20
Gero, Japan	D10	40
Geroliménas, Grc.	G5	28
Gerona see Girona, Spain	B13	20
Geronimo, Ok., U.S.	G10	128
Gers, state, Fr.	F6	18
Gers, stm., Fr.	F6	18
Gêrzê, China	B10	54
Geseke, Ger.	E4	16
Geser, Indon.	F9	44
Getafe, Spain	D7	20
Gettysburg, Pa., U.S.	E8	114
Getúlio Vargas, Braz.	C11	92
Geumpang, Indon.	J2	48
Gevgelija, Mac.	B5	28
Geyikli, Tur.	D9	28
Geyser, Mt., U.S.	C16	136
Geyserville, Ca., U.S.	E3	134
Geyve, Tur.	C13	28
Ghaapplato, plat., S. Afr.	E7	70
Ghadāmis, Libya	B1	62
Ghagghar, stm., India	D5	54
Ghāghara (Kauriālā), stm., Asia	E9	54
Ghāghra see Ghāghara, stm., Asia	E9	54
Ghakhar, Pak.	B4	54
Ghana, ctry., Afr.	H4	64
Ghanzi, Bots.	B5	70
Ghanzi, state, Bots.	C6	70
Gharandal, hist., Jord.	H6	58
Gharaunda, India	D6	54
Ghardaïa, Alg.	C5	64
Ghardimaou, Tun.	H2	24
Gharyān, Libya	A2	62
Ghāt, Libya	C2	62
Ghatere, Mount, mtn., Sol. Is.	d8	79b
Ghātprabha, stm., India	C2	53
Ghātsīla, India	G11	54
Għawdex (Gozo), i., Malta	H8	24
Ghazāl, Bahr al-, stm., Sudan	F6	62
Ghāziābād, India	D6	54
Ghāzīpur, India	F9	54
Ghazlūna, Pak.	C1	54
Ghaznī, Afg.	C10	56
Ghaznī, state, Afg.	B1	54
Ghaznī, stm., Afg.	B2	54
Ghazzah (Gaza), Gaza	G5	58
Ghazzah, Leb.	E6	58
Ghent see Gent, Bel.	C12	14
Gheorgheni, Rom.	C12	26
Gherla, Rom.	C10	26
Gheroo, Geziret, i., Egypt	G1	58
Ghīnah, Wādī al-, stm., Sau. Ar.	H9	58
Ghisonaccia, Fr.	H15	18
Ghizo see Gizo Island, i., Sol. Is.	e7	79b
Ghizunabeana Islands, is., Sol. Is.	d8	79b
Ghotki, Pak.	E2	54
Ghubaysh, Sudan	E5	62
Ghūriān, Afg.	C9	56
Gianh, stm., Viet.	C7	48
Giannitsá, Grc.	C5	28
Giant Mountain, mtn., N.Y., U.S.	F3	110
Giant's Castle, mtn., S. Afr.	F9	70
Giant's Castle Game Reserve, S. Afr.	F9	70
Gia Rai, Viet.	H7	48
Giarre, Italy	G9	24
Gibara, Cuba	B9	102
Gibbon, Mn., U.S.	G4	118
Gibbons, Ab., Can.	C17	138
Gibbonsville, Id., U.S.	E13	136
Gibb River, Austl.	C5	74
Gibeon, Nmb.	D3	70
Gibraleón, Spain	G3	20
Gibraltar, Gib.	H5	20
Gibraltar, dep., Eur.	H5	20
Gibraltar, Strait of, strt.	B3	64
Gibraltar Point, c., Eng., U.K.	H13	12
Gibsland, La., U.S.	E5	122
Gibson City, Il., U.S.	D9	120
Gibson Desert, des., Austl.	D4	74
Gibsons, B.C., Can.	G7	138
Giddalūr, India	D4	53
Giddings, Tx., U.S.	D11	130
Gidgi, Lake, l., Austl.	E5	74
Giedraičiai, Lith.	E8	10
Gien, Fr.	G11	14
Giessen, Ger.	F4	16
Gifatîn, Gezira, is., Egypt	K4	58
Gifford, Fl., U.S.	I5	116
Gifford, stm., Nu., Can.	A14	106
Gifford Creek, Austl.	D3	74
Gifgâfa, Bîr, well, Egypt	H4	58
Gifhorn, Ger.	D6	16
Gifu, Japan	D9	40
Gifu, state, Japan	D10	40
Giganta, Sierra de la, mts., Mex.	C3	100
Gigena see Alcira, Arg.	F5	92
Gigha Island, i., Scot., U.K.	F7	12
Giglio, Isola del, i., Italy	H7	22
Gihu see Gifu, Japan	D9	40
Gijón, Spain	A5	20
Gila, stm., U.S.	K2	132
Gila Bend, Az., U.S.	K4	132
Gila Cliff Dwellings National Monument, p.o.i., N.M., U.S.	J8	132
Gilbert, La., U.S.	E7	122
Gilbert, stm., Austl.	C8	74
Gilbert Islands see Kiribati, ctry., Oc.	D9	72
Gilbert Islands, is., Kir.	D8	72
Gilbert Peak, mtn., Wa., U.S.	D5	136
Gilbert Plains, Mb., Can.	C13	124
Gilbués, Braz.	E3	88
Gildford, Mt., U.S.	B16	136
Gilford Island, i., B.C., Can.	F4	138
Gilgandra, Austl.	H7	76
Gilgil, Kenya	E7	66
Gil Gil Creek, stm., Austl.	G8	76
Gilgit, Pak.	B11	56
Gilirang, Indon.	E12	50
Gil Island, i., B.C., Can.	C1	138
Giljuj, stm., Russia	F14	34
Gillam, Mb., Can.	D12	106
Gillen, Lake, l., Austl.	E5	74
Gillespie, Il., U.S.	E8	120
Gillett, Ar., U.S.	C7	122
Gillette, Wy., U.S.	C7	126
Gillian, Lake, l., Nu., Can.	B16	106
Gillingham, Eng., U.K.	J13	12
Gills Rock, Wi., U.S.	C3	112
Gilman, Il., U.S.	D10	120
Gilman, Wi., U.S.	F8	118
Gilmer, Tx., U.S.	E4	122
Gilmore City, Ia., U.S.	B3	120
Gilroy, Ca., U.S.	F4	134
Giltner, Ne., U.S.	G14	126
Giluwe, Mount, mtn., Pap. N. Gui.	b3	79a
Gīmbī, Eth.	F7	62
Gimcheon see Kimch'ŏn, Kor., S.	F8	38
Gimie, Mount, vol., St. Luc.	m6	105c
Gimli, Mb., Can.	D16	124
Gimpu, Indon.	D12	50
Gineina, Râs el-, mtn., Egypt	I4	58
Gin Gin, Austl.	E8	76
Gingoog, Phil.	F5	52
Gīnīr, Eth.	F8	62
Ginosa, Italy	D10	24
Gioia, Golfo di, b., Italy	F9	24
Gioia del Colle, Italy	D10	24
Gioia Tauro, Italy	F9	24
Giong Rieng, Viet.	H7	48
Gipuzkoako, co., Spain	A8	20
Girafi, Wadi (Paran, Nahal), stm.	I5	58
Giralia, Austl.	D2	74
Girard, Il., U.S.	E8	120
Girard, Ks., U.S.	G3	120
Girard, Oh., U.S.	C5	114
Girard, Pa., U.S.	C5	114
Girardot, Col.	E4	86
Giraud, Pointe, c., Dom.	j6	105c
Girgarre, Austl.	K5	76
Girīdīh, India	F11	54
Girna, stm., India	H5	54
Gir National Park, p.o.i., India	H3	54
Girne (Kyrenia), N. Cyp.	C4	58
Girón, Ec.	D2	84
Girona, Spain	B13	20
Girona, co., Spain	B13	20
Gironde, state, Fr.	E5	18
Gironde, est., Fr.	D5	18
Gīr Range, mts., India	H3	54
Giru, Austl.	B6	76
Giruá, Braz.	D10	92
Girvan, Scot., U.K.	F8	12
Gisborne, N.Z.	D8	80
Giscome, B.C., Can.	B8	138
Gislaved, Swe.	H5	8
Gisors, Fr.	E10	14
Gitarama, Rw.	E5	66
Gitega, Bdi.	E5	66
Giulianova, Italy	H10	22
Giurgiu, Rom.	F12	26
Giurgiu, state, Rom.	E13	26
Giuvala, Pasul, p., Rom.	D12	26
Givet, Fr.	D13	14
Givors, Fr.	D10	18
Giyon, Eth.	F7	62
Giza see El-Gîza, Egypt	H1	58
Gijduvan, Uzb.	F10	32
Gižiga, Russia	D21	34
Gižiginskaja guba, b., Russia	D20	34
Gizo, Sol. Is.	e7	79b
Gizo Island, i., Sol. Is.	e7	79b
Giżycko, Pol.	B17	16
Gjirokastër, Alb.	D14	24
Gjirokastra see Gjirokastër, Alb.	D14	24
Gjoa Haven, Nu., Can.	B11	106
Gjøvik, Nor.	F4	8
Gjuhëzës, Kepi i, c., Alb.	D13	24
Gjumri, Arm.	A5	56
Glace Bay, N.S., Can.	D17	110
Glacier, B.C., Can.	E13	138
Glacier Bay, b., Ak., U.S.	E12	140
Glacier National Park, p.o.i., B.C., Can.	E13	138
Glacier National Park, p.o.i., Mt., U.S.	B12	136
Glacier Peak, vol., Wa., U.S.	B5	136
Glacier Strait, strt., Nu., Can.	B10	141
Glad', Russia	A15	10
Gladbrook, Ia., U.S.	B5	120
Gladewater, Tx., U.S.	E4	122
Gladstone, Austl.	D8	76
Gladstone, Mb., Can.	D14	124
Gladstone, Mi., U.S.	C2	112
Gladstone, Mo., U.S.	E3	120
Glåma, stm., Nor.	F4	8
Glan, Phil.	H5	52
Glaris see Glarus, Switz.	C5	22
Glarner Alpen, mts., Switz.	D6	22
Glarus, Switz.	C5	22
Glarus Alps see Glarner Alpen, mts., Switz.	D6	22
Glasco, Ks., U.S.	B11	128
Glasgow, Scot., U.K.	F8	12
Glasgow, Ky., U.S.	G12	120
Glasgow, Mo., U.S.	E5	120
Glasgow, Mt., U.S.	F7	124
Glasgow, Va., U.S.	G6	114
Glassboro, N.J., U.S.	E10	114
Glastonbury, Eng., U.K.	J10	12
Glauchau, Ger.	F8	16
Glazov, Russia	C8	32
Glazunovka, Russia	H19	10
Gleichen, Ab., Can.	F17	138
Glen Alpine, N.C., U.S.	A4	116
Glenavon, Sk., Can.	D10	124
Glenboro, Mb., Can.	E14	124
Glenburn, N.D., U.S.	F12	124
Glen Burnie, Md., U.S.	E9	114
Glen Canyon, val., U.S.	F6	132
Glen Canyon Dam, dam, Az., U.S.	G5	132
Glen Canyon National Recreation Area, p.o.i., U.S.	F6	132
Glencoe, On., Can.	F8	112
Glencoe, S. Afr.	F9	70
Glencoe, Mn., U.S.	G4	118
Glen Cove, N.Y., U.S.	D12	114
Glendale, Az., U.S.	J4	132
Glendale, Ca., U.S.	I7	134
Glendale, Ms., U.S.	F9	122
Glendale, Ut., U.S.	F4	132
Glendale, Wi., U.S.	A10	120
Glendive, Mt., U.S.	G9	124
Glendo, Wy., U.S.	E7	126
Glendon, Ab., Can.	B19	138
Glendo Reservoir, res., Wy., U.S.	E8	126
Glen Elder, Ks., U.S.	B10	128
Glenelg, stm., Austl.	K3	76
Glengarriff, Ire.	J3	12
Glengyle, Austl.	E2	76
Glen Innes, Austl.	G8	76
Glenmora, La., U.S.	G6	122
Glennallen, Ak., U.S.	D10	140
Glenns Ferry, Id., U.S.	H11	136
Glenoma, Wa., U.S.	D4	136
Glenormiston, Austl.	D7	74
Glenreagh, Austl.	G9	76
Glen Robertson, On., Can.	E2	110
Glen Rock, Pa., U.S.	E9	114
Glenrock, Wy., U.S.	E7	126
Glen Rose, Tx., U.S.	B10	130
Glenrothes, Scot., U.K.	E9	12
Glens Falls, N.Y., U.S.	G3	110
Glenville, Mn., U.S.	H5	118
Glenwood, Ab., Can.	G17	138
Glenwood, Al., U.S.	F12	122
Glenwood, Ar., U.S.	C5	122
Glenwood, Ga., U.S.	D3	116
Glenwood, Ia., U.S.	C2	120
Glenwood, Mn., U.S.	F3	118
Glenwood, Va., U.S.	H6	114
Glenwood City, Wi., U.S.	F6	118
Glenwood Springs, Co., U.S.	D9	132
Glidden, Wi., U.S.	E8	118
Glide, Or., U.S.	G3	136
Glina, Cro.	E13	22
Glittertind see Glittertinden, mtn., Nor.	F3	8
Glittertinden, mtn., Nor.	F3	8
Gliwice, Pol.	F14	16
Gljadjanskoe, Russia	D10	32
Globe, Az., U.S.	J6	132
Glodeni, Mol.	B14	26
Głogów, Pol.	E11	16
Głogów Małopolski, Pol.	F17	16
Glomma see Glåma, stm., Nor.	F4	8
Glommersträsk, Swe.	D8	8
Glorieta, N.M., U.S.	F3	128
Glorieuses, Îles, is., Reu.	C8	68
Glorioso Islands see Glorieuses, Îles, is., Reu.	C8	68
Gloucester, Austl.	H9	76
Gloucester, Eng., U.K.	J10	12
Gloucester, Ma., U.S.	B15	114
Gloucester, Va., U.S.	G9	114
Gloucester Island, i., Austl.	B7	76
Glouster, Oh., U.S.	E3	114
Gloversville, N.Y., U.S.	A11	114
Głowno, Pol.	E15	16
Głubczyce, Pol.	F13	16
Glubokoe, Kaz.	D14	32
Glubokoje see Glubokoe, Kaz.	D14	32
Głuchołazy, Pol.	F13	16
Glücksburg, Ger.	B5	16
Glückstadt, Ger.	C5	16
Glucomanka, gora, mtn., Russia	B11	38
Glyndon, Mn., U.S.	E2	118
Gmünd, Aus.	D10	22
Gmünd, Aus.	B12	22
Gmunden, Aus.	C10	22
Gnalta, Austl.	H4	76
Gnezdovo, Russia	F14	10
Gniew, Pol.	C14	16
Gniezno, Pol.	D13	16
Gnilec, Russia	H19	10
Gnjilane, Yugo.	G8	26
Gnowangerup, Austl.	F3	74
Gō, stm., Japan	E5	40
Goa, state, India	D2	53
Goālpāra, India	E13	54
Goaso, Ghana	H4	64
Goat Island, i., Antig.	e4	105b
Goat Point, c., Antig.	e4	105b
Goba, Eth.	F8	62
Gobabis, Nmb.	C4	70
Göbel, Tur.	D11	28
Gobernador Gregores, Arg.	I2	90
Gobernador Ingeniero Valentín Virasoro, Arg.	D9	92
Gobernador Juan E. Martínez, Arg.	D8	92
Gobernador Vera see Vera, Arg.	D7	92
Gobi Desert, des., Asia	C5	36
Gobō, Japan	F8	40
Goce Delčev, Blg.	H10	26
Goch, Ger.	E2	16
Goðafoss, wtfl, Ice.	k31	8a
Godāvari, stm., India	C5	53
Godāvari, Mouths of the, mth., India	C5	53
Godbout, Qc., Can.	A9	110
Goderich, On., Can.	E8	112
Godfrey, Il., U.S.	F7	120
Godhavn (Qeqertarsuaq), Grnld.	D15	141
Godhra, India	G4	54
Gödöllő, Hung.	B6	26
Godoy Cruz, Arg.	F3	92
Gods, stm., Mb., Can.	D12	106
Gods Lake, Mb., Can.	E12	106
Gods Lake, l., Mb., Can.	E12	106
Gods Mercy, Bay of, b., Nu., Can.	C13	106
Godthåb (Nuuk), Grnld.	E15	141
Godwin Austen see K2, mtn., Asia	B12	56
Goeie Hoop, Kaap die see Good Hope, Cape of, c., S. Afr.	I4	70
Goéland, Lac au, l., Qc., Can.	E15	106
Goes, Neth.	C12	14
Goffstown, N.H., U.S.	G5	110
Gogebic, Lake, res., Mi., U.S.	E9	118
Gogoi, Moz.	B11	70
Gogrial, Sudan	F5	62
Gohad, India	E7	54
Gohpur, India	E14	54
Goiana, Braz.	D8	88
Goianésia, Braz.	H1	88
Goiânia, Braz.	I1	88
Goianinha, Braz.	D8	88
Goiás, Braz.	G7	84
Goiás, state, Braz.	C7	90
Goiatuba, Braz.	J1	88
Goio-Erê, Braz.	B11	92
Gôio-Erê, stm., Braz.	B11	92
Góis, Port.	D2	20
Gojō, Japan	E8	40
Gojra, Pak.	C4	54
Gokāk, India	C2	53
Gökçeada, i., Tur.	C8	28
Gökova Körfezi (Kerme, Gulf of), b., Tur.	G10	28
Göksu, stm., Tur.	B4	58
Göksu, stm., Tur.	A6	58
Göktepe, Tur.	F11	28
Gokwe, Zimb.	D4	68
Golāghāt, India	C7	46
Gola Gokarannāth, India	D8	54
Gołańcz, Pol.	D13	16
Gölbaşı, Tur.	D15	28
Gölbası, Tur.	A8	58
Golcanda, hist., India	C4	53
Golconda, Il., U.S.	G9	120
Golconda, Nv., U.S.	C8	134
Gölcük, Tur.	C12	28
Gołdap, Pol.	B18	16
Gold Bridge, B.C., Can.	F8	138
Gold Coast see Southport, Austl.	F9	76
Gold Coast, cst., Ghana	I4	64
Golden, B.C., Can.	E13	138
Golden, Co., U.S.	B3	128
Golden, Il., U.S.	D7	120
Golden Bay, b., N.Z.	E5	80
Golden City, Mo., U.S.	G3	120
Goldendale, Wa., U.S.	E6	136
Golden Gate Highlands National Park, p.o.i., S. Afr.	F9	70
Golden Hinde, mtn., B.C., Can.	G5	138
Golden Lake, l., On., Can.	C12	112
Golden Meadow, La., U.S.	H8	122
Goldfield, Ia., U.S.	B3	120
Goldfield, Nv., U.S.	F8	134
Gold Mountain, mtn., Nv., U.S.	F8	134
Goldonna, La., U.S.	E5	122
Gold River, B.C., Can.	G4	138
Gold Rock, On., Can.	B6	118
Goldsboro, N.C., U.S.	A7	116
Goldston, N.C., U.S.	A6	116
Goldsworthy, Austl.	D3	74
Goldthwaite, Tx., U.S.	C9	130
Goleniów, Pol.	C10	16
Goleta, Ca., U.S.	I6	134
Golfito, C.R.	H6	102
Golfo de Santa Clara, Mex.	F5	98
Gölhisar, Tur.	F12	28
Goliad, Tx., U.S.	F10	130
Golicyno, Russia	E19	10
Golina, Pol.	D13	16
Golin Baixing, China	B4	38
Gölmarmara, Tur.	E10	28
Golmud, China	D3	36
Golmud, stm., China	A7	46
Golodnaja Guba, ozero, l., Russia	C24	8
Golovin, Ak., U.S.	D7	140
Golpāyegān, Iran	C7	56
Gölpazarı, Tur.	C13	28
Golub-Dobrzyń, Pol.	C14	16
Golva, N.D., U.S.	A8	126
Golyšmanovo, Russia	C11	32
Goma, D.R.C.	E5	66
Gomang Co, l., China	C12	54
Gomati, stm., India	E8	54
Gombe, Nig.	G7	64
Gombi, Nig.	G7	64
Gómez Farías, Mex.	A5	100
Gómez Palacio, Mex.	C7	100
Gómez Plata, Col.	D4	86
Gomo Co, l., China	B10	54
Gomogomo, Indon.	b1	79a
Gomoh, India	G10	54
Gonābād, Iran	C8	56
Gonaïves, Haiti	C11	102
Gonam, Russia	E15	34
Gonam, stm., Russia	E14	34
Gonarezhou National Park, p.o.i., Zimb.	B10	70
Gonâve, Golfe de la, b., Haiti	C11	102
Gonâve, Île de la, i., Haiti	C11	102
Gonbad-e Qābūs, Iran	B8	56
Gonda, India	E8	54
Gondal, India	G3	54
Gondar see Gonder, Eth.	E7	62
Gondarbal, India	A5	54
Gonder, Eth.	E7	62
Gondia, India	H8	54
Gönen, Tur.	C10	28
Gong, stm., China	I6	42
Gong'an, China	F4	42
Gongcheng, China	I4	42
Gongchenqiao, China	F8	42
Gonggar, China	D13	54
Gonghe, China	D5	36
Gongliu, China	F14	32
Gongola, stm., Nig.	G7	64
Gongshiya, China	C10	54
Gongxi, China	H6	42
Gongxian, China	D5	42
Gongzhuling, China	C6	38
Goñi, Ur.	F9	92
Goniądz, Pol.	C18	16
Gōnoura, Japan	F2	40
Gonzales, Ca., U.S.	G4	134
Gonzales, La., U.S.	G8	122
González, Mex.	D9	100
González Moreno, Arg.	G6	92
Goochland, Va., U.S.	G8	114
Goodenough Island, i., Pap. N. Gui.	b5	79a
Gooderham, On., Can.	D11	112
Goodeve, Sk., Can.	C10	124
Good Hope, Cape of (Goeie Hoop, Kaap die), c., S. Afr.	I4	70
Good Hope Mountain, mtn., B.C., Can.	E6	138
Goodhue, Mn., U.S.	G6	118
Goodland, Fl., U.S.	K4	116
Goodland, In., U.S.	K11	118
Goodland, Ks., U.S.	B7	128
Goodlands, Mb., Can.	E13	124
Goodman, Wi., U.S.	C1	112
Goodnews Bay, Ak., U.S.	E7	140
Goodnight, Co., U.S.	C4	128
Goodooga, Austl.	G6	76
Goodrich, N.D., U.S.	G13	124
Good Spirit Lake, l., Sk., Can.	C11	124
Goodview, Mn., U.S.	G7	118
Goodwater, Al., U.S.	D12	122
Goodyear, Az., U.S.	J4	132
Goole, Eng., U.K.	H12	12
Goolgowi, Austl.	I5	76
Goonda, Moz.	A11	70
Goondiwindi, Austl.	G8	76
Goongarrie, Austl.	F4	74
Goose, stm., N.D., U.S.	G17	124
Goose Creek, S.C., U.S.	C6	116
Goose Island, i., B.C., Can.	E2	138
Goose Lake, l., Sk., Can.	C6	124
Goose Lake, l., U.S.	B5	134
Gooty, India	D3	53
Gopālganj, Bngl.	G12	54
Gopālganj, India	E10	54
Gopichettipālaiyam, India	F3	53
Göppingen, Ger.	H5	16
Goqên, China	F4	36
Go Quao, Viet.	H7	48
Góra Kalwaria, Pol.	E17	16
Gorakhpur, India	E9	54
Goražde, Bos.	F5	26
Gorda, Punta, c., Cuba	A6	102
Gorda, Punta, c., Nic.	E6	102
Gordeevka, Russia	H14	10
Gordion, hist., Tur.	D15	28
Gordo, Al., U.S.	D11	122
Gordon, Ga., U.S.	D2	116
Gordon, Wi., U.S.	E7	118
Gordon, Lake, res., Austl.	o13	77a
Gordon Creek, stm., Ne., U.S.	E11	126
Gordon Downs, Austl.	C5	74
Gordon Horne Peak, mtn., B.C., Can.	E12	138
Gordonsville, Va., U.S.	F7	114
Gordonvale, Austl.	A5	76
Gore, N.S., Can.	E13	110
Goré, Chad	F3	62
Gorē, Eth.	F7	62
Gore, N.Z.	H3	80
Goreda, Indon.	F9	44
Goree, Tx., U.S.	H9	128
Gore Range, mts., Co., U.S.	H6	126
Goreville, Il., U.S.	G8	120
Gorgān, Iran	B7	56
Gorgona, Isla, i., Col.	F2	86
Gorgota, Rom.	E13	26
Gorham, Me., U.S.	G6	110
Gori, Geor.	F6	32
Gorica see Gorizia, Italy	E10	22
Goricy, Russia	C19	10
Gorinchem, Neth.	C14	14
Gorizia (Gorica), Italy	E10	22
Gorj, state, Rom.	E10	26
Gorkhā, Nepal	E10	54
Gorki see Nižnij Novgorod, Russia	H21	8
Gorki, Russia	A11	32
Gorkiy Reservoir see Gor'kovskoe vodohranilišče, res., Russia	H20	8
Gor'kovskoe vodohranilišče (Gorkiy Reservoir), res., Russia	H20	8
Gorlice, Pol.	G17	16
Görlitz, Ger.	E10	16
Gorman, Tx., U.S.	B9	130
Gorna Orjahovica, Blg.	F12	26
Gornjak, Russia	D14	32
Gornji Vakuf, Bos.	F4	26
Gorno-Altajsk, Russia	D15	32
Gornozavodsk, Russia	B13	36
Gornye Ključi, Russia	B10	38
Gorodec, Russia	H20	8
Gorodec, Russia	B12	10
Gorodno, Russia	C12	10
Goroka, Pap. N. Gui.	b4	79a
Gorong, Pulau, i., Indon.	F9	44
Gorongosa, stm., Moz.	B12	70
Gorongosa, Serra da, mtn., Moz.	D5	68
Gorontalo, Indon.	E7	44
Górowo Iławeckie, Pol.	B16	16
Gorškovo, Russia	F20	10
Görükle, Tur.	C11	28
Gorutuba, stm., Braz.	H4	88
Gorzów, state, Pol.	D11	16
Gorzów Śląski, Pol.	E14	16
Gorzów Wielkopolski (Landsberg), Pol.	D11	16
Goschen Strait, strt., Pap. N. Gui.	c5	79a
Gosen, Japan	B12	40
Gosford, Austl.	I8	76
Goshen, N.S., Can.	E15	110
Goshen, Ca., U.S.	G6	134
Goshen, In., U.S.	G4	112
Goshen, N.Y., U.S.	C11	114
Goshute Lake, l., Nv., U.S.	C2	132
Goshute Valley, val., Nv., U.S.	C2	132
Goslar, Ger.	E6	16
Gosnells, Austl.	F3	74
Gossinga, Sudan	F5	62
Gostivar, Mac.	B3	28
Gostynin, Pol.	D15	16
Göta, stm., Swe.	G5	8
Gotebo, Ok., U.S.	F10	128
Göteborg (Gothenburg), Swe.	H4	8
Gotemba, Japan	D11	40
Gotești, Mol.	C15	26
Gotha, Ger.	F6	16
Gothenburg see Göteborg, Swe.	H4	8
Gothenburg, Ne., U.S.	G12	126
Gothèye, Niger	G5	64
Gotland, state, Swe.	G8	8
Gotland, i., Swe.	H8	8
Gotō-rettō, is., Japan	F1	40
Gotska Sandön, i., Swe.	G8	8
Gōtsu, Japan	D5	40
Göttingen, Ger.	E5	16
Goubangzi, China	D4	38

Name	Map Ref.	Page
Gouda, Neth.	B13	14
Goudge, Arg.	G3	92
Goudiri, Sen.	G2	64
Gough Island, i., St. Hel.	K5	60
Gough Lake, l., Ab., Can.	D18	138
Gouin, Réservoir, res., Qc., Can.	B1	110
Goulais, stm., On., Can.	B6	112
Goulburn, Austl.	J7	76
Goulburn Islands, is., Austl.	B6	74
Goulburn River National Park, p.o.i., Austl.	I7	76
Gould, Ar., U.S.	D7	122
Goulds, Fl., U.S.	K5	116
Goumbou, Mali	G3	64
Goundam, Mali	F4	64
Goundi, Chad	F3	62
Gourbeyre, Guad.	h5	105c
Gourdon, Fr.	E7	18
Gouré, Niger	G7	64
Gourma-Rharous, Mali	F4	64
Gournay-en-Bray, Fr.	E10	14
Gouro, Chad	D3	62
Gouverneur, N.Y., U.S.	D14	112
Govan, Sk., Can.	C9	124
Gove, Ks., U.S.	C8	128
Govena, mys, c., Russia	E22	34
Govenlock, Sk., Can.	E4	124
Governador Valadares, Braz.	J5	88
Govind Ballabh Pant Reservoir see Govind Ballabh Pant Sāgar, res., India	F9	54
Govind Ballabh Pant Sāgar, res., India	F9	54
Govind Reservoir see Govind Sāgar, res., India	C6	54
Govind Sāgar, res., India	C6	54
Gowanda, N.Y., U.S.	B7	114
Gower, Mo., U.S.	E3	120
Gowmal (Gumal), stm., Asia	B2	54
Gowmal Kalay, Afg.	B2	54
Gowrie, Ia., U.S.	B3	120
Goya, Arg.	D8	92
Goyaves, Îlets à, is., Guad.	h5	105c
Göyçay, Azer.	A6	56
Goz Beïda, Chad	E4	62
Gozdnica, Pol.	E11	16
Gozha Co, l., China	A5	46
Gozo see Għawdex, i., Malta	H8	24
Graaff-Reinet, S. Afr.	H7	70
Grabo, C. Iv.	I3	64
Grabow, Ger.	C7	16
Grabów nad Prosną, Pol.	E13	16
Gračac, Cro.	F12	22
Gračanica, Bos.	E5	26
Grace, Id., U.S.	H15	136
Gracefield, Qc., Can.	B13	112
Graceville, Fl., U.S.	G13	122
Gracias a Dios, Cabo, c., N.A.	E6	102
Gradaús, Braz.	E7	84
Grado, Italy	E10	22
Grado, Spain	A4	20
Grad Sofija, state, Blg.	G10	26
Grady, Ar., U.S.	C7	122
Grady, N.M., U.S.	G5	128
Graettinger, Ia., U.S.	H4	118
Grafenau, Ger.	H9	16
Gräfenhainichen, Ger.	E8	16
Grafing bei München, Ger.	H7	16
Grafton, Austl.	G9	76
Grafton, Il., U.S.	F7	120
Grafton, N.D., U.S.	F16	124
Grafton, W.V., U.S.	E5	114
Grafton, Wi., U.S.	E2	112
Grafton, Cape, c., Austl.	A5	76
Graham, N.C., U.S.	H6	114
Graham, Mount, mtn., Az., U.S.	K7	132
Graham Island, i., B.C., Can.	E4	106
Graham Island, i., Nu., Can.	B7	141
Graham Lake, res., Me., U.S.	F8	110
Graham Land, reg., Ant.	B34	81
Graham Moore, Cape, c., Nu., Can.	A15	106
Grahamstad see Grahamstown, S. Afr.	H8	70
Grahamstown, S. Afr.	H8	70
Grain Coast, cst., Lib.	I3	64
Grainfield, Ks., U.S.	B8	128
Grajaú, Braz.	C2	88
Grajaú, stm., Braz.	B3	88
Grajewo, Pol.	C18	16
Gramada, Blg.	F9	26
Grambling, La., U.S.	E6	122
Gramilla, Arg.	C5	92
Grammichele, Italy	G8	24
Grampian Mountains, mts., Scot., U.K.	E9	12
Grampians National Park, p.o.i., Austl.	K3	76
Gramsh, Alb.	D14	24
Granada, Col.	F5	86
Granada, Nic.	G5	102
Granada, Spain	G7	20
Granada, Co., U.S.	C6	128
Granada, co., Spain	G7	20
Granadella see La Granadella, Spain	C11	20
Granbury, Tx., U.S.	B10	130
Granbury, Lake, res., Tx., U.S.	B10	130
Granby, Qc., Can.	E4	110
Granby, Co., U.S.	A3	128
Granby, Mo., U.S.	H3	120
Granby, stm., B.C., Can.	G12	138
Granby, Lake, res., Co., U.S.	A2	128
Gran Chaco, reg., S.A.	D5	90
Grand, stm., On., Can.	E9	112
Grand, stm., U.S.	E4	120
Grand, stm., Mi., U.S.	E3	112
Grand, stm., Oh., U.S.	C4	114
Grand, stm., S.D., U.S.	B12	126
Grand, East Fork, stm., U.S.	D3	120
Grand, Lac, l., Qc., Can.	A12	112
Grand, North Fork, stm., U.S.	B10	126
Grand, South Fork, stm., S.D., U.S.	B9	126
Grandas, Spain	A4	20
Grand Bahama, i., Bah.	B9	96
Grand Ballon, mtn., Fr.	G16	14
Grand Bank, Nf., Can.	j22	107a
Grand-Bassam, C. Iv.	H4	64
Grand Bay, Al., U.S.	G10	122
Grand Beach, Mb., Can.	D17	124
Grand Bend, On., Can.	E8	112
Grand-Bourg, Guad.	i6	105c
Grand Caille Point, c., St. Luc.	m6	105c
Grand Calumet, Île du, i., Qc., Can.	C13	112
Grand Canal see Da Yunhe, can., China	E8	42
Grand Canal, can., Ire.	H6	12
Grand Cane, La., U.S.	E5	122
Grand Canyon, Az., U.S.	G4	132
Grand Canyon, val., Az., U.S.	G4	132
Grand Canyon National Park, p.o.i., Az., U.S.	G4	132
Grand Case, Guad.	A1	105a
Grand Cayman, i., Cay. Is.	C7	102
Grand Cess, Lib.	I3	64
Grand Chenier, La., U.S.	H6	122
Grand Coulee Dam, dam, Wa., U.S.	C8	136
Grand Cul de Sac, Guad.	B2	105a
Grande, stm., Arg.	H3	92
Grande, stm., Arg.	A5	92
Grande, stm., Bol.	C4	90
Grande, stm., Braz.	F4	88
Grande, stm., Braz.	C7	90
Grande, stm., S.A.	J3	90
Grande, stm., Ven.	C11	86
Grande, Arroyo, stm., Ur.	F9	92
Grande, Bahía, b., Arg.	J3	90
Grande, Boca, mth., Ven.	C11	86
Grande, Cerro, mtn., Mex.	E7	100
Grande, Cerro, mtn., Mex.	G2	130
Grande, Ilha, i., Braz.	L3	88
Grande, Ilha, i., Braz.	A11	92
Grande, Ponta, c., Braz.	I6	88
Grande, Rio see Rio Grande, stm., N.A.	H13	98
Grande, Serra, mts., Braz.	D5	88
Grande-Anse, Qc., Can.	C4	110
Grande Cache, Ab., Can.	C11	138
Grande Cayemite, i., Haiti	C11	102
Grande de Manacapuru, Lago, l., Braz.	I11	86
Grande de Matagalpa, stm., Nic.	F6	102
Grande de Santiago, stm., Mex.	E6	100
Grande do Gurupá, Ilha, i., Braz.	D7	84
Grande-Entrée, Qc., Can.	C15	110
Grande Prairie, Ab., Can.	A12	138
Grand Erg de Bilma, des., Niger	F7	64
Grand Erg Occidental, des., Alg.	C5	64
Grand Erg Oriental, des., Alg.	C6	64
Grande-Rivière, Qc., Can.	B12	110
Grande Rivière, La, stm., Qc., Can.	E15	106
Grande Ronde, stm., U.S.	E9	136
Grandes, Salinas, pl., Arg.	A4	92
Grandes, Salinas, pl., Arg.	D5	92
Grand-Étang, N.S., Can.	D15	110
Grande-Terre, i., Guad.	h6	105c
Grande Vigie, Pointe de la, c., Guad.	g6	105c
Grand Falls, N.B., Can.	C9	110
Grandfather Mountain, mtn., N.C., U.S.	H4	114
Grandfield, Ok., U.S.	G10	128
Grand Forks, B.C., Can.	G12	138
Grand Forks, N.D., U.S.	D1	118
Grand Haven, Mi., U.S.	E3	112
Grandin, Lac, l., N.T., Can.	C7	106
Grand Island, Ne., U.S.	G14	126
Grand Island, i., Mi., U.S.	B3	112
Grand Isle, La., U.S.	H9	122
Grand Junction, Co., U.S.	D8	132
Grand Junction, Ia., U.S.	B3	120
Grand Lake, Co., U.S.	A3	128
Grand Lake, l., N.B., Can.	D11	110
Grand Lake, l., N.A.	E9	110
Grand Lake, l., La., U.S.	H6	122
Grand Lake, l., Mi., U.S.	C6	112
Grand Lake, res., Oh., U.S.	D1	114
Grand Ledge, Mi., U.S.	B1	114
Grand Manan, N.B., Can.	F10	110
Grand Manan Island, i., N.B., Can.	F10	110
Grand Marais, Mi., U.S.	B4	112
Grand Meadow, Mn., U.S.	H6	118
Grand-Mère, Qc., Can.	D4	110
Grand Morin, stm., Fr.	F12	14
Grand Portage, Mn., U.S.	D9	118
Grand Portage National Monument, p.o.i., Mn., U.S.	C9	118
Grand Prairie, Tx., U.S.	B11	130
Grand Rapids, Mb., Can.	A14	124
Grand Rapids, Mi., U.S.	F4	112
Grand Rapids, Mn., U.S.	D5	118
Grand Rhône, stm., Fr.	F10	18
Grand Saline, Tx., U.S.	E3	122
Grand Staircase--Escalante National Monument, p.o.i., Ut., U.S.	F5	132
Grand Teton, mtn., Wy., U.S.	G16	136
Grand Teton National Park, p.o.i., Wy., U.S.	F16	136
Grand Tower, Il., U.S.	G8	120
Grand Traverse Bay, b., Mi., U.S.	C4	112
Grand Turk, T./C. Is.	B12	102
Grandview, Mb., Can.	C13	124
Grandview, Mo., U.S.	F3	120
Grandview, Tx., U.S.	B10	130
Grandview, Wa., U.S.	D6	136
Grand View, Wi., U.S.	E7	118
Grand Wash Cliffs, clf, Az., U.S.	H3	132
Grañén, Spain	C10	20
Graneros, Chile	G2	92
Granger, Wa., U.S.	D6	136
Granger, Wy., U.S.	B6	132
Granger Draw, stm., Tx., U.S.	D7	130
Granger Lake, res., Tx., U.S.	D10	130
Granges see Grenchen, Switz.	C4	22
Grangeville, Id., U.S.	E10	136
Granite City, Il., U.S.	F7	120
Granite Falls, Mn., U.S.	G3	118
Granite Falls, N.C., U.S.	I4	114
Granite Falls, Wa., U.S.	B5	136
Granite Pass, p., Wy., U.S.	C5	126
Granite Peak, Austl.	E4	74
Granite Peak, mtn., Mt., U.S.	E14	136
Granite Peak, mtn., Mt., U.S.	E17	136
Granite Peak, mtn., Nv., U.S.	C6	134
Graniteville, S.C., U.S.	C4	116
Granitola, Capo, c., Italy	G6	24
Granja, Braz.	B5	88
Gran Laguna Salada, l., Arg.	H3	90
Gränna, Swe.	G6	8
Granollers, Spain	C13	20
Gran Paradiso, mtn., Italy	E4	22
Gran Paradiso, Parco Nazionale del, p.o.i., Italy	E4	22
Gran Rio, stm., Sur.	C6	84
Gran Sasso d'Italia, mts., Italy	H10	22
Gransee, Ger.	C9	16
Grant, Fl., U.S.	I5	116
Grant, Mi., U.S.	E4	112
Grant City, Mo., U.S.	D3	120
Grantham, Eng., U.K.	I12	12
Grantley Adams International Airport, Barb.	n9	105d
Grant Park, Il., U.S.	C10	120
Grant Point, c., Nu., Can.	B11	106
Grants, N.M., U.S.	H9	132
Grantsburg, Wi., U.S.	F6	118
Grants Pass, Or., U.S.	A2	134
Grant-Suttie Bay, b., Nu., Can.	B15	106
Grantsville, W.V., U.S.	F4	114
Grantville, Ga., U.S.	D14	122
Granum, Ab., Can.	G17	138
Granville, Fr.	F7	14
Granville, Il., U.S.	J9	118
Granville, N.D., U.S.	F13	124
Granville, W.V., U.S.	E5	114
Granville Lake, l., Mb., Can.	D10	106
Granvin, Nor.	F2	8
Grão Mogol, Braz.	I4	88
Grapeland, Tx., U.S.	F3	122
Grapevine Lake, res., Tx., U.S.	B10	130
Grapevine Peak, mtn., Nv., U.S.	G8	134
Gras, Lac de, l., N.T., Can.	C8	106
Gräsö, i., Swe.	F8	8
Grasonville, Md., U.S.	F9	114
Grass, stm., N.Y., U.S.	D15	112
Grass Creek, Wy., U.S.	D4	126
Grasse, Fr.	F12	18
Grassflat, Pa., U.S.	D7	114
Grasslands National Park, p.o.i., Sk., Can.	E6	124
Grass Valley, Ca., U.S.	D4	134
Grass Valley, Or., U.S.	E6	136
Grassy, Austl.	n12	77a
Grassy Plains, B.C., Can.	C4	138
Graulhet, Fr.	F7	18
Gravelbourg, Sk., Can.	E7	124
Gravelines, Fr.	D11	14
Gravelotte, S. Afr.	C10	70
Gravenhage, 's- see 's-Gravenhage, Neth.	B12	14
Gravenhurst, On., Can.	D10	112
Gravesend, Eng., U.K.	J13	12
Gravette, Ar., U.S.	H3	120
Gravina in Puglia, Italy	D10	24
Gray, Fr.	G14	14
Gray, Ga., U.S.	D2	116
Grayback Mountain, mtn., Or., U.S.	A2	134
Grayiske alper, mts., Eur.	D13	18
Grayling, Mi., U.S.	D5	112
Grays, Eng., U.K.	J13	12
Grays Harbor, b., Wa., U.S.	D2	136
Grays Lake, sw., Id., U.S.	G15	136
Grayson, Sk., Can.	D11	124
Grayson, Al., U.S.	C11	122
Grayson, La., U.S.	E6	122
Grays Peak, mtn., Co., U.S.	B3	128
Graysville, Tn., U.S.	B13	122
Grayville, Il., U.S.	F9	120
Graz, Aus.	C12	22
Grdelica, Yugo.	G9	26
Great Artesian Basin, bas., Austl.	E3	76
Great Australian Bight, b., Austl.	F5	74
Great Barrier Island, i., N.Z.	C6	80
Great Barrier Reef, rf., Austl.	C9	74
Great Basin, bas., U.S.	C4	108
Great Basin National Park, p.o.i., Nv., U.S.	E2	132
Great Bear, stm., N.T., Can.	B6	106
Great Bear Lake, l., N.T., Can.	B6	106
Great Beaver Lake, l., B.C., Can.	B7	138
Great Belt see Storebælt, strt., Den.	I4	8
Great Bend, Ks., U.S.	C10	128
Great Bitter Lake see Murrat el-Kubra, Buheirat, l., Egypt	H3	58
Great Britain see United Kingdom, ctry., Eur.	D8	6
Great Camanoe, i., Br. Vir. Is.	e8	104b
Great Central, B.C., Can.	G6	138
Great Channel, strt., Asia	G7	46
Great Dismal Swamp, sw., U.S.	H9	114
Great Divide Basin, bas., Wy., U.S.	F4	126
Great Dividing Range, mts., Austl.	C8	74
Great Driffield, Eng., U.K.	G12	12
Greater Antilles, is., N.A.	H15	94
Greater Khingan Range see Da Hinggan Ling, mts., China	B9	36
Greater Sunda Islands, is., Asia	F4	44
Great Exuma, i., Bah.	C9	96
Great Falls, Mb., Can.	D18	124
Great Falls, Mt., U.S.	C15	136
Great Falls, S.C., U.S.	B4	116
Great Himalayan National Park, p.o.i., India	C6	54
Great Inagua, i., Bah.	B11	102
Great Indian Desert (Thar Desert), des., Asia	D3	54
Great Karroo (Groot Karroo), plat., S. Afr.	H6	70
Great La Cloche Island, i., On., Can.	B8	112
Great Lake, res., Austl.	n13	77a
Great Malvern, Eng., U.K.	I10	12
Great Miami, stm., U.S.	E13	120
Great Namaqualand (Groot Namaland), hist. reg., Nmb.	D3	70
Great Nicobar, i., India	G7	46
Great Ouse, stm., Eng., U.K.	I13	12
Great Palm Island, i., Austl.	B6	76
Great Pee Dee, stm., S.C., U.S.	C6	116
Great Plain of the Koukdjuak, pl., Nu., Can.	B16	106
Great Plains, pl., N.A.	C4	108
Great Point, c., Ma., U.S.	C15	114
Great Ruaha, stm., Tan.	F7	66
Great Sacandaga Lake, res., N.Y., U.S.	G2	110
Great Sale Cay, i., Bah.	I7	116
Great Salt Lake, l., Ut., U.S.	B4	132
Great Salt Lake Desert, des., Ut., U.S.	C3	132
Great Salt Plains Lake, res., Ok., U.S.	E10	128
Great Sand Dunes National Monument, p.o.i., Co., U.S.	D3	128
Great Sand Hills, hills, Sk., Can.	D4	124
Great Sandy Desert, des., Austl.	D4	74
Great Sandy National Park, p.o.i., Austl.	E9	76
Great Scarcies, stm., Afr.	H2	64
Great Sea Reef, rf., Fiji	p19	79e
Great Slave Lake, l., N.T., Can.	C8	106
Great Smoky Mountains, mts., U.S.	A2	116
Great Smoky Mountains National Park, p.o.i., U.S.	A2	116
Great Tenasserim, stm., Mya.	F4	48
Great Thatch Island, i., Br. Vir. Is.	e7	104b
Great Tobago, i., Br. Vir. Is.	e7	104b
Great Victoria Desert, des., Austl.	E5	74
Great Wall see Chang Cheng, misc. cult., China	D6	36
Great Yarmouth, Eng., U.K.	I14	12
Gréboun, mtn., Niger	F6	64
Grecco, Ur.	F9	92
Gredos, Sierra de, mts., Spain	D5	20
Greece, N.Y., U.S.	E12	112
Greece, ctry., Eur.	H13	6
Greeley, Co., U.S.	G8	126
Greeley, Ks., U.S.	F2	120
Greeleyville, S.C., U.S.	C6	116
Greely Fiord, b., Nu., Can.	A9	141
Green, stm., U.S.	E7	132
Green, stm., Il., U.S.	C8	120
Green, stm., Ky., U.S.	G10	120
Green, stm., N.D., U.S.	G17	136
Green, stm., Wa., U.S.	C5	136
Green Bay, Wi., U.S.	D1	112
Green Bay, b., U.S.	D2	112
Greenbrier, Ar., U.S.	B6	122
Green Brier, Tn., U.S.	H11	120
Greenbrier, stm., W.V., U.S.	F5	114
Greenburg, La., U.S.	G8	122
Greenbush, Mn., U.S.	C2	118
Greencastle, In., U.S.	E10	120
Greencastle, Pa., U.S.	E8	114
Green Cove Springs, Fl., U.S.	G4	116
Greendale, In., U.S.	E13	120
Greene, Ia., U.S.	B5	120
Greeneville, Tn., U.S.	H3	114
Greenfield, Ca., U.S.	B13	114
Greenfield, Il., U.S.	E7	120
Greenfield, Ia., U.S.	C3	120
Greenfield, Ma., U.S.	H4	110
Greenfield, Mo., U.S.	G4	120
Greenfield, Oh., U.S.	E2	114
Greenfield, Ok., U.S.	F10	128
Green Forest, Ar., U.S.	H4	120
Green Island Bay, b., Phil.	E2	52
Green Islands, is., Pap. N. Gui.	D6	72
Green Lake, Wi., U.S.	H10	118
Green Lake, l., B.C., Can.	E9	138
Green Lake, l., Wi., U.S.	H9	118
Greenland, Ar., U.S.	I3	120
Greenland, dep., N.A.	B19	94
Greenland Basin, unds.	A14	144
Greenland Sea	B21	94
Greenleaf, Ks., U.S.	B11	128
Green Lookout Mountain, mtn., Wa., U.S.	E4	136
Green Mountains, mts., N.A.	G4	110
Greenock, Scot., U.K.	F8	12
Greenore Point, c., Ire.	I6	12
Greenough, stm., Austl.	E3	74
Greenport, N.Y., U.S.	C13	114
Green River, Pap. N. Gui.	a3	79a
Green River, Ut., U.S.	D7	132
Green River, Wy., U.S.	B7	132
Green River Lake, res., Ky., U.S.	G12	120
Greensboro, Fl., U.S.	G14	122
Greensboro, Ga., U.S.	C2	116
Greensboro, N.C., U.S.	H6	114
Greensburg, In., U.S.	E12	120
Greensburg, Ks., U.S.	D9	128
Greensburg, Pa., U.S.	D6	114
Green Springs, Oh., U.S.	C2	114
Green Swamp, sw., N.C., U.S.	B7	116
Greentown, In., U.S.	H4	112
Greenup, Il., U.S.	E9	120
Greenup, Ky., U.S.	F3	114
Greenvale, Austl.	B5	76
Green Valley, Az., U.S.	L6	132
Greenville, Lib.	H3	64
Greenville, Al., U.S.	F12	122
Greenville, Ga., U.S.	D14	122
Greenville, Il., U.S.	F8	120
Greenville, Ky., U.S.	G10	120
Greenville, Me., U.S.	E7	110
Greenville, Mi., U.S.	E4	112
Greenville, Ms., U.S.	D7	122
Greenville, Mo., U.S.	G7	120
Greenville, N.C., U.S.	A8	116
Greenville, Oh., U.S.	D1	114
Greenville, Pa., U.S.	C5	114
Greenville, S.C., U.S.	B3	116
Greenville, Tx., U.S.	D2	122
Greenwater Lake, l., On., Can.	C8	118
Greenwich, Ct., U.S.	C12	114
Greenwich, Oh., U.S.	C3	114
Greenwood, B.C., Can.	G12	138
Greenwood, Ar., U.S.	B4	122
Greenwood, In., U.S.	E11	120
Greenwood, Ms., U.S.	D8	122
Greenwood, S.C., U.S.	B3	116
Greenwood, Wi., U.S.	G8	118
Greenwood, Lake, res., S.C., U.S.	B4	116
Greer, S.C., U.S.	B3	116
Greers Ferry Lake, res., Ar., U.S.	B6	122
Greeson, Lake, res., Ar., U.S.	C5	122
Gregório, stm., Braz.	E3	84
Gregory, Mi., U.S.	B1	114
Gregory, S.D., U.S.	D13	126
Gregory, Tx., U.S.	G10	130
Gregory, stm., Austl.	C7	74
Gregory, Lake, l., Austl.	E3	74
Gregory, Lake, l., Austl.	D5	74
Gregory, Lake, l., Austl.	G2	76
Gregory Range, mts., Austl.	B4	76
Greifswald, Ger.	B9	16
Greifswalder Bodden, b., Ger.	B9	16
Greiz, Ger.	F8	16
Gremiha, Russia	B18	8
Grenå, Den.	H4	8
Grenada, Ms., U.S.	D9	122
Grenada, ctry., N.A.	q11	105e
Grenada Lake, res., Ms., U.S.	D9	122
Grenadines, is., N.A.	p11	105e
Grenchen, Switz.	C4	22
Grenen, c., Den.	H4	8
Grenfell, Austl.	I7	76
Grenoble, Fr.	D11	18
Grenola, Ks., U.S.	D12	128
Grenora, N.D., U.S.	F10	124
Grenville, Gren.	q10	105e
Gresham, Or., U.S.	E4	136
Gresik, Indon.	G8	50
Gresik, Indon.	E3	50
Gressåmoen Nasjonalpark, p.o.i., Nor.	D5	8
Gretna, Mb., Can.	E16	124
Gretna, La., U.S.	H8	122
Gretna, Va., U.S.	H6	114
Gretna Green, Scot., U.K.	F9	12
Greven, Ger.	D3	16
Grevená, Grc.	C4	28
Grevenbroich, Ger.	E2	16
Grevesmühlen, Ger.	C7	16
Greybull, stm., Wy., U.S.	C4	126
Grey Eagle, Mn., U.S.	F4	118
Grey Islands, is., Nf., Can.	i22	107a
Greylock, Mount, mtn., Ma., U.S.	B12	114
Greymouth, N.Z.	F4	80
Grey Range, mts., Austl.	F4	76
Greytown, S. Afr.	F10	70
Gribbel Island, i., B.C., Can.	C1	138
Gribingui, stm., C.A.R.	C3	66
Gridley, Ca., U.S.	D4	134
Gridley, Il., U.S.	D9	120
Griesheim, Ger.	G4	16
Griffin, Sk., Can.	E10	124
Griffin, Ga., U.S.	C1	116
Griffin, Lake, l., Fl., U.S.	H4	116
Griffith, Austl.	J5	76
Griggsville, Il., U.S.	E7	120
Grignols, Fr.	E5	18
Grigoriopol, Mol.	B16	26
Grijalva (Cuilco), stm., N.A.	G12	100
Grim, Cape, c., Austl.	n12	77a
Grimari, C.A.R.	C3	66
Grimma, Ger.	E8	16
Grimmen, Ger.	B9	16
Grimsby, On., Can.	E10	112
Grimsby, Eng., U.K.	H12	12
Grimsel Pass, p., Switz.	D5	22
Grímsey, i., Ice.	j30	8a
Grimshaw, Ab., Can.	D7	106
Grimstad, Nor.	G3	8
Grímsvötn, vol., Ice.	k31	8a
Grindelwald, Switz.	D5	22
Grinnell, Ia., U.S.	C5	120
Grinnell Peninsula, pen., Nu., Can.	B7	141
Grintavec, mtn., Slvn.	D11	22
Griqualand East, hist. reg., S. Afr.	G9	70
Griqualand West, hist. reg., S. Afr.	F6	70
Grise Fiord, Nu., Can.	B9	141
Gris-Nez, Cap, c., Fr.	D10	14
Griswold, Mb., Can.	E13	124
Griswold, Ia., U.S.	C2	120
Grizzly Bear Mountain, mtn., N.T., Can.	B6	106
Grizzly Mountain, mtn., Id., U.S.	C10	136
Grjadcy, Russia	D14	10
Grjazovec, Russia	G18	8
Groaíras, Braz.	B5	88
Groblersdal, S. Afr.	D9	70
Grodków, Pol.	F13	16
Grodzisk Mazowiecki, Pol.	D16	16
Groen, stm., S. Afr.	G6	70
Groesbeck, Tx., U.S.	F2	122
Grofa, hora, mtn., Ukr.	A10	26
Groix, Fr.	G5	14
Groix, Île de, i., Fr.	G5	14
Grójec, Pol.	E16	16
Grombalia, Tun.	H4	24
Gronau, Ger.	D3	16
Grong, Nor.	D5	8
Groningen, Neth.	A15	14
Groningen, Sur.	B6	84
Groom, Tx., U.S.	F7	128
Groot, stm., S. Afr.	H7	70
Groot-Berg, stm., S. Afr.	H4	70
Groot-Brakrivier, S. Afr.	I6	70
Grootdraaidam, res., S. Afr.	E9	70
Groote Eylandt, i., Austl.	B7	74
Grootfontein, Nmb.	D2	68
Grootgeluk, S. Afr.	C8	70
Groot Karasberge, mts., Nmb.	E4	70
Groot Karroo see Great Karroo, plat., S. Afr.	H6	70
Groot-Kei, stm., S. Afr.	H9	70
Groot Laagte, stm., Afr.	B5	70
Groot Namaland see Great Namaqualand, hist. reg., Nmb.	D3	70
Groot-Swartberge, mts., S. Afr.	H6	70
Groot-Vis, stm., S. Afr.	H8	70
Grootvloer, pl., S. Afr.	F5	70
Gros Islet, St. Luc.	I7	105c
Gros-Morne, Mart.	k6	105c
Gros Morne, mtn., Nf., Can.	j22	107a
Gros Piton, vol., St. Luc.	m6	105c
Grossenhain, Ger.	E9	16
Grosse Pointe, Mi., U.S.	B3	114
Grosse Pointe, c., Guad.	h6	105c
Grosser Beerberg, mtn., Ger.	F6	16
Grosseto, Italy	H7	22
Gross-Gerau, Ger.	G4	16
Grossglockner, mtn., Aus.	C9	22
Grossos, Braz.	C7	88
Grossvenediger, mtn., Aus.	C9	22
Groton, N.Y., U.S.	F13	112
Groton, S.D., U.S.	B14	126
Grottaglie, Italy	D11	24
Grottammare, Italy	G11	22
Grottoes, Va., U.S.	F7	114
Grouard Mission, Ab., Can.	D7	106
Groundhog, stm., On., Can.	F14	106
Grove City, Mn., U.S.	F4	118
Grove City, Oh., U.S.	E2	114
Grove City, Pa., U.S.	C5	114
Grove Hill, Al., U.S.	F11	122
Grove Mountains, mts., Ant.	C12	81
Grover City, Ca., U.S.	H5	134
Groves, Tx., U.S.	H5	122
Groveton, N.H., U.S.	F5	110
Groveton, Tx., U.S.	F3	122
Grovetown, Ga., U.S.	C3	116
Growa Point, c., Lib.	I3	64
Growler Peak, mtn., Az., U.S.	K3	132
Groznyj, Russia	F7	32
Grubišno Polje, Cro.	E14	22
Grudziądz, Pol.	C14	16
Grulla, Tx., U.S.	H9	130
Grumo Appula, Italy	D10	24
Grundy, Va., U.S.	G3	114
Grundy Center, Ia., U.S.	B5	120
Grušino, Russia	G21	8
Gruver, Tx., U.S.	E7	128
Gruznovka, Russia	E10	34
Gryfice, Pol.	C11	16
Gryfino, Pol.	C10	16
Grytviken, S. Geor.	J9	90
Guacanayabo, Golfo de, b., Cuba	B9	102
Guacara, Ven.	B7	86
Guacarí, Col.	F3	86
Gu Achi, Az., U.S.	K4	132
Guachiría, stm., Col.	E6	86
Guachochi, Mex.	B5	100
Guadajoz, stm., Spain	G6	20
Guadalajara, Mex.	E7	100
Guadalajara, Spain	D7	20
Guadalajara, co., Spain	D8	20
Guadalcanal, state, Sol. Is.	f8	79b
Guadalcanal, i., Sol. Is.	e9	79b
Guadalete, stm., Spain	H4	20
Guadalhorce, stm., Spain	G6	20
Guadalimar, stm., Spain	F7	20
Guadalmena, stm., Spain	F8	20
Guadalope, stm., Spain	D10	20
Guadalquivir, stm., Spain	H4	20
Guadalquivir, Marismas del, sw., Spain	G4	20
Guadalupe, Mex.	D7	100
Guadalupe, Mex.	C8	100
Guadalupe, Ca., U.S.	I5	134
Guadalupe, stm., Tx., U.S.	F11	130
Guadalupe, Isla, i., Mex.	G3	98
Guadalupe Bravos, Mex.	C1	130
Guadalupe Mountains, mts., U.S.	B3	130
Guadalupe Mountains National Park, p.o.i., Tx., U.S.	C3	130
Guadalupe Peak, mtn., Tx., U.S.	C3	130
Guadalupe Victoria, Mex.	C6	100
Guadalupe Victoria, Mex.	G6	130
Guadarrama, Puerto de, p., Spain	D6	20
Guadarrama, Sierra de, mts., Spain	D6	20
Guadeloupe, dep., N.A.	h15	96a
Guadeloupe Passage, strt., N.A.	g5	105c
Guadiana, stm., Eur.	G3	20
Guadiana Menor, stm., Spain	G7	20
Guadiato, stm., Spain	F5	20
Guadiela, stm., Spain	D8	20
Guadix, Spain	G7	20
Guafo, Isla, i., Chile	H1	90
Guaíba, Braz.	E12	92
Guaíba, est., Braz.	E12	92
Guaimaca, Hond.	E4	102
Guainía, state, Col.	F7	86
Guainía, stm., S.A.	F8	86
Guaiquinima, Cerro, mtn., Ven.	E10	86
Guaíra, Braz.	K1	88
Guaíra, Braz.	B10	92
Guairá, state, Para.	B9	92
Guairá, Salto del (Sete Quedas, Salto das), wtfl, S.A.	B10	92
Guáitara, stm., Col.	G3	86
Guaitecas, Islas, is., Chile	H2	90
Guajaba, Cayo, i., Cuba	B9	102
Guajará-Açu, Braz.	A1	88
Guajará-Mirim, Braz.	F4	84
Guaje, Laguna del, l., Mex.	B7	100
Gualaca, Pan.	H6	102
Gualaceo, Ec.	I2	86
Gualala, Ca., U.S.	E2	134
Gualdo Tadino, Italy	G9	22
Gualeguay, Arg.	F8	92
Gualeguay, stm., Arg.	F8	92
Gualeguaychú, Arg.	F8	92
Gualicho, Salina del, pl., Arg.	H4	90
Guam, dep., Oc.	j10	78c
Guamá, stm., Braz.	A1	88
Guamal, Col.	F5	86
Guamal, Col.	C4	86
Guaminí, Arg.	H6	92
Guam International Airport, Guam	i10	78c
Guamote, Ec.	H2	86
Guamúchil, Mex.	C4	100
Guamués, stm., Col.	G3	86
Gua Musang, Malay.	J5	48
Guanacaste, Cordillera de, mts., C.R.	G5	102
Guanaceví, Mex.	C6	100
Guanahacabibes, Golfo de, b., Cuba	A5	102
Guana Island, i., Br. Vir. Is.	e8	104b
Guanaja, Hond.	D5	102
Guanaja, Isla de, i., Hond.	D5	102
Guanajuato, Mex.	E8	100
Guanajuato, state, Mex.	E8	100
Guanambi, Braz.	H4	88
Guanaparo, Caño, stm., Ven.	C7	86
Guañape, Islas, is., Peru	E2	84
Guanare, Ven.	C7	86
Guanare, stm., Ven.	C7	86
Guanarito, Ven.	C7	86
Guandacol, Arg.	D3	92
Guandu, China	I5	42
Guane, Cuba	A5	102
Guang'an, China	F2	42
Guangchang, China	H7	42
Guangde, China	F8	42
Guangdong, state, China	J6	42
Guangfeng, China	G8	42
Guangji, China	G6	42
Guangling, China	B6	42
Guangming Ding, mtn., China	F7	42
Guangnan, China	G5	36
Guangxi, state, China	G6	36
Guangxi Zhuangzu Zizhiqu see Guangxi, state, China	G6	36
Guangyuan, China	E1	42
Guangze, China	H7	42
Guangzhou (Canton), China	J5	42
Guanhães, Braz.	J4	88
Guánica, P.R.	C2	104a
Guanipa, stm., Ven.	C10	86
Guanta, Ven.	B9	86
Guantánamo, Cuba	B10	102
Guantao, China	C6	42
Guanting Shuiku, res., China	A6	42
Guanxian, China	E5	36
Guanxian, China	C6	42
Guanyun, China	D8	42
Guapi, Col.	F3	86
Guapiara, Braz.	B13	92
Guápiles, C.R.	G6	102
Guaporé, Braz.	D11	92
Guaporé (Iténez), stm., S.A.	F5	84
Guaqui, Bol.	C3	90
Guará, stm., Braz.	G3	88
Guarabira, Braz.	D8	88
Guaraciaba do Norte, Braz.	C5	88
Guaraciana, Braz.	I4	88
Guaranda, Ec.	H2	86
Guaraniaçu, Braz.	B11	92
Guarapari, Braz.	K5	88
Guarapuava, Braz.	B12	92
Guaraqueçaba, Braz.	B13	92
Guaratinguetá, Braz.	L3	88
Guaratuba, Braz.	B13	92
Guarda, Port.	D3	20
Guarda, state, Port.	D3	20
Guardafui, Cape see Gwardafuy, Gees, c., Som.	B10	66
Guardia Escolta, Arg.	D6	92
Guardiagrele, Italy	H11	22
Guardia Mitre, Arg.	H4	90
Guardo, Spain	B6	20
Guareña, Spain	F4	20
Guarenas, Ven.	B8	86
Guárico, state, Ven.	C8	86
Guárico, stm., Ven.	C8	86
Guárico, Embalse del, l., Ven.	C8	86
Guariquito, stm., Ven.	C8	86
Guarulhos, Braz.	L2	88
Guasare, stm., Ven.	B5	86
Guasave, Mex.	C4	100
Guasdualito, Ven.	D6	86
Guasipati, Ven.	D11	86
Guastalla, Italy	F7	22
Guatemala, Guat.	E2	102
Guatemala, ctry., N.A.	E2	102
Guatemala Basin, unds.	H29	142
Guateque, Col.	E5	86
Guatimozín, Arg.	F6	92
Guatopo, Parque Nacional, p.o.i., Ven.	B8	86
Guatuaro Point, c., Trin.	s13	105f
Guaviare, state, Col.	G5	86
Guaviare, stm., Col.	E8	86
Guaxupé, Braz.	K2	88
Guayabal, Cuba	B9	102
Guayabal, Ven.	D8	86
Guayabero, stm., Col.	F5	86
Guayacán, Chile	D2	92
Guayaguayare, Trin.	s12	105f
Guayama, P.R.	C3	104a
Guayana see Guyana, ctry., S.A.	C6	84
Guayana, Macizo de (Guiana Highlands), mts., S.A.	E10	86
Guayaneco, Archipiélago, is., Chile	I1	90
Guayanilla, P.R.	B2	104a
Guayape, stm., Hond.	E4	102
Guayapo, stm., Ven.	E8	86
Guayaquil, Ec.	I1	86
Guayaquil, Golfo de, b., S.A.	D1	84
Guayaramerín, Bol.	B3	90
Guayas, state, Ec.	H1	86
Guayas, stm., Ec.	I2	86
Guaymallén, Arg.	F3	92
Guaymas, Mex.	B3	100
Guaynabo, P.R.	B3	104a
Guayquiraró, stm., Arg.	E8	92
Guazapares, Mex.	B4	100
Guazárachi, Mex.	B5	100
Guba, D.R.C.	G5	66
Gubaha, Russia	C9	32
Gûbâi, Madîq (Jubal, Strait of), strt., Egypt	K4	58
Gubavica, wtfl, Cro.	G13	22
Gubbi, India	E3	53
Gubbio, Italy	G9	22
Guben, Ger.	E10	16
Gubin, Pol.	E10	16
Gucheng, China	E4	42
Gūdalūr, India	G3	53
Gúdar, Sierra de, mts., Spain	D10	20
Gudauta, Geor.	F6	32
Gudermes, Russia	F7	32
Gudivāda, India	C5	53

Name | Map Ref. | Page

Gudiyāttam, India E4 53
Güdül, Tur. C15 28
Gūdūr, India D4 53
Guebwiller, Fr. G16 14
Güéjar, stm., Col. F5 86
Guékédou, Gui. H2 64
Guélengdeng, Chad E3 62
Guelma, Alg. B6 64
Guelmime, Mor. D2 64
Guelph, On., Can. E9 112
Guérande, Fr. G6 14
Guercif, Mor. C4 64
Guerdjoumane, Djebel, mtn., Alg. H13 20
Güere, stm., Ven. C9 86
Guéréda, Chad E4 62
Guéret, Fr. C7 18
Guerla Mendata Shan, mtn., China C8 54
Guernesey see Guernsey, dep., Eur. L10 12
Guerneville, Ca., U.S. E3 134
Guernica see Gernika, Spain A8 20
Guernica y Luno see Gernika, Spain A8 20
Guernsey, dep., Eur. E6 14
Guernsey, i., Guern. E6 14
Guerrero, Mex. A5 100
Guerrero, Mex. F7 130
Guerrero, state, Mex. G8 100
Guerrero Negro, Mex. B1 100
Gueydan, La., U.S. G6 122
Guga, Russia F16 34
Gugē, mtn., Eth. F7 62
Guguan, i., N. Mar. Is. B5 72
Gui, stm., China I4 42
Guiana Basin, unds. G9 144
Guiana Highlands (Guayana, Macizo de), mts., S.A. E10 86
Güicán, Col. D5 86
Guichi, China F7 42
Guide, China D5 36
Guidimouni, Niger G6 64
Guiding, China H2 42
Guier, Lac de, l., Sen. F1 64
Guijuelo, Spain D5 20
Guilarte, Monte, mtn., P.R. B2 104a
Guildford, Eng., U.K. J12 12
Guildhall, Vt., U.S. F5 110
Guilford, Me., U.S. E7 110
Guilin, China I4 42
Guillaume-Delisle, Lac, l., Qc., Can. D15 106
Guillestre, Fr. E12 18
Guimarães, Braz. B3 88
Guimaras Island, i., Phil. E4 52
Guimba, Phil. C3 52
Guin, Al., U.S. D11 122
Guinan, China D5 36
Guindulman, Phil. F5 52
Guinea, ctry., Afr. G2 64
Guinea, Gulf of, b., Afr. I6 64
Guinea Basin, unds. H13 144
Guinea-Bissau, ctry., Afr. G1 64
Güines, Cuba A7 102
Guingamp, Fr. F5 14
Güinope, Hond. F4 102
Guiping, China J4 42
Guipúzcoa see Gipuzkoako, co., Spain A8 20
Guiratinga, Braz. G7 84
Güiria, Ven. B10 86
Guitry, C. Iv. H3 64
Guiuan, Phil. E5 52
Guixian, China J3 42
Guiyang, China I5 42
Guiyang, China H2 42
Güiza, stm., Col. G2 86
Guizhou, state, China F6 36
Gujarāt, state, India G3 54
Gūjar Khān, Pak. B4 54
Gujrānwāla, Pak. B4 54
Gujrāt, Pak. B4 54
Gukou, China H8 42
Gulargambone, Austl. H7 76
Gulbarga, India C3 53
Gulbene, Lat. C9 10
Güldüzü, Tur. B8 58
Guledagudda, India C2 53
Gülek Boğazı, p., Tur. A5 58
Gulf Islands National Seashore, p.o.i., U.S. G10 122
Gulfport, Ms., U.S. G9 122
Gulf Shores, Al., U.S. G11 122
Gulgong, Austl. I7 76
Gulian, China F13 34
Gulistan, Uzb. F11 32
Gulkana, Ak., U.S. D10 140
Gull, stm., On., Can. B9 118
Gullfoss, wtfl, Ice. k29 8a
Gull Lake, Sk., Can. D5 124
Gull Lake, l., Ab., Can. D17 138
Gull Lake, l., Mn., U.S. E4 118
Güllük, Tur. F10 28
Güllük Körfezi, b., Tur. F10 28
Gülpınar, Tur. D9 28
Gulu, Ug. D6 66
Guluogongba, China A10 54
Gumaca, Phil. D4 52
Gumal (Gowmal), stm., Asia B2 54
Gumbalie, Austl. G5 76
Gumdag, Turkmen. B7 56
Gumel, Nig. G6 64
Gumia, India G10 54
Gumma, state, Japan C11 40
Gummersbach, Ger. E3 16
Gümüşhane, Tur. A4 56
Gümüşsu, Tur. E12 28
Guna, India F6 54
Gundagai, Austl. J7 76
Gundji, D.R.C. D4 66
Gundlupet, India F3 53
Güney, Tur. C9 28
Güney, Tur. E12 28
Gungu, D.R.C. F3 66
Gunmi, Nig. G6 64
Gunnar, Sk., Can. D9 106
Gunnarn, Swe. D7 8
Gunnbjørn Fjeld, mtn., Grnld. D19 141
Gunnedah, Austl. H7 76
Gunnison, Ut., U.S. D5 132
Gunnison, stm., Co., U.S. E8 132
Gunong Mulu National Park, p.o.i., Malay. A9 50
Gun Point, c., Gren. p11 105e
Gunpowder Creek, stm., Austl. B2 76
Gunsan see Kunsan, Kor., S. F7 38
Guntakal, India D3 53
Guntersville, Al., U.S. C12 122
Guntersville Dam, dam, Al., U.S. C12 122
Guntersville Lake, res., Al., U.S. C12 122
Guntūr, India C5 53
Gunungkencana, Indon. G4 50
Gunungsahilan, Indon. C2 50
Gunungsitoli, Indon. L3 48
Gunupur, India B6 53
Günzburg, Ger. H6 16
Gunzenhausen, Ger. G6 16
Guo, stm., China E7 42
Guoyang, China E7 42
Guoyangzhen, China B5 42
Gupis, Pak. B11 56
Gurabo, P.R. B4 104a
Gura Humorului, Rom. B12 26
Gurais, India A5 54
Gurdāspur, India B5 54
Gurdon, Ar., U.S. D5 122
Güre, Tur. E12 28
Gurevsk, Russia D15 32
Gurgueia, stm., Braz. D4 88
Gurha, India F3 54
Guri, Embalse de, res., Ven. D10 86
Gurskoe, Russia F16 34
Gurskøya, i., Nor. E1 8
Gürsu, Tur. C12 28
Gurupá, Braz. D7 84
Gurupi, Braz. F1 88
Gurupi, stm., Braz. D8 84
Guru Sikhar, mtn., India F4 54
Gurvan Sayhan uul, mts., Mong. C5 36
Gusau, Nig. G6 64
Gusev, Russia F5 10
Gušgy, Turkmen. B9 56
Gushan, China B10 42
Gushi, China E6 42
Gus'-Hrustal'nyj, Russia I19 8
Gusino, Russia F14 10
Gusinoozersk, Russia F10 34
Gus'-Khrustal'nyy see Gus'-Hrustal'nyj, Russia I19 8
Guspini, Italy E2 24
Güssing, Aus. C13 22
Gustav Holm, Kap, c., Grnld. D19 141
Gustavus, Ak., U.S. E12 140
Gustine, Ca., U.S. F5 134
Gustine, Tx., U.S. C9 130
Güstrow, Ger. C8 16
Gütersloh, Ger. E4 16
Guthrie, Ok., U.S. F11 128
Guthrie, Tx., U.S. H8 128
Guthrie Center, Ia., U.S. C3 120
Gutian, China H8 42
Gutiérrez Zamora, Mex. E10 100
Guttenberg, Ia., U.S. B6 120
Guwāhāti, India E13 54
Guxian, China E5 42
Guyana, ctry., S.A. C6 84
Guyang, China A4 42
Guye, China B8 42
Guy Fawkes River National Park, p.o.i., Austl. H9 76
Guymon, Ok., U.S. E7 128
Guyot, Mount, mtn., U.S. I2 114
Guyra, Austl. H8 76
Guyton, Ga., U.S. D4 116
Guyuan, China D2 42
Guzar, Uzb. G11 32
Güzelyurt, N. Cyp. C3 58
Güzelyurt Körfezi, b., N. Cyp. C3 58
Guzhen, China E7 42
Guzmán, Mex. F9 98
Guzmán, Mex. F7 100
Gvardejsk, Russia F4 10
Gwa, Mya. D2 48
Gwaai, Zimb. D4 68
Gwādar, Pak. D9 56
Gwalia, Austl. E4 74
Gwalior (Lashkar), India E7 54
Gwanda, Zimb. B9 70
Gwane, D.R.C. D5 66
Gwangju see Kwangju, Kor., S. G7 38
Gwardafuy, Gees, c., Som. B10 66
Gwātar Bay, b., Asia E9 56
Gwayi, stm., Zimb. D4 68
Gwda, stm., Pol. C12 16
Gweedore, Ire. F4 12
Gweru, Zimb. D4 68
Gwinn, Mi., U.S. B2 112
Gwydir, stm., Austl. G7 76
Gyangtse see Gyangzê, China D12 54
Gyangzê, China D12 54
Gyaring Co, l., China C12 54
Gyaring Hu, l., China E4 36
Gyda, Russia B4 34
Gydanskaja guba, b., Russia B4 34
Gydanskij poluostrov, pen., Russia B4 34
Gyeongju see Kyŏngju, Kor., S. D2 40
Gyirong, China D10 54
Gyldenløves Fjord, b., Grnld. E17 141
Gym Peak, mtn., N.M., U.S. K9 132
Gympie, Austl. F9 76
Gyobingauk, Mya. C2 48
Gyoma, Hung. C7 26
Gyöngyös, Hung. B6 26
Győr (Raab), Hung. B4 26
Győr-Moson-Sopron, state, Hung. B4 26
Gypsum, Co., U.S. D10 132
Gypsum, Ks., U.S. C11 128
Gypsumville, Mb., Can. C15 124
Gyula, Hung. C8 26
Gyulafehérvár see Alba Iulia, Rom. C10 26
Gyzylarbat, Turkmen. B8 56

H

Haag in Oberbayern, Ger. H8 16
Haaksbergen, Neth. D2 16
Haapiti, Fr. Poly. v20 78h
Haapsalu, Est. G10 8
Haar, Ger. H7 16
Ha'Arava ('Arabah, Wādī al-), val., Asia H6 58
Ha'Arava (Jayb, Wādī al-), stm., Asia H6 58
Haarlem, Neth. B13 14
Habaqila, China C6 36
Habarovsk, Russia G16 34
Habary, Russia D13 32
Habashīyah, Jabal, mts., Yemen F7 56
Habbān, Yemen G6 56
Habermehl Peak, mtn., Ant. C6 81
Habiganj, Bngl. F13 54
Habomai Islands see Malaja Kuril'skaja Grjada, is., Russia C17 38
Hachijō-jima, i., Japan F12 40
Hachiman, Japan D9 40
Hachinohe, Japan D14 38
Hachiōji, Japan D12 40
Hackberry, La., U.S. H5 122
Hackberry Creek, stm., Ks., U.S. C8 128
Hackett, Ar., U.S. B4 122
Hackettstown, N.J., U.S. D11 114
Hadāli, Pak. B4 54
HaDarom, state, Isr. H5 58
Hadd, Ra's al-, c., Oman E8 56
Haddam, Ks., U.S. B11 128
Haddington, Scot., U.K. F10 12
Haddock, Ga., U.S. C2 116
Haddon Downs, Austl. F3 76
Hadejia, Nig. G7 64
Hadejia, stm., Nig. G6 64
Haden, Austl. F8 76
Hadera, Isr. F5 58
Haderslev, Den. I3 8
Hadībū, Yemen G7 56
Hadīthah, Iraq C5 56
Hadley Bay, b., Nu., Can. A9 106
Hadlock, Wa., U.S. B4 136
Ha Dong, Viet. B7 48
Hadramawt, reg., Yemen F6 56
Hadrian's Wall, misc. cult., Eng., U.K. G10 12
Hadzilavičy, Bela. G13 10
Haeju, Kor., N. E6 38
Haenam, Kor., S. G7 38
Haerhpin see Harbin, China B7 38
Haffner Bjerg, mtn., Grnld. B13 141
Hafford, Sk., Can. B6 124
Haffouz, Tun. I3 24
Hāfizābād, Pak. B4 54
Hāflong, India F14 54
Hafnarfjörður, Ice. k28 8a
Haft Gel, Iran C6 56
Hagan, Ga., U.S. D3 116
Hagari, stm., India D3 53
Hagemeister Island, i., Ak., U.S. E7 140
Hagen, Ger. E3 16
Hagenow, Ger. C7 16
Hagensborg, B.C., Can. D4 138
Hagerman, N.M., U.S. A3 130
Hagerstown, In., U.S. I4 112
Hagerstown, Md., U.S. E8 114
Hagersville, On., Can. F9 112
Hagfors, Swe. F5 8
Haggin, Mount, mtn., Mt., U.S. D13 136
Hagi, Japan E4 40
Ha Giang, Viet. A7 48
Hagondange, Fr. E15 14
Hags Head, c., Ire. I3 12
Hague, Sk., Can. B7 124
Hague, Cap de la, c., Fr. E7 14
Haguenau, Fr. F16 14
Hagues Peak, mtn., Co., U.S. G7 126
Hahira, Ga., U.S. F2 116
Hai'an, China E9 42
Haibei, China B10 36
Haicheng, China A10 42
Haichow Bay see Haizhou Wan, b., China D8 42
Haidargarh, India E8 54
Hai Duong, Viet. B8 48
Haifa see Hefa, Isr. F5 58
Haifa see Hefa, state, Isr. F5 58
Haifeng, China J6 42
Haig, Austl. F5 74
Haigler, Ne., U.S. A7 128
Haikang, China K3 42
Haikou, China K4 42
Haikou, China G9 42
Hā'il, Sau. Ar. D5 56
Hailākāndi, India F14 54
Hailar, China B8 36
Hailar, stm., China B8 36
Haileyville, Ok., U.S. C3 122
Hailin, China B8 38
Hailun, China B10 36
Hailuoto, i., Fin. D11 8
Haimen, China J7 42
Haimen, China G9 42
Hainan, state, China L3 42
Hainan Dao (Hainan Island), i., China L4 42
Hainan Island see Hainan Dao, i., China L4 42
Hainan Strait see Qiongzhou Haixia, strt., China K4 42
Haines, Ak., U.S. E12 140
Haines, Or., U.S. F8 136
Haines City, Fl., U.S. H4 116
Haines Junction, Yk., Can. C3 106
Haining, China F9 42
Hai Ninh, Viet. B8 48
Hai Phong, Viet. B8 48
Haiphong see Hai Phong, Viet. B8 48
Haiti, ctry., N.A. C11 102
Haitun, China D4 36
Haivoron, Ukr. A16 26
Haiyuan, China C1 42
Haizhou, China D8 42
Haizhou Wan, b., China D8 42
Hajdú-Bihar, state, Hung. B8 26
Hajdúböszörmény, Hung. B8 26
Hajdúnánás, Hung. B8 26
Hajdúszoboszló, Hung. B8 26
Hājīpur, India F10 54
Hajnówka, Pol. D19 16
Hakasija, state, Russia D16 32
Hakha, Mya. A1 48
Hakken-san, mtn., Japan E8 40
Hakodate, Japan D14 38
Hakone-yama, vol., Japan D12 40
Hakui, Japan C9 40
Haku-san, vol., Japan C9 40
Haku-san-kokuritsu-kōen, p.o.i., Japan C9 40
Hal see Halle, Bel. D13 14
Halab (Aleppo), Syria B8 58
Halab, state, Syria B8 58
Halachó, Mex. B2 102
Halahai, China B6 38
Halā'ib, Sudan C7 62
Halawa, Cape, c., Hi., U.S. B5 78a
Halberstadt, Ger. E7 16
Halbrite, Sk., Can. E10 124
Halcon, Mount, mtn., Phil. D3 52
Halden, Nor. G4 8
Haldensleben, Ger. D7 16
Haldimand, On., Can. F10 112
Haldwāni, India D7 54
Hale, Mo., U.S. E4 120
Haleakala Crater, crat., Hi., U.S. C5 78a
Haleakala National Park, p.o.i., Hi., U.S. C5 78a
Hale Center, Tx., U.S. G7 128
Halenkov, Czech Rep. G14 16
Halfmoon Bay, B.C., Can. G6 138
Halfway, Md., U.S. E8 114
Halfway, Or., U.S. F9 136
Halicarnassus, hist., Tur. F10 28
Halifax, Austl. B6 76
Halifax, N.S., Can. F13 110
Halifax, Eng., U.K. H11 12
Halifax, N.C., U.S. H8 114
Halifax, Va., U.S. H6 114
Halifax Bay, b., Austl. B6 76
Haliyāl, India D2 53
Halkapınar, Tur. A5 58
Halland, state, Swe. H5 8
Hallandale, Fl., U.S. K5 116
Hallānīyah, Juzur al- (Kuria Muria Islands), is., Oman F8 56
Halla-san, mtn., Kor., S. H7 38
Hall Basin, b., N.A. A13 141
Halle, Bel. D13 14
Halle, Ger. E7 16
Hällefors, Swe. G6 8
Hallein, Aus. C10 22
Hallettsville, Tx., U.S. E11 130
Halley, sci., Ant. C2 81
Halligen, is., Ger. B4 16
Hall in Tirol, Aus. C8 22
Hall Islands, is., Micron. C6 72
Hall Lake, l., Nu., Can. B14 106
Hall Land, reg., Grnld. A14 141
Hall Mountain, mtn., Wa., U.S. B9 136
Hallock, Mn., U.S. C2 118
Hallowell, Me., U.S. F7 110
Hall Peninsula, pen., Nu., Can. C17 106
Halls, Tn., U.S. I8 120
Hallsberg, Swe. G6 8
Halls Creek, Austl. C5 74
Hallstahammar, Swe. G7 8
Hallstavik, Swe. F8 8
Hallstead, Pa., U.S. C10 114
Hallsville, Mo., U.S. E5 120
Halmahera, i., Indon. E8 44
Halmahera, Laut (Halmahera Sea), Indon. F8 44
Halmahera Sea see Halmahera, Laut, Indon. F8 44
Hal'mer-Ju, Russia A10 32
Halmstad, Swe. H5 8
Haloŭčyn, Bela. F12 10
Hal'šany, Bela. F8 10
Halsey, Ne., U.S. F12 126
Halsey, Or., U.S. F3 136
Halstead, Ks., U.S. D11 128
Haltern, Ger. E3 16
Haltiatunturi, mtn., Eur. B9 8
Haltom City, Tx., U.S. B10 130
Halton Hills see Georgetown, On., Can. E9 112
Halvorson, Mount, mtn., B.C., Can. C10 138
Ham, stm., Nmb. F4 70
Hamada, Japan E4 40
Hamadān, Iran C6 56
Hamāh, Syria C7 58
Hamāh, state, Syria C8 58
Hamamatsu, Japan E10 40
Haman, Kor., S. D1 40
Hamana-ko, l., Japan E10 40
Hamar, Nor. F4 8
Ha Marakabei, Leso. F9 70
Hamar-Daban, hrebet, mts., Russia F9 34
Hamburg, Ger. C6 16
Hamburg, Ar., U.S. D7 122
Hamburg, Ia., U.S. D2 120
Hamburg, N.J., U.S. C11 114
Hamburg, N.Y., U.S. B7 114
Hamburg, state, Ger. C6 16
Hamden, Ct., U.S. C13 114
Hamden, Oh., U.S. E3 114
Häme, state, Fin. F11 8
Hämeenlinna (Tavastehus), Fin. F10 8
Hamelin, Austl. E2 74
Hameln, Ger. D5 16
HaMerkaz, state, Isr. F5 58
Hamersley Range, mts., Austl. D3 74
Hamgyŏng-sanjulgi, mts., Kor., N. D8 38
Hamhŭng, Kor., N. E7 38
Hami, China C3 36
Hamilton, Austl. K4 76
Hamilton, Ber. k15 104e
Hamilton, On., Can. E10 112
Hamilton, N.Z. C6 80
Hamilton, Scot., U.K. F8 12
Hamilton, Al., U.S. C11 122
Hamilton, Ga., U.S. E14 122
Hamilton, Il., U.S. D6 120
Hamilton, Mi., U.S. F4 112
Hamilton, Mo., U.S. E3 120
Hamilton, Mt., U.S. D12 136
Hamilton, N.Y., U.S. B10 114
Hamilton, Oh., U.S. E1 114
Hamilton, stm., Austl. D3 76
Hamilton, Lake, res., Ar., U.S. C5 122
Hamilton, Mount, mtn., Ca., U.S. F4 134
Hamilton City, Ca., U.S. D3 134
Hamilton Dome, Wy., U.S. D4 126
Hamilton Hotel, Austl. D3 76
Hamilton Mountain, mtn., N.Y., U.S. G2 110
Hamina, Fin. F12 8
Hamiota, Mb., Can. D13 124
Hamīrpur, India F7 54
Hamlin, Tx., U.S. B7 130
Hamlin, W.V., U.S. F3 114
Hamlin Valley Wash, stm., U.S. E3 132
Hamm, Ger. E3 16
Hammamet, Tun. H4 24
Hammamet, Golfe de, b., Tun. H4 24
Hammam Lif, Tun. H4 24
Hammelburg, Ger. F5 16
Hammerdal, Swe. E6 8
Hammerfest, Nor. A10 8
Hammon, Ok., U.S. F9 128
Hammond, In., U.S. G2 112
Hammond, La., U.S. G8 122
Hammondsport, N.Y., U.S. F12 112
Hampden, Me., U.S. F8 110
Hampden, N.D., U.S. F15 124
Hampi, India D3 53
Hampshire, Il., U.S. I10 118
Hampstead, N.C., U.S. B8 116
Hampton, N.B., Can. E11 110
Hampton, Ar., U.S. D6 122
Hampton, Fl., U.S. G3 116
Hampton, Ga., U.S. C1 116
Hampton, Ne., U.S. G15 126
Hampton, N.H., U.S. H6 110
Hampton, Tn., U.S. H3 114
Hampton, Va., U.S. G9 114
Hampton Butte, mtn., Or., U.S. G6 136
Hampton Tableland, plat., Austl. F5 74
Hamra, Swe. F6 8
Hamrā', Al-Hamādah al-, des., Libya B2 62
Hamra, As Saquia al, stm., W. Sah. D2 64
Hamsara, stm., Russia D16 32
Hams Fork, stm., Wy., U.S. F2 126
Hamta, Gebel (Hamāṭah, Jabal), mtn., Egypt C6 62
Ham Tan, Viet. G8 48
Hāmūn, Daryācheh-ye, l., Iran C9 56
Han, stm., China I7 42
Han, stm., China F6 42
Han, Nong, l., Thai. D7 48
Hana, Hi., U.S. C6 78a
Hanahan, S.C., U.S. D5 116
Hanamaki, Japan E14 38
Hanauni see Anglem, Mount, mtn., N.Z. H2 80
Hanapepe, Hi., U.S. B2 78a
Hanateio, Fr. Poly. s18 78g
Hanatetena, Fr. Poly. s18 78g
Hanau am Main, Ger. F4 16
Hanbury, stm., N.T., Can. C9 106
Hancavičy, Bela. H9 10
Hânceşti, Mol. C15 26
Hanceville, Al., U.S. C12 122
Hancheng, China D7 36
Hanchuang, China D4 42
Hanchung see Hanzhong, China E2 42
Hancock, Md., U.S. E7 114
Hancock, Mi., U.S. D10 118
Hancock, Mn., U.S. F3 118
Hancock, N.Y., U.S. C10 114
Handa, Japan E9 40
Handan, China C6 42
Handlová, Slov. H14 16
Handsworth, Sk., Can. E10 124
Handyga, Russia D16 34
HaNegev (Negev Desert), reg., Isr. H5 58
Hanford, Ca., U.S. G6 134
Hanga Roa, Chile e29 78l
Hangayn nuruu, mts., Mong. B4 36
Hangchou see Hangzhou, China F9 42
Hangchow see Hangzhou, China F9 42
Hangchow Bay see Hangzhou Wan, b., China F9 42
Hanggin Houqi, China A2 42
Hanggin Qi, China B3 42
Hangman Creek, stm., U.S. C9 136
Hangö see Hanko, Fin. G10 8
Hangu, China B7 42
Hangu, Pak. B3 54
Hanguang, China I5 42
Hangzhou, China F9 42
Hangzhou Wan, b., China F9 42
Hanino, Russia F19 10
Hanīsh, is., Yemen G5 56
Hanish Islands see Hanīsh, is., Yemen G5 56
Hanjiang, China I8 42
Hankinson, N.D., U.S. E2 118
Hanko, Fin. G10 8
Hankow see Wuhan, China F6 42
Hanku see Hangu, China B7 42
Hānle, India B7 54
Hanley, Sk., Can. C7 124
Hanna, Ab., Can. E19 138
Hanna, Ok., U.S. B3 122
Hanna, Wy., U.S. B10 132
Hanna City, Il., U.S. D8 120
Hannah, N.D., U.S. F15 124
Hannah Bay, b., On., Can. E14 106
Hannibal, Mo., U.S. E6 120
Hannover, Ger. D5 16
Ha Noi (Hanoi), Viet. B7 48
Hanoi see Ha Noi, Viet. B7 48
Hanover, On., Can. D8 112
Hanover see Hannover, Ger. D5 16
Hanover, S. Afr. G7 70
Hanover, Il., U.S. B7 120
Hanover, In., U.S. F12 120
Hanover, N.H., U.S. G4 110
Hanover, N.M., U.S. K8 132
Hanover, Pa., U.S. E9 114
Hanover, Va., U.S. G8 114
Hanover, Isla, i., Chile J2 90
Hansdiha, India F11 54
Hānsi, India D5 54
Hanska, Mn., U.S. G4 118
Hantajskoe, ozero, l., Russia C6 34
Hantan see Handan, China C6 42
Hantau, Kaz. F12 32
Hantsport, N.S., Can. E12 110
Hanty-Mansijsk, Russia B11 32
Hantzsch, stm., Nu., Can. B16 106
Hanumāngarh, India C3 46
Hanumangarh, India D4 54
Hanuy, stm., Mong. B5 36
Hanyin, China E3 42
Hanzhong, China E2 42
Hanzhuang, China D7 42
Haojiadian, China F5 42
Haoli see Hegang, China B11 36
Hāora, India G12 54
Haparanda, Swe. D10 8
Hapčeranga, Russia G11 34
Happy, Tx., U.S. G7 128
Happy Jack, Az., U.S. I5 132
Happy Valley-Goose Bay, Nf., Can. E18 106
Hāpur, India D6 54
Haql, Sau. Ar. I5 58
Harad, Sau. Ar. E6 56
Haradok, Bela. E13 10
Haradzec, Bela. H7 10
Haradzec, Bela. G13 10
Haradzišča, Bela. G9 10
Haramachi, Japan B13 40
Haranor, Russia A8 36
Harar see Härer, Eth. F8 62
Harare, Zimb. D5 68
Harazé Mangueigne, Chad E4 62
Harbala, Russia D13 34
Harbavičy, Bela. G13 10
Harbin, China B7 38
Harbiye, Tur. B7 58
Harbor, Or., U.S. A1 134
Harbor Beach, Mi., U.S. E7 112
Harbour Breton, Nf., Can. j22 107a
Harbourville, N.S., Can. E12 110
Harda, India G6 54
Hardangerfjorden, b., Nor. F2 8
Hardangerjøkulen, ice, Nor. F2 8
Hardangervidda Nasjonalpark, p.o.i., Nor. F2 8
Hardap, state, Nmb. D3 70
Hardeeville, S.C., U.S. D4 116
Harderwijk, Neth. B14 14
Hardin, Il., U.S. E7 120
Hardin, Mt., U.S. B5 126
Harding, S. Afr. G9 70
Harding, Lake, res., U.S. E13 122
Hardinsburg, Ky., U.S. G11 120
Hardisty Lake, l., N.T., Can. C7 106
Hardoi, India E7 54
Hardtner, Ks., U.S. D10 128
Hardwick, Ga., U.S. C2 116
Hardwick, Vt., U.S. F4 110
Hardy, Ar., U.S. H6 120
Hardy, Ne., U.S. A11 128
Hardy Bay, b., N.T., Can. B16 140
Hare Bay, b., Nf., Can. i22 107a
Hare Indian, stm., N.T., Can. B5 106
Hareøen, i., Grnld. C14 141
Härer, Eth. F8 62
Hargeysa, Som. C8 66
Harghita, state, Rom. C12 26
Har Hu, l., China D4 36
Hari, stm., Indon. D3 50
Harib, Yemen G6 56
Haridwār, India D7 54
Harihar, India D2 53
Harim, Syria B7 58
Harīpur, Pak. B4 54
Harīrūd (Tedžen), stm., Asia C9 56
Harischandra Range, mts., India B1 53
Haritonovo, Russia F22 8
Harkers Island, N.C., U.S. B9 116
Harlan, Ky., U.S. H2 114
Harlan County Lake, res., Ne., U.S. A9 128
Harlem, Fl., U.S. J5 116
Harlem, Ga., U.S. C3 116
Harleton, Tx., U.S. E4 122
Harlingen, Neth. A14 14
Harlingen, Tx., U.S. H10 130
Harlovka, Russia B17 8
Harlow, Eng., U.K. J13 12
Harlowton, Mt., U.S. D17 136
Harman, W.V., U.S. F6 114
Harmancık, Tur. D12 28
Harmanli, Blg. H12 26
Harmony, In., U.S. E10 120
Harnai, India C1 53
Harney Basin, bas., Or., U.S. G8 136
Harney Lake, l., Or., U.S. G7 136
Harney Peak, mtn., S.D., U.S. D9 126
Härnösand, Swe. E8 8
Har nuur, l., Mong. B3 36
Haro, Spain B8 20
Haro, Cabo, c., Mex. B3 100
Harovsk, Russia F18 8
Harpanahalli, India D3 53
Harper, Lib. I3 64
Harper, Ks., U.S. D10 128
Harper, Tx., U.S. D8 130
Harper, Mount, mtn., Ak., U.S. D11 140
Harqin Qi, China D3 38
Harrai, India G7 54
Harricana, stm., Can. E15 106
Harriman, Tn., U.S. I13 120
Harrington, De., U.S. F10 114
Harrington, Me., U.S. F9 110
Harris, Sk., Can. C6 124
Harris, Monts. D3 105a
Harris, Mn., U.S. F5 118
Harris, reg., Scot., U.K. D6 12
Harris, Lake, l., Fl., U.S. H4 116
Harrisburg, Ar., U.S. B8 122
Harrisburg, Il., U.S. F9 120
Harrisburg, Or., U.S. F3 136
Harrisburg, Pa., U.S. D8 114
Harrismith, S. Afr. F9 70
Harrison, Ar., U.S. H4 120
Harrison, Mi., U.S. D5 112
Harrison, Ne., U.S. E9 126
Harrison Bay, b., Ak., U.S. B9 140
Harrisonburg, La., U.S. F7 122
Harrisonburg, Va., U.S. F6 114
Harrison Islands, is., Nu., Can. B13 106
Harrison Lake, l., B.C., Can. G9 138
Harriston, On., Can. E9 112
Harriston, Ms., U.S. F7 122
Harrisville, N.Y., U.S. D14 112
Harrisville, W.V., U.S. E4 114
Harrodsburg, Ky., U.S. G13 120
Harrogate, Eng., U.K. H11 12
Harrold, Tx., U.S. G9 128
Harrowsmith, On., Can. D13 112
Harry S. Truman Reservoir, res., Mo., U.S. F4 120
Har Sai Shan, mtn., China D4 36
Harsīn, Iran C6 56
Hârşova, Rom. E14 26
Harstad, Nor. B7 8
Harsūd, India G6 54
Hart, Mi., U.S. E3 112
Hart, Tx., U.S. G6 128
Hart, stm., Yk., Can. B3 106
Hartbees, stm., S. Afr. F5 70
Hartberg, Aus. C12 22
Hartford, Ar., U.S. C4 122
Hartford, Ct., U.S. C13 114
Hartford, Ks., U.S. F2 120
Hartford, Mi., U.S. F3 112
Hartford, S.D., U.S. H2 118
Hartford, Wi., U.S. H10 118
Hartford City, In., U.S. H4 112
Hartland, N.B., Can. D9 110
Hartland, Me., U.S. F7 110
Hartlepool, Eng., U.K. G11 12
Hartley, Ia., U.S. H3 118
Hartley Bay, B.C., Can. C1 138
Hart Mountain, mtn., Mb., Can. B12 124
Hartney, Mb., Can. E13 124
Harts, stm., S. Afr. E7 70
Hartselle, Al., U.S. C12 122
Hartshorne, Ok., U.S. C3 122
Hartsville, S.C., U.S. B5 116
Hartville, Mo., U.S. G5 120
Hartwell, Ga., U.S. B3 116
Hartwell Lake, res., U.S. B2 116
Hartz Mountains National Park, p.o.i., Austl. o13 77a
Hārūnābād, Pak. D4 54
Haruniye, Tur. A7 58
Harūr, India E4 53
Har-Us nuur, l., Mong. B3 36
Hārūt, stm., Afg. C9 56
Harvard, Ne., U.S. G14 126
Harvey, N.B., Can. E12 110
Harvey, Il., U.S. G2 112
Harvey, N.D., U.S. G14 124
Harwich, Eng., U.K. J14 12
Haryāna, state, India D6 54
Haryn', stm., Eur. H10 10
Harz, mts., Ger. E6 16
Hasavjurt, Russia F7 32
Hasdo, stm., India G9 54
Hase, stm., Ger. D3 16
Hasenkamp, Arg. E8 92
Hashima, Japan D9 40
Hashimoto, Japan E8 40
Hāsilpur, Pak. D4 54
Haskell, Ok., U.S. I2 120
Haskell, Tx., U.S. A8 130
Haskovo, Blg. H12 26
Haskovo, state, Blg. H12 26
Haslemere, Eng., U.K. J12 12
Hasperos Canyon, val., N.M., U.S. H3 128
Haşş, Jabal al-, hill, Syria C8 58
Hassa, Tur. B7 58
Hassan, India E3 53
Hassayampa, stm., Az., U.S. J4 132
Hassel Sound, strt., Nu., Can. B6 141
Hasselt, Bel. D14 14
Hassfurt, Ger. F6 16
Hassi Messaoud, Alg. C6 64
Hässleholm, Swe. H5 8
Hastings, Barb. n8 105d
Hastings, On., Can. D11 112
Hastings, N.Z. D7 80
Hastings, Eng., U.K. K13 12
Hastings, Mi., U.S. F4 112
Hastings, Mn., U.S. G6 118
Hastings, Ne., U.S. G14 126
Haswell, Co., U.S. C5 128
Hatanga, Russia B9 34
Hatanga, stm., Russia B9 34
Hatangskij zaliv, b., Russia B10 34
Hatay (Antioch), Tur. B7 58
Hatay, state, Tur. B7 58
Hatch, N.M., U.S. K9 132
Hatch, Ut., U.S. F4 132
Hat Chao Mai National Park, p.o.i., Thai. I4 48
Hatchie, stm., U.S. B9 122
Hatfield, Austl. I4 76
Hatfield, Ar., U.S. C4 122
Hatfield, Ma., U.S. B13 114
Hatgal, Mong. F9 34
Hāthras, India E7 54
Ha Tien, Viet. G7 48
Hatillo, P.R. A2 104a
Ha Tinh, Viet. C7 48
Hatip, Tur. F15 28
Hato, Bocht van, b., Neth. Ant. p21 104g
Hato Mayor del Rey, Dom. Rep. C13 102
Hāt Pīplia, India G6 54
Hatta, India F7 54
Hatteras, N.C., U.S. A10 116
Hatteras, Cape, c., N.C., U.S. A10 116
Hatteras Island, i., N.C., U.S. A10 116
Hattiesburg, Ms., U.S. F9 122
Hatton, Al., U.S. C11 122
Hatton, N.D., U.S. G16 124
Hatunsaray, Tur. A3 58
Hatvan, Hung. B6 26
Hat Yai, Thai. I5 48
Hatyrka, Russia D24 34
Haugesund, Nor. G1 8
Haukeligrend, Nor. G2 8
Haukivesi, l., Fin. E12 8
Hauraki Gulf, b., N.Z. C6 80
Hausach, Ger. H4 16
Haut, Isle au, i., Me., U.S. F8 110
Haut Atlas, mts., Mor. C3 64
Haute-Corse, state, Fr. G15 18
Haute-Garonne, state, Fr. F7 18
Haute-Loire, state, Fr. D9 18
Haute-Marne, state, Fr. F14 14
Hautes-Alpes, state, Fr. E12 18
Haute-Saône, state, Fr. G14 14
Haute-Savoie, state, Fr. C12 18
Hautes-Pyrénées, state, Fr. F6 18
Haute-Vienne, state, Fr. D7 18
Haut-Rhin, state, Fr. G16 14
Haut Sheila, N.B., Can. C11 110
Hauts Plateaux, reg., Afr. C5 64
Hauula, Hi., U.S. B4 78a
Hauwāret el-Maqta', Egypt I1 58
Havana see La Habana, Cuba A6 102
Havana, Fl., U.S. G14 122
Havana, Il., U.S. D7 120
Havana, N.D., U.S. B15 126
Havannah, Canal de la, strt., N. Cal. n16 79d
Havant, Eng., U.K. K12 12

Name — Map Ref. — Page

Havast, Uzb. F11 32
Havasu, Lake, res., U.S. I2 132
Havasu Creek, stm., Az., U.S. H4 132
Havel, stm., Ger. D8 16
Havelberg, Ger. D8 16
Haveli, Pak. C4 54
Havelland, reg., Ger. D8 16
Havelock, On., Can. D12 112
Havelock, N.C., U.S. B8 116
Haverfordwest, Wales, U.K. J7 12
Haverhill, Eng., U.K. I13 12
Haverhill, Ma., U.S. B14 114
Hāveri, India D2 53
Haviland, Ks., U.S. D9 128
Havířov, Czech Rep. G14 16
Havlíčkův Brod, Czech Rep. G11 16
Havre see Le Havre, Fr. E8 14
Havre, Mt., U.S. B17 136
Havre-Aubert, Qc., Can. C15 110
Havre Aubert, Île du, i., Qc., Can. C14 110
Havre de Grace, Md., U.S. E9 114
Havre North, Mt., U.S. B17 136
Havsa, Tur. B9 28
Haw, stm., N.C., U.S. A7 116
Hawaii, state, U.S. B5 78a
Hawaii, i., Hi., U.S. C6 78a
Hawaiian Islands, is., Hi., U.S. C4 78a
Hawaiian Ridge, unds. G21 142
Hawaii Volcanoes National Park, p.o.i., Hi., U.S. D6 78a
Hawarden, Sk., Can. C7 124
Hawea, Lake, l., N.Z. G3 80
Hawera, N.Z. D6 80
Hawesville, Ky., U.S. G11 120
Hawi, Hi., U.S. C6 78a
Hawick, Scot., U.K. F10 12
Hawke, Cape, c., Austl. I9 76
Hawke Bay, b., N.Z. D7 80
Hawker, Austl. H2 76
Hawkes, Mount, mtn., Ant. D36 81
Hawkesbury, On., Can. E2 110
Hawkesbury Island, i., B.C., Can. C1 138
Hawkeye, Ia., U.S. B6 120
Hawkins, Tx., U.S. E3 122
Hawkins, Wi., U.S. F8 118
Haw Knob, mtn., U.S. A1 116
Hawksbill Creek, b., Bah. J7 116
Hawkwood, Austl. E8 76
Hawley, Mn., U.S. E2 118
Hawley, Pa., U.S. C10 114
Hawthorne, Fl., U.S. G3 116
Hawthorne, Nv., U.S. E7 134
Hawwâret'Adlan, Egypt I1 58
Hay, Austl. J5 76
Hay, stm., Austl. D7 74
Hay, stm., Can. D7 106
Hay, Cape, c., N.T., Can. B17 140
Hayang, Kor., S. D1 40
Hayange, Fr. E14 14
Haybān, Jabal, mtn., Sudan E6 62
Haydarlı, Tur. E13 28
Hayden, Co., U.S. C9 132
Haydenville, Oh., U.S. E3 114
Hayes, La., U.S. G6 122
Hayes, stm., Mb., Can. D12 106
Hayes, stm., Nu., Can. B11 106
Hayes, Mount, mtn., Ak., U.S. D10 140
Hayes Center, Ne., U.S. G11 126
Hayesville, Or., U.S. F4 136
Hayfield, Mn., U.S. H6 118
Hayford Peak, mtn., Nv., U.S. G1 132
Hayfork, Ca., U.S. C2 134
Hay Lakes, Ab., Can. C17 138
Haynes, Ar., U.S. C8 122
Hayneville, Al., U.S. E12 122
Hayrabolu, Tur. B10 28
Hay River, N.T., Can. C7 106
Hays, Ab., Can. F19 138
Hays, Ks., U.S. C9 128
Hays, Mt., U.S. F5 124
Hay Springs, Ne., U.S. E10 126
Haystack Mountain, mtn., Nv., U.S. B1 132
Hayti, Mo., U.S. H8 120
Hayti, S.D., U.S. C15 126
Hayward, Ca., U.S. F3 134
Hayward, Wi., U.S. E7 118
Haywards Heath, Eng., U.K. J13 12
HaZafon, state, Isr. F6 58
Hazard, Ky., U.S. G2 114
Hazārībāg, India G10 54
Ḥazawzā, Sabkhat, l., Sau. Ar. H9 58
Hazebrouck, Fr. D11 14
Hazel Green, Wi., U.S. I8 118
Hazelton, B.C., Can. A3 138
Hazelton, N.D., U.S. A12 126
Hazelton Mountains, mts., B.C., Can. B3 138
Hazelwood, N.C., U.S. A2 116
Hazen, Ar., U.S. C7 122
Hazen, N.D., U.S. G12 124
Hazen, Lake, l., Nu., Can. A11 141
Hazlehurst, Ms., U.S. F8 122
Hazlet, Sk., Can. D5 124
Hazleton, Ia., U.S. B6 120
Hazleton, Pa., U.S. D9 114
Hazlett, Lake, l., Austl. D5 74
Ḥazor HaGelilit, Isr. E6 58
He, stm., China H6 42
He, stm., China I4 42
Healdsburg, Ca., U.S. E2 134
Healdton, Ok., U.S. G11 128
Healesville, Austl. K5 76
Healy, Ks., U.S. C8 128
Heard Island, i., Austl. O10 142
Hearst, On., Can. F14 106
Heart, stm., N.D., U.S. H12 124
Heart Lake, l., Ab., Can. A19 138
Heath, Pointe, c., Qc., Can. A15 110
Heathcote, Austl. K5 76
Heath Springs, S.C., U.S. B5 116
Heathsville, Va., U.S. G9 114
Heavener, Ok., U.S. C4 122
Hebei, state, China D8 36
Hebel, Austl. G6 76
Heber, Az., U.S. I6 132
Heber City, Ut., U.S. C5 132
Heber Springs, Ar., U.S. B6 122
Hebgen Lake, res., Mt., U.S. F15 136
Hebi, China D6 42
Hebrides, is., Scot., U.K. D5 12
Hebrides, Sea of the, Scot., U.K. D6 12
Hebron, Nf., Can. F13 141
Hebron, Il., U.S. B9 120
Hebron, Ne., U.S. A11 128
Hebron, N.D., U.S. H11 124
Hebron see Al-Khalīl, W.B. G5 58
Hecate Strait, strt., B.C., Can. E4 106
Hecelchakán, Mex. B2 102
Hechi, China I3 42
Hechiceros, Mex. F4 130
Hechingen, Ger. H4 16
Hechuan, China G2 42
Hecla, Mb., Can. C17 124
Hecla, Cape, c., Nu., Can. A13 141
Hecla Island, i., Mb., Can. D17 124
Hectanooga, N.S., Can. F10 110
Hector, Mn., U.S. G4 118
Hede, Swe. E5 8
Hedemora, Swe. F6 8
He Devil, mtn., Id., U.S. E10 136
Hedley, Tx., U.S. G8 128
Hedmark, state, Nor. F4 8
Hedrick, Ia., U.S. C5 120
Heerenveen, Neth. B14 14
Heerlen, Neth. D15 14
Ḥefa (Haifa), Isr. F5 58
Ḥefa, state, Isr. F5 58
Hefei, China F7 42
Heflin, Al., U.S. D13 122
Hegang, China B11 36
Heho, Mya. B3 48
Hei, stm., China A7 42
Heide, Ger. B5 16
Heidelberg, Ger. G4 16
Heidelberg, S. Afr. E9 70
Heidelberg, Ms., U.S. F10 122
Heidenheim, Ger. G6 16
Heihe, China A10 36
Heilbad Heiligenstadt, Ger. E6 16
Heilbron, S. Afr. E8 70
Heilbronn, Ger. G5 16
Heiligenhafen, Ger. B6 16
Heilong (Amur), stm., Asia F14 34
Heilongguan, China C4 42
Heilongjiang, state, China B10 36
Heilungkiang see Heilongjiang, state, China B8 38
Heimaey, i., Ice. I29 8a
Heinola, Fin. F12 8
Heishan, China D4 38
Heishuisi, China C3 42
Hejaz see Al-Ḥijāz, reg., Sau. Ar. D4 56
Hejian, China B7 42
Hejiang, China G1 42
Hejing, China C2 36
Hekla, vol., Ice. k30 8a
Hekou, China G4 42
Hekou, China A6 48
Helagsfjället, mtn., Swe. E5 8
Helan Mountains see Helan Shan, mts., China B1 42
Helan Shan, mts., China B1 42
Helbra, Ger. E7 16
Helder see Den Helder, Neth. B13 14
Helder, Den see Den Helder, Neth. B13 14
Helen, Mount, hill, Austl. C3 76
Helena, Ar., U.S. C8 122
Helena, Mt., U.S. D14 136
Helena, Ok., U.S. E10 128
Helensburgh, Scot., U.K. E8 12
Helenwood, Tn., U.S. H13 120
Helgoland, i., Ger. B3 16
Helgoländer Bucht, b., Ger. C4 16
Heli, China B11 36
Heliopolis, hist., Egypt H2 58
Helixi, China F8 42
Hellesylt, Nor. E2 8
Hellín, Spain F9 20
Hells Canyon, val., U.S. E10 136
Hells Canyon National Recreation Area, p.o.i., Or., U.S. E10 136
Hells Gate, val., B.C., Can. G9 138
Helmand, stm., Asia C9 56
Helmcken Falls, wtfl, B.C., Can. E10 138
Helmond, Neth. C14 14
Helmstedt, Ger. D6 16
Helong, China C8 38
Helper, Ut., U.S. D6 132
Helsingborg, Swe. H5 8
Helsingfors see Helsinki, Fin. F11 8
Helsingør, Den. H5 8
Helsinki (Helsingfors), Fin. F11 8
Helska, Mierzeja, pen., Pol. B14 16
Helston, Eng., U.K. K7 12
Helvecia, Arg. E7 92
Helwan, Egypt I2 58
Helwan Observatory, sci., Egypt I2 58
Hemau, Ger. G7 16
Hemāvati, stm., India E2 53
Hemel Hempstead, Eng., U.K. J12 12
Hemet, Ca., U.S. J9 134
Hemingford, Ne., U.S. E9 126
Hemingway, S.C., U.S. C6 116
Hemphill, Tx., U.S. F5 122
Hemsön, i., Swe. E8 8
Henan, state, China E5 42
Henares, stm., Spain D7 20
Henbury, Austl. D6 74
Hendek, Tur. C13 28
Henderson, Ky., U.S. G10 120
Henderson, Mn., U.S. G5 118
Henderson, Ne., U.S. G15 126
Henderson, Nv., U.S. G1 132
Henderson, N.C., U.S. H7 114
Henderson, Tn., U.S. B10 122
Henderson, Tx., U.S. E4 122
Hendersonville, Tn., U.S. H11 120
Hendricks, Mn., U.S. G2 118
Hendricks, W.V., U.S. E6 114
Henefer, Ut., U.S. B5 132
Henganofi, Pap. N. Gui. b4 79a
Hengchow see Hengyang, China H5 42
Hengdaozi, China C7 38
Hengelo, Neth. B15 14
Hengfeng, China G7 42
Henglu, China D7 38
Hengshan, China C3 42
Hengshan, China H5 42
Heng Shan, mts., China B5 42
Hengshui, China C6 42
Hengxian, China J3 42
Hengyang, China H5 42
Hénin-Beaumont, Fr. D11 14
Henlopen, Cape, c., De., U.S. F10 114
Hennebont, Fr. G5 14
Hennef, Ger. F3 16
Hennessey, Ok., U.S. E11 128
Henniker, N.H., U.S. G5 110
Henning, Mn., U.S. E3 118
Henrietta, N.Y., U.S. A8 114
Henrietta, Tx., U.S. H10 128
Henrietta Island see Genrietty, ostrov, i., Russia A20 34
Henrietta Maria, Cape, c., On., Can. D14 106
Henri Pittier, Parque Nacional, p.o.i., Ven. B8 86
Henry, Il., U.S. C8 120
Henry, Cape, c., Va., U.S. H10 114
Henry, Mount, mtn., Mt., U.S. B11 136
Henryetta, Ok., U.S. B2 122
Henry Kater, Cape, c., Nu., Can. B17 106
Henrys Fork, stm., Id., U.S. F15 136
Hensall, On., Can. E8 112
Hensley, Ar., U.S. C6 122
Henslow, Cape, c., Sol. Is. e9 79b
Hentiesbaai, Nmb. C2 70
Hentiyn nuruu, mts., Mong. G10 34
Henzada, Mya. D2 48
Hephzibah, Ga., U.S. C3 116
Heping, China H7 42
Heppenheim, Ger. G4 16
Heppner, Or., U.S. E7 136
Hepu, China K3 42
Hequ, China B4 42
Héraðsflói, b., Ice. k32 8a
Herāt, Afg. C9 56
Hérault, state, Fr. F9 18
Hérault, stm., Fr. F9 18
Herbert, Sk., Can. D6 124
Herberton, Austl. A5 76
Herbertsdale, S. Afr. H5 70
Herborn, Ger. F4 16
Herceg-Novi, Yugo. G5 26
Hércules, Mex. A7 100
Herðubreið, vol., Ice. k31 8a
Heredia, C.R. G5 102
Hereford, Eng., U.K. I10 12
Hereford, Az., U.S. L6 132
Hereford, Tx., U.S. G6 128
Hereke, Tur. C12 28
Herencia, Spain E7 20
Herford, Ger. D4 16
Herington, Ks., U.S. C11 128
Herisau, Switz. C6 22
Herkimer, N.Y., U.S. E15 112
Hermagor, Aus. D10 22
Herman, Mn., U.S. F2 118
Herman, Ne., U.S. C1 120
Hermanas, Mex. G6 130
Hermanns-Denkmal, hist., Ger. E4 16
Hermansverk, Nor. F2 8
Hermansville, Mi., U.S. C2 112
Hermanus, S. Afr. I4 70
Hermanville, Ms., U.S. F8 122
Hermiston, Or., U.S. E7 136
Hermitage, Ar., U.S. D6 122
Hermit Islands, is., Pap. N. Gui. a4 79a
Hermleigh, Tx., U.S. B7 130
Hermon, Mount (Shaykh, Jabal ash-), mtn., Asia E6 58
Hermosillo, Mex. A3 100
Hermyingyi, Mya. E4 48
Hernád (Hornad), stm., Eur. H17 16
Hernandarias, Arg. E8 92
Hernandarias, Para. B10 92
Hernando, Arg. F6 92
Hernando, Fl., U.S. H3 116
Hernando, Ms., U.S. C9 122
Herndon, Pa., U.S. D9 114
Herne Bay, Eng., U.K. J14 12
Herning, Den. H3 8
Heroica Zitácuaro, Mex. F8 100
Heron Island, i., Austl. D8 76
Heron Lake, Mn., U.S. H3 118
Hérouville-Saint-Clair, Fr. E8 14
Herradura, Arg. C8 92
Herreid, S.D., U.S. B12 126
Herrera de Pisuerga, Spain B6 20
Herrick, Austl. n13 77a
Herrin, Il., U.S. G8 120
Hersbruck, Ger. G7 16
Herschel, Sk., Can. C5 124
Herschel, S. Afr. G8 70
Herschel Island, i., Yk., Can. C12 140
Herscher, Il., U.S. C9 120
Hershey, Ne., U.S. F11 126
Hershey, Pa., U.S. D9 114
Herstal, Bel. D14 14
Hertford, Eng., U.K. J12 12
Hertogenbosch, 's- see 's-Hertogenbosch, Neth. C14 14
Herval d'Oeste, Braz. C12 92
Hervás, Spain D5 20
Hervey Bay, b., Austl. E9 76
Hervey-Jonction, Qc., Can. D4 110
Herzberg, Ger. E9 16
Herzberg am Harz, Ger. E6 16
Heshan, China J3 42
Heshui, China J4 42
Heshun, China C5 42
Hesperia, Mi., U.S. E3 112
Hesperus Mountain, mtn., Co., U.S. F8 132
Hess, stm., Yk., Can. C4 106
Hessen, state, Ger. F5 16
Hesston, Ks., U.S. C11 128
Het, stm., Laos B6 48
Heta, stm., Russia B8 34
Hetang, China H8 42
Heṭauṇḍā, Nepal E10 54
Hetch Hetchy Aqueduct, aq., Ca., U.S. F4 134
Hetögeln, l., Swe. D6 8
Hettstedt, Ger. E7 16
Heuvelton, N.Y., U.S. D14 112
Heves, Hung. B7 26
Heves, state, Hung. A7 26
Hewanorra International Airport, St. Luc. m6 105c
Hewu, China H5 42
Hexham, Eng., U.K. F11 12
Hexian, China I4 42
Heyang, China D3 42
Heyburn, Id., U.S. H13 136
Heysham, Eng., U.K. G10 12
Heyuan, China J6 42
Heywood, Austl. L3 76
Heyworth, Il., U.S. D9 120
Heze, China D6 42
Hezheng, China D5 36
Hialeah, Fl., U.S. K5 116
Hiawatha, Ks., U.S. E2 120
Hiawatha, Ut., U.S. D6 132
Hibbard, Qc., Can. C2 110
Hibbing, Mn., U.S. D5 118
Hickman, Ky., U.S. H8 120
Hickory, Ms., U.S. E9 122
Hickory, N.C., U.S. I4 114
Hickory Flat, Ms., U.S. C9 122
Hicks, Point, c., Austl. K7 76
Hico, Tx., U.S. C9 130
Hida see Hita, Japan F3 40
Hidalgo, Mex. B8 100
Hidalgo, Mex. C9 100
Hidalgo, Mex. B9 100
Hidalgo, state, Mex. E9 100
Hidalgo del Parral, Mex. B6 100
Hida-sammyaku, mts., Japan C10 40
Hidrolândia, Braz. I1 88
Hieflau, Aus. C11 22
Hienghène, N. Cal. m15 79d
Hierapolis see Pamukkale, hist., Tur. F12 28
Higashīhiroshima, Japan E5 40
Higashiichiki, Japan H3 40
Higashine, Japan A13 40
Higashiōsaka, Japan E8 40
Higgins, Tx., U.S. E8 128
Higgins Lake, l., Mi., U.S. D5 112
Higginsville, Mo., U.S. E4 120
Highbury, Austl. C8 74
Highland, Il., U.S. F8 120
Highland, In., U.S. G2 112
Highland, Ks., U.S. E2 120
Highland Park, Il., U.S. F2 112
Highlands, N.J., U.S. D12 114
Highlands, N.C., U.S. A2 116
Highlands, Tx., U.S. H3 122
High Level, Ab., Can. D7 106
High Point, N.C., U.S. I5 114
High Point, mtn., N.J., U.S. C11 114
High Point, mtn., Wy., U.S. B9 132
High Point, c., Ber. I15 104e
High River, Ab., Can. F17 138
Highrock Lake, l., Mb., Can. D10 106
Highrock Lake, l., Sk., Can. D9 106
High Rock Lake, res., N.C., U.S. A5 116
High Springs, Fl., U.S. G3 116
Hightstown, N.J., U.S. D11 114
High Willhays, mtn., Eng., U.K. K9 12
Highwood, Mt., U.S. C16 136
Highwood, stm., Ab., Can. F17 138
Highwood Baldy, mtn., Mt., U.S. C16 136
High Wycombe, Eng., U.K. J11 12
Higuera de Abuya, Mex. C5 100
Higueras, Mex. I8 130
Higüero, Punta, c., P.R. B1 104a
Higüey, Dom. Rep. C13 102
Hiiumaa, i., Est. G10 8
Hikari, Japan F4 40
Hikone, Japan D9 40
Hilbert, Wi., U.S. D1 112
Hilda, Ab., Can. D3 124
Hildburghausen, Ger. F6 16
Hildesheim, Ger. D5 16
Hiliotaluwa, Indon. L3 48
Hillaby, Mount, mtn., Barb. n8 105d
Hill Bank, Belize D3 102
Hill City, Ks., U.S. B9 128
Hill City, S.D., U.S. D9 126
Hillcrest Mines, Ab., Can. G16 138
Hillerød, Den. I4 8
Hilliard, Fl., U.S. F4 116
Hill Island Lake, l., N.T., Can. C9 106
Hillister, Tx., U.S. G4 122
Hills, Mn., U.S. H2 118
Hillsboro, Il., U.S. E8 120
Hillsboro, Ks., U.S. C11 128
Hillsboro, Mo., U.S. F7 120
Hillsboro, N.D., U.S. D1 118
Hillsboro, Oh., U.S. E2 114
Hillsboro, Or., U.S. E3 136
Hillsboro, Wi., U.S. H8 118
Hillsboro Canal, can., Fl., U.S. J5 116
Hillsborough, Gren. q10 105e
Hillsborough, N.C., U.S. H6 114
Hillsborough, stm., Fl., U.S. H3 116
Hillsborough, Cape, c., Austl. C7 76
Hillsborough Bay, b., P.E., Can. D13 110
Hillsdale, Mi., U.S. G5 112
Hillston, Austl. I5 76
Hillsville, Va., U.S. H5 114
Hillswick, Scot., U.K. n18 12a
Hilo, Hi., U.S. D6 78a
Hilok, Russia F11 34
Hilok, stm., Russia F10 34
Hilton, N.Y., U.S. E12 112
Hilton Head Island, i., S.C., U.S. D5 116
Hilvan, Tur. A9 58
Hilversum, Neth. B14 14
Himāchal Pradesh, state, India B6 54
Himalayas, mts., Asia F10 142
Himarë, Alb. D13 24
Himatnagar, India G4 54
Himeji, Japan E7 40
Himi, Japan C9 40
Himki, Russia E20 10
Ḥimṣ (Homs), Syria D7 58
Ḥimṣ, state, Syria D8 58
Hinchinbrook Island, i., Austl. B6 76
Hinchinbrook Island, i., Ak., U.S. D10 140
Hinchinbrook Island National Park, p.o.i., Austl. B6 76
Hinckley, Il., U.S. C9 120
Hinckley, Mn., U.S. E5 118
Hinckley, Ut., U.S. D4 132
Hindang, Phil. E5 52
Hindaun, India E6 54
Hindmarsh, Lake, l., Austl. J3 76
Hindu Kush, mts., Asia B10 56
Hindupur, India E3 53
Hines, Or., U.S. G7 136
Hinesville, Ga., U.S. E4 116
Hinganghāt, India H7 54
Hingham, Ma., U.S. B15 114
Hingol, stm., Pak. D10 56
Hingoli, India B3 53
Hinigaran, Phil. E4 52
Hinnøya, i., Nor. B6 8
Hinojosa del Duque, Spain F5 20
Hinokage, Japan G4 40
Hinsdale, Mt., U.S. F6 124
Hinterrhein, stm., Switz. D6 22
Hinton, Ab., Can. C13 138
Hinton, Ok., U.S. F10 128
Hinton, W.V., U.S. G5 114
Hipólito, Mex. C8 100
Hipólito Yrigoyen, Arg. F4 92
Hirado, Japan F2 40
Hirado-shima, i., Japan F2 40
Hīrākud, India H9 54
Hīrākud Reservoir, res., India H10 54
Hirara, Japan G10 36
Hirata, Japan D5 40
Hiratsuka, Japan D12 40
Hiriyūr, India E3 53
Hirosaki, Japan D14 38
Hiroshima, Japan E5 40
Hiroshima, state, Japan E5 40
Hirosima see Hiroshima, Japan E5 40
Hirovo, Russia B16 10
Hirson, Fr. E13 14
Hisār, India D5 54
Hisarönü, Tur. B14 28
Hispaniola, i., N.A. D10 96
Hisua, India F10 54
Ḥisyah, Syria D7 58
Hita, Japan F3 40
Hitachi, Japan C13 40
Hitachi-ōta, Japan C13 40
Hitchcock, Tx., U.S. H3 122
Hitchins, Ky., U.S. F3 114
Hitiaa, Fr. Poly. v22 78h
Hitoyoshi, Japan G3 40
Hitra, i., Nor. E3 8
Hiuchiga-take, vol., Japan C12 40
Hiuchi-nada, Japan E6 40
Hiva, Uzb. F10 32
Hiva Oa, i., Fr. Poly. s19 78g
Hiwannee, Ms., U.S. F10 122
Hiwasa, Japan F7 40
Hiwassee, stm., U.S. B14 122
Hiwassee Lake, res., N.C., U.S. A1 116
Hixson, Tn., U.S. B13 122
Hjälmaren, l., Swe. G6 8
Hjo, Swe. G6 8
Hjørring, Den. H3 8
Hkakabo Razi, mtn., Mya. C8 46
Hkok (Kok), stm., Asia B4 48
Hlaingbwe, Mya. D3 48
Hlathikulu, Swaz. E10 70
Hlinsko, Czech Rep. G11 16
Hlohovec, Slov. H13 16
Hlotse, Leso. F9 70
Hluhluwe, S. Afr. F11 70
Hluhluwe Game Reserve, S. Afr. F10 70
Hluša, Bela. G11 10
Hlyboka, Ukr. A12 26
Hlybokae, Bela. E10 10
Hmelita, Russia E16 10
H. Neely Henry Lake, res., Al., U.S. D12 122
Ho, Ghana H5 64
Hoa Binh, Viet. B7 48
Hoare Bay, b., Nu., Can. D13 141
Hobart, Austl. o13 77a
Hobart, Ok., U.S. F9 128
Hobbs, N.M., U.S. B4 130
Hobbs Coast, cst., Ant. C28 81
Hobe Sound, Fl., U.S. I5 116
Hobgood, N.C., U.S. H8 114
Hobq Shamo, des., China A2 42
Hobson Lake, l., B.C., Can. D10 138
Hobyo, Som. C9 66
Hochalmspitze, mtn., Aus. C10 22
Hochfeld, Nmb. B3 70
Ho Chi Minh City see Thanh Pho Ho Chi Minh, Viet. G8 48
Hochkönig, mtn., Aus. C10 22
Höchstadt an der Aisch, Ger. G6 16
Hochstetter Forland, pen. B21 141
Hoch'uan see Hechuan, China G2 42
Ḥocimsk, Bela. G15 10
Hockenheim, Ger. G4 16
Hocking, stm., Oh., U.S. E15 120
Ḥôḍ, reg., Maur. F3 64
Hodal, India E6 54
Hodeida see Al-Ḥudaydah, Yemen G5 56
Hodge, La., U.S. E6 122
Hodgenville, Ky., U.S. G12 120
Hodgeville, Sk., Can. D7 124
Hódmezővásárhely, Hung. C7 26
Hodna, Chott el, l., Alg. B6 64
Hodonín, Czech Rep. H12 16
Hodžanur'jah, gora, mtn., Uzb. G11 32
Hodžejli, Uzb. F9 32
Hœdic, Île de, i., Fr. G6 14
Hoehne, Co., U.S. D4 128
Hoei see Huy, Bel. D14 14
Hoek van Holland, Neth. C12 14
Hoeryŏng-ŭp, Kor., N. C8 38
Hoeyang-ŭp, Kor., N. E7 38
Hof, Ger. F7 16
Hof, Ice. k32 8a
Hofei see Hefei, China F7 42
Hoffman, Mn., U.S. F3 118
Hofgeismar, Ger. E5 16
Hofheim am Taunus, Ger. F4 16
Hofheim in Unterfranken, Ger. F6 16
Hofors, Swe. F7 8
Hofsjökull, ice, Ice. k30 8a
Hōfu, Japan E4 40
Hofuf see Al-Hufūf, Sau. Ar. D6 56
Hogansville, Ga., U.S. D14 122
Hogback Mountain, mtn., Ne., U.S. F9 126
Hogback Mountain, mtn., S.C., U.S. A3 116
Högsby, Swe. H6 8
Hohenwald, Tn., U.S. B11 122
Hoher Dachstein, mtn., Aus. C10 22
Hohe Tauern, mts., Aus. C9 22
Hohhot, China A4 42
Hohoe, Ghana H5 64
Hōhoku, Japan E3 40
Hoh Xil Hu, l., China D3 36
Hoh Xil Shan, mts., China D2 36
Hoi An, Viet. E9 48
Hoihong see Haikang, China K3 42
Hoihow see Haikou, China K4 42
Hoima, Ug. D6 66
Hoisington, Ks., U.S. C10 128
Hojāi, India E14 54
Højer, Den. B4 16
Hōjō, Japan F5 40
Hokah, Mn., U.S. H7 118
Hokang see Hegang, China B11 36
Hokitika, N.Z. F4 80
Hokkaidō, i., Japan C15 38
Holalkere, India D3 53
Holberg, B.C., Can. F2 138
Holbrook, Austl. J6 76
Holbrook, Az., U.S. I6 132
Holbrook, Ne., U.S. A8 128
Holden, Ab., Can. C18 138
Holden, Mo., U.S. F4 120
Holden, W.V., U.S. G3 114
Holden Village, Wa., U.S. B6 136
Holder, Fl., U.S. H3 116
Holderness, pen., Eng., U.K. H12 12
Holdfast, Sk., Can. D8 124
Holdingford, Mn., U.S. F4 118
Hold With Hope, reg., Grnld. C22 141
Hole in the Mountain Peak, mtn., Nv., U.S. C1 132
Hole Narsipur, India E2 53
Holetown, Barb. n8 105d
Holgate, Oh., U.S. C1 114
Holguín, Cuba B9 102
Holíč, Slov. H13 16
Hollabrunn, Aus. B13 22
Holland, Mi., U.S. F3 112
Holland, Tx., U.S. D10 130
Holland, hist. reg., Neth. B13 14
Holland see Netherlands, ctry., Eur. B15 14
Hollandale, Ms., U.S. D8 122
Hollandia see Jayapura, Indon. F11 44
Hollandsbird Island, i., Nmb. D2 70
Holley, N.Y., U.S. E11 112
Holliday, Tx., U.S. H10 128
Hollins, Va., U.S. G6 114
Hollister, Ca., U.S. G4 134
Hollow Rock, Tn., U.S. H9 120
Holly, Co., U.S. C6 128
Holly Grove, Ar., U.S. C7 122
Holly Hill, Fl., U.S. G4 116
Holly Springs, Ms., U.S. C9 122
Hollywood, Fl., U.S. J5 116
Holm, Russia C14 10
Holman, N.T., Can. A7 106
Hólmavík, Ice. k28 8a
Holmen, Wi., U.S. H7 118
Holmes, Mount, mtn., Wy., U.S. F16 136
Holm Land, pen., Grnld. A22 141
Holm Ø, i., Grnld. C14 141
Holmogorskaja, Russia E19 8
Holmsk, Russia G17 34
Holmsund, Swe. E9 8
Ḥolon, Isr. F5 58
Holoog, Nmb. E4 70
Holovanivs'k, Ukr. A17 26
Holstebro, Den. H3 8
Holstein, Ia., U.S. B2 120
Holsteinsborg (Sisimiut), Grnld. D15 141
Holston, stm., Tn., U.S. H2 114
Holston, North Fork, stm., U.S. H3 114
Holsworthy, Eng., U.K. K8 12
Holt, Fl., U.S. G12 122
Holt, Mi., U.S. B1 114
Holton, Ks., U.S. E2 120
Holts Summit, Mo., U.S. F5 120
Holy Cross, Ak., U.S. D8 140
Holy Cross Mountain, mtn., B.C., Can. C10 138
Holyhead, Wales, U.K. H8 12
Holy Island, i., Eng., U.K. F11 12
Holyoke, Co., U.S. G10 126
Holyoke, Ma., U.S. B13 114
Holyrood, Ks., U.S. C10 128
Holzkirchen, Ger. I7 16
Holzminden, Ger. E5 16
Hom, stm., Nmb. F4 70
Homa Bay, Kenya E6 66
Homalin, Mya. D7 46
Homathko, stm., B.C., Can. E6 138
Homathko Icefield, ice, B.C., Can. E6 138
Homberg, Ger. E5 16
Hombori Tondo, mtn., Mali F4 64
Hombre Muerto, Salar del, pl., Arg. B4 92
Homburg, Ger. G3 16
Home Bay, b., Nu., Can. B17 106
Home Hill, Austl. B6 76
Homel', Bela. H13 10
Homel', state, Bela. H12 10
Homeland Park, S.C., U.S. B3 116
Homer, Ak., U.S. E9 140
Homer, Ga., U.S. B2 116
Homer, La., U.S. E5 122
Homer, Ne., U.S. B1 120
Homer City, Pa., U.S. D6 114
Homerville, Ga., U.S. E3 116
Homestead, Fl., U.S. K5 116
Homestead National Monument of America, p.o.i., Ne., U.S. A11 128
Homewood, Al., U.S. D12 122
Hommura, Japan E12 40
Homnābād, India C3 53
Homochitto, stm., Ms., U.S. F7 122
Homoíne, Moz. C12 70
Homosassa, Fl., U.S. H3 116
Homs see Al-Khums, Libya A2 62
Homs see Ḥimṣ, Syria D7 58
Honaker, Va., U.S. H4 114
Honan see Luoyang, China D5 42
Honan see Henan, state, China E5 42
Honāvar, India D2 53
Hon Chong, Viet. G7 48
Honda, Col. E4 86
Honda, Bahía, b., Col. A5 86
Honda Bay, b., Phil. F2 52
Hondeklipbaai, S. Afr. G3 70
Hon Dien, Nui, mtn., Viet. G9 48
Hondo, Ab., Can. A16 138
Hondo, Japan G3 40
Hondo, N.M., U.S. H3 128
Hondo, stm., N.A. C3 102
Hondo Creek, stm., Tx., U.S. E8 130
Honduras, ctry., N.A. E4 102
Honduras, Cabo de, c., Hond. D5 102
Honduras, Gulf of, b., N.A. D4 102
Honea Path, S.C., U.S. B3 116
Hønefoss, Nor. F4 8
Honesdale, Pa., U.S. C10 114
Honey Grove, Tx., U.S. D3 122
Honey Lake, l., Ca., U.S. C5 134
Honeyville, Ut., U.S. B4 132
Honfleur, Fr. E9 14
Hong, stm., China E6 42
Hong, Song see Red, stm., Asia D9 46
Hon Gai, Viet. B8 48
Hong Hu, l., China F5 42
Hongjiang, China H4 42
Hong Kong see Xianggang, China J6 42
Hongliuyuan, China F17 32
Hong Ngu, Viet. G7 48
Hongqi, China B7 38
Hongshi, China C7 38
Hongshui, stm., China J3 42
Hongtong, China C4 42
Honguedo, Détroit d', strt., Qc., Can. A12 110
Hongze, China E8 42
Hongze Hu, l., China E8 42
Honiara, Sol. Is. e8 79b
Honjō, Japan E13 38
Honningsvåg, Nor. A11 8
Honokaa, Hi., U.S. C6 78a
Honolulu, Hi., U.S. B4 78a
Honomu, Hi., U.S. D6 78a
Hon Quan, Viet. G8 48
Honshū, i., Japan G12 38
Honuu, Russia C17 34
Hood, stm., Nu., Can. B9 106
Hood, Mount, vol., Or., U.S. E5 136
Hood Canal, b., Wa., U.S. C4 136
Hoodoo Peak, mtn., Wa., U.S. B6 136
Hood Point, c., Austl. F3 74
Hoodsport, Wa., U.S. C3 136
Hoogeveen, Neth. B15 14
Hoogeveense Vaart, can., Neth. B15 14
Hooker, Ok., U.S. E7 128
Hook Head, c., Ire. I6 12
Hookina, Austl. H2 76
Hook Island, i., Austl. C7 76
Hook Point, c., Austl. E9 76
Hooks, Tx., U.S. D4 122
Hoonah, Ak., U.S. E12 140
Hoopa, Ca., U.S. B2 134
Hooper, Ne., U.S. C1 120
Hooper Bay, Ak., U.S. D6 140
Hoople, N.D., U.S. F16 124
Hoopstad, S. Afr. E7 70
Hoorn, Neth. B14 14
Hoosick Falls, N.Y., U.S. H3 110
Hoover Dam, dam, U.S. G2 132
Hooversville, Pa., U.S. H11 112
Hopatcong, N.J., U.S. D11 114
Hope, B.C., Can. G9 138
Hope, Ar., U.S. D5 122
Hope, In., U.S. E12 120
Hope, Ben, mtn., Scot., U.K. C8 12
Hope, Point, c., Ak., U.S. C6 140
Hopedale, La., U.S. H9 122
Hopeh see Hebei, state, China D8 36
Ho-pei see Hebei, state, China D8 36
Hopelchén, Mex. C3 102
Hope Mills, N.C., U.S. B7 116
Hopër, stm., Russia E17 6
Hopes Advance, Cap, c., Qc., Can. C17 106
Hopetoun, Austl. F4 74
Hopetoun, Austl. J4 76
Hopetown, S. Afr. F6 70
Hope Valley, R.I., U.S. C14 114
Hopewell, Va., U.S. G8 114
Hopewell Culture National Historic Park, p.o.i., Oh., U.S. E2 114
Hopewell Islands, is., Nu., Can. D14 106
Hopi see Hebi, China D6 42
Hopkins, Mo., U.S. D3 120
Hopkins, stm., Austl. K4 76
Hopkinsville, Ky., U.S. H10 120
Hopkinton, Ia., U.S. B6 120
Hopólite Bouchard, Arg. G6 92
Hoppo see Hepu, China K3 42
Hopwood, Mount, hill, Austl. C5 76
Hoquiam, Wa., U.S. C2 136
Hor, Russia G16 34
Hor, stm., Russia G16 34
Hor, stm., Russia B12 36
Horatio, Ar., U.S. D4 122
Hordaland, state, Nor. F2 8
Horezu, Rom. D10 26
Horicon, Wi., U.S. H10 118
Horinger, China A4 42
Horinsk, Russia F10 34
Horizontina, Braz. C10 92
Horlick Mountains, mts., Ant. D29 81
Horlivka, Ukr. E5 32
Horlovo, Russia E21 10
Hormigueros, P.R. B1 104a
Hormuz, Strait of, strt., Asia D8 56
Horn, Aus. B12 22
Horn, c., Ice. j28 8a
Horn, stm., N.T., Can. C7 106
Horn, Cape see Hornos, Cabo de, c., Chile K3 90
Hornad (Hernád), stm., Eur. H17 16
Hornaday, stm., Can. B6 106
Hornafjörður, b., Ice. k32 8a
Hornavan, l., Swe. C7 8
Hornbeck, La., U.S. F5 122
Hornbrook, Ca., U.S. B3 134
Hornby Bay, b., N.T., Can. B7 106
Hornell, N.Y., U.S. B8 114
Hornepayne, On., Can. F13 106
Horn Island, i., Ms., U.S. G10 122
Horn Lake, Ms., U.S. C8 122
Hornos, Cabo de (Horn, Cape), c., Chile K3 90
Horn Plateau, plat., N.T., Can. C6 106

Name | Map Ref. | Page

Hornsea, Eng., U.K. H12 12
Horodkivka, Ukr. A15 26
Horodok, Ukr. G19 16
Horog, Taj. B11 56
Horol', Russia B10 38
Horqin Youyi Qianqi, China B9 36
Horqin Youyi Zhongqi, China B4 38
Horqin Zuoyi Houqi, China C4 38
Horqin Zuoyi Zhongqi, China B5 38
Horqueta, Para. D5 90
Horse Cave, Ky., U.S. G12 120
Horse Creek, stm., U.S. F8 126
Horse Creek, stm., Co., U.S. C5 128
Horsefly, B.C., Can. D9 138
Horsefly Lake, l., B.C., Can. D10 138
Horseheads, N.Y., U.S. B9 114
Horse Islands, is., Nf., Can. i22 107a
Horsens, Den. I3 8
Horseshoe Bend, Id., U.S. G10 136
Horsham, Austl. K4 76
Horsham, Eng., U.K. J12 12
Horšovský Týn, Czech Rep. G8 16
Horten, Nor. G4 8
Hortobágy, reg., Hung. B8 26
Hortobágyi Nemzeti Park, p.o.i., Hung. B8 26
Horton, Ks., U.S. E2 120
Horton, stm., N.T., Can. B6 106
Horton Lake, l., N.T., Can. B6 106
Hortonville, Wi., U.S. G10 118
Hory, Bela. F14 10
Hosa'ina, Eth. F7 62
Hösbach, Ger. F5 16
Hosedahard, Russia A9 32
Hosford, Fl., U.S. G14 122
Hoshāb, Pak. D9 56
Hoshangābād, India G6 54
Hoshiārpur, India C5 54
Hosh Isa, Egypt H1 58
Hosmer, B.C., Can. G15 138
Hospers, Ia., U.S. A2 120
Hospet, India D3 53
Hospitalet see L'Hospitalet de Llobregat, Spain C13 20
Hossegor, Fr. F4 18
Hosston, La., U.S. E5 122
Hosta Butte, mtn., N.M., U.S. H8 132
Hoste, Isla, i., Chile K3 90
Hosūr, India E3 53
Hotagen, l., Swe. E5 8
Hotaka-dake, mtn., Japan C10 40
Hotamış, Tur. A4 58
Hotan, China A5 46
Hotazel, S. Afr. E6 70
Hotevilla, Az., U.S. H6 132
Hotilovo, Russia C17 10
Hot'kovo, Russia G18 10
Hot'kovo, Russia D21 10
Hot Springs, Ar., U.S. C5 122
Hot Springs, N.C., U.S. I3 114
Hot Springs, S.D., U.S. D9 126
Hot Springs, Va., U.S. F6 114
Hot Springs National Park see Hot Springs, Ar., U.S. C5 122
Hot Springs Peak, mtn., Nv., U.S. B8 134
Hot Sulphur Springs, Co., U.S. A2 128
Hottah Lake, l., N.T., Can. B7 106
Hottentotsbaai, b., Nmb. E2 70
Hotynec, Russia G18 10
Houaïlou, N. Cal. m15 79d
Houat, Île de, i., Fr. G6 14
Houdan, Fr. F10 14
Houghton, Mi., U.S. D10 118
Houghton, N.Y., U.S. B7 114
Houghton Lake, l., Mi., U.S. D4 112
Houlka, Ms., U.S. C10 122
Houlton, Me., U.S. D9 110
Houma, China D4 42
Houma, Tonga n13 78e
Houma, La., U.S. H8 122
Hou-pei see Hubei, state, China F5 42
Hourtin, Étang d', l., Fr. D4 18
Housatonic, Ma., U.S. B12 114
House, N.M., U.S. G5 128
Houston, B.C., Can. B4 138
Houston, Mn., U.S. H7 118
Houston, Mo., U.S. G6 120
Houston, Tx., U.S. H3 122
Houston, Lake, res., Tx., U.S. H3 122
Hout, stm., S. Afr. C9 70
Houtman Abrolhos, is., Austl. E2 74
Houxinqiu, China C5 38
Hovd, Mong. B3 36
Hovd, Mong. C5 36
Hovd, stm., Mong. E16 32
Hove, Eng., U.K. K12 12
Hoven, S.D., U.S. B13 126
Hovenweep National Monument, p.o.i., U.S. F7 132
Hoverla, hora, mtn., Ukr. A11 26
Hovgaard Ø, i., Grnld. A22 141
Hövsgöl nuur, l., Mong. F9 34
Hovu-Aksy, Russia D16 32
Howar, Wādī, val., Afr. D5 62
Howard, Austl. E9 76
Howard, Ks., U.S. D12 128
Howard, Pa., U.S. D8 114
Howard, S.D., U.S. C15 126
Howard City, Mi., U.S. E4 112
Howard Draw, stm., Tx., U.S. D6 130
Howard Lake, Mn., U.S. F4 118
Howe, In., U.S. G4 112
Howe, Cape, c., Austl. K7 76
Howe Island, i., On., Can. D13 112
Howell, Mi., U.S. B2 114
Howells, Ne., U.S. F15 126
Howick, S. Afr. F10 70
Howitt, Mount, mtn., Austl. K6 76
Howland Island, i., Oc. C9 72
Howser, B.C., Can. F13 138
Howson Peak, mtn., B.C., Can. B3 138
Hoxie, Ar., U.S. H6 120
Hoxie, Ks., U.S. B8 128
Höxter, Ger. E5 16
Hoxtolgay, China B2 36
Hoy, i., Scot., U.K. C9 12
Hoyerswerda, Ger. E10 16
Hoyos, Spain D4 20
Höytiäinen, l., Fin. E13 8
Hoyt Lakes, Mn., U.S. D6 118
Hradec Králové, Czech Rep. F11 16
Hradzjanka, Bela. G11 10
Hranice, Czech Rep. G13 16
Hrèsk, Bela. G10 10
Hristoforovo, Russia F22 8
Hrodna, Bela. G6 10
Hrodna, state, Bela. G7 10
Hroma, stm., Russia B17 34
Hron, stm., Slov. H14 16
Hronov, Czech Rep. F12 16
Hrubieszów, Pol. F19 16
Hrustal'nyj, Russia B11 38
Hsiakuan see Dali, China F5 36
Hsiamen see Xiamen, China I7 42
Hsian see Xi'an, China D3 42
Hsiangt'an see Xiangtan, China H5 42
Hsiangyang see Xiangfan, China F4 42
Hsienyang see Xianyang, China D3 42
Hsi-hseng, Mya. B3 48
Hsilo, Tai. J9 42
Hsim, stm., Mya. B4 48
Hsinchu, Tai. I9 42
Hsinghua see Xinghua, China E8 42
Hsingt'ai see Xingtai, China C6 42
Hsinhailien see Lianyungang, China D8 42
Hsinhsiang see Xinxiang, China D5 42
Hsining see Xining, China D5 36
Hsinking see Changchun, China C6 38
Hsinp'u see Lianyungang, China D8 42
Hsintien, Tai. I9 42
Hsinyang see Xinyang, China E6 42
Hsipaw, Mya. A3 48
Hsüanhua see Xuanhua, China A6 42
Hsüch'ang see Xuchang, China D5 42
Hsüchou see Xuzhou, China D7 42
Hua'an, China I7 42
Huab, stm., Nmb. B2 70
Huacaraje, Bol. B4 90
Huacho, Peru F2 84
Huachuca City, Az., U.S. L6 132
Huadian, China C7 38
Huading Shan, mtn., China G9 42
Hua Hin, Thai. F4 48
Huai, stm., China C6 42
Huai, stm., China E8 42
Huai'an, China E8 42
Huai'an, China A6 42
Huaibin, China E6 42
Huaicheng see Huai'an, China E8 42
Huaidezhen, China C6 38
Huaiji, China I5 42
Huailai, China A6 42
Huainan, China E7 42
Huairou, China A7 42
Huaite see Gongzhuling, China C6 38
Huaiyang, China E6 42
Huai Yot, Thai. I4 48
Huaiyuan, China E7 42
Huajuapan de León, Mex. G10 100
Hualahuises, Mex. C9 100
Hualalai, vol., Hi., U.S. D6 78a
Hualañé, Chile G2 92
Hualfín, Arg. C4 92
Hualien, Tai. J9 42
Huallaga, stm., Peru E2 84
Huallanca, Peru E2 84
Hualong, China D5 36
Huambo, Ang. C2 68
Huamei Shan, mtn., China I5 42
Huan, stm., China F6 42
Huanan, China B11 36
Huancabamba, Peru E2 84
Huancané, Peru G4 84
Huancavelica, Peru F2 84
Huancayo, Peru F2 84
Huang (Yellow), stm., China D8 36
Huangchuan, China E6 42
Huanggai Hu, l., China G5 42
Huanggang, China F6 42
Huanggangliang, mtn., China C2 38
Huanghua, China B7 42
Huangjinbu, China G7 42
Huangling, China D3 42
Huanglong, China D3 42
Huangnihe, China C7 38
Huangpi, China F6 42
Huangqi, China H8 42
Huangshahe, China H4 42
Huangshan, China G8 42
Huangshan see Guangming Ding, mtn., China F7 42
Huangshi, China F6 42
Huangshi, China G4 42
Huangtang Hu, l., China G6 42
Huangtuliangzi, China A8 42
Huanguelén, Arg. H6 92
Huangxian, China C9 42
Huangyan, China G9 42
Huangyuan, China D5 36
Huangzhong, China D5 36
Huangzhu, China L4 42
Huanjiang, China I3 42
Huanren, China D6 38
Huánuco, Peru E2 84
Huanuni, Bol. C3 90
Huanxian, China C2 42
Huara, Chile C3 90
Huaral, Peru F2 84
Huaraz, Peru E2 84
Huariaca, Peru F2 84
Huarmey, Peru F2 84
Huarong, China G5 42
Huasaga, stm., S.A. I3 86
Hua Sai, Thai. H5 48
Huascarán, Nevado, mtn., Peru E2 84
Huasco, Chile D2 92
Huasco, stm., Chile D2 92
Huatabampo, Mex. B4 100
Huating, China D2 42
Huatong, China A9 42
Huauchinango, Mex. E9 100
Huautla, Mex. C5 96
Huaxian, China J5 42
Huaxian, China D3 42
Huaxian, China D6 42
Huaynamota, stm., Mex. D6 100
Huazamota, Mex. D6 100
Huazhou, China K4 42
Hubbard, Ia., U.S. B4 120
Hubbard Creek Reservoir, l., Tx., U.S. B8 130
Hubbard Lake, l., Mi., U.S. D6 112
Hubbards, N.S., Can. F12 110
Hubbell, Mi., U.S. D10 118
Hubei, state, China F5 42
Huberdeau, Qc., Can. E2 110
Hubli-Dhārwār, India D2 53
Hubuleng, China A4 42
Huchow see Huzhou, China F9 42
Huckleberry Mountain, mtn., Or., U.S. G4 136
Hucknall, Eng., U.K. H11 12
Huddersfield, Eng., U.K. H11 12
Huddinge, Swe. G8 8
Huder, China A9 36
Hudiksvall, Swe. F7 8
Hudson, Fl., U.S. H3 116
Hudson, Ia., U.S. B5 120
Hudson, N.Y., U.S. H3 110
Hudson, N.C., U.S. I4 114
Hudson, Oh., U.S. C4 114
Hudson, S.D., U.S. H2 118
Hudson, Wy., U.S. E4 126
Hudson, stm., U.S. G16 112
Hudson, Baie d' see Hudson Bay, b., Can. C13 106
Hudson Bay, Sk., Can. B11 124
Hudson Bay, b., Can. C13 106
Hudson Falls, N.Y., U.S. G3 110
Hudson's Hope, B.C., Can. D6 106
Hudson Strait, strt., Can. C16 106
Hudžand, Taj. A10 56
Hue, Viet. D8 48
Huebra, stm., Spain D4 20
Huehuetenango, Guat. E2 102
Huejutla de Reyes, Mex. E9 100
Huelgoat, Fr. F5 14
Huelva, Spain G3 20
Huelva, co., Spain G4 20
Huentelauquén, Chile E2 92
Huércal-Overa, Spain G8 20
Huerfano, stm., Co., U.S. C4 128
Huerlumada, China B13 54
Huerva, stm., Spain C9 20
Huesca, Spain B10 20
Huesca, co., Spain B10 20
Huéscar, Spain G8 20
Huetamo de Núñez, Mex. F8 100
Hueytown, Al., U.S. D11 122
Hufrat an-Nahās, Sudan F4 62
Hughenden, Austl. C4 76
Hughes, Ak., U.S. C9 140
Hughes, Ar., U.S. C8 122
Hughes Springs, Tx., U.S. E4 122
Hugh Keenleyside Dam, dam, B.C., Can. G12 138
Hughson, Ca., U.S. F5 134
Hugh Town, Eng., U.K. L6 12
Hugli, stm., India G12 54
Hugo, Co., U.S. B5 128
Hugo, Ok., U.S. C3 122
Hugoton, Ks., U.S. D7 128
Huhar, stm., China B4 38
Huhehaote see Hohhot, China A4 42
Huhehot see Hohhot, China A4 42
Huichang, China I6 42
Huicheng see Huilai, China J7 42
Hŭich'ŏn, Kor., N. D7 38
Huichou see Huizhou, China J6 42
Huila, state, Col. F4 86
Huila, Nevado del, vol., Col. F3 86
Huilai, China J7 42
Huili, China F5 36
Huillapima, Arg. D4 92
Huimin, China C7 42
Huinan, China C7 38
Huisachal, Mex. H6 130
Huishui, China H2 42
Huisne, stm., Fr. F9 14
Huitong, China H3 42
Huitzo, Mex. G10 100
Huitzuco de los Figueroa, Mex. F9 100
Huixian, China E2 42
Huixian, China D5 42
Huixtla, Mex. H12 100
Huize, China F5 36
Huizhou, China J6 42
Hŭksan-chedo, is., Kor., S. G6 38
Hukuntsi, Bots. D5 70
Hulan, China B7 38
Hulan Ergi, China B9 36
Hulbert, Mi., U.S. B4 112
Hulett, Wy., U.S. C8 126
Hulga, stm., Russia B10 32
Hulin, China B11 36
Hulin, stm., China B4 38
Huliu, stm., China A6 42
Hull, Qc., Can. C14 112
Hull, Il., U.S. E6 120
Hull, Ia., U.S. H2 118
Hullo, Est. A6 10
Hulun see Hailar, China B8 36
Hulun Nur, l., China B8 36
Huma, China F14 34
Huma, Tonga o15 78e
Humacao, P.R. B4 104a
Humahuaca, Arg. D3 90
Humaitá, Braz. E5 84
Humaitá, Para. C8 92
Humansdorp, S. Afr. I7 70
Humansville, Mo., U.S. G4 120
Humara, Jabal al-, hill, Sudan D6 62
Humbe, Ang. D1 68
Humber, stm., Eng., U.K. H12 12
Humbird, Wi., U.S. G8 118
Humboldt, Sk., Can. B8 124
Humboldt, Az., U.S. I4 132
Humboldt, Il., U.S. E9 120
Humboldt, Ia., U.S. B3 120
Humboldt, Ne., U.S. D2 120
Humboldt, S.D., U.S. D15 126
Humboldt, stm., Nv., U.S. C7 134
Humboldt, North Fork, stm., Nv., U.S. B1 132
Humboldt, South Fork, stm., Nv., U.S. C1 132
Humboldt Gletscher, ice, Grnld. B13 141
Humboldt Lake, l., Nv., U.S. D7 134
Hume, Ca., U.S. G7 134
Hume, Lake, res., Austl. J6 76
Humeburn, Austl. F5 76
Humenné, Slov. H17 16
Humeston, Ia., U.S. D4 120
Hummi, ozero, l., Russia F16 34
Humphrey, Ne., U.S. F15 126
Humphreys, Mount, mtn., Ca., U.S. F7 134
Humphreys Peak, mtn., Az., U.S. H5 132
Humpolec, Czech Rep. G11 16
Humpty Doo, Austl. B6 74
Hūn, Libya B3 62
Hun, stm., China D5 38
Hun, stm., China D6 38
Húnaflói, b., Ice. j29 8a
Hunan, state, China H4 42
Hunchun, China C9 38
Hundred, W.V., U.S. E5 114
Hunedoara, Rom. D9 26
Hunedoara, state, Rom. C9 26
Hünfeld, Ger. F5 16
Hungary, ctry., Eur. B6 26
Hungchiang see Hongjiang, China H4 42
Hŭngdŏki-dong, Kor., N. E7 38
Hungerford, Austl. G5 76
Hungerford, Tx., U.S. H2 122
Hungry Horse Dam, dam, Mt., U.S. B13 136
Hungry Horse Reservoir, res., Mt., U.S. B12 136
Hung Yen, Viet. B8 48
Hunjiang, China C7 38
Hunlen Falls, wtfl, B.C., Can. D5 138
Hunsberge, mts., Nmb. E3 70
Hunsrück, mts., Ger. G3 16
Hunsūr, India E3 53
Hunte, stm., Ger. D4 16
Hunter, N.D., U.S. D1 118
Hunter, stm., Austl. I8 76
Hunter Island, i., Austl. n12 77a
Hunter Island, i., B.C., Can. E2 138
Hunter Mountain, mtn., N.Y., U.S. B11 114
Hunter River, P.E., Can. D13 110
Hunters, Wa., U.S. B8 136
Hunters Bay, b., Mya. C1 48
Huntingdon, Qc., Can. E2 110
Huntingdon, Eng., U.K. I12 12
Huntingdon, Pa., U.S. D7 114
Huntingdon, Tn., U.S. I9 120
Huntington, In., U.S. H4 112
Huntington, Tx., U.S. F4 122
Huntington, Ut., U.S. D5 132
Huntington, W.V., U.S. F3 114
Huntington Beach, Ca., U.S. J7 134
Huntland, Tn., U.S. B12 122
Huntley, Mt., U.S. B4 126
Huntly, N.Z. C6 80
Huntly, Scot., U.K. D10 12
Huntsville, On., Can. C10 112
Huntsville, Al., U.S. C12 122
Huntsville, Mo., U.S. E5 120
Huntsville, Tn., U.S. H13 120
Huntsville, Tx., U.S. G3 122
Huntsville, Ut., U.S. B5 132
Hunyuan, China B5 42
Huong Hoa, Viet. D8 48
Huon Gulf, b., Pap. N. Gui. b4 79a
Huon Peninsula, pen., Pap. N. Gui. b4 79a
Huonville, Austl. o13 77a
Huoqiu, China E7 42
Huoshan, China F7 42
Huoxian, China C4 42
Hurd, Cape, c., On., Can. C8 112
Hüren Tovon uul, mtn., Mong. C4 36
Hure Qi, China C4 38
Hurghada, Egypt K4 58
Hurley, N.M., U.S. K8 132
Hurley, S.D., U.S. D15 126
Hurley, Wi., U.S. E8 118
Huron, Ca., U.S. G5 134
Huron, Oh., U.S. C3 114
Huron, S.D., U.S. C14 126
Huron, stm., Mi., U.S. B2 114
Huron, Lake, l., N.A. D7 112
Huron Mountains, hills, Mi., U.S. B2 112
Hurricane, Ut., U.S. F3 132
Hurstbridge, Austl. K5 76
Hurtado, stm., Chile E2 92
Hurtsboro, Al., U.S. E13 122
Hurunui, stm., N.Z. F5 80
Husainīwāla, India C5 54
Húsavík, Far. Is. n34 8b
Húsavík, Ice. j31 8a
Hushitai, China C5 38
Huşi, Rom. C15 26
Huslia, Ak., U.S. C8 140
Hussar, Ab., Can. E18 138
Husum, Ger. B4 16
Hutag, Mong. B5 36
Hutanopan, Indon. C1 50
Hutchinson, S. Afr. G6 70
Hutchinson, Ks., U.S. C11 128
Hutchinson, Mn., U.S. G4 118
Hutch Mountain, mtn., Az., U.S. I5 132
Hutsonville, Il., U.S. E10 120
Huttig, Ar., U.S. D6 122
Hutto, Tx., U.S. D10 130
Hutuo, stm., China B5 42
Huwei, Tai. J9 42
Huxi, China H6 42
Huxian, China D3 42
Huxley, Ab., Can. E17 138
Huy, Bel. D14 14
Huzhen, China G9 42
Huzhou, China F9 42
Hvannadalshnúkur, mtn., Ice. k31 8a
Hvar, Cro. G13 22
Hvar, Otok, i., Cro. G13 22
Hveragerði, Ice. k29 8a
Hvolsvöllur, Ice. l29 8a
Hwainan see Huainan, China E7 42
Hwange, Zimb. D4 68
Hwang Ho see Huang, stm., China D8 36
Hwangju-ŭp, Kor., N. E6 38
Hwangshih see Huangshi, China F6 42
Hyannis, Ma., U.S. C15 114
Hyannis, Ne., U.S. F11 126
Hyargas nuur, l., Mong. B3 36
Hyattville, Wy., U.S. C5 126
Hyden, Austl. F3 74
Hyden, Ky., U.S. G2 114
Hyde Park, Guy. B6 84
Hyde Park, N.Y., U.S. C12 114
Hyde Park, Vt., U.S. F4 110
Hyderābād, India C4 53
Hyderābād, Pak. F2 54
Hydra see Ýdra, i., Grc. F6 28
Hydraulic, B.C., Can. D9 138
Hydro, Ok., U.S. F10 128
Hydrographers Passage, strt., Austl. C8 76
Hyères, Fr. F12 18
Hyères, Îles d', is., Fr. G12 18
Hyesan, Kor., N. D8 38
Hyland, stm., Can. C5 106
Hyndman, Pa., U.S. E7 114
Hyndman Peak, mtn., Id., U.S. G12 136
Hyōgo, state, Japan D7 40
Hyrum, Ut., U.S. B5 132
Hysham, Mt., U.S. A5 126
Hythe, Eng., U.K. J13 12
Hyūga, Japan G4 40
Hyūga-nada, Japan G4 40
Hyvinge see Hyvinkää, Fin. F11 8
Hyvinkää, Fin. F11 8

I

Iaciara, Braz. H2 88
Iaco (Yaco), stm., S.A. F4 84
Iaçu, Braz. G5 88
Iaeger, W.V., U.S. G4 114
Ialomița, state, Rom. E14 26
Ialomița, stm., Rom. E13 26
Ialomiței, Balta, sw., Rom. E14 26
Iamonia, Lake, l., Fl., U.S. F1 116
Iapu, Braz. J4 88
Iargara, Mol. C15 26
Iași, Rom. B14 26
Iași, state, Rom. B14 26
Iatt, Lake, res., La., U.S. F6 122
Ib, stm., India G10 54
Iba, Phil. C2 52
Ibadan, Nig. H5 64
Ibagué, Col. E4 86
Ibaiti, Braz. A12 92
Ibănești, Rom. A13 26
Ibapah Peak, mtn., Ut., U.S. D3 132
Ibar, stm., Yugo. F7 26
Ibaraki, state, Japan C13 40
Ibarra, Ec. G2 86
Ibarreta, Arg. B8 92
Ibb, Yemen G5 56
Ibbenbüren, Ger. D3 16
Ibembo, D.R.C. D4 66
Iberá, Esteros del, sw., Arg. D8 92
Iberia, Mo., U.S. F5 120
Iberian Mountains see Ibérico, Sistema, mts., Spain D8 20
Iberian Peninsula, pen., Eur. D12 4
Ibérico, Sistema (Iberian Mountains), mts., Spain D8 20
Ibiá, Braz. J2 88
Ibiapina, Braz. B5 88
Ibicaraí, Braz. H6 88
Ibicuí, Braz. H5 88
Ibicuí, stm., Braz. D9 92
Ibiquera, Braz. G5 88
Ibiraçu, Braz. J5 88
Ibirapuã, Braz. I5 88
Ibirapuitã, stm., Braz. D10 92
Ibirataia, Braz. H6 88
Ibirubá, Braz. D11 92
Ibitiara, Braz. G4 88
Ibitinga, Braz. K1 88
Ibiza see Eivissa, Spain F12 20
Ibiza see Eivissa, i., Spain F12 20
Ibotirama, Braz. G4 88
İbriktepe, Tur. B9 28
Ibshawâi, Egypt I1 58
Ibusuki, Japan H3 40
Ica, Peru F2 84
Içá (Putumayo), stm., S.A. D4 84
Icabarú, stm., Ven. E10 86
Icacos Point, c., Trin. s11 105f
Icamaquã, stm., Braz. D10 92
Icamole, Mex. I7 130
Içana, Braz. G8 86
Içana (Isana), stm., S.A. G7 86
Icaño, Arg. D5 92
Icatu, Braz. B3 88
Iceberg Pass, p., Co., U.S. G7 126
İçel (Mersin), Tur. B5 58
İçel, state, Tur. B4 58
Iceland, ctry., Eur. k30 8a
Iceland Basin, unds. C11 144
Ice Mountain, mtn., B.C., Can. B9 138
Ichaikaronji, India C2 53
Ichchāpuram, India B7 53
Ichikawa, Japan D12 40
Ichinomiya, Japan D9 40
Ichkeul, Lac, l., Tun. G3 24
Ichnia, Ukr. D4 32
Ich'un see Yichun, China B10 36
Ičinskaja Sopka, vulkan, vol., Russia E20 34
Icó, Braz. D6 88
Icy Cape, c., Ak., U.S. B7 140
Ida, Mount see Ídhi Óros, mtn., Grc. H7 28
Idabel, Ok., U.S. D4 122
Ida Grove, Ia., U.S. B2 120
Idah, Nig. H6 64
Idaho, state, U.S. G12 136
Idaho City, Id., U.S. G11 136
Idaho Falls, Id., U.S. G14 136
Idaho National Engineering Laboratory, sci., Id., U.S. G14 136
Idalou, Tx., U.S. H7 128
Idanha-a-Nova, Port. E3 20
Idāppādi, India F3 53
Idar, India G4 54
Idar-Oberstein, Ger. G3 16
Idelès, Alg. E6 64
Ídhi Óros, mtn., Grc. H7 28
Idi, Indon. J3 48
Idiofa, D.R.C. F3 66
Idku, Bahra el-, l., Egypt G1 58
Idlib, Syria C7 58
Idlib, state, Syria C7 58
Idolo, Isla del, i., Mex. E10 100
Idoûkâl-en-Taghès, mtn., Niger F6 64
Idre, Swe. F5 8
Idrija, Slvn. D11 22
Idutywa, S. Afr. H9 70
Iecava, stm., Lat. D7 10
Ieper, Bel. D11 14
Ierápetra, Grc. H8 28
Ierzu, Italy E3 24
Iesolo, Italy E9 22
Ifakara, Tan. F7 66
Ife, Nig. H5 64
Iferouâne, Niger F6 64
Iferten see Yverdon-les-Bains, Switz. D3 22
Ifôghas, Adrar des, mts., Afr. F5 64
Igan, Malay. B7 50
Igan, stm., Malay. B7 50
Iganga, Ug. D6 66
Igaporã, Braz. G4 88
Igara, Braz. F5 88
Igara Paraná, stm., Col. H5 86
Igarapé-Açu, Braz. D8 84
Igarapé-Miri, Braz. B1 88
Igarka, Russia A15 32
Igatpuri, India B1 53
Igboho, Nig. H5 64
Igharghar, Oued, stm., Alg. D6 64
Igiugig, Ak., U.S. E8 140
Iglesias, Italy E2 24
Iglesias, Cerro las, mtn., Mex. B5 100
Iglesiente, reg., Italy E2 24
Igloolik, Nu., Can. B14 106
Igma, Gebel el-, mts., Egypt I4 58
Ignacio, Co., U.S. F9 132
Ignalina, Lith. E9 10
Ignatei, Mol. B15 26
Igoumenítsa, Grc. D3 28
Igra, Russia C8 32
Iguaçu (Iguazú), stm., S.A. B10 92
Iguaçu, Parque Nacional do, p.o.i., Braz. B11 92
Iguaí, Braz. H5 88
Iguala, Mex. F9 100
Igualada, Spain C12 20
Iguana, stm., Ven. D9 86
Iguape, Braz. B14 92
Iguape, stm., Braz. B13 92
Iguassu Falls, wtfl, S.A. B10 92
Iguatemi, stm., Braz. A10 92
Iguatu, Braz. D6 88
Iguazú (Iguaçu), stm., S.A. B10 92
Iguazú, Parque Nacional, p.o.i., S.A. B10 92
Iguéla, Gabon E1 66
Iguéla, Lagune, b., Gabon E1 66
Iguîdi, 'Erg, sand, Afr. D3 64
Igžej, Russia D18 32
Iharaña, Madag. C9 68
Iheya-shima, i., Japan I18 39a
Ihnâsiya el-Madina, Egypt I1 58
Ihosy, Madag. E8 68
Ihtiman, Blg. G10 26
Iida, Japan D10 40
Iisalmi, Fin. E12 8
Iiyama, Japan C11 40
Iizuka, Japan F3 40
Ijâfene, des., Maur. E3 64
Ijebu-Ode, Nig. H5 64
IJmuiden, Neth. B13 14
IJssel, stm., Neth. B15 14
IJsselmeer, l., Neth. B14 14
Ijuí, Braz. D11 92
Ijuí, stm., Braz. D10 92
Ika, Russia C19 32
Ikali, D.R.C. E4 66
Ikaría, i., Grc. F9 28
Ikatskij hrebet, mts., Russia F11 34
Ikeda, Japan E6 40
Ikej, Russia D17 32
Ikeja, Nig. H5 64
Ikela, D.R.C. E4 66
Ikerre, Nig. H6 64
İkizce, Tur. D15 28
Ikom, Nig. H6 64
Ikot-Ekpene, Nig. H6 64
Ikuno, Japan D7 40
Ikurangi, hill, Cook Is. a26 78j
Ila, Nig. H6 64
Ilagan, Phil. B3 52
Ilaiyānkudi, India G4 53
Īlām, Iran C6 56
Ilām, Nepal E11 54
Ilan, Tai. I9 42
Ilanskij, Russia C17 32
Ilaro, Nig. H5 64
Iława, Pol. C15 16
Ilbenge, Russia D13 34
Île-à-la-Crosse, Sk., Can. D9 106
Ilebo, D.R.C. E4 66
Île-de-France, hist. reg., Fr. E11 14
Île de France, i., Grnld. B22 141
Île-du-Prince-Édouard see Prince Edward Island, state, Can. D13 110
Ilek, stm., Asia D8 32
Ilesha, Nig. H5 64
Îles Loyauté, state, N. Cal. m16 79d
Île Tintamarre, i., Anguilla A2 105a
Ilevskij Pogost, Russia F20 8
Ileza, Russia F20 8
Ilfracombe, Austl. D5 76
Ilfracombe, Eng., U.K. J8 12
Ilhabela, Braz. L3 88
Ilha Grande, Baía da, b., Braz. L3 88
Ilha Solteira, Represa de, res., Braz. D6 90
Ilhea Point, c., Nmb. C2 70
Ilhéus, Braz. H6 88
Ilia, Rom. D9 26
Iliamna, Ak., U.S. E8 140
Iliamna Lake, l., Ak., U.S. D9 140
Il'ič, Kaz. F11 32
Ilicinea, Braz. K3 88
Iliff, Co., U.S. G9 126
Iligan, Phil. F5 52
Iligan Bay, b., Phil. F4 52
Iliniza, vol., Ec. H2 86
Ilion, N.Y., U.S. A10 114
Ilir, Russia C18 32
Ilizi, Alg. D6 64
Il'ja, Bela. F10 10
Iljino, Russia E14 10
Iljinskij, Russia G17 34
Iljinskoe, Russia D19 10
Iljinsko-Podomskoe, Russia F23 8
Iljiny gory, hills, Russia D17 10
Ilkal, India D2 53
Ilkley, Eng., U.K. H11 12
Illampu, Nevado, mtn., Bol. C3 90
Illana Bay, b., Phil. G4 52
Illapel, Chile E2 92
Ille-et-Vilaine, state, Fr. F7 14
Illéla, Niger G6 64
Iller, stm., Ger. I6 16
Illertissen, Ger. H6 16
Illescas, Mex. D7 100
Illichivs'k, Ukr. C17 26
Illimani, Nevado, mtn., Bol. C3 90
Illinois, state, U.S. D8 120
Illinois, stm., U.S. B3 122
Illinois, stm., Il., U.S. E7 120
Illinois, stm., Or., U.S. H3 136
Il'men', ozero, l., Russia B14 10
Ilo, Peru G3 84
Iloilo, Phil. E4 52
Ilomantsi, Fin. E14 8
Ilorin, Nig. H5 64
Il'pyrskij, Russia D21 34
Ilūkste, Lat. E9 10
Ilulissat see Jakobshavn, Grnld. D15 141
Ilwaki, Indon. G8 44
Ilwŏl-san, mtn., Kor., S. C1 40
Imabari, Japan E5 40
Imaichi, Japan C12 40
Imandra, ozero, l., Russia C14 8
Imari, Japan F2 40
Imaruí, Braz. D13 92
Imaruí, Lagoa do, l., Braz. D13 92
Imatra, Fin. F13 8
Imavere, Est. B8 10
Imbabura, state, Ec. G2 86
Imbituba, Braz. D13 92
Imeni Cjurupy, Russia E21 10
Imeni Kirova, Russia E14 34
Imeni Poliny Osipenko, Russia F16 34
Imeni Stepana Razina, Russia I21 8
Imeni Željabova, Russia A19 10
Īmī, Eth. F8 62
Imías, Cuba B10 102
Imilac, Chile B3 92
Imlay, Nv., U.S. C7 134
Imlay City, Mi., U.S. E6 112
Immenstadt, Ger. I6 16
Immokalee, Fl., U.S. J4 116
Imnaha, stm., Or., U.S. E10 136
Imola, Italy F8 22
Imonda, Pap. N. Gui. a3 79a
Impasugong, Phil. F5 52
Imperatriz, Braz. C2 88
Imperia, Italy G5 22
Imperial, Sk., Can. C8 124
Imperial, Ca., U.S. K10 134
Imperial, Tx., U.S. C5 130
Imperial Beach, Ca., U.S. K8 134
Imperial Dam, dam, U.S. K2 132
Imperial de Aragón, Canal, can., Spain C9 20
Imperial Valley, val., Ca., U.S. E5 98
Impfondo, Congo D3 66
Imphāl, India D7 46
Imroz, Tur. C8 28
Imst, Aus. C7 22
Imuris, Mex. F7 98
Ina, Japan D10 40
Ina, Il., U.S. F9 120
Inajá, Braz. E7 88
I-n-Amenas, Alg. D6 64
Iñapari, Peru F4 84
Inarajan, Guam j10 78c
Inari, Fin. B12 8
Inarigda, Russia B19 32
Inarijärvi, l., Fin. B12 8
Inawashiro-ko, l., Japan B12 40
Inca, Spain E13 20
Inca de Oro, Chile C3 92
Incahuasi, Cerro de, mtn., S.A. C3 92
İnce Burun, c., Tur. C10 28
İncekum Burnu, c., Tur. B4 58
Inchelium, Wa., U.S. B8 136
Inch'ŏn, Kor., S. F7 38
İncirliova, Tur. F10 28
Incomati (Komati), stm., Afr. E10 70
Incudine, Monte, mtn., Fr. H15 18
Incy, Russia D19 8
Indaiá, stm., Braz. J3 88
Indalsälven, stm., Swe. E6 8
Indé, Mex. I2 130
Independence, Ca., U.S. G7 134
Independence, Ia., U.S. B6 120
Independence, Ks., U.S. G2 120
Independence, Ky., U.S. F13 120
Independence, La., U.S. G8 122
Independence, Mo., U.S. E3 120
Independence, Va., U.S. H4 114
Independence, Wi., U.S. G7 118
Independence Fjord, b., Grnld. A20 141
Independencia, Bol. C3 90
Independência, Braz. C5 88
Inderborskij, Kaz. E8 32
Indi, India C2 53
India, ctry., Asia D4 46
Indialantic, Fl., U.S. H5 116
Indiana, Pa., U.S. D6 114
Indiana, state, U.S. D11 120
Indiana Dunes National Lakeshore, p.o.i., In., U.S. G2 112
Indianapolis, In., U.S. I3 112
Indian Bayou, stm., Ar., U.S. C7 122
Indian Church, Belize D3 102
Indian Head, Sk., Can. D10 124
Indian Lake, N.Y., U.S. G2 110
Indian Lake, l., On., Can. A7 112
Indian Lake, l., Mi., U.S. B3 112
Indian Ocean K11 142
Indianola, Ia., U.S. C4 120
Indianola, Ms., U.S. D8 122
Indianola, Ne., U.S. A8 128
Indian Peak, mtn., Ut., U.S. E3 132
Indian River, Mi., U.S. C5 112
Indian Rock, mtn., Wa., U.S. E6 136
Indiantown, Fl., U.S. I5 116
Indiera Alta, P.R. B2 104a
Indiga, Russia C23 8
Indigirka, stm., Russia C18 34
Indin, Mya. H14 54
Indio, Ca., U.S. J9 134
Indira Gandhi Canal, can., India E4 54
Indispensable Strait, strt., Sol. Is. e9 79b
Indochina, reg., Asia D7 48
Indonesia, ctry., Asia J16 30
Indore, India G5 54
Indragiri, stm., Indon. D2 50
Indramayu, Indon. G6 50
Indrāvati, stm., India B5 53

Name	Map Ref.	Page
Indravati Tiger Reserve, p.o.i., India	B5	53
Indre, state, Fr.	C7	18
Indre, stm., Fr.	G10	14
Indre-et-Loire, state, Fr.	G9	14
Indus, stm., Asia	D2	46
Industry, Tx., U.S.	H2	122
İnece, Tur.	B10	28
In Ecker, Alg.	E6	64
İnegöl, Tur.	C12	28
Ineu, Rom.	C8	26
Inez, Ky., U.S.	G3	114
Inez, Tx., U.S.	F11	130
Inferior, Laguna, b., Mex.	G11	100
Infiernillo, Canal del, strt., Mex.	G6	98
Infiernillo, Presa del, res., Mex.	F7	100
Ing, stm., Thai.	C5	48
Ingá, Braz.	D8	88
Ingabu, Mya.	D2	48
Ingal, Niger	F6	64
Ingall Point, c., On., Can.	B10	118
Ingelheim, Ger.	G4	16
Ingende, D.R.C.	E3	66
Ingeniero Jacobacci, Arg.	H3	90
Ingeniero Luiggi, Arg.	G5	92
Ingham, Austl.	B6	76
Inglefield Land, reg., Grnld.	B12	141
Ingleside, Tx., U.S.	G10	130
Inglewood, Austl.	G8	76
Inglewood, Austl.	K4	76
Inglewood, Ca., U.S.	J7	134
Inglis, Mb., Can.	D12	124
Ingolf Fjord, b., Grnld.	A22	141
Ingolstadt, Ger.	H7	16
Ingonish, N.S., Can.	D16	110
Ingrāj Bāzār, India	F12	54
Ingrid Christensen Coast, cst., Ant.	B12	81
In Guezzam, Alg.	F6	64
Ingušetija, state, Russia	F6	32
Ingushetia see Ingušetija, state, Russia	F6	32
Inhaca, Ilha da, i., Moz.	E11	70
Inhambane, Moz.	C12	70
Inhambane, state, Moz.	C12	70
Inhambane, Baía de, b., Moz.	C12	70
Inhambupe, Braz.	F6	88
Inhaminga, Moz.	D5	68
Inhapim, Braz.	J4	88
Inharrime, Moz.	D12	70
Inhassoro, Moz.	B12	70
Inhuma, Braz.	D5	88
Inhumas, Braz.	I1	88
Inimutaba, Braz.	J3	88
Ining see Yining, China	F14	32
Inírida, stm., Col.	F7	86
Inis see Ennis, Ire.	I3	12
Inis Córthaidh see Enniscorthy, Ire.	I6	12
Inishbofin, i., Ire.	H2	12
Inishmore, i., Ire.	H3	12
Inishowen, pen., Ire.	F5	12
Inishturk, i., Ire.	H2	12
Inja, Russia	E17	34
Inja, stm., Russia	D18	34
Injune, Austl.	E7	76
Inkom, Id., U.S.	H14	136
Inkster, N.D., U.S.	F16	124
Inland Lake, l., Mb., Can.	B14	124
Inland Sea see Seto-naikai, Japan	E5	40
Inle Lake, l., Mya.	B3	48
Inman, Ks., U.S.	C11	128
Inman Mills, S.C., U.S.	A3	116
Inn, stm., Eur.	B10	22
Innamincka, Austl.	F3	76
Inner Channel, strt., Belize	D3	102
Inner Hebrides, is., Scot., U.K.	E6	12
Inner Mongolia see Nei Monggol, state, China	C7	36
Inner Sister Island, i., Austl.	m13	77a
Innisfail, Austl.	A6	76
Innisfail, Ab., Can.	D17	138
Innisfree, Ab., Can.	C19	138
Innokentevka, Russia	G16	34
Innoko, stm., Ak., U.S.	D8	140
Innoshima, Japan	E6	40
Innsbruck, Aus.	C8	22
Innviertel, reg., Aus.	B10	22
Inola, Ok., U.S.	H2	120
Inongo, D.R.C.	E3	66
İnönü, Tur.	D13	28
Inowrocław, Pol.	D14	16
In Salah, Alg.	D5	64
Instow, Sk., Can.	E5	124
Inta, Russia	A10	32
Intendente Alvear, Arg.	G6	92
İntepe, Tur.	D9	28
Interlaken, Switz.	D4	22
Interlândia, Braz.	I1	88
International Falls, Mn., U.S.	C5	118
Inthanon, Doi, mtn., Thai.	C4	48
Intiyaco, Arg.	D7	92
Intracoastal Waterway, strt., U.S.	L5	116
Intracoastal Waterway, strt., U.S.	H10	130
Intu, Indon.	D9	50
Inubō-saki, c., Japan	D13	40
Inukjuak, Qc., Can.	D15	106
Inuvik, N.T., Can.	B4	106
Inverbervie, Scot., U.K.	E10	12
Invercargill, N.Z.	H3	80
Inverell, Austl.	G8	76
Inverloch, Austl.	L5	76
Invermay, Sk., Can.	C10	124
Invermere, B.C., Can.	F14	138
Inverness, N.S., Can.	D15	110
Inverness, Scot., U.K.	D8	12
Inverness, Ca., U.S.	E3	134
Inverness, Fl., U.S.	H3	116
Inverurie, Scot., U.K.	D10	12
Inverway, Austl.	C5	74
Investigator Strait, strt., Austl.	G7	74
Inwood, Mb., Can.	D16	124
Inyangani, mtn., Zimb.	D5	68
Inyathi, Zimb.	D4	68
Inyo, Mount, mtn., Ca., U.S.	G8	134
Inyokern, Ca., U.S.	H8	134
Inyo Mountains, mts., Ca., U.S.	G7	134
Inzana Lake, l., B.C., Can.	B6	138
Ioánnina, Grc.	D3	28
Iokanga, stm., Russia	C18	8
Iola, Ks., U.S.	G2	120
Ioma, Pap. N. Gui.	b4	79a
Iona, Ang.	D1	68
Iona, N.S., Can.	D16	110
Iona, Id., U.S.	G15	136
Iona, i., Scot., U.K.	E6	12
Ione, Ca., U.S.	E5	134
Ione, Wa., U.S.	B9	136
Ionia, Mi., U.S.	E4	112
Ionian Islands see Iónioi Nísoi, is., Grc.	E3	28
Ionian Sea, Eur.	F11	24
Iónioi Nísoi, state, Grc.	E3	28
Iónioi Nísoi (Ionian Islands), is., Grc.	E3	28
Iony, ostrov, i., Russia	E17	34
Íos, i., Grc.	G8	28
Iosegun Lake see Fox Creek, Ab., Can.	B14	138
Iowa, La., U.S.	G5	122
Iowa, state, U.S.	I5	118
Iowa, stm., Ia., U.S.	C6	120
Iowa City, Ia., U.S.	C6	120
Iowa Falls, Ia., U.S.	B4	120
Iowa Park, Tx., U.S.	H10	128
Ipameri, Braz.	I1	88
Ipanema, stm., Braz.	E7	88
Ipanguaçu, Braz.	C7	88
Ipatinga, Braz.	J4	88
Ipatovo, Russia	E6	32
Ipaumirim, Braz.	D6	88
Ípeiros, state, Grc.	D3	28
Ípeiros, hist. reg., Grc.	D3	28
Ipel' (Ipoly), stm., Eur.	I14	16
Ipiales, Col.	G3	86
Ipiaú, Braz.	H6	88
Ipin see Yibin, China	F5	36
Ipirá, Braz.	G6	88
Ipixuna, Braz.	C3	88
Ipoh, Malay.	J5	48
Ipojuca, stm., Braz.	E7	88
Ipoly (Ipel'), stm., Eur.	I14	16
Iporã, Braz.	G7	84
Iporã, Braz.	A11	92
Ipota, Vanuatu	I17	79d
İpsala, Tur.	C9	28
Ipswich, Austl.	F9	76
Ipswich, Eng., U.K.	I14	12
Ipswich, Ma., U.S.	B15	114
Ipswich, S.D., U.S.	B13	126
Ipu, Braz.	C5	88
Ipubi, Braz.	D5	88
Ipuc' (Iput'), stm., Eur.	H14	10
Ipueiras, Braz.	C5	88
Iput' (Ipuc'), stm., Eur.	H14	10
Iqaluit, Nu., Can.	C17	106
Iqfahs, Egypt	J1	58
Iquique, Chile	D2	90
Iquitos, Peru	D3	84
Ira, Tx., U.S.	B7	130
Iracema, Braz.	C6	88
Irákleia, i., Grc.	G8	28
Irákleio, Grc.	H8	28
Iran, ctry., Asia	C7	56
Iran Mountains, mts., Asia	C9	50
Īrānshahr, Iran	D9	56
Irapa, Ven.	B10	86
Irapuato, Mex.	E8	100
Iraq, ctry., Asia	C5	56
Irará, Braz.	F6	88
Irati, Braz.	B12	92
Irazú, Volcán, vol., C.R.	G6	102
Irbejskoe, Russia	C17	32
Irbid, Jord.	F6	58
Irbid, state, Jord.	F6	58
Irbīl, Iraq	B5	56
Irbit, Russia	C10	32
Irdning, Aus.	C11	22
Irebu, D.R.C.	E3	66
Irecê, Braz.	F5	88
Ireland, ctry., Eur.	H4	12
Ireland Island North, i., Ber.	k15	104e
Irene, S.D., U.S.	D15	126
Ireng (Maú), stm., S.A.	F12	86
Ireton, Ia., U.S.	B1	120
Irgiz, Kaz.	E10	32
Iri, Kor., S.	G7	38
Iriba, Chad	E4	62
Iriga, Phil.	D4	52
Irîgui, reg., Afr.	F3	64
Iringa, Tan.	F7	66
Irinjālakuda, India	F3	53
Iriomote-jima, i., Japan	G9	36
Iriri, stm., Braz.	D7	84
Irish, Mount, mtn., Nv., U.S.	F1	132
Irish Sea, Eur.	H7	12
Irituia, Braz.	A2	88
Irkutsk, Russia	D18	32
Irma, Ab., Can.	D19	138
Irminger Basin, unds.	B10	144
Irnijärvi, l., Fin.	D13	8
Iroise, b., Fr.	F4	14
Iron Bottom Sound, strt., Sol. Is.	e8	79b
Iron Bridge, On., Can.	B6	112
Iron City, Tn., U.S.	B11	122
Irondale, Al., U.S.	D12	122
Irondale, Mo., U.S.	G7	120
Irondequoit, N.Y., U.S.	E12	112
Iron Gate, val., Eur.	E9	26
Iron Knob, Austl.	F7	74
Iron Mountain, Mi., U.S.	C1	112
Iron Range, Austl.	B8	74
Iron River, Mi., U.S.	E10	118
Ironton, Mn., U.S.	E4	118
Ironton, Mo., U.S.	G7	120
Ironton, Oh., U.S.	F3	114
Ironwood, Mi., U.S.	E8	118
Iroquois, On., Can.	D14	112
Iroquois, stm., U.S.	H2	112
Iroquois Falls, On., Can.	F14	106
Irō-zaki, c., Japan	E11	40
Irrawaddy see Ayeyarwady, stm., Mya.	E8	46
Irricana, Ab., Can.	E17	138
Irrigon, Or., U.S.	E7	136
Irshava, Ukr.	A10	26
Irsina, Italy	D10	24
Irtyš see Irtysh, stm., Asia	C11	32
Irtysh (Irtyš) (Ertix), stm., Asia	C11	32
Irtyšsk, Kaz.	D12	32
Irún, Spain	A9	20
Iruña see Pamplona, Spain	B9	20
Irurzun, Spain	B9	20
Irú Tepuy, mtn., Ven.	E11	86
Irvine, Ab., Can.	E3	124
Irvine, Scot., U.K.	F8	12
Irvines Landing, B.C., Can.	G6	138
Irving, Tx., U.S.	B10	130
Irvington, Ky., U.S.	G11	120
Isa, Nig.	G6	64
Isaac, stm., Austl.	D7	76
Isaac Lake, l., B.C., Can.	C10	138
Isabel, state, Sol. Is.	d8	79b
Isabela, Phil.	G3	52
Isabela, P.R.	A1	104a
Isabela, Cabo, c., Dom. Rep.	C12	102
Isabela, Isla, i., Ec.	i11	84a
Isabelia, Cordillera, mts., Nic.	F5	102
Isaccea, Rom.	D15	26
Isachsen, Nu., Can.	B5	141
Isachsen, Cape, c., Nu., Can.	B4	141
Ísafjarðardjúp, b., Ice.	j28	8a
Ísafjörður, Ice.	j28	8a
Isahaya, Japan	G3	40
Isak, Indon.	J3	48
Isaka, Tan.	E6	66
Īsa Khel, Pak.	B3	54
Işalniţa, Rom.	E10	26
Isana (Içana), stm., S.A.	G7	86
Isangel, Vanuatu	I17	79d
Isanti, Mn., U.S.	F5	118
Isar, stm., Eur.	H8	16
Isarog, Mount, vol., Phil.	D4	52
İscehisar, Tur.	E13	28
Ischia, Italy	D7	24
Ischia, Isola d', i., Italy	D7	24
Ise, Japan	E9	40
Iseo, Lago d', l., Italy	E6	22
Isère, state, Fr.	D11	18
Isère, stm., Fr.	D11	18
Iserlohn, Ger.	E3	16
Isernia, Italy	C8	24
Isesaki, Japan	C12	40
Ise-shima-kokuritsu-kōen, p.o.i., Japan	E9	40
Ise-wan, b., Japan	E9	40
Iseyin, Nig.	H5	64
Isezaki see Isesaki, Japan	C12	40
Isfahan see Eşfahān, Iran	C7	56
Isfara, Taj.	A11	56
Isherton, Guy.	F12	86
Ishigaki, Japan	G9	36
Ishikari, stm., Japan	C14	38
Ishikari-wan, b., Japan	C14	38
Ishikawa, state, Japan	C9	40
Ishim (Išim), stm., Asia	C12	32
Ishinomaki, Japan	A14	40
Ishioka, Japan	C13	40
Ishizuchi-san, mtn., Japan	F5	40
Ishpeming, Mi., U.S.	B2	112
Ishurdi, Bngl.	F12	54
Isigny-sur-Mer, Fr.	E7	14
Işıklı, Tur.	E12	28
Isil'kul', Russia	C12	32
Išim, Russia	C11	32
Išimskaja ravnina, pl., Asia	C11	32
Isiolo, Kenya	D7	66
Isipingo, ngh., S. Afr.	G10	70
Isiro, D.R.C.	D5	66
Isis, Austl.	E9	76
Iskăr, stm., Blg.	F11	26
Iskăr, Jazovir, res., Blg.	G10	26
İskenderun (Alexandretta), Tur.	B6	58
İskenderun Körfezi, b., Tur.	B6	58
Iskitim, Russia	D14	32
Iskut, stm., B.C., Can.	D4	106
Isla, Mex.	G11	100
Isla, Salar de la, pl., Chile	B3	92
İslâhiye, Tur.	A7	58
Islāmābād, Pak.	B4	54
Islāmkot, Pak.	F3	54
Islāmpur, India	C2	53
Islāmpur, India	F10	54
Islāmpur, India	E12	54
Island, Ky., U.S.	G10	120
Island Falls, Me., U.S.	E8	110
Island Harbour, Anguilla	A1	105a
Island Lake, l., Mb., Can.	E12	106
Island Park, Id., U.S.	F15	136
Island Pond, Vt., U.S.	F5	110
Islands, Bay of, b., Nf., Can.	j22	107a
Isla Patrulla, Ur.	F10	92
Isla Vista, Ca., U.S.	I5	134
Islay, i., Scot., U.K.	F6	12
Isle, Mn., U.S.	E5	118
Isle, stm., Fr.	E5	18
Isle of Man, dep., Eur.	G8	12
Isle of Wight, Va., U.S.	H9	114
Isle Royale National Park, p.o.i., Mi., U.S.	C10	118
Islesboro Island, i., Me., U.S.	F8	110
Isleta, N.M., U.S.	I10	132
Isleton, Ca., U.S.	E4	134
Islón, Chile	D2	92
Ismailia (Al-Ismā'īlīyah), Egypt	H3	58
Isna, Egypt	B6	62
Isny, Ger.	I5	16
Isoka, Zam.	C5	68
Isola del Liri, Italy	I10	22
Isola di Capo Rizzuto, Italy	F11	24
Isonzo, stm., Eur.	E10	22
Isparta, Tur.	F13	28
Isparta, state, Tur.	F13	28
Ispica, Italy	H8	24
Israel, ctry., Asia	G5	58
Isrā'īl see Israel, ctry., Asia	G5	58
Issa, stm., Russia	D11	10
Isser, Oued, stm., Alg.	H14	20
Issia, C. Iv.	H3	64
Issoire, Fr.	D9	18
Issoudun, Fr.	H10	14
Issuna, Tan.	F6	66
Issyk-Kul', Kyrg.	F13	32
Issyk-Kul, Lake see Issyk-Kul', ozero, l., Kyrg.	F13	32
Issyk-Kul', ozero, l., Kyrg.	F13	32
Īstādeh-ye Moqor, Āb-e, l., Afg.	B2	54
İstanbul, Tur.	B12	28
İstanbul, state, Tur.	B11	28
İstanbul Boğazı (Bosporus), strt., Tur.	B12	28
Istiaía, Grc.	E6	28
Istmina, Col.	E3	86
Isto, Mount, mtn., Ak., U.S.	C11	140
Istra, Russia	E19	10
Istria, pen., Eur.	E10	22
Itá, Para.	B9	92
Itabaiana, Braz.	D8	88
Itabaiana, Braz.	F7	88
Itabaianinha, Braz.	F7	88
Itabapoana, Braz.	K5	88
Itaberaba, Braz.	G5	88
Itaberaí, Braz.	G8	84
Itabi, Braz.	F7	88
Itabira, Braz.	J4	88
Itabuna, Braz.	H6	88
Itacajá, Braz.	E2	88
Itacambiruçu, stm., Braz.	I4	88
Itacoatiara, Braz.	D6	84
Itacurubí del Rosario, Para.	B9	92
Itaeté, Braz.	G5	88
Itaguajé, Braz.	D6	90
Itaguara, Braz.	K3	88
Itaguari, stm., Braz.	H3	88
Itagüí, Col.	D4	86
Itaí, Braz.	A13	92
Itaiçaba, Braz.	C7	88
Itaim, stm., Braz.	D5	88
Itainópolis, Braz.	D5	88
Itaipu Reservoir, res., S.A.	B10	92
Itäisen Suomenlahden kansallispuisto, p.o.i., Fin.	F12	8
Itaituba, Braz.	D6	84
Itajaí, Braz.	C13	92
Itajubá, Braz.	L3	88
Itaju do Colônia, Braz.	H6	88
Itajuípe, Braz.	H6	88
Itala Game Reserve, S. Afr.	E10	70
Itálica, hist., Spain	G4	20
Italy, Tx., U.S.	B11	130
Italy, ctry., Eur.	G11	6
Itamaraju, Braz.	I6	88
Itamarandiba, Braz.	I4	88
Itamarandiba, stm., Braz.	I4	88
Itamari, Braz.	G6	88
Itambacuri, Braz.	I5	88
Itambé, Braz.	H5	88
Itami, Japan	E8	40
Itampolo, Madag.	E7	68
Itānagar, India	E14	54
Itanhaém, Braz.	B14	92
Itanhém, Braz.	I5	88
Itaobim, Braz.	I5	88
Itapagipe, Braz.	J1	88
Itapajé, Braz.	B6	88
Itaparica, Ilha de, i., Braz.	G6	88
Itaparica, Represa de, res., Braz.	E6	88
Itapebi, Braz.	H6	88
Itapecerica, Braz.	K3	88
Itapecuru-Mirim, Braz.	B3	88
Itapemirim, Braz.	K5	88
Itaperuna, Braz.	K5	88
Itapetim, Braz.	D7	88
Itapetinga, Braz.	H5	88
Itapetininga, Braz.	L1	88
Itapetininga, stm., Braz.	A14	92
Itapeva, Braz.	L1	88
Itapicuru, Braz.	F6	88
Itapicuru, stm., Braz.	B3	88
Itapicuru, stm., Braz.	F6	88
Itapipoca, Braz.	B6	88
Itapiranga, Braz.	D6	84
Itapirapuã, Braz.	G7	84
Itapiúna, Braz.	C6	88
Itápolis, Braz.	K1	88
Itaporã de Goiás, Braz.	D1	88
Itaporanga, Braz.	D6	88
Itaporanga d'Ajuda, Braz.	F7	88
Itapúa, state, Para.	C10	92
Itaquara, Braz.	G6	88
Itaquari, Braz.	K5	88
Itaqui, Braz.	D9	92
Itarantim, Braz.	H5	88
Itararé, Braz.	B13	92
Itararé, stm., Braz.	A13	92
Itārsi, India	G6	54
Itarumã, Braz.	C6	90
Itasca, Tx., U.S.	B10	130
Itasca, Lake, l., Mn., U.S.	D3	118
Itata, stm., Chile	H1	92
Itatinga, Braz.	L1	88
Itatira, Braz.	C6	88
Itatupã, Braz.	D7	84
Itaueira, Braz.	D4	88
Itaueira, stm., Braz.	D4	88
Itaúna, Braz.	K3	88
Itbayat Island, i., Phil.	K9	42
Itéa, Grc.	E5	28
Iténez (Guaporé), stm., S.A.	F5	84
Ithaca, Mi., U.S.	E5	112
Ithaca, N.Y., U.S.	B9	114
Ithaca see Itháki, i., Grc.	E3	28
Itháki, i., Grc.	E3	28
Itimbiri, stm., D.R.C.	D4	66
Itinga, Braz.	I5	88
Itiquira, stm., Braz.	G6	84
Itiruçu, Braz.	G5	88
Itiúba, Braz.	F5	88
Itla el-Bâsha, hill, Egypt	K3	58
Itō, Japan	E12	40
Itoigawa, Japan	B10	40
Iton, stm., Fr.	F9	14
Itororó, Braz.	H5	88
Itsuki, Japan	G3	40
Ittiri, Italy	D2	24
Ittoqqortoormiit see Scoresbysund, Grnld.	C21	141
Itu, Braz.	L2	88
Itu, stm., Braz.	D10	92
Ituaçu, Braz.	G5	88
Ituango, Col.	D4	86
Ituberá, Braz.	G6	88
Itueta, Braz.	J5	88
Ituí, stm., Braz.	E3	84
Ituiutaba, Braz.	J1	88
Itumbiara, Braz.	J1	88
Ituna, Sk., Can.	C10	124
Itupiranga, Braz.	E8	84
Ituporanga, Braz.	C13	92
Iturama, Braz.	C6	90
Iturbide, Mex.	C3	102
Iturup, ostrov (Etorofu-tō), i., Russia	B17	38
Ituverava, Braz.	K2	88
Ituxi, stm., Braz.	E4	84
Ituzaingó, Arg.	C9	92
Itzehoe, Ger.	C5	16
Iuka, Ms., U.S.	C10	122
Iul'tin, Russia	C25	34
Iúna, Braz.	K5	88
Ivacèvičy, Bela.	H8	10
Ivačovo, Russia	F17	8
Ivaí, stm., Braz.	D6	90
Ivaiporã, Braz.	B12	92
Ivalo, Fin.	B12	8
Ivalojoki, stm., Fin.	B12	8
Ivanava, Bela.	H8	10
Ivančice, Czech Rep.	G12	16
Ivangorod, Russia	A11	10
Ivangrad, Yugo.	G6	26
Ivanhoe, Austl.	I5	76
Ivanhoe, Ca., U.S.	G6	134
Ivanhoe, Mn., U.S.	G2	118
Ivanhoe, Va., U.S.	H4	114
Ivanišči, Russia	D18	10
Ivanjica, Yugo.	F7	26
Ivan'kovo, Russia	F20	10
Ivan'kovskoe vodohranilišče, res., Russia	D19	10
Ivano-Frankivs'k, Ukr.	F13	6
Ivano-Frankivs'k, co., Ukr.	A11	26
Ivanovka, Russia	F14	34
Ivanovo, Russia	H19	8
Ivanovskaja oblast', co., Russia	H19	8
Ivanovskoe, Russia	A11	10
Ivanpah Lake, l., Ca., U.S.	H1	132
Ivdel', Russia	B9	32
Ivigtut, Grnld.	E16	141
Ivindo, stm., Gabon	D2	66
Ivinheima, stm., Braz.	D6	90
Iviza see Eivissa, Spain	F12	20
Ivjanec, Bela.	G9	10
Ivohibe, Madag.	E8	68
Ivory Coast see Cote d'Ivoire, ctry., Afr.	H3	64
Ivory Coast, cst., C. Iv.	I3	64
Ivrea, Italy	E4	22
İvrindi, Tur.	D10	28
Ivujivik, Qc., Can.	C15	106
Iwaki, Japan	B13	40
Iwaki-san, vol., Japan	D14	38
Iwakuni, Japan	E5	40
Iwami, Japan	D7	40
Iwanuma, Japan	A13	40
Iwata, Japan	E10	40
Iwate, state, Japan	A14	40
Iwate-san, vol., Japan	E14	38
'Iweibid, Gebel, mtn., Egypt	H3	58
Iwo, Nig.	H5	64
Ixmiquilpan, Mex.	E9	100
Ixopo, S. Afr.	G10	70
Ixtapa, Mex.	G8	100
Ixtepec, Mex.	G11	100
Ixtlán del Río, Mex.	E6	100
Iyang see Yiyang, China	G5	42
Iyo, Japan	F5	40
Iyo-mishima, Japan	F6	40
Iyo-nada, Japan	F5	40
Izabal, Lago de, l., Guat.	E3	102
Izamal, Mex.	B3	102
Izapa, hist., Mex.	H12	100
Izberbaš, Russia	F7	32
Izbica, Pol.	F19	16
Izegem, Bel.	D12	14
Iževsk, Russia	C8	32
Izium, Ukr.	E5	32
Ižma, stm., Russia	B8	32
Izmaïl, Ukr.	D15	26
Izmalkovo, Russia	H21	10
Izmayil see Izmaïl, Ukr.	D15	26
İzmir (Smyrna), Tur.	E10	28
İzmir, state, Tur.	E10	28
İzmir Körfezi, b., Tur.	E9	28
İzmit (Kocaeli), Tur.	C12	28
İzmit Körfezi, b., Tur.	C12	28
İznik, Tur.	C12	28
İznik Gölü, l., Tur.	C12	28
Iznoski, Russia	E18	10
Izozog, Bañados del, sw., Bol.	C4	90
Izra', Syria	F7	58
Izsák, Hung.	C6	26
Iztaccíhuatl, Volcán, vol., Mex.	F9	100
Iztaccíhuatl y Popocatéptl, Parques Nacionales, p.o.i., Mex.	F9	100
Izucar de Matamoros, Mex.	F9	100
Izu-hantō, pen., Japan	E11	40
Izuhara, Japan	E2	40
Izu Islands see Izu-shotō, is., Japan	E12	40
Izumi, Japan	G3	40
Izumi, Japan	A13	40
Izumi, Japan	E8	40
Izumo, Japan	D5	40
Izu-shotō (Izu Islands), is., Japan	E12	40
Izu Trench, unds.	G17	142
Izvestij CIK, ostrova, is., Russia	A5	34
Izvorul Muntelui, Lacul, l., Rom.	C12	26

J

Name	Map Ref.	Page
Jabal, Baḩr al- see Mountain Nile, stm., Afr.	F6	62
Jabal al-Awliyā', Sudan	D6	62
Jabal Lubnān, state, Leb.	D6	58
Jabalón, stm., Spain	F7	20
Jabalpur, India	G7	54
Jabālyah, Gaza	G5	58
Jabbūl, Sabkhat al-, l., Syria	C8	58
Jabiru, Austl.	B6	74
Jablah, Syria	C6	58
Jablanica, Bos.	F4	26
Jablaničko jezero, res., Bos.	F4	26
Jablonec nad Nisou, Czech Rep.	F11	16
Jabłonka, Pol.	G15	16
Jablonovyj hrebet, mts., Russia	F11	34
Jablunkov, Czech Rep.	G14	16
Jaboticabal, Braz.	K1	88
Jaca, Spain	B10	20
Jacala, Mex.	E9	100
Jacaré, stm., Braz.	F5	88
Jacareí, Braz.	L2	88
Jacarezinho, Braz.	D7	90
Jáchal, stm., Arg.	E4	92
Jaciara, Braz.	G6	84
Jacinto, Braz.	I5	88
Jacinto Aráuz, Arg.	I6	92
Jacinto City, Tx., U.S.	H3	122
Jackfish Lake, l., Sk., Can.	A5	124
Jackhead Harbour, Mb., Can.	C16	124
Jack Mountain, mtn., Mt., U.S.	D14	136
Jackpot, Nv., U.S.	B2	132
Jacksboro, Tn., U.S.	H1	114
Jacksboro, Tx., U.S.	H10	128
Jackson, Ca., U.S.	E5	134
Jackson, Ky., U.S.	G2	114
Jackson, La., U.S.	G7	122
Jackson, Mi., U.S.	B1	114
Jackson, Mn., U.S.	H4	118
Jackson, Ms., U.S.	E8	122
Jackson, N.C., U.S.	H8	114
Jackson, Oh., U.S.	E3	114
Jackson, S.C., U.S.	C4	116
Jackson, Tn., U.S.	B10	122
Jackson, Wy., U.S.	G16	136
Jackson, stm., Va., U.S.	G6	114
Jackson, Mount, mtn., Ant.	C34	81
Jackson, Mount, mtn., Austl.	F3	74
Jackson Creek, stm., Can.	E12	124
Jackson Lake, l., Wy., U.S.	G16	136
Jacksonville, Al., U.S.	D13	122
Jacksonville, Ar., U.S.	C6	122
Jacksonville, Fl., U.S.	F4	116
Jacksonville, Il., U.S.	E7	120
Jacksonville, N.C., U.S.	B8	116
Jacksonville, Or., U.S.	A2	134
Jacksonville, Tx., U.S.	F3	122
Jacksonville Beach, Fl., U.S.	F4	116
Jacmel, Haiti	C11	102
Jaco, Mex.	B6	100
Jacobābād, Pak.	D2	54
Jacobina, Braz.	F5	88
Jacobsdal, S. Afr.	F7	70
Jacques-Cartier, Mont, mtn., Qc., Can.	A11	110
Jacu, stm., Braz.	D8	88
Jacuí, stm., Braz.	D11	92
Jacuípe, stm., Braz.	F5	88
Jacumba, Ca., U.S.	K9	134
Jacundá, Braz.	D8	84
Jacupiranga, Braz.	B13	92
Jacuriaí, stm., Braz.	F6	88
Jadebusen, b., Ger.	C4	16
J.A.D. Jensens Nunatakker, mtn., Grnld.	E16	141
Jadraque, Spain	D8	20
Jādū, Libya	A2	62
Jaén, Peru	E2	84
Jaén, Spain	G7	20
Jaén, co., Spain	G7	20
Jāfarābād, India	H3	54
Jaffa, Cape, c., Austl.	K2	76
Jaffna, Sri L.	G4	53
Jaffna Lagoon, b., Sri L.	G4	53
Jaffrey, N.H., U.S.	B13	114
Jafr, Qā' al-, depr., Jord.	H7	58
Jagalūr, India	D3	53
Jagannāthganj Ghāt, Bngl.	F12	54
Jagatsingpur, India	H11	54
Jagdalpur, India	B6	53
Jageljurta, gora, hill, Russia	C17	8
Jagersfontein, S. Afr.	F7	70
Jaggayyapeta, India	C5	53
Jagodnoe, Russia	D18	34
Jagraon, India	C5	54
Jagtiāl, India	B4	53
Jaguaquara, Braz.	G6	88
Jaguarão, Braz.	F11	92
Jaguarão (Yaguarón), stm., S.A.	F11	92
Jaguarari, Braz.	F5	88
Jaguari, Braz.	D10	92
Jaguariaíva, Braz.	B13	92
Jaguaribara, Braz.	C6	88
Jaguaribe, Braz.	C6	88
Jaguaribe, stm., Braz.	C7	88
Jaguaruna, Braz.	D13	92
Jagüey Grande, Cuba	A7	102
Jahānābād, India	F10	54
Jahrom, Iran	D7	56
Jahroma, Russia	D20	10
Jaicós, Braz.	D5	88
Jailolo, Indon.	E8	44
Jaintiāpur, Bngl.	F14	54
Jaipur, India	E5	54
Jaipur Hāt, Bngl.	F12	54
Jais, India	E8	54
Jaisalmer, India	E3	54
Jaito, India	C5	54
Jaja, Russia	C15	32
Jājapur, India	H11	54
Jajce, Bos.	E4	26
Jakarta, Indon.	G5	50
Jakarta, Teluk, b., Indon.	F5	50
Jakaulevičy, Bela.	F13	10
Jakhāu, India	G2	54
Jakobshavn (Ilulissat), Grnld.	D15	141
Jakobstad see Pietarsaari, Fin.	E10	8
Jakovlevka, Russia	B10	38
Jakša, Russia	B9	32
Jakutija, state, Russia	C14	34
Jakutsk, Russia	D14	34
Jal, N.M., U.S.	B4	130
Jalaid Qi, China	B9	36
Jalālābād, Afg.	C11	56
Jalālpur, India	E9	54
Jalandhar, India	C5	54
Jalapa, Guat.	E3	102
Jalapa see Xalapa, Mex.	F10	100
Jālaun, India	E7	54
Jales, Braz.	D6	90
Jalesar, India	E7	54
Jaleshwar, India	H11	54
Jālgaon, India	H5	54
Jālgaon, India	H6	54
Jalingo, Nig.	H7	64
Jalisco, state, Mex.	E6	100
Jālna, India	B2	53
Jalón, stm., Spain	C9	20
Jālor, India	F4	54
Jalostotitlán, Mex.	E7	100
Jalpa, Mex.	E7	100
Jalpāiguri, India	E12	54
Jaluit, at., Marsh. Is.	C7	72
Jalutorovsk, Russia	C11	32
Jamaame, Som.	E8	66
Jamaica, ctry., N.A.	D8	102
Jamaica Channel, strt., N.A.	D9	102
Jamal, poluostrov, pen., Russia	B2	34
Jam-Alin', hrebet, mts., Russia	F15	34
Jamālpur, Bngl.	F12	54
Jamālpur, India	F11	54
Jamanota, hill, Aruba	o20	104g
Jamantau, gora, mtn., Russia	D9	32
Jamanxim, stm., Braz.	E6	84
Jamari, stm., Braz.	E5	84
Jamarovka, Russia	F11	34
Jambelí, Canal de, strt., Ec.	I2	86
Jambi, Indon.	D3	50
Jambi, state, Indon.	D3	50
Jamboaye, stm., Indon.	J3	48
Jambol, Blg.	G13	26
Jambongan, Pulau, i., Malay.	G1	52
Jambuair, Tanjung, c., Indon.	J3	48
Jambusar, India	G4	54
James, stm., U.S.	C8	108
James, stm., Mo., U.S.	H4	120
James, stm., Va., U.S.	G8	114
James, Isla, i., Chile	H2	90
James Bay, b., Can.	E14	106
James City, N.C., U.S.	A8	116
James Craik, Arg.	F6	92
James Island, S.C., U.S.	D5	116
James Point, c., Bah.	K9	116
Jamesport, Mo., U.S.	E4	120
James Ross, Cape, c., N.T., Can.	B17	140
James Ross Island, i., Ant.	B35	81
James Ross Strait, strt., Nu., Can.	A11	106
Jamestown, Austl.	I2	76
Jamestown, S. Afr.	G8	70
Jamestown, Ca., U.S.	F5	134
Jamestown, Ky., U.S.	H12	120
Jamestown, N.Y., U.S.	B6	114
Jamestown, N.C., U.S.	I6	114
Jamestown, N.D., U.S.	H15	124
Jamestown, Tn., U.S.	H13	120
Jamestown, misc. cult., Va., U.S.	G9	114
Jām Jodhpur, India	H3	54
Jamkhandi, India	C2	53
Jamm, Russia	B10	10
Jammerbugten, b., Den.	H3	8
Jammu, India	B5	54
Jammu and Kashmir see Kashmir, hist. reg., Asia	B4	46
Jamnagar (Navanagar), India	G3	54
Jampang-kulon, Indon.	G5	50
Jāmpur, Pak.	D3	54
Jämsä, Fin.	F11	8
Jamshedpur, India	G10	54
Jamsk, Russia	E19	34
Jämtland, state, Swe.	E6	8
Jamūi, India	F11	54
Jamuna, stm., Bngl.	F12	54
Jana, stm., Russia	C16	34
Janaúba, Braz.	H4	88
Janaucu, Ilha, i., Braz.	C7	84
Jand, Pak.	B4	54
Jandaia, Braz.	G7	84
Jandiāla, India	C5	54
Jandowae, Austl.	F8	76
Jándula, stm., Spain	F7	20
Janeiro, stm., Braz.	F3	88
Janesville, Ca., U.S.	C5	134
Janesville, Mn., U.S.	G5	118
Janesville, Wi., U.S.	B9	120
Jangamo, Moz.	D12	70
Jangeru, Indon.	E10	50
Jangijul', Uzb.	F11	32
Jangīpur, India	F11	54
Jangoon, India	C4	53
Janīn, W.B.	F6	58
Janisjarvi, ozero, l., Russia	E14	8
Janiuay, Phil.	E4	52
Jankan, hrebet, mts., Russia	E12	34
Jan Kempdorp, S. Afr.	E7	70
Janlohong, Indon.	B10	50
Jan Mayen, i., Nor.	B22	94
Janos, Mex.	F8	98
Jánosháza, Hung.	B4	26
Janowiec Wielkopolski, Pol.	D13	16
Janskij, Russia	C15	34
Janskij zaliv, b., Russia	B16	34
Jantra, stm., Blg.	F12	26
Januária, Braz.	H3	88
Januário Cicco, Braz.	D8	88
Jaora, India	G5	54
Japan, ctry., Asia	E12	38
Japan, Sea of (East Sea), Asia	D11	38
Japan Basin, unds.	E16	142
Japan Trench, unds.	F17	142
Japaratinga, Braz.	E8	88
Japi, Braz.	D7	88
Japonskoje more see East Sea, Asia	D11	38
Japonskoje more see Japan, Sea of, Asia	D11	38
Japtiksalja, Russia	C3	34
Japurá, Braz.	H8	86
Japurá (Caquetá), stm., S.A.	D5	84
Jaqué, Pan.	D2	86
Jarābulus, Syria	B9	58
Jaraguá, Braz.	H1	88
Jaraguá do Sul, Braz.	C13	92
Jaraíz de la Vera, Spain	D5	20
Jarales, N.M., U.S.	I10	132
Jarama, stm., Spain	D7	20
Jaramānah, Syria	E7	58
Jaransk, Russia	C7	32
Jarānwāla, Pak.	C4	54
Jarash, Jord.	F6	58
Jarash, hist., Jord.	F6	58
Jarcevo, Russia	E15	10
Jardim, Braz.	D6	88
Jardim, Braz.	D5	90
Jardim de Piranhas, Braz.	D7	88
Jardín América, Arg.	C10	92
Jardines de la Reina, Archipiélago de los, is., Cuba	B8	102
Jardinópolis, Braz.	K1	88
Jarej-Uliga-Delap, Marsh. Is.	C8	72
Jarenga, Russia	E23	8
Jarensk, Russia	E23	8
Jargalant, Mong.	B4	36
Jari, stm., Braz.	C7	84
Jaridih, India	G11	54
Jarkand see Shache, China	B12	56
Jarkino, Russia	C17	32
Jarocin, Pol.	D13	16
Jarohta, Russia	C17	32
Jaroměř, Czech Rep.	F11	16
Jaroslavl', Russia	H19	8
Jaroslavskaja oblast', co., Russia	H18	8
Jarosław, Pol.	F18	16
Jarratt, Va., U.S.	H8	114
Jar-Sale, Russia	A12	32
Jartai Yanchi, l., China	B1	42
Jarud Qi, China	B4	38
Järvakandi, Est.	G11	8
Järvenpää, Fin.	F11	8
Jarvie, Ab., Can.	B17	138
Jarvis, On., Can.	F9	112
Jarvisburg, N.C., U.S.	H10	114
Jarvis Island, i., Oc.	D10	72
Jasdan, India	G3	54
Jasel'da, stm., Bela.	H8	10
Jashpurnagar, India	D5	46
Jasień, Pol.	E11	16
Jāsk, Iran	D8	56
Jaškul', Russia	E7	32

Name — Map Ref. — Page

Jasło, Pol. G17 16
Jasnogorsk, Russia F20 10
Jasnyj, Russia F14 34
Jason Islands, is., Falk. Is. J4 90
Jasper, Ab., Can. D12 138
Jasper, Al., U.S. D11 122
Jasper, Ar., U.S. I4 120
Jasper, Fl., U.S. F3 116
Jasper, Ga., U.S. B1 116
Jasper, In., U.S. F10 120
Jasper, Mn., U.S. H2 118
Jasper, Mo., U.S. G3 120
Jasper, Tn., U.S. B13 122
Jasper Lake, l., Ab., Can. C13 138
Jasper National Park, p.o.i., Ab., Can. D13 138
Jastarnia, Pol. B14 16
Jászapáti, Hung. B7 26
Jászberény, Hung. B6 26
Jász-Nagykun-Szolnok, state, Hung. B7 26
Jataí, Braz. G7 84
Jatapu, stm., Braz. D6 84
Jataté, stm., Mex. G13 100
Jati, Braz. D6 88
Jāti, Pak. F2 54
Játiva see Xàtiva, Spain F10 20
Jatni, India H10 54
Jaú, Braz. L1 88
Jaú, stm., Braz. H11 86
Jaú, Parque Nacional do, p.o.i., Braz. I10 86
Jauaperi, stm., Braz. H11 86
Jauá Sarisariñama, Parque Nacional, p.o.i., Ven. E9 86
Jauja, Peru F2 84
Jaunjelgava, Lat. D7 10
Jaunpiebalga, Lat. C9 10
Jaunpur, India F9 54
Java see Jawa, i., Indon. H6 50
Javalambre, mtn., Spain D9 20
Java Sea see Jawa, Laut, Indon. F6 50
Java Trench, unds. J13 142
Jávea see Xàbia, Spain F11 20
Javorník, Czech Rep. F13 16
Javorová skála, mtn., Czech Rep. G10 16
Jawa (Java), i., Indon. H6 50
Jawa, Laut (Java Sea), Indon. F6 50
Jawa Barat, state, Indon. G5 50
Jawa Tengah, state, Indon. G7 50
Jawa Timur, state, Indon. G8 50
Jawhar, Som. D9 66
Jawi, Indon. D6 50
Jawor, Pol. E12 16
Jaworzno, Pol. F15 16
Jay, Fl., U.S. G11 122
Jay, Ok., U.S. H3 120
Jaya, Puncak (Jaya Peak), mtn., Indon. F10 44
Jaya Peak see Jaya, Puncak, mtn., Indon. F10 44
Jayapura, Indon. F11 44
Jayb, Wādī al- (Ha'Arava), stm., Asia H6 58
Jaynes, Az., U.S. K5 132
Jaypur, India B6 53
Jayuya, P.R. B2 104a
Jažełbicy, Russia B15 10
Jažma, Russia C21 8
Jeanerette, La., U.S. H7 122
Jeannette Island see Žannetty, ostrov, i., Russia A20 34
Jebba, Nig. H5 64
Jebel, Rom. D8 26
Jedburgh, Scot., U.K. F10 12
Jeddah see Jiddah, Sau. Ar. E4 56
Jędrzejów, Pol. F16 16
Jeffara (Al-Jifārah), pl., Afr. C7 64
Jeffers, Mn., U.S. G3 118
Jefferson, Ga., U.S. B2 116
Jefferson, Oh., U.S. C5 114
Jefferson, Or., U.S. F3 136
Jefferson, S.C., U.S. B5 116
Jefferson, S.D., U.S. B1 120
Jefferson, Wi., U.S. A9 120
Jefferson, Mount, mtn., U.S. F15 136
Jefferson, Mount, mtn., Nv., U.S. E8 134
Jefferson, Mount, vol., Or., U.S. F5 136
Jefferson City, Mo., U.S. F5 120
Jefferson City, Tn., U.S. H2 114
Jeffersontown, Ky., U.S. F12 120
Jeffersonville, Ga., U.S. D2 116
Jeffersonville, In., U.S. F12 120
Jeffrey City, Wy., U.S. E5 126
Jega, Nig. G5 64
Jehol see Chengde, China A7 42
Jejsk see Ejsk, Russia E5 32
Jeju see Cheju, Kor., S. H7 38
Jēkabpils, Lat. D8 10
Jekyll Island, i., Ga., U.S. E4 116
Jelai, stm., Indon. E7 50
Jelenia Góra, Pol. F11 16
Jelenia Góra, state, Pol. E11 16
Jelgava, Lat. D6 10
Jelgavkrasti, Lat. C7 10
Jellicoe, On., Can. B11 118
Jelm Mountain, mtn., Wy., U.S. F7 126
Jemaja, Pulau, i., Indon. B4 50
Jember, Indon. H8 50
Jemez Canyon Reservoir, res., N.M., U.S. H9 132
Jemez Springs, N.M., U.S. H10 132
Jemnice, Czech Rep. H11 16
Jempang, Kenohan, l., Indon. D9 50
Jena, Ger. F7 16
Jena, La., U.S. F6 122
Jendouba, Tun. H2 24
Jeneponto, Indon. F11 50
Jenks, Ok., U.S. H2 120
Jennings, Fl., U.S. F2 116
Jennings, La., U.S. G6 122
Jensen, Ut., U.S. C7 132
Jens Munk Island, i., Nu., Can. B14 106
Jens Munks Ø, i., Grnld. E17 141
Jenu, Indon. D6 50
Jeonju see Chŏnju, Kor., S. G7 38
Jepara, Indon. G7 50
Jeparit, Austl. K4 76
Jeptha Knob, hill, Ky., U.S. F12 120
Jequié, Braz. G5 88
Jequitinhonha, Braz. I5 88
Jequitinhonha, stm., Braz. H5 88
Jerada, Mor. C4 64
Jerba, Île de, i., Tun. C7 64
Jerécuaro, Mex. E8 100
Jérémie, Haiti C10 102
Jeremoabo, Braz. F6 88
Jerevan see Yerevan, Arm. A5 56
Jerez de García Salinas, Mex. D7 100
Jerez de la Frontera, Spain H4 20
Jerez de los Caballeros, Spain F4 20
Jericho, Austl. D5 76
Jericho see Arīḥā, Gaza G6 58
Jericó, Braz. D7 88
Jerid, Chott, l., Tun. C6 64
Jerimoth Hill, hill, R.I., U.S. C14 114
Jeroaquara, Braz. G7 84
Jerome, Az., U.S. I4 132
Jerome, Id., U.S. H12 136
Jersey, dep., Eur. E6 14
Jersey, i., Jersey E6 14
Jersey City, N.J., U.S. D11 114
Jerseyville, Il., U.S. E7 120
Jerumenha, Braz. D4 88
Jerusalem see Yerushalayim, Isr. G6 58
Jervis, Cape, c., Austl. J1 76
Jervis Bay, b., Austl. J8 76
Jervis Bay Territory, co., Austl. J8 76
Jervis Inlet, b., B.C., Can. F7 138
Jesenice, Czech Rep. F9 16
Jeseník, Czech Rep. F13 16
Jesi (Iesi), Italy G10 22
Jessen, Ger. E9 16
Jessore, Bngl. G12 54
Jesup, Ga., U.S. E4 116
Jesup, Ia., U.S. B5 120
Jesús Carranza, Mex. G11 100
Jesús María, Arg. E5 92
Jesús Menéndez, Cuba B9 102
Jet, Ok., U.S. E10 128
Jetmore, Ks., U.S. C9 128
Jetpur, India H3 54
Jeune Landing, B.C., Can. F3 138
Jever, Ger. C3 16
Jewel Cave National Monument, p.o.i., S.D., U.S. D8 126
Jewell, Ks., U.S. B10 128
Jewell Ridge, Va., U.S. G4 114
Jewett, Il., U.S. E9 120
Jewett City, Ct., U.S. C13 114
Jezercës, maja e, mtn., Alb. B13 24
Jeziorany, Pol. B16 16
Jhābua, India G5 54
Jha Jha, India F11 54
Jhālakāti, Bngl. G13 54
Jhālāwār, India F6 54
Jhang Sadar, Pak. C4 54
Jhānsi, India F7 54
Jhārgrām, India G11 54
Jharia, India G11 54
Jhārsuguda, India H10 54
Jhelum, Pak. B4 54
Jhelum, stm., Asia C4 54
Jhinkpāni, India G10 54
Jhok Rind, Pak. C3 54
Jhunjhunūn, India D5 54
Jiaban, China I2 42
Jiading, China F9 42
Jiāganj, India F12 54
Jiahe, China I5 42
Jiali, China C14 54
Jialing, stm., China G2 42
Jialu, stm., China E5 42
Jiamusi, China B11 36
Ji'an, China D7 38
Ji'an, China H6 42
Jian, stm., China H8 42
Jianchang, China A8 42
Jianchang, China B10 42
Jianchuan, China F4 36
Jiande, China G8 42
Jiang'an, China G1 42
Jiangcheng, China A5 48
Jiangdu, China E8 42
Jiange, China E1 42
Jianghua, China I4 42
Jiangjin, China G2 42
Jiangkou, China J4 42
Jiangkou, China H3 42
Jiangkou, China F4 42
Jiangle, China H7 42
Jiangling, China F4 42
Jiangmen, China J5 42
Jiangmifeng, China B7 38
Jiangshan, China G8 42
Jiangsu, state, China E8 42
Jiangtun, China J5 42
Jiangxi, state, China H6 42
Jiangya, China G4 42
Jiangyin, China F9 42
Jiangyou, China F1 42
Jiangzhong, China D14 54
Jianli, China G5 42
Jianning, China H7 42
Jian'ou, China H8 42
Jianping, China D3 38
Jianshi, China F3 42
Jianshui, China G5 36
Jianyang, China E5 36
Jianyang, China H8 42
Jiaocheng, China C4 42
Jiaohe, China C7 38
Jiaolai, stm., China C4 38
Jiaonan, China D8 42
Jiaoxian, China C8 42
Jiaozhou Wan, b., China C9 42
Jiaozuo, China D5 42
Jiashan, China E7 42
Jiashi, China B12 56
Jiashun Hu, l., China A10 54
Jiawang, China D7 42
Jiaxian, China D5 42
Jiaxian, China B4 42
Jiaxing, China F9 42
Jiazi, China J6 42
Jibuti see Djibouti, Dji. E8 62
Jicarón, Isla, i., Pan. I7 102
Jičín, Czech Rep. F11 16
Jiddah (Jeddah), Sau. Ar. E4 56
Jidingxilin, China B14 54
Jieshi Wan, b., China J6 42
Jieshou, China E6 42
Jiexi, China J6 42
Jiexiu, China C4 42
Jieyang, China J7 42
Jieznas, Lith. F7 10
Jiguaní, Cuba B9 102
Jigüey, Bahía de, strt., Cuba A8 102
Jigzhi, China E5 36
Jihlava, Czech Rep. G11 16
Jihlava, stm., Czech Rep. G12 16
Jihočeský kraj, state, Czech Rep. G10 16
Jihomoravský kraj, state, Czech Rep. G12 16
Jijia, stm., Rom. B14 26
Jijiga, Eth. F8 62
Jilantai, China B1 42
Jilib, Som. D8 66
Jili Hu, l., China B2 36
Jilin, China C7 38
Jilin, state, China C10 36
Jill, Kediet ej, mtn., Maur. E2 64
Jiloca, stm., Spain C9 20
Jīma, Eth. F7 62
Jimbolia, Rom. D7 26
Jimena de la Frontera, Spain H5 20
Jiménez, Mex. B6 100
Jiménez, Mex. A8 100
Jiménez del Téul, Mex. D7 100
Jimeta, Nig. H7 64
Jim Ned Creek, stm., Tx., U.S. C8 130
Jimo, China C9 42
Jimsar, China C2 36
Jim Thorpe, Pa., U.S. D10 114
Jin (Gam), stm., Asia A7 48
Jin, stm., China H7 42
Jinan (Tsinan), China C7 42
Jincang, China C9 38
Jincheng, China D5 42
Jīnd, India D6 54
Jindabyne, Austl. K7 76
Jindřichův Hradec, Czech Rep. G11 16
Jing, stm., China D3 42
Jing'an, China G6 42
Jingbian, China C3 42
Jingbohu, res., China C8 38
Jingde, China F8 42
Jingdezhen, China G7 42
Jinggangshan, China H6 42
Jinghai, China B7 42
Jinghe, China F14 32
Jinghong, China B5 48
Jingle, China B4 42
Jingmen, China F5 42
Jingning, China D1 42
Jingxi, China J2 42
Jingxian, China F8 42
Jingxian, China C7 42
Jingxian, China H3 42
Jingxin, China I6 42
Jingyu, China C7 38
Jingzhi, China C8 42
Jinhae see Chinhae, Kor., S. D1 40
Jinhua, China G8 42
Jining, China D7 42
Jining, China A5 42
Jinja, Ug. D6 66
Jinjiazhen, China C5 38
Jinju see Chinju, Kor., S. G7 38
Jinmu Jiao, c., China L3 42
Jinning, China G5 36
Jinotega, Nic. F5 102
Jinotepe, Nic. G4 102
Jinping, China H3 42
Jinqian, stm., China E3 42
Jinsha, China H1 42
Jinsha (Yangtze), stm., China F5 36
Jinshi, China G4 42
Jintian, China H6 42
Jintotolo Channel, strt., Phil. E4 52
Jinxi, China A9 42
Jinxi, China H7 42
Jinxian, China G7 42
Jinxian, China B6 42
Jinzhou, China B9 42
Jinzhou, China A9 42
Ji-Paraná, Braz. F5 84
Jipijapa, Ec. H1 86
Jiquiriçá, stm., Braz. G6 88
Jiri, stm., India F14 54
Jirkov, Czech Rep. F9 16
Jishou, China G3 42
Jisr ash-Shughūr, Syria C7 58
Jitaúna, Braz. G6 88
Jiu, stm., Rom. F10 26
Jiudaoliang, China F4 42
Jiufeng, China I7 42
Jiujiang, China G6 42
Jiulian Shan, mts., China I6 42
Jiuliguan, China F6 42
Jiuling Shan, mts., China G6 42
Jiulong, China J5 42
Jiulong, stm., China I7 42
Jiuquan, China D4 36
Jiutai, China B6 38
Jiuyuanqu, China D4 42
Jiuzhan, China C7 38
Jiuzhen, China I7 42
Jiwen, China A9 36
Jixi, China B9 38
Jixi, China F8 42
Jixian, China A7 42
Jixian, China D6 42
Jiyi, China D4 42
Jiyuan, China D5 42
Jiyun, stm., China B7 42
Jīzān, Sau. Ar. F5 56
Jizl, Wādī al-, stm., Sau. Ar. K8 58
J. J. Castelli see Castelli, Arg. B7 92
J.M. Lencinas see Las Catitas, Arg. F3 92
Joaçaba, Braz. C12 92
Joana Coeli, Braz. A1 88
Joanes, Braz. D8 84
João Câmara, Braz. C8 88
João Monlevade, Braz. J4 88
João Pessoa, Braz. D8 88
João Pinheiro, Braz. I2 88
Joaquim Távora, Braz. A12 92
Joaquin, Tx., U.S. F4 122
Joaquín V. González, Arg. B5 92
Jobos, P.R. C3 104a
Job Peak, mtn., Nv., U.S. D7 134
Jocolí, Arg. F3 92
Jódar, Spain G7 20
Jodhpur, India E4 54
Jodiya, India G3 54
Joensuu, Fin. E13 8
Joetsu, Japan B11 40
Jõgeva, Est. G12 8
Jog Falls, wtfl, India D2 53
Joggins, N.S., Can. E12 110
Jogjakarta see Yogyakarta, Indon. G7 50
Jōhana, Japan C9 40
Johannesburg, S. Afr. E8 70
John Day, Or., U.S. F8 136
John Day, stm., Or., U.S. E6 136
John Day, Middle Fork, stm., Or., U.S. F8 136
John Day, North Fork, stm., Or., U.S. F8 136
John Day Fossil Beds National Monument, p.o.i., Or., U.S. F7 136
John F. Kennedy Space Center, sci., Fl., U.S. H5 116
John H. Kerr Reservoir, res., U.S. H7 114
John Martin Reservoir, res., Co., U.S. C6 128
John o' Groats, Scot., U.K. C9 12
John Redmond Reservoir, res., Ks., U.S. F1 120
Johns Island, i., S.C., U.S. D5 116
Johnson, Ar., U.S. H3 120
Johnson, Ks., U.S. D7 128
Johnsonburg, Pa., U.S. C7 114
Johnson City, N.Y., U.S. B10 114
Johnson City, Tn., U.S. H3 114
Johnson City, Tx., U.S. D9 130
Johnsondale, Ca., U.S. H7 134
Johnson Draw, stm., Tx., U.S. D6 130
Johnson Point, c., St. Vin. o11 105e
Johnsonville, S.C., U.S. C6 116
Johnston, Ia., U.S. C4 120
Johnston, S.C., U.S. C4 116
Johnston, Lake, l., Austl. F4 74
Johnston Atoll, at., Oc. B10 72
Johnstown, Co., U.S. G8 126
Johnstown, N.Y., U.S. G2 110
Johnstown, Oh., U.S. D3 114
Johnstown, Pa., U.S. D7 114
Johor, state, Malay. L6 48
Johor Bahru, Malay. L6 48
Joigny, Fr. G12 14
Joiner, Ar., U.S. B8 122
Joinville, Braz. C13 92
Joinville Island, i., Ant. B35 81
Jojogan, Indon. G7 50
Jokkmokk, Swe. C8 8
Jökulsá á Brú, stm., Ice. k32 8a
Jökulsårgljúfur Nasjonalpark, p.o.i., Ice. k32 8a
Joliet, Il., U.S. C9 120
Joliette, Qc., Can. D3 110
Jolo, Phil. G3 52
Jolo Group, is., Phil. G3 52
Jolo Island, i., Phil. H3 52
Jombang, Indon. G8 50
Jomda, China E4 36
Jonava, Lith. E7 10
Jones, Ok., U.S. F11 128
Jonesboro, Ar., U.S. I7 120
Jonesboro, Ga., U.S. C1 116
Jonesboro, Il., U.S. G8 120
Jonesboro, La., U.S. E6 122
Jonesborough, Tn., U.S. H3 114
Jones Mill, Ar., U.S. C6 122
Jonesport, Me., U.S. F9 110
Jones Sound, strt., Nu., Can. B8 141
Jonestown, Ms., U.S. C8 122
Jonesville, La., U.S. F7 122
Jonesville, Mi., U.S. B1 114
Jonglei Canal, can., Sudan F6 62
Joniškėlis, Lith. D6 10
Joniškis, Lith. D6 10
Jönköping, Swe. H6 8
Jönköping, state, Swe. H6 8
Jonquière, Qc., Can. B5 110
Jonuta, Mex. F12 100
Jonzac, Fr. D5 18
Joplin, Mo., U.S. G3 120
Joplin, Mt., U.S. B16 136
Joppa, Il., U.S. G9 120
Jora, India E6 54
Jordan, Mn., U.S. G5 118
Jordan, Mt., U.S. G6 124
Jordan, ctry., Asia H7 58
Jordan (Al-Urdunn) (HaYarden), stm., Asia F6 58
Jordan, stm., Ut., U.S. C5 132
Jordan Creek, stm., U.S. H10 136
Jordânia, Braz. H5 88
Jordan Valley, Or., U.S. G10 136
Jordão, stm., Braz. B12 92
Jorge Montt, Isla, i., Chile J2 90
Jorhāt, India C7 46
Jornado del Muerto, des., N.M., U.S. J10 132
Joroinen, Fin. E12 8
Jos, Nig. G6 64
Jose Abad Santos, Phil. H5 52
José Batlle y Ordóñez, Ur. F10 92
José Bonifácio, Braz. K1 88
José de Freitas, Braz. C4 88
José de San Martín, Arg. H2 90
José Pedro Varela, Ur. F10 92
Joseph, Or., U.S. E9 136
Joseph, Lac, l., Nf., Can. E17 106
Joseph Bonaparte Gulf, b., Austl. B5 74
Joshīmath, India C7 54
Jōshin-Etsu-kōgen-kokuritsu-kōen, p.o.i., Japan C11 40
Joshua, Tx., U.S. B10 130
Joshua Tree, Ca., U.S. I9 134
Joshua Tree National Park, p.o.i., Ca., U.S. J10 134
Jostedalsbreen, ice, Nor. F2 8
Jostedalsbreen Nasjonalpark, p.o.i., Nor. F2 8
Jotunheimen Nasjonalpark, p.o.i., Nor. F2 8
Joubertina, S. Afr. H6 70
Jourdanton, Tx., U.S. F9 130
Joutsijärvi, Fin. C13 8
Joviânia, Braz. I1 88
Jowai, India F14 54
Joya, Mex. H6 130
Joyce, La., U.S. F6 122
Joyuda, P.R. B1 104a
J. Percy Priest Lake, res., Tn., U.S. H11 120
J. Strom Thurmond Reservoir, res., U.S. C3 116
Juami, stm., Braz. I7 86
Juana Díaz, P.R. B2 104a
Juan Aldama, Mex. C7 100
Juan Bautista Alberdi, Arg. C5 92
Juan de Fuca, Strait of, strt., N.A. B2 136
Juan de Garay, Arg. I5 92
Juan de Nova, Île, i., Reu. D7 68
Juan E. Barra, Arg. H7 92
Juan Fernández, Archipiélago, is., Chile I6 82
Juanjuí, Peru E2 84
Juan N. Fernández, Arg. I8 92
Juan Viñas, C.R. H6 102
Juárez see Benito Juárez, Arg. H8 92
Juárez, Mex. F8 98
Juárez, Mex. B8 100
Juatinga, Ponta de, c., Braz. L3 88
Juazeirinho, Braz. D7 88
Juazeiro, Braz. E5 88
Juazeiro do Norte, Braz. D6 88
Juba, Sudan G6 62
Juba see Genalē, stm., Afr. C8 66
Juba see Jubba, stm., Afr. D8 66
Jubal, Strait of see Gûbâl, Madîq, strt., Egypt K4 58
Jubayl, Leb. D6 58
Jubba (Genalē), stm., Afr. D8 66
Juby, Cap, c., Mor. D2 64
Júcar (Xúquer), stm., Spain E10 20
Juchipila, Mex. E7 100
Juchitán de Zaragoza, Mex. G11 100
Jucurucu, stm., Braz. I5 88
Jucurutu, Braz. C7 88
Judenburg, Aus. C11 22
Judino, Russia B22 10
Judique, N.S., Can. E15 110
Judith, stm., Mt., U.S. C17 136
Judith Gap, Mt., U.S. D17 136
Judith Peak, mtn., Mt., U.S. C17 136
Judoma, stm., Russia E16 34
Jufari, stm., Braz. H10 86
Jug, stm., Russia G21 8
Jugorskij poluostrov, pen., Russia A10 32
Juhnov, Russia F18 10
Juidongshan, China J7 42
Juigalpa, Nic. F5 102
Juist, i., Ger. C2 16
Juiz de Fora, Braz. K4 88
Jujuy, state, Arg. D3 90
Jukagirskoe ploskogor'e, plat., Russia C19 34
Jukta, Russia B19 32
Jula, stm., Russia E21 8
Julesburg, Co., U.S. G10 126
Juliaca, Peru G3 84
Julia Creek, Austl. C3 76
Julia Creek, stm., Austl. C3 76
Julianadorp, Neth. Ant. p22 104g
Julian Alps, mts., Eur. D10 22
Juliana Top, mtn., Sur. C6 84
Julianehåb (Qaqortoq), Grnld. E16 141
Jülich, Ger. F2 16
Juliette, Lake, res., Ga., U.S. D2 116
Julimes, Mex. A6 100
Júlio de Castilhos, Braz. D11 92
Juma, Russia D15 8
Juma, stm., China B6 42
Jumba, Som. E8 66
Jumilla, Spain F9 20
Jumlā, Nepal D9 54
Jūnāgadh, India H3 54
Juncos, P.R. B4 104a
Junction, Tx., U.S. D8 130
Junction City, Ar., U.S. E6 122
Junction City, Ks., U.S. B12 128
Junction City, Ky., U.S. G13 120
Jundah, Austl. E4 76
Jundiaí, Braz. L2 88
Juneau, Ak., U.S. E13 140
Juneau, Wi., U.S. H10 118
Junee, Austl. J6 76
June Lake, Ca., U.S. F6 134
Jungar Qi, China B4 42
Jungfrau, mtn., Switz. D4 22
Junggar Pendi, bas., China B2 36
Juniata, Ne., U.S. G14 126
Juniata, stm., Pa., U.S. D8 114
Junín, Arg. G7 92
Junín, Ec. H1 86
Junín de los Andes, Arg. G2 90
Juniper, N.B., Can. D9 110
Junipero Serra Peak, mtn., Ca., U.S. G4 134
Jūniyah, Leb. E6 58
Junlian, China F5 36
Junnar, India B1 53
Junqueiro, Braz. E7 88
Junxian, China E4 42
Juodkrantė, Lith. E3 10
Juozapinės kalnas, hill, Lith. F8 10
Juparanã, Lagoa, l., Braz. J5 88
Jupiter, Fl., U.S. J5 116
Juquiá, Braz. B14 92
Juquiá, Ponta do, c., Braz. B14 92
Jur, Russia E16 34
Jur, stm., Sudan F5 62
Jura, Mol. B16 26
Jura, state, Fr. C11 18
Jura, mts., Eur. B12 18
Jura, i., Scot., U.K. F7 12
Jūra, stm., Lith. E5 10
Jurbarkas, Lith. E5 10
Jurenino, Russia G20 8
Jurevec, Russia H20 8
Jurga, Russia C15 32
Juriti, Braz. D6 84
Jūrmala, Lat. C6 10
Jurong, China F8 42
Juruá, stm., S.A. D4 84
Juruena, stm., Braz. E6 84
Jurumirim, Represa de, res., Braz. L1 88
Jusepín, Ven. C10 86
Juškovo, Russia G21 8
Justiniano Posse, Arg. F6 92
Justino Solari see Mariano I. Loza, Arg. D8 92
Justo Daract, Arg. F5 92
Jutaí, stm., Braz. D4 84
Jüterbog, Ger. D9 16
Jutiapa, Guat. E3 102
Juticalpa, Hond. E4 102
Jutland see Jylland, reg., Den. H3 8
Jutrosin, Pol. E13 16
Juventud, Isla de la (Pines, Isle of), i., Cuba B6 102
Juxian, China D8 42
Juye, China D6 42
Juža, Russia H20 8
Južna Morava, stm., Yugo. F8 26
Južno-Enisejskij, Russia C17 32
Južno-Sahalinsk, Russia G17 34
Južno-Ural'sk, Russia D10 32
Južnyj, mys, c., Russia E20 34
Južnyj Ural, mts., Russia D9 32
Jwayyā, Leb. E6 58
Jyekundo see Yushu, China E4 36
Jylland (Jutland), reg., Den. H3 8
Jyväskylä, Fin. E11 8

K

K2, mtn., Asia B12 56
Kaabong, Ug. D6 66
Kaahka, Turkmen. B8 56
Kaala, mtn., Hi., U.S. B3 78a
Kaala-Gomen, N. Cal. m15 79d
Kaapstad see Cape Town, S. Afr. H4 70
Kaarli, Est. A9 10
Kaatoan, Mount, mtn., Phil. F5 52
Kabacan, Phil. G5 52
Kabaena, Pulau, i., Indon. G7 44
Kabah, hist., Mex. B3 102
Kabala, S.L. H2 64
Kabale, Ug. E5 66
Kabalega Falls, wtfl, Ug. D6 66
Kabalo, D.R.C. F5 66
Kabambare, D.R.C. E5 66
Kabanjahe, Indon. K4 48
Kabankalan, Phil. F4 52
Kabardin-Balkaria see Kabardino-Balkarija, state, Russia F6 32
Kabardino-Balkarija, state, Russia F6 32
Kabba, Nig. H6 64
Kabbani, stm., India F3 53
Kåbdalis, Swe. C8 8
Kabetogama Lake, l., Mn., U.S. C5 118
Kab-hegy, mtn., Hung. B4 26
Kabinda, D.R.C. F4 66
Kabinu, Indon. A9 50
Kabīr Kūh, mts., Iran C6 56
Kabna, Sudan D6 62
Kābol, Afg. C10 56
Kābol, state, Afg. A2 54
Kabompo, Zam. C3 68
Kabompo, stm., Zam. C3 68
Kabongo, D.R.C. F5 66
Kābul see Kābol, Afg. C10 56
Kabul (Kābol), stm., Asia A4 54
Kabwe, Zam. C4 68
Kabylie, reg., Alg. H14 20
Kačanik, Yugo. G8 26
Kačerginė, Lith. F6 10
Kachchh, Gulf of, b., India G2 54
Kačiry, Kaz. D13 32
Kačkanar, Russia C10 32
Kačug, Russia D19 32
Kadaiyanallūr, India G3 53
Kadaň, Czech Rep. F9 16
Kadan Kyun, i., Mya. F4 48
Kadapongan, Pulau, i., Indon. F9 50
Kaddam, res., India B4 53
Kade, Ghana H4 64
Kadéï, stm., Afr. G2 62
Kadi, India G4 54
Kadina, Austl. F7 74
Kading, stm., Laos C7 48
Kadınhanı, Tur. E15 28
Kadiolo, Mali G3 64
Kādīpur, India E9 54
Kadiri, India D4 53
Kadirli, Tur. A7 58
Kadoka, S.D., U.S. D11 126
Kadoma, Zimb. D4 68
Kaduj, Russia A20 10
Kaduna, Nig. G6 64
Kaduna, stm., Nig. G6 64
Kāduqlī, Sudan E5 62
Kadūr, India E3 53
Kaduvu, i., Fiji q19 79e
Kaduvu Passage, strt., Fiji q18 79e
Kadyj, Russia H20 8
Kadžerom, Russia B9 32
Kaédi, Maur. F2 64
Kaélé, Cam. B2 66
Kaena Point, c., Hi., U.S. B3 78a
Kaesŏng, Kor., N. F7 38
Kafanchan, Nig. H6 64
Kaffrine, Sen. G1 64
Kafia Kingi, Sudan F4 62
Kafr el-Dauwar, Egypt G1 58
Kafr el-Sheikh, Egypt G1 58
Kafr el-Zaiyât, Egypt H1 58
Kafr Sa'd, Egypt G2 58
Kafue, Zam. D4 68
Kafue, stm., Zam. D4 68
Kaga, Japan C9 40
Kaga Bandoro, C.A.R. C3 66
Kāgān, Pak. A4 54
Kagan, Uzb. G10 32
Kagawa, state, Japan E6 40
Kagawong, Lake, l., On., Can. C7 112
Kagaznagar, India B4 53
Kagera, stm., Afr. E6 66
Kagmar, Sudan E6 62
Kagoshima, Japan H3 40
Kagoshima, state, Japan H3 40
Kagoshima-wan, b., Japan H3 40
Kahama, Tan. E6 66
Kahayan, stm., Indon. D8 50
Ka-Hem see Malyj Enisej, stm., Russia F8 34
Kahemba, D.R.C. F3 66
Kahiu Point, c., Hi., U.S. B5 78a
Kahoka, Mo., U.S. D6 120
Kahoolawe, i., Hi., U.S. C5 78a
Kahouanne, Îlet à, i., Guad. h5 105c
Kahramanmaraş (Maraş), Tur. A7 58
Kahraman Maraş, state, Tur. A7 58
Kahuku Point, c., Hi., U.S. B4 78a
Kahului, Hi., U.S. C5 78a
Kai, Kepulauan (Kai Islands), is., Indon. G9 44
Kaiapoi, N.Z. F5 80
Kaibab Plateau, plat., Az., U.S. G4 132
Kaidu, stm., China F15 32
Kaieteur Fall, wtfl, Guy. E12 86
Kaieteur National Park, p.o.i., Guy. E12 86
Kaifeng, China D6 42
Kaihua, China G8 42
Kai Islands see Kai, Kepulauan, is., Indon. G9 44
Kaijian, China J4 42
Kaijiang, China F2 42
Kai Kecil, i., Indon. G9 44
Kaikoura, N.Z. F5 80
Kailahun, S.L. H2 64
Kailas see Kangrinboqê Feng, mtn., China C8 54
Kailāshahar, India F14 54
Kailas Range see Gangdisê Shan, mts., China C9 54
Kaili, China H2 42
Kailu, China C4 38
Kailua, Hi., U.S. B4 78a
Kailua Kona, Hi., U.S. D6 78a
Kaïmaktsalán (Kajmakčalan), mtn., Eur. C15 24
Kaimana, Indon. F9 44
Kaimon-dake, vol., Japan H3 40
Kainabrivier, stm., Nmb. E4 70
Kainan, Japan E8 40
Kainantu, Pap. N. Gui. b4 79a
Kainji Reservoir, res., Nig. G5 64
Kaipara Harbour, b., N.Z. C5 80
Kaiparowits Plateau, plat., Ut., U.S. F5 132
Kaiping, China J5 42
Kairouan, Tun. I3 24
Kairuku, Pap. N. Gui. b4 79a
Kaiserslautern, Ger. G3 16
Kaišiadorys, Lith. F7 10
Kait, Tanjung, c., Indon. E5 50
Kaitangata, N.Z. H3 80
Kaithal, India D6 54
Kaituma, stm., Guy. D12 86
Kaiwi Channel, strt., Hi., U.S. B4 78a
Kaixian, China F3 42
Kaiyang, China H2 42
Kaiyuan, China G5 36
Kaiyuan, China C6 38
Kaiyuancheng, China C6 38
Kaiyuh Mountains, mts., Ak., U.S. D8 140
Kajaani, Fin. D12 8
Kajabbi, Austl. B2 76
Kajakī, Band-e, res., Afg. C10 56
Kajang, Malay. K5 48
Kajga, Kaz. D10 32
Kajmysovy, Russia C13 32
Kajo Kaji, Sudan G6 62
Kaka, Sudan E6 62
Kakabeka Falls, wtfl, On., Can. C9 118
Kakagi Lake, l., On., Can. B5 118
Kakamas, S. Afr. F5 70
Kakamega, Kenya D6 66
Kakamigahara, Japan D9 40
Kakata, Lib. H2 64
Kākdwīp, India H12 54
Kakegawa, Japan E10 40
Kakhonak, Ak., U.S. E9 140
Kakhovka Reservoir see Kakhovs'ke vodoskhovyshche, res., Ukr. E4 32
Kakhovs'ke vodoskhovyshche, res., Ukr. E4 32
Kākināda (Cocanada), India C6 53
Kakisa Lake, l., N.T., Can. C7 106
Kakizaki, Japan B11 40
Kakogawa, Japan E7 40
Kakšaal-Too, hrebet, mts., Asia F13 32
Kaktovik, Ak., U.S. B11 140
Kakuda, Japan B13 40
Kakus, stm., Malay. B8 50
Kakwa, stm., Ab., Can. B12 138
Kala, stm., Sri L. G4 53
Kalaa Kebira, Tun. I4 24
Kalabahi, Indon. G7 44
Kalabakan, Malay. A10 50
Kalabo, Zam. D3 68
Kalač, Russia D6 32
Kalačinsk, Russia D12 32
Kalač-na-Donu, Russia E6 32
Kaladan, stm., Asia G14 54
Ka Lae, c., Hi., U.S. E6 78a
Kalahari Desert, des., Afr. C5 70
Kalahari Gemsbok National Park, p.o.i., S. Afr. D5 70
Kalajoki, Fin. D10 8
Kalakan, Russia E12 34
Kalām, Pak. B11 56
Kalama, Wa., U.S. D4 136
Kalamalka Lake, l., B.C., Can. F11 138
Kalamáta, Grc. F5 28
Kalamazoo, Mi., U.S. F4 112
Kalamazoo, stm., Mi., U.S. F4 112
Kalamb, India B1 53
Kalampising, Indon. B10 50
Kalao, Pulau, i., Indon. G12 50
Kalaotoa, Pulau, i., Indon. G7 44
Kalar, stm., Russia E12 34
Kalasin, Thai. D6 48
Kalašnikovo, Russia C18 10
Kalāt, Pak. D10 56
Kalávryta, Grc. E5 28
Kalaw, Mya. B3 48
Kalbarri, Austl. E2 74
Kale, Tur. F11 28
Kale, Tur. G12 28
Kaleden, B.C., Can. G11 138
Kalegauk Island, i., Mya. E3 48
Kalehe, D.R.C. E5 66
Kalemie, D.R.C. F5 66
Kalemyo, Mya. D7 46
Kaletwa, Mya. H14 54
Kalevala, Russia D14 8
Kalewa, Mya. D7 46
Kálfafell, Ice. k31 8a
Kalgan see Zhangjiakou, China A6 42
Kalgoorlie-Boulder, Austl. F4 74
Kaliakra, nos, c., Blg. F15 26
Kalianda, Indon. F4 50
Kalibo, Phil. E4 52
Kalima, D.R.C. E5 66
Kalimantan (Borneo), i., Asia F5 44

I•28 Kali-Kenh

Name	Map Ref.	Page
Kalimantan Barat, state, Indon.	D7	50
Kalimantan Selatan, state, Indon.	E9	50
Kalimantan Tengah, state, Indon.	D8	50
Kalimantan Timur, state, Indon.	C10	50
Kālimpang, India	E12	54
Kālīnadi, stm., India	D2	53
Kalinin see Tver', Russia	D18	10
Kaliningrad (Königsberg), Russia	F3	10
Kaliningradskaja oblast', co., Russia	F4	10
Kalinkavičy, Bela.	H12	10
Kaliro, Ug.	D6	66
Kalisat, Indon.	H8	50
Kāli Sindh, stm., India	F6	54
Kalispell, Mt., U.S.	B12	136
Kalisz, Pol.	E14	16
Kalisz, state, Pol.	E13	16
Kalisz Pomorski, Pol.	C11	16
Kaliua, Tan.	E6	66
Kaliveli Tank, l., India	E4	53
Kalixälven, stm., Swe.	C9	8
Kaljazin, Russia	C20	10
Kālka, India	C6	54
Kalkaska, Mi., U.S.	D4	112
Kalkfonteindam, res., S. Afr.	F7	70
Kalkım, Tur.	D10	28
Kalkrand, Nmb.	D3	70
Kallar Kahār, Pak.	B4	54
Kallavesi, l., Fin.	E12	8
Kallsjön, l., Swe.	E5	8
Kalmar, Swe.	H6	8
Kalmar, state, Swe.	H7	8
Kalmarsund, strt., Swe.	H7	8
Kalmykia see Kalmykija, state, Russia	E7	32
Kalmykija, state, Russia	E7	32
Kalmykovo, Kaz.	E8	32
Kālna, India	G12	54
Kalocsa, Hung.	C5	26
Kalofer, Blg.	G12	26
Kalohi Channel, strt., Hi., U.S.	B4	78a
Kalol, India	G4	54
Kālol, India	G4	54
Kalomo, Zam.	D4	68
Kalona, Ia., U.S.	J7	118
Kalone Peak, mtn., B.C., Can.	D4	138
Kalpeni Island, i., India	F1	53
Kālpi, India	E7	54
Kalpin, China	A12	56
Kalsūbai, mtn., India	B1	53
Kaltag, Ak., U.S.	D8	140
Kaluga, Russia	F19	10
Kalukalukuang, Pulau, i., Indon.	F10	50
Kalumburu, Austl.	B5	74
Kałuszyn, Pol.	D17	16
Kalutara, Sri L.	H4	53
Kalužskaja oblast', co., Russia	F18	10
Kalyān, India	B1	53
Kalyāndurg, India	D3	53
Kálymnos, Grc.	G9	28
Kálymnos, i., Grc.	F9	28
Kama, stm., Russia	C8	32
Kamae, Japan	G4	40
Kamaishi, Japan	E14	38
Kamakou, mtn., Hi., U.S.	B5	78a
Kamakura, Japan	D12	40
Kamālia, Pak.	C4	54
Kamamaung, Mya.	D3	48
Kaman, stm., Laos	E8	48
Kamanjab, Nmb.	D1	68
Kamarān, i., Yemen	F5	56
Kāmāreddi, India	B4	53
Kama Reservoir see Kamskoe vodohranilišče, res., Russia	C9	32
Kamas, Ut., U.S.	C5	132
Kamay, Tx., U.S.	H10	128
Kambalda, Austl.	F4	74
Kambam, India	G3	53
Kambarka, Russia	C8	32
Kambja, Est.	B9	10
Kambove, D.R.C.	G5	66
Kamčatka, stm., Russia	E21	34
Kamčatka, poluostrov, pen., Russia	E19	34
Kamčatskij poluostrov, pen., Russia	E21	34
Kamčatskij zaliv, b., Russia	E21	34
Kamchatka Peninsula see Kamčatka, poluostrov, pen., Russia	E20	34
Kameda, Japan	B12	40
Kamen', gora, mtn., Russia	C8	34
Kameng, stm., India	E14	54
Kamenjak, Rt, c., Cro.	F10	22
Kamenka, Kaz.	D11	32
Kamenka, Russia	D21	8
Kamenka, Russia	D6	32
Kamen'-na-Obi, Russia	D14	32
Kameno, Blg.	G14	26
Kamen-Rybolov, Russia	B9	38
Kamenskoe, Russia	D22	34
Kamensk-Ural'skij, Russia	C10	32
Kamenz, Ger.	E10	16
Kāmet, mtn., Asia	C7	54
Kam'ians'ke, Ukr.	D16	26
Kamień Krajeński, Pol.	C13	16
Kamienna Góra, Pol.	F12	16
Kamieńsk, Pol.	E15	16
Kamieskroon, S. Afr.	G3	70
Kamiiso, Japan	D14	38
Kamilukuak Lake, l., Can.	C10	106
Kamina, D.R.C.	F4	66
Kaminak Lake, l., Nu., Can.	C12	106
Kaminoyama, Japan	A13	40
Kaminuriak Lake, l., Nu., Can.	C12	106
Kamioka, Japan	C10	40
Kámiros, hist., Grc.	G10	28
Kamjanec, Bela.	H6	10
Kamkhat Muḥaywir, hill, Jord.	G7	58
Kamloops, B.C., Can.	F10	138
Kamnik, Slvn.	D11	22
Kamo, Japan	B12	40
Kamoa Mountains, mts., Guy.	C6	84
Kamojima, Japan	E7	40
Kāmoke, Pak.	B5	54
Kampala, Ug.	D6	66
Kampar, Malay.	J5	48
Kampar, stm., Indon.	C3	50
Kamparkalns, hill, Lat.	C5	10
Kampar Kanan, stm., Indon.	C2	50
Kampen, Neth.	B14	14
Kamphaeng Phet, Thai.	D4	48
Kampinoski Park Narodowy, p.o.i., Pol.	D16	16
Kâmpóng Cham, Camb.	F7	48
Kâmpóng Chhnăng, Camb.	F7	48
Kâmpóng Kântuŏt, Camb.	G7	48
Kâmpóng Saôm, Camb.	G6	48
Kâmpóng Saôm, Chhâk, b., Camb.	G6	48
Kâmpóng Thum, Camb.	F7	48
Kampong Ulu, Mya.	G4	48
Kâmpôt, Camb.	G7	48
Kampsville, Il., U.S.	E7	120
Kampti, Burkina	G4	64
Kampuchea see Cambodia, ctry., Asia	C3	48
Kampungbaru, Indon.	D3	50
Kampung Litang, Malay.	A11	50
Kamrau, Teluk, b., Indon.	F9	44
Kamsack, Sk., Can.	C12	124
Kamskoe vodohranilišče, res., Russia	C9	32
Kāmthi, India	H7	54
Kamuela, Hi., U.S.	D6	78a
Kámuk, Cerro, mtn., C.R.	H6	102
Kamundan, stm., Indon.	F9	44
Kamyšin, Russia	D7	32
Kamyšlov, Russia	C10	32
Kan, stm., Russia	C17	32
Kanaaupscow, stm., Qc., Can.	E15	106
Kanab, Ut., U.S.	F4	132
Kanab Creek, stm., U.S.	G4	132
Kanaga Island, i., Ak., U.S.	g23	140a
Kanagawa, state, Japan	D12	40
Kanakapura, India	E3	53
Kananga (Luluabourg), D.R.C.	F4	66
Kananggar, Indon.	I12	50
Kanangra-Boyd National Park, p.o.i., Austl.	I7	76
Kanaš, Russia	C7	32
Kanawha, Ia., U.S.	B4	120
Kanawha, stm., W.V., U.S.	F4	114
Kanazawa, Japan	C9	40
Kanbauk, Mya.	E3	48
Kanchanaburi, Thai.	F4	48
Kanchanjanggā (Kānchenjunga), mtn., Asia	E11	54
Kānchenjunga (Kanchanjanggā), mtn., Asia	E11	54
Kānchipuram, India	E4	53
Kanchow see Ganzhou, China	I6	42
Kańczuga, Pol.	F18	16
Kanda, Japan	F3	40
Kandahar, Sk., Can.	C9	124
Kandalakša, Russia	C15	8
Kandalakšskaja guba, b., Russia	C15	8
Kandale, D.R.C.	F3	66
Kandang, Indon.	K3	48
Kandangan, Indon.	E9	50
Kandanghaur, Indon.	G6	50
Kandé, Togo	H5	64
Kandhkot, Pak.	D2	54
Kandi, India	G12	54
Kandi, Tanjung, c., Indon.	E7	44
Kandıra, Tur.	B13	28
Kandla, India	G3	54
Kandos, Austl.	I7	76
Kandreho, Madag.	D8	68
Kandy, Sri L.	H5	53
Kane, Pa., U.S.	C7	114
Kane Basin, b., N.A.	B12	141
Kanem, state, Chad	E3	62
Kaneohe, Hi., U.S.	B4	78a
Kanëvka, Russia	C18	8
Kang, Bots.	C6	70
Kangaba, Mali	G3	64
Kangalassy, Russia	D15	34
Kangâmiut, Grnld.	D15	141
Kangān, Iran	D7	56
Kangar, Malay.	I5	48
Kangaroo Island, i., Austl.	G7	74
Kangāvar, Iran	C6	56
Kangbao, China	C7	36
Kangding, China	C9	46
Kangean, Kepulauan (Kangean Islands), is., Indon.	G9	50
Kangean, Pulau, i., Indon.	G9	50
Kangean Islands see Kangean, Kepulauan, is., Indon.	G9	50
Kangeeak Point, c., Nu., Can.	B18	106
Kangerlussuaq, b., Grnld.	D19	141
Kangersuatsiaq see Prøven, Grnld.	C14	141
Kanger Valley National Park, p.o.i., India	B6	53
Kanggye, Kor., N.	D7	38
Kanghwa-do, i., Kor., S.	F7	38
Kangiqsualujjuaq, Qc., Can.	D17	106
Kangiqsujuaq, Qc., Can.	C16	106
Kangirsuk, Qc., Can.	C17	106
Kangmar, China	D12	54
Kangnŭng, Kor., S.	B1	40
Kango, Gabon	D2	66
Kangping, China	C5	38
Kangpu, China	F4	36
Kangrinboqê Feng, mtn., China	C8	54
Kangshan, Tai.	J9	42
Kangsŏ, Kor., N.	E6	38
Kangto, mtn., Asia	D14	54
Kangwŏn-do, state, Kor., S.	B1	40
Kanha National Park, p.o.i., India	G8	54
Kanhar, stm., India	F9	54
Kanhsien see Ganzhou, China	I6	42
Kani, Mya.	A2	48
Kaniama, D.R.C.	F4	66
Kanibadam, Taj.	A11	56
Kaniet Islands, is., Pap. N. Gui.	a4	79a
Kanigiri, India	D4	53
Kanin, poluostrov, pen., Russia	C21	8
Kanin-Kamen', mts., Russia	B21	8
Kanin Nos, Russia	B20	8
Kanin Nos, mys, c., Russia	B20	8
Kaniva, Austl.	K3	76
Kanjiža, Yugo.	C7	26
Kankaanpää, Fin.	F10	8
Kankakee, Il., U.S.	G2	112
Kankan, Gui.	G3	64
Kānker, India	H8	54
Kankunskij, Russia	E14	34
Kanmaw Kyun, i., Mya.	G4	48
Kannack, Viet.	E9	48
Kannad, India	H5	54
Kannapolis, N.C., U.S.	A5	116
Kannauj, India	E7	54
Kanniyākumari, India	G3	53
Kannod, India	G6	54
Kannur see Cannanore, India	F2	53
Kannus, Fin.	E10	8
Kano, Nig.	G6	64
Kanonji, Japan	E6	40
Kanopolis, Ks., U.S.	C10	128
Kanorado, Ks., U.S.	B6	128
Kanosh, Ut., U.S.	E4	132
Kanoya, Japan	H3	40
Kanpetlet, Mya.	B1	48
Kānpur (Cawnpore), India	E7	54
Kansas, state, U.S.	C10	128
Kansas, stm., Ks., U.S.	B13	128
Kansas City, Ks., U.S.	E3	120
Kansas City, Mo., U.S.	E3	120
Kansk, Russia	C17	32
Kansŏng, Kor., S.	A1	40
Kan-sou see Gansu, state, China	D5	36
Kansu see Gansu, state, China	D5	36
Kantang, Thai.	I4	48
Kantchari, Burkina	G5	64
Kānth, India	D7	54
Kantishna, stm., Ak., U.S.	D9	140
Kantō-heiya, pl., Japan	D12	40
Kanton, i., Kir.	D9	72
Kantō-sanchi, mts., Japan	D11	40
Kantu-long, Mya.	C3	48
Kantunilkin, Mex.	B4	102
Kanuku Mountains, mts., Guy.	F12	86
Kanuma, Japan	C12	40
Kanye, Bots.	D7	70
Kanyutkwin, Mya.	C3	48
Kaohiung see Kaohsiung, Tai.	J8	42
Kaohsiung, Tai.	J8	42
Kaohsiunghsien, Tai.	J9	42
Kaoka Bay, b., Sol. Is.	e9	79b
Kaoko Veld, plat., Nmb.	D1	68
Kaolack, Sen.	G1	64
Kaolinovo, Blg.	F14	26
Kaoma, Zam.	C3	68
Kaouar, reg., Niger	F7	64
Kapaa, Hi., U.S.	A2	78a
Kapadvanj, India	G4	54
Kapanga, D.R.C.	F4	66
Kapaonik, mts., Yugo.	G8	26
Kapatkevičy, Bela.	H11	10
Kapčagaj, Kaz.	F13	32
Kapčagajskoe vodohranilišče, res., Kaz.	F13	32
Kapchagay Reservoir see Kapčagajskoe vodohranilišče, res., Kaz.	F13	32
Kapfenberg, Aus.	C12	22
Kapıdağ Yarımadası, pen., Tur.	C10	28
Kapikotongwa, stm., On., Can.	A11	118
Kapingamarangi, at., Micron.	C6	72
Kapiri Mposhi, Zam.	C4	68
Kapisigdlit, Grnld.	E16	141
Kapiskau, stm., On., Can.	E14	106
Kapit, Malay.	C8	50
Kaplan, La., U.S.	G6	122
Kaplice, Czech Rep.	H10	16
Kapoeta, Sudan	G6	62
Kapona, D.R.C.	F5	66
Kapos, stm., Hung.	C5	26
Kaposvár, Hung.	C4	26
Kaposvar Creek, stm., Sk., Can.	D11	124
Kappeln, Ger.	B5	16
Kaptai, Bngl.	G14	54
Kaptai Lake see Karnaphuli Reservoir, res., Bngl.	G14	54
Kapuas, stm., Indon.	D6	50
Kapuas, stm., Indon.	E9	50
Kapunda, Austl.	J2	76
Kapūrthala, India	C5	54
Kapuskasing, On., Can.	F14	106
Kapuvár, Hung.	B4	26
Kapyl', Bela.	G9	10
Kara, Russia	C1	34
Kara-Balta, Kyrg.	F12	32
Karabanovo, Russia	D21	10
Karabaš, Russia	C9	32
Kara-Bogaz-Gol, zaliv, b., Turkmen.	A7	56
Kara-Bogaz-Gol Gulf see Kara-Bogaz-Gol, zaliv, b., Turkmen.	A7	56
Karabük, Tur.	B15	28
Karabula, Russia	C17	32
Karaburun, Tur.	E9	28
Karabutak, Kaz.	D10	32
Karacabey, Tur.	C11	28
Karačaevo-Čerkesija, state, Russia	F6	32
Karacasu, Tur.	F11	28
Karačev, Russia	G17	10
Karachay see Karačaevo-Čerkesija, state, Russia	F6	32
Karachay-Cherkessia see Karačaevo-Čerkesija, state, Russia	F6	32
Karāchi, Pak.	E10	56
Karād, India	C2	53
Karaftit, Russia	F11	34
Karaganda, Kaz.	E12	32
Karagayly see Karkaralinsk, Kaz.	E13	32
Karaginskij, ostrov, i., Russia	E21	34
Karaginskij zaliv, b., Russia	E21	34
Karagoš, gora, mtn., Russia	D15	32
Karahallı, Tur.	E12	28
Kāraikkudi, India	F4	53
Karaisalı, Tur.	A6	58
Karaj, Iran	B7	56
Kara-Kala, Turkmen.	B8	56
Karakaralong, Pulau, is., Indon.	E8	44
Karakax, stm., China	A7	54
Karakojyn, ozero, l., Kaz.	E11	32
Karakol, Kyrg.	F13	32
Karakoram Pass, p., Asia	A6	54
Karakoram Range, mts., Asia	A4	46
Karakul', Uzb.	G10	32
Kara-Kum Canal see Garagumskij kanal, can., Turkmen.	B9	56
Karama, stm., Indon.	E11	50
Karamai see Karamay, China	B1	36
Karaman, Tur.	A4	58
Karaman, state, Tur.	A4	58
Karamanlı, Tur.	F12	28
Karamay, China	B1	36
Karamea Bight, b., N.Z.	E4	80
Karamürsel, Tur.	C12	28
Karamyševo, Russia	C18	32
Karamzino, Russia	D17	10
Karangasem, Indon.	H9	50
Karangnunggal, Indon.	G6	50
Kāranja, India	H6	54
Karanjia, India	H10	54
Karapınar, Tur.	A4	58
Karas, state, Nmb.	E3	70
Karaşar, Tur.	C14	28
Karasburg, Nmb.	F4	70
Kara Sea see Karskoe more, Russia	B10	30
Karasjok, Nor.	B11	8
Karasu, Tur.	B13	28
Karasu, stm., Tur.	B4	56
Karasuk, Russia	D13	32
Karatal, Kaz.	E15	32
Karatal, stm., Kaz.	E13	32
Karataş Burun, c., Tur.	B6	58
Karatau, Kaz.	F11	32
Karatau, hrebet, mts., Kaz.	F11	32
Karatau Range see Karatau, hrebet, mts., Kaz.	F11	32
Karatobe, Kaz.	E8	32
Karaton, Kaz.	E8	32
Karatsu, Japan	F2	40
Karaul, Kaz.	E13	32
Karaul, Russia	B5	34
Karauli, India	E6	54
Karawa, D.R.C.	D4	66
Karawang, Indon.	G5	50
Karawang, Tanjung, c., Indon.	F5	50
Karawanken, mts., Eur.	D11	22
Karažal, Kaz.	E12	32
Karbalā', Iraq	C5	56
Kårböle, Swe.	E6	8
Karcag, Hung.	B7	26
Kardámaina, Grc.	G9	28
Kardeljevo, Cro.	G14	22
Kárditsa, Grc.	D4	28
Kärdla, Est.	G10	8
Kărdžali, Blg.	H12	26
Karelia see Karelija, state, Russia	D15	8
Karelia, hist. reg., Eur.	E14	8
Karelija, state, Russia	D15	8
Karelija see Karelia, hist. reg., Eur.	E14	8
Karel'skij Gorodok, Russia	B19	10
Karema, Tan.	F6	66
Karen, India	F7	46
Karesuando, Swe.	B9	8
Kärevere, Est.	B9	10
Kargasok, Russia	C14	32
Kargat, Russia	C14	32
Kargil, India	A5	54
Kargopol', Russia	F18	8
Kariba, Zimb.	D4	68
Kariba, Lake, res., Afr.	D4	68
Karibib, Nmb.	B2	70
Kariega, stm., S. Afr.	H6	70
Karimata, Kepulauan, is., Indon.	D6	50
Karimata, Selat, strt., Indon.	E6	50
Karīmganj, India	F14	54
Karīmnagar, India	B4	53
Karimunjawa, Kepulauan, is., Indon.	F7	50
Karimunjawa, Pulau, i., Indon.	F7	50
Karisimbi, vol., Afr.	E5	66
Káristos, Grc.	E7	28
Kariya, Japan	D10	40
Kārkal, India	E2	53
Karkaralinsk, Kaz.	E13	32
Karkar Island, i., Pap. N. Gui.	a4	79a
Karkonoski Park Narodowy, p.o.i., Pol.	F11	16
Karkūk, Iraq	B5	56
Karleby see Kokkola, Fin.	E10	8
Karlino, Pol.	B11	16
Karl-Marx-Stadt see Chemnitz, Ger.	F8	16
Karlovac, Cro.	E12	22
Karlovo, Blg.	G11	26
Karlovy Vary, Czech Rep.	F8	16
Karlsborg, Swe.	D10	8
Karlsburg see Alba Iulia, Rom.	C10	26
Karlshamn, Swe.	H6	8
Karlskoga, Swe.	G6	8
Karlskrona, Swe.	H6	8
Karlsruhe, Ger.	G4	16
Karlstad, Swe.	G5	8
Karlstadt, Ger.	G5	16
Karluk, Ak., U.S.	E9	140
Karma, Bela.	H14	10
Karma, Niger	G5	64
Karmah an Nuzul, Sudan	D6	62
Karmāla, India	B2	53
Karmøy, i., Nor.	G1	8
Karnack, Tx., U.S.	E4	122
Karnak, Il., U.S.	G9	120
Karnāl, India	D6	54
Karṇālī, stm., Asia	D8	54
Karnāli, stm., Nepal	D8	54
Karnaphuli Reservoir, res., Bngl.	G14	54
Karnātaka, state, India	D2	53
Karnobat, Blg.	G13	26
Kärnten, state, Aus.	D10	22
Karoli, India	G7	54
Karonga, Mwi.	B5	68
Karoo National Park, p.o.i., S. Afr.	H6	70
Karoonda, Austl.	J2	76
Karor, Pak.	C3	54
Kárpathos, Grc.	H10	28
Kárpathos, i., Grc.	H10	28
Karpats'kyi Pryrodnyi Natsional'nyi Park, p.o.i., Ukr.	A11	26
Karpenísi, Grc.	E4	28
Karpogory, Russia	D21	8
Karpuzlu, Tur.	F10	28
Karratha, Austl.	D3	74
Karrats Fjord, b., Grnld.	C14	141
Kars, Tur.	A5	56
Karsakpaj, Kaz.	E11	32
Karsantı, Tur.	A6	58
Karši, Uzb.	G11	32
Karsin, Pol.	C13	16
Karskoe more (Kara Sea), Russia	B10	30
Kartala, vol., Com.	C7	68
Kartaly, Russia	D10	32
Kartārpur, India	C5	54
Karthaus, Pa., U.S.	C7	114
Kartuzy, Pol.	B14	16
Karufa, Indon.	F9	44
Karumba, Austl.	A3	76
Karungi, Swe.	C10	8
Karunjie, Austl.	C5	74
Karūr, India	F4	53
Karviná, Czech Rep.	G14	16
Kārwār, India	D1	53
Karyés, Grc.	C7	28
Karymskoe, Russia	F11	34
Kasai (Cassai), stm., Afr.	E3	66
Kasaji, D.R.C.	G4	66
Kasama, Japan	C13	40
Kasama, Zam.	C5	68
Kasane, Bots.	D3	68
Kasanga, Tan.	F6	66
Kasangulu, D.R.C.	E3	66
Kasaoka, Japan	E6	40
Kāsaragod, India	E2	53
Kasba, India	F11	54
Kasba Lake, l., Can.	C10	106
Kascjukouka, Bela.	H13	10
Kascjukovičy, Bela.	G14	10
Kaseda, Japan	H3	40
Kasempa, Zam.	C4	68
Kasenga, D.R.C.	G5	66
Kasenye, D.R.C.	D6	66
Kasese, D.R.C.	E5	66
Kasese, Ug.	D6	66
Kaset Sombun, Thai.	D5	48
Kāsganj, India	E7	54
Kāshān, Iran	C7	56
Kashgar see Kashi, China	B12	56
Kashi, China	B12	56
Kashihara, Japan	E8	40
Kashima, Japan	F3	40
Kashima-nada, Japan	C13	40
Kashing see Jiaxing, China	F9	42
Kāshīpur, India	D7	54
Kashiwazaki, Japan	B11	40
Kāshmar, Iran	B8	56
Kashmir, hist. reg., Asia	A3	46
Kasia, India	E9	54
Kasimbar, Indon.	D12	50
Kasimov, Russia	I19	8
Kašin, Russia	C20	10
Kašira, Russia	F21	10
Kasiruta, Pulau, i., Indon.	F8	44
Kaskaskia, stm., Il., U.S.	E9	120
Kaskinen, Fin.	E9	8
Kaslo, B.C., Can.	G13	138
Kasnja, Russia	E17	10
Kasongo, D.R.C.	E5	66
Kasongo-Lunda, D.R.C.	F3	66
Kásos, i., Grc.	H9	28
Kasota, Mn., U.S.	G5	118
Kaspijsk, Russia	F7	32
Kaspijskij, Russia	E7	32
Kaspijskoje more see Caspian Sea	F7	32
Kasplja, stm., Eur.	E13	10
Kasr, Ra's, c., Afr.	D7	62
Kassab, Syria	C6	58
Kassalā, Sudan	D7	62
Kassándra, pen., Grc.	C6	28
Kassandra, Gulf of see Kassándras, Kólpos, b., Grc.	C6	28
Kassándras, Kólpos, b., Grc.	C6	28
Kassel, Ger.	E5	16
Kasserine, Tun.	B6	64
Kastamonu, Tur.	A3	56
Kastamonu, state, Tur.	B16	28
Kastélli, Grc.	H6	28
Kastoría, Grc.	C4	28
Kastorías, Límni, l., Grc.	C4	28
Kastrakíou, Technití Límni, res., Grc.	E4	28
Kasugai, Japan	D9	40
Kasulu, Tan.	E6	66
Kasumi, Japan	D7	40
Kasumiga-ura, l., Japan	C13	40
Kasungan, Indon.	E8	50
Kasūr, Pak.	C5	54
Kaszuby, hist. reg., Pol.	B13	16
Kataba, Zam.	D4	68
Katahdin, Mount, mtn., Me., U.S.	E7	110
Katako-Kombe, D.R.C.	E4	66
Katanga, hist. reg., D.R.C.	F4	66
Katanga, stm., Russia	C18	32
Katangi, India	G7	54
Katangli, Russia	F17	34
Katanning, Austl.	F3	74
Katchall Island, i., India	G7	46
Katepwa Beach, Sk., Can.	D10	124
Kateríni, Grc.	C5	28
Kates Needle, mtn., N.A.	D4	106
Katete, Zam.	C5	68
Katha, Mya.	D8	46
Katherîna, Gebel, mtn., Egypt	J4	58
Katherine, Austl.	B6	74
Katherine, stm., Austl.	B6	74
Katherine Creek, stm., Austl.	D4	76
Kāthiāwār Peninsula, pen., India	H3	54
Kathla, India	C6	54
Kāṭhmāṇḍau (Kathmandu), Nepal	E10	54
Kathmandu see Kāṭhmāṇḍau, Nepal	E10	54
Kathor, India	H4	54
Kathua, India	B5	54
Kati, Mali	G3	64
Katibas, stm., Malay.	C8	50
Katihār, India	F11	54
Katimik Lake, l., Mb., Can.	B14	124
Katiola, C. Iv.	H4	64
Katipunan, Phil.	F4	52
Ka Tiriti o te Moana see Southern Alps, mts., N.Z.	F4	80
Katmai, Mount, vol., Ak., U.S.	E8	140
Káto Achaía, Grc.	E4	28
Kātol, India	H7	54
Katoomba, Austl.	I8	76
Katowice, Pol.	F14	16
Katowice, state, Pol.	F15	16
Katrineholm, Swe.	G7	8
Katsina, Nig.	G6	64
Katsina Ala, stm., Afr.	H6	64
Katsuta, Japan	C13	40
Katsuura, Japan	D13	40
Katsuyama, Japan	C9	40
Katsuyama, Japan	D6	40
Kattakurgan, Uzb.	G11	32
Kattegat, strt., Eur.	H4	8
Katul, Jabal, mtn., Sudan	E5	62
Katun', stm., Russia	D15	32
Katunino, Russia	G21	8
Kātwa, India	G11	54
Katwijk aan Zee, Neth.	B13	14
Katyn, Russia	F14	10
Katzenbuckel, mtn., Ger.	G5	16
Kauai, i., Hi., U.S.	B2	78a
Kauai Channel, strt., Hi., U.S.	B3	78a
Kaufbeuren, Ger.	I6	16
Kaufman, Tx., U.S.	E2	122
Kaukauna, Wi., U.S.	D1	112
Kaukau Veld, plat., Afr.	D3	68
Kaulakahi Channel, strt., Hi., U.S.	B2	78a
Kaumalapau, Hi., U.S.	C4	78a
Kaunas, Lith.	F6	10
Kaura-Namoda, Nig.	G6	64
Kauriālā (Ghāghara), stm., Asia	D8	54
Kautokeino, Nor.	B10	8
Kau-ye Kyun, i., Mya.	G4	48
Kavača, Russia	D23	34
Kavadarci, Mac.	B5	28
Kavaja see Kavajë, Alb.	C13	24
Kavajë, Alb.	C13	24
Kavaklıdere, Tur.	F11	28
Kavála, Grc.	C7	28
Kavalerovo, Russia	B11	38
Kāvali, India	D4	53
Kavaratti, India	F3	46
Kavaratti Island, i., India	F3	46
Kāveri (Cauvery), stm., India	F4	53
Kāveri Falls, wtfl, India	E3	53
Kavieng, Pap. N. Gui.	a5	79a
Kavīr, Dasht-e, des., Iran	C8	56
Kaw, Ok., U.S.	E12	128
Kawa, Mya.	D3	48
Kawagama Lake, l., On., Can.	C10	112
Kawagoe, Japan	D12	40
Kawaguchi, Japan	D12	40
Kawaihoa, c., Hi., U.S.	B1	78a
Kawaikini, mtn., Hi., U.S.	A2	78a
Kawambwa, Zam.	B4	68
Kawanoe, Japan	E6	40
Kawardha, India	H8	54
Kawasaki, Japan	D12	40
Kawatana, Japan	F2	40
Kawdut, Mya.	E3	48
Kaweenakumik Lake, l., Mb., Can.	B14	124
Kawhia Harbour, b., N.Z.	D6	80
Kawich Peak, mtn., Nv., U.S.	F9	134
Kawkareik, Mya.	D4	48
Kaw Lake, res., Ok., U.S.	E12	128
Kawludo, Mya.	C3	48
Kawnipi Lake, l., On., Can.	C7	118
Kawthaung, Mya.	H4	48
Kaxgar, stm., China	B12	56
Kaya, Burkina	G4	64
Kayah, state, Mya.	C3	48
Kayak Island, i., Ak., U.S.	E11	140
Kāyalpattinam, India	G4	53
Kayan, Mya.	D3	48
Kayan, stm., Indon.	B10	50
Kāyankulam, India	G3	53
Kaycee, Wy., U.S.	D6	126
Kayenta, Az., U.S.	G6	132
Kayes, Mali	G2	64
Kayin, state, Mya.	D3	48
Kaymaz, Tur.	D14	28
Kayseri, Tur.	B4	56
Kaysville, Ut., U.S.	B4	132
Kayuadi, Pulau, i., Indon.	G12	50
Kayuagung, Indon.	E4	50
Kayumas, Indon.	G9	50
Kazače, Russia	B16	34
Kazačinskoe, Russia	C19	32
Kazačinskoe, Russia	E7	34
Kazahskij melkosopočnik (Kazakh Hills), hills, Kaz.	D12	32
Kazakh Hills see Kazahskij melkosopočnik, hills, Kaz.	D12	32
Kazaki, Russia	H21	10
Kazakstan, ctry., Asia	E10	32
Kazalinsk, Kaz.	E10	32
Kazan', Russia	C7	32
Kazan, stm., Can.	C11	106
Kazanlăk, Blg.	G12	26
Kazanlı, Tur.	B5	58
Kazan-rettō, is., Japan	G18	30
Kazanskoe, Russia	C11	32
Kāzerūn, Iran	D7	56
Kazimierza Wielka, Pol.	F16	16
Kazincbarcika, Hung.	A7	26
Kaziranga National Park, p.o.i., India	E14	54
Kazlų Rūda, Lith.	F6	10
Kaztalovka, Kaz.	E7	32
Kazula, Moz.	D5	68
Kazym, Russia	B11	32
Kazym, stm., Russia	B11	32
Kazyr, stm., Russia	D16	32
Kbal Dâmrei, Camb.	E7	48
Kdyně, Czech Rep.	G9	16
Kéa, Grc.	F7	28
Kéa, i., Grc.	F7	28
Keahole Point, c., Hi., U.S.	D5	78a
Kealaikahiki Channel, strt., Hi., U.S.	C5	78a
Keams Canyon, Az., U.S.	H6	132
Keanapapa Point, c., Hi., U.S.	C4	78a
Kearney, Mo., U.S.	E3	120
Kearney, Ne., U.S.	G13	126
Kearns, Ut., U.S.	C4	132
Kearny, Az., U.S.	J6	132
Keban Barajı, res., Tur.	B4	56
Keban Reservoir see Keban Barajı, res., Tur.	B4	56
Kébèmer, Sen.	F1	64
Kebnekaise, mtn., Swe.	B8	8
K'ebrī Dehar, Eth.	F8	62
Kech, stm., Pak.	D9	56
Kechika, stm., B.C., Can.	D5	106
Keçiborlu, Tur.	F13	28
Kecskemét, Hung.	C6	26
Kedah, state, Malay.	J5	48
Kėdainiai, Lith.	E6	10
Kediri, Indon.	G8	50
Kedon, Russia	D20	34
Kédougou, Sen.	G2	64
Kędzierzyn-Koźle, Pol.	F14	16
Keefers, B.C., Can.	F9	138
Keele, stm., N.T., Can.	C5	106
Keele Peak, mtn., Yk., Can.	C4	106
Keeling Islands see Cocos Islands, dep., Oc.	K12	142
Keelung see Chilung, Tai.	I9	42
Keene, Ky., U.S.	G13	120
Keene, N.H., U.S.	B13	114
Keene, Tx., U.S.	B10	130
Keeney Knob, mtn., W.V., U.S.	G5	114
Keer-Weer, Cape, c., Austl.	B8	74
Keeseville, N.Y., U.S.	F3	110
Keetmanshoop, Nmb.	E3	70
Keewatin, On., Can.	B4	118
Keewatin, Mn., U.S.	D5	118
Kefallinía, i., Grc.	E3	28
Kefamenanu, Indon.	G7	44
Kefar Naḥum (Capernaum), hist., Isr.	F6	58
Kefar Sava, Isr.	F5	58
Keffi, Nig.	H6	64
Keflavík, Ice.	k28	8a
Ke Ga, Mui, c., Viet.	F9	48
Kegalla, Sri L.	H5	53
Keg River, Ab., Can.	D7	106
Kegums, Lat.	D7	10
Ke-hsi Mānsām, Mya.	B3	48
Keighley, Eng., U.K.	H10	12
Keila, Est.	G11	8
Keimoes, S. Afr.	F5	70
Keith, Scot., U.K.	D9	12
Keith Arm, b., N.T., Can.	B6	106
Keithley Creek, B.C., Can.	D9	138
Keithsburg, Il., U.S.	J8	118
Keiyasi, Fiji	p18	79e
Keizer, Or., U.S.	F3	136
Kejimkujik National Park, p.o.i., N.S., Can.	F11	110
Kejvy, mts., Russia	C17	8
Kekaha, Hi., U.S.	B2	78a
Kékes, mtn., Hung.	B7	26
Kekri, India	E5	54
K'elafo, Eth.	F8	62
Kelai, stm., Indon.	C10	50
Kelani, stm., Sri L.	H5	53
Kelantan, state, Malay.	J6	48
Kelantan, stm., Malay.	J6	48
Kelapa, Indon.	D4	50
Kelbia, Sebkhet, l., Tun.	I4	24
Kelheim, Ger.	H7	16
Kelibia, Tun.	H5	24
Kéllé, Congo	E2	66
Kellerberrin, Austl.	F3	74
Keller Lake, l., N.T., Can.	C6	106
Kellett, Cape, c., N.T., Can.	B14	140
Kelleys Island, i., Oh., U.S.	C3	114
Kellogg, Id., U.S.	C10	136
Kellogg, Ia., U.S.	C5	120
Kellogg, Mn., U.S.	G6	118
Kelloselkä, Fin.	C13	8
Kells, Ire.	H6	12
Kelmė, Lith.	E5	10
Kélo, Chad	F3	62
Kelolokan, Indon.	C10	50
Kelowna, B.C., Can.	G11	138
Kelsey Bay, B.C., Can.	F5	138
Kelseyville, Ca., U.S.	D3	134
Kelso, Scot., U.K.	F10	12
Kelso, Wa., U.S.	D4	136
Keluang, Malay.	K6	48
Kelvington, Sk., Can.	B10	124
Kelvin Island, i., On., Can.	B10	118
Kem', Russia	D16	8
Kem', stm., Russia	D15	8
Kemano, B.C., Can.	C2	138
Kemena, stm., Malay.	B8	50
Kemer, Tur.	F13	28
Kemer Barajı, res., Tur.	F11	28
Kemerhisar, Tur.	A5	58
Kemerovo, Russia	C15	32
Kemi, Fin.	D11	8
Kemijärvi, Fin.	C12	8
Kemijärvi, l., Fin.	C12	8
Kemijoki, stm., Fin.	C12	8
Kemmerer, Wy., U.S.	B6	132
Kemmuna (Comino), i., Malta	H8	24
Kemnath, Ger.	G7	16
Kemp, Tx., U.S.	E2	122
Kemp, Lake, res., Tx., U.S.	H9	128
Kempner, Tx., U.S.	C9	130
Kempsey, Austl.	H9	76
Kempt, Lac, l., Qc., Can.	F16	106
Kempten, Ger.	I6	16
Kemptville, On., Can.	C14	112
Kemujan, Pulau, i., Indon.	F7	50
Kemul, Kong, mtn., Indon.	C9	50
Ken, stm., India	F8	54
Kenai, Ak., U.S.	D9	140
Kenai Mountains, mts., Ak., U.S.	E9	140
Kenai Peninsula, pen., Ak., U.S.	E9	140
Kenansville, Fl., U.S.	I5	116
Kenansville, N.C., U.S.	B7	116
Kenbridge, Va., U.S.	H7	114
Kendal, Sk., Can.	D10	124
Kendal, Indon.	G7	50
Kendal, Eng., U.K.	G10	12
Kendall, Austl.	H9	76
Kendall, Fl., U.S.	K5	116
Kendall, Wi., U.S.	H8	118
Kendall, Cape, c., Nu., Can.	C13	106
Kendari, Indon.	F7	44
Kendawangan, Indon.	E7	50
Kendrāparha, India	H11	54
Kendrew, S. Afr.	H7	70
Kendrick, Fl., U.S.	G3	116
Kendrick, Id., U.S.	D10	136
Kendujhargarh, India	H10	54
Kenedy, Tx., U.S.	F10	130
Kenema, S.L.	H2	64
Kenga, Russia	C14	32
Kenge, D.R.C.	E3	66
Keng Hkam, Mya.	B3	48
Kēng Tung, Mya.	B4	48
Kenhardt, S. Afr.	F5	70

Name	Map Ref.	Page
Kenilworth, Ut., U.S.	D6	132
Kénitra, Mor.	C3	64
Kenly, N.C., U.S.	A7	116
Kenmare, Ire.	J3	12
Kenmare, N.D., U.S.	F11	124
Kennard, Tx., U.S.	F3	122
Kennebec, stm., Me., U.S.	F7	110
Kennebecasis Bay, b., N.B., Can.	E11	110
Kennebunk, Me., U.S.	G6	110
Kennedy, Al., U.S.	D11	122
Kennedy, Cape see Canaveral, Cape, c., Fl., U.S.	H5	116
Kennedy, Mount, mtn., B.C., Can.	F5	138
Kennedy, Mount, mtn., Yk., Can.	C3	106
Kennedy Lake, l., B.C., Can.	G5	138
Kenner, La., U.S.	G8	122
Kennetcook, N.S., Can.	E13	110
Kennett, Mo., U.S.	H7	120
Kennewick, Wa., U.S.	D7	136
Kenney Dam, dam, B.C., Can.	C6	138
Kenogami, stm., On., Can.	E13	106
Kénogami, Lac, res., Qc., Can.	B5	110
Keno Hill, Yk., Can.	C3	106
Kenora, On., Can.	B4	118
Kenosha, Wi., U.S.	F2	112
Kenozero, ozero, l., Russia	E18	8
Kensal, N.D., U.S.	G15	124
Kensett, Ar., U.S.	B7	122
Kensington, Ks., U.S.	B9	128
Kensington Park, Fl., U.S.	I3	116
Kent, Oh., U.S.	C4	114
Kent, Wa., U.S.	C4	136
Kentau, Kaz.	F11	32
Kent Group, is., Austl.	L6	76
Kentland, In., U.S.	H2	112
Kenton, Mi., U.S.	E10	118
Kenton, Tn., U.S.	H8	120
Kent Peninsula, pen., Nu., Can.	B9	106
Kentrikí Makedonía, state, Grc.	C6	28
Kentucky, state, U.S.	G12	120
Kentucky, stm., Ky., U.S.	F13	120
Kentucky, Middle Fork, stm., Ky., U.S.	G2	114
Kentucky, North Fork, stm., Ky., U.S.	G2	114
Kentucky Lake, res., U.S.	H9	120
Kentville, N.S., Can.	E12	110
Kentwood, La., U.S.	G8	122
Kenya, ctry., Afr.	D7	66
Kenya, Mount see Kirinyaga, mtn., Kenya	E7	66
Kenyon, Mn., U.S.	G6	118
Keokuk, Ia., U.S.	D6	120
Keoladeo National Park, p.o.i., India	E6	54
Keo Nua, Deo, p., Asia	C7	48
Keosauqua, Ia., U.S.	D5	120
Keota, Ia., U.S.	C6	120
Keota, Ok., U.S.	B4	122
Keowee, Lake, res., S.C., U.S.	B2	116
Kepi, Indon.	G10	44
Kepina, Russia	D19	8
Kępno, Pol.	E13	16
Keppel Bay, b., Austl.	D8	76
Kepsut, Tur.	D11	28
Kerala, state, India	F3	53
Keramadoo, mtn., Palau	f8	78b
Keramian, Pulau, i., Indon.	F9	50
Kerang, Austl.	J4	76
Keratéa, Grc.	F6	28
Keravat, Pap. N. Gui.	a5	79a
Kerch, Ukr.	E5	32
Kerec, mys, c., Russia	D18	8
Kerema, Pap. N. Gui.	b4	79a
Keremeos, B.C., Can.	G11	138
Keren, Erit.	D7	62
Kerens, Tx., U.S.	E2	122
Keret', Russia	C15	8
Keret', ozero, l., Russia	D15	8
Kerewan, Gam.	G1	64
Kerguelen, Îles, is., Afr.	J17	4
Kerguelen Plateau, unds.	O10	142
Keri, Grc.	F3	28
Kericho, Kenya	E7	66
Kerinci, Gunung, vol., Indon.	D2	50
Kerkenna, Îles, is., Tun.	C7	64
Kerkhoven, Mn., U.S.	F3	118
Kerkiči, Turkmen.	B10	56
Kerkrade, Neth.	F2	16
Kérkyra (Corfu), Grc.	D2	28
Kérkyra (Corfu), i., Grc.	D2	28
Kermadec Islands, is., N.Z.	F9	72
Kermadec Ridge, unds.	M20	142
Kermadec Trench, unds.	M21	142
Kermān, Iran	C8	56
Kermānshāh (Bākhtarān), Iran	C6	56
Kerme, Gulf of see Gökova Körfezi, b., Tur.	G10	28
Kermit, Tx., U.S.	C4	130
Kern, stm., Ca., U.S.	H7	134
Kern, South Fork, stm., Ca., U.S.	H7	134
Kernersville, N.C., U.S.	H5	114
Kernville, Ca., U.S.	H7	134
Kérouané, Gui.	H3	64
Kerrobert, Sk., Can.	C4	124
Kerrville, Tx., U.S.	D8	130
Kerry, state, Ire.	I2	12
Kerry Head, c., Ire.	I2	12
Kershaw, S.C., U.S.	B5	116
Kersley, B.C., Can.	D8	138
Kertamulia, Indon.	D6	50
Kerulen, stm., Asia	B7	36
Kesagami Lake, l., On., Can.	E14	106
Keşan, Tur.	C9	28
Kesennuma, Japan	E14	38
Keshan, China	B10	36
Keshod, India	H3	54
Keski-Suomi, state, Fin.	E11	8
Kes'ma, Russia	B20	10
Kesova Gora, Russia	C20	10
Kestell, S. Afr.	F9	70
Keswick, Eng., U.K.	G9	12
Keszthely, Hung.	C4	26
Ket', stm., Russia	C14	32
Keta, Ghana	H5	64
Keta, ozero, l., Russia	C6	34
Ketapang, Indon.	F4	50
Ketapang, Indon.	D6	50
Ketchikan, Ak., U.S.	E13	140
Ketchum, Id., U.S.	G12	136
Kete-Krachi, Ghana	H4	64
Ketoj, ostrov, i., Russia	G19	34
Kętrzyn, Pol.	B17	16
Kettering, Eng., U.K.	I12	12
Kettering, Oh., U.S.	E1	114
Kettle, stm., N.A.	H12	138
Kettle Falls, Wa., U.S.	B8	136
Kęty, Pol.	G15	16
Keudeteunom, Indon.	J2	48
Keuka Lake, l., N.Y., U.S.	B8	114
Keukenhof, misc. cult., Neth.	B13	14
Keul', Russia	C18	32
Kevelaer, Ger.	E2	16
Kevin, Mt., U.S.	B14	136
Kew, T./C. Is.	A12	102
Kewanee, Il., U.S.	C7	120
Kewaunee, Wi., U.S.	D2	112
Keweenaw Bay, b., Mi., U.S.	E10	118
Keweenaw Peninsula, pen., Mi., U.S.	D11	118
Keweenaw Point, c., Mi., U.S.	D11	118
Key, Lough, l., Ire.	G4	12
Keya Paha, stm., U.S.	E13	126
Keyes, Ok., U.S.	E6	128
Keyhole Reservoir, res., Wy., U.S.	C8	126
Key Largo, Fl., U.S.	K5	116
Key Largo, i., Fl., U.S.	K5	116
Keyser, W.V., U.S.	E7	114
Keystone, S.D., U.S.	D9	126
Keystone, W.V., U.S.	G4	114
Keystone Lake, res., Ok., U.S.	A2	122
Keystone Peak, mtn., Az., U.S.	L5	132
Keysville, Va., U.S.	G7	114
Keytesville, Mo., U.S.	E5	120
Key West, Fl., U.S.	L4	116
Kezi, Zimb.	B9	70
Kežma, Russia	C18	32
Kežmarok, Slov.	G16	16
Kgalagadi, state, Bots.	D5	70
Kgatleng, state, Bots.	D8	70
Khadki, India	B1	53
Khadzhybeis'kyi lyman, l., Ukr.	C17	26
Khagaria, India	F11	54
Khairāgarh, India	H8	54
Khairpur, Pak.	E2	54
Khairpur, Pak.	D4	54
Khajrāho, India	F8	54
Khakassia see Hakasija, state, Russia	D16	32
Kha Khaeng, stm., Thai.	E4	48
Khakhea, Bots.	D6	70
Khalatse, India	A6	54
Khālidī, Khirbat al-, hist., Jord.	I6	58
Khalîya, Gebel, mtn., Egypt	I3	58
Khalūf, Oman	E8	56
Khambhāliya, India	G2	54
Khambhāt, India	G4	54
Khambhāt, Gulf of, b., India	H3	54
Khāmgaon, India	H6	54
Khāmis, Ash-Shallāl al- (Fifth Cataract), wtfl, Sudan	D6	62
Khamīs Mushayṭ, Sau. Ar.	F5	56
Khammam, India	C5	53
Khan, stm., Laos	C6	48
Khan, stm., Nmb.	C2	70
Khānābād, Afg.	B10	56
Khān Abū Shāmāt, Syria	E7	58
Khānaqīn, Iraq	C6	56
Khancoban, Austl.	K7	76
Khandela, India	E5	54
Khandwa, India	H6	54
Khānewāl, Pak.	C3	54
Khāngarh, Pak.	D3	54
Khangchendzonga National Park, p.o.i., India	E12	54
Khangkhai, Laos	C6	48
Khania, Gulf of see Chanión, Kólpos, b., Grc.	H6	28
Khanka, Lake, l., Asia	B10	38
Khanna, India	C6	54
Khānpur, Pak.	D3	54
Khansiir, Raas, c., Som.	B9	66
Khān Yūnus, Gaza	G5	58
Khao Laem Reservoir, res., Thai.	E4	48
Khao Sok National Park, p.o.i., Thai.	H4	48
Khao Yoi, Thai.	F4	48
Kharagpur, India	G11	54
Khārān, Pak.	D10	56
Kharāyij, Sabkhat al-, l., Syria	C8	58
Kharg Island see Khārk, Jazīreh-ye, i., Iran	D7	56
Khargon, India	H5	54
Khāriān Cantonment, Pak.	B4	54
Khārk, Jazīreh-ye, i., Iran	D7	56
Kharkiv, Ukr.	D5	32
Kharmanli see Harmanli, Blg.	H12	26
Khartoum see Al-Kharṭūm, Sudan	D6	62
Khartoum North see Al-Kharṭūm Baḥrī, Sudan	D6	62
Khasebake, Bots.	B7	70
Khāsh, Afg.	C9	56
Khāsh, Iran	D9	56
Khashm al-Qirbah, Sudan	D7	62
Khaskovo see Haskovo, Blg.	H12	26
Khatanga see Hatanga, Russia	B9	34
Khatanga see Hatanga, stm., Russia	B9	34
Khatauli, India	D6	54
Khatt, Oued al, stm., W. Sah.	D2	64
Khavast see Havast, Uzb.	F11	32
Khawsa, Mya.	E3	48
Khayung, stm., Thai.	E7	48
Khed, India	C1	53
Kheil, Katîb el-, sand, Egypt	H3	58
Khemis el Khechna, Alg.	H14	20
Khemis Melyana, Alg.	H13	20
Khemmarat, Thai.	D7	48
Khenchla, Alg.	B6	64
Khenifra, Mor.	C3	64
Kherson, Ukr.	F15	6
Kheta see Heta, stm., Russia	B8	34
Khetia, India	H5	54
Khimki see Himki, Russia	E20	10
Khipro, Pak.	F2	54
Khisfīn, Golan	F6	58
Khiva see Hiva, Uzb.	F10	32
Khlong Thom, Thai.	I4	48
Khlung, Thai.	F6	48
Khok Kloi, Thai.	H4	48
Khok Samrong, Thai.	E5	48
Kholm, Afg.	B10	56
Khomas, state, Nmb.	C3	70
Khomeynīshahr, Iran	C7	56
Khondmāl Hills, hills, India	H10	54
Khong see Mekong, stm., Asia	E10	46
Khon Kaen, Thai.	D6	48
Khordha, India	H10	54
Khorixas, Nmb.	B2	70
Khorog see Horog, Taj.	B11	56
Khorramābād, Iran	C6	56
Khorramshahr, Iran	C6	56
Khotyn, Ukr.	A13	26
Khouribga, Mor.	C3	64
Khowai, India	F13	54
Khowst, Afg.	C10	56
Khrisokhoús, Kólpos, b., Cyp.	C3	58
Khuis, Bots.	E5	70
Khuīyāla, India	E3	54
Khulna, Bngl.	G12	54
Khulna, state, Bngl.	G12	54
Khun Tan, Doi, mtn., Thai.	C4	48
Khunti, India	G10	54
Khurai, India	F7	54
Khurja, India	D6	54
Khushāb, Pak.	B4	54
Khust, Ukr.	A10	26
Khuzdār, Pak.	D10	56
Khvoy, Iran	B6	56
Khwae Noi, stm., Thai.	E4	48
Khyber Pass, p., Asia	A3	54
Khyriv, Ukr.	G18	16
Kiama, Austl.	J8	76
Kiama, D.R.C.	F3	66
Kiamba, Phil.	H5	52
Kiambi, D.R.C.	F5	66
Kiamichi, stm., Ok., U.S.	C3	122
Kiamusze see Jiamusi, China	B11	36
Kian see Ji'an, China	H6	42
Kiangarow, Mount, mtn., Austl.	F8	76
Kiang-si see Jiangxi, state, China	H6	42
Kiangsi see Jiangxi, state, China	H6	42
Kiang-sou see Jiangsu, state, China	E8	42
Kiangsu see Jiangsu, state, China	E8	42
Kiaohsien see Jiaoxian, China	C8	42
Kibangou, Congo	E2	66
Kibombo, D.R.C.	E5	66
Kibondo, Tan.	E6	66
Kibre Mengist, Eth.	F7	62
Kıbrıs see Cyprus, ctry., Asia	C4	58
Kıbrısçık, Tur.	C14	28
Kibuye, Rw.	E5	66
Kičevo, Mac.	B3	28
Kickapoo, stm., Wi., U.S.	H8	118
Kicking Horse Pass, p., Can.	E14	138
Kidal, Mali	F5	64
Kidapawan, Phil.	G5	52
Kidatu, Tan.	F7	66
Kidderminster, Eng., U.K.	I10	12
Kidira, Sen.	G2	64
Kidnappers, Cape, c., N.Z.	D7	80
Kidston, Austl.	B5	76
Kiefersfelden, Ger.	I8	16
Kiel, Ger.	B6	16
Kiel, Wi., U.S.	H10	118
Kiel Bay see Kieler Bucht, b., Ger.	B6	16
Kiel Canal see Nord-Ostsee-Kanal, can., Ger.	B5	16
Kielce, Pol.	F16	16
Kielce, state, Pol.	F16	16
Kieler Bucht, b., Ger.	B6	16
Kiester, Mn., U.S.	H5	118
Kiev see Kyïv, Ukr.	D4	32
Kievka, Kaz.	D12	32
Kiev Reservoir see Kyïvs'ke vodoskhovyshche, res., Ukr.	D4	32
Kiffa, Maur.	F2	64
Kifisiá, Grc.	E6	28
Kigali, Rw.	E6	66
Kigoma, Tan.	E5	66
Kihčik, Russia	F20	34
Kihei, Hi., U.S.	C5	78a
Kihniö, Fin.	E10	8
Kihnu, i., Est.	G10	8
Kii-hantō, pen., Japan	F8	40
Kiik, Kaz.	E12	32
Kii-suidō, strt., Japan	F7	40
Kikerino, Russia	A12	10
Kikinda, Yugo.	D7	26
Kikládhes (Cyclades), is., Grc.	F7	28
Kikori, Pap. N. Gui.	b3	79a
Kikori, stm., Pap. N. Gui.	b3	79a
Kikuchi, Japan	G3	40
Kikwit, D.R.C.	F3	66
Kīlakkarai, India	G4	53
Kilauea, Hi., U.S.	A2	78a
Kilauea Crater, crat., Hi., U.S.	D6	78a
Kılbasan, Tur.	A4	58
Kilbuck Mountains, mts., Ak., U.S.	D8	140
Kilchu-ŭp, Kor., N.	D8	38
Kilcoy, Austl.	F9	76
Kildare, state, Ire.	H6	12
Kildare, Cape, c., P.E., Can.	D13	110
Kildurk, Austl.	C5	74
Kilembe, D.R.C.	F3	66
Kilgore, Tx., U.S.	E4	122
Kilian Island, i., Nu., Can.	B18	140
Kılıç, Tur.	C12	28
Kiliia, Ukr.	D16	26
Kilikollūr, India	G3	53
Kilimanjaro, mtn., Tan.	E7	66
Kilimli, Tur.	B14	28
Kilindoni, Tan.	F7	66
Kilis, Tur.	B8	58
Kilkee, Ire.	I3	12
Kilkenny, Ire.	I5	12
Kilkenny, state, Ire.	I5	12
Kilkís, Grc.	C5	28
Killaloe, Ire.	I4	12
Killaloe Station, On., Can.	C12	112
Killam, Ab., Can.	D19	138
Killarney, Austl.	G9	76
Killarney, Mb., Can.	E14	124
Killarney, On., Can.	C8	112
Killarney, Ire.	I3	12
Killdeer, N.D., U.S.	G11	124
Killeen, Tx., U.S.	C10	130
Killen, Al., U.S.	C11	122
Killington Peak, mtn., Vt., U.S.	G4	110
Killiniq Island, i., Can.	E13	141
Killybegs, Ire.	G4	12
Kilmarnock, Scot., U.K.	F8	12
Kilmarnock, Va., U.S.	G9	114
Kilmore, Austl.	K5	76
Kilo, Indon.	H11	50
Kilombero, stm., Tan.	F7	66
Kilomines, D.R.C.	D5	66
Kilosa, Tan.	F7	66
Kilrush, Ire.	I3	12
Kilttān Island, i., India	F3	46
Kilwa, D.R.C.	F5	66
Kilwa Kivinje, Tan.	F7	66
Kim, Co., U.S.	D5	128
Kimba, Austl.	F7	74
Kimball, Ne., U.S.	F9	126
Kimball, S.D., U.S.	D13	126
Kimbe Bay, b., Pap. N. Gui.	b5	79a
Kimberley, B.C., Can.	G15	138
Kimberley, S. Afr.	F7	70
Kimberley Downs, Austl.	C4	74
Kimberley Plateau, plat., Austl.	C5	74
Kimberling City, Mo., U.S.	H4	120
Kimberly, Id., U.S.	H12	136
Kimberly, Wi., U.S.	G10	118
Kimch'aek, Kor., N.	D8	38
Kimch'ŏn, Kor., S.	F8	38
Kimhae, Kor., S.	D1	40
Kimito, Fin.	F10	8
Kim-me-ni-oli Wash, stm., N.M., U.S.	H8	132
Kimmirut, Nu., Can.	C17	106
Kímolos, i., Grc.	G7	28
Kimovsk, Russia	F21	10
Kimpō-zan, mtn., Japan	D11	40
Kimry, Russia	D20	10
Kinabalu, Gunong (Kinabalu, Mount), mtn., Malay.	G1	52
Kinabalu National Park, p.o.i., Malay.	H1	52
Kinabatangan, stm., Malay.	H2	52
Kinbasket Lake, res., B.C., Can.	D12	138
Kincaid, Sk., Can.	E6	124
Kincardine, On., Can.	D8	112
Kinchafoonee Creek, stm., Ga., U.S.	F14	122
Kinchega National Park, p.o.i., Austl.	I4	76
Kinda, D.R.C.	F4	66
Kinde, Mi., U.S.	E7	112
Kinder, La., U.S.	G6	122
Kindersley, Sk., Can.	C4	124
Kindia, Gui.	G2	64
Kindu, D.R.C.	E5	66
Kinešma, Russia	H19	8
King, N.C., U.S.	H5	114
King and Queen Court House, Va., U.S.	G9	114
Kingaroy, Austl.	F8	76
King City, On., Can.	E10	112
King City, Ca., U.S.	G4	134
Kingfield, Me., U.S.	F6	110
Kingfisher, Ok., U.S.	F10	128
King George, Va., U.S.	F8	114
King George, Mount, mtn., B.C., Can.	F15	138
King George Islands, is., Nu., Can.	D14	106
King George Sound, strt., Austl.	G3	74
King Hill, Id., U.S.	G11	136
Kingisepp, Russia	A11	10
King Island, i., Austl.	m12	77a
King Island, i., B.C., Can.	D3	138
King Leopold Ranges, mts., Austl.	C4	74
Kingman, Az., U.S.	H2	132
Kingman, Ks., U.S.	D10	128
Kingman Reef, rf., Oc.	C10	72
King Mountain, mtn., Or., U.S.	H3	136
Kingombe, D.R.C.	E5	66
Kingoonya, Austl.	F7	74
King Peak, mtn., Ca., U.S.	C1	134
Kings, stm., Ca., U.S.	G6	134
Kings Beach, Ca., U.S.	D5	134
Kingsbridge, Eng., U.K.	K9	12
Kingsburg, Ca., U.S.	G6	134
Kings Canyon National Park, p.o.i., Ca., U.S.	G7	134
Kingsford, Mi., U.S.	C1	112
Kingshill, V.I.U.S.	h10	104c
Kingsland, Ar., U.S.	D6	122
Kingsland, Ga., U.S.	F4	116
Kingsley, S. Afr.	E10	70
Kingsley, Ia., U.S.	B2	120
Kingsley, Mi., U.S.	D4	112
Kingsley Dam, dam, Ne., U.S.	F11	126
King's Lynn, Eng., U.K.	I13	12
Kings Mountain, N.C., U.S.	A4	116
King Solomon's Mines see Mikhrot Timna', hist., Isr.	I5	58
King Sound, strt., Austl.	C4	74
Kings Peak, mtn., Ut., U.S.	C6	132
Kingsport, Tn., U.S.	H3	114
Kingston, N.S., Can.	E11	110
Kingston, On., Can.	D13	112
Kingston, Jam.	i14	104d
Kingston, N.Z.	G3	80
Kingston, Norf. I.	y25	78i
Kingston, Ga., U.S.	C14	122
Kingston, Mo., U.S.	E3	120
Kingston, N.Y., U.S.	C11	114
Kingston, Ok., U.S.	C2	122
Kingston, Pa., U.S.	C9	114
Kingston, Tn., U.S.	I13	120
Kingston Southeast, Austl.	K2	76
Kingston upon Hull, Eng., U.K.	H12	12
Kingston upon Thames, Eng., U.K.	J12	12
Kingstown, St. Vin.	o11	105e
Kingstree, S.C., U.S.	C6	116
Kingsville, On., Can.	G7	112
Kingsville, Tx., U.S.	G10	130
Kingtechen see Jingdezhen, China	G7	42
King William Island, i., Nu., Can.	B11	106
King William's Town, S. Afr.	H8	70
Kinhwa see Jinhua, China	G8	42
Kınık, Tur.	D10	28
Kinira, stm., S. Afr.	G9	70
Kinistino, Sk., Can.	B9	124
Kinkala, Congo	E2	66
Kinlochleven, Scot., U.K.	E8	12
Kinnaird Head, c., Scot., U.K.	D10	12
Kinneret, Yam (Galilee, Sea of), l., Isr.	F6	58
Kinosaki, Japan	D7	40
Kinpoku-san, mtn., Japan	A11	40
Kinross, Scot., U.K.	E9	12
Kinsale, Monts.	D3	105a
Kinsale, Old Head of, c., Ire.	J4	12
Kinsarvik, Nor.	F2	8
Kinshasa (Léopoldville), D.R.C.	E3	66
Kinsley, Ks., U.S.	D9	128
Kinsman, Oh., U.S.	C5	114
Kinston, N.C., U.S.	A8	116
Kintampo, Ghana	H4	64
Kintyre, pen., Scot., U.K.	F7	12
Kintyre, Mull of, c., Scot., U.K.	F7	12
Kinuseo Falls, wtfl, B.C., Can.	B9	138
Kinuso, Ab., Can.	A15	138
Kinyangiri, Tan.	E6	66
Kinyeti, mtn., Sudan	G6	62
Kinzia, D.R.C.	E3	66
Kinzua, Or., U.S.	E7	136
Kinzua Dam, dam, Pa., U.S.	C6	114
Kiowa, Co., U.S.	B4	128
Kiowa, Ok., U.S.	C3	122
Kiowa Creek, stm., Co., U.S.	A4	128
Kipawa, stm., Qc., Can.	B11	112
Kipawa, Lac, res., Qc., Can.	A10	112
Kipembawe, Tan.	F6	66
Kipengere Range, mts., Tan.	F6	66
Kipili, Tan.	F6	66
Kipini, Kenya	E8	66
Kipling, Sk., Can.	D11	124
Kipnuk, Ak., U.S.	E7	140
Kipushi, D.R.C.	G5	66
Kirakira, Sol. Is.	f9	79b
Kirandul, India	B5	53
Kiraușk, Bela.	G12	10
Kirazlı, Tur.	C9	28
Kirbla, Est.	B6	10
Kirchberg, Ger.	G5	16
Kirchmöser, Ger.	D8	16
Kireevsk, Russia	G20	10
Kirejkovo, Russia	G18	10
Kirenga, stm., Russia	C19	32
Kirensk, Russia	C19	32
Kirghizia see Kyrgyzstan, ctry., Asia	F12	32
Kirgiz Range, mts., Asia	F12	32
Kirgiz Soviet Socialist Republic see Kyrgyzstan, ctry., Asia	F12	32
Kiri, D.R.C.	E3	66
Kiribati, ctry., Oc.	D9	72
Kırıkhan, Tur.	B7	58
Kırıkkale, Tur.	B3	56
Kirillovo, Russia	H21	8
Kirin see Jilin, China	C7	38
Kirin see Jilin, state, China	C10	36
Kirinyaga (Kenya, Mount), mtn., Kenya	E7	66
Kirishima-Yaku-kokuritsu-kōen, p.o.i., Japan	H3	40
Kirishima-yama, vol., Japan	H3	40
Kiriši, Russia	A15	10
Kiritimati (Christmas Island), at., Kir.	C11	72
Kiriwina Islands (Trobriand Islands), is., Pap. N. Gui.	b5	79a
Kırka, Tur.	D13	28
Kırkağaç, Tur.	D10	28
Kirkcaldy, Scot., U.K.	E9	12
Kirkcudbright, Scot., U.K.	G8	12
Kirkenes, Nor.	B14	8
Kirkland, Il., U.S.	B9	120
Kirkland, Tx., U.S.	G8	128
Kirkland, Wa., U.S.	C4	136
Kirkland Lake, On., Can.	F14	106
Kırklareli, Tur.	B10	28
Kırklareli, state, Tur.	B10	28
Kirklin, In., U.S.	H3	112
Kirkpatrick, Mount, mtn., Ant.	D21	81
Kirksville, Mo., U.S.	D5	120
Kirkwall, Scot., U.K.	B9	12
Kirkwood, S. Afr.	H7	70
Kirkwood, Mo., U.S.	F7	120
Kirmir, stm., Tur.	C15	28
Kirn, Ger.	G3	16
Kirov, Russia	F17	10
Kirov, Russia	C7	32
Kirovakan see Vanadzor, Arm.	A5	56
Kirovohrad, Ukr.	E4	32
Kirovohrad, co., Ukr.	A17	26
Kirovsk, Russia	C15	8
Kirovsk, Turkmen.	B9	56
Kirovskaja oblast', co., Russia	F22	8
Kirovskij, Kaz.	F13	32
Kirovskij, Russia	F20	34
Kirovskij, Russia	B10	38
Kirriemuir, Scot., U.K.	E9	12
Kirs, Russia	C8	32
Kirsanov, Russia	D6	32
Kırşehir, Tur.	B3	56
Kīrthar Range, mts., Pak.	D10	56
Kirtland, N.M., U.S.	G8	132
Kiruna, Swe.	C8	8
Kirundu, D.R.C.	E5	66
Kirwin, Ks., U.S.	B9	128
Kiryū, Japan	C12	40
Kirżač, Russia	D21	10
Kisa, Swe.	G6	8
Kisangani (Stanleyville), D.R.C.	D5	66
Kisar, Pulau, i., Indon.	G8	44
Kisaran, Indon.	B1	50
Kisarazu, Japan	D12	40
Kisbey, Sk., Can.	E11	124
Kiselëvsk, Russia	D15	32
Kīsh, Jazīreh-ye, i., Iran	D7	56
Kishanganj, India	E11	54
Kishangarh, India	E3	54
Kishangarh Bās, India	E5	54
Kishi, Nig.	H5	64
Kishinev see Chișinău, Mol.	B15	26
Kishiwada, Japan	E8	40
Kishorganj, Bngl.	F13	54
Kisii, Kenya	E6	66
Kisiju, Tan.	F7	66
Kisiwada see Kishiwada, Japan	E8	40
Kiska Island, i., Ak., U.S.	g22	140a
Kiskatinaw, stm., B.C., Can.	A10	138
Kiska Volcano, vol., Ak., U.S.	g22	140a
Kiskörei-viztároló, res., Hung.	B7	26
Kiskőrös, Hung.	C6	26
Kiskunfélegyháza, Hung.	C6	26
Kiskunhalas, Hung.	C6	26
Kiskunmajsa, Hung.	C6	26
Kiskunsági Nemzeti Park, p.o.i., Hung.	C6	26
Kislovodsk, Russia	F6	32
Kismaayo, Som.	E8	66
Kiso, stm., Japan	D9	40
Kiso-sammyaku, mts., Japan	D10	40
Kissidougou, Gui.	H2	64
Kissimmee, Fl., U.S.	H4	116
Kissimmee, stm., Fl., U.S.	I4	116
Kissimmee, Lake, l., Fl., U.S.	I4	116
Kississing Lake, l., Mb., Can.	D10	106
Kisújszállás, Hung.	B7	26
Kisuki, Japan	D5	40
Kisumu, Kenya	E6	66
Kisvárda, Hung.	A9	26
Kita, Mali	G3	64
Kitaa see Vestgrønland, state, Grnld.	D16	141
Kitaibaraki, Japan	C13	40
Kitakami, stm., Japan	E14	38
Kitakata, Japan	B12	40
Kitakyūshū, Japan	F3	40
Kitale, Kenya	D7	66
Kitami, Japan	C15	38
Kitangiri, Lake, l., Tan.	E6	66
Kitchener, On., Can.	E9	112
Kithārah, Khirbat, hist., Jord.	I6	58
Kitimat, B.C., Can.	B2	138
Kitimat Ranges, mts., B.C., Can.	C2	138
Kitinen, stm., Fin.	C12	8
Kitíou, Akrotírion, c., Cyp.	D4	58
Kitridge Point, c., Barb.	n9	105d
Kitsuki, Japan	F4	40
Kittanning, Pa., U.S.	D6	114
Kittitas, Wa., U.S.	D6	136
Kitt Peak National Observatory, sci., Az., U.S.	K5	132
Kitui, Kenya	E7	66
Kitunda, Tan.	F6	66
Kitwanga, B.C., Can.	A2	138
Kitwe, Zam.	C4	68
Kityang see Jieyang, China	J7	42
Kitzbühel, Aus.	C9	22
Kitzingen, Ger.	G6	16
Kiukiang see Jiujiang, China	G6	42
Kiunga, Pap. N. Gui.	b3	79a
Kiuruvesi, Fin.	E12	8
Kivalina, Ak., U.S.	C7	140
Kivijärvi, l., Fin.	E11	8
Kiviõli, Est.	G12	8
Kivu, Lake, l., Afr.	E5	66
Kıyıköy, Tur.	B11	28
Kiyiu Lake, l., Sk., Can.	C5	124
Kızıl Adalar, is., Tur.	C11	28
Kızılcabölük, Tur.	F11	28
Kızılcahamam, Tur.	C15	28
Kızıldağ Milli Parkı, p.o.i., Tur.	F14	28
Kızılırmak, stm., Tur.	A4	56
Kızılören, Tur.	F15	28
Kizimkazi, Tan.	F7	66
Kızkalesi, hist., Tur.	B4	58
Kizljar, Russia	F7	32
Kizyl-Atrek, Turkmen.	B7	56
Kizyl-Su, Turkmen.	B7	56
Kjahta, Russia	F10	34
Kjungej-Ala-Too, hrebet, mts., Asia	F13	32
Kjusjur, Russia	B14	34
Kjustendil, Blg.	G9	26
Klabat, Gunung, vol., Indon.	E8	44
Kladno, Czech Rep.	F10	16
Kladovo, Yugo.	E9	26
Klagan, Malay.	G1	52
Klagenfurt, Aus.	D11	22
Klaipėda (Memel), Lith.	E3	10
Klakah, Indon.	G8	50
Klamath, stm., U.S.	B2	134
Klamath Falls, Or., U.S.	A3	134
Klamath Marsh, sw., Or., U.S.	H5	136
Klamath Mountains, mts., U.S.	B2	134
Klamono, Indon.	F9	44
Klang, Malay.	K5	48
Klangenan, Indon.	G6	50
Klangenang, Indon.	G6	50
Klangpi, Mya.	G14	54
Klatovy, Czech Rep.	G9	16
Klawer, S. Afr.	G4	70
Kleck, Bela.	G9	10
Kleczew, Pol.	D14	16
Kleena Kleene, B.C., Can.	E5	138
Klein Curaçao, i., Neth. Ant.	q22	104g
Klein Karroo see Little Karroo, plat., S. Afr.	H5	70
Klein Namaland see Little Namaqualand, hist. reg., S. Afr.	F3	70
Klekovača, mtn., Bos.	E3	26
Klemme, Ia., U.S.	A4	120
Klemtu, B.C., Can.	D2	138
Klerksdorp, S. Afr.	E8	70
Kletnja, Russia	G16	10
Kleve, Ger.	E2	16
Klickitat, stm., Wa., U.S.	E5	136
Klimavičy, Bela.	G14	10
Klimino, Russia	C17	32
Klimovo, Russia	H15	10
Klimovsk, Russia	E20	10
Klimpfjäll, Swe.	D6	8
Klin, Russia	D19	10
Klinaklini, stm., B.C., Can.	E5	138
Klincy, Russia	H15	10
Klingenthal, Ger.	F8	16
Klínovec, mtn., Czech Rep.	F8	16
Klintehamn, Swe.	H8	8
Klip, stm., S. Afr.	E9	70
Klipdale, S. Afr.	I4	70
Klipplaat, S. Afr.	H7	70
Klisura, Blg.	G11	26
Kljazma, stm., Russia	E21	10
Ključ, Bos.	E3	26
Ključevskaja Sopka, vulkan, vol., Russia	E21	34
Ključi, Russia	E21	34
Kljukvenka, Russia	C15	32
Kłobuck, Pol.	F14	16
Kłodawa, Pol.	D14	16
Kłodzko, Pol.	F12	16
Klondike, hist. reg., Yk., Can.	C3	106
Klooga, Est.	A7	10
Klosterneuburg, Aus.	B13	22
Kloten, Switz.	C5	22
Klotz, Lac, l., Qc., Can.	C16	106
Klötze, Ger.	D7	16
Kluane Lake, l., Yk., Can.	C3	106
Kluczbork, Pol.	F14	16
Klungkung, Indon.	H9	50
Knaddah, Syria	C7	58
Knapp, Wi., U.S.	G6	118
Kneehills Creek, stm., Ab., Can.	E17	138
Knee Lake, l., Mb., Can.	D12	106
Kneža, Blg.	F11	26
Knić, Yugo.	F7	26
Knickerbocker, Tx., U.S.	C7	130
Knife, stm., N.D., U.S.	G12	124
Knight Inlet, b., B.C., Can.	F4	138
Knights Landing, Ca., U.S.	E4	134
Knin, Cro.	F13	22
Knippa, Tx., U.S.	E8	130
Knittelfeld, Aus.	C11	22
Knjaževac, Yugo.	F9	26
Knob Noster, Mo., U.S.	F4	120
Knokke-Heist, Bel.	C12	14
Knosós, hist., Grc.	H8	28
Knox, Pa., U.S.	C6	114
Knox, Cape, c., B.C., Can.	E4	106
Knox City, Tx., U.S.	H9	128
Knox Coast, cst., Ant.	B15	81
Knoxville, Ga., U.S.	D2	116
Knoxville, Il., U.S.	D7	120
Knoxville, Tn., U.S.	I2	114
Knuckles, mtn., Sri L.	H5	53
Knud Rasmussen Land, reg., Grnld.	A14	141
Knysna, S. Afr.	I6	70
Knyszyn, Pol.	C18	16
Kob', Russia	C18	32
Kobar Sink, depr., Eth.	E8	62
Kobayashi, Japan	H3	40
Kōbe, Japan	E8	40
København (Copenhagen), Den.	I4	8
København, state, Den.	I5	8
Kobjaj, Russia	D14	34
Koblenz, Ger.	F3	16
K'obo, Eth.	E7	62
Koboža, Russia	B18	10
Koboža, stm., Russia	A18	10
Kobroor, Pulau, i., Indon.	G10	44
Kobryn, Bela.	H7	10
Kobuk, Ak., U.S.	C8	140
Kobuk, stm., Ak., U.S.	C8	140
Kobuleti, Geor.	F6	32
Kobylin, Pol.	E13	16
Kocaali, Tur.	B13	28
Kocaavşar, stm., Tur.	D10	28
Kocaeli, state, Tur.	C12	28
Kočani, Mac.	B5	28
Koçarlı, Tur.	F10	28
Kočečum, stm., Russia	C8	34
Kočevje, Slvn.	E11	22
Kočevo, Russia	C8	32
Kŏch'ang, Kor., S.	G7	38
Koch Bihār, India	E12	54
Kocher, stm., Ger.	G5	16
Kochi (Cochin), India	G3	53
Kōchi, Japan	F6	40
Kōchi, state, Japan	F6	40
Koch Island, i., Nu., Can.	B15	106
Kochiu see Gejiu, China	G5	36
Kodaikānal, India	F3	53
Kodar, hrebet, mts., Russia	E12	34
Kodāri, Nepal	E10	54
Kodarma, India	F10	54
Kodiak, Ak., U.S.	E9	140
Kodiak Island, i., Ak., U.S.	E9	140
Kodinār, India	H3	54
Kodok, Sudan	F6	62
Kodyma, Ukr.	A16	26
Kodyma, stm., Ukr.	B17	26
Koës, Nmb.	D4	70
Köflach, Aus.	C11	22
Koforidua, Ghana	H4	64
Kōfu, Japan	D11	40
Koga, Japan	C12	40
Kogaluc, stm., Qc., Can.	D15	106
Kogaluc, Baie, b., Qc., Can.	D15	106
Kogan, Austl.	F8	76
Køge, Den.	I5	8
Kogon, stm., Gui.	G2	64
Kohanava, Bela.	F12	10
Kohāt, Pak.	B3	54
Kohīma, India	C7	46
Kohler, Wi., U.S.	E2	112
Kohtla-Järve, Est.	G12	8
Kohyl'nyk (Cogâlnic), stm., Eur.	C15	26
Koide, Japan	B11	40
Koigi, Est.	B8	10
Koindu, S.L.	H2	64
Koiva (Gauja), stm., Eur.	C7	10
Kojda, Russia	C20	8
Kŏje-do, i., Kor., S.	E1	40
Kojgorodok, Russia	B8	32
Kojonup, Austl.	F3	74
Kok (Hkok), stm., Asia	B4	48
Kokalaat, Kaz.	E10	32
Kokand, Uzb.	F12	32
Kokas, Indon.	F9	44
Kokčetav, Kaz.	D12	32
Kokemäki, Fin.	F9	8
Kokenau, Indon.	F10	44
Kokhav HaYarden, hist., Isr.	F6	58
Kokiu see Gejiu, China	G5	36
Kokkilai Lagoon, b., Sri L.	G5	53
Kokkola, Fin.	E10	8
Kokoda, Pap. N. Gui.	b4	79a
Kokomo, In., U.S.	H3	112
Kokomo, Ms., U.S.	F8	122
Kokong, Bots.	D6	70
Kokopo, Pap. N. Gui.	a5	79a
Kokorevka, Russia	H17	10
Koksan-ŭp, Kor., N.	E7	38
Kökshetaū see Kokčetav, Kaz.	D12	32

Name	Map Ref.	Page
Koksoak, stm., Qc., Can.	D17	106
Kokstad, S. Afr.	G9	70
Kokubu, Japan	H3	40
Kola, Russia	B15	8
Kolachel, India	G3	53
Kolaka, Indon.	F7	44
Kolangār, Afg.	A2	54
Kola Peninsula see Kol'skij poluostrov, pen., Russia	C17	8
Kolār, India	E3	53
Kolāras, India	F6	54
Kolār Gold Fields, India	E4	53
Kolárovo, Slov.	I13	16
Kolašin, Yugo.	G6	26
Kolbio, Kenya	E8	66
Kolbuszowa, Pol.	F17	16
Kol'čugino, Russia	D22	10
Kolda, Sen.	G2	64
Kolding, Den.	I3	8
Kole, D.R.C.	E4	66
Kolea, Alg.	H13	20
Kolguev, ostrov, i., Russia	B18	6
Kolhāpur, India	C4	53
Kolhāpur, India	C1	53
Koli, Russia	A17	10
Kolín, Czech Rep.	F11	16
Koljubakino, Russia	E19	10
Kollam see Quilon, India	G3	53
Kollegāl, India	E3	53
Kolleru Lake, l., India	C5	53
Kolmogorovo, Russia	C16	32
Köln (Cologne), Ger.	E2	16
Kolno, Pol.	C17	16
Koło, Pol.	D14	16
Koloa, Hi., U.S.	B2	78a
Kołobrzeg, Pol.	B11	16
Kolodnja, Russia	F15	10
Kolokani, Mali	G3	64
Kolombangara Island, i., Sol. Is.	d7	79b
Kolomna, Russia	E21	10
Kolomyia, Ukr.	A12	26
Kolonga, Tonga	n14	78e
Kolonia, Micron.	m11	78d
Kolonodale, Indon.	F7	44
Kolosib, India	F14	54
Kolosovka, Russia	C12	32
Kolovai, Tonga	n13	78e
Kolozsvár see Cluj-Napoca, Rom.	C10	26
Kolp', stm., Russia	A19	10
Kolpaševo, Russia	C14	32
Kolpino, Russia	A13	10
Kolpny, Russia	H19	10
Kol'skij poluostrov (Kola Peninsula), pen., Russia	C17	8
Koluton, Kaz.	D11	32
Kolwezi, D.R.C.	G5	66
Kolyma, stm., Russia	C20	34
Kolyma Plain see Kolymskaja nizmennost', pl., Russia	C19	34
Kolymskaja, Russia	C20	34
Kolymskaja nizmennost' (Kolyma Plain), pl., Russia	C19	34
Kom, mtn., Blg.	F10	26
Koma, Mya.	E4	48
Komadugu Gana, stm., Nig.	G7	64
Komagane, Japan	D10	40
Komandorskie ostrova, is., Russia	D20	30
Komandorski Islands see Komandorskie ostrova, is., Russia	D20	30
Komárno, Slov.	I13	16
Komarnyky, Ukr.	G19	16
Komárom, Hung.	B5	26
Komárom-Esztergom, state, Hung.	B5	26
Komati (Incomati), stm., Afr.	E10	70
Komatipoort, S. Afr.	D10	70
Komatsu, Japan	C9	40
Komatsushima, Japan	E7	40
Kome Island, i., Ug.	E6	66
Komering, stm., Indon.	E4	50
Komfane, Indon.	G9	44
Komi, state, Russia	B8	32
Komissarovo, Russia	B9	38
Komló, Hung.	C5	26
Kommunizma, pik, mtn., Taj.	B11	56
Komodo, Pulau, i., Indon.	H11	50
Komodo National Park, p.o.i., Indon.	H11	50
Komoé, stm., Afr.	H4	64
Kom Ombo, Egypt	C6	62
Komoran, Pulau, i., Indon.	G10	44
Komoro, Japan	C11	40
Komotiní, Grc.	B8	28
Kompasberg, mtn., S. Afr.	G7	70
Komsomolec, Kaz.	D10	32
Komsomolec, zaliv, b., Kaz.	E8	32
Komsomol'sk, Russia	H18	8
Komsomol'sk, Russia	C15	32
Komsomol'sk-na-Amure, Russia	F16	34
Komsomol'skoj Pravdy, ostrova, is., Russia	A10	34
Konakovo, Russia	D19	10
Konakpınar, Tur.	D10	28
Konar, stm., Asia	A3	54
Konārak, India	I11	54
Konawa, Ok., U.S.	C2	122
Konch, India	F7	54
Konda, stm., Russia	B10	32
Kondagaon, India	B5	53
Kondega, Russia	F15	8
Kondinin, Austl.	F3	74
Kondoa, Tan.	E7	66
Kondopoga, Russia	E16	8
Kondrovo, Russia	F18	10
Kondukūr, India	D4	53
Kondūz, Afg.	B10	56
Koné, N. Cal.	m15	79d
Kong, stm., Asia	F8	48
Kŏng, Kaôh, i., Camb.	G6	48
Kongcheng, China	F7	42
Kong Christian IX Land, reg., Grnld.	D18	141
Kong Christian X Land, reg., Grnld.	C19	141
Kong Frederik VIII Land, reg., Grnld.	B19	141
Kong Frederik VI Kyst, cst., Grnld.	E17	141
Kongjiawopeng, China	B5	38
Kongju, Kor., S.	F7	38
Kongmoon see Jiangmen, China	J5	42
Kongolo, D.R.C.	F5	66
Kongor, Sudan	F6	62
Kong Oscar Fjord, strt., Grnld.	C21	141
Kongsvinger, Nor.	F5	8
Kongur Shan, mtn., China	G13	32
Kong Wilhelms Land, reg., Grnld.	B21	141
Konice, Czech Rep.	G12	16
Königsberg see Kaliningrad, Russia	F3	10
Königswinter, Ger.	F3	16
Konin, Pol.	D14	16
Konin, state, Pol.	D14	16
Konispol, Alb.	E14	24
Kónitsa, Grc.	C3	28
Konjic, Bos.	F4	26
Konkiep, stm., Nmb.	E3	70
Konkouré, stm., Gui.	G2	64
Konna, Mali	G4	64
Konnevesi, l., Fin.	E12	8
Konnur, India	C2	53
Konoša, Russia	F18	8
Kōnosu, Japan	C12	40
Konotop, Ukr.	E15	6
Końskie, Pol.	E16	16
Konstantinovskij, Russia	C22	10
Konstanz, Ger.	I4	16
Kontagora, Nig.	G5	64
Kontcha, Cam.	C2	66
Kontha, Mya.	C3	48
Kontseba, Ukr.	A16	26
Kon Tum, Viet.	E8	48
Konya, Tur.	F15	28
Konya, state, Tur.	E15	28
Konz, Ger.	G2	16
Konza, Kenya	E7	66
Konžakovskij Kamen', gora, mtn., Russia	C9	32
Koocanusa, Lake, res., N.A.	B11	136
Kookynie, Austl.	E4	74
Koolatah, Austl.	C8	74
Kooloonong, Austl.	J4	76
Koontz Lake, In., U.S.	G3	112
Koorawatha, Austl.	J7	76
Koosa, Est.	B9	10
Kooskia, Id., U.S.	D11	136
Kootenai (Kootenay), stm., N.A.	G13	138
Kootenay (Kootenai), stm., N.A.	G13	138
Kootenay Lake, l., B.C., Can.	G14	138
Kootenay National Park, p.o.i., B.C., Can.	F14	138
Kopāganj, India	E9	54
Kopargaon, India	B2	53
Kópavogur, Ice.	k29	8a
Kopejsk, Russia	C10	32
Koper, Slvn.	E10	22
Kopervik, Nor.	G1	8
Kopet Mountains, mts., Asia	B8	56
Köping, Swe.	G6	8
Koplik, Alb.	B13	24
Koppal, India	D3	53
Koppang, Nor.	F4	8
Koppies, S. Afr.	E8	70
Koprivnica, Cro.	D13	22
Köprü, stm., Tur.	F14	28
Köprülü Kanyon Milli Parkı, p.o.i., Tur.	F14	28
Kopylovo, Russia	F21	8
Korab (Korabit, Maja e), mtn., Eur.	C14	24
Korabit, Maja e (Korab), mtn., Eur.	C14	24
Korāput, India	B6	53
Korarou, Lac, l., Mali	F4	64
Koratla, India	B4	53
Korba, India	G9	54
Korba, Tun.	H4	24
Korbach, Ger.	E4	16
Korça see Korçë, Alb.	D14	24
Korçë, Alb.	D14	24
Korčula, Cro.	H14	22
Korčula, Otok, i., Cro.	H13	22
Korea, North, ctry., Asia	D7	38
Korea, South, ctry., Asia	G8	38
Korea Bay, b., Asia	E5	38
Korea Strait, strt., Asia	E2	40
Korelakša, Russia	D15	8
Korenovsk, Russia	E5	32
Korf, Russia	D22	34
Korhogo, C. Iv.	H3	64
Korientzé, Mali	F4	64
Korim, Indon.	F10	44
Korinthiakós Kólpos (Corinth, Gulf of), b., Grc.	E5	28
Kórinthos, Grc.	F5	28
Kōriyama, Japan	B13	40
Korjakskaja Sopka, vulkan, vol., Russia	F20	34
Korjakskoe nagor'e, mts., Russia	D22	34
Korjažma, Russia	F22	8
Korkino, Russia	D10	32
Korkuteli, Tur.	F13	28
Korla, China	C2	36
Korliki, Russia	B14	32
Körmend, Hung.	C3	26
Kornat, Otok, i., Cro.	G12	22
Kornati, Nacionalni Park, p.o.i., Cro.	G12	22
Korner, Mt., U.S.	A14	136
Korneuburg, Aus.	B13	22
Koro, i., Fiji	p19	79e
Köroğlu Tepesi, mtn., Tur.	C14	28
Korogwe, Tan.	F7	66
Koroleve, Ukr.	H19	16
Koromere see East Cape, c., N.Z.	C8	80
Koronadal, Phil.	G5	52
Koróni, Grc.	G4	28
Korónia, Límni, l., Grc.	C6	28
Korópi, Grc.	F6	28
Koror, Palau	g8	78b
Körös, stm., Hung.	C7	26
Koro Sea, Fiji	p20	79e
Korosten', Ukr.	E14	6
Koro Toro, Chad	D3	62
Korotyš, Russia	H20	10
Korovin Volcano, vol., Ak., U.S.	g24	140a
Korovou, Fiji	p19	79e
Koroyanitu, mtn., Fiji	p18	79e
Korsakov, Russia	G17	34
Korsakovo, Russia	G20	10
Korsør, Den.	I4	8
Koršunovo, Russia	C20	32
Kortrijk, Bel.	D12	14
Korucam, Cape see Koruçam Burnu, c., N. Cyp.	C3	58
Koruçam Burnu, c., N. Cyp.	C3	58
Korucu, Tur.	D10	28
Korumburra, Austl.	L5	76
Koryak Mountains see Korjakskoe nagor'e, mts., Russia	D22	34
Koryŏng, Kor., S.	D1	40
Kos (Cos), i., Grc.	G10	28
Kosa, Russia	C8	32
Kosa, Russia	F10	34
Kosai, Japan	E10	40
Kosaja Gora, Russia	F20	10
Koščagyl, Kaz.	E8	32
Kościan, Pol.	D12	16
Kościerzyna, Pol.	B14	16
Kosciusko, Ms., U.S.	D9	122
Kosciusko, Mount, mtn., Austl.	K6	76
Kosciusko National Park, p.o.i., Austl.	K6	76
Kose, Est.	A8	10
Koshikijima-rettō, is., Japan	H2	40
Koshkonong, Lake, l., Wi., U.S.	B9	120
Kōshoku, Japan	C11	40
Košice, Slov.	H17	16
Kosi Kalan, India	E6	54
Kosimeer, l., S. Afr.	E11	70
Kosiv, Ukr.	A12	26
Köşk, Tur.	F11	28
Koslan, Russia	E23	8
Kosŏng, Kor., S.	E1	40
Kosŏng-ŭp, Kor., N.	E8	38
Kosovo-Metohija, co., Yugo.	G7	26
Kosovska Mitrovica, Yugo.	G7	26
Kosrae, i., Micron.	C7	72
Kösreli, Tur.	A6	58
Kosse, Tx., U.S.	F2	122
Kossou, Lac de, res., C. Iv.	H3	64
Kostenec, Blg.	G10	26
Koster, S. Afr.	D8	70
Kostomukša, Russia	D14	8
Kostonjärvi, l., Fin.	D12	8
Kostroma, Russia	H19	8
Kostroma, stm., Russia	G19	8
Kostromskaja oblast', co., Russia	G20	8
Kostrzyn, Pol.	D10	16
Kosum Phisai, Thai.	D6	48
Koszalin, Pol.	B12	16
Koszalin, state, Pol.	C12	16
Kőszeg, Hung.	B3	26
Kota, India	G9	54
Kota, India	F5	54
Kotaagung, Indon.	F4	50
Kotabangun, Indon.	D10	50
Kotabaru, Indon.	E10	50
Kota Belud, Malay.	G1	52
Kota Bharu, Malay.	I6	48
Kotabumi, Indon.	F4	50
Kotadabok, Indon.	D4	50
Kot Addu, Pak.	C3	54
Kota Kinabalu, Malay.	G1	52
Kotamobagu, Indon.	E7	44
Kotapinang, Indon.	C1	50
Kota Tinggi, Malay.	L6	48
Kotawaringin, Indon.	E7	50
Kotcho Lake, l., B.C., Can.	D6	106
Kot Chutta, Pak.	D3	54
Kotel'nič, Russia	C7	32
Kotel'nikovo, Russia	E6	32
Kotel'nyj, ostrov, i., Russia	A16	34
Kotelnyj, ostrov, i., Russia	B3	34
Köthen, Ger.	E7	16
Kotikovo, Russia	G17	34
Kotka, Fin.	F12	8
Kot Kapūra, India	C5	54
Kotlas, Russia	F22	8
Kotli, Pak.	B4	54
Kotlik, Ak., U.S.	D7	140
Kôtomo, Île, i., N. Cal.	n16	79d
Kotor, Yugo.	G5	26
Kotoriba, Cro.	D13	22
Kotovs'k, Ukr.	B16	26
Kot Pūtli, India	E6	54
Kotri, Pak.	F2	54
Kottagūdem, India	C5	53
Kottayam, India	G3	53
Kotto, stm., C.A.R.	C4	66
Kottūru, India	D3	53
Kotuj, stm., Russia	B9	34
Kotzebue, Ak., U.S.	C7	140
Kotzebue Sound, strt., Ak., U.S.	C7	140
Kötzting, Ger.	G8	16
Kouang-si see Guangxi, state, China	G6	36
Kouang-tong see Guangdong, state, China	J6	42
Kouaoua, N. Cal.	m15	79d
Kouchibouguac National Park, p.o.i., N.B., Can.	D11	110
Koudougou, Burkina	G4	64
Kouei-tcheou see Guizhou, state, China	H2	42
Kouga, stm., S. Afr.	H7	70
Kougaberge, mts., S. Afr.	H6	70
Koukdjuak, stm., Nu., Can.	B16	106
Kouki, C.A.R.	C3	66
Koúklia, Cyp.	D3	58
Koulamoutou, Gabon	E2	66
Koulikoro, Mali	G3	64
Koumala, Austl.	C7	76
Koumbia, Gui.	G2	64
Koumpentoum, Sen.	G2	64
Koumra, Chad	F3	62
Koundâra, Gui.	G2	64
Kounradskij, Kaz.	E12	32
Kourou, Fr. Gu.	B7	84
Kouroussa, Gui.	G3	64
Kousséri, Cam.	B2	66
Koussi, Emi, mtn., Chad	D3	62
Koutiala, Mali	G3	64
Kouts, In., U.S.	G2	112
Kouvola, Fin.	F12	8
Kova, Russia	C18	32
Kovada Milli Parkı, p.o.i., Tur.	F13	28
Kovarskas, Lith.	E7	10
Kovdor, Russia	C14	8
Kovdozero, ozero, res., Russia	C14	8
Kovilpatti, India	G3	53
Kovrov, Russia	H19	8
Kovūr, India	D5	53
Kovža, Russia	F18	8
Kowalewo Pomorskie, Pol.	C14	16
Kowloon see Jiulong, China	J5	42
Kowŏn-ŭp, Kor., N.	E7	38
Kowt-e'Ashrow, Afg.	C10	56
Koxtag, China	A4	46
Köyceğiz Gölü, l., Tur.	G11	28
Koyna Reservoir, res., India	C1	53
Koyuk, Ak., U.S.	D7	140
Koyukuk, Ak., U.S.	D8	140
Koyukuk, stm., Ak., U.S.	C8	140
Kō-zaki, c., Japan	E2	40
Kozan, Tur.	A6	58
Kozáni, Grc.	C4	28
Kožany, Russia	H14	10
Kozel'sk, Russia	F18	10
Koževnikovo, Russia	C14	32
Kozhikode (Calicut), India	F2	53
Kozienice, Pol.	E17	16
Kozlov Bereg, Russia	B10	10
Kozlovo, Russia	D19	10
Kozlu, Tur.	B14	28
Koz'mino, Russia	F22	8
Kožposëlok, Russia	E17	8
Kōzu-shima, i., Japan	E12	40
Kpalimé, Togo	H5	64
Kra, Isthmus of, isth., Asia	H4	48
Kraai, stm., S. Afr.	G8	70
Krabi, Thai.	H4	48
Krâchéh, Camb.	F8	48
Kraeva, Russia	B9	38
Kragan, Indon.	G7	50
Kragujevac, Yugo.	F7	26
Krajenka, Pol.	C13	16
Krakatoa see Rakata, Pulau, i., Indon.	G4	50
Krakovets', Ukr.	G19	16
Kraków, Pol.	F15	16
Kraków, state, Pol.	G15	16
Kralendijk, Neth. Ant.	p23	104g
Kraljevo, Yugo.	F7	26
Kralovice, Czech Rep.	G9	16
Kralupy nad Vltavou, Czech Rep.	F10	16
Kramators'k, Ukr.	E5	32
Kramfors, Swe.	E7	8
Kranídi, Grc.	F6	28
Kranj (Krainburg), Slvn.	D11	22
Kranskop, S. Afr.	F10	70
Krapivna, Russia	G18	10
Krasavino, Russia	F22	8
Krasieo, stm., Thai.	E4	48
Krasivaja Meča, stm., Russia	G20	10
Krāslava, Lat.	E10	10
Krasnae, Bela.	F10	10
Krasnaja Gorbatka, Russia	I19	8
Krasnaja Slabada, Bela.	H9	10
Krasnaluki, Bela.	F11	10
Krasneno, Russia	D23	34
Kraśnik, Pol.	F18	16
Kraśnik Fabryczny, Pol.	F18	16
Krasni Okny, Ukr.	B16	26
Krasnoarmejsk, Russia	D21	10
Krasnoarmejskij, Russia	C23	34
Krasnobród, Pol.	F19	16
Krasnodar, Russia	E5	32
Krasnoe, ozero, l., Russia	D23	34
Krasnoe Selo, Russia	A12	10
Krasnoe Znamja, Russia	C18	10
Krasnogorodskoe, Russia	D11	10
Krasnogorsk, Russia	E20	10
Krasnogorsk, Russia	G17	34
Krasnojarovo, Russia	F14	34
Krasnojarsk, Russia	C16	32
Krasnojarskoe vodohranilišče, res., Russia	D16	32
Krasnokamsk, Russia	C8	32
Krasnomajskij, Russia	C17	10
Krasnoščele, Russia	C17	8
Krasnosel'kup, Russia	A14	32
Krasnoturjinsk, Russia	C10	32
Krasnoufimsk, Russia	C9	32
Krasnoural'sk, Russia	C10	32
Krasnovišersk, Russia	B9	32
Krasnovodskij poluostrov, pen., Turkmen.	A7	56
Krasnozavodsk, Russia	D20	10
Krasnozërskoe, Russia	D14	32
Krasnoznamensk, Russia	F5	10
Krasnoznamenskoe, Kaz.	D11	32
Krasnye Gory, Russia	B12	10
Krasnyj Čikoj, Russia	F10	34
Krasnyj Gorodok, Russia	C16	10
Krasnyj Jar, Russia	C12	32
Krasnyj Luč, Russia	C13	10
Krasnyj Oktjabr', Russia	D21	10
Krasnyj Tkač, Russia	E22	10
Krasnystaw, Pol.	E19	16
Kratovo, Mac.	A5	28
Krâvanh, Chuŏr Phnum, mts., Camb.	F6	48
Krbava, reg., Cro.	F12	22
Krečetovo, Russia	F18	8
Krefeld, Ger.	E2	16
Kremastón, Technití Límni, res., Grc.	E4	28
Kremenchug Reservoir see Kremenchuts'ke vodoskhovyshche, res., Ukr.	E4	32
Kremenchuk, Ukr.	E4	32
Kremenchuts'ke vodoskhovyshche, res., Ukr.	E4	32
Kremenskoe, Russia	E18	10
Kremmling, Co., U.S.	C10	132
Krems an der Donau, Aus.	B12	22
Kress, Tx., U.S.	G7	128
Kresta, zaliv, b., Russia	C25	34
Krestcy, Russia	B22	10
Krestcy, Russia	B15	10
Krest-Maër, Russia	C17	34
Kretinga, Lith.	E4	10
Kribi, Cam.	D1	66
Křimice, Czech Rep.	G9	16
Krishna, stm., India	C5	53
Krishna, Mouths of the, mth., India	D5	53
Krishnagiri, India	E4	53
Krishnanagar, India	G12	54
Krishnarāja Sāgara, res., India	E3	53
Krishnarājpet, India	E3	53
Kristiansand, Nor.	G3	8
Kristianstad, Swe.	I6	8
Kristiansund, Nor.	E2	8
Kristiinankaupunki (Kristinestad), Fin.	E9	8
Kristinehamn, Swe.	G6	8
Kristinestad see Kristiinankaupunki, Fin.	E9	8
Kríti, state, Grc.	H7	28
Kríti (Crete), i., Grc.	H7	28
Kritikón Pélagos (Crete, Sea of), Grc.	H8	28
Kriva Palanka, Mac.	A5	28
Krivodol, Blg.	F10	26
Križevci, Cro.	D13	22
Krjukovo, Russia	E20	10
Krjukovo, Russia	C20	34
Krk, Otok, i., Cro.	E11	22
Krnov, Czech Rep.	F13	16
Krobia, Pol.	E12	16
Krøderen, l., Nor.	F3	8
Krokodil, stm., S. Afr.	D8	70
Krom, stm., S. Afr.	G4	70
Kroměříž, Czech Rep.	G13	16
Kromy, Russia	H18	10
Kronach, Ger.	F7	16
Krŏng Kaôh Kŏng, Camb.	G6	48
Krŏng Kêb, Camb.	G7	48
Kronoberg, state, Swe.	H6	8
Kronockaja Sopka, vulkan, vol., Russia	F21	34
Kronockij zaliv, b., Russia	F21	34
Kronoki, Russia	F21	34
Kronprins Christian Land, reg., Grnld.	A22	141
Kronštadt, Russia	A12	10
Kroonstad, S. Afr.	E8	70
Kropotkin, Russia	E6	32
Kropotkin, Russia	E12	34
Krośniewice, Pol.	D14	16
Krosno, Pol.	G17	16
Krosno, state, Pol.	G17	16
Krotoszyn, Pol.	E13	16
Krotz Springs, La., U.S.	G7	122
Kroya, Indon.	G6	50
Krško, Slvn.	E12	22
Kruger National Park, p.o.i., S. Afr.	C10	70
Krugersdorp, S. Afr.	E8	70
Kruhlae, Bela.	F12	10
Krui, Indon.	F3	50
Kruisfontein, S. Afr.	H7	70
Kruja see Krujë, Alb.	C13	24
Krujë, Alb.	C13	24
Krumbach, Ger.	H6	16
Krumovgrad, Blg.	H12	26
Krung Thep (Bangkok), Thai.	F5	48
Kruså, Den.	B5	16
Kruševac, Yugo.	F8	26
Krušinovka, Bela.	G12	10
Krutcy, Russia	C12	10
Krutoe, Russia	H20	10
Kruzenšterna, proliv, strt., Russia	G19	34
Kruzof Island, i., Ak., U.S.	E12	140
Kryčau, Bela.	G14	10
Kryms'kyi pivostriv (Crimean Peninsula), pen., Ukr.	E4	32
Krynica, Pol.	G16	16
Krynychne, Ukr.	D15	26
Kryve Ozero, Ukr.	B17	26
Kryvošyn, Bela.	H8	10
Kryvyj Rih, Ukr.	E4	32
Kryzhopil', Ukr.	A15	26
Krzeszowice, Pol.	F15	16
Krzyż, Pol.	D11	16
Ksenevka, Russia	F12	34
Kstovo, Russia	H20	8
Kuah, Malay.	I4	48
Kuai, stm., China	E7	42
Kualacenako, Indon.	D3	50
Kuala Kangsar, Malay.	J5	48
Kualakapuas, Indon.	E9	50
Kuala Krai, Malay.	J6	48
Kuala Kubu Baharu, Malay.	K5	48
Kualakurun, Indon.	D8	50
Kualalangsa, Indon.	J4	48
Kuala Lipis, Malay.	J5	48
Kuala Lumpur, Malay.	K5	48
Kuala Nerang, Malay.	I5	48
Kualapesaguan, Indon.	E6	50
Kuala Pilah, Malay.	K6	48
Kuala Rompin, Malay.	K6	48
Kuala Sepetang, Malay.	J5	48
Kualasimpang, Indon.	J3	48
Kuala Terengganu, Malay.	J6	48
Kualu, stm., Indon.	B1	50
Kuamut, stm., Malay.	A10	50
Kuancheng, China	A8	42
Kuandian, China	D6	38
Kuan Shan, mtn., Tai.	J9	42
Kuantan, Malay.	K6	48
Kuanyün see Guanyun, China	D8	42
Kuban', stm., Russia	E6	32
Kubenskoe, ozero, l., Russia	G18	8
Kubokawa, Japan	F6	40
Kubrat, Blg.	F13	26
Kučema, Russia	D20	8
Kuchaiburi, India	G11	54
Kuchāman, India	E5	54
Kuching, Malay.	C7	50
Kūchnay Darweyshān, Afg.	C9	56
Kuchurhan, stm., Eur.	B16	26
Kuçova see Kuçovë, Alb.	D13	24
Kuçovë, Alb.	D13	24
Kūd, India	B5	54
Kudamatsu, Japan	F4	40
Kudat, Malay.	G1	52
Kudever', Russia	D12	10
Kudirkos Naumiestis, Lith.	F5	10
Kudus, Indon.	G7	50
Kudymkar, Russia	C8	32
Kuee Ruins, hist., Hi., U.S.	D6	78a
Kueisui see Hohhot, China	A4	42
Kueiyang see Guiyang, China	H2	42
K'uerhlo see Korla, China	C2	36
Kufstein, Aus.	C9	22
Kugluktuk, Nu., Can.	B8	106
Kugmallit Bay, b., N.T., Can.	C13	140
Kuhësi see Kukës, Alb.	B14	24
Kuhmoinen, Fin.	F11	8
Kuhn Ø, i., Grnld.	C22	141
Kuial'nyts'kyi lyman, l., Ukr.	C17	26
Kuiseb, stm., S. Afr.	C2	70
Kuitan, China	J7	42
Kuito, Ang.	C2	68
Kuiu Island, i., Ak., U.S.	E13	140
Kuivastu, Est.	G10	8
Kuja, Russia	D18	8
Kujang-ŭp, Kor., N.	E7	38
Kujawy, reg., Pol.	D14	16
Kujbyšev, Russia	C13	32
Kujbyševskoe vodohranilišče, res., Russia	D7	32
Kujgan, Kaz.	E12	32
Kujū-san, vol., Japan	F4	40
Kukalaya, stm., Nic.	F6	102
Kukawa, Nig.	G7	64
Kukës, Alb.	B14	24
Kukoboj, Russia	B22	10
Kükong see Shaoguan, China	I5	42
Kukshi, India	G5	54
Kukuj, Russia	A15	10
Kukukus Lake, l., On., Can.	B7	118
Kukurtli, Turkmen.	B8	56
Kula, Blg.	F9	26
Kula, Tur.	E11	28
Kula, Yugo.	D6	26
Kulagi, Russia	H15	10
Kula Gulf, strt., Sol. Is.	e7	79b
Kulai, Malay.	L6	48
Kula Kangri, mtn., Bhu.	E13	54
Kular, Russia	B15	34
Kulaura, Bngl.	F13	54
Kuldīga, Lat.	D5	10
Kuldja see Yining, China	F14	32
Kule, Bots.	C5	70
Kulebaki, Russia	I20	8
Kulen Vakuf, Bos.	E3	26
Kulim, Malay.	J5	48
Kuljab, Taj.	B10	56
Kulkyne Creek, stm., Austl.	H5	76
Kullu, India	B6	54
Kulm, N.D., U.S.	A13	126
Kulmbach, Ger.	F7	16
Kuloj, Russia	D20	8
Kuloj, Russia	F20	8
Kuloj, stm., Russia	D20	8
Kul'sary, Kaz.	E8	32
Kulti, India	G11	54
Kultuk, Russia	D18	32
Kulu, Tur.	D16	28
Kulunda, Russia	D13	32
Kulundinskaja ravnina, pl., Asia	D13	32
Kulundinskoe, ozero, l., Russia	D13	32
Kulwin, Austl.	J4	76
Kumagaya, Japan	C12	40
Kumai, Indon.	E8	50
Kumai, Teluk, b., Indon.	E7	50
Kumajri see Gjumri, Arm.	A5	56
Kumamoto, Japan	G3	40
Kumamoto, state, Japan	G3	40
Kumano, Japan	F9	40
Kumano-nada, Japan	F9	40
Kumanovo, Mac.	A4	28
Kumara, Russia	F14	34
Kumārghāt, India	F14	54
Kumasi, Ghana	H4	64
Kumba, Cam.	D1	66
Kumbakonam, India	F4	53
Kumbarilla, Austl.	F8	76
Kumdanlı, Tur.	E13	28
Kume-jima, i., Japan	I18	39a
Kŭm-gang, stm., Kor., S.	F7	38
Kumla, Swe.	G6	8
Kumluca, Tur.	B15	28
Kumluca, Tur.	G13	28
Kumo, Nig.	H7	64
Kumon Range, mts., Mya.	C8	46
Kumora, Russia	E11	34
Kumta, India	D2	53
Kumu, D.R.C.	D5	66
Kumukahi, Cape, c., Hi., U.S.	o16	135a
Kümüx, China	C2	36
Kŭmya-ŭp, Kor., N.	E7	38
Kuna, Id., U.S.	G10	136
Kunašir, ostrov (Kunashiri-tō), i., Russia	C16	38
Kunda, Est.	G12	8
Kunda Hills, hills, India	F3	53
Kundāpura, India	E2	53
Kundar, stm., Asia	C2	54
Kunderu, stm., India	D4	53
Kundiān, Pak.	B3	54
Kundiawa, Pap. N. Gui.	b3	79a
Kundla, India	H3	54
Kundur, Pulau, i., Indon.	C3	50
Kunene, state, Nmb.	B2	70
Kunene (Cunene), stm., Afr.	D1	68
Kunes, Nor.	A12	8
Kungchuling see Gongzhuling, China	C6	38
Kunggyü Yumco, l., China	C9	54
Kunghit Island, i., B.C., Can.	E4	106
Kungrad, Uzb.	F9	32
Kungsbacka, Swe.	H4	8
Kungur, Russia	C9	32
Kunhegyes, Hung.	B7	26
Kuningan, Indon.	G6	50
Kunisaki, Japan	F4	40
Kunisaki-hantō, pen., Japan	F4	40
Kunja, Russia	D13	10
Kunja, stm., Russia	D13	10
Kunlong, Mya.	D8	46
Kunlun Mountains see Kunlun Shan, mts., China	A5	46
Kunlun Shan, mts., China	A5	46
Kunming, China	F5	36
Kunnamkulam, India	F2	53
Kunsan, Kor., S.	F7	38
Kunshan, China	F9	42
Kunting, China	G9	42
Kununurra, Austl.	C5	74
Kunwi, Kor., S.	C1	40
Kunya, Nig.	G6	64
Künzelsau, Ger.	G5	16
Kuopio, Fin.	E12	8
Kuopio, state, Fin.	E12	8
Kupa, stm., Eur.	E12	22
Kupang, Indon.	H7	44
Kupanskoe, Russia	D21	10
Kup'ians'k, Ukr.	E5	32
Kupino, Russia	D13	32
Kupiškis, Lith.	E7	10
Kupreanof Island, i., Ak., U.S.	E13	140
Kuqa, China	F14	32
Kuqa, China	F14	32
Kuragino, Russia	D16	32
Kuranec, Bela.	F9	10
Kurashiki, Japan	E6	40
Kurasiki see Kurashiki, Japan	E6	40
Kurauli, India	E7	54
Kuraymah, Sudan	D6	62
Kurayoshi, Japan	D6	40
Kurčatov, Russia	D5	32
Kurčum, Kaz.	E14	32
Kurdistān, hist. reg., Asia	B5	56
Kurdistan see Kurdistān, hist. reg., Asia	B5	56
Kurdufān, state, Sudan	E6	62
Kurduvādi, India	B2	53
Kure, Japan	E5	40
Kurejka, stm., Russia	C7	34
Kuresaare, Est.	G10	8
Kurgal'džinskij, Kaz.	D12	32
Kurgan, Russia	C11	32
Kurgan-Tjube, Taj.	B10	56
Kuria, i., Kir.	C8	72
Kuria Muria Islands see Hallānīyah, Juzur al-, is., Oman	F8	56
Kuridala, Austl.	C3	76
Kurīgrām, Bngl.	F12	54
Kurikka, Fin.	E10	8
Kuril Islands see Kuril'skie ostrova, is., Russia	E19	30
Kuril'sk, Russia	B14	36
Kuril'skie ostrova (Kuril Islands), is., Russia	E19	30
Kuril Strait see Pervyj Kuril'skij proliv, strt., Russia	F20	34
Kuril Trench, unds.	E18	142
Kurinjippadi, India	F4	53
Kurinwás, stm., Nic.	F5	102
Kurjanovskaja, Russia	F19	8
Kurkliai, Lith.	E8	10
Kurmuk, Sudan	E6	62
Kurnool, India	D3	53
Kurobe, Japan	C10	40
Kurort Schmalkalden, Ger.	F6	16
Kurovskoe, Russia	E21	10
Kurow, N.Z.	G4	80
Kuršėnai, Lith.	D6	10
Kurseong, India	E12	54
Kuršiu nerija (Kurššskaja kosa), spit, Eur.	E3	10
Kursk, Russia	D5	32
Kurskaja oblast', co., Russia	H19	10
Kurššskaja kosa (Kuršiu nerija), spit, Eur.	E3	10
Kuršumlija, Yugo.	F8	26
Kurşunlu, Tur.	C16	28
Kūrtī, Sudan	D6	62
Kurtistown, Hi., U.S.	D6	78a
Kurtoğlu Burnu, c., Tur.	G11	28
Kuruktag, mts., China	C2	36
Kuruman, S. Afr.	E6	70
Kuruman, stm., S. Afr.	E5	70
Kurumanheuwels, mts., S. Afr.	E6	70
Kurume, Japan	F3	40
Kurumkan, Russia	F11	34
Kurunegala, Sri L.	H5	53
Kuruqi, China	B9	36
Kuryongp'o, Kor., S.	C2	40
Kuşadası, Tur.	F10	28
Kuşadası Körfezi, b., Tur.	F9	28
Kusan-ni, Kor., S.	B1	40
Kusawa Lake, l., Yk., Can.	D12	140
Kuş Gölü, l., Tur.	C10	28
Kuş Gölü Milli Parkı, p.o.i., Tur.	C10	28
Kushālgarh, India	G5	54
Kusheriki, Nig.	G6	64
Kushikino, Japan	H3	40
Kushima, Japan	H4	40
Kushiro, Japan	C16	38
Kushnytsia, Ukr.	A10	26
Kushtia, Bngl.	G12	54
Kushui, China	C3	36
Kusiro see Kushiro, Japan	C16	38
Kusiyāra, stm., Bngl.	F13	54
Kuskokwim, stm., Ak., U.S.	D7	140
Kuskokwim Bay, b., Ak., U.S.	E7	140
Kuskokwim Mountains, mts., Ak., U.S.	D8	140
Kuśmā, Nepal	D9	54
Kušmurun, Kaz.	D10	32
Kušmurun, ozero, l., Kaz.	D10	32
Kustanaj, Kaz.	D10	32
Kūstī, Sudan	E6	62
Kusu, Japan	F4	40
Kut, Ko, i., Thai.	G6	48
Kutabaru, Indon.	D3	50
Kutacane, Indon.	K3	48
Kütahya, Tur.	D13	28
Kütahya, state, Tur.	D12	28
Kutaisi, Geor.	F6	32
Kutch, Rann of (Kachchh, Rann of), reg., Asia	D2	46
Kutima, Russia	C19	32
Kutina, Cro.	E13	22
Kutiyāna, India	H3	54
Kutná Hora, Czech Rep.	G11	16
Kutno, Pol.	D15	16
Kutse Game Reserve, Bots.	C7	70
Kutu, D.R.C.	E3	66
Kutubdia Island, i., Bngl.	H13	54
Kutum, Sudan	E4	62
Kúty, Slov.	H13	16
Kuujjuaq, Qc., Can.	D17	106
Kuuli-Majak, Turkmen.	A7	56
Kuusamo, Fin.	D13	8
Kuusankoski, Fin.	F12	8
Kuvango, Ang.	C2	68
Kuvšinovo, Russia	C16	10
Kuwait see Al-Kuwayt, Kuw.	D6	56
Kuwait, ctry., Asia	D6	56
Kuwana, Japan	D9	40
Kuybyshev Reservoir see Kujbyševskoe vodohranilišče, res., Russia	D7	32
Kuye, stm., China	B4	42
Kuženkino, Russia	C16	10
Kuz'miniči, Russia	F16	10
Kuz'movka, Russia	B16	32
Kuzneck, Russia	D7	32
Kuzneckij Alatau, mts., Russia	D15	32
Kuznecovka, Russia	D11	10
Kuznetsk see Kuzneck, Russia	D7	32
Kuzomen', Russia	C17	8
Kvænangen, b., Nor.	A9	8
Kvaløya, i., Nor.	B8	8
Kvaløya, i., Nor.	A10	8
Kvam, Nor.	F3	8
Kvarnbergsvattnet, l., Swe.	D5	8
Kvarner, b., Cro.	F11	22
Kvarnerić, b., Cro.	F11	22
Kverkfjöll, vol., Ice.	k31	8a
Kvichak Bay, b., Ak., U.S.	E8	140
Kwa, stm., D.R.C.	E3	66
Kwai see Khwae Noi, stm., Thai.	E4	48

Name	Map Ref.	Page
Kwajalein, at., Marsh. Is.	C7	72
Kwakoegron, Sur.	B6	84
Kwamisa, mtn., Ghana	H4	64
Kwamouth, D.R.C.	E3	66
Kwando (Cuando), stm., Afr.	D3	68
Kwangchow see Guangzhou, China	J5	42
Kwangju, Kor., S.	G7	38
Kwango (Cuango), stm., Afr.	E3	66
Kwangsi Chuang see Guangxi, state, China	G6	36
Kwangtung see Guangdong, state, China	J6	42
KwaZulu-Natal, state, S. Afr.	F10	70
Kweichow see Guizhou, state, China	F6	36
Kweihwa see Hohhot, China	A4	42
Kweilin see Guilin, China	I4	42
Kweisui see Hohhot, China	A4	42
Kweiyang see Guiyang, China	H2	42
Kwekwe, Zimb.	D4	68
Kweneng, state, Bots.	C7	70
Kwenge (Caengo), stm., Afr.	B2	68
Kwethluk, Ak., U.S.	D7	140
Kwidzyn, Pol.	C14	16
Kwigillingok, Ak., U.S.	E7	140
Kwilu (Cuilo), stm., Afr.	F3	66
Kyabra, Austl.	F4	76
Kyabra Creek, stm., Austl.	E4	76
Kyabram, Austl.	K5	76
Kyaikkami, Mya.	D3	48
Kyaiklat, Mya.	D2	48
Kyaikto, Mya.	D3	48
Kya-in, Mya.	D4	48
Kyalite, Austl.	J4	76
Kyancutta, Austl.	F7	74
Ky Anh, Viet.	C8	48
Kyaukhnyat, Mya.	C3	48
Kyaukme, Mya.	A3	48
Kyaukpa, Mya.	F4	48
Kyaukpyu, Mya.	C1	48
Kyaukse, Mya.	B2	48
Kyauktaw, Mya.	D7	46
Kyaunggon, Mya.	D2	48
Kybartai, Lith.	F5	10
Kyebang-san, mtn., Kor., S.	B1	40
Kyeikdon, Mya.	E4	48
Kyidaunggan, Mya.	C3	48
Kyiv (Kiev), Ukr.	D4	32
Kyïvs'ke vodoskhovyshche, res., Ukr.	D4	32
Kyjov, Czech Rep.	G13	16
Kykotsmovi Village, Az., U.S.	H6	132
Kyle, Sk., Can.	D5	124
Kyle, S.D., U.S.	D10	126
Kyle, Lake, res., Zimb.	B10	70
Kyllíni, Grc.	F4	28
Kymi, state, Fin.	F12	8
Kyneton, Austl.	K5	76
Kynšperk nad Ohří, Czech Rep.	F8	16
Kyoga, Lake, l., Ug.	D6	66
Kyogle, Austl.	G9	76
Kyŏngju, Kor., S.	D2	40
Kyŏngsan, Kor., S.	D1	40
Kyŏngsang-bukto, state, Kor., S.	C1	40
Kyŏngsang-namdo, state, Kor., S.	D1	40
Kyŏngsŏng-ŭp, Kor., N.	D8	38
Kyônkadun, Mya.	D2	48
Kyonpyaw, Mya.	D2	48
Kyōto, Japan	D8	40
Kyōto, state, Japan	D8	40
Kyparissía, Grc.	F4	28
Kyparissiakós Kólpos, b., Grc.	F4	28
Kyra, Russia	G11	34
Kyren, Russia	D18	32
Kyrgyzstan, ctry., Asia	F12	32
Kyritz, Ger.	D8	16
Kyrönjoki, stm., Fin.	E10	8
Kyrösjärvi, l., Fin.	F10	8
Kyštym, Russia	C10	32
Kýthira, Grc.	G5	28
Kýthira, i., Grc.	G5	28
Kýthnos, i., Grc.	F7	28
Kyundon, Mya.	B2	48
Kyungyi, i., Mya.	E3	48
Kyuquot, B.C., Can.	F3	138
Kyūshū, i., Japan	G2	40
Kyushu-Palau Ridge, unds.	H16	142
Kyūshū-sanchi, mts., Japan	G4	40
Kywong, Austl.	J6	76
Kyyjärvi, Fin.	E11	8
Kyyvesi, l., Fin.	E12	8
Kyzyl, Russia	D16	32
Kyzylbair, Turkmen.	B8	56
Kyzyl-Kija, Kyrg.	F12	32
Kyzylkum, des., Asia	F10	32
Kyzyluj, Kaz.	E11	32
Kzyl-Orda, Kaz.	F11	32
Kzyltu, Kaz.	D12	32

L

Name	Map Ref.	Page
La Aguja, Cabo de, c., Col.	B4	86
La Albuera, Spain	F4	20
La Alcarria, reg., Spain	D8	20
La Algaba, Spain	G4	20
La Almunia de Doña Godina, Spain	C9	20
La Antigua, Salina, pl., Arg.	D4	92
La Araucanía, state, Chile	I1	92
Laascaanood, Som.	C9	66
La Ascención, hill, Mex.	C8	100
La Asunción, Ven.	B10	86
Laau Point, c., Hi., U.S.	B4	78a
Laayoune see El Aaiún, W. Sah.	D2	64
La Azufrosa, Mex.	F7	130
La Babia, Mex.	A7	100
Labadieville, La., U.S.	H8	122
La Baie, Qc., Can.	B6	110
La Banda, Arg.	C5	92
La Bandera, Cerro, mtn., Mex.	C6	100
La Bañeza, Spain	B4	20
La Barca, Mex.	E7	100
La Barge, Wy., U.S.	H16	136
Labasa, Fiji	p19	79e
La Baule-Escoublac, Fr.	G6	14
Labé, Gui.	G2	64
Labe (Elbe), stm., Eur.	C5	16
Labelle, Qc., Can.	D2	110
La Belle, Mo., U.S.	D5	120
Laberge, Lake, l., Yk., Can.	C4	106
Labi, Bru.	A9	50
Labian, Tanjong, c., Malay.	A11	50
La Biche, stm., Ab., Can.	B18	138
Labis, Malay.	K6	48
La Bisbal d'Empordà, Spain	C13	20
Łabiszyn, Pol.	D13	16
La Blanca Grande, Laguna, l., Arg.	I5	92
Labná, hist., Mex.	B3	102
Laboe, Ger.	B6	16
Laborde, Arg.	F6	92
Laborie, St. Luc.	m7	105c
La Bostonnais, Qc., Can.	C4	110
Laboulaye, Arg.	G6	92
Labrador, reg., Nf., Can.	E18	106
Labrador Basin, unds.	C9	144
Labrador City, Nf., Can.	E17	106
Labrador Sea, N.A.	D17	94
Lábrea, Braz.	E5	84
La Brea, Trin.	s12	105f
Labuan, Malay.	A9	50
Labuan, state, Malay.	A9	50
Labuan, Pulau, i., Malay.	A9	50
Labuchongshan, mts., China	C10	54
La Bufadora, Mex.	L9	134
Labuhan, Indon.	G4	50
Labuhanbajo, Indon.	H11	50
Labuhanbilik, Indon.	B2	50
Labuhanpandan, Indon.	H10	50
Labuhanruku, Indon.	B1	50
Labuk, stm., Malay.	H1	52
Labuk, Telukan, b., Malay.	G1	52
Labu Kananga, Indon.	H10	50
Labutta, Mya.	D2	48
Labytnangi, Russia	A11	32
Laç, Alb.	C13	24
Lača, ozero, l., Russia	F18	8
Lac-à-Beauce, Qc., Can.	C4	110
La Cadena, Mex.	I3	130
La Calera, Chile	F2	92
La Campana, Spain	G5	20
La Canada Flintridge, Ca., U.S.	I7	134
La Candelaria, Arg.	C5	92
La Candelaria, Mex.	C1	130
Lacantum, stm., Mex.	D2	102
La Capelle-en-Thiérache, Fr.	D12	14
La Carlota, Arg.	F6	92
La Carlota, Phil.	E4	52
La Carolina, Spain	F7	20
Lacaune, Fr.	F8	18
Laccadive Islands see Lakshadweep, is., India	F3	46
Lac-Édouard, Qc., Can.	C4	110
La Ceiba, Hond.	E4	102
Lacepede Bay, b., Austl.	K2	76
Lac-Etchemin, Qc., Can.	D6	110
Lacey, Wa., U.S.	C4	136
Lac-Frontière, Qc., Can.	D6	110
La Chapelle-d'Angillon, Fr.	G11	14
La Châtaigneraie, Fr.	C5	18
La Chaux-de-Fonds, Switz.	C3	22
Lachhmangarh Sīkar, India	E5	54
Lachine, Qc., Can.	E3	110
Lachlan, stm., Austl.	J5	76
La Chorrera, Col.	H5	86
La Chorrera, Pan.	H8	102
Lachute, Qc., Can.	E2	110
Laçi see Laç, Alb.	C13	24
La Ciénaga, Arg.	C4	92
La Ciotat, Fr.	F11	18
La Citadelle, hist., Haiti	C11	102
La Ciudad, Mex.	D6	100
Lackawanna, N.Y., U.S.	B6	114
Lac La Biche, Ab., Can.	B18	138
Lac la Hache, B.C., Can.	E9	138
Laclede, Id., U.S.	B10	136
Laclede, Mo., U.S.	E4	120
La Clotilde, Arg.	C7	92
Lac-Mégantic, Qc., Can.	E6	110
La Colorada, Mex.	A3	100
La Coma, Mex.	C9	100
Lacombe, Ab., Can.	D17	138
Lacombe, La., U.S.	G9	122
Lacona, Ia., U.S.	C4	120
La Concepción, Pan.	H6	102
La Concepción, Ven.	B5	86
Laconi, Italy	E2	24
Laconia, N.H., U.S.	G5	110
Laconia, Gulf of see Lakonikós Kólpos, b., Grc.	G5	28
La Consulta, Arg.	F3	92
Lacoochee, Fl., U.S.	H3	116
La Coruña see A Coruña, Spain	A2	20
La Coruña see A Coruña, co., Spain	A2	20
La Coste, Tx., U.S.	E9	130
La Courtine, Fr.	D8	18
La Crescent, Mn., U.S.	H7	118
La Crosse, Ks., U.S.	C9	128
La Crosse, Va., U.S.	H7	114
Lacrosse, Wa., U.S.	D9	136
La Crosse, Wi., U.S.	H7	118
La Cruz, Arg.	D9	92
La Cruz, Col.	G3	86
La Cruz, C.R.	E7	96
La Cruz, Mex.	G2	130
La Cruz de Río Grande, Nic.	F5	102
Lac Seul, On., Can.	A6	118
La Cuesta, P.R.	B2	104a
La Cumbre, Arg.	E5	92
La Cygne, Ks., U.S.	F3	120
Ladākh, hist. reg., Pak.	A6	54
Ladākh Range, mts., Asia	A6	54
Ladder Creek, stm., Ks., U.S.	C7	128
Laddonia, Mo., U.S.	E6	120
La Désirade, i., Guad.	h6	105c
La Digue, i., Sey.	j13	69b
Ladismith, S. Afr.	H5	70
Ladispoli, Italy	I8	22
Lādīz, Iran	D9	56
Ladner, B.C., Can.	G7	138
Lādnūn, India	E5	54
Ladoga, In., U.S.	I3	112
Ladoga, Lake see Ladožskoe ozero, l., Russia	F14	8
La Dorada, Col.	E4	86
La Dormida, Arg.	F4	92
Ladožskoe ozero (Ladoga, Lake), l., Russia	F14	8
Laduškin, Russia	F3	10
Ladva-Vetka, Russia	F15	8
Lady Ann Strait, strt., Nu., Can.	B10	141
Lady Barron, Austl.	n14	77a
Ladybrand, S. Afr.	F8	70
Lady Elliot Island, i., Austl.	E9	76
Ladysmith, B.C., Can.	H7	138
Ladysmith, S. Afr.	F9	70
Ladysmith, Wi., U.S.	F7	118
Lae, Pap. N. Gui.	b4	79a
La Encantada, Mex.	C8	100
La Escondida, Mex.	H8	130
La Esmeralda, Mex.	B7	100
Læsø, i., Den.	H4	8
La Esperanza, Cuba	A5	102
La Esperanza, Hond.	E3	102
La Esperanza, Mex.	H4	130
La Esperanza, P.R.	B3	104a
La Estrada see A Estrada, Spain	B2	20
Lafa, China	C7	38
La Falda, Arg.	E5	92
La Farge, Wi., U.S.	H8	118
Lafayette, Al., U.S.	E13	122
Lafayette, Ca., U.S.	F3	134
Lafayette, Co., U.S.	A3	128
Lafayette, Ga., U.S.	C13	122
Lafayette, In., U.S.	H3	112
Lafayette, La., U.S.	G6	122
Lafayette, Tn., U.S.	H11	120
Lafayette, Mount, mtn., N.H., U.S.	F5	110
La Feria, Tx., U.S.	H10	130
La Ferté-Bernard, Fr.	F9	14
La Ferté-Saint-Aubin, Fr.	G10	14
Lafia, Nig.	H6	64
Lafiagi, Nig.	H6	64
Lafleche, Sk., Can.	E7	124
La Flèche, Fr.	G8	14
La Florida, Guat.	D2	102
La Foa, N. Cal.	m15	79d
La Follette, Tn., U.S.	H1	114
Lafourche, Bayou, stm., La., U.S.	H8	122
La Fragua, Arg.	C5	92
La Fría, Ven.	C5	86
La Fuente de San Esteban, Spain	D4	20
La Galite, i., Tun.	G2	24
La Gallareta, Arg.	D7	92
Lagan, stm., Swe.	E3	8
Lagarto, Braz.	F7	88
Lagawe, Phil.	B3	52
Lage, China	D10	54
Lågen, stm., Nor.	F4	8
Lages, Braz.	C12	92
Laghmān, state, Afg.	A3	54
Laghouat, Alg.	C5	64
Lagkadás, Grc.	C5	28
Lagoa da Prata, Braz.	K3	88
Lagoa Vermelha, Braz.	D12	92
Lago da Pedra, Braz.	C3	88
Lago Kolonie, Aruba	p20	104g
Lagolândia, Braz.	H1	88
Lagonegro, Italy	D9	24
Lagonoy Gulf, b., Phil.	D4	52
Lago Posadas, Arg.	I2	90
Lagos, Nig.	H5	64
Lagos, Port.	G2	20
Lagos de Moreno, Mex.	E8	100
La Gouèra, W. Sah.	E1	64
La Goulette, Tun.	H4	24
Lago Viedma, Arg.	I2	90
La Granadella, Spain	C11	20
La Grande, Or., U.S.	E8	136
La Grande Deux, Réservoir, res., Qc., Can.	E15	106
La Grande Quatre, Réservoir, res., Qc., Can.	E16	106
LaGrange, Austl.	C4	74
La Grange, Ga., U.S.	D13	122
La Grange, Ky., U.S.	F12	120
La Grange, Mo., U.S.	D6	120
La Grange, Tx., U.S.	E11	130
Lagrange, Wy., U.S.	F8	126
Lagrange Bay, b., Austl.	C4	74
La Gran Sabana, pl., Ven.	E10	86
La Guadeloupe, Qc., Can.	E6	110
La Guajira, state, Col.	G11	102
La Guajira, Península de, pen., S.A.	A6	86
La Guardia, Arg.	D5	92
La Guardia, Bol.	C4	90
La Guardia see A Guardia, Spain	C1	20
La Guerche-sur-l'Aubois, Fr.	G11	14
Laguiole, Fr.	E8	18
Laguna, Braz.	D13	92
Laguna, N.M., U.S.	H9	132
Laguna, Ilha da, i., Braz.	D7	84
Laguna Beach, Ca., U.S.	J8	134
Laguna Dam, dam, U.S.	K2	132
Laguna de Jaco, Mex.	G4	130
Laguna Larga, Arg.	E6	92
Laguna Paiva, Arg.	E7	92
Lagunas, Peru	E2	84
Lagunas de Chacagua, Parque Nacional, p.o.i., Mex.	H9	100
Lagunillas, Bol.	C4	90
Laha, China	B9	36
La Habana (Havana), Cuba	A6	102
Lahad Datu, Malay.	A11	50
Lahad Datu, Telukan, b., Malay.	A11	50
La Harpe, Il., U.S.	K7	118
La Harpe, Ks., U.S.	G2	120
Lahat, Indon.	E3	50
Lahdenpohja, Russia	F14	8
Lahemaa rahvus, p.o.i., Est.	G11	8
Lahewa, Indon.	L3	48
Lahfân, Bîr, well, Egypt	G4	58
Lahij, Yemen	G5	56
Lāhījān, Iran	B7	56
Lahnstein, Ger.	F3	16
Laholm, Swe.	H5	8
Lahontan Reservoir, res., Nv., U.S.	D6	134
Lahore, Pak.	C5	54
La Horqueta, Col.	F5	86
Lahr, Ger.	H3	16
Lahti, Fin.	F11	8
La Huerta, N.M., U.S.	B3	130
Lahva, Bela.	H10	10
Laï, Chad	F3	62
Laiagam, Pap. N. Gui.	b3	79a
Laibin, China	J3	42
Lai Chau, Viet.	A6	48
Laichow Bay see Laizhou Wan, b., China	C8	42
Laifeng, China	G3	42
L'Aigle, Fr.	F9	14
Laihia, Fin.	E9	8
Laïmbélé, Mont, mtn., Vanuatu	k16	79d
Laingsburg, S. Afr.	H5	70
Laingsburg, Mi., U.S.	B1	114
Lainioälven, stm., Swe.	C10	8
Lainsitz see Lužnice, stm., Eur.	G10	16
Laird Hill, Tx., U.S.	E3	122
Lais, Indon.	C12	50
Lais, Indon.	E3	50
Lais, Phil.	G5	52
Laitila, Fin.	F9	8
Laiwu, China	C7	42
Laixi, China	C9	42
Laiyang, China	C9	42
Laizhou Bay see Laizhou Wan, b., China	C8	42
Laizhou Wan (Laizhou Bay), b., China	C8	42
Laja, stm., Chile	H2	92
Laja, Laguna de la, l., Chile	H2	92
Laja, Salto del, wtfl, Chile	H2	92
La Jara, Co., U.S.	D2	128
La Jara, reg., Spain	E5	20
La Jara Canyon, val., N.M., U.S.	G9	132
La Jarita, Mex.	F4	130
Lajas, P.R.	B1	104a
Laje, Braz.	G6	88
Lajeado, Braz.	D11	92
Lajedo, Braz.	E7	88
Lajes, Braz.	C7	88
Lajinha, Braz.	K5	88
Laji Shan, mts., China	D5	36
Lajosmizse, Hung.	B6	26
Lajta (Leitha), stm., Eur.	H12	16
La Junta, Co., U.S.	D5	128
Lakar Kūh, mtn., Iran	C8	56
Lakatoro, Vanuatu	k16	79d
Lake, Ms., U.S.	E9	122
Lake Alfred, Fl., U.S.	H4	116
Lake Andes, S.D., U.S.	D14	126
Lake Arthur, La., U.S.	G6	122
Lakeba, i., Fiji	q20	79e
Lakeba Passage, strt., Fiji	q20	79e
Lake Benton, Mn., U.S.	G2	118
Lake Brownwood, Tx., U.S.	C8	130
Lake Cargelligo, Austl.	I6	76
Lake Charles, La., U.S.	G5	122
Lake Chelan National Recreation Area, p.o.i., Wa., U.S.	B6	136
Lake City, Ar., U.S.	B8	122
Lake City, Co., U.S.	E9	132
Lake City, Fl., U.S.	F3	116
Lake City, Mi., U.S.	D4	112
Lake City, Pa., U.S.	B5	114
Lake City, S.C., U.S.	C6	116
Lake City, Tn., U.S.	H1	114
Lake Cowichan, B.C., Can.	H6	138
Lake Crystal, Mn., U.S.	G4	118
Lake Dallas, Tx., U.S.	A10	130
Lake Delton, Wi., U.S.	H9	118
Lake District National Park, p.o.i., Eng., U.K.	G9	12
Lake Elsinore, Ca., U.S.	J8	134
Lakefield, On., Can.	D11	112
Lakefield, Mn., U.S.	H3	118
Lake Forest, Il., U.S.	F2	112
Lake Fork Reservoir, res., Tx., U.S.	E3	122
Lake Geneva, Wi., U.S.	B9	120
Lake George, N.Y., U.S.	G3	110
Lake Harbor, Fl., U.S.	J5	116
Lake Havasu City, Az., U.S.	I2	132
Lake Helen, Fl., U.S.	H4	116
Lakehurst, N.J., U.S.	D11	114
Lake Jackson, Tx., U.S.	E12	130
Lake King, Austl.	F3	74
Lakeland, Fl., U.S.	H3	116
Lakeland, Ga., U.S.	E2	116
Lake Linden, Mi., U.S.	D10	118
Lake Louise, Ab., Can.	E14	138
Lake Mead National Recreation Area, p.o.i., U.S.	G2	132
Lake Mills, Wi., U.S.	A8	120
Lake Minchumina, Ak., U.S.	D9	140
Lake Mohawk see Sparta, N.J., U.S.	C11	114
Lake Nash, Austl.	D7	74
Lake Norden, S.D., U.S.	C15	126
Lake Oswego, Or., U.S.	E4	136
Lake Ozark, Mo., U.S.	F5	120
Lake Park, Fl., U.S.	J5	116
Lake Park, Ia., U.S.	H3	118
Lake Placid, Fl., U.S.	I4	116
Lake Placid, N.Y., U.S.	F3	110
Lake Pleasant, N.Y., U.S.	G2	110
Lakeport, Ca., U.S.	D3	134
Lakeport, Mi., U.S.	E7	112
Lake Preston, S.D., U.S.	C15	126
Lakes Entrance, Austl.	K7	76
Lakeshore, Ms., U.S.	G9	122
Lakeside, Ca., U.S.	K8	134
Lakeside, Mt., U.S.	B12	136
Lake Stevens, Wa., U.S.	B4	136
Laketown, Ut., U.S.	B5	132
Lake View, Ar., U.S.	C8	122
Lake View, Ia., U.S.	B2	120
Lakeview, Mi., U.S.	E4	112
Lakeview, Mi., U.S.	F4	112
Lakeview, Oh., U.S.	D2	114
Lakeview, Or., U.S.	A5	134
Lake Village, Ar., U.S.	D7	122
Lakeville, Mn., U.S.	G5	118
Lake Wales, Fl., U.S.	I4	116
Lake Wilson, Mn., U.S.	G2	118
Lakewood, Co., U.S.	B3	128
Lakewood, N.J., U.S.	D11	114
Lakewood, Oh., U.S.	C4	114
Lakewood, Wa., U.S.	C4	136
Lakewood, Wi., U.S.	C1	112
Lakewood Park, N.D., U.S.	F15	124
Lake Worth, Fl., U.S.	J5	116
Lakhdaria, Alg.	H14	20
Lākheri, India	F5	54
Lakhīmpur, India	D8	54
Lakhipur, India	F14	54
Lakhnādon, India	G7	54
Lakinsk, Russia	H18	8
Lakonikós Kólpos (Laconia, Gulf of), b., Grc.	G5	28
Lakota, N.D., U.S.	F15	124
Laksefjorden, b., Nor.	A12	8
Lakshadweep, state, India	F3	46
Lakshadweep, is., India	F3	46
Lakshadweep Sea, Asia	G3	46
Lākshām, Bngl.	G13	54
Lakshmeshwar, India	D2	53
La Laja, Chile	H1	92
Lāla Mūsa, Pak.	B4	54
Lâlapaşa, Tur.	B9	28
L'Albufera, l., Spain	E10	20
Laleham, Austl.	D7	76
La Leona, Mex.	I6	130
La Leonesa, Arg.	C8	92
Lālganj, India	F10	54
Lalībela, Eth.	E7	62
La Libertad, Guat.	D2	102
La Ligua, Chile	F2	92
La Lima, Hond.	E3	102
Lalin, stm., China	B7	38
Lalindi, Indon.	I12	50
La Línea de la Concepción, Spain	H5	20
Lalitpur, India	F7	54
Lalitpur, Nepal	E10	54
Lalla Khedidja, Tamgout de, mtn., Alg.	H14	20
Lālmanir Hāt, Bngl.	F12	54
La Loche, Sk., Can.	D9	106
La Lora, plat., Spain	B7	20
La Louvière, Bel.	D13	14
L'Alpe-d'Huez, Fr.	D12	18
Lālpur, India	G2	54
Lālsot, India	E6	54
La Luz, Mex.	C10	100
La Luz, Mex.	I10	130
Lama, ozero, l., Russia	C7	34
La Macarena, Parque Nacional, p.o.i. Col.	F5	86
La Macarena, Serranía de, mts., Col.	F5	86
La Maddalena, Italy	C3	24
La Madrid, Arg.	C5	92
Lamadrid, Mex.	G6	130
La Magdalena, Mex.	H1	130
Lama-Kara, Togo	H5	64
La Malbaie, Qc., Can.	C6	110
La Mancha, reg., Spain	E8	20
Lamandau, stm., Indon.	E7	50
Lamap, Vanuatu	k16	79d
Lamar, Co., U.S.	C6	128
Lamar, Mo., U.S.	G3	120
Lamarche, Fr.	F14	14
La Marmora, Punta, mtn., Italy	D3	24
La Maroma, Mex.	F7	130
La Marque, Tx., U.S.	H4	122
La Marsa, Tun.	H4	24
La Martre, Qc., Can.	A10	110
Lamas, Peru	E2	84
Lamballe, Fr.	F6	14
Lambaréné, Gabon	E1	66
Lambari, stm., Braz.	J3	88
Lambayeque, Peru	E2	84
Lambay Island, i., Ire.	H7	12
Lambert, Ms., U.S.	C8	122
Lambert, Mt., U.S.	G9	124
Lambert, Cape, c., Pap. N. Gui.	a5	79a
Lambert Glacier, ice, Ant.	C11	81
Lambert Land, reg., Grnld.	B21	141
Lamberton, Mn., U.S.	G3	118
Lambertsbaai see Lambert's Bay, S. Afr.	H3	70
Lambert's Bay, S. Afr.	H3	70
Lambton, Cape, c., N.T., Can.	A6	106
Lame Deer, Mt., U.S.	B6	126
La Media Luna, Arrecifes de, rf., Hond.	E6	102
Lamentin, Guad.	h5	105c
Lamèque, N.B., Can.	C12	110
Lamèque, Île, i., N.B., Can.	C12	110
La Merced, Arg.	B5	92
La Merced, Arg.	D5	92
Lameroo, Austl.	J3	76
La Mesa, Ca., U.S.	K8	134
Lamesa, Tx., U.S.	B6	130
Lamía, Grc.	E5	28
Lamine, stm., Mo., U.S.	F5	120
Lamington National Park, p.o.i., Austl.	G9	76
La Misión, Mex.	K9	134
Lamitan, Phil.	G4	52
Lamlam, Mount, hill, Guam	j9	78c
Lammeulo, Indon.	J2	48
La Moille, Il., U.S.	C8	120
Lamoille, Nv., U.S.	C1	132
Lamoille, stm., Vt., U.S.	F4	110
Lamon Bay, b., Phil.	C4	52
Lamone, stm., Italy	F9	22
Lamongan, Indon.	G8	50
Lamoni, Ia., U.S.	D3	120
Lamont, Ca., U.S.	H6	134
Lamont, Ia., U.S.	I7	118
Lamont, Ok., U.S.	E11	128
La Monte, Mo., U.S.	F4	120
La Mothe, Lac, l., Qc., Can.	B5	110
La Mothe-Achard, Fr.	H7	14
Lamotrek, at., Micron.	C5	72
Lamotte-Beuvron, Fr.	G10	14
Lampang, Thai.	C4	48
Lampasas, Tx., U.S.	C9	130
Lampasas, stm., Tx., U.S.	C9	130
Lampazos de Naranjo, Mex.	B8	100
Lampedusa, Isola di, i., Italy	I6	24
Lampertheim, Ger.	G4	16
Lamphun, Thai.	C4	48
Lampman, Sk., Can.	E11	124
Lampung, state, Indon.	F4	50
Lamskoe, Russia	H21	10
Lamu, Kenya	E8	66
La Mure, Fr.	E11	18
Lan', stm., Bela.	H10	10
Lana, Italy	D8	22
Lanai, i., Hi., U.S.	C4	78a
Lanai City, Hi., U.S.	C4	78a
Lanaihale, mtn., Hi., U.S.	C5	78a
Lanalhue, Lago, l., Chile	I1	92
Lanark, On., Can.	C13	112
Lanark, Scot., U.K.	F9	12
Lanbi Kyun, i., Mya.	G4	48
Lancang, China	A4	48
Lancang see Mekong, stm., Asia	D9	46
Lancaster, Eng., U.K.	G10	12
Lancaster, Ca., U.S.	I7	134
Lancaster, Mn., U.S.	C2	118
Lancaster, Mo., U.S.	D5	120
Lancaster, N.H., U.S.	F5	110
Lancaster, Oh., U.S.	E3	114
Lancaster, Pa., U.S.	D9	114
Lancaster, S.C., U.S.	B5	116
Lancaster, Tx., U.S.	E2	122
Lancaster, Va., U.S.	G9	114
Lancaster, Wi., U.S.	B7	120
Lancaster Sound, strt., Nu., Can.	C8	141
Lance Creek, Wy., U.S.	D8	126
Lancelin, Austl.	F2	74
Lanchou see Lanzhou, China	D5	36
Lanchow see Lanzhou, China	D5	36
Lanciano, Italy	H11	22
Lancun, China	C9	42
Łańcut, Pol.	F18	16
Lândana, Ang.	B1	68
Landau an der Isar, Ger.	H8	16
Landau in der Pfalz, Ger.	G4	16
Landeck, Aus.	C7	22
Lander, Wy., U.S.	E4	126
Landerneau, Fr.	F4	14
Landes, state, Fr.	F5	18
Landes, reg., Fr.	E5	18
Landete, Spain	E9	20
Landis, Sk., Can.	B5	124
Lando, S.C., U.S.	B4	116
Land O'Lakes, Wi., U.S.	E9	118
Landösjön, l., Swe.	E5	8
Landri Sales, Braz.	D3	88
Landrum, S.C., U.S.	A3	116
Landsborough Creek, stm., Austl.	D5	76
Land's End, c., Eng., U.K.	K7	12
Landshut, Ger.	H7	16
Landskrona, Swe.	I5	8
Lane, mth., Fr.	G9	14
Lanesboro, Mn., U.S.	H6	118
Lanett, Al., U.S.	E13	122
Lanezi Lake, l., B.C., Can.	C10	138
La'nga Co, l., China	C8	54
Langa-Langa, D.R.C.	E3	66
Langbank, Sk., Can.	D11	124
Lang Bay, B.C., Can.	G6	138
Langdale, Al., U.S.	E13	122
Langdon, N.D., U.S.	F15	124
Langeac, Fr.	D9	18
Langeberg, mts., S. Afr.	H5	70
Langeland, i., Den.	I4	8
Langenhagen, Ger.	D5	16
Langenthal, Switz.	C4	22
Langfang, China	B7	42
Langford, S.D., U.S.	B15	126
Langgam, Indon.	C2	50
Langham, Sk., Can.	B6	124
Langhe, hist. reg., Italy	F5	22
Langholm, Scot., U.K.	F9	12
Langjökull, ice, Ice.	k29	8a
Langkawi, Pulau, i., Malay.	I4	48
Langley, B.C., Can.	G8	138
Langley, Ok., U.S.	A3	122
Langlo, stm., Austl.	E5	76
Langnau im Emmental, Switz.	C4	22
Langogne, Fr.	E9	18
Langøya, i., Nor.	B6	8
Langping, China	F4	42
Langreo, Spain	A5	20
Langres, Fr.	G14	14
Langruth, Mb., Can.	D15	124
Langsa, Indon.	J3	48
Langsa, Teluk, b., Indon.	J4	48
Langshan, China	A2	42
Lang Son, Viet.	B8	48
Lang Suan, Thai.	H4	48
Languedoc, hist. reg., Fr.	F8	18
L'Anguille, stm., Ar., U.S.	C8	122
Langxi, China	F8	42
Langzhong, China	F1	42
Lanigan, Sk., Can.	C8	124
Lanigan Creek, stm., Sk., Can.	C9	124
Lanín, Volcán, vol., S.A.	G2	90
Länkäran, Azer.	B6	56
Länkipohja, Fin.	F11	8
Lannemezan, Fr.	F6	18
Lannion, Fr.	F5	14
Lanping, China	F4	36
Lansdowne, India	D7	54
Lansdowne House, On., Can.	E13	106
L'Anse, Mi., U.S.	B1	112
Lansing, Ia., U.S.	H7	118
Lansing, Mi., U.S.	B1	114
Lantana, Fl., U.S.	J5	116
Lantau Island, i., China	J6	42
Lanta Yai, Ko, i., Thai.	I4	48
Lantian, China	D3	42
La Nurra, reg., Italy	D2	24
Lanusei, Italy	E3	24
Lanxi, China	G8	42
Lan Yü, i., Tai.	J9	42
Lanzhou, China	D5	36
Lanzo Torinese, Italy	E4	22
Lao, stm., Thai.	C4	48
Laoag, Phil.	A3	52
Laoang, Phil.	D5	52
Lao Cai, Viet.	A6	48
Laodao, stm., China	G5	42
Laofu, China	C3	38
Laoha, stm., China	C4	38
Laohekou, China	E4	42
Laohokow see Laohekou, China	E4	42
Laois, state, Ire.	I5	12
Lao Ling, mtn., China	C9	38
Laon, Fr.	E12	14
Laona, Wi., U.S.	F10	118
La Orchila, Isla, i., Ven.	B8	86
La Oroya, Peru	F2	84
Laos, ctry., Asia	C6	48
Laoshan Wan, b., China	C9	42
Lapa, Braz.	B13	92
Lapai, Nig.	H6	64
Lapalisse, Fr.	C9	18
La Palma, Col.	E4	86
La Palma, Pan.	H8	102
La Palma, Pan.	I7	102
La Palma del Condado, Spain	G4	20
La Paloma, Ur.	G10	92
La Pampa, state, Arg.	G3	90
La Paragua, Ven.	D10	86
La Pasión, stm., Guat.	D2	102
La Paya, Parque Nacional, p.o.i., Col.	G4	86
La Paz, Arg.	E8	92
La Paz, Arg.	F4	92
La Paz, Bol.	C3	90
La Paz, Col.	B5	86
La Paz, Hond.	E4	102
La Paz, Mex.	C3	100
La Paz, Mex.	D8	100
La Paz, Ur.	G9	92
La Paz, Bahía de, b., Mex.	C3	100
La Perla, Mex.	A6	100
La Perouse, Bahía, b., Chile	e30	78l
La Perouse Strait, strt., Asia	B13	36
La Pesca, Mex.	D10	100
La Piedad de Cabadas, Mex.	E7	100
La Pine, Or., U.S.	G5	136
La Place, La., U.S.	G8	122
Lap Lae, Thai.	D4	48
Lapland, hist. reg., Eur.	C11	8
La Plata, Arg.	G8	92
La Plata, Col.	F4	86
La Plata, Md., U.S.	F9	114
La Plata, Mo., U.S.	D5	120
La Plata Peak, mtn., Co., U.S.	D10	132
La Pobla de Segur, Spain	B11	20
La Pocatière, Qc., Can.	C6	110
Lapominka, Russia	D19	8
Laporte, Co., U.S.	G7	126
La Porte, In., U.S.	G3	112
Laporte, Pa., U.S.	C9	114
La Porte City, Ia., U.S.	B5	120
La Potherie, Lac, l., Qc., Can.	D16	106
La Poza Grande, Mex.	C2	100
Lappajärvi, l., Fin.	E10	8
Lappeenranta, Fin.	F12	8
Lappi, state, Fin.	C12	8
Laprida, Arg.	D5	92
Laprida, Arg.	H7	92
La Pryor, Tx., U.S.	F8	130
Lapta, N. Cyp.	C4	58
Laptev Sea see Laptevyh, more, Russia	B4	32
Laptevyh, more, Russia	B4	32
La Puebla de Montalbán, Spain	E6	20
La Puerta, Arg.	D5	92
La Puerta de Cabrera, Mex.	H2	130
Lapu-Lapu, Phil.	E4	52
La Purísima, Mex.	B2	100
Lăpuș, Rom.	B11	26
Lapwai, Id., U.S.	D10	136
La Quiaca, Arg.	D3	90
L'Áquila, Italy	H10	22
Lār, Iran	D7	56
Lara, state, Ven.	B7	86
Laracha, Spain	A2	20
Larache, Mor.	B3	64
Laramie, Wy., U.S.	F7	126
Laramie, stm., U.S.	E8	126
Laramie Mountains, mts., Wy., U.S.	F7	126
Laramie Peak, mtn., Wy., U.S.	E7	126
Laranjal, Braz.	K4	88
Laranjeiras, Braz.	F7	88
Laranjeiras do Sul, Braz.	B11	92
Larantuka, Indon.	G7	44
Larap, Phil.	C4	52
Larat, Indon.	G9	44
Larat, Pulau, i., Indon.	G9	44
Larche Pass, p., Eur.	E12	18
Larchwood, Ia., U.S.	H2	118
Larde, Moz.	D6	68
L'Ardoise, N.S., Can.	E16	110
Laredo, Spain	A7	20
Laredo, Tx., U.S.	G8	130
La Reforma, Mex.	C4	100
Lares, P.R.	B2	104a
Larga, Mol.	A13	26
Larga, Laguna, l., Tx., U.S.	G10	130
Largo, Fl., U.S.	I3	116
Largo, Cañon, val., N.M., U.S.	G9	132
Largo, Cayo, i., Cuba	B7	102
Largs, Scot., U.K.	F8	12
Lariang, stm., Indon.	D11	50
Larimore, N.D., U.S.	G16	124
Larino, Italy	I11	22
Lario see Como, Lago di, l., Italy	D6	22
La Rioja, Arg.	D4	92
La Rioja, state, Arg.	D4	92
La Rioja, state, Spain	B8	20
Lárisa, Grc.	D5	28
Larjak, Russia	B14	32
Lārkāna, Pak.	D10	56
Lárnakos, Kólpos, b., Cyp.	D4	58
Larne, N. Ire., U.K.	G7	12
Larned, Ks., U.S.	C9	128
La Robla, Spain	B5	20
La Rochefoucauld, Fr.	D6	18
La Rochelle, Fr.	C4	18
La Roche-sur-Yon, Fr.	H7	14
La Roda, Spain	E8	20
La Romaine, Qc., Can.	i21	107a
La Romana, Dom. Rep.	C13	102
La Ronge, Sk., Can.	D10	106
Laroquebrou, Fr.	D8	18
Larose, Pointe, c., Mart.	k7	105c
Larroque, Arg.	F8	92
Larrys River, N.S., Can.	E15	110
Larsen Ice Shelf, ice, Ant.	B34	81
La Rubia, Arg.	E7	92
La Rue, Oh., U.S.	D2	114
Larvik, Nor.	G3	8
Larzac, Causse du, plat., Fr.	F9	18
La Sabanilla, Mex.	C8	100
La Sal, Ut., U.S.	E7	132
La Salle, Co., U.S.	G8	126
La Salle, Il., U.S.	C8	120
La Salle, stm., Mb., Can.	E16	124
Lasan, Indon.	C9	50
Las Animas, Co., U.S.	C5	128
Las Arenas, P.R.	B1	104a
La Sarre, Qc., Can.	F15	106
Las Arrias, Arg.	E6	92
Las Ballenas, Canal de, strt., Mex.	G6	98
Las Breñas, Arg.	C7	92
Las Cabezas de San Juan, Spain	G5	20
Las Cabras, Chile	G2	92
Lascano, Ur.	F10	92
Las Casitas, mtn., Mex.	D4	100
Las Catitas, Arg.	F3	92
Las Choapas, Mex.	G11	100
Las Chorreras, Mex.	A6	100
Las Cruces, N.M., U.S.	K10	132
Las Cuatas, Mex.	D1	130
Las Cuevas, Mex.	A8	100
Las Cumaraguas, Ven.	p20	104g
La Selle, Morne, mtn., Haiti	C11	102
La Serena, Chile	D2	92
La Serena, reg., Spain	F5	20
La Seu d'Urgell, Spain	B12	20
La Seyne, Fr.	F11	18
La Seyne, Fr.	F11	18
Las Flores, Arg.	G8	92

I • 32 Lasf-Ling

Name — Map Ref. — Page

Las Flores, P.R. B3 104a
Las Flores, Arroyo, stm., Arg. H7 92
Las Garcitas, Arg. C7 92
Las Guayabas, Mex. C10 100
Lashburn, Sk., Can. A4 124
Las Heras, Arg. I3 90
Las Heras, Arg. F3 92
Lashio, Mya. A3 48
Lashkar Gāh, Afg. C9 56
Las Hormigas, Mex. C9 100
Lasia, Pulau, i., Indon. K3 48
Łasin, Pol. C15 16
La Sirena, Ven. p20 104g
Łaskarzew, Pol. E17 16
Las Lajas, Arg. I2 92
Las Lajas, Pan. H7 102
Las Lomitas, Arg. B7 92
Las Malvinas, Arg. G3 92
Las Mareas, P.R. C3 104a
Las Margaritas, Mex. G13 100
Las Marianas, Arg. G8 92
Las Marías, P.R. B1 104a
Las Minas, Cerro, mtn., Hond. E3 102
Las Nopaleras, Cerro, mtn., Mex. C7 100
La Solana, Spain F7 20
Las Ovejas, Arg. H2 92
Las Palmas, Arg. C8 92
Las Palmas, P.R. C3 104a
Las Palomas, Mex. F9 98
La Spezia, Italy F6 22
Las Piedras, P.R. B4 104a
Las Piedras, Ur. G9 92
Las Piedras, stm., Peru F3 84
Las Plumas, Arg. H3 90
Lasqueti Island, i., B.C., Can. G6 138
Las Rosas, Arg. F7 92
Las Rosas, Mex. G12 100
Lassance, Braz. I3 88
Lassen Peak, vol., Ca., U.S. C4 134
Lassen Volcanic National Park, p.o.i., Ca., U.S. C4 134
L'Assomption, stm., Qc., Can. D3 110
Las Tablas, Pan. I7 102
Las Tinajas, Arg. C6 92
Last Mountain Lake, l., Sk., Can. C8 124
Las Tórtolas, Cerro (Tórtolas, Cerro de las), mtn., S.A. D2 92
Lastoursville, Gabon E2 66
Las Tunas, Cuba B9 102
Las Tunas Grandes, Laguna, l., Arg. H6 92
Las Varas, Mex. G8 98
Las Varas, Mex. E6 100
Las Varillas, Arg. E6 92
Las Vegas, P.R. B1 104a
Las Vegas, Nv., U.S. G1 132
Las Vegas, N.M., U.S. F3 128
Las Vegas, Ven. C7 86
Latacunga, Ec. H2 86
La Tagua, Col. H4 86
Latakia see Al-Lādhiqīyah, Syria C6 58
Lata Mountain, vol., Am. Sam. h13 79c
Latehar, India G10 54
La Teste-de-Buch, Fr. E4 18
Lāthi, India H3 54
Lathrop, Mo., U.S. E3 120
Latimer, Ia., U.S. I5 118
Latina, Italy C6 24
Latisana, Italy E10 22
Latium see Lazio, state, Italy B6 24
Latjuga, Russia D23 8
La Torrecilla, mtn., P.R. B3 104a
La Tortuga, Isla, i., Ven. B9 86
Latouche Treville, Cape, c., Austl. C4 74
La Tour-d'Auvergne, Fr. D8 18
La Trimouille, Fr. C7 18
La Trinidad, Nic. F4 102
La Trinidad, Phil. B3 52
La Trinidad de Orichuna, Ven. D7 86
La Trinité, Mart. k6 105c
Latrobe, Pa., U.S. D6 114
Latta, S.C., U.S. B6 116
La Tuque, Qc., Can. C4 110
Lātūr, India B3 53
Latvia, ctry., Eur. D7 10
Lau, Nig. H7 64
Lauchhammer, Ger. E9 16
Lauenburg, Ger. C6 16
Lauf an der Pegnitz, Ger. G7 16
Lauge Koch Kyst, cst., Grnld. B13 141
Laughlin, Nv., U.S. H2 132
Laughlin Peak, mtn., N.M., U.S. E4 128
Lau Group, is., Fiji p20 79e
Lauis see Lugano, Switz. D5 22
Laukaa, Fin. E11 8
Laun, Thai. G4 48
Launceston, Austl. n13 77a
Launceston, Eng., U.K. K8 12
La Unión, Chile H2 90
La Unión, El Sal. F4 102
La Unión, Mex. G8 100
La Unión, Spain G10 20
La Union, N.M., U.S. L10 132
La Unión, Ven. C8 86
Laupheim, Ger. H5 16
Laura, Austl. C8 74
La Urbana, Ven. D8 86
Laurel, Fl., U.S. I3 116
Laurel, In., U.S. E12 120
Laurel, Md., U.S. E9 114
Laurel, Ms., U.S. F9 122
Laurel, Mt., U.S. B4 126
Laurel, Ne., U.S. E15 126
Laurel Bay, S.C., U.S. D5 116
Laureldale, Pa., U.S. D10 114
Laureles, Ur. E9 92
Laurel River Lake, res., Ky., U.S. G1 114
Laurelville, Oh., U.S. E15 120
Laurencekirk, Scot., U.K. E10 12
Laurens, S.C., U.S. B3 116
Laurentides, Les, plat., Qc., Can. F16 106
Lau Ridge, unds. L21 142
Laurier, Mb., Can. D14 124
Laurier-Station, Qc., Can. D5 110
Laurinburg, N.C., U.S. B6 116
Laurium, Mi., U.S. D10 118
Lausanne, Switz. D3 22
Lausitzer Neisse (Nysa Łużycka), stm., Eur. F10 16
Laut, Pulau, i., Indon. A5 50
Laut, Pulau, i., Indon. E10 50
Laut, Selat, strt., Indon. E9 50
Lauta, Ger. E9 16
Lautaro, Chile I1 92
Lauterbach, Ger. F5 16
Lauter Sachsen, Ger. F8 16
Laut Kecil, Kepulauan, is., Indon. F9 50
Lautoka, Fiji p18 79e
Lauzerte, Fr. E7 18
Lava (Łyna), stm., Eur. B16 16
Lava Beds National Monument, p.o.i., Ca., U.S. B4 134
Lavaca, stm., Tx., U.S. E11 130
Laval, Qc., Can. E3 110
Laval, Fr. F8 14
La Vall d'Uixó, Spain E10 20
Lavalle, Arg. D5 92
Lavalle, Arg. D8 92
Lavapié, Punta, c., Chile H1 92
Lavassaare, Est. G11 8
La Vega, Dom. Rep. C12 102
La Vela de Coro, Ven. B7 86
Lavelanet, Fr. G7 18
Lavello, Italy C9 24
La Venada, Mex. I10 130
La Venta, hist., Mex. F11 100
La Ventura, Mex. C8 100
La Vera, reg., Spain D5 20
La Vergne, Tn., U.S. H11 120
Laverne, Ok., U.S. E9 128
Laverton, Austl. E4 74
La Veta, Co., U.S. D4 128
Lavieille, Lake, l., On., Can. C11 112
La Vila Joiosa, Spain F10 20
Lavillette, N.B., Can. C11 110
La Viña, Arg. B5 92
Lavina, Mt., U.S. A4 126
La Vista, Ne., U.S. C1 120
La Voulte-sur-Rhône, Fr. E10 18
Lavras, Braz. K3 88
Lávrio, Grc. F7 28
Lavumisa, Swaz. E10 70
Lawang, Indon. G8 50
Lawas, Malay. A9 50
Lawdar, Yemen G6 56
Lawers, Ben, mtn., Scot., U.K. E8 12
Lawgi, Austl. E8 76
Lawksawk, Mya. B3 48
Lawler, Ia., U.S. A5 120
Lawn, Tx., U.S. B8 130
Lawndale, N.C., U.S. A4 116
Lawn Hill, Austl. C7 74
Lawn Hill Creek, stm., Austl. C7 74
Lawrence, In., U.S. I3 112
Lawrence, Ks., U.S. F2 120
Lawrence, Ma., U.S. B14 114
Lawrenceburg, In., U.S. E12 120
Lawrenceburg, Ky., U.S. F12 120
Lawrenceburg, Tn., U.S. B11 122
Lawrenceville, Il., U.S. F10 120
Lawrenceville, N.J., U.S. D11 114
Lawson, Mo., U.S. E3 120
Lawtey, Fl., U.S. F3 116
Lawton, N.D., U.S. F15 124
Lawton, Ok., U.S. G10 128
Lawu, Gunung, vol., Indon. G7 50
Lawz, Jabal al-, mtn., Sau. Ar. J6 58
Laxå, Swe. G6 8
Laxe, Spain A1 20
Lay Lake, res., Al., U.S. D12 122
Layou, St. Vin. o11 105e
Layton, Ut., U.S. B4 132
Laytonville, Ca., U.S. D2 134
La Zarca, Mex. C6 100
Lazarev, Russia F17 34
Lázaro Cárdenas, Mex. G7 100
Lázaro Cárdenas, Presa, res., Mex. C6 100
Lazdijai, Lith. F6 10
Lazio, state, Italy B6 24
Léach, Camb. F6 48
Leachville, Ar., U.S. I7 120
Lead, S.D., U.S. C9 126
Leadbetter Point, c., Wa., U.S. D2 136
Leader, Sk., Can. D4 124
Lead Hill, hill, Mo., U.S. H4 120
Leadore, Id., U.S. F13 136
Leadville, Co., U.S. D10 132
Leaf, stm., Ms., U.S. F10 122
Leaf Lake, l., Sk., Can. A11 124
Leaghur, Lake, l., Austl. I4 76
League City, Tx., U.S. H3 122
Leakey, Tx., U.S. E8 130
Leaksville, N.C., U.S. H5 114
Lealman, Fl., U.S. I3 116
Leamington, On., Can. F7 112
Le'an, China H6 42
Leandro, Braz. C3 88
Leandro N. Alem, Arg. C10 92
Leary, Ga., U.S. F14 122
Leatherman Peak, mtn., Id., U.S. F13 136
Leavenworth, Ks., U.S. E2 120
Leavenworth, Wa., U.S. C6 136
Leawood, Ks., U.S. F3 120
Lebak, Phil. G5 52
Lebam, Wa., U.S. D3 136
Lebanon, In., U.S. H3 112
Lebanon, Ks., U.S. B10 128
Lebanon, Ky., U.S. G12 120
Lebanon, N.H., U.S. G4 110
Lebanon, Oh., U.S. E1 114
Lebanon, Or., U.S. F3 136
Lebanon, Pa., U.S. D9 114
Lebanon, S.D., U.S. B13 126
Lebanon, Tn., U.S. H11 120
Lebanon, Va., U.S. H3 114
Lebanon, ctry., Asia E6 58
Lebec, Ca., U.S. I7 134
Lebesby, Nor. A12 8
Le Bic, Qc., Can. B8 110
Lebjaže, Kaz. D13 32
Le Blanc, Fr. H10 14
Lebo, D.R.C. D4 66
Lebo, Ks., U.S. F2 120
Lębork, Pol. B13 16
Lebrija, Spain H4 20
Lebrija, stm., Col. D5 86
Łebsko, Jezioro, l., Pol. B13 16
Lebu, Chile H1 92
Le Carbet, Mart. k6 105c
Lecce, Italy D12 24
Lecco, Italy E6 22
Le Center, Mn., U.S. G5 118
Lech, stm., Eur. H6 16
Lechainá, Grc. F4 28
Lechang, China I5 42
Le Chesne, Fr. E13 14
Lechiguanas, Islas de las, is., Arg. F8 92
Lechuguilla, Cerro, mtn., Mex. D6 100
Lecompte, La., U.S. F6 122
Le Creusot, Fr. H13 14
Le Croisic, Fr. G6 14
Łęczyca, Pol. D15 16
Ledesma, Spain C4 20
Le Diamant, Mart. I6 105c
Ledjanaja, gora, mtn., Russia D23 34
Ledo, India C8 46
Ledo, Indon. C6 50
Ledong, China L3 42
Le Dorat, Fr. C7 18
Ledu, China D5 36
Leduc, Ab., Can. C17 138
Leechburg, Pa., U.S. D6 114
Leech Lake, l., Mn., U.S. D4 118
Leedey, Ok., U.S. F9 128
Leeds, Eng., U.K. H11 12
Leeds, Al., U.S. D12 122
Leek, Eng., U.K. H10 12
Leelanau, Lake, l., Mi., U.S. D4 112
Leelanau Peninsula, pen., Mi., U.S. C4 112
Leer, Ger. C3 16
Leesburg, Fl., U.S. H4 116
Leesburg, Ga., U.S. E1 116
Leesburg, Va., U.S. E8 114
Lees Summit, Mo., U.S. F3 120
Leesville, La., U.S. F5 122
Leesville, Tx., U.S. E10 130
Leeton, Austl. J6 76
Leeu-Gamka, S. Afr. H6 70
Leeuwarden, Neth. A14 14
Leeuwin, Cape, c., Austl. F2 74
Lee Vining, Ca., U.S. F6 134
Leeward Islands, is., N.A. h15 96a
Lefkáda, Grc. E3 28
Lefkáda, i., Grc. E3 28
Lefke, N. Cyp. C3 58
Lefkosía see Nicosia, Cyp. C4 58
Lefors, Tx., U.S. F8 128
Le François, Mart. k7 105c
Lefroy, Lake, l., Austl. F4 74
Legal, Ab., Can. C17 138
Leganés, Spain D7 20
Legaspi, Phil. D4 52
Leggett, Ca., U.S. D2 134
Leghorn see Livorno, Italy G7 22
Legion, Zimb. B9 70
Legionowo, Pol. D16 16
Legnago, Italy E8 22
Legnano, Italy E5 22
Legnica, Pol. E12 16
Legnica, state, Pol. E12 16
Le Gosier, Guad. h6 105c
Le Grand, Ca., U.S. F5 134
Le Guelta, Alg. H11 20
Legume, Austl. G9 76
Leh, India A6 54
Le Havre, Fr. E8 14
Lehčevo, Blg. F10 26
Lehigh, Ia., U.S. B3 120
Lehigh, Ok., U.S. C2 122
Lehigh Acres, Fl., U.S. J4 116
Lehighton, Pa., U.S. D10 114
Lehrte, Ger. D5 16
Lehtse, Est. A8 10
Lehua, i., Hi., U.S. A1 78a
Lehututu, Bots. C5 70
Lei, stm., China H5 42
Leiah, Pak. C3 54
Leibnitz, Aus. D12 22
Leicester, Eng., U.K. I11 12
Leichhardt, stm., Austl. A2 76
Leichhardt Falls, wtfl, Austl. B2 76
Leiden (Leyden), Neth. B13 14
Leigh Creek South, Austl. H2 76
Leighton, Al., U.S. C11 122
Leighton Buzzard, Eng., U.K. J12 12
Leinan, Sk., Can. D6 124
Leine, stm., Ger. D5 16
Leinster, hist. reg., Ire. I6 12
Leinster, Mount, mtn., Ire. I6 12
Leipalingis, Lith. F6 10
Leipsic, Oh., U.S. C2 114
Leipzig, Ger. E8 16
Leiria, Port. E2 20
Leiria, state, Port. E2 20
Leisler, Mount, mtn., Austl. D6 74
Leitariegos, Puerto de, p., Spain A4 20
Leitha (Lajta), stm., Eur. H12 16
Leitrim, Ire. H4 12
Leitrim, state, Ire. H5 12
Leivádia, Grc. E5 28
Leiyang, China H5 42
Leizhou Bandao, pen., China K3 42
Lejasciems, Lat. C9 10
Lekeitio, Spain A8 20
Leksozero, ozero, l., Russia E14 8
Le Lamentin, Mart. k6 105c
Leland, Il., U.S. C9 120
Leland, Mi., U.S. C4 112
Leland, Ms., U.S. D8 122
Leleiwi Point, c., Hi., U.S. D7 78a
Leleque, Arg. H2 90
Leles, Indon. G5 50
Leli Shan, mtn., China B8 54
Le Locle, Switz. C3 22
Lelystad, Neth. B14 14
Le Maire, Estrecho de, strt., Arg. J4 90
Le Mans, Fr. G9 14
Le Marin, Mart. I7 105c
Le Mars, Ia., U.S. B1 120
Lema Shilindi, Eth. G8 62
Lemay, Mo., U.S. F7 120
Lembak, Indon. C10 50
Lemdiyya, Alg. H13 20
Leme, Braz. L2 88
Lemesós (Limassol), Cyp. D4 58
Lemhi, stm., Id., U.S. F13 136
Lemhi Pass, p., U.S. F13 136
Lemhi Range, mts., Id., U.S. F13 136
Lemieux Islands, is., Nu., Can. E13 141
Leming, Tx., U.S. E9 130
Lemitar, N.M., U.S. I10 132
Lemmatsi, Est. B9 10
Lemmenjoen kansallispuisto, p.o.i., Fin. B11 8
Lemmon, S.D., U.S. B10 126
Lemmon, Mount, mtn., Az., U.S. K6 132
Lemnos see Límnos, i., Grc. D8 28
Lemoncove, Ca., U.S. G7 134
Le Mont-Dore, N. Cal. n16 79d
Lemoore, Ca., U.S. G6 134
Le Moule, Guad. h6 105c
Lempa, stm., N.A. F3 102
Lempe, Indon. D12 50
Lemro, stm., Mya. B1 48
Le Murge, hills, Italy D10 24
Le Muy, Fr. F12 18
Lemyethna, Mya. D2 48
Lena, Il., U.S. B8 120
Lena, Wi., U.S. D1 112
Lena, stm., Russia B14 34
Lenart, Slvn. D12 22
Lençóis, Braz. G5 88
Lençois Maranhenses, Parque Nacional dos, p.o.i., Braz. B4 88
Lendery, Russia E14 8
Lendinara, Italy E8 22
Lenger, Kaz. F12 32
Lenggor, stm., Malay. K6 48
Lenghu, China D3 36
Lengshuitan, China H4 42
Lenhovda, Swe. H6 8
Leningrad see Sankt-Peterburg, Russia A13 10
Leningradskaja oblast', co., Russia G15 8
Leninogor see Leninogorsk, Kaz. D14 32
Leninogorsk, Kaz. D14 32
Lenin Peak, mtn., Asia B11 56
Leninsk, Kaz. E10 32
Leninsk, Uzb. F12 32
Leninskij, Russia F20 10
Leninsk-Kuzneckij, Russia D15 32
Leninskoe, Russia G15 34
Lennonville, Austl. E3 74
Lennox, S.D., U.S. H2 118
Lennox, Isla, i., Chile K3 90
Lennoxville, Qc., Can. E5 110
Lenoir, N.C., U.S. I4 114
Lenora, Czech Rep. H9 16
Lenore Lake, l., Sk., Can. B9 124
Lenox, Ga., U.S. E2 116
Lenox, Ia., U.S. D3 120
Lenox, Tn., U.S. H8 120
Lens, Fr. D11 14
Lensk, Russia B20 32
Lenti, Hung. C3 26
Lentini, Italy G9 24
Lentua, l., Fin. D13 8
Lentvaris, Lith. F8 10
Lenya, stm., Mya. G4 48
Léo, Burkina G4 64
Leoben, Aus. C12 22
Léogâne, Haiti C11 102
Leola, Ar., U.S. C6 122
Leola, S.D., U.S. B14 126
Leominster, Eng., U.K. I10 12
Leominster, Ma., U.S. B14 114
Léon, Fr. F4 18
León, Mex. E8 100
León, Nic. F4 102
León, Spain B5 20
Leon, Ks., U.S. D12 128
León, co., Spain B5 20
Leon, stm., Tx., U.S. C10 130
León, Montes de, mts., Spain B4 20
Leona, stm., Tx., U.S. F8 130
Leonard, Tx., U.S. D2 122
Leonardtown, Md., U.S. F9 114
Leonardville, Ks., U.S. B11 128
Leonberg, Ger. H4 16
Leones, Arg. F6 92
Leonforte, Italy G8 24
Leongatha, Austl. L5 76
Leoniha, Russia G18 8
Leonora, Austl. E4 74
Leopold and Astrid Coast, cst., Ant. B13 81
Leopoldina, Braz. K4 88
Leopoldo de Bulhões, Braz. I1 88
Léopoldville see Kinshasa, D.R.C. E3 66
Leoti, Ks., U.S. C7 128
Leova, Mol. C15 26
Lepanto see Náfpaktos, Grc. E4 28
Lepanto, Ar., U.S. B8 122
Lepar, Pulau, i., Indon. E5 50
Lepe, Spain G3 20
Lepel', Bela. F11 10
Leping, China G7 42
L'Épiphanie, Qc., Can. E3 110
Lepontine Alps, mts., Eur. C14 18
Lepreau, Point, c., N.B., Can. E10 110
Le Prêcheur, Mart. k6 105c
Lepsi see Lepsy, Kaz. E13 32
Lepsy, Kaz. E13 32
Le Puy, Fr. D9 18
Lequeitio see Lekeitio, Spain A8 20
Lercara Friddi, Italy G7 24
Lerdo, Mex. C7 100
Lerici, Italy F6 22
Lérida, Col. G6 86
Lérida see Lleida, Spain C11 20
Lerma, stm., Mex. E8 100
Le Roy, Il., U.S. D9 120
Le Roy, Ks., U.S. F2 120
Le Roy, N.Y., U.S. B7 114
Lerum, Swe. H5 8
Lerwick, Scot., U.K. n18 12a
Les Abymes, Guad. h5 105c
Le Saint-Esprit, Mart. k7 105c
Les Andelys, Fr. E10 14
Les Anses-d'Arlets, Mart. I6 105c
Les Borges Blanques, Spain C11 20
Lesbos see Lésvos, i., Grc. D9 28
Les Cayes, Haiti C11 102
Leshan, China F5 36
Les Herbiers, Fr. H7 14
Lesina, Lago di, b., Italy I12 22
Lesko, Pol. G18 16
Leskovac, Yugo. F8 26
Leskov Island, i., S. Geor. K12 82
Les Laurentides see Laurentides, Les, plat., Qc., Can. F16 106
Leslie, Ar., U.S. I5 120
Leslie, Mi., U.S. B1 114
Leslie, W.V., U.S. F5 114
Lesneven, Fr. F4 14
Lesnoe, Russia B18 10
Lesogorsk, Russia G17 34
Lesosibirsk, Russia E7 34
Lesotho, ctry., Afr. F9 70
Lesozavodsk, Russia B10 38
Lesozavodskij, Russia C15 8
Les Sables-d'Olonne, Fr. H7 14
Les Saintes, is., Guad. i5 105c
Lesser Antilles, is. D8 82
Lesser Khingan Range see Xiao Hinggan Ling, mts., China B10 36
Lesser Slave, stm., Ab., Can. A16 138
Lesser Slave Lake, l., Ab., Can. D8 106
Lesser Sunda Islands see Tenggara, Nusa, is., Indon. G6 44
L'Esterre, Gren. q10 105e
Lestock, Sk., Can. C9 124
Le Sueur, Mn., U.S. G4 118
Le Sueur, stm., Mn., U.S. G5 118
Lešukonskoe, Russia D21 8
Lésvos (Lesbos), i., Grc. D9 28
Leszno, Pol. E12 16
Leszno, state, Pol. E12 16
Letaba, stm., S. Afr. C10 70
Letcher, S.D., U.S. D14 126
Letea, Ostrovul, i., Rom. D16 26
Letenye, Hung. C3 26
Lethbridge, Ab., Can. G18 138
Lethem, Guy. F12 86
Le Thillot, Fr. B12 18
Leti, Kepulauan, is., Indon. G8 44
Leticia, Col. D4 84
Letlhakane, Bots. B7 70
Letlhakeng, Bots. D7 70
Letnjaja Zolotica, Russia D17 8
Letpadan, Mya. D2 48
Le Tréport, Fr. D10 14
Letsôk-aw Kyun, i., Mya. G3 48
Letung, Indon. B4 50
Leucas see Lefkáda, i., Grc. E3 28
Leucate, Étang de, l., Fr. G9 18
Leuk, Switz. D4 22
Leuser, Gunung, mtn., Indon. K3 48
Leutkirch, Ger. I6 16
Leuven, Bel. D13 14
Levack, On., Can. B8 112
Levan, Ut., U.S. D5 132
Levanger, Nor. E4 8
Levante, Riviera di, cst., Italy F6 22
Levanzo, Isola di, i., Italy F6 24
Le Vauclin, Mart. k7 105c
Levelland, Tx., U.S. H6 128
Leveque, Cape, c., Austl. C4 74
Leverkusen, Ger. E3 16
Levice, Slov. H14 16
Levin, N.Z. E6 80
Lévis, Qc., Can. D5 110
Levisa Fork, stm., U.S. G3 114
Levittown, P.R. B3 104a
Levittown, N.Y., U.S. D12 114
Levittown, Pa., U.S. D11 114
Levkosía see Nicosia, Cyp. C4 58
Levoča, Slov. H16 16
Levski, Blg. F12 26
Levuka, Fiji p19 79e
Lėvuo, stm., Lith. E7 10
Lewe, Mya. C2 48
Lewellen, Ne., U.S. F10 126
Lewer, stm., Nmb. D3 70
Lewes, De., U.S. F10 114
Lewin Brzeski, Pol. F13 16
Lewis, Ia., U.S. J3 118
Lewis, Butt of, c., Scot., U.K. C6 12
Lewis, Isle of, i., Scot., U.K. C6 12
Lewis, Mount, mtn., Nv., U.S. C8 134
Lewis and Clark Lake, res., U.S. E15 126
Lewis and Clark Range, mts., Mt., U.S. C13 136
Lewisburg, Ky., U.S. H10 120
Lewisburg, Pa., U.S. D8 114
Lewisburg, Tn., U.S. B12 122
Lewis Range, mts., N.A. B13 136
Lewis Run, Pa., U.S. C7 114
Lewis Smith Lake, res., Al., U.S. C11 122
Lewiston, Ca., U.S. C3 134
Lewiston, Id., U.S. D10 136
Lewiston, Me., U.S. F6 110
Lewiston, Mi., U.S. D5 112
Lewiston, Mn., U.S. H7 118
Lewiston, Ut., U.S. B5 132
Lewiston Orchards, Id., U.S. D10 136
Lewistown, Il., U.S. D7 120
Lewistown, Mt., U.S. C17 136
Lewistown, Pa., U.S. D8 114
Lewisville, N.B., Can. D12 110
Lewisville, Ar., U.S. D5 122
Lewisville, Tx., U.S. A10 130
Lewisville Lake, res., Tx., U.S. H12 128
Lewvan, Sk., Can. D9 124
Lexa, Ar., U.S. C8 122
Lexington, Ga., U.S. C2 116
Lexington, Il., U.S. D9 120
Lexington, Ky., U.S. F1 114
Lexington, Ma., U.S. B14 114
Lexington, Mi., U.S. E7 112
Lexington, Ms., U.S. D8 122
Lexington, N.C., U.S. I5 114
Lexington, Ok., U.S. F11 128
Lexington, Or., U.S. E7 136
Lexington, S.C., U.S. C4 116
Lexington, Tx., U.S. D10 130
Lexington, Va., U.S. G6 114
Lexington Park, Md., U.S. F9 114
Leyden see Leiden, Neth. B13 14
Leye, China I2 42
Leyte, i., Phil. E5 52
Leyte Gulf, b., Phil. E5 52
Lezhë, Alb. C13 24
Lezhi, China F1 42
Lëzna, Bela. E13 10
L'gov, Russia D5 32
Lhasa, China D13 54
Lhasa, stm., China C13 54
Lhazê, China D11 54
Lhoknga, Indon. J2 48
Lhokseumawe, Indon. J3 48
Lhoksukon, Indon. J3 48
Lhorong, China E4 36
L'Hospitalet de Llobregat, Spain C13 20
Lhuntsi Dzong, Bhu. E13 54
Li, Thai. D4 48
Li, stm., China G4 42
Li, stm., Thai. D4 48
Liamuiga, Mount, vol., St. K./N. C2 105a
Lian, stm., China I5 42
Liancheng, China I7 42
Lianga, Phil. F6 52
Liangbao, China D4 42
Liangbuaya, Indon. C10 50
Liangdang, China E1 42
Lianghekou, China G3 42
Liangmentou, China G9 42
Liangping, China F2 42
Liangyuan, China E7 42
Liangzi Hu, l., China F6 42
Lianhuapao, China B8 38
Lianhua Shan, mts., China J6 42
Lianjiang, China K4 42
Liannan, China I5 42
Lianshui, China E8 42
Lianxian, China I5 42
Lianyuan, China H4 42
Lianyungang, China D8 42
Liao, stm., China D5 38
Liaocheng, China C7 42
Liaodong Bandao (Liaotung Peninsula), pen., China D5 38
Liaodong Wan (Liaotung, Gulf of), b., China A9 42
Liaoning, state, China D5 38
Liaotung, Gulf of see Liaodong Wan, b., China A9 42
Liaotung Peninsula see Liaodong Bandao, pen., China E5 38
Liaoyang, China D5 38
Liaoyuan, China C6 38
Liaozhong, China D5 38
Liard, stm., Can. C6 106
Liat, Pulau, i., Indon. E5 50
Libagon, Phil. E5 52
Líbano, Col. E4 86
Libby, Mt., U.S. B11 136
Libby Dam, dam, Mt., U.S. B11 136
Libenge, D.R.C. D3 66
Liberal, Ks., U.S. D7 128
Liberal, Mo., U.S. G3 120
Liberec, Czech Rep. F11 16
Liberia, C.R. G5 102
Liberia, ctry., Afr. H3 64
Liberta, Antig. f4 105b
Libertad, Ven. C7 86
Libertad, Ven. C7 86
Libertador General Bernardo O'Higgins, state, Chile G2 92
Liberty, Ms., U.S. F8 122
Liberty, Mo., U.S. E3 120
Liberty, N.Y., U.S. C11 114
Liberty, N.C., U.S. I6 114
Liberty, S.C., U.S. B3 116
Liberty, Tx., U.S. G4 122
Liberty Center, Oh., U.S. G5 112
Libertyville, Il., U.S. B9 120
Libo, China I2 42
Libobo, Tanjung, c., Indon. F8 44
Libode, S. Afr. G9 70
Libourne, Fr. E5 18
Librazhd, Alb. C14 24
Libres, Mex. F10 100
Libreville, Gabon D1 66
Liburung, Indon. F12 50
Libya, ctry., Afr. B3 62
Libyan Desert, des., Afr. C5 62
Libyan Plateau, plat., Afr. A4 62
Licancábur, Volcán, vol., S.A. D3 90
Licantén, Chile G1 92
Licata, Italy G7 24
Lich, Ger. F4 16
Licheng, China C5 42
Licheng see Liyang, China F8 42
Lichfield, Eng., U.K. I11 12
Lichinga, Moz. C6 68
Lichtenau, Ger. E5 16
Lichtenburg, S. Afr. E7 70
Lichtenfels, Ger. F7 16
Lichuan, China H7 42
Lichuan, China F3 42
Licking, Mo., U.S. G6 120
Licking, stm., Ky., U.S. F1 114
Ličko Polje, val., Cro. F12 22
Lida, Bela. G8 10
Liddon Gulf, b., N.T., Can. B17 140
Liden, Swe. E7 8
Lidgerwood, N.D., U.S. E1 118
Lidköping, Swe. G5 8
Lido di Ostia, Italy I9 22
Lidzbark, Pol. C15 16
Lidzbark Warmiński, Pol. B16 16
Liebenbergsvlei, stm., S. Afr. E9 70
Liebig, Mount, mtn., Austl. D6 74
Liechtenstein, ctry., Eur. C6 22
Liège (Luik), Bel. D14 14
Lielais Liepu kalns, hill, Lat. D10 10
Lielvārde, Lat. D7 10
Lienchou see Hepu, China K3 42
Lienz, Aus. D9 22
Liepāja, Lat. D3 10
Liepājas ezers, l., Lat. D4 10
Lier, Bel. C13 14
Lierre see Lier, Bel. C13 14
Liestal, Switz. C4 22
Liești, Rom. D14 26
Liévin, Fr. D11 14
Lièvre, stm., Qc., Can. C14 112
Liezen, Aus. C11 22
Liffey, stm., Ire. H6 12
Lifford, Ire. G5 12
Lifou, i., N. Cal. m16 79d
Līgatne, Lat. C7 10
Lighthouse Point, Fl., U.S. J5 116
Lighthouse Point, c., Fl., U.S. H14 122
Lighthouse Point, c., Mi., U.S. C4 112
Lightning Creek, stm., Wy., U.S. D7 126
Lightning Ridge, Austl. G6 76
Lignite, N.D., U.S. F11 124
Ligny-en-Barrois, Fr. F14 14
Ligonha, stm., Moz. D6 68
Ligonier, In., U.S. G4 112
Ligonier, Pa., U.S. H10 112
Liguria, state, Italy F5 22
Ligurian Sea, Eur. G5 22
Lihir Island, i., Pap. N. Gui. a5 79a
Lihoslavl', Russia C18 10
Lihou Reefs and Cays, rf., Austl. A8 76
Lihue, Hi., U.S. B2 78a
Lihuel Calel, Parque Nacional, p.o.i., Arg. H5 92
Lihula, Est. B6 10
Lijiang, China F5 36
Lik, stm., Laos C6 48
Likasi (Jadotville), D.R.C. G5 66
Likati, D.R.C. D4 66
Likely, B.C., Can. D9 138
Liki, Indon. D2 50
Likino-Dulevo, Russia E21 10
Lilbourn, Mo., U.S. H8 120
Lilibeo, Capo see Boeo, Capo, c., Italy G6 24
Lilienfeld, Aus. B12 22
Liling, China H5 42
Lille, Fr. D12 14
Lillebælt, strt., Den. I3 8
Lillebonne, Fr. E9 14
Lillehammer, Nor. F3 8
Lillers, Fr. D11 14
Lillestrøm, Nor. F4 8
Lillhärdal, Swe. F6 8
Lillington, N.C., U.S. A7 116
Lillooet, B.C., Can. F9 138
Lillooet, stm., B.C., Can. G8 138
Lillooet Lake, l., B.C., Can. F8 138
Lilongwe, Mwi. C5 68
Liloy, Phil. F4 52
Lilydale, Austl. n13 77a
Lim, stm., Eur. G16 22
Lima, Para. A9 92
Lima, Peru F2 84
Lima, Mt., U.S. F14 136
Lima, N.Y., U.S. B8 114
Lima, Oh., U.S. D1 114
Lima (Limia), stm., Eur. C2 20
Limarí, stm., Chile E2 92
Limas, Indon. C4 50
Limassol see Lemesós, Cyp. D4 58
Limavady, N. Ire., U.K. F6 12
Limay, stm., Arg. G3 90
Limay Mahuida, Arg. H4 92
Limbang, Malay. A9 50
Limbang, stm., Malay. A9 50
Līmbdi, India G3 54
Limbe, Cam. D1 66
Limbé, Haiti C11 102
Limbujan see Pio V. Corpuz, Phil. E5 52
Limburg an der Lahn, Ger. F4 16
Limeira, Braz. L2 88
Limerick, Sk., Can. E7 124
Limerick (Luimneach), Ire. I4 12
Limerick, state, Ire. I4 12
Limestone, Me., U.S. D9 110
Limestone, Lake, res., Tx., U.S. F2 122
Limfjorden, l., Den. H3 8
Limia (Lima), stm., Eur. C2 20
Limingen, l., Nor. D5 8
Limmared, Swe. H5 8
Limmen Bight, b., Austl. B7 74
Límnos, i., Grc. D8 28
Limoeiro, Braz. D8 88
Limoeiro do Norte, Braz. C6 88
Limoges, Fr. D7 18
Limón, Hond. E5 102
Limone Piemonte, Italy F4 22
Limoux, Fr. F8 18
Limpopo, stm., Afr. D8 70
Linahamari, Russia B14 8
Lin'an, China F8 42
Linapacan Island, i., Phil. E2 52
Linares, Chile G2 92
Linares, Mex. C9 100
Linares, Spain F7 20
Linch, Wy., U.S. D6 126
Lincheng, China C6 42
Linch'ing see Linqing, China C6 42
Lincoln, Arg. G7 92
Lincoln, Eng., U.K. H12 12
Lincoln, Ar., U.S. I3 120
Lincoln, Ca., U.S. E4 134
Lincoln, Il., U.S. D8 120
Lincoln, Mi., U.S. D6 112
Lincoln, Mo., U.S. F4 120
Lincoln, Mt., U.S. D14 136
Lincoln, Ne., U.S. K2 118
Lincoln, N.H., U.S. F5 110
Lincoln, Mount, mtn., Co., U.S. B2 128
Lincoln City, Or., U.S. F2 136
Lincoln Creek, stm., Ne., U.S. F15 126
Lincoln Park, Co., U.S. C3 128
Lincoln Park, Mi., U.S. B2 114
Lincoln Sea, N.A. A13 141
Lincolnton, Ga., U.S. C3 116
Lincolnton, N.C., U.S. A4 116
Lincoln Village, Ca., U.S. F4 134
Lindale, Ga., U.S. C13 122
Lindale, Tx., U.S. E3 122
Lindau, Ger. I5 16
Linde, stm., Russia C13 34
Linden, Guy. B6 84
Linden, Al., U.S. E11 122
Linden, In., U.S. H3 112
Linden, Mi., U.S. B2 114
Linden, Tn., U.S. B11 122
Lindesnes, c., Nor. H2 8
Lindi, Tan. F7 66
Lindi, stm., D.R.C. D5 66
Líndos, hist., Grc. G10 28
Lind Point, c., V.I.U.S. e7 104b
Lindsay, On., Can. D11 112
Lindsay, Ca., U.S. G6 134
Lindsay, Ne., U.S. F15 126
Lindsay, Ok., U.S. G11 128
Line Islands, is., Oc. D11 72
Linesville, Pa., U.S. C5 114
Lineville, Al., U.S. D13 122
Lineville, Ia., U.S. D4 120
Linfen, China C4 42
Linganamakki Reservoir, res., India D2 53
Lingao, China L3 42
Lingayen, Phil. B3 52
Lingayen Gulf, b., Phil. B3 52
Lingbi, China E7 42
Lingbo, Swe. F7 8
Lingchuan, China D5 42

Name	Map Ref.	Page
Lingen, Ger.	D3	16
Lingfengwei, China	I6	42
Lingga, Kepulauan, is., Indon.	C4	50
Lingga, Pulau, i., Indon.	D4	50
Lingomo II, D.R.C.	D4	66
Lingqiu, China	B6	42
Lingshan, China	J3	42
Lingshi, China	C4	42
Lingshui, China	L4	42
Linguère, Sen.	F2	64
Lingwu, China	B2	42
Lingxian, China	H5	42
Lingyuan, China	A8	42
Linh, Ngoc, mtn., Viet.	E9	48
Linhai, China	G9	42
Linhares, Braz.	J5	88
Linhe, China	A2	42
Linhsia see Linxia, China	D5	36
Lini see Linyi, China	D8	42
Linjiang, China	D7	38
Linköping, Swe.	G6	8
Linkou, China	B9	38
Linksmakalnis, Lith.	F6	10
Linkuva, Lith.	D6	10
Linn, Ks., U.S.	B11	128
Linn, Mo., U.S.	F6	120
Linnansaaren kansallispuisto, p.o.i., Fin.	E13	8
Linnhe, Loch, b., Scot., U.K.	E7	12
Linqi, China	D5	42
Linqing, China	C6	42
Linqu, China	C8	42
Linquan, China	E6	42
Linru, China	D5	42
Lins, Braz.	K1	88
Linstead, Jam.	i13	104d
Lintan, China	E5	36
Linton, In., U.S.	E10	120
Linton, N.D., U.S.	A12	126
Lintong, China	D3	42
Linwu, China	I5	42
Linxi, China	C8	36
Linxi, China	C3	38
Linxia, China	D5	36
Linxian, China	C4	42
Linxian, China	C5	42
Linyi, China	D8	42
Linyi, China	C7	42
Linyü see Shanhaiguan, China	A8	42
Linz, Aus.	B11	22
Lio Matoh, Malay.	B9	50
Lion, Golfe du, b., Fr.	G10	18
Lion, Gulf of see Lion, Golfe du, b., Fr.	G10	18
Lionel Town, Jam.	j13	104d
Liouesso, Congo	D3	66
Lipa, Phil.	D3	52
Lipan, Tx., U.S.	B9	130
Lipari, Italy	F8	24
Lipari, Isola, i., Italy	F9	24
Lipari, Isole see Eolie, Isole, is., Italy	F8	24
Lipcani, Mol.	A13	26
Lipeck, Russia	D6	32
Lípez, Cerro, mtn., Bol.	D3	90
Lipicy, Russia	G20	10
Liping, China	H3	42
Lipki, Russia	G20	10
Lipník nad Bečvou, Czech Rep.	G13	16
Lipno, Pol.	D15	16
Lipno, údolní nádrž, res., Czech Rep.	H10	16
Lipova, Rom.	C8	26
Lipovcy, Russia	B9	38
Lippe, stm., Ger.	E2	16
Lippstadt, Ger.	E4	16
Lipscomb, Tx., U.S.	E8	128
Lipsoí, i., Grc.	F9	28
Liptovská Teplička, Slov.	G15	16
Liptovský Mikuláš, Slov.	G15	16
Liptrap, Cape, c., Austl.	L5	76
Lipu, China	I4	42
Lira, Ug.	D6	66
Liri, stm., Italy	C7	24
Liria see Llíria, Spain	E10	20
Liro, Vanuatu	k17	79d
Lisala, D.R.C.	D4	66
Lisboa (Lisbon), Port.	F1	20
Lisboa, state, Port.	E1	20
Lisbon see Lisboa, Port.	F1	20
Lisbon, N.H., U.S.	F5	110
Lisbon, N.D., U.S.	A15	126
Lisbon, Oh., U.S.	D5	114
Lisburn, N. Ire., U.K.	G6	12
Lisburne, Cape, c., Ak., U.S.	C6	140
Lishi, China	C4	42
Lishu, China	C6	38
Lishui, China	G8	42
Lishuzhen, China	B9	38
Lisicy, Russia	D19	10
Lisieux, Sk., Can.	E7	124
Lisieux, Fr.	E9	14
Liski, Russia	D5	32
L'Isle-Jourdain, Fr.	C6	18
Lisman, Al., U.S.	E10	122
Lismore, Austl.	G9	76
Lismore, N.S., Can.	E14	110
Lišov, Czech Rep.	G10	16
Listowel, On., Can.	E9	112
Listowel, Ire.	I3	12
Litang, China	F5	36
Litang, China	J3	42
Litchfield, Il., U.S.	E8	120
Litchfield, Mn., U.S.	F4	118
Litchfield, Ne., U.S.	F13	126
Litchville, N.D., U.S.	A14	126
Lithgow, Austl.	I8	76
Líthinon, Ákra, c., Grc.	I7	28
Lithonia, Ga., U.S.	D14	122
Lithuania, ctry., Eur.	E7	10
Litija, Slvn.	D11	22
Lititz, Pa., U.S.	D9	114
Litoměřice, Czech Rep.	F10	16
Litomyšl, Czech Rep.	G12	16
Litovko, Russia	G16	34
Little, stm., U.S.	D5	122
Little, stm., U.S.	B8	122
Little, stm., Ga., U.S.	C3	116
Little, stm., N.C., U.S.	A7	116
Little, stm., Ok., U.S.	F11	128
Little, stm., Tx., U.S.	D11	130
Little, Mountain Fork, stm., U.S.	C4	122
Little Abaco, i., Bah.	B9	96
Little Andaman, i., India	F7	46
Little Arkansas, stm., Ks., U.S.	C11	128
Little Beaver Creek, stm., U.S.	A8	126
Little Beaver Creek, stm., U.S.	B7	128
Little Belt see Lillebælt, strt., Den.	I3	8
Little Belt Mountains, mts., Mt., U.S.	D16	136
Little Bighorn, stm., U.S.	B5	126
Little Bighorn Battlefield National Monument, p.o.i., Mt., U.S.	B5	126
Little Blue, stm., U.S.	G15	126
Little Buffalo, stm., Can.	C8	106
Little Carpathians see Malé Karpaty, mts., Slov.	H13	16
Little Cayman, i., Cay. Is.	C7	102
Little Chute, Wi., U.S.	D1	112
Little Colorado, stm., Az., U.S.	H5	132
Little Current, On., Can.	C8	112
Little Current, stm., On., Can.	A12	118
Little Deep Creek, stm., N.D., U.S.	F12	124
Little Deschutes, stm., Or., U.S.	G5	136
Little Desert, des., Austl.	K3	76
Little Desert National Park, p.o.i., Austl.	K3	76
Little Dry Creek, stm., Mt., U.S.	G7	124
Little Falls, Mn., U.S.	E4	118
Little Falls, N.Y., U.S.	E15	112
Littlefork, Mn., U.S.	C5	118
Little Fork, stm., Mn., U.S.	C5	118
Little Hurricane Creek, stm., Ga., U.S.	E3	116
Little Inagua, i., Bah.	B11	102
Little Kanawha, stm., W.V., U.S.	E4	114
Little Karroo (Klein Karroo), plat., S. Afr.	H5	70
Little Lake, l., La., U.S.	H8	122
Little London, Jam.	i12	104d
Little Lost, stm., Id., U.S.	F13	136
Little Mexico, Tx., U.S.	D4	130
Little Missouri, stm., U.S.	B7	108
Little Missouri, stm., Ar., U.S.	D5	122
Little Namaqualand (Klein Namaland), hist. reg., S. Afr.	F3	70
Little Nicobar, i., India	G7	46
Little Osage, stm., U.S.	G3	120
Little Pee Dee, stm., S.C., U.S.	B6	116
Little Pic, stm., On., Can.	C12	118
Little Powder, stm., U.S.	B7	126
Little Quill Lake, l., Sk., Can.	C10	124
Little Rann of Kachchh, reg., India	G3	54
Little Red, stm., Ar., U.S.	B7	122
Little Red, Middle Fork, stm., Ar., U.S.	B6	122
Little Red Deer, stm., Ab., Can.	E16	138
Little River, Ks., U.S.	C10	128
Little Rock, Ar., U.S.	C6	122
Little Rock, stm., U.S.	H2	118
Little Sable Point, c., Mi., U.S.	E3	112
Little Saint Bernard Pass, p., Eur.	D12	18
Little Sandy Creek, stm., Wy., U.S.	E3	126
Little Sioux, stm., U.S.	J3	118
Little Sioux, West Fork, stm., Ia., U.S.	B2	120
Little Smoky, stm., Ab., Can.	A14	138
Little Snake, stm., U.S.	C8	132
Littlestown, Pa., U.S.	E8	114
Little Tallapoosa, stm., U.S.	D13	122
Little Tennessee, stm., U.S.	A1	116
Little Tobago, i., Trin.	r13	105f
Littleton, Co., U.S.	B3	128
Littleton, N.H., U.S.	F5	110
Littleton, W.V., U.S.	E5	114
Little Valley, N.Y., U.S.	B7	114
Little Wabash, stm., Il., U.S.	F9	120
Little White, stm., S.D., U.S.	D12	126
Little Wood, stm., Id., U.S.	G12	136
Litvínov, Czech Rep.	F9	16
Liu, stm., China	C6	38
Liu, stm., China	C5	38
Liu, stm., China	I3	42
Liuaniua see Ontong Java, at., Sol. Is.	D7	72
Liuba, China	E2	42
Liuboml', Ukr.	E20	16
Liuchen, China	J4	42
Liucheng, China	I3	42
Liuchow see Liuzhou, China	I3	42
Liucura, Chile	I2	92
Liufang, China	H7	42
Liuhe, China	C6	38
Liuheng Dao, i., China	G10	42
Liujiazi, China	A9	42
Liupan Shan, mts., China	D2	42
Liushuquan, China	F16	32
Liuxi, stm., China	J5	42
Liuyang, China	G5	42
Liuyang, stm., China	G5	42
Liuzhou, China	I3	42
Livada, Rom.	B10	26
Livadija, Russia	C10	38
Līvāni, Lat.	D9	10
Livanjsko Polje, val., Bos.	F3	26
Lively, On., Can.	B8	112
Lively Island, i., Falk. Is.	J5	90
Live Oak, Ca., U.S.	D4	134
Live Oak, Fl., U.S.	F2	116
Liveringa, Austl.	C4	74
Livermore, Ca., U.S.	F4	134
Livermore, Ia., U.S.	B3	120
Livermore, Ky., U.S.	G10	120
Livermore, Mount, mtn., Tx., U.S.	D3	130
Livermore Falls, Me., U.S.	F6	110
Liverpool, N.S., Can.	F12	110
Liverpool, Eng., U.K.	H10	12
Liverpool, Cape, c., Nu., Can.	C10	141
Liverpool Bay, b., N.T., Can.	A5	106
Liverpool Bay, b., Eng., U.K.	H9	12
Lívingston, Guat.	E3	102
Livingston, Al., U.S.	E10	122
Livingston, Il., U.S.	F8	120
Livingston, La., U.S.	G8	122
Livingston, Mt., U.S.	E16	136
Livingston, Tn., U.S.	H12	120
Livingston, Tx., U.S.	G4	122
Livingston, Wi., U.S.	B7	120
Livingston, Lake, res., Tx., U.S.	G3	122
Livingstone, Zam.	D4	68
Livingstone Falls, wtfl, Afr.	A1	68
Livingstonia, Mwi.	C5	68
Livingston Manor, N.Y., U.S.	C11	114
Livno, Bos.	F4	26
Livny, Russia	H20	10
Livonia, La., U.S.	G7	122
Livonia, Mi., U.S.	B2	114
Livonia, N.Y., U.S.	B8	114
Livorno (Leghorn), Italy	G7	22
Livramento do Brumado, Braz.	G5	88
Liwale, Tan.	F7	66
Lixi, China	G6	42
Lixian, China	G4	42
Lixian, China	D1	42
Lixian see Black, stm., Asia	D9	56
Lixin, China	E7	42
Lixoúri, Grc.	E3	28
Liyang, China	F8	42
Lizarda, Braz.	E2	88
Lizard Point, c., Eng., U.K.	L7	12
Lizarra see Estella, Spain	B8	20
Ljady, Bela.	F14	10
Ljahavičy, Bela.	G9	10
Ljahovskie ostrova, is., Russia	B17	34
Ljamca, Russia	D17	8
Ljaskavičy, Bela.	H11	10
Ljasnaja, Bela.	G8	10
Ljuban', Bela.	H10	10
Ljuban', Russia	A14	10
Ljubercy, Russia	E20	10
Ljubimec, Blg.	H12	26
Ljubljana, Slvn.	D11	22
Ljubnica, Russia	C15	10
Ljubohna, Russia	G17	10
Ljubuški, Bos.	F4	26
Ljudinovo, Russia	G17	10
Ljudkovo, Russia	F17	10
Ljungan, stm., Swe.	E5	8
Ljungby, Swe.	H5	8
Ljusdal, Swe.	F7	8
Ljusina, Bela.	H9	10
Ljusnan, stm., Swe.	F6	8
Llancanelo, Laguna, l., Arg.	G3	92
Llandeilo, Wales, U.K.	J8	12
Llandrindod Wells, Wales, U.K.	I9	12
Llandudno, Wales, U.K.	H9	12
Llanelli, Wales, U.K.	J8	12
Llangefni, Wales, U.K.	H8	12
Llanidloes, Wales, U.K.	I9	12
Llano, stm., Tx., U.S.	D8	130
Llano Colorado, Mex.	L9	134
Llanos, pl., S.A.	E7	86
Llanquihue, Lago, l., Chile	H2	90
Lleida, Spain	C11	20
Lleida, co., Spain	B12	20
Llera de Canales, Mex.	D9	100
Llerena, Spain	F4	20
Lleulleu, Lago, l., Chile	I1	92
Llico, Chile	G1	92
Llíria, Spain	E10	20
Llivia, Spain	B12	20
Llobregat, stm., Spain	C12	20
Lloydminster, Sk., Can.	E9	106
Llucena, Spain	D10	20
Lluchmayor see Llucmajor, Spain	E13	20
Llucmajor, Spain	E13	20
Llullaillaco, Volcán, vol., S.A.	B3	92
Lo (Panlong), stm., Asia	A7	48
Loa, Ut., U.S.	E5	132
Loa, stm., Chile	D3	90
Loanda, Braz.	D6	90
Loange (Luangue), stm., Afr.	F3	66
Lobamba, Swaz.	E10	70
Lobanovo, Russia	G21	10
Lobatse, Bots.	D7	70
Löbau, Ger.	E10	16
Lobaye, stm., C.A.R.	D3	66
Lobelville, Tn., U.S.	B11	122
Lobería, Arg.	I8	92
Lobnja, Russia	D20	10
Lobos, Arg.	G8	92
Lobos, Cay, i., Bah.	A9	102
Lobos, Isla, i., Mex.	B3	100
Lobskoe, Russia	E16	8
Łobżenica, Pol.	C13	16
Locarno, Switz.	D5	22
Loches, Fr.	G10	14
Loch Garman see Wexford, Ire.	I6	12
Lochinver, Scot., U.K.	C7	12
Lochsa, stm., Id., U.S.	D12	136
Lock, Austl.	F7	74
Lockeport, N.S., Can.	G11	110
Lockerbie, Scot., U.K.	F9	12
Lockesburg, Ar., U.S.	D4	122
Lockhart, Austl.	J6	76
Lock Haven, Pa., U.S.	C8	114
Lockney, Tx., U.S.	G7	128
Lockport, Il., U.S.	C9	120
Lockport, La., U.S.	H8	122
Lockport, N.Y., U.S.	E11	112
Lockwood, Mo., U.S.	G4	120
Locminé, Fr.	G6	14
Loc Ninh, Viet.	G8	48
Locust Creek, stm., U.S.	D4	120
Locust Fork, stm., Al., U.S.	D11	122
Locust Grove, Ok., U.S.	H2	120
Lod (Lydda), Isr.	G5	58
Lodalskåpa, mtn., Nor.	F2	8
Loddon, stm., Austl.	K4	76
Lodejnoe Pole, Russia	F15	8
Lodève, Fr.	F9	18
Lodge Creek, stm., N.A.	F4	124
Lodge Grass, Mt., U.S.	B5	126
Lodgepole, Ab., Can.	C15	138
Lodgepole, Ne., U.S.	F10	126
Lodgepole Creek, stm., U.S.	F10	126
Lodhrān, Pak.	D3	54
Lodi, Italy	E6	22
Lodi, Ca., U.S.	E4	134
Lodi, Wi., U.S.	H9	118
Lodja, D.R.C.	E4	66
Lodwar, Kenya	D7	66
Łódź, Pol.	E15	16
Łódź, state, Pol.	E15	16
Loei, Thai.	D5	48
Loei, stm., Thai.	D5	48
Loeriesfontein, S. Afr.	G4	70
Lofer, Aus.	C9	22
Lofoten, is., Nor.	B5	8
Lofoten Basin, unds.	A14	144
Loga, Niger	G5	64
Logan, Ia., U.S.	C2	120
Logan, Ks., U.S.	B9	128
Logan, Oh., U.S.	E3	114
Logan, Ut., U.S.	B5	132
Logan, W.V., U.S.	G4	114
Logan, Mount, mtn., Yk., Can.	C2	106
Logan Creek, stm., Ne., U.S.	E15	126
Logan Island, i., On., Can.	A10	118
Logan Martin Lake, res., Al., U.S.	D12	122
Logan Mountains, mts., Yk., Can.	C5	106
Logan Pass, p., Mt., U.S.	B13	136
Logansport, In., U.S.	H3	112
Logansport, La., U.S.	F5	122
Loganville, Ga., U.S.	C2	116
Logone, stm., Afr.	F3	62
Logroño, Spain	B8	20
Løgstør, Den.	H3	8
Logudoro, reg., Italy	D2	24
Lohārdaga, India	G10	54
Lohiniva, Fin.	C11	8
Lohne, Ger.	D4	16
Loho see Luohe, China	E6	42
Lohrville, Ia., U.S.	B3	120
Loi (Nanlei), stm., Asia	B4	48
Loi, Phou, mtn., Laos	B6	48
Loi-kaw, Mya.	C3	48
Loi Mwe, Mya.	B4	48
Loing, stm., Fr.	F11	14
Loing, Canal du, can., Fr.	F11	14
Loir, stm., Fr.	G8	14
Loire, state, Fr.	D10	18
Loire, stm., Fr.	B4	18
Loire, Canal latéral à la, can., Fr.	C9	18
Loire-Atlantique, state, Fr.	G7	14
Loiret, state, Fr.	F11	14
Loir-et-Cher, state, Fr.	G10	14
Loja, Ec.	D2	84
Loja, Spain	G6	20
Lokandu, D.R.C.	E5	66
Lokan Reservoir see Lokan tekojärvi, res., Fin.	C12	8
Lokan tekojärvi, res., Fin.	C12	8
Lokeren, Bel.	C13	14
Loket, Czech Rep.	F8	16
Lokichar, Kenya	D7	66
Lokichokio, Kenya	D6	66
Loknja, Russia	D13	10
Lokoja, Nig.	H6	64
Lokolama, D.R.C.	E3	66
Lokot', Russia	H17	10
Loksa, Est.	A8	10
Loks Land, i., Nu., Can.	E13	141
Lola, Gui.	H3	64
Loleta, Ca., U.S.	C1	134
Loliondo, Tan.	E7	66
Lolita, Tx., U.S.	F11	130
Lolland, i., Den.	I4	8
Lolo, Mt., U.S.	D12	136
Lolodorf, Cam.	D2	66
Lolo Pass, p., U.S.	D12	136
Lolowai, Vanuatu	j16	79d
Loltong, Vanuatu	j16	79d
Lolvavana, Passage, strt., Vanuatu	j16	79d
Lom, Blg.	F10	26
Lom, Nor.	F3	8
Lom, stm., Afr.	F2	62
Lomami, stm., D.R.C.	D4	66
Lomas de Zamora, Arg.	G8	92
Lomax, Il., U.S.	D6	120
Łomazy, Pol.	E19	16
Lombardia, state, Italy	E6	22
Lombardy see Lombardia, state, Italy	E6	22
Lomblen, Pulau, i., Indon.	G7	44
Lombok, Indon.	H10	50
Lombok, i., Indon.	H10	50
Lombok, Selat, strt., Indon.	H9	50
Lomé, Togo	H5	64
Lomela, D.R.C.	E4	66
Lomela, stm., D.R.C.	E4	66
Lometa, Tx., U.S.	C9	130
Lomié, Cam.	D2	66
Lomira, Wi., U.S.	H10	118
Lommel, Bel.	C14	14
Lomond, Loch, l., Scot., U.K.	E8	12
Lomonosov, Russia	A12	10
Lomonosovka, Kaz.	D11	32
Lomovoe, Russia	D19	8
Lompobatang, Gunung, mtn., Indon.	F11	50
Lompoc, Ca., U.S.	I5	134
Lom Sak, Thai.	D5	48
Łomża, Pol.	C18	16
Łomża, state, Pol.	C18	16
Lonaconing, Md., U.S.	E7	114
Lonāvale, India	B1	53
Loncoche, Chile	G2	90
Loncopué, Arg.	I2	92
London, On., Can.	F8	112
London, Eng., U.K.	J12	12
London, Ar., U.S.	B5	122
London, Ky., U.S.	G1	114
London, Tx., U.S.	D8	130
Londonderry, N.S., Can.	E13	110
Londonderry (Derry), N. Ire., U.K.	F6	12
Londonderry, Cape, c., Austl.	B5	74
Londonderry, Isla, i., Chile	K2	90
Londrina, Braz.	D6	90
Lone Grove, Ok., U.S.	G11	128
Lone Oak, Ky., U.S.	G9	120
Lone Pine, Ca., U.S.	G7	134
Lone Rock, Wi., U.S.	A7	120
Lone Tree, Ia., U.S.	C6	120
Lone Wolf, Ok., U.S.	G9	128
Long, stm., China	I3	42
Longa, Ang.	C2	68
Longá, stm., Braz.	B5	88
Longa, proliv, strt., Russia	B24	34
Long Akah, Malay.	B9	50
Longana, Vanuatu	j17	79d
Longarone, Italy	D9	22
Longaví, Chile	G2	92
Longbangun, Indon.	C9	50
Long Bay, b., U.S.	C7	116
Long Beach, Ca., U.S.	J7	134
Long Beach, Ms., U.S.	G9	122
Long Beach, N.Y., U.S.	D12	114
Long Beach, Wa., U.S.	D2	136
Long Beach, cst., N.J., U.S.	E11	114
Longboat Key, Fl., U.S.	I3	116
Long Branch, N.J., U.S.	D12	114
Long Cay, i., Bah.	m18	104f
Longchang, China	G1	42
Longchuan, China	I6	42
Long Creek, stm., N.A.	E10	124
Longde, China	D2	42
Long Eaton, Eng., U.K.	I11	12
Longford, Austl.	L6	76
Longford, Ire.	H5	12
Longford, state, Ire.	H5	12
Long Hu, l., China	F6	42
Longhua, China	A7	42
Longhui, China	H4	42
Longiram, Indon.	C9	50
Long Island, i., Antig.	f4	105b
Long Island, i., Austl.	D7	76
Long Island, i., Bah.	A10	102
Long Island, i., Nu., Can.	E14	106
Long Island, i., N.S., Can.	F10	110
Long Island, i., N.Y., U.S.	D12	114
Long Island Sound, strt., U.S.	D12	114
Longitudinal, Valle, val., Chile	H1	92
Longjiang, China	B9	36
Longkou, China	C9	42
Long Lake, N.Y., U.S.	G2	110
Long Lake, l., On., Can.	B11	118
Longleaf, La., U.S.	F6	122
Long Leaf Park, N.C., U.S.	B8	116
Longli, China	H2	42
Longlin, China	G6	36
Longling, China	G4	36
Longmeadow, Ma., U.S.	B13	114
Long Moc, Viet.	C7	48
Longmont, Co., U.S.	A3	128
Long Mountain, mtn., Mo., U.S.	H5	120
Longnan, China	I6	42
Longnawan, Indon.	C9	50
Long Pine, Ne., U.S.	E13	126
Long Point, c., Bah.	n18	104f
Long Point, c., N.S., Can.	D16	110
Long Point, pen., Mb., Can.	A15	124
Long Point, pen., On., Can.	F9	112
Long Point Bay, b., On., Can.	F9	112
Longquan, China	G8	42
Long Range Mountains, mts., Nf., Can.	j22	107a
Longreach, Austl.	D5	76
Long-Sault, On., Can.	E2	110
Longsegah, Indon.	B10	50
Longshan, China	G3	42
Longsheng, China	I3	42
Longs Peak, mtn., Co., U.S.	A3	128
Long Swamp, Br. Vir. Is.	e8	104b
Long Thanh, Viet.	G8	48
Longton, Ks., U.S.	G1	120
Longtown, Eng., U.K.	F10	12
Longueuil, Qc., Can.	E3	110
Longuyon, Fr.	E14	14
Longview, Ab., Can.	F16	138
Long View, N.C., U.S.	I4	114
Longview, Tx., U.S.	E4	122
Longview, Wa., U.S.	D4	136
Longwai, Indon.	C10	50
Longwy, Fr.	E14	14
Longxi, China	E5	36
Longxian, China	D2	42
Long Xuyen, Viet.	G7	48
Longyan, China	I7	42
Longyou, China	G8	42
Longzhen, China	B10	36
Longzhou, China	J2	42
Lonigo, Italy	E8	22
Löningen, Ger.	D3	16
Lonja, stm., Cro.	E13	22
Lonoke, Ar., U.S.	C7	122
Lonquimay, Volcán, vol., Chile	I2	92
Lonsdale, Mn., U.S.	G5	118
Lons-le-Saunier, Fr.	H14	14
Lontra, stm., Braz.	D1	88
Loogootee, In., U.S.	F11	120
Lookout, Cape, c., N.C., U.S.	B9	116
Lookout Mountain, mts., U.S.	C13	122
Lookout Pass, p., U.S.	C11	136
Lookout Ridge, mts., Ak., U.S.	C8	140
Loolmalassin, vol., Tan.	E7	66
Loomis, Ne., U.S.	G13	126
Loomis, Wa., U.S.	B7	136
Loop, Tx., U.S.	B5	130
Loop Head, c., Ire.	I2	12
Lop, China	A5	46
Lop, stm., Viet.	F8	48
Lopatina, gora, mtn., Russia	F17	34
Lopatka, mys, c., Russia	F20	34
Lopatovo, Russia	D12	10
Lop Buri, Thai.	E5	48
Lopévi, i., Vanuatu	k17	79d
Lopez, Cap, c., Gabon	E1	66
Lop Nur, l., China	C3	36
Loptjuga, Russia	E22	8
Lora, Hāmūn-i-, l., Asia	D9	56
Lora del Río, Spain	G5	20
Lorain, Oh., U.S.	C3	114
Loraine, Tx., U.S.	B7	130
Loralai, Pak.	C2	54
Lorca, Spain	G9	20
Lord Howe Island, i., Austl.	G6	72
Lord Howe Rise, unds.	L19	142
Lord Mayor Bay, b., Nu., Can.	B12	106
Lordsburg, N.M., U.S.	K8	132
Loreauville, La., U.S.	G7	122
Loreley, misc. cult., Ger.	F3	16
Lorena, Braz.	L3	88
Lorengau, Pap. N. Gui.	a4	79a
Lorenzo, Tx., U.S.	H7	128
Lorenzo Geyres, Ur.	F9	92
Loreto, Arg.	C9	92
Loreto, Mex.	D8	100
Loreto, Mex.	B3	100
Loreto, state, Peru	H4	86
Loretto, Ky., U.S.	G12	120
Loretto, Tn., U.S.	B11	122
Lorica, Col.	C4	86
Lorient, Fr.	G5	14
Lorimor, Ia., U.S.	C3	120
Loriol-sur-Drôme, Fr.	E10	18
Loris, S.C., U.S.	B7	116
Lorman, Ms., U.S.	F7	122
Lorn, Firth of, b., Scot., U.K.	E7	12
Lorne, Austl.	L5	76
Lorne, N.B., Can.	C10	110
Lörrach, Ger.	I3	16
Lorraine, hist. reg., Fr.	F14	14
Los, Îles de, is., Gui.	H2	64
Losada, stm., Col.	F4	86
Los Alamos, N.M., U.S.	F2	128
Los Aldamas, Mex.	B9	100
Los Andes, Chile	F2	92
Los Angeles, Chile	H1	92
Los Angeles, Ca., U.S.	I7	134
Los Angeles Aqueduct, aq., Ca., U.S.	H7	134
Los Antiguos, Arg.	I2	90
Los Banos, Ca., U.S.	F5	134
Los Blancos, Arg.	D4	90
Los Bolones, Cerro, mtn., Mex.	G12	100
Los Cerrillos, Arg.	E5	92
Los Conquistadores, Arg.	E8	92
Los Fresnos, Tx., U.S.	H10	130
Los Garza, Mex.	H8	130
Los Gatos, Ca., U.S.	F4	134
Loshan see Leshan, China	F5	36
Los Hermanos, Islas, is., Ven.	B9	86
Łosice, Pol.	D18	16
Los Idolos, Parque Arquelógico de, hist., Col.	G3	86
Lošinj, Otok, i., Cro.	F11	22
Losinoborskaja, Russia	C15	32
Los Juríes, Arg.	D6	92
Los Lagos, Chile	G2	90
Los Llanos, P.R.	B3	104a
Los López, Mex.	H8	130
Los Lunas, N.M., U.S.	I10	132
Los Mochis, Mex.	C4	100
Los Nogales, Mex.	H8	130
Losolava, Vanuatu	j16	79d
Los Padillas, N.M., U.S.	I10	132
Los Palacios, Arg.	D3	92
Los Palacios, Cuba	A6	102
Los Palacios y Villafranca, Spain	G4	20
Los Picachos, Parque Nacional, p.o.i., Col.	F4	86
Los Rábanos, P.R.	B2	104a
Los Ríos, state, Ec.	H2	86
Los Roques, Islas, is., Ven.	B8	86
Los Sauces, Chile	H1	92
Lossiemouth, Scot., U.K.	D9	12
Lost, stm., U.S.	A4	134
Los Taques, Ven.	B6	86
Los Teques, Ven.	B8	86
Los Testigos, Islas, is., Ven.	B10	86
Lost Hills, Ca., U.S.	H6	134
Lost Nation, Ia., U.S.	C7	120
Lost River Range, mts., Id., U.S.	F13	136
Lost Trail Pass, p., U.S.	E13	136
Losuia, Pap. N. Gui.	b5	79a
Los Vidrios, Mex.	F6	98
Los Vilos, Chile	E2	92
Los Yébenes, Spain	E6	20
Lot, state, Fr.	E7	18
Lot, stm., Fr.	E7	18
Lota, Chile	H1	92
Lot-et-Garonne, state, Fr.	E6	18
Lothair, S. Afr.	E10	70
Lotošino, Russia	D18	10
Lotsane, stm., Bots.	C8	70
Lotta, stm., Eur.	B13	8
Lotuke, Jabal, mtn., Sudan	G6	62
Lotung, Tai.	I9	42
Louang Namtha, Laos	B5	48
Louangphrabang, Laos	C6	48
Loubomo, Congo	E2	66
Loudon, Tn., U.S.	A1	116
Loudonville, Oh., U.S.	D3	114
Loudun, Fr.	G9	14
Loue, stm., Fr.	H14	14
Louga, Sen.	F1	64
Louge, Arg.	H7	92
Loughborough, Eng., U.K.	I11	12
Loughrea, Ire.	H4	12
Louhi, Russia	C15	8
Louin, Ms., U.S.	E9	122
Louisa, Ky., U.S.	F3	114
Louisbourg, N.S., Can.	E16	110
Louisburg, Ks., U.S.	F3	120
Louisburg, N.C., U.S.	H7	114
Louise, Ms., U.S.	D8	122
Louise, Tx., U.S.	H2	122
Louiseville, Qc., Can.	D3	110
Louisiade Archipelago, is., Pap. N. Gui.	B10	74
Louisiana, Mo., U.S.	E6	120
Louisiana, state, U.S.	F6	122
Louis Trichardt, S. Afr.	C9	70
Louisville, Al., U.S.	F13	122
Louisville, Ga., U.S.	C3	116
Louisville, Ky., U.S.	F12	120
Louisville, Ne., U.S.	D1	120
Louisville, Oh., U.S.	D4	114
Louisville Ridge, unds.	M22	142
Louis-XIV, Pointe, c., Qc., Can.	E14	106
Loulé, Port.	G2	20
Loum, Cam.	D1	66
Lount Lake, l., On., Can.	A4	118
Louny, Czech Rep.	F9	16
Loup, stm., Ne., U.S.	F14	126
Loup City, Ne., U.S.	F14	126
Loups Marins, Lacs des, l., Qc., Can.	D16	106
Lourdes, Fr.	F5	18
Lourenço Marques see Maputo, Moz.	D11	70
Lourinhã, Port.	E1	20
Lousã, Port.	D2	20
Louth, Austl.	H5	76
Louth, Ire.	H6	12
Louth, Eng., U.K.	H13	12
Louth, state, Ire.	H6	12
Loutrá Aidhipsoú, Grc.	E6	28
Louvain see Leuven, Bel.	D13	14
Louviers, Fr.	E10	14
Louviers, Co., U.S.	B4	128
Lovat', stm., Russia	B14	10
Loveč, Blg.	F11	26
Loveč, state, Blg.	F11	26
Loveland, Co., U.S.	G7	126
Lovell, Wy., U.S.	C4	126
Lovell Village, St. Vin.	p11	105e
Lovelock, Nv., U.S.	C7	134
Lovely, Ky., U.S.	G3	114
Lovere, Italy	E6	22
Loves Park, Il., U.S.	B8	120
Loving, N.M., U.S.	B3	130
Loving, Tx., U.S.	H10	128
Lovingston, Va., U.S.	G7	114
Lovington, N.M., U.S.	B4	130
Lovosice, Czech Rep.	F9	16
Lovozero, Russia	D13	8
Lovozero, ozero, l., Russia	C16	8
Lóvua, Ang.	B3	68
Low, Qc., Can.	C14	112
Low, Cape, c., Nu., Can.	C13	106
Lowa, D.R.C.	E5	66
Lowa, stm., D.R.C.	E5	66
Lowden, Ia., U.S.	C7	120
Lowell, Ar., U.S.	H3	120
Lowell, In., U.S.	G2	112
Lowell, Ma., U.S.	B14	114
Lowell, Or., U.S.	G4	136
Lowell, Lake, res., Id., U.S.	G10	136
Löwen, stm., Nmb.	E3	70
Löwenberg, Ger.	D8	16
Lower Arrow Lake, res., B.C., Can.	G12	138
Lower Austria see Niederösterreich, state, Aus.	B12	22
Lower California see Baja California, pen., Mex.	B2	96
Lower Egypt see Misr el-Bahrî, hist. reg., Egypt	G2	58
Lower Glenelg National Park, p.o.i., Austl.	L3	76
Lower Hutt, N.Z.	E6	80
Lower Lake, l., U.S.	B5	134
Lower Manitou Lake, l., On., Can.	B6	118
Lower Post, B.C., Can.	D5	106
Lower Red Lake, l., Mn., U.S.	D3	118
Lower Saxony see Niedersachsen, state, Ger.	D4	16
Lower Trajan's Wall, misc. cult., Eur.	D15	26
Lower West End Point, c., Anguilla	A1	105a
Lower Woods Harbour, N.S., Can.	G10	110
Lowestoft, Eng., U.K.	I14	12
Lowgar, state, Afg.	A2	54
Łowicz, Pol.	D15	16
Lowmoor, Va., U.S.	G6	114
Low Rocky Point, c., Austl.	o12	77a
Lowry City, Mo., U.S.	F4	120
Lowville, N.Y., U.S.	E14	112
Loxton, Austl.	J3	76
Loyal, Wi., U.S.	G8	118
Loyalton, Ca., U.S.	D5	134
Loyalty Islands see Loyauté, Îles, is., N. Cal.	m16	79d
Loyang see Luoyang, China	D5	42
Loyauté, Îles (Loyalty Islands), is., N. Cal.	m16	79d
Loyoro, Ug.	D6	66
Lozère, state, Fr.	E9	18
Loznica, Yugo.	E6	26
Lualaba, stm., Afr.	E5	66
Luama, stm., D.R.C.	E5	66
Lu'an, China	F7	42
Luan, stm., China	E3	38
Luancheng, China	J3	42
Luanda, Ang.	B1	68
Luando, stm., Ang.	C2	68
Luang, Khao (Maw Taung), mtn., Asia	G4	48
Luang, Thale, l., Thai.	I5	48
Luang Chiang Dao, Doi, mtn., Thai.	C4	48
Luanginga, stm., Afr.	G4	66
Luang Prabang see Louangphrabang, Laos	C6	48
Luangue (Loange), stm., Afr.	F3	66
Luangwa, stm., Afr.	C5	68
Luanping, China	A7	42
Luanshya, Zam.	C4	68
Luan Toro, Arg.	H5	92
Luanxian, China	B8	42
Luapula, stm., Afr.	C4	68
Luar, Danau, l., Indon.	C8	50
Luarca, Spain	A4	20
Luba, Eq. Gui.	I6	64
Lubaantun, hist., Belize	D3	102
Lubań, Pol.	E11	16
Lubāna, Lat.	D9	10
Lubang Islands, is., Phil.	D2	52
Lubango, Ang.	C1	68
Lubāns, l., Lat.	D9	10
Lubartów, Pol.	E18	16
Lübben, Ger.	E9	16
Lübbenau, Ger.	E9	16
Lubbock, Tx., U.S.	H7	128
Lübeck, Ger.	C6	16
Lubefu, D.R.C.	E4	66
Lubefu, stm., D.R.C.	E4	66
Lubień Kujawski, Pol.	D15	16
Lubilash, stm., D.R.C.	F4	66
Lubin, Pol.	E12	16
Lublin, Pol.	E18	16
Lublin, state, Pol.	E18	16
Lubliniec, Pol.	F14	16
Lubny, Ukr.	E4	32
Luboń, Pol.	D12	16
Lubsko, Pol.	E10	16
Lübtheen, Ger.	C7	16
Lubuagan, Phil.	B3	52
Lubudi, D.R.C.	G5	66
Lubukbatang, Indon.	F3	50
Lubuklinggau, Indon.	E3	50
Lubukpakam, Indon.	B1	50
Lubuksikaping, Indon.	C1	50
Lubumbashi (Élisabethville), D.R.C.	G5	66
Lubutu, D.R.C.	E5	66
Lübz, Ger.	C7	16
Lucan, On., Can.	E8	112
Lucanas, Peru	F3	84
Lucania, hist. reg., Italy	D10	24
Lucania, Mount, mtn., Yk., Can.	C3	106
Lucapa, Ang.	B3	68
Lucas, Ia., U.S.	C4	120
Lucas, Ks., U.S.	B10	128
Lucban, Phil.	C3	52
Lucca, Italy	G7	22
Lucea, Jam.	i12	104d
Luce Bay, b., Scot., U.K.	G8	12
Lucedale, Ms., U.S.	G10	122
Lucena, Phil.	D3	52
Lucena, Spain	G6	20
Lucena del Cid see Llucena, Spain	D10	20
Lučenec, Slov.	H15	16
Lucera, Italy	C9	24

Name — Map Ref. — Page

Lucerne see Luzern, Switz. C5 22
Lucerne, Ca., U.S. D3 134
Lucerne, Lake of see Vierwaldstätter See, l., Switz. D5 22
Luchou see Luzhou, China G1 42
Luchow see Luzhou, China G1 42
Lüchow, Ger. C7 16
Luchuan, China J4 42
Lucinda, Austl. B6 76
Lucira, Ang. C1 68
Luckau, Ger. E9 16
Luckenwalde, Ger. D9 16
Luckhoff, S. Afr. F7 70
Luck Lake, l., Sk., Can. C6 124
Lucknow, On., Can. E8 112
Lucknow, India E8 54
Lucky Lake, Sk., Can. D6 124
Luçon, Fr. C4 18
Lucusse, Ang. C3 68
Luda Kamčija, stm., Blg. G14 26
Ludao, China C8 38
Lüdenscheid, Ger. E3 16
Lüderitz, Nmb. E2 70
Ludhiāna, India C5 54
Ludian, China F5 36
Ludington, Mi., U.S. E3 112
Ludlow, Eng., U.K. I10 12
Ludlow, Ma., U.S. B13 114
Ludogorie, reg., Blg. F13 26
Ludowici, Ga., U.S. E4 116
Luduş, Rom. C11 26
Ludvika, Swe. F6 8
Ludwigsburg, Ger. H4 16
Ludwigsfelde, Ger. D9 16
Ludwigshafen am Rhein, Ger. G4 16
Ludwigslust, Ger. C7 16
Ludza, Lat. D10 10
Luebo, D.R.C. F4 66
Lueders, Tx., U.S. B8 130
Luena, Ang. C3 68
Luena, D.R.C. F5 66
Luena, stm., Ang. C3 68
Luepa, Ven. E11 86
Lueyang, China E2 42
Lufeng, China J6 42
Lufico, Ang. B1 68
Lufira, stm., D.R.C. F5 66
Lufkin, Tx., U.S. F4 122
Luga, Russia B12 10
Luga, stm., Russia A11 10
Lugano, Switz. D5 22
Lugano, Lago di, l., Eur. D14 18
Luganville, Vanuatu j16 79d
Lugards Falls, wtfl, Kenya E7 66
Lugenda, stm., Moz. C6 68
Luggarus see Locarno, Switz. D5 22
Lugnaquillia Mountain, mtn., Ire. I6 12
Lugo, Italy F8 22
Lugo, Spain A3 20
Lugo, co., Spain B3 20
Lugoj, Rom. D8 26
Lugovoj, Kaz. F12 32
Lugovskij, Russia E11 34
Luhans'k, Ukr. E5 32
Luhe, China E8 42
Luhovicy, Russia F21 10
Luhsien see Luzhou, China G1 42
Luiana, Ang. D3 68
Luido, Moz. B12 70
Luik see Liège, Bel. D14 14
Luimneach see Limerick, Ire. I4 12
Luino, Italy D5 22
Luishia, D.R.C. G5 66
Luis L. León, Presa, res., Mex. F2 130
Luis Muñoz Marin, Aeropuerto Internacional, P.R. B3 104a
Luitpold Coast, cst., Ant. C1 81
Luiza, D.R.C. F4 66
Luján, Arg. F4 92
Luján de Cuyo, Arg. F3 92
Lujiang, China F7 42
Lukang, Tai. I9 42
Lukenie, stm., D.R.C. E3 66
Lukeville, Az., U.S. L4 132
Lukojanov, Russia I21 8
Lukolela, D.R.C. E3 66
Lukolela, D.R.C. F4 66
Lukovit, Blg. F11 26
Łuków, Pol. E18 16
Lukuga, stm., D.R.C. F5 66
Lukula, D.R.C. F2 66
Lukulu, Zam. C3 68
Lulaka, stm., D.R.C. E4 66
Luleå, Swe. D10 8
Luleälven, stm., Swe. C9 8
Lüleburgaz, Tur. B10 28
Lules, Arg. C5 92
Luliang, China G5 36
Lüliang Shan, mts., China C4 42
Luling, Tx., U.S. E10 130
Lulonga, stm., D.R.C. D3 66
Lulua, stm., D.R.C. F4 66
Luluabourg see Kananga, D.R.C. F4 66
Lumajang, Indon. H8 50
Lumajangdong Co, l., China B8 54
Lumaku, Gunong, mtn., Malay. A9 50
Lumana, D.R.C. E5 66
Lumbala Kaquengue, Ang. C3 68
Lumbala N'guimbo, Ang. C3 68
Lumber, stm., U.S. B6 116
Lumber City, Ga., U.S. E3 116
Lumberport, W.V., U.S. E5 114
Lumberton, N.C., U.S. B7 116
Lumberton, Tx., U.S. G4 122
Lumbis, Indon. A10 50
Lumbrales, Spain D4 20
Lumby, B.C., Can. F12 138
Lumding, India F14 54
Lumpkin, Ga., U.S. E14 122
Lumu, Indon. E11 50
Lumut, Malay. J5 48
Lumut, Tanjung, c., Indon. E4 50
Luna Pier, Mi., U.S. C2 114
Lūnāvāda, India G4 54
Lund, B.C., Can. G6 138
Lund, Swe. I5 8
Lund, Nv., U.S. E2 132
Lundazi, Zam. C5 68
Lundy, i., Eng., U.K. J8 12
Lüneburg, Ger. C6 16
Lüneburger Heide, reg., Ger. D6 16
Lunel, Fr. F10 18
Lünen, Ger. E3 16
Lunenburg, N.S., Can. F12 110
Lunenburg, Va., U.S. H7 114
Lunéville, Fr. F15 14
Lungch'i see Zhangzhou, China I7 42
Lunge'nake, China C10 54
Lunglei, India G14 54
Lungtsin see Longzhou, China J2 42
Lungué-Bungo (Lungwebungu), stm., Afr. C3 68
Lungwebungu (Lungué-Bungo), stm., Afr. C3 68
Lūni, India E4 54
Lūni, stm., India F4 54
Luninec, Bela. H9 10
Luninets see Luninec, Bela. H9 10
Lūnkaransar, India D4 54
Luntai, China F14 32
Luo, stm., China D4 42
Luo, stm., China D4 42
Luobei, China B11 36
Luobu, China I3 42
Luocheng, China I3 42
Luoding, China J4 42
Luofu, D.R.C. E5 66
Luohe, China E6 42
Luoji, China E7 42
Luonan, China D4 42
Luoning, China D4 42
Luoqi, China G2 42
Luotian, China F6 42
Luowenba, China F2 42
Luoxiao Shan, mts., China H6 42
Luoyang, China D5 42
Luoyuan, China H8 42
Luozi, D.R.C. F2 66
Lupanshui, China F5 36
Lupar, stm., Malay. C7 50
Łupawa, Pol. B13 16
Lupeni, Rom. D10 26
Lupin see Manzhouli, China B8 36
Luputa, D.R.C. F4 66
Luqiao, China E7 42
Luqiao, China G9 42
Luqu, China E5 36
Luque, Spain G6 20
Luquillo, P.R. B4 104a
Lure, Fr. G15 14
Luremo, Ang. B2 68
Lurgan, N. Ire., U.K. G6 12
Luribay, Bol. C3 90
Lurín, Peru F2 84
Lúrio, Moz. C7 68
Lúrio, stm., Moz. C6 68
Lusaka, Zam. D4 68
Lusambo, D.R.C. E4 66
Lusanga, D.R.C. E3 66
Lusangi, D.R.C. E5 66
Luscar, Ab., Can. C13 138
Luseland, Sk., Can. B4 124
Lushan, China E5 42
Lu Shan, mtn., China G6 42
Lushnja see Lushnjë, Alb. D13 24
Lushnjë, Alb. D13 24
Lushoto, Tan. E7 66
Lüshun (Port Arthur), China E4 38
Lusk, Wy., U.S. E8 126
Lussac-les-Châteaux, Fr. C6 18
Lūt, Dasht-e, des., Iran C8 56
Lü-ta see Dalian, China B9 42
Lü Tao, i., Tai. J9 42
Lutembo, Ang. C3 68
Lutesville, Mo., U.S. G7 120
Luther, Mi., U.S. D4 112
Luther, Ok., U.S. F11 128
Lutherstadt Eisleben, Ger. E7 16
Lutherstadt Wittenberg, Ger. E8 16
Luti, Sol. Is. d7 79b
Luton, Eng., U.K. J12 12
Lutong, Malay. A8 50
Łutselk'e, N.T., Can. C8 106
Lutz, Fl., U.S. H3 116
Lützow, Ger. C7 16
Lutzow-Holm Bay, b., Ant. B8 81
Luuq, Som. D8 66
Luverne, Al., U.S. F12 122
Lu Verne, Ia., U.S. I4 118
Luverne, Mn., U.S. H2 118
Luvua, stm., D.R.C. F5 66
Luvuvhu, stm., S. Afr. C10 70
Luwegu, stm., Tan. F7 66
Luwingu, Zam. C4 68
Luwuk, Indon. F7 44
Luxapallila Creek, stm., U.S. D11 122
Luxembourg, Lux. E14 14
Luxembourg, ctry., Eur. E15 14
Luxemburg, Wi., U.S. D2 112
Luxeuil-les-Bains, Fr. G15 14
Luxi, China G4 36
Luxor see El-Uqsor, Egypt B6 62
Luz, Braz. J3 88
Luza, Russia F22 8
Luža, Russia A14 10
Luzern (Lucerne), Switz. C5 22
Luzhai, China I3 42
Luzhou, China G1 42
Luziânia, Braz. I2 88
Luzilândia, Braz. B4 88
Lužki, Bela. E10 10
Lužnice, stm., Eur. G10 16
Luzon, i., Phil. B3 52
Luzon Strait, strt., Asia G16 30
L'viv, Ukr. F13 6
L'viv, co., Ukr. G19 16
L'vovskij, Russia E20 10
Lwówek, Pol. D12 16
Lyallpur see Faisalabad, Pak. C4 54
Lyčkovo, Russia C15 10
Lycksele, Swe. D8 8
Lydenburg, S. Afr. D10 70
Lydia Mills, S.C., U.S. B3 116
Lyell, Mount, mtn., Can. E13 138
Lyerly, Ga., U.S. C13 122
Lyford, Tx., U.S. H10 130
Lykošino, Russia B16 10
Lyle, Mn., U.S. H6 118
Lyman, Ne., U.S. F8 126
Lyman, S.C., U.S. B3 116
Lymans'ke, Ukr. C17 26
Lyme Bay, b., Eng., U.K. K9 12
Łyna (Lava), stm., Eur. B16 16
Lynch, Ne., U.S. E14 126
Lynchburg, Oh., U.S. E2 114
Lynchburg, S.C., U.S. B5 116
Lynchburg, Tn., U.S. B12 122
Lynchburg, Va., U.S. G6 114
Lynd, stm., Austl. A4 76
Lynden, Wa., U.S. B4 136
Lyndhurst, Austl. B5 76
Lyndon, Ks., U.S. F2 120
Lyndon, Ky., U.S. F12 120
Lyndon, stm., Austl. D2 74
Lyndon B. Johnson, Lake, res., Tx., U.S. D9 130
Lyndon B. Johnson Space Center, sci., Tx., U.S. H3 122
Lyngen, b., Nor. B9 8
Lyngseidet, Nor. B8 8
Lynn, Al., U.S. C11 122
Lynn, Ma., U.S. B14 114
Lynndyl, Ut., U.S. D4 132
Lynn Haven, Fl., U.S. G13 122
Lynn Lake, Mb., Can. D10 106
Lyntupy, Bela. E9 10
Lynx Lake, l., N.T., Can. C9 106
Lyon, Fr. D10 18
Lyon Inlet, b., Nu., Can. B14 106
Lyon Mountain, N.Y., U.S. F2 110
Lyonnais, hist. reg., Fr. D10 18
Lyons, In., U.S. F10 120
Lyons, Ks., U.S. C10 128
Lyons, Mi., U.S. F5 112
Lyons, Ne., U.S. C1 120
Lyons, N.Y., U.S. E13 112
Lyons, stm., Austl. D3 74
Lysa Hora, Ukr. A18 26
Łysica, mtn., Pol. F16 16
Lyskovo, Russia H21 8
Lys'va, Russia C9 32
Lysychans'k, Ukr. E5 32
Lytham Saint Anne's, Eng., U.K. H9 12
Lytle, Tx., U.S. E9 130

M

Ma, stm., Asia C7 48
Ma'ān, Jord. H6 58
Ma'ān, state, Jord. H7 58
Ma'anshan, China F8 42
Maardu, Est. G11 8
Maarianhamina (Mariehamn), Fin. F9 8
Ma'arrat an-Nu'mān, Syria C7 58
Maas (Meuse), stm., Eur. D14 14
Maasin, Phil. E5 52
Maastricht, Neth. D14 14
Mabalane, Moz. C11 70
Mabank, Tx., U.S. E2 122
Mabaruma, Guy. C12 86
Mabeleapodi, Bots. B6 70
Mabel Lake, l., B.C., Can. F12 138
Maben, Ms., U.S. D9 122
Mablethorpe, Eng., U.K. H13 12
Mableton, Ga., U.S. D14 122
Mabton, Wa., U.S. D6 136
Mabuasehube Game Reserve, Bots. D6 70
Mača, Russia E12 34
Maca, Cerro, vol., Chile H2 90
Macachín, Arg. H6 92
Macaé, Braz. L5 88
Macaíba, Braz. C8 88
Macajuba, Braz. G5 88
Macalister, B.C., Can. D8 138
Macalister, stm., Austl. K6 76
Macalister, Mount, mtn., Austl. J7 76
MacAlpine Lake, l., Nu., Can. B10 106
Macan, Kepulauan, is., Indon. G12 50
Macao see Macau, dep., Asia J5 42
Macapá, Braz. C7 84
Macará, Ec. D2 84
Macareo, Caño, stm., Ven. C11 86
MacArthur, Phil. E5 52
Macas, Ec. I2 86
Macau, Braz. C7 88
Macau, Macau J5 42
Macau, dep., Asia J5 42
Macaúbas, Braz. G4 88
MacClenny, Fl., U.S. F3 116
Macclesfield, Eng., U.K. H10 12
Macdhui, Ben, mtn., Afr. G9 70
Macdonald, Lake, l., Austl. D5 74
MacDonald Pass, p., Mt., U.S. D14 136
MacDonnell Ranges, mts., Austl. D6 74
Macdui, Ben, mtn., Scot., U.K. D9 12
Macedonia, hist. reg., Eur. H10 26
Macedonia, ctry., Eur. B4 28
Maceió, Braz. E8 88
Macenta, Gui. H3 64
Maceo, Col. D4 86
Macerata, Italy G10 22
MacFarlane, stm., Sk., Can. D9 106
Macgillycuddy's Reeks, mts., Ire. J3 12
MacGregor, Mb., Can. D15 124
Machado, Braz. K3 88
Machado, stm., Braz. F5 84
Machagai, Arg. C7 92
Machaila, Moz. C11 70
Machakos, Kenya E7 66
Machala, Ec. D2 84
Machalí, Chile G2 92
Machalilla, Parque Nacional, p.o.i., Ec. H1 86
Machanga, Moz. B12 70
Machaquilá, stm., Guat. D3 102
Machattie, Lake, l., Austl. E2 76
Machaze, Moz. B11 70
Macheng, China F6 42
Mācherla, India C4 53
Machias, Me., U.S. F9 110
Machilīpatnam (Bandar), India C5 53
Machiques, Ven. B5 86
Machkund, res., India B6 53
Macho, Arroyo del, stm., N.M., U.S. H4 128
Machu Picchu see Machupicchu, hist., Peru F3 84
Machupicchu, hist., Peru F3 84
Maciá, Arg. F8 92
Macia, Moz. D11 70
Măcin, Rom. D15 26
Macintyre, stm., Austl. G7 76
Mackay, Austl. C7 76
Mackay, Id., U.S. G13 136
Mackay, Lake, l., Austl. D5 74
MacKay Lake, l., N.T., Can. C8 106
Mackenzie, stm., Austl. D7 76
Mackenzie, stm., N.T., Can. B4 106
Mackenzie Bay, b., Can. C12 140
Mackenzie King Island, i., Can. B3 141
Mackenzie Mountains, mts., Can. C4 106
Mackinac, Straits of, strt., Mi., U.S. C4 112
Mackinac Bridge, Mi., U.S. C5 112
Mackinac Island, Mi., U.S. C5 112
Mackinaw, stm., Il., U.S. D9 120
Mackinaw City, Mi., U.S. C5 112
Mackinnon Road, Kenya E7 66
Macklin, Sk., Can. B4 124
Macksville, Austl. H9 76
Macksville, Ks., U.S. C9 128
Maclean, Austl. G9 76
Maclear, S. Afr. G9 70
Macleay, stm., Austl. H9 76
Macleod, Lake, l., Austl. D2 74
Macmillan, stm., Yk., Can. C4 106
Macomb, Il., U.S. D7 120
Macomer, Italy D2 24
Mâcon, Fr. C10 18
Macon, Ga., U.S. D2 116
Macon, Il., U.S. E9 120
Macon, Ms., U.S. D10 122
Macon, Mo., U.S. E5 120
Macon, Bayou, stm., U.S. E7 122
Macondo, Ang. C3 68
Macorís, Cabo, c., Dom. Rep. C12 102
Macoupin Creek, stm., Il., U.S. E8 120
Macovane, Moz. B12 70
Macquarie, stm., Austl. H6 76
Macquarie, stm., Austl. n13 77a
Macquarie, Lake, l., Austl. I8 76
Macquarie Harbour, b., Austl. o12 77a
Macquarie Island, i., Austl. A20 81
Macquarie Marshes, sw., Austl. H6 76
Macquarie Ridge, unds. O18 142
Mac. Robertson Land, reg., Ant. B10 81
Macucuau, stm., Braz. H11 86
Macugnaga, Italy E4 22
Macumba, stm., Austl. E7 74
Macuro, Ven. B10 86
Macusani, Peru F3 84
Macuspana, Mex. G12 100
Mad, stm., Ca., U.S. C2 134
Mādabā, Jord. G6 58
Madagascar, ctry., Afr. D8 68
Madagascar Basin, unds. L8 142
Madagascar Plateau, unds. M7 142
Madan, Blg. H11 26
Madanapalle, India E4 53
Madang, Pap. N. Gui. b4 79a
Madaoua, Niger G6 64
Mādārīpur, Bngl. G13 54
Madawaska, Me., U.S. C8 110
Madawaska, stm., On., Can. C13 112
Madawaska Highlands, plat., On., Can. C12 112
Madaya, Mya. A3 48
Maddalena, Isola, i., Italy C3 24
Maddaloni, Italy C8 24
Maddock, N.D., U.S. G14 124
Madeira, i., Port. C1 64
Madeira, stm., S.A. E5 84
Madeira, Arquipélago da (Madeira Islands), is., Port. C1 64
Madeira Islands see Madeira, Arquipélago da, is., Port. C1 64
Mädelegabel, mtn., Eur. I6 16
Madeleine, Îles de la, is., Qc., Can. C15 110
Madeleine-Centre, Qc., Can. A11 110
Madeline Island, i., Wi., U.S. E8 118
Madera, Mex. A4 100
Madera, Ca., U.S. G5 134
Madera see Madeira, stm., S.A. E5 84
Madgaon, India D1 53
Madhepura, India F11 54
Madhubani, India E10 54
Madhugiri, India E3 53
Madhupur, India F11 54
Madhya Pradesh, state, India D4 46
Madibogo, S. Afr. E7 70
Madida, China C9 38
Madidi, stm., Bol. B3 90
Madill, Ok., U.S. C2 122
Madimba, D.R.C. E3 66
Madīnat ash-Sha'b, Yemen G5 56
Madingo-Kayes, Congo E2 66
Madingou, Congo E2 66
Madirovalo, Madag. D8 68
Madison, Al., U.S. C12 122
Madison, Fl., U.S. F2 116
Madison, Ga., U.S. C2 116
Madison, In., U.S. F12 120
Madison, Me., U.S. F6 110
Madison, Mn., U.S. F2 118
Madison, Mo., U.S. E5 120
Madison, Ne., U.S. F15 126
Madison, N.C., U.S. H5 114
Madison, S.D., U.S. C15 126
Madison, W.V., U.S. F4 114
Madison, Wi., U.S. A8 120
Madison, stm., U.S. E15 136
Madison Heights, Va., U.S. G6 114
Madison Range, mts., Mt., U.S. E15 136
Madisonville, Ky., U.S. G10 120
Madisonville, La., U.S. G8 122
Madisonville, Tn., U.S. A1 116
Madisonville, Tx., U.S. G2 122
Madiun, Indon. G7 50
Madiyi, China G4 42
Mado Gashi, Kenya D7 66
Madoi, China E4 36
Madona, Lat. D9 10
Madora, Bela. G13 10
Madrakah, Ra's al-, c., Oman F8 56
Madras see Chennai, India E5 53
Madras, Or., U.S. F5 136
Madre, Laguna, b., Mex. C10 100
Madre, Laguna, b., Tx., U.S. H10 130
Madre, Sierra, mts., Phil. B3 52
Madre de Chiapas, Sierra, mts., N.A. G12 100
Madre de Dios, stm., S.A. F4 84
Madre de Dios, Isla, i., Chile J1 90
Madre del Sur, Sierra, mts., Mex. G9 100
Madre Occidental, Sierra, mts., Mex. B3 96
Madre Oriental, Sierra, mts., Mex. C8 100
Madrid, Spain D7 20
Madrid, Al., U.S. F13 122
Madrid, Ne., U.S. G11 126
Madrid, state, Spain D7 20
Madridejos, Spain E7 20
Madura, i., Indon. G8 50
Madura, Selat, strt., Indon. G8 50
Madurai, India G4 53
Madurāntakam, India E4 53
Maduru, stm., Sri L. H5 53
Maebashi, Japan C11 40
Mae Hong Son, Thai. C3 48
Mae Klong, stm., Thai. E4 48
Mae Ping Mae Hat Mae Kor National Park, p.o.i., Thai. D4 48
Mae Ramat, Thai. D4 48
Mae Sariang, Thai. C3 48
Maeser, Ut., U.S. C7 132
Mae Sot, Thai. D4 48
Maestra, Sierra, mts., Cuba B9 102
Maestu, Spain B8 20
Mae Tha, Thai. C4 48
Maevatanana, Madag. D8 68
Maéwo, i., Vanuatu j17 79d
Mafeking, Mb., Can. B12 124
Mafeking see Mafikeng, S. Afr. D7 70
Mafeteng, Leso. F8 70
Maffra, Austl. K6 76
Mafia Island, i., Tan. F8 66
Mafikeng, S. Afr. D7 70
Mafra, Braz. C13 92
Magadan, Russia E19 34
Magadi, Kenya E7 66
Magaguadavic Lake, l., N.B., Can. E9 110
Magalhães de Almeida, Braz. B4 88
Magallanes, Phil. D4 52
Magangué, Col. C4 86
Magaria, Niger G6 64
Magazine Mountain, mtn., Ar., U.S. B5 122
Magdagači, Russia F14 34
Magdalena, Arg. G9 92
Magdalena, Bol. B4 90
Magdalena, Mex. E7 100
Magdalena, N.M., U.S. I9 132
Magdalena, state, Col. B4 86
Magdalena, stm., Col. B4 86
Magdalena, stm., Mex. F7 98
Magdalena, Bahía, b., Mex. C2 100
Magdalena, Isla, i., Chile H2 90
Magdalena, Punta, c., Col. F3 86
Magdalena de Kino, Mex. F7 98
Magdeburg, Ger. D7 16
Magelang, Indon. G7 50
Magellen, Strait of, strt., S.A. J2 90
Magenta, Italy E5 22
Magetan, Indon. G7 50
Maggiore, Lago, l., Eur. C14 18
Maghâgha, Egypt J1 58
Maghama, Maur. F2 64
Mágina, mtn., Spain G7 20
Maglaj, Bos. E5 26
Maglić, mtn., Bos. F5 26
Maglie, Italy D12 24
Magnet, Mb., Can. C14 124
Magnetawan, stm., On., Can. C10 112
Magnetic Island, i., Austl. B6 76
Magnitogorsk, Russia D9 32
Magnolia, Ar., U.S. D5 122
Magnolia, Ms., U.S. F8 122
Mago, i., Fiji p20 79e
Magog, Qc., Can. E4 110
Magozal, Mex. E10 100
Magrath, Ab., Can. G18 138
Maguan, China A7 48
Maguari, Cabo, c., Braz. D8 84
Magumeri, Nig. G7 64
Māgura, Bngl. G12 54
Maguse Lake, l., Nu., Can. C12 106
Magway, Mya. B2 48
Magway, state, Mya. B2 48
Mahābād, Iran B6 56
Mahābaleshwar, India C1 53
Mahabe, Madag. D8 68
Mahābhārat Lek, mts., Nepal E11 54
Mahabharat Range see Mahābhārat Lek, mts., Nepal E11 54
Mahabo, Madag. E7 68
Mahačkala, Russia F7 32
Mahād, India B1 53
Mahādeo Range, mts., India C2 53
Mahagi, D.R.C. D6 66
Mahajamba, stm., Madag. D8 68
Mahājan, India D4 54
Mahajanga, Madag. D8 68
Mahākālī (Sārda), stm., Asia D8 54
Mahakam, stm., Indon. D9 50
Mahalapye, Bots. E4 68
Maham, India D6 54
Mahānadi, stm., India H10 54
Mahanoro, Madag. D8 68
Mahanoy City, Pa., U.S. D9 114
Maharagama, Sri L. H4 53
Mahārājganj, India E10 54
Mahārājpur, India F7 54
Mahārāshtra, state, India E4 46
Mahāsamund, India H9 54
Maha Sarakham, Thai. D6 48
Mahaut, Dom. j6 105c
Mahaweli, stm., Sri L. H5 53
Mahaxai, Laos D7 48
Mahbūbābād, India C4 53
Mahbūbnagar, India C4 53
Mahd adh-Dhahab, Sau. Ar. E5 56
Mahdia, Guy. E12 86
Mahe, India F2 53
Mahé, i., Sey. j13 69b
Mahébourg, Mrts. i10 69a
Mahendra Giri, mtn., India B7 53
Mahendranagar, Nepal D7 54
Mahenge, Tan. F7 66
Mahesāna, India G4 54
Maheshwar, India G5 54
Mahi, stm., India G4 54
Mahia Peninsula, pen., N.Z. D7 80
Mahilëu, Bela. G13 10
Mahilëu, state, Bela. G13 10
Mahina, Fr. Poly. u21 78h
Mahlabatini, S. Afr. F10 70
Mahmūdābād, India E8 54
Mahmudiye, Tur. D14 28
Mahoba, India F7 54
Mahogany Mountain, mtn., Or., U.S. G9 136
Mahogany Tree, Anguilla A1 105a
Mahomet, Il., U.S. D9 120
Mahón see Maó, Spain E15 20
Mahone Bay, N.S., Can. F12 110
Mahone Bay, b., N.S., Can. F12 110
Mahood Lake, l., B.C., Can. E10 138
Mahora, Spain E9 20
Mahrāt, Jabal, plat., Yemen F7 56
Mahrauni, India F7 54
Mahuva, India H3 54
Maiaky, Ukr. C17 26
Maicao, Col. B5 86
Maichen, China K3 42
Maicuru, stm., Braz. D7 84
Maiden, N.C., U.S. A4 116
Maidenhead, Eng., U.K. J12 12
Maidstone, Sk., Can. A4 124
Maidstone, Eng., U.K. J13 12
Maiduguri, Nig. G7 64
Maihar, India F8 54
Maijoma, Mex. F3 130
Maikala Range, mts., India G8 54
Maikoor, Pulau, i., Indon. G9 44
Mailāni, India D8 54
Main, stm., Ger. F4 16
Maināguri, India E12 54
Mainburg, Ger. H7 16
Main Channel, strt., On., Can. C8 112
Mai-Ndombe, Lac, l., D.R.C. E3 66
Main-Donau-Kanal, can., Ger. G7 16
Maine, state, U.S. E7 110
Maine, hist. reg., Fr. F8 14
Maine, Gulf of, b., N.A. G8 110
Maine-et-Loire, state, Fr. G8 14
Maïné-Soroa, Niger G7 64
Mainhardt, Ger. G5 16
Mainland, i., Scot., U.K. B9 12
Mainland, i., Scot., U.K. n18 12a
Mainpuri, India E7 54
Maintirano, Madag. D7 68
Mainz, Ger. G4 16
Maio, i., C.V. k10 65a
Maipo, stm., Chile F2 92
Maipo, Volcán, vol., S.A. G3 92
Maipú, Arg. F3 92
Maipú, Arg. H8 92
Maipú, ngh., Chile F2 92
Maiqihamiao, China C4 38
Maiquetía, Ven. B8 86
Maišiagala, Lith. F8 10
Maiskhāl Island, i., Bngl. H13 54
Maitembge, Bots. E4 68
Maitland, Austl. F7 74
Maitland, Austl. I8 76
Maitland, stm., On., Can. E8 112
Maitri, sci., Ant. C6 81
Maíz, Islas del, is., Nic. F6 102
Maizuru, Japan D8 40
Maja, stm., Russia E15 34
Majari, stm., Braz. F11 86
Majene, Indon. E11 50
Majī, Eth. F7 62
Majia, stm., China C7 42
Majiang, China J4 42
Majiangzong, China C12 54
Majja, Russia D15 34
Majkain, Kaz. D13 32
Majkop, Russia F6 32
Major, Puig, mtn., Spain E13 20
Majorca see Mallorca, i., Spain E13 20
Majskij, Russia F14 34
Majskoe, Kaz. D13 32
Majuro, at., Marsh. Is. C8 72
Maka, Sen. G2 64
Makabana, Congo E2 66
Makale, Indon. E11 50
Makallé, Arg. C8 92
Makālu, mtn., Asia E11 54
Makanči, Kaz. E14 32
Makapuu Head, c., Hi., U.S. B4 78a
Makarakomburu, Mount, mtn., Sol. Is. e8 79b
Makarev, Russia H20 8
Makarov, Russia G17 34
Makasar, Selat (Makassar Strait), strt., Indon. D11 50
Makassar Strait see Makasar, Selat, strt., Indon. D11 50
Makat, Kaz. E8 32
Makawao, Hi., U.S. C5 78a
Makeni, S.L. H2 64
Makgadikgadi, pl., Bots. E4 68
Makgadikgadi Pans Game Reserve, Bots. B7 70
Makhaleng, stm., Afr. G8 70
Makham, Thai. F5 48
Maki, Indon. F9 44
Makiivka, Ukr. E5 32
Makindu, Kenya E7 66
Makinsk, Kaz. D11 32
Makira, state, Sol. Is. f10 79b
Makira Harbour, b., Sol. Is. f9 79b
Makkah (Mekka), Sau. Ar. E4 56
Makkovik, Nf., Can. D19 106
Makó, Hung. C7 26
Makokou, Gabon D2 66
Makongolosi, Tan. F6 66
Makoua, Congo E3 66
Maków Mazowiecki, Pol. D16 16
Makrai, India G6 54
Makrāna, India E5 54
Makrān Coast, cst., Asia D9 56
Maksatiha, Russia C18 10
Maksimkin Jar, Russia C15 32
Maktar, Tun. I3 24
Makumbi, D.R.C. F4 66
Makung, Tai. J8 42
Makurdi, Nig. H6 64
Makushin Volcano, vol., Ak., U.S. F6 140
Makušino, Russia C11 32
Makwassie, S. Afr. E8 70
Māl, India E12 54
Mala see Mallow, Ire. I4 12
Mala, Punta, c., Pan. I8 102
Malabang, Phil. G5 52
Malabar Coast, cst., India F2 53
Malabo, Eq. Gui. I6 64
Malacacheta, Braz. I4 88
Malacca see Melaka, Malay. K6 48
Malacca, Strait of, strt., Asia B2 50
Malacky, Slov. H13 16
Malad, stm., U.S. H14 136
Malad City, Id., U.S. A4 132
Maladzečna, Bela. F9 10
Málaga, Col. D5 86
Málaga, Spain H6 20
Málaga, co., Spain H6 20
Malagarasi, Tan. F6 66
Malagash, N.S., Can. E13 110
Malagasy Republic see Madagascar, ctry., Afr. D8 68
Malagón, Spain E7 20
Malaimbandy, Madag. E8 68
Malaita, state, Sol. Is. d9 79b
Malaita, i., Sol. Is. e9 79b
Malaja Kuril'skaja Grjada (Habomai-shotō), is., Russia C17 38
Malaja Višera, Russia B15 10
Malaka, Sempitan, strt., Indon. J2 48
Malakāl, Sudan F6 62
Malākand, Pak. A3 54
Malakoff, Tx., U.S. E3 122
Malakula, state, Vanuatu k16 79d
Malakula, i., Vanuatu k16 79d
Malambo, Col. B4 86
Malang, Indon. H8 50
Malanggwā, Nepal E10 54
Malanje, Ang. B2 68
Malanville, Benin G5 64
Malanzán, Arg. E4 92
Mała Panew, stm., Pol. F14 16
Mälaren, l., Swe. G7 8
Malargüe, Arg. G3 92
Malaspina, Arg. H3 90
Malaspina Glacier, ice, Ak., U.S. E11 140
Malatya, Tur. B4 56
Malau, Vanuatu j16 79d
Malaut, India C5 54
Malavalli, India E3 53
Malawali, Pulau, i., Malay. G1 52
Malawi, ctry., Afr. C5 68
Malaŵi, Lake see Nyasa, Lake, l., Afr. C5 68
Malaya see Semenanjung Malaysia, hist. reg., Malay. K6 48
Malayagiri, mtn., India H10 54
Malaybalay, Phil. F5 52
Malāyer, Iran C6 56
Malay Peninsula, pen., Asia J5 48
Malay Reef, rf., Austl. B7 76
Malaysia, ctry., Asia E3 44
Malbon, Austl. C3 76
Malbork, Pol. B15 16
Malbrán, Arg. D6 92
Malchin, Ger. C8 16
Malchow, Ger. C8 16
Malcolm, Austl. E4 74
Malcolm Island, i., B.C., Can. F4 138
Malcom, Ia., U.S. C5 120
Malczyce, Pol. E12 16
Malden, i., Kir. D11 72
Mal di Ventre, Isola di, i., Italy E2 24
Maldives, ctry., Asia I11 30
Maldonado, Ur. G10 92
Male', Mald. i12 46a
Male, Mya. A2 48
Maléas, Ákra, c., Grc. G6 28
Male' Atoll, at., Mald. i12 46a
Mālegaon, India H5 54
Malé Karpaty (Little Carpathians), mts., Slov. H13 16
Malema, Moz. C6 68
Malente, Ger. B6 16
Māler Kotla, India C5 54
Malesherbes, Fr. F11 14
Malgomaj, l., Swe. D6 8
Malhanskij hrebet, mts., Russia F10 34
Malheur, stm., Or., U.S. F9 136
Malheur, South Fork, stm., Or., U.S. G8 136
Malheur Lake, l., Or., U.S. G8 136
Mali, Gui. G2 64
Mali, ctry., Afr. F4 64
Mali, stm., Mya. C8 46
Malīk, Sudan F6 62
Malik, Wādī al-, val., Sudan D5 62
Mali Kyun, i., Mya. F4 48
Malili, Indon. E12 50
Malin, Or., U.S. A4 134
Malinaltepec, Mex. G9 100
Malinau, Indon. B10 50
Malindi, Kenya E8 66
Malines see Mechelen, Bel. C13 14
Malingping, Indon. G4 50
Malin Head, c., Ire. F5 12
Malino, Bukit, mtn., Indon. C12 50
Malita, Phil. G5 52
Malizhen, China A7 48
Maljamar, N.M., U.S. B4 130
Malka, Russia F20 34
Malkāpur, India H5 54
Malkara, Tur. C9 28
Mallāh, Syria F7 58
Mallan luonnonpuisto, p.o.i., Fin. B9 8
Mallawi, Egypt K1 58
Mallersdorf-Pfaffenberg, Ger. H8 16
Mallery Lake, l., Nu, Can. C11 106
Mallet, Braz. B12 92
Malligasta, Arg. D4 92
Mallorca (Majorca), i., Spain E13 20
Mallow, Ire. I4 12
Malm, Nor. D4 8
Malmberget, Swe. C8 8
Malmesbury, S. Afr. H4 70
Malmö, Swe. I5 8
Malmok, c., Neth. Ant. p23 104g
Malo, i., Vanuatu j16 79d
Maloelap, at., Marsh. Is. C8 72
Maloe Skuratovo, Russia G19 10
Malojaroslavec, Russia E19 10
Malolos, Phil. C3 52
Malone, Fl., U.S. G13 122
Malone, N.Y., U.S. F2 110
Malonga, D.R.C. G4 66
Małopolska, reg., Pol. F17 16
Malošujka, Russia E17 8
Malott, Wa., U.S. B7 136

Name	Map Ref.	Page
Małowice, Pol.	E11	16
Måløy, Nor.	E1	8
Malozemel'skaja Tundra, reg., Russia	C24	8
Malpas, Austl.	J3	76
Malpe, India	E2	53
Malpeque Bay, b., P.E., Can.	D13	110
Malprabha, stm., India	D2	53
Mālpura, India	E5	54
Malta, Braz.	D7	88
Malta, Lat.	D10	10
Malta, Mt., U.S.	F6	124
Malta, ctry., Eur.	I8	24
Malta, i., Malta	I8	24
Malta Channel, strt., Eur.	H8	24
Maltahöhe, Nmb.	D3	70
Maluku (Moluccas), is., Indon.	F8	44
Maluku, Laut (Molucca Sea), Indon.	F8	44
Ma'lūlā, Syria	E7	58
Malu Mare, Rom.	E10	26
Malunda, Indon.	E11	50
Mālvan, India	C1	53
Malvern, Ar., U.S.	C6	122
Malvern, Ia., U.S.	K3	118
Malvern, Oh., U.S.	D4	114
Malvérnia, Moz.	C10	70
Malvinas Sur, Arg.	D8	92
Malý Dunaj, stm., Slov.	H13	16
Malyja Haradzjačiсy, Bela.	H11	10
Malyj Anjuj, stm., Russia	C21	34
Malyj Enisej, stm., Russia	F8	34
Malyj Tajmyr, ostrov, i., Russia	A10	34
Mama, Russia	E11	34
Mamaia, Rom.	E15	26
Mamanguape, Braz.	D8	88
Mamasa, Indon.	E11	50
Mamasa, stm., Indon.	E11	50
Mambajao, Phil.	F5	52
Mambasa, D.R.C.	D5	66
Mamberamo, stm., Indon.	F10	44
Mamburao, Phil.	D3	52
Mamehaktebo, Indon.	C9	50
Mameigwess Lake, l., On., Can.	B6	118
Ma-Me-O Beach, Ab., Can.	C17	138
Mamfe, Cam.	C1	66
Mamljutka, Kaz.	D11	32
Mammoth, Az., U.S.	K6	132
Mammoth Cave National Park, p.o.i., Ky., U.S.	G11	120
Mammoth Lakes, Ca., U.S.	F7	134
Mammoth Spring, Ar., U.S.	H6	120
Mamonovo, Russia	F2	10
Mamoré, stm., S.A.	F4	84
Mamou, Gui.	G2	64
Mampikony, Madag.	D8	68
Mamry, Jezioro, l., Pol.	B17	16
Mamuju, Indon.	E11	50
Mamuno, Bots.	C5	70
Man, C. Iv.	H3	64
Man, W.V., U.S.	G4	114
Man, Isle of see Isle of Man, dep., Eur.	G8	12
Mana, Hi., U.S.	A2	78a
Manabí, state, Ec.	H2	86
Manacacías, stm., Col.	F5	86
Manacapuru, Braz.	I11	86
Manacapuru, stm., Braz.	I11	86
Manacor, Spain	E14	20
Manado (Menado), Indon.	E7	44
Manaenki, Russia	G19	10
Managua, Nic.	F4	102
Managua, Lago de, l., Nic.	F4	102
Manakara, Madag.	E8	68
Manakau, mtn., N.Z.	F5	80
Manāli, India	B6	54
Manama see Al-Manāmah, Bahr.	D7	56
Manam Island, i., Pap. N. Gui.	a4	79a
Mánamo, Caño, stm., Ven.	C10	86
Mananara Avaratra, Madag.	D8	68
Mananjary, Madag.	E8	68
Manantenina, Madag.	E8	68
Manapire, stm., Ven.	D8	86
Manappārai, India	F4	53
Manār, stm., India	B3	53
Manas, China	C2	36
Manās, stm., Asia	E13	54
Manasarowar Lake see Mapam Yumco, l., China	C8	54
Manas Hu, l., China	B2	36
Manāslu, mtn., Nepal	D10	54
Manasquan, N.J., U.S.	D11	114
Manassas, Va., U.S.	F8	114
Mânăstirea, Rom.	E13	26
Manatí, Col.	B4	86
Manatí, P.R.	B3	104a
Manatuto, Indon.	G8	44
Manaung, Mya.	C1	48
Manaus, Braz.	D5	84
Manavgat, Tur.	G14	28
Manawa, Wi., U.S.	G10	118
Manāwar, India	G5	54
Manawoka, Pulau, i., Indon.	F9	44
Manban, China	A6	48
Manbij, Syria	B8	58
Mancelona, Mi., U.S.	D4	112
Mancha Real, Spain	G7	20
Manche, state, Fr.	E7	14
Mancheng, China	B6	42
Mancherāl, India	B4	53
Manchester, Eng., U.K.	H10	12
Manchester, Ct., U.S.	C13	114
Manchester, Ga., U.S.	E14	122
Manchester, Ia., U.S.	B6	120
Manchester, Ky., U.S.	G2	114
Manchester, N.H., U.S.	H5	110
Manchester, Oh., U.S.	F2	114
Manchester, Vt., U.S.	G3	110
Manchioneal, Jam.	i14	104d
Manchouli see Manzhouli, China	B8	36
Manchuria see Dong San Shen, hist. reg., China	B5	38
Manciano, Italy	H8	22
Mancos, Co., U.S.	F8	132
Mancos, stm., U.S.	F8	132
Mānd, stm., India	G9	54
Mand, stm., Iran	D7	56
Manda, Tan.	G6	66
Manda, Jabal, mtn., Sudan	F4	62
Mandabe, Madag.	E7	68
Mandaguari, Braz.	A12	92
Manda Island, i., Kenya	E8	66
Mandal, Mong.	B6	36
Mandala, Puncak, mtn., Indon.	F10	44
Mandalay, Mya.	A2	48
Mandalay, state, Mya.	B2	48
Mandan, N.D., U.S.	A11	126
Mandar, Teluk, b., Indon.	E11	50
Mandara, Monts (Mandara Mountains), mts., Afr.	G7	64
Mandara Mountains (Mandara, Monts), mts., Afr.	G7	64
Mandas, Italy	E3	24
Mandaue, Phil.	E4	52
Mandeb, Bab el, strt.	E8	62
Mandera, Kenya	D8	66
Manderson, Wy., U.S.	C5	126
Mandeville, Jam.	i13	104d
Mandi, India	C6	54
Mandi Bahāuddīn, Pak.	B4	54
Mandi Būrewāla, Pak.	C4	54
Mandi Dabwāli, India	D5	54
Mandimba, Moz.	C6	68
Mandioli, Pulau, i., Indon.	F8	44
Mandioré, Lagoa (Mandioré, Laguna), l., S.A.	G6	84
Mandioré, Laguna (Mandioré, Lagoa), l., S.A.	G6	84
Mandla, India	G8	54
Mandlakazi, Moz.	D11	70
Mandora, Austl.	C4	74
Mandra, Pak.	B4	54
Mandritsara, Madag.	D8	68
Mandsaur, India	F5	54
Mandun, China	A4	48
Manduria, Italy	D11	24
Māndvi, India	H4	54
Māndvi, India	G2	54
Mandya, India	E3	53
Manendragarh, India	G9	54
Manfalût, Egypt	K1	58
Manfredonia, Italy	I12	22
Manfredonia, Golfo di, b., Italy	C10	24
Manga, Braz.	H3	88
Manga, reg., Niger	F7	64
Mangabeiras, Chapada das, hills, Braz.	E2	88
Mangagoy, Phil.	F6	52
Mangai, D.R.C.	E3	66
Mangalagiri, India	C5	53
Mangaldai, India	E14	54
Mangalia, Rom.	F15	26
Mangalore, India	E2	53
Mangalvedha, India	C2	53
Mangchang, China	I2	42
Mange, China	B9	54
Mangela, Mount see Nanggala Hill, mtn., Sol. Is.	e7	79b
Manggar, Indon.	E6	50
Mangham, La., U.S.	E7	122
Mangin Range, mts., Mya.	C8	46
Mangkalihat, Tanjung, c., Indon.	C11	50
Manglares, Cabo, c., Col.	G2	86
Mangla Reservoir, res., Pak.	B4	54
Mangnai, China	G16	32
Mangochi, Mwi.	C6	68
Mangoky, stm., Madag.	E7	68
Mangole, Pulau, i., Indon.	F8	44
Mangrol, India	H2	54
Mangrūl Pīr, India	H6	54
Mangsang, Indon.	E4	50
Mangshi see Luxi, China	G4	36
Mangueira, Lagoa, b., Braz.	F11	92
Mangueirinha, Braz.	B11	92
Mangum, Ok., U.S.	G9	128
Mangya, China	D3	36
Manhattan, Ks., U.S.	B12	128
Manhattan, Mt., U.S.	E15	136
Manhiça, Moz.	D11	70
Mān Hpāng, Mya.	A4	48
Manhuaçu, Braz.	K4	88
Manhuaçu, stm., Braz.	J5	88
Manhumirim, Braz.	K4	88
Maniago, Italy	D9	22
Manica, Moz.	D5	68
Manica, state, Moz.	B11	70
Manicaland, state, Zimb.	B11	70
Manic Deux, Réservoir, res., Qc., Can.	A8	110
Manicoré, Braz.	E5	84
Manicouagan, stm., Qc., Can.	E17	106
Manicouagan, Réservoir, res., Qc., Can.	E17	106
Maniganggo, China	E4	36
Manigotagan, Mb., Can.	C17	124
Manigotagan, stm., Can.	C17	124
Manihiki, at., Cook Is.	E10	72
Maniitsoq see Sukkertoppen, Grnld.	D15	141
Mānikganj, Bngl.	G13	54
Mānikpur, India	F8	54
Manila, Phil.	C3	52
Manila, Ar., U.S.	I7	120
Manila, Ut., U.S.	C7	132
Manila Bay, b., Phil.	C3	52
Manilla, Austl.	H8	76
Manily, Russia	D22	34
Maningrida, Austl.	B6	74
Maninjau, Danau, l., Indon.	D1	50
Manipa, Selat, strt., Indon.	F8	44
Manipur, state, India	C7	46
Manipur, stm., Asia	A1	48
Manisa, Tur.	E10	28
Manisa, state, Tur.	E11	28
Manistee, Mi., U.S.	D3	112
Manistee, stm., Mi., U.S.	D3	112
Manistique, Mi., U.S.	C3	112
Manistique Lake, l., Mi., U.S.	B4	112
Manito, Il., U.S.	K9	118
Manitoba, state, Can.	D11	106
Manitoba, Lake, l., Mb., Can.	D15	124
Manitou, stm., On., Can.	B5	118
Manitou, Lake, l., On., Can.	C7	112
Manitou Beach, Sk., Can.	C8	124
Manitou Lake, l., Sk., Can.	B4	124
Manitoulin Island, i., On., Can.	C7	112
Manitou Springs, Co., U.S.	C3	128
Manitowaning, On., Can.	C8	112
Manitowoc, Wi., U.S.	D2	112
Maniwaki, Qc., Can.	B13	112
Manizales, Col.	E4	86
Manja, Madag.	E7	68
Manjakandriana, Madag.	D8	68
Manjeri, India	F3	53
Mānjra, stm., India	B3	53
Mankanza, D.R.C.	D3	66
Mankato, Ks., U.S.	B10	128
Mankato, Mn., U.S.	G4	118
Mankera, Pak.	C3	54
Mankota, Sk., Can.	E6	124
Manley Hot Springs, Ak., U.S.	D9	140
Manlleu, Spain	B13	20
Manmād, India	H5	54
Manna, Indon.	F3	50
Mannahill, Austl.	I3	76
Mannar, Sri L.	G4	53
Mannar, Gulf of, b., Asia	G4	53
Mannārgudi, India	F4	53
Mannford, Ok., U.S.	A2	122
Mannheim, Ger.	G4	16
Manning, N.D., U.S.	G11	124
Manning, S.C., U.S.	C5	116
Manning Strait, strt., Sol. Is.	d7	79b
Mannum, Austl.	J2	76
Mannville, Ab., Can.	C19	138
Manoharpur, India	G10	54
Manokwari, Indon.	F9	44
Manombo Atsimo, Madag.	E7	68
Manono, D.R.C.	F5	66
Manor, Sk., Can.	E11	124
Manor, Tx., U.S.	D10	130
Manosque, Fr.	F11	18
Manouane, Lac, l., Qc., Can.	C2	110
Manouane, Lac, res., Qc., Can.	E16	106
Manp'o, Kor., N.	D7	38
Mānpur, India	H8	54
Manra, at., Kir.	D9	72
Manresa, Spain	C12	20
Mānsa, India	C5	54
Mansa, Zam.	C4	68
Mansafīs, Egypt	J1	58
Mānsehra, Pak.	A4	54
Mansel Island, i., Nu., Can.	C14	106
Mansfield, Eng., U.K.	H11	12
Mansfield, Ga., U.S.	C2	116
Mansfield, Il., U.S.	D9	120
Mansfield, La., U.S.	E5	122
Mansfield, Mo., U.S.	G5	120
Mansfield, Oh., U.S.	D3	114
Mansfield, Pa., U.S.	C8	114
Mansfield, Tx., U.S.	B10	130
Mansfield, Mount, mtn., Vt., U.S.	F4	110
Mansion, St. K./N.	C2	105a
Mansôa, Gui.-B.	G1	64
Manson, Ia., U.S.	B3	120
Mansucum, Pan.	H9	102
Mansura, La., U.S.	F6	122
Manta, Ec.	H1	86
Manta, Bahía de, b., Ec.	H1	86
Mantagao, stm., Mb., Can.	C16	124
Mantalingajan, Mount, mtn., Phil.	F1	52
Mantanani Besar, Pulau, i., Malay.	G1	52
Manteca, Ca., U.S.	F4	134
Mantecal, Ven.	D7	86
Mantena, Braz.	J5	88
Manteo, N.C., U.S.	I10	114
Mantes-la-Jolie, Fr.	F10	14
Manti, Ut., U.S.	D5	132
Mantiqueira, Serra da, mts., Braz.	L3	88
Manton, Mi., U.S.	D4	112
Mántova, Italy	E7	22
Mantua, Cuba	A5	102
Mantua see Mántova, Italy	E7	22
Mantua, Oh., U.S.	C4	114
Manturovo, Russia	G21	8
Mäntyharju, Fin.	F12	8
Manu, Peru	F3	84
Manuae, at., Cook Is.	E11	72
Manuae, at., Fr. Poly.	E11	72
Manua Islands, is., Am. Sam.	h13	79c
Manuel, Mex.	D9	100
Manuel Alves, stm., Braz.	F2	88
Manuel Alves Grande, stm., Braz.	D2	88
Manuel Benavides, Mex.	A6	100
Manuel F. Mantilla see Pedro R. Fernández, Arg.	D8	92
Manuguru, India	B5	53
Manui, Pulau, i., Indon.	F7	44
Manukau, N.Z.	C6	80
Manukau Harbour, b., N.Z.	C6	80
Manus Island, i., Pap. N. Gui.	a4	79a
Mānwat, India	B3	53
Many, La., U.S.	F5	122
Manyara, Lake, l., Tan.	E7	66
Manyberries, Ab., Can.	E3	124
Many Island Lake, l., Can.	D3	124
Manyoni, Tan.	F6	66
Many Peaks, Austl.	E8	76
Manza, D.R.C.	F5	66
Manzala, Bahra el-, l., Egypt	G3	58
Manzanares, Spain	E7	20
Manzanilla Point, c., Trin.	s13	105f
Manzanillo, Cuba	B9	102
Manzanillo, Mex.	F6	100
Manzanillo Bay, b., N.A.	C11	102
Manzano, N.M., U.S.	G2	128
Manzano Peak, mtn., N.M., U.S.	G2	128
Manzhouli, China	B8	36
Manzini, Swaz.	E10	70
Mao, Chad	E3	62
Mao, Dom. Rep.	C12	102
Maó, Spain	E15	20
Maoba, China	F3	42
Maoke, Pegunungan, mts., Indon.	a2	79a
Maolin, China	C5	38
Maoming, China	K4	42
Mapaga, Indon.	D11	50
Mapam Yumco, l., China	C8	54
Mapane, Indon.	D12	50
Mapari, stm., Braz.	I8	86
Mapastepec, Mex.	H12	100
Mapi, Indon.	G10	44
Mapimí, Mex.	C6	100
Mapimí, Bolsón de, des., Mex.	B6	100
Mapire, Ven.	D9	86
Mapiri, Bol.	C3	90
Mapixari, Ilha, i., Braz.	I9	86
Maple, stm., Ia., U.S.	B2	120
Maple, stm., Mi., U.S.	E5	112
Maple, stm., N.D., U.S.	H16	124
Maple Creek, Sk., Can.	E4	124
Maple Lake, Mn., U.S.	F4	118
Maple Mount, Ky., U.S.	G10	120
Maple Ridge, B.C., Can.	G8	138
Mapleton, Ia., U.S.	B2	120
Mapleton, Or., U.S.	F3	136
Mapleton, Ut., U.S.	C5	132
Mapuera, stm., Braz.	C6	84
Maputo, Moz.	D11	70
Maputo, state, Moz.	D11	70
Maputo, stm., Afr.	E11	70
Maqên Gangri, mtn., China	E4	36
Maqna, Sau. Ar.	J5	58
Maquan, stm., China	D10	54
Maquela do Zombo, Ang.	B2	68
Maquereau, Pointe au, c., Qc., Can.	B12	110
Maquinchao, Arg.	H3	90
Maquoketa, Ia., U.S.	B7	120
Maquoketa, stm., Ia., U.S.	B7	120
Maquoketa, North Fork, stm., Ia., U.S.	B7	120
Mar, Serra do, mts., Braz.	B13	92
Mara, stm., Afr.	E7	66
Maraã, Braz.	H9	86
Maraa, Fr. Poly.	v21	78h
Marabá, Braz.	C1	88
Marabahan, Indon.	E9	50
Maraboon, Lake, res., Austl.	D6	76
Maracá, Ilha de, i., Braz.	C7	84
Maracá, Ilha de, i., Braz.	F11	86
Maracaçumé, stm., Braz.	A3	88
Maracaibo, Ven.	B5	86
Maracaibo, Lago de, l., Ven.	C6	86
Maracaju, Braz.	D5	90
Maracanaú, Braz.	B6	88
Maracás, Braz.	G5	88
Maracay, Ven.	B8	86
Marādah, Libya	B3	62
Maradi, Niger	G6	64
Marāghah, Sabkhat al-, l., Syria	C8	58
Marāgheh, Iran	B6	56
Maragogipe, Braz.	G6	88
Maragoji, Braz.	E8	88
Marahuaca, Cerro, mtn., Ven.	F9	86
Maraial, Braz.	E8	88
Marais des Cygnes, stm., U.S.	F3	120
Marajó, Baía de, b., Braz.	D8	84
Marajó, Ilha de, i., Braz.	D8	84
Maralal, Kenya	D7	66
Marali, C.A.R.	C3	66
Maralinga, Austl.	F6	74
Marambio, sci., Ant.	B35	81
Marampa, S.L.	H2	64
Maramsilli Reservoir, res., India	H8	54
Maramureș, state, Rom.	B10	26
Maran, Malay.	K6	48
Marana, Az., U.S.	K5	132
Marand, Iran	B6	56
Marang, Malay.	J6	48
Marangas, Phil.	F1	52
Maranguape, Braz.	B6	88
Maranhão, state, Braz.	C3	88
Maranhão, stm., Braz.	D9	84
Marano, Laguna di, b., Italy	E10	22
Maranoa, stm., Austl.	F7	76
Marañón, stm., Peru	D2	84
Marasende, Pulau, i., Indon.	F10	50
Mărășești, Rom.	D14	26
Maratasã, stm., Braz.	C4	88
Marathon, Austl.	C4	76
Marathon, On., Can.	C12	118
Marathon, Tx., U.S.	D4	130
Marathon, Wi., U.S.	G9	118
Marathónas, Grc.	E6	28
Maratua, Pulau, i., Indon.	B11	50
Maraú, Braz.	H6	88
Marau, Braz.	D11	92
Marauiá, stm., Braz.	H9	86
Maravilha, Braz.	C11	92
Maravillas, Mex.	B6	100
Maravillas Creek, stm., Tx., U.S.	E4	130
Marav Lake, l., Pak.	D2	54
Maravovo, Sol. Is.	e8	79b
Marawi, Phil.	F5	52
Marawwah, i., U.A.E.	E7	56
Marayes, Arg.	E4	92
Marbella, Spain	H6	20
Marble, N.C., U.S.	A2	116
Marble Bar, Austl.	D3	74
Marble Canyon, val., Az., U.S.	G5	132
Marble Falls, Tx., U.S.	D9	130
Marble Hall, S. Afr.	D9	70
Marble Hill, Mo., U.S.	G8	120
Marblemount, Wa., U.S.	B5	136
Marble Rock, Ia., U.S.	I6	118
Marburg, Ger.	F4	16
Marburg, S. Afr.	G10	70
Marca, Ponta da, c., Ang.	D1	68
Marcal, stm., Hung.	B4	26
Marcelin, Sk., Can.	B7	124
Marceline, Mo., U.S.	E5	120
March, Eng., U.K.	I12	12
March (Morava), stm., Eur.	H12	16
Marche, state, Italy	G10	22
Marche, hist. reg., Fr.	C8	18
Marche-en-Famenne, Bel.	D14	14
Marchena, Spain	G5	20
Marches see Marche, state, Italy	G10	22
Mar Chiquita, Laguna, b., Arg.	H9	92
Mar Chiquita, Laguna, l., Arg.	E6	92
Marcigny, Fr.	C10	18
Marco, Braz.	B5	88
Marcos Juárez, Arg.	F6	92
Marcus, Ia., U.S.	B2	120
Marcus Baker, Mount, mtn., Ak., U.S.	D10	140
Marcus Island see Minami-Tori-shima, i., Japan	G19	30
Marcy, Mount, mtn., N.Y., U.S.	F2	110
Mardān, Pak.	A4	54
Mardarivka, Ukr.	B16	26
Mar del Plata, Arg.	H9	92
Mardin, Tur.	B5	56
Maré, i., N. Cal.	m17	79d
Mare a Brăilei, Insula, i., Rom.	D14	26
Marea de Portillo, Cuba	C9	102
Marechal Cândido Rondon, Braz.	B10	92
Marechal Deodoro, Braz.	E8	88
Maree, Loch, l., Scot., U.K.	D7	12
Mareeba, Austl.	A5	76
Maremma, reg., Italy	H8	22
Marengo, Il., U.S.	B9	120
Marengo, Ia., U.S.	C5	120
Marenisco, Mi., U.S.	E9	118
Marennes, Fr.	D4	18
Marettimo, Isola, i., Italy	G5	24
Marfa, Tx., U.S.	D3	130
Margai Caka, l., China	A6	46
Margaree Harbour, N.S., Can.	D15	110
Margaret, stm., Austl.	C5	74
Margaret Bay, B.C., Can.	E3	138
Margaret River, Austl.	F2	74
Margaretville, N.Y., U.S.	B11	114
Margarita, Isla de, i., Ven.	B9	86
Margate, S. Afr.	G10	70
Margate, Eng., U.K.	J14	12
Margate, Fl., U.S.	J5	116
Margecany, Slov.	H16	16
Margelan see Margilan, Uzb.	F12	32
Margherita di Savoia, Italy	C10	24
Margherita Peak, mtn., Afr.	D5	66
Margilan, Uzb.	F12	32
Margonin, Pol.	D13	16
Margosatubig, Phil.	G4	52
Mārgow, Dasht-e, des., Afg.	C9	56
Marha, Russia	D13	34
Marha, stm., Russia	C12	34
Maria, Îles, is., Fr. Poly.	F11	72
María Cleofas, Isla, i., Mex.	E5	100
María Elena, Chile	D3	90
María Grande, Arg.	E8	92
María Ignacia, Arg.	H8	92
Maria Island, i., Austl.	B7	74
Maria Island National Park, p.o.i., Austl.	o14	77a
Mariakani, Kenya	E7	66
María Madre, Isla, i., Mex.	E5	100
María Magdalena, Isla, i., Mex.	E5	100
Mariana, Braz.	K4	88
Mariana Islands, is., Oc.	B5	72
Mariana Ridge, unds.	H17	142
Mariana Trench, unds.	H17	142
Marian Lake, l., N.T., Can.	C7	106
Marianna, Ar., U.S.	C8	122
Marianna, Fl., U.S.	G13	122
Mariano I. Loza, Arg.	D8	92
Mariánské Lázně, Czech Rep.	G8	16
Marias, stm., Mt., U.S.	B16	136
Marias Pass, p., Mt., U.S.	B13	136
María Teresa, Arg.	G6	92
Mariato, Punta, c., Pan.	I7	102
Maribo, Den.	B7	16
Maribor, Slvn.	D12	22
Maricao, P.R.	B2	104a
Marico, stm., Afr.	D8	70
Maricopa, Az., U.S.	J4	132
Maricunga, Salar de, pl., Chile	C3	92
Marié, stm., Braz.	H8	86
Marie Byrd Land, reg., Ant.	C29	81
Marie-Galante, i., Guad.	i6	105c
Mariehamn see Maarianhamina, Fin.	F9	8
Mariental, Nmb.	D4	70
Marienville, Pa., U.S.	C6	114
Mariestad, Swe.	G5	8
Marieta, stm., Ven.	E8	86
Marietta, Ga., U.S.	D14	122
Marietta, Mn., U.S.	G2	118
Marietta, Oh., U.S.	E4	114
Marieville, Qc., Can.	E3	110
Marignane, Fr.	F11	18
Marigot, Dom.	i6	105c
Marigot, Guad.	A1	105a
Mariinsk, Russia	C15	32
Mariinskoe, Russia	F17	34
Marijampolė, Lith.	F6	10
Marij El, state, Russia	C7	32
Marília, Braz.	D7	90
Marimba, Ang.	B2	68
Marín, Mex.	I7	130
Marín, Spain	B2	20
Marina di Ravenna, Italy	F9	22
Marina Fall, wtfl, Guy.	E12	86
Mar''ina Horka, Bela.	G11	10
Marinduque, i., Phil.	D3	52
Marine City, Mi., U.S.	B3	114
Marinette, Wi., U.S.	C2	112
Maringá, Braz.	D6	90
Marino, Vanuatu	j16	79d
Marintu, Indon.	C6	50
Marion, Al., U.S.	E11	122
Marion, Ar., U.S.	B8	122
Marion, Il., U.S.	G9	120
Marion, In., U.S.	H4	112
Marion, Ia., U.S.	B6	120
Marion, Ks., U.S.	C12	128
Marion, Ky., U.S.	G9	120
Marion, La., U.S.	E6	122
Marion, Ms., U.S.	E10	122
Marion, N.C., U.S.	I4	114
Marion, N.D., U.S.	A14	126
Marion, Oh., U.S.	D2	114
Marion, S.C., U.S.	B6	116
Marion, Va., U.S.	H4	114
Marion, Lake, res., S.C., U.S.	C5	116
Marion Bay, b., Austl.	o13	77a
Marion County Lake, res., Ks., U.S.	C11	128
Marion Downs, Austl.	D2	76
Marion Junction, Al., U.S.	E11	122
Marion Reef, rf., Austl.	B9	76
Marionville, Mo., U.S.	G4	120
Maripa, Ven.	D9	86
Mariposa, Ca., U.S.	F5	134
Mariquita, Col.	E4	86
Mariscal Estigarribia, Para.	D4	90
Maritime Alps, mts., Eur.	E12	18
Maritsa (Évros) (Marica) (Meriç), stm., Eur.	C9	28
Mariupol', Ukr.	E5	32
Mariusa, Caño, stm., Ven.	C11	86
Mariveles, Phil.	C3	52
Mariyampole see Marijampolė, Lith.	F6	10
Marjanovka, Russia	D12	32
Marka, Som.	D8	66
Markakol', ozero, l., Kaz.	E15	32
Mārkāpur, India	D4	53
Markaryd, Swe.	H5	8
Markdale, On., Can.	D9	112
Marked Tree, Ar., U.S.	B8	122
Markesan, Wi., U.S.	H10	118
Market Harborough, Eng., U.K.	I12	12
Markham, On., Can.	E10	112
Markham, Tx., U.S.	F11	130
Markham Bay, b., Nu., Can.	C16	106
Markit, China	B12	56
Markle, In., U.S.	H4	112
Markleeville, Ca., U.S.	E6	134
Markovo, Russia	D23	34
Marks, Russia	D7	32
Marks, Ms., U.S.	C8	122
Marktheidenfeld, Ger.	G5	16
Marktoberdorf, Ger.	I6	16
Marktredwitz, Ger.	G8	16
Mark Twain Lake, res., Mo., U.S.	E6	120
Marlboro, Ab., Can.	C14	138
Marlboro, N.Y., U.S.	C11	114
Marlborough, Austl.	D7	76
Marlborough, Guy.	B6	84
Marlborough, Ma., U.S.	B14	114
Marlette, Mi., U.S.	E6	112
Marlinton, W.V., U.S.	F5	114
Marlow, Ok., U.S.	G11	128
Marmaduke, Ar., U.S.	H7	120
Marmande, Fr.	E6	18
Marmara, Sea of see Marmara Denizi, Tur.	C11	28
Marmara Adası, i., Tur.	C10	28
Marmara Denizi (Marmara, Sea of), Tur.	C11	28
Marmara Ereğlisi, Tur.	C10	28
Marmara Gölü, l., Tur.	E10	28
Marmaris, Tur.	G11	28
Marmaton, stm., U.S.	G3	120
Marmelos, stm., Braz.	E5	84
Marmet, W.V., U.S.	F4	114
Marmion Lake, l., On., Can.	C7	118
Marmolada, mtn., Italy	D8	22
Marmora, On., Can.	D12	112
Marnay, Fr.	G14	14
Marne, Ger.	C4	16
Marne, Mi., U.S.	E4	112
Marne, state, Fr.	E13	14
Marne, stm., Fr.	E11	14
Marne à la Saône, Canal de la, can., Fr.	F14	14
Maroa, Ven.	F8	86
Maroantsetra, Madag.	D8	68
Maromandia, Madag.	C8	68
Maromme, Fr.	E10	14
Maromokotro, mtn., Madag.	C8	68
Marondera, Zimb.	D5	68
Maroni (Marowijne), stm., S.A.	C7	84
Maros, Indon.	F11	50
Maros (Mureș), stm., Eur.	C7	26
Maroua, Cam.	B2	66
Marovoay, Madag.	D8	68
Marowijne (Maroni), stm., S.A.	C7	84
Marquand, Mo., U.S.	G7	120
Marquard, S. Afr.	F8	70
Marquesas Islands see Marquises, Îles, is., Fr. Poly.	D12	72
Marquesas Keys, is., Fl., U.S.	L3	116
Marquette, Ks., U.S.	C11	128
Marquette, Mi., U.S.	B2	112
Marquis, Gren.	q10	105e
Marquises, Îles, is., Fr. Poly.	D12	72
Marradi, Italy	F8	22
Marrah, Jabal, hill, Sudan	E4	62
Marrakech, Mor.	C3	64
Marrakesh see Marrakech, Mor.	C3	64
Marrawah, Austl.	n12	77a
Marree, Austl.	E7	74
Marrero, La., U.S.	H8	122
Marromeu, Moz.	D6	68
Marrupa, Moz.	C6	68
Marsá al-Burayqah, Libya	A3	62
Marsabit, Kenya	D7	66
Marsala, Italy	G6	24
Marsciano, Italy	H9	22
Marseille, Fr.	F11	18
Marseilles, Il., U.S.	C9	120
Marsfjället, mtn., Swe.	D6	8
Marshall, Lib.	H2	64
Marshall, Ak., U.S.	D7	140
Marshall, Ar., U.S.	I5	120
Marshall, Mi., U.S.	B1	114
Marshall, Mn., U.S.	G3	118
Marshall, Mo., U.S.	E4	120
Marshall, N.C., U.S.	I3	114
Marshall, Tx., U.S.	E4	122
Marshall, Va., U.S.	F8	114
Marshall, stm., Austl.	D7	74
Marshallberg, N.C., U.S.	B9	116
Marshall Islands, ctry., Oc.	H19	142
Marshall Islands, is., Marsh. Is.	B7	72
Marshalltown, Ia., U.S.	B5	120
Marshfield, Mo., U.S.	G4	120
Marshfield, Wi., U.S.	G8	118
Mars Hill, Me., U.S.	D9	110
Mars Hill, N.C., U.S.	I3	114
Marsh Island, i., La., U.S.	H7	122
Marshville, N.C., U.S.	A5	116
Marsing, Id., U.S.	G10	136
Märsta, Swe.	G7	8
Marstal, Den.	B6	16
Martaban, Gulf of, b., Mya.	D3	48
Martapura, Indon.	E9	50
Martapura, Indon.	F4	50
Marte R. Gómez, Presa, res., Mex.	H9	130
Marthaguy Creek, stm., Austl.	H6	76
Martha's Vineyard, i., Ma., U.S.	C15	114
Martí, Cuba	B9	102
Martigny, Switz.	D4	22
Martigues, Fr.	F11	18
Martin, Slov.	G14	16
Martin, Ky., U.S.	G3	114
Martin, Mi., U.S.	F4	112
Martin, N.D., U.S.	G13	124
Martin, Tn., U.S.	H9	120
Martín, stm., Spain	C10	20
Martina Franca, Italy	D11	24
Martindale, Tx., U.S.	E10	130
Mărtinești, Rom.	D14	26
Martinez, Ca., U.S.	E3	134
Martinez, Ga., U.S.	C3	116
Martínez de la Torre, Mex.	E10	100
Martinho Campos, Braz.	J3	88
Martinique, dep., N.A.	i15	96a
Martinique Passage, strt., N.A.	k6	105c
Martin Lake, res., Al., U.S.	E12	122
Martinópole, Braz.	B5	88
Martinsberg, Aus.	B12	22
Martinsburg, W.V., U.S.	E7	114
Martins Ferry, Oh., U.S.	D5	114
Martinsville, Il., U.S.	E10	120
Martinsville, In., U.S.	E11	120
Martinsville, Va., U.S.	H5	114
Martin Vaz, Ilhas, is., Braz.	H12	82
Martos, Spain	G7	20
Martre, Lac la, l., N.T., Can.	C7	106
Martti, Fin.	C13	8
Marudi, Malay.	A9	50
Marudu, Telukan, b., Malay.	G1	52
Marugame, Japan	E6	40
Maruim, Braz.	F7	88
Maruoka, Japan	C9	40
Marutea, at., Fr. Poly.	E12	72
Marv Dasht, Iran	D7	56
Marvine, Mount, mtn., Ut., U.S.	E5	132
Mārwār, India	F4	54
Mary, Turkmen.	B9	56
Mary, stm., Austl.	E9	76
Maryborough, Austl.	E9	76
Maryborough, Austl.	K4	76
Marydale, S. Afr.	F5	70
Maryfield, Sk., Can.	E12	124
Mary Kathleen, Austl.	C2	76
Maryland, state, U.S.	E8	114
Maryneal, Tx., U.S.	B7	130
Maryport, Eng., U.K.	G9	12
Marysvale, Ut., U.S.	E4	132
Marysville, N.B., Can.	D10	110
Marysville, Ca., U.S.	D4	134
Marysville, Ks., U.S.	L2	118
Marysville, Mi., U.S.	B3	114
Marysville, Oh., U.S.	D2	114
Marysville, Wa., U.S.	B4	136
Maryville, Mo., U.S.	D3	120
Maryville, Tn., U.S.	I2	114
Marzagão, Braz.	I1	88
Marzo, Punta, c., Col.	D3	86
Masada see Mezada, Horvot, hist., Isr.	G6	58
Masai Mara Game Reserve, Kenya	E7	66
Masai Steppe, plat., Tan.	E7	66
Masaka, Ug.	E6	66
Masalembu Besar, Pulau, i., Indon.	F9	50
Masamba, Indon.	E12	50
Masan, Kor., S.	D1	40
Masasi, Tan.	G7	66
Masatepe, Nic.	G4	102
Masaya, Nic.	G4	102
Masbate, Phil.	D4	52
Masbate, i., Phil.	E4	52
Mascarene Basin, unds.	K8	142
Mascarene Islands, is., Afr.	i10	69a
Mascarene Plateau, unds.	J8	142
Mascot, Tn., U.S.	H2	114
Mascota, Mex.	E6	100
Mascoutah, Il., U.S.	F8	120
Maseru, Leso.	F8	70
Mashan, China	J3	42
Mashava, Zimb.	D5	68
Mashhad, Iran	B8	56
Mashi, China	G6	42
Mashiko, Japan	C13	40
Mashra'ar Raqq, Sudan	F5	62
Masi-Manimba, D.R.C.	E3	66
Masindi, Ug.	D6	66
Masira, Gulf of see Maṣīrah, Khalīj, b., Oman	F8	56
Maṣīrah, i., Oman	E8	56
Maṣīrah, Khalīj, b., Oman	F8	56
Masisea, Peru	E3	84
Masjed-e Soleymān, Iran	C6	56
Mask, Lough, l., Ire.	H3	12
Maskanah, Syria	B8	58
Masljanino, Russia	D14	32
Mason, Mi., U.S.	F5	112
Mason, Oh., U.S.	E1	114
Mason, Tx., U.S.	D8	130
Mason, W.V., U.S.	E3	114
Mason City, Il., U.S.	D8	120
Mason City, Ia., U.S.	A4	120
Mason City, Ne., U.S.	F13	126
Masqaṭ (Muscat), Oman	E8	56
Massa, Italy	F7	22
Massachusetts, state, U.S.	B14	114
Massachusetts Bay, b., Ma., U.S.	B15	114
Massafra, Italy	D11	24
Massaguet, Chad	E3	62
Massa Marittima, Italy	G7	22
Massangena, Moz.	B11	70
Massawa (Mitsiwa), Erit.	D7	62
Massena, Ia., U.S.	C3	120
Massena, N.Y., U.S.	F2	110
Massenya, Chad	E3	62
Massey, On., Can.	B7	112
Massey Sound, strt., Nu., Can.	B7	141
Massiac, Fr.	D9	18
Massillon, Oh., U.S.	D4	114
Massina, reg., Mali	G4	64
Massinga, Moz.	C12	70
Massingir, Moz.	C11	70
Massive, Mount, mtn., Co., U.S.	D10	132
Masson Island, i., Ant.	B14	81
Mastābah, Sau. Ar.	E4	56
Masterson, Tx., U.S.	F6	128
Masterton, N.Z.	E6	80
Mastic Point, Bah.	K8	116
Mastung, Pak.	D10	56
Masty, Bela.	G7	10
Masuda, Japan	E4	40
Masurai, Gunung, mtn., Indon.	E2	50
Masuria see Mazury, reg., Pol.	C16	16
Masvingo, Zimb.	E5	68
Masvingo, state, Zimb.	B10	70
Maṣyāf, Syria	C7	58
Mata Amarilla, Arg.	I2	90
Matabeleland North, state, Zimb.	A9	70
Matabeleland South, state, Zimb.	B9	70
Matabuena, Spain	C7	20
Matacuni, stm., Ven.	F9	86
Mata de São João, Braz.	G6	88
Matadi, D.R.C.	F2	66
Matagalpa, Nic.	F5	102
Matagami, Qc., Can.	F15	106
Matagorda, Tx., U.S.	F12	130

I•36 Mata-Mian

Name — Map Ref. — Page

Matagorda Island, i., Tx., U.S. F11 130
Matagorda Peninsula, pen., Tx., U.S. F11 130
Matahiae, Pointe, c., Fr. Poly. w22 78h
Matâi, Egypt J1 58
Mataiea, Fr. Poly. w22 78h
Mataiva, at., Fr. Poly. E12 72
Matak, Pulau, i., Indon. B5 50
Matakana, Austl. I5 76
Matale, Sri L. H5 53
Matam, Sen. F2 64
Matamoros, Mex. C10 100
Matamoros, Mex. C7 100
Matan, Indon. D7 50
Matandu, stm., Tan. F7 66
Matane, Qc., Can. B9 110
Matanni, Pak. B3 54
Matanzas, Cuba A7 102
Matanzas, Mex. E8 100
Matapan, Cape see Taínaro, Ákra, c., Grc. G5 28
Matape, stm., Mex. A3 100
Matapédia, Qc., Can. C9 110
Matapédia, Lac, l., Qc., Can. B9 110
Mataquito, stm., Chile G2 92
Matara, Sri L. I5 53
Mataram, Indon. H9 50
Mataranka, Austl. B6 74
Mataró, Spain C13 20
Matasiri, Pulau, i., Indon. F9 50
Matatiele, S. Afr. G9 70
Matatula, Cape, c., Am. Sam. h12 79c
Matâ'utu, Wal./F. E9 72
Matavera, Cook Is. a27 78j
Mataveri, Chile e29 78l
Mataveri, Aeropuerto, Chile f29 78l
Mataveri Airstrip see Mataveri, Aeropuerto, Chile f29 78l
Matehuala, Mex. D8 100
Mateke Hills, hills, Zimb. B10 70
Matera, Italy D10 24
Mateur, Tun. G3 24
Matha, Fr. D5 18
Mather, Mb., Can. E14 124
Mather, Pa., U.S. E5 114
Matheson, On., Can. F14 106
Mathews, Va., U.S. G9 114
Mathis, Tx., U.S. F10 130
Mathura (Muttra), India E6 54
Matias Barbosa, Braz. K4 88
Matías Romero, Mex. G11 100
Matícora, stm., Ven. B6 86
Matinha, Braz. B3 88
Matipó, Braz. K4 88
Matiyure, stm., Ven. D7 86
Mātli, Pak. F2 54
Mato, Cerro, mtn., Ven. D9 86
Mato Grosso, state, Braz. F6 84
Mato Grosso, Planalto do, plat., Braz. B5 90
Mato Grosso, Plateau of see Mato Grosso, Planalto do, plat., Braz. B5 90
Mato Grosso do Sul, state, Braz. C6 90
Matola Rio, Moz. D11 70
Matopos, Zimb. B9 70
Matosinhos, Port. C2 20
Matouying, China B8 42
Matozinhos, Braz. J3 88
Maṭraḥ, Oman E8 56
Matsudo, Japan D12 40
Matsue, Japan D6 40
Matsumoto, Japan C10 40
Matsusaka, Japan E9 40
Matsu Tao, i., Tai. H8 42
Matsutō, Japan C9 40
Matsuura, Japan F2 40
Matsuyama, Japan F5 40
Mattagami, stm., On., Can. F14 106
Mattamuskeet, Lake, l., N.C., U.S. A9 116
Mattaponi, stm., Va., U.S. G8 114
Mattawa, On., Can. B11 112
Mattawa, Wa., U.S. D7 136
Mattawamkeag, stm., Me., U.S. E8 110
Matterhorn, mtn., Eur. D13 18
Matterhorn, mtn., Nv., U.S. B1 132
Matthews Mountain, hill, Mo., U.S. G7 120
Matthew Town, Bah. C10 96
Mattighofen, Aus. B10 22
Mattoon, Il., U.S. E9 120
Mattoon, Wi., U.S. F9 118
Mattydale, N.Y., U.S. E13 112
Matua, Indon. E7 50
Matudo see Matsudo, Japan D12 40
Matue see Matsue, Japan D6 40
Matuku, i., Fiji q19 79e
Matumoto see Matsumoto, Japan C10 40
Maturín, Ven. C10 86
Matutina, Braz. J2 88
Matuzaka see Matsusaka, Japan E9 40
Maú (Ireng), stm., S.A. F12 86
Maúa, Moz. C6 68
Mau Aimma, India F8 54
Maubeuge, Fr. D12 14
Maud, Tx., U.S. D4 122
Maudaha, India F7 54
Maude, Austl. J5 76
Maués, Braz. D6 84
Maués, stm., Braz. D6 84
Mauganj, India F8 54
Maui, i., Hi., U.S. C5 78a
Mauk, Indon. F5 50
Mauldin, S.C., U.S. B3 116
Maule, state, Chile G2 92
Maule, stm., Chile G1 92
Maule, Laguna del, l., Chile G2 92
Mauléon-Licharre, Fr. F5 18
Maumee, Oh., U.S. G6 112
Maumee, stm., U.S. G6 112
Maumelle, Lake, res., Ar., U.S. C6 122
Maumere, Indon. G7 44
Maun, Bots. D3 68
Maunabo, P.R. B4 104a
Mauna Kea, vol., Hi., U.S. D6 78a
Maunaloa, Hi., U.S. B4 78a
Mauna Loa, vol., Hi., U.S. D6 78a
Maunath Bhanjan, India F9 54
Maungdaw, Mya. H14 54
Maungmagan, Mya. E3 48
Maunoir, Lac, l., N.T., Can. B6 106
Maupihaa, at., Fr. Poly. E11 72
Mau Rānīpur, India F7 54
Maurepas, Lake, l., La., U.S. G8 122
Maurice, Lake, l., Austl. E6 74
Mauricie, Parc national de la, p.o.i., Qc., Can. D3 110
Mauritania, ctry., Afr. F2 64
Mauritanie see Mauritania, ctry., Afr. F2 64
Mauritius, ctry., Afr. h10 69a
Mauron, Fr. F6 14
Mauston, Wi., U.S. H8 118
Mautau, c., Fr. Poly. r19 78g
Mauterndorf, Aus. C10 22
Mauthen, Aus. D9 22
Mauvais Coulee, stm., N.D., U.S. F14 124
Mava, Pap. N. Gui. b3 79a
Maverick, Az., U.S. J7 132
Mavinga, Ang. D3 68
Mavrovo Nacionalni Park, p.o.i., Mac. B3 28
Mavuradonha Mountains, mts., Zimb. D5 68
Mawchi, Mya. C3 48
Mawlaik, Mya. D7 46
Mawlamyine (Moulmein), Mya. D3 48
Mawson, sci., Ant. B11 81
Maw Taung (Luang, Khao), mtn., Asia G4 48
Max, N.D., U.S. G12 124
Maxaranguape, Braz. C8 88
Maxcanú, Mex. B3 102
Maxixe, Moz. C12 70
Maxville, On., Can. E2 110
Maxwell, Ca., U.S. D3 134
Maxwell, Ne., U.S. F12 126
Maxwell, N.M., U.S. E4 128
May, Tx., U.S. B9 130
May, Cape, pen., N.J., U.S. F11 114
May, Mount, mtn., Ab., Can. B11 138
Maya, Pulau, i., Indon. D6 50
Mayaguana, i., Bah. A11 102
Mayaguana Passage, strt., Bah. A11 102
Mayagüez, P.R. B1 104a
Mayang, China H3 42
Mayarí, Cuba B10 102
Maybole, Scot., U.K. F8 12
Maydena, Austl. o13 77a
Maydh, Som. B9 66
Mayen, Ger. F3 16
Mayenne, Fr. F8 14
Mayenne, state, Fr. F8 14
Mayenne, stm., Fr. F8 14
Mayer, Az., U.S. I4 132
Mayerthorpe, Ab., Can. C15 138
Mayfield, Ky., U.S. H9 120
Mayfield, Ut., U.S. D5 132
Mayflower, Ar., U.S. C6 122
Māyir, Syria B8 58
Maykain see Majkain, Kaz. D13 32
Maymyo, Mya. A3 48
Maynard, Ia., U.S. B6 120
Maynardville, Tn., U.S. H2 114
Mayne, stm., Austl. D3 76
Mayo, Yk., Can. C3 106
Mayo, Fl., U.S. F2 116
Mayo, state, Ire. H3 12
Mayo, stm., Arg. I3 90
Mayo, stm., Mex. B4 100
Mayon Volcano, vol., Phil. D4 52
Mayor Buratovich, Arg. G4 90
Mayotte, dep., Afr. C8 68
Mayoyoque, Col. G4 86
May Pen, Jam. j13 104d
Mayreau, i., St. Vin. p11 105e
Mays Landing, N.J., U.S. E11 114
Maysville, Ky., U.S. F2 114
Maysville, Mo., U.S. E3 120
Maysville, N.C., U.S. B8 116
Maysville, Ok., U.S. G11 128
Mayumba, Gabon E2 66
Māyūram, India F4 53
Mayville, Mi., U.S. E6 112
Mayville, N.Y., U.S. B6 114
Mayville, N.D., U.S. G16 124
Maywood, Ne., U.S. G12 126
Maza, Arg. H6 92
Mazabuka, Zam. D4 68
Mazagão, Braz. D7 84
Mazamet, Fr. F8 18
Mazán, stm., Peru I4 86
Mazara, Val di, reg., Italy G7 24
Mazara del Vallo, Italy G6 24
Mazār-e Sharīf, Afg. B10 56
Mazarrón, Golfo de, b., Spain G9 20
Mazaruni, stm., Guy. D11 86
Mazatenango, Guat. E2 102
Mazatlán, Mex. D5 100
Mažeikiai, Lith. D5 10
Mazenod, Sk., Can. E7 124
Mazinga, mtn., Neth. Ant. C2 105a
Mazirbe, Lat. C5 10
Mazon, Il., U.S. C9 120
Mazowe, stm., Afr. D5 68
Mazury (Masuria), reg., Pol. C16 16
Mazyr, Bela. D3 32
Mbabane, Swaz. E10 70
M'bahiakro, C. Iv. H4 64
Mbaïki, C.A.R. D3 66
Mbaké, Sen. G1 64
Mbala, Zam. B5 68
Mbalabala, Zimb. B9 70
Mbale, Ug. D6 66
Mbalmayo, Cam. D2 66
Mbamba Bay, Tan. G7 66
Mbandaka (Coquilhatville), D.R.C. D3 66
Mbanga, Cam. D1 66
Mbanika Island, i., Sol. Is. e8 79b
M'banza Congo, Ang. B1 68
Mbanza-Ngungu, D.R.C. F3 66
Mbarara, Ug. E6 66
Mbashe, stm., S. Afr. H9 70
Mbava Island, i., Sol. Is. d7 79b
Mbé, Cam. C2 66
Mberengwa, Zimb. B9 70
Mbeya, Tan. F6 66
Mbigou, Gabon E2 66
Mbinda, Congo E2 66
Mbini, Eq. Gui. I6 64
Mbini, stm., Afr. I6 64
Mboi, D.R.C. F4 66
Mboki, C.A.R. C5 66
Mbola, Sol. Is. e9 79b
Mborokua, i., Sol. Is. e8 79b
Mborong, Indon. H12 50
Mbouda, Cam. C2 66
Mbour, Sen. G1 64
Mbout, Maur. F2 64
Mbuji-Mayi (Bakwanga), D.R.C. F4 66
Mbuluzi, stm., Swaz. E10 70
Mbwemkuru, stm., Tan. F7 66
McAdam, N.B., Can. E9 110
McAdoo, Pa., U.S. D9 114
McAlester, Ok., U.S. C3 122
McAllen, Tx., U.S. H9 130
McArthur, Oh., U.S. E3 114
McArthur, stm., Austl. C7 74
McArthur River, Austl. C7 74
McBain, Mi., U.S. D4 112
McBee, S.C., U.S. B5 116
McBeth Fjord, b., Nu., Can. B17 106
McBride, B.C., Can. C10 138
McCall Creek, Ms., U.S. F8 122
McCamey, Tx., U.S. C5 130
McCammon, Id., U.S. H14 136
McCauley Island, i., B.C., Can. E4 106
McCleary, Wa., U.S. C3 136
McClellan Creek, stm., Tx., U.S. F8 128
McClellanville, S.C., U.S. C6 116
McClintock, Mount, mtn., Ant. D21 81
McCloud, Ca., U.S. B3 134
McCloud, stm., Ca., U.S. B3 134
McClure, Il., U.S. G8 120
Mcclusky, N.D., U.S. G13 124
McColl, S.C., U.S. B6 116
McComb, Ms., U.S. F8 122
McConaughy, Lake, res., Ne., U.S. F11 126
McConnellsburg, Pa., U.S. E7 114
McConnelsville, Oh., U.S. E4 114
McCook, Ne., U.S. A8 128
McCormick, S.C., U.S. C3 116
McCreary, Mb., Can. D14 124
McCullough Mountain, mtn., Nv., U.S. H1 132
McCune, Ks., U.S. G2 120
McCurtain, Ok., U.S. B4 122
McDade, Tx., U.S. D10 130
McDermitt, Nv., U.S. B8 134
McDermott, Oh., U.S. F2 114
McDonald, Ks., U.S. B7 128
McDonald, Lake, l., Mt., U.S. B12 136
McDowell Peak, mtn., Az., U.S. J4 132
Mcensk, Russia G19 10
McEwen, Tn., U.S. H10 120
McFadden, Wy., U.S. B10 132
McFarland, Ca., U.S. H6 134
McGehee, Ar., U.S. D7 122
McGill, Nv., U.S. D2 132
McGrath, Ak., U.S. D8 140
McGraw, N.Y., U.S. B9 114
McGregor, Tx., U.S. C10 130
McGregor, stm., B.C., Can. B9 138
McGregor Lake, l., Ab., Can. F18 138
McHenry, Il., U.S. B9 120
McHenry, Ms., U.S. G9 122
Mchinji, Mwi. C5 68
McIntosh, Al., U.S. F10 122
McIntosh, Mn., U.S. D3 118
McIntyre Bay, b., On., Can. B10 118
McKeand, stm., Nu., Can. C17 106
McKee, Ky., U.S. G2 114
McKeesport, Pa., U.S. D6 114
McKenzie, Tn., U.S. H9 120
McKenzie, stm., Or., U.S. F4 136
McKenzie Bridge, Or., U.S. F4 136
McKenzie Island, On., Can. E12 106
McKinlay, Austl. C3 76
McKinlay, stm., Austl. C3 76
McKinley, Mount, mtn., Ak., U.S. D9 140
McKinleyville, Ca., U.S. C1 134
McKinney, Tx., U.S. D2 122
McKittrick Summit, mtn., Ca., U.S. H6 134
McLain, Ms., U.S. F10 122
McLaurin, Ms., U.S. F9 122
McLean, Il., U.S. D8 120
McLean, Tx., U.S. F8 128
McLeansboro, Il., U.S. F9 120
McLennan, Ab., Can. D7 106
McLeod, stm., Ab., Can. C15 138
McLeod Bay, b., N.T., Can. C8 106
McLeod Lake, B.C., Can. B7 138
M'Clintock Channel, strt., Nu., Can. A10 106
McLoughlin, Mount, mtn., Or., U.S. A3 134
McLouth, Ks., U.S. E2 120
M'Clure Strait, strt., N.T., Can. B16 140
McMahon, Sk., Can. D6 124
McMinnville, Or., U.S. E3 136
McMinnville, Tn., U.S. B13 122
McMurdo, sci., Ant. C22 81
McMurdo Sound, strt., Ant. C22 81
McNary, Az., U.S. I7 132
McNeil, Ar., U.S. D5 122
McPherson, Ks., U.S. C11 128
McQueeney, Tx., U.S. E9 130
McRae, Ar., U.S. B7 122
McRae, Ga., U.S. D3 116
McVeigh, Ky., U.S. G3 114
McVille, N.D., U.S. G15 124
McWilliams, Al., U.S. F11 122
Mdantsane, S. Afr. H8 70
M'drak, Viet. F9 48
Mead, Ne., U.S. C1 120
Mead, Lake, res., U.S. G2 132
Meade, Ks., U.S. D8 128
Meaden Peak, mtn., Co., U.S. C9 132
Meadow, Ut., U.S. E4 132
Meadow Lake, Sk., Can. E9 106
Meadow Valley Wash, stm., Nv., U.S. F2 132
Meadowview, Va., U.S. H3 114
Meadville, Ms., U.S. F7 122
Meadville, Mo., U.S. E4 120
Meadville, Pa., U.S. C5 114
Meaford, On., Can. D9 112
Mealhada, Port. D2 20
Meandarra, Austl. F7 76
Meander River, Ab., Can. D7 106
Mearim, stm., Braz. B3 88
Meath, state, Ire. H6 12
Meath, hist. reg., Ire. H6 12
Meaux, Fr. F11 14
Mecaya, stm., Col. G4 86
Mecca see Makkah, Sau. Ar. E4 56
Mechanicsburg, Oh., U.S. D2 114
Mechanicsville, Ia., U.S. C6 120
Mechanicsville, Va., U.S. G8 114
Mechanicville, N.Y., U.S. B12 114
Mechelen (Malines), Bel. C13 14
Mecklenburg, hist. reg., Ger. C7 16
Mecklenburger Bucht, b., Ger. B7 16
Mecklenburg-Vorpommern, state, Ger. C8 16
Mecubúri, Moz. C6 68
Mecula, Moz. C6 68
Meda, Port. D3 20
Medak, India B4 53
Medan, Indon. B1 50
Medanosa, Punta, c., Arg. I3 90
Mede, Italy E5 22
Medeiros Neto, Braz. I5 88
Medellín, Col. D4 86
Médenine, Tun. C6 64
Mederdra, Maur. F1 64
Medford, Ok., U.S. E11 128
Medford, Or., U.S. A2 134
Medford, Wi., U.S. F8 118
Medgidia, Rom. E15 26
Mediapolis, Ia., U.S. C6 120
Mediaş, Rom. C11 26
Medicine Bow, Wy., U.S. B10 132
Medicine Bow, stm., Wy., U.S. A10 132
Medicine Bow Mountains, mts., U.S. F6 126
Medicine Creek, stm., Mo., U.S. E4 120
Medicine Hat, Ab., Can. D3 124
Medicine Lake, Mt., U.S. F9 124
Medicine Lodge, Ks., U.S. D10 128
Medicine Lodge, stm., U.S. D10 128
Medina, Braz. I5 88
Medina see Al-Madīnah, Sau. Ar. E4 56
Medina, N.Y., U.S. E11 112
Medina, Oh., U.S. C4 114
Medina, Tx., U.S. E8 130
Medina, stm., Tx., U.S. E9 130
Medinaceli, Spain C8 20
Medina del Campo, Spain C6 20
Medina-Sidonia, Spain H5 20
Medinīpur, India G11 54
Medio, Punta, c., Chile C2 92
Medio Creek, stm., Tx., U.S. F10 130
Mediterranean Sea A4 62
Medje, D.R.C. D5 66
Medjez el Bab, Tun. H3 24
Medkovec, Blg. F10 26
Mednogorsk, Russia D9 32
Médoc, reg., Fr. D4 18
Medora, N.D., U.S. H10 124
Médouneu, Gabon D2 66
Meductic, N.B., Can. E9 110
Medveđa, Yugo. G8 26
Medvedica, stm., Russia C19 10
Medvedica, stm., Russia D6 32
Medvėgalis, hill, Lith. E5 10
Medvežegorsk, Russia E15 8
Medvežji ostrova, is., Russia B21 34
Medyn', Russia F18 10
Meekatharra, Austl. E3 74
Meeker, Co., U.S. C8 132
Meeks Bay, Ca., U.S. D5 134
Meeladeen, Som. B9 66
Meerane, Ger. F8 16
Meersburg, Ger. I5 16
Meerut, India D6 54
Mēga, Eth. G7 62
Mega, Pulau, i., Indon. E2 50
Megalópoli, Grc. F4 28
Mégantic, Lac, l., Qc., Can. E5 110
Mégara, Grc. E6 28
Megargel, Tx., U.S. H9 128
Meghālaya, state, India F13 54
Meghna, stm., Bngl. G13 54
Megísti, i., Grc. G12 28
Megra, Russia C19 8
Mehakit, Indon. E9 50
Meharry, Mount, mtn., Austl. D3 74
Mehedinți, state, Rom. E10 26
Mehekar, India H6 54
Meherrin, stm., U.S. H7 114
Mehidpur, India G5 54
Mehikoorma, Est. B10 10
Mehndāwal, India E9 54
Mehren'ga, Russia F19 8
Mehrenga, stm., Russia E19 8
Mehtarlām, Afg. C11 56
Mehun-sur-Yèvre, Fr. G11 14
Mei, stm., China I7 42
Mei, stm., China H7 42
Meia Meia, Tan. F7 66
Meia Ponte, stm., Braz. I1 88
Meichuan, China F6 42
Meiganga, Cam. C2 66
Meighen Island, i., Nu., Can. A5 141
Meigs, Ga., U.S. E1 116
Meihekou, China C6 38
Meihsien see Meizhou, China I7 42
Meikeng, China J6 42
Meiktila, Mya. B2 48
Meiners Oaks, Ca., U.S. I6 134
Meiningen, Ger. F6 16
Meishan, China E5 36
Meissen, Ger. E9 16
Meitan, China H2 42
Meizhou, China I7 42
Mejillones, Chile D2 90
Mejillones, Península, pen., Chile A2 92
Mejnypil'gyno, Russia D24 34
Mékambo, Gabon D2 66
Mek'elē, Eth. E7 62
Mékhé, Sen. F1 64
Mekhtar, Pak. C2 54
Mekka see Makkah, Sau. Ar. E4 56
Meknès, Mor. C3 64
Mekong (Mékôngk) (Khong) (Lancang), stm., Asia F9 46
Mekongga, Gunung, mtn., Indon. F7 44
Mékôngk see Mekong, stm., Asia F10 46
Melado, stm., Chile H2 92
Melaka, Malay. K6 48
Melaka, state, Malay. K6 48
Melanesia, is., Oc. D7 72
Melawi, stm., Indon. D8 50
Melbourne, Austl. K5 76
Melbourne, Ar., U.S. H6 120
Melbourne, Fl., U.S. H5 116
Melbourne, Ia., U.S. J5 118
Melbourne Island, i., Nu., Can. B10 106
Melcher, Ia., U.S. C4 120
Melchor, Isla, i., Chile I2 90
Melchor Múzquiz, Mex. B8 100
Meldorf, Ger. B4 16
Meldrum Bay, On., Can. C6 112
Meldrum Creek, B.C., Can. D8 138
Mélé, Baie, b., Vanuatu k17 79d
Melekeok, Palau g8 78b
Melenki, Russia I19 8
Meleuz, Russia D9 32
Mélèzes, stm., Qc., Can. D16 106
Melfi, Chad E3 62
Melfi, Italy C9 24
Melfort, Sk., Can. B9 124
Meliane, Oued, stm., Tun. H4 24
Meliau, Indon. D7 50
Meligalás, Grc. F4 28
Melilla, Sp. N. Afr. B4 64
Melimoyu, Cerro, vol., Chile H2 90
Melincué, Arg. F7 92
Melita, Mb., Can. E12 124
Melitopol', Ukr. E5 32
Melívoia, Grc. D5 28
Mellansel, Swe. E7 8
Mellen, Wi., U.S. E8 118
Mellerud, Swe. G5 8
Mellish Reef, at., Austl. C11 74
Mellit, Sudan E5 62
Mělník, Czech Rep. F10 16
Melo, Ur. F10 92
Melolo, Indon. H12 50
Melos see Mílos, i., Grc. G7 28
Melrhir, Chott, l., Alg. C6 64
Melrose, Austl. E4 74
Melrose, Austl. I6 76
Melrose, Mn., U.S. F4 118
Melrose, N.M., U.S. G5 128
Melrose, Wi., U.S. G8 118
Melsungen, Ger. E5 16
Meltaus, Fin. C11 8
Melton Mowbray, Eng., U.K. I12 12
Melun, Fr. F11 14
Melūr, India F4 53
Melvern, Ks., U.S. F2 120
Melvern Lake, res., Ks., U.S. F2 120
Melville, Sk., Can. D11 124
Melville, La., U.S. G7 122
Melville, Cape, c., Austl. B9 74
Melville Bugt, b., Grnld. B12 141
Melville Hall Airport, Dom. i6 105c
Melville Hills, hills, Can. B7 106
Melville Island, i., Austl. B6 74
Melville Island, i., Can. A17 140
Melville Peninsula, pen., Nu., Can. B14 106
Melvin, Ky., U.S. G3 114
Melvin, Tx., U.S. C8 130
Melyana, Alg. H13 20
Mélykút, Hung. C6 26
Mêmar Co, l., China A9 54
Memba, Moz. C7 68
Membalong, Indon. E5 50
Memboro, Indon. H11 50
Memel see Klaipėda, Lith. E3 10
Memel, S. Afr. E9 70
Mēmele (Nemunėlis), stm., Eur. D7 10
Memmingen, Ger. I5 16
Mempawah, Indon. C6 50
Memphis, Fl., U.S. I3 116
Memphis, Mi., U.S. B3 114
Memphis, Tn., U.S. B8 122
Memphis, Tx., U.S. G8 128
Memphrémagog, Lac (Memphremagog, Lake), l., N.A. E4 110
Memphremagog, Lake (Memphrémagog, Lac), l., N.A. E4 110
Memramcook, N.B., Can. D12 110
Mena, Ar., U.S. C4 122
Menado see Manado, Indon. E7 44
Ménaka, Mali F5 64
Menan, Id., U.S. G15 136
Menard, Tx., U.S. D8 130
Menasha, Wi., U.S. G10 118
Menate, Indon. D8 50
Mendawai, Indon. E8 50
Mendawai, stm., Indon. E8 50
Mende, Fr. E9 18
Mendebo, mts., Eth. F7 62
Mendenhall, Ms., U.S. F9 122
Mendī, Eth. F7 62
Mendi, Pap. N. Gui. b3 79a
Mendocino, Ca., U.S. D2 134
Mendocino, Cape, c., Ca., U.S. C1 134
Mendocino Fracture Zone, unds. E24 142
Mendon, Il., U.S. D6 120
Mendota, Ca., U.S. G5 134
Mendoza, Arg. F3 92
Mendoza, state, Arg. G3 92
Mendoza, stm., Arg. F3 92
Mene de Mauroa, Ven. B6 86
Mene Grande, Ven. C6 86
Menemen, Tur. E9 28
Menen, Bel. D12 14
Menfi, Italy G6 24
Mengban, China A5 48
Mengcheng, China E7 42
Mengellang, Palau f8 78b
Menggala, Indon. F4 50
Menggudai, China B2 42
Menghai, China B5 48
Mengjiawan, China B3 42
Mengla, China B5 48
Menglian, China A4 48
Mengxian, China D5 42
Mengyin, China D7 42
Mengzi, China A6 48
Menihek Lakes, l., Nf., Can. E17 106
Menin see Menen, Bel. D12 14
Menindee, Austl. I4 76
Menjuša, Russia B13 10
Menlo Park, Ca., U.S. F3 134
Menno, S.D., U.S. D15 126
Meno, Ok., U.S. E10 128
Menominee, Mi., U.S. C2 112
Menominee, stm., U.S. C2 112
Menomonee Falls, Wi., U.S. A9 120
Menomonie, Wi., U.S. G7 118
Menongue, Ang. C2 68
Menor, Mar, b., Spain G10 20
Menorca (Minorca), i., Spain D15 20
Mentasta Lake, Ak., U.S. D11 140
Mentawai, Kepulauan, is., Indon. E1 50
Mentawai, Selat, strt., Indon. D2 50
Menton, Fr. F13 18
Mentor, Oh., U.S. C4 114
Menyapa, Gunung, mtn., Indon. C9 50
Menzel Bourguiba, Tun. G3 24
Menzel Bou Zelfa, Tun. H4 24
Menzelinsk, Russia C8 32
Menzel Temime, Tun. H5 24
Menzies, Austl. E4 74
Menzies, Mount, mtn., Ant. C10 81
Meobbaai, b., Nmb. D2 70
Meoqui, Mex. A6 100
Meota, Sk., Can. A5 124
Meppel, Neth. B15 14
Meppen, Ger. D3 16
Meqerghane, Sebkha, pl., Alg. D5 64
Mequinenza, Embalse de, res., Spain C10 20
Mequon, Wi., U.S. E2 112
Merah, Indon. C10 50
Meramec, stm., Mo., U.S. F7 120
Meran see Merano, Italy D8 22
Merangin, stm., Indon. E3 50
Merano (Meran), Italy D8 22
Meratus, Pegunungan, mts., Indon. E9 50
Merauke, Indon. G11 44
Merbau, Indon. C3 50
Merbein, Austl. J4 76
Mercaderes, Col. G3 86
Mercāra, India E2 53
Merced, Ca., U.S. F5 134
Merced, stm., Ca., U.S. F5 134
Mercedario, Cerro, mtn., Arg. E2 92
Mercedes, Arg. D8 92
Mercedes, Arg. G8 92
Mercedes, Tx., U.S. H10 130
Mercedes, Ur. F8 92
Mercer, Mo., U.S. D4 120
Mercer, Pa., U.S. C5 114
Mercersburg, Pa., U.S. E7 114
Merchants Bay, b., Nu., Can. D13 141
Mercoal, Ab., Can. C13 138
Mercury, Nv., U.S. G10 134
Mercury Islands, is., N.Z. C6 80
Mercy, Cape, c., Nu., Can. E13 141
Mercy Bay, b., N.T., Can. B16 140
Meredith, Lake, res., Tx., U.S. F7 128
Meredosia, Il., U.S. E7 120
Mereeg, Som. D9 66
Méré Lava, i., Vanuatu j17 79d
Merevari, stm., Ven. E9 86
Merëža, Russia A19 10
Mergui, Mya. F4 48
Mergui Archipelago, is., Mya. G3 48
Meribah, Austl. J3 76
Mérida, Mex. B3 102
Mérida, Spain F4 20
Mérida, Ven. C6 86
Mérida, state, Ven. C6 86
Mérida, Cordillera de, mts., Ven. C6 86
Meridian, Ga., U.S. E4 116
Meridian, Ms., U.S. E10 122
Meridian, Tx., U.S. C10 130
Meridianville, Al., U.S. C12 122
Mérignac, Fr. E5 18
Merigold, Ms., U.S. D8 122
Merikarvia, Fin. F9 8
Merimbula, Austl. K7 76
Merín, Laguna (Mirim, Lagoa), b., S.A. F11 92
Merinda, Austl. B6 76
Merino, Co., U.S. G9 126
Merinos, Ur. F9 92
Merizo, Guam j9 78c
Merkinė, Lith. F7 10
Merkys, stm., Lith. F8 10
Merlin, On., Can. F7 112
Merlin, Or., U.S. H3 136
Merna, Ne., U.S. F13 126
Meron, Har (Meron, Mount), mtn., Isr. E6 58
Meron, Mount see Meron, Har, mtn., Isr. E6 58
Merouane, Chott, l., Alg. C6 64
Merredin, Austl. F3 74
Merrick, mtn., Scot., U.K. F8 12
Merrill, Ia., U.S. B1 120
Merrill, Mi., U.S. E5 112
Merrill, Or., U.S. A4 134
Merrillan, Wi., U.S. G8 118
Merrillville, In., U.S. G2 112
Merrimack, stm., U.S. H5 110
Merriman, Ne., U.S. E11 126
Merritt, B.C., Can. F10 138
Merritt Island, Fl., U.S. H5 116
Merriwa, Austl. I8 76
Mer Rouge, La., U.S. E7 122
Merrygoen, Austl. H7 76
Merryville, La., U.S. G5 122
Mersa Matruh, Egypt A5 62
Mersea Island, i., Eng., U.K. J13 12
Merseburg, Ger. E7 16
Mersey, stm., Austl. n13 77a
Mersey, stm., N.S., Can. F12 110
Mersing, Malay. K6 48
Mērsrags, Lat. C6 10
Merta, India E5 54
Merthyr Tydfil, Wales, U.K. J9 12
Mértola, Port. G3 20
Mertz Glacier Tongue, ice, Ant. B19 81
Méru, Fr. E11 14
Meru, Kenya D7 66
Meruoca, Braz. B5 88
Merweville, S. Afr. H5 70
Merzifon, Tur. A4 56
Merzig, Ger. G2 16
Mesa, Az., U.S. J5 132
Mesabi Range, hills, Mn., U.S. D6 118
Mesagne, Italy D11 24
Mesáras, Órmos, b., Grc. I7 28
Mesa Verde National Park, p.o.i., Co., U.S. F8 132
Mescalero, N.M., U.S. H3 128
Meščerino, Russia G20 10
Meschede, Ger. E4 16
Meščura, Russia E24 8
Mesewa see Massawa, Erit. D7 62
Mesgouez, Lac, l., Qc., Can. E16 106
Mesick, Mi., U.S. D4 112
Mesilla, N.M., U.S. K10 132
Meškuičiai, Lith. D6 10
Mesolóngi, Grc. E4 28
Mesopotamia, hist. reg., Asia C5 56
Mesquite, Tx., U.S. E2 122
Messalo, stm., Moz. C6 68
Messina, Italy F9 24
Messina, S. Afr. C9 70
Messina, Gulf of see Messiniakós Kólpos, b., Grc. G5 28
Messina, Stretto di, strt., Italy F9 24
Messíni, Grc. F4 28
Messíni, hist., Grc. F4 28
Messiniakós Kólpos, b., Grc. G5 28
Messix Peak, mtn., Ut., U.S. B4 132
Messkirch, Ger. H5 16
Messojaha, stm., Russia C4 34
Mesta (Néstos), stm., Eur. B6 28
Mestghanem, Alg. B4 64
Mestre, ngh., Italy E9 22
Mesuji, stm., Indon. E4 50
Meta, state, Col. F5 86
Meta, stm., S.A. D7 86
Métabetchouan, Qc., Can. B5 110
Métabetchouane, stm., Qc., Can. B4 110
Meta Incognita Peninsula, pen., Nu., Can. C17 106
Metairie, La., U.S. H8 122
Metaline Falls, Wa., U.S. B9 136
Metamora, Il., U.S. D8 120
Metán, Arg. B5 92
Metangula, Moz. C5 68
Metapán, El Sal. E3 102
Metaponto, hist., Italy D10 24
Metapontum see Metaponto, hist., Italy D10 24
Meteor Crater, crat., Az., U.S. H6 132
Metharaw, Mya. D4 48
Methow, Wa., U.S. B7 136
Methow, stm., Wa., U.S. B6 136
Methven, N.Z. F4 80
Metica, stm., Col. E5 86
Metiskow, Ab., Can. B3 124
Metlakatla, Ak., U.S. E13 140
Metlika, Slvn. E12 22
Meto, Bayou, stm., Ar., U.S. C7 122
Metropolis, Il., U.S. G9 120
Metropolitan, Mi., U.S. C2 112
Metter, Ga., U.S. D3 116
Mettuppālaiyam, India F3 53
Mettūr, India F3 53
Metz, Fr. E15 14
Metzingen, Ger. H5 16
Meu, stm., Fr. F7 14
Meulaboh, Indon. J2 48
Meureudu, Indon. J3 48
Meurthe, stm., Fr. F15 14
Meurthe-et-Moselle, state, Fr. F15 14
Meuse, state, Fr. E14 14
Meuse (Maas), stm., Eur. D14 14
Meuselwitz, Ger. E8 16
Mexiana, Ilha, i., Braz. C8 84
Mexicali, Mex. K10 134
Mexican Hat, Ut., U.S. F7 132
México see Ciudad de México, Mex. F9 100
Mexico, Me., U.S. F6 110
Mexico, Mo., U.S. E6 120
Mexico, N.Y., U.S. E13 112
México, state, Mex. F9 100
Mexico, ctry., N.A. C4 96
Mexico, Gulf of, b., N.A. B6 96
Mexico Basin, unds. F5 144
Mexico Bay, b., N.Y., U.S. E13 112
Mexico City see Ciudad de México, Mex. F9 100
Meycauayan, Phil. C3 52
Meydān Khvolah, Afg. B2 54
Meyersdale, Pa., U.S. E6 114
Meymaneh, Afg. B9 56
Meyronne, Sk., Can. E7 124
Meyungs, Palau g7 78b
Mëža (M'oža), stm., Eur. E14 10
Meẕada, Ḥorvot (Masada), hist., Isr. G6 58
Mezcala, Mex. G9 100
Mezcalapa, stm., Mex. G12 100
Meždurečensk, Russia D15 32
Meždurečenskij, Russia C10 32
Mèze, Fr. F9 18
Mezen', Russia D21 8
Mezen', stm., Russia D21 8
Mezenskaja guba, b., Russia C20 8
Mežica, Slvn. D11 22
Mezőberény, Hung. C8 26
Mezőcsát, Hung. B7 26
Mezőkövesd, Hung. B7 26
Mezőtúr, Hung. B7 26
Mezquital, stm., Mex. D6 100
Mfangano Island, i., Kenya E6 66
Mgači, Russia F17 34
M'Goun, Irhil, mtn., Mor. C3 64
M'hai, B'nom, mtn., Viet. G8 48
Mhasvād, India C2 53
Mhow, India G5 54
Mi, stm., China H5 42
Mi, stm., China C8 42
Mia, Oued, stm., Alg. D5 64
Miahuatlán de Porfirio Díaz, Mex. G10 100
Miajadas, Spain E4 20
Miaméré, C.A.R. C4 66
Miami, Mb., Can. E15 124
Miami, Az., U.S. J6 132
Miami, Fl., U.S. K5 116
Miami, Ok., U.S. H3 120
Miami, Tx., U.S. F8 128
Miami Beach, Fl., U.S. K5 116
Miami Canal, can., Fl., U.S. J5 116
Miamisburg, Oh., U.S. E1 114
Miami Springs, Fl., U.S. K5 116
Miān Channūn, Pak. C4 54
Mianchi, China D4 42
Miandrivazo, Madag. D8 68
Mianduhe, China B9 36
Mīāneh, Iran B6 56
Miang, Phu, mtn., Thai. D5 48
Mianning, China F5 36
Miānwāli, Pak. B3 54

Name	Map Ref.	Page
Mianxian, China	E2	42
Mianyang, China	F1	42
Mianzhu, China	E5	36
Miaodao Qundao, is., China	B9	42
Miaoli, Tai.	I9	42
Miao Ling, mts., China	H2	42
Miass, Russia	C10	32
Miass, stm., Russia	C10	32
Miastko, Pol.	B12	16
Micang Shan, mts., China	E2	42
Michalovce, Slov.	H17	16
Michaud, Point, c., N.S., Can.	E16	110
Micheal Peak, mtn., B.C., Can.	C4	138
Michel, B.C., Can.	G16	138
Miches, Dom. Rep.	C13	102
Michigan, N.D., U.S.	F15	124
Michigan, state, U.S.	C10	108
Michigan, stm., Co., U.S.	G6	126
Michigan, Lake, l., U.S.	E2	112
Michigan City, In., U.S.	G3	112
Michipicoten Island, i., On., Can.	F13	106
Michoacán, state, Mex.	F8	100
Micoud, St. Luc.	m7	105c
Micronesia, is., Oc.	B6	72
Micronesia, Federated States of, ctry., Oc.	C6	72
Mičurinsk, Russia	D6	32
Midai, Pulau, i., Indon.	B5	50
Midale, Sk., Can.	E10	124
Mid-Atlantic Ridge, unds.	F9	144
Middelburg, Neth.	C12	14
Middelburg, S. Afr.	G7	70
Middelburg, S. Afr.	D9	70
Middle, stm., B.C., Can.	B5	138
Middle, stm., Ia., U.S.	C3	120
Middle, stm., Mn., U.S.	C2	118
Middle Alkali Lake, l., Ca., U.S.	B5	134
Middle America Trench, unds.	H29	142
Middle Andaman, i., India	F7	46
Middleboro, Ma., U.S.	C15	114
Middlebourne, W.V., U.S.	E5	114
Middleburg, N.Y., U.S.	B11	114
Middleburg, Pa., U.S.	D8	114
Middlebury, Vt., U.S.	F3	110
Middle Caicos, i., T./C. Is.	B12	102
Middle Fabius, stm., Mo., U.S.	D5	120
Middlefield, Oh., U.S.	C4	114
Middlegate, Norf. I.	y25	78i
Middle Loup, stm., Ne., U.S.	F14	126
Middlemount, Austl.	D7	76
Middle Musquodoboit, N.S., Can.	E13	110
Middleport, Oh., U.S.	E3	114
Middle Raccoon, stm., Ia., U.S.	J4	118
Middlesboro, Ky., U.S.	H2	114
Middlesbrough, Eng., U.K.	G11	12
Middlesex, Belize	D3	102
Middle Stewiacke, N.S., Can.	E13	110
Middleton, N.S., Can.	F11	110
Middleton, Mi., U.S.	E5	112
Middleton, Wi., U.S.	A8	120
Middleton Island, i., Ak., U.S.	E10	140
Middleton Reef, at., Austl.	E11	74
Middletown, Ca., U.S.	E3	134
Middletown, Ct., U.S.	C13	114
Middletown, Il., U.S.	K9	118
Middletown, In., U.S.	H4	112
Middletown, Ky., U.S.	F12	120
Middletown, Md., U.S.	E8	114
Middletown, N.Y., U.S.	C11	114
Middletown, Oh., U.S.	E1	114
Middletown, Pa., U.S.	D9	114
Middletown, R.I., U.S.	C14	114
Middleville, Mi., U.S.	F4	112
Midgic, N.B., Can.	E12	110
Midi, Canal du, can., Fr.	F9	18
Midi de Bigorre, Pic du, mtn., Fr.	G5	18
Mid-Indian Basin, unds.	J10	142
Mid-Indian Ridge, unds.	L10	142
Midland, On., Can.	D9	112
Midland, Ca., U.S.	J2	132
Midland, Mi., U.S.	E5	112
Midland, S.D., U.S.	C11	126
Midland, Tx., U.S.	C5	130
Midlands, state, Zimb.	B10	70
Midleton, Ire.	J4	12
Midlothian, Tx., U.S.	B11	130
Midnapore, Ab., Can.	F16	138
Midongy Atsimo, Madag.	E8	68
Mid-Pacific Mountains, unds.	G19	142
Midsayap, Phil.	G5	52
Midville, Ga., U.S.	D3	116
Midway, B.C., Can.	G12	138
Midway, Al., U.S.	E13	122
Midway, Ky., U.S.	F13	120
Midway, Tx., U.S.	F3	122
Midway Islands, dep., Oc.	G22	30
Midway Park, N.C., U.S.	B8	116
Midwest City, Ok., U.S.	F11	128
Midyan, reg., Sau. Ar.	J6	58
Midžur (Midžor), mtn., Eur.	F9	26
Mie, Japan	G4	40
Mie, state, Japan	E9	40
Międzybórz, Pol.	E13	16
Międzylesie, Pol.	F12	16
Międzyrzec Podlaski, Pol.	D18	16
Międzyrzecz, Pol.	D11	16
Mielan, Fr.	F6	18
Mielec, Pol.	F17	16
Mier, Mex.	B9	100
Miercurea-Ciuc, Rom.	C12	26
Mieres, Spain	A5	20
Mieroszów, Pol.	F12	16
Mier y Noriega, Mex.	D8	100
Miesbach, Ger.	I7	16
Mīēso, Eth.	F8	62
Mieszkowice, Pol.	D10	16
Mifflinburg, Pa., U.S.	H12	112
Miguel Alemán, Presa, res., Mex.	F10	100
Miguel Alves, Braz.	C4	88
Miguel Auza, Mex.	C7	100
Miguel Calmon, Braz.	F5	88
Miguel Hidalgo, Presa, res., Mex.	B4	100
Miguelópolis, Braz.	K1	88
Miguel Riglos, Arg.	H6	92
Mihăești, Rom.	D12	26
Mihajlovka, Russia	D6	32
Mihajlovka, Russia	D14	32
Mihajlovka, Russia	C10	38
Mihajlovskij, Russia	F20	8
Mihalgazi, Tur.	C13	28
Mihanavičy, Bela.	G10	10
Mihara, Japan	E5	40
Mihara-yama, vol., Japan	E12	40
Mihninskaja, Russia	F21	8
Mikame, Japan	F5	40
Mikasa, Japan	C14	38
Mikaševičy, Bela.	H10	10
Mikhrot Timna' (King Solomon's Mines), hist., Isr.	I5	58
Mikindani, Tan.	G8	66
Mikkeli (Sankt Michel), Fin.	F12	8
Mikkeli, state, Fin.	F12	8
Mikołajki, Pol.	C17	16
Mikołów, Pol.	F14	16
Mikrá Préspa, Límni, l., Eur.	D15	24
Mikšino, Russia	C18	10
Mikulino, Russia	E14	10
Mikumi, Tan.	F7	66
Mikun', Russia	E23	8
Mikuni, Japan	C9	40
Miladummadulu Atoll, at., Mald.	h12	46a
Milagro, Arg.	E5	92
Milagro, Ec.	I2	86
Milagros, Phil.	D4	52
Milan see Milano, Italy	E6	22
Milan, Ga., U.S.	D2	116
Milan, In., U.S.	E12	120
Milan, Mi., U.S.	B2	114
Milan, Mn., U.S.	F3	118
Milan, Mo., U.S.	D4	120
Milan, N.M., U.S.	H8	132
Milang, Austl.	J2	76
Milange, Moz.	D6	68
Milano (Milan), Italy	E6	22
Milâs, Tur.	F10	28
Milavidy, Bela.	H8	10
Milazzo, Italy	F9	24
Milazzo, Golfo di, b., Italy	F9	24
Milbank, S.D., U.S.	F2	118
Milburn, Ok., U.S.	C2	122
Milden, Sk., Can.	C6	124
Mildmay, On., Can.	D8	112
Mildura, Austl.	J4	76
Mile, China	G5	36
Miles, Austl.	F8	76
Miles, Tx., U.S.	C7	130
Miles City, Mt., U.S.	A7	126
Milestone, Sk., Can.	E9	124
Milet, hist., Tur.	F10	28
Milford, De., U.S.	F10	114
Milford, Ia., U.S.	H3	118
Milford, Me., U.S.	F8	110
Milford, Ma., U.S.	B14	114
Milford, Mi., U.S.	B2	114
Milford, N.H., U.S.	B14	114
Milford, Pa., U.S.	C11	114
Milford, Ut., U.S.	E4	132
Milford Center, Oh., U.S.	D2	114
Milford Haven, Wales, U.K.	J7	12
Milford Lake, res., Ks., U.S.	B11	128
Milford Sound, strt., N.Z.	G2	80
Mili, at., Marsh. Is.	C8	72
Milian, stm., Malay.	A10	50
Milicz, Pol.	E13	16
Miljatino, Russia	F17	10
Milk, stm., N.A.	B6	108
Milk, North Fork (North Milk), stm., N.A.	B13	136
Mil'kovo, Russia	F20	34
Milk River, Ab., Can.	G18	138
Millard, Ne., U.S.	C1	120
Millau, Fr.	E9	18
Millboro, Va., U.S.	F6	114
Millbrook, N.Y., U.S.	C12	114
Mill City, Or., U.S.	F4	136
Millcreek, Pa., U.S.	B5	114
Millcreek, Ut., U.S.	C5	132
Mill Creek, W.V., U.S.	F5	114
Milledgeville, Ga., U.S.	C2	116
Milledgeville, Il., U.S.	C8	120
Mille Lacs, Lac des, l., On., Can.	C8	118
Mille Lacs Lake, l., Mn., U.S.	E5	118
Millen, Ga., U.S.	D4	116
Miller, Mo., U.S.	G4	120
Miller, S.D., U.S.	C14	126
Miller Mountain, mtn., Nv., U.S.	E7	134
Millerovo, Russia	E6	32
Millersburg, Ky., U.S.	F1	114
Millersburg, Mi., U.S.	C5	112
Millersburg, Oh., U.S.	D4	114
Millersport, Oh., U.S.	I7	112
Millerton, N.Y., U.S.	C12	114
Millet, Ab., Can.	C17	138
Millevaches, Plateau de, plat., Fr.	D7	18
Millicent, Austl.	K3	76
Milligan, Fl., U.S.	G12	122
Milligan, Ne., U.S.	G15	126
Millington, Mi., U.S.	E6	112
Millington, Tn., U.S.	B9	122
Millinocket, Me., U.S.	E8	110
Mill Island, i., Ant.	B15	81
Mill Island, i., Nu., Can.	C15	106
Millry, Al., U.S.	F10	122
Mills, Wy., U.S.	E6	126
Mills Creek, stm., Austl.	D4	76
Mills Lake, l., N.T., Can.	C7	106
Millstream, Austl.	D3	74
Milltown, Mt., U.S.	D13	136
Milltown, Wi., U.S.	F6	118
Milltown Malbay, Ire.	I3	12
Mill Valley, Ca., U.S.	F3	134
Millville, N.J., U.S.	E10	114
Millwood, Va., U.S.	E7	114
Millwood Lake, res., Ar., U.S.	D4	122
Milne Land, i., Grnld.	C20	141
Milnor, N.D., U.S.	A15	126
Milo, Ab., Can.	F18	138
Mílos, i., Grc.	G7	28
Miłosław, Pol.	D13	16
Milparinka, Austl.	G3	76
Milroy, In., U.S.	E12	120
Milroy, Pa., U.S.	D8	114
Miltenberg, Ger.	G5	16
Milton, On., Can.	E10	112
Milton, N.Z.	H4	80
Milton, Fl., U.S.	G11	122
Milton, Ia., U.S.	D5	120
Milton, Pa., U.S.	G13	112
Milton, Wi., U.S.	B9	120
Milton-Freewater, Or., U.S.	E8	136
Milton Keynes, Eng., U.K.	I12	12
Miltonvale, Ks., U.S.	B11	128
Miltou, Chad	E3	62
Miluo, stm., China	G5	42
Milwaukee, Wi., U.S.	E2	112
Milwaukee, stm., Wi., U.S.	H11	118
Milwaukie, Or., U.S.	E4	136
Mimbres, stm., N.M., U.S.	K9	132
Mimizan-les-Bains, Fr.	E4	18
Mimoň, Czech Rep.	F10	16
Mimoso do Sul, Braz.	K5	88
Mims, Fl., U.S.	H5	116
Min, stm., China	F5	36
Min, stm., China	I8	42
Mina, Mex.	H7	130
Mina, Nv., U.S.	E7	134
Mīnā' al-Aḥmadī, Kuw.	D6	56
Mīnāb, Iran	D8	56
Minahasa, pen., Indon.	E7	44
Minakuchi, Japan	E9	40
Minamata, Japan	G3	40
Minami-Alps-kokuritsu-kōen, p.o.i., Japan	D11	40
Minami-Tori-shima, i., Japan	G19	30
Minas, Cuba	B9	102
Minas, Indon.	C2	50
Minas, Ur.	G10	92
Minas Basin, b., N.S., Can.	E12	110
Minas de Barroterán, Mex.	B8	100
Minas de Corrales, Ur.	E10	92
Minas de Matahambre, Cuba	A5	102
Minas Gerais, state, Braz.	C8	90
Minas Novas, Braz.	I4	88
Minatare, Ne., U.S.	F9	126
Minatitlán, Mex.	F11	100
Minbu, Mya.	B2	48
Minbya, Mya.	B1	48
Minbyin, Mya.	C1	48
Mincio, stm., Italy	E7	22
Minco, Ok., U.S.	F10	128
Minčol, mtn., Slov.	G17	16
Mindanao, i., Phil.	G5	52
Mindanao, stm., Phil.	G5	52
Mindelheim, Ger.	H6	16
Mindelo, C.V.	k10	65a
Mindemoya, On., Can.	C7	112
Minden, On., Can.	D11	112
Minden, Ger.	D4	16
Minden, La., U.S.	E5	122
Minden, Ne., U.S.	G14	126
Minden, Nv., U.S.	E6	134
Minden City, Mi., U.S.	E7	112
Mindoro, i., Phil.	D3	52
Mindoro Strait, strt., Phil.	D3	52
Mine, Japan	E4	40
Mine Centre, On., Can.	C6	118
Minehead, Eng., U.K.	J9	12
Mineiros, Braz.	G7	84
Mineola, Tx., U.S.	E3	122
Mineral, Wa., U.S.	D4	136
Mineral Point, Wi., U.S.	B7	120
Mineral Springs, Ar., U.S.	D5	122
Mineral Wells, Tx., U.S.	B9	130
Minersville, Pa., U.S.	H13	112
Minerva, Oh., U.S.	D4	114
Minervino Murge, Italy	C9	24
Mineville, N.Y., U.S.	F3	110
Minfeng, China	A5	46
Minga, D.R.C.	G5	66
Mingäçevir, Azer.	A6	56
Mingāora, Pak.	C11	56
Mingary, Austl.	I3	76
Mingene, Austl.	E3	74
Mingin, Mya.	A2	48
Minglanilla, Spain	E9	20
Mingo Junction, Oh., U.S.	D5	114
Mingo Lake, l., Nu., Can.	C16	106
Mingshui, China	B10	36
Mingulay, i., Scot., U.K.	E5	12
Mingyuegou, China	C8	38
Minhang, China	F9	42
Minh Hai, Viet.	H7	48
Minhla, Mya.	B2	48
Minhla, Mya.	C2	48
Minho, hist. reg., Port.	C2	20
Minho (Miño), stm., Eur.	B2	20
Minićevo, Yugo.	F9	26
Minicoy Island, i., India	G3	46
Minigwal, Lake, l., Austl.	E4	74
Minija, stm., Lith.	E4	10
Minilya, Austl.	D2	74
Minilya, stm., Austl.	D2	74
Miniota, Mb., Can.	D12	124
Minitonas, Mb., Can.	B12	124
Minle, China	D5	36
Minna, Nig.	H6	64
Minneapolis, Ks., U.S.	B11	128
Minneapolis, Mn., U.S.	G5	118
Minnedosa, Mb., Can.	D13	124
Minneola, Ks., U.S.	D8	128
Minneota, Mn., U.S.	G2	118
Minnesota, state, U.S.	E4	118
Minnesota, stm., Mn., U.S.	G5	118
Minnesota Lake, Mn., U.S.	H5	118
Minnewanka, Lake, res., Ab., Can.	E15	138
Minnitaki Lake, l., On., Can.	B6	118
Mino, Japan	D9	40
Miño (Minho), stm., Eur.	B2	20
Minocqua, Wi., U.S.	F9	118
Minong, Wi., U.S.	E7	118
Minonk, Il., U.S.	D8	120
Minorca see Menorca, i., Spain	D15	20
Minot, N.D., U.S.	F12	124
Minqing, China	H8	42
Minquan, China	D6	42
Minquiers, Plateau des, is., Jersey	E6	14
Min Shan, mts., China	E5	36
Minsk, Bela.	G10	10
Minsk, state, Bela.	G10	10
Minskae uzvyšša, plat., Bela.	G10	10
Mińsk Mazowiecki, Pol.	D17	16
Minta, Cam.	D2	66
Minto, Mb., Can.	E13	124
Minto, Yk., Can.	C3	106
Minto, N.D., U.S.	C1	118
Minto, Lac, l., Qc., Can.	D16	106
Minto, Mount, mtn., Ant.	C22	81
Minto Inlet, b., N.T., Can.	A7	106
Minton, Sk., Can.	E9	124
Minturn, Co., U.S.	D10	132
Minûf, Egypt	H1	58
Minusinsk, Russia	D16	32
Minvoul, Gabon	D2	66
Minxian, China	E5	36
Minya see El-Minya, Egypt	J1	58
Minya el-Qamh, Egypt	H2	58
Mio, Mi., U.S.	D5	112
Miquan, China	F15	32
Mir, Bela.	G9	10
Mira, stm., Col.	G2	86
Mīrābād, Afg.	C9	56
Mirabella, Gulf of see Mirampéllou, Kólpos, b., Grc.	H8	28
Miracema do Tocantins, Braz.	E1	88
Mirador, Braz.	D3	88
Miradouro, Braz.	K4	88
Miraflores, Col.	E5	86
Miraflores, Col.	G5	86
Miraj, India	C2	53
Miramar, Arg.	I9	92
Miramar, Moz.	C12	70
Miramas, Fr.	F10	18
Miramichi Bay, b., N.B., Can.	C11	110
Mirampéllou, Kólpos, b., Grc.	H8	28
Mīrān, Pak.	C3	54
Miranda, Braz.	D5	90
Miranda, Col.	F3	86
Miranda, state, Ven.	B8	86
Miranda, stm., Braz.	D5	90
Miranda de Ebro, Spain	B7	20
Mirande, Fr.	F6	18
Mirando City, Tx., U.S.	G8	130
Mirandola, Italy	F8	22
Mira Táglio, Italy	E9	22
Miravalles, Volcán, vol., C.R.	G5	102
Miravete, Puerto de, p., Spain	E5	20
Mirbāṭ, Oman	F7	56
Mirecourt, Fr.	F14	14
Miri, Malay.	A9	50
Miria, Niger	G6	64
Miriam Vale, Austl.	E8	76
Mirim, Lagoa (Merín, Laguna), b., S.A.	F11	92
Miriñay, stm., Arg.	D9	92
Miritiparaná, stm., Col.	H6	86
Miriyama, Pap. N. Gui.	a3	79a
Mirnoe Ozero, Russia	C13	32
Mirny, sci., Ant.	B14	81
Mirnyj, Russia	D11	34
Mirnyy, sci., Ant.	B14	81
Miroslav, Czech Rep.	H12	16
Mirow, Ger.	C8	16
Mīrpur, Bngl.	G13	54
Mīrpur, Pak.	B4	54
Mīrpur Batoro, Pak.	F2	54
Mīrpur Khās, Pak.	F2	54
Mirror, Ab., Can.	D17	138
Mirtóon Pélagos, Grc.	G6	28
Miryang, Kor., S.	D1	40
Mirzāpur, India	F9	54
Misantla, Mex.	F10	100
Misawa, Japan	D14	38
Miscou Centre, N.B., Can.	C12	110
Miscou Island, i., N.B., Can.	C12	110
Miscou Point, c., N.B., Can.	B12	110
Mishan, China	B9	38
Mishawaka, In., U.S.	G3	112
Mishicot, Wi., U.S.	D2	112
Misima Island, i., Pap. N. Gui.	B10	74
Misiones, state, Arg.	C10	92
Misiones, state, Para.	C9	92
Misión Santa Rosa, Para.	D4	90
Misión San Vicente, Mex.	F4	98
Miskitos, Cayos, is., Nic.	E6	102
Miskolc, Hung.	A7	26
Mišnëvo, Russia	G19	10
Misool, Pulau, i., Indon.	F9	44
Miṣrātah, Libya	A3	62
Misr el-Bahrî (Lower Egypt), hist. reg., Egypt	G2	58
Misrikh, India	E8	54
Missinaibi, stm., On., Can.	E14	106
Missinaibi Lake, l., On., Can.	F14	106
Mission, B.C., Can.	G8	138
Mission, S.D., U.S.	D12	126
Mission, Tx., U.S.	H9	130
Mission Mountain, hill, Ok., U.S.	H3	120
Mission Viejo, Ca., U.S.	J8	134
Mississagi, stm., On., Can.	B6	112
Mississauga, On., Can.	E10	112
Mississinewa, stm., U.S.	H4	112
Mississippi, state, U.S.	D9	122
Mississippi, stm., On., Can.	C13	112
Mississippi, stm., U.S.	E9	108
Mississippi Lake, l., On., Can.	C13	112
Mississippi River Delta, La., U.S.	H9	122
Mississippi Sound, strt., U.S.	G10	122
Mississippi State, Ms., U.S.	D10	122
Missoula, Mt., U.S.	D12	136
Missouri, state, U.S.	F5	120
Missouri, stm., U.S.	D9	108
Missouri City, Tx., U.S.	H3	122
Mistake Creek, stm., Austl.	D6	76
Mistassibi, stm., Qc., Can.	A4	110
Mistassini, Qc., Can.	E16	106
Mistassini, Qc., Can.	B4	110
Mistassini, stm., Qc., Can.	B4	110
Mistassini, Lac, l., Qc., Can.	E16	106
Mistatim, Sk., Can.	B10	124
Mistelbach an der Zaya, Aus.	B13	22
Misterbianco, Italy	G9	24
Misti, Volcán, vol., Peru	G3	84
Misumi, Japan	E4	40
Mišutino, Russia	A19	10
Mita, Punta de, c., Mex.	E6	100
Mitchell, Austl.	F6	76
Mitchell, On., Can.	E8	112
Mitchell, In., U.S.	F11	120
Mitchell, Or., U.S.	F6	136
Mitchell, S.D., U.S.	D14	126
Mitchell, stm., Austl.	C8	74
Mitchell, stm., Austl.	K6	76
Mitchell, Mount, mtn., N.C., U.S.	I3	114
Mitchinamecus, stm., Qc., Can.	C2	110
Mitchinamecus, Réservoir, res., Qc., Can.	C1	110
Mît Ghamr, Egypt	H2	58
Mithapur, India	G2	54
Mithi, Pak.	F2	54
Mitidja, Plaine de la, pl., Alg.	H14	20
Mitiškovo, Russia	F16	10
Mitla, hist., Mex.	G10	100
Mito, Japan	C13	40
Mitsio, Nosy, i., Madag.	C8	68
Mitsukaidō, Japan	C13	40
Mitsuke, Japan	B11	40
Mittellandkanal, can., Ger.	D5	16
Mittenwald, Ger.	I7	16
Mittersill, Aus.	C9	22
Mittweida, Ger.	E9	16
Mitú, Col.	G6	86
Mitumba, Monts, mts., D.R.C.	F5	66
Mitwaba, D.R.C.	F5	66
Mitzic, Gabon	D2	66
Miura, Japan	D12	40
Miura-hantō, pen., Japan	D12	40
Mixian, China	D5	42
Miyagi, state, Japan	A13	40
Miyake-jima, i., Japan	E12	40
Miyako, Japan	E14	38
Miyako-jima, i., Japan	G10	36
Miyakonojō, Japan	H4	40
Miyama, Japan	E9	40
Miyanojō, Japan	H3	40
Miyazaki, Japan	H4	40
Miyazaki, state, Japan	G4	40
Miyazu, Japan	D8	40
Miyoshi, Japan	E5	40
Miyun, China	A7	42
Miyun Shuiku, res., China	A7	42
Mīzan Teferī, Eth.	F7	62
Mizdah, Libya	A2	62
Mize, Ms., U.S.	F9	122
Mizen Head, c., Ire.	I6	12
Mizen Head, c., Ire.	J3	12
Mizhhir'ia, Ukr.	A10	26
Mizhi, China	C4	42
Mizil, Rom.	E13	26
Mizoram, state, India	G14	54
Mizpah Creek, stm., Mt., U.S.	A7	126
Mizque, Bol.	C3	90
Mizukaidō see Mitsukaidō, Japan	C13	40
Mizusawa, Japan	E14	38
Mjadzel, Bela.	F9	10
Mjakit, Russia	D19	34
Mjaksa, Russia	B21	10
Mjölby, Swe.	G6	8
Mjøsa, l., Nor.	F4	8
Mkalama, Tan.	E6	66
Mkhondvo, stm., Afr.	E10	70
Mkokotoni, Tan.	F7	66
Mkomazi, stm., S. Afr.	G10	70
Mkulwe, Tan.	F6	66
Mkuze, S. Afr.	E10	70
Mkuze, stm., S. Afr.	E11	70
Mkuze Game Reserve, S. Afr.	E11	70
Mladá Boleslav, Czech Rep.	F11	16
Mladenovac, Yugo.	E7	26
Mlava, stm., Yugo.	E8	26
Mława, Pol.	C16	16
Mljet, Otok, i., Cro.	H14	22
Mljet Nacionalni Park, p.o.i., Cro.	H14	22
Mmabatho, S. Afr.	D7	70
Mmadinare, Bots.	B8	70
Moa, stm., Afr.	H2	64
Moab, Ut., U.S.	E7	132
Moala, i., Fiji	q18	79e
Moama, Austl.	K5	76
Moamba, Moz.	D11	70
Moanda, Gabon	E2	66
Moar Lake, l., Can.	C18	124
Moate, Ire.	H5	12
Moba, D.R.C.	F5	66
Mobara, Japan	D13	40
Mobaye, C.A.R.	D4	66
Mobeetie, Tx., U.S.	F8	128
Moberly, Mo., U.S.	E5	120
Mobile, Al., U.S.	G10	122
Mobile, Az., U.S.	J4	132
Mobile, stm., Al., U.S.	G11	122
Mobile Bay, b., Al., U.S.	G10	122
Mobridge, S.D., U.S.	B12	126
Moca, Dom. Rep.	C12	102
Mocajuba, Braz.	B1	88
Mo Cay, Viet.	G8	48
Mocha see Al-Mukhā, Yemen	G5	56
Mochudi, Bots.	D8	70
Mocksville, N.C., U.S.	I5	114
Moclips, Wa., U.S.	C2	136
Môco, Morro de, mtn., Ang.	C2	68
Mocoa, Col.	G3	86
Mococa, Braz.	K2	88
Mocodoene, Moz.	C12	70
Mocoretá, Arg.	E8	92
Moctezuma, Mex.	G8	98
Moctezuma, stm., Mex.	G8	98
Moctezuma, stm., Mex.	E9	100
Mocuba, Moz.	D6	68
Modane, Fr.	D12	18
Modāsa, India	G4	54
Modder, stm., S. Afr.	F7	70
Módena, Italy	F7	22
Modeste, Mount, mtn., B.C., Can.	H6	138
Modesto, Ca., U.S.	F4	134
Modica, Italy	H8	24
Mödling, Aus.	B13	22
Modowi, Indon.	F9	44
Modra, Slov.	H13	16
Moe, Austl.	L6	76
Moeda, Braz.	K3	88
Moei (Thaungyin), stm., Asia	D3	48
Moema, Braz.	J3	88
Moengo, Sur.	B7	84
Moen-jo-Daro, hist., Pak.	D10	56
Moenkopi, Az., U.S.	G5	132
Moenkopi Wash, stm., Az., U.S.	G6	132
Moeris, Lake see Qârûn, Birket, l., Egypt	I1	58
Moeskroen see Mouscron, Bel.	D12	14
Moffat, Scot., U.K.	F9	12
Moga, India	C5	54
Mogadiscio see Muqdisho, Som.	D9	66
Mogadishu see Muqdisho, Som.	D9	66
Mogalakwena, stm., S. Afr.	C9	70
Mogami, stm., Japan	A13	40
Mogaung, Mya.	C8	46
Mogdy, Russia	F15	34
Mogilno, Pol.	D13	16
Mogincual, Moz.	D7	68
Mogoča, Russia	F12	34
Mogočin, Russia	C14	32
Mogogh, Sudan	F6	62
Mogok, Mya.	A3	48
Mogollon Rim, clf, Az., U.S.	I6	132
Mogor, Afg.	B1	54
Mogotes, Col.	D5	86
Mogotón, mtn., N.A.	F4	102
Moguer, Spain	G4	20
Mogzon, Russia	F11	34
Mohács, Hung.	C5	26
Mohall, N.D., U.S.	F12	124
Mohammed, Râs, c., Egypt	K5	58
Mohammedia, Mor.	C3	64
Mohania, India	F9	54
Mohawk, Mi., U.S.	D10	118
Mohawk, stm., N.Y., U.S.	B11	114
Mohe, China	F13	34
Mohéli see Mwali, i., Com.	C7	68
Mohnyin, Mya.	D8	46
Mohokare (Caledon), stm., Afr.	F8	70
Mohyliv-Podil's'kyi, Ukr.	A14	26
Moi, Nor.	G2	8
Moinești, Rom.	C13	26
Moira, stm., On., Can.	D12	112
Moiraba, Braz.	B1	88
Mo i Rana, Nor.	C5	8
Moiseevka, Russia	C13	32
Moisés Ville, Arg.	E7	92
Moisie, Qc., Can.	E17	106
Moisie, stm., Qc., Can.	E17	106
Moitaco, Ven.	C9	86
Mojácar, Spain	G9	20
Mojave, Ca., U.S.	H7	134
Mojave, stm., Ca., U.S.	H9	134
Mojave Desert, des., Ca., U.S.	D4	98
Mojero, stm., Russia	C9	34
Mojiguaçu, stm., Braz.	K2	88
Mojikit Lake, res., On., Can.	A10	118
Moji-Mirim, Braz.	L2	88
Mojo, Eth.	F7	62
Moju, Braz.	A1	88
Moju, stm., Braz.	D8	84
Mōka, Japan	C12	40
Mokāma, India	F10	54
Mokapu Peninsula, pen., Hi., U.S.	B4	78a
Mokau, stm., N.Z.	D6	80
Mokelumne, stm., Ca., U.S.	E5	134
Moknine, Tun.	B7	64
Mokochu, Khao, mtn., Thai.	E4	48
Mokokchūng, India	C7	46
Mokolo, Cam.	B2	66
Mokolo, stm., S. Afr.	C8	70
Mokpalin, Mya.	D3	48
Mokp'o, Kor., S.	G7	38
Mokša, stm., Russia	D6	32
Mokwa, Nig.	H5	64
Mol, Bel.	C14	14
Mola di Bari, Italy	C11	24
Molat, Otok, i., Cro.	F11	22
Moldary, Kaz.	D13	32
Moldau see Vltava, stm., Czech Rep.	F10	16
Moldavia, hist. reg., Rom.	C13	26
Molde, Nor.	E2	8
Moldova, ctry., Eur.	B15	26
Moldova, stm., Rom.	C13	26
Moldoveanu, Vârful, mtn., Rom.	D11	26
Môle, Cap du, c., Haiti	C11	102
Mole Creek, Austl.	n13	77a
Molega Lake, l., N.S., Can.	F12	110
Molène, Île de, i., Fr.	F3	14
Molepolole, Bots.	D7	70
Molėtai, Lith.	E8	10
Molfetta, Italy	C10	24
Molina, Chile	G2	92
Molina de Aragón, Spain	D9	20
Molina de Segura, Spain	F9	20
Moline, Il., U.S.	C7	120
Moline, Ks., U.S.	D12	128
Molino, Fl., U.S.	G11	122
Molino de Valdo de Piedras, Mex.	E3	130
Molinos, Arg.	B4	92
Molise, state, Italy	C8	24
Mollendo, Peru	G3	84
Mölln, Ger.	C6	16
Mölndal, Swe.	H4	8
Molodežnaja, sci., Ant.	B9	81
Molodogvardejskoe, Kaz.	D11	32
Mologa, stm., Russia	B19	10
Molokai, i., Hi., U.S.	B5	78a
Molokai Fracture Zone, unds.	G24	142
Molokovo, Russia	B19	10
Molong, Austl.	I7	76
Molopo, stm., Afr.	E5	70
Moloundou, Cam.	D3	66
Molson Lake, l., Mb., Can.	E11	106
Molu, Pulau, i., Indon.	G9	44
Moluccas see Maluku, is., Indon.	F8	44
Molucca Sea see Maluku, Laut, Indon.	F8	44
Molvoticy, Russia	C15	10
Moma, Moz.	D6	68
Moma, stm., Russia	C17	34
Mombaça, Braz.	C6	88
Mombasa, Kenya	E7	66
Mombetsu, Japan	B15	38
Momčilgrad, Blg.	H12	26
Momi, Fiji	p18	79e
Momotombo, Volcán, vol., Nic.	F4	102
Mompono, D.R.C.	D4	66
Mompós, Col.	C4	86
Momskij hrebet, mts., Russia	C18	34
Mon, state, Mya.	E3	48
Møn, i., Den.	I5	8
Mona, Ut., U.S.	D5	132
Mona, Isla de, i., P.R.	h14	96a
Mona, Punta, c., C.R.	H6	102
Monaca, Pa., U.S.	D5	114
Monach Islands, is., Scot., U.K.	D5	12
Monaco, Mon.	G4	22
Monaco, ctry., Eur.	F13	18
Monadnock Mountain, mtn., N.H., U.S.	B13	114
Monagas, state, Ven.	C10	86
Monaghan, Ire.	G6	12
Monaghan, state, Ire.	G6	12
Monahans, Tx., U.S.	C5	130
Monakino, Russia	C10	38
Mona Passage, strt., N.A.	C13	102
Monapo, Moz.	C7	68
Monarch, S.C., U.S.	B4	116
Monarch Mountain, mtn., B.C., Can.	E5	138
Monarch Pass, p., Co., U.S.	E10	132
Monashee Mountains, mts., B.C., Can.	F12	138
Monastir, Tun.	I4	24
Moncalieri, Italy	F4	22
Moncalvo, Italy	E5	22
Monção, Braz.	B3	88
Mončegorsk, Russia	B15	8
Mönchengladbach, Ger.	E2	16
Monchique, Port.	G2	20
Moncks Corner, S.C., U.S.	C5	116
Monclova, Mex.	B8	100
Moncton, N.B., Can.	D12	110
Monday, stm., Para.	B10	92
Mondego, stm., Port.	D3	20
Mondjamboli, D.R.C.	D4	66
Mondoubleau, Fr.	F9	14
Mondovi, Wi., U.S.	G7	118
Mondragone, Italy	C7	24
Monemvasía, Grc.	G6	28
Monessen, Pa., U.S.	D5	114
Monesterio, Spain	F4	20
Monett, Mo., U.S.	H4	120
Monette, Ar., U.S.	I7	120
Monfalcone, Italy	E10	22
Monferrato, hist. reg., Italy	F5	22
Monforte de Lemos, Spain	B3	20
Monga, D.R.C.	D4	66
Mongaguá, Braz.	B14	92
Mongalla, Sudan	F6	62
Mongers Lake, l., Austl.	E3	74
Monggon Qulu, China	B8	36
Möng Hai, Mya.	B4	48
Möng Hsat, Mya.	B4	48
Mongibello see Etna, Monte, vol., Italy	G8	24
Möng Küng, Mya.	B3	48
Möng Ma, Mya.	B4	48
Möng Nai, Mya.	B3	48
Mongo, Chad	E3	62
Mongol Altayn nuruu, mts., Asia	E16	32
Mongolia, ctry., Asia	E14	30
Mongonu, Nig.	G7	64
Möng Pai, Mya.	C3	48
Möng Pawn, Mya.	B3	48
Mongu, Zam.	D3	68
Möng Yai, Mya.	A4	48
Monico, Wi., U.S.	F9	118
Monida Pass, p., U.S.	F14	136
Monino, Russia	E21	10
Moniquirá, Col.	E5	86
Mõniste, Est.	H12	8
Monitor Valley, val., Nv., U.S.	E9	134
Mońki, Pol.	C18	16
Monkira, Austl.	E3	76
Monmouth, Wales, U.K.	J10	12
Monmouth, Or., U.S.	F3	136
Monmouth Mountain, mtn., B.C., Can.	E7	138
Mono, stm., Afr.	H5	64
Mono, Caño, stm., Col.	E7	86
Mono Island, i., Sol. Is.	d6	79b
Mono Lake, l., Ca., U.S.	E7	134
Monon, In., U.S.	H3	112
Monona, Ia., U.S.	H7	118
Monona, Wi., U.S.	A8	120
Monongahela, stm., U.S.	E6	114
Monopoli, Italy	D11	24
Monor, Hung.	B6	26
Monreal del Campo, Spain	D9	20
Monreale, Italy	F7	24
Monroe, La., U.S.	E6	122
Monroe, Mi., U.S.	C2	114
Monroe, N.Y., U.S.	C11	114
Monroe, N.C., U.S.	B5	116
Monroe, Or., U.S.	F3	136
Monroe, Ut., U.S.	E4	132
Monroe, Va., U.S.	G6	114
Monroe, Wa., U.S.	C4	136
Monroe, Wi., U.S.	B8	120
Monroe City, In., U.S.	F10	120
Monroe Lake, res., In., U.S.	E11	120
Monroeville, Al., U.S.	F11	122
Monroeville, In., U.S.	D1	114
Monroeville, Oh., U.S.	C3	114
Monroeville, Pa., U.S.	D6	114
Monrovia, Lib.	H2	64
Mons, Bel.	D12	14
Monsefú, Peru	E2	84
Monselice, Italy	E8	22
Monsenhor Hipólito, Braz.	D5	88
Monsenhor Tabosa, Braz.	C5	88
Mönsterås, Swe.	H7	8
Montabaur, Ger.	F3	16
Montagne, Neth. Ant.	p23	104g
Montagu, S. Afr.	H5	70
Montague, P.E., Can.	D14	110
Montague, Mi., U.S.	E3	112
Montague, Tx., U.S.	H11	128
Montague, Isla, i., Mex.	F5	98
Montague Island, i., Ak., U.S.	E10	140
Montagu Island, i., S. Geor.	K12	82
Montaigu, Fr.	H7	14
Montalbano Ionico, Italy	D10	24
Montalegre, Port.	C3	20
Montana, Blg.	F10	26
Montana, state, Blg.	F10	26
Montana, state, U.S.	B6	108
Montaña de Covadonga, Parque Nacional de la, p.o.i., Spain	A5	20
Montánchez, Spain	E4	20
Montanha, Braz.	J5	88
Montargis, Fr.	G11	14
Montauban, Fr.	E7	18
Montauk Point, c., N.Y., U.S.	C14	114
Montbard, Fr.	G13	14
Montbéliard, Fr.	G15	14
Mont Belvieu, Tx., U.S.	H3	122
Montblanc, Spain	C11	20
Montblanch see Montblanc, Spain	C11	20
Montbrison, Fr.	D9	18
Montbron, Fr.	D6	18
Montceau-les-Mines, Fr.	H13	14
Montclair, Ca., U.S.	I8	134
Mont-de-Marsan, Fr.	F5	18
Montdidier, Fr.	E11	14
Monte, Laguna del, l., Arg.	H6	92
Monteagudo, Bol.	C4	90
Monte Albán, hist., Mex.	G10	100
Monte Alegre, Braz.	D7	84
Monte Alegre de Goiás, Braz.	G2	88

I•38 Mont-Murd

Name | Map Ref. | Page

Monte Alegre de Minas, Braz. J1 88
Monte Alegre de Sergipe, Braz. F7 88
Monte Azul, Braz. H4 88
Montebello, Qc., Can. C14 112
Montebello, P.R. B2 104a
Montecarlo, Arg. C10 92
Monte Carmelo, Braz. J2 88
Monte Caseros, Arg. E8 92
Montecassino, Abbazia di, Italy C7 24
Montecatini Terme, Italy G7 22
Montecito, Ca., U.S. I6 134
Monte Comán, Arg. G4 92
Monte Creek, B.C., Can. F11 138
Monte Cristi, Dom. Rep. C12 102
Monte Cristo, Bol. B4 90
Montecristo, Isola di, i., Italy H7 22
Monte do Carmo, Braz. F1 88
Monte Escobedo, Mex. D7 100
Montefalco, Italy H9 22
Montefiascone, Italy H8 22
Montego Bay, Jam. i12 104d
Monteiro, Braz. D7 88
Montejicar, Spain G7 20
Montejinni, Austl. C6 74
Montelíbano, Col. C4 86
Montélimar, Fr. E10 18
Monte Lindo, stm., Para. A9 92
Montellano, Spain H5 20
Montello, Nv., U.S. B2 132
Montello, Wi., U.S. H9 118
Monte Maíz, Arg. F6 92
Montemayor, Meseta de, plat., Arg. H3 90
Montemorelos, Mex. C9 100
Montemor-o-Velho, Port. D2 20
Montemuro, mtn., Port. C2 20
Montenegro, Braz. D12 92
Montenegro see Crna Gora, state, Yugo. G6 26
Monte Pascoal, Parque Nacional de, p.o.i., Braz. I5 88
Monte Patria, Chile E2 92
Montepuez, Moz. C6 68
Montepulciano, Italy G8 22
Monte Quemado, Arg. B6 92
Montereau-Faut-Yonne, Fr. F11 14
Monterey, Ca., U.S. G3 134
Monterey, Va., U.S. F6 114
Monterey Bay, b., Ca., U.S. G3 134
Montería, Col. C3 86
Monteros, Arg. C5 92
Monterotondo, Italy H9 22
Monterrey, Mex. C8 100
Montesano, Wa., U.S. C3 136
Monte Sant'Angelo, Italy I12 22
Monte Santu, Capo di, c., Italy D3 24
Montes Claros, Braz. I3 88
Montesilvano Marina, Italy H11 22
Montevallo, Al., U.S. D12 122
Montevarchi, Italy G8 22
Montevideo, Mn., U.S. G3 118
Montevideo, Ur. G9 92
Monte Vista, Co., U.S. D2 128
Montezuma, Ga., U.S. D1 116
Montezuma, In., U.S. I2 112
Montezuma, Ks., U.S. D8 128
Montezuma Castle National Monument, p.o.i., Az., U.S. I4 132
Montgenèvre, Col de, p., Fr. E12 18
Montgomery, Al., U.S. E12 122
Montgomery, La., U.S. F6 122
Montgomery, Mn., U.S. G5 118
Montgomery, Pa., U.S. C8 114
Montgomery, Tx., U.S. G3 122
Montgomery City, Mo., U.S. E6 120
Montguyon, Fr. D5 18
Monthey, Switz. D3 22
Monticello, Ar., U.S. D7 122
Monticello, Fl., U.S. F2 116
Monticello, Il., U.S. D9 120
Monticello, In., U.S. H3 112
Monticello, Ky., U.S. H13 120
Monticello, Mn., U.S. F5 118
Monticello, Ms., U.S. F8 122
Monticello, Mo., U.S. D6 120
Monticello, N.Y., U.S. C11 114
Monticello, Ut., U.S. F7 132
Monticello, hist., Va., U.S. G7 114
Montigny-le-Roi, Fr. G14 14
Montigny-lès-Metz, Fr. E15 14
Montijo, Pan. I7 102
Montijo, Port. F2 20
Montijo, Spain F4 20
Montijo, Golfo de, b., Pan. I7 102
Montilla, Spain G6 20
Montivilliers, Fr. E9 14
Mont-Joli, Qc., Can. B8 110
Mont-Laurier, Qc., Can. B14 112
Montluçon, Fr. C8 18
Montmagny, Qc., Can. D6 110
Montmédy, Fr. E14 14
Montmorillon, Fr. C6 18
Monto, Austl. E8 76
Montoro, Spain F6 20
Montour Falls, N.Y., U.S. B9 114
Montpelier, Jam. i13 104d
Montpelier, Id., U.S. H15 136
Montpelier, In., U.S. H4 112
Montpelier, Oh., U.S. C1 114
Montpelier, Vt., U.S. F4 110
Montpellier, Fr. F9 18
Montréal, Qc., Can. E3 110
Montreal, Wi., U.S. E8 118
Montreal, stm., On., Can. A10 112
Montreal Lake, l., Sk., Can. E9 106
Montreuil-sur-Mer, Fr. D10 14
Montreux, Switz. D3 22
Montrose, Scot., U.K. E10 12
Montrose, Co., U.S. E9 132
Montrose, Mi., U.S. E6 112
Montrose, Pa., U.S. C9 114
Montrose, S.D., U.S. D15 126
Montross, Va., U.S. F9 114
Monts, Pointe des, c., Qc., Can. A9 110
Mont-Saint-Michel, Qc., Can. D1 110
Mont-Saint-Michel, Baie du, b., Fr. F7 14
Mont-Saint-Michel, Le, Fr. F7 14
Montserrat, dep., N.A. h15 96a
Mont-Tremblant, Parc de récréation du, p.o.i., Qc., Can. D2 110
Monument, Or., U.S. F7 136
Monument Draw, stm., U.S. B5 130
Monument Peak, mtn., Co., U.S. D9 132
Monument Valley, val., U.S. F6 132
Monviso, mtn., Italy F4 22
Monyo, Mya. C2 48
Monywa, Mya. A2 48
Monza, Italy E6 22
Monze, Zam. D4 68
Monzen, Japan B9 40
Monzón, Spain C11 20
Mooi, stm., S. Afr. F10 70
Moolawatana, Austl. G2 76
Moon, Mountains of the see Ruwenzori, mts., Afr. D6 66
Moonie, Austl. F8 76
Moonie, stm., Austl. G7 76
Moora, Austl. F3 74
Moorcroft, Wy., U.S. C8 126
Moore, Id., U.S. G13 136
Moore, Ok., U.S. F11 128
Moore, Tx., U.S. E8 130
Moore, Lake, l., Austl. E3 74
Moorea, i., Fr. Poly. v20 78h
Moorefield, W.V., U.S. E7 114
Moore Haven, Fl., U.S. J4 116
Mooreland, Ok., U.S. E9 128
Mooresville, N.C., U.S. A5 116
Moorhead, Mn., U.S. E2 118
Moorhead, Ms., U.S. D8 122
Mooringsport, La., U.S. E5 122
Moornanyah Lake, l., Austl. I4 76
Moorreesburg, S. Afr. H4 70
Moosburg an der Isar, Ger. H7 16
Moosehead Lake, l., Me., U.S. E7 110
Moose Island, i., Mb., Can. C16 124
Moose Jaw, Sk., Can. D8 124
Moose Jaw, stm., Sk., Can. D8 124
Moose Lake, Mn., U.S. E6 118
Moose Lake, l., Ab., Can. B19 138
Mooselookmeguntic Lake, l., Me., U.S. F5 110
Moose Mountain, mtn., Sk., Can. E11 124
Moose Mountain Creek, stm., Sk., Can. E11 124
Moose Pass, Ak., U.S. D10 140
Moosomin, Sk., Can. D12 124
Moosonee, On., Can. E14 106
Mootwingee National Park, p.o.i., Austl. H4 76
Mopane, S. Afr. C9 70
Mopipi, Bots. B7 70
Moppo see Mokp'o, Kor., S. G7 38
Mopti, Mali G4 64
Moquegua, Peru G3 84
Mór, Hung. B5 26
Mòr, Glen, val., Scot., U.K. D8 12
Mora, Cam. B2 66
Mora, Port. F2 20
Mora, Swe. F6 8
Mora, Mn., U.S. F5 118
Mora, stm., N.M., U.S. F4 128
Morač, stm., Bela. H10 10
Morādābād, India D7 54
Morada Nova, Braz. C6 88
Morada Nova de Minas, Braz. J3 88
Morąg, Pol. C15 16
Moral de Calatrava, Spain F7 20
Moraleda, Canal, strt., Chile H2 90
Morales, Laguna de, b., Mex. D10 100
Moramanga, Madag. D8 68
Moran, Ks., U.S. G2 120
Moran, Mi., U.S. B5 112
Moran, Tx., U.S. B8 130
Morant Bay, Jam. j14 104d
Morant Cays, is., Jam. D10 102
Morant Point, c., Jam. j14 104d
Morar, Loch, l., Scot., U.K. E7 12
Moratalla, Spain F9 20
Moratuwa, Sri L. H4 53
Morava, hist. reg., Czech Rep. G13 16
Morava (March), stm., Eur. H12 16
Moravia, N.Y., U.S. B9 114
Moravské Budějovice, Czech Rep. G11 16
Morawa, Austl. E3 74
Morawhanna, Guy. C12 86
Moray Firth, b., Scot., U.K. D9 12
Morbi, India G3 54
Morbihan, state, Fr. G6 14
Morcenx, Fr. E5 18
Morden, Mb., Can. E15 124
Mordovia see Mordovija, state, Russia D6 32
Mordovija, state, Russia D6 32
Mordves, Russia F21 10
Mordvinia see Mordovija, state, Russia D6 32
Mordy, Pol. D18 16
More, Ben, mtn., Scot., U.K. E7 12
Moreau, stm., S.D., U.S. B12 126
Moreau, North Fork, stm., S.D., U.S. B9 126
Moreau, South Fork, stm., S.D., U.S. B9 126
Moreau Peak, mtn., S.D., U.S. B9 126
Moreauville, La., U.S. F7 122
Morecambe, Eng., U.K. G9 12
Morecambe Bay, b., Eng., U.K. H9 12
Moree, Austl. G7 76
Morehead, Ky., U.S. F2 114
Morehead City, N.C., U.S. B9 116
Moreland, Ga., U.S. D14 122
Moreland, Ky., U.S. G13 120
Morelia, Mex. F8 100
Morell, P.E., Can. D14 110
Morella, Austl. D4 76
Morelos, Mex. B5 100
Morelos, Mex. I2 130
Morelos, state, Mex. F9 100
Morena, India E6 54
Morena, Sierra, mts., Spain F5 20
Morenci, Az., U.S. J7 132
Moreni, Rom. D12 26
Moreno, Bahía, b., Chile A2 92
Møre og Romsdal, state, Nor. E2 8
Moresby Island, i., B.C., Can. E4 106
Moreton, Austl. B8 74
Moreton Island, i., Austl. F9 76
Moreuil, Fr. E11 14
Morez, Fr. H14 14
Morgan, Mn., U.S. G3 118
Morgan, Mt., U.S. F6 124
Morgan, Tx., U.S. B10 130
Morgan, Ut., U.S. B5 132
Morgan City, Al., U.S. C12 122
Morgan City, La., U.S. H7 122
Morganfield, Ky., U.S. G10 120
Morgan Hill, Ca., U.S. F4 134
Morganito, Ven. E8 86
Morganton, N.C., U.S. I4 114
Morgantown, In., U.S. E11 120
Morgantown, Ms., U.S. F8 122
Morgantown, Ms., U.S. F7 122
Morgantown, W.V., U.S. E6 114
Morgenzon, S. Afr. E9 70
Morghāb (Murgab), stm., Asia B9 56
Moriah, Mount, mtn., Nv., U.S. D2 132
Moriarty, N.M., U.S. G2 128
Morice, stm., B.C., Can. B4 138
Morice Lake, l., B.C., Can. B3 138
Morichal Largo, stm., Ven. C10 86
Moricsala rezervāts, Lat. C5 10
Moriki, Nig. G6 64
Morino, Russia C13 10
Morinville, Ab., Can. C17 138
Morioka, Japan E14 38
Morīri, Tso, l., India B6 54
Morisset, Austl. I8 76
Morjakovskij Zaton, Russia C14 32
Morkoka, stm., Russia D11 34
Morlaix, Fr. F5 14
Morley, Mi., U.S. E4 112
Mormal', Bela. H12 10
Mormugao, India D1 53
Morne-à-l'Eau, Guad. h5 105c
Morne du Vitet, hill, Guad. B2 105a
Morne Trois Pitons National Park, p.o.i., Dom. j6 105c
Morney, Austl. E3 76
Morning Sun, Ia., U.S. C6 120
Mornington, Austl. L5 76
Mornington, Isla, i., Chile I1 90
Mornington Island, i., Austl. C7 74
Morobe, Pap. N. Gui. b4 79a
Morocco, In., U.S. H2 112
Morocco, ctry., Afr. C3 64
Moro Creek, stm., Ar., U.S. D6 122
Morogoro, Tan. F7 66
Moro Gulf, b., Phil. G4 52
Moroleón, Mex. E8 100
Morombe, Madag. E7 68
Morón, Arg. G8 92
Morón, Cuba A8 102
Mörön, Mong. B5 36
Morón, Ven. B7 86
Morona, stm., S.A. I3 86
Morona Santiago, state, Ec. I3 86
Morondava, Madag. E7 68
Morón de Almazán, Spain C8 20
Morón de la Frontera, Spain G5 20
Moroni, Com. C7 68
Moroni, Ut., U.S. D5 132
Moron Us, stm., China E3 36
Morošečnoe, Russia E20 34
Morotai, i., Indon. E8 44
Moroto, Ug. D6 66
Moroto, mtn., Ug. D6 66
Morovis, P.R. B3 104a
Morozovsk, Russia E6 32
Morpeth, Eng., U.K. F11 12
Morrilton, Ar., U.S. B6 122
Morrin, Ab., Can. E18 138
Morrinhos, Braz. B5 88
Morrinhos, Braz. I1 88
Morrinsville, N.Z. C6 80
Morris, Mb., Can. E16 124
Morris, Il., U.S. C9 120
Morris, Mn., U.S. F2 118
Morrisburg, On., Can. D14 112
Morris Jesup, Kap, c., Grnld. A19 141
Morrison, Arg. F6 92
Morrison, Il., U.S. C8 120
Morrisonville, Il., U.S. E8 120
Morristown, Az., U.S. J4 132
Morristown, In., U.S. E12 120
Morristown, S.D., U.S. B11 126
Morristown, Tn., U.S. H2 114
Morrisville, Pa., U.S. H15 112
Morro, Punta, c., Mex. C2 102
Morro Bay, Ca., U.S. H5 134
Morro do Chapéu, Braz. F5 88
Morros, Braz. B3 88
Morrosquillo, Golfo de, b., Col. C3 86
Morrow, La., U.S. G6 122
Morrumbala, Moz. D6 68
Morrumbene, Moz. C12 70
Morse, La., U.S. G6 122
Morse, Tx., U.S. E7 128
Morsi, India H6 54
Mörskom see Myrskylä, Fin. F11 8
Morson, On., Can. B4 118
Mortagne-sur-Sèvre, Fr. H8 14
Mortara, Italy E5 22
Morteau, Fr. G15 14
Morteros, Arg. E6 92
Mortes, stm., Braz. F7 84
Mortlach, Sk., Can. D7 124
Mortlock Islands, is., Micron. C6 72
Morton, Il., U.S. D8 120
Morton, Mn., U.S. G4 118
Morton, Tx., U.S. H6 128
Morton, Wa., U.S. D4 136
Morton National Park, p.o.i., Austl. J7 76
Morua, Vanuatu k17 79d
Moruya, Austl. J7 76
Morvan, mts., Fr. G13 14
Morvant, Trin. s12 105f
Morven, Austl. F6 76
Morven, Ga., U.S. F2 116
Morven, N.C., U.S. B5 116
Morwell, Austl. L6 76
Moryń, Pol. D10 16
Moržovec, ostrov, i., Russia C20 8
Mosal'sk, Russia F17 10
Mosbach, Ger. G5 16
Moscos Islands, is., Mya. E3 48
Moscow see Moskva, Russia E20 10
Moscow, Id., U.S. D10 136
Moscow see Moskva, stm., Russia E21 10
Mosel (Moselle), stm., Eur. G2 16
Moselebe, stm., Bots. D7 70
Moselle, Ms., U.S. F9 122
Moselle, state, Fr. F15 14
Moselle (Mosel), stm., Eur. G2 16
Moses Lake, Wa., U.S. C7 136
Moses Point, Ak., U.S. D7 140
Moshaweng, stm., S. Afr. E6 70
Mosheim, Tn., U.S. H3 114
Moshi, Tan. E7 66
Mosinee, Wi., U.S. G9 118
Mosjøen, Nor. D5 8
Moskalvo, Russia F17 34
Moskenesøya, i., Nor. C5 8
Moskovskaja oblast', co., Russia D19 10
Moskovskaja vozvyšennost', plat., Russia E19 10
Moskva (Moscow), Russia E20 10
Moskva, stm., Russia E21 10
Moskvy, kanal imeni, can., Russia D20 10
Mosomane, Bots. C8 70
Mosonmagyaróvár, Hung. B4 26
Mosopa, Bots. D7 70
Mosqueiro, Braz. D8 84
Mosquera, Col. F2 86
Mosquito Coast see Mosquitos, Costa de, hist. reg., Nic. F6 102
Mosquitos, Costa de, hist. reg., Nic. F6 102
Mosquitos, Golfo de los, b., Pan. H7 102
Moss, Nor. G4 8
Mossaka, Congo E3 66
Mossbank, Sk., Can. E7 124
Mossburn, N.Z. G2 80
Mosselbaai (Mossel Bay), S. Afr. I6 70
Mossel Bay see Mosselbaai, S. Afr. I6 70
Mossleigh, Ab., Can. F17 138
Mossman, Austl. C9 74
Moss Mountain, mtn., Ar., U.S. C6 122
Mossoró, Braz. C7 88
Moss Point, Ms., U.S. G10 122
Moss Vale, Austl. J8 76
Mossy, stm., Mb., Can. C13 124
Most, Czech Rep. F9 16
Mostar, Bos. F4 26
Mostardas, Braz. E12 92
Møsting, Kap, c., Grnld. E17 141
Mostovaja, Russia D16 10
Mostyn, Malay. A11 50
Mosul see Al-Mawṣil, Iraq B5 56
Møsvatnet, l., Nor. G2 8
Mot'a, Eth. E7 62
Mota del Cuervo, Spain E8 20
Mota del Marqués, Spain C5 20
Motagua, stm., N.A. E3 102
Motal', Bela. H8 10
Motala, Swe. G6 8
Mota Lava, i., Vanuatu i16 79d
Motaze, Moz. D11 70
Moteve, Cap, c., Fr. Poly. s18 78g
Motherwell, Scot., U.K. F9 12
Motihāri, India E10 54
Motloutse, stm., Bots. B9 70
Motopu, Fr. Poly. s18 78g
Motozintla de Mendoza, Mex. H12 100
Motril, Spain H7 20
Motru, Rom. E10 26
Mott, N.D., U.S. A10 126
Motu, stm., N.Z. C7 80
Motueka, N.Z. E5 80
Motul de Felipe Carrillo Puerto, Mex. B3 102
Motutapu, i., Cook Is. a27 78j
Motygino, Russia C17 32
Motyklejka, Russia E18 34
Mouaskar, Alg. B5 64
Mouchoir Passage, strt., N.A. B12 102
Moudjéria, Maur. F2 64
Moúdros, Grc. D8 28
Mouila, Gabon E2 66
Mould Bay, N.T., Can. A16 140
Moule à Chique, Cap, c., St. Luc. m7 105c
Moulins, Fr. H12 14
Moulmein see Mawlamyine, Mya. D3 48
Moulmeingyun, Mya. D2 48
Moulouya, Oued, stm., Mor. C4 64
Moulton, Al., U.S. C11 122
Moulton, Ia., U.S. D5 120
Moulton, Tx., U.S. E10 130
Moultrie, Ga., U.S. E2 116
Moultrie, Lake, res., S.C., U.S. C5 116
Mouly, N. Cal. m16 79d
Mounana, Gabon E2 66
Mound City, Ks., U.S. F3 120
Mound City, Mo., U.S. D2 120
Mound City, S.D., U.S. B12 126
Moundou, Chad F3 62
Moundridge, Ks., U.S. C11 128
Mounds, Ok., U.S. B2 122
Moundsville, W.V., U.S. E5 114
Moundville, Al., U.S. E11 122
Mounlapamôk, Laos E7 48
Mountain, Wi., U.S. C1 112
Mountain, stm., N.T., Can. C5 106
Mountainair, N.M., U.S. G2 128
Mountainaire, Az., U.S. H5 132
Mountain Brook, Al., U.S. D12 122
Mountain City, Ga., U.S. B2 116
Mountain City, Nv., U.S. B1 132
Mountain Creek, Al., U.S. E12 122
Mountain Grove, Mo., U.S. G5 120
Mountain Home, Ar., U.S. H5 120
Mountain Home, Id., U.S. G11 136
Mountain Iron, Mn., U.S. D6 118
Mountain Lake, Mn., U.S. H3 118
Mountain Nile, stm., Afr. F6 62
Mountain Park, Ab., Can. D13 138
Mountain Pine, Ar., U.S. C5 122
Mountain View, Ar., U.S. I5 120
Mountain View, Ca., U.S. F3 134
Mountain View, Ok., U.S. F10 128
Mountain View, Wy., U.S. E6 126
Mountain Village, Ak., U.S. D7 140
Mountain Zebra National Park, p.o.i., S. Afr. H7 70
Mount Airy, N.C., U.S. H5 114
Mount Alida, S. Afr. F10 70
Mount Angel, Or., U.S. E4 136
Mount Aspiring National Park, p.o.i., N.Z. G3 80
Mount Athos see Ágio Óros, state, Grc. C7 28
Mount Ayliff, S. Afr. G9 70
Mount Ayr, Ia., U.S. D3 120
Mount Barker, Austl. F3 74
Mount Barker, Austl. J2 76
Mount Berry, Ga., U.S. C13 122
Mount Buffalo National Park, p.o.i., Austl. K5 76
Mount Calm, Tx., U.S. C11 130
Mount Carmel, Il., U.S. F10 120
Mount Carmel, Pa., U.S. D9 114
Mount Carroll, Il., U.S. B7 120
Mount Clemens, Mi., U.S. B3 114
Mount Cook National Park, p.o.i., N.Z. F4 80
Mount Dora, Fl., U.S. H4 116
Mount Enterprise, Tx., U.S. F4 122
Mount Field National Park, p.o.i., Austl. o13 77a
Mount Forest, On., Can. D9 112
Mount Frere, S. Afr. G9 70
Mount Gambier, Austl. K3 76
Mount Garnet, Austl. A5 76
Mount Gay, W.V., U.S. G3 114
Mount Hagen, Pap. N. Gui. b3 79a
Mount Holly, N.C., U.S. A4 116
Mount Holly Springs, Pa., U.S. H12 112
Mount Hope, Austl. F7 74
Mount Hope, Ks., U.S. D11 128
Mount Horeb, Wi., U.S. B8 120
Mount Ida, Ar., U.S. C5 122
Mount Isa, Austl. C2 76
Mount Jackson, Va., U.S. F7 114
Mount Juliet, Tn., U.S. H11 120
Mount Kaputar National Park, p.o.i., Austl. H8 76
Mount Lebanon, Pa., U.S. D6 114
Mount Lofty Ranges, mts., Austl. I2 76
Mount Magnet, Austl. E3 74
Mount Manara, Austl. I4 76
Mount Margaret, Austl. F4 76
Mount Morgan, Austl. D8 76
Mount Morris, Il., U.S. I9 118
Mount Morris, Mi., U.S. E6 112
Mount Olive, Il., U.S. E8 120
Mount Olive, Ms., U.S. F9 122
Mount Olive, N.C., U.S. A7 116
Mount Orab, Oh., U.S. E2 114
Mount Perry, Austl. E8 76
Mount Pleasant, On., Can. E9 112
Mount Pleasant, Ia., U.S. D6 120
Mount Pleasant, Mi., U.S. E5 112
Mount Pleasant, Pa., U.S. D6 114
Mount Pleasant, S.C., U.S. D6 116
Mount Pleasant, Tn., U.S. B11 122
Mount Pleasant, Tx., U.S. D4 122
Mount Pleasant, Ut., U.S. D5 132
Mount Pulaski, Il., U.S. D8 120
Mount Rainier National Park, p.o.i., Wa., U.S. D5 136
Mount Revelstoke National Park, p.o.i., B.C., Can. E12 138
Mount Riddock, Austl. D6 74
Mount Saint Helens National Volcanic Monument, p.o.i., Wa., U.S. D5 136
Mount Selinda, Zimb. B11 70
Mount Somers, N.Z. F4 80
Mount Sterling, Il., U.S. E7 120
Mount Sterling, Ky., U.S. F2 114
Mount Sterling, Oh., U.S. E2 114
Mount Uniacke, N.S., Can. F12 110
Mount Union, Pa., U.S. D8 114
Mount Vernon, Austl. D3 74
Mount Vernon, Al., U.S. F10 122
Mount Vernon, Ga., U.S. D3 116
Mount Vernon, Il., U.S. F8 120
Mount Vernon, Ia., U.S. C6 120
Mount Vernon, Ky., U.S. G1 114
Mount Vernon, Mo., U.S. G4 120
Mount Vernon, Oh., U.S. D3 114
Mount Vernon, Or., U.S. F7 136
Mount Vernon, S.D., U.S. D14 126
Mount Vernon, Wa., U.S. B4 136
Mount Vernon, hist., Va., U.S. F8 114
Mount William National Park, p.o.i., Austl. n13 77a
Mount Willoughby, Austl. E6 74
Mount Wolf, Pa., U.S. H13 112
Moura, Braz. H11 86
Moura, Port. F3 20
Mourdi, Dépression du, depr., Chad D4 62
Mourdiah, Mali G3 64
Mourne Mountains, mts., N. Ire., U.K. G6 12
Mouscron, Bel. D12 14
Moussa 'Ali, mtn., Afr. B8 66
Moussoro, Chad E3 62
Moutier, Switz. C4 22
Moutong, Indon. E7 44
Mouzáki, Grc. D4 28
Movenda, D.R.C. D4 66
Moweaqua, Il., U.S. E8 120
Moxotó, stm., Braz. E7 88
Moyahua, Mex. E7 100
Moyale, Kenya D7 66
Moyamba, S.L. H2 64
Moyen Atlas, mts., Mor. C4 64
Moyeuvre-Grande, Fr. E14 14
Moyie, B.C., Can. G15 138
Moyie, stm., N.A. H14 138
Moyo, Pulau, i., Indon. H10 50
Moyobamba, Peru E2 84
Moyu, China A4 46
M'oža (Měža), stm., Eur. E14 10
Možajsk, Russia E18 10
Mozambique, ctry., Afr. D5 68
Mozambique Channel, strt., Afr. D7 68
Mozambique Plateau, unds. M6 142
Mozdok, Russia F6 32
Mozolevo, Russia A16 10
Mpala, D.R.C. F5 66
Mpanda, Tan. F6 66
Mphoengs, Zimb. B8 70
Mpika, Zam. C5 68
Mporokoso, Zam. B5 68
Mpui, Tan. F6 66
Mpumalanga, state, S. Afr. E9 70
Mpwapwa, Tan. F7 66
Mqanduli, S. Afr. G9 70
Mrągowo, Pol. C17 16
Mrkonjić Grad, Bos. E3 26
M'Saken, Tun. I4 24
Mscislaụ, Bela. F14 10
Msciž, Bela. F11 10
Msta, Russia C17 10
Msta, stm., Russia B15 10
Mszczonów, Pol. E16 16
Mtama, Tan. G7 66
Mtamvuna, stm., S. Afr. G9 70
Mtwara, Tan. G8 66
Mu, N. Cal. m16 79d
Mu, stm., Mya. A2 48
Mu, Cerro, mtn., S.A. C5 86
Mu'a, Tonga n14 78e
Mualang, Indon. C7 50
Muanda, D.R.C. F2 66
Muang Hay, Laos B5 48
Muang Hôngsa, Laos C5 48
Muang Hounxianghoung, Laos B6 48
Muang Khammouan, Laos D7 48
Muang Khao, Laos C6 48
Muang Không, Laos E7 48
Muang Khôngxédôn, Laos E7 48
Muang La, Laos B6 48
Muang Long, Laos B5 48
Muang Ngoy, Laos B6 48
Muang Nong, Laos D8 48
Muang Ou Tai, Laos A5 48
Muang Pak-Lay, Laos C5 48
Muang Paktha, Laos B5 48
Muang Pakxan, Laos C6 48
Muang Phalan, Laos D7 48
Muang Phônthong, Laos E7 48
Muang Sam Sip, Thai. E7 48
Muang Sing, Laos B5 48
Muang Souvannakhili, Laos E7 48
Muang Sung, Laos B6 48
Muang Thatèng, Laos E8 48
Muang Va, Laos B6 48
Muang Vangviang, Laos C6 48
Muang Xaignabouri, Laos C5 48
Muang Xamtong, Laos C6 48
Muang Xépôn, Laos D7 48
Muang Yo, Laos B5 48
Muar, Malay. L6 48
Muar, stm., Malay. K6 48
Muara, Bru. A9 50
Muaraancalung, Indon. C10 50
Muarabenangin, Indon. D9 50
Muarabungo, Indon. D2 50
Muaradua, Indon. F4 50
Muaraenim, Indon. E3 50
Muarajuloi, Indon. D8 50
Muarakelingi, Indon. E3 50
Muaralabuh, Indon. D2 50
Muaralakitan, Indon. E3 50
Muaralembu, Indon. D2 50
Muarapangean, Indon. B10 50
Muarapayang, Indon. D9 50
Muarasabak, Indon. D3 50
Muarasiberut, Indon. D1 50
Muaratebo, Indon. D3 50
Muarateladang, Indon. E4 50
Muaratembesi, Indon. D3 50
Muaratewe, Indon. D9 50
Muaratunan, Indon. D10 50
Mubārakpur, India E9 54
Mubende, Ug. D6 66
Mubi, Nig. G7 64
Mubur, Pulau, i., Indon. B4 50
Mucaitá, stm., Braz. D4 88
Mucajaí, stm., Braz. F11 86
Muchinga Escarpment, clf, Zam. C4 68
Muchinga Mountains, mts., Zam. C5 68
Muckadilla, Austl. F7 76
Mučkas, Russia D23 8
Mucojo, Moz. C7 68
Muconda, Ang. C3 68
Mucujê, Braz. G5 88
Muçum, Braz. D11 92
Mucuri, Braz. J6 88
Mucuri, stm., Braz. J6 88
Muda, stm., Malay. J5 48
Mudan, stm., China B10 36
Mudanjiang, China B8 38
Mudanya, Tur. C11 28
Mud Creek, stm., Ne., U.S. F13 126
Mud Creek, stm., Tx., U.S. E3 122
Muddus Nationalpark, p.o.i., Swe. C9 8
Muddy, stm., Nv., U.S. G2 132
Muddy Boggy Creek, stm., Ok., U.S. C3 122
Muddy Creek, stm., Ut., U.S. E6 132
Mudgee, Austl. I7 76
Mudhol, India C2 53
Mudjuga, Russia E18 8
Mud Lake, l., Nv., U.S. F8 134
Mudon, Mya. D3 48
Mudurnu, Tur. C14 28
Muelle de los Bueyes, Nic. G5 102
Muenster, Tx., U.S. H11 128
Muerto, Mar, l., Mex. G11 100
Mufulira, Zam. C4 68
Mufu Shan, mtn., China G5 42
Mufu Shan, mts., China G6 42
Mughal Sarāi, India F9 54
Mugi, Japan F7 40
Mu Gia, Deo, p., Asia D7 48
Muğla, Tur. F11 28
Muğla, state, Tur. F11 28
Muḥammad Qawl, Sudan C7 62
Muhanovo, Russia D21 10
Muḥavec, stm., Bela. H7 10
Muhino, Russia F14 34
Mühlacker, Ger. H4 16
Mühldorf am Inn, Ger. H8 16
Mühlhausen, Ger. E6 16
Muhlig-Hofmann Mountains, mts., Ant. C5 81
Mühlviertel, reg., Aus. B11 22
Muḥradah, Syria C7 58
Muhu, i., Est. G10 8
Muié, Ang. C3 68
Mui Hopohoponga Point, c., Tonga n14 78e
Muineachán see Monaghan, Ire. G6 12
Muine Bheag, Ire. I6 12
Muite, Moz. C6 68
Muja, Russia E12 34
Mujnak, Uzb. F9 32
Mukah, Malay. B8 50
Mukalla see Al-Mukallā, Yemen G6 56
Mukatsjeve, Ukr. A9 26
Mukāwir, hist., Jord. G6 58
Mukdahan, Thai. D7 48
Mukden see Shenyang, China D5 38
Mukeriān, India C5 54
Mukharram al-Fawqānī, Syria D7 58
Mukilteo, Wa., U.S. C4 136
Mukinbudin, Austl. F3 74
Mukomuko, Indon. E2 50
Mukry, Turkmen. B10 56
Muktsar, India C5 54
Mūl, India A4 53
Mula, China F5 36
Mula, Spain F9 20
Mula, stm., India B2 53
Mula, stm., India B1 53
Mulaku Atoll, at., Mald. i12 46a
Mulan, China B10 36
Mulas, Punta de, c., Cuba B10 102
Mulatos, Mex. A4 100
Mulbāgal, India E4 53
Mulberry, Ar., U.S. B4 122
Mulberry, Fl., U.S. I4 116
Mulberry Fork, stm., Al., U.S. D12 122
Mulberry Mountain, mtn., Ar., U.S. I5 120
Mulchatna, stm., Ak., U.S. D8 140
Mulchén, Chile H1 92
Mulde, stm., Ger. E8 16
Muldoon, Tx., U.S. E10 130
Muldraugh, Ky., U.S. G12 120
Muldrow, Ok., U.S. B4 122
Muleshoe, Tx., U.S. G6 128
Mulgowie, Austl. F9 76
Mulgrave, N.S., Can. E15 110
Mulhacén, mtn., Spain G7 20
Mulhall, Ok., U.S. E11 128
Mulhouse, Fr. G16 14
Muling, China B9 38
Muling, China B9 38
Muling, stm., China B9 38
Mulinu'u, Cape, c., Samoa g11 79c
Mūlki, India E2 53
Mull, Island of, i., Scot., U.K. E6 12
Mullengudgery, Austl. H6 76
Muller, Pegunungan, mts., Indon. C8 50
Mullet Peninsula, pen., Ire. G2 12
Mullet Pond Bay, Neth. Ant. A1 105a
Mullett Lake, l., Mi., U.S. C5 112
Mullewa, Austl. E3 74
Müllheim, Ger. I3 16
Mullin, Tx., U.S. C9 130
Mullingar, Ire. H5 12
Mullins, S.C., U.S. B6 116
Mulobezi, Zam. D4 68
Mulongo, D.R.C. F5 66
Mulshi Lake, res., India B1 53
Multai, India H7 54
Multān, Pak. C3 54
Multé, Mex. D2 102
Mulumbe, Monts, mts., D.R.C. F5 66
Mulvane, Ks., U.S. D11 128
Mumbai (Bombay), India B1 53
Mumbwa, Zam. D4 68
Mumen, China E2 42
Mumeng, Pap. N. Gui. b4 79a
Mumford, Tx., U.S. G2 122
Mun, stm., Thai. E7 48
Muna, stm., Russia C13 34
Muna, Pulau, i., Indon. F7 44
Muncar, Indon. H9 50
Münchberg, Ger. F7 16
München (Munich), Ger. H7 16
Munchique, Cerro, mtn., Col. F3 86
Munchique, Parque Nacional, p.o.i., Col. F3 86
Muncie, In., U.S. H4 112
Muncy, Pa., U.S. C9 114
Mundare, Ab., Can. C18 138
Munday, Tx., U.S. H9 128
Mundelein, Il., U.S. B9 120
Münden, Ger. E5 16
Mundra, India G2 54
Mundrabilla, Austl. F5 74
Mundubbera, Austl. E8 76
Munfordville, Ky., U.S. G12 120
Mungallala Creek, stm., Austl. F6 76
Mungana, Austl. C8 74
Mungar Junction, Austl. E9 76
Mungbere, D.R.C. D5 66
Mungeli, India G8 54
Munger, India F11 54
Mungindi, Austl. G7 76
Mungo, Ang. C2 68
Mungo National Park, p.o.i., Austl. I4 76
Munhango, Ang. C2 68
Munich see München, Ger. H7 16
Muniesa, Spain C10 20
Munim, stm., Braz. B3 88
Munising, Mi., U.S. B3 112
Muniz Freire, Braz. K5 88
Munku-Sardyk, gora, mtn., Asia D17 32
Münsingen, Ger. H5 16
Munson, Ab., Can. E18 138
Münster, Ger. D3 16
Munster, Ger. C6 16
Munster, hist. reg., Ire. I3 12
Munte, Indon. C11 50
Muntok, Indon. E4 50
Munuscong Lake, l., N.A. B5 112
Muong Hinh, Viet. C7 48
Muong Saiapoun, Laos C5 48
Muonio, Fin. C10 8
Muping, China C9 42
Muqdisho (Mogadiscio), Som. D9 66
Muqui, Braz. K5 88
Mur (Mura), stm., Eur. D12 22
Mura (Mur), stm., Eur. D12 22
Murajá, Braz. D8 84
Murakami, Japan A12 40
Murana, Indon. F9 44
Muraši, Russia C7 32
Murat, Fr. D8 18
Murat, stm., Tur. H17 6
Murat Dağı, mtn., Tur. E12 28
Muratlı, Tur. B10 28
Muravera, Italy E3 24
Murayama, Japan A13 40
Murça, Port. C3 20
Murchison, Tx., U.S. E3 122
Murchison, stm., Austl. E2 74
Murchison, Mount, mtn., N.Z. F4 80
Murcia, Spain G9 20
Murcia, state, Spain G9 20
Mur-de-Barrez, Fr. E8 18

Name | Map Ref. | Page

Murdo, S.D., U.S. D12 126
Mürefte, Tur. C10 28
Mureş, state, Rom. C11 26
Mureş (Maros), stm., Eur. C7 26
Muret, Fr. F7 18
Murewa, Zimb. D5 68
Murfreesboro, Ar., U.S. C5 122
Murfreesboro, Tn., U.S. I11 120
Murgab, Taj. B11 56
Murgab (Morghāb), stm., Asia B9 56
Murgha Kibzai, Pak. C2 54
Murgon, Austl. F8 76
Muri, Cook Is. a27 78j
Muriaé, Braz. K4 88
Muriaé, stm., Braz. K5 88
Muribeca dos Guararapes, Braz. E8 88
Murici, Braz. E8 88
Muricizal, stm., Braz. D1 88
Murīdke, Pak. C5 54
Muriege, Ang. C3 68
Müritz, l., Ger. C8 16
Murmansk, Russia B15 8
Murmanskaja oblast', co., Russia C16 8
Murnau, Ger. I7 16
Muro Lucano, Italy D9 24
Murom, Russia I19 8
Muromcevo, Russia C13 32
Muroran, Japan C14 38
Muroto, Japan F7 40
Muroto-zaki, c., Japan F7 40
Murowana Goślina, Pol. D13 16
Murphy, Id., U.S. G10 136
Murphy, N.C., U.S. A1 116
Murphys, Ca., U.S. E5 134
Murra Murra, Austl. G6 76
Murrat el-Kubra, Buheirat (Great Bitter Lake), l., Egypt H3 58
Murray, Ia., U.S. C3 120
Murray, Ky., U.S. H9 120
Murray, Ut., U.S. C5 132
Murray, stm., Austl. J2 76
Murray, stm., B.C., Can. B9 138
Murray, Lake, l., Pap. N. Gui. b3 79a
Murray, Lake, res., S.C., U.S. B4 116
Murray Bridge, Austl. J2 76
Murray Fracture Zone, unds. F24 142
Murray Harbour, P.E., Can. E14 110
Murray Maxwell Bay, b., Nu., Can. A14 106
Murray River, P.E., Can. D14 110
Murraysburg, S. Afr. G6 70
Murree, Pak. B4 54
Murrhardt, Ger. H5 16
Murrumbidgee, stm., Austl. J4 76
Murrumburrah, Austl. J7 76
Murrupula, Moz. D6 68
Mursala, Pulau, i., Indon. L4 48
Murshidābād, India F12 54
Murska Sobota, Slvn. D13 22
Murtajāpur, India H6 54
Murtee, Austl. H4 76
Murter, Otok, i., Cro. G12 22
Murtle Lake, l., B.C., Can. D11 138
Murtoa, Austl. K4 76
Murtosa, Port. D2 20
Muru, Capu di, c., Fr. H14 18
Murud, India B1 53
Murud, Gunong, mtn., Malay. B9 50
Murukta, Russia C9 34
Murung, stm., Indon. C9 50
Mururoa, at., Fr. Poly. F13 72
Murwāra (Katni), India G8 54
Murwillumbah, Austl. G9 76
Murzuq, Libya B2 62
Murzūq, Idhān, des., Libya C2 62
Mürzzuschlag, Aus. C12 22
Muş, Tur. B5 56
Mūsa (Mūša), stm., Eur. D6 10
Mūša (Mūsa), stm., Eur. D6 10
Mûsa, Gebel (Sinai, Mount), mtn., Egypt J5 58
Musadi, D.R.C. E4 66
Musā'id, Libya A4 62
Musala, mtn., Blg. G10 26
Musan-ŭp, Kor., N. C8 38
Muscat see Masqaṭ, Oman E8 56
Muscat and Oman see Oman, ctry., Asia F8 56
Muscatine, Ia., U.S. C6 120
Muscle Shoals, Al., U.S. C11 122
Musclow, Mount, mtn., B.C., Can. C3 138
Muscoda, Wi., U.S. A7 120
Musgrave, Austl. B8 74
Mus-Haja, gora, mtn., Russia D17 34
Mushie, D.R.C. E3 66
Mushin, Nig. H5 64
Mūsi, stm., India C4 53
Musi, stm., Indon. E4 50
Musicians Seamounts, unds. F22 142
Muskegon, Mi., U.S. E3 112
Muskegon, stm., Mi., U.S. E4 112
Muskingum, stm., Oh., U.S. E4 114
Muskogee, Ok., U.S. I2 120
Muskoka, Lake, l., On., Can. D10 112
Musoma, Tan. E6 66
Musquodoboit Harbour, N.S., Can. F13 110
Mussau Island, i., Pap. N. Gui. a4 79a
Musselshell, stm., Mt., U.S. G6 124
Mussende, Ang. C2 68
Mussidan, Fr. D6 18
Mussomeli, Italy G7 24
Mussuma, Ang. C3 68
Mustafakemalpaşa, Tur. C11 28
Mustafa Kemal Paşa, stm., Tur. D11 28
Mustahīl, Eth. F8 62
Mustāng, Nepal D9 54
Mustang Draw, stm., Tx., U.S. B5 130
Mustang Island, i., Tx., U.S. G10 130
Musters, Lago, l., Arg. I3 90
Mustla, Est. B8 10
Mustvee, Est. B9 10
Muswellbrook, Austl. I8 76
Mût, Egypt B5 62
Mut, Tur. B4 58
Mutá, Ponta do, c., Braz. G6 88
Mutanchiang see Mudanjiang, China B8 38
Mutankiang see Mudanjiang, China B8 38
Mutare, Zimb. D5 68
Mutlu (Rezovska), stm., Eur. G14 26
Mutoko, Zimb. D5 68
Mutoraj, Russia B17 32
Mutsamudu, Com. C7 68
Mutshatsha, D.R.C. G4 66
Mutsu, Japan D14 38
Mutsu-wan, b., Japan D14 38
Mutton Bay, Qc., Can. i22 107a
Mutuípe, Braz. G6 88
Mutum, Braz. J5 88
Mu Us Shamo (Ordos Desert), des., China B3 42
Mūvattupula, India F3 53
Muxima, Ang. B1 68
Muyinga, Bdi. E6 66
Muyumba, D.R.C. F5 66
Muzaffarābād, Pak. A4 54
Muzaffargarh, Pak. C3 54
Muzaffarnagar, India D6 54
Muzaffarpur, India E10 54
Muzat, stm., China C2 36
Muži, Russia A10 32
Muzillac, Fr. G6 14
Muztag, mtn., China D2 36
Muztag, mtn., China A5 46
Mvolo, Sudan F6 62
Mvoti, stm., S. Afr. F10 70
Mvuma, Zimb. D5 68
Mwadui, Tan. E6 66
Mwali, i., Com. C7 68
Mwanza, Tan. E6 66
Mweelrea, mtn., Ire. H3 12
Mweka, D.R.C. E4 66
Mwene-Ditu, D.R.C. F4 66
Mwenezi, Zimb. B10 70
Mwenezi, stm., Afr. B10 70
Mweru, Lake, l., Afr. B4 68
Mweru Wantipa, Lake, l., Zam. B4 68
Mwilitau Islands (Purdy Islands), is., Pap. N. Gui. a4 79a
Mwinilunga, Zam. C3 68
Myājlār, India E3 54
Myall Lakes National Park, p.o.i., Austl. I9 76
Myanaung, Mya. C2 48
Myanmar (Burma), ctry., Asia D8 46
Myaungmya, Mya. D2 48
Mycenae see Mykínes, hist., Grc. F5 28
Myebon, Mya. B1 48
Myingyan, Mya. B2 48
Myitkyinā, Mya. C8 46
Myitnge, stm., Mya. B3 48
Myitta, Mya. E4 48
Myittha, Mya. B2 48
Myittha, stm., Mya. B2 48
Myjava, Slov. H13 16
Mykines, i., Far. Is. m34 8b
Mykínes, hist., Grc. F5 28
Mykolaïv, Ukr. F15 6
Mykolaïv, co., Ukr. B17 26
Mykolaïvka, Ukr. C16 26
Mýkonos, i., Grc. F8 28
Myla, Russia D24 8
Mymensingh (Nasirābād), Bngl. F13 54
Mynaral, Kaz. E12 32
Mynfontein, S. Afr. G6 70
Myohaung, Mya. B1 48
Myohyang-san, mtn., Kor., N. D7 38
Myōkō-san, vol., Japan C11 40
Myra, hist., Tur. G12 28
Mýrdalsjökull, ice, Ice. I30 8a
Myrskylä, Fin. F11 8
Myrtle Beach, S.C., U.S. C7 116
Myrtle Creek, Or., U.S. G3 136
Myrtle Grove, Fl., U.S. G11 122
Myrtle Point, Or., U.S. G2 136
Myrtletowne, Ca., U.S. C1 134
Myškino, Russia C21 10
Myślenice, Pol. G15 16
Myślibórz, Pol. D10 16
Mysłowice, Pol. F15 16
Mysore, India E3 53
Mysore see Karnātaka, state, India F4 46
Mystic, Ct., U.S. C14 114
Mystrás, hist., Grc. F5 28
Mys Vhodnoj, Russia B6 34
Myszków, Pol. F15 16
Myt, Russia H20 8
My Tho, Viet. G8 48
Mytilíni, Grc. D9 28
Mytišči, Russia E20 10
Myton, Ut., U.S. C6 132
Mývatn, l., Ice. k31 8a
Mzimba, Mwi. C5 68
Mzimvubu, stm., S. Afr. G9 70
Mzintlava, stm., S. Afr. G9 70
Mzuzu, Mwi. C5 68

N

Na (Tengtiao), stm., Asia A6 48
Naab, stm., Ger. G7 16
Naalehu, Hi., U.S. D6 78a
Naas, Ire. H6 12
Nababeep, S. Afr. F3 70
Nabari, Japan E9 40
Nabberu, Lake, l., Austl. E4 74
Nabburg, Ger. G8 16
Naberežnye Čelny, Russia C8 32
Nabeul, Tun. H4 24
Nābha, India C6 54
Nabire, Indon. F10 44
Nabī Shu'ayb, Jabal an-, mtn., Yemen F5 56
Nabouwalu, Fiji p19 79e
Nabq, Egypt J5 58
Nabula, China C7 54
Nābulus, W.B. F6 58
Nacala-a-Velha, Moz. C7 68
Nachingwea, Tan. G7 66
Nāchna, India E3 54
Náchod, Czech Rep. F12 16
Nachvak Fiord, b., Nf., Can. F13 141
Nacimiento, Chile H1 92
Nacimiento, Lake, res., Ca., U.S. H5 134
Naco, Mex. F8 98
Naco, Az., U.S. L6 132
Nacogdoches, Tx., U.S. F4 122
Nácori Chico, Mex. G8 98
Nacozari de García, Mex. F8 98
Ñacunday, Para. B10 92
Nadarivatu, Fiji p18 79e
Nadela, Spain B3 20
Nadiād, India G4 54
Nadi Bay, b., Fiji p18 79e
Nădlac, Rom. C7 26
Naduri, Fiji p19 79e
Nadvoicy, Russia E16 8
Nadym, Russia A12 32
Nadym, stm., Russia A12 32
Naenwa, India F5 54
Nærbø, Nor. G1 8
Næstved, Den. I4 8
Nafada, Nig. G7 64
Nafī, Sau. Ar. D5 56
Náfpaktos, Grc. E4 28
Náfplio, Grc. F5 28
Nafūsah, Jabal, hills, Libya A2 62
Naga, Phil. D4 52
Nagahama, Japan D9 40
Nagahama, Japan F5 40
Naga Hills, mts., Asia C7 46
Nagai, Japan A12 40
Nagai Island, i., Ak., U.S. F7 140
Nāgāland, state, India C7 46
Nagano, Japan C11 40
Nagano, state, Japan C11 40
Nagaoka, Japan B11 40
Nagaon, India E14 54
Nāgappattinam, India F4 53
Nagara, stm., Japan D9 40
Nagarhole Tiger Reserve, India E2 53
Nāgārjuna Sāgar, res., India C4 53
Nagarote, Nic. F4 102
Nagasaki, Japan G2 40
Nagasaki, state, Japan G2 40
Nagato, Japan E4 40
Nāgaur, India E4 54
Nāgāvali, stm., India B6 53
Nagda, India G5 54
Nāgercoil, India G3 53
Nagīna, India D7 54
Nagłowice, Pol. F15 16
Nago, Japan I19 39a
Nagold, Ger. H4 16
Nagornyj, Russia E13 34
Nagoya, Japan D9 40
Nāgpur, India H7 54
Nagqu, China C14 54
Nagua, Dom. Rep. C12 102
Naguabo, P.R. B4 104a
Nagyatád, Hung. C4 26
Nagybánya see Baia Mare, Rom. B10 26
Nagyecsed, Hung. B9 26
Nagykanizsa, Hung. C4 26
Nagykáta, Hung. B6 26
Nagykőrös, Hung. B6 26
Naha, Japan I18 39a
Nahabuan, Indon. C9 50
Nāhan, India C6 54
Nahanni Butte, N.T., Can. C6 106
Nahariyya, Isr. E5 58
Nahāvand, Iran C6 56
Nahe, China B9 36
Nahe, stm., Ger. G3 16
Nahma, Mi., U.S. C3 112
Nahodka, Russia A13 32
Nahodka, Russia C10 38
Nahoe, Fr. Poly. r19 78g
Nahoï, Cap, c., Vanuatu j16 79d
Nahuel Huapi, Lago, l., Arg. H2 90
Nahuel Niyeu, Arg. H3 90
Naica, Mex. B6 100
Naicam, Sk., Can. B9 124
Naila, Ger. F7 16
Naiman Qi, China C4 38
Nā'īn, Iran C7 56
Naini Tāl, India D7 54
Nainpur, India G8 54
Nairai, i., Fiji p19 79e
Nairn, La., U.S. H9 122
Nairobi, Kenya E7 66
Naitauba, i., Fiji p20 79e
Naivasha, Kenya E7 66
Naizishan, China C7 38
Najac, Fr. E8 18
Najafābād, Iran C7 56
Najasa, stm., Cuba B9 102
Najd (Nejd), hist. reg., Sau. Ar. D5 56
Najībābād, India D7 54
Najin, Kor., N. C9 38
Naka, stm., Japan C13 40
Nakajō, Japan A12 40
Nakama, Japan F3 40
Nakaminato, Japan C13 40
Nakamura, Japan G5 40
Nakano, Japan C11 40
Nakano-shima, i., Japan k19 39a
Nakasongola, Ug. D6 66
Nakatsu, Japan F4 40
Nakatsugawa, Japan D10 40
Nakhl, Egypt I4 58
Nakhon Nayok, Thai. E5 48
Nakhon Pathom, Thai. F5 48
Nakhon Phanom, Thai. D7 48
Nakhon Ratchasima, Thai. E6 48
Nakhon Sawan, Thai. E4 48
Nakhon Si Thammarat, Thai. H5 48
Nakhon Thai, Thai. D5 48
Nakina, On., Can. A12 118
Nakło nad Notecią, Pol. C13 16
Nakodar, India C5 54
Nakonde, Zam. B5 68
Nakskov, Den. I4 8
Naktong-gang, stm., Kor., S. C1 40
Nakuru, Kenya E7 66
Nakusp, B.C., Can. F13 138
Nālanda, India F10 54
Nalayh, Mong. B6 36
Nalbāri, India E13 54
Nal'čik, Russia F6 32
Nałęczów, Pol. E18 16
Nalgonda, India C4 53
Nallamalla Hills, mts., India D4 53
Nallıhan, Tur. C14 28
Nalón, stm., Spain A5 20
Nalong, China J2 42
Nālūt, Libya A2 62
Nam (Nan'a), stm., Asia B4 48
Namaacha, Moz. D10 70
Namacurra, Moz. D6 68
Namadgi National Park, p.o.i., Austl. J7 76
Namak, Daryācheh-ye, l., Iran C7 56
Namakan Lake, l., N.A. C6 118
Nāmakkal, India F4 53
Namangan, Uzb. F12 32
Namanyere, Tan. F6 66
Namapa, Moz. C6 68
Namarrói, Moz. D6 68
Namatanai, Pap. N. Gui. a5 79a
Nambour, Austl. F9 76
Nam Co, l., China C13 54
Nam Dinh, Viet. B7 48
Nam Du, Quan Dao, is., Viet. H6 48
Nameh, Indon. B10 50
Namen see Namur, Bel. D13 14
Namerikawa, Japan C10 40
Nametil, Moz. D6 68
Nam-gang, stm., Kor., N. E7 38
Namhae-do, i., Kor., S. G8 38
Namhan-gang, stm., Kor., S. F7 38
Namhkam, Mya. D8 46
Namib Desert, des., Nmb. E1 68
Namibe, Ang. D1 68
Namibia, ctry., Afr. E2 68
Namib Naukluft Park, p.o.i., Nmb. D2 70
Namie, Japan B14 40
Namies, S. Afr. F4 70
Namji-ri, Kor., S. D1 40
Namlea, Indon. F8 44
Namling, China D12 54
Nam Nao National Park, p.o.i., Thai. D5 48
Nam Ngum Reservoir, res., Laos C6 48
Namnoi, Khao, mtn., Mya. G4 48
Namoi, stm., Austl. H7 76
Nampa, Id., U.S. G10 136
Nampala, Mali F3 64
Nam Pat, Thai. D5 48
Nampawng, Mya. A3 48
Nam Phan (Cochin China), hist. reg., Viet. G8 48
Namp'o, Kor., N. E6 38
Nampula, Moz. D6 68
Namsang, Mya. B3 48
Namsen, stm., Nor. D5 8
Namsos, Nor. D4 8
Nam Tok, Thai. E4 48
Nam Tok Mae Surin National Park, p.o.i., Thai. C4 48
Namtu, Mya. A3 48
Namu, B.C., Can. E3 138
Namuka-I-Lau, i., Fiji q20 79e
Namúli, Serra, mts., Moz. D6 68
Namur (Namen), Bel. D13 14
Namutoni, Nmb. D2 68
Namwala, Zam. D4 68
Namwŏn, Kor., S. G7 38
Namysłów, Pol. E13 16
Nan, Thai. C5 48
Nan, stm., Thai. D5 48
Nan'a (Nam), stm., Asia B4 48
Nanaimo, B.C., Can. G6 138
Nanam, Kor., N. D8 38
Nan'an, China I8 42
Nanango, Austl. F8 76
Nanao, Japan B9 40
Nanatsu-jima, is., Japan B9 40
Nanbu, China F1 42
Nancha, China B10 36
Nanchang, China G6 42
Nancheng, China H7 42
Nancheng see Hanzhong, China E2 42
Nanching see Nanjing, China E8 42
Nanchong, China F2 42
Nanchuan, China G2 42
Nanch'ung see Nanchong, China F2 42
Nancowry Island, i., India G7 46
Nancy, Fr. F15 14
Nanda Devi, mtn., India C8 54
Nandaime, Nic. G4 102
Nandan, Japan E7 40
Nānded, India B3 53
Nāndgaon, India H5 54
Nandi Drug, mtn., India E3 53
Nandikotkūr, India D4 53
Nandu, China F8 42
Nandu, stm., China L4 42
Nāndūra, India H6 54
Nandurbār, India H4 54
Nandyāl, India D4 53
Nanfen, China D5 38
Nanfeng, China H7 42
Nanga-Eboko, Cam. D2 66
Nangakelawit, Indon. C8 50
Nangamau, Indon. D7 50
Nangaobat, Indon. C8 50
Nanga Parbat, mtn., Pak. B11 56
Nangapinoh, Indon. D7 50
Nangarhār, state, Afg. A3 54
Nangatayap, Indon. D7 50
Nanggala Hill, mtn., Sol. Is. e7 79b
Nangin, Mya. G4 48
Nangnim-ŭp, Kor., N. D7 38
Nangong, China C6 42
Nang Rong, Thai. E6 48
Nanguan, China C5 42
Nanhua, China F5 36
Nan Hulsan Hu, l., China D4 36
Nanika Lake, l., B.C., Can. C3 138
Nanjangūd, India E3 53
Nanjiang, China E2 42
Nanjing, China I7 42
Nanjing (Nanking), China E8 42
Nankang, China I6 42
Nanking see Nanjing, China E8 42
Nankoku, Japan F6 40
Nankye, Mya. E3 48
Nanle, China C6 42
Nanlei (Loi), stm., Asia A4 48
Nanling, China F8 42
Nan Ling, mts., China I5 42
Nanliu, stm., China J3 42
Nanlou Shan, mtn., China C7 38
Nannine, Austl. E3 74
Nanning, China J3 42
Na Noi, Thai. C5 48
Nanortalik, Grnld. E16 141
Nanpan, stm., China G5 36
Nānpāra, India E8 54
Nanpiao, China A9 42
Nanping, China E5 36
Nanping, China H8 42
Nansei, Japan E9 40
Nansei-shotō (Ryukyu Islands), is., Japan k19 39a
Nan Shan see Qilian Shan, mts., China D4 36
Nanshan Island, i., Asia C6 44
Nantais, Lac, l., Qc., Can. C16 106
Nantai-zan, vol., Japan C12 40
Nanterre, Fr. F11 14
Nantes, Fr. G7 14
Nantes à Brest, Canal de, can., Fr. F5 14
Nanticoke, Pa., U.S. C9 114
Nanto, Japan E9 40
Nanton, Ab., Can. F17 138
Nantong, China E9 42
Nant'ou, Tai. J9 42
Nantucket, Ma., U.S. C15 114
Nantucket Island, i., Ma., U.S. C15 114
Nantucket Sound, strt., Ma., U.S. C15 114
Nantulo, Moz. C6 68
Nantung see Nantong, China E9 42
Nanty Glo, Pa., U.S. H11 112
Nanu, Pap. N. Gui. b3 79a
Nanuku Passage, strt., Fiji p20 79e
Nanumea, at., Tuvalu D8 72
Nanuque, Braz. I5 88
Nanusa, Kepulauan, is., Indon. E8 44
Nanxi, China G1 42
Nanxian, China G5 42
Nanxiang, China F9 42
Nanxiong, China I6 42
Nanyang, China E5 42
Nanyang Hu, l., China D7 42
Nanyi Hu, l., China F8 42
Nan-yō, Japan A13 40
Nanyuki, Kenya D7 66
Nanzamu, China C6 38
Nanzhao, China E5 42
Nao, Cabo de la see Nau, Cap de la, c., Spain F11 20
Naococane, Lac, l., Qc., Can. E16 106
Naogaon, Bngl. F12 54
Naokot, Pak. F2 54
Náousa, Grc. C5 28
Napa, Ca., U.S. E3 134
Napa, stm., Ca., U.S. E3 134
Napaku, Indon. B9 50
Napalkovo, Russia C3 34
Napanee, On., Can. D12 112
Napassoq, Grnld. D15 141
Naperville, Il., U.S. C9 120
Napido, Indon. F10 44
Napier, N.Z. D7 80
Napier, Mount, hill, Austl. C5 74
Napier Mountains, mts., Ant. B10 81
Naples see Napoli, Italy D8 24
Naples, Fl., U.S. J4 116
Naples, Id., U.S. B10 136
Naples, N.Y., U.S. B8 114
Naples, Tx., U.S. D4 122
Napo, state, Ec. H3 86
Napo, stm., S.A. D3 84
Napoleon, N.D., U.S. A13 126
Napoleonville, La., U.S. H7 122
Napoli (Naples), Italy D8 24
Napoli, Golfo di, b., Italy D8 24
Nappamerrie, Austl. F3 76
Nappanee, In., U.S. G4 112
Napu, Indon. H11 50
Nara, Japan E8 40
Nara, Mali F3 64
Nara, state, Japan E8 40
Nāra, stm., Pak. F2 54
Nara, stm., Russia E20 10
Narač, vozero, l., Bela. F9 10
Naracoorte, Austl. K3 76
Naradhan, Austl. I6 76
Naraini, India F8 54
Naramata, B.C., Can. G11 138
Naranjal, Ec. I2 86
Naranjito, P.R. B3 104a
Narasannapeta, India B7 53
Narasapur, India C5 53
Narasaraopet, India C4 53
Narasun, Russia A7 36
Narathiwat, Thai. I5 48
Naraŭ (Narew), stm., Eur. D17 16
Nārāyanganj, Bngl. G13 54
Nārāyani (Gandak), stm., Asia E10 54
Nārāyanpet, India C3 53
Narbonne, Fr. F8 18
Nardò, Italy D11 24
Nares Strait, strt., N.A. B11 141
Narew (Naraŭ), stm., Eur. D17 16
Nargund, India D2 53
Nariño, state, Col. G3 86
Narita, Japan D13 40
Nariva Swamp, sw., Trin. s12 105f
Nar'jan-Mar, Russia C25 8
Narkatiāganj, India E10 54
Narlı, Tur. A8 58
Narmada, stm., India H4 54
Nārnaul, India D6 54
Narodnaja, gora, mtn., Russia B10 32
Narodnaya, Mount see Narodnaja, gora, mtn., Russia B10 32
Naro-Fominsk, Russia E19 10
Narol, Pol. F19 16
Narooma, Austl. K8 76
Nārowāl, Pak. B5 54
Narrabri, Austl. H7 76
Narran, stm., Austl. G7 76
Narrandera, Austl. J6 76
Narraway, stm., Can. B11 138
Narrogin, Austl. F3 74
Narromine, Austl. I6 76
Narsaq see Narssaq, Grnld. E16 141
Narsimhapur, India G7 54
Narsinghgarh, India G6 54
Narsīpatnam, India C6 53
Narssaq, Grnld. E16 141
Naru, Japan G1 40
Naruto, Japan E7 40
Narva, Est. G13 8
Narva, Russia C16 32
Narva, stm., Eur. A11 10
Narvik, Nor. B7 8
Narvskij zaliv, b., Eur. A10 10
Narvskoe vodohranilišče, l., Eur. A10 10
Narwāna, India D6 54
Narwietooma, Austl. D6 74
Narym, Russia C14 32
Naryn, Kyrg. F13 32
Naryn, stm., Asia F13 32
Narynkol, Kaz. F13 32
Näsåker, Swe. E7 8
Na San, Thai. H4 48
Nasawa, Vanuatu j17 79d
Nasbinals, Fr. E9 18
Nasca, Peru F2 84
Nase see Naze, Japan k19 39a
Nash, Tx., U.S. D4 122
Nāshik, India H4 54
Nashua, Ia., U.S. B5 120
Nashua, N.H., U.S. B14 114
Nashville, Ar., U.S. D5 122
Nashville, Il., U.S. F8 120
Nashville, In., U.S. E11 120
Nashville, Mi., U.S. F4 112
Nashville, N.C., U.S. I8 114
Nashville, Tn., U.S. H11 120
Nashwaak, stm., N.B., Can. D10 110
Nashwauk, Mn., U.S. D5 118
Nasielsk, Pol. D16 16
Näsijärvi, l., Fin. F10 8
Nāṣir, Sudan F6 62
Nāṣir, Buheirat see Nasser, Lake, res., Afr. C6 62
Nasīrābād, India E5 54
Nasr, Egypt H1 58
Nass, stm., B.C., Can. E5 106
Nassarawa, Nig. H6 64
Nassau, Bah. m18 104f
Nassau, N.Y., U.S. B12 114
Nassau International Airport, Bah. m18 104f
Nassau Island, i., Cook Is. E10 72
Nassawadox, Va., U.S. G10 114
Nasser, Lake (Nâsir, Buheirat), res., Afr. C6 62
Nässjö, Swe. H6 8
Nastapoka Islands, is., Nu., Can. D15 106
Nasu, Japan B13 40
Nasu-dake, vol., Japan B12 40
Nasukoin Mountain, mtn., Mt., U.S. B12 136
Nasva, Russia D13 10
Nata, Bots. E4 68
Nata, stm., Afr. B8 70
Natal, Braz. C8 88
Natal, B.C., Can. G16 138
Natal, Indon. C1 50
Natal see KwaZulu-Natal, state, S. Afr. F10 70
Natalia, Tx., U.S. E9 130
Natalkuz Lake, res., B.C., Can. C5 138
Natanes Plateau, plat., Az., U.S. J6 132
Natashquan, stm., Can. i21 107a
Natchez, Ms., U.S. F7 122
Natchez Trace Parkway, p.o.i., U.S. E9 122
Natchitoches, La., U.S. F5 122
Natewa Bay, b., Fiji p19 79e
Nāthdwāra, India F4 54
Natimuk, Austl. K3 76
Nation, stm., B.C., Can. A7 138
National City, Ca., U.S. K8 134
Natitingou, Benin G5 64
Native Bay, b., Nu., Can. C14 106
Natividade, Braz. F2 88
Natkyizin, Mya. E3 48
Natoma, Ks., U.S. B9 128
Nator, Bngl. F12 54
Natori, Japan A13 40
Natron, Lake, l., Afr. E7 66
Natrûn, Wadi el-, val., Egypt H1 58
Nattaung, mtn., Mya. C3 48
Natuna Besar, i., Indon. A6 50
Natuna Besar, Kepulauan, is., Indon. A5 50
Natuna Selatan, Kepulauan, is., Indon. B6 50
Natural Bridge, misc. cult., Va., U.S. G6 114
Natural Bridges National Monument, p.o.i., Ut., U.S. F6 132
Naturaliste, Cape, c., Austl. F2 74
Naturno, Italy D7 22
Nau, Cap de la, c., Spain F11 20
Naucelle, Fr. E8 18
Naucratis, hist., Egypt H1 58
Nauen, Ger. D8 16
Naugatuck, Ct., U.S. C12 114
Naughton, On., Can. B8 112
Naujamiestis, Lith. E6 10
Naujan, Lake, l., Phil. D3 52
Naujoji Akmenė, Lith. D5 10
Naumburg, Ger. E7 16
Naunglon, Mya. D3 48
Nā'ūr, Jord. G6 58
Nauru, state, Oc. p17 78f
Nauru International Airport, Nauru q17 78f
Nauški, Russia F10 34
Nausori, Fiji p19 79e
Nauta, Peru D3 84
Nautanwa, India E9 54
Nautla, Mex. E10 100
Nauvoo, Il., U.S. D6 120
Nava, Mex. A8 100
Navadwip, India G12 54
Navael'nja, Bela. G8 10
Navahrudak, Bela. G8 10
Navajo, N.M., U.S. H7 132
Navajo Mountain, mtn., Ut., U.S. F6 132
Navajo National Monument, p.o.i., Az., U.S. G6 132
Navajo Reservoir, res., U.S. G9 132
Naval, Phil. C7 44
Navalmoral de la Mata, Spain E5 20
Navan, Ire. H6 12
Navapolack, Bela. E11 10
Navāpur, India H4 54
Navarin, mys, c., Russia D24 34
Navarino, Isla, i., Chile K3 90
Navarra, state, Spain B9 20
Navarro Mills Lake, res., Tx., U.S. F2 122
Navasëlki, Bela. H7 10
Navasota, Tx., U.S. G2 122
Navasota, stm., Tx., U.S. D11 130
Navassa, N.C., U.S. B7 116
Navassa Island, i., N.A. C10 102
Navesnoe, Russia H20 10
Navia, Arg. G4 92
Navia, stm., Spain A4 20
Navidad, Chile F1 92
Navidad, stm., Tx., U.S. E11 130
Navio, Riacho do, stm., Braz. E6 88
Naviti, i., Fiji p18 79e
Navlja, Russia H17 10
Năvodari, Rom. E15 26
Navoi, Uzb. F11 32
Navojoa, Mex. B4 100
Navolato, Mex. C5 100
Navsāri, India H4 54
Nawa see Naha, Japan I18 39a
Nawābganj, Bngl. F12 54
Nawābganj, India E8 54
Nawābshāh, Pak. E2 54
Nawāda, India F10 54
Nāwah, Afg. B1 54
Nawalgarh, India E5 54
Nawāpāra, India H8 54
Naxçıvan, Azer. B6 56
Naxi, China G1 42
Náxos, i., Grc. F8 28
Nayāgarh, India H10 54
Nayarit, state, Mex. E6 100
Nāy Band, Kūh-e, mtn., Iran C8 56
Naylor, Mo., U.S. H7 120
Nayoro, Japan B15 38
Nazaré, Braz. D2 88
Nazaré, Port. E1 20
Nazaré da Mata, Braz. D8 88
Nazaré do Piauí, Braz. D4 88
Nazareth see Naẕerat, Isr. F6 58
Nazarovo, Russia C16 32
Nazas, Mex. C6 100
Nazas, stm., Mex. C6 100
Nazca Ridge, unds. K5 144
Naze, Japan k19 39a
Naze, The see Lindesnes, c., Nor. H2 8
Naẕerat (Nazareth), Isr. F6 58
Naẕerat 'Illit, Isr. F6 58
Nazija, Russia A14 10
Nazilli, Tur. F11 28
Nazina, Russia B13 32
Nazko, stm., B.C., Can. D7 138
Nazlet el-'Amûdein, Egypt J1 58
Nazran', Russia F7 32
Nazrēt, Eth. F7 62
Nazwá, Oman E8 56
Nazyvaevsk, Russia C12 32
N'dalatando, Ang. B1 68
Ndali, Benin H5 64
Ndélé, C.A.R. C4 66
Ndendé, Gabon E2 66
N'Djamena (Fort-Lamy), Chad E3 62
Ndjolé, Gabon E2 66
Ndogo, Lagune, l., Gabon E2 66
Ndola, Zam. C4 68
Ndumu Game Reserve, S. Afr. E11 70
Neabul Creek, stm., Austl. F6 76
Neagh, Lough, l., N. Ire., U.K. G6 12
Neah Bay, Wa., U.S. B2 136
Neale, Lake, l., Austl. D6 74
Neamţ, state, Rom. B13 26
Néa Páfos (Paphos), Cyp. D3 58
Neápoli, Grc. G6 28
Near Islands, is., Ak., U.S. g21 140a
Neath, Wales, U.K. J9 12
Nebine Creek, stm., Austl. G6 76
Nebitdag, Turkmen. B7 56
Neblina, Cerro de la see Neblina, Pico da, mtn., S.A. G9 86
Neblina, Pico da, mtn., S.A. G9 86
Nebo, Il., U.S. E7 120
Nebo, Mount, mtn., Ut., U.S. D5 132
Nebolči, Russia A16 10
Nebraska, state, U.S. C7 108
Nebraska City, Ne., U.S. D1 120
Necedah, Wi., U.S. G8 118
Nechako, stm., B.C., Can. C7 138
Nechako Reservoir, res., B.C., Can. C5 138
Neches, Tx., U.S. F3 122
Neches, stm., Tx., U.S. G4 122
Nechí, Col. C4 86
Nechí, stm., Col. D4 86
Nechranice, vodní nádrź, res., Czech Rep. F9 16
Neckarsulm, Ger. G5 16
Necker Island, i., Br. Vir. Is. d9 104b
Necochea, Arg. I8 92
Nederland, Tx., U.S. H4 122
Nêdong, China D13 54
Needhams Point, c., Barb. n8 105d
Needle Mountain, mtn., Wy., U.S. F17 136
Needles, Ca., U.S. I2 132
Needville, Tx., U.S. H3 122
Neegro, Qooriga, b., Som. C10 66
Ñeembucú, state, Para. C8 92
Neenah, Wi., U.S. G10 118
Neepawa, Mb., Can. D14 124
Nefëdovo, Russia C12 32
Nefta, Tun. C6 64
Neftçala, Azer. B6 56
Neftejugansk, Russia B12 32
Nefza, Tun. H3 24
Negage, Ang. B2 68
Negara, Indon. H9 50
Negara, stm., Indon. E9 50
Negaunee, Mi., U.S. B2 112
Negēlē, Eth. F7 62
Negeribatin, Indon. F4 50
Negeri Sembilan, state, Malay. K6 48
Negev Desert see HaNegev, reg., Isr. H5 58
Negombo, Sri L. H4 53
Negra, Laguna, l., Ur. G11 92
Negreira, Spain B2 20
Nègres, Pointe des, c., Mart. k6 105c
Negrești-Oaș, Rom. B10 26
Negritos, Peru D1 84
Negro, stm., Arg. H4 90
Negro, stm., Braz. C13 92
Negro, stm., Col. E4 86
Negro, stm., Para. B9 92
Negro, stm., S.A. I11 86
Negro, stm., S.A. F9 92
Negros, i., Phil. F4 52
Nehalem, stm., Or., U.S. E3 136
Neharèlae, Bela. G9 10
Nehawka, Ne., U.S. D1 120
Nehbandān, Iran C8 56
Nehe see Nahe, China B9 36
Néhoué, Baie de, b., N. Cal. m14 79d
Neiba, Dom. Rep. C12 102

Name	Map Ref.	Page
Neichiang see Neijiang, China	G1	42
Neidpath, Sk., Can.	D6	124
Neiges, Piton des, mtn., Reu.	i10	69a
Neijiang, China	G1	42
Neikiang see Neijiang, China	G1	42
Neilburg, Sk., Can.	B4	124
Neillsville, Wi., U.S.	G8	118
Nei Monggol, state, China	C7	36
Nei Mongol see Nei Monggol, state, China	C7	36
Neiqiu, China	C6	42
Neira, Col.	E4	86
Neisse see Lausitzer Neisse, stm., Eur.	F10	16
Neisse see Nysa Łużycka, stm., Eur.	E10	16
Neiva, Col.	F4	86
Neixiang, China	E4	42
Neja, Russia	G20	8
Nejapa de Madero, Mex.	G11	100
Nejd see Najd, hist. reg., Sau. Ar.	D5	56
Nejdek, Czech Rep.	F8	16
Nek'emtē, Eth.	F7	62
Nelichu, mtn., Sudan	F6	62
Nelidovo, Russia	D15	10
Neligh, Ne., U.S.	E14	126
Neljaty, Russia	E12	34
Nel'kan, Russia	E16	34
Nellikuppam, India	F4	53
Nellore, India	D4	53
Nel'ma, Russia	G16	34
Nelson, B.C., Can.	G13	138
Nelson, N.Z.	E5	80
Nelson, Ne., U.S.	A10	128
Nelson, stm., Mb., Can.	D12	106
Nelson, Cape, c., Austl.	L3	76
Nelson, Estrecho, strt., Chile	J2	90
Nelson Lakes National Park, p.o.i., N.Z.	E5	80
Nelson's Dockyard, hist., Antig.	f4	105b
Nelsonville, Oh., U.S.	E3	114
Nelspoort, S. Afr.	H6	70
Nelspruit, S. Afr.	D10	70
Néma, Maur.	F3	64
Nemadji, stm., U.S.	E6	118
Neman, Russia	E4	10
Neman (Nemunas), stm., Eur.	E4	10
Nembe, Nig.	I6	64
Nemenčinė, Lith.	F8	10
Nemeriči, Russia	G16	10
Nemours, Fr.	F11	14
Nemunas (Neman), stm., Eur.	E4	10
Nemunėlis (Mēmele), stm., Eur.	D7	10
Nemuro, Japan	C16	38
Nemuro Strait, strt., Asia	C16	38
Nen, stm., China	B9	36
Nenagh, Ire.	I4	12
Nenana, Ak., U.S.	D10	140
Nenana, stm., Ak., U.S.	D10	140
Nendo, i., Sol. Is.	E7	72
Nene, stm., Eng., U.K.	I13	12
Neneckij avtonomnyj okrug, Russia	C23	8
Nenets see Neneckij avtonomnyj okrug, Russia	C23	8
Nenetsia see Neneckij avtonomnyj okrug, Russia	C23	8
Nenggiri, stm., Malay.	J5	48
Neodesha, Ks., U.S.	G2	120
Neoga, Il., U.S.	E9	120
Néo Karlovási, Grc.	F9	28
Neola, Ut., U.S.	C6	132
Neopit, Wi., U.S.	G10	118
Neosho, Mo., U.S.	H3	120
Neosho, stm., U.S.	H2	120
Nepa, stm., Russia	C19	32
Nepal, ctry., Asia	E9	54
Nepālgañj, Nepal	D8	54
Nepa Nagar, India	H6	54
Nepeña, Peru	E2	84
Nephin, mtn., Ire.	G3	12
Nepisiguit, stm., N.B., Can.	C10	110
Nepisiguit Bay, b., N.B., Can.	C11	110
Neptune, N.J., U.S.	D11	114
Neptune Beach, Fl., U.S.	F4	116
Nérac, Fr.	E6	18
Nerča, stm., Russia	F12	34
Nerčinsk, Russia	F12	34
Nerčinskij Zavod, Russia	F12	34
Nerehta, Russia	H19	8
Neretva, stm., Eur.	G15	22
Neriquinha, Ang.	D3	68
Neris (Vilija), stm., Eur.	F6	10
Nerja, Spain	H7	20
Nerjungri, Russia	E13	34
Nerl', Russia	C20	10
Nerl', stm., Russia	D22	10
Nerópolis, Braz.	I1	88
Nerussa, stm., Russia	H16	10
Nerva, Spain	G4	20
Nes, Neth.	C1	16
Nesbyen, Nor.	F3	8
Neščarda, vozero, l., Bela.	E12	10
Neskaupstaður, Ice.	k32	8a
Nesna, Nor.	C5	8
Nespelem, Wa., U.S.	B7	136
Ness, Loch, l., Scot., U.K.	D8	12
Ness City, Ks., U.S.	C8	128
Nesselrode, Mount, mtn., N.A.	D4	106
Nesterkovo, Russia	A13	10
Nestoïta, Ukr.	B16	26
Netanya, Isr.	F5	58
Netherdale, Austl.	C7	76
Netherlands, ctry., Eur.	B14	14
Netherlands Antilles, dep., N.A.	i14	96a
Netherlands Guiana see Surinam, ctry., S.A.	C6	84
Netrakona, Bngl.	F13	54
Nettilling Fiord, b., Nu., Can.	B17	106
Nettilling Lake, l., Nu., Can.	B17	106
Nett Lake, l., Mn., U.S.	C5	118
Nettuno, Italy	C6	24
Neubrandenburg, Ger.	C9	16
Neuburg an der Donau, Ger.	H7	16
Neuchâtel, Switz.	D3	22
Neuchâtel, Lac de, l., Switz.	D3	22
Neudorf, Sk., Can.	D11	124
Neuenburg see Neuchâtel, Switz.	D3	22
Neuenhagen, Ger.	D9	16
Neuerburg, Ger.	F2	16
Neufchâteau, Fr.	F14	14
Neufchâtel-en-Bray, Fr.	E10	14
Neu-Isenburg, Ger.	F4	16
Neumarkt in der Oberpfalz, Ger.	G7	16
Neumünster, Ger.	B6	16
Neun, stm., Laos	C6	48
Neunkirchen, Aus.	C13	22
Neuquén, Arg.	G3	90
Neuquén, state, Arg.	G2	90
Neuquén, stm., Arg.	G3	90
Neurara, Chile	B3	92
Neuruppin, Ger.	D8	16
Neuse, stm., N.C., U.S.	A8	116
Neusiedl am See, Aus.	C13	22
Neuss, Ger.	E2	16
Neustadt, Ger.	F7	16
Neustadt an der Aisch, Ger.	G6	16
Neustadt an der Weinstrasse, Ger.	G3	16
Neustadt bei Coburg, Ger.	F6	16
Neustadt in Holstein, Ger.	B6	16
Neustrelitz, Ger.	C9	16
Neutral Hills, hills, Ab., Can.	B3	124
Neu-Ulm, Ger.	H6	16
Neuvic, Fr.	D8	18
Neuwied, Ger.	F3	16
Neva, stm., Russia	A13	10
Nevada, Ia., U.S.	B4	120
Nevada, Mo., U.S.	G3	120
Nevada, state, U.S.	D4	108
Nevada, Sierra, mts., Spain	G7	20
Nevada, Sierra, mts., Ca., U.S.	F6	134
Nevada City, Ca., U.S.	D4	134
Nevado, Cerro, mtn., Arg.	G3	92
Nevado, Cerro, mtn., Col.	E4	86
Nevado de Colima, Parque Nacional del, p.o.i., Mex.	F7	100
Nevado de Toluca, Parque Nacional, p.o.i., Mex.	F8	100
Neve, Serra da, mts., Ang.	C1	68
Nevel', Russia	D12	10
Nevel'sk, Russia	G17	34
Nevel'skogo, proliv, strt., Russia	F17	34
Never, Russia	F13	34
Nevers, Fr.	G12	14
Nevesinje, Bos.	F5	26
Nevinnomyssk, Russia	F6	32
Nevis, i., St. K./N.	C2	105a
Nevis, Ben, mtn., Scot., U.K.	E7	12
Nevis Peak, vol., St. K./N.	C2	105a
Nevjansk, Russia	C10	32
Nevşehir, Tur.	B3	56
New, stm., Belize	D3	102
New, stm., Guy.	C6	84
New, stm., U.S.	F4	114
New, stm., S.C., U.S.	D4	116
Newala, Tan.	G7	66
New Albany, In., U.S.	F12	120
New Albany, Ms., U.S.	C9	122
New Amsterdam, Guy.	B6	84
New Angledool, Austl.	G6	76
Newark, Ar., U.S.	B7	122
Newark, De., U.S.	E10	114
Newark, N.J., U.S.	D11	114
Newark, N.Y., U.S.	A8	114
Newark, Oh., U.S.	D3	114
Newark Lake, l., Nv., U.S.	D1	132
Newark-on-Trent, Eng., U.K.	H12	12
Newark Valley, N.Y., U.S.	B9	114
New Athens, Il., U.S.	F8	120
New Augusta, Ms., U.S.	F9	122
New Baden, Il., U.S.	F8	120
New Bedford, Ma., U.S.	C15	114
Newberg, Or., U.S.	E4	136
New Berlin, Il., U.S.	E7	120
New Berlin, N.Y., U.S.	B10	114
New Berlin, Wi., U.S.	F1	112
Newbern, Al., U.S.	E11	122
New Bern, N.C., U.S.	A8	116
Newbern, Tn., U.S.	H8	120
Newberry, Fl., U.S.	G3	116
Newberry, S.C., U.S.	B4	116
Newberry National Volcanic Monument, p.o.i., Or., U.S.	G5	136
New Bethlehem, Pa., U.S.	D6	114
New Bloomfield, Pa., U.S.	H12	112
New Boston, Oh., U.S.	F3	114
New Boston, Tx., U.S.	D4	122
New Braunfels, Tx., U.S.	E9	130
New Britain, Ct., U.S.	C13	114
New Britain, i., Pap. N. Gui.	b5	79a
New Brockton, Al., U.S.	F12	122
Newbrook, Ab., Can.	B17	138
New Brunswick, N.J., U.S.	D11	114
New Brunswick, state, Can.	D10	110
Newburg, Mo., U.S.	G6	120
Newburgh, In., U.S.	G10	120
Newburgh, N.Y., U.S.	C11	114
Newbury, Eng., U.K.	J11	12
Newburyport, Ma., U.S.	B15	114
New Caledonia, dep., Oc.	F7	72
New Caledonia see Nouvelle-Calédonie, i., N. Cal.	m15	79d
New Caledonia Basin, unds.	L19	142
New Carlisle, Qc., Can.	B11	110
New Carlisle, Oh., U.S.	E2	114
New Castille see Castilla la Nueva, hist. reg., Spain	E7	20
Newcastle, Austl.	I8	76
Newcastle, N.B., Can.	C11	110
Newcastle, St. K./N.	C2	105a
Newcastle, S. Afr.	E9	70
Newcastle, N. Ire., U.K.	G7	12
New Castle, Co., U.S.	D9	132
New Castle, De., U.S.	E10	114
New Castle, In., U.S.	I4	112
Newcastle, Ne., U.S.	I2	118
Newcastle, Ok., U.S.	F11	128
New Castle, Pa., U.S.	D5	114
Newcastle, Tx., U.S.	A9	130
New Castle, Va., U.S.	G5	114
Newcastle, Wy., U.S.	D8	126
Newcastle Bay, b., Austl.	B8	74
Newcastle-under-Lyme, Eng., U.K.	I10	12
Newcastle upon Tyne, Eng., U.K.	G10	12
Newcastle Waters, Austl.	C6	74
Newcastle West, Ire.	I3	12
New City, N.Y., U.S.	C11	114
Newcomerstown, Oh., U.S.	D4	114
New Concord, Oh., U.S.	D4	114
New Cumberland, W.V., U.S.	D5	114
Newdegate, Austl.	F3	74
New Delhi, India	D6	54
New Denver, B.C., Can.	F13	138
New Edinburg, Ar., U.S.	D6	122
New Effington, S.D., U.S.	F1	118
Newell, Ia., U.S.	B2	120
Newell, W.V., U.S.	D5	114
Newell, Lake, l., Ab., Can.	F19	138
New Ellenton, S.C., U.S.	C4	116
Newellton, La., U.S.	E7	122
New England, N.D., U.S.	A10	126
New England National Park, p.o.i., Austl.	H9	76
Newfane, N.Y., U.S.	E11	112
Newfane, Vt., U.S.	A13	114
New Florence, Pa., U.S.	D6	114
Newfound Gap, p., U.S.	I2	114
Newfoundland, state, Can.	j22	107a
Newfoundland, i., Nf., Can.	j22	107a
Newfoundland Basin, unds.	D9	144
New Franklin, Mo., U.S.	E5	120
New Freedom, Pa., U.S.	E9	114
New Galloway, Scot., U.K.	F8	12
Newgate, B.C., Can.	G15	138
New Georgia, i., Sol. Is.	e7	79b
New Georgia Group, is., Sol. Is.	d7	79b
New Georgia Sound, strt., Sol. Is.	e8	79b
New Germany, N.S., Can.	F12	110
New Glasgow, N.S., Can.	E14	110
New Guinea, i.	b3	79a
Newhalem, Wa., U.S.	B5	136
New Hamburg, On., Can.	E9	112
New Hampshire, state, U.S.	G5	110
New Hampton, Ia., U.S.	A5	120
New Hanover, S. Afr.	F10	70
New Hanover, i., Pap. N. Gui.	a4	79a
New Harmony, In., U.S.	F10	120
New Hartford, Ia., U.S.	I6	118
Newhaven, Eng., U.K.	K13	12
New Haven, Ct., U.S.	C13	114
New Haven, Il., U.S.	G9	120
New Haven, Ky., U.S.	G12	120
New Haven, Mo., U.S.	F6	120
New Hazelton, B.C., Can.	A3	138
New Hebrides see Vanuatu, ctry., Oc.	k16	79d
New Hebrides, is., Vanuatu	k16	79d
New Hebrides Trench, unds.	L20	142
Newhebron, Ms., U.S.	F9	122
New Holland, Oh., U.S.	E2	114
New Holland, Pa., U.S.	D9	114
New Holstein, Wi., U.S.	E1	112
New Hope, Al., U.S.	C12	122
New Iberia, La., U.S.	G7	122
New Ireland, i., Pap. N. Gui.	a5	79a
New Jersey, state, U.S.	D11	114
New Johnsonville, Tn., U.S.	H10	120
New Kensington, Pa., U.S.	D6	114
New Kent, Va., U.S.	G9	114
Newkirk, Ok., U.S.	E11	128
New Kowloon see Xinjiulong, China	J6	42
Newlands, Austl.	C6	76
New Lexington, Oh., U.S.	E3	114
New Lisbon, Wi., U.S.	H8	118
New Liskeard, On., Can.	F14	106
New Llano, La., U.S.	F5	122
New London, Ct., U.S.	C13	114
New London, Mo., U.S.	E6	120
New London, N.H., U.S.	G5	110
New London, Oh., U.S.	C3	114
New London, Tx., U.S.	E4	122
New London, Wi., U.S.	G10	118
New Madrid, Mo., U.S.	H8	120
Newman, Austl.	D3	74
Newman, Ca., U.S.	F4	134
Newman Grove, Ne., U.S.	F15	126
Newmarket, On., Can.	D10	112
Newmarket, Eng., U.K.	I13	12
New Market, Al., U.S.	C12	122
New Market, Ia., U.S.	D3	120
Newmarket, N.H., U.S.	G5	110
New Market, Va., U.S.	F7	114
New Martinsville, W.V., U.S.	E4	114
New Mexico, state, U.S.	D9	98
New Milford, Ct., U.S.	C12	114
New Milford, Pa., U.S.	C10	114
Newnan, Ga., U.S.	D14	122
New Norfolk, Austl.	o13	77a
New Norway, Ab., Can.	D18	138
New Orleans, La., U.S.	G8	122
New Paris, Oh., U.S.	I5	112
New Philadelphia, Oh., U.S.	D4	114
New Pine Creek, Or., U.S.	A5	134
New Plymouth, N.Z.	D5	80
New Plymouth, Id., U.S.	G10	136
Newport, Eng., U.K.	K11	12
Newport, Wales, U.K.	J10	12
Newport, Ar., U.S.	B7	122
Newport, Ky., U.S.	E1	114
Newport, Me., U.S.	F7	110
Newport, N.H., U.S.	G4	110
Newport, N.C., U.S.	B8	116
Newport, Or., U.S.	F2	136
Newport, Pa., U.S.	D8	114
Newport, R.I., U.S.	C14	114
Newport, Tn., U.S.	I2	114
Newport, Vt., U.S.	F4	110
Newport Beach, Ca., U.S.	J7	134
Newport News, Va., U.S.	G9	114
New Port Richey, Fl., U.S.	H3	116
New Providence, i., Bah.	C9	96
Newquay, Eng., U.K.	K7	12
New Richland, Mn., U.S.	H5	118
New Richmond, Qc., Can.	B10	110
New Richmond, Wi., U.S.	F6	118
New River, St. K./N.	C2	105a
New Road, N.S., Can.	F13	110
New Roads, La., U.S.	G7	122
New Rochelle, N.Y., U.S.	D12	114
New Ross, N.S., Can.	F12	110
New Ross, Ire.	I6	12
Newry, N. Ire., U.K.	G6	12
Newry, S.C., U.S.	B3	116
New Salem, N.D., U.S.	A11	126
New Schwabenland, reg., Ant.	C5	81
New Sharon, Ia., U.S.	C5	120
New Siberian Islands see Novosibirskie ostrova, is., Russia	A18	34
New Smyrna Beach, Fl., U.S.	G5	116
New South Wales, state, Austl.	I6	76
New Tazewell, Tn., U.S.	H2	114
New Tecumseth, On., Can.	D9	112
Newton, Ga., U.S.	F14	122
Newton, Il., U.S.	F9	120
Newton, Ia., U.S.	C4	120
Newton, Ks., U.S.	C11	128
Newton, Ma., U.S.	B14	114
Newton, Ms., U.S.	E9	122
Newton, N.J., U.S.	C11	114
Newton, Tx., U.S.	G5	122
Newton Falls, N.Y., U.S.	F2	110
Newton Stewart, Scot., U.K.	G8	12
New Town, N.D., U.S.	F11	124
Newtownabbey, N. Ire., U.K.	G6	12
Newtownards, N. Ire., U.K.	G7	12
New Ulm, Mn., U.S.	G4	118
New Ulm, Tx., U.S.	H2	122
New Washington, Oh., U.S.	D3	114
New Waterford, N.S., Can.	D16	110
New Waverly, Tx., U.S.	G3	122
New Westminster, B.C., Can.	G8	138
New Whiteland, In., U.S.	E11	120
New York, N.Y., U.S.	D12	114
New York, state, U.S.	C12	108
New York Mills, Mn., U.S.	E3	118
New York State Barge Canal, can., N.Y., U.S.	E12	112
New Zealand, ctry., Oc.	D4	80
Neyrīz, Iran	D7	56
Neyshābūr, Iran	B8	56
Neyveli, India	F4	53
Neyyāttinkara, India	G3	53
Nezahualcóyotl, Presa, res., Mex.	G12	100
Nezavertailovca, Mol.	C16	26
Nezperce, Id., U.S.	D10	136
Ngabang, Indon.	C6	50
Ngabé, Congo	E3	66
Ngambé, Cam.	D2	66
Ngami, Lake, l., Bots.	B6	70
Ngamiland, state, Bots.	B6	70
Ngan-chouei see Anhui, state, China	F7	42
Ngangla Ringco, l., China	C9	54
Nganglong Kangri, mts., China	B9	54
Ngangzê Co, l., China	C11	54
Nganjuk, Indon.	G7	50
Ngao, Thai.	C5	48
Ngaoui, Mont, mtn., Afr.	F3	62
Ngaoundéré, Cam.	C2	66
Ngape, Mya.	B2	48
Ngaputaw, Mya.	D2	48
Ngara, Tan.	E6	66
Ngatangiia, Cook Is.	a27	78j
Ngatangiia Harbour, b., Cook Is.	a27	78j
Ngawi, Indon.	G7	50
Ngay Nua, Laos	B5	48
Ngcheangel, is., Palau	D9	44
Ngeaur, i., Palau	D9	44
Ngereklmadel, Palau	g7	78b
Ngerkeai, Palau	g8	78b
Ngermetengel, Palau	f7	78b
Ngeruktabel, i., Palau	h7	78b
Ngetbong, Palau	f8	78b
Nggatokae Island, i., Sol. Is.	e8	79b
Nggela Pile, i., Sol. Is.	e9	79b
Nghia Hanh, Viet.	E9	48
Ngiap, stm., Laos	C6	48
Ngidinga, D.R.C.	F3	66
Ng'iro, mtn., Kenya	D7	66
Ngiro, Ewaso, stm., Kenya	D7	66
Ngo, Congo	E3	66
Ngoko, stm., Afr.	D3	66
Ngom, stm., China	B8	46
Ngomeni, Ras, c., Kenya	E8	66
Ngong, Kenya	E7	66
Ngoring Hu, l., China	E4	36
Ngounié, stm., Gabon	E2	66
Ngouri, Chad	E3	62
Nguigmi, Niger	G7	64
Ngulu, at., Micron.	C4	72
Ngum, stm., Laos	C6	48
Nguna, Île, i., Vanuatu	k17	79d
Nguru, Nig.	G7	64
Nhacoongo, Moz.	D12	70
Nhamundá, stm., Braz.	D6	84
Nha Trang, Viet.	F9	48
Nhill, Austl.	K3	76
Nhoma, stm., Afr.	D2	68
Niafounké, Mali	F4	64
Niagara, Wi., U.S.	C1	112
Niagara Falls, On., Can.	E10	112
Niagara Falls, N.Y., U.S.	A6	114
Niagara Falls, wtfl, N.A.	E10	112
Niagara-on-the-Lake, On., Can.	E10	112
Niagassola, Gui.	G3	64
Niah, Malay.	B8	50
Niamey, Niger	G5	64
Niangara, D.R.C.	D5	66
Niangay, Lac, l., Mali	F4	64
Niangoloko, Burkina	G4	64
Niangua, stm., Mo., U.S.	G5	120
Nia-Nia, D.R.C.	D5	66
Niantic, Il., U.S.	E8	120
Nianyushan, China	G7	42
Nianzishan, China	B9	36
Niari, stm., Congo	E2	66
Nias, Pulau, i., Indon.	L3	48
Nicaragua, ctry., N.A.	F5	102
Nicaragua, Lago de, l., Nic.	G5	102
Nicaragua, Lake see Nicaragua, Lago de, l., Nic.	G5	102
Nicastro, Italy	F10	24
Nice, Fr.	F13	18
Niceville, Fl., U.S.	G12	122
Nichinan, Japan	H4	40
Nicholas Channel (San Nicolás, Canal de), strt., N.A.	G11	108
Nicholasville, Ky., U.S.	G13	120
Nicholls, Ga., U.S.	E3	116
Nicholl's Town, Bah.	B9	96
Nicholson, Pa., U.S.	C10	114
Nickel Centre, On., Can.	B8	112
Nickerson, Ks., U.S.	C10	128
Nicobar Islands, is., India	G7	46
Nicola, B.C., Can.	F10	138
Nicola, stm., B.C., Can.	F9	138
Nicolae Bălcescu, Rom.	B13	26
Nicolet, Qc., Can.	D4	110
Nicolet, Lake, l., Mi., U.S.	B5	112
Nicolet Sud-Ouest, stm., Qc., Can.	E5	110
Nicollet, Mn., U.S.	G4	118
Nicosia (Levkosía), Cyp.	C4	58
Nicosia, Italy	G8	24
Nicoya, Golfo de, b., C.R.	H5	102
Nicoya, Península de, pen., C.R.	H5	102
Nida, Lith.	E3	10
Nida, stm., Pol.	F16	16
Nidadavole, India	C5	53
Nidzica, Pol.	C16	16
Niebüll, Ger.	B4	16
Niedere Tauern, mts., Aus.	C10	22
Niederösterreich, state, Aus.	B12	22
Niedersachsen, state, Ger.	D4	16
Niekerkshoop, S. Afr.	F6	70
Niemba, D.R.C.	F5	66
Niemodlin, Pol.	F13	16
Nienburg, Ger.	D5	16
Niers, stm., Eur.	C15	14
Niesky, Ger.	E10	16
Nieszawa, Pol.	D14	16
Nieu-Bethesda, S. Afr.	G7	70
Nieuport see Nieuwpoort, Bel.	C11	14
Nieuw Amsterdam, Sur.	B6	84
Nieuw Nickerie, Sur.	B6	84
Nieuwpoort, Bel.	C11	14
Nieuwpoort, Neth. Ant.	p22	104g
Nièvre, state, Fr.	G12	14
Nifisha, Egypt	H3	58
Niğde, Tur.	H15	6
Niğde, state, Tur.	A5	58
Nigei Island, i., B.C., Can.	F3	138
Nigel, S. Afr.	E9	70
Niger, ctry., Afr.	F6	64
Niger, stm., Afr.	H6	64
Niger Delta, Nig.	I6	64
Nigeria, ctry., Afr.	H6	64
Nightcaps, N.Z.	G3	80
Nighthawk, Wa., U.S.	B7	136
Nigríta, Grc.	C6	28
Niheidât el-Sûd, Gebel el-, mtn., Egypt	J3	58
Nihommatsu, Japan	B13	40
Nihuil, Embalse del, res., Arg.	G3	92
Niigata, Japan	B11	40
Niigata, state, Japan	B11	40
Niihama, Japan	F6	40
Niihau, i., Hi., U.S.	B1	78a
Nii-jima, i., Japan	E12	40
Niitsu, Japan	B12	40
Níjar, Spain	H8	20
Nijmegen, Neth.	C14	14
Nijvel see Nivelles, Bel.	D13	14
Nikel', Russia	B14	8
Nikki, Benin	G5	64
Nikkō, Japan	C12	40
Nikkō-kokuritsu-kōen, p.o.i., Japan	B12	40
Nikolaevo, Russia	B12	10
Nikolaevsk-na-Amure, Russia	F17	34
Nikol'sk, Russia	G21	8
Nikol'sk, Russia	C6	32
Nikolski, Ak., U.S.	F6	140
Nikol'skij, Russia	F15	8
Nikol'skoe, Russia	H19	10
Nikol'skoe, Russia	E22	34
Nikopol', Ukr.	E4	32
Nīkshahr, Iran	D9	56
Nikšić, Yugo.	G5	26
Nikumaroro, at., Kir.	D9	72
Nikunau, i., Kir.	D8	72
Nīl, Bahr el- see Nile, stm., Afr.	B6	62
Nīl, Nahr an- see Nile, stm., Afr.	D6	62
Nila, Pulau, i., Indon.	G9	44
Nilakka, l., Fin.	E12	8
Nile, stm., Afr.	D6	62
Nile Delta, Egypt	H1	58
Niles, Il., U.S.	B10	120
Niles, Mi., U.S.	G3	112
Niles, Oh., U.S.	C5	114
Nīlgiri, India	H11	54
Nilka, China	F14	32
Nilsiä, Fin.	E12	8
Nīmach, India	F5	54
Nimba, Mount, mtn., Afr.	H3	64
Nimbāhera, India	F5	54
Nîmes, Fr.	F10	18
Nimpkish Lake, l., B.C., Can.	F3	138
Nimule, Sudan	G6	62
Ninda, Ang.	C3	68
Nindigully, Austl.	G7	76
Nine Degree Channel, strt., India	G3	46
Ninette, Mb., Can.	E14	124
Ninetyeast Ridge, unds.	K11	142
Ninety Mile Beach, cst., Austl.	L6	76
Ninety Six, S.C., U.S.	B3	116
Ninfas, Punta, c., Arg.	H4	90
Ninga, Mb., Can.	E14	124
Ning'an, China	B8	38
Ningbo, China	G9	42
Ningcheng, China	D3	38
Ningde, China	H8	42
Ningdu, China	H6	42
Ningguo, China	F8	42
Ninghai, China	G9	42
Ning-hia see Ningxia, state, China	D6	36
Ninghua, China	H7	42
Ningi, Nig.	G6	64
Ningjing Shan, mts., China	F4	36
Ningming, China	J2	42
Ningnan, China	F5	36
Ningpo see Ningbo, China	G9	42
Ningqiang, China	E2	42
Ningshan, China	E3	42
Ningsia see Yinchuan, China	B2	42
Ningsia Hui see Ningxia, state, China	D6	36
Ningsia Hui Autonomous Region see Ningxia, state, China	D6	36
Ningwu, China	B4	42
Ningxia, state, China	D6	36
Ningxiang, China	G5	42
Ningyuan, China	I4	42
Ninh Binh, Viet.	B7	48
Ninh Hoa, Viet.	F9	48
Ninhue, Chile	H1	92
Ninigo Group, is., Pap. N. Gui.	a3	79a
Ninnescah, North Fork, stm., Ks., U.S.	D10	128
Ninnescah, South Fork, stm., Ks., U.S.	D10	128
Ninohe, Japan	D14	38
Nioaque, Braz.	D5	90
Niobrara, stm., U.S.	E14	126
Nioghalvfjerdsfjorden, ice, Grnld.	B22	141
Nioki, D.R.C.	E3	66
Niono, Mali	G3	64
Nioro, Mali	F3	64
Niort, Fr.	C5	18
Niota, Tn., U.S.	B14	122
Nipāni, India	C2	53
Nipawin, Sk., Can.	E10	106
Nipe, Bahía de, b., Cuba	B10	102
Nipigon, On., Can.	B10	118
Nipigon, Lake, res., On., Can.	B10	118
Nipigon Bay, b., On., Can.	C10	118
Nipissing, Lake, l., On., Can.	B10	112
Nipomo, Ca., U.S.	H5	134
Niquelândia, Braz.	H1	88
Niquero, Cuba	B9	102
Niquivil, Arg.	E3	92
Nīra, stm., India	B2	53
Nirasaki, Japan	D11	40
Nirgua, Ven.	B7	86
Nirmal, India	B4	53
Nirmāli, India	E11	54
Niš, Yugo.	F8	26
Nişāb, Yemen	G6	56
Nišava, stm., Eur.	F9	26
Niscemi, Italy	G8	24
Nishio, Japan	E10	40
Nishiwaki, Japan	E7	40
Nisporeni, Mol.	B15	26
Nisqually, stm., Wa., U.S.	D4	136
Nisswa, Mn., U.S.	E4	118
Nītaure, Lat.	C8	10
Niterói, Braz.	L4	88
Nith, stm., On., Can.	E9	112
Nitinat Lake, l., B.C., Can.	H6	138
Nitra, Slov.	H14	16
Nitra, stm., Slov.	H14	16
Nitro, W.V., U.S.	F4	114
Niue, dep., Oc.	E10	72
Niulakita, i., Tuvalu	E8	72
Niut, Gunung, mtn., Indon.	C6	50
Niutao, i., Tuvalu	D8	72
Niutoushan, China	B7	38
Niutou Shan, i., China	G9	42
Niuzhuang, China	A10	42
Nive, stm., Austl.	E6	76
Nivelles, Bel.	D13	14
Nivernais, hist. reg., Fr.	G12	14
Niverville, Mb., Can.	E16	124
Nixa, Mo., U.S.	G4	120
Nixon, Nv., U.S.	D6	134
Niža, Russia	C20	8
Nizāmābād, India	B4	53
Nizām Sāgar, res., India	C3	53
Nižegorodskaja oblast', co., Russia	H21	8
Nizip, Tur.	A8	58
Nízke Tatry, Narodny Park, p.o.i., Slov.	H15	16
Nižneangarsk, Russia	E10	34
Nižnee Kujto, ozero, l., Russia	D14	8
Nižneilimsk, Russia	C18	32
Nižnekamsk, Russia	C8	32
Nižnekamskoe vodohranilišče, res., Russia	C8	32
Nižneudinsk, Russia	D17	32
Nižnevartovsk, Russia	B13	32
Nižnij Casučej, Russia	F12	34
Nižnij Kuranah, Russia	E14	34
Nižnij Novgorod (Gorki), Russia	H21	8
Nižnij Pjandž, Taj.	B10	56
Nižnij Tagil, Russia	C10	32
Nižnjaja Peša, Russia	C22	8
Nižnjaja Pojma, Russia	C17	32
Nižnjaja Tavda, Russia	C11	32
Nižnjaja Tunguska, stm., Russia	B16	32
Nizza Monferrato, Italy	F5	22
Njandoma, Russia	F19	8
Njasviž, Bela.	G9	10
Njazidja, i., Com.	C7	68
Njesuthi, mtn., Afr.	F9	70
Njombe, stm., Tan.	F7	66
Njuhča, Russia	E22	8
Njuja, Russia	D12	34
Njuja, stm., Russia	B20	32
Njuk, ozero, l., Russia	D14	8
Njuksenica, Russia	F21	8
Njurba, Russia	D12	34
Njuvčim, Russia	B8	32
Nkambe, Cam.	C2	66
Nkawkaw, Ghana	H4	64
Nkayi, Zimb.	D4	68
Nkhata Bay, Mwi.	C5	68
Nkhotakota, Mwi.	C5	68
Nkomi, Lagune, l., Gabon	E1	66
Nkongsamba, Cam.	D2	66
Nkwalini, S. Afr.	F10	70
Nmai, stm., Mya.	C8	46
Noākhāli, Bngl.	G13	54
Noatak, Ak., U.S.	C7	140
Noatak, stm., Ak., U.S.	C8	140
Nobeoka, Japan	G4	40
Noble, Il., U.S.	F9	120
Noblesville, In., U.S.	H3	112
Noboribetsu, Japan	C14	38
Nobres, Braz.	F6	84
Nocatee, Fl., U.S.	I4	116
Noce, stm., Italy	D8	22
Nocera Inferiore, Italy	D8	24
Nockatunga, Austl.	F4	76
Nocona, Tx., U.S.	H11	128
Nocupétaro, Mex.	F8	100
Noetinger, Arg.	F6	92
Nogales, Mex.	F7	98
Nogales, Az., U.S.	L5	132
Nogent-le-Rotrou, Fr.	F9	14
Nogent-sur-Seine, Fr.	F12	14
Noginsk, Russia	E21	10
Nogliki, Russia	F17	34
Nogoa, stm., Austl.	E6	76
Nogoyá, Arg.	F7	92
Nógrád, state, Hung.	B6	26
Noguera Pallaresa, stm., Spain	B12	20
Noguera Ribagorçana, stm., Spain	B11	20
Nohar, India	D5	54
Noia, Spain	B2	20
Noir, Causse, plat., Fr.	E9	18
Noir, Isla, i., Chile	J2	90
Noire, stm., Qc., Can.	B13	112
Noirmoutier, Île de, i., Fr.	H6	14
Noirmoutier-en-l'Île, Fr.	H6	14
Nojima-zaki, c., Japan	E12	40
Nokha Mandi, India	E4	54
Nokia, Fin.	F10	8
Nokomis, Sk., Can.	C8	124
Nokomis, Fl., U.S.	I3	116
Nokomis, Il., U.S.	E8	120
Nokou, Chad	E2	62
Nokuku, Vanuatu	j16	79d
Nola, C.A.R.	D3	66
Nola, Italy	D8	24
Nolichucky, stm., U.S.	H2	114
Nolin, stm., Ky., U.S.	G11	120
Nolin Lake, res., Ky., U.S.	G11	120
Nolinsk, Russia	C8	32
Nólsoy, i., Far. Is.	n34	8b
Nombre de Dios, Pan.	H8	102
Nome, Ak., U.S.	D6	140
Nomozaki, Japan	G2	40
Nomtsas, Nmb.	D3	70
Nonacho Lake, l., N.T., Can.	C8	106
Nonburg, Russia	D24	8
Nondalton, Ak., U.S.	D8	140
Nong'an, China	B6	38
Nong Han, Thai.	D6	48
Nong Khai, Thai.	D6	48
Nongoma, S. Afr.	E10	70
Nongpoh, India	F13	54
Nongstoin, India	F13	54
Nonoava, Mex.	B5	100
Nonogasta, Arg.	D4	92
Nonouti, at., Kir.	D8	72
Nonsuch Bay, b., Antig.	f4	105b
Nonthaburi, Thai.	F5	48
Nooksack, Wa., U.S.	B4	136
Noonkanbah, Austl.	C4	74
Noordoostpolder, reg., Neth.	B14	14
Noordpunt, c., Neth. Ant.	p21	104g
Noordwijk aan Zee, Neth.	B13	14
Noorvik, Ak., U.S.	C7	140
Nootka Island, i., B.C., Can.	G4	138
Nóqui, Ang.	B1	68
Norah, is., Erit.	D7	62
Nora Islands see Norah, is., Erit.	D7	62
Noralee, B.C., Can.	B4	138
Nora Springs, Ia., U.S.	A5	120
Norcatur, Ks., U.S.	B8	128
Norcia, Italy	H10	22
Norcross, Ga., U.S.	D14	122
Nord, Grnld.	A22	141
Nord, state, Fr.	D12	14
Nord, state, N. Cal.	m15	79d
Nord, Canal du, can., Fr.	D12	14
Nord, Canal du, can., Fr.	E11	14
Nordaustlandet, i., Nor.	B29	141
Nordborg, Den.	A5	16
Nordegg, Ab., Can.	D14	138
Nordegg, stm., Ab., Can.	D15	138
Norden, Ger.	C3	16
Nordenham, Ger.	C4	16
Nordenšel'da, arhipelag, is., Russia	A8	34
Nordenskjold Archipelago see Nordenšel'da, arhipelag, is., Russia	A8	34
Norderstedt, Ger.	C6	16
Nordfjord, b., Nor.	F1	8
Nordfold, Nor.	C6	8
Nordgrønland (Avanersuaq), state, Grnld.	B15	141
Nordhausen, Ger.	E6	16
Nordhorn, Ger.	D2	16
Nordjylland, state, Den.	H4	8
Nordkapp (North Cape), c., Nor.	A11	8
Nordkinnhalvøya, pen., Nor.	A12	8
Nordland, state, Nor.	C6	8
Nördlingen, Ger.	H6	16
Nordmaling, Swe.	E8	8
Nordman, Id., U.S.	B9	136
Nordostrundingen, c., Grnld.	A23	141
Nord-Ostsee-Kanal (Kiel Canal), can., Ger.	B5	16
Nordrhein-Westfalen, state, Ger.	E4	16
Nordstrand, i., Ger.	B4	16
Nord-Trøndelag, state, Nor.	D5	8
Nordvik, Russia	B11	34
Norfolk, Ne., U.S.	E15	126
Norfolk, Va., U.S.	H9	114
Norfolk Island, dep., Norf. I.	x25	78i
Norfolk Island National Park, p.o.i., Norf. I.	y25	78i
Norfolk Ridge, unds.	L19	142
Norfork Lake, res., U.S.	H5	120
Norikura-dake, vol., Japan	C10	40
Noril'sk, Russia	C6	34
Norlina, N.C., U.S.	H7	114
Normal, Il., U.S.	D9	120
Norman, Ar., U.S.	C5	122
Norman, Ok., U.S.	F11	128
Norman, stm., Austl.	B3	76
Norman, Lake, res., N.C., U.S.	A4	116
Normanby Island, i., Pap. N. Gui.	c5	79a
Normandes, Îles see Channel Islands, is., Eur.	L10	12
Normandie, hist. reg., Fr.	F8	14
Normandie, Collines de, hills, Fr.	F8	14
Normandin, Qc., Can.	B4	110
Normandy see Normandie, hist. reg., Fr.	F8	14
Normandy, Hills of see Normandie, Collines de, hills, Fr.	F8	14
Normangee, Tx., U.S.	F2	122
Norman Island, i., Br. Vir. Is.	e8	104b
Normanton, Austl.	A3	76
Norman Wells, N.T., Can.	B5	106
Norogachi, Mex.	B5	100
Norquay, Sk., Can.	C11	124
Ñorquinco, Arg.	H2	90
Norra Storfjället, mtn., Swe.	D6	8
Norrbotten, state, Swe.	C9	8
Nørresundby, Den.	H3	8
Norridgewock, Me., U.S.	F7	110
Norris, Tn., U.S.	H1	114
Norris Lake, res., Tn., U.S.	H2	114
Norristown, Pa., U.S.	D10	114
Norrköping, Swe.	G7	8
Norrtälje, Swe.	G8	8
Norseman, Austl.	F4	74
Norsjö, Swe.	D8	8
Norsjø, l., Nor.	G3	8
Norsk, Russia	F15	34
Norske Øer, is., Grnld.	B22	141

Name	Map Ref.	Page
Norsup, Vanuatu	k16	79d
Norte, Cabo, c., Braz.	C8	84
Norte, Serra do, plat., Braz.	F6	84
Norte de Santander, state, Col.	C5	86
Nortelândia, Braz.	F6	84
North, S.C., U.S.	C4	116
North, stm., Ia., U.S.	C3	120
North, Cape, c., N.S., Can.	C16	110
North Adams, Ma., U.S.	B12	114
North Adams, Mi., U.S.	C1	114
North Albany, Or., U.S.	F3	136
Northallerton, Eng., U.K.	G11	12
Northam, Austl.	F3	74
North America, cont.	C5	4
North American Basin, unds.	E7	144
Northampton, Austl.	E2	74
Northampton, Eng., U.K.	I12	12
Northampton, Ma., U.S.	B13	114
North Andaman, i., India	F7	46
North Atlanta, Ga., U.S.	C1	116
North Augusta, S.C., U.S.	C4	116
North Aulatsivik Island, i., Nf., Can.	F13	141
North Australian Basin, unds.	K14	142
North Baltimore, Oh., U.S.	C2	114
North Battleford, Sk., Can.	B5	124
North Bay, On., Can.	B10	112
North Bend, B.C., Can.	G9	138
North Bend, Ne., U.S.	J2	118
North Bennington, Vt., U.S.	B12	114
North Berwick, Scot., U.K.	E10	12
North Berwick, Me., U.S.	G6	110
North Borneo see Sabah, state, Malay.	H1	52
North Bourke, Austl.	H5	76
North Branch, Mi., U.S.	E6	112
North Caicos, i., T./C. Is.	B11	102
North Canadian, stm., Ok., U.S.	F12	128
North Canton, Ga., U.S.	C14	122
North Canton, Oh., U.S.	D4	114
North Cape, c., P.E., Can.	C13	110
North Cape, c., N.Z.	B5	80
North Cape see Nordkapp, c., Nor.	A11	8
North Caribou Lake, l., On., Can.	E12	106
North Carolina, state, U.S.	D11	108
North Cascades National Park, p.o.i., Wa., U.S.	B5	136
North Channel, strt., On., Can.	B7	112
North Channel, strt., U.K.	F7	12
North Charleston, S.C., U.S.	D5	116
North Chicago, Il., U.S.	F2	112
North Chungcheong see Ch'ungch'ŏng-bukto, state, Kor., S.	B1	40
Northcliffe, Austl.	F3	74
North College Hill, Oh., U.S.	E13	120
North Collins, N.Y., U.S.	F11	112
North Concho, stm., Tx., U.S.	C7	130
North Conway, N.H., U.S.	F5	110
North Crossett, Ar., U.S.	D6	122
North Cyprus see Cyprus, North, ctry., Asia	C4	58
North Dakota, state, U.S.	G13	124
North Downs, hills, Eng., U.K.	J13	12
North Eagle Butte, S.D., U.S.	B11	126
North East, Md., U.S.	E9	114
North-East, state, Bots.	B8	70
Northeast Cape, Ak., U.S.	D6	140
Northeast Cape Fear, stm., N.C., U.S.	B8	116
North East Point, c., Bah.	A11	102
Northeast Providence Channel, strt., Bah.	B9	96
Northeim, Ger.	E6	16
North English, Ia., U.S.	C5	120
Northern see HaZafon, state, Isr.	F6	58
Northern, state, S. Afr.	C9	70
Northern Cape, state, S. Afr.	G5	70
Northern Cook Islands, is., Cook Is.	E10	72
Northern Division, state, Fiji	p20	79e
Northern Donets, stm., Eur.	F16	6
Northern Dvina see Severnaja Dvina, stm., Russia	E19	8
Northern Indian Lake, l., Mb., Can.	D11	106
Northern Ireland, state, U.K.	G6	12
Northern Marianas, dep., Oc.	B6	72
Northern Sporades see Vórioi Sporádhes, is., Grc.	D6	28
Northern Territory, state, Austl.	D6	74
North Fabius, stm., U.S.	D6	120
Northfield, Ma., U.S.	B13	114
Northfield, Mn., U.S.	G5	118
Northfield, Vt., U.S.	F4	110
North Fiji Basin, unds.	K20	142
North Flinders Range, mts., Austl.	H2	76
North Fond du Lac, Wi., U.S.	H10	118
North Foreland, c., Eng., U.K.	J14	12
North Fork, Ca., U.S.	F6	134
North Fork, stm., U.S.	H5	120
North Fort Myers, Fl., U.S.	J4	116
North Frisian Islands, is., Eur.	B3	16
Northglenn, Co., U.S.	B4	128
North Gulfport, Ms., U.S.	G9	122
North Gyeongsang see Kyŏngsang-bukto, state, Kor., S.	C1	40
North Henik Lake, l., Nu., Can.	C11	106
North Hero, Vt., U.S.	F3	110
North Highlands, Ca., U.S.	E4	134
North Horr, Kenya	D7	66
North Island, i., N.Z.	C5	80
North Judson, In., U.S.	G3	112
North Kent Island, i., Nu., Can.	B7	141
North Kingsville, Oh., U.S.	C5	114
North Knife Lake, l., Mb., Can.	D11	106
North Korea see Korea, North, ctry., Asia	D7	38
North Lakhimpur, India	C7	46
North Las Vegas, Nv., U.S.	G1	132
North La Veta Pass, p., Co., U.S.	D3	128
North Little Rock, Ar., U.S.	C6	122
North Llano, stm., Tx., U.S.	D8	130
North Logan, Ut., U.S.	B5	132
North Loup, Ne., U.S.	F14	126
North Loup, stm., Ne., U.S.	F14	126
North Magnetic Pole, misc. cult.	B4	141
North Mamm Peak, mtn., Co., U.S.	D9	132
North Manchester, In., U.S.	H4	112
North Manitou Island, i., Mi., U.S.	C3	112
North Mankato, Mn., U.S.	G4	118
North Miami, Fl., U.S.	K5	116
North Miami Beach, Fl., U.S.	K5	116
North Milk (Milk, North Fork), stm., N.A.	B13	136
North Myrtle Beach, S.C., U.S.	C7	116
North New River Canal, can., Fl., U.S.	J5	116
North Newton, Ks., U.S.	C11	128
North Ogden, Ut., U.S.	B5	132
North Ossetia see Severnaja Osetija, state, Russia	F6	32
North Palisade, mtn., Ca., U.S.	F7	134
North Palm Beach, Fl., U.S.	J5	116
North Park, Il., U.S.	B8	120
North Peninsula, pen., On., Can.	A10	118
North Plains, pl., N.M., U.S.	I8	132
North Platte, Ne., U.S.	F12	126
North Platte, stm., U.S.	F11	126
North Point, c., Barb.	n8	105d
North Pole, misc. cult.	A4	94
Northport, Al., U.S.	D11	122
Northport, Mi., U.S.	C4	112
Northport, Wa., U.S.	B9	136
North Portal, Sk., Can.	E11	124
North Raccoon, stm., Ia., U.S.	C3	120
North Rhine-Westphalia see Nordrhein-Westfalen, state, Ger.	E4	16
North Richland Hills, Tx., U.S.	B10	130
North Rim, Az., U.S.	G4	132
North Ronaldsay, i., Scot., U.K.	B10	12
North Rustico, P.E., Can.	D13	110
North Salt Lake, Ut., U.S.	C5	132
North Saskatchewan, stm., Can.	E9	106
North Sea, Eur.	D9	6
North Shoal Lake, l., Mb., Can.	D16	124
North Shore City, N.Z.	C6	80
North Shoshone Peak, mtn., Nv., U.S.	D8	134
North Siberain Lowland see Severo-Sibirskaja nizmennost', pl., Russia	B6	34
North Skunk, stm., Ia., U.S.	C5	120
North Solitary Island, i., Austl.	G9	76
North Solomons, state, Pap. N. Gui.	d7	79b
North Spicer Island, i., Nu., Can.	B15	106
North Stradbroke Island, i., Austl.	F9	76
North Sumatra see Sumatera Utara, state, Indon.	K4	48
North Sydney, N.S., Can.	D16	110
North Taranaki Bight, b., N.Z.	D5	80
North Terre Haute, In., U.S.	E10	120
North Thompson, stm., B.C., Can.	F10	138
North Troy, Vt., U.S.	F4	110
North Tunica, Ms., U.S.	C8	122
North Uist, i., Scot., U.K.	D5	12
Northumberland Isles, is., Austl.	C7	76
Northumberland National Park, p.o.i., Eng., U.K.	F10	12
Northumberland Strait, strt., Can.	D12	110
North Umpqua, stm., Or., U.S.	G4	136
North Vancouver, B.C., Can.	G7	138
North Vietnam see Vietnam, ctry., Asia	E9	48
Northville, N.Y., U.S.	G2	110
North-West, state, S. Afr.	E7	70
North West Bluff, c., Monts.	D3	105a
North West Cape, c., Austl.	D2	74
North-West Frontier, state, Pak.	A4	54
Northwest Miramichi, stm., N.B., Can.	C10	110
Northwest Pacific Basin, unds.	F18	142
Northwest Providence Channel, strt., Bah.	m17	104f
Northwest Territories, state, Can.	B10	106
North Wichita, stm., Tx., U.S.	H9	128
North Wilkesboro, N.C., U.S.	H4	114
North Windham, Me., U.S.	G6	110
Northwood, Ia., U.S.	H5	118
Northwood, N.D., U.S.	G16	124
North York, ngh., On., Can.	E10	112
North York Moors National Park, p.o.i., Eng., U.K.	G12	12
North Zulch, Tx., U.S.	G2	122
Norton, Ks., U.S.	B9	128
Norton, Va., U.S.	H3	114
Norton Shores, Mi., U.S.	E3	112
Norton Sound, strt., Ak., U.S.	D6	140
Nortonville, Ks., U.S.	E2	120
Norvegia, Cape, c., Ant.	C3	81
Norwalk, Ct., U.S.	C12	114
Norwalk, Ia., U.S.	C4	120
Norwalk, Oh., U.S.	C3	114
Norway, Ia., U.S.	C6	120
Norway, Me., U.S.	F6	110
Norway, ctry., Eur.	E3	8
Norway Bay, b., Nu., Can.	A10	106
Norway House, Mb., Can.	E11	106
Norwegian Basin, unds.	B13	144
Norwegian Sea, Eur.	C3	30
Norwich, On., Can.	E9	112
Norwich, Eng., U.K.	I14	12
Norwich, Ct., U.S.	C13	114
Norwich, N.Y., U.S.	B10	114
Norwood, On., Can.	D11	112
Norwood, Co., U.S.	E8	132
Norwood, Ma., U.S.	B14	114
Norwood, Mn., U.S.	G5	118
Norwood, N.C., U.S.	A5	116
Norwood, Oh., U.S.	E1	114
Noshiro, Japan	D13	38
Nosop (Nossob), stm., Afr.	D5	70
Nosovaja, Russia	B26	8
Nosovščina, Russia	E17	8
Nossa Senhora das Dores, Braz.	F7	88
Nossob (Nosop), stm., Afr.	D5	70
Nosy-Varika, Madag.	E8	68
Notasulga, Al., U.S.	E13	122
Notch Hill, B.C., Can.	F11	138
Noteć, stm., Pol.	D11	16
Nótio Aigaío, state, Grc.	G9	28
Noto, Italy	H9	24
Noto, Japan	B10	40
Noto, Golfo di, b., Italy	H9	24
Noto-hantō, pen., Japan	B10	40
Notozero, ozero, l., Russia	C14	8
Notre-Dame, N.B., Can.	D12	110
Notre-Dame, Monts, mts., Qc., Can.	B9	110
Notre Dame Bay, b., Nf., Can.	j22	107a
Notre-Dame-du-Laus, Qc., Can.	B14	112
Notrees, Tx., U.S.	C5	130
Nottawasaga, stm., On., Can.	D10	112
Nottawasaga Bay, b., On., Can.	D9	112
Nottaway, stm., Qc., Can.	E15	106
Nottingham, Eng., U.K.	I11	12
Nottingham Island, i., Nu., Can.	C15	106
Nottoway, stm., Va., U.S.	H8	114
Notukeu Creek, stm., Sk., Can.	E6	124
Notwane, stm., Afr.	D8	70
Nouâdhibou, Maur.	E1	64
Nouâdhibou, Râs, c., Afr.	E1	64
Nouakchott, Maur.	F1	64
Nouâmghâr, Maur.	F1	64
Nouméa, N. Cal.	n16	79d
Noupoort, S. Afr.	G7	70
Nouveau-Québec, Cratère du, crat., Qc., Can.	C16	106
Nouvelle, Qc., Can.	B10	110
Nouvelle-Calédonie (New Caledonia), i., N. Cal.	m15	79d
Nouvelle-Écosse see Nova Scotia, state, Can.	G18	106
Nouvelle-France, Cap de, c., Qc., Can.	C16	106
Nova Andradina, Braz.	D6	90
Nová Baňa, Slov.	H14	16
Nova Caipemba, Ang.	B1	68
Nova Era, Braz.	J4	88
Nova Friburgo, Braz.	L4	88
Nova Gorica, Slvn.	D10	22
Nova Gradiška, Cro.	E14	22
Nova Granada, Braz.	K1	88
Nova Iguaçu, Braz.	L4	88
Novaja Kazanka, Kaz.	E7	32
Novaja Ladoga, Russia	F14	8
Novaja Maluksa, Russia	A14	10
Novaja Sibir', ostrov, i., Russia	B19	34
Novaja Zemlja, is., Russia	B8	30
Nova Kakhovka, Ukr.	E4	32
Nova Lamego, Gui.-B.	G2	64
Nova Lima, Braz.	K4	88
Novalukoml', Bela.	F11	10
Nova Mambone, Moz.	B12	70
Nova Olinda, Braz.	D6	88
Nová Paka, Czech Rep.	F11	16
Nova Ponte, Braz.	J2	88
Nova Prata, Braz.	D12	92
Novara, Italy	E5	22
Nova Roma, Braz.	G2	88
Nova Russas, Braz.	C5	88
Nova Scotia, state, Can.	G18	106
Nova Soure, Braz.	F6	88
Novato, Ca., U.S.	E3	134
Nova Venécia, Braz.	J5	88
Nova Vida, Braz.	F5	84
Novaya Zemlya see Novaja Zemlja, is., Russia	B8	30
Nova Zagora, Blg.	G13	26
Nové Hrady, Czech Rep.	H10	16
Novelda, Spain	F10	20
Nové Město nad Váhom, Slov.	H13	16
Nové Město na Moravě, Czech Rep.	G12	16
Nové Zámky, Slov.	I14	16
Novgorod, Russia	B14	10
Novgorodskaja oblast', co., Russia	B15	10
Novi Bečej, Yugo.	D7	26
Novi Beograd, Yugo.	E7	26
Novice, Tx., U.S.	C8	130
Novigrad, Cro.	E10	22
Novikovo, Russia	G17	34
Novi Ligure, Italy	F5	22
Novinger, Mo., U.S.	D5	120
Novi Pazar, Blg.	F14	26
Novi Pazar, Yugo.	F7	26
Novi Sad, Yugo.	D6	26
Novo, Lago, l., Braz.	C7	84
Novo Airão, Braz.	H11	86
Novoaltajsk, Russia	D14	32
Novo Aripuanã, Braz.	E5	84
Novočerkassk, Russia	E6	32
Novodvinsk, Russia	D19	8
Novoe, Russia	C11	32
Novoenisejsk, Russia	C16	32
Novo Hamburgo, Braz.	D12	92
Novo Horizonte, Braz.	K1	88
Novoizborsk, Russia	C10	10
Novokačalinsk, Russia	B10	38
Novokaširsk, Russia	F21	10
Novokazalinsk, Kaz.	F10	32
Novokujbyševsk, Russia	D7	32
Novokuzneck, Russia	D15	32
Novolazarevskaja, sci., Ant.	C6	81
Novo Mesto, Slvn.	E12	22
Novomoskovsk (Stalinogorsk), Russia	F21	10
Novo Oriente, Braz.	C5	88
Novopetrovskoe, Russia	E19	10
Novorossijsk, Russia	F5	32
Novorybnoe, Russia	B10	34
Novoržev, Russia	C12	10
Novošahtinsk, Russia	E6	32
Novošelovo, Russia	E7	34
Novoselytsia, Ukr.	A13	26
Novosergievka, Russia	D8	32
Novosibirsk, Russia	C14	32
Novosibirskie ostrova, is., Russia	A18	34
Novosibirskoe vodohranilišče, res., Russia	D14	32
Novosil's'ke, Ukr.	D15	26
Novosokol'niki, Russia	D12	10
Novotroick, Russia	D9	32
Novotroickoe, Kaz.	F12	32
Novouzensk, Russia	D7	32
Novovjatsk, Russia	C7	32
Novozavidovskij, Russia	D19	10
Novozybkov, Russia	H14	10
Novska, Cro.	E13	22
Nový Bohumín, Czech Rep.	G14	16
Nový Bor, Czech Rep.	F10	16
Novyja Valosavičy, Bela.	F11	10
Nový Jičín, Czech Rep.	G13	16
Novyj Nekouz, Russia	C20	10
Novyj Port, Russia	A12	32
Novyj Uzen', Kaz.	F8	32
Novyj Vasjugan, Russia	C13	32
Novy Pahost, Bela.	E10	10
Nowa Ruda, Pol.	F12	16
Nowa Sól, Pol.	E11	16
Nowe, Pol.	C14	16
Nowe Miasto nad Pilicą, Pol.	E16	16
Nowendoc, Austl.	H8	76
Nowgong, India	F7	54
Nowitna, stm., Ak., U.S.	D9	140
Nowogard, Pol.	C11	16
Nowogrodziec, Pol.	E11	16
Nowood, stm., Wy., U.S.	C5	126
Nowra, Austl.	J8	76
Nowrangapur, India	B6	53
Nowshāk, mtn., Asia	B11	56
Nowshera, Pak.	B4	54
Nowshera, Pak.	C11	56
Nowy Dwór Mazowiecki, Pol.	D16	16
Nowy Sącz, Pol.	G16	16
Nowy Sącz, state, Pol.	G16	16
Nowy Staw, Pol.	B15	16
Nowy Targ, Pol.	G15	16
Noxapater, Ms., U.S.	E9	122
Noxen, Pa., U.S.	C9	114
Noxon, Mt., U.S.	B11	136
Noxubee, stm., U.S.	D10	122
Noy, stm., Laos	D7	48
Noya see Noia, Spain	B2	20
Noyant, Fr.	G9	14
Noyon, Fr.	E11	14
Nsanje, Mwi.	D6	68
Nsawam, Ghana	H4	64
Nsok, Eq. Gui.	I7	64
Nsukka, Nig.	H6	64
Nsuta, Ghana	H4	64
Ntwetwe Pan, pl., Bots.	B7	70
Nu see Salween, stm., Asia	C8	46
Nūbah, Jibāl an-, mts., Sudan	E6	62
Nubian Desert, des., Sudan	C6	62
Ñuble, stm., Chile	H2	92
Nucet, Rom.	C9	26
Nudol'-Šarino, Russia	D19	10
Nueces, stm., Tx., U.S.	G10	130
Nueces Plains, pl., Tx., U.S.	F8	130
Nueltin Lake, l., Can.	C11	106
Nuestra Señora de Talavera, Arg.	B6	92
Nueva, Isla, i., Chile	K3	90
Nueva Antioquia, Col.	D7	86
Nueva Ciudad Guerrero, Mex.	B9	100
Nueva Esparta, state, Ven.	B9	86
Nueva Galia, Arg.	G5	92
Nueva Germania, Para.	A9	92
Nueva Gerona, Cuba	B6	102
Nueva Imperial, Chile	G2	90
Nueva Italia de Ruiz, Mex.	F7	100
Nueva Loja, Ec.	G3	86
Nueva Palmira, Ur.	F8	92
Nueva Rosita, Mex.	A8	100
Nueva San Salvador, El Sal.	F3	102
Nueva Toltén, Chile	G2	90
Nueve, Canal Numero, can., Arg.	H8	92
Nueve de Julio, Arg.	G7	92
Nuevitas, Cuba	B9	102
Nuevo, Bajo, unds., Col.	E8	102
Nuevo, Cayo, i., Mex.	E12	100
Nuevo, Golfo, b., Arg.	H4	90
Nuevo Camarón, Mex.	G8	130
Nuevo Casas Grandes, Mex.	F9	98
Nuevo Delicias, Mex.	B7	100
Nuevo Laredo, Mex.	B9	100
Nuevo León, state, Mex.	B8	100
Nuevo Primero de Mayo, Mex.	H9	130
Nuevo Progreso, Mex.	F12	100
Nuevo Rocafuerte, Ec.	H4	86
Nuevo San Lucas, Mex.	F2	130
Nûgssuaq, pen., Grnld.	C15	141
Nugu, res., India	F3	53
Nui, at., Tuvalu	D8	72
Nuku'alofa, Tonga	n14	78e
Nukuhu, Pap. N. Gui.	b4	79a
Nukus, Uzb.	F9	32
Nul, Vanuatu	k17	79d
Nulato, Ak., U.S.	D8	140
Nullagine, Austl.	D4	74
Nullarbor, Austl.	F6	74
Nullarbor Plain, pl., Austl.	F5	74
Numan, Nig.	H7	64
Numancia (Numantia), hist., Spain	C8	20
Numantia see Numancia, hist., Spain	C8	20
Numata, Japan	C12	40
Numazu, Japan	D11	40
Numfoor, Pulau, i., Indon.	F10	44
Nunavut, state, Canada	B11	106
Nunda, N.Y., U.S.	B7	114
Nuneaton, Eng., U.K.	I11	12
Nuñez, Cape, c., S. Geor.	J9	90
Nunivak Island, i., Ak., U.S.	D6	140
Nunjiang, China	B10	36
Nunkun, mtn., India	A6	54
Nunnelly, Tn., U.S.	I10	120
Nuomin, stm., China	B10	36
Nuoro, Italy	D3	24
Nuquí, Col.	E3	86
Nura, Kaz.	E12	32
Nura, stm., Kaz.	E12	32
Nur Dağları, mts., Tur.	B7	58
Nuremberg see Nürnberg, Ger.	G6	16
Nuremburg see Nürnberg, Ger.	G6	16
Nuriootpa, Austl.	J2	76
Nürnberg (Nuremberg), Ger.	G6	16
Nūrpur, India	B5	54
Nürtingen, Ger.	H5	16
Nusa Tenggara Barat, state, Indon.	G10	50
Nusa Tenggara Timur, state, Indon.	H12	50
Nuṣayrīyah, Jabal an-, mts., Syria	C7	58
Nu Shan, mts., China	F4	36
Nüshan Hu, l., China	E8	42
Nushki, Pak.	D10	56
Nutrioso, Az., U.S.	J7	132
Nutter Fort, W.V., U.S.	E5	114
Nuuk see Godthåb, Grnld.	E15	141
Nuwerus, S. Afr.	G4	70
Nuweveldberge, mts., S. Afr.	H5	70
Nūzvīd, India	C5	53
Nyabéssan, Cam.	D2	66
Nyabing, Austl.	F3	74
Nyack, N.Y., U.S.	C12	114
Nyahanga, Tan.	E6	66
Nyainqêntanglha Feng, mtn., China	C13	54
Nyainqêntanglha Shan, mts., China	C6	46
Nyainrong, China	B14	54
Nyakanazi, Tan.	E6	66
Nyala, Sudan	E5	62
Nyalam, China	D10	54
Nyamlell, Sudan	F5	62
Nyamtumbo, Tan.	G7	66
Nyang, stm., China	D14	54
Nyanga, stm., Afr.	J7	64
Nyasa, Lake, l., Afr.	C5	68
Nyaunglebin, Mya.	C3	48
Nyboe Land, reg., Grnld.	A14	141
Nyborg, Den.	I4	8
Nybro, Swe.	H6	8
Nyda, Russia	A12	32
Nyêmo, China	C7	46
Nyeri, Kenya	E7	66
Nyerol, Sudan	F6	62
Nyimba, Zam.	C5	68
Nyingchi, China	F3	36
Nyírbátor, Hung.	B9	26
Nyíregyháza, Hung.	B8	26
Nykøbing, Den.	I4	8
Nyköping, Swe.	G7	8
Nyland see Uusimaa, state, Fin.	F11	8
Nylstroom, S. Afr.	D9	70
Nymboida, stm., Austl.	G9	76
Nymburk, Czech Rep.	F11	16
Nynäshamn, Swe.	G7	8
Nyngan, Austl.	H6	76
Nyon, Switz.	D3	22
Nyons, Fr.	E11	18
Nýrsko, Czech Rep.	G9	16
Nyš, Russia	F17	34
Nysa, Pol.	F13	16
Nysa Kłodzka, stm., Pol.	F12	16
Nysa Łużycka (Lausitzer Neisse), stm., Eur.	E10	16
Nyslott see Savonlinna, Fin.	F13	8
Nysted, Den.	B7	16
Nyunzu, D.R.C.	F5	66
Nyūzen, Japan	C10	40
Nyvrovo, Russia	F17	34
Nzébéla, Gui.	H3	64
Nzérékoré, Gui.	H3	64
N'zeto, Ang.	B1	68
Nzwani, i., Com.	C7	68
O		
Oahe, Lake, res., U.S.	A12	126
Oahe Dam, dam, S.D., U.S.	C12	126
Oahu, i., Hi., U.S.	B4	78a
Oakbank, Austl.	I3	76
Oak Bay, B.C., Can.	H7	138
Oak Bluffs, Ma., U.S.	C15	114
Oakburn, Mb., Can.	D13	124
Oak City, N.C., U.S.	I8	114
Oak City, Ut., U.S.	D4	132
Oakdale, Ca., U.S.	F5	134
Oakdale, La., U.S.	G6	122
Oakdale, Ne., U.S.	E14	126
Oakes, N.D., U.S.	A14	126
Oakesdale, Wa., U.S.	C9	136
Oakey, Austl.	F8	76
Oakfield, Me., U.S.	D8	110
Oakfield, Wi., U.S.	H10	118
Oak Grove, La., U.S.	E7	122
Oak Harbor, Wa., U.S.	B4	136
Oak Hill, Fl., U.S.	H5	116
Oak Hill, Oh., U.S.	F3	114
Oak Hill, W.V., U.S.	G4	114
Oakhurst, Ca., U.S.	F6	134
Oak Knolls, Ca., U.S.	I5	134
Oak Lake, Mb., Can.	E13	124
Oak Lake, l., Mb., Can.	E13	124
Oak Lake, l., On., Can.	A5	118
Oakland, Ca., U.S.	F3	134
Oakland, Ia., U.S.	C2	120
Oakland, Me., U.S.	F7	110
Oakland, Md., U.S.	E6	114
Oakland, Ms., U.S.	C9	122
Oakland, Ne., U.S.	C1	120
Oakland, Or., U.S.	G3	136
Oakland City, In., U.S.	F10	120
Oakland Park, Fl., U.S.	J5	116
Oak Lawn, Il., U.S.	G2	112
Oakley, Id., U.S.	H13	136
Oakley, Ks., U.S.	B8	128
Oakman, Al., U.S.	D11	122
Oakohay Creek, stm., Ms., U.S.	F9	122
Oakover, stm., Austl.	D4	74
Oak Park, Il., U.S.	G2	112
Oak Ridge, Tn., U.S.	H1	114
Oak Ridge National Laboratory, sci., Tn., U.S.	H1	114
Oaktown, In., U.S.	F10	120
Oak View, Ca., U.S.	I6	134
Oakville, Mb., Can.	E15	124
Oakville, On., Can.	E10	112
Oakwood, Oh., U.S.	C1	114
Oamaru, N.Z.	G4	80
Oancea, Rom.	D14	26
Ōarai, Japan	C13	40
Oatman, Az., U.S.	H2	132
Oaxaca, state, Mex.	G10	100
Oaxaca de Juárez, Mex.	G10	100
Ob', stm., Russia	A11	32
Obabika Lake, l., On., Can.	A9	112
Obal', stm., Bela.	E12	10
Obala, Cam.	D2	66
Obama, Japan	D8	40
Obama, Japan	G3	40
Oban, Austl.	C2	76
Oban, Scot., U.K.	E7	12
Obanazawa, Japan	A13	40
O Barco de Valdeorras, Spain	B3	20
Ob Bay see Obskaja guba, b., Russia	A12	32
Obed, Ab., Can.	C13	138
Obeliai, Lith.	E8	10
Oberá, Arg.	C10	92
Oberhausen, Ger.	E2	16
Oberlin, La., U.S.	G6	122
Oberlin, Oh., U.S.	C3	114
Oberösterreich, state, Aus.	B10	22
Oberpullendorf, Aus.	C13	22
Oberursel, Ger.	F4	16
Oberviechtach, Ger.	G8	16
Ob Gulf see Obskaja guba, b., Russia	A12	32
Obi, Kepulauan, is., Indon.	F8	44
Obi, Pulau, i., Indon.	F8	44
Obi, Selat, strt., Indon.	F8	44
Óbidos, Braz.	D6	84
Obihiro, Japan	C15	38
Obi Islands see Obi, Kepulauan, is., Indon.	F8	44
Obion, Tn., U.S.	H8	120
Obion, stm., Tn., U.S.	H8	120
Obion, Middle Fork, stm., Tn., U.S.	H9	120
Oblačnaja, gora, mtn., Russia	C11	38
Oblong, Il., U.S.	F9	120
Obluče, Russia	G15	34
Obninsk, Russia	E19	10
Obnova, Blg.	F12	26
Obo, C.A.R.	C5	66
Obock, Dji.	E8	62
Obokote, D.R.C.	E5	66
Obozërskij, Russia	E19	8
O'Brien, Or., U.S.	A2	134
Obrovac, Cro.	F12	22
Obša, stm., Russia	E16	10
Obščij syrt, mts., Eur.	D8	32
Obskaja guba, b., Russia	A12	32
Obuasi, Ghana	H4	64
Obudu, Nig.	H6	64
Ocala, Fl., U.S.	G3	116
Ocamo, stm., Ven.	F9	86
Ocampo, Mex.	A4	100
Ocaña, Col.	C5	86
Ocaña, Spain	E7	20
Occhito, Lago di, res., Italy	C8	24
Occidental, Cordillera, mts., Col.	E3	86
Oceana, W.V., U.S.	G4	114
Ocean Cape, c., Ak., U.S.	E12	140
Ocean City, Md., U.S.	F10	114
Ocean City, N.J., U.S.	E11	114
Ocean Falls, B.C., Can.	D3	138
Ocean Island see Banaba, i., Kir.	D7	72
Ocean Park, Wa., U.S.	D2	136
Oceanside, Ca., U.S.	J8	134
Ocean Springs, Ms., U.S.	G10	122
Ocheyedan, Ia., U.S.	H3	118
Ōchi, Japan	E7	40
Ochlocknee, Ga., U.S.	F1	116
Ochlockonee, stm., U.S.	G14	122
Ocho Rios, Jam.	i13	104d
Ochsenfurt, Ger.	G5	16
Ocilla, Ga., U.S.	E2	116
Ockelbo, Swe.	F7	8
Ocmulgee National Monument, p.o.i., Ga., U.S.	D2	116
Ocnita, Mol.	A14	26
Ocoa, Bahía de, b., Dom. Rep.	C12	102
Ocoee, Fl., U.S.	H4	116
Ocoña, stm., Peru	G3	84
Oconee, stm., Ga., U.S.	D3	116
Oconee, Lake, res., Ga., U.S.	C2	116
Oconomowoc, Wi., U.S.	A9	120
Oconto, Wi., U.S.	D2	112
Oconto Falls, Wi., U.S.	D1	112
Ocosingo, Mex.	G12	100
Ocotal, Nic.	F4	102
Ocotes, Cerro, mtn., Mex.	B5	100
Ocotlán, Mex.	E7	100
Ocotlán de Morelos, Mex.	G10	100
Ocozocuautla, Mex.	G12	100
Ocracoke Island, i., N.C., U.S.	A10	116
Ocumare del Tuy, Ven.	B8	86
Oda, Ghana	H4	64
Ōda, Japan	D5	40
Oda, Jabal, mtn., Sudan	C7	62
Odaka, Japan	B14	40
Ōdate, Japan	D14	38
Odawara, Japan	D12	40
Odebolt, Ia., U.S.	B2	120
Odell, Il., U.S.	D9	120
Odell, Tx., U.S.	G9	128
Odem, Tx., U.S.	G10	130
Odemira, Port.	G2	20
Ödemiş, Tur.	E10	28
Odendaalsrus, S. Afr.	E8	70
Odense, Den.	I3	8
Odenwald, mts., Ger.	G4	16
Oder (Odra), stm., Eur.	D10	16
Oderzo, Italy	E9	22
Odesa, Ukr.	C17	26
Odesa, co., Ukr.	C16	26
Odessa see Odesa, Ukr.	C17	26
Odessa, Mo., U.S.	F3	120
Odessa, Tx., U.S.	C5	130
Odessa, Wa., U.S.	C8	136
Odesskoe, Russia	D12	32
Odiel, stm., Spain	G4	20
Odienné, C. Iv.	H3	64
Odin, Mount, mtn., B.C., Can.	F12	138
Odincovo, Russia	E20	10
Odobeşti, Rom.	D13	26
Odolanów, Pol.	E13	16
Odon, In., U.S.	F11	120
O'Donnell, Tx., U.S.	B6	130
Odorheiu Secuiesc, Rom.	C12	26
Odra (Oder), stm., Eur.	D10	16
Odrzywół, Pol.	E16	16
Odum, Ga., U.S.	E3	116
Odžaci, Yugo.	D6	26
Oebisfelde, Ger.	D6	16
Oeiras, Braz.	D4	88
Oelsnitz, Ger.	F8	16
Oelwein, Ia., U.S.	B6	120
Oenpelli, Austl.	B6	74
Oetz, Aus.	C7	22
O'Fallon, Mo., U.S.	F7	120
Ofanto, stm., Italy	D9	24
Ofaqim, Isr.	G5	58
Offa, Nig.	H5	64
Offaly, state, Ire.	H5	12
Offenbach am Main, Ger.	F4	16
Offenburg, Ger.	H3	16
Oficina Alemania, Chile	B3	92
Ofu, i., Am. Sam.	h13	79c
Ogaden, reg., Afr.	F8	62
Ōgaki, Japan	D9	40
Ogallala, Ne., U.S.	F11	126
Ogan, stm., Indon.	E4	50
Ogasawara-guntō, is., Japan	G18	30
Ogatsu, Japan	A14	40
Ogawa, Japan	G3	40
Ogbomosho, Nig.	H5	64
Ogden, Ks., U.S.	B12	128
Ogden, Ut., U.S.	B5	132
Ogdensburg, N.Y., U.S.	D14	112
Ogeechee, stm., Ga., U.S.	D4	116
Ogema, Sk., Can.	E8	124
Ogidaki Mountain, hill, On., Can.	A6	112
Ogilvie, Mn., U.S.	F5	118
Ogilvie Mountains, mts., Yk., Can.	C3	106
Oglesby, Il., U.S.	C8	120
Oglethorpe, Ga., U.S.	D1	116
Ogliastra, reg., Italy	E3	24
Oglio, stm., Italy	E6	22
Ogmore, Austl.	D7	76
Ognon, stm., Fr.	G15	14
Ogoja, Nig.	H6	64
Ogoki, stm., On., Can.	E13	106
Ogooué, stm., Afr.	I7	64
Ogōri, Japan	E4	40
Ogosta, stm., Blg.	F10	26
Ogre, Lat.	D7	10
Ogre, stm., Lat.	D8	10
O Grove, Spain	B2	20
Ogulin, Cro.	E12	22
Ogunquit, Me., U.S.	G6	110
Ogurdžaly, ostrov, i., Turkmen.	B7	56
Oğuzeli, Tur.	B8	58
Oha, Russia	F17	34
Ohanet, Alg.	D6	64
Ōhara, Japan	D13	40
O'Higgins, Cabo, c., Chile	e30	78l
O'Higgins, Lago (San Martín, Lago), l., S.A.	I2	90
Ohio, state, U.S.	D3	114
Ohio, stm., U.S.	G9	120
Ohio Peak, mtn., Co., U.S.	E9	132
'Ohonua, Tonga	o15	78e
Ohoopee, stm., Ga., U.S.	D3	116
Ohota, stm., Russia	E17	34
Ohotsk, Russia	E17	34
Ohře, stm., Eur.	F9	16
Ohrid, Mac.	B3	28
Ohrid, Lake, l., Eur.	D14	24
Ohrigstad, S. Afr.	D10	70
Öhringen, Ger.	G5	16
Ohuira, Bahía de, l., Mex.	C4	100
Ōi, stm., Japan	E11	40
Oiapoque, Braz.	C7	84
Oiapoque (Oyapok), stm., S.A.	C7	84
Oies, Île aux, i., Qc., Can.	C6	110
Oil Center, N.M., U.S.	B4	130
Oil City, La., U.S.	E4	122
Oil City, Pa., U.S.	C6	114
Oildale, Ca., U.S.	H7	134
Oilton, Ok., U.S.	A2	122
Oilton, Tx., U.S.	G9	130
Oil Trough, Ar., U.S.	B7	122
Oise, state, Fr.	E11	14
Oise, stm., Eur.	E11	14
Oistins, Barb.	n8	105d
Ōita, Japan	F4	40
Ōita, state, Japan	F4	40
Oituz, Pasul, p., Rom.	C13	26
Ojat', stm., Russia	F16	8
Öje, Swe.	F5	8
Ojinaga, Mex.	A6	100
Ojiya, Japan	B11	40
Ojmjakon, Russia	D17	34
Ojocaliente, Mex.	D7	100
Ojo de la Casa, Mex.	C1	130
Ojo del Carrizo, Mex.	E2	130
Ojo de Liebre, Laguna, b., Mex.	B1	100
Ojos del Salado, Nevado, mtn., S.A.	C3	92
Ojos Negros, Mex.	L9	134
Oka, stm., Russia	D6	32
Oka, stm., Russia	D18	32
Okaba, Indon.	G10	44
Okahandja, Nmb.	B3	70
Okaihau, N.Z.	B5	80
Okak Islands, is., Nf., Can.	F13	141
Okanagan (Okanogan), stm., N.A.	G11	138
Okanagan Falls, B.C., Can.	G11	138
Okanagan Lake, l., B.C., Can.	G10	138
Okanagan Landing, B.C., Can.	F11	138
Okanogan, Wa., U.S.	B7	136
Okanogan (Okanagan), stm., N.A.	G11	138
Okanogan Range, mts., Can.	A6	136
Okāra, Pak.	C4	54
Okaukuejo, Nmb.	D2	68
Okavango (Cubango), stm., Afr.	D2	68
Okavango Delta, Bots.	D3	68
Ōkawa, Japan	F3	40
Okawville, Il., U.S.	F8	120
Okaya, Japan	C11	40
Okayama, Japan	E6	40
Okayama, state, Japan	E6	40
Okazaki, Japan	E10	40
Okeechobee, Fl., U.S.	I5	116
Okeechobee, Lake, l., Fl., U.S.	J5	116

Name	Map Ref.	Page
Okeene, Ok., U.S.	E10	128
Okefenokee Swamp, sw., U.S.	F3	116
Okemos, Mi., U.S.	B1	114
Okene, Nig.	H6	64
Okhaldunggā, Nepal	E11	54
Okhotsk, Sea of, Asia	D18	30
Okhotsk Basin, unds.	D17	142
Okhtyrka, Ukr.	D4	32
Okiep, S. Afr.	F3	70
Okinawa, Japan	I18	39a
Okinawa Island see Okinawa-jima, i., Japan	I19	39a
Okinawa-jima, i., Japan	I19	39a
Okinawa-shotō, is., Japan	I18	39a
Okino-Erabu-shima, i., Japan	I19	39a
Oki-shotō, is., Japan	C6	40
Okitipupa, Nig.	H5	64
Oklahoma, state, U.S.	F11	128
Oklahoma City, Ok., U.S.	F11	128
Oklawaha, Fl., U.S.	G4	116
Oklee, Mn., U.S.	D3	118
Okmulgee, Ok., U.S.	B3	122
Okollo, Ug.	D6	66
Okolona, Ar., U.S.	D5	122
Okolona, Ky., U.S.	F12	120
Okondja, Gabon	E2	66
Okonek, Pol.	C12	16
Okotoks, Ab., Can.	F16	138
Okoyo, Congo	E2	66
Oktjabr', Russia	C20	10
Oktjabr'sk, Kaz.	E9	32
Oktjabr'skij, Russia	F20	8
Oktjabr'skij, Russia	G21	8
Oktjabr'skij, Russia	D8	32
Oktjabr'skij, Russia	F14	34
Oktjabr'skoe, Kaz.	D11	32
Oktjabr'skoe, Russia	B10	32
Ōkuchi, Japan	G3	40
Okulovka, Russia	B16	10
Okunëv Nos, Russia	C25	8
Okushiri-tō, i., Japan	C13	38
Okuta, Nig.	H5	64
Okwa, stm., Afr.	C6	70
Ola, Russia	E19	34
Ola, Ar., U.S.	B5	122
Ólafsfjörður, Ice.	j30	8a
Olancha, Ca., U.S.	G8	134
Olancha Peak, mtn., Ca., U.S.	G7	134
Olanchito, Hond.	E4	102
Öland, i., Swe.	H7	8
Olanta, S.C., U.S.	C6	116
Olary, Austl.	I3	76
Olathe, Co., U.S.	E8	132
Olathe, Ks., U.S.	F3	120
Olavarría, Arg.	H7	92
Oława (Ohlau), Pol.	F13	16
Olbia, Italy	D3	24
Olcott, N.Y., U.S.	E11	112
Old Castille see Castilla la Vieja, hist. reg., Spain	C7	20
Old Cork, Austl.	D3	76
Old Crow, Yk., Can.	C12	140
Old Crow, stm., N.A.	C11	140
Olden, Tx., U.S.	B9	130
Oldenburg, Ger.	C3	16
Oldenburg, hist. reg., Ger.	C4	16
Oldenburg in Holstein, Ger.	B6	16
Oldenzaal, Neth.	B15	14
Old Faithful Geyser, gysr., Wy., U.S.	F16	136
Old Forge, Pa., U.S.	C10	114
Old Fort Bay see Vieux-Fort, Qc., Can.	i22	107a
Oldham, Eng., U.K.	H10	12
Oldham, S.D., U.S.	C15	126
Old Harbor, Ak., U.S.	E9	140
Old Harbour, Jam.	j13	104d
Old Hickory Lake, res., Tn., U.S.	H11	120
Oldman, stm., Ab., Can.	G19	138
Old Mkushi, Zam.	C4	68
Old Norwood, Monts.	D3	105a
Old Road, Antig.	f4	105b
Old Road Bluff, c., Antig.	f4	105b
Old Road Town, St. K./N.	C2	105a
Olds, Ab., Can.	E16	138
Old Saybrook, Ct., U.S.	C13	114
Old Speck Mountain, mtn., Me., U.S.	F5	110
Old Tate, Bots.	B8	70
Old Town, Me., U.S.	F8	110
Olduvai Gorge, val., Tan.	E7	66
Old Wives Lake, l., Sk., Can.	D8	124
Olean, N.Y., U.S.	B7	114
O'Leary, P.E., Can.	D12	110
Olecko, Pol.	B18	16
Olëkma, stm., Russia	E13	34
Olekminsk, Russia	D13	34
Olëkminskij Stanovik, mts., Russia	F12	34
Ølen, Nor.	G1	8
Olenegorsk, Russia	B15	8
Olenëk, Russia	C11	34
Olenëk, stm., Russia	C12	34
Olenëkskij zaliv, b., Russia	B13	34
Olenij, ostrov, i., Russia	B4	34
Olenino, Russia	D16	10
Oléron, Île d', i., Fr.	D4	18
Oleśnica, Pol.	E13	16
Olesno, Pol.	F14	16
Ol'ga, Russia	C11	38
Olga, Mount, mtn., Austl.	D6	74
Olgastretet, strt., Nor.	B30	141
Ölgiy, Mong.	E16	32
Olhão, Port.	G3	20
Olho d'Água das Flores, Braz.	E7	88
Ol'hon, ostrov, i., Russia	F10	34
Olib, Otok, i., Cro.	F11	22
Olifants (Elefantes), stm., Afr.	D10	70
Olifants, stm., S. Afr.	H6	70
Olifants, stm., S. Afr.	H4	70
Olifantshoek, S. Afr.	E6	70
Ólimbos (Olympus), mtn., Cyp.	C3	58
Olímpia, Braz.	K1	88
Olin, Ia., U.S.	B6	120
Olinda, Braz.	D8	88
Olio, Austl.	C4	76
Olite, Spain	B9	20
Oliva, Arg.	F6	92
Oliva, Spain	F10	20
Oliva de la Frontera, Spain	F3	20
Olivares, Cerro de, mtn., S.A.	E2	92
Olive Branch, Ms., U.S.	C9	122
Olivees Mountain, mtn., St. K./N.	C2	105a
Olive Hill, Ky., U.S.	F2	114
Olivehurst, Ca., U.S.	D4	134
Oliveira, Braz.	K3	88
Oliveira dos Brejinhos, Braz.	G4	88
Olivenza, Spain	F3	20
Oliver Springs, Tn., U.S.	H13	120
Olivet, Mi., U.S.	B1	114
Olivet, S.D., U.S.	D15	126
Olji Moron, stm., China	B4	38
Oljutorskij, mys, c., Russia	E23	34
Oljutorskij zaliv, b., Russia	D22	34
Olla, La., U.S.	F6	122
Ollagüe, Chile	D3	90
Ollagüe, Volcán, vol., S.A.	D3	90
Ollei, Palau	f8	78b
Olmedo, Spain	C6	20
Olmos, Peru	E2	84
Olney, Mt., U.S.	B12	136
Olney, Tx., U.S.	H10	128
Olomouc, Czech Rep.	G13	16
Olonec, Russia	F15	8
Olongapo, Phil.	C2	52
Oloron-Sainte-Marie, Fr.	F5	18
Olot, Spain	B13	20
Olovjannaja, Russia	F12	34
Olpe, Ger.	E3	16
Olpe, Ks., U.S.	F1	120
Olsufevo, Russia	G16	10
Olsztyn, Pol.	C16	16
Olsztyn, state, Pol.	C16	16
Olt, state, Rom.	E11	26
Olt, stm., Rom.	D11	26
Olta, Arg.	E4	92
Olten, Switz.	C4	22
Olteni, Rom.	E12	26
Oltenița, Rom.	E13	26
Oltet, stm., Rom.	E10	26
Olton, Tx., U.S.	G6	128
Oluan Pi, c., Tai.	K9	42
Olustee, Fl., U.S.	F3	116
Olutanga Island, i., Phil.	G4	52
Olvera, Spain	H5	20
Olympia, Wa., U.S.	C3	136
Olympiá, hist., Grc.	F4	28
Olympia see Olympiá, hist., Grc.	F4	28
Olympic Mountains, mts., Wa., U.S.	C3	136
Olympic National Park, p.o.i., Wa., U.S.	C3	136
Ólympos (Olympus, Mount), mtn., Grc.	C5	28
Olympus see Ólimbos, mtn., Cyp.	C3	58
Olympus, Mount see Ólympos, mtn., Grc.	C5	28
Olympus, Mount, mtn., Wa., U.S.	C3	136
Om', stm., Russia	D13	32
Ōmachi, Japan	C10	40
Omae-zaki, c., Japan	E11	40
Ōmagari, Japan	E14	38
Omagh, N. Ire., U.K.	G5	12
Omaha, Ne., U.S.	C2	120
Omaha, Tx., U.S.	D4	122
Omaheke, state, Nmb.	C4	70
Omak, Wa., U.S.	B7	136
Oman, ctry., Asia	F8	56
Oman, Gulf of, b., Asia	E8	56
Omaruru, Nmb.	B3	70
Omaruru, stm., Nmb.	B2	70
Omatako, mtn., Nmb.	B3	70
Omatako, stm., Nmb.	B3	70
Omate, Peru	G3	84
Omboué, Gabon	E1	66
Ombrone, stm., Italy	H8	22
Omčak, Russia	D18	34
Omdurman see Umm Durmān, Sudan	D6	62
Ōme, Japan	D12	40
Omega, Ga., U.S.	E2	116
Omegna, Italy	E5	22
Omemee, On., Can.	D11	112
Omeo, Austl.	K6	76
Ömerköy, Tur.	D10	28
Ömerli Barajı, res., Tur.	C12	28
Ometepe, Isla de, i., Nic.	G5	102
Ometepec, Mex.	G9	100
Ōmi-hachiman, Japan	D8	40
Omineca, stm., B.C., Can.	D6	106
Omineca Mountains, mts., B.C., Can.	D5	106
Ōmiya, Japan	D12	40
Ommaney, Cape, c., Ak., U.S.	E13	140
Ommanney Bay, b., Nu., Can.	A10	106
Omo, stm., Afr.	F7	62
Omoloj, stm., Russia	B15	34
Omolon, stm., Russia	C20	34
Omsk, Russia	C12	32
Omsukčan, Russia	D20	34
Omul, Vârful, mtn., Rom.	D12	26
Ōmura, Japan	G2	40
Omurtag, Blg.	F13	26
Ōmuta, Japan	F3	40
Omutinskij, Russia	C11	32
Omutninsk, Russia	C8	32
Onabas, Mex.	A4	100
Onaga, Ks., U.S.	E1	120
Onaman Lake, l., On., Can.	A11	118
Onamia, Mn., U.S.	E5	118
Onangué, Lac, l., Gabon	E1	66
Onaping Lake, l., On., Can.	A8	112
Onarga, Il., U.S.	D10	120
Onatchiway, Lac, res., Qc., Can.	A5	110
Onawa, Ia., U.S.	B1	120
Onaway, Mi., U.S.	C5	112
Oncativo, Arg.	E6	92
Once, Canal Numero, can., Arg.	H8	92
Oncócua, Ang.	D1	68
Onda, Spain	E10	20
Ondangwa, Nmb.	D2	68
Ondas, stm., Braz.	G3	88
Ondava, stm., Slov.	H17	16
Ondjiva, Ang.	D2	68
Ondo, Japan	E5	40
Ondo, Nig.	H5	64
Öndörhaan, Mong.	B7	36
Ondozero, ozero, l., Russia	E15	8
Oneco, Fl., U.S.	I3	116
Onega, Russia	E17	8
Onega, stm., Russia	E18	8
Onega, Lake see Onežskoe ozero, l., Russia	F16	8
Onega Bay see Onežskaja guba, b., Russia	D17	8
One Hundred and Two, stm., Mo., U.S.	D3	120
One Hundred Fifty Mile House, B.C., Can.	D9	138
One Hundred Mile House, B.C., Can.	E9	138
Oneida, Il., U.S.	C7	120
Oneida, N.Y., U.S.	E14	112
Oneida, Tn., U.S.	H13	120
Oneida Lake, l., N.Y., U.S.	E14	112
O'Neill, Ne., U.S.	E14	126
Onekama, Mi., U.S.	D3	112
Onekotan, ostrov, i., Russia	G20	34
Oneonta, Al., U.S.	D12	122
Oneonta, N.Y., U.S.	B10	114
Onești, Rom.	C13	26
Onevai, i., Tonga	n14	78e
Onežskaja guba (Onega Bay), b., Russia	D17	8
Onežskij poluostrov, pen., Russia	D17	8
Onežskoe ozero (Onega, Lake), l., Russia	F16	8
Ongjin-ŭp, Kor., N.	F6	38
Ongniud Qi, China	C3	38
Ongole, India	D5	53
Onilahy, stm., Madag.	F7	68
Onion Creek, stm., Tx., U.S.	D10	130
Onitsha, Nig.	H6	64
Ōno, Japan	D9	40
Onoda, Japan	F4	40
Onomichi, Japan	E6	40
Onon, Mong.	B7	36
Onon Gol, stm., Asia	G11	34
Onoto, Ven.	C9	86
Onotoa, at., Kir.	D8	72
Onoway, Ab., Can.	C16	138
Ons, Illa de, i., Spain	B1	20
Onset, Ma., U.S.	C15	114
Onslow, Austl.	D3	74
Onslow Bay, b., N.C., U.S.	B8	116
On-take, vol., Japan	H3	40
Ontake-san, vol., Japan	D10	40
Ontario, Ca., U.S.	I8	134
Ontario, Or., U.S.	F10	136
Ontario, state, Can.	E13	106
Ontario, Lake, l., N.A.	E11	112
Ontinyent, Spain	F10	20
Ontojärvi, l., Fin.	D13	8
Ontonagon, Mi., U.S.	E9	118
Ontong Java, at., Sol. Is.	D7	72
Onverwacht, Sur.	B6	84
Oodnadatta, Austl.	E7	74
Ooldea, Austl.	F6	74
Oologah, Ok., U.S.	H2	120
Oologah Lake, res., Ok., U.S.	H2	120
Oorlogskloof, stm., S. Afr.	G4	70
Oos-Londen see East London, S. Afr.	H8	70
Oostburg, Wi., U.S.	E2	112
Oostelijk Flevoland, reg., Neth.	B14	14
Oostende, Bel.	C11	14
Oosterhout, Neth.	C13	14
Oosterschelde, est., Neth.	C12	14
Ootsa Lake, B.C., Can.	C4	138
Ootsa Lake, res., B.C., Can.	C4	138
Opaka, Blg.	F13	26
Opala, D.R.C.	E4	66
Oparino, Russia	G22	8
Opatija, Cro.	E11	22
Opava, Czech Rep.	G13	16
Opawica, stm., Qc., Can.	A2	110
Opečenskij Posad, Russia	B17	10
Opelika, Al., U.S.	E13	122
Opelousas, La., U.S.	G6	122
Opeongo, stm., On., Can.	C12	112
Opeongo Lake, l., On., Can.	C11	112
Ophir, Ak., U.S.	D8	140
Ophir, Or., U.S.	H2	136
Opihikao, Hi., U.S.	D7	78a
Opinaca, stm., Qc., Can.	E15	106
Opiscotéo, Lac, l., Qc., Can.	E17	106
Opobo, Nig.	I6	64
Opočka, Russia	D11	10
Opoczno, Pol.	E16	16
Opole, Pol.	F13	16
Opole, state, Pol.	F13	16
Opotiki, N.Z.	D7	80
Oppdal, Nor.	E3	8
Oppland, state, Nor.	F3	8
Opportunity, Mt., U.S.	D14	136
Opportunity, Wa., U.S.	C9	136
Optima Lake, res., Ok., U.S.	E7	128
Opua, N.Z.	B6	80
Opunake, N.Z.	D5	80
Opuwo, Nmb.	D1	68
Oquawka, Il., U.S.	K7	118
Or, Côte d', mts., Fr.	G13	14
Oracle, Az., U.S.	K6	132
Oradea, Rom.	B8	26
Öræfajökull, ice, Ice.	k31	8a
Orahovica, Cro.	E14	22
Orai, India	F7	54
Oraibi Wash, stm., Az., U.S.	H6	132
Oral see Ural'sk, Kaz.	D8	32
Oran see Wahran, Alg.	B4	64
Orange, Austl.	I7	76
Orange, Fr.	E10	18
Orange, Ma., U.S.	B13	114
Orange, Tx., U.S.	G5	122
Orange, Va., U.S.	F7	114
Orange (Oranje) (Senqu), stm., Afr.	F3	70
Orange, Cabo, c., Braz.	C7	84
Orangeburg, S.C., U.S.	C4	116
Orange City, Ia., U.S.	A1	120
Orange Cove, Ca., U.S.	G6	134
Orange Free State see Free State, state, S. Afr.	F8	70
Orange Grove, Tx., U.S.	G9	130
Orange Lake, Fl., U.S.	G3	116
Orange Lake, l., Fl., U.S.	G3	116
Orangeville, On., Can.	E9	112
Orangeville, Ut., U.S.	D5	132
Orange Walk, Belize	C3	102
Orango, Ilha de, i., Gui.-B.	G1	64
Orani, Phil.	C3	52
Oranienburg, Ger.	D8	16
Oranje see Orange, stm., Afr.	F3	70
Oranje Gebergte, mts., Sur.	C6	84
Oranjemund, Nmb.	F3	70
Oranjestad, Aruba	o19	104g
Oranjestad, Neth. Ant.	C1	105a
Oranje Vrijstaat see Free State, state, S. Afr.	F8	70
Orăștie, Rom.	D10	26
Orba Co, l., China	A8	54
Orbetello, Italy	H8	22
Órbigo, stm., Spain	B5	20
Orbisonia, Pa., U.S.	D8	114
Orbost, Austl.	K7	76
Örbyhus, Swe.	F7	8
Orcadas, sci., Ant.	B36	81
Orchard City, Co., U.S.	E8	132
Orchard Homes, Mt., U.S.	D12	136
Orchard Mesa, Co., U.S.	E8	132
Orchard Park, N.Y., U.S.	B7	114
Ord, Ne., U.S.	F14	126
Ord, stm., Austl.	C5	74
Ord, Mount, mtn., Austl.	C5	74
Ordenes see Ordes, Spain	A2	20
Orderville, Ut., U.S.	F4	132
Ordes, Spain	A2	20
Ordesa y Monte Perdido, Parque Nacional de, p.o.i., Spain	B10	20
Ord Mountain, mtn., Ca., U.S.	I9	134
Ordos Desert see Mu Us Shamo, des., China	B3	42
Ord River, Austl.	C5	74
Ordu, Tur.	A4	56
Ordway, Co., U.S.	C5	128
Ordžonikidzeabad, Taj.	B10	56
Örebro, Swe.	G6	8
Örebro, state, Swe.	G6	8
Oredež, Russia	B13	10
Oredež, stm., Russia	B13	10
Oregon, Il., U.S.	B8	120
Oregon, Mo., U.S.	D2	120
Oregon, Oh., U.S.	C2	114
Oregon, state, U.S.	G6	136
Oregon Caves National Monument, p.o.i., Or., U.S.	A2	134
Oregon City, Or., U.S.	E4	136
Oregon Dunes National Recreation Area, p.o.i., Or., U.S.	G2	136
Orehovo-Zuevo, Russia	E21	10
Orel, Russia	G18	10
Orel', ozero, l., Russia	F16	34
Orellana, Peru	E2	84
Orellana, Embalse de, res., Spain	E5	20
Orem, Ut., U.S.	C5	132
Ore Mountains, mts., Eur.	F8	16
Orenburg, Russia	D8	32
Örencik, Tur.	D12	28
Orense, Arg.	I8	92
Orense see Ourense, Spain	B3	20
Orense see Ourense, co., Spain	B3	20
Oreor, i., Palau	g8	78b
Orestes Pereyra, Mex.	B6	100
Orestiáda, Grc.	B9	28
Orford Ness, c., Eng., U.K.	I14	12
Organ Pipe Cactus National Monument, p.o.i., Az., U.S.	K4	132
Orgelet, Fr.	H14	14
Orgosolo, Italy	D3	24
Orgūn, Afg.	C10	56
Orhangazi, Tur.	C12	28
Orhei, Mol.	B15	26
Orhon, stm., Mong.	B5	36
Orichuna, stm., Ven.	D7	86
Orick, Ca., U.S.	B1	134
Orient, Ia., U.S.	C3	120
Orient, Wa., U.S.	B8	136
Oriental, Cordillera, mts., Col.	E5	86
Oriental, Cordillera, mts., Peru	F3	84
Orientos, Austl.	G3	76
Orihuela see Oriola, Spain	F10	20
Orillia, On., Can.	D10	112
Orimattila, Fin.	F11	8
Orinduik, Guy.	E11	86
Orinoco, stm., S.A.	C10	86
Orinoco, Delta del, Ven.	C11	86
Oriola, Spain	F10	20
Orion, Il., U.S.	C7	120
Oriskany, N.Y., U.S.	E14	112
Orissa, state, India	D5	46
Orissaare, Est.	B5	10
Oristano, Italy	E2	24
Oristano, Golfo di, b., Italy	E2	24
Orituco, stm., Ven.	C8	86
Orivesi, l., Fin.	E13	8
Oriximiná, Braz.	D6	84
Orizaba, Mex.	F10	100
Orjahovo, Blg.	F10	26
Orjen, mtn., Yugo.	G5	26
Orkney, Sk., Can.	E5	124
Orkney, S. Afr.	E8	70
Orkney Islands, is., Scot., U.K.	C10	12
Orlândia, Braz.	K1	88
Orlando, Fl., U.S.	H4	116
Orléanais, hist. reg., Fr.	F11	14
Orleans, On., Can.	C14	112
Orléans, Fr.	G10	14
Orleans, Ca., U.S.	B2	134
Orleans, Ma., U.S.	C15	114
Orleans, Ne., U.S.	A9	128
Orleans, Vt., U.S.	F4	110
Orléans, Canal d', can., Fr.	G11	14
Orléans, Île d', i., Qc., Can.	D6	110
Orlik, Russia	D18	32
Orlovskaja oblast', co., Russia	H19	10
Orly, Fr.	F11	14
Ormāra, Pak.	D9	56
Ormiston, Sk., Can.	E8	124
Ormoc, Phil.	E5	52
Ormond Beach, Fl., U.S.	G4	116
Ornain, stm., Fr.	F14	14
Ornans, Fr.	G15	14
Orne, state, Fr.	F8	14
Orne, stm., Fr.	E14	14
Orne, stm., Fr.	F8	14
Ornö, i., Swe.	G8	8
Örnsköldsvik, Swe.	E8	8
Oročen, Russia	E14	34
Orocovis, P.R.	B3	104a
Orocué, Col.	E6	86
Orofino, Id., U.S.	D10	136
Orog nuur, l., Mong.	B5	36
Orohena, Mont, mtn., Fr. Poly.	v22	78h
Oroluk, at., Micron.	C6	72
Oromocto, N.B., Can.	E10	110
Oromocto Lake, l., N.B., Can.	E10	110
Oron, Nig.	I6	64
Orona, at., Kir.	D9	72
Orono, On., Can.	D11	112
Orono, Me., U.S.	F8	110
Orontes (Asi), stm., Asia	B7	58
Oroquieta, Phil.	F4	52
Orós, Braz.	D6	88
Orós, Açude, res., Braz.	D6	88
Orosei, Italy	D3	24
Orosei, Golfo di, b., Italy	D3	24
Orosháza, Hung.	C7	26
Oroszlány, Hung.	B5	26
Orote Peninsula, pen., Guam	j9	78c
Oroville, Ca., U.S.	D4	134
Oroville, Lake, res., Ca., U.S.	D4	134
Orpheus Island, i., Austl.	B6	76
Orrick, Mo., U.S.	E3	120
Orrin, N.D., U.S.	F13	124
Orroroo, Austl.	I2	76
Orrs Island, Me., U.S.	G7	110
Orša, Bela.	F13	10
Orsk, Russia	D9	32
Orșova, Rom.	E9	26
Ortaca, Tur.	G11	28
Ortakent, Tur.	F10	28
Ortaklar, Tur.	F10	28
Orta Nova, Italy	C9	24
Ortega, Col.	F4	86
Ortegal, Cabo, c., Spain	A2	20
Orteguaza, stm., Col.	G4	86
Orthon, stm., Bol.	B3	90
Ortigueira, Spain	A3	20
Orting, Wa., U.S.	C4	136
Ortiz, Mex.	A3	100
Ortiz, Ven.	C8	86
Ortona, Italy	H11	22
Ortonville, Mn., U.S.	F2	118
Orūmīyeh, Iran	B6	56
Orūmīyeh, Daryācheh-ye (Urmia, Lake), l., Iran	B6	56
Orust, i., Swe.	G4	8
Orvieto, Italy	H9	22
Orwell, Oh., U.S.	C5	114
Orxon, stm., China	B8	36
Orzinuovi, Italy	E6	22
Orzyc, stm., Pol.	D17	16
Oš, Kyrg.	F12	32
Os, Nor.	E4	8
Osa, Península de, pen., C.R.	H6	102
Osage, Ia., U.S.	H6	118
Osage, Wy., U.S.	D8	126
Osage, stm., Mo., U.S.	F5	120
Osage Beach, Mo., U.S.	F5	120
Osage City, Ks., U.S.	F2	120
Ōsaka, Japan	E8	40
Ōsaka, state, Japan	E8	40
Osakarovka, Kaz.	D12	32
Ōsaka-wan, b., Japan	E8	40
Osăm, stm., Blg.	F11	26
Osawatomie, Ks., U.S.	F3	120
Osborne, Ks., U.S.	B10	128
Osburn, Id., U.S.	C11	136
Osceola, Ar., U.S.	B8	122
Osceola, Ia., U.S.	C4	120
Osceola, Mo., U.S.	F4	120
Osceola, Wi., U.S.	F6	118
Osceola Mills, Pa., U.S.	D7	114
Oschatz, Ger.	E8	16
Oschersleben, Ger.	D7	16
Osečina, Yugo.	E6	26
Osëtr, stm., Russia	F21	10
Osetrovo, Russia	E10	34
Osgood, In., U.S.	E12	120
Oshawa, On., Can.	E11	112
Oshika, Japan	A14	40
Oshika-hantō, pen., Japan	A14	40
Ō-shima, i., Japan	E12	40
Oshima-hantō, pen., Japan	C14	38
Oshkosh, Ne., U.S.	F10	126
Oshkosh, Wi., U.S.	G10	118
Oshogbo, Nig.	H5	64
Oshwe, D.R.C.	E3	66
Osica de Jos, Rom.	E11	26
Osijek, Cro.	E15	22
Osilo, Italy	D2	24
Osimo, Italy	G10	22
Osinniki, Russia	D15	32
Osipovo Selo, Russia	D13	10
Osire Süd, Nmb.	B3	70
Oskaloosa, Ia., U.S.	C5	120
Oskaloosa, Ks., U.S.	E2	120
Oskarshamn, Swe.	H7	8
Oskolkovo, Russia	B26	8
Oslo, Nor.	G4	8
Oslo, state, Nor.	F4	8
Oslofjorden, b., Nor.	G4	8
Osmānābād, India	B3	53
Osmaneli, Tur.	C12	28
Osmaniye, Tur.	A7	58
Os'mino, Russia	A11	10
Osmussaar, i., Est.	A6	10
Osnabrück, Ger.	D4	16
Osorno, Chile	H2	90
Osorno, Spain	B6	20
Osoyoos, B.C., Can.	G11	138
Oss, Neth.	C14	14
Ossa, Mount, mtn., Austl.	n13	77a
Ossabaw Island, i., Ga., U.S.	E4	116
Osseo, Wi., U.S.	G7	118
Ossian, Ia., U.S.	A6	120
Ossining, N.Y., U.S.	C12	114
Ossipee, N.H., U.S.	G5	110
Ossjøen, l., Nor.	F4	8
Ossora, Russia	E21	34
Ostaškov, Russia	C16	10
Ostašovo, Russia	E18	10
Ostende see Oostende, Bel.	C11	14
Ostër (Ascör), stm., Eur.	G15	10
Osterburg, Ger.	D7	16
Östergötland, state, Swe.	G7	8
Osterholz-Scharmbeck, Ger.	C4	16
Osterode am Harz, Ger.	E6	16
Osterøyni, i., Nor.	F1	8
Östersund, Swe.	E6	8
Osterwieck, Ger.	E6	16
Østfold, state, Nor.	G4	8
Ostfriesische Inseln (East Frisian Islands), is., Ger.	C3	16
Ostfriesland, hist. reg., Ger.	C3	16
Østgrønland (Tunu), state, Grnld.	C18	141
Östhammar, Swe.	F8	8
Ostpreussen, hist. reg., Eur.	F4	10
Ostrava, Czech Rep.	G14	16
Ostróda, Pol.	C15	16
Ostrogožsk, Russia	D5	32
Ostrołęka, Pol.	C17	16
Ostrołęka, state, Pol.	D17	16
Ostroróg, Pol.	D12	16
Ostrov, Czech Rep.	F8	16
Ostrov, Russia	C11	10
Ostrov, i., Slov.	I13	16
Ostrov-Zalit, Russia	B11	10
Ostrowiec Świętokrzyski, Pol.	F17	16
Ostrów Mazowiecka, Pol.	D17	16
Ostrów Wielkopolski, Pol.	E13	16
Ostrzeszów, Pol.	E13	16
Ostuni, Italy	D11	24
O'Sullivan Lake, l., On., Can.	A11	118
Osum, stm., Alb.	D14	24
Ōsumi-hantō, pen., Japan	H3	40
Osumi Islands see Ōsumi-shotō, is., Japan	I9	38
Ōsumi-kaikyō, strt., Japan	I9	38
Ōsumi-shotō, is., Japan	I9	38
Osuna, Spain	G5	20
Oswego, Il., U.S.	C9	120
Oswego, Ks., U.S.	G2	120
Oswego, N.Y., U.S.	E13	112
Oswestry, Eng., U.K.	I9	12
Oświęcim (Auschwitz), Pol.	F15	16
Osyka, Ms., U.S.	F8	122
Ōta, Japan	C12	40
Otaci, Mol.	A14	26
Ōtake, Japan	E5	40
Otaki, N.Z.	E6	80
Otaru, Japan	C14	38
Otautau, N.Z.	H2	80
Otava, Fin.	F12	8
Otava, stm., Czech Rep.	G9	16
Otavalo, Ec.	G2	86
Otavi, Nmb.	D2	68
Ōtawara, Japan	C12	40
Otego Creek, stm., N.Y., U.S.	G3	110
Oteotea, Sol. Is.	e9	79b
Oteros, stm., Mex.	B4	100
Otinapa, Mex.	C6	100
Otis, Co., U.S.	A6	128
Otis, Ks., U.S.	C9	128
Otish, Monts, mts., Qc., Can.	E16	106
Otjimbingwe, Nmb.	C2	70
Otjinene, Nmb.	B4	70
Otjiwarongo, Nmb.	B3	70
Otjozondjou, stm., Nmb.	B5	70
Otjozondjupa, state, Nmb.	B3	70
Otočac, Cro.	F12	22
Otoskwin, stm., On., Can.	E13	106
Otra, stm., Nor.	G2	8
Otradnyj, Russia	D8	32
Otranto, Italy	D12	24
Otranto, Strait of, strt., Eur.	D12	24
Otrokovice, Czech Rep.	G13	16
Otrøya, i., Nor.	E2	8
Ötscher, mtn., Aus.	C12	22
Ōtsu, Japan	D8	40
Otta, Nor.	F3	8
Ottawa, On., Can.	C14	112
Ottawa, Il., U.S.	C9	120
Ottawa, Ks., U.S.	F2	120
Ottawa, Oh., U.S.	C1	114
Ottawa (Outaouais), stm., Can.	C15	112
Ottawa Islands, is., Nu., Can.	D14	106
Otterburne, Mb., Can.	E16	124
Otter Creek, Fl., U.S.	G3	116
Otter Creek, stm., Vt., U.S.	F3	110
Otter Lake, Mi., U.S.	E6	112
Otterøya see Otrøya, i., Nor.	E2	8
Otter Tail, stm., Mn., U.S.	E2	118
Otter Tail Lake, l., Mn., U.S.	E2	118
Otterville, Mo., U.S.	F5	120
Ottosdal, S. Afr.	E7	70
Ottoshoop, S. Afr.	D8	70
Ottoville, Oh., U.S.	D1	114
Ottumwa, Ia., U.S.	C5	120
Ottweiler, Ger.	G3	16
Otway, Cape, c., Austl.	L4	76
Otwock, Pol.	D17	16
Ötztaler Alpen (Venoste, Alpi), mts., Eur.	D7	22
Ou, stm., China	G9	42
Ou, stm., China	I5	42
Ou, stm., Laos	B6	48
Ouacha, Niger	G6	64
Ouachita, stm., U.S.	F7	122
Ouachita, Lake, res., Ar., U.S.	C5	122
Ouachita Mountains, mts., U.S.	C4	122
Ouaco, N. Cal.	m15	79d
Ouadda, C.A.R.	C4	66
Ouagadougou, Burkina	G4	64
Ouahigouya, Burkina	G4	64
Ouahran see Wahran, Alg.	B4	64
Ouaka, stm., C.A.R.	C4	66
Oualâta, Maur.	F3	64
Ouallene, Alg.	E5	64
Ouanary, Fr. Gu.	C7	84
Ouanda Djallé, C.A.R.	C4	66
Ouango, C.A.R.	D4	66
Ouangolodougou, C. Iv.	H3	64
Ouarâne, reg., Maur.	E2	64
Ouarkziz, Jbel, mts., Afr.	D3	64
Ouarzazate, Mor.	C3	64
Ouasiemsca, stm., Qc., Can.	A4	110
Oubangui (Ubangi), stm., Afr.	E3	66
Oudenaarde, Bel.	D12	14
Oudtshoorn, S. Afr.	H6	70
Oued Fodda, Alg.	H12	20
Oued-Zem, Mor.	C3	64
Ouémé, stm., Benin	H5	64
Ouen, Île, i., N. Cal.	n16	79d
Ouessant, Île d' (Ushant), i., Fr.	F3	14
Ouesso, Congo	D3	66
Ouezzane, Mor.	C3	64
Ouham, stm., Afr.	F3	62
Ouidah, Benin	H5	64
Ouimet Canyon, misc. cult., On., Can.	C10	118
Ouistreham, Fr.	E8	14
Oujda, Mor.	C4	64
Oulangan kansallispuisto, p.o.i., Fin.	C13	8
Oulu (Uleåborg), Fin.	D11	8
Oulu, state, Fin.	D12	8
Oulujärvi, l., Fin.	D12	8
Oum-Chalouba, Chad	D4	62
Oumé, C. Iv.	H3	64
Oum-Hadjer, Chad	E3	62
Oumiao, China	F5	42
Ounasjoki, stm., Fin.	C11	8
Ounianga Kébir, Chad	D3	62
Ourém, Braz.	A2	88
Ourense, Spain	B3	20
Ourense, co., Spain	B3	20
Ouricuri, Braz.	D5	88
Ourinhos, Braz.	D7	90
Ouro Branco, Braz.	D7	88
Ouro Fino, Braz.	L2	88
Ouro Preto, Braz.	K4	88
Ours, Grande chute à l', wtfl, Qc., Can.	B4	110
Ourthe, stm., Bel.	D14	14
Ōu-sammyaku, mts., Japan	E14	38
Oust, can., Fr.	F6	14
Outaouais (Ottawa), stm., Can.	C15	112
Outardes, stm., Qc., Can.	E17	106
Outer Hebrides, is., Scot., U.K.	D5	12
Outer Island, i., Wi., U.S.	D8	118
Outer Santa Barbara Passage, strt., Ca., U.S.	J7	134
Outjo, Nmb.	B3	70
Outlook, Sk., Can.	C6	124
Outlook, Mt., U.S.	F9	124
Out Skerries, is., Scot., U.K.	n19	12a
Ouvéa, i., N. Cal.	m16	79d
Ouyen, Austl.	J4	76
Ovacık, Tur.	B15	28
Ovada, Italy	F5	22
Ovalle, Chile	E2	92
Ovana, Cerro, mtn., Ven.	E8	86
Ovar, Port.	D2	20
Ovejas, Col.	C4	86
Overbrook, Ks., U.S.	F2	120
Overflowing, stm., Can.	A12	124
Overland Park, Ks., U.S.	F3	120
Overton, Ne., U.S.	G13	126
Overton, Tx., U.S.	E4	122
Overton Arm, b., Nv., U.S.	G2	132
Övertorneå, Swe.	C10	8
Ovett, Ms., U.S.	F9	122
Ovid, N.Y., U.S.	B9	114
Ovidiopol', Ukr.	C17	26
Oviedo, Spain	A5	20
Ovinišče, Russia	B20	10
Ovīši, Lat.	C4	10
Ovoot, Mong.	B7	36
Øvre Anárjohka Nasjonalpark, p.o.i., Nor.	B13	8
Øvre Dividal Nasjonalpark, p.o.i., Nor.	B8	8
Ovstug, Russia	G16	10
Owando, Congo	E3	66
Owase, Japan	E9	40
Owasso, Ok., U.S.	H2	120
Owatonna, Mn., U.S.	G5	118
Owbeh, Afg.	C9	56
Owego, N.Y., U.S.	B9	114
Owen, Wi., U.S.	G8	118
Owendo, Gabon	D1	66
Owens, stm., Ca., U.S.	F7	134
Owensboro, Ky., U.S.	G10	120
Owens Lake, l., Ca., U.S.	G8	134
Owen Sound, On., Can.	D8	112
Owen Sound, b., On., Can.	D9	112
Owen Stanley Range, mts., Pap. N. Gui.	b4	79a
Owensville, In., U.S.	F10	120
Owensville, Mo., U.S.	F6	120
Owerri, Nig.	H6	64
Owikeno Lake, l., B.C., Can.	E3	138
Owingsville, Ky., U.S.	F2	114
Owl, stm., Ab., Can.	A19	138
Owl, stm., Mb., Can.	D12	106
Owo, Nig.	H6	64
Owosso, Mi., U.S.	E5	112
Owyhee, Nv., U.S.	B9	134
Owyhee, stm., U.S.	G9	136
Owyhee, Lake, res., Or., U.S.	G9	136
Owyhee, South Fork, stm., U.S.	H10	136
Öxarfjörður, b., Ice.	j31	8a
Oxbow, Sk., Can.	E11	124
Oxelösund, Swe.	G7	8
Oxford, N.S., Can.	E13	110
Oxford, N.Z.	F5	80
Oxford, Eng., U.K.	J11	12
Oxford, Al., U.S.	D13	122
Oxford, In., U.S.	H2	112
Oxford, Ks., U.S.	D11	128
Oxford, Me., U.S.	F6	110
Oxford, Md., U.S.	F9	114
Oxford, Ms., U.S.	C9	122
Oxford, N.Y., U.S.	B10	114
Oxford, N.C., U.S.	H7	114
Oxford, Oh., U.S.	E13	120
Oxford, Pa., U.S.	I14	112
Oxford, Wi., U.S.	H9	118
Oxford Junction, Ia., U.S.	J8	118
Oxford Lake, l., Mb., Can.	E11	106
Oxford Peak, mtn., Id., U.S.	H14	136
Oxkutzcab, Mex.	B3	102
Oxley Downs, Austl.	J4	76
Oxley Wild Rivers National Park, p.o.i., Austl.	H8	76
Oxnard, Ca., U.S.	I6	134
Oxus see Amu Darya, stm., Asia	F10	32
Oya, stm., Malay.	B8	50
Oyabe, Japan	C9	40
Oyama, Japan	C12	40
Ōyano, Japan	G3	40
Oyapok (Oiapoque), stm., S.A.	C7	84
Oyem, Gabon	D2	66
Oyen, Ab., Can.	C3	124
Oyo, Nig.	H5	64
Oyonnax, Fr.	C11	18
Oyster Creek, mth., Tx., U.S.	E12	130
Ozamis, Phil.	F4	52
Ozark, Al., U.S.	F13	122
Ozark, Ar., U.S.	B5	122
Ozark, Mo., U.S.	G4	120
Ozark Plateau, plat., U.S.	H4	120
Ozarks, Lake of the, res., Mo., U.S.	F5	120
Ózd, Hung.	A7	26
Ožerele, Russia	F21	10
Ozernovskij, Russia	F20	34
Ozërnyj, Russia	D10	32
Ozery, Russia	F21	10
Ozette Lake, l., Wa., U.S.	B2	136
Ozieri, Italy	D2	24
Ozimek, Pol.	F14	16
Ozinki, Russia	D7	32
Ozorków, Pol.	E15	16

Name — Map Ref. — Page

Ōzu, Japan F5 40
Ozuluama, Mex. E9 100
Ozurgeti, Geor. F6 32

P

Paagoumène, N. Cal. m14 79d
Paama, state, Vanuatu k17 79d
Paama, i., Vanuatu k17 79d
Paamiut see Frederikshåb, Grnld. E15 141
Paarl, S. Afr. H4 70
Paauilo, Hi., U.S. C6 78a
Pabbay, i., Scot., U.K. D5 12
Pabbiring, Kepulauan, is., Indon. F11 50
Pabean, Indon. G9 50
Pabellón, Ensenada del, b., Mex. C4 100
Pabianice, Pol. E15 16
Pablo, Mt., U.S. C12 136
Pābna, Bngl. G12 54
Pabradė, Lith. F8 10
Pacaás Novos, Serra dos, mts., Braz. F5 84
Pacajus, Braz. C6 88
Pacasmayo, Peru E2 84
Pacatuba, Braz. C6 88
Pachino, Italy H9 24
Pachitea, stm., Peru E3 84
Pachmarhi, India G7 54
Pāchora, India H5 54
Pachuca de Soto, Mex. E9 100
Pacific, B.C., Can. B2 138
Pacific, Mo., U.S. F7 120
Pacifica, Ca., U.S. F3 134
Pacific-Antarctic Ridge, unds. P22 142
Pacific Grove, Ca., U.S. G3 134
Pacific Ocean F20 142
Pacific Ranges, mts., B.C., Can. E5 138
Pacific Rim National Park, p.o.i., B.C., Can. H5 138
Paciran, Indon. G8 50
Pacitan, Indon. H7 50
Pacora, Pan. C2 86
Pacov, Czech Rep. G11 16
Pacuí, stm., Braz. I3 88
Padada, Phil. G5 52
Padamo, stm., Ven. F9 86
Padampur, India H9 54
Padang, Indon. D6 50
Padang, Indon. G12 50
Padang, Indon. D2 50
Padang, Pulau, i., Indon. C3 50
Padang Endau, Malay. K6 48
Padangpanjang, Indon. D2 50
Padangsidempuan, Indon. C1 50
Padany, Russia E15 8
Padas, stm., Malay. A9 50
Padauari, stm., Braz. G9 86
Paddle, stm., Ab., Can. B16 138
Paddle Prairie, Ab., Can. D7 106
Paderborn, Ger. E4 16
Padjelanta Nationalpark, p.o.i., Swe. C7 8
Padloping Island, i., Nu., Can. D13 141
Padma see Ganges, stm., Asia G13 54
Pádova (Padua), Italy E8 22
Pādra, India G4 54
Padrauna, India E9 54
Padre Bernardo, Braz. H1 88
Padre Island, i., Tx., U.S. G10 130
Padre Island National Seashore, p.o.i., Tx., U.S. G10 130
Padre Paraíso, Braz. I5 88
Padstow, Eng., U.K. K8 12
Padua see Pádova, Italy E8 22
Paducah, Ky., U.S. G9 120
Paducah, Tx., U.S. G8 128
Paea, Fr. Poly. v21 78h
Paedun, Kor., S. D1 40
Paektu-san, mtn., Asia C10 36
Paestum, hist., Italy D8 24
Páez, stm., Col. F4 86
Pafúri, Moz. C10 70
Pag, Otok, i., Cro. F11 22
Pagadenbaru, Indon. G5 50
Pagadian, Phil. G4 52
Pagai Selatan, Pulau, i., Indon. E2 50
Pagai Utara, Pulau, i., Indon. E2 50
Pagan, Mya. B2 48
Pagan, i., N. Mar. Is. B5 72
Pagaralam, Indon. E3 50
Pagasitikós Kólpos, b., Grc. D5 28
Page, Az., U.S. G5 132
Page, N.D., U.S. G16 124
Pagėgiai, Lith. E4 10
Pagerdewa, Indon. E4 50
Paget, Mount, mtn., S. Geor. J9 90
Pagoda Peak, mtn., Co., U.S. C9 132
Pagoda Point, c., Mya. E2 48
Pagon, Bukit, mtn., Asia A9 50
Pago Pago, Am. Sam. h12 79c
Pagosa Springs, Co., U.S. F9 132
Paguate, N.M., U.S. H9 132
Pagudpud, Phil. A3 52
Pahača, Russia D22 34
Pahala, Hi., U.S. D6 78a
Pahang, state, Malay. K6 48
Pahang, stm., Malay. K6 48
Pahokee, Fl., U.S. J5 116
Pahost, Bela. G12 10
Pahrump, Nv., U.S. G10 134
Pai, Thai. C4 48
Pai, stm., Asia C3 48
Paico, Peru F3 84
Paide, Est. B8 10
Paige, Tx., U.S. D10 130
Paignton, Eng., U.K. K9 12
Paiguano, Chile E2 92
Päijänne, l., Fin. F11 8
Paikü Co, l., China D10 54
Pailolo Channel, strt., Hi., U.S. B5 78a
Paimpol, Fr. F5 14
Painan, Indon. D2 50
Painesdale, Mi., U.S. D10 118
Painesville, Oh., U.S. C4 114
Paint, stm., Mi., U.S. E10 118
Paint Creek, stm., Oh., U.S. E14 120
Painted Desert, des., Az., U.S. H5 132
Painted Rock Reservoir, res., Az., U.S. K3 132
Paintsville, Ky., U.S. G3 114
Paisley, Scot., U.K. F8 12
Paisley, Or., U.S. H6 136
Païta, N. Cal. n16 79d
Paita, Peru E1 84
Paitan, Telukan, b., Malay. G1 52
Paiton, Indon. G8 50
Pajala, Swe. C10 8
Paján, Ec. H1 86
Pajares, Puerto de, p., Spain B5 20
Pajaros Point, c., Br. Vir. Is. d9 104b
Pajęczno, Pol. E14 16
Pajer, gora, mtn., Russia C1 34
Pajeú, stm., Braz. E6 88
Paj-Hoj, hills, Russia A10 32
Paka, Malay. J6 48
Pākāla, India E4 53
Pakaraima Mountains, mts., S.A. E11 86
Pakashkan Lake, l., On., Can. B8 118
Pākaur, India F11 54
Pak Chong, Thai. E5 48
Pākhāl, l., India C5 53
Pákhna, Cyp. D3 58
Pakhoi see Beihai, China K3 42
Pakistan, ctry., Asia C2 46
Paklenica Nacionalni Park, p.o.i., Cro. F12 22
Pakokku, Mya. B2 48
Pakowki Lake, l., Ab., Can. E2 124
Pākpattan, Pak. C4 54
Pak Phanang, Thai. H5 48
Pak Phayun, Thai. I5 48
Pak Phraek, Thai. H5 48
Pakrac, Cro. E14 22
Pakruojis, Lith. E6 10
Paks, Hung. C5 26
Paktīā, state, Afg. B2 54
Paktīkā, state, Afg. B2 54
Pakwash Lake, l., On., Can. A5 118
Pakxé, Laos E7 48
Pala, Chad F2 62
Pala, Mya. F4 48
Palacios, Tx., U.S. F11 130
Palagruža, Otoci, is., Cro. H13 22
Palai, India G3 53
Palaiochóra, Grc. H6 28
Pālakodu, India C5 53
Palamós, Spain C14 20
Pālampur, India B6 54
Palamu National Park, p.o.i., India G10 54
Palamut, Tur. D10 28
Palana, Russia E20 34
Palanan Bay, b., Phil. B4 52
Palanga, Lith. E3 10
Palangkaraya, Indon. E8 50
Palani, India F3 53
Pālanpur, India F4 54
Palaoa Point, c., Hi., U.S. C4 78a
Palapye, Bots. C8 70
Pālār, stm., India E4 53
Palas de Rei, Spain B3 20
Palatka, Russia D19 34
Palatka, Fl., U.S. G4 116
Palau, Italy C3 24
Palau, ctry., Oc. g8 78b
Palau Islands, is., Palau D10 44
Palauk, Mya. F4 48
Palaw, Mya. F4 48
Palawan, i., Phil. F2 52
Palawan Passage, strt., Phil. F1 52
Palayan, Phil. C3 52
Pālayankottai, India G3 53
Palembang, Indon. E4 50
Palena, Italy I11 22
Palena, stm., S.A. H2 90
Palencia, Spain B6 20
Palencia, co., Spain B6 20
Palen Lake, l., Ca., U.S. J1 132
Palenque, Mex. G13 100
Palenque, hist., Mex. G12 100
Palermo, Col. F4 86
Palermo, Italy F7 24
Palermo, Ur. F10 92
Palestina, Mex. E6 130
Palestine, Ar., U.S. B7 122
Palestine, Il., U.S. E10 120
Palestine, Tx., U.S. F3 122
Palestine, hist. reg., Asia G6 58
Palestine, Lake, res., Tx., U.S. E3 122
Palestrina, Italy I9 22
Paletwa, Mya. D7 46
Pālghāt, India F3 53
Palgrave Point, c., Nmb. E1 68
Palhano, stm., Braz. C6 88
Pāli, India F4 54
Palima, Indon. F12 50
Palinuro, Capo, c., Italy D9 24
Palisade, Ne., U.S. A7 128
Palisades, Id., U.S. G15 136
Palisades Reservoir, res., U.S. G15 136
Pālitāna, India H3 54
Palivere, Est. A6 10
Palizada, Mex. F12 100
Palk Bay, b., Asia G4 53
Palkino, Russia G20 8
Pālkonda, India B6 53
Pālkonda Range, mts., India D4 53
Palk Strait, strt., Asia G4 53
Pallastunturi, mtn., Fin. B11 8
Palliser, Cape, c., N.Z. E6 80
Palma, Braz. K4 88
Palma, Moz. C7 68
Palma, stm., Braz. G2 88
Palma, Badia de, b., Spain E13 20
Palmácia, Braz. C6 88
Palma del Río, Spain G5 20
Palma de Mallorca, Spain E13 20
Palma di Montechiaro, Italy G7 24
Palmar, stm., Ven. B6 86
Palmar, Lago Artificial del, res., Ur. F9 92
Palmar Camp, Belize D3 102
Palmarejo, P.R. B1 104a
Palmares, Braz. E8 88
Palmarito, Ven. D6 86
Palmarola, Isola, i., Italy D6 24
Palmas, Braz. F1 88
Palmas, Braz. C12 92
Palmas Bellas, Pan. H7 102
Palmas de Monte Alto, Braz. H4 88
Palma Soriano, Cuba B9 102
Palm Bay, Fl., U.S. H5 116
Palm Beach, Fl., U.S. J5 116
Palmdale, Ca., U.S. I7 134
Palm Desert, Ca., U.S. J9 134
Palmeira, Braz. B13 92
Palmeira das Missões, Braz. C11 92
Palmeira dos Índios, Braz. E7 88
Palmeiras, stm., Braz. F2 88
Palmeirinhas, Ponta das, c., Ang. B1 68
Palmelo, Braz. I1 88
Palmer, P.R. B4 104a
Palmer, Ak., U.S. D10 140
Palmer, Ma., U.S. B13 114
Palmer, Ne., U.S. F14 126
Palmer, Tn., U.S. B13 122
Palmer, sci., Ant. B34 81
Palmer Lake, Co., U.S. B3 128
Palmer Land, reg., Ant. C34 81
Palmerston, N.Z. G4 80
Palmerston, at., Cook Is. E10 72
Palmerston, Cape, c., Austl. C7 76
Palmerston North, N.Z. E6 80
Palmerton, Pa., U.S. D10 114
Palmetto, Ga., U.S. D14 122
Palmetto, La., U.S. G6 122
Palmetto Point, c., Antig. e4 105b
Palmi, Italy F9 24
Palmira, Col. F3 86
Palmira, Cuba A7 102
Palmira, Ec. I2 86
Palmitas, Ur. F9 92
Palm Springs, Ca., U.S. J9 134
Palmyra see Tudmur, Syria D9 58
Palmyra, Il., U.S. E7 120
Palmyra, Mo., U.S. E6 120
Palmyra, N.Y., U.S. A8 114
Palmyra, Va., U.S. G7 114
Palmyra, hist., Syria D9 58
Palmyra Atoll, at., Oc. C10 72
Palo Alto, Mex. H8 130
Palo Alto, Ca., U.S. F3 134
Palo Blanco, P.R. B2 104a
Palo Flechado Pass, p., N.M., U.S. E3 128
Paloh, Malay. B7 50
Paloich, Sudan E6 62
Palojoensuu, Fin. B10 8
Palomar Mountain, mtn., Ca., U.S. J9 134
Palomas, Mex. F4 130
Palo Pinto, Tx., U.S. B9 130
Palopo, Indon. E12 50
Palos, Cabo de, c., Spain G10 20
Palo Santo, Arg. B8 92
Palos Verdes Point, c., Ca., U.S. J7 134
Palouse, stm., U.S. D8 136
Palo Verde, Ca., U.S. J2 132
Palpa, Peru F2 84
Palpalá, Arg. B5 92
Palu, Indon. D11 50
Palu, Teluk, b., Indon. D11 50
Paluga, Russia D21 8
Palwal, India D6 54
Pama, Burkina G5 64
Pamanukan, Indon. G5 50
Pāmban Channel, strt., India G4 53
Pāmban Island, i., India G4 53
Pamekasan, Indon. G8 50
Pamenang, Indon. E3 50
Pameungpeuk, Indon. G5 50
Pamiers, Fr. F7 18
Pamir, mts., Asia B11 56
Pamlico Sound, strt., N.C., U.S. A10 116
Pampa, Tx., U.S. F8 128
Pampã, stm., Braz. I5 88
Pampa (Pampas), reg., Arg. G4 90
Pampa Almirón, Arg. C8 92
Pampa del Chañar, Arg. E3 92
Pampa del Indio, Arg. B7 92
Pampanga, stm., Phil. C3 52
Pampanua, Indon. F12 50
Pampas, Peru F3 84
Pampas, stm., Peru F3 84
Pampas see Pampa, reg., Arg. F4 90
Pamplico, S.C., U.S. B6 116
Pamplona, Col. D5 86
Pamplona, Spain B9 20
Pamukkale (Hierapolis), hist., Tur. F12 28
Pamukova, Tur. C13 28
Pana, Il., U.S. E8 120
Panabá, Mex. B3 102
Panabo, Phil. G5 52
Panacea, Fl., U.S. G14 122
Panadura, Sri L. H4 53
Panagjurište, Blg. G11 26
Panaitan, Pulau, i., Indon. G4 50
Panaji, India D1 53
Panamá, Pan. H8 102
Panama, Ok., U.S. B4 122
Panama, ctry., N.A. F9 96
Panamá, Bahía de, b., Pan. H8 102
Panamá, Canal de (Panama Canal), can., Pan. H8 102
Panamá, Golfo de, b., Pan. D2 86
Panama, Gulf of see Panamá, Golfo de, b., Pan. D2 86
Panama, Isthmus of see Panamá, Istmo de, isth., Pan. H8 102
Panamá, Istmo de (Panama, Isthmus of), isth., Pan. H8 102
Panama Basin, unds. H5 144
Panama Canal see Panamá, Canal de, can., Pan. H8 102
Panama City, Fl., U.S. G13 122
Panambi, Braz. D11 92
Panamint Range, mts., Ca., U.S. G8 134
Panamint Valley, val., Ca., U.S. G8 134
Panao, Peru E2 84
Panarea, Isola, i., Italy F9 24
Panaro, stm., Italy F8 22
Panay, i., Phil. E4 52
Panay Gulf, b., Phil. E4 52
Pančevo, Yugo. E7 26
Panciu, Rom. D14 26
Panda, Moz. D12 70
Pandaria, India G8 54
Pan de Azúcar, Ur. G10 92
Pandėlys, Lith. D8 10
Pāndharkawada, India A4 53
Pandharpur, India C2 53
Pāndhurna, India H7 54
Pando, Ur. G10 92
Panevėžys, Lith. E7 10
Panfilov, Kaz. F13 32
Pāng, stm., Mya. B4 48
Panga, D.R.C. D5 66
Pangala, Congo E2 66
Pangandaran, Indon. G6 50
Pangani, Tan. F7 66
Pangani, stm., Tan. E7 66
Pangburn, Ar., U.S. B7 122
Pangfou see Bengbu, China E7 42
Panghkam, Mya. D8 46
Pangi, D.R.C. E5 66
Pangkajene, Indon. F11 50
Pangkalanbrandan, Indon. J4 48
Pangkalanbuun, Indon. E7 50
Pangkalpinang, Indon. E5 50
Pangnirtung, Nu., Can. B17 106
Pango Aluquem, Ang. B1 68
Pangŏjin, Kor., S. D2 40
Pangong Tso, l., Asia B7 54
Panguiranan, Phil. D4 52
Panguitch, Ut., U.S. F4 132
Pangutaran, Phil. G3 52
Pangutaran Group, is., Phil. G3 52
Panhandle, Tx., U.S. F7 128
Paniau, mtn., Hi., U.S. B1 78a
Panié, Mont, mtn., N. Cal. m15 79d
Pānīpat, India D6 54
Panitan, Phil. E4 52
Panj (Pjandž), stm., Asia B11 56
Panjang, Indon. F4 50
Panjang, Selat, strt., Indon. C3 50
Pankshin, Nig. H6 64
Panlong (Lo), stm., Asia A7 48
P'anmunjŏm-ni, Kor., N. E7 38
Panna, India F8 54
Panna National Park, p.o.i., India F7 54
Pannawonica, Austl. D3 74
Panola, U.S. E10 122
Páno Lévkara, Cyp. D4 58
Panopah, Indon. D7 50
Panorama, Braz. D6 90
Panovo, Russia C18 32
Panruti, India F4 53
Panshan, China D4 38
Pantanal, reg., S.A. C5 90
Pantanaw, Mya. D2 48
Pantar, Pulau, i., Indon. G7 44
Pantelleria, Isola di, i., Italy H6 24
Pantonlabu, Indon. J3 48
Pánuco, Mex. E10 100
Pánuco, stm., Mex. E9 100
Panxian, China F5 36
Panyam, Nig. H6 64
Panzós, Guat. E3 102
Pao, stm., Thai. D6 48
Pao, stm., Ven. C8 86
Pao, stm., Ven. C9 86
Paochi see Baoji, China D2 42
Paoki see Baoji, China D2 42
Paola, Italy E9 24
Paola, Ks., U.S. F3 120
Paoli, In., U.S. F11 120
Paopao, Fr. Poly. v20 78h
Paoting see Baoding, China B6 42
Paotou see Baotou, China A4 42
Paotow see Baotou, China A4 42
Pápa, Hung. B4 26
Papagaio, stm., Braz. I10 86
Papagaios, Braz. D3 88
Papagayo, Golfo de, b., C.R. G4 102
Papaikou, Hi., U.S. D6 78a
Papantla de Olarte, Mex. E10 100
Papara, Fr. Poly. v22 78h
Papa Stour, i., Scot., U.K. n18 12a
Papeari, Fr. Poly. w22 78h
Papeete, Fr. Poly. v21 78h
Papenburg, Ger. C3 16
Papetoai, Fr. Poly. v20 78h
Paphos see Néa Páfos, Cyp. D3 58
Papigochic, stm., Mex. G8 98
Papillion, Ne., U.S. C1 120
Paposo, Chile B2 92
Papua, Gulf of, b., Pap. N. Gui. D5 72
Papua New Guinea, ctry., Oc. D5 72
Papulovo, Russia F23 8
Papun, Mya. C3 48
Papunáua, stm., Col. G6 86
Papurí (Papuri), stm., S.A. G6 86
Papuri (Papurí), stm., S.A. G6 86
Pará, state, Braz. D7 84
Pará, stm., Braz. A1 88
Pará, stm., Braz. J3 88
Parabel', Russia C14 32
Paraburdoo, Austl. D3 74
Paracatu, Braz. I2 88
Paracatu, stm., Braz. I3 88
Paracel Islands see Xisha Qundao, is., China B5 50
Pārachinār, Pak. B3 54
Paracho de Verduzco, Mex. F7 100
Parachute, Co., U.S. D8 132
Paraćin, Yugo. F8 26
Paracuru, Braz. B6 88
Parada, Punta, c., Peru G2 84
Paradise, Ca., U.S. D4 134
Paradise, Mt., U.S. C12 136
Paradise, Nv., U.S. G1 132
Paradise Island, i., Bah. m18 104f
Paradise Valley, Az., U.S. J5 132
Paradise Valley, Nv., U.S. B8 134
Pāradwīp, India H11 54
Paragonah, Ut., U.S. F4 132
Paragould, Ar., U.S. H7 120
Paraguá, stm., Bol. B4 90
Paragua, stm., Ven. D10 86
Paraguaçu, stm., Braz. G6 88
Paraguai (Paraguay), stm., S.A. D5 90
Paraguaipoa, Ven. B6 86
Paraguaná, Península de, pen., Ven. A6 86
Paraguarí, Para. B9 92
Paraguarí, state, Para. C9 92
Paraguay, ctry., S.A. D5 90
Paraguay (Paraguai), stm., S.A. E5 90
Paraíba, state, Braz. D7 88
Paraíba do Sul, stm., Braz. K5 88
Paraibano, Braz. D3 88
Parainen, Fin. F9 8
Paraíso, Mex. F12 100
Paraiso, Pan. H8 102
Parakou, Benin H5 64
Paramakkudi, India G4 53
Paramaribo, Sur. B6 84
Parambu, Braz. D5 88
Paramillo, Parque Nacional, p.o.i., Col. D3 86
Paramirim, Braz. G4 88
Paramirim, stm., Braz. F4 88
Páramo de Masa, Puerto de, p., Spain B7 20
Paramušir, ostrov, i., Russia F20 34
Paramythiá, Grc. D3 28
Paran, Naḥal (Girafi, Wadi), stm. I5 58
Paraná, Arg. E7 92
Paranã, Braz. G1 88
Paraná, state, Braz. D6 90
Paranã, stm., Braz. G1 88
Paraná, stm., S.A. F5 90
Paranaguá, Braz. B13 92
Paranaguá, Baía de, b., Braz. B13 92
Paranaíba, Braz. C6 90
Paranaíba, stm., Braz. C6 90
Paranaidji, Braz. D2 88
Paranapanema, stm., Braz. D6 90
Paranapiacaba, Serra do, mts., Braz. B13 92
Paranavaí, Braz. D6 90
Parang, Phil. G5 52
Parang, Pulau, i., Indon. F7 50
Parângu Mare, Vârful, mtn., Rom. D10 26
Paranhos, Braz. A10 92
Paranoá, Lago do, res., Braz. H2 88
Paraopeba, Braz. J3 88
Parapetí, stm., Bol. C4 90
Parara, Indon. E12 50
Paratinga, Braz. G4 88
Paratoo, Austl. I2 76
Paray-le-Monial, Fr. C9 18
Pārbati, stm., India F6 54
Pārbatipur, Bngl. F12 54
Parbhani, India B3 53
Parchim, Ger. C7 16
Pardeeville, Wi., U.S. H9 118
Pārdi, India H4 54
Parding, China B12 54
Pardo, stm., Braz. K1 88
Pardo, stm., Braz. H6 88
Pardo, stm., Braz. L1 88
Pardo, stm., Braz. D6 90
Pardo, stm., Braz. D11 92
Pardubice, Czech Rep. F11 16
Paredón, Mex. C8 100
Parelhas, Braz. D7 88
Paren', Russia D21 34
Paren', stm., Russia D21 34
Parent, Qc., Can. C2 110
Parentis-en-Born, Fr. E4 18
Parepare, Indon. E11 50
Parera, Arg. G5 92
Parfenevo, Russia F20 8
Párga, Grc. D3 28
Parham, Antig. f4 105b
Paria, Gulf of, b. B10 86
Paria, Península de, pen., Ven. B10 86
Pariaguán, Ven. C9 86
Pariaman, Indon. D1 50
Paricutín, vol., Mex. F7 100
Parigi, Indon. D12 50
Parika, Guy. B6 84
Parikkala, Fin. F13 8
Parima, stm., Braz. F10 86
Parima, Serra (Parima, Sierra), mts., S.A. F9 86
Parima, Sierra (Parima, Serra), mts., S.A. F9 86
Parima Tapirapecó, Parque Nacional, p.o.i., Ven. F9 86
Parintins, Braz. D6 84
Paris, On., Can. E9 112
Paris, Fr. F11 14
Paris, Ar., U.S. B5 122
Paris, Il., U.S. I2 112
Paris, Ky., U.S. F1 114
Paris, Mo., U.S. E5 120
Paris, Tn., U.S. H9 120
Paris, Tx., U.S. D3 122
Parisienne, Ile, i., On., Can. B5 112
Parita, Bahía de, b., Pan. H7 102
Parit Buntar, Malay. J5 48
Parkano, Fin. E10 8
Park City, Mt., U.S. B3 126
Park City, Ut., U.S. C5 132
Parkdale, Or., U.S. E5 136
Parker, Az., U.S. I2 132
Parker, Co., U.S. B4 128
Parker, Fl., U.S. G13 122
Parker, Cape, c., Nu., Can. B10 141
Parker City, In., U.S. H4 112
Parker Dam, Ca., U.S. I2 132
Parker Dam, dam, U.S. I2 132
Parkersburg, Il., U.S. F9 120
Parkersburg, Ia., U.S. B5 120
Parkersburg, W.V., U.S. E4 114
Parkes, Austl. I7 76
Park Falls, Wi., U.S. F8 118
Park Forest, Il., U.S. G2 112
Parkhill, On., Can. E8 112
Parkland, Wa., U.S. C4 136
Park Range, mts., Co., U.S. C10 132
Park Rapids, Mn., U.S. E3 118
Parkrose, Or., U.S. E4 136
Park Rynie, S. Afr. G10 70
Parksley, Va., U.S. G10 114
Parkston, S.D., U.S. D14 126
Parksville, B.C., Can. G6 138
Parkville, Md., U.S. E9 114
Parkville, Mo., U.S. E3 120
Parla, Spain D7 20
Parlākimidi, India B7 53
Parli, India B3 53
Parma, Italy F7 22
Parma, Mo., U.S. H8 120
Parma, Oh., U.S. C4 114
Parnaguá, Braz. F3 88
Parnaíba, Braz. B5 88
Parnaíba, stm., Braz. B5 88
Parnaibinha, stm., Braz. E2 88
Parnamirim, Braz. E6 88
Parnassós, mtn., Grc. E5 28
Párnitha, mtn., Grc. E6 28
Pärnu, Est. G11 8
Pärnu laht, b., Est. G11 8
Paro, Bhu. E12 54
Pārola, India H5 54
Paromaj, Russia F17 34
Paroo, stm., Austl. G5 76
Páros, i., Grc. F8 28
Parowan, Ut., U.S. F4 132
Parque Nacional da Chapada da Diamantina, p.o.i., Braz. G4 88
Parral, Chile H2 92
Parral, stm., Mex. B6 100
Parramatta, Austl. I8 76
Parras de la Fuente, Mex. C7 100
Parrish, Fl., U.S. I3 116
Parrsboro, N.S., Can. E12 110
Parry, Cape, c., N.T., Can. A6 106
Parry Bay, b., Nu., Can. B14 106
Parry Island, i., On., Can. C9 112
Parry Peninsula, pen., N.T., Can. B6 106
Parry Sound, On., Can. C9 112
Parsberg, Ger. G7 16
Parsęta, stm., Pol. B11 16
Parshall, N.D., U.S. G11 124
Paršino, Russia C20 32
Parsnip, stm., B.C., Can. A8 138
Parsons, Ks., U.S. G2 120
Parsons, Tn., U.S. B10 122
Pärsti, Est. B8 10
Partanna, Italy G6 24
Parthenay, Fr. H8 14
Partinico, Italy F7 24
Partizansk, Russia C10 38
Partizánske, Slov. H14 16
Paru, stm., Braz. D7 84
Parú, stm., Ven. E9 86
Paru de Oeste, stm., Braz. C6 84
Parūr, India F3 53
Pārvatīpuram, India B6 53
Paryang, China C9 54
Parys, S. Afr. E8 70
Pasadena, Ca., U.S. I7 134
Pasadena, Tx., U.S. H3 122
Pasaje, Ec. D2 84
Pa Sak, stm., Thai. E5 48
Paşaköy, N. Cyp. C4 58
Pasarbantal, Indon. E2 50
Pasawng, Mya. C3 48
Pascagoula, Ms., U.S. G10 122
Pascagoula, stm., Ms., U.S. G10 122
Paşcani, Rom. B13 26
Pasco, Wa., U.S. D7 136
Pascoag, R.I., U.S. C14 114
Pascua, Isla de (Easter Island) (Rapa Nui), i., Chile f30 78l
Pas-de-Calais, state, Fr. D11 14
Pasewalk, Ger. C10 16
Pasir Mas, Malay. J6 48
Pasirpengarayan, Indon. C2 50
Pasir Puteh, Malay. J6 48
Paškovo, Russia G15 34
Pasłęka, stm., Pol. C16 16
Pasley Bay, b., Nu., Can. A11 106
Pašman, Otok, i., Cro. G12 22
Pasmore, stm., Austl. H2 76
Pasni, Pak. D9 56
Paso de Indios, Arg. H3 90
Paso del Cerro, Ur. E9 92
Paso de los Libres, Arg. D9 92
Paso de los Toros, Ur. F9 92
Paso de Patria, Para. C8 92
Paso de San Antonio, Mex. E3 130
Paso Hondo, Mex. H13 100
Paso Robles, Ca., U.S. H5 134
Pašozero, Russia F16 8
Pasquia Hills, hills, Sk., Can. A11 124
Pasrūr, Pak. B5 54
Passadumkeag, Me., U.S. E8 110
Passadumkeag Mountain, hill, Me., U.S. E8 110
Passage Point, c., N.T., Can. B16 140
Passaic, N.J., U.S. H15 112
Passamaquoddy Bay, b., N.A. E10 110
Passau, Ger. H9 16
Passero, Capo, c., Italy H9 24
Passo Fundo, Braz. D11 92
Passo Real, Represa do, res., Braz. D11 92
Passos, Braz. K2 88
Pastavy, Bela. E9 10
Pastaza, state, Ec. H3 86
Pastaza, stm., S.A. D2 84
Pastillo, P.R. B3 104a
Pasto, Col. G3 86
Pastos Bons, Braz. D3 88
Pasuruan, Indon. G8 50
Pasvalys, Lith. D7 10
Pásztó, Hung. B6 26
Patacamaya, Bol. C3 90
Patadkal, hist., India C3 53
Patagonia, Az., U.S. L6 132
Patagonia, reg., Arg. I2 90
Pātan, India G3 54
Patchogue, N.Y., U.S. D13 114
Patea, N.Z. D6 80
Pategi, Nig. H6 64
Pate Island, i., Kenya E8 66
Patensie, S. Afr. H7 70
Paterna, Spain E10 20
Paternion, Aus. D10 22
Paternò, Italy G8 24
Paterson, N.J., U.S. D11 114
Pathānkot, India B5 54
Pathein, Mya. D2 48
Pathfinder Reservoir, res., Wy., U.S. E5 126
Pathiu, Thai. G4 48
Pathum Thani, Thai. E5 48
Pati, Indon. G7 50
Patía, Col. F3 86
Patía, stm., Col. F2 86
Patiāla, India C6 54
Patillas, P.R. B3 104a
Pati Point, c., Guam i10 78c
Pativilca, Peru F2 84
Pātkai Range, mts., Asia F4 36
Pat Mayse Lake, res., Tx., U.S. D3 122
Pátmos, i., Grc. F9 28
Patna, India F10 54
Patna, India H11 54
Patnāgarh, India H9 54
Patnanongan Island, i., Phil. C4 52
Pato Branco, Braz. C11 92
Patoka, Il., U.S. F8 120
Patoka, stm., In., U.S. F10 120
Patoka Lake, res., In., U.S. F11 120
Patomskoe nagor'e, plat., Russia E12 34
Patonga, Ug. D6 66
Patos, Braz. D7 88
Patos, stm., Arg. E3 92
Patos, Lagoa dos, b., Braz. E12 92
Patos de Minas, Braz. J2 88
Patquía, Arg. D4 92
Pátra, Grc. E4 28
Patrai, Gulf of see Patraikós Kólpos, b., Grc. E4 28
Patraikós Kólpos, b., Grc. E4 28
Patricio Lynch, Isla, i., Chile I1 90
Patrocínio, Braz. J2 88
Pattani, Thai. I5 48
Pattaya, Thai. F5 48
Patten, Me., U.S. D8 110
Patterson, Ca., U.S. F4 134
Patterson, Ga., U.S. E3 116
Patterson, Mount, mtn., Yk., Can. C4 106
Patti, Golfo di, b., Italy F9 24
Pattison, Ms., U.S. F8 122
Pattoki, Pak. C4 54
Pattonsburg, Mo., U.S. D3 120
Pattukkottai, India F4 53
Pattullo, Mount, mtn., B.C., Can. D5 106
Patuākhāli, Bngl. G13 54
Patuca, stm., Hond. E5 102
Pātūr, India H6 54
Patusi, Pap. N. Gui. a4 79a
Patuxent, stm., Md., U.S. F9 114
Pátzcuaro, Mex. F8 100
Pau, Fr. F5 18
Pau, Gave de, stm., Fr. F5 18
Pau Brasil, Braz. H6 88
Pau dos Ferros, Braz. D6 88
Pauh, Indon. E3 50
Pauini, stm., Braz. E4 84
Pauini, stm., Braz. H10 86
Pauk, Mya. B2 48
Pauksa Taung, mtn., Mya. C2 48
Paul, Id., U.S. H13 136
Paulding, Ms., U.S. E9 122
Paulicéia, Braz. D6 90
Paulina Peak, mtn., Or., U.S. G5 136
Pauline, Mount, mtn., Can. C11 138
Paulino Neves, Braz. B4 88
Paulistana, Braz. E5 88
Paulistas, Braz. J4 88
Paullina, Ia., U.S. B2 120
Paulo Afonso, Braz. E6 88
Paulo Afonso, Cachoeira de, wtfl, Braz. E6 88
Paulpietersburg, S. Afr. E10 70
Pauls Valley, Ok., U.S. G11 128
Paung, Mya. D3 48
Paungde, Mya. C2 48
Pauri, India C7 54
Paute, Ec. I2 86
Paute, stm., Ec. I2 86
Pauto, stm., Col. E6 86
Pavia, Italy E6 22
Pavilion, B.C., Can. F9 138
Pāvilosta, Lat. D4 10
Pavlikeni, Blg. F12 26
Pavlodar, Kaz. D13 32
Pavlof Volcano, vol., Ak., U.S. E7 140
Pavlovo, Russia I20 8
Pavlovsk, Russia A13 10
Pavlovsk, Russia D14 32
Pavlovskij Posad, Russia E21 10
Pavo, Ga., U.S. F2 116
Pavullo nel Frignano, Italy F7 22
Pavuvu Island, i., Sol. Is. e8 79b
Pawan, stm., Indon. D7 50
Pawhuska, Ok., U.S. E12 128
Pawn, stm., Mya. C3 48
Pawnee, Il., U.S. E8 120
Pawnee, Ok., U.S. A2 122
Pawnee, stm., Ks., U.S. C9 128
Pawnee Rock, Ks., U.S. C9 128
Pawni, India H7 54
Pawota, Mya. D3 48
Paw Paw, Il., U.S. C8 120
Paw Paw, Mi., U.S. F4 112
Pawtucket, R.I., U.S. C14 114
Paxoí, i., Grc. D3 28
Paxson, Ak., U.S. D10 140
Paxton, Ne., U.S. F11 126
Paya, Hond. E5 102
Payakumbuh, Indon. D2 50
Payamlı, Tur. A9 58
Payerne, Switz. D3 22
Payeti, Indon. H12 50
Payette, Id., U.S. F10 136
Payette, stm., Id., U.S. G10 136
Payette, North Fork, stm., Id., U.S. F11 136
Payette, South Fork, stm., Id., U.S. F11 136
Payne, Oh., U.S. C1 114
Payne, Lac, l., Can. D16 106
Paynes Find, Austl. E3 74
Paynton, Sk., Can. A5 124
Paysandú, Ur. F8 92
Payson, Az., U.S. I5 132
Payson, Il., U.S. E6 120
Payson, Ut., U.S. C5 132
Payún, Cerro, mtn., Arg. H3 92
Pazarbaşı Burnu, c., Tur. B13 28
Pazarcık, Tur. A8 58
Pazardžik, Blg. G11 26
Pazaryeri, Tur. D12 28
Paz de Ariporo, Col. E6 86
Pčevža, Russia A15 10
Pe, Mya. F4 48
Pea, stm., U.S. F12 122
Peabody, Ks., U.S. C11 128
Peabody, Ma., U.S. B14 114
Peace, stm., Can. D8 106
Peace, stm., Fl., U.S. I4 116
Peace River, Ab., Can. D7 106
Peachland, B.C., Can. G11 138
Peach Orchard, Ga., U.S. C3 116
Peach Springs, Az., U.S. H3 132
Peak District National Park, p.o.i., Eng., U.K. H11 12
Peak Downs, Austl. D7 76
Peak Hill, Austl. E3 74
Peak Hill, Austl. I7 76
Peäldoajvi, mtn., Fin. B12 8
Peale, Mount, mtn., Ut., U.S. E7 132
Pearisburg, Va., U.S. G5 114
Pearl, Il., U.S. E7 120
Pearl, Ms., U.S. E8 122
Pearl, stm., U.S. G9 122
Pearland, Tx., U.S. H3 122
Pearl Harbor, b., Hi., U.S. B3 78a
Pearl Peak, mtn., Nv., U.S. C1 132
Pearl River, La., U.S. G9 122
Pearson, Ga., U.S. E3 116

Name — Map Ref. — Page

Peary Land, reg., Grnld. A18 141
Pease, stm., Tx., U.S. G9 128
Pebane, Moz. D6 68
Pebas, Peru D3 84
Pebble Island, i., Falk. Is. J5 90
Peć, Yugo. G7 26
Pecan Gap, Tx., U.S. D3 122
Peçanha, Braz. J4 88
Peças, Ilha das, i., Braz. B13 92
Pecatonica, Il., U.S. B8 120
Pecatonica, stm., U.S. B8 120
Pečenga, Russia B14 8
Pechenizhyn, Ukr. A11 26
Pechora see Pečora, stm., Russia C25 8
Pechora Bay see Pečorskaja guba, b., Russia A8 32
Pečora, Russia A9 32
Pečora (Pechora), stm., Russia A8 32
Pecoraro, Monte, mtn., Italy F10 24
Pečorskaja guba, b., Russia A8 32
Pečorskoe more, Russia A8 32
Pečory, Russia C10 10
Pecos, N.M., U.S. F3 128
Pecos, Tx., U.S. C4 130
Pecos, stm., U.S. F12 98
Pecos National Monument, p.o.i., N.M., U.S. F3 128
Pécs, Hung. C5 26
Pedana, India C5 53
Pedasí, Pan. I7 102
Pedder, Lake, res., Austl. o12 77a
Peddie, S. Afr. H8 70
Pededze, stm., Eur. C10 10
Pedernales, Dom. Rep. C12 102
Pedernales, Ven. C10 86
Pedernales, stm., Tx., U.S. D9 130
Pedernales, Salar de, pl., Chile C3 92
Pedra Azul, Braz. I5 88
Pedra Branca, Braz. C6 88
Pedra Lume, C.V. k10 65a
Pedras de Fogo, Braz. D8 88
Pedras Salgadas, Port. C3 20
Pedraza, Col. B4 86
Pedregal, Ven. B6 86
Pedreiras, Braz. C3 88
Pedriceña, Mex. C6 100
Pedro, Point, c., Sri L. G5 53
Pedro Afonso, Braz. E1 88
Pedro Avelino, Braz. C7 88
Pedro Cays, is., Jam. D9 102
Pedro Gomes, Braz. G7 84
Pedro II, Braz. C5 88
Pedro II, Ilha, i., S.A. G8 86
Pedro Juan Caballero, Para. D5 90
Pedro Leopoldo, Braz. J3 88
Pedro Osório, Braz. E11 92
Pedro R. Fernández, Arg. D8 92
Pedro Velho, Braz. D8 88
Peebles, Scot., U.K. F9 12
Peebles, Oh., U.S. F2 114
Pee Dee, stm., U.S. A6 116
Peekskill, N.Y., U.S. C12 114
Peel, I. of Man G8 12
Peel, stm., Can. B4 106
Peel Point, c., N.T., Can. B17 140
Peel Sound, strt., Nu., Can. A11 106
Peene, stm., Ger. C9 16
Peerless, Mt., U.S. F8 124
Peesane, Sk., Can. B10 124
Peetz, Co., U.S. G9 126
Pegasus Bay, b., N.Z. F5 80
Pegnitz, Ger. G7 16
Pegu, stm., Mya. D3 48
Pegu Yoma, mts., Mya. C2 48
Pegyš, Russia E24 8
Pehlivanköy, Tur. B9 28
Pehuajó, Arg. G7 92
Peian see Bei'an, China B10 36
Peiching see Beijing, China B7 42
Peihai see Beihai, China K3 42
Peikang, Tai. J9 42
Peine, Ger. D6 16
Peine, Pointe à, c., Dom. j6 105c
Peinnechaung, i., Mya. I14 54
Peip'ing see Beijing, China B7 42
Peipus, Lake, l., Eur. B10 10
Peiraiás (Piraeus), Grc. F6 28
Peissenberg, Ger. I7 16
Peixe, Braz. G1 88
Peixe, stm., Braz. D6 90
Peixian, China D7 42
Peixoto, Represa de, res., Braz. K2 88
Pekalongan, Indon. G6 50
Pekan, Malay. K6 48
Pekanbaru, Indon. C2 50
Pekin, Il., U.S. D8 120
Pekin, In., U.S. F11 120
Peking see Beijing, China B7 42
Peklino, Russia G16 10
Pekul'nej, hrebet, mts., Russia C24 34
Pelabohan Klang, Malay. K5 48
Pelabuhanratu, Indon. G5 50
Pelagie, Isole, is., Italy I6 24
Pelaihari, Indon. E9 50
Pelat, Mont, mtn., Fr. E12 18
Pełczyce, Pol. C11 16
Peleduj, Russia C20 32
Pelée, Montagne, vol., Mart. k6 105c
Pelee, Point, c., On., Can. G7 112
Pelee Island, i., On., Can. G7 112
Pelega, Vârful, mtn., Rom. D9 26
Peleliu see Beliliou, i., Palau D9 44
Peleng, Pulau, i., Indon. F7 44
Pelham, Al., U.S. D12 122
Pelham, Ga., U.S. E1 116
Pelhřimov, Czech Rep. G11 16
Pelican, Ak., U.S. E12 140
Pelican Bay, b., Mb., Can. B13 124
Pelican Lake, Wi., U.S. F9 118
Pelican Lake, l., Mb., Can. E14 124
Pelican Lake, l., Mb., Can. B13 124
Pelican Lake, l., Mn., U.S. C5 118
Pelican Rapids, Mb., Can. B13 124
Pelican Rapids, Mn., U.S. E2 118
Pelister Nacionalni Park, p.o.i., Mac. B4 28
Peljekaise Nationalpark see Pieljekaise Nationalpark, p.o.i., Swe. C6 8
Pelješac, Poluotok, pen., Cro. H14 22
Peljušnja, Russia B15 10
Pella, Ia., U.S. C5 120
Pélla, hist., Grc. C5 28
Pell City, Al., U.S. D12 122
Pellegrini, Arg. H6 92
Pellegrini, Lago, l., Arg. I4 92
Pello, Fin. C11 8
Pellworm, i., Ger. B4 16
Pelly, Sk., Can. C12 124
Pelly, stm., Yk., Can. C4 106
Pelly Bay, b., Nu., Can. B12 106
Pelly Crossing, Yk., Can. C3 106
Pelly Lake, l., Nu., Can. B10 106
Pelly Mountains, mts., Yk., Can. C4 106
Pelón de Nado, mtn., Mex. E9 100
Peloponnesus see Pelopónnisos, pen., Grc. F5 28
Pelopónnisos, state, Grc. F5 28
Pelopónnisos (Peloponnesus), pen., Grc. F5 28
Pelotas, Braz. E11 92
Pelotas, stm., Braz. C12 92
Pelusium Bay see Tîna, Khalîg el-, b., Egypt G3 58
Pemadumcook Lake, l., Me., U.S. E7 110
Pemalang, Indon. G6 50
Pemangkat, Indon. C6 50
Pematangsiantar, Indon. B1 50
Pemba, Moz. C7 68
Pemba, Zam. D4 68
Pemba, i., Tan. F7 66
Pemberton, Austl. F3 74
Pemberton, B.C., Can. F8 138
Pembina, N.D., U.S. C1 118
Pembina, stm., Ab., Can. B16 138
Pembina, stm., N.A. F16 124
Pembina Hills, hills, N.A. E15 124
Pembroke, On., Can. C12 112
Pembroke, Wales, U.K. J7 12
Pembroke, Ga., U.S. D4 116
Pembroke, Ky., U.S. H10 120
Pembroke, Me., U.S. F9 110
Pembroke, N.C., U.S. B6 116
Pembroke, Cape, c., Nu., Can. C14 106
Pembroke Pines, Fl., U.S. K5 116
Pembrokeshire Coast National Park, p.o.i., Wales, U.K. J7 12
Pembuang, Indon. E7 50
Pembuang, stm., Indon. D8 50
Pemigewasset, stm., N.H., U.S. G5 110
Pemuco, Chile H1 92
Penafiel, Port. C2 20
Peñalara, Pico de, mtn., Spain D6 20
Penalva, Braz. B3 88
Penang see George Town, Malay. J4 48
Peñaranda de Bracamonte, Spain D5 20
Pen Argyl, Pa., U.S. D10 114
Peñarroya-Pueblonuevo, Spain F5 20
Peñas, Cabo de, c., Spain A5 20
Penas, Golfo de, b., Chile I2 90
Penasco, N.M., U.S. E3 128
Pench National Park, p.o.i., India H7 54
Pendembu, S.L. H2 64
Pendembu, S.L. H2 64
Pendências, Braz. C7 88
Pendleton, In., U.S. H4 112
Pendleton, Or., U.S. E8 136
Pendleton, S.C., U.S. B3 116
Pendolo, Indon. E12 50
Pend Oreille, stm., N.A. B9 136
Pend Oreille, Lake, l., Id., U.S. B10 136
Pendžikent, Taj. B10 56
Penebel, Indon. H9 50
Penedo, Braz. F7 88
Penetanguishene, On., Can. D9 112
Peneus see Pineiós, stm., Grc. D5 28
Penfield, Pa., U.S. C7 114
Penganga, stm., India H6 54
Pengchia Yü, i., Tai. I8 42
P'enghu Ch'üntao (Pescadores), is., Tai. J8 42
P'enghu Shuitao, strt., Tai. J8 42
Pengkou, China I7 42
Penglai, China C9 42
Pengpu see Bengbu, China E7 42
Pengshui, China G2 42
Pengwaluote Shan, mtn., China B11 54
Pengxi, China F1 42
Pengxian, China E5 36
Pengze, China G7 42
Penha, Braz. C13 92
Penhsi see Benxi, China D5 38
Penibética, Cordillera, mts., Spain G8 20
Peniche, Port. E1 20
Penicuik, Scot., U.K. F9 12
Penida, Nusa, i., Indon. H9 50
Peninsular Malaysia see Semenanjung Malaysia, hist. reg., Malay. K6 48
Peníscola, Spain D11 20
Penki see Benxi, China D5 38
Pennant Station, Sk., Can. D5 124
Penne, Italy H10 22
Penneru, stm., India D4 53
Penn Hills, Pa., U.S. H10 112
Pennine Alps, mts., Eur. C13 18
Pennines, mts., Eng., U.K. G10 12
Pennington Gap, Va., U.S. H2 114
Pennsboro, W.V., U.S. E4 114
Pennsylvania, state, U.S. C8 114
Penn Yan, N.Y., U.S. B8 114
Penny Ice Cap, ice, Nu., Can. B17 106
Penny Strait, strt., Nu., Can. B6 141
Peno, Russia D15 10
Penobscot, stm., Me., U.S. F8 110
Penobscot, East Branch, stm., Me., U.S. D8 110
Penobscot, West Branch, stm., Me., U.S. D7 110
Penobscot Bay, b., Me., U.S. F7 110
Penola, Austl. K3 76
Peñón de Ifac see Penyal d'Ifac, misc. cult., Spain F11 20
Penong, Austl. F6 74
Penonomé, Pan. H7 102
Penrhyn, at., Cook Is. D11 72
Penrith, Austl. I8 76
Penrith, Eng., U.K. G10 12
Pensacola, Fl., U.S. G11 122
Pensacola Bay, b., Fl., U.S. G11 122
Pensacola Mountains, mts., Ant. D36 81
Pense, Sk., Can. D9 124
Pensilvania, Col. E4 86
Pentagon Mountain, mtn., Mt., U.S. C13 136
Pentecostes, Braz. B6 88
Pentecost Island see Pentecôte, i., Vanuatu j17 79d
Pentecôte, state, Vanuatu j17 79d
Pentecôte (Pentecost Island), i., Vanuatu j17 79d
Penticton, B.C., Can. G11 138
Pentland, Austl. C5 76
Pentland Firth, strt., Scot., U.K. C9 12
Pentwater, Mi., U.S. E3 112
Penuba, Indon. D4 50
Peñuelas, P.R. B2 104a
Penuguan, Indon. E4 50
Penukonda, India D3 53
Penyal d'Ifac, misc. cult., Spain F11 20
Penza, Russia D7 32
Penzance, Eng., U.K. K7 12
Penzberg, Ger. I7 16
Penžina, stm., Russia D22 34
Penžinskaja guba, b., Russia D21 34
Penžinskij hrebet, mts., Russia D22 34
Peoples Creek, stm., Mt., U.S. F5 124
People's Democratic Republic of Korea see Korea, North, ctry., Asia D7 38
Peoria, Az., U.S. J4 132
Peoria, Il., U.S. D8 120
Peoria Heights, Il., U.S. K9 118
Peotone, Il., U.S. G2 112
Pepel, S.L. H2 64
Pepin, Wi., U.S. G6 118
Pepin, Lake, l., U.S. G6 118
Peqin, Alb. C13 24
Perabumulih, Indon. E4 50
Perak, state, Malay. J5 48
Perak, stm., Malay. J5 48
Perak, Kuala, b., Malay. J5 48
Perales de Alfambra, Spain D9 20
Peralillo, Chile G2 92
Peralta, N.M., U.S. I10 132
Perambalur, India F4 53
Percé, Qc., Can. B12 110
Perchas, P.R. B2 104a
Perche, Collines du, hills, Fr. F9 14
Percival Lakes, l., Austl. D4 74
Percy Isles, is., Austl. C8 76
Perdida, stm., Braz. E2 88
Perdido, stm., U.S. G11 122
Perdido, Monte, mtn., Spain B10 20
Perdizes, Braz. J2 88
Perdue, Sk., Can. B6 124
Perechyn, Ukr. H18 16
Pereez'na, Russia G22 8
Pereira, Col. E4 86
Perelazy, Russia G14 10
Peremyšl', Russia F18 10
Pereslavl'-Zalesskij, Russia D21 10
Pérez, Arg. F7 92
Pergamino, Arg. F7 92
Pergamum, hist., Tur. D10 28
Pergine Valsugana, Italy D8 22
Perham, Mn., U.S. E3 118
Péribonka, Qc., Can. B4 110
Péribonka, stm., Qc., Can. B5 110
Péribonka, Lac, l., Qc., Can. E16 106
Perico, Arg. B5 92
Pericumã, stm., Braz. B3 88
Peridot, Az., U.S. J6 132
Perigiraja, Indon. D3 50
Périgord, hist. reg., Fr. D6 18
Périgueux, Fr. D6 18
Perijá, Serranía de, mts., S.A. C5 86
Perim see Barīm, i., Yemen G5 56
Peri-Mirim, Braz. B3 88
Perito Moreno, Arg. I2 90
Peritoró, Braz. C3 88
Periyār, stm., India G3 53
Periyar Tiger Reserve, India G3 53
Perkasie, Pa., U.S. D10 114
Perkins, Ok., U.S. A2 122
Perlas, Archipiélago de las, is., Pan. H8 102
Perlas, Laguna de, b., Nic. F6 102
Perleberg, Ger. C7 16
Perlez, Yugo. D7 26
Perlis, state, Malay. I5 48
Perm', Russia C9 32
Përmet, Alb. D14 24
Pernambuco, state, Braz. E6 88
Pernik, Blg. G10 26
Péronne, Fr. E11 14
Perote, Mex. F10 100
Perow, B.C., Can. B4 138
Perpignan, Fr. G8 18
Perrault Falls, On., Can. A5 118
Perrin, Tx., U.S. A9 130
Perrine, Fl., U.S. K5 116
Perris, Ca., U.S. J8 134
Perro, Laguna del, l., N.M., U.S. G3 128
Perro, Punta del, c., Spain H4 20
Perros, Bahía de, b., Cuba A8 102
Perros-Guirec, Fr. F5 14
Perry, Fl., U.S. F2 116
Perry, Ia., U.S. C3 120
Perry, Ks., U.S. E2 120
Perry, Mi., U.S. B1 114
Perry, Mo., U.S. E6 120
Perry, N.Y., U.S. B7 114
Perry, Kap, c., Grnld. B11 141
Perry Lake, res., Ks., U.S. E2 120
Perrysburg, Oh., U.S. C2 114
Perry's Victory and International Peace Memorial, hist., Oh., U.S. C2 114
Perrysville, Oh., U.S. D3 114
Perryton, Tx., U.S. E8 128
Perryville, Ak., U.S. E8 140
Perryville, Ar., U.S. B6 122
Perryville, Ky., U.S. G12 120
Perryville, Mo., U.S. G8 120
Perseverancia, Bol. B4 90
Persia, Ia., U.S. C2 120
Persia see Iran, ctry., Asia C7 56
Persian Gulf, b., Asia D7 56
Perth, Austl. F3 74
Perth, On., Can. D13 112
Perth, Scot., U.K. E9 12
Perth Amboy, N.J., U.S. D11 114
Perth Basin, unds. L13 142
Pertominsk, Russia D18 8
Peru, Il., U.S. C8 120
Peru, In., U.S. H3 112
Peru, Ne., U.S. D2 120
Peru, N.Y., U.S. F3 110
Peru, ctry., S.A. E2 84
Peru Basin, unds. J5 144
Perućac, Jezero, res., Eur. G16 22
Peru-Chile Trench, unds. K6 144
Perugia, Italy G9 22
Perugorría, Arg. D8 92
Peruíbe, Braz. B14 92
Perušić, Cro. F12 22
Pervomais'k, Ukr. A17 26
Pervomajsk, Russia I20 8
Pervomajskij, Russia F15 10
Pervoural'sk, Russia C9 32
Pervyj Kuril'skij proliv, strt., Russia F20 34
Pes', Russia B17 10
Pesaro, Italy G9 22
Pescadores see P'enghu Ch'üntao, is., Tai. J8 42
Pescadores Channel see P'enghu Shuitao, strt., Tai. J8 42
Pescara, Italy H11 22
Pescara, stm., Italy H11 22
Pescasseroli, Italy C7 24
Pescia, Italy G7 22
Pesé, Pan. D1 86
Peshāwar, Pak. B3 54
Peshkopi, Alb. C14 24
Peshkopija see Peshkopi, Alb. C14 24
Peshtigo, Wi., U.S. C2 112
Peshtigo, stm., Wi., U.S. F10 118
Peski, Bela. G7 10
Pesočnoe, Russia B22 10
Peso da Régua, Port. C3 20
Pesquería, stm., Mex. I8 130
Pessac, Fr. E5 18
Pest, state, Hung. B6 26
Peštera, Blg. G11 26
Pestovo, Russia B18 10
Pëstraja Dresva, Russia D20 34
Petacalco, Bahía, b., Mex. G7 100
Petah Tiqwa, Isr. F5 58
Petal, Ms., U.S. F9 122
Petalcingo, Mex. G12 100
Petalión, Kólpos, b., Grc. F7 28
Petaluma, Ca., U.S. E3 134
Petare, Ven. B8 86
Petatlán, Mex. G8 100
Petawawa, On., Can. C12 112
Petén Itzá, Lago, l., Guat. D2 102
Petenwell Lake, res., Wi., U.S. G8 118
Peterborough, Austl. I2 76
Peterborough, On., Can. D11 112
Peterborough, Eng., U.K. I12 12
Peterhead, Scot., U.K. D11 12
Peter Island, i., Br. Vir. Is. e8 104b
Peter Isøy, i., Ant. B31 81
Peter Lake, l., Nu., Can. C12 106
Peterlee, Eng., U.K. G11 12
Peterman, Al., U.S. F11 122
Peter Pond Lake, l., Sk., Can. D9 106
Petersburg, Ak., U.S. E13 140
Petersburg, Il., U.S. K9 118
Petersburg, In., U.S. F10 120
Petersburg, Tn., U.S. B12 122
Petersburg, Tx., U.S. H7 128
Petersburg, Va., U.S. G8 114
Petersburg, W.V., U.S. F6 114
Petersfield, Eng., U.K. J12 12
Peterson, Ia., U.S. B2 120
Peter the Great Bay see Petra Velikogo, zaliv, b., Russia C9 38
Petilia Policastro, Italy E10 24
Pétion-Ville, Haiti C11 102
Petit-Bourg, Guad. h5 105c
Petitcodiac, N.B., Can. E11 110
Petite Rivière Noire, Piton de la, mtn., Mrts. i10 69a
Petites-Anses, Guad. i5 105c
Petit-Goâve, Haiti C11 102
Petit Jean, stm., Ar., U.S. B5 122
Petitot, stm., Can. D6 106
Petit Piton, vol., St. Luc. m6 105c
Petitsikapau Lake, l., Nf., Can. E17 106
Petlād, India G4 54
Peto, Mex. B3 102
Petoskey, Mi., U.S. C5 112
Petra see Al-Batrā', hist., Jord. H6 58
Petra Velikogo, zaliv (Peter the Great Bay), b., Russia C9 38
Petre, Point, c., On., Can. E12 112
Petrič, Blg. H10 26
Petrified Forest National Park, p.o.i., Az., U.S. I7 132
Petrila, Rom. D10 26
Petrinja, Cro. E13 22
Petriščevo, Russia E19 10
Petrodvorec, Russia A12 10
Petrolândia, Braz. E6 88
Petrolea, Col. C5 86
Petrolia, Tx., U.S. G10 128
Petrolina, Braz. E5 88
Petrolina de Goiás, Braz. I1 88
Petrona, Punta, c., P.R. C3 104a
Petropavl see Petropavlovsk, Kaz. D11 32
Petropavlovka, Russia F10 34
Petropavlovsk, Kaz. D11 32
Petropavlovsk-Kamčatskij, Russia F20 34
Petrópolis, Braz. L4 88
Petros, Tn., U.S. H13 120
Petroșani, Rom. D10 26
Petrovac, Yugo. E8 26
Petrovsk, Russia D6 32
Petrovskij, Russia H18 8
Petrovsk-Zabajkal'skij, Russia F10 34
Petrozavodsk, Russia F15 8
Petrusburg, S. Afr. F7 70
Petrusville, S. Afr. G7 70
Petrykau, Bela. H11 10
Pettus, Tx., U.S. F10 130
Petuhovo, Russia C11 32
Peuetsagoe, Gunung, vol., Indon. J3 48
Peureulak, Indon. J3 48
Peusangan, stm., Indon. J3 48
Pevek, Russia C23 34
Peza, stm., Russia D23 8
Pezawa Taung, mtn., Mya. C2 48
Pézenas, Fr. F9 18
Pezinok, Slov. H13 16
Pfarrkirchen, Ger. H8 16
Pforzheim, Ger. H4 16
Pfronten, Ger. I6 16
Pfunds, Aus. D7 22
Pfungstadt, Ger. G4 16
Pha-an, Mya. D3 48
Phagwāra, India C5 54
Phalaborwa, S. Afr. C10 70
Phalodi, India E4 54
Phaltan, India C2 53
Phan, Thai. C4 48
Phanat Nikhom, Thai. F5 48
Phangan, Ko, i., Thai. H5 48
Phangnga, Thai. H4 48
Phaniang, stm., Thai. D6 48
Phanom Dongrak Range (Dângrêk, Chuŏr Phnum), mts., Asia C3 44
Phan Rang, Viet. G9 48
Phan Thiet, Viet. G9 48
Phan Thong, Thai. F5 48
Pharenda, India E9 54
Pharr, Tx., U.S. H9 130
Phat Diem, Viet. B8 48
Phatthalung, Thai. I5 48
Phayao, Thai. C4 48
Phelps, N.Y., U.S. B8 114
Phelps, Wi., U.S. E9 118
Phelps Lake, l., N.C., U.S. I9 114
Phenix City, Al., U.S. E13 122
Phepane, stm., S. Afr. E6 70
Phet Buri, stm., Thai. F4 48
Phetchabun, Thai. D5 48
Phetchabun, Thiu Khao, mts., Thai. D5 48
Phetchaburi, Thai. F4 48
Phibun Mangsahan, Thai. E7 48
Phichai, Thai. D5 48
Phichit, Thai. D5 48
Philadelphia, Ms., U.S. E9 122
Philadelphia, N.Y., U.S. D14 112
Philadelphia, Pa., U.S. E10 114
Phil Campbell, Al., U.S. C11 122
Philip, S.D., U.S. C11 126
Philippeville see Skikda, Alg. B6 64
Philippeville, Bel. D13 14
Philippi, W.V., U.S. E5 114
Philippi see Fílippoi, hist., Grc. B7 28
Philippi, Lake, l., Austl. E2 76
Philippine Basin, unds. H15 142
Philippines, ctry., Asia C4 52
Philippine Sea H15 142
Philippine Trench, unds. I15 142
Philippolis, S. Afr. G7 70
Philipsburg, Mt., U.S. D13 136
Philipsburg, Pa., U.S. D7 114
Philip Smith Mountains, mts., Ak., U.S. C10 140
Philipstown, S. Afr. G7 70
Phillaur, India C5 54
Phillip Island, i., Austl. L5 76
Phillips, Me., U.S. F6 110
Phillips, Tx., U.S. F7 128
Phillips, Wi., U.S. F8 118
Phillipsburg, Ga., U.S. E2 116
Phillipsburg, N.J., U.S. D10 114
Philo, Il., U.S. E9 120
Philo, Oh., U.S. E4 114
Philpots Island, i., Nu., Can. C10 141
Phimai, Thai. E6 48
Phitsanulok, Thai. D5 48
Phnom Penh see Phnum Pénh, Camb. G7 48
Phnum Pénh (Phnom Penh), Camb. G7 48
Phoenix, Az., U.S. J4 132
Phoenix, N.Y., U.S. E13 112
Phoenix, Or., U.S. A3 134
Phoenix Islands, is., Kir. D9 72
Phoenixville, Pa., U.S. D10 114
Phofung (Sources, Mont-aux-), mtn., Afr. F9 70
Phon, Thai. E6 48
Phong, stm., Thai. D6 48
Phôngsali, Laos B6 48
Phon Phisai, Thai. D6 48
Phra Chedi Sam Ong, p., Asia E4 48
Phrae, Thai. C5 48
Phra Nakhon Si Ayutthaya, Thai. E5 48
Phran Kratai, Thai. D4 48
Phrom Phiram, Thai. D5 48
Phu Cat, Viet. E9 48
Phuket, Thai. I4 48
Phuket, Ko, i., Thai. I4 48
Phu Ly, Viet. B7 48
Phum Duang, stm., Thai. H4 48
Phumĭ Bå Khâm, Camb. F8 48
Phumĭ Béng, Camb. F7 48
Phumĭ Châmbák, Camb. G7 48
Phumĭ Chhuk, Camb. G7 48
Phumĭ Chruŏy Slêng, Camb. F8 48
Phumĭ Kâmpóng Srâlau, Camb. E7 48
Phumĭ Kâmpóng Trâbêk, Camb. F7 48
Phumĭ Kaôh Kért, Camb. F7 48
Phumĭ Khpôb, Camb. G7 48
Phumĭ Lvéa Kraôm, Camb. F6 48
Phumĭ Narŭng, Camb. F7 48
Phumĭ Prêk Kák, Camb. F7 48
Phumĭ Puŏk Chás, Camb. F6 48
Phumĭ Sâmraông, Camb. E6 48
Phumĭ Srê Kôkir, Camb. F8 48
Phumĭ Thbêng, Camb. F7 48
Phumĭ Thmâ Pôk, Camb. F6 48
Phumĭ Tœk Choŭ, Camb. F6 48
Phu My, Viet. E9 48
Phuoc Long, Viet. G8 48
Phuoc Long, Viet. H7 48
Phu Pan National Park, p.o.i., Thai. D6 48
Phu Quoc, Dao, i., Viet. G6 48
Phu Tho, Viet. B7 48
Phu Vang, Viet. D8 48
Pi, stm., China F7 42
Piaçabuçu, Braz. F7 88
Piacenza, Italy E6 22
Pialba, Austl. E9 76
Piancó, Braz. D7 88
Pianosa, Isola, i., Italy H12 22
Pianosa, Isola, i., Italy H6 22
Piapot, Sk., Can. E4 124
Piaseczno, Pol. D16 16
Piaski, Pol. E18 16
Piatã, Braz. G5 88
Piatra-Neamț, Rom. B13 26
Piauí, state, Braz. D4 88
Piauí, stm., Braz. D4 88
Piauí, Morro do, mtn., Braz. H2 88
Piave, stm., Italy E9 22
Piaxtla, stm., Mex. D5 100
Piazza Armerina, Italy G8 24
Pibor Post, Sudan F6 62
Pic, stm., On., Can. B12 118
Picacho, Az., U.S. K5 132
Picardie, hist. reg., Fr. E11 14
Picardy see Picardie, hist. reg., Fr. E11 14
Picayune, Ms., U.S. G9 122
Pichanal, Arg. D4 90
Picher, Ok., U.S. H3 120
Pichilemu, Chile G1 92
Pichimá, Col. E3 86
Pichi Mahuida, Arg. I5 92
Pichincha, state, Ec. H2 86
Pichucalco, Mex. G12 100
Pickardville, Ab., Can. C17 138
Pickens, Ms., U.S. E9 122
Pickens, S.C., U.S. B3 116
Pickensville, Al., U.S. D10 122
Pickerel Lake, l., Mb., Can. B14 124
Pickering, Eng., U.K. G12 12
Pickle Lake, On., Can. E12 106
Pickstown, S.D., U.S. D14 126
Pickton, Tx., U.S. D3 122
Pickwick Lake, res., U.S. B10 122
Pico, mtn., C.V. I10 65a
Pico, i., Port. C3 60
Pico da Neblina, Parque Nacional, p.o.i., Braz. G9 86
Pico de Orizaba, Parque Nacional, p.o.i., Mex. F10 100
Pico de Orizaba, Volcán (Citlaltépetl, Volcán), vol., Mex. F10 100
Picos, Braz. D5 88
Picquigny, Fr. E11 14
Picton, On., Can. D12 112
Picton, N.Z. E6 80
Picton, Isla, i., Chile K3 90
Pictou, N.S., Can. E14 110
Pictou Island, i., N.S., Can. E14 110
Picture Butte, Ab., Can. G18 138
Pictured Rocks National Lakeshore, p.o.i., Mi., U.S. B3 112
Picuí, Braz. D7 88
Picún Leufú, Arg. G3 90
Pidálion, Akrotírion, c., Cyp. D5 58
Pidhorodna, Ukr. A17 26
Pidurutalagala, mtn., Sri L. H5 53
Piedecuesta, Col. D5 86
Piedimonte Matese, Italy C8 24
Piedmont, Al., U.S. D13 122
Piedmont, Mo., U.S. G7 120
Piedmont see Piemonte, state, Italy F5 22
Piedra, stm., Co., U.S. F9 132
Piedra, Cerro, mtn., Chile H1 92
Piedra del Águila, Arg. H3 90
Piedrafita, Puerto de, p., Spain B3 20
Piedrahita, Spain D5 20
Piedras, Punta, c., Arg. G9 92
Piedras, Punta, c., Ven. B11 86
Piedras Blancas, Arg. E8 92
Piedras Negras, Guat. D2 102
Piedras Negras, Mex. A8 100
Pieksämäki, Fin. E12 8
Pielinen, l., Fin. E13 8
Pieljekaise Nationalpark, p.o.i., Swe. C6 8
Piemonte, state, Italy F5 22
Pienaarsrivier, S. Afr. D8 70
Pieniężno, Pol. B16 16
Pieniński Park Narodowy, p.o.i., Pol. G16 16
Pienza, Italy G8 22
Pierce, Co., U.S. G8 126
Pierce, Id., U.S. D11 136
Pierce City, Mo., U.S. E14 128
Pierpont, S.D., U.S. B15 126
Pierre, S.D., U.S. C12 126
Pierre, Bayou, stm., La., U.S. F5 122
Pierre, Bayou, stm., Ms., U.S. E8 122
Pierre Part, La., U.S. G7 122
Pierreville, Trin. s13 105f
Pierz, Mn., U.S. F4 118
Piešťany, Slov. H13 16
Pietarsaari, Fin. E10 8
Pietermaritzburg, S. Afr. F10 70
Pietersburg, S. Afr. C9 70
Pietrasanta, Italy F7 22
Piet Retief, S. Afr. E10 70
Pietrosu, Vârful, mtn., Rom. B12 26
Pigeon, Mi., U.S. E6 112
Pigeon, stm., Mb., Can. B17 124
Pigeon Forge, Tn., U.S. I2 114
Pigeon Lake, l., Ab., Can. C16 138
Pigeon Lake, l., On., Can. D11 112
Piggs Peak, Swaz. E10 70
Pigs, Bay of see Cochinos, Bahía de, b., Cuba B7 102
Pigüé, Arg. H6 92
Pihāri, India E8 54
Pihlajavesi, l., Fin. F13 8
Pihtipudas, Fin. E11 8
Pijijiapan, Mex. H12 100
Pikalëvo, Russia A17 10
Pikangikum, On., Can. E12 106
Pikes Peak, mtn., Co., U.S. C3 128
Pikes Rocks, hill, Pa., U.S. C6 114
Pikesville, Md., U.S. E9 114
Piketberg, S. Afr. H4 70
Piketon, Oh., U.S. E2 114
Pikeville, Tn., U.S. B13 122
Pikou, China B10 42
Pikounda, Congo D3 66
Piła, Pol. C12 16
Piła, state, Pol. C12 16
Pilanesberg Game Reserve, p.o.i., S. Afr. D8 70
Pilão Arcado, Braz. E4 88
Pilar, Arg. E5 92
Pilar, Braz. E8 88
Pilar, Para. C8 92
Pilar de Goiás, Braz. H1 88
Pilar do Sul, Braz. A14 92
Pilares, Mex. D3 130
Pilas Group, is., Phil. G3 52
Pilawa, Pol. D17 16
Pilcomayo, stm., S.A. D4 90
Pilcomayo, Brazo Norte, stm., Para. B8 92
Pilcomayo, Brazo Sur del, stm., S.A. B8 92
Pilcomayo, Parque Nacional, p.o.i., Arg. B8 92
Pilger, Ne., U.S. E15 126
Pilgrim's Rest, S. Afr. D10 70
Pili, Phil. D4 52
Pīlībhīt, India D7 54
Pilica, stm., Pol. E16 16
Pilliga, Austl. H7 76
Pilot, The, mtn., Austl. K7 76
Pilot Butte, Sk., Can. D9 124
Pilot Knob, Mo., U.S. G7 120
Pilot Knob, mtn., Id., U.S. E11 136
Pilot Mound, Mb., Can. E15 124
Pilot Mountain, N.C., U.S. H5 114
Pilot Peak, mtn., Nv., U.S. E8 134
Pilot Peak, mtn., Wy., U.S. F16 136
Pilot Rock, Or., U.S. E8 136
Pilottown, La., U.S. H9 122
Pilsen see Plzeň, Czech Rep. G9 16
Pilu, stm., Mya. B3 48
Pilzno, Pol. G17 16
Pima, Az., U.S. K7 132
Pimba, Austl. F7 74
Pimenteira, Vereda, stm., Braz. F4 88
Pimentel, Braz. B3 88
Pinang, Pulau, i., Malay. J4 48
Pinarbaşı, Tur. B16 28
Pinar del Río, Cuba A5 102
Pinarello, Fr. H15 18
Pinarhisar, Tur. B10 28
Pinas, Arg. E5 92
Pinatubo, Mount, vol., Phil. C3 52
Pincher Creek, Ab., Can. G17 138
Pinchi Lake, l., B.C., Can. B6 138
Pinckneyville, Il., U.S. F8 120
Pinconning, Mi., U.S. E5 112
Pindale, Mya. B2 48
Pindamonhangaba, Braz. L3 88
Pindaré, stm., Braz. B3 88
Pindaré-Mirim, Braz. B3 88
Píndhos Óros (Pindus Mountains), mts., Grc. D4 28
Pindi Gheb, Pak. B4 54
Pindobaçu, Braz. F5 88
Pindus Mountains see Píndhos Óros, mts., Grc. D4 28
Pindwāra, India F4 54
Pine, stm., Mi., U.S. E5 112
Pine Apple, Al., U.S. F11 122
Pine Barrens, reg., N.J., U.S. E11 114
Pine Bluff, Ar., U.S. C7 122
Pine Bush, N.Y., U.S. C11 114
Pine Castle, Fl., U.S. H4 116
Pine City, Mn., U.S. F6 118
Pine Creek, Austl. B6 74
Pine Creek, stm., Nv., U.S. C9 134
Pine Creek, stm., Pa., U.S. C8 114
Pine Falls, Mb., Can. D17 124
Pinega, Russia D20 8
Pinega, stm., Russia D20 8
Pine Grove, W.V., U.S. E5 114
Pine Hill, Austl. D6 76
Pine Hill, Al., U.S. F11 122
Pine Hills, Fl., U.S. H4 116
Pinehouse Lake, l., Sk., Can. D9 106
Pinehurst, Ga., U.S. D2 116
Pinehurst, Id., U.S. E10 136
Pinehurst, N.C., U.S. A6 116
Pinehurst Lake, l., Ab., Can. B19 138
Pineiós (Peneus), stm., Grc. D5 28
Pine Island, Mn., U.S. G6 118
Pine Island, i., Fl., U.S. J3 116
Pine Island Bay, b., Ant. C30 81
Pinellas Park, Fl., U.S. I3 116
Pine Mountain, mtn., Ca., U.S. H4 134
Pine Pass, p., B.C., Can. A8 138
Pine Point, N.T., Can. C8 106
Pine Ridge, S.D., U.S. D10 126
Pine River, Mb., Can. C13 124
Pine River, Mn., U.S. E4 118
Pinerolo, Italy F4 22
Piñeros, Isla, i., P.R. B4 104a
Pines, Isle of see Juventud, Isla de la, i., Cuba B6 102
Pines, Lake O' The, res., Tx., U.S. E4 122
Pine Swamp Knob, mtn., W.V., U.S. E6 114
Pinetop-Lakeside, Az., U.S. I6 132
Pinetops, N.C., U.S. I8 114
Pinetown, S. Afr. F10 70
Pine Valley, val., Ut., U.S. E3 132
Pineville, Ky., U.S. H2 114
Pineville, La., U.S. F6 122
Pineville, Mo., U.S. H3 120
Pineville, W.V., U.S. G4 114
Pinewood, S.C., U.S. C5 116
Ping, stm., Thai. E5 48
Ping'an, China B5 38
Pingba, China H2 42
Pingchang, China F2 42
Pingding, China C5 42
Pingdingshan, China E5 42
Pingdu, China C8 42
Pingelly, Austl. F3 74
Pinghe, China A6 48
Pinghu, China F9 42
Pingjiang, China G5 42
Pingle, China I4 42
Pingli, China E3 42
Pingliang, China D2 42
Pingluo, China B2 42
Pingnan, China H8 42
Pingnan, China J4 42
Pingquan, China A8 42
Pingshi, China I5 42
Pingtan, China I8 42
Pingtan Dao, i., China I8 42
P'ingtung, Tai. J9 42
Pingwu, China E5 36
Pingxiang, China H5 42
Pingxiang, China J2 42
Pingyang, China H9 42
Pingyao, China C5 42
Pingyi, China D7 42
Pingyin, China C7 42
Pingyuan, China I6 42

Name	Map Ref.	Page
Pinhão, Braz.	F7	88
Pinheiro, Braz.	B3	88
Pinheiros, Braz.	J5	88
Pinhel, Port.	D3	20
Pini, Pulau, i., Indon.	E2	44
Pinillos, Col.	C4	86
Pinjarra, Austl.	F3	74
Pinjug, Russia	F22	8
Pinkiang see Harbin, China	B7	38
Pink Mountain, B.C., Can.	D6	106
Pinnacle, mtn., Va., U.S.	E7	114
Pinnacle Buttes, mtn., Wy., U.S.	G17	136
Pinnacles National Monument, p.o.i., Ca., U.S.	G4	134
Pinnaroo, Austl.	J3	76
Pinneberg, Ger.	C5	16
Pinos, Mex.	D8	100
Pinos, Isla de see Juventud, Isla de la, i., Cuba	B6	102
Pinos, Mount, mtn., Ca., U.S.	I6	134
Pinos Puente, Spain	G7	20
Pinrang, Indon.	E11	50
Pins, Île des, i., N. Cal.	n16	79d
Pins, Pointe aux, c., On., Can.	F8	112
Pinsk, Bela.	H9	10
Pinsk Marshes see Pripet Marshes, reg., Eur.	H12	10
Pinson, Al., U.S.	D12	122
Pinta, Isla, i., Ec.	h11	84a
Pintada Arroyo, stm., N.M., U.S.	G3	128
Pintados, Chile	D3	90
Pintasan, Malay.	A10	50
Pinto Butte, mtn., Sk., Can.	E6	124
Pintoyacu, stm., Ec.	H3	86
Pin Valley National Park, p.o.i., India	C6	54
Pioche, Nv., U.S.	F2	132
Piombino, Italy	H7	22
Pioneer Mine, B.C., Can.	F8	138
Pionerskij, Russia	F3	10
Pionki, Pol.	E17	16
Piorini, stm., Braz.	D5	84
Piorini, Lago, l., Braz.	D5	84
Piotrków, state, Pol.	E15	16
Piotrków Trybunalski, Pol.	E15	16
Pio V. Corpuz, Phil.	E5	52
Piove di Sacco, Italy	E8	22
Pio XII, Braz.	B3	88
Pipanaco, Salar de, pl., Arg.	D4	92
Pīpār, India	E4	54
Piparia, India	G7	54
Pīpar Road, India	E4	54
Pipe Spring National Monument, p.o.i., Az., U.S.	G4	132
Pipestem Creek, stm., N.D., U.S.	G14	124
Pipestone, Mn., U.S.	H2	118
Pipestone, stm., On., Can.	E12	106
Pipestone Creek, stm., Can.	E12	124
Pipestone National Monument, p.o.i., Mn., U.S.	G2	118
Pipinas, Arg.	G9	92
Piplān, Pak.	B3	54
Pipmuacan, Réservoir, res., Qc., Can.	A6	110
Piqua, Oh., U.S.	D1	114
Piquet Carneiro, Braz.	C6	88
Piquiri, stm., Braz.	B11	92
Piracanjuba, Braz.	I1	88
Piracanjuba, stm., Braz.	I1	88
Piracicaba, Braz.	L2	88
Piracicaba, stm., Braz.	L1	88
Piracuruca, Braz.	B5	88
Pirae, Fr. Poly.	v21	78h
Piraeus see Peiraiás, Grc.	F6	28
Piraí do Sul, Braz.	B12	92
Piraju, Braz.	L1	88
Pirajuí, Braz.	L1	88
Piram Island, i., India	H4	54
Piran, Slvn.	E10	22
Pirané, Arg.	B8	92
Piranga, Braz.	K4	88
Piranhas, Braz.	G7	84
Piranhas, stm., Braz.	E1	88
Piranhas, stm., Braz.	C7	88
Piranji, stm., Braz.	C6	88
Pirapemas, Braz.	B3	88
Pirapora, Braz.	I3	88
Piraquara, Braz.	B13	92
Pirassununga, Braz.	K2	88
Pirata, Monte, hill, P.R.	B4	104a
Piratinga, stm., Braz.	H2	88
Piratini, Braz.	E11	92
Piratini, stm., Braz.	D10	92
Piratuba, Braz.	C11	92
Pires do Rio, Braz.	I1	88
Piriápolis, Ur.	G10	92
Pirin, Parki Narodowe, p.o.i., Blg.	H10	26
Piripiri, Braz.	C5	88
Píritu, Ven.	C7	86
Pirmasens, Ger.	G3	16
Pirna, Ger.	F9	16
Pirojpur, Bngl.	G12	54
Pirot, Yugo.	F9	26
Pirovano, Arg.	H7	92
Pirovskoe, Russia	C16	32
Pīr Panjāl Range, mts., Asia	B5	54
Pirtleville, Az., U.S.	L7	132
Pirttikylä, Fin.	E9	8
Piru, Indon.	F8	44
Pisa, Italy	G7	22
Pisagua, Chile	C2	90
Pisco, Peru	F2	84
Pişcolt, Rom.	B9	26
Písek, Czech Rep.	G10	16
Pishan, China	A4	46
Pishchanka, Ukr.	A15	26
Pisinemo, Az., U.S.	K4	132
Pismo Beach, Ca., U.S.	H5	134
Pisticci, Italy	D10	24
Pistoia, Italy	G7	22
Pisuerga, stm., Spain	C6	20
Pit, stm., Ca., U.S.	B4	134
Pit, North Fork, stm., Ca., U.S.	B5	134
Pita, Gui.	G2	64
Pitalito, Col.	G4	86
Pitanga, Braz.	B12	92
Pitangui, Braz.	J3	88
Pitcairn, dep., Pit.	c28	78k
Piteå, Swe.	D9	8
Piteälven, stm., Swe.	D8	8
Piteşti, Rom.	E11	26
Pithāpuram, India	C6	53
Pithiviers, Fr.	F11	14
Pithom, hist., Egypt	H2	58
Pithorāgarh, India	D8	54
Pitinga, stm., Braz.	H12	86
Pitiquito, Mex.	F6	98
Pitkjaranta, Russia	F14	8
Pitljar, Russia	C2	34
Pitomača, Cro.	D14	22
Pitrufquén, Chile	G2	90
Pitt Island, i., B.C., Can.	E5	106
Pitt Lake, l., B.C., Can.	G8	138
Pittsboro, N.C., U.S.	I6	114
Pittsburg, Ks., U.S.	G3	120
Pittsburg, Tx., U.S.	E4	122
Pittsburgh, Pa., U.S.	D6	114
Pittsfield, Il., U.S.	E7	120
Pittsfield, Me., U.S.	F7	110
Pittsfield, Ma., U.S.	B12	114
Pittsford, Mi., U.S.	C1	114
Pittston, Pa., U.S.	C10	114
Pittsview, Al., U.S.	E13	122
Pittsworth, Austl.	F8	76
Pituil, Arg.	D4	92
Pium, Braz.	F1	88
Piura, Peru	E1	84
Piute Peak, mtn., Ca., U.S.	H7	134
Pivan', Russia	F16	34
Pivdennyy Buh, stm., Ukr.	A17	26
Pizarro, Col.	E3	86
Pizzo, Italy	F10	24
Pjakupur, stm., Russia	B13	32
Pjalka, Russia	C19	8
Pjandž (Panj), stm., Asia	B11	56
Pjaozero, ozero, l., Russia	C14	8
Pjasina, stm., Russia	B6	34
Pjasino, ozero, l., Russia	B6	34
Pjasinskij zaliv, b., Russia	B5	34
Pjatigorsk, Russia	F6	32
Pjatovskij, Russia	F19	10
Pjažieva Sel'ga, Russia	F16	8
Placentia Bay, b., Nf., Can.	j23	107a
Placerville, Ca., U.S.	E5	134
Placetas, Cuba	A8	102
Plácido Rosas, Ur.	F11	92
Plai Mat, stm., Thai.	E6	48
Plain City, Ut., U.S.	B4	132
Plain Dealing, La., U.S.	E5	122
Plainfield, Ct., U.S.	C13	114
Plainfield, In., U.S.	I3	112
Plainfield, N.J., U.S.	D11	114
Plains, Ga., U.S.	E14	122
Plains, Ks., U.S.	D8	128
Plains, Mt., U.S.	C12	136
Plainview, Mn., U.S.	G6	118
Plainview, Ne., U.S.	E15	126
Plainview, Tx., U.S.	G7	128
Plainville, In., U.S.	F10	120
Plainwell, Mi., U.S.	F4	112
Plakhtiïvka, Ukr.	C16	26
Plamondon, Ab., Can.	B18	138
Plampang, Indon.	H10	50
Planá, Czech Rep.	G8	16
Plana, L'Illa, i., Spain	F10	20
Planada, Ca., U.S.	F5	134
Planalto, Braz.	C11	92
Planchón, Cerro del (El Planchón, Volcán), vol., S.A.	G2	92
Planeta Rica, Col.	C4	86
Plano, Il., U.S.	C9	120
Plano, Tx., U.S.	D2	122
Plantagenet, On., Can.	E2	110
Plantation, Fl., U.S.	J5	116
Plant City, Fl., U.S.	I3	116
Plantersville, Ms., U.S.	C10	122
Plantsite, Az., U.S.	J7	132
Plaquemine, La., U.S.	G7	122
Plasencia, Spain	D4	20
Plaster Rock, N.B., Can.	D9	110
Plasy, Czech Rep.	G9	16
Plata, Isla de la, i., Ec.	H1	86
Plata, Río de la, est., S.A.	G9	92
Plato, Col.	C4	86
Platte, stm., U.S.	E3	120
Platte, stm., Ne., U.S.	C7	108
Platte, Île, i., Sey.	k13	69b
Platte Center, Ne., U.S.	F15	126
Platte City, Mo., U.S.	E3	120
Platteville, Co., U.S.	A4	128
Platteville, Wi., U.S.	B7	120
Plattsburgh, N.Y., U.S.	F3	110
Plattsmouth, Ne., U.S.	D2	120
Plau, Ger.	C8	16
Plauen, Ger.	F8	16
Plav, Yugo.	G6	26
Plavsk, Russia	G20	10
Playa Azul, Mex.	G7	100
Playa de Fajardo, P.R.	B4	104a
Playa de Guayanilla, P.R.	B2	104a
Playa de Naguabo, P.R.	B4	104a
Playa de Ponce, P.R.	C2	104a
Playa Noriega, Laguna, l., Mex.	A3	100
Playa Vicente, Mex.	G11	100
Playgreen Lake, l., Mb., Can.	E11	106
Play Ku, Viet.	F8	48
Plaza, N.D., U.S.	F12	124
Pleasant, Mount, hill, N.B., Can.	E9	110
Pleasant Bay, N.S., Can.	D16	110
Pleasantdale, Sk., Can.	B9	124
Pleasant Grove, Ut., U.S.	C5	132
Pleasant Hill, Il., U.S.	E7	120
Pleasant Hill, La., U.S.	F5	122
Pleasant Hill, Mo., U.S.	F3	120
Pleasanton, Ks., U.S.	F3	120
Pleasanton, Tx., U.S.	F9	130
Pleasantville, N.J., U.S.	E11	114
Pleasantville, Pa., U.S.	C6	114
Pleaux, Fr.	D8	18
Plehanovo, Russia	F20	10
Plenty, Sk., Can.	C5	124
Plenty, Bay of, b., N.Z.	C7	80
Plentywood, Mt., U.S.	F9	124
Pleščeevo, ozero, l., Russia	D21	10
Pleseck, Russia	E19	8
Plessisville, Qc., Can.	D5	110
Pleszew, Pol.	E13	16
Plétipi, Lac, l., Qc., Can.	E16	106
Plettenbergbaai, S. Afr.	I6	70
Pleven, Blg.	F11	26
Plevna, Mt., U.S.	A8	126
Plitvička Jezera Nacionalni Park, p.o.i., Cro.	F12	22
Pljevlja, Yugo.	F6	26
Pljuskovo, Russia	H16	10
Pljussa, stm., Russia	A11	10
Płock, Pol.	D15	16
Płock, state, Pol.	D15	16
Ploërmel, Fr.	G6	14
Ploieşti, Rom.	E12	26
Plomb du Cantal, mtn., Fr.	D8	18
Plomer, Point, c., Austl.	H9	76
Plön, Ger.	B6	16
Płońsk, Pol.	D16	16
Ploskoe, Russia	H21	10
Plotnica, Bela.	H9	10
Ploudalmézeau, Fr.	F4	14
Plovdiv, Blg.	G11	26
Plovdiv, state, Blg.	G11	26
Plumerville, Ar., U.S.	B6	122
Plummer, Id., U.S.	C9	136
Plumridge Lakes, l., Austl.	E5	74
Plumtree, Zimb.	B8	70
Plungė, Lith.	E4	10
Plutarco Elías Calles, Presa, res., Mex.	G8	98
Plymouth, Monts.	D3	105a
Plymouth, Eng., U.K.	K8	12
Plymouth, Ca., U.S.	E5	134
Plymouth, Il., U.S.	D6	120
Plymouth, Ma., U.S.	C15	114
Plymouth, Ne., U.S.	A11	128
Plymouth, N.H., U.S.	G5	110
Plymouth, N.C., U.S.	I9	114
Plymouth, Oh., U.S.	C3	114
Plymouth, Pa., U.S.	C10	114
Plzeň, Czech Rep.	G9	16
Pô, Burkina	G4	64
Po, stm., Italy	F8	22
Po, Foci del, mth., Italy	F9	22
Po, Mouths of the see Po, Foci del, mth., Italy	F9	22
Poarta Orientală, Pasul, p., Rom.	D9	26
Pobè, Benin	H5	64
Pobeda, gora, mtn., Russia	C18	34
Pobedino, Russia	G17	34
Pobedy, pik, mtn., Asia	F14	32
Poblado Cerro Gordo, P.R.	A3	104a
Poblado Jacaguas, P.R.	B2	104a
Poblado Medianía Alta, P.R.	B4	104a
Poblado Santana, P.R.	B2	104a
Pobra de Trives, Spain	B3	20
Pocahontas, Ar., U.S.	H6	120
Pocahontas, Ia., U.S.	B3	120
Poção, Braz.	E7	88
Pocatello, Id., U.S.	H14	136
Počep, Russia	H16	10
Počinok, Russia	D4	32
Pocitos, Salar, pl., Arg.	B4	92
Poço da Cruz, Açude, res., Braz.	E7	88
Poções, Braz.	H5	88
Pocola, Ok., U.S.	B4	122
Pocomoke City, Md., U.S.	F10	114
Poconé, Braz.	G6	84
Pocono Mountains, hills, Pa., U.S.	C10	114
Pocono Summit, Pa., U.S.	C10	114
Poço Redondo, Braz.	E7	88
Poços de Caldas, Braz.	K2	88
Pocrane, Braz.	J5	88
Podbereze, Russia	D13	10
Podborove, Russia	A18	10
Poddębice, Pol.	E14	16
Poddore, Russia	C13	10
Poděbrady, Czech Rep.	F11	16
Podgorica (Titograd), Yugo.	G6	26
Podjuga, Russia	F19	8
Podkamennaja Tunguska, Russia	B16	32
Podkamennaja Tunguska, stm., Russia	B16	32
Podlasie, reg., Pol.	D19	16
Podol'sk, Russia	E20	10
Podor, Sen.	F2	64
Podporože, Russia	F16	8
Podravina, reg., Cro.	E15	22
Podtësovo, Russia	C16	32
Podujevo, Yugo.	G8	26
Poel, i., Ger.	B7	16
Poelela, Lagoa, l., Moz.	D12	70
Pofadder, S. Afr.	F4	70
Pogar, Russia	H16	10
Poggibonsi, Italy	G8	22
Pogoanele, Rom.	E13	26
Pogoreloe Gorodišče, Russia	D17	10
Pogradec, Alb.	D14	24
Pogradeci see Pogradec, Alb.	D14	24
Pograničnyj, Russia	B9	38
P'ohang, Kor., S.	C2	40
Pohjanmaa, reg., Fin.	D11	8
Pohjois-Karjala, state, Fin.	E14	8
Pohnpei, i., Micron.	I11	78d
Pohri, India	F6	54
Pohvistnevo, Russia	D8	32
Pöide, Est.	B6	10
Poinsett, Cape, c., Ant.	B16	81
Poinsett, Lake, l., S.D., U.S.	C15	126
Point, Tx., U.S.	E3	122
Point Arena, Ca., U.S.	E2	134
Point Au Fer Island, i., La., U.S.	H7	122
Point Baker, Ak., U.S.	E13	140
Pointe-à-la-Garde, Qc., Can.	B10	110
Pointe a la Hache, La., U.S.	H9	122
Pointe-à-Pitre, Guad.	h5	105c
Pointe-à-Pitre-le Raizet, Aéroport de, Guad.	h5	105c
Pointe du Canonnier, c., Guad.	A1	105a
Point Edward, On., Can.	E7	112
Pointe-Noire, Congo	E2	66
Pointe-Noire, Guad.	h5	105c
Point Fortin, Trin.	s12	105f
Point Hope, Ak., U.S.	C6	140
Point Jupiter, c., St. Vin.	p11	105e
Point Lake, l., N.T., Can.	B8	106
Point Marion, Pa., U.S.	E5	114
Point Pelee National Park, p.o.i., On., Can.	G7	112
Point Pleasant, N.J., U.S.	D11	114
Point Reyes National Seashore, p.o.i., Ca., U.S.	E2	134
Point Roberts, Wa., U.S.	B3	136
Point Salines International Airport, Gren.	q10	105e
Point Sapin, N.B., Can.	D12	110
Poisson Blanc, Lac du, res., Qc., Can.	B14	112
Poissy, Fr.	F10	14
Poitiers, Fr.	H9	14
Poitou, hist. reg., Fr.	C5	18
Poivre Atoll, i., Sey.	k12	69b
Pojarkovo, Russia	G14	34
Pojoaque Valley, N.M., U.S.	F2	128
Pojuca, Braz.	G6	88
Pojuca, stm., Braz.	G6	88
Pokaran, India	E3	54
Pokataroo, Austl.	G7	76
Pokharā, Nepal	D10	54
Poko, D.R.C.	D5	66
Pokrovsk, Russia	D14	34
Pokrovskoe, Russia	H19	10
Pola, stm., Russia	C14	10
Polacca Wash, stm., Az., U.S.	H6	132
Polack, Bela.	E11	10
Pola de Lena, Spain	A5	20
Pola de Siero, Spain	A5	20
Poland, ctry., Eur.	D15	16
Polanów, Pol.	B12	16
Polatlı, Tur.	D15	28
Polcura, Chile	H2	92
Poldnevica, Russia	G22	8
Polebridge, Mt., U.S.	B12	136
Pol-e Khomrī, Afg.	B10	56
Polese see Pripet Marshes, reg., Eur.	H12	10
Polesine, reg., Italy	E8	22
Polewali, Indon.	E11	50
Polgár, Hung.	B8	26
Poli, Cam.	C2	66
Poli, China	D8	42
Policastro, Golfo di, b., Italy	E9	24
Police (Pölitz), Pol.	C10	16
Polička, Czech Rep.	G12	16
Polillo Island, i., Phil.	C3	52
Polillo Islands, is., Phil.	C4	52
Pólis, Cyp.	C3	58
Polist', stm., Russia	C14	10
Polistena, Italy	F10	24
Poljarnyj, Russia	B15	8
Poljarnyj, Russia	C24	34
Poljarnyj Ural, mts., Russia	A10	32
Polk, Ne., U.S.	F15	126
Polk, Pa., U.S.	C6	114
Pol'kino, Russia	B8	34
Pollāchi, India	F3	53
Pöllau, Aus.	C12	22
Pollino, Monte, mtn., Italy	E10	24
Pollock, La., U.S.	F6	122
Pollock, S.D., U.S.	B12	126
Polnovo-Seliger, Russia	C15	10
Polo, Il., U.S.	B8	120
Polomet', stm., Russia	C15	10
Polonnaruwa, Sri L.	H5	53
Polonnaruwa, hist., Sri L.	H5	53
Polotnjanyj, Russia	F19	10
Polotsk see Polack, Bela.	E11	10
Polski Trămbeš, Blg.	F12	26
Polson, Mt., U.S.	C12	136
Poltava, Ukr.	E4	32
Poltimore, Qc., Can.	C14	112
Põltsamaa, Est.	G12	8
Poluj, stm., Russia	A11	32
Polunočnoe, Russia	B10	32
Polur, India	E4	53
Polvijärvi, Fin.	E13	8
Polýaigos, i., Grc.	G7	28
Polynesia, is., Oc.	J22	142
Polysajevo, Russia	F6	34
Pomarkku, Fin.	F9	8
Pombal, Braz.	D7	88
Pomerania, hist. reg., Eur.	C11	16
Pomeranian Bay, b., Eur.	B10	16
Pomerene, Az., U.S.	K6	132
Pomerode, Braz.	C13	92
Pomeroy, Ia., U.S.	B3	120
Pomeroy, Wa., U.S.	D9	136
Pomfret, S. Afr.	D6	70
Pomi, Rom.	B10	26
Pomme de Terre, stm., Mn., U.S.	F3	118
Pomme de Terre, stm., Mo., U.S.	G4	120
Pomme de Terre Lake, res., Mo., U.S.	G4	120
Pomona, Ca., U.S.	I8	134
Pomona, Ks., U.S.	F2	120
Pomona Lake, res., Ks., U.S.	F2	120
Pomorskij proliv, strt., Russia	B24	8
Pompano Beach, Fl., U.S.	J5	116
Pompei, hist., Italy	D8	24
Pompejevka, Russia	G15	34
Pompéu, Braz.	J3	88
Pomquet, N.S., Can.	E15	110
Ponass Lakes, l., Sk., Can.	B9	124
Ponazyrevo, Russia	G22	8
Ponca, Ne., U.S.	B1	120
Ponca City, Ok., U.S.	E11	128
Ponca Creek, stm., U.S.	E14	126
Ponce, P.R.	B2	104a
Ponce, Aeropuerto, P.R.	B2	104a
Ponce de Leon, Fl., U.S.	G12	122
Poncha Pass, p., Co., U.S.	C2	128
Pond Creek, Ok., U.S.	E11	128
Ponderay, Id., U.S.	B10	136
Pondicherry (Puduchcheri), India	F4	53
Pondicherry, state, India	E5	53
Pond Inlet, Nu., Can.	A15	106
Pond Inlet, b., Nu., Can.	A15	106
Pondosa, Ca., U.S.	B4	134
Ponente, Riviera di, cst., Italy	F5	22
Ponérihouen, N. Cal.	m15	79d
Ponferrada, Spain	B4	20
Pongolo, stm., S. Afr.	E10	70
Poniatowa, Pol.	E17	16
Ponizove, Russia	E14	10
Ponnaiyār, stm., India	E4	53
Ponnāni, India	F2	53
Ponnūru Nidubrolu, India	C5	53
Ponoj, Russia	C19	8
Ponoj, stm., Russia	C18	8
Ponoka, Ab., Can.	D17	138
Ponorogo, Indon.	G7	50
Pons, Fr.	D5	18
Ponta Delgada, Port.	C3	60
Ponta Grossa, Braz.	B12	92
Pontalina, Braz.	I1	88
Ponta Porã, Braz.	D5	90
Pontarlier, Fr.	H15	14
Pontas de Pedra, Braz.	D8	88
Pontassieve, Italy	G8	22
Pontchartrain, Lake, l., La., U.S.	G8	122
Pontchâteau, Fr.	G6	14
Pont-de-Vaux, Fr.	C10	18
Ponte Alta do Bom Jesus, Braz.	G2	88
Ponte-Caldelas, Spain	B2	20
Ponte de Lima, Port.	C2	20
Pontedera, Italy	G7	22
Pontedeume, Spain	A2	20
Ponte do Púngoè, Moz.	A12	70
Ponteix, Sk., Can.	E6	124
Ponte Nova, Braz.	K4	88
Ponte Serrada, Braz.	C12	92
Pontevedra, Spain	B2	20
Pontevedra, co., Spain	B2	20
Pontiac, Il., U.S.	D9	120
Pontiac, Mi., U.S.	B2	114
Pontianak, Indon.	C6	50
Pontine Islands see Ponziane, Isole, is., Italy	D6	24
Pontivy, Fr.	F5	14
Pontoise, Fr.	E11	14
Pontotoc, Ms., U.S.	C9	122
Pontotoc, Tx., U.S.	D9	130
Pontremoli, Italy	F6	22
Pontresina, Switz.	D6	22
Pont-Rouge, Qc., Can.	D5	110
Ponts, Spain	C12	20
Pont-sur-Yonne, Fr.	F12	14
Pontus Mountains see Doğu Karadeniz Dağları, mts., Tur.	A5	56
Pontypridd, Wales, U.K.	J9	12
Ponyri, Russia	H19	10
Ponziane, Isole (Pontine Islands), is., Italy	D6	24
Poole, Eng., U.K.	K11	12
Pooley Island, i., B.C., Can.	D2	138
Poolville, Tx., U.S.	B10	130
Pooncarie, Austl.	I4	76
Poopó, Bol.	C3	90
Poopó, Lago, l., Bol.	C3	90
Popayán, Col.	F3	86
Pope, Ms., U.S.	C8	122
Popeşti-Leordeni, Rom.	E13	26
Popham Bay, b., Nu., Can.	C17	106
Popigaj, Russia	B11	34
Popigaj, stm., Russia	B10	34
Popiltah Lake, l., Austl.	I3	76
Poplar, Mt., U.S.	F8	124
Poplar, stm., Can.	B16	124
Poplar, stm., N.A.	F8	124
Poplar, West Fork (West Poplar), stm., N.A.	F8	124
Poplar Bluff, Mo., U.S.	H7	120
Poplar Hill, On., Can.	E12	106
Poplar Point, Mb., Can.	D16	124
Poplarville, Ms., U.S.	G9	122
Popocatépetl, Volcán, vol., Mex.	F9	100
Popoh, Indon.	H7	50
Popokabaka, D.R.C.	F3	66
Popoli, Italy	H10	22
Popondetta, Pap. N. Gui.	b4	79a
Popovo, Blg.	F13	26
Poprad, Slov.	G16	16
Poprad, stm., Eur.	G16	16
Popricani, Rom.	B14	26
Pŏptong-ŭp, Kor., N.	E7	38
Poquoson, Va., U.S.	G9	114
Porangatu, Braz.	G1	88
Porbandar, India	H2	54
Porce, stm., Col.	D4	86
Porcher Island, i., B.C., Can.	E4	106
Porco, Bol.	C3	90
Porcos, stm., Braz.	G3	88
Porcuna, Spain	G6	20
Porcupine, stm., N.A.	B3	106
Pordenone, Italy	D9	22
Pordim, Blg.	F11	26
Poreče, Russia	E18	10
Poreče-Rybnoe, Russia	C22	10
Porhov, Russia	C12	10
Pori (Björneborg), Fin.	F9	8
Porjaguba, Russia	C15	8
Porlamar, Ven.	B10	86
Porog, Russia	E18	8
Poronajsk, Russia	G17	34
Poroshkove, Ukr.	H18	16
Porpoise Bay, b., Ant.	B17	81
Porrentruy, Switz.	C3	22
Porretta Terme, Italy	F7	22
Porsangen, b., Nor.	A11	8
Porsangerhalvøya, pen., Nor.	A11	8
Porsgrunn, Nor.	G3	8
Porsuk, stm., Tur.	D13	28
Portachuelo, Bol.	C4	90
Port Adelaide, Austl.	J2	76
Portadown, N. Ire., U.K.	G6	12
Portage, Mi., U.S.	F4	112
Portage, Ut., U.S.	B4	132
Portage Bay, b., Mb., Can.	C15	124
Portage Lake, l., Mi., U.S.	D10	118
Portage la Prairie, Mb., Can.	E15	124
Portageville, Mo., U.S.	H8	120
Portal, Ga., U.S.	D4	116
Portal, N.D., U.S.	F11	124
Port Alberni, B.C., Can.	G6	138
Portalegre, Port.	E3	20
Portalegre, state, Port.	E3	20
Portales, N.M., U.S.	G5	128
Port Alfred, S. Afr.	H8	70
Port Alice, B.C., Can.	F3	138
Port Allen, La., U.S.	G7	122
Port Alma, Austl.	D8	76
Port Angeles, Wa., U.S.	B3	136
Port Antonio, Jam.	i14	104d
Port Aransas, Tx., U.S.	G10	130
Portarlington, Ire.	H5	12
Port Arthur, Austl.	o13	77a
Port Arthur see Lüshun, China	E4	38
Port Arthur, Tx., U.S.	H4	122
Port Askaig, Scot., U.K.	F6	12
Port Augusta, Austl.	F7	74
Port au Port Peninsula, pen., Nf., Can.	B17	110
Port-au-Prince, Haiti	C11	102
Port-au-Prince, Baie de, b., Haiti	C11	102
Port Austin, Mi., U.S.	D6	112
Port Blair, India	F7	46
Port Borden, P.E., Can.	D13	110
Port Byron, Il., U.S.	J8	118
Port Canning, India	G12	54
Port-Cartier, Qc., Can.	E17	106
Port Chalmers, N.Z.	G4	80
Port Charlotte, Fl., U.S.	J3	116
Port Clinton, Oh., U.S.	C3	114
Port Clyde, Me., U.S.	G7	110
Port Colborne, On., Can.	F10	112
Port Coquitlam, B.C., Can.	G8	138
Port-de-Paix, Haiti	C11	102
Port Dickson, Malay.	K5	48
Porte Crayon, Mount, mtn., W.V., U.S.	F6	114
Port Edward see Weihai, China	C10	42
Port Edward, S. Afr.	G10	70
Port Edwards, Wi., U.S.	G9	118
Porteirinha, Braz.	H4	88
Portel, Braz.	D7	84
Port Elgin, N.B., Can.	D12	110
Port Elgin, On., Can.	D8	112
Port Elizabeth, S. Afr.	H7	70
Port-en-Bessin, Fr.	E8	14
Porter, Tx., U.S.	G3	122
Port Erin, I. of Man	G8	12
Porter Point, c., St. Vin.	o11	105e
Porterville, S. Afr.	H4	70
Porterville, Ca., U.S.	G7	134
Porterville, Ms., U.S.	E10	122
Portete, Bahía, b., Col.	A6	86
Port Fairy, Austl.	L4	76
Port Gamble, Wa., U.S.	C4	136
Port-Gentil, Gabon	E1	66
Port Gibson, Ms., U.S.	F8	122
Port Graham, Ak., U.S.	E9	140
Port-Harcourt, Nig.	I6	64
Port Hardy, B.C., Can.	F3	138
Port Hawkesbury, N.S., Can.	E15	110
Port Hedland, Austl.	D3	74
Port Heiden, Ak., U.S.	E8	140
Port Hill, P.E., Can.	D13	110
Porthmadog, Wales, U.K.	I8	12
Port Hood, N.S., Can.	D15	110
Port Hope, On., Can.	E11	112
Port Hope, Mi., U.S.	E7	112
Port Huron, Mi., U.S.	B3	114
Portimão, Port.	G2	20
Port Isabel, Tx., U.S.	H10	130
Port Jervis, N.Y., U.S.	C11	114
Port Kembla, Austl.	J8	76
Port Lairge see Waterford, Ire.	I5	12
Portland, Austl.	I7	76
Portland, Austl.	L3	76
Portland, Ar., U.S.	D7	122
Portland, In., U.S.	H5	112
Portland, Me., U.S.	G6	110
Portland, N.D., U.S.	G16	124
Portland, Or., U.S.	E4	136
Portland, Tn., U.S.	H11	120
Portland, Tx., U.S.	G10	130
Portland, Bill of, c., Eng., U.K.	K10	12
Portland, Cape, c., Austl.	n13	77a
Portland, Isle of, i., Eng., U.K.	K10	12
Portland Bay, b., Austl.	L3	76
Portland Bight, b., Jam.	j13	104d
Portland Point, c., Jam.	j13	104d
Portlaoise, Ire.	H5	12
Port Lavaca, Tx., U.S.	F11	130
Port Leyden, N.Y., U.S.	E14	112
Port Lincoln, Austl.	F7	74
Port Loko, S.L.	H2	64
Port-Louis, Guad.	h5	105c
Port Louis, Mrts.	h10	69a
Port-Lyautey see Kénitra, Mor.	C3	64
Port MacDonnell, Austl.	L3	76
Port Macquarie, Austl.	H9	76
Port Maria, Jam.	i14	104d
Port McNeill, B.C., Can.	F3	138
Port McNicoll, On., Can.	D10	112
Port Moller, Ak., U.S.	E7	140
Port Morant, Jam.	j14	104d
Portmore, Jam.	j13	104d
Port Moresby, Pap. N. Gui.	b4	79a
Port Morien, N.S., Can.	D17	110
Port Neches, Tx., U.S.	H4	122
Port Nelson, Mb., Can.	D12	106
Portneuf, stm., Qc., Can.	B7	110
Portneuf, stm., Id., U.S.	H14	136
Port Neville, B.C., Can.	F4	138
Port Nolloth, S. Afr.	F3	70
Port Norris, N.J., U.S.	E10	114
Porto, Port.	C2	20
Porto, state, Port.	C2	20
Porto Acre, Braz.	E4	84
Porto Alegre, Braz.	E12	92
Porto Alegre, S. Tom./P.	J6	64
Porto Amboim, Ang.	C1	68
Portobelo, Pan.	H8	102
Porto Calvo, Braz.	E8	88
Porto de Moz, Braz.	D7	84
Porto de Pedras, Braz.	E8	88
Porto dos Gaúchos, Braz.	F6	84
Porto Empedocle, Italy	G7	24
Porto Esperança, Braz.	C5	90
Porto Esperidião, Braz.	G6	84
Porto Feliz, Braz.	L2	88
Portoferraio, Italy	H7	22
Porto Ferreira, Braz.	K2	88
Port of Ness, Scot., U.K.	C6	12
Porto Franco, Braz.	D2	88
Port of Spain, Trin.	s12	105f
Portogruaro, Italy	E9	22
Portola, Ca., U.S.	D5	134
Portomaggiore, Italy	F8	22
Porto Mendes, Braz.	B10	92
Porto Murtinho, Braz.	D5	90
Porto Nacional, Braz.	F1	88
Porto-Novo, Benin	H5	64
Porto Novo, India	F4	53
Port Orange, Fl., U.S.	G5	116
Port Orchard, Wa., U.S.	C4	136
Port Orford, Or., U.S.	H2	136
Porto San Giorgio, Italy	G10	22
Porto Santana, Braz.	D7	84
Porto Santo, i., Port.	C1	64
Porto Santo Stefano, ngh., Italy	H7	22
Porto Seguro, Braz.	I6	88
Porto Tolle, Italy	F9	22
Porto Torres, Italy	D2	24
Porto União, Braz.	C12	92
Porto Válter, Braz.	E3	84
Porto-Vecchio, Fr.	H15	18
Porto Velho, Braz.	E5	84
Portoviejo, Ec.	H1	86
Port Patrick, Vanuatu	m17	79d
Port Perry, On., Can.	D11	112
Port Phillip Bay, b., Austl.	L5	76
Port Pirie, Austl.	F7	74
Portree, Scot., U.K.	D6	12
Port Renfrew, B.C., Can.	H6	138
Port Rowan, On., Can.	F9	112
Port Royal, Jam.	j14	104d
Port Royal, Pa., U.S.	D8	114
Port Royal, S.C., U.S.	D5	116
Port Said see Bûr Sa'îd, Egypt	G3	58
Port Saint Joe, Fl., U.S.	H13	122
Port Saint Johns, S. Afr.	G9	70
Port Saint Lucie, Fl., U.S.	I5	116
Port Sanilac, Mi., U.S.	E7	112
Port Saunders, Nf., Can.	i22	107a
Portsea, Austl.	L5	76
Portsmouth, Dom.	i6	105c
Portsmouth, Eng., U.K.	K11	12
Portsmouth, N.H., U.S.	G6	110
Portsmouth, Oh., U.S.	F2	114
Portsmouth, Va., U.S.	H9	114
Portsoy, Scot., U.K.	D10	12
Port Stanley, On., Can.	F8	112
Port Sudan see Būr Sūdān, Sudan	D7	62
Port Sulphur, La., U.S.	H9	122
Port Talbot, Wales, U.K.	J9	12
Porttipahdan tekojärvi, l., Fin.	B12	8
Port Townsend, Wa., U.S.	B4	136
Portugal, ctry., Eur.	D3	20
Portugalete, Spain	A7	20
Portuguesa, state, Ven.	C7	86
Portuguesa, stm., Ven.	C8	86
Portuguese Guinea see Guinea-Bissau, ctry., Afr.	G1	64
Port Vila, Vanuatu	k17	79d
Portville, N.Y., U.S.	B7	114
Port-Vladimir, Russia	B15	8
Port Wentworth, Ga., U.S.	D4	116
Port Wing, Wi., U.S.	E7	118
Porus, Jam.	i13	104d
Porvenir, Chile	J2	90
Porvoo, Fin.	F11	8
Porzuna, Spain	E6	20
Posadas, Arg.	C9	92
Posadas, Spain	G5	20
Posavina, val., Eur.	E14	22
Pošehon'e, Russia	B22	10
Poseidon, Temple of, hist., Grc.	F6	28
Posen, Mi., U.S.	C6	112
Poshan see Boshan, China	C7	42
Posio, Fin.	C12	8
Poso, Indon.	D12	50
Poso, Danau, l., Indon.	D12	50
Poso, Teluk, b., Indon.	D12	50
Pospeliha, Russia	D14	32
Posse, Braz.	H2	88
Possession Island, i., Nmb.	E2	70
Pössneck, Ger.	F7	16
Possum Kingdom Lake, res., Tx., U.S.	B9	130
Post, Tx., U.S.	A6	130
Posta de Jihuites, Mex.	I2	130
Postelle, Tn., U.S.	A1	116
Postmasburg, S. Afr.	F6	70
Postojna, Slvn.	E11	22
Postrervalle, Bol.	C4	90
Postville, Ia., U.S.	A6	120
Potaro, stm., Guy.	E12	86
Potaro-Siparuni, state, Guy.	E12	86
Potchefstroom, S. Afr.	E8	70
Poté, Braz.	I5	88
Poteau, Ok., U.S.	B4	122
Poteet, Tx., U.S.	E9	130
Potenza, Italy	D9	24
Potgietersrus, S. Afr.	D9	70
Poth, Tx., U.S.	E9	130
Potholes Reservoir, res., Wa., U.S.	D7	136
Poti, Geor.	F6	32
Poti, stm., Braz.	C4	88
Potiraguá, Braz.	H6	88
Potiskum, Nig.	G7	64
Potomac, Il., U.S.	H2	112
Potomac, stm., U.S.	F9	114
Potomac, North Fork South Branch, stm., U.S.	F6	114
Potomac, South Branch, stm., U.S.	E7	114
Potomac Heights, Md., U.S.	F8	114
Potosí, Bol.	C3	90
Potosi, Mo., U.S.	G7	120
Potrerillos, Chile	C3	92
Potro, Cerro del (El Potro, Cerro), mtn., S.A.	D3	92
Potsdam, Ger.	D9	16
Potsdam, N.Y., U.S.	F2	110
Pott, Île, i., N. Cal.	I14	79d
Potter, Ne., U.S.	F9	126
Potterville, Mi., U.S.	B1	114
Potts Camp, Ms., U.S.	C9	122
Pottstown, Pa., U.S.	D10	114
Pottsville, Pa., U.S.	D9	114
Pouancé, Fr.	G7	14
Poughkeepsie, N.Y., U.S.	C11	114
Poulan, Ga., U.S.	E2	116
Poulsbo, Wa., U.S.	C4	136
Poultney, Vt., U.S.	G3	110
Poum, N. Cal.	m14	79d
Pouso Alegre, Braz.	L3	88
Poŭthĭsăt, Camb.	F6	48
Poŭthĭsăt, stm., Camb.	F6	48
Poutini see Westland National Park, p.o.i., N.Z.	F3	80
Poutrincourt, Lac, l., Qc., Can.	A2	110
Považská Bystrica, Slov.	G14	16
Povenec, Russia	E16	8
Póvoa de Varzim, Port.	C2	20
Povorino, Russia	D6	32
Povorotnyj, mys, c., Russia	C10	38
Povungnituk, Qc., Can.	C15	106
Povungnituk, stm., Qc., Can.	C15	106
Powassan, On., Can.	B10	112
Poway, Ca., U.S.	K9	134
Powder, stm., U.S.	A7	126
Powder, stm., Or., U.S.	F9	136
Powder, South Fork, stm., Wy., U.S.	D6	126
Powderly, Tx., U.S.	D3	122
Powder River Pass, p., Wy., U.S.	C5	126
Powell, Wy., U.S.	C4	126
Powell, stm., U.S.	H2	114
Powell, Lake, res., U.S.	F5	132
Powell Creek, stm., Austl.	E5	76
Powellhurst, Or., U.S.	E4	136
Powell Lake, l., B.C., Can.	F6	138
Powell River, B.C., Can.	G6	138
Powers, Mi., U.S.	C2	112
Powers, Or., U.S.	H2	136
Powers Lake, N.D., U.S.	F11	124
Powhatan, Va., U.S.	G7	114
Powhatan Point, Oh., U.S.	E4	114
Poxoréu, Braz.	G7	84

I•46 Poya-Quin

Name	Map Ref.	Page
Poya, N. Cal.	m15	79d
Poyang Hu, l., China	G7	42
Poyen, Ar., U.S.	C6	122
Poygan, Lake, l., Wi., U.S.	G9	118
Požarevac, Yugo.	E8	26
Poza Rica de Hidalgo, Mex.	E10	100
Požega, Cro.	E14	22
Požega, Yugo.	F7	26
Poznań, Pol.	D12	16
Poznań, state, Pol.	D12	16
Pozoblanco, Spain	F6	20
Pozo-Cañada, Spain	F9	20
Pozo del Molle, Arg.	F6	92
Pozo del Tigre, Arg.	B7	92
Pozuelos, Ven.	B9	86
Pozzallo, Italy	H8	24
Pozzuoli, Italy	D8	24
Prachatice, Czech Rep.	G10	16
Prachin Buri, Thai.	E5	48
Prachuap Khiri Khan, Thai.	G4	48
Pradera, Col.	F3	86
Prado, Braz.	I6	88
Prados, Braz.	K3	88
Præstø, Den.	A8	16
Prague see Praha, Czech Rep.	F10	16
Prague, Ne., U.S.	F16	126
Prague, Ok., U.S.	B2	122
Praha (Prague), Czech Rep.	F10	16
Praha, state, Czech Rep.	F10	16
Praha, mtn., Czech Rep.	G9	16
Prahova, state, Rom.	D13	26
Prahova, stm., Rom.	E13	26
Praia, C.V.	I10	65a
Praia Grande, Braz.	D13	92
Prainha Nova, Braz.	E5	84
Prairie, Austl.	C5	76
Prairie, stm., Mi., U.S.	G4	112
Prairie City, Il., U.S.	D7	120
Prairie City, Ia., U.S.	C4	120
Prairie Creek, stm., Ne., U.S.	F15	126
Prairie Dog Creek, stm., Ks., U.S.	B8	128
Prairie du Chien, Wi., U.S.	A6	120
Prairie du Sac, Wi., U.S.	H9	118
Prairie River, Sk., Can.	B11	124
Prairies, Coteau des, hills, U.S.	C16	126
Prairies, Lake of the, res., Can.	C12	124
Prairie View, Tx., U.S.	G3	122
Prairie Village, Ks., U.S.	B14	128
Pran Buri, Thai.	F4	48
Pran Buri, stm., Thai.	F4	48
Prānhita, stm., India	B5	53
Praslin, i., Sey.	j13	69b
Prasonísi, Ákra, c., Grc.	H10	28
Praszka, Pol.	E14	16
Prata, Braz.	J1	88
Prata, stm., Braz.	J1	88
Prata, stm., Braz.	I2	88
Pratāpgarh, India	F5	54
Pratápolis, Braz.	K2	88
Pratas Island see Tungsha Tao, i., Tai.	K7	42
Prat de Llobregat see El Prat de Llobregat, Spain	C12	20
Prato, Italy	G8	22
Pratt, Ks., U.S.	D10	128
Prattville, Al., U.S.	E12	122
Pratudão, stm., Braz.	H3	88
Pravdinskij, Russia	D20	10
Pravia, Spain	A4	20
Praya, Indon.	H10	50
Preajba, Rom.	E12	26
Prečistoe, Russia	G19	8
Predeal, Rom.	D12	26
Preeceville, Sk., Can.	C11	124
Preetz, Ger.	B6	16
Pregolja, stm., Russia	F3	10
Pregonero, Ven.	D6	86
Preguiças, stm., Braz.	B4	88
Preila, Lith.	E4	10
Prěk Poŭthĭ, Camb.	G7	48
Prelate, Sk., Can.	D4	124
Premnitz, Ger.	D8	16
Premont, Tx., U.S.	G9	130
Premuda, Otok, i., Cro.	F11	22
Prenjasi see Prrenjas, Alb.	C14	24
Prentiss, Ms., U.S.	F9	122
Prenzlau, Ger.	C9	16
Preobraženie, Russia	C10	38
Preparis Island, i., Mya.	F7	46
Preparis North Channel, strt., Mya.	E7	46
Preparis South Channel, strt., Mya.	F7	46
Přerov, Czech Rep.	G13	16
Prescott, On., Can.	D14	112
Prescott, Az., U.S.	I4	132
Prescott, Ar., U.S.	D5	122
Prescott, Wi., U.S.	G6	118
Prescott Island, i., Nu., Can.	A11	106
Presidencia de la Plaza, Arg.	C7	92
Presidencia Roca, Arg.	C8	92
Presidencia Roque Sáenz Peña, Arg.	C7	92
Presidente Dutra, Braz.	C3	88
Presidente Epitácio, Braz.	D6	90
Presidente Hayes, state, Para.	B8	92
Presidente Prudente, Braz.	D6	90
Presidio, Tx., U.S.	E3	130
Presidio, stm., Mex.	D6	100
Presnogor'kovka, Kaz.	D11	32
Prešov, Slov.	H17	16
Prespa, Lake, l., Eur.	D14	24
Presque Isle, Me., U.S.	D8	110
Presque Isle, pen., Pa., U.S.	B5	114
Prestea, Ghana	H4	64
Preston, Eng., U.K.	H10	12
Preston, Id., U.S.	A5	132
Preston, Ia., U.S.	B7	120
Preston, Ks., U.S.	D10	128
Preston, Mn., U.S.	H6	118
Prestonsburg, Ky., U.S.	G3	114
Prestwick, Scot., U.K.	F8	12
Preto, stm., Braz.	I9	86
Preto, stm., Braz.	I2	88
Preto, stm., Braz.	F3	88
Preto, stm., Braz.	B4	88
Preto, stm., Braz.	G1	88
Preto, stm., Braz.	K1	88
Preto, stm., Braz.	L4	88
Preto do Igapó-açu, stm., Braz.	E5	84
Pretoria, S. Afr.	D9	70
Pretty Prairie, Ks., U.S.	D10	128
Préveza, Grc.	E3	28
Prey Lvéa, Camb.	G7	48
Prey Vêng, Camb.	G7	48
Pribilof Islands, is., Ak., U.S.	E5	140
Priboj, Yugo.	F6	26
Příbram, Czech Rep.	G10	16
Price, Ut., U.S.	D6	132
Price, stm., Ut., U.S.	D6	132
Price Island, i., B.C., Can.	D2	138
Prichard, Al., U.S.	G10	122
Prickly Pear Cays, is., Anguilla	A1	105a
Priddy, Tx., U.S.	C9	130
Priego de Córdoba, Spain	G6	20
Priekule, Lat.	D4	10
Priekule, Lith.	E4	10
Prieska, S. Afr.	F6	70
Priest, stm., Id., U.S.	B10	136
Priest Lake, res., Id., U.S.	B9	136
Priest River, Id., U.S.	B10	136
Prieta, Peña, mtn., Spain	A6	20
Prieto Diaz, Phil.	D5	52
Prievidza, Slov.	H14	16
Prijedor, Bos.	E3	26
Prilep, Mac.	B4	28
Priluki, Russia	A22	10
Primeira Cruz, Braz.	B4	88
Primera, Tx., U.S.	H10	130
Primero, stm., Arg.	E6	92
Primghar, Ia., U.S.	A2	120
Primorsk, Russia	F13	8
Primorskij, Russia	C9	38
Primorskij hrebet, mts., Russia	F10	34
Primo Tapia, Mex.	K8	134
Primrose Lake, l., Can.	E9	106
Prince Albert, Sk., Can.	A8	124
Prince Albert, S. Afr.	H6	70
Prince Albert Sound, strt., N.T., Can.	A7	106
Prince Alfred, Cape, c., N.T., Can.	B15	140
Prince Charles Island, i., Nu., Can.	B15	106
Prince Charles Mountains, mts., Ant.	C11	81
Prince Edward Island, state, Can.	D13	110
Prince Edward Island, i., P.E., Can.	F18	106
Prince Edward Island National Park, p.o.i., P.E., Can.	D13	110
Prince Frederick, Md., U.S.	F9	114
Prince George, B.C., Can.	C8	138
Prince George, Va., U.S.	G8	114
Prince Gustaf Adolf Sea, Can.	B4	141
Prince of Wales Island, i., Austl.	B8	74
Prince of Wales Island, i., Nu., Can.	A11	106
Prince of Wales Island, i., Ak., U.S.	E13	140
Prince of Wales Strait, strt., N.T., Can.	B15	140
Prince Olav Coast, cst., Ant.	B9	81
Prince Patrick Island, i., N.T., Can.	A16	140
Prince Regent Inlet, b., Nu., Can.	A12	106
Prince Rupert, B.C., Can.	E4	106
Prince Rupert Bluff Point, c., Dom.	i5	105c
Princes Islands see Kızıl Adalar, is., Tur.	C11	28
Princess Anne, Md., U.S.	F10	114
Princess Astrid Coast, cst., Ant.	C6	81
Princess Charlotte Bay, b., Austl.	B8	74
Princess Martha Coast, cst., Ant.	C4	81
Princess Ragnhild Coast, cst., Ant.	C7	81
Princess Royal Island, i., B.C., Can.	C1	138
Princes Town, Trin.	s12	105f
Princeton, B.C., Can.	G10	138
Princeton, Ca., U.S.	D3	134
Princeton, In., U.S.	F10	120
Princeton, Ky., U.S.	G9	120
Princeton, Me., U.S.	E9	110
Princeton, Mi., U.S.	B2	112
Princeton, N.J., U.S.	D11	114
Princeton, N.C., U.S.	A7	116
Princeton, W.V., U.S.	G4	114
Princeton, Wi., U.S.	H9	118
Princeville, Qc., Can.	D4	110
Princeville, Il., U.S.	D8	120
Prince William Sound, strt., Ak., U.S.	D10	140
Príncipe, i., S. Tom./P.	I6	64
Príncipe da Beira, Braz.	F5	84
Prineville, Or., U.S.	F6	136
Pringsewu, Indon.	F4	50
Prinses Margrietkanaal, can., Neth.	A14	14
Prins Karls Forland, i., Nor.	B27	141
Prinzapolka, stm., Nic.	F5	102
Priozërnyj, Kaz.	E14	32
Priozersk, Russia	F14	8
Pripet (Prypjac'), stm., Eur.	H10	10
Pripet Marshes, reg., Eur.	H12	10
Pripoljarnyj Ural, mts., Russia	A9	32
Priština, Yugo.	G8	26
Pritchett, Co., U.S.	D6	128
Pritzwalk, Ger.	C8	16
Privas, Fr.	E10	18
Priverno, Italy	C7	24
Privodino, Russia	F22	8
Prizren, Yugo.	G7	26
Prjaža, Russia	F15	8
Probolinggo, Indon.	G8	50
Probstzella, Ger.	F7	16
Procida, Isola di, i., Italy	D7	24
Procter, B.C., Can.	G13	138
Proctor, Mn., U.S.	E6	118
Proctor Lake, res., Tx., U.S.	C9	130
Proddatūr, India	D4	53
Proença-a-Nova, Port.	E2	20
Progreso, Mex.	B8	100
Progreso, Mex.	B3	102
Progreso, Mex.	K10	134
Progreso, Ur.	G9	92
Prohladnyj, Russia	F6	32
Project City, Ca., U.S.	C3	134
Prokopevsk, Russia	D15	32
Prokuplje, Yugo.	F8	26
Prokuševo, Russia	G16	8
Proletarskij, Russia	E20	10
Prome (Pyè), Mya.	C2	48
Pronja, stm., Bela.	G14	10
Pronja, stm., Russia	F21	10
Prony, Baie de, b., N. Cal.	n16	79d
Prophet, stm., B.C., Can.	D6	106
Prophetstown, Il., U.S.	C8	120
Propriá, Braz.	F7	88
Propriano, Fr.	H14	18
Proserpine, Austl.	C7	76
Prosna, stm., Pol.	E14	16
Prospect, Oh., U.S.	D2	114
Prosperidad, Phil.	F5	52
Prosser, Wa., U.S.	D7	136
Prostějov, Czech Rep.	G12	16
Prostki, Pol.	C18	16
Proston, Austl.	F8	76
Proszowice, Pol.	F16	16
Protection, Ks., U.S.	D9	128
Protem, S. Afr.	I5	70
Protva, stm., Russia	F20	10
Provadija, Blg.	F14	26
Prøven (Kangersuatsiaq), Grnld.	C14	141
Provence, hist. reg., Fr.	F12	18
Providence, Ky., U.S.	G10	120
Providence, R.I., U.S.	C14	114
Providence, Ut., U.S.	B5	132
Providence, Atoll de, i., Sey.	k12	69b
Providence, Cape, c., N.Z.	H2	80
Providencia, Mex.	G4	130
Providencia, Isla de, i., Col.	F7	102
Providenciales, i., T./C. Is.	B11	102
Providenija, Russia	D26	34
Provincetown, Ma., U.S.	B15	114
Provins, Fr.	F12	14
Provo, Ut., U.S.	C5	132
Provo, stm., Ut., U.S.	C5	132
Provost, Ab., Can.	B3	124
Prrenjas, Alb.	C14	24
Prudentópolis, Braz.	B12	92
Prudhoe Bay, Ak., U.S.	B10	140
Prudhoe Island, i., Austl.	C7	76
Prudnik, Pol.	F13	16
Pruszków, Pol.	D16	16
Prut, stm., Eur.	D15	26
Pružany, Bela.	H7	10
Prydz Bay, b., Ant.	B12	81
Pryluky, Ukr.	D4	32
Pryor, Ok., U.S.	H2	120
Przasnysz, Pol.	D16	16
Przedbórz, Pol.	E15	16
Przemyśl, Pol.	G18	16
Przemyśl, state, Pol.	F18	16
Przeworsk, Pol.	F18	16
Psachná, Grc.	E6	28
Pskov, Russia	C11	10
Pskov, Lake, l., Eur.	B11	10
Pskovskaja oblast', co., Russia	C11	10
Pszczyna, Pol.	G14	16
Ptarmigan, Cape, c., N.T., Can.	A7	106
Ptolemaída, Grc.	C4	28
Ptuj, Slvn.	D12	22
Puakatike, Volcán, vol., Chile	e30	78l
Puán, Arg.	H6	92
Pucallpa, Peru	E3	84
Pucará, Bol.	C4	90
Pučeveem, stm., Russia	C23	34
Pučež, Russia	H20	8
Pucheng, China	H8	42
Pucheng, China	D3	42
Púchov, Slov.	G14	16
Pučišća, Cro.	G13	22
Pudasjärvi, Fin.	D12	8
Pudož, Russia	F17	8
Puduari, stm., Braz.	I11	86
Puduchcheri see Pondicherry, India	F4	53
Pudukkottai, India	F4	53
Puebla, state, Mex.	F10	100
Puebla de Don Fadrique, Spain	G8	20
Puebla de Sanabria, Spain	B4	20
Puebla de Zaragoza, Mex.	F9	100
Pueblito, Mex.	E2	130
Pueblito de Ponce, P.R.	B1	104a
Pueblo, Co., U.S.	C4	128
Pueblonuevo, Col.	C4	86
Pueblo Nuevo, P.R.	B2	104a
Pueblo Nuevo, Ven.	B7	86
Pueblo Viejo, Laguna, l., Mex.	D10	100
Pueblo Yaqui, Mex.	B4	100
Puente-Caldelas see Ponte-Caldelas, Spain	B2	20
Puente del Arzobispo, Spain	E5	20
Puentedeume see Pontedeume, Spain	A2	20
Puente Genil, Spain	G6	20
Puerca, Punta, c., P.R.	B4	104a
Puerco, stm., U.S.	I7	132
Puerco, stm., N.M., U.S.	I10	132
Puerto Acosta, Bol.	C3	90
Puerto Adela, Para.	B10	92
Puerto Aisén, Chile	I2	90
Puerto Alegre, Bol.	B4	90
Puerto Ángel, Mex.	H10	100
Puerto Arista, Mex.	H11	100
Puerto Armuelles, Pan.	H6	102
Puerto Asís, Col.	G3	86
Puerto Ayacucho, Ven.	E8	86
Puerto Baquerizo Moreno, Ec.	i12	84a
Puerto Barrios, Guat.	E3	102
Puerto Bermúdez, Peru	F3	84
Puerto Berrío, Col.	D4	86
Puerto Bolívar, Col.	A5	86
Puerto Boyacá, Col.	E4	86
Puerto Cabello, Ven.	B7	86
Puerto Cabezas, Nic.	F6	102
Puerto Carreño, Col.	D8	86
Puerto Chicama, Peru	E2	84
Puerto Colombia, Col.	B4	86
Puerto Cortés, Hond.	E3	102
Puerto Cumarebo, Ven.	B7	86
Puerto Deseado, Arg.	I3	90
Puerto Escondido, Mex.	H10	100
Puerto Escondido, c., Ven.	p20	104g
Puerto Esperanza, Arg.	B10	92
Puerto Fonciere, Para.	D5	90
Puerto Francisco de Orellana, Ec.	H3	86
Puerto Heath, Bol.	B3	90
Puerto Iguazú, Arg.	B10	92
Puerto Ingeniero Ibáñez, Chile	I2	90
Puerto Inírida, Col.	F7	86
Puerto Juárez, Mex.	B4	102
Puerto la Cruz, Ven.	B9	86
Puerto Leguízamo, Col.	H4	86
Puerto Libertad, Mex.	G6	98
Puerto Limón, Col.	F5	86
Puerto Limón, C.R.	G6	102
Puertollano, Spain	F6	20
Puerto Lobos, Arg.	H4	90
Puerto López, Col.	E5	86
Puerto Madero, Mex.	H12	100
Puerto Madryn, Arg.	H3	90
Puerto Maldonado, Peru	F4	84
Puerto Montt, Chile	H2	90
Puerto Morelos, Mex.	B4	102
Puerto Natales, Chile	J2	90
Puerto Padre, Cuba	B9	102
Puerto Páez, Ven.	D8	86
Puerto Palmer, Pico, mtn., Mex.	G6	130
Puerto Peñasco, Mex.	F6	98
Puerto Pinasco, Para.	D5	90
Puerto Pirámides, Arg.	H4	90
Puerto Piray, Arg.	C10	92
Puerto Píritu, Ven.	B9	86
Puerto Plata, Dom. Rep.	C12	102
Puerto Princesa, Phil.	F2	52
Puerto Real, P.R.	B1	104a
Puerto Real, Spain	H4	20
Puerto Rico, Arg.	C10	92
Puerto Rico, Bol.	B3	90
Puerto Rico, Col.	G4	86
Puerto Rico, dep., N.A.	b3	104a
Puerto Rico Trench, unds.	G7	144
Puerto Rondón, Col.	D6	86
Puerto San José, Guat.	F2	102
Puerto San Julián, Arg.	I3	90
Puerto Santa Cruz, Arg.	J3	90
Puerto Sastre, Para.	D5	90
Puerto Suárez, Bol.	C5	90
Puerto Tejada, Col.	F3	86
Puerto Tolosa, Col.	H4	86
Puerto Umbría, Col.	G3	86
Puerto Vallarta, Mex.	E6	100
Puerto Varas, Chile	H2	90
Puerto Victoria, Arg.	C10	92
Puerto Viejo, C.R.	G5	102
Puerto Villamil, Ec.	i11	84a
Puerto Villamizar, Col.	C5	86
Puerto Wilches, Col.	D5	86
Puerto Ybapobó, Para.	D5	90
Pueyrredón, Lago (Cochrane, Lago), l., S.A.	I2	90
Pugačov, Russia	D7	32
Puget Sound, strt., Wa., U.S.	C4	136
Puglia, state, Italy	C10	24
Pugŏ-ri, Kor., N.	D9	38
Puhi-waero see South West Cape, c., N.Z.	H2	80
Puhja, Est.	B9	10
Puiești, Rom.	C14	26
Puigcerdá, Spain	B12	20
Puigmal d' Err (Puigmal), mtn., Eur.	G8	18
Pujiang, China	G8	42
Pujilí, Ec.	H2	86
Puka see Pukë, Alb.	B13	24
Pukaki, Lake, l., N.Z.	F3	80
Pukch'ŏng-ŭp, Kor., N.	D8	38
Pukë, Alb.	B13	24
Pukekohe, N.Z.	C6	80
Pukhrāyān, India	E7	54
Pukou, China	H8	42
Puksoozero, Russia	E19	8
Pula, Cro.	F10	22
Pula, Italy	F3	24
Pulacayo, Bol.	D3	90
Pulantien see Xinjin, China	B9	42
Pulap, at., Micron.	C5	72
Púlar, Cerro, vol., Chile	B3	92
Pulaski, N.Y., U.S.	E13	112
Pulaski, Tn., U.S.	B11	122
Pulaski, Va., U.S.	G5	114
Pulau, stm., Indon.	G10	44
Pulaukida, Indon.	E3	50
Pulau Pinang, state, Malay.	J5	48
Puławy, Pol.	E18	16
Pulgaon, India	H7	54
Puli, Tai.	J9	42
Pulicat, India	E5	53
Pulicat Lake, l., India	E4	53
Puliyangudi, India	G3	53
Pullman, Wa., U.S.	D9	136
Pulog, Mount, mtn., Phil.	B3	52
Pulon'ga, Russia	C18	8
Pułtusk, Pol.	D16	16
Puma Yumco, l., China	D13	54
Pumei, China	A7	48
Pumpkin Buttes, mtn., Wy., U.S.	D7	126
Pumpkin Creek, stm., Mt., U.S.	B7	126
Pumpkin Creek, stm., Ne., U.S.	F10	126
Puná, Isla, i., Ec.	I1	86
Punaauia, Fr. Poly.	v21	78h
Punakha, Bhu.	E12	54
Punan, Indon.	B10	50
Punata, Bol.	C3	90
Pūnch, India	B5	54
Punchaw, B.C., Can.	C7	138
Pune (Poona), India	B1	53
Punganūru, India	E4	53
P'ungsan-ŭp, Kor., N.	D7	38
Pungué, stm., Afr.	A12	70
Punia, D.R.C.	E5	66
Punilla, Sierra de la, mts., Arg.	D3	92
Punitaqui, Chile	E2	92
Punjab, state, India	C5	54
Punjab, state, Pak.	C4	54
Punnichy, Sk., Can.	C9	124
Puno, Peru	G3	84
Punta, Cerro de, mtn., P.R.	B2	104a
Punta Alta, Arg.	I6	92
Punta Arenas, Chile	J2	90
Punta Banda, Cabo, c., Mex.	L9	134
Punta Cardón, Ven.	B6	86
Punta Colnett, Mex.	F4	98
Punta de Agua Creek (Tramperos Creek), stm., U.S.	E5	128
Punta de Díaz, Chile	C2	92
Punta del Cobre, Chile	C2	92
Punta del Este, Ur.	G10	92
Punta Delgada, Arg.	H4	90
Punta de los Llanos, Arg.	E4	92
Punta de Piedras, Ven.	B9	86
Punta Gorda, Nic.	G6	102
Punta Gorda, Fl., U.S.	J3	116
Punta Gorda, Bahía de, b., Nic.	G6	102
Punta Negra, Salar de, pl., Chile	B3	92
Punta Prieta, Mex.	A1	100
Puntarenas, C.R.	G5	102
Punta Santiago, P.R.	B4	104a
Punto Fijo, Ven.	B6	86
Punung, Indon.	H7	50
Puper, Indon.	F9	44
Puppy's Point, c., Norf. I.	y24	78i
Puqi, China	G5	42
Puqian, China	L4	42
Puquio, Peru	F3	84
Pur, stm., Russia	A13	32
Puracé, Volcán, vol., Col.	F3	86
Pūranpur, India	D7	54
Purcell, Ok., U.S.	F11	128
Purcell Mountains, mts., N.A.	F14	138
Purcellville, Va., U.S.	E8	114
Purdy, Mo., U.S.	H3	120
Puré (Puruí), stm., S.A.	I6	86
Purgatoire, stm., Co., U.S.	D5	128
Puri, India	I10	54
Purificación, Col.	F4	86
Purificación, stm., Mex.	C9	100
Purísima, Mex.	E7	130
Purmerend, Neth.	B13	14
Pūrna, stm., India	H5	54
Pūrna, stm., India	H6	54
Pūrnia, India	F11	54
Puronga, Russia	F19	8
Puruí (Puré), stm., S.A.	I6	86
Puruliya, India	G11	54
Puruni, stm., Guy.	D12	86
Purús, stm., S.A.	E4	84
Puruvesi, l., Fin.	F13	8
Purvis, Ms., U.S.	F9	122
Purwakarta, Indon.	G5	50
Purwodadi, Indon.	G6	50
Purwodadi, Indon.	G7	50
Purwokerto, Indon.	G6	50
Purworejo, Indon.	G6	50
Pusa, Malay.	C7	50
Pusad, India	B3	53
Pusan (Fusan), Kor., S.	D2	40
Pusan-jikhalsi, state, Kor., S.	D2	40
Pusat Gayo, Pegunungan, mts., Indon.	J3	48
Pushkar, India	E5	54
Puškin, Russia	A13	10
Puškino, Russia	D20	10
Püspökladány, Hung.	B8	26
Püssi, Est.	A10	10
Pustozersk, Russia	C25	8
Putaendo, Chile	F2	92
Putao, Mya.	C8	46
Putian, China	G6	42
Putian, China	I8	42
Putignano, Italy	D10	24
Puting, Tanjung, c., Indon.	E7	50
Putla de Guerrero, Mex.	D5	96
Putnam, Ct., U.S.	C14	114
Putney, Ga., U.S.	E1	116
Putney, Vt., U.S.	B13	114
Putorana, plato, plat., Russia	C7	34
Puttalam, Sri L.	G4	53
Puttalam Lagoon, b., Sri L.	G4	53
Puttūr, India	E4	53
Putú, Chile	G1	92
Putumayo, state, Col.	G4	86
Putumayo (Içá), stm., S.A.	D3	84
Putuo, China	F10	42
Putussibau, Indon.	C8	50
Putyla, Ukr.	B12	26
Puula, l., Fin.	F12	8
Puurmani, Est.	B9	10
Puyallup, Wa., U.S.	C4	136
Puyang, China	D6	42
Puy-de-Dôme, state, Fr.	D9	18
Puymorens, Col de, p., Fr.	G7	18
Puyo, Ec.	H3	86
Pweto, D.R.C.	F5	66
Pwinbyu, Mya.	B2	48
Pyalo, Mya.	C2	48
Pyapon, Mya.	D2	48
Pyawbwe, Mya.	B3	48
Pyhäjärvi, l., Fin.	E11	8
Pyhäjärvi, l., Fin.	F9	8
Pyhäjoki, Fin.	D10	8
Pyhäjoki, stm., Fin.	D11	8
Pyhäselkä, l., Fin.	E13	8
Pyhätunturi, mtn., Fin.	C12	8
Pyinbongyi, Mya.	D3	48
Pyinmana, Mya.	C3	48
Pyin Oo Lwin see Maymyo, Mya.	A3	48
Pýlos, Grc.	G4	28
Pymatuning Reservoir, res., U.S.	C5	114
Pyŏktong-ŭp, Kor., N.	D6	38
P'yŏngch'ang, Kor., S.	B1	40
P'yonghae, Kor., S.	C2	40
P'yŏngt'aek, Kor., S.	F7	38
P'yŏngyang, Kor., N.	E6	38
Pyote, Tx., U.S.	C4	130
Pyramid Lake, l., Nv., U.S.	D6	134
Pyramid Peak, mtn., Wy., U.S.	G16	136
Pyrenees, mts., Eur.	G6	18
Pyrénées-Atlantiques, state, Fr.	F5	18
Pyrénées Occident, Parc National des, p.o.i., Fr.	G5	18
Pyrénées-Orientales, state, Fr.	G8	18
Pýrgos, Grc.	F4	28
Pytalovo, Russia	C10	10
Pyu, Mya.	C3	48
Pyūthān, Nepal	D9	54

Q

Name	Map Ref.	Page
Qaanaaq see Thule, Grnld.	B12	141
Qabbāsīn, Syria	B8	58
Qacentina (Constantine), Alg.	B6	64
Qā'en, Iran	C8	56
Qagan Moron, stm., China	C3	38
Qagan Nur, l., China	C7	36
Qahar Youyi Zhongqi, China	A5	42
Qaidam, stm., China	D4	36
Qaidam Pendi, bas., China	D3	36
Qalāt, Afg.	C10	56
Qal'at ash-Shaqīf (Beaufort Castle), hist., Leb.	E6	58
Qal'at Bīshah, Sau. Ar.	E5	56
Qal'at Ṣāliḥ, Iraq	C6	56
Qal'eh-ye Now, Afg.	C9	56
Qallābāt, Sudan	E7	62
Qalyûb, Egypt	H2	58
Qamar, Ghubbat al-, b., Yemen	F7	56
Qamdo, China	E4	36
Qamea, i., Fiji	p20	79e
Qamīnis, Libya	A3	62
Qānā, Leb.	E6	58
Qandahār, Afg.	C10	56
Qandala, Som.	B9	66
Qaqortoq see Julianehåb, Grnld.	E16	141
Qārah, Syria	D7	58
Qarazhal see Karažal, Kaz.	E12	32
Qardho, Som.	C9	66
Qarqan, stm., China	G15	32
Qârûn, Birket (Moeris, Lake), l., Egypt	I1	58
Qarwāw, Ra's, c., Oman	F8	56
Qasigiannguit see Christanshåb, Grnld.	D15	141
Qaṣr al-Azraq, hist., Jord.	G7	58
Qaṣr al-Kharānah, hist., Jord.	G7	58
Qaṣr al-Mushattá, hist., Jord.	G7	58
Qaṣr aṭ-Ṭūbah, hist., Jord.	G7	58
Qaṣr Ḍab'ah, hist., Jord.	G7	58
Qaṣr-e Shīrīn, Iran	C6	56
Qasr Farâfra, Egypt	B5	62
Qaṭanā, Syria	E6	58
Qatar, ctry., Asia	D7	56
Qatrani, Gebel, hill, Egypt	I1	58
Qattâra, Munkhafad el- (Qattara Depression), depr., Egypt	B5	62
Qattara Depression see Qattâra, Munkhafad el-, depr., Egypt	B5	62
Qaṭṭīnah, Buḥayrat, res., Syria	D7	58
Qāzigund, India	B5	54
Qazımämmäd, Azer.	B6	56
Qazvīn, Iran	B6	56
Qena, Egypt	B6	62
Qena, Wadi (Qinā, Wādī), stm., Egypt	K3	58
Qeqertarsuaq see Godhavn, Grnld.	D15	141
Qesari, Ḥorbat (Caesarea), hist., Isr.	F5	58
Qeshm, Jazīreh-ye, i., Iran	D8	56
Qetura, Isr.	I5	58
Qezel Owzan, stm., Iran	B6	56
Qian, stm., China	J3	42
Qian'an, China	B6	38
Qian Gorlos, China	B6	38
Qianning, China	E5	36
Qianshan, China	F7	42
Qianwei, China	F5	36
Qianxi, China	H1	42
Qianyang, China	H3	42
Qiaolima, China	A8	54
Qiaowan, China	C4	36
Qidong, China	H5	42
Qiemo, China	G15	32
Qigong, China	F5	36
Qijiang, China	G2	42
Qila Saifullāh, Pak.	C2	54
Qilian Shan, mtn., China	D4	36
Qilian Shan, mts., China	D4	36
Qimen, China	G7	42
Qin, stm., China	D5	42
Qing, stm., China	F4	42
Qingcheng, China	C7	42
Qingchengzi, China	D5	38
Qingdao (Tsingtao), China	C9	42
Qingfeng, China	D6	42
Qinggang, China	B10	36
Qinghai, state, China	D4	36
Qinghai Hu, l., China	D5	36
Qingjiang, China	G6	42
Qingjiang, China	E8	42
Qinglong, China	F6	36
Qinglonggang, China	F9	42
Qingshen, China	F5	36
Qingshui, China	D4	36
Qingshui, China	D2	42
Qingshui, stm., China	H3	42
Qingshui, stm., China	C2	42
Qingtang, China	I5	42
Qingyang, China	B8	38
Qingyang, China	F7	42
Qingyang, China	C2	42
Qingyuan, China	C6	38
Qingyuan, China	J5	42
Qingyuan, China	H8	42
Qingyuan, China	I3	42
Qing Zang Gaoyuan (Tibet, Plateau of), plat., China	B6	46
Qingzhen, China	H2	42
Qinhuangdao, China	B8	42
Qin Ling, mts., China	E3	42
Qinshihuang Mausoleum (Terra Cotta Army), hist., China	D3	42
Qinshui, China	D5	42
Qinxian, China	C5	42
Qinyang, China	D5	42
Qinyuan, China	C5	42
Qinzhou, China	J3	42
Qionghai, China	L4	42
Qionglai, China	E5	36
Qionglaishan, mts., China	E5	36
Qiongzhong, China	L3	42
Qiongzhou Haixia, strt., China	K4	42
Qiqian, China	F13	34
Qiqihar, China	B9	36
Qira, China	A5	46
Qiryat Ata, Isr.	F6	58
Qiryat Gat, Isr.	G5	58
Qiryat Shemona, Isr.	E6	58
Qishn, Yemen	F7	56
Qitai, China	C2	36
Qitaihe, China	B11	36
Qitamu, China	B7	38
Qixia, China	C9	42
Qixian, China	D6	42
Qiyang, China	H4	42
Qizhou, China	F6	42
Qizil Jilga, China	A7	54
Qom, Iran	C7	56
Qomsheh, Iran	C7	56
Qonggyai, China	D13	54
Qôrnoq, Grnld.	E15	141
Qostanay see Kustanaj, Kaz.	D10	32
Qowowuyag (Chopu), mtn., Asia	D11	54
Qu, stm., China	F2	42
Qu, stm., China	G8	42
Quabbin Reservoir, res., Ma., U.S.	B13	114
Quadra Island, i., B.C., Can.	F5	138
Quadros, Lagoa dos, l., Braz.	D12	92
Quakenbrück, Ger.	D3	16
Qualicum Beach, B.C., Can.	G6	138
Quambatook, Austl.	J4	76
Quang Ngai, Viet.	E9	48
Quang Trach, Viet.	D8	48
Quantico, Va., U.S.	F8	114
Quanyang, China	C7	38
Quanzhou, China	I8	42
Qu'Appelle, Sk., Can.	D10	124
Qu'Appelle, stm., Can.	D12	124
Qu'Appelle Dam, dam, Sk., Can.	D7	124
Quaraí, Braz.	E9	92
Quaraí (Cuareim), stm., S.A.	E9	92
Quarles, Pegunungan, mts., Indon.	E11	50
Quarryville, Pa., U.S.	E9	114
Quartier d'Orléans, Guad.	A1	105a
Quartu Sant'Elena, Italy	E3	24
Quartz Lake, l., Nu., Can.	A14	106
Quartz Mountain, mtn., Or., U.S.	G4	136
Quartzsite, Az., U.S.	J2	132
Quba, Azer.	A6	56
Qūchān, Iran	B8	56
Quchijie, China	G4	42
Queanbeyan, Austl.	J7	76
Québec, Qc., Can.	D5	110
Québec, state, Can.	E16	106
Quebeck, Tn., U.S.	I12	120
Quebra-Anzol, stm., Braz.	J2	88
Quebracho, Ur.	E9	92
Quebrada Seca, P.R.	B4	104a
Quedal, Cabo, c., Chile	H2	90
Quedlinburg, Ger.	E7	16
Queen Charlotte Islands, is., B.C., Can.	E4	106
Queen Charlotte Sound, strt., B.C., Can.	E2	138
Queen Charlotte Strait, strt., B.C., Can.	F3	138
Queen City, Mo., U.S.	D5	120
Queen City, Tx., U.S.	D4	122
Queen Elizabeth Islands, is., Can.	B13	94
Queen Mary Coast, cst., Ant.	B14	81
Queen Maud Gulf, b., Nu., Can.	B10	106
Queen Maud Land, reg., Ant.	C4	81
Queen Maud Mountains, mts., Ant.	D23	81
Queenscliff, Austl.	L5	76
Queensland, state, Austl.	D8	74
Queensport, N.S., Can.	E15	110
Queenstown, Austl.	o12	77a
Queenstown, N.Z.	G3	80
Queenstown, S. Afr.	G8	70
Queguay Grande, stm., Ur.	F9	92
Queimada Nova, Braz.	E5	88
Queimadas, Braz.	F6	88
Queimados, Braz.	L4	88
Quela, Ang.	B2	68
Quelelevu, i., Fiji	p20	79e
Quelimane, Moz.	D6	68
Quelpart Island see Cheju-do, i., Kor., S.	H7	38
Quemado, Tx., U.S.	F7	130
Quemado, Punta de, c., Cuba	B10	102
Quemoy see Chinmen Tao, i., Tai.	I8	42
Quemú Quemú, Arg.	H6	92
Quequén, Arg.	I8	92
Querary, stm., Col.	G6	86
Quercy, hist. reg., Fr.	E7	18
Querétaro, Mex.	E8	100
Querétaro, state, Mex.	E8	100
Querobabi, Mex.	F7	98
Quesada, C.R.	E8	96
Quesada, Spain	G7	20
Queshan, China	E5	42
Quesnel, B.C., Can.	C8	138
Quesnel, stm., B.C., Can.	D8	138
Quesnel Lake, l., B.C., Can.	D9	138
Que Son, Viet.	E9	48
Questa, N.M., U.S.	E3	128
Quetico Lake, l., On., Can.	C7	118
Quetta, Pak.	C10	56
Quetzaltenango, Guat.	E2	102
Quevedo, Ec.	H2	86
Quezon City, Phil.	C3	52
Qufu, China	D7	42
Quibala, Ang.	C2	68
Quibdó, Col.	E3	86
Quiberon, Fr.	G5	14
Quíbor, Ven.	C7	86
Quiculungo, Ang.	B2	68
Quila, Mex.	C5	100
Quilengues, Ang.	C1	68
Quilimarí, Chile	F2	92
Quillabamba, Peru	F3	84
Quillacollo, Bol.	C3	90
Quill Lake, Sk., Can.	B9	124
Quillota, Chile	F2	92
Quilon, India	G3	53
Quilpie, Austl.	F5	76
Quilpué, Chile	F2	92
Quimarí, Alto de, mtn., Col.	C3	86
Quimaria, Ang.	B1	68
Quimby, Ia., U.S.	B2	120
Quimilí, Arg.	C6	92
Quimper (Kemper), Fr.	F5	14
Quimperlé, Fr.	G5	14
Quinault, stm., Wa., U.S.	C3	136
Quince Mil, Peru	F3	84
Quincy, Ca., U.S.	D4	134
Quincy, Fl., U.S.	G14	122
Quincy, Il., U.S.	E6	120
Quincy, Ma., U.S.	B14	114
Quincy, Wa., U.S.	C7	136
Quindío, state, Col.	E4	86
Quines, Arg.	F5	92
Quinhagak, Ak., U.S.	E7	140
Quinlan, Tx., U.S.	E2	122
Quinn, stm., Nv., U.S.	B7	134

Name — Map Ref. — Page

Quintanar de la Orden, Spain E7 20
Quintana Roo, state, Mex. C3 102
Quinte, Bay of, b., On., Can. D12 112
Quinto, Spain C10 20
Quinto, stm., Arg. G5 92
Quinton, Ok., U.S. B3 122
Quipapá, Braz. E7 88
Quirauk Mountain, mtn., Md., U.S. E8 114
Quiriguá, hist., Guat. E3 102
Quirihue, Chile H1 92
Quirindi, Austl. H8 76
Quirinópolis, Braz. C6 90
Quiriquire, Ven. C10 86
Quiroga, Mex. F8 100
Quiros, Cap, c., Vanuatu j16 79d
Quissanga, Moz. C7 68
Quissico, Moz. D12 70
Quitaque, Tx., U.S. G7 128
Quitasueño, unds., Col. E7 102
Quitasueño, Banco see Quitasueño, unds., Col. E7 102
Quita Sueno Bank see Quitasueño, unds., Col. E7 102
Quiterajo, Moz. C7 68
Quitilipi, Arg. C7 92
Quitman, Ga., U.S. F2 116
Quitman, Tx., U.S. E3 122
Quito, Ec. H2 86
Quixadá, Braz. C6 88
Quixeramobim, Braz. C6 88
Qujiadian, China C5 38
Qujing, China F5 36
Qujiu, China J2 42
Qulin, Mo., U.S. H7 120
Qumarlêb, China E4 36
Qumrān, Khirbat, hist., W.B. G6 58
Quoich, stm., Nu., Can. C12 106
Quorn, Austl. F7 74
Quoxo, stm., Bots. C7 70
Qurdūd, Sudan E5 62
Qus, Egypt B6 62
Quseir, Egypt B6 62
Qutdligssat, Grnld. C15 141
Quthing, Leso. G8 70
Quweisna, Egypt H2 58
Quxian, China F2 42
Qüxü, China D13 54
Quyang, China B6 42
Quy Nhon, Viet. F9 48
Quyon, Qc., Can. C13 112
Quyquyó, Para. C9 92
Quzhou, China G8 42
Quzhou, China C6 42
Qyzylorda see Kzyl-Orda, Kaz. F11 32

R

Raab (Rába), stm., Eur. D12 22
Raalte, Neth. B15 14
Ra'ananna, Isr. F5 58
Raas, Pulau, i., Indon. G9 50
Raasay, i., Scot., U.K. D6 12
Raasiku, Est. A8 10
Rab, Otok, i., Cro. F11 22
Raba, Indon. H11 50
Rába (Raab), stm., Eur. D12 22
Rábade, Spain A3 20
Rabak, Sudan E6 62
Rabat, Malta I8 24
Rabat, Malta H8 24
Rabat, Mor. C3 64
Rabaul, Pap. N. Gui. a5 79a
Rabbit Creek, stm., S.D., U.S. B10 126
Rabbit Ears Pass, p., Co., U.S. C10 132
Rabi, i., Fiji p20 79e
Rābi', Ash-Shallāl ar- (Fourth Cataract), wtfl, Sudan D6 62
Rābigh, Sau. Ar. E4 56
Rabka, Pol. G15 16
Rabkavi Banhatti, India C2 53
Râbnita, Mol. B16 26
Rabočeostrovsk, Russia D16 8
Rabwāh, Pak. C4 54
Rabyānah, Ramlat, des., Libya C4 62
Raccoon, stm., Ia., U.S. C4 120
Raccoon Creek, stm., Oh., U.S. E15 120
Race, Cape, c., Nf., Can. j23 107a
Race Point, c., Ma., U.S. B15 114
Rach Gia, Viet. G7 48
Rach Gia, Vinh, b., Viet. H7 48
Raciąż, Pol. D16 16
Racibórz, Pol. F14 16
Racine, Wi., U.S. F2 112
Radaškovičy, Bela. F10 10
Rădăuți, Rom. B12 26
Radcliff, Ky., U.S. G12 120
Radeberg, Ger. E9 16
Radebeul, Ger. E9 16
Radford, Va., U.S. G5 114
Rādhanpur, India G3 54
Rădinești, Rom. E10 26
Radisson, Sk., Can. B6 124
Radium Hot Springs, B.C., Can. F14 138
Radnice, Czech Rep. G9 16
Radofinnikovo, Russia A13 10
Radom, Pol. E17 16
Radom, state, Pol. E16 16
Radomsko, Pol. E15 16
Radomyśl Wielki, Pol. F17 16
Radoviš, Mac. B5 28
Radstadt, Aus. C10 22
Radutino, Russia H17 10
Radviliškis, Lith. E6 10
Radville, Sk., Can. E9 124
Radymno, Pol. G18 16
Radzyń Chełmiński, Pol. C14 16
Rae, N.T., Can. C7 106
Rae, stm., Nu., Can. B7 106
Rāe Bareli, India E8 54
Raeford, N.C., U.S. B6 116
Rae Isthmus, isth., Nu., Can. B13 106
Rae Strait, strt., Nu., Can. B12 106
Rafaela, Arg. E7 92
Rafael Freyre, Cuba B10 102
Rafah, Gaza G5 58
Rafḥā', Sau. Ar. D5 56
Rafsanjān, Iran C8 56
Raft, stm., U.S. H13 136
Raga, Sudan F5 62
Ragay Gulf, b., Phil. D4 52
Ragged Island, i., Bah. A10 102
Ragged Island Range, is., Bah. A10 102
Ragged Top Mountain, mtn., Wy., U.S. F7 126
Ragland, Al., U.S. D12 122
Raguva, Lith. E7 10
Rahačou, Bela. G12 10
Rahad al-Bardī, Sudan E4 62
Rāhatgarh, India G7 54
Rahimatpur, India C1 53
Rahīm Ki Bāzār, Pak. F2 54
Rahīmyār Khān, Pak. D3 54
Rāichūr, India C3 53
Raiganj, India F12 54
Raigarh, India H9 54
Rāikot, India C5 54
Railroad Valley, val., Nv., U.S. E10 134
Railton, Austl. n13 77a
Rainbow Bridge National Monument, p.o.i., Ut., U.S. F6 132
Rainbow Falls, wtfl, B.C., Can. D11 138
Rainelle, W.V., U.S. G5 114
Rainier, Mount, vol., Wa., U.S. D5 136
Rainy, stm., N.A. C4 118
Rainy Lake, l., N.A. C5 118
Rainy River, On., Can. C4 118
Raipur, India H8 54
Raipur Uplands, plat., India H9 54
Raisen, India G6 54
Raisin, stm., Mi., U.S. G6 112
Raivavae, i., Fr. Poly. F12 72
Rajabasa, Indon. F4 50
Rājahmundry, India C5 53
Rājaldesar, India E5 54
Rājampet, India D4 53
Rajang, stm., Malay. B7 50
Rājapālaiyam, India G3 53
Rājāpur, India C1 53
Rājasthān, state, India E4 54
Rājbāri, Bngl. G12 54
Rajčihinsk, Russia G14 34
Rāj Gangpur, India G10 54
Rājgarh, India E6 54
Rājgarh, India G6 54
Rājgarh, India D5 54
Rajik, Indon. E4 50
Rājkot, India G3 54
Rāj Nāndgaon, India H8 54
Rājpipla, India H4 54
Rājpur, India G5 54
Rājpura, India C6 54
Rājshāhi, Bngl. F12 54
Rājshāhi, state, Bngl. F12 54
Rājula, India H3 54
Raka, stm., China D11 54
Rakamaz, Hung. A8 26
Rakaposhi, mtn., Pak. B11 56
Rakata, Pulau (Krakatoa), i., Indon. G4 50
Rakhine, state, Mya. C1 48
Rakhiv, Ukr. A11 26
Rakitnoe, Russia B11 36
Rakiura see Stewart Island, i., N.Z. H3 80
Rakoniewice, Pol. D12 16
Rakops, Bots. B7 70
Rakovník, Czech Rep. F9 16
Råkvåg see Råkvågen, Nor. E4 8
Råkvågen, Nor. E4 8
Rakvere, Est. G12 8
Raleigh, Ms., U.S. E9 122
Raleigh, N.C., U.S. I7 114
Ralik Chain, is., Marsh. Is. C7 72
Ralls, Tx., U.S. H7 128
Ralston, Pa., U.S. C9 114
Ramah, N.M., U.S. H8 132
Rām Allāh, W.B. G6 58
Rāmanagaram, India E3 53
Rāmanāthapuram, India G4 53
Rāmānuj Ganj, India G9 54
Ramat Gan, Isr. F5 58
Ramat HaSharon, Isr. F5 58
Ramatlabama, Bots. D7 70
Rambervillers, Fr. F15 14
Rambouillet, Fr. F10 14
Rambutyo Island, i., Pap. N. Gui. a4 79a
Rām Dās, India B5 54
Rāmdurg, India C2 53
Ramea, Nf., Can. j22 107a
Ramene, Russia F20 8
Ramenskoe, Russia E21 10
Rāmeswaram, India G4 53
Rāmgarh, Bngl. G13 54
Rāmgarh, India E5 54
Rāmgarh, India G10 54
Ram Head, c., V.I.U.S. e8 104b
Rāmhormoz, Iran C6 56
Ramírez, Mex. I10 130
Ramírez, Mex. G7 130
Ramla, Isr. G5 58
Ramlu, mtn., Afr. E8 62
Ramm, Jabal, mtn., Jord. I6 58
Rāmnagar, India F9 54
Rāmnagar, India D7 54
Râmnicu Sărat, Rom. D14 26
Râmnicu Vâlcea, Rom. D11 26
Ramona, Ca., U.S. J9 134
Ramona, S.D., U.S. C15 126
Ramos, Mex. D8 100
Ramos, stm., Mex. C6 100
Ramotswa, Bots. D7 70
Rampart, Ak., U.S. C9 140
Ramparts, stm., N.T., Can. B4 106
Rāmpur, India D7 54
Rāmpur, India C6 54
Rāmpura, India F5 54
Rāmpur Hāt, India F11 54
Ramree Island, i., Mya. C1 48
Ramseur, N.C., U.S. I6 114
Ramsey, I. of Man G8 12
Ramsey Lake, l., On., Can. A7 112
Ramsgate, Eng., U.K. J14 12
Ramshorn Peak, mtn., Mt., U.S. E15 136
Rāmtek, India H7 54
Rāmu, Bngl. H14 54
Ramu, stm., Pap. N. Gui. a3 79a
Ramville, Îlet, i., Mart. k7 105c
Ramygala, Lith. E7 10
Rānāghāt, India G12 54
Rana Kao, Volcán, vol., Chile f29 78l
Rāna Pratāp Sāgar, res., India F5 54
Ranau, Malay. H1 52
Ranau, Danau, l., Indon. F3 50
Ranburne, Al., U.S. D13 122
Rancagua, Chile G2 92
Rancah, Indon. G6 50
Rancevo, Russia D16 10
Rancharia, Braz. D6 90
Ranchería, stm., Col. B5 86
Ranchester, Wy., U.S. C5 126
Rānchi, India G10 54
Ranchillos, Arg. C5 92
Ranch Lake, l., Sk., Can. B9 124
Rancho Cordova, Ca., U.S. E4 134
Rancho Nuevo, Mex. H7 130
Ranchos, Arg. G8 92
Ranco, Lago, l., Chile H2 90
Rancul, Arg. G5 92
Randazzo, Italy G8 24
Randers, Den. H4 8
Randleman, N.C., U.S. I6 114
Randlett, Ok., U.S. G10 128
Randolph, Az., U.S. K5 132
Randolph, Me., U.S. F7 110
Randolph, Ne., U.S. E15 126
Randolph, N.Y., U.S. B7 114
Randolph, Ut., U.S. B5 132
Random Lake, Wi., U.S. E2 112
Randsfjorden, l., Nor. F3 8
Ranfurly, N.Z. G4 80
Rāngāmāti, Bngl. G13 54
Rangantemiang, Indon. D8 50
Rangas, Tanjung, c., Indon. E11 50
Rangasa, Tanjung, c., Indon. E11 50
Rangaunu Bay, b., N.Z. B5 80
Rangeley, Me., U.S. E6 110
Ranger, Tx., U.S. B9 130
Rangia, India E13 54
Rangitaiki, stm., N.Z. D7 80
Rangitata, stm., N.Z. F4 80
Rangitikei, stm., N.Z. D7 80
Rangkasbitung, Indon. G4 50
Rangoon see Yangon, Mya. D2 48
Rangoon, stm., Mya. D3 48
Rangpur, Bngl. F12 54
Rangpur, Pak. C3 54
Rangsang, Pulau, i., Indon. C3 50
Rānībennur, India D2 53
Rānīganj, India G11 54
Rānikhet, India D7 54
Rankamhaeng National Park, p.o.i., Thai. D4 48
Ranken, stm., Austl. D7 74
Ranken Store, Austl. C7 74
Rankin, Il., U.S. H2 112
Rankin, Tx., U.S. C6 130
Rankin Inlet, Nu., Can. C12 106
Rankins Springs, Austl. I6 76
Rann of Kutch see Kutch, Rann of, reg., Asia D2 46
Ranong, Thai. H4 48
Ranongga Island, i., Sol. Is. e7 79b
Ranot, Thai. I5 48
Ransiki, Indon. F9 44
Ransom, Ks., U.S. C8 128
Ranson, W.V., U.S. E8 114
Rantabe, Madag. D8 68
Rantaukampar, Indon. C2 50
Rantaupanjang, Indon. D2 50
Rantauprapat, Indon. B1 50
Rantekombola, Bulu, mtn., Indon. E12 50
Rantepao, Indon. E11 50
Rantoul, Il., U.S. D9 120
Raohe, China B11 36
Raoping, China J7 42
Raoul, Ga., U.S. B2 116
Raoul-Blanchard, Mont, mtn., Qc., Can. C6 110
Raoul Island, i., N.Z. F9 72
Rapa, i., Fr. Poly. F12 72
Rapallo, Italy F6 22
Rapang, Indon. E11 50
Rapa Nui see Pascua, Isla de, i., Chile f30 78l
Rāpar, India G3 54
Rapel, stm., Chile F2 92
Rapel, Embalse, res., Chile G2 92
Rapelli, Arg. C5 92
Raper, Cape, c., Nu., Can. B17 106
Rapidan, stm., Va., U.S. F7 114
Rapid City, Mb., Can. D13 124
Rapid City, S.D., U.S. C9 126
Rapid Creek, stm., S.D., U.S. D9 126
Rapide-Blanc, Qc., Can. C4 110
Rapid River, Mi., U.S. C2 112
Räpina, Est. G12 8
Rappahannock, stm., Va., U.S. G9 114
Rāpti, stm., Asia E9 54
Rapu Rapu Island, i., Phil. D5 52
Raraka, at., Fr. Poly. E12 72
Rarotonga, i., Cook Is. a26 78j
Rarotonga International Airport, Cook Is. a26 78j
Rasa, Punta, c., Arg. H9 92
Ra's al-Khaymah, U.A.E. D8 56
Ra's Ba'labakk, Leb. D7 58
Râșcani, Mol. B14 26
Rașcov, Mol. B15 26
Ras Dashen Terara, mtn., Eth. E7 62
Ras Dejen see Ras Dashen Terara, mtn., Eth. E7 62
Ras Djebel, Tun. G4 24
Raseiniai, Lith. E5 10
Râs el-Barr, Egypt G2 58
Rashād, Sudan E6 62
Rashid (Rosetta), Egypt G1 58
Rashid, Masabb (Rosetta Mouth), mth., Egypt G1 58
Rasht, Iran B6 56
Raška, Yugo. F7 26
Rās Koh, mtn., Pak. D10 56
Rasm al-Arwām, Sabkhat, l., Syria C8 58
Râșnov, Rom. D12 26
Rasra, India F9 54
Rassua, ostrov, i., Russia G19 34
Rast, Rom. F10 26
Rastatt, Ger. H4 16
Rastede, Ger. C4 16
Rastenburg see Kętrzyn, Pol. B17 16
Rásttigáisá, mtn., Nor. A12 8
Ratak Chain, is., Marsh. Is. C8 72
Ratamka, Bela. G10 10
Ratangarh, India D5 54
Rat Buri, Thai. F4 48
Rāth, India F7 54
Rathbun Lake, res., Ia., U.S. D4 120
Rathdrum, Id., U.S. C9 136
Rathenow, Ger. D8 16
Rathkeale, Ire. I3 12
Ráth Luirc, Ire. I4 12
Rathwell, Mb., Can. E15 124
Rat Island, i., Ak., U.S. g22 140a
Rat Islands, is., Ak., U.S. g22 140a
Ratlām, India G5 54
Ratmanova, ostrov, i., Russia C27 34
Ratnāgiri, India C1 53
Ratnapura, Sri L. H5 53
Raton, N.M., U.S. E4 128
Raton Pass, p., N.M., U.S. E4 128
Rats, stm., Qc., Can. A4 110
Rattanaburi, Thai. E6 48
Rattaphum, Thai. I5 48
Rattlesnake, Mt., U.S. D13 136
Rattlesnake Creek, stm., Ks., U.S. D10 128
Ratz, Mount, mtn., B.C., Can. D4 106
Ratzeburg, Ger. C6 16
Rau, Indon. C2 50
Raub, Malay. K5 48
Rauch, Arg. H8 92
Raul Soares, Braz. K4 88
Rauma, Fin. F9 8
Rauma, stm., Nor. E2 8
Rauna, Lat. C8 10
Raung, Gunung, vol., Indon. H9 50
Raurkela, India G10 54
Răut, stm., Mol. B14 26
Ravalgaon, India H5 54
Ravanusa, Italy G7 24
Ravena, N.Y., U.S. B12 114
Ravenna, Italy F9 22
Ravenna, Ky., U.S. G2 114
Ravenna, Ne., U.S. F13 126
Ravenna, Oh., U.S. G8 112
Ravensburg, Ger. I5 16
Ravenscrag, Sk., Can. E4 124
Ravenshoe, Austl. A5 76
Ravensthorpe, Austl. F4 74
Ravenswood, W.V., U.S. F4 114
Rāvi, stm., Asia C4 54
Ravnina, Turkmen. B9 56
Rāwah, Iraq C5 56
Rawaki, at., Kir. D9 72
Rāwalpindi, Pak. B4 54
Rawas, stm., Indon. E3 50
Rawdon, Qc., Can. D3 110
Rawicz, Pol. E12 16
Rawlinna, Austl. F4 74
Rawlins, Wy., U.S. B9 132
Rawson, Arg. H4 90
Rawson, Arg. G7 92
Raxāul, India E10 54
Ray, Cape, c., Nf., Can. C17 110
Raya, Indon. C11 50
Raya, Bukit, mtn., Indon. D8 50
Rāyachoti, India D4 53
Rāyadurg, India D3 53
Rāyagarha, India B6 53
Ray Hubbard, Lake, res., Tx., U.S. E2 122
Raymond, Ab., Can. G18 138
Raymond, Il., U.S. E8 120
Raymond, Mn., U.S. F3 118
Raymond, Wa., U.S. D3 136
Raymond Terrace, Austl. I8 76
Raymondville, Tx., U.S. H10 130
Raymore, Sk., Can. C9 124
Rayne, La., U.S. G6 122
Rayones, Mex. C8 100
Rayong, Thai. F5 48
Rayside-Balfour, On., Can. B8 112
Raytown, Mo., U.S. E3 120
Rayville, La., U.S. E7 122
Raz, Pointe du, c., Fr. F4 14
Războieni, Rom. B13 26
Razdolinsk, Russia C16 32
Răzeni, Mol. C15 26
Razgrad, Blg. F13 26
Razim, Lacul, l., Rom. E15 26
Rāznas ezers, l., Lat. D10 10
Razorback Mountain, mtn., B.C., Can. E6 138
Răzvani, Rom. E13 26
Ré, Île de, i., Fr. C4 18
Reading, Eng., U.K. J11 12
Reading, Mi., U.S. C1 114
Reading, Oh., U.S. E1 114
Reading, Pa., U.S. D9 114
Readlyn, Ia., U.S. B5 120
Readstown, Wi., U.S. H8 118
Real, stm., Braz. F6 88
Real, Cordillera, mts., S.A. G4 84
Real del Castillo, Mex. L9 134
Real del Padre, Arg. G4 92
Realicó, Arg. G5 92
Reardan, Wa., U.S. C8 136
Reata, Mex. B8 100
Reay, Scot., U.K. C9 12
Rebecca, Lake, l., Austl. F4 74
Rebiana Sand Sea see Rabyānah, Ramlat, des., Libya C4 62
Reboly, Russia E14 8
Rebouças, Braz. B12 92
Rebun-tō, i., Japan B14 38
Recanati, Italy G10 22
Recherche, Archipelago of the, is., Austl. F4 74
Recife, Braz. E8 88
Recinto, Chile H2 92
Recklinghausen, Ger. E2 16
Reconquista, Arg. D8 92
Recreio, Braz. K4 88
Recreo, Arg. D5 92
Rector, Ar., U.S. H7 120
Rècyča, Bela. H13 10
Recz, Pol. C11 16
Red (Hong, Song) (Yuan), stm., Asia D9 46
Red, stm., N.A. A2 118
Red, stm., U.S. E9 108
Red, stm., U.S. H10 120
Red, Elm Fork, stm., U.S. F8 128
Red, North Fork, stm., U.S. G9 128
Red, Prairie Dog Town Fork, stm., U.S. H7 122
Red, Salt Fork, stm., U.S. G9 128
Redang, Pulau, i., Malay. J6 48
Red Bank, N.J., U.S. D11 114
Red Bank, Tn., U.S. B13 122
Red Bay, Nf., Can. i22 107a
Red Bay, Al., U.S. C10 122
Redbay, Fl., U.S. G12 122
Redberry Lake, l., Sk., Can. B6 124
Red Bluff, Ca., U.S. C3 134
Red Bluff Reservoir, res., U.S. C4 130
Red Boiling Springs, Tn., U.S. H12 120
Red Canyon, val., S.D., U.S. D9 126
Redcar, Eng., U.K. G11 12
Red Cedar, stm., Mi., U.S. F5 112
Red Cedar Lake, l., On., Can. B9 112
Redcliff, Ab., Can. D3 124
Red Cliff, Co., U.S. D10 132
Redcliff see Red Cliff, Co., U.S. D10 132
Redcliffe, Austl. F9 76
Redcliffe, Mount, mtn., Austl. E4 74
Red Cliffs, Austl. J3 76
Red Cloud, Ne., U.S. A10 128
Red Creek, stm., Ms., U.S. G10 122
Red Deer, Ab., Can. D17 138
Red Deer, stm., Can. B12 124
Red Deer, stm., Can. F19 138
Red Deer Lake, l., Mb., Can. B12 124
Reddersburg, S. Afr. F8 70
Red Devil, Ak., U.S. D8 140
Redding, Ca., U.S. C3 134
Redditch, Eng., U.K. I10 12
Redenção, Braz. C6 88
Redfield, S.D., U.S. C14 126
Redford, Tx., U.S. E3 130
Redhead, Trin. s13 105f
Redja, stm., Russia C14 10
Redkey, In., U.S. H4 112
Redkino, Russia D19 10
Red Lake, On., Can. E12 106
Red Lake, l., On., Can. E12 106
Red Lake, l., Az., U.S. H2 132
Red Lake, stm., Mn., U.S. D2 118
Red Lake Falls, Mn., U.S. D2 118
Red Lake Road, On., Can. B5 118
Redlands, Ca., U.S. I8 134
Redlands, Co., U.S. D8 132
Red Level, Al., U.S. F12 122
Red Lion, Pa., U.S. E9 114
Red Lodge, Mt., U.S. B3 126
Redmond, Or., U.S. F5 136
Redmond, Ut., U.S. D5 132
Redmond, Wa., U.S. C4 136
Red Mountain, mtn., Mt., U.S. C14 136
Red Mountain Pass, p., Co., U.S. F9 132
Red Oak, Ia., U.S. D2 120
Redon, Fr. G6 14
Redonda, Isla, i., Ven. t12 105f
Redonda Islands, is., B.C., Can. F6 138
Redondela, Spain B2 20
Redondo, Port. F3 20
Redondo Beach, Ca., U.S. J7 134
Redoubt Volcano, vol., Ak., U.S. D9 140
Red Pass, B.C., Can. D11 138
Red Rock, B.C., Can. C8 138
Red Rock, On., Can. C10 118
Red Rock, stm., Mt., U.S. F14 136
Red Rock, Lake, res., Ia., U.S. C4 120
Redruth, Eng., U.K. K7 12
Red Sea C7 62
Redvers, Sk., Can. E12 124
Redwater, Ab., Can. C17 138
Redwater, stm., Mt., U.S. G8 124
Redwillow, stm., Can. A11 138
Red Willow Creek, stm., Ne., U.S. G12 126
Red Wing, Mn., U.S. G6 118
Redwood, stm., Mn., U.S. G3 118
Redwood Falls, Mn., U.S. G3 118
Redwood National Park, p.o.i., Ca., U.S. B1 134
Ree, Lough, l., Ire. H5 12
Reed City, Mi., U.S. E4 112
Reeder, N.D., U.S. A10 126
Reed Lake, l., Sk., Can. D6 124
Reedley, Ca., U.S. G6 134
Reedsburg, Wi., U.S. H8 118
Reedsville, Wi., U.S. D2 112
Reefton, N.Z. F4 80
Reelfoot Lake, l., Tn., U.S. H8 120
Rees, Ger. E2 16
Reese, Mi., U.S. E6 112
Reese, stm., Nv., U.S. C9 134
Reeseville, Wi., U.S. H10 118
Refuge Cove, B.C., Can. F6 138
Refugio, Tx., U.S. F10 130
Rega, stm., Pol. C11 16
Regência, Braz. J6 88
Regeneração, Braz. D4 88
Regensburg, Ger. H8 16
Regent, N.D., U.S. A10 126
Reggâne, Alg. D5 64
Reggio di Calabria, Italy F9 24
Reggio nell'Emilia, Italy F7 22
Reghin, Rom. C11 26
Regina, Sk., Can. D9 124
Región Metropolitana, state, Chile F2 92
Registan see Rīgestān, reg., Afg. C9 56
Registro, Braz. B14 92
Regozero, Russia D14 8
Rehau, Ger. F7 16
Rehoboth, Nmb. C3 70
Rehoboth Beach, De., U.S. F10 114
Rehovot, Isr. G5 58
Reichenbach, Ger. F8 16
Reidsville, Ga., U.S. D3 116
Reidsville, N.C., U.S. H6 114
Reigate, Eng., U.K. J12 12
Reihoku, Japan G2 40
Reims (Rheims), Fr. E12 14
Rein Anteriur (Vorderrhein), stm., Switz. D6 22
Reinbeck, Ia., U.S. B5 120
Reindeer Lake, l., Can. D10 106
Reinga, Cape, c., N.Z. B5 80
Reinosa, Spain A6 20
Reisa Nasjonalpark, p.o.i., Nor. B10 8
Reisterstown, Md., U.S. E9 114
Reitz, S. Afr. E9 70
Reliance, N.T., Can. C9 106
Remada, Tun. C7 64
Remagen, Ger. F3 16
Remanso, Braz. E4 88
Rembang, Indon. G7 50
Remedios, Col. D4 86
Remedios, Pan. H7 102
Remedios, Punta, c., El Sal. F2 102
Remer, Mn., U.S. D5 118
Remington, Va., U.S. F8 114
Rémiré, Fr. Gu. C7 84
Remiremont, Fr. G15 14
Remoulins, Fr. F10 18
Rempang, Pulau, i., Indon. C3 50
Remscheid, Ger. E3 16
Remsen, Ia., U.S. B1 120
Remus, Mi., U.S. E4 112
Renaix see Ronse, Bel. D12 14
Renata, B.C., Can. G12 138
Rencēni, Lat. C8 10
Rende, Italy E10 24
Rend Lake, res., Il., U.S. F8 120
Rendova Island, i., Sol. Is. e7 79b
Rendsburg, Ger. B5 16
Renfrew, On., Can. C13 112
Rengat, Indon. D3 50
Rengel, Indon. G8 50
Rengo, Chile G2 92
Reng Tlāng, mtn., Asia H14 54
Renheji, China F6 42
Renhuai, China H2 42
Reni, Ukr. D15 26
Renland, reg., Grnld. C20 141
Renmark, Austl. J3 76
Rennell, i., Sol. Is. E7 72
Rennell, Islas, is., Chile J2 90
Rennell and Bellona, state, Sol. Is. f9 79b
Rennes, Fr. F7 14
Rennie, Mb., Can. E18 124
Reno, Nv., U.S. D6 134
Reno, stm., Italy F8 22
Reno Hill, mtn., Wy., U.S. E6 126
Renoster, stm., S. Afr. G5 70
Renous, N.B., Can. D11 110
Renovo, Pa., U.S. C8 114
Rensjön, Swe. B8 8
Rensselaer, In., U.S. H2 112
Rensselaer, N.Y., U.S. B12 114
Rentería, Spain A9 20
Renton, Wa., U.S. C4 136
Renville, Mn., U.S. G3 118
Renwick, Ia., U.S. B4 120
Reo, Indon. H12 50
Repetek, Turkmen. B9 56
Repton, Al., U.S. F11 122
Republic, Mi., U.S. B1 112
Republic, Mo., U.S. G4 120
Republic, Wa., U.S. B8 136
Republican, stm., U.S. B11 128
Republican, North Fork, stm., U.S. A6 128
Republican, South Fork, stm., U.S. B7 128
Republic of Korea see Korea, South, ctry., Asia G8 38
Repulse Bay, Nu., Can. B13 106
Repulse Bay, b., Austl. C7 76
Repvåg, Nor. A11 8
Requena, Spain E9 20
Reriutaba, Braz. C5 88
Reșadiye Yarımadası, pen., Tur. G10 28
Reschenpass (Resia, Passo di), p., Eur. C16 18
Reschenscheideck see Reschenpass, p., Eur. C16 18
Reschenscheideck see Resia, Passo di, p., Eur. C16 18
Resen, Mac. B4 28
Reserva, Braz. B12 92
Reserve, La., U.S. G8 122
Reserve, N.M., U.S. J8 132
Resia, Passo di (Reschenpass), p., Eur. C16 18
Resistencia, Arg. C8 92
Reșița, Rom. D8 26
Resko, Pol. C11 16
Resolute (Kaujuitoq), Nu., Can. C7 141
Resolution Island, i., Nu., Can. E12 141
Resolution Island, i., N.Z. G2 80
Resplendor, Braz. J5 88
Restigouche, stm., Can. C9 110
Restinga Seca, Braz. D11 92
Reston, Mb., Can. E12 124
Retalhuleu, Guat. E2 102
Retamosa, Ur. F10 92
Retezat, Parcul Național, p.o.i., Rom. D9 26
Rethel, Fr. E13 14
Réthymno, Grc. H7 28
Rettihovka, Russia B10 38
Reunion, dep., Afr. I11 60
Reus, Spain C12 20
Reuss, stm., Switz. C5 22
Reuterstadt Stavenhagen, Ger. C8 16
Reutlingen, Ger. H5 16
Revda, Russia C16 8
Revelstoke, B.C., Can. F12 138
Revelstoke, Lake, res., B.C., Can. E12 138
Reventazón, Peru E1 84
Revilla del Campo, Spain B7 20
Revillagigedo, Islas, is., Mex. F2 100
Revillagigedo Island, i., Ak., U.S. E13 140
Revillagigedo Islands see Revillagigedo, Islas, is., Mex. F2 100
Revin, Fr. E13 14
Revolución, Mex. H2 130
Rewa, India F8 54
Rewāri, India D6 54
Rexburg, Id., U.S. G15 136
Rexford, Ks., U.S. B8 128
Rexford, Mt., U.S. B11 136
Rey, Isla del, i., Pan. H8 102
Rey, Laguna del, l., Mex. B7 100
Reyes, Bol. B3 90
Reyes, Point, c., Ca., U.S. F2 134
Reyhanlı, Tur. B7 58
Reykjanes Ridge, unds. C10 144
Reykjavík, Ice. k28 8a
Reyno, Ar., U.S. H7 120
Reynolds, Ga., U.S. D1 116
Reynolds, N.D., U.S. G16 124
Reynosa, Mex. B9 100
Rezé, Fr. G7 14
Rēzekne, Lat. D10 10
Rezina, Mol. B15 26
Rezovo, Blg. G15 26
Rezovska (Mutlu), stm., Eur. G14 26
Rhaetian Alps, mts., Eur. C15 18
Rhame, N.D., U.S. A9 126
Rheda-Wiedenbrück, Ger. E4 16
Rheims see Reims, Fr. E12 14
Rhein, Sk., Can. C11 124
Rhein see Rhine, stm., Eur. C15 14
Rheine, Ger. D3 16
Rheinland-Pfalz, state, Ger. G3 16
Rhine, Ga., U.S. E2 116
Rhine (Rhein) (Rhin), stm., Eur. C15 14
Rhinelander, Wi., U.S. F9 118
Rhineland-Palatinate see Rheinland-Pfalz, state, Ger. G3 16
Rhinns Point, c., Scot., U.K. F6 12
Rhir, Cap, c., Mor. C2 64
Rho, Italy E5 22
Rhode Island, state, U.S. C14 114
Rhode Island Sound, strt., U.S. C14 114
Rhodes see Ródos, Grc. G11 28
Rhodes see Ródos, i., Grc. G10 28
Rhodesia see Zimbabwe, ctry., Afr. D4 68
Rhodes Matopos National Park, p.o.i., Zimb. B8 70
Rhodes' Tomb, hist., Zimb. B9 70
Rhodope Mountains, mts., Eur. H11 26
Rhön, mts., Ger. F5 16
Rhondda, Wales, U.K. J9 12
Rhône, state, Fr. D10 18
Rhône, stm., Eur. F10 18
Rhyl, Wales, U.K. H9 12
Riachão, Braz. D2 88
Riachão do Jacuípe, Braz. F6 88
Riacho de Santana, Braz. G4 88
Riachos, Islas de los, is., Arg. H4 90
Riamkanan, Waduk, res., Indon. E9 50
Riaño, Spain A6 20
Riau, state, Indon. D2 50
Riau, Kepulauan, is., Indon. C4 50
Riaza, Spain C7 20
Ribadeo, Spain A3 20
Ribas do Rio Pardo, Braz. D6 90
Ribáuè, Moz. C6 68
Ribe, Den. I3 8
Ribe, state, Den. I3 8
Ribeira, Braz. B13 92
Ribeira do Pombal, Braz. F6 88
Ribeirão, Braz. E8 88
Ribeirão Preto, Braz. K2 88
Ribeirão Vermelho, Braz. K3 88
Ribeiro Gonçalves, Braz. D3 88
Ribera, Italy G7 24
Riberalta, Bol. B3 90
Rib Lake, Wi., U.S. F8 118
Ribnica, Slvn. E11 22
Ribnitz-Damgarten, Ger. B8 16
Ribstone Creek, stm., Ab., Can. D19 138
Ricardo Flores Magón, Mex. F9 98
Riccione, Italy F9 22
Rice, Tx., U.S. E2 122
Rice Lake, l., On., Can. D11 112
Riceville, Ia., U.S. H6 118
Riceville, Tn., U.S. B14 122
Richan, On., Can. B6 118
Richard B. Russell Lake, res., U.S. B3 116
Richard Collinson Inlet, b., N.T., Can. B17 140
Richards, Tx., U.S. G3 122
Richards Bay, S. Afr. F11 70
Richards Bay, b., S. Afr. F11 70
Richards Island, i., N.T., Can. C13 140
Richardson, Tx., U.S. E2 122
Richardson, Wa., U.S. B4 136
Richardson Mountains, mts., Can. B3 106
Richard Toll, Sen. F1 64
Riche, Pointe, c., Nf., Can. i22 107a
Richelieu, Fr. G9 14
Richelieu, stm., Qc., Can. E3 110
Richer, Mb., Can. E17 124
Richey, Mt., U.S. G8 124
Richfield, Mn., U.S. G5 118
Richfield, Pa., U.S. D8 114
Richfield, Ut., U.S. E4 132
Richfield Springs, N.Y., U.S. B11 114
Richford, Vt., U.S. F4 110
Rich Hill, Mo., U.S. F3 120
Richibucto, N.B., Can. D12 110
Richland, Ga., U.S. E14 122
Richland, Mi., U.S. F4 112
Richland, Mt., U.S. F7 124
Richland, Wa., U.S. D7 136
Richland Center, Wi., U.S. H8 118
Richland Creek, stm., Tx., U.S. C11 130
Richlands, Va., U.S. G4 114
Richland Springs, Tx., U.S. C9 130
Richmond, Austl. C4 76
Richmond, Austl. I8 76
Richmond, B.C., Can. G7 138
Richmond, On., Can. C14 112
Richmond, Qc., Can. E4 110
Richmond, N.Z. E5 80
Richmond, S. Afr. G6 70
Richmond, S. Afr. F10 70
Richmond, Eng., U.K. G11 12
Richmond, Ca., U.S. F3 134
Richmond, In., U.S. I5 112
Richmond, Ky., U.S. G1 114
Richmond, Me., U.S. F7 110
Richmond, Mi., U.S. B3 114
Richmond, Mn., U.S. F4 118
Richmond, Mo., U.S. E4 120
Richmond, Tx., U.S. H3 122
Richmond, Ut., U.S. B5 132
Richmond, Va., U.S. G8 114
Richmond Heights, Fl., U.S. K5 116
Richmond Highlands, Wa., U.S. C4 136
Richmond Hill, On., Can. E10 112
Richmond Hill, Ga., U.S. E4 116
Richmond Peak, mtn., St. Vin. o11 105e
Richton, Ms., U.S. F9 122
Richwood, Oh., U.S. D2 114
Richwood, W.V., U.S. F5 114

Name Map Ref. Page

Ricobayo, Embalse de, res., Spain C4 20
Riddle, Or., U.S. H3 136
Rideau, stm., On., Can. C14 112
Ridgecrest, Ca., U.S. H8 134
Ridgedale, Sk., Can. A9 124
Ridgeland, Ms., U.S. E8 122
Ridgeland, S.C., U.S. D4 116
Ridgetown, On., Can. F8 112
Ridgeville, Mb., Can. E16 124
Ridgeville, S.C., U.S. C5 116
Ridgeway, Mo., U.S. D4 120
Ridgway, Co., U.S. E9 132
Ridgway, Il., U.S. G9 120
Ridgway, Pa., U.S. C7 114
Riding Mountain National Park, p.o.i., Mb., Can. D13 124
Riegelwood, N.C., U.S. B7 116
Riesa, Ger. E9 16
Riesco, Isla, i., Chile J2 90
Riesi, Italy G8 24
Riet, stm., S. Afr. F7 70
Riet, stm., S. Afr. H5 70
Rietavas, Lith. E4 10
Rietfontein (Buitsivango), stm., Afr. B4 70
Rieti, Italy H9 22
Rif, mts., Mor. C4 64
Riffe Lake, res., Wa., U.S. D4 136
Rifle, Co., U.S. D9 132
Rifstangi, c., Ice. j31 8a
Rift Valley, val., Afr. F7 62
Rīga, Lat. D7 10
Riga, Gulf of, b., Eur. C6 10
Rigaih, Indon. J2 48
Rigby, Id., U.S. G14 136
Rīgestān, reg., Afg. C9 56
Riggins, Id., U.S. E10 136
Rigi, mtn., Switz. C5 22
Rigo, Pap. N. Gui. b4 79a
Rig-Rig, Chad E2 62
Riihimäki, Fin. F11 8
Riiser-Larsen Peninsula, pen., Ant. B8 81
Riječki Zaljev, b., Cro. E11 22
Rijeka (Fiume), Cro. E11 22
Rijssen, Neth. D2 16
Rillito, Az., U.S. K5 132
Rimatara, i., Fr. Poly. F11 72
Rimavská Sobota, Slov. H15 16
Rimbey, Ab., Can. D16 138
Rimersburg, Pa., U.S. C6 114
Rimini, Italy F9 22
Rimouski, Qc., Can. B8 110
Rimouski, stm., Qc., Can. B8 110
Rinbung, China C7 46
Rinca, Pulau, i., Indon. H11 50
Rincon, Ga., U.S. D4 116
Rincon, N.M., U.S. K9 132
Rinconada, Arg. D3 90
Rincón del Bonete, Lago Artificial de, res., Ur. F9 92
Rincón de Romos, Mex. D7 100
Rīngas, India E5 54
Ringdove, Vanuatu k16 79d
Ringebu, Nor. F4 8
Ringgold, Ga., U.S. C13 122
Ringim, Nig. G6 64
Ringkøbing, Den. H2 8
Ringkøbing, state, Den. H3 8
Ringkøbing Fjord, b., Den. H2 8
Ringling, Ok., U.S. G11 128
Ringsted, Ia., U.S. H4 118
Ringvassøya, i., Nor. A8 8
Rinjani, Gunung, vol., Indon. H10 50
Rinteln, Ger. D5 16
Rio, Wi., U.S. H9 118
Riobamba, Ec. H2 86
Río Blanco, Chile F2 92
Rio Branco, Braz. E4 84
Río Branco, Ur. F11 92
Río Bravo, Mex. C9 100
Río Bravo, Parque Internacional del, p.o.i., Mex. F5 130
Rio Brilhante, Braz. D6 90
Río Bueno, Chile H2 90
Rio Casca, Braz. K4 88
Río Ceballos, Arg. E5 92
Río Chico, Ven. B9 86
Rio Claro, Braz. L2 88
Rio Claro, Trin. s12 105f
Río Colorado, Arg. I5 92
Río Cuarto, Arg. F5 92
Rio das Pedras, Moz. C12 70
Rio de Janeiro, Braz. L4 88
Rio de Janeiro, state, Braz. L4 88
Rio Dell, Ca., U.S. C1 134
Río de Oro, Col. C5 86
Rio do Sul, Braz. C13 92
Rio Espera, Braz. K4 88
Rio Felix, stm., N.M., U.S. H3 128
Río Gallegos, Arg. J3 90
Río Grande, Arg. J3 90
Rio Grande, Braz. F11 92
Río Grande, Mex. D7 100
Río Grande, Nic. F4 102
Río Grande, P.R. B4 104a
Rio Grande (Bravo), stm., N.A. H13 98
Rio Grande do Norte, state, Braz. C7 88
Rio Grande do Sul, state, Braz. D11 92
Ríohacha, Col. B5 86
Río Hato, Pan. H7 102
Rio Hondo, Tx., U.S. H10 130
Rio Hondo, stm., N.M., U.S. H3 128
Rio Hondo, Embalse, res., Arg. C5 92
Río Jueyes, P.R. B3 104a
Riolândia, Braz. D6 90
Rio Largo, Braz. E8 88
Riom, Fr. D9 18
Río Mayo, Arg. I2 90
Río Mulatos, Bol. C3 90
Riondel, B.C., Can. G14 138
Rio Negro, Braz. C13 92
Ríonegro, Col. D5 86
Río Negro, state, Arg. G3 90
Rio Negro, Pantanal do, sw., Braz. C5 90
Rionero in Vulture, Italy D9 24
Riópar, Spain F8 20
Rio Pardo, Braz. E11 92
Rio Pardo de Minas, Braz. H4 88
Río Piedras, P.R. B3 104a
Rio Piracicaba, Braz. J4 88
Rio Pomba, Braz. K4 88
Rio Preto, Braz. L3 88
Rio Rancho, N.M., U.S. H10 132
Rio Real, Braz. F6 88
Río Segundo, Arg. E5 92
Ríosucio, Col. E4 86
Río Tercero, Arg. F5 92
Rio Tinto, Braz. D8 88
Rio Verde, Braz. G7 84
Ríoverde, Mex. E8 100
Rio Verde de Mato Grosso, Braz. C6 90
Rio Vista, Ca., U.S. E4 134
Riozinho, stm., Braz. D4 84
Riozinho, stm., Braz. E3 88
Ripley, N.Y., U.S. B6 114
Ripley, Oh., U.S. F2 114
Ripley, Tn., U.S. B9 122
Ripoll, Spain B13 20
Ripon, Qc., Can. E1 110
Ripon, Eng., U.K. G11 12
Ripon, Ca., U.S. F4 134
Ripon, Wi., U.S. H10 118
Riposto, Italy G9 24
Risaralda, state, Col. E3 86
Risbäck, Swe. D6 8
Rishīkesh, India C7 54
Rishiri-suidō, strt., Japan B14 38
Rishiri-tō, i., Japan B14 38
Rishon LeẔiyyon, Isr. G5 58
Rising Star, Tx., U.S. B9 130
Rising Sun, In., U.S. F12 120
Rising Sun, Md., U.S. E9 114
Risle, stm., Fr. E9 14
Risnjak, mtn., Cro. E11 22
Risti, Est. A7 10
Ristna, Est. G9 8
Rita Blanca Creek, stm., Tx., U.S. F6 128
Ritchie, S. Afr. F7 70
Ritidian Point, c., Guam i10 78c
Ritter, Mount, mtn., Ca., U.S. F6 134
Rittman, Oh., U.S. D4 114
Ritzville, Wa., U.S. C8 136
Rivadavia, Arg. E3 92
Rivadavia, Arg. G6 92
Rivadavia, Chile D2 92
Riva del Garda, Italy E7 22
Rivas, Nic. G5 102
Rive-de-Gier, Fr. D10 18
Rivera, Arg. H6 92
Rivera, Ur. E10 92
River Cess, Lib. H3 64
Riverdale, Ca., U.S. G6 134
Riverdale, N.D., U.S. G12 124
River Falls, Al., U.S. F12 122
River Falls, Wi., U.S. G6 118
Riverhead, N.Y., U.S. D13 114
Riverhurst, Sk., Can. D7 124
Riverina, reg., Austl. J5 76
River John, N.S., Can. E13 110
River Jordan, B.C., Can. H6 138
River Road, Or., U.S. F3 136
Rivers, Mb., Can. D13 124
Riversdale, S. Afr. I5 70
Riverside, Ca., U.S. J8 134
Riverside, Ia., U.S. C6 120
Riverside, Tx., U.S. G3 122
Riverside, Wa., U.S. B7 136
Rivers Inlet, B.C., Can. E3 138
Riversleigh, Austl. C7 74
Riverton, N.Z. H2 80
Riverton, Il., U.S. E8 120
Riverton, Ne., U.S. A10 128
Riverton, Ut., U.S. C4 132
Riverton, Va., U.S. F7 114
Riverton, Wy., U.S. D4 126
Riverton Heights, Wa., U.S. C4 136
River View, Al., U.S. E13 122
Rives, Tn., U.S. H8 120
Rivesville, W.V., U.S. E5 114
Riviera, Tx., U.S. G10 130
Riviera Beach, Fl., U.S. J5 116
Rivière-à-Pierre, Qc., Can. C5 110
Rivière-Bleue, Qc., Can. C7 110
Rivière-de-la-Chaloupe, Qc., Can. A14 110
Rivière-du-Loup, Qc., Can. C7 110
Rivière-Matawin, Qc., Can. D3 110
Rivière-Pilote, Mart. I7 105c
Rivière-Salée, Mart. k7 105c
Rivne, Ukr. E14 6
Rivoli, Italy E4 22
Rivoli Bay, b., Austl. K2 76
Riyadh see Ar-Riyāḍ, Sau. Ar. E6 56
Rīyāq, Leb. E7 58
Rize, Tur. A5 56
Rizzuto, Capo, c., Italy F11 24
Rjad, Russia C18 10
Rjazan', Russia D5 32
Rjazancevo, Russia D22 10
Rjazanskaja oblast', co., Russia I19 8
Rjažsk, Russia D6 32
Rjukan, Nor. G3 8
Ro, N. Cal. m16 79d
Roachdale, In., U.S. I3 112
Road Town, Br. Vir. Is. e8 104b
Roan Mountain, Tn., U.S. H3 114
Roanne, Fr. C9 18
Roanoke, Al., U.S. D13 122
Roanoke, Il., U.S. D8 120
Roanoke, Va., U.S. G6 114
Roanoke, stm., U.S. H8 114
Roanoke Island, i., N.C., U.S. I10 114
Roanoke Rapids, N.C., U.S. H8 114
Roanoke Rapids Lake Dam, dam, N.C., U.S. H8 114
Roan Plateau, plat., U.S. D7 132
Roaring Spring, Pa., U.S. D7 114
Roaring Springs, Tx., U.S. H7 128
Roatán, Isla de, i., Hond. D4 102
Robbins, N.C., U.S. A6 116
Robbins, Tn., U.S. H13 120
Robbins Island, i., Austl. n12 77a
Robbinsville, N.C., U.S. A2 116
Robe, Austl. K2 76
Robe, Mount, hill, Austl. H3 76
Röbel, Ger. C8 16
Robersonville, N.C., U.S. I8 114
Roberta, Ga., U.S. D1 116
Robert Lee, Tx., U.S. C7 130
Robert Louis Stevenson's Tomb, hist., Samoa g12 79c
Roberts, Id., U.S. G14 136
Roberts, Mt., U.S. B3 126
Robertsdale, Al., U.S. G11 122
Robertsfors, Swe. D9 8
Robert S. Kerr Lake, res., Ok., U.S. B3 122
Robertson, S. Afr. H4 70
Roberts Peak, mtn., B.C., Can. D10 138
Roberts Port, Lib. H2 64
Roberval, Qc., Can. B4 110
Robinson, Il., U.S. E10 120
Robinson, Tx., U.S. C10 130
Róbinson Crusoe, Isla, i., Chile I7 82
Robinvale, Austl. J4 76
Robledo, Spain F8 20
Roblin, Mb., Can. C12 124
Roboré, Bol. C5 90
Rob Roy Island, i., Sol. Is. d7 79b
Robson, Mount, mtn., B.C., Can. C11 138
Robstown, Tx., U.S. G10 130
Roby, Tx., U.S. B7 130
Roca, Cabo da, c., Port. F1 20
Roçado, Braz. D3 88
Rocafuerte, Ec. H1 86
Roca Partida, Isla, i., Mex. F2 100
Rocas, Atol das, at., Braz. F11 82
Rocciamelone, mtn., Italy E4 22
Rocha, Ur. G10 92
Rochdale, Eng., U.K. H10 12
Rochechouart, Fr. D6 18
Rochefort, Fr. D5 18
Rochelle, Ga., U.S. E2 116
Rochelle, Il., U.S. C8 120
Roche-Percée, Sk., Can. E10 124
Rochester, In., U.S. G3 112
Rochester, Mi., U.S. B2 114
Rochester, Mn., U.S. G6 118
Rochester, N.H., U.S. G5 110
Rochester, N.Y., U.S. E12 112
Rochester, Tx., U.S. H9 128
Rochlitz, Ger. E8 16
Rock, stm., U.S. H2 118
Rock, stm., U.S. J8 118
Rockall, i., Scot., U.K. D6 6
Rockall Rise, unds. C12 144
Rock Bay, B.C., Can. F5 138
Rock Creek, B.C., Can. G11 138
Rock Creek, stm., N.A. F7 124
Rock Creek, stm., Mt., U.S. D13 136
Rock Creek, stm., Nv., U.S. C9 134
Rock Creek Butte, mtn., Or., U.S. F8 136
Rockdale, Il., U.S. C9 120
Rockdale, Tx., U.S. D11 130
Rockefeller Plateau, plat., Ant. D27 81
Rockenhausen, Ger. G3 16
Rock Falls, Il., U.S. C8 120
Rockford, Il., U.S. B8 120
Rockford, Ia., U.S. A5 120
Rockford, Oh., U.S. D1 114
Rockford, Tn., U.S. B15 122
Rockglen, Sk., Can. E8 124
Rockhampton, Austl. D8 76
Rockhampton Downs, Austl. C7 74
Rock Hill, S.C., U.S. B4 116
Rockingham, N.C., U.S. B6 116
Rockingham Bay, b., Austl. B6 76
Rock Island, Il., U.S. C7 120
Rocklake, N.D., U.S. F14 124
Rockland, On., Can. C14 112
Rockland, Id., U.S. H14 136
Rockland, Me., U.S. F7 110
Rockland, Ma., U.S. B15 114
Rocklands Reservoir, l., Austl. K3 76
Rockledge, Fl., U.S. H5 116
Rocklin, Ca., U.S. E4 134
Rockmart, Ga., U.S. D13 122
Rockport, In., U.S. G10 120
Rockport, Ky., U.S. G11 120
Rockport, Me., U.S. F7 110
Rockport, Ma., U.S. B15 114
Rock Port, Mo., U.S. D2 120
Rock Rapids, Ia., U.S. H2 118
Rock River, Wy., U.S. F6 126
Rocksprings, Tx., U.S. E7 130
Rock Springs, Wy., U.S. B7 132
Rockstone, Guy. B6 84
Rock Tombs see Speos, hist., Egypt K1 58
Rock Valley, Ia., U.S. H2 118
Rockville, In., U.S. I2 112
Rockville, Md., U.S. E8 114
Rockwall, Tx., U.S. E2 122
Rockwell, Ia., U.S. B4 120
Rockwell, N.C., U.S. A5 116
Rockwood, Me., U.S. E7 110
Rockwood, Pa., U.S. I10 112
Rockwood, Tn., U.S. I13 120
Rocky Cape National Park, p.o.i., Austl. n12 77a
Rockyford, Ab., Can. E17 138
Rocky Ford, Co., U.S. C5 128
Rocky Mount, N.C., U.S. I8 114
Rocky Mount, Va., U.S. H5 114
Rocky Mountain, mtn., Mt., U.S. C14 136
Rocky Mountain House, Ab., Can. D16 138
Rocky Mountain National Park, p.o.i., Co., U.S. G7 126
Rocky Mountains, mts., N.A. D6 106
Rocky Mountain Trench, val., N.A. G15 138
Rocky Point, c., Bah. K8 116
Rodalben, Ger. G3 16
Rødbyhavn, Den. I4 8
Rodeo, Arg. E3 92
Rodeo, Mex. C6 100
Rodeo, N.M., U.S. L7 132
Roderick Island, i., B.C., Can. D2 138
Rodewisch, Ger. F8 16
Rodez, Fr. E8 18
Roding, Ger. G8 16
Rodino, Russia G21 8
Rodney, On., Can. F8 112
Rodney, Cape, c., Ak., U.S. D6 140
Rodniki, Russia H19 8
Ródos (Rhodes), Grc. G11 28
Ródos (Rhodes), i., Grc. G10 28
Rodrigues, i., Mrts. K9 142
Roebourne, Austl. D3 74
Roebuck Bay, b., Austl. C4 74
Roeland Park, Ks., U.S. E3 120
Roermond, Neth. C14 14
Roeselare, Bel. D11 14
Roes Welcome Sound, strt., Nu., Can. C13 106
Roff, Ok., U.S. C2 122
Rogačevo, Russia D20 10
Rogagua, Laguna, l., Bol. B3 90
Rogaguado, Laguna, l., Bol. B3 90
Rogaland, state, Nor. G2 8
Rogaška Slatina, Slvn. D12 22
Rogers, Ar., U.S. H3 120
Rogers, Tx., U.S. D10 130
Rogers, Mount, mtn., Va., U.S. H4 114
Rogers Lake, l., Ca., U.S. I8 134
Rogers Pass, p., B.C., Can. E13 138
Rogersville, N.B., Can. D11 110
Rogersville, Al., U.S. C11 122
Rogersville, Tn., U.S. H3 114
Roggewein, Cabo, c., Chile e30 78l
Rogliano, Fr. G15 18
Rognedino, Russia G16 10
Rogue, stm., Or., U.S. H2 136
Rohri, Pak. E2 54
Rohtak, India D6 54
Roi Et, Thai. E6 48
Roi Georges, Îles du, is., Fr. Poly. E12 72
Roilianka, Ukr. C16 26
Rojas, Arg. G7 92
Rojo, Cabo, c., Mex. E10 100
Rojo, Cabo, c., P.R. C1 104a
Rokan, Indon. C2 50
Rokan, stm., Indon. C2 50
Rokel, stm., S.L. H2 64
Rokiškis, Lith. E8 10
Rokycany, Czech Rep. G9 16
Roland, Mb., Can. E16 124
Roland, Ar., U.S. C6 122
Roland, Ia., U.S. B4 120
Rolândia, Braz. D6 90
Roldanillo, Col. E3 86
Rolfe, Ia., U.S. B3 120
Roll, Az., U.S. K2 132
Rolla, Mo., U.S. G6 120
Rolla, N.D., U.S. F14 124
Rolling Fork, Ms., U.S. E8 122
Rolling Fork, stm., Ky., U.S. G12 120
Rollingstone, Austl. B6 76
Rollins, Mt., U.S. C12 136
Rolvsøya, i., Nor. A10 8
Roma, Austl. F7 76
Roma (Rome), Italy I9 22
Roma, Leso. F8 70
Roma, Tx., U.S. H8 130
Romagna, hist. reg., Italy F9 22
Roman, Rom. C13 26
Romanche Gap, unds. I12 144
Romang, Pulau, i., Indon. G8 44
Romania, ctry., Eur. D11 26
Roman Nose Mountain, mtn., Or., U.S. G3 136
Romano, Cape, c., Fl., U.S. K4 116
Romano, Cayo, i., Cuba A9 102
Romans-sur-Isère, Fr. D10 18
Romanzof Mountains, mts., Ak., U.S. C11 140
Romblon, Phil. D4 52
Rome see Roma, Italy I9 22
Rome, Ga., U.S. C13 122
Rome, N.Y., U.S. E14 112
Romeo, Mi., U.S. B2 114
Romilly-sur-Seine, Fr. F12 14
Romney, W.V., U.S. E7 114
Romny, Ukr. D4 32
Romont, Switz. D3 22
Romorantin-Lanthenay, Fr. G10 14
Rompin, stm., Malay. K6 48
Romsey, Eng., U.K. J11 12
Ron, Mui, c., Viet. C8 48
Rona, i., Scot., U.K. D7 12
Rona, i., Scot., U.K. B7 12
Ronan, Mt., U.S. C12 136
Roncador, Banco see Roncador, Cayos de, unds., Col. F7 102
Roncador, Cayos de, unds., Col. F7 102
Roncador, Serra do, plat., Braz. F7 84
Roncador Bank see Roncador, Cayos de, unds., Col. F7 102
Ronda, Spain H5 20
Ronda, Serranía de, mts., Spain H5 20
Rondane Nasjonalpark, p.o.i., Nor. F3 8
Ronde, Pointe, c., Dom. i5 105c
Rondônia, state, Braz. F5 84
Rondonópolis, Braz. G7 84
Rong, stm., China I3 42
Rong'an, China I3 42
Rongcheng, China C10 42
Ronge, Lac la, l., Sk., Can. D10 106
Rongelap, at., Marsh. Is. B7 72
Rongjiang, China I3 42
Rongkop, Indon. H7 50
Rongshui, China I3 42
Rongxian, China J4 42
Rønne, Den. I6 8
Ronneby, Swe. H6 8
Ronne Ice Shelf, ice, Ant. C34 81
Ronse, Bel. D12 14
Ronuro, stm., Braz. F7 84
Roodhouse, Il., U.S. E7 120
Roof Butte, mtn., Az., U.S. G7 132
Rooiboklaagte, stm., Nmb. B5 70
Roorkee, India D6 54
Roosendaal, Neth. C13 14
Roosevelt, Mn., U.S. C3 118
Roosevelt, Ok., U.S. G9 128
Roosevelt, Ut., U.S. C6 132
Roosevelt, stm., Braz. E5 84
Roosevelt Campobello International Park, p.o.i., N.B., Can. F10 110
Roosevelt Island, i., Ant. C24 81
Root, stm., Mn., U.S. H7 118
Ropaži, Lat. C7 10
Roper, N.C., U.S. I9 114
Roper, stm., Austl. B6 74
Roper Valley, Austl. B6 74
Ropesville, Tx., U.S. H6 128
Roque, Braz. B3 88
Roquefort, Fr. E5 18
Roraima, state, Braz. C5 84
Roraima, Mount, mtn., S.A. E11 86
Røros, Nor. E4 8
Rosa, Lake, l., Bah. B11 102
Rosales, Mex. A6 100
Rosalia, Wa., U.S. C9 136
Rosamond, Ca., U.S. I7 134
Rosamond Lake, l., Ca., U.S. I7 134
Rosario, Arg. F7 92
Rosário, Braz. B3 88
Rosario, Mex. B4 100
Rosario, Mex. D5 100
Rosario, Para. B9 92
Rosario, Ur. G9 92
Rosario, stm., Arg. B5 92
Rosario, Bahía del, b., Mex. G4 98
Rosario, Islas del, is., Col. B4 86
Rosario de Arriba, Mex. F4 98
Rosario de la Frontera, Arg. B5 92
Rosario de Lerma, Arg. B5 92
Rosario del Tala, Arg. F8 92
Rosário do Sul, Braz. E10 92
Rosário Oeste, Braz. F6 84
Rosarito, Mex. A2 100
Rosarito, Mex. K8 134
Rosarno, Italy F9 24
Rosas, Mex. H4 130
Roscoe, S.D., U.S. B13 126
Roscoe, Tx., U.S. B7 130
Roscommon, Ire. H4 12
Roscommon, state, Ire. H4 12
Roscrea, Ire. I5 12
Rose, Mount, mtn., Nv., U.S. D5 134
Roseau, Dom. j6 105c
Roseau, Mn., U.S. C3 118
Roseau, stm., N.A. C2 118
Roseberth, Austl. E2 76
Rosebery, Austl. n12 77a
Roseboro, N.C., U.S. B7 116
Rosebud, Mt., U.S. A6 126
Rosebud, S.D., U.S. D12 126
Rosebud, Tx., U.S. C11 130
Rosebud, stm., Ab., Can. E17 138
Rosebud Creek, stm., Mt., U.S. A6 126
Roseburg, Or., U.S. G3 136
Rosebush, Mi., U.S. E5 112
Rose City, Mi., U.S. D5 112
Rosedale, Austl. E8 76
Rosedale, Ab., Can. E18 138
Rosedale, La., U.S. G7 122
Rosedale, Ms., U.S. D7 122
Rose Hill, N.C., U.S. B7 116
Rose Hill, Va., U.S. H2 114
Rose Island, i., Bah. K8 116
Rosemary, Ab., Can. F18 138
Rosenberg, Tx., U.S. H3 122
Rosenheim, Ger. I8 16
Rosepine, La., U.S. G5 122
Roses, Golf de, b., Spain B14 20
Roses, Golfo de see Roses, Golf de, b., Spain B14 20
Roseto degli Abruzzi, Italy H11 22
Rosetown, Sk., Can. C6 124
Rosetta see Rashid, Egypt G1 58
Rosetta Mouth see Rashid, Masabb, mth., Egypt G1 58
Rose Valley, Sk., Can. B10 124
Roseville, Il., U.S. D7 120
Roseville, Mi., U.S. F7 112
Roseville, Mn., U.S. F5 118
Rosholt, S.D., U.S. F2 118
Rosholt, Wi., U.S. G9 118
Rosica, stm., Blg. F12 26
Rosiclare, Il., U.S. G9 120
Rosignol, Guy. B6 84
Roșiori de Vede, Rom. E12 26
Roskilde, Den. I4 8
Roskilde, state, Den. I5 8
Roslavl', Russia G15 10
Rosman, N.C., U.S. A3 116
Rosmead, S. Afr. G7 70
Ros Mhic Thriúin see New Ross, Ire. I6 12
Ross, Austl. o13 77a
Ross, stm., Yk., Can. C4 106
Rossano, Italy E10 24
Rossasna, Bela. F13 10
Rossburn, Mb., Can. D13 124
Rosseau, Lake, l., On., Can. C10 112
Rossel, Cap, c., N. Cal. m16 79d
Rossell y Rius, Ur. F10 92
Rossford, Oh., U.S. C2 114
Ross Ice Shelf, ice, Ant. D23 81
Rossignol, Lake, l., N.S., Can. F11 110
Ross Island, i., Ant. C22 81
Ross Lake, res., N.A. B5 136
Rossland, B.C., Can. G13 138
Rosslau, Ger. E8 16
Rosso, Maur. F1 64
Ross-on-Wye, Eng., U.K. J10 12
Rossoš', Russia D5 32
Ross R. Barnett Reservoir, res., Ms., U.S. E9 122
Ross River, Yk., Can. C4 106
Ross Sea, Ant. C23 81
Røssvatnet, l., Nor. D5 8
Rossville, Ga., U.S. C13 122
Rossville, Il., U.S. H2 112
Rossville, Ks., U.S. E2 120
Røst, is., Nor. C4 8
Rosthern, Sk., Can. B7 124
Roštkala, Taj. B11 56
Rostock, Ger. B7 16
Rostov, Russia C22 10
Rostov-na-Donu, Russia E6 32
Rosvinskoe, Russia C24 8
Roswell, Ga., U.S. B1 116
Roswell, N.M., U.S. H4 128
Rota, i., N. Mar. Is. B5 72
Rotan, Tx., U.S. B7 130
Rotenburg, Ger. C5 16
Roth, Ger. G7 16
Rothenburg ob der Tauber, Ger. G6 16
Rothera, sci., Ant. B34 81
Rotherham, Eng., U.K. H11 12
Rothesay, N.B., Can. E11 110
Rothesay, Scot., U.K. F7 12
Rothsay, Mn., U.S. E2 118
Rothwell, N.B., Can. D10 110
Roti, Pulau, i., Indon. H7 44
Roto, Austl. I5 76
Rotondella, Italy D10 24
Rotorua, N.Z. D7 80
Rottenburg, Ger. H4 16
Rottenburg an der Laaber, Ger. H8 16
Rotterdam, Neth. C13 14
Rotterdam, N.Y., U.S. B11 114
Rottweil, Ger. H4 16
Rotuma, i., Fiji E8 72
Roubaix, Fr. D12 14
Roudnice nad Labem, Czech Rep. F9 16
Rouen, Fr. E10 14
Rouge, stm., Qc., Can. E2 110
Rough, stm., Ky., U.S. G11 120
Rough River Lake, res., Ky., U.S. G11 120
Rouleau, Sk., Can. D9 124
Roulers see Roeselare, Bel. D11 14
Roulette, Pa., U.S. C7 114
Round Hill Head, c., Austl. E8 76
Round Lake, Mn., U.S. H3 118
Round Lake, l., On., Can. C12 112
Round Mound, hill, Ks., U.S. C9 128
Round Mountain, Nv., U.S. E8 134
Round Mountain, mtn., Austl. H9 76
Round Rock, Tx., U.S. D10 130
Roundup, Mt., U.S. A4 126
Rousay, i., Scot., U.K. B9 12
Rouses Point, N.Y., U.S. E3 110
Roussillon, hist. reg., Fr. G8 18
Routhierville, Qc., Can. B9 110
Rouyn-Noranda, Qc., Can. F15 106
Rovaniemi, Fin. C11 8
Rovenskaja Slabada, Bela. H13 10
Rovereto, Italy E8 22
Roversi, Arg. C6 92
Rovigo, Italy E8 22
Rovuma (Ruvuma), stm., Afr. C6 68
Rowan Lake, l., On., Can. B5 118
Rowena, Austl. G7 76
Rowland, N.C., U.S. B6 116
Rowley, stm., Nu., Can. A15 106
Rowley Island, i., Nu., Can. B14 106
Roxas, Phil. E4 52
Roxboro, N.C., U.S. H7 114
Roxborough, Trin. r13 105f
Roxburgh, N.Z. G3 80
Roxton, Tx., U.S. D3 122
Roy, N.M., U.S. F4 128
Roy, Ut., U.S. B4 132
Roy, Wa., U.S. C4 136
Royal Bardiyā Wild Life Reserve, India D8 54
Royal Canal, can., Ire. H6 12
Royal Center, In., U.S. H3 112
Royal Chitwan National Park, p.o.i., Nepal E10 54
Royal City, Wa., U.S. D7 136
Royale, Isle, i., Mi., U.S. D10 118
Royal Gorge, val., Co., U.S. C3 128
Royal Leamington Spa, Eng., U.K. I11 12
Royal Natal National Park, p.o.i., S. Afr. F9 70
Royal Oak, Mi., U.S. B2 114
Royalton, Mn., U.S. F4 118
Royal Tunbridge Wells, Eng., U.K. J13 12
Royan, Fr. D5 18
Roye, Fr. E11 14
Royston, Eng., U.K. I12 12
Royston, Ga., U.S. B2 116
Różan, Pol. D17 16
Roždestveno, Russia C20 10
Rozdil'na, Ukr. C17 26
Rozewie, Przylądek, c., Pol. B14 16
Rožňava, Slov. H16 16
Roznov, Rom. C13 26
Rożnów, Pol. G16 16
Roztocze, hills, Eur. F19 16
Roztoky, Czech Rep. F10 16
Rrogozhina see Rrogozhinë, Alb. C13 24
Rrogozhinë, Alb. C13 24
Rtiščevo, Russia D6 32
Ru, stm., China E6 42
Ruacana Falls, wtfl, Afr. D1 68
Ruahine Range, mts., N.Z. D7 80
Ruapehu, Mount, vol., N.Z. D6 80
Ruapuke Island, i., N.Z. H3 80
Rubbestadneset, Nor. G1 8
Rubcovsk, Russia D14 32
Rubi, stm., D.R.C. D5 66
Rubio, Ven. D5 86
Rubondo Island, i., Tan. E6 66
Ruby, Ak., U.S. D8 140
Ruby, stm., Mt., U.S. E14 136
Ruby Dome, mtn., Nv., U.S. C1 132
Ruby Lake, sw., Nv., U.S. C1 132
Ruby Mountains, mts., Nv., U.S. C1 132
Ruby Valley, val., Nv., U.S. C1 132
Rucheng, China I5 42
Ruciane-Nida, Pol. C17 16
Ruda Śląska, Pol. F14 16
Rudauli, India E8 54
Rūdbār, Afg. C9 56
Rüdersdorf, Ger. D9 16
Rudkøbing, Den. B6 16
Rudnaja Pristan', Russia B11 38
Rudnja, Russia F14 10
Rudnyj, Kaz. D10 32
Rudnyj, Russia B11 38
Rūdnyy see Rudnyj, Kaz. D10 32
Rudo, Bos. F6 26
Rudolf, Lake (Turkana, Lake), l., Afr. D7 66
Rudolf Hāyk' see Rudolf, Lake, l., Afr. D7 66
Rudolstadt, Ger. F7 16
Rudong, China E9 42
Rudozem, Blg. H11 26
Rudyard, Mi., U.S. B5 112
Rue, Fr. D10 14
Rufā'ah, Sudan E6 62
Ruffin, S.C., U.S. C5 116
Rufiji, stm., Tan. F7 66
Rufino, Arg. G6 92
Rufisque, Sen. G1 64
Rufunsa, Zam. D4 68
Rufus, Or., U.S. E6 136
Rugāji, Lat. D10 10
Rugao, China E9 42
Rugby, Eng., U.K. I11 12
Rugby, N.D., U.S. F14 124
Rügen, i., Ger. B9 16
Rugged Mountain, mtn., B.C., Can. F4 138
Ruhan', Russia G15 10
Ruhengeri, Rw. E5 66
Ruhpolding, Ger. I8 16
Ruhr, stm., Ger. E3 16
Ruhunu National Park, p.o.i., Sri L. H5 53
Rui'an, China H9 42
Ruidoso, N.M., U.S. H3 128
Ruidoso, stm., N.M., U.S. H3 128
Ruihong, China G7 42
Ruijin, China I6 42
Ruiz, Mex. D6 100
Ruiz, Nevado del, vol., Col. E4 86
Ruiz de Montoya, Arg. C10 92
Ruki, stm., D.R.C. E3 66
Rukwa, Lake, l., Tan. F6 66
Rule, Tx., U.S. A8 130
Ruleville, Ms., U.S. D8 122
Rulo, Ne., U.S. D2 120
Rúm, i., Scot., U.K. D6 12
Rum, stm., Mn., U.S. F5 118
Ruma, Yugo. D6 26
Rumbek, Sudan F5 62
Rum Cay, i., Bah. C10 96
Rumia, Pol. B14 16
Rumigny, Fr. E13 14
Rum Jungle, Austl. B6 74
Rumoi, Japan B14 38
Runan, China E6 42
Runanga, N.Z. F4 80
Runde, stm., Zimb. B10 70
Rundēni, Lat. D10 10
Rundu, Nmb. D2 68
Rŭng, Kaôh, i., Camb. G6 48
Runge, Tx., U.S. F10 130
Rungwa, Tan. F6 66
Rungwa, stm., Tan. F6 66
Running Water Draw, stm., U.S. G6 128
Ruo, stm., China C4 36
Ruoqiang, China D2 36
Ruoxi, China G6 42
Rupat, Pulau, i., Indon. C2 50
Rupert, Id., U.S. H13 136
Rupert, W.V., U.S. G5 114
Rupert, stm., Qc., Can. E15 106
Rupert Creek, stm., Austl. C4 76
Rupununi, stm., Guy. F12 86
Rur, stm., Eur. D15 14
Rural Retreat, Va., U.S. H4 114
Rurrenabaque, Bol. B3 90
Rurutu, i., Fr. Poly. F11 72
Rusape, Zimb. D5 68
Ruṣayriṣ, Khazzān ar-, res., Afr. E6 62
Ruse, Blg. F12 26
Ruse, state, Blg. F13 26
Rusera, India F11 54
Rushan, China C9 42
Rush Center, Ks., U.S. C9 128
Rush City, Mn., U.S. F5 118
Rush Creek, stm., Co., U.S. C5 128
Rushford, Mn., U.S. H7 118
Rushmore, Mn., U.S. H3 118
Rushville, Il., U.S. D7 120
Rushville, In., U.S. E12 120
Rusinga Island, i., Kenya E6 66
Rusizi, stm., Afr. E5 66
Rusk, Tx., U.S. F3 122
Ruskin, Fl., U.S. I3 116
Rusnė, Lith. E4 10
Russas, Braz. C6 88
Russell, Mb., Can. D12 124
Russell, Ia., U.S. D4 120
Russell, Ks., U.S. C10 128
Russell, Ky., U.S. F3 114
Russell, Cape, c., N.T., Can. A16 140
Russell Cave National Monument, p.o.i., Al., U.S. C13 122
Russell Islands, is., Sol. Is. e8 79b
Russellkonda, India I10 54
Russells Point, Oh., U.S. D2 114
Russell Springs, Ky., U.S. G12 120
Russellville, Al., U.S. C11 122
Russellville, Ar., U.S. B5 122
Russellville, Ky., U.S. H11 120
Rüsselsheim, Ger. G4 16
Russia, ctry., Eur. B18 2
Russian, stm., Ca., U.S. E2 134
Russiaville, In., U.S. H3 112
Russkij, Russia C9 38
Rust, Aus. C13 22
Rustavi, Geor. F7 32
Rustburg, Va., U.S. G6 114
Rustenburg, S. Afr. D8 70
Ruston, La., U.S. E6 122
Rutana, Bdi. E6 66
Rute, Spain G6 20
Ruteng, Indon. H12 50
Ruth, Nv., U.S. D1 132
Rutherford, Tn., U.S. H8 120
Rutherfordton, N.C., U.S. A3 116
Ruthin, Wales, U.K. H9 12
Ruthven, Ia., U.S. H4 118
Rutland, B.C., Can. G11 138
Rutland, N.D., U.S. A15 126
Rutland, Vt., U.S. G4 110
Rutledge, Ga., U.S. C2 116
Rutog, China B7 54
Rutshuru, D.R.C. E5 66
Rutter, On., Can. B9 112
Ruvuma (Rovuma), stm., Afr. C6 68
Ruwenzori, mts., Afr. D6 66
Ruwenzori Range see Ruwenzori, mts., Afr. D6 66
Ruy Barbosa, Braz. G5 88
Ruza, Russia E19 10
Ruza, stm., Russia E18 10
Ruzaevka, Russia D7 32
Ružany, Bela. H7 10
Ružomberok, Slov. G15 16
Rwanda, ctry., Afr. E6 66
Ryan, Ok., U.S. G11 128
Ryan Peak, mtn., Id., U.S. G12 136
Rybače, Kaz. E14 32
Rybačij, poluostrov, pen., Russia B15 8
Rybinsk, Russia B21 10
Rybinskoe vodohranilišče (Rybinsk Reservoir), res., Russia B21 10
Rybinsk Reservoir see Rybinskoe vodohranilišče, res., Russia B21 10
Rybnik, Pol. F14 16
Rybnoje, Russia E7 34
Ryde, Eng., U.K. K11 12
Ryderwood, Wa., U.S. D3 136
Rydzyna, Pol. E12 16
Ryegate, Mt., U.S. A3 126
Rye Patch Reservoir, res., Nv., U.S. C7 134
Ryfoss, Nor. F3 8
Ryley, Ab., Can. C18 138
Rylovići, Russia H15 10
Ryl'sk, Russia D4 32
Rýmařov, Czech Rep. G13 16
Ryōhaku-sanchi, mts., Japan C9 40
Ryōtsu, Japan A11 40
Rysy, mtn., Eur. G15 16

Ryug-Sama I•49

Name	Map Ref.	Page
Ryūgasaki, Japan	D13	40
Ryukyu Islands see Nansei-shotō, is., Japan	k19	39a
Ryukyu Trench, unds.	G15	142
Ržanica, Russia	G16	10
Rzeszów, Pol.	F18	16
Rzeszów, state, Pol.	F17	16
Ržev, Russia	D17	10

S

Name	Map Ref.	Page
Sa, Thai.	C5	48
Saale, stm., Ger.	E7	16
Saalfeld, Ger.	F7	16
Saar see Saarland, state, Ger.	G2	16
Saarbrücken, Ger.	G2	16
Saarburg, Ger.	G2	16
Saaremaa, i., Est.	G9	8
Saarijärvi, Fin.	E11	8
Saaristomeren kansallispuisto, p.o.i., Fin.	G9	8
Saarland, state, Ger.	G2	16
Saarlouis, Ger.	G2	16
Saavedra, Arg.	H6	92
Saba, i., Neth. Ant.	B1	105a
Šabac, Yugo.	E6	26
Sabadell, Spain	C13	20
Sabae, Japan	D9	40
Sabah, state, Malay.	H1	52
Sabah, hist. reg., Malay.	D6	44
Sabak, Malay.	K5	48
Sabalana, Kepulauan, is., Indon.	G11	50
Sabana, Archipiélago de, is., Cuba	A7	102
Sabana de la Mar, Dom. Rep.	C13	102
Sabana de Mendoza, Ven.	C6	86
Sabanagrande, Hond.	F4	102
Sabana Grande, P.R.	B2	104a
Sabanalarga, Col.	B4	86
Sabana Llana, P.R.	B3	104a
Sabang, Indon.	J2	48
Sabang, Indon.	C11	50
Sabarei, Kenya	D7	66
Sābari, stm., India	C5	53
Sābarmati, stm., India	G4	54
Sab'atayn, Ramlat as-, sand, Yemen	F6	56
Sabbioneta, Italy	E7	22
Şāberī, Hāmūn-e, l., Asia	C9	56
Sabetha, Ks., U.S.	E2	120
Sabhā, Libya	B2	62
Sabidana, Jabal, mtn., Sudan	D7	62
Sabie, S. Afr.	D10	70
Sabié, stm., Afr.	D10	70
Sabile, Lat.	C5	10
Sabina, Oh., U.S.	E2	114
Sabina, hist. reg., Italy	H9	22
Sabinal, Tx., U.S.	E8	130
Sabinal, stm., Tx., U.S.	E8	130
Sabinal, Cayo, i., Cuba	B9	102
Sabiñánigo, Spain	B10	20
Sabinas, Mex.	B8	100
Sabinas, stm., Mex.	B8	100
Sabinas, stm., Mex.	B9	100
Sabinas Hidalgo, Mex.	B8	100
Sabine, stm., U.S.	G5	122
Sabine Bay, b., Can.	A17	140
Sabine Lake, l., U.S.	H5	122
Sabine Pass, strt., U.S.	H5	122
Sabinópolis, Braz.	J4	88
Şabiote, Spain	F7	20
Šabla, Blg.	F15	26
Sable, Cape, c., N.S., Can.	G11	110
Sable, Cape, pen., Fl., U.S.	K4	116
Sable Island, i., N.S., Can.	G16	110
Sablūkah, Shallāl as- (Sixth Cataract), wtfl, Sudan	D6	62
Šablykino, Russia	H18	10
Sabor, stm., Port.	C4	20
Sabou, Burkina	G4	64
Sabrina Coast, cst., Ant.	B16	81
Şabyā, Sau. Ar.	F5	56
Sabyin, Mya.	C2	48
Sabzevār, Iran	B8	56
Sac, stm., Mo., U.S.	G4	120
Sacaton, Az., U.S.	J5	132
Sac City, Ia., U.S.	B3	120
Săcele, Rom.	D12	26
Sachayoj, Arg.	C6	92
Sachsen, state, Ger.	F9	16
Sachsen (Saxony), hist. reg., Ger.	D5	16
Sachsen-Anhalt, state, Ger.	D7	16
Şachs Harbour, N.T., Can.	B14	140
Šack, Bela.	G10	10
Sackets Harbor, N.Y., U.S.	E13	112
Sackville, N.B., Can.	E12	110
Saco, Me., U.S.	G6	110
Saco, stm., U.S.	F5	110
Sacramento, Braz.	J2	88
Sacramento, Ca., U.S.	E4	134
Sacramento, stm., Ca., U.S.	E4	134
Sacramento Mountains, mts., N.M., U.S.	E10	98
Sacramento Valley, val., Ca., U.S.	D3	134
Sacramento Wash, stm., Az., U.S.	H2	132
Sacred Heart, Mn., U.S.	G3	118
Sádaba, Spain	B9	20
Şa'dah, Yemen	F5	56
Sadaik Taung, mtn., Mya.	E4	48
Sada-misaki, c., Japan	F4	40
Sada-misaki-hantō, pen., Japan	F5	40
Sadang, stm., Indon.	E11	50
Sa Dao, Thai.	I5	48
Sadda, Pak.	B3	54
Saddle Mountain, mtn., Co., U.S.	C3	128
Saddle Mountain, mtn., Or., U.S.	E3	136
Saddle Peak, mtn., India	F7	46
Sa Dec, Viet.	G7	48
Sādiqābād, Pak.	D3	54
Sadiya, India	C8	46
Sadlers, St. K./N.	C2	105a
Sado, i., Japan	A11	40
Sado, stm., Port.	F2	20
Sado-kaikyō, strt., Japan	B11	40
Sadowara, Japan	G4	40
Şādri, India	F4	54
Šadrinsk, Russia	C10	32
Sädvaluspen, Swe.	C7	8
Saegertown, Pa., U.S.	C5	114
Şaerluojia Hu, l., China	B11	54
Šafárikovo, Slov.	H16	16
Säffle, Swe.	G5	8
Saffron Walden, Eng., U.K.	I13	12
Safi, Mor.	C3	64
Safīd Kūh, Selseleh-ye, mts., Afg.	C9	56
Safonovo, Russia	D22	8
Safonovo, Russia	E16	10
Safranbolu, Tur.	B15	28
Saga, China	D10	54
Saga, Japan	F3	40
Saga, state, Japan	F3	40
Sagae, Japan	A13	40
Sagaing, Mya.	B2	48
Sagaing, state, Mya.	A2	48
Sagamihara, Japan	D12	40
Sagami-nada, b., Japan	D12	40
Saganaga Lake, l., N.A.	C7	118
Saganoseki, Japan	F4	40
Saganthit Kyun, i., Mya.	F4	48
Sāgar, India	D2	53
Sāgar, India	G7	54
Sagara, Japan	E11	40
Sagaranten, Indon.	G5	50
Sagavanirktok, stm., Ak., U.S.	C10	140
Sagay, Phil.	E4	52
Sage, Mount, mtn., Br. Vir. Is.	e8	104b
Sage Creek, stm., Mt., U.S.	B16	136
Sagerton, Tx., U.S.	A8	130
Saginaw, Mi., U.S.	E6	112
Saginaw, stm., Mi., U.S.	E5	112
Saginaw Bay, b., Mi., U.S.	E6	112
Sağkaya, Tur.	A6	58
Sagleipie, Lib.	H3	64
Şaglek Bay, b., Nf., Can.	F13	141
Šagonar, Russia	D16	32
Şagu, Rom.	C8	26
Saguache, Co., U.S.	C2	128
Saguache Creek, stm., Co., U.S.	C2	128
Sagua de Tánamo, Cuba	B10	102
Sagua la Grande, Cuba	A7	102
Saguaro National Park, p.o.i., Az., U.S.	K5	132
Saguenay, stm., Qc., Can.	B7	110
Sagunt, Spain	E10	20
Sagunto see Sagunt, Spain	E10	20
Sāgwāra, India	G4	54
Sa'gya, China	D12	54
Sahagún, Col.	C4	86
Sahagún, Spain	B5	20
Sahalin, ostrov, i., Russia	F17	34
Sahalinskij zaliv, b., Russia	F17	34
Sahara, des., Afr.	E5	64
Sahāranpur, India	C6	54
Saharsa, India	F11	54
Sahel see Sudan, reg., Afr.	E4	62
Sāhibganj, India	F11	54
Sāhīwāl, Pak.	C4	54
Şāhīwāl, Pak.	C4	54
Şahovskaja, Russia	D18	10
Şahrisabz, Uzb.	G11	32
Şahtinsk, Kaz.	E12	32
Şahtjorsk, Russia	G17	34
Šahty, Russia	E6	32
Sahuaripa, Mex.	A4	100
Sahuarita, Az., U.S.	L5	132
Sahuayo de José María Morelos, Mex.	E7	100
Şahunja, Russia	H22	8
Šahy, Slov.	H14	16
Sai Buri, Thai.	I5	48
Sai Buri, stm., Thai.	I5	48
Saidor, Pap. N. Gui.	b4	79a
Saidpur, Bngl.	F12	54
Saidu, Pak.	C11	56
Saigō, Japan	C6	40
Saigon see Thanh Pho Ho Chi Minh, Viet.	G8	48
Saijō, Japan	F6	40
Şaiki, Japan	G4	40
Šaim, Russia	B10	32
Saimaa, l., Fin.	F13	8
Sainte Agathe, Mb., Can.	E16	124
Sainte-Agathe-des-Monts, Qc., Can.	D2	110
Saint-Agrève, Fr.	D10	18
Saint Alban's, Nf., Can.	j22	107a
Saint Albans, Eng., U.K.	J12	12
Saint Albans, Vt., U.S.	F3	110
Saint Albans, W.V., U.S.	F4	114
Saint Albert, Ab., Can.	C17	138
Saint Aldhelm's Head, c., Eng., U.K.	K10	12
Saint-Alexis-des-Monts, Qc., Can.	D3	110
Saint-Amand-Mont-Rond, Fr.	H11	14
Saint-André-Avellin, Qc., Can.	E1	110
Saint Andrew, Barb.	n8	105d
Saint Andrew, Mount, mtn., St. Vin.	o11	105e
Saint Andrews, N.B., Can.	E9	110
Saint Andrews, Scot., U.K.	E10	12
Saint Andrews, S.C., U.S.	D5	116
Sainte-Anne, Guad.	h6	105c
Sainte-Anne, Mart.	I7	105c
Sainte Anne, Lac, l., Ab., Can.	C16	138
Sainte-Anne-de-Beaupré, Qc., Can.	C5	110
Sainte-Anne-de-Madawaska, N.B., Can.	C8	110
Sainte-Anne-des-Monts, Qc., Can.	A10	110
Sainte-Anne-du-Lac, Qc., Can.	D1	110
Saint Ann's Bay, Jam.	i13	104d
Saint-Anselme, Qc., Can.	D6	110
Saint Ansgar, Ia., U.S.	H5	118
Saint Anthony, Nf., Can.	i22	107a
Saint Anthony, Id., U.S.	G15	136
Saint Arnaud, Austl.	K4	76
Saint Augustin, Qc., Can.	i22	107a
Saint Augustine, Fl., U.S.	G4	116
Saint Austell, Eng., U.K.	K8	12
Saint-Avold, Fr.	E15	14
Saint-Barthélemy, i., Guad.	B2	105a
Saint-Basile, N.B., Can.	C8	110
Saint Bathans, Mount, mtn., N.Z.	G3	80
Saint Bees Head, c., Eng., U.K.	G9	12
Saint-Boniface-de-Shawinigan, Qc., Can.	D3	110
Saint-Bonnet, Fr.	E11	18
Saint Brides Bay, b., Wales, U.K.	J7	12
Saint-Brieuc, Fr.	F6	14
Saint-Brieuc, Baie de, b., Fr.	F6	14
Saint Catharines, On., Can.	E10	112
Saint Catherine, Mount, vol., Gren.	q10	105e
Saint Catherines Island, i., Ga., U.S.	E4	116
Saint Catherine's Point, c., Eng., U.K.	K11	12
Saint-Céré, Fr.	E7	18
Saint-Chamond, Fr.	D10	18
Saint Charles, Id., U.S.	A5	132
Saint Charles, Il., U.S.	C9	120
Saint Charles, Mi., U.S.	E5	112
Saint Charles, Mn., U.S.	H6	118
Saint Charles, Mo., U.S.	F7	120
Saint Charles Mesa, Co., U.S.	C4	128
Saint Christopher (Saint Kitts), i., St. K./N.	C2	105a
Saint Christopher and Nevis see Saint Kitts and Nevis, ctry., N.A.	C2	105a
Saint Clair, Mi., U.S.	B3	114
Saint Clair, Mo., U.S.	F6	120
Saint Clair, stm., N.A.	B3	114
Saint Clair, Lake, l., N.A.	B3	114
Saint Clair Shores, Mi., U.S.	B3	114
Saint-Claud, Fr.	D6	18
Saint Claude, Mb., Can.	E15	124
Saint-Claude, Fr.	C11	18
Saint-Claude, Guad.	h5	105c
Saint Cloud, Fl., U.S.	H4	116
Saint Cloud, Mn., U.S.	F4	118
Sainte-Croix, Qc., Can.	D5	110
Saint Croix, i., V.I.U.S.	g10	104c
Saint Croix, stm., N.A.	E9	110
Saint Croix, stm., U.S.	G6	118
Saint Croix Falls, Wi., U.S.	F6	118
Saint Croix Island National Monument, p.o.i., Me., U.S.	E10	110
Saint-Cyr, stm., Qc., Can.	A1	110
Saint David, Az., U.S.	L6	132
Saint David's, Wales, U.K.	J7	12
Saint David's Head, c., Wales, U.K.	J7	12
Saint David's Island, i., Ber.	k16	104e
Saint-Denis, Fr.	E11	14
Saint-Denis, Reu.	i10	69a
Saint-Dié, Fr.	F15	14
Saint-Dizier, Fr.	F13	14
Saint-Donat-de-Montcalm, Qc., Can.	D2	110
Saint Edward, Ne., U.S.	F15	126
Saint Elias, Cape, c., Ak., U.S.	E11	140
Saint Elias, Mount, mtn., N.A.	C2	106
Saint Elias Mountains, mts., N.A.	D12	140
Saint-Élie, Fr. Gu.	C7	84
Saint Elmo, Il., U.S.	E9	120
Saint-Étienne, Fr.	D10	18
Saint-Étienne-du-Rouvray, Fr.	E10	14
Saint-Eugène, Qc., Can.	B4	110
Saint-Eustache, Qc., Can.	E2	110
Saint-Fabien, Qc., Can.	B8	110
Saint-Félicien, Qc., Can.	B4	110
Saint-Félix-de-Valois, Qc., Can.	D3	110
Saint-Florent-sur-Cher, Fr.	G11	14
Saint-Flour, Fr.	D9	18
Sainte-Foy, Qc., Can.	D5	110
Sainte-Foy-la-Grande, Fr.	E6	18
Saint Francis, Ks., U.S.	B7	128
Saint Francis, Wi., U.S.	I11	118
Saint Francis, stm., N.A.	C7	110
Saint Francis, stm., U.S.	C8	122
Saint Francis, Cape, c., S. Afr.	I7	70
Saint Francis Bay, b., S. Afr.	I7	70
Saint Francisville, Il., U.S.	F10	120
Saint Francisville, La., U.S.	G7	122
Saint-François, Guad.	h6	105c
Saint-François, stm., Qc., Can.	D4	110
Saint-François, Lac, l., Can.	E2	110
Saint-François, Lac, res., Qc., Can.	E5	110
Saint-Gabriel, Can.	B8	110
Saint-Gabriel-de-Gaspé, Qc., Can.	B12	110
Saint-Gall see Sankt Gallen, Switz.	C6	22
Saint-Gaudens, Fr.	F6	18
Sainte Genevieve, Mo., U.S.	G7	120
Saint George, Austl.	G7	76
Saint George, Ber.	k16	104e
Saint George, N.B., Can.	E10	110
Saint George, On., Can.	E9	112
Saint George, Ut., U.S.	F3	132
Saint George, Cape, c., Fl., U.S.	H13	122
Saint George, Point, c., Ca., U.S.	B1	134
Saint George Island, i., Fl., U.S.	H14	122
Saint-Georges, Qc., Can.	D4	110
Saint-Georges, Qc., Can.	D6	110
Saint-Georges, Fr. Gu.	C7	84
Saint George's, Gren.	q10	105e
Saint George's Bay, b., Nf., Can.	j22	107a
Saint Georges Bay, b., N.S., Can.	E15	110
Saint George's Channel, strt., Eur.	J7	12
Saint George's Channel, strt., Pap. N. Gui.	a5	79a
Saint-Gilles-Croix-de-Vie, Fr.	H6	14
Saint Gotthard Pass see San Gottardo, Passo del, p., Switz.	D5	22
Saint Helena, Ca., U.S.	E3	134
Saint Helena, dep., Afr.	H5	60
Saint Helena Bay see Sint Helenabaai, b., S. Afr.	H3	70
Saint Helens, Eng., U.K.	H10	12
Saint Helens, Or., U.S.	E4	136
Saint Helens, Mount, vol., Wa., U.S.	D4	136
Saint Helier, Jersey	E6	14
Saint-Hilaire-du-Harcouët, Fr.	F7	14
Saint-Hyacinthe, Qc., Can.	E4	110
Saint Ignace Island, i., On., Can.	C11	118
Saint Ignatius, Guy.	F12	86
Saint Ignatius, Mt., U.S.	C12	136
Saint-Isidore, N.B., Can.	C11	110
Saint Ives, Eng., U.K.	K7	12
Saint James, Mi., U.S.	C4	112
Saint James, Mn., U.S.	G4	118
Saint James, Mo., U.S.	G6	120
Saint James, Cape, c., B.C., Can.	E4	106
Saint James Islands, is., V.I.U.S.	e7	104b
Saint-Jean, Guad.	B2	105a
Saint-Jean, Lac, res., Qc., Can.	B4	110
Saint Jean Baptiste, Mb., Can.	E16	124
Saint-Jean-d'Angély, Fr.	C5	18
Saint-Jean-de-Luz, Fr.	F4	18
Saint-Jean-de-Maurienne, Fr.	D12	18
Saint-Jean-du-Gard, Fr.	E9	18
Saint-Jean-Port-Joli, Qc., Can.	C6	110
Saint-Jean-sur-Richelieu, Qc., Can.	E3	110
Saint-Jérôme, Qc., Can.	E3	110
Saint Jo, Tx., U.S.	H11	128
Saint Joe, stm., Id., U.S.	C11	136
Saint John, N.B., Can.	E10	110
Saint John, N.D., U.S.	F14	124
Saint John, Wa., U.S.	C9	136
Saint John, i., V.I.U.S.	e8	104b
Saint John, stm., N.A.	E10	110
Saint John, Cape, c., Nf., Can.	E19	106
Saint John's, Antig.	f4	105b
Saint John's, Nf., Can.	j23	107a
Saint Johns, Az., U.S.	I7	132
Saint Johns, Mi., U.S.	E5	112
Saint Johns, stm., Fl., U.S.	G4	116
Saint Johnsbury, Vt., U.S.	F4	110
Saint Joseph, Dom.	j6	105c
Saint Joseph, Il., U.S.	D9	120
Saint Joseph, Mi., U.S.	F3	112
Saint Joseph, Mn., U.S.	F4	118
Saint Joseph, Mo., U.S.	E3	120
Saint Joseph, stm., U.S.	G3	112
Saint Joseph, stm., U.S.	G5	112
Saint Joseph, Lake, l., On., Can.	E12	106
Saint-Joseph-de-Beauce, Qc., Can.	D6	110
Saint Joseph Island, i., On., Can.	B6	112
Saint-Jovite, Qc., Can.	D2	110
Saint-Julien-en-Born, Fr.	E4	18
Sainte-Julienne, Qc., Can.	E3	110
Saint-Junien, Fr.	D6	18
Saint Just, P.R.	B4	104a
Saint Kilda, i., Scot., U.K.	D4	12
Saint Kitts see Saint Christopher, i., St. K./N.	C2	105a
Saint Kitts and Nevis, ctry., N.A.	C2	105a
Saint-Lambert, Qc., Can.	E3	110
Saint Landry, La., U.S.	G6	122
Saint Laurent, Mb., Can.	D16	124
Saint-Laurent (Saint Lawrence), stm., N.A.	B8	110
Saint-Laurent du Maroni, Fr. Gu.	B7	84
Saint Lawrence, Austl.	D7	76
Saint Lawrence (Saint-Laurent), stm., N.A.	B8	110
Saint Lawrence, Gulf of, b., Can.	F18	106
Saint Lawrence Island, i., Ak., U.S.	D5	140
Saint-Léandre, Qc., Can.	B9	110
Saint-Léonard, N.B., Can.	C9	110
Saint-Lô, Fr.	E7	14
Saint Louis, Sk., Can.	B8	124
Saint-Louis, Guad.	i6	105c
Saint-Louis, Sen.	F1	64
Saint Louis, Mi., U.S.	E5	112
Saint Louis, Mo., U.S.	F7	120
Saint Louis, stm., U.S.	E6	118
Saint-Louis, Lac, l., Qc., Can.	E3	110
Saint-Louis de Kent, N.B., Can.	D12	110
Saint Louis Park, Mn., U.S.	G5	118
Saint-Loup-sur-Semouse, Fr.	G14	14
Sainte-Luce, Mart.	I7	105c
Saint Lucia, ctry., N.A.	m6	105c
Saint Lucia, Cape, c., S. Afr.	F11	70
Saint Lucia, Lake, l., S. Afr.	E11	70
Saint Lucia Channel, strt., N.A.	I6	105c
Saint Lucia Game Reserve, S. Afr.	F11	70
Saint Lucie Canal, can., Fl., U.S.	J5	116
Saint Magnus Bay, b., Scot., U.K.	n18	12a
Saint-Malo, Fr.	F7	14
Saint-Malo, Golfe de, b., Fr.	F6	14
Saint-Marc, Haiti	C11	102
Saint-Marc, Canal de, strt., Haiti	C11	102
Saint-Marc-des-Carrières, Qc., Can.	D4	110
Sainte-Marie, Mart.	k7	105c
Sainte Marie, Nosy, i., Madag.	D9	68
Saint Maries, Id., U.S.	C10	136
Saint Marks, stm., Fl., U.S.	F1	116
Saint-Martin (Sint Maarten), i., N.A.	A1	105a
Saint-Martin, Cap, c., Mart.	k6	105c
Saint Martin, Lake, l., Mb., Can.	C15	124
Saint Martins, N.B., Can.	E11	110
Saint Martinville, La., U.S.	G7	122
Saint Mary, Mo., U.S.	G8	120
Saint Mary, stm., N.A.	G18	138
Saint Mary Peak, mtn., Austl.	H2	76
Saint Mary Reservoir, res., Ab., Can.	G17	138
Saint Marys, Austl.	n14	77a
Saint Marys, Ak., U.S.	D7	140
Saint Marys, Ga., U.S.	F4	116
Saint Marys, Ks., U.S.	E1	120
Saint Marys, Pa., U.S.	C7	114
Saint Marys, W.V., U.S.	E4	114
Saint Mary's, i., Eng., U.K.	L6	12
Saint Marys, stm., U.S.	H5	112
Saint Marys, stm., U.S.	F4	116
Saint Mary's Bay, b., Nf., Can.	j23	107a
Saint Marys Bay, b., N.S., Can.	F10	110
Saint Marys City, Md., U.S.	F9	114
Saint-Mathieu, Fr.	D6	18
Saint Matthew Island, i., Ak., U.S.	D5	140
Saint Matthews, Ky., U.S.	F12	120
Saint-Maurice, stm., Qc., Can.	D4	110
Sainte-Maxime, Fr.	F12	18
Saint Meinrad, In., U.S.	F11	120
Saint Michael, Ak., U.S.	D7	140
Saint Michaels, Md., U.S.	F9	114
Saint-Michel-des-Saints, Qc., Can.	D2	110
Saint-Mihiel, Fr.	F14	14
Saint Moritz see Sankt Moritz, Switz.	D6	22
Saint-Nazaire, Fr.	G6	14
Saint-Nicolas see Sint-Niklaas, Bel.	C12	14
Saint-Omer, Fr.	D11	14
Saintonge, hist. reg., Fr.	D5	18
Saint-Pacôme, Qc., Can.	C7	110
Saint-Pamphile, Qc., Can.	D7	110
Saint Paris, Oh., U.S.	D2	114
Saint-Patrice, Lac, l., Qc., Can.	B12	112
Saint Paul, Ab., Can.	B19	138
Saint-Paul, Reu.	i10	69a
Saint Paul, In., U.S.	E12	120
Saint Paul, Ks., U.S.	G2	120
Saint Paul, Mn., U.S.	G5	118
Saint Paul, Va., U.S.	H3	114
Saint Paul, stm., Lib.	H2	64
Saint-Paul, Île, i., Afr.	M10	142
Saint Paul Island, i., Ak., U.S.	E6	140
Saint Paul's, St. K./N.	C2	105a
Saint Pauls, N.C., U.S.	B7	116
Saint Paul's Point, c., Pit.	c28	78k
Saint Peter, Mn., U.S.	G4	118
Saint Peter Port, Guern.	E6	14
Saint Peters, N.S., Can.	E16	110
Saint Peters Bay, P.E., Can.	D14	110
Saint Petersburg see Sankt-Peterburg, Russia	A13	10
Saint Petersburg, Fl., U.S.	I3	116
Saint-Pierre, Mart.	k6	105c
Saint-Pierre, Reu.	i10	69a
Saint-Pierre, St. P./M.	j22	107a
Saint Pierre, i., Sey.	k12	69b
Saint-Pierre, Lac, l., Qc., Can.	D3	110
Saint Pierre and Miquelon, dep., N.A.	j22	107a
Saint Pierre-Jolys, Mb., Can.	E16	124
Saint-Pierre-sur-Dives, Fr.	E8	14
Saint-Pol-sur-Ternoise, Fr.	D11	14
Saint-Pons-de-Thomères, Fr.	F8	18
Saint-Prime, Qc., Can.	B4	110
Saint-Prosper-de-Dorchester, Qc., Can.	D6	110
Saint-Quentin, N.B., Can.	C9	110
Saint-Quentin, Fr.	E12	14
Saint-Raphaël, Fr.	F12	18
Saint-Raymond, Qc., Can.	D5	110
Saint Regis Falls, N.Y., U.S.	F2	110
Saint-Rémy-de-Provence, Fr.	F10	18
Saint Robert, Mo., U.S.	G5	120
Saint-Roch-de-Mékinac, Qc., Can.	D3	110
Saint-Romuald, Qc., Can.	D5	110
Sainte-Rose-du-dégelis see Dégelis, Can.	C8	110
Sainte Rose du Lac, Mb., Can.	C14	124
Saintes, Fr.	D5	18
Saint-Savin, Fr.	H9	14
Saint-Siméon, Qc., Can.	C6	110
Saint Simons Island, Ga., U.S.	E4	116
Saint Simons Island, i., Ga., U.S.	E4	116
Saintes-Maries-de-la-Mer, Fr.	F10	18
Saint Stephen, S.C., U.S.	C6	116
Sainte-Thérèse-de-Blainville, Qc., Can.	E3	110
Saint Thomas, On., Can.	F8	112
Saint Thomas, N.D., U.S.	F16	124
Saint Thomas, i., V.I.U.S.	e7	104b
Saint-Tite, Qc., Can.	D4	110
Saint-Trond see Sint-Truiden, Bel.	D14	14
Saint-Tropez, Fr.	F12	18
Saint-Ubalde, Qc., Can.	D4	110
Saint-Urbain-de-Charlevoix, Qc., Can.	C6	110
Saint-Valéry-en-Caux, Fr.	E9	14
Saint-Vallier, Fr.	D10	18
Sainte-Véronique, Qc., Can.	D2	110
Saint Vincent, Mn., U.S.	C1	118
Saint Vincent, i., St. Vin.	o11	105e
Saint-Vincent, Baie de, b., N. Cal.	n15	79d
Saint Vincent, Gulf, b., Austl.	J2	76
Saint Vincent and the Grenadines, ctry., N.A.	p10	105e
Saint Vincent Passage, strt., N.A.	m7	105c
Saint-Vith, Bel.	D14	14
Saint Walburg, Sk., Can.	E9	106
Saint-Yrieix-la-Perche, Fr.	D7	18
Saint-Yvon, Qc., Can.	A12	110
Saipan, i., N. Mar. Is.	B5	72
Saiqi, China	H8	42
Saitama, state, Japan	C12	40
Saito, Japan	G4	40
Sai Yok National Park, p.o.i., Thai.	E4	48
Sajama, Nevado, mtn., Bol.	C3	90
Sajanogorsk, Russia	D16	32
Şajat, Turkmen.	B9	56
Šajman, Taj.	B11	56
Sajószentpéter, Hung.	A7	26
Sak, stm., S. Afr.	G5	70
Sa Kaeo, Thai.	F6	48
Sakai, Japan	E8	40
Sakaide, Japan	E6	40
Sakaiminato, Japan	D6	40
Sakakawea, Lake, res., N.D., U.S.	G12	124
Sakala, Pulau, i., Indon.	G10	50
Sakami, stm., Qc., Can.	E15	106
Sakami, Lac, l., Qc., Can.	E15	106
Sakania, D.R.C.	G5	66
Sakaraha, Madag.	E7	68
Sakarya, Tur.	C13	28
Sakarya, state, Tur.	C13	28
Sakarya (Sangarius), stm., Tur.	B13	28
Sakata, Japan	A12	40
Sakawa, Japan	F6	40
Sakchu-ŭp, Kor., N.	D6	38
Sakété, Benin	H5	64
Sakhalin see Sahalin, ostrov, i., Russia	F17	34
Sakhnin, Isr.	F6	58
Şakht Sar, Iran	B7	56
Šakiai, Lith.	E6	10
Sakiet Sidi Youssef, Tun.	H2	24
Sakishima-shotō, is., Japan	G9	36
Sakon Nakhon, Thai.	D6	48
Sakrand, Pak.	E2	54
Saks, Al., U.S.	D13	122
Sakti, India	H9	54
Saku, Japan	C11	40
Sakuma, Japan	D10	40
Sakurai, Japan	E8	40
Şal, i., C.V.	k10	65a
Šal'a, Slov.	H13	16
Sala, Swe.	F7	8
Salaberry-de-Valleyfield, Qc., Can.	E2	110
Salacgrīva, Lat.	C7	10
Sala Consilina, Italy	D9	24
Salada, Laguna, l., Mex.	F5	98
Saladas, Arg.	D8	92
Saladillo, Arg.	G8	92
Saladillo, stm., Arg.	D6	92
Saladillo Dulce, Arroyo, stm., Arg.	E7	92
Salado, stm., Arg.	D4	92
Salado, stm., Arg.	E7	92
Salado, stm., Arg.	I5	92
Salado, stm., Arg.	G9	92
Salado, stm., Cuba	B9	102
Salado, stm., Mex.	B9	100
Salado, stm., N.M., U.S.	I9	132
Salaga, Ghana	H4	64
Salairskij krjaž, mts., Russia	D14	32
Şălaj, state, Rom.	B10	26
Šalakuša, Russia	E19	8
Salal, Chad	E3	62
Şalālah, Oman	F7	56
Şalālah, Sudan	C7	62
Salamanca, Chile	E2	92
Salamanca, Mex.	E8	100
Salamanca, Spain	D5	20
Salamanca, N.Y., U.S.	F11	112
Salamanca, co., Spain	D4	20
Salamanga, Moz.	E11	70
Salamat, Bahr, stm., Chad	F3	62
Salamina, Col.	E4	86
Salamína, Grc.	F6	28
Salamína, i., Grc.	F6	28
Salamis, hist., N. Cyp.	C4	58
Salamīyah, Syria	C8	58
Salamonie, stm., In., U.S.	H4	112
Salantai, Lith.	D4	10
Salaquí, Col.	D3	86
Salaquí, stm., Col.	D3	86
Salas, Peru	E2	84
Salas de los Infantes, Spain	B7	20
Salatiga, Indon.	G7	50
Salavat, Russia	D9	32
Salaverry, Peru	E2	84
Salawati, i., Indon.	F9	44
Salāya, India	G2	54
Sala y Gómez, Isla, i., Chile	L28	142
Sala y Gomez Ridge, unds.	L29	142
Şalbani, India	G11	54
Šalčininkai, Lith.	F8	10
Salcombe, Eng., U.K.	K9	12
Saldaña, Spain	B6	20
Saldaña, stm., Col.	F4	86
Saldanha, S. Afr.	H3	70
Saldungaray, Arg.	I7	92
Saldus, Lat.	D5	10
Sale, Austl.	L6	76
Salé, Mor.	C3	64
Sale Creek, Tn., U.S.	B13	122
Saleh, Teluk, b., Indon.	H10	50
Salehard, Russia	A11	32
Salem, India	F4	53
Salem, Monts.	D3	105a
Salem, Ar., U.S.	H6	120
Salem, Il., U.S.	F9	120
Salem, Ia., U.S.	D6	120
Salem, Ma., U.S.	B15	114
Salem, Mo., U.S.	G6	120
Salem, N.H., U.S.	B14	114
Salem, N.J., U.S.	E10	114
Salem, N.Y., U.S.	G3	110
Salem, Oh., U.S.	D5	114
Salem, Or., U.S.	F3	136
Salem, S.D., U.S.	D15	126
Salem, Va., U.S.	G5	114
Salem, W.V., U.S.	E5	114
Salemi, Italy	G6	24
Salem Upland, plat., Mo., U.S.	G6	120
Salentina, Penisola, pen., Italy	D12	24
Salerno, Italy	D8	24
Salerno, Golfo di, b., Italy	D8	24
Salers, Fr.	D8	18
Salgar, Col.	D4	86
Salgótarján, Hung.	A6	26
Salgueiro, Braz.	E6	88
Salher, mtn., India	H4	54
Sali, Cro.	G12	22
Salida, Co., U.S.	C3	128
Salihli, Tur.	E11	28
Salihorsk, Bela.	H10	10
Salima, Mwi.	C5	68
Salimbatu, Indon.	B10	50
Salin, Mya.	B2	48
Salina, Ks., U.S.	C11	128
Salina, Ut., U.S.	E5	132
Salina Cruz, Mex.	G11	100
Salina Point, c., Bah.	A10	102
Salinas, Braz.	I4	88
Salinas, Ec.	I1	86
Salinas, Mex.	G5	130
Salinas, P.R.	C3	104a
Salinas, Ca., U.S.	G4	134
Salinas, stm., Braz.	I4	88
Salinas, stm., N.A.	D2	102
Salinas, stm., Ca., U.S.	G4	134
Salinas, Pampa de las, pl., Arg.	E4	92
Salinas de Hidalgo, Mex.	D8	100
Salinas Pueblo Missions National Monument, p.o.i., N.M., U.S.	G2	128
Salinas Victoria, Mex.	I7	130
Saline, Mi., U.S.	B2	114
Saline, stm., Ar., U.S.	D6	122
Saline, stm., Ar., U.S.	C4	122
Saline, stm., Ks., U.S.	C11	128
Saline Bayou, stm., La., U.S.	E6	122
Saline Lake, l., La., U.S.	F6	122
Salines, Cap de ses, c., Spain	E14	20
Salines, Point, c., Gren.	r10	105e
Salines, Pointe des, c., Mart.	I7	105c
Salinópolis, Braz.	D8	84
Salipolo, Indon.	E11	50
Salisbury, Austl.	J2	76
Salisbury, Eng., U.K.	J11	12
Salisbury, Md., U.S.	F10	114
Salisbury, Mo., U.S.	E5	120
Salisbury, N.C., U.S.	I5	114
Salisbury, Pa., U.S.	E6	114
Salisbury see Harare, Zimb.	D5	68
Salisbury Island, i., Nu., Can.	C15	106
Salisbury Plain, pl., Eng., U.K.	J11	12
Salish Mountains, mts., Mt., U.S.	B12	136
Salitpa, Al., U.S.	F10	122
Salitre, stm., Braz.	E5	88
Şalkhad, Syria	F7	58
Salles-Curan, Fr.	E8	18
Sallisaw, Ok., U.S.	B4	122
Salluit, Qc., Can.	C15	106
Salmi, Russia	F14	8
Salmo, B.C., Can.	G13	138
Salmon, stm., B.C., Can.	B8	138
Salmon, stm., N.B., Can.	D11	110
Salmon, stm., Id., U.S.	E10	136
Salmon, Middle Fork, stm., Id., U.S.	E12	136
Salmon, South Fork, stm., Id., U.S.	E11	136
Salmon Arm, B.C., Can.	F11	138
Salmon Falls Creek, stm., U.S.	H12	136
Salmon Gums, Austl.	F4	74
Salmon Peak, mtn., Tx., U.S.	E7	130
Salmon River Mountains, mts., Id., U.S.	F12	136
Salmon Valley, B.C., Can.	B8	138
Salo, Fin.	F10	8
Salò, Italy	E7	22
Salome, Az., U.S.	J3	132
Salomon, Cap, c., Mart.	I6	105c
Salon-de-Provence, Fr.	F11	18
Salonga, Parc National de la, p.o.i., D.R.C.	E4	66
Salonika see Thessaloníki, Grc.	C6	28
Salonika, Gulf of see Thermaïkós Kólpos, b., Grc.	C6	28
Salonta, Rom.	C8	26
Salor, stm., Spain	E4	20
Salpaussel'kja, mts., Eur.	B3	32
Sal Rei, C.V.	k10	65a
Salsacate, Arg.	E5	92
Salsipuedes, Canal, strt., Mex.	A2	100
Sal'sk, Russia	E6	32
Salsomaggiore Terme, Italy	F6	22
Salt, stm., Az., U.S.	J4	132
Salt, stm., Mo., U.S.	E6	120
Salt, Middle Fork, stm., Mo., U.S.	E5	120
Salt, North Fork, stm., Mo., U.S.	E5	120
Salta, Arg.	B5	92
Salta, state, Arg.	D4	90
Saltanovka, Russia	H17	10
Saltash, Eng., U.K.	K8	12
Salt Basin, l., Tx., U.S.	C2	130
Salt Cay, i., Bah.	m18	104f
Saltcoats, Sk., Can.	C11	124
Salt Creek, stm., Il., U.S.	D8	120
Saltee Islands, is., Ire.	I6	12
Saltfjellet Svartisen Nasjonalpark, p.o.i., Nor.	C6	8
Saltillo, Mex.	C8	100
Saltillo, Tn., U.S.	B10	122
Salt Lake City, Ut., U.S.	C4	132
Salto, Arg.	G7	92
Salto, Ur.	E9	92
Salto del Guairá, Para.	A10	92
Salto Grande, Embalse, res., S.A.	E8	92
Salton City, Ca., U.S.	J9	134
Salton Sea, l., Ca., U.S.	J10	134
Salto Santiago, Represa de, res., Braz.	B11	92
Saltspring Island, i., B.C., Can.	H7	138
Saltville, Va., U.S.	H4	114
Saluda, Va., U.S.	G9	114
Saluda, stm., S.C., U.S.	B4	116
Salûm, Egypt	A5	62
Sālūmbar, India	F5	54
Sālūr, India	B6	53
Saluzzo, Italy	F4	22
Salvador, Braz.	G6	88
Salvador, El see El Salvador, ctry., N.A.	F3	102
Salvador, Lake, l., La., U.S.	H8	122
Salvatierra, Mex.	E8	100
Salviac, Fr.	E7	18
Salween (Nu) (Khong) (Thanlwin), stm., Asia	E8	46
Salyan, Azer.	B6	56
Salyān, Nepal	D9	54
Salyer, Ca., U.S.	C2	134
Salyersville, Ky., U.S.	G2	114
Salzach, stm., Eur.	B9	22
Salzburg, Aus.	C10	22
Salzburg, state, Aus.	C10	22
Salzgitter, Ger.	D6	16
Salzkammergut, reg., Aus.	C10	22
Salzwedel, Ger.	D7	16
Samacá, Col.	E5	86
Samacèvičy, Bela.	G14	10
Samagaltaj, Russia	D16	32
Samah, Libya	B3	62
Samales Group, is., Phil.	G3	52
Samalga Pass, strt., Ak., U.S.	g25	140a
Samal Island, i., Phil.	G5	52
Sāmalkot, India	C6	53
Samâlût, Egypt	J1	58
Samaná, Dom. Rep.	C13	102
Samāna, India	C5	54

Name	Map Ref.	Page
Samaná, Bahía de, b., Dom. Rep.	C13	102
Samaná, Cabo, c., Dom. Rep.	C13	102
Samana Cay, i., Bah.	A11	102
Samandağı, Tur.	B6	58
Samaniego, Col.	G3	86
Samaqua, stm., Qc., Can.	A4	110
Samar, i., Phil.	E5	52
Samara, Russia	D8	32
Samara, stm., Russia	D8	32
Samarai, Pap. N. Gui.	c5	79a
Samaria, Id., U.S.	A4	132
Samaria Gorge see Samariás, Farángi, val., Grc.	H6	28
Samariapo, Ven.	E8	86
Samariás, Farángi (Samaria Gorge), val., Grc.	H6	28
Samarinda, Indon.	D10	50
Samarka, Russia	B10	38
Samarkand, Uzb.	G11	32
Sāmarrā', Iraq	C5	56
Samastīpur, India	F10	54
Samaúna, Braz.	E5	84
Samba Caju, Ang.	B2	68
Sambaíba, Braz.	D3	88
Sambalpur, India	H9	54
Sambar, Tanjung, c., Indon.	E7	50
Sambas, Indon.	C6	50
Sambava, Madag.	C9	68
Şambayat, Tur.	A9	58
Sambhal, India	D7	54
Sāmbhar, India	E5	54
Sāmbhar Lake, l., India	E5	54
Sambir, Ukr.	G19	16
Sambit, Pulau, i., Indon.	C11	50
Sambito, stm., Braz.	D5	88
Samboja, Indon.	D10	50
Sâmbor, Camb.	F7	48
Samborombón, stm., Arg.	G9	92
Samborombón, Bahía, b., Arg.	G9	92
Sambre, stm., Eur.	D12	14
Sambre à l'Oise, Canal de la, can., Fr.	E12	14
Sambriāl, Pak.	B5	54
Samch'ŏk, Kor., S.	B2	40
Sam Chom, Khao, mtn., Thai.	H4	48
Same, Tan.	E7	66
Sam Ford Fiord, b., Nu., Can.	A16	106
Samfya, Zam.	C4	68
Samka, Mya.	B3	48
Samnangjin, Kor., S.	D1	40
Sam Ngao, Thai.	D4	48
Samoa, ctry., Oc.	g12	79c
Samoa Islands, is., Oc.	h12	79c
Samo Alto, Chile	E2	92
Samobor, Cro.	E12	22
Samoded, Russia	E19	8
Samokov, Blg.	G10	26
Sámos, i., Grc.	F9	28
Samoset, Fl., U.S.	I3	116
Samosir, Pulau, i., Indon.	B1	50
Samothrace see Samothráki, i., Grc.	C8	28
Samothráki, Grc.	C8	28
Samothráki (Samothrace), i., Grc.	C8	28
Sampacho, Arg.	F5	92
Sampanahan, Indon.	E10	50
Sampang, Indon.	G8	50
Sampit, Indon.	E8	50
Sampit, stm., Indon.	E8	50
Sampit, Teluk, b., Indon.	E8	50
Sampwe, D.R.C.	F5	66
Sam Rayburn Reservoir, res., Tx., U.S.	F4	122
Samro, ozero, l., Russia	B11	10
Sam Son, Viet.	C7	48
Samsun, Tur.	A4	56
Samsu-ŭp, Kor., N.	D7	38
Samtown, La., U.S.	F6	122
Samuhú, Arg.	C7	92
Samui, Ko, i., Thai.	H5	48
Samundri, Pak.	C4	54
Samut Prakan, Thai.	F5	48
Samut Sakhon, Thai.	F5	48
Samut Songkhram, Thai.	F5	48
San, Mali	G3	64
San (Xan), stm., Asia	F8	48
San, stm., China	E8	42
San (Syan), stm., Eur.	F18	16
Saña, Peru	E2	84
Şan'ā', Yemen	F5	56
Sana, stm., Bos.	E3	26
Sanaa see Şan'ā', Yemen	F5	56
Sanabu, Egypt	K1	58
Sanaga, stm., Cam.	D2	66
San Agustín, Arg.	E5	92
San Agustín, Arg.	I8	92
San Agustín, Mex.	C1	130
San Agustin, Cape, c., Phil.	G6	52
Sanak Islands, is., Ak., U.S.	F7	140
San Alberto, Mex.	G6	130
San Ambrosio, Isla, i., Chile	H7	82
Sanana, Pulau, i., Indon.	F8	44
Sānand, India	G4	54
Sanandaj, Iran	B6	56
San Andreas, Ca., U.S.	E5	134
San Andrés, Col.	F7	102
San Andrés, Isla de, i., Col.	F7	102
San Andres Mountains, mts., N.M., U.S.	H2	128
San Andrés Sajcabajá, Guat.	E2	102
San Andrés Tuxtla, Mex.	F11	100
San Andrés y Providencia, state, Col.	F7	102
Sananduva, Braz.	C12	92
San Angelo, Tx., U.S.	C7	130
San Antero, Col.	C4	86
San Antonio, Arg.	D5	92
San Antonio, Chile	F2	92
San Antonio, Col.	F4	86
San Antonio, N.M., U.S.	F2	128
San Antonio, N.M., U.S.	J9	132
San Antonio, Tx., U.S.	E9	130
San Antonio, Ur.	E9	92
San Antonio, stm., Tx., U.S.	F10	130
San Antonio, Cabo, pen., Arg.	H9	92
San Antonio, Cabo de, c., Cuba	B5	102
San Antonio, Lake, res., Ca., U.S.	H4	134
San Antonio, Mount, mtn., Ca., U.S.	I8	134
San Antonio, Punta, c., Mex.	B3	100
San Antonio Abad see Sant Antoni de Portmany, Spain	F12	20
San Antonio Bay, b., Tx., U.S.	F11	130
San Antonio de Bravo, Mex.	D3	130
San Antonio de La Paz see San Antonio, Arg.	D5	92
San Antonio de los Baños, Cuba	A6	102
San Antonio de los Cobres, Arg.	B4	92
San Antonio del Táchira, Ven.	D5	86
San Antonio de Tamanaco, Ven.	C8	86
San Antonio el Grande, Mex.	F2	130
San Antonio Mountain, mtn., N.M., U.S.	E2	128
San Antonio Oeste, Arg.	H4	90
Sanatorium, Ms., U.S.	F9	122
San Augustine, Tx., U.S.	F4	122
San Augustin Pass, p., N.M., U.S.	K10	132
Sanāw, Yemen	F7	56
Sanāwad, India	G6	54
San Bartolomeo in Galdo, Italy	C9	24
San Benedetto del Tronto, Italy	H10	22
San Benedetto Po, Italy	E7	22
San Benedicto, Isla, i., Mex.	F3	100
San Benito, Tx., U.S.	H10	130
San Benito, stm., Ca., U.S.	G4	134
San Benito Mountain, mtn., Ca., U.S.	G5	134
San Bernard, stm., Tx., U.S.	E12	130
San Bernardino, Ca., U.S.	I8	134
San Bernardino Mountains, mts., Ca., U.S.	I9	134
San Bernardino Strait, strt., Phil.	D5	52
San Bernardo, Chile	F2	92
San Bernardo, Islas de, is., Col.	C3	86
San Bernardo del Viento, Col.	C3	86
Sanbe-yama, vol., Japan	D5	40
San Blas, Mex.	E6	100
San Blas, Mex.	B4	100
San Blas, Cape, c., Fl., U.S.	H13	122
San Blas, Golfo de, b., Pan.	H8	102
San Blas, Serranía de, mts., Pan.	H8	102
San Borja, Bol.	B3	90
Sanborn, Ia., U.S.	H3	118
Sanborn, N.D., U.S.	H15	124
San Bruno, Ca., U.S.	F3	134
San Buenaventura, Bol.	B3	90
San Buenaventura, Mex.	B8	100
San Buenaventura see Ventura, Ca., U.S.	I6	134
San Carlos, Chile	H2	92
San Carlos, Mex.	C9	100
San Carlos, Mex.	A8	100
San Carlos, Nic.	G5	102
San Carlos, Phil.	E4	52
San Carlos, Phil.	C3	52
San Carlos, Az., U.S.	J6	132
San Carlos, Ca., U.S.	F3	134
San Carlos, Ur.	G10	92
San Carlos, Ven.	C7	86
San Carlos, stm., C.R.	G5	102
San Carlos, stm., Ven.	C7	86
San Carlos Centro, Arg.	E7	92
San Carlos de Bariloche, Arg.	H2	90
San Carlos de Bolívar, Arg.	H7	92
San Carlos de Guaroa, Col.	F5	86
San Carlos del Zulia, Ven.	C5	86
San Carlos de Río Negro, Ven.	G8	86
San Carlos Reservoir, res., Az., U.S.	J6	132
San Cataldo, Italy	G7	24
San Cayetano, Arg.	I8	92
Sancha, stm., China	H1	42
Sanchahe, China	B7	38
Sanchenglong, China	B4	38
San Ciro de Acosta, Mex.	E9	100
San Clemente, Spain	E8	20
San Clemente, Ca., U.S.	J8	134
San Clemente Island, i., Ca., U.S.	K7	134
San Cristóbal, Arg.	E7	92
San Cristóbal, Dom. Rep.	C12	102
San Cristóbal, Ven.	D5	86
San Cristobal, i., Sol. Is.	f9	79b
San Cristóbal, Bahía, b., Mex.	B1	100
San Cristóbal, Isla, i., Ec.	i12	84a
San Cristóbal, Volcán, vol., Nic.	F4	102
San Cristóbal de las Casas, Mex.	G12	100
Sancti Spíritus, Cuba	A8	102
Sancy, Puy de, mtn., Fr.	D8	18
Sand, Nor.	G2	8
Sand, stm., Ab., Can.	B19	138
Sand, stm., S. Afr.	F8	70
Sand, stm., S. Afr.	C9	70
Sandai, Indon.	D7	50
Sandakan, Malay.	H2	52
Sândăn, Camb.	F8	48
Sandaré, Mali	G2	64
Sand Arroyo, stm., U.S.	D7	128
Sanday, i., Scot., U.K.	B10	12
Sandefjord, Nor.	G4	8
Sanderson, Tx., U.S.	D5	130
Sandersville, Ga., U.S.	D3	116
Sandersville, Ms., U.S.	F9	122
Sand Fork, W.V., U.S.	F5	114
Sand Hill, stm., Mn., U.S.	D2	118
Sand Hills, hills, Ne., U.S.	F11	126
Sāndi, India	E8	54
Sandia, Peru	F4	84
San Diego, Ca., U.S.	K8	134
San Diego, Tx., U.S.	G9	130
San Diego, Cabo, c., Arg.	J3	90
San Diego Aqueduct, aq., Ca., U.S.	J8	134
Sandıklı, Tur.	E13	28
Sandīla, India	E8	54
Sandilands Village, Bah.	m18	104f
Sand Key, i., Fl., U.S.	I3	116
Sand Lake, l., On., Can.	A4	118
Sandnes, Nor.	G1	8
Sandoa, D.R.C.	F4	66
Sandomierz, Pol.	F17	16
Sandoná, Col.	G3	86
San Donà di Piave, Italy	E9	22
Sandovo, Russia	B19	10
Sandoway, Mya.	C2	48
Sandown, Eng., U.K.	K11	12
Sand Point, Ak., U.S.	E7	140
Sandpoint, Id., U.S.	B10	136
Sandringham, Austl.	E2	76
Sandspit, B.C., Can.	E4	106
Sand Springs, Ok., U.S.	A2	122
Sand Springs, Tx., U.S.	B6	130
Sandstone, Austl.	E3	74
Sandstone, Mn., U.S.	E5	118
Sandu Ao, b., China	H8	42
Sandusky, Mi., U.S.	E7	112
Sandusky, Oh., U.S.	C3	114
Sandvika, Nor.	G4	8
Sandviken, Swe.	F7	8
Sandwich, Eng., U.K.	J14	12
Sandwich Bay, b., Nmb.	C2	70
Sandwick, B.C., Can.	G5	138
Sandwīp Island, i., Bngl.	G13	54
Sandy, Or., U.S.	E4	136
Sandy, Ut., U.S.	C5	132
Sandy Bay Mountain, mtn., Me., U.S.	E6	110
Sandy Cape, c., Austl.	E9	76
Sandy Cape, c., Austl.	n12	77a
Sandy Creek, stm., Austl.	I5	76
Sandy Hook, Ky., U.S.	F2	114
Sandy Hook, spit, N.J., U.S.	D12	114
Sandykači, Turkmen.	B9	56
Sandy Lake, l., On., Can.	E12	106
Sandy Point, c., Trin.	r13	105f
Sandy Point Town, St. K./N.	C2	105a
Sandy Springs, Ga., U.S.	C1	116
Sandžak, reg., Yugo.	F6	26
San Elizario, Tx., U.S.	C1	130
San Enrique, Arg.	G7	92
San Estanislao, Para.	B9	92
San Esteban, Isla, i., Mex.	A2	100
San Esteban de Gormaz, Spain	C7	20
San Felipe, Chile	F2	92
San Felipe, Col.	G8	86
San Felipe, Mex.	F5	98
San Felipe, Mex.	E8	100
San Felipe, Ven.	B7	86
San Felipe, Cayos de, is., Cuba	B6	102
San Felipe Nuevo Mercurio, Mex.	C7	100
San Felipe Pueblo, N.M., U.S.	F2	128
San Felíu de Guixols see Sant Feliu de Guíxols, Spain	C14	20
San Félix, Isla, i., Chile	H6	82
San Fernando, Chile	G2	92
San Fernando, Mex.	C9	100
San Fernando, Mex.	F6	130
San Fernando, Phil.	B2	52
San Fernando, Phil.	C3	52
San Fernando, Spain	H4	20
San Fernando, Trin.	s12	105f
San Fernando, Ca., U.S.	I7	134
San Fernando de Apure, Ven.	D8	86
San Fernando de Atabapo, Ven.	E8	86
San Fernando del Valle de Catamarca, Arg.	D4	92
Sånfjällets Nationalpark, p.o.i., Swe.	E5	8
Sanford, Co., U.S.	D2	128
Sanford, Fl., U.S.	H4	116
Sanford, Me., U.S.	G6	110
Sanford, N.C., U.S.	A6	116
Sanford, Tx., U.S.	F7	128
Sanford, stm., Austl.	E3	74
Sanford, Mount, vol., Ak., U.S.	D11	140
San Francisco, Arg.	E6	92
San Francisco, El Sal.	F3	102
San Francisco, Ca., U.S.	F3	134
San Francisco, stm., Arg.	B5	92
San Francisco, stm., U.S.	J8	132
San Francisco, Paso de, p., S.A.	C3	92
San Francisco Bay, b., Ca., U.S.	F3	134
San Francisco Creek, stm., Tx., U.S.	E5	130
San Francisco de Borja, Mex.	B5	100
San Francisco de Horizonte, Mex.	I4	130
San Francisco del Chañar, Arg.	D5	92
San Francisco del Oro, Mex.	B5	100
San Francisco del Rincón, Mex.	E7	100
San Francisco de Macorís, Dom. Rep.	C12	102
San Francisco de Mostazal, Chile	F2	92
San Gabriel, Ec.	G3	86
San Gabriel Chilac, Mex.	F10	100
San Gabriel Mountains, mts., Ca., U.S.	I8	134
Sangamankanda Point, c., Sri L.	H5	53
Sangamner, India	B1	53
Sangamon, stm., Il., U.S.	D7	120
Sangar, Russia	D14	34
Sangasanga-dalam, Indon.	D10	50
San Gavino Monreale, Italy	E2	24
Sangay, vol., Ec.	I2	86
Sangay, Parque Nacional, p.o.i., Ec.	H3	86
Sange, D.R.C.	F5	66
Sangeang, Pulau, i., Indon.	H11	50
Sanger, Ca., U.S.	G6	134
Sanger, Tx., U.S.	H11	128
Sângera, Mol.	B15	26
Sangerhausen, Ger.	E7	16
San Germán, P.R.	B1	104a
Sangerville, Me., U.S.	E7	110
Sanggan, stm., China	A6	42
Sanggau, Indon.	C7	50
Sangha, stm., Afr.	E3	66
Sanghar, Pak.	E2	54
Sangihe, Kepulauan, is., Indon.	E7	44
Sangihe, Pulau, i., Indon.	E8	44
San Gil, Col.	D5	86
Sangilen, hrebet, mts., Russia	D17	32
San Gimignano, Italy	G7	22
San Giovanni in Fiore, Italy	E10	24
San Giovanni in Persiceto, Italy	F8	22
San Giovanni Rotondo, Italy	C9	24
San Giovanni Valdarno, Italy	G8	22
Sangiyn Dalay nuur, l., Mong.	B4	36
Sangju, Kor., S.	F8	38
Sangkapura, Indon.	F8	50
Sângkê, stm., Camb.	F6	48
Sangkulirang, Indon.	C10	50
Sāngli, India	C2	53
Sangmélima, Cam.	D2	66
Sāngole, India	C2	53
Sangolquí, Ec.	H2	86
San Gorgonio Mountain, mtn., Ca., U.S.	I9	134
San Gottardo, Passo del, p., Switz.	D5	22
Sangre de Cristo Mountains, mts., U.S.	E3	128
San Gregorio, Arg.	G6	92
Sangre Grande, Trin.	s12	105f
Sangro, stm., Italy	H11	22
Sangrūr, India	C5	54
Sangsang, China	D11	54
Sangue, stm., Braz.	F6	84
Sangutane, stm., Moz.	C11	70
Sangya, China	C13	54
San Hipólito, Punta, c., Mex.	B1	100
Sanhu, China	H6	42
Sânhûr, Egypt	I1	58
Sanibel Island, i., Fl., U.S.	J3	116
San Ignacio, Arg.	C10	92
San Ignacio, Mex.	D8	100
San Ignacio, Mex.	B2	100
San Ignacio, Para.	C9	92
San Ignacio, Isla, i., Mex.	C4	100
San Ignacio, Laguna, b., Mex.	B2	100
San Ignacio de Moxo, Bol.	B3	90
San Ignacio de Velasco, Bol.	C4	90
San Isidro, Arg.	D5	92
San Isidro, Arg.	G8	92
San Isidro del General, C.R.	H5	102
San Jacinto, Col.	C4	86
San Jacinto, Ca., U.S.	J9	134
San Jacinto Peak, mtn., Ca., U.S.	J9	134
San Jaime, Arg.	E8	92
San Javier, Arg.	C10	92
San Javier, Arg.	E8	92
San Javier, Bol.	C4	90
San Javier, Chile	G2	92
San Javier, Mex.	H8	130
San Javier, Ur.	F8	92
San Javier, stm., Arg.	E8	92
Sanjay National Park, p.o.i., India	G8	54
San Jerónimo, Guat.	E2	102
Sanjiang, China	I3	42
Sanjō, Japan	B11	40
San Joaquín, Bol.	B4	90
San Joaquín, stm., Bol.	B4	90
San Joaquin, stm., Ca., U.S.	E4	134
San Joaquín de Omaguas, Peru	D3	84
San Joaquin Valley, val., Ca., U.S.	G5	134
San Jorge, Arg.	E6	92
San Jorge, stm., Col.	C4	86
San Jorge, Bahía de, b., Mex.	F6	98
San Jorge, Golfo, b., Arg.	I3	90
San Jorge Island, i., Sol. Is.	e8	79b
San José, C.R.	H5	102
San José, Mex.	F7	130
San Jose, Phil.	E3	52
San Jose, Ca., U.S.	F4	134
San Jose, Il., U.S.	D8	120
San Jose, N.M., U.S.	F3	128
San José, Ven.	q19	104g
San Jose, stm., N.M., U.S.	I9	132
San José, Cerro, mtn., Mex.	H2	130
San José, Isla, i., Mex.	C3	100
San José, Isla, i., Pan.	H8	102
San José, Laguna, b., P.R.	B3	104a
San José de Bácum, Mex.	B3	100
San José de Batuc, Mex.	A3	100
San José de Chiquitos, Bol.	C4	90
San José de Feliciano, Arg.	E8	92
San José de Guanipa, Ven.	C9	86
San José de Jáchal, Arg.	E3	92
San José de la Popa, Mex.	H7	130
San José de las Lajas, Cuba	A6	102
San José del Cabo, Mex.	D4	100
San José del Guaviare, Col.	F5	86
San José de Mayo, Ur.	G9	92
San José de Ocuné, Col.	E6	86
San José de Tiznados, Ven.	C8	86
San Jose Island, i., Tx., U.S.	G11	130
San Juan, Arg.	E3	92
San Juan, Mex.	E3	130
San Juan, P.R.	B3	104a
San Juan, state, Arg.	E3	92
San Juan, stm., Arg.	F4	92
San Juan, stm., Col.	E3	86
San Juan, stm., Mex.	H8	130
San Juan, stm., N.A.	G5	102
San Juan, stm., U.S.	F6	132
San Juan, stm., Ven.	B10	86
San Juan, Cabezas de, c., P.R.	B4	104a
San Juan, Cabo, c., Arg.	J4	90
San Juan Basin, bas., N.M., U.S.	G8	132
San Juan Bautista, Mex.	H6	130
San Juan Bautista, Para.	C9	92
San Juan Bautista see Sant Joan de Labritja, Spain	E12	20
San Juan Bautista, Ca., U.S.	G4	134
San Juan Creek, stm., Ca., U.S.	H5	134
San Juan de Colón, Ven.	C5	86
San Juan de Guadalupe, Mex.	C7	100
San Juan de la Maguana, Dom. Rep.	C12	102
San Juan del Norte, Nic.	G6	102
San Juan de los Cayos, Ven.	B7	86
San Juan de los Morros, Ven.	C8	86
San Juan del Río, Mex.	C6	100
San Juan del Río, Mex.	E8	100
San Juan del Sur, Nic.	G4	102
San Juan de Micay, stm., Col.	F3	86
San Juan de Payara, Ven.	D8	86
San Juan de Sabinas, Mex.	G6	130
San Juanico, Mex.	B2	100
San Juan Islands, is., Wa., U.S.	B3	136
San Juanito, Isla, i., Mex.	E5	100
San Juan Mountains, mts., Co., U.S.	C9	98
San Juan Nepomuceno, Col.	C4	86
San Juan Nepomuceno, Para.	C9	92
San Justo, Arg.	E7	92
Sankarani, stm., Afr.	G3	64
Sankeshwar, India	C2	53
Sankh, stm., India	G10	54
Sankheda, India	G4	54
Sankosh, stm., Asia	E13	54
Sankt Anton am Arlberg, Aus.	C7	22
Sankt Gallen, Switz.	C6	22
Sankt Goarshausen, Ger.	F3	16
Sankt Ingbert, Ger.	G3	16
Sankt Michel see Mikkeli, Fin.	F12	8
Sankt Moritz, Switz.	D6	22
Sankt-Peterburg (Saint Petersburg), Russia	A13	10
Sankt Peter-Ording, Ger.	B4	16
Sankt Pölten, Aus.	B12	22
Sankt Veit an der Glan, Aus.	D11	22
Sankt-Vith see Saint-Vith, Bel.	D14	14
Sankt Wendel, Ger.	G3	16
Sankuru, stm., D.R.C.	E4	66
San Lázaro, Cabo, c., Mex.	C2	100
San Leandro, Ca., U.S.	F3	134
San Leonardo, Mex.	G3	130
Şanlıurfa (Urfa), Tur.	A9	58
Şanlıurfa, state, Tur.	A9	58
San Lorenzo, Arg.	D8	92
San Lorenzo, Arg.	F7	92
San Lorenzo, Bol.	D4	90
San Lorenzo, Ec.	G2	86
San Lorenzo, Mex.	C7	100
San Lorenzo, P.R.	B4	104a
San Lorenzo, stm., Mex.	C5	100
San Lorenzo, Cabo, c., Ec.	H1	86
San Lorenzo, Isla, i., Mex.	A2	100
San Lorenzo, Monte (Cochrane, Cerro), mtn., S.A.	I2	90
San Lorenzo de la Parrilla, Spain	E8	20
Sanlúcar de Barrameda, Spain	H4	20
San Lucas, Bol.	D3	90
San Lucas, Mex.	D3	100
San Lucas, Cabo, c., Mex.	D4	100
San Luis, Arg.	F4	92
San Luis, Cuba	B10	102
San Luis, Guat.	D3	102
San Luis, Co., U.S.	D3	128
San Luis, Ven.	B7	86
San Luis, state, Arg.	F5	92
San Luís, Laguna, l., Bol.	B4	90
San Luis, Sierra de, mts., Arg.	F5	92
San Luis Creek, stm., Co., U.S.	C3	128
San Luis de la Paz, Mex.	E8	100
San Luis Gonzaga, Mex.	C3	100
San Luis Gonzaga, Bahía, b., Mex.	G5	98
San Luis Jilotepeque, Guat.	E3	102
San Luis Obispo, Ca., U.S.	H5	134
San Luis Potosí, Mex.	D8	100
San Luis Potosí, state, Mex.	D8	100
San Luis Reservoir, res., Ca., U.S.	F4	134
San Luis Río Colorado, Mex.	E5	98
San Luis Valley, val., Co., U.S.	D3	128
San Manuel, Arg.	H8	92
San Manuel, Az., U.S.	K6	132
San Marcial, stm., Mex.	A3	100
San Marcos, Col.	C4	86
San Marcos, Mex.	G9	100
San Marcos, Tx., U.S.	E9	130
San Marcos, Isla, i., Mex.	B2	100
San Marino, S. Mar.	G9	22
San Marino, ctry., Eur.	G9	22
San Martín, Arg.	D5	92
San Martín, Arg.	F3	92
San Martín, Col.	F5	86
San Martín, stm., Bol.	B4	90
San Martin, sci., Ant.	B34	81
San Martín, Lago (O'Higgins, Lago), l., S.A.	I2	90
San Martín de los Andes, Arg.	H2	90
San Martino di Castrozza, ngh., Italy	D8	22
San Mateo, Mex.	G1	130
San Mateo see Sant Mateu del Maestrat, Spain	D10	20
San Mateo, Ca., U.S.	F3	134
San Mateo, Fl., U.S.	G4	116
San Mateo, N.M., U.S.	H9	132
San Matías, Bol.	C5	90
San Matías, Golfo, b., Arg.	H4	90
Sanmen, China	G9	42
Sanmenhsia see Sanmenxia, China	D4	42
Sanmenxia, China	D4	42
San Miguel, Ec.	H2	86
San Miguel, El Sal.	F3	102
San Miguel, Mex.	A8	100
San Miguel, Pan.	H8	102
San Miguel, stm., Bol.	B4	90
San Miguel, stm., S.A.	G3	86
San Miguel, stm., Co., U.S.	E8	132
San Miguel, Golfo de, b., Pan.	H8	102
San Miguel de Allende, Mex.	E8	100
San Miguel de Cruces, Mex.	C6	100
San Miguel del Monte, Arg.	G8	92
San Miguel de Salcedo, Ec.	H2	86
San Miguel de Tucumán, Arg.	C4	92
San Miguel Island, i., Ca., U.S.	I5	134
Sanming, China	H7	42
San Miniato, Italy	G7	22
Sannār, Sudan	E6	62
Sannicandro Garganico, Italy	I12	22
San Nicolás, Peru	G2	84
San Nicolas, Phil.	A3	52
San Nicolás de los Arroyos, Arg.	F7	92
San Nicolás de los Garza, Mex.	C8	100
San Nicolas Island, i., Ca., U.S.	J6	134
Sânnicolau Mare, Rom.	C7	26
Sannieshof, S. Afr.	E7	70
Sannikova, proliv, strt., Russia	B16	34
Sano, Japan	C12	40
Sanok, Pol.	G18	16
Sânon, stm., Fr.	F15	14
San Pablo, Phil.	C3	52
San Pablo Bay, b., Ca., U.S.	E3	134
San Pasqual, Punta, c., Mex.	C3	100
San Pedro, Arg.	B5	92
San Pedro, Arg.	C5	92
San Pedro, Arg.	F8	92
San Pedro, Chile	F2	92
San Pedro, Col.	C4	86
San-Pédro, C. Iv.	I3	64
San Pedro, Neth. Ant.	A1	105a
San Pedro, state, Para.	B9	92
San Pedro, stm., Mex.	F8	98
San Pedro, stm., Mex.	G2	130
San Pedro, stm., N.A.	D2	102
San Pedro, stm., N.A.	K6	132
San Pedro, Punta, c., Chile	B2	92
San Pedro, Volcán, vol., Chile	D3	90
San Pedro Carchá, Guat.	E2	102
San Pedro de Jujuy see San Pedro, Arg.	B5	92
San Pedro de las Colonias, Mex.	C7	100
San Pedro del Gallo, Mex.	C6	100
San Pedro del Paraná, Para.	C9	92
San Pedro de Macorís, Dom. Rep.	C13	102
San Pedro de Ycuamandiyú, Para.	B9	92
San Pedro Peaks, mtn., N.M., U.S.	G10	132
San Pedro Sula, Hond.	E3	102
San Pedro Tabasco, Mex.	D2	102
San Pellegrino Terme, Italy	E6	22
San Pietro, Isola di, i., Italy	E2	24
San Pitch, stm., Ut., U.S.	D5	132
Sanquhar, Scot., U.K.	F9	12
Sanquianga, Parque Nacional, p.o.i., Col.	F2	86
San Quintín, Cabo, c., Mex.	F4	98
San Rafael, Arg.	G3	92
San Rafael, Chile	G2	92
San Rafael, Mex.	C8	100
San Rafael, Ca., U.S.	E3	134
San Rafael, N.M., U.S.	H8	132
San Rafael, Ven.	B6	86
San Rafael, stm., Mex.	F5	98
San Rafael, stm., Ut., U.S.	E6	132
San Rafael del Norte, Nic.	F4	102
San Rafael Swell, plat., Ut., U.S.	E6	132
San Ramón, Arg.	C5	92
San Ramón, Bol.	B4	90
San Ramón de la Nueva Orán, Arg.	D4	90
San Remo, Italy	G4	22
San Rodrigo, stm., Mex.	F6	130
San Roque, Arg.	D8	92
San Roque, Punta, c., Mex.	B1	100
San Saba, Tx., U.S.	C9	130
San Saba, stm., Tx., U.S.	C9	130
San Salvador, Arg.	E8	92
San Salvador, El Sal.	F3	102
San Salvador, i., Bah.	C10	96
San Salvador de Jujuy, Arg.	A5	92
Sansanné-Mango, Togo	G5	64
San Sebastián, P.R.	B1	104a
San Sebastián see Donostia, Spain	A9	20
San Sebastián, Bahía, b., Arg.	J3	90
Sansepolcro, Italy	G9	22
San Severo, Italy	I12	22
Sansha, China	H9	42
San Simon, Az., U.S.	K7	132
San Simon, stm., Az., U.S.	K7	132
San Simon Wash, stm., Az., U.S.	K4	132
Sanski Most, Bos.	E3	26
San Solano, Arg.	E4	92
Sans-Souci, hist., Haiti	C11	102
Santa, stm., Peru	E2	84
Santa Adélia, Braz.	K1	88
Santa Amalia, Spain	E4	20
Santa Ana, Bol.	B3	90
Santa Ana, Ec.	H1	86
Santa Ana, El Sal.	E3	102
Santa Ana, Mex.	F7	98
Santa Ana, Mex.	C8	100
Santa Ana, Ca., U.S.	J8	134
Santa Ana, Ven.	C9	86
Santa Ana del Alto Beni, Bol.	C3	90
Santa Anna, Tx., U.S.	C8	130
Santa Bárbara, Chile	H2	92
Santa Barbara, Col.	E4	86
Santa Bárbara, Hond.	E3	102
Santa Bárbara, Mex.	B6	100
Santa Barbara, Ca., U.S.	I6	134
Santa Bárbara, Ven.	D6	86
Santa Barbara Channel, strt., Ca., U.S.	I6	134
Santa Barbara Island, i., Ca., U.S.	J7	134
Santa Catalina, Gulf of, b., Ca., U.S.	J7	134
Santa Catalina, Isla, i., Mex.	C3	100
Santa Catalina Island, i., Ca., U.S.	J7	134
Santa Catarina, Mex.	C8	100
Santa Catarina, Mex.	L10	134
Santa Catarina, state, Braz.	C12	92
Santa Catarina, Ilha de, i., Braz.	C13	92
Santa Cecília, Braz.	C12	92
Santa Clara, Col.	I7	86
Santa Clara, Cuba	A7	102
Santa Clara, Ca., U.S.	F3	134
Santa Clara, Ut., U.S.	F3	132
Santa Clara, stm., Ca., U.S.	I7	134
Santa Clarita, Ca., U.S.	I7	134
Santa Clotilde, Peru	D3	84
Santa Coloma de Farners, Spain	C13	20
Santa Coloma de Farnés see Santa Coloma de Farners, Spain	C13	20
Santa Comba, Spain	A2	20
Santa Cruz, Braz.	J5	88
Santa Cruz, Braz.	D8	88
Santa Cruz, C.R.	G5	102
Santa Cruz, Phil.	C2	52
Santa Cruz, Phil.	D4	52
Santa Cruz, Phil.	C3	52
Santa Cruz, Ca., U.S.	G3	134
Santa Cruz, state, Arg.	I2	90
Santa Cruz, stm., Arg.	J3	90
Santa Cruz, stm., N.A.	J4	132
Santa Cruz, Isla, i., Ec.	i11	84a
Santa Cruz Cabrália, Braz.	I6	88
Santa Cruz de la Sierra, Bol.	C4	90
Santa Cruz del Quiché, Guat.	E2	102
Santa Cruz del Sur, Cuba	B9	102
Santa Cruz de Mudela, Spain	F7	20
Santa Cruz do Capibaribe, Braz.	D7	88
Santa Cruz do Piauí, Braz.	D5	88
Santa Cruz do Rio Pardo, Braz.	L1	88
Santa Cruz do Sul, Braz.	D11	92
Santa Cruz Island, i., Ca., U.S.	J6	134
Santa Cruz Islands, is., Sol. Is.	E7	72
Santa Elena, Arg.	E8	92
Santa Elena, Ec.	I1	86
Santa Elena, Mex.	B7	100
Santa Elena, Bahía de, b., Ec.	H1	86
Santa Elena, Cabo, c., C.R.	G4	102
Santa Eufemia, Spain	F6	20
Santa Eulalia, Spain	D9	20
Santa Eulalia del Río see Santa Eulària del Riu, Spain	E12	20
Santa Eulària del Riu, Spain	E12	20
Santa Fe, Arg.	E7	92
Santa Fe, Spain	G7	20
Santa Fe, N.M., U.S.	F3	128
Santa Fe, state, Arg.	D7	92
Santa Fe, stm., Fl., U.S.	G3	116
Santa Fe Baldy, mtn., N.M., U.S.	F3	128
Santa Fe de Bogotá, Col.	E4	86
Santa Fe de Minas, Braz.	I3	88
Santa Fé do Sul, Braz.	D6	90
Santa Filomena, Braz.	E3	88
Sant'Agata di Militello, Italy	F8	24
Santa Gertrudis, Mex.	G2	130
Santa Helena, Braz.	B3	88
Santa Helena de Goiás, Braz.	G7	84
Santai, China	F1	42
Santa Inês, Braz.	G5	88
Santa Inés, Bahía, b., Mex.	B3	100
Santa Inés, Isla, i., Chile	J2	90
Santa Isabel, Arg.	H4	92
Santa Isabel, P.R.	C3	104a
Santa Isabel, i., Sol. Is.	e8	79b
Santa Isabel, stm., Mex.	F1	130
Santa Isabel, Pico de, mtn., Eq. Gui.	I6	64
Santa Isabel Creek, stm., Tx., U.S.	G8	130
Santa Juliana, Braz.	J2	88
Santal, Baie du, b., N. Cal.	m16	79d
Santa Lucía, Arg.	D8	92
Santa Lucía, Ur.	G9	92
Santa Lucia Range, mts., Ca., U.S.	G4	134
Santaluz, Braz.	F6	88
Santa Luzia, Braz.	D7	88
Santa Magdalena, Arg.	G6	92
Santa Magdalena, Isla, i., Mex.	C2	100
Santa Margarita, Ca., U.S.	H5	134
Santa Margarita, Isla, i., Mex.	C2	100
Santa Margherita Ligure, Italy	F6	22
Santa María, Arg.	C4	92
Santa Maria, Braz.	D10	92
Santa María, Mex.	F6	130
Santa Maria, Ca., U.S.	I5	134
Santa Maria, i., Vanuatu	j16	79d
Santa Maria, stm., Braz.	E10	92
Santa María, stm., Mex.	F9	98
Santa María, stm., Mex.	E8	100
Santa Maria, stm., Az., U.S.	I3	132
Santa María, Bahía, b., Mex.	C4	100
Santa María, Cabo, c., Ur.	G10	92
Santa Maria, Cabo de, c., Ang.	C1	68
Santa Maria, Cabo de, c., Port.	H3	20
Santa María, Isla, i., Chile	H1	92
Santa María, Isla, i., Ec.	i11	84a
Santa María, Laguna de, l., Mex.	F9	98
Santa María Asunción Tlaxiaco, Mex.	G10	100
Santa Maria Capua Vetere, Italy	C7	24
Santa María Colotepec, Mex.	H10	100
Santa Maria da Boa Vista, Braz.	E5	88
Santa Maria da Vitória, Braz.	G3	88
Santa Maria de Itabira, Braz.	J4	88
Santa María del Oro, Mex.	C6	100
Santa María del Río, Mex.	E8	100
Santa Maria di Leuca, Capo, c., Italy	E12	24
Santa Maria do Suaçuí, Braz.	J4	88
Santa María la Real de Nieva, Spain	C6	20
Santa Marinella, Italy	H8	22
Santa Marta, Col.	B4	86
Santa Marta, Cabo de, c., Ang.	C1	68
Santa Marta, Ciénaga Grande, b., Col.	B4	86
Santa Mónica, Mex.	F7	130
Santa Monica, Ca., U.S.	I7	134
Santa Monica Bay, b., Ca., U.S.	J7	134
Santan, Indon.	D10	50
Santana, Braz.	G3	88
Santana, Coxilha de (Santa Ana, Cuchilla de), hills, S.A.	E10	92
Santana, Ilha de, i., Braz.	B4	88
Santana da Boa Vista, Braz.	E11	92
Santana do Ipanema, Braz.	E7	88
Santana do Livramento, Braz.	E9	92

Name Map Ref. Page

Santander, Col. F3 86
Santander, Phil. F4 52
Santander, Spain A7 20
Santander, state, Col. D5 86
Santander Jiménez, Mex. C9 100
Sant'Andrea, Isola, i., Italy D11 24
Santanghu, China C3 36
Santanilla, Islas, is., Hond. D6 102
Sant'Antine, Nuraghe, hist., Italy D2 24
Sant'Antioco, Italy E2 24
Sant'Antioco, Isola di, i., Italy E2 24
Sant Antoni de Portmany, Spain F12 20
Santanyí, Spain E14 20
Santa Paula, Ca., U.S. I6 134
Santaquin, Ut., U.S. D5 132
Santa Quitéria, Braz. C5 88
Santa Quitéria do Maranhão, Braz. B4 88
Santarcangelo di Romagna, Italy F9 22
Santarém, Braz. D7 84
Santarém, Port. E2 20
Santarém, state, Port. E2 20
Santaren Channel, strt., Bah. C9 96
Santa Rita, Braz. D8 88
Santa Rita, Col. G5 86
Santa Rita, Hond. E3 102
Santa Rita, Mex. G7 130
Santa Rita, Mt., U.S. B14 136
Santa Rita, Ven. B6 86
Santa Rosa, Arg. H5 92
Santa Rosa, Braz. H2 88
Santa Rosa, Braz. C10 92
Santa Rosa, Col. F7 86
Santa Rosa, Ec. D2 84
Santa Rosa, Ca., U.S. E3 134
Santa Rosa, Tx., U.S. H10 130
Santa Rosa, Ven. C7 86
Santa Rosa, Ven. D7 86
Santa Rosa, Mount, hill, Guam i10 78c
Santa Rosa Beach, Fl., U.S. G12 122
Santa Rosa de Copán, Hond. E3 102
Santa Rosa del Conlara, Arg. F5 92
Santa Rosa de Leales, Arg. C5 92
Santa Rosa de Osos, Col. D4 86
Santa Rosa de Sucumbíos, Ec. G3 86
Santa Rosa de Viterbo, Col. E5 86
Santa Rosa Island, i., Ca., U.S. J5 134
Santa Rosalía, Mex. B2 100
Santa Rosalía, Mex. H9 130
Santa Rosalía, Ven. C7 86
Santa Rosa Wash, stm., Az., U.S. K5 132
Šantarskie ostrova, is., Russia E16 34
Santa Sylvina, Arg. C7 92
Santa Teresa, Braz. J5 88
Santa Teresa, Mex. C9 100
Santa Teresa, stm., Braz. G1 88
Santa Teresa, Embalse de, res., Spain D5 20
Santa Teresa, Fortaleza de, hist., Ur. F11 92
Santa Uxía, Spain B1 20
Santa Vitória do Palmar, Braz. F11 92
Santee, Ca., U.S. K8 134
Santee, stm., S.C., U.S. C6 116
Santee Dam, dam, S.C., U.S. C5 116
Sant'Eufemia, Golfo di, b., Italy F9 24
Sant Feliu de Guíxols, Spain C14 20
Santhià, Italy E5 22
Santiago, Braz. D10 92
Santiago, Chile F2 92
Santiago, Mex. D4 100
Santiago, Pan. H7 102
Santiago, Para. C9 92
Santiago, i., C.V. I10 65a
Santiago, stm., Mex. C6 100
Santiago, stm., S.A. D2 84
Santiago, Isla, i., Ec. I11 84a
Santiago de Compostela, Spain B2 20
Santiago de Cuba, Cuba C9 102
Santiago del Estero, Arg. C5 92
Santiago del Estero, state, Arg. C5 92
Santiago de los Caballeros, Dom. Rep. C12 102
Santiago Island, i., Phil. B2 52
Santiago Ixcuintla, Mex. E6 100
Santiago Jamiltepec, Mex. G10 100
Santiago Larre, Arg. G8 92
Santiago Papasquiaro, Mex. C6 100
Santiago Peak, mtn., Ca., U.S. J8 134
Santiago Peak, mtn., Tx., U.S. E4 130
Santiaguillo, Laguna, l., Mex. C6 100
Santiam Pass, p., Or., U.S. F5 136
Säntis, mtn., Switz. C6 22
Santisteban del Puerto, Spain F7 20
Sant Joan de Labritja, Spain E12 20
Sant Jordi, Golf de, b., Spain D11 20
Sant Mateu del Maestrat, Spain D10 20
Santo Amaro, Braz. G6 88
Santo Amaro, Braz. B4 88
Santo André, Braz. L2 88
Santo Ângelo, Braz. D10 92
Santo Antão, i., C.V. k10 65a
Santo Antônio, Braz. D8 88
Santo Antônio, S. Tom./P. I6 64
Santo Antônio, stm., Braz. I3 88
Santo Antônio, stm., Braz. F1 88
Santo Antônio da Patrulha, Braz. D12 92
Santo Antônio de Jesus, Braz. G6 88
Santo Antônio de Pádua, Braz. K4 88
Santo Antônio do Amparo, Braz. K3 88
Santo Antônio do Içá, Braz. D4 84
Santo Augusto, Braz. C11 92
Santo Domingo, Cuba C8 96
Santo Domingo, Dom. Rep. C13 102
Santo Domingo, Mex. D8 100
Santo Domingo, Mex. C2 100
Santo Domingo, Mex. I3 130
Santo Domingo, Ven. D5 86
Santo Domingo de la Calzada, Spain B7 20
Santo Domingo de los Colorados, Ec. H1 86
Santo Domingo Pueblo, N.M., U.S. F2 128
Santo Domingo Tehuantepec, Mex. G11 100
Santo Domingo Zanatepec, Mex. G11 100
Santo Estêvão, Braz. G6 88
Santo / Malo, state, Vanuatu j16 79d
San Tomé, Ven. C9 86
Santo Onofre, stm., Braz. G4 88
Santorini see Thíra, i., Grc. G8 28
Santos, Braz. L2 88
Santos Dumont, Braz. K4 88
Santo Tirso, Port. C2 20
Santo Tomás, Mex. L9 134
Santo Tomás, Punta, c., Mex. L9 134
Santo Tomé, Arg. E7 92
Santo Tomé, Arg. D9 92
San Vicente de Alcántara, Spain E3 20
San Vicente de Baracaldo see Barakaldo, Spain A8 20
San Vicente del Caguán, Col. F4 86
San Vincente, Arg. D5 92
San Vincenzo, Italy G7 22
San Vito, Capo, c., Italy F6 24
Sanya, China L3 42
Sanyati, stm., Zimb. D4 68
Sanyō, Japan E4 40
Sanyuan, China D3 42
Sanzao Dao, i., China K5 42
Sanza Pombo, Ang. B2 68
São Benedito, Braz. C5 88
São Benedito do Rio Preto, Braz. B3 88
São Bento, Braz. B3 88
São Bento do Norte, Braz. C7 88
São Bento do Sul, Braz. C13 92
São Bento do Una, Braz. E7 88
São Borja, Braz. D10 92
São Caetano do Sul, Braz. L2 88
São Carlos, Braz. L2 88
São Cristóvão, Braz. F7 88
São Domingos, Braz. G2 88
São Domingos, Braz. C11 92
São Domingos, Gui.-B. G1 64
São Domingos do Maranhão, Braz. C3 88
São Felipe, Braz. H5 88
São Félix de Balsas, Braz. D3 88
São Francisco, Braz. H3 88
São Francisco, stm., Braz. E6 88
São Francisco, stm., Braz. H5 88
São Francisco, Baía de, b., Braz. C13 92
São Francisco, Ilha de, i., Braz. C13 92
São Francisco de Assis, Braz. D10 92
São Francisco de Goiás, Braz. H1 88
São Francisco de Paula, Braz. D12 92
São Francisco do Maranhão, Braz. D4 88
São Francisco do Sul, Braz. C13 92
São Gabriel, Braz. F5 88
São Gabriel, Braz. E10 92
São Gabriel da Palha, Braz. J5 88
São Gabriel de Goiás, Braz. H2 88
São Gonçalo do Sapucaí, Braz. K3 88
São Gonçalo dos Campos, Braz. G6 88
Sao Hill, Tan. F7 66
São Jerônimo, Braz. E12 92
São Jerônimo da Serra, Braz. A12 92
São João da Aliança, Braz. H2 88
São João da Barra, Braz. K5 88
São João da Boa Vista, Braz. L2 88
São João de Cortês, Braz. B3 88
São João Del Rei, Braz. K3 88
São João do Araguaia, Braz. C1 88
São João do Jaguaribe, Braz. C6 88
São João do Piauí, Braz. E4 88
São João dos Patos, Braz. D4 88
São Joaquim, Braz. D12 92
São Joaquim, Parque Nacional de, p.o.i., Braz. D13 92
São Joaquim da Barra, Braz. K1 88
São José, Braz. C13 92
São José, stm., Braz. J5 88
São José da Laje, Braz. E7 88
São José das Piranhas, Braz. D6 88
São José de Anauá, Braz. G11 86
São José do Cedro, Braz. C11 92
São José do Egito, Braz. D7 88
São José do Gurupi, Braz. A2 88
São José do Mipibu, Braz. D8 88
São José do Peixe, Braz. D4 88
São José do Rio Preto, Braz. K1 88
São José dos Campos, Braz. L3 88
São José dos Pinhais, Braz. B13 92
São Leopoldo, Braz. D12 92
São Lourenço, Braz. L3 88
São Lourenço, Pantanal de, sw., Braz. C5 90
São Lourenço do Sul, Braz. E12 92
São Luís, Braz. B3 88
São Luís do Curu, Braz. B6 88
São Luís do Quitunde, Braz. E8 88
São Luís Gonzaga, Braz. D10 92
São Manuel, Braz. L1 88
São Manuel, stm., Braz. E6 84
São Marcos, stm., Braz. I2 88
São Marcos, Baía de, b., Braz. B3 88
São Mateus, Braz. J6 88
São Mateus, Braço Norte, stm., Braz. J5 88
São Mateus do Sul, Braz. B12 92
São Miguel, Braz. D6 88
São Miguel, i., Port. C3 60
São Miguel do Araguaia, Braz. F7 84
São Miguel d'Oeste, Braz. C11 92
São Miguel do Guamá, Braz. A2 88
São Miguel dos Campos, Braz. E7 88
São Miguel do Tapuio, Braz. C5 88
Saona, Isla, i., Dom. Rep. C13 102
Saône, stm., Fr. C10 18
Saône-et-Loire, state, Fr. C10 18
Saoner, India H7 54
São Nicolau, i., C.V. k10 65a
São Nicolau, stm., Braz. C5 88
São Paulo, Braz. L2 88
São Paulo, state, Braz. D7 90
São Paulo de Olivença, Braz. D4 84
São Paulo do Potengi, Braz. C7 88
São Pedro do Piauí, Braz. C4 88
São Pedro do Sul, Port. D2 20
São Raimundo das Mangabeiras, Braz. D3 88
São Raimundo Nonato, Braz. E4 88
São Romão, Braz. I3 88
São Roque, Braz. L2 88
São Roque, Cabo de, c., Braz. C8 88
São Sebastião, Braz. L3 88
São Sebastião, Ilha de, i., Braz. L3 88
São Sebastião, Ponta, c., Moz. C12 70
São Sebastião do Paraíso, Braz. K2 88
São Sepé, Braz. E11 92
São Simão, Braz. K2 88
São Simão, Represa de, res., Braz. C7 90
São Timóteo, Braz. G4 88
São Tomé, Braz. C7 88
São Tomé, S. Tom./P. I6 64
São Tomé, i., S. Tom./P. I6 64
São Tomé, Cabo de, c., Braz. L5 88
São Tomé, Pico de, mtn., S. Tom./P. I6 64
Sao Tome and Principe, ctry., Afr. I6 64
Saoura, Oued, stm., Alg. D4 64
São Valério, stm., Braz. F1 88
São Vicente, Braz. M2 88
São Vicente, i., C.V. k9 65a
São Vicente, Cabo de, c., Port. H1 20
Sapanca, Tur. C13 28
Sape, Selat, strt., Indon. H11 50
Sapele, Nig. H6 64
Sapelo Island, i., Ga., U.S. E4 116
Sápes, Grc. B8 28
Šapitwa, mtn., Mwi. D6 68
Šapki, Russia A14 10
Šapkina, stm., Russia C26 8
Sapockin, Bela. G6 10
Sappa Creek, stm., U.S. A9 128
Sappa Creek, South Fork, stm., Ks., U.S. B8 128
Sappho, Wa., U.S. B2 136
Sapporo, Japan C14 38
Sap Songkhla, Thale, l., Thai. I5 48
Saptakośī, stm., Nepal E11 54
Sapudi, Pulau, i., Indon. G9 50
Sapulpa, Ok., U.S. A2 122
Sapwe, D.R.C. G5 66
Saqqâra, Egypt I2 58
Saqqâra, Pyramides de (Step Pyramid), hist., Egypt I1 58
Saqqez, Iran B6 56
Saraana, Baie, b., Qc., Can. B1 110
Sarāb, Iran B6 56
Saraburi, Thai. E5 48
Saracura, stm., Braz. G5 88
Saraféré, Mali F4 64
Saragosa, Tx., U.S. C4 130
Saragossa see Zaragoza, Spain C10 20
Sarāi Naurang, Pak. B3 54
Saraipāli, India H9 54
Sarajevo, Bos. F5 26
Saraji, Austl. D7 76
Sarakhs, Iran B9 56
Saraktaš, Russia D9 32
Saraland, Al., U.S. G10 122
Saran', Kaz. E12 32
Saran, Gunung, mtn., Indon. D7 50
Saranac, Mi., U.S. F4 112
Saranac, stm., N.Y., U.S. F3 110
Saranda see Sarandë, Alb. E13 24
Sarandë, Alb. E13 24
Sarandi, Braz. C11 92
Sarandí del Yí, Ur. F10 92
Sarandí Grande, Ur. F9 92
Sarangani Bay, b., Phil. H5 52
Sarangani Islands, is., Phil. H5 52
Sarangani Strait, strt., Phil. H5 52
Sārangarh, India H9 54
Sārangpur, India G6 54
Saranpaul', Russia B10 32
Saransk, Russia D6 32
Saraphi, Thai. C4 48
Sarapul, Russia C8 32
Sarāqib, Syria C7 58
Sarare, stm., Ven. D6 86
Sarasota, Fl., U.S. I3 116
Sarata, Ukr. C16 26
Saratoga, Ca., U.S. F3 134
Saratoga, Tx., U.S. G4 122
Saratoga, Wy., U.S. B10 132
Saratoga Springs, N.Y., U.S. G2 110
Saratov, Russia D7 32
Saratov Reservoir see Saratovskoe vodohranilišče, res., Russia D7 32
Saratovskoe vodohranilišče, res., Russia D7 32
Sarāvān, Iran D9 56
Saravan, Laos E8 48
Saravena, Col. D5 86
Sarawak, state, Malay. B8 50
Sarawak, hist. reg., Malay. E5 44
Saray, Tur. B10 28
Saraya, Gui. G2 64
Sarayevo see Sarajevo, Bos. F5 26
Sarayköy, Tur. F11 28
Sarayönü, Tur. E15 28
Sarbāz, Iran D9 56
Sarcelle, Passe de la, strt., N. Cal. n16 79d
Sarcidano, reg., Italy E3 24
Sarcoxie, Mo., U.S. G3 120
Sārda (Mahākālī), stm., Asia D8 54
Sardah, Bngl. F12 54
Sardārpur, India G5 54
Sardārshahr, India D5 54
Sardegna, state, Italy D4 24
Sardegna (Sardinia), i., Italy D3 24
Sardinata, Col. H11 102
Sardinia see Sardegna, state, Italy D4 24
Sardinia see Sardegna, i., Italy D3 24
Sardis, Al., U.S. E12 122
Sardis, Ga., U.S. D4 116
Sardis, Ms., U.S. C9 122
Sardis, Tn., U.S. B10 122
Sardis, hist., Tur. E10 28
Sardis Lake, res., Ms., U.S. C9 122
Sardis Lake, res., Ok., U.S. C3 122
Šardonem', Russia E21 8
Sarek, mtn., Swe. C7 8
Sareks Nationalpark, p.o.i., Swe. C7 8
Sar-e Pol, Afg. B10 56
Sarepta, La., U.S. E5 122
Sargent, Ga., U.S. D14 122
Sargent, Ne., U.S. F13 126
Sargodha, Pak. B4 54
Sarh, Chad F3 62
Sārī, Iran B7 56
Saria, i., Grc. H10 28
Sarıgöl, Tur. E11 28
Sarıkaya, Tur. E15 28
Sarikei, Malay. B7 50
Sarina, Austl. C7 76
Sariñena, Spain C10 20
Sariska Tiger Reserve, India E6 54
Sarita, Tx., U.S. G10 130
Sariwŏn, Kor., N. E6 38
Sarıyar Barajı, res., Tur. D14 28
Sarja, Russia G21 8
Sark, i., Guern. E6 14
Sarkand, Kaz. E13 32
Šarkaŭščyna, Bela. E10 10
Şarkikaraağaç, Tur. E14 28
Şarköy, Tur. C10 28
Sarles, N.D., U.S. F15 124
Sarlyk, Russia D9 32
Sarmi, Indon. F10 44
Sarmiento, Arg. I3 90
Särna, Swe. F5 8
Sarnia, On., Can. F7 112
Sarno, Italy D8 24
Sarolangun, Indon. E3 50
Saronic Gulf see Saronikós Kólpos, b., Grc. F6 28
Saronikós Kólpos, b., Grc. F6 28
Saronno, Italy E6 22
Saros Körfezi, b., Tur. C9 28
Sárospatak, Hung. A8 26
Sarowbī, Afg. C10 56
Sarpsborg, Nor. G4 8
Sarralbe, Fr. E15 14
Sarre (Saar), stm., Eur. E15 14
Sarrebourg, Fr. F16 14
Sarreguemines, Fr. E16 14
Šarscin, Bela. H14 10
Sartang, stm., Russia C15 34
Sartell, Mn., U.S. F4 118
Sartène, Fr. H14 18
Sarthe, state, Fr. G9 14
Sarthe, stm., Fr. G8 14
Saruhanlı, Tur. E10 28
Sárvár, Hung. B3 26
Sárviz, can., Hung. C5 26
Saryg-Sep, Russia D17 32
Sarykamyšskoe ozero, l., Asia A8 56
Sarykopa, ozero, l., Kaz. E10 32
Saryozek, Kaz. F13 32
Sarypovo, Russia C15 32
Sarysu, stm., Kaz. E11 32
Sary-Taš, Kyrg. G12 32
Sarzana, Italy F6 22
Sasabeneh, Eth. F8 62
Sasaginnigak Lake, l., Mb., Can. C17 124
Sasakwa, Ok., U.S. C2 122
Sasamungga, Sol. Is. d7 79b
Sāsarām, India F9 54
Sasayama, Japan D8 40
Sásd, Hung. C5 26
Sasebo, Japan F2 40
Saseginaga, Lac, l., Qc., Can. A11 112
Saskatchewan, state, Can. E9 106
Saskatchewan, stm., Can. E10 106
Saskatoon, Sk., Can. B7 124
Saskylah, Russia B11 34
Sasolburg, S. Afr. E8 70
Sasovo, Russia D6 32
Saspamco, Tx., U.S. E9 130
Sassafras, Ky., U.S. G2 114
Sassafras Mountain, mtn., U.S. A3 116
Sassandra, C. Iv. I3 64
Sassandra, stm., C. Iv. I3 64
Sassari, Italy D2 24
Sassnitz, Ger. B9 16
Sasso Marconi, Italy F8 22
Sassuolo, Italy F7 22
Sasyk, ozero, l., Ukr. D16 26
Sasykkol', ozero, l., Kaz. E14 32
Satadougou, Mali G2 64
Satah Mountain, vol., B.C., Can. D6 138
Sata-misaki, c., Japan H3 40
Satāna, India H5 54
Sátão, Port. D3 20
Sātāra, India C1 53
Satara Ruskamp, S. Afr. D10 70
Satélite, Mex. C1 130
Satellite Beach, Fl., U.S. H5 116
Satengar, Pulau, i., Indon. G10 50
Satevó, Mex. G1 130
Satevó, stm., Mex. G1 130
Satilla, stm., Ga., U.S. E4 116
Sátiro Dias, Braz. F6 88
Šaţţ (Tekezē), stm., Afr. E7 62
Satki, Russia I20 8
Satluj see Sutlej, stm., Asia C5 54
Satna, India F8 54
Sátoraljaújhely, Hung. A8 26
Sātpura Range, mts., India H6 54
Satsuma-hantō, pen., Japan H3 40
Satsunan-shotō, is., Japan k19 39a
Sattahip, Thai. F5 48
Satui, Indon. E9 50
Satu Mare, Rom. B10 26
Satu Mare, state, Rom. B10 26
Šatun, Thai. I4 48
Šatura, Russia I18 8
Saturnino M. Laspiur, Arg. E6 92
Satyamangalam, India F3 53
Sauce, Arg. E8 92
Sauce Corto, Arroyo, stm., Arg. H7 92
Saucier, Ms., U.S. G9 122
Saucillo, Mex. A6 100
Sauðárkrókur, Ice. k30 8a
Saudi Arabia, ctry., Asia E5 56
Sauerland, reg., Ger. E4 16
Saueruiná, stm., Braz. F6 84
Saugatuck, Mi., U.S. F3 112
Saugeen, stm., On., Can. D8 112
Saugerties, N.Y., U.S. B12 114
Saugstad, Mount, mtn., B.C., Can. D4 138
Saujil, Arg. D4 92
Sauk, stm., Mn., U.S. F4 118
Sauk Centre, Mn., U.S. F3 118
Sauk City, Wi., U.S. H9 118
Sauk Rapids, Mn., U.S. F4 118
Saukville, Wi., U.S. E1 112
Saül, Fr. Gu. C7 84
Sauldre, Canal de la, can., Fr. B8 18
Saulgau, Ger. I5 16
Saulieu, Fr. G13 14
Sault aux Cochons, stm., Qc., Can. A7 110
Sault-de-Vaucluse, Fr. E11 18
Saulteaux, stm., Ab., Can. B16 138
Sault Sainte Marie, On., Can. B5 112
Sault Sainte Marie, Mi., U.S. B5 112
Saumarez Reef, rf., Austl. C9 76
Saumlaki, Indon. G9 44
Saumur, Fr. G8 14
Saunders Island, i., Falk. Is. J4 90
Saunders Island, i., S. Geor. K12 82
Sauquoit, N.Y., U.S. B10 114
Saurimo, Ang. B3 68
Sausar, India H7 54
Sausu, Indon. D12 50
Sautar, Ang. C2 68
Sauteurs, Gren. q10 105e
Sauveterre-de-Guyenne, Fr. E5 18
Sauwald, for., Aus. B10 22
Sauzal, Mex. C1 130
Sava, stm., Eur. F16 22
Savai'i, i., Samoa g11 79c
Savalou, Benin H5 64
Savanna, Il., U.S. B7 120
Savanna, Ok., U.S. C3 122
Savannah, Ga., U.S. D5 116
Savannah, Mo., U.S. E3 120
Savannah, Tn., U.S. B10 122
Savannah, stm., U.S. D4 116
Savannah River Plant, sci., S.C., U.S. C4 116
Savannah Sound, Bah. K9 116
Savannakhét, Laos D7 48
Savanna-la-Mar, Jam. i12 104d
Savant Lake, On., Can. A8 118
Savant Lake, l., On., Can. A8 118
Sāvantvādi, India D1 53
Savanūr, India D2 53
Savaştepe, Tur. D10 28
Savè, Benin H5 64
Save (Sabi), stm., Afr. E5 68
Sāveh, Iran B7 56
Savelugu, Ghana H4 64
Savenay, Fr. G7 14
Saverdun, Fr. F7 18
Savigliano, Italy F4 22
Savino-Borisovskaja, Russia E21 8
Savinskij, Russia E19 8
Savissivik, Grnld. B13 141
Šavnik, Yugo. G6 26
Savoie, state, Fr. D12 18
Savoie, hist. reg., Fr. D12 18
Savo Island, i., Sol. Is. e8 79b
Savona, B.C., Can. F10 138
Savona, Italy F5 22
Savonlinna, Fin. F13 8
Savoy, Tx., U.S. D2 122
Savoy see Savoie, hist. reg., Fr. D12 18
Savran', Ukr. A17 26
Savusavu Bay, b., Fiji p19 79e
Savu Sea see Sawu, Laut, Indon. G7 44
Sawah, Indon. B9 50
Sawahlunto, Indon. D2 50
Sawāi Mādhopur, India E6 54
Sawākin, Sudan D7 62
Sawankhalok, Thai. D4 48
Sawara, Japan D13 40
Sawata, Japan A11 40
Sawatch Range, mts., Co., U.S. B2 128
Sawdā', Jabal, mtn., Sau. Ar. F5 56
Sawdā', Jabal as-, hills, Libya A4 62
Sawdā', Qurnat as-, mtn., Leb. D7 58
Sawdirī, Sudan E5 62
Sawqirah, Oman F8 56
Sawqirah, Dawhat, b., Oman F8 56
Sawtooth National Recreation Area, p.o.i., Id., U.S. F12 136
Sawu, Laut (Savu Sea), Indon. G7 44
Sawu, Pulau, i., Indon. H7 44
Sawyer, Mi., U.S. G3 112
Sawyer, N.D., U.S. F12 124
Saxby, stm., Austl. B3 76
Saxon, Wi., U.S. E8 118
Saxony see Sachsen, state, Ger. F9 16
Saxony see Sachsen, hist. reg., Ger. D5 16
Saxony-Anhalt see Sachsen-Anhalt, state, Ger. D7 16
Saxton, Pa., U.S. D7 114
Say, Niger G5 64
Sayan Mountains, mts., Asia D17 32
Sayaxché, Guat. D2 102
Şaydā (Sidon), Leb. E6 58
Şaydā, state, Leb. E6 58
Sayhūt, Yemen F7 56
Sayil, hist., Mex. B3 102
Saylac, Som. B8 66
Saylūn, Khirbat (Shiloh), hist., W.B. F6 58
Saynshand, Mong. C7 36
Sayram Hu, l., China F14 32
Sayre, Ok., U.S. F9 128
Sayre, Pa., U.S. C9 114
Sayreville, N.J., U.S. D11 114
Sayward, B.C., Can. F5 138
Saywūn, Yemen F6 56
Saza, Japan F2 40
Sba, Alg. D4 64
Ščadryn, Bela. H12 10
Scafell Pike, mtn., Eng., U.K. G9 12
Scalea, Italy E9 24
Scammon Bay, Ak., U.S. D6 140
Scandia, Ks., U.S. B11 128
Scanlon, Mn., U.S. E6 118
Scapa Flow, b., Scot., U.K. C9 12
Scapegoat Mountain, mtn., Mt., U.S. C14 136
Ščapino, Russia E20 34
Scappoose, Or., U.S. E3 136
Ščara, stm., Bela. G8 10
Scarborough, St. K./N. C2 105a
Scarborough, Trin. r13 105f
Scarborough, Eng., U.K. G12 12
Scarborough, ngh., On., Can. E10 112
Scărișoara, Rom. F11 26
Scarp, i., Scot., U.K. C5 12
Scawfell Island, i., Austl. C7 76
Ščedro, Otok, i., Cro. G13 22
Ščekino, Russia F20 10
Ščelkovo, Russia E20 10
Sceptre, Sk., Can. D4 124
Ščerbakovo, Russia C21 34
Ščerbakty, Kaz. D13 32
Ščerbinka, Russia E20 10
Schaffhausen, Switz. C5 22
Schaffhouse see Schaffhausen, Switz. C5 22
Schärding, Aus. B10 22
Schefferville, Qc., Can. E17 106
Scheinfeld, Ger. G6 16
Schelde, stm., Eur. C13 14
Schell Creek Range, mts., Nv., U.S. D2 132
Schenectady, N.Y., U.S. B11 114
Schenevus Creek, stm., N.Y., U.S. B11 114
Schertz, Tx., U.S. E9 130
Schiedam, Neth. C13 14
Schiermonnikoog, i., Neth. C2 16
Schiltigheim, Fr. F16 14
Schio, Italy E8 22
Schkeuditz, Ger. E8 16
Schladming, Aus. C10 22
Schlater, Ms., U.S. D8 122
Schleiden, Ger. F2 16
Schleswig, Ger. B5 16
Schleswig, Ia., U.S. B2 120
Schleswig-Holstein, state, Ger. B6 16
Schlitz, Ger. F5 16
Schlüchtern, Ger. F5 16
Schmölln, Ger. F8 16
Schneeberg, Ger. F8 16
Schneeberg, mtn., Ger. F7 16
Schneverdingen, Ger. C5 16
Schœlcher, Mart. k6 105c
Schofield, Wi., U.S. G9 118
Schoharie, N.Y., U.S. B11 114
Schoharie Creek, stm., N.Y., U.S. B11 114
Schönebeck, Ger. D7 16
Schongau, Ger. I6 16
Schopfheim, Ger. I3 16
Schorndorf, Ger. H5 16
Schouten, Kepulauan, is., Indon. F10 44
Schouten Island, i., Austl. o14 77a
Schouten Islands, is., Pap. N. Gui. a3 79a
Schramberg, Ger. H4 16
Schreiber, On., Can. C11 118
Schriever, La., U.S. H8 122
Schrobenhausen, Ger. H7 16
Schulenburg, Tx., U.S. E11 130
Schultz Lake, l., Nu., Can. C11 106
Schuyler, Va., U.S. G7 114
Schuylkill, stm., Pa., U.S. D10 114
Schuylkill Haven, Pa., U.S. D9 114
Schwabach, Ger. G7 16
Schwaben, hist. reg., Ger. H5 16
Schwäbische Alb, mts., Ger. H5 16
Schwäbisch Gmünd, Ger. H5 16
Schwäbisch Hall, Ger. G5 16
Schwabmünchen, Ger. H6 16
Schwandorf in Bayern, Ger. G7 16
Schwaner, Pegunungan, mts., Indon. D8 50
Schwarzach im Pongau, Aus. C10 22
Schwarzwald (Black Forest), mts., Ger. H4 16
Schwatka Mountains, mts., Ak., U.S. C8 140
Schwaz, Aus. C8 22
Schwechat, Aus. B13 22
Schwedt, Ger. C10 16
Schweinfurt, Ger. F5 16
Schweizer Nationalpark, p.o.i., Switz. D7 22
Schweizer-Reineke, S. Afr. E7 70
Schwerin, Ger. C7 16
Schweriner See, l., Ger. C7 16
Schwyz, Switz. C5 22
Sciacca, Italy G6 24
Scicli, Italy H8 24
Scilly, Isles of, is., Eng., U.K. L6 12
Scio, Oh., U.S. D4 114
Scio, Or., U.S. F4 136
Scioto, stm., Oh., U.S. E3 114
Šćit, mtn., Bos. E4 26
Scobey, Mt., U.S. F8 124
Scone, Austl. I8 76
Scooba, Ms., U.S. E10 122
Scordia, Italy G8 24
Scoresby Land, reg., Grnld. C21 141
Scoresbysund (Ittoqqortoormiit), Grnld. C21 141
Scoresby Sund, strt., Grnld. C21 141
Scotia, N.Y., U.S. B12 114
Scotia Ridge, unds. N8 144
Scotia Sea K10 82
Scotland, On., Can. E9 112
Scotland, S.D., U.S. D15 126
Scotland, Tx., U.S. H10 128
Scotland, state, U.K. E8 12
Scotlandville, La., U.S. G7 122
Scotsburn, N.S., Can. E14 110
Scott, Sk., Can. B5 124
Scott, Ms., U.S. D7 122
Scott, stm., Ca., U.S. B3 134
Scott, Cape, c., B.C., Can. F2 138
Scott, Mount, mtn., Or., U.S. H4 136
Scott Base, sci., Ant. C22 81
Scott City, Mo., U.S. G8 120
Scott Coast, cst., Ant. C20 81
Scottdale, Pa., U.S. D6 114
Scott Island, i., Ant. B23 81
Scott Islands, is., B.C., Can. F2 138
Scott Peak, mtn., Id., U.S. F14 136
Scott Reef, rf., Austl. B4 74
Scottsbluff, Ne., U.S. F9 126
Scotts Bluff National Monument, p.o.i., Ne., U.S. F9 126
Scottsboro, Al., U.S. C12 122
Scottsdale, Austl. n13 77a
Scottsdale, Az., U.S. J5 132
Scotts Head, c., Dom. j6 105c
Scotts Hill, Tn., U.S. B10 122
Scottsville, Ky., U.S. H11 120
Scottville, Mi., U.S. E3 112
Scourie, Scot., U.K. C7 12
Scout Lake, Sk., Can. E8 124
Scranton, N.D., U.S. A9 126
Scranton, Pa., U.S. C10 114
Screven, Ga., U.S. E3 116
Scribner, Ne., U.S. J2 118
Scrub Island, i., Anguilla A2 105a
Ščuče, Russia C10 32
Ščučinsk, Kaz. D12 32
Ščučyn, Bela. G7 10
Scugog, Lake, l., On., Can. D11 112
Scunthorpe, Eng., U.K. H12 12
Scutari, Lake, l., Eur. H16 22
Ščytkavičy, Bela. G10 10
Seabrook, Lake, l., Austl. F3 74
Seaford, De., U.S. F10 114
Seaforth, On., Can. E8 112
Seahorse Point, c., Nu., Can. C15 106
Sea Islands, is., U.S. E5 116
Sea Isle City, N.J., U.S. E11 114
Seal, stm., Mb., Can. D11 106
Seal, Cape, c., S. Afr. I6 70
Sea Lake, Austl. J4 76
Sealark Channel, strt., Sol. Is. e9 79b
Seal Cays, is., T./C. Is. B12 102
Seale, Al., U.S. E13 122
Sealevel, N.C., U.S. B9 116
Seal Island, i., N.S., Can. G10 110
Sealy, Tx., U.S. H2 122
Seara, Braz. C11 92
Searcy, Ar., U.S. B7 122
Searles Lake, l., Ca., U.S. H8 134
Searsport, Me., U.S. F7 110
Seaside, Ca., U.S. G4 134
Seaside, Or., U.S. D3 136
Seaside Park, N.J., U.S. E11 114
Seattle, Wa., U.S. C4 136
Sebago Lake, l., Me., U.S. G6 110
Se Bai, stm., Thai. E7 48
Sebakung, Indon. D10 50
Sebangan, Teluk, b., Indon. E8 50
Sebangka, Pulau, i., Indon. C4 50
Sebastian, Tx., U.S. H10 130
Sebastian, Cape, c., Or., U.S. A1 134
Sebastián Vizcaíno, Bahía, b., Mex. A1 100
Sebastopol, Ca., U.S. E3 134
Sebastopol, Ms., U.S. E9 122
Sebec Lake, l., Me., U.S. E7 110
Šebekino, Russia D5 32
Seben, Tur. C14 28
Sebeș, Rom. D10 26
Sebes Körös (Crișul Repede), stm., Eur. B8 26
Sebewaing, Mi., U.S. E6 112
Sebež, Russia D11 10
Sebino see Iseo, Lago d', l., Italy E6 22
Sebnitz, Ger. F10 16
Sebree, Ky., U.S. G10 120
Sebring, Fl., U.S. I4 116
Sebuku, Indon. A10 50
Sebuku, Teluk, b., Indon. A11 50
Sebuyau, Malay. C7 50
Secchia, stm., Italy F7 22
Sechura, Peru E1 84
Sechura, Desierto de, des., Peru E1 84
Seclantás, Arg. B4 92
Sečovská Polianka, Slov. H17 16
Section, Al., U.S. C13 122
Security, Co., U.S. C4 128
Seda, China E5 36
Seda, Lith. D5 10
Sedah, Indon. B4 74
Sedalia, Ab., Can. C3 124
Sedalia, Mo., U.S. F4 120
Sedan, Fr. E13 14
Sedanovo, Russia C18 32
Sedayu, Indon. G8 50
Seddon, Kap, c., Grnld. B14 141
Sedel'nikovo, Russia C13 32
Séderon, Fr. E11 18
Sedgewick, Ab., Can. D19 138
Sedgwick, Co., U.S. G10 126
Sedgwick, Ks., U.S. D11 128
Sédhiou, Sen. G1 64
Sedlčany, Czech Rep. G10 16
Sedom (Sodom), hist., Isr. G6 58
Sedro Woolley, Wa., U.S. B4 136
Šeduva, Lith. E6 10
Seehausen, Ger. D7 16
Seeheim, Nmb. E3 70
Seeis, Nmb. C3 70
Seekoei, stm., S. Afr. G7 70
Seeley Lake, Mt., U.S. C13 136
Seelyville, In., U.S. E10 120
Sées, Fr. F9 14
Seesen, Ger. E6 16
Sefadu, S.L. H2 64
Seferihisar, Tur. E9 28
Segama, stm., Malay. A11 50
Segamat, Malay. K6 48
Ségbana, Benin G5 64
Segeri, Indon. F11 50
Segesta, hist., Italy G6 24
Segeža, Russia E15 8
Segorbe, Spain E10 20

Name | Map Ref. | Page

Ségou, Mali G3 64
Segovary, Russia E20 8
Segovia, Spain D6 20
Segovia, co., Spain C6 20
Segozero, ozero, l., Russia E15 8
Segre, stm., Eur. H6 18
Seguam Island, i., Ak., U.S. g24 140a
Séguédine, Niger E7 64
Séguéla, C. Iv. H3 64
Seguí, Arg. E7 92
Seguin, Tx., U.S. E10 130
Segundo, stm., Arg. E6 92
Seguntur, Indon. C10 50
Segura, stm., Spain F10 20
Segura, Sierra de, mts., Spain G8 20
Sehithwa, Bots. B6 70
Sehore, India G6 54
Sehwān, Pak. D10 56
Seibert, Co., U.S. B6 128
Seikpyu, Mya. B2 48
Seiland, i., Nor. A10 8
Seiling, Ok., U.S. E9 128
Seim, stm., Eur. D4 32
Seinäjoki, Fin. E10 8
Seine, stm., Mb., Can. E17 124
Seine, stm., On., Can. C6 118
Seine, stm., Fr. E9 14
Seine, Baie de la, b., Fr. E8 14
Seine, Bay of the see Seine, Baie de la, b., Fr. E8 14
Seine-et-Marne, state, Fr. F12 14
Seine-Maritime, state, Fr. E9 14
Seixal, Port. F1 20
Seixas, Ponta do, c., Braz. D8 88
Sejmčan, Russia D19 34
Sejny, Pol. B19 16
Sekayam, stm., Indon. C7 50
Sekayu, Indon. E3 50
Sekeladi, Indon. E3 50
Seki, Azer. A6 56
Seki, Japan D9 40
Sekiu, Wa., U.S. B2 136
Sekoma, Bots. D6 70
Sekondi, Ghana I4 64
Seksna, Russia A21 10
Selagskij, mys, c., Russia B23 34
Selama, Malay. J5 48
Selangor, state, Malay. K5 48
Selaru, Pulau, i., Indon. G9 44
Selatan, Tanjung, c., Indon. F9 50
Selatpanjang, Indon. C3 50
Selawik, Ak., U.S. C8 140
Selawik Lake, l., Ak., U.S. C7 140
Selayar, Pulau, i., Indon. G12 50
Selayar, Selat, strt., Indon. F12 50
Selb, Ger. F8 16
Selbusjøen, l., Nor. E4 8
Selby, Eng., U.K. H11 12
Selby, S.D., U.S. B12 126
Selbyville, De., U.S. F10 114
Sel'co, Russia E19 8
Sel'co, Russia G17 10
Selçuk, Tur. F10 28
Seldovia, Ak., U.S. E9 140
Selebi-Phikwe, Bots. C9 70
Selečnja, Russia H17 10
Selehov, Russia D18 32
Selemdža, stm., Russia F14 34
Selemdžinsk, Russia F15 34
Selenduma, Russia F10 34
Selenge, D.R.C. E3 66
Selenge, stm., Asia G9 34
Selenicë, Alb. D13 24
Selennjah, stm., Russia C16 34
Sélestat, Fr. F16 14
Seleznëvo, Russia F13 8
Selfoss, Ice. l29 8a
Selfridge, N.D., U.S. A11 126
Sel'gon, Russia G16 34
Sélibabi, Maur. F2 64
Seliger, ozero, l., Russia C15 10
Seligman, Az., U.S. H4 132
Selihova, zaliv, b., Russia D20 34
Selimbau, Indon. C8 50
Selinsgrove, Pa., U.S. D8 114
Selinunte, hist., Italy G6 24
Selišče, Russia D16 10
Seližarovo, Russia D16 10
Selkirk, Mb., Can. D17 124
Selkirk, Scot., U.K. F10 12
Selkirk Mountains, mts., N.A. F13 138
Sellers, S.C., U.S. B6 116
Sellersburg, In., U.S. F12 120
Selles-sur-Cher, Fr. G10 14
Selm, Ger. E3 16
Selma, Al., U.S. E11 122
Selma, Ca., U.S. G6 134
Selma, N.C., U.S. A7 116
Selmer, Tn., U.S. B10 122
Selmont, Al., U.S. E11 122
Selon', stm., Russia B13 10
Selong, Indon. H10 50
Selva, Arg. D6 92
Selvagens, Ilhas, is., Port. C1 64
Selvas, for., Braz. F8 82
Selway, stm., Id., U.S. D11 136
Selwyn, Austl. C3 76
Selwyn, Passage, strt., Vanuatu k16 79d
Selwyn Lake, l., Can. D10 106
Selwyn Mountains, mts., Can. C4 106
Selwyn Range, mts., Austl. C3 76
Seman, stm., Alb. D13 24
Semangka, Teluk, b., Indon. F4 50
Semara, W. Sah. D2 64
Semarang, Indon. G7 50
Semayang, Kenohan, l., Indon. D10 50
Sembakung, stm., Indon. B10 50
Semcy, Russia H16 10
Semenanjung Malaysia, hist. reg., Malay. K6 48
Semenov, Russia H21 8
Semeru, Gunung, vol., Indon. H8 50
Semey see Semipalatinsk, Kaz. D13 32
Semežava, Bela. H10 10
Semichi Islands, is., Ak., U.S. g21 140a
Semiluki, Russia D5 32
Semily, Czech Rep. F11 16
Seminary, Ms., U.S. F9 122
Seminoe Reservoir, res., Wy., U.S. A9 132
Seminole, Ok., U.S. B2 122
Seminole, Tx., U.S. B5 130
Seminole, Lake, res., U.S. G14 122
Seminole Draw, stm., U.S. B5 130
Semiozërnoe, Kaz. D10 32
Semipalatinsk, Kaz. D13 32
Semitau, Indon. C7 50
Semizbuga, Kaz. D13 32
Semliki, stm., Afr. D6 66
Semnān, Iran B7 56
Semois, stm., Eur. E13 14
Semonaiha, Kaz. D14 32
Semporna, Malay. A11 50
Semuda, Indon. E8 50
Semža, Russia C21 8
Sên, stm., Camb. F7 48
Sena, Bol. B3 90
Senador Canedo, Braz. I1 88
Senador Pompeu, Braz. C6 88
Senaki, Geor. F6 32
Sena Madureira, Braz. E4 84
Senanayake Samudra, res., Sri L. H5 53
Senanga, Zam. D3 68
Senath, Mo., U.S. H7 120
Senatobia, Ms., U.S. C8 122
Senber, Kaz. E11 32
Sendai, Japan H3 40
Sendai, Japan A13 40
Sendelingsdrif, Nmb. F3 70
Sendhwa, India H5 54
Sendurjana, India H7 54
Senduruhan, Indon. D7 50
Senebui, Tanjung, c., Indon. B2 50
Seneca, Il., U.S. C9 120
Seneca, Ks., U.S. E1 120
Seneca, Mo., U.S. H3 120
Seneca, S.C., U.S. B3 116
Seneca, Mount, mtn., N.Y., U.S. B7 114
Seneca Falls, N.Y., U.S. B9 114
Seneca Lake, l., N.Y., U.S. B8 114
Senegal, ctry., Afr. G2 64
Sénégal, stm., Afr. F2 64
Senekal, S. Afr. F8 70
Senetosa, Capu di (Senetosa, Punta di), c., Fr. H14 18
Senetosa, Punta di see Senetosa, Capu di, c., Fr. H14 18
Senftenberg, Ger. E10 16
Sengés, Braz. B13 92
Sênggê, stm., China B8 54
Senhor do Bonfim, Braz. F5 88
Senica, Slov. H13 16
Senigallia, Italy G10 22
Senirkent, Tur. E13 28
Senise, Italy D10 24
Senja, i., Nor. B7 8
Senkaku-shotō, is., Japan F9 36
Şenköy, Tur. B7 58
Senkursk, Russia E20 8
Senlis, Fr. E11 14
Senmonorom, Camb. F8 48
Senneterre, Qc., Can. F15 106
Senoia, Ga., U.S. D14 122
Senpazar, Tur. B16 28
Sens, Fr. F12 14
Senta, Yugo. D7 26
Sentarum, Danau, l., Indon. C7 50
Sentinel, Ok., U.S. F9 128
Sentinel Butte, mtn., N.D., U.S. A8 126
Senyavin Islands, is., Micron. C6 72
Seo de Urgel see La Seu d'Urgell, Spain B12 20
Seonāth, stm., India H8 54
Seoni, India G7 54
Seoni Mālwa, India G6 54
Seoul see Sŏul, Kor., S. F7 38
Sepanjang, Pulau, i., Indon. G9 50
Sepasu, Indon. C10 50
Sepetiba, Baía de, b., Braz. L4 88
Sepi, Sol. Is. e8 79b
Sepik, stm., Pap. N. Gui. a3 79a
Sępopol, Pol. B17 16
Sept-Îles, Qc., Can. E17 106
Sepúlveda, Spain C7 20
Seputih, stm., Indon. F4 50
Sequatchie, stm., Tn., U.S. B13 122
Sequillo, stm., Spain C5 20
Sequim, Wa., U.S. B3 136
Sequoia National Park, p.o.i., Ca., U.S. G7 134
Şerabad, Uzb. B10 56
Serafimovič, Russia E6 32
Seraing, Bel. D14 14
Seram (Ceram), i., Indon. F8 44
Seram, Laut (Ceram Sea), Indon. F8 44
Serang, Indon. G5 50
Serasan, Pulau, i., Indon. B6 50
Serasan, Selat, strt., Indon. B6 50
Serayevo see Sarajevo, Bos. F5 26
Serbeulangit, Pegunungan, mts., Indon. K3 48
Serbia see Srbija, state, Yugo. E7 26
Serdo, Eth. E8 62
Serdobsk, Russia D6 32
Séré'ama, Mont, mtn., Vanuatu i16 79d
Serebrjansk, Kaz. E14 32
Serebrjanye Prudy, Russia F21 10
Sered', Slov. H13 16
Seredejskij, Russia F18 10
Serëdka, Russia B11 10
Seremban, Malay. K5 48
Serengeti National Park, p.o.i., Tan. E6 66
Serengeti Plain, pl., Tan. E6 66
Serengka, Indon. D7 50
Serenje, Zam. C5 68
Seret (Siret), stm., Eur. A12 26
Sergač, Russia I21 8
Sergeevka, Kaz. D11 32
Sergeevka, Russia C10 38
Sergeja Kirova, ostrova, is., Russia A6 34
Sergen, Tur. B10 28
Sergiev Posad, Russia D21 10
Serginskij, Russia B10 32
Sergipe, state, Braz. F7 88
Sergozero, ozero, l., Russia C17 8
Seria, Bru. A9 50
Serian, Malay. C7 50
Seribudolok, Indon. B1 50
Seridó, stm., Braz. D7 88
Sérifos, i., Grc. F7 28
Serik, Tur. G14 28
Serinyol, Tur. B7 58
Serkovo, Russia A15 32
Serlovaja Gora, Russia F12 34
Serov, Russia C10 32
Serowe, Bots. C8 70
Serpejsk, Russia F17 10
Serpentine Lakes, l., Austl. E5 74
Serpents Mouth, strt. C11 86
Serpuhov, Russia F20 10
Serra, Braz. K5 88
Serra Branca, Braz. D7 88
Serra da Canastra, Parque Nacional da, p.o.i., Braz. K2 88
Serra da Capivara, Parque Nacional da, p.o.i., Braz. E4 88
Serra de Outes, Spain B1 20
Serra do Navio, Braz. C7 84
Serra do Salitre, Braz. J2 88
Serra dos Órgãos, Parque Nacional da, p.o.i., Braz. L4 88
Serrana, Braz. K2 88
Serrana, Cayo de, unds., Col. E7 102
Serrana Bank see Serrana, Cayo de, unds., Col. E7 102
Serranía, Braz. K2 88
Serranía de la Neblina, Parque Nacional, p.o.i., Ven. G8 86
Serranilla, Banco see Serranilla, Cayo de, unds., Col. E8 102
Serranilla, Cayo de, unds., Col. E8 102
Serranilla Bank see Serranilla, Cayo de, unds., Col. E8 102
Serrano, Banco see Serrana, Cayo de, unds., Col. E7 102
Serra Talhada, Braz. E6 88
Serres, Fr. E11 18
Sérres, Grc. B6 28
Serrezuela, Arg. E5 92
Serrinha, Braz. F6 88
Serrita, Braz. D6 88
Sertânia, Braz. E7 88
Sertãozinho, Braz. K1 88
Serui, Indon. F10 44
Serule, Bots. B8 70
Serutu, Pulau, i., Indon. D6 50
Seruwai, Indon. J4 48
Sêrxü, China E4 36
Seryševo, Russia F14 34
Sesayap, stm., Indon. B10 50
Sesayap Lama, Indon. B10 50
Seseganaga Lake, l., On., Can. A8 118
Sese Islands, is., Ug. E6 66
Sesfontein, Nmb. D1 68
Sesheke, Zam. D3 68
Sesia, stm., Italy E5 22
Sesibu, Indon. A10 50
Sessa Aurunca, Italy C7 24
Sestao, Spain A7 20
Sestri Levante, Italy F6 22
Sestroreck, Russia F14 8
Šešupė, stm., Eur. F5 10
Šeta, Lith. E7 10
Sète, Fr. F9 18
Sete Barras, Braz. B13 92
Sete Cidades, Parque Nacional de, p.o.i., Braz. C5 88
Sete Lagoas, Braz. J3 88
Sete Quedas, Parque Nacional de, p.o.i., Braz. A11 92
Sete Quedas, Salto das (Guairá, Salto del), wtfl, S.A. B10 92
Seth Ward, Tx., U.S. G7 128
Seto, Japan D10 40
Seto-naikai (Inland Sea), Japan E5 40
Seton Portage, B.C., Can. F8 138
Settat, Mor. C3 64
Setté Cama, Gabon E1 66
Sette-Daban, hrebet, mts., Russia D16 34
Settlers, S. Afr. D9 70
Setúbal, Port. F1 20
Setúbal, state, Port. F2 20
Setúbal, Baía de, b., Port. F2 20
Seul, Lac, l., On., Can. A6 118
Seul Choix Point, c., Mi., U.S. C4 112
Seulimeum, Indon. J2 48
Sevan, Lake see Sevana Lich, l., Arm. A6 56
Sevana Lich, l., Arm. A6 56
Sevastopol', Ukr. G15 6
Ševelevskaja, Russia F20 8
Seven Persons, Ab., Can. E3 124
Seven Sisters Peaks, mtn., B.C., Can. B2 138
Seventy Mile House, B.C., Can. E9 138
Severn, stm., On., Can. E12 106
Severn, stm., U.K. J10 12
Severnaja Dvina (Northern Dvina), stm., Russia E19 8
Severnaja Osetija, state, Russia F6 32
Severnaja Sos'va, stm., Russia B10 32
Severnaja Zemlja, is., Russia B12 30
Severna Park, Md., U.S. E9 114
Severnoe, Russia C13 32
Severnye uvaly, hills, Russia C7 32
Severnyj Ural, mts., Russia B9 32
Severočeský, state, Czech Rep. F10 16
Severodvinsk (Molotovsk), Russia D18 8
Severo-Enisejskij, Russia B16 32
Severo-Kuril'sk, Russia F20 34
Severomoravský, state, Czech Rep. G13 16
Severomorsk, Russia B15 8
Severo-Sibirskaja nizmennost' (North Siberain Lowland), pl., Russia B6 34
Severoural'sk (Severouralsk), Russia B9 32
Severo-Zadonsk, Russia F21 10
Severy, Ks., U.S. D12 128
Sevettijärvi, Fin. B13 8
Sevier, stm., Ut., U.S. D4 132
Sevier, East Fork, stm., Ut., U.S. F5 132
Sevier Desert, des., Ut., U.S. D4 132
Sevier Lake, l., Ut., U.S. B6 98
Sevierville, Tn., U.S. I2 114
Sevilla, Col. E4 86
Sevilla (Seville), Spain G5 20
Sevilla, co., Spain G5 20
Seville see Sevilla, Spain G5 20
Seville, Fl., U.S. G4 116
Sevlievo, Blg. F12 26
Sewāni, India D5 54
Seward, Ak., U.S. D10 140
Seward, Ne., U.S. G15 126
Seward, Pa., U.S. D7 114
Seward Peninsula, pen., Ak., U.S. C7 140
Sexsmith, Ab., Can. A12 138
Sextín, stm., Mex. B6 100
Seybaplaya, Mex. C2 102
Seychelles, ctry., Afr. k12 69b
Seychelles, is., Sey. k13 69b
Seydişehir, Tur. F14 28
Seydisfjörður, Ice. k32 8a
Seyhan (Sarus), stm., Tur. B6 58
Seyhan Barajı, res., Tur. A6 58
Seymour, Austl. K5 76
Seymour, S. Afr. H8 70
Seymour, Ct., U.S. C12 114
Seymour, In., U.S. F12 120
Seymour, Mo., U.S. G5 120
Seymour, Tx., U.S. H9 128
Seymour, Wi., U.S. D1 112
Sežana, Slvn. E10 22
Sézanne, Fr. F12 14
Sfákia, Grc. H7 28
Sfântu Gheorghe, Rom. D12 26
Sfântu Gheorghe, Brațul, stm., Rom. E16 26
Sfântu Gheorghe, Ostrovul, i., Rom. D16 26
Sfax, Tun. C7 64
's-Gravenhage (The Hague), Neth. B13 14
Sha, stm., China H7 42
Sha, stm., China E6 42
Shaanxi, state, China E3 42
Shabeelle (Shebelē Wenz, Wabē), stm., Afr. D8 66
Shabunda, D.R.C. E5 66
Shabwah, Yemen F6 56
Shache (Yarkant), China B12 56
Shackleton Ice Shelf, ice, Ant. B14 81
Shackleton Range, mts., Ant. D2 81
Shady Cove, Or., U.S. A3 134
Shady Grove, Fl., U.S. F2 116
Shadyside, Oh., U.S. E5 114
Shageluk, Ak., U.S. D8 140
Shag Rocks, r., S. Geor. J8 90
Shāhābād, India C3 53
Shāhābād, India C6 54
Shāhābād, India E7 54
Shāhāda, India H5 54
Shah Alam, Malay. K5 48
Shāhdādpur, Pak. F2 54
Shahdol, India G8 54
Shahe, China J3 42
Shahezhen, China A7 42
Shāhjahānpur, India E7 54
Shāh Kot, Pak. C4 54
Shāhpur, India C3 53
Shāhpur, Pak. B8 54
Shāhpura, India G8 54
Shāhpura, India E5 54
Shāhpura, India F5 54
Shahr-e Kord, Iran C7 56
Shaighālu, Pak. C2 54
Shājāpur, India G6 54
Shakawe, Bots. D3 68
Shaker Heights, Oh., U.S. G8 112
Shakespeare Island, i., On., Can. B10 118
Shaki, Nig. H5 64
Shakopee, Mn., U.S. G5 118
Shakotan-hantō, pen., Japan C14 38
Shaktoolik, Ak., U.S. D7 140
Shala, Lake see Shala Hāyk', l., Eth. F7 62
Shala Hāyk', l., Eth. F7 62
Shalalth, B.C., Can. F8 138
Shaler Mountains, mts., Can. A8 106
Shallowater, Tx., U.S. H6 128
Shaluli Shan, mts., China E4 36
Shām, Jabal ash-, mtn., Oman E8 56
Shamattawa, Mb., Can. D12 106
Shambe, Sudan F6 62
Shambu, Eth. F7 62
Shāmli, India D6 54
Shamokin, Pa., U.S. D9 114
Shamrock, Fl., U.S. G2 116
Shamrock, Tx., U.S. F8 128
Shamva, Zimb. D5 68
Shan, state, Mya. B4 48
Shancheng, China C2 42
Shandan, China D5 36
Shandī, Sudan D6 62
Shandong, state, China C7 42
Shandong Bandao (Shantung Peninsula), pen., China C9 42
Shand uul, mtn., Mong. C5 36
Shangani, Zimb. A9 70
Shangani, stm., Zimb. D4 68
Shangbahe, China F6 42
Shangcheng, China F6 42
Shangch'iu see Shangqiu, China D6 42
Shangchuan Dao, i., China K5 42
Shangdu, China C7 36
Shanghai, China F9 42
Shanghai, state, China F9 42
Shanghai Shih see Shanghai, state, China I4 38
Shanghang, China I7 42
Shanghe, China C7 42
Shangjao see Shangrao, China G7 42
Shangjin, China E4 42
Shanglin, China J3 42
Shangqing, China I8 42
Shangqiu, China D6 42
Shangqiu, China D6 42
Shangrao, China G7 42
Shangshui, China E6 42
Shangsi, China J2 42
Shangxian, China E3 42
Shangyi, China A6 42
Shangying, China B7 38
Shangyou Shuiku, res., China I6 42
Shangyu, China F9 42
Shangzhi, China B8 38
Shanhaiguan, China A8 42
Shanhaikwan see Shanhaiguan, China A8 42
Shanhetun, China B7 38
Shankou, China K3 42
Shannon, Il., U.S. B8 120
Shannon, Ms., U.S. C10 122
Shannon, stm., Ire. I3 12
Shannon Ø, i., Grnld. B22 141
Shannontown, S.C., U.S. C5 116
Shanshan, China C3 36
Shansi see Shanxi, state, China B5 42
Shantar Islands see Šantarskie ostrova, is., Russia E16 34
Shāntipur, India G12 54
Shantou, China J7 42
Shantung see Shandong, state, China C7 42
Shantung Peninsula see Shandong Bandao, pen., China C9 42
Shanwei, China J6 42
Shanxi, state, China B5 42
Shanyang, China E3 42
Shanyin, China B5 42
Shaoguan, China I5 42
Shaohing see Shaoxing, China G9 42
Shaohsing see Shaoxing, China G9 42
Shaokuan see Shaoguan, China I5 42
Shaoleng, stm., China C3 38
Shaowu, China H7 42
Shaoxing, China G9 42
Shaoyang, China H4 42
Shaqqā, Syria F7 58
Shaqrā', Sau. Ar. D6 56
Shaqrā', Yemen G6 56
Shara, gora, mtn., Asia A5 56
Shari-dake, mtn., Japan C16 38
Sharīn Gol, Mong. B6 36
Sharjah see Ash-Shāriqah, U.A.E. D8 56
Shark Bay, b., Austl. E2 74
Sharktooth Mountain, mtn., B.C., Can. D5 106
Sharm el-Sheikh, Egypt K5 58
Sharon, N.D., U.S. G16 124
Sharon, Pa., U.S. C5 114
Sharon, Tn., U.S. H9 120
Sharon, Wi., U.S. B9 120
Sharpe, Lake, res., S.D., U.S. C12 126
Shashe, stm., Afr. B9 70
Shashemenē, Eth. F7 62
Shashi, China F5 42
Shasi see Shashi, China F5 42
Shasta, Ca., U.S. C3 134
Shasta, Mount, vol., Ca., U.S. B3 134
Shasta Lake, res., Ca., U.S. C3 134
Shaṭṭ al-'Arab (Shaṭṭ ash-, stm., Asia D8 56
Shatt al-'Arab see Arvand ... B2 62
Shats'k, Ukr. E19 16
Shats'kyi Pryrodnyi Natsional'nyi Park, p.o.i., Ukr. E19 16
Shattuck, Ok., U.S. E9 128
Shaunavon, Sk., Can. E5 124
Shaw, Ms., U.S. D8 122
Shawan, China C2 36
Shawano, Wi., U.S. D1 112
Shawinigan, Qc., Can. D4 110
Shawinigan-Sud, Qc., Can. D4 110
Shawnee, Ks., U.S. E3 120
Shawnee, Oh., U.S. E3 114
Shawnee, Ok., U.S. B2 122
Shawneetown, Il., U.S. G9 120
Shawville, Qc., Can. C13 112
Shaxian, China H7 42
Shayang, China F5 42
Shay Gap, Austl. D4 74
Shaykh Miskīn, Syria F7 58
Shaykh 'Uthmān, Yemen G6 56
Shchūchinsk see Ščučinsk, Kaz. D12 32
She, stm., China F6 42
Shebelē Wenz, Wabē (Shabeelle), stm., Afr. C8 66
Sheberghān, Afg. B10 56
Sheboygan, Wi., U.S. E2 112
Sheboygan, stm., Wi., U.S. E1 112
Sheboygan Falls, Wi., U.S. E1 112
Shechem, hist., W.B. F6 58
Shediac, N.B., Can. D12 110
Shedin Peak, mtn., B.C., Can. D5 106
Sheenjek, stm., Ak., U.S. C11 140
Sheep Mountain, mtn., Az., U.S. K2 132
Sheerness, Eng., U.K. J13 12
Sheet Harbour, N.S., Can. F14 110
Sheffield, N.Z. F4 80
Sheffield, Eng., U.K. H11 12
Sheffield, Al., U.S. C11 122
Sheffield, Il., U.S. J9 118
Sheffield, Ia., U.S. B4 120
Sheffield, Pa., U.S. C6 114
Shegaon, India H6 54
Sheho, Sk., Can. C10 124
Shehong, China F1 42
Shekhupura, India F10 54
Shekhūpura, Pak. C5 54
Shekki see Zhongshan, China J5 42
Shelagyote Peak, mtn., B.C., Can. D5 106
Shelbina, Mo., U.S. E5 120
Shelburne, N.S., Can. G11 110
Shelburne, On., Can. D9 112
Shelburne Falls, Ma., U.S. B13 114
Shelby, Ia., U.S. C2 120
Shelby, Mi., U.S. E3 112
Shelby, Ms., U.S. D8 122
Shelby, Mt., U.S. B15 136
Shelby, Ne., U.S. F15 126
Shelby, N.C., U.S. A4 116
Shelbyville, Il., U.S. E9 120
Shelbyville, In., U.S. E12 120
Shelbyville, Mo., U.S. E5 120
Shelbyville, Tn., U.S. B12 122
Shelbyville, Lake, res., Il., U.S. E8 120
Sheldon, Ia., U.S. H3 118
Sheldon, Mo., U.S. G3 120
Shelek see Čilik, Kaz. F13 32
Shelekhov, Gulf of see Šelihova, zaliv, b., Russia D20 34
Shelikof Strait, strt., Ak., U.S. E9 140
Shell, stm., Mb., Can. C12 124
Shellbrook, Sk., Can. A7 124
Shell Creek, stm., Ne., U.S. F15 126
Shelley, B.C., Can. C8 138
Shellharbour, Austl. J8 76
Shell Lake, Wi., U.S. F7 118
Shellman, Ga., U.S. F14 122
Shellmouth Dam, dam, Mb., Can. D12 124
Shell Rock, Ia., U.S. B5 120
Shell Rock, stm., U.S. I6 118
Shellsburg, Ia., U.S. B5 120
Shelton, Ct., U.S. C12 114
Shelton, Ne., U.S. G14 126
Shemogue, N.B., Can. D12 110
Shemonaikha see Semonaiha, Kaz. D14 32
Shenandoah, Ia., U.S. D2 120
Shenandoah, Va., U.S. F7 114
Shenandoah, stm., U.S. E8 114
Shenandoah, North Fork, stm., Va., U.S. F7 114
Shenandoah, South Fork, stm., Va., U.S. F7 114
Shenandoah National Park, p.o.i., Va., U.S. F7 114
Shenchi, China B4 42
Shencottah, India G3 53
Shendam, Nig. H6 64
Shenge, S.L. H2 64
Shengsi Liedao, is., China I5 38
Shengxian, China G9 42
Shengze, China F9 42
Shenjing, China J5 42
Shenmu, China B4 42
Shenqiu, China E6 42
Shensi see Shaanxi, state, China E3 42
Shenton, Mount, mtn., Austl. E4 74
Shenxian, China C6 42
Shenyang (Mukden), China D5 38
Shenzhen, China J6 42
Sheoganj, India F4 54
Sheopur, India F6 54
Shepard, Ab., Can. E17 138
Shepherd, Mi., U.S. E5 112
Shepherd, state, Vanuatu k17 79d
Shepherd, Îles, is., Vanuatu k17 79d
Shepherdstown, W.V., U.S. E7 114
Shepherdsville, Ky., U.S. F12 120
Shepparton, Austl. K5 76
Sheppey, Isle of, i., Eng., U.K. J13 12
Sheqi, China E5 42
Sherard, Cape, c., Nu., Can. C10 141
Sherard Osborn Fjord, b., Grnld. A14 141
Sherborne, Eng., U.K. K10 12
Sherbro Island, i., S.L. H2 64
Sherbrooke, N.S., Can. E14 110
Sherbrooke, Qc., Can. E5 110
Sherburn, Mn., U.S. H4 118
Sherburne, N.Y., U.S. B10 114
Sheridan, Ar., U.S. C6 122
Sheridan, In., U.S. H3 112
Sheridan, Or., U.S. E3 136
Sheridan, Tx., U.S. E11 130
Sheridan, Wy., U.S. C6 126
Sherman, N.Y., U.S. B6 114
Sherman, Tx., U.S. D2 122
Sherman Mills, Me., U.S. E8 110
Sherman Mountain, mtn., Ar., U.S. I4 120
Sherman Station, Me., U.S. E8 110
Sherpur, Bngl. F12 54
Sherpur, Bngl. G13 54
Sherridon, Mb., Can. E10 106
Sherrill, N.Y., U.S. E14 112
Shertallai, India G3 53
's-Hertogenbosch, Neth. C14 14
Sherwood, Ar., U.S. C6 122
Sherwood, Oh., U.S. C1 114
Sherwood, Tn., U.S. B12 122
Sherwood Park, Ab., Can. C17 138
Sherwood Shores, Tx., U.S. D9 130
Shesh Gāv, Afg. B2 54
Shetland Islands, is., Scot., U.K. n17 12a
Shetrunji, stm., India H3 54
Shexian, China G8 42
Sheyang, China E9 42
Sheyenne, N.D., U.S. G14 124
Sheyenne, stm., N.D., U.S. H16 124
Sheykhābād, Afg. A2 54
Shiant Islands, is., Scot., U.K. D6 12
Shibām, Yemen F6 56
Shibata, Japan B12 40
Shibīn el-Kôm, Egypt H1 58
Shibing, China H2 42
Shibukawa, Japan C12 40
Shicheng, China H7 42
Shickley, Ne., U.S. G15 126
Shidai, China F7 42
Shidao, China C10 42
Shidler, Ok., U.S. E12 128
Shiga, state, Japan D9 40
Shigezhuang, China B6 42
Shigouyi, China C2 42
Shiguaigou, China A4 42
Shihch'i see Zhongshan, China J5 42
Shihchiachuang see Shijiazhuang, China C6 42
Shihkiachwang see Shijiazhuang, China C6 42
Shijiabao, China F1 42
Shijiazhuang, China C6 42
Shijiu Hu, l., China F8 42
Shikārpur, India D2 53
Shikārpur, Pak. E2 54
Shikohābād, India E7 54
Shikoku, i., Japan F6 40
Shikoku-sanchi, mts., Japan F6 40
Shikotsu-ko, l., Japan C14 38
Shiliguri, India E12 54
Shillelagh, Ire. I6 12
Shillington, Pa., U.S. H13 112
Shillong, India F13 54
Shiloh, Oh., U.S. I5 112
Shiloh see Saylūn, Khirbat, hist., W.B. F6 58
Shilong, China J5 42
Shima, Japan E9 40
Shimabara, Japan G3 40
Shimada, Japan E11 40
Shimane, state, Japan D5 40
Shimbiris, mtn., Som. B9 66
Shimen, China G4 42
Shimian, China F5 36
Shimizu, Japan D11 40
Shimla, India C6 54
Shimminato, Japan C10 40
Shimoda, Japan E11 40
Shimodate, Japan C13 40
Shimoga, India E2 53
Shimonoseki, Japan F3 40
Shimono-shima, i., Japan E2 40
Shin, Loch, l., Scot., U.K. C8 12
Shinano, stm., Japan B11 40
Shīndand, Afg. C9 56
Shingbwiyang, Mya. C8 46
Shingū, Japan F9 40
Shingū, Japan E7 40
Shingwidzi, S. Afr. C10 70
Shingwidzi (Singuédeze), stm., Afr. C10 70
Shinji-ko, l., Japan D5 40
Shinjō, Japan A13 40
Shinyanga, Tan. E6 66
Shiocton, Wi., U.S. G10 118
Shiogama, Japan A14 40
Shiojiri, Japan C10 40
Shiono-misaki, c., Japan F8 40
Shioya-zaki, c., Japan C13 40
Shiping, China G5 36
Shiping, China G2 42
Shipka Pass see Šipčenski Prohod, p., Blg. G12 26
Shipman, Va., U.S. G7 114
Shippegan, N.B., Can. C12 110
Shippensburg, Pa., U.S. D8 114
Shiprock, N.M., U.S. G8 132
Ship Rock, mtn., N.M., U.S. G8 132
Shipshaw, stm., Qc., Can. B6 110
Shipu, China G9 42
Shiquan, China E3 42
Shirahama, Japan F8 40
Shirakawa, Japan B13 40
Shīrāz, Iran D7 56
Shirbīn, Egypt G2 58
Shiretoko-misaki, c., Japan B16 38
Shīr Kūh, mtn., Iran C7 56
Shirley, In., U.S. I4 112
Shiroishi, Japan A13 40
Shirone, Japan B11 40
Shirpur, India H5 54
Shīrvān, Iran B8 56
Shisanzhan, China F14 34
Shishaldin Volcano, vol., Ak., U.S. F7 140
Shishi, China I8 42
Shishmaref, Ak., U.S. C6 140
Shishou, China G5 42
Shitang, China I4 42
Shiv, India E3 54
Shively, Ky., U.S. F12 120
Shivpuri, India F6 54
Shivta, Horvot (Subeita), hist., Isr. H5 58
Shivwits Plateau, plat., Az., U.S. G3 132
Shiwu, China C6 38
Shiyan, China E4 42
Shizhu, China G8 42
Shizugawa, Japan A14 40
Shizui, China C6 38
Shizunai, Japan C15 38
Shizuoka, Japan E11 40
Shizuoka, state, Japan E10 40
Shkodër, Alb. B13 24
Shkodra see Shkodër, Alb. B13 24
Shkumbin, stm., Alb. C14 24
Shō, stm., Japan C10 40
Shoal, stm., Fl., U.S. G12 122
Shoal Creek, stm., U.S. H3 120
Shoal Creek, stm., Mo., U.S. E4 120
Shoalhaven, stm., Austl. J8 76
Shoal Lake, l., Can. B3 118
Shoals, In., U.S. F11 120
Shoalwater Bay, b., Austl. D8 76
Shōbara, Japan E6 40
Shōdo-shima, i., Japan E7 40
Sholingnur, India E4 53
Shorāpur, India C3 53
Shoreacres, B.C., Can. G13 138
Shorewood, Wi., U.S. E2 112
Shorkot, Pak. C3 54
Shortland Island, i., Sol. Is. d6 79b
Shortland Islands, is., Sol. Is. d6 79b
Shoshone, Id., U.S. H12 136
Shoshone, stm., Wy., U.S. C4 126
Shoshone, South Fork, stm., Wy., U.S. G17 136
Shoshone Lake, l., Wy., U.S. F15 136
Shoshone Mountains, mts., Nv., U.S. E8 134
Shoshone Peak, mtn., Nv., U.S. G9 134
Shoshone Range, mts., Nv., U.S. C9 134
Shoshong, Bots. C8 70
Shostka, Ukr. D4 32
Shouchang, China G8 42
Shouguang, China C8 42
Shouning, China H8 42
Shouxian, China E7 42
Shouyang, China C5 42
Show Low, Az., U.S. I6 132
Shqipëria see Albania, ctry., Eur. C14 24
Shreve, Oh., U.S. D4 114
Shreveport, La., U.S. E5 122
Shrewsbury, Eng., U.K. I10 12
Shri Dūngargarh, India D4 54
Shri Mohangarh, India E3 54
Shū see Šu, Kaz. F12 32
Shū see Ču, stm., Asia F11 32
Shu, stm., China D8 42
Shuajingsi, China B9 46
Shuangcheng, China B7 38
Shuangfeng, China H5 42
Shuanggou, China E5 42
Shuanggou, China D7 42
Shuangji, stm., China D5 42
Shuangjiang, China G4 36
Shuangliao, China C5 38
Shuangpai, China I4 42

Name | Map Ref. | Page

Shuangshutai, China C4 38
Shuangyang, China C6 38
Shuangyashan, China B11 36
Shubrâ el-Kheima, Egypt H1 58
Shubuta, Ms., U.S. F10 122
Shucheng, China F7 42
Shuibatang, China G2 42
Shuiji, China H8 42
Shuijingtang, China G2 42
Shuikoushan, China H5 42
Shuitou, China I8 42
Shuiye, China C5 42
Shujāābād, Pak. D3 54
Shujālpur, India G6 54
Shuksan, Mount, mtn., Wa., U.S. B5 136
Shulan, China B7 38
Shulaps Peak, mtn., B.C., Can. F8 138
Shule, China B12 56
Shule, stm., China C4 36
Shumagin Islands, is., Ak., U.S. F7 140
Shunchang, China H7 42
Shunde, China J5 42
Shungnak, Ak., U.S. C8 140
Shunyi, China A7 42
Shuqualak, Ms., U.S. E10 122
Shurkhua, Mya. A1 48
Shurugwi, Zimb. D5 68
Shūshtar, Iran C6 56
Shuswap, stm., B.C., Can. F12 138
Shuswap Lake, l., B.C., Can. F11 138
Shuwak, Sudan E7 62
Shuyak Island, i., Ak., U.S. E9 140
Shuyang, China D8 42
Shwangliao see Liaoyuan, China C6 38
Shwebo, Mya. A2 48
Shwegun, Mya. D3 48
Shwegyin, Mya. D3 48
Shymkent see Šymkent, Kaz. F11 32
Shyok, India A7 54
Shyok, stm., Asia B4 46
Si, stm., China D7 42
Sia, Indon. G9 44
Siāhān Range, mts., Pak. D9 56
Siak, stm., Indon. C2 50
Siak Sri Indrapura, Indon. C3 50
Siālkot, Pak. B5 54
Siam see Thailand, ctry., Asia E5 48
Siam, Gulf of see Thailand, Gulf of, b., Asia G5 48
Sian see Xi'an, China D3 42
Siangtan see Xiangtan, China H5 42
Sianów, Pol. B12 16
Siantan, Pulau, i., Indon. B4 50
Siapa, stm., Ven. G9 86
Siargao Island, i., Phil. F6 52
Siasconset, Ma., U.S. C15 114
Siasi, Phil. H3 52
Siasi Island, i., Phil. H3 52
Siaškotan, ostrov, i., Russia G19 34
Siau, Pulau, i., Indon. E7 44
Šiauliai, Lith. E6 10
Sibaj, Russia D9 32
Sibayi, Lake, l., S. Afr. E11 70
Šibenik, Cro. G12 22
Siberia see Sibir', reg., Russia C12 34
Siberut, Pulau, i., Indon. D1 50
Sibi, Pak. D10 56
Sibigo, Indon. K2 48
Sibir', reg., Russia C12 34
Sibircevo, Russia B10 38
Sibirjakova, ostrov, i., Russia B4 34
Sibiti, Congo E2 66
Sibiu, Rom. D11 26
Sibiu, state, Rom. D11 26
Sibley, Ia., U.S. H3 118
Sibley, La., U.S. E5 122
Sibley, Ms., U.S. F7 122
Sibley Peninsula, pen., On., Can. C10 118
Sibolga, Indon. C1 50
Sibsāgar, India C7 46
Sibu, Malay. B7 50
Sibuguey Bay, b., Phil. G4 52
Sibut, C.A.R. C3 66
Sibutu Island, i., Phil. H2 52
Sibutu Passage, strt., Asia H2 52
Sibuyan Island, i., Phil. D4 52
Sibuyan Sea, Phil. D4 52
Sicapoo, Mount, mtn., Phil. B3 52
Siccus, stm., Austl. H2 76
Sichang see Xichang, China F5 36
Si Chon, Thai. H4 48
Sichuan, state, China E5 36
Sichuan Pendi, bas., China F1 42
Sichuanzhai, China A5 48
Sicilia, state, Italy F8 24
Sicilia (Sicily), i., Italy G7 24
Sicily see Sicilia, state, Italy F8 24
Sicily see Sicilia, i., Italy G7 24
Sicily, Strait of, strt. G5 24
Sicily Island, La., U.S. F7 122
Sicuani, Peru F3 84
Sidareja, Indon. G6 50
Sidas, Indon. C6 50
Siddhapur, India G4 54
Siddipet, India B4 53
Sidéradougou, Burkina G4 64
Siderno, Italy F10 24
Sideròpolis, Braz. D13 92
Síderos, Ákra, c., Grc. H9 28
Sidhauli, India E8 54
Sidhi, India F8 54
Sîdi Barrâni, Egypt A5 62
Sidi bel Abbès, Alg. B4 64
Sidi-Ifni, Mor. D2 64
Siding Spring Mountain, mtn., Austl. H7 76
Sidirókastro, Grc. B6 28
Sidi Sâlim, Egypt G1 58
Sidlaghatta, India E3 53
Sidley, Mount, mtn., Ant. C28 81
Sidmouth, Eng., U.K. K9 12
Sidnaw, Mi., U.S. E10 118
Sidney, B.C., Can. H7 138
Sidney, Il., U.S. D9 120
Sidney, Mt., U.S. G9 124
Sidney, Ne., U.S. F10 126
Sidney, N.Y., U.S. B10 114
Sidney, Oh., U.S. D1 114
Sidney Lanier, Lake, res., Ga., U.S. B2 116
Sidon see Şaydā, Leb. E6 58
Sidon, Ms., U.S. D8 122
Sidorovsk, Russia A14 32
Sidra, Gulf of see Surt, Khalīj, b., Libya A3 62
Sidrolândia, Braz. D6 90
Siedlce, Pol. D18 16
Siedlce, state, Pol. D17 16
Siegburg, Ger. F3 16
Siegen, Ger. F4 16
Siemianowice Śląskie, Pol. F15 16
Siĕmpang, Camb. E8 48
Siĕmréab, Camb. F6 48
Siena, Italy G8 22
Sienyang see Xianyang, China D3 42
Sieradz, Pol. E14 16
Sieradz, state, Pol. E14 16
Sieraków, Pol. D12 16
Sierpc, Pol. D15 16
Sierra Blanca, Tx., U.S. C2 130
Sierra Blanca Peak, mtn., N.M., U.S. H3 128
Sierra Chica, Arg. H7 92
Sierra Colorada, Arg. H3 90
Sierra Gorda, Chile D3 90
Sierra Leone, ctry., Afr. H2 64
Sierra Mojada, Mex. G4 130
Sierra Nevada see Nevada, Sierra, mts., Ca., U.S. F6 134
Sierra Nevada, Parque Nacional, p.o.i., Ven. C6 86
Sierra Vista, Az., U.S. L6 132
Sierre, Switz. D4 22
Siesta Key, Fl., U.S. I3 116
Sífnos, i., Grc. F7 28
Sifón Villanueva, Mex. G7 130
Sig, Russia D16 8
Sigatoka, Fiji q18 79e
Sigep, Indon. D1 50
Sighetu Marmației, Rom. B10 26
Sighișoara, Rom. C11 26
Siglan, Russia E19 34
Sigli, Indon. J2 48
Siglufjördur, Ice. j30 8a
Sigmaringen, Ger. H5 16
Signal Mountain, Tn., U.S. B13 122
Signal Mountain, mtn., Vt., U.S. F4 110
Signy, sci., Ant. B36 81
Sigourney, Ia., U.S. C5 120
Sigsig, Ec. D2 84
Siguanea, Ensenada de la, b., Cuba B6 102
Siguatepeque, Hond. E3 102
Sigüenza, Spain C8 20
Siguiri, Gui. G3 64
Sigulda, Lat. C7 10
Sigurd, Ut., U.S. E5 132
Siguri Falls, wtfl, Tan. F7 66
Sihabuhabu, Dolok, mtn., Indon. B1 50
Sihanoukville see Kâmpóng Saôm, Camb. G6 48
Sihor, India H3 54
Sihorā, India G8 54
Sihote-Alin', mts., Russia E17 30
Sihtovo, Russia E15 10
Sihui, China J5 42
Siirt, Tur. B5 56
Sija, Russia E19 8
Sijunjung, Indon. D2 50
Sikandarābād, India D6 54
Sikanni Chief, stm., B.C., Can. D6 106
Sikao, Thai. I4 48
Sīkar, India E5 54
Sikasso, Mali G3 64
Sikeston, Mo., U.S. H8 120
Sikhote-Alin Mountains see Sihote-Alin', mts., Russia E17 30
Sikiang see Xi, stm., China J5 42
Siking see Xi'an, China D3 42
Síkinos, i., Grc. G8 28
Sikkim, state, India E12 54
Sikonge, Tan. F6 66
Sikotan, ostrov (Shikotan-tō), i., Russia C17 38
Siktjah, Russia B13 34
Sikuati, Malay. G1 52
Sikyón, hist., Grc. F5 28
Sil, stm., Spain B3 20
Šila, Russia E7 34
Šilalė, Lith. E5 10
Silao, Mex. E8 100
Silas, Al., U.S. F10 122
Silaut, Indon. E2 50
Silay, Phil. E4 52
Silchar, India F14 54
Şile, Tur. B12 28
Siler City, N.C., U.S. I6 114
Sileru, stm., India C5 53
Silesia, hist. reg., Eur. F13 16
Siletyteniz, ozero, l., Kaz. D12 32
Siletz, Or., U.S. F3 136
Siletz, stm., Or., U.S. F3 136
Silgadhī, Nepal D8 54
Silghāt, India E14 54
Silhouette, i., Sey. j13 69b
Siliana, Tun. H3 24
Siliana, Oued, stm., Tun. I3 24
Silifke, Tur. B4 58
Siling Co, l., China C12 54
Silistra, Blg. E14 26
Silivri, Tur. B11 28
Siljan, l., Swe. F6 8
Šilka, Russia F12 34
Šilka, stm., Russia F12 34
Silkeborg, Den. H3 8
Sillamäe, Est. A10 10
Sillem Island, i., Nu., Can. A16 106
Sillian, Aus. D9 22
Sillon de Talbert, pen., Fr. F5 14
Šilovići, Russia E15 10
Silsbee, Tx., U.S. G4 122
Silton, Sk., Can. D9 124
Siluas, Indon. C6 50
Šilutė, Lith. E4 10
Silvânia, Braz. I1 88
Silvassa, India H4 54
Silver, Tx., U.S. B7 130
Silver Bank Passage, strt., N.A. B12 102
Silver Bell, Az., U.S. K5 132
Silver City, N.M., U.S. K8 132
Silver City, N.C., U.S. B6 116
Silver Creek, Ms., U.S. F9 122
Silver Creek, Ne., U.S. F15 126
Silver Creek, stm., Az., U.S. I6 132
Silver Creek, stm., Or., U.S. G7 136
Silverdale, Wa., U.S. C4 136
Silver Lake, Ks., U.S. E2 120
Silver Lake, Mn., U.S. G4 118
Silver Lake, Wi., U.S. F1 112
Silver Lake, l., Or., U.S. G7 136
Silver Lake, l., Or., U.S. G5 136
Silver Spring, Md., U.S. E8 114
Silver Star Mountain, mtn., Wa., U.S. B6 136
Silverthrone Mountain, vol., B.C., Can. E4 138
Silverton, Austl. H3 76
Silverton, B.C., Can. G13 138
Silverton, Co., U.S. F9 132
Silverton, Tx., U.S. G7 128
Silvi, Italy H11 22
Silvia, Col. F3 86
Silvies, stm., Or., U.S. G7 136
Šimanovsk, Russia F14 34
Simao, China A5 48
Simão Dias, Braz. F6 88
Simav, Tur. D11 28
Simav, stm., Tur. C11 28
Simbach, Ger. H8 16
Simbo Island, i., Sol. Is. e7 79b
Simcoe, On., Can. F9 112
Simcoe, Lake, l., On., Can. D10 112
Simdega, India G10 54
Simeria, Rom. D10 26
Simeulue, Pulau, i., Indon. K2 48
Simferopol', Ukr. G15 6
Simikot, Nepal C8 54
Similkameen, stm., N.A. G10 138
Simití, Col. D4 86
Simi Valley, Ca., U.S. I7 134
Simizu see Shimizu, Japan D11 40
Simla, Co., U.S. B4 128
Simmern, Ger. G3 16
Simmie, Sk., Can. E5 124
Simms, Mt., U.S. C15 136
Simnas, Lith. F6 10
Simoca, Arg. C5 92
Simões, Braz. D5 88
Simojärvi, l., Fin. C12 8
Simojovel, Mex. G12 100
Simon, Lac, l., Qc., Can. E1 110
Simonette, stm., Ab., Can. A12 138
Simonoseki see Shimonoseki, Japan F3 40
Simonstad see Simon's Town, S. Afr. I4 70
Simon's Town, S. Afr. I4 70
Simoom Sound, B.C., Can. F4 138
Simpang, Indon. D3 50
Simpang-kiri, stm., Indon. K3 48
Simplon Pass, p., Switz. D4 22
Simpson Desert, des., Austl. D7 74
Simpson Island, i., On., Can. C11 118
Simpson Peninsula, pen., Nu., Can. B13 106
Simpson Strait, strt., Nu., Can. B11 106
Simpsonville, S.C., U.S. B3 116
Simrishamn, Swe. I6 8
Simsonbaai, Neth. Ant. A1 105a
Simunjan, Malay. C7 50
Simušir, ostrov, i., Russia G19 34
Sīna, stm., India B2 53
Sinabang, Indon. K3 48
Sinabung, Gunung, vol., Indon. K4 48
Sinai (Sinai Peninsula), pen., Egypt J4 58
Sinai, Mount see Mûsa, Gebel, mtn., Egypt J5 58
Sinai, Mount, vol., Gren. q10 105e
Sinaia, Rom. D12 26
Sinai Peninsula see Sinai, pen., Egypt J4 58
Sinajana, Guam j10 78c
Sinaloa, state, Mex. C5 100
Sinaloa, stm., Mex. C5 100
Sinamaica, Ven. B6 86
Sinan, China H3 42
Sinanpaşa, Tur. E13 28
Sīnāwin, Libya A2 62
Sincan, Tur. D15 28
Sincé, Col. B2 84
Sincelejo, Col. C4 86
Sinch'ang-ŭp, Kor., N. D8 38
Sin-ch'on, Kor., N. E6 38
Sinclair, Wy., U.S. B9 132
Sinclair, Lake, res., Ga., U.S. C2 116
Sinclair Mills, B.C., Can. B9 138
Sind, state, Pak. F2 54
Sind, stm., India F7 54
Sindañgan, Phil. F4 52
Sindangbarang, Indon. G5 50
Sindara, Gabon E2 66
Sindari, India F3 54
Sindelfingen, Ger. H4 16
Sindhnūr, India D3 53
Sindhulī Māñdi, Nepal E10 54
Sindingale, Mya. C2 48
Sindor, Russia B8 32
Sines, Port. G2 20
Sinfra, C. Iv. H3 64
Singalamwe, Nmb. D3 68
Singapore, Sing. C3 50
Singapore, ctry., Asia L6 48
Singapore, Strait of, strt., Asia C4 50
Singaraja, Indon. H9 50
Sing Buri, Thai. E5 48
Singen, Ger. I4 16
Singida, Tan. E6 66
Singitic Gulf see Ayíou Órous, Kólpos, b., Grc. C6 28
Singkaling Hkāmti, Mya. C8 46
Singkang, Indon. F11 50
Singkawang, Indon. C6 50
Singkep, Pulau, i., Indon. D4 50
Singkil, Indon. K3 48
Singkuang, Indon. C1 50
Singleton, Austl. I8 76
Singleton, Mount, mtn., Austl. E3 74
Singuédeze (Shingwidzi), stm., Afr. C10 70
Sining see Xining, China D5 36
Sinj, Cro. G13 22
Sinjah, Sudan E6 62
Sinjai, Indon. F12 50
Sinjaja, stm., Eur. D11 10
Sinjaja, stm., Russia D14 34
Sinjuga, Russia E12 34
Sinkāt, Sudan D7 62
Sinkiang see Xinjiang, state, China A5 46
Sinnamahoning, Pa., U.S. C7 114
Sinnamary, Fr. Gu. B7 84
Sinnar, India B2 53
Sinnûris, Egypt I1 58
Sinnyŏng, Kor., S. C1 40
Sinoie, Lacul, l., Rom. E15 26
Sinop, Tur. A4 56
Sinsheim, Ger. G4 16
Sinsiang see Xinxiang, China D5 42
Sinskoe, Russia D14 34
Sintang, Indon. C7 50
Sint Christoffelberg, hill, Neth. Ant. p21 104g
Sint Eustatius, i., Neth. Ant. B1 105a
Sint Helenabaai, b., S. Afr. H3 70
Sint Kruis, Neth. Ant. p21 104g
Sint Maarten (Saint-Martin), i., N.A. A1 105a
Sint Nicolaas, Aruba p20 104g
Sint-Niklaas, Bel. C12 14
Sintra, Port. F1 20
Sint-Truiden, Bel. D14 14
Sinú, stm., Col. C4 86
Sinŭiju, Kor., N. D6 38
Sió, stm., Hung. C5 26
Siocon, Phil. G4 52
Siófok, Hung. C5 26
Sion, Switz. D4 22
Siorapaluk, Grnld. B12 141
Sioux Center, Ia., U.S. H2 118
Sioux City, Ia., U.S. B1 120
Sioux Falls, S.D., U.S. H2 118
Sioux Lookout, On., Can. A6 118
Sioux Narrows, On., Can. B4 118
Sioux Rapids, Ia., U.S. B2 120
Sipalay, Phil. F4 52
Šipan, Otok, i., Cro. H14 22
Sipapo, stm., Ven. E8 86
Siparia, Trin. s12 105f
Šipčenski Prohod (Shipka Pass), p., Blg. G12 26
Šipicyno, Russia F22 8
Siping, China C6 38
Sipiwesk Lake, l., Mb., Can. D11 106
Siple, Mount, mtn., Ant. C28 81
Siple Island, i., Ant. C28 81
Si Prachan, Thai. E4 48
Sipsey, stm., Al., U.S. D10 122
Šipunskij, mys, c., Russia F21 34
Sipura, Pulau, i., Indon. E1 50
Siqueira Campos, Braz. A12 92
Siquia, stm., Nic. F5 102
Siquijor, Phil. F4 52
Siquijor Island, i., Phil. F4 52
Siquirres, C.R. G6 102
Sira, India E3 53
Šira, Russia D16 32
Sira, stm., Nor. G2 8
Si Racha, Thai. F5 48
Siracusa, Italy G9 24
Sirāhā, Nepal E11 54
Sirājganj, Bngl. F12 54
Şīr Banī Yās, i., U.A.E. E7 56
Sirdar, B.C., Can. G14 138
Sir Douglas, Mount, mtn., Can. F15 138
Sir Edward Pellew Group, is., Austl. C7 74
Siret, Rom. B12 26
Siret (Seret), stm., Eur. A12 26
Sirḥān, Wādī as-, val., Sau. Ar. H8 58
Sirik, Tanjong, c., Malay. B7 50
Sirikit Reservoir, res., Thai. D5 48
Sirino, Monte, mtn., Italy D9 24
Sir James MacBrien, Mount, mtn., N.T., Can. C4 106
Sīrjān, Iran D8 56
Sirkeli, Tur. C15 28
Sirocina, Bela. E12 10
Şirohi, India F4 54
Širokovo, Russia C17 32
Sironj, India F6 54
Sırpsındığı, Tur. B9 28
Sīrrī, Jazīreh-ye, i., Iran D7 56
Sirsa, India D5 54
Sir Sandford, Mount, mtn., B.C., Can. E13 138
Sirsi, India D2 53
Sirsilla, India B4 53
Sirte, Gulf of see Surt, Khalīj, b., Libya A3 62
Sir Timothy's Hill, hill, St. K./N. C2 105a
Şirupa, stm., Mex. G8 98
Širvintos, Lith. E7 10
Sir Wilfrid Laurier, Mount, mtn., B.C., Can. D11 138
Sisaba, mtn., Tan. F6 66
Sisak, Cro. E13 22
Si Sa Ket, Thai. E7 48
Sishen, S. Afr. E6 70
Sishilijie, China G7 42
Sishui, China D7 42
Sisib Lake, l., Mb., Can. B14 124
Sisimiut see Holsteinsborg, Grnld. D15 141
Siskiyou Pass, p., Or., U.S. A3 134
Sisseton, S.D., U.S. F1 118
Sīstān, reg., Asia C9 56
Sister Bay, Wi., U.S. C2 112
Sisteron, Fr. E11 18
Sisters, Or., U.S. F5 136
Sistersville, W.V., U.S. E5 114
Sit', stm., Russia B20 10
Sītāmarhi, India E10 54
Sītāpur, India E8 54
Siteia, Grc. H9 28
Siteki, Swaz. E10 70
Si Thep, hist., Thai. E5 48
Sithoniá, pen., Grc. C6 28
Sitidgi Lake, l., N.T., Can. B4 106
Sítio d'Abadia, Braz. H2 88
Sitka, Ak., U.S. E12 140
Sitkalidak Island, i., Ak., U.S. E9 140
Sittard, Neth. C14 14
Sitten see Sion, Switz. D4 22
Sittoung, stm., Mya. C3 48
Sittwe, Mya. D7 46
Siuri, India G11 54
Siuslaw, stm., Or., U.S. G3 136
Sivaganga, India G4 53
Sivakāsi, India G3 53
Sivaki, Russia F14 34
Şivas, Tur. B4 56
Šiveluč, vulkan, vol., Russia E21 34
Siverek, Tur. B4 56
Siverskij, Russia A12 10
Sivrihisar, Tur. D14 28
Siwa, Egypt B5 62
Siwalik Range, mts., India C6 54
Siwān, India E10 54
Sixian, China E7 42
Sixth Cataract see Sablūkah, Shallāl as-, wtfl, Sudan D6 62
Siyang, China E8 42
Sizuoka see Shizuoka, Japan E11 40
Sjælland, i., Den. I4 8
Sjalec, Bela. G13 10
Sjamža, Russia F19 8
Sjarheevičy, Bela. G10 10
Sjas', stm., Russia A15 10
Sjas'stroj, Russia F15 8
Sjenica, Yugo. F7 26
Sjuzikozero, Russia F17 8
Skærfjorden, b., Grnld. B22 141
Skaftafell Nasjonalpark, p.o.i., Ice. k31 8a
Skagafjörður, b., Ice. j31 8a
Skagen, Den. H4 8
Skagerrak, strt., Eur. H3 8
Skagit, stm., N.A. H8 138
Skagway, Ak., U.S. E12 140
Skaistkalne, Lat. D7 10
Skalbmierz, Pol. F16 16
Skalino, Russia G18 8
Skalistyj Golec, gora, mtn., Russia E12 34
Skalka, l., Swe. C8 8
Skåne, state, Swe. H5 8
Skārdu, Pak. B12 56
Skarszewy, Pol. B14 16
Skarżysko-Kamienna, Pol. E16 16
Skaudvilė, Lith. E5 10
Skawina, Pol. F15 16
Skeena, stm., B.C., Can. B1 138
Skeena Crossing, B.C., Can. A3 138
Skeena Mountains, mts., B.C., Can. D5 106
Skegness, Eng., U.K. H13 12
Skei, Nor. F2 8
Skeleton Coast, cst., Nmb. B1 70
Skellefteå, Swe. D9 8
Skellefteälven, stm., Swe. D8 8
Skellytown, Tx., U.S. F7 128
Skerryvore, r., Scot., U.K. E5 12
Ski, Nor. G4 8
Skiatook, Ok., U.S. H1 120
Skibbereen, Ire. J3 12
Skidal', Bela. G7 10
Skiddaw, mtn., Eng., U.K. G9 12
Skidmore, Tx., U.S. F10 130
Skien, Nor. G3 8
Skierniewice, Pol. E16 16
Skierniewice, state, Pol. D16 16
Skikda, Alg. B6 64
Skilak Lake, l., Ak., U.S. D9 140
Skillet Fork, stm., Il., U.S. F9 120
Skinnastaðir, Ice. j31 8a
Skipton, Austl. K4 76
Skipton, Eng., U.K. H10 12
Skive, Den. H3 8
Skjálfandafljót, stm., Ice. k31 8a
Šklad, Russia B13 34
Šklou, Bela. F13 10
Škofja Loka, Slvn. D11 22
Skoganvarre, Nor. B11 8
Skoganvarri see Skoganvarre, Nor. B11 8
Skokie, Il., U.S. F2 112
Skón, Camb. F7 48
Skópelos, i., Grc. D6 28
Skopin, Russia D5 32
Skopje, Mac. A4 28
Skoplje see Skopje, Mac. A4 28
Skórcz, Pol. C14 16
Skövde, Swe. G5 8
Skowhegan, Me., U.S. F7 110
Skownan, Mb., Can. C14 124
Skriplivka, Russia C13 10
Skrudaliena, Lat. E9 10
Skudeneshavn, Nor. G1 8
Skukuza, S. Afr. D10 70
Skull Valley, Az., U.S. I4 132
Skuna, can., Ms., U.S. D9 122
Skunk, stm., Ia., U.S. D6 120
Skuodas, Lith. D4 10
Skuratovskij, Russia F20 10
Skwierzyna, Pol. D11 16
Skye, Island of, i., Scot., U.K. D6 12
Skyland, N.C., U.S. A3 116
Skyring, Península, pen., Chile I1 90
Skyring, Seno, strt., Chile J2 90
Skýros, i., Grc. E7 28
Slabada, Bela. G11 10
Slagelse, Den. I4 8
Slagnäs, Swe. D8 8
Slamet, Gunung, vol., Indon. G6 50
Slancy, Russia A11 10
Slaney, stm., Ire. H6 12
Slănic, Rom. D12 26
Slano, Cro. H14 22
Slaný, Czech Rep. F10 16
Slater, Ia., U.S. C4 120
Slater, Mo., U.S. E4 120
Slatina, Cro. E14 22
Slatina, Rom. E11 26
Slaughter, La., U.S. G7 122
Slaunae, Bela. F12 10
Slautnoe, Russia D22 34
Slave, stm., Can. C8 106
Slave Coast, cst., Afr. H5 64
Slave Lake, Ab., Can. A16 138
Slavgorod, Russia D13 32
Slavjanka, Russia C9 38
Slavjansk-na-Kubani, Russia E5 32
Slavkoviči, Russia C12 10
Slavonia see Slavonija, hist. reg., Cro. E14 22
Slavonija, hist. reg., Cro. E14 22
Slavonski Brod, Cro. E15 22
Slavsk, Russia E4 10
Sławno, Pol. B12 16
Slayton, Mn., U.S. G3 118
Sleaford, Eng., U.K. H12 12
Sledge, Ms., U.S. C8 122
Sledzjuki, Bela. G13 10
Sleeper Islands, is., Nu., Can. D14 106
Sleeping Bear Dunes National Lakeshore, p.o.i., Mi., U.S. D3 112
Sleepy Eye, Mn., U.S. G4 118
Ślesin, Pol. D14 16
Slidell, La., U.S. G9 122
Slide Mountain, mtn., N.Y., U.S. B11 114
Sliema, Malta I8 24
Slievekimalta, mtn., Ire. I4 12
Sligeach see Sligo, Ire. G4 12
Sligo, Ire. G4 12
Sligo, Pa., U.S. C6 114
Sligo, state, Ire. G4 12
Sligo Bay, b., Ire. G4 12
Slinger, Wi., U.S. H10 118
Slino, ozero, l., Russia C16 10
Slippery Rock, Pa., U.S. C5 114
Šlissel'burg, Russia A13 10
Slīteres Rezervāts, Lat. C5 10
Sliven, Blg. G13 26
Sljudjanka, Russia D18 32
Sloan, Nv., U.S. H1 132
Slobidka, Ukr. B16 26
Slobodskoj, Russia C8 32
Slobozia, Mol. C16 26
Slobozia, Rom. E14 26
Slobozia, Rom. F12 26
Slocan, B.C., Can. G13 138
Slocan Lake, l., B.C., Can. G13 138
Slocomb, Al., U.S. F13 122
Słomniki, Pol. F15 16
Slonim, Bela. G8 10
Slough, Eng., U.K. J12 12
Slovakia, ctry., Eur. H14 16
Slovenia, ctry., Eur. E11 22
Slovenija see Slovenia, ctry., Eur. E11 22
Slovenské rudohorie, mts., Slov. H15 16
Slov'ians'k, Ukr. E5 32
Slovinka, Russia G20 8
Słowiński Park Narodowy, p.o.i., Pol. B13 16
Słubice, Pol. D10 16
Sluč, stm., Bela. H10 10
Sluck, Bela. G10 10
Šluknov, Czech Rep. E10 16
Słupca, Pol. D13 16
Słupia, stm., Pol. B13 16
Słupsk (Stolp), Pol. B13 16
Słupsk, state, Pol. B13 16
Slutsk see Sluck, Bela. G10 10
Smålandsfarvandet, b., Den. I4 8
Smalininkai, Lith. E5 10
Smaljavičy, Bela. F10 10
Smallwood Reservoir, res., Nf., Can. E18 106
Smalouka, Bela. E13 10
Smarhon', Bela. F9 10
Smederevo, Yugo. E7 26
Smeralda, Costa, cst., Italy C3 24
Smethport, Pa., U.S. C7 114
Šmidovič, Russia G15 34
Šmidta, poluostrov, pen., Russia F17 34
Śmigiel, Pol. D12 16
Smila, Ukr. E4 32
Smiley, Sk., Can. C4 124
Smiley, Tx., U.S. E10 130
Smiltene, Lat. C8 10
Smith, Ab., Can. A16 138
Smith, stm., U.S. H5 114
Smith, stm., Ca., U.S. B2 134
Smith, stm., Mt., U.S. C15 136
Smith, stm., Or., U.S. G2 136
Smith Arm, b., N.T., Can. B6 106
Smith Bay, b., Nu., Can. B10 141
Smith Bay, b., Ak., U.S. B9 140
Smith Canyon, val., Co., U.S. D5 128
Smithers, B.C., Can. B3 138
Smithfield, S. Afr. G8 70
Smithfield, N.C., U.S. A7 116
Smithfield, Va., U.S. G9 114
Smith Island see Sumisu-jima, i., Japan E13 36
Smith Island, i., N.C., U.S. C8 116
Smithland, Ky., U.S. G9 120
Smith Mountain Lake, res., Va., U.S. G6 114
Smith Point, c., N.S., Can. E13 110
Smith River, Ca., U.S. B1 134
Smiths, Al., U.S. E13 122
Smiths Falls, On., Can. D13 112
Smiths Grove, Ky., U.S. G11 120
Smithton, Austl. n12 77a
Smithville, Ga., U.S. E1 116
Smithville, Ms., U.S. C10 122
Smithville, Tn., U.S. I12 120
Smithville, Tx., U.S. D10 130
Smithville Lake, res., Mo., U.S. E3 120
Smoke Creek Desert, des., Nv., U.S. C6 134
Smokey, Cape, c., N.S., Can. D16 110
Smoky, stm., Ab., Can. A12 138
Smoky Cape, c., Austl. H9 76
Smoky Dome, mtn., Id., U.S. G12 136
Smoky Hill, stm., U.S. B12 128
Smoky Hill, North Fork, stm., U.S. B7 128
Smoky Lake, Ab., Can. B18 138
Smøla, i., Nor. E2 8
Smolensk, Russia F15 10
Smolenskaja-Moskovskaja vozvyšennost', plat., Eur. F16 10
Smolenskaja oblast', co., Russia F15 10
Smoljan, Blg. H11 26
Smoot, Wy., U.S. H16 136
Smoothrock Lake, l., On., Can. A9 118
Smorodovka, Russia C12 10
Smyrna see İzmir, Tur. E10 28
Smyrna, De., U.S. E10 114
Smyrna, Ga., U.S. D14 122
Smyrna, Tn., U.S. I11 120
Smythe, Mount, mtn., B.C., Can. D6 106
Snæfell, mtn., Ice. k32 8a
Snaefell, mtn., I. of Man G8 12
Snæfellness, pen., Ice. k28 8a
Snag, Yk., Can. C3 106
Snake, stm., Yk., Can. B4 106
Snake, stm., U.S. D8 136
Snake, stm., Mn., U.S. E5 118
Snake, stm., Ne., U.S. E11 126
Snake Creek, stm., S.D., U.S. B14 126
Snake River Plain, pl., Id., U.S. G13 136
Snake Valley, val., U.S. D3 132
Snares Islands, is., N.Z. H2 80
Snåsavatnet, l., Nor. D4 8
Sneads, Fl., U.S. G13 122
Sneedville, Tn., U.S. H2 114
Sneek, Neth. A14 14
Sněžka, mtn., Czech Rep. F11 16
Śniardwy, Jezioro, l., Pol. C17 16
Sniatyn, Ukr. A12 26
Snina, Slov. G18 16
Snipe Lake, l., Ab., Can. A14 138
Snjadin, Bela. H11 10
Snøhetta, mtn., Nor. E3 8
Snohomish, Wa., U.S. C4 136
Snoqualmie Pass, p., Wa., U.S. C5 136
Snøtinden, mtn., Nor. C5 8
Snov, stm., Eur. H15 10
Snover, Mi., U.S. E7 112
Snowbird Lake, l., N.T., Can. C10 106
Snowdon, mtn., Wales, U.K. H8 12
Snowdonia National Park, p.o.i., Wales, U.K. I8 12
Snowflake, Az., U.S. I6 132
Snow Hill, Md., U.S. F10 114
Snow Hill, N.C., U.S. A8 116
Snow Lake, Mb., Can. E10 106
Snowmass Mountain, mtn., Co., U.S. D9 132
Snow Mountain, mtn., Ca., U.S. D3 134
Snowtown, Austl. I2 76
Snowy, stm., Austl. K7 76
Snowy Mountain, mtn., N.Y., U.S. G2 110
Snowy Mountains, mts., Austl. K7 76
Snowy River National Park, p.o.i., Austl. K6 76
Snuŏl, Camb. F8 48
Snyder, Ok., U.S. G10 128
Snyder, Tx., U.S. B7 130
Soacha, Col. E4 86
Soalala, Madag. D8 68
Soap Lake, Wa., U.S. C7 136
Soavinandriana, Madag. D8 68
Sobaek-sanmaek, mts., Kor., S. C1 40
Soběslav, Czech Rep. G10 16
Sobinka, Russia I19 8
Sobradinho, Braz. D11 92
Sobradinho, Represa de, res., Braz. E5 88
Sobral, Braz. B5 88
Sobrance, Slov. H18 16
Sobrarbe, hist. reg., Spain B10 20
Sochaczew, Pol. D16 16
Soch'e see Shache, China B12 56
Soči, Russia F5 32
Société, Archipel de la (Society Islands), is., Fr. Poly. E11 72
Society Hill, S.C., U.S. B6 116
Society Islands see Société, Archipel de la, is., Fr. Poly. E11 72
Soco, stm., Dom. Rep. C13 102
Socompa, Paso (Socompa, Portezuelo de), p., S.A. B3 92
Socompa, Portezuelo de (Socompa, Paso), p., S.A. B3 92
Soconusco, Sierra de see Madre de Chiapas, Sierra, mts., N.A. G12 100
Socorro, Col. D5 86
Socorro, N.M., U.S. I10 132
Socorro, Tx., U.S. C1 130
Socorro, Isla, i., Mex. F3 100
Socotra see Suquṭrā, i., Yemen G7 56
Soc Trang, Viet. H8 48
Socuéllamos, Spain E8 20
Soda Creek, B.C., Can. D8 138
Soda Lake, l., Ca., U.S. H9 134
Sodankylä, Fin. C12 8
Soda Springs, Id., U.S. H15 136
Söderhamn, Swe. F7 8
Södermanland, state, Swe. G7 8
Södertälje, Swe. G7 8
Sodo, Eth. F7 62
Sodom see Sedom, hist., Isr. G6 58
Sodus, N.Y., U.S. E12 112
Sodwana Bay National Park, p.o.i., S. Afr. E11 70
Soe, Indon. G7 44
Soekmekaar, S. Afr. C9 70
Soest, Ger. E4 16
Soest, Neth. B14 14
Sofala, Moz. B12 70
Sofala, state, Moz. B12 70
Sofia see Sofija, Blg. G10 26
Sofija (Sofia), Blg. G10 26
Sofija, state, Blg. G10 26
Sofijsk, Russia F16 34
Sofjanga, Russia D14 8
Sofrino, Russia D20 10
Sogamoso, Col. E5 86
Sogamoso, stm., Col. D5 86
Soğanlı, stm., Tur. C15 28
Sogcho see Sokch'o, Kor., S. A1 40
Sogda, Russia F15 34
Sognefjorden, b., Nor. F1 8
Sogn og Fjordane, state, Nor. F2 8
Sogod, Phil. E5 52
Sogo Nur, l., China C5 36
Sogoža, stm., Russia B22 10
Soğuksu Milli Parkı, p.o.i., Tur. C15 28
Söğüt Gölü, l., Tur. F12 28
Söğütlü, Tur. C13 28
Sog Xian, China E3 36
Sohāgpur, India G6 54
Sohna, India D6 54
Sohor, gora, mtn., Russia F10 34
Soignies, Bel. D12 14
Sointula, B.C., Can. F4 138
Soira, mtn., Erit. E7 62
Soissons, Fr. E12 14
Sojana, Russia D20 8
Şojat, India F4 54
Šojna, Russia C20 8
Sŏjosŏn-man, b., Kor., N. E6 38
Sokch'o, Kor., S. A1 40
Söke, Tur. F10 28

Name | Map Ref. | Page

Sokele, D.R.C. F4 66
Sokodé, Togo H5 64
Sokol, Russia G19 8
Sokol, Russia B14 34
Sokółka, Pol. C19 16
Sokolov, Czech Rep. F8 16
Sokołów Małopolski, Pol. F18 16
Sokone, Sen. G1 64
Sokoto, Nig. G5 64
Sokoto, stm., Nig. G5 64
Sokyriany, Ukr. A14 26
Sol, Costa del, cst., Spain H5 20
Sola, Vanuatu i16 79d
Solacolu, Rom. E13 26
Solai, Kenya D7 66
Solan, India C6 54
Solana, Fl., U.S. J3 116
Solânea, Braz. D8 88
Solano, Phil. B3 52
Solāpur, India C2 53
Solca, Rom. B12 26
Sol'cy, Russia B13 10
Solda Gölü, l., Tur. F12 28
Sol de Julio, Arg. D6 92
Soldiers Grove, Wi., U.S. H8 118
Soldotna, Ak., U.S. D9 140
Soledad, Col. B4 86
Soledad, Ca., U.S. G4 134
Soledad, Ven. C10 86
Soledad, Picacho, mtn., Mex. B5 100
Soledad Díez Gutiérrez, Mex. D8 100
Soledade, Braz. D11 92
Soledad Pass, p., Ca., U.S. I7 134
Solen, N.D., U.S. A12 126
Solenzara, Fr. H15 18
Soleure see Solothurn, Switz. C4 22
Solihull, Eng., U.K. I11 12
Solikamsk, Russia C9 32
Sol'-Ileck, Russia D8 32
Soliman, Tun. H4 24
Solingen, Ger. E3 16
Solís de Mataojo, Ur. G10 92
Sollefteå, Swe. E7 8
Sollentuna, Swe. G7 8
Sóller, Spain E13 20
Solnečnogorsk, Russia D19 10
Sologne, reg., Fr. G10 14
Sologoncy, Russia C11 34
Solok, Indon. D2 50
Solomennoe, Russia F16 8
Solomon, Az., U.S. K7 132
Solomon, stm., Ks., U.S. B11 128
Solomon, North Fork, stm., Ks., U.S. B10 128
Solomon, South Fork, stm., Ks., U.S. B10 128
Solomon Basin, unds. J18 142
Solomon Islands, ctry., Oc. D7 72
Solomon Islands, is., Oc. d7 79b
Solomon Sea, Oc. D6 72
Solomon's Pools see Sulaymān, Birak, hist., W.B. G5 58
Solon, China B9 36
Solon, Ia., U.S. C6 120
Solon, Me., U.S. F7 110
Solothurn, Switz. C4 22
Soloveckie ostrova, is., Russia D16 8
Solov'evsk, Russia F12 34
Solov'evsk, Russia F13 34
Şolsona, Spain C12 20
Šolta, Otok, i., Cro. G13 22
Solṭānābād, Iran B8 56
Soltau, Ger. C5 16
Solvang, Ca., U.S. I5 134
Solvay, N.Y., U.S. A9 114
Sol'vyčegodsk, Russia F22 8
Solway Firth, b., U.K. G9 12
Solwezi, Zam. C4 68
Solza, Russia D18 8
Sōma, Japan B13 40
Soma, Tur. D10 28
Somabhula, Zimb. D4 68
Somalia, ctry., Afr. D9 66
Somali Basin, unds. I8 142
Somaliland see Somalia, ctry., Afr. D9 66
Somali Republic see Somalia, ctry., Afr. D9 66
Sombo, Ang. B3 68
Sombor, Yugo. D6 26
Sombrerete, Mex. D7 100
Sombreretillo, Mex. H7 130
Sombrero Channel, strt., India G7 46
Sombrio, Braz. D13 92
Sombrio, Lagoa do, l., Braz. D13 92
Somdari, India F4 54
Somerset, Austl. n12 77a
Somerset, Co., U.S. E9 132
Somerset, Ky., U.S. G13 120
Somerset, Oh., U.S. E3 114
Somerset, Pa., U.S. D6 114
Somerset, Tx., U.S. E9 130
Somerset East, S. Afr. H7 70
Somerset Island, i., Nu., Can. A12 106
Somerset West, S. Afr. I4 70
Somers Point, N.J., U.S. E11 114
Somersworth, N.H., U.S. G5 110
Somerton, Az., U.S. K2 132
Somerville, N.J., U.S. D11 114
Somerville, Tn., U.S. B9 122
Somerville, Tx., U.S. G2 122
Somerville Lake, res., Tx., U.S. D11 130
Someș (Szamos), stm., Eur. B9 26
Somino, Russia A17 10
Somme, state, Fr. D11 14
Somme, stm., Fr. E11 14
Somme, Baie de la, b., Fr. D10 14
Sommen, l., Swe. H6 8
Sömmerda, Ger. E7 16
Somogy, state, Hung. C4 26
Somosierra, Puerto de, p., Spain C7 20
Somosomo, Fiji p20 79e
Somosomo Strait, strt., Fiji p19 79e
Somoto, Nic. F4 102
Somovo, Russia H17 10
Somport, Col du (Somport, Puerto de), p., Eur. G5 18
Somport, Puerto de (Somport, Col du), p., Eur. G5 18
Sompuis, Fr. F13 14
Son, stm., India F10 54
Sonāmarg, India A5 54
Sonāmukhi, India G11 54
Sŏnch'ŏn-ŭp, Kor., N. E6 38
Sønderborg, Den. I3 8
Sønderjylland, state, Den. I3 8
Sondershausen, Ger. E6 16
Søndre Strømfjord, Grnld. D15 141
Sondrio, Italy D6 22
Sonepur, India H9 54
Song, Nig. H7 64
Song, Thai. C5 48
Song Bay Hap, Cua, b., Viet. H7 48
Song Cau, Viet. F9 48
Song Da see Black, stm., Asia D9 46
Songe, Nor. G3 8
Songea, Tan. G7 66
Song Hong see Red, stm., Asia D9 46
Songhua, stm., China B11 36
Songhua Hu, res., China C7 38
Songjiang, China F9 42
Songjŏng, Kor., S. G7 38
Sŏngju, Kor., S. D1 40
Songkhla, Thai. I5 48
Songkhram, stm., Thai. D6 48
Songlinba, China I6 42
Sŏngnam, Kor., S. F7 38
Songnim, Kor., N. E6 38
Songpan, China E5 36
Song Phi Nong, Thai. E4 48
Songtao, China G3 42
Songxi, China H8 42
Songxian, China D4 42
Sonid Youqi, China C7 36
Sonid Zuoqi, China C7 36
Sonīpat, India D6 54
Son La, Viet. B6 48
Sonmiāni, Pak. D10 56
Sonmiāni Bay, b., Pak. D10 56
Sonneberg, Ger. F7 16
Sonningdale, Sk., Can. B6 124
Sono, stm., Braz. I3 88
Sono, stm., Braz. E1 88
Sonoma, Ca., U.S. E3 134
Sonora, Ca., U.S. F5 134
Sonora, Tx., U.S. D7 130
Sonora, state, Mex. G7 98
Sonora, stm., Mex. G7 98
Sonora, Desierto de, des., N.A. F6 98
Sonoyta, Mex. F6 98
Sonqor, Iran C6 56
Sŏnsan, Kor., S. C1 40
Sonseca, Spain E6 20
Sonsón, Col. E4 86
Sonsonate, El Sal. F3 102
Sonsorol Islands, is., Palau D9 44
Sonstraal, S. Afr. E6 70
Son Tay, Viet. B7 48
Sonthofen, Ger. I6 16
Soochow see Suzhou, China F9 42
Sooke, B.C., Can. H7 138
Sooner Lake, res., Ok., U.S. A1 122
Sopchoppy, Fl., U.S. G14 122
Soperton, Ga., U.S. D3 116
Sopki, Russia C13 10
Sopot, Pol. B14 16
Sop Pong, Laos A6 48
Sopron, Hung. B3 26
Sopur, India A5 54
Sora, Italy I10 22
Sorada, India I10 54
Sorata, Bol. C3 90
Sorbhog, India E13 54
Sorel, Qc., Can. D3 110
Sorell, Cape, c., Austl. o12 77a
Sørfold, Nor. C6 8
Sorgues, Fr. E10 18
Soria, Spain C8 20
Soria, co., Spain C8 20
Soriano, Ur. F8 92
Sørli, Nor. D5 8
Sorø, Den. I4 8
Soro, India H11 54
Soro, Monte, mtn., Italy G8 24
Soroca, Mol. A15 26
Sorocaba, Braz. L2 88
Soročinsk, Russia D8 32
Soroco, P.R. B4 104a
Sorol, at., Micron. C5 72
Soron, India E7 54
Sorong, Indon. F9 44
Sororó, stm., Braz. C1 88
Sorot', stm., Russia C12 10
Soroti, Ug. D6 66
Sørøya, i., Nor. A10 8
Sorrento, Italy D8 24
Sorrento, La., U.S. G8 122
Sorris-Sorris, Nmb. B2 70
Sor Rondane Mountains, mts., Ant. C7 81
Sorsk, Russia D16 32
Sorso, Italy D2 24
Sorsogon, Phil. D4 52
Şort, Spain B12 20
Sortandy, Kaz. D12 32
Sortavala, Russia F14 8
Sør-Trøndelag, state, Nor. E4 8
Sõrve neem, c., Est. C4 10
Šoša, stm., Russia D18 10
Sos del Rey Católico, Spain B9 20
Soskovo, Russia H18 10
Sosna, stm., Russia H21 10
Sosneado, Cerro, mtn., Arg. G3 92
Sosnogorsk, Russia B8 32
Sosnovec, Russia D15 8
Sosnovka, Kaz. D13 32
Sosnovka, Russia C19 8
Sosnovo-Ozërskoe, Russia F11 34
Sosnovskoe, Russia I20 8
Sosnovyj Bor, Russia A11 10
Sosnowiec, Pol. F15 16
Soso, Ms., U.S. F9 122
Sos'va, Russia B10 32
Sotkamo, Fin. D13 8
Soto, Mex. F1 130
Soto la Marina, Mex. D9 100
Soto la Marina, Barra, i., Mex. C10 100
Sotra see Store Sotra, i., Nor. F1 8
Sotteville-lès-Rouen, Fr. E9 14
Souanké, Congo D2 66
Soubré, C. Iv. H3 64
Soudan, Austl. D7 74
Souderton, Pa., U.S. D10 114
Soufrière, St. Luc. m6 105c
Soufrière, vol., Guad. h5 105c
Soufrière, vol., St. Vin. o11 105e
Soufrière Hills, vol., Monts. d3 105a
Souillac, Fr. E7 18
Sŏul (Seoul), Kor., S. F7 38
Soulac-sur-Mer, Fr. D4 18
Sound, The, strt., Eur. I5 8
Sounding Creek, stm., Ab., Can. E19 138
Sounding Lake, l., Ab., Can. B3 124
Sources, Mont-aux- (Phofung), mtn., Afr. F9 70
Soure, Braz. D8 84
Sour el Ghozlane, Alg. H14 20
Souris, Mb., Can. E13 124
Souris, stm., N.A. E13 124
Sourlake, Tx., U.S. G4 122
Sourland Mountain, hill, N.J., U.S. D11 114
Sousa, Braz. D6 88
Sousel, Port. F3 20
Sousse, Tun. I4 24
Sout, stm., S. Afr. H6 70
South, stm., N.C., U.S. B7 116
South Africa, ctry., Afr. F7 70
South America, cont. G9 4
Southampton, On., Can. D8 112
Southampton, Eng., U.K. K11 12
Southampton, N.Y., U.S. D13 114
Southampton, Cape, c., Nu., Can. C13 106
Southampton Island, i., Nu., Can. C14 106
South Andaman, i., India F7 46
South Anna, stm., Va., U.S. G8 114
South Antler Creek see Antler, stm., N.A. E12 124
South Australia, state, Austl. E6 74
South Australian Basin, unds. M15 142
Southaven, Ms., U.S. B8 122
South Baldy, mtn., N.M., U.S. J9 132
Southbank, B.C., Can. C5 138
South Bay, Fl., U.S. J5 116
South Bay, b., Nu., Can. C14 106
South Bay, b., On., Can. C8 112
South Baymouth, On., Can. C7 112
South Bend, In., U.S. G3 112
South Bend, Wa., U.S. D3 136
South Bohemia see Jihočeský kraj, state, Czech Rep. G10 16
South Borneo see Kalimantan Selatan, state, Indon. E9 50
South Boston, Va., U.S. H6 114
Southbridge, N.Z. F5 80
Southbridge, Ma., U.S. B13 114
South Brookfield, N.S., Can. F11 110
South Bruny Island, i., Austl. o13 77a
South Burlington, Vt., U.S. F3 110
South Carolina, state, U.S. C5 116
South Celebes see Sulawesi Selatan, state, Indon. E11 50
South Charleston, W.V., U.S. F4 114
South China Basin, unds. H14 142
South China Sea, Asia H15 30
South Dakota, state, U.S. C12 126
South Downs, hills, Eng., U.K. K12 12
South East, state, Bots. D7 70
South East Cape, c., Austl. o13 77a
Southeast Indian Ridge, unds. N12 142
Southeast Pacific Basin, unds. P25 142
South East Point, c., Austl. L6 76
Southend-on-Sea, Eng., U.K. J13 12
Southern, state, Bots. D7 70
Southern see HaDarom, state, Isr. H5 58
Southern Alps, mts., N.Z. F4 80
Southern Bug see Pivdennyy Buh, stm., Ukr. A17 26
Southern Cook Islands, is., Cook Is. E10 72
Southern Cross, Austl. F3 74
Southern Ghāts, mts., India G3 53
Southern Indian Lake, l., Mb., Can. D10 106
Southern Ocean N13 142
Southern Pines, N.C., U.S. A6 116
South Esk, stm., Austl. n13 77a
South Fabius, stm., Mo., U.S. E6 120
South Fallsburg, N.Y., U.S. C11 114
Southfield, Mi., U.S. B2 114
South Fiji Basin, unds. L20 142
South Foreland, c., Eng., U.K. J14 12
South Fork, Co., U.S. F10 132
South Fulton, Tn., U.S. H8 120
Southgate, Mi., U.S. B2 114
South Georgia, i., S. Geor. J9 90
South Georgia and the South Sandwich Islands, dep., S.A. K11 82
South Grand, stm., Mo., U.S. F3 120
South Hātia Island, i., Bngl. G13 54
South Haven, Mi., U.S. F3 112
South Henderson, N.C., U.S. H7 114
South Henik Lake, l., Nu., Can. C11 106
South Hero, Vt., U.S. F3 110
South Hill Village, Anguilla A1 105a
South Holston Lake, res., U.S. H3 114
South Honshu Ridge, unds. G16 142
South Houston, Tx., U.S. H3 122
South Indian Basin, unds. O12 142
South Indian Lake, Mb., Can. D11 106
South International Falls, Mn., U.S. C5 118
South Island, i., N.Z. G5 80
South Konkan Hills, hills, India C1 53
South Korea see Korea, South, ctry., Asia G8 38
South Lake Tahoe, Ca., U.S. E5 134
Southland, Tx., U.S. H7 128
Southlawn, Il., U.S. E8 120
South Llano, stm., Tx., U.S. D8 130
South Loup, stm., Ne., U.S. F13 126
South Lyon, Mi., U.S. F6 112
South Magnetic Pole, misc. cult. B18 81
South Manitou Island, i., Mi., U.S. C3 112
South Miami, Fl., U.S. K5 116
South Milwaukee, Wi., U.S. F2 112
South Moravia see Jihomoravský kraj, state, Czech Rep. G12 16
South Nahanni, stm., N.T., Can. C5 106
South Nation, stm., On., Can. C14 112
South Negril Point, c., Jam. i12 104d
South Ogden, Ut., U.S. B5 132
South Orkney Islands, is., Ant. B36 81
South Paris, Me., U.S. F6 110
South Pass, p., Wy., U.S. E4 126
South Pekin, Il., U.S. D8 120
South Pittsburg, Tn., U.S. B13 122
South Platte, stm., U.S. F11 126
South Point, c., Barb. n8 105d
South Pole, misc. cult., Ant. D1 81
Southport (Gold Coast), Austl. F9 76
Southport, Austl. o13 77a
Southport, Eng., U.K. H9 12
Southport, In., U.S. E11 120
Southport, N.C., U.S. C7 116
South Portland, Me., U.S. G6 110
South Range, Mi., U.S. D10 118
South River, On., Can. C10 112
South Ronaldsay, i., Scot., U.K. C10 12
South Sandwich Islands, is., S. Geor. K11 82
South Sandwich Trench, unds. N11 144
South Saskatchewan, stm., Can. A8 124
South Shetland Islands, is., Ant. B35 81
South Sioux City, Ne., U.S. I2 118
South Skunk, stm., Ia., U.S. C5 120
South Slocan, B.C., Can. G13 138
South Sound, b., Br. Vir. Is. e9 104b
South Spicer Island, i., Nu., Can. B15 106
South Sulphur, stm., Tx., U.S. D3 122
South Sumatra see Sumatera Selatan, state, Indon. E4 50
South Taranaki Bight, b., N.Z. D5 80
South Tasman Rise, unds. N17 142
South Thompson, stm., B.C., Can. F11 138
South Torrington, Wy., U.S. E8 126
South Uist, i., Scot., U.K. D5 12
South Umpqua, stm., Or., U.S. G3 136
South Ventana Cone, mtn., Ca., U.S. G4 134
South Vietnam see Vietnam, ctry., Asia E9 48
South West Africa see Namibia, ctry., Afr. E2 68
South West Cape, c., Austl. o12 77a
South West Cape, c., N.Z. H2 80
South West City, Mo., U.S. H3 120
Southwest Harbor, Me., U.S. F8 110
Southwest Indian Ridge, unds. M8 142
Southwest Miramichi, stm., N.B., Can. D10 110
Southwest National Park, p.o.i., Austl. o12 77a
Southwest Pacific Basin, unds. M23 142
Southwest Point, c., Bah. K8 116
South Whitley, In., U.S. G4 112
South Wichita, stm., Tx., U.S. H9 128
South Windham, Me., U.S. G6 110
Southwold, Eng., U.K. I14 12
Soutpansberg, mts., S. Afr. C9 70
Sovata, Rom. C11 26
Sovetsk, Russia G20 10
Sovetsk, Russia E4 10
Sovetsk, Russia C7 32
Sovetskaja Gavan', Russia G17 34
Sovetskij, Russia F13 8
Sovpole, Russia D20 8
Sowa Pan, pl., Bots. B7 70
Soweto, S. Afr. E8 70
Sōya-misaki, c., Japan B14 38
Soyang-chŏsuji, res., Kor., S. F7 38
Soyo, Ang. B1 68
Sož, stm., Eur. H13 10
Sozimskij, Russia C8 32
Sozopol, Blg. G14 26
Spa, Bel. D14 14
Spain, ctry., Eur. E7 20
Spalding, Sk., Can. B9 124
Spalding, Eng., U.K. I12 12
Spanish, On., Can. B7 112
Spanish, stm., On., Can. B8 112
Spanish Fork, Ut., U.S. C5 132
Spanish Point, c., Ber. k15 104e
Spanish Sahara see Western Sahara, dep., Afr. E2 64
Spanish Town, Br. Vir. Is. e9 104b
Spanish Town, Jam. i13 104d
Spánta, Ákra, c., Grc. H6 28
Sparkman, Ar., U.S. D6 122
Sparks, Nv., U.S. D6 134
Sparland, Il., U.S. C8 120
Sparlingville, Mi., U.S. F7 112
Sparrows Point, Md., U.S. E9 114
Sparta see Spárti, Grc. F5 28
Sparta, Ga., U.S. C3 116
Sparta, Il., U.S. F8 120
Sparta, Ky., U.S. F13 120
Sparta, N.J., U.S. C11 114
Sparta, N.C., U.S. H4 114
Sparta, Tn., U.S. I12 120
Sparta, Wi., U.S. H8 118
Spartanburg, S.C., U.S. B4 116
Spárti, Grc. F5 28
Spartivento, Capo, c., Italy F2 24
Spartivento, Capo, c., Italy G10 24
Spas-Klepiki, Russia I19 8
Spassk-Dal'nij, Russia B10 38
Spearfish, S.D., U.S. C8 126
Spearville, Ks., U.S. D9 128
Spednic Lake, l., N.A. E9 110
Speedway, In., U.S. I3 112
Speightstown, Barb. n8 105d
Speikkogel, mtn., Aus. C12 22
Speke Gulf, b., Tan. E6 66
Spencer, In., U.S. E11 120
Spencer, Ia., U.S. H3 118
Spencer, Ne., U.S. E14 126
Spencer, W.V., U.S. F4 114
Spencer, Wi., U.S. G8 118
Spencer, Cape, c., Austl. G7 74
Spencer, Cape, c., N.B., Can. E11 110
Spencer Gulf, b., Austl. F7 74
Spencerville, Oh., U.S. D1 114
Spences Bridge, B.C., Can. F9 138
Speos (Rock Tombs), hist., Egypt K1 58
Sperryville, Va., U.S. F7 114
Spétses, i., Grc. F6 28
Spey, stm., Scot., U.K. D9 12
Speyer, Ger. G4 16
Spezia see La Spezia, Italy F6 22
Spezzano Albanese, Italy E10 24
Sphinx see Abū el-Ḥul, hist., Egypt I1 58
Spickard, Mo., U.S. D4 120
Spilimbergo, Italy D9 22
Spillville, Ia., U.S. A5 120
Spinazzola, Italy D10 24
Spindale, N.C., U.S. A4 116
Spires see Speyer, Ger. G4 16
Spirit Lake, Ia., U.S. H3 118
Spirit River, Ab., Can. D7 106
Spiro, Ok., U.S. B4 122
Spišská Nová Ves, Slov. H16 16
Spitsbergen, i., Nor. B4 30
Spitsbergen Bank, unds. B5 142
Spittal an der Drau, Aus. D10 22
Split, Cro. G13 22
Split Lake, res., Mb., Can. D11 106
Špogi, Lat. D9 10
Spokane, Wa., U.S. C9 136
Spokane, stm., U.S. C8 136
Spoleto, Italy H9 22
Spoon, stm., Il., U.S. D7 120
Spooner, Wi., U.S. F7 118
Sporava, Bela. H8 10
Spornoe, Russia D19 34
Spotsylvania, Va., U.S. F8 114
Sprague, Wa., U.S. C9 136
Spratly Islands, is., Asia D5 44
Spray, Or., U.S. F7 136
Spree, stm., Ger. E10 16
Spremberg, Ger. E10 16
Spring, stm., U.S. H3 120
Spring, stm., Ar., U.S. H6 120
Spring, South Fork, stm., U.S. H6 120
Springbok, S. Afr. F3 70
Spring City, Tn., U.S. B14 122
Spring City, Ut., U.S. D5 132
Spring Creek, stm., Austl. D3 76
Spring Creek, stm., N.D., U.S. G11 124
Spring Creek, stm., S.D., U.S. C8 134
Springdale, Nf., Can. j22 107a
Springdale, Ar., U.S. H3 120
Springdale, Ut., U.S. F4 132
Springdale, Wa., U.S. B9 136
Springe, Ger. D5 16
Springerville, Az., U.S. I7 132
Springfield, N.S., Can. F12 110
Springfield, Co., U.S. D6 128
Springfield, Fl., U.S. G13 122
Springfield, Ga., U.S. D4 116
Springfield, Il., U.S. E8 120
Springfield, Ma., U.S. B13 114
Springfield, Mn., U.S. G4 118
Springfield, Mo., U.S. G4 120
Springfield, Oh., U.S. E2 114
Springfield, Or., U.S. F3 136
Springfield, S.C., U.S. C4 116
Springfield, S.D., U.S. E14 126
Springfield, Tn., U.S. H10 120
Springfontein, S. Afr. G7 70
Spring Glen, Ut., U.S. D5 132
Spring Green, Wi., U.S. A7 120
Spring Grove, Mn., U.S. H7 118
Springhill, N.S., Can. E12 110
Springhill, La., U.S. D5 122
Spring Hope, N.C., U.S. I7 114
Springhouse, B.C., Can. E8 138
Spring Lake, N.C., U.S. A7 116
Springs, S. Afr. E9 70
Springsure, Austl. E7 76
Springvale, Austl. D3 76
Springvale, Me., U.S. G6 110
Spring Valley, Ca., U.S. K9 134
Spring Valley, Il., U.S. J9 118
Spring Valley, N.Y., U.S. C11 114
Spring Valley, Wi., U.S. G6 118
Spring Valley, val., Nv., U.S. D2 132
Springview, Ne., U.S. E13 126
Springville, Al., U.S. D12 122
Springville, Ca., U.S. G7 134
Springville, Ut., U.S. C5 132
Sproat Lake, l., B.C., Can. G5 138
Spruce Grove, Ab., Can. C17 138
Spruce Knob, mtn., W.V., U.S. F6 114
Spruce Mountain, mtn., Az., U.S. I4 132
Spruce Pine, Al., U.S. C11 122
Spruce Pine, N.C., U.S. I3 114
Spulico, Capo, c., Italy E10 24
Spurfield, Ab., Can. A16 138
Spurger, Tx., U.S. G4 122
Spurn Head, c., Eng., U.K. H13 12
Spuzzum, B.C., Can. G9 138
Squamish, B.C., Can. G7 138
Squamish, stm., B.C., Can. F7 138
Squam Lake, l., N.H., U.S. G5 110
Square Lake, l., Me., U.S. D8 110
Squatec, Qc., Can. C8 110
Squaw Cap Mountain, mtn., N.B., Can. C10 110
Squaw Peak, mtn., Mt., U.S. C12 136
Squilax, B.C., Can. F11 138
Squillace, Golfo di, b., Italy F10 24
Squinzano, Italy D12 24
Sragen, Indon. G7 50
Srbija (Serbia), state, Yugo. E7 26
Srbobran, Yugo. D6 26
Srê Âmbĕl, Camb. G6 48
Sredinnyj hrebet, mts., Russia E20 34
Sredna Gora, mts., Blg. G11 26
Srednee Kujto, ozero, l., Russia D14 8
Srednekolymsk, Russia C19 34
Srednerusskaja vozvyšennost', plat., Russia D5 32
Srednesibirskoe ploskogor'e (Central Siberian Uplands), plat., Russia C10 34
Srednij Ural, mts., Russia C9 32
Srednij Vasjugan, Russia C13 32
Şrednjaja Olëkma, Russia E13 34
Śrem, Pol. D13 16
Srê Moăt, Camb. F8 48
Sremska Mitrovica, Yugo. E6 26
Sremski Karlovci, Yugo. D6 26
Srêng, stm., Camb. F6 48
Srêpŏk, stm., Camb. F8 48
Sretensk, Russia F12 34
Sri Aman, Malay. C7 50
Sri Jayawardenepura (Kotte), Sri L. H5 53
Srīkākulam, India B6 53
Sri Kālahasti, India E4 53
Sri Lanka, ctry., Asia G5 53
Srīnagar, India A5 54
Srīrampur, India B2 53
Srīrangam, India F4 53
Srīvardhan, India B1 53
Şrīvilliputtūr, India G3 53
Środa Śląska, Pol. E12 16
Środa Wielkopolska, Pol. D13 16
Sseu-tch'ouan see Sichuan, state, China E5 36
Ssup'ing see Siping, China C6 38
Staaten, stm., Austl. C8 74
Stacyville, Ia., U.S. H6 118
Stade, Ger. C5 16
Stadlandet, pen., Nor. E1 8
Stadl-Paura, Aus. B10 22
Stadskanaal, Neth. A16 14
Stadtallendorf, Ger. F5 16
Stadtoldendorf, Ger. E5 16
Stafford, Eng., U.K. I10 12
Stafford, Ks., U.S. D10 128
Stafford Springs, Ct., U.S. C13 114
Staffordsville, Ky., U.S. G14 120
Stagen, Indon. E10 50
Staines, Eng., U.K. J12 12
Staked Plain see Estacado, Llano, pl., U.S. H6 128
Stakhanov, Ukr. E5 32
Stalać, Yugo. F8 26
Stalowa Wola, Pol. F18 16
Stamford, Austl. C4 76
Stamford, Eng., U.K. I12 12
Stamford, Ct., U.S. C12 114
Stamford, N.Y., U.S. B11 114
Stamford, Tx., U.S. B8 130
Stamford, Lake, res., Tx., U.S. A8 130
Stamps, Ar., U.S. D5 122
Stanaford, W.V., U.S. G4 114
Stanberry, Mo., U.S. D3 120
Stancionno-Ojašinskij, Russia C14 32
Standard, Ab., Can. E18 138
Standerton, S. Afr. E9 70
Standish, Mi., U.S. E6 112
Stanfield, Or., U.S. E7 136
Stanford, Ky., U.S. G13 120
Stanford, Mt., U.S. C16 136
Stanger, S. Afr. F10 70
Stanislaus, stm., Ca., U.S. F5 134
Stanley, Austl. n12 77a
Stanley, N.B., Can. D10 110
Stanley, Falk. Is. J5 90
Stanley, N.C., U.S. A4 116
Stanley, N.D., U.S. F11 124
Stanley, Wi., U.S. G7 118
Stanley Falls, wtfl, D.R.C. D4 66
Stanley Reservoir, res., India F3 53
Stanleyville see Kisangani, D.R.C. D5 66
Stanovoe nagor'e, mts., Russia E11 34
Stanovoj hrebet, mts., Russia E14 34
Stanovoy Mountains see Stanovoe nagor'e, mts., Russia E11 34
Stanthorpe, Austl. G8 76
Stanton, Ky., U.S. G2 114
Stanton, Mi., U.S. E4 112
Stanton, Ne., U.S. F15 126
Stanton, N.D., U.S. G12 124
Stanton, Tn., U.S. B9 122
Stantonsburg, N.C., U.S. A8 116
Stanwood, Wa., U.S. B4 136
Staples, Mn., U.S. E4 118
Stapleton, Al., U.S. G11 122
Stąporków, Pol. E16 16
Star, Ms., U.S. E8 122
Star, N.C., U.S. A6 116
Starachowice, Pol. E17 16
Staraja Rudnja, Bela. H13 10
Staraja Russa, Russia B14 10
Stara Pazova, Yugo. D7 26
Stara Zagora, Blg. G12 26
Starbuck, Mb., Can. E16 124
Starbuck, Wa., U.S. D8 136
Starbuck, i., Kir. D11 72
Star City, Sk., Can. B9 124
Star City, Ar., U.S. D7 122
Stargard Szczeciński, Pol. C11 16
Stargo, Az., U.S. J7 132
Star Harbour, b., Sol. Is. f10 79b
Starica, Russia D17 10
Stari Grad, Cro. G13 22
Starij Rjad, Russia B17 10
Stari Vlah, reg., Yugo. F7 26
Starke, Fl., U.S. G3 116
Starkville, Ms., U.S. D10 122
Starnberg, Ger. H7 16
Starnberger See, l., Ger. I7 16
Starodub, Russia H15 10
Staroe Rahino, Russia B15 10
Starogard Gdański, Pol. C14 16
Starokozache, Ukr. C16 26
Star Peak, mtn., Nv., U.S. C7 134
Start Point, c., Eng., U.K. K9 12
Staryja Darohi, Bela. G11 10
Staryj Medved', Russia B13 10
Staryj Oskol, Russia D5 32
Stary Sącz, Pol. G16 16
Stassfurt, Ger. E7 16
State College, Pa., U.S. D7 114
State Line, Ms., U.S. F10 122
Stateline, Nv., U.S. E5 134
Staten Island see Estados, Isla de los, i., Arg. J4 90
State Road, N.C., U.S. H4 114
Statesboro, Ga., U.S. D4 116
Statesville, N.C., U.S. I5 114
Staubun, Bela. H14 10
Staunton, Il., U.S. E8 120
Staunton, Va., U.S. F6 114
Staunton see Roanoke, stm., U.S. H8 114
Stavanger, Nor. G1 8
Stave Lake, l., B.C., Can. G8 138
Stavely, Ab., Can. F17 138
Stavne, Ukr. G18 16
Stavropol', Russia E6 32
Stawell, Austl. K4 76
Stawell, stm., Austl. C4 76
Stawiszyn, Pol. E14 16
Stayner, On., Can. D9 112
Steamboat Springs, Co., U.S. C10 132
Stearns, Ky., U.S. H13 120
Stębark, Pol. C16 16
Steele, Mo., U.S. H8 120
Steele, N.D., U.S. H14 124
Steele, Mount, mtn., Wy., U.S. B9 132
Steels Point, c., Norf. I. y25 78i
Steelville, Mo., U.S. G6 120
Steensby Inlet, b., Nu., Can. A15 106
Steenwijk, Neth. B15 14
Steep Rock, Mb., Can. C15 124
Stefanie, Lake, l., Afr. G7 62
Stefansson Island, i., Nu., Can. A9 106
Ştefan Vodă, Rom. E14 26
Ştege, Den. B8 16
Stehekin, Wa., U.S. B6 136
Steiermark, state, Aus. C11 22
Steinach, Aus. C8 22
Steinbach, Mb., Can. E17 124
Steinfurt, Ger. D3 16
Steinhausen, Nmb. B4 70
Steinkjer, Nor. D4 8
Stekljanka, Russia G19 8
Stella, S. Afr. E7 70
Stellarton, N.S., Can. E14 110
Stellenbosch, S. Afr. H4 70
Stelvio, Parco Nazionale dello, p.o.i., Italy D7 22
Stelvio, Passo dello, p., Italy D7 22
Stendal, Ger. D7 16
Stende, Lat. C5 10
Stephen, Mn., U.S. C2 118
Stephens, Ar., U.S. D5 122
Stephens, Port, b., Austl. I9 76
Stephens City, Va., U.S. E7 114
Stephens Creek, Austl. H3 76
Stephens Lake, res., Mb., Can. D11 106
Stephenville, Nf., Can. j22 107a
Stephenville, Tx., U.S. B9 130
Stepnjak, Kaz. D12 32
Step Pyramid see Saqqâra, Pyramides de, hist., Egypt I1 58
Steptoe Valley, val., Nv., U.S. D2 132
Stepurino, Russia D18 10
Steréa Elláda, state, Grc. E5 28
Sterkstroom, S. Afr. G8 70
Sterling, Co., U.S. G9 126
Sterling, Il., U.S. C8 120
Sterling, Ks., U.S. C10 128
Sterling, Mi., U.S. D5 112
Sterling, Ne., U.S. D1 120
Sterling City, Tx., U.S. C7 130
Sterlington, La., U.S. E6 122
Şterlitamak, Russia D9 32
Šternberk, Czech Rep. G13 16
Sterzing see Vipiteno, Italy D8 22
Stettin Lagoon, b., Eur. C10 16
Stettler, Ab., Can. D18 138
Steubenville, Oh., U.S. D5 114
Stevenage, Eng., U.K. J12 12
Stevenson, Al., U.S. C13 122
Stevenson Entrance, strt., Ak., U.S. E9 140
Stevens Pass, p., Wa., U.S. C5 136
Stevens Peak, mtn., Id., U.S. C11 136
Stevens Point, Wi., U.S. G9 118
Stevensville, Mi., U.S. F3 112
Stevensville, Mt., U.S. D12 136
Stewardson, Il., U.S. E9 120
Stewart, B.C., Can. D4 106
Stewart, stm., Yk., Can. C3 106
Stewart, Isla, i., Chile J2 90
Stewart Island, i., N.Z. H3 80
Stewartstown, Pa., U.S. E9 114
Stewartsville, Mo., U.S. E3 120
Stewart Valley, Sk., Can. D6 124
Stewartville, Mn., U.S. H6 118
Stewiacke, N.S., Can. E13 110
Steyr, Aus. B11 22
Steytlerville, S. Afr. H7 70
Stickney, S.D., U.S. D14 126
Stiene, Lat. C7 10
Stif, Alg. B6 64
Stigler, Ok., U.S. B3 122
Stih, hora, mtn., Ukr. A10 26
Stikine, stm., N.A. D4 106
Stikine Ranges, mts., B.C., Can. D4 106
Stilbaai, S. Afr. I5 70
Stilfontein, S. Afr. E8 70
Stilís, Grc. E5 28
Stillhouse Hollow Lake, res., Tx., U.S. D10 130
Stillwater, B.C., Can. G6 138
Stillwater, Mn., U.S. F6 118
Stillwater, Ok., U.S. A1 122
Stillwell, Ok., U.S. I3 120
Stînca-Costești, Lacul, res., Eur. B14 26
Stine Mountain, mtn., Mt., U.S. E13 136
Stinking Water Creek, stm., Ne., U.S. G11 126
Ştinnett, Tx., U.S. F7 128
Štip, Mac. B5 28
Stirling, Austl. F3 74
Stirling, On., Can. D12 112
Stirling, Scot., U.K. E8 12
Stirling City, Ca., U.S. D4 134
Stirrat, W.V., U.S. G15 120
Stjernøya, i., Nor. A9 8
Stobi, hist., Mac. B4 28
Stockach, Ger. I5 16
Stockbridge, Ga., U.S. C1 116
Stockbridge, Mi., U.S. B1 114
Stockdale, Tx., U.S. E9 130
Stockerau, Aus. B13 22

Name	Map Ref.	Page
Stockholm, Swe.	G8	8
Stockholm, Me., U.S.	C8	110
Stockholm, state, Swe.	G8	8
Stockport, Eng., U.K.	H10	12
Stockton, Al., U.S.	G11	122
Stockton, Ca., U.S.	F4	134
Stockton, Il., U.S.	B8	120
Stockton, Ks., U.S.	B9	128
Stockton, Mo., U.S.	G4	120
Stockton-on-Tees, Eng., U.K.	G11	12
Stockton Plateau, plat., Tx., U.S.	D5	130
Stockton Reservoir, res., Mo., U.S.	G4	120
Stockton Springs, Me., U.S.	F8	110
Stoczek Łukowski, Pol.	D18	16
Stœng Trêng, Camb.	F8	48
Stoffberg, S. Afr.	D9	70
Stojba, Russia	F15	34
Stoke-on-Trent, Eng., U.K.	I11	12
Stokes Point, c., Austl.	n11	77a
Stolberg, Ger.	F2	16
Stolbovo, Russia	H17	10
Stolbovoj, ostrov, i., Russia	B16	34
Stoneboro, Pa., U.S.	C5	114
Stone Harbor, N.J., U.S.	E11	114
Stonehaven, Scot., U.K.	E10	12
Stonehenge, Austl.	E4	76
Stonehenge, hist., Eng., U.K.	J11	12
Stone Mountain, Ga., U.S.	C1	116
Stone Mountain, mtn., Vt., U.S.	F5	110
Stoner, B.C., Can.	C8	138
Stoneville, N.C., U.S.	H6	114
Stonewall, Mb., Can.	D16	124
Stonewall, Ms., U.S.	E10	122
Stonewall, Ok., U.S.	C2	122
Stoney Creek, On., Can.	E10	112
Stonington, Il., U.S.	E8	120
Stonington, Me., U.S.	F8	110
Stony Creek, stm., Ca., U.S.	D3	134
Stony Lake, l., Mb., Can.	D11	106
Stony Lake, l., On., Can.	D11	112
Stony Plain, Ab., Can.	C16	138
Stony Point, N.C., U.S.	I4	114
Stony Rapids, Sk., Can.	D9	106
Stony River, Ak., U.S.	D8	140
Stopnica, Pol.	F16	16
Stora Lulevatten, l., Swe.	C8	8
Storavan, l., Swe.	D8	8
Stord, i., Nor.	G1	8
Storebælt, strt., Den.	I4	8
Store Koldewey, i., Grnld.	B22	141
Støren, Nor.	E4	8
Store Sotra, i., Nor.	F1	8
Storkerson Bay, b., N.T., Can.	B14	140
Storkerson Peninsula, pen., Nu., Can.	A9	106
Storlien, Swe.	E5	8
Storm Bay, b., Austl.	o13	77a
Storm Lake, Ia., U.S.	B2	120
Stornoway, Scot., U.K.	C6	12
Storozhynets', Ukr.	A12	26
Storrs, Ct., U.S.	C13	114
Storsjøen, l., Nor.	F4	8
Storsjön, l., Swe.	E5	8
Storstrøm, state, Den.	I5	8
Storthoaks, Sk., Can.	E12	124
Storuman, Swe.	D7	8
Storuman, l., Swe.	D6	8
Storvindeln, l., Swe.	D7	8
Storvreta, Swe.	F7	8
Story City, Ia., U.S.	B4	120
Stosch, Isla, i., Chile	I1	90
Stoŭbcy, Bela.	G9	10
Stoughton, Sk., Can.	E10	124
Stoughton, Ma., U.S.	B14	114
Stoughton, Wi., U.S.	B8	120
Stoŭng, stm., Camb.	F7	48
Stow, Oh., U.S.	C4	114
Stowe, Vt., U.S.	F4	110
Stowell, Tx., U.S.	H4	122
Stowmarket, Eng., U.K.	I14	12
Stoyoma Mountain, mtn., B.C., Can.	G9	138
Stradella, Italy	E6	22
Stradzečy, Bela.	I6	10
Strahan, Austl.	o12	77a
Strakonice, Czech Rep.	G9	16
Stralsund, Ger.	B9	16
Strand, S. Afr.	I4	70
Stranraer, Scot., U.K.	G8	12
Strasbourg, Sk., Can.	C9	124
Strasbourg, Fr.	F16	14
Strasburg, Ger.	C9	16
Strasburg, N.D., U.S.	A12	126
Strasburg, Oh., U.S.	D4	114
Strasburg, Pa., U.S.	E9	114
Strășeni, Mol.	B15	26
Stratford, On., Can.	E8	112
Stratford, N.Z.	D6	80
Stratford, Ca., U.S.	G6	134
Stratford, Ct., U.S.	C12	114
Stratford, Ia., U.S.	B4	120
Stratford, Ok., U.S.	C2	122
Stratford, Wi., U.S.	G8	118
Stratford-upon-Avon, Eng., U.K.	I11	12
Strathalbyn, Austl.	J2	76
Strathclair, Mb., Can.	D13	124
Strathgordon, Austl.	o12	77a
Strathlorne, N.S., Can.	D15	110
Strathmore, Ab., Can.	E17	138
Strathmore, val., Scot., U.K.	E9	12
Strathroy, On., Can.	F8	112
Strathy Point, c., Scot., U.K.	C8	12
Stratton, Co., U.S.	B6	128
Stratton, Me., U.S.	E6	110
Stratton, Ne., U.S.	A7	128
Straubing, Ger.	H8	16
Strausberg, Ger.	D9	16
Strawberry, stm., Ar., U.S.	H6	120
Strawberry, stm., Ut., U.S.	C6	132
Strawberry Mountain, mtn., Or., U.S.	F8	136
Strawberry Reservoir, res., Ut., U.S.	C5	132
Strawn, Tx., U.S.	B9	130
Strážnice, Czech Rep.	H13	16
Streaky Bay, b., Austl.	F6	74
Streatham, B.C., Can.	C4	138
Streator, Il., U.S.	C9	120
Středočeský, state, Czech Rep.	G10	16
Stredoslovenský Kraj, state, Slov.	H15	16
Streeter, N.D., U.S.	A13	126
Streetsboro, Oh., U.S.	C4	114
Streetsville, On., Can.	E10	112
Strehaia, Rom.	E10	26
Strelka-Čunja, Russia	B18	32
Strel'na, stm., Russia	C18	8
Strel'skaja, Russia	G22	8
Strenči, Lat.	C8	10
Strèšyn, Bela.	H13	10
Strickland, stm., Pap. N. Gui.	b3	79a
Strimon, Gulf of see Strymonikós Kólpos, b., Grc.	C6	28
Strjama, stm., Blg.	G11	26
Stroeder, Arg.	H4	90
Strofádes, is., Grc.	F3	28
Stromboli, Isola, i., Italy	F9	24
Strome, Ab., Can.	D18	138
Stromeferry, Scot., U.K.	D7	12
Stromsburg, Ne., U.S.	F15	126
Strömstad, Swe.	G4	8
Strömsund, Swe.	E6	8
Strong City, Ks., U.S.	C12	128
Stronghurst, Il., U.S.	D7	120
Stronsay, i., Scot., U.K.	B10	12
Stropkov, Slov.	G17	16
Stroud, Austl.	I8	76
Stroud, Eng., U.K.	J10	12
Stroud, Ok., U.S.	B2	122
Stroudsburg, Pa., U.S.	D10	114
Struga, Mac.	B3	28
Struma, stm., Eur.	H10	26
Strumble Head, c., Wales, U.K.	I7	12
Strumica, Mac.	B5	28
Strunino, Russia	D21	10
Struthers, Oh., U.S.	C5	114
Stryi, stm., Ukr.	H19	16
Stryker, Mt., U.S.	B12	136
Stryker, Oh., U.S.	G5	112
Stryków, Pol.	E15	16
Strymonikós Kólpos (Strimon, Gulf of), b., Grc.	C6	28
Strzegom, Pol.	F12	16
Strzelce Krajeńskie, Pol.	D11	16
Strzelce Opolskie, Pol.	F14	16
Strzelecki Creek, stm., Austl.	G3	76
Strzelecki Desert, des., Austl.	F3	76
Strzelecki National Park, p.o.i., Austl.	n13	77a
Strzelin, Pol.	F12	16
Strzyżów, Pol.	G17	16
Stuart, Fl., U.S.	I5	116
Stuart, Ia., U.S.	C3	120
Stuart, Va., U.S.	H5	114
Stuart, stm., B.C., Can.	B7	138
Stuart Island, i., Ak., U.S.	D7	140
Stuart Lake, l., B.C., Can.	B5	138
Stuarts Draft, Va., U.S.	G6	114
Studen Kladenec, Jazovir, res., Blg.	H12	26
Stuie, B.C., Can.	D4	138
Stupino, Russia	F20	10
Stura di Demonte, stm., Italy	F4	22
Sturge Island, i., Ant.	B21	81
Sturgeon, stm., On., Can.	B9	112
Sturgeon, stm., Mi., U.S.	E10	118
Sturgeon Bay, Wi., U.S.	D2	112
Sturgeon Bay, b., Mb., Can.	B15	124
Sturgeon Falls, On., Can.	B10	112
Sturgeon Lake, l., Ab., Can.	A13	138
Sturgeon Lake, l., On., Can.	D11	112
Sturgeon Lake, l., On., Can.	A7	118
Sturgis, Sk., Can.	C11	124
Sturgis, Ky., U.S.	G10	120
Sturgis, Mi., U.S.	G4	112
Sturgis, S.D., U.S.	C9	126
Štúrovo, Slov.	I14	16
Sturt, Mount, mtn., Austl.	G3	76
Sturtevant, Wi., U.S.	F2	112
Sturt National Park, p.o.i., Austl.	G3	76
Sturt Stony Desert, des., Austl.	G3	76
Stutterheim, S. Afr.	H8	70
Stuttgart, Ger.	H5	16
Stuttgart, Ar., U.S.	C7	122
Styr, stm., Eur.	H9	10
Styria see Steiermark, state, Aus.	C11	22
Šu, Kaz.	F12	32
Suaçuí Grande, stm., Braz.	J4	88
Suai, Malay.	B8	50
Suaita, Col.	D5	86
Suapure, stm., Ven.	D8	86
Suaqui Grande, Mex.	A4	100
Subah, Indon.	G6	50
Subang, Indon.	G5	50
Subansiri, stm., Asia	D14	54
Šubarkuduk, Kaz.	E9	32
Subarnarekha, stm., India	G11	54
Sūbāṭ, stm., Sudan	F6	62
Subate, Lat.	D8	10
Subei, China	D3	36
Subeita see Shivta, Ḥorvot, hist., Isr.	H5	58
Subiaco, Italy	I10	22
Sublette, Ks., U.S.	D8	128
Sublett Range, mts., Id., U.S.	H14	136
Subotica, Yugo.	C6	26
Sucarnoochee, stm., U.S.	E10	122
Succotah, hist., Egypt	H3	58
Suceava, Rom.	B13	26
Suceava, state, Rom.	B12	26
Suchań, Pol.	C11	16
Suchou see Suzhou, China	F9	42
Süchow see Xuzhou, China	D7	42
Sucio, stm., Col.	D3	86
Sucre, Bol.	C3	90
Sucre, Col.	C4	86
Sucre, state, Col.	C4	86
Sucre, state, Ven.	B10	86
Sucuaro, Col.	E7	86
Sucumbíos, state, Ec.	H3	86
Sucuriju, Braz.	C8	84
Sucuriú, stm., Braz.	C6	90
Sud, state, N. Cal.	m16	79d
Sud, Canal du, strt., Haiti	C11	102
Suda, Russia	A20	10
Suda, stm., Russia	A20	10
Sudan, Tx., U.S.	G6	128
Sudan, ctry., Afr.	E5	62
Sudan, reg., Afr.	E4	62
Sudbišči, Russia	H20	10
Sudbury, On., Can.	B8	112
Sudbury, Eng., U.K.	I13	12
Sudd see As-Sudd, reg., Sudan	F6	62
Sudetes, mts., Eur.	F11	16
Sudogda, Russia	H19	8
Sudomskaja vozvyšennost', plat., Russia	C12	10
Sudost', stm., Eur.	H16	10
Südtirol see Trentino-Alto Adige, state, Italy	D8	22
Suðuroy, i., Far. Is.	n34	8b
Sue, stm., Sudan	F5	62
Sueca, Spain	E10	20
Suez see El-Suweis, Egypt	I3	58
Suez, Gulf of see Suweis, Khalîg el-, b., Egypt	J4	58
Suez Canal see Suweis, Qanâ el-, can., Egypt	H3	58
Suffield, Ab., Can.	D2	124
Suffolk, Va., U.S.	H9	114
Sufu see Kashi, China	B12	56
Sugar City, Id., U.S.	G15	136
Sugar Hill, Ga., U.S.	B1	116
Sugar Island, i., Mi., U.S.	B5	112
Sugar Land, Tx., U.S.	H3	122
Sugarloaf, hill, Oh., U.S.	C4	114
Sugarloaf Mountain, mtn., Me., U.S.	E6	110
Sugarloaf Point, c., Austl.	I9	76
Suğla Gölü, l., Tur.	F14	28
Sugoj, stm., Russia	D20	34
Sugut, stm., Malay.	G1	52
Suhag, Egypt	B6	62
Suhai Hu, l., China	G16	32
Suhana, Russia	C12	34
Ṣuḥār, Oman	E8	56
Sühbaatar, Mong.	A6	36
Suhindol, Blg.	F12	26
Suhiniči, Russia	F18	10
Suhl, Ger.	F6	16
Suhodol'skij, Russia	G21	10
Suhona, stm., Russia	F22	8
Suhoverkovo, Russia	D18	10
Suhumi, Geor.	F6	32
Şuhut, Tur.	E13	28
Suiá-Miçu, stm., Braz.	F7	84
Suichuan, China	H6	42
Suide, China	C4	42
Suifu see Yibin, China	F5	36
Suihua, China	B10	36
Suijiang, China	F5	36
Suileng, China	B10	36
Suining, China	E7	42
Suining, China	F1	42
Suipacha, Arg.	G8	92
Suiping, China	E5	42
Suippes, Fr.	E13	14
Suir, stm., Ire.	I5	12
Suixi, China	E7	42
Suiyang, China	B9	38
Suiyang, China	H2	42
Suiyangdian, China	E5	42
Suizhong, China	A9	42
Suizhou, China	F5	42
Šuja, Russia	H19	8
Šuja, stm., Russia	E15	8
Sujāngarh, India	E5	54
Sujāwal, Pak.	F2	54
Sukabumi, Indon.	G5	50
Sukadana, Indon.	D6	50
Sukadana, Indon.	F4	50
Sukadana, Teluk, b., Indon.	D6	50
Sukagawa, Japan	B13	40
Sukamara, Indon.	E7	50
Sukaraja, Indon.	E7	50
Sukau, Malay.	A11	50
Sukhothai, Thai.	D4	48
Sukhumi see Suhumi, Geor.	F6	32
Sukkertoppen (Maniitsoq), Grnld.	D15	141
Sukkozero, Russia	E14	8
Sukkur, Pak.	E2	54
Sukoharjo, Indon.	G7	50
Sukromlja, Russia	D17	10
Sukses, Nmb.	B3	70
Sukumo, Japan	G5	40
Sukunka, stm., B.C., Can.	A9	138
Sul, Baía, b., Braz.	C13	92
Sula, i., Nor.	F1	8
Sula, stm., Russia	C23	8
Sula, Kepulauan (Sula Islands), is., Indon.	F8	44
Sulaimān Range, mts., Pak.	C3	54
Sula Islands see Sula, Kepulauan, is., Indon.	F8	44
Sulawesi (Celebes), i., Indon.	F7	44
Sulawesi Selatan, state, Indon.	E11	50
Sulawesi Tengah, state, Indon.	D12	50
Sulawesi Tenggara, state, Indon.	E12	50
Sulaymān, Birak (Solomon's Pools), hist., W.B.	G5	58
Sulcis, reg., Italy	E2	24
Sulechów, Pol.	D11	16
Sulęcin, Pol.	D11	16
Sulejówek, Pol.	D17	16
Sulen, Mount, mtn., Pap. N. Gui.	a3	79a
Sulina, Rom.	D16	26
Sulina, Braţul, stm., Rom.	D16	26
Sulingen, Ger.	D4	16
Sulitelma, mtn., Eur.	C7	8
Sullana, Peru	D1	84
Sulligent, Al., U.S.	D10	122
Sullivan, Il., U.S.	E9	120
Sullivan, In., U.S.	E10	120
Sullivan Lake, l., Ab., Can.	E18	138
Sulmona, Italy	H10	22
Sulphur, La., U.S.	G5	122
Sulphur, Ok., U.S.	C2	122
Sulphur, stm., U.S.	D5	122
Sulphur Springs, Tx., U.S.	D3	122
Sulphur Springs Draw, stm., U.S.	H6	128
Sulphur Springs Valley, val., Az., U.S.	L7	132
Sultan, Wa., U.S.	C5	136
Sultan Alonto, Lake, l., Phil.	G5	52
Sultandağı, Tur.	E14	28
Sultanhisar, Tur.	F11	28
Sultan Kudarat, Phil.	G4	52
Sultānpur, India	E8	54
Sulu Archipelago, is., Phil.	H3	52
Sulu Chi, l., China	C11	54
Sulūq, Libya	A4	62
Sulu Sea, Asia	F2	52
Sulzbach-Rosenberg, Ger.	G7	16
Šum, Russia	A14	10
Šumadija, reg., Yugo.	E7	26
Sumangat, Tanjong, c., Malay.	G1	52
Sumatera (Sumatra), i., Indon.	E3	44
Sumatera Barat, state, Indon.	D2	50
Sumatera Selatan, state, Indon.	E4	50
Sumatera Utara, state, Indon.	K4	48
Sumatra see Sumatera, i., Indon.	E3	44
Sumba, Far. Is.	n34	8b
Sumba, i., Indon.	H11	50
Sumba, Selat, strt., Indon.	H11	50
Sumbawa, i., Indon.	H10	50
Sumbawa Besar, Indon.	H10	50
Sumbawanga, Tan.	F6	66
Sumbe, Ang.	C1	68
Sumburgh Head, c., Scot., U.K.	o18	12a
Sumé, Braz.	D7	88
Sumedang, Indon.	G5	50
Sümeg, Hung.	B4	26
Šumen, Blg.	F13	26
Sumenep, Indon.	G8	50
Šumerlja, Russia	C7	32
Sumisu-jima (Smith Island), i., Japan	E13	36
Šumjači, Russia	G15	10
Summerfield, Fl., U.S.	G3	116
Summerfield, N.C., U.S.	H6	114
Summer Lake, l., Or., U.S.	H6	136
Summerland, B.C., Can.	G11	138
Summerside, P.E., Can.	D13	110
Summersville, Mo., U.S.	G6	120
Summerton, S.C., U.S.	C5	116
Summerville, Ga., U.S.	C13	122
Summerville, S.C., U.S.	C5	116
Summit, S.D., U.S.	F1	118
Summit Lake, B.C., Can.	B8	138
Summit Mountain, mtn., Nv., U.S.	D9	134
Sumner, Ia., U.S.	B5	120
Sumner, Ms., U.S.	D8	122
Sumner, Wa., U.S.	C4	136
Sumoto, Japan	E7	40
Sumpangbinangae, Indon.	F11	50
Šumperk, Czech Rep.	G13	16
Sumpiuh, Indon.	G6	50
Sumqayıt, Azer.	A6	56
Šumšu, ostrov, i., Russia	F20	34
Sumter, S.C., U.S.	C5	116
Sumusta el-Waqf, Egypt	J1	58
Sumy, Ukr.	D4	32
Sumzom, China	F4	36
Sun, stm., Mt., U.S.	C14	136
Sunāmganj, Bngl.	F13	54
Sunbright, Tn., U.S.	H13	120
Sunburst, Mt., U.S.	B14	136
Sunbury, Austl.	K5	76
Sunbury, Oh., U.S.	D3	114
Sunbury, Pa., U.S.	D9	114
Sunchales, Arg.	E7	92
Suncho Corral, Arg.	C6	92
Sunch'ŏn, Kor., S.	G7	38
Sunch'ŏn-ŭp, Kor., N.	E6	38
Sun City, Az., U.S.	J4	132
Suncook, N.H., U.S.	G5	110
Sunda, Selat (Sunda Strait), strt., Indon.	G4	50
Sundance, Wy., U.S.	C8	126
Sundarbans, reg., Asia	H12	54
Sundargarh, India	G9	54
Sunda Shelf, unds.	I13	142
Sunda Strait see Sunda, Selat, strt., Indon.	G4	50
Sundays, stm., S. Afr.	H7	70
Sunde, Nor.	G1	8
Sunderland, Eng., U.K.	G11	12
Sundown, Tx., U.S.	H6	128
Sundridge, On., Can.	C10	112
Sundsvall, Swe.	E7	8
Sunflower, Ms., U.S.	D8	122
Sunflower, Mount, mtn., Ks., U.S.	B7	128
Sungaianyar, Indon.	E10	50
Sungaibuntu, Indon.	F5	50
Sungaidareh, Indon.	D2	50
Sungaiguntung, Indon.	C3	50
Sungai Kolok, Thai.	I5	48
Sungailangsat, Indon.	D2	50
Sungailimau, Indon.	D1	50
Sungaipenuh, Indon.	E2	50
Sungai Petani, Malay.	J5	48
Sungaipinang, Indon.	D8	50
Sungairotan, Indon.	E4	50
Sungaiselan, Indon.	E5	50
Sungari see Songhua, stm., China	B11	36
Sungari Reservoir see Songhua Hu, res., China	C7	38
Sungchiang see Songjiang, China	F9	42
Sungguminasa, Indon.	F11	50
Sungsang, Indon.	E4	50
Sunland Park, N.M., U.S.	L10	132
Sunne, Swe.	G5	8
Sunnynook, Ab., Can.	E19	138
Sunnyside, Ut., U.S.	D6	132
Sunnyside, Wa., U.S.	D7	136
Sunnyslope, Ab., Can.	E17	138
Sunnyvale, Ca., U.S.	F3	134
Sun Prairie, Wi., U.S.	A8	120
Sunrise, Fl., U.S.	J5	116
Sunrise, Wy., U.S.	E8	126
Sunrise Manor, Nv., U.S.	G1	132
Sunset, La., U.S.	G6	122
Sunset, Tx., U.S.	H11	128
Sunset Country, reg., Austl.	J3	76
Sunset Crater National Monument, p.o.i., Az., U.S.	H5	132
Sunshine, Austl.	K5	76
Suntar, Russia	D12	34
Suntar-Hajata, hrebet, mts., Russia	D17	34
Sun Valley, Id., U.S.	G12	136
Sunwu, China	B10	36
Sunwui see Jiangmen, China	J5	42
Sunyani, Ghana	H4	64
Suojarvi, Russia	E15	8
Suomussalmi, Fin.	D13	8
Suō-nada, Japan	F4	40
Suordah, Russia	C15	34
Supamo, stm., Ven.	D10	86
Supaul, India	E11	54
Superí see La Merced, Arg.	D5	92
Superior, Az., U.S.	J5	132
Superior, Mt., U.S.	C12	136
Superior, Wi., U.S.	E6	118
Superior, Wy., U.S.	B7	132
Superior, Laguna, b., Mex.	G11	100
Superior, Lake, l., N.A.	B10	108
Supetar, Cro.	G13	22
Suphan Buri, Thai.	E4	48
Suphan Buri, stm., Thai.	E5	48
Suponevo, Russia	G17	10
Supung Reservoir, res., Asia	D6	38
Suqian, China	E8	42
Sūq Suwayq, Sau. Ar.	E4	56
Suquṭrā (Socotra), i., Yemen	G7	56
Ṣūr (Tyre), Leb.	E6	58
Ṣūr, Oman	E8	56
Sur, Point, c., Ca., U.S.	G4	134
Sura, stm., Russia	C7	32
Surabaya, Indon.	G8	50
Surakarta, Indon.	G7	50
Ṣūrān, Syria	C7	58
Šurany, Slov.	H14	16
Surat, Austl.	F7	76
Sūrat, India	H4	54
Sūratgarh, India	D4	54
Surat Thani, Thai.	H4	48
Suraž, Bela.	E13	10
Suraž, Russia	G15	10
Surendranagar, India	G3	54
Surf City, N.J., U.S.	E11	114
Surfers Paradise, Austl.	G9	76
Surgères, Fr.	C5	18
Surgoinsville, Tn., U.S.	H3	114
Surgut, Russia	B12	32
Suriāpet, India	C4	53
Surigao, Phil.	F5	52
Surin, Thai.	E6	48
Surinam, ctry., S.A.	C6	84
Suring, Wi., U.S.	D1	112
Surprise Valley, val., U.S.	B5	134
Surrency, Ga., U.S.	E3	116
Surrey, N.D., U.S.	F12	124
Surry, Va., U.S.	G9	114
Sursee, Switz.	C5	22
Surt, Libya	A3	62
Surt, Khalīj (Sidra, Gulf of), b., Libya	A3	62
Surtanāhu, Pak.	E2	54
Surtsey, i., Ice.	I29	8a
Suru, Pap. N. Gui.	b3	79a
Sürüç, Tur.	A9	58
Suruga-wan, b., Japan	E11	40
Surulangun, Indon.	E3	50
Surumu, stm., Braz.	F11	86
Šuryškary, Russia	A10	32
Susa, Italy	E4	22
Sušac, Otok, i., Cro.	H13	22
Sūsah, Libya	A4	62
Susaki, Japan	F6	40
Susanino, Russia	G19	8
Susanino, Russia	F17	34
Susanville, Ca., U.S.	C5	134
Šušenskoe, Russia	D16	32
Susitna, stm., Ak., U.S.	D9	140
Susleni, Mol.	B15	26
Susoh, Indon.	K3	48
Susong, China	F7	42
Suspiro del Moro, Puerto, p., Spain	G7	20
Susquehanna, Pa., U.S.	C10	114
Susquehanna, stm., U.S.	E9	114
Susquehanna, West Branch, stm., Pa., U.S.	C8	114
Susques, Arg.	D3	90
Sussex, N.B., Can.	E11	110
Sussex, N.J., U.S.	C11	114
Sussex, Va., U.S.	H8	114
Susuman, Russia	D18	34
Susurluk, Tur.	D11	28
Susuzmüsellim, Tur.	B9	28
Šušvė, stm., Lith.	E6	10
Sutak, India	B6	54
Sutherland, S. Afr.	H5	70
Sutherland, Ia., U.S.	A2	120
Sutherlin, Or., U.S.	G3	136
Sutjeska Nacionalni Park, p.o.i., Bos.	F5	26
Sutlej (Langqên) (Satluj), stm., Asia	D3	54
Sutter, Ca., U.S.	D4	134
Sutter Buttes, mtn., Ca., U.S.	D4	134
Sutter Creek, Ca., U.S.	E5	134
Sutton, Ak., U.S.	D10	140
Sutton, W.V., U.S.	F5	114
Sutton, Monts see Green Mountains, mts., N.A.	G4	110
Sutton in Ashfield, Eng., U.K.	H11	12
Sutton West, On., Can.	D10	112
Suttor, stm., Austl.	C6	76
Sutwik Island, i., Ak., U.S.	E8	140
Suure-Jaani, Est.	B8	10
Suur Munamägi, hill, Est.	C9	10
Suur Pakri, i., Est.	A6	10
Suva, Fiji	q19	79e
Suvadiva Atoll, at., Mald.	i12	46a
Suvarlı, Tur.	A8	58
Suvasvesi, l., Fin.	E12	8
Suvorov, Russia	F19	10
Suwa, Japan	C11	40
Suwałki, Pol.	B18	16
Suwałki, state, Pol.	C18	16
Suwannaphum, Thai.	E6	48
Suwannee, stm., U.S.	G2	116
Suwanose-jima, i., Japan	k19	39a
Suwarrow, at., Cook Is.	E10	72
Suweis, Khalîg el- (Suez, Gulf of), b., Egypt	J4	58
Suweis, Qanâ el- (Suez Canal), can., Egypt	H3	58
Suwŏn, Kor., S.	F7	38
Suzak, Kaz.	F11	32
Suzaka, Japan	C11	40
Suzdal', Russia	H19	8
Suzhou, China	F9	42
Suzhou, China	E7	42
Suzigou, China	A10	42
Suzuka, Japan	E9	40
Suzuka-sammyaku, mts., Japan	D9	40
Suzu-misaki, c., Japan	B10	40
Suzun, Russia	D14	32
Suzzara, Italy	F7	22
Svalbard, dep., Eur.	B6	30
Svaliava, Ukr.	A10	26
Svapa, stm., Russia	H18	10
Svappavaara, Swe.	C9	8
Svärdsjö, Swe.	F6	8
Svartenhuk, pen., Grnld.	C15	141
Svartisen, ice, Nor.	C5	8
Svataj, Russia	C19	34
Svay Riĕng, Camb.	G7	48
Svėdasai, Lith.	E8	10
Svegssjön, l., Swe.	E5	8
Švėkšna, Lith.	E4	10
Svelvik, Nor.	G4	8
Svenčionėliai, Lith.	E8	10
Svenčionys, Lith.	E9	10
Svendborg, Den.	A6	16
Sventoji, Lith.	D3	10
Sventoji, stm., Lith.	E7	10
Sverdlovsk see Ekaterinburg, Russia	C10	32
Sverdrup, ostrov, i., Russia	B4	34
Sverdrup Channel, strt., Nu., Can.	A6	141
Sverdrup Islands, is., Nu., Can.	B5	141
Sveti Nikole, Mac.	B4	28
Svetlahorsk, Bela.	H12	10
Svetlaja, Russia	B12	36
Svetlogorsk, Russia	F2	10
Svetlograd, Russia	E6	32
Svetlyj, Russia	F3	10
Svetlyj, Russia	D10	32
Svetlyj, Russia	E12	34
Svetogorsk, Russia	F13	8
Svetozarevo, Yugo.	F8	26
Svidník, Slov.	G17	16
Svilengrad, Blg.	H13	26
Svínoy, i., Far. Is.	m34	8b
Svir, Bela.	F9	10
Svir', stm., Russia	F16	8
Svirica, Russia	F15	8
Svirsk, Russia	D18	32
Svislač, stm., Bela.	G11	10
Svištov, Blg.	F12	26
Svit, Slov.	G16	16
Svitavy, Czech Rep.	G12	16
Svjacilavičy, Bela.	H14	10
Svjatoj Nos, mys, c., Russia	B18	8
Svjatoj Nos, mys, c., Russia	B17	34
Svobodnyj, Russia	F14	34
Svolvær, Nor.	B6	8
Svratka, stm., Czech Rep.	G12	16
Swabia see Schwaben, hist. reg., Ger.	H5	16
Swain Reefs, rf., Austl.	C9	76
Swainsboro, Ga., U.S.	D3	116
Swains Island, at., Am. Sam.	E9	72
Swakop, stm., Nmb.	C2	70
Swakopmund, Nmb.	C2	70
Swale, stm., Eng., U.K.	G11	12
Swan, stm., Can.	B13	124
Swan, stm., Ab., Can.	A15	138
Swan, stm., Mt., U.S.	C13	136
Swanage, Eng., U.K.	K11	12
Swanee see Suwannee, stm., U.S.	G2	116
Swan Hill, Austl.	J4	76
Swan Hills, Ab., Can.	B15	138
Swan Islands see Santanilla, Islas, is., Hond.	D6	102
Swan Lake, Mb., Can.	E15	124
Swan Lake, l., Mb., Can.	B13	124
Swan Lake, l., Mn., U.S.	G4	118
Swannanoa, N.C., U.S.	I3	114
Swan Peak, mtn., Mt., U.S.	C13	136
Swanquarter, N.C., U.S.	A9	116
Swan Range, mts., Mt., U.S.	C13	136
Swan Reach, Austl.	J2	76
Swan River, Mb., Can.	B12	124
Swansboro, N.C., U.S.	B8	116
Swansea, Austl.	o13	77a
Swansea, Wales, U.K.	J8	12
Swanton, Vt., U.S.	F3	110
Swanville, Mn., U.S.	F4	118
Swart-Mfolozi, stm., S. Afr.	F10	70
Swartz Creek, Mi., U.S.	F6	112
Swarzędz, Pol.	D13	16
Swāt, stm., Pak.	A3	54
Swatow see Shantou, China	J7	42
Swaziland, ctry., Afr.	E10	70
Sweden, ctry., Eur.	E6	8
Swedish Knoll, mtn., Ut., U.S.	D5	132
Swedru, Ghana	H4	64
Sweeny, Tx., U.S.	E12	130
Sweet Briar, Va., U.S.	G6	114
Sweetgrass, Mt., U.S.	A15	136
Sweet Grass Hills, hills, Mt., U.S.	B15	136
Sweet Home, Tx., U.S.	E10	130
Sweet Springs, Mo., U.S.	F4	120
Sweetwater, Tn., U.S.	A1	116
Sweetwater, Tx., U.S.	B7	130
Sweetwater, stm., Wy., U.S.	E5	126
Swellendam, S. Afr.	H5	70
Świdnica, Pol.	F12	16
Świdnik, Pol.	E18	16
Świdwin, Pol.	C11	16
Świebodzice, Pol.	F12	16
Świebodzin, Pol.	D11	16
Świecie, Pol.	C14	16
Świerzawa, Pol.	E11	16
Świętokrzyski Park Narodowy, p.o.i., Pol.	F16	16
Swift Current, Sk., Can.	D6	124
Swift Current Creek, stm., Sk., Can.	D6	124
Swinburne, Cape, c., Nu., Can.	A11	106
Swindle Island, i., B.C., Can.	D2	138
Swindon, Eng., U.K.	J11	12
Swinford, Ire.	H4	12
Świnoujście (Swinemünde), Pol.	C9	16
Switzerland, ctry., Eur.	C14	18
Swords, Ire.	H6	12
Syalah, Russia	C13	34
Syan (San), stm., Eur.	F18	16
Sycamore, Ga., U.S.	E2	116
Sycamore, Il., U.S.	C9	120
Sycamore, Oh., U.S.	D2	114
Syčovka, Russia	E17	10
Sydenham, stm., On., Can.	F7	112
Sydney, Austl.	I8	76
Sydney, N.S., Can.	D16	110
Sydney Bay, b., Norf. I.	y25	78i
Sydney Lake, l., On., Can.	A4	118
Sydney Mines, N.S., Can.	D16	110
Syičy, Bela.	H12	10
Syke, Ger.	D4	16
Sykesville, Pa., U.S.	C7	114
Syktyvkar, Russia	B8	32
Sylacauga, Al., U.S.	D12	122
Sylhet, Bngl.	F13	54
Syloga, Russia	E20	8
Sylt, i., Ger.	B4	16
Sylva, N.C., U.S.	A2	116
Sylvan Grove, Ks., U.S.	C10	128
Sylvania, Ga., U.S.	D4	116
Sylvania, Oh., U.S.	C2	114
Sylvan Lake, Ab., Can.	D16	138
Sylvan Lake, l., Ab., Can.	D16	138
Sylvan Pass, p., Wy., U.S.	F16	136
Sylvester, Ga., U.S.	E2	116
Sylvester, Tx., U.S.	B7	130
Sym, Russia	B15	32
Syme see Sými, i., Grc.	G10	28
Sými, i., Grc.	G10	28
Šymkent, Kaz.	F11	32
Synevir, Ukr.	A10	26
Syowa, sci., Ant.	C9	81
Syracuse, In., U.S.	G4	112
Syracuse, Ks., U.S.	C7	128
Syracuse, Ne., U.S.	D1	120
Syracuse, N.Y., U.S.	A9	114
Syrdarja, Uzb.	A10	56
Syr Darya (Syrdar'ja), stm., Asia	F11	32
Syria, ctry., Asia	B4	56
Syriam, Mya.	D3	48
Syrian Desert (Shām, Bādiyat ash-), des., Asia	C4	56
Sýrna, i., Grc.	G9	28
Sýros, i., Grc.	F7	28
Sysmä, Fin.	F11	8
Sysola, stm., Russia	B8	32
Syt'kovo, Russia	D16	10
Syväri, l., Fin.	E13	8
Syzran', Russia	D7	32
Szabolcs-Szatmár-Bereg, state, Hung.	A9	26
Szamos (Someș), stm., Eur.	B9	26
Szamotuły, Pol.	D12	16
Szarvas, Hung.	C7	26
Szczawnica, Pol.	G16	16
Szczecin (Stettin), Pol.	C10	16
Szczecin, state, Pol.	C11	16
Szczecinek, Pol.	C12	16
Szczuczyn, Pol.	C18	16
Szczytno, Pol.	C17	16
Szechwan see Sichuan, state, China	E5	36
Szechwan Basin see Sichuan Pendi, bas., China	F1	42
Szeged, Hung.	C7	26
Szeghalom, Hung.	B8	26
Székesfehérvár, Hung.	B5	26
Szekszárd, Hung.	C5	26
Szentendre, Hung.	B5	26
Szentes, Hung.	C7	26
Szeping see Siping, China	C6	38
Szerencs, Hung.	A8	26
Szob, Hung.	B5	26
Szolnok, Hung.	B7	26
Szombathely, Hung.	B3	26
Szprotawa, Pol.	E11	16
Szubin, Pol.	C13	16
Szypliszki, Pol.	B19	16

T

Name	Map Ref.	Page
Taal, Lake, l., Phil.	D3	52
Tábara, Spain	C5	20
Tabar Islands, is., Pap. N. Gui.	a5	79a
Tabarka, Tun.	H2	24
Tabasco, state, Mex.	D6	96
Tabelbala, Alg.	D4	64
Taber, Ab., Can.	G18	138
Tabernes de Valldigna see Tavernes de la Valldigna, Spain	E10	20
Tabira, Braz.	D7	88
Tablas de Daimiel, Parque Nacional de las, p.o.i., Spain	E7	20
Tablas Island, i., Phil.	D4	52
Tablas Strait, strt., Phil.	D3	52
Tablat, Alg.	H14	20
Table Mountain, mtn., Az., U.S.	K6	132
Table Rock, Ne., U.S.	D1	120
Table Rock Lake, res., U.S.	H4	120
Table Top, mtn., Az., U.S.	K4	132
Tablones, P.R.	B4	104a
Taboi, Mount, hill, St. Vin.	p11	105e
Tábor, Czech Rep.	G10	16
Tabor, Russia	B19	34
Tabor, Ia., U.S.	D2	120
Tabora, Tan.	E6	66
Tabor City, N.C., U.S.	B7	116
Tabou, C. Iv.	I3	64
Tabrīz, Iran	B6	56
Tabuaeran, at., Kir.	C11	72
Tabu-dong, Kor., S.	C1	40
Tabuk, Phil.	B3	52
Tabūk, Sau. Ar.	J7	58
Tabuleiro do Norte, Braz.	C6	88
Tabwémasana, Mont, mtn., Vanuatu	j16	79d
Tacámbaro de Codallos, Mex.	F8	100
Tacaná, Volcán, vol., N.A.	H12	100
Tacañitas, Arg.	D6	92
Taché, Lac, l., N.T., Can.	C7	106
Tacheng, China	B1	36
Tachia, stm., Tai.	I9	42
Tachichitlte, Isla de, i., Mex.	C4	100
Tachie, stm., B.C., Can.	B6	138
Táchira, state, Ven.	D6	86
Tachoshui, Tai.	I9	42
Tacima, Braz.	D8	88
Tacloban, Phil.	E5	52
Taclobo, Phil.	D4	52
Tacna, Peru	G3	84
Tacna, Az., U.S.	K3	132
Tacoma, Wa., U.S.	C4	136
Taconic Range, mts., U.S.	B12	114
Taco Pozo, Arg.	B6	92
Tacuarembó, Ur.	E9	92
Tacuarembó, stm., Ur.	E10	92
Tacuarí, stm., Ur.	F10	92
Tacutu (Takutu), stm., S.A.	F11	86
Tademaït, Plateau du, plat., Alg.	D5	64
Tādepallegūdem, India	C5	53
Tadjemout, Alg.	D5	64
Tadjerouine, Tun.	I2	24
Tadjoura, Dji.	E8	62
Tadotsu, Japan	E6	40
Tadoule Lake, l., Mb., Can.	D11	106
Tadoussac, Qc., Can.	B7	110

Name	Map Ref.	Page
Tādpatri, India	D4	53
T'aean, Kor., S.	F7	38
T'aebaek-sanmaek, mts., Asia	F8	38
Taech'ŏn, Kor., S.	F7	38
Taedong-gang, stm., Kor., N.	E6	38
Taegu, Kor., S.	D1	40
Taejin, Kor., S.	C2	40
Taejŏn, Kor., S.	F7	38
Taeng, stm., Thai.	C4	48
Tafahi, i., Tonga	E9	72
Tafalla, Spain	B9	20
Tafanlieh, Tai.	J9	42
Tafassâsset, Oued, stm., Afr.	E6	64
Tafassasset, Ténéré du, des., Niger	E7	64
Taféa, state, Vanuatu	I17	79d
Tafelberg, hill, Neth. Ant.	p22	104g
Tafí Viejo, Arg.	C5	92
Tafo, Ghana	H4	64
Taft, Ca., U.S.	H6	134
Taft, Tx., U.S.	F10	130
Taftān, Kūh-e, vol., Iran	D9	56
Taga, Samoa	g11	79c
Tagajō, Japan	A14	40
Taganrog, Russia	E5	32
Tagânt, reg., Maur.	F2	64
Tagawa, Japan	F3	40
Tagaytay, Phil.	C3	52
Tagbilaran, Phil.	F4	52
Tage, Pap. N. Gui.	b3	79a
Tagish Lake, l., Can.	C3	106
Tagliamento, stm., Italy	E9	22
Taglio di Po, Italy	E9	22
Taguatinga, Braz.	G2	88
Taguke, China	B10	54
Tagula Island, i., Pap. N. Gui.	B10	74
Tagum, Phil.	G5	52
Tagus (Tajo) (Tejo), stm., Eur.	E2	20
Tahakopa, N.Z.	H3	80
Tahan, Gunong, mtn., Malay.	J6	48
Tahat, mtn., Alg.	E6	64
Tahiataš, Uzb.	F9	32
Tahifet, Alg.	E6	64
Tahiryuak Lake, l., N.T., Can.	A8	106
Tahiti, i., Fr. Poly.	v23	78h
Tahiti-Faaa, Aéroport International de, Fr. Poly.	v21	78h
Tahkuna nina, c., Est.	A5	10
Tahlequah, Ok., U.S.	I3	120
Tahoe, Lake, l., U.S.	E5	134
Tahoe City, Ca., U.S.	D5	134
Tahoe Lake, l., Nu., Can.	A8	106
Tahoka, Tx., U.S.	A6	130
Tahoua, Niger	F5	64
Tahquamenon, stm., Mi., U.S.	B4	112
Tahta, Egypt	L2	58
Tahta, Russia	E6	32
Tahta-Bazar, Turkmen.	B9	56
Tahtaköprü, Tur.	D12	28
Tahtamygda, Russia	F13	34
Tahtsa Lake, res., B.C., Can.	C3	138
Tahtsa Peak, mtn., B.C., Can.	C3	138
Tahuata, i., Fr. Poly.	s18	78g
Tahulandang, Pulau, i., Indon.	E7	44
Tahuna, Indon.	E8	44
Tai'an, China	C7	42
Taiarapu, Presqu'île de, pen., Fr. Poly.	w22	78h
Taibai Shan, mtn., China	E2	42
Taibilla, Sierra de, mts., Spain	F8	20
Taibus Qi, China	C8	36
Taicang, China	F9	42
T'aichou see Taizhou, China	E8	42
T'aichung, Tai.	I9	42
Taieri, stm., N.Z.	G4	80
Taigu, China	C5	42
Taihang Shan, mts., China	C5	42
Taihape, N.Z.	D6	80
Taihe, China	H6	42
Taihe, China	E6	42
Taihezhen, China	B5	38
T'aihsien see Taizhou, China	E8	42
Taihu, China	F7	42
Tai Hu, l., China	F9	42
Taikang, China	D6	42
Taikou, China	F4	42
Tailai, China	B9	36
Tai Lake see Tai Hu, l., China	F9	42
Tailem Bend, Austl.	J2	76
Taimba, Russia	B17	32
T'ainan, Tai.	J8	42
Taínaro, Ákra, c., Grc.	G5	28
Taining, China	H7	42
Taiobeiras, Braz.	H4	88
T'aipei, Tai.	I9	42
T'aipeihsien, Tai.	I9	42
Taiping, China	J2	42
Taiping, Malay.	J5	48
Taipingdian, China	E4	42
Taipu, Braz.	C8	88
Tais, Indon.	F3	50
Taisha, Japan	D5	40
Taishan, China	J5	42
Tai Shan see Yuhuang Ding, mtn., China	C9	42
Taishun, China	H8	42
Taitao, Península de, pen., Chile	I2	90
T'aitung, Tai.	J9	42
Taivalkoski, Fin.	D12	8
Taiwan, ctry., Asia	J9	42
Taiwan Strait, strt., Asia	I8	42
Taixian, China	E9	42
Taixing, China	E9	42
Ṭaiyiba, Isr.	F6	58
Taiyuan, China	C5	42
Taizhao, China	D14	54
Taizhou, China	E8	42
Taizi, stm., China	D5	38
Tajbola, Russia	B15	8
Tajga, Russia	C15	32
Tajgonos, mys, c., Russia	D21	34
Tajgonos, poluostrov, pen., Russia	D21	34
Tajikistan, ctry., Asia	B11	56
Tajima, Japan	B12	40
Tajimi, Japan	D10	40
Tajique, N.M., U.S.	G2	128
Tajitos, Mex.	F6	98
Tāj Mahal, hist., India	E7	54
Tajmura, stm., Russia	B18	32
Tajmyr, ozero, l., Russia	B9	34
Tajmyr, poluostrov, pen., Russia	B7	34
Tajšet, Russia	C17	32
Tajumulco, Volcán, vol., Guat.	E2	102
Tajuña, stm., Spain	D7	20
Tak, Thai.	D4	48
Takachu, Bots.	C5	70
Takahagi, Japan	C13	40
Takahashi, Japan	E6	40
Takahe, Mount, mtn., Ant.	C29	81
Takaka, N.Z.	E5	80
Takakkaw Falls, wtfl, B.C., Can.	E14	138
Takalar, Indon.	F11	50
Takamatsu, Japan	E7	40
Takanabe, Japan	G4	40
Takaoka, Japan	C9	40
Takasago, Japan	E7	40
Takasaki, Japan	C11	40
Takatsuki, Japan	E8	40
Ta-kaw, Mya.	B4	48
Takayama, Japan	C10	40
Takefu, Japan	D9	40
Takenake, China	A8	54
Takengon, Indon.	J3	48
Takeo, Japan	F3	40
Take-shima, is., Asia	B4	40
Taketa, Japan	G4	40
Takêv, Camb.	G7	48
Takhatpur, India	G8	54
Takhli, Thai.	E5	48
Takhta-Bazar see Tahta-Bazar, Turkmen.	B9	56
Takijuq Lake, l., Nu., Can.	B8	106
Takikawa, Japan	C14	38
Takla Lake, l., B.C., Can.	A5	138
Takla Landing, B.C., Can.	D5	106
Takla Makan Desert see Taklimakan Shamo, des., China	G14	32
Taklimakan Shamo (Takla Makan Desert), des., China	G14	32
Takolekaju, Pegunungan, mts., Indon.	E11	50
Taksimo, Russia	F10	34
Taku, Japan	F3	40
Takuan, Mount, vol., Pap. N. Gui.	d6	79b
Takum, Nig.	H7	64
Takutea, i., Cook Is.	E11	72
Takutu (Tacutu), stm., S.A.	F11	86
Talačyn, Bela.	F12	10
Talagang, Pak.	B4	54
Talagante, Chile	F2	92
Talaimannar, Sri L.	G4	53
Talāja, India	H4	54
Talak, reg., Niger	F6	64
Tālāla, India	H3	54
Talang, Gunung, vol., Indon.	D2	50
Talangbetutu, Indon.	E4	50
Talangpadang, Indon.	F4	50
Talangrimbo, Indon.	E4	50
Talara, Peru	D1	84
Talas, Kyrg.	F12	32
Talasea, Pap. N. Gui.	b4	79a
Tal'at al-Jamā'ah, Rujm, mtn., Jord.	H6	58
Talata Mafara, Nig.	G6	64
Talaud, Kepulauan (Talaud Islands), is., Indon.	E8	44
Talaud Islands see Talaud, Kepulauan, is., Indon.	E8	44
Talavera de la Reina, Spain	D5	20
Talawanta, Austl.	B3	76
Talawdī, Sudan	E6	62
Talayan, Phil.	G5	52
Talbotton, Ga., U.S.	E14	122
Talbragar, stm., Austl.	I7	76
Talca, Chile	G2	92
Talcahuano, Chile	H1	92
Tālcher, India	H10	54
Talco, Tx., U.S.	D3	122
Taldom, Russia	D20	10
Taldykorgan, Kaz.	F13	32
Taldyqorghan see Taldykorgan, Kaz.	F13	32
Talence, Fr.	E5	18
Talent, Or., U.S.	A3	134
Talgar, Kaz.	F13	32
Talghar see Talgar, Kaz.	F13	32
Talhār, Pak.	F2	54
Taliabu, Pulau, i., Indon.	F7	44
Talibon, Phil.	E5	52
Talibong, Ko, i., Thai.	I4	48
Talica, Russia	C10	32
Talien see Dalian, China	B9	42
Tālīkota, India	C3	53
Taliparamba, India	E2	53
Talisay, Phil.	E4	52
Taliwang, Indon.	H10	50
Talkeetna, Ak., U.S.	D9	140
Talkeetna Mountains, mts., Ak., U.S.	D10	140
Talla, Egypt	J1	58
Talladega, Al., U.S.	D12	122
Tallahala Creek, stm., Ms., U.S.	F9	122
Tallahassee, Fl., U.S.	F1	116
Tallahatchie, stm., Ms., U.S.	D8	122
Tallangatta, Austl.	K6	76
Tallapoosa, Ga., U.S.	D13	122
Tallapoosa, stm., U.S.	E12	122
Tallard, Fr.	E11	18
Tallassee, Al., U.S.	E12	122
Tall as-Sulṭān, hist., Gaza	G6	58
Tall Bīsah, Syria	D7	58
Tallinn, Est.	G11	8
Tallmadge, Oh., U.S.	C4	114
Tall Rif'at, Syria	B8	58
Tallulah, La., U.S.	E7	122
Talmage, Ca., U.S.	D2	134
Talmage, Ne., U.S.	K2	118
Tal'menka, Russia	D14	32
Talnah, Russia	C6	34
Taloda, India	H5	54
Taloga, Ok., U.S.	E10	128
Talok, Indon.	C11	50
Tāloqān, Afg.	B10	56
Talovka, Russia	F7	32
Taloyoak, Nu., Can.	B12	106
Talquin, Lake, res., Fl., U.S.	G14	122
Talsi, Lat.	C5	10
Taltal, Chile	B2	92
Taltson, stm., N.T., Can.	C8	106
Talu, Indon.	C1	50
Taluk, Indon.	D2	50
Talumphuk, Laem, c., Thai.	H5	48
Talvikjulja, Russia	B13	8
Talwood, Austl.	G7	76
Tama, Arg.	E4	92
Tama, Ia., U.S.	C5	120
Tamalameque, Col.	C5	86
Tamale, Ghana	H4	64
Tamalea, Indon.	E11	50
Tamalpais, Mount, mtn., Ca., U.S.	F3	134
Tamana, Japan	G3	40
Tamana, Mount, hill, Trin.	s12	105f
Tamanaco, stm., Ven.	C9	86
Tamaniquá, Braz.	I9	86
Taman Negara, p.o.i., Malay.	J6	48
Tamano, Japan	E6	40
Tamanquaré, Ilha, i., Braz.	H9	86
Tamapatz, Mex.	E9	100
Tamar, stm., Austl.	n13	77a
Tamarac, stm., Mn., U.S.	C2	118
Tamaroa, Il., U.S.	F8	120
Tamási, Hung.	C5	26
Tamaulipas, state, Mex.	C9	100
Tamazulapan del Progreso, Mex.	G9	100
Tamazunchale, Mex.	E9	100
Tambacounda, Sen.	G2	64
Tambakboyo, Indon.	G7	50
Tamba-kōchi, plat., Japan	D8	40
Tambangsawah, Indon.	E3	50
Tambara, Moz.	D5	68
Tāmbaram, India	E5	53
Tambej, Russia	B3	34
Tambelan, Kepulauan, is., Indon.	C5	50
Tamberías, Arg.	E3	92
Tambo, stm., Austl.	K6	76
Tambohorano, Madag.	D7	68
Tambolongang, Pulau, i., Indon.	G12	50
Tambora, Gunung, vol., Indon.	H10	50
Tamboril, Braz.	C5	88
Tamboryacu, stm., Peru	H4	86
Tambov, Russia	D6	32
Tambre, stm., Spain	B2	20
Tambu, Teluk, b., Indon.	C11	50
Tambunan, Malay.	H1	52
Tambura, Sudan	F5	62
Tâmchekkeṭ, Maur.	F2	64
Tame, Col.	D6	86
Tameapa, Mex.	C5	100
Tâmega, stm., Port.	C3	20
Tamel Aike, Arg.	I2	90
Tamenghest, Alg.	E6	64
Tamenghest, Oued, stm., Alg.	E5	64
Tamga, Russia	B10	38
Tamgak, Adrar, mtn., Niger	F6	64
Tamiahua, Mex.	E10	100
Tamiahua, Laguna de, l., Mex.	E10	100
Tamiami Canal, can., Fl., U.S.	K4	116
Tamil Nādu, state, India	F4	53
Tamiš (Timiș), stm., Eur.	D7	26
Tâmîya, Egypt	I1	58
Tamkūhi, India	E10	54
Tam Ky, Viet.	E9	48
Tammerfors see Tampere, Fin.	F10	8
Tammisaari, Fin.	G10	8
Tamms, Il., U.S.	G8	120
Tampa, Fl., U.S.	I3	116
Tampa Bay, b., Fl., U.S.	I3	116
Tampang, Indon.	F4	50
Tampaon, stm., Mex.	E9	100
Tampere (Tammerfors), Fin.	F10	8
Tampico, Mex.	D10	100
Tampico, Il., U.S.	C8	120
Tampin, Malay.	K6	48
Tamsagbulag, Mong.	B8	36
Tamshiyacu, Peru	D3	84
Tamsweg, Aus.	C10	22
Tamu, Mya.	D7	46
Tamuning, Guam	i10	78c
Tamworth, Austl.	H8	76
Tamworth, Eng., U.K.	I11	12
Tana (Teno), stm., Eur.	B12	8
Tana, stm., Kenya	D8	66
Tana, Lake see T'ana Hāyk', l., Eth.	E7	62
Tanabe, Japan	F8	40
Tanabi, Braz.	K1	88
Tana bru, Nor.	A12	8
Tanacross, Ak., U.S.	D11	140
Tanafjorden, b., Nor.	A13	8
Tanaga Island, i., Ak., U.S.	g23	140a
T'ana Hāyk', l., Eth.	E7	62
Tanahbala, Pulau, i., Indon.	F2	44
Tanahgrogot, Indon.	D10	50
Tanahjampea, Pulau, i., Indon.	G12	50
Tanahmasa, Pulau, i., Indon.	F2	44
Tanahmerah, Indon.	G10	44
Tanah Merah, Malay.	J6	48
Tanahputih, Indon.	C2	50
Tanakeke, Pulau, i., Indon.	F11	50
Tanakpur, India	D7	54
Tanami Desert, des., Austl.	C5	74
Tan An, Viet.	G8	48
Tanana, Ak., U.S.	C9	140
Tanana, stm., Ak., U.S.	D10	140
Tananarive see Antananarivo, Madag.	D8	68
Tanbar, Austl.	E3	76
Tan Chau, Viet.	G7	48
Tanch'ŏn-ŭp, Kor., N.	D8	38
Tancítaro, Pico de, mtn., Mex.	F7	100
Tanda, Egypt	K1	58
Tānda, India	E9	54
Tānda, India	C5	54
Tandag, Phil.	F6	52
Tandaltī, Sudan	E6	62
Țăndărei, Rom.	E14	26
Tandil, Arg.	H8	92
Tando Ādam, Pak.	F2	54
Tando Allāhyār, Pak.	F2	54
Tandou Lake, l., Austl.	I3	76
Tandula Tank, res., India	H8	54
Tandun, Indon.	C2	50
Tāndūr, India	C3	53
Tanega-shima, i., Japan	I9	38
Tanezrouft, des., Afr.	E4	64
Tang, stm., China	E7	42
Tang, stm., China	E5	42
Tang, stm., China	B6	42
Tanga, Russia	F11	34
Tanga, Tan.	F7	66
Tangail, Bngl.	F12	54
Tanga Islands, is., Pap. N. Gui.	a5	79a
Tanga Langua, c., Gren.	q10	105e
Tanganyika see Tanzania, ctry., Afr.	F6	66
Tanganyika, Lake, l., Afr.	F6	66
Tangarana, stm., Peru	I4	86
Tangarare, Sol. Is.	e8	79b
Tanger (Tangier), Mor.	B3	64
Tangerang, Indon.	G5	50
Tangerhütte, Ger.	D7	16
Tangermünde, Ger.	D7	16
Tanggu, China	B7	42
Tanggulashan, China	A14	54
Tanggula Shan, mts., China	E3	36
Tanggula Shankou, p., China	B13	54
Tanghe, China	E5	42
Tangi, Pak.	A3	54
Tangier, N.S., Can.	F14	110
Tangier see Tanger, Mor.	B3	64
Tangier, Va., U.S.	G10	114
Tangipahoa, stm., U.S.	G8	122
Tangjiagou, China	F7	42
Tangkou, China	F8	42
Tangmai, China	E4	36
Tango-hantō, pen., Japan	D8	40
Tangra Yumco, l., China	C11	54
Tangshan, China	B8	42
Tangtou, China	D8	42
Tangyan, Mya.	A4	48
Tangyin, China	D6	42
Tangyuan, China	B10	36
Tanhoj, Russia	F10	34
Taniantaweng Shan, mts., China	F4	36
Tanigawa-dake, mtn., Japan	C11	40
Tanimbar, Kepulauan, is., Indon.	G9	44
Tanintharyi, state, Mya.	F3	48
Tanis, hist., Egypt	H2	58
Tanjay, Phil.	F4	52
Tanjung, Indon.	H10	50
Tanjung, Indon.	E9	50
Tanjungbalai, Indon.	B1	50
Tanjungbatu, Indon.	C3	50
Tanjungbatu, Indon.	B11	50
Tanjungkarang-Telukbetung, Indon.	F4	50
Tanjunglabu, Indon.	E5	50
Tanjungpandan, Indon.	E5	50
Tanjungpinang, Indon.	C4	50
Tanjungpura, Indon.	K4	48
Tanjungraja, Indon.	E4	50
Tanjungredep, Indon.	B10	50
Tanjungselor, Indon.	B10	50
Tanjunguban, Indon.	C4	50
Tānk, Pak.	B3	54
Tankwa, stm., S. Afr.	H5	70
Tanna, i., Vanuatu	I17	79d
Tannenberg see Stębark, Pol.	C16	16
Tanner, Mount, mtn., B.C., Can.	G12	138
Tannu-Ola, hrebet, mts., Asia	D16	32
Tannūrah, Ra's, c., Sau. Ar.	D7	56
Tanon Strait, strt., Phil.	E4	52
Tanout, Niger	F6	64
Tanquinho, Braz.	G6	88
Tanshui, Tai.	I9	42
Tanta, Egypt	H2	58
Tan-Tan, Mor.	D2	64
Tantoyuca, Mex.	E9	100
Tanuku, India	C5	53
Tanvald, Czech Rep.	F11	16
Tanyang, Kor., S.	C1	40
Tanzania, ctry., Afr.	F6	66
Tao'er, stm., China	B5	38
Taohuazhen, China	A6	42
Taole, China	B2	42
Taonan, China	B5	38
Taongi, at., Marsh. Is.	B7	72
Taormina, Italy	G9	24
Taos, Mo., U.S.	F5	120
Taos, N.M., U.S.	E3	128
Taos Pueblo, N.M., U.S.	E3	128
Taoudenni, Mali	E4	64
Taounate, Mor.	C4	64
Taourirt, Mor.	C4	64
Taoyuan, China	G4	42
Taoyüan, Tai.	I9	42
Tapa, Est.	G11	8
Tapachula, Mex.	H12	100
Tapaga, Cape, c., Samoa	h12	79c
Tapah, Malay.	J5	48
Tapajós, stm., Braz.	D6	84
Tapaktuan, Indon.	K3	48
Tapalqué, Arg.	H7	92
Tapauá, stm., Braz.	E4	84
Tapejara, Braz.	D12	92
Taperoá, Braz.	D7	88
Tapes, Braz.	E12	92
Tapeta, Lib.	H3	64
Taphan Hin, Thai.	D5	48
Taphoen, stm., Thai.	E4	48
Tāpi, stm., India	H4	54
Ta Pi, stm., Thai.	H4	48
Tapiche, stm., Peru	E3	84
Tapini, Pap. N. Gui.	b4	79a
Taplan National Park, p.o.i., Thai.	E6	48
Tāplejungg, Nepal	E11	54
Tappen, N.D., U.S.	H14	124
Tapuae-o-Uenuku, mtn., N.Z.	E5	80
Tapuio, stm., Braz.	C3	88
Tapul Group, is., Phil.	H3	52
Tapun, Mya.	C2	48
Tapuruquara, Braz.	H9	86
Taqāṭu' Hayyā, Sudan	D7	62
Taquara, Braz.	D12	92
Taquaras, Ponta das, c., Braz.	C13	92
Taquari, stm., Braz.	D12	92
Taquari Novo, stm., Braz.	C5	90
Taquaritinga, Braz.	K1	88
Tar, stm., N.C., U.S.	I8	114
Tara, Austl.	F8	76
Tara, Russia	C12	32
Tara, stm., Eur.	G16	22
Tara, stm., Russia	C13	32
Taraba, stm., Nig.	H7	64
Tarabuco, Bol.	C3	90
Ṭarābulus (Tripoli), Leb.	D6	58
Ṭarābulus (Tripoli), Libya	A2	62
Ṭarābulus (Tripolitania), hist. reg., Libya	A2	62
Taraclia, Mol.	D15	26
Tarago, Austl.	J7	76
Taraira (Traíra), stm., S.A.	H7	86
Taraju, Indon.	G6	50
Tarakan, Indon.	B10	50
Tarakan, Pulau, i., Indon.	B10	50
Taralga, Austl.	J7	76
Tara Nacionalni Park, p.o.i., Yugo.	F6	26
Tārānagar, India	D5	54
Taranaki, Mount (Egmont, Mount), vol., N.Z.	D6	80
Tarancón, Spain	D8	20
Taranto, Italy	D11	24
Taranto, Golfo di, b., Italy	E10	24
Tarapoto, Peru	E2	84
Taraquá, Braz.	G7	86
Tarare, Fr.	D10	18
Tarariras, Ur.	G9	92
Tarāsa Dwīp, i., India	G7	46
Tarascon, Fr.	F10	18
Tarascon-sur-Ariège, Fr.	G7	18
Tarasovo, Russia	C19	32
Tarat, Alg.	D6	64
Tarata, Bol.	C3	90
Taratakbuluh, Indon.	C2	50
Tarauacá, stm., Braz.	E3	84
Taravao, Isthme de, isth., Fr. Poly.	v22	78h
Tarawa, at., Kir.	C8	72
Tarawera, N.Z.	D7	80
Tarazona, Spain	C9	20
Tarbagataj, hrebet, mts., Asia	E14	32
Tarbagatay Shan see Tarbagataj, hrebet, mts., Asia	E14	32
Tarbela Reservoir, res., Pak.	A4	54
Tarbert, Scot., U.K.	D6	12
Tarbes, Fr.	F6	18
Tarboro, N.C., U.S.	I8	114
Tarbū, Libya	B3	62
Tarcoola, Austl.	F6	74
Tardoki-Jani, gora, mtn., Russia	G16	34
Taree, Austl.	H9	76
Tareja, Russia	B7	34
Tärendö, Swe.	C10	8
Tarentum, Pa., U.S.	D6	114
Tarfa, Wadi el-, stm., Egypt	J2	58
Tarfaya, Mor.	D2	64
Targhee Pass, p., U.S.	F15	136
Tărgovište, Blg.	F13	26
Târgoviște, Rom.	E12	26
Târgu Bujor, Rom.	D14	26
Târgu Frumos, Rom.	B14	26
Târgu Jiu, Rom.	D10	26
Târgu Mureș, Rom.	C11	26
Târgu-Neamț, Rom.	B13	26
Târgu Ocna, Rom.	C13	26
Târgu Secuiesc, Rom.	D12	26
Tarifa, Spain	H5	20
Tarifa, Punta de, c., Spain	H5	20
Tarija, Bol.	D4	90
Tarikere, India	E2	53
Tarim, stm., China	F14	32
Tarim Pendi, bas., China	F12	30
Taritatu, stm., Indon.	F10	44
Tarkastad, S. Afr.	G8	70
Tarkio, Mo., U.S.	D2	120
Tarkio, stm., U.S.	D2	120
Tarko-Sale, Russia	B13	32
Tarkwa, Ghana	H4	64
Tarlac, Phil.	C3	52
Tarm, Den.	I3	8
Tarma, Peru	F2	84
Tarn, state, Fr.	F8	18
Tarn, stm., Fr.	F7	18
Tärnaby, Swe.	D6	8
Tarnak, stm., Afg.	B1	54
Târnava Mare, stm., Rom.	C11	26
Târnăveni, Rom.	C11	26
Tarn-et-Garonne, state, Fr.	F7	18
Tarnobrzeg, Pol.	F17	16
Tarnobrzeg, state, Pol.	F17	16
Tarnogród, Pol.	F18	16
Târnova, Mol.	A14	26
Tarnów, Pol.	G16	16
Tarnów, state, Pol.	G16	16
Tarnowskie Góry, Pol.	F14	16
Taro, Sol. Is.	d7	79b
Taro, stm., Italy	F7	22
Taron, Pap. N. Gui.	a5	79a
Tarong, Austl.	F8	76
Taroom, Austl.	E7	76
Taroudannt, Mor.	C3	64
Ta Roun, Co, mtn., Viet.	D8	48
Tarpon Springs, Fl., U.S.	H3	116
Tarquinia, Italy	H8	22
Tarra, stm., S.A.	C5	86
Tarrafal, C.V.	k10	65a
Tarragona, Spain	C12	20
Tarragona, co., Spain	D11	20
Tarraleah, Austl.	o13	77a
Tarrasa see Terrassa, Spain	C13	20
Tàrrega, Spain	C12	20
Tárrega see Tàrrega, Spain	C12	20
Tarsus, Tur.	B5	58
Tartagal, Arg.	D4	90
Tartu, Est.	G12	8
Ṭarṭūs, Syria	D6	58
Ṭarṭūs, state, Syria	D7	58
Tarum, stm., Indon.	G5	50
Tarumirim, Braz.	J5	88
Tarumizu, Japan	H3	40
Tarutao, Ko, i., Thai.	I4	48
Tarutao National Park, p.o.i., Thai.	I4	48
Tarutino, Russia	E19	10
Tarutung, Indon.	B1	50
Tarvisio, Italy	D10	22
Tarzan, Tx., U.S.	B6	130
Taşağıl, Tur.	B2	58
Tasāwah, Libya	B2	62
Tasbuget, Kaz.	F11	32
Taseeva, stm., Russia	C16	32
Taseevo, Russia	C17	32
Taseko Lakes, l., B.C., Can.	E7	138
Taseko Mountain, mtn., B.C., Can.	E7	138
Tāsgaon, India	C2	53
Tashi Gang Dzong, Bhu.	E13	54
Ṭashk, Daryācheh-ye, l., Iran	D7	56
Tasikmalaya, Indon.	G5	50
Tåsinge, i., Den.	B6	16
Taškent, Uzb.	F11	32
Taškepri, Turkmen.	B9	56
Taš-Kumyr, Kyrg.	F12	32
Tasman Basin, unds.	N18	142
Tasman Bay, b., N.Z.	E5	80
Tasmania, state, Austl.	n13	77a
Tasmania, i., Austl.	o13	77a
Tasman Peninsula, pen., Austl.	o13	77a
Tasman Sea, Oc.	G7	72
Tășnad, Rom.	B9	26
Tassialouc, Lac, l., Qc., Can.	D16	106
Taštagol, Russia	D15	32
Tastiota, Mex.	A3	100
Tata, Hung.	B5	26
Tata, Mor.	D3	64
Tatabánya, Hung.	B5	26
Tatarbunary, Ukr.	D16	26
Tatarija, state, Russia	C8	32
Tatarinka, Russia	E16	10
Tatarsk, Russia	C13	32
Tatarskij proliv, strt., Russia	G17	34
Tatarskoe-Maklakovo, Russia	I21	8
Tatarstan see Tatarija, state, Russia	C8	32
Tatar Strait see Tatarskij proliv, strt., Russia	G17	34
Tate, Ga., U.S.	B1	116
Tate, stm., Austl.	A4	76
Tateyama, Japan	E12	40
Tate-yama, vol., Japan	C10	40
Tathlina Lake, l., N.T., Can.	C7	106
Tatlayoko Lake, B.C., Can.	E6	138
Tatlayoko Lake, l., B.C., Can.	E6	138
Tatlow, Mount, mtn., B.C., Can.	E7	138
Tatnam, Cape, c., Mb., Can.	D12	106
Tatranský Narodny Park, p.o.i., Slov.	G15	16
Tatrzański Park Narodowy, p.o.i., Pol.	G15	16
Tatsuno, Japan	E7	40
Tatsuno, Japan	D10	40
Tatuí, Braz.	L1	88
Tatum, N.M., U.S.	H5	128
Tatum, Tx., U.S.	E4	122
Tat'ung see Datong, China	A5	42
Tatvan, Tur.	B5	56
Tau, Am. Sam.	h13	79c
Tau, Nor.	G1	8
Tau, i., Am. Sam.	h13	79c
Tauá, Braz.	C5	88
Taubaté, Braz.	L3	88
Tauberbischofsheim, Ger.	G5	16
Taučik, Kaz.	F8	32
Taujskaja guba, b., Russia	E18	34
Taumarunui, N.Z.	D6	80
Taumaturgo, Braz.	E3	84
Taum Sauk Mountain, mtn., Mo., U.S.	G7	120
Taungbon, Mya.	E3	48
Taungdwingyi, Mya.	B2	48
Taunggyi, Mya.	B3	48
Taungnyo Range, mts., Mya.	E3	48
Taungup, Mya.	C2	48
Taungup Pass, p., Mya.	C2	48
Taunsa, Pak.	C3	54
Taunton, Eng., U.K.	J9	12
Taunton, Ma., U.S.	C14	114
Taupo, N.Z.	D6	80
Taupo, Lake, l., N.Z.	D7	80
Tauragė, Lith.	E5	10
Tauranga, N.Z.	C7	80
Taurianova, Italy	F9	24
Taurisano, Italy	E12	24
Tauroa Point, c., N.Z.	B5	80
Taurus Mountains see Toros Dağları, mts., Tur.	A3	58
Tautira, Fr. Poly.	v23	78h
Tavan-Bogdo-Ula, gora, mtn., Asia	E15	32
Tavares, Braz.	D7	88
Tavas, Tur.	F12	28
Tavastehus see Hämeenlinna, Fin.	F10	8
Tavda, Russia	C11	32
Tavda, stm., Russia	C11	32
Tavernes de la Valldigna, Spain	E10	20
Tavernier, Fl., U.S.	K5	116
Taveuni, i., Fiji	p20	79e
Taviano, Italy	E11	24
Tavira, Port.	G3	20
Tavistock, On., Can.	E9	112
Tavistock, Eng., U.K.	K8	12
Tavolara, Isola, i., Italy	D3	24
Tavoliere, reg., Italy	C9	24
Tavolžan, Kaz.	D13	32
Tavor, Har, mtn., Isr.	F6	58
Tavoy Point, c., Mya.	F3	48
Tavşanlı, Tur.	D12	28
Tavua, Fiji	p18	79e
Tawaeli, Indon.	D11	50
Tawakoni, Lake, res., Tx., U.S.	E2	122
Tawas City, Mi., U.S.	D6	112
Tawau, Malay.	A10	50
Tawîla, Gezira, is., Egypt	K4	58
Tawitawi Group, is., Phil.	H3	52
Tawitawi Island, i., Phil.	H2	52
Ṭawkar, Sudan	D7	62
Taxco de Alarcón, Mex.	F8	100
Taxkorgan Tajik Zizhixian, China	B12	56
Tay, stm., Scot., U.K.	E9	12
Tay, Firth of, b., Scot., U.K.	E9	12
Tay, Loch, l., Scot., U.K.	E8	12
Tayabamba, Peru	E2	84
Tayabas Bay, b., Phil.	D3	52
Tayan, Indon.	C7	50
Taylor, Az., U.S.	I6	132
Taylor, Ne., U.S.	F13	126
Taylor, Tx., U.S.	D10	130
Taylor, Mount, mtn., N.M., U.S.	H9	132
Taylors, S.C., U.S.	B3	116
Taylorsville, Ky., U.S.	F12	120
Taylorsville, Ms., U.S.	F9	122
Taylorsville, N.C., U.S.	I4	114
Taylorville, Il., U.S.	E8	120
Taymā', Sau. Ar.	K9	58
Taymouth, N.B., Can.	D10	110
Taymyr Peninsula see Tajmyr, poluostrov, pen., Russia	B7	34
Tay Ninh, Viet.	G8	48
Taytay, Phil.	E2	52
Tayu, Indon.	G7	50
Taz, stm., Russia	A14	32
Taza, Mor.	C4	64
Tazewell, Tn., U.S.	H2	114
Tazewell, Va., U.S.	G4	114
Tazin, stm., Can.	C8	106
Tazin Lake, l., Sk., Can.	D9	106
Tazovskaja guba, b., Russia	A13	32
Tazovskij, Russia	A13	32
Tazovskij poluostrov, pen., Russia	C4	34
Tbessa, Alg.	B6	64
Tbilisi, Geor.	F6	32
Tchaourou, Benin	H5	64
Tchentlo Lake, l., B.C., Can.	A5	138
Tchesinkut Lake, l., B.C., Can.	B5	138
Tchibanga, Gabon	E2	66
Tcho-kiang see Zhejiang, state, China	G8	42
Tchollíré, Cam.	C2	66
Tchula, Ms., U.S.	D8	122
Tczew, Pol.	B14	16
Té, stm., Camb.	F8	48
Teá, stm., Braz.	H9	86
Teaca, Rom.	C11	26
Teaehoa, c., Fr. Poly.	s18	78g
Teague, Tx., U.S.	F2	122
Teahupoo, Fr. Poly.	w22	78h
Te Anau, Lake, l., N.Z.	G2	80
Teapa, Mex.	G12	100
Te Awamutu, N.Z.	C6	80
Teba, Spain	H5	20
Tebakang, Malay.	C7	50
Tebicuary, stm., Para.	C9	92
Tebicuary-mí, stm., Para.	C9	92
Tebingtinggi, Indon.	B1	50
Tebingtinggi, Indon.	E3	50
Tebingtinggi, Pulau, i., Indon.	C3	50
Tébourba, Tun.	H3	24
Téboursouk, Tun.	H3	24
Tecalitlán, Mex.	F7	100
Tecate, Mex.	K9	134
Techirghiol, Rom.	E15	26
Techlé, W. Sah.	E2	64
Techou see Dezhou, China	C7	42
Tecka, Arg.	H2	90
Tecka, stm., Arg.	H2	90
Tecomán, Mex.	F7	100
Tecopa, Ca., U.S.	H9	134
Tecpan de Galeana, Mex.	G8	100
Tecuala, Mex.	D6	100
Tecuci, Rom.	D14	26
Tecumseh, Ok., U.S.	B2	122
Tedžen, Turkmen.	B9	56
Tedžen (Harīrūd), stm., Asia	B9	56
Teec Nos Pos, Az., U.S.	G7	132
Teeli, Russia	D16	32
Tees, stm., Eng., U.K.	G11	12
Teeswater, On., Can.	D8	112
Tefé, Braz.	D5	84
Tefé, stm., Braz.	D4	84
Tefenni, Tur.	F12	28
Tegal, Indon.	G6	50
Tégama, reg., Niger	F6	64
Tegéa, hist., Grc.	F5	28
Tegineneng, Indon.	F4	50
Tegucigalpa, Hond.	E4	102
Tegul'det, Russia	C15	32
Tehachapi, Ca., U.S.	H7	134
Tehachapi Pass, p., Ca., U.S.	H7	134
Tehek Lake, l., Nu., Can.	C12	106
Tehrān (Teheran), Iran	B7	56
Tehrathum, Nepal	E11	54
Tehuacán, Mex.	F10	100
Tehuantepec, Golfo de, b., Mex.	H11	100
Tehuantepec, Gulf of see Tehuantepec, Golfo de, b., Mex.	H11	100
Tehuantepec, Isthmus of see Tehuantepec, Istmo de, isth., Mex.	G11	100
Tehuantepec, Istmo de, isth., Mex.	G11	100
Teignmouth, Eng., U.K.	K9	12
Teixeira, Braz.	D7	88
Teixeira Pinto, Gui.-B.	G1	64
Tejakula, Indon.	H9	50
Tejkovo, Russia	H19	8
Tejon Pass, p., Ca., U.S.	I7	134
Tejupilco de Hidalgo, Mex.	F8	100
Tekamah, Ne., U.S.	C1	120
Tekapo, Lake, l., N.Z.	F4	80
Tekax, Mex.	B3	102
Teke, Tur.	B12	28
Teke Burnu, c., Tur.	E9	28
Tekeli, Kaz.	F13	32
Tekezē (Satīt), stm., Afr.	E7	62
Tekirdağ, Tur.	C10	28
Tekirdağ, state, Tur.	B10	28
Tekkali, India	B7	53
Tekoa, Wa., U.S.	C9	136
Tekonsha, Mi., U.S.	B1	114
Te Kuiti, N.Z.	D6	80
Tel, stm., India	A6	53
Tela, Hond.	E4	102
Telaopengsha Shan, mtn., China	C11	54
Telavi, Geor.	F7	32
Tel Aviv-Jaffa see Tel Aviv-Yafo, Isr.	F5	58
Tel Aviv-Yafo, Isr.	F5	58
Telč, Czech Rep.	G11	16
Teleckoe, ozero, l., Russia	D15	32
Telefomin, Pap. N. Gui.	b3	79a
Telegraph Creek, B.C., Can.	D4	106
Telêmaco Borba, Braz.	B12	92
Telemark, state, Nor.	G3	8
Telembí, stm., Col.	G2	86
Telén, Arg.	H5	92
Telen, stm., Indon.	C10	50
Telenești, Mol.	B15	26
Teleno, mtn., Spain	B4	20
Teleorman, state, Rom.	E12	26
Teleorman, stm., Rom.	E12	26
Telescope Point, c., Gren.	q10	105e
Telese, Italy	C8	24
Telford, Eng., U.K.	I10	12
Télimélé, Gui.	G2	64
Telire, stm., C.R.	H6	102
Teljo, Jabal, mtn., Sudan	E5	62
Telkwa, B.C., Can.	B3	138
Tell Basta, hist., Egypt	H2	58
Tell City, In., U.S.	G11	120
Tell El-Amarna, hist., Egypt	K1	58
Tellel Rub, hist., Egypt	H2	58
Teller, Ak., U.S.	C6	140

Name	Map Ref.	Page
Tellicherry, India	F2	53
Tellier, Arg.	I3	90
Tello, Col.	F4	86
Telluride, Co., U.S.	F9	132
Tel Megiddo, hist., Isr.	F6	58
Telmen nuur, l., Mong.	B4	36
Teloloapan, Mex.	F8	100
Telos see Tílos, i., Grc.	G10	28
Telsen, Arg.	H3	90
Telšiai, Lith.	E5	10
Teltow, Ger.	D9	16
Telukbayur, Indon.	D2	50
Telukbayur, Indon.	B10	50
Telukdalem, Indon.	L3	48
Teluk Intan, Malay.	K5	48
Tema, Ghana	H5	64
Temagami, Lake, l., On., Can.	A9	112
Temaju, Pulau, i., Indon.	C6	50
Te Manga, mtn., Cook Is.	a26	78j
Temangga, Indon.	C7	50
Tematangi, at., Fr. Poly.	F12	72
Temax, Mex.	B3	102
Tembeling, stm., Malay.	J6	48
Tembenči, stm., Russia	A17	32
Tembesi, stm., Indon.	D3	50
Tembilahan, Indon.	D3	50
Temblador, Ven.	C10	86
Temblor Range, mts., Ca., U.S.	H6	134
Teme, stm., Eng., U.K.	I10	12
Temecula, Ca., U.S.	J8	134
Temelli, Tur.	D15	28
Temengor, Tasik, res., Malay.	J5	48
Temetiu, mtn., Fr. Poly.	s18	78g
Temir, Kaz.	E9	32
Temirtau, Kaz.	D12	32
Témiscaming, Qc., Can.	B10	112
Témiscamingue, Lac (Timiskaming, Lake), res., Can.	B10	112
Témiscouata, Lac, l., Qc., Can.	C7	110
Tëmkino, Russia	E17	10
Temora, Austl.	J6	76
Temosachic, Mex.	A5	100
Tempe, Az., U.S.	J5	132
Tempe, Danau, l., Indon.	F12	50
Tempino, Indon.	D3	50
Tempio Pausania, Italy	D2	24
Temple, Tx., U.S.	C10	130
Templi, Valle dei, hist., Italy	G7	24
Templin, Ger.	C9	16
Tempoal, stm., Mex.	E9	100
Tempoal de Sánchez, Mex.	E9	100
Tempy, Russia	D20	10
Temuco, Chile	G2	90
Temwen, i., Micron.	m12	78d
Tena, Ec.	H3	86
Tenabo, Mex.	B2	102
Tenaha, Tx., U.S.	F4	122
Tena Kourou, mtn., Burkina	G4	64
Tenāli, India	C5	53
Tenasserim, Mya.	F4	48
Tendaho, Eth.	E8	62
Tende, Col de, p., Eur.	E13	18
Ten Degree Channel, strt., India	G7	46
Tendō, Japan	A13	40
Ténenkou, Mali	G3	64
Ténéré, des., Niger	F7	64
Ténès, Alg.	H12	20
Ténès, Cap, c., Alg.	H12	20
Teng, stm., Mya.	B3	48
Tengah, Kepulauan, is., Indon.	G10	50
Tengchong, China	G4	36
Tenggara, Nusa (Lesser Sunda Islands), is., Indon.	G6	44
Tenggara Celebes see Sulawesi Tenggara, state, Indon.	E12	50
Tenggarong, Indon.	D10	50
Tengger Shamo, des., China	D5	36
Tenghilan, Malay.	G1	52
Tengiz, ozero, l., Kaz.	D11	32
Tengréla, C. Iv.	G3	64
Tengtiao (Na), stm., Asia	A6	48
Tengxian, China	J4	42
Tengxian, China	D7	42
Tenkāsi, India	G3	53
Tenke, D.R.C.	G5	66
Tenkeli, Russia	B17	34
Tenkiller Ferry Lake, res., Ok., U.S.	B4	122
Tenkodogo, Burkina	G4	64
Tennant Creek, Austl.	C6	74
Tennessee, state, U.S.	D10	108
Tennessee, stm., U.S.	A11	122
Tennille, Ga., U.S.	D3	116
Teno, Chile	G2	92
Teno (Tana), stm., Eur.	B12	8
Tenom, Malay.	A9	50
Tenos see Tínos, Grc.	F8	28
Tenos see Tínos, i., Grc.	F8	28
Tenosique, Mex.	D2	102
Tenryū, Japan	E10	40
Tenryū, stm., Japan	E10	40
Tensas, stm., La., U.S.	F7	122
Tensed, Id., U.S.	C10	136
Ten Sleep, Wy., U.S.	C5	126
Tenterfield, Austl.	G8	76
Ten Thousand Islands, is., Fl., U.S.	K4	116
Tentolomatinan, Gunung, mtn., Indon.	E7	44
Teocaltiche, Mex.	E7	100
Teodelina, Arg.	G7	92
Teófilo Otoni, Braz.	I5	88
Teo Lakes, l., Sk., Can.	C4	124
Teotihuacán, hist., Mex.	F9	100
Tepa, Indon.	G8	44
Tepalcatepec, Mex.	F7	100
Tepebaşı, Tur.	B3	58
Tepehuanes, Mex.	C6	100
Tepehuanes, stm., Mex.	C6	100
Tepeji de Ocampo, Mex.	F9	100
Tepelenë, Alb.	D13	24
Tepic, Mex.	E6	100
Teplice, Czech Rep.	F9	16
Tepoca, Bahía de, b., Mex.	F6	98
Tepoca, Punta, c., Mex.	G6	98
Ter, stm., Spain	B14	20
Téra, Niger	G5	64
Tera, stm., Spain	C4	20
Teradomari, Japan	B11	40
Teraina, i., Kir.	C11	72
Teramo, Italy	H10	22
Terbuny, Russia	H21	10
Terceira, i., Port.	C3	60
Tercero, stm., Arg.	F6	92
Terdal, India	C2	53
Terek, stm., Russia	G18	6
Terempa, Indon.	B5	50
Terengganu, state, Malay.	J6	48
Terengganu, stm., Malay.	J6	48
Terenos, Braz.	D6	90
Teresina, Braz.	C4	88
Teresópolis, Braz.	L4	88
Terespol, Pol.	D19	16
Terevaka, Cerro, mtn., Chile	e29	78l
Tergüün Bogd uul, mtn., Mong.	C5	36
Teriang, stm., Malay.	K6	48
Teriberka, Russia	B16	8
Terihi, i., Fr. Poly.	t19	78g
Terlingua, Tx., U.S.	E4	130
Terlingua Creek, stm., Tx., U.S.	E4	130
Termas del Arapey, Ur.	E9	92
Termas de Río Hondo, Arg.	C5	92
Termez, Uzb.	B10	56
Termini Imerese, Italy	G7	24
Termini Imerese, Golfo di, b., Italy	F7	24
Terminillo, Monte, mtn., Italy	H9	22
Términos, Laguna de, b., Mex.	C2	102
Termoli, Italy	H11	22
Termonde see Dendermonde, Bel.	C12	14
Ternej, Russia	B12	38
Terneuzen, Neth.	C12	14
Terni, Italy	H9	22
Ternitz, Aus.	C12	22
Ternopil', Ukr.	F14	6
Terpenija, mys, c., Russia	G17	34
Terpenija, zaliv, b., Russia	G17	34
Terra Alta, W.V., U.S.	E6	114
Terra Bella, Ca., U.S.	H6	134
Terrace, B.C., Can.	B2	138
Terracina, Italy	C7	24
Terra Cotta Army (Qinshihuang Mausoleum), hist., China	D3	42
Terral, Ok., U.S.	H11	128
Terralba, Italy	E2	24
Terra Santa, Braz.	D6	84
Terrassa, Spain	C13	20
Terrebonne Bay, b., La., U.S.	H8	122
Terre-de-Bas, Guad.	i5	105c
Terre-de-Haut, Guad.	i5	105c
Terre-de-Haut, i., Guad.	i5	105c
Terre Haute, In., U.S.	E10	120
Terrell, Tx., U.S.	E2	122
Terre-Neuve see Newfoundland, state, Can.	B17	110
Territoire du Yukon see Yukon, state, Can.	B3	106
Territoires du Nord-Ouest see Northwest Territories, state, Can.	B10	106
Terry, Ms., U.S.	E8	122
Terry, Mt., U.S.	A7	126
Terschelling, i., Neth.	A14	14
Terskej-Alatau, hrebet, mts., Kyrg.	F13	32
Teruel, Col.	F4	86
Teruel, Spain	D9	20
Teruel, co., Spain	D10	20
Terujak, Indon.	J3	48
Tervola, Fin.	C11	8
Terzaghi Dam, dam, B.C., Can.	F8	138
Tes, stm., Asia	D16	32
Tescott, Ks., U.S.	B11	128
Teseney, Erit.	D7	62
Teshekpuk Lake, l., Ak., U.S.	B9	140
Teshio, Japan	E14	38
Teshio, stm., Japan	E15	38
Teslin, Yk., Can.	C4	106
Teslin, stm., Can.	C4	106
Teslin Lake, l., Can.	C4	106
Tësovo, Russia	E17	10
Tësovo-Netyl'skij, Russia	B13	10
Tësovskij, Russia	B13	10
Tessalit, Mali	E5	64
Tessaoua, Niger	G6	64
Testa, Capo, c., Italy	C3	24
Testour, Tun.	H3	24
Tetachuck Lake, res., B.C., Can.	C4	138
Tete, Moz.	D5	68
Tête Jaune Cache, B.C., Can.	D11	138
Tetepare Island, i., Sol. Is.	e7	79b
Teterow, Ger.	C8	16
Tetica, mtn., Spain	G8	20
Teton, Id., U.S.	G15	136
Teton, stm., Id., U.S.	G15	136
Teton, stm., Mt., U.S.	C15	136
Tetonia, Id., U.S.	G15	136
Teton Range, mts., Wy., U.S.	G16	136
Tetouan, Mor.	B4	64
Tetovo, Mac.	A4	28
Tetufera, Mont, mtn., Fr. Poly.	v22	78h
Teuco, stm., Arg.	D4	90
Teulada, Italy	F2	24
Teulada, Capo, c., Italy	F2	24
Teulon, Mb., Can.	D16	124
Teutoburger Wald, hills, Ger.	D4	16
Teuva, Fin.	E9	8
Tevere (Tiber), stm., Italy	H9	22
Teverya, Isr.	F6	58
Te Waewae Bay, b., N.Z.	H2	80
Tewah, Indon.	D8	50
Tewantin-Noosa, Austl.	F9	76
Tewkesbury, Eng., U.K.	I11	12
Texada Island, i., B.C., Can.	G6	138
Texana, Lake, res., Tx., U.S.	F11	130
Texarkana, Ar., U.S.	D4	122
Texarkana, Tx., U.S.	D4	122
Texas, Austl.	G8	76
Texas, state, U.S.	E8	108
Texas City, Tx., U.S.	H4	122
Texel, i., Neth.	A13	14
Texhoma, Ok., U.S.	E7	128
Texico, N.M., U.S.	G5	128
Texoma, Lake, res., U.S.	H11	128
Teyateyaneng, Leso.	F8	70
Teywarah, Afg.	C9	56
Teziutlán, Mex.	F10	100
Tezpur, India	E14	54
Tezzeron Lake, l., B.C., Can.	B6	138
Tha, stm., Laos	B5	48
Tha-anne, stm., Nu., Can.	C11	106
Thabana-Ntlenyana, mtn., Leso.	F9	70
Thabaung, Mya.	D2	48
Thabazimbi, S. Afr.	D8	70
Thabyu, Mya.	E4	48
Thagyettaw, Mya.	F3	48
Thai Binh, Viet.	B8	48
Thailand, ctry., Asia	E5	48
Thailand, Gulf of, b., Asia	G5	48
Thai Nguyen, Viet.	B7	48
Thak, Pak.	C3	54
Thal, Pak.	B3	54
Thala, Tun.	I2	24
Thal Desert, des., Pak.	C3	54
Thalfang, Ger.	G2	16
Tha Li, Thai.	D5	48
Thalia, Tx., U.S.	H9	128
Thālith, Ash-Shallāl ath- (Third Cataract), wtfl, Sudan	D6	62
Thalwil, Switz.	C5	22
Thames, N.Z.	C6	80
Thames, stm., On., Can.	F8	112
Thames, stm., Eng., U.K.	J13	12
Thames, Firth of, b., N.Z.	C6	80
Thamesford, On., Can.	E8	112
Thamesville, On., Can.	F7	112
Thāna, India	B1	53
Thandaung, Mya.	C3	48
Thangoo, Austl.	C4	74
Thangool, Austl.	E8	76
Thanh Hoa, Viet.	C7	48
Thanh Pho Ho Chi Minh (Saigon), Viet.	G8	48
Thanjāvūr, India	F4	53
Thann, Fr.	B12	18
Thap Than, stm., Thai.	E6	48
Tharabwin West, Mya.	F4	48
Tharād, India	F3	54
Thar Desert (Great Indian Desert), des., Asia	D3	54
Thargomindah, Austl.	F5	76
Tharrawaddy, Mya.	D2	48
Tha Sala, Thai.	H4	48
Thásos, Grc.	C7	28
Thásos, i., Grc.	C7	28
Thásos, hist., Grc.	C7	28
Thaton, Mya.	D3	48
Tha Tum, Thai.	E6	48
Thau, Bassin de, l., Fr.	F9	18
Thaungyin (Moei), stm., Asia	D3	48
Thaya (Dyje), stm., Eur.	H12	16
Thayawthadangyi Kyun, i., Mya.	F3	48
Thayer, Ks., U.S.	G2	120
Thayer, Mo., U.S.	H6	120
Thayetchaung, Mya.	F4	48
Thayetmyo, Mya.	C2	48
Thazi, Mya.	B3	48
Thebes see Thíva, Grc.	E6	28
The Bottom, Neth. Ant.	B1	105a
The Cheviot, mtn., Eng., U.K.	F10	12
The Dalles, Or., U.S.	E5	136
Thedford, Ne., U.S.	E12	126
The Father see Ulawun, Mount, vol., Pap. N. Gui.	b5	79a
The Fens, reg., Eng., U.K.	I12	12
The Fishing Lakes, l., Sk., Can.	D10	124
The Granites, hill, Austl.	D6	74
The Hague see 's-Gravenhage, Neth.	B12	14
The Heads, c., Or., U.S.	H2	136
Theinkun, Mya.	G4	48
The Lakes National Park, p.o.i., Austl.	L6	76
The Little Minch, strt., Scot., U.K.	D6	12
Thelon, stm., Can.	C11	106
The Lynd, Austl.	B5	76
The Minch, strt., Scot., U.K.	D6	12
Thenia, Alg.	H14	20
Theodore, Austl.	E8	76
Theodore, Sk., Can.	C10	124
Theodore, Al., U.S.	G10	122
Theodore Roosevelt National Park North Unit, p.o.i., N.D., U.S.	G10	124
Theodore Roosevelt National Park South Unit, p.o.i., N.D., U.S.	G10	124
The Pas, Mb., Can.	E10	106
Thepha, Thai.	I5	48
The Pinnacle, hill, Mo., U.S.	E6	120
The Rand see Witwatersrand, mts., S. Afr.	D8	70
Theresa Creek, stm., Austl.	D6	76
The Rhins, pen., Scot., U.K.	G7	12
Thermaïkós Kólpos (Salonika, Gulf of), b., Grc.	C6	28
Thermopolis, Wy., U.S.	D4	126
Thermopylae see Thermopýles, hist., Grc.	E5	28
Thermopýles (Thermopylae), hist., Grc.	E5	28
The Rock, Austl.	J6	76
The Rockies, mtn., Wa., U.S.	D4	136
The Rope, clf, Pit.	c28	78k
Thesiger Bay, b., N.T., Can.	B15	140
The Slot see New Georgia Sound, strt., Sol. Is.	e8	79b
Thessalía, state, Grc.	D5	28
Thessalía, hist. reg., Grc.	D5	28
Thessalon, On., Can.	B6	112
Thessaloníki (Salonika), Grc.	C6	28
Thessaly see Thessalía, hist. reg., Grc.	D5	28
Thetford, Eng., U.K.	I13	12
Thetford Mines, Qc., Can.	D5	110
Theunissen, S. Afr.	F8	70
The Valley, Anguilla	A1	105a
The Village, Ok., U.S.	F11	128
The Wash, b., Eng., U.K.	I13	12
The Weald, reg., Eng., U.K.	J13	12
Thibodaux, La., U.S.	H8	122
Thief Lake, l., Mn., U.S.	C3	118
Thief River Falls, Mn., U.S.	C2	118
Thiene, Italy	E8	22
Thiers, Fr.	D9	18
Thiès, Sen.	G1	64
Thika, Kenya	E7	66
Thimphu, Bhu.	E12	54
Thingvallavatn, l., Ice.	k29	8a
Thingvellir, Ice.	k29	8a
Thingvellir Nasjonalpark, p.o.i., Ice.	k29	8a
Thio, N. Cal.	m16	79d
Thionville, Fr.	E15	14
Thíra, Grc.	G8	28
Thíra (Santorini), i., Grc.	G8	28
Third Cataract see Thālith, Ash-Shallāl ath-, wtfl, Sudan	D6	62
Thiruvananthapuram see Trivandrum, India	G3	53
Thiruvārūr, India	F4	53
Thistilfjörður, b., Ice.	j32	8a
Thíva, Grc.	E6	28
Thiviers, Fr.	D6	18
Thjórsá, stm., Ice.	k30	8a
Thohoyandou, S. Afr.	C10	70
Thoi Binh, Viet.	H7	48
Thomas, Ok., U.S.	F10	128
Thomas, W.V., U.S.	E6	114
Thomaston, Al., U.S.	E11	122
Thomaston, Ga., U.S.	D1	116
Thomaston, Me., U.S.	F7	110
Thomasville, Ga., U.S.	F2	116
Thomasville, N.C., U.S.	I5	114
Thompson, Mb., Can.	D11	106
Thompson, Ia., U.S.	H5	118
Thompson, N.D., U.S.	D1	118
Thompson, stm., B.C., Can.	F9	138
Thompson, stm., U.S.	E4	120
Thompson Falls, Mt., U.S.	C11	136
Thompson Peak, mtn., Ca., U.S.	B3	134
Thomsen, stm., N.T., Can.	B16	140
Thomson, Ga., U.S.	C3	116
Thomson, Il., U.S.	C7	120
Thomson, stm., Austl.	E4	76
Thongwa, Mya.	D3	48
Thonon-les-Bains, Fr.	C12	18
Thonotosassa, Fl., U.S.	H3	116
Thonze, Mya.	D2	48
Thorhild, Ab., Can.	B17	138
Thórisvatn, l., Ice.	k30	8a
Thorlákshöfn, Ice.	l29	8a
Thornaby-on-Tees, Eng., U.K.	G11	12
Thornbury, On., Can.	D9	112
Thorndale, Tx., U.S.	D10	130
Thornton, Co., U.S.	B4	128
Thornton, Tx., U.S.	F2	122
Thorntonville, Tx., U.S.	C4	130
Thorp, Wi., U.S.	G8	118
Thorsby, Ab., Can.	C16	138
Thorshavn see Tórshavn, Far. Is.	n34	8b
Thórshöfn, Ice.	j32	8a
Thouars, Fr.	H8	14
Thoune see Thun, Switz.	D4	22
Thousand Lake Mountain, mtn., Ut., U.S.	E5	132
Thousand Oaks, Ca., U.S.	I7	134
Thousand Ships Bay, b., Sol. Is.	e8	79b
Thousand Springs Creek, stm., U.S.	B2	132
Thrace, hist. reg., Eur.	H13	26
Thrakikó Pélagos, Grc.	C8	28
Three Forks, Mt., U.S.	E15	136
Three Gorges Dam, dam, China	F4	42
Three Hills, Ab., Can.	E17	138
Three Hummock Island, i., Austl.	n12	77a
Three Kings Islands, is., N.Z.	B5	80
Three Mile Plains, N.S., Can.	F12	110
Three Points, Cape, c., Ghana	I4	64
Three Rivers, Mi., U.S.	G4	112
Three Rivers, Tx., U.S.	F9	130
Three Sisters, mtn., Or., U.S.	F5	136
Three Sisters Islands, is., Sol. Is.	f10	79b
Three Springs, Austl.	E3	74
Thrissur see Trichūr, India	F3	53
Throssel, Lake, l., Austl.	E4	74
Thu, Cu Lao, i., Viet.	G9	48
Thuan Chau, Viet.	B6	48
Thu Dau Mot, Viet.	G8	48
Thuin, Bel.	D13	14
Thule (Qaanaaq), Grnld.	B12	141
Thun, Switz.	D4	22
Thun Chang, Thai.	C5	48
Thunder Bay, On., Can.	C9	118
Thunder Bay, b., On., Can.	C9	118
Thunderbird, Lake, res., Ok., U.S.	F11	128
Thunderbolt, Ga., U.S.	D4	116
Thunder Butte Creek, stm., S.D., U.S.	B10	126
Thunder Creek, stm., Sk., Can.	D7	124
Thuner See, l., Switz.	D4	22
Thung Salaeng Luang National Park, p.o.i., Thai.	D5	48
Thung Wa, Thai.	I4	48
Thüringen, state, Ger.	F7	16
Thüringer Wald, mts., Ger.	F6	16
Thuringia see Thüringen, state, Ger.	F7	16
Thurles, Ire.	I5	12
Thurmont, Md., U.S.	E8	114
Thursday Island, Austl.	B8	74
Thurso, Scot., U.K.	C9	12
Thurston Island, i., Ant.	C31	81
Thusis, Switz.	D6	22
Thylungra, Austl.	F4	76
Thyolo, Mwi.	D5	68
Thysville see Mbanza-Ngungu, D.R.C.	F3	66
Tiachiv, Ukr.	A10	26
Tianchang, China	E8	42
Tiandeng, China	J2	42
Tiandong, China	J2	42
Tian'e, China	I2	42
Tiangang, China	C7	38
Tianguá, Braz.	B5	88
Tianjin (Tientsin), China	B7	42
Tianjin, state, China	B7	42
Tianjun, China	D4	36
Tianlin, China	I2	42
Tian Ling, mtn., China	B8	38
Tianmen, China	F5	42
Tianqiaoling, China	C8	38
Tianshifu, China	D6	38
Tianshui, China	D1	42
Tiantai, China	G9	42
Tiantang, China	J4	42
Tianwangsi, China	F8	42
Tianyang, China	J2	42
Tianzhen, China	A6	42
Tianzhu, China	D5	36
Tianzhu, China	H3	42
Tiarei, Fr. Poly.	v22	78h
Tiaro, Austl.	E9	76
Tiassalé, C. Iv.	H4	64
Ti'avea, Samoa	g12	79c
Tibaji, stm., Braz.	A12	92
Tibal-og, Phil.	G5	52
Tibasti, Sarīr, des., Libya	C3	62
Tibati, Cam.	C2	66
Tibbie, Al., U.S.	F10	122
Tiber see Tevere, stm., Italy	H9	22
Tiberias, Lake see Kinneret, Yam, l., Isr.	F6	58
Tibesti, mts., Afr.	C3	62
Tibet see Xizang, state, China	B5	46
Tibet, Plateau of see Qing Zang Gaoyuan, plat., China	B6	46
Tiblawan, Phil.	G6	52
Tibnīn, Leb.	E6	58
Tibooburra, Austl.	G4	76
Tiburón, Cabo, c.	C3	86
Tiburón, Isla, i., Mex.	G6	98
Tiča, Jazovir, res., Blg.	F13	26
Ticao Island, i., Phil.	D4	52
Tîchît, Maur.	F3	64
Ticino, stm., Eur.	D14	18
Tickfaw, stm., U.S.	G8	122
Ticonderoga, N.Y., U.S.	G3	110
Ticul, Mex.	B3	102
Tidioute, Pa., U.S.	C6	114
Tidiquin, Jbel, mtn., Mor.	C4	64
Tidjikja, Maur.	F2	64
Tiébissou, C. Iv.	H3	64
T'iehling see Tieling, China	C5	38
Tiel, Neth.	C14	14
Tieli, China	B10	36
Tieling, China	C5	38
Tielt, Bel.	C12	14
Tiémé, C. Iv.	H3	64
T'ienching see Tianjin, China	B7	42
Tien Giang see Mekong, stm., Asia	F9	46
Tien Shan, mts., Asia	F13	32
T'ienshui see Tianshui, China	D1	42
Tientsin see Tianjin, China	B7	42
Tientsin see Tianjin, state, China	B7	42
Tien Yen, Viet.	B8	48
Tie Plant, Ms., U.S.	D9	122
Tierp, Swe.	F7	8
Tierra Amarilla, Chile	C2	92
Tierra Blanca, Mex.	F10	100
Tierra Blanca, Mex.	G3	130
Tierra Blanca Creek, stm., U.S.	G6	128
Tierra de Campos, reg., Spain	C5	20
Tierra del Fuego, Arg.	J3	90
Tierra del Fuego, i., S.A.	J3	90
Tiétar, stm., Spain	E5	20
Tietê, Braz.	L2	88
Tietê, stm., Braz.	D6	90
Tiéti, N. Cal.	m15	79d
Tiffany Mountain, mtn., Wa., U.S.	B7	136
Tiffin, Oh., U.S.	C2	114
Tifton, Ga., U.S.	E2	116
Tiga, Île, i., N. Cal.	m16	79d
Tigalda Island, i., Ak., U.S.	F7	140
Tigapuluh, Pegunungan, mts., Indon.	D3	50
Tighina, Mol.	C16	26
Tigil', Russia	E20	34
Tignall, Ga., U.S.	C3	116
Tignish, P.E., Can.	D12	110
Tigoda, stm., Russia	A14	10
Tigre, Col.	F7	86
Tigre, stm., Peru	D2	84
Tigre, stm., Ven.	C10	86
Tigris (Dicle) (Dijlah), stm., Asia	C5	56
Tiguentourine, Alg.	D6	64
Tihany, hist., Hung.	C4	26
Tihert, Alg.	B5	64
Tihon, Russia	G22	8
Tihookeanskij, Russia	C10	38
Tihoreck, Russia	E6	32
Tihua see Ürümqi, China	C2	36
Tihuatlán, Mex.	E10	100
Tihvin, Russia	A16	10
Tijuana, Mex.	K8	134
Tijuana, stm., N.A.	K9	134
Tijucas, Braz.	C13	92
Tijucas do Sul, Braz.	B13	92
Tijuco, stm., Braz.	J1	88
Tikal, hist., Guat.	D3	102
Tikal, Parque Nacional, p.o.i., Guat.	D3	102
Tikrīt, Iraq	C5	56
Tikša, Russia	D15	8
Tikšeozero, ozero, l., Russia	C14	8
Tiksi, Russia	B14	34
Tiladummati Atoll, at., Mald.	h12	46a
Tilburg, Neth.	C14	14
Tilbury, On., Can.	F7	112
Tilcha, Austl.	G3	76
Tilden, Il., U.S.	F8	120
Tilden, Ne., U.S.	E15	126
Tilden, Tx., U.S.	F9	130
Tilhar, India	D7	54
Tilimsen, Alg.	C4	64
Tilin, Mya.	B2	48
Tillabéri, Niger	G5	64
Tilley, Ab., Can.	F19	138
Tillia, Niger	F5	64
Tillmans Corner, Al., U.S.	G10	122
Tillson, N.Y., U.S.	C11	114
Tillsonburg, On., Can.	F9	112
Tílos, i., Grc.	G10	28
Tilpa, Austl.	H5	76
Tilton, N.H., U.S.	G5	110
Tiltonsville, Oh., U.S.	D5	114
Tima, Egypt	L2	58
Timaná, Col.	G3	86
Timanskij krjaž, hills, Russia	B8	32
Timaru, N.Z.	G4	80
Timbalier Bay, b., La., U.S.	H8	122
Timbaúba, Braz.	D8	88
Timbavati Game Reserve, S. Afr.	D10	70
Timbedgha, Maur.	F3	64
Timber Lake, S.D., U.S.	B11	126
Timbiras, Braz.	C4	88
Timbó, Braz.	C13	92
Timbo, Lib.	H3	64
Timbuktu see Tombouctou, Mali	F4	64
Timétrine, Mali	F4	64
Timétrine, mts., Mali	F4	64
Timimoun, Alg.	D5	64
Timirist, Râs, c., Maur.	F1	64
Timirjazevo, Russia	E4	10
Timiș, state, Rom.	D8	26
Timiș (Tamiš), stm., Eur.	D7	26
Timiskaming, Lake (Témiscamingue, Lac), res., Can.	B10	112
Timișoara, Rom.	D8	26
Timmendorfer Strand, Ger.	B7	16
Timmins, On., Can.	F14	106
Timmonsville, S.C., U.S.	B6	116
Timms Hill, mtn., Wi., U.S.	F8	118
Timna' see Mikhrot Timna', hist., Isr.	I5	58
Timok, stm., Eur.	E9	26
Timon, Braz.	C4	88
Timor, i., Indon.	G8	44
Timor Sea	K15	142
Timošino, Russia	H21	8
Timotes, Ven.	C6	86
Timpanogos Cave National Monument, p.o.i., Ut., U.S.	C5	132
Timpton, stm., Russia	E14	34
Timšer, Russia	B9	32
Tims Ford Lake, res., Tn., U.S.	B12	122
Tina, stm., S. Afr.	G9	70
Tîna, Khalîg el- (Pelusium Bay), b., Egypt	G3	58
Tinaca Point, c., Phil.	H5	52
Tinambung, Indon.	E11	50
Tinapagee, Austl.	G5	76
Tinaquillo, Ven.	C7	86
Tindivanam, India	E4	53
Tindouf, Alg.	D3	64
Tineba, Pegunungan, mts., Indon.	D12	50
Tineg, stm., Phil.	B3	52
Ting, stm., China	I7	42
Tinggi, Pulau, i., Malay.	K7	48
Tingha, Austl.	G8	76
Tinghert, Ḥamādat (Tinghert, Plateau du), plat., Afr.	D7	64
Tinghert, Plateau du (Tinghert, Ḥamādat), plat., Afr.	D6	64
Tinghsien see Dingxian, China	B6	42
Tinglev, Den.	B5	16
Tingo María, Peru	E2	84
Tingri, China	D11	54
Tingri see Dinggyê, China	D11	54
Tinguiririca, Volcán, vol., Chile	G2	92
Tinharé, Ilha de, i., Braz.	G6	88
Tinh Bien, Viet.	G7	48
Tinian, i., N. Mar. Is.	B5	72
Tinjar, stm., Malay.	B9	50
Tínos, Grc.	F8	28
Tínos, i., Grc.	F8	28
Tinsley, Ms., U.S.	E8	122
Tinsukia, India	C8	46
Tintagel, B.C., Can.	B5	138
Tintina, Arg.	C6	92
Tintinara, Austl.	J3	76
Tio, Erit.	E8	62
Tiobrad Árann see Tipperary, Ire.	I4	12
Tioga, N.D., U.S.	F11	124
Tiojala, Fin.	F10	8
Tioman, Pulau, i., Malay.	K7	48
Tionesta, Pa., U.S.	C6	114
Tipasa, Alg.	H13	20
Tipitapa, Nic.	F4	102
Tippecanoe, stm., In., U.S.	H3	112
Tipperary, Ire.	I4	12
Tipperary, state, Ire.	I5	12
Tipton, Ca., U.S.	G6	134
Tipton, Ia., U.S.	C6	120
Tipton, Mo., U.S.	F5	120
Tipton, Ok., U.S.	G9	128
Tipton, Mount, mtn., Az., U.S.	H2	132
Tiptonville, Tn., U.S.	H8	120
Tip Top Mountain, mtn., On., Can.	F13	106
Tiptūr, India	E3	53
Tiputini, stm., Ec.	H4	86
Tira, Isr.	F5	58
Tīrān, i., Sau. Ar.	K5	58
Tiran, Strait of, strt.	K5	58
Tirana see Tiranë, Alb.	C13	24
Tiranë, Alb.	C13	24
Tirano, Italy	D7	22
Tiraspol, Mol.	C16	26
Tire, Tur.	E10	28
Tiree, i., Scot., U.K.	E6	12
Tirich Mīr, mtn., Pak.	B11	56
Tirna, stm., India	B3	53
Tírnavos, Grc.	D5	28
Tirodi, India	H7	54
Tirol, state, Aus.	C8	22
Tiros, Braz.	J3	88
Tirso, stm., Italy	E2	24
Tīrthahalli, India	E2	53
Tiruchchirāppalli, India	F4	53
Tiruchengodu, India	F3	53
Tirukkalukkunram, India	E5	53
Tirukkovilūr, India	F4	53
Tiruliai, Lith.	E6	10
Tirunelveli, India	G3	53
Tirupati, India	E4	53
Tiruppattūr, India	E4	53
Tiruppur, India	F3	53
Tirūr, India	F2	53
Tirutturaippūndi, India	F4	53
Tiruvalla, India	G3	53
Tiruvannāmalai, India	E4	53
Tirūvottiyūr, India	E5	53
Tiruvur, India	C5	53
Tisa (Tisza) (Tysa), stm., Eur.	D7	26
Tisaiyanvilai, India	G3	53
Tisdale, Sk., Can.	B9	124
Tishomingo, Ok., U.S.	C2	122
Tīsīyah, Syria	F7	58
Tiskilwa, Il., U.S.	C8	120
Tisovec, Slov.	H15	16
Tīsta, stm., Asia	F12	54
Tisza (Tisa) (Tysa), stm., Eur.	C7	26
Tiszaföldvár, Hung.	C7	26
Tiszaújváros, Hung.	B7	26
Tiszavasvári, Hung.	A8	26
Titaf, Alg.	D4	64
Tit-Ary, Russia	B14	34
Titicaca, Lake, l., S.A.	G4	84
Titilāgarh, India	H9	54
Titonka, Ia., U.S.	H4	118
Titov Veles, Mac.	B4	28
Titran, Nor.	E2	8
Tittabawassee, stm., Mi., U.S.	E5	112
Tittmoning, Ger.	H8	16
Titule, D.R.C.	D5	66
Titusville, Fl., U.S.	H5	116
Titusville, Pa., U.S.	C6	114
Tiuni, India	C6	54
Tivaouane, Sen.	F1	64
Tiverton, Eng., U.K.	K9	12
Tivoli, Italy	I9	22
Tivoli, Tx., U.S.	F11	130
Tiyās, Syria	D8	58
Tizimín, Mex.	B3	102
Tizi-Ouzou, Alg.	B5	64
Tizmant el-Zawâya, Egypt	I1	58
Tiznados, stm., Ven.	C8	86
Tiznit, Mor.	D3	64
Tjörn, i., Swe.	G4	8
Tjukalinsk, Russia	C12	32
Tjul'gan, Russia	D9	32
Tjumen', Russia	C10	32
Tjung, stm., Russia	D13	34
Tjuva-Guba, Russia	B15	8
Tlacotalpan, Mex.	F11	100
Tlacotepec, Mex.	G9	100
Tlahualilo de Zaragoza, Mex.	B7	100
Tlalnepantla, Mex.	F9	100
Tlaltenango de Sánchez Román, Mex.	E7	100
Tlapaneco, stm., Mex.	G9	100
Tlaquepaque, Mex.	E7	100
Tlaxcala, state, Mex.	F9	100
Tlaxcala de Xicohténcatl, Mex.	F9	100
Tłuszcz, Pol.	D17	16
Tmassah, Libya	B3	62
Tnâot, stm., Camb.	G7	48
Toa Alta, P.R.	B3	104a
Toa Baja, P.R.	B3	104a
Toachi, stm., Ec.	H2	86
Toahayana, Mex.	B5	100
Toamasina, Madag.	D8	68
Toba, Japan	E9	40
Toba, Danau, l., Indon.	K4	48
Tobago, i., Trin.	r13	105f
Toba Inlet, b., B.C., Can.	F6	138
Toba Kākar Range, mts., Pak.	C10	56
Tobarra, Spain	F9	20
Tobas, Arg.	D6	92
Toba Tek Singh, Pak.	C4	54
Tobejuba, Isla, i., Ven.	C11	86
Tobermorey, Austl.	D7	74
Tobermory, On., Can.	C8	112
Tobermory, Scot., U.K.	E6	12
Tobias, Ne., U.S.	G15	126
Tobias Barreto, Braz.	F6	88
Tobin, Mount, mtn., Nv., U.S.	C8	134
Tobique, stm., N.B., Can.	C9	110
Toboali, Indon.	E5	50
Tobol, Kaz.	D10	32
Tobol, stm., Asia	C11	32
Toboli, Indon.	D12	50
Tobol'sk, Russia	C11	32
Toboso, Phil.	E4	52
Tobruk see Ṭubruq, Libya	A4	62
Tobseda, Russia	B25	8
Tobyhanna, Pa., U.S.	C10	114
Tobyš, stm., Russia	C24	8
Tocantínia, Braz.	E1	88
Tocantinópolis, Braz.	D2	88
Tocantins, state, Braz.	F8	84
Tocantins, stm., Braz.	D8	84
Tocantins, stm., Braz.	F1	88
Tocantinzinho, stm., Braz.	H1	88
Tochcha Lake, l., B.C., Can.	B5	138
Tochigi, Japan	C12	40
Tochigi, state, Japan	C12	40
Tochio, Japan	B12	40
Toco, Trin.	s13	105f
Tocoa, Hond.	E5	102
Toconao, Chile	D3	90
Tocopilla, Chile	D2	90
Tocuco, stm., Ven.	C5	86
Tocumwal, Austl.	J5	76
Tocuyo, stm., Ven.	B7	86
Tocuyo de la Costa, Ven.	B7	86
Toda Rāisingh, India	E5	54
Todi, Italy	H9	22
Todos os Santos, Baia de, b., Braz.	G6	88
Todos Santos, Bol.	C3	90
Todos Santos, Mex.	D3	100
Todos Santos, Bahía de, b., Mex.	L8	134
Tofino, B.C., Can.	G5	138
Toga, i., Vanuatu	i16	79d
Togi, Japan	B9	40
Togiak, Ak., U.S.	E7	140
Togian, Kepulauan, is., Indon.	F7	44
Togo, ctry., Afr.	H5	64
Togtoh, China	A4	42
Togučin, Russia	C14	32
Togur, Russia	C14	32
Togwotee Pass, p., Wy., U.S.	G15	136
Tōhaku, Japan	D6	40
Tohiea, Mont, mtn., Fr. Poly.	v20	78h
Tohopekaliga, Lake, l., Fl., U.S.	H4	116
Tohtamyš, Taj.	B11	56
Toi-misaki, c., Japan	H4	40
Toiyabe Range, mts., Nv., U.S.	D8	134
Tōjō, Japan	E6	40
Tojtepa, Uzb.	F11	32
Tok, Ak., U.S.	D11	140
Tokachi, stm., Japan	C15	38
Tokachi-dake, vol., Japan	C15	38
Tokaj, Hung.	A8	26
Tōkamachi, Japan	B11	40
Tokara-kaikyō, strt., Japan	j19	39a
Tokara-rettō, is., Japan	k19	39a
Tokat, Tur.	A4	56
Tŏkchŏk-kundo, is., Kor., S.	F6	38
Tokelau, dep., Oc.	D9	72

I•58 Tokk-Tuni

Name Map Ref. Page

Tokko, Russia D12 34
Tokma, Russia C19 32
Tokmak, Kyrg. F13 32
Tokoro, stm., Japan C15 38
Tokoroa, N.Z. D6 80
Tok-to, is., Asia B4 40
Toktogul, Kyrg. F12 32
Tokuno-shima, i., Japan I19 39a
Tokur, Russia F15 34
Tokushima, Japan E7 40
Tokushima, state, Japan F7 40
Tokuyama, Japan E4 40
Tokwe, stm., Zimb. B10 70
Tōkyō, Japan D12 40
Tōkyō, state, Japan D12 40
Tokyo Bay see Tōkyō-wan, b., Japan D12 40
Tōkyō-daigaku-uchūkūkan-kenkyūsho, sci., Japan H4 40
Tōkyō-wan, b., Japan D12 40
Tôlañaro, Madag. F8 68
Tolbo, Mong. B3 36
Toledo, Braz. B11 92
Toledo, Col. D5 86
Toledo, Phil. E4 52
Toledo, Spain E6 20
Toledo, Il., U.S. E9 120
Toledo, Oh., U.S. C2 114
Toledo, Or., U.S. F3 136
Toledo, co., Spain E6 20
Toledo, Montes de, mts., Spain E6 20
Toledo Bend Reservoir, res., U.S. F4 122
Tolentino, Italy G10 22
Toli, China B1 36
Toliara, Madag. E7 68
Tolima, state, Col. E4 86
Tolima, Nevado del, vol., Col. E4 86
Tolitoli, Indon. C12 50
Toljatti, Russia D7 32
Tol'ka, Russia B14 32
Tolleson, Az., U.S. J4 132
Tolloche, Arg. B6 92
Tolmači, Russia C18 10
Tolmezzo, Italy D10 22
Tolmin, Slvn. D10 22
Tolna, state, Hung. C5 26
Tolo, Teluk, b., Indon. F7 44
Tolosa, Spain A8 20
Tolstoj, mys, c., Russia E20 34
Tolti, Pak. A6 54
Tolú, Col. C4 86
Toluca, Il., U.S. D8 120
Toluca, Nevado de, vol., Mex. F9 100
Toluca de Lerdo, Mex. F9 100
Tolybaj, Kaz. D10 32
Tom', stm., Russia C14 32
Tomah, Wi., U.S. H8 118
Tomahawk, Wi., U.S. F9 118
Tomakomai, Japan C14 38
Tomanivi, mtn., Fiji p19 79e
Tomar, Port. E2 20
Tomari, Russia G17 34
Tomás Gomensoro, Ur. E9 92
Tomasine, stm., Qc., Can. B13 112
Tomaszów Lubelski, Pol. F19 16
Tomaszów Mazowiecki, Pol. E15 16
Tombador, Serra do, plat., Braz. F6 84
Tomball, Tx., U.S. G3 122
Tombigbee, stm., U.S. F10 122
Tombos, Braz. K5 88
Tombouctou (Timbuktu), Mali F4 64
Tombstone, Az., U.S. L6 132
Tombstone Mountain, mtn., Yk., Can. C3 106
Tombua, Ang. D1 68
Tom Burke, S. Afr. C9 70
Tomé, Chile H1 92
Tomé-Açu, Braz. B1 88
Tomelilla, Swe. I5 8
Tomelloso, Spain E8 20
Tomichi Creek, stm., Co., U.S. C2 128
Tomini, Indon. C12 50
Tomini, Teluk, b., Indon. F7 44
Tomioka, Japan C11 40
Tommot, Russia E14 34
Tomo, stm., Col. E7 86
Tompkins, Sk., Can. D5 124
Tompkinsville, Ky., U.S. H12 120
Tompo, Indon. C12 50
Tom Price, Austl. D3 74
Tomptokan, Russia E15 34
Tomsk, Russia C15 32
Toms River, N.J., U.S. E11 114
Tonalá, Mex. G12 100
Tonami, Japan C9 40
Tonantins, Braz. I7 86
Tonantins, stm., Braz. I7 86
Tonasket, Wa., U.S. B7 136
Tonawanda, N.Y., U.S. B6 114
Tonbo, Mya. C2 48
Tonbridge, Eng., U.K. J13 12
Tondano, Indon. E8 44
Tønder, Den. B4 16
Tondi, India G4 53
Tone, stm., Japan D13 40
Tonekābon, Iran B7 56
Tonga, ctry., Oc. E9 72
Tongaat, S. Afr. F10 70
Tong'an, China I7 42
Tonganoxie, Ks., U.S. E2 120
Tonga Ridge, unds. K21 142
Tongariro National Park, p.o.i., N.Z. D6 80
Tongatapu, state, Tonga o14 78e
Tongatapu, i., Tonga n13 78e
Tonga Trench, unds. L21 142
Tongbai, China E5 42
Tongbai Shan, mts., China E5 42
Tongbei, China B10 36
Tongcheng, China F7 42
Tongchuan, China D3 42
Tongde, China D5 36
Tongeren, Bel. D14 14
Tongguan, China G5 42
Tongguan, China D3 42
Tonghai, China G5 36
Tonghe, China B10 36
Tonghua, China D6 38
Tongjiang, China B11 36
Tongjiang, China F2 42
Tongjosŏn-man, b., Kor., N. E7 38
Tongliang, China G1 42
Tongliao, China C4 38
Tongling, China F7 42
Tongling, China J3 42
Tonglu, China G8 42
Tongnae, Kor., S. D2 40
Tongnan, China F1 42
Tongo, Austl. H4 76
Tongoa, i., Vanuatu k17 79d
Tongoy, Chile E2 92
Tongren, China D5 36
Tongren, China H3 42
Tongres see Tongeren, Bel. D14 14
Tongsa Dzong, Bhu. E13 54
Tongtian, stm., China E4 36
Tongue, Scot., U.K. C8 12
Tongue, stm., U.S. A7 126
Tongue of the Ocean, unds. C9 96
Tongwei, China D1 42
Tongxian, China B7 42
Tongxin, China C1 42
Tongxu, China D6 42
Tongyu, China B5 38
Tongzi, China G2 42
Tonj, Sudan F5 62
Tonk, India E5 54
Tonkawa, Ok., U.S. E11 128
Tonkin see Bac Phan, hist. reg., Viet. A7 48
Tonkin, Gulf of, b., Asia C8 48
Tônlé Sab, Bœng, l., Camb. F6 48
Tonle Sap see Tônlé Sab, Bœng, l., Camb. F6 48
Tonneins, Fr. E6 18
Tonopah, Nv., U.S. E8 134
Tonoshō, Japan E7 40
Tonosí, Pan. D1 86
Tonotha, Bots. B8 70
Tons, stm., India F8 54
Tønsberg, Nor. G4 8
Tonstad, Nor. G2 8
Tonto Creek, stm., Az., U.S. I5 132
Tonto National Monument, p.o.i., Az., U.S. J5 132
Toodyay, Austl. F3 74
Tooele, Ut., U.S. C4 132
Toogoolawah, Austl. F9 76
Toomsboro, Ga., U.S. D2 116
Toora-Hem, Russia D17 32
Toowoomba, Austl. F8 76
Topeka, Ks., U.S. E2 120
Top Hill, hill, Gren. q11 105e
Topia, Mex. C5 100
Topki, Russia C15 32
Topko, gora, mtn., Russia E16 34
Topley, B.C., Can. B4 138
Toplița, Rom. C12 26
Topocalma, Punta, c., Chile G1 92
Topol'čany, Slov. H14 16
Topolobampo, Mex. C4 100
Topolovățu Mare, Rom. D8 26
Toporok, Russia B16 10
Topozero, ozero, l., Russia D14 8
Toppenish, Wa., U.S. D6 136
Topsa, Russia E20 8
Top Springs, Austl. C6 74
Tor, Eth. F6 62
Torbalı, Tur. E10 28
Torbat-e Ḥeydarīyeh, Iran B8 56
Torbat-e Jām, Iran B9 56
Torbrook, N.S., Can. F12 110
Torch Lake, l., Mi., U.S. C4 112
Tordesillas, Spain C5 20
Töre, Swe. C10 8
Torgau, Ger. E8 16
Torhout, Bel. C12 14
Toribulu, Indon. D11 50
Torino (Turin), Italy E4 22
Torit, Sudan G6 62
Tormes, stm., Spain C5 20
Torna, Russia B20 8
Torna, mtn., India B1 53
Torneälven (Tornionjoki), stm., Eur. C10 8
Torneträsk, l., Swe. B8 8
Torngat Mountains, mts., Can. F13 141
Tornillo, Tx., U.S. C1 130
Tornionjoki (Torneälven), stm., Eur. C10 8
Tornquist, Arg. I6 92
Toro, Spain C5 20
Toro, mtn., Mex. F6 100
Toro, Lago del, l., Chile J2 90
Toro, Punta, c., Chile F1 92
Törökszentmiklós, Hung. B7 26
Torom, Russia F16 34
Toronto, On., Can. E10 112
Toronto, Ks., U.S. G1 120
Toronto, S.D., U.S. G2 118
Toropec, Russia D14 10
Tororo, Ug. D6 66
Toros Dağları (Taurus Mountains), mts., Tur. A3 58
Torosozero, Russia E18 8
Toroume, hill, Cook Is. b26 78j
Torquay, Sk., Can. E10 124
Torquay (Torbay), Eng., U.K. K9 12
Torrance, Ca., U.S. J7 134
Torrão, Port. F2 20
Torreblanca, Spain D11 20
Torre del Greco, Italy D8 24
Torredonjimeno, Spain G6 20
Torrejoncillo, Spain E4 20
Torrejón de Ardoz, Spain D7 20
Torrejón-Tiétar, Embalse de, res., Spain E5 20
Torrelavega, Spain A6 20
Torremolinos, Spain H6 20
Torrens, Lake, l., Austl. F7 74
Torrens Creek, Austl. C5 76
Torrens Creek, stm., Austl. D5 76
Torrent, Arg. D9 92
Torrent, Spain E10 20
Torrente see Torrent, Spain E10 20
Torrenueva, Spain F7 20
Torreón, Mex. C7 100
Torre Pellice, Italy F4 22
Torreperojil, Spain F7 20
Torres, Braz. D13 92
Torres, Îles, is., Vanuatu i16 79d
Torres Islands see Torres, Îles, is., Vanuatu i16 79d
Torres Strait, strt., Oc. b3 79a
Torres Vedras, Port. E1 20
Torrevella, Spain G10 20
Torrevieja see Torrevella, Spain G10 20
Torridon, Scot., U.K. D7 12
Torrijos, Spain D6 20
Torrington, Ct., U.S. C12 114
Torrington, Wy., U.S. E8 126
Torröjen, l., Swe. E5 8
Torsa (Amo), stm., Asia E12 54
Torsby, Swe. F5 8
Tórshavn (Thorshavn), Far. Is. n34 8b
Tortola, i., Br. Vir. Is. e8 104b
Tórtolas, Cerro de las (Las Tórtolas, Cerro), mtn., S.A. D2 92
Tortona, Italy F5 22
Tortorici, Italy F8 24
Tortosa, Spain D11 20
Tortosa, Cap de, c., Spain D11 20
Tortue, Île de la, i., Haiti B11 102
Tortuga Island see Tortue, Île de la, i., Haiti B11 102
Tortuguero, Laguna, b., P.R. B2 104a
Toruń, Pol. C14 16
Toruń, state, Pol. C15 16
Torup, Swe. H5 8
Toržok, Russia C17 10
Torzym, Pol. D11 16
Tosa, Japan F6 40
Tosa-shimizu, Japan G5 40
Tosa-wan, b., Japan F6 40
Tosca, S. Afr. D6 70
Toscana, state, Italy G8 22
Toses, Collada de, p., Spain B12 20
Tosno, Russia A13 10
Toson Hu, l., China D4 36
Tosontsengel, Mong. B4 36
Tostado, Arg. D7 92
Tõstamaa, Est. G10 8
Tosu, Japan F3 40
Totana, Spain G9 20
Toteng, Bots. B6 70
Totiyas, Som. D8 66
Tot'ma, Russia F20 8
Totness, Sur. B6 84
Totoya, i., Fiji q20 79e
Tottenham, Austl. I6 76
Tottenham, On., Can. D10 112
Tottori, Japan D7 40
Tottori, state, Japan D6 40
Touba, C. Iv. H3 64
Toubkal, Jebel, mtn., Mor. C3 64
Touchet, stm., Wa., U.S. D8 136
Touchwood Lake, l., Ab., Can. B19 138
Toudao, stm., China C7 38
Touggourt, Alg. C6 64
Touho, N. Cal. m15 79d
Toul, Fr. F14 14
Touliu, Tai. J9 42
Toulon, Fr. F11 18
Toulon-sur-Arroux, Fr. H13 14
Toulouse, Fr. F7 18
Toumodi, C. Iv. H3 64
Tounassine, Hamada, des., Alg. D3 64
Toungo, Nig. H7 64
Toungoo, Mya. C3 48
Touraine, hist. reg., Fr. G9 14
Tourcoing, Fr. D11 14
Touriñan, Cabo, c., Spain A1 20
Tournai, Bel. D12 14
Tournon, Fr. D10 18
Tournus, Fr. H13 14
Touros, Braz. C8 88
Tours, Fr. G9 14
Toussidé, Pic, vol., Chad C3 62
Touws, stm., S. Afr. H5 70
Toužim, Czech Rep. F9 16
Tovar, Ven. C6 86
Tovarkovskij, Russia G21 10
Tovuz, Azer. A6 56
Tow, Tx., U.S. D9 130
Towada, Japan D14 38
Towanda, Ks., U.S. D12 128
Towanda, Pa., U.S. C9 114
Tower, Mn., U.S. D6 118
Tower City, Pa., U.S. D9 114
Tower Hill, Austl. D5 76
Tower Hill, Il., U.S. E9 120
Towerhill Creek, stm., Austl. C5 76
Towla, Mount, mtn., Zimb. B9 70
Town and Country, Wa., U.S. C9 136
Town Hill, hill, Ber. k16 104e
Townsend, Mt., U.S. D15 136
Townshend Island, i., Austl. D8 76
Townsville, Austl. B6 76
Towson, Md., U.S. E9 114
Towuti, Danau, l., Indon. F7 44
Toyah, Tx., U.S. C4 130
Toyah Creek, stm., Tx., U.S. D4 130
Toyama, Japan C10 40
Toyama, state, Japan C10 40
Toyama-wan, b., Japan C10 40
Tōyo, Japan F6 40
Tōyō, Japan F7 40
Toyohashi, Japan E10 40
Toyokawa, Japan E10 40
Toyonaka, Japan E8 40
Toyooka, Japan D7 40
Toyosaka, Japan B12 40
Toyota, Japan D10 40
Toyoura, Japan E3 40
Tozeur, Tun. C6 64
Trabzon, Tur. A4 56
Tracadie, N.B., Can. C12 110
Tracy, Qc., Can. E3 110
Tracy, Ca., U.S. F4 134
Tracy City, Tn., U.S. B13 122
Tradewater, stm., Ky., U.S. G10 120
Traer, Ia., U.S. B5 120
Trafalgar, Cabo, c., Spain H4 20
Traíd, Spain D9 20
Tráighlí see Tralee, Ire. I3 12
Traiguén, Chile I1 92
Trail, B.C., Can. G13 138
Traill Ø, i., Grnld. C21 141
Traipu, Braz. E7 88
Traira (Taraira), stm., S.A. H7 86
Trairi, Braz. B6 88
Trakai, Lith. F7 10
Tralee, Ire. I3 12
Trá Lí see Tralee, Ire. I3 12
Trammel, Va., U.S. G3 114
Tramperos Creek (Punta de Agua Creek), stm., U.S. E5 128
Tramping Lake, l., Sk., Can. B5 124
Tra My, Viet. E9 48
Trăn, Blg. G9 26
Tranås, Swe. G6 8
Trancas, Arg. C5 92
Tranco de Beas, Embalse de, res., Spain F8 20
Trang, Thai. I4 48
Trangan, Pulau, i., Indon. G9 44
Trang Dinh, Viet. A8 48
Trani, Italy C10 24
Tran Ninh see Xiangkhoang, Plateau de, plat., Laos C6 48
Tranqueras, Ur. E9 92
Transantarctic Mountains, mts., Ant. D30 81
Transkei, hist. reg., S. Afr. G8 70
Transylvania, hist. reg., Rom. C10 26
Transylvanian Alps see Carpații Meridionali, mts., Rom. D11 26
Trapani, Italy F6 24
Trapper Peak, mtn., Mt., U.S. E12 136
Traralgon, Austl. L6 76
Trârza, reg., Maur. F1 64
Trasimeno, Lago, l., Italy G9 22
Trás-os-Montes, hist. reg., Port. C3 20
Trat, Thai. F6 48
Traun, Aus. B11 22
Traun, stm., Aus. B11 22
Traunstein, Ger. I8 16
Travellers Lake, l., Austl. I4 76
Traverse, Lake, res., U.S. F2 118
Traverse City, Mi., U.S. D4 112
Tra Vinh, Viet. H8 48
Travis, Lake, l., Tx., U.S. D10 130
Travnik, Bos. E4 26
Trayning, Austl. F3 74
Trbovlje, Slvn. D12 22
Třebíč, Czech Rep. G11 16
Trebinje, Bos. G5 26
Trebišov, Slov. H17 16
Treblinka, Pol. D18 16
Trece Martires, Phil. C3 52
Tregosse Islets, is., Austl. A8 76
Tregubovo, Russia B14 10
Treinta y Tres, Ur. F10 92
Trélazé, Fr. G8 14
Trelew, Arg. H3 90
Trelleborg, Swe. I5 8
Tremadog Bay, b., Wales, U.K. I8 12
Tremblant, Mont, mtn., Qc., Can. D2 110
Trembleur Lake, l., B.C., Can. B5 138
Tremiti, Isole, is., Italy H12 22
Tremont, Il., U.S. K9 118
Tremonton, Ut., U.S. B4 132
Tremp, Spain B11 20
Trempealeau, Wi., U.S. G7 118
Trenche, stm., Qc., Can. B4 110
Trenčín, Slov. H14 16
Trenel, Arg. G5 92
Trêng, Camb. F6 48
Trenggalek, Indon. H7 50
Trenque Lauquen, Arg. G6 92
Trent, stm., On., Can. D12 112
Trent, stm., Eng., U.K. H12 12
Trente et Un Milles, Lac des, l., Qc., Can. B13 112
Trentino-Alto Adige, state, Italy D8 22
Trento (Trent), Italy D7 22
Trenton, N.S., Can. E14 110
Trenton, On., Can. D12 112
Trenton, Fl., U.S. G3 116
Trenton, Ga., U.S. C13 122
Trenton, Mo., U.S. D4 120
Trenton, Ne., U.S. A8 128
Trenton, N.J., U.S. D11 114
Trenton, N.C., U.S. A8 116
Trentwood, Wa., U.S. C9 136
Trepassey, Nf., Can. j23 107a
Tres Algarrobos, Arg. G6 92
Tres Arroyos, Arg. I7 92
Três Corações, Braz. K3 88
Três Coroas, Braz. D12 92
Três de Maio, Braz. C10 92
Tres Esquinas, Col. G4 86
Três Lagoas, Braz. D6 90
Tres Lagos, Arg. I2 90
Tres Lomas, Arg. H6 92
Três Marias, Braz. J3 88
Tres Marías, Islas, is., Mex. E5 100
Três Marias, Represa de, res., Braz. J3 88
Tres Montes, Península, pen., Chile I1 90
Tres Montosas, mtn., N.M., U.S. I9 132
Tres Palos, Laguna, l., Mex. G9 100
Três Passos, Braz. C11 92
Tres Picos, Cerro, mtn., Arg. I6 92
Três Pontas, Braz. K3 88
Tres Puntas, Cabo, c., Arg. I3 90
Três Rios, Braz. L4 88
Tres Vírgenes, Volcán de las, vol., Mex. B2 100
Tres Zapotes, hist., Mex. F11 100
Tretten, Nor. F4 8
Treuchtlingen, Ger. H6 16
Treuenbrietzen, Ger. D8 16
Treviglio, Italy E6 22
Treviso, Italy E9 22
Trevorton, Pa., U.S. D9 114
Trgovište, Yugo. G9 26
Triabunna, Austl. o13 77a
Triberg, Ger. H4 16
Tribugá, Ensenada de, b., Col. E3 86
Tribune, Sk., Can. E10 124
Tribune, Ks., U.S. C7 128
Tricarico, Italy D10 24
Tricase, Italy E12 24
Trichonída, Límni, l., Grc. E4 28
Trichūr, India F3 53
Tri County Supply Canal, can., Ne., U.S. G12 126
Trida, Austl. I5 76
Trident Peak, mtn., Nv., U.S. B7 134
Trier, Ger. G2 16
Trieste (Trst), Italy E10 22
Trieste, Gulf of, b., Eur. E10 22
Triglav, mtn., Slvn. D10 22
Triglavski narodni park, p.o.i., Slvn. D10 22
Trigueros, Spain G4 20
Tríkala, Grc. D4 28
Trikora, Puncak, mtn., Indon. F10 44
Trilby, Fl., U.S. H3 116
Triman, Pak. D2 54
Trincheras, Mex. F7 98
Trincomalee, Sri L. G5 53
Trindade, Braz. I1 88
Trindade, i., Braz. H12 82
Třinec, Czech Rep. G14 16
Trinidad, Bol. B3 90
Trinidad, Col. E6 86
Trinidad, Cuba B8 102
Trinidad, Co., U.S. D4 128
Trinidad, Tx., U.S. E2 122
Trinidad, Ur. F9 92
Trinidad, i., Trin. s13 105f
Trinidad, Isla, i., Arg. I7 92
Trinidad and Tobago, ctry., N.A. s13 105f
Trinity, Tx., U.S. G3 122
Trinity, stm., Ca., U.S. C2 134
Trinity, stm., Tx., U.S. D13 130
Trinity, Elm Fork, stm., Tx., U.S. H11 128
Trinity, South Fork, stm., Ca., U.S. C2 134
Trinity, West Fork, stm., Tx., U.S. H11 128
Trinity Bay, b., Nf., Can. j23 107a
Trinity Bay, b., Tx., U.S. H4 122
Trinity Islands, is., Ak., U.S. E9 140
Trinity Peak, mtn., Nv., U.S. C7 134
Trinity Site, hist., N.M., U.S. H2 128
Trino, Italy E5 22
Tripa, stm., Indon. J3 48
Trípoli, Grc. F5 28
Tripoli see Ṭarābulus, Leb. D6 58
Tripoli see Ṭarābulus, Libya A2 62
Tripoli, Ia., U.S. I6 118
Tripolis, hist., Tur. F12 28
Tripp, S.D., U.S. D15 126
Tripura, state, India G13 54
Tristan da Cunha Group, is., St. Hel. J4 60
Tristao, Îles, is., Gui. G2 64
Triste, Spain B10 20
Triste, Golfo, b., Ven. B7 86
Tri Ton, Viet. G7 48
Triumph, La., U.S. H9 122
Trivandrum, India G3 53
Trnava, Slov. H13 16
Trobriand Islands, is., Pap. N. Gui. b5 79a
Trogir, Cro. G13 22
Troia, Italy C9 24
Troick, Russia D10 32
Troickoe, Russia D15 32
Troickoe, Russia G16 34
Troicko-Pečorsk, Russia B9 32
Troina, Italy G8 24
Troisdorf, Ger. F2 16
Trois-Pistoles, Qc., Can. B7 110
Trois Pitons, Morne, vol., Dom. j6 105c
Trois-Rivières, Qc., Can. D4 110
Trois-Rivières, Guad. i5 105c
Trojan, Blg. G11 26
Trojanova Tabla, hist., Yugo. E9 26
Trollhättan, Swe. G5 8
Trombetas, stm., Braz. C6 84
Troms, state, Nor. B8 8
Tromsø, Nor. B8 8
Trona, Ca., U.S. H8 134
Tronador, Cerro, mtn., S.A. H2 90
Trondheim, Nor. E4 8
Trondheimsfjorden, b., Nor. E4 8
Troödos, Cyp. D3 58
Troodos Mountains, mts., Cyp. D3 58
Troon, Scot., U.K. F8 12
Trophy Mountain, vol., B.C., Can. E11 138
Tropic, Ut., U.S. F4 132
Tropojë, Alb. B14 24
Troškūnai, Lith. E7 10
Trosna, Russia H18 10
Trotuș, stm., Rom. C13 26
Troup, Tx., U.S. E3 122
Trout, La., U.S. F6 122
Trout, stm., N.T., Can. C6 106
Trout Creek, Mi., U.S. E9 118
Trout Creek Pass, p., Co., U.S. C3 128
Trout Lake, l., N.T., Can. C6 106
Trout Lake, l., On., Can. E12 106
Troutville, Va., U.S. G6 114
Trouville-sur-Mer, Fr. E9 14
Trowbridge, Eng., U.K. J10 12
Troy, Al., U.S. F13 122
Troy, Id., U.S. D10 136
Troy, Mo., U.S. F7 120
Troy, N.H., U.S. B13 114
Troy, N.Y., U.S. B12 114
Troy, N.C., U.S. A6 116
Troy, Oh., U.S. D1 114
Troy, Pa., U.S. C9 114
Troy, Tn., U.S. H8 120
Troy, Tx., U.S. C10 130
Troy see Truva, hist., Tur. D9 28
Troyes, Fr. F13 14
Troy Peak, mtn., Nv., U.S. E1 132
Trst see Trieste, Italy E10 22
Trstená, Slov. G15 16
Truax, Sk., Can. E8 124
Trubč'evsk, Russia H16 10
Truchas, N.M., U.S. E3 128
Truchas Peak, mtn., N.M., U.S. E3 128
Trucial States see United Arab Emirates, ctry., Asia E7 56
Truckee, Ca., U.S. D5 134
Truckee, stm., U.S. D6 134
Trud, Russia C16 10
Trujillo, Col. E3 86
Trujillo, Hond. E4 102
Trujillo, Peru E2 84
Trujillo, Spain E5 20
Trujillo, Ven. C6 86
Trujillo, state, Ven. C6 86
Trujillo Alto, P.R. B4 104a
Truk Islands see Chuuk, is., Micron. C6 72
Truman, Mn., U.S. H4 118
Trumann, Ar., U.S. B8 122
Trumansburg, N.Y., U.S. B9 114
Trumbull, Ct., U.S. C12 114
Trumbull, Mount, mtn., Az., U.S. G3 132
Trundle, Austl. I6 76
Trung Phan (Annam), hist. reg., Viet. D8 48
Truro, N.S., Can. E13 110
Truro, Eng., U.K. K7 12
Trusan, stm., Malay. A9 50
Truscott, Tx., U.S. H9 128
Trușeni, Mol. B15 26
Truth or Consequences, N.M., U.S. J9 132
Trutnov, Czech Rep. F11 16
Truva (Troy), hist., Tur. D9 28
Truxton Wash, stm., Az., U.S. H3 132
Truyère, stm., Fr. E8 18
Tryduby, Ukr. A17 26
Tryon, Ne., U.S. F12 126
Tryon, N.C., U.S. A3 116
Trzcianka, Pol. C12 16
Trzciel, Pol. D11 16
Trzebiatów, Pol. B11 16
Trzebinia, Pol. F15 16
Trzebnica, Pol. E13 16
Tsagaannuur, Mong. E15 32
Tsaidam Basin see Qaidam Pendi, bas., China D3 36
Tsala Apopka Lake, l., Fl., U.S. H3 116
Tsamkong see Zhanjiang, China K4 42
Ts'anghsien see Cangzhou, China B7 42
T'sangwu see Wuzhou, China J4 42
Tsaratanana, Madag. D8 68
Tsaratanana, mts., Madag. C8 68
Tsau, Bots. E3 68
Tsavo, Kenya E7 66
Tsaydaychuz Peak, mtn., B.C., Can. C4 138
Tsebrykove, Ukr. B17 26
Tses, Nmb. D4 70
Tsetserleg, Mong. B5 36
Tsévié, Togo H5 64
Tshabong, Bots. D6 70
Tshane, Bots. D5 70
Tshela, D.R.C. E2 66
Tshidilamolomo, S. Afr. D7 70
Tshikapa, D.R.C. F4 66
Tshofa, D.R.C. F5 66
Tshuapa, stm., D.R.C. E4 66
Tshumbe (Chiumbe), stm., Afr. B3 68
Tsiafajavona, vol., Madag. D8 68
Tsiigehtchic, N.T., Can. B4 106
Tsimlyansk Reservoir see Cimljanskoe vodohranilišče, res., Russia E6 32
Tsinan see Jinan, China C7 42
Tsineng, S. Afr. E6 70
Tsinghai see Qinghai, state, China D4 36
Tsingkiang see Qingjiang, China E8 42
Tsingtao see Qingdao, China C9 42
Tsingyuan see Baoding, China B6 42
Ts'in-hai see Qinghai, state, China D4 36
Tsining see Jining, China D7 42
Tsinling Shan see Qin Ling, mts., China E3 42
Tsintsabis, Nmb. D2 68
Tsiombe, Madag. F8 68
Tsipa see Cipa, stm., Russia F11 34
Tsiribihina, stm., Madag. D7 68
Tsiroanomandidy, Madag. D8 68
Tsitsihar see Qiqihar, China B9 36
Tsna see Cna, stm., Russia D6 32
Tsomo, stm., S. Afr. H8 70
Tsomog, Mong. B6 36
Tsu, Japan E9 40
Tsubame, Japan B11 40
Tsuchiura, Japan C13 40
Tsugaru-kaikyō, strt., Japan D14 38
Tsukumi, Japan F4 40
Tsukushi-sanchi, mts., Japan F3 40
Tsumeb, Nmb. D2 68
Tsumkwe, Nmb. D3 68
Tsuni see Zunyi, China H2 42
Tsuruga, Japan D9 40
Tsurugi-san, mtn., Japan F7 40
Tsuruoka, Japan A12 40
Tsushima, is., Japan E2 40
Tsushima-kaikyō (Eastern Channel), strt., Japan F2 40
Tsuyama, Japan D7 40
Tswaane, Bots. C6 70
Ttruchchendūr, India G4 53
Tua, D.R.C. E3 66
Tua, stm., Port. C3 20
Tua, Tanjung, c., Indon. F4 50
Tua Chua, Viet. B6 48
Tual, Indon. G9 44
Tuam, Ire. H4 12
Tuamotu, Îles, is., Fr. Poly. E12 72
Tuamotu Archipelago see Tuamotu, Îles, is., Fr. Poly. E12 72
Tuamotu Ridge, unds. K24 142
Tuanan, Indon. E9 50
Tuangku, Pulau, i., Indon. K3 48
Tuapse, Russia F5 32
Tuasivi, Cape, c., Samoa g11 79c
Tuba, Russia C18 32
Tuba, stm., Russia D16 32
Tubac, Az., U.S. L5 132
Tuban, Indon. G8 50
Tubarão, Braz. D13 92
Ṭūbās, W.B. F6 58
Tübingen, Ger. H4 16
Ṭubruq, Libya A4 62
Tubuai, i., Fr. Poly. F12 72
Tucacas, Ven. B7 86
Tucano, Braz. F6 88
Tucheng, China G2 42
Tuchów, Pol. G17 16
Tuckerman, Ar., U.S. B7 122
Tuckerton, N.J., U.S. E11 114
Tučkovo, Russia E19 10
Tucson, Az., U.S. K5 132
Tucumán, state, Arg. C5 92
Tucumcari, N.M., U.S. F5 128
Tucunuco, Arg. E3 92
Tucupido, Ven. C9 86
Tucupita, Ven. C11 86
Tucuruí, Braz. D8 84
Tucuruí, Represa de, res., Braz. D8 84
Tudela, Phil. F4 52
Tudela, Spain B9 20
Tudmur (Palmyra), Syria D9 58
Tufānganj, India E12 54
Tufi, Pap. N. Gui. b4 79a
Tugela, stm., S. Afr. F10 70
Tug Fork, stm., U.S. G3 114
Tuggerah Lake, b., Austl. I8 76
Tuguegarao City, Phil. B3 52
Tugur, Russia F16 34
Tuhai, stm., China C7 42
Tuhuangba, China F3 42
Tui, Spain B2 20
Tuibo, China C7 38
Tuira, stm., Pan. D3 86
Tujmazy, Russia D8 32
Tukangbesi, Kepulauan, is., Indon. G7 44
Tukituki, stm., N.Z. D7 80
Tukosméra, Mont, mtn., Vanuatu I17 79d
Tūkrah, Libya A4 62
Tuktoyaktuk, N.T., Can. B4 106
Tukums, Lat. D6 10
Tukuringra, hrebet, mts., Russia F14 34
Tukuyu, Tan. F6 66
Tula, Mex. D9 100
Tula, Russia F20 10
Tulach Mhór see Tullamore, Ire. H5 12
Tulaghi, Sol. Is. e8 79b
Tulancingo, Mex. E9 100
Tulangbawang, stm., Indon. F4 50
Tulare, Ca., U.S. G6 134
Tulare, S.D., U.S. C14 126
Tulare Lake Bed, reg., Ca., U.S. G6 134
Tulare Lake Canal, can., Ca., U.S. G6 134
Tularosa, N.M., U.S. H2 128
Tularosa Valley, bas., N.M., U.S. E9 98
Tulbagh, S. Afr. H4 70
Tulcán, Ec. G3 86
Tulcea, Rom. D15 26
Tulcea, state, Rom. D15 26
Tulelake, Ca., U.S. B4 134
Tule Lake, l., Ca., U.S. B4 134
Tulemalu Lake, l., Nu., Can. C11 106
Tule Valley, val., Ut., U.S. D3 132
Tuli, Zimb. B9 70
Tuliszków, Pol. D14 16
Tulita, N.T., Can. C5 106
Ṭūlkarm, W.B. F6 58
Tullahoma, Tn., U.S. B12 122
Tullamore, Ire. H5 12
Tulle, Fr. D7 18
Tullibigeal, Austl. I6 76
Tulln, Aus. B13 22
Tullos, La., U.S. F6 122
Tullus, Sudan E4 62
Tully, Austl. A5 76
Tulsa, Ok., U.S. H2 120
Tulsequah, B.C., Can. D4 106
Tul'skaja oblast', co., Russia G20 10
Tuluá, Col. E3 86
Tulum, Mex. B4 102
Tulum, hist., Mex. B4 102
Tulun, Russia D18 32
Tulungagung, Indon. H7 50
Tulungselapan, Indon. E4 50
Tuma, stm., Nic. F5 102
Tumacacori National Historical Park, p.o.i., Az., U.S. L5 132
Tumaco, Col. G2 86
Tumaco, Rada de, b., Col. G2 86
Tuman-gang (Tumen), stm., Asia C8 38
Tumanskij, Russia D24 34
Tumany, Russia D20 34
Tumbarumba, Austl. J6 76
Tumbes, Peru D1 84
Tumbes, Punta, c., Chile H1 92
Tumbler Ridge, B.C., Can. A10 138
Tumen, China C8 38
Tumen (Tuman-gang), stm., Asia C8 38
Tumeremo, Ven. D11 86
Tumiritinga, Braz. J5 88
Tumkūr, India E3 53
Tumoteqi, China A4 42
Tumpat, Malay. I6 48
Tumsar, India H7 54
Tumtum, Wa., U.S. C9 136
Tumu, Ghana G4 64
Tumuc-Humac Mountains, mts., S.A. C6 84
Tumut, Austl. J7 76
Tun, stm., Thai. D4 48
Tunapuna, Trin. s12 105f
Tunari, Cerro, mtn., Bol. C3 90
Tunas de Zaza, Cuba B8 102
Tunchang, China L3 42
T'unch'i see Huangshan, China G8 42
Tunduru, Tan. G7 66
Tundža, stm., Eur. G13 26
Tungabhadra, stm., India D3 53
Tungabhadra Reservoir, res., India D2 53
Tungaru, Sudan E6 62
T'ungchou see Tongxian, China B7 42
T'ungch'uan see Tongchuan, China D3 42
Tung Hai see East China Sea, Asia F9 36
T'unghsien see Tongxian, China B7 42
T'unghua see Tonghua, China D6 38
Tunghwa see Tonghua, China D6 38
Tungkal, stm., Indon. D3 50
Tungku, Malay. A11 50
Tungla, Nic. F5 102
T'ungliao see Tongliao, China C4 38
Tungsha Tao (Pratas Island), i., Tai. K7 42
Tungshih, Tai. I9 42
Tungsten, N.T., Can. C5 106
Tungurahua, state, Ec. H2 86
Tungurahua, vol., Ec. H2 86
Tuni, India C6 53
Tunia, stm., Col. G5 86
Tunis, Tun. H4 24
Tunis, Golfe de, b., Tun. G4 24
Tunis, Gulf of see Tunis, Golfe de, b., Tun. G4 24
Tunisia, ctry., Afr. C6 64
Tunisie see Tunisia, ctry., Afr. C6 64

Name — Map Ref. — Page

Tunja, Col. E5 86
Tunkhannock, Pa., U.S. C9 114
Tunliu, China C5 42
Tunnel Hill, Ga., U.S. C13 122
Tunnelton, W.V., U.S. E6 114
Tunnsjøen, l., Nor. D5 8
Tuntum, Braz. C3 88
Tunu see Østgrønland, state, Grnld. C18 141
Tununak, Ak., U.S. D6 140
Tunuyán, Arg. F3 92
Tunuyán, stm., Arg. F4 92
Tunxi, China G8 42
Tuo, stm., China G1 42
Tuo, stm., China E7 42
Tuobalage, China C12 54
Tuobuja, Russia D13 34
Tuoj-Haja, Russia B20 32
Tuokusidawan Ling, mtn., China A6 46
Tuolumne, can., Ca., U.S. F5 134
Tuong Duong, Viet. C7 48
Tuotuo, stm., China A13 54
Tupã, Braz. D6 90
Tupaciguara, Braz. J1 88
Tupanciretã, Braz. D10 92
Tuparro, stm., Col. E7 86
Tupelo, Ms., U.S. C10 122
Tupelo, Ok., U.S. C2 122
Tupik, Russia F13 34
Tupinambarana, Ilha, i., Braz. D6 84
Tupiraçaba, Braz. H1 88
Tupiza, Bol. D3 90
Tupper Lake, N.Y., U.S. F2 110
Tupungato, Cerro, mtn., S.A. F2 92
Tuquan, China B9 36
Túquerres, Col. G3 86
Tura, India F13 54
Tura, Russia B18 32
Tura, stm., Russia C11 32
Turabah, Sau. Ar. E5 56
Turaiyūr, India F4 53
Turan, Russia D16 32
Ţurāq al-'Ilab, hills, Syria E9 58
Turau, Bela. H10 10
Turbaco, Col. B4 86
Turbat, Pak. D9 56
Turbo, Col. C3 86
Turčasovo, Russia E18 8
Turda, Rom. C10 26
Turek, Pol. D14 16
Turfan see Turpan, China C2 36
Turfan Depression see Turpan Pendi, depr., China C2 36
Turgaj, Kaz. E10 32
Turgaj, stm., Kaz. E10 32
Turgajskaja ložbina, reg., Kaz. D10 32
Turgajskoe plato, plat., Kaz. D10 32
Turgay see Turgaj, stm., Kaz. E10 32
Turginovo, Russia D18 10
Turgoš, Russia A18 10
Turgutlu, Tur. E10 28
Türi, Est. B8 10
Turia (Túria), stm., Spain D9 20
Túria (Turia), stm., Spain D9 20
Turiaçu, Braz. A3 88
Turiaçu, stm., Braz. B3 88
Turimiquire, Cerro, mtn., Ven. B10 86
Turin, Ab., Can. F18 138
Turin see Torino, Italy E4 22
Turinsk, Russia C10 32
Turka, Ukr. G19 16
Turkana, Lake see Rudolf, Lake, l., Afr. D7 66
Turkestan, Kaz. F11 32
Turkestanskij hrebet, mts., Asia B10 56
Túrkeve, Hung. B7 26
Turkey, ctry., Asia B3 56
Turkey, stm., Ia., U.S. I7 118
Turkey Creek, stm., Ne., U.S. K2 118
Turkish Republic of Northern Cyprus see Cyprus, North, ctry., Asia C4 58
Turkmenbaši, Turkmen. B7 56
Turkmenia see Turkmenistan, ctry., Asia B8 56
Turkmenistan, ctry., Asia B8 56
Türkoğlu, Tur. A7 58
Turks and Caicos Islands, dep., N.A. A12 102
Turks Island Passage, strt., T./C. Is. B12 102
Turks Islands, is., T./C. Is. B12 102
Turku (Åbo), Fin. F9 8
Turku ja Pori, state, Fin. F10 8
Turkwel, stm., Kenya D7 66
Turley, Ok., U.S. H2 120
Turlock, Ca., U.S. F5 134
Turmalina, Braz. I4 88
Turmantas, Lith. E9 10
Turnagain, stm., B.C., Can. D5 106
Turneffe Islands, is., Belize D4 102
Turner, Mt., U.S. F5 124
Turner, Or., U.S. F4 136
Turners Falls, Ma., U.S. B13 114
Turnhout, Bel. C13 14
Turnov, Czech Rep. F11 16
Turnu Măgurele, Rom. F11 26
Turnu Roşu, Pasul, p., Rom. D11 26
Turočak, Russia D15 32
Turon, Ks., U.S. D10 128
Turpan, China C2 36
Turpan Pendi (Turfan Depression), depr., China C2 36
Turquino, Pico, mtn., Cuba C9 102
Turrell, Ar., U.S. B8 122
Turret Peak, mtn., Az., U.S. I5 132
Turtle, stm., Mb., Can. D14 124
Turtle-Flambeau Flowage, res., Wi., U.S. E8 118
Turtle Islands, is., S.L. H2 64
Turtle Lake, N.D., U.S. G13 124
Turtle Lake, Wi., U.S. F6 118
Turu, stm., Russia B18 32
Turuhan, stm., Russia A14 32
Turuhansk, Russia C6 34
Turvo, Braz. D13 92
Turvo, stm., Braz. K1 88
Turwi, stm., Zimb. B10 70
Turzovka, Slov. G14 16
Tuscaloosa, Al., U.S. D11 122
Tuscaloosa, Lake, res., Al., U.S. D11 122
Tuscany see Toscana, state, Italy G8 22
Tuscarora Mountain, mts., Pa., U.S. D8 114
Tuscola, Tx., U.S. B8 130
Tuscumbia, Al., U.S. C11 122
Tuscumbia, Mo., U.S. F5 120
Tuskegee, Al., U.S. E13 122
Tustumena Lake, l., Ak., U.S. D9 140
Tutaev, Russia C22 10
Tuticorin, India G4 53
Tutin, Yugo. F7 26
Tutóia, Braz. B4 88
Tutoko, Mount, mtn., N.Z. G3 80
Tutrakan, Blg. E13 26
Tuttle, N.D., U.S. G14 124
Tuttle Creek Lake, res., Ks., U.S. B12 128
Tutuala, Indon. G8 44
Tutuila, i., Am. Sam. h12 79c
Tutupaca, Volcán, vol., Peru G3 84
Tutwiler, Ms., U.S. C8 122
Tutzing, Ger. I7 16
Tuul, stm., Mong. B6 36
Tuva, state, Russia D16 32
Tuvalu, ctry., Oc. D8 72
Tuvuca, i., Fiji p20 79e
Ţuwayq, Jabal, mts., Sau. Ar. E6 56
Tuxford, Sk., Can. D8 124
Tuxpan, Mex. E6 100
Tuxpan de Rodríguez Cano, Mex. E10 100
Tuxtepec, Mex. F10 100
Tuxtla Gutiérrez, Mex. G12 100
Túy see Tui, Spain B2 20
Tuy, stm., Ven. B8 86
Tuyen Hoa, Viet. D8 48
Tuyen Quang, Viet. B7 48
Tuy Hoa, Viet. F9 48
Tuyün see Duyun, China H2 42
Ţuyūr, Burj aţ-, hill, Sudan C5 62
Tuz, Iraq C5 56
Tuz Gölü, l., Tur. B3 56
Tuzigoot National Monument, p.o.i., Az., U.S. I4 132
Tuzla, Bos. E5 26
Tuzly, Ukr. D17 26
Tvardiţa, Mol. C15 26
Tver' (Kalinin), Russia D18 10
Tverca, stm., Russia D18 10
Tverskaja oblast', co., Russia D16 10
Tweed, On., Can. D12 112
Tweed, stm., U.K. F10 12
Tweed Heads, Austl. G9 76
Twee Rivieren, S. Afr. E5 70
Twelve Mile Lake, l., Sk., Can. E7 124
Twenthekanaal, can., Neth. B15 14
Twentynine Palms, Ca., U.S. I9 134
Twin Buttes, mtn., Or., U.S. F4 136
Twin Buttes Reservoir, res., Tx., U.S. C7 130
Twin City, Ga., U.S. D3 116
Twin Falls, Id., U.S. H12 136
Twin Lakes, Ga., U.S. F2 116
Twin Lakes, Wi., U.S. B9 120
Twinsburg, Oh., U.S. C4 114
Twisp, Wa., U.S. B6 136
Twitchell Reservoir, res., Ca., U.S. H5 134
Twitya, stm., N.T., Can. C5 106
Two Butte Creek, stm., Co., U.S. D6 128
Twofold Bay, b., Austl. K7 76
Two Harbors, Mn., U.S. D7 118
Two Medicine, stm., Mt., U.S. B14 136
Two Rivers, Wi., U.S. D2 112
Tybee Island, Ga., U.S. D5 116
Tychy, Pol. F14 16
Tyczyn, Pol. G18 16
Tye, Tx., U.S. B8 130
Tygda, Russia F14 34
Tyler, Mn., U.S. G2 118
Tyler, Tx., U.S. E3 122
Tylertown, Ms., U.S. F8 122
Tylihul, stm., Ukr. B17 26
Tylihul's'kyi lyman, l., Ukr. B17 26
Tym, stm., Russia C14 32
Tymovskoe, Russia F17 34
Tynda, Russia E13 34
Tyndall, S.D., U.S. D15 126
Tyndaris, hist., Italy F8 24
Tynemouth, Eng., U.K. F11 12
Tynset, Nor. E4 8
Tyre see Şūr, Leb. E6 58
Tyrifjorden, l., Nor. F3 8
Tyrma, Russia F15 34
Tyrma, stm., Russia F15 34
Tyrone, Ok., U.S. E7 128
Tyrrell, Lake, l., Austl. J4 76
Tyrrhenian Sea, Eur. G11 6
Tysa (Tisa) (Tisza), stm., Eur. A10 26
Tysnesøya, i., Nor. F1 8
Tysse, Nor. F1 8
Tytuvėnai, Lith. E6 10
Ty Ty, Ga., U.S. E2 116
Tyva see Tuva, state, Russia D16 32
Tzaneen, S. Afr. C9 70
Tzekung see Zigong, China F5 36
Tzeliutsing see Zigong, China F5 36
Tzucacab, Mex. B3 102
Tzukung see Zigong, China F5 36
Tzupo see Boshan, China C7 42
Tzupo see Zibo, China C8 42

U

Uatumã, stm., Braz. D6 84
Uauá, Braz. E6 88
Uaupés, Braz. H8 86
Uaupés (Vaupés), stm., S.A. G7 86
Uaxactún, hist., Guat. D3 102
Ubá, Braz. K4 88
Ubagan, stm., Kaz. D10 32
Ubaidullaganj, India G6 54
Ubaitaba, Braz. H6 88
Ubajara, Parque Nacional de, p.o.i., Braz. B5 88
Ubangi (Oubangui), stm., Afr. E3 66
Ubatã, Braz. H6 88
Ubaté, Col. E5 86
Ubatuba, Braz. L3 88
Ube, Japan F4 40
Úbeda, Spain F7 20
Uberaba, Braz. J2 88
Uberlândia, Braz. J1 88
Überlingen, Ger. I5 16
Ubiña, Peña, mtn., Spain B4 20
Ubl'a, Slov. H18 16
Ubly, Mi., U.S. E7 112
Ubombo, S. Afr. E11 70
Ubon Ratchathani, Thai. E7 48
Ubrique, Spain H5 20
Ubundu, D.R.C. E5 66
Učaly, Russia D9 32
Učami, Russia B17 32
Učaral, Kaz. E14 32
Ucayali, stm., Peru D3 84
Uchinoura, Japan H4 40
Uchiura-wan, b., Japan C14 38
Uchiza, Peru E2 84
Uchoa, Braz. K1 88
Uckermark, reg., Ger. C9 16
Ucon, Id., U.S. G15 136
Učur, stm., Russia E15 34
Uda, stm., Russia C17 32
Uda, stm., Russia F15 34
Udagamandalam, India F3 53
Udaipur, India F4 54
Udalguri, India E13 54
Udall, Ks., U.S. D11 128
Udamalpet, India F3 53
Udankudi, India G4 53
Udaquiola, Arg. H8 92
Udaypur, Nepal E11 54
Uddevalla, Swe. G4 8
Uddjaur, l., Swe. D8 8
Udgīr, India B3 53
Udhampur, India B5 54
Udimskij, Russia F21 8
Udine, Italy D10 22
Udmurtia see Udmurtija, state, Russia C8 32
Udmurtija, state, Russia C8 32
Udokan, hrebet, mts., Russia E12 34
Udomlja, Russia C17 10
Udon Thani, Thai. D6 48
Udskaja guba, b., Russia F16 34
Udskoe, Russia F15 34
Udupi, India E2 53
Udža, Russia B12 34
Ueckermünde, Ger. C10 16
Ueda, Japan C11 40
Uele, stm., D.R.C. D4 66
Uelen, Russia C26 34
Uel'kal', Russia C25 34
Uelzen, Ger. C6 16
Ueno, Japan E9 40
Uere, stm., D.R.C. D5 66
Uetersen, Ger. C5 16
Ufa, Russia D9 32
Ufa, stm., Russia C9 32
Uffenheim, Ger. G6 16
Ugab, stm., Nmb. E2 68
Uganda, ctry., Afr. D6 66
Ugărčin, Blg. F11 26
Ugarit, hist., Syria C6 58
Ugashik, Ak., U.S. E8 140
Uglegorsk, Russia G17 34
Uglekamensk, Russia C10 38
Uglič, Russia C21 10
Ugljan, Otok, i., Cro. F12 22
Ugodiči, Russia C22 10
Ugodskij Zavod, Russia E19 10
Ugra, stm., Russia F18 10
Uherské Hradiště, Czech Rep. G13 16
Uherský Brod, Czech Rep. H13 16
Uhlenhorst, Nmb. C3 70
Uhra, stm., Russia B22 10
Uhta, Russia F18 8
Uhta, Russia B8 32
Uíge, Ang. B1 68
Uil, Kaz. E8 32
Uinebona, stm., Ven. E10 86
Uinta Mountains, mts., Ut., U.S. C6 132
Uiraúna, Braz. D6 88
Uisŏng, Kor., S. C1 40
Uitenhage, S. Afr. H7 70
Uithuizermeeden, Neth. A15 14
Uj, stm., Asia D10 32
Ujandina, stm., Russia C17 34
Ujar, Russia C16 32
Ujelang, at., Marsh. Is. C7 72
Újfehértó, Hung. B8 26
Ujhāni, India D7 54
Uji, Japan E8 40
Uji-guntō, is., Japan H2 40
Ujiji, Tan. E5 66
Ujjain, India G5 54
Ujung, Indon. G12 50
Ujunggenteng, Indon. G5 50
Ujungkulon National Park, p.o.i., Indon. G4 50
Ujungpandang (Makasar), Indon. F11 50
Uk, Russia C17 32
Uka, Russia E21 34
Ukara Island, i., Tan. E6 66
Ukerewe Island, i., Tan. E6 66
Ukiah, Ca., U.S. D2 134
Uki Ni Masi Island, i., Sol. Is. f9 79b
Ukmergė, Lith. E7 10
Ukraine, ctry., Eur. F15 6
Ukui, Indon. D3 50
Ukyr, Russia G10 34
Ula, Bela. E12 10
Ulaanbaatar, Mong. B6 36
Ulaangom, Mong. G7 34
Ulan, Austl. I7 76
Ulan Bator see Ulaanbaatar, Mong. B6 36
Ulan Buh Shamo, des., China A2 42
Ulan-Burgasy, hrebet, mts., Russia F10 34
Ulanów, Pol. F18 16
Ulansuhai Nur, l., China A3 42
Ulan-Ude, Russia F10 34
Ulawa Island, i., Sol. Is. e9 79b
Ulawun, Mount (The Father), vol., Pap. N. Gui. b5 79a
Ulchin, Kor., S. B2 40
Ulcinj, Yugo. H6 26
Ulco, S. Afr. F7 70
Uldz, stm., Asia B8 36
Uleåborg see Oulu, Fin. D11 8
Ulen, Mn., U.S. D2 118
Ulety, Russia F11 34
Ulëz, Alb. C13 24
Ulhāsnagar, India B1 53
Ul'ianovka, Ukr. A17 26
Uliastay, Mong. B4 36
Ulindi, stm., D.R.C. E5 66
Ulja, Russia E17 34
Uljanovo, Russia G18 10
Uljanovsk, Russia D7 32
Ul'kan, Russia C19 32
Ulla, stm., Spain B2 20
Ulladulla, Austl. J8 76
Ullin, Il., U.S. G8 120
Ullŭng-do, i., Kor., S. B3 40
Ulm, Ger. H5 16
Ulm, Mt., U.S. C15 136
Ulmarra, Austl. G9 76
Ulmeni, Rom. D13 26
Ulóngue, Moz. C5 68
Ulsan, Kor., S. D2 40
Ulster, hist. reg., Eur. G5 12
Ulster Canal, can., Eur. G5 12
Ulu, Indon. E8 44
Ulu, Russia D14 34
Ulúa, stm., Hond. E3 102
Ulubat Gölü, l., Tur. C11 28
Uluborlu, Tur. E13 28
Uluçınar, Tur. B6 58
Uludağ, mtn., Tur. C12 28
Uludağ Yarımdası Milli Parkı, p.o.i., Tur. C12 28
Ulukışla, Tur. A5 58
Ulul, i., Micron. C5 72
Ulungur, stm., China B2 36
Ulungur Hu, l., China B2 36
Ulunhan, Russia F11 34
Uluru (Ayers Rock), mtn., Austl. E6 74
Ulutau, gory, mts., Kaz. E11 32
Ulverston, Eng., U.K. G9 12
Ulverstone, Austl. n12 77a
Ulysses, Ks., U.S. D7 128
Uma, China F13 34
Umán, Mex. B3 102
Umanak, Grnld. C15 141
Umanak Fjord, b., Grnld. C15 141
Umargāon, India H4 54
Umaria, India G8 54
Umarizal, Braz. D7 88
Umarkot, Pak. F2 54
Umatac, Guam j9 78c
Umatilla, Fl., U.S. H4 116
Umatilla, Or., U.S. E7 136
Umatilla, stm., Or., U.S. E7 136
Umatilla, Lake, res., U.S. E4 136
Umba, Russia C16 8
Umbertide, Italy G9 22
Umboi Island, i., Pap. N. Gui. b4 79a
Umbria, state, Italy G9 22
Umbukul, Pap. N. Gui. a4 79a
Umbuzero, ozero, l., Russia C16 8
Umeå, Swe. E9 8
Umeälven, stm., Swe. D8 8
Umfolozi Game Reserve, S. Afr. F10 70
Umfors, Swe. C6 8
Umfreville Lake, res., On., Can. A3 118
Umkomaas, S. Afr. G10 70
Umm al-Arānib, Libya B2 62
Umm al-Jimāl, Khirbat, hist., Jord. F7 58
Umm al-Qaywayn, U.A.E. D8 56
Umm as-Sa'd, hist., Syria E7 58
Umm Bel, Sudan E5 62
Umm Durmān (Omdurman), Sudan D6 62
Umm el Faḥm, Isr. F6 58
Umm Lajj, Sau. Ar. D4 56
Umm Mitmam, sand, Egypt H3 58
Umm Omeiyid, Râs, mtn., Egypt K3 58
Umm Ruwābah, Sudan E6 62
Umm Sayyālah, Sudan E6 62
Umnak Island, i., Ak., U.S. g25 140a
Umpqua, stm., Or., U.S. G3 136
Umpulo, Ang. C2 68
'Umrān, Yemen F5 56
Umraniye, Tur. D14 28
Umred, India H7 54
Umreth, India G4 54
Umtata, S. Afr. G9 70
Umuarama, Braz. A11 92
Umzingwani, stm., Zimb. B9 70
Umzinto, S. Afr. G10 70
Una, Braz. H6 88
Una, India H3 54
Una, stm., Eur. E13 22
Unac, stm., Bos. E3 26
Unadilla, Ga., U.S. D2 116
Unadilla, N.Y., U.S. B10 114
Unaí, Braz. I2 88
Unalakleet, Ak., U.S. D7 140
Unalaska, Ak., U.S. F6 140
Unalaska Island, i., Ak., U.S. F6 140
Unare, stm., Ven. C9 86
'Unayzah, Sau. Ar. D5 56
Uncia, Bol. C3 90
Uncompahgre Peak, mtn., Co., U.S. E9 132
Uncompahgre Plateau, plat., Co., U.S. E8 132
Unden, l., Swe. G5 8
Underberg, S. Afr. F9 70
Undva nina, c., Est. B4 10
Uneča, Russia H15 10
Uneiuxi, stm., Braz. H9 86
Unga Island, i., Ak., U.S. E7 140
Ungava, Péninsule d', pen., Qc., Can. D16 106
Ungava Bay, b., Can. D17 106
Ungava Peninsula see Ungava, Péninsule d', pen., Qc., Can. D16 106
Ungch'ŏn, Kor., S. D1 40
Unggi-ŭp, Kor., N. C9 38
Ungheni, Mol. B14 26
União, Braz. C4 88
União dos Palmares, Braz. E7 88
Unicoi, Tn., U.S. H3 114
Uniejów, Pol. D14 16
Unimak Island, i., Ak., U.S. F7 140
Unimak Pass, strt., Ak., U.S. F6 140
Unini, stm., Braz. H11 86
Unión, Arg. G5 92
Unión, Para. B9 92
Union, Ia., U.S. B4 120
Union, La., U.S. G8 122
Union, N.J., U.S. D11 114
Union, Or., U.S. E9 136
Union, S.C., U.S. B4 116
Union, Wa., U.S. C3 136
Union, W.V., U.S. G5 114
Union Bay, B.C., Can. G6 138
Union City, Ga., U.S. D14 122
Union City, Mi., U.S. F4 112
Union City, Oh., U.S. D1 114
Union City, Pa., U.S. C6 114
Union City, Tn., U.S. H8 120
Unión de Reyes, Cuba A7 102
Unión de Tula, Mex. E7 100
Union Flat Creek, stm., U.S. D9 136
Union Grove, Wi., U.S. F1 112
Union Island, i., St. Vin. p10 105e
Union Point, Ga., U.S. C2 116
Union Springs, Al., U.S. E13 122
Uniontown, Al., U.S. E11 122
Uniontown, Ky., U.S. G10 120
Uniontown, Pa., U.S. E6 114
Unionville, Mi., U.S. E6 112
United, Pa., U.S. D6 114
United Arab Emirates, ctry., Asia E7 56
United Arab Republic see Egypt, ctry., Afr. B5 62
United Kingdom, ctry., Eur. D8 6
United States, ctry., N.A. C10 102
Unity, Sk., Can. B4 124
Universal City, Tx., U.S. E9 130
University, Ms., U.S. C9 122
University City, Mo., U.S. F7 120
University Park, N.M., U.S. K10 132
University Park, Tx., U.S. E2 122
Unjha, India G4 54
Unnão, India E8 54
Uno, Canal Numero, can., Arg. H9 92
Unquillo, Arg. E5 92
Unst, i., Scot., U.K. n19 12a
Unstrut, stm., Ger. E7 16
Unža, stm., Russia G21 8
Unzen-dake, vol., Japan G3 40
Uong Bi, Viet. B8 48
Uozu, Japan C10 40
Upa, stm., Russia G20 10
Upanema, Braz. C7 88
Upata, Ven. C10 86
Upemba, Lac, l., D.R.C. F5 66
Upernavik, Grnld. C14 141
Upía, stm., Col. E5 86
Upington, S. Afr. F5 70
Upland, Ne., U.S. A10 128
Upleta, India H3 54
Upolu, i., Samoa h11 79c
Upolu Point, c., Hi., U.S. C6 78a
Upper Arlington, Oh., U.S. D2 114
Upper Arrow Lake, l., B.C., Can. F13 138
Upper Austria see Oberösterreich, state, Aus. B10 22
Upper Blackville, N.B., Can. D10 110
Upper Darby, Pa., U.S. E10 114
Upper Egypt see El-Sa'īd, hist. reg., Egypt J2 58
Upper Fraser, B.C., Can. B8 138
Upper Ganga Canal (Upper Ganges Canal), can., India D6 54
Upper Iowa, stm., U.S. H7 118
Upper Kapuas Mountains, mts., Asia C8 50
Upper Klamath Lake, l., Or., U.S. H5 136
Upper Lake, Ca., U.S. D3 134
Upper Lake, l., Ca., U.S. B5 134
Upper Manitou Lake, l., On., Can. B5 118
Upper Musquodoboit, N.S., Can. E14 110
Upper Red Lake, l., Mn., U.S. C4 118
Upper Sandusky, Oh., U.S. D2 114
Upper Takutu-Upper Essequibo, state, Guy. F12 86
Upper Trajan's Wall, misc. cult., Mol. C15 26
Upper Volta see Burkina Faso, ctry., Afr. G4 64
Uppsala, Swe. G7 8
Uppsala, state, Swe. F7 8
Upshi, India B6 54
Upton, Ky., U.S. G12 120
Urabá, Golfo de, b., Col. C3 86
Uracoa, Ven. C10 86
Uraj, Russia B10 32
Urakawa, Japan C15 38
Ural, stm. E8 32
Ural Mountains see Ural'skie gory, mts., Russia C9 32
Ural'sk, Kaz. D8 32
Ural'skie gory (Ural Mountains), mts., Russia C9 32
Urana, Austl. J6 76
Urandangi, Austl. D7 74
Urangan, Austl. E9 76
Urania, La., U.S. F6 122
Uranium City, Sk., Can. D9 106
Uraricaá, stm., Braz. F10 86
Uraricoera, Braz. F11 86
Uraricoera, stm., Braz. F11 86
Ura-Tjube, Taj. B10 56
Uravakonda, India D3 53
Uravan, Co., U.S. E8 132
Urawa, Japan D12 40
Urbana, Ar., U.S. D6 122
Urbana, Il., U.S. D9 120
Urbana, Oh., U.S. D2 114
Urbandale, Ia., U.S. C4 120
Urbania, Italy G9 22
Urbino, Italy G9 22
Urcos, Peru F3 84
Urdinarrain, Arg. F8 92
Urdžar, Kaz. E14 32
Ure, stm., Eng., U.K. G11 12
Urèčča, Bela. H10 10
Uren', Russia H21 8
Ureña, Ven. D5 86
Ures, Mex. G7 98
Ureshino, Japan F2 40
Urewera National Park, p.o.i., N.Z. D7 80
Urgenč, Uzb. F10 32
Urho Kekkosen kansallispuisto, p.o.i., Fin. B12 8
Uriah, Al., U.S. F11 122
Uriah, Mount, mtn., N.Z. E4 80
Uribante, stm., Ven. D6 86
Uribe, Col. F4 86
Uribia, Col. B5 86
Urich, Mo., U.S. F4 120
Urickij, Kaz. D11 32
Urique, stm., Mex. B5 100
Urjung-Haja, Russia B11 34
Urjupinsk, Russia D6 32
Urla, Tur. E9 28
Urlaţi, Rom. D13 26
Urlings, Antig. f4 105b
Urmia see Orūmīyeh, Iran B6 56
Urmia, Lake see Orūmīyeh, Daryācheh-ye, l., Iran B6 56
Uromi, Nig. H6 64
Uroševac, Yugo. G8 26
Urrao, Col. D3 86
Ursa, Il., U.S. D6 120
Uruaçu, Braz. H1 88
Uruapan, Mex. L9 134
Uruapan del Progreso, Mex. F7 100
Urubamba, Peru F3 84
Urubamba, stm., Peru F3 84
Urubaxi, stm., Braz. H9 86
Urubu, stm., Braz. D6 84
Urubu, stm., Braz. F1 88
Uruburetama, Braz. B6 88
Urucará, Braz. D6 84
Urucu, stm., Braz. D5 84
Uruçuca, Braz. H6 88
Uruçuí, Serra da, hills, Braz. E3 88
Urucuia, stm., Braz. I3 88
Uruçui-preto, stm., Braz. E3 88
Uruguai (Uruguay), stm., S.A. F8 92
Uruguaiana, Braz. D9 92
Uruguay, ctry., S.A. F10 92
Uruguay (Uruguai), stm., S.A. F8 92
Urumchi see Ürümqi, China C2 36
Ürümqi, China C2 36
Urup, ostrov, i., Russia G19 34
Urupês, Braz. K1 88
Urutaí, Braz. I1 88
Uruwira, Tan. F6 66
Urziceni, Rom. E13 26
Uržum, Russia C7 32
Usa, Japan F4 40
Usa, stm., Russia A9 32
Uşak, Tur. E12 28
Uşak, state, Tur. E12 28
Ušaki, Russia A13 10
Usakos, Nmb. B2 70
Usborne, Mount, mtn., Falk. Is. J5 90
Uščerpe, Russia H14 10
U.S. Department of Energy Hanford Site, sci., Wa., U.S. D7 136
Usedom, i., Eur. B10 16
Ushant see Ouessant, Île d', i., Fr. F3 14
Ushashi, Tan. E6 66
Ushtobe see Uštobe, Kaz. E13 32
Ushuaia, Arg. J3 90
Usingen, Ger. F4 16
Usinsk, Russia A9 32
Usk, Wa., U.S. B9 136
Usk, stm., Wales, U.K. J9 12
Uslar, Ger. E5 16
Usmas ezers, l., Lat. C4 10
Usole, Russia C9 32
Usole-Sibirskoe, Russia D18 32
Uspallata, Arg. F3 92
Uspanapa, stm., Mex. G11 100
Ussuri (Wusuli), stm., Asia C11 36
Ussurijsk, Russia C10 38
Ust'-Barguzin, Russia F10 34
Ust'-Belaja, Russia C23 34
Ust'-Bol'šereck, Russia F20 34
Ust'-Čaun, Russia C23 34
Ust'-Chorna, Ukr. A10 26
Ust'-Cil'ma, Russia D25 8
Uste, Russia G18 8
Uster, Switz. C5 22
Ustica, Isola di, i., Italy F7 24
Ust'-Ilimsk, Russia C18 32
Ust'-Ilimskoe vodohraniliišče, res., Russia C18 32
Ústí nad Labem, Czech Rep. F10 16
Ústí nad Orlicí, Czech Rep. G12 16
Ust'-Išim, Russia C12 32
Ustja, stm., Russia F21 8
Ust'-Javron'ga, Russia E21 8
Ustjuckoe, Russia B18 10
Ustjužna, Russia B19 10
Ustka, Pol. B12 16
Ust'-Kamčatsk, Russia E21 34
Ust'-Kamenogorsk, Kaz. E14 32
Ust'-Koksa, Russia D15 32
Ust'-Kujda, Russia B16 34
Ust'-Kulom, Russia B8 32
Ust'-Kut, Russia C19 32
Ust'-Lyža, Russia A9 32
Ust'-Maja, Russia D15 34
Ust'-Man'ja, Russia B10 32
Ust'-Nera, Russia D17 34
Ust'-Njukža, Russia E13 34
Uštobe, Kaz. E13 32
Ust'-Omčug, Russia D18 34
Ust'-Ordynskij, Russia D18 32
Ust'-Ozërnoe, Russia C15 32
Ust'-Pinega, Russia D19 8
Ust'-Reki, Russia E22 8
Ustroń, Pol. G14 16
Ust'-Sumy, Russia D14 32
Ust'-Tym, Russia D24 6
Ust'-Ulagan, Russia D15 32
Ust'-Urgal, Russia F15 34
Ust-Urt Plateau, plat., Asia F9 32
Ust-Vyjskaja, Russia E22 8
Usu, China C1 36
Usuki, Japan F4 40
Usulután, El Sal. F3 102
Usumacinta, stm., N.A. D2 102
Usumbura see Bujumbura, Bdi. E5 66
Ušumun, Russia F14 34
Usvjaty, Russia E13 10
Utah, state, U.S. D5 132
Utah Lake, l., Ut., U.S. C5 132
Utata, Russia D18 32
Ute, Ia., U.S. B2 120
Ute Creek, stm., N.M., U.S. F5 128
Utegi, Tan. E6 66
Utena, Lith. E8 10
Utete, Tan. F7 66
Uthai Thani, Thai. E4 48
Uthal, Pak. D10 56
U Thong, Thai. E4 48
Utiariti, Braz. F6 84
Utica, Ks., U.S. C8 128
Utica, Mi., U.S. F6 112
Utica, Ms., U.S. E8 122
Utica, N.Y., U.S. E14 112
Utica, Oh., U.S. D3 114
Utica see Utique, hist., Tun. G3 24
Utiel, Spain E9 20
Utila, Isla de, i., Hond. D4 102
Utinga, stm., Braz. G5 88
Utique (Utica), hist., Tun. G3 24
Uto, Japan G3 40
Utopia, Tx., U.S. E8 130
Utorgoš, Russia B13 10
Utraula, India E9 54
Utrecht, Neth. B14 14
Utrecht, S. Afr. E10 70
Utrera, Spain G5 20
Utrik, at., Marsh. Is. B7 72
Utroja, stm., Eur. D10 10
Utsunomiya, Japan C12 40
Uttamapālaiyam, India G3 53
Uttaradit, Thai. D4 48
Uttarkāshi, India C7 54
Uttar Pradesh, state, India E7 54
Utuado, P.R. B2 104a
Utukok, stm., Ak., U.S. C7 140
Utupua, i., Sol. Is. E7 72
Uulu, Est. B7 10
Uusimaa, state, Fin. F11 8
Uvá, stm., Col. F7 86
Uvalda, Ga., U.S. D3 116
Uvalde, Tx., U.S. E8 130
Uvaravičy, Bela. H13 10
Uvarovo, Russia D6 32
Uvdal, Nor. F3 8
Uvinza, Tan. F6 66
Uvira, D.R.C. E5 66
Uvs Lake see Uvsu-Nur, ozero, l., Asia F7 34
Uvsu-Nur, ozero, l., Asia F7 34
Uvworé, c., Vanuatu I17 79d
Uwa, Japan F5 40
Uwajima, Japan F5 40
Uwayl, Sudan F5 62
Uxbridge, On., Can. D10 112
Uxmal, hist., Mex. B3 102
Uyo, Nig. H6 64
Uyuni, Bol. D3 90
Uyuni, Salar de, pl., Bol. D3 90
Uzbekistan, ctry., Asia E10 30
Uzda, Bela. G10 10
Uzerche, Fr. D7 18
Uzgen, Kyrg. F12 32
Uzhhorod, Ukr. A9 26
Užice, Yugo. F6 26
Uzlovaja, Russia F20 10
Üzümlü, Tur. G12 28
Uzun Ada, i., Tur. E9 28
Uzunköprü, Tur. B9 28
Uzunkuduk, Uzb. F11 32
Užur, Russia C16 32
Užventis, Lith. E5 10

V

Vaal, stm., S. Afr. F7 70
Vaaldam, res., S. Afr. E8 70
Vaalwater, S. Afr. D8 70
Vaasa (Vasa), Fin. E9 8
Vaasa, state, Fin. E10 8
Vabalninkas, Lith. D7 10
Vác, Hung. B6 26
Vacacaí, stm., Braz. E11 92
Vacaria, Braz. D12 92
Vacaria, stm., Braz. I4 88
Vacaville, Ca., U.S. E4 134
Vaccarès, Étang de, l., Fr. F10 18
Vache, Île à, i., Haiti C11 102
Vad, Russia I21 8
Vadakara see Badagara, India F2 53
Vădeni, Rom. D14 26
Vadnagar, India G4 54
Vado, N.M., U.S. K10 132
Vadodara (Baroda), India G4 54
Vado Ligure, Italy F5 22
Vadsø, Nor. A13 8
Vaduz, Liech. C6 22
Vaga, stm., Russia F20 8
Vågåmo, Nor. F3 8
Vágar, i., Far. Is. m34 8b
Vaghena Island, i., Sol. Is. d7 79b
Vah, stm., Russia B13 32
Váh, stm., Slov. H13 16
Vahsel, Cape, c., S. Geor. J9 90
Vaiden, Ms., U.S. D9 122
Vaigai, stm., India G4 53
Vaigat, strt., Grnld. C15 141
Vaijāpur, India B2 53
Vaikam, India G3 53
Väike-Maarja, Est. A9 10
Vail, Co., U.S. D10 132
Vail, Ia., U.S. B2 120
Vaimali, Vanuatu k17 79d
Vaippār, stm., India G4 53
Vaison-la-Romaine, Fr. E11 18
Vaitahu, Fr. Poly. s18 78g
Vākhān, hist. reg., Afg. B11 56
Valaam, Russia F14 8
Valadeces, Mex. H9 130
Valandovo, Mac. B5 28
Valašské Meziříčí, Czech Rep. G13 16
Valatie, N.Y., U.S. B12 114
Vâlcea, state, Rom. E11 26
Vălčedrăm, Blg. F10 26
Valcheta, Arg. H3 90
Valdagno, Italy E8 22
Valdai Hills see Valdajskaja vozvyšennost', hills, Russia C15 10
Valdaj, Russia E16 8
Valdaj, Russia B16 10
Valdajskaja vozvyšennost' (Valdai Hills), hills, Russia C15 10
Valdarno, val., Italy G8 22
Val-de-Cães, Braz. A1 88
Valdecañas, Embalse de, res., Spain E5 20
Valdemarsvik, Swe. G7 8
Valdepeñas, Spain F7 20
Valderaduey, stm., Spain C5 20
Valdés, Península, pen., Arg. H4 90
Val-des-Bois, Qc., Can. C14 112
Valdez, Ak., U.S. D10 140
Valdivia, Chile G2 90

Name | Map Ref. | Page

Valdivia, Col. D4 86
Valdobbiadene, Italy E8 22
Val-d'Oise, state, Fr. E10 14
Val-d'Or, Qc., Can. F15 106
Valdosta, Ga., U.S. F2 116
Valdoviño see Aviño, Spain A2 20
Vale, Or., U.S. G9 136
Valemount, B.C., Can. D11 138
Valença, Braz. L4 88
Valença, Braz. G6 88
Valença, Port. B2 20
Valença do Piauí, Braz. D4 88
Valence, Fr. E10 18
Valencia, Phil. F5 52
València, Spain E10 20
Valencia, Ven. B7 86
València, state, Spain E10 20
València, co., Spain E10 20
València, Golf de, b., Spain E10 20
Valencia, Golfo de see València, Golf de, b., Spain E10 20
Valencia, Gulf of see València, Golf de, b., Spain E10 20
Valencia, Lago de, l., Ven. B8 86
Valencia de Alcántara, Spain E3 20
Valencia de Don Juan, Spain B5 20
Valencia Island, i., Ire. J2 12
Valenciennes, Fr. D12 14
Valente, Braz. F6 88
Valentin, Russia C11 38
Valentine, Ne., U.S. E12 126
Valentine, Tx., U.S. D3 130
Valenza, Italy F5 22
Valera, Ven. C6 86
Valga, Est. H12 8
Valiente, Península, pen., Pan. H7 102
Valili, mtn., Fiji p19 79e
Valjevo, Yugo. E6 26
Valkeakoski, Fin. F11 8
Valkenswaard, Neth. C14 14
Valkininkas, Lith. F7 10
Valladares, Mex. H7 130
Valladolid, Mex. B3 102
Valladolid, Spain C6 20
Valladolid, co., Spain C6 20
Vall de Uxó see La Vall d'Uixó, Spain E10 20
Valle, Lat. D7 10
Vallecillo, Mex. H7 130
Valle d'Aosta, state, Italy E4 22
Valle de Allende, Mex. H2 130
Valle de la Pascua, Ven. C8 86
Valle del Cauca, state, Col. F3 86
Valle del Rosario, Mex. G1 130
Valle de Olivos, Mex. B5 100
Valle de Santiago, Mex. E8 100
Valledupar, Col. B5 86
Vallée d'Aoste see Valle d'Aosta, state, Italy E4 22
Valle Edén, Ur. E9 92
Vallegrande, Bol. C4 90
Valle Hermoso, Mex. C10 100
Vallejo, Ca., U.S. E3 134
Vallenar, Chile D2 92
Valle Redondo, Mex. K9 134
Valletta, Malta I8 24
Valley, Al., U.S. E13 122
Valley, Ne., U.S. C1 120
Valley, Wa., U.S. B9 136
Valley, stm., Mb., Can. C13 124
Valley Bend, W.V., U.S. F6 114
Valley City, N.D., U.S. H16 124
Valley East, On., Can. B8 112
Valley Falls, Ks., U.S. E2 120
Valley Farms, Az., U.S. K5 132
Valley Head, Al., U.S. C13 122
Valley Mills, Tx., U.S. C10 130
Valley of the Kings, hist., Egypt B6 62
Valley Springs, S.D., U.S. H2 118
Valley Station, Ky., U.S. F12 120
Valleyview, Ab., Can. A13 138
Valley View, Tx., U.S. H11 128
Vallimanca, Arroyo, stm., Arg. H7 92
Vallorbe, Switz. D3 22
Valls, Spain C12 20
Valmeyer, Il., U.S. F7 120
Valmiera, Lat. C8 10
Valoria la Buena, Spain C6 20
Valožyn, Bela. F9 10
Vālpārai, India F3 53
Valparaíso, Chile F2 92
Valparaíso, Mex. D7 100
Valparaiso, Fl., U.S. G12 122
Valparaiso, In., U.S. G2 112
Valparaiso, Ne., U.S. F16 126
Valparaíso, state, Chile F2 92
Valréas, Fr. E10 18
Vals, stm., S. Afr. E8 70
Vals, Tanjung, c., Indon. G10 44
Valsbaai see False Bay, b., S. Afr. I4 70
Valtimo, Fin. E13 8
Valujki, Russia D5 32
Valverde del Camino, Spain G4 20
Valyncy, Bela. E11 10
Vamori Wash, stm., Az., U.S. L5 132
Van, Tur. B5 56
Van, Lake see Van Gölü, l., Tur. B5 56
Vanadzor, Arm. A5 56
Vanajavesi, l., Fin. F10 8
Van Alstyne, Tx., U.S. D2 122
Vananda, B.C., Can. G6 138
Vanavara, Russia B18 32
Van Bruyssel, Qc., Can. C4 110
Van Buren, Ar., U.S. B4 122
Van Buren, Me., U.S. C8 110
Vanceboro, Me., U.S. E9 110
Vanceburg, Ky., U.S. F2 114
Vancouver, B.C., Can. G7 138
Vancouver, Wa., U.S. E4 136
Vancouver Island, i., B.C., Can. G4 138
Vancouver Island Ranges, mts., B.C., Can. G5 138
Vandalia, Il., U.S. F8 120
Vandalia, Mo., U.S. E6 120
Vandalia, Oh., U.S. E1 114
Vandavāsi, India E4 53
Vanderbijlpark, S. Afr. E8 70
Vanderbilt, Tx., U.S. F11 130
Vanderhoof, B.C., Can. B6 138
Vanderkloof Dam, res., S. Afr. F7 70
Vanderlin Island, i., Austl. C7 74
Vandervoort, Ar., U.S. C4 122
Van Diemen Gulf, b., Austl. B6 74
Vandry, Qc., Can. C3 110
Vandžiogala, Lith. E6 10
Vanegas, Mex. D8 100
Vänern, l., Swe. G5 8
Vänersborg, Swe. G5 8
Vangaindrano, Madag. E8 68
Van Gölü, l., Tur. B5 56
Vangunu Island, i., Sol. Is. e8 79b
Van Horn, Tx., U.S. C3 130
Van Horne, Ia., U.S. B5 120
Vanier, On., Can. C14 112
Vanikolo, i., Sol. Is. E7 72
Vanimo, Pap. N. Gui. a3 79a
Vanino, Russia G17 34
Vānīvilāsa Sāgara, res., India E3 53
Vāniyambādi, India E4 53
Vankarem, Russia C25 34
Vankleek Hill, On., Can. E2 110
Van Lear, Ky., U.S. G3 114
Vanna, i., Nor. A8 8
Vännäs, Swe. E8 8
Vanndale, Ar., U.S. B8 122
Vannes, Fr. G6 14
Van Ninh, Viet. F9 48
Van Phong, Vung, b., Viet. F9 48
Van Phong Bay see Van Phong, Vung, b., Viet. F9 48
Van Reenen, S. Afr. F9 70
Van Rees, Pegunungan, mts., Indon. F10 44
Vanrhynsdorp, S. Afr. G4 70
Vansant, Va., U.S. G3 114
Vansittart Island, i., Nu., Can. B14 106
Vanskoe, Russia B19 10
Vanthali, India H3 54
Vanua Balavu, i., Fiji p20 79e
Vanua Lava, i., Vanuatu i16 79d
Vanua Levu, i., Fiji p19 79e
Vanuatu (New Hebrides), ctry., Oc. k16 79d
Van Wert, Oh., U.S. D1 114
Van Wyksdorp, S. Afr. H5 70
Van Zylsrus, S. Afr. E6 70
Vao, N. Cal. n16 79d
Var, state, Fr. F12 18
Var, stm., Fr. F13 18
Varada, stm., India D2 53
Varallo, Italy E5 22
Vārānasi (Benares), India F9 54
Varandej, Russia A9 32
Varangerfjorden, b., Nor. A14 8
Varangerhalvøya, pen., Nor. A13 8
Varano, Lago di, l., Italy I12 22
Varaždin, Cro. D13 22
Varazze, Italy F5 22
Varberg, Swe. H5 8
Vardak, state, Afg. A2 54
Vardar (Axiós), stm., Eur. B5 28
Varde, Den. I3 8
Vardø, Nor. A14 8
Varel, Ger. C4 16
Varela, Arg. G4 92
Varėna, Lith. F7 10
Varennes-sur-Allier, Fr. C9 18
Varese, Italy E5 22
Vârfurile, Rom. C9 26
Vargem, Riacho da, stm., Braz. E6 88
Vargem Grande, Braz. B3 88
Varginha, Braz. K3 88
Varkallai, India G3 53
Varkaus, Fin. E12 8
Värmeln, l., Swe. G5 8
Värmland, state, Swe. G5 8
Varna, Blg. F14 26
Varna, Russia D10 32
Varna, state, Blg. F14 26
Värnamo, Swe. H6 8
Varniai, Lith. E5 10
Varnjany, Bela. F9 10
Varnsdorf, Czech Rep. F10 16
Varnville, S.C., U.S. D4 116
Várpalota, Hung. B5 26
Värska, Est. C10 10
Varvarin, Yugo. F8 26
Várzea, stm., Braz. C11 92
Várzea Alegre, Braz. D6 88
Várzea da Palma, Braz. I3 88
Várzea Grande, Braz. G6 84
Varzino, Russia B17 8
Vas, state, Hung. B3 26
Vasa see Vaasa, Fin. E9 8
Vasa see Vaasa, state, Fin. E10 8
Vasai, India E3 46
Vasalemma, Est. A7 10
Vasco, País see Euskal Herriko, state, Spain A8 20
Vashkivtsi, Ukr. A12 26
Vashkivtsi, Ukr. A14 26
Vashon Island, i., Wa., U.S. C4 136
Vasilevičy, Bela. H12 10
Vasilevskij Moh, Russia C18 10
Vasiliká, Grc. C6 28
Vasjugan, stm., Russia C13 32
Vaška, stm., Russia D21 8
Vaskelovo, Russia F14 8
Vaslui, Rom. C14 26
Vaslui, state, Rom. C14 26
Vass, N.C., U.S. A6 116
Vassar, Mi., U.S. E6 112
Västerås, Swe. G7 8
Västerbotten, state, Swe. D8 8
Västernorrland, state, Swe. E7 8
Västervik, Swe. H7 8
Västmanland, state, Swe. G7 8
Vasto, Italy H11 22
Västra Götaland, state, Swe. G4 8
Vasvár, Hung. B3 26
Vatan, Fr. G10 14
Vatican see Vatican City, ctry., Eur. I9 22
Vatican City, ctry., Eur. I9 22
Vaticano, Capo, c., Italy F9 24
Vatnajökull, ice, Ice. k31 8a
Vatomandry, Madag. D8 68
Vatra Dornei, Rom. B12 26
Vättern, l., Swe. G6 8
Vatu-i-ra Channel, strt., Fiji p19 79e
Vatukoula, Fiji p18 79e
Vauclin, Montagne du, mtn., Mart. k7 105c
Vaucluse, state, Fr. F11 18
Vaucouleurs, Fr. F14 14
Vaughan, On., Can. E10 112
Vaughn, N.M., U.S. G3 128
Vaukavysk, Bela. G7 10
Vaupés, state, Col. G6 86
Vaupés (Uaupés), stm., S.A. G7 86
Vava'u, i., Tonga E9 72
Vavoua, C. Iv. H3 64
Vavuniya, Sri L. G5 53
Växjö, Swe. H6 8
Vaza-barris, stm., Braz. E6 88
Vazante, Braz. J2 88
Vazuza, stm., Russia E17 10
Vazuzskoe vodohranilišče, res., Russia E16 10
Veazie, Me., U.S. F8 110
Veblen, S.D., U.S. B15 126
Vecht (Vechte), stm., Eur. B15 14
Vechta, Ger. D4 16
Vechte (Vecht), stm., Eur. B15 14
Vecpiebalga, Lat. C8 10
Vecsés, Hung. B6 26
Veddige, Swe. H4 8
Vedea, stm., Rom. F12 26
Vedia, Arg. G7 92
Vednoe, Russia C19 10
Veedersburg, In., U.S. H2 112
Veendam, Neth. A15 14
Veenendaal, Neth. C14 14
Vega, i., Nor. D4 8
Vega Alta, P.R. B3 104a
Vega Baja, P.R. B3 104a
Vegreville, Ab., Can. C18 138
Veguita, N.M., U.S. I10 132
Veinticinco de Mayo, Arg. G7 92
Veiros, Braz. D7 84
Veisiejai, Lith. F6 10
Vejle, Den. I3 8
Vejle, state, Den. I3 8
Vela Luka, Cro. H13 22
Velas, Cabo, c., C.R. G4 102
Velázquez, Ur. G10 92
Velden, Ger. H8 16
Veleka, stm. G14 26
Veleuščina, Bela. F11 10
Vélez, Col. D5 86
Vélez-Málaga, Spain H6 20
Vel'gija, Russia B17 10
Velhas, stm., Braz. I3 88
Velikaja, stm., Russia C11 10
Velikaja, stm., Russia D23 34
Velikaja Kema, Russia B12 38
Velika Morava, stm., Yugo. E8 26
Velikie Luki, Russia D13 10
Velikij Ustjug, Russia F21 8
Veliki Vitorog, mtn., Bos. E4 26
Velikoe, Russia G17 8
Velikoe, ozero, l., Russia C19 10
Velikonda Hills, hills, India D4 53
Veliko Tărnovo, Blg. F12 26
Velikovisočnoe, Russia C25 8
Veli Lošinj, Cro. F11 22
Vélingara, Sen. G2 64
Veliž, Russia E14 10
Vel'ké Kapušany, Slov. H18 16
Velké Meziříčí, Czech Rep. G12 16
Vella Gulf, strt., Sol. Is. d7 79b
Vella Lavella, i., Sol. Is. d7 79b
Vellār, stm., India F4 53
Velletri, Italy I9 22
Vellore, India E4 53
Velma, Ok., U.S. G11 128
Vel'sk, Russia F20 8
Velten, Ger. D9 16
Velva, N.D., U.S. F13 124
Velyka Mykhailivka, Ukr. B16 26
Velykodolyns'ke, Ukr. C17 26
Velykoplos'ke, Ukr. C16 26
Velykyi Bychkiv, Ukr. B11 26
Velykyj Kuialnyk, stm., Ukr. B17 26
Venadillo, Col. E4 86
Venado Tuerto, Arg. F6 92
Venafro, Italy C8 24
Venâncio Aires, Braz. D11 92
Vence, Fr. F13 18
Venda, hist. reg., S. Afr. C10 70
Vendas Novas, Port. F2 20
Vendée, state, Fr. C4 18
Vendéen, Bocage, reg., Fr. C4 18
Vendôme, Fr. G10 14
Vendrell see El Vendrell, Spain C12 20
Veneta, Laguna, b., Italy E9 22
Venetie, Ak., U.S. C10 140
Veneto, state, Italy E8 22
Venev, Russia F21 10
Venézia (Venice), Italy E9 22
Venezuela, ctry., S.A. B4 84
Venezuela, Golfo de, b., S.A. A3 84
Venezuela, Gulf of see Venezuela, Golfo de, b., S.A. A3 84
Venezuelan Basin, unds. G7 144
Vengerovo, Russia C13 32
Vengurla, India D1 53
Veniaminof, Mount, vol., Ak., U.S. E8 140
Venice see Venézia, Italy E9 22
Venice, Fl., U.S. I3 116
Venice, La., U.S. H9 122
Venice, Gulf of, b., Eur. E9 22
Vénissieux, Fr. D10 18
Venkatagiri, India E4 53
Venlo, Neth. C15 14
Venosa, Italy D9 24
Venoste, Alpi (Ötztaler Alpen), mts., Eur. D7 22
Venray, Neth. C15 14
Venta, stm., Eur. C4 10
Ventanas, Ec. H2 86
Ventersdorp, S. Afr. E8 70
Venterstad, S. Afr. G7 70
Ventimiglia, Italy G4 22
Ventotene, Isola, i., Italy D7 24
Ventspils, Lat. C4 10
Ventuari, stm., Ven. E8 86
Ventura, Ca., U.S. I6 134
Venturia, N.D., U.S. B13 126
Venustiano Carranza, Mex. G12 100
Venustiano Carranza, Presa, res., Mex. B8 100
Vera, Arg. D7 92
Vera, Spain G9 20
Vera, Cape, c., Nu., Can. B8 141
Veracruz, Mex. F10 100
Veracruz, state, Mex. F10 100
Veranópolis, Braz. D12 92
Verāval, India H3 54
Verbania, Italy E5 22
Verbano see Maggiore, Lago, l., Eur. C14 18
Verbeek, Pegunungan, mts., Indon. E12 50
Verbilki, Russia D20 10
Vercelli, Italy E5 22
Vercors, reg., Fr. E11 18
Verde, stm., Braz. F6 84
Verde, stm., Braz. F4 88
Verde, stm., Braz. J1 88
Verde, stm., Braz. H1 88
Verde, stm., Braz. D4 90
Verde, stm., Mex. E7 100
Verde, stm., Az., U.S. J5 132
Verde, Cape, c., Bah. A10 102
Verde Grande, stm., Braz. H4 88
Verden, Ger. D5 16
Verden, Ok., U.S. F10 128
Verde Pequeno, stm., Braz. H4 88
Verdi, Nv., U.S. D5 134
Verdigre, Ne., U.S. E14 126
Verdigris, stm., U.S. E13 128
Verdon, stm., Fr. F12 18
Verdun, Qc., Can. E3 110
Verdun-sur-Garonne, Fr. F7 18
Verdun-sur-Meuse, Fr. E14 14
Vereeniging, S. Afr. E9 70
Veregin, Sk., Can. C11 124
Vereja, Russia E19 10
Vereščagino, Russia B15 32
Vergemont Creek, stm., Austl. D4 76
Vergennes, Vt., U.S. F3 110
Verhnedneprovskij, Russia E16 10
Verhneimbatsk, Russia B15 32
Verhnemulomskoe vodohranilišče, res., Russia B14 8
Verhneural'sk, Russia D9 32
Verhneviljujsk, Russia D13 34
Verhnij Baskunčak, Russia E7 32
Verhnij Most, Russia C11 10
Verhnij Ufalej, Russia C10 32
Verhnjaja Amga, Russia E14 34
Verhnjaja Angara, stm., Russia E11 34
Verhnjaja Inta, Russia A10 32
Verhnjaja Salda, Russia C10 32
Verhnjaja Tajmyra, stm., Russia B8 34
Verhnjaja Tojma, Russia E21 8
Verhojansk, Russia C15 34
Verhojanskij hrebet (Verkhoyansk Mountains), mts., Russia C14 34
Verhopuja, Russia F19 8
Verhove, Russia H20 10
Verigin see Veregin, Sk., Can. C11 124
Verín, Spain C3 20
Veríssimo, Braz. J1 88
Verkhovyna, Ukr. A11 26
Verkhoyansk Mountains see Verhojanskij hrebet, mts., Russia C14 34
Vermelho, stm., Braz. E2 88
Vermilion, Oh., U.S. C3 114
Vermilion, stm., Ab., Can. C19 138
Vermilion, stm., On., Can. B8 112
Vermilion, stm., Mn., U.S. C6 118
Vermilion Bay, b., La., U.S. H6 122
Vermilion Lake, l., On., Can. A6 118
Vermilion Lake, l., Mn., U.S. D5 118
Vermilion Pass, p., Can. E14 138
Vermillion, S.D., U.S. E16 126
Vermillion, stm., S.D., U.S. E15 126
Vermillion, East Fork, stm., S.D., U.S. D15 126
Vermillon, stm., Qc., Can. C3 110
Vermont, Il., U.S. D7 120
Vermont, state, U.S. F4 110
Vernal, Ut., U.S. C7 132
Verndale, Mn., U.S. E3 118
Verneuil, Fr. F9 14
Vernon, B.C., Can. F11 138
Vernon, Fr. E10 14
Vernon, Al., U.S. D10 122
Vernon, Ct., U.S. C13 114
Vernon, In., U.S. F12 120
Vernon, Tx., U.S. G9 128
Vernon, Ut., U.S. C4 132
Vernonia, Or., U.S. E3 136
Vernon Lake, res., La., U.S. F5 122
Vernon River, P.E., Can. D13 110
Vero Beach, Fl., U.S. I5 116
Véroia, Grc. C5 28
Verona, On., Can. D13 112
Verona, Italy E8 22
Verona, Ms., U.S. C10 122
Verónica, Arg. G9 92
Versailles, Fr. F11 14
Versailles, Il., U.S. E7 120
Versailles, Ky., U.S. F13 120
Versailles, Mo., U.S. F5 120
Versailles, Oh., U.S. D1 114
Veršino-Darasunskij, Russia F12 34
Veršino-Šahtaminskij, Russia F12 34
Vertedero, P.R. B3 104a
Vertientes, Cuba B8 102
Verulam, S. Afr. F10 70
Verviers, Bel. D14 14
Verwoerd Reservoir see Gariep Dam, res., S. Afr. G7 70
Vescovato, Fr. G15 18
Veselí nad Lužnicí, Czech Rep. G10 16
Vesëlyj Jar, Russia C11 38
Vesole, Monte, mtn., Italy D9 24
Vesoul, Fr. G15 14
Vespasiano, Braz. J4 88
Vesta, C.R. H6 102
Vest-Agder, state, Nor. G2 8
Vestavia Hills, Al., U.S. D12 122
Vesterålen, is., Nor. B6 8
Vestfjorden, b., Nor. C5 8
Vestfold, state, Nor. G4 8
Vestgrønland (Kitaa), state, Grnld. D16 141
Vestmannaeyjar, Ice. I29 8a
Vestsjælland, state, Den. I4 8
Vestvågøya, i., Nor. B5 8
Vesuvio (Vesuvius), vol., Italy D8 24
Vesuvius see Vesuvio, vol., Italy D8 24
Veszprém, Hung. B4 26
Veszprém, state, Hung. B4 26
Vésztő, Hung. C8 26
Vet, stm., S. Afr. F8 70
Vetapālem, India D5 53
Vetju, Russia E24 8
Vetlanda, Swe. H6 8
Vetluga, Russia H21 8
Vetluga, stm., Russia C7 32
Vetlužskij, Russia G21 8
Vetlužskij, Russia H21 8
Vetrişoaia, Rom. C15 26
Vetschau, Ger. E9 16
Veurne, Bel. C11 14
Vevey, Switz. D3 22
Veynes, Fr. E11 18
Vézère, stm., Fr. D7 18
Viacha, Bol. C3 90
Viadana, Italy F7 22
Viale, Arg. E8 92
Viamão, Braz. E12 92
Viamonte, Arg. F6 92
Vian, Ok., U.S. B4 122
Viana, Braz. B3 88
Viana do Bolo, Spain B3 20
Viana do Castelo, Port. C1 20
Viana do Castelo, state, Port. C2 20
Viangchan (Vientiane), Laos D6 48
Viareggio, Italy G7 22
Vibank, Sk., Can. D10 124
Viborg, Den. H3 8
Viborg, S.D., U.S. D15 126
Viborg, state, Den. H3 8
Vibo Valentia, Italy F10 24
Vic, Spain C13 20
Vícam, Mex. B3 100
Vicebsk, Bela. E13 10
Vicebsk, state, Bela. E11 10
Vicente Guerrero, Mex. D6 100
Vicente Guerrero, Presa, res., Mex. D9 100
Vicenza, Italy E8 22
Viceroy, Sk., Can. E8 124
Vich see Vic, Spain C13 20
Vichada, state, Col. E7 86
Vichada, stm., Col. E7 86
Vichadero, Ur. E10 92
Vichra, stm., Eur. F14 10
Vichuquén, Chile G1 92
Vichy, Fr. C9 18
Vici, Ok., U.S. E9 128
Vicksburg, Ms., U.S. E8 122
Viçosa, Braz. K4 88
Viçosa do Ceará, Braz. B5 88
Vic-sur-Cère, Fr. E8 18
Victor, Id., U.S. G15 136
Victor, Ia., U.S. C5 120
Victor, Mt., U.S. D12 136
Victor Harbor, Austl. J2 76
Victoria, Arg. F7 92
Victoria, B.C., Can. H7 138
Victoria, P.E., Can. D13 110
Victoria, Chile I1 92
Victoria see Labuan, Malay. A9 50
Victoria see Rabat, Malta H8 24
Victoria, Sey. j13 69b
Victoria, Ks., U.S. C9 128
Victoria, Tx., U.S. F11 130
Victoria, Va., U.S. G7 114
Victoria, state, Austl. K4 76
Victoria, stm., Austl. C6 74
Victoria, Chutes see Victoria Falls, wtfl, Afr. D4 68
Victoria, Lake, l., Afr. E6 66
Victoria, Lake, l., Austl. I3 76
Victoria, Mount, mtn., Mya. B1 48
Victoria, Mount, mtn., Pap. N. Gui. b4 79a
Victoria Falls, wtfl, Afr. D4 68
Victoria Fjord, b., Grnld. A16 141
Victoria Harbour, On., Can. D10 112
Victoria Island, i., Can. A8 106
Victoria Land, reg., Ant. C20 81
Victoria Nile, stm., Afr. D6 66
Victoria Peak, mtn., Belize D3 102
Victoria Peak, mtn., B.C., Can. F4 138
Victoria River Downs, Austl. C6 74
Victorias, Phil. E4 52
Victoria Strait, strt., Nu., Can. B10 106
Victoriaville, Qc., Can. D4 110
Victoria West, S. Afr. G6 70
Victorica, Arg. H5 92
Victorino, Ven. F8 86
Victorville, Ca., U.S. I8 134
Vičuga, Russia H19 8
Vicuña, Chile E2 92
Vicuña Mackenna, Arg. F5 92
Vidalia, Ga., U.S. D3 116
Vidalia, La., U.S. F7 122
Vidal Ramos, Braz. C13 92
Videira, Braz. C12 92
Vidigueira, Port. F3 20
Vidin, Blg. E9 26
Vidisha, India G6 54
Vidor, Tx., U.S. G4 122
Viđoy, i., Far. Is. m34 8b
Vidra, Rom. E13 26
Vidsel, Swe. D9 8
Vidzeme, hist. reg., Lat. C8 10
Viechtach, Ger. G8 16
Viedma, Arg. H4 90
Viedma, Lago, l., Arg. I2 90
Vieille Case, Dom. i6 105c
Viejo, Cerro, mtn., Peru D2 84
Viella, Spain B11 20
Vienna see Wien, Aus. B13 22
Vienna, Ga., U.S. D2 116
Vienna, Il., U.S. G9 120
Vienna, Mo., U.S. F5 120
Vienna, W.V., U.S. E4 114
Vienna see Wien, state, Aus. B13 22
Vienna Woods see Wienerwald, mts., Aus. B13 22
Vienne, Fr. D10 18
Vienne, state, Fr. C6 18
Vienne, stm., Fr. C6 18
Vientiane see Viangchan, Laos D6 48
Vieques, P.R. B5 104a
Vieques, Aeropuerto, P.R. B5 104a
Vieques, Isla de, i., P.R. B5 104a
Vieremä, Fin. E12 8
Vierwaldstätter See (Lucerne, Lake of), l., Switz. D5 22
Vierzon, Fr. G11 14
Viesca, Mex. C7 100
Vieste, Italy I13 22
Vietnam, ctry., Asia E9 48
Viet Tri, Viet. B7 48
Vieux-Fort, Qc., Can. i22 107a
Vieux Fort, St. Luc. m7 105c
Vieux-Fort, Pointe du, c., Guad. i5 105c
Vieux-Habitants, Guad. h5 105c
Vievis, Lith. F7 10
Vigala, Est. B7 10
Vigan, Phil. B3 52
Vigevano, Italy E5 22
Vigie Airport, St. Luc. I6 105c
Vignola, Italy F7 22
Vigo, Spain B2 20
Vigo, Ría de, est., Spain B1 20
Vihāri, Pak. D4 54
Vihorevka, Russia C18 32
Vihowa, Pak. C3 54
Vihren, mtn., Blg. H10 26
Viinijärvi, Fin. E13 8
Viivikonna, Est. A10 10
Vijāpur, India G4 54
Vijayawāda, India C5 53
Vikārābād, India C3 53
Viking, Ab., Can. C19 138
Vikna, Nor. D4 8
Vikna, i., Nor. D4 8
Vikramasingapuram, India G3 53
Vikulovo, Russia C12 32
Vila da Ribeira Brava, C.V. k10 65a
Vila de Sena, Moz. D5 68
Vila do Bispo, Port. G1 20
Vila do Conde, Port. C2 20
Vila Fontes, Moz. D6 68
Vilafranca del Panadés see Vilafranca del Penedès, Spain C12 20
Vilafranca del Penedès, Spain C12 20
Vila Franca de Xira, Port. F2 20
Vila Gamito, Moz. C5 68
Vilagarcía de Arousa, Spain B1 20
Vilaine, stm., Fr. G7 14
Vilaka, Lat. C10 10
Vilalba, Spain A3 20
Vilanandro, Tanjona, c., Madag. D7 68
Vilāni, Lat. D9 10
Vilankulo, Moz. B12 70
Vila Nova de Famalicão, Port. C2 20
Vila Nova de Gaia, Port. C2 20
Vilanova i la Geltrú, Spain C12 20
Vila Real, Port. C3 20
Vila-Real, Spain E10 20
Vila Real, state, Port. C3 20
Vila Velha, Braz. K5 88
Vila Verde, Port. C2 20
Vilcabamba, Cordillera de, mts., Peru F3 84
Vilejka, Bela. F9 10
Vilelas, Arg. C6 92
Vilhelmina, Swe. D7 8
Vilhena, Braz. F5 84
Vilija (Neris), stm., Eur. F6 10
Viljandi, Est. G11 8
Viljuj, stm., Russia D13 34
Viljujsk, Russia D13 34
Viljujskoe vodohranilišče, res., Russia B20 32
Vilkaviškis, Lith. F6 10
Vil'kickogo, ostrov, i., Russia A19 34
Vil'kickogo, proliv, strt., Russia A9 34
Vilkija, Lith. E6 10
Villa Abecia, Bol. D3 90
Villa Ana, Arg. D8 92
Villa Ángela, Arg. C7 92
Villa Atamisqui, Arg. D6 92
Villa Bella, Bol. B3 90
Villa Berthet, Arg. C7 92
Villablino, Spain B4 20
Villa Bruzual, Ven. C7 86
Villa Cañás, Arg. G7 92
Villacañas, Spain E7 20
Villa Carlos Paz, Arg. E5 92
Villacarrillo, Spain F7 20
Villacastín, Spain D6 20
Villach, Aus. D10 22
Villacidro, Italy E2 24
Villa Clara, Arg. E8 92
Villa Concepción del Tío, Arg. E6 92
Villa Constitución, Arg. F7 92
Villa de Arista, Mex. D8 100
Villa de Cos, Mex. D7 100
Villa de Cura, Ven. B8 86
Villa del Carmen, Arg. F5 92
Villa del Río, Spain G6 20
Villa del Rosario, Arg. E8 92
Villa del Rosario, Arg. E6 92
Villa del Rosario, Ven. B5 86
Villa de Soto, Arg. E5 92
Villadiego, Spain B7 20
Villa Dolores, Arg. E5 92
Villa Flores, Mex. G12 100
Villa Florida, Para. C9 92
Villafranca de los Barros, Spain F4 20
Villafranca di Verona, Italy E7 22
Villagarcía de Arosa see Vilagarcía de Arousa, Spain B1 20
Village see The Village, Ok., U.S. F11 128
Villa General Roca, Arg. F4 92
Villa Gesell, Arg. H9 92
Villagrán, Mex. C9 100
Villa Grove, Il., U.S. E9 120
Villaguay, Arg. E8 92
Villa Guerrero, Mex. F9 100
Villa Hayes, Para. B9 92
Villahermosa, Mex. G12 100
Villa Hidalgo, Mex. H3 130
Villa Huidobro, Arg. G5 92
Villa Insurgentes, Mex. C3 100
Villa Iris, Arg. I6 92
Villajoyosa see La Vila Joiosa, Spain F10 20
Villa Juárez, Mex. B3 100
Villa Krause, Arg. E3 92
Villalba, P.R. B3 104a
Villalba see Vilalba, Spain A3 20
Villaldama, Mex. B8 100
Villalon, Phil. E5 52
Villalonga, Arg. G4 90
Villalpando, Spain C5 20
Villa Mainero, Mex. C9 100
Villa María, Arg. F6 92
Villamartín, Spain H5 20
Villa Mazán, Arg. D4 92
Villa Media Agua, Arg. E3 92
Villa Mercedes, Arg. F5 92
Villa Montes, Bol. D4 90
Villa Nueva, Arg. F6 92
Villanueva, Col. B5 86
Villanueva, N.M., U.S. F3 128
Villanueva de Córdoba, Spain F6 20
Villanueva de la Serena, Spain F5 20
Villanueva de la Sierra, Spain D4 20
Villanueva de los Infantes, Spain F8 20
Villanueva del Río y Minas, Spain G4 20
Villanueva y Geltrú see Vilanova i la Geltrú, Spain C12 20
Villa Ocampo, Arg. D8 92
Villa Ocampo, Mex. H2 130
Villa Oliva, Para. B8 92
Villa Pérez, P.R. B2 104a
Villapinzón, Col. E5 86
Villarcayo, Spain B7 20
Villa Regina, Arg. G3 90
Villa Reynolds, Arg. F5 92
Villa Rica, Ga., U.S. D14 122
Villarreal see Vila-Real, Spain E10 20
Villarrica, Para. B9 92
Villarrobledo, Spain E8 20
Villarrubia de los Ojos, Spain E7 20
Villas, N.J., U.S. E10 114
Villa San Giovanni, Italy F9 24
Villa Santa Rita de Catuna, Arg. E4 92
Villasayas, Spain C8 20
Villa Serrano, Bol. C4 90
Villasis, Phil. C3 52
Villa Unión, Arg. D3 92
Villa Unión, Arg. D6 92
Villa Unión, Mex. D5 100
Villa Valeria, Arg. G5 92
Villavicencio, Col. E5 86
Villaviciosa de Córdoba, Spain F5 20
Villazón, Bol. D3 90
Villefranche-de-Rouergue, Fr. E8 18
Villefranche-sur-Saône, Fr. C10 18
Villena, Spain F10 20
Villeneuve-sur-Lot, Fr. E6 18
Villeneuve-sur-Yonne, Fr. F12 14
Ville Platte, La., U.S. G6 122
Villers-Cotterêts, Fr. E12 14
Villerupt, Fr. E14 14
Villeta, Col. E4 86
Villeurbanne, Fr. D10 18
Villiers, S. Afr. E9 70
Villingen-Schwenningen, Ger. H4 16
Villisca, Ia., U.S. D3 120
Villmanstrand see Lappeenranta, Fin. F12 8
Vilnius, Lith. F8 10
Vilsbiburg, Ger. H8 16
Vil'shanka, Ukr. A17 26
Vilshofen, Ger. H9 16
Viluppuram, India E4 53
Vilvoorde, Bel. D13 14
Vilvorde see Vilvoorde, Bel. D13 14
Vimmerby, Swe. H6 8
Vimperk, Czech Rep. G9 16
Vina, Ca., U.S. D3 134
Vina, stm., Cam. C2 66
Viña del Mar, Chile F2 92
Vinalhaven, Me., U.S. F8 110
Vinalhaven Island, i., Me., U.S. F8 110
Vinaròs, Spain D11 20
Vinaroz see Vinaròs, Spain D11 20
Vincennes, In., U.S. F10 120
Vincennes Bay, b., Ant. B15 81
Vincent, Al., U.S. D12 122
Vinces, Ec. H2 86
Vindelälven, stm., Swe. D8 8
Vindhya Range, mts., India G6 54
Vinegar Hill, mtn., Or., U.S. F8 136
Vineland, N.J., U.S. E10 114
Vinemont, Al., U.S. C12 122
Vineyard Haven, Ma., U.S. C15 114
Vineyard Sound, strt., Ma., U.S. C15 114
Ving Ngün, Mya. A4 48
Vinh, Viet. C7 48
Vinhais, Port. C4 20
Vinh Long, Viet. G8 48
Vinh Yen, Viet. B7 48
Vinita, Ok., U.S. H2 120
Vinkovci, Cro. E15 22
Vinnytsia, Ukr. F14 6
Vinnytsia, co., Ukr. A16 26
Vinson Massif, mtn., Ant. C32 81
Vintilă Vodă, Rom. D13 26
Vinton, La., U.S. G5 122
Vinton, Va., U.S. G6 114
Viola, Il., U.S. C7 120
Vioolsdrif, S. Afr. F3 70
Vipiteno, Italy D8 22
Vir, Otok, i., Cro. F11 22
Virac, Phil. D5 52
Viramgām, India G3 54
Vīrarājendrapet, India E2 53
Virbalis, Lith. F5 10
Virden, Mb., Can. E13 124
Virden, Il., U.S. E8 120
Virden, N.M., U.S. K8 132
Vire, Fr. F8 14
Virgem da Lapa, Braz. I4 88
Vírgenes, Cabo, c., S.A. J3 90
Virgil, Ks., U.S. C13 128
Virgin, stm., U.S. G2 132
Virgin Gorda, i., Br. Vir. Is. e9 104b
Virginia, S. Afr. F8 70
Virginia, Il., U.S. E7 120
Virginia, Mn., U.S. D6 118
Virginia, state, U.S. G7 114
Virginia Beach, Va., U.S. H10 114
Virginia City, Mt., U.S. E14 136
Virginia City, Nv., U.S. D6 134
Virginia Falls, wtfl, N.T., Can. C5 106
Virginia Peak, mtn., Nv., U.S. D6 134
Virgin Islands, dep., N.A. h14 96a
Virgin Islands, is., N.A. e7 104b
Virgin Islands National Park, p.o.i., V.I.U.S. e7 104b
Virgin Passage, strt., N.A. B5 104a
Virihaure, l., Swe. C7 8
Virje, Cro. D13 22
Virojoki, Fin. F12 8
Viroqua, Wi., U.S. H7 118
Virovitica, Cro. E14 22

Virr-Weix I•61

Name — Map Ref. — Page

Virrat, Fin. E10 8
Virtaniemi, Fin. B13 8
Virtsu, Est. G10 8
Virú, Peru E2 84
Virudunagar, India G3 53
Virunga, Parc National de, p.o.i., D.R.C. D5 66
Viru-Nigula, Est. A9 10
Virvytė, stm., Lith. D5 10
Vis see Visrivier, stm., Nmb. E3 70
Vis, stm., S. Afr. G5 70
Vis, Otok, i., Cro. G13 22
Visale, Sol. Is. e8 79b
Visalia, Ca., U.S. G6 134
Visayan Islands, is., Phil. E4 52
Visayan Sea, Phil. E4 52
Visby, Swe. H8 8
Viscount, Sk., Can. C8 124
Viscount Melville Sound, strt., Can. B11 94
Višegrad, Bos. F6 26
Viseu, Port. D3 20
Viseu, state, Port. D3 20
Vishākhapatnam, India C6 53
Visnagar, India G4 54
Višneva, Bela. F9 10
Visoko, Bos. E5 26
Visokoi Island, i., S. Geor. K12 82
Visp, Switz. D4 22
Visrivier, stm., Nmb. E3 70
Vista, Ca., U.S. J8 134
Vistina, Russia A11 10
Vistula see Wisła, stm., Pol. B14 16
Vistula Lagoon, b., Eur. B16 16
Vita, Mb., Can. E17 124
Vita, stm., Col. E7 86
Vitarte, Peru F2 84
Vite, India C2 53
Viterbo, Italy H8 22
Viti see Fiji, ctry., Oc. E8 72
Vitiaz Strait, strt., Pap. N. Gui. b4 79a
Vitigudino, Spain C4 20
Viti Levu, i., Fiji p19 79e
Vitim, Russia E11 34
Vitim, stm., Russia E12 34
Vitimskoe ploskogor'e, plat., Russia F11 34
Vitinja, p., Blg. G10 26
Vítkov, Czech Rep. G13 16
Vitória, Braz. D7 84
Vitória, Braz. K5 88
Vitoria see Gasteiz, Spain B8 20
Vitória da Conquista, Braz. H5 88
Vitória de Santo Antão, Braz. E8 88
Vitória do Mearim, Braz. B3 88
Vitorino Freire, Braz. C3 88
Vitré, Fr. F7 14
Vitry-le-François, Fr. F13 14
Vitteaux, Fr. G13 14
Vittoria, Italy H8 24
Vittorio Veneto, Italy D9 22
Viveiro, Spain A3 20
Viver, Spain E10 20
Vivero see Viveiro, Spain A3 20
Vivi, stm., Russia D8 34
Vivian, La., U.S. E4 122
Vizcaíno, Desierto de, des., Mex. B2 100
Vizcaya see Bizkaiko, co., Spain A8 20
Vize, Tur. B10 28
Vizianagaram, India B6 53
Vizille, Fr. D11 18
Vizinga, Russia B7 32
Vjalikaja Maščanica, Bela. G12 10
Vjalikija Radvaničy, Bela. H7 10
Vjaseja, Bela. G10 10
Vjatka, stm., Russia C8 32
Vjatskie Poljany, Russia C8 32
Vjazemskij, Russia G15 34
Vjaz'ma, Russia E17 10
Vjazniki, Russia H20 8
Vjazyn', Bela. F10 10
Vjosës (Aóös), stm., Eur. D13 24
Vlaardingen, Neth. C13 14
Vlădeasa, Vârful, mtn., Rom. C9 26
Vladičin Han, Yugo. G8 26
Vladikavkaz, Russia F6 32
Vladimir, Russia H18 8
Vladimirskaja oblast', co., Russia I19 8
Vladimirskij Tupik, Russia E16 10
Vladivostok, Russia C9 38
Vlasenica, Bos. E5 26
Vlasotince, Yugo. G9 26
Vlasovo, Russia B16 34
Vlieland, i., Neth. A13 14
Vlissingen, Neth. C12 14
Vlora see Vlorë, Alb. D13 24
Vlorë, Alb. D13 24
Vltava (Moldau), stm., Czech Rep. F10 16
Vnukovo, Russia E20 10
Vöcklabruck, Aus. C10 22
Vo Dat, Viet. G8 48
Vodla, stm., Russia F17 8
Vodlozero, ozero, l., Russia E16 8
Vodosalma, Russia D14 8
Voël, stm., S. Afr. H7 70
Voghera, Italy F6 22
Voh, N. Cal. m15 79d
Vohimena, Tanjona, c., Madag. F8 68
Vohipeno, Madag. E8 68
Võhma, Est. G11 8
Voi, Kenya E7 66
Voinești, Rom. B14 26
Voinjama, Lib. H3 64
Voiron, Fr. D11 18
Voitsberg, Aus. C12 22
Vojmsjön, l., Swe. D6 8
Vojnica, Russia D14 8
Vojvodina, co., Yugo. D7 26
Volcán, Pan. H6 102
Volcano, Hi., U.S. D6 78a
Volcano Islands see Kazan-rettō, is., Japan G18 30
Volčiha, Russia D14 32
Volda, Nor. E2 8
Volga, S.D., U.S. G2 118
Volga, stm., Russia E7 32
Volga-Baltic Canal see Volgo-Baltijskij kanal, can., Russia G17 8
Volgino, Russia B16 10
Volgo, ozero, l., Russia C16 10
Volgo-Baltijskij kanal, can., Russia G17 8
Volgodonsk, Russia E6 32
Volgograd, Russia E6 32
Volgograd Reservoir see Volgogradskoe vodohranilišče, res., Russia E7 32
Volgogradskoe vodohranilišče, res., Russia D7 32
Volhov, Russia A15 10
Volhov, stm., Russia G14 8
Volissós, Grc. E8 28
Völkermarkt, Aus. D11 22
Völklingen, Ger. G2 16
Volksrust, S. Afr. E9 70
Voločanka, Russia B7 34
Volodarskoe, Kaz. D11 32
Voloe, Russia F17 10
Vologda, Russia A22 10
Vologda, stm., Russia A22 10
Vologodskaja oblast', co., Russia G19 8
Volokolamsk, Russia D18 10
Volonga, Russia C22 8
Vólos, Grc. D5 28
Volos, Gulf of see Pagasitikós Kólpos, b., Grc. D5 28
Vološka, Russia F19 8
Volosovo, Russia A12 10
Volot, Russia C13 10
Volovo, Russia G21 10
Vol'sk, Russia D7 32
Volta, stm., Ghana H5 64
Volta Blanche (White Volta), stm., Afr. G4 64
Volta Lake, res., Ghana H4 64
Volta Noire (Black Volta) (Mouhoun), stm., Afr. G4 64
Volta Redonda, Braz. L3 88
Volterra, Italy G7 22
Vol'teva, Russia D21 8
Voltri, ngh., Italy F5 22
Volturno, stm., Italy C8 24
Vólvi, Límni, l., Grc. C6 28
Volyn', co., Ukr. E20 16
Volžsk, Russia C7 32
Volžskij, Russia E6 32
Vonavona Island, i., Sol. Is. e7 79b
Vonda, Sk., Can. B7 124
Vondanka, Russia G22 8
Vondrozo, Madag. E8 68
Von Frank Mountain, mtn., Ak., U.S. D8 140
Vopnafjörður, Ice. k32 8a
Vopnafjörður, b., Ice. k32 8a
Vorarlberg, state, Aus. C6 22
Vorau, Aus. C12 22
Vorderrhein see Rein Anteriur, stm., Switz. D6 22
Vordingborg, Den. I4 8
Vóreio Aigaío, state, Grc. D8 28
Vórioi Sporádhes, is., Grc. D6 28
Vórios Evvoïkós Kólpos, b., Grc. E5 28
Vorkuta, Russia A10 32
Vormsi, i., Est. G10 8
Vorobevo, Russia C13 32
Voroncov, Mol. B16 26
Voroncovo, Russia C11 10
Voronež, Russia D5 32
Voronežskaja oblast', co., Russia H21 10
Voronja, stm., Russia B16 8
Voronok, Russia H15 10
Voronovo, Russia E5 34
Vorpommern, hist. reg., Ger. C9 16
Vorsma, Russia H20 8
Vørterkaka Nunatak, mtn., Ant. C8 81
Võrtsjärv, l., Est. G12 8
Võru, Est. H12 8
Vosburg, S. Afr. G6 70
Vosges, state, Fr. F15 14
Vosges, mts., Fr. F15 14
Voskresensk, Russia E21 10
Voskresenskoe, Russia C20 10
Voskresenskoe, Russia B21 10
Voss, Nor. F2 8
Vostočno-Kounradskij, Kaz. E13 32
Vostočno-Sibirskoe more, Russia B20 34
Vostočnyj Sajan, mts., Russia D17 32
Vostok, i., Kir. E11 72
Vostok, sci., Ant. C15 81
Votice, Czech Rep. G10 16
Votkinsk, Russia C8 32
Votuporanga, Braz. D7 90
Vouga, stm., Port. D2 20
Vouziers, Fr. E13 14
Voyageurs National Park, p.o.i., Mn., U.S. C6 118
Voyeykov Ice Shelf, ice, Ant. B17 81
Vože, ozero, l., Russia F18 8
Vožega, Russia F19 8
Voznesene, Russia F16 8
Vozroždenija, ostrov, i., Asia E9 32
Vraca, Blg. F10 26
Vradyïvka, Ukr. B17 26
Vrancea, state, Rom. D13 26
Vrangelja, ostrov (Wrangel Island), i., Russia B24 34
Vranje, Yugo. G8 26
Vratsa see Vraca, Blg. F10 26
Vrbas, Yugo. D6 26
Vrbas, stm., Bos. E4 26
Vrbovec, Cro. E13 22
Vrchlabí, Czech Rep. F11 16
Vrede, S. Afr. E9 70
Vredenburg, S. Afr. H3 70
Vredenburgh, Al., U.S. F11 122
Vredenburg-Saldanha see Vredenburg, S. Afr. H3 70
Vredendal, S. Afr. G4 70
Vriddhāchalam, India F4 53
Vrindāvan, India E6 54
Vršac, Yugo. D8 26
Vrútky, Slov. G14 16
Vryburg, S. Afr. E7 70
Vryheid, S. Afr. E10 70
Vselug, ozero, l., Russia C14 10
Vsetín, Czech Rep. G13 16
Vsevidof, Mount, mtn., Ak., U.S. F6 140
Vučitrn, Yugo. G7 26
Vukovar, Cro. E16 22
Vulcan, Ab., Can. F17 138
Vulcan, Rom. D10 26
Vulcănești, Mol. D15 26
Vulcano, Isola, i., Italy F8 24
Vulsino see Bolsena, Lago di, l., Italy H9 22
Vung Tau, Viet. G8 48
Vunidawa, Fiji p19 79e
Vunisea, Fiji q18 79e
Vuohijärvi, l., Fin. F11 8
Vuyyūru, India C5 53
Vyāra, India H4 54
Vyborg (Viipuri), Russia F13 8
Vyčegda, stm., Russia B7 32
Vyčegodskij, Russia F22 8
Východočeský, state, Czech Rep. F11 16
Východoslovenský Kraj, state, Slov. H17 16
Vygoniči, Russia G16 10
Vygozero, ozero, l., Russia E16 8
Vyksa, Russia I20 8
Vylkove, Ukr. D16 26
Vynohradiv, Ukr. A10 26
Vypolzovo, Russia C16 10
Vyrica, Russia A13 10
Vyšgorodok, Russia C11 10
Vyskod', Russia C13 10
Vyškov, Czech Rep. G12 16
Vyšneol'šanoe, Russia H20 10
Vyšnevolockoe vodohranilišče, res., Russia C16 10
Vyšnij Voloček, Russia C17 10
Vysoké Mýto, Czech Rep. G12 16
Vysokiniči, Russia F19 10
Vysokoe, Russia D17 10
Vysokogornyj, Russia G16 34
Vysokovsk, Russia D19 10
Vytebet', stm., Russia G18 10
Vytegra, Russia F17 8
Vyzhnytsia, Ukr. A12 26

W

Wa, Ghana G4 64
Waal, stm., Neth. C14 14
Waalwijk, Neth. C14 14
Wabag, Pap. N. Gui. b3 79a
Wabakimi Lake, l., On., Can. A8 118
Wabamun, Ab., Can. C16 138
Wabamun Lake, l., Ab., Can. C15 138
Wabana, Nf., Can. j23 107a
Wabasca, stm., Ab., Can. D7 106
Wabasca-Desmarais, Ab., Can. D8 106
Wabash, In., U.S. H4 112
Wabash, stm., U.S. F9 120
Wabasha, Mn., U.S. G6 118
Wabasso, Mn., U.S. G3 118
Wabeno, Wi., U.S. F10 118
Wabera, Eth. F8 62
Wabowden, Mb., Can. E11 106
Wąbrzeźno, Pol. C14 16
Wabu Hu, l., China E7 42
Waccamaw, stm., U.S. C7 116
Waccamaw, Lake, l., N.C., U.S. B7 116
Wachapreague, Va., U.S. G10 114
Wachau, reg., Aus. B12 22
Wacissa, Fl., U.S. F2 116
Waco, Tx., U.S. C10 130
Waco Lake, res., Tx., U.S. C10 130
Waconda Lake, res., Ks., U.S. B10 128
Wadayama, Japan D7 40
Wad Bandah, Sudan E5 62
Wadbilliga National Park, p.o.i., Austl. K7 76
Waddenzee, strt., Neth. A14 14
Waddington, N.Y., U.S. D14 112
Waddington, Mount, mtn., B.C., Can. E5 138
Wadena, Sk., Can. C10 124
Wadena, Mn., U.S. E3 118
Wadesboro, N.C., U.S. B5 116
Wādī as-Sīr, Jord. G6 58
Wādī Halfā', Sudan C6 62
Wadley, Al., U.S. D13 122
Wadley, Ga., U.S. D3 116
Wad Madanī, Sudan E6 62
Wadowice, Pol. G15 16
Wadsworth, Nv., U.S. D6 134
Wadsworth, Oh., U.S. C4 114
Wafangdian, China B9 42
Wageningen, Neth. C14 14
Wager Bay, b., Nu., Can. B13 106
Wagga Wagga, Austl. J6 76
Wagin, Austl. F3 74
Waging am See, Ger. I8 16
Wagner, S.D., U.S. D14 126
Wagoner, Ok., U.S. I2 120
Wagon Mound, N.M., U.S. F4 128
Wagontire Mountain, mtn., Or., U.S. G7 136
Wagrien, reg., Ger. B6 16
Wągrowiec, Pol. D13 16
Waha, Libya B4 62
Wahai, Indon. F8 44
Wāh Cantonment, Pak. B4 54
Wahiawa, Hi., U.S. B3 78a
Wahpeton, N.D., U.S. E2 118
Wahran (Oran), Alg. B4 64
Wai, India B1 53
Waialua, Hi., U.S. B3 78a
Waianae, Hi., U.S. B3 78a
Waiau, N.Z. F5 80
Waiau, stm., N.Z. G2 80
Waiau, stm., N.Z. F5 80
Waiblingen, Ger. H5 16
Waidhofen an der Thaya, Aus. B12 22
Waidhofen an der Ybbs, Aus. C11 22
Waigeo, Pulau, i., Indon. E9 44
Waihi, N.Z. C6 80
Waikabubak, Indon. H11 50
Waikato, stm., N.Z. C6 80
Waikelo, Indon. H11 50
Waikerie, Austl. J2 76
Wailuku, Hi., U.S. C5 78a
Waimate, N.Z. G4 80
Waimea, Hi., U.S. A2 78a
Wainganga, stm., India H7 54
Waingapu, Indon. H12 50
Waini, stm., Guy. D12 86
Wainunu Bay, b., Fiji p19 79e
Wainwright, Ab., Can. B3 124
Wainwright, Ak., U.S. B7 140
Waipukurau, N.Z. E7 80
Wairarapa, Lake, l., N.Z. E6 80
Wairau, stm., N.Z. E5 80
Wairoa, N.Z. D7 80
Wairoa, stm., N.Z. B6 80
Waïsisi, Vanuatu I17 79d
Waitaki, stm., N.Z. G4 80
Waitara, N.Z. D6 80
Waitemata, N.Z. C6 80
Waite Park, Mn., U.S. F4 118
Waitotara, N.Z. D6 80
Waitsburg, Wa., U.S. D8 136
Waiwo, Indon. F9 44
Wajima, Japan B9 40
Wajir, Kenya D8 66
Waka, D.R.C. D4 66
Waka, Eth. F7 62
Wakarusa, In., U.S. G3 112
Wakasa-wan, b., Japan D8 40
Wakatipu, Lake, l., N.Z. G3 80
Wakaw, Sk., Can. B8 124
Wakayama, Japan E8 40
Wakayama, state, Japan F8 40
WaKeeney, Ks., U.S. B9 128
Wakefield, Eng., U.K. H11 12
Wakefield, Ks., U.S. B11 128
Wakefield, Ne., U.S. E15 126
Wakefield, Va., U.S. H8 114
Wake Forest, N.C., U.S. I7 114
Wake Island, dep., Oc. B7 72
Wake Island, at., Wake I. H19 142
Wakema, Mya. D2 48
Waki, Japan E7 40
Wakis, Pap. N. Gui. b5 79a
Wakita, Ok., U.S. E10 128
Wakkanai, Japan B14 38
Wakomata Lake, l., On., Can. B6 112
Wakonda, S.D., U.S. E15 126
Waku Kungo, Ang. C2 68
Walachia, hist. reg., Rom. E11 26
Walanae, stm., Indon. F12 50
Walawe, stm., Sri L. H5 53
Wałbrzych, Pol. F12 16
Wałbrzych, state, Pol. F12 16
Walcha, Austl. H8 76
Walcott, Ia., U.S. C7 120
Walcott, N.D., U.S. E1 118
Walcott, Lake, res., Id., U.S. H13 136
Wałcz, Pol. C12 16
Waldbröl, Ger. F3 16
Walden, On., Can. B8 112
Walden, Co., U.S. C10 132
Waldheim, Sk., Can. B7 124
Waldkirchen, Ger. H9 16
Waldmünchen, Ger. G8 16
Waldo, B.C., Can. G15 138
Waldoboro, Me., U.S. F7 110
Waldorf, Md., U.S. F9 114
Waldport, Or., U.S. F2 136
Waldron, Sk., Can. D11 124
Waldron, Ar., U.S. C4 122
Waldron, In., U.S. E12 120
Waldshut-Tiengen, Ger. I4 16
Waldviertel, reg., Aus. B12 22
Wales, state, U.K. I9 12
Wales Island, i., Nu., Can. B13 106
Walewale, Ghana G4 64
Walgett, Austl. G6 76
Walgreen Coast, cst., Ant. C30 81
Walhachin, B.C., Can. F10 138
Walhalla, N.D., U.S. F15 124
Walhalla, S.C., U.S. B2 116
Walhalla, hist., Ger. G8 16
Walker, Ia., U.S. B6 120
Walker, stm., Nv., U.S. D7 134
Walker Bay, b., S. Afr. I4 70
Walker Lake, l., Nv., U.S. E7 134
Walkerton, On., Can. D8 112
Walkerton, In., U.S. G3 112
Walkertown, N.C., U.S. H5 114
Walkerville, Mt., U.S. D14 136
Wall, S.D., U.S. D10 126
Wallace, Id., U.S. C11 136
Wallace, Ne., U.S. G11 126
Wallace, N.C., U.S. B7 116
Wallaceburg, On., Can. F7 112
Wallal Downs, Austl. C4 74
Wallam Creek, stm., Austl. G6 76
Wallangarra, Austl. G8 76
Wallaroo, Austl. F7 74
Wallasey, Eng., U.K. H9 12
Walla Walla, Wa., U.S. D8 136
Wallingford, Ct., U.S. C13 114
Wallingford, Vt., U.S. G4 110
Wallis, Tx., U.S. H2 122
Wallis, Îles, is., Wal./F. E9 72
Wallis and Futuna, dep., Oc. E9 72
Wallisville Lake, res., Tx., U.S. H4 122
Wall Lake, Ia., U.S. I3 118
Wallowa, Or., U.S. E9 136
Wallowa, stm., Or., U.S. E9 136
Walls of Jericho National Park, p.o.i., Austl. n13 77a
Walnut, Il., U.S. C8 120
Walnut, Ia., U.S. C2 120
Walnut, Ms., U.S. C10 122
Walnut, N.C., U.S. I3 114
Walnut, stm., Ks., U.S. D11 128
Walnut Canyon National Monument, p.o.i., Az., U.S. H5 132
Walnut Cove, N.C., U.S. H5 114
Walnut Creek, stm., Ks., U.S. C9 128
Walnut Grove, Mn., U.S. G3 118
Walnut Grove, Ms., U.S. E9 122
Walnut Ridge, Ar., U.S. H7 120
Walnut Springs, Tx., U.S. B10 130
Walpole, Austl. G3 74
Walpole, N.H., U.S. G4 110
Walsall, Eng., U.K. I11 12
Walsenburg, Co., U.S. D4 128
Walsh, Austl. C8 74
Walsh, Ab., Can. E3 124
Walsh, stm., Austl. A5 76
Walsrode, Ger. D5 16
Walterboro, S.C., U.S. D5 116
Walters, Ok., U.S. G10 128
Waltershausen, Ger. F6 16
Walthall, Ms., U.S. D9 122
Walthill, Ne., U.S. B1 120
Walton, N.S., Can. E13 110
Walton, In., U.S. H3 112
Walton, N.Y., U.S. B10 114
Walvisbaai see Walvis Bay, Nmb. C2 70
Walvis Bay (Walvisbaai), Nmb. C2 70
Walvis Bay, b., Nmb. C2 70
Walvis Ridge, unds. K14 144
Walworth, Wi., U.S. B9 120
Wamba, D.R.C. D5 66
Wamba, Nig. H6 64
Wamba (Uamba), stm., Afr. F3 66
Wampsville, N.Y., U.S. A10 114
Wampú, Hond. E5 102
Wampú, stm., Hond. E5 102
Wampum, Pa., U.S. D5 114
Wamsutter, Wy., U.S. B9 132
Wanaka, N.Z. G3 80
Wanaka, Lake, l., N.Z. G3 80
Wan'an, China H6 42
Wanapa, Neth. Ant. p23 104g
Wanapitei, stm., On., Can. B9 112
Wanapitei Lake, l., On., Can. B8 112
Wanbaoshan, China B6 38
Wanbi, Austl. J3 76
Wanblee, S.D., U.S. D11 126
Wanchese, N.C., U.S. I10 114
Wandel Hav, Grnld. A22 141
Wandering, stm., Ab., Can. A18 138
Wanfoxia, China C4 36
Wang, stm., Thai. D4 48
Wanganui, N.Z. D6 80
Wanganui, stm., N.Z. D6 80
Wangaratta, Austl. K6 76
Wangcun, China C7 42
Wangdu Phodrang, Bhu. E12 54
Wangiwangi, Pulau, i., Indon. G7 44
Wang Noi, Thai. E5 48
Wangpan Yang, b., China F9 42
Wangqing, China C8 38
Wangtai, China H7 42
Wangyehmiao see Horqin Youyi Qianqi, China B9 36
Wanhedian, China E5 42
Wanhsien see Wanxian, China F3 42
Wani, India A4 53
Wanie-Rukula, D.R.C. D5 66
Wanigela, Pap. N. Gui. b4 79a
Wanipigow, stm., Can. C18 124
Wānkāner, India G3 54
Wanneroo, Austl. F3 74
Wannian, China G7 42
Wanning, China L4 42
Wanparti, India C4 53
Wantan, China F4 42
Wanxian, China F3 42
Wanyuan, China E3 42
Wanzai, China G6 42
Wanzleben, Ger. D7 16
Wapakoneta, Oh., U.S. D1 114
Wapanucka, Ok., U.S. C2 122
Wapato, Wa., U.S. D6 136
Wapello, Ia., U.S. C6 120
Wāpi, India H4 54
Wapiti, stm., Can. A12 138
Wappingers Falls, N.Y., U.S. C12 114
Wapsipinicon, stm., U.S. J8 118
War, W.V., U.S. G4 114
Warangal, India B4 53
Wārāseoni, India H7 54
Waratah, Austl. n12 77a
Waratah Bay, b., Austl. L5 76
Warburg, Ger. E4 16
Warburton, Austl. K5 76
Warburton Bay, b., N.T., Can. C8 106
Ward, stm., Austl. E6 76
Warden, S. Afr. E9 70
Wardha, India H7 54
Wardha, stm., India H7 54
Ward Hill, hill, Scot., U.K. C9 12
Wardlow, Ab., Can. F19 138
Wardner, B.C., Can. G15 138
Wardswell Draw, stm., U.S. B5 130
Waremme, Bel. D14 14
Waren, Ger. C8 16
Waren, Indon. F10 44
Warenai, stm., Indon. F10 44
Warenda, Austl. D3 76
Warendorf, Ger. E3 16
Ware Shoals, S.C., U.S. B3 116
Wargla, Alg. C6 64
Warialda, Austl. G8 76
Warin Chamrap, Thai. E7 48
Warkworth, On., Can. D11 112
Warman, Sk., Can. B7 124
Warmandi, Indon. F9 44
Warmbad, Nmb. F4 70
Warmbad, S. Afr. D9 70
Warm Baths see Warmbad, S. Afr. D9 70
Warminster, Eng., U.K. J10 12
Warminster, Pa., U.S. D10 114
Warm Springs, Ga., U.S. E14 122
Warm Springs, Mt., U.S. D14 136
Warm Springs, Or., U.S. F5 136
Warnemünde, ngh., Ger. B7 16
Warner, Ab., Can. G18 138
Warner, N.H., U.S. G5 110
Warner Lakes, l., Or., U.S. H6 136
Warner Mountains, mts., U.S. B5 134
Warner Peak, mtn., Or., U.S. A6 134
Warner Robins, Ga., U.S. D2 116
Warnow, stm., Ger. B8 16
Warra, Austl. F8 76
Warracknabeal, Austl. K4 76
Warragul, Austl. L5 76
Warrawagine, Austl. D4 74
Warrego, stm., Austl. G5 76
Warren, Ar., U.S. D6 122
Warren, In., U.S. H4 112
Warren, Mi., U.S. B2 114
Warren, Mn., U.S. C2 118
Warren, Oh., U.S. C5 114
Warren, Pa., U.S. C6 114
Warrens, Wi., U.S. G8 118
Warrensburg, Mo., U.S. F4 120
Warrensburg, N.Y., U.S. G3 110
Warrenton, S. Afr. F7 70
Warrenton, Mo., U.S. F6 120
Warrenton, N.C., U.S. H7 114
Warrenton, Or., U.S. D2 136
Warri, Nig. H6 64
Warrington, Eng., U.K. H10 12
Warrington, Fl., U.S. G11 122
Warrior, Al., U.S. D12 122
Warrnambool, Austl. L4 76
Warroad, Mn., U.S. C3 118
Warrumbungle National Park, p.o.i., Austl. H7 76
Warsaw see Warszawa, Pol. D16 16
Warsaw, Il., U.S. D6 120
Warsaw, In., U.S. G4 112
Warsaw, Ky., U.S. F13 120
Warsaw, Mo., U.S. F4 120
Warsaw, N.Y., U.S. B7 114
Warsaw, N.C., U.S. A7 116
Warspite, Ab., Can. B18 138
Warszawa (Warsaw), Pol. D16 16
Warszawa, state, Pol. D16 16
Warta, Pol. E14 16
Warta, stm., Pol. D11 16
Wartburg, Tn., U.S. H13 120
Wartrace, Tn., U.S. B12 122
Warud, India H7 54
Warwick, Austl. G9 76
Warwick, Eng., U.K. I11 12
Warwick, R.I., U.S. C14 114
Warwick Channel, strt., Austl. B7 74
Wasaga Beach, On., Can. D10 112
Wasagu, Nig. G6 64
Wasatch Range, mts., Ut., U.S. C5 132
Wasbank, S. Afr. F10 70
Wascana Creek, stm., Sk., Can. D9 124
Wasco, Ca., U.S. H6 134
Wasco, Or., U.S. E6 136
Waseca, Mn., U.S. G5 118
Wasgomuwa National Park, p.o.i., Sri L. H5 53
Washademoak Lake, l., N.B., Can. E11 110
Washburn, Il., U.S. D8 120
Washburn, N.D., U.S. G12 124
Washburn, Wi., U.S. E7 118
Washburn, Mount, mtn., Wy., U.S. F16 136
Washburn Lake, l., Nu., Can. A9 106
Wāshīm, India H6 54
Washington, D.C., U.S. F8 114
Washington, Ga., U.S. C3 116
Washington, Il., U.S. D8 120
Washington, In., U.S. F10 120
Washington, Ia., U.S. C6 120
Washington, La., U.S. G6 122
Washington, Mo., U.S. F6 120
Washington, N.C., U.S. A8 116
Washington, Pa., U.S. D5 114
Washington, Tx., U.S. G2 122
Washington, Ut., U.S. F3 132
Washington, Va., U.S. F7 114
Washington, state, U.S. C6 136
Washington, Mount, mtn., N.H., U.S. F5 110
Washington Court House, Oh., U.S. E2 114
Washington Island, i., Wi., U.S. C3 112
Washington Land, reg., Grnld. A12 141
Washington Terrace, Ut., U.S. B5 132
Washita, stm., U.S. G12 128
Washow Bay, b., Mb., Can. C17 124
Washpool National Park, p.o.i., Austl. G9 76
Washtucna, Wa., U.S. D8 136
Wasian, Indon. F9 44
Wasilków, Pol. C19 16
Wasior, Indon. F9 44
Waskada, Mb., Can. E13 124
Waskaganish, Qc., Can. E15 106
Waskahigan, stm., Ab., Can. B13 138
Waskom, Tx., U.S. E4 122
Waspam, Nic. E5 102
Wassenaar, Neth. B13 14
Wasseralfingen, Ger. H6 16
Wassy, Fr. F13 14
Watampone, Indon. F12 50
Watansopeng, Indon. F11 50
Watatic, Mount, mtn., Ma., U.S. B14 114
Waterberge, mts., S. Afr. D8 70
Waterbury, Ct., U.S. C12 114
Wateree Lake, res., S.C., U.S. B5 116
Waterford (Port Lairge), Ire. I5 12
Waterford, Ca., U.S. F5 134
Waterford, Pa., U.S. C6 114
Waterford, Wi., U.S. B9 120
Waterford, state, Ire. I5 12
Waterhen Lake, l., Mb., Can. B14 124
Water Island, i., V.I.U.S. e7 104b
Waterloo, Austl. C5 74
Waterloo, Bel. D13 14
Waterloo, On., Can. E9 112
Waterloo, Qc., Can. E4 110
Waterloo, Al., U.S. C10 122
Waterloo, Il., U.S. F7 120
Waterloo, Ia., U.S. B5 120
Waterloo, N.Y., U.S. B8 114
Waterloo, Wi., U.S. A9 120
Waterman, Il., U.S. C9 120
Waterproof, La., U.S. F7 122
Watersmeet, Mi., U.S. E9 118
Waterton-Glacier International Peace Park, p.o.i., N.A. B13 136
Waterton Lakes National Park, p.o.i., Ab., Can. G16 138
Watertown, N.Y., U.S. E14 112
Watertown, S.D., U.S. C15 126
Watertown, Wi., U.S. A9 120
Waterval Boven, S. Afr. D10 70
Water Valley, Ms., U.S. C9 122
Waterville, N.S., Can. E12 110
Waterville, Ks., U.S. B12 128
Waterville, Me., U.S. F7 110
Waterville, Oh., U.S. C2 114
Waterville, Wa., U.S. C6 136
Watervliet, N.Y., U.S. B12 114
Watford, Eng., U.K. J12 12
Watford City, N.D., U.S. G10 124
Wathena, Ks., U.S. E2 120
Watkins Glen, N.Y., U.S. B9 114
Watkinsville, Ga., U.S. C2 116
Watling Island see San Salvador, i., Bah. C10 96
Watonga, Ok., U.S. F10 128
Watrous, Sk., Can. C8 124
Watsa, D.R.C. D5 66
Watseka, Il., U.S. H2 112
Watsikengo, D.R.C. E4 66
Watson, Sk., Can. B9 124
Watson Lake, Yk., Can. C5 106
Watsonville, Ca., U.S. G4 134
Watt Mountain, vol., Dom. j6 105c
Watts Bar Lake, res., Tn., U.S. B14 122
Watts Mills, S.C., U.S. B4 116
Wattwil, Switz. C5 22
Watubela, Kepulauan, is., Indon. F9 44
Watzmann, mtn., Ger. I8 16
Waubay Lake, l., S.D., U.S. B15 126
Wauchope, Austl. D6 74
Wauchula, Fl., U.S. I4 116
Wauconda, Wa., U.S. B7 136
Waugh, Mb., Can. B3 118
Waukara, Bukit, mtn., Indon. D11 50
Waukaringa, Austl. I2 76
Waukarlycarly, Lake, l., Austl. D4 74
Waukegan, Il., U.S. F2 112
Waukesha, Wi., U.S. A9 120
Waukon, Ia., U.S. H7 118
Waunakee, Wi., U.S. A8 120
Wauneta, Ne., U.S. G11 126
Waupun, Wi., U.S. H10 118
Waurika, Ok., U.S. G11 128
Waurika Lake, res., Ok., U.S. G10 128
Wausa, Ne., U.S. E15 126
Wausau, Wi., U.S. G9 118
Wauseon, Oh., U.S. C1 114
Wautoma, Wi., U.S. G9 118
Wauwatosa, Wi., U.S. E1 112
Wauzeka, Wi., U.S. A7 120
Wave Hill, Austl. C6 74
Waverly, Ia., U.S. B5 120
Waverly, Mo., U.S. E4 120
Waverly, Ne., U.S. D1 120
Waverly, N.Y., U.S. B9 114
Waverly, Oh., U.S. E2 114
Waverly, Tn., U.S. H10 120
Waverly, Va., U.S. G8 114
Waverly Hall, Ga., U.S. E14 122
Wāw, Sudan F5 62
Wawa, On., Can. F14 106
Wawa, Nig. H5 64
Wawa, stm., Nic. E5 102
Wāw al-Kabīr, Libya B3 62
Wawanesa, Mb., Can. E14 124
Waxahachie, Tx., U.S. B11 130
Waxhaw, N.C., U.S. B5 116
Way, Lake, l., Austl. E4 74
Waya, i., Fiji p18 79e
Waycross, Ga., U.S. E3 116
Wayland, Ia., U.S. C6 120
Wayland, Ky., U.S. G3 114
Wayland, Mi., U.S. F4 112
Waylyn, S.C., U.S. D6 116
Wayne, Ab., Can. E18 138
Wayne, Mi., U.S. B2 114
Wayne, Ne., U.S. E15 126
Wayne, N.J., U.S. D11 114
Wayne, W.V., U.S. F3 114
Wayne City, Il., U.S. F9 120
Waynesboro, Ms., U.S. F10 122
Waynesboro, Tn., U.S. B11 122
Waynesboro, Va., U.S. F6 114
Waynesville, Il., U.S. D8 120
Waynesville, N.C., U.S. A3 116
Waynoka, Ok., U.S. E10 128
Wāzah Khwāh, Afg. B2 54
Wazīrābād, Pak. B5 54
Wda, stm., Pol. C14 16
Wé, N. Cal. m16 79d
We, Pulau, i., Indon. J2 48
Weatherford, Ok., U.S. F10 128
Weatherford, Tx., U.S. B10 130
Weatherly, Pa., U.S. D10 114
Weaubleau, Mo., U.S. G4 120
Weaver Lake, l., Mb., Can. B17 124
Weaverville, Ca., U.S. C3 134
Weaverville, N.C., U.S. I3 114
Webb, Sk., Can. D5 124
Webb, Ms., U.S. D8 122
Webbwood, On., Can. B7 112
Weber, stm., Ut., U.S. B5 132
Weber City, Va., U.S. H3 114
Webster, Ab., Can. A12 138
Webster, Fl., U.S. H3 116
Webster, Ma., U.S. B14 114
Webster, Wi., U.S. F6 118
Webster City, Ia., U.S. B4 120
Weda, Indon. E8 44
Weddell Island, i., Falk. Is. J4 90
Weddell Sea, Ant. B36 81
Wedderburn, Austl. K4 76
Wedgeport, N.S., Can. G11 110
Wedowee, Al., U.S. D13 122
Weed, Ca., U.S. B3 134
Weems, Va., U.S. G9 114
Weenen, S. Afr. F10 70
Weeping Water, Ne., U.S. D1 120
Weert, Neth. C14 14
Wee Waa, Austl. H7 76
Węgorzewo, Pol. B17 16
Węgrów, Pol. D17 16
Wei, stm., China C8 42
Wei, stm., China D3 42
Wei, stm., China C6 42
Weichang, China C2 38
Weichuan, China D6 42
Weida, Ger. F8 16
Weiden in der Oberpfalz, Ger. G7 16
Weifang, China C8 42
Weihai, China C10 42
Weihaiwei see Weihai, China C10 42
Weihe, China B8 38
Weilburg, Ger. F4 16
Weilheim, Ger. I7 16
Weilmoringle, Austl. G6 76
Weimar, Ger. E7 16
Weimar, Tx., U.S. E11 130
Weinan, China D3 42
Weinheim, Ger. G4 16
Weipa, Austl. B8 74
Weippe, Id., U.S. D11 136
Weir, Ks., U.S. D14 128
Weir, Ms., U.S. D9 122
Weir, stm., Austl. G8 76
Weirton, W.V., U.S. D5 114
Weisburd, Arg. C6 92
Weiser, Id., U.S. F10 136
Weiser, stm., Id., U.S. F10 136
Weishan Hu, l., China D7 42
Weishi, China D6 42
Weisner Mountain, mtn., Al., U.S. C13 122
Weissenburg in Bayern, Ger. G7 16
Weissenfels, Ger. E7 16
Weiss Lake, res., U.S. C13 122
Weisswasser, Ger. E10 16
Weitra, Aus. B11 22
Weixi, China F4 36

Name — Map Ref. — Page

Weixian, China C6 42
Weiyuan, stm., China A5 48
Weiz, Aus. C12 22
Wejherowo, Pol. B14 16
Wekoewa Punt, c., Neth. Ant. p23 104g
Welaka, Fl., U.S. G4 116
Welch, Ok., U.S. H2 120
Welch, Tx., U.S. B5 130
Welcome, Mn., U.S. H4 118
Weldiya, Eth. E7 62
Weldon, Sk., Can. A8 124
Weldon, Il., U.S. D9 120
Weldon, stm., U.S. D4 120
Weleetka, Ok., U.S. B2 122
Welk'īte, Eth. F7 62
Welkom, S. Afr. E8 70
Welland, On., Can. F10 112
Welland, stm., Eng., U.K. I12 12
Wellborn, Fl., U.S. F3 116
Wellborn, Tx., U.S. G2 122
Wellesley Islands, is., Austl. C8 74
Wellingborough, Eng., U.K. I12 12
Wellington, Austl. I7 76
Wellington, On., Can. E12 112
Wellington, N.Z. E6 80
Wellington, S. Afr. H4 70
Wellington, Eng., U.K. K9 12
Wellington, Co., U.S. G7 126
Wellington, Mo., U.S. E4 120
Wellington, Oh., U.S. C3 114
Wellington, Tx., U.S. G8 128
Wellington, Ut., U.S. D6 132
Wellington, Isla, i., Chile I2 90
Wellington Bay, b., Nu., Can. B9 106
Wellington Channel, strt., Nu., Can. B7 141
Wellman, Ia., U.S. C6 120
Wellman, Tx., U.S. A5 130
Wells, Eng., U.K. J10 12
Wells, Mi., U.S. C2 112
Wells, Mn., U.S. H5 118
Wells, N.Y., U.S. G2 110
Wells, Tx., U.S. F3 122
Wells, Lake, l., Austl. E4 74
Wells, Mount, hill, Austl. C5 74
Wellsboro, Pa., U.S. C8 114
Wellsburg, Ia., U.S. B4 120
Wellsburg, W.V., U.S. D5 114
Wellsford, N.Z. C6 80
Wells-next-the-Sea, Eng., U.K. I13 12
Wellston, Oh., U.S. E3 114
Wellsville, Ks., U.S. C13 128
Wellsville, Mo., U.S. E6 120
Wellsville, N.Y., U.S. B8 114
Wellsville, Oh., U.S. D5 114
Wellton, Az., U.S. K2 132
Wels, Aus. B10 22
Welsford, N.B., Can. E10 110
Welshpool, Wales, U.K. I9 12
Welwyn Garden City, Eng., U.K. J12 12
Wembley, Ab., Can. A11 138
Wena, D.R.C. E4 66
Wenatchee, Wa., U.S. C6 136
Wenatchee Mountains, mts., Wa., U.S. C6 136
Wenceslau Braz, Braz. L1 88
Wenchang, China L4 42
Wencheng, China H8 42
Wenchi, Ghana H4 64
Wenchou see Wenzhou, China F9 36
Wenchow see Wenzhou, China F9 36
Wendell, Id., U.S. H12 136
Wenden, Az., U.S. J3 132
Wendeng, China C10 42
Wendover, Ut., U.S. C2 132
Weng, stm., China I6 42
Weng'an, China H2 42
Wenling, China G9 42
Wenlock, stm., Austl. B8 74
Wenquan, China E14 32
Wenshan, China A7 48
Wenshang, China D7 42
Wenshui, China C4 42
Wenshui, China G2 42
Wensleydale, val., Eng., U.K. G11 12
Wentworth, Austl. J3 76
Wentworth, S.D., U.S. G2 118
Wenxi, China D4 42
Wenxian, China D5 42
Wenzhou, China F9 36
Wepener, S. Afr. F8 70
Werda, Bots. D6 70
Werdau, Ger. F8 16
Werder, Ger. D8 16
Wernadinga, Austl. B2 76
Wernigerode, Ger. E6 16
Werra, stm., Ger. E5 16
Werribee, Austl. K5 76
Werrikimbe National Park, p.o.i., Austl. H9 76
Werris Creek, Austl. H8 76
Wertheim, Ger. G5 16
Wesel, Ger. E2 16
Weser, stm., Ger. C4 16
Weskan, Ks., U.S. C7 128
Weslaco, Tx., U.S. H10 130
Weslemkoon Lake, l., On., Can. C12 112
Wesley, Dom. i6 105c
Wesleyville, Pa., U.S. B5 114
Wessel, Cape, c., Austl. B7 74
Wessel Islands, is., Austl. B7 74
Wessington, S.D., U.S. C14 126
Wessington Springs, S.D., U.S. C14 126
West, Ms., U.S. D9 122
West, Tx., U.S. C10 130
West Allis, Wi., U.S. B9 120
West Antarctica, reg., Ant. D30 81
Westbank, B.C., Can. G11 138
West Bank, dep., Asia F6 58
West Bay, N.S., Can. E15 110
West Bay, b., Tx., U.S. E1 122
West Bend, Ia., U.S. B3 120
West Bend, Wi., U.S. E1 112
West Bengal, state, India G11 54
West Blocton, Al., U.S. D11 122
West Bohemia see Západočeský kraj, state, Czech Rep. G9 16
West Borneo see Kalimantan Barat, state, Indon. D7 50
West Branch, Ia., U.S. C6 120
Westbridge, B.C., Can. G11 138
West Bromwich, Eng., U.K. I11 12
Westbrook, Me., U.S. G6 110
Westbrook, Mn., U.S. G3 118
Westbrook, Tx., U.S. B6 130
West Burlington, Ia., U.S. D6 120
West Burra, i., Scot., U.K. n18 12a
Westby, Austl. J6 76
Westby, Wi., U.S. H8 118
West Cache Creek, stm., Ok., U.S. G10 128
West Caicos, i., T./C. Is. B11 102
West Cape, c., N.Z. G2 80
West Cape Howe, c., Austl. G3 74
West Carlisle, Tx., U.S. H6 128
West Caroline Basin, unds. I16 142
West Chester, Pa., U.S. E10 114
Westchester Station, N.S., Can. E13 110
Westcliffe, Co., U.S. C3 128
West Columbia, S.C., U.S. B4 116
West Columbia, Tx., U.S. H3 122
West Cote Blanche Bay, b., La., U.S. H7 122
West Des Moines, Ia., U.S. C4 120
West Dolores, stm., Co., U.S. F8 132
West Elk Peak, mtn., Co., U.S. E9 132
West End, Ar., U.S. C6 122
West End, N.C., U.S. A6 116
Westerland, Ger. B4 16
Westerly, R.I., U.S. C14 114
Western, state, Sol. Is. e7 79b
Western, stm., Austl. D4 76
Western Australia, state, Austl. D4 74
Western Cape, state, S. Afr. H5 70
Western Channel, strt., Asia E2 40
Western Desert, des., Egypt B5 62
Western Division, state, Fiji p18 79e
Western Dvina (Daugava) (Zahodnjaja Dzvina) (Zapadnaja Dvina), stm., Eur. D7 10
Western Ghāts, mts., India E3 46
Westernport, Md., U.S. E6 114
Western Sahara, dep., Afr. E2 64
Western Samoa see Samoa, ctry., Oc. g12 79c
Western Sayans see Zapadnyj Sajan, mts., Russia D16 32
Western Shore, N.S., Can. F12 110
Westerschelde, est., Neth. C12 14
Westerstede, Ger. C3 16
Westerville, Oh., U.S. D3 114
Westerwald, mts., Ger. F3 16
West European Basin, unds. D12 144
West Falkland, i., Falk. Is. J4 90
West Fargo, N.D., U.S. E1 118
Westfield, Il., U.S. E9 120
Westfield, In., U.S. H3 112
Westfield, Ma., U.S. H4 110
Westfield, N.J., U.S. D11 114
Westfield, Pa., U.S. C8 114
Westfield, Wi., U.S. H9 118
West Fork, Ar., U.S. I3 120
West Frankfort, Il., U.S. G9 120
West Friese Eilanden, is., Neth. A14 14
West Frisian Islands see West Friese Eilanden, is., Neth. A14 14
Westgate, Austl. F6 76
West Grand Lake, res., Me., U.S. E8 110
West Hamlin, W.V., U.S. F3 114
West Hartford, Ct., U.S. C13 114
West Haven, Ct., U.S. C13 114
West Helena, Ar., U.S. C8 122
Westhoff, Tx., U.S. E10 130
Westhope, N.D., U.S. F12 124
West Ice Shelf, ice, Ant. B13 81
West Indies, is. C7 82
West Java see Jawa Barat, state, Indon. G5 50
West Jefferson, N.C., U.S. H4 114
West Jordan, Ut., U.S. C4 132
West Kettle, stm., B.C., Can. G11 138
West Kingston, R.I., U.S. C14 114
West Laramie, Wy., U.S. F7 126
West Lafayette, In., U.S. H2 112
Westlake, La., U.S. G5 122
Westland National Park, p.o.i., N.Z. F3 80
West Lebanon, In., U.S. H2 112
West Liberty, Ky., U.S. G2 114
West Liberty, Oh., U.S. D2 114
Westlock, Ab., Can. B16 138
West Lorne, On., Can. F8 112
Westmeath, state, Ire. H5 12
West Memphis, Ar., U.S. B8 122
Westminster, Co., U.S. B3 128
Westminster, Md., U.S. E9 114
West Monroe, La., U.S. E6 122
Westmoreland, Ks., U.S. B12 128
Westmoreland, Tn., U.S. H11 120
Westmorland, Ca., U.S. J10 134
West Nicholson, Zimb. B9 70
West Nishnabotna, stm., Ia., U.S. C2 120
West Nueces, stm., Tx., U.S. E7 130
West Nusa Tenggara see Nusa Tenggara Barat, state, Indon. G10 50
Weston, Id., U.S. A4 132
Weston, Mo., U.S. E3 120
Weston, Oh., U.S. C2 114
Weston, Or., U.S. E8 136
Weston, W.V., U.S. E5 114
Weston-super-Mare, Eng., U.K. J9 12
West Orange, Tx., U.S. G5 122
Westover, Tn., U.S. B10 122
West Palm Beach, Fl., U.S. J5 116
West Palm Beach Canal, can., Fl., U.S. J5 116
West Pensacola, Fl., U.S. G11 122
Westphalia, Ks., U.S. F2 120
West Plains, Mo., U.S. H6 120
West Point, Ga., U.S. E13 122
West Point, Ia., U.S. D6 120
West Point, Ky., U.S. F11 120
West Point, Ms., U.S. D10 122
West Point, Ne., U.S. J2 118
West Point, N.Y., U.S. C11 114
West Point, Va., U.S. G9 114
West Point Lake, res., U.S. D13 122
West Poplar (Poplar, West Fork), stm., N.A. F8 124
Westport, N.S., Can. F10 110
Westport, On., Can. D13 112
Westport, Ire. H3 12
Westport, Ct., U.S. C12 114
Westport, In., U.S. E12 120
Westport, Or., U.S. D3 136
Westpunt, c., Aruba o19 104g
West Quoddy Head, c., Me., U.S. F10 110
Westray, i., Scot., U.K. B9 12
West Richland, Wa., U.S. D7 136
West Road, stm., B.C., Can. C7 138
West Rutland, Vt., U.S. G3 110
West Salem, Il., U.S. F9 120
West Salem, Oh., U.S. D3 114
West Shoal Lake, l., Mb., Can. D16 124
West Siberian Plain see Zapadno-Sibirskaja ravnina, pl., Russia B12 32
West Slovakia see Západoslovenský Kraj, state, Slov. H14 16
West Spanish Peak, mtn., Co., U.S. D4 128
West Sumatra see Sumatera Barat, state, Indon. D2 50
West Terre Haute, In., U.S. E10 120
West Union, Ia., U.S. B6 120
West Union, Oh., U.S. F2 114
West Unity, Oh., U.S. C1 114
West Valley City, Ut., U.S. C4 132
West Vancouver, B.C., Can. G7 138
Westville, N.S., Can. E14 110
Westville, In., U.S. G3 112
West Virginia, state, U.S. F5 114
West Walker, stm., U.S. E6 134
West Warwick, R.I., U.S. C14 114
West Webster, N.Y., U.S. E12 112
Westwold, B.C., Can. F11 138
Westwood, Ca., U.S. C5 134
Westwood Lakes, Fl., U.S. K5 116
West Wyalong, Austl. I6 76
West Yellowstone, Mt., U.S. F15 136
Wetar, Pulau, i., Indon. G8 44
Wetar, Selat, strt., Indon. G8 44
Wetaskiwin, Ab., Can. C17 138
Wete, Tan. E7 66
Wethersfield, Ct., U.S. C13 114
Wetmore, Ks., U.S. E2 120
Wetumpka, Al., U.S. E12 122
Wetzlar, Ger. F4 16
Wewahitchka, Fl., U.S. G13 122
Wewak, Pap. N. Gui. a3 79a
Wewoka, Ok., U.S. B2 122
Wexford, Ire. I6 12
Wexford, state, Ire. I6 12
Weyburn, Sk., Can. E10 124
Weymontachie, Qc., Can. C3 110
Weymouth, N.S., Can. F10 110
Weymouth, Eng., U.K. K10 12
Weymouth, Ma., U.S. B15 114
Whakatane, N.Z. C7 80
Whangarei, N.Z. B6 80
Whapmagoostui, Qc., Can. D15 106
Wharfe, stm., Eng., U.K. H11 12
Wharton, W.V., U.S. G4 114
Wharton Basin, unds. K12 142
Wharton Lake, l., Nu., Can. C10 106
Whataroa, N.Z. F4 80
What Cheer, Ia., U.S. C5 120
Whatley, Al., U.S. F11 122
Wheatland, Ca., U.S. D4 134
Wheatland, Ia., U.S. C7 120
Wheatley, On., Can. F7 112
Wheatley, Ar., U.S. C7 122
Wheaton, Il., U.S. C9 120
Wheaton, Md., U.S. E8 114
Wheat Ridge, Co., U.S. B3 128
Wheeler, Ms., U.S. C10 122
Wheeler, Tx., U.S. F8 128
Wheeler, stm., Qc., Can. D17 106
Wheeler Lake, res., Al., U.S. C11 122
Wheeler Peak, mtn., Nv., U.S. D2 132
Wheeler Peak, mtn., N.M., U.S. E3 128
Wheeling, W.V., U.S. D5 114
Wheelwright, Arg. F7 92
Wheelwright, Ky., U.S. G3 114
Whidbey Island, i., Wa., U.S. B4 136
Whiskey Peak, mtn., Wy., U.S. E5 126
Whistler, B.C., Can. F8 138
Whitakers, N.C., U.S. H8 114
Whitby, On., Can. E11 112
Whitby, Eng., U.K. G12 12
Whitchurch, Eng., U.K. H10 12
Whitchurch-Stouffville, On., Can. E10 112
White, Ga., U.S. C14 122
White, stm., N.A. C2 106
White, stm., Ar., U.S. C7 122
White, stm., U.S. D13 126
White, stm., U.S. C7 132
White, stm., Az., U.S. J6 132
White, stm., In., U.S. F10 120
White, stm., Nv., U.S. F1 132
White, stm., Tx., U.S. H7 128
White, stm., Wa., U.S. C5 136
White, East Fork, stm., In., U.S. F10 120
White, Lake, l., Austl. D5 74
White Bay, b., Nf., Can. i22 107a
White Bear Lake, Mn., U.S. F6 118
White Bluff, Tn., U.S. H10 120
White Butte, mtn., N.D., U.S. A9 126
White Castle, La., U.S. G7 122
White City, Ks., U.S. C12 128
White Cliffs, Austl. H4 76
Whitecourt, Ab., Can. B15 138
White Deer, Tx., U.S. F7 128
Whiteface, stm., Mn., U.S. D6 118
Whiteface Mountain, mtn., N.Y., U.S. F3 110
Whitefield, N.H., U.S. F5 110
Whitefish, Mt., U.S. B12 136
Whitefish Bay, Wi., U.S. A10 120
Whitefish Bay, b., On., Can. B4 118
Whitefish Bay, b., N.A. B5 112
Whitefish Lake, l., Ab., Can. B18 138
Whitefish Lake, l., N.T., Can. C9 106
Whitefish Point, Mi., U.S. B4 112
Whitefish Point, c., Mi., U.S. B4 112
White Hall, Ar., U.S. C6 122
White Hall, Il., U.S. E7 120
Whitehall, Mi., U.S. E3 112
Whitehall, N.Y., U.S. G3 110
Whitehall, Wi., U.S. G7 118
Whitehaven, Eng., U.K. G9 12
Whitehorse, Yk., Can. C4 106
White House, Tn., U.S. H11 120
Whitehouse, Tx., U.S. E3 122
White Island, i., Nu., Can. B13 106
White Island, i., N.Z. C7 80
White Lake, S.D., U.S. D14 126
White Lake, Wi., U.S. F10 118
White Lake, l., On., Can. C13 112
White Lake, l., La., U.S. H6 122
Whitemark, Austl. n13 77a
White Mountain Peak, mtn., Ca., U.S. F7 134
White Mountains, mts., N.H., U.S. F5 110
Whitemouth, stm., Mb., Can. E18 124
Whitemouth Lake, l., Mb., Can. E18 124
Whitemud, stm., Mb., Can. D15 124
White Nile (Abyad, Al-Bahr al-), stm., Afr. E6 62
White Oak, Tx., U.S. E4 122
White Oak Creek, stm., Tx., U.S. D3 122
White Otter Lake, l., On., Can. B6 118
White Pigeon, Mi., U.S. G4 112
Whitepine, Mt., U.S. C11 136
White Pine, Tn., U.S. H2 114
White Plains, N.Y., U.S. C12 114
White Plains, N.C., U.S. H5 114
Whiteriver, Az., U.S. J6 132
White River, S.D., U.S. D12 126
White River Junction, Vt., U.S. G4 110
White Rock, B.C., Can. G8 138
White Russia see Belarus, ctry., Eur. E14 6
Whitesail Lake, res., B.C., Can. C3 138
Whitesand, stm., Sk., Can. C11 124
White Sands National Monument, p.o.i., N.M., U.S. B1 130
Whitesboro, Tx., U.S. D2 122
Whitesburg, Ky., U.S. H3 114
White Sea see Beloe more, Russia D18 8
White Settlement, Tx., U.S. B10 130
White Springs, Fl., U.S. F3 116
White Sulphur Springs, Mt., U.S. D16 136
White Sulphur Springs, W.V., U.S. G5 114
Whitesville, Ky., U.S. G11 120
Whiteville, N.C., U.S. B7 116
Whiteville, Tn., U.S. B9 122
White Volta (Volta Blanche), stm., Afr. G4 64
Whitewater, Mt., U.S. F6 124
Whitewater, Wi., U.S. B9 120
Whitewater, stm., U.S. E13 120
Whitewater Baldy, mtn., N.M., U.S. J8 132
Whitewater Creek, stm., N.A. F6 124
Whitewater Lake, l., Mb., Can. E13 124
White Woman Creek, stm., U.S. C7 128
Whitewood, Austl. C4 76
Whitewood, Sk., Can. D11 124
Whitewood, S.D., U.S. C9 126
Whithorn, Jam. i12 104d
Whithorn, Scot., U.K. G8 12
Whiting, Ia., U.S. B1 120
Whiting, Ks., U.S. E2 120
Whitley City, Ky., U.S. H13 120
Whitman, Ma., U.S. B15 114
Whitmire, S.C., U.S. B4 116
Whitmore Mountains, mts., Ant. D31 81
Whitney, On., Can. C11 112
Whitney, Lake, res., Tx., U.S. C10 130
Whitney, Mount, mtn., Ca., U.S. G7 134
Whitney Point, N.Y., U.S. B9 114
Whitsunday Island, i., Austl. C7 76
Whittemore, Ia., U.S. A3 120
Whittemore, Mi., U.S. D6 112
Whittle, Cap, c., Qc., Can. i22 107a
Whittlesea, Austl. K5 76
Whittlesey, Mount, hill, Wi., U.S. E8 118
Whitwell, Tn., U.S. B13 122
Wholdaia Lake, l., N.T., Can. C9 106
Whyalla, Austl. F7 74
Whycocomagh, N.S., Can. E15 110
Wiang Phan, Thai. B4 48
Wiarton, On., Can. D8 112
Wichian Buri, Thai. E5 48
Wichita, Ks., U.S. D11 128
Wichita, stm., Tx., U.S. G10 128
Wichita Falls, Tx., U.S. H10 128
Wick, Scot., U.K. C9 12
Wickenburg, Az., U.S. J4 132
Wickepin, Austl. F3 74
Wickett, Tx., U.S. C5 130
Wickham, Austl. D3 74
Wickiup Reservoir, res., Or., U.S. G5 136
Wickliffe, Ky., U.S. H8 120
Wicklow, Ire. H6 12
Wicklow, state, Ire. H7 12
Wicklow Head, c., Ire. I7 12
Wicklow Mountains, mts., Ire. H6 12
Widgeegoara Creek, stm., Austl. F6 76
Więcbork, Pol. C13 16
Wieleń, Pol. D12 16
Wieliczka, Pol. F16 16
Wielkopolska, reg., Pol. E13 16
Wielkopolski Park Narodowy, p.o.i., Pol. D12 16
Wieluń, Pol. E14 16
Wien (Vienna), Aus. B13 22
Wien, state, Aus. B13 22
Wiener Neustadt, Aus. C13 22
Wienerwald, mts., Aus. B13 22
Wieprz, stm., Pol. E18 16
Wieprz, stm., Pol. B12 16
Wieprz-Krzna, Kanał, can., Pol. E19 16
Wierden, Neth. D2 16
Wiergate, Tx., U.S. F5 122
Wieruszów, Pol. E14 16
Wierzyca, stm., Pol. B14 16
Wiesbaden, Ger. F4 16
Wiesloch, Ger. G4 16
Wigan, Eng., U.K. H10 12
Wiggins, Co., U.S. A4 128
Wiggins, Ms., U.S. G9 122
Wight, Isle of, i., Eng., U.K. K11 12
Wigtown, Scot., U.K. G8 12
Wilbur, Wa., U.S. C8 136
Wilburton, Ok., U.S. C3 122
Wilcannia, Austl. H4 76
Wilcox, Sk., Can. D9 124
Wilcox, Ne., U.S. A9 128
Wildcat Creek, stm., In., U.S. H3 112
Wildcat Hill, mtn., Sk., Can. A11 124
Wild Coast, cst., S. Afr. H9 70
Wilder, Id., U.S. G9 136
Wilderness of Judaea (Midbar Yehuda), des., Asia G6 58
Wildhay, stm., Ab., Can. C13 138
Wildhorse Creek, stm., U.S. G10 126
Wild Horse Lake, l., Mt., U.S. B17 136
Wild Rice, stm., Mn., U.S. D2 118
Wild Rice, stm., N.D., U.S. H17 124
Wildrose, N.D., U.S. F10 124
Wild Rose, Wi., U.S. D9 118
Wildwood, Ab., Can. C15 138
Wildwood, N.J., U.S. F11 114
Wilge, stm., S. Afr. E9 70
Wilhelm, Mount, mtn., Pap. N. Gui. b3 79a
Wilhelmina Gebergte, mts., Sur. C6 84
Wilhelmshaven, Ger. C4 16
Wilhelmstal, Nmb. B3 70
Wilkerson Pass, p., Co., U.S. B3 128
Wilkes-Barre, Pa., U.S. C10 114
Wilkesboro, N.C., U.S. H4 114
Wilkes Land, reg., Ant. C16 81
Wilkie, Sk., Can. B5 124
Willacoochee, Ga., U.S. E2 116
Willamette, stm., Or., U.S. E4 136
Willamette, Middle Fork, stm., Or., U.S. G4 136
Willamina, Or., U.S. E3 136
Willandra Billabong Creek, stm., Austl. I5 76
Willandra National Park, p.o.i., Austl. I5 76
Willapa Bay, b., Wa., U.S. D2 136
Willard, Mo., U.S. G4 120
Willard, Oh., U.S. C3 114
Willard, Ut., U.S. B4 132
Willard, Punta, c., Mex. A2 100
Willcox, Az., U.S. K7 132
Willcox Playa, l., Az., U.S. K7 132
Willemstad, Neth. Ant. p22 104g
Willeroo, Austl. C6 74
William, Mount, mtn., Austl. K4 76
William Bill Dannelly Reservoir, res., Al., U.S. E11 122
Williams, Ca., U.S. D3 134
Williams, Ia., U.S. I5 118
Williams, Mn., U.S. C3 118
Williams, stm., Austl. C3 76
Williamsburg, Ia., U.S. C5 120
Williamsburg, Ky., U.S. H1 114
Williamsburg, Va., U.S. G9 114
Williams Lake, B.C., Can. D8 138
Williamson, N.Y., U.S. E12 112
Williamson, W.V., U.S. G3 114
Williamson, stm., Or., U.S. H5 136
Williamson, Mount, mtn., Ca., U.S. G7 134
Williamsport, Pa., U.S. C8 114
Williamston, Mi., U.S. F5 112
Williamston, S.C., U.S. B3 116
Williamstown, Ky., U.S. F1 114
Williamstown, N.J., U.S. E11 114
Williamstown, W.V., U.S. E4 114
Williamsville, Il., U.S. L9 118
Willikies, Antig. f4 105b
Willimantic, Ct., U.S. C13 114
Willingboro, N.J., U.S. D10 114
Willis, Tx., U.S. G3 122
Willis Group, is., Austl. C10 74
Williston, Fl., U.S. G3 116
Williston, N.D., U.S. F10 124
Williston, S.C., U.S. C4 116
Williston Lake, res., B.C., Can. D6 106
Willits, Ca., U.S. D2 134
Willmar, Mn., U.S. F3 118
Willoughby, Oh., U.S. C4 114
Willoughby Bay, b., Antig. f4 105b
Willow, Ak., U.S. D10 140
Willow, stm., B.C., Can. C8 138
Willowbrook, Sk., Can. C10 124
Willow Bunch, Sk., Can. E8 124
Willow Bunch Lake, l., Sk., Can. E8 124
Willow Creek, Ca., U.S. C2 134
Willow Creek, Mt., U.S. E15 136
Willow Creek, stm., Ab., Can. F17 138
Willow Creek, stm., Or., U.S. F9 136
Willow Creek, stm., Or., U.S. E7 136
Willow Lake, S.D., U.S. C15 126
Willow Lake, l., N.T., Can. C7 106
Willowmore, S. Afr. H6 70
Willowra, Austl. D6 74
Willow Reservoir, res., Wi., U.S. F9 118
Willows, Ca., U.S. D3 134
Willow Springs, Mo., U.S. H6 120
Willowvale, S. Afr. H9 70
Wills Creek, stm., Austl. D2 76
Wills Point, Tx., U.S. E2 122
Wilmar, Ar., U.S. D6 122
Wilmer, Al., U.S. G10 122
Wilmer, Tx., U.S. E2 122
Wilmette, Il., U.S. F2 112
Wilmington, De., U.S. E10 114
Wilmington, N.C., U.S. B7 116
Wilmington, Oh., U.S. E2 114
Wilmington, Vt., U.S. H4 110
Wilmore, Ky., U.S. G13 120
Wilmot, S.D., U.S. F2 118
Wilpattu National Park, p.o.i., Sri L. G4 53
Wilsall, Mt., U.S. D16 136
Wilson, Austl. H2 76
Wilson, Ar., U.S. B8 122
Wilson, La., U.S. G7 122
Wilson, N.Y., U.S. E11 112
Wilson, N.C., U.S. I8 114
Wilson, Ok., U.S. G11 128
Wilson, Tx., U.S. H7 128
Wilson, stm., Austl. F4 76
Wilson, Cape, c., Nu., Can. B14 106
Wilson, Mount, mtn., Az., U.S. H2 132
Wilson, Mount, mtn., Ca., U.S. I7 134
Wilson, Mount, mtn., Co., U.S. F8 132
Wilson Lake, res., Al., U.S. C11 122
Wilson Lake, res., Ks., U.S. C10 128
Wilsons Promontory, pen., Austl. L6 76
Wilsons Promontory National Park, p.o.i., Austl. L6 76
Wilsonville, Ne., U.S. A8 128
Wilton, Eng., U.K. J11 12
Wilton, Me., U.S. F6 110
Wilton, N.H., U.S. B14 114
Wilton, Wi., U.S. H8 118
Wilton, stm., Austl. B6 74
Wiluna, Austl. E4 74
Wimauma, Fl., U.S. I3 116
Wimberley, Tx., U.S. D9 130
Winamac, In., U.S. G3 112
Winburg, S. Afr. F8 70
Winchendon, Ma., U.S. B13 114
Winchester, On., Can. C14 112
Winchester, Eng., U.K. J11 12
Winchester, Il., U.S. E7 120
Winchester, In., U.S. H5 112
Winchester, Ky., U.S. G1 114
Winchester, Tn., U.S. B12 122
Winchester, Va., U.S. E7 114
Wind, stm., Yk., Can. B3 106
Wind, stm., Wy., U.S. D4 126
Wind Cave National Park, p.o.i., S.D., U.S. D9 126
Winder, Ga., U.S. B2 116
Windermere, B.C., Can. F15 138
Windermere, Eng., U.K. G10 12
Windfall, Ab., Can. B14 138
Windhoek, Nmb. C3 70
Windigo, stm., Qc., Can. C3 110
Windom, Mn., U.S. H3 118
Windorah, Austl. E4 76
Window Rock, Az., U.S. H7 132
Wind River Peak, mtn., Wy., U.S. E3 126
Wind River Range, mts., Wy., U.S. D3 126
Windsor, Austl. I8 76
Windsor, N.S., Can. E12 110
Windsor, On., Can. F6 112
Windsor, Qc., Can. E5 110
Windsor, Eng., U.K. J12 12
Windsor, Ca., U.S. E3 134
Windsor, Ct., U.S. C13 114
Windsor, Il., U.S. E9 120
Windsor, Mo., U.S. F4 120
Windsor, N.C., U.S. I9 114
Windsor, Va., U.S. H9 114
Windsor Forest, Ga., U.S. E4 116
Windsor Locks, Ct., U.S. C13 114
Windthorst, Tx., U.S. H10 128
Windward, Gren. p11 105e
Windward Islands, is., N.A. k6 105c
Windward Passage, strt., N.A. C11 102
Windy Peak, mtn., Co., U.S. C2 128
Winfield, Al., U.S. D11 122
Winfield, Ks., U.S. D12 128
Winfield, Mo., U.S. E7 120
Winfield, W.V., U.S. F4 114
Wing, N.D., U.S. G13 124
Wingate, N.C., U.S. B5 116
Wingham, Austl. H9 76
Wingham, On., Can. E8 112
Wingo, Ky., U.S. H9 120
Winisk, On., Can. D13 106
Winisk, stm., On., Can. E13 106
Winisk Lake, l., On., Can. E13 106
Wink, Tx., U.S. C4 130
Winkana, Mya. E4 48
Winkelman, Az., U.S. K6 132
Winkler, Mb., Can. E16 124
Winlock, Wa., U.S. D3 136
Winneba, Ghana H4 64
Winnebago, Mn., U.S. H4 118
Winnebago, Ne., U.S. B1 120
Winnebago, stm., Ia., U.S. H5 118
Winnebago, Lake, l., Wi., U.S. G10 118
Winneconne, Wi., U.S. G10 118
Winnemucca, Nv., U.S. B8 134
Winnemucca Lake, l., Nv., U.S. C6 134
Winner, S.D., U.S. D13 126
Winnetka, Il., U.S. F2 112
Winnett, Mt., U.S. H5 124
Winnibigoshish, Lake, res., Mn., U.S. D4 118
Winnie, Tx., U.S. H4 122
Winning, Austl. D2 74
Winnipeg, Mb., Can. E16 124
Winnipeg, stm., Can. E11 106
Winnipeg, Lake, l., Mb., Can. E11 106
Winnipeg Beach, Mb., Can. D17 124
Winnipegosis, Mb., Can. C13 124
Winnipegosis, Lake, l., Mb., Can. B13 124
Winnipesaukee, Lake, l., N.H., U.S. G5 110
Winnsboro, S.C., U.S. B4 116
Winnsboro, Tx., U.S. E3 122
Winnsboro Mills, S.C., U.S. B4 116
Winona, Ks., U.S. B7 128
Winona, Mn., U.S. G7 118
Winona, Ms., U.S. D9 122
Winona, Mo., U.S. G6 120
Winooski, stm., Vt., U.S. F4 110
Winschoten, Neth. A15 14
Winschoterdiep, can., Neth. A15 14
Winsen, Ger. C6 16
Winslow, Az., U.S. H6 132
Winslow, In., U.S. F10 120
Winslow, Me., U.S. F7 110
Winsted, Mn., U.S. G4 118
Winston, Fl., U.S. H3 116
Winston, Or., U.S. G3 136
Winston-Salem, N.C., U.S. H5 114
Winter, Wi., U.S. F8 118
Winter Garden, Fl., U.S. H4 116
Winter Harbor, Me., U.S. F8 110
Winter Harbour, B.C., Can. F2 138
Winterhaven, Ca., U.S. K2 132
Winter Haven, Fl., U.S. I4 116
Winter Island, i., Nu., Can. B14 106
Winter Park, Fl., U.S. H4 116
Winters, Ca., U.S. E3 134
Winters, Tx., U.S. C8 130
Winterset, Ia., U.S. C4 120
Winterswijk, Neth. B15 14
Winterthur, Switz. C5 22
Winterville, Ga., U.S. C2 116
Winterville, Ms., U.S. D7 122
Winthrop, Me., U.S. F7 110
Winthrop, Wa., U.S. B6 136
Winthrop Harbor, Il., U.S. F2 112
Wintinna, Austl. E6 74
Winton, Austl. D4 76
Winton, N.Z. H3 80
Winton, N.C., U.S. H8 114
Wirātnagar, Nepal E11 54
Wirgañj, Nepal E10 54
Wisbech, Eng., U.K. I12 12
Wiscasset, Me., U.S. G7 110
Wisconsin, state, U.S. G9 118
Wisconsin, stm., Wi., U.S. I8 118
Wisconsin Dells, Wi., U.S. H9 118
Wisconsin Dells, misc. cult., Wi., U.S. H9 118
Wisconsin Rapids, Wi., U.S. G8 118
Wisdom, Mt., U.S. E13 136
Wise, Va., U.S. G3 114
Wiseman, Ak., U.S. C9 140
Wishek, N.D., U.S. A13 126
Wishram, Wa., U.S. E5 136
Wisła, Pol. G14 16
Wisła (Vistula), stm., Pol. B14 16
Wiślany, Mierzeja, spit, Eur. B15 16
Wisłok, stm., Pol. F18 16
Wisłoka, stm., Pol. F17 16
Wismar, Ger. C7 16
Wisner, La., U.S. F7 122
Wister, Ok., U.S. C4 122
Wisznice, Pol. E19 16
Witbank, S. Afr. D9 70
Witham, stm., Eng., U.K. H12 12
Withlacoochee, stm., U.S. F2 116
Witkowo, Pol. D13 16
Wit-Mfolozi, stm., S. Afr. F10 70
Witney, Eng., U.K. J11 12
Wit Nossob, stm., Nmb. C4 70
Witsand, S. Afr. I5 70
Witt, Il., U.S. E8 120
Wittenberg, Wi., U.S. G9 118
Wittenberge, Ger. C7 16
Wittenburg, Ger. C6 16
Wittenoom, Austl. D3 74
Wittingen, Ger. D6 16
Wittlich, Ger. G2 16
Wittmund, Ger. C3 16
Wittstock, Ger. C8 16
Witu Islands, is., Pap. N. Gui. a5 79a
Witvlei, Nmb. C4 70
Witwatersrand, mts., S. Afr. D8 70
Witzenhausen, Ger. E5 16
Wiżajny, Pol. B18 16
Wkra, stm., Pol. C15 16
Wleń, Pol. E11 16
Włocławek, Pol. D15 16
Włocławek, state, Pol. D14 16
Włoszczowa, Pol. F15 16
Woburn, Ma., U.S. B14 114
Wodonga, Austl. K6 76
Wodzisław Śląski, Pol. F14 16
Wokam, Pulau, i., Indon. G10 44
Woking, Eng., U.K. J12 12
Wokingham Creek, stm., Austl. C4 76
Wolbrom, Pol. F15 16
Wolcott, In., U.S. D10 120
Wolcott, N.Y., U.S. E13 112
Wolcottville, In., U.S. G4 112
Woleai, at., Micron. C5 72
Wolf, stm., U.S. B9 122
Wolf, stm., Ms., U.S. G9 122
Wolf, stm., Wi., U.S. G10 118
Wolf, Volcán, vol., Ec. h11 84a
Wolfach, Ger. H4 16
Wolf Creek, Or., U.S. H3 136
Wolf Creek, stm., U.S. E9 128
Wolf Creek, stm., Mt., U.S. C17 136
Wolf Creek Pass, p., Co., U.S. F10 132
Wolf Creek Reservoir, res., Ks., U.S. F2 120
Wolfeboro, N.H., U.S. G5 110
Wolfe Island, i., On., Can. D13 112
Wolfen, Ger. E8 16
Wolfenbüttel, Ger. D6 16
Wolfenden, Mount, mtn., B.C., Can. F3 138
Wolfforth, Tx., U.S. H6 128
Wolfhagen, Ger. E4 16
Wolf Lake, Mi., U.S. E3 112
Wolf Lake, l., Ab., Can. B20 138
Wolf Point, Mt., U.S. F8 124
Wolfratshausen, Ger. I7 16
Wolf Rock, r., Eng., U.K. L7 12
Wolfsberg, Aus. D11 22
Wolfsburg, Ger. D6 16
Wolfville, N.S., Can. E12 110
Wolgast, Ger. B9 16
Woliński Park Narodowy, p.o.i., Pol. C10 16
Wollaston Lake, l., Sk., Can. D10 106
Wollaston Peninsula, pen., Can. B7 106
Wollemi National Park, p.o.i., Austl. I7 76
Wollongong, Austl. J8 76
Wołomin, Pol. D17 16
Wołów, Pol. E12 16
Wolseley, Sk., Can. D10 124
Wolsey, S.D., U.S. C14 126
Wolverhampton, Eng., U.K. I10 12
Wolverton, Eng., U.K. I11 12
Wondai, Austl. F8 76
Wonderland, Ca., U.S. C4 134
Wondinong, Austl. E3 74
Wonewoc, Wi., U.S. H8 118
Wŏnju, Kor., S. F7 38
Wonogiri, Indon. G7 50
Wonosari, Indon. H7 50
Wonosobo, Indon. G6 50
Wŏnsan, Kor., N. E7 38
Wonthaggi, Austl. L5 76
Wood, S.D., U.S. D12 126

Wood-Youn I•63

Name — Map Ref. — Page

Wood, stm., Ne., U.S. G13 126
Wood, Mount, mtn., Mt., U.S. E17 136
Woodall Mountain, hill, Ms., U.S. C10 122
Woodbine, Ga., U.S. F4 116
Woodbine, Ia., U.S. C2 120
Woodbridge, Eng., U.K. I14 12
Woodbridge, Va., U.S. F8 114
Woodburn, Or., U.S. E4 136
Woodbury, Ga., U.S. E14 122
Woodbury, N.J., U.S. E10 114
Woodbury, Tn., U.S. I11 120
Woodhull, Il., U.S. C7 120
Woodlake, Ca., U.S. G6 134
Wood Lake, Ne., U.S. E12 126
Woodland, Ca., U.S. E4 134
Woodland, Me., U.S. E9 110
Woodland, N.C., U.S. H8 114
Woodland Park, Co., U.S. C3 128
Woodridge, Mb., Can. E17 124
Wood River, Il., U.S. F7 120
Wood River, Ne., U.S. G14 126
Woodroffe, Mount, mtn., Austl. E6 74
Woodruff, Az., U.S. I6 132
Woodruff, S.C., U.S. B3 116
Woodruff, Wi., U.S. F9 118
Woods, Lake, l., Austl. C6 74
Woods, Lake of the, l., N.A. B3 118
Woodsboro, Tx., U.S. F10 130
Woodsfield, Oh., U.S. E4 114
Woods Hole, Ma., U.S. C15 114
Woodside, Austl. L6 76
Woodson, Tx., U.S. A8 130
Woodstock, Austl. D3 76
Woodstock, N.B., Can. D9 110
Woodstock, On., Can. E9 112
Woodstock, Eng., U.K. J11 12
Woodstock, Il., U.S. B9 120
Woodstock, N.Y., U.S. B11 114
Woodstock, Vt., U.S. G4 110
Woodsville, N.H., U.S. F4 110
Woodville, N.Z. E6 80
Woodville, Al., U.S. C12 122
Woodville, Ga., U.S. C2 116
Woodville, Ms., U.S. F7 122
Woodville, Oh., U.S. G6 112
Woodville, Tx., U.S. G4 122
Woodward, Ok., U.S. E9 128
Woody, stm., Can. B12 124
Woody Head, c., Austl. G9 76
Woolmarket, Ms., U.S. G9 122
Woomera, Austl. F7 74
Woonsocket, R.I., U.S. B14 114
Woonsocket, S.D., U.S. C14 126
Woorabinda, Austl. E7 76
Wooramel, Austl. E2 74
Wooramel, stm., Austl. E2 74
Wooster, Oh., U.S. D3 114
Worcester, S. Afr. H4 70
Worcester, Eng., U.K. I10 12
Worcester, Ma., U.S. B14 114
Worden, Mt., U.S. A4 126
Wörgl, Aus. C9 22
Workington, Eng., U.K. G9 12
Worksop, Eng., U.K. H11 12
Worland, Wy., U.S. C5 126
Worms, Ger. G4 16
Worthing, Eng., U.K. K12 12
Worthington, In., U.S. E11 120
Worthington, Mn., U.S. H3 118
Worthington, Oh., U.S. D3 114
Worthington Peak, mtn., Nv., U.S. E1 132
Wotho, at., Marsh. Is. B7 72
Wotu, Indon. E12 50
Wouhnta, Nic. F6 102
Wounded Knee, S.D., U.S. D10 126
Wounded Knee Creek, stm., S.D., U.S. D10 126
Wowan, Austl. D8 76
Wowoni, Pulau, i., Indon. F7 44
Woy Woy, Austl. I8 76
Wrangel Island see Vrangelja, ostrov, i., Russia B24 34
Wrangell, Ak., U.S. E13 140
Wrangell, Cape, c., Ak., U.S. g21 140a
Wrangell Mountains, mts., Ak., U.S. D11 140
Wrath, Cape, c., Scot., U.K. C8 12
Wrens, Ga., U.S. C3 116
Wrentham, Ab., Can. G18 138
Wrexham, Wales, U.K. H10 12
Wright, Mount, mtn., Mt., U.S. B14 136
Wright City, Mo., U.S. F6 120
Wright Patman Lake, res., Tx., U.S. D4 122
Wrightson, Mount, mtn., Az., U.S. L6 132
Wrightstown, Wi., U.S. D1 112
Wrightsville, Ga., U.S. D3 116
Wrightsville Beach, N.C., U.S. B8 116
Wrigley, N.T., Can. C6 106
Wrigley, Tn., U.S. I10 120
Wrocław (Breslau), Pol. E13 16
Wrocław, state, Pol. E13 16
Wrong Lake, l., Mb., Can. B17 124
Wrottesley, Cape, c., N.T., Can. B15 140
Wroxton, Sk., Can. C12 124
Września, Pol. D13 16
Wschowa, Pol. E12 16
Wu, stm., China H3 42
Wu, stm., China G2 42
Wu, stm., China H4 42
Wu, stm., China G7 42
Wu, stm., China I5 42
Wubu, China C4 42
Wuchang, China B7 38
Wuchang Hu, l., China F7 42
Wuchin see Changzhou, China F8 42
Wuchou see Wuzhou, China J4 42
Wuchow see Wuzhou, China J4 42
Wuchuan, China K4 42
Wuchuan, China A4 42
Wuchung see Wuzhong, China C2 42
Wuda, China B2 42
Wudaoliang, China D3 36
Wudi, China C7 42
Wuding, China F5 36
Wuding, stm., China C4 42
Wudu, China E5 36
Wufeng, China F4 42
Wugang, China H4 42
Wugong, China D2 42
Wugong Shan, mts., China H5 42
Wuhai, China B2 42
Wuhan (Hankow), China F6 42
Wuhsi see Wuxi, China F9 42
Wuhsing see Huzhou, China F9 42
Wuhu, China F8 42
Wuhua, China J6 42
Wuhuanchi, China C4 38
Wüjang, China B7 54
Wujia, stm., China A3 42
Wujiangdu, China H2 42
Wukang, China F8 42
Wukari, Nig. H6 64
Wukeshu, China B7 38
Wulateqianqi, China A3 42
Wuliang Shan, mts., China G5 36
Wulong, China G2 42
Wuluhan, Indon. H8 50
Wulumuch'i see Ürümqi, China C2 36
Wuluo, China H3 42
Wuming, China J3 42
Wundwin, Mya. B2 48
Wunnummin Lake, l., On., Can. E13 106
Wunstorf, Ger. D5 16
Wupatki National Monument, p.o.i., Az., U.S. H5 132
Wuppertal, Ger. E3 16
Wuppertal, S. Afr. H4 70
Wuqi, China C3 42
Wuqia, China B12 56
Wuqiang, China B6 42
Wurno, Nig. G6 64
Würzburg, Ger. G5 16
Wurzen, Ger. E8 16
Wushan, China F3 42
Wusheng, China F2 42
Wushenqi, China B3 42
Wushi, China J4 42
Wusih see Wuxi, China F9 42
Wusuli (Ussuri), stm., Asia B11 36
Wutai, China B5 42
Wutai Shan, mtn., China B5 42
Wutong, China I3 42
Wutongqiao, China F5 36
Wutsin see Changzhou, China F8 42
Wut'ungch'iao see Wutongqiao, China F5 36
Wutungkiao see Wutongqiao, China F5 36
Wuvulu Island, i., Pap. N. Gui. a3 79a
Wuwei, China D5 36
Wuwei, China F7 42
Wuxi, China F9 42
Wuxi, China F3 42
Wuxiang, China C5 42
Wuyang, China H4 42
Wuyi, China G8 42
Wuyi Shan, mts., China H7 42
Wuyuan, China A3 42
Wuyuan, China G7 42
Wuzhai, China B4 42
Wuzhi Shan (Wuzhi Peak), mtn., China L3 42
Wuzhong, China C2 42
Wuzhou, China J4 42
Wyaconda, Mo., U.S. D6 120
Wyandotte, Mi., U.S. B2 114
Wyandra, Austl. F5 76
Wyangala, Lake, res., Austl. J7 76
Wyatt, Mo., U.S. H8 120
Wycheproof, Austl. K4 76
Wye, stm., U.K. J10 12
Wyeville, Wi., U.S. G8 118
Wyk, Ger. B4 16
Wykoff, Mn., U.S. H6 118
Wylie, Lake, res., U.S. A4 116
Wymark, Sk., Can. D6 124
Wymondham, Eng., U.K. I13 12
Wymore, Ne., U.S. K2 118
Wyndham, Austl. C5 74
Wyndmere, N.D., U.S. E1 118
Wynne, Ar., U.S. B8 122
Wynnewood, Ok., U.S. G11 128
Wynniatt Bay, b., Can. A8 106
Wynona, Ok., U.S. E12 128
Wynot, Ne., U.S. E15 126
Wynyard, Austl. n12 77a
Wynyard, Sk., Can. C9 124
Wyodak, Wy., U.S. C7 126
Wyoming, On., Can. F7 112
Wyoming, Ia., U.S. B6 120
Wyoming, Mi., U.S. F4 112
Wyoming, state, U.S. E5 126
Wyoming Peak, mtn., Wy., U.S. H16 136
Wyong, Austl. I8 76
Wyperfield National Park, p.o.i., Austl. J3 76
Wyśmierzyce, Pol. E16 16
Wysokie Mazowieckie, Pol. D18 16
Wyszków, Pol. D17 16
Wytheville, Va., U.S. H4 114

X

Xaafuun, Raas, c., Som. B10 66
Xàbia, Spain F11 20
Xaidulla, China A4 46
Xainza, China C12 54
Xai-Xai, Moz. D11 70
Xalapa (Jalapa), Mex. F10 100
Xalin, Som. C9 66
Xam (Chu), stm., Asia B7 48
Xambioá, Braz. D1 88
Xambrê, stm., Braz. A11 92
Xam Nua, Laos B7 48
Xá-Muteba, Ang. B2 68
Xan (San), stm., Asia E8 48
Xangongo, Ang. D2 68
Xankändi, Azer. B6 56
Xánthi, Grc. B7 28
Xanxerê, Braz. C11 92
Xapecó, stm., Braz. C11 92
Xapuri, Braz. F4 84
Xar Moron, stm., China C3 38
Xàtiva, Spain F10 20
Xau, Lake, pl., Bots. B7 70
Xavantina, Braz. D6 90
Xaxim, Braz. C11 92
Xcalak, Mex. C4 102
X-Can, Mex. B4 102
Xelva, Spain E9 20
Xenia, Oh., U.S. E2 114
Xepenehe, N. Cal. m16 79d
Xhumo, Bots. B7 70
Xi, stm., China J5 42
Xiachuan Dao, i., China K5 42
Xiagaixin, China A5 48
Xiamen (Amoy), China I7 42
Xi'an (Sian), China D3 42
Xianfeng, China G3 42
Xiang, stm., China G5 42
Xiangcheng, China E5 42
Xiangfan, China F4 42
Xianggang (Hong Kong), China J6 42
Xiangkhoang, Laos C6 48
Xiangkhoang, Plateau de (Tran Ninh), plat., Laos C6 48
Xiangning, China D4 42
Xiangride, China D4 36
Xiangshan, China G9 42
Xiangtan, China H5 42
Xiangxiang, China H5 42
Xiangyin, China G5 42
Xiangyuan, China C5 42
Xiangzhou, China J3 42
Xianju, China G9 42
Xianshui, stm., China B9 46
Xiantao, China F5 42
Xianyang, China D3 42
Xianyang, China G8 42
Xianyou, China I8 42
Xiao, stm., China G8 42
Xiaochengzi, China C5 38
Xiaogan, China F5 42
Xiaoguai, China B1 36
Xiao Hinggan Ling (Lesser Khingan Range), mts., China B10 36
Xiaojin, China E5 36
Xiaojiu, China B7 38
Xiaoluan, stm., China D2 38
Xiaopingyang, China J3 42
Xiaoshan, China F9 42
Xiaoxian, China D7 42
Xiaoyi, China C4 42
Xiapu, China H9 42
Xiawa, China C4 38
Xiaxian, China D4 42
Xibo, stm., China D3 38
Xichang, China F5 36
Xichong, China F1 42
Xicoténcatl, Mex. D9 100
Xié, stm., Braz. G8 86
Xifei, stm., China E7 42
Xifeng, China C6 38
Xifeng, China H2 42
Xigazê, China D12 54
Xihan, stm., China D1 42
Xihe, China F5 42
Xiheying, China B6 42
Xihua, China E6 42
Xiji, China D1 42
Xiliao, stm., China C5 38
Xilin, China D11 54
Xilinhot, China C2 38
Ximakou, China F5 42
Ximalin, China A6 42
Ximiao, China C5 36
Xin, stm., China G7 42
Xin'an, China C6 38
Xin'anjiang Shuiku, res., China G8 42
Xinavane, Moz. D11 70
Xin Barag Youqi, China B8 36
Xin Barag Zuoqi, China B8 36
Xinbin, China D6 38
Xincai, China E6 42
Xinchang, China G9 42
Xincheng, China G6 36
Xincheng, China B6 42
Xindu, China I4 42
Xinfeng, China I6 42
Xinfeng Shuiku, res., China J6 42
Xing'an, China I4 42
Xingcheng, China A9 42
Xingguo, China H6 42
Xinghai, China D4 36
Xinghe, China A5 42
Xinghua, China E8 42
Xinglong, China D1 42
Xingren, China F6 36
Xingrenbu, China C1 42
Xingtai, China C6 42
Xingtang, China B6 42
Xingu, stm., Braz. D7 84
Xingxian, China B4 42
Xingyi, China F5 36
Xinhe, China C6 42
Xinhua, China H4 42
Xinhui, China J5 42
Xining, China D5 36
Xinji, China C6 42
Xinjiang, China D4 42
Xinjiang, state, China A5 46
Xinjin, China E5 36
Xinjin, China B9 42
Xinjiulong (New Kowloon), China J6 42
Xinkai, stm., China C5 38
Xinli, China B7 38
Xinlitun, China D5 38
Xinmin, China C5 38
Xinning, China H4 42
Xinshao, China H4 42
Xintian, China I5 42
Xinwen, China D7 42
Xinxian, China B5 42
Xinxian, China F6 42
Xinxiang, China D5 42
Xinxing, China C8 38
Xinyang, China E6 42
Xinye, China E5 42
Xinyi, China D8 42
Xinyu, China H6 42
Xinzhou, China L3 42
Xiongyuecheng, China A9 42
Xiping, China E6 42
Xiping, China G8 42
Xiqing Shan, mts., China E5 36
Xique-Xique, Braz. F4 88
Xırdalan, Azer. A6 56
Xishanqiao, China F8 42
Xisha Qundao (Paracel Islands), is., China B5 50
Xishui, China F6 42
Xiti, China B9 54
Xiu, stm., China G6 42
Xi Ujimqin Qi, China B2 38
Xiushui, China G6 42
Xiuyan, China A10 42
Xiva, Spain E10 20
Xixabangma Feng, mtn., China D10 54
Xixi, China H8 42
Xixian, China E6 42
Xixiang, China E2 42
Xixona, Spain F10 20
Xiyang, China C5 42
Xizang (Tibet), state, China B5 46
Xizi, China D3 38
Xochicalco, hist., Mex. F9 100
Xochistlahuaca, Mex. G9 100
Xu, stm., China H7 42
Xuancheng, China F8 42
Xuan'en, China F3 42
Xuang, stm., Laos B6 48
Xuanhan, China F2 42
Xuanhua, China A6 42
Xuanwei, China F5 36
Xuchang, China D5 42
Xun, stm., China J4 42
Xungru, China D10 54
Xunwu, China I6 42
Xupu, China H4 42
Xúquer see Júcar, stm., Spain E10 20
Xuwen, China K4 42
Xuyi, China E8 42
Xuyong, China G1 42
Xuzhou, China D7 42
Xylókastro, Grc. E5 28

Y

Yaak, Mt., U.S. B11 136
Yaan, China E5 36
Yaapeet, Austl. J3 76
Yablonovy Range see Jablonovyj hrebet, mts., Russia F11 34
Yabluniv, Ukr. A12 26
Yabrīn, Sau. Ar. E6 56
Yabucoa, P.R. B4 104a
Yabuli, China B8 38
Yacambu, Parque Nacional, p.o.i., Ven. C7 86
Yacata, i., Fiji p20 79e
Yacheng, China L3 42
Yachi, stm., China H2 42
Yaco see Iaco, stm., S.A. F4 84
Yacuiba, Bol. D4 90
Yacyretá, Isla, i., Para. C9 92
Yādgīr, India C3 53
Yadkin, stm., N.C., U.S. H4 114
Yadkinville, N.C., U.S. H5 114
Yadong, China E12 54
Yafran, Libya A2 62
Yagasa Cluster, i., Fiji q20 79e
Yagoua, Cam. B3 66
Yagradagzê Shan, mtn., China D4 36
Yaguajay, Cuba A8 102
Yaguarón (Jaguarão), stm., S.A. F11 92
Yaguas, stm., S.A. I6 86
Yahe, China B9 38
Yahk, B.C., Can. G14 138
Yahualica, Mex. E7 100
Yai, Khao, mtn., Thai. E4 48
Yainax Butte, mtn., Or., U.S. A4 134
Yaita, Japan C12 40
Yaitopya see Ethiopia, ctry., Afr. F7 62
Yaizu, Japan E11 40
Yajiang, China E5 36
Yakacık, Tur. B7 58
Yakeshi, China B9 36
Yakima, Wa., U.S. D6 136
Yakima, stm., Wa., U.S. D7 136
Yakmach, Pak. D9 56
Yako, Burkina G4 64
Yakoma, D.R.C. D4 66
Yakumo, Japan C14 38
Yaku-shima, i., Japan I9 38
Yakutat Bay, b., Ak., U.S. E11 140
Yakutia see Jakutija, state, Russia D14 34
Yala, Thai. I5 48
Yalahau, Laguna de, b., Mex. B4 102
Yale, B.C., Can. G9 138
Yale, Mi., U.S. E7 112
Yale, Ok., U.S. A2 122
Yale, Mount, mtn., Co., U.S. C2 128
Yalgoo, Austl. E3 74
Yalinga, C.A.R. C4 66
Yalobusha, stm., Ms., U.S. D9 122
Yalong, stm., China E5 36
Yalova, Tur. C12 28
Yalpuh, ozero, l., Ukr. D15 26
Yalu (Amnok-kang), stm., Asia D7 38
Yalu, stm., China D6 38
Yalvaç, Tur. E14 28
Yamaga, Japan F3 40
Yamagata, Japan A13 40
Yamagata, state, Japan A13 40
Yamaguchi, Japan E4 40
Yamaguchi, state, Japan E4 40
Yamal Peninsula see Jamal, poluostrov, pen., Russia B2 34
Yamanaka, Japan C9 40
Yamanashi, state, Japan D11 40
Yamasaki, Japan D7 40
Yamaska, stm., Qc., Can. E4 110
Yamatengwumulu, China D4 36
Yamba, Austl. G9 76
Yambio, Sudan G5 62
Yamdena, Pulau, i., Indon. G9 44
Yame, Japan F3 40
Ya Men, b., China J5 42
Yamethin, Mya. B3 48
Yamma Yamma, Lake, l., Austl. F3 76
Yamoussoukro, C. Iv. H4 64
Yampa, stm., Co., U.S. C8 132
Yampil', Ukr. A15 26
Yamsay Mountain, mtn., Or., U.S. H5 136
Yamuna, stm., India F8 54
Yamzho Yumco, l., China D13 54
Yan, stm., China C4 42
Yan, stm., Sri L. G5 53
Yanac, Austl. K3 76
Yanagawa, Japan F3 40
Yanai, Japan F5 40
Yanam, India C6 53
Yan'an, China C3 42
Yanbu' al-Bahr, Sau. Ar. E4 56
Yanceyville, N.C., U.S. H6 114
Yanchang, China C3 42
Yancheng, China E9 42
Yanchi, China C2 42
Yanco Creek, stm., Austl. J5 76
Yanda Creek, stm., Austl. H5 76
Yandama Creek, stm., Austl. G3 76
Yandé, Île, i., N. Cal. m14 79d
Yandina, Sol. Is. e8 79b
Yandoon, Mya. D2 48
Yanfolila, Mali G3 64
Yang, stm., Thai. D7 48
Yangambi, D.R.C. D4 66
Yan'gang, China I7 42
Yangbajain, China C13 54
Yangcheng, China D5 42
Yangchiang see Yangjiang, China K4 42
Yangchou see Yangzhou, China E8 42
Yangchow see Yangzhou, China E8 42
Yangch'üan see Yangquan, China C5 42
Yangchun, China J4 42
Yangdachengzi, China B6 38
Yanggao, China A5 42
Yanghexi, China G3 42
Yangjiang, China K4 42
Yangkü see Taiyuan, China C5 42
Yangliuqing, China B7 42
Yangon (Rangoon), Mya. D2 48
Yangon, state, Mya. D3 48
Yangpingguan, China E1 42
Yangquan, China C5 42
Yangriwan, China F4 42
Yangsan, Kor., S. D2 40
Yangshan, China I5 42
Yangshuo, China I4 42
Yangtze see Chang, stm., China F8 36
Yangtze see Jinsha, stm., China F5 36
Yangxian, China E2 42
Yangxin, China G6 42
Yangyang, Kor., S. A1 40
Yangyuan, China A5 42
Yangzhou, China E8 42
Yanhe, China G3 42
Yanji, China C8 38
Yanji, China C8 38
Yanjiadian, China B9 42
Yankeetown, Fl., U.S. G3 116
Yankton, S.D., U.S. E15 126
Yanqi, China C2 36
Yanqing, China A6 42
Yanshou, China B8 38
Yantabulla, Austl. G5 76
Yantai, China C9 42
Yantan, China G9 42
Yanting, China F1 42
Yantongshan, China C6 38
Yanyuan, China F5 36
Yanzhou, China D7 42
Yao, Chad E3 62
Yaoundé, Cam. D2 66
Yaoxian, China D3 42
Yao Yai, Ko, i., Thai. I4 48
Yap, i., Micron. C4 72
Yapacana, Parque Nacional, p.o.i., Ven. F8 86
Yapacaní, Bol. C4 90
Yapen, Pulau, i., Indon. F10 44
Yapen, Selat, strt., Indon. F10 44
Yappar, stm., Austl. B4 76
Yaque del Norte, stm., Dom. Rep. C12 102
Yaqui, stm., Mex. G8 98
Yaquina, stm., Or., U.S. F3 136
Yaracuy, state, Ven. B7 86
Yaraka, Austl. E5 76
Yardımcı, Tur. A10 58
Yardımcı Burnu, c., Tur. G13 28
Yarí, stm., Col. H5 86
Yariga-take, mtn., Japan C10 40
Yarīm, Yemen G5 56
Yaring, Thai. I5 48
Yaritagua, Ven. B7 86
Yarkand see Shache, China B12 56
Yarkand see Yarkant, stm., China G13 32
Yarkant see Shache, China B12 56
Yarkant, stm., China G13 32
Yarloop, Austl. F3 74
Yarmouth, N.S., Can. G10 110
Yarmouth, Me., U.S. G6 110
Yarmu, Pap. N. Gui. a3 79a
Yarram, Austl. L6 76
Yarraman, Austl. F9 76
Yarrawonga, Austl. K5 76
Yarumal, Col. D4 86
Yasawa Group, is., Fiji p18 79e
Yashiro-jima, i., Japan F5 40
Yasinia, Ukr. A11 26
Yasothon, Thai. E6 48
Yass, Austl. J7 76
Yasugi, Japan D6 40
Yasuní, stm., Ec. H3 86
Yasuni, Parque Nacional, p.o.i., Ec. H4 86
Yata, stm., Bol. B3 90
Yatağan, Tur. F11 28
Yaté, N. Cal. n16 79d
Yates City, Il., U.S. D7 120
Yathkyed Lake, l., Nu., Can. C11 106
Yating, China I2 42
Yatsuga-take, mtn., Japan D11 40
Yatsuo, Japan C10 40
Yatsushiro, Japan G3 40
Yatsushiro-kai, b., Japan G3 40
Yatuá, stm., Ven. G8 86
Yauca, Peru G3 84
Yauco, P.R. B2 104a
Yautepec, Mex. F9 100
Yavarí (Javari), stm., S.A. D3 84
Yavaros, Mex. B4 100
Yavatmāl, India H7 54
Yaví, Cerro, mtn., Ven. E9 86
Yavita, Ven. F8 86
Yaviza, Pan. H9 102
Yavoriv, Ukr. G19 16
Yavuzeli, Tur. A8 58
Yaw, stm., Mya. B2 48
Yawatahama, Japan F5 40
Yaxchilán, hist., Mex. D2 102
Yayladağı, Tur. C7 58
Yayuan, China D7 38
Yazd, Iran C7 56
Yazoo, stm., Ms., U.S. E8 122
Yazoo City, Ms., U.S. E8 122
Ybbs an der Donau, Aus. B12 22
Ýding Skovhøj, hill, Den. I3 8
Ýdra (Hydra), i., Grc. F6 28
Ye, Mya. E3 48
Yebyu, Mya. E4 48
Yecheng, China B12 56
Yech'ŏn, Kor., S. C1 40
Yecla, Spain F9 20
Yedashe, Mya. C3 48
Yedi Göller Milli Parkı, p.o.i., Tur. B14 28
Yedseram, stm., Nig. G7 64
Yeeda, Austl. C4 74
Yeghegnador, Arm. B6 56
Yei, Sudan G6 62
Yeji, China F6 42
Yela Island, i., Pap. N. Gui. B10 74
Yelarbon, Austl. G8 76
Yell, i., Scot., U.K. n18 12a
Yellandu, India C5 53
Yellow see Huang, stm., China D8 36
Yellow, stm., Wi., U.S. G8 118
Yellow, stm., Wi., U.S. F7 118
Yellow Grass, Sk., Can. E9 124
Yellowhead Pass, p., Can. D12 138
Yellow House Draw, stm., Tx., U.S. H3 122
Yellowknife, N.T., Can. C8 106
Yellowknife, stm., N.T., Can. C8 106
Yellow Sea, Asia G5 38
Yellowstone, stm., U.S. B7 108
Yellowstone, Clarks Fork, stm., U.S. B3 126
Yellowstone Falls, wtfl, Wy., U.S. F16 136
Yellowstone Lake, l., Wy., U.S. F16 136
Yellowstone National Park, Wy., U.S. F16 136
Yellowstone National Park, p.o.i., U.S. F16 136
Yellowtail Dam, dam, Mt., U.S. B4 126
Yellville, Ar., U.S. H5 120
Yelverton Bay, b., Nu., Can. A9 141
Yemen, ctry., Asia F6 56
Yenagoa, Nig. H6 64
Yenangyaung, Mya. B2 48
Yenanma, Mya. C2 48
Yen Bai, Viet. B7 48
Yench'eng see Yancheng, China E9 42
Yenchi see Yanji, China C8 38
Yenda, Austl. J6 76
Yendéré, Burkina G4 64
Yendi, Ghana H4 64
Ye-ngan, Mya. B3 48
Yengisar, China B12 56
Yengo National Park, p.o.i., Austl. I8 76
Yenice, Tur. A6 58
Yenice, stm., Tur. B15 28
Yenicekale, Tur. A7 58
Yenierenköy, N. Cyp. C5 58
Yenimehmetli, Tur. D15 28
Yenipazar, Tur. C13 28
Yenişehir, Tur. C12 28
Yenisey see Enisej, stm., Russia C6 34
Yenshuichen, Tai. J9 42
Yentai see Yantai, China C9 42
Yeola, India H5 54
Yeo Lake, l., Austl. E4 74
Yeovil, Eng., U.K. K10 12
Yepachic, Mex. A4 100
Yeppoon, Austl. D8 76
Yerevan (Erivan), Arm. A5 56
Yerington, Nv., U.S. E6 134
Yerköy, Tur. B3 56
Yerlisu, Tur. C9 28
Yermo, Ca., U.S. I9 134
Yerupaja, Nevado, mtn., Peru F2 84
Yerushalayim (Jerusalem), Isr. G6 58
Yesa, Embalse de, res., Spain B9 20
Yeşildere, Tur. A4 58
Yeşilköy, Tur. C11 28
Yeşiltepe, Tur. A3 58
Yeso, N.M., U.S. G4 128
Yetman, Austl. G8 76
Yetti, reg., Afr. D3 64
Ye-u, Mya. A2 48
Yeu, Île d', i., Fr. H6 14
Yevlax, Azer. A6 56
Yexian, China E5 42
Yexian, China C8 42
Yeywa, Mya. B3 48
Ygatimí, Para. B10 92
Yguazú, stm., Para. B10 92
Yhú, Para. B10 92
Yi, stm., China B6 42
Yi, stm., China D8 42
Yi, stm., China D5 42
Yi, stm., Ur. F10 92
Yi'allaq, Gebel, mtn., Egypt H4 58
Yi'an, China B10 36
Yibin, China F5 36
Yibug Caka, l., China B11 54
Yichang, China F4 42
Yicheng, China F5 42
Yichuan, China D5 42
Yichuan, China C3 42
Yichuan see Yinchuan, China B2 42
Yichun, China B10 36
Yichun, China H6 42
Yidie, China C4 42
Yidu, China C8 42
Yidu, China F4 42
Yifeng, China G6 42
Yığılca, Tur. C14 28
Yilan, China B10 36
Yilaxi, China C7 38
Yiliang, China F5 36
Yilong, China F2 42
Yin, stm., Mya. B2 48
Yinbaing, Mya. D3 48
Yinchuan, China B2 42
Ying, stm., China E6 42
Yingcheng see Yingchengzi, China B6 38
Yingcheng, China F5 42
Yingchengzi, China B6 38
Yingde, China I5 42
Yingjin, stm., China C3 38
Yingkou, China A10 42
Yingkou, China A9 42
Yingpan, China I2 42
Yingshang, China E6 42
Yingshouyingzi, China A7 42
Yingtan, China G7 42
Yining, China F14 32
Yinjiang, China G3 42
Yinkeng, China H6 42
Yinmatu, stm., China D2 38
Yinnyein, Mya. D3 48
Yin Shan, mts., China C6 36
Yi'ong, stm., China E3 36
Yirga'Alem, Eth. F7 62
Yirol, Sudan F6 62
Yishan, China I3 42
Yishui, China D8 42
Yisuhe, China H5 42
Yitong, stm., China C6 38
Yitulihe, China A9 36
Yiwu, China G8 42
Yiwu, China A5 48
Yixian, China D4 38
Yixing, China F8 42
Yixun, stm., China D2 38
Yiyang, China G5 42
Yiyang, China D4 42
Yiyang, China G7 42
Yiyuan, China C8 42
Yizhang, China I5 42
Yli-Kitka, l., Fin. C13 8
Ylivieska, Fin. D11 8
Ymer Ø, i., Grnld. C21 141
Ynykčanskij, Russia D16 34
Yoakum, Tx., U.S. E10 130
Yocona, stm., Ms., U.S. C9 122
Yog Point, c., Phil. C5 52
Yogyakarta, Indon. G7 50
Yogyakarta, state, Indon. H7 50
Yoho National Park, p.o.i., B.C., Can. E14 138
Yōka, Japan D7 40
Yokadouma, Cam. D2 66
Yōkaichi, Japan D9 40
Yokkaichi, Japan D9 40
Yoko, Cam. C2 66
Yokoate-jima, i., Japan k19 39a
Yokohama, Japan D12 40
Yokosuka, Japan D12 40
Yokote, Japan E14 38
Yola, Nig. H7 64
Yolombo, D.R.C. E4 66
Yom, stm., Thai. D5 48
Yonago, Japan D6 40
Yoncalla, Or., U.S. G3 136
Yonezawa, Japan B12 40
Yong'an, China I7 42
Yongchang, China D5 36
Yongcheng, China D7 42
Yŏngch'ŏn, Kor., S. D1 40
Yongchuan, China G1 42
Yongding, China I7 42
Yongding, stm., China A6 42
Yŏngdŏk, Kor., S. C2 40
Yŏngdong, Kor., S. F7 38
Yongfeng, China H6 42
Yonggi, Kor., S. C1 40
Yongi, China C7 38
Yŏngil-man, b., Kor., S. C2 40
Yŏngju, Kor., S. C1 40
Yongkang, China G9 42
Yongle, stm., China H5 42
Yongnian, China C6 42
Yongning, China J3 42
Yongning, China B1 42
Yongping, China F4 36
Yongren, China F5 36
Yongshan, China F5 36
Yongshou, China D2 42
Yongtai, China I8 42
Yŏngwŏl, Kor., S. B1 40
Yongxing, China B4 42
Yongxing, China H5 42
Yongxiu, China G6 42
Yŏngyang, Kor., S. C2 40
Yongzhou, China H4 42
Yonibana, S.L. H2 64
Yonkers, N.Y., U.S. D12 114
Yonne, state, Fr. G12 14
Yonne, stm., Fr. F12 14
Yopal, Col. E5 86
Yopurga, China B12 56
York, Austl. F3 74
York, Eng., U.K. H11 12
York, Al., U.S. E10 122
York, N.D., U.S. F14 124
York, Pa., U.S. E9 114
York, S.C., U.S. A4 116
York, Cape, c., Austl. B8 74
York, Kap, c., Grnld. B12 141
Yorke Peninsula, pen., Austl. F7 74
Yorketown, Austl. G7 74
York Factory, Mb., Can. D12 106
Yorkshire Dales National Park, p.o.i., Eng., U.K. G10 12
York Sound, strt., Austl. B4 74
Yorkton, Sk., Can. C11 124
Yorktown, Tx., U.S. E10 130
Yorktown, Va., U.S. G9 114
Yorkville, Il., U.S. J10 118
Yorkville, N.Y., U.S. E14 112
Yoro, Hond. E4 102
Yoron-jima, i., Japan I19 39a
Yosemite National Park, p.o.i., Ca., U.S. F6 134
Yosemite Village, Ca., U.S. F6 134
Yoshii, stm., Japan E7 40
Yösöbulag see Altay, Mong. B4 36
Yos Sudarso, Pulau, i., Indon. G10 44
Yŏsu, Kor., S. G7 38
You, stm., China G6 36
You, stm., China G4 42
Youanmi, Austl. E3 74
Youghal, Ire. J5 12
Young, Austl. J7 76
Young, Sk., Can. C8 124
Young, Az., U.S. I5 132
Young, Ur. F9 92
Younghusband Peninsula, pen., Austl. K2 76
Young Island, i., Ant. B21 81
Youngs Rock, r., Pit. c28 78k
Youngstown, Ab., Can. C2 124
Youngstown, N.Y., U.S. E10 112
Youngstown, Oh., U.S. C5 114
Youngsville, La., U.S. G6 122
Youngsville, N.C., U.S. H7 114
Yountville, Ca., U.S. E3 134

Name	Map Ref.	Page
Youssoufia, Mor.	C3	64
Youxian, China	H5	42
Youyang, China	G3	42
Yŏyang-ni, Kor., S.	B1	40
Yozgat, Tur.	B3	56
Ypres see Ieper, Bel.	D11	14
Ypsilanti, Mi., U.S.	B2	114
Yreka, Ca., U.S.	B3	134
Ysabel Channel, strt., Pap. N. Gui.	a4	79a
Ystad, Swe.	I5	8
Ytterhogdal, Swe.	E6	8
Yu, stm., China	J3	42
Yuam, stm., Thai.	C3	48
Yuan see Red, stm., Asia	D9	46
Yuan, stm., China	H6	42
Yuan, stm., China	G4	42
Yuanling, China	G4	42
Yuanmou, China	F5	36
Yuantan, China	J5	42
Yuanyang, China	D5	42
Yuasa, Japan	E8	40
Yuba City, Ca., U.S.	D4	134
Yūbari, Japan	C15	38
Yucaipa, Ca., U.S.	I8	134
Yucatán, state, Mex.	B3	102
Yucatán, Península de (Yucatan Peninsula), pen., N.A.	C3	102
Yucatan Channel, strt., N.A.	B4	102
Yucatan Peninsula see Yucatán, Península de, pen., N.A.	C3	102
Yucca, Az., U.S.	I2	132
Yucca Mountain, mtn., Nv., U.S.	G9	134
Yucca Valley, Ca., U.S.	I9	134
Yucheng, China	C7	42
Yuci, China	C5	42
Yudu, China	I6	42
Yuechi, China	F2	42
Yueqing, China	G9	42
Yuexi, China	F5	36
Yueyang, China	G5	42
Yufa, China	B7	42
Yugan, China	G7	42
Yugoslavia, ctry., Eur.	F7	26
Yuhebu, China	C3	42
Yuhuan Dao, i., China	G9	42
Yuhuang Ding, mtn., China	C9	42
Yukon, Ok., U.S.	F11	128
Yukon, state, Can.	B3	106
Yukon, stm., N.A.	D7	140
Yukon Flats, sw., Ak., U.S.	C11	140
Yukuhashi, Japan	F3	40
Yuli, China	F15	32
Yüli, Tai.	J9	42
Yulin, China	B3	42
Yulin, China	J3	42
Yulin, China	L3	42
Yuma, Az., U.S.	K2	132
Yuma, Co., U.S.	A6	128
Yuma, Bahía de, b., Dom. Rep.	C13	102
Yumare, Ven.	B7	86
Yumbel, Chile	H1	92
Yumbo, Col.	F3	86
Yumen, China	D4	36
Yumt uul, mtn., Mong.	C4	36
Yun, stm., China	F5	42
Yuna, stm., Dom. Rep.	C13	102
Yunak, Tur.	E14	28
Yunan, China	J4	42
Yuncheng, China	D4	42
Yuncheng, China	D6	42
Yungay, Chile	H2	92
Yungchi see Jilin, China	C7	38
Yungchia see Wenzhou, China	F9	36
Yungning see Nanning, China	J3	42
Yunkai Dashan, mts., China	J4	42
Yun Ling, mts., China	F4	36
Yunnan, state, China	G5	36
Yunnanfu see Kunming, China	F5	36
Yunta, Austl.	I2	76
Yunwu Shan, mtn., China	A7	42
Yunxi, China	E4	42
Yunxian, China	E4	42
Yunxiao, China	I7	42
Yunyang, China	F3	42
Yunyang see Yunxian, China	E4	42
Yunzalin, stm., Mya.	D3	48
Yuping, China	H3	42
Yuqing, China	H2	42
Yurimaguas, Peru	E2	84
Yuriria, Laguna de, l., Mex.	E8	100
Yuruá see Juruá, stm., S.A.	D4	84
Yuruarí, stm., Ven.	D11	86
Yurubi, Parque Nacional, p.o.i., Ven.	B7	86
Yurungkax, stm., China	A5	46
Yuscarán, Hond.	F4	102
Yûsef, Bahr (Yūsuf, Baḥr), can., Egypt	K1	58
Yushan, China	G8	42
Yü Shan, mtn., Tai.	J9	42
Yushanzhen, China	G3	42
Yushu, China	E4	36
Yushu, China	B7	38
Yutian, China	B7	42
Yutian, China	A5	46
Yuty, Para.	C9	92
Yütz'u see Yuci, China	C5	42
Yuxian, China	B6	42
Yuxian, China	B5	42
Yuxian, China	D5	42
Yuyao, China	F9	42
Yuzawa, Japan	E14	38
Yvelines, state, Fr.	F10	14
Yverdon-les-Bains, Switz.	D3	22
Ywathagyi, Mya.	A2	48

Z

Name	Map Ref.	Page
Zaandam see Zaanstad, Neth.	B13	14
Zaanstad, Neth.	B13	14
Zabalac', Bela.	G7	10
Zăbalț, Rom.	C8	26
Zabīd, Yemen	G5	56
Žabinka, Bela.	H6	10
Ząbkowice Śląskie, Pol.	F12	16
Žabljak, Yugo.	F6	26
Żabno, Pol.	F16	16
Zābol, Iran	C9	56
Zābol, state, Afg.	C1	54
Zabolotiv, Ukr.	A12	26
Zabor''e, Bela.	E12	10
Zabore, Russia	F15	10
Zabory, Russia	E15	10
Zabrze, Pol.	F14	16
Zabyčanne, Bela.	G14	10
Zacapa, Guat.	E3	102
Zacapu, Mex.	F8	100
Zacatecas, Mex.	D7	100
Zacatecas, state, Mex.	D7	100
Zacatlán, Mex.	F10	100
Zacoalco de Torres, Mex.	E7	100
Zacualtipan, Mex.	E9	100
Zadar (Zara), Cro.	F12	22
Zadetkale Kyun, i., Mya.	G3	48
Zadetkyi Kyun, i., Mya.	H3	48
Zadoi, China	B8	46
Za'farâna, well, Egypt	I3	58
Zafer Burnu, c., N. Cyp.	C5	58
Zafirovo, Blg.	F13	26
Zafra, Spain	F4	20
Żagań, Pol.	E11	16
Žagare, Lith.	D6	10
Zagazig, Egypt	H2	58
Zaghouan, Tun.	H4	24
Zaghouan, Jebel, mtn., Tun.	H4	24
Zagora, Mor.	C3	64
Zagórz, Pol.	G18	16
Zagreb, Cro.	E12	22
Zāgros, Kūhhā-ye, mts., Iran	C7	56
Zagros Mountains see Zāgros, Kūhhā-ye, mts., Iran	C7	56
Za'gya, stm., China	B13	54
Zāhedān, Iran	D9	56
Zahīrābād, India	C3	53
Zahlah, Leb.	E6	58
Zahnitkiv, Ukr.	A15	26
Zahrebetnoe, Russia	B17	8
Žailma, Kaz.	D10	32
Zaire see Congo, Democratic Republic of the, ctry., Afr.	E4	66
Zaïre see Congo, stm., Afr.	F2	66
Zaječar, Yugo.	F9	26
Zajsan, Kaz.	E14	32
Zajsan, ozero, l., Kaz.	E14	32
Zaka, Zimb.	B10	70
Zakamensk, Russia	F9	34
Zakarpattia, co., Ukr.	A10	26
Zakhidnyy Buh (Bug) (Buh), stm., Eur.	D17	16
Zakliczyn, Pol.	G16	16
Zakopane, Pol.	G16	16
Zakouma, Chad	E3	62
Zakroczym, Pol.	D16	16
Zákynthos, Grc.	F3	28
Zákynthos, i., Grc.	F3	28
Zala, state, Hung.	C3	26
Zala, stm., Hung.	C4	26
Zalaegerszeg, Hung.	C3	26
Zalamea de la Serena, Spain	F5	20
Zalantun, China	B9	36
Zalari, Russia	D18	32
Zalaszentgrót, Hung.	C4	26
Zalău, Rom.	B10	26
Zalese, Russia	F4	10
Zalim, Sau. Ar.	E5	56
Zalingei, Sudan	E4	62
Žaltyr, Kaz.	D12	32
Žaludok, Bela.	G7	10
Zama, Ms., U.S.	E9	122
Zamakh, Yemen	F6	56
Zamantı, stm., Tur.	A6	58
Zambeze, stm., Afr.	C3	68
Zambezi, Zam.	C3	68
Zambezi, stm., Afr.	D5	68
Zambezi Escarpment, clf, Zimb.	D4	68
Zambia, ctry., Afr.	C4	68
Zamboanga, Phil.	G3	52
Zamboanga Peninsula, pen., Phil.	G3	52
Zambrów, Pol.	C18	16
Žambyl, Kaz.	F12	32
Žambyl, Kaz.	E12	32
Zamežnaja, Russia	D24	8
Zami, stm., Mya.	D4	48
Zamora, Ec.	D2	84
Zamora, Spain	C5	20
Zamora, co., Spain	C5	20
Zamora de Hidalgo, Mex.	F7	100
Zamość, Pol.	F19	16
Zamość, state, Pol.	F19	16
Zanaga, Congo	E2	66
Žanatas, Kaz.	F11	32
Záncara, stm., Spain	E8	20
Zanda, China	C7	54
Zanesville, Oh., U.S.	E3	114
Zanjān, Iran	B6	56
Zanjón, Arg.	C5	92
Žannetty, ostrov, i., Russia	A20	34
Zante see Zákynthos, i., Grc.	F3	28
Zanthus, Austl.	F4	74
Zanzibar, Tan.	F7	66
Zanzibar, i., Tan.	F7	66
Zanzibar Channel, strt., Tan.	F7	66
Zaostrove, Russia	F14	8
Zaō-zan, vol., Japan	A13	40
Zaozërnyj, Russia	C16	32
Zaozhuang, China	D7	42
Zap, N.D., U.S.	G12	124
Zapadnaja Dvina, Russia	D15	10
Zapadna Morava, stm., Yugo.	F8	26
Zapadno-Sibirskaja ravnina (West Siberian Plain), pl., Russia	B12	32
Zapadnyj hrebet, mts., Russia	F17	34
Zapadnyj Sajan, mts., Russia	D16	32
Západočeský kraj, state, Czech Rep.	G9	16
Západoslovenský Kraj, state, Slov.	H14	16
Zapala, Arg.	G2	90
Zapata, Tx., U.S.	H8	130
Zapata, Península de, pen., Cuba	A7	102
Zapatoca, Col.	D5	86
Zapatosa, Ciénaga de, l., Col.	C5	86
Zapljuse, Russia	B12	10
Zapole, Russia	B12	10
Zapoljarnyj, Russia	B14	8
Zapopan, Mex.	E7	100
Zaporizhzhia, Ukr.	E5	32
Zapovednyj, Russia	C10	38
Zaprudnja, Russia	D20	10
Zaqatala, Azer.	A6	56
Zaragoza, Mex.	A8	100
Zaragoza, Mex.	C1	130
Zaragoza (Saragossa), Spain	C10	20
Zaragoza, co., Spain	C9	20
Zarajsk, Russia	F21	10
Zaranj, Afg.	C9	56
Zarasai, Lith.	E9	10
Zárate, Arg.	G8	92
Zarautz, Spain	A8	20
Zarauz see Zarautz, Spain	A8	20
Zaraza, Ven.	C9	86
Zareče, Russia	E21	8
Zarečensk, Russia	C14	8
Zarghūn Shahr, Afg.	C10	56
Zaria, Nig.	G6	64
Żarki, Pol.	F15	16
Žarma, Kaz.	E14	32
Zărnești, Rom.	D12	26
Žarsuat, Kaz.	E12	32
Zarubino, Russia	C9	38
Zarumilla, Peru	D1	84
Żary, Pol.	E11	16
Zarzaïtine, Alg.	D6	64
Zarzal, Col.	E4	86
Zasa, Lat.	D8	10
Zāskār, stm., India	B6	54
Zāskār Mountains, mts., Asia	B7	54
Zaslaue, Bela.	F10	10
Zastava, Russia	G22	8
Zasule, Russia	D22	8
Žatec, Czech Rep.	F9	16
Zatyshshya, Ukr.	B16	26
Zavalla, Tx., U.S.	F4	122
Zave, Zimb.	D5	68
Zavet, Blg.	F13	26
Zavodoukovsk, Russia	C11	32
Zavodovski Island, i., S. Geor.	K12	82
Zavolžsk, Russia	H20	8
Zawadzkie, Pol.	F14	16
Zawiercie, Pol.	F15	16
Zāwiyat al-Mukhaylá, Libya	A4	62
Zaydābād, Afg.	A2	54
Zaysan see Zajsan, Kaz.	E14	32
Zaysan, Lake see Zajsan, ozero, l., Kaz.	E14	32
Zayü, stm., China	C8	46
Zayzan see Zajsan, Kaz.	E14	32
Zaza, stm., Cuba	B8	102
Zaza, Presa, res., Cuba	B8	102
Zbąszynek, Pol.	D11	16
Zbraslav, Czech Rep.	G10	16
Žd'ár nad Sazavou, Czech Rep.	G11	16
Ždiar, Slov.	G16	16
Zduńska Wola, Pol.	E14	16
Zearing, Ia., U.S.	B4	120
Zeballos, B.C., Can.	G4	138
Zebedelia, S. Afr.	D9	70
Zebulon, Ga., U.S.	C1	116
Zedang, China	D13	54
Zeebrugge, Bel.	C11	14
Zeehan, Austl.	n12	77a
Zeeland, Mi., U.S.	F4	112
Zeeland, N.D., U.S.	B13	126
Zeerust, S. Afr.	D7	70
Zefat, Isr.	F6	58
Zehdenick, Ger.	D9	16
Zeil, Mount, mtn., Austl.	D6	74
Zeist, Neth.	B14	14
Zeitz, Ger.	E8	16
Zeja, Russia	F14	34
Zeja, stm., Russia	F14	34
Zejskoe vodohranilišče, res., Russia	F14	34
Zelee, Cape, c., Sol. Is.	e9	79b
Zelenoborskij, Russia	C14	8
Zelenogorsk, Russia	F13	8
Zelenograd, Russia	D20	10
Zelenogradsk, Russia	F3	10
Zelenokumsk, Russia	F6	32
Železinka, Kaz.	D13	32
Železnodorožnyj, Russia	F4	10
Železnodorožnyj, Russia	B8	32
Železnogorsk, Russia	H18	10
Železnogorsk-Ilimskij, Russia	C18	32
Zelienople, Pa., U.S.	D5	114
Zella-Mehlis, Ger.	F6	16
Zell am See, Aus.	C9	22
Zell am Ziller, Aus.	C8	22
Zèl'va, Bela.	G7	10
Želva, Lith.	E8	10
Zemaitijos nacionalnis parkas, p.o.i., Lith.	D4	10
Zembin, Bela.	F11	10
Zembra, Île, i., Tun.	G4	24
Zémio, C.A.R.	C4	66
Zempoala, hist., Mex.	F10	100
Zemun, Yugo.	E7	26
Zeng, stm., China	J5	42
Zenica, Bos.	E4	26
Zenon Park, Sk., Can.	A10	124
Zentsūji, Japan	E6	40
Zenza do Itombe, Ang.	B1	68
Zephyr, Tx., U.S.	C9	130
Zephyrhills, Fl., U.S.	H3	116
Zepu, China	B12	56
Zeravšan, stm., Asia	B10	56
Zeravšanskij hrebet, mts., Asia	B10	56
Zerbst, Ger.	D8	16
Żerków, Pol.	D13	16
Zerqan, Alb.	C14	24
Žešart, Russia	E23	8
Zeulenroda, Ger.	F7	16
Zeven, Ger.	C5	16
Zevenaar, Neth.	E2	16
Zeytinbağı, Tur.	C11	28
Žezdy, Kaz.	E11	32
Zêzere, stm., Port.	E2	20
Žezkazgan, Kaz.	E11	32
Zgierz, Pol.	E15	16
Zgorzelec, Pol.	E11	16
Zhabuchaka Hu, l., China	C9	54
Zhakou, China	F5	42
Zhambyl see Žambyl, Kaz.	F12	32
Zhang, stm., China	I6	42
Zhang, stm., China	C5	42
Zhangaözen see Novyj Uzen', Kaz.	F8	32
Zhangaqazaly see Novokazalinsk, Kaz.	F10	32
Zhangbei, China	A6	42
Zhangguangcai Ling, mts., China	B8	38
Zhanghuang, China	K3	42
Zhangjiakou, China	A6	42
Zhangping, China	I7	42
Zhangpu, China	I7	42
Zhangqiu, China	C7	42
Zhangshuping, China	F4	42
Zhangwu, China	C5	38
Zhangye, China	D5	36
Zhangzhou, China	I7	42
Zhanjiang, China	K4	42
Zhanyu, China	B5	38
Zhao'an, China	J7	42
Zhaodong, China	A7	38
Zhaojue, China	C9	46
Zhaoping, China	I4	42
Zhaoqing, China	J5	42
Zhaotong, China	F5	36
Zhaoxing, China	B11	36
Zhaoyuan, China	B10	36
Zhari Namco, l., China	C10	54
Zharma see Žarma, Kaz.	E14	32
Zhaxi Co, l., China	B10	54
Zhaxigang, China	B7	54
Zhayyq see Ural, stm.	E8	32
Zhecheng, China	D6	42
Zhegu, China	D13	54
Zhejiang, state, China	G8	42
Zhelin, China	F9	42
Zhem see Emba, stm., Kaz.	E9	32
Zhenbeikou, China	B2	42
Zheng'an, China	G2	42
Zhengding, China	B6	42
Zhenghe, China	H8	42
Zhenglan Qi, China	C8	36
Zhengning, China	D3	42
Zhengyang, China	E6	42
Zhengzhou, China	D5	42
Zhenhai, China	G9	42
Zhenjiang, China	E8	42
Zhenlai, China	B9	36
Zhenning, China	H1	42
Zhenping, China	E5	42
Zhentou, stm., China	E6	42
Zhenxiong, China	F5	36
Zhenyu, China	H9	42
Zhenyuan, China	H3	42
Zhenyuan, China	D2	42
Zherong, China	H8	42
Zhetiqara see Džetygara, Kaz.	D10	32
Zhijiang, China	H3	42
Zhixia, China	G8	42
Zhob, Pak.	C2	54
Zhob, stm., Pak.	C10	56
Zhongba, China	C5	46
Zhongdian, China	F4	36
Zhongning, China	C1	42
Zhongpingchang, China	F3	42
Zhongshan, China	J5	42
Zhongshan, China	I4	42
Zhongshan, sci., Ant.	B12	81
Zhongtiao Shan, mts., China	D4	42
Zhongwei, China	C1	42
Zhongxian, China	F3	42
Zhongxiang, China	F5	42
Zhongyaozhan, China	F14	34
Zhoucun, China	C7	42
Zhouning, China	H8	42
Zhoushan Dao, i., China	F9	42
Zhoushan Qundao, is., China	F10	42
Zhouzhi, China	D3	42
Zhuanghe, China	B10	42
Zhuanglang, China	D1	42
Zhucang, China	H2	42
Zhucheng, China	D8	42
Zhuhe, China	G5	42
Zhuji, China	G9	42
Zhujia Jian, i., China	G10	42
Zhujiang Kou, est., Asia	J5	42
Zhumadian, China	E5	42
Zhuolu, China	A6	42
Zhuozhou, China	B6	42
Zhuozi, China	A5	42
Zhushan, China	E4	42
Zhuxi, China	E3	42
Zhuzhou, China	H5	42
Zhytomyr, Ukr.	E14	6
Zi, stm., China	C8	42
Zi, stm., China	G4	42
Ziārat, Pak.	C10	56
Žiar nad Hronom, Slov.	H14	16
Zibo, China	C8	42
Zichang, China	C3	42
Ziębice, Pol.	F13	16
Zielona Góra, Pol.	E11	16
Zielona Góra, state, Pol.	D11	16
Zierikzee, Neth.	C12	14
Ziesar, Ger.	D8	16
Zifta, Egypt	H2	58
Žigalovo, Russia	D19	32
Žigansk, Russia	C13	34
Zigong, China	F5	36
Zigui, China	F4	42
Ziguinchor, Sen.	G1	64
Zihuatanejo, Mex.	G8	100
Ziiyang, China	E3	42
Zijin, China	J6	42
Zikhron Ya'aqov, Isr.	F5	58
Žilaja Tambica, Russia	E17	8
Žilina, Slov.	G14	16
Žilino, Russia	F4	10
Zillah, Libya	B3	62
Zillertaler Alpen (Aurine, Alpi), mts., Eur.	C8	22
Zilupe, Lat.	D11	10
Zilwaukee, Mi., U.S.	E6	112
Zima, Russia	D18	32
Zimapán, Mex.	E9	100
Zimbabwe, ctry., Afr.	D4	68
Zimbabwe Ruins, hist., Zimb.	B10	70
Zimi, S.L.	H2	64
Zimnicea, Rom.	F12	26
Zimonino, Russia	G14	10
Zinder, Niger	G6	64
Zinga Mulike, Tan.	F7	66
Zinnik see Soignies, Bel.	D12	14
Zion, Il., U.S.	F2	112
Zion National Park, p.o.i., Ut., U.S.	F4	132
Zionsville, In., U.S.	I3	112
Zipaquirá, Col.	E5	86
Zirbitzkogel, mtn., Aus.	C11	22
Žirjatino, Russia	G16	10
Žirovnice, Czech Rep.	G11	16
Zitong, China	F1	42
Zittau, Ger.	F10	16
Ziway, Lake see Ziway Hāyk', l., Eth.	F7	62
Ziway Hāyk', l., Eth.	F7	62
Zixi, China	G7	42
Ziya, stm., China	B7	42
Ziyuan, China	I4	42
Žizdra, stm., Russia	F19	10
Zizhong, China	G1	42
Zizhou, China	C3	42
Žižica, Russia	D14	10
Žižickoe, ozero, l., Russia	D14	10
Zlaté Moravce, Slov.	H14	16
Zlatoust, Russia	C9	32
Zlatoustovsk, Russia	F15	34
Zlín, Czech Rep.	G13	16
Zlītan, Libya	A2	62
Žlobin, Bela.	H13	10
Złoczew, Pol.	E14	16
Złotoryja, Pol.	E11	16
Złotów, Pol.	C13	16
Zlynka, Russia	H14	10
Zmeinogorsk, Russia	D14	32
Żmigród, Pol.	E12	16
Zmiïnyi, ostriv, i., Ukr.	D17	26
Znamenka, Russia	F17	10
Znamensk, Russia	F4	10
Znamenskoe, Russia	C12	32
Żnin, Pol.	D13	16
Znojmo, Czech Rep.	H12	16
Zoar, S. Afr.	H5	70
Žodzina, Bela.	F11	10
Zoétélé, Cam.	D2	66
Zogang, China	F4	36
Žohova, ostrov, i., Russia	A19	34
Zohreh, stm., Iran	C7	56
Zolotaja Gora, Russia	F14	34
Žolymbet, Kaz.	D12	32
Zomba, Mwi.	D6	68
Zonguldak, Tur.	B14	28
Zonguldak, state, Tur.	B15	28
Zonza, Fr.	H15	18
Zorita, Spain	E5	20
Zorra, Arroyo de la, stm., Mex.	E6	130
Zouar, Chad	C3	62
Zouérat, Maur.	E2	64
Zoug see Zug, Switz.	C5	22
Zouxian, China	D7	42
Zovka, Russia	B11	10
Zrenjanin, Yugo.	D7	26
Žuantobe, Kaz.	F11	32
Zuata, stm., Ven.	C9	86
Zubaydīyah, Jabal az-, mtn., Syria	E8	58
Zubovo, Russia	F17	8
Zudáñez, Bol.	C4	90
Zuera, Spain	C10	20
Zufar (Dhofar), reg., Oman	F7	56
Zug, Switz.	C5	22
Zugdidi, Geor.	F6	32
Zuger See, l., Switz.	C5	22
Zugspitze, mtn., Eur.	I6	16
Zújar, stm., Spain	F5	20
Žukopa, Russia	D15	10
Žukovka, Russia	G16	10
Žukovskij, Russia	E21	10
Zuli, stm., China	D1	42
Zulia, state, Ven.	C5	86
Zulia, stm., S.A.	C5	86
Zululand, hist. reg., S. Afr.	F10	70
Zumbo, Moz.	D5	68
Zumbrota, Mn., U.S.	G6	118
Zungeru, Nig.	H6	64
Zunhua, China	A7	42
Zuni, stm., U.S.	I7	132
Zuni Pueblo, N.M., U.S.	H8	132
Zunyi, China	H2	42
Zuo, stm., China	J2	42
Zuodeng, China	J2	42
Zuomuchedong Hu, l., China	D12	54
Zuoyun, China	A5	42
Žuravičy, Bela.	G13	10
Zurich, On., Can.	E8	112
Zürich (Zurigo), Switz.	C5	22
Zurich, Lake see Zürichsee, l., Switz.	C5	22
Zürichsee, l., Switz.	C5	22
Zurigo see Zürich, Switz.	C5	22
Zurmi, Nig.	G6	64
Zuša, stm., Russia	G19	10
Žut, Otok, i., Cro.	G12	22
Zutphen, Neth.	B15	14
Zuwārah, Libya	A2	62
Zuwayzā, Jord.	G6	58
Zvenigorod, Russia	E19	10
Zvezdec, Blg.	G14	26
Zvezdnyj, Russia	C19	32
Zvishavane, Zimb.	B9	70
Zvolen, Slov.	H15	16
Zwedru, Lib.	H3	64
Zweibrücken, Ger.	G3	16
Zweisimmen, Switz.	D4	22
Zwickau, Ger.	F8	16
Zwierzyniec, Pol.	F18	16
Zwoleń, Pol.	E17	16
Zwolle, Neth.	B14	14
Zwolle, La., U.S.	F5	122
Żyrardów, Pol.	D16	16
Zyrjanka, Russia	C19	34
Zyrjanovsk, Kaz.	E14	32
Zyrjanskoe, Russia	C15	32
Zyryan see Zyrjanovsk, Kaz.	E14	32
Žytkavičy, Bela.	H10	10
Żywiec, Pol.	G15	16